NOTABLE AMERICAN WOMEN

A Biographical Dictionary

Completing the Twentieth Century

Susan Ware, *Editor*

Stacy Braukman, *Assistant Editor*

The Belknap Press of Harvard University Press

Cambridge, Massachusetts, and London, England

2004

Printed in the United States of America

Library of Congress Cataloging-in-Publication Data
Notable American women : a biographical dictionary completing the twentieth century / Susan Ware, editor ; Stacy Braukman, assistant editor.
p. cm.
"Prepared under the auspices of the Radcliffe Institute for Advanced Study, Harvard University."
Includes bibliographical references and indexes.
ISBN 0-674-01488-X (cloth)
1. Women—United States—Biography—Dictionaries.
2. United States—Biography—Dictionaries.
I. Ware, Susan, 1950– II. Braukman, Stacy Lorraine.
III. Radcliffe Institute for Advanced Study.
CT3260.N5725 2004
920.72′0973—dc22 2004048859

ADVISORY COMMITTEE

Funding for research and editing provided in part by grants from:

The National Endowment for the Humanities
The Spencer Foundation
The John D. and Catherine T. MacArthur Foundation
The Brown Foundation
The H. W. Wilson Foundation
The Gladys Krieble Delmas Foundation
The Foundation for Child Development in honor of Karen Gerard
Harvard History Department Publication Fund
The Scott Family Endowment Fund
The New Hampshire Charitable Foundation
David H. Taylor, Jr.
Carole Turner Reading
Barbara Newman Kravitz
Prudence Linder Steiner
Joan Challinor
Marilynn Wood Hill

CONTENTS

PREFACE

When Radcliffe College decided in the 1950s to sponsor the research to produce a comprehensive biographical dictionary on American women, few could have predicted what a huge impact the volumes, collectively known as *Notable American Women*, would have on the field of history and the expectations of what a biographical dictionary should encompass. At that time, most biographical dictionaries and general reference books, like the historical profession in general, almost completely excluded the achievements of women. When the first three volumes of *Notable American Women* appeared in 1971, covering 1,359 women who died between 1607 and 1950, they uncovered and documented through individual biographies the enormous contributions that women had made throughout American history. The research contained in this collection provided many of the intellectual and factual underpinnings for the emergence of women's history as an important and recognized field in American history. The publication in 1980 of *Notable American Women: The Modern Period*, which covered 442 women who had died between 1951 and 1975, continued this process, once again encouraging and fostering exciting new research and fundamentally shaping the way that historians thought and wrote about American history.

Notable American Women: Completing the Twentieth Century, which profiles 483 women who died between January 1, 1976, and December 31, 1999, represents the culmination of the premise behind the initial volumes: to uncover and document women's contributions to politics and culture during historical periods when their significance was generally unrecognized by the society at large. Documentation of the enormous demographic and social changes in American women's lives since the 1970s will have to wait for later volumes, precisely because many women who have been most affected by those changes are still alive. Though it is of course impossible to predict what *Notable American Women*'s future incarnations might look like, it seems reasonable to anticipate a qualitative difference in the careers and experiences of women whose adult lives were spent in a society where opportunities and options for women were significantly broader than they had been in earlier periods. In this sense, the publication of *Notable American Women: Completing the Twentieth Century* signals the end of an era, with the five volumes comprising a distinct intellectual and historical entity that completes the mission begun in the 1950s to bring women into the mainstream of American history.

Notable American Women has become a standard reference book found in practically every library and on many scholars' bookshelves. "Start with *Notable*," teachers often tell students, knowing that the entries will provide not just biographical facts but also a stimulating interpretative essay on a woman and her times. Few other reference books can offer as much in a short format as *Notable American Women* does, with its scope and size enhancing its usefulness. The roughly contemporaneous life spans of the women covered allow glimpses of major events and periods from a variety of perspectives. The volume also provides comprehensive coverage of women's contributions from a variety of fields, not just a single area like science or music. Few people sit down and read the volume from beginning to end, but the high quality of the entries and the inherent appeal of these women's life stories encourage a certain amount of browsing. Very often checking one entry leads a reader to another, and then another, and then perhaps to an earlier volume to look up a woman who had a significant effect on the subject's life, and so forth. A comprehensive index by field facilitates these linkages

Informed by the recognition that gender is central for understanding women's lives, the essays in *Notable American Women* provide integrated treatments of women's professional and personal lives that are often missing from other standard reference works, even those devoted to women. This volume also presents an important opportunity to continue and expand the historical profession's commitment to representing the diversity of American women's experiences—a central focus of contemporary scholarship on women—with a biographical dictionary that is truly inclusive. The volume's emphasis on notable (rather than just "famous") women allows it to identify the accomplishments of previously overlooked leaders and activists and integrate these individuals' stories into the larger patterns of modern American history. The commitment to diversity also includes representation of women from a broad spectrum of political views, ideologies, and party affiliations, and acknowledgment of the rich diversity of American women's religious heritage. With its wide range of subjects, *Notable American Women* thus documents differences (of race, ethnicity, region, class, sexual orientation, and political ideology) that have divided women over the course of the twentieth century at the same time it highlights the potential commonalities of gender in shaping women's lives.

Who exactly is a notable American woman? Following the methodology of earlier volumes, the editors employed these criteria for inclusion: the subject's influence on her times or field; the subject's innovative or pioneering work; and the relevance of her career for the history of women. The editors first faced the challenge, as had their predecessors, of defining the parameters of "notability." An incentive to employ a somewhat expansive definition was the chance to recognize the contributions of community activists who left their mark in more localized arenas, such as María Latigo Hernández's education advocacy in San Antonio, Helen Lake Kanahele's labor activism in Hawaii, or Muriel Snowden's longtime association with Freedom House in Boston. Another consideration was a desire to include biographies such as those of astronauts Christa McAuliffe and Judith Resnik, who were killed in the *Challenger* disaster in 1986. Though these women made contributions to the fields of education and engineering, respectively, they likely would not have been included (in this volume, at least) were it not for the public impact of their deaths. But just being in the news isn't enough, as the case of First Ladies proves. Following the precedent of the last volume (which reversed the standard employed in the first three), wives of presidents were not automatically included. In our estimation, Jacqueline Kennedy Onassis met the criteria for inclusion, but Mamie Eisenhower, Bess Truman, and Pat Nixon (all of whom died within our timeframe) did not.

The editors next tackled the question of what constituted an American. Seventy-three women in the volume were born outside the United States, mainly in Europe but also in Canada, Mexico, the Caribbean, China, Korea, and Japan. Most, but not all, were confirmed to have attained U.S. citizenship. Even if their citizenship remained in question, the editors decided to include some women, like actresses Dolores del Río and Lynn Fontanne, who spent most of their adult lives in the United States and whose contributions to American life and culture were too great to be ignored. Similarly, the editors chose not to leave out such significant figures as art collector Peggy Guggenheim and writer Janet Flanner, American-born women who spent decades living abroad. Not fitting into our definition of American was Golda Meir, whose family emigrated to Milwaukee from Russia when she was a young girl but who spent her entire adult life in Palestine and, later, Israel.

The editors even had to confront what should have been the easiest word in our title—who was a woman?—when faced with several examples of transsexuals or people of indeterminate gender: in particular, Stella Walsh, the Olympic athlete who had both female and male chromosomes, and Christine Jorgensen, the nation's first publicly known male-to-female transsexual. In the end, neither woman met the general criteria for inclusion.

Finally, as contemporary women's historians and race and gender theorists have amply demonstrated, the very categories of race and sexual orientation are fraught with the sort of ambiguities and complexities that do not always fit neatly into the short biographical form. Many women in this volume claimed multiple racial and ethnic identities, and wherever possible the authors of their biographies have noted the mixed ancestry of their subjects and have faithfully described the identities by which the subjects lived their lives—as in the case of Effa Manley, the multiracial Negro League baseball owner who, though her father was white and her mother was German and Asian Indian, chose to live as an African American so that she could safely marry a black man. One of the most persistent problems facing women's historians, a problem that confronts us still, has been how to characterize women who had female life companions or who lived women-centered lives but who never identified as lesbians. There are numerous examples in this volume: Katharine Burr Blodgett, Laura Gilpin, and Berenice Abbott, to name a few. In each instance, the editors have respected contributors' decisions to avoid labeling their subjects as "lesbian" or "bisexual" and to describe their personal relationships without speculating about their sexual or romantic nature.

The broad sweep of women profiled in this volume of *Notable American Women* demonstrates not just the breadth of women's contributions to twentieth-century American life but also the tenacity of our search procedure. The selection process started with the creation of a large database of potential subjects, beginning with reading all the obituaries of women that appeared in the *New York Times* between 1976 and 1999, as well as samples from newspapers such as the *Washington Post, Chicago Tribune,* and *Los Angeles Times* for regional comparison. Other major sources included professional journals, yearbooks, and reference works that contained obituary notices or death dates. Calls for nomination were placed in the newsletters of the *American Historical Review,* the *Journal of American History,* the Coordinating Council on Women's History, and others. We also contacted state and local libraries, representatives of political, labor, cultural, social, scientific, religious, racial, ethnic, and educational organizations, as well as historians, distinguished practitioners in many fields, and persons connected with specialized branches of women's studies. In addition we publicized the project and recruited suggestions and nominations through Radcliffe's website.

This large computerized database (which eventually included more than two thousand names) was winnowed down by the editors after extensive consultation, first with the advisory board and then with hundreds of consultants in approximately fifty specialized fields. Lists were circulated widely in an attempt to avoid regional, ethnic, or racial bias. At all stages a special effort was made to elicit the names of members of minority groups, among them African Americans, Native Americans, Asian Americans, and Latinas. All prospective minority subjects were also included on the lists in their own specialized fields, such as religion, labor, or voluntary associations. In the end, approximately one quarter of the biographies in the book (sixty-nine African Americans, twenty-one Latinas, sixteen Asian Americans, and thirteen Native Americans) is devoted to the lives and contributions of nonwhite women.

The editors also actively sought out subjects from every region of the country, a decision that reflected both the shift among historians toward studying women's lives and experiences from a regional perspective and the editors' self-conscious desire to steer away from a perceived northeastern bias in earlier volumes. Still, the careers of more than half of the women in the volume were centered in the Northeast, mainly in New York and Massachusetts. Western women make up about a quarter of the book (a figure somewhat skewed by the large number of actors and singers based in California), and women from the Midwest and the South (excluding Washington, D.C.) each represent 10 to 13 percent of the total. Not surprisingly, as the cultural and intellectual capitals of the country, New York and California loom large here, but the presence of women from the rural South, the Plains states, and such places as Hawaii, the Pacific Northwest, and Puerto Rico is a critically important element in the book's depiction of the diversity of American women's opportunities and experiences.

As soon as subjects were chosen, the editors worked to match them with appropriate authors, a process we called "matchmaking." Contributors include historians, distinguished scholars and journalists, and specialists in various fields, as well as graduate students doing advanced dissertation research and one Supreme Court justice. Historian Anne Firor Scott deserves special mention for being the only author to contribute an essay to each of the three *Notable* editions. The lengths assigned for articles were based on the editors' assessment of the importance of the subject, the complexity of her life, and the availability (or lack) of sources.

Every contributor was expected to provide a standardized set of biographical details about her or his subject, including date and place of birth; full names of the subject's parents; birth order and number of children in the family; parents' nationality and geographical origins, occupation, and socioeconomic status; subject's education, including high schools, colleges, and universities attended and degrees received; religious affiliation, if relevant; marital status and history; children's full names, including adopted children and stepchildren, and years of birth; date and place of death; and cause of death, if available. In the rare instances when such pieces of information are not included in the essay, it is because authors and editors were unable to track them down, no matter how diligent our search. Each entry also includes a full bibliography identifying primary manuscript sources and published secondary works, as well as the subject's major published works. Cross-references to other entries in the volume and in previous volumes are indicated by SMALL CAPITAL letters. The volume also includes an index of biographies by field and an index of contributors.

The goal of the editing process was to preserve each author's style and interpretation as much as possible. All essays were rigorously fact-checked by a team of graduate students to insure that they conformed to standards of historical accuracy and comprehensiveness. The result, we hope, is a volume that is both factually accurate and stimulating to read. The short biographical form, demanding both breadth and brevity and making even the most stalwart author feel like an encyclopedist, is one of the most difficult genres there is, and we trust that readers appreciate that the essays by necessity only scratch the surface of the lives of fascinating and complex women whose experiences are well worth further study and reflection.

A project of this scope was possible only through the efforts of hundreds of scholars and the enthusiastic support from a wide range of institutions, beginning with the authors who contributed essays, some more than one, to the volume. Dedicated, gracious, and patient as they were ushered through the many stages it took to bring their words to the printed page, to them we offer heartfelt thanks and congratulations for their hard work. We also thank our extensive group of consultants, who were extremely generous with their time and expertise at each phase of the project and who gave us the confidence to decide who made the cut and who didn't.

This volume could have never come to fruition without the initial support and sponsorship of President Linda Wilson of Radcliffe College, which Drew Gilpin Faust then continued when she became Dean of the Radcliffe Institute for Advanced Study, Harvard University. Just as fortunate was our association with the Arthur and Elizabeth Schlesinger Library on the History of Women in America. The library generously opened its doors—and its precious office space—to our small but tenacious operation. For nearly five years, we had the good fortune and the great pleasure to work in one of the most distinguished repositories of women's history in the country. Thank you to the directors—Mary Maples Dunn, Jane Knowles, Nancy Cott, and Megan Sniffin-Marinoff—and the entire staff for making us feel at home, and for allowing us to take full advantage of your resources and services.

Our next largest debt is to the National Endowment for the Humanities. It took us four tries, but once we received funding in 2000, the timely completion of the project was assured. Thanks especially to program officers Martha Chomiak and Barbara Paulson for their enthusiasm and support at all stages of the process. We are also delighted to acknowledge support from the foundations and individuals listed on the page preceding the Contents, as well as many others who responded generously to our fundraising appeals. Thank you all.

The project benefited greatly from a first-rate advisory committee, also listed earlier. Special thanks go to Barbara Sicherman and Carol Hurd Green for giving us the meticulously edited *Notable American Women: The Modern Period* to follow as our model. We also had the good fortune to work with Jennifer Snodgrass of Harvard University Press.

Jennifer was available whenever we needed her, always patient and ready with an answer to any question (no matter how minute), and quick with praise for the editorial team's uncanny ability to stay on—or ahead of—schedule.

Last, we thank the many graduate students who worked tirelessly as fact-checkers and research assistants for *Notable American Women.* Their meticulous research, their relentless quest to confirm the accuracy of biographical information and bibliographic citations, and their good humor through occasionally frustrating and wearying searches across Harvard's—and Boston's—labyrinthine library systems are beyond commendable. In many ways, their work made up the backbone of this project; their enthusiasm was contagious. This formidable team included Melissa Carlson, Haley Duschinski, Malinda Ellwood, Meredith Greene, Carrie Haberstroh, Laura Lisy, Alison Maynard, Elizabeth More, Robin Morris, Julia Ott, Daniel Sargent, Sheri Shepherd, David Wagner, and Katja Zelljadt. Matthew Kaliner's talents as a statistician were indispensable. Special thanks go to those whom the editors called upon to do more than check facts: Annie Bergen, Amanda Bird, Jennifer Cote, and Kimberly Sims. And finally, we owe a special debt of gratitude to our succession of research assistants: Aimee Brown, who created the database and began the arduous process of inputting names; Rachel Keegan, who continued the process while doing outreach to a variety of professional groups and organizations; and Deborah Levine and Kathryn Losavio, who compiled and annotated bibliographies, performed extensive research in all of the major categories, and assisted in the process of matching authors to subjects. This volume is all the better for the talents, intellect, creativity, and vision of everyone who contributed to it.

Stacy Braukman
Susan Ware

INTRODUCTION: A CENTURY OF WOMEN

"I'm a conductor, period." Antonia Brico's blunt statement speaks for many of the women profiled in this volume of *Notable American Women,* who wanted nothing more than the chance to be taken seriously as individuals and compete on an equal basis with men. When they succeeded (which was often, as is amply documented here), it was because of individual merit and talent. When they failed, they blamed themselves, not society. And yet such an individualistic stance had definite limits: sometimes merit wasn't enough to break down the barriers society put in women's way; often race or class made the struggle even harder. In Brico's case, stonewalling by the male-dominated musical establishment in the 1930s and 1940s effectively kept her from practicing her craft at a level that matched her ability. Despite her brave protestations, no amount of talent or perseverance could change the conditions that marginalized her in her chosen field.

Brico's dilemma—living a woman's life but trying to make it in a man's world—is also the dilemma of modern women's history. As such, it is one of the most prominent themes running through this volume. When reading these essays, it is important to have (adapting a phrase of historian Joan Kelly's) a certain "doubled vision": to be aware of all the changes that had already taken place that made women's collective accomplishments possible, while at the same time never losing sight of the attitudes and barriers that kept women from being full and equal participants in modern society. Though the essays certainly contain their share of horror stories of discrimination and prejudice, on balance they provide even more evidence of how women, individually and collectively, have been able to challenge and subvert those gender expectations as part of one of the twentieth century's most significant social revolutions: the expansion of opportunities for women in almost all aspects of American public life.

For a book about a cohort of women whose careers mainly unfolded in the middle decades of the twentieth century, a period without an active feminist movement, this volume contains a surprising amount of activity for women by women, and not just when the story reaches the 1960s and 1970s. A strong thread of gender consciousness—the willingness to think of women as "we," often accompanied by a tendency to link women's struggles with a broader agenda for social change—runs through many of the stories, as individual women tried to improve conditions for other women in their communities, their professions, and the nation at large. At the same time, an even stronger theme of individualism—the desire, like Antonia Brico's, to be treated as human beings, rather than women—animates the volume. Acting as if equality had already been accomplished, such women achievers were not blind to barriers, but just pushed forward and got on with it. If Harvard Law School doesn't admit women, then enroll at Columbia. This no-nonsense approach served them well as they crafted their exceptional careers.

These two strands—one focused on gender consciousness, the other on individual achievement—coexist throughout this volume, indeed sometimes within the same individual. They come into even greater relief after the resurgence of feminism in the 1960s and 1970s. For many successful women, the noisy feminist revival was unwelcome and unappealing: after all, they had made it on their own without consciousness-raising, protest marches, or legislation. Invested in their own strategies for personal and professional success, they were often unwilling or unable to link their individual accomplishments with broader patterns for women as a whole. When the director Dorothy Arzner was rediscovered by feminists in the 1970s, she confounded their desire to make her into a victim of Hollywood sexism by announcing that her decision to opt out of the studio system was hers alone and that she had never been hampered by gender during her career.

And yet for other women the revival of feminism, and the civil rights revolution that preceded it, tapped a gender consciousness they had quietly harbored for years, allowing them to take their careers in exciting new directions as a host of new issues were suddenly thrust onto the national agenda. Sex discrimination had been something women just learned to live with and work around, but a network of feminists in the federal government made sure it became illegal under Title VII of the Civil Rights Act of 1964. When women scholars realized that their disciplines studied the activities of men only, they immediately set out to correct the imbalance. Labor organizers loudly pronounced that a woman's place was in her union.

The ability to illuminate larger patterns such as the fortunes of feminism in twentieth-century America through individual lives suggests the value of a biographical dictionary such as *Notable American Women.* Though fewer than five hundred women hardly constitute a representative sample of American womanhood as a whole, looking collectively at these lives reveals many trends and themes that enrich our understanding of countless other aspects of American history and women's lives. Individual essays stand alone, but the whole adds up to more than the sum of its parts.

Before looking at the broader trends, it is helpful to compile a composite portrait of the 483 women themselves. To begin with, approximately one-third were born in the nineteenth century, and the remaining two-thirds in the twentieth. More than one-third of the women profiled were the firstborn in their families; 11 percent were only children. Their birth dates span almost one hundred years: from Wyoming governor Nellie Tayloe Ross, born in 1876, to Tejana singer Selena Perez Quintanilla, born in 1971. More than three-quarters of the women were born in the thirty-year span from 1890 to 1920, and that cohort comprises the biographical core of the volume. Three-quarters of the women were white, with the remainder comprised of African Americans, Latinas, Native Americans, and Asian Americans.

In terms of demographics, it is hard not to be struck by the long lives of these women: more than three-fifths lived past the age of eighty, and almost one-third made it to ninety or beyond, at a time when the life expectancy of a woman born in 1900 was less than fifty years. Seven hardy women reached the century mark, with the Everglades activist Marjorie Stoneman Douglas taking the prize for a life that stretched to 108 years. This correlation between notable lives and longevity did not hold as clearly for women born past

1920, for an obvious reason: they had to die at a younger age in order to make our cutoff date of December 31, 1999. Possibly the combination of robust health and lengthy careers (quite a few of the women worked almost up to the day they died) proved an advantage when amassing notable accomplishments. Still, the strong representation of women who died at younger ages (fourteen women under the age of fifty; another twenty-five in their fifties) suggests that it was possible to cram enough into a shorter lifespan to merit inclusion. Sadly, some of the youngest women represented are the victims of violence (Selena, Anna Mae Aquash, Ana Mendieta, Theresa Cha) or accident, as in the case of *Challenger* astronauts Christa McAuliffe and Judith Resnik.

If gender truly were a recognized principle when it came to writing entries for biographical dictionaries, then essays on men would pay prominent attention to marital status, numbers of children, and domestic responsibilities, and assess how these personal details affected the subject's professional accomplishments. Whether or not that standard is met in general reference works, in *Notable American Women* the essays do pay attention to such issues. There is a fine line here. Since so much earlier historical writing relegated women to their roles as wives, mothers, and keepers of the home, it might seem like going backward to insist that such details occupy a prominent place in the narrative of each woman's life. And yet whether a woman chose to marry and whether she chose to have children (and how many) often did have a significant effect on the course of her professional life. Learning about how earlier generations of women juggled marriage, childbearing, and career still has resonance today as new generations of women (and men) face similar challenges.

The general breakdown of the volume shows that more than three-quarters of the women married at least once, while just under one-quarter (106 women, or 22 percent) never married. The percentage of women who married in this volume is significantly higher than in the previous volume, where it was closer to 60 percent, a shift which suggests two trends: a growing willingness to try to combine marriage with professional work or activism as the twentieth century unfolded, coupled with a continued commitment on the part of a substantial minority of these women to remaining single, at a rate far higher than that in the general population.

The range of life choices and lifestyles among the women who remained single shows the continued vibrancy of a historical tradition of women living independent of men. Few of the women in the volume openly called themselves lesbians, although historians have had little difficulty applying that label to women such as Janet Flanner, Elizabeth Bishop, Eva Le Gallienne, Berenice Abbott, or Dorothy Arzner. More common were women who steered clear of the label, consciously or not, and shared either a lifelong committed same-sex partnership or serial monogamous relationships with other women. This unmarried group also includes women who identified themselves as heterosexual but chose not to marry. The historical point is that women could participate in a variety of living arrangements and relationships because women's employment opportunities offered them the chance to be economically self-sufficient.

The pattern that emerges concerning marriage is similarly complex. Since almost four out of five women in the volume were married at some point in their lives, the institution of heterosexual marriage was a widespread experience that these notable women shared with American women at large. And yet almost half of the women who married were divorced, often more than once. Divorce still carried a certain stigma in the middle years of the twentieth century, but that did not stop these women from terminating relationships that no longer suited them personally or professionally. Their percentage of failed marriages is much higher than the prevailing divorce rate, suggesting a certain incompatibility between high-achieving women and the institution of marriage.

Seeing these notable women's lives as precursors of late-twentieth-century divorce patterns is one way to interpret the figures, but another is to look at the majority (54 percent of the ever-married women) who did remain married until the proverbial "death do us part." The importance of these relationships comes through clearly in the essays, especially in the surprisingly high number of marriages where the husband and wife worked together. This trend is most evident among scientists, but is also seen in a variety of other fields: psychologists Mamie Phipps and Kenneth Clark, designers Ray and Charles Eames, and screenwriters Frances Goodrich and Albert Hackett, to name a few. One possible conclusion is that women found an easier route to professional success when their careers were coupled with successful men. Another might be that some of the potential conflicts between marriage and career were muted when the couple was working as well as living together. (As someone once said of the famous acting couple Lynn Fontanne and Alfred Lunt, "No one can be as good as the Lunts. They rehearse in bed.") But there are also examples, especially from the performing arts, where such combined working and personal relationships became untenable, especially when the wife's success outstripped her husband's.

One of the most striking demographic characteristics of the volume is the large number of women who did not have children: more than half (52 percent) of the total, including 40 percent of the married women. Among the rest of the ever-married women, 40 percent had either one child or two. Additionally, four single women had one child each. While there were a smattering of women who had large families (ranging all the way up to thirteen children), the average number of children per married woman is 1.45, significantly below the national norm. (In 1900 American women had an average of 3.5 children; by the 1930s the average had dropped to 2.4, rising to 3.2 at the height of the baby boom in the 1950s.) This marked divergence from the general pattern seems to indicate that women's professional aspirations, and the difficulty of combining child-rearing responsibilities with the demands of a successful career, conflicted with reproduction. Having said that, it is also important to note (as the essays abundantly confirm) the joy and pride that many women took in their offspring. Long before feminists in the 1970s promoted childbearing as a conscious choice, these women were making individual decisions in a similar manner.

As has held true in all previous volumes, the women profiled enjoyed significant access to higher education. More than half (55 percent) of the women earned a bachelor's degree, and many of the rest took some college-level classes. A total of 118 women in this volume earned 90 doctorates, 15 medical degrees, and 15 law degrees, while approximately half that number earned terminal master's degrees. Long before the postwar expansion of higher education allowed wider access for men and women, this collective record represents an impressive educational accomplishment, and one directly related to the professional success that won many of these women inclusion in this volume.

Historians of women's education have long noted the significance of the Seven Sisters women's colleges in producing large numbers of women leaders, and this trend is confirmed by this cohort of women as well. Seventy-one women graduated from Seven Sisters colleges, more than one-quarter of all the undergraduate degrees earned. Unlike in the previous volume, where Bryn Mawr and Smith dominated, Vassar College produced by far the largest number of graduates (nineteen), followed by Barnard with twelve and Radcliffe and Bryn Mawr with ten each. Of the remaining Seven Sisters, Smith had nine graduates, Wellesley eight, and Mount Holyoke three. Other colleges or universities that produced significant numbers of graduates included Hunter College, the University of California at Berkeley, and Howard University.

The influence of Howard University deserves special mention. Howard not only consistently nurtured future leaders in its undergraduate and graduate programs, but it also offered black women a welcome place for professional employment. The list of women who spent all or part of their careers at Howard includes Dorothy Porter Wesley, Letitia Brown, Dorothy Boulding Ferebee, Gwendolyn Bennett, Flemmie Kittrell, and Lois Mailou Jones. Howard's preeminence should be placed within the broader importance of historically black colleges and universities for the careers of African Americans in the twentieth century. At a time when many colleges and universities were closed to blacks because of either race or cost, institutions such as Atlanta University, Bennett College, Tuskegee Institute, Spelman College, and Bethune-Cookman College trained the rising generations of African Americans. That story too is well documented in this volume.

In the graduate education of these women, one institution stands head and shoulders above the rest: Columbia University, with forty-one women receiving graduate degrees from the university. In part this is because of the importance of Teachers College in the educational careers of many of the women in the volume, but the dominance of Columbia extends to a wide range of fields from history to bacteriology to law. The next cluster of well-represented graduate institutions includes the University of Chicago (fourteen degrees), Harvard University and Radcliffe College (thirteen), Yale University (ten), and the University of California at Berkeley (nine). Combined with the strong showing of Barnard College and Hunter College in this composite educational profile, the predominance of Columbia University confirms the importance of New York City as a site for educational opportunities for women on a par with its dominant role in the areas of literature, the arts, and many professions.

Demographic factors like longevity, marital status, and number of children are common to all women, and help to highlight the ways in which the women profiled in *Notable American Women* marked general milestones in the female life cycle at the same time they struck off in new directions. Another reward of looking collectively at these individual lives is the ability to determine the fields where women have found the greatest opportunities—and the greatest barriers—and then place those accomplishments within the broader patterns of twentieth-century women's history.

Though there are obvious continuities with previous volumes in the areas where women have excelled (literature and the arts are a ready example), there are some rather striking differences. If the ups and downs were put in the language of stock market trading, the ticker would go something like this: settlement house leaders markedly down, film stars and modern dancers way up. Leaders of women's voluntary associations and education leaders decline, while popular musicians and journalists gain. Scientists and writers remain unchanged.

Within that shorthand are profound changes in women's history over the past century. For example, the shift toward popular culture is emblematic of its growing importance in modern American life. As the century unfolded, Americans had more time for leisure, and they avidly followed fields like sports, aviation, entertainment, and the movies, all areas where women had toeholds or, in the case of Hollywood, practically dominated. In fact, the women who excelled in popular culture often attained the cultural and social status that previously belonged to female leaders like Harriet Beecher Stowe, Jane Addams, and Eleanor Roosevelt, who had made their marks in more traditional areas such as literature, settlement work, or politics.

In a corresponding trend, the growing acceptance by the modern state of responsibilities for social and child welfare and social security, areas that previously had been the province of women's voluntary associations, created paid professional opportunities for women at various levels of government. Unlike social reformers such as Jane Addams or Lillian Wald who helped shaped the Progressive-era public agenda as truly national leaders, settlement leaders and social workers by mid-century were increasingly tied to bureaucratic structures that allowed them to pioneer and implement significant social welfare programs but without the national visibility of earlier leaders. Because the expansion of state responsibility for welfare was seen as a dramatic step forward from earlier voluntary initiatives, leaders saw this as progress, not loss. This overall growth in the state—one of the twentieth century's most important developments—is a major reason why categories like social reform and social welfare, so prominent in earlier volumes, are much less visible here. Instead, women's activism found new realms and challenges in government and the professions.

Amidst the breadth and range of individual women's accomplishments represented in this volume are patterns that suggest numerous areas for further research. One of the most interesting categories is science and medicine. This distinguished group includes two Nobel Prize winners (Gertrude Elion and Barbara McClintock) and many members of the National Academy of Sciences. It also presents some of the most graphic demonstrations of the systematic, widespread discrimination that women faced for most of the twentieth century. Research universities and laboratories hardly held out a welcome mat for these aspiring scientists: physicist Leona Marshall Libby's advisor warned her that as a woman going into science she might starve. Unfazed, Libby went on to play an important role in experimental nuclear physics. Like so many women throughout the volume, she was not about to be stopped by hostility or by barriers placed in her way.

That many women scientists married other scientists added an interesting twist to the problem. The strong anti-nepotism rules in most academic settings made it impossible for a husband and wife both to secure full-time employment in the same department or laboratory, which meant that the wife often worked as an unpaid research assistant in her husband's lab. This of course allowed her to do her work, but cut her off from salary and other professional benefits. Rather than be thwarted by such circumstances, the neuroscientist Berta Scharrer, whose scientist husband became the breadwinner in the family, found a creative solution to compensate for her lack of research funds: there were plenty of cockroaches in the basement of the University of Chicago laboratory where they worked, so she made cockroaches the basis of her experimental (and highly influential) research. There is another "happy ending" for many of these marginalized women scientists: when the women's movement started to question why there were so few tenured women professors, many of these scientists went from unpaid research associates to full professors practically overnight.

In the humanities and social sciences, women faced similar problems finding academic appointments, but certain institutions, notably the women's colleges and especially Barnard College, proved good havens. So did Columbia University, which played a prominent role in training and nurturing scholars in the expanding field of anthropology, with Margaret Mead leading the way. Women continued to excel in the field of education, long a focus of women's activism and energy, although not quite at the level of the charismatic leaders and institution founders of earlier generations. Glimmerings of the feminist challenge to the academy are seen in the lives of visionaries like Radcliffe president Mary Bunting, who realized that women in the 1950s were limited by a "climate of unexpectation," and the career of sociologist Mirra Komarovsky, who pioneered the study of gender long before the term was in common use.

A related cluster of activism concerns child advocacy. When broadly defined, this cluster shows the continuation of an interest in early childhood, especially but not limited to education, that has long been an important part of women's history. Examples of child-centered professional lives include nursery school pioneer Abigail Adams Eliot; Icie Macy Hoobler of the Michigan Children's Fund; children's librarians (a new specialty) such as Virginia Haviland and Augusta Baker; and Elizabeth Coatsworth and Ursula Nordstrom, both influential figures in the development of children's literature as a distinct area of publishing. New York City Family Court judge Justine Wise Polier championed the interests of children in the courts, psychologists Susan Gray and Louise Bates Ames explored the lives of young children, and psychiatrists and psychoanalysts Selma Fraiberg and Margaret Mahler looked at mother-child bonds.

Two other clusters deserve mention. The first is conservatism, an important intellectual tradition in twentieth-century America and a generally understudied and under-documented area in women's history, although it is beginning to draw more study. One place to start is by noting the influence of women in the Republican Party through the careers of Mary Louise Smith, Marion Martin, and Margaret Chase Smith. All of these women were allied with the moderate wing of the party and often combined their partisan politicking with a commitment to expanding roles for women. Important examples of libertarianism are found in the writer Ayn Rand, who reached a huge popular audience for her ideas with *Atlas Shrugged* and *The Fountainhead,* and Suzanne La Follette, who with William F. Buckley Jr. blended conservatism and anti-communism into a major cultural force at the *National Review* in the 1950s. Foreign policy specialist Dorothy Fosdick helped shaped the anti-communist agenda of Washington Senator Henry "Scoop" Jackson, an instructive example of a woman wielding enormous power but remaining practically invisible behind a famous man. A bit later, Nixon appointee Dixy Lee Ray pushed a pro-nuclear, anti-environmentalist agenda in office and out. What is missing from the volume is documentation of the tremendous growth of conservative women's organizations in the 1970s and beyond, headed by such women as Phyllis Schlafly and Beverly Le Haye, plus the influence of conservative women in the Bush and

Reagan administrations. Because these women are still alive, assessment of their influence will have to wait for future volumes.

Another fascinating cluster involves religious activism. The Catholic Church underwent enormous changes over the course of the century, and the impact of these changes on individual women in the church—and the impact of women's voices in pushing for further reform—is well represented in the lives of Catholic activists such as Sister Annette Walters of the Sister Formation Conference, theologian Thea Bowman, artist Corita Kent, and activist Dorothy Day. The atheist Madalyn O'Hair outraged both the left and the right with her assertion, upheld by the Supreme Court in 1963, that school prayer was unconstitutional. Under pressure from feminists, most major denominations were challenged to open the ministry, priesthood, or rabbinate to women starting in the 1960s. While this volume does not document the role of women as rabbis (this too will have to wait), it does touch on the ordination of women as Episcopal priests through the lives of Jeannette Piccard and Pauli Murray. Trude Weiss-Rosmarin's focus on educating Jewish women through the *Jewish Spectator,* Catherine Marshall's best-selling religious tracts, and Cynthia Clark Wedel's activism within United Church Women and the National Council of Churches suggest other ways of expanding the roles of women within religious traditions. Finally, the life of faith healer Kathryn Kuhlman demonstrates that even in evangelical religious traditions, which tend to encourage submissive roles for women, there is room for charismatic female leadership.

Women have always been an important part of both the arts and literature, and their participation is well documented in this volume. Because of the broad sweep of the lives profiled, it is possible to demonstrate trends and shifting fashions over time. For example, the social realism of painters such as Alice Neel and Isabel Bishop from the 1930s is followed by the postwar emergence of abstract expressionism, a field generally associated with men but represented here in the careers of Lee Krasner, Joan Mitchell, and Elaine de Kooning. Taking the story even further, the performance art and installations of artists such as Nancy Graves and Ana Mendieta show new directions art was taking in the 1970s and beyond.

A similar pattern is at work in literature, with well-known writers and public intellectuals such as Mary McCarthy, Diana Trilling, Barbara Tuchman, Lillian Hellman, and Elizabeth Bishop followed by younger experimental writers such as Kathy Acker or Theresa Cha. An emerging lesbian sensibility is suggested in the works of May Sarton, Muriel Rukeyser, and Djuna Barnes. The importance of Southern writers is confirmed by Harriette Arnow, Sarah Patton Boyle, and Katharine Du Pre Lumpkin. Other literary trends well represented are the vibrancy of the African American literary tradition through the lives of writers such as Dorothy West and Ann Petry (with links to the Harlem Renaissance) and Margaret Walker, and the important contributions of Latinas such as Estela Trambley and Lourdes Casal and Native American writer Mary TallMountain in bridging worlds and cultures through words.

One of the most innovative sectors in the arts, and one of the most dynamic fields represented in this volume, is dance, a quintessentially modern form with its focus on creative expression and physicality linked to the key social and political issues of the day, including the changing status of women. Glimpses of the modern dance revolution appeared in the last volume with the biographies of Ruth St. Denis and Doris Humphrey, but the real flowering is here. In addition to Martha Graham, a seminal artist of the past century, the lives of Agnes de Mille, Hanya Holm, Pearl Primus, and Bessie Schönberg demonstrate the centrality of women to this expanding—and expansive—field. Flourishing alongside modern dance (and sometimes cross-pollinating with it, as in the career of Agnes de Mille) is ballet, represented in the lives of American Ballet Theatre leader Lucia Chase and ballerinas Nora Kaye and Alexandra Danilova. A fascinating subset of ethnic dance performance is documented in the lives of Ragini Devi (born Esther Sherman), who became one of the prime interpreters of dance from India; ethnological dancer and interpreter La Meri (born Russell Meriwether Hughes); and Molly Spotted Elk, who kept Penobscot tribal traditions alive by bringing them to wider audiences through dance. Finally, the strong influence of dance educators such as Margaret H'Doubler and Martha Hill laid the foundations for the teaching of dance in both academic and popular settings. The vibrancy of these careers, and their interconnections and broader outreach, suggest multiple opportunities for future research.

Women's continued influence, indeed dominance, in the fields of twentieth-century film, theater, and popular music is also illustrated in this volume. The period covered encompasses the Golden Era of Hollywood, and includes the careers of actresses ranging from the silent era (Lillian Gish, Louise Brooks, and Mary Pickford) to stars of the 1930s and 1940s (Bette Davis, Joan Crawford, Ginger Rogers, and, of course, Mae West) to African American activists such as Fredi Washington and Butterfly McQueen, who challenged the racial typecasting that limited their roles. Women's contributions behind the camera are also well documented, including pioneering director Dorothy Arzner, editor Barbara McLean, animator Mary Ellen Bute, and documentary filmmaker Shirley Clarke. Even though radio and television never had quite the golden age for women that film did, women's contributions there are represented in the biographies of Lucille Ball, Dinah Shore, Mary Margaret McBride, and Pauline Frederick.

Many performers made their mark on the live stage, although by the 1960s Broadway was losing the battle for cultural dominance to television and film. Still, the careers of superb actresses such as Helen Hayes, Lynn Fontanne, and Ruth Gordon, as well as theatrical producers such as Eva Le Gallienne and Cheryl Crawford, show the ongoing vitality of this medium. Though vaudeville was fast receding, Molly Picon struggled to keep the tradition of Yiddish theater alive.

Women had been on stage for centuries, but tradition-bound fields such as classical music were less welcoming, as conductors Antonia Brico and Margaret Hillis discovered when they tried to break into that very male-dominated field. Marian Anderson, Maria Callas, and Rosa Ponselle found opportunities in concert and operatic singing, although Anderson was barred by her race from singing at the Metropolitan Opera until the 1950s, past the peak of her career. Composers such as Elinor Remick Warren, Miriam Gideon, and Louise Talma also took their places within twentieth-century American classical music.

Just as it is hard to imagine Hollywood without women in starring roles, it is almost impossible to imagine the field of popular music without its female singers. Where would jazz and blues be without Ethel Waters, Pearl Bailey, Mary Lou Williams, Sarah Vaughan, Willie Mae Thornton, Melba Liston, Alberta Hunter, and Victoria Spivey? Many of these women essentially had two careers: one from the 1920s through the

1950s, when jazz and blues were the dominant forms of popular music, and then again in the 1960s and 1970s, when the performers were rediscovered by younger audiences. Able to sustain their connection with listeners over decades and changing musical tastes, singers like Kate Smith, Ethel Merman, and Ella Fitzgerald were major figures in mid-century popular culture. In the field of country and western music, the lives of Minnie Pearl, Maybelle Carter, and Tammy Wynette show the importance of women performers within what became one of the century's fastest-growing and influential musical traditions. While the country stars were white, popular music overall shows a high degree of racial intermixing, both of artists and of musical styles.

When faced with so many success stories, at times it may seem that women were on a relentless and inevitable climb toward equal participation in all facets of American life, but there were certain areas where women did not make as much progress as might be expected. The field of business is one. Individual women had opportunities to found their own companies, but rarely were able to translate that initiative into sustained corporate success. Barred from corporate culture, women did not even have a chance to hit the glass ceiling, and they often found opportunities in small business uncertain at best. For example, chemist Hazel Bishop (who invented "kiss proof" lipstick), Bette Graham (who invented Liquid Paper), and Brownie Wise (who helped popularize Tupperware in the 1950s) all were forced to relinquish control of their companies while at the peak of their success. More successful in the long term was Olive Beech, who took over her husband's aviation company after his death and built it into a diversified and profitable postwar corporation. Women such as Olga Erteszek, Vera Maxwell, and Lilly Daché also found success as fashion designers and entrepreneurs.

A final profession where women excelled was journalism, an expanding field that offered the opportunity to work side-by-side with men in the camaraderie of the newsroom. Journalism provided a range of possibilities, ranging from women who co-owned or inherited newspapers (Dorothy Schiff, Mary Bingham, Dorothy Chandler) to foreign correspondents (Ruth Baldwin Cowan, Sigrid Schultz, Irene Corbally Kuhn) to syndicated columnists (Erma Bombeck, Sylvia Porter). Nancy Woodhull served as the first managing editor of *USA Today,* the pioneering national newspaper launched in the 1980s, and Meg Greenfield became a respected editorial voice at the *Washington Post* and *Newsweek.* Feature and investigative reporting continued to offer professional opportunities for women, ranging from Emma Bugbee, who got her break covering Eleanor Roosevelt's press conferences for women reporters in the 1930s, to Charlotte Curtis, who wrote about society and style in new, hipper ways in the 1970s. In magazines, Ruth Whitney served as the longtime editor of *Glamour,* Diana Vreeland led *Vogue* during the fashion heyday of the 1960s, and Ruth Ross broke new ground with the debut of *Essence* in 1970. Especially noteworthy is how African American women, Latinas, and Asian American women used journalism to promote a combined professional and civil rights agenda. For this phenomenon, see the careers of Ethel Payne, Hazel Garland, and Alice Dunnigan, as well as the activist journalism practiced by Louise Leung Larson, Michi Weglyn, and Francisca Flores. Also of note is the importance of newspapers such as the *Chicago Defender* and the *Pittsburgh Courier* in fostering the careers of minority journalists.

* * *

Another benefit of a biographical dictionary with a defined time span is the opportunity to look at important historical events and movements through the lens of biography. This volume of *Notable American Women* richly demonstrates women's activism and participation across a broad sweep of public life, ranging from the peace movement to birth control and sex education, conservation, community activism, and partisan politics, especially from the 1930s through the 1970s, the chronological core of the volume. A pattern first observed in the last volume—women joining the federal government during the New Deal in the 1930s—continues apace, with women serving at the national level in every presidential administration from Franklin Roosevelt to Bill Clinton.

It is especially interesting to cut across the essays chronologically and see what is happening in a variety of fields and professions at the same point in time. Take the Great Depression of the 1930s. The gravest economic crisis the United States had ever faced occurred just as many women were completing their schooling or trying to get started in a profession, causing disruption and delay in careers. In cases such as those of Pearl Primus, Lee Krasner, and Harriette Arnow, temporary employment by the Works Progress Administration or Federal Art Project tided them over. At the same time, the Depression opened up opportunities for many women, especially those trained in social welfare, who found jobs in the expanding federal and state bureaucracies; Clara Beyer, Eveline Burns, Gay Bolling Shepperson, and Hilda Worthington Smith demonstrate this trend. The Depression was also a global phenomenon, and a factor in the rise of Nazism in Germany that caused the flight of many trained professionals, especially in the medical and scientific fields, to the United States. American women's history was enriched by the arrival of Helene Deutsch, Margaret Mahler, and Helen Wolff, among others.

An especially vibrant area represented in the volume is labor activism and radicalism in the 1930s, as women took leading roles in the attempt to propose alternatives to a capitalist system in disarray. The decade witnessed the height of the influence of the Communist Party in the United States, and women such as Peggy Dennis, Vera Weisbord, Emma Tenayuca, and Louise Alone Thompson Patterson joined up. Writers including Mary McCarthy, Diana Trilling, Martha Gellhorn, Lillian Hellman, Meridel Le Sueur, and Muriel Rukeyser were deeply involved in left-wing politics. The decade also saw a surge in the strength of organized labor, and once again women were centrally involved: Emma Tenayuca in Texas, Luisa Moreno in California, Myra Wolfgang in Detroit, Rose Norwood in Boston, Jennie Matyas and Sue Ko Lee in San Francisco, and Pauline Newman in New York, to name a few. For a woman like Clara Lemlich Shavelson, her activism in the 1930s was part of a lifelong commitment to radical social change which began in the great garment workers' strike of 1909–1910, continued through grassroots groups like the United Council of Working-Class Women in the 1930s, and ended in her nineties when she helped organize the orderlies in her nursing home. The white southern tenant farmer Myrtle Lawrence shows another side of labor activism with her participation in the Southern Tenant Farmers' Union. One thing that is distinctive about most of these labor activists and radicals is that they also shared a feminist perspective, or at least a concern for women workers and women's issues, making them examples of what is sometimes referred to as labor feminism.

The next great challenge that the United States faced was World War II. Historians debate whether the war permanently changed the status of women, but for many of those included in this volume, the war definitely opened up new opportunities. Scientists like Gertrude Elion and Charlotte Friend could suddenly get jobs or research positions that were held by men in peacetime; economist Alice Bourneuf and foreign affairs specialist Eleanor Lansing Dulles participated in the Bretton Woods Conference, which restructured the postwar global economy. The best example of widening horizons concerns the status of women in the military. Grace Hopper started her pioneering work on computers with the United States Naval Reserve in 1943. Mildred McAfee Horton, Nancy Harkness Love, Ruth Streeter, Jacqueline Cochran, and Joy Bright Hancock all led branches of the armed services that were opened to women during the wartime emergency. After the war, these leaders worked with congresswoman Frances Bolton to pass legislation giving women a permanent place in the armed services. Another wartime breakthrough described in the volume concerned the racial integration of the armed services' nursing staffs, thanks to the persistent prodding of the National Association of Colored Graduate Nurses and its leaders, Mabel Keaton Staupers and Estelle Massey Osborne.

The wartime experience looks quite different, however, when viewed from the perspective of Japanese Americans. Every single Japanese American woman in this volume was incarcerated under Executive Order #9066, issued by President Franklin D. Roosevelt in February 1942. Poet Teiko Tomita was the oldest, born in Japan in 1896; fearing that her poetry would be seen as subversive, with much pain she destroyed her manuscripts before she was incarcerated at Tule Lake, California, and later Heart Mountain, Wyoming. Physician Kazue Togasaki, American-born and around the same age as Tomita, served as the director of medical services in the various assembly areas and camps where she was detained. Younger women like Aki Kurose, Miyoko Ito, Michi Weglyn, and Yoshiko Uchida were still in high school or college when the war broke out, and their stays in the camps were of shorter duration, as they qualified for release to continue their schooling outside the West Coast war zone. Additionally, two non-Japanese women married to Japanese American men, Elaine Black Yoneda and Estelle Peck Ishigo, spent time in the camps to keep their families together, even though their surrender was not legally required. In many cases wartime internment set in motion lifelong activism. Michi Weglyn, who published the first comprehensive history of the internment camps in 1976, campaigned for restitution and redress; Estelle Ishigo's watercolors from Heart Mountain helped raise public awareness about the denial of civil liberties during wartime; and Yoshiko Uchida wrote about the wartime experience of Japanese Americans in books for young readers.

The activism of the women during the Depression and war years came back to haunt them during the late 1940s and 1950s during the McCarthy period of anti-Communist hysteria. Personal or political trauma is a common thread in many of the entries, confirming the effect this moment had across many fields and professions. Labor activists and radicals were especially hard hit, their organizing during the 1930s and 1940s now seen as linked to Communist-front activities; both Luisa Moreno and Josefina Fierro left the country rather than face possible deportation, and Florence Luscomb and Jessie Lloyd O'Connor had their passports seized because of alleged radical activities. Academics were under special pressure, and women ranging from biologist Ruth Bleier to sociologist Helen Merrell Lynd were called before the House Committee on Un-American Activities (HUAC) or one of its state offshoots. Composer Miriam Gideon and her husband lost teaching positions at Brooklyn College because of his activism. HUAC went after Hollywood with a vengeance: Joan Crawford, Lucille Ball, and screenwriter Frances Goodrich were among those forced to testify before the committee. In the federal government, Mary Dublin Keyserling and Esther Peterson were investigated by loyalty committees, although later cleared.

In these times of recrimination, accusation, and innuendo, there were moments of personal courage and conscience. Senator Margaret Chase Smith spoke out against her fellow senator Joseph McCarthy on the Senate floor in 1950. Representative Helen Gahagan Douglas waged a valiant, if unsuccessful, campaign that year against the red-baiting Richard Nixon, who called his opponent pink right down to her underwear. Lillian Hellman refused to cooperate with HUAC when called to testify in 1952, and suffered the consequences when she was blacklisted. Physicist Katharine Way spoke out against the unfounded accusations sabotaging careers in her field, charges often rooted in the secret wartime conditions necessary to develop the atomic bomb. Meridel Le Sueur kept on writing, even though no publisher would touch her books.

Many more women were not called before committees, but silently feared the exposure of their links to radical associations, the potential loss of livelihood, or other professional consequences. Historian Eleanor Flexner, for example, took great pains to conceal the radical roots of the activism that led her to undertake *Century of Struggle*, a pioneering survey of the woman suffrage movement published in 1959. One wonders how many other women might also have hidden (perhaps even from the authors of these essays) the full extent of their radical pasts out of fear of exposure, even long after the threat of McCarthyism had died down. This topic is ripe for future research.

The other major development of the 1950s—the rise of the civil rights movement—is probably the most far-reaching story in the entire volume. The civil rights revolution has already received much attention from historians, but the actions and campaigns documented here deepen and complicate the story in some very interesting ways. At the very least, the range of activism suggests the need for a history that recognizes, indeed gives center stage to, the roles that women, black and white, played in grassroots and national organizations, supporting the men who took the public leadership roles. The critical contributions of organizers such as Ella Baker and Ruby Hurley to the National Association for the Advancement of Colored People (NAACP), the Southern Christian Leadership Conference, and the Student Non-Violent Coordinating Committee give a grassroots perspective on how and why a movement arises. Add to them the contributions of women like Daisy Bates in Arkansas, Mary Modjeska Simkins and Septima Poinsette Clark in South Carolina, and Fannie Lou Hamer in Mississippi, and the range of activism becomes clearer. Also important are liberal white Southerners such as Virginia Foster Durr, Hazel Brannon Smith, and Sarah Patton Boyle, who at great personal and professional cost cast their lot with the forces that would fundamentally change the South they had grown up in.

The civil rights story is not just limited to the South, however, nor to the 1950s and early 1960s. Many of the individual biographies record activism in the NAACP dating back to the 1930s and 1940s. This social movement had been incubating for quite a while before public events like *Brown v. Board of Education*, the Birmingham bus boycott, or Little Rock forced it into public consciousness. The battle was national, as seen in the activism of Frances Albrier in the San Francisco Bay Area, Edith Spurlock Sampson in Chicago, Muriel Snowden in Boston, and Sadie Alexander in Philadelphia. Northern white allies pushed for civil rights, including Elizabeth Wood's fight for integrated public housing in Chicago in the 1940s and Judge Justine Wise Polier's pathbreaking rulings challenging school segregation in New York City in the 1950s.

This volume also provides much evidence for expanding the discussion of civil rights beyond its traditional formulation as a black-white, North-South struggle. The story of Chicana/o activism is especially instructive. As seen in the lives of Luisa Moreno and Josefina Fierro, the 1939 founding of *El Congreso de Pueblos de Hablan Española,* an organization dedicated to expanding the civil rights of Mexican Americans in the United States, launched it on a trajectory similar to the more familiar story of the NAACP agitating for civil rights for African Americans. The organization was also one in which women played central leadership roles. Two decades later, Francisca Flores was a founding member of the Mexican American Political Association in 1960. Further examples of Chicana activism include María Latigo Hernández's organizing with *La Raza Unida* in Texas in the 1970s and the environmental activism of Aurora Castillo and Mothers of East Los Angeles in the 1980s and 1990s.

Less fully represented but still significant is the story of Native American activism spanning the period from the 1930s to the present. Well-placed government administrators such as Ruth Muskrat Bronson and her white ally Ruth Underhill tried as early as the 1930s to make the Bureau of Indian Affairs more responsive to tribal sovereignty and governance. Historian Angie Debo devoted her career to applying an Indian-centered perspective to the federal government's century-long attempt to deal with its indigenous peoples. Activist Annie Dodge Wauneka mobilized around the issue of better access to health care on reservations and Lucy Covington led a successful battle to win recognition for the Colville Indian tribe in Washington state. Anna Mae Aquash, murdered in 1976, represents the radicalism of the American Indian Movement as it tried to build a pan-Indian identity. These struggles too should be seen as part of the broader civil rights struggle of the twentieth century.

The effects of the civil rights movement rippled though the postwar period, and nowhere is the legacy more clear than in its effect on the emergence of the other profound social movement amply documented in this volume: the revival of feminism in the 1960s, 1970s, and beyond. In some ways it is surprising how well represented the feminist movement is in this volume, as many of the women who were its instigators and many more who were its beneficiaries are still alive. And yet, like civil rights, feminism had been incubating, either within individuals or within organizations, for quite a while. "This is the most important movement of the century," explained Wilma Scott Heide, an early president of the National Organization for Women, in 1967. "I've been waiting for it all my life."

Historians often divide the emergence of the women's movement into the women's rights branch and the women's liberation branch. This volume does an excellent job of documenting the women's rights branch, but with the exception of Valerie Solanas, Gloria Martin, and visionaries like Audre Lorde, does less well with women's liberation and radical feminism. One obvious reason is that the women involved in women's rights tended to be older, and thus more likely to die in time for inclusion. Catherine East, Kathryn Clarenbach, Esther Peterson, and Mary Dublin Keyserling represent a pattern of women employed in the federal government who informally networked to advance women's causes starting in the 1960s through initiatives like the President's Commission on the Status of Women in the Kennedy Administration and its state offshoots. Many of these women went on to become founders or early members of the National Organization for Women in 1966 and later participated in a range of government-related feminist activity, including the National Women's Conference in Houston in 1977.

The breadth of the feminist vision can only be hinted at by pointing to the various areas beyond government where it had an impact. National political life certainly looked and sounded different with the addition of Bella Abzug, Millicent Fenwick, Ella Grasso, and Barbara Jordan. Barbara Wertheimer, Olga Madar, and Myra Wolfgang joined feminist and labor concerns in the Coalition of Labor Union Women, founded in 1974. Francisca Flores prioritized women's issues in the Chicano movement as the first president of La Comisíon Femenil Mexicana Nacional. Within the scientific and medical communities, patient-activists like Rose Kushner challenged standard ways of treating breast cancer, while books like *Our Bodies, Ourselves* (represented in the entry on Esther Rome) encouraged women to take a more active role in their medical and physical wellbeing. Every discipline in the humanities and social sciences was affected by the rise of feminist scholarship, as seen in the careers of historian Joan Kelly, sociologists Eleanor Leacock and Jessie Bernard, and literary scholars Ellen Moers and Elaine Hedges. Myra Sadker challenged the way that girls were taught in the classroom. Activists like Tish Sommers and Maggie Kuhn tackled issues facing aging women and displaced homemakers, and Johnnie Tillmon reminded the public and policymakers alike that welfare was a women's issue.

Finally, the volume documents the links between the two waves of feminist activism in the twentieth century—the suffrage movement of the 1910s and the revival of feminism in the 1960s—though the life of Alice Paul, whose lifelong activism for the vote and then for the Equal Rights Amendment spans the period covered in the volume. Paul is joined by many other women who aligned themselves with the feminist cause, through the National Woman's Party, women's professional or voluntary associations, or more informally. But this observation brings us back to where this discussion started: to the conflict between women who had made it as individuals and had little or no gender consciousness, and those who were willing to reach out to other women as a group and stress the similarities of their shared experiences. That schism continues to define women today, and no doubt will for the foreseeable future.

In the end, all roads lead to Pauli Murray. In a volume this rich with women's stories, it might seem unlikely that one life could embody so many of its themes, but just as Eleanor Roosevelt emerged as the dominant figure of the last volume, so Pauli Murray became the epicenter of this one. It is not hard to see why. Pauli Murray was involved in practically all the major developments that historians write about when they try to make sense of the twentieth century, especially the movements for social change that have been so central to its history. Civil rights, feminism, religion, literature, law, sexuality—no matter the subject, she was there. Her wide-ranging activism conjures up images of a cartoon poster from the 1920s, usually referred to as the "Spider Web Chart," which purported to link all the major women's organizations to left-wing and radical causes in sinister and subversive ways. On a Spider Web Chart of the key issues and concerns of this volume, almost every line would go through Pauli Murray.

Pauli Murray is well known to historians but not to the general public. An African American born in the segregated south in 1910, Murray was raised in Durham, North Carolina, by an extended family of strong women who valued education. She went north to attend Hunter College, graduating in 1933. A brief marriage during college was later annulled, and for the rest of her life she struggled with her own gender identity and attraction to women. Jobs were scarce in the worst year of the Depression, when she graduated, and even scarcer for black women. Murray eventually found a position with the Works Progress Administration, striking up a friendship with Eleanor Roosevelt along the way. Denied admission to the graduate school of the University of North Carolina because of her race, she earned a law degree from Howard University in 1944, where she articulated the connection (based in part on her personal experience) between Jim Crow discrimination against African Americans and "Jane Crow" discrimination against women. When Harvard Law School turned down her application for further graduate study, saying she was "not of the sex entitled to be admitted," her feminist consciousness solidified.

Murray worked as a lawyer and researcher in the 1950s and was asked to join the President's Commission on the Status of Women, where she promulgated the view that the Fourteenth Amendment could be used to challenge sex discrimination as well as race discrimination. A founder of the National Organization for Women, she later taught at Benedict College and Brandeis University before fulfilling a lifelong calling to become an Episcopal priest, something that became a possibility only in the 1970s. She was ordained in 1977 and served several congregations before dying in 1985 at the age of seventy-four.

Not every woman in this volume touches on so many of the twentieth century's major themes as Pauli Murray, but each one serves as a window on the broader historical period in which she was such a notable participant.

Susan Ware

NOTABLE AMERICAN WOMEN

A

ABBOTT, Berenice. July 17, 1898–December 9, 1991. Photographer.

Berenice Abbott was an innovative and pioneering photographer in three genres: portraiture, urban landscape, and science. She was born in Springfield, Ohio, the youngest of five children of Alice Bunn and Charles E. Abbott. Her name was originally spelled Bernice. She was raised by her mother after her parents separated when she was three months old, and she grew up in extreme poverty while her mother worked as a milliner and seamstress. In 1917 Abbott briefly attended Ohio State University; after one term she moved to New York City. She enrolled at Columbia University to study journalism, but stayed only one week.

Small in stature, with large intense eyes and close-cropped hair, the energetic Abbott soon found herself in the midst of the exciting emerging Greenwich Village avant-garde scene, meeting such powerful writers as DJUNA BARNES and Eugene O'Neill. She supported herself with odd jobs, including modeling for artists, and in her spare time played minor roles at the Provincetown Playhouse. After nearly dying from influenza, she began to learn sculpture and made the acquaintance of Man Ray, Marcel Duchamp, and the eccentric Baroness Elsa von Freytag-Loringhoven, all three affiliated with the irreverent attitudes of Dada.

In the winter of 1921 Abbott went to Paris, where she lived in poverty for two years. Her luck turned in 1923 when Man Ray hired her as his assistant in his successful portrait photography business. At his suggestion, she began taking photographs on her lunch break; photography soon became her consuming occupation. Abbott held her first one-person exhibition in 1926 and in 1928 was invited to join the First Salon of Independent Photographers, where critics singled out her work for praise. Her portraits of Paris intellectuals in the 1920s were based on principles that motivated her throughout her life—simplicity of setting, attention to light, and allowing the sitters to emerge on their own terms, what she called "a good likeness, character, and spontaneity" (*A Guide to Better Photography*, p. 133). Abbott's portraits of Djuna Barnes, *Little Review* editors JANE HEAP and MARGARET ANDERSON, publisher SYLVIA BEACH, writer James Joyce, art collector PEGGY GUGGENHEIM, and poet Jean Cocteau are often regarded as the definitive images of those famous personalities. She also photographed well-known African Americans like singer Huddie Ledbetter and successful Harlem businesswoman A'LELIA WALKER.

In 1929 Abbott went to New York for a brief visit and was thrilled by the city's transformation since the late teens. She moved there immediately and decided to begin a portrait of New York City, an endeavor that obsessed her for the next ten years. Part of her inspiration came from the work of Eugene Atget, whose photographic portrait of Paris is now recognized as one of the great achievements in the history of photography. Abbott bought all of Atget's negatives and prints when he died, unknown, in 1927 and energetically promoted him for many years.

In 1934, after several years of sparse freelance assignments, Abbott accepted a summer job as the photographer for books on Henry Hobson Richardson and pre–Civil War architecture with the architectural historian Henry Russell Hitchcock. This experience refined her technical understanding of the subtleties of her 8×10 Century Universal view camera. In the fall of 1934 the Museum of the City of New York exhibited forty-one of her New York photographs. Elizabeth McCausland, the art critic and journalist, reviewed the exhibition and the two women became lifelong partners. In the spring of 1935 they traveled to Pennsylvania, West Virginia, Tennessee, Arkansas, Missouri, Illinois, and Ohio in a journey that would later become a ritual itinerary for Farm Security Administration (FSA) photographers. That fall they jointly, but unsuccessfully, applied to the Guggenheim Foundation to create a "Portrait of America" with photographs and text.

Abbott finally gained support from the Federal Art Project for her New York City project in late 1935. She worked on it exclusively for the next three years, along with a team of researchers supervised by McCausland. Abbott avoided romanticism, emphasizing instead themes like changing transportation and food distribution systems, with images of shopkeepers and pushcart operators set in contrast to the impersonal buildings of the corporate world. In 1939 E. P. Dutton published a selection of the photographs, with texts by

McCausland, as *Changing New York*—the only document of their collaboration.

When her government support ended in 1939, Abbott turned to the difficult endeavor of creating photographic visualizations of scientific concepts, a decision probably influenced by her relationship with McCausland, who had written about cutting-edge scientific ideas earlier in her career. Abbott may also have felt the intense pressure on the Left that began in the summer of 1938 with the creation of the Special Committee on Un-American Activities, also known as the Dies Committee (later the House Committee on Un-American Activities). In 1936 Abbott had been a founding board member of the radical Photo League, an organization committed to photography of workers and social causes, and also had participated in the American Artists Congress, the Popular Front gathering of artists and critics that opposed fascism. The hunt for Communists and the disillusioning 1939 Nazi-Soviet pact probably contributed to Abbott's new enthusiasm, shared by many artists at this time, for abstract principles rather than social realism.

For the next twenty years Abbott remained based in New York, where she invented new systems of lighting and projection in order to create visual images of concepts such as magnetism or gravity in photographs. The resulting images were technically complex and aesthetically stunning. In 1944 she was hired as photography editor at *Science Illustrated* magazine, and her first scientific images appeared in a high school textbook, *American High School Biology*, in 1948. Abbott was also a pioneering teacher and writer on photography. From 1935 until 1958 she taught at the New School for Social Research and organized their photography program. She also wrote a popular textbook, *A Guide to Better Photography* (1941). In 1954 she photographed U.S. Route One from Maine to Florida and back, taking more than four hundred photographs documenting the changing American landscape. After the Soviet Union launched Sputnik in 1957, she was invited to join the Physical Science Study Committee, a group who were reorganizing the study of high school physics. She worked there from 1958 to 1960, and a series of her photographs was used to illustrate their textbook, *Physics* (1960).

After the death of Elizabeth McCausland in 1965, Abbott moved permanently to Maine, although she kept an ongoing association with the New York Public Library, which mounted a major retrospective of her work in 1989. She continued to make prints from her negatives and oversaw the publication of nine limited-edition portfolios of her work between 1974 and 1982. Berenice Abbott has a major place in the history of photography as an artist, a teacher, a writer, and an inventor, but above all for her vision, initiative, and perseverance. She died in Monson, Maine, on December 9, 1991, at the age of ninety-three. Her work continues to be featured frequently in special exhibitions throughout the country.

Bibliography: The primary Berenice Abbott archive is privately held by Ron Kurtz, Commerce Graphics in East Rutherford, New Jersey. The New York Public Library and the Museum of the City of New York each holds a complete archival set of the "Changing New York" photographs. The Museum of the City of New York also has archival documents based on Abbott's Works Progress Administration–supported "Changing New York" project. The George Eastman House in Rochester, New York, has a 1975 interview with Abbott by James McQuaid that cannot be photocopied. *Changing New York*, with a text by Elizabeth McCausland (1939), was republished as *New York in the Thirties* (1973). Abbott's other publications include *A Guide to Better Photography* (1941), *The View Camera Made Simple* (1948), and *A New Guide to Better Photography* (1953). Abbott also published two works on Eugene Atget: *Eugene Atget Portfolio: Twenty Photographic Prints from His Original Glass Negatives* (1956) and *The World of Atget* (1964). Her scientific photographs were most prominently published in three books with texts by E. G. Valens: *Magnet* (1964), *Motion* (1965), and *The Attractive Universe* (1969). Her later American scene work appears in *Greenwich Village Today and Yesterday* (1949), text by Henry Wysham Lanier; and *A Portrait of Maine* (1968), text by Chenoweth Hall.

Secondary works on Berenice Abbott include three books by Hank O'Neal: *Berenice Abbott: The Red River Photographs* (1979); *Berenice Abbott, American Photographer* (1982); and *The Beauty of Physics* (1986). See also Michael G. Sundell, *Berenice Abbott: Documentary Photographs of the 1930s; An Exhibition*, New Gallery of Contemporary Art, Cleveland, Ohio (1980); Julia van Haaften, ed., *Berenice Abbott, Photographer: A Modern Vision* (1989); and Bonnie Yochelson, *Berenice Abbott's Changing New York* (1997). Another useful article is Elizabeth McCausland, "The Photography of Berenice Abbott," *Trend* 3, no. 1 (March–April 1935). An obituary appeared in the *New York Times* on December 11, 1991.

SUSAN NOYES PLATT

ABEL, Theodora Mead. September 9, 1899–December 2, 1998. Clinical psychologist.

Theodora Mead Abel was a clinical psychologist and educator who brought an anthropological sensibility—an awareness that culture has an indelible effect on a therapist's treatment and a patient's response—to her work in mental testing, psychoanalysis, and family therapy. A pioneer in cross-cultural psychology, Abel devoted her long career to understanding and solving the problems faced by mental health professionals in a multicultural society.

Theodora Mead was born in Newport, Rhode

Island, the only child of Robert Gillespie Mead, a New York City lawyer, and Elizabeth Manning Cleveland, a welfare worker who helped fund the American Cancer Society and raised money for hospitals. Mead grew up in Manhattan, spending childhood summers on the family's farm in Ossining, New York, and before the age of twelve had taken several trips to Europe. In 1917 she graduated from Miss Chapin's, a private high school in New York City, and in 1921 she received a BA in history from Vassar College, where she studied psychology with Margaret Washburn.

In the fall of 1921 she enrolled in graduate school in psychology at Columbia University but withdrew to play the violin with a professional string quartet. Back at Columbia in 1922, she began working with luminaries in her field. Mead took courses with LETA HOLLINGWORTH and Robert Woodworth, and in 1923 she studied at the Sorbonne with Pierre Janet. She returned to Columbia to continue her work in experimental psychology, receiving an MA in 1924 and a PhD in 1925. While at Columbia, Mead worked part-time at the Manhattan Trade School for Girls, of which her mother had been an early supporter; the mental tests she administered there on "subnormal" girls (girls with mental retardation) formed the basis for her PhD thesis, published in 1925.

In the midst of her graduate training, on November 9, 1924, Theodora Mead married Theodore Abel, a Polish-born graduate student in sociology at Columbia whom she had met while traveling in Poland in 1921. The marriage lasted until his death in 1988. The couple had three children: Peter, Caroline, and Zita.

Abel began her professional career in 1925 at the University of Illinois at Urbana-Champaign (UIUC) when her husband became a professor in the UIUC sociology department; she did research on the galvanic skin reflex, testing the electrical activity and conductivity of skin, using electrodes. The following year the Abels moved to Cornell, where she continued her research in experimental psychology with the support of a National Research Council Fellowship. The couple moved back to New York in 1929, and she was hired to teach psychology at Sarah Lawrence College. Beginning in 1936, Abel served for four years as director of research at the Manhattan Trade School for Girls, continuing the testing work she had begun as a graduate student. Abel later published her findings in *The Subnormal Adolescent Girl* (1942), co-authored with Elaine F. Kinder. From 1940 to 1946, she worked as a research psychologist at Letchworth Village, an experimental farm community created in 1909 to care for adults and children with mental retardation and other developmental disabilities.

In 1947, Abel shifted her research focus when she collaborated with anthropologists RUTH BENEDICT, MARGARET MEAD, and Rhoda Metraux on studies of "national character" in the Columbia University Research in Contemporary Cultures project, which was started by Benedict and funded by the Office of Naval Research. A cross-disciplinary research group investigated the patterning of behavior in seven different cultures, through open-ended interviewing, analyses of themes in novels and films, and use of projective techniques like the Rorschach test. Abel carried out Rorschach analyses on Chinese and Mexican subjects, and analyzed Syrian culture with Mead and French culture with Metraux. Cross-cultural study, both on foreign cultures and on ethnic minorities within the United States, became the major emphasis of her career. Occasionally it involved fieldwork: in 1953–54, while Metraux was doing field research on Montserrat in the British West Indies, Abel lived briefly in the village under study and administered a series of testing procedures on adults and adolescents. But Abel devoted most of her time to working with patients and research subjects in New York.

Abel brought this anthropological angle to her work as director of psychology at the Postgraduate Center for Mental Health in New York City, a position she held between 1947 and 1971. There, beginning in the 1960s, she and Metraux established one of the earliest training programs in cross-cultural psychotherapy. Aspiring therapists were asked to write their own personal histories and to discuss cases from their practices where they were having trouble understanding a patient's beliefs or ideas. Discussion often focused on how to interpret communication, verbal or nonverbal, by a patient from a culture unfamiliar to the therapist. In addition to teaching, Abel also carried out therapy and diagnostic testing on patients from a wide range of ethnic groups. From 1951 to 1962 she taught psychology at Long Island University and maintained a private practice. By 1969 she was also teaching and practicing family psychotherapy at the Postgraduate Center for Mental Health.

In 1971, Abel and her husband relocated from New York City to Albuquerque, New Mexico. There she started a new private practice, and combined her concentration on cross-cultural psychology with a new research interest: family therapy. Abel became chief of family therapy at the Child Guidance Center and was appointed assistant (later associate and full) professor of clinical psychology at the University of New Mexico. Throughout the 1970s and 1980s, she lectured on and demonstrated family therapy all over the world, including in Mexico, Japan, Egypt, and Iran. She had come to believe that family (rather than individual) therapy revealed the cultural variables in behavior most clearly. Abel became especially renowned for using family therapy with the Indians of New Mexico, including the Mescalero and Jicarilla Apaches, the Navajo, and other native groups in northern New Mexico. In a display of their respect for Abel, several tribes in Albuquerque gave her the title "grandmother."

Two of her major works reflect Abel's lifelong interest in cross-cultural psychology. *Psychological Testing in Cultural Contexts* (1973) revealed the culture-boundedness of all mental and personality tests, even as it offered guidance to psychologists on how to use the tests sensitively. *Psychotherapy and Culture* (1987) addressed the impact of cultural beliefs and modes of behavior on various aspects of psychotherapy.

Abel continued to see patients into her nineties. In 1997 she received the American Psychological Foundation's Gold Medal Award for Life Achievement in the Practice of Psychology. She died at the age of ninety-nine at her home in Forestburgh, New York.

Bibliography: Abel's papers are held at the Archives of the History of American Psychology at the University of Akron, Ohio. Her dissertation was published as *Tested Mentality as Related to Success in Skilled Trade Training* (New York, *Columbia University Archives of Psychology* 12, no. 77 [1925]). Her books include *Psychological Testing in Cultural Contexts* (1973); *Culture and Psychotherapy* (1974), with Rhoda Metraux and an introduction by Margaret Mead; and *Psychotherapy and Culture,* with Rhoda Metraux and Samuel Roll (1987). The latter is a revised edition of *Culture and Psychotherapy.* An assessment of Abel's life and work can be found in the report on her award from the American Psychological Foundation (*American Psychologist* 52, no. 8 [August 1997], pp. 803–5), which includes a portrait. J. Leroy Gabaldon's PhD dissertation, "Patterns of an Age: The Psychological Writings of Theodora M. Abel" (Fielding Institute, 1980), examines the stages of her career in experimental, applied, and clinical psychology as reflections of broader trends within the discipline of psychology, and considers her connections to anthropology. An obituary appeared in the *New York Times* on December 13, 1998.

NADINE M. WEIDMAN

ABZUG, Bella. July 24, 1920–March 31, 1998. U.S. Representative, feminist.

Born "yelling," according to her family, in the year that marked the passage of the suffrage amendment, Bella Abzug liked to say that she had been a feminist since the day she was born. A lifelong activist, Abzug protested injustices against women and minorities and organized campaigns for women's rights, human rights, and peace—movements she saw as integrally related. Forceful, bold, and always outspoken, Abzug brought a pioneering vision as well as practical organizing and political skills to these causes. Her leadership helped promulgate second-wave feminism and the antinuclear and global ecology movements as powerful forces for social change.

The second daughter of Russian immigrants Esther Tanklefsky and Emanuel Savitzky, Bella was born and grew up in the Bronx. Her father left Czarist Russia in 1905 to protest the outbreak of the Russo-Japanese War. His pacifism—reflected in his renaming his Manhattan butcher shop the "Live and Let Live Meat Market"—did not inspire commercial success but became a formative influence on Bella, as did his love of music. After his death, when Bella was thirteen, Esther Savitzky became the family's main breadwinner by working as a department store saleswoman and cashier. Esther's fierce determination served Bella as a model of female competence and strength, and her continuing, unconditional support helped Bella mold her own untraditional career.

Another early influence was Judaism. The Savitzkys kept a kosher home, and as a young child Bella frequently accompanied her maternal grandfather to synagogue, although she considered it unjust that women had to sit separately in the balcony. When after her father's death she was forbidden to say the prayer of mourning traditionally reserved for males, she stood alone in synagogue each day for a year to say the *kaddish* anyway. She viewed her determination as an early blow on behalf of the liberation of Jewish women.

Judaism also became the inspiration for her political activism. When she was twelve, Bella joined Hashomer Hatzair, a Labor Zionist youth group she admired because of its idealism and militancy, and dreamed of going to Palestine to build a Jewish homeland. She became part of a group of uniformed youths who collected pennies for the Jewish National Fund by shaking cans outside subway stops. Zionism, she said, "made me a political activist, it kept me a rebel" (*Moment,* February 1976, pp. 26–29).

Bella entered Walton High, an all-girls public school, in 1934 and was elected senior class president. Deeply affected by the Depression and by Franklin Roosevelt's message of social uplift, she thought seriously of pursuing a legal career defending poor people and alleviating public misery. In 1938 she enrolled in tuition-free Hunter College. Elected president of her class several times and president of the entire student body, she led numerous demonstrations against fascism. With America at war when she graduated in 1942, she began working for a defense contractor, but decided that she could make a greater contribution to the war effort through the law. Rejected at Harvard Law School because of her sex, she entered Columbia University Law School on scholarship, one of a handful of women in her class. An outstanding student, she become an editor of the *Columbia Law Review.* In 1944, while still in law school, she married Martin Abzug, a young businessman and aspiring novelist she had met on a trip to visit relatives in Florida. A gentle and witty man, madly in love with Bella, Martin typed the drafts of her law papers. After the birth of their two daughters—Eve Gail (Eegee) in 1949 and Isobel Jo (Liz) in 1952—and throughout their loving forty-two-year marriage, he was her staunchest supporter.

After graduation, Abzug joined a law office specializing in labor union cases. To ensure that she was recognized as a working woman, she began wearing distinctive wide-brimmed hats, which, along with her gravelly voice and blunt and colorful language, became Abzug trademarks. She soon opened her own office to handle tenants' rights and civil liberties cases; her clients included Jewish schoolteachers, actors, and others accused of "un-American" activities. Abzug's most notable client was Willie McGee, a black Mississippian condemned to death after being convicted of raping a white woman with whom he had a long-standing consensual relationship. Abzug twice secured a stay of execution, but when the third attempt failed, McGee was executed.

After the United States and Soviet Union renewed nuclear testing in the early 1960s, Abzug helped found Women Strike for Peace in 1961, serving as its national legislative and political director. When the Abzugs moved from Mt. Vernon to Greenwich Village in 1965, Bella began to organize peace action committees in the city. An early opponent of the Vietnam War, Abzug founded the Coalition for a Democratic Alternative, and with Allard Lowenstein helped organize the "Dump Johnson" campaign. Supported by women from the peace movement and other New Left allies, she challenged the party machine and ran for Congress in 1970, scoring an upset primary victory over the Democratic incumbent from Manhattan's 19th Congressional District. In the general election, she defeated Republican-Liberal nominee Barry Farber by almost ten thousand votes, becoming one of only twelve women in the House and the first elected on a women's rights/peace platform. After her first term, her district was gerrymandered, and she succeeded in winning election in her new district only after its popular liberal congressman, William Ryan, died after the primary. Abzug was returned to the House for a third term in 1974 by an overwhelming majority.

Abzug used her congressional position to further her long-held views about pacifism, women's rights, and the rights of poor people and minorities. Speaker Thomas O'Neill considered her the hardest-working member of the House; skilled in coalition building, she was also one of its most effective power players. Abzug wrote the Equal Credit Act, providing women with fair access to consumer credit, and authored pioneering legislation on comprehensive child care, Social Security for homemakers, family planning, abortion rights, and Title IX regulations enforcing equal opportunity for women in federally funded educational institutions; she also introduced an amendment to the Civil Rights Act to include gay and lesbian rights. She organized the congressional caucus on women's issues, and co-founded the National Women's Political Caucus in 1971.

Abzug's legislative achievements extended beyond women's rights. As chair of the House Subcommittee on Government Information and Individual Rights, she co-authored the Freedom of Information Act, the Right to Privacy Act, and the "Government in the Sunshine" Act, which opened up government agencies to public scrutiny. The first to call for President Nixon's impeachment during the Watergate scandal, she conducted inquiries into covert and illegal activities of the CIA, FBI, and other federal agencies. A committed environmentalist, she co-authored the Water Pollution Act of 1972. Abzug also sponsored pioneering legislation to permit the free emigration of Soviet Jewry, and throughout her three terms was a leading supporter of economic and military aid to Israel. In 1975, she led the fight to condemn the UN General Assembly's resolution equating Zionism with racism, and as congressional adviser to the U.S. delegation to the UN Decade for Women Conference in Mexico that year, she played an important role in publicly condemning anti-Zionist and anti-Jewish attacks.

Abzug's career as an elected official ended in 1976, when she left the House to run for the Senate. In a four-way race, she lost by a fraction of a percentage point to Daniel Patrick Moynihan. The following year she lost a close race for New York City mayor, and she failed in two later congressional bids. In 1977, she presided over the first National Women's Conference, in Houston; as a congresswoman, she had authored the bill that secured its funding. In 1978 President Carter appointed Abzug co-chair of the National Advisory Committee on Women, although he fired her when she criticized cutbacks in the group's funding. In 1979, Abzug established WOMEN USA, co-founded with congresswomen Patsy Mink, Maxine Waters, and others to mobilize women as lobbyists on behalf of economic, environmental, and political issues. In 1984, with close friend and colleague Mim Kelber, she wrote *Gender Gap:*

Bella Abzug's Guide to Political Power for American Women.

In 1990, with Mim Kelber and others, Abzug founded and co-chaired WEDO, the Women's Environment and Development Organization, an international advocacy group supporting women's empowerment, economic development, and environmental security. Through WEDO, she organized and led the World Women's Congress for a Healthy Planet, which produced a blueprint for incorporating women's perspectives into local, national, and international decision making. From its leading role in the 1995 Beijing World Conference on Women to co-sponsoring the First World Conference on Breast Cancer, WEDO became a powerful international women's network. As the movement spread, so did Abzug's influence; activists in remote corners of the globe began to refer to themselves as the "Bella Abzugs" of their respective countries. In declining health from heart disease and breast cancer, Abzug nonetheless remained an active leader of the international women's movement. She died of complications following heart surgery in New York City on March 31, 1998, at the age of seventy-seven.

"If you combined Churchill, Oprah, Dr. Ruth, and EMMA GOLDMAN, you'd get a picture of Bella," Abzug's good friend Gloria Steinem put it. One of the few American women who transcended U.S. politics to address the global nature of women's issues, Abzug remained true to the vision of justice and equality that motivated her earliest public actions. In private, she was a loving daughter, wife, and mother, with a wide circle of loyal friends. Passionate and uncompromising, she played a pivotal role in securing women's rights, locally and globally, in the twentieth century.

Bibliography: The Bella Abzug Papers Collection at the Columbia University Rare Book & Manuscript Library contains congressional correspondence, memoranda, speeches, reports, and photographs relating to her terms in office, 1970–76, as well as draft transcripts of an oral history, appointment books, and subject files. Primary documents, photographs and exhibits, and biographical narrative and chronology can be found at the Jewish Women's Archive, Brookline, Massachusetts. In addition to *Gender Gap* (1984), Abzug's own writings include *Bella! Ms. Abzug Goes to Washington,* a diary of her first year in office edited by Mel Ziegler (1972); and "Bella on Bella," *Moment* 1, no. 7 (February 1976), pp. 26–29. See also her "Martin, What Should I Do Now?" *Ms.* July/August 1990, pp. 94–96. Further biographical information can be found in Doris Faber, *Bella Abzug* (1976); Amy Swerdlow, *Women Strike for Peace: Traditional Motherhood and Radical Politics in the 1960s* (1993); Gloria Steinem, "Bella Abzug," *Ms.*, January/February 1996, p. 63; and Joyce Antler, *The Journey Home: How Jewish Women Shaped Modern America* (1997). The author's interview with Bella Abzug on March 29, 1996, at Brandeis University also provided helpful information. An obituary appeared in the *New York Times* on April 1, 1998. See also tributes by Ellen Goodman in the *Boston Globe* (which contains the Steinem quote) and Myra MacPherson in the *Washington Post,* both on April 2, 1998.

JOYCE ANTLER

ACKER, Kathy. April 18, 1947–November 30, 1997. Writer, performance artist, playwright.

In her life, death, and art, Kathy Acker held herself up against the commonplace yet incomprehensible reality of embodiment. Forever insistent on the value of bodily experience, her novels have been called crude, revolting, pornographic, brittle, and fatalistic. Dealing explicitly with sex as the meeting place of power and identity, her writing strove to break boundaries of narrative, linguistic, and social convention.

Acker's literary persona stands at odds with her upper-middle-class background. Born Karen Lehman in New York City, she was the daughter of Claire Kathleen Weill and Donal M. Lehman. Her parents' families, both of German Jewish extraction, were of such standing that their wedding merited note in the society pages. Her father, a World War II veteran, left her mother three months into her pregnancy. His daughter never knew him.

Growing up in New York's exclusive Sutton Place with a trust fund and her grandmother for support, she was raised by her mother and stepfather, Albert A. Alexander Jr., whom she later claimed had made sexual advances toward her. In her teens she married her friend Robert Acker, whose name, despite their rapid divorce, she was stubbornly to retain the rest of her life. She studied classics at Brandeis University, then moved to the University of California at San Diego to work with neo-Marxist philosopher Herbert Marcuse. She graduated in 1968. No longer supported by her parents, at some point she entered the sex industry as a stripper and live-show performer. After returning to New York, she did graduate work at New York University and City University of New York and began writing. She always credited novelist William S. Burroughs as her model and mentor.

Acker's early work was self-published and self-distributed at local bookstores. Her first published work, *Politics* (1972), excited little comment at the time. Her pseudonymous novel, *The Childlike Life of the Black Tarantula: Some Lives of Murderesses* (1973), with its melding of ecstatic sexual violence and linguistic subversion, laid the foundation for her future notoriety. Over the next decade she published five novels, as well as various chapbooks, unpublished works of poetry, and articles. Though *New York City in 1979* (1981) won the

Pushcart Prize, Acker gained a reputation in New York City primarily as a performance artist. She was friends with photographer Robert Mapplethorpe and singer Patti Smith, and studied with Black Mountain School poet Jerome Rothenberg. By the time she moved to London in the 1980s, she was well established in the New York literary scene.

The publication of *Blood and Guts in High School* (1984), with its combination of graphic sexual imagery, cut-up, disjointed narrative, and savage indictments of the political and social order, caused quite a stir among critics. The press perhaps paid more attention to her image than to the merit of her works. Tattooed, with short spiked hair and numerous piercings, Acker found herself trapped within a persona that was partly media exaggeration but partly her real self. Regarding her own body, Acker often spoke of it as a work of art.

In London, Acker did collaborations with the famed Riverside Studios and wrote prolifically. *Don Quixote, Which Was a Dream* was published in 1986, followed by *Empire of the Senseless* (1988) and *In Memoriam to Identity* (1990). She also wrote the screenplay for *Variety,* the play *Lulu Unchained,* and the libretto for the opera *The Birth of the Poet,* on which she collaborated with experimental composer Peter Gordon (to whom she was briefly married) and director Richard Foreman.

Acker's writing was not about plot per se; instead, Acker focused on examining ideas she found compelling, and, perhaps foremost, on breaking down literary conventions to explore the power relationships implicit in the ordinary use of language. She often borrowed from and rewrote classic literature. As with the earlier *Great Expectations,* her *Don Quixote* emphatically abandoned the inherited literary tradition. From the bleakly matter-of-fact incest that opens *Blood and Guts in High School,* to the sadistic techniques of control of *My Mother: Demonology* (1993), to the delirious violence of *Pussy, King of the Pirates* (1996), Acker also confronted what she saw as the hypocrisy of the nuclear family. Long estranged from her mother, Acker briefly forged a reconciliation with her in the 1970s, but her mother committed suicide shortly afterward. Acker claimed that though her novels were usually written in first person, the only truly autobiographical parts of them were those that dealt with her mother.

By the time Acker moved to California in 1990 to launch the writing department at the San Francisco Art Institute, she had proclaimed herself a staunch proponent of a feminism that celebrated women's sexuality in and of itself. Her books abound in graphic descriptions of sex. She forever sought a world in which inherited roles would give way to genuine relationships between individuals. And in her life and art, she insisted on the importance of the language of the body in bringing about that change.

When in 1996 her own body rebelled against her, Acker was confronted with the possibility that, in her words, "my death, and so my life, would be meaningless." Diagnosed with breast cancer, she underwent a double mastectomy. A post-surgery biopsy revealed that the cancer had spread to her lymph nodes. Her position at the San Francisco Art Institute did not carry health insurance, and she was left to fight her cancer with her own resources. Acker turned to alternative therapies and at one point publicly declared herself free of cancer, convinced that her mind had cured her body. She moved back to London to be with her lover, writer Charles Shaar Murray, but returned to San Francisco at the end of the summer of 1997. As her cancer spread to her bones and major organs, she entered an alternative therapy center in Tijuana, Mexico. In the course of intensive treatment, she died there on November 30, 1997, at the age of fifty.

Acker died as she had lived. Her writing explored the junctures of bodily experience, language, and power, raging against the society that negates the value of all of them by separating each from the others. As she wrote in *Empire of the Senseless,* her aim was always one thing: that "one day, maybe, there'ld [*sic*] be a human society in the world which is beautiful, a society which wasn't just disgust" (p. 227).

Bibliography: Duke University's Special Collections Library contains selected correspondence, manuscript drafts, artwork, and miscellaneous recordings of Acker made from around 1970 to 1994. Acker's *The Childlike Life of the Black Tarantula: Some Lives of Murderesses* (1973) was republished, with additions, as *The Childlike Life of the Black Tarantula by the Black Tarantula* in 1975. Other books not mentioned in the text include *I Dreamt I Was a Nymphomaniac: Imagining* (1974); *Florida* (1978); *Kathy Goes to Haiti* (1978); *The Adult Life of Toulouse Lautrec by Henri Toulouse Lautrec* (1978); *Great Expectations* (1982); *Hello, I'm Erica Jong* (chapbook, 1982); *My Life, My Death, by Pier Paolo Passolini* (1984); and *Algeria: A Series of Invocations Because Nothing Else Works* (1984). See also *Bodies of Work: Essays* (1997) and Amy Scholder and Dennis Cooper, eds., *Essential Acker: The Selected Writings of Kathy Acker* (2002), with an introduction by Jeanette Winterson. Two of Acker's novels were published posthumously in one volume as *Rip-Off Red, Girl Detective* and *The Burning Bombing of America: The Destruction of the U.S.* (2002). Dramatic and cinematic works include *Lulu Unchained* (1983), *Variety* (1985), *Birth of the Poet* (1985), and *Eurydice in the Underworld* (1997). Acker also wrote two books of poetry, *I Don't Expect You'll Do the Same, by Clay Fear* (1974) and *Persian Poems* (1978). Additionally, Acker appears in the 1990 film *The Golden Boat* by Chilean director Raoul Ruiz, and is featured in a 1998 documentary, *The Falconer,* about artist Peter Whitehead. One of the few sustained critical treatments of her works is Nicola Pitchford, *Tactical Readings: Feminist Postmodernism in the Novels of Kathy Acker and Angela Carter* (2001). Acker discusses her illness in the *London Guardian,* January 18, 1997, which contains the quotation in the text. See also Charles Shaar Murray's description of her last year in the *Observer Review,* December 7, 1997. Obituaries appeared in the *London Guardian* on December 1, 1997, and the *New York Times* on December 3, 1997.

GREGORY L. FORD

ADAMS, Harriet Stratemeyer. December 11, 1892–March 27, 1982. Children's author, publishing executive.

Born in Newark, New Jersey, Harriet Stratemeyer was the elder of two daughters of Magdalene Baker Van Camp and Edward Stratemeyer. Harriet's mother was a homemaker and clubwoman, and her father was the unseen hand behind perennially popular series books for adolescents, including the Bobbsey Twins, Tom Swift, the Hardy Boys, and Nancy Drew. He created a rationalized system of literary production in which he farmed out a list of characters and plot outlines to ghost writers who wrote books under a host of pseudonyms that he owned.

Harriet attended school in Newark and graduated from Barringer High School in 1910. Later that fall, she entered Wellesley College, where she studied German, English composition, music, religion, and economics. She also played piano for the symphony orchestra and served as college correspondent to the *Newark Evening News, Newark Sunday Call,* and *Boston Globe.* In her senior year, Harriet became president of the Press Club.

Following her graduation in 1914, she received a job offer from the *Boston Globe,* but her father, who held old-fashioned ideas about women working, would not allow his daughter to take the position. When she persisted, he finally offered to let her work for him, although not in his New York office. Instead, he brought manuscripts and page proofs home for her to work on. She later recalled how much she had learned from this experience.

With her 1915 marriage to Russell Vroom Adams, an investment banker, and the birth of her first son in 1916, Harriet turned her attention to her family. She, like many of her Wellesley classmates, became engaged with women's club work. In 1922, she reported in an alumnae publication that she worked for the Maplewood Woman's Club and the New York Wellesley Club, and served as the superintendent of the Sunday school, all while keeping "house with 'two kiddies'"—Russell Jr. and Patricia (born 1921). The births of Camilla (1923) and Edward (1925) brought her children to four.

On May 10, 1930, Edward Stratemeyer died. As executors of the estate, Harriet and her sister Edna initially considered selling the literary syndicate, but the sour economy meant that few were interested in buying and those who were could not afford to pay. Later that fall, their mother granted them the exclusive right to use Stratemeyer's pen names and to add new stories to the series he had established, which they did under the name Stratemeyer Syndicate. Harriet, then thirty-eight years old and with young children still at home, hired a nurse, moved the company's headquarters nearer to her New Jersey home, and enthusiastically threw herself into her new role.

Despite the Depression's impact on the publishing industry, the Stratemeyer sisters successfully managed to continue their father's venture, maintaining many of their father's series while adding six new lines of books. Harriet and Edna utilized their father's production methods—developing characters, drafting plot outlines, making contracts with ghost writers and publishers, revising manuscripts, proofing galleys, hiring illustrators, and shepherding the Syndicate books through production. They also adhered to his policy of discretion and secrecy about who actually wrote the books.

Under the leadership of the Stratemeyer daughters, the content and style of Syndicate books shifted more toward juvenile mystery. Perhaps the most marked change occurred in the design of girls' adventure series. Edward Stratemeyer first offered books expressly for adolescent female readers when he introduced the Motor Girls, Ruth Fielding, and the Outdoor Girls series in the 1910s. Though publishers advertised this latter series as featuring active and fun-loving girls who shared a fondness for outdoor life and adventure, Stratemeyer included romantic subplots in each volume. As the series matured, he allowed his heroines to age and marry, substituting new adolescent Outdoor Girls for the married protagonists.

As the daughters developed the plots for the Nancy Drew series, which their father had originated in 1930, they decided to perpetuate Nancy's adolescent status and her independence, endowing the plucky and level-headed protagonist with a loving and approving father, a devoted housekeeper who provided maternal comforts with little oversight, and an affable but undemanding boyfriend. Harriet believed that marrying off Nancy Drew would be disastrous. "Nancy will never get married," she told *Redbook* magazine, "because Ned Nickerson can't corner her long enough to ask her. And I don't plan to give him the opportunity" (April 1980, p. 44).

As syndicate head, Harriet Stratemeyer Adams created new series, outlined stories, and edited the work of her ghostwriters. Occasionally, she plotted an adventure and fleshed it out herself. By perfecting her father's corporate system of created authorship, she nurtured scores of adolescent adventure stories under such pseudonyms as Carolyn Keene, Laura Lee Hope, and Franklin W. Dixon.

Nancy Drew's perpetual status as a teenager had profound consequences for book sales. By the mid 1930s, the sisters found that their girls' books outsold boys' books. At the close of the decade, Nancy Drew had her screen debut in a Warner Brothers production called *Nancy Drew—Detective.* By 1979, publishers had sold more than 53 million volumes in the Nancy Drew series.

In 1942, Edna married Charles Wesley Squier and retired from her role as active partner in the Syndicate. Harriet steered the Syndicate through the remainder of World War II and the resulting paper shortage that led to the conclusion of the original Tom Swift series. During the 1950s and 1960s, she devoted herself to her publishing work and her avocation—running an organic farm in New Jersey. Adams traveled extensively, visiting Asia, Israel, Greece, South Africa, Central and South America, and Europe. She used some of these locales as settings for her adventure stories. Beginning in the 1960s, she brought colleagues into partnership with her.

For many years, Adams had chafed at the low royalties paid by Grosset & Dunlap to the Stratemeyer Syndicate. In 1979, she gave Simon & Schuster exclusive rights to all future titles, a move that Grosset & Dunlap challenged in court. Adams emerged from the legal battle victorious and in 1980 celebrated her fiftieth anniversary as head of the Stratemeyer Syndicate. She died in Pottersville, New Jersey, in 1982 at the age of eighty-nine, and in 1984 Simon & Schuster purchased the Stratemeyer Syndicate and all rights to its literary property.

Bibliography: There are five principal collections of materials that pertain to Harriet Stratemeyer Adams's personal and professional life. The Wellesley College Archives contains yearbooks, reunion publications, news clippings, and alumnae news issued by the Class of 1914, as well as a documentary film script, "Harriet S. Adams and the Stratemeyer Syndicate." Yale University's Beinecke Rare Book and Manuscript Library holds a collection of Stratemeyer Syndicate records that includes business correspondence, as well as legal and financial records relating to the 1984 sale of the Syndicate to Simon & Schuster. The collection also contains drafts of speeches given by Adams to various organizations. The New York Public Library's Manuscripts and Archives Division maintains an immense collection of Stratemeyer family and Stratemeyer Syndicate material, including correspondence, financial papers, and photographs. The University of Oregon Special Collections contains correspondence from readers in the late 1920s, a Nancy Drew manuscript and outline attributed to Harriet S. Adams, as well as early writings by Edward Stratemeyer. Extensive information about the business practices of the Stratemeyer Syndicate, and Adams's role in it, is found in the records pertaining to the 1979 court case *Grosset & Dunlap, Inc. vs. Gulf & Western Corporation and Stratemeyer Syndicate, a partnership, 79 Civ. 2242,* found at the National Archives–Federal Records Center in New York. Deidre Johnson's *Stratemeyer Pseudonyms and Series Books* (1982) provides a detailed list of publications issued by Edward Stratemeyer and the Stratemeyer Syndicate. See also Johnson, *Edward Stratemeyer and the Stratemeyer Syndicate* (1993). Trudi Johanna Abel provides an extensive introduction to the development of the Stratemeyer Syndicate and the origins of girls' series books in "A Man of Letters, a Man of Business: Edward Stratemeyer and the Adolescent Readers, 1890–1930" (PhD dissertation, Rutgers University, 1993). An obituary appeared in the *New York Times* on March 29, 1982.

TRUDI JOHANNA ABEL

ADLER, Stella. February 10, 1901–December 21, 1992. Actress, acting teacher.

Stella Adler was born on New York City's Lower East Side, where Yiddish theater flourished. Her parents, Sara Levitzky and Jacob Adler, were among the theatrical elite. Both fled their native Russia after the 1883 prohibition of Yiddish plays. Sara divorced her first husband, actor/manager Maurice Heine, and became Jacob's third wife in 1891 and his leading lady at the Independent Yiddish Artists Company in 1892. They produced theater that enlightened the audience, and excelled in plays by Shakespeare, Tolstoy, and Jacob Gordin, whose adaptation of *King Lear* (1892) provided Jacob Adler with his signature role. From them, Stella learned that the "soul finds itself in art."

Stella grew up under what she called extravagant circumstances. She was the fourth of five children born to Jacob and Sara, each of whom had other children from their previous marriages. The family lived in a brownstone filled with children, pets, plants, and guests, but never enough beds. The youngest slept on the floor or in beds vacated by siblings away on theatrical tours. A loving father, Jacob was less than loyal as a husband. Sara pulled away from the family emotionally, serving as Stella's model for deep psychological acting, but not for mothering.

The Adler family was lower middle class, but theater had bred in them aristocratic manners, and Stella always retained her royal demeanor. The whole family acted in Jacob's company. Stella debuted at age four in *Broken Hearts.* As a child, she played boys as well as girls; as she grew, she became the ingénue in classical plays. Stella enjoyed learning through reading and travel. When her acting allowed, she attended public school, the socialist Workers School, and later New York University. But, as she said, "when surrounded by the great language of Tolstoy, Shakespeare, etc., school pales in comparison."

Stella Adler debuted in London in 1919 with

her father's company, playing Naomi in Gordin's *Elisha ben Avuya.* While in London, she met her first husband, Englishman Horace Eliashcheff. Their brief marriage ended in divorce. Adler made her English-language debut on Broadway in 1922 as the Butterfly in *The World We Live In* and spent one season on the vaudeville circuit. In 1923–24, she saw the great Russian actor and director Konstantin Stanislavsky perform with the Moscow Art Theatre. Inspired by the Russians, she enrolled in 1925 at the new American Laboratory Theatre to study with two former Moscow Art Theatre actors, Richard Boleslavsky and Maria Ouspenskaya. Returning to her roots, from 1927 to 1931 she acted with Jacob Ben Ami at the Irving Place Theatre on New York's Lower East Side and toured with Maurice Schwartz and the Yiddish Art Theatre throughout Europe and South America.

Unhappy with the Broadway system, Adler joined the Group Theatre, founded by Harold Clurman, Lee Strasberg, and CHERYL CRAWFORD in 1931. This young, idealistic collective produced plays that addressed essential American social concerns during a ten-year period that coincided with the Great Depression and the death of Yiddish theater. While Adler admired Clurman's vision, the Group did not suit her. With more theatrical experience than the others, she bristled at the democratic spirit that equalized them, and she argued with Strasberg's interpretation of Stanislavsky's teachings. In 1934, she traveled to Paris, where she studied with Stanislavsky himself for five weeks. On her return she openly challenged Strasberg's emphasis on emotional memory, reporting that Stanislavsky favored the actor's creative imagination and the play's given circumstances. Her report prodded Strasberg into saying that he taught his own Method, a term now inextricably linked with American acting. Her challenge thus opened a rift in actor training that still exists.

Adler's work with the Group established her as a leading American actress, even when her innate nobility seemed unsuited to their gritty, realistic plays. She especially resisted playing the matronly Bessie Berger in Clifford Odets's *Awake and Sing!* (1935), displaying her temper at every curtain call by pulling off her gray wig to flaunt her beauty, youth, and golden hair. Other notable roles included Gwyn Ballantine in John Howard Lawson's *Gentlewoman* (1934), the role on which she worked with Stanislavsky, and Clara in Odets's *Paradise Lost* (1935), her last role with the Group.

Adler briefly experimented with screen acting, appearing in three films: *Love on Toast* (1938), *The Shadow of the Thin Man* (1941), and *My Girl Tisa* (1948). She also played on Broadway, appearing in Max Reinhardt's production of *Sons and Soldiers* (1943) and as the flamboyant lion tamer in *He Who Gets Slapped* (1946).

During the 1940s, Adler turned to teaching as her primary occupation, laying the foundation for her most enduring legacy. She began by coaching actors at the Group Theatre. In 1940–42 she developed the Dramatic Workshop at the New School for Social Research under the auspices of German director Erwin Piscator. In 1949, she set forth a comprehensive two-year curriculum and opened the Stella Adler Acting Studio (later renamed the Stella Adler Conservatory of Acting) in New York. In 1966–67, she taught at Yale University's School of Drama, and in 1985 she opened the Stella Adler Academy and Theatre in Los Angeles, commuting between the coasts. Her book, *The Technique of Acting,* which summarized her theories, appeared in 1988. As a teacher, she inspired, cajoled, praised, and upbraided three generations of actors, reminding them that her criticisms were not about them personally but about the work. Many respected actors, including Marlon Brando and Robert De Niro, profited from her pragmatic approach to technique and her impassioned lectures on plays.

Stella Adler met her second husband, director Harold Clurman, in 1926 and worked with him throughout the 1930s. They married in 1943. Having grown up on the Lower East Side with Jacob Adler as his childhood idol, Clurman shared Stella's belief in theater as a cultural force. Though their respect for one another's professional opinions never faltered, their stormy personal relationship ended in divorce in 1960. Her third and happiest marriage, to atomic physicist and novelist Mitchell Wilson, ended with his death in 1973. Stella Adler died at the age of ninety-one in her home in Los Angeles and was buried in the Adler family plot at Mount Carmel Cemetery in New York.

Bibliography: The New York Public Library houses three collections that provide information about Stella Adler: the Billy Rose Theatre Collection contains theater reviews, newspaper interviews, obituaries, photographs, and theater programs; the Theatre on Film and Tape Archive holds a videotaped interview with Stella Adler by John Gruen, conducted on March 10, 1981, which is the source for the quotes in the text; the American Jewish Committee Oral History Collection includes interviews with Leon Schachter and Lulla Rosenfeld about the Adler family. In addition to her book *The Technique of Acting* (1988), Adler's lectures on script analysis were edited by Barry Paris as *Stella Adler on Ibsen, Strindberg and Chekhov* (1999); her master class notes were compiled and edited by Howard Kissel in *Stella Adler: The Art of Acting* (2000). Information about Adler's childhood appears in Lulla Rosenfeld's two books, *Bright Star of Exile: Jacob Adler and the Yiddish Theatre* (1977) and *The Yiddish Theatre and Jacob P. Adler* (1988). Stella Adler's work in the Group Theatre is treated in Harold Clurman, *The Fervent Years* (1957); Helen Krich Chinoy, ed., "Reunion: A Self-Portrait of the Group Theatre," a special issue of *Educational Theatre Journal* 28, no. 4 (December 1976); and Wendy

Smith, *Real Life Drama* (1990). *Stella Adler: Awake and Dream* (1989), an R. M. Arts Video documentary, includes biographical and pedagogical information as well as clips from her films. Her teaching methods are examined in Richard Brestoff, *The Great Acting Teachers and Their Methods* (1995); Mark Hammer, "The Stella Adler Conservatory," in David Krasner, ed., *Method Acting Reconsidered* (2000); David Krasner, "Strasberg, Adler, and Meisner: Method Acting," in Alison Hodge, ed., *Twentieth Century Actor Training* (2000); and Joanna Rotté, *Acting with Adler* (2000). An obituary appeared in the *New York Times* on December 22, 1992.

SHARON MARIE CARNICKE

AGOSTINI DE DEL RÍO, Amelia. 1896–December 11, 1996. Writer, educator, scholar of Puerto Rican history.

Born in the mountain town of Yauco, Puerto Rico, Amelia Agostini was for more than four decades a prominent member of New York's Hispanic intellectual circles and had an established reputation in the literary and artistic world of her native country. In this sense, her contributions bridge the Puerto Rican/Hispanic communities on the island and in the States. She received her elementary and secondary schooling in her Puerto Rican hometown. An excellent student, she was awarded a scholarship to study at the University of Puerto Rico's Normal School. She graduated in 1917 and began working as a high school teacher.

At the Normal School, Agostini was part of a select group of women students being trained mostly as teachers, but her exposure to academic life at Puerto Rico's main center of learning allowed her to develop many friendships with prominent female and male writers and intellectuals of this period. In 1918 she left the island to further her education at Vassar College, where she graduated Phi Beta Kappa in 1922 with a BA in Spanish literature. Back in Puerto Rico, she taught in Santurce's high school for several years, but also was involved in writing, directing, and performing in some theater productions.

In 1926, she married well-known Spanish literary critic Angel del Río, who had been her professor at the University of Puerto Rico. They moved to New York City, where her husband taught first at New York University and then at the Hispanic Institute of Columbia University. During these years they had two children, Carmen and Mike. Angel del Río and several other intellectuals from Spain were living in exile in New York and Puerto Rico during the years of the Spanish civil war and the long Francisco Franco fascist dictatorship. These Spanish exiles played a key role in founding Columbia's Hispanic Institute and a prestigious Department of Hispanic Studies at the University of Puerto Rico.

Agostini received a master's degree from Columbia University in 1932 and a doctorate from the University of Madrid in 1958, both in Spanish. Agostini's broad intellectual formation and close contact with Spanish and Latin American literary circles is reflected in many of her writings. She would spend forty years living in New York involved in teaching, scholarly pursuits, and creative writing. She was a professor of Spanish language and literature at Barnard College for many years and chaired the Spanish department from 1941 to 1962. Along with her husband, she taught at Middlebury College's Spanish immersion summer program. The couple also co-edited the widely used textbook *Antología General de la Literatura Española* (1960). From her experiences in the New York City Latino community, she wrote the book of narrative profiles *Puertorriqueños en Nueva York* (1970).

Agostini returned to Puerto Rico in the late 1960s, a few years after the death of her husband. On the island, she continued teaching and writing, and she became a frequent cultural columnist for the Puerto Rican newspaper *El Imparcial.* Her articles from this period are collected in the book *Rosa de los Vientos* (1980). Most of these articles relate personal anecdotes involving distinguished literary figures from Puerto Rico and other Spanish-speaking countries. These writings present a mixture of cultural commentary, autobiographical account, and literary criticism, but most of all they show how numerous intellectual friendships shaped and enriched Agostini's life.

Viñetas de Puerto Rico (1965), Agostini's intimate recollection of growing up in the small town of Yauco, Puerto Rico, describes a few of the town's most picturesque characters. Her connection to the homeland is also reflected in her poetry volume *Canto a San Juan de Puerto Rico y otros poemas* (1974). She also authored several books of children's stories and songs.

For her many literary and cultural contributions, Agostini was honored in 1973 by the Puerto Rico chapter of the American Women's Union. She was also elected president of the Sociedad de Autores Puertorriqueños. After a long and productive life, she died at the age of one hundred in Spring Lake, New Jersey, where she had lived with her daughter.

Bibliography: Amelia Agostini de del Río was a prolific scholar and writer who produced more than forty books of poetry, essays, short stories, and plays. In addition to those mentioned in the text, see *Nuestras Vidas Son Los Ríos* (1974) and *Duerme, Hijo* (1978). Biographical information can be found in Josefina Rivera de Alvarez, ed., *Diccionario de Literatura Puertorriqueña*, vol. 2, book 1 (1974). An obituary appeared in the *New York Times* on December 14, 1996, with a correction on December 17.

EDNA ACOSTA-BELÉN

AINSWORTH, Dorothy Sears. March 8, 1894–December 2, 1976. Physical education leader.

Dorothy Sears Ainsworth, physical education's and sports' "First Lady of the World," was born in Moline, Illinois, the youngest of three daughters of Stella Davidson and Harry Ainsworth. Her mother, a teacher, and father, an 1887 Harvard Law School graduate, met as students at Oberlin College. After their 1889 marriage, they settled in Moline, where Harry succeeded his father as president of William White and Company, a manufacturer of machinery, tools, and mill equipment. "Dot" enjoyed a secure childhood in a loving, affluent midwestern family that valued individual dignity, education, community service, sport, and exercise. She spent weekends in Sunday school at the First Congregational Church and summers at her family's cottage on the shores of Lake Michigan.

Dorothy attended Moline public schools, where the large but graceful young woman enjoyed German gymnastics classes and excelled in basketball. She graduated from Moline High School in 1912 and enrolled at Smith College in Northampton, Massachusetts, where she majored in history. An excellent athlete, Dorothy played basketball and tennis. Also a good actress with a strong speaking voice, she was active in drama, frequently playing men's roles. Popular among her peers, she gave rides in her Willys Knight (one of two automobiles on the Smith campus in 1916) and was elected president of Chapin House residence.

After graduating from Smith, Ainsworth returned to Moline, trained as a nurse's aide, and worked as a teacher-coach at Moline High School. In the summer of 1918, she helped American soldiers preparing for European service in World War I at a camp on Long Island. One year later, Ainsworth resigned her teaching position and sailed to Europe with eighteen women in the Smith College Relief Unit assigned to Grecourt, France, where she assisted needy families by driving a truck filled with critical food and supplies across the French countryside. The experience in France inspired her to commit herself to promoting international understanding when she returned home in 1920.

To advance her goal, Ainsworth first obtained professional experience and additional education. She worked for two years as an instructor of physical education at Smith and then completed a master's degree at Teachers College, Columbia University. After one year at Skidmore College, she was rehired by Smith as director of physical education, a position she held for thirty-four years. Returning to Columbia for a doctorate, she adopted the theory that physical education can help children develop the values, skills, and character required in a democratic society. When Ainsworth completed her doctorate in 1930, she published *The History of Physical Education in Twelve Colleges for Women,* a tribute to her predecessor at Smith, Senda Berenson, and a profile of physical education at Barnard, Bryn Mawr, Elmira, Goucher, Mills, Mount Holyoke, Radcliffe, Rockford, Smith, Vassar, Wellesley, and Wells Colleges.

The educational theory Ainsworth embraced at Columbia informed her future academic and professional endeavors. She became a leader of the twentieth-century school of thought concerning the "science" of physical education and sport that promoted women's and girls' health not through athletic competition but through broad opportunities to be physically active. Under her direction, physical education became an integral part of undergraduate life at Smith. By means of course work, intramural programs, and special events, "Miss A" expanded Smith's athletic and recreational facilities and, during 1935–36, developed a graduate course in physical education. In 1937 Smith's trustees granted her a full professorship. So great was Ainsworth's popularity by 1937 that she ran (unsuccessfully) for mayor of Northampton. Continuing to teach and write, she authored numerous newspaper and journal articles and co-edited *Individual Sports for Women* (1943). In 1945, at Ainsworth's insistence, Smith approved a Master of Science in Education degree that soon attracted women scholars from around the world, many of whom were influenced by Ainsworth and her philosophy.

While ascending as an academic innovator, Ainsworth became a leader within her profession. She served as president of the National Association of Directors of Physical Education for College Women (1937–41) and the American Association of Health, Physical Education and Recreation (1950–51). She chaired the U.S. Joint Council on International Affairs in Health, Physical Education and Recreation from 1950 to 1957, and cofounded and led its international arm from 1959 to 1965. She participated in the 1952 creation of the affiliated World Confederation of Organizations of the Teaching Profession (WCOTP), which adopted her philosophy of developing every person rather than archetypal athletes and Olympic competitors.

During the cold war era, Ainsworth continued her internationalist approach to sports. In July 1949, she organized the first, historic International Congress in Physical Education for Girls and Women, in Copenhagen, with 235 delegates from twenty-four countries. Four years later, the Congress reconvened in Paris and established the International Association of Physical Education and Sport for Girls and Women (IAPESGW). As president of IAPESGW for eight years and WCOTP for six, Ainsworth traveled and lectured extensively, dedicating herself to promoting health through physical activity, peace through understanding, and the acceptance of women as representatives of their nations on issues of human welfare.

Scholar, teacher, author, administrator, and ambassador, Dorothy Sears Ainsworth visited all fifty states and nearly every country in the world during her long career. Of all her honors and awards, she was most pleased by her 1956 honorary Doctor of Science degree from Smith. She never married but was a caring aunt and dedicated friend. She remained active professionally until her late seventies, then returned to Illinois in failing health. Ainsworth died peacefully in Moline at age eighty-two on December 2, 1976.

Bibliography: Dorothy Ainsworth authored or edited three books: *The History of Physical Education in Twelve Colleges for Women* (1930); *Individual Sports for Women* (ed.) (1943, and later editions); and *Basic Rhythms* (co-editor with Ruth Evans) (1955). Between 1930 and 1968 she also wrote numerous articles, speeches, and reports about international relations, health, physical education, sport, and recreation. A copy of Ainsworth's complete bibliography can be found in the Dorothy Sears Ainsworth Collection, 1916–1975, in the Smith College Archives in Northampton, Massachusetts. This extensive archival collection includes a 1974 oral history, collected correspondence, photographs, speeches and writings, as well as reports and records of many of the organizations she was involved in. Hazel C. Peterson provided a comprehensive overview of Ainsworth's importance in *Dorothy S. Ainsworth: Her Life, Professional Career and Contributions to Physical Education* (1968). See also Edith Betts and Hazel Peterson, "Dorothy Sears Ainsworth: Pioneer in International Relations," *Journal of Physical Education, Recreation and Dance* 56, no. 5 (May/June 1985), pp. 63–67. Ainsworth's obituary was released by the *Smith College News* on December 3, 1976, and appeared in the *New York Times* on December 4, 1976.

MARY G. TURCO

AINSWORTH, Mary Dinsmore Salter. December 1, 1913–March 21, 1999. Psychologist.

Mary Dinsmore Salter was born in Glendale, Ohio, the oldest of Charles and Mary Dinsmore Salter's three daughters. Her mother undertook training as a nurse, but did not pursue a career after marriage. After Mary's father, a successful businessman, was transferred by his firm to Toronto at the end of World War I, the family became Canadian citizens.

Mary, a precocious child, learned to read at the age of three and graduated from high school at sixteen. In 1929 she enrolled at the University of Toronto, where she was accepted into the challenging honors course in psychology two years later. She earned her bachelor's degree in 1935, continuing with graduate studies in psychology under the guidance of William Blatz, whose security theory had sparked her interest. According to this theory, the family is the secure base that enables a developing child to explore new interests and acquire new skills. She completed her doctoral dissertation, "An Evaluation of Adjustment Based on the Concept of Security," in 1939.

After serving as instructor at the University of Toronto until 1942, Mary decided to enlist in the Canadian Women's Army Corps, where she quickly rose to the rank of major. As director of personnel selection, she gained considerable clinical and diagnostic skills. She built upon these skills after returning to the University of Toronto as assistant professor in 1946, co-authoring a widely used clinical book, *Developments in the Rorschach Technique,* with Bruno Klopfer, an acclaimed expert in this field.

In 1950, Mary Salter married Leonard Ainsworth, a World War II veteran and graduate student who was completing his master's degree in psychology at Toronto. The couple decided that Leonard should complete the doctorate in London. Mary applied for and was offered a research position on John Bowlby's team at the Tavistock Institute of Human Relations. This event changed the direction of her life.

Bowlby, together with James Robertson, was conducting observational studies of the devastating effects of separation from the mother on institutionalized and hospitalized young children. Ainsworth's task was to help analyze Robertson's data. At the same time, she was exposed to Bowlby's emerging ideas about the evolutionary foundation of infant-mother attachment, inspired by the burgeoning field of ethology. Although fascinated by ethology herself, Ainsworth did not initially find Bowlby's newfangled propositions particularly persuasive. Like the majority of psychologists and psychoanalysts at the time, she believed that babies learn to love their mothers because mothers satisfy babies' needs.

In the beginning of 1954, after completing his doctorate, Leonard Ainsworth accepted a two-year position at the East African Institute of Social Research in Kampala, Uganda. Mary was not particularly eager to interrupt her career again, but once in Kampala she managed to garner funds for a short-term longitudinal study of twenty-six mothers and infants who lived in six surrounding villages. Suddenly, Bowlby's ethological notions about attachment began to seem relevant. Thus the first study exploring Bowlby's ideas about attachment was undertaken several years before he made his first formal presentation of the theory to colleagues at the British Psycho-Analytical Society in 1958. Upon receiving a preprint of this presentation, Ainsworth reestablished her close collaboration with Bowlby, albeit mostly by correspondence. Because of other commitments, Ainsworth did not publish a book on her Uganda findings until 1967.

In late 1955, Leonard Ainsworth accepted a position as forensic psychologist in Baltimore. Mary lectured part-time at Johns Hopkins University and supervised clinical students while also serving as diagnostician at Sheppard and Enoch Pratt Psychiatric Hospital. In 1958, she was promoted to associate professor in clinical psychology. In 1960, the Ainsworths divorced. They had no children.

When the focus of her position at Johns Hopkins switched to developmental psychology, Ainsworth was able to launch a groundbreaking sequel to her Uganda study. Families for the Baltimore study were recruited through local pediatricians. Extensive monthly home observations began shortly after the child's birth. Mothers' and infants' behavior was recorded in shorthand, dictated into a tape recorder immediately after each visit, and transcribed. The last observation, at twelve months, included a laboratory procedure now famous as "the Strange Situation" (devised with her research associate, Barbara Wittig). It consists of several brief episodes during which an infant is observed when the mother is present and when she is absent. Infants' behavior, especially upon reunion with their mothers, revealed important individual differences that were strongly correlated with observations of maternal sensitivity to infant signals during feeding, close bodily contact, face-to-face play, and crying during the first three months and to a more harmonious and secure mother-infant relationship during the last three months of the first year.

Bowlby incorporated findings from the Uganda study and preliminary insights from the Baltimore project into the first volume (1969) of his trilogy, *Attachment and Loss.* Over the next decade or so, Ainsworth published influential journal articles and a book, *Patterns of Attachment* (1978), describing the findings of the Baltimore study. As a consequence, the Strange Situation began to be used as a shortcut method for assessing infant-parent attachment patterns as predictors of development beyond infancy. Several longitudinal studies in the United States, Germany, and Israel supported and extended Ainsworth's discoveries, but she occasionally expressed regret that the Strange Situation had stolen the limelight from her highly original analyses of naturalistic home observations.

In 1974, Ainsworth accepted a position at the University of Virginia, becoming a Commonwealth Professor of Psychology in 1975. In 1984, at seventy, the mandatory retirement age, she reluctantly retired as professor emerita. Ainsworth remained professionally active until 1992, when her health began to fail. During these later years, she retained a deep interest in the research projects of her former students, now influential academicians, who had begun to study attachment beyond infancy. In 1998, a few months before her death, she received one of the highest honors psychology can bestow, the Gold Medal Award for Life Achievement in the Science of Psychology from the American Psychological Foundation. In the same year, she was the first recipient of the newly instituted Mentor Award of the APA's developmental division.

Mary Ainsworth died of a massive stroke on March 21, 1999, in Charlottesville at the age of eighty-five, and her ashes were interred in the cemetery of the University of Virginia. Her conceptual contributions and empirical findings have revolutionized developmental and social psychologists' thinking about infant-caregiver attachment, and by extension about close human relationships at all ages.

Bibliography: Mary Ainsworth's correspondence is held by the Archives of the History of American Psychology, Akron University, Ohio. Materials related to her Baltimore Study, including transcriptions of observations, can be accessed at the data archive of Murray Research Center, Radcliffe Institute for Advanced Study, Harvard University. Two books summarize her two short-term longitudinal studies: *Infancy in Uganda: Infant Care and the Growth of Love* (1967); and *Patterns of Attachment: A Psychological Study of the Strange Situation* (1978), written with Mary Blehar, Everett Waters, and Sally Wall. In addition, Ainsworth published many empirical and theoretical articles in premier journals, such as *Child Development* and *Developmental Psychology,* and in influential edited books. A brief autobiography appeared in Agnes N. O'Connell and Nancy Felipe Russo, eds., *Models of Achievement: Reflections of Eminent Women in Psychology* (1983). An interview (coauthored with Robert S. Marvin), "On the Shaping of Attachment Theory and Research: An Interview with Mary D. S. Ainsworth," was published in *Monographs of the Society for Research in Child Development* 60 (1995), pp. 3–21. Additional information can be gleaned from two brief biographies by former students: Mary Main's article, "Mary D. Salter Ainsworth: Tribute and Portrait," *Psychoanalytic Inquiry* 19, no. 5 (1999), pp. 682–736; and Inge Bretherton's chapter, "Mary Ainsworth: Insightful Observer and Courageous Theoretician," in Gregory A. Kimble and Michael Wertheimer, eds., *Portraits of Pioneers of Psychology, Volume Five* (2003). See also Bretherton, "The Origins of Attachment Theory: John Bowlby and Mary Ainsworth," *Developmental Psychology* 28, no. 5 (September 1992), pp. 759–75; and Robert Karen, *Becoming Attached* (1994). Ainsworth's obituary appeared in the *New York Times* on April 7, 1999. A longer obituary, written by Bretherton and Main, was published in the *American Psychologist* 55, no. 10 (October 2000), pp. 1148–49.

INGE BRETHERTON

ALBERS, Anni. June 12, 1899–May 9, 1994. Textile designer and fiber artist, printmaker.

Annelise Else Frieda Fleischmann was born in Berlin, the eldest of three children of Antonie "Toni" Ullstein and Siegfried Fleischmann. Hers was a privileged childhood. Her father was a furniture manufacturer, and her mother was a member of a prominent publishing family. From birth, an inherited deformity of the arch of her foot set her apart from others and limited her mobility. She was educated by private tutors as a child and then attended the lyceum. Her interest in art was evident early, and her mother arranged for art lessons. From 1916 to 1919, she studied art with Martin Brandenburg. She enrolled briefly at the Kunstgewerbeschule in Hamburg but left dissatisfied.

On April 21, 1922, at the age of twenty-three, Annelise Fleischmann enrolled at the Bauhaus in Weimar. For a young woman who had known only comfort and protection, this was a courageous decision. After completing the *Vorkurs* (preliminary course), she would have preferred studying painting but was assigned, along with other women, to the Weaving Workshop. She was an influential member, participating in the transition from the craft-oriented activities in Weimar to the industry-oriented program in Dessau. In 1930 she was awarded the Bauhaus diploma on the basis of a sound-absorbing, light-reflecting wall-covering material she designed for the auditorium of the Allgemeinen Deutschen Gewerkschaftbundesschule in Bernau. Throughout her career, she enjoyed the challenge of integrating aesthetic concerns, the limitations and possibilities of the woven fabric, and the functional demands of specific situations. She assisted in the running of the Weaving Workshop when needed and also taught the Design Theory course.

In 1925 Annelise Fleischmann married Josef Albers, an artist who taught in the *Vorkurs* at the Bauhaus. The couple did not have children. From then on she was known as Anni Albers, and the two shared an acute awareness of and fascination with the visual world and a commitment to the experimental spirit of modernism. Although Anni Albers assumed a traditional role by promoting her husband's work before her own, essential to their relationship was a mutual respect for each other's artistic accomplishments, and their work is often the subject of two-person exhibitions.

When, in August 1933, the Bauhaus closed under pressure from the Nationalist Socialist Party, the Alberses were eager to leave Germany. Although her family had converted to Christianity, Anni Albers's lineage was Jewish, and Josef Albers was at risk because of both his association with the Bauhaus and his abstract art. Through the efforts of Philip Johnson at the Museum of Modern Art, Josef Albers was invited to teach art at the new Black Mountain College, an experimental college that thrived in the mountains of North Carolina near Asheville from 1933 to 1957. They arrived in November 1933, and Anni Albers received her United States citizenship on May 17, 1939.

Although Josef held the official appointment, Anni was quickly enlisted to teach classes in weaving and textile design. In March 1934 she was appointed instructor in weaving, and in 1938, assistant professor. Unlike the Bauhaus, Black Mountain College was a liberal arts school in which the arts were to be an integral part of college life and the learning process. Unencumbered by a preexisting program, Anni Albers created a weaving curriculum emphasizing design for industrial production. This curriculum is described in her book *On Weaving* (1965), a basic text for weaving studies.

During this period Albers designed some of her finest textiles, including the drapery for the Rockefeller guest house in New York City. A one-person exhibition of her textiles at the Museum of Modern Art in 1949 was the first exhibition at the museum devoted solely to textiles. Jewelry designed with a student, Alex Reed, was exhibited throughout the United States. On frequent trips to Mexico, Albers formed a collection of textiles from Mexico and Central America, and together the Alberses formed an important collection of pre-Columbian miniatures. Anni Albers was in the forefront of bringing recognition to the high achievement of the pre-Columbian weavers.

Josef and Anni Albers left Black Mountain in 1949, and in 1950 he was appointed chair of the Department of Design at Yale University. For the next two decades, free of the responsibilities of teaching, Anni focused her attention on her writing and weaving. During the 1950s she wove most of her pictorial weavings. She created the ark panels for Temple Emanu-El in Dallas in 1956 and was commissioned by Walter Gropius to design bedspreads and partitions for dormitories at the Harvard Graduate Center.

In 1963, Josef Albers was invited to make a series of prints at the Tamarind Lithography Workshop. The workshop director encouraged Anni Albers to make a lithograph. She returned the following year to produce her first print portfolio, *Line Involvements,* a portfolio of seven lithographs. She later worked with Ken Tyler at Gemini G.E.L. in Los Angeles and at Tyler Graphics in New York using screenprinting and etching. Until 1970, Albers continued to weave, completing two major commissions: the ark panels for the Temple B'nai Israel in Woonsocket, Rhode Island (1962),

peared in the *Voice* on August 27, 1987, and in the *San Francisco Chronicle* and the *Daily Californian* on August 28, 1987.

KEONA K. ERVIN

ALEXANDER, Margaret Walker. *See* Walker, Margaret.

ALEXANDER, Sadie Tanner Mossell. January 2, 1898–November 1, 1989. Lawyer, civil rights activist.

Sadie Tanner Mossell Alexander, a prominent Philadelphia lawyer and nationally known civil rights advocate, was the youngest of three children of Mary Louise Tanner and Aaron Albert Mossell. Her family had a singular history of accomplishment. Aaron Mossell and his brother Nathan were the first black graduates of the University of Pennsylvania's law and medical schools, respectively. Nathan's wife, Gertrude E. H. Bustill Mossell, was the author of *The Work of the Afro-American Woman* (1894), an important work of nineteenth-century black feminism. Sadie's maternal grandfather, Bishop Benjamin Tucker Tanner of the African Methodist Episcopal Church, founded the *A.M.E. Church Review,* one of the leading journals of African American intellectual life in the late nineteenth century. Bishop Tanner's accomplished children included Henry Ossawa Tanner, the well-known expatriate painter.

When Sadie Mossell was a year old, her father left his family and returned to his hometown of Lockport, New York. Afterward, she and her mother shuttled back and forth between residences in Philadelphia, where they lived with Bishop Tanner, and Washington, D.C., where they lived with her maternal uncle by marriage, Lewis Baxter Moore, a dean at Howard University. Sadie attended Washington's prestigious M Street High School, and returned to Philadelphia to attend college at the University of Pennsylvania, where she earned her BS in education in 1918 and her PhD in economics in 1921. Her doctoral dissertation, entitled "The Standard of Living among One Hundred Negro Migrant Families in Philadelphia," was an important analysis of the Great Migration of southern blacks to the North. Alexander was the second African American woman to earn a doctorate (Georgiana Simpson was awarded hers one day earlier at the University of Chicago), and the first in economics. In 1919, while at Penn, she was elected the first national president of Delta Sigma Theta sorority; she served until 1923.

Sadie Mossell had much difficulty finding employment, but she finally obtained a position as an assistant actuary with the North Carolina Mutual Life Insurance Company, a black-owned corporation in Durham, North Carolina. After two years in Durham she returned to Philadelphia, where she and Raymond Pace Alexander were married on November 29, 1923. The two had met while studying at Penn, and she agreed to marry him following his graduation from Harvard Law School in 1923. She soon found herself dissatisfied with the duties of a housewife, and in 1924 she enrolled in the law school at Penn. Her grades earned her election to the prestigious University of Pennsylvania Law Review, where she was the first black woman to serve as an editor. After graduating and being admitted to the bar in 1927, she joined her husband's law firm, becoming the first African American woman admitted to the practice of law in Pennsylvania. She and Raymond had two daughters: Mary Elizabeth (1934) and Rae Pace (1937).

Alexander initially had to content herself with "office practice"—matters that did not involve many appearances in court, the typical fare of a woman attorney in the 1920s. She started with trusts and estates work in the city's orphan's court, and pro forma, uncontested divorces, impressing judges with her mastery of the technical details of pleading and practice. A staunch Republican, she used her party connections to secure appointments as an assistant city solicitor from 1927 to 1931, and again from 1936 to 1940. In the late 1940s and the 1950s, she drew institutional clients like the African Methodist Episcopal Church to the Alexander firm and developed into a tough negotiator in increasingly complicated divorce proceedings.

In 1959, when her husband became the first black judge appointed to the Philadelphia Court of Common Pleas, Alexander struck out on her own. At a time when most women lawyers in the city still played subordinate roles in the offices of men, she opened her own law office and received a steady flow of family law clients. Alexander was one of the leading practitioners of family law in the city, and a number of local firms referred their domestic relations matters to her. In 1976, she joined the firm of Atkinson, Myers, and Archie, as counsel.

It was Sadie Alexander's activities in the civil rights arena that earned her a national reputation. Local and visiting blacks, including Jackie Robinson, often sought the Alexanders' counsel and advocacy when encountering the racial segregation and exclusion that was still widely practiced in Philadelphia's hotels, restaurants, theaters, and schools. Sadie and Raymond Alexander helped draft the 1935 state civil rights act, which strengthened the nondiscrimination provisions of the state public accommodations laws. Sadie Alexander served for more than two decades as the secretary of the National Urban League, and held the same post in the National Bar Association, the black lawyers' professional group, from 1943 to 1947.

Her rise to national prominence began in earnest in 1946, when President Truman named her to his President's Committee on Civil Rights. The committee's report, *To Secure These Rights* (1947), recommended strong federal action to enforce civil rights and foreshadowed much of the next twenty years of federal activity in this area. In 1948, she helped found the Philadelphia chapter of the American Civil Liberties Union (ACLU) and was soon elected to the organization's national board. (During that same year, she was instrumental in desegregating the dining facilities at Washington National Airport when, after being refused service, she filed suit and wrote a letter of protest to President Truman.) In the late 1940s, the Alexanders joined the Democratic Party and allied themselves with a group of reform Democrats in the city. In 1952, after the reformers took over city government, Sadie Alexander was selected as a member of the newly formed Philadelphia Commission on Human Relations. She became the commission's chairwoman in 1962 and remained active in local and national civil rights movements, but she was forced to resign from the commission in 1968 because of her aggressive stances against housing discrimination and police brutality. In 1978, she began her last stint in public service when President Carter appointed her to chair the White House Conference on Aging, but President Reagan removed her from office before the conference took place.

Raymond Pace Alexander died in 1974. In 1983 Sadie Alexander moved to Cathedral Village, a retirement community in Philadelphia, where she spent the last years of her life combating Alzheimer's disease before dying in 1989 at the age of ninety-one.

Bibliography: The Alexander family papers are housed at the University Archives and Records Center, University of Pennsylvania, in Philadelphia; they include the personal and professional papers of Sadie T. M. and Raymond Pace Alexander. The collection also includes the papers of Elizabeth Mossell Anderson and Raymond's sister, Virginia Alexander, both of whom kept up an active correspondence with Sadie. Sadie Alexander's autobiographical publications include "A Clean Sweep: Reflections on the Rocky Road to Winning a 'Broom Award' in 1918," *Pennsylvania Gazette,* March 1972, pp. 30–32; "The Best of Times and the Worst of Times," *Law Alumni Journal* 12 (Spring 1977), pp. 19–21; and "Forty-five Years a Woman Lawyer," in J. Clay Smith Jr., ed., *Rebels in Law: Voices in History of Black Women Lawyers* (1998). An informative published interview with Alexander, with useful information on her family background, home life, and career, may be found in Ruth Edmonds Hill, ed., *The Black Women Oral History Project,* vol. 2 (1991). Alexander's doctoral dissertation was published as Sadie Tanner Mossell, "The Standard of Living among One Hundred Negro Migrant Families in Philadelphia," *Annals of the American Academy of Political and Social Science* 98 (November 1921), pp. 173–218. Her other major published writings include "Women as Practitioners of Law in the United States," *National Bar Journal* 1 (1941), pp. 56–64; and "Negro Women in Our Economic Life," *Opportunity* 8 (July 1930), pp. 201–3.

For commentary on Alexander's dissertation by a modern-day economist, see Julianne Malveaux, "Missed Opportunity: Sadie Tanner Mossell Alexander and the Economics Profession," *American Economic Review* 81 (1991), pp. 307–10. An analysis of Alexander's civil rights career is contained in Charles Lewis Nier III, "Sweet Are the Uses of Adversity: The Civil Rights Activism of Sadie Tanner Mossell Alexander," *Temple Political and Civil Rights Law Review* 8 (1998), pp. 59–86. For more on Alexander's life and career, see Kenneth W. Mack, "A Social History of Everyday Practice: Sadie T. M. Alexander and the Incorporation of Black Women into the American Legal Profession, 1925–60," *Cornell Law Review* 87 (2002), pp. 1405–74. Alexander's birth certificate, obtained from the Philadelphia City Archives, lists her first name as "Sarah." She was named after her maternal grandmother, Sarah, who was also known as "Sadie" (or "Sadee"). Alexander appears to have used the first name "Sadie" for her entire life. Obituaries appeared in the *New York Times* and the *Philadelphia Inquirer* on November 3, 1989.

KENNETH WALTER MACK

ALLEN, Donna. August 19, 1920–July 19, 1999. Labor economist, peace and media activist.

Donna Rehkopf Allen, a peace activist in Women Strike for Peace and the founder of the Women's Institute for Freedom of the Press, was born in Petoskey, Michigan, to Louise Densmore and Caspar Rehkopf. She was the second of three children and the only girl. Her self-supporting grandmother had an early and enduring influence on her, as did her mother, a 1915 graduate of the University of Michigan who was a Detroit schoolteacher. While Donna was a child, her father enrolled in Michigan State College to earn an engineering degree, which he could not have done without his wife's support and financial backing. Flexible gender roles and the importance of lifelong education were central tenets in Donna Allen's life.

In 1929 the family moved to Chicago, where Caspar Rehkopf found work as an metallurgical engineer. Donna graduated from Morton High School, in the Chicago suburb of Cicero. She went on to Morton Junior College, where she majored in history and edited the college newspaper, and in 1941 transferred to Duke University to study history and economics. In 1943 she graduated and married Russell Allen, with whom she would have four children: Dana (1945), Indra (1946), Martha (1948), and Mark (1950). While her husband served with the U.S. Air Corps in the Pacific during World War

II, Allen moved to Washington, D.C., to become assistant to the director of research at the Metal Trades Department of the American Federation of Labor (1944–45). In 1948 she conducted research on the Railway Brotherhoods for the National Labor Bureau. She also worked for the Presidential Emergency Board and was appointed by President Truman under the Railway Labor Act to hear emergency cases in industrial labor relations.

In the fall of 1949 the family moved to Albany, New York, where Russell Allen became research and education director for the International Brotherhood of Paper Makers. Donna Allen finished her thesis, "Collective Bargaining under the Railway Labor Act," and in June 1952 received an MA degree in economics from the University of Chicago. She taught at the Cornell School of Industrial Relations from 1953 to 1955. In 1957 the Allens moved to Washington, D.C., when her husband accepted a position as education director of the Industrial Union Department of the AFL-CIO. The family rented a house in Cleveland Park where Donna lived for the rest of her life. In Washington, she continued her academic studies, eventually obtaining a PhD in history from Howard University in 1971.

At the height of the cold war arms race in the late 1950s, Allen turned her attention to the pollution of children's milk from nuclear fallout due to atmospheric tests by the United States and the Soviet Union. She was active in the Women's International League for Peace and Freedom (WILPF) and the Committee for a Sane Nuclear Policy (SANE), but she was also one of a handful of Washington women who were impatient for more militant action against the nuclear threat than those organizations were ready to assume. These women called for a women's strike for peace in November 1961 under the slogans "End the Arms Race, Not the Human Race" and "No Tests East or West." Tens of thousands of women in communities across the country turned out for the strike, which developed into a national movement. Thus Allen became a founder of Women Strike for Peace (WSP), a leader in the struggle against nuclear proliferation, and a key woman in the successful campaign for the 1963 atmospheric nuclear test ban treaty. In the ensuing years, Allen was known as the movement's expert on the economics of disarmament and the social costs of the arms race and the Vietnam War, of which she was an outspoken critic.

When Russell Allen took a post at Michigan State University in 1964, Allen decided to remain in Washington. By mutual agreement their two younger children, still in high school, moved to Michigan with their father. Donna and Russell Allen divorced in 1968 but remained friends throughout her life.

In November 1964, Allen, along with Dagmar Wilson, the national spokesperson for WSP, and Russ Nixon, general manager of the *National Guardian,* a leftist weekly published in New York City, were subpoenaed to testify before an executive session of the House Committee on Un-American Activities (HUAC) concerning visits they had made to the State Department in 1963 to urge that an entry permit be granted to a Japanese law school dean and peace leader who had been invited to lecture in the United States. All three refused to testify in secret session and called for an open hearing. HUAC refused and cited them for contempt. They were tried in federal court on April 7, 1965, convicted, and sentenced in June. The conviction was overturned on August 2, 1966.

In addition to her leading role in Women Strike for Peace and on the national board of WILPF, Allen was also an active participant in the National Women's Political Caucus, the National Woman's Party, and the National Organization for Women. Frustrated by the difficulties that the women's and peace movements faced in raising their concerns and issues in the media, in 1972 Allen founded the Women's Institute for Freedom of the Press. This organization still pioneers in research, education, and publishing and operates as a national and international network for women working in communications and the public arena who want to restructure the media system. From 1972 to 1987 Allen edited *The Media Report to Women* while her daughter (and colleague) Martha edited the annual *Directory of Women's Media* (1974–89). Working long hours and without salary, Allen devoted twenty-seven years of her life to ceaselessly campaigning for a democratic media system that would give equal treatment to people of all genders, classes, and races. By the time of her death, Allen and her associates had created a significant network of women dedicated to protesting media bias and creating new kinds of independent media and communications systems. Donna Allen died in Washington, D.C., on July 19, 1999, at the age of seventy-eight.

Bibliography: The Donna Allen Papers are part of the National Women and Media Collection located at the University of Missouri, Columbia. Allen's publications are available from the Women's Institute for Freedom of the Press, Washington, D.C. The Swarthmore College Peace Collection contains articles by Donna Allen and news of her projects on the economics of disarmament, as well as *Memo,* the national publication of Women Strike for Peace. Secondary sources include Maurine H. Beasley, "Donna Allen and the Women's Institute: A Feminist Perspective on the First Amendment," *American Journalism* 9, nos. 3–4 (Summer/Fall 1992), pp. 154–66; Martha Allen, "Address at the Dr. Donna Allen Memorial Symposium," Freedom

Forum, Arlington, Virginia, August 3, 2001; and Amy Swerdlow, *Women Strike for Peace: Traditional Motherhood and Radical Politics in the 1960s* (1993). An obituary appeared in the *New York Times* on July 26, 1999.

AMY SWERDLOW

ALLEN, Elsie. September 22, 1899–December 31, 1990. Pomo basket maker and educator.

Elsie Allen was a pivotal figure in the effort to preserve and revitalize Pomo culture, particularly the production of exquisite baskets made from native plants. The Pomo Indians lived in northern California in what would become Sonoma, Mendocino, and Lake counties. Even though these peoples spoke seven related but very different languages and lived in more than seventy politically independent groups, white anthropologists designated them "the Pomo." Pomo baskets are highly regarded for their quality construction, superb technique, and transcendent beauty. Allen wove baskets, collected the baskets of others, and taught basket weaving, producing a lasting cultural legacy.

Allen was born in a hop field near Santa Rosa, California, the only child of Annie Tomasia Ramon and George Gomachu (anglicized to Comanche). Like many native people in the region, her parents worked as laborers on white-owned farms. Elsie lived with her grandmother, Mary Arnold, near the village of Cloverdale until she was eight years old. Following George's death, her mother married Richard Burke, who was half Pomo and half English, and the entire family moved to the area around Hopland, in southern Mendocino County. They lived in a wooden house during the winter but spent the summer on the banks of the Russian River in a traditional house of leaves over willow branch frames.

As a child, Elsie helped her family pick hops and other crops. She grew up speaking only the language of her people and learning traditional life skills such as fishing, hunting, and gathering acorns and other wild plants. Although she was baptized Catholic in Santa Rosa and considered herself a nominal Catholic, she also learned many traditional religious beliefs and blended them into the new religion. For example, fasting was a custom in both traditions, and she learned to fast for purification before starting an important project such as a new basket. This blending of traditional with new customs was characteristic of her approach to life.

When Elsie was eleven, a government agent convinced her mother to send her to the Indian boarding school on the Round Valley Reservation in northeastern Mendocino County, where children were forbidden to speak their own languages. Elsie found it difficult to learn in this environment and returned to her family after about a year. When she was thirteen, an Indian day school opened on the Hopland Rancheria and she attended for three years, finally learning English.

By the time she was a teenager, Elsie had learned basket making from her mother and her maternal grandmother, but there was little time for making baskets because she had to help support the family. At the age of eighteen, wanting to learn something better than farm labor, she found work in San Francisco with the help of a local priest. She worked as a domestic servant in a private home and later at Saint Joseph's Hospital. After six months at the hospital, she contracted the flu during the 1918 epidemic, which ended her adventure in the city.

On May 1, 1919, Elsie married Arthur Allen, a northern Pomo and ranch worker, at Saint Mary's Catholic Church in Ukiah. After the Christian ceremony, the family also held a traditional Pomo wedding. The couple's first child, Genevieve, was born in 1920, the year the family moved to the Pinoleville Indian Rancheria near Ukiah. Three more children followed: Leonard (1922), Dorothy (1924), and George (1928).

Continuing to work in the fields while raising her family left Allen little time to weave baskets, although she did make a few, which were buried with family members. When her grandmother, Mary Arnold, died in 1924, Allen lost not only her teaching but also the example of her baskets because tradition required that a woman's baskets be buried with her.

During the 1940s, Allen and her mother joined other Pomo women in organizing the Pomo Women's Club. The goal of the organization was to ease discrimination against their people by educating non-Indians about Pomo culture and traditions. Exhibitions and demonstrations of basket making proved effective at this, and Allen became chair of the basket committee. Soon requests for exhibitions were pouring in, but the supply of baskets was limited. This led Elsie's mother to question the burial tradition, and she asked her daughter not to bury her own life's work with her. Although many people were shocked by this defiance of tradition, Elsie's mother's baskets were valuable models for Allen when she began to weave again.

Her mother's death in 1962 helped Allen make the decision to return to basket making and to communicate the significance of this art to the world. She was then in her early sixties. For almost the next thirty years, Elsie Allen gathered materials, wove and exhibited baskets, and became a collector of other weavers' work. She taught basket weaving to both Indian and non-Indian students and consulted for museums and scholars. In 1972,

Allen's book, *Pomo Basketmaking: A Supreme Art for the Weaver,* was published.

As she became a public person, Allen endured criticism from some members of the Pomo community. Some believed that she was wrong to share her knowledge with a wide, non-Indian public, while others believed that dwelling on past traditions would undermine efforts to adapt to a white-dominated world. Allen never wavered in her belief that the living culture of a people could ease that process of adaptation.

In the last three decades of her life, Allen became one of the best-known teachers and representatives of Pomo culture, passing on her knowledge and wisdom to many students. She demonstrated her work at the Festival of American Folklife on the Washington Mall in 1974, and helped identify and label baskets at the Smithsonian Institution. From 1979 to 1981 she participated in Sonoma State University's Warm Springs Cultural Resources Study, a cultural record of the Makahmo and Mahilakawna (Dry Creek/West Creek) Pomo. She also participated in an ethnobotanical study that resulted in the relocation of endangered plants from an area to be flooded by a proposed dam. Her most significant legacy is the Elsie Allen Collection of 131 baskets, which is the only collection of Pomo baskets that is documented with the names of individual weavers. It resides in the Jesse Peter Museum at Santa Rosa Junior College in California. Elsie Allen died in Sebastopol, California, in 1990 at the age of ninety-one.

Bibliography: The best account of Elsie Allen's life is in her book, *Pomo Basketmaking: A Supreme Art for the Weaver* (1972). See also Suzanne Abel-Vidor, Dot Brovarney, and Susan Billy, *Remember Your Relations: The Elsie Allen Baskets, Family and Friends* (1996), which contains wonderful information about Allen and many other Pomo basket makers. Also of interest is Ralph T. Coe, *Lost and Found Traditions: Native American Art 1965–85* (1986). Other sources include two articles by Barbara Winther: "Pomo Banded Baskets and Their Dau Marks," *American Indian Art Magazine* 10, no. 4 (Autumn 1985), pp. 50–58; and "More About Dau Marks: Visiting Four Pomo Basket Makers," *American Indian Art Magazine* 21, no. 4 (Autumn 1996), pp. 44–51. Allen is briefly discussed in Sherrie Ann Smith-Ferri, "Weaving a Tradition: Pomo Indian Baskets from 1850 through 1996" (PhD dissertation, University of Washington, 1998). Brief biographies of Allen are found in Roger Matuz, ed., *St. James Guide to Native North American Artists* (1998); and Liz Sonneborn, *A to Z of Native American Women* (1998). Allen is also profiled in the video *Pomo Basketweavers: A Tribute to Three Elders* (1994).

LINDA PACINI PITELKA

AMES, Louise Bates. October 29, 1908–October 31, 1996. Child psychologist.

Louise Bates was born in Portland, Maine, the oldest of three children and the only daughter of Annie Earle Leach and Samuel Lewis Bates. Her father was a highly respected lawyer and judge in the community; her mother taught school prior to marriage. Both parents valued education, literature, and outdoor activities. Whether collecting wildflowers or reading Dickens around the fireplace, the family provided Louise with a safe and stimulating haven for nurturing her intellect and creativity.

Bates attended public schools in Portland, where she developed talents in debate, literature, and history. After graduation in 1926, she attended Wheaton College in Norton, Massachusetts, but she balked at the cloistered and elite atmosphere of the all-female institution. In 1928 she transferred to the University of Maine, where she had a much happier experience, both socially and intellectually.

As a young girl Louise Bates had planned to become a lawyer like her father, but a course in psychology with Charles A. Dickinson spurred her to further study in this area. After marrying fellow student and future psychophysiologist Smith Ames on May 22, 1930, at the end of her senior year, she decided that a career as a psychologist would provide her with more flexibility for family life. Following graduation, Ames took a year off to give birth to her only child, Joan, and therewith began a family legacy in child psychology. Joan would become a child psychologist like her mother, and together they would co-author *Don't Push Your Preschooler* (1974). In turn, Joan's daughter Carol would also become a psychologist, writing parenting books with Louise Bates Ames after her mother died. In all of their works, the three generations of women stressed the importance of biology in shaping patterns of child development.

Shortly after her daughter's birth, Ames returned to the University of Maine, where she completed her master's degree in 1933. She then chose to attend Yale University to work with Arnold Gesell, who had founded the Yale Clinic of Child Development in 1911. She entered Yale's doctoral program in psychology in 1933 and became Gesell's research assistant. In 1936, Ames completed her doctorate, and in 1937 she divorced her husband. Her dissertation on crawling in infants introduced the themes of maturation and development that would preoccupy her for a lifetime. Starting early in her career, she drew on cinematography to film and then analyzed patterns of behavior in her young research subjects.

After receiving her PhD, Ames continued at the Clinic, working with many talented researchers, especially pediatrician Frances Ilg, a close friend and colleague until Ilg's death in 1981. The mostly female researchers were exceptionally collaborative, a tradition that Ames maintained throughout her writing career. Of the approximately fifty monographs she published, at least thirty-five were co-authored. Her most influential publications include *The First Five Years of Life* (1940), *Infant and Child in the Culture of Today* (1943), and *The Child from Five to Ten* (1946). Ames was that rare academic writer who could address both scholarly and popular audiences in her work. Her books charted the progress of child development, explaining the characteristics and behaviors children may be expected to acquire as they age. The idea of the "terrible twos"—now a mainstay of popular culture—was a product of the Gesell group's work on norms. Ames also urged parents to be accepting of children who displayed unconventional gender characteristics, contending that individual differences are biologically based and that it would be undemocratic to seek to eradicate such differences.

In 1948 Gesell retired and the university disbanded the Clinic and opened a child study center whose approach was more psychoanalytical than biological. In response, Ames, Ilg, and Janet Rodell founded the Gesell Institute of Child Development in New Haven in 1950. With the Institute initially languishing for want of funds (it was not affiliated with Yale), in 1952 Ames was enticed into publishing a syndicated newspaper column with Frances Ilg as a source of revenue. The column, "Child Behavior," and later "Parents Ask," was published in sixty-five major newspapers, from the *Boston Globe* to the *Los Angeles Times*, and included parents' letters and the researchers' responses. Thousands of parents wrote to the authors, and Ames personally responded to each writer with the mixture of science and common sense that informed all of her work.

Because of the success of the column, Ames became a celebrity who gave public lectures, hosted her own television and radio shows, and appeared on talk shows. During the 1960s, Ames used her public platform to espouse her views on the importance of school readiness. In all of her work, she remained staunchly committed to the idea that children should begin school when they are developmentally ready—not simply at a designated chronological age—even when the tides of scholarly opinion shifted in a different direction.

A lesser-known but distinctive contribution to psychology was Ames's research on age in relation to Rorschach responses. Prior to Ames's work, clinicians had been using a single standard to judge the normality of Rorschach responses. Ames demonstrated that both children and the elderly have patterns of response that are different from those of all other age groups. This research fit in well with Ames's basic idea that age must be considered when evaluating the significance of differences in behavior.

Although she was not always in favor with colleagues of differing theoretical inclinations, especially those who stressed the role of the environment in shaping individual behavior, during the 1950s and 1960s Louise Ames was viewed as one of the preeminent publicizers of developmental psychology. In 1974 she was honored by the Society for Projective Techniques and the Rorschach Institute for her distinguished contributions. Always taking great pleasure and interest in her work, she maintained an active retirement of research and writing in New Haven until the last few months of her life. Louise Bates Ames died of thyroid cancer at her granddaughter's home in Cincinnati at the age of eighty-eight.

Bibliography: Louise Bates Ames's voluminous personal and professional papers are at the Library of Congress and include much information about the Yale Clinic of Child Development and Ames's own work, as well as her correspondence with parents who wrote to her via her newspaper column. Ames published two autobiographical essays: "Louise Bates Ames" in Dennis Thompson and John D. Hogan, eds., *A History of Developmental Psychology in Autobiography* (1996); and "Child Development and Clinical Psychology," in Eugene Walker, ed., *The History of Clinical Psychology in Autobiography*, vol. 2, (1993). See also Gwendolyn Stevens and Sheldon Gardner, *The Women of Psychology*, vol. 2 (1982). Ames's own text, *Arnold Gesell: Themes of His Work* (1989), yields some interesting information about the genesis of the Gesell Institute. In addition to the books mentioned in the essay, significant other monographs by Ames include *Youth: The Years from Ten to Sixteen*, written with Frances L. Ilg and Arnold Gesell (1956); *Child Behavior: From the Gesell Institute of Human Development*, written with Frances L. Ilg and Sidney Baker (1981); *Child Rorschach Responses: Developmental Trends from Two to Ten Years*, written with Ruth W. Metraux, Janet Learned Rodell, and Richard Walker (1974); and *Stop School Failure*, written with Clyde Gillespie and John W. Streff (1972). With Ilg, Joan Ames Chase, and Carol Chase Haber, she also published a series of books on the various ages of children. For samples of the newspaper column and of parents' letters to Ames, see *Child Behavior* (1955) and *Parents Ask* (1962), both of which Ames co-authored with Frances Ilg. Obituaries appeared in the *Washington Post* on November 4, 1996, and the *New York Times* on November 7, 1996. Richard N. Walker's obituary of Ames, published in *American Psychologist* 54 (July 1999), p. 516, provides a colleague's view.

JULIA GRANT

ANDERSON, Marian. February 27, 1897–April 8, 1993. Contralto.

Marian Anderson was born in Philadelphia, the oldest of three daughters of Anna Delilah Rucker and John Berkeley Anderson. Her father was employed in the refrigerator room at the Reading

Terminal Market and sold coal in the winter. Her mother, who was a qualified teacher in Virginia, could not afford the time or money to acquire accreditation in Pennsylvania, and worked during the family's neediest period as a cleaner at the John Wanamaker department store. Anderson's musical talent was recognized very early at the Union Baptist Church, where the choir director, Alexander Robinson, was astounded by her singing in the lower register and by her range, both very unusual for a child.

Her father died in 1909, and she and her mother and sisters moved to her grandparents' house, where her aunts also lived. Her grandfather died in 1910, leaving a household of powerful but poor women and nothing to spare for music lessons. Indeed, the money she began to earn singing informally at social gatherings or fund-raisers for African American charities soon became an important part of family income—so important that she could not be spared to attend high school. Thus the objectives of greatest importance throughout her life emerged in her childhood. One was the need to support her family; another was an intense determination to acquire standard schooling and musical training (she finally graduated from South Philadelphia High School for Girls in 1921, with the help of her church); a third was a drive to perform. Equally present were the obstacles placed in her way because she was an African American, experienced very early in rejection by white music teachers and a Philadelphia music academy.

Perhaps the most important early musical influences on her were Roland Hayes, the African American tenor, who introduced her to the world of the art song, and Giuseppe Boghetti, one of her early teachers who taught her new vocal techniques, provided some language instruction, and enlarged her early repertory. A poorly attended debut at New York's Town Hall in 1924 almost caused her to give up singing. But in August 1925 she got her first big break when she won a contest that gave her a (well-received) solo performance at Lewisohn Stadium with the New York Philharmonic Orchestra.

Anderson and her first accompanist, William "Billy" King, had begun touring in 1922. At first they toured generally within an African American circle; after the Lewisohn success they performed for a wider audience. In these early years they were compelled to manage their own concert schedule. They were frequently excluded from hotels, sometimes refused sleeping accommodation on trains, and forced to maintain an exhausting schedule in order to pay touring bills and help support her family.

Like many aspiring American artists, Anderson decided to study abroad to improve her musical education and reputation, and in 1927 she went to London. In 1930 and 1931 she visited Berlin and Scandinavia, where she sang to enthusiastic audiences and expanded her repertory to include German lieder and Scandinavian songs, which remained thereafter an important part of her programs. Brahms and Schubert were particularly beloved by her—her recording of Brahms's challenging *Four Serious Songs* (*Vier ernste Gesänge*) is still regarded by some critics as the most powerful performance ever recorded.

After 1932 Anderson returned repeatedly to Europe. In 1935, now a famous singer, she signed a contract with Sol Hurok, the powerful American impresario. She was booked for seventy concerts for the 1937–38 season, and ninety for the next year; she also was heard on radio and on records. Her rich, vibrant contralto, her exceptional volume, and the intensity of her passion for her music, together with her unique programming that combined classical art songs with Negro spirituals, drew diverse audiences that responded to her with fervor.

Marian Anderson became an even greater celebrity in 1939 when the Daughters of the American Revolution refused to allow her to sing in Constitution Hall in Washington, D.C., a refusal that led to ELEANOR ROOSEVELT's highly publicized resignation from the organization. In an outdoor concert on Easter Sunday at the Lincoln Memorial, Anderson sang to an integrated crowd of seventy-five thousand and a national radio audience. Although Anderson was a reluctant crusader on matters of race, her dignified and powerful performance was an important moment in the struggle for racial equality and cemented her place as one of America's leading concert artists.

After World War II she was invited more frequently to perform with orchestras, and on January 7, 1955, she made her debut at the Metropolitan Opera, singing Ulrica in Verdi's *Un Ballo in Maschera.* She was the first African American to sing at the Met, an event of great importance in the history of black participation in opera. Her tours now took her around the world, including a forty-thousand-mile goodwill trip through Asia for the U.S. State Department in 1957. She was briefly a delegate to the United Nations in its thirteenth session (1958). In 1964 Hurok announced a farewell tour, which culminated in a Carnegie Hall concert on Easter Sunday in 1965. After her retirement from concert performances, she continued to do narratives with music (especially Aaron Copeland's *A Lincoln Portrait*) and give lectures.

In 1943 Anderson married Orpheus (King) Fisher, an architect whom she first met in Philadelphia around World War I. They did not have children. Together they created a farm retreat in Danbury, Connecticut, called Marianna, where she recuperated from the rigors of her performing schedule. Anderson remained in Danbury until 1992, when she moved to Portland, Oregon, to live with her nephew, the conductor James DePriest. She died the next year at the age of ninety-six.

During her long life Anderson received many prizes and honors, including the 1938 Spingarn Medal from the NAACP, the Philadelphia Award (also known as the Bok Medal), which she used to set up a scholarship fund in the 1940s, and the Presidential Medal of Freedom in 1963. She was extremely loyal to her family, especially to her beloved mother, who lived until 1964, and she was a generous mentor to young African American singers. She loved fashion and clothes, and often traveled with her sewing machine. She had great dignity and reserve, too, and when speaking in public frequently referred to herself in the third person. Perhaps this was because she regarded her voice as an instrument: she once said that she wasn't interested in presenting herself as an individual but "as a medium thru which the composers' messages are best transmitted." Her nephew, after her death, epitomized her as "someone blessed with a voice and a burning desire to sing."

Bibliography: The bulk of Marian Anderson's papers, including clippings, memorabilia, family correspondence (including particularly affecting letters from her mother), and a rich collection of photographs, are at the Annenberg Rare Book and Manuscript Library, University of Pennsylvania, Philadelphia. Her quotation comes from a letter to Harry Burleigh, September 21, 1935, which is part of the collection. The best, and most recent, biography is Allan Keiler, *Marian Anderson: A Singer's Journey* (2000), which includes detailed coverage of the intricate negotiations over Constitution Hall, a complete list of the songs in Anderson's repertory, as well as a complete discography. Also useful is Janet L. Sims, *Marian Anderson: An Annotated Bibliography and Discography* (1981). For a glimpse of Anderson herself, see her autobiography written with Harold Taubman: *My Lord, What a Morning: An Autobiography* (1956). The autobiography has been reprinted several times; the most recent edition (2002) has an affectionate and perceptive introduction by her nephew, James Anderson DePriest, which contains the final quote on p. xiii. Also of interest is Kosti Vehanen, *Marian Anderson: A Portrait* (1941), a firsthand account by the Finnish accompanist who was with her during her early triumphs in Europe. An obituary appeared in the *New York Times* on April 9, 1993.

MARY MAPLES DUNN

AQUASH, Anna Mae. March 27, 1945–c. January 1976. Activist.

Now recognized as a founder of Native American radical activism, Anna Mae Aquash, a full-blooded member of the Micmac people, was born Anna Mae Pictou in a Micmac village near Shubenacadie, Nova Scotia, Canada. Her father, Francis Thomas Levi, abandoned the family before Anna Mae's birth. In 1949, her mother, Mary Ellen Pictou, married Noel Sapier, and the couple raised the girl and her two older sisters at Pictou's Landing, a poverty-stricken Micmac reserve. Her stepfather tried to make a living with seasonal labor, but Anna Mae Pictou suffered a hardscrabble childhood punctuated by poverty and multiple attacks of tuberculosis. Sapier, a Micmac traditionalist committed to preserving tribal traditions, language, and religion, did pass on to her a strong sense of Micmac identity. Off-reservation schools, where non-Indian children subjected Anna Mae to relentless racism and harassment, also endowed her with a fierce sense of being Indian, not just Micmac, and paved the way for the pan-Indian identity so common to Native American radicals in the 1960s and 1970s.

In 1956, Sapier died, and Anna Mae's mother later married a drifter. The couple abandoned the children, and Anna Mae took to the road, supporting herself harvesting potatoes, blueberries, and cranberries on New England's migrant labor circuit. At the age of seventeen, she met Jake Maloney, another Micmac, and they moved to Boston, where Aquash gave birth to two daughters, Denise (1964) and Deborah (1965). Over the course of the next decade they moved back and forth between Boston and Micmac reserves in Nova Scotia. During a stay in New Brunswick, they married.

Back in Boston in 1968, Anna Mae Pictou became active in Native American politics. Working in a factory during the day, she volunteered at night with the Boston Indian Council, a group dedicated to help young, urban Indians avoid the pitfalls of alcoholism. There she heard about the American Indian Movement (AIM), an activist group recently founded in Minneapolis. Although key AIM leaders such as Dennis Banks and George Mitchell were Anishinabes (Chippewas), they promoted a pan-Indian identity. Pictou was thrilled in 1970 when Banks and Russell Means, an Oglala Sioux, staged a Thanksgiving protest at the Mayflower II, a tourist site at Plymouth, Massachusetts. For Anna Mae, Pilgrims were the advance party of a mass European migration to North America that all but wiped out indigenous civilizations.

One month later, Pictou and her daughters moved to Bar Harbor, Maine, where she went to work for the Teaching and Research in Bicultural Education School Project (TRIBES), which helped Indian dropouts resume their education. When TRIBES lost funding in 1972, she returned to Boston, took courses at Wheelock College, and worked at a day-care center in an African American neighborhood. The problems of poverty, drugs, and violence in the black community broadened Pictou's perspective about the challenges facing people of color. She also fell in love with Nogeeshik Aquash, a Chippewa artist and activist. Together they became leaders in AIM's Boston chapter.

In 1972, they joined the Trail of Broken Treaties, a caravan and march on Washington, D.C., where hundreds of AIM activists and other interested Indian people descended on the Bureau of Indian Affairs (BIA) offices. When the BIA failed to provide promised housing, they occupied and then trashed the BIA building and issued a series of demands that included revival of tribal sovereignty, restoration of treaty-making status to individual tribes, and restitution for past treaty violations. The occupation ended one week later when the Nixon administration promised to review their demands.

Pictou and Aquash returned to Boston and stayed there until April 1973, when AIM sent two hundred Indian people to Wounded Knee, South Dakota, the site of the army's 1890 massacre of three hundred Miniconjou Sioux. Oglala Sioux traditionalists there resented the leadership of Richard Wilson, who presided over a tribal government AIM considered nothing more than a puppet of the BIA. The traditionalists asked AIM for support. AIM protestors arrived at Pine Ridge, South Dakota, and on February 28, 1973, an armed confrontation began in the village of Wounded Knee. The occupation started as a symbolic protest of Oglala Sioux politics, but once the FBI sent in 250 agents, it became broader based, highlighting the plight of American Indians. The standoff, in which Pictou and Aquash both participated, lasted seventy-one days. While they were there, Anna Mae Pictou and Nogeeshik Aquash married in a traditional Oglala ceremony, on April 12, 1973.

The Aquashes returned to Boston but separated permanently in the summer of 1974, when Anna Mae, now recognized as a talented and courageous organizer, took a job with AIM's national office in St. Paul, Minnesota. She had also come under FBI surveillance as an insurgent radical. The surveillance tightened in 1975 when Anna Mae Aquash joined forces with Leonard Peltier, AIM's chief of security, in backing Navajo protests against commercial coal mining near the reservation. From New Mexico, in the Navajo reservation at Four Corners, they headed north to Pine Ridge, where AIM had established an encampment to protest Richard Wilson's continuing, heavy-handed treatment of Oglala traditionalists. Federal agents joined forces with Wilson's Guardians of the Oglala Nation and attacked the encampment. During the confrontation, a firefight took place. One AIM member and two federal agents were killed. The FBI launched a nationwide manhunt for AIM leaders involved in the protest. Three AIM members—Bob Robideau, Darrele Butler, and Leonard Peltier—were brought to trial. An all-non-Indian jury acquitted Robideau and Butler, but Peltier was convicted of murder and given two life sentences.

In September and again in November, federal agents arrested Anna Mae Aquash. Convinced that her life was in danger, she jumped bail, disappearing on November 24, 1975. Two months later, on February 24, 1976, her body was discovered on the reservation. An autopsy performed by Public Health Service pathologists declared exposure the cause of death, but Anna Mae's family and AIM insisted on a second autopsy, which revealed a bullet hole at the base of her skull. Anna Mae Aquash had been murdered at the age of thirty-one. The crime remains unsolved, and Native American radical activists still cite her murder as a rallying cry. What few question, however, is that during her life Aquash carved out a prominent place in the history of American radicalism.

Bibliography: For early narratives of Aquash's life, see Johanna Brand, *The Life and Death of Anna Mae Aquash* (1978), and Lowell Bergman and David Weir, "The Killing of Anna Mae Aquash," *Rolling Stone*, April 7, 1977, pp. 51–55. A more recent interpretation is Devon A. Mihesuah, "Anna Mae Pictou-Aquash: An American Indian Activist," in Theda Perdue, ed., *Sifters: Native American Women's Lives* (2000). John William Sayer, *Ghost Dancing the Law: The Wounded Knee Trials* (1997), discusses the legal cases that grew out of the occupation. Peter Matthiessen's *In the Spirit of Crazy Horse* (1980) is a general history of AIM. For more general discussions of the surveillance and harassment faced by Native American activists, see Ward Churchill, *Agents of Repression: The FBI's Secret War against the Black Panther Party and the American Indian Movement* (1988), and Kenneth Stern, *Loud Hawk: The United States versus the American Indian Movement* (1994).

JAMES S. OLSON

ARCHAMBAUD, Mary Alice Nelson. *See* Spotted Elk, Molly.

ARDEN, Eve. April 30, 1909–November 12, 1990. Actress.

Eve Arden was born Eunice Quedens in California, the only child of Lucille Frank and Charles Patrick Quedens. After her father deserted the family early on, she was reared by a trio of strong female relatives—her mother, a local actress and milliner; her grandmother, Louisa Frank, who had emigrated as a teenager to California from Germany; and her paternal aunt, Elsie Quedens. Eunice first lived in her grandmother's San Francisco boarding house and then in her aunt's Mill Valley home.

In 1926, she graduated from nearby Tamalpais

Arden

High School, where she had flourished in the drama society. That same year, Eve Arden's autobiography reports, the trio conspired her entrée into professional theater by plunking her down at the stage door of Henry Duffy's San Francisco stock company, where she auditioned for an apprenticeship. Having succeeded, Quedens debuted as a walk-on in *Alias the Deacon* and was promoted to a speaking role in *The Patsy* (1928). She had the guts, fortified by invaluable stock experience, to remain in Los Angeles at tour's end. After fits and starts, this aspiring actress connected with the BandBox, a repertory theater making the hotel and resort rounds of the "citrus circuit," and over the next five years continued to hone her comedic skills of timing and delivery, culminating in a noteworthy performance as Amanda in Noel Coward's *Private Lives* (1933). During this same time, Quedens appeared in at least two movies—*Song of Love* (1929) and *Dancing Lady* (1933).

Her big break came in 1933 while appearing with Tyrone Power in *Lo and Behold* at the Pasadena Playhouse: she was discovered by Lee Shubert, who contracted her for Billie Burke's upcoming "Ziegfeld Follies." Thrilled beyond measure, she adopted the name Eve Arden, relocated to New York, and debuted as a showgirl on January 4, 1934. For seven years, Arden sought to make a name in Broadway musicals, and succeeded, but that name never appeared above the title.

Returning to California in 1937 after her mother's death, Eve Arden hoped to transfer her extensive theatrical talents to celluloid. In *Stage Door* (1937), Arden took the initiative to magnify her secondary role, thereby creating an unforgettable Hollywood image: a wisecracking would-be starlet effortlessly sporting a live cat for a fur piece. Audiences appreciated this catty but cool portrayal for its arched eyebrows and equally arched delivery, exquisitely timed. Arden worked steadily thereafter, appearing with such stars as the Marx Brothers (*At the Circus,* 1939), Clark Gable (*Comrade X,* 1940), MARLENE DIETRICH (*Manpower,* 1941), and Bob Hope (*Let's Face It!* 1943, reprising her 1941 stage role opposite Danny Kaye).

Playing the featured but jaundiced best friend never was a starring role, however. After convincing a producer that no other performer could best her Russian dialect, Arden won not only the role she coveted as a hilarious Russian sniper in *The Doughgirls* (1944) but also a seven-year contract. The year 1945 brought Arden an Academy Award nomination for *Mildred Pierce*, where she played Ida, the best friend and the perfect foil to the maternal excesses of JOAN CRAWFORD's character. Dozens of contract movies ensued, notably *The Voice of the Turtle* (1947) and *One Touch of Venus* (1948).

The role of "The Fairest of All English Teachers," and not the caustic, wisecracking best friend, brought Arden enduring fame. First broadcast on radio in July 1948, *Our Miss Brooks* starred Eve Arden as Connie Brooks, a teacher smarter than the principal and wiser than the biology teacher (her love interest). Immediately recognizing the signature Arden delivery, the audience found that her character resonated with the postwar times, and many a woman identified with an unattached but still attractive heroine a bit past her prime. And teachers responded in kind, flooding Arden with gratitude for depicting their profession's humanity. The popular showed moved to television in 1952, premiering on CBS on October 3 in its Friday-night lineup. Now at the height of fame, Arden earned $200,000 a year—and awards: Woman of the Year in Radio (1952), Emmy (1953), Top Female TV Star (1954). *Our Miss Brooks* aired its final episode in 1956 but was soon reincarnated as a movie, with a decidedly different twist: a marriage proposal at the end for Connie Brooks.

Thereafter, Eve Arden alternated among three entertainment media. On stage, her first love, she played the title role in the 1958 national tour of *Auntie Mame* and starred in a 1967 national tour of *Hello, Dolly!* In regional and summer theater, where countless fans demanded bow upon bow, she thrived. On screen, Arden played notably against type in *Anatomy of a Murder* (1959) and *The Dark at the Top of the Stairs* (1960), before finally being promoted to principal in *Grease* (1978) and reprising the role in its sequel (1982). Sandwiched in between were television roles—*The Eve Arden Show* (1957–58), *The Mothers-in-Law* (1967–69), and *Faerie Tale Theatre* (1985).

"Alligators have the right idea: they eat their young," Arden's most memorable line from *Mildred Pierce,* bore no resemblance to Arden's own maternal instincts. In fact, the lion's share of her autobiography lovingly details her treasured family, always with the odd animal tossed in for memorable measure. In 1947, after divorcing Edward Bergen, a literary agent whom she had married eight years before, Eve Arden became a single parent to two daughters, Liza (1945) and Constance (1947). She married actor Brooks West in 1951; the couple adopted one son, Duncan (1953), and had another, Douglas (1954). Widowed in 1984, Eve Arden died in Los Angeles of cardiac arrest in 1990. She is buried in Westwood Memorial Park, beneath a most apt epitaph: "The world will remember."

In Hollywood's Golden Age, Eve Arden gilded many a secondary role. A victim of her own success, she often reprised a cinematic stereotype for which she is remembered—the sardonic, unattached, but worldly friend of the female lead. In the golden days of 1950s comedy, however, she became a glittering broadcast star for disassembling a more pervasive stereotype—that of the old maid schoolteacher.

Bibliography: The New York Public Library for the Performing Arts at Lincoln Center holds files of theater clippings, playbills, and stills. The Museum of Radio and Television, New York, houses a range of video and audio recordings featuring Arden; its Chicago counterpart, the Museum of Broadcast Communications, houses video recordings of *Our Miss Brooks*. Scripts of that series are located in the UCLA Film & Television Archive. Arden's autobiography, *Three Phases of Eve* (1985), includes a rich store of personal and professional photographs but few dates. For biographical accounts, see Cary O'Dell, "Our Miss Brooks," in Horace Newcomb, ed., *Encyclopedia of Television* (1997); and Liz Sonneborn, *A to Z of American Women in the Performing Arts* (2002). *Current Biography* (1953) presents a snazzy snapshot of Arden while mysteriously omitting any reference to her Oscar nomination. Raymond D. McGill, ed., *Notable Names in the American Theatre* (1976), includes extensive credits for her stage, movie, radio, and television appearances to that date. Sources vary on her date of birth, ranging from 1907 to 1912; the year 1909 was inferred from the 1920 U.S. Census and from the Social Security Death Index. Additional family information was supplied by Douglas Brooks West. Obituaries appeared in the *New York Times* on November 13, 1990, and *Variety* on November 19, 1990.

HARRIETTE L. WALKER

ARMSTRONG, Barbara Nachtrieb. August 4, 1890–January 18, 1976. Law professor, legal scholar, social insurance advocate.

Barbara Nachtrieb was born in San Francisco, the third of four children of Anna Day and John Jacob Nachtrieb. Her parents, both of German stock and born in the Midwest, had made the trek west with their parents in their childhoods. Like her two brothers (whom she adored) and her sister, Barbara attended public schools. She earned her BA in economics from the University of California at Berkeley in 1913 and her JD in 1915 from Boalt Hall, the University of California's School of Jurisprudence; she was one of only two women in her law school class. She was admitted to the California Bar the same year.

After graduation, Barbara Nachtrieb practiced law sporadically with a law school classmate, Louise Cleveland, and worked as executive secretary of the California Social Insurance Commission, where she became interested in workmen's compensation and other government-sponsored mechanisms for preventing poverty. In 1917 she enrolled in the doctoral program in economics at Berkeley. When she took a joint appointment in the school of law and department of economics in 1919, she was the first woman in the country to become a member of a law faculty at a law school approved by the American Bar Association (ABA). She earned her PhD in 1921 and was promoted to assistant professor in 1923. In 1928, when she became associate professor, she moved to Boalt Hall full-time. And in 1935 (somewhat later than the norm for her male colleagues) she became a full professor. At the time, she was one of only two women on the law faculty. Her salary was very low; her dean is reported to have said that no professor deserved to earn so little. She remained at Boalt Hall until 1965, becoming the A. F. and May T. Morrison Professor of Law in 1955. A beloved teacher and an influential member of the law school faculty, she continued to teach even after her formal retirement in 1957.

Barbara Nachtrieb married her first husband, Lymon Grimes, in 1920. A daughter, Patricia Grimes, was born in 1922, but the marriage ended in divorce in 1925. The next year she married Ian Armstrong, an importer. The second marriage proved durable, and by all accounts was extraordinarily loving and supportive. Ian typed her manuscripts, cared for Patricia, and daily snipped a rose from their garden, which Barbara wore in her lapel with a matching hat on her head. Barbara Armstrong was an avid gardener and deeply devoted to her family, and her vitality, radiant enthusiasms, and joyful and energetic persona attracted a wide range of friends and a loyal following among students.

Armstrong's joint specialties in economics and law were a magical combination, serving as the linchpins for her lifelong commitment to social insurance in and outside the law school. Convinced by her early experience with the California Social Insurance Commission that reforming poverty was of far greater importance than relieving it, Armstrong committed herself to achieving publicly supported minimum insurance against catastrophic economic and personal disaster. In 1926–27, she spent a year in Europe investigating the social insurance polices of thirty-four industrial countries. Returning to the United States, she began to teach and write about social insurance, publishing *Insuring the Essentials: Minimum Wage, Plus Social Insurance—A Living Wage Program* in 1932. This book forcefully proposed a solution to problems of economic dependence, arguing for a minimum "living" wage for all workers, and for national programs to insure workers and their families against workplace accidents and the expenses of health care, unemployment, old age, disability, and death.

In the Depression-era United States, this work catapulted Armstrong to the attention of Washington policy makers, and in the summer of 1934 she was invited to serve as a consultant to President

Franklin Delano Roosevelt's Committee on Economic Security (CES). Her tenacious spirit and provocative ideas proved to be something of a problem for the more cautious members of the CES. She ran afoul of both its executive director, Edwin Witte, and Secretary of Labor FRANCES PERKINS. But strong support from business and the public persuaded the CES to accept a nationally based old-age insurance program that would ultimately be financed on a pay-as-you-go basis. Armstrong is now generally regarded as the architect of the U.S. Social Security program and as a shaper of U.S. unemployment insurance.

Armstrong was deeply committed to universal health insurance, but never succeeded in achieving that goal. After it was dropped by the CES in 1935, she continued to work on the issue, publishing *The Health Insurance Doctor: His Role in Great Britain, Denmark and France* (1939). In the 1940s she led an unsuccessful movement to create compulsory universal health insurance in California. She was more successful at affecting rent regulations. During World War II she took a leave from her job at Berkeley to head the Rent Enforcement Division of the San Francisco District Office of the U.S. Office of Price Controls. Later she codified her interest in family law, publishing her most influential book, *California Family Law: Persons and Domestic Relations, the Community Property System,* in 1953. Frequently revised, the two-volume *California Family Law* remains a standard law text in the subject.

Inside the walls of Boalt Hall, Armstrong was a remarkable presence. Her course "The Law and Problems of Poverty," first taught in 1928, introduced to the curriculum the notion that law could facilitate social change. Subsequent courses in industrial and labor law, domestic and family law, and in landlord–tenant relations continued this tradition. Known for her brilliant intellect, barbed wit, and passionate opinions, she fostered spirited debate and activist commitments among her students. Midafternoon tea and discussion sessions in her office confirmed her reputation as an inspiring and committed teacher, particularly engaged with women who were serious about careers in law.

At seventy-nine, still an active presence in Boalt Hall, Barbara Nachtrieb Armstrong was attacked and beaten by three hoodlums in Berkeley. She spent the last six years of her life bound to a wheelchair and in great pain. True to her indomitable spirit, she turned her energies to exploring ways to develop cooperative measures against crime. She died at her home in Oakland on January 18, 1976, at the age of eighty-five.

Bibliography: Armstrong destroyed most of her own papers, claiming that she had no room to keep them. In their absence, the most important single source of information comes from an interview with her in the Oral History Collection, Social Security Project, at Columbia University, completed in 1965. Sandra P. Epstein, *Law at Berkeley: The History of Boalt Hall* (1997), provides the best source of information about her teaching career. Her early views are documented in two reports: Social Insurance Commission of the State of California, *Social Insurance in California* (1916); and Social Insurance Commission of the State of California, *California's Need of Social Health Insurance* (1917). Her experience with the New Deal is explored by Alice Kessler-Harris, *In Pursuit of Equity: Women, Men, and the Quest for Economic Citizenship in 20th-Century America* (2001). Armstrong's views of the legislation can be found in "The Federal Social Security Act," *American Bar Association Journal* 21 (December 1935), pp. 786–97; and "Old Age Security Abroad: The Background of Titles II and VIII of the Social Security Act," *Law and Contemporary Problems* 3, no. 2 (April 1936), pp. 175–85. Insight into Armstrong's persona comes from Roger J. Traynor, Richard Dinkelspiel, et al., "Barbara Nachtrieb Armstrong: In Memoriam," *California Law Review* 65, no. 5 (September 1977), pp. 920–36. Also useful are papers written for the Women's Legal History Biography Project at Stanford Law School, including Beth Hollenberg, "Full of Zoom: Barbara Nachtrieb Armstrong, First Woman Professor of Law" (Spring 1997); Lea Rappaport Geller, "Insuring Our Future: The Work of Barbara Nachtrieb Armstrong" (April 2000); and Courtney Towle, "Barbara Nachtrieb Armstrong: A Driving Force behind Social Security" (Fall 2000). An obituary appeared in the *New York Times* on January 21, 1976.

ALICE KESSLER-HARRIS

ARNOW, Harriette Simpson. July 7, 1908–March 22, 1986. Writer.

Growing up in the southern Appalachian mountains of Kentucky along the Big South Fork of the Cumberland River shaped the life and fiction of Harriette Simpson Arnow. Born Harriette Louisa Simpson in Wayne County, Kentucky, she was the second daughter of Mollie Jane Denney and Elias Thomas Simpson. Both parents were also born in Wayne County and were schoolteachers before they married in 1905. The family included five girls and one boy, the youngest, who was born when Harriette was thirteen years old. Elias Simpson, discovering he could not support his growing family on a teacher's salary, held a number of manual labor jobs, including one on the Kentucky oil fields and another in a veneer factory in Burnside, Kentucky, the Simpsons' hometown. Harriette grew up in a family of storytellers who could trace both sides of the family back to the American Revolutionary War. Her parents' and grandparents' stories made her eager to learn history. She wanted to be a writer before she started school.

Harriette attended public school in Burnside

until 1918, when she and her sisters were taught at home by their mother during the Spanish influenza epidemic. She later attended two private boarding schools in Kentucky, St. Helens Academy and Stanton Academy. She graduated from Burnside High School in 1924 and then attended Berea College from 1924 to 1926, where she earned a teaching certificate. She accepted her first teaching job in a one-room school in Pulaski County, Kentucky. While a teacher, she took her only creative writing course, a University of Kentucky extension course in 1926–27. She left rural Kentucky to earn a BS in education at the University of Louisville in 1931, then taught again until she decided that she "would rather starve as a writer than a teacher" (Miller, p. 34).

She moved to Cincinnati in 1934 and held a variety of jobs—primarily waitress, clerk, and typist—to support herself as a writer. Initially she wrote short fiction, publishing a few stories in the 1930s and 1940s. She also began a novel about a young woman, Louisa, who runs out of money for college, accepts a teaching job in a rural one-room school, and boards with the family of one of her pupils (as she had). This first novel, *Mountain Path* (1936), received favorable reviews in the *New York Times* and *Saturday Review*. She then began her second novel, *Between the Flowers* (posthumously published in 1999), the compelling story of a marriage between partners with incompatible desires.

While working for the Works Progress Administration (WPA) as a researcher and writer in Cincinnati in 1938, she met newspaperman Harold Arnow, whom she married on March 22, 1939. The couple bought a farm at the edge of the Cumberland National Forest, in the small community of Keno, Kentucky, and lived there for five years. Their first child, a son, was stillborn there on December 11, 1939. Their daughter, Marcella Jane Arnow, was born on September 22, 1941. Another daughter lived for only minutes after she was born.

Because farming and maintaining a home without running water and electricity took more time than Arnow had imagined it would, she did very little writing on the farm. During World War II, her husband left Kentucky to find work in Detroit, and soon she and their daughter joined him. A son, Thomas Louis Arnow, was born in a Detroit hospital on December 15, 1946. While the family lived in crowded Detroit wartime housing, Arnow completed her novel *Hunter's Horn* (1949) and began her best-known novel, *The Dollmaker* (1954). *Saturday Review*'s National Critics' Poll named *Hunter's Horn* the best novel of the year, and the *New York Times Book Review* listed it as one of the ten best novels of 1949. *The Dollmaker*, also a best seller, received recognition as runner-up (to Faulkner's *A Fable*) for the National Book Award.

Hunter's Horn, which Arnow wanted to title "End of the Gravel," focuses on an untold American story—that of rural Kentucky hill families who watch gravel roads bring changes to their community. Her novel also redefines the American hunting story by juxtaposing the story of a farmer obsessed with killing King Devil, a red fox of mythic proportions, with equally realistic domestic scenes of childbirth and family life in the late 1930s.

The Dollmaker, which Arnow thought of titling "Highway," focuses on what happened to Appalachian people during World War II. As roads and "progress" arrived, people left the southern mountains in record numbers for northern industrial centers. The central character, Gertie Nevels, who had been the epitome of self-sufficiency in Kentucky, must learn how to survive when her family moves to Detroit. Joyce Carol Oates has called the novel "our most unpretentious American masterpiece." The television movie of *The Dollmaker* aired in May 1984, and Jane Fonda won an Emmy for her performance as Gertie.

Harriette Arnow is known for the historical authenticity of her fiction and the compelling storytelling in her histories. *Seedtime on the Cumberland* (1960) and *Flowering of the Cumberland* (1963) reconstruct the transitional years of early exploration and settlement along the Cumberland River from 1780 to 1803. Arnow described these as companion books, not sequels; the central subject of *Seedtime* is the lone pioneer, while *Flowering* focuses on social groups of pioneers during the same time period. *Old Burnside* (1977), Arnow's only published memoir, is a valuable account of her childhood. In *The Weedkiller's Daughter* (1970), her only novel set entirely outside of Kentucky, Arnow examines themes of environmentalism, McCarthyism, the Vietnam War, civil rights, and adolescent angst and alienation. Her last book, *The Kentucky Trace: A Novel of the American Revolution* (1974), returns to a Kentucky setting. The story concerns a surveyor with the androgynous name Leslie. He adopts a child, forms a nontraditional family, and becomes covertly involved as a patriot in the American Revolution. At the time of her death, Arnow was revising *Belle*, a Civil War novel.

The Arnows never sold their land in Kentucky, though in 1950 they bought a home in Ann Arbor, Michigan, where Harriette continued to write fiction. Her husband, Harold, who worked as a newspaper reporter for the *Detroit Times* and retired as public relations director for the Michigan Heart Association, died on February 20, 1985. Harriette Simpson Arnow died at home on March 22, 1986, the couple's wedding anniversary. They are buried in the Cassada family cemetery in Keno, Kentucky.

Bibliography: The principal collection of Arnow's manuscripts and personal correspondence is in the Margaret I. King Library Special Collections & Archives at the University of Kentucky in Lexington. Smaller collections of letters and other materials are located at Berea College in Berea, Kentucky; the University of Louisville in Kentucky; the George Arents Research Library for Special Collections at Syracuse University; the Bentley Historical Library at the University of Michigan in Ann Arbor; and Eastern Kentucky University Library. Two bibliographies cover important primary and secondary sources through the mid 1980s: Sandra L. Ballard, "Harriette Simpson Arnow," *Appalachian Journal* 14, no. 4 (Summer 1987), pp. 360–72; and Mary Anne Brennan, "Harriette Simpson Arnow: A Checklist," *Bulletin of Bibliography* 46, no. 1 (March 1989), pp. 46–52. Two book-length studies focus on Arnow: Wilton Eckley's *Harriette Arnow* (1974), and Haeja Chung, ed., *Harriette Simpson Arnow: Critical Essays on Her Work* (1995), the most comprehensive collection of Arnow scholarship to date. In addition, Joyce Carol Oates's landmark essay on *The Dollmaker* appears as the afterword in the Avon edition (1972), pp. 601–8; the quotation is on p. 601. Dissertations devoted to Arnow include Glenda Kay Hobbs, "Harriette Arnow's Literary Journey: From the Parish to the World" (Harvard University, 1975); Charlotte Haines, "To Sing Her Own Song: The Literary Work of Harriette Simpson Arnow" (University of Massachusetts at Amherst, 1993); and Martha Billips Turner, "Agrarianism and Loss: The Kentucky Novels of Harriette Simpson Arnow" (University of Kentucky, 1997). Sandra L. Ballard's essay "Harriette Simpson Arnow's Unpublished Final Novel, *Belle*" appeared in *Appalachian Journal* 25, no. 1 (Fall 1997), pp. 48–61.

Important interviews include Danny Miller's in *MELUS* 9 (Summer 1982), pp. 83–97; Alex Kotlowitz's in the *Detroit News,* December 4, 1983, pp. 14+; John Flynn's in the *Michigan Quarterly Review* 29, no. 2 (Spring 1991), pp. 241–60; the Appalshop documentary film *Harriette Simpson Arnow: 1908–1986* (1987); and the unpublished Kentucky Oral History Program interview with Harriette Arnow conducted by John Douglass in Ann Arbor, Michigan, on October 5, 1982 (the tapes are available at the University of Kentucky). An obituary appeared in the *New York Times* on March 25, 1986.

SANDRA L. BALLARD

ARZNER, Dorothy. January 3, 1897–October 1, 1979. Film director.

Dorothy Arzner was the only female director working in the Hollywood studio system at its height. She directed sixteen films between 1927 and 1943 and co-directed at least three more. Known for her efficiency and calm demeanor on the set, Arzner fashioned the first boom microphone and a megaphone topped by a rectangular frame to allow simultaneous framing and directing. Single-minded in pursuit of her craft, she always claimed that she never was hampered by her sex.

Born in San Francisco, Dorothy Arzner moved to Los Angeles after the 1906 earthquake. Her birth certificate was lost and she later gave various dates for her birth; her mother's name is unknown. In Los Angeles, her father, Louis Arzner, opened a Hollywood restaurant frequented by silent film personalities, which seems to have demystified filmmaking for his daughter at an early age. Dorothy Arzner was raised in an affluent home as an only child, having lost a brother at a young age. Her father doted on the tomboyish Arzner, who attended Westlake School, an exclusive private high school for girls in Los Angeles. In 1915, she entered the University of Southern California as a pre-med student. When the United States entered World War I, Arzner left college to serve as a volunteer ambulance driver but never went overseas.

After the war, William De Mille, a filmmaker at Paramount and head of the Los Angeles Emergency Ambulance Corps, invited Arzner to observe the workings of the Paramount–Famous Players–Lasky studio, the largest and most powerful studio in Hollywood. Willing to give her a start, De Mille asked Arzner what she might like to do. Arzner decided that ultimately she wanted to become a director but that the best place to start was at the bottom in the script (scenario) department.

Arzner's film career should have been exceptionally brief: she was hired as a script typist but could not type. Furthermore, the scenario department was typically a dead end for women. Despite her rough start, Arzner was quickly promoted to "script girl," an employee who kept continuity by observing the script and the placement of objects and actors on the set. Her first job as a script girl for exotic Russian star Alla Nazimova would have been particularly instructive, as Nazimova tightly controlled her films and eventually became an independent filmmaker in her own right.

Before 1920 ended, Arzner was cutting film under the guidance of female editor Nan Heron. She proved exceptionally talented. From 1920 to 1922, Arzner edited films for Realart, a subsidiary of Paramount, where her efficiency initially caught and then kept the attention of Hollywood studio heads. Paramount recalled her to edit the Rudolph Valentino film *Blood and Sand* (1922), and her seamless integration of inexpensive stock footage of real bullfights with close-ups of Valentino—the latter filmed by Arzner herself—won acclaim. Esteemed Paramount director James Cruze put Arzner on his own staff, and she edited the highly successful Western *The Covered Wagon* (1923), among other films. Arzner also wrote freelance screenplays, a typical spare-time pursuit in Hollywood.

Arzner was ready to direct by the mid 1920s, a time when there were no other women making movies in mainstream Hollywood. Female filmmakers had disappeared in the early 1920s, when the roles of director and producer became masculinized within the newly bureaucratized studio system. Arzner's talent as an editor, her experience as a screenwriter, her proven efficiency, and perhaps even her mannish attire (unmarried and childless, she dressed in suits and wore her hair short) worked to overcome any doubts about her abilities based on her sex. Columbia, a "poverty row" company that produced several of Arzner's screenplays, offered Arzner a job writing and directing. Paramount executives countered with a promise that she would get her chance to direct when the right picture came along. Arzner responded with a successful ultimatum: she wanted a major picture to direct in two weeks or she would leave the studio. The result was *Fashions for Women* (1927). Through the 1930s she remained the only woman directing in Hollywood on a regular basis.

Arzner directed ten films for Paramount in 1927 through 1931. All were considered "woman's films." The most enduring was *The Wild Party* (1929), which marked the transition to sound for Paramount's flapper star CLARA BOW. It was to relax Bow that Arzner devised a microphone dangling from a fishing pole. In 1931, Arzner left Paramount for independent production after a studio-wide pay cut. She next directed Katharine Hepburn as an independent but doomed aviatrix in *Christopher Strong* (1933) for RKO. In 1933, Samuel Goldwyn hired Arzner to direct Anna Sten, a Russian actress he hoped would be the next Garbo. *Nana* (1934) was a disappointment, but Arzner was put under contract as an associate producer at Columbia. This contract led to her direction of *Craig's Wife* (1936), a successful melodrama starring Rosalind Russell.

Next Arzner directed JOAN CRAWFORD in *The Bride Wore Red* for MGM. Much to Arzner's dismay, Louis B. Mayer demanded that the originally dark story conclude with a happy ending. Arzner refused the next few scripts and was labeled difficult by Mayer. Three years passed before Arzner took up the megaphone again to replace a director on RKO's *Dance, Girl, Dance* (1940), featuring LUCILLE BALL. Feminist film critics later celebrated *Dance, Girl, Dance* for the way its female characters reverse the male gaze. Arzner's last film was *First Comes Courage* (1943), a Columbia production about a female spy (Merle Oberon). Stricken with pneumonia, Arzner stepped down from the production before it was finished and retired from feature filmmaking. She was in her mid forties.

Arzner did not completely retire. She made training films for the Women's Army Corps during World War II, created a radio program, and taught at UCLA. She also filmed a series of Pepsi-Cola advertisements at the request of her friend Joan Crawford, who was then married to the chair of Pepsi's board. In the early 1950s she moved to La Quinta, California.

In the 1970s Arzner was rediscovered by feminists and celebrated as a pioneer by the Director's Guild of America in 1975. She lived long enough to complicate early feminist appraisals of her career by rejecting the notion that her climb up the Hollywood ladder was arduous, or that she had been forced out of Hollywood. Intriguingly, Arzner said that movies were always secondary in her life. Perhaps she was referring to her long relationship with choreographer Marion Morgan, her partner from 1927 until Morgan's death in 1971. A unique success in a man's world, an unsettling figure in a heterosexual world, and a woman who resisted her own exceptionalism, Arzner was, and is, an anomaly. She died in La Quinta in 1979 at the age of eighty-two.

Bibliography: Primary sources on Arzner are held at the Dorothy Arzner Collection, Arts Library Special Collections, University Research Library, University of California, Los Angeles. Among the books and articles chronicling Arzner's film career are Claire Johnston, *The Work of Dorothy Arzner: Towards a Feminist Cinema* (1975); Judith Mayne, *Directed by Dorothy Arzner* (1994); Pam Cook, "Approaching the Work of Dorothy Arzner," in Patricia Erens, ed., *Sexual Stratagems: The World of Women in Film* (1979); Beverle Houston, "Missing in Action: Notes on Dorothy Arzner," *Wide Angle* 6, no. 3 (1984), pp. 24–31; Russell Cousins, "Sanitizing Zola: Dorothy Arzner's Problematic Nana," *Literature/Film Quarterly* 23, no. 3 (1995), pp. 209–15; Francine Parker, "Approaching the Art of Arzner," *Action* 8, no. 4 (July–August 1973), pp. 9–14; and "Dorothy Arzner," in John Wakeman, ed., *World Film Directors* (1987), pp. 3–8. See also Deborah Derow's Barnard College senior thesis (May 1976) with marginal notes by Dorothy Arzner, in the UCLA Library Department of Special Collections; and Jami Nicole Cope, "The Woman behind the Camera: An Auteur Study of the Films of Dorothy Arzner" (MA thesis, University of Northern Iowa, 2001). Arzner's career is also documented in the Ally Acker film *Early Women Directors on Directing* (1991). An obituary appeared in the *New York Times* on October 12, 1979.

KAREN WARD MAHAR

B

BABÍN, María Teresa. May 31, 1910–December 19, 1989. Literary critic, educator.

To a large extent, the life and writings of María Teresa Babín were emblematic of the profound changes experienced by Puerto Rican society after the U.S. occupation following the Spanish-Cuban-American War of 1898. The social effects of this political dislocation particularly informed how and why Babín understood Spanish-derived traditions to be an anchor in the midst of Puerto Rican uncertainty and the disarray caused by increasingly dominant U.S. cultural and linguistic influences. As a writer she identified with the perspectives and legacy of a select group of intellectuals known locally as the *Generación del Treinta* (the 1930s Generation). The literary production of this group attempted to define and counterbalance how Puerto Rican identity and culture were being understood—especially within educated circles in Puerto Rico, the Americas, and Europe—during a decade in which starvation, social unrest, and political insecurity reached unprecedented levels on that island.

María Teresa Babín was the oldest of six children born to a relatively well-off Catholic family in the southern seaport and planter capital of Ponce, then the second largest city in Puerto Rico. Her father, Emmanuel Babín Satgé, was a chemist for the sugar corporations, and her mother, Joaquina Cortés Marrero, who remained a central force and presence throughout her daughter's adult life, was a housewife. As a child Babín went for elementary school in the southern coffee-exporting port of Yauco, Puerto Rico, where she had the reputation of being a very responsible and bright student. She went back to Ponce to finish high school, graduating in 1928. At age nineteen she underwent major surgery that made her unable to bear children.

Moving to San Juan, María Teresa Babín enrolled at the University of Puerto Rico. She graduated with honors in 1931 with a BA in Hispanic studies. Between 1932 and 1939, at a time when more than half of the local population was unemployed, owing to the Great Depression, she found work as a Spanish and French teacher in several municipal high schools in the island's interior (Coamo and Isabela) and at Central High School in the Santurce sector of San Juan. From 1935 to 1937 she was also the director of the educational radio program *Programa de la Escuela del Aire* (the School Program of the Air Waves).

In 1939 she finished her master's in Hispanic studies at the University of Puerto Rico's Río Piedras campus. There she studied under some of the leading figures of the *Generación del Treinta,* including Antonio S. Pedreira, Margot Arce, Rafaél Ramírez, and Nilita Vientós Gastón, who remained her lifelong friends. She also studied with two other leading island intellectuals, Lidio Cruz Monclova and PILAR BARBOSA DE ROSARIO. Her MA thesis, "Federico García Lorca y su obra," analyzed the work of the Spanish poet murdered in 1936 during the Spanish civil war. María Teresa Babín was a poet in her own right, and her master's thesis reflected her immense passion—and that of the *Generación del Treinta*—for Iberian civilization and for what they saw as the stabilizing influence of Spanish values.

From the late 1930s to the 1950s, Babín shifted back and forth between Puerto Rico and the United States, between the world of high school education and the world of the university, and between being a university professor and being a university student. After teaching at Easton High School in Pennsylvania from 1939 to 1940, she returned to Puerto Rico as assistant professor and director of the Spanish Department at the University of Puerto Rico. In 1944 she married the Spanish painter Esteban Vicente, and the next year she returned to the United States to teach at Long Island Garden City High School. During her stay in the United States she studied at Columbia University, where she earned a doctorate in literature in 1951.

Her dissertation, "El Mundo Poético de Federico García Lorca," built on her master's-level research. García Lorca's signature combination of modernist longings, venerable folk traditions, and deep-felt angst held significant appeal for someone like María Teresa Babín who—as García Lorca once had—frequently found herself to be a cultured Hispanic expatriate in New York City. She later expanded this dissertation into *García Lorca Vida y Obra* (1955) and *La Prosa Mágica de García Lorca* (1962). These last two works established María Teresa Babín as one of the most important Puerto Rican critics of the work of García Lorca during the postwar era.

During the late 1950s and early 1960s her literary criticism scholarship diversified to encompass other Iberian writers, such as Miguel de Unamuno, Garcilaso de la Vega, Juan Ramón Jiménez, and José Ortega y Gasset. These essays were subsequently collected in her anthology *Siluetas Literarias* (1967). In 1958 she published the book-length essay *Panorama de la Cultura Puertorriqueña,* which once more definitively grounded Puerto Rican character and peoplehood on the basis of Spain's patrimony and, albeit to a lesser extent, the island's pre-Columbian inhabitants. Following again in the footsteps of the

Generación del Treinta, this book rapidly became one of the postwar foundational texts authenticating the content, meaning, and boundaries of Puerto Rican heritage and customs.

For many years María Teresa Babín taught at New York University's Washington Square College. In 1963 she returned to Puerto Rico, becoming director of the Spanish program in the local government's Department of Public Education. In 1966 she became professor and director of the Department of Hispanic Studies at the University of Puerto Rico's Mayagüez campus. Divorced from her first husband in 1961, she married writer and philosopher José Nieto Iglesias in 1964; this marriage lasted until his death in 1978.

During the 1970s and 1980s she continued to shuttle between the United States and Puerto Rico. From 1969 to 1978 she was the founder and director of the Department of Puerto Rican Studies at Herbert H. Lehman College of the City University of New York. She also was professor of Spanish literature at New York University. In both positions she saw herself as a staunch and tireless champion for Hispanic purity in the midst of the deracinating metropolis's cultural muddle. By 1977 she reappeared in the island, this time as professor of Puerto Rican literature at the Centro de Estudios Avanzados de Puerto Rico y el Caribe located in San Juan, a position she held until 1983. By now widely recognized for her contributions as an important Puerto Rican writer and educator, María Teresa Babín died of cancer at the age of seventy-nine in the Río Piedras sector of San Juan.

Bibliography: In addition to the books mentioned in the text, Babín's publications include *Introducción a la Cultura Hispánica* (1949); *Fantasia Boricua: Estampas de mi Tierra* (1956); *La Hora Colmada* (1960); *Las Voces de tu Voz* (poetry, 1962); *Jornadas Literarias* (1967); *La Crítica Literaria en Puerto Rico* (1960); *La Cultura de Puerto Rico* (1970); *The Puerto Ricans' Spirit* (1971); *Borinquen: An Anthology of Puerto Rican Literature* (1974, with Stan Steiner); *Genio y Figura de Nemesio Canales* (1978); and *La Barca Varada* (1982). An inordinately prolific writer, María Teresa Babín also published numerous articles in important journals and periodicals in Puerto Rico, including *Asomante, Ateneo Puertorriqueño, Brújula, Revista del Instituto de Cultura, Revista Interamericana, Sin Nombre, La Torre, Atenea, Books Abroad, Educación, Repertorio Americano,* and *Revista Hispánica Moderna.* She also edited anthologies of other important Island authors such as Francisco Gonzalo Marín (1958) and Evaristo Ribera Chevremont (1967, with Jaime Luis Rodríguez). Also of interest is her 1976 essay, "El Jíbaro: Símbolo y Síntesis," which was presented at the January 1976 Comparative Literature Symposium at Texas Tech University and later was published in *Revista del Instituto de Cultura Puertorriqueña* (April–June, 1977).

The most complete biographical and bibliographical information is contained in Josefina Rivera de Alvarez, *Diccionario de literatura puertorriqueña* (1967), pp. 158–60. See also Maria E. Ramos Rosado, "La obra ensayistica de María Teresa Babín y sus implicaciones en la enseñanza del español en Puerto Rico" (ME thesis, University of Puerto Rico, 1977). Additional valuable personal information for this article was provided by her niece, Carmen Elena Rivera Babín. An obituary appeared in *El Nuevo Dia* on December 20, 1989.

GLADYS M. JIMÉNEZ-MUÑOZ

BAILEY, Pearl. March 29, 1918–August 17, 1990. Jazz and blues singer, actress.

Pearl Bailey was born in Newport News, Virginia, the youngest of four children of Joseph James Bailey, an evangelical preacher, and Ella Mae, a housewife. Her parents, both of Creek Indian and African American descent, divorced when Pearl was four years old. By that time, the family had moved to Washington, D.C. Pearl (who called herself Pearlie Mae) stayed with her father briefly, then joined her mother, brother, and two sisters in Philadelphia.

Pearl attended William Penn High School and considered becoming a teacher. But her older brother, Willie, who performed tap dance as Bill Bailey (and later became a minister), inspired her to follow in his footsteps—literally. In 1933, he shooed her away from the Pearl Theater in Philadelphia, where he was performing. Undaunted, at age fifteen she entered an amateur contest there and won the five-dollar first prize by singing "Poor Butterfly." The theater offered her a two-week engagement but closed before she could collect her first paycheck. Pearl's brother then steered her to the Apollo Theater's amateur-night contest in Harlem. She won the contest, and the victory convinced her to drop out of school to pursue a career as an entertainer in Philadelphia nightclubs. She moved on to saloons in Pennsylvania mining towns for fifteen dollars a week plus tips. By the early 1940s she was playing in New York's Village Vanguard, where the owner advised her to relax during her performances. This prompted her to develop a languorous singing style for which she would become famous.

Renowned bandleader Cab Calloway heard her sing at the Blue Angel, an elegant Upper East Side supper club, in 1945. Bailey was already performing her drawling version of "Tired," one of her trademark songs, and audiences adored her. She had a distinctive way of talk-singing and embellishing her songs; few performances went by without her addressing the crowd as "Oh, honey," in a sly, offhanded manner. When a singer in Cab's show at the Strand Theater in New York became ill, he asked Pearl to substitute. She was shaking when she walked onstage, but the audience cheered for her. "Applause will never again sound like that to me," she later said (*Raw Pearl,* p. 41).

The role launched Bailey's career. In 1946, she

had a part in a stage production of *St. Louis Woman* and made her first of many successful tours in England. She appeared in the Hollywood movie *Variety Girl* in 1947. In 1950, she starred on Broadway in the Theatre Guild production of *Arms and the Girl.* She also recorded with prominent bandleaders Edgar Hayes, Cootie Williams, and Count Basie, and in the 1950s began starring in leading New York clubs such as the Empire Room at the Waldorf-Astoria and the Royal Box at the Americana.

On November 19, 1952, Pearl became a highly publicized bride at London's Registry Office when she married Louis Bellson Jr., a white drummer in Duke Ellington's band. Newspapers reported that Bellson's father sent Pearl a telegram opposing the marriage. She was thirty-four, and Bellson, of Italian ancestry, was twenty-eight. Not only was the marriage interracial, but she had been married before (estimates ran from two to five times), while it was Bellson's first marriage. Bellson's mother Carmen sent a congratulatory telegram to the couple.

Bellson quit Ellington's band and for many years led Pearl's backup groups, which ranged from quartets to big bands. They gave up their little apartment in Greenwich Village, moved to California, then Lake Havasu, Arizona, and adopted two children, first Tony in 1955, and several years later his sister Dee Dee. Pearl said the Bellson marriage succeeded because she and Louis never stepped on each other's toes.

Her acting career flourished. In 1954, she appeared in the film *Carmen Jones,* based on *Carmen,* with an all–African American cast, then headed to Broadway for a role in the comedy *House of Flowers.* In 1955, she performed with her brother on *Toast of the Town,* the premier variety show of the era, on CBS. She had memorable roles in Paramount's *That Certain Feeling* (1956), *St. Louis Blues* (1958), and *Porgy and Bess* (1959). Bailey won a Tony Award in 1968 for her role as a lively, pushy matchmaker in the all–African American production of *Hello, Dolly!* Columnist Walter Winchell gushed that her opening night was the greatest he had ever seen. The show ran for two years, and then Bailey took it on the road. In Washington, D.C., she waved to President Lyndon B. Johnson in the audience and invited him onstage. Her sensual, languid sense of humor and charm endeared her to audiences.

In the 1960s, she began suffering from narrowing of the coronary arteries; several times she collapsed during and after performances. But she always rebounded and continued to work. She made several movies in the 1970s but became better known as a special adviser to the U.S. Mission to the United Nations, appointed by President Gerald Ford, then reappointed by Presidents Ronald Reagan and George Bush. She made numerous trips abroad as an official goodwill ambassador. In 1978 she received an honorary doctorate from Georgetown University, and the next year she entered the university as a student and earned a bachelor's degree in theology. "I made the dean's list," she said joyfully in 1985. She received the Presidential Medal of Freedom in 1988, and in the course of her career published six books, including several memoirs and a cookbook.

Above all, she thought of herself as a singer. Leading jazz critics praised her rapport with audiences and her command of every nuance as a comedy artist. As late as June 1990, she danced, strutted, and belted her way through a concert at Carnegie Hall. Soon after, she had surgery to replace her arthritic left knee. Recuperating in a hotel room in Philadelphia, where her sisters lived, Pearl collapsed and was taken to the hospital on August 17, 1990. She was pronounced dead, probably from a heart attack. She was seventy-two. Nearly two thousand people attended her funeral at the Deliverance Evangelistic Church in Philadelphia. She was buried at Rolling Green Memorial Park in nearby West Chester, alongside her mother and brother.

Bibliography: Many articles about Bailey, dating from the 1940s to 1990, have been collected in the files of the Institute of Jazz Studies, Dana Library, Rutgers University. Among the most useful are "Three Who Sing for Laughs," *Vogue,* August 1, 1946, p. 140; "Pearl Bailey," *Ebony,* May 1950, p. 71; "Just Crazy . . . We're Happy," *Life,* December 1, 1952, p. 89; "This Time It's Love," *Ebony,* May 1953, pp. 123–27. See also the *New York Times,* January 17, 1964, and June 27, 1990. A tribute to Bailey written by Cab Calloway, "Unforgettable," appears in *Reader's Digest,* August 1991, pp. 153–58. Bailey's own books include *Raw Pearl* (1968); *Talking to Myself* (1971); *Pearl's Kitchen: An Extraordinary Cookbook* (1973); *Duey's Tale* (1975); *Hurry Up, America, & Spit* (1976); and *Between You and Me: A Heartfelt Memoir on Learning, Loving, and Living* (1989). Obituaries appeared in dozens of leading magazines and newspapers around the world, including the *New York Times* and the *Los Angeles Times* on August 18, 1990.

LESLIE GOURSE

BAKER, Augusta. April 1, 1911–February 23, 1998. Librarian, storyteller.

In the course of her career, the indefatigable Augusta Baker influenced public library policy, altered the course of American publishing for children, and inspired a generation of youth services librarians. She was born Augusta Braxston in Baltimore, the only child of Mabel Gough and Winfort J. Braxston. Her parents were educators (her mother was an elementary school teacher; her father taught mathematics) who placed a strong emphasis on the value of education and the joys of reading. Her earliest recollections were of her mother's teaching and her grandmother's storytelling, which may well have planted the seeds of her later interest in storytelling. She attended all-black public schools in Baltimore and graduated from Frederick Douglass High School at age sixteen.

Encouraged by her father to seek an integrated educational setting, she enrolled at the University of Pittsburgh in 1927. At the end of her sophomore year she married fellow student James Baker, and together they moved to Albany, New York. Her transfer to the New York College for Teachers (now the School of Education at the State University of New York at Albany) was delayed when she refused their suggestion that she train in an all-black school instead of the customary university high school. She finally gained admission after intercession by University of Pittsburgh officials and ELEANOR ROOSEVELT, who was then living in Albany while her husband was governor. Baker's experiences in the school and public libraries in Albany led her to appreciate the relative freedom of public libraries with regard to the services they could provide. Baker earned a BA in education in 1933 and a BS in library science in 1934, and shortly thereafter she and her husband moved to New York City. Baker worked briefly as a teacher, but the Depression limited her employment opportunities. She gave birth to her son, James Henry "Buddy" Baker III, in September 1936. Later, after an amicable divorce from her husband, she married Gordon Alexander in 1944.

In 1937 Anne Carroll Moore, influential supervisor of youth services for the New York Public Library, hired Baker as a children's librarian at the 135th Street Harlem Branch (now the Countee Cullen Regional Branch on 136th Street). Baker initially took the job on a temporary basis (her son had just been born), but she found that she loved the work and ultimately took a permanent position. The manager of Baker's branch, Ernestine Rose, insisted that the branch act as an arts and community center for the Harlem neighborhood. The library had a sizable collection of nonfiction titles on African American history and culture, but Baker found the juvenile fiction collection to be far from adequate. In 1939 she began assembling a collection of titles that would fairly represent African American culture and give children of all races a realistic picture of African American life. Baker wrote letters and gave speeches to prominent publishers and editors; her influence motivated several leading publishers to identify authors and illustrators who could produce materials with positive images of African Americans. Baker's efforts to develop the collection at the 135th Street Harlem Branch resulted in what was ultimately christened the James Weldon Johnson Memorial Collection, a library of titles on which she later based her groundbreaking bibliography *Books about Negro Life for Children,* published in 1946.

Being a children's librarian at the New York Public Library (NYPL) meant telling stories in library programs for youth. To that end, Baker trained as a storyteller with the renowned Mary Gould Davis, who was then supervisor of storytelling for the NYPL. Baker's storytelling style was either dryly witty or humorously inclusive, depending upon her story and her audience. Her delivery was smooth, her manner confident, her timing impeccable. Her storytelling was the epitome of enthusiastic control, and her reputation as a master teller was well deserved.

With her appointment as supervisor of storytelling and assistant coordinator of Children's Services in 1953, Baker became the first African American librarian to have an administrative position in the NYPL. Her love of traditional folktales and her desire to promote them among children and other librarians and storytellers inspired Baker to compile four collections of stories: *The Talking Tree* (1955); *The Golden Lynx* (1960); *Young Years: Best Loved Stories and Poems for Little Children* (1960); and *Once Upon a Time* (1964). Two of these titles, *The Talking Tree* and *The Golden Lynx,* are still recognized by contemporary library professionals as classic world folktale collections.

In 1961 Augusta Baker became coordinator of Children's Services for the New York Public Library, a position that put her in charge of programming for youth and the policies governing that programming in all eighty-two branches of the NYPL. Baker seized the opportunity to improve the quality of the library's juvenile collections, emphasizing culturally inclusive books and audiovisual materials. Her influence grew beyond the public library to training schools and professional organizations. She presented at national and international conferences, and lectured extensively on storytelling, children's literature, and library programming. She consulted for the television program *Sesame Street,* acted as an adviser to Weston Woods Media Company, and moderated the weekly radio program "The World of Children's Literature." Baker also served the American Library Association in various capacities, including president of the Children's Services Division (which later became the Association of Library Services to Children) and chair of what was then the combined Newbery and Caldecott Awards committee.

In 1974, after thirty-seven years with the New York Public Library, Augusta Baker retired as coordinator of Children's Services, but she did not retire from storytelling, libraries, or professional life. In 1977, with co-author Ellin Greene, Baker published *Storytelling: Art and Technique,* the definitive handbook on storytelling in libraries. In 1980 she and her husband moved to Columbia, South Carolina, where her son lived; there, at the University of South Carolina, she became storyteller-in-residence, a position created specifically for her. In 1986, "A(ugusta) Baker's Dozen: A Celebration of Stories," an annual festival, was established in her honor by the University of South Carolina College of Library and Information Science and the Richland County Public Library. Augusta Baker told stories in honor of longtime friend and colleague Charlemae Hill Rollins at the 1989 dedication of the Charlemae Hill Rollins Children's Room at the Hall Branch Library of the Chicago Public Library. Baker retired from her University of South Carolina position in 1994 and died in Columbia, South Carolina, on February 23, 1998, at the age of eighty-six.

Bibliography: The papers of Augusta Baker are located in the South Caroliniana Library at the University of South Carolina, Columbia. See also the Augusta Baker Collection of African American Children's Literature and Folklore located at Thomas Cooper Library, University of South Carolina, which contains more than 1,600 first-edition children's books (many inscribed), together with papers and illustrative materials that provide an in-depth look at children's literature in the twentieth-century United States. For biographical information, see *The American Library Association Yearbook of Library and Information Service* (1980); E. J. Josey, ed., *The Black Librarian in America* (1970); Henrietta M. Smith, "An Interview with Augusta Baker," *Horn Book Magazine* 71, no. 3 (May–June 1995), pp. 292–95; and Robert V. Williams, "Interview with Augusta Baker" (May 7, 1989), conducted for the South Carolina Library History Project under the auspices of the School of Library and Information Science, University of South Carolina. In addition to the publications mentioned in the text, Augusta Baker's books include *The Black Experience in Children's Books* (1971), a revised and expanded version of *Books about Negro Life for Children* (1946); and, with Ellin Greene, *Storytelling: Art and Technique* (2nd ed., 1987). Baker also contributed numerous articles and book reviews to such periodicals as *American Unity, Horn Book, Junior Libraries, Library Journal, Saturday Review of Literature, School Library Quarterly,* and *Wilson Library Bulletin.* An obituary by Andrea Glick, "Storyteller Leaves Lasting Legacy," appeared in the *School Library Journal* 44, no. 4 (April 1998), pp. 13–15.

JANICE M. DEL NEGRO

BAKER, Ella. December 13, 1903–December 13, 1986. Civil rights activist, community organizer.

Miss Baker, as she was known throughout the civil rights movement, was a dignified, elegant woman, short in stature but imposing. She was much admired for her deep and compelling voice and her ability to deliver stirring orations at a moment's notice. Her real talent, however, lay not in speechmaking but in grassroots organizing. "Strong people don't need strong leaders" was her guiding principle for a career of activism that spanned fifty years. Ella Baker is a prime example of the often unheralded roles women played in the emergence of the civil rights movement.

Ella Josephine Baker was born in Norfolk, Virginia, the middle child of three children of Georgianna Ross and Blake Baker. Her father worked as a waiter on a steamship that ran between Norfolk and Washington, D.C. Her mother, a former schoolteacher, taught Ella and her siblings to read before they started school and stressed to them the importance of expressing themselves in correct English, and of conveying substance, not just sound. From her father she learned to have fun. He always remembered when the circus was in town, and he took the children on frequent outings. Another important influence was her maternal grandfather, Mitchell Ross, a Baptist minister and respected community leader.

Much of Baker's way of working came out of her family background. When she was seven years old, the Bakers moved to the family homestead in rural Littleton, North Carolina. On family lands that had been part of the plantation on which her forebears had worked as slaves, Ella Baker grew up hearing stories of rebellion from the aunts, uncles, cousins, and grandparents in her extended family. From them she learned the importance of sharing and the ongoing nature of the struggle for freedom and justice, and she gained a profound sense of community.

Baker took these precepts with her into her movement work. Because there was no secondary school for blacks in Littleton, her parents sent her to high school at Shaw University in Raleigh, North Carolina. She remained there for college, graduating as valedictorian in 1927. Her mother wanted her to be a schoolteacher, but Baker decided against it and moved to New York City to continue her education in the streets of what to her was a vibrant, vitalizing atmosphere. She traveled all over the city and attended street meetings of all political and cultural varieties. She was often the only black person, and the only woman, present. Compared to later years, she felt that the political atmosphere during those years was much freer—that it was a time of meaningful dialogue when many alliances were formed.

Observing firsthand the impact of the Depression on Harlem, Baker plunged into what was to be her life's work: organizing the unorganized, helping develop grassroots leadership, and forming local action groups. Supporting herself with odd jobs, she became a founding member of the Young Negroes' Cooperative League (YNCL), a group established in 1930 by George Schuyler, a leading black newspaper writer, to increase economic power for blacks through consumer cooperatives. In 1931 she became the YNCL's national director. An important influence on her emerging political consciousness was her job with the workers education program of the Works Progress Administration (WPA), where she worked on consumer and labor issues. During this period she also worked with women's groups such as the Harlem Housewives Cooperative and the Harlem Young Women's Christian Association (YWCA).

In 1941 she joined the National Association for the Advancement of Colored People (NAACP) and became a full-time civil rights worker. Initially hired as a field secretary, she traveled for six months of the year, mostly in the South, a lone black woman in the segregated conditions of the 1940s, setting up or buttressing local NAACP chapters. She encouraged activists to focus on local issues and develop local leadership. On these field trips she made invaluable contacts throughout the South that laid the groundwork for much of the civil rights activism of the decades to come. She was named director of branches in 1943 and carried on in that role until 1946, when she resigned in protest over the way the organization functioned. She wrote in her letter of resignation that the full capacities of the staff had not been utilized and that there was a lack of appreciation for collective thinking in the group. She had also just taken responsibility for raising her nine-year-old niece, Jacqueline, which made it difficult for her to travel. During the 1940s she married Thomas J. Roberts, a refrigeration mechanic who had been her classmate at Shaw and later joined the Brotherhood of Sleeping Car Porters. He helped rear Jacqueline, but his emotional problems disrupted the marriage, which ended in 1959.

During the early 1950s, Baker fought de facto segregation in New York City schools and ran unsuccessfully for the New York City Council on the Liberal Party ticket—the only time she enrolled in a political party. Then came the dramatic action of Rosa Parks on a city bus in Montgomery, Alabama, which set in motion the Montgomery bus boycott of 1955–56. Baker, who along with veteran civil rights activists Stanley Levison and Bayard Rustin had already established In Friendship, a support organization for school desegregation in the South, thought that a new group ought to come out of the Montgomery movement, one that would make the most of the outpouring of ordinary people who had participated in the boycott. In 1957, Baker, Levison, and Rustin started the organization that was to become the Southern Christian Leadership Conference (SCLC), headed by the Reverend Martin Luther King Jr. Rustin drafted the working papers adopted by the SCLC, and Baker edited them.

In 1958 Baker agreed (reluctantly, for she had been drafted without consultation) to organize the SCLC's Crusade for Citizenship, a voter registration project. What was supposed to be a temporary six-week assignment in Atlanta stretched into more than two years, with Baker eventually becoming executive director of the SCLC. Her organizational skills and contacts were critical to the emerging civil rights movement, but she found herself increasingly restive under King, who seemed to be driven to establish the SCLC as a major player on the civil rights scene rather than to develop a mass movement made up of local people and community organizers. Baker realized, not for the first time, that her lack of deference to male leadership, outspoken manner, and insistence on expressing her opinions antagonized many men, particularly southern black ministers.

Student sit-ins erupted spontaneously in Greensboro, North Carolina, in early 1960 and spread rapidly across the South. Believing that this outburst of activism needed to be coordinated, Baker convinced the SCLC to put up the money for a meeting of sit-in groups to be held at her alma mater, Shaw University. The students welcomed the idea; out of this meeting the Student Nonviolent Coordinating Committee (SNCC) was born, and the shock troops of the 1960s movement came into being, primarily at Baker's instigation. The young people's innovativeness, their courage, their daring, and their originality inspired Miss Baker. And she inspired them, even though they were decades younger than she. What she gave them was a belief in their abilities and the abilities of others, a belief in the importance of developing local organizations and local leaders. She counseled them on the need to be independent from organizations like the SCLC, but helped them understand that they were not to be merely a self-perpetuating institution.

In August 1960 Baker resigned from the SCLC and went to work, part-time, for the Atlanta office of the National Student YWCA. This gave her free time to work closely with SNCC, which from the beginning was organized nonhierarchically around the principles of decentralized group-centered leadership, consensus decision making, and grassroots organizing. She worked with the students throughout the 1960s, providing not just a bridge across generations but a powerful role model of political engagement and activism that was especially important to the women, black and white, in the movement. After the 1964 Freedom Summer in Mississippi, in which northern students came south to work on voter registration drives, Baker helped SNCC establish the Mississippi Freedom Democratic Party (MFDP), which staged a major challenge to the Democratic Party's adherence to an all-white southern party at the 1964 national convention in Atlantic City. FANNIE LOU HAMER became the movement's most visible public orator, but Baker played a crucial behind-the-scenes role, working to persuade delegations to support the MFDP. The maneuverings in Atlantic City, which failed to unseat the all-white Mississippi delegation, left the MFDP devastated, but educated.

Despite failing health in the 1970s and 1980s, Ella Baker continued her lifelong commitment to social change. Moving back to New York City, she served on the board of the Puerto Rican Solidarity Committee and was vice chair of the Mass Party Organizing Committee. What Baker had hoped to leave behind were local groups that would carry on the work—the development of local campaigns on local issues, the development of local leaders, and the burgeoning of local organizations. Ella Baker died in New York City in 1986 on her eighty-third birthday.

Bibliography: Ella Baker's papers are in the Schomburg Center for Research in Black Culture in New York City. Important biographical sources are Ellen Cantarow and Susan Gushee O'Malley, *Moving the Mountain: Women Working for Social Change* (1980); and Joanne Grant, *Ella Baker, Freedom Bound* (1998). See also Grant's 1981 documentary film, *Fundi: The Story of Ella Baker.* Baker's speech at the SNCC organizing conference, "Bigger than a Hamburger," appeared in the *Southern Patriot,* May 1960, p. 4. General sources on the civil rights movement that treat Baker's role include Clayborne Carson, *In Struggle: SNCC and the Black Awakening of the 1960s* (1981); James Forman, *The Making of Black Revolutionaries* (1972); Mary King, *Freedom Song* (1987); David J. Garrow, *Bearing the Cross: Martin Luther King, Jr. and the Southern Christian Leadership Conference* (1986); Adam Fairclough, *To Redeem the Soul of America: The Southern Christian Leadership Conference and Martin Luther King, Jr.* (1987); Taylor Branch, *Parting the Waters: America in the King Years, 1954–63* (1989); and John Dittmer, *Local People: The Struggle for Civil Rights in Mississippi* (1994). Also of interest is Anne Braden, "The Southern Freedom Movement in Perspective," a special issue of the *Monthly Review* 17, no. 3 (1965–66), pp. 1–92. An obituary appeared in the *New York Times* on December 17, 1986.

JOANNE GRANT

BALL, Lucille. August 6, 1911–April 26, 1989. Comedian, actress, studio executive.

Lucille Ball was born in Jamestown, New York, the first child and only daughter of Henry Durrell Ball, a telephone lineman, and Desiree "DeDe" Hunt, a factory worker. The family moved to Montana, then to Wyandotte, Michigan, where Henry died of typhoid when Lucille was three and her mother was pregnant with her brother Fred. After DeDe married Ed Peterson, a factory worker, in 1918, the couple spent several years in Detroit, leaving Lucille with Ed's mother, who raised the child according to the strict principles of her own Swedish childhood. The experience left the girl with a fear of being alone and a sense that she had to work to make others like her. In 1922 the family reunited in Celoron, New York, although financial reverses and legal troubles caused them to lose their home and the friendship of their neighbors.

Local vaudeville shows provided Lucille a respite from her personal turmoil and suggested a way of focusing her talents. She left Jamestown High to enroll at the Robert Minton–John Murray Anderson School of Drama in New York City, where the star pupil was BETTE DAVIS. Lucille, outgoing and brash in Jamestown (she was the first girl to bob her hair and wear slacks), was stunned into silence in New York. After six weeks, school officials suggested she leave. For the next several years, she moved back and forth from Jamestown to New York City, trying unsuccessfully to get steady work as a showgirl. Flat-chested, skinny, and shy, she finally succeeded as a model. A chance meeting with a theatrical agent in 1933 got her a ticket to Hollywood.

Having learned from her New York experience, she spoke up in Hollywood. While making her first film, *Roman Scandals* (1933) starring Eddie Cantor, she persuaded the writers to give her a few lines. Director Ed Sedgwick recognized her talents immediately and told her she could become the greatest female comedian in America, but she did not take him seriously. Ball worked briefly at Columbia, and then moved on to RKO, where she had small roles in *Top Hat* (1935) and *Follow the Fleet* (1936), with GINGER ROGERS and Fred Astaire, and was the third lead in the film *Stage Door* (1937) starring Rogers and Katharine Hepburn, where she played an aspiring actress.

Ball was one of the hardest-working players on the lot, appearing in several major RKO pictures a year. In 1940 RKO put her in its film adaptation of the Broadway hit musical *Too Many Girls* with Desi Arnaz, a Cuban bandleader who was making his film debut. She and Arnaz, six years her junior, began a tempestuous courtship on the set, which led to their marriage on November 30, 1940, in Greenwich, Connecticut. Arnaz's film career faltered, and he took his band back on the road before enlisting in the army. Lucille and Desi separated in 1944, reuniting a day before the divorce became final.

Meanwhile Ball had moved to MGM, where her hair color was changed from medium brown to vivid red to take advantage of improvements in Technicolor. She was soon relegated to supporting roles. Even though she had worked with the Three Stooges, the Marx Brothers, Edgar Bergen, and Harold Lloyd, no one recognized her gift for physical comedy, not even Ball herself. When Buster

Keaton tried to convince Louis B. Mayer that Ball was a brilliant comedian, the studio head replied that only glamorous actresses sold tickets.

As her disappointing MGM career came to a close, Ball switched to radio, starring in a successful CBS show called *My Favorite Husband* (1947). In 1950 Ball agreed to CBS's request to transfer the show to television. Determined to preserve her marriage by working with Arnaz, she insisted that he be given a co-starring role and that the show, now called *I Love Lucy,* be filmed in Hollywood rather than done live in New York as was then standard practice. After fevered negotiations, Ball and Arnaz ended up owning the show and being responsible for its production. They also became parents: after several miscarriages, and three weeks before her fortieth birthday, Ball gave birth to Lucie Arnaz on July 17, 1951.

Writers Jess Oppenheimer, Madelyn Pugh, and Bob Carroll Jr. drew on Ball's personality and comedic talents to develop Lucy Ricardo, a homebound housewife determined to defy her Cuban bandleader husband and find a place in show business. Ball's gift for physical, knockabout comedy, her expressive rubber face, and madcap plots involving overly expansive bread loaves and hyperactive conveyor belts drew an audience of 14 million Americans, one in nine, to the show. As Arnaz developed the couple's Desilu Studios into a major force in television production, Ball gave birth to their son Desi Jr. on January 19, 1953; her pregnancy was worked into the story line of the hit show. In February she won her first Emmy and signed an $8 million contract with sponsor Phillip Morris. Ball also survived an investigation in 1952 by the deadly House Committee on Un-American Activities. She had registered to vote as a Communist in 1936 at the insistence of her grandfather, but did not vote. The public supported her.

The Arnaz marriage was strained by Desi's drinking and womanizing, and by his discomfort with Lucille's phenomenal popularity. She filed for divorce the day after their last show filmed in May 1960. Ball went to Broadway, where she starred in *Wildcat* (1960), and married Gary Morton, a comedian. Returning to Hollywood, she bought out Arnaz's interest in Desilu in 1962, and set about building up the faltering studio. Ball was uncomfortable as company president but approved production of two groundbreaking shows, *Mission Impossible* and *Star Trek.* In 1967, Ball sold Desilu to Paramount for $17 million. As majority stockholder, her personal share was $10 million.

In 1962, Ball had also returned to television, costarring in *The Lucy Show* with Vivian Vance, who had played her sidekick Ethel on *I Love Lucy.* Ball continued to do "Lucy" shows until 1974, when she made the film *Mame,* which was a personal disappointment and critical disaster. She emerged from semi-retirement in 1985 to play a homeless woman in *Stone Pillow,* which her fans rejected. Her last series, *Life with Lucy,* was dropped after a few episodes because of poor ratings.

A total extrovert, an admitted workaholic, and a perfectionist, Ball found her greatest happiness in work. Aside from backgammon and word games, she was unable to fill her last days happily. She died at Cedars-Sinai Medical Center of an acute rupture of the abdominal aorta on April 26, 1989, at the age of seventy-seven.

Television allowed Lucille Ball to unleash extraordinary gifts that were never called for in movies. Although the character Lucy Ricardo offends those who see her as a thwarted housewife, Ricardo is in the great comic tradition of the subversive underling. Ball proved that stardom is not reserved for the glamorous and that talent can burst forth after the age of forty.

Bibliography: Lucille Ball's correspondence, as well as various newspaper and magazine clippings, can be found widely scattered in collections at a variety of institutions: in California, at the University of Southern California, UCLA, San Diego State University, and the Margaret Herrick Library of the Academy of Motion Picture Arts and Sciences in Beverly Hills; in New York, at the New York Public Library for the Performing Arts at Lincoln Center, and at the Fenton Historical Society of Jamestown and the Lucy-Desi Museum, also located in Jamestown. Full-length scholarly and journalistic works on Ball include Kathleen Brady, *Lucille: The Life of Lucille Ball* (1994); Bart Andrews, *The "I Love Lucy" Book* (1985); Warren G. Harris, *Lucy & Desi: The Legendary Love Story of Television's Most Famous Couple* (1991); and Eleanor Harris, *The Real Story of Lucille Ball* (1954). Obituaries appeared in the *Los Angeles Times* on April 26, 1989, and the *New York Times* on April 27, 1989.

KATHLEEN BRADY

BAMBARA, Toni Cade. March 25, 1939–December 9, 1995. Writer, filmmaker, community activist.

Toni Cade Bambara once remarked: "I work every day, all the time, because it is a compulsion. It is also because there is much for us to consider. . . . I always have ten or fifteen projects cooking because I never know which one is going to fly first or which one is going to get past that bend in the tunnel where the light is stuck" (Chandler, pp. 348–49). Named for her father's employer, Miltona Mirkin Cade was the second of two children born to Helen Brent Henderson and Walter Cade in New York City. She was raised primarily by her mother, whom she credited as a major influence on her writing. Never fond of her given name, Cade renamed herself Toni in kindergarten. In 1970, she adopted the surname Bambara after encountering it in a sketchbook inside her great-grandmother's trunk.

Toni and her older brother, Walter Cade III (also an artist), grew up in Harlem, Bedford Stuyvesant, Queens, and Jersey City, New Jersey. Formally educated in public and private schools, she graduated in 1959 from Queens College with a BA in theater arts and English. She continued to study theater, film, and dance at New York University, the New School for Social Research, the Studio Museum of Harlem Film Institute, and later, the University of Florence and the École de Mime Étienne Decroux in Paris. She earned a master's degree from City College of New York (CCNY) in 1965. Thereafter, she held a number of academic posts, including at CCNY from 1965 to 1969 and at Livingston College of Rutgers University from 1969 to 1974. At CCNY, Cade was active in the college's SEEK (Search for Education, Elevation, and Knowledge) program designed to recruit black and Latino students. She advised various publications sponsored by the program and also mentored students involved in the 1968–69 campus uprisings. On and off campus, Cade was involved in organizing numerous community workshops, rallies, and study groups. She also served as director-adviser for the Theater of the Black Experience.

In 1970 she gave birth to her only child, a daughter, Karma Bene Bambara. That same year, under the name Toni Cade, she published *The Black Woman,* an anthology of writings by black women that was one of the first to raise the politics of gender as a critical concern in the black liberation struggle. The volume's insistent melding of feminist and nationalist desire challenged masculinist assumptions implicit in much of 1960s black radical discourse. In 1971, now known as Toni Cade Bambara, she edited *Tales and Stories for Black Folks,* which was designed to introduce young readers to storytelling and African American folklore. It featured the work of well-known writers such as Langston Hughes and Alice Walker alongside that of Bambara's students at Livingston College.

Bambara insists that she began to take writing seriously only around the mid to late 1960s. Eventually convinced that writing was not frivolous but "a perfectly legitimate way to participate in struggle," Bambara focused on creating stories with "usable lessons" (Guy-Sheftall, p. 245). In 1972, she authored her first collection of short fiction, *Gorilla, My Love,* which was widely reviewed and won the Black Rose Award for Literature from *Encore* magazine. Many of the stories are notable for their sassy child narrators, whose sharp insight and poignant social commentary belie their protagonists' tender years.

In 1974 Bambara and her daughter relocated to Atlanta, where Bambara was writer in residence at Spelman College until 1977. She immersed herself in the city's arts scene and was a founding member both of the Southern Collective of African-American Writers and of the Conference Committee on Black South Literature and Art. She also directed the Pomoja Writers Guild and was affiliated with the Institute of the Black World.

By the time her second volume of short fiction, *The Sea Birds Are Still Alive* (1977), appeared, Bambara had become interested in larger social forces shaping human experience. In writing *Seabirds,* Bambara contemplated the kinds of sociocultural changes necessary to sustain black life after the 1960s. She credited her travels to Cuba (1973) and Vietnam (1975), combined with her increasing involvement in community organizing, with expanding her political vision. While in Atlanta, Bambara published her first novel, *The Salt Eaters* (1980), which explored how some ancestral traditions and ways of knowing might be adapted to the contemporary context in order to restore individual psychic health and communal wholeness. The novel won an American Book Award and the Langston Hughes Society Award in 1981.

By the 1980s Bambara had grown increasingly interested in film as a more compelling medium for her own artistic expression. In 1985, she moved from Atlanta to Philadelphia, where she joined the Scribe Video Center, which was dedicated to using video as a tool for progressive social change and thus ideally suited to her politics. At Scribe, Bambara taught script writing, lectured, and wrote about film. Her involvement with the center led to collaboration on several documentary films for video and TV during the 1980s and 1990s. Bambara was known as a major supporter of and participant in the Black Independent Cinema Movement and as a particularly enthusiastic supporter of black women filmmakers.

Though passionate about filmmaking, Bambara nevertheless continued to write fiction and essays until her death. She once characterized herself as less a researcher (given her penchant for fictionalizing) than a nosey detective "willing to go anywhere to get the information" (Salaam, p. 49). Although this self-disclosure was in reference to *Salt Eaters,* she might easily have been describing her approach to *Those Bones Are Not My Child* (1999), a haunting fictional account of the still largely unsolved 1979–82 Atlanta child murders. Bambara spent the last twelve years of her life working on *Those Bones,* which was completed by Toni Morrison, who had first met Bambara while working as a senior editor at Random House in the 1970s. Morrison also edited *Deep Sightings and Rescue Missions: Fictions, Essays, and Conversa-*

tions (1996), a collection of short fiction, critical essays, and interviews by and with Bambara. Both books were published posthumously. In 1993 Bambara was diagnosed with colon cancer. She died of the disease two years later in Philadelphia at the age of fifty-six.

Bibliography: In addition to the books mentioned in the essay, Bambara also wrote, with Julie Dash and bell hooks, *Daughters of the Dust: The Making of an African American Woman's Film* (1992). Her essays include "Salvation Is the Issue," in Mari Evans, ed., *Black Women Writers (1950–1980): A Critical Evaluation* (1983); "School Daze," in *Five for Five: The Films of Spike Lee* (1991); the foreword to Cherrie Moraga and Gloria Anzaldúa, eds., *This Bridge Called My Back: Writings by Radical Women of Color* (1981); and "What Is It I Think I'm Doing Anyhow," in Janet Sternburg, ed., *The Writer on Her Work* (1980). Also of interest is "Thinking about My Mother," *Redbook*, September 1973, pp. 73, 155–56.

Interviews with Bambara include Zala Chandler, "Voices beyond the Veil: An Interview with Toni Cade Bambara and Sonia Sanchez," in Joanne M. Braxton and Andrée Nicola McLaughlin, eds., *Wild Women in the Whirlwind: Afra-American Culture and the Contemporary Literary Renaissance* (1990); Beverly Guy-Sheftall, "Commitment: Toni Cade Bambara Speaks," in Roseann P. Bell, Bettye J. Parker, and Beverly Guy-Sheftall, eds., *Sturdy Black Bridges: Visions of Black Women in Literature* (1979); Kalamu Ya Salaam, "Searching for the Mother Tongue," *First World* 2, no. 4 (1980), pp. 48–52; and Claudia Tate, ed., *Black Women Writers at Work* (1983).

Biographical information about Toni Cade Bambara can be found in Thadious M. Davis and Trudier Harris, eds., *Afro-American Writers after 1955: Dramatists and Prose Writers* (1985); Patrick Meanor and Gwen Crane, eds., *American Short-Story Writers Since World War II* (2000); Valerie Smith, ed., *African American Writers* (2nd ed., 2001); and James P. Draper, ed., *Black Literature Criticism* (1992). See also Margo Perkins, "Getting Basic: Bambara's Re-visioning of the Black Aesthetic," in Berel Lang, ed., *Race and Racism in Theory and Practice* (2000). An obituary appeared in the *New York Times* on December 11, 1995.

MARGO V. PERKINS

BARBOSA DE ROSARIO, Pilar. July 4, 1897–January 22, 1997. Historian, educator.

Pilar Barbosa de Rosario was born in San Juan, Puerto Rico, and passed away in that city just months short of her hundredth birthday. During her lifetime, she served as a direct link between the early Puerto Rican statehood movement founded by her father, José Celso Barbosa, and the island's contemporary campaign to make Puerto Rico part of the United States as the fifty-first state. Upon her death, the pro-statehood governor of Puerto Rico, Pedro Rosselló, decreed three days of mourning.

One of twelve children of José Celso Barbosa and Belén Sánchez, she attended the University of Puerto Rico (UPR). In 1921 she was the first woman to teach at the university as an undergraduate; in 1924 she received a BA in education. She then obtained an MA in history in 1925 from Clark University in Worcester, Massachusetts. She later returned to the University of Puerto Rico, where in 1929 she founded the Department of History and Social Science, which she directed for fourteen years. She was the first woman to chair an academic department at UPR. Her teaching career at the university spanned the years from 1926 until her retirement in 1967.

Besides her career as an educator, Pilar Barbosa de Rosario, a gregarious and vivacious woman with a magnetic personality, is best remembered for her work as a historian. Affectionately known as Doña Pilar, she was a recognized authority on Puerto Rican political history, particularly the history of the campaign for autonomy from Spain in the late nineteenth century and the movement for U.S. statehood in the early twentieth. She published more than twenty books on Puerto Rican history and politics, including *De Baldorioty a Barbosa* (1957); *La comisión autonomista de 1896* (1957); *El ensayo de la autonomía* (1975); and *Raíces del proceso político puertorriqueño* (1981). Four of her books (a record number) won first-prize awards from the Instituto de Literatura Puertorriqueña.

Pilar Barbosa de Rosario dedicated her life to revealing her father's story and perpetuating his political ideals. In promoting her father's legacy, she was motivated by the fact that many of her students' peers viewed him with contempt and spoke of him as a traitor to his race and his country because of his staunch support for U.S. statehood for Puerto Rico. Dr. José Celso Barbosa, a physician, journalist, and politician, was an Afro-Puerto Rican who, after being denied a college education in Puerto Rico because of his race, studied in the United States and graduated as a medical doctor from the University of Michigan in 1882. He then went on to become a prominent leader of the island's movement for autonomy from Spain. In the aftermath of the U.S. annexation of Puerto Rico, he founded the statehood movement because he believed that only as a state of the union would the people of Puerto Rico be guaranteed racial and civil justice. Pilar based many of her books on a large collection of documents, newspapers, and articles written by her father, which, according to her own account, she found in a trunk in her house after a dream in which he told her to look there.

Loved and esteemed by her students, many of whom went on to positions of power and prominence in the Puerto Rican government, she had a particularly close association with the leaders of the island's New Progressive Party. Many of them looked upon her as a mentor. Pilar Barbosa educated many generations of young people in Puerto Rico. Considered the dean of Puerto Rican historians and an outstanding teacher, she influenced the careers of many who subsequently became leading historians and educators in their own right, among them Arturo Morales Carrión, Luis M. Díaz Soler, and Rafael Picó. The recipient of many honors and awards during her lifetime, Barbosa de Rosario was a member of the Real Academia de la Historia de España and of the Academia de Artes y Ciencias de Puerto Rico.

In the late 1920s, Doña Pilar married José Ezequiel Rosario, an economics professor, who passed away in 1963. They never had children. She was, however, extremely devoted to her students. She received them regularly at her home on Saturday afternoons for informal discussions and after her retirement welcomed them warmly any day of the week. In 1984 President Ronald Reagan presented her with an Outstanding Leadership Award for her work in education, and in 1993 the Commonwealth of Puerto Rico named her the island's Official Historian. She became the first woman to be so honored and held the position until her death. Pilar Barbosa de Rosario is buried in Magdalena de Pazzi cemetery in Old San Juan, Puerto Rico.

Bibliography: For an introduction to the life of Pilar Barbosa de Rosario, see the entry in the *Enciclopedia Puertorriquena Siglo XXI* (1998), p. 213. Articles about her career include Aurelio Tió, "Semblanza de la Dra. Pilar Barbosa de Rosario," *Revista de la Academia de Artes y Ciencias de Puerto Rico* 1, no. 1 (1986), pp. 118–24; Eneld Routté-Gómez, "Pilar Barbosa, the Other Side of History," *San Juan Star,* September 1, 1991; and Luis M. Díaz Soler, "Homenaje, Pilar Barbosa, Una Semblanza," *Cultura* 1, no. 11 (1997), pp. 4–6. An obituary appeared in the *New York Times* on January 24, 1997. See also Rosario Fajardo, "Pilar Barbosa de Rosario Remembered as Scholar, Patriot," *San Juan Star,* July 5, 1997.

CARLOS SANABRIA

BARNES, Djuna. June 12, 1892–June 19, 1982. Writer, journalist, artist.

Djuna Chappell Barnes was born in Cornwall-on-Hudson, New York, where she grew up in an unusual family. Her father, born Henry Budington but later called Wald Barnes, was a talented musician and inventor whose sporadic work habits kept his family in poverty. He also was a bigamist and libertine, establishing two families living in the same household and venturing frequently into other sexual liaisons. The second of five children and the only girl, Djuna helped her mother, Elizabeth Chappell, with child care and other household duties, burdens that later contributed to her decision not to have children of her own. Her unconventional upbringing extended to her education, which took place mainly at home. Barnes spent much time in the outdoors, participated in family musical gatherings, read widely, and wrote poetry, plays, and fiction from an early age.

Djuna was deeply influenced by her paternal grandmother, Zadel Barnes Gustafson, a suffragist, spiritualist, and temperance advocate who helped her hone her writing skills. They often slept in the same bed together, and they kept up an extensive correspondence when Zadel was traveling. Barnes later suggested that she associated her grandmother with her attraction to women. Strangely, when Djuna was seventeen Zadel encouraged her to marry the brother of her father's second wife, Percy Faulkner (who was three times her age and a soap salesman), in an unofficial ceremony. Barnes left him after two months. In 1912, Barnes's parents divorced; Djuna, her mother, and her brothers moved to the Bronx, while her father stayed with his second family. Bitter and impoverished, Djuna entered adulthood struggling to help her family survive difficult times. Barnes's novel *Ryder* (1928), about a maniacal father, and her drama *The Antiphon* (1958) portrayed her family experience as both complex and damaging.

Barnes supported herself and her family as a professional writer. She was hired as a reporter for several newspapers, including the Brooklyn *Daily Eagle* and the *New York Press,* and became a regular contributor to major magazines such as *McCall's* and *Vanity Fair.* She also developed her talents as an illustrator. In 1912, Barnes enrolled as an art student at Pratt Institute in New York, and in 1915–16 she took classes at the Art Students League of New York. Between 1913 and 1919, Barnes published *The Book of Repulsive Women* (1915), some twenty-five plays and short stories, and more than a hundred articles, many of them accompanied by her ribald drawings. She also published many pieces in experimental literary magazines, including the *Dial, Little Review,* and *Smart Set,* and wrote several plays for the Provincetown Players, an innovative theater group.

Barnes's journalism, primarily features and interviews, covered the motley, dynamic culture of early-twentieth-century New York City in prose that was both laconic and witty, filled with surprising aphorisms and odd turns of phrase. Part of the reason she could capture the texture and spirit of bohemian Greenwich Village so well was that she lived there and had become friends with many of its famous representatives, including photographer BERENICE ABBOTT, poet EDNA ST. VINCENT MILLAY, and playwright Eugene O'Neill. Barnes became known for her distinct beauty—she was tall, with rippling auburn hair, sharp tilted features, and cat-shaped eyes—and her distinctive style. She often wore a black hat and cape and ruffled blouses, and strode through the neighborhood in high heels, brandishing a long cane. She lived with Courtenay Lemon, a theater critic and philosopher, from 1917 to 1919.

In 1920, Barnes sailed to Paris, on assignment for *McCall's* magazine to chronicle the activities of writers and artists searching for community and expressive freedom in Europe. Barnes was paid very well for her interviews and sketches. This income, along with later royalties from the publication of *Ryder,* enabled her to purchase an apartment on Rue St. Romain. Her most famous interview was with author James Joyce, whose novel *Ulysses* (1922) she revered. Barnes often could be seen alone, writing in a café, or among the many writers who gathered at GERTRUDE STEIN's salon or at SYLVIA BEACH's bookstore, Shakespeare and Company. Barnes lived in Paris for most of the decade, though she returned to the United States several times and traveled often in Europe.

In Paris, Barnes met heiress NATALIE CLIFFORD BARNEY, who was the center of a vibrant circle of lesbian writers and artists. In characteristic style, Barnes both celebrated and poked fun at Barney and her salon, in 1928 privately printing a bawdy Elizabethan zodiac titled *Ladies Almanack* that satirized Barney and her set. In later years, when Barnes had little financial security, Barney helped support her. In 1921, Barnes met artist Thelma Wood and fell deeply in love. They lived and worked together for most of the decade, each year marked by a doll Barnes gave to Wood to symbolize her devotion. But Wood's alcoholism and frequent infidelities compelled a despairing Barnes to break off the relationship in the early 1930s. Barnes had several heterosexual relationships over the next ten years, but by then she had resigned herself to living in solitude.

Barnes wrote most of her novel *Nightwood* (1936) while in residence at Hayford Hall, an English mansion rented by art collector PEGGY GUGGENHEIM. (Guggenheim, too, supported Barnes for many years.) *Nightwood* evoked a sexual and cultural underworld with characters who each expressed a sense of painful marginality and loneliness. Barnes's difficult breakup with Thelma Wood, who is represented in the novel as a character who is both depraved and alluring, was one source of the novel's themes; Barnes's familiarity with Paris's gay subculture was another. *Nightwood* is considered a masterpiece for its language of loss and subversion and its indictment of moral and political forces that suppress the full range of human expression. T. S. Eliot supplied an introduction.

In 1939, Barnes returned to the United States. For most of the rest of her life she lived in an apartment at Patchin Place in Greenwich Village—reclusive, alcoholic, and ill. She eventually stopped drinking, but she was plagued by arthritis, emphysema, asthma, and intestinal troubles. She nevertheless maintained an extensive correspondence with friends and established new connections, including one with United Nations Secretary-General Dag Hammarskjöld, who helped her publish and mount the Swedish stage production of *The Antiphon.* Often on the edge of poverty, she was supported by royalties, small stipends from friends, bequests, and the sale of her papers to the University of Maryland. At the time of her death in 1982 in New York City at the age of ninety, she was completing a bestiary, *Creatures in an Alphabet,* which was published that year.

Barnes was a famous member of the literary avant-garde in the 1910s, 1920s, and 1930s. Commentary on her looks, wit, and presence sometimes overshadowed serious considerations of her literary art, but her contributions as both a journalist and a writer have received fresh and powerful interpretations by feminist literary critics and historians since the 1980s. Her representations of marginality and social transgression, though rooted in a painful family past, express important themes of twentieth-century modernity.

Bibliography: The papers and manuscripts of Djuna Barnes are housed in the University of Maryland Libraries Special Collections, which also contain family photographs and many photographs and drawings of Barnes. Her major books, in addition to those cited above, include *A Book* (1923), revised in 1929 as *A Night among the Horses* and in 1962 as *Spillway and Other Stories;* early fiction, journalism, and interviews collected in *New York* (1989); *Smoke and Other Early Stories* (1982); and *Interviews* (1985). An interview with Barnes was published in *Time* magazine in 1943: "The Barnes among Women," January 18, 1943, p. 55. Biographical information and critical perspectives on Djuna Barnes can be found in Phillip Herring, *Djuna: The Life and Work of Djuna Barnes* (1995); Mary Lynn Broe, ed., *Silence and Power: A Reevaluation of Djuna Barnes* (1991); Shari Benstock, *Women of the Left Bank: Paris, 1900–1940* (1986); and Bridget Elliott and Jo-Ann Wallace, *Women Artists and Writers: Modernist (Im)positionings* (1994). See also Douglas Messerli, *Djuna Barnes: A Bibliography* (1975). An obituary appeared in the *New York Times* on June 20, 1982.

ELIZABETH FRANCIS

BATES, Daisy Lee Gatson. November 11, 1914–November 4, 1999. Journalist, publisher, civil rights activist.

When Daisy Gatson was eight years old, she learned that while she was still an infant her mother, an African American, had been murdered by three white men in an attempted rape. This knowledge filled her with a hatred of all white people and shaped her destiny as a civil rights activist. Born in the tiny sawmill town of Huttig in southern Arkansas, Daisy Lee Gatson was abandoned by her natural father, Hezekiah "Babe" Gatson, after the death of her mother, Millie Riley, and she grew up in the home of Orlee and Susie Smith. On his deathbed, her adoptive father pleaded with her to move beyond hatred to a determination to change the conditions of racial discrimination in the South. She accepted his challenge.

In the early 1930s, shortly after Orlee Smith's death, Daisy Gatson married Lucius Christopher (L.C.) Bates and settled in Memphis, Tennessee, for several years. In a late-in-life interview, Bates stated that she had attended classes at Le Moyne College, but no records survive to document this claim. Although trained in journalism at Wilberforce College, L.C. sold insurance after losing his first newspaper job during the Depression. Finally in 1941 the Bateses were able to move to Little Rock, Arkansas, and inaugurate a weekly newspaper, the *State Press*. The young couple were crusading journalists, and their paper prospered. Daisy Bates briefly attended both Philander Smith College and Shorter Business College. The Bateses became active in the National Association for the Advancement of Colored People (NAACP), and in 1952 Daisy was elected president of the Arkansas State Conference of NAACP branches.

Although the couple had no children of their own (L.C. had a daughter by a previous marriage who did not live with them), in the early 1950s Daisy Bates created an NAACP youth council of about one hundred young people, which met at her house once a week to discuss major issues of the day. Through this effort she was able to instill in these youngsters an understanding of the need for changes in the South's racial practices, the opportunities that now existed as a result of recent Supreme Court decisions, and a vision of their own participation in that process. All of the students whom white officials would handpick to desegregate Central High School in 1957 were members of this youth council. Bates was therefore a natural choice, selected by the students themselves, to be the mentor and advocate of the "Little Rock Nine."

When Arkansas Governor Orval Faubus attempted to prevent the desegregation of Little Rock Central High School in 1957, President Dwight Eisenhower sent U.S. Army paratroopers to escort the nine black children into the school. Through the remainder of the school year, the Little Rock Nine required the protection of soldiers to help fend off escalating attacks from segregationist students within the school. Every afternoon the nine gathered at the Bates home to discuss the day's activities and abuses and to renew their resolve. Daisy Bates was a major force, perhaps the major force, in preventing the black students' capitulation to both the segregationist onslaught and the attempts of Little Rock's white leadership to impose a "cooling off period" that would involve the black students' withdrawal from Central High. For two years Bates served as the students' advisor and "therapy group" leader, and she also functioned as the conduit between the school authorities and the nine black children and their families.

Daisy Bates consequently became a prime target of the segregationists' wrath in Little Rock. Her home was attacked repeatedly, requiring armed volunteers to protect it for two years. The campaign of intimidation extended to the Bateses' newspaper, eventually forcing it to shut down in 1959, wiping out the couple's life savings. Daisy Bates also suffered a significant loss of support from Little Rock's black community. While some of the city's African Americans admired her tenacity and her commitment to the struggle for equality, many black professionals and church leaders felt she was moving "too fast," and others thought she enjoyed the spotlight of publicity too much.

The strain took a toll on both her health and her marriage. Hospitalized repeatedly, Bates finally moved to New York in 1960 to write her autobiography, which was published in 1962 as *The Long Shadow of Little Rock* with an introduction by ELEANOR ROOSEVELT. She also took courses in creative writing at New York University. Bates accepted an appointment from President John F. Kennedy to work for the Democratic National Committee, and under President Lyndon B. Johnson she worked to promote voter education and registration throughout the Midwest, especially among women. She divorced L.C. in 1963 but remarried him in 1965, and they remained married until his death in 1980.

In 1965 Daisy Bates suffered the first of a series of strokes, but she continued to work for the Office of Economic Opportunity in the tiny Arkansas community of Mitchellville. In 1968 she became the Arkansas director of the Equal Employment Opportunity Commission. Through the 1970s her health deteriorated further, and she dedicated most of her time to caring for her ailing husband. After L.C.'s death Daisy attempted to restart the *State Press*, but her failing health forced her to sell the paper in 1988. Daisy Bates died on November 4, 1999; her body lay in state in the rotunda of the Arkansas State Capitol, a rare tribute for any Arkansan, and she was the only woman to be so honored. Later that month her home became a national historic landmark, and in 2001 the Arkansas General Assembly created a state holiday in her honor.

Poised, refined, and graceful, in her stylish clothes, careful makeup, and coiffed hair, Daisy

Bates was equally strong-willed and outspoken. With courage and tenacity she broke down barriers all around her, in Arkansas and beyond, that had limited what African Americans and women could do and be, and her finest legacy is that she broadened the common understanding of the dignity and worth of every American.

Bibliography: A collection of Daisy Bates's correspondence and assorted memorabilia from the 1950s and 1960s is located at the Wisconsin Historical Society in Madison. Additional manuscript materials can be found in the Daisy Bates Papers at the University of Arkansas Library, Special Collections, at Fayetteville; materials here include records pertaining to Bates's work for the Office of Economic Opportunity in Arkansas. Her autobiography, *The Long Shadow of Little Rock* (1962; second ed., 1986), contains an introduction by Eleanor Roosevelt as well as photographs of Daisy and L. C. Bates. For an interesting and revealing interview with Daisy Bates, see Linda S. Caillouet, "Daisy Lee Gatson Bates," *Arkansas Democrat-Gazette,* January 12, 1992; see also the Elizabeth Jacoway interview with Daisy Bates conducted on October 11, 1976, in the papers of the Southern Oral History Program, University of North Carolina at Chapel Hill. Numerous articles can be found in *Ebony, Jet,* and *The Crisis* tracing Bates's activities during the Little Rock ordeal. A biographical sketch of Daisy Bates can be found in Erma Glasco Davis and Faustine Childress Wilson, eds., *The Arkansas African American Hall of Fame* (1993). Obituaries appeared in the *New York Times* and the *Arkansas Democrat-Gazette* on November 5, 1999.

ELIZABETH JACOWAY

BAUMGARTNER, Leona. August 18, 1902–January 15, 1991. Public health official.

Leona Baumgartner was born in Chicago and raised in Lawrence, Kansas. She was the daughter of Olga Leisy and William J. Baumgartner, a zoology professor at the University of Kansas. A 1919 graduate of Lawrence High School, Leona attended the University of Kansas as an undergraduate, receiving her BA in 1923 and an MS in 1925. After stints as a high school biology teacher, coordinator of nursing education at a junior college, and head of the division of bacteriology and hygiene at the University of Montana, she won a Rockefeller Research Fellowship to study at Kaiser Wilhelm Institute in Munich. Following her time in Germany, she went to Yale on a Sterling Fellowship, earning her PhD in immunology in 1932 and her medical degree in 1934. After an internship and residency in pediatrics at New York Hospital, she took a position with the U.S. Public Health Service.

In 1937 Baumgartner joined the New York City Department of Health, where she emerged as one of the most dynamic innovators of the twentieth century. Beginning as a medical instructor in child and school hygiene, she soon became director of the Bureau of Child Health. In the midst of the Depression and with the support of the administration of Mayor Fiorello LaGuardia, she embarked on an energetic effort to establish child health clinics, day nurseries, and neighborhood clinics throughout the city. No other city in the nation had established such an extensive set of services for women and children, and these institutions have been credited with helping reduce the city's infant mortality rates substantially, despite the hardships of the Depression. Determined to distinguish these centers from the traditionally run-down public services for the poor, Baumgartner made sure that they provided safe and clean environments staffed by well-trained and friendly adults who recognized the special emotional needs of individual children. The popular clinics, which treated nearly 35 percent of the city's children, became models of efficient, first-class public care throughout the country. During World War II, Baumgartner also organized emergency medical programs for the mothers and children of military personnel. She married Nathaniel Elias, a chemical engineer, in 1942 and helped him raise his two children, Peter and Barbara, from a previous marriage.

Baumgartner was a forceful advocate of public health and sought to humanize the activities of the NYC Department of Health and make them a critical part of the city's social and political life. She also was an early advocate for a variety of plans for national health insurance. She worked hard to reach out to the public through radio addresses and newspaper press releases. Throughout her long life she found time to publish numerous newspaper columns, advice brochures, and scholarly analyses of pressing public health concerns. In 1949–50 she served as associate chief of the U.S. Children's Bureau in Washington.

From 1954 to 1962, during the mayoralty of Robert Wagner Jr., Baumgartner served as New York City's commissioner of health, the first woman to be so named. She is remembered as being one of the most innovative commissioners in the city's history. During her tenure she initiated one of the earliest campaigns in the nation against childhood smoking. In 1954, shortly after the publication of articles linking smoking to cancer, she announced her concerns about tobacco smoke, and in 1960, four years before the famous U.S. surgeon general's report that linked smoking to lung cancer, New York City began a campaign in the public school system to discourage teenage smoking. Sex education classes, anti-rat campaigns, and efforts to curb teenage pregnancies through the use of birth control were all hallmarks of her sustained effort to create a healthful environment through community education and public health campaigns.

Child and teenage health were a special focus of her years as commissioner of health. An early proponent of the Salk vaccine for immunization against polio, Baumgartner organized a city-wide effort to vaccinate all of the city's children. In May and June 1962, some 238,142 doses of vaccine were administered to children in New York City through the Department of Health clinics, leading to the near eradication of polio as a serious threat to New York children's health in the 1960s and 1970s. Baumgartner was also among the first in the nation to initiate a pilot project on coronary heart disease that identified diet as an important component in its prevalence. Later she advocated fluoridating the city's water supply to reduce tooth decay.

In 1962 President Kennedy appointed Baumgartner to head the Office of Technical Cooperation and Research for the Agency for International Development (AID), where she helped improve standards for public health programs internationally and successfully advocated for the inclusion of birth control in AID health programs. In 1966 she was named a visiting professor of social medicine at Harvard Medical School. She also served as executive director of the Medical Care and Education Foundation. Widowed in 1964, she married Alexander Langmuir, an epidemiologist, in 1970 and retired from Harvard in 1972. In retirement Baumgartner remained a passionate advocate of the importance of public health activities, continuing to call for both greater resources for public health and an integration of the private, voluntary, and public hospital systems into a cohesive system of prevention and service.

Baumgartner was one of the most prominent women in American medicine and public health during the middle decades of the twentieth century. In light of her professional attainments, her advocacy of child and maternal health issues, and her strong advocacy for public health in general, she was awarded the Sedgwick Medal by the American Public Health Association and the Lasker Award, the nation's premier award for advances in medical and public health science. Leona Baumgartner died of polycythemia, a blood disease, in 1991 in Chilmark, Massachusetts, at the age of eighty-eight.

Bibliography: Leona Baumgartner's extensive papers are held at Countway Medical Library at Harvard Medical School. Among her numerous policy papers, public statements, journal articles, and magazine and newspaper articles, see "A Doctor Diagnoses Soviet Medicine," *New York Times Magazine,* May 17, 1959, pp. 42–47; "How Will We Get Well and Keep Healthy?" *Nursing Outlook* 16, no. 3 (March 1968), pp. 40–42; "One Hundred Years of Health: New York City, 1866–1966," *Bulletin of New York Academy of Medicine,* 45 (June 1969), pp. 555–86; "But What about the People?" *American Journal of Public Health* 57 (1967), pp. 610–16; "Optimal Utilization of Medical Womanpower," *Journal of the American Medical Women's Association* 21, no. 10 (October 1966), pp. 832–37; and "Better Communication for Better Health," *National Tuberculosis Association Bulletin* 52, no. 9 (October 1966), pp. 3–6. Biographical information can be found in *Current Biography* (1950), pp. 22–24, and Julia Bess Frank, "A Personal History of Dr. Leona Baumgartner Covering the Years 1902–1962" (MD dissertation, Yale University, 1977), which also contains a bibliography. An obituary appeared in the *New York Times* on January 17, 1991.

DAVID ROSNER

BEECH, Olive Ann Mellor. September 25, 1903–July 6, 1993. Aviation industry leader, business executive.

Olive Ann Mellor was born in Waverly, Kansas, the youngest of four daughters of Suzanne Miller and Frank B. Mellor. Her mother's and father's ancestors emigrated from England to the United States between 1795 and 1804. Olive Ann spent most of her childhood in the farming community of Paola, Kansas, where her father was a carpenter and building contractor. Her mother was a farm woman who also took care of foster children from the Wichita Children's Home.

Olive Ann Mellor was educated in public schools in Paolo. At an early age, she demonstrated a keen business acumen. When she was seven she had her own bank account, and four years later her mother arranged with the local bank for Olive Ann to write checks and pay the family bills. In 1917, when Olive Ann was fourteen, the family moved to Wichita, where she later attended the American Secretarial and Business College. In 1921, at the age of eighteen, Olive Ann moved to Augusta, Kansas, to work as an office manager for Staley Electrical Company, an appliance and contracting firm.

Following the death of her Augusta employer, she returned to Wichita, where, in 1925, she began work as a secretary and bookkeeper for the newly formed Travel Air Manufacturing Company. Commercial aviation was in its infancy, and the business of manufacturing small aircraft was risky and uncertain. The brainchild of Walter Herschel Beech, a former World War I pilot, engineer, and barnstorming aviator, Travel Air became the world's leading producer of commercial airplanes by the late 1920s. When Olive Ann joined Travel Air as its twelfth employee, she had never flown in an airplane and knew nothing about the airline industry. As the only woman and only non-pilot employed by Travel Air, she immediately set out to learn the airplane manufacturing industry from the ground up. She rapidly earned the respect, admiration, and love of Walter H. Beech. On February 24, 1930, the couple married.

After a brief residence in New York City, where Walter was vice president of Curtiss-Wright Airplane Company, the couple returned to Wichita in 1932 to become more closely allied with designing and producing airplanes. Employing a handful of former Travel Air employees, they co-founded the Beech Aircraft Company. Walter served as president and Olive Ann as secretary-treasurer.

Established at the height of the Depression, Beech Aircraft faced numerous challenges during its early years. At first a good year might mean the sale of a single aircraft. Still, two airplanes that would become the company's foundation for years to come were produced during the 1930s: the classic Model 17 single-engine Staggerwing biplane and the Model 18 Twin Beech. Olive Beech convinced her husband that a winning performance of the Beechcraft Model 17 in the Bendix Transcontinental Trophy Race, America's most famous cross-country race, would be even more impressive if piloted by a woman, arguing that a win by a woman pilot "would be convincing proof that unlike some airplanes of that day, brute strength was not required to operate a Beechcraft" (McDaniel, 1971, p. 20). LOUISE THADEN and Blanche Noyes flew the Model 17 in the 1936 race and won the coveted Bendix trophy.

In 1937, Beech gave birth to their first daughter, Suzanne. A second daughter, Mary Lynn, was born in 1940. Beech continued her role as a business executive while her daughters were young, taking on additional responsibility for running the company when her husband was hospitalized in September 1940 with encephalitis. By then Beech Aircraft had suspended all commercial production and had shifted its focus to defense manufacturing.

The outbreak of World War II resulted in spectacular growth for Beech Aircraft. Demand for military versions of the Model 17 and Model 18 soared: more than 90 percent of all United States bombardiers and navigators learned their skills in the Beechcraft Model 18. Employment jumped from 235 in 1939 to a wartime peak of 14,000. Because of her husband's illness, Beech continued in her leadership position as the head of the company throughout the war years.

Following World War II, Beech Aircraft turned to diversified manufacturing, producing corn harvesters, cotton pickers, and washing machines. In 1946, the single-engine V-tail Beechcraft Bonanza was introduced and became the leader in its field. Three years later, in 1949, the rugged Beechcraft Twin-Bonanza was first produced. Military demand for that plane soared after the outbreak of the Korean War in June 1950.

After Walter Beech suffered a fatal heart attack on November 29, 1950, Olive Ann, at the age of forty-seven, was elected president and chairman of the board of Beech Aircraft. Under her energetic leadership, Beech Aircraft continued its policies of growth and diversification in the post–World War II period. It made an early entry into the nation's space program, developed a line of missile targets for training, and acquired a wide variety of subcontracts from other aerospace manufacturers. Olive Ann skillfully led the company until 1968, when she recommended that her nephew, Frank I. Hendrick, become president. Beech remained chairman and CEO until 1982, when she was made chairman emeritus of the company. In February 1980, Beech Aircraft merged with Raytheon, and she was elected to its board of directors.

Universally recognized as the "the first lady of aviation" even though she never learned to fly, Olive Ann Mellor Beech received numerous awards, including selection by *Fortune* magazine as one of the ten highest ranking women in business in the 1970s, the prestigious Wright Brothers Memorial Trophy in 1980, induction into the National Aviation Hall of Fame in 1981, and an honorary doctorate in business administration from Wichita State University in 1982. Appointed to national boards by Presidents Eisenhower, Johnson, and Nixon, Beech was widely respected as a philanthropist and patron of the arts. Well known for her strong leadership abilities and financial aptitude, she also demonstrated impeccable taste in fashion. She died of congestive heart failure on July 6, 1993, at her home in Wichita, Kansas, at the age of eighty-nine.

Bibliography: The Walter H. and Olive Ann Beech Collection in the Department of Special Collections, Wichita State University Libraries, contains correspondence, scrapbooks, financial documentation, photographs, clippings, publications, reports, memos, certificates, and plaques, most of which concern the life and career of Olive Ann Beech. A number of articles about Beech have been published in the popular press. See, for example, Peter Wyden, "Danger: Boss Lady at Work," *Saturday Evening Post,* August 8, 1959, p. 26. An essay by Beech, "The Woman Executive," appears in Peter Krass, ed., *The Book of Leadership Wisdom: Classic Writings by Legendary Business Leaders* (1998). Biographical information appears in *Current Biography* (1956), pp. 41–43. For information about Olive Ann Beech and the history of Beech Aircraft, see A. J. Pelletier, *Beech Aircraft and Their Predecessors* (1995); and William H. McDaniel, *The History of Beech* (1971; 2nd ed., 1976). Mary Lynn Oliver of Wichita, Kansas, provided biographical information about her mother's family. An obituary appeared in the *New York Times* on July 7, 1993.

JUDY BARRETT LITOFF

BENEDEK, Therese F. November 8, 1892–October 27, 1977. Psychoanalyst, psychiatrist.

Born in Eger, Hungary, Therese Friedmann was the third of four children of Ignatius Friedmann, a successful businessman, and Charlotte Link, a homemaker. At age six, she moved with her family to Budapest. As a teenager, determined to pursue a medical education, she gained admission to the local gymnasium and later attended the University of Budapest, where she received her medical degree in 1916.

As a medical student, Therese Friedmann became interested in the psychology of children, especially the emotional reaction of infants to separation from their mothers. After fulfilling her residency requirements in pediatrics in 1918, she became an assistant physician at the pediatric clinic of St. Elizabeth University in what is now Bratislava, Slovakia. Days after resigning this position in 1919, she married Tibor Benedek, a fellow medical student. Political turmoil in Hungary prompted the young Jewish couple to leave for Germany. In February 1920, the month when the anti-Semitic Horthy regime took power in Hungary, Tibor began a residency in dermatology at the University of Leipzig medical school. Two months later, Therese joined the staff of the psychiatric clinic affiliated with the university and launched what would soon become a remarkable career in psychoanalysis.

Earlier, during her student days in Budapest, a course of lectures by Freud's associate Sandor Ferenczi opened to her the possibility of psychoanalysis as a vocation, and she underwent a five-month training analysis. Only after moving to Leipzig, however, did Benedek gain access to the most instrumental group of psychoanalysts outside Freud's immediate circle. The nearby Berlin Psychoanalytic Society had established the first training institute and clinic in 1920 and set the standards for training in therapeutic techniques. The women who would soon emerge at the forefront of the new profession—KAREN HORNEY, Melanie Klein, HELENE DEUTSCH, and Alice Balint—all trained there. Benedek, who meanwhile had organized and presided over a small psychoanalytic circle in Leipzig, first attracted attention by presenting several well-received papers at the meetings of the Berlin Psychoanalytic Society. Later (1932–35) she served as a faculty member of the institute and developed expertise in psychoanalytic training. During these busy years she gave birth to her two children, Thomas G. in 1926 and Judith in 1929.

In April 1936 the Benedek family fled Nazi Germany and found refuge in the United States. Tibor Benedek secured a faculty position at Northwestern University School of Medicine, and Therese Benedek joined the staff of the Institute for Psychoanalysis in Chicago. She resumed her work as a training analyst and built a clinical practice that flourished for the next forty years. She became a naturalized citizen in 1942.

Working with Franz Alexander, who directed the Institute for Psychoanalysis in Chicago, Benedek became a leading researcher in the burgeoning field of psychosomatic medicine. Freud's theories of hysteria linked specific physical symptoms to underlying emotional trauma. By the 1930s these theories had become a foundation for speculations about chronic diseases (such as ulcers, asthma, and hypertension) that appeared to lack a clear or simple biological or organic cause. Very early in her career, Benedek began to speculate about the role of drives or instincts in producing both mental and physical problems and sought to establish a correlation between psychological and endocrine factors. Her 1934 essay "Mental Processes in Thyrotoxic States," based on clinical case studies conducted in Germany, explored the relationship between anxiety or aggression and the hormonal action of the thyroid gland. After joining the staff of the Institute for Psychoanalysis, she pursued a similar line of investigation, including a five-year project focused on the psychosomatic aspects of diabetes mellitus.

Female sexuality, including pregnancy and childbirth, became the subject of Benedek's signature research. With Boris B. Rubenstein, an endocrinologist, she conducted a major study of the relationship between the sexual drive, including the desire for motherhood, and hormonal fluctuations during the menstrual cycle. The extensive data she collected from vaginal smears, basal body temperature, and daily psychoanalysis with fifteen patients yielded a strong correlation between the physiological processes of ovulation and emotions. Benedek concluded that the female sexual drive fluctuates with estrogen levels and that passivity and narcissism vary with the activity of progesterone. Equally important, she surmised that her investigation disclosed "an instinctual core" in woman, a desire for heterosexual intercourse that in turn stimulates a desire for pregnancy and, ultimately, for motherhood. The results of this landmark study were published in 1942 as a monograph entitled *The Sexual Cycle in Women: The Relation between Ovarian Function and Psychodynamic Processes.*

Benedek held fast to her theories concerning female sexuality and the biological aim of motherhood. In the late 1960s, when many psychoanalysts and feminists turned to examine women's capacity for orgasm as a function distinct from women's procreative role, Benedek continued to insist that reproductive goals were central to the psychic makeup of women. The procreative act, she believed, which delimited male sexual behavior, was for women only the prelude to a prolonged reproductive role that culminated in the nurturing behavior associated with motherhood.

In addition to her research in various aspects of psychosomatic medicine and female sexuality,

Benedek excelled as an investigator of emotional dynamics in the family. She considered, for example, twentieth-century changes in family organization that fostered a greater degree of equality between husband and wife and the impact of modern marriage on reproductive functions and on relationships between parents and child in personality development. At the close of World War II, she published *Insight and Personality Adjustment: A Study of the Psychological Effects of War* (1946), which discusses the emotional dynamics of separation and psychological challenges to sexual relationships prompted by expanding democracy. Considering herself a "psychoanalytic educator," she developed these themes in her numerous publications, many written late in life, including two books edited with E. James Anthony: *Parenthood: Its Psychology and Pathology* (1970) and *Depression and Human Existence* (1975).

Therese Benedek died in 1977 at age eighty-four after suffering a heart attack on her way home from her office, where she had continued to practice psychoanalysis. A colleague recalled that at the time of her death Benedek was reading widely on the social history of women and female sexuality in preparation for a book she was planning to write on the ambivalent relationship between the sexes.

Bibliography: The Institute for Psychoanalysis in Chicago holds the papers of Therese Benedek, including personal correspondence, research and case notes, course syllabi, and materials related to her publications. Benedek edited, with Joan Fleming, *Psychoanalytic Education* (1966). She published numerous essays in books and in journals, including the prestigious *Journal of the American Psychoanalytic Association.* She collected and introduced her major essays written between 1931 and 1968 in *Psychoanalytic Investigations: Selected Papers* (1973). Her publications, including books, articles, and book chapters, are listed in Alexander Grinstein, ed., *The Index of Psychoanalytic Writings* (1956–58, 1964). Her early career in Hungary and Germany is covered in Thomas G. Benedek, "A Psychoanalytic Career Begins: Therese F. Benedek, M.D.—A Documentary Biography," *Annual of Psychoanalysis* 7(1979), pp. 3–15. Brief biographies appear in Joan Fleming, "Therese Benedek, M.D. 1892–1977," *Psychoanalytic Quarterly* 47, no. 2 (1978), pp. 289–92; Gwendolyn Stevens and Sheldon Gardner, *Women of Psychology: Volume 2* (1982), pp. 46–48; and Catherine M. Coppolillo, "Benedek, Therese Friedmann," in Rima Lunin Schultz and Adele Hast, eds., *Women Building Chicago 1790–1990* (2001), pp. 73–75. Thomas G. Benedek, MD, professor of medicine, University of Pittsburgh, supplied information on the background of his mother's family. Obituaries appeared in the *New York Times* and the *Chicago Tribune* on October 29, 1977.

MARI JO BUHLE

BENNETT, Gwendolyn. July 8, 1902–May 30, 1981. Writer, artist.

Born in Giddings, Texas, Gwendolyn Bennett was the only child of Joshua Robin Bennett and Mayme Frank Abernathy. Both parents were African American, and Mayme was also of Native American heritage. For a time they taught on a Paiute Reservation in Wadsworth, Nevada, before moving to Washington, D.C., where Joshua Bennett studied law and his wife trained as a manicurist and beautician. The couple divorced when Gwendolyn was a child, and her mother was awarded custody. In retaliation, Joshua Bennett kidnapped his daughter, separating her from her mother. Remarried (his new wife proved to be a good stepmother to Gwendolyn), Bennett moved the family frequently to avoid detection before finally settling in Brooklyn, New York. There Gwendolyn attended Brooklyn Girls' High School, graduating in 1921.

By the age of twenty Gwendolyn Bennett had achieved recognition as a writer and illustrator, and she would win further accolades from the literary lions of the nascent "New Negro" arts movement of the 1920s. At first she set out to be a painter. She took fine arts classes at Columbia before earning her degree from Pratt Institute in 1924. She then accepted a teaching position in the Fine Arts Department of Howard University in Washington, D.C., where she was finally reunited with her mother, and spent the following year studying art in Paris.

Upon her return she changed direction. Charles S. Johnson, who had earlier chosen her poem "To Usward" to be read at a banquet as a call to young black writers, appointed her as his assistant editor at *Opportunity* magazine, the influential African American journal. There, from 1926 to 1928, Bennett wrote a monthly column called "The Ebony Flute" (after a poem by William Rose Benet), which was avidly read for news about literary activity in Harlem.

All of Bennett's activities and associations placed her at the epicenter of what is now called the Harlem Renaissance, and she found mentors in Charles Johnson, James Weldon Johnson, Langston Hughes, and AUGUSTA SAVAGE. She also belonged to the informal and close-knit Harlem Writers Guild, along with Hughes, Countee Cullen, Eric Walrond, Helene Johnson, Wallace Thurman, Bruce Nugent, and Aaron and Alta Douglass. Artistically, Bennett's drawings, inspired by art nouveau, graced several magazine covers from 1923 to 1930. Countee Cullen assured her a place in Harlem Renaissance history when he published eight of her poems in his historic anthology, *Caroling Dusk* (1927).

Bennett's literary output in her chosen genres, poetry and short prose, is puzzlingly meager—despite its high quality, it is undeniably spare. The discontinuity of this brilliant and versatile woman's artistic life confounds and disconcerts. Her personal journals, however, shed light on the paradox of her uneven career. In the handwritten pages of a journal kept first in Paris, then sporadically from 1936 to 1937, and again in 1958, Bennett emerges as an idealistic and passionate, yet contradictory, woman.

Her literary production can be periodized by charting her life through singlehood, an unsuccessful marriage, to remarriage and death. From 1923 to 1928, her artistic heyday, Bennett produced most of her significant work: some twenty-two poems, two short stories, and an unknown number of paintings and drawings. Her oeuvre was small, yet it was central to the Harlem Renaissance, as it resonated with the movement's aesthetic goals and added a new female voice to the panoply of mostly male poets. The lyrical Bennett is exemplified in "Quatrains," where the poet blends her two artistic inclinations: "Brushes and paints are all I have / To speak the music of in my soul / While silently there laughs at me / A copper jar beside a pale green bowl" (*Caroling Dusk*, p. 155).

During this time Bennett also produced book reviews, articles, and pen-and-ink drawings for the covers of *Opportunity* and *Crisis* magazines. Her short stories ("Tokens" and "Wedding Day") are gems, evoking the dreams and disappointments of black expatriates in Paris during the 1920s. The republication of "Tokens" in *Ebony and Topaz: A Collectanea* (1927) placed her prose before a crossover audience, but she did not go on to publish a collected volume of her work. When a fire in her stepmother's basement destroyed Bennett's canvases, she also lost the incentive to continue with her art. Bennett's brilliant first act was to have no sequel, and by the late 1930s her career as a publishing writer and exhibiting visual artist was waning.

While teaching art at Howard University, Bennett met and married a medical student, Alfred Joseph Jackson, in 1928. Jackson moved to Eustis, Florida, to establish a practice, and Gwendolyn joined him several months later. The role of country doctor's wife was stifling, and her marriage a disappointment; the couple did not have children. The Promised Land of course lay in New York, which she missed sorely. At Bennett's urging, Jackson took the New York medical boards so that they could return to New York. In the early 1930s they bought a home in Hempstead, Long Island, but marital conflict and financial difficulties ensued. The Great Depression was crushing the vibrancy of Harlem and bringing the New Negro movement to a close. Furthermore, Jackson did not support Bennett's career aspirations, preferring that she pull in income from her job with the Department of Information and Education of the Welfare Council of New York.

Jackson died unexpectedly in 1936. Newly single, Bennett became assistant director of the Harlem Art Center, sponsored by the WPA Federal Art Project, and embraced the cause of education as a means to empower people. She founded and directed both the George Washington Carver Community School and the Jefferson School for Democracy. It was her misfortune that the House Committee on Un-American Activities (HUAC) investigated both schools as "Red Fronts" and closed them in the 1940s. Despite a political climate inimical to her ideals, Bennett forged on as a leader in the arts and social organizations and at the Harlem Art Center.

Bennett's 1940 marriage to fellow School of Democracy teacher Richard Crosscup, who was white, initiated the last phase in her life. Bennett finally achieved a harmonious union with a man who shared her political ideals. She also gave up artistic endeavors and retired from public life. In 1968 the couple moved to Kutztown, Pennsylvania, where they ran a successful antique business. Richard died in 1980. Gwendolyn died eighteen months later in Reading, Pennsylvania, at the age of seventy-eight.

Bibliography: The Gwendolyn Bennett Papers are held by the Manuscripts, Archives and Rare Books Division, the Schomburg Center for Research in Black Culture, New York Public Library. The fullest biographical study of Bennett is Sandra Y. Govan, "Gwendolyn Bennett: Portrait of an Artist Lost" (PhD dissertation, Emory University, 1980). See also Govan's "After the Renaissance: Gwendolyn Bennett and the WPA Years," *Mid-Atlantic Writers Association* 3, no. 2 (December 1988), pp. 27–31; and "A Blend of Voices: Composite Narrative Strategies in Biographical Reconstruction," in Dolan Hubbard, ed., *Recovered Writers/Recovered Texts: Race, Class, and Gender in Black Women's Literature* (1997), pp. 90–104. For a general introduction to the intellectual currents of the time, see Lorraine Elena Roses and Ruth Elizabeth Randolph, eds., *The Harlem Renaissance and Beyond: Literary Biographies of 100 Black Women Writers, 1900–1945* (1990). General sources include Cheryl A. Wall, *Women of the Harlem Renaissance* (1995); and Steven Watson, *The Harlem Renaissance: Hub of African-American Culture, 1920–1930* (1995).

LORRAINE ELENA ROSES

BERNARD, Jessie Shirley. June 8, 1903–October 6, 1996. Sociologist, feminist.

Jessie Bernard was a prolific writer, a leading sociologist, an active feminist, a single mother of three, and a beloved mentor. Born and raised in Minneapolis, Jessie Sarah (later changed to Shirley) Ravitch was the third of four children of Bessie Kanter and David Solomon Ravitch, who had immigrated separately to the United States from Transylvania (later Romania) in the 1880s.

Bernard

While mastering English, David Ravitch delivered dairy products throughout Minneapolis. Later he became a haberdasher and invested in real estate. While Jessie was growing up, the Ravitches were the only Jewish family in a middle-class neighborhood of first- and second-generation immigrants.

Throughout her life, Jessie struggled exceptionally well to steer her own course. Writing was her first love, and she dated her career as a published author to the fourth grade when several of her pieces appeared in the *Minneapolis Journal.* Despite her parents' belief that she should attend business school until getting married, she entered the University of Minnesota at sixteen. Like many prominent early women sociologists, Jesse Ravitch married a sociologist, having fallen in love simultaneously with sociology and her first sociology professor, Luther L. Bernard (known as "LLB"), for whom she worked as a research assistant. She received her BA (1923) and MA (1924) from the University of Minnesota, and at twenty-two published her first professional sociological article. In 1925, contradicting cultural and familial norms, she married LLB, who was twenty-three years her senior and not Jewish. She then followed her husband to professorships at Cornell (1924–25), Tulane (1927–28), the University of North Carolina (1928–29), and Washington University (1929–46).

Jessie completed her PhD in sociology and psychology in 1935, when the Bernards were at Washington University. Struggling to attain professional and personal independence within her marriage, she separated from her husband for four years and worked in Washington, D.C., until the couple reconciled. Overcoming her husband's objections, she fulfilled her goal to have children when their daughter, Dorothy Lee, was born in 1941. She was thirty-eight, and LLB was sixty-one. Their sons, Claude and David, followed in 1945 and 1950 respectively. While pregnant with Dorothy, Jessie began teaching sociology at Lindenwood College, where she remained for seven years. In 1947, LLB, who had retired from Washington University, negotiated a lectureship for himself and an assistant professorship for Jessie at Pennsylvania State University. Four years after joining the university and seven months after David's birth, LLB died of cancer. Jessie raised their three children as a single mother while quickly rising to the rank of full professor. She remained at Penn State until 1964, the year she published *Academic Women,* a study of women faculty members' personal and professional lives. For the rest of her life, she was based in Washington, D.C.

Despite her traditional training as a sociologist, Bernard was among the first to demonstrate important leadership as a feminist scholar. At sixty-two, Bernard chose to retire and become "a sociologist at large." Penn State officially awarded her the title Research Scholar *Honoris Causa.* Following her retirement, Bernard authored, coauthored, or edited thirteen books, wrote many articles, and frequently lectured at professional meetings and universities around the world.

Jessie Bernard's largest scholarly contributions centered on increasing our understanding of the effects of sexism on sociology and women's experience of marriage, parenting, education, and ultimately all aspects of global culture and economic life. She argued that owing to the gendered nature of social structures, women and men live in different worlds. Bernard observed that women and men not only perceive their marriages differently, but have two different marriages. By statistically examining a large array of health and mortality data, she found that marriage was generally good for men and bad for women. This research, initially published in "The Paradox of the Happy Marriage" (1971) and *The Future of Marriage* (1972), was reported widely in the popular press, replicated by others, and served as the jumping-off point for further related studies.

Building on her previous work and extensive new research, Bernard published *The Female World* (1981) and *The Female World from a Global Perspective* (1987). In the former, which spans prehistoric times to the 1970s, she points out that although women and men move geographically in the same workplaces, households, and political and economic arenas, they live in essentially different, single-sex worlds. In the latter volume, her last, she maps global differences among females in life expectancy, nutrition, wealth, literacy, work, and politics and examines how racism, classism, and imperialism divide their world. Bernard's analysis of extensive micro and macro sociological data is enriched by her experiences visiting women from all over the world and her participation in numerous international women's meetings.

Prior to her involvement in feminist scholarship, Bernard had contributed to three major "revolutions" in sociology. As a graduate student in the 1920s, she participated in the injection of empirical research into meetings of the American Sociological Society. In the 1930s, she helped challenge the dominance of the University of Chicago over the field through the creation of the *American Sociological Review.* In 1951, as a Pennsylvania State University professor, she was a founding member of the Society for the Study of Social Problems. With her "fourth—feminist—revolution," Bernard advanced social science and lay understanding of gender and helped legitimize feminist studies. She did so not only through her pioneering books, dozens of conference papers, and leadership of professional associations, but through writing hundreds of well-argued letters recommending the hiring, tenuring, and promotion of junior colleagues who were studying gender. Because Bernard was a respected scholar, her advocacy was especially important in legitimizing the new field.

Along with advancing women's studies, Bernard was a beloved mentor of dozens of feminist scholars and a major influence for innumerable others. Many feminist sociologists who were never officially her students benefited greatly from her wise and affectionate encouragement as well as from her writings. As an energetic, enthusiastic founding member of Sociologists for Women in Society (SWS) in 1971, she helped attract many new members. She was also a founding board member of the Center for Women Policy Studies and a member of the boards of the Urban Institute's Woman's Program and the Women's Equity Action League. In 1976, the American Sociological Association, pressed by Sociologists for Women in Society, established the Jessie Bernard Award for the best work on gender. Numerous other associations and institutions of higher education recognized the importance of Bernard's contributions with their highest awards. She died in Washington, D.C., in 1996 at the age of ninety-three.

Bibliography: The Jessie Bernard Papers are at the Pennsylvania State University Library. The most complete collected bibliography of her work is "Vitae of Jessie Bernard" compiled by Muriel Cantor and Linda Kalof, Department of Sociology, American University, Washington, D.C. A "Selected Bibliography" is contained in Robert C. Bannister, *Jessie Bernard: The Making of a Feminist* (1991), pp. 255–62. See also Gwendolyn Styrvoky Safier, "Jessie Bernard: Sociologist" (PhD dissertation, University of Kansas, 1972). Publications by Jessie Bernard not fully cited in the text include "Relative Rate of Change in Custom and Beliefs of Modern Jews," *Proceedings of the American Sociological Society: Trends of Our Civilization* 19 (1925), pp. 171–76; *American Community Behavior* (1949, rev. 1962); *Social Problems at Mid-century: Role, Status, and Stress in a Context of Abundance* (1957); *Marriage and Family among Negroes* (1966); *Remarriage: A Study of Marriage* (1956, rev. 1971); *The Sex Game: Communication between the Sexes* (1968, rev. 1972); *Women and the Public Interest: An Essay on Policy and Protest* (1971); "The Paradox of the Happy Marriage" in Vivian Gornick and Barbara K. Moran, eds., *Woman in Sexist Society* (1971); *The Future of Marriage* (1972, rev. 1982); *The Future of Motherhood* (1974); *Women, Wives, Mothers: Values and Options* (1975); "My Four Revolutions: An Autobiographical History of the ASA," *American Journal of Sociology* 78, no. 4 (January 1973), pp. 773–91; *Self-Portrait of a Family* (1978); and "A Woman's Twentieth Century," in Bennett M. Berger, ed., *Authors of Their Own Lives: Intellectual Autobiographies by Twenty American Sociologists* (1990). The September 1988 issue of *Gender & Society* was conceived as an homage to Bernard on the occasion of her eighty-fifth birthday. See also Arlene Kaplan Daniels, "Jessie Bernard: The Making of a Feminist," *American Journal of Sociology* 97, no. 2 (September 1991), pp. 555–57; Barbara Laslett, "Jessie Bernard: The Making of a Woman's Life," *Contemporary Sociology* 20, no. 5 (September 1991), pp. 679–82; Jean Lipman-Blumen, "Jessie Bernard," in *The International Encyclopedia of Social and Behavioral Sciences* (1979), pp. 49–56; and Pamela Roby, "Women and the ASA: Degendering Organizational Structures and Processes, 1964–1974," *American Sociologist* 23, no. 1 (Spring 1992), pp. 18–48. Obituaries appeared in the *Washington Post* on October 10, 1996, and the *New York Times* on October 11, 1996.

PAMELA ANN ROBY

BERNAYS, Doris E. Fleischman. July 18, 1892–July 10, 1980. Feminist, journalist, public relations counsel.

Born and raised in New York City, Doris Elsa Fleischman was one of three children of Samuel E. Fleischman, an attorney, and Harriet Rosenthal. Fleischman graduated from the Horace Mann School for Girls in 1909 and from Barnard College in 1913. A talented painter and singer, she pursued a career in journalism, taking a job as a feature writer at the *New York Tribune* in 1914. She eventually became assistant editor of the woman's page and assistant Sunday editor. During her time at the paper, Fleischman marched in the first Women's Peace Parade in 1917 and wrote articles about factory girls and women's reform work. An ardent feminist, she interviewed women accomplished in politics, business, and science and emphasized not only women's talents but the very real opportunities for their professional achievement. In her semi-autobiographical book *A Wife Is Many Women* (1955), she recalled the *Tribune*'s woman's page as "a leading influence in the Feminist movement and in the fight for Woman's Suffrage" (p. 169).

In 1919, Edward L. Bernays lured her away from the *Tribune* to become the staff writer for his new public relations firm, and she excelled in her new position. When the couple married in 1922, she became an equal partner in the firm, Edward L. Bernays, Counsel on Public Relations. Although Edward Bernays is frequently identified as the "father of public relations," Fleischman's considerable contributions to the profession have often been overlooked. Together the couple defined and expanded the profession beyond publicity into an appreciation of public opinion and behavior. Their client list included not only the U.S. government and major corporations like American Tobacco and General Electric, but also Sigmund Freud (Edward's uncle), Samuel Goldwyn, CLARE BOOTHE LUCE, and Henry Miller.

Fleischman proved herself early in her public relations career. In 1920, she traveled to Atlanta, Georgia, to publicize the national convention of the National Association for the Advancement of

Colored People (NAACP), the first to be held south of the Mason-Dixon Line. Oblivious to insult (white men threw pennies at her feet to imply that she was a prostitute) and the threat of violence, Fleischman persuaded the Atlanta press to cover the convention as it would any other newsworthy event. She also conceived of, edited, and published *Contact,* the firm's house publication that explained the nature and value of public relations to clients and media leaders nationwide. Edward Bernays credited Fleischman with the idea for *Contact* and noted in his autobiography how important it had been to the growth and success of the firm. Describing her as his most valuable asset, Bernays always acknowledged her equal contributions to the policies and strategies the firm devised for its clients. Nonetheless, only Bernays met with clients, while Fleischman worked behind the scenes. The rationale was that many businessmen were hesitant to deal with a woman, and both partners seemingly accepted this division of labor.

Fleischman's professional accomplishments may also have been overshadowed by her sometimes provocative private life. She and Edward had hoped to keep their marriage a secret, but when the new bride registered at the Waldorf-Astoria under her maiden name the story made the newspapers. Both husband and wife were members of the Lucy Stone League, and Doris, with Edward's encouragement, pursued her right to use her birth name after marriage. She even persuaded the Secretary of State to issue a passport in her own name, becoming in 1925 the first American married woman to travel overseas with such documentation. When her daughter Doris was born in 1929, Fleischman shocked her nurse by using her maiden name on the birth certificate. A second daughter, Anne, was born the next year.

By 1949, however, Fleischman was rethinking the meaning of these efforts. "Notes of a Retiring Feminist" appeared in the *American Mercury* with "Doris E. Fleischman (Bernays)" as its author. In what became her best-known article she addressed the "formidable confusions concerning her name" and poked fun at her early feminist belief that an independent name might safeguard an independent life. She concluded, "Miss will now endeavor to turn herself into Mrs. She will secure a new passport, a new checkbook, a new letterhead. . . . [But] there will be no change in the inner life or external motions of an ex-miss" (p. 168).

The interplay between Doris Fleischman Bernays's private life and her career illuminates the innocence, compromises, and transformations of feminism during the first half of the twentieth century. In her 1928 edited book, *An Outline of Careers for Women: A Practical Guide to Achievement,* Doris Fleischman was optimistic, emphasizing the opportunities and choices available to young women in business and the professions. In 1955 *A Wife Is Many Women* picked up where this earlier book left off, examining the implications of these new opportunities and describing the work involved in managing career and family. Drawing on her own experiences, she playfully recounted the difficulties of juggling home and work and considered the choices she had made—from going in to work late so that she could arrange the flowers at home to deciding to forego meeting with clients. Referring to this second choice, she wrote, "Have I been a coward to withdraw from such active company? Perhaps I have. But if I were to start in as [a] public relations woman today, I think I would have less opportunity to share counsel table than when I began this work in the early twenties" (p. 171).

As a mature feminist, Bernays seemed to have rejected boldness for its own stake and emphasized instead the everyday give-and-take of career, marriage, and running a household. This insight may ultimately explain why her husband's career overshadowed her own. Although her autobiography credits Edward with inventing the name "public relations counsel," his memoir claims that he and Doris coined the phrase together. What at first appears a slight discrepancy or a failure of memory may instead be a rare glimpse inside a feminist marriage at mid-century.

In 1961, the couple relocated to Cambridge, Massachusetts, to be near their daughters. Retirement did not suit either of them, and they kept up their public relations work from home. Doris Fleischman Bernays continued to work and remain active in feminist causes until her death in Cambridge in 1980 at the age of eighty-seven.

Bibliography: The Doris Fleischman Bernays Papers are housed at the Schlesinger Library, Radcliffe Institute for Advanced Study, Harvard University. Additional material can be found in the Edward L. Bernays Papers at the Library of Congress. See also Edward Bernays, *Biography of an Idea: Memoirs of Public Relations Counsel Edward L. Bernays* (1965). For another view of life within the Bernays family, see Anne Bernays and Justin Kaplan, *Back Then: Two Lives in 1950's New York* (2002). Doris E. Fleischman (Bernays), "Notes of a Retiring Feminist" appeared in *American Mercury* 68 (February 1949), pp. 161–68. For references to her many other newspaper and magazine articles, consult Keith A. Larson, *Public Relations: The Edward L. Bernayses and the American Scene; A Bibliography* (1978). See also two articles by Susan Henry: "Anonymous in Her Own Name: Public Relations Pioneer Doris E. Fleischman," *Journalism History* 23, no. 2 (Summer 1997), pp. 50–62; and "Dissonant Notes of a Retiring Feminist: Doris E. Fleischman's Later Years," *Journal of Public Relations Research* 10, no. 1 (Winter 1998), pp. 1–33. Obituaries appeared in the *New York Times* and *Boston Globe* on July 12, 1980.

AMY G. RICHTER

BEYER, Clara Mortenson. April 13, 1892–Sept. 25, 1990. Labor law specialist, federal official.

Clara Mortenson Beyer, who worked on labor legislation for more than half a century, was born in Middletown, California, to Danish immigrants Mary Frederickson, a farm wife, and Morten Mortenson, a carpenter and unsuccessful chicken farmer. The sixth of nine children, she was fifteen when her father was killed in a freak trolley accident. She took a number of jobs, including fruit picking and domestic work, to put herself through high school and the University of California at Berkeley, where she earned a BA in 1915 and an MA in economics in 1916. These jobs gave her a lifelong interest in working conditions.

After Berkeley, where she had studied new theories of labor economics, she took a job teaching at Bryn Mawr College's new labor school. Impressed by the young instructor when he lectured on campus, Felix Frankfurter, head of the War Labor Policies Board, recruited Clara Mortenson to study wages, hours, working conditions, and compensation. With no regrets, she abandoned her academic career for the opportunity to influence public policy. In Washington, D.C., she became friends with Supreme Court Justice Louis Brandeis and his daughter, Elizabeth, with whom she worked after the war. As secretary of the District of Columbia's Minimum Wage Board, Mortenson conducted cost-of-living studies and argued successfully with employers for raising women's minimum wage to one of the highest minimums in the country. In 1923, the U.S. Supreme Court ruled that minimum wage laws for women were unconstitutional.

In 1920 she married Otto Beyer, an engineer who became an expert in labor-management relations. He was supportive of her career, and they often worked closely together. Their son Morten was born in 1921, followed by Donald in 1924 and Richard in 1925. While her children were small, Beyer held a number of part-time jobs, including executive secretary of the Women's Joint Committee for the Minimum Wage and Hour Legislation, researcher for the American Federation of Labor, and executive secretary of the New York Consumers' League, where she worked with FRANCES PERKINS and MARY (MOLLY) DEWSON. In 1928 she returned to the Labor Department to work in the Children's Bureau, serving from 1931 to 1934 as director of its Industrial Division. In 1933 she and Dewson successfully lobbied President Franklin D. Roosevelt to appoint Perkins secretary of labor, making her the first woman in a U.S. president's cabinet.

Beginning in 1934, Beyer worked closely with Perkins, serving as associate director of the new Bureau of Labor Standards (BLS). Beyer was eager for the chance to build an organization from the beginning. Perkins did not feel she could name another woman to head an important Labor Department division, but Beyer was content with the considerable power and prestige she had as associate director under Verne Zimmer. In the Labor Department, Beyer focused on apprenticeships, vocational education, liaison with state governments, programs for elderly and migrant laborers, occupational accident and disease controls, and industrial home work abuses. She also worked closely with Perkins and Arthur Altmeyer to develop the provisions that went into the Social Security Act of 1935.

Beyer's principal legislative accomplishment was her role in the Fair Labor Standards Act of 1938, which set minimum wage and maximum hour standards nationwide. Her bureau helped Ben Cohen and Thomas Corcoran draft the legislation. She met considerable resistance from organized labor, who felt that a minimum wage would depress wages overall, so she and Congresswoman MARY T. NORTON (D-NJ) lobbied William Green, president of the American Federation of Labor, whose support was crucial to getting the law passed. Beyer also helped prepare the government's successful defense of the law when it was challenged and appealed to the Supreme Court.

Beginning in the 1920s, Beyer had worked to abolish child labor as secretary to an umbrella organization promoting ratification of the Child Labor Amendment. When that failed, she sought to outlaw child labor through the National Industrial Recovery Act (1933), only to see that law struck down. In 1938, an anti-child-labor provision was finally included in the Fair Labor Standards Act. During World War II, Beyer, through her good relationship with state governors, negotiated agreements to set aside state laws limiting hours for the duration of the war. Later, she helped tighten regulations to curb abuses of veterans' education funds.

Although Frances Perkins left Labor in 1945, Beyer continued to work at the BLS until 1958. During her last year, she served as acting director. She earned a reputation as a tireless and creative administrator who was frank but not always diplomatic. On her retirement from the Department of Labor, she joined the International Cooperation Administration, later the U.S. Agency for International Development (USAID). She visited thirty-two countries, mostly developing nations, to study labor conditions and advise on policies before retiring in 1972.

In 1925, Otto and Clara Beyer had purchased "Spring Hill," a 100-acre farm in McLean, Virginia, where they raised their children and entertained friends from the capital. Otto died in 1948.

In the 1960s, Beyer helped found an organization to improve race relations in her community, serving as its first president. She especially worked to secure voting rights for African Americans, whose attempts to register to vote were often frustrated by poll taxes and other impediments.

Even after her second retirement, Beyer continued to work for USAID as a consultant. In 1973, concerned that women's issues were virtually ignored in foreign aid programs, she lobbied to include a mandatory provision, sponsored by Senator Charles Percy (R-IL), for programs to benefit women in the Foreign Assistance Act. Her part in securing the Percy Amendment, like much of her work in the BLS, never received the recognition it deserved. She claimed this did not matter to her, "because I got the work done" (Murray, p. 230).

Clara Beyer was part of what syndicated columnist Drew Pearson called a "Ladies Brain Trust" in the New Deal that included Beyer, Frances Perkins, Molly Dewson, Mary Norton, and of course ELEANOR ROOSEVELT. These women made substantive contributions to the New Deal, but they worked, Beyer said, not for self-advancement but out of social consciousness. Clara Beyer lived to be ninety-eight. She died in 1990 at her home in Washington of acute cardiac arrhythmia, and was buried in Arlington National Cemetery beside her husband.

Bibliography: The principal manuscript collection is the Clara Mortenson Beyer Collection at the Schlesinger Library, Radcliffe Institute for Advanced Study, Harvard University, which includes correspondence from 1911 to 1974. Also at Schlesinger is a 1983 interview with Beyer. Beyer correspondence can also be found in the Mary (Molly) Dewson collection at Schlesinger, and in the Paul A. and Elizabeth Brandeis Raushenbush Papers at the State Historical Society of Wisconsin Archives in Madison. Records of her work for the various agencies can be found in the National Archives, Washington, D.C. At the U.S. Department of Labor, Beyer authored two books: *A History of Labor Legislation for Women in Three States* (1929) and *Children of Working Mothers in Philadelphia: Part 1, Working Mothers* (1931). A chapter on Beyer, "The Work Got Done: An Interview with Clara Mortenson Beyer," appears in Meg McGavran Murray, ed., *Face to Face: Fathers, Mothers, Masters, Monsters; Essays for a Nonsexist Future* (1983). For a longer profile, see Sue Blumenthal, *Clara Mortenson Beyer: A Life of Clear Direction* (privately printed, 1990). Descriptions of Beyer's role in the New Deal can be found in Susan Ware, *Beyond Suffrage: Women in the New Deal* (1981); and Vivien Hart, "Feminism and Bureaucracy: The Minimum Wage Experiment in the District of Columbia," *Journal of American Studies* 26, no. 1 (April 1992), pp. 1–22. Her community work in McLean is described in Mary S. Gardiner with Clara M. Beyer, Victor Dunbar, and Agnes Sollenberger, *Neighbors for a Better Community: Its History, Aims, and Achievements* (privately printed, 1980). Obituaries appeared in the *Washington Post* on September 27, 1990, and the *New York Times* on September 28, 1990.

KRISTIE MILLER

BIEBER, Margarete. July 31, 1879–February 25, 1978. Archaeologist, art historian.

A respected leader in the field of ancient Greek and Roman art and archaeology, Margarete Bieber was born in Schoenau, Germany (now Przechowo, Poland), the second of four children (three girls and a boy) of Jacob Bieber, a Jewish mill owner, and Valli Bukofzer. At first cared for by a governess, she later studied in Dresden at a boarding school for young ladies. Her desire to study medicine was discouraged by her family, but she was allowed to pursue further studies intending to become a teacher. She then turned to the study of antiquity.

The achievement of higher education and the attainment of academic renown was difficult for a woman and relatively rare when Bieber was young, but her perseverance and dedication made her success possible. At a time when scholarship of Greek and Roman art was rapidly developing, she played a prominent role in the field of study and demonstrated how women could become scholars and academic professionals.

Bieber studied ancient history, philosophy, and philology at Berlin University from 1901 to 1904 and received her PhD in 1907 from the University of Bonn. Her dissertation examined the history of tragic costume in Greek art. In 1910 she served as an assistant in archaeology at the German Archaeological Institute in Athens, and her early travels took her to classical sites in Italy and Turkey as well as to London and Paris. In the same decade she became an assistant at the Cassel Museum, where she published a catalogue of the museum's ancient sculpture collections, and in 1915–16 she assisted at the Berlin Archaeological Institute. In Berlin her students included Erwin Panofsky, who later became a noted art historian. In 1919 she completed a qualifying essay on ancient theater and became a lecturer at Justus Liebig University, Giessen. At that time she was the only woman on the faculty. By the early 1930s she had been promoted to the rank of professor and head of the department of archaeology.

Bieber never married, but in 1933 when she was in her early fifties she adopted a six-year-old girl, Ingebord. In that same year she was dismissed from the university because of her Jewish descent. She and Ingebord left Germany for England, and she became an Honorary Fellow at Somerville College at Oxford during 1933–34. She came to the United States at the invitation of Barnard College and by 1936 had become a visiting professor at Columbia University. In 1937 she was named associate professor of fine arts and archaeology. After her reluctant retirement from Columbia in 1948, she lectured at the School of General Studies at Columbia and at Princeton University. She continued to work informally with graduate students for the rest of her life.

In 1940 Bieber became a U.S. citizen. It has been said that she stood between two worlds in both her personal life and her professional life. Grateful for the opportunities her American academic career offered her, she was sympathetic to the suffering of friends and family in Europe during the war and involved in the German refugee effort. Because she bridged the two cultures, she could provide much needed communication between German and American scholarship. To help her English-speaking students read important German scholarship on ancient art, she wrote *German Readings: A Short Survey of Greek and Roman Art for Students of German and Fine Arts,* first published in 1946 and reissued in 1950 and 1958.

The subjects of her books reveal both her broad scholarly interests and her dedication to students and the general public. *The History of the Greek and Roman Theater* (1939; 2nd ed. 1961) presents a synthetic history of the theater in the ancient world, drawing on literary, architectural, and figurative sources. The photography for this work was supported by a fellowship from the American Association of University Women. *Laocoon: The Influence of the Group since Its Rediscovery* (1942) illustrates what she called the "need for small books to illustrate single important works of art with pictures and discussions from all possible angles, in order to introduce students and laymen to the spirit of special periods of art and to lead them to historical knowledge as well as to art appreciation" (p. 5). After Bieber's retirement from Columbia, the Bollingen Foundation provided support that allowed her to write *The Sculpture of the Hellenistic Age* (1955; rev. ed., 1961). Her next book, *Alexander the Great in Greek and Roman Art* (1964), is a chronological study of representations of Alexander that illustrate varied conceptions of him from the time of his youth to late antiquity.

Her final book, *Ancient Copies: Contributions to the History of Greek and Roman Art,* published in 1977 when Bieber was ninety-six years old, is a major contribution on a broad and complex subject. In this book she returned to her earlier interest in Greek dress as she confronted the issue of how Roman copies reflect and transform earlier, and usually lost, Greek works. She had begun work on this manuscript in Germany prior to her enforced emigration, but when the colleague who was providing the illustrations committed suicide because of Nazi persecution, she abandoned the project. Only when she was settled in America, aided by grants from the American Philosophical Society that enabled her to do research in Italy, did she return to this study.

A compilation of Bieber's impressive list of more than three hundred publications was published in 1969 and presented to her in honor of her ninetieth birthday. In 1971 Bieber was named to the American Academy of Arts and Sciences. In 1974 she received the Gold Medal Award for Distinguished Archaeological Achievement from the Archaeological Institute of America. Bieber was unable to attend the ceremony because of her frail physical condition, but her presence was felt through slides and a recorded acceptance speech. A remark she made to a reporter earlier in her nineties captures her indomitable spirit: "I am to archaeologists what the Statue of Liberty is to tourists. They keep coming to see if the old lady is still around. And working." She died in New Canaan, Connecticut, at the age of ninety-eight.

Bibliography: An archive of Bieber's papers from the period 1907 to 1974 is housed at Special Collections, Howard-Tilton Memorial Library, Tulane University, New Orleans. The collection includes notes, publications, student records, poetry, and other writings, as well as personal letters and correspondence to and from scholars in art history, archaeology, and classics. It also includes correspondence from Germany describing Berlin after the war and informing her of the fates of German scholars. For Bieber's extensive publications, see Larissa Bonfante Warren and Rolf Winkes, eds., *Bibliography of the Works of Margarete Bieber, for her 90th Birthday, July 31, 1969* (1969). For biographical information, see Bonfante's chapter on Bieber in Claire Richter Sherman, ed., *Women as Interpreters of the Visual Arts, 1820–1970* (1981), which draws on an unpublished memoir Bieber wrote when she turned eighty. Also of interest is Rita Reif, "At 91, a Historian Relates the Story of Her Own Life," *New York Times,* May 22, 1971, which contains the final quotation. Obituaries appeared in the *New York Times* on February 28, 1978, and the *New Canaan Advertiser* on March 3, 1978. See also the tribute by Evelyn Harrison in the *American Journal of Archaeology* 82, no. 4 (Autumn 1978), pp. 573–75.

ANN THOMAS WILKINS

BINGHAM, Mary Clifford Caperton. December 24, 1904–April 18, 1995. Newspaper publisher, philanthropist.

Mary Bingham was the matriarch of the most powerful newspaper family in Kentucky for more than a half century. She revered the power of the word, and her greatest legacies are the cultural programs and library innovations she brought to the state.

Mary Clifford Caperton was the fifth child of

Helena Lefroy, a homemaker and writer, and Clifford Caperton, a telegraph operator and later an advertising agency representative. Along with five sisters and a brother, she grew up in a genteelly poor household in Richmond, Virginia. The book-loving Mary won a prize for Latin at Miss Virginia Randolph Ellett's School for Girls, followed by a scholarship to study classics at Radcliffe College. She bested students there and at Harvard to become the first woman to win the Charles Eliot Norton Fellowship, which enabled her to study for a year at the American School of Classical Studies at Athens after she graduated in 1928. After returning to the states, she worked as an editorial assistant at Little, Brown publishers in Boston. In 1931, she married Harvard graduate George Barry Bingham Sr., whom she had met when they auditioned for a student play. The couple returned to Louisville, where Barry worked for the *Louisville Courier-Journal* and *Louisville Times,* newspapers his father Robert Worth Bingham had bought in 1918.

Barry soon took the helm of the media companies, including a large printing house and radio station WHAS, while Mary stayed home to tend Robert Worth Bingham III, who was born in 1932, followed by George (1933), Sarah (1938), Jonathan (1942), and Eleanor (1946). A sixth child was stillborn. Mary managed family life with the help of five servants at Melcombe, the family's massive red-brick Georgian mansion overlooking the Ohio River. Her role changed during World War II when her husband served overseas in the navy. Several times a week during Barry's four-year absence, Mary took a bus downtown to write editorials. Both Binghams were strong Democrats, and when the solid New Dealer questioned one of Franklin Roosevelt's policies, the president called her to the White House to confer. After Barry returned, Mary retired to Melcombe, although she edited the Sunday book page into the 1960s. She also served as a vice president and director of the companies from 1942 to 1985.

Mary Bingham influenced all aspects of newspaper policy enacted by her high-profile husband. The Binghams had an unusually close marriage: one observer said the couple seemed more welded than wedded. They read and discussed the newspapers daily over breakfast in their bedroom and forged policy on long walks in the country. Having defied convention ever since she opted for a college diploma instead of a society debut, Mary provided Barry with the backbone to chart the newspaper's progressive editorial policies. The Bingham newspapers won eight Pulitzer Prizes and shepherded the South's first integrated city schools. They earned a national reputation for integrity and leadership in the civil rights movement, including support for court-ordered busing in the 1970s. Mary pushed the papers' successful campaign for laws forcing strip miners to restore the land they mined. In 1967, the Binghams hired the nation's first ombudsman to handle reader concerns and later instituted one of the nation's strictest conflict-of-interest policies.

Many hostile Kentuckians reviled the Binghams as members of a liberal elite, or even communists, but Mary Bingham's steely resolve and conservative Episcopalian faith helped her shrug off such criticism as an inevitable byproduct of upholding the venerable newspaper mission to enlighten readership, even after circulation began to plummet in the 1970s. After her husband retired to the chairman's office, she continued to influence the newspapers' editorial direction via sheaves of memos to her son Barry Jr. and others. Usually witty, sometimes acid, and always incisive, the memos also offered nuts-and-bolts advice on story placement, wording of columns, and staff hires.

As a philanthropist, Bingham focused on improving Louisville's cultural and intellectual climate. She was instrumental in introducing bookmobiles to the state's rural poor and crusaded nationally to improve education. She and Barry campaigned to resurrect downtown Louisville as a cultural oasis, raising funds to build the cavernous Kentucky Center for the Arts with its own orchestra, ballet, and opera companies. They also contributed generously to the renowned Actors Theatre of Louisville, most notably toward its showcase Bingham Theatre.

A pencil-thin, blue-eyed blonde, Bingham's patrician looks, Old World manners, and blistering candor often masked her infectious laugh and gleeful sense of irony. Intimates relished her skills as both a rapt listener and a rollicking raconteur unafraid to mock herself in her aristocratic Tidewater accent. One of Bingham's nine grandchildren pinpointed ethics and quality rather than wealth as her grandparents' defining characteristics. In her seventies, Bingham still savored slipping off to an island near their Cape Cod summer home to skinny dip with her husband. She epitomized a pre-feminist generation of women whose sizable influence remained hidden behind their husbands' public personas. Although her daughter Sallie found her mother's backstage role wanting, *Washington Post* publisher Katharine Graham said Mary Bingham was an inspiration to all women.

The Binghams' power and privilege were offset by personal tragedy. Their youngest son Jonathan died at twenty-two when he accidentally electrocuted himself at Melcombe in 1964. Two years later, Robert Worth, heir to the publisher's office, died in another freak accident. Relationships with their remaining children occasionally were strained, which biographers (including Sallie) blame on Mary and Barry's rigid standards and emotional distance from them during childhood, an ironic contrast to the couple's emotional intimacy. When Barry Jr., Sallie, and Eleanor fought over how to divide the media empire, their parents chose to sell it all. Gannett Co. bought the newspapers for more than $300 million in 1986, and the other businesses fetched around $133 million. Widowed in 1988, Bingham took over administration of the Mary and Barry Bingham Sr. Fund, which distributed more than $59 million before she died in 1995.

Mary Bingham was ninety when, during an address before a Louisville Rotary International dinner in her honor, she collapsed of a heart attack and died. Fittingly, her last public words called for more responsible journalism and for money to bring the Louisville library into the computer age.

Bibliography: Manuscript material, including photographs, is found in the Mary Caperton Bingham and Barry Bingham Papers at the Schlesinger Library, Radcliffe Institute for Advanced Study, Harvard University. See also the files of the *Louisville Courier-Journal* library. Books surveying the Bingham media dynasty include Marie Brenner, *House of Dreams: The Bingham Family of Louisville* (1988); David Leon Chandler, *The Binghams of Louisville: The Dark History behind One of America's Great Fortunes* (1987); and Susan E. Tifft and Alex S. Jones, *The Patriarch: The Rise and Fall of the Bingham Dynasty* (1991). A more personal view of the Bingham family and Mary's role in it is found in Sallie Bingham, *Passion and Prejudice: A Family Memoir* (1989). Obituaries appeared in the *Louisville Courier-Journal* on April 19, 1995, and the *New York Times* on April 20, 1995. See also various tributes in the *Courier-Journal,* including Katharine Graham, "A Woman of Consequence," April 21, 1995.

LINDA J. LUMSDEN

BIRD, Rose Elizabeth. November 2, 1936–December 4, 1999. Lawyer, Chief Justice of the Supreme Court of California.

Rose Elizabeth Bird was born outside Tucson, Arizona. She was the third child and first daughter born into a family, which, like so many families during the Great Depression, had fallen on hard times. Her father, Harry O. Bird, a bankrupt hat supplies salesman, and her mother, Anne, a former schoolteacher, were running a chicken farm when Rose was born. Bird's father left the family when she was five years old, and died soon after. Bird's mother, left with the task of raising three children on her own, took a job installing windows on transport planes at a local air force base. Sometime around 1950 she moved her family back to New York, her home state, and took a job in a plastics factory.

When Bird graduated from Sea Cliff High School in 1954, she was given a full-tuition scholarship to Long Island University. She planned on becoming a journalist and majored in English and minored in economics and history. When she graduated in 1958, she received a fellowship to attend the University of California at Berkeley, but before heading west, she spent a year working as a secretary to save money for her living expenses.

At Berkeley, still planning a career in journalism, Bird studied political science and earned a Ford Foundation grant to intern at the California state legislature in Sacramento after her first year. While she was there, she helped draft legislation to establish a statewide testing program for public schools, and this experience convinced her to become a lawyer.

She graduated near the top of her class at Boalt Hall School of Law at Berkeley in 1965, and from that moment on her career became a list of firsts. She was the first woman to clerk for the Nevada Supreme Court. In 1966 she became the first female deputy public defender in the Santa Clara County District Attorney's Office, where she gained a reputation as a talented attorney and a compassionate human being. During this time, she also taught law at Stanford University.

In 1974 she left the DA's office intending to open her own practice, but that summer she volunteered on the California gubernatorial campaign of her friend Edmund (Jerry) Brown. Once elected governor, Brown appointed Bird as secretary of agriculture and services—making her the first woman in the state of California to hold a cabinet position. She quickly made enemies in California's politically powerful agribusiness circles by securing legislation that allowed agriculture workers to use collective bargaining and banning the short-handled hoe, which had forced field workers to labor while stooped over for hours at a time.

In 1977, Governor Brown appointed Bird chief justice of the California Supreme Court. She was the first woman to serve as chief justice and the first woman to serve on that court. Her appointment was controversial from the moment it was announced. Critics cited her lack of experience on the bench, her youth (she was forty), her position as a public defender (which many claimed was proof she was "soft on crime"), as well as her gender. It was her track record of being pro-labor, however, that troubled many people in the business community.

As chief justice, Rose Bird cut back on many luxuries that other justices took for granted and sold the limousine designated for the chief justice's use; when she traveled, she chose modest accommodations. Bird also wrote her own opinions rather than leaving the task to her staff, and she often wrote concurring opinions, wanting to make sure her argument was distinguished from the court's. Even legal scholars who disagreed with her have admired the thoroughness of her opinions.

In 1978, Bird stood for retention in the state's general election—standard procedure for appointed judges in California and usually a mere formality. In Bird's case, a campaign to remove her was launched and she was confirmed by a majority of 51.7 percent, the smallest margin of victory in a retention vote in California's history.

In 1986 her opponents found a way to capture the public's attention and connect Chief Justice Bird to an issue Californians would rally against. While she served on the Supreme Court, Justice Bird had voted against every death sentence that came before the court—sixty-four in total. She had voted with the majority of the court on sixty-one of these cases, but her opponents singled out her voting record as soft on crime and out of touch with the wishes of the California citizenry.

Before 1986, it had been understood that politics would not enter judiciary elections. Conservatives in California, however, organized to make Justice Bird's retention a political issue, and Bird had to campaign for her job. She campaigned so reluctantly that a citizens' group was formed to campaign on her behalf. Bird lost the election by a 2–1 margin and left the court in January 1987.

Her life after the bench was quiet. Law firms and law schools did not make offers. After a short lecture tour with Robert Bork and a brief stint commentating for a local television station, she settled into a very private life. She volunteered at a community law center in Palo Alto, read to the blind, and took care of her ailing mother until her mother's death in 1991. Bird never married.

Bird was first diagnosed with breast cancer in 1976, and over the next four years she underwent surgery four times. She refused chemotherapy and radiation and treated herself with a strict vegetarian diet, exercise, and large doses of vitamin C. In November 1996 she had a radical mastectomy on her other breast. But the cancer came back, and she died at Stanford University Hospital on December 4, 1999, at the age of sixty-three.

In the last speech she gave as chief justice, Bird said, "Our humanity informs us and instructs us in what it is to live lives of decency and dignity. As lawyers and judges, we bring unique perspective to our humanity that, if used wisely and well, can enhance the quality of justice in our society" (*In Memoriam,* p. 1316). Just as it is clear that Rose Bird's career broke new ground for women in law, it is also clear that Bird dedicated her life to enhancing the quality of justice for all Americans.

Bibliography: For an overview of Rose Elizabeth Bird's life and legal career, see Peggy Lamson, *In the Vanguard: Six American Women in Public Life* (1979). Betty Medsger, *Framed: The New Right Attack on Chief Justice Rose Bird and the Courts* (1983), responds to some of the irresponsible press coverage of Bird and the investigation of the Supreme Court that this coverage led to during Bird's tenure there. The *Los Angeles Times Sunday Magazine* published a profile of Bird by Frank Clifford on October 5, 1986. The campaign to unseat her was covered extensively by many newspapers, including the *Los Angeles Times, San Francisco Chronicle,* and *New York Times.* A transcript of the memorial service held at the California Supreme Court, titled "In Memoriam: Chief Justice Rose Elizabeth Bird (1936–1999), was published in 22 *Official California Reports* 4th, 1275–79 (2000). Obituaries appeared in the *New York Times, Washington Post,* and *Los Angeles Times,* all on December 6, 1999.

MARY MALINDA POLK

BISHOP, Elizabeth. February 8, 1911–October 6, 1979. Poet.

Elizabeth Bishop was born in Worcester, Massachusetts, an only child in a wealthy family. Her father, William T. Bishop, was the oldest son and heir to John W. Bishop, owner of a prominent contracting firm and builders of such Boston landmarks as the Boston Public Library and the Museum of Fine Arts. Her mother, Gertrude May Boomer (sometimes spelled "Bulmer"), came from a relatively poor family in rural Nova Scotia. Eight months after Elizabeth's birth, the death of her father from Bright's disease shattered the family. Gertrude Bishop felt deeply disoriented by her husband's death and spent the next five years in and out of mental institutions. Her daughter endured the absences and general unreliability of her mother until, in 1916, Gertrude was permanently institutionalized. She lived for eighteen more years, and her daughter never saw her again.

Little Elizabeth immediately managed, with the uncanny resourcefulness of a child, to construct for herself a secure and apparently timeless world in the home of her maternal grandparents in Canada. But her father's family, worried that their grandchild would miss out on important opportunities, uprooted her a year later and she began what would be a lifetime of living as a guest in other people's homes. Her stay with the Bishop grandparents was miserable. There in the Worcester mansion, among her grown aunts and uncles and the Swedish-speaking household staff, she developed a debilitating depression that she would never really overcome, as well as chronic, severe asthma and eczema.

After nine excruciating months, the Bishops abandoned this experiment and arranged for Elizabeth to live with her mother's sister, Maud, near Boston, and to reacquaint herself with her Canadian roots and grandparents by spending summers in Nova Scotia. Because of her illnesses, she had little formal schooling until 1925, and in 1927 she was sent by the Bishop family to the Walnut Hill School for Girls in Natick, Massachusetts. In 1930, she enrolled at Vassar College, where her fellow students included MARY MCCARTHY, Eleanor Clark, and MURIEL RUKEYSER. Bishop was a small woman, with a round face and wiry brown hair. In college she came to see herself as a writer among gifted women writers, and received a first-rate education in English literature and classics. She also began to drink, first moderately under the fashionable impetus of Prohibition, and then heavily and secretively. Alarmingly for her, she also fell deeply in love with her college roommate and had to confront the idea that she would not have a "normal" life as she was raised to imagine one. She graduated in 1934. For the remaining decades of her life, she would suffer from depression, asthma, and alcoholism, she would wander the world in search of a home, the passion in her life would be for women, and she would feel debilitating shame about all of these things. And she would be a poet.

Bishop began publishing short stories and poems in school literary magazines from the start of her formal education. In college, she co-founded an underground literary magazine, *Con Spirito*, and was well known as a poet and short story writer. Several of her poems appeared in national publications. Her early work was highly accomplished and mannered, influenced by baroque prose writers, seventeenth-century English poets, and Gerard Manley Hopkins. In the spring of her senior year, she was introduced to the poet MARIANNE MOORE, whose work she admired. This relationship effectively launched Bishop's career as a poet, as she found in Moore a model for how to conduct that career and discovered a range of subject matter beyond romantic love and picturesque nature. In 1935, she published her first characteristic poem, "The Map," in an anthology called *Trial Balances*, which Moore had recommended. (The poem was one of several of Bishop's to be included in the volume.) Although she struggled in the years before it was published, her first book, *North & South*, was warmly received when it appeared in 1946, and the literary world took notice. One of the reviewers of *North & South*, young poet Robert Lowell, became Bishop's closest literary friend and the most important influence on her mature work.

Despite the success of her book, Bishop continued to struggle with depression and alcoholism, until, desperate, she left the States in November 1951 for a trip around the world. Her first port of call was Brazil, where she remained for the next fifteen years. She fell in love with a Brazilian, Lota de Macedo Soares, and together they made a home such as Bishop had literally never known. She drank less, wrote more, and relaxed in the relatively open and easy Brazilian social world. The body of work Bishop produced while she flourished in Brazil—the volumes *Poems: North & South: A Cold Spring* (1955), *Questions of Travel* (1965), and the *Complete Poems* (1969)—would earn her glowing reviews and nearly all of the honors and prizes available to American poets, including the Pulitzer Prize (1956), the National Book Award (1970), and the Books Abroad/Neustadt International Prize for Literature (1976). She also did important translations of Brazilian writers and co-edited a collection of their work.

In 1967, after several years of ill health, Soares, then fifty-seven, suffered a breakdown; on the advice of her doctors, Bishop left Brazil for New York. Two months later Soares followed her to New York and died, an apparent suicide, on the night she arrived. Bishop was once again cast out. After three difficult years, she managed, with Lowell's help, to secure a teaching position at Harvard University. She spent the last years of her life teaching, living in Boston under the loving care of her friend Alice Methfessel, spending summers at North Haven, Maine, and writing what most critics consider her finest work. The short volume *Geography III* (1976) collects poems she had been considering for many years (the great poem "The Moose," for example, had been with her since 1946), as well as poems it is difficult to imagine the modern American canon without: "In the Waiting Room," "Crusoe in England," "One Art." She died in Boston of a ruptured cerebral aneurysm at the age of sixty-eight, and was buried in the Bishop family plot in Worcester.

Bibliography: Elizabeth Bishop's papers, which include many photographs of the poet, are in the Vassar College Library Special Collections, Poughkeepsie, New York. There are also important collections of her letters to Marianne Moore at the Rosenbach Museum and Library in Philadelphia and to Robert Lowell at Houghton Library, Harvard University. In addition to the books mentioned in the text, collections of her published work include *The Complete Poems 1927–1979* (1983) and *The Collected Prose* (1984). A selection of her letters was published under the title *One Art: Letters*, selected and edited by Robert Giroux, in 1994.

Important critical and biographical studies of the poet include Bonnie Costello, *Elizabeth Bishop: Questions of Mastery* (1991); Gary Fountain and Peter Brazeau, *Remembering Elizabeth Bishop* (1994); Lorrie Goldensohn, *Elizabeth Bishop: The Biography of a Poetry* (1992); Victoria Harrison, *Elizabeth Bishop's Poetics of Intimacy* (1993); David Kalstone, *Becoming a Poet* (1989); Marilyn May Lombardi, ed., *Elizabeth Bishop: The Geography of Gender* (1993); Brett Millier, *Elizabeth Bishop: Life and the Memory of It* (1993); Adrienne Rich, "The Eye of the Outsider: The Poetry of Elizabeth Bishop," *Boston Review*, April, 1983, pp. 15–17; Lloyd Schwartz and Sybil Estess, eds., *Elizabeth Bishop and Her Art* (1983); Anne Stevenson, *Elizabeth Bishop* (1966); and Thomas Travisano, *Elizabeth Bishop: Her Artistic Development* (1988). See also Candace W. MacMahon, *Elizabeth Bishop: A Bibliography, 1927–1979* (1980). An obituary appeared in the *New York Times* on October 8, 1979.

BRETT C. MILLIER

BISHOP, Hazel Gladys. August 17, 1906–December 5, 1998. Cosmetic chemist, entrepreneur.

Hazel Gladys Bishop was born in Hoboken, New Jersey, the second of two children of Mabel Billington and Henry Bishop. Her father owned a number of business ventures that were managed by her mother, and conversation at home often revolved around what made a business successful. "Open your own business," advised her mother, "even if it's a peanut stand" (Drachman, p. 92). After attending Bergen School for Girls in Jersey City, Hazel Bishop enrolled at Barnard College, graduating with a BA in chemistry in 1929. When the Depression ended her hopes of a medical career, she went to work first as a chemical technician and then from 1935 to 1942 as a research assistant in a dermatology laboratory at Columbia Medical Center. Her two inventions in the 1930s, mentholated tissues and a pimple stick disguiser, were not marketed. The war opened up more varied employment opportunities for women, and Bishop took a position first at Standard Oil, where she worked on the development of aviation fuel for jet engines from 1942 to 1945, and subsequently at Socony Vacuum Oil Company (1945–50).

A chance meeting with a lawyer hoping to market a French "Rouge Baiser" (kissable lipstick) encouraged her to experiment in her own kitchen with a lipstick that would not rub off or leave a stain. After two years and more than three hundred experiments, she developed the first lipstick that was smear-proof and long lasting. "Stays on you, not on him" was the advertisement developed by the Hecht Company. Not for her the exotic names of rival companies—Bishop's shades made up by the Kolmar Company to her recipe were called simply pink, red, or dark red.

In 1950 she founded and became president of Hazel Bishop Inc. This was a propitious time to launch a new cosmetic. By 1948 an estimated 80 to 90 percent of women wore lipstick. Rivals ELIZABETH ARDEN and HELENA RUBINSTEIN employed their own sales forces to market an array of products through their own salons or in department stores. Bishop's business strategy, in contrast, was based on advertising a limited product line, direct sales, and mass drugstore distribution.

Because Bishop was short of capital, she had no choice but to offer a partnership to a businessman in return for equity in the company. She made a deal with an advertising agent, Raymond Spector, who began an aggressive advertising campaign, adding a hot embrace to the advertisements to show that the lipstick was truly "kissable." Within the first three months of 1950, Hazel Bishop Inc. had made cosmetics history with sales of $50,000. By 1953 sales topped $10 million and the company had captured 25 percent of the lipstick market.

Hazel Bishop had launched an exciting new product, overcome her lack of capital, and adopted a successful marketing strategy. But her meteoric success did not last long. While Bishop took charge of marketing, her partner Spector bought out the other stockholders and recapitalized the company so that her shares dwindled to only 8 percent of the stock. A policy disagreement gave Spector the chance to fire Bishop. Two years of litigation left her, in 1954, with a small settlement that barely covered her legal costs. She lost her company and her income, and she had to agree to the loss of her name and to stay out of the cosmetics industry in the future.

Nevertheless, Bishop went on to found three more companies and to invent a glove cleaner (Leather Lav), a foot spray, and a perfume stick (Perfemme). In 1961 she embarked on a second career as a stockbroker in the field of health and cosmetics. As an analyst of the cosmetics industry at Bache Company (1962–68) and then Evans & Company (1968–81), she had a rare perspective on everything from product development to management, marketing, and sales.

Bishop had an abiding interest in chemistry. In an interview in 1963 she said, "I'm still essentially a chemist and I expect I shall always be one. It lets you deal with the facts" (*Petroleum Today,* Spring 1963, p. 12). In 1954, she was elected a fellow of the American Institute of Chemists and a member of the New York Academy of Sciences. For ten years she was active on the lecture circuit, speaking about the chemistry of cosmetics to the American Chemical Society, business groups, and chemistry students. In 1976, she was honored by the New York chapter of the American Institute of Chemists and in 1981 was named Cosmetic Executive Woman of the Year.

In 1978, Hazel Bishop embarked on her third and last career at the Fashion Institute of Technology (FIT) in New York City. She was excited about being an entrepreneur again, this time producing new talent for leadership in the cosmetics industry. Of all her careers, she said, she relished her last the most. She taught case studies from concept to product launch, distribution, and retail, out of her own experience. In 1980 she was appointed the first holder of the Revlon Chair in Cosmetics Marketing at FIT. Charles Revlon, her former competitor, publicly acknowledged her accomplishments in business, in finance, and in academia.

Bishop, who never married and lived with her mother until her death in 1954, entered a retirement community in 1990 in Rye, New York, and died there eight years later at the age of ninety-two. In a 1982 oral history interview, she described her career as "a tossed salad," but one that had changed the industry. She was, she judged, an example of how not to run a business but of how to live a life. She was an inventive, creative woman who always moved on to the next venture. "If you're willing to strive and have no fear of failure, you can never fail as long as you are on to the next step."

Bibliography: The Hazel Bishop papers in the Schlesinger Library, Radcliffe Institute for Advanced Study, Harvard University, include photographs, early examples of lipsticks, personal and business correspondence, advertisements of Hazel Bishop Inc. legal records, clippings, and teaching notes and lectures from the Fashion Institute of Technology. An unpublished oral history, "The Reminiscences of Hazel Bishop," January 1982, from which the final quotation comes, is at the Archives of the Fashion Institute of Technology, New York City. Biographical sketches are found in Virginia G. Drachman, *Enterprising Women: 250 Years of American Business* (2002), and *Current Biography* (1957), pp. 56–58. Selected news articles include the *New York Herald Tribune,* August 8, 1951, and *Business Week,* March 17, 1951, pp. 42+. An obituary appeared in the *New York Times* on December 10, 1998.

JANE S. KNOWLES

BISHOP, Isabel. March 3, 1902–February 19, 1988. Artist.

Isabel Bishop, whose images of youthful urban women earned her career-long acclaim in mainstream art circles, was born in Cincinnati, Ohio. She was the youngest child by thirteen years, preceded by two sets of twins. Her mother, Anna Newbold Bartram, was an aspiring though unpublished author and early suffragist whose inability to pursue a career strengthened her desires for her daughter's independence. Isabel's father, John Remsen Bishop, taught Greek and Latin and served as principal at the Walnut Hills High School. In 1903 he moved his family from Cincinnati to Detroit, where he took up a succession of poorly paid urban teaching posts. Isabel thus spent her childhood in a family disaffected by the loss of class status and financial security, culminating in her father's dismissal from a principal's post when she was fifteen.

With strong beliefs in the educational value of classical literature and the arts, Bishop's parents supported her interests, enrolling her in her first life-drawing class at Detroit's Wicker School of Fine Arts when she was only twelve. Isabel graduated from high school shortly after her father's job loss, and her parents encouraged her to be financially self-sufficient. Her father's wealthy cousin, James Bishop Ford, promised tuition and living expenses for Bishop to study graphic design and illustration in the practically oriented New York School of Applied Design for Women. After two years, Bishop felt restricted in all but her life-drawing classes and longed to become a painter. At age eighteen, she made her case to Ford, who generously agreed to continue her stipend for what would become a thirteen-year apprenticeship of long hours in small studio apartments alternating with classes at New York's Art Students League.

From 1920 to 1923, Bishop sampled from every available artistic style offered at the League: academic classes with Frank Vincent DuMond, late cubism with the modernist Max Weber, lectures from the urban realist Robert Henri, and summer study with the figurative realist Guy Pène du Bois. From 1927 to 1931 she settled into mural-painting classes with Kenneth Hayes Miller, her most serious mentor. Her study culminated with summer trips in 1931 and 1933 to visit museums in Paris, London, Madrid, and Munich. Accompanied by Miller on both trips, they were joined in 1933 by her other close friend and longtime Miller protégé, artist Reginald Marsh. These three artists shared both a reverence for the old masters and subject matter from the Union Square/14th Street New York neighborhood, the thriving office and retail district where all had studios. From 1926 to 1934 Bishop lived and worked at 9 West 14th Street, directly across from Hearn's Department Store. From that vantage point she painted the middle-class shoppers that were also Miller's subjects, although critics faulted her work's too-close adherence to her teacher's choice of subjects. In 1934 she moved three blocks to 857 Broadway, a studio she occupied until 1984. There she discovered the young, generally lower-middle-class office workers and students, and the intellectual and stylistic frameworks, that would guide her work for the next fifty years.

The mid-1930s studio relocation also marked both professional recognition and personal change. The Midtown Cooperative Gallery invited her to join in 1932, and in 1933 it put on her first exhibition; it would represent her work with regular solo shows for her entire life. In 1936 the Metropolitan Museum of Art, which was only beginning to acquire American art, purchased her *Two Girls;* virtually every major museum in the country would eventually own Bishop paintings or prints. In 1941 the National Academy of Design elected her full Academician. Bishop was elected to membership in the National Institute of Arts and Letters in 1944; two years later she became its first woman officer.

In 1934 Bishop met and married Harold Wolff, a successful neurologist. Having observed several marriages in which close women artist friends sacrificed their own career ambitions for their husbands, Bishop had been apprehensive about marriage. In Wolff she found much-needed financial support just as James Ford was terminating his patronage. Her husband admired and encouraged her achievements and the marriage was a union of mutual respect; their six-day-per-week work schedules and career aims meshed comfortably. When their only son, Remsen, was born in 1940, Bishop's mother-in-law helped with childcare responsibilities. Their twenty-eight-year marriage ended when Wolff died suddenly of a cerebral hemorrhage in 1962.

Quiet spoken and modest in behavior, elegant and dignified in bearing, meticulous and disciplined in artistic practice, Bishop gained respect in all camps of the art world. Her art attained a remarkable synthesis of traditional, modern, and even avant-garde pictorial modes. As with old master works, the artist adopted a muted earth-toned palette and took a humanist approach, with the figure taking on the burden of emotional and pictorial expression. But her working girls, idle men, and students were always contemporary, public, and urban. And by her late walking pictures, figures and ground had merged into colorful veiled grids emphasizing paint and surface, showing her accommodation to the concerns of advanced postwar painting. In 1975 the Whitney Museum of American Art mounted a major retrospective of her work.

Like many "new women" of her generation, Bishop negotiated the complex rhetoric of female accomplishment in art by adopting a model of professionalized self-sufficiency and seeking recognition based on individual merit. "I didn't want to be a woman artist, I just wanted to be an artist," she stated in 1982. But in supporting feminist claims to equality, she also acknowledged difference and hoped that because she spoke in her authentic voice her art would be "recognizable as being by a woman." In 1979 she received major recognition for both sides of this complex equation with her two most important honors. President Jimmy Carter presented her with the Outstanding Achievement in the Arts Award, and the Women's Caucus for Art of the College Art Association selected Bishop, along with fellow artists SELMA BURKE, GEORGIA O'KEEFFE, ALICE NEEL, and LOUISE NEVELSON, to receive the first of their lifetime achievement awards. In such distinguished company the words of art critic Emily Genauer resonated as strongly as they had when she wrote them in 1936: "Isabel Bishop, we say with vehemence and conviction, is one of the most important woman painters in America today." Bishop was able to savor these honors for almost another decade, until her death at her home in Riverdale, New York, from Parkinson's disease at the age of eighty-five.

Bibliography: A major collection of Isabel Bishop papers, including correspondence, early criticism, and exhibition catalogs from the Midtown Cooperative Gallery, can be found at the Archives of American Art, Smithsonian Institution, Washington, D.C. Bishop published two discussions of her approaches to art: "Concerning Edges," *Magazine of Art* 38 (May 1945), pp. 168–73; and "Isabel Bishop Discusses Genre Drawings," *American Artist* 17 (Summer 1953), pp. 46–47. Major works on the artist include Karl Lunde, *Isabel Bishop* (1975); University of Arizona Museum of Art, *Isabel Bishop* (first retrospective exhibition, 1974); Bruce St. John, *Isabel Bishop: The Affectionate Eye* (1985); *Isabel Bishop, Etchings and Aquatints: A Catalogue Raisonné of the Prints,* compiled and edited by Susan Pirpiris Teller (1981); Ellen Wiley Todd, *The New Woman Revised: Painting and Gender Politics on Fourteenth Street* (1993); and Helen Yglesias, *Isabel Bishop* (1989). See also Lawrence Alloway, "Isabel Bishop: The Grand Manner and the Working Girl," *Art in America* (September–October 1975), pp. 61–65; Emily Genauer, "Miss Bishop Ranks High as a Painter," *New York World-Telegram,* February 15, 1936, p. 15; and John Russell, "A Novelist's Eye in Isabel Bishop's Art," *New York Times,* April 12, 1975. The first quote on being a woman artist comes from my unpublished interview with her on December 16, 1982, and the second from interviews with Bishop by Patricia Depew for the film *Isabel Bishop: Portrait of an Artist* (1980). See also Louis M. Starr's interviews with the artist conducted in 1957 for the Oral History Research Office at Columbia University; and Cindy Nemser, "Conversation with Isabel Bishop," *Feminist Art Journal* 1 (Spring 1976), pp. 14–20. An obituary appeared in the *New York Times* on February 22, 1988.

ELLEN WILEY TODD

BLACKSTON, Johnnie Tillmon. *See* Tillmon, Johnnie.

BLAMAUER, Karoline Wilhemine Charlotte. *See* Lenya, Lotte.

BLEIER, Ruth Harriet. November 17, 1923–January 4, 1988. Neuroanatomist, physician, feminist scholar.

Ruth Bleier was a physician who practiced medicine at a time when women constituted only 6 percent of all American physicians, a noted neuroanatomist who published three major mammalian brain atlases, and a feminist scholar who used her scientific training to examine gender bias in scientific research on sex differences. She was also a mother, a musician, an athlete, and a political activist.

The only child of Hungarian-born pharmacist Abe H. Bleier and Sadie Sima Linder, the American-born daughter of Russian immigrants, Ruth grew up in New Kensington, Pennsylvania, outside Pittsburgh. After graduating from Goucher College (BA, 1945) and the Woman's Medical College of Pennsylvania (MD, 1949), Bleier trained at Sinai Hospital in Baltimore. She practiced general medicine in Baltimore, concentrating her work among those who could least afford medical care.

She was married to Leon Eisenberg, a physician and child psychiatrist, from 1949 until their divorce in 1966. They had two children: Mark Philip Eisenberg (1952) and Kathy Bleier Eisenberg (1955). Bleier was active in the civil rights movement and with the Maryland Committee for Peace; for the latter involvement she was subpoenaed to testify before the House Committee on Un-American Activities (HUAC) in 1951. She refused to cooperate with the committee's attempts to intimidate the peace movement and instead delivered a spirited defense of liberty and justice.

As a result, Bleier became a victim of McCarthyism. Denied her hospital privileges, she continued her political activity and her medical practice, ending the latter when she entered the laboratory of Jerzy Rose at Johns Hopkins University School of Medicine for postdoctoral training in neuroanatomy, which she completed in 1961. She published studies of the hypothalamus of the cat (1961), the guinea pig (1983), and the rhesus monkey (1984), which together established her as an authority on the hypothalamus. One reviewer commented that her cat study "is to the experimentalist what the Pilot's Guide to the English Channel is to the navigator—indispensable."

Following her fellowship, Bleier became a research instructor in the departments of psychiatry and physiology at the Johns Hopkins University School of Medicine. She joined the faculty at the University of Wisconsin, Madison, in 1967, in the Department of Neurophysiology, with concurrent appointments in the Waisman Center of Mental Retardation and Human Development and the Wisconsin Regional Primate Center. From 1975 until her death from cancer in Madison in 1988, she was also a faculty member of the Women's Studies Program.

At Wisconsin she continued her research on the hypothalamus and discovered unusual cells in the adjacent brain ventricles. In a series of elegant and detailed anatomical experiments, she determined that these are macrophages, or scavenger cells. She postulated that they form the first line of defense against bacteria and viruses invading the brain. A segment of her research—one that brought her to the cutting edge at the interface of feminist thought, sociobiology, and hard neuroscience—was on brain sexual dimorphism: male/female differences in brain structure. She and her colleagues elucidated the structural dimorphisms in the hypothalamic areas of rodents, and she was preparing a study of this kind in primates. Shortly before her death, she entered the debate on the presence and relevance of sex differences in the size of the human corpus callosum, the major anatomical connection between the two cerebral hemispheres, and challenged studies claiming to demonstrate such differences.

In the early 1970s, Bleier became one of the first scientists in the world to critically examine the foundations of the modern biological sciences from a feminist perspective. She demonstrated how science, gender, and sexuality, rather than being objective and value free, are constructs embedded within historical and cultural contexts, ever changing in response to social values and ideas. Her studies in this area culminated in the critically acclaimed book *Science and Gender* in 1984 and, two years later, her edited volume, *Feminist Approaches to Science*, which uncovered systematic gender biases in the structure, processes, and language of science. Her experience as a working scientist gave her an important vantage point from which she authoritatively discussed the interaction between neurological development and human experience.

During the 1970s, as her academic work proceeded, Bleier joined the women's movement's efforts to improve the lot of women in higher education. At the University of Wisconsin, she was a founder of the Association of Faculty Women (AFW), a campus group that agitated for university compliance with affirmative action requirements. The AFW won an equity salary raise for faculty women, integrated the gymnasium with a media-worthy "shower-in" at the men's locker room, and helped create the Women's Studies Program in 1975. In a time of growing lesbian separatism within feminism, Bleier, herself a lesbian, rejected that model, instead working assiduously for lesbian rights within the larger women's movement, where she served as an effective bridge between lesbians and heterosexual women. Bleier wrote that these years of political activity brought a "sense of exhilaration. . . . The experience for most of us has been like stepping on an endless escalator that goes up only—an ever-heightening sense of awareness, self identity, direction, and strength."

Bleier's political and academic interests came together in her teaching and research in the Women's Studies Program, which she chaired from 1982 through 1986. During this period, she negotiated a significant expansion of the women's studies faculty, actualizing her commitment to minority and third-world issues in the academy and expanding the science component of the women's studies curriculum. Racing through the hallways in her white lab coat or whimsically donning her famous pink flapper hat and tinkling her crystal bell to call the women's studies meetings to order, she knit a diverse group of people into a community.

Throughout her career, Bleier made a profound commitment to political and social justice. She worked for equal opportunity for all and retained enormous optimism that justice was an attainable goal. She brought her passion to the community outside the university, where she helped start Lysistrata, a feminist restaurant, organized lesbian-friendly community activities, worked for abortion rights (alongside her partner and Madison abortion-provider, Dr. Elizabeth Karlin), supported A Room of One's Own feminist bookstore, and fostered campus–community connections. Bleier was an unflagging friend to people who faced discrimination and a generous contributor to women's causes.

Bibliography: Ruth Bleier's three anatomical atlases of the mammalian brain are *The Hypothalamus of the Cat: A Cytoarchitectonic Atlas in the Horsely-Clarke Coordinate System* (1961), *The Hypothalamus of the Guinea Pig: A Cytoarchitectonic Atlas* (1983), and *The Hypothalamus of the Rhesus Monkey: A Cytoarchitectonic Atlas* (1984). Her feminist science can most easily be seen in her *Science and Gender: A Critique of Biology and Its Theories on Women* (1984) and her edited volume, *Feminist Approaches to Science* (1986). Her final overview of feminism and science can be found in Judith Walzer Leavitt and Linda Gordon, "A Decade of Feminist Critiques in the Natural Sciences: An Address by Ruth Bleier," *Signs: Journal of Women in Culture and Society* 14, no. 1 (1988), pp. 182–95. Quotations in this article are from Peter Daniel's review of her first book in the *Journal of Mental Science* 108 (May 1962), p. 378, and from Ruth Bleier, "History of the Association of Faculty Women in Madison," in *University Women: A Series of Essays*, ed. Marian J. Swoboda and Audrey J. Roberts, vol. 3 (1980), p. 19. Obituaries appeared in the *Capital Times*, January 4, 1988, and the *Wisconsin State Journal*, January 5, 1988.

JUDITH WALZER LEAVITT

BLODGETT, Katharine Burr. January 10, 1898–October 12, 1979. Physicist, physical chemist, inventor.

Katharine Burr Blodgett was born in Schenectady, New York, the second child and only daughter of Katharine Buchanan Burr and George Reddington Blodgett. Her life began amid tragedy, as her father, the chief patent attorney for General Electric, was shot by an intruder in his home just weeks before she was born. The murder was never solved. His widow sold their house and took her children to New York City, then to Europe to absorb culture and languages. Except for a winter's tutoring by her mother and one public-school year, Katharine attended the exclusive Rayson School in New York.

Entering Bryn Mawr on scholarship in 1913 at the age of fifteen, she was inspired by physics professor James Barnes to major in physics. She also excelled in math. Blodgett graduated second in her class in 1917.

Touring GE during her senior year—her tour guide was her future director and collaborator Irving Langmuir—she was urged to get further training. At the University of Chicago, Blodgett worked with Harvey Lemon on gas-adsorption to charcoal, research important for the development of gas masks. She received her master's degree in 1918. Though the Blodgett name and wartime manpower shortages doubtless helped her get hired at GE that year, Katharine Blodgett soon proved herself. Langmuir, who won the 1932 Nobel Prize in Chemistry, credited her with most of the experimental work for his important paper "The Mechanism of the Surface Phenomena of Flotation" (1920).

He also strongly encouraged her admission to Cambridge University in 1924. There she worked with Sir Ernest Rutherford at the famous Cavendish Laboratory, publishing under her own name and becoming, in 1926, the first woman PhD in physics from Cambridge. Her thesis dealt with the path of electrons in mercury vapor. Upon her return to GE, she and Langmuir worked on improving tungsten filaments for electric lamps.

Katharine Blodgett is best known for her work on thin films, specifically for inventing "invisible" (nonreflective) glass. She was the first to realize, in the early 1930s, that multiple layers of films just one molecule thick could be built up on a solid surface like glass. By controlling the number of layers, and thus the film's thickness with relation to the wavelength of visible light, one could make reflections from the top and from the bottom of the film layer cancel each other out. Thus was created the kind of glass now prevalent in eyeglasses, picture frames, shop windows, windshields, television and computer screens, cameras, and telescopes. Her initial paper on the topic appeared in the *Journal of the American Chemical Society* in 1934, and GE announced the process in 1938.

Langmuir and Blodgett are credited with starting the field of optical coatings—indeed, with revolutionizing optics—and one whole category of thin films is called Langmuir-Blodgett films. (Their research built on the work of the gifted German amateur Agnes Pockels, who discovered surface tension and invented methods and apparatus for measuring it in the 1880s.) Partly because she was the only woman researcher at GE, but mainly because of the myriad uses of her "invisible" glass, Blodgett was featured in both *Time* and *Life* in 1939. One such use of her glass was in the stunning cinematography of the wildly popular *Gone with the Wind* (1939).

Blodgett contributed to the American cause in two world wars. Besides her gas-mask research during World War I, her denser and longer-lasting smoke screens saved thousands of lives in Italy and North Africa during World War II, and her nonreflective glass was used in submarine periscopes, range finders, and aerial cameras. She also worked on de-icing airplane wings. Later she devised humidity monitors for high-altitude military weather balloons.

One of her best-known inventions, and the one that pleased her most, was an elegant and precise color gauge for measuring the thickness of monomolecular coatings on glass, patented in 1952. She also built the first controlled-thickness X-ray "grating," three thousand layers of stearic acid barium-copper stearate. In her last years at GE, Blodgett worked on electrically conductive glass and on using electrical discharges in gases to remove surface impurities, both important in fabricating semiconductors.

Though an inveterate problem solver, holding nine patents and famous for applied research, she had important basic discoveries to her credit as well. For example, her work on aircraft icing advanced the understanding of the physics of precipitation. Irving Langmuir called Blodgett "a gifted experimenter" with a "rare combination of theoretical and practical ability" (MacDonald, p. 309). Fellow of the American Physical Society and member of the Optical Society of America, she was starred (outstanding in her discipline) in *American Men of Science* in 1944 and was often called the country's foremost woman scientist. She received four honorary doctorates (1939–44), and the AAUW Annual Achievement Award in 1945. Schenectady declared a Katharine Blodgett Day in 1951, the year she became the first industrial scientist to win a Garvan Medal. In 1972 she became the first woman to win the Photographic Society of America's Progress Medal.

Never married, and obviously devoting major energy to research, Katharine Blodgett was no one-dimensional workaholic. She was involved in amateur dramatics, community service, and conservation projects. Gregarious and witty (challenged, she once found a rhyme for *polyvinyl*), she was well known around Schenectady for such kindnesses as shopping for shut-ins on Saturday mornings. She lived quietly in a small house, shared for many years with Gertrude Brown, who came from an old Schenectady family, and also for a time with Elsie Errington, English-born director of a nearby girls' school. The household arrangement freed Blodgett from most domestic responsibilities—except for making her famous applesauce and popovers.

She delighted in her summer retreat at Lake George, New York, where she kept a fast motorboat. In 1963 Blodgett retired from General Electric to enjoy interests ranging from gardening, antiques, and bridge to astronomy and the study of wild ferns. She died at home on October 12, 1979, after a long illness, the immediate cause of death being cerebral thrombosis. She was buried in Mount Auburn Cemetery in Cambridge, Massachusetts. In 1983 an entire issue of the journal *Thin Solid Films* was dedicated to her, with papers inspired by her work.

Bibliography: Katharine Blodgett left no personal papers to any archive, but her laboratory notebooks and some biographical material are found at the General Electric Research and Development Center, Schenectady, New York. For her PhD thesis, "A Determination of the Mean Free Path of Electrons in Mercury Vapor," see *Philosophical Magazine* 4 (1927), p. 164. Among her notable scientific publications are (with Langmuir) "Built-Up Films of Barium Stearate and Their Optical Properties," *Physical Review* 51, no. 11 (June 1, 1937), pp. 964–82; and "Use of Interference to Extinguish Reflection of Light from Glass," *Physical Review* 55, no. 4 (February 15, 1939), pp. 391–404. Praised for the clarity and precision of her writing, Blodgett also wrote for the nonspecialist: see "A Method of Extinguishing the Reflection of Light from Glass," *Science* 89 (1939); and "A Gauge That Measures Millionths of an Inch," in Neil B. Reynolds and Ellis L. Manning, eds., *Excursions in Science* (1939).

Books containing chapters or sections on Blodgett include Edna Yost, *American Women of Science* (1943); Alice Goff, *Women Can Be Engineers* (1946); Lois Decker O'Neill, *The Women's Book of World Records and Achievements* (1979); Anne Macdonald, *Feminine Ingenuity* (1992); Louise S. Grinstein, Rose K. Rose, and Miriam H. Rafailovich, eds., *Women in Chemistry and Physics: A Biobibliographic Sourcebook* (1993); Benjamin F. Shearer and Barbara S. Shearer, eds., *Notable Women in the Physical Sciences: A Biographical Dictionary* (1997); and Marlene Rayner-Canham and Geoffrey Rayner-Canham, *Women in Chemistry: Their Changing Roles from Alchemical Times to the Mid-Twentieth Century* (1998). For Blodgett's nationwide fame, see *Life*, January 23, 1939, pp. 24–25; *Time*, January 9, 1939, p. 33; and Jo Chamberlin, "Mistress of the Thin Films," *Science Illustrated*, December 1947, pp. 8–11. An obituary appeared in the *New York Times* on October 14, 1979. See also the tribute by her GE colleagues Vincent Schaefer and George Gaines in the *Journal of Colloid and Interface Science* (July 1980) and *Thin Solid Films* 99 (1983). Additional information was provided by the Bryn Mawr Alumnae Association; Chris Hunter at the Schenectady Museum and Virginia Lagoy, librarian at the Schenectady County Historical Society; Gary Williams, Department of Physics and Astronomy, UCLA; and George Wise, former GE historian.

AUTUMN STANLEY

BOLTON, Frances Payne Bingham. March 29, 1885–March 9, 1977. U.S. Representative, nursing advocate, philanthropist.

Frances Payne Bingham was born in Cleveland, Ohio, the fourth of five children of banker-industrialist Charles William Bingham and homemaker and volunteer Mary Perry Payne. Her upper-class family was well established in Ohio business and politics. Her uncle, Oliver H. Payne, was a partner in Standard Oil with John D. Rockefeller. Frances was educated by tutors and private schools in Cleveland and France, and graduated from Miss

Spence's School for Girls in New York City in 1904. Her mother died when she was thirteen, and her older brother Oliver died just two years later. In 1907 Frances married Chester Castle Bolton, son of another prominent Cleveland family, and they had four children: Charles Bingham (1909); Kenyon Castle (1912); Oliver Payne (1917); and Elizabeth (1919), who died in infancy. Her son Oliver joined her in Congress in 1952 when he was elected from Ohio's 11th district.

Well before her congressional career, Frances Payne Bolton (as she preferred to be known) was involved in public life as a philanthropist. Charitable work for the Visiting Nurse Association brought the young woman of privilege to the worst sections of Cleveland and into the homes of the desperately poor. This intimate view of poverty made a deep impression on Bolton and inspired her lifelong commitment to nursing education and social welfare.

Early in the twentieth century, when nursing leaders and feminists struggled to organize nursing as a profession with standards and educational requirements, Bolton became an influential ally. During World War I, her influence was key in the army's decision to establish a school of nursing. In 1923, she provided an endowment to build a school of nursing at Western Reserve University (named the Frances Payne Bolton School of Nursing in 1935). At a time when many nursing schools and organizations were racially segregated, Bolton provided financial support for the National Association of Colored Graduate Nurses (NACGN) and helped the group establish a national headquarters in New York City in 1934. Later, as a congresswoman, Bolton continued to work with NACGN executive secretary MABEL KEATON STAUPERS in efforts to desegregate the Army Nurse Corps.

Her husband Chester Bolton was elected to Congress in 1928 as a Republican from the 22nd district of Ohio, where he served until his death in 1939. Frances Payne Bolton served the remainder of his term and was reelected fourteen times, serving twenty-nine years before she was defeated in 1968. Bolton's political career allowed her to introduce and support legislation for causes she already focused on as a philanthropist. Her greatest political contributions were relentlessly advocating racial equality, increasing federal funds and support for nursing education and public health, and raising American awareness of the emerging nations of Africa.

Even before the bombing of Pearl Harbor, a Bolton amendment to an appropriations bill set aside $1.2 million to increase enrollment in nursing schools. Bolton introduced and pushed through the 1943 Nurse Training Act (also called the Bolton Act), creating the Cadet Nurse Corps. The Bolton Act provided federal funds but prohibited discrimination by race or marital status, inspiring many previously all-white nursing schools to accept black nurses in order to qualify. The Cadet Nurse Corps was significant in ensuring the Army Nurse Corps a supply of well-trained nurses for the duration of the war. Bolton's persistent lobbying to upgrade army nurses to full military rank was instrumental in its eventual enactment by Congress.

Early in 1941 Bolton was assigned to the House Committee on Foreign Affairs, where she served throughout her congressional career, eventually becoming the ranking Republican member. Bolton conducted study tours to the Soviet Union, the Near East, and Africa to gain firsthand knowledge, and her appointment as a United Nations delegate in 1953 increased her interest in world conditions. The African continent, long ignored by the United States, was undergoing tremendous change as its peoples struggled to decolonize and create independent states after the war and throughout the 1950s and 1960s. In 1955 Bolton spent more than three months observing the living conditions and political situations in twenty-four African nations, and funded the production of three films to educate Americans. Bolton was influential in shaping U.S. policy in Africa and promoting humanitarian aid, and was one of the first U.S. representatives to speak out against apartheid in South Africa.

The Foreign Affairs Committee also prepared influential reports on communist movements throughout the world, and Bolton voted with the majority in 1950 to require communist organizations in the United States to register. She voted with the minority, however, in 1945 against a permanent committee on un-American activities. Bolton believed that good relations, humanitarian efforts, and astute foreign policy were the best strategies to impede the spread of communism.

Bolton introduced equal-pay legislation and worked for the inclusion of women in federal bans on discrimination, and even advocated including women in the military draft. Unlike many of her congresswomen contemporaries, however, Bolton opposed an equal rights amendment to the Constitution. CLARE BOOTHE LUCE, elected in 1942, also worked for racial equality in the military. HELEN GAHAGAN DOUGLAS, a supporter of Roosevelt and the New Deal (unlike Bolton), was another strong voice for civil rights and desegregation. Bolton also found a frequent ally in MARGARET CHASE SMITH on issues of public health and the status of women in the military, and seconded Smith's nomination for president at the 1964 Republican National Convention.

Bolton used her considerable energy and personal wealth to create a legacy of ongoing institutions dedicated to education and learning, and set up the Payne Fund in 1927 to serve as her primary granting agency. Her friendship with Irish psychic Eileen Garrett led to the establishment of the Parapsychology Foundation in New York in 1951. She enjoyed studying world religions and was a lifelong practitioner of yoga. She formed the Accokeek Foundation in 1957 to preserve land directly across the Potomac from Mount Vernon for historic interpretation and education. Frances Payne Bolton died at her home in Lyndhurst, Ohio, just short of her ninety-second birthday, and is buried at Lakeview Cemetery in Cleveland.

Bibliography: The Frances Payne Bolton Papers, Frances Payne Bolton Audio-Visual Collection, Payne Fund Records, and Chester Castle Bolton Papers are housed in the Library of the Western Reserve Historical Society in Cleveland, Ohio. A finding guide and biographical summary by project archivist Leslie Ann Solotko is available. Other resources include Susan Cramer Winters, "Enlightened Citizen: Frances Payne Bolton and the Nursing Profession" (PhD dissertation, University of Virginia, School of Nursing, 1997); the documentary film, *Reaching Out for Liberty and Light: The Life of Frances Payne Bolton* (2000), produced with support of the Payne Fund; and David Loth, *A Long Way Forward: The Biography of Congresswoman Frances Payne Bolton* (1957), which covers her career through the mid 1950s. An obituary appeared in the *New York Times* on March 10, 1977.

ROSEMARY A. BYRNE

BOMBECK, Erma. February 21, 1927–April 22, 1996. Writer, humorist.

About the same time as Betty Friedan deplored the domestic life of American married women in *The Feminine Mystique* (1963), Erma Bombeck began mining the same material for lighthearted humor in popular newspaper columns that quickly reached wide syndication. She would continue to do so for another thirty years in books and magazines as well, and on national television, where she became a familiar and beloved personality.

Born Erma Louise Fiste in Dayton, Ohio, she was named after her sixteen-year-old mother, Erma Haines, who had grown up in an orphanage, left school in the sixth grade, and at fourteen married Cassius Edwin Fiste, a thirty-three-year-old crane operator who already had a daughter, Thelma, seven years older than Erma Louise. When the future writer was nine, her father died of complications from polycystic kidney disease, an inherited disease that she also suffered from for most of her life. Thelma went to live with her birth mother, and Erma and her mother moved in with the girl's paternal grandparents in the Haymarket district of Dayton, an industrial area filled with immigrants and a community Erma would remember fondly. Her mother found work at the Leland Electric Factory and then at a General Motors plant, where she met and married Albert "Tom" Harris when Erma was eleven.

Inspired by child star Shirley Temple, Erma's mother focused on tap-dancing lessons for her daughter as the route to her success, but Erma had other career ambitions. Her future fame was foreshadowed in junior high school when she wrote a humor column that criticized bad cafeteria food and poked fun at teachers, predictable teenage targets. Erma then attended Patterson Vocational High School, where students alternated two weeks of classes with two weeks of outside work. Encouraged by her English teacher, she again got her own column in the school newspaper and talked her way into a job as a gofer at the *Dayton Journal-Herald.* At the paper, Erma met her future husband, William Lawrence Bombeck, a Catholic high school student who worked as a copyboy.

After graduating in 1944, Erma wanted to go to college, a goal not supported by her parents, who believed that girls of her class should work until they married. To pay her own way, Erma worked for the newspaper as a full-time copygirl by day and at Wright-Patterson Air Force Base at night, where she edited proofs for airplane manuals. At the end of a year she had earned enough to enroll at Ohio University in Athens. Here, in contrast to previous school experiences, Erma received low grades, was rejected by the school newspaper, and was discouraged by her college counselor from attempting a writing career.

She returned to Dayton, where in 1945 she enrolled at the University of Dayton, a Catholic college with a relaxed, supportive atmosphere that suited her and moved her to convert to Catholicism in 1949, the same year she married Bill Bombeck. After graduating, she began a full-time job at the *Dayton Journal-Herald* writing obituaries and articles on such female-oriented topics as gardening and cooking, about which she knew next to nothing. Eventually she realized that journalism was not her calling, confessing that she was far more interested in expressing opinions than in marshalling facts.

The Bombecks longed for a family, and after experiencing years of infertility adopted a seven-month-old daughter, Betsy, in 1954 when Bill was a high school science teacher earning extra money as a neighborhood handyman. Deciding to become a full-time homemaker, Bombeck quit her job on the paper and soon became pregnant with son Andy, born in 1955, and again with Matthew, born in 1958. Her years at home were to become fertile grounds for future trademark columns that irreverently poked fun at housework at a time when postwar America was taking homemaking and child rearing very seriously.

When her children were all in school, Bombeck found work with the *Kettering-Oakwood Times,* a weekly suburban newspaper, where she wrote humor columns at three dollars each. In 1965, she was noticed by Glenn Thompson, then executive editor of the *Dayton Journal-Herald* and the person she always acknowledged had helped her most. He assigned her three "At Wit's End" columns a week, at fifteen dollars each, and within three weeks dispatched her columns to the Newsday Syndicate on Long Island, which carried her columns until 1988, when she moved to the Universal Press Syndicate. She would eventually appear nationally in more than seven hundred newspapers.

Erma Bombeck's driving ambition and writing discipline led her to publish a dozen books; some were collections of her columns but most were original writing. Her 1976 novel, *The Grass Is Always Greener over the Septic Tank,* sold half a million copies in hardcover. From 1969 to 1975 she wrote a column for *Good Housekeeping* in addition to her syndicated newspaper column, and in 1975 she began appearing on ABC's daily television show *Good Morning America,* offering two or three minutes of humorous observations two mornings a week for eleven years. Though she otherwise avoided political topics throughout her career, Bombeck actively supported the equal rights amendment (ERA). As a humorous chronicler of family life, Bombeck endeared herself to legions of American women who identified with the good-natured figure she cut in her columns but also shared her concerns that militant feminism disrespected domesticity.

In 1992, after a diagnosis of breast cancer, Bombeck went through a modified radical mastectomy. The following year her kidneys failed, from the same disease that had killed her father. For the next few years she was confined to her home, where she received at-home dialysis while waiting for a kidney transplant. A match was found in 1996, and she flew to San Francisco, where she died of complications from the surgery. She was sixty-nine.

In what is probably her most famous column, called "If I Had My Life to Live Over," made all the more poignant to readers aware of her health problems, Bombeck compiled a list of life's simplest pleasures, like eating popcorn in the "good" living room or sitting on the lawn without worrying about grass stains. Bombeck's status as an admired writer and public personality was acknowledged at a University of Dayton conference in her honor in 2000. With such nationally recognized humorists as Art Buchwald in attendance, the meeting established Erma Bombeck's place in the rich historical context of America's most cherished comic writers.

Bibliography: Erma Bombeck's papers have been promised to the University of Dayton. In addition to the books mentioned in the text, she was the author of *At Wit's End* (1967); *"Just Wait Till You Have Children of Your Own!"* (1971); *I Lost Everything in the Post-Natal Depression* (1973); *If Life Is a Bowl of Cherries, What Am I Doing in the Pits?* (1978); *Aunt Erma's Cope Book* (1979); *Motherhood: The Second Oldest Profession* (1983); *Family: The Ties That Bind . . . and Gag!* (1987); *When You Look Like Your Passport Photo, It's Time to Go Home* (1991); *A Marriage Made in Heaven—or, Too Tired for an Affair* (1993); and *All I Know about Animal Behavior I Learned in Loehmann's Dressing Room* (1995). See also *Forever, Erma: Best-Loved Writing from America's Favorite Humorist* (1996). Briefly departing from her lighthearted topics, in 1989 she published *I Want to Grow Hair, I Want to Grow Up, I Want to Go to Boise,* a book about child cancer patients. No scholarly biography has yet appeared, but Lynn Hutner Colwell, *Erma Bombeck: Writer and Humorist* (1992), and Susan Edwards, *Erma Bombeck: A Life in Humor* (1997), are both useful. An obituary appeared in the *New York Times* on April 23, 1996.

BARBARA HABER

BOUCHER, Connie. July 15, 1923–December 20, 1995. Copyright licensing pioneer, conservationist.

Connie Klingborg Boucher is best known for her role as a pioneer in the character merchandising industry. She was born in Seattle, the elder of two daughters, to parents of Swedish descent, Frans O. Klingborg, a cabinetmaker, and Eve Heiner Klingborg, who later worked for her daughter's company for nearly thirty years. A graduate of San Mateo High School in San Mateo, California, Connie Klingborg attended the Chouinard Art Institute (later a part of the California Institute of the Arts) in Los Angeles in 1941–42. On September 23, 1943, she married John F. Boucher, and the couple had two sons: Douglas (1945) and Theodore (1948). The Bouchers moved to San Francisco, where Connie worked at the department store I. Magnin. It was at I. Magnin that she met Jim Young, a fellow window designer who became a significant part of her professional life and, later, her personal life.

Connie Boucher and Jim Young's first major business venture came when Boucher grew unhappy with the quality of the coloring books available to her two sons. Obtaining the rights to Winnie the Pooh, Boucher and Young published a giant-size Winnie the Pooh coloring book in 1959 that sold fifty thousand copies in six months. Buoyed by this success, Determined Productions, as their new company was called, began publishing a series of coloring books based on characters from children's literary classics, including *The Wind in the Willows* and *The Tale of Peter Rabbit.*

The project that proved the most significant to

Determined Productions' future growth developed in 1961, when Boucher approached Charles M. Schulz, creator of the *Peanuts* comic strip, with her idea for a calendar that featured *Peanuts* characters. Schulz agreed to the proposal, and the collaborative effort resulted in the first-ever *Peanuts* product. A year later, Boucher again approached Schulz. Having seen a *Peanuts* strip with Snoopy hugging Charlie Brown and the text "Happiness is a Warm Puppy," Boucher convinced a reluctant Schulz that he had created a theme for a possible book. Schulz drew up the rest of the panels, and Determined published *Happiness Is a Warm Puppy* in 1962. The book spent forty-five weeks on the *New York Times* best-seller list.

Boucher divorced her first husband just as Determined Productions enjoyed these initial achievements. Boucher, as president, continued to steer Determined with Jim Young as vice president and artistic director. The two later married, after working together for many years.

Other *Peanuts* books followed *Happiness,* as did the first Snoopy plush doll in 1968, as well as a host of other products (including posters, games, clothing, and housewares) shortly thereafter. According to Schulz, Boucher's vision differed from that of other publishers and companies, who had previously wanted simply to reprint his comic strips. Capitalizing on her initial success with *Peanuts*, Boucher obtained the rights to numerous other cartoon, literary, and entertainment characters—including, eventually, the Beatles—giving them life beyond the printed page and the movie and television screens. Boucher's efforts were revolutionary, as she created the process whereby copyrights could be licensed and used in the manufacture and sale of products. Unheard of in the 1950s, by the 1970s copyright licensing had become standard practice in the marketing world.

As the company grew, Young gradually scaled back his formal involvement in the company, while Boucher developed another area of the character merchandising market, one that combined her interest in children's books with her interest in book-related merchandise. Previously, dolls based on book characters had primarily been sold in retail outlets such as toy stores; Boucher designed and packaged dolls with the books on which they were based and sold them in bookstores. One of her earliest, and most successful, undertakings in this arena was a book-and-doll project based on Maurice Sendak's *Where the Wild Things Are* (1963).

To ensure the quality of Determined's merchandise, Boucher built a company that controlled the entire productive process, from design to manufacturing to marketing. Boucher's business acumen also led the San Francisco–based company into international markets early on. Determined Productions established manufacturing operations in Japan, where merchandise could be produced inexpensively for American markets. Recognizing the growth of a vibrant consumer economy there, Boucher converted the manufacturing operations to sales operations in the 1970s, establishing a subsidiary that made Japanese *Peanuts* products for Japanese consumers. Using the same strategy, Boucher set up markets for Determined Productions' items in other Asian countries as well.

Boucher was personally concerned about the environment, conservation, and animal welfare, and she helped pioneer another aspect of the licensing industry in the 1980s—cause-related marketing. Determined Productions was named the licensing agent for the World Wildlife Fund and began by producing a series of plush toys that represented endangered species. Portions of the profits from these and other conservation-related products went directly to the Fund's programs. Throughout the 1980s, Boucher expanded this side of Determined's business, developing licensing programs and products for UNICEF, the Humane Society of the United States, the Jane Goodall Institute, and the Rainforest Action Network.

Boucher's interest in ecological issues took her beyond the walls of her company. In the late 1980s, she financed and helped produce *Elephant Diary,* a film that focused on the brutal killing of African elephants for their ivory tusks. The film won a Genesis Award in 1990, an annual honor given by the Ark Trust, a national animal protection organization. The next year, Boucher traveled to the Amazon rain forest to document the devastation wrought by human activity in this ecosystem. The movie that resulted, *Amazon Diary,* was nominated for a 1990 Academy Award for Short Live Action Film.

Toward the end of her career, Boucher sponsored a traveling exhibition that illustrated her impact in the character merchandising industry. Having convinced more than thirty top fashion designers to create outfits for the Snoopy plush doll, as well as for his sister Belle, starting in 1984 Boucher and Determined Productions took the fashion show to cities in the United States and Europe. In 1990, the "Snoopy in Fashion" exhibit opened at the Louvre in Paris. Still an active company president, Boucher died five years later in San Francisco at the age of seventy-two from complications after heart surgery.

Bibliography: Biographical details about Boucher's life come from press information from her company, Determined Productions, and personal correspondence with Determined Productions executives. Boucher's publishing credits include *Happiness Is a Warm Puppy* (1962) and

Snoopy in Fashion (1984); her film productions are *Elephant Diary* (1989) and *Amazon Diary* (1990). Obituaries appeared in the *San Francisco Chronicle* on December 23, 1995, and the *New York Times* on December 27, 1995.

BLAIN ROBERTS

BOURNEUF, Alice. October 2, 1912–December 7, 1980. Economist.

In an age when career opportunities for women were significantly limited in economics and other disciplines, Alice Bourneuf by merit and force of character earned entrance into the elite group of Harvard-Radcliffe scholars when the Age of Schumpeter was replacing the venerable age of Taussig. She was born in Haverhill, Massachusetts, the tenth of eleven children in a very religious family, and she remained a devoted Catholic all her life. Her ancestry stemmed from early Acadian settlers. Her Canadian-born father, Volusien Modeste Bourneuf, was a carpenter who ran a successful construction business. Her mother, Jessie Marie d'Entremont, had been trained as a teacher before she left her native Nova Scotia. After Alice's father died, when she was two, the family moved to the Boston area, where Alice graduated from Newton High School in 1929. During her Radcliffe College years she was a commuter; she graduated Phi Beta Kappa and magna cum laude in 1933.

With the encouragement of her professors, she decided to continue her graduate studies at Harvard. Bourneuf belonged to two minorities: she was a woman; and in the epoch when Boston Cardinal O'Connell and Harvard president A. Lawrence Lowell had guarded interrelations, Bourneuf, like Joseph Kennedy, was the rather rare Catholic who chose to go to Harvard. In Professor Frank Taussig's famous graduate course, the few women were relegated to the rear rows; deemed even worse than children, they were to be neither seen nor heard in Taussig's famous Socratic dialogues. Taussig had a reputation for automatically giving women students the grade of C, while in Joseph Schumpeter's succeeding graduate seminar the grade was transformed into the perfunctory "woman's A," but Bourneuf later confided to a fellow economist that Taussig had in fact given her an A. Among her Harvard classmates were John Kenneth Galbraith and Paul Samuelson.

Job prospects were bleak during the Great Depression, especially for women economists, and Bourneuf took a job teaching at Rosemont College in Pennsylvania from 1937 to 1939. After receiving her MA from Radcliffe in 1939, she went to Belgium to undertake research for her doctoral dissertation. Her stay ended abruptly in May 1940 when the Germans invaded Belgium, forcing her to leave her research notes behind as she fled Hitler's war. Then at Harvard she became Professor Seymour Harris's research assistant prior to joining federal government service in Washington. Her first position was with the Office of Price Administration, specializing in wartime administration of export-import prices. Her stature as an economist soared at the Federal Reserve Board, where she worked on international monetary plans for the postwar period. At the famous Bretton Woods conference in 1944 that set up the International Monetary Fund (IMF) and the World Bank, there were only two women economists: Bourneuf from the Federal Reserve and the State Department's ELEANOR LANSING DULLES.

After the war Bourneuf worked in the research department of the IMF in Washington from 1946 to 1948, and then moved to Oslo, Norway, to represent there the Marshall Plan's program of large-scale economic and military aid to European economies devastated by the war. Many colleagues believe she regarded her work in Oslo, where she served as local representative of executive director Richard Bissell, to have been the high point in her public policy career. Important too was her tour of duty from 1951 to 1953 in the Paris office of the Marshall Plan as guardian helper for Norway's amazing postwar recovery. Her 1958 book, *Norway: The Planned Revival,* won kudos as a definitive work on the Marshall Plan's Scandinavian efforts.

When Bourneuf left government service in 1953, she returned to academic life, which may have seemed something of an anticlimax—a common experience for many of her generation. A Littauer School of Public Administration Fellowship at Harvard in 1953–54 allowed her to write up her Norway research and receive the PhD from Radcliffe in 1955. She joined the economics department of Mount Holyoke College in 1954, and was appointed a visiting associate professor at the University of California at Berkeley from 1957 to 1959.

Bourneuf's finest moment, however, was perhaps still to come—when she chose to accept the challenge of an important role in bringing Boston College's adequate economics department up into the very frontier of modern mainstream economics. Before World War II, the leading Catholic colleges were largely staffed by ordained Jesuits; some of Joseph Schumpeter's best graduate students had been recruited from their ranks. With the postwar explosion in student numbers, both undergraduate and graduate, the center of gravity was to shift more toward lay careerists; and with the permanent slowdown in recruitment of ordained orders, the secular component had continued to increase in the various Catholic universities. In 1959 Alice Bourneuf became the first woman appointed a full professor in the College of Arts and Sciences at Boston College.

At Boston College, the team of department-head Father Robert McEwen and Professor Bourneuf must have seemed, if not like a hurricane, at least like a Grade 3 tropical storm. Aside from Bourneuf's expertise, energy, and creative public research in the field of macroeconomics, her major asset was guileless devotion to excellence. What she lost in the short run from adhering to stubborn meritocracy, she and her colleagues more than won in the long run. What you saw in her was what you got. Her fulfilled life disproved Leo Durocher's Darwinian maxim, "Good guys end up last."

Alice Bourneuf never married, but she always maintained an amazingly wide circle of friends. After her retirement from Boston College in 1977, she moved to Ogunquit, Maine, stoically battling terminal cancer while still maintaining her research and training activities. She died in Boston on December 7, 1980, at the age of sixty-eight. Her many scholarly co-workers and students kept alive the memory of an important player in what is remembered as a golden age in economics.

Bibliography: Biographical material about Alice Bourneuf is found in the Radcliffe College Archives at the Schlesinger Library, Radcliffe Institute for Advanced Study, Harvard University. The Boston College Archives also contains material about her career. In addition to *Norway: The Planned Revival* (1958), Bourneuf published extensively in journals such as the *American Economic Review*, the *Review of Economic Statistics*, and the *Review of Social Economy*. Bourneuf's own account of her wartime experience appeared as "Chestnut Hill Girl Tells Thrilling Story of Fleeing Belgium," *Boston Daily Globe*, June 1, 1940. David A. Belsley, Edward J. Kanes, Paul A. Samuelson, and Robert M. Solow, eds., *Inflation, Trade and Taxes: Essays in Honor of Alice Bourneuf* (1976), includes a tribute by Samuelson. An obituary appeared in the *Boston Globe* on December 12, 1980.

PAUL A. SAMUELSON

BOWMAN, Thea. December 29, 1937–March 30, 1990. Catholic nun, teacher, activist.

Thea J. Bowman, the first black Catholic member of the Franciscan Sisters of Perpetual Adoration, played a crucial role in helping the Catholic church engage issues of interracial justice and intercultural understanding. As an accomplished and charismatic gospel singer, dancer, writer, scholar, and teacher, she mentored church and lay leaders, and helped incorporate Catholicism into the culture and religious practices of black communities.

The future Catholic nun was born Bertha J. Bowman in Yazoo City, Mississippi, the granddaughter of a slave and the only child of Mary Esther Coleman and Theon Edward Bowman. Growing up in the racially segregated and economically poor black community of Canton, Mississippi, Bertha called herself an "old folk's child," shaped by the music, songs, stories, and religious practices of the elders in her neighborhood. Bowman learned an ethic of service from her father, who worked long hours as a medical doctor caring for black patients shunned by Mississippi's white physicians. Her mother, a high school music teacher, taught her the importance of racial pride and groomed her as a cultured young woman.

Bowman was baptized into the Episcopal church and as a child attended a variety of Protestant churches. She first experienced Catholicism at age ten through the missions of the Franciscan Sisters of Perpetual Adoration, a Catholic order of nuns based in La Crosse, Wisconsin. During the 1940s, the sisters created a stir in Bowman's segregated town for crossing racial lines to teach black children at Holy Child Jesus School. Bowman decided to become Catholic largely due to her admiration for their charitable work. On June 8, 1947, Father Justin Furman, ST, formally baptized Bertha Bowman into the Catholic church.

In 1949, the Bowman family sent their daughter to Holy Child Jesus School. Within this Catholic environment, by age twelve she felt called to become a nun. Against the advice of her priest, who encouraged her to join one of the predominantly black orders of nuns, Bowman decided to enter the Franciscan Sisters of Perpetual Adoration. In August 1953, she traveled to Wisconsin to begin her formation as a woman religious. Upon entering the novitiate, she took the name "Thea" to honor her father. She graduated magna cum laude from the order's Viterbo College in 1965, majoring in English and minoring in speech and drama.

In 1968, Bowman began graduate school at Catholic University in Washington, D.C., earning her MA in English the next year and completing her doctoral dissertation, a rhetorical analysis of Thomas More's *A Dyalogue of Comforte Agaynst Tribulacyon*, in 1972. Bowman's graduate school years proved to be a turning point in her intellectual, personal, and spiritual development. Her experience in the black churches of Washington, D.C., reconnected her to the worship styles, spirituality, and liturgy of her youth in Canton. She found parallels between the oral tradition in English renaissance culture, her area of graduate research, and the oral traditions of African Americans. She began to study the black musical and literary traditions and presented on these topics at Catholic University and eventually at other colleges, schools, and churches.

After completing her doctorate, Thea Bowman

became a well-known gospel singer, a teacher at Viterbo College, and an advocate for racial justice and a greater role for women within the church. Trading the traditional Franciscan habit for a dashiki and a head wrap, she led workshops and gave presentations utilizing spoken word, song, and dance. Her dynamic and charismatic presentations at churches, schools, and conferences allowed Catholics to explore the richness of black spiritual and cultural practices. In part because of her own positive experiences with Catholic education, she became a strong proponent of the responsibilities of Catholic schools to serve poor communities and communities of color.

The reforms of Vatican II (1962–65), which encouraged greater lay participation in the church and sanctioned diversity in liturgical practices, provided Bowman with an opportunity to weave together Catholic practices with black religious and cultural traditions. The activism of the civil rights movement, the black power movement, and the black arts movement, which advanced the appreciation and study of black culture, also contributed to a resurgence of organizational efforts among black Catholics for greater recognition and self-determination within the church. In 1968, Bowman became a charter member of the First National Black Sisters Conference. She helped establish and teach at the Institute for Black Catholic Studies at Xavier University in New Orleans, the only predominantly black Catholic University in the United States and a center for the study and formation of black Catholic theology, liturgy, and social thought. In 1987, she helped organize the National Black Catholic Congress to allow blacks within the Church to address issues of racial inequality and to recognize and develop their contributions to the Catholic church. And she drew upon her study of black music to write a history of African American music for *Lead Me, Guide Me* (1987), the Catholic hymnal for black communities.

In 1978 Bowman returned to Mississippi to care for her ailing parents. The next year she took a position as director of intercultural awareness for the Diocese of Jackson, Mississippi. In 1984, the same year both her parents died, she was diagnosed with breast cancer, which eventually spread to her bones and lymph nodes. Despite the pain of cancer and the weakening effects of chemotherapy, she continued a rigorous speaking schedule. Through television and magazine interviews and a popular videotape about her experiences with cancer called *Almost Home: Living with Suffering and Dying* (1989), Bowman became an advocate for the sick and helped guide others through the process of caregiving. The American Cancer Society presented her with its national Courage Award in 1988.

The most galvanizing public moment of Bowman's career was her speech to the National Council of Catholic Bishops on June 17, 1989. Weak from cancer, Bowman challenged the bishops to confront racism within the church and society, to recognize black cultural and religious traditions as resources for the church, and to become more accountable to the communities they served. The speech ended with Bowman urging the bishops, many of them tearful, to stand and join hands while she led them in singing "We Shall Overcome."

Thea Bowman died on March 30, 1990, in Canton, Mississippi, at the age of fifty-two. She was buried near her parents in Memphis, Tennessee. For her contributions to American Catholicism, she was posthumously awarded the Laetare Medal from the University of Notre Dame.

Bibliography: The Franciscan Sisters of Perpetual Adoration in La Crosse, Wisconsin, are collecting Thea Bowman's papers and correspondence. The Catholic Diocese of Jackson, Mississippi, has also archived Bowman's correspondence and writing. Overviews of Bowman's life include John Bookser-Feister, "We Are All Children of God," *Extension*, April/May 1989, pp. 24–27; Celestine Cepress, FSPA, *Sister Thea Bowman, Shooting Star: Selected Writings and Speeches* (1993); and Christian Koontz, RSM, *Thea Bowman: Handing On Her Legacy* (1991). See also the videocassettes *Almost Home: Living with Suffering and Dying* (1989) and *Sr. Thea, Her Own Story: A Video Autobiography* (1992). For her scholarship and advocacy, see Thea Bowman, "Black History and Culture," *U.S. Catholic Historian* 7 (Spring–Summer, 1989), pp. 307–10; "The Gift of African American Sacred Song," in *Lead Me, Guide Me: The African American Catholic Hymnal* (1987); and ed., *Families: Black and Catholic, Catholic and Black—Readings, Resources, and Family Activities* (1985). On Bowman's religious practices and place within black Catholicism, see Joseph A. Brown, SJ, *A Retreat with Thea Bowman and Bede Abram: Leaning on the Lord* (1997); Joseph A. Brown, SJ, *To Stand on the Rock: Meditations on Black Catholic Identity* (1998); Mary E. McGann and Eva Marie Lumas, "The Emergence of African American Catholic Worship," *U.S. Catholic Historian* 19 (Spring 2001), pp. 27–65; and M. Shawn Copeland, "The *African American Catholic Hymnal* and the African American Spiritual," *U.S. Catholic Historian* 19, no. 2 (Spring 2001), pp. 67–82. An obituary appeared in the *New York Times* on April 1, 1990.

PAUL JOHN SCHADEWALD

BOYLE, Kay. February 19, 1902–December 27, 1992. Writer, political activist.

Kay Boyle, a short story writer, novelist, and poet whose work spanned the twentieth century, was born in St. Paul, Minnesota, the second of two daughters of Katherine Evans and Howard Peterson Boyle. The family lived well, thanks to her paternal grandfather, who founded the West Publishing Company. Her father worked in the family business and other ventures, while her self-educated mother, who had aspired to be a photographer before her marriage, was active in political causes such as suffrage and socialism. Kay received virtually no formal education and was educated at home by her mother. Hoping to be an architect, in 1918 she studied mechanical drawing at Ohio Mechanics Institute in Cincinnati, where her family had moved after suffering financial reverses. She also briefly attended Parsons School of Fine and Applied Arts in New York City in 1919.

Kay Boyle's literary career was centered first, briefly, in New York and then for the next thirty years in France, Austria, and Germany. Among her mentors was the poet Lola Ridge, New York editor of Harold Loeb's avant-garde literary magazine *Broom,* which was publishing revolutionary modernists such as William Carlos Williams, GERTRUDE STEIN, Hart Crane, and Sherwood Anderson. Through Ridge, Boyle met the author and publisher Robert McAlmon; through the good offices of Harold Loeb, Paris opened its literary doors, and before long Boyle was writing for Eugene Jolas's magazine *transition.* She was also being published in Harriet Monroe's magazine *Poetry.* Her first book, *Short Stories,* was published in 1929 by Black Sun Press, owned by Harry and Caresse Crosby, whom she befriended. It was followed by *Wedding Day and Other Stories* in 1930.

The typical Kay Boyle story of the twenties and thirties begins in medias res, eschewing exposition to orient the reader. One dramatic, situational moment replaces the old-fashioned imperatives of plot, rising action, and resolution—invariably her stories have none of these. A single psychological tableau replaced the linear plot. As with the greatest of the modernists, the chaos of the unconscious replaced the predictabilities of realism, and a happy ending was not to be expected. From 1931, when Harold Ross, another of Kay Boyle's mentors, published his first Boyle story in the *New Yorker,* until the mid 1950s, she was the most distinguished and consistent writer of short stories in that magazine. Kay Boyle might even be considered the creator of what came to be known as the *New Yorker* story.

In her personal life Kay Boyle was a romantic, tempestuous, often willful, and defiant of social obligation. She married three times, but her happiest times were with lovers, or with her husbands before she married them. To escape the Midwest and the confines of her grandfather's wealth, in 1922 she married Richard Brault, a French exchange student. In 1926 Boyle left Brault for Ernest Walsh, the poet-editor of *This Quarter* and the biological father of her first child, Sharon, who was born in 1927 while Boyle was still married to Brault. Walsh was the love of her life, but he died prematurely before they could marry. Five more children would follow over the years, as Kay Boyle viewed motherhood as another form of creativity. By the time she divorced Brault in 1931, she was already living with her next husband, surrealist writer Laurence Vail, who had previously been married to heiress and art collector PEGGY GUGGENHEIM. In 1932 Boyle and Vail married; this relationship produced three children: Apple-Joan (1929), Kathe (1934), and Clover (1939). Her final marriage, to Baron Joseph von Franckenstein, which occurred in 1943 immediately after her divorce from Vail became final, produced two more children: Faith Carson (1942) and Ian Savin (1943).

The political upheavals of the thirties, forties, and fifties in Europe inspired Kay Boyle's richest short stories, among them two O. Henry Award winners, "The White Horses of Vienna" (1935), published in *Harper's,* and "Defeat" (1941). So brilliantly does Kay Boyle capture the rise of fascism in "The White Horses of Vienna" that she was accused of being sympathetic to fascism, although nothing could have been further from the truth. After World War II, Boyle lived again in Europe, this time as a foreign correspondent for the *New Yorker.* Her most brilliant short story collection, *The Smoking Mountain: Stories of Postwar Germany* (1951), describes a postwar Germany riddled by a surviving Nazism. During these years she also published novels, although they were never as well received as her short stories.

Later, her passion turned to politics—to, as she would say, speaking for those who lacked the opportunity to voice their own needs. In the 1950s she fought for and gained Joseph Franckenstein's vindication after her husband, a victim of McCarthyism, was fired from the foreign service for his relationship with her. The *New Yorker* also fired her for her political views, despite the protests of her friend JANET FLANNER. During the Vietnam War, her participation in anti-war demonstrations in Oakland led to a jail sentence. She also became one of the leaders of the 1968 strike at San Francisco State, where she had a distinguished teaching career from 1963 (the year of her third husband's death) until her retirement in 1979. Virtually to the end of her life, she added both her defiant prose and her physical presence to a variety of causes, from oppression in Iran to student grievances. *The Underground Woman* (1975), her last novel, pictured her as a woman alone during the tumultuous 1960s when she became a political activist.

Kay Boyle has not been lauded like two other Paris writers, DJUNA BARNES and ANAÏS NIN, although many believe she was a far more distinguished writer than either of them. Her career evolved from the sensibilities of modernism. As history moved forward, her writing, like her life, took on fierce tones of commitment and a more strident realism; she seemed out of fashion, although her writing always reflected the tensions of the epoch in which she lived. After a long series of illnesses, including cancer and heart disease, Kay Boyle died at the age of ninety in Mill Valley, California.

Bibliography: Kay Boyle's papers are housed in the Special Collections Research Center at Southern Illinois University, Carbondale. They include audiotapes of interviews with Boyle and members of her family as well as her FBI files released by the Department of Justice. Southern Illinois University also holds the letters of Kay Boyle's agent, Ann Watkins, and the papers of Boyle's friend Robert Carlton Brown, as well as the Black Sun Archive and the papers of Caresse Crosby. An exhaustive bibliography of Kay Boyle's work was compiled by David V. Koch, the curator of Special Collections at Southern Illinois. The Harry Ransom Humanities Research Center at the University of Texas at Austin contains papers of Robert McAlmon, Marcel Duchamp, Evelyn Scott, and William Carlos Williams, all of them Boyle's friends, as well as the correspondence between Boyle and author Samuel Beckett. The Berg Collection at the New York Public Library contains a portion of Kay Boyle's papers. Biographies and studies of her writing include Sandra Whipple Spanier, *Kay Boyle: Artist and Activist* (1986), and Joan Mellen, *Kay Boyle: Author of Herself* (1994). Two other interesting studies of Boyle are Hugh Ford, *Four Lives in Paris* (1987), and John Glassco, *Memoirs of Montparnasse* (1970), where she appears as "May Fry." See also the 1968 edition of Robert McAlmon's *Being Geniuses Together, 1920–1930,* to which Boyle added her own memories of living in Paris. Obituaries appeared in the *New York Times* and the *San Francisco Chronicle* on December 29, 1992.

JOAN MELLEN

BOYLE, Sarah Lindsay Patton. May 9, 1906–February 20, 1994. Writer, civil rights activist.

Sarah Lindsay Patton was born in Lindsay, Virginia, on the remnants of an Albemarle County plantation originally granted to her father's family in the colonial era. Her mother, Jane Stringfellow Patton, taught her and her older sister to be proud of their family tree, which included Revolutionary war hero General Hugh Mercer and other military and political leaders. Her father, Robert Williams Patton, an Episcopal clergyman, emphasized social responsibility over the social register. From 1920 until his retirement in 1940, he served as director of the American Church Institute for Negroes, which oversaw and raised funds for St. Augustine's College, Bishop Payne Divinity School, and normal and industrial schools for blacks in seven southern states. Although she admired her father, Sarah resented his frequent absences when she was a child and did not embrace his comparatively progressive (though paternalistic) racial views. She also rebelled against her rigid Episcopal training and experimented with a variety of religious beliefs, including spiritualism and Buddhism, as a young adult.

"Patty," as she was always known, was educated at home by a private tutor but did not learn to read until her late teens because of undiagnosed dyslexia. In 1926, she enrolled in the Corcoran School of Art in Washington, D.C., where she studied painting. In 1932, she married Eldridge Roger Boyle II, a speech and drama instructor at the University of Virginia in Charlottesville. After her marriage, Boyle took up freelance writing in addition to work as a portrait painter to supplement her husband's Depression-era income, selling an average of one article per week on topics such as manners and household management to popular women's magazines. Her two sons, E. Roger Boyle III and Patton Lindsay Boyle, were born in 1939 and 1943.

In the late 1940s, Boyle and her husband began to recognize incompatibilities that would contribute to their eventual divorce in 1965. Their disagreements touched off a spiritual crisis, encouraging Boyle to return to the Episcopal teachings of her childhood. Her renewed faith was an important prerequisite for the political awakening she experienced soon after.

In the summer of 1950, when Gregory H. Swanson, an African American, won his legal battle for admission to the University of Virginia law school, Boyle suddenly realized that segregation was unchristian and unjust. She contacted Swanson to welcome him to Charlottesville and wrote a magazine article about his case. The rough draft of the article offended Swanson deeply, however, and he ended their acquaintance. Puzzled, Boyle asked Thomas Jerome Sellers, editor of a black weekly newspaper, the *Charlottesville Tribune,* to explain her offense. Sellers criticized the article's patronizing tone and informed Boyle that the gradualism she embraced was unacceptable to blacks who were stepping up their efforts to end segregation. Although shaken by his criticism, Boyle soon turned to Sellers for a reeducation on race through frequent conversations that they jokingly called the "T. J. Sellers Course for Backward Southern Whites."

As her contact with Sellers reshaped her opinions, Boyle began to write and speak in support of immediate integration and better communication between blacks and whites. In dozens of articles and letters to the editors of Virginia newspapers, as well as in the weekly column "From Behind the Curtain," which she contributed to Sellers's newspaper in 1952 and early 1953, Boyle assured black and white audiences alike that much racial tension was simply the result of misunderstanding and that the majority of white southerners would renounce segregation as soon as they realized that the system was unjust. Although she later considered her first efforts idealistic and naive, she always maintained that strong leadership in the early 1950s could have allowed integration to proceed more peacefully than it ultimately did.

Boyle's civil rights activities attracted little attention until late 1954, when she spoke in favor of school integration at a highly publicized hearing of the Virginia General Assembly's Commission on Public Education. Then an article that she had called "We Are Readier Than We Think" appeared in the *Saturday Evening Post* on February 19, 1955, under the inflammatory title "Southerners Will *Like* Integration." Segregationists' response was immediate and hostile, including hate mail, threatening phone calls, and, in August 1956 in the midst of a local school desegregation crisis, a cross burned on Boyle's lawn. To Boyle, the social isolation she experienced as white acquaintances in Charlottesville avoided her and resisted integration was even more distressing. Far fewer white southerners were ready to awaken to and oppose injustice than she had expected.

Despite her disillusionment, Boyle continued to write, speak, and organize in the late 1950s, touring the state for the interracial Virginia Council on Human Relations and working with the National Association for the Advancement of Colored People and other civil rights organizations. In 1962, she published *The Desegregated Heart: A Virginian's Stand in Time of Transition,* a spiritual autobiography in which she described her upbringing as a "typical southern lady," her conversion and reeducation on race, and her efforts to overcome the despair she had felt in the late 1950s as southerners seemed incapable of living up to her high ideals for human fellowship. Her solution, outlined in the third part of her narrative (which was also published on its own as *The Back Together Heart*), was to expect less of human beings and put her faith entirely in God.

A strong seller, *The Desegregated Heart* solidified Boyle's national reputation as a civil rights advocate. She received numerous awards and was appointed to advisory committees of the National Council of the Protestant Episcopal Church and the U.S. Commission on Civil Rights. She also participated in a number of marches and nonviolent protests, including a June 1964 demonstration in St. Augustine, Florida, where she was arrested and jailed. Her second book, an interracial etiquette manual titled *For Human Beings Only: A Primer for Human Understanding,* appeared in 1964.

By the mid 1960s, however, Boyle began to feel that her call for communication and Christian fellowship was no longer relevant to a movement that was increasingly turning away from nonviolence and toward black nationalism. She retired from her civil rights crusade in 1967. Her retirement years and particularly her struggle against age discrimination are the subject of her third book, *The Desert Blooms: A Personal Adventure in Growing Old Creatively* (1983). Boyle died in 1994 at the age of eighty-seven at her apartment in Arlington, Virginia, and was buried near her birthplace.

Bibliography: The Sarah Patton Boyle Papers at the University of Virginia at Charlottesville contain biographical data, extensive correspondence, copies of Boyle's writings and speeches, and other materials centering on the period from 1950 to 1968. Correspondence also survives in the Benjamin Muse Papers at the University of Virginia and the James McBride Dabbs Papers at the University of North Carolina at Chapel Hill. The Bronislaw Makeilski Papers at the University of Virginia contain manuscripts of her stories. Some personal correspondence and photographs are in the author's possession, as are the audiotapes of an interview conducted on January 4, 1994. For fuller biographical treatments, see Jennifer Ritterhouse's introduction to the 2001 reprint of *The Desegregated Heart: A Virginian's Stand in Time of Transition;* Fred Hobson, *But Now I See: The White Southern Racial Conversion Narrative* (1999); Kathleen Murphy Dierenfield, "One 'Desegregated Heart': Sarah Patton Boyle and the Crusade for Civil Rights in Virginia," *Virginia Magazine of History and Biography* 104 (1996), pp. 251–84; Joanna Bowen Gillespie, "Sarah Patton Boyle's Desegregated Heart," in Janet L. Coryell et al., eds., *Beyond Image and Convention: Explorations in Southern Women's History* (1998), pp. 158–83; Ritterhouse, "Speaking of Race: Sarah Patton Boyle and the 'T. J. Sellers Course for Backward Southern Whites,'" in Martha Hodes, ed., *Sex, Love, Race: Crossing Boundaries in North American History* (1999), pp. 491–513; and John Egerton, *A Mind to Stay Here: Profiles from the South* (1970). Obituaries appeared in the *New York Times* and *Charlottesville Daily Progress* on March 5, 1994.

JENNIFER RITTERHOUSE

BRICO, Antonia Louisa. June 26, 1902–August 3, 1989. Conductor, pianist.

Despite adversity and barriers, Antonia Brico was one of the earliest American women to have a professional career as an orchestral conductor. Born in Rotterdam, the Netherlands, as a young child Antonia was placed with foster parents, who brought her to the United States in 1906. She was raised as Wilhelmina Wolthus in California. Antonia learned about her birth family years later and resumed her birth name in 1924.

Despite unhappiness and abuse she endured as a child, Antonia received piano lessons as a cure for fingernail biting and found encouragement from her high school choral teacher, who took her to summer band concerts conducted by Berkeley professor Paul Steindorff, who later gave her piano lessons. After graduating from Technical High

School in Oakland, Brico enrolled at the University of California at Berkeley in the fall of 1919. She supported herself by teaching piano, playing dances, and performing on the radio. In 1923 she received a BA in music with minors in Asian philosophy and foreign languages. After an additional year at Berkeley, she traveled to New York to study piano with Sigismond Stojowski, a noted Polish pianist and teacher. Though Brico received considerable support and encouragement as a musician during her collegiate years, her desire to be a conductor continued to meet resistance, amazement, and even hostility. A chance encounter with Swami Yogananda and his self-realization teachings in the spring of 1925 led Brico to develop much-needed self-esteem and intensified her aspiration to be a conductor.

In 1926 Brico joyfully reunited with members of her birth family in Holland. While in Amsterdam, she met the concertmaster of the Amsterdam Philharmonic—one of the few people to support her ambitions—who urged her to study conducting with Karl Muck, a leading Wagner conductor in Germany, which she did the following summer. Brico spent the next five years in Germany. She was one of two students selected for the prestigious conducting program at the Berlin Hochschule für Musik, the first American and the first woman admitted. She graduated in 1929, but school officials delayed her postgraduation professional debut because she was a woman. Brico finally sponsored herself in a concert with the Berlin Philharmonic in early 1930, to positive reviews. This success was quickly followed by an appearance with the Los Angeles Philharmonic, after which Brico returned to Europe for guest engagements with several major orchestras. With the rise of Nazism making it difficult for foreigners to stay in Germany, she returned to New York in September 1932.

Despite the Depression, Brico remained optimistic about her conducting career. She made her New York debut with an orchestra of out-of-work professional musicians in performances at the Metropolitan Opera House. In 1934, she founded the Women's Orchestra of New York (later called New York Women's Symphony Orchestra) and, with the assistance of ELEANOR ROOSEVELT and Mayor Fiorello La Guardia and his wife, assembled important financial supporters. This orchestra was a critical and fiscal success, performing at major venues such as Carnegie Hall and Town Hall. Despite opposition by a prominent woman donor, on July 25, 1938, Brico became the first woman to conduct the New York Philharmonic in a performance at Lewisohn Stadium. In 1939, believing she had proven that women were capable musicians, Brico transformed the Women's Symphony into the Brico Symphony Orchestra, one of the first truly mixed orchestras. This ensemble of fifty-eight women and twenty-five men performed several critically acclaimed concerts during the first season, including one at the 1939 New York World's Fair. However, the board of directors withdrew financial support because of the inclusion of men, and the orchestra disbanded in 1940.

Brico continued with guest conducting, primarily in the Midwest and California, but her engagements dwindled. In the early 1940s she moved to Denver thinking she would be appointed permanent conductor of the Denver Symphony, but in 1945 the board rejected her without audition because she was a woman. Brico's name resurfaced each time the Denver Symphony searched for a new conductor, but nothing ever materialized. To support herself, she took church jobs and developed a private studio of conducting, piano, and voice students. In 1947, she was hired as conductor for the Denver Businessmen's Orchestra and continued with this amateur group of women and men until 1985.

Brico never married; during her last twenty-six years, however, Elizabeth Jans lived with her as her "companion, cook, housekeeper, and friend" (Collins, p. 58). Throughout her life she also maintained particularly intense friendships with several prominent men she admired or idolized: her mentor-teachers, Steindorff and Stojowski; the guru Yogananda; Finnish composer Jean Sibelius; and Dr. Albert Schweitzer. Brico's friendship with Sibelius lasted from 1937 until his death in 1957. He helped her secure guest conducting in Europe, and she was a noted interpreter and advocate for his symphonic works. Her annotated scores with markings from the composer as well as her own ideas offer much musical insight into Sibelius's music. Desiring to discuss Bach's music, Brico arranged to meet Schweitzer in 1949, and their extensive correspondence lasted until his death in 1965. Brico visited Schweitzer twice in Europe and made five trips to his hospital in Lambaréné, French Equatorial Africa (Gabon).

The film *Antonia: A Portrait of the Woman* (1974), co-directed by folksinger Judy Collins and Jill Godmilow, briefly revitalized a career that had languished during the years in Denver. Collins had studied with Brico from 1949 to 1955 and later described her teacher as a major musical influence. The film combines poignant and bitter interview material with rehearsal and concert footage of Brico conducting. After the film premiered, Brico was engaged as guest conductor at Lincoln Center's Mostly Mozart Festival, the Kennedy Center, and the Hollywood Bowl, plus made her first international appearances in nearly two decades. She conducted her final New York concert with the Brooklyn Philharmonic in 1977. In 1988, Brico fell and fractured her hip while leaving a Judy Collins concert. She remained bedridden in a Denver nursing home until her death the next year at the age of eighty-seven.

Brico repeatedly denied being a feminist, yet her story as it became known through the film touched many women, and she was in demand as a speaker for feminist gatherings and women's studies conferences. In a 1975 lecture she exclaimed: "And don't anybody ever say Brico [is] a 'woman conductor' . . . I am *a* conductor, period" (Christensen, p. 99). Although Brico's professional life never developed as she had hoped or as her skills would have predicted, her example modeled professional possibilities for a current generation of women conductors.

Bibliography: The Antonia Brico Collection at the Colorado Historical Society in Denver is the largest collection of archival materials (1919–89), including sixty boxes of printed material, clippings, scrapbooks, oral history tapes; many audio and video recordings of interviews, concerts, and lectures; and a finding aid by Christopher B. Gerboth. Scrapbooks of the Brico Symphony (1948–82) in the Denver Public Library contain programs, clippings, reviews, repertory, and some correspondence (including a letter from Sibelius). The Library of Congress holds a reel-to-reel tape of a 1977 interview with Brico and Joyce Barthelson done for the Voice of America. Lance Eugene Christensen, "'I Will *Not* Be Deflected from My Course': The Life of Dr. Antonia Brico" (MH thesis, University of Colorado at Denver, 2000), and Beth Abelson Macleod, *Women Performing Music: The Emergence of American Women as Classical Instrumentalists and Conductors* (2001), offer particularly detailed information and draw on different primary sources.

For further biographical information, see Jane Weiner LePage, *Women Composers, Conductors, and Musicians of the Twentieth Century: Selected Biographies* (1980); Charles E. Samson, "Antonia Brico and Jean Sibelius" (MA thesis, University of Northern Colorado, 1991); Patricia Stanley, "Dr. Antonia Brico and Dr. Albert Schweitzer: A Chronicle of Their Friendship," in *Literary and Musical Notes: A Festschrift for Wm. A. Little* (1995); and Tenesa Rasmussen, "Antonia Brico and the New York Women's Symphony Orchestra: 1934–1939" (MM thesis, Southern Methodist University, 1997). See also Judy Collins, *Singing Lessons* (1998); Carol Neuls-Bates, *Women in Music: An Anthology of Source Readings from the Middle Ages to the Present* (rev. ed. 1996); and Jan Bell Groh, *Evening the Score: Women in Music and the Legacy of Frédérique Petrides* (1991), which reproduces all thirty-seven issues of *Women in Music* (1935–40). Obituaries appeared in the *Denver Post* on August 4, 1989, and the *New York Times* on August 5, 1989, with a correction on August 18, 1989.

J. MICHELE EDWARDS

BRIGHT, Josefina Fierro. *See* Fierro, Josefina.

BRODIE, Fawn McKay. September 15, 1915–January 10, 1981. Writer, historian.

Fawn McKay Brodie was a fourth-generation Utah Mormon who began life firmly within the church and ended as a secular, liberal, self-made success story equally far removed from it. She was born in Huntsville, Utah, and grew up in an elite but financially struggling family. Her paternal uncle David O. McKay would eventually be president of the church. Her father, Thomas Evans McKay, served as Republican majority leader in the state senate and chairman of the State Utility Commission, as well as assistant to the Council of Twelve for the Church. She described her mother, Fawn Brimhall McKay, as a "quiet heretic." Both her mother and her mother's father (who had served as president of Brigham Young University) would take their own lives. Fawn was the second of five children. All three of her sisters would grow up to be "Jack Mormons," inactive but nonetheless still members of the church. Her brother carried on the family tradition actively. Only Fawn would be completely on the outside.

A precocious student who was placed in fourth grade at age six and published two poems at age ten, she remained devout through high school, giving testimonies at local ward meetings, including one on the divine origins of the Book of Mormon. She entered two-year Weber College in Ogden at the start of the Depression, but it was not until she moved to the secular University of Utah in the fall of 1932 that she began to turn from devout to doubtful. After a brief teaching stint at Weber, she arrived at the University of Chicago in 1935 for graduate study, where "the confining aspects of the Mormon religion dripped off within a few weeks," as she remembered it. "It was like taking off a hot coat in the summertime." Six weeks before graduation in 1936 she met Bernard Brodie, a son of antireligious Latvian Jewish immigrants, who wooed her despite her parents' horror, and their efforts, including fasting, prayer, and an anti-Semitic letter, to put a stop to it. Fawn and Bernard were married on the morning of the day she was awarded a master's degree in English.

They moved as demanded by his career as a national defense and weapons analyst—from Chicago to Princeton to Dartmouth, ending up in Washington, D.C., in 1943. Fawn took what jobs she could and spent all available time studying her former church. In 1943, for her partial manuscript on Joseph Smith, she won an Alfred Knopf fellowship that included a small stipend and a book contract. Two years later, shortly before the Brodies moved yet again, to New Haven, she had finished *No Man Knows My History: The Life of Joseph Smith, The Mormon Prophet,* which is still regarded outside the church as the most significant Smith biography and was widely praised when it was published in 1945. Within the church, however, her depiction of Smith as a well-meaning impostor was denounced, and in the following year she was excommunicated.

She would never look back, and she would never again be without a biography project. Some took longer than others, and there were distractions. The family moved several more times, eventually settling in California; she was a devoted mother to three children, Dick (born 1942), Bruce (1946), and Pamela (1950); and she took on shorter projects, including a collaborative textbook on weaponry with Bernard. Her biography of Thaddeus Stevens took thirteen years, only to be rejected by Knopf before being published to good reviews but very modest sales by W. W. Norton as *Thaddeus Stevens: Scourge of the South* in 1959.

Her trajectory as a biographer was driven partly by politics, partly by a Freudian fascination with the motivations of great men. Though she remained close to her family, and they to her, she had rejected not only her parents' faith, but also their steadfast Republicanism. By 1952 she was an ardent supporter of Adlai Stevenson; by 1966 she was so stunned by Ronald Reagan's election as governor of California that she considered dropping everything in order to work against him. (She did not, however, identify with contemporary feminists, whom she called "shrews.") Meanwhile, beginning in the early 1950s when Bernard joined the RAND corporation, the Brodies were increasingly drawn into psychoanalytic circles and both underwent psychoanalysis, in her case focusing on depression and sexual issues.

Her twin influences are visible for both good and ill in all of her post-Smith books. She gave Thaddeus Stevens, whose uncompromising Reconstruction-era politics had been criticized by many previous writers, a sympathetic treatment and focused on how his clubfoot might have driven his ambition and fierce radicalism. She next explored the restless rebelliousness of adventurer, explorer, and poet Sir Richard Burton. The critical success of *The Devil Drives: A Life of Sir Richard Burton* (1967)—not to mention its commercial triumph as a *New York Times* best seller and a main selection of the Literary Guild Book Club—helped earn Brodie a teaching position at UCLA in 1968, where she would remain until her early retirement in 1977.

Today she is most remembered for *Thomas Jefferson: An Intimate History* (1974), in which, without ignoring Jefferson's political career or philosophy, she chiefly sought to illuminate his "inner life." She pondered the influence of his parents on his rebelliousness. She asked why he never freed his slaves, answering with the then-controversial claim that he was in love with his domestic slave (and wife's half-sister) Sally Hemings and would lose her by freeing her. The book spent thirteen weeks on the *New York Times* best-seller list. Denunciations of her claim that Jefferson had a love affair with Hemings—a charge first made in Jefferson's lifetime—continued for decades, until a 1998 DNA test proved it right.

Sadly, she moved from her greatest triumph to her worst mistake. Her last book, a biography of Richard Nixon's pre-presidential years (*Richard Nixon: The Shaping of His Character*), was rushed to a finish just weeks before her death and was published posthumously in 1981. A full-bore attack on Nixon's "pathologies" and the most Freudian of her books, it was criticized by many reviewers for facile theorizing, scandal-mongering, and lack of perspective. It was both an unfortunate postscript to Brodie's life and a coincidental indication of the decline of psychobiography.

Fawn Brodie died of cancer in Santa Monica, California, at the age of sixty-five. Her passion for evidence, her accessible yet high-toned style, and her ability to look at her subjects with fresh eyes no matter how zealously guarded their reputations, still stand as models and ensure that her books will remain vital for years to come.

Bibliography: The Special Collections Department of the University of Utah's Marriott Library houses the Fawn McKay Brodie papers. A 1975 oral history (the source of all quotes above) can be obtained from the Oral History Program at California State University, Fullerton. Newell G. Bringhurst's *Fawn McKay Brodie: A Biographer's Life* (1999) is an excellent biography. In addition to Brodie's biographies and the textbook (*From Crossbow to H-Bomb*, 1962; rev. and enlarged ed., 1973), she edited two diaries—Richard Burton, *The City of the Saints and Across the Rocky Mountains to California* (1963), and Frederick Hawkins, *Piercy's Route from Liverpool to the Great Salt Lake Valley* (1963)—and compiled two wartime reference volumes, *Our Far Eastern Record: A Reference Digest on American Policy* (1942) and *Peace Aims and Postwar Planning: A Bibliography* (1942). From 1946 to 1977 she also published occasional articles on history and contemporary politics in popular magazines and newspapers. An obituary appeared in the *New York Times* on January 13, 1981.

BRUCE NICHOLS

BRONSON, Ruth Muskrat. October 3, 1897–June 12, 1982. Indian rights activist, federal official.

Ruth Muskrat was born and raised on a farm in the Delaware District of the Cherokee Nation, Indian Territory, near what is now Grove, Oklahoma. Her father, James Ezekial Muskrat, descended from Cherokees who had been forced to leave their ancestral home in Georgia earlier in the nineteenth century. Her Irish and English mother, Ida Lenora Kelly, came from southwestern Missouri. Ruth Muskrat, the fourth of their seven children, identified most strongly with the Cherokee community in which she was raised. At the age of ten, she witnessed the destruction caused by an Oklahoma statehood movement that dissolved Cherokee national institutions, divided up the Cherokee estate, and replaced Cherokee citizenship with United States citizenship. Against the odds, the Muskrats held on to their farmland and escaped the poverty and despair that statehood brought to many Cherokees.

Cherokee tribal dissolution would have a profound influence on the development of Ruth Muskrat's philosophy of Indian cultural survival. As she matured, she began to articulate a position that accepted the fact of conquest but not of powerlessness. Moreover, she rejected the prevailing assumption that American Indians must choose between complete assimilation or cultural isolation. Instead, she insisted that American Indians had a legitimate, legal claim to both a tribal identity and an American identity.

In the early twentieth century, restrictive racial laws and attitudes reached high levels. Paradoxically, women of color discovered expanded opportunities within the crusade for social justice. The subsequent development of Ruth Muskrat's race consciousness and leadership skills was rooted in these dual conditions of restriction and opportunity.

The Muskrats, like Cherokees generally, supported formal schooling, and all their children would eventually attend college. To attend high school, Muskrat left home for Oklahoma Institute of Technology in Tonkawa. After graduating in 1916, she pursued teacher training at Henry Kendall Academy in Tulsa and Northeastern State Teachers College in Tahlequah. After two years teaching in rural schools, Muskrat spent three semesters at the University of Oklahoma, followed by three semesters at the University of Kansas. In 1923 she enrolled with advanced standing at Mount Holyoke College, graduating with a BA in 1925.

Her first experience working with Indian youth outside of Oklahoma came in 1921, when the Young Women's Christian Association sent her to the Mescalero Apache Indian Reservation in New Mexico to organize a recreation program for girls. The report Muskrat submitted about her efforts led to an offer to attend a World's Student Christian Federation Conference in Beijing in 1922. Muskrat's participation in this international conference taught her much about student leadership around the world. Once home, she spoke repeatedly of the need to develop a new generation of Indian leaders. Viable solutions to Indian problems, argued Muskrat, could be found only by Indians themselves. She presented her philosophy of Indian leadership before a prominent gathering of Indian rights activists known as the Committee of One Hundred during their meeting with President Calvin Coolidge in 1923.

In 1925 Muskrat accepted a teaching position at Haskell Indian Institute in Lawrence, Kansas, the nation's largest federal Indian boarding school. She quickly worked her way up in the Bureau of Indian Affairs (BIA) Education Division. In a few short years, she went from teaching eighth-grade English to coordinating an expanded placement program for boarding-school graduates. On July 15, 1928, Ruth Muskrat married John Franklin Bronson, a mechanical engineer from Waterbury, Connecticut. Early in their life together, John began referring to his wife as Lady. This endearment came to symbolize, for family and friends alike, his lifelong support of his wife's Indian rights activism.

In 1932, Ruth Muskrat Bronson began recruiting qualified Indian students to participate in a new federal higher education loan program. Although the official government line emphasized the race-based assumption that vocational training for Indian students was most appropriate, the loans could be used to attend any accredited postsecondary program. As the administrator of the fund, Bronson routinely encouraged qualified applicants to seek academic training and leadership opportunities. Moreover, she purposefully encouraged applicants who hoped to use their education for the benefit of American Indian communities.

In 1935 the federal loan program Bronson administered expanded, and the family soon relocated to Washington, D.C. When a dear friend, Verna Nori of Laguna Pueblo, died unexpectedly in the late 1930s, the Bronsons adopted her twenty-one-month-old daughter, Dolores. In 1943, Bronson left the BIA after its offices were moved to Chicago. She spent the next year writing *Indians Are People Too* (1944), an educational text designed for youth groups.

In 1945, Bronson emerged as an important leader in the newly established National Congress of American Indians (NCAI). In its formative years, the NCAI sought to provide assistance to American Indian tribes who were being pressured to terminate their treaty rights. During the next ten years, Bronson served as the NCAI's executive secretary, established a legislative news service, and otherwise helped build the NCAI into an organization that demanded the attention of politicians and bureaucrats alike. She coped with a shoestring budget by turning her home into the NCAI's Washington office.

By the mid 1950s, Bronson had grown weary of the contentious nature of national politics and welcomed an opportunity to work with Indian leaders at the community level. In 1957 she became a health education specialist for the Indian Health Service on the San Carlos Apache Indian Reservation in Arizona. For the next five years, and through a variety of development projects, Bronson encouraged Apache women and girls to assume leadership roles at San Carlos. In 1962 she became a consultant to the Save the Children Federation's Indian Community Development Program in the Southwest. Now living in Tucson, Bronson suffered a personal loss when her husband died one day before their thirty-eighth wedding anniversary in 1966. Her activism slowed dramatically when she suffered a stroke in 1972. Despite her disabilities, Bronson continued to work for the development of Indian leadership in whatever ways she could until her death in Tucson in 1982 at the age of eighty-four.

Ruth Muskrat Bronson deserves a prominent place among the influential and important Indian leaders of the twentieth century. She claimed a legal and moral high ground from which she asserted her right to be both Cherokee and American. Her devotion to the development of Indian leadership mattered in her own time, and her words and actions paved the way for American Indian leaders who followed.

Bibliography: There is no published biography of Ruth Muskrat Bronson. The most comprehensive portrait to date is Gretchen G. Harvey, "Cherokee and American: Ruth Muskrat Bronson, 1897–1982" (PhD dissertation, Arizona State University, 1996). Bronson published one book, *Indians Are People Too* (1944). Her correspondence and a record of her activities are scattered throughout several manuscript and archival collections, the most significant of them being the Ruth Muskrat Bronson file in the Archives at Mount Holyoke College Library; the Records of the Bureau of Indian Affairs at the National Archives; the D'Arcy McNickle Papers at the Newberry Library in Chicago; and the Papers of the National Congress of American Indians in the National Anthropological Archives, Suitland, Maryland. Interviews and personal papers from her daughter, Dolores Bronson Tidrick of Denver, and a fellow Indian rights activist, Elizabeth Clark Rosenthal of Santa Fe, provided indispensable context for understanding the importance of Bronson's life.

GRETCHEN G. HARVEY

BROOKS, Louise. November 14, 1906–August 8, 1985. Actress, writer.

An American actress who became a star through the roles she played in European films, Louise Brooks experienced a renaissance as a writer on film culture decades after her film career was over. Famous for her hairstyle—a modern bob—Brooks endured as an icon of the late 1920s, her striking image and attitude the basis for a cult of fans in the United States and in Europe.

Born Mary Louise Brooks in Cherryvale, Kansas, she was the second of four children of Leonard Porter Brooks and Myra Rude. Her father was a lawyer; her mother, the eldest of six surviving children out of ten, was a strong-willed woman interested in the arts and eager to escape her large family. Unsatisfied with playing a conventional maternal role, Myra encouraged her daughter to be a dancer. At fifteen, Louise left Kansas for New York, where she became a student in the Denishawn Dancers, a modern, experimental troupe (MARTHA GRAHAM was also a member) with which she toured in 1922 and 1923. After leaving Denishawn, she danced in the chorus of George White's *Scandals* on Broadway in 1924 and later in the Florenz Ziegfeld musical *Louie the 14th* in 1925. Brooks then debuted in her first film, *Street of Forgotten Men* (1925). Her last musical appearance was in Ziegfeld's famous *Follies.* She married director Edward Sutherland in 1926 but divorced him in 1928. Another marriage, to socialite Deering Davis in 1933, was even briefer (six months). Neither marriage, nor the numerous long-term liaisons she had throughout her life, produced any children.

Before her debut in Europe, Brooks appeared in fourteen American films. The most significant of these included Howard Hawks's *A Girl in Every Port* (1928), William Wellman's *Beggars of Life* (1928), and Malcolm St. Clair's *The Canary Murder Case* (1929). Each of these films played an important role in Brooks's life. *A Girl in Every Port* inspired G. W. Pabst to invite her to audition for *Pandora's Box* (1929), and these two films together ensured her revival more than two decades later; *Beggars of Life* motivated an essay she wrote on director Wellman long after her career as an actress was over; and *The Canary Murder Case* effectively ended her successful run in the U.S. film industry when she flatly refused to dub a sound version of the film, claiming she wanted nothing to do with Hollywood. She got her wish: she became known as an overly demanding star, and rumors circulated that her voice was not good enough for sound film.

For a headstrong actress who had little patience with what she saw as the superficiality of Hollywood culture, this blacklisting could not have come at a better time. Brooks was invited to Germany to test for G. W. Pabst's adaptation of Frank Wedekind's *The Lulu Plays,* entitled *Pandora's Box.* This was literally the role of a lifetime for Brooks; not only did she become most famous for her portrayal of Lulu, but she also identified strongly with the part of the sexually uninhibited woman. Pabst, too, felt that Brooks *was* Lulu; according to Brooks, he prophesied to her, "Your life is exactly like Lulu's, and you will end the same way" (*Lulu in Hollywood,* p. 105).

His prophecy was partly right; unlike Lulu, she did not die young, but her life as an actress was cut short. After two more films in Europe (*Diary of a Lost Girl,* 1929, and *Prix de Beauté,* 1930), Brooks returned to Hollywood. She was no longer as successful as before or during her stint in Europe. Working mainly for lesser studios in B-movie roles, her last film, *Overland Stage Raiders,* was in 1938, co-starring with John Wayne. For the next fifteen years Brooks floundered. She returned briefly to Kansas, where she taught dance, and then held a series of odd jobs in New York City, which left her almost destitute.

During this time two men conspired to revive her work. In 1953 James Card, motion picture curator of the George Eastman House and a fan of Brooks since his teens, asked to see *Pandora's Box* and *Diary of a Lost Girl* at the Cinémathèque Française in Paris. Upon watching Brooks's performance, Henri Langlois, the institution's founding director, became fascinated with the star himself. The two men joined forces to restore *Pandora's Box,* and when Langlois organized an exhibition of *Sixty Years of Cinema* at the Cinémathèque in 1955, one of the two enormous photographs he hung in the lobby to represent cinema was of Brooks. After corresponding with Brooks, Card finally met her in New York City; in 1956 he persuaded her to move to Rochester, New York, where the Eastman House is located. In 1958 Brooks traveled to Paris, where Langlois was presenting a series of films entitled "Hommage à Louise Brooks."

Through Card's encouragement, Brooks began to write a series of articles describing her work in film. Of the approximately twenty-eight pieces she authored, she published twenty in American and European venues. Some of these essays were later collected in *Lulu in Hollywood* (1982). Though not a traditional memoir, these works make up a partial autobiography and present Brooks's take on other figures in film history. A self-proclaimed "inhumane executioner of the bogus" (*Lulu in Hollywood,* p. 6), Brooks was committed to painting what she considered a truthful picture of Hollywood film culture. Her sharp-witted essays reveal her as a serious critic of how films are made and received, and of how film history is written.

Brooks remained in Rochester for the rest of her life. Bedridden and rarely able to leave her home, she continued to be a subject of fascination for the filmmakers, film critics, and film fans whose works kept the Louise Brooks cult alive. Much of what interests and energizes the cult is speculation about her bisexuality, as well as her combined intellect and striking image. She died at her Rochester home in 1985 at the age of seventy-eight. Her death was front-page news throughout Europe, but her life and death were less commemorated in the United States. In 2000 a new edition of *Lulu in Hollywood* was published, testifying to Brooks's importance to film history and to the fact that the star lives on through her writings.

Bibliography: The George Eastman House in Rochester, New York, holds a large portion of Brooks's papers, photographs, and private library. Some of the most significant writings on Brooks are authored by the star herself, especially *Lulu in Hollywood* (1982, 2nd ed. 2000); and everyone to subsequently write on Brooks has drawn on her own words. Barry Paris's biography, *Louise Brooks* (1989), offers a rich and exhaustive history of her life. Other works focus on her as a visual icon yet also depend on her own self-descriptions. This category would include Roland Jaccard, ed., *Louise Brooks, Portrait of an Anti-Star* (1977, English ed. 1986); Kenneth Tynan's influential essay "The Girl in the Black Helmet," *New Yorker,* June 11, 1979, pp. 45–78; and Richard Leacock's documentary *Lulu in Berlin* (1984), which is essentially a documentation of conversations with the aging star. Also of interest is Donald McNamara's interview with Brooks, "Lulu in Rochester: Self-Portrait of an Anti-Star," *Missouri Review* 6, no. 3 (Summer 1983), pp. 63–82, which responds to the Tynan essay. Scholarly essays on Brooks include Mary Ann Doane, "The Erotic Barter," in *Femmes Fatales: Feminism, Film Theory, and Psychoanalysis* (1991); Thomas Elsaesser, "Lulu and the Meter Man: Louise Brooks, Pabst, and 'Pandora's Box'," *Screen* 24, nos. 4–5 (July–October 1983), pp. 4–36; Amelie Hastie, "Louise Brooks, Star Witness," *Cinema Journal* 36, no. 3 (1997), pp. 3–24; and Peter Wollen, "Brooks and the Bob," *Sight and Sound* 4, no. 2 (1994), pp. 22–25. Obituaries appeared in the *New York Times,* the *Washington Post,* the *Guardian (London),* and the *Times* (London), all on August 10, 1985.

AMELIE HASTIE

BROWN, Letitia Woods. October 24, 1915–August 3, 1976. Historian, community activist.

Letitia Christine Woods was born in Tuskegee, Alabama, the middle of three daughters of Evadne Clark Adams and Matthew Woods. Her father was educated at Tuskegee Institute, the industrial college founded by Booker T. Washington. Evadne Woods's parents were Theodosia Evadne Clark and the former slave Lewis Adams, who in 1881 became a commissioner and trustee of the Tuskegee Normal School. Together they raised twelve children, all of whom became educators throughout the South. Evadne and Matthew Woods and their children enjoyed middle-class status among the African American elite of the community, where both parents taught at the Institute.

Like her father, Letitia attended Tuskegee Institute. In the midst of the Great Depression she graduated with a BS degree in education from the normal school in 1935, then taught briefly in the segregated school system of Macon County, Alabama. During a time when few African American women were fortunate enough to pursue degrees in higher education, Letitia Woods continued her education at Ohio State University, where she earned an MA in history in 1937.

Upon returning to Alabama, Woods taught history at Tuskegee Institute from 1937 to 1940. From there she moved to Memphis, Tennessee, where she accepted a position teaching history at LeMoyne-Owen College from 1940 to 1945. Like most African American educators of her era, she found that the teaching positions available to her in higher education were limited primarily to historically black colleges and universities, mainly in the segregated South. Letitia remained in Tennessee until she moved to Cambridge, Massachusetts, to pursue a PhD in history at Harvard. There she met Theodore Edward Brown, a doctoral student in economics. The couple married in 1947 and moved to Harlem, where they lived with Brown's family. After the birth of two children, Lucy Evadne Brown (1948) and Theodore Edward Brown Jr. (1951), the family relocated to Mount Vernon, New York. There Letitia Brown served on the local Health and Welfare Council and successfully campaigned to elect an African American, Harold Wood, to the Westchester County Board of Supervisors.

The family moved again in 1956, this time to Washington, D.C., where Brown worked as an economist in the Bureau of Technical Assistance, which was part of the State Department's Agency for International Development. While raising a family in the nation's capital, Letitia Woods Brown developed an interest in the history of African Americans of the District of Columbia, a subject that would be the topic of her research and lectures for the remaining years of her career. When her children were young, Brown sent them to Tuskegee to visit with relatives during the summers, while she researched and wrote her Harvard dissertation, which she completed in 1966. In the course of pursuing her doctorate, Brown taught at Howard University, first in the social science department and later in history. She earned the rank of associate professor and taught history at the university from 1961 to 1970. In 1961, Brown and her husband helped train the first group of Peace Corps volunteers destined for Ghana.

While at Howard, she networked with other pioneering African American women historians who would go on to earn doctorate degrees, such as Elsie Lewis, who earned her PhD in history from the University of Chicago and chaired the history department at Howard during the 1960s. Brown also worked with Lorraine Anderson Williams, who earned her PhD in history from American University and headed the social science department and later the history department at Howard University during the 1970s.

Letitia Brown and her colleagues were among the few African Americans in higher education who not only researched and taught in the field of black history in the late 1960s but had also earned PhDs. Consequently, Brown was sought after by mainstream colleges and universities, which previously had not hired black faculty. George Washington University recruited her, and she joined the American Studies Department as a full professor in 1971. Her scholarly publications continued to focus on Washington, D.C. With Elsie Lewis, she co-authored *Washington from Banneker to Douglass, 1791–1870* for the National Portrait Gallery in 1971. Brown's major work, *Free Negroes in the District of Columbia, 1790–1846,* was published in 1972.

Actively engaged in professional organizations, Brown served on an American Historical Association (AHA) committee from 1971 to 1973 to restructure and reorganize the AHA. While a Fulbright lecturer in Australia, she collaborated with foreign scholars to build networks through the American Studies Association. In addition, she was involved in the effort to improve educational achievement among the largely African American school-age population in Washington, D.C., through the National Assessment for Educational Progress. Brown was also actively involved with the development of the Columbia Historical Society of Washington, D.C., which was founded in 1973, and she served as vice chair of the Joint Commission on Landmarks of the National Capital, pressing for recognition of sites relevant to the history of Washington's black community.

During the later years of her career, Brown championed the use of oral history as an important tool for historians. She became a primary consultant to the Schlesinger Library Black Women Oral History Project at Radcliffe. The project team located and interviewed seventy-two black women of achievement from an earlier generation in various arenas in the United States. The pathbreaking and compelling interviews helped spur the developing field of black women's history.

Letitia Woods Brown died of cancer at her home in Washington, D.C., at the age of sixty. In 1983 the Association of Black Women Historians established the Letitia Woods Brown Memorial Publication Prize to honor excellence in scholarly publications in the field of black women's history.

Bibliography: Interviews with her daughter, Lucy Brown Murray, were the major source of information about Letitia Woods Brown's personal life. Her papers are not yet cataloged and are still maintained by family members at her former home in the District of Columbia. Obituaries appeared in the *New York Times* and *Washington Post* on August 5, 1976. See also Roderick S. French, "Letitia Woods Brown, 1915–1976," *Records of the Columbia Historical Society* 50 (1980), pp. 522–24.

ROSALYN TERBORG-PENN

BROWN, Rachel Fuller. November 23, 1898–January 14, 1980. Biochemist.

Rachel Fuller Brown was born in Springfield, Massachusetts, the only daughter of Annie Fuller and George Hamilton Brown, a real estate and insurance man. Her father's business interests drew them to Webster Groves, Missouri, but a few years later George left the family in poverty. Annie moved Rachel and her younger brother, Sumner Jerome, back to Springfield, where, as director of religious education in various Episcopal churches, Annie supported her two children and her grandparents. In an effort to help family finances, Rachel enrolled in a vocational high school to become a wage earner, but her mother insisted that she change schools to gain a classical education. Annie wanted her children to go to college, as she was never able to do. Rachel did well at Central High School and set her sights on attending nearby Mount Holyoke, a women's college known for its rigorous academic standards and its history of fostering women leaders. Tuition was far beyond her family's meager means, but Henrietta F. Dexter, a good friend of Rachel's grandmother, offered Rachel the unimaginable: four years of support to attend the college, starting in 1916.

Brown at first chose to major in history, but she also came to love chemistry, a strong tradition at Mount Holyoke since the days of founder MARY LYON. Outside the classroom she kept busy with religious study, drama, and sports. She earned her BA in chemistry and history in 1920. A faculty mentor, EMMA PERRY CARR, urged her to attend the University of Chicago for graduate work in chemistry. After Brown was awarded her MS in organic chemistry in 1921, she taught for three years at the Frances Shimer School near Chicago. Realizing she did not want to spend her life teaching, she returned to Chicago for further graduate work in organic chemistry, with a minor in bacteriology.

Although she submitted her PhD thesis in 1926, her committee members were unable to schedule her oral exam. Desperate for a job and having rapidly exhausted her meager savings, Brown left Chicago without her degree to start a career at the Division of Laboratories and Research of the New York Department of Health in Albany. The Division was already famous for discovering the causes of diseases, developing tests for them, and if possible, creating treatments. It was also known for recruiting women for its staff, an unusual practice at the time. Brown was immediately immersed in research, and for seven years she worked without her PhD until Division Director Augustus Wadsworth personally arranged for her to take her orals when she was in Chicago for a meeting. She received her doctorate in 1933 and was elected to Sigma Xi, the honor society for science and engineering.

Brown maintained her mother's Episcopal affiliation throughout her life. In Albany, she joined St. Peter's Episcopal Church, where she met Dorothy Wakerley, a manager for an insurance company who became her lifetime companion. The home they shared soon included Rachel's grandmother and mother, as well as various nieces and nephews and a succession of visiting women scientists from China. The women lived together until Brown's death.

In Albany, Brown first worked on antigen research to improve tests for syphilis and then on extracting polysaccharides for research on pneumonia. In 1948 she began her famous postal collaboration with ELIZABETH LEE HAZEN, a microbiologist also with the Division but based in New York City. Searching for an antifungal antibiotic, they shared information and samples through the U.S. mail. Fungal diseases were still a little-recognized yet serious source of sickness and death, and there were no antifungal agents safe for human use. Hazen first cultured soil samples for possible antifungal organisms, then sent promising ones to Brown to purify and find the particular chemical agents capable of arresting or killing fungal growth.

Hazen collected microorganism No. 48240 from some soil on a friend's farm, and it yielded two antifungal substances, called Fractions N and AN. Fraction N was too toxic for human use, but Fraction AN proved effective against two pathogenic fungi—one of which is responsible for the chronic disease cryptococcosis, which affects lungs, skin, and the central nervous system, and the other of which causes candidiasis, a serious systemic infection developing in patients treated with broad-spectrum antibiotics. Nystatin (they chose the name in honor of New York State) was the first antibiotic to be safe and effective in treating a range of human fungal diseases. Later it proved effective in stopping fungal growth on flood-damaged works of art in Florence, Italy, and also somewhat helped slow Dutch elm disease.

Brown presented their joint work at the National Academy of Sciences regional meeting in 1950, and its commercial possibilities excited pharmaceutical companies—which had the abilities to manufacture and test the compound in humans that the New York State lab lacked. E. R. Squibb & Sons won the production license and produced the first tablets for human use in 1954 under the name mycostatin. Neither woman profited financially from the discovery. The patent royalties were assigned to the Research Corporation of New York, a nonprofit foundation for the advancement of science. Royalties eventually totaled $13.4 million; the Research Corporation used half for grants to further scientific research and the other half to support the Brown-Hazen Fund for research in the biomedical sciences, especially mycology. Between 1957 and 1978 the fund supported training and research in biomedical sciences, and encouraged women to take up careers in science. For several years it was the largest single source of nonfederal funds for medical mycology in the United States.

Brown and Hazen received many major awards for their collaborative work, beginning with the Squibb Award in Chemotherapy (1955). In 1975 they were the first women to receive the American Institute of Chemists Chemical Pioneer Award. On Brown's retirement in 1968, she received the Distinguished Service Award of the New York State Department of Health.

Rachel Brown always felt that although a scientific career demanded special sacrifices, it yielded deep rewards. For more than fifty years she was active in the American Association of University Women and strongly supported the participation of women in science, though she was sometimes frustrated by the lack of response on campuses. She gave generously both to her alma mater and to scholarships for high school and college women to become scientists. She died in 1980 in Albany at the age of eighty-one.

Bibliography: Richard S. Baldwin, in *The Fungus Fighters: Two Women Scientists and Their Discovery* (1981), provides a well-crafted tale of Brown's scientific collaboration with Elizabeth Lee Hazen. Original papers used by Baldwin on both Brown and Hazen and the Brown-Hazen Fund are now held by the Schlesinger Library, Radcliffe Institute for Advanced Study, Harvard University. Mount Holyoke College holds a manuscript collection that includes course records, correspondence, writings, memorabilia, biographical information, and photographs. The Special Collections Research Center at the University of Chicago Library has Brown's student notes and chemistry notebooks from 1920 to 1926. Details of her life and accomplishments are included in Edna Yost, *Women of Modern Science* (1959), and Louis Haber, *Women Pioneers of Science* (1979). An obituary appeared in the *New York Times* on January 16, 1980.

SARA F. TJOSSEM

BROWNE, Marjorie Lee. September 9, 1914–October 19, 1979. Mathematician, educator.

Marjorie Lee Browne was one of the first African American women to earn a PhD in mathematics. She then spent thirty years on the faculty of North Carolina Central University (NCCU), twenty-five of them as the only person with a doctorate in math, and nineteen as department chair. "I always, always, always liked mathematics," she said shortly before her death. "As a child I was rather introverted, and mathematics was a lonely subject, something I could do alone. As an adult, I do have plenty of friends and I talk with them for hours at a time. But I also like to be alone, and mathematics is something I can do completely alone. If I had my life to live again, I wouldn't do anything else. I *love* mathematics" (Kenschaft, 1981, p. 594).

She was born in Memphis, Tennessee, the second child of Mary Taylor and Lawrence Johnson Lee, a railway postal clerk. He had attended Leland College in northern Louisiana for two years, and loved math. A "whiz" at mental arithmetic, he followed his daughter's mathematical studies as long as he could. Mary Taylor Lee died before her daughter was two years old, so the children were raised by their stepmother, Lottie Taylor Lee, a schoolteacher. She also enthusiastically encouraged Marjorie's interest in mathematics.

Marjorie Lee's early formal education was in the LaRose Elementary School in Memphis. She then attended LeMoyne High School, a private school started after the Civil War by the Methodist and Congregational churches, where she was influenced by its excellent teachers. She enrolled at LeMoyne College in Memphis but longed to go to Howard University. Her father helped her fulfill that dream, and she graduated cum laude from Howard with a BS in 1935.

Teaching jobs were scarce during the Depression. From 1935 to 1939 she taught at Gilbert Academy in New Orleans, a Methodist secondary school. (Her grandfather Taylor was a Methodist minister, and she remained affiliated with the Methodist church throughout her life.) While teaching at the academy, she married James Browne, an English teacher there, but they were divorced after a few years. They had no children.

During her summers off from teaching, Browne began taking graduate courses at the University of Michigan. In 1939 she received her MS degree and began teaching at Wiley College in Marshall, Texas, while she continued to work toward her doctorate at Michigan under the direction of G. Y. Rainich. In 1947–48 she returned to Michigan as a teaching fellow to finish her graduate studies. In 1949 she defended her thesis, "On the One Parameter Subgroups in Certain Topological and Matrix Groups," and was officially awarded the PhD in 1950.

Browne joined the faculty at North Carolina Central University in Durham, North Carolina, in 1949. Her talents were quickly recognized, and she served as chair of the Department of Mathematics from 1951 to 1970. During her tenure as chair, Browne won a $60,000 grant from IBM for NCCU's first academic computer, one of the first such grants awarded to a historically black institution. She supervised its installation, and it went on line in March 1962. In October 1974 the North Carolina chapter of the National Council of Teachers of Mathematics made her one of the first two honorees to receive the W. W. Rankin Award for Excellence in Mathematics Education; the other was the late Dr. Rankin himself.

An important part of Browne's mathematical career was work conducted under the auspices of the National Science Foundation (NSF). Under her leadership, North Carolina Central University received grants from the NSF from 1957 to 1971 for an Institute for Secondary Teachers of Science and Mathematics to be held on campus each summer. In 1964–65 Browne was also the director of an NSF Undergraduate Research Participation Program at NCCU. She served on NSF advisory panels in 1966, 1967, and 1973, and also served as a faculty consultant in mathematics for the Ford Foundation in 1968–69.

Browne later observed that she had pursued "the life of an academic nomad" (Fletcher, p. 460), referring to the three postdoctoral fellowships she held. Browne's first foreign travel was in 1952–53 to Western Europe, in conjunction with a year as a Ford Fellow at Cambridge University studying combinatorial topology. In 1958–59 she was an NSF Faculty Fellow at UCLA, where she studied numerical analysis and computing. She spent the year 1965–66 at Columbia University studying Lie groups and Lie algebras, again as an NSF Faculty Fellow. She also spent a summer at Stanford in 1957.

Along with being department chair and professionally active, Browne taught fifteen hours a week, both graduate and undergraduate courses, and supervised ten master's theses. This left little time for research or writing, but in August 1955 her "Note on the Classical Groups" was published in the *American Mathematical Monthly*. She also wrote four sets of lecture notes for the NCCU NSF institutes: "Sets, Logic and Mathematical Thought" (1957), "Introduction to Linear Algebra" (1959), "Algebraic Structures" (1964), and "Elementary Matrix Algebra" (1969).

In the classroom, Marjorie Lee Browne was known as a rigorous teacher whose love of mathematics and personal warmth inspired numerous students. During her later years she often helped pay for the education of gifted young people. After thirty years at North Carolina Central University, she retired in 1979. She intended to write about the real number system, but had a sudden heart attack on October 19 and died in her home in Durham at the age of sixty-five. In a time when few women and fewer African Americans pursued high-level careers in mathematics, Browne's life was a pioneering beacon.

Bibliography: Biographical and professional information for this article was drawn from conversations and supporting material sent by Browne to the author in October 1979. Additional information was provided by William Thomas Fletcher, a student of Browne's at NCCU who succeeded her as department chair. See his "Marjorie Lee Browne—A Biography," in Jack Salzman, David Lionel Smith, and Cornel West, eds., *Encyclopedia of African American Culture and History* (1996); and "Marjorie Lee Browne—An American Mathematician," *Twentieth-Century Scientists* (1994). Additional material on Browne is found in Patricia C. Kenschaft, "Black Women in Mathematics in the United States," *American Mathematical Monthly* 88, no. 8 (October 1981), pp. 592–604; and Kenschaft, "Marjorie Lee Browne: In Memoriam," *Association for Women in Mathematics Newsletter* 10, no. 5 (September–October 1980), pp. 8–11. Additional information was supplied by colleagues Virginia Knight and Scott Williams, and Browne's cousins Lavern Taylor Pierce and Thaddeus Taylor.

PATRICIA CLARK KENSCHAFT

BRUCH, Hilde. March 11,1904–December 15, 1984. Physician, psychiatrist.

Hilde Bruch was born in Duelken (now Viersen), Germany, the third of seven children of Hirsch and Adele Rath Bruch. Her parents, who were Jewish, ran a successful livestock business in predominantly Catholic Duelken. Until the age of ten, Hilde attended a one-room Jewish school and then advanced to a local secular school. At twelve, she commuted by train to a *gymnasium* in München-Gladbach where she took the college preparatory course. Despite the dislocations of World War I, she graduated in 1923 and began the study of medicine. After graduation from the medical school at Albert Ludwig University (Freiberg) in 1929, she did an internship at the Physiolog Institut, University of Kiel, and also began pediatric training.

In 1930, Bruch began a two-year residency at Leipzig's Children's Hospital, which she never completed because of anti-Semitism associated with the rise of Nazism. In August 1932, when clinic work became untenable for her, she tried to establish a private pediatric practice in Düsseldorf but was thwarted by the escalating restrictions on non-Aryan physicians. Bruch returned to her hometown, but the situation there was no better. Leaving Germany for London in June 1933 under the pretext of attending an international pediatric conference, she declared herself a student of midwifery in order to circumvent employment restrictions in England. Bruch spent one year in London; with the help of the Jewish Refugees Committee, she secured work as a research assistant in a child guidance clinic in London's East End. Finding England staid and its medicine old-fashioned, she asked her mother's cousin, David Kaufmann, a Kansas businessman, to sponsor her immigration to the United States. She arrived in New York in October 1934.

Through contacts made on the Atlantic crossing, Bruch quickly secured an interview with

Rustin McIntosh, chief of pediatrics at Columbia University's College of Physicians and Surgeons, who recognized that her training in physiology would be desirable in the laboratory of Donovan J. McCune, an infant researcher. Bruch was appointed assistant in pediatrics at Babies Hospital but the position carried no salary. She depended on the Emergency Committee in Aid of Displaced Foreign Physicians for wages, and on the National Council of Jewish Women for personal support.

Although her adjustment to life in the United States appeared successful, Bruch was fearful about her family's survival and distressed by her lack of funds to help bring them to safety. She was also anxious to become a citizen so she could provide her family with preferred immigration status, but the process was slow and would not be finalized until 1940. She attempted suicide in March 1935 and spent a number of months as a psychiatric patient at Bloomingdale Hospital. The experience sensitized her to the problem of mental illness and provided her initial experience with American psychiatry.

After recovering, Bruch developed an endocrine clinic for children at the College of Physicians and Surgeons, where her new work on childhood obesity was supported by the Josiah Macy Jr. Foundation. Bruch was skeptical of the hormonal explanations of disease that were popular in the 1930s, and began to look instead for emotional and intrafamilial contributions to both overweight and underweight. She gained prominence in the medical profession in 1939 for proving that Froelich's syndrome, a disorder in boys, does not originate in a pituitary abnormality and is responsive to psychotherapy.

Bruch's ideas about the origin of appetite disorders led her to pursue training in psychiatry and psychoanalysis at Johns Hopkins University Hospital, the Henry Phipps Psychiatric Clinic, and the Baltimore-Washington Institute of Psychoanalysis, where she studied with Harry Stack Sullivan and FRIEDA FROMM-REICHMANN from 1941 to 1943. Fromm-Reichmann, also a refugee from Nazi Germany, became Bruch's analyst and later a close personal friend, providing access to a community of women physicians as well as emotional support as Bruch tried to rescue her family. Bruch's mother and two younger brothers escaped with her help, but her older brother and sister died in concentration camps. In 1946, Bruch brought her nephew, Herbert, the son of her oldest brother, to the United States and eventually adopted him. Although she had been involved in romantic relationships in Germany and the United States, she never married.

From 1943 to 1964, Bruch practiced psychoanalysis in New York City, taught at Columbia's College of Physicians and Surgeons, and directed the Children's Service at the New York State Psychiatric Institute (1954–56). In *The Importance of Overweight* (1957) and in articles in popular magazines, she described how obesity can be generated by parental misconceptions of the child's needs, leading to confusion, anger, and misinterpretation of bodily sensations. By the 1960s, Bruch was a leading expert on both overeating and not eating, which she regarded as points on a spectrum. She published extensively on anorexia nervosa in medical journals, and outlined the process of diagnosis for American doctors as the disorder became more common.

In 1964, Bruch became a professor of psychiatry at Baylor University School of Medicine in Houston, where she devoted herself increasingly to the treatment of anorexia nervosa. Physicians, parents, and young women from across the nation wrote seeking her advice. Dismayed by the paucity of knowledge and the use of inappropriate therapies, she published *Eating Disorders: Obesity, Anorexia Nervosa and the Person Within* (1973), intended for mental health professionals. She also began to write about anorexia nervosa for popular magazines for women and girls. *The Golden Cage: The Enigma of Anorexia Nervosa* (1978) sold over 150,000 copies and was translated into German, French, Italian, Swedish, and Japanese. Based on seventy case histories drawn from her clinical practice, it was the first book to provide a clear and largely sympathetic account of how anorexia nervosa is related to psychosexual issues in adolescence and why anorectics insist on bodily control through dieting.

Widely recognized for her work on eating disorders in the late 1970s and early 1980s, Hilde Bruch was eulogized as "Lady Anorexia" when she died in Houston in 1984 from the effects of Parkinson's disease at the age of eighty. A tall woman with a large frame who loved to cook and eat, Bruch was known to colleagues and friends for her firm opinions and willingness to confront controversy. She displayed sensitivity in her clinical conversations with anorectics and provided the medical profession and lay public with a diagnostic and therapeutic model for the disease. Her work was a bellwether that marked the beginning of a rise in the number of diagnosed cases of anorexia nervosa, a disorder that was associated increasingly with adolescent girls in the late twentieth century.

Bibliography: Hilde Bruch's papers are located at the Texas Medical Center Library in Houston. Randy J. Sparks, ed., *The Papers of Hilde Bruch: A Manuscript Collection in the Harris County Medical Archive* (1985), is a guide to that collection and contains a complete bibliography of Bruch's published professional and popular writing on anorexia nervosa and eating disorders. The Texas Medical Center Library also contains an oral history interview with Bruch done by Jane Preston and Hannah Decker

(November 1974–January 1975). Joanne Hatch Bruch, *Unlocking* The Golden Cage: *An Intimate Biography of Hilde Bruch, M.D.* (1996), is an intimate and nonscholarly biography of the subject's life by the wife of Bruch's adopted nephew. Other biographical material is found in Reinhard Heitkamp, "Hilde Bruch: Leben und Werk" (PhD dissertation, University of Cologne Medical School, 1987); and Theodore Lidz, "Hilde Bruch, 1904–84" *American Journal of Psychiatry* 142, no. 7 (July 1985), pp. 869–70.

In addition to *The Importance of Overweight* (1957), *Eating Disorders* (1973), and *The Golden Cage* (1978), Bruch's vast medical publications include "Psychiatric Aspects of Obesity in Childhood," *American Journal of Psychiatry* 99 (1943), pp. 752–57; "Hunger and Instinct," *Journal of Nervous and Mental Disease* 149, no. 2 (August 1969), pp. 91–114; and "Anorexia Nervosa: Therapy and Theory," *American Journal of Psychiatry* 139 (1982), pp. 1531–38. Completed before her death, but published posthumously, Danita Czyzewski and Melanie Suhr, eds., *Conversations with Anorexics* (1988), is a summary of Bruch's fifty years of experience with anorexia nervosa. Joan Jacobs Brumberg, *Fasting Girls: The Emergence of Anorexia Nervosa as a Modern Disease* (1988), places the disease within late-nineteenth- and twentieth-century popular and medical history. Bruch's work in endocrinology is given cultural meaning in Paula Saukko, "Fat Boys and Goody Girls: Hilde Bruch's Work on Eating Disorders and the American Anxiety about Democracy, 1930–1960," in Jeffrey Sobal and Donna Maurer, eds., *Weighty Issues: Fatness and Thinness as Social Problems* (1999).

JOAN JACOBS BRUMBERG

BUCH, Vera. *See* Weisbord, Vera Buch.

BUGBEE, Emma. May 19, 1888–October 6, 1981. Journalist.

A New York City reporter for fifty-five years, Emma Bugbee established herself as a quiet feminist who loved newspaper work and helped other women enter the male-dominated field. Born in Shippensburg, Pennsylvania, she was a Bugbee on both sides of the family, but her parents were not believed to be relatives. Her father, Edward Howard Bugbee, dated his family back to his grandfather, Howard Bugbee, who arrived in Cornish, New Hampshire, in 1811. Her mother, Emma A. J. Bugbee, was descended from Edward Bugbee, who came to Massachusetts from England in 1634.

Emma was the only girl in the family; she had younger twin brothers and an older brother. Both of her parents were high school teachers who likely had attended state normal schools in New York. Her mother declined to wear a wedding ring because she thought it denoted female subjugation, and she influenced her only daughter to believe in woman's rights. Emma's father died when Emma was eleven years old, and her mother replaced him as a high school teacher in Port Jervis, New York, to complete the school term. She then moved her family to Methuen, Massachusetts, her parents' home, where she took a job teaching French at the public high school that Bugbee attended.

After graduation Bugbee enrolled in Barnard College, living with an aunt who was a New York City schoolteacher. Drawn to journalism, she volunteered to be campus correspondent for the *Tribune.* She received her bachelor's degree in 1909 and returned to Methuen to teach Greek for one year at her former high school, but she was unhappy. When a Barnard friend, Eva vom Baur Hansl, asked Bugbee to be a vacation substitute for her at the *Tribune* in July 1910, she quickly agreed. Hansl, later the woman's editor for the *New York Sun,* traveled longer than expected in Germany, and Bugbee was hired permanently. She remained at the *Tribune,* which became the *Herald Tribune* in 1924, until her retirement two days before it stopped publication in 1966, setting a record of longevity for a woman reporter in New York City. She was then seventy-seven years old.

During her first years at the newspaper, Bugbee was not allowed to sit with male reporters in the newsroom but was forced to occupy separate quarters. Her first major assignment was covering a three-week winter march of suffragists from New York City to Albany in 1911: she trudged along with the group through the snow by day and filed her stories each night. Bugbee gained her first byline in 1914 when she posed as a Salvation Army worker and rang a bell to attempt to collect money for the poor at Christmas. Her story began, "Is it the hearts or the hands of New Yorkers that are so cold?" In spite of being a token woman on the city staff, Bugbee loved her job and valued her friendships with women on other newspapers. "We thought it [newspaper work] was *wonderful,*" she told an interviewer late in life (Collins, *She Was There,* p. 13). "Everybody thinks I was high in journalism, but there were eleven newspapers in New York, and they all had at least one woman on the staff" (ibid., p. 15).

A steady but not spectacular performer, Bugbee covered subjects ranging from murder trials to religion, which was her assignment at the time she retired, but editors confined her chiefly to topics aimed at women readers, including women in politics. Starting in 1928 she specialized in reporting on the career of ELEANOR ROOSEVELT, who had attracted press attention as the wife of New York governor Franklin D. Roosevelt; Bugbee covered Roosevelt until 1962, when Eleanor died. Sent to Washington in 1933 to report on Roosevelt's role during her husband's inauguration, Bugbee became a key participant in Eleanor Roosevelt's women-only press conferences. Although the *Herald Tribune* was staunchly Republican, the editors were so impressed when Roosevelt invited her to lunch at the White House that they kept Bugbee in the capital for four months. Subsequently, from time to time she took the train from New York to Washington to attend the conferences. In 1934 Bugbee was one of four women journalists who accompanied Roosevelt on a tour of Puerto Rico and the Virgin Islands to inspect conditions for women garment workers.

Bugbee's coverage of Eleanor Roosevelt pictured her as a role model for women. Bugbee's final story for the *Herald Tribune* was on the dedication of a Roosevelt memorial bench at the United Nations. It ran in the newspaper's last issue, April 24, 1966, with a picture of Bugbee on the bench and a caption calling her a "Devoted Reporter." The story was accompanied by a tribute from another staff member to Bugbee herself. A tall woman with a big smile and a motherly air, Bugbee was said to resemble Roosevelt.

Throughout her career Bugbee worked to improve the status of women journalists. Serving three terms as president of the Newspaper Women's Club of New York, which she helped found in 1922 to bring together women who had covered the suffrage movement, she may have been responsible for Roosevelt's club membership. Another prominent member was HELEN ROGERS REID, president of the *Herald Tribune*, with whom Bugbee had a warm relationship. Reid wrote the introduction for the first of Bugbee's five "Peggy" books, a popular series for adolescent readers about the fictional adventures of a woman reporter in New York, Washington, London, and World War II. Roosevelt figured prominently in one volume. With proceeds from the books, Bugbee, who loved the outdoors, built a weekend house in Bethel, Connecticut.

Bugbee never married. Her religious affiliation was Unitarian Universalist. Surrounded by paintings she painted after retirement, she spent the last eleven years of her life in a nursing home in Warwick, Rhode Island, where she died at age ninety-three. She is buried in Lawrence, Massachusetts. Her significance lay in her ability to display a quiet competence in the rough-and-tumble world of New York journalism for a half century while never losing sight of the fact that women in journalism needed to band together to open the door wider for other women.

Bibliography: There are no manuscript sources for Bugbee, although correspondence with Eleanor Roosevelt can be found at the Franklin D. Roosevelt Library, Hyde Park, New York, which also has pictures of Bugbee with Eleanor Roosevelt. The Library of Congress has a copy of a 1950 episode of the NBC television series *Today with Mrs. Roosevelt* in which Roosevelt interviewed five reporters, including Bugbee, on freedom of the press. Genealogical information can be located in Justin Coy Bugbee, compiler, *The Family of Edward Bugbee* (1982). Bugbee's books for juveniles contain considerable information about conditions for women in metropolitan journalism in the 1930s and 1940s. They are: *Peggy Covers the News* (1936), *Peggy Covers Washington* (1937), *Peggy Covers London* (1939), *Peggy Covers the Clipper* (1941), and *Peggy Goes Overseas* (1945). Oral history interviews with Bugbee appear in Jean E. Collins, *She Was There: Stories of Pioneering Women Journalists* (1980) and "Two of Barnard's Nellie Blys," *Barnard Alumnae* 65, no. 2 (Winter 1976), pp. 2–4. Other references can be found in Richard Kluger, *The Paper: The Life and Death of the New York Herald Tribune* (1986); Ishbel Ross, *Ladies of the Press* (1936); and Bess Furman, *Washington By-Line* (1949). Family information was obtained from David Starr of Cranston, Rhode Island, whose wife was a niece of Bugbee. An obituary appeared in the *New York Times* on October 10, 1981.

MAURINE H. BEASLEY

BUNTING, Mary (Polly) Ingraham. July 10, 1910–January 21, 1998. Educator, microbiologist, feminist.

Mary Ingraham Bunting, known all her life as Polly, was born into an old, established Brooklyn family, the eldest of four children. Her father, Henry Andrews Ingraham, was a lawyer, but also an expert trout fisherman, a lover of literature, and a trustee of his alma mater, Wesleyan University. Her mother, Mary Shotwell Ingraham, was president of the national Young Women's Christian Association and a longtime member of the New York City Board of Higher Education.

As a child, Polly was a tomboy and an enthusiastic rider who competed once in Madison Square Garden. Because of a succession of illnesses, she missed most of elementary school, educating herself in her father's extensive library. She graduated from Packer Collegiate Institute, an all-girls Brooklyn school, in 1927 and went directly to Vassar, where she discovered bacteriology and knew she had found her life's work. She graduated Phi Beta Kappa, with honors, in 1931 and was awarded the college's most prestigious fellowship for graduate study. She completed her PhD at the University of Wisconsin in agricultural bacteriology in only three years—because, she came to understand, her professors thought it less important to give her the necessary grounding since they did not expect a woman to accomplish much in science.

After Polly received her PhD in 1933, she taught biology, genetics, and bacteriology for two years at Bennington as a nontenured instructor. In June 1937 she married Henry Bunting, whom she had met when he was a medical student at Wisconsin. During Henry's internship and residency at Baltimore City Hospital, Polly taught at Goucher College. When they went to New Haven, where he completed his residency in pathology at

Yale Medical School, she did research in bacterial genetics and published several papers in the *Journal of Bacteriology*. She and Henry lived in Bethany, Connecticut, where they set up a small but self-sufficient farm. When the first of their four children, Mary, was born in 1940, Bunting decided to temporarily abandon her scientific work and be a full-time mother and farmer. Three sons followed: Charles (1942), William (1945), and John (1947). Nonetheless, Polly was active in the community, serving as a 4-H leader and helping establish a regional high school.

In 1946, Salvador Luria, who later won the Nobel Prize, invited her to present a paper at the first major conference in her discipline after World War II. She was the only woman on the program, and Luria insisted they could not hold the conference without her. She had pioneered a convenient and effective system to track and measure generational changes (analogous to gene mutations in higher organisms) in a bright red strain of bacteria, *Serratia marcescens,* which threw off pink and white mutants. Previously no one had believed bacteria had nuclei, genes, or mutations.

Polly Bunting's rural life ended abruptly when, in April 1954, just weeks after his forty-fourth birthday, Henry Bunting died suddenly of a malignant brain tumor. Now she had four young children to support, and Yale was unwilling to offer any woman a full-time position. At this difficult moment in her life the president of Rutgers University, Lewis Webster Jones, whom she had known at Bennington, offered her the deanship of Douglass College, the women's division of Rutgers. At the age of forty-five, abandoning the country life she and her children loved, she embarked on an entirely new career.

At Douglass, she almost immediately proposed a revolutionary program permitting older women to be part-time students. Faculty objected, fearing these women would not be serious and would erode academic standards. Bunting's answer was that people need opportunities, not prejudgment. The program was established and still flourishes.

In 1957, she was appointed to a committee of the National Science Foundation. In the wake of Sputnik, the committee wanted to find out why so many scientifically talented high school students in America were not going to college. It found that 90 percent of these were female. When the other members of the committee—all men—expressed no interest in this statistic, Polly realized that they, like her graduate school professors, did not expect women to accomplish anything professionally. That "awakening," as she called it, led to her realization that American women were living in "a climate of unexpectation." For the rest of her career, she devoted herself to changing that climate.

In 1960, Bunting assumed the presidency of Radcliffe College. She transformed the college, which had been a group of arid barracks housing students who commuted to classes at Harvard, into an integral component of the university—raising the money for a library at the quadrangle, establishing a house system commensurate with Harvard's, and gaining women access to Harvard's graduate schools and financial aid. At her first trustees meeting she announced her plan for the Radcliffe Institute for Independent Study (later renamed the Bunting Institute), a pathbreaking fellowship program that offered married women who had abandoned promising careers to raise families an opportunity to pick up where they had left off. In 1971 she helped negotiate a new agreement between Radcliffe and Harvard, which integrated offices, personnel, and housing and laid the groundwork for the eventual merger of the two institutions in 1999.

Bunting was at Radcliffe for twelve years, taking a leave in 1964–65 to complete the unfinished term of a commissioner at the Atomic Energy Commission. She was the first woman on the AEC, but preferred to be remembered as the first biologist. In this capacity, she raised questions about the environmental impact of atomic testing.

When she left Radcliffe in 1972, she became a special assistant to William Bowen, the new president of Princeton, with the primary responsibility of establishing a continuing education program. She stayed in that position until 1975, when she turned sixty-five.

Having been single for twenty-five years, in 1979 she astonished her family and friends by announcing that she was going to marry Clement A. Smith, a retired pediatrician of Harvard Medical School. They were married for nine and a half years until his death in 1988. She spent her final years in a retirement community in Hanover, New Hampshire, coping with Alzheimer's disease, which eroded her formidable faculties but which she endured with humor and good grace. She died there in 1998. Her family interred her ashes at Clem Smith's farmhouse in Peacham, Vermont.

Polly Bunting was a quiet, unpretentious, almost unintentional revolutionary. Though her own career had suffered from the "climate of unexpectation," she never expected to give her life to the struggle against that climate until she realized how much damage it was doing to the lives of other women. She made a crucial difference for thousands of those lives.

Bibliography: The archives of the Schlesinger Library at the Radcliffe Institute for Advanced Study, Harvard University, contain extensive files of papers relating to Polly Bunting. An extensive oral history completed in 1978 by Jeannette Bailey Cheek discusses her life, background, ideas, and goals; the quotations in the text are found there. The archives also contain copies of almost all of her scientific papers as well as both formal and informal speeches. Of particular interest are her address at Vassar's centennial, "Education and Evolution," October 12, 1961; her speech to the American Society for Microbiology, "From *Serratia* to Women's Lib and a Bit Beyond," May 5, 1971; and "Women: Resource for a Changing World," April 17, 1972, delivered at an invitational conference at Radcliffe. She laid out her principles effectively in "A Huge Waste: Educated Womanpower," *New York Times Magazine,* May 7, 1961, pp. 23, 109, 112. Useful secondary sources are the *Time* magazine cover story "One Woman, Two Lives," November 3, 1961, pp. 68–73; Elizabeth Moot O'Hern, *Profiles of Pioneer Women Scientists* (1985); and Margaret Rossiter, *Women Scientists in America before Affirmative Action, 1940–1972* (1995). Obituaries appeared in the *New York Times* and *Boston Globe* on January 23, 1998.

ELAINE YAFFE

BUNZEL, Ruth Leah. April 18, 1898–January 14, 1990. Anthropologist.

Ruth Bunzel was a noted cultural anthropologist who specialized in Pueblo societies, especially Zuni. She was one of a cadre of distinguished women anthropologists (with RUTH BENEDICT, Esther Goldfrank, MARGARET MEAD, and GLADYS REICHARD) who worked in New York City, under the tutelage of Franz Boas and ELSIE CLEWS PARSONS, and shared an interest in the ethnography of the American Southwest. Benedict, Mead, and Bunzel were especially close; their personal and professional lives were intertwined in a remarkable network of women anthropologists from the 1920s through the 1960s.

Ruth Leah Bunzel was born in New York City to Hattie Bernheim and Jonas Bunzel, well-educated Jews of German and Czech heritage. The youngest of four children, she was raised by her mother after her father, a successful retailer, died in 1908 from heart problems. Her mother was independent and financially comfortable with a trust fund from her family's business importing Cuban tobacco. Bunzel was raised as a reformed Jew in a household in which English was spoken as a first language and German as a second.

Bunzel graduated in 1918 from Barnard College, where she was an inquisitive but shy student. Without specific career goals, she initially majored in German but changed to European history due to the political atmosphere and anti-German sentiment in New York during World War I. She also took classes in anthropology from Franz Boas, one of America's premier anthropologists, who was then taking a strong anti-war stance. Bunzel, however, remained generally apolitical.

After graduating, Bunzel held a series of temporary clerical jobs before becoming Boas's secretary in 1922, when Esther Goldfrank, a friend of Bunzel's sister Madeleine, left to pursue full-time study in anthropology and conduct fieldwork in the American Southwest. In 1924 Boas traveled to Europe for the summer and Bunzel accompanied Ruth Benedict, an anthropologist at Columbia University, to Zuni Pueblo in New Mexico. At Boas's suggestion, Bunzel conducted her own research project in addition to serving as Benedict's assistant. She studied the relationship of the artist to her craft, and how women potters interpreted aesthetic styles. Employing participant observation and projective interviewing techniques, the study was both culturally sensitive and appropriate because it dealt with women's culture. *The Pueblo Potter: A Study of Creative Imagination in Primitive Art* (1929) became Bunzel's dissertation and a classic in the anthropology of art, the first anthropological work to combine aesthetic analysis and psychology. As Bunzel modestly noted years later, "I was too ignorant at the time to know that I was pioneering" (*Daughters of the Desert,* p. 41).

On her return, Bunzel became a doctoral candidate in anthropology at Columbia. She returned to New Mexico for several more fieldwork seasons in the 1920s and 1930s to study Zuni culture and values, making more than ten trips, lasting four to twelve months each, and received her PhD in 1929. Many of her most important publications in ritual, mythology, texts, and ritual poetry were based on this research. She concentrated on culture and personality, a new area of anthropology to which she made several theoretical contributions. She also was a noted linguist (she studied with Edward Sapir) who learned the language with such fluency that Zuni elders consider her works on Zuni songs, prayers, and stories accurate today. As a result, many Zuni feel that her publications are important mechanisms to preserve their culture.

As important as her theoretical and descriptive publications is the esteem Zunis hold for Bunzel. In an era when American Indians often felt besieged by outside researchers, Bunzel fit in well at Zuni Pueblo and established lifelong relationships with her Zuni family. Bunzel also never violated Zuni prohibitions against taking photographs of ceremonies or attempted to gain access to areas considered inviolate. She participated in women's work, such as grinding corn, baking bread, and presenting ceremonial food, and became a good potter. Her sponsor, Flora Zuni, a sewing teacher at the Zuni Day School, formally adopted her. She received a Zuni name, Maiatitsa (blue bird, for the blue smock she wore) from Flora's Badger clan, and another, Tsatitsa, from Nick Dumaka, a Zuni governor.

Back in New York, Bunzel earned a modest living teaching evening and summer courses in anthropology at Columbia and Barnard for the university extension service, supplementing this income with fellowships and research grants. She was never given a tenure-track position. There were few during the Depression years, and Bunzel felt that her gender also marginalized her—with Benedict and Reichard on the faculty at Columbia and Barnard, there were no more slots for women academicians in anthropology. In general, she preferred fieldwork and writing to teaching.

During the mid 1930s, Bunzel continued her study of behavior. Supported by a Guggenheim Fellowship to travel to Guatemala, she centered her research on the Mayan village of Santo Tomas Chichicastenango, an important ceremonial and market center. Her monograph is considered one of the first community studies. She also conducted a comparative study of alcoholism in Mexico and Guatemala, the first anthropologist to work on this subject.

In 1936 Bunzel extended her research endeavors to Spain in order to assess the culture's impact on American Indian communities, but had to leave because of the Spanish Civil War. During World War II she remained in England working for the Office of War Information as a Spanish intelligence translator. From 1947 to 1951 she participated in the cultures-at-a-distance project called Research in Contemporary Cultures, sponsored by the Office of Naval Research, which studied the cultures of nations thought to be relevant to the rebuilding of the postwar world. Bunzel directed the group working on China and the Chinese living in New York City. Final reports were completed but never published.

Bunzel remained in government service until 1951, when she returned to Columbia as an adjunct professor; she taught in the university's extension service until her retirement in 1972. A quiet, private individual who never married or had children, she was never good at self-promotion and always considered herself an accidental anthropologist, having come into the field by chance. In retrospect she felt lucky to have been sponsored by Franz Boas and Ruth Benedict and to have been part of the network of female scholars based at Columbia University. As a social scientist who had a varied career, she hoped that her work in cross-cultural values would help American culture understand its own dynamics. Ruth Bunzel died at her home in Greenwich Village in 1990 at the age of ninety-one.

Bibliography: Information on Bunzel is from a 1985 oral interview for the Daughters of the Desert Project under the direction of Barbara A. Babcock and Nancy J. Parezo, archived at the Wenner-Gren Foundation for Anthropological Research, New York. Reference works about Bunzel include Babcock and Parezo, *Daughters of the Desert: Women Anthropologists and the Native American Southwest* (1988); David M. Fawcett and Teri McLuhan, "Ruth Leah Bunzel," in Ute Gacs, Aisha Khan, Jerrie McIntyre, and Ruth Weinberg, eds., *Women Anthropologists: A Biographical Dictionary* (1988); Margaret Mead, "Apprenticeship under Boas," in Walter Goldschmidt, ed., *The Anthropology of Franz Boas* (1959); and Triloki Pandey, "Anthropologists at Zuni," *Proceedings of the American Philosophical Society* 116, no. 4 (1972), pp. 321–37. Also of interest is Margaret Ann Hardin, "Zuni Potters and *The Pueblo Potter:* The Contributions of Ruth Bunzel," in Nancy J. Parezo, ed., *Hidden Scholars: Women Anthropologists and the Native American Southwest* (1993).

Major works by Ruth Bunzel include "Notes on the Kachina Cult in San Felipe," *Journal of American Folklore* 41 (1928), pp. 290–92; *The Pueblo Potter: A Study of Creative Imagination in Primitive Art* (1929); "Introduction: Zuni Ceremonialism," "Zuni Origin Myths," and "Zuni Ritual Poetry," all in *Bureau of American Ethnology 47th Annual Report for 1929–1930* (1932); *Zuni Texts* (1933); "Zuni," in Franz Boas, ed., *Handbook of American Indian Languages*, vol. 4 (1935); "Art" and "The Economic Organization of Primitive Peoples," in Boas, ed., *General Anthropology* (1938); *Chichicastenango, a Guatemalan Village* (1952); *The Golden Age of American Anthropology* (co-edited with Margaret Mead) (1960); and *Zuni Ceremonialism: Three Studies* (1992), which contains an introduction by Parezo. An obituary appeared in the *New York Times* on January 17, 1990.

NANCY J. PAREZO

BURKE, Selma. December 31, 1900–August 29, 1995. Sculptor, art educator.

Selma Hortense Burke was born in Mooresville, North Carolina, the seventh of ten children of African American parents, Mary Jackson and Neal Burke. Neal Burke was primarily a Methodist minister, although he also held outside jobs as a railroad brakeman and a cruise ship chef. Selma Burke's great-grandfather was reportedly owned by the family of Stonewall Jackson. After gaining his freedom, he attended college, setting an example for his descendants. Although Selma's father died when she was twelve, her mother lived a long life, beginning work on her college degree at age seventy-five.

Burke was interested in art from a very young age. The objects her father brought back from his ocean journeys were subjects for her models, made from the white clay of a local riverbed. She was also fascinated by a trunk full of African artifacts that was shipped back to North Carolina after the deaths of two paternal uncles who had served as missionaries abroad. Burke's father eagerly encouraged his daughter's artistic aspirations, but her mother, who wanted her to become a nurse, was more hesitant. After graduating from the Slater Industrial and State Normal School (later Winston-Salem State University), Burke went on to Saint Agnes Training School for Nurses, where she earned her RN in 1924.

In the late 1920s Burke worked as a private nurse for Amelia Waring, heiress of the Otis Elevator empire, who opened cultural doors for her employee. Protected from the Great Depression by Waring's wealth, Burke regularly attended operas at the Met and Carnegie Hall, hobnobbing with society people and artists. When Waring died, Burke resolved to go back to her true love, sculpture. She spent time working in New York City and studying at Sarah Lawrence College, modeling to pay for her classes. She visited Europe to hone her skills before attending Columbia University on scholarship, earning a master's of fine arts in 1941. In these years she also worked on the Federal Art Project and taught at Harlem Community Art Center under the supervision of sculptor AUGUSTA SAVAGE. Burke had her first solo exhibit at a New York City gallery in 1941.

To support the war effort, Burke took a job at Brooklyn Navy Yard but was injured driving a truck there. While she recuperated, she decided to participate in a competition to create a profile of Franklin Delano Roosevelt. After receiving the commission in 1943, she found two-dimensional sources inadequate and requested a sitting with the president. This was granted in 1944, and Burke sketched the image for which she is most famous. President Harry Truman unveiled the resulting plaque, sculpted in relief, at the dedication of the Recorder of Deeds Building in Washington, D.C., in September 1945. Burke's profile is largely accepted as the basis for the United States "Roosevelt" dime. The artist herself certainly put forward this view, despite occasional claims to the contrary.

Burke's personal life mirrored the changes she underwent professionally. She was involved with three men, although she usually only referred to the last two when recounting her life. Her first marriage was to childhood friend Durant Woodward in 1928. He was a mortician; they wed while she was an advanced nursing student at the Women's Medical College in Philadelphia. This marriage ended with Woodard's untimely death less than a year later from blood poisoning. After Burke settled in New York on her own, she became deeply involved in the burgeoning artistic community of the Harlem Renaissance. Around 1935 she met one of its stars, poet Claude McKay, with whom she had a significant but stormy relationship. (She stated that they had married and divorced, but biographies of McKay do not support that claim.) In 1949, she married architect Herman Kobbe; they moved to an artists' colony in New Hope, Pennsylvania, where they lived until his death in 1955. Burke did not have children in any of these relationships, and she did not marry again. She remained in Pennsylvania for the rest of her life, serving on numerous art and civic councils in Bucks County before moving to Pittsburgh.

Burke's work included portraits of numerous other well-known figures, including striking representations of MARY MCLEOD BETHUNE, Booker T. Washington, and Martin Luther King Jr. Other motifs included less well-known individuals, such as the German Jewish model she sculpted abroad during the Nazi ascension, as well as explorations of human emotion and families. "[My work] is of a woman's interest," she once reflected, a "labor of love." Burke most often focused her work on the human body, and she desired to create art that could be appreciated by all and not just by those who had an art education. Burke also sought to bring art education to more people. She taught at various places in New York and Pennsylvania, including the Selma Burke School of Sculpture in New York, which she founded in 1940. She also opened the Selma Burke Art Center in Pittsburgh, and operated it from the early 1970s until 1981. She wanted to teach children how to approach sculpture as a vibrant, lively art form, and believed they ought to touch these works to really understand them. Her school allowed her to connect her primary love of sculpting with thousands of eager recipients.

Selma Burke received numerous honorary degrees and awards up until the end of her life. Her works are housed in a wide variety of places, from the Mooresville Public Library in her North Carolina hometown to the Holy Rosary Church in Pittsburgh to the Museum of Modern Art in Miami, Florida. She spent her later years in a retirement home in New Hope, Pennsylvania, where she died of cancer at age ninety-four. Her remains were cremated, but her art stands as a timeless monument to her life.

Bibliography: Burke's papers were donated to Spelman College in Atlanta, Georgia. There is no full-length treatment of Burke's life, but useful biographies can be found in Darlene Clark Hine, ed., *Black Women in America* (1993); Jules Heller and Nancy G. Heller, eds., *North American Women Artists of the Twentieth Century: A Biographical Dictionary* (1995); and Jessie Carney Smith, ed., *Notable Black American Women* (1992). See also Robert J. Gangwere, "An Interview with Selma Burke," *Carnegie Magazine,* January 1975, pp. 6–12; the quotation in the text is found on p. 12. For the relationship between Burke and Claude McKay, see Wayne F. Cooper, *Claude McKay: Rebel Sojourner in the Harlem Renaissance* (1987). When Burke received an Essence award in 1989, *Essence* magazine ran a profile of her that included a wonderful photograph of the artist (October 1989, p. 68). A lengthy obituary appeared in the Pittsburgh *Post-Gazette* on August 30, 1995; the *New York Times* ran a much shorter one on September 2, 1995.

JENNIFER COTE

BURNS, Eveline M. March 16, 1900–September 2, 1985. Economist, Social Security expert.

Eveline M. Burns was one of the twentieth century's foremost scholars on social insurance and was among the small group of experts who helped design the U.S. Social Security Act of 1935. Born and educated in London, Eveline Mabel Richardson was the only child of Eveline Maud Falkner and Frederick Haig Richardson. Her mother died of complications from Eveline's birth, and her father remarried a year later. Her father and stepmother had three more children. Eveline and her siblings grew up in an apolitical, nonreligious, middle-class household. Frederick ran the London office of the Richardson family's Sheffield silversmith business.

After attending Streatham Secondary School, Eveline entered London School of Economics (LSE) at age sixteen. While still in school she held her first career job—as an administrative officer in the British Ministry of Labor—where she worked from 1917 to 1920. Eveline graduated from LSE with first-class honors in economics in 1920. In school she met her future husband, Arthur Robert Burns, who was also an economics student at LSE. The couple married in April 1922; they did not have children.

Eveline Burns was hired as an assistant lecturer in economics at LSE in 1921 and earned her doctorate in 1926. Later that year, she and Arthur moved to the United States when Eveline was awarded a Laura Spelman Rockefeller Fellowship to study abroad. They decided to make the trans-Atlantic move permanent, and Eveline Burns became a lecturer in economics at Columbia University and Arthur Burns joined the faculty at Barnard College. Most of the economics faculty at Columbia were opposed to appointing a woman, but the chairman at the time, E. R. A. Seligman, was actively seeking to do so, and he believed that a foreign-born woman with degrees from LSE would be less controversial. (The couple did become naturalized U.S. citizens in 1937.) Burns remained on the Columbia economics faculty for fourteen years, taking a leave of absence from 1939 to 1942 to serve on President Roosevelt's National Resources Planning Board (NRPB). In 1939, Arthur also joined the Columbia economics faculty—this unusual arrangement may have contributed to the university's declining to renew Eveline's contract in 1942.

Eveline Burns's role as a technical expert for the Committee on Economic Security (CES) was the defining opportunity of her professional career, starting a lifelong involvement with Social Security. The CES, established in 1934 by President Franklin D. Roosevelt at the instigation of Labor Secretary FRANCES PERKINS, designed the Social Security Act of 1935. When the Social Security Board was established in 1935, Burns became its initial training consultant. Her first book on Social Security, *Toward Social Security: An Explanation of the Social Security Act and a Survey of the Larger Issues* (1936), became the indispensable guide for the first generation of Social Security officials.

Burns served as a senior staff member on the Social Science Research Council, then took a temporary position at the NRPB in 1939. Working until 1942 as director of research for its Committee on Long-Range and Relief Policies, and as chief of the Economic, Security and Health Section from 1942 until the NRPB was abolished in 1943, Burns was the primary author of the board's 640-page report "Security, Work and Relief Policies." Submitted just three days prior to the attack on Pearl Harbor, the report provided a blueprint for an expanded federal system of social welfare, but it fell on ears deafened by the thunder of war. Although the NRPB report was not released until 1943, and the government took no action on it, the report became a standard reference source on social insurance. Burns judged the NRPB report to be one of her best and most satisfying achievements.

After she completed her NRPB assignment and Columbia terminated her teaching contract, Burns did a stint as a consultant to the National Planning Association in Washington, D.C., and held a temporary academic appointment at Bryn Mawr. When she returned to Columbia in 1946, it was as a professor in the School of Social Work, where she created the doctoral program and served as the program's first chair. She also taught an influential course on comparative Social Security systems. Frustrated by the lack of a reliable textbook, she wrote her own, *The American Social Security System* (1949), which quickly became the standard text in the field. Three of her six books, and most of her more than one hundred published articles, focus on Social Security. Burns frequently worked as a consultant to the government on the Social Security Act, and to other government agencies—including the Federal Reserve, the Treasury Department, and the State Department—on a range of topics involving social welfare and economic security.

Eveline Burns had close working relationships with many social welfare figures of her time, but most especially with MARY (MOLLY) DEWSON, a social reformer and member of the Social Security Board whom Burns considered her "American godmother." In addition, Burns was prominent in many professional organizations, including the American Association of University Women, the Consumers' League of New York, the American Economic Association, and the National Conference on Social Welfare. At the American Public Welfare Association she collaborated closely with Loula Dunn and served for many years on the association's executive boards.

When Dwight Eisenhower came into office in 1953, the Chamber of Commerce tried to convince the president to replace contributory social insurance under Social Security with a flat-rate system that would severely limit benefits. Eisenhower's secretary of Health, Education and Welfare, OVETA CULP HOBBY, formed a small cadre of informal advisors, known as the Hobby lobby, to consider the various proposals. The only pro—Social Security member of the original five-person group was Eveline Burns, and it was partly thanks to her advocacy that Hobby and Eisenhower declined to support the proposed flat-rate system and even sponsored an expansion of Social Security in 1954.

In addition to her teaching at Columbia, Burns was a visiting professor at Princeton and Bryn Mawr, and at Manchester University in England on a Guggenheim Fellowship during 1954–55. Following her retirement from Columbia in 1967, she held professorships at New York University and Barnard College. Eveline Burns continued to work as author, consultant, and lecturer until 1981, following her husband's death. In 1985, she helped mark the fiftieth anniversary of Social Security by participating in scholarly conferences and ceremonial observances. Just nineteen days before her death, Burns made a final public appearance at an anniversary event at the Social Security headquarters in Baltimore. Following the ceremony, she returned to the Quaker retirement community in Newton, Pennsylvania, that had been her home since 1981. She fell ill a few days later and died in Newton's St. Mary's Hospital on September 2, 1985, at the age of eighty-five.

Bibliography: Eveline Burns's papers are in the Social Welfare History Archives, University of Minnesota Libraries, Minneapolis–St. Paul. For biographical information, see Linda R. Wolf Jones, *Eveline M. Burns and the American Social Security System, 1935–1960* (1991), and *Current Biography* (1960), pp. 64–66. Also of interest is Shirley Jenkins, ed., *Social Security in International Perspective: Essays in Honor of Eveline M. Burns* (1969), which contains a full bibliography. There is a lengthy 1965 oral history interview with Peter Corning in the Social Security Project collection at the Oral History Research Office, Columbia University; and a brief 1985 oral history with Blanche Coll, which is available through the Social Security Administration History Archives in Baltimore, Maryland. Books by Burns not mentioned in the text include *Wages and the State: A Comparative Study of the Problems of State Wage Regulation* (1926); *The Economic World: A Survey* (with A. R. Burns, 1927); *Social Security and Public Policy* (1956); and *Health Services for Tomorrow: Trends and Issues* (1973). See also Linda Gordon, *Pitied but Not Entitled: Single Mothers and the History of Welfare, 1890–1935* (1994). Obituaries appeared in the *New York Times* on September 6, 1985, and the *London Times* on September 7, 1985.

LARRY DEWITT

BUTE, Mary Ellen. November 21, 1906–October 17, 1983. Filmmaker.

Texas-born artist Mary Ellen Bute deserves a special place in film history as America's foremost innovator of abstract animation starting in the early 1930s, and as world pioneer in electronic imagery in the early 1950s. Bute then turned to live-action productions, notably the feature-length *Passages from Finnegans Wake* (1965) and an unfinished work on Walt Whitman. Throughout her fifty-year career she headed her own New York–based production company called Expanding Cinema, which her letterhead described as "a company doing research, experimental and creative work in motion pictures."

Mary Ellen was the first of six children born to the Butes, a prominent Houston family. Her father, James House Bute, gave up a medical practice in favor of cattle ranching and oil well options. Her mother, Claire Robinson, made her debut into Houston society a year before she married. Undoubtedly the young daughter was expected to adopt her parents' privileged lifestyle, but Mary Ellen turned to the arts to express her independent and exuberant personality.

At age sixteen, before completing her last two years of high school, Bute left home with a scholarship to Pennsylvania Academy of Fine Arts in Philadelphia, expecting to become a painter of flowers and horses in the style of Rosa Bonheur. Once there, Bute saw abstract paintings by Mondrian, Braque, and other European modernists, and her artistic aspirations were turned upside down. Kandinsky's beautiful configurations reminded her of "frozen music" and she longed to see them developed in time-continuity.

For the next dozen years, Bute traveled, studied, and experimented with ways to create a new kinetic art. She studied modern stage-lighting techniques in New York City, which became her permanent home, and at Yale's newly opened School of Drama in 1925–26, as one of the first ten women admitted. In an effort to integrate science and art, Bute worked and conferred with such luminaries as color organist Thomas Wilfred, electronics wizard Leon Theremin, and mathematician and musicologist Joseph Schillinger. Asked to create abstract drawings for a never-completed film Schillinger was working on with filmmaker-historian Lewis Jacobs, Bute soon realized that with expert technical help she could make motion pictures that would synchronize light and sound.

Help came from avant-garde filmmaker Melville J. Webber and special-effects cameraman Theodore "Ted" Nemeth. With their collaboration Mary Ellen Bute created the five-minute *Rhythm in Light* (1934), the first publicly shown American abstract motion picture. Filmed in Bute's small midtown apartment, *Rhythm in Light* has as its musical accompaniment Grieg's familiar "Anitra's Dance" from *Peer Gynt.* It was the first of Bute's three black-and-white productions that cinematically explored the abstract spaces and shapes of everyday objects (eggbeaters, crumpled cellophane, table-tennis balls) and models of large objects (staircases, archways) with rhythmically moving lights.

In the next two decades Bute created more than a dozen short abstract films with Nemeth's invaluable technical collaboration. The films ran three to nine minutes, with music by such composers as Wagner, Bach, Shostakovich and Aaron Copland. Starting in 1937 with *Escape,* Bute introduced color, for which she generally painted individual flat geometric forms, using a continuum of graphs to correlate pictures and sound. To enhance the popular appeal of these films, she called them the "Seeing Sound" series. Most of the films were widely shown in major movie theaters such as the prestigious Radio City Music Hall (where in June 1935 some eighteen thousand people a day saw *Rhythm in Light* before the feature presentation) and in the growing number of art houses around the country.

On October 15, 1940, Mary Ellen Bute and Ted Nemeth eloped. Soon afterward he opened Ted Nemeth Studio, which provided what he called their "bread-and-butter" income and which also distributed all of Bute's films. Between her *Tarantella* (1940) and *Polka Graph* (1947), Bute gave birth to their two sons: Theodore Jr. (1941) and James (1947).

Starting in 1952, Bute began experimenting with a specially modified oscilloscope that permitted her to create abstract drawings with a beam of light as freely as with a pencil. Her *Abstronic* (1952) and *Mood Contrasts* (1953) were among the world's first films to use electronically generated imagery and were also her last "visual music" productions. In 1956, Bute turned to live action with a half-hour dramatic film entitled *The Boy Who Saw Through,* which cast teenager Christopher Walken as the boy who could see through walls (and adults' posturings and pretenses).

One of Bute's gifts was her ability to find talented collaborators and assistants: sculptor Rutherford Boyd, whose three-dimensional artwork provided substance for her film *Parabola* (1937); animator Norman McLaren, who hand-painted on film the character designs for her popular *Spook Sport* (1939); conductor Leopold Stokowski, whose music opened and closed Bute's *Pastorale* (1950); and film editor Thelma Schoonmaker, who served as general factotum for six months or so on Bute's most ambitious production, *Passages from Finnegans Wake,* which took six years to complete. Like the off-Broadway play on which it was based, her cinematic adaptation dramatized bits and pieces of James Joyce's monumental, enigmatic work, adding some of Ted Nemeth's animation tricks. The film won an award at the Cannes Film Festival, but without stars or a straightforward narrative it was limited to art houses and failed to earn back its cost, estimated at $230,000.

In her seventies, amicably separated from Ted Nemeth and having depleted her inheritance, Mary Ellen Bute lived at a Salvation Army residence for women, located on New York's fashionable Gramercy Park. During that period Bute lectured and presented her films at numerous East Coast, midwestern, and Canadian venues, trying to earn enough money to finish her Walt Whitman film. Easily recognized by her relentless Texas accent, resounding laugh, red hair, and high heels (she was just over five feet tall), she still enjoyed dressing up, sometimes in a sequined split skirt or leopard-print leather pants, borrowed or rented for special occasions. Although she was never part of the burgeoning avant-garde scene, typified by MAYA DEREN, Marie Menken, and SHIRLEY CLARKE, Bute was a founding member and ardent supporter of the Women's Independent Film Exchange, which co-sponsored her Cineprobe presentation at the Museum of Modern Art six months before her death.

Mary Ellen Bute died of heart failure in New York City shortly before her seventy-seventh birthday. She had often predicted that, like music, her films would have a long life, and they continue to reach new generations of admiring filmmakers, avant-garde and electronic arts enthusiasts, and James Joyce aficionados around the world.

Bibliography: Mary Ellen Bute's films and papers, including photographs, stills, videotapes, and miscellaneous materials, are scattered around the country, in Yale University's Film Study Center and Beinecke Rare Book and Manuscript Library; the Museum of Modern Art and Anthology Film Archives, both in New York City; the George Eastman House in Rochester, New York; the Golda Meir Library at the University of Wisconsin–Milwaukee; the iotaCenter in Los Angeles; and the University of Minnesota. Some materials are also in the private collections of Kit Basquin, Cecile Starr, and Larry Mollott, who over many years have been working on a documentary film about Bute's life and films.

Articles by Bute appeared in *Design* 42 (April 1941), p. 25; *Film Music* 12, no. 4 (March–April 1953), pp. 15–18; and *Films in Review* 5, no. 6 (June–July 1954), pp. 263–66. Major sources for information about Bute include interviews in *Film Culture* (Winter 1964–65) and *AFI Report* (Summer 1974); Robert Russett and Cecile Starr, eds., *Experimental Animation, Origins of a New Art* (1976); Jayne Pilling, ed., *Women and Animation: A Compendium*

(1992); and Lauren Rabinovitz, "Mary Ellen Bute," in Jan-Christopher Horak, ed., *Lovers of Cinema, The First American Film Avant-Garde, 1919–1945* (1995). Research assistance was provided by Kit Basquin. Obituaries appeared in the *New York Times* on October 19, 1983, and *Variety* on November 2, 1983.

CECILE STARR

C

CABRERA, Lydia. May 20, 1900–September 19, 1991. Writer, ethnographer, artist.

Lydia Cabrera, born in Havana, Cuba, was the youngest of eight children of Raimundo Cabrera y Bosch and Elisa Bilbao Marcaida y Casanova, members of the upper classes. Raimundo Cabrera was writer and publisher of the prestigious magazine *Cuba y América,* where starting at age fourteen Cabrera wrote the social column "Nena en sociedad" (A Child in Society). Her twenty-seven entries mark the development of an ironic and humorous writing style perfected in later years in her short stories. Until his death in 1923, she was mentored by her father to become his intellectual heir. In 1917, Cabrera, studying on her own, obtained her baccalaureate diploma after having completed the required examinations.

From early in her childhood, she pursued interests in art and the preservation of colonial architecture and culture. In 1915–16, behind her father's back, she attended the Havana art school, Academia de San Alejandro. In 1922, Salón de Bellas Artes showed her works. Also in 1922 she participated in the foundation of "Asociación Cubana de Arte Retrospectivo" (Cuban Association of Retrospective Art), to raise awareness about the cultural value of colonial architecture. The same year, she founded a commercial firm, Alyds, dedicated to interior decoration. With the income derived from this venture she financed her studies in Asian art at L'École du Louvre in Paris (1927–30). In the end, she spent more than a decade in Europe, living in France, Spain, and Italy with sporadic visits back to Havana, until she returned to Cuba in 1938. Soon after, Cabrera and her life companion María Teresa de Rojas, a historical researcher and editor who shared her interest in colonial architecture, began the restoration of their home, the Quinta San José in Havana. Intended to become a colonial museum, the house was destroyed by fire after Cabrera and Rojas left Havana in 1960.

Cabrera's youthful interest in Afro-Cuban stories had flourished during her stay in Europe in the late twenties and thirties as she participated in the avant-garde movements with their search for the exotic and the primitive in Asian and African arts. On her return to Cuba, she became part of the Afro-Cuban movement, which included poet Nicolás Guillén, novelist Alejo Carpentier, ethnographer Fernando Ortiz, and painter Wifredo Lam.

Cabrera's greatest legacy is her ethnographic work based on conversations with Afro-Cuban informants in the Pogolotti neighborhood adjacent to her home in Havana, and in the province of Matanzas. Writings such as *Cuentos Negros de Cuba* (Negro Stories from Cuba), published in French in 1936 and Spanish in 1940, record the cultural integration of Spanish and African-derived popular traditions originating in Yoruba, Fon, Kongo, and Ejagham African cultures. In his introduction to the Spanish edition of her stories, Ortiz characterizes them as a collaboration between black folklore and its Spanish translator. In them, Cabrera rescues countless Yoruba songs and legends in a matter-of-fact, humorous narrative style that came to be recognized as Magical Realism. Of her work, Isabel Castellanos notes, "If Cabrera's short stories surprise the reader by the overflowing nature of a fabulous imagination, where all the boundaries of recognized conventional categories disappear, her investigative work astonishes due to the abundance and depth of information, strictly verifiable and documented" (*Páginas Sueltas,* p. 64).

Although Cabrera published more than twenty books, her most important was her 600-page magnum opus, *El Monte* [The Sacred Wild], which appeared in 1954. Subtitled "Notes on religions, magic, superstitions, and folklore of the Creole Negroes and the People of Cuba," *El Monte* vacillates between presenting the material from a European perspective (as the words *superstitions* and *folklore* indicate) and from that of the multiple voices of her informants. Her introduction to *El Monte* anticipates all the elements of the Latin American narrative genre, to be labeled *testimonio* [testimony] by the Cuban writer and ethnographer Miguel Barnet in the 1960s. *Testimonio* represents an arrangement between a knowledgeable informant and a member of the intelligentsia, capable of disseminating cultural information narrated by illiterate members of society.

Ethnographer Morton Marks asserts, "The remarkable achievement of Lydia Cabrera is that her works can be read as literature, folklore, ethnography, ethnohistory, ethnobotany and ethnopharmacology" (*En torno a Lydia Cabrera,* p. 244). *El Monte,* here presented as a paradigm for her entire ethnographic work, consists of ten chapters that define Afro-Cuban beliefs, rituals, song and language, plus a collection of the names of more than 450 plants used by practitioners for medicinal and spiritual purposes. Cabrera's books, in the able hands of priests and priestesses in the United States, have become useful tools in the difficult task of adaptation of Afro-Cuban religion to a culture defined by its individualism, mobility, and pluralism, rather than house, community, and family.

On July 20, 1960, Lydia Cabrera, along with María Teresa de Rojas, left Cuba to settle in Miami, Florida. For several years Cabrera retreated from public life. Her memoir, *Itinerario del insomnio: Trinidad de Cuba* (Itinerary of Insomnia: Trinidad of Cuba) (1977), records her difficult transition, with humor. In 1968 she worked on a new edition of *El Monte* and in 1970, ten years after leaving Cuba, she resumed her writing. From 1972 to 1974 she and Rojas lived in Spain. Cabrera's later ethnographic works published in the United States, based on field notes she brought with her in a trunk from the island nation, developed from and amplified cultural practices first recorded in *El Monte.* The multiple volumes of ethnographic work that she published are the best source of recorded testimonies on Afro-Cuban culture. In recognition of her monumental contribution, the Congress of Afro-American Literature was held in her honor in 1976. Her life and works attest to her desire to highlight the complexity of national culture by giving voice to practices previously considered marginal. She died in Miami on September 19, 1991.

Bibliography: The Archives and Special Collections Department of the Otto Richter Library at the University of Miami holds Lydia Cabrera's papers. The most complete bibliographies may be found in Isabel Castellanos, ed., *Lydia Cabrera: Páginas Sueltas* (1994); and Mariela Gutiérrez, *Lydia Cabrera: Aproximaciones* (1997). Lydia Cabrera, *El Monte: Igbo-Finda; Ewe Orisha, Vititi Nfinda (Notas sobre las religiones, la magia, las supersticiones y el folklore de los negros criollos y del pueblo de Cuba),* originally published in 1954, has gone through numerous editions, although no English translation exists. In addition to the books mentioned in the text, other important works by Cabrera include *Anaforuana* (1975) (ethnography); *Ayapá: Cuentos de jicotea* (1971) (fiction); *La medicina popular de Cuba* (1984) (ethnography); and *Páginas Sueltas* (1994) (collected writings and letters, Isabel Castellanos, ed.).

Books written about Cabrera include Isabel Castellanos and Josefina Inclán, eds., *En Torno a Lydia Cabrera (Cincuentenario de "Cuentos Negros de Cuba") 1936–1986* (1987); Mariela Gutiérrez, *Lydia Cabrera: Aproximaciones* (1997); Rosario Hiriart, *Lydia Cabrera: Vida Hecha Arte* (1978); and Reinaldo Sanchez and José A. Madrigal, eds., *Homenaje a Lydia Cabrera* (1977). *Lydia Cabrera: An Intimate Portrait May 14–July 13, 1984,* curated by Ana María Simo for the Intar Latin American Gallery in New York City, includes Cabrera's story "Obbara Lies but Doesn't Lie," translated by Suzanne Jill Levine. Lydia Cabrera's birth date is uncertain. She used 1900, but some sources suggest it was 1899. An obituary appeared in the *New York Times* on September 25, 1991.

FLORA GONZÁLEZ MANDRI

CADE, Toni. *See* Bambara, Toni Cade.

CALDERONE, Mary Steichen. July 1, 1904–October 24, 1998. Physician, sex education advocate.

In 1967, Dr. Mary Steichen Calderone told a reporter, "Too many people think you complete sex education by teaching reproduction. Sex education has to be far more than that. Sex involves something you are, not just something you do." With these words, Calderone threw down the gauntlet to parents, physicians, and teachers: education for what she termed "healthy sexuality" must become part of the birthright of every child. The foremost American proponent for greater acceptance of sexuality as a natural human good, Calderone helped create a language by which Americans could publicly discuss this contentious subject.

Calderone's path to preeminence in the field of sexuality education originated in early childhood. The daughter of Luxembourg-born photographer Edward Steichen, Mary was raised to appreciate the beauty and scientific wonder of nature—including the human body. Yet her mother, Clara Smith Steichen, raised on the Ozarks frontier, was steeped in the common Victorian sentiment that sexuality—particularly masturbation—was embarrassing and shameful. To Mary's everlasting shame and fury, Clara equipped Mary with metal "mittens" to prevent nighttime masturbation. She often cited these early experiences as formative influences on her later career.

Mary Steichen was born in New York City, but her parents moved to France with her when she was two years old. Her younger sister, Kate, was born in 1908. By the outbreak of World War I in 1914, her parents' marriage was fraying. Although the entire family left for the safety of New York,

Clara soon returned to France with young Kate. Mary insisted on staying in the United States, close to her father. She never again lived with her mother, who was divorced from Edward in 1922. Boarding with family friends, Mary attended the progressive upper-crust private school Brearley. She matriculated at Vassar College in 1921, majoring in chemistry as preparation for a career in medicine but also dabbling in theatrical productions, and graduated in 1925.

There followed four tumultuous years. She returned to New York and joined the American Laboratory Theatre, an offshoot of the Moscow Art Theatre, where in 1926 she met and married her first husband, a fellow actor, W. Lon Martin. Their first child, Nell, born that year, was probably conceived prior to their marriage. By 1928, when their second child, Linda Joan, was born, Mary realized she was not cut out for an acting career. When Linda was still a baby, the couple separated, divorcing in the early 1930s.

After undergoing psychoanalysis and completing a course of aptitude tests at the Stevens Institute of Technology, Steichen turned back to a career in medicine. In 1934 she took a year of premedical courses at Columbia University's College of Physicians and Surgeons. In May 1935, just as she was about to complete her exams, eight-year-old Nell contracted pneumonia at boarding school and died, precipitating a period of deep depression for Mary. Nevertheless, she entered the University of Rochester School of Medicine and Dentistry in the fall of that year. After graduating in 1939, she completed an internship in pediatrics at Bellevue Hospital in New York City but declined to pursue a residency because of her need to be an active parent to Linda, now age twelve. Instead she undertook a combined fellowship and master's in public health at the Columbia University School of Public Health. During fieldwork on the Lower East Side in New York City, she met her second husband, Dr. Frank Calderone, who became first deputy health commissioner of New York City from 1943 to 1946 and medical director of health services for the UN Secretariat from 1951 to 1954. They married in 1941 and had two children, Francesca Calderone-Steichen (1943) and Maria Steichen Calderone (1946).

Calderone spent a few years raising her new family in Old Brookville, Long Island, and working part-time as a school physician in Great Neck. During this period she became a Quaker, a faith she credited with stiffening her lifelong resistance to intolerance. She also lectured to groups of parents and teachers on sex education for young people. By 1953, when the Planned Parenthood Federation of America (PPFA) was looking for a medical director (then a part-time job), Calderone's public health connections made her a natural choice. Besides, as she often said, she had "no established practice, and nothing to lose, and no *qualified* male physician would have taken it" (More, p. 207).

Calderone's tenure at Planned Parenthood from 1953 to 1964 coincided with some of the most profound changes in American society's attitudes toward family planning and contraception. Her goal at the organization, in which she brilliantly succeeded, was to reshape its reputation in the image of a professionally run voluntary health organization. She engaged in much behind-the-scenes persuasion to encourage organized medicine, notably the American Public Health Association (APHA) and the American Medical Association (AMA), to incorporate family planning into the definition of good general medical care and public health, which both organizations did, in 1959 and 1964, respectively.

The subject of abortion also began to enter public policy discussions, albeit *sotto voce.* Recognizing the subject's importance, but also the risk of associating Planned Parenthood with so volatile an issue, in 1955 Calderone organized a conference of physicians, scientists, and statisticians, including Alfred Kinsey, to discuss abortion as a public health challenge. The resulting edited volume, *Abortion in the United States* (1958), provided the first systematic assessment of the impact of illegal abortion on women's health.

Eventually, Calderone decided that her "part-time" position and salary at PPFA were not commensurate with her growing responsibilities there, nor with her increasing national and international reputation. More fundamentally, her interests began to shift from contraception to sex education, a shift reflected in her 1960 book, *Release from Sexual Tensions.* Looking back, she credited a 1961 meeting of the North American Conference on Church and Family sponsored by the National Council of Churches of Christ as the moment when she realized that sexuality education had moved to the top of her personal agenda for social change.

In 1964, Calderone resigned from Planned Parenthood. With a colleague from the National Council of Churches and others from medicine, law, health education, and family life education, she organized a small nonprofit public health organization called SIECUS—the Sex Information and Education Council of the U.S. Calderone was its executive director until 1975 and president from 1975 to 1982. SIECUS disseminated information and educational materials to anyone wishing to expand the current state of sex education through research or teaching.

Calderone was used to the limelight, but she never expected the storm of publicity—some of it exceedingly ugly—unleashed by her efforts on behalf of SIECUS. By 1968 SIECUS's straightforward progress confronted the organized hostility of groups like the Ku Klux Klan, the Christian Crusade, and the John Birch Society. SIECUS's new, more liberal approach to sex education provided the perfect foil for a resurgent right-wing political movement, which claimed that Calderone was a communist and that SIECUS countenanced pedophilia and child pornography. Calderone's relationship with radical feminism was only somewhat smoother than her dealings with the religious right. Her support for Hugh Hefner, a SIECUS donor, and her reluctance to incorporate gender conflict into her ideas about sexuality made some feminists uneasy.

Calderone and her husband separated in 1979, but never divorced. In her later years Calderone took up the cause of sexuality among the aged and the disabled. She also was hired in 1982 as an adjunct professor in the Program on Human Sexuality of the Department of Health Education at New York University. She was particularly keen to raise the scientific status of sexuality research among medical researchers. Less visible in the last decade of her life after the onset of Alzheimer's disease, Mary Steichen Calderone died in Kennett Square, Pennsylvania, in 1998 at the age of ninety-four.

Bibliography: The principal source for Mary Steichen Calderone's papers, books, and audio and videotapes is the Schlesinger Library, Radcliffe Institute for Advanced Study, Harvard University. The transcript of a 1974 oral history interview with Calderone, conducted by James W. Reed for the Family Planning Oral History Project, is also at the Schlesinger Library. Other materials may be found in the Frank Calderone collection located in Archives & Special Collections, Columbia University Health Sciences Library, and at the SIECUS Library, New York City. Materials pertaining to Calderone's activities at Planned Parenthood are also located in the Planned Parenthood Federation papers at the Sophia Smith Collection, Smith College Library, and in the Alan Guttmacher papers at the Countway Medical Library at Harvard. Letters pertaining to Calderone's childhood may be found in the Alfred Stieglitz Archive, Beinecke Rare Book and Manuscript Library, Yale University.

Calderone wrote or edited many books, including *Release from Sexual Tensions* (with Phyllis and Robert P. Goldman, 1960), *The Family Book about Sexuality* (with Eric W. Johnson, 1981), and *Talking with Your Child about Sex* (with James W. Ramey, 1982). She edited *Abortion in the United States* (1958), *Manual of Family Planning and Contraceptive Practice* (1964), and *Sexuality and Human Values* (1974). She contributed chapters to Ruth B. Kundsin, ed., *Successful Women in the Sciences* (1973); Clive M. Davis, ed., *Challenges in Sexual Science* (1983); and Carole Vance, ed., *Pleasure and Danger: Exploring Female Sexuality* (1984). She also wrote countless articles in the *SIECUS Newsletter* and *SIECUS Report,* in medical journals, and in popular magazines such as the *Ladies' Home Journal, Redbook,* and *Bride's Magazine.* The opening quote appeared in *Parade,* June 18, 1967, p. 19.

Chapter-length studies of Calderone's life and achievements are found in Lynn Gilbert and Gaylen Moore, *Particular Passions: Talks with Women Who Have Shaped Our Times* (1981); and David Mace, "Mary Steichen Calderone: Interpreter of Human Sexuality," in Leonard S. Kenworthy, ed., *Living in the Light: Some Quaker Pioneers of the 20th Century,* vol. 1 (1984). Discussions of Calderone's career in the larger context of her family and professional ties are contained in Penelope Niven, *Steichen: A Biography* (1997); Ellen S. More, *Restoring the Balance: Women Physicians and the Profession of Medicine, 1850–1995* (1999); and Jeffrey Moran, *Teaching Sex: The Shaping of Adolescence in the 20th Century* (2000). A valuable, if critical, assessment of Calderone from a feminist perspective is provided by Mary Breasted in *Oh! Sex Education* (1970). An obituary appeared in the *New York Times* on October 25, 1998.

ELLEN S. MORE

CALLAS, Maria. December 2, 1923–September 16, 1977. Operatic soprano.

One of the most important musicians of the twentieth century, the soprano Maria Callas was born Maria Anna Sophia Cecilia Kalogeropoulos in Manhattan to Greek immigrant parents, pharmacist Georges Kalogeropoulos (who shortened the family name to Callas) and the former Evangelia Dimitroadou. Callas began her musical training as a child and attended public schools in New York City; her eighth-grade graduation in 1937 marked the end of her formal education. Later that year, along with her mother and older sister Iakinthy, she moved to Athens to further her studies at the National Conservatory, singing her first leading role (Santuzza in Mascagni's *Cavalleria Rusticana*) at the age of fifteen. In 1939, she began training under Elvira de Hidalgo, a coloratura soprano of some repute. De Hidalgo honed Callas's huge, ungainly voice by means of a rigorous training in *bel canto,* a method of singing that cultivates flexibility and ease of execution rather than powerful sound. Callas made her professional operatic debut with the Athens Opera in 1941 and sang leading roles until 1945, when she returned to the United States.

After several false starts, Callas's "big career" (as she called it) began in Italy in 1947, when she sang the title role in Ponchielli's *La Gioconda.* In Verona she accepted the patronage of Giovanni Battista Meneghini, a local businessman whom she married in 1949 and who would manage her career for more than a decade. She first won widespread renown in 1949 when, at the behest of conductor Tullio Serafin (her other great mentor), she alternated performances of Wagner's Brünnhilde, a part calling for immense vocal power, and Elvira in Bellini's *I Puritani,* a florid, high-flying role that generally requires a very different kind of voice. Callas's fame exploded as a result of this uncanny versatility combined with her command of the stage, which blossomed following a dramatic weight loss. In little more than a year, Callas transformed herself from a heavy, awkward woman into a sylph no less comely than the heroines she portrayed on stage, becoming one of the most photographed women in the world.

Her exceptional combination of gifts drew leading directors from the legitimate theater to the opera house, among them Luchino Visconti, who mounted for Callas several productions (including Verdi's *La Traviata* at La Scala in 1955) that are widely considered unsurpassed. The growing popularity of the long-playing record, Callas's willingness to take on any artistic challenge, and the media's fascination with her "rags to riches," "ugly duckling turned swan" life story were among the factors that brought her career and celebrity to an astonishing pitch of intensity in the mid 1950s.

By the end of the decade, though, Callas's voice was growing worn and her cancellations began to mount, largely on account of sheer exhaustion. Widely publicized run-ins with impresarios (due in part to Meneghini's clumsy management) also sapped her energies. In 1959 she left her husband and began a nine-year relationship with shipping magnate Aristotle Onassis. At the same time she radically curtailed her appearances; she was not yet forty-two when she last performed on the operatic stage, in 1965. The next year she gave up her American citizenship, retaining her Greek nationality exclusively. During the remaining years of her life, which she spent living mainly in Paris, she starred in a 1969 film (Pier Paolo Pasolini's *Medea*), taught master classes at the Juilliard School of Music from 1971 to 1972, and undertook an ill-advised comeback tour in 1973 and 1974, but never recaptured the drive and confidence that had once carried her to the pinnacle of the musical world. She died in Paris at the age of fifty-three of apparent heart failure.

The popular caricature of Callas the "singing actress" depicts her as a wild vocalist heedless of musical values and given to over-the-top histrionics. In reality, she was by temperament a classicist, deploying her sometimes unruly voice with instrumental precision, measured but telling in her movements on stage. Her dark, reedy timbre was not conventionally beautiful, but it burned with emotion: in the words of John Ardoin, it was "better than beautiful, for it was a voice that once heard could not easily be forgotten" (*The Callas Legacy*, p. 205). It encompassed the sulfurous outpourings of a Lady Macbeth, the dainty filigree of Bellini's *La Sonnambula,* and the slashing rage of a Medea: no music for soprano, it seemed, was beyond Callas's means. Coaches and scholars, though, insist that no singer can take on works of such extreme and varied demands without compromising her vocal longevity, an assertion that would seem to be borne out by the shocking brevity of Callas's prime. Still, as Ardoin wrote, "Had she put herself in less peril, had she taken fewer chances or remained within safer limits, she would never have been Callas. You cannot achieve as she achieved by halfway measures" (ibid., p. 203). Half a century after their original release, her recordings outsell those of any living operatic soprano.

No less than Callas the musician, Callas the individual remains a lightning rod for controversy. A woman who utterly dominated her profession, a working-class girl who made herself as wealthy and regal as any aristocrat, Callas rattled the gender and class paradigms of her time. To the popular press the bold, fiercely ambitious soprano was a "tigress." The power of her artistry forced the musical establishment to reconsider works by nineteenth-century Italian composers previously dismissed as shallow and lacking in substance, discrediting hallowed assumptions and paving the way for the likes of Beverly Sills and Cecilia Bartoli.

There was no great happiness in Callas's private life: she never had the children for which she longed, and she was estranged from her family for many years. All the same, the fact that biographers still seek to make her life conform to B-movie clichés (Callas is alleged to have died of a broken heart, by her own hand, or as a junkie alone and forgotten) may offer the most eloquent proof that her genius remains to this day disconcerting and unfathomable. In the words of baritone Tito Gobbi: "She shone for all too brief a while in the world of opera, like a vivid flame attracting the attention of the whole world, and she had a strange magic which was all her own. I always thought she was immortal—and she is."

Bibliography: The starting point for those wishing to learn about Maria Callas is John Ardoin, *The Callas Legacy: The Complete Guide to Her Recordings on Compact Disc* (4th ed., 1995), a detailed, chronological study of her studio and live recordings. The volume also includes a bibliography, a list of recorded interviews, and a videography. Matthew Gurewitsch, "Forget the Callas Legend," *Atlantic Monthly,* April 1999, pp. 98–104, and Will Crutchfield, "The Story of a Voice," *New Yorker,* November 13, 1995, p. 94, offer succinct and perceptive overviews of her career. See also J. B. Steane's assessment of Callas in *The Grand Tradition: Seventy Years of Singing on Record* (2nd ed., 1993). Wayne Koestenbaum's *The Queen's Throat: Opera, Homosexuality, and the Mystery of Desire* (1993) includes an intriguing chapter entitled "The Callas Cult." Catherine Clément's invaluable *Opera, or the Undoing of Women* (1979; English translation, 1988) discusses Callas briefly and examines her most famous roles in depth.

Callas biographies are, by and large, shoddy affairs. Two exceptions are Stelios Galatopoulos, *Maria Callas: Sacred Monster* (1998); and Nicholas Petsalis-Diomidis, *The Unknown Callas: The Greek Years* (2000), a meticulously documented study of her life limited to the years 1937 to 1945. David A. Lowe's *Callas: As They Saw Her* (1986) is an indispensable collection of reviews, essays, and reminiscences. Tito Gobbi, *My Life* (1979), pp. 132–33, contains the final quote. Attila Csampai's *Callas: Images of a Legend* (1996), a large-format volume, gathers dozens of striking photographs of Callas on stage and off, as does André Tubeuf's diminutive *La Callas* (1999). Callas claimed her birthday was December 4, her mother said December 3, but her birth certificate lists December 2, 1923. An obituary appeared in the *New York Times* on September 17, 1977.

MARION LIGNANA ROSENBERG

CANNON, Sarah Ophelia Colley. *See* Pearl, Minnie.

CANSINO, Margarita Carmen. *See* Hayworth, Rita.

CARABILLO, Virginia (Toni). March 26, 1926–October 28, 1997. Feminist, writer, graphic designer.

Virginia Anne Carabillo was born in Brooklyn the second of two children and only daughter of Anne V. Woods and Anthony S. Carabillo, an Italian immigrant. In 1937, the family moved to Wappingers Falls, New York, where her father ran a pharmacy; her mother did not work outside the home. Carabillo was known from her teenage years as Toni. Her life was affected by women's limited career opportunities after World War II and by the feminist movement of the 1960s. As an adult, she worked in corporate public relations jobs before pursuing a career as a writer, graphic artist, and publisher. Her experiences with sex discrimination motivated her more than twenty-five years of activism on behalf of women's issues.

Carabillo attended Middlebury College in Vermont, completing a double major in English and American literature and earning a BA with honors in 1948. Her Catholic Italian family encouraged her pursuit of education and a professional career, despite the popular assumption that women sought higher education only as a step toward marriage. The next year, she received an MA from Teachers College, Columbia University.

Although she encountered employers who wanted to hire her only for secretarial positions, Carabillo pursued a career in public relations. From 1949 to 1959, she worked in public relations at Vassar College and at Daystrom Electric Corporation (later Daystrom Weston Industrial), in Poughkeepsie, New York. She also worked briefly as a freelance greeting card designer. In 1959, following a breakup with her fiancé, Carabillo moved to Southern California. After employment at *Empire Magazine,* a short-lived business journal, Carabillo went to work for System Development Corporation, a designer of national defense systems. Although she rose to assistant manager of corporate communications, she experienced the discrimination common to women in the professional world, including infrequent promotions, lack of secretarial support, and exclusion from networking opportunities. Soon after she began gathering data documenting sex discrimination in salaries and promotions at the company, she lost her job. In 1969 she co-founded the Women's Heritage Corporation, a publishing firm, with Judith Meuli. The two partners also founded Women's Graphic Communications, a graphics arts company, in 1970.

Carabillo's departure from the corporate world coincided with her involvement in the women's movement. Indeed, her professional experiences stimulated her interest in feminism. She joined the National Organization for Women (NOW) in 1966, shortly after its inception. Carabillo believed NOW offered an important opportunity for professional women to work collectively to eliminate employment discrimination. Later, her concerns included passage of the equal rights amendment (ERA) and the legalization of abortion. In 1967, Carabillo became a founding member of the newly formed Southern California chapter of NOW (later reorganized as the Los Angeles chapter). She served as the chapter's corresponding secretary, public relations chair, chair of the speaker's bureau, and president in 1968–70 and 1980–82. During her first term as president, the group established a resource center. During her second term, the Los Angeles chapter spearheaded West Coast efforts to ratify the ERA, coordinating marches and organizing fund-raisers.

Carabillo also participated in NOW's national leadership. She sat on NOW's board of directors from 1968 to 1977, served as vice president for public relations from 1971 to 1974, and chaired the advisory committee between 1975 and 1977. In these positions, she publicized NOW's agenda and activities, creating slide shows, producing videotapes, and writing position papers, pamphlets, and press releases. In 1973, for example, she testified before the National Association of Broadcasters Television Code Review Board and the Radio Code Review Board regarding the media's depiction of women and the women's movement. As a leader in NOW, Carabillo also sought to reform the organization's administrative structure and encourage more activism at the local level.

In the early 1970s, some of NOW's leaders, including former president and founder Betty Friedan, depicted lesbians as a threat to feminism. The L.A. chapter, over which Carabillo had presided, proposed that NOW support lesbianism as an essential expression of women's right to self-determination. The chapter's resolution in support of this position was adopted by NOW's membership at its 1971 convention. Although Carabillo backed this campaign, in a 1997 interview she indicated that she did not help draft the resolution.

Carabillo's activism was supported by her almost thirty-year personal and business partnership with Judith Meuli. A writer, graphic designer, real estate broker, and former research scientist at UCLA, Meuli held numerous offices in the L.A. chapter of NOW and on NOW's national board of directors. Together they edited NOW's national newsletter, *NOW Acts,* from 1970 to 1973 and NOW's national newspaper, the *National NOW Times,* from 1977 to 1985. As writers and graphic artists, they published women's history calendars and biographies, and designed and distributed logos and images for feminist posters, buttons, and T-shirts.

Carabillo also collaborated with Eleanor Smeal, who served as president of NOW in 1977–82, and again in 1985–87. In 1983, Smeal began publishing a newsletter about feminism and politics, the *Eleanor Smeal Report,* which Carabillo edited. In 1987, Carabillo, Smeal, and Meuli joined Peg Yorkin and Katherine Spillar to establish the Fund for the Feminist Majority (later the Feminist Majority) and the Feminist Majority Foundation. Carabillo later served as vice president of the Feminist Majority. The organizations offered strategic assistance to encourage women to run for office and supported the legalization of the early abortion medication RU-486.

Beyond her role as a longtime member and officer of NOW and the Feminist Majority, Carabillo served as a documentarian and historian of the movement. She co-authored several books, including *The Feminization of Power* (1988), with Judith Meuli, and produced two videos: *Abortion: For Survival* (1989) and *Abortion Denied: Shattering Young Women's Lives* (1990). Carabillo's extensive library on American feminism became the basis for the *Feminist Chronicles, 1953–1993* (1993), a chronology of the feminist movement in the United States she wrote with Meuli and June Bundy Csida. Toni Carabillo died at her home in Los Angeles in 1997 after a seven-year struggle with lymphoma and lung cancer. She was seventy-one. At the time of her death, she was at work on a book documenting the history of feminism in the twentieth century.

Bibliography: Interviews with Toni Carabillo are available in the Tully-Crenshaw Feminist Oral History Project at Schlesinger Library, Radcliffe Institute for Advanced Study, Harvard University, and the Center for Oral and Public History at California State University–Fullerton. Archival material on Carabillo is found in the National Organization for Women papers at the Schlesinger Library, as well as in a small collection of material Carabillo and Judith Meuli donated regarding a split within NOW in the 1970s. Carabillo donated her extensive library and research materials to the Feminist Majority Foundation. Obituaries appeared in the *New York Times* on November 5, 1997; *Feminist Majority Newsletter,* Fall 1997; and *National NOW Times,* January 1998.

ANNE M. VALK

CARTER, Maybelle Addington. May 10, 1909–October 23, 1978. Country music guitarist, singer.

Mother Maybelle, a pioneer in country and folk music, was a member of the original Carter Family, a group that brought the mountain music of their ancestors to the radio and recorded music of the early twentieth century. Maybelle Addington, Alvin Pleasant "A. P." Delaney Carter, and his wife Sara Dougherty descended from English settlers who had brought their culture to the mountains of Virginia after the Revolutionary War. Living in an area known as Poor Valley, the families lived much like those before them, farming and cutting timber. It was an environment in which songs and instrumental skills were nurtured and passed down.

Maybelle Addington was born in Scott County, Virginia, the sixth of ten children of Hugh Jack Addington, a farmer who also ran a general store and lumber mill, and Margaret Elizabeth Kilgore. Raised in a household in which everyone played music, Maybelle showed musical promise early in life and learned to play the banjo and the autoharp. When she was thirteen, she took up the guitar. Her mother knew an exhaustive repertoire of songs, and the Addingtons hosted many musical parties and dances.

In 1915, when Maybelle was six, she attended the wedding of her cousin Sara Dougherty and A. P. Carter, a local musician and salesman. Sara, with her haunting deep alto voice, was also musically gifted. Sara and A.P. started performing together locally, even as they started a family of their own. By the 1920s, with a wife and three children to support, A.P. began to see music as a way out of the grinding poverty and backbreaking labor of their lives. In 1925 Maybelle joined Sara and A.P. at local events, having dropped out of Midway High School to work. That December, Maybelle and A.P.'s brother, Ezra Carter, began a whirlwind courtship; they married in March 1926. This cemented family ties and led to the trio known as the Carter Family.

In 1927, Ralph Peer, a talent scout for Victor Talking Machine Company who had successfully commercially marketed blues music, went on an exploring trip to Bristol, Tennessee. He was looking for the kinds of old-time tunes by authentic performers that were beginning to find commercial success. A.P. convinced Sara and Maybelle to make the hot and dusty journey to Bristol on July 31, 1927. Maybelle was eighteen years old, and seven months pregnant, when they made the grueling eight-hour car trip across twenty-six miles of dirt roads. What came to be known as the "Bristol Sessions" were some of the most important events in the history of country music. Jimmie Rodgers, an equally important figure in country music history, recorded at the same sessions two days later. The Carter Family's three-part harmony singing and their unique instrumental style impressed Peer, and he recorded six songs with the group.

The records were released in November, and their popularity, as well as A.P.'s ability to find uncopyrighted songs, led to a busy recording career for the family group. The second recording session was in Camden, New Jersey, in May 1928. Most of the songs were commercial successes and became country standards. During this session they recorded "Wildwood Flower," a song that Maybelle had learned from her mother and that had entered into oral tradition from vaudeville. Sara sang and Maybelle played guitar. "Wildwood Flower" was released on January 4, 1929, and sold over 120,000 copies. Its sales were ten times higher than for other records of the time. Over the next fourteen years they would record hundreds of songs, including such defining classics as "Will the Circle Be Unbroken," "Keep on the Sunny Side," and "Wabash Cannonball."

Their records established the Carter Family, and Maybelle Carter in particular, as the premiere old-time music artists. Maybelle was among the first to use the guitar as a lead instrument. She translated her banjo playing to the guitar and developed a unique style that influenced country guitarists for decades. Her "Carter Scratch," or thumb-brushing technique, involved playing the bass line with the thumb while the fingers strummed the rhythm. This widely imitated style had a unique and inventive quality that made the Carter Family sound unmistakable.

After the original Carter Family disbanded in 1943, Maybelle Carter kept the family tradition alive by forming a new musical group, Mother Maybelle and the Carter Sisters. With her drive and the support of Ezra, the all-female band now featured the daughters—Helen (born in September 1927), the instrumentalist on accordion; June (born in June 1929), the natural comedian on autoharp; and Anita (born in March 1933), the featured singer on bass. They were a fixture on the radio program *The Old Dominion Barn Dance* in Richmond, Virginia, from 1946 to 1948, and in 1948–49 they appeared on WNOX in Knoxville, Tennessee, where they were joined by legendary guitarist Chet Atkins.

In 1950, Mother Maybelle and the Carter Sisters and Chet Atkins joined Nashville's Grand Ole Opry and continued to record sentimental ballads. With the emergence in the early 1960s of an interest in folk music, a new generation of fans discovered Maybelle Carter. Joan Baez, Bob Dylan, and Emmylou Harris covered Carter Family songs. Mother Maybelle's appearance at the Newport Folk Festival in 1963 was a success, and in 1966 she and Sara recorded what is now a classic album, *An Historic Reunion: Sara and Maybelle, the Original Carters.* As the folk revival gained momentum, singer-songwriter Johnny Cash hired the Carters to tour college campuses with him, and he married June in 1968. From 1969 to 1971 Mother Maybelle and the Carter Sisters appeared on ABC-TV's *Johnny Cash Show.* In 1970, Maybelle, Sara, and A. P. Carter were elected to the Country Music Hall of Fame. In poor health since her husband's death in 1975, Maybelle Carter died on October 23, 1978, at the age of sixty-nine.

Maybelle Carter achieved legendary status before her death. Her rich repertoire and distinctive musicianship influenced generations of performers. With openness and grace she bridged the gap from isolated mountain family entertainment to commercial country music to the folk rock of the 1970s, always projecting the dignity, artistry, and heartfelt emotion of hardworking people.

Bibliography: Live recordings and an interview with Maybelle Carter can be found in the Mike Seeger Collection in the Southern Folklife Collection, Library of the University of North Carolina–Chapel Hill. Biographies of Maybelle and the Carter Family include John Atkins, ed., *The Carter Family* (1973); Janette Carter, *Living with Memories* (1983); and Mark Zwonitzer with Charles Hirshberg, *Will You Miss Me When I'm Gone? The Carter Family and Their Legacy in American Music* (2002). See also Mary A. Bufwack and Robert K. Oermann, *Finding Her Voice: The Saga of Women in Country Music* (1993). A landmark twelve-CD box set, *In the Shadow of Clinch Mountain* (2000), includes a biographical essay on the Carter Family by Charles Wolfe, as well as extensive photographs, liner notes, song lyrics, and a complete discography. An obituary appeared in the *New York Times* on October 24, 1978.

MARY A. BUFWACK

CASAL, Lourdes. April 5, 1938–February 1, 1981. Poet, literary critic, activist.

Lourdes Casal, one of the earliest and perhaps finest post-1959 Cuban American writers, was born in Havana to middle-class parents. Her father, Pedro Casal, was a physician and her mother, Emilia Valdés, a schoolteacher. A light-skinned *china mulata,* Lourdes embodied all three "races" represented on the island—black, white, and Asian (Chinese).

Lourdes attended private primary and secondary schools, where she early distinguished herself as an excellent pupil with a quick, original mind and a quiet and introverted manner. In 1954 she enrolled at la Universidad Católica de Santo Tomas de Villanueva in Marianao, where she began a course of study in chemical engineering. During her third and fourth years at Villanueva, Casal abandoned applied science for psychology. She became politicized through her associations with various members of the 26 of July Movement, an anti-Batista group composed largely of university students, most notably Fidel Castro.

After the revolution of 1959, Casal joined the Directorio Revolucionario Estudiantil (DRE; Cuban Student Directorate). Soon, even revolutionary Catholics came to oppose the new Castro government, and she determined that it was best to leave the country rather than risk being charged with conspiring against the government. She left the country soon thereafter and traveled to Africa—purportedly at the behest of the Central Intelligence Agency (CIA)—as a delegate of the DRE and director of the Consejo Revolucionario Cubano (Cuban Revolutionary Council). In 1962 she moved to New York City, where she completed her clinical training, began teaching and writing professionally, and became a naturalized citizen.

In the first decade of her career, Casal published *Los Fundadores: Alfonso y Otros Cuentos* (The Founders: Alfonso and Other Stories, 1973)—one of the few extant works that give voice to Chinese Cuban history. In 1971 she published *El Casa Padilla* (The Padilla Case)—her most stridently anti-Castro piece. Casal's experiences in the United States, including her participation in the civil rights movement, politicized her. She began to collaborate with *Nueva Generación* (New Generation), a progressive journal founded by young Cuban Americans, and attended the first and second Cuban Studies conferences, whose members tended toward the radical desire for a dialogue with Cuba. In 1972, she helped found the Institute for Cuban Studies at Rutgers—an institute dedicated to free and open exchange between Cuba and the United States. The center, a clearinghouse for balanced, reliable information on Cuba, has served as a vital communication link between the two countries through publications, exchange programs, and art projects.

In the early seventies, Casal renounced her Catholic activism and evidenced a kind of agnosticism marked by experimentation in santería. She finished her graduate work at the New School for Social Research, receiving her PhD in 1975. In these years, she began to reconsider her position toward the Cuban revolution. She was instrumental in founding *Arieto,* a literary magazine that published the work of young Cubans both on and off the island. Their work was the first collection of post-1959 Cuban American literature—poetry and fiction written by young authors who had arrived in the United States as children or young adults and who expressed a distinctly bicultural sense of self complicated by historical dislocation.

Lourdes Casal was a marvelously talented essayist, poet, fiction writer, and organizer-activist who found her place in the many bridge-building projects she initiated and nurtured. Her poems, including "For Lourdes Velar," first express a distinct sense of dislocation—the feeling of being "forever a stranger among the stones" (line 36). Other poems include "Contra la Razon y por la Fuerza" ("By Reason or By Force") and a series of poems collected in *Palabras Juntan Revolución* (Words Join Revolution, 1981), including "Obbatala," "Havana 1968," and "Definition"—one of her better-known poems. Her short stories include "Rodrigo de Triana" (1971), "Maria Valdes or Colina Universitaria" (1973), a satire of Cecilia Valdes, and "Love Story, Segun Cyrano Prufrock" (1973). Casal's essays, too, have a kind of poetic quality about them.

Lourdes Casal was one of the first of her generation to return to post-revolutionary Cuba, making her first trip in 1973. She returned to the island again a few months later for an academic conference and was converted to the revolution. On her return, the editorial board of *Arieto* voted to adopt an attitude of open support for the revolution. *Arieto* became a meeting point for Cuban Americans supportive of the Cuban revolution. This nucleus helped form the controversial Antonio Maceo Brigades, which allowed Cuban Americans, many of whom could hardly remember Cuba, to return to the island to reestablish familial, artistic, and intellectual connections. As a result of their willingness to engage in *el dialago,* however, she and other *Arieto* writers were often marked for harassment in the Cuban exile community. Even today, Casal's work is rarely included in anthologies of Cuban American literature, which tend to define Cuban American identity as a distinctly "exile" sensibility.

Despite being intensely private about her personal life, Casal was gregarious and social, initiating and nurturing many important collaborative projects and friendships both in the United States and in Cuba, including long associations with artist ANA MENDIETA and poet Nancy Morejon. Those who knew Casal describe her as having been fearless, honest, and loyal. Her genius lay in the realm of human relationships and bridge building. Some would say she built this bridge on her back—that is, at the expense of her body. By the time she began to help organize *el dialago,* her health suffered. She was plagued by kidney problems, which earlier cortisone treatments—then considered the best course—had exacerbated. By 1978, Casal required dialysis. In December 1979, she fell ill during a trip to Cuba, where she was hospitalized. Settling permanently in Havana, she died there in 1981 and was buried in the pantheon of exiled revolutionaries, near the mother of Jose Martí. Fidel Castro sent a wreath.

In the early years of the twenty-first century, those who continued the project of normalizing relations between Cuba and the United States began to claim Lourdes Casal as their own. Excluded from anthologies of Cuban American literature for decades, her voice led the way for those who would attempt to defy, disrupt, and challenge geopolitical, artistic, and emotional borders between Cubans on both sides of the Florida Straits—the ninety-mile border that has represented more than a geographic boundary. Casal devoted her life to undoing the effects of that artificial separation.

Bibliography: Lourdes Casal's published works include *El Caso Padilla* (1971); *Los Fundadores: Alfonso y Otros Cuentos* (1973); *Revolution and Race: Blacks in Contemporary Cuba* (1979); *The Role of the Urban Working Class in the Cuban Revolution: Insurrectional Stage* (1979); *Cuba: On the Political Organization of Socialist Democracy* (1979); and *Palabras Juntan Revolución* (1981). "For Ana Velford" opens Ruth Behar's anthology, *Puentes a Cuba/Bridges to Cuba* (1995); and "A Love Story according to Cyrano Prufrock" is found in Juana Ponce de Leon and Estaban Rios Rivera, eds., *Dream with No Name: Contemporary Fiction from Cuba* (1999).

Secondary sources include Ruth Behar and Lucia Suarez, "Two Conversations with Nancy Morejon," in Behar, *Bridges to Cuba/Puentes a Cuba;* Silvia Burunat, "El Arte Literaro de Lourdes Casal," *Revista Hispanica de Cultural y Literatura* 1, no. 1 (Fall 1985), pp. 107–11; Olga Connor, "Tres Poetas Cubanas: Criticos y Textos," *El Nuevo Herald,* August 6, 2000; Leonel A. de la Cuesta and Maria Cristina Herrera, eds., *Itinerario Ideológico: Antologia* (1982); Maria Cristina Garcia, "Hardliners vs. 'Dialagueros': Cuban Exile Political Groups and United States–Cuba Policy," *Journal of American Ethnic History* (Summer 1998), pp. 3–28; and Julio Matas, "La Nostalgia es Absurda: Review of *Los Fundadores,*" *Caribe* 1, no. 2 (Autumn 1976), pp. 127–29.

MARIA MARTINEZ

CASTILLO, Aurora. August 15, 1913–April 30, 1998. Community activist, environmentalist.

In 1985, community activist Aurora Castillo helped co-found Mothers of East Los Angeles (MELA), a political organization opposed to the construction of a state prison in East Los Angeles. With the help of Castillo, MELA broadened its scope to address issues of quality of life and environmental racism, on the assumption that minority and poor communities bear the brunt of environmental problems. In 1995 Castillo gained national distinction when she was awarded the prestigious Goldman Environmental Prize for her work in grassroots organizing; she was the first Latina and the oldest person to receive the $75,000 award.

Aurora Castillo was born in East Los Angeles. She was the daughter of Joaquin Peter Castillo and Frances Sanchez, working-class Latinos who were both laundry workers. Castillo, who had a twin sister, Bertha, and at least one other sister, was a fourth-generation Mexican American whose family held a long tradition of political activism. Her great-great-grandfather, Augustine Olvera, was the first county judge of Los Angeles and the man for whom historic Olvera Street is named.

From a young age, Castillo was shaped into a vocal spokesperson for Latino rights by her experiences growing up in the predominantly Latino and working-class community of Boyle Heights. At Garfield High School in East Los Angeles, guidance counselors encouraged her to pursue a "practical" course of study with classes in home economics; Castillo attributed this advice to the tendency to track Latino students away from college-prep courses. Instead she enrolled in business classes, a decision that enabled her to remain self-sufficient and independent throughout her life. For most of her career, she worked as a secretary at Douglas Aircraft.

Castillo also had a strong interest in the cultural life of Los Angeles, and after high school she financed dance lessons from instructor Trinidad Goni by performing office work in return for the lessons. She also enrolled in drama and voice classes at Los Angeles City College. Her interest in the arts would later lead her to champion the integration of East Los Angeles into the cultural life of greater Los Angeles. She fought for the restoration of the historic Golden Gate Theater, and helped establish a shuttle service from East Los Angeles to the Hollywood Bowl concert venue.

Aurora Castillo is most noted for her work with Mothers of East Los Angeles. In spring 1985, the pastor of the Church of the Resurrection, which Castillo attended regularly, told her that Governor George Deukmejian planned to build another (the sixth) state prison in the area. Accounts vary regarding the events that led to the formation of MELA, but soon Castillo and a group of parish women, which also included Juana Gutiérrez, joined together to oppose the governor's plan to build another prison in their community. Moral outrage over the prison increased when the group learned that the California Department of Corrections had failed to test the Boyle Heights site for hazardous waste, develop an Environmental Impact Report detailing the environmental costs of the prison to the community, or provide the residents with adequate notice prior to the selection of the site. Together with a coalition of other groups opposed to the construction of the prison, MELA joined in weekly marches against the prison, lobbied politicians, and traveled to Sacramento to make their position known. In 1992 their efforts succeeded; Governor Pete Wilson ended the project and expanded existing facilities instead.

The work of Castillo and MELA did not end with the struggle against the prison. The organization had already branched out into issues of environmental justice affecting the Latino and working-class communities surrounding Boyle Heights. MELA, together with the Coalition Against the Pipeline, successfully opposed the building of a hundred-mile pipeline that would have carried oil south from Santa Barbara to Long Beach. As originally planned, the pipeline would have detoured twenty miles inland through East Los Angeles, bypassing affluent communities and placing East Los Angeles at risk in case of a leak. In 1990, MELA also successfully defeated a proposal to build a toxic waste incinerator in the neighboring city of Vernon.

Castillo's strong disposition, her involvement with the Catholic Church, and her bilingual skills all marked her as a natural spokesperson and leader in MELA. She was responsible for rallying community support and was the guardian of the organization's contact list. She met with both the English- and the Spanish-language press, explaining MELA's positions on issues. Besides serving MELA in a professional capacity, Castillo also became a mentor and role model to many of the younger women in the organization, some of whom had followed more traditional paths than Castillo. Ironically, despite the name of the organization, Castillo never married or had children of her own. Instead, "motherhood" in MELA came to represent the symbolic responsibility the community had to its children. The women (and later, men) of the organization used their role as caretakers of the family to challenge measures they viewed as threatening the welfare of their community.

Mothers of East Los Angeles continued its work for community improvement long after it successfully defeated the prison proposal, and despite its eventual split in 1990 along parish lines into two independent branches. Together with MELA, Castillo helped mobilize a community into active political participation. She is significant not only for her ability to effect political change, but also for her role in an organization that empowered local women. Aurora Castillo continued her work with MELA until her death in Los Angeles, from complications related to leukemia, on April 30, 1998, at the age of eighty-four.

Bibliography: Information about Mothers of East Los Angeles can be found in Mary S. Pardo, *Mexican American Women Activists: Identity and Resistance in Two Los Angeles Communities* (1998). See also Gabriel Gutiérrez, "Mothers of East Los Angeles Strike Back," in Robert D. Bullard, ed., *Unequal Protection: Environmental Justice and Communities of Color* (1994); Mary S. Pardo, "Mexican American Women Grassroots Community Activists: 'Mothers of East Los Angeles,'" *Frontiers* 11, no. 1 (1990), pp. 1–7; and Kamala Platt, "Chicana Strategies for Success and Survival: Cultural Poetics of Environmental Justice from the Mothers of East Los Angeles," *Frontiers* 18, no. 2 (1997), pp. 48–72. The *Los Angeles Times* regularly published material concerning the community activism of Mothers of East Los Angeles, as did the Spanish-language press, especially *La Opiníon* (Los Angeles). Juana Gutiérrez provided information about Mothers of East Los Angeles during a conversation with the author on August 8, 2003, in Los Angeles; Mary Lou Trevis and Frank Villalobos provided information about Aurora Castillo during telephone conversations on August 28, 2003, and September 16, 2003. An obituary appeared in the *Los Angeles Times* on May 15, 1998.

LUPE GARCÍA

CHA, Theresa Hak Kyung. March 4, 1951–November 5, 1982. Artist, writer.

From the perspective of her life as an artist, we might open the story of Theresa Hak Kyung Cha with her murder at age thirty-one. It was not until after her tragic death that *Dictée,* her most widely known and significant work, was released; only posthumously did Cha become an influential figure in both postmodern and Asian American arts and letters. Cha's notoriety continues to climb as a growing body of critical texts engages her work from a variety of perspectives and disciplines, including feminism, Asian American studies, postmodern theory, postcolonial theory, media studies, fine art, and art history. This variety of interests speaks to the hybrid nature of Cha's oeuvre, a hybridity certainly arising from the tremendous cultural and political changes surrounding her life—starting with the sudden geopolitical centrality of her native country at the time of her birth in 1951.

The third of five children, Cha was born in Pusan, in southernmost Korea, where her family had moved to flee from advancing North Korean and Chinese armies. This was not the first or last move for her parents, Hyung Sang and Hyung Soon Cha. Raised in Manchuria among other ethnic Koreans, they had moved to Korea during World War II, seeking refuge from Japanese terror in China. In 1962 the Cha family again sought to escape repression, this time from the South Korean government, by moving to Hawaii and then settling in San Francisco a year later.

Cha's parents, who had been teachers in Manchuria, enrolled all of their children in Catholic school. Theresa excelled in her schoolwork at San Francisco's Convent of the Sacred Heart, where her studies included Greek and Roman classics, French, and the Catholic catechism. Though these subjects would influence her later work, her studies at the University of California, Berkeley, which she began in 1969, directly fed into her artistic pursuits. Berkeley in the sixties and seventies has become synonymous with student political activism, the counterculture, and academic innovation. The same year Cha enrolled, the university formed its Ethnic Studies department, which included Asian American studies, soon followed by Afro-American Studies and Women's Studies departments. And in the local art scene, valuable opportunities opened for experimentation in performance, video, and installation. In this fertile environment, Cha would produce a great variety of work while obtaining four different degrees: BAs in comparative literature (1973) and art (1975), an MA in art (1977), and an MFA in art (1978).

During those years she read widely in cultural theory and avant-garde literature and through her work at Berkeley's Pacific Film Archive was exposed to a wealth of classic and avant-garde films and filmmakers. Her earliest archived work, *Earth,* a 1973 artist book of symbolist-like poetry, combined French and English to explore the ability to transform language through repetition, isolation, changes in context, font choice, and layout. She continued this linguistic/design exploration in her other artist books, mail art, videos, and even her performances. *Barren Cave Mute* (1974) and *Aveugle Voix* (*Blind Voice,* 1975) both feature the artist uncovering written words in ways that highlight the struggle as a woman and a "foreigner" to communicate and to be heard.

Indeed, Cha herself experienced a kind of silencing when she had to abandon a project she began filming in Korea because governmental officials suspected her of spying for North Korea.

This experience became part of the personal, familial, and political history Cha draws on in her densely layered, extended prose poem *Dictée.* This book captures the sense of alienation resulting from being a foreigner—in one's country of birth and in one's country of residence. But the text also captures the possibility of empowerment located within all of these "alien" cultures. Thus, the text uses the muses as a frame around which to tell the stories of, among others, Cha's mother; a young Korean revolutionary woman, Yu Guan Soon; and the martyrs Joan of Arc and Therese of Lisieux. This work combs the past to restore ignored histories or redefine past events from the perspectives of the forgotten participants, especially colonized Koreans and women. The aim of the book is to "open avenues to MEMORY, to the elemental process of recollection" in order to conduct "experiments with time; Time which the characters experience . . . in Korean history, in 'mythological' Time" (Tanam Press broadside, 1982).

Just a few weeks before *Dictée* was released, Cha was murdered at the Puck Building in lower Manhattan. She had gone there to meet photographer Richard Barnes, her husband of six months whom she had met at Berkeley. The two had moved to New York City two years earlier in hopes of furthering their careers. From the number and diversity of projects Cha was pursuing at the time of her death, it is likely she would have produced other memorable works. To describe the art she did complete, we can turn to her description of her video project *Passages Paysages:* "The images are absent of the object, they are sequences of implied events, for what is present to the viewer is only the remnant, the memory. The point of view is from a delayed time and space, either in the past or the future, there is a sense of lost time and space, and the desire to retrieve it, to know again."

Bibliography: The Berkeley Art Museum maintains a comprehensive archive of Cha's works and research materials such as slides, notebooks, and documentation (including the Tanam Press broadside for *Dictée* and Cha's typewritten description of *Passages Paysages,* from which the quotations in the text are taken). Cha's solo exhibitions, excluding performances, were all mounted after her death: *Theresa Hak Kyung Cha (1951–1982): Echoes,* at Mills College Art Gallery, Oakland (1989); *Theresa Hak Kyung Cha, MATRIX/Berkeley 137,* Berkeley Art Museum and Pacific Film Archive, University of California, Berkeley (1990); and *Theresa Hak Kyung Cha: Other Things Seen, Other Things Heard* (1993) and *Theresa Hak Kyung Cha: Exilee* (1995), both at the Whitney Museum of American Art, New York City. Cha's work has also been included in numerous group exhibitions. Cha edited *Apparatus, Cinematographic Apparatus: Selected Writings* for Tanam Press (1980), and included her own text and photo piece, "Commentaire." Cha's *Dictée* was originally published in 1982; it was reprinted by Third Woman Press in 1995, and again by the University of California Press in 2001.

The most significant analysis of *Dictee* remains Elaine Kim and Norma Alarcon, eds., *Writing Self, Writing Nation: Essays on Theresa Hak Kyung Cha's Dictée* (1994). The collection includes a narrative chronology assembled by Moira Roth based on interviews and thorough research. Lawrence Rinder, "The Theme of Displacement in the Art of Theresa Hak Kyung Cha and a Catalogue of the Artist's Oeuvre" (MA thesis, Hunter College, 1990), stands as an important early exploration of Cha's work. The most comprehensive analysis of Cha's oeuvre, including a detailed chronology of Cha's life with photos of the artist and many of her works, is Constance Lewallen, *The Dream of the Audience: Theresa Hak Kyung Cha 1951–1982,* the eponymous catalogue for an exhibit organized by the Berkeley Art Museum (2001). Trinh T. Minh-Ha includes a chapter on Cha, "Grandma's Story," in her celebrated *Woman, Native, Other* (1989), and Anne Anlin Cheng's *The Melancholy of Race* (2000) offers insights into Cha's work from an interdisciplinary perspective that focuses on race and identity.

PATRICIA VENTURA

CHADWICK, Florence May. November 9, 1918–March 15, 1995. Swimmer.

Florence May Chadwick, who gained lasting fame with channel swims around the globe, was born in San Diego, California. She was the second child and first daughter of Richard Chadwick, a police officer who became a member of the California Board of Narcotics, and Mary Lacko, a homemaker who later ran a restaurant in downtown San Diego. Although the Chadwicks were not sport enthusiasts, they encouraged Florence to begin swimming at an early age and she competed in her first race when she was six. She finished last. Chadwick bounced back with an attitude that would carry her across the English Channel twenty-six years later: "I made up my mind to become the best swimmer in California if I could" (Chadwick, p. 56). Once she realized her swimming forte rested with long-distance ocean events, not pool races, she fulfilled that goal. At the age of ten she swam the channel at the mouth of San Diego Bay, the youngest person to do so. She won the 2.5-mile swim race off La Jolla, California, ten times in the next eighteen years.

A 1936 graduate of Point Loma Junior and Senior High School in San Diego, where she swam competitively, Chadwick attended San Diego State College and studied law at Southwestern University of Law in Los Angeles and Balboa Law School in San Diego. She also attended Dickenson Business College. She was married twice, once before World War II and once during, but was never willing to trade her swimming ambitions for married life. Referring to both marriages as "detours," she admitted, "If I were married I'd have to devote full time to it. I'd have to be the best cook, the best housekeeper and the best whatever . . . and I don't have the time" (Melnick, p. 14). The names of her husbands are unknown and she never had children.

In 1926 Gertrude Ederle became the first American, male or female, to swim the English Channel, a feat that made her one of the best-known sport celebrities of the 1920s. Crossing the English Channel was a challenge Florence Chadwick had also dreamed of since her first race. Solidly built and five foot six, Chadwick had the perfect physique for long-distance swimming. In 1948, at the age of thirty, she departed for Saudi Arabia to save money and train. Chadwick began working as a comptometer for Aramco, an Arabian-American oil company in Dhahran. She trained in the Persian Gulf twice daily and two years later had saved the five thousand dollars necessary to attempt the English Channel swim.

Chadwick had applied to enter a contest sponsored by the London *Daily Mail,* but her application was rejected and she decided to go it alone. At 2:37 AM on August, 8, 1950, Chadwick entered the chilly waters at Cape Gris-Nez, France. Along the way Chadwick's father fed her sugar cubes and two friends from Saudi Arabia wrote jokes in Arabic on a blackboard to keep her spirits high. Chadwick arrived on the shores of Dover, England, thirteen hours and twenty minutes later as two fishermen—the only bystanders—watched in amazement. Chadwick had clipped Gertrude Ederle's twenty-four-year-old world record by an hour and eleven minutes.

Chadwick went on to complete sixteen channel swims and hold a number of world records. After swimming the English Channel from France to England, Chadwick was the first woman to make the more difficult swim in the opposite direction, crossing from England to France three times for a total of four English Channel swims. Chadwick was also the first woman to complete the Catalina Channel in southern California, which connects Catalina Island to Palo Verdes. She set a world record for crossing the Straits of Gibraltar in Spain, mastered the Bristol Channel between England and Wales, and easily completed both the Bosporus and Dardanelles in Turkey. The only channel that defeated her was the Irish Sea, connecting Ireland and Scotland. She attempted this crossing twice, the last time in 1960, but was unable to conquer the chilling 45-degree water.

Channel swimming offers few monetary rewards, so Chadwick found other ways to earn a living. In 1944 she worked with "America's mermaid," Esther Williams, on water ballet scenes for the movie *Bathing Beauty.* In 1946 she was director of aquatics at the La Jolla Beach and Tennis Club in California. Chadwick did a number of radio and television endorsements and was the spokesperson for Catalina Swimwear. From 1953 to 1963 she worked at Grossingers, a resort in New York's Catskill Mountains. Following her resort debut, she opened swimming schools in a Manhattan hotel and in Fort Lee, New Jersey. When the hotel closed in 1966, Chadwick taught private swimming lessons and was a credit counselor for Manufacturer's Hanover Bank on Wall Street. Chadwick returned to San Diego in 1968 to take care of her ailing mother and worked as a stockbroker with F. I. duPont, Glore Forgan & Co.

Florence Chadwick mastered open-water swimming better than any other woman and most men, and her love for the sea never dwindled. "I'm happiest in the water," she declared later in life. "Some people go for a walk. I go for a swim" (ibid., p. 14). Often called the greatest female distance swimmer in history, she was inducted into the International Swimming Hall of Fame in 1970. Florence Chadwick died of leukemia in San Diego in 1995 at the age of seventy-six, and her ashes were scattered in the Pacific Ocean off Point Loma.

Bibliography: The Henning Library at the International Swimming Hall of Fame in Fort Lauderdale, Florida, and the Research Archives at the San Diego Historical Society contain articles and newspaper clippings that profile Florence Chadwick. The most helpful are Norman Melnick, "Whatever Happened to Florence Chadwick?" *San Francisco Sunday Examiner and Chronicle,* September 13, 1970; and Florence Chadwick, as told to Seth Kantor, "The Sea Is My Home," both found at the Henning Library. Biographical material can also be found in Janet Woolum, *Outstanding Women Athletes: Who They Are and How They Influenced Sports in America* (1998); and Victoria Sherrow, *Encyclopedia of Women and Sports* (1996). General interest articles on Florence Chadwick include Mitchell Smyth, "Whatever happened to Florence Chadwick? . . . She's Swimming in a Treacherous Sea," *Toronto Star,* December 14, 1986; and Jay Horning, "English Channel Crosser Now Swims in 'Sea of Finance,'" *St. Petersburg Times,* February 8, 1987. Some of her trophies are at the Hall of Champions in San Diego's Balboa Park. Obituaries appeared in the *New York Times* and *Toronto Star* on March 19, 1995.

KAREN CHRISTEL KRAHULIK

CHALL, Jeanne Sternlicht. January 1, 1921–November 27, 1999. Psychologist, reading specialist.

Educational psychologist and reading researcher Jeanne Sternlicht Chall, whose work and advocacy helped shift the field of reading to a wider embrace of phonics, was born Jeanne Sternlicht in Shendishov, Poland. She did not meet her father, Hyman Sternlicht, who had immigrated to America, until she was seven years old, when she moved to New York City with her mother, Eva Kreinik Sternlicht, and three older sisters. Her father, whom she loved dearly, was always a major influence in her life. Her mother was her first pupil. Raised speaking Yiddish, Jeanne learned to speak English in school and taught her mother to speak and read the language so that she could pass the citizenship test.

Growing up in New York City and attending New York public schools, Jeanne's favorite place was the public library where she developed her love affair with books, reading, and children's literature. Over her lifetime she acquired a personal library of over ten thousand books, spanning more than two hundred years of American education history.

The first member of her family to attend college, Jeanne planned to become a teacher. She entered City College of New York in 1937 and received her bachelor's degree cum laude in 1941. Her student teaching experience in the Bronx confirmed that she loved teaching, but she was unable to secure a teaching position because of the lingering effects of the Great Depression. Considering herself lucky to be offered a research assistantship to work with Irving Lorge at the Institute of Educational Research, Teachers College, Columbia University, she discovered that educational research combined her love of teaching with her insatiable curiosity and love of inquiry.

In 1946 Jeanne married Leo Chall and accompanied him to Ohio State University, where she secured a research assistantship to work with Edgar Dale and earned a master's degree in 1947. Watching her classmates successfully sitting for the examination to enter doctoral studies, she decided to try for herself, and was subsequently admitted to the doctoral program, from which she graduated in 1952. The Challs did not have children (she always said the schoolchildren of America were her children), and they divorced in 1964.

Chall's work with Edgar Dale, her teacher and mentor, included her master's thesis on the readability of health materials, collaboration on several vocabulary studies, and the development of the Dale-Chall Readability Formula (1948), still used in its revised form (1995) by publishers today. He taught her to conquer her terror of writing, to view research from multiple perspectives, to value historical synthesis, and always to connect educational research to practice.

Returning to New York City in 1950, Chall joined the faculty of City College, where she taught and conducted research until 1965, progressing in rank from instructor to professor. Here she wrote *Readability: An Appraisal of Research and Application* (1958). Interested in helping teachers improve children's reading, she collaborated with a longtime colleague and friend, Florence Roswell, in developing diagnostic reading tests for word analysis (1956) and for auditory blending (1962).

In 1961 the Carnegie Foundation commissioned Chall to conduct a three-year study of the effectiveness of phonics and innovative programs for beginning reading instruction, particularly for inner-city children. Her synthesis of relevant research and observed instructional practices is presented in *Learning to Read: The Great Debate* (1967), a classic for understanding the importance of phonics in teaching beginning reading. This book, which introduced the term *decoding,* shifted the national conversation about how beginning reading should be taught. Throughout her life, as controversy swirled around phonics versus whole language instruction, Chall held fast to her research-based conviction that instruction should introduce children early to systematic phonics and then move beyond it.

In the fall of 1965 Chall moved to Cambridge, where she had been appointed professor of education at Harvard University. She held this position until 1991, when she retired as professor emerita. At Harvard, Chall founded the Reading Laboratory in 1966 and directed it for more than twenty-five years. Later she founded the Harvard Adult Literacy Lab.

In 1967, she was invited to join researchers, educators, and television producers to develop a new concept for television, *Sesame Street.* Chall insisted that they teach the ABCs and phonics and not just focus on self-esteem. She continued as an advisor and educational consultant for the Children's Television Workshop on *The Electric Company* and helped develop PBS's *Between the Lions.*

Jeanne Chall's work was always at the cusp of the reading field. Interested in connecting research, practice, and public policy, she joined John Carroll in leading the U.S. Department of Education's "Right to Read" effort, resulting in their edited volume, *Toward a Literate Society* (1975). In the 1970s she developed an explanatory model for how reading develops over the life span, *Stages of Reading Development* (1983). This synthesis of her work on readability and reading research describes six qualitatively different stages of reading, each needing different instructional practices.

Concerned about declining reading achievement, as indicated by declining SAT scores, she studied the difficulty levels of textbooks used in elementary classrooms, concluding in *An Analysis of Textbooks in Relation to Declining SAT Scores* (1977) that the achievement decline was related to the use of increasingly easier reading materials. Her subsequent study of this phenomenon for the Spencer Foundation was presented in *Should Textbooks Challenge Students? The Case for Easier or Harder Books* (1991).

Retirement in 1991 did not slow her down, but increasingly failing health began to reduce her pace. Collaborating with former colleagues and students, she spent her time writing a comprehensive diagnostic reading test, a series of phonics workbooks, a guide to testing and teaching, a guide for volunteer tutors, a set of qualitative readability scales, three textbooks, and revised editions of her earlier pathbreaking works. Jeanne Chall died at her Cambridge home at age seventy-eight on November 27, 1999, having just completed the final revision of a synthesis of American educational practice and research, *The Academic Achievement Challenge: What Really Works in the Classroom* (2000).

Jeanne Chall is remembered by her colleagues and students as the consummate teacher who taught them to take risks, think deeply, question, look for evidence from many sources, connect research to practice, and be generous with ideas. Through her books, articles, lectures, conference presentations, and courses, she taught college professors, educational researchers, classroom teachers and scholars, and through them, the children of the United States. She consistently demonstrated that to be a teacher is the most challenging, worthy, and important of all professions.

Bibliography: Jeanne S. Chall was a prolific scholar, whose publications beyond those mentioned in the text included books, edited volumes, book chapters, research reports, and articles for professional journals. Gail Kearns, "Jeanne S. Chall: A Memorial Tribute," *Perspectives* (Fall 2000), includes an extensive, though not complete, bibliography of her work. Insights into Jeanne Chall's relationships with her students and colleagues come from the special themed issue of the International Dyslexia Association newsletter, "Jeanne Sternlicht Chall: The Difference One Life Can Make," *Perspectives* 26, no. 4 (Fall 2000); five of these tributes were reprinted in *American Educator* 25, no. 1 (Spring 2001), pp. 16–28. See also Steven A. Stahl, "Jeanne S. Chall (1921–1999): An Appreciation," *Educational Researcher* 29, no. 5 (June–July 2000), pp. 41–43. Also of interest is Jeanne S. Chall's two-part "My Fascination with the Teaching and Psychology of Reading," *History of Reading News* 17, no. 1 (Fall 1993), and 17, no. 2 (Spring 1994). This essay draws on the author's personal conversations held with Chall over twenty-three years as student, colleague, and friend. Obituaries appeared in the *Boston Globe* on December 2, 1999, and the *New York Times* on December 12, 1999.

SUSAN H. HARRIS-SHARPLES

CHANDLER, Dorothy Buffum. May 19, 1901–July 6, 1997. Civic and cultural leader, newspaper executive.

Dorothy Buffum was born in Lafayette, Illinois, the youngest of three children of Fern Smith and Charles Abel Buffum. When she was about one year old, her parents moved to Long Beach, California, where her father opened a dry-goods store, which later became the first of a chain of popular department stores known as Buffum's. Active in civic affairs, he served for a time as mayor of Long Beach. Dorothy inherited her love of music from her mother, who had studied music at Knox College in Illinois and taught piano.

Lively and outgoing, "Buff" was known for her freckles and boundless energy. After graduating with honors from Long Beach High School in 1919, she became a campus favorite at Stanford University. During her junior year, she met Norman Chandler, son (and heir apparent) of *Los Angeles Times* publisher Harry Chandler. When the couple dropped out of school and wed on August 20, 1922, Dorothy gained entry to a dynastic powerhouse, the Chandler family.

Harrison Grey Otis, the founder of the dynasty,

had acquired the *Times* when he came to Los Angeles after the Civil War. He made the newspaper an instrument for nonstop boosterism to convert the unpromising, dusty town on a coastal plain into a bustling metropolis. Otis's concept of orderly, conservative, civic life was carried forward by the second publisher of the *Times,* his son-in-law, Harry Chandler, who supported land development and business expansion and fought socialism and the unions. Following his father's death in 1944, Norman became the third publisher of the *Times* and head of the Times Mirror Company, directing the Chandler family's multimillion-dollar holdings in paper manufacturing, real estate, securities, commercial printing, ranching, and oil. The Chandlers were not just a newspaper family; as major landholders, they fostered the growth, development, and promotion of the region.

In the early years of her marriage, Dorothy Chandler found it difficult to adjust to the traditional role expected of her as a social figure, wife, and mother to daughter Camilla, born in 1925, and son Otis, born two years later. In the early 1930s she was successfully treated for clinical depression. This period, she said later, was a turning point in her life. Taking a new view of herself and her abilities, she took up work in civic affairs as an active volunteer and fund-raiser for Los Angeles's Children's Hospital. At the Times Mirror Company she assumed the title of vice president for corporate relations and worked in partnership with her husband to remake the *Times* into a paper with high-quality journalism. She strengthened the coverage of women's news and the arts and created the annual Times Women of the Year Awards. She never considered herself a feminist, and in fact disliked the term, but she was a woman of strong will, immense energy, and great organizational abilities who felt that women's talents were underutilized.

On the board of the Southern California Symphony Association, Chandler won the appreciation of music lovers for her campaign in 1950 to save the city's landmark Hollywood Bowl from financial collapse. From the mid 1950s on, she focused primarily on an ambitious plan for a grand concert hall for Los Angeles that would bring to the city not only fine music but also the cultural and social life that surrounds a fine symphony orchestra—and that would invigorate the declining downtown core of the city.

After three county bond issues for the concert hall failed at the polls, Chandler resolved to raise private money and build a performing arts center herself. Her remarkable campaign to fund the project ultimately raised $45 million for construction of the three-building complex, with $18.5 million coming entirely from private donations. In its cover story on the Los Angeles matriarch, *Time* magazine called Dorothy Chandler's fund drive "perhaps the most impressive display of virtuoso money-raising and civic citizenship in the history of U.S. womanhood."

In the years it took to see her dream realized, Chandler came into her own as a major figure in Los Angeles. Candid, forceful, and charming in pursuit of her single-minded goal, she worked in defiance of city planners who opposed the "recentering" of downtowns in favor of new centers outside the old city cores. Chandler wanted a cultural center that would be identified with Los Angeles as a whole, one that all parts of the city would patronize with pride.

During her campaign for the Music Center, Chandler not only sought contributions from the area's influential old-money families, but also turned to "new money" sources in the city's show-business Westside and among Jewish business leaders. Her actions were not immediately appreciated by the old-guard elite, who had resisted community involvement with movie industry people and had quietly excluded Jews from their social life. Chandler brought together people who had not previously shared one another's company, and she could say with unabashed pride that what she had done "did more to break down the barriers against Hollywood, against Jews, against newtimers than anything that's happened in our city." When the Music Center for the Performing Arts opened in December 1964, Dorothy Chandler was credited with reversing the decay of the downtown core, revitalizing the cultural heritage of Los Angeles, and uniting the city's diverse citizens in a common goal. The next year the center's main auditorium was named the Dorothy Chandler Pavilion.

In 1960 she was instrumental with her husband in launching a hugely successful diversification program at Times Mirror. That same year, her son Otis was named fourth publisher of the *Los Angeles Times,* an occasion that Dorothy Chandler considered the most important day of her life. Otis continued the new direction that Dorothy and Norman Chandler had laid out for the paper and brought it in subsequent years to journalistic excellence. Dorothy Chandler's husband died in 1974, and her last years were spent in poor health and isolation in her Los Angeles home. In 1985 President Ronald Reagan selected her as one of the first recipients of the National Medal of Arts. Chandler died in a convalescent hospital in Hollywood in 1997 at the age of ninety-six, having left an indelible mark on modern Los Angeles.

Bibliography: The Dorothy Chandler papers are located at the Department of Special Collections, Charles E. Young Research Library, UCLA. The collection consists of correspondence and papers related to Dorothy Chandler's involvement with the Music Center of Los Angeles, the Southern California Symphony Association, the Center Theater Group of Los Angeles, and the Hollywood Bowl Association. Anita J. Klaz's oral history of Dorothy Chandler (January 1980) is included in Klaz's "An Oral History of Dorothy Buffum Chandler" (master's thesis, California State University at Northridge, 1981); the quotation in the text appears on p. 148. Other useful sources include *Current Biography* (1957), pp. 101–4; David Halberstam, *The Powers That Be* (1979); and Robert Gottlieb and Irene Wolt, *Thinking Big: The Story of the* Los Angeles Times, *Its Publishers, and Their Influence on Southern California* (1977). A cover story on Dorothy Chandler called "Brightness in the Air" appeared in *Time,* December 18, 1964, pp. 54–58; the quotation about her "virtuoso fund-raising" is found on p. 54. A history of the Music Center of Los Angeles can be found in Tamara Constance Asseyev, "The Development of the Los Angeles Music Center Project," (MA thesis, University of California at Los Angeles, 1968). See also "The Music Center Story," privately published by the Music Center Foundation. Obituaries appeared in the *Los Angeles Times* on July 7, 1997, and the *New York Times* on July 8, 1997.

MARGARET LESLIE DAVIS

CHARTERS, Jennie Matyas. *See* Matyas, Jennie.

CHASE, Lucia. March 24, 1897–January 9, 1986. Ballet dancer, patron and co-director of American Ballet Theatre.

Lucia Hosmer Chase, one of the most prominent members of the American dance world, was born in Waterbury, Connecticut, the third of five daughters of Elizabeth Hosmer Kellogg and Irving Hall Chase. Both her parents traced their lineage back to the earliest American settlements. After her father graduated from Yale in 1880, he began working at the Waterbury Clock Company (later Timex), assuming its presidency in 1912. Her mother was born in Waterbury and was an 1881 graduate of St. Margaret's School, a private girls' school that all her daughters attended. Lucia entered the Primary Room in 1904, remaining through graduation in 1913. Designated class orator and playing the role of Rosalind in *As You Like It* senior year, she was described in the yearbook with a prophetic inscription: "Lucia is our actress . . . if she followed the stage as a profession she would be unequalled." She entered Bryn Mawr in September 1914, leaving in January 1917 without a degree.

The early entries in Chase's extant diaries and her correspondence with her family reveal the life of a young woman of privilege, but there were always references to ballet, acting, and voice classes. A petite, blue-eyed brunette, Lucia Chase began the study of ballet when she was sixteen. She enrolled in the one-year course at Theatre Guild School in 1926–27 to study with noted director Rouben Mamoulian.

On December 28, 1926, Lucia Chase married Thomas Ewing Jr. In 1929 her husband, who enjoyed a reputation as a polo player, inherited the bulk of his uncle's estate from the Alexander Smith & Sons Carpet Company. The couple had two sons, Thomas Ewing III (1929) and Alexander (1931), before Ewing died of pneumonia in 1933 at the age of thirty-five, leaving a life estate of $1 million to his wife and $1 million to each of their sons. After other bequests were paid, she also inherited the remainder of her husband's more than $7 million estate.

After Ewing's death, Lucia Chase returned to ballet classes with Mikhail Mordkin, a Russian-born dancer, choreographer, and teacher. Mordkin, who had danced with the Bolshoi Ballet and the Diaghilev Ballets Russes, and partnered Anna Pavlova (1909–1911), opened his New York school in 1927. Chase appeared as Princess Aurora in Mordkin's production of *The Sleeping Beauty,* later dancing the leads in *La Fille Mal Gardee* and *Giselle.* The Mordkin Ballet, a forty-seven-member company financed by Chase, who was one of its principal dancers, toured the United States throughout 1937 and 1938.

Drawing on her experience with Mordkin, Chase was ready to move forward with the institution most closely associated with her name. Although she credited the inception of Ballet Theatre to Richard Pleasant, who had been administrator of the Mordkin company and school, she was the new company's primary financial patron. Four members of Mordkin's corps de ballet and eight principal dancers, including Chase, joined Ballet Theatre when it was formed in 1939.

Ballet Theatre's mission was international in scope, featuring choreographers from the major European traditions plus emerging talented Americans. There were separate wings for the Classical, American, and British repertories. The company opened a four-week season to critical acclaim at New York's Center Theater on January 11, 1940. Later that year the troupe performed in Philadelphia and Chicago, forecasting its future as a touring company. For the first time dancers in America were on salary for rehearsal weeks, and the performers' union, the American Guild of Musical Artists, recognized a ballet management. Ballet Theatre choreographers in 1940 included Michael Fokine, Adolph Bolm, Anton Dolin, Antony Tudor, AGNES DE MILLE, and Eugene Loring. Mordkin contributed one ballet and then was dropped. Chase said that he never spoke to her again.

In her early forties, when most ballerinas have already retired, and with two small children at home, Lucia Chase's performing career flourished. (She shaved ten years off her age while she was dancing, even managing to fool some of her obituary writers.) She was probably the happiest as a principal dancer during the first five years of Ballet Theatre, when she drew praise for her acting abilities in Tudor's and de Mille's works. She was less pleased about the number of checks she had to write as the company's chief source of funds.

In 1945 Chase and Oliver Smith were appointed co-directors of Ballet Theatre; she initially considered the job temporary, but it lasted for the next thirty-five years. Because Smith was also a working theatrical designer, Chase took responsibility for the day-to-day management. Her duties included choosing the ballets and choreographers, hiring the dancers, scheduling rehearsals and performances, and casting. (A vivid portrait of Chase's life was depicted in the role of the ballet director, Adelaide, in the 1977 film *The Turning Point.*) Ballet Theatre was an artistic success, but ticket sales never covered expenses. By 1948, Chase had contributed more than a million dollars, continuing to support the company throughout her tenure as director, although other donors and subsequently the National Foundation for the Arts supplemented her contributions. In 1957 the troupe changed its name to American Ballet Theatre to reflect the range of the company's national and international tours. Chase performed regularly with the company until 1960; she continued mime roles such as the Queen Mother in *Swan Lake* into the 1970s.

When Chase began her career, ballet was a fledgling art in America, dominated by the various Ballets Russes troupes. The Chase years at Ballet Theatre saw the founding and establishment of a company that is considered one of the major international ballet troupes. Chase can be credited with supporting the American phase of Antony Tudor's career, fostering Jerome Robbins's early works, encouraging Agnes de Mille's ballet career, and mounting a full-length *Swan Lake* (1967), which led the company to supremacy as a keeper of the classical flame. She also welcomed the Soviet émigré superstars and commissioned works by young American choreographers such as Twyla Tharp and Eliot Feld. Under the Chase-Smith management, international ballet stars including Mikhail Baryshnikov, Alicia Alonso, Erik Bruhn, Anton Dolin, Carla Fracci, Alicia Markova, and many others found a home, and American talents like NORA KAYE, John Kriza, Fernando Bujones, and Cynthia Gregory were groomed to stardom.

Lucia Chase always kept her private life separate from the professional demands of Ballet Theatre. In addition to her Park Avenue apartment, she kept homes in Waterbury and Narragansett Pier, Rhode Island. She never remarried, but remained close to her extended family. She retired from Ballet Theatre in 1980 and suffered a stroke several years later. Lucia Chase died of pneumonia at her New York apartment in 1986 at the age of eighty-eight and was buried in the Ewing family plot at Woodlawn Cemetery in Yonkers.

Bibliography: The Lucia Chase papers, a gift of her estate, are deposited at the Dance Collection, New York Public Library for the Performing Arts at Lincoln Center. The papers span the years 1899 to 1982, and include personal and business records and correspondence, including letters to and from members of her family, diaries, and personal financial papers. The Dance Collection holdings also include 900 photographs, three scrapbooks, three cartons of clippings, sixteen cartons of costumes, three reels of audiotape, and fifteen reels of film. The American Ballet Theatre Records held at the Dance Collection cover the period 1936–67. There are extensive files relating to Chase, particularly regarding financial and business correspondence. The yearbook quote appears in the *Salmagundi,* the yearbook of St. Margaret's School, from 1913 (information provided by St. Margaret's). The *Waterbury (Connecticut) Republican-American* has extensive clippings relating to Lucia Chase and the Chase family. Charles Payne's *American Ballet Theatre* (1978) is the most complete history in print of Chase's involvement with the company. Among the most useful periodical articles are Emily Coleman, "Lucia Chase: Director in Spite of Herself," *Theatre Arts* 42 (September 1958), pp. 63–65; "Lucia Chase Remembered," *Ballet Review* 26 (Spring 1990), pp. 54–66; and Olga Maynard, "Lucia Chase: First Lady of American Ballet," *Dance Magazine* 45, no. 8 (August 1971), pp. 28–33. Lucia Chase's son, Alexander Ewing, and her former secretary, Florence Pettan, supplied information for this essay. Obituaries appeared in the *New York Times* on January 10, 1986, and in *Dance Magazine* (March 1986).

IRIS FANGER

CHEN, Joyce. September 14, 1917–August 23, 1994. Restaurateur, cookbook author, entrepreneur.

Through her cooking classes, restaurants, and television programs, Joyce Chen influenced American cooks and diners who had previously known only highly inauthentic versions of Cantonese cuisine, or dishes like chop suey and chow mein, which are unknown in China. She was born Liao Jia-ai in Beijing into a high-ranking family in the Chin dynasty, the youngest child and seventh daughter in a family of nine. One grandfather was a governor, and her father, Hsin-Shih Liao, was a government administrator who was decorated for his services during a famine. The family, which moved to Shanghai when she was in her teens, enjoyed good food and entertained extensively. Unusually for such a wealthy family, her mother did some of the cooking herself, and the young child was encouraged to plan meals and received instruction in cooking techniques. She later recalled, "Whenever I entered the kitchen, my mother never forgot to remind me that I should learn how to cook so I wouldn't eat raw rice in case I couldn't afford a family cook in the future."

When she was in high school, one of her teachers, following the fashion for using English names, called her Joyce, because she was so joyful. She did not attend college. In 1943 she married Thomas Chen, born Chen Da-chong, in Hangzhou. They had three children: Henry (1944), Helen (1948), and Stephen (1952). The first two children were born in Shanghai; the last was born in Cambridge, Massachusetts, where the family settled in May 1949 after fleeing the Chinese Revolution and becoming American citizens. Thomas Chen continued to follow his trade as a leather salesman after the family moved to the United States. He went on to import ivory and curios for gift shops, and subsequently Chinese antiques. The Chens divorced in 1966.

Once in Cambridge, it was not long before Joyce Chen began to continue her family's hospitable tradition by entertaining students and members of the academic community with home-cooked Chinese meals. Soon her cooking began to find a wider American audience, starting with her daughter's Buckingham School in Cambridge. When the two dozen egg rolls she made for the school bazaar sold out in five minutes, the mother who was in charge of the food table asked her to make more. Her egg rolls continued to sell out many years thereafter.

Joyce Chen opened the first of her four restaurants in Cambridge in May 1958, hoping that the restaurant would be "a place to enjoy truly authentic Chinese food, but may also serve as a cultural exchange center." It was an immediate success with local diners. It soon received critical attention from food writers as well, who praised the tasteful décor, the good service, and a menu that offered a great variety of interesting dishes, particularly from northern China. When she was unable to hire local cooks who could prepare sufficiently authentic dishes, she used her influence with Cambridge academics serving in the Kennedy administration to get permission for cooks from China to emigrate.

As her cooking became better known, Joyce Chen began to teach classes at the Boston and Cambridge Centers for Adult Education starting in 1960. In addition to teaching cooking techniques, she led her students on visits to Boston's Chinatown, visiting bean-sprouting and tofu-making operations as well as food markets. She was a meticulous teacher, demonstrating the correct technique for making Peking duck and its accompanying pancakes, as well as stir-fried and simmered dishes at a time when these things were considered quite exotic.

Her first book, the *Joyce Chen Cook Book,* was originally self-published and sold to diners at her restaurants; it was commercially published by Lippincott in 1962. The cookbook began with a description of specifically Chinese ingredients and cooking equipment, which were then unfamiliar to the American cook, and featured the recipes she had been teaching as well as an introductory essay about her own life and experiences. At a time when traditional Chinese restaurant food in the United States was notoriously greasy, she emphasized the use of minimum amounts of fats and oils. Ever resourceful, she recruited Paul Dudley White of Harvard Medical School to supply an introduction, in which he praised her recipes for their healthfulness as well as their flavor.

Joyce Chen's business ventures grew out of difficulties she faced in operating her restaurants. Classically trained chefs were in short supply, and less-skilled cooks lacked both the talent and the experience to carry out Chen's carefully prepared master recipes with consistency and judgment. To deal with this problem, she prepared a series of bottled mixtures for her recipes that could be used by these lesser cooks. They proved such a success at the restaurant that customers wanted to buy them to use at home, a desire Chen was happy to fulfill. She formed a series of companies, of which Joyce Chen Specialty Foods was perhaps the best known. She also sold cooking equipment, such as bamboo spatulas, Japanese cleavers, and the first flat-bottomed wok, whose virtue was that it could sit flat on the cooking elements of American stoves without tipping over. She also hosted a nationally syndicated television program, *Joyce Chen Cooks,* which was produced by the same public television station as the popular *French Chef* program featuring Julia Child, a frequent diner at her restaurant. In 1972 Chen was featured in a documentary about a trip back to China she took with her family; they were among the first Americans to visit that country after President Nixon's historic visit that year.

In 1985 Joyce Chen was diagnosed with Alzheimer's disease. She died in Lexington, Massachusetts, on August 23, 1994, at the age of seventy-six.

Bibliography: Biographical information, as well as recipes and cooking techniques, can be found in *The Joyce Chen Cook Book* (1962), which contains both quotations from the text. A revised edition appeared in 1983. For additional material about the family, see Helen Chen, *Helen Chen's Chinese Home Cooking* (1994). Articles on Chen and her restaurant appeared in the *Boston Globe* on October 13, 1988; May 19, 1994; and July 8, 1994. This article draws on the author's experiences as a student in her cooking classes and as a diner at her restaurants. Obituaries appeared in the *Boston Globe* on August 25, 1994, and the *New York Times* on August 26, 1994.

BARBARA KETCHAM WHEATON

CHILDRESS, Alice. October 12, 1916–August 14, 1994. Playwright, writer, actress.

Alice Childress was born in Charleston, South Carolina. Little is known about her father or her mother, Florence. When her parents separated, Alice was sent at the age of five to live with her maternal grandmother, Eliza Campbell White, on 118th Street between Lenox and Fifth Avenues in Harlem. Her grandmother was the first to encourage Alice's literary imagination. Teachers at New York Public School 81, the Julia Ward Howe Junior High School, and Wadleigh High School later exposed her to the writings of Paul Laurence Dunbar, Sean O'Casey, Guy de Maupassant, Sholom Aleichem, William Shakespeare, and others. Wednesday night testimonials at Harlem's Salem Church taught her the art of dramatic storytelling.

Childress's formal education ended at the conclusion of her second year of high school when both her grandmother and her mother died. Forced prematurely into adulthood, Childress assumed responsibility for supporting herself. Her status as a working-class Harlemite—photo retoucher, insurance agent, and maid—and the simple settings of her employments became the grist for her later plays and novels. Most of her plots center on the lives of the "genteel poor"—domestics, porters, seamstresses, dancers, washerwomen, artists, and the unemployed—that unfold in train stations, backyards, parks, and tenements.

Acting became the focus of Childress's life in the 1940s. Her first roles were as Dolly in John Silvera and Abram Hill's comedy of manners *On Strivers' Row* (1940) and as Polly Ann in Theodore Browne's folk drama *Natural Man* (1941). Her role as Blanche in the original American version of Philip Yordan's Polish play *Anna Lucasta,* which Abram Hill suggested be adapted to portray an African American family, went to Broadway in August 1944 and earned Childress a Tony Award nomination. Staged at the Mansfield Theatre, *Anna Lucasta* ran for 957 performances. Its success launched the acting careers of Ossie Davis, Ruby Dee, Sidney Poitier, and Canada Lee.

The American Negro Theatre (ANT), headquartered in Harlem's Schomburg Center for Research in Black Culture (New York Public Library), served as Childress's training ground during her acting years. After the success of *Anna Lucasta,* radio and television work followed, but she fell victim to a racially doubly-biased system: her light complexion marked her as unacceptable for African American roles, while her race foreclosed casting in roles written for women of European ancestry. After an eleven-year apprenticeship, she was disillusioned with a black artistic aesthetic that privileged male issues and a theater governed by colorism and the stock casting of African American women, and she felt compelled to write her own plays.

Childress's first play, *Florence,* appeared in 1949, initiating a phase of her writing where she focused on female-centered interracial conflict. The treatment of African American women resisting Euro-American control and domination inside and outside the theater informs *Trouble in Mind* (1955) and *Wedding Band: A Love/Hate Story in Black and White* (1966), her two major plays of the period. *Trouble in Mind,* a protest against the racial inequities in the theater, earned Childress a Village Voice Obie Award for the best off-Broadway play of the 1955–56 season. *Wedding Band* drew Broadway speculation, but because Childress was unwilling to reconfigure the plot to accommodate dominant-culture tastes, it was never produced. In 1973, ABC televised a two-hour prime-time performance, but the depiction of an interracial, common-law marriage caused eight network affiliates to cancel their broadcasts; others aired it after midnight. A nondramatic publication, *Like One of the Family . . . Conversations from a Domestic's Life* (1956), a collection of sixty-two conversations that were first serialized in the *Baltimore Afro-American,* complemented the gendered, interracial politics of her plays during this inaugural phase.

From 1966 to 1968, Childress had a fellowship at the Radcliffe Institute for Independent Study. As the 1960s concluded, a second phase of her writing—the probing of intra-racial conflict—commenced. The plays *String* (1969), *Wine in the Wilderness* (1969), and *Mojo* (1970) indict classism and Euro-American acculturation as artificial and divisive appropriations that undermine African American solidarity.

A Hero Ain't Nothin' but a Sandwich (1973), Childress's most recognized and controversial work, ushered in the third phase of her writing, a period primarily devoted to young adult fiction. Labeled offensive because of its treatment of sex, drugs, and profane language, *A Hero,* a novel about a thirteen-year-old drug addict, was banned by school libraries in Georgia and New York. Its popularity soared among readers of all ages when New World Pictures released a film version in 1978. Childress wrote the screenplay. Her first novel for adults, *A Short Walk,* appeared in 1979.

Childress's acute social consciousness and commitment to a young adult readership continued with the publication of *Rainbow Jordan* (1981) and *Those Other People* (1989), novels featuring young adults grappling with peer pressure, parental abandonment, physical abuse, and sexual awakening. Assembling a gallery of characters and weaving intricate plots and subplots, Childress challenged the pervasive notion that good young adult fiction must be stylistically stark and linear in narration to accommodate inexperienced readers. Two plays for young children, *When the Rattlesnake Sounds* (1975), chronicling the commitment of Harriet Tubman, and *Let's Hear It for the Queen* (1976), a lesson on crime and punishment, expanded the age range of Childress's audience. One concession to adult theater, a dramatization of the life of Jackie "Moms" Mabley called *Moms: A Praise Play for a Black Comedienne* (1987), appeared during this period.

A private woman, Alice Childress safeguarded many personal details of her life. Articles usually identify her birth year as 1920, but at her death the family released the date as 1916. She married Nathan Woodard, a jazz musician, on July 17, 1957, but was silent about her earlier union with Alvin Childress, an actor who played Amos in the television series *Amos 'n Andy* (1951–53). Facts about her daughter, Jean Childress, who was born in 1935 and predeceased her mother in 1990, were similarly obscured. At the time of her death in Queens, New York, at the age of seventy-seven, Childress was working on an account of her maternal and paternal great-grandparents as a prelude to writing about her own life. A pioneer in the American theater, Alice Childress assisted in the dismantling of racial and gender stereotypes and led the way for other women's plays to receive public and influential staging.

Bibliography: Some of Alice Childress's correspondence is included in the American Negro Theatre Records collection in the Manuscripts, Archives and Rare Books Division, Schomburg Center for Research in Black Culture, New York Public Library. An oral history interview with Childress is part of the Hatch-Billops Collection of Oral Histories at the City University of New York Archives. In addition to the published plays and novels mentioned in the text, her unpublished plays, which are held by the Childress Estate, include "Hell's Alley," with Alvin Childress (1938); "Just a Little Simple" (1950); "Gold through the Trees" (1952); "The Freedom Drum" (1969); "Sea Island Song" (1977); and "A Man Bearing a Pitcher" (date unknown). A screenplay of *A Hero Ain't Nothin' but a Sandwich* (1978) and an edited work, *Black Scenes* (1971), complement a number of articles, essays, and interviews. La Vinia Delois Jennings's *Alice Childress* (1995) offers a critical introduction to her life and work. An obituary appeared in the *New York Times* on August 19, 1994.

LA VINIA DELOIS JENNINGS

CHINN, May Edward. April 15, 1896–December 1, 1980. Physician.

May Edward Chinn was born in Great Barrington, Massachusetts, the only child of Lulu Ann Evans and William Lafayette Chinn. Her father had been born a slave on the Chinn plantation in Lancaster County, Virginia, in 1852, and she believed that her fair-skinned father was the son of a white slaveholder and a slave woman. When he was eleven, William Chinn had escaped from slavery and found his way to Great Barrington, where he worked a variety of low-income jobs. He met his wife, twenty-five years his junior, after she moved to the town to work as a housekeeper. Lulu Ann Evans, the daughter of an ex-slave father and a Chickahominy Indian mother, had been born on the Chickahominy reservation near Norfolk, Virginia, in 1876. Acknowledging her mixed racial background, May Chinn called herself an Afro-American/American Indian.

Her parents had a tension-filled marriage with periodic separations. When their daughter was three, the family moved to New York City. William Chinn had a history of alcohol abuse, which his daughter blamed on his inability to secure steady employment because of his race. The family lived a hardscrabble life; Lulu Chinn's income as a domestic often was the only financial support for the family. Determined that her five-year-old daughter would receive a first-class education, she saved enough money from her meager wages to send May to the Manual Training and Industrial School, a school for black children in Bordentown, New Jersey. May stayed less than a year because she contracted osteomyelitis (a bone infection) in her lower jaw. Upon her return home, May moved in with her mother at the Irvington, New York, estate of Charles E. Tiffany, the jeweler, where her mother worked as a housekeeper until Tiffany's death in 1902. Chinn and her mother then returned to New York City, where her parents tenuously reconciled and where she attended the city's public schools.

Chinn attended Washington Irving High School for a year before transferring to Morris High School in the Bronx. She dropped out in eleventh grade. A year later she passed the entrance exam for Teachers College at Columbia University and qualified for admission. In contrast to her husband, Lulu Chinn tenaciously supported her daughter's intellectual endeavors. Despite several proposals, May Chinn never married—in part because of lingering bitterness toward her father.

An accomplished pianist, Chinn entered college in 1917 planning on majoring in music; but she changed her major after a racist music professor mistreated her. Fortuitously, she took a course from Jean Broadhurst, a bacteriology professor who in 1937 would become the first to identify the measles virus. Broadhurst recognized Chinn's scientific aptitude and convinced her to switch her major. Chinn received her BS in 1921 and then worked for a year in a clinical pathology laboratory. For four years in the early 1920s she also worked as an accompanist for Paul Robeson, the black artist and activist.

While an undergraduate, Chinn had decided to become a physician, prompted by her own childhood illness and her awareness of the poor health status of Harlem residents. In 1922, Chinn became the first black woman admitted to Bellevue Hospital Medical School (now New York University School of Medicine). Following her graduation in 1926, she continued her professional trailblazing when she became the first black woman intern at Harlem Hospital, which had just opened its doors to black physicians. She also was the first woman to ride with the Harlem Hospital ambulance service on emergency calls.

Upon the completion of her internship in 1927, Chinn became the only African American woman physician in Harlem and a member of a very small medical sorority: the 1930 census found only ninety-two black women physicians practicing in the United States. As a pioneering black woman physician, Chinn faced obstacles based on her race and gender. At first her black male colleagues questioned her abilities, and even some black patients were apprehensive about receiving care from a black woman. The prestigious Rockefeller Institute withdrew a research fellowship after it was discovered that she was not Chinese. Chinn also discovered other ways racial discrimination hindered the careers and work conditions of black physicians; for instance, they could not admit their patients to most New York hospitals, which forced them to perform even major surgeries in patients' homes. Her experiences as an African American woman physician led her in 1975 to become one of the founders of the Susan Smith McKinney Steward Medical Society, one of the first organizations of black women physicians.

Despite professional hurdles, Chinn practiced medicine in Harlem for over fifty years. Initially she maintained a general medical practice, but she became increasingly interested in cancer prevention and detection because so many of her patients were in advanced stages of the disease. For five years beginning in 1928 she studied with George Papanicolaou, the inventor of the Pap smear for cervical cancer detection. In 1933, she received a master's degree in public health from Columbia. In 1944, she secured a position at the Strang Clinic, one of the country's top cancer facilities—a remarkable achievement, given that it occurred before the advent of the postwar civil rights movement. Her work focused on the early detection of cancer, and she remained on staff for almost thirty years. In recognition of her work there, the Society of Surgical Oncology elected her as a member in 1958. Ill health forced Chinn to close her office in 1977, but she continued to practice medicine until her death. She conducted cancer-screening examinations at health fairs and served as a medical consultant to the Phelps-Stokes Fund.

Chinn was a legendary figure in Harlem, but when she reached her eighties she gained renown beyond its borders. In April 1979, *New York Times Magazine* profiled her life in "A Healing Hand in Harlem." In 1980 she received honorary degrees from both Columbia University and New York University and the Distinguished Alumnus Award from Teachers College. On December 1, 1980, while attending a reception at Columbia University, May Edward Chinn collapsed and died at the age of eighty-four. Following her wishes, there was no funeral for the physician whom generations of Harlem residents affectionately called Dr. May.

Bibliography: The May Edward Chinn Papers in the Manuscripts, Archives, and Rare Books Division at Schomburg Center for Research in Black Culture, New York Public Library, are not extensive but contain correspondence, clippings, curriculum vitae, speeches, her will, and photographs. They also include a very useful, but brief, manuscript, "Autobiography of Dr. May Edward Chinn." A copy of her oral history conducted by Ellen Craft Dammond can be found in the Black Women Oral History Project, Schlesinger Library, Radcliffe Institute for Advanced Study, Harvard University. Among Chinn's publications are "Cancer and the Negro," *Opportunity* 15 (February 1937), pp. 51–53, and "A Vaginal Smear Screening Program for the Diagnosis of Uterine Carcinoma," *Harlem Hospital Bulletin* 8 (September 1955), pp. 52–61.

The only book-length biography of Chinn is for young adults: Ellen Rubinstein Butts and Joyce R. Schwartz, *May Chinn: The Best Medicine* (1995). Accounts of her life are presented in George Davis, "A Healing Hand in Harlem," *New York Times Magazine*, April 22, 1979, pp. 40 ff.; and Nadine Brozan, "For a Doctor at 84, a Day to Remember," *New York Times*, May 17, 1980. For her work with Paul Robeson, see Martin Bauml Duberman, *Paul Robeson* (1988), and Paul Robeson Jr., *The Undiscovered Paul Robeson: An Artist's Journey, 1898–1939* (2001). Her work with the Susan Smith McKinney Medical Society is discussed in Charlayne Hunter-Gault, "Black Women M.D.s: Spirit and Endurance," *New York Times*, November 16, 1977. Further information about black physicians in Harlem can be found in Gerald A. Spencer, *Medical Symphony* (1947), and Aubre de L. Maynard, *Surgeons to the Poor: The Harlem Hospital Story* (1978). Obituaries appeared in the *New York Times* on December 3, 1980, and the *Amsterdam News* on December 6, 1980.

VANESSA N. GAMBLE

CHU, Grace Zia. August 23, 1899–April 15, 1999. Chinese culinary instructor.

Grace Zia Chu, who helped teach Americans that there is more to Chinese cooking than chop suey and chow mein, was born in Shanghai, China, the first daughter of nine children of Hong-Lai Zia and Sochen Sze. Her father was a Christian educator and editor, and her mother was active in the Young Women's Christian Association (YWCA). Grace graduated from the McTyeire School for Girls in Shanghai in 1918. Recently orphaned, she came to the United States in 1920 after receiving a scholarship as well as support from various missionary families to attend Wellesley College. She later recalled her college years as "far from home, in a world full of tall strangers and inedible food." Although she loved ice cream, she was able to tolerate little else; salads and cheese had been all but unknown to her. Growing up in a wealthy Chinese family with servants, she had never cooked; but once she found herself at Wellesley, she began to try to replicate Chinese cooking to cure her unrelenting homesickness. She would later claim that she invented Chinese cooking because she figured out how to cook Chinese food with a few Chinese cooking utensils (a wok, a Chinese slicing cleaver, a steamer, and chopsticks) and the ingredients found in American supermarkets.

After earning a bachelor's degree in biology in 1924 and receiving a certificate from Wellesley's Department of Hygiene and Physical Education the following year, Grace returned to China, where she taught physical education at the McTyeire School and Ginling College in Nanjing for the next thirteen years. In 1928 she married Shi-ming Chu, whom she had met in Boston while he was a student at MIT. Although he had received a degree in engineering, Chu's husband opted to follow a military career, and quickly became a major general in the Chinese Nationalist army when he went back to China. Their first son, Samuel, was born in Shanghai in 1929, and their second son, Daniel, was born in Nanjing in 1933.

Grace Chu's life changed dramatically when her husband became an interpreter and aide-de-camp to Nationalist leader Chiang Kai-shek in 1937. She became acquainted with Madame Chiang Kai-shek, a fellow Wellesley alumna, and she began to work closely with her through the Women's Advisory Committee in Chunking. At this point the Nationalist government was engaged in a bitter civil war with Communist forces led by Mao Zedong. After her husband was posted as a military attaché to the Chinese Embassy in Washington, D.C., in 1941, Grace Chu became not just a representative of the increasingly beleaguered Nationalist government but also a self-described "ambassador for Chinese food" through her entertaining as a diplomat's wife. The family spent the war years in Washington. In 1946, with their teenage sons enrolled in American schools, the Chus returned to China, but they separated two years later. She came back to the United States as a refugee in 1948, and he settled in Tokyo, where he lived until his death in 1965. They never divorced.

Struggling to make a living to support herself and her two sons, Chu first attempted to run a gift shop in Florida, then later worked as a chef at the Hotel New Yorker. She also worked briefly as a secretary at Columbia University. She began teaching cooking lessons at the China Institute in New York City through a friend's invitation in 1955. Although she had never formally been trained as a chef or a culinary teacher, she acquainted herself with chefs at various Chinese restaurants in the city and soon began her own cooking school in her apartment on West 111th Street in Manhattan and through the Mandarin House Restaurant. Seeing herself as a cultural diplomat, she used her expertise on Chinese cooking to familiarize her students and readers with Chinese culture. "I have a missionary spirit about Chinese cooking," she told thousands of students. "I want you to become thoroughly absorbed with Chinese culture and history and philosophy as it relates to food."

Through her best-selling book, *The Pleasures of Chinese Cooking* (1962), Chu successfully reached a large readership as she became the first culinary teacher to contextualize Chinese recipes for an American audience. She interspersed her culinary teaching with history lessons as she explained the origins of tea drinking in China and the reason Chinese ingredients are chopped or sliced into small pieces (a severe shortage of fuel throughout Chinese history made it necessary to cut food into very small pieces in order to cook it quickly). She exposed Chinese-food-lovers to the regional diversity of China as she explained the distinctions (not widely recognized in America at that time) among Sichuan, Hunan, Fukien, and Cantonese cooking styles. Although her classes and cookbooks included complex recipes, she was best known for her ability to encourage beginners.

In addition to her teaching, Chu often appeared on radio and television and lectured throughout the United States and Europe. In 1975, she wrote another cookbook, *Madame Chu's Cooking School,* because she felt that the popularization of Chinese food in the 1960s and 1970s, and the proliferation of Chinatowns in cities throughout the nation, demanded an expanded collection of her recipes.

In 1986, Grace Chu moved to Columbus, Ohio, to be near her sister Ruth Zia and her son Samuel. She lived in the First Community Village in Upper Arlington, Ohio, where she died in 1999 just short of her hundredth birthday. Her legacy as a culinary instructor and a cultural diplomat will endure much longer in America. Craig Claiborne, eminent restaurant writer for the *New York Times,* called Chu "the doyenne of Chinese cooking teachers" and added, "there is probably no one, certainly no one on the New York scene, who has done more to familiarize the public with the food of her homeland than Madame Grace Chu."

Bibliography: There is a small collection of Grace Chu papers at the Schlesinger Library, Radcliffe Institute for Advanced Study, Harvard University. In addition to her books, see Grace Chu, "Many Knowing Gourmets Place Chinese Food Right Up There with French," *The Continental,* Spring–Summer 1971, p. 23; and Chu and Irene Sax, "From Alumnae Kitchens: Soy Sauce, Scallions, and Hospitality," *Wellesley Alumnae Magazine,* Winter 1982, pp. 24–28, which contains the quotation about her college years. Articles about Chu include Irene Sax, "Grace Chu and the Pleasures of Chinese Entertaining," *Food & Wine,* March 1981, pp. 44–46; Marcia Seligson, "The Eggroll and I," *Newsday,* July 3, 1971, which includes the quotation about her missionary spirit; and Karin A. Welzel, "Madame Chu Wrote the Book on Chinese Cuisine," *Columbus Dispatch,* April 28, 1999, which has Craig Claiborne's final quotation. An obituary appeared in the *New York Times* on April 19, 1999.

SONIA LEE

CLAMPITT, Amy. June 15, 1920–September 10, 1994. Poet, critic, editor.

The *New York Times* headlined Amy Clampitt's obituary "Late Bloomer." In a world where poetry was mostly the province of the young, her first full-length book, *The Kingfisher* (1983), appeared to astonishing acclaim when she was sixty-three years old. In the eleven years before her death she published four more volumes of poetry—*What the Light Was Like* (1985), *Archaic Figure* (1987), *Westward* (1990), and *A Silence Opens* (1994)—and a book of critical essays, *Predecessors, Et Cetera* (1991); she also edited *The Essential [John] Donne* (1988). But the brilliance of her craftsmanship and the resonance of her ideas did not simply represent the accomplishments of age. Clampitt's poetic achievements grew out of a lifetime of sensibility. At the New School for Social Research in 1977 she won an award for poetry; and she won a fellowship from the Academy of American Poets in 1981. A Guggenheim Fellowship in 1982 and a MacArthur grant in 1992 crowned her long toil in what she called "the poetry factory" (Salter, p. xxi).

Amy Clampitt's first memory as a child was of the intensity of a bed of violets suggestive of all nature and art. She was born in New Providence, Iowa (population 200), the oldest of five children of Lutie Pauline Felt and Roy Justin Clampitt. Her farming family lived first on her grandfather's comfortable homestead, and then, when she was ten, moved to bleaker acreage nearby. She once called herself a "poet of place," then changed her mind to say "displacement" (*New York Times,* September 12, 1994). But she remained proud of her identity with a courageous community of pioneers. New Providence, settled by Quakers from North Carolina, also provided a religious background that mixed Quaker values with hymns, sermons, and Bible readings. Although Clampitt attended Sunday school with the rest of the town, she came to believe organized religion was obsolete. Later the beauty of church ritual drew her to the Episcopalians until the Vietnam War when, reflecting her Quaker background, she felt church leaders were too slow to speak out against violence. Yet the first poet she loved—Gerard Manley Hopkins, an ardent believer—remained an inspiration.

Clampitt attended Consolidated School in New Providence for twelve grades, then went to Grinnell College, graduating with honors in 1941. She attended graduate school for a time at Columbia University and took classes at the New School for Social Research, but soon gave up formal education to earn her living and to write. She worked as a secretary at Oxford University Press from 1943 to 1951 and as reference librarian at the National Audubon Society from 1952 to 1959. She then supported herself as a freelance editor and researcher before joining E. P. Dutton as an editor from 1977 to 1982. Although she put most of her literary energy into writing three novels during the 1950s, she eventually put prose aside to print two small volumes of poetry: *Multitudes, Multitudes* (1974) and *The Isthmus* (1981). When the elegance of her work caught the attention of Howard Moss, poetry editor of the *New Yorker,* she gained an audience. Over a number of years Clampitt also worked on a play primarily about Dorothy Wordsworth called *Mad with Joy,* which was produced by the Poets' Theater in Cambridge, Massachusetts, in 1993, but her main concern became writing and organizing her poetry.

At one point she won a trip to England in a company-sponsored essay contest and later returned to Europe to confirm another aspect of her complex self: her belief in "the *livingness* of the past" (Salter, p. xviii). Many of the English writers Clampitt loved, such as Wordsworth, Keats, Hopkins, and George Eliot, remained a deeper part of her as she visited the places that shaped them. Small wonder that Helen Vendler suggested that a century from now Amy Clampitt's work might be seen as a document of "what, in the twentieth century, made up the stuff of culture" (Vendler, p. 22). Clampitt's collected poems, annotated to make their complex references easier for readers, include a vast range of everyday experiences, from Greyhound buses and boysenberry pie to the five-and-dime and the Statue of Liberty—"crass icon of the possible"—and to religious assertions and political testimonies (*Collected Poems,* p. 406). When she became famous overnight as a poet, she gave many readings and she also taught at Wisconsin, Smith, Amherst, and the College of William and Mary.

Clampitt's heritage of protest continued to define her life. Picketing the White House against bombing in Southeast Asia in 1971, she chose the sign "Poet," clarifying her profession for the first time. A number of her poems reflected the anxieties of the Vietnam era; especially powerful was "The Dahlia Gardens," an elegy for Norman Morrison, who had immolated himself in protest. In the late 1960s at a party for Democrats she met Harold (Hal) Korn, the Columbia Law School professor with whom she shared the next twenty-five years of her life. Although Clampitt kept her tiny Greenwich Village apartment as a measure of independence, she lived uptown with Hal and dedicated *The Kingfisher* to him. When she discovered she had ovarian cancer with little time ahead, they married—five days before her seventy-fourth birthday.

Amy Clampitt's nature was outgoing and nurturing even as she praised women's inner strength. In her poems she celebrated the archaic power of Medusa, the magical bravery of POCAHONTAS (Matoaka), and the revolutionary satisfaction of MARGARET FULLER. Her essays and her poems about other women pay homage to many who found liberation in their writing. Margaret Fuller, EDITH WHARTON, Stevie Smith, MARIANNE MOORE, EMILY DICKINSON, and Dorothy Wordsworth appear in her gallery of heroines. The strong sense of place and the complexity of feeling about nature and culture emerging in her poems claimed the attention of readers hungry for the richness of language and intellectual challenge in her poems.

When Amy Clampitt received a MacArthur Fellowship in 1992, she bought a small house in Lenox, Massachusetts. She and Hal lived there until her death in 1994 at the age of seventy-four. Her ashes were buried in the garden under a favorite birch. After her death, Harold Korn with several of her close friends formed the Amy Clampitt Foundation to benefit poetry and the literary arts.

Bibliography: No biography of Amy Clampitt exists. The best essay on her life is the foreword to *The Collected Poems of Amy Clampitt* (1997) by Mary Jo Salter. Her papers are being assembled for the Henry W. and Albert A. Berg Collection of English and American Literature at the New York Public Library. Basic facts may be found in *Contemporary Authors,* vol. 110 (1984). Particularly helpful essays are Helen Vendler, "On the Thread of Language," *New York Review of Books,* March 1983, pp. 19–22; Paul Olson, "The Marryings of All Likeness," *Prairie Schooner* 51, no. 1 (Spring 1983), pp. 99–102; Richard Howard, "The Hazardous Definition of Structures," *Parnassus: Poetry in Review* 11, no. 1 (Spring–Summer 1983), pp. 271–75; Peter Porter, "Painting in Words," *Observer,* June 17, 1984, p. 22; and Willard Spiegelman, "Amy Clampitt's Drama of Syntax," *Verse* 10, no. 3 (Winter 1993), pp. 18–33. Tapes of Clampitt reading from her works in 1987 are available from the Academy of American Poets Audio Archive, New York City. An obituary appeared in the *New York Times* on September 12, 1994.

EUGENIA KALEDIN

CLARENBACH, Kathryn (Kay) Frederick. October 7, 1920–March 4, 1994. Educator, feminist.

Having been born the same year as the Nineteenth Amendment granting women the right to vote was ratified, Kay Clarenbach did not take her birthright lightly. Columnist Jacquelyn Mitchard described her as "one of the quiet architects of the women's movement" (*Milwaukee Journal,* November 6, 1988). Indeed, Clarenbach helped build the modern women's movement beginning in 1964 when she took a key leadership position in Wisconsin before becoming a founding member of the National Organization for Women (NOW). Contemporaries credited Clarenbach with bringing organizational acumen and strategic sophistication to feminist groups. Her penchant for behind-the-scenes organizing and talent for encouraging others to accept leadership roles suited her modest personal style but made her significant contributions to the women's movement less well known.

Kathryn Dorothy Frederick was born in Sparta, Wisconsin, the third of four children and only daughter of Nina Vivian Hubbell and Alexander Ernst Frederick. Her father, an ordained Methodist minister and lawyer, served in the Wisconsin State Assembly from 1912 to 1916 and made an unsuccessful bid for Congress in the mid 1920s. Her mother, a 1907 graduate of Sparta High School, taught school and served on the Sparta School Board for many years. A. E. Frederick's ministerial duties and work as a state humane and parole and probation officer encouraged his children to appreciate and be curious about the wider, more diverse world beyond rural Wisconsin, a perspective Clarenbach brought to her career as an educator and social activist.

Kay's educational and professional experience prepared her well for her later role as a social movement leader. Like her father, she attended the University of Wisconsin, graduating with a BA in political science in 1941, followed by an MA in the same subject in 1942. To support the war effort, she took the federal Civil Service Exam and moved to Washington, D.C., to work as an administrative analyst with the War Production Board. In 1944 she returned to Madison to pursue a PhD in political science. After completing her PhD in August 1946, she married Henry G. Clarenbach, a fellow graduate student, on September 5, and then reported to Purdue University ten days later to teach political science as an instructor. Purdue wanted her to remain for another year, but Clarenbach moved to New York City to be with her husband while he pursued a PhD at Columbia University. While there, the couple worked on Henry Wallace's 1948 presidential campaign.

Like many white, middle-class women in the 1950s, Clarenbach left the labor market to raise children and pursue volunteer work, which included a position on the state board of the Missouri League of Women Voters. She and Henry had three children: Sara (1949), David (1953), and Janet (1957). Work on women's issues became a true calling in 1962 when Clarenbach renewed her career as an educator. As director of University Education for Women at the University of Wisconsin, she became a pioneer in the field of continuing education for women. She described her work there as life-changing: "I was not particularly conscious of disadvantages to women until I began working in the University's extension program. Once I began questioning the system, of asking the 'whys,' a whole new world unfolded" (*Green Bay Press Gazette,* March 29, 1979).

From her position at the University of Wisconsin, Clarenbach had the resources to encourage the nascent women's movement. After a continuing education conference in February 1963 in which ESTHER PETERSON—primary organizer of John F. Kennedy's President's Commission on the Status of Women—gave the keynote address, Clarenbach arranged a meeting between Peterson and leaders of women's groups to discuss the formation of a Wisconsin state commission. Governor John Reynolds appointed her as the first chair of the subsequent commission, the Wisconsin Governor's Commission on the Status of Women (WGCSW), a post she held from 1964 to 1969 and from 1971 to 1979.

At a national conference for state commissions on the status of women in 1966, Clarenbach joined a small group of conference attendees to form the group that became NOW. During the next two years she worked as a founding member and first chair of the NOW board of directors. She remained a feminist organizer throughout the 1970s, most notably as the first president of the National Association of Commissions for Women in 1970, as the chair of the national organizing conference of the National Women's Political Caucus in 1971, and as the executive director of the National Commission on the Observance of International Women's Year in 1977.

Clarenbach guided the deliberations of the inadequately funded WGCSW and sustained the fledgling NOW from her University of Wisconsin office, where her dignified bearing and academic credentials lent credibility to feminist demands. She applied her love of writing, a gift she attributed to her mother, to feminist activism by writing numerous reports for the WGCSW and by publishing scholarly articles on women's education. Friends especially appreciated Clarenbach's graciousness, equanimity, and sense of humor in the midst of the tumultuous early years of the modern women's movement. She retired from University of Wisconsin–Extension in 1988 as a professor of political science.

Speaking to a reporter on the tenth anniversary of the International Women's Year Conference, which she had helped organize, Clarenbach said, "I'm hopeful. You have to be or else you leave this movement" (*Los Angeles Times,* November 30, 1987). Her belief that the women's movement would lead to meaningful social change sustained her work as one of Wisconsin's—and the nation's—leading feminists. She not only headed numerous organizations but was in great demand as a public speaker and radio commentator. She was particularly proud of her role as the first lay president of the board of trustees of Alverno College, a Catholic women's college in Milwaukee. Kay Clarenbach's eloquence, keen intellect, and pragmatic approaches to social change inspired great respect and loyalty among her friends and colleagues. She died in Madison, Wisconsin, in 1994 at the age of seventy-three.

Bibliography: The Kathryn F. Clarenbach Papers in the University of Wisconsin–Madison Archives include the records of the Wisconsin Governor's Commission on the Status of Women as well as personal correspondence and newspaper clippings related to the activities of women's organizations Clarenbach helped organize, particularly in Wisconsin, during the 1970s and 1980s. The papers also include records related to Clarenbach's career at the University of Wisconsin–Extension. The University of Wisconsin Archives' Oral History Project has a finding aid and an unbound transcript of two oral history interviews with Clarenbach conducted in 1987 and 1989. Scholarly publications by Clarenbach include *The Green Stubborn Bud: Women's Culture at Century's Close,* edited with Edward Kamarck (1987); "Unfinished Business of Women's Rights," *Journal of Intergroup Relations* 7, no. 2 (September 1979), pp. 41–47; "Women in Legal Perspective," in Joan I. Roberts, ed., *Beyond Intellectual Sexism: A New Woman, a New Reality* (1976); and "Can Continuing Education Adapt?" *AAUW Journal* 63, no. 2 (January 1970), pp. 62–65. Additional sources on Clarenbach's work in Wisconsin are Marie Laberge, "'Seeking a Place to Stand': Political Power and Activism among Wisconsin Women, 1945–1963" (PhD dissertation, University of Wisconsin–Madison, 1995), and the documentary film *Step By Step: Building a Feminist Movement, 1941–1977* (1998). Additional information for this article was provided by Sara

Clarenbach, filmmaker Joyce Follet, and friends Gene Boyer Sr., Austin Doherty, Mary Eastwood, Joel Read, and Constance Fuller Threinen. Obituaries appeared in the *New York Times* on March 10, 1994, and the *Washington Post* on March 16, 1994.

KATHLEEN A. LAUGHLIN

CLARK, Georgia Neese. January 27, 1898–October 26, 1995. Banker, U.S. Treasurer, Kansas civic leader.

Born in Richland, Kansas, Georgia Neese Clark built an early career as a New York–based stage actress in the 1920s. After returning to her home in Kansas during the Depression to help run the family banking business, Clark became active in state and national Democratic Party affairs. In 1949, President Harry Truman appointed her to serve as U.S. Treasurer. When her political appointment ended, Clark returned to Kansas and pursued a successful business career. In the last decades of her life she was a well-known patron of the theater arts in Topeka, Kansas, as well as a voice for women's political involvement and leadership.

Early family circumstances influenced her to pursue uncommon interests, and she would later encourage other women to do the same. The second of two daughters born to Ellen O'Sullivan and Albert Neese in the small town of Richland in northeastern Kansas, she grew up in a Presbyterian household. Her father, an entrepreneur of Dutch descent, had founded the town's bank and also operated a lumberyard, grain elevator, insurance agency, and general store; her mother was a housewife. Albert Neese told his daughters that he wished they had been sons, but he nevertheless encouraged and schooled them in the family's enterprises. Before reaching adulthood, Georgia Neese contemplated leaving home to become an actress, but her parents advised her to complete her education. After graduating from high school in 1917, she briefly attended the College of the Sisters of Bethany in nearby Topeka and then pursued a BA in economics at Washburn College (later Washburn University). She graduated in 1921.

Later that year, she moved to New York City and began studies at Sargent's Dramatic School (which later became the American Academy of Dramatic Arts). In the next decade, she developed a career with touring companies and a fondness for comedic roles. In 1929 she married theatrical manager George M. Clark and thereafter was known professionally as Georgia Neese Clark. The onset of the Depression caused a steep downturn in the entertainment industry, and Clark returned to Kansas in 1930 to help manage the Neese family businesses, a career change prompted in part by her father's failing health.

Directing her energies toward banking, she became president of the Richland State Bank in 1938, following her father's death the previous year. A supporter of Franklin D. Roosevelt, she also rose in political prominence, serving as national committeewoman for the Kansas Democratic Party beginning in 1936. As a state delegate to every national Democratic convention from 1936 to 1964, Clark befriended many party activists, including ELEANOR ROOSEVELT and INDIA EDWARDS, who in the 1940s served as director of the Women's Division of the Democratic National Committee.

Edwards's dedicated involvement in making use of women's political talents helped launch the public service career of Georgia Neese Clark and many other women of her generation. Clark had actively supported Harry Truman's re-election bid in 1948, and in her predominantly Republican home state of Kansas, she was well regarded as an articulate speaker on behalf of Democratic issues and candidates. In 1949, when U.S. Treasurer William A. Julian sustained fatal injuries in an automobile accident, President Truman, mindful of Democratic women's critical support during the recent close election, asked Edwards for advice on naming a suitable successor. Edwards suggested Clark, the banker from Kansas, and Truman offered her the position. Although no woman had ever been named U.S. Treasurer, her appointment was confirmed unanimously by the U.S. Senate.

As Treasurer, Clark and her staff were responsible for the accounting of federal monetary accounts, as well as issuing U.S. currency, and Clark's signature appeared on paper currency printed during her tenure in office, from June 1949 to early 1953. Clark viewed her public position as an opportunity to encourage women to enter business and political arenas, and she spoke frequently on this topic. By the time Dwight D. Eisenhower named a Republican successor, IVY BAKER PRIEST, in 1953, the precedent had been set: since then, the position of U.S. Treasurer has usually been held by a woman.

Georgia Neese Clark's first marriage was childless and ended in divorce in the 1940s. In 1953 Clark married for a second time. Her husband, Andrew J. Gray, a journalist and public relations executive, moved with her to Kansas, where she resumed oversight of the Richland State Bank. The marriage lasted more than forty years, until his death in 1994.

Meanwhile Clark's successful career in Kansas continued. In 1964 she moved the family bank to Topeka, reorganizing and renaming it Capital City State Bank and Trust. Her Democratic Party leadership at the local and state level, punctuated with occasional national appointments, continued well into her eighties. She served on the White House Advisory Committee on Aging, and in 1967 chaired the Small Business Administration Advisory Council. She also served on the boards of the Harry Truman Library Institute and the Sex Information and Education Council of the U.S. (SIECUS). In her home community of Topeka, a range of civic, educational, and philanthropic organizations benefited from her leadership and support, especially local arts organizations and her alma mater, Washburn University.

Admired for her business acumen, sharp wit, and long-standing commitment to her community, Georgia Neese Clark died in a Topeka retirement home on October 26, 1995. A longtime public figure, she had enjoyed keeping one fact of her personal life enigmatic: her age. Many published accounts list an inaccurate birth date, a phenomenon she apparently did not mind. Image-conscious and broadly interested in business, politics, and drama to the end, she was ninety-seven years old when she died.

Bibliography: Primary source collections, including photographs, for Georgia Neese Clark are housed at the Kansas State Historical Library, Topeka, Kansas; the Mabee Library, Washburn University, Topeka; the Topeka and Shawnee County Public Library; and the Harry S. Truman Library at Independence, Missouri. Biographical information can be found in *Current Biography* (1949), pp. 114–16; and Ann Gardner, *Kansas Women* (1986), pp. 23–24. Feature articles on Clark from the *Topeka Capital-Journal* include "An Update with . . . Georgia Neese Gray," December 11, 1981; "Arts Center Patroness Honored," May 17, 1988; and "Georgia: Staged for Success," May 20, 1988. For general background on women in Democratic Party politics in the Truman era, see India Edwards, *Pulling No Punches: Memoirs of a Woman in Politics* (1977), and Jo Freeman, *A Room at a Time: How Women Entered Politics* (2000). Obituaries appeared in the *New York Times* and *Topeka Capital-Journal* on October 28, 1995.

RACHEL WALTNER GOOSSEN

CLARK, Mamie Phipps. October 18, 1917–August 11, 1983. Psychologist, child advocate, community mental health pioneer.

Mamie Clark was born Mamie Katherine Phipps in Hot Springs, Arkansas, the second of two children and only daughter of Harold Hilton Phipps, a physician and resort operator born in St. Kitts, and Katie Florence Phipps, a homemaker who was born in Hot Springs. By her own report, the young Mamie grew up happy, comfortable, privileged, and sheltered during the Great Depression. Although she attended segregated schools, graduating from Langston High School in 1934, she loved school and excelled in math. Her parents encouraged her from an early age to pursue higher education.

Mamie left Hot Springs for Howard University in Washington, D.C., in 1934, at the age of sixteen. At that time, Howard was the preeminent university for African Americans. Several crucial events at Howard shaped the direction of her future and set the stage for the accomplishments and activities for which she later became best known. Although she originally majored in math, she changed to psychology under the influence of Kenneth Bancroft Clark, then a senior psychology major and popular campus activist with whom she ultimately eloped. The couple married on April 14, 1938, in Stafford, Virginia.

Clark obtained her BS degree in 1938 (magna cum laude and Phi Beta Kappa) and her MS in 1939, both from Howard. Before attending graduate school, she worked briefly in the offices of Charles Hamilton Houston, vice dean of Howard Law School, legal mastermind behind school desegregation, and mentor to many of its principals, including Thurgood Marshall. She later described it as the most marvelous learning experience she had ever had. In 1940, shortly after the birth of her first child, Kate Miriam, Clark joined her husband in the psychology doctoral program at Columbia University. In 1944, only months after the birth of her second child, Hilton Bancroft, in October 1943, she completed her PhD.

Kenneth and Mamie Clark became the first two African Americans to enter and complete the Columbia doctoral program in psychology, and only the seventeenth and twenty-second African Americans, respectively, to obtain psychology doctoral degrees in the United States. Although neither wrote a race-related dissertation, together they published a series of groundbreaking studies of children's racial self-concept. These studies, which assessed children's responses to a series of questions about black or white pictures and dolls, and later became a foundation for the social science evidence presented in the 1954 *Brown v. Board of Education* Supreme Court case, were based on a paradigm developed by Mamie Clark while she was a graduate student at Howard.

In the mid 1940s, Clark worked briefly for the American Public Health Association, then as a research psychologist for the U.S. Armed Forces Institute at Teachers College, and finally at the Riverdale Children's Association, formerly the Colored Orphans Asylum, a center for neglected and dependent children. While working within the established child advocacy and guidance system of New York City, the frustrated Clark came to the conclusion that she needed to venture out on her own and start something in which her unique vision for promoting the development and well-being of children, particularly black and poor children, could be realized. With the encouragement of her husband, who was then an assistant professor of psychology at City College of New York, the couple decided to co-found a child guidance clinic. The Northside Center for Child Development (originally called the Northside Testing and Consultation Center) was established in 1946 in the basement of Dunbar Apartments on 155th Street in Harlem, where Kenneth and Mamie Clark lived with their children.

Mamie's father provided the original start-up grant of $936. The Center's racially mixed staff—all friends and academic associates of the Clarks—consisted of a small group of psychiatrists, social workers, and psychologists who worked either part-time or as volunteers (in addition to one paid clerical worker). The philosophy of its directors, known affectionately as Dr. Mamie and Dr. Ken, was decidedly integrationist, multicultural, and eclectic, combining psychology, psychiatry, remedial education, social services, medical assistance, nutrition, and recreation—all designed for the mental hygiene of the whole child. Unlike most clinics at the time, the Clarks acknowledged and emphasized the effects of racism and economic inequalities on the lives of children and their families, and advocated for social change along with child welfare as a way of treating communities, families, and children simultaneously.

In addition to her leadership of the Northside Center, Mamie Clark became deeply involved in the cultural, economic, political, and educational life of New York City by serving on the boards of such diverse organizations as Mount Sinai Medical Center, Teachers College of Columbia University, the New York Public Library, the Museum of Modern Art, and the New York City Mission Society. She served on advisory groups for the National Headstart Planning Committee of the Office of Economic Opportunity and the Special Allocations Fund Committee of the United Fund of Greater New York. She was a fellow of both the American Psychological Association and the American Association of Orthopsychiatry, and a visiting professor at Yeshiva University from 1958 to 1960. She received numerous awards, fellowships, and honorary degrees during her lifetime. Mamie Clark retired from Northside in 1980. That year she became treasurer of the family-run human relations consulting firm of Clark, Phipps, Clark & Harris.

Mamie Katherine Phipps Clark died in 1983 of lung cancer. She was sixty-five. Her funeral services were held at Riverside Church in Manhattan, and she was buried in Mount Hope Cemetery in the town of Hastings-on-Hudson, New York, where she and her husband had lived for many decades. During her lifetime, she was known as graceful and gracious, principled and tenacious, pragmatic and visionary. She left a legacy of innovative and comprehensive child guidance and advocacy as well as lasting contributions to the field of psychology and its role in dismantling racial desegregation in the United States.

Bibliography: Mamie Clark's papers are archived in two locations: the New York Public Library (along with other papers associated with the Northside Center for Child Development) and the Library of Congress (with Kenneth Bancroft Clark's papers). Other papers related to the Northside Center are archived with the Rockefeller Brothers Fund Papers in the Rockefeller Archive Center in North Tarrytown, New York. An oral history of Mamie Clark is available from the Columbia University Oral History Research Office under the title "Reminiscences of Mamie Clark" (dated 1991, although the interview was conducted in 1976). Also available at Columbia University is Mamie Clark's doctoral dissertation, "Changes in Primary Mental Abilities with Age" (1944). Her master's thesis, "The Development of Consciousness of Self of Negro Pre-school Children" (1939), is available at Howard University. Among the articles published jointly by Kenneth and Mamie Clark, the most significant are "The Development of Consciousness of Self and the Emergence of Racial Identification in Negro Preschool Children," *Journal of Social Psychology* 10, no. 4 (November 1939), pp. 591–99; and "Skin Color as a Factor in Racial Identification of Negro Preschool Children," *Journal of Social Psychology* 11, no. 1 (February 1940), pp. 159–69. Robert V. Guthrie, *Even the Rat Was White: A Historical View of Psychology* (1976; rev. ed., 1998), includes a brief biography of Mamie Clark as one of the first fifty African Americans to receive a doctorate in psychology. Agnes N. O'Connell and Nancy Felipe Russo, eds., *Models of Achievement: Reflections of Eminent Women in Psychology* (1983), contains some of Mamie Clark's reflections. Shafali Lal, "Giving Children Security: Mamie Phipps Clark and the Racialization of Child Psychology," *Psychological Bulletin* 57, no. 1 (January 2002), pp. 20–29, examines Clark's legacy as a psychologist. Gerald Markowitz and David Rosner, *Children, Race, and Power: Kenneth and Mamie Clark's Northside Center* (1996), is an excellent historical treatment of the Clarks' child guidance clinic. An obituary appeared in the *New York Times* on August 12, 1983. Additional information for this article was obtained via personal communication with Hilton Clark and from the staff of the Northside Center.

LAYLI PHILLIPS

CLARK, Septima Poinsette. May 3, 1898–December 15, 1987. Educator, civil rights activist.

Septima Poinsette Clark spent her life fighting for justice, equality, and freedom. For four decades she combined teaching with a commitment to social change, engaging herself in community-based projects in South Carolina that empowered poor, illiterate blacks and opened opportunities for them to experience full citizenship. When her teaching career ended because of her membership in the National Association for the Advancement of Colored People (NAACP), she moved on, by way of the Highlander Folk School and the Southern Christian Leadership Conference (SCLC), to play a vital role in the civil rights movement that reshaped the South and the nation in the 1950s and beyond.

This mission of service was inherited from her parents, a former slave and a free woman raised in Haiti, who instilled racial accountability. Septima was born in Charleston, South Carolina, the second of eight children of Victoria Warren Anderson and Peter Porcher Poinsette, a cook and caterer. Helping care for her younger siblings while her mother took in laundry earned Septima the title "Little Ma." She began her education in Charleston's inferior segregated public schools, spending most of the day sitting or playing. After a brief stint in a private school, she enrolled in Avery Institute, graduating in 1916 with a certificate to teach in the black schools of the state's Sea Islands. When she began her teaching career in 1916 on Johns Island at the Promise Land School, blacks were not allowed to teach in South Carolina's regular school systems. But in 1920, as the result of a successful NAACP campaign in which she participated, teaching positions were opened to black educators.

In 1920 Septima Poinsette married Nerie Clark, a navy cook, and they had two children: Victoria, who died in infancy, and Nerie Jr. Widowed in 1925, she never remarried. Her son lived with his paternal grandparents in North Carolina for part of his youth, and Clark eventually settled in Columbia, South Carolina, where she taught at the Booker T. Washington School until 1946, when she returned to Charleston to care for her ailing mother. Low wages, inadequate facilities, no bus transportation, and limited sessions were common in schools in both cities under the "separate but equal" banner. Despite teaching full-time, Clark was able to earn an undergraduate degree from Benedict College (1942) and a master's from Hampton University (during the summers of 1945–47), and attend summer sessions at Atlanta and Columbia universities. In Atlanta, she studied with noted scholar W. E. B. DuBois.

When the U.S. Supreme Court outlawed segregation in *Brown v. Board of Education* (1954), southern legislatures enacted measures to dilute, stall, or prevent its implementation. In a covert effort to destroy the NAACP, South Carolina passed a law stipulating that no city employee could affiliate with any civil rights organization and that all persons who refused to give up their membership would be dismissed. Clark, a longtime member of the NAACP, attempted to rally her black colleagues in Charleston, but their fear of losing their jobs and pensions kept them silent and invisible. Clark's contract was not renewed. She had taught for forty years and was fifty-eight years old. But new opportunities quickly came her way.

Starting in the summer of 1954, Clark had attended workshops at the Highlander Folk School in Tennessee, then the only place in the South where blacks and whites could discuss strategies for social change in an interracial setting. In 1956, Highlander founder Myles Horton invited Clark to become the director of workshops. In the post-*Brown* climate, workshops centered around how local leaders—black and white—could implement public school desegregation, a first step in the quest for full citizenship. Clark encouraged local leaders from South Carolina such as Esau Jenkins and Bernice Robinson to come to Highlander. Then she helped them set up a literacy program on Johns Island that became the prototype for the citizenship schools that dotted the South in later years. Adult classes used daily activities as subject matter in training the eager students to read, write, and pass the literacy test. Between 1956 and 1961 Clark traveled across the South helping to spread citizenship education. Seven hundred teachers worked in the schools and thousands registered to vote. The political landscape in the region was indeed changing.

In 1961 the Citizenship School Program was transferred to the Southern Christian Leadership Conference after the state of Tennessee forced Highlander to close. Clark moved to Atlanta and became the SCLC's director of education and teaching. Though she continued to travel widely, most of the organization's training sessions took place in Dorchester County, Georgia. The McIntosh Center allowed persons identified as local leaders to spend a week in the program and then return to their communities to establish citizenship schools that focused on voting, citizenship training, and literacy. Clark endured threats and harassment from groups such as the Ku Klux Klan and the White Citizens Council, but was never deterred from her objective—full citizenship for African Americans. Following the passage of the Civil Rights Act in 1964 and the Voting Rights Act of 1965, Clark personally witnessed the impact of the citizenship program on the political empowerment of black southerners as blacks not only registered to vote but also won elected and appointive offices. In 1975 Clark was elected to the same Charleston school board that had fired her nineteen years earlier.

In 1970, Clark retired from the SCLC and conducted workshops for the American Friends Service Committee, organized day-care sites, raised funds for scholarships, and was sought after as a speaker on civil rights and women's rights. In her later years she began to reevaluate her own role and the position of women generally in the civil rights movement: despite the enormous contributions women had made to the movement, she realized, they had seldom been recognized and appreciated at the time. Clark herself received many national and regional awards, including South Carolina's highest award, the Order of the Palmetto, in 1982. Septima Poinsette Clark, freedom fighter, educator, community activist, and crusader, died in Charleston, South Carolina, at the age of eighty-nine.

Bibliography: Archival material is found in the Septima P. Clark Papers, Special Collections, Robert Scott Small Library, College of Charleston, South Carolina. Clark wrote an autobiography with LeGette Blythe, *Echo in My Soul* (1962), and also contributed to Cynthia S. Brown, ed., *Ready from Within: Septima Clark and the Civil Rights Movement* (1990). Two articles documenting Clark's life and influence are Jacqueline A. Rouse, "We Seek to Know . . . in Order to Speak the Truth: Nurturing Seeds of Discontent—Septima P. Clark and Participatory Leadership," in Bettye Collier Thomas and V. P. Franklin, eds., *Sisters in the Struggle: African American Women in the Civil Rights–Black Power Movement* (2001); and Grace Jordan McFadden, "Septima P. Clark and the Struggle for Human Rights," in Vicki L. Crawford, Jacqueline Anne Rouse, and Barbara Woods, eds., *Women in the Civil Rights Movement: Trailblazers and Torchbearers, 1941–1965* (1993). An obituary appeared in the *New York Times* on December 17, 1987.

JACQUELINE A. ROUSE

CLARKE, Shirley. October 2, 1919–September 23, 1997. Filmmaker, video artist.

Independent filmmaker Shirley Clarke, a founding figure in American avant-garde cinema in the 1950s and 1960s, was born Shirley Brimberg in New York City. Her father, Samuel Nathan Brimberg, was a Polish immigrant who made his fortune as a women's clothing manufacturer. Samuel married Florence Rosenberg, whose own father was a Latvian immigrant who had also amassed a sizable fortune in the United States as an industrial inventor and entrepreneur. Shirley was the eldest of three daughters, all of whom attended the progressive Lincoln School in Manhattan and enjoyed a privileged childhood that included chauffeurs, nannies, and governesses. This lifestyle was temporarily disrupted by the stock market crash of 1929, but their father went into metal-shelving manufacturing and quickly recouped his losses.

Shirley attended several colleges, including Stephens College, Bennington College, the University of North Carolina, and Johns Hopkins University, but never graduated. In 1943, she returned to New York City to study modern dance with the most prominent figures in the field: MARTHA GRAHAM, Anna Sokolow, and HANYA HOLM.

In 1942 she married lithographer Bert Clarke, and the couple moved into a brownstone on East 87th Street. Their daughter, Wendy, was born in 1944. Bert encouraged Shirley as she continued her dance lessons, and she made her first films with a movie camera she received as a wedding present. In 1952, Clarke wanted to learn more about filmmaking, so she and Bert, along with some friends, hired filmmaker Peter Glushanok to teach them. The next summer she made her first short film, *Dance in the Sun* (1953), in which she incorporated her interest in choreography and movement.

Success in the film world came quickly for her. Barely five years after picking up a camera, Clarke was the only woman in a group of filmmakers chosen by the U.S. Information Agency to produce a series of short films for the World's Fair in Brussels. Her documentary, *Skyscraper,* produced along with Irving Jacoby and Willard Van Dyke, garnered a 1959 Academy Award nomination in the category Best Short Film in the Live Action.

In 1960, Clarke graduated from short films to feature-length films with her adaptation of Jack Gelber's controversial play *The Connection,* which depicts the seedy underworld of heroin addiction in New York. To fund the film, Clarke initiated a profit-sharing plan with about a hundred investors, an arrangement that was common in theater but unheard of in film at the time. The New York State censor board objected to the film's liberal use of the word *shit* (slang for heroin), and for more than a year prevented it from opening. *The Connection* won the Critic's Prize at Cannes and established Clarke as one of the most important experimental filmmakers in American cinema.

While filming *The Connection,* Clarke fell in love with the principal actor, Carl Lee, a professionally trained African American actor and son of actor Canada Lee. Lee helped Clarke transform Warren Miller's novel *The Cool World* into a screenplay. *The Cool World* was the first fiction feature film to be shot entirely on location in Harlem, and eventually it played at the 1963 Venice Film Festival. Clarke divorced her husband and entered into a tumultuous relationship with Carl that lasted more than twenty years until his death in 1986 from AIDS, contracted through a dirty hypodermic needle.

In 1960, Clarke was the only woman among twenty-three filmmakers who came together to promote the production, distribution, and exhibition of avant-garde films. The group, which included directors like Albert Maysles, Jonas Mekas, Gregory Markopoulos, and Emile de Antonio, became known as the New American Cinema Group. In 1962, she co-founded the Film-Makers' Cooperative with Mekas. This nonprofit center provided an outlet that circumvented Hollywood's monopoly on distribution. The filmmaker received 75 percent of the rental fee for a movie; the co-op kept only 25 percent for operational costs. In 1963, Clarke co-directed the short documentary *Robert Frost: A Lover's Quarrel with the World,* which went on to win an Oscar for best feature documentary.

Shirley Clarke moved to the Chelsea Hotel in 1965, and her apartment became a sort of salon for independent filmmakers. Clarke wanted the New American Cinema films to have a wider commercial release, so in 1966 she, Louis Brigante, and Jonas Mekas formed the Film-Makers' Distribution Center—an outgrowth of the Film-Makers' Cooperative—which distributed films to more mainstream venues. The Distribution Center encountered difficulties in its attempts to release Clarke's film *Portrait of Jason,* due to its explicit portrayal of a black homosexual hustler. Clarke resorted to personally taking the film around the country to show at colleges and universities. The Center folded in 1970 after numerous financial struggles.

In 1969, Clarke played herself in French director Agnès Varda's film *Lions Love.* The movie shows her traveling to California to negotiate a contract with a Hollywood studio, only to be frustrated by the demands of an industry ruled by market forces. Varda's film reflected Clarke's real-life discouragement with her inability to find a producer who would accept her scripts on her own terms. She once said, "Who says a film has to cost a million dollars, and be safe and innocuous to satisfy every twelve-year-old in America?"

Attracted by the new medium of video, she began working alongside her daughter, Wendy, herself a noted video artist, in the Video Space Troupe, a collaborative group of artists and technicians whose work influenced the face of experimental video in the United States. Clarke's active involvement in the group lasted until 1975, when she moved to California to teach film and video at UCLA for the next decade. In her final documentary, *Ornette: Made in America* (1985), a portrait of jazz great Ornette Coleman, Clarke combines abstract video imagery with black-and-white film footage of Coleman's early performances.

Shirley Clarke's filmmaking and teaching careers ended with the onset of Alzheimer's disease. Longtime friend David Cort and his wife Piper took care of her when she became incapacitated. She died on September 23, 1997, in Boston, at the age of seventy-seven. After her death, the Museum of Modern Art and the American Film Institute held retrospectives of her work.

Bibliography: Shirley Clarke's papers are primarily located at the Wisconsin Center for Film and Theater Research at the Wisconsin Historical Society in Madison. Transcripts contained in *Film Culture* 42 (Autumn 1966), pp. 44–54, document group discussions with artists involved with the Film-Makers' Cooperative, including Clarke and Strom de Hirsch. In 1975, the American Film Institute held a seminar on Clarke's work; transcripts are located at the New York Public Library for the Performing Arts at Lincoln Center. Her sister, Elaine Dundy, provides insight into Clarke's personal life in her autobiography, *Life Itself!* (2001). Clarke's work in film and video is detailed in Lauren Rabinovitz, *Points of Resistance: Women, Power and Politics in the New York Avant-Garde Cinema, 1943–1971* (1991). Additional information was provided by James Kreul. An obituary appearing in the *New York Times* on September 26, 1997, contains the quotation from Clarke.

BETH MAULDIN

COATSWORTH, Elizabeth Jane. May 31, 1893–August 31, 1986. Children's author, poet.

Elizabeth Jane Coatsworth was born in Buffalo, New York, to Ida Reid and William T. Coatsworth, a prosperous family of grain merchants. Her sister, Margaret, was born in 1890; two other siblings died in infancy. Elizabeth lived with her parents, sister, and paternal grandmother, Electa Weller Coatsworth. She loved books, and recalled that her grandmother frequently read to her. Her maternal grandfather, Adam Reid, had memorized a great deal of poetry and was perhaps an early influence on Elizabeth as well. Summers were spent at Bay Beach on the shore of Lake Erie, where the family owned four cottages. The Coatsworth family frequently traveled, taking Elizabeth to Europe and Egypt when she was five. This trip established for her the beginnings of a powerful sense of geography, an important theme in much of her writing.

From 1906 until 1909, the family lived in Pasadena, California, where Elizabeth attended high school for two years. Returning to Buffalo, she graduated from the Buffalo Seminary in 1911. Later the same year, she enrolled at Vassar College, where she met and became lifelong friends with Louise Seaman—who, as the first children's editor in America, would later publish many of Coatsworth's books. After the death of her father in 1912, the Buffalo home was sold and Elizabeth traveled with her mother and sister when her schedule at Vassar allowed. She spent the summer of 1914 in England, when she began writing poetry in earnest. After graduating with a BA from Vassar in 1915, she took an MA from Columbia in 1916. She traveled again, spending thirteen months in 1916–17 in what today are Thailand, China, the Philippines, Korea, Japan, and Hawaii.

When her sister Margaret married and moved east in 1919, Elizabeth and her mother moved to Cambridge, and Elizabeth studied at Radcliffe. Later, they purchased an eighteenth-century home near Hingham, Massachusetts. During the 1920s, Coatsworth traveled widely, visiting

France, England, Scotland, and later, Greece, Italy, Egypt, and Morocco. Her early work consisted of poetry, beginning with *Fox Footprints* (1923), followed by *Atlas and Beyond* (1924) and *Compass Rose* (1929). Thereafter she began writing prose. Her first juvenile title, *The Cat and the Captain* (1927), established a long and fruitful career in writing for children.

She married author and naturalist Henry Beston on June 18, 1929. Beston was educated at Harvard and authored ten books. The year before their marriage, he published one of his best-known books, *The Outermost House,* the journal of a year he spent alone on Cape Cod. He is also known for his book *Herbs and the Earth* (1935). The Bestons's first daughter, Margaret (Meg), was born in June 1930. Their second daughter, Catherine (Kate), was born in April 1932. In 1931, the Bestons bought Chimney Farm in Nobleboro, Maine, overlooking Damariscotta Lake, where they lived for the rest of their lives.

Elizabeth Coatsworth's writing career spanned several decades, and she authored over ninety books, more than half of which were published by Macmillan and many of which appeared in Europe as well as America. She also contributed short stories and poetry to magazines, including *Atlantic Monthly, Dial,* and the *Horn Book.* She is best known for *The Cat Who Went to Heaven* (1930), illustrated by Lynd Ward, in which the cat belonging to an artist painting the Buddha becomes part of the painting, thereby achieving eternal happiness. This book won the Newbery Medal for the best children's book in 1931.

Many of her prose works retain a lyrical quality, and some, like *The Cat Who Went to Heaven,* contain verse. The *Sally* series, illustrated by Helen Sewell, consisting of five books beginning with *Away Goes Sally* (1934), describes the life of a family after the American Revolution. Some of her books contain autobiographical references; for instance, *Bess and the Sphinx* (1967) is loosely based on her childhood travels. Of writing for children, Coatsworth says: "[The author] is like a man walking with his family who suddenly sees ahead of him an unexpected mountain, a monkey in the branches of a tree, or comes upon a house in the woods where a little while ago there was only a glade. His first impulse is to turn and say, 'Look!' . . . and if he is lucky, the children look" (*Horn Book,* 1948, p. 389).

By the late 1930s, Coatsworth began writing for older readers, producing such novels as *Here I Stay* (1938), about a girl who remains on the family farm in Maine despite the popularity of moving west, and *The Trunk* (1941). Despite its wide variety of settings and attention to travel, her writing reveals a powerful connection to New England, evidenced by several sketches of that region, including *Country Neighborhood* (1944), *Maine Ways* (1947), *The White Room* (1958), and *Maine Memories* (1968). She co-authored *Chimney Farm Bedtime Stories* (1966) with Henry Beston, two years before his death on April 15, 1968.

Coatsworth's last book of fiction, published while she was in her eighties, was *Marra's World* (1975). At eighty-three, she authored *Personal Geography: Almost an Autobiography* (1976), a unique, introspective memoir in which her life with Beston figures prominently. During the last years of her life she seemed content to remain at Chimney Farm, generally alone, as she explained in *Personal Geography:* "The world in which I live is enough for me. After so many travels, I am home, and my happiness here is no less than it was in foreign lands and my sense of wonder has not dulled with all these years. I am as happy as an old dog stretched out in the sunlight" (p. 166). Elizabeth Coatsworth died at Chimney Farm on August 31, 1986, at the age of ninety-three. Her contribution to children's literature is especially significant in the context of rapid changes in the field beginning in the 1920s. She helped establish a tone and pace for children's books in the "new" literature at the precise moment when women, as editors of children's literature, were entering the publishing profession in larger numbers.

Bibliography: For a complete listing of Coatsworth's published writing, including publisher, date of publication, and illustrator, see *Twentieth Century Children's Writers* (3rd ed., 1989). Other helpful references can be found in *American Women Writers: A Critical Reference Guide from Colonial Times to the Present* (vol.1, 2nd ed., 2000); *American Writers for Children, 1900–1960* (1983); and *Contemporary Authors* (vols. 5–8, 1963). The Kerlan Collection at the University of Minnesota contains original manuscripts, published and unpublished, from 1930 to 1976. The Beston Family Papers are located at Bowdoin College Library in Brunswick, Maine. The Louise Seaman Bechtel Collection at Vassar College contains personal correspondence between Bechtel and Coatsworth, especially from 1915 to 1925, some of which contains illustrations of Coatsworth's journeys abroad. The Bechtel Collection also contains some of her published articles, and book reviews. In addition to her books of poetry and prose for both children and adults, Coatsworth also contributed to the *Horn Book,* an important periodical during the early years of professionalization for individuals connected to children's publishing. See, for example, "Upon Writing for Children," *Horn Book* 24, no. 6 (September 1948), pp. 389–95; and "Laura E. Richards," *Horn Book* 19, no. 2 (March 1943), p. 79. Her death certificate, obtainable from the Department of Human Services, Augusta, Maine, confirms the date of August 31, 1986, rather than September 2nd which appears in some sources. Obituaries appeared in the *Portland Press Herald* on September 2, 1986, the *New York Times* on September 3, 1986, and *Publishers Weekly* on September 19, 1986.

JACALYN EDDY

COCHRAN, Jacqueline. May 11, 1906–August 8, 1980. Aviator, entrepreneur.

Jacqueline Cochran was born in Muscogee, Florida. In her autobiography she described herself as an orphan, raised as a foster child, but 1910 census records list her as Bessie Pittman, the last of five children of Ira and Molly Grant Pittman. She received only two years of elementary school education while her father, an illiterate lumberman, moved from town to town in search of work. At the age of eight she went with her family to Columbus, Georgia, where she worked in a textile mill. At ten she became a housekeeper and hairdresser's apprentice in her employer's shop. At fourteen she married Robert M. Cochran and gave birth to a son, Robert Jr., on February 21, 1921.

While the child was left with the Pittmans in Florida, Bessie Pittman Cochran worked as a hairdresser in Montgomery, Alabama, and then as a doctor's assistant back in Florida. After the death of her son in 1925, she moved to Mobile, Alabama, again working as a beautician. Her husband divorced her in 1927, and she moved on to Pensacola, Florida, where she was part owner of a beauty shop.

Her next move was to New York City in 1929, where she was employed by Antoine's, a fashionable salon. There she retained the surname of Cochran and chose the name Jacqueline from a telephone book. While working at Antoine's branch in Miami, she met Floyd Bostwick Odlum, forty-year-old millionaire financier who became her business adviser and companion. He suggested she gain mobility and publicity for her planned cosmetics line by becoming a flying saleswoman.

In the summer of 1932 she took lessons at Roosevelt Field on Long Island, qualifying for a pilot's license in twenty days. From the start Cochran seemed born to fly, eager to solve technical problems and willing to endure intense physical pain to push an aircraft to the limits of its performance. In addition to her remarkable intelligence and good looks, Jackie Cochran was always a commanding presence, appreciative of ability in others but impatient with ignorance. She was loyal and generous to friends—her dearest was AMELIA EARHART—and feared by her enemies.

In 1935 she founded Jacqueline Cochran Cosmetics, Inc., and the following year she married Odlum, who was to become increasingly crippled by severe attacks of rheumatoid arthritis. Odlum financed her business undertakings and reveled in her ambition to become the world's leading woman pilot. In her first international race, the McRobertson International from England to Australia in 1934, she was forced down by mechanical difficulties in Bucharest, Romania. In 1936 she entered the prestigious Bendix cross-country race, open to men and women, but was grounded by mechanical failures. In 1937 she placed third, and in 1938 she won the coveted Bendix trophy.

After flying a bomber to Britain in June 1941, she returned to the United States in July and recruited twenty-five American woman pilots to ferry planes for the British Air Transport Auxiliary. In 1942, with the approval of General H. H. Arnold, chief of the Army Air Force, she founded the Women's Pilot Training Program at Houston, soon moving it to Avenger Air Field in Sweetwater, Texas. In July 1943 it merged with the Auxiliary Ferry Squadron, Air Transport Command, a contingent of more experienced woman pilots organized by NANCY LOVE, to form the Women's Airforce Service Pilots (WASPs), with Cochran as director. The WASPs, who were classified as civilian employees of the army, were disbanded in 1944 when the need for ferrying pilots lessened. Not until 1977 did Congress grant the WASPs military status with its accompanying honors and benefits.

The winner of the Clifford Burke Harmon trophy of the International League of Aviators as the world's outstanding woman pilot every year from 1938 through 1949 and again in 1953 and 1961, Cochran set more aviation records than any other woman pilot in the world. In 1953, flying a Keynoter F-86 Sabre jet, she reached the speed of 652.337 miles per hour, breaking through the sonic barrier at Mach 1. In 1962 she set nine international speed, altitude, and distance records in a Northrop T-38 military jet, and the following year, at the age of fifty-seven, she flew a Lockheed F-104 Starfighter at 1263.686 miles per hour—Mach 2. Cochran was both friend and pupil of General Charles Yeager, the first man to break the sound barrier. Yet in twenty-five years of record-setting flights she never neglected her cosmetics business, traveling from the luxurious Cochran-Odlum ranch in Indio, California, to her offices in New York and salons in Chicago and Los Angeles. She sold the business in 1963.

Friend of leading figures in aviation, business, and scientific circles, Cochran was politically conservative and an anti-feminist who preferred the company of men, especially aviators. With the exception of Earhart and Mesenna Howard, she had few close friends among woman aviators, although she did serve as the president of the Ninety-Nines, the international women's aviation organization, from 1941 to 1943. In 1952 she campaigned for Dwight D. Eisenhower and in 1956 she ran unsuccessfully on the Republican ticket for a congressional seat in California. After initially helping to finance the testing and training of thirteen woman astronaut candidates, she testified at a 1963 congressional hearing that there was no need for women in space at that time, and the idea was dropped until 1978.

In 1971 Cochran was grounded, unable to pass the physical test for renewal of her flying license. In 1973 the ranch, with its main house, five guest houses, golf course, and swimming pool, was sold and Cochran and Odlum moved across the street to a smaller house. She bought a huge trailer and traveled with her ailing husband until a year before his death in 1976. During the last four years of her life she became increasingly ill and was confined to a wheelchair. Refusing to sleep and insisting that she would never die in bed, she died in the chair in 1980 at the age of seventy-four. In March 1996 the U.S. Postal Service issued an international airmail stamp in her honor, a fitting tribute to one of America's most talented and courageous aviation pioneers.

Bibliography: The largest collection of Jacqueline Cochran papers is found at the Dwight D. Eisenhower Library at the Eisenhower Presidential Center in Abilene. The Lyndon Baines Johnson Library, the Florida State Archives, Texas Woman's University, the National Air and Space Museum, and the Coachella Valley Historical Society contain additional archival material. The U.S. Air Force Academy holds an oral history with Cochran. See also the Kenneth W. Leish interview with Cochran, 1960, at the Columbia University Oral History Research Office. For autobiographical information (not always reliable), see Jacqueline Cochran, *The Stars at Noon* (1954), and Cochran and Maryann Bucknum Brinley, *Jackie Cochran: The Autobiography of the Greatest Woman Pilot in Aviation History* (1987). Obituaries appeared on August 10, 1980, in the *New York Times, Los Angeles Times,* and *Washington Post.*

DORIS L. RICH

COIT, Elisabeth. September 7, 1892–April 2, 1987. Architect, affordable housing advocate.

Born into a comfortable life in Winchester, Massachusetts, a leafy suburb of Boston, Elisabeth Coit would dedicate much of her life to addressing the housing problems of the urban poor. The second child of native New Englanders Eliza Richmond Atwood and Robert Coit, a successful architect who designed homes for Boston's elite, Elisabeth enjoyed an idyllic early childhood, developing a passion for sailing during family summers on the Massachusetts coast. Widowed before Elisabeth was in her teens, her father raised the children with the help of his parents. A poet and essayist in his time away from the drafting table, he encouraged his son and three daughters to pursue a broad education in the arts and sciences. After graduating from Winchester High School, Coit enthusiastically followed her father's advice: she took courses in art and design at Radcliffe College from 1909 to 1911 and at the Boston Museum of Fine Arts from 1911 to 1913. In 1919, she received a BS in architecture from MIT and set out to become a practicing architect. Like her father, as a professional she remained devoted to many hobbies, including painting, aviation, and writing poetry. She never married.

Shortly after graduation, Coit moved to New York City to work as a draftsman for Grosvenor Atterbury, an architect best known for planning a philanthropically funded housing development in Queens. She quickly fell in love with the city, an affair that lasted a lifetime. Coit proved to be a quick learner and an adept employee; she rose through the ranks to become a supervisor of draftsmen and then persuaded Atterbury to give her afternoons off to begin building her own practice. She became a licensed architect in New York State in 1926 and was working full-time on her own projects by the early 1930s.

As one of a small number of female architects in the 1920s, Coit initially found it difficult to attract clients. Many of the commissions she received during this period were for restaurants, offices, and small vacation homes. Free to bring an individual sensibility to her designs, Coit focused closely on her clients' needs and fashioned practical, attractive spaces with whimsical touches, such as squirrel stencil cutouts in window shutters. Several of the projects Coit developed in her private practice attracted notice from the architectural press. She won an award from the journal *Pencil Points* in 1930, was listed in the *Architectural Record* as a winner of the 1932 Better Homes in America Small House Architectural Competition, and a house she fashioned for Mary Burnham of Yorktown Heights, New York, appeared in 1940 on *House and Garden*'s list of exceptional homes costing under $10,000.

Since working for Atterbury, a pioneer in the field of low-cost housing, Coit had become increasingly attuned to the difficulties involved in constructing homes for people of modest means. Time spent in Europe, where she studied art history and ceramics at the Collège de France in 1923–24, convinced her that Germany, Austria, and France had done a far better job than the United States in providing shelter for the poor. Determined to improve this situation, in 1937 Coit applied for and won an American Institute of Architects (AIA) Langley Scholarship to investigate how architects might create low-cost apartments and single-family homes that best suited the needs of working-class residents.

As the federal government made its first forays into subsidizing housing during the lean years of the Depression, Coit tackled the enormous task of exploring the varied approaches to inexpensive housing that had been taken in the United States, visiting more than a hundred private and publicly funded developments in the eastern states. While attempting to determine the future of public housing, Coit, unlike many of her contemporaries, focused on the tenants themselves rather than on architectural theory. Her report explored what people of limited means most wanted from the places where they cooked, washed, played, and slept, touching on everything from outdoor living space to closets to paint materials.

The AIA journal *Octagon* published the results of her two-year study as "Notes on the Design and Construction of the Dwelling Unit for the Lower-Income Family" in October and November 1941, and the response was immediate. Coit's resident-centric approach to the study of low-cost housing garnered accolades in both mainstream newspapers and architectural journals, and she became known as a leading authority on the low-income tenant. In 1942 she left her practice to concentrate on public housing, lending her expertise to the Federal Public Housing Authority in Washington during wartime by collecting and analyzing the available information on federal housing projects.

Coit returned to her beloved New York City in 1947 and, after a brief stint with the firm of Mayer-Whittlesey as a research associate, joined the New York City Housing Authority (NYCHA), where she would serve as principal project planner in the Design Division until her retirement. This was an extremely active period for the NYCHA as it scrambled to meet the need for low-cost housing by erecting more than 150 projects and developments throughout the five boroughs. Coit was in the forefront of all the activity, serving as a liaison between the Authority and the architects hired to plan public developments, overseeing drawings for projects in progress, and regularly revising the "Memo to Architects," which informed contractors of ever-changing building standards and regulations.

Even after retirement in 1962 at the age of seventy, Coit showed no signs of slowing down. She continued to write professionally, conducting a study for the Public Housing Administration whose results were published as "Report on Family Living in High Apartment Buildings" in 1965. In 1970, Mayor John Lindsay appointed her to the Landmark Preservation Commission, which was instrumental in preserving such historically and aesthetically significant buildings as Grand Central Station, Carnegie Hall, and Radio City Music Hall. Now in her eighties, Coit still insisted on using public transportation to visit every site under consideration.

When her health began to fail, Coit returned to Massachusetts and moved into a nursing home in Amherst. She died there on April 2, 1987, at the age of ninety-four, not far from where she had spent her earliest days.

Bibliography: The Schlesinger Library at Radcliffe Institute for Advanced Study, Harvard University, holds a collection of Elisabeth Coit's personal correspondence, architectural drawings, photographs, poems, and paintings. Other archival materials relating to Coit can be found at the American Institute of Architects Library and Archives in Washington, D.C. Her study of low-income housing was included in the exhibit "Women in American Architecture: A Historic and Contemporary Perspective," which appeared in 1977 at the Brooklyn Museum and at MIT's Hayden Gallery. Nancy Jane Olive's "Elisabeth Coit: Pioneer in Architecture" (MA thesis, Michigan State University, 1989), and Susana Torre, ed., *Women in American Architecture: A Historic and Contemporary Perspective* (1977), include extensive discussions of Coit's contributions to public housing. Rich sources of information on her early career are the many articles Coit published in newspapers and magazines, including "Steps toward Modernization," *American Architect* 147 (September 1935), pp. 17–18; "Inspired by Cows and Milk Bottles: The New York Offices of Walker-Gordon Company," *American Architect* 139 (April 1931), pp. 56–57, 86, 88; and "Housing from the Tenant's Viewpoint," *Architectural Record* 91, no. 4 (April 1942), pp. 71–85. Stories about Coit's designs and her studies of low-income housing also frequently appeared in New York newspapers. During her time at the FHA and the NYCHA she contributed to several published reports, including *Manual of Instruction for Erecting Temporary Dwellings* (1945); *Public Housing: A Review of Experience in Low Rent Housing* (1946); and *The Significance of the Work of the New York City Housing Authority* (1949). Obituaries appeared in the *Boston Globe* on April 7, 1987, and the *New York Times* on April 8, 1987.

KIMBERLY SIMS

COLLETT, Glenna. June 20, 1903–February 3, 1989. Athlete.

Born in New Haven, Connecticut, Glenna Collett was the daughter of George Collett, an insurance salesman, and Ada Wilkinson, a homemaker. When Glenna was six years old, her father moved the family to Providence, Rhode Island, where she grew up, attended school, and took up golf. Collett later wrote that there was not a time when she was not interested in some kind of sport. She could swim and dive at nine years old and drove her first automobile the following year. As a child she most enjoyed playing baseball with her brother, Edwin "Ned" Collett, and his friends; but when Collett was fourteen her mother encouraged her to take up a game more suitable for a young girl. After a brief try at tennis, Glenna discovered golf.

Inspired by the accomplishments of America's earliest female golf standouts Alexa Stirling, Elaine Rosenthal, and Marion Hollins, Glenna Collett determined to become a champion. In the pre–World War I period, golf was extremely exclusive and played by only a handful of affluent, socially connected Americans. Because it was an individual sport that emphasized rhythm and balance over brute strength, golf was also one of the few athletic outlets available to women in that period. A member of the Metacomet Golf Club, George Collett had the wherewithal to introduce his daughter to the game and pay for her to receive lessons from two golf professionals, John Anderson and Alex Smith. The family even traveled to Florida in the winter so that Glenna could play and receive instruction from Smith year-round.

Despite all of the resources poured into Glenna's golf career, her competitive game took time to develop. For several years, she flashed occasional brilliance against a background of inconsistency. In 1921, for example, she shot an 85 to win the qualifying medal of the U.S. Women's Championship but was eliminated in the first round of match play. Collett finally broke through the following season, capturing the prestigious North and South Championship, then the Eastern, and her first U.S. Women's Championship. By the close of 1922, the nineteen-year-old Collett had emerged as one of America's top golfers.

Noted golf historian Herbert Warren Wind considered Collett the best woman golfer in America in the 1920s. Between 1922 and 1935, Collett collected an all-time record six U.S. Women's Championships, including three in a row from 1928 through 1930. She also won two Canadian Women's Amateurs, one French Amateur, six North and South titles, and approximately forty-nine championships overall. Although she made it to the final match of the British Ladies' Amateur in 1929 and 1930, Collett failed to win that event, the only important title she never held. From 1932 to 1948, Collett played in the Curtis Cup, a biennial Anglo-American team competition that paralleled the men's Walker Cup and Ryder Cup series.

Because of her remarkable record and popular image, sportswriters dubbed Collett the Bobby Jones of women's golf. Of course the label underscores the second-class position of even the top female athletes in the Golden Age of sports. Yet it also reveals much about Collett's outstanding reputation. Jones was unquestionably the finest male golfer of the period; the public adored his all-American boyish looks, amateur idealism, sportsmanship, self-discipline, and competitive dominance. On every point, Collett was his counterpart, arguably doing more than any other player to popularize women's golf. She was especially long and accurate from the tee, capable of driving the ball 300 yards. Like Jones, she sometimes overwhelmed the competition, winning final matches in major events by lopsided scores while displaying a steely determination.

Collett was also unassuming, self-controlled, and consistently gracious in victory or defeat. Although she challenged Victorian convention just by becoming a famous, competitive athlete, Collett projected a modest image that made Americans feel comfortable with her athleticism. If her long drives were sometimes called mannish, her appearance and demeanor were overtly feminine by the standards of her day. Often described in the press as "tomboyish" or "outdoorsy" rather than "muscular," Collett possessed dark hair and eyes, stood five foot six, and maintained a slim figure.

In 1931, while still in her competitive prime, Collett reinforced her image by marrying Edwin H. Vare Jr., a prominent businessman who was the son of a former Republican Pennsylvania state senator. The couple settled in Philadelphia, and Glenna reduced her golf schedule and made plans to start a family. By 1935, when she won her sixth U.S. championship, Collett was the mother of two, Glenna Kalen (1933) and Edwin Collett (1934). Collett was golf's version of "the American Girl"; her public persona was like that of contemporaries HELEN WILLS MOODY and Gertrude Ederle and nearly the opposite from that of flamboyant Frenchwoman Suzanne Lenglen or the aggressively competitive MILDRED (BABE) DIDRIKSON. In her roles as wife, mother, and competitive golfer, Collett embodied much of the broader social conflict between change and continuity that marked American life in the 1920s.

In 1950, the Ladies Professional Golf Association (LPGA) honored Collett by making her a charter member of their hall of fame. Two years later, the LPGA began awarding the Vare Trophy at the end of each season to the player with the lowest scoring average. Collett, who never turned professional, entered a few ladies' senior events throughout the next decade before retiring from competitive golf in 1962. She spent the final years of her life in Florida, near the place where her father had taken her for winter lessons before World War I. Right up to the end she occasionally scored rounds in the eighties that matched her age. Glenna Collett died in Gulf Stream, Florida, in 1989 at the age of eighty-five.

Bibliography: Collett's autobiography, *Ladies in the Rough* (1929), provides good coverage of her early competitive career, as well as her views on women in golf, but offers little about her background, childhood, or personal life. She wrote several articles for popular magazines, among them "For Wearing on the Green," *Collier's*, October 25, 1930, pp. 24+; "From Tee and Fairway," *Ladies' Home Journal*, June 1931, pp. 13+; and "Golf We Women Play," *Saturday Evening Post*, July 9, 1927, pp. 12–13. Solid historical treatments of Collett's career and public image include Herbert Warren Wind, *The Story of American Golf, Its Champions and Its Championships*, 3rd ed. (1975); Peter Alliss, *The Who's Who of Golf* (1983); and Rhonda Glenn, *The Illustrated History of Women's Golf* (1991). An obituary appeared in the *New York Times* on February 6, 1989.

STEPHEN R. LOWE

COOK, Alice Hanson. November 28, 1903–February 7, 1998. Labor educator and activist, feminist.

Alice Hanson Cook devoted her life to helping working people, and especially working women, on four continents. What she called her patchwork career included social work, adult education, labor organizing, a tour of foreign service at the end of World War II, twenty years teaching in Cornell's School of Industrial and Labor Relations, and authoring numerous books and articles. She was one of the pioneers in bringing attention to issues such as comparable worth, maternity leave, and pay equity. Known for both her scholarly writings and her activism on behalf of working women around the world, Cook's personal life reflected many of the concerns examined in her academic work.

Alice Hanson was born in Alexandria, Virginia, the first of three children of August Hanson, a Swedish American railway clerk, and Flora Kays, an Anglo-Scots graduate of Northwestern University's Cumnock School of Oratory. Both Alice's mother and her maternal grandmother were part of the nineteenth-century tradition of white middle-class women's activism and set early role models for Alice's lifelong devotion to reform and revolution in society. They also gave Alice models for her insistence on her own personal independence and career.

Virtually blind in her right eye, Alice wore glasses from the age of three. Her family moved around in her youth, and she attended high schools in Evanston, Illinois, and East Green Bay, Wisconsin, graduating in 1920. She then enrolled at her mother's alma mater, Northwestern University's School of Speech, gaining her only formal degree in 1924. While at Northwestern, Alice began her studies of both economics and social work and also began her lifelong attachment to the ideals of socialism. In 1926 she married Wesley Cook, a divinity student who later became a union organizer.

Throughout the 1920s and '30s, Cook linked her employment with various forms of community activism. Early jobs with the Industrial Department of the Young Women's Christian Association (YWCA) in Philadelphia and Chicago led her to find ways to use the YW for both union support efforts and attempts to organize women workers previously ignored by unions, such as domestic servants. Her work with the YWCA also led to her involvement with adult labor education efforts such as the Bryn Mawr Summer School for Women Workers, Arkansas's Commonwealth College, the Southern Summer School for Workers in North Carolina, and the Hudson Shore School. From 1937 to 1939 she also was directly employed by the union movement, working as education director for the early Congress of Industrial Organizations' Textile Workers' Organizing Committee. From 1940 to 1943, she served as assistant to the manager of the Philadelphia Joint Board of the Amalgamated Clothing Workers of America.

The 1930s and '40s marked the beginning of Cook's interests in similar developments around the world. From 1929 to 1931, she studied in Germany under a DAAD (Deutscher Akademischer Austauschdienst) fellowship, beginning her long association with the German system of adult and labor education. She would return to Germany after World War II, when she became the chief of adult education in Germany's American Zone for the Education Division of the High Commission, Germany, from 1950 to 1952. Her travels through Germany, combined with her own personal experiences, led her to become intrigued with questions of comparative systems of labor education. She would ultimately travel throughout Western and Eastern Europe as well as Asia in order to carry out her research.

While her career was blossoming, Cook was also modeling unconventional living situations. Her first experience with collective living came in the 1920s with her association with Commonwealth College, an adult labor-education program in which participants produced their own housing and food. When she moved to Philadelphia in 1931, she and her husband became core members of a collective household of Socialist Party members known as "Soviet House." In 1939 she gave birth to their only biological son, Philip. Initially she attempted to continue full-time work, but the outbreak of World War II made it impossible to find child care. By then living in a large house on the outskirts of Philadelphia, her solution was to take in more living companions. Through the forties, she lived in a household of two to four adults and upward of four pre-school-age children.

Through most of her life, Cook evinced little concern with the creation of a traditional nuclear family, preferring to open her home to biologically unrelated people and live collectively. After her divorce from Wesley in 1952 and when her son was in high school, she took in two more teenagers, Richard Bernstein and Adelheid (Adi) Troscher, children of German friends. Both considered themselves her children as well. From the late 1970s until the mid 1990s, when she moved to a retirement community, Cook lived in a loosely collective community in Ithaca, New York, known as Longhouse.

Cook's academic career began in 1952, when she was hired by the New York State School of Industrial and Labor Relations at Cornell University. She began as a researcher in the school's extension division, but moved into a full academic teaching position in 1955. She was a well-respected teacher in the school up to her retirement in 1972. She also became an important figure on the Cornell campus, fighting to open the faculty club to women, serving as the university's first ombudsman, and helping to establish Cornell's Women's Studies Program.

After officially retiring, Cook began her most important feminist works. From the early 1970s until shortly before her death, she split her time between Ithaca and the Industrial Relations Center at the University of Hawaii. After she became a professor emerita, she published most of her best-known works. These include *The Working Mother: A Survey of Problems and Programs in Nine Countries* (1975); *Working Women in Japan: Discrimination, Resistance, and Reform* (1980, with Hiroko Hayashi); *The Most Difficult Revolution: Women and Trade Unions* (1992); and, with Val Lorwin and Arlene Kaplan Daniels as co-editors, *Women and Trade Unions in Eleven Industrialized Countries* (1984). She also wrote myriad articles on a wide range of topics, including comparable worth, work and family issues, labor education, union democracy, and the role of unions in communities. In these works, she wed her long-standing socialist principles with what seemed to be her inbred feminism to provide insight into working women's situations around the world. Alice Hanson Cook died in Ithaca at the age of ninety-four.

Bibliography: The papers of Alice Hanson Cook are deposited at the Kheel Center for Labor-Management Documentation & Archives of the Catherwood Library, School of Industrial and Labor Relations at Cornell University, Ithaca, New York. The Feminist Press published *A Lifetime of Labor: The Autobiography of Alice H. Cook* in 1998. A documentary on her life, *Never Done: The Working Life of Alice H. Cook, Part I,* by Marilyn Rivchin, Sandra Pollack, and Diane McPherson, appeared in 1993. Additional information was provided by Cornell University professor emerita Fran Herman as well as friends, colleagues, and former students. An obituary appeared in the *New York Times* on February 15, 1998.

ILEEN A. DEVAULT

COTTEN, Elizabeth (Libba). January 5, 1893–June 29, 1987. Singer, songwriter, musician.

Born in Chapel Hill, North Carolina, the daughter of George Nevills (sometimes spelled Nevilles), an African American miner, and Louise Price, a housekeeper and midwife, Elizabeth was the second of four children, two girls and two boys. When she was about eight, she began borrowing her older brother's banjo, then his guitar, and she wrote her first and most famous song, "Freight Train," when she was eleven. Around this time she quit school and began doing housework and babysitting, and after five months she could afford the $3.75 to purchase her own guitar. She easily picked up new songs, but when she joined the Baptist Church a few years later she abandoned secular music and would not play a guitar or banjo again for many years.

She married Frank Cotten in February 1910 and had a daughter—her only child, Lillie—in 1911. The family moved between Chapel Hill, Washington, D.C., and New York City, where Frank owned a successful chauffeur business and garage and Elizabeth worked in a furniture shop. When Lillie was grown and moved away, Elizabeth obtained a divorce and returned to Washington, D.C., to be near her daughter. During World War II she lived with Lillie and her five grandchildren. She had various jobs, including working at Lansburgh's Department Store.

In 1948, while working at Lansburgh's, she found a lost child, Peggy Seeger, whom she returned to her mother, RUTH CRAWFORD SEEGER, a prominent composer and the wife of musicologist Charles Seeger. Elizabeth soon began working for the Seeger family in Chevy Chase, Maryland, doing the cooking and ironing once a week. In the Seeger household she was surrounded by music, and one day Elizabeth, now referred to as Libba (a family nickname), began playing one of the family's guitars. Peggy heard her, and she and her brother Mike began to encourage Cotten to perform, including her own composition "Freight Train." The family of folk musicians and collectors (which also included older brother Pete) greatly enjoyed her wealth of southern songs, including "Snake Bake a Hoecake" and "Old Cow Died," which Ruth Crawford Seeger included in her book *Animal Folk Songs for Children* (1951). Although Cotten was initially uncomfortable in her dual capacity as housekeeper and musical informant, she soon became familiar with her new role and returned to her youthful style of playing the banjo and then the guitar upside down, since she was left-handed and had never changed the strings on her brother's instruments.

Mike Seeger began tape-recording her at home in 1952 and issued her first album for Folkways Records in 1958, *Folksongs and Instrumentals with Guitar* (reissued on CD as *Freight Train and Other North Carolina Folk Songs and Tunes* in 1989). "Freight Train" became a hit first in England, as performed by Nancy Whisky. Libba Cotten secured the copyright following a legal battle once the song had become popular; it was later recorded by Peter, Paul, and Mary, among others. Cotten played for visitors to the Seeger household, where she worked until 1955, and her public career was launched in 1960 when she appeared with Mike Seeger at Swarthmore College. She was then sixty-seven years old.

Soon she was performing in concerts, coffeehouses, and festivals, beginning with the University of Chicago Folk Festival in 1961, followed by the Philadelphia Folk Festival (1963, 1972), the UCLA Folk Festival (1964), the Newport Folk Festival (1964, 1968), and the Festival of American Folklife in Washington, D.C. (1968–71). She often shared the stage with other blues musicians, such as Mississippi John Hurt, Skip James, Muddy Waters, Otis Span, and Taj Mahal. Her second album for Folkways, *Elizabeth Cotten, Volume II: Shake Sugaree,* appeared in 1967, followed by *Elizabeth Cotten, Volume III: When I'm Gone* (1975) and *Elizabeth Cotten Live!* (Arhoolie, 1983), which won a Grammy for Best Traditional Folk Recording. In 1972 she received the Burl Ives Award from the National Folk Festival Association, and in 1984 she was named a National Endowment for the Arts National Heritage Fellow. Meanwhile, in 1978 she purchased a house in Syracuse, New York, where she lived with her daughter and grandchildren. In 1989 she was selected as one of seventy-five influential African American women to be included in a photo documentary, *I Dream a World.* Although her hands were becoming weak, she continued to perform into her nineties; she appeared at the Philadelphia Folk Festival in 1986. She played her last concert in Harlem on February 22, 1987, not long before her death on June 29 in Syracuse at the age of ninety-four.

Vestapol/Rounder issued a video of her life in 1994, and she has been honored by a road named the Elizabeth Cotten Bikeway in North Carolina, along with many honors from the city of Syracuse. Her banjo and guitar reside in the permanent collection of the Smithsonian Institution. She appears on numerous compilation albums, including *Close to Home: Old Time Music from Mike Seeger's Collection 1952–1967* (Smithsonian Folkways, 1997). Libba Cotten is remembered not only because of her influential songs, combining blues, traditional, and religious tunes, but also for her unique guitar and banjo styles, which came to be widely copied.

Bibliography: Brief biographies of Elizabeth Cotten, which often disagree on basic factual information, are found in Kristin Baggelaar and Donald Milton, *Folk Music: More Than a Song* (1976); Sheldon Harris, *Blues Who's Who: A Biographical Dictionary of Blues Singers* (1979); Jessie Carney Smith, ed., *Notable Black American Women* (1992); and Irwin Stambler and Lyndon Stambler, *Folk and Blues: The Encyclopedia* (2001). The birth date used here is found in the Social Security Death Index; other published sources sometimes give it as 1895. A short interview with Cotten appears in Brian Lasker, *I Dream a World: Portraits of Black Women Who Changed America* (1989). Also of interest are the articles on the occasion of her ninetieth birthday concert celebration by Richard Harrington in the *Washington Post* and Jon Pareles in the *New York Times,* both on January 7, 1983.

RONALD COHEN

COVINGTON, Lucy Friedlander. November 24, 1910–September 20, 1982. Political activist, tribal leader.

Lucy Friedlander Covington was over forty when she assumed the role that would make her a hero of the struggle for American Indian self-determination. During the 1950s the federal government proposed to abolish the Colville Indian Reservation in Washington State, and Covington, a native and resident of the reservation, resolved to resist. For the next two decades, in tribal council chambers, congressional hearing rooms, and national Indian conventions, Covington worked effectively to preserve her reservation and make the United States fulfill its trust responsibility to Indians.

Lucy Covington may not have aspired to political leadership in her early years, but she was a descendant of chiefs and tried to embody those ancestors' honorable qualities. Her upbringing instilled pride in her Indian heritage and a sense of responsibility for kin, tribe, tribal land, and posterity. She entered the political arena at the request of an older brother and community elders.

The center of Lucy's first community was Nespelem, a reservation town. She was born near there, in a teepee on land allotted to Mary Moses. Lucy's maternal great-grandfather was Chief Moses, who had skillfully bargained with American officials, first to keep his people in their mid-Columbia homeland and then for other reserved land. Moses's father-in-law was Owhi, a leader of Yakama and Palus Indians who rebelled against treaties imposed on them in the 1850s. The daughter of Moses's first wife married a son of the Yakama chief Kamiakin and gave birth to Lucy's mother Nellie.

Lucy was the fourth of five children born to Nellie and Louis T. Friedlander Sr., a rancher of Nez Perce and Okanagan Indian and German descent. After Louis died, when Lucy was two, Nellie remarried and had four more children, who did not live long. Because intertribal marriage was common among distinguished native families, Lucy also had Wenatchi, Sanpoil, Palus, and Entiat ancestors. Lucy credited Mary Moses, who was the chief's second wife and sister to Lucy's grandmother, with raising her. In addition to learning from elders, Lucy attended reservation schools through tenth grade, finished high school in 1931 at the Haskell Institute, an Indian boarding school in Kansas, and took courses at Kinman Business College in Spokane.

In 1935 Lucy married John J. Covington, another Colville tribe member. The newlyweds moved several times as John took construction jobs. During World War II, employment opportunities drew them to Portland, Oregon, where both worked as shipyard welders. When John joined the Navy Seabees and went to the Pacific front, Lucy kept welding. After the war, the couple returned to the reservation, settled on Mary Moses's allotment, and raised cattle. A car wreck ended John's life in 1958. Although Lucy never remarried and bore no children, her home was hardly lonely or childless: she shared it with and mothered several nieces and nephews, who remember her as a firm but warmhearted matriarch. Related or not, many people called her Auntie, Mother, and Grandmother.

In 1956 voters of the Nespelem district elected Covington to the Colville Tribes' governing council. Except for a two-year break, she sat on the council until 1980. For one term she was council chair—the first woman in that position. She also served as vice-chair and headed the planning committee for years.

A U.S. proposal to terminate the reservation launched Covington into political orbit. Officials described termination, which was national policy in the 1950s, as Indian emancipation from oppressive supervision, and some Colville Indians said they relished that prospect. But Covington opposed termination because it would entail the liquidation of tribal property and dissipate her people's most precious heritage, their land. In her opinion, surrendering the land her elders had suffered for was tantamount to forfeiting Indian identity.

Controversy about termination divided Colville Indians for years. From Covington's first term until 1970, few council members shared her view. Undaunted, Covington advocated her position in numerous forums. Financing her efforts by selling her cattle, she traveled to Washington, D.C., and elsewhere to buttonhole lawmakers and presidents, testify against termination bills, and recruit allies at intertribal meetings. Her charisma was apparent to many. Colleagues have described Covington as smart, frank, dignified, selfless, beautiful, and a commanding presence. The Affiliated Tribes of Northwest Indians and the Association on American Indian Affairs (AAIA) each made her an officer, and AAIA established an award in her honor.

Many people credit Covington with reversing the drive for Colville termination. Through the 1960s, most of the tribal council's fourteen members favored termination and claimed to speak for a majority of tribe members, who expected large individual payments if tribal assets were liquidated. Covington and her allies countered the protermination arguments with a publication called *Our Heritage.* Each time other councilors submitted a termination plan to Congress, Covington was among those who raised objections that deterred legislation. She also pressured the Bureau of Indian Affairs (BIA) to replace its unsympathetic local agent with Sherwin Broadhead, who favored tribal development. Finally in 1971, Covington's campaign succeeded, both with the BIA and with tribal voters. Anti-termination candidates won nine council seats. After a long, often lonely struggle, Covington had reason to believe that her beloved reservation would endure.

During her remaining active years, Covington worked with characteristic determination to protect tribal rights and resources, develop tribal services, govern the reservation for the benefit of tribe members, and promote intertribal cooperation. She also mentored younger tribal leaders. And Covington's advocacy played a crucial part in persuading U.S. officials to endorse Indian self-determination in the 1970s.

In 1982, at the age of seventy-one, Lucy Covington died of pulmonary fibrosis at her home in Nespelem, Washington. National lawmakers and officials joined hundreds of other mourners at Catholic funeral services followed by traditional Seven Drums ceremonies in her honor. A *Colville Tribal Tribune* obituary of the Colvilles' "First Lady" declared that her "unfaltering caring for her native lands and Colville peoples; her outstanding leadership qualities; her keen sense of business developments for the Colville Reservation; and her support for higher education and training for American Indians afforded her the respect and admiration of the . . . tribal membership and . . . throughout America's Indian Country."

Bibliography: Lucy Covington: Native American Indian, a film produced by Encyclopedia Britannica Education Corporation in 1978, features Covington explaining her political and cultural activism. For vital statistics and other facts, this essay relied on telephone interviews with Covington's niece, Barbara Aripa; an obituary in the *Colville Tribal Tribune,* October 29, 1982, p. 1; a death certificate filed with the Washington State Department of Health; Haskell enrollment data supplied by the National Archives, Central Plains Branch; and census rolls of the Colville Indian Agency for 1920 and 1937, supplied by the Colville Confederated Tribes. A delayed birth registration, filed with Washington State in 1942, lists November 23, 1910, as her date of birth. References to personal traits also drew on telephone interviews with Covington's political colleagues—Mel Tonasket, Sherwin Broadhead, and LaDonna Harris. Family members have placed unpublished documents by and about Covington in the archives of the Colville Confederated Tribes, but public access is restricted.

Evidence of Covington's role in preventing the termination of the Colville Reservation is varied and scattered. Primary sources include the transcripts of several congressional hearings, such as S. 282, U.S. Senate, 90th Cong., 1st session (1967); articles in the *Wenatchee* [Washington] *Daily World* newspaper during the years 1965–71; Hilda Bryant, "Drowns Indians in Mainstream," *Seattle Post-Intelligencer*, December 11, 1969, pp. 5–6; and Robert May, "The Indian Wars Are On Again," *Northwest Indian Times* 4, no. 1 (March 1972), p. 14. Secondary sources include Kathleen A. Dahl, "The Battle over Termination on the Colville Indian Reservation," *American Indian Culture and Research Journal* 18 (1994), pp. 29–53; John Fahey, *Saving the Reservation: Joe Garry and the Battle to Be Indian* (2001), p. 195, note 18; and Alexandra Harmon, "A History of the Colville Indian Reservation and Its Peoples" (unpublished manuscript, 2000).

ALEXANDRA HARMON

COWAN, Ruth Baldwin. June 15, 1901–February 5, 1993. Journalist.

Ruth Baldwin Cowan, one of the first accredited woman war correspondents during World War II, was born in Salt Lake City, the only child of Ida Baldwin and William Henry Cowan, a mining prospector. After her father's death when she was about eight, Cowan and her mother moved to Florida, where her mother attempted to homestead acres of grapefruit and orange trees. Failing at that, they moved back to Salt Lake City and then on to San Antonio, where Cowan attended high school. She graduated from the University of Texas at Austin in 1923 and for several years taught algebra at Main Avenue High School in San Antonio, where she herself had gone to school.

Cowan began her journalism career in 1928 through the intercession of a family friend, Mary Carter, who was working for the *San Antonio Evening News*. Carter wanted to go out on dates with her boyfriend, and she passed on to Cowan assignments to review films and plays that she did not want to attend. From there, Cowan began taking on other assignments, including coverage of the San Antonio Board of Education. She then resigned from teaching and secured a regular job on the newspaper, where she juggled several bylines: "Ruth Cowan" if she was writing stories for women, but "if it was a real honest-to-God he-man story, it was R. Baldwin Cowan or Baldwin Cowan," she reminisced years later.

With the *Evening News*'s permission, she also began freelancing for other newspapers and covered the 1928 Democratic Convention for the *Houston Chronicle*. Her work at the convention attracted the attention of the local United Press (UP) bureau, and she was hired as R. Baldwin Cowan, a job she successfully filled for months. When the UP superiors discovered that Cowan was a woman, however, she was promptly fired. She next wired the general manager of the Associated Press (AP) in New York, explaining what had happened and asking if they had any openings for a woman. The AP offered her a job in Chicago, but once she was there the editors, who were unaccustomed to having a woman on staff, did not know what to do with her. So Cowan created her own niche, covering national conventions in Chicago, the World's Fair, and other national stories, including the trial of gangster Al Capone. When the Washington bureau had an opening in 1940, Cowan transferred there.

In Washington, Cowan represented the AP at First Lady ELEANOR ROOSEVELT's weekly news conferences and joined in the wire service's Washington coverage of the Japanese attack on Pearl Harbor. As part of the Washington press corps, Cowan became interested in war coverage, and one of her assignments was covering the Women's Auxiliary Army Corps (WAAC), which was headed by her longtime friend and fellow Texan, OVETA CULP HOBBY. But what she really wanted was to be transferred to London. With the backing of Hobby and Eleanor Roosevelt, Cowan eventually convinced the AP to let her accompany the WAACs when they were being shipped out to their presumed destination of London in early 1943. She was joined on the journey by Inez Callaway Robb, a reporter for the International News Service.

They were midway across the Atlantic Ocean when they learned that the WAAC contingent was headed not to London but to Africa, where the war was heating up. They landed in Algiers. Cowan was greeted by a disgruntled AP bureau chief, Wes Gallagher, who wanted nothing to do with her, a sentiment that was also representative of how the military viewed her presence. Cowan, however, refused to budge. She dispatched a telegram back to Eleanor Roosevelt in Washington, saying: "Don't encourage more women to come to Africa. The men don't want us here" (Edwards, p. 151). She doubted the telegram would make it past the censors but still hoped it might have some effect, and she believed that her welcome improved in Algiers after that. When Gallagher refused to give her assignments, she thought up story ideas on her own (including a visit to a sheik's harem in Morocco) and flourished despite his disfavor.

After other correspondents returned to the United States, Cowan remained in Europe, making her way to London, Gibraltar, Rome, and Paris. In London, the editors again had no idea how to use her, so she was free to travel the countryside pursuing her own story ideas. At one point she was detained by military personnel who thought she might be a spy, but she was released when it became clear that somebody else had been using her name. She later participated in the aftermath of the Normandy invasion in June and July 1944, flying in hospital planes to evacuate the wounded and sharing her experiences in first-person dispatches for readers back in the States. She also covered part of the Battle of the Bulge in December 1944.

Throughout her time as war correspondent, Cowan and other women journalists were subjected to the indignity of being unwanted by their own colleagues and unwelcome by the military personnel they were covering. Men correspondents were given jeeps, press housing, and regular briefings; the women had to find their own rides, stay in military hospitals with nurses, and cultivate their own sources who were hospitable to them. Cowan and other women correspondents succeeded despite this adversity.

Cowan stayed in Europe two and a half years, returning to the United States shortly before V-E Day (May 8, 1945). Reassigned to the AP bureau in Washington, she covered the White House, the Capitol, and the House Armed Services Committee. In 1947–48 she was president of the National Women's Press Club. In 1956 she retired from the AP and at the age of fifty-five married Bradley C. Nash, then undersecretary of commerce in the Eisenhower administration. She later worked as a public relations consultant for the Women's Division of the Republican National Committee and then as an assistant undersecretary in the Department of Health, Education and Welfare. In 1961 she and her husband retired to Harpers Ferry, West Virginia. She died there in 1993 at the age of ninety-one.

Bibliography: Ruth Baldwin Cowan's personal papers are housed at the Schlesinger Library, Radcliffe Institute for Advanced Study, Harvard University. An important source on her life is an interview conducted on September 26, 1987, and March 21, 1988, by Margot Knight for the Women in Journalism oral history project of the Washington Press Club Foundation, which is found in the Oral History Collection of Columbia University and other repositories. The oral history is the source for all the unattributed quotations in the text. An example of Cowan's AP war coverage can be found in Lilya Wagner, *Women War Correspondents of World War II* (1989). See also Nancy Caldwell Sorel, *Women Who Wrote the War* (1999); and Julia Edwards, *Women of the World: The Great Foreign Correspondents* (1988). A feature about Cowan, "Capital Press Woman," was published in *Newsweek*, June 16, 1947, p. 66. An obituary appeared in the *New York Times* on February 6, 1993.

AGNES HOOPER GOTTLIEB

CRAWFORD, Cheryl. September 24, 1902–October 7, 1986. Theater producer.

Born in Akron, Ohio, and raised in a puritanical, religious family with roots that reached back to pre-Revolutionary America, Cheryl Crawford hardly seemed destined for a glittering theatrical career. Her father, Robert Kingsley Crawford, owned a successful real estate company and her mother, Luella Elizabeth Parker, was a homemaker. A poker-faced, exceedingly plain tomboy, the eldest child and the only daughter in a family of four children, young Cheryl was stagestruck from an early age. In her autobiography, *One Naked Individual: My Fifty Years in the Theatre* (1977), Crawford described her childhood as normal and happy, but nonetheless she escaped from her conservative family environment as soon as she could. In 1921, she entered Smith College as a drama major, then spent a summer working in theater in Provincetown, Massachusetts. After graduation in 1925 she went to New York, determined to secure a place for herself on Broadway. From the beginning, she demonstrated an extraordinary talent for being in the right place at the right time and for cultivating associations with theatrical visionaries.

Although she knew she wanted to be a producer, she enrolled in the Theatre Guild's acting school. Soon thereafter she applied for a job as assistant stage manager for the Guild, at the time the most prestigious producing organization on Broadway. Sensing Crawford's strong will, Theresa Helburn, a Guild co-founder and one of the few women in an executive position in the theater, hired her. Taking on a variety of jobs, including casting, Crawford exhibited administrative skills and an ability to forge relationships with potential investors that would mark her long and productive career.

At the Guild, Crawford met two young firebrands, Harold Clurman and Lee Strasberg, who were dissatisfied with the kind of theater the Guild offered, mostly European plays acted in the grand manner. Early in 1931, alight with plans for a distinctly American repertory theater, Crawford resigned from the Theatre Guild to join Clurman and Strasberg in co-founding the Group Theatre. Their intention was to train a band of young actors to perform new American plays that would illuminate the rips and tears of a country in the grip of the Great Depression. Clurman, an inspiring orator, became the Group's principal director, its tireless booster and final arbiter in choice of plays. Strasberg, with a priestly devotion to truthful acting, was placed in charge of actor training. To Crawford fell the responsibility of raising funds and overseeing the company's daily operations—toilsome tasks in which she felt stifled. Creatively, her only fulfilling moment with the Group came when, working with émigré composer Kurt Weill and playwright Paul Green, she was instrumental in developing the Group's sole musical, *Johnny Johnson* (1936). Faced with conflicts with her two high-strung co-founders and with escalating financial setbacks, Crawford resigned from the Group in 1937 to pursue a career as an independent producer.

Her first five productions were failures, but characteristically she persevered. In 1940, she launched the first of what were to become three legendary seasons of summer stock at the Maplewood Theatre in New Jersey. Among her offerings were ETHEL BARRYMORE in *The School for Scandal* (1940), Paul Robeson in O'Neill's *Emperor Jones* (1940), *Twelfth Night* with HELEN HAYES (1941), and *Anna Christie* with Ingrid Bergman (1941). Her most notable production, however, was a new version of George Gershwin's Broadway folk opera *Porgy and Bess,* which became her first independent success when she moved it to Broadway.

Throughout the 1940s Crawford produced a number of innovative landmark musicals. On *One Touch of Venus* (1943) she worked again with Kurt Weill and supervised musical theater neophytes, humorists S. J. Perelman and Ogden Nash, on the show's book and lyrics. In 1947, working with composer Frederick Loewe and librettist Alan Jay Lerner, she produced *Brigadoon,* a musical fantasy that was her biggest hit. In 1949 Crawford presented *Regina,* a courageous Broadway opera by Marc Blitzstein based on LILLIAN HELLMAN'S *Little Foxes.*

Also in the 1940s, collaborating with Margaret Webster and EVA LE GALLIENNE, who shared her commitment to repertory and to Shakespeare, Crawford organized the short-lived American Repertory Theatre; its failure after only two seasons convinced Crawford of the virtual impossibility of sustaining a true repertory company within the American system. Around the same period Crawford served as the vice president of the board of directors of the American National Theatre and Academy (ANTA) and presented a number of distinguished productions for the group, including Charles Laughton in Brecht's *Galileo* (1947) and John Garfield in Ibsen's *Peer Gynt* (1951).

In the fall of 1947, with Group Theatre colleagues Elia Kazan and Robert Lewis, she established the Actors Studio to provide performers struggling through the boredom of long runs in the theater with a laboratory in which they could sharpen their craft. Lee Strasberg, who was to become the Studio's guru in residence, did not join until 1949, and under his autocratic direction the Studio gained fame as the high temple of the Method (an adaptation of ideas about an actor's creative process first enunciated by Russian director Konstantin Stanislavsky). At the Actors Studio, as at the Group, Crawford was again responsible for keeping the wolf from the door. And again, she chafed because she felt overworked and unappreciated. When the opportunity for an Actors Studio Theatre became a possibility in the early 1960s, she became its producer, although she later claimed she should have known better. Despite worthy plays (including *Strange Interlude* [1963] and *Three Sisters* [1964]) and illustrious casts drawn from the Studio's extraordinary roster, the Theatre proved maddeningly short-lived, expiring in 1965.

While she was dedicating herself to idealistic ventures, Crawford continued her career as an independent producer in the commercial arena. Her most notable work was a quartet of Tennessee Williams plays: *The Rose Tattoo* (1951), *Camino Real* (1953), *Sweet Bird of Youth* (1959), and *Period of Adjustment* (1960). She had few successes in the 1960s and 1970s, but often her misfires, such as Jerome Robbins's 1963 production of Brecht's *Mother Courage* with Anne Bancroft, represented the highest intentions. Until her death in New York in 1986 at the age of eighty-four she never stopped searching for challenging plays and musicals.

Although Crawford announced in her autobiography that her private life would remain private, it was well known and accepted in theater circles that Crawford was a lesbian. Her longest relationship was with Dorothy Patten, a Group Theatre actress who was emotionally unstable. Friends claimed the producer's seemingly forbidding veneer—her expressionless face and eyes and her flat, dry voice—was a mask to conceal shyness, but Crawford's absence of personal showmanship may well have shrouded her legacy. Given her central participation in some of the most influential institutions of the twentieth-century American theater, she deserves to be much better known than she is. Frugal and canny, Cheryl Crawford was a producer of a kind the theater unfortunately can no longer accommodate. A crucial figure in establishing a place for women in the theater, Crawford competed with distinction in a field dominated by men.

Bibliography: Cheryl Crawford's papers are in the Billy Rose Theatre Collection of the New York Public Library for the Performing Arts at Lincoln Center. *One Naked Individual: My Fifty Years in the Theatre* (1977) is the only sustained account of Crawford's entire career. The most complete account of the Group Theatre, which contains a balanced portrait of Crawford, is Wendy Smith's *Real Life Drama: The Group Theatre and America, 1931–1940* (1990). The author had two long interviews with Crawford: the first on October 15, 1983, for a book, *A Method to Their Madness: The History of the Actors Studio* (1984); the second in November 1985 for an article, "Still Savvy after All These Years," in *American Theatre* 2 (March 1986), pp. 12–15. An obituary appeared in the *New York Times* on October 8, 1986.

FOSTER HIRSCH

CRAWFORD, Joan. March 23, 1905–May 10, 1977. Actress.

Joan Crawford was one of only a handful of female actresses to maintain star status within the Hollywood system over nearly five decades. She achieved her place as one of "Hollywood's Legendary Ladies" through a combination of intense ambition, unwavering self-discipline, hard work, and professionalism. Crawford delighted audiences with her portrayals of passionate dancing flappers in the late silent and early sound era, street-smart working girls in the Depression, failed mothers and femmes fatales in the 1940s, and female grotesques in the 1950s and 1960s, prolonging her celebrity with assiduous attention to her star image.

Although she often played an heiress or sparkling upper-class sophisticate, her most memorable screen characterizations cast her as a girl from the wrong side of the tracks who fought for respect, a plot deeply entwined with her biography. Crawford was born Lucille Fay Le Sueur in San Antonio, Texas, the third child and first daughter to live beyond infancy of Thomas Le Sueur, a handsome French-Canadian laborer, and Anna Belle Johnson, a waitress of Irish and Swedish descent. Apparently Tom LeSueur deserted the family shortly before Lucille was born. As her mother picked up odd jobs and an occasional husband (Henry Cassin) to support the family, Lucille spent her childhood in San Antonio; Lawton, Oklahoma; and Kansas City, Missouri. To pay for her tuition at a Catholic primary school and the Rockingham Academy, Lucille waited on tables and did housework at school. She later spent one semester in the business course at Stephens College in 1922.

The hurts of social exclusion dominated her memories, but what sustained Lucille, laboring as a telephone operator and then in a series of department store jobs, was the social transformation promised by nightlife. By 1921, she began to win local dance contests, excelling at the Black Bottom, the Fox Trot, and the Cakewalk. By 1924, nightlife was providing her salary, first as a dancer in cheap bar rooms in Chicago and Oklahoma City, then in the chorus of a swanky Detroit floor show, and eventually in the chorus of a Broadway revue in New York. Learning the Charleston from black dancers at Harlem nightclubs, she won a coveted solo spot at a popular New York speakeasy. A starting contract from MGM brought her to Hollywood in January 1925. Renamed by a movie fan magazine contest, MGM's Lucille LeSueur became Joan Crawford.

The social promise and sexual dangers nightlife offered to women provided the dramatic tension in Crawford's first starring vehicle, *Our Dancing Daughters* (1928), written by Josephine Lovett. Several women screenwriters prominent in Hollywood's early pre-Code years, including Bess Meredyth, Auarania Rouverol, Leonore Coffee, and ANITA LOOS, wrote other early scripts that cast her as the exemplar of female modernity and unabashed sexuality and established her stardom.

Crawford's 1930s films, featuring her sympathetic depiction of characters transcending working-class limits, delighted audiences, especially urban working women—who remained devoted fans throughout Crawford's career. Now she was guided on screen by more prestigious directors, including Clarence Brown and George Cukor, and partnered with a range of male stars, including John Gilbert, William Haines, and Clark Gable. Exhibitors placed her on the top ten stars list of the *Motion Picture Herald* from 1932 to 1936, but later in the decade, after her name appeared on the "box office poison list" along with Katharine Hepburn and GRETA GARBO, the studio began offering its best scripts to a new crop of younger actresses. By 1943, women's film and Crawford seemed dated and she was forced out of MGM.

Crawford staged a working actress's triumphant comeback in *Mildred Pierce* (1945), a stylish Warner Brothers hybrid combining elements of dark mystery and women's melodrama. The part of a housewife forced by her husband's desertion to work as a waitress who then rises as a restaurant owner, failing as a sacrificing mother but winning a reprieve as a wife, won Crawford an Oscar for Best Actress. In the 1950s Crawford did the best she could with the parts offered to her, often playing powerful and destructive women, and then moving into the horror genre, most notably portraying a former film star opposite BETTE DAVIS in *What Ever Happened to Baby Jane?* (1962).

In addition to her many affairs, Crawford married four times. To the delight of publicists and fans, her first marriage to Douglas Fairbanks Jr., film star and the son of Hollywood's first family, provided a storybook romance as long as it lasted (1929–33), and an education for Joan on the mores of the wealthy. Her 1935–39 marriage to Franchot Tone, an actor on Broadway and a founding member of the left-wing Group Theatre, introduced her to classic drama, rare books, and the Hollywood left-wing community. Her activities as an early member of the Screen Actors Guild and her support for Hollywood anti-fascist activities and Russian war relief earned her an FBI dossier for "subversive activities." Her marriage to actor Philip Terry took place in 1942 during a low point in her career; she divorced him in 1946. After she married Alfred Steele, president of the Pepsi-Cola Company, in 1955, she traveled more than a hundred thousand miles throughout the world with him to promote Pepsi. After his death in 1959, she filled his slot as the first woman appointed to the

Pepsi-Cola board of directors. In addition to working occasionally in television, she appeared on film for the last time in 1970.

Although the standards for Hollywood female stardom emphasized romance more than motherhood, Crawford wanted to have children. After numerous miscarriages and the end of her marriage to Tone, she adopted a daughter, Christina, in 1939. She and Terry adopted a son, Philip Jr., in 1943, whom she renamed Christopher after the divorce. Again on her own, she adopted two more girls, Cathy and Cynthia, in 1947.

Named America's Most Glamorous Mother in 1949, Crawford's childrearing emphasized discipline, consistency, and rigid scheduling, values promoted in the childrearing literature of the day and consistent with the Christian Science she practiced. Her relationships with her two older children were especially contentious and punitive. Crawford's daughter's popular memoir articulately described the extreme dissonance associated with her childhood experiences of the star-making machinery, material affluence, and emotional deprivation, themes common in many stars' children's accounts of growing up in Hollywood. In hindsight Crawford wondered whether the stars of her time should have had children: "A part of us wanted a real personal private life . . . but the biggest part of us wanted the career" (Newquist, pp. 145–46).

Crawford spent her final years in contact with friends and loyal fans, appearing in public as long as she felt she could still present an image befitting a movie star. She died at her home in New York on May 10, 1977, at the age of seventy-two.

Bibliography: Joan Crawford's life and career have been analyzed by several serious Hollywood biographers. Bob Thomas, *Joan Crawford: A Biography* (1978), relies primarily on materials from MGM, Los Angeles, and New York film archives, and extensive interviews with Crawford and those who knew and worked with her. It includes the credits and cast lists for all Crawford's films and a list of her television appearances. David Houston's research for *Jazz Baby: A Biography of Joan Crawford* (1983) drew primarily on local records, newspapers, and interviews to trace Crawford's childhood in Lawton, Oklahoma, and Kansas City, Missouri, ending with Crawford's MGM contract in 1925; he offers the birth date of March 23, 1905, three years earlier than the one Crawford used. Christina Crawford's *Mommie Dearest* (1978) was an effort to come to terms with growing up as the star's daughter. Fred Lawrence Guiles's biography, *Joan Crawford: The Last Word* (1995), attempted to shift the focus from maternal failure back to Crawford's films and dramatic accomplishments, appending a full filmography. Roy Newquist, a Chicago celebrity journalist and book reviewer, conducted a series of interviews with Crawford between 1962 and 1977, which he published as *Conversations with Joan Crawford* (1980). Crawford wrote two autobiographies, *A Portrait of Joan*, co-authored by Jane Kesner Ardmore (1962); and *My Way of Life* (1971). Jeanine Basinger, *A Woman's View: How Hollywood Spoke to Women, 1930–1960* (1993) provides an expansive and sympathetic analysis of the film genre with which Crawford was most closely identified, and includes discussion of many of her films. An obituary appeared in the *New York Times* on May 11, 1977.

JUDITH E. SMITH

CUNNINGHAM, Imogen. April 12, 1883–June 23, 1976. Photographer.

Imogen Cunningham was born in Portland, Oregon, the eldest of six children of Isaac Burns Cunningham and his second wife, Susan Elizabeth Johnson, both of Scottish ancestry and both born in Missouri. Her family also included three half-siblings from her father's first marriage. Isaac Cunningham, a self-educated freethinker and avid reader, made a spartan living, first as a farmer and later in a small wood and coal business. Susan Cunningham ran the large household, which was moved from Portland to a remote area of Seattle, Washington, around 1889.

Throughout her long life, Cunningham was a feisty individualist. As a young child, she was taught to read by her father, who encouraged her to pursue creative and intellectual studies. She attended a local elementary school and Broadway High School. In 1903, she enrolled at the University of Washington, where she majored in chemistry and supported herself working as secretary to a professor. Recognizing that photography might afford a viable profession, in 1905 she acquired a 4×5 camera and wrote her senior thesis, "Modern Processes of Photography." Completing her course work in three and a half years, she was the only child in the family to graduate from a university.

From 1907 to 1909, Cunningham was employed at the studio of Edward S. Curtis, the well-known Seattle-based photographer who was engaged in a vast chronicle of Native American life. There she improved and expanded her technical skills and became acquainted with the most advanced camera expression of her time through the periodical *Camera Work*, edited and published by Alfred Stieglitz. Her introduction to the wider world of pictorialist photography and modern artistic culture, in particular the work of photographer Gertrude Käsebier, was to have a significant effect on the style and content of her own early work. Awarded a scholarship by her college sorority in 1909, Cunningham was able to study abroad at the Technische Hochschule in Dresden, Germany.

On her return to Seattle in 1910, after meeting with Stieglitz and Käsebier in New York, Cunningham opened a professional portrait studio at 1117 Terry Avenue. She photographed sitters both in her artistically furnished studio and in their own homes and gardens because upper-class clients had shown a preference for less formal work than was being done by most commercial studios. Similarly, her artful handling of lighting effects was meant to create an artistic product rather than merely a facial map. Cunningham also kept up a lively correspondence with several notables in pictorialist photography, and wrote articles. "Photography as a Profession for Women," published in 1913, was significant for its recognition of the problems facing women entering the field.

Cunningham also found time for her own creative work. Many were costume pieces, conceived in the pictorialist style. With such titles as "The Vision" or "The Dream," these images, made out-of-doors in a soft, romantic manner, are reminiscent of the earlier work of English Victorian photographer Julia Margaret Cameron. This work was exhibited in New York in 1914 at the Brooklyn Institute of Arts and Sciences and at the Portland Art Museum in Oregon.

Though Cunningham was not conventionally beautiful, her abundant head of hair and interesting features were nonetheless attractive. In February 1915, she married George Roy Partridge (called Roi), a Seattle artist she had met through corresponding with him to arrange an exhibition of his work at the Seattle Fine Arts Society. Their son Gryffyd was born in December, followed by twin sons, Rondal and Padraic, born in September 1917 after the family had moved to San Francisco. As Cunningham noted, she seemed always to have "one hand in the dishpan and the other in the darkroom." Living in the Bay Area also gave her more opportunities to associate with others in the medium, among them California photographers Francis Bruguière (in whose studio she briefly worked), DOROTHEA LANGE, and Edward Weston.

In 1921, after Partridge took a faculty position at Mills College and the family had moved to Oakland, Cunningham was able to resume her professional career as a portraitist. Though still tied to domestic duties, for the first time she found her own expressive voice. Using a large-format camera, during the 1920s she made a series of sharply focused close-ups of botanical and organic matter, the best known of which are images of magnolia blossoms and calla lilies. Her new highly delineated approach recommended her to Group f/64, which included only photographers dedicated to highly focused imagery and nonmanipulative printing techniques.

Nevertheless, Cunningham's interest in a diverse range of photographic practices inspired her to experiment with negative prints, double exposures, light abstractions, and montages. She was a member of Pictorial Photographers of America, and her work was included in 1928 in that organization's exhibition at the California Palace of the Legion of Honor, San Francisco, as well as in *Film und Foto,* a celebrated exhibition of avant-garde photography held in Stuttgart, Germany, in 1929. Between 1929 and 1938, Cunningham had one-person exhibitions at the Berkeley Art Museum (1929); the M. H. deYoung Memorial Museum, San Francisco (1931); the Julien Levy Gallery, New York City (1931); the Los Angeles Museum (1932); the Dallas Art Museum (1935); and the E. B. Crocker Art Gallery, Sacramento (1936).

The excellence of Cunningham's portraits of dancer MARTHA GRAHAM recommended her to *Vanity Fair* magazine, which commissioned her in 1934 to photograph Hollywood celebrities. Her increased professional stature and duties precipitated marital difficulties, ending in a divorce from Partridge in June 1934.

In 1947, Cunningham moved from Oakland to San Francisco and taught at the California School of Fine Arts for the next four years; a later teaching stint was at the San Francisco Art Institute from 1965 to 1967.

Cunningham continued to photograph throughout the remainder of her life, producing many portraits of artists, some street photography, and some interiors, including the well-known *Unmade Bed* (1957). She maintained an interest in the nude figure and in montages and double exposures. Her work was seen in more than thirty one-person shows between 1951 and 1976, as well as in numerous group exhibitions. She won a Guggenheim Fellowship in her early eighties. For her last project, entitled *After Ninety,* Cunningham photographed elderly people—friends and strangers—hoping to find some meaning in the advanced age that she herself was impatiently bearing. In June 1975, the photographer established the Imogen Cunningham Trust to preserve and promote her work after her death, which occurred at St. Francis Hospital in San Francisco when she was ninety-three.

Bibliography: Imogen Cunningham's correspondence, lecture notes, and unpublished writings are to be found mainly in the Imogen Cunningham Archives, part of the Imogen Cunningham Trust, Berkeley, California. Other material is at the Center for Creative Photography, University of Arizona, Tucson; Mills College Art Gallery, Oakland, California; and the Roi Partridge Collection at the Bancroft Library, University of California, Berkeley. Writings by Cunningham include "Photography as a Profession for Women," *The Arrow* 29, no. 2 (January 1913), pp. 203–9; and "Imogen Cunningham" (a statement) in John Paul Edwards, "Group f/64," *Camera Craft* 42, no. 3 (March 1935), p. 113.

Amy Rule, ed., *Imogen Cunningham: Selected Texts and Bibliography* (1992), offers the most complete bibliography pertaining to the photographer. Richard Lorenz, *Imogen Cunningham: Ideas without End* (1993), is the most thoroughly researched biography; the quote is from p. 24. Earlier monographs include Judy Dater, *Imogen Cunningham: A Portrait* (1979). Margaretta Mitchell, *After Ninety* (1977), is based on Cunningham's last series of portraits. The earliest catalog of a one-person exhibition of Cunningham's work is "'Impressions in Silver' by Imogene [sic] Cunningham," *Los Angeles Museum Art News*, April 1932. Other catalogs are *Imogen Cunningham, Photographs 1921–1967,* foreword by Beaumont Newhall (1967); and *Imogen Cunningham, Frontiers: Photographs 1906–1976,* text by Richard Lorenz for the Imogen Cunningham Trust, Berkeley, California, and the United States Information Agency (1987).

Cunningham's work is included in all major general histories of photography as well as in works that deal specifically with women photographers. Among them are Olivia Lahs-Gonzales, *Defining Eye: Women Photographers of the 20th Century—Selections from the Helen Kornblum Collection* (1997); Judith Fryer Davidov, *Women's Camera Work: Self/Body/Other in American Visual Culture* (1998); Martha Kreisel, *American Women Photographers: A Selected and Annotated Bibliography* (1999); and Naomi Rosenblum, *A History of Women Photographers* (2nd ed., 2000). An obituary appeared in the *New York Times* on June 26, 1976.

NAOMI ROSENBLUM

CURTIS, Charlotte Murray. December 19, 1928–April 16, 1987. Journalist.

As an innovative and iconoclastic writer and editor of society news during the 1960s and 1970s, Charlotte Curtis transformed journalism's approach to writing about the rich and famous. Taking her topic as seriously as others might treat politics or economics, Curtis used a deadpan style and fine sense of irony to neither celebrate nor skewer her subjects, but to display them in midflight with all their charms and foibles on view, mirrors of the culture that produced and sustained them.

Charlotte Murray Curtis was born in Chicago, the elder of two daughters of Lucile Atcherson and George Morris Curtis. She grew up in Columbus, Ohio, where her mother's family had deep roots as socially prominent owners of residential and commercial real estate. Curtis's early exposure to lives of wealth and privilege was useful preparation for her career.

An equally important influence was the model of achievement offered by her mother, a Smith College graduate and suffragist who in 1922 became the first woman to be a field officer in the foreign service. The Senate's initial refusal to confirm Lucile Atcherson's appointment, on the ground that a young single woman should not represent the United States abroad, provoked a flood of letters and telegrams that persuaded the senators to change their minds. During her first posting, in Bern, Switzerland, Atcherson met George Morris Curtis, an American medical school professor on a research project there. She resigned from the foreign service in 1927 to marry Dr. Curtis. In 1932, after Charlotte and her sister Mary were born, the family moved from Chicago, where Dr. Curtis was teaching, to Columbus, where he joined the medical faculty at Ohio State University.

Curtis graduated from the Columbus School for Girls in 1946 and entered Vassar College, graduating in 1950 with a major in American history. During her senior year, she had become engaged to a Yale student, Dwight Fullerton Jr., the son of an Ohio judge. By the time of their wedding on July 7, 1950, Curtis was privately expressing doubts about the marriage. They had no children and divorced three years later.

During college summers, Curtis had worked at the *Columbus Citizen,* one of the city's three daily newspapers. She did not at first have a career in journalism in mind, but she enjoyed the work and the newsroom atmosphere. Following graduation, she became a full-time reporter and was named society editor two years later. She remained at the Columbus paper, later called the *Citizen-Journal,* until 1961, when she moved to New York to take a job in the women's section of the *New York Times.* The *Times* was to be her home for the next twenty-five years.

Curtis's deft portraits of eminent figures in the world of New York fashion, unusual for the absence of awe with which she approached her subjects and for her penchant for quoting their unconsciously revealing observations, attracted the attention of Clifton Daniel, a senior *Times* editor who wanted to expand the definition of society news. Although Curtis was eager to move on to ordinary news reporting, Daniel persuaded her to accept a new and highly visible society beat.

Her initial reluctance to forgo "real" reporting reflected the lowly status of the women's page in American journalism: it was not just a ghetto for female reporters but a home for marginal stories unlikely to attract serious readers of either sex. By the end of her nine-year reign (1965–74) as editor of the women's page, Curtis not only had renamed the page "Family/Style" but had broadened its content and made it must-reading for anyone who wanted to "catch society in the act," as Curtis explained in the introduction to *The Rich and Other Atrocities*, a collection of her articles published in 1976 (p. ix).

Her method was deceptively simple: let rich people talk, and faithfully report their words, including the often startling lack of irony and self-awareness with which the words were uttered. For example, she quoted Estée Lauder's explanation for wearing an elaborate gold and diamond crown to the opening of the Metropolitan Opera House: "You know how it is. You have to wear something" (p. 78). She reported this comment from the owner of a Palm Beach mansion: "I'm here all alone with my maid, the butler and the cook" (p. 11).

Her approach drew enormous attention, and Curtis soon became almost as much a celebrity as those she wrote about. A petite figure, impeccably dressed with her auburn hair carefully styled, she looked as if she belonged at all the right parties. In 1966 Curtis obtained and printed the secret guest list for the masked ball Truman Capote gave for *Washington Post* publisher Katharine Graham. Her best-known story was her account of the fund-raising party thrown by Leonard Bernstein and his wife, Felicia Montealegre, for the Black Panthers in 1970, an event that captured a white liberal mentality run fatuously amok.

In 1974 she left Family/Style to supervise the Op-Ed page. As an associate editor, Curtis was the first woman to have her name on the paper's masthead. Her eight-year tenure there did not match the creativity of her writing years. Her relationship with other women at the paper was tense because she withheld her support when female staff members organized and sued the *Times* for sex discrimination. In 1982, Curtis left the editor's job to begin a weekly society column for the news pages; lacking prominent display, it did not have the impact of her earlier reporting.

Curtis married for the second time on June 15, 1972, to Dr. William E. Hunt, a neurosurgeon and former student of her father's. He remained in Columbus, where he was a professor at Ohio State University College of Medicine, while she kept her small penthouse apartment in Greenwich Village. They visited on weekends and holidays, and Hunt helped her through a breast cancer diagnosis and treatment in 1972. After cancer recurred in 1986, Curtis suspended her column and moved to be with her husband in Columbus, where she died at the age of fifty-eight.

Bibliography: The Schlesinger Library, Radcliffe Institute for Advanced Study, Harvard University, holds both Charlotte Curtis's papers and those of her mother, Lucile Atcherson Curtis. Neither collection has been processed. The New York Times Archives contains an oral history interview with Curtis, conducted by Susan Dryfoos on June 21, 1983. Charlotte Curtis wrote two books: *First Lady* (1962), an account of Jacqueline Kennedy's first year in the White House; and *The Rich and Other Atrocities* (1976), a collection of Curtis's society reporting, annotated by the author. The only full-length biography is Marilyn S. Greenwald, *A Woman of the Times: Journalism, Feminism, and the Career of Charlotte Curtis* (1999). A provocative, if not flattering, review of this book and of Curtis's career appears in Judith Martin, "Too Much a Lady?" *New York Times,* August 29, 1999. For a perspective on Curtis's stance toward women's issues at the *Times*, see Nan Robertson, *The Girls in the Balcony: Women, Men, and the New York Times* (1992). Gay Talese, *The Kingdom and the Power* (1969), is a useful account of life at the *New York Times* during Curtis's rise to prominence there. Tom Wolfe, *Radical Chic & Mau-Mauing the Flak Catchers* (1970), an account of the Bernstein Black Panther party, discusses the impact of Curtis's reporting. An obituary appeared in the *New York Times* on April 17, 1987.

LINDA GREENHOUSE

CUTHBERT, Marion Vera. March 15, 1896–May 5, 1989. Educator, YWCA official.

Marion Cuthbert devoted her life to the education, leadership, and training of women and girls, particularly African Americans. She was born in St. Paul, Minnesota, the third child of Thomas Cuthbert, a waiter from New Jersey, and Victoria Means, a housewife who hailed from New Orleans. Cuthbert grew up with a strong desire to attain a college education. After graduating from Central High School in St. Paul in 1913, she attended the University of Minnesota in Minneapolis from 1913 to 1915. Because of financial difficulties, she left college to serve as a governess to the young daughter of a St. Paul family. When the family relocated to Boston, Cuthbert accompanied them to continue taking care of their daughter, and enrolled in Boston University. In 1917–18, she was a student in the university's Teachers College but in 1918 transferred to the College of Liberal Arts, where she majored in English and philosophy. Cuthbert received a BA degree in 1920 and went to Florence, Alabama, where she worked first as an English teacher and later as the principal of Burrell Normal School, a private high school for African Americans sponsored by the Congregational Church.

Cuthbert was part of a small, elite group of black women who had earned liberal arts degrees from northern universities in the late nineteenth and early twentieth centuries. Despite their superb training and education, many employment opportunities were closed to them because of their race. Many did, however, find meaningful work teaching at segregated black schools throughout the South. In 1923, Cuthbert participated in the creation of the National Association of College Women (NACW), an organization aimed at developing leadership among black women graduates of accredited liberal arts colleges and universities.

Cuthbert's life and career were greatly influenced by another prominent African American woman, Juliette Derricotte, who became her close friend. In 1918 Derricotte graduated from

Talladega College, a school in Alabama founded by the American Missionary Association, and became its first woman trustee. She later served as secretary of the National Student Council of the Young Women's Christian Association (YWCA). In 1927 Cuthbert joined Derricotte at Talladega when she was hired as dean of women, a position she held until 1930. Beginning in 1928, Cuthbert attended Columbia University for four successive summers and earned a master's in psychology in 1931. In November of that year, Derricotte, who was working as dean of women at prestigious Fisk University in Nashville, Tennessee, was tragically killed in a car accident. Derricotte's death infuriated the black community when it became known that she had been denied admission to a white hospital.

Her death also had a profound effect upon Cuthbert. By the fall of 1931, Cuthbert had left the South for good to enroll full-time in a doctoral program in psychology at Columbia, where her studies were supported by the National Council on Religion in Higher Education. There she carried on Derricotte's work. In 1932, Cuthbert became a secretary of the National Board of the YWCA, focusing her efforts in the fields of professional development and counseling. She organized and led many institutes on leadership development for the volunteers and professionals of the national YWCA, traveled throughout the United States and Europe, and became much sought after as a speaker.

Cuthbert continued to take summer courses at Columbia between 1932 and 1935. In 1940, after receiving a Julius Rosenwald Graduate Fellowship, she was finally able to return to Columbia full-time to complete her dissertation. "Education and Marginality: A Study of the Negro Woman College Graduate" was a pathbreaking study of black women graduates in forty communities across the country. Cuthbert examined the marginality that many black college-educated women experienced in the professional world, and suggested that they should take the lead in the betterment of the black community and also do more interracial work with liberal white women. Her work remains a classic in the study of black higher education. She received her doctorate from Teachers College in 1942.

In 1944, Charles S. Johnson, the first African American president of Fisk University, aggressively pursued Cuthbert for a position as associate director of the new Race Relations Institute that was being established at Fisk. Cuthbert turned down the offer, explaining that she preferred to work on racial issues in her personal rather than her professional life. She chose instead to join the faculty of Brooklyn College in 1944 and became one of the few African American professors there and the first black woman to serve as dean of women.

In 1961, Cuthbert, who remained single throughout her life, retired from Brooklyn College and moved to her country home in Plainfield, New Hampshire, where she devoted her days to writing and activism. Cuthbert authored numerous volumes of poetry, children's books, and short stories. Locally, she served on the board of the Plainfield library, the College Women's Club, and the Community Baptist Church. She also made a profound contribution to many national organizations concerned with social and racial justice, human rights, and world peace. She was on the board of the National Association for the Advancement of Colored People (NAACP), a fellow of the National Council on Religion in Higher Education, a member of the Council of Church Women United, and the National Conference of Christians and Jews. When Cuthbert's health began to fail, she lived in a series of nursing homes in Concord, New Hampshire, and Windsor, Vermont. In 1989, Marion Cuthbert died at the age of ninety-three in Claremont, New Hampshire. She requested that her ashes be scattered from the top of nearby Mount Ascutney.

Bibliography: The Marion Vera Cuthbert Papers are housed at the Spelman College Archives in Atlanta, Georgia. The collection includes Cuthbert's correspondence, YWCA writings, published and unpublished creative and academic writings, photographs, address books, speeches, and memorial service tapes. Information regarding her Rosenwald Fellowship is located in the Julius Rosenwald Papers, Special Collections, Fisk University, Nashville, Tennessee. Correspondence with Charles S. Johnson is found in the Charles S. Johnson Papers, Special Collections at Fisk University; YWCA information is available in Cuthbert's Personnel file, National YWCA Papers, Smith College Archives, Northampton, Massachusetts. Some of Cuthbert's writings include *Juliette Derricotte* (1933); *We Sing America* (1936); *Democracy and the Negro* (1936); *April Grasses* (1936); *Education and Marginality: A Study of the Negro Woman College Graduate* (originally her PhD thesis, Columbia University, 1942; reprinted 1987); and *Songs of Creation* (1949).

LINDA M. PERKINS

D

DACHÉ, Lilly. ca. 1892–December 31, 1989. Milliner, merchandiser.

Hats with cherries and hats without; sleek-fitting cloches, exotic turbans, glamorous snoods; even something called the half-hat—such was the stock-in-trade of Lilly Daché, one of America's leading milliners in the years prior to and following World War II. In those days respectable women did not leave the house without wearing something atop their heads, and Daché crowned many of them. "Believe me, I have made many hats," she wrote in her breezy 1946 autobiography, *Talking through My Hats.* "Perhaps I have made more hats than any other one woman in the world" (p. 4). Daché was guilty of only slight exaggeration. Producing as many as nine thousand hats a year during her heyday in the 1940s, she not only generated millions of dollars in sales (at a time when a decent hat could be had for $2.95, run-of-the-line Daché creations ranged in price from $39.50 to $79.50) but also set the nation's millinery styles.

Chic, excitable, and "highly perfumed," Daché was "everybody's idea of a French woman," related Margaret Case Harriman in a 1942 *New Yorker* profile of the milliner (p. 20). From time to time, however, doubts about Daché's origins surfaced, and it was speculated that she was Polish, or Romanian, or Jewish. Daché, however, would have none of it, doggedly clinging to her identity as the daughter of a French Catholic farmer from Bordeaux and his style-conscious wife. Her parents' names are not known, but she did volunteer that she was born in Bègles, France, and was the first of five children. Whatever her roots, Daché remained her own, and probably most successful, creation.

According to Daché, her childhood alternated between the urban Parisian world her mother loved and the rural life in Bordeaux preferred by her father. After serving an apprenticeship with some of Paris's leading milliners, Daché arrived in the United States in 1924. Following a series of low-paying jobs as a salesgirl, including a brief stint at Macy's where she didn't take to the monotony of filling out sales slips, the young French milliner, then in her early thirties, found herself on Manhattan's affluent Upper West Side, a neighborhood liberally sprinkled with all kinds of stores from florists to dress shops. In one of these stores, the Bonnet Shop at Broadway and 77th Street, her career took off. Upon learning that the store's owner was planning to leave the business, Daché, together with a co-worker, bought it on installment for a thousand dollars. A few months later, she bought out her partner. By 1926, within two years of arriving in the New World, Lilly Daché had her own shop where her fanciful, custom-made chapeaux soon attracted a considerable local following.

In short order, one store quickly grew to two and then to three, prompting Daché in 1928 to consolidate her operations into one establishment in midtown Manhattan. In 1937, Daché built what she liked to call the "house that is made of hats" (Daché, *Talking through My Hats,* p. 5): the Daché Building at 78 East 56th Street, a swanky, nine-story building whose glass-bricked facade and air-conditioned interiors were the very latest in architectural fashion. Each floor in the Daché Building was given over to a different aspect of the business: one floor for wholesale trade, another for retail customers, a third for workrooms. The top two floors were reserved for the private use of Daché along with her husband, Jean Despres, a vice president at Coty whom she married in 1931, and their adopted daughter, Suzanne.

The interior of the Daché Building was as luxurious as its exterior. Thickly carpeted, heavily mirrored, and upholstered in pink silk and leopard prints, the selling floors more closely resembled the rooms of a fancy private home or a Hollywood film set than a place where money exchanged hands. In fact, all fixtures that even remotely smacked of a business transaction—counters, display cases, adding machines—were deliberately hidden from sight.

Despite the Depression and World War II, Lilly Daché prospered throughout the 1930s and 1940s as American women found that a new hat was a relatively inexpensive way to refresh a wardrobe and their spirits. Not even a strike by the Millinery Workers' Union, which lasted for two years in the early 1940s, adversely affected her business. Hats are an emotional thing, she once wrote, explaining their hold on American women. Daché's continued success was also largely built upon her customer base, which was drawn from the well-connected and the deep-pocketed, from show-business personalities and socialites to those in the news. Its ranks included Gertrude Lawrence, marlene dietrich (who wore Daché's hats in her movie *Desire*), Carmen Miranda, LOUELLA PARSONS, and DOROTHY PARKER. ELEANOR ROOSEVELT called on Daché to create a hat that would require no fuss or bother. Women used to fight for her hats, the milliner proudly recalled in a 1967 interview.

Daché's success was also a function of her ongoing inventiveness and market savvy. Awarded a Lord & Taylor design prize in 1941, Daché was hailed for being one of the first to make use of plastic vinyl, or "vinylite" as it was then called. During the war years, when traditional millinery materials were in short supply, Daché used lucite in lieu of ribbon and kitchen twine instead of straw. A decade later, hoping to appeal to a younger generation of American woman, she created a number of lower-priced hat lines variously called "Dachettes," "Lilly's Dillies," and "Mlle. Lilly." In the mid 1950s and into the 1960s, as hats began to disappear along with white gloves and other conventions of ladylike behavior, Daché turned to the manufacture of clothing, beauty products, hair ornaments, and perfume, including two scents called "Drifting" and "Dashing."

"America's foremost milliner" retired in 1968 and then divided her time between Florida and France. She died in 1989 at the age of ninety-seven in a nursing home in Louvecienne, France. Lilly Daché is no longer a household word nor do too many women these days sport a hat, let alone a Daché creation. All the same, Daché's contribution to American business history and to the interior life of America's women endures, reminding us, as she herself put it, that the "right hat on the right head is poetry" (Daché, *Talking through My Hats*, p. 234).

Bibliography: Lilly Daché, *Talking through My Hats,* edited by Dorothy Roe Lewis (1946), offers a lighthearted, autobiographical account of the milliner's rise to success. "$200,000,000 Worth of Hats," *Fortune,* January 1935, pp. 50–55, 82–84, profiles the millinery industry, detailing Daché's involvement in it; "Milliner Builds Multi-Story Establishment," *Architectural Record* 83 (March 1938), pp. 52–56, describes the glories of the house that Daché built. Margaret Case Harriman, "Hats Will Be Worn," *New Yorker,* April 4, 1942, pp. 20–25, provides a witty and insightful look at the colorful milliner. Hambla Bauer, "Lady, Where Did You Get That Hat!" *Saturday Evening Post,* April 13, 1946, pp. 26–7, 110–16, analyzes the relationship between custom milliners such as Daché and the manufacturers of inexpensive, mass-produced hats. Bernadine Morris, "The Everlasting Lilly Daché," *New York Times,* October 14, 1967, salutes Daché for her steadfastness. *Women's Wear Daily* is an indispensable source for insights into Daché's collections and millinery fashion more generally. Jenna Weissman Joselit, *A Perfect Fit: Clothes, Character, and the Promise of America* (2001), explores pre–World War II America's growing fascination with clothing and accessories. Daché's hats, along with a series of her sketches, can be found at the Fashion Institute of Technology. Her hats can also be found at the Parsons School of Design and the Costume Institute of the Metropolitan Museum of Art, and in the private hands of costume collectors. An obituary appeared in the *New York Times* on January 2, 1990.

JENNA WEISSMAN JOSELIT

DAHL-WOLFE, Louise. November 19, 1895–December 11, 1989. Photographer.

Louise Emma Augusta Dahl—her mother believed that it was lucky to have initials that spelled a word—was born in boomtown San Francisco. Her parents, Emma O. Wilberg and Knut Martin Dahl, had emigrated from Norway. The youngest of three daughters, she vividly recalled the San Francisco earthquake of 1906, particularly the refugees escaping to the hills and the ash that descended on their house when the city burned. Her father, a marine engineer, took his daughters to ship christenings as recreation on Sunday afternoons.

Louise Dahl first trained in art at the San Francisco Institute of Art, starting in 1914. Art training at that time was dominated by academic copies of classical casts, but she later commented that learning color theory from Rudolph Schaeffer, a recently arrived German teacher, was the most important part of her training there. When Diaghilev's Ballet Russe came to San Francisco, she was dazzled by their avant-garde dance, music, sets, and costumes. Discouraged from pursuing painting by a teacher, she planned to study interior decorating in New York, but when her father died unexpectedly in 1919 she decided to stay in San Francisco designing electric signs.

Dahl's interest in photography began when she met well-known pictorial photographer Annie Brigman around 1921. Pictorialism, with its soft-focus romantic images of nude figures in nature, was still prominent in those years, but sharp-focus photography and close-ups were already emerging as the modern style of art photography. Louise Dahl began working with a reflex camera under the guidance of her friend Consuelo Kanaga, a pioneering photojournalist, and she learned to do her own enlarging. She also met photographers like the experimentalist Francis Bruguierre and the modernist Edward Weston.

In 1923 she moved to New York City to study interior decorating, then returned to work for a prestigious decorating firm in San Francisco the following year. In 1926 her mother was killed in a car accident while she was in the car. To recover from her grief, she went on an extended trip to Europe. While traveling with Consuelo Kanaga she met her future husband, the artist Meyer "Mike" Wolfe, in Kairouan, Tunisia, in 1928. They married in New York the same year and remained happily married until his death in 1985. They did not have children.

In 1929–30 she worked as a photographer for interior decorators in New York and San Francisco, then spent a summer in a log cabin in the Smoky Mountains in 1932. Her first focused documentary works were intense but informal portraits of the mountain people of Tennessee. When she returned to New York in the winter of 1933, one of her Tennessee photographs was published in *Vanity Fair.*

After three years of freelance photography in

food and fashion, she became the staff photographer for *Harper's Bazaar* in 1936, a position that she was to hold for twenty-two years. Both location and color photography were in their infancy when Dahl-Wolfe joined *Harper's*. Sportswear and the healthy active woman who wore it were just emerging as subjects in fashion photography. With her background in art, Dahl-Wolfe revolutionized the look of fashion photography, brilliantly matching the model, fashion, and setting. Long before Andy Warhol, Dahl-Wolfe bridged the worlds of high and low art, of fashion, and of the women for whom the elegant clothes were made. Her 1943 photograph of seventeen-year-old Lauren Bacall launched the film star's career.

The Dahl-Wolfe model is statuesque and classical in her features and bearing. These svelte women have features as smooth as glass. They are independent women who pursue sports and leisure with elegance. They do not actually engage in any activity, except perhaps meditation on artwork, but they appear to command all that they survey, and to have a real sense of their own power, gained through their magnificent and perfect clothes. Hair is tightly coiffed; hats and turbans are defining accessories. Sexuality is contained by sleek, tailored, buttoned-up suits and dresses. Dahl-Wolfe's cool, elegant women are not about bodies (except legs) but about clothes and pose. Dahl-Wolfe herself was short and squat, and not at all beautiful in her appearance, a striking contrast to her models. Frequently she used a sharp upward angle for the photograph, making her models seem larger than life.

Dahl-Wolfe frequently combined fashion with art. Her models posed against backgrounds inspired by contemporary art (often created in collaboration with her husband) or with artworks that ranged from Noguchi lamps to a pre-Columbian Chac-mool in a temple in the Yucatan. She pioneered the idea of posing models at the Museum of Modern Art or in art galleries. In one outstanding example, taken during World War II, she posed a model in front of the head of an Etruscan warrior at the Metropolitan Museum of Art. The silhouette of the model brilliantly echoes the silhouette and colors (earthen tones) of the masked soldier's face.

She meticulously crafted the cropping and color of her image as well as the layout in the magazine, working in collaboration with *Harper's* editor, Carmel Snow, and fashion editor DIANA VREELAND. Dahl-Wolfe's sense of color was impeccable, achieved by hours of looking for the right location and adjusting color balance in the printing process. She highlighted pale beiges, browns, or blues with a splash of red, brilliant lighting, and angular compositions. Buildings, landscapes or art subtly complemented the colors of the dress. When she left *Harper's* in 1958, it was the end of an era.

Her portrait photography is also sensitive, displaying an ability to convey the character of her sitter through clothes and pose. Her early portraits of people from Tennessee are both personal and respectful. While working for *Harper's*, she was asked to photograph Hollywood stars like Orson Wells, writers like Eudora Welty, and celebrity designers such as her friend Cecil Beaton.

In 1957 Dahl-Wolfe began to work for *Sports Illustrated*, producing a series of photographs of gourmet cooks and sports fashions. She made photographs for *Vogue* in 1959, and traveled to Rome for *Sports Illustrated* in 1960, before she retired from photography. She moved to Frenchtown, New Jersey, in 1961. She died of pneumonia at age ninety-four in a nursing home in Allendale, New Jersey, on December 11, 1989.

Bibliography: Archival manuscript sources documenting Louise Dahl-Wolfe's career are found at the Center for Creative Photography, University of Arizona, Tucson; at the Fashion Institute of Technology, New York City; and in private papers in the hands of the artist's niece Else and her husband Hans Ege. The Staley-Wise Gallery, New York City, has a complete inventory of her photographs. The main sources of writings by Louise Dahl-Wolfe are *Louise Dahl-Wolfe: A Photographer's Scrapbook* (1984), and Margaretta K. Mitchell, ed., *Recollections: Ten Women of Photography* (1979). Exhibition catalogs with major essays on Louise Dahl-Wolfe include Sally Eauclaire, *Louise Dahl-Wolfe: A Retrospective Exhibition* (National Museum of Women in the Arts, Washington, D.C., 1987), and *Louise Dahl-Wolfe* (2000), with a foreword by Dorothy Twining Globus, essays by Vicki Goldberg and Nan Richardson, and a complete bibliography. Useful articles are by John A. Cuadrado, "The Fashion Image: Louise Dahl-Wolfe, A Pioneering Photographer's Eye for Style," *Architectural Digest*, September 1988, p. 66+; John Duka, "A Chronicler of Fashion, at 88, Reflects on Change," *New York Times*, September 28, 1984; Peter Estersohn, "First Lady of Fashion Photography Louise Dahl Wolfe," *Interview*, February 1981, p. 30; and Vicki Goldberg, "Profile: Louise Dahl-Wolfe," *American Photographer* 6, no. 6 (June 1981), pp. 38–47. An obituary appeared in the *New York Times* on December 13, 1989.

SUSAN NOYES PLATT

DANILOVA, Alexandra. November 20, 1903–July 13, 1997. Ballet dancer and teacher.

Alexandra Dionisievna Danilova, one of the twentieth century's most celebrated ballerinas, was born in Peterhof, Russia, a town west of St. Petersburg. Danilova later wrote that her father, Dionis Danilov, caught a fatal illness while hunting and that her mother, Claudia Gotovtzeva, died while nursing him when Alexandra was two years old. Alexandra and her older sister Elena remained in Peterhof with their grandmother until her death two years later. When Alexandra was about four, she was adopted by Lidia Mstislavna Gototsova. Elena, adopted by another family, remained in Russia after the Revolution and wrote regularly to Danilova in later years, but the letters stopped during the siege of Leningrad in World War II and Danilova was never able to trace her after that.

Soon after adopting Danilova, Gototsova married General Mikhail Ivanovitch Batianov, one of Russia's leading military figures. The family had no connection with the arts, and it was unheard of for girls in her class to train professionally, but when Danilova was seven her school put on a Christmas recital with her as a butterfly. She was so enthralled by dancing that one of her stepbrothers suggested she apply to the Imperial Ballet School in St. Petersburg, which was attached to the Maryinsky Theatre. She was accepted into the cloistered, dedicated boarding school and began training in August 1911. She studied with a series of former Maryinsky dancers, including Elisaveta Gerdt and Olga Preobrazhenskaya, and one of her fellow students was the choreographer George Balanchine.

The outbreak of World War I did not have much effect on the Imperial Ballet School, but the 1917 Russian Revolution did. Despite the privation and disruption it caused in her training, Danilova graduated in 1920 and joined the State Academic Theatre for Opera and Ballet, as the Maryinsky was then called. She became a soloist in 1922. The minister of fine arts, Anatoly Lunacharsky, supported the ballet as a Russian art form, and the pre-Revolutionary works of Marius Petipa and Lev Ivanov continued in the repertoire. Danilova's first solo role was Prayer in the 1870 ballet *Coppélia,* a ballet with which she was associated for many years.

George Balanchine had already begun choreographing experimental works, and Danilova took part in his small group, Young Ballet. In 1924 four members of that group, including Danilova and Balanchine, received permission to tour Germany for the summer recess, expecting to return for the fall ballet season. They attracted the interest of Serge Diaghilev, the expatriate director of the Ballets Russes, and he asked them to join his company; they did, and were then permanently exiled from Russia. Danilova danced for Diaghilev until his death in 1929, performing in ballets by Michel Fokine, Balanchine, Bronislava Nijinska, and Léonide Massine, whose works became closely associated with her. As a dancer she considered herself a *soubrette,* someone with a classical technique who could convey character.

She and Balanchine had been living together as wife and husband since 1927, but Diaghilev's dancers scattered after his death and the couple drifted apart, finally separating in 1931. Danilova danced with the Monte Carlo Opera for the next two years and from 1931 to 1932 danced in the musical *Waltzes from Vienna* on London's West End stage. Whenever possible, she continued studying with Russian émigré teachers, including Lubov Egorova, Nikolai Legat, and Nijinska, who taught her to be expressive without using the old formal mime. While she was in London, she married Guiseppe Massera, an Italian engineer, in 1932 or 1933; he did not want her to continue dancing, and they soon separated. He died in 1936.

Several impresarios—inheritors of the Diaghilev repertory, if not of his taste—attracted the members of the former Diaghilev company as well as students emerging from the Russian émigré schools in Paris. In 1933 Massine asked Danilova to join one of these groups, de Basil's Ballets Russes. There she assumed the role of the Street Dancer in Massine's *Le Beau Danube.* Danilova was not happy in the company and left in 1938 to join Massine and Serge Denham, a Russian American émigré and former banker who had formed the Ballet Russe de Monte Carlo. One of Massine's early creations for the company was *Gaîte Parisienne,* and Danilova soon assumed the part of the Glove Seller, another of her signature roles. Massine also invited Nicholas Sergeyev, formerly from the Maryinsky, to mount the full-length *Coppélia* for her.

World War II meant that the company lost its Monte Carlo base, and it moved to the United States. Lacking a permanent home, they mainly toured, usually in a series of one- or two-night stands in small towns on problematic stages introducing ballet to countless audiences. Danilova was the leading dancer from 1938 to 1951, often partnered by Frederick Franklin. Her professionalism and dedication in difficult circumstances were legendary, as were her legs. Her February 14, 1941, marriage to Ballet Russe soloist Kasimir Kokich was annulled on July 15, 1948, though she remained on good terms with him and his new wife, and was their daughter's godmother; she never had children of her own. Her final appearance as a regular member of the Ballet Russe was as the Glove Seller on December 30, 1951, in Dallas.

After she left the Ballet Russe, she danced with the Slavenska-Franklin Ballet for a year, and then went to Dallas to teach. In 1956 she formed a small troupe, Great Moments of Ballet, which toured the United States and several foreign countries. Her last stage appearance as a dancer was as Raymonda in Tokyo in September 1957, though she appeared on Broadway in the 1958 musical *Oh*

Captain! She also appeared in the 1977 film *The Turning Point.*

In 1963 Balanchine invited her to teach classical variations to students at the School of American Ballet, and in 1964 she joined the faculty there; she taught until her retirement in 1989, and staged ballets for the school's annual workshops. Though as a dancer she often worked with twentieth-century choreographers, as a teacher and stager she emphasized the classical ballet of her youth. In 1974 she and Balanchine staged *Coppélia* for the New York City Ballet; the first two acts, Danilova's responsibility, were based on the old Ballet Russe production.

Alexandra Danilova became a U.S. citizen in the late 1940s, was awarded the Capezio Prize in 1958, and was a Kennedy Center honoree in 1989. She died at her home in Manhattan in 1997 at the age of ninety-three and is buried at Oakland Cemetery, in Sag Harbor, near her compatriot and frequent collaborator George Balanchine.

Bibliography: The Alexandra Danilova Collection at the Library of Congress has her personal letters, class notebooks, and clipping files. The Dance Collection at the New York Public Library for the Performing Arts at Lincoln Center has Danilova's oral history (taped in 1975, 1977–78, and 1992), which recounts primarily her professional life. The Dance Collection also has letters and documents dealing with her career with the Ballet Russe de Monte Carlo as well as many photographs and videos. Danilova's autobiography, *Choura: The Memoirs of Alexandra Danilova* (1986), written with Holly Bruback, is chatty and evocative, as is the earlier *Alexandra Danilova* by A. E. Twysden (1947), written by a devotee of Danilova's with her cooperation. Jack Anderson's *The One and Only: The Ballet Russe de Monte Carlo* (1981) contains vivid descriptions of life on tour. Joan Acocella's biography of Danilova in the *International Encyclopedia of Dance* (1998) was prepared with Danilova's assistance. Danilova was also the subject of Anne Belle's documentary film, *Reflections of a Dancer* (1981). An obituary appeared in the *New York Times* on July 15, 1997.

MARY CARGILL

DAVIS, Bette. April 5, 1908–October 6, 1989. Actress.

At her best, Bette Davis put complicated, conflicted women on the screen at a time when most screen characters were still melodramatic simplifications. A small (five foot three) blue-eyed blonde, she was unfazed by the cant of her era that considered screen acting inferior to acting on the stage. An actress first and a star second—and in no way a conventional beauty—she invented a jagged, sincere, many-sided style of film acting that continues to reverberate through the generations.

Born Ruth Elizabeth Davis in Lowell, Massachusetts, she was the elder of two daughters of Harlow Morrell Davis, a patent lawyer from a Yankee family of long standing, and Ruth Favor, a homemaker of French Huguenot descent. The couple, incompatible almost from the start, divorced when Betty was ten. As a result, she and her younger sister, Barbara, were educated in a patchwork of public and private schools in New York, New Jersey, and Massachusetts—wherever Ruth Davis could find work as a professional photographer or housemother. Popular and active as child, Betty changed the spelling of her name in imitation of Balzac's *La Cousine Bette* and finally graduated from Cushing Academy, a boarding school in Ashburnham, Massachusetts, in 1926.

By 1927, a nineteen-year-old Bette Davis was attending the John Murray Anderson–Robert Milton School of Theatre and Dance in New York. Although she starred in term plays and studied with MARTHA GRAHAM, Davis was temperamentally restless and eager to earn a living. She left school before her first year was over, rushing headlong into professional engagements on and off Broadway, on tour, and with numerous stock companies, among them George Cukor's repertory theater in Rochester, New York.

After opening on Broadway in *Solid South* (1930), she received her first offer from a Hollywood film studio. With a few exceptions—most notably *Cabin in the Cotton* (1932)—Davis's first years in Hollywood produced nothing extraordinary. Then, in 1934, after a long campaign, she convinced Warners to loan her to RKO to play the sociopathic cockney Mildred Rogers in their adaptation of *Of Human Bondage,* and got her first star-making notices. The next year she won an Oscar for Best Actress for *Dangerous* (1935), in which she played an alcoholic actress patterned on the Broadway legend Jeanne Eagels.

In 1936, Warners had to sue to prevent her from violating her contract and making a film in England for the Italian producer Ludovico Toeplitz. When she returned to Warners, however, she was treated generously, starring next in *Jezebel* (1938), a finely wrought study of the anger and ambivalence of a southern belle. The performance—fueled by an adulterous affair with the film's director, William Wyler—brought her a second Oscar, as best actress of 1938. The next year she played the role that she sometimes referred to as her favorite, Judith Traherne, the mortally ill heroine of *Dark Victory* (1939). After *Dark Victory,* Bette Davis starred in an unbroken string of sixteen box-office successes, playing everything from genteel novelists to murderous housewives to self-hateful spinsters to a sexagenarian Queen Elizabeth I. Her most memorable films from this remarkably productive period included *The Old Maid* (1939), *The*

Little Foxes (1941), *Now, Voyager* (1942), *Watch on the Rhine* (1943), and *The Corn Is Green* (1945).

In 1932 she had married her high school sweetheart, Harmon Nelson, a freelance musician. But the marriage was as rocky as her parents', and in 1938 Nelson found her with Howard Hughes and divorced her. Davis married again in 1940, to New England hotelier Arthur Farnsworth; he died in 1943 from a mysterious compound skull fracture.

The war years were Bette Davis's prime, and not only on screen. In 1941 she became the first woman president of the Academy of Motion Picture Arts and Sciences, quitting when she realized she was little more than a figurehead. In 1942, with John Garfield, she co-founded the Hollywood Canteen. Totally committed to her role as the organization's president, she danced, ate, and clowned almost nightly with the servicemen passing through Los Angeles.

Yet after the war, Davis's career began to sink, with terrible films such as *Beyond the Forest* (1949), more parodies of Davis vehicles than the real thing. Released from her Warners contract, she freelanced. At forty-two, she seriously believed her career was over, until her performance in *All about Eve* (1950), where she played, not coincidentally, an explosive theatrical prima donna who was terrified of aging. For her performance as Margo Channing, New York Film Critics named her the year's best actress.

Having divorced William Grant Sherry, a painter whom she had married in 1945, in 1950 she married *All about Eve*'s leading man, Gary Merrill. With Sherry, Davis had had one child, a daughter, Barbara Davis Sherry, nicknamed B.D. (1947). With Merrill, she adopted two others, Margot Mosher Merrill (1951), who was brain damaged, and Michael Woodman Merrill (1952). The Merrills lived in Cape Elizabeth, Maine.

By 1960, while Davis and Merrill were touring together in *The World of Carl Sandburg*, it became clear that that marriage was finished, and they divorced. In her best-selling autobiography, *The Lonely Life* (1962), she took responsibility for her failed marriages, but wondered if somewhere there wasn't a man who could tame her. In the book's coda, a long, agonized meditation on women and freedom, Davis ruefully compared herself to her character Julie Marsden in *Jezebel* and confessed that in her relationships with men, she had always had to remain in charge, but inevitably lost respect for them when they allowed her to.

In 1962, no longer a box-office name, she took a role in an offbeat, low-budget psychological thriller, *What Ever Happened to Baby Jane?*, poignantly playing a homicidally demented middle-aged former child star alongside co-star JOAN CRAWFORD. The film was a megahit, bringing Davis her tenth, and final, Oscar nomination. The downside of this comeback was that for years afterward, she was offered almost nothing but lurid films about decrepit gorgons, and in films like *The Nanny* (1965) became something of a laughingstock.

In the new era of made-for-TV films and miniseries, however, worthwhile roles came to her again, including a part as a pathetic recluse in *Strangers* (1979), for which she won a best-actress Emmy. In 1977, the American Film Institute bestowed on her its Life Achievement Award; she was the first woman to receive it. Almost more prominent than she had been at her zenith, she now found herself hailed by a new generation of film critics who were seeing her classic films for the first time, while new stars—most notably Jane Fonda—praised her warmly as an influence and a role model.

In 1983, she suffered breast cancer and a stroke. Despite permanent damage to her speech and gait, she continued making films. In 1985, Davis was shattered when her daughter, B. D. Hyman, published a contemptuous family memoir, *My Mother's Keeper.* She feebly tried to respond in her own book, *This 'n That* (1987). Then, looking dismayingly frail, she played a scrappy octogenarian opposite LILLIAN GISH in *The Whales of August* (1987), a sensitive study of old age.

Bette Davis died of cancer in Paris in 1989, having gone to Europe to accept an award at a Spanish film festival. Eighty-one at the time of her death, she left behind on film a brilliant constellation of contrasting and vibrant figures, the legacy of sixty years of hard work and dedication to what she liked to call total realism on the screen.

Bibliography: A collection of Davis's personal papers, photographs, scripts, and scrapbooks is located at the Twentieth Century Archives, Boston University. An outstanding source of information is Randall Riese, *All about Bette* (1993), which contains a filmography and a complete list of Davis's awards. Biographies include Shaun Considine, *Bette and Joan: The Divine Feud* (1989); Charles Higham, *Bette: The Life of Bette Davis* (1981); Barbara Leaming, *Bette Davis: A Biography* (1992); and James Spada, *More than a Woman* (1993). Davis wrote two autobiographies, *The Lonely Life* (1962), with Sanford Dody, and *This 'n That* (1987), with Michael Herskowitz. Memoirs wholly or in part about Bette Davis include Sanford Dody, *Giving Up the Ghost* (1980); Elizabeth Fuller, *Me and Jezebel: When Bette Davis Came for Dinner—and Stayed* (1992); Vincent Sherman, *Studio Affairs* (1996); and Whitney Stine, *I'd Love to Kiss You . . .* (1990). See also *Time*, March 28, 1938, pp. 33–34; *Current Biography* (1941, 1953); and Janet Flanner, "Cotton-Dress Girl," *New Yorker*, February 20, 1943, pp. 19–24. Some information in this essay is taken from a taped interview with Bette Davis by Elliott Sirkin on April 25, 1980. Obituaries appeared in the *Los Angeles Times* and *New York Times* on October 8, 1989, and in *Variety* on October 9, 1989.

ELLIOTT L. SIRKIN

DAWIDOWICZ, Lucy S. June 16, 1915–December 5, 1990. Historian, writer.

Lucy Dawidowicz, whose pioneering scholarship on the Nazi destruction of European Jewry shaped the field of Holocaust studies, was born Lucy Schildkret in New York City, the eldest of two daughters of Polish Jewish immigrants, Dora Ofnaem and Max Schildkret. Dawidowicz's family struggled financially—her mother worked mainly as a millinery operator and her father as a salesman and shop owner—but their home was rich in books, newspapers, and ideas. Avowed secularists, Dawidowicz's parents stressed Yiddish language and culture as the basis of their children's Jewish identities. Max and Dora Schildkret were members of the socialist yiddishist organization, the Workmen's Circle, and they spoke both Yiddish and English with their children at home. Dawidowicz also received a bilingual education. During the day she attended public schools in New York City; on afternoons and weekends, she attended the yiddishist Sholem Aleichem *folkshuln* (folk schools), where she discovered the Jewish history and culture to which she would devote so much of her career.

Still, as a student at all-girls Hunter College High School (1928–32) and Hunter College (1932–36), Dawidowicz's main love was reading and writing English literature and poetry. She graduated from Hunter with a BA in English literature and briefly continued her literary studies as a master's student at Columbia University. Dropping out of the program in 1936, Dawidowicz grew preoccupied with the crisis facing European Jewry, particularly the Jews of Poland. Nazism, fascism, and anti-Semitism were on the rise, and Eastern European Jewry was facing economic and social isolation. On the suggestion of Jacob Shatsky, a former Yiddish school teacher, Dawidowicz redirected her studies to the Jewish experience. In 1937, she re-enrolled at Columbia University as a master's student in history and planned to write a thesis on the Yiddish press of England.

After completing her course work, Dawidowicz embarked for a fellowship year at the Yiddish Scientific Institute (YIVO), the preeminent research institution of East European Jewry, in Vilna, Poland. The experience transformed Dawidowicz's agenda as a Jew and a historian. Arriving in August 1938, as Europe was falling swiftly under Nazi domination, Dawidowicz daily encountered Polish Jewry's perilous situation. Vilna was regarded as the "Jerusalem of the West" and center of Yiddish life, but its Jewish community was increasingly threatened by poverty and anti-Semitism. Dawidowicz left Poland late in the summer of 1939 fearing for the future of Eastern European Jewry and determined to preserve its legacy through her research.

Dawidowicz pursued this mission with her characteristic boldness and energy, becoming one of the foremost Jewish historians of her time and for decades one of only a handful of women in her field. From 1940 to 1946, she worked in the New York offices of YIVO as assistant to the research director, Max Weinreich. YIVO had moved its headquarters from Vilna to New York in 1940, and Dawidowicz helped the organization reconstitute its mission and archival holdings in the United States. In 1946–47, under the auspices of the Joint Distribution Committee, Dawidowicz served as an education officer in Germany's displaced persons camps. Her main responsibility was to supply the camps with school, library, and newspaper supplies, but she also worked to recover books and manuscripts that the Nazis had stolen from YIVO's Vilna library.

Dawidowicz spent the next two decades, from 1948 to 1969, as a research analyst and ultimately research director for the American Jewish Committee, one of the premier Jewish communal organizations in the United States. She moved next to Yeshiva University in New York, where from 1969 to 1978 she served as professor of social history and held an endowed chair in Holocaust studies. Dawidowicz left Yeshiva University in 1978 to devote herself full-time to writing.

Dawidowicz published widely on topics in modern Jewish history and culture but is best known for helping to create the field of Holocaust studies. Her pathbreaking account of the Nazi persecution of European Jewry, *The War against the Jews, 1933–1945* (1975), positioned her as a leading Holocaust historian and articulator of the "intentionalist" school of Holocaust scholarship. In contrast to the "functionalists," who contended that the plan to murder European Jewry arose from piecemeal decisions and institutional factors over the course of World War II, Dawidowicz argued that genocidal anti-Semitism was always essential to Hitler's and the Nazis' war aims. *The War against the Jews* also draws from Jewish sources to illuminate the Holocaust from the perspective of its victims. Most significantly, Dawidowicz challenges claims made in the early 1960s and 1970s that Jews behaved passively in the ghettoes and camps. She demonstrates, rather, that Jews mounted resistance efforts in the face of insurmountable odds. She reiterates these themes in a companion volume, *A Holocaust Reader*

(1976), a compilation of documents tracing the origins and implementation of the "final solution."

Though much of Dawidowicz's research focused on the Holocaust, she was also committed to illuminating the Jewish communities and culture that had flourished before the Nazi era. In *The Golden Tradition: Jewish Life and Thought in Eastern Europe* (1967), Dawidowicz captures the vibrant and dynamic community of rabbis and radicals, socialists and Zionists, through a kaleidoscopic collection of pre–World War II Jewish writing. She devotes more than half of her memoir, *From That Place and Time* (1989), to her year in Poland because "Vilna exists now only in memory and in history. I wanted to reconstruct, as best I could, the Vilna I knew . . . to bestow upon it and its Jews a posthumous life" (pp. xiii–xiv).

Although raised in a secular and socialist-leaning home and a member of the Young Communist League in college, Dawidowicz became an observant Jew and outspoken neo-conservative later in life. She was an active public intellectual whose views on topics from Jewish identity to Israel to the relationship between feminism and Judaism appeared on the pages of major American periodicals and newspapers. Dawidowicz was married to Szymon M. Dawidowicz, a Polish Jewish refugee, from 1948 to his death in 1979. They had no children. She died in New York City from cancer on December 5, 1990, at the age of seventy-five. At the time of her death, Dawidowicz was working on a comprehensive history of American Jewry.

Bibliography: The Lucy Dawidowicz Papers are housed at the American Jewish Historical Society in New York City. The collection includes source materials from Dawidowicz's studies of American Jewish history, anti-Semitism, Holocaust denial, European Jewish history, and her memoir; clippings about her publications; biographical sketches; and photographs. Select materials on Dawidowicz can also be found at the American Jewish Archives, Hebrew Union College, Cincinnati. Her memoir, *From That Place and Time: A Memoir, 1938–1947* (1989), covers her time in Vilna through her work with displaced persons in Germany after the war. In addition to the works cited above, her books include *The Jewish Presence: Essays on Identity and History* (1977); *The Holocaust and the Historians* (1981); and *On Equal Terms: Jews in America 1881–1981* (1982). Her essays are collected in Neal Kozodoy, ed., *What Is the Use of Jewish History?* (1992), which also contains a useful introduction. Dawidowicz co-authored *Politics in a Pluralist Democracy* (1963) with Leon J. Goldstein, and co-edited *For Max Weinreich on His Seventieth Birthday: Studies in Jewish Language, Literature, and Society* (1964). Dawidowicz was a frequent contributor to *Commentary* magazine and other periodicals and newspapers. Additional information on Dawidowicz can be found in the *American Jewish Year Book* (1992), pp. 593–94; and the interview with Dawidowicz in *Publishers Weekly,* May 12, 1989, pp. 264–66. Obituaries appeared in several domestic and foreign newspapers, including the *New York Times* on December 6, 1990, and the *Guardian* on December 14, 1990.

RONA SHERAMY

DAY, Dorothy May. November 8, 1897–November 29, 1980. Journalist, spiritual leader, activist.

On May 1, 1933, Dorothy Day walked among the Communist demonstrators in Union Square in New York City, distributing the first issue of the *Catholic Worker.* The floundering that had characterized her life, and that she later documented in *The Long Loneliness* (1952), had come to an end. Through the *Catholic Worker*—the newspaper she co-founded and edited and the revolutionary religious and social movement that she embodied for more than four decades—Day would bring to the American Catholic Church a prophetic challenge: to truly be servant of the poor and peacemaker. Many in her lifetime called her a saint. Day responded that she did not want to be dismissed that easily.

The Long Loneliness is the conversion narrative of a woman always "haunted by God" (p. 9). Also an account of her coming of age, the book has shaped subsequent accounts of her early life. She was born in Brooklyn, New York, the third of five children of Grace Satterlee and John Day, a sports journalist who was well known in the horse-racing world. Always distant from her patriarchal and narrow-minded father, Day remained close to her mother, who provided a model of gentility even in hard times, and who depended on her daughter for emotional and practical support. Dorothy was also close to her younger sister, Della.

After living for two years in California, the Days moved to Chicago in 1906, where for a time they lived in poverty. Importantly, Chicago introduced Dorothy to the lives of the poor as she explored the world of Upton Sinclair's novels, and also to religious faith, personified especially in the mother of a school friend. Day graduated from Robert Waller High School and in 1914 went to the University of Illinois at Urbana on a scholarship. There she further developed her socialist consciousness and rejoiced in her independence. Eager to begin a writing career, Day left school in 1916 and moved to New York City, where her family was now living. Defying her father's disapproval, she went to work for the socialist paper *The Call,* and later, until its suppression for sedition, *The Masses,* and lived on the edge, financially and personally, of the literary and artistic bohemia of Greenwich Village. Her closest friendship was with Jewish writer Michael Gold, later editor of the Communist *Daily Worker.*

In 1917 a journalistic adventure led to the first of her many political arrests and imprisonments:

she was jailed with a group of suffragists after a Washington, D.C., protest, and went on a hunger strike with them. Day sympathized with the suffragists' resistance to oppression but not their solution: a philosophical anarchist, she never voted. The following year, troubled by what seemed a pointless life in a time of war and epidemic, she and Della entered nurses' training. At the hospital she met Lionel Moise, a journalist and adventurer. A doomed and desperate love affair marked by passion and humiliation led to pregnancy and an abortion; he deserted her. Day tells the story of the affair in her only published novel, the self-revelatory *The Eleventh Virgin* (1924), which is full of unfiltered detail of its heroine's life. Neither the affair nor her brief marriage (1920–21) to Barkeley Tobey appear in her later autobiography.

The Eleventh Virgin was sold to the movies, allowing Day—who loved the sea and wrote lyrically of the beauty of nature—to buy a cottage in a community of immigrant workers and radicals on Staten Island. She was living there in a common-law marriage with naturalist and anarchist Forster Batterham when she discovered she was pregnant. Having thought that she was unable to have children, her joy at the birth of her daughter, Tamar Teresa, on March 4, 1926, compelled the conversion toward which the narrative of her autobiography moves. Determined that her child would not repeat her disorderly life, and seeing the Catholic Church as the church of immigrants and the poor, Day had her daughter baptized as a Catholic. In 1927 Day sought baptism for herself. Batterham, adamantly opposed to organized religion and to marriage, resisted angrily and the relationship ended.

Day struggled to support her daughter and herself. She worked briefly in Hollywood as a screenwriter, did freelance journalism in Mexico, and depended on commissions from such liberal Catholic magazines as *America* and *Commonweal.* In Washington in December 1932 to cover the Hunger March of the Unemployed Councils, she yearned to join the demonstrators, wept with frustration at the incompatibility of her new faith and her political beliefs, and prayed for a solution. Waiting for her in New York, sent by the editor of *Commonweal,* was itinerant French philosopher and worker Peter Maurin, the improbable answer to her prayer.

He brought her news of a Catholic social teaching that she could reconcile with her radicalism. Maurin envisioned a Catholic lay movement based on voluntary poverty, a philosophy of labor, and the practice of the Works of Mercy. His call to a personalist revolution and the practice of voluntary poverty was congenial to Day's temperament and her political convictions, but she primarily focused on his proposal for a Catholic newspaper for the unemployed.

The first (May 1933) issue of the *Catholic Worker*—the name deliberately echoed the *Daily Worker*—reflected Dorothy Day's lifetime commitment to labor and to racial justice. The *Catholic Worker*'s call for a revolutionary response to the Depression based in the gospel and the practice of the Works of Mercy rapidly found an audience. There were 2500 copies of the first issue; within five years there were over 150,000 copies per issue, and Day found herself the voice of a new movement. Soon increasing numbers of the poor and hungry came seeking the freely given hospitality that the paper described, volunteers came to share the life of voluntary poverty, and the long history of the Catholic Worker houses of hospitality began. The first, opened in December 1933, was an apartment for ten women; within ten years, there were thirty Catholic Worker houses in American cities.

Philosophically resistant to asserting authority, Day was driven by her desire to serve the poor and to encourage others to do so. Financial neediness was a constant. The *Catholic Worker* never took funds from the state and never registered as a charitable organization for tax purposes, and Day begged ceaselessly for contributions. She worried, too, especially in the early years, about balancing responsibilities to her daughter and her work. Her sources of strength were the rituals, sacraments, and theology of the Catholic Church—daily Mass, the spiritual community of the doctrine of the Mystical Body—her wide reading, and the tangible community of the Catholic Worker houses.

From 1933 on, Day defined her professional role as editor and her vocation as writer, and she wrote into being the most important lay movement in the American Catholic Church. She sustained the movement with regular columns in the *Catholic Worker,* numerous articles in other publications, and her books: *From Union Square to Rome* (1938), an explanation of her conversion shaped to the objections of her Communist brother and friends; two accounts of the Catholic Worker's growth, *House of Hospitality* (1939) and *Loaves and Fishes* (1963); and a biography of her beloved Saint Thérèse of Lisieux (1960). Two compilations of her journals and columns—*On Pilgrimage* (1948; a "woman's book") and *On Pilgrimage: The Sixties* (1972)—include accounts of months spent with her daughter, who had married at eighteen and had nine children. Day was a lifelong source of support for Tamar and an enthusiastic grandmother.

Attributing her lucid and personal style to her newspaper training, Day wrote lovingly of the destitute, often deeply disturbed guests of the Catholic Worker. She welcomed scholars and students who were increasingly drawn to the movement. Jacques Maritain was a frequent visitor to the New York houses and an important influence. A young Michael Harrington came in 1951; *The Other America* (1962) had its source in his two years there. As the movement grew, Day was increasingly in demand as a speaker; she traveled widely by bus or in ramshackle donated cars. A memorable presence, she compelled the attention of audiences through the clarity and uncompromising directness of her message.

Dorothy Day's deep love for and loyalty to the Church did not silence her. Drawing on her convert's conviction of the responsibility and rights of laypersons, she criticized the institutional church when it failed to meet its own ideals. Deeply engaged throughout her life in the cause of racial justice, she urged lay Catholics to take personal responsibility to act boldly against racial discrimination. Most controversially, she rejected Catholic just-war theory and maintained the pacifism that she had first adopted during World War I.

On Pilgrimage: The Sixties tracks Day's many journeys. She went on a controversial visit to Cuba in 1962, eager to see the socialist revolution. In 1963 she traveled to Rome on a women's peace pilgrimage (Mothers for Peace) to thank Pope John XXIII for his encyclical *Pacem in Terris* (Peace on Earth), returning there in 1965 during the final session of the Second Vatican Council when the bishops were debating questions of war and peace. There Day joined a group of nineteen women in a ten-day fast for peace. The Council statement, *The Pastoral Constitution on the Church in the Modern World,* embraced many of the *Catholic Worker*'s goals: it validated the right of conscientious objection, recognized the witness of gospel-based nonviolence, and condemned indiscriminate warfare.

Dorothy Day's passionate convictions shaped Catholic pacifism. The logic of the Works of Mercy underlay her conviction: love and violence are incompatible. At the time of the Spanish civil war, when the Church was supporting Franco and the American left was supporting the rebels, the *Catholic Worker* announced a position of neutrality. The anger from both sides at that position was relatively mild compared to the response both within and outside the movement to the *Catholic Worker*'s declaration of opposition to United States involvement in World War II. Some longtime Workers left, some houses closed, and the paper's circulation dropped drastically. For Day no compromise was possible. Clear about the evils of Nazism, and always a fierce opponent of anti-Semitism, she endorsed the obligation to resist by any means except violence. Her position called her to the attention of the FBI, and surveillance continued for several decades.

In the 1950s, the *Catholic Worker* opposed the war in Korea and resisted the repression of the McCarthy era. Day also joined in the failed attempts to prevent the execution of Julius and ETHEL ROSENBERG. The movement's antinuclear activism inspired a civil disobedience campaign in the late 1950s: Catholic Workers defied New York City orders to go into civil defense shelters during air raid drills, arguing that cooperation would endorse war preparedness. Imprisoned four times in the Women's House of Detention, Day wrote movingly about women's prison experience and tried to use her influence to improve prison conditions.

In the 1960s, as opposition grew to the war in Vietnam, the *Catholic Worker*'s steady resistance to conscription and war attracted many young people to its houses and farms. Although sometimes uncomfortable with their social behaviors, Day welcomed the young radicals' enthusiasm for justice and supported the draft-card burnings originated by young Catholic Worker men. She also continued to travel: to Australia in 1970 to speak out against the war, and to California in 1973, where she was imprisoned for supporting a strike by the United Farm Workers.

Dorothy Day died in New York City in 1980 at the age of eighty-three of heart disease, at Maryhouse, the last of the many homes she had struggled to establish for the homeless. In 1983, when the American bishops issued their groundbreaking peace pastoral (*The Challenge of Peace*), they acknowledged the profound impact of Dorothy Day. In 1997 Cardinal John O'Connor of New York City proposed the cause of her beatification, the first step in the formal process toward canonization.

Bibliography: The Dorothy Day Papers and the New York Catholic Worker Records are in the Department of Special Collections and University Archives at Marquette University, Milwaukee, Wisconsin. The collection includes photographs, audio and videotapes of talks by Dorothy Day, oral history interviews, films, and documentaries (see especially "Still a Rebel," a 1973 interview of Day by Bill Moyers for WNET). *The Long Loneliness* was originally published in 1952; the quotation is from the 1959 Image Books edition. Anne Klejment and Alice Klejment, *Dorothy Day and the Catholic Worker* (1986), contains a bibliography of Day's published writings, a listing of *Catholic Worker* articles, and selected secondary sources. Robert Ellsberg, ed., *By Little and By Little: The Selected Writings of Dorothy Day* (1983; reprinted 1992 as *Selected Writings*), is an indispensable collection. Rosalie Riegle Troester, *Voices from the Catholic Worker* (1993), is a compilation of oral histories with Catholic Workers from many eras. Stanley Vishnewski, *Wings of the Dawn* (1985), is a memoir by Day's colleague and friend who joined the Worker at sixteen and remained all his life. Biographies include William Miller, *Dorothy Day: A Biography* (1982), and Jim Forest, *Love Is the Measure* (1986; rev. ed 1994). See also Miller, *A Harsh and Dreadful Love: Dorothy Day and the Catholic Worker Movement* (1973). Important secondary sources include Robert Coles, *Dorothy Day: A Radical Devotion* (1987); Eileen Egan, *Peace Be with You: Justified War or the Way of Nonviolence* (1999); Marc Ellis, *A Year at the Catholic Worker* (1978); Michael Harrington, *The Other America* (1962); Anne Klejment and Nancy Roberts, eds., *American Catholic Pacifism: The Influence of Dorothy Day and the Catholic Worker Movement* (1996), especially articles by Patricia McNeal, William H. Shannon, and the editors; Brigid O'Shea Merriman, OSF, *Searching for Christ: The Spirituality of Dorothy Day* (1994); June O'Connor, *The Moral Vision of Dorothy Day: A Feminist Perspective* (1991); Mel Piehl, *Breaking Bread: The Catholic Worker and the Origin of Catholic Radicalism in America* (1982); and Nancy Roberts, *Dorothy Day and the Catholic Worker* (1984). An obituary appeared in the *New York Times* on December 1, 1980.

CAROL HURD GREEN

DEBO, Angie Elbertha. January 30, 1890–February 21, 1988. Historian.

Born in Beattie, Kansas, where her parents, Edward P. and Lina Cooper Debo, were homesteaders, Angie Debo liked to observe that her birth date coincided with the closing of the American frontier. She spent a lifetime examining the historical implications of that settlement for Native American Indians. Debo's father, a descendant of French and German immigrants, and her mother, the daughter of Kansas pioneers, migrated to Oklahoma in 1899, ten years after the land run opened the territory to white settlement. They arrived in covered wagons with Angie, Edwin (her younger brother by one year), and members of Mrs. Debo's extended family, settling in Marshall, Oklahoma. Angie remained in Marshall for most of the rest of her life, with brief periods away for work, travel, and schooling.

Debo acquired her common school education in a one-room schoolhouse that was in session only a few months a year, and used her ninth-grade education to teach in nearby rural schools between 1907 and 1910 until Marshall High School opened. She graduated in 1913 at the age of twenty-three. Strongly influenced by the independent women in her family, Debo early announced her intention to become "an old maid and teach school" (Leckie, p. 16). She never married, but her school teaching career was interrupted by a bout with typhoid fever in 1915. When it was over, Debo enrolled at the University of Oklahoma in Norman.

There she came under the influence of history professor Edward Everett Dale, who had studied at Harvard University with Frederick Jackson Turner. Although she would reject Dale's optimistic view of the encounter between Native Americans and whites, Debo embraced her teacher's interest in Oklahoma's Five Civilized Tribes as well as his emphasis on social history and local study. An outstanding student, Debo earned her bachelor's degree in three years, graduating in 1918. She taught school in Enid, Oklahoma, until 1923 when at age thirty-three she enrolled as a graduate student at the University of Chicago.

Debo's master's thesis examined the historical roots of American isolationism; she earned her degree in 1924. Despite a superb record at Chicago and the rapid publication of her thesis, Debo faced the extremely discouraging prospects for academic employment that confronted most women historians of her generation. While male classmates at Chicago such as Henry Steele Commager embarked on distinguished academic careers, Debo accepted an appointment in the high school affiliated with West Texas State Teachers College in Canyon, Texas. An energetic woman who hiked and enjoyed the outdoors, she loved the rough natural beauty of the high plains but could not accept her marginal status at the college. To the end of her life, Debo expressed shock and dismay at the pervasiveness of sex discrimination in the academy.

Still, Debo decided to pursue a PhD in history at the University of Oklahoma; she completed her doctorate in 1933. At Dale's suggestion, Debo crafted a dissertation based on recently acquired manuscripts on the Choctaw Nation. When her thesis was published in 1934 as *The Rise and Fall of the Choctaw Republic,* the book was awarded the Dunning Prize by the American Historical Association for the outstanding monograph in American history. A work of striking originality, it examined the tribe's experience from an Indian-centered perspective even as it laid bare the story of unrelenting white depredations. With this first full-scale immersion into Native American history, Debo found her life's work.

Despite lavish praise from professional historians for her scholarship, Debo labored in tremendous isolation for most of her career with only sporadic financial support for her efforts. A grant from the Social Science Research Council in 1934 enabled her to write her most important book, *And Still the Waters Run,* which carefully detailed the "criminal conspiracy" that defrauded Oklahoma's Five Civilized Tribes of their lands through manipulation of the allotment system. The University of Oklahoma refused to publish the book for fear that its revelations would alienate potential donors. Princeton University Press issued the work in 1940; in time the book would earn recognition as an extraordinary scholarly achievement.

Debo's years of painstaking research on *And Still the Waters Run* coincided with the Great Depression, a fact that exacerbated her struggle to survive as a scholar and historian. She returned to West Texas State Teachers College in 1931 and briefly taught in the history department in 1932–33 but was dismissed amid financial cutbacks. Soon after she returned home to Marshall to pursue her research and writing independently. Now forty-four years old, she lived with her parents and supported herself with some part-time teaching and a short stint with the Indian-Pioneer Project sponsored by the Works Progress Administration (WPA). Yet Debo still managed to complete a history of the Creek Indians entitled *The Road to Disappearance* (1941). She also served briefly as director of the Federal Writers' Project for Oklahoma in 1940–1941.

In the 1940s, Debo published several regionally focused studies, including *Tulsa: From Creek Town to Oil Capital* (1943); *Oklahoma: Foot-Loose and Fancy-Free* (1949); and a work of fiction, *Prairie City: The Story of an American Community* (1944), based on Marshall and its pioneers. None had great commercial success, but each enhanced Debo's reputation in Oklahoma as an insightful student of the state's history and progress. She taught occasionally at Oklahoma A&M, and in the summer of 1967 at the University of Oklahoma, but she never held a regular appointment in a history department. In 1947, she accepted a position as curator of maps at the Oklahoma A&M College Library, where she remained until her retirement in 1955 at the age of sixty-five.

Her passion for Native American history grew more overtly political in retirement as her Social Security pension and a small inheritance gave her some financial freedom. An active participant in the Indian Rights Association and the Association on American Indian Affairs, she lectured and wrote widely on federal policy toward Native American tribes, often opposing termination of government trusteeship in the 1950s as a fateful step toward abandonment of Native American rights, lands, and interests. Starting in the late 1960s, she lobbied aggressively on behalf of measures to protect the rights of Alaska's indigenous peoples. A lifelong Democrat and active member of the American Civil Liberties Union, she opposed the war in Vietnam as a lamentable example of American imperialism.

Even in old age and declining health, Debo continued her scholarly work on Native American history, tracing the contours of white imperialism from the Native American viewpoint in her far-reaching *History of the Indians of the United States* (1970) and completing a sympathetic biography of Geronimo when she was eighty-six years old. The rise of the "new history" and the sweeping political changes of the 1960s and 1970s led to her rediscovery by a new generation of historians and activists. In the last two decades of her life, virtually every year brought awards and honors, including an Award for Scholarly Distinction from the American Historical Association in 1987. The following year, Debo was the subject of an award-winning documentary film entitled *Indians, Outlaws and Angie Debo* that chronicled her courageous pursuit of a truthful and compassionate Native American history. She died in 1988 at the age of ninety-eight and is buried in Marshall, Oklahoma.

Bibliography: The extensive Angie Debo Papers are located at Oklahoma State University in Stillwater. Additional Debo material can be found in the Western History Collections at the University of Oklahoma and in the Grant and Carolyn Foreman Manuscript Collection at the Oklahoma Historical Society in Oklahoma City. See also Richard Lowitt, "Dear Miss Debo: The Correspondence of E. E. Dale and Angie Debo," *Chronicles of Oklahoma* 77, no. 4 (Winter 1999–2000), pp. 372–405.

Debo was the author of numerous books and essays; salient works in addition to those listed in the text include her MA thesis, "The Historical Background of the American Policy of Isolation," *Smith College Studies in History* 9 (April–July 1924), pp. 71–165; *The Five Civilized Tribes: Report on Social and Economic Conditions* (1951); *Geronimo: The Man, His Time, His Place* (1976); and *Oklahoma: A Guide to the Sooner State* (1941), edited with John M. Oskison.

There is only one full biography of Angie Debo, Shirley Leckie's excellent *Angie Debo: Pioneering Historian* (2000). Barbara Abrash and Martha Sandlin's documentary film *Indians, Outlaws and Angie Debo* (1988) offers a compelling account of Debo's life and work, as well as interviews with Debo herself. Additional discussions of her life and work may be found in Glenna Matthews and Gloria Valencia-Weber, "Against Great Odds: The Life of Angie Debo," *OAH Newsletter* 13 (May 1985), pp. 8–11; Kenneth McIntosh, "Geronimo's Friend: Angie Debo and the New History," *Chronicles of Oklahoma* 66 (Summer 1988), pp. 164–77; Suzanne Schrems and Cynthia Wolff, "Politics and Libel: Angie Debo and the Publication of *And Still the Waters Run*," *Western Historical Quarterly* 22 (May 1991), pp. 184–203; and Ellen Fitzpatrick, *History's Memory: Writing America's Past 1880–1980* (2002). A portrait of Angie Debo painted by Charles Wilson hangs in the Capitol rotunda in Oklahoma City.

ELLEN FITZPATRICK

DeGAETANI, Jan. July 10, 1933–September 15, 1989. Mezzo-soprano.

Jan DeGaetani, mezzo-soprano, was one of the leading concert singers of the twentieth century, excelling in a broad range of repertoire, and becoming especially well known as a champion of new music. Her vocal flexibility and range enabled her to conquer the challenges of the extended techniques that were popular among composers in the years from 1960 to 1980. She sang the premieres of numerous works by George Crumb, Peter Maxwell Davies, Elliott Carter, György Ligeti, Richard Wernick, Jacob Druckman, and other leading composers.

DeGaetani was born Janice Ruetz in Massillon, Ohio, the third of four daughters of Cora Eleanor Hayman, a housewife, and Earl D. Ruetz, a lawyer. Her father encouraged her singing in church choirs and supported her decision to study in New York City at the Juilliard School after her graduation from high school in Massillon in 1951. At Juilliard her primary teacher was the coach, composer, and editor Sergius Kagan, who was not known as a voice teacher per se, but who agreed to work as a vocal coach with the talented youngster because of her evident intelligence and eagerness to learn. DeGaetani credited his openness and high musical standards for much of her growth as a singer. She also credited weekly reading sessions, supervised by Norman Lloyd, singing part-songs and madrigals from the Renaissance and Baroque, with helping expand her musical vocabulary and skills.

Work with such groups as the Gramercy Chamber Ensemble and the Waverly Consort followed her graduation in 1955, but it was her association with the Contemporary Chamber Ensemble, under the direction of Arthur Weisberg, and that group's pianist, Gilbert Kalish, that proved to be pivotal in bringing DeGaetani fame as an interpreter of new music and a trendsetter among musicians. While doing the usual jobs of a young singer in New York City—waitressing, secretarial work, an occasional radio commercial or early music concert—DeGaetani devoted a great deal of her time in 1958–59 to learning Arnold Schoenberg's *Pierrot Lunaire.* She first performed this seminal work in 1960 in the Carnegie Recital Hall with Robert Cole and the Grammercy Chamber Ensemble. Numerous performances followed, culminating in a recording on the Nonesuch label with Weisberg and the Contemporary Chamber Ensemble in 1970.

Another important performance in Jan DeGaetani's career came on October 31, 1970, with the premiere of George Crumb's *Ancient Voices of Children* at the Library of Congress in Washington, D.C. Crumb had a growing reputation as a composer of experimental music for piano or chamber ensemble; upon receiving a commission for a new work, he asked DeGaetani if he might set some texts of Federico García Lorca for her and the ensemble. The premiere was a sensational success, and DeGaetani was propelled into a position as one of the leading performers of new music, joining such stars of extended vocalism as Bethany Beardslee and Cathy Berberian. Important premieres followed, including Druckman's *Lamia* (1974), Davies's *Dark Angels* (1974), Carter's *Syringa* (1978), Wernick's *Visions of Terror and Wonder* (1977), and Crumb's *Apparition* (1979).

With Gilbert Kalish as her partner, DeGaetani concertized extensively and recorded a wide range of repertoire, much of it under the watchful care of Teresa Sterne of Nonesuch Records. She was a regular guest with leading orchestras, frequently singing Bach or Mahler, but also venturing into Wagner (*Erda* with Sir Georg Solti and the Chicago Symphony) and Falla (*The Three-Cornered Hat* with Pierre Boulez and the New York Philharmonic).

DeGaetani was a longtime member of the artist faculty of the Aspen Music Festival, teaching a class of young singers and performing. These performances included opera (Blind Mary in Peter Maxwell Davies's *The Martyrdom of Saint Magnus,* Baba in Gian Carlo Menotti's *The Medium*), oratorio (Handel's *Semele,* Schoenberg's *Gurrelieder,* Mozart's *Requiem*), and solo works ranging from Schubert to Cole Porter.

Jan DeGaetani's performances were marked by an unusually wide spectrum of vocal colors, dynamics, and expressive timbres and shadings. In Ravel's *Chansons Madécasses* she moved with seeming effortlessness from the yearning of the first song to the savage violence of the second, and then on to the gentle languor of the third song. She imbued a Stephen Foster song like "Beautiful Child of Song" with affectionate love that enabled it to become a direct communication with the listener, even from a recording. Her stage persona was natural and welcoming; audiences were presented with candor and were directed by DeGaetani's obvious focus and commitment to concentrate their attention on the artwork being presented.

Her vocal technique was firmly classical in its grounding, so she could venture without fear into the extreme reaches of her range without doing harm to her instrument. She did not possess "perfect pitch," but the lack of this crutch made her study of new scores fresh, thorough, and supremely intelligent.

DeGaetani taught voice for brief periods as adjunct faculty at the State College of New York at Purchase and at Bennington College. In 1973 she joined the faculty of the Eastman School of Music in Rochester, New York, where she made her home. Among her students at Aspen, Eastman, and these other schools are many successful performers and pedagogues, including Pamela Coburn, Renee Fleming, Carmen Pelton, William Sharp, and Lucy Shelton.

Students and colleagues alike treasured

DeGaetani's openness and enthusiasm. Her teaching was characterized by devotion to the music, firm technical and musical values, and personalized concern for the needs of each student. She was a steadfast friend and inspiring colleague whose high standards for herself and others were matched by her devotion to the well-being of those around her. She required the best of herself and of her fellow musicians, but treated those with whom she worked with remarkable generosity and consideration. She was one of those special musicians who was always eager to learn new concepts, new music, and new ideas.

In 1958 she married Thomas DeGaetani, a stage manager, and the couple had two children: Francesca (1961) and Mark (1963). They divorced in 1966, and DeGaetani, now singing professionally under her first husband's name, married oboist Philip West in 1969. West later adopted both children. After a three-year battle with leukemia, DeGaetani died on September 15, 1989, in Rochester, New York, at the age of fifty-six.

Bibliography: The Sibley Music Library at the Eastman School of Music in Rochester, New York, has a collection of material pertaining to Jan DeGaetani, including her personal library of scores. DeGaetani was a co-author, with Norman Lloyd and Ruth Lloyd, of *The Complete Sightsinger: A Stylistic and Historical Approach* (1980). *Current Biography* (1977), pp. 125–28, provides biographical material and excerpts from reviews. See also Barbara Staropoli, "If You Encounter a Great Teacher: Remembrances of Jan DeGaetani," *Journal of Singing* 50 (November 1993), pp. 27–34; the volume also includes a partial discography by Teresa Sterne. *A Tribute to Jan DeGaetani at the Kathryn Bache Miller Theatre* (1992), presented by the Fritz Reiner Center for Contemporary Music at Columbia University, includes biographical information, tributes, and a discography. An obituary appeared in the *New York Times* on September 17, 1989.

ROBERT SPILLMAN

DE KOONING, Elaine. March 12, 1918–February 1, 1989. Artist, art critic.

Elaine Marie Catherine Fried was born in Brooklyn, the first of four children of Mary Ellen O'Brien and Charles Fried. Elaine's mother was a descendant of Irish immigrants and identified strongly with her Celtic heritage. Elaine's father, who was of German descent, grew up on a farm in upstate New York. Though he became a CPA, he passed on his love of nature and animals to his children. Mary Ellen Fried, who briefly studied law at Hunter College, conveyed her appreciation of art to her children by taking them to museums, the opera, and theater. She also decorated their home with reproductions by Raphael, Rembrandt, Elisabeth-Louise Vigée-Lebrun, and Rosa Bonheur. Mary Ellen's choice to showcase two male and two female artists provided Elaine with an important, but false, assumption that "half the painters in the world were women" (Munro, p. 250).

Elaine excelled in school, especially at Erasmus Hall High School, whose strong art program and supportive female teachers encouraged the young aspiring artist. She enrolled at Hunter College in 1936, but in 1937 began taking classes at the Leonardo da Vinci Art School. That same year, she transferred to the American Artists School because, as she commented, "I loved the conviviality of the school, the endless arguments over politics after class in cafeterias or parks. I had been brought up as a Roman Catholic, but I felt at home with members of the Young Communist League or the opposing Trotskyite groups. Our discussions would rage on and on, night after night" (Munro, p. 252).

In 1937 she met Willem de Kooning, a Dutch-born painter fourteen years her senior who took on the role of mentor. De Kooning would become one of the leading abstract expressionists, and soon the two were painting alongside one another in Willem's studio. On December 9, 1943, they were married at City Hall. Theirs was never a conventional marriage. Elaine was not interested in playing the role of the traditional wife because her focus was art, and yet during certain periods of her life, such as the 1940s before her husband had received wide recognition, she worked hard to promote his career. They never had any children, although in 1956 Willem had a daughter, Lisa, with Joan Ward. The couple separated amicably the next year, but reconciled in 1975, at which time Elaine bought a house near her husband's in East Hampton.

In the 1940s and 1950s, Elaine de Kooning devoted energy to the family of artists, dubbed the Abstract Expressionists, that developed near East Tenth Street in downtown Manhattan. Here cheap studio spaces and the Cedar Bar provided a nucleus. In 1949, the artists established The Club, a place where they met regularly to discuss ideas and socialize, with Elaine and Mercedes Matter the only women charter members. Her membership reveals the important position she held within this predominantly male enclave. Likewise, her paintings were exhibited at important group exhibitions such as the 1951 *Ninth Street Show* and the 1953–56 Stable Gallery shows. Beginning in 1951, the de Koonings spent the first of three summers in East Hampton. In 1954 the couple shared the "Red House" in Bridgehampton with fellow artists Franz Kline and Nancy Ward. Long Island had become the summer hub for many of the downtown artists.

Elaine de Kooning also held an important position within the larger art establishment as an art critic for *Art News.* In 1948, she took a job as editorial associate and became one of the first artists of this period to write critically about art. Her articles on Arshile Gorky, Franz Kline, and Mark Rothko are among the first to acknowledge the importance of these artists. Some of her articles reveal the critical debates taking place in the 1950s as well. In "Subject: What, How, or Who?" (1955), for example, she defends modern painters who continue to work from nature, challenging the influential critic Clement Greenberg, who argued that anyone who creates representational paintings is a minor artist.

De Kooning also defied Greenberg's myopic critical perspective by creating both nonrepresentational and representational paintings. She used the fluid brushwork of abstract expressionism to create portraits of her friends, or to capture the movement of sport figures in action or the beauty of a bull. De Kooning particularly excelled at portraiture because she could accurately capture a sitter's likeness in a rapid manner, and for this reason, in 1962, she was commissioned to paint President Kennedy's portrait. From 1963 to 1964 de Kooning taught at the University of California at Davis, where she experimented with sculpture because she was unable to paint, devastated by Kennedy's assassination. Although she later returned to portraiture, in the summer of 1976 while teaching in Paris for the New York Studio School, she was captivated by a nineteenth-century sculpture of Bacchus. She began a six-year investigation of the subject through paintings and lithographs, while at the same time teaching at the University of Georgia (1976–78). In 1983, another trip to France inspired a new series based on cave paintings, in which she employed both thin washes of acrylic paint and sumi ink.

Earlier in her career, especially in the 1950s, it was extremely difficult for a female to be considered more than a good "woman artist." The macho painter, exemplified by Jackson Pollock, represented the quintessential image of an abstract expressionist. Even though Elaine de Kooning adopted this persona by drinking, smoking, and swearing, her petite five-foot, five-inch frame, accented by her auburn hair, sparkling brown eyes, and lipstick-lined mouth, made her look more like a 1950s movie star than a tough, rugged painter. Furthermore, de Kooning's artistic contributions have been overshadowed by the status of her husband, relegating her work to a secondary position in the abstract expressionism canon. The further the art world moves away from Greenberg's narrow model, however, the more artists who were deemed "inferior" are being reevaluated. De Kooning's work as a painter and critic has been acknowledged through a retrospective in 1992–93 and in a book that features some of her most important articles from *Art News*. Elaine de Kooning died of lung cancer on February 1, 1989, in Southampton, Long Island, at the age of seventy.

Bibliography: Most of the information about her family is taken from an interview in Eleanor Munro, *Originals: American Women Artists* (1979). However, the date of Elaine de Kooning's birth, 1918, comes from the artist's sister, Marjorie Luyckx. Information about Elaine de Kooning's position within the artists' community and an in-depth bibliography can be found in Celia Stahr, "The Social Relations of Abstract Expressionism: An Alternative History" (PhD dissertation, University of Iowa, 1997). The best source for information about and reproductions of her artwork is *Elaine de Kooning*, Georgia Museum of Art, traveling retrospective (1992–1993), with an introduction by Jane K. Bledsoe, a chronology by Marjorie Luyckx, and texts by Helen A. Harrison, Lawrence Campbell, and Rose Slivka. For an overview of her art criticism, see *Elaine de Kooning, the Spirit of Abstract Expressionism* (1994), which contains a preface by Marjorie Luyckx and an introductory essay by Rose Slivka. A taped interview with Karl Fortress (1971) and correspondence and other papers can be found at the Archives of American Art, Smithsonian Institution, Washington, D.C. For a detailed bibliography, see Françoise S. Puniello and Halina R. Rusak, *Abstract Expressionist Women Painters: An Annotated Bibliography* (1991). See also *Elaine de Kooning: Portraits,* Salander-O'Reilly Galleries, New York, January 5–30, 1999, with an essay by Bill Berkson. Also of interest are Elaine de Kooning, "Painting a Portrait of the President," *Art News,* Summer 1964, pp. 37, 64–65; "De Kooning Memories," *Vogue,* December 1983, pp. 352–353, 393–394; and, with Rosalyn Drexler, "Dialogue," *Art News,* January 1971, reprinted in Elizabeth C. Baker and Thomas B. Hess, eds., *Art and Sexual Politics* (1973). An obituary appeared in the *New York Times* on February 2, 1989.

CELIA S. STAHR

DEL RÍO, Dolores. August 3, 1904–April 11, 1983. Actress.

Dolores del Río, one of the first Mexican film personalities to achieve international stardom, was born Maria Dolores Asúnsolo López Negrete in Durango, Mexico. Her father, Jesus Leonardo Asúnsolo, was a banker, and both he and his wife, Antonia López Negrete, were from wealthy Mexican families. The outbreak of the Mexican Revolution in 1910 jeopardized their position in Durango, and Asúnsolo fled the city for the United States. Negrete and her young daughter moved to Mexico City, where the protection of the first president of the Republic of Mexico—Negrete's distant cousin—ensured that their way of living would continue. Young Dolores took art and dance classes, and studied at the local convent school.

At age seventeen, she married Jaime Martínez del Río, a lawyer eighteen years her senior. He also was from a wealthy family, and had been educated in England. The pair enjoyed a two-year European honeymoon, hobnobbing with members of the Continent's high society. They settled in Chihuahua and then Mexico City, where they entertained many prominent visitors. Among these was Edwin Carewe, an American director of silent films. Impressed by del Río's beauty and her dancing ability at the 1925 party at which they met, he insisted she come to Hollywood. The del Ríos left for California shortly thereafter—she to act, and he to work as a screenwriter.

Carewe offered the young woman a contract and advised her to shorten her lengthy married name to Dolores del Río. She appeared in a minor role in his 1925 film *Joanna.* In 1926, she was one of the numerous winners, along with JOAN CRAWFORD and Mary Astor, of the WAMPAS (Western Association of Motion Picture Advertisers) Baby Stars beauty pageant. Del Río made her debut as a lead actress in *What Price Glory* (1926), a film about World War I directed by Raoul Walsh. Her striking good looks, considered exotic by much of Hollywood and the U.S. cinema audience, launched her to fame. She was cast in a number of roles, not unexpectedly of various ethnicities—a French barmaid in *What Price Glory,* a Russian peasant in an adaptation of Tolstoy's *Resurrection* (1927), a Spanish–Native American woman in *Ramona* (1928). By this time, del Río's childless marriage had fallen apart, and she and Jaime divorced in 1928. He died shortly thereafter.

Although in her numerous publicity spreads del Río was depicted as a thoroughly modern woman with a trendy wardrobe, her on-camera image was frequently as a barefoot foreigner, a type of role only solidified by her accented English once Hollywood made the transition to talkies. In *Bird of Paradise* (1932), one of her early sound roles, she played a Polynesian who throws herself into a volcano. She appeared in numerous musicals about Latin America, much like Brazilian actress Carmen Miranda in the 1940s and 1950s. These song-and-dance movies included *Flying Down to Rio* (1933), where she danced with Fred Astaire, and *In Caliente* (1935), which was choreographed by Busby Berkely.

Del Río did not remain single for long. In 1930 she married Cedric Gibbons, an art director at Metro-Goldwyn-Mayer. Their marriage ended in divorce in 1941. By then Del Río had begun an affair with Orson Welles. She starred in his film *Journey into Fear* (1942), although he ended up deserting both her and the project. Director Norman Foster stepped in to complete the movie, but del Río had had enough of Hollywood. After having made well over twenty American films, she returned to her native Mexico.

Once home, del Río became part of the nascent Mexican film scene. She teamed up with Emilio Fernandez, and the two made a number of movies, beginning with *Flor Silvestre (Wild Flower)* in 1943. She again played barefoot and downtrodden women, but this time, despite her resistance and at Fernandez's insistence, it was to prove she was "Mexican, and proud of it." Her most famous Mexican role was in *Maria Candelaria* (1943), where she played the title character—a woman who was stoned to death after being mistakenly identified as the subject of a nude portrait, although she had only modeled for its face. The film received the Palme d'Or at Cannes in 1946, and brought international attention to Mexico's thriving film culture. Despite a subsequent break with Fernandez, del Río went on to win three of the five Ariels (Mexico's highest film award) she was nominated for as Mejor Actuacion Femenina (best actress).

Altogether, del Río made fifty-six films in Mexico and the United States. In 1947 she appeared alongside Henry Fonda in John Ford's *The Fugitive,* based on Graham Greene's novel *The Power and the Glory.* She did not make another American film until *Flaming Star* (1960), in which she played Elvis Presley's mother. She appeared as Sal Mineo's mother in John Ford's last western, *Cheyenne Autumn* (1964), and played a role in the Italian film *C'era una volta* (*More than a Miracle*) in 1967.

Del Río's last marriage was to Lewis Riley, an American businessman, in 1959. Her film career essentially ended by the late 1960s, and she began charitable work, most notably establishing the Estancia Infantil, which offered day care for the children of Mexican actors. Del Río spent much of the 1970s tending to both the center's board and the young people who attended the center, making one last (largely unnoticed) film in 1978, *The Children of Sanchez.*

Dolores del Río died on April 11, 1983, in Newport Beach, California, at the age of seventy-eight.

Bibliography: A collection of photographs, including stills from some of Dolores del Río's early films, is located at the Museum of Modern Art, New York City. Del Río contributed a chapter, "Achieving Stardom," to Charles Reed Jones, ed., *Breaking into the Movies* (1927). The most inclusive biography of del Río is the three-volume Spanish work by David Ramon, *Dolores del Río* (1997). Another Spanish-language biography is Aurelio de los Reyes and Garcia Rojas, *Dolores del Río* (1996). For a filmography, see Allen L. Woll, *The Films of Dolores del Rio* (1978). Joanne Hershfield presents a scholarly deconstruction of the racialization and exoticization behind the icon of del Rio in *The Invention of Dolores del Rio* (2000). See also Carl J. Mora, *Mexican Cinema: Reflections of a Society* (rev. ed. 1989). Mexican writer Carlos Monsivais features a critical chapter about del Río in *Mexican Postcards* (1997), translated by John Kraniauskas; the book contains the quotation on p. 80. An obituary appeared in the *New York Times* on April 13, 1983.

JENNIFER COTE

DEMING, Barbara. July 23, 1917–August 2, 1984. Writer, activist.

Barbara Deming was one of America's most important radical activists for peace, justice, and equality. Her life and interests spanned the major movements of this century: she marched and worked for disarmament and then for civil rights; she protested the war in Vietnam; she struggled finally for women's rights, and lesbian and gay rights. Deming rejected the notion that the various movements of her time were separate or unconnected. All of her struggles for justice followed from the premise of respect for one's fellow human, the basis, she believed, for all human rights.

In spite of her mother's artistic influence and her Quaker schooling, Barbara Deming's upbringing could not have predicted her later involvement in all of the major social justice movements of her generation. Born in New York City, Barbara was the second of four children and the only girl. Her mother, Katherine Burritt, was a singer, raised in Europe and the United States, tutored by her father who was also a singer. Katherine gave up her career in 1913 to marry Harold Deming, a lawyer from a family of lawyers and Republican politicians. All four Deming children began school in New York City at Friends Seminary attached to the Fifteenth Street Quaker Meeting. Barbara thrived in that community and was considered the brightest student in her class. She began to write poetry and published several poems in the Friends Seminary literary journal before her graduation in 1934. Many of her poems in this early period were passionate love poems written for her first lover, Norma Millay, sister of the poet EDNA ST. VINCENT MILLAY.

At Bennington College, Deming continued to write, although one of her professors, Genevieve Taggard, criticized her poetry for its references to same-sex love. After that, she began writing heavily metaphorical poems that concealed her true subjects. It was also at Bennington that Deming met the women who were to become the first and last of three significant adult relationships in her life—Vida Ginsberg and Jane Gapen. Barbara and Vida were lovers from about 1938 until Vida married Barbara's younger brother Quentin (Chip) in 1948.

Deming graduated from college in 1938 as the war in Europe was intensifying and the economic depression in the United States was deepening. She wanted to live as a writer, but her father—whose fortunes seemed to have survived the Depression largely intact—refused on principle; he believed all of his children should work and earn their own livings. Harold Deming also refused to support his daughter's desire to study writing at Tulane University in Louisiana and insisted that she take a degree in Theater Arts at Case Western Reserve. After finishing her MA there, Barbara took a job as a film reviewer for the Library of Congress and began cataloging war films. During this time, she wrote a draft of her first book, *Running Away from Myself: A Dream Portrait of America Drawn from the Films of the Forties* (1969). She was known in a small circle of literary, artistic people for her work in film criticism and her stories in several national magazines, including the *New Yorker* and *Vogue*.

Deming had been working on a novel since 1951, encouraged by people like Truman Capote, but it remained unfinished until shortly before her death. When she looked back on that period, she would say that she was discouraged because the main character was identifiable as a lesbian, although she did not identify herself as a lesbian at that time. In 1954 Barbara met painter Mary Meigs, who became her partner and lifelong friend. Mary was the first woman Barbara met who called herself a lesbian. They settled in a home in Wellfleet, Massachusetts, where Mary painted and Barbara wrote poems, stories, and essays. Their relationship lasted for fourteen years, and during this period Deming began her long involvement in politics.

In 1960, Deming was a forty-three-year-old woman who had achieved modest success as a writer. On vacation in Cuba in March, shortly after the Cuban revolution, she found herself arguing with her companions about Fidel Castro and resolved to talk with him herself regarding her reservations about the execution of men loyal to the dictator Castro had overthrown. She was able to find and interview him on a street corner where other reporters eventually found them. Photographs of that meeting show two intense people of nearly the same height: Castro, dark, slim, and bearded; Barbara, willowy, rail-thin, her straight dark hair framing large, inquiring eyes. The published account in the *Nation* of her spontaneous interview with Castro was the beginning of her political writing and personal activism. Within a few weeks, she was regularly attending meetings of the Committee for Nonviolent Action and joined some of the protests against nuclear weapons testing. On a disarmament peace march through the southern United States, she was arrested and jailed for walking in an integrated group. *Prison Notes* (1966), her first published book, is an account of this and subsequent imprisonments during civil rights protests.

The positive response to her political writing gave Deming the energy and direction she had not found in her literary career. Her next book, *Revolution and Equilibrium* (1971), detailed the anti–

Vietnam War movement, particularly her own travels to North Vietnam where she witnessed and experienced the U.S. bombing of Hanoi.

In 1969, Deming began living with her third long-term lover and companion, Jane Gapen. A difficult custody dispute with Jane's husband over Jane's two children precipitated both women into a feminist awareness and simultaneously into a more public lesbian identity. After years of suppressing what she considered her "personal" life, Deming was finally forced into disclosure to friends. In 1974, realizing at last that her personal life as a lesbian had political implications, she dedicated her book on the emerging feminism, *We Cannot Live without Our Lives,* to "all those seeking the courage to assert 'I am'—and especially to my lesbian sisters." *Remembering Who We Are* (1981) was a collection of letters and essays that carried further her earlier feminist explorations.

In 1983 Deming was part of the Women's Encampment for a Future of Peace and Justice and joined a demonstration near the Seneca Army Depot in upstate New York, where she was arrested and jailed for the last time. Her essay about this protest is included in the reprinted *Prison Notes* under the title *Prisons That Could Not Hold* (1995). In 1984 Deming was diagnosed with advanced ovarian cancer. She died at the age of sixty-seven at home in Sugarloaf Key, Florida, surrounded by a community of women.

Bibliography: Barbara Deming's papers are primarily housed at the Schlesinger Library, Radcliffe Institute for Advanced Study, Harvard University; they include extensive correspondence, photographs, news clippings, calendars, and other documents and memorabilia. Some of her early civil rights papers are at Boston University's Mugar Library. The University of Georgia Press reissued *Prison Notes* under the title *Prisons That Could Not Hold* in 1995. Deming's novel, *A Humming under My Feet,* was published posthumously in England by the Women's Press in 1985, and her collection of poems, *I Change, I Change,* edited by Judith McDaniel, was published by New Victoria Press in 1996. The most complete account of Barbara Deming's relationships—with her three significant partners and others—is McDaniel's introduction to the poetry volume. A brief obituary appeared in the *New York Times* on August 4, 1984.

JUDITH MCDANIEL

DE MENIL, Dominique. March 23, 1908–December 31, 1997. Art collector, philanthropist, human rights advocate.

Dominique de Menil, who with her husband built one of the greatest private art collections in the United States, was born Dominique Schlumberger in Paris, where her family had emigrated from Alsace after the Franco-Prussian War in 1871. Her mother, Louise Delpech, cared for Dominique and her two sisters while her father, Conrad Schlumberger, a physics professor, and her uncle Marcel, a mechanical engineer, invented a way to identify minerals according to their degree of electrical resistance. Their magnetic sounding device is still used worldwide to log the potential of oil fields when prospecting.

Fifty years after new laws secured a secular system of primary and secondary education, Dominique graduated from the University of Paris in 1927; she pursued advanced degrees in mathematics and physics from the Sorbonne in 1928. Although her parents were strict Protestants, Dominique became a Catholic shortly before her marriage in 1931 to Jean de Menil. A Catholic but ecumenical in his approach to religion, Jean did not ask for Dominique's conversion; she maintained that she had already planned it.

Dominique's younger sister, Sylvie, married Eric Boissonnas, who, like Jean de Menil, joined the Schlumberger corporation in 1936 when Conrad Schlumberger died. When World War II erupted in Europe in 1939, de Menil and Boissonnas were managing Schlumberger operations in Romania, where Jean sabotaged railroads and destroyed Schlumberger equipment to decommission it before the advancing Nazis. Dominique left Paris for the Schlumberger estate in Normandy, taking their two daughters: Marie-Christophe, who was born in 1933, and Adelaide, born in 1935. When German troops entered Paris in 1940, Dominique, pregnant with her son Georges, drove her daughters and her sister Sylvie, who was also pregnant, to Toulouse. Earlier in the war, Dominique's elder sister, Annette, and her husband had moved to Houston, Texas, where Schlumberger had its American headquarters. In 1941 Dominique and the children were reunited with Jean in Havana, Cuba, before eventually arriving in Houston, which the couple called home until their deaths. Two more children were born in Houston: François (1945) and Philippa (1947). Although Jean and Dominique were devoted to each other's life and work, their children sometimes felt their absence. A business trip to Venezuela in the 1940s led to an extended separation; all the children attended boarding school. "We got used to being orphans," Christophe said (Tomkins, p. 55).

Jean, who anglicized his name to John when the couple became American citizens in 1962, and Dominique had begun collecting art in Paris, when they commissioned the young surrealist painter Max Ernst to paint a portrait of Dominique. She did not like what Ernst produced, claiming she looked too stiff, and the portrait remained hidden in their Paris apartment until she returned after the war to reclaim their possessions. The de Menils had learned about art from Marie-Alain Couturier, a Dominican priest they met in Paris. During trips to New York from 1943 through 1945, the de Menils visited exhibitions and art dealers with Father Couturier and made the seminal purchase of the collection, a Cézanne watercolor. De Menil claimed that she never would have started collecting so much art had they not moved to Houston, a city that lacked galleries, museums, and dealers at the time. "That is why I developed this physical need to acquire," she said (Browning, p. 218).

Dominique de Menil first became involved with teaching and exhibiting art at St. Thomas University in Houston with the help of museum director Dr. Jermayne MacAgy, who greatly influenced Dominique's emergence as a curator and collector before MacAgy's death in 1964. De Menil taught art history using art from her collection rather than from slides, sometimes pulling a priceless object from her handbag. When the university wanted to expand, the de Menils hired architect Philip Johnson to design a master plan, which was finished in 1957. (Johnson was an unknown architect in 1948 when he received his first residential commission—to design the de Menils' flat-roofed Houston house.) After a disagreement over issues of control in 1968, de Menil moved her operations to Rice University, where she and John built a media center and exhibition hall. The exhibitions she mounted there established her national reputation as a curator.

The Menil Foundation was established in 1954 as a charitable organization dedicated to promoting understanding through the arts. One of the foundation's best-known projects was the Rothko Chapel, dedicated in 1971, which houses fourteen paintings by the abstract artist Mark Rothko commissioned by the de Menils in 1964. A nondenominational center for meditation and prayer, the chapel was designed by Philip Johnson and completed by Howard Barnstone and Gene Aubry.

When John died in 1973, Dominique temporarily postponed her plans to build a museum to house their art collection. The Menil Collection opened in 1987, with an innovative design by Italian architect Renzo Piano that uses a complex skylight system to fill the galleries with natural light. The collection focuses on antiquities, Byzantine and medieval art, tribal art, and twentieth-century art, especially surrealism. Other legacies of the Menil Foundation include the Byzantine Fresco Chapel Museum, designed by François de Menil, and Richmond Hall, featuring the work of minimalist sculptor Dan Flavin. The Cy Trombley Gallery, also designed by Renzo Piano, was Dominique's final commission.

Committed to modernism and art's spiritual influence, the de Menils progressed from art to the advocation of diversity; they were strong and early supporters of the emerging civil rights movement. They mentored Mickey Leland, an African American Houstonian who served five years in the Texas legislature and followed BARBARA JORDAN for three terms as U.S. congressman. With former president Jimmy Carter, Dominique de Menil initiated the Carter-Menil Human Rights Foundation in 1985. During her lifetime, the foundation awarded the $100,000 Carter-Menil Human Rights Prize biannually. The Rothko Chapel celebrated its twentieth anniversary in 1991 with a keynote address by Nelson Mandela, who received the $10,000 Rothko Chapel Award for Commitment to Truth and Freedom.

A tall, elegant woman with a spectacular smile, Dominique de Menil was driven by a passion that transformed Houston's cultural landscape. Her strength was matched only by her generosity; her energetic spirit awed and inspired others. "She could sleep standing up," a friend said at her death. "She was from another world" (Browning, p. 216). She died at her home in 1997 at the age of eighty-nine.

Bibliography: A complete bibliography of Dominique de Menil's writings is not available; most of her essays, catalog introductions, and other work is collected by the Menil Foundation, Houston, Texas. A profile of Dominique de Menil by Calvin Tomkins entitled "The Benefactor" appeared in the *New Yorker* on June 8, 1998, pp. 52–67. Other biographical information can be found in Dominique Browning, "Dominique in Full Bloom," *Town & Country,* February 1984, pp. 166–67; Clifford Pugh, "The Magnificent Obsession: Dominique de Menil's Life in the Arts," *Magazine of the Houston Post,* May 31, 1987; and Patricia C. Johnson, "Dominique de Menil's Passion for Art," *Houston Chronicle,* July 29, 1990. See also Grace Glueck, "The De Menil Family: The Medici of Modern Art," *New York Times Magazine,* May 18, 1986, p. 28. Obituaries appeared in the *Houston Chronicle* and *New York Times* on January 1, 1998.

RENATA GOLDEN

DE MILLE, Agnes. September 18, 1905–October 7, 1993. Dancer, choreographer, writer.

Agnes George de Mille was born at 357 W. 118th Street in New York City, the first child of William Churchill de Mille, a playwright, and Anna Angela George, the youngest child of Henry George, the distinguished American writer and thinker who devised the "Single Tax" theory. Her younger sister, Margaret, was born in 1908. The de Mille family was Episcopalian, except for Agnes's grandmother, Beatrice "Bebe" Samuels, born to a German Jewish family that had immigrated to New York in 1871. She converted after her marriage, later becoming a theatrical playbroker who promoted women dramatists. Agnes attended the

Horace Mann School, where both her parents had been educated. Summers meant vacations at Merriewold in Sullivan County, New York, her family's summer home at the foot of the Catskills. Agnes would return to Merriewold for rest and respite during her entire life and later record her memories in *Where the Wings Grow* (1978).

In 1914 William de Mille moved his family to Hollywood to join his brother, producer and director Cecil B. DeMille, in the fledgling silent film industry. Agnes and Margaret attended Hollywood School for Girls, from which Agnes graduated in 1922. The children grew up immersed in the world of film.

Agnes began dancing as a three-year-old, later making up plays and dance pageants in which she performed and directed the neighborhood children. A performance by Anna Pavlova that she attended at age thirteen inspired her future career, even though dance was not considered a proper profession for daughters of upper-class American families. At age fourteen, Agnes began ballet classes with the Russian immigrant Theodore Kosloff, a former member of the famed Diaghilev Ballet Russe. This late start, coupled with her build—five foot one at adulthood, with heavy bust, wide hips, and short legs—meant she would never have a traditional ballet career, but she would not be deterred. She carved a unique niche in the dance world from her strengths: determination, intelligence, an understanding of theatrical narrative, and a keen sense of humor. She also honed an essential tool for a prospective choreographer by studying and practicing piano intensively during her teenage years.

De Mille continued to create and perform dances at the University of California at Los Angeles, where she pledged Kappa Alpha Theta, a social sorority. She graduated cum laude with a degree in English in 1926.

Her parents' separation in 1926 and divorce in 1927 transformed her life. She moved with her mother and sister to New York City, re-enrolled in ballet classes, and began to choreograph and perform in dance recitals with a succession of partners. Her self-produced concert career, subsidized by an allowance from her father and her mother's funds, continued in the United States and Europe for over a decade. In 1931, she appeared on a program with modern dance innovators MARTHA GRAHAM, DORIS HUMPHREY, Charles Weidman, and HELEN TAMIRIS.

De Mille moved to London in 1932, where she studied with Marie Rambert, who invited her to study at the Ballet Club, an incubator of ballet talent. A fellow pupil was the seminal twentieth-century choreographer Antony Tudor, who was creating psychologically driven ballets. De Mille danced roles in the premieres of Tudor's *Dark Elegies, Gallant Assembly,* and *The Judgment of Paris.* She also recommended to the fledgling Ballet Theatre when it was formed in 1939 that Tudor join her as one of its choreographers. De Mille's contribution to Ballet Theatre inaugural season (1940) was *Black Ritual,* followed by *Three Virgins and a Devil* (1941). LUCIA CHASE, patroness and later director of Ballet Theatre, became her friend and adversary from 1940 on.

When the Ballet Russe de Monte Carlo asked de Mille for a new ballet, she accepted with *Rodeo,* choreographed to a score commissioned from Aaron Copland, and cast herself in the leading role of The Cowgirl on opening night, October 16, 1942, at the Metropolitan Opera House. *Rodeo,* which remains her most significant contribution to the ballet repertory, led directly to the assignment as choreographer for the Richard Rodgers–Oscar Hammerstein II Broadway show *Oklahoma!* After its Broadway premiere on March 31, 1943, de Mille became one of the most sought-after dance makers in show business. The innovation of the Act I finale, the dream ballet, and the use of dance to tell the story, helped transform the structure of the American musical.

In 1942 MARTHA GRAHAM, her much admired friend, introduced Agnes to her future husband, Walter Foy Prude. The couple married in 1943; because Prude served in the military until 1945, they had little time together until the war ended. Their only child, Jonathan de Mille Prude, was born in April 1946. Prude managed concert artists' careers for the Sol Hurok organization.

The de Mille era on Broadway lasted through 1951 with hits such as *One Touch of Venus* (1943), *Bloomer Girl* (1944), *Carousel* (1945), *Brigadoon* (1947), *Allegro* (1947), *Gentlemen Prefer Blondes* (1949), and *Paint Your Wagon* (1951), followed by five less popular shows, ending with the flop *Come Summer* (1970). *Oklahoma!* (1955) was the only film de Mille made of her commercial stage works, no doubt because her fights for optimum work conditions gave her a reputation for being difficult among the men in control of the team-oriented world of Broadway.

De Mille continued to create ballets for Ballet Theatre, but only her danced-out version of the Lizzie Borden tale, *Fall River Legend* (1948), is often revived. She segued into a career as a television personality with three programs for *Omnibus* (1956–57), considered models for explaining dance to a wider public. In 1980, PBS-TV presented *Conversations about the Dance,* based on her dance history lecture commissioned by the Harvard Summer Dance Center in 1974.

Her career as an author was launched by her best seller *Dance to the Piper* (1952). The stream of books ended in 1991 with the publication of her massive biography of Martha Graham. She also thrived on the lecture circuit because of her straight-talking, witty, and gossipy style. Her evangelical fervor about the importance of the arts in American society led to her appointment to the original National Council of the Arts and as chairperson of its first dance panel in 1965.

Twice she formed her own dance company, the Agnes de Mille Dance Theatre (which toured in 1953 and 1954) and the Agnes de Mille Heritage Dance Theatre (which toured in 1973 and 1974, closing in 1975), the latter drawn from students at North Carolina School of the Arts where she served as adviser. She invested her own money in these projects and raised additional funds but could not sustain either troupe.

On May 15, 1975, in the midst of a busy round of lectures and choreography assignments, she was felled by a massive stroke that left the right side of her body paralyzed and impaired her vision, speech, memory, and mobility. Through her indomitable spirit and will to succeed, she learned to walk again and to write with her left hand. Within a year she picked up her career to choreograph *The Informer* (1988) and *The Other* (1992), a revised version of *Summer* created in 1975 for the Boston Ballet and subsequently restaged under various names for the American Ballet Theatre; she also wrote several more books and continued to deliver her eloquent lectures. Agnes de Mille died of a stroke at her Greenwich Village apartment on October 7, 1993, at the age of eighty-eight. Her ashes are buried at Merriewold beside those of her husband, who died in 1988. Among her many honors and seventeen honorary degrees is the Kennedy Center Career Achievement Award (1980).

Bibliography: The Agnes de Mille Collection, housed at the Dance Collection of the New York Public Library for the Performing Arts at Lincoln Center, contains films and videotapes of her ballets and appearances on television, her diaries, business papers, choreographic notes, photographs, papers, and thousands of pieces of correspondence relating to her private life and her career, plus diaries and papers of her husband, Walter Foy Prude. A smaller collection of de Mille materials is kept at the Sophia Smith Collection, Smith College Library, Northampton, Massachusetts; a clipping file is held at the Harvard Theatre Collection, Pusey Library. There are also records, letters, and photographs pertinent to de Mille's career in the American Ballet Theatre Collection and the Lucia Chase Collection at the Dance Collection of the New York Public Library for the Performing Arts at Lincoln Center.

Books and publications by de Mille not mentioned in the text include *And Promenade Home* (1958); *To a Young Dancer* (1962); *The Book of the Dance* (1963); *Russian Journals* (1970); *Lizzie Borden: A Dance of Death* (1968); *Speak to Me, Dance with Me* (1973); *America Dances* (1980); *Reprieve: A Memoir* (1981); *Portrait Gallery* (1990); and *Martha: The Life and Work of Martha Graham* (1991). Carol Easton's excellent biography, *No Intermission: The Life of Agnes de Mille* (1996), includes a full danceography. See also Charles Payne, *American Ballet Theatre* (1978). Gemze de Lappe, one of de Mille's lead dancers, contributed to this article. An obituary appeared in the *New York Times* on October 8, 1993.

IRIS FANGER

DENNIS, Peggy. January 1, 1909–September 25, 1993. Journalist, Communist activist.

Peggy Dennis, best known as an author, a journalist, and an organizer for the Communist Party USA (CPUSA), was born Regina Karasick in New York City. Her parents, Meyer and Berta Karasick, were Russian Jewish revolutionaries who had immigrated to the United States in 1904 from a small village near Kiev. In 1912 the family, which also included her older sister, Mini, moved to Los Angeles and settled into the local immigrant radical community. As children, Regina and her sister attended the Socialist Party Sunday school, marched on picket lines, attended political meetings, and, thanks to their mother's explicitly feminist encouragement, became self-confident activists who intended to avoid conventional marriage and motherhood. In 1922, at age thirteen, Regina Karasick joined the local Communist children's group, which had been organized by her sixteen-year-old sister. After her graduation from Roosevelt High School at age sixteen, in 1925 she joined the Young Communist League and adopted the name Reggie Carson. Although she enrolled in Teachers College of the University of California, she left after only one year to devote herself to her Communist Party (CP) assignment—working in the Communist children's movement.

At age eighteen she married a fellow Communist named Bill (last name unknown), but the marriage dissolved shortly thereafter when she became involved with Frank Waldron, the charismatic twenty-three-year-old educational director for the Communist Party in Southern California who would later be known as Eugene Dennis. In this new relationship Peggy Dennis held firm to her rejection of legal marriage, but she and Gene spent the next thirty-three years together. Despite her mother's warning that children would "change your life, not his," Dennis gave in to Gene's desire to have a child (*Autobiography of an American Communist,* p. 37). Their first son, Tim, was born in November 1929 while they were organizing agricultural workers in California's Central Valley. When Gene was indicted in 1930 for his labor activities, he fled to the Soviet Union. Peggy and Tim joined him the next year.

The couple spent the years 1931–35 working with the international Communist movement in Moscow. During that time Gene represented the Comintern, traveling around the world to provide aid to struggling Communist parties. In 1933 the Comintern recognized Peggy's political talents and made her an official traveling courier as well. In 1935 Peggy and Gene were directed to return to the United States. In an act that reveals the personal sacrifices professional revolutionaries were forced to make at the time, the couple reluctantly complied with the Soviets' demand that five-year-old Tim, who spoke only Russian, remain in Moscow. The family never lived together in the United States again, although they did see their son (who grew up in the Soviet Union and became known as Timor Timofeev) on several occasions.

Upon their return to the States the pair adopted the names Peggy and Gene Dennis and settled in Milwaukee, Wisconsin, where Gene became state CP secretary and Peggy was appointed state educational director. In 1938 they moved to New York City, where Gene joined the national leadership of the CPUSA and Peggy did research for him and worked on a CP magazine about national issues. The Dennises' second son, Eugene Jr., was born in New York in December 1942.

Despite Peggy's efforts to protect young Gene from the upheavals his older brother had experienced, his father's election as general secretary of the CPUSA at the dawn of the cold war led to further disruptions for the family. In 1948 Gene Dennis and ten other CPUSA leaders were indicted under the Smith Act for conspiring to teach or advocate the overthrow of the United States government. Found guilty in 1949 after a contentious political trial in New York City (the conviction was upheld by the U.S. Supreme Court in 1951), Gene spent the next five years in prison. During this period Peggy Dennis gained increasing recognition for her own political work, both as a vocal opponent of McCarthyism and as the first editor of the women's pages of the CPUSA's Sunday newspaper, *The Worker.* She was also active with the Families Committee set up to support the children of CP leaders who either were in prison or had gone underground during these years. Although Gene and Peggy Dennis were disturbed by revelations in 1956 confirming the horrors of Stalin's regime in the Soviet Union, they remained in the party and Gene resumed a leadership role after his release from prison.

After her husband's death in January 1961 at the age of fifty-five, Peggy Dennis moved to San Francisco and became foreign affairs editor of the CP's West Coast newspaper, *People's World.* In that position, and in articles she wrote for magazines such as the *Progressive* and the *Nation,* she became an increasingly vocal critic of the Soviet Union and of the CPUSA's isolation from the burgeoning U.S. Left. In 1976 Dennis abandoned her long struggle to reform the Communist Party from within and resigned from the organization. She continued to work as a freelance writer. Her 1977 memoir, *The Autobiography of an American Communist: A Personal View of a Political Life,* stands as a unique and important contribution to knowledge about the history of the American Communist Party and the intertwined personal and political experiences of its women leaders.

Disabled by a severe stroke in 1989, Peggy Dennis died four years later at the Jewish Home for the Aged in San Francisco at the age of eighty-four. She was buried next to Gene Dennis at the German Waldheim Cemetery in Chicago in a plot reserved for Communist leaders.

Bibliography: The papers of Peggy and Eugene Dennis are housed at the Library Division of the State Historical Society of Wisconsin in Madison. They cover the years 1923–89 and include newspaper clippings, correspondence, articles, unpublished writings, research notes, audiotapes, and material obtained from the federal government through the Freedom of Information Act. Dennis's memoir, *The Autobiography of an American Communist: A Personal View of a Political Life* (1977), is a valuable source for information about her life through 1975. Dennis's response to Ellen Kay Trimberger's essay, "Women in the Old and New Left: The Evolution of the Politics of Personal Life," *Feminist Studies* 5, no. 3 (Fall 1979) (see pp. 432–61 for both), provides additional insight into Dennis's life. On the larger question of women's experiences in the Communist Party, see Robert Shaffer, "Women and the Communist Party USA, 1930–1940," *Socialist Review* 45 (1975), pp. 73–118, and Kate Weigand, *Red Feminism: American Communism and the Making of Women's Liberation* (2001). The documentary film, *Love in the Cold War* (1991), by Eric Stange and David Dugan, details Peggy and Eugene Dennis's relationship and the ways their political commitments both enhanced and complicated their family life. See also John Stanley, "American Communists Left Out in the Cold—Film Traces Couple's Turbulent Years in the Party," *San Francisco Chronicle,* January 12, 1992. Obituaries appeared in the *San Francisco Chronicle* on September 28, 1993, and the *New York Times* on October 12, 1993.

KATE WEIGAND

DENNY, Dorothy Detzer. *See* Detzer, Dorothy.

DETZER, Dorothy. December 1, 1893–January 7, 1981. Peace activist, lobbyist.

From 1924 until her retirement in 1946, Dorothy Detzer, the national (or executive) secretary of the Women's International League for Peace and Freedom (WILPF), was recognized as one of the most effective "cause" lobbyists in Washington, D.C. Detzer was born in Fort Wayne, Indiana, to Laura Goshorn, a librarian, club woman, and suffragist, and August Jacob Detzer, a drugstore owner. Dorothy had a twin brother, Donald, as well as older and younger brothers, and her parents actively exposed their children to the political, social, and cultural worlds of the Progressive era. Although raised as Christians, the family embraced no specific sect.

After graduating from Fort Wayne High School in 1914, Detzer traveled to Hawaii, China, Japan, and the Philippines, where she resided for a year. (The trip was financed by money her parents had been saving for her college education.) She then moved to Chicago to work at Hull House. Detzer was assigned to the Juvenile Protective Association and the Juvenile Court, where she investigated infractions against child labor laws. At the same time, she took courses at the Chicago School of Civics and Philanthropy, but did not complete any degree.

Dorothy Detzer's career took shape as a result of U.S. participation in World War I. In 1918, her brother Donald enlisted in the army. While serving in a field hospital unit, he suffered a dousing of mustard gas that damaged his lungs; ten years later he died from resultant tuberculosis. Detzer claimed that her twin's long illness as a result of war motivated her to become a professional peace activist. In 1920, JANE ADDAMS recommended Detzer to the American Friends Service Committee for relief missions in war-torn Austria and Russia. In late 1924, Detzer accepted the position to work with WILPF and moved to Washington, D.C.

WILPF, which grew out of the anti–World War I efforts of pacifist suffragists, became an official international organization in 1919. With headquarters in Geneva, and Jane Addams as its first president, it represented the voice of women who desired a world devoid of violence—whether physical, economic, psychological, racial, ethnic, or other. It also stood for women's equality, justice for the underdogs of the world, and freedom to express oneself and to live without oppression. Detzer's job was primarily to lobby senators and representatives in Washington, D.C., although she frequently represented the U.S. branch at international peace movement and League of Nations conferences. As a self-supporting woman with no outside income, Detzer relied on the WILPF women for a living wage; individuals often bought her clothes and other items to make up for her low salary. Legislators respected Detzer for her thorough research, persuasive manner, and great integrity, knowing full well that the fashionable, outspoken "Lady Lobbyist" (as she was known) would accept no personal favors, private dinners, or backroom deals that would compromise her work.

Detzer's lobbying efforts touched practically every major foreign policy issue of the times. On behalf of WILPF, she lobbied Congress for legislation to allow alien conscientious objectors to become U.S. citizens, to end lynching, for the removal of U.S. troops and U.S. governmental pressure in Haiti and Nicaragua, and for the 1928 Kellogg-Briand Pact, which established negotiation rather than battle as the preferred method of international cooperation. From late 1930 through 1931, along with MABEL VERNON, Detzer coordinated the petition campaign that collected more than half a million U.S. signatures in support of universal disarmament. In 1932, WILPF successfully lobbied to have a female representative, MARY WOOLLEY, in the U.S. delegation to the Geneva League of Nations Disarmament Conference. Perhaps Detzer's greatest success was the 1934 establishment of Senator Gerald Nye's Special Committee Investigating the Munitions Industry's Work, which determined that arms dealers had tried to influence the congressional vote for war in 1917.

The Nye Committee led WILPF and Detzer to an issue that was one of the most controversial for WILPF members: the organization's support for President Franklin D. Roosevelt's neutrality acts, which they believed would restrict the arms trade and therefore prevent war. When the first act failed to prevent the 1935 Italian conquest of Ethiopia, several WILPF members, particularly African American women, resigned, but Detzer supported it anyway. When in 1936 the second act prevented the United States from shipping even humanitarian aid to the Loyalists in the Spanish civil war, others resigned, claiming that the organization was turning a blind eye to the spread of fascism. Detzer had in fact tried to prevent the selling of weapons to secondary powers, such as Germany and Italy, that continued to supply Franco with arms. In spite of the neutrality acts, she and WILPF contributed funds for Spanish relief.

As Nazi Germany and fascist Italy and Spain pushed human rights aside, Detzer lobbied harder for U.S. neutrality and a possible role as mediator while at the same time using her considerable influence in Washington to achieve aid for refugees and rescue for those in flight, including European WILPF members. Once the United States officially joined the war effort in 1941, Detzer and WILPF turned their efforts toward domestic injustices—the internment of Japanese Americans, racism in the U.S. military, relief work, and the exclusion of Jewish refugees from the United States.

In 1946, Detzer decided to leave WILPF and public life, primarily because the financially depleted organization had decided to consolidate its national office by moving it to Philadelphia, a city Detzer had no desire to live in. After a few years of living with her aging parents and writing her memoirs, she joined Norman Thomas's Postwar World Council. In 1954, at the age of sixty-one, she married Ludwell H. Denny, the well-to-do foreign editor of the Scripps-Howard newspaper chain and a close friend since her European days in the 1920s. Except for authoring some articles for Scripps-Howard, Detzer retired from the working world altogether. The couple remained together until his death in 1970. Dorothy Detzer died on January 7, 1981, at the age of eighty-seven, in Monterey, California, where she had moved in 1969 from Washington, D.C.

Bibliography: Dorothy Detzer's memoir, *Appointment on the Hill* (1948), is one of the best sources on her work and her feelings about it. Manuscript collections include the Dorothy Detzer Papers, a relatively small offering, at the Swarthmore College Peace Collection. Detzer's lobbying is also well documented in the Women's International League for Peace and Freedom Papers at the Swarthmore College Peace Collection and the University of Colorado, Boulder. Most of both collections are available on microfilm. An audiotape of an oral history by Rosemary Rainbolt (June 28, 1974) is in the Swarthmore College Peace Collection.

Karl Detzer's memoir, *Myself When Young* (1968), sheds light on Detzer's young home environment. Excellent Detzer sources include Carrie A. Foster, *The Women and the Warriors: The U.S. Section of the Women's International League for Peace and Freedom, 1915–1946* (1995); Anne Marie Pois, "The Politics and Process of Organizing for Peace: The United States Section of the Women's International League for Peace and Freedom" (PhD dissertation, University of Colorado, 1988); Rosemary Rainbolt, "Women and War in the United States: The Case of Dorothy Detzer, National Secretary, WILPF," *Peace and Change: A Journal of Peace Research* 4, no. 3 (Fall 1977), pp. 18–22; and Berenice A. Carroll, "The Outsiders: Comments on Fukuda Hideko, Catherine Marshall and Dorothy Detzer," *Peace and Change: A Journal of Peace Research* 4, no. 3 (Fall 1977), pp. 23–26. An obituary appeared in the *Washington Post* on January 17, 1981.

HARRIET HYMAN ALONSO

DEUTSCH, Helene. October 9, 1884–March 29, 1982. Psychoanalyst, psychiatrist.

Helene Deutsch was born in Przemysl, Poland, the youngest of four children of Wilhelm Rosenbach, a lawyer and legal scholar, and Regina Fass, a homemaker. Both parents were Jewish. She embraced her father's Polish nationalism and commitment to social justice and considered him the guiding influence in her life. She grew up hating her mother, who was physically and emotionally abusive. Around the age of fourteen, partly to defy her overbearing mother, Helene began a romantic relationship with a much older, married man, Herman Lieberman. A prominent socialist, Lieberman drew Helene into politics and also encouraged her to pursue a formal education. In 1907 she accompanied him to Vienna, where he began a term in the Austrian parliament and she became one of the first women medical students at the university. Their relationship ended in 1910 when she moved to Munich to continue her medical education. There she met Felix Deutsch, an internist her own age. She married him on April 14, 1912, and one year later received her medical degree from the University of Vienna. On January 29, 1917, she gave birth to their only child, Martin.

During World War I, while working at the Wagner-Jauregg Clinic for Psychiatry and Nervous Diseases at the University of Vienna, Deutsch began to specialize in psychiatry and psychoanalysis. In February 1918 she became one of the first women elected to the Vienna Psychoanalytic Society, and later that year she undertook a course of analysis with Sigmund Freud. Although, much to her dismay, Freud suspended their sessions after only one year, she remained enthralled by his theories and therapeutic techniques. He became, she later recalled, "the center of [her] intellectual sphere" (Deutsch, p. 131).

Deutsch delivered her first formal paper on psychoanalysis, "On the Psychology of Mistrust," to the 1920 meeting of the International Psychoanalytic Association. Four years later, at the invitation of the Vienna Psychoanalytic Society, she accepted a position as the first director of its training institute. In 1930 she published a major essay, translated as *Psychoanalysis of the Neuroses,* which established her as an outstanding clinician.

Aware of the dangers posed to Jews by Hitler's rise to power, and enticed by career opportunities in the United States, Helene and Felix Deutsch, along with their son, fled central Europe and resettled in the Boston area. By 1941, when she became an American citizen, she had established herself as a prominent member and training analyst of the Boston Psychoanalytic Institute. Reserved in public but warm among her friends and students, Deutsch was an extraordinarily effective therapist as well as teacher and lecturer. Her colleagues described her as devoid of egotistic traits and capable of deep empathy with her patients.

Deutsch achieved distinction as a principal theorist of female psychosexual development. Her papers on this subject, along with those of KAREN HORNEY, engaged Freud in a prolonged and heated discussion focused on the Oedipus complex in girls, particularly the role of penis envy in establishing the course of feminine development. Although Deutsch considered herself Freud's loyal disciple, she played down the "trauma of anatomical deficiency" and emphasized instead the psychic emergence of the vagina, which she described as the pathway to motherhood. She named not orgasm but childbirth as the pinnacle of woman's sexual pleasure and identified the capacity for motherhood as the defining marker of her difference from man.

Unlike Freud, who advanced a father-centered

theory of development, Deutsch reasoned from the mother's point of view. She held out childbirth and especially nursing as the source of genuine psychic bliss, because these acts alone hold out the possibility of restoring the sense of unity that infants experience at their mother's breast. In both her theoretical writings and her clinical practice, she focused on biological rites of passage, such as onset of menstruation, pregnancy, and menopause, events that, in her opinion, induced conflicts between narcissistic self-love and the love of others.

These ideas came together to constitute the heart of Deutsch's major, two-volume publication, *The Psychology of Women* (1944, 1945). She incorporated her original outline of female development from infancy to old age and renewed her emphasis on motherhood, devoting one entire volume to this topic. After reaffirming the instinctual basis of psychoanalytic theory, she updated her presentation to account for recent trends, notably ego psychology, and acknowledged the importance of cultural and social factors. Alongside her long-established theories about the basic traits of femininity (narcissism, passivity, and masochism), Deutsch branched out to explore the new problems associated with women's expanding opportunities to work outside the home. As women joined men in the realm of intellectual achievement, she reasoned, they ran the risk of endangering their femininity and capacity for motherliness.

After receiving positive reviews when it first appeared, *The Psychology of Women* generated considerable criticism in the late 1960s and early 1970s from second-wave feminists such as Kate Millett and Germaine Greer. Millett, for example, accused Deutsch of promoting the "doctrine of female subjection" (Millett, *Sexual Politics* [1970], p. 206). Late in her life, Deutsch responded to such objections by reaffirming both her advocacy of equality of opportunity and her belief in the indispensable psychic rewards of motherhood.

Over the next several decades, later feminists reevaluated Deutsch's contribution and noted that she had laid a strong foundation for a theory of psychic development that deviated sharply from Freud's phallocentric schema. By emphasizing the lasting importance of the mother–infant bond and the trauma of separation, she anticipated the discussions of the problems of separation and individuation that would mark the rise of psychoanalytic feminism in the works of theorists such as Nancy Chodorow, Jessica Benjamin, and Carol Gilligan.

Although Deutsch devoted less time to writing after the publication of *The Psychology of Women*, she continued to achieve distinction for her clinical work and role as a teacher. She served as president of the Boston Psychoanalytic Society from 1939 to 1941 and affiliated with its training institute and the psychiatry department of the Massachusetts General Hospital in Boston. Meanwhile, Felix Deutsch distinguished himself in the field of psychosomatic medicine.

Until his death in 1964, Felix and Helene Deutsch lived together in a small house in Cambridge, Massachusetts, and at their weekend retreat, a small farm near Lake Winnipesaukee in New Hampshire. They worked together closely, although not always comfortably, throughout their lives. She overshadowed her husband in both professional and social realms. Outliving him by nearly two decades, she continued to take pleasure in her friends, including the many former students who visited her regularly. In her autobiography, *Confrontations with Myself* (1973), Deutsch expressed her enduring belief that "psychoanalysis is *par excellence* a profession for women" (p. 209). She died in Cambridge at age ninety-seven.

Bibliography: Helene Deutsch's papers are at the Schlesinger Library, Radcliffe Institute for Advanced Study, Harvard University. *Psychoanalysis of the Sexual Functions of Women*, her first book, was published in Germany in 1925; it was translated into English by Eric Mosbacher, edited by Paul Roazen, and published in the United States in 1991. Her major writings on psychoanalysis are *Neuroses and Character Types* (1965), *Selected Problems of Adolescence* (1967), and *A Psychoanalytic Study of the Myth of Dionysus and Apollo* (1969). After her death, Paul Roazen collected and edited additional essays on psychoanalysis under the title *The Therapeutic Process, the Self, and Female Psychology* (1992). Deutsch's autobiography, *Confrontations with Myself* (1973), focuses on her experiences in Europe; her authorized biography, *Helene Deutsch, A Psychoanalyst's Life* (1985; reprinted, with a new introduction, 1992), written by Paul Roazen, covers the entire span of her life and professional career. Feminist appraisals of Deutsch's contributions are Brenda S. Webster, "Helene Deutsch: A New Look," *Signs* 10, no. 3 (Spring 1985), pp. 553–571; and Janet Sayers, *Mothers of Psychoanalysis: Helene Deutsch, Karen Horney, Anna Freud, Melanie Klein* (1991). An interview by Anne Roiphe, "What Women Psychoanalysts Say about Women's Liberation," appeared in the *New York Times Magazine*, February 13, 1972. Deutsch's work in relation to other women in Freud's circle is examined by Mari Jo Buhle in *Feminism and Its Discontents: A Century of Struggle with Psychoanalysis* (1998). An obituary appeared in the *New York Times* on April 1, 1982.

MARI JO BUHLE

DEVI, Ragini. August 18, 1893–January 23, 1982. Dancer, dance ethnographer.

Esther Luella Sherman was born in the lakeside town of Petoskey, Michigan. Her mother, Ida Bell Parker, a housewife, was born in Iosco, Michigan; her father, Alexander Otto Sherman, born in Newstead, Ontario, to German parents, was an immigrant tailor. Soon after Esther's birth, her family moved to Minneapolis, where she would spend her formative years learning to be a well-behaved, cultured, middle-class white American. She and her younger brother, DeWitt, grew up in a clapboard house near Lake Harriet, played Bach and Beethoven on the piano, and learned to swim and canoe. Not much else is known about her childhood. Sherman skillfully concealed the details of her early life, and what little she did say about it revolved largely around her love for dance: "I remember dancing as a child of eight," she wrote in the introduction to her pioneering ethnographic survey of folk and classical Indian dances, *Dance Dialects of India* (1972). "I would slip out of the house after dark when I heard music and dance barefoot on the lawn" (p. 15). Later she sought out formal instruction from a local dance teacher.

By the time she graduated from high school in the 1910s, her passion for dance, now well established, led her to engage a local man (a Russian immigrant) to teach her ballet. Soon the two were performing a revue of "international" dances at local cabarets and small theaters around Minneapolis. Using the stage names "Rita Cassilas" and "Todi Ragini," Sherman spent her nights performing an array of Russian folk dances and self-styled Greek- and Egyptian-themed pieces, and her days studying Indian history and culture at the University of Minnesota at St. Paul (most likely as a nonmatriculating student). At the university she met the young scientist from Nagpur, India, whom she would eventually marry. A committed Indian nationalist, Ramlal Balaram Bajpai was wanted by the British, as family legend had it, for defacing a public statue of Queen Victoria. He managed to evade capture by escaping to the United States, where he enrolled at the University of Minnesota in 1916. In 1921 (against her parents' wishes), Sherman married Bajpai in a civil ceremony in Wilmington, Delaware, and they moved to Brooklyn, New York.

There she found some work in silent films, but her career turned a corner on April 28, 1922, when she gave a solo performance onstage at Manhattan's Greenwich Village Theater. Dancing supposedly authentic Indian entertainments, she made her debut as Ragini Devi—telling her American audiences that she was a Kashmiri Hindu born, raised, and trained to dance in India. From then on, she was known, on stage and off, as Ragini Devi (in India, though, she never passed for anything other than a Westerner well versed in Indian attitudes and culture). Between 1922 and 1930, her self-styled performances earned praise from American dance critics and exotica-seekers alike. In 1928, she published her pioneering first book, *Nritanjali,* an introduction to Hindu dancing for American readers, which earned critical acclaim in the States as well as in India.

In 1930, seizing on her new international fame, Devi decided to travel to India, which she had been long eager to do. Committed to dance above all else, Devi permanently left her husband and set sail for South India—where, upon arrival, she gave birth both to her only daughter, Indrani (September 19, 1930), and to a new phase of her career.

Eager to study Indian dance at its source, she traveled furiously about, seeking out teachers. In Madras she studied *sadir* (which was later transformed into India's best-known classical dance, Bharata Natyam) with famed ex-Devadesi Mylapore Gauri Amma; traveling to the southwestern coastal state of Kerala, she became the first woman to study Kathakali at the legendary Kerala Kalamandalam. Eager to join the young, nationalism-inspired effort to revive and reinvent indigenous Indian arts, she persuaded a youthful Kathakali master, Gopinath, to partner her on a national tour aimed at introducing audiences in the rest of India to Kathakali. Shortening the length of the dances, streamlining the costumes, and staging them on an indoor, proscenium stage, Devi and Gopinath gained prominence by transforming Kathakali into evening entertainment for urban theatergoers.

From 1933 to 1936 they toured India, presenting their adapted Kathakali "dance dramas" to entranced audiences and rave reviews. In 1938, Devi set sail (without Gopinath) for a European tour—which had barely begun when the escalation of European hostilities forced her to return, with her daughter, to the United States. Stranded in New York City, she established the India Dance Theatre, a dance school and company on West 57th Street, where she profited from the growing American rage for "ethnic" and "exotic" dance. In 1947 she traveled back to India (where her daughter, now married, was living) and in 1949 won a Rockefeller Foundation grant to support her ethnographic work. For the next several years she traveled the young nation, documenting regional classical and folk dance forms. Meanwhile, carrying on the family torch, Indrani soon became one of India's best-loved cultural ambassadors, performing before world leaders such as Mao Zedong and John F. Kennedy the dances her mother had fought to preserve. Devi half-jokingly lamented this state of affairs: "My daughter has already pushed me to the background. There was a time when I was known in my own right!" (*Evening News of India,* August 8, 1952).

Throughout the late 1950s and 1960s, Devi lived in Bombay, compiling the results of her research. In 1972 she finally saw *Dance Dialects of India* published; in 1978 she left India, tearfully, to retire at the assisted living facility in Englewood, New Jersey—the Actor's Fund Home—where she would die, from a stroke, on January 23, 1982. Her final performance, held at New York University, had taken place just a few years before, in 1979. Sharing the stage with her daughter and granddaughter, both accomplished performers in their own right, she expressed delight in seeing the fruits of her lifelong labors displayed by three generations of her own family. Many consider Devi's greatest achievement to be the introduction of the dances of India to the United States. It is clear that in addition to her artistic and ethnographic achievements, Ragini Devi's life is also notable for what it suggests about the history of Americans' fascination with "the East."

Bibliography: There are two principal manuscript collections of Ragini Devi's papers: one, consisting largely of news clippings and photographs, is housed in the Dance Collection at the New York Public Library for the Performing Arts at Lincoln Center; the other, which contains a range of personal and professional correspondence, notes, clippings, and more photographs, is in the Mohan Khokar Dance Collection, in Chennai, Tamil Nadu, India. Together, these collections preserve copies of Devi's various magazine and newspaper profiles, reviews of her performances in India, Europe, and the United States, and an incomplete assortment of her published ethnographic and unpublished personal writings. They also contain detailed oral interviews with Devi's daughter, Indrani Rahman, who died in 1999. Another small collection of oral testimonies, gathered from an assortment of Devi's surviving colleagues and acquaintances in 2001 and 2002, remains in the author's possession.

Other important sources of biographical information include *Dancing in the Family: An Unconventional Memoir of Three Women* (2001), an anecdotally rich family memoir written by Devi's granddaughter Sukanya Rahman; and Susheela Misra's *Some Dancers of India* (1992), which opens with a lengthy combined entry on Ragini Devi, Indrani, and Gopinath. See also Marianne Elizabeth Jirgal Fainstadt, "Dance of India in USA, 1906–1970" (MA thesis, UCLA, 1970). Rachel Mattson, "The Seductions of Dissonance: Ragini Devi and the Idea of India in the US, 1893–1965" (PhD dissertation, New York University, 2003), places Devi's unusual story into a critical analytical and historical context. An obituary appeared in the *New York Times* on January 26, 1982.

RACHEL MATTSON

DEWHURST, Colleen. June 3, 1924–August 22, 1991. Actress.

Colleen Dewhurst was born with no theatrical lineage whatever and had no contacts in the profession to exploit. She was not a stagestruck or even an extroverted child and had no youthful ambitions to any sort of career in the arts. Yet for more than thirty years she was at the very pinnacle of her profession, as highly esteemed by the public as she was by her peers.

Dewhurst was born in Montreal, the only child of Fred Dewhurst, a onetime professional hockey and football player, and Frances Dewhurst, who was, variously, a receptionist and a Christian Science practitioner. Her parents relocated often when Colleen was a child, first to the Boston area and then to various towns north of Milwaukee; she rarely attended a school for more than a year. The elder Dewhursts divorced when Colleen was thirteen, and thereafter she had little contact with her father. After high school, she enrolled in Milwaukee Downer College, with her only real ambition being to become an aviator. After two years, however, stimulated by some college skits she both wrote and performed, she persuaded her mother to allow her to relocate in New York in 1945 and attend the American Academy of Dramatic Arts.

Once Dewhurst was part of the Manhattan theatrical scene, her life followed a stereotypical pattern: acting classes (one instructor was the legendary Harold Clurman), low-wage jobs, auditions, and small-scale performances. Her only steady work was in the quite extensive network of summer stock theaters.

In 1956 Dewhurst accidentally came to the notice of Joseph Papp, who had recently inaugurated his project (then widely regarded as outlandish) to provide free performances of Shakespeare in working-class New York neighborhoods. He included Dewhurst in his company, first as the barbaric Tamora in *Titus Andronicus* and then, in her breakthrough role, as Kate in *The Taming of the Shrew.* There followed Gertrude, Lady Macbeth, and Cleopatra. She was at last becoming an actress with a reputation, at least in the realm of classical theater.

She attracted further notice in dramas of the sort that in the 1950s mostly appeared off-Broadway. Among her successes were Edwin Justus Mayer's *Children of Darkness* (1958), where she first worked with her favorite director and lifelong friend, José Quintero. Three years later, on Broadway, came Tad Mosel's *All the Way Home,* an adaptation of James Agee's novel *A Death in the Family.* For her interpretation of the heroic Mary Follet, Dewhurst would earn an Antoinette Perry ("Tony") Award for best actress in 1961.

The dramatist with whom she would always be most identified, however, was Eugene O'Neill. Her first Broadway appearance had been as a neighbor in *Desire under the Elms* in 1952; there would follow *More Stately Mansions* (1967), *Mourning Becomes Electra* (1972), and *Long Day's Journey into Night* (1988). But she received her greatest acclaim for the O'Neill role that some had called "unplayable": Josie Hogan—simultaneously virgin, whore, and mother—in *A Moon for the Misbegotten* in 1973. Her triumph in Quintero's production earned her near-universal praise and a second Tony.

Although often called the consummate O'Neill actress, Dewhurst might have claimed the same honor for the plays of Edward Albee. She had a personal (if not a box office) triumph as the hulking recluse Amelia Evans in his adaptation of CARSON MCCULLERS's story *The Ballad of the Sad Café* (1963). A decade later she starred in *All Over* (1971) under John Gielgud's direction, and in 1976 in a revival under the playwright's direction of *Who's Afraid of Virginia Woolf?*

The weightiness of most of these plays led to Dewhurst's reputation as a solemn tragedian: at five foot eight and possessed of a forceful baritone, she evoked substance, a solidity of appearance. But the infectious laugh and antic sense of humor that so delighted her friends also appealed to audiences in her comic performances. These included revivals of Kaufman and Hart's *You Can't Take It with You* in 1983, in which she contributed a climactic cameo as the Grand Duchess Olga, opposite her longtime friend and co-star, Jason Robards, and O'Neill's only comedy, *Ah, Wilderness!* in 1988.

Although Dewhurst always insisted that the stage was her one natural milieu, her credits include a long list of films and television appearances. Most of her film roles were cameos, a few notable examples being *A Fine Madness* (1966), *The Cowboys* (1972), *Annie Hall* (1977), *Tribute* (1980), and *Dying Young* (1991), opposite her younger son, Campbell Scott. Her numerous television appearances included works of such major dramatists as Arthur Miller, Jean-Paul Sartre, and Euripides, as well as two for which she won Emmy Awards for best supporting actress: *Between Two Women* (1986) and *Those She Left Behind* (1989). She was honored twice with Emmys as Avery Brown, the memorable mother of Candice Bergen's character in the television sitcom *Murphy Brown*.

Although Dewhurst will be remembered in the main as a superb performer, she set her social activism at an equal value. Serving for two terms as president of Actors' Equity, the 39,000-member union of stage actors, she was outspoken in favor of increasing opportunities for ethnic minorities and was arrested for demonstrating against the planned demolition of the Helen Hayes and Morosco Theatres. When the specter of AIDS first began to afflict the theatrical community, she was a vigorous activist in favor of government-funded research and was instrumental in the creation of Broadway Cares and Equity Fights AIDS.

Dewhurst was married in 1947 to fellow actor James Vickery; they divorced in 1959. She married her *Children of Darkness* co-star George C. Scott in 1959; their two sons, Alexander and Campbell, were born in 1960 and 1961. The couple divorced in 1963, remarried in 1967, and divorced for the second time in 1971. Her companion over her last years was theatrical producer Ken Marsolais. After a period of severe discomfort during which she tried to keep performing (her final appearance was opposite Robards in A. R. Gurney's *Love Letters*), Dewhurst died of cervical cancer in 1991 in her beloved farmhouse in South Salem, New York. She was sixty-seven.

Playgoers who were fortunate to see Dewhurst in her prime roles are unlikely to forget her, but the surest indicator of her stature as an actress comes from her peers and colleagues. Cherry Jones, who would herself appear in the role of Josie Hogan twenty years later, exclaimed, "Colleen Dewhurst in *A Moon for the Misbegotten* made the earth stop spinning."

Bibliography: Colleen Dewhurst: Her Autobiography was in very rough form at the time of her death; it was completed by her editor, Tom Viola, and published in 1997. Though not seriously inaccurate, it provides a rather sanitized account. The Billy Rose Theatre Collection at the New York Public Library for the Performing Arts, Lincoln Center, includes an extensive clipping file and also a videotaped interview with Dewhurst conducted by Edwin Wilson for City University Television in 1991. For biographical information, see *Current Biography* (1974), pp. 110–13; Emily McMurray, ed., *Contemporary Theatre, Film, and Television*, vol. 11 (1994), which also includes a full list of stage, film, and television credits for Dewhurst; and Barbara Lee Horn, *Colleen Dewhurst: A Bio-Bibliography* (1993). José Quintero's *If You Don't Dance, They Beat You* (1974) provides a useful personal account. Susan Pizzolato provided very helpful research assistance. The final quote is found in Jackson R. Bryer and Richard A. Davison, eds., *The Actor's Art: Conversations with Contemporary American Stage Performers* (2001), p. 141. Obituaries appeared in the *New York Times* on August 24, 1991, and *Variety* on August 26, 1991.

JOHN D. SHOUT

DICKERSON, Nancy. January 27, 1927–October 18, 1997. Television news correspondent, producer.

Nancy Conners Hanschman never expected to have a career in the media. Born in Wauwatosa, Wisconsin, she was one of two daughters of Florence Conners and Frederick R. Hanschman, a successful architectural engineer. After graduating from Wauwatosa High School in 1944, she attended Clarke College, a small Catholic women's college in Dubuque, Iowa, where she studied piano. Transferring to the University of Wisconsin in 1946, she majored in Spanish and Portuguese and got her degree in 1948, after which she spent several years in Milwaukee as a teacher. But she couldn't forget the conference she had attended in Europe while a United Nations student delegate: since then, she had wanted to find a way to help improve global communication.

After moving to Washington, D.C., she took a job in the spring of 1951 doing research and writing reports and speeches for members of the Senate Foreign Relations Committee. Working with the committee taught her about politics and brought her into contact with some of the most powerful men in America, but because she was a woman, she was excluded from opportunities to advance. As she noted in her 1976 memoir, *Among Those Present,* "Since I was young and female, I was told there was no chance for me to make investigative trips on my own, as male staff members did. Also, since I did not have my doctorate and was a woman, there was no chance that I could ever become chief of staff" (p. 19).

By 1954, she had decided to enter the field of journalism. After turning down a newspaper job on the women's page, she got a job producing two public affairs radio shows for CBS, *The Leading Question* and *Capitol Cloakroom.* Television was overtaking radio in popularity, but thanks to the good contacts she had made while working for the Senate, she was usually able to get important guests and come up with interesting topics for them to discuss. Her next job took her to television, where she became the associate producer of *Face the Nation,* a new show created as competition for NBC-TV's very successful *Meet the Press.* She also became a fixture in Washington's social scene, dating some of the most eligible bachelors in town and developing long-standing friendships with numerous influential political figures and their wives.

After six years of producing and doing special projects for CBS radio and television (including working as an assistant for Edward R. Murrow), she was determined to get on the air, even though few women, such as PAULINE FREDERICK, had been able to do so up to that point. In February 1960, she succeeded, becoming CBS's first woman correspondent, covering the political conventions and the presidential election. Later that year she also hosted her own CBS radio show, *One Woman's Washington.*

In 1962 she married real estate tycoon C. Wyatt Dickerson, a widower with three children, and continued to work as a reporter. But she felt that many of the men at CBS were jealous when she got scoops or handled big stories, and in 1963 she decided to change networks. Becoming a correspondent for NBC, she covered the assassination of President Kennedy and the administration of Lyndon B. Johnson, who was already a friend. Over the years, she reported on such major events as Martin Luther King's "I Have a Dream" speech, the anti-war demonstrations in Chicago, and the inauguration of President Nixon. She also anchored occasional newscasts, the first woman on NBC to do so. Although she went on assignment all over the world and expanded the public's acceptance of a woman doing news, the print media of her day seemed more fascinated by what she wore than by what she achieved. Numerous articles dwelled on her extensive wardrobe; one reporter praised her for maintaining the balance between being authoritative yet feminine.

Nancy Dickerson, by her own account, was a very intense and driven person who preferred to be busy. In her personal life, she had two sons (Michael and John, born in 1963 and 1968) with her husband and helped raise his three daughters, Elizabeth, Ann, and Jane. A well-known hostess, her dinner parties at the Dickerson's Kalorama Triangle townhouse or Merrywood, their estate in McLean, Virginia, attracted Washington's political elite. But her journalism career was also important to her, and she continued to work for NBC. As a result of all this, she was under considerable stress. "I was always controversial at the networks. Aside from being the only female in my position, I irked some people. I was raising five children, working a full day and often at night and on Sundays, and I simply did not have time to waste. As a result I could be excessively abrupt, even arrogant, which naturally prompted retribution" (*Among Those Present,* p. 151).

After she left NBC in 1970, she became a syndicated producer of news programs and documentaries; her work appeared regularly on PBS and elsewhere. A 1982 documentary she produced, *784 Days That Changed America—From Watergate to Resignation,* won a Peabody Award. She also interviewed major newsmakers, such as Egyptian President Anwar Sadat and Israeli Prime Minister Manachem Begin, and did specials about such topics as the role of women in Islam. Her style of reporting, common now but unusual at the time, humanized many of the newsmakers. Her first marriage ended in divorce in 1983, and in 1989 she married John Whitehead, former deputy secretary of state. She was a commentator for the Fox Network from 1986 through 1991, and continued to do some work for PBS after that. She died in New York City on October 18, 1997, of complications from a stroke at the age of seventy.

In a 1983 interview with Marian Christy, Nancy Dickerson remarked, "I have to tell you this: It's corny, but I think it's everyone's duty to make the world a better place." She saw journalism as a calling, not just a way of earning money, and she tried to do her job ethically and honestly. Above all, Nancy Dickerson proved that a woman could be a credible TV reporter at a time when newswomen were not widely accepted.

Bibliography: The best introduction to Nancy Dickerson is her autobiography, *Among Those Present: A Reporter's View of Twenty-five Years in Washington* (1976). Additional biographical information can be found in Nancy Signorelli, ed., *Women in Communication: A Biographical Sourcebook* (1996). Articles about Dickerson and her career include Marian Christy, "There's No Time to Squander; Nancy Dickerson's Old-Fashioned Work Ethic," *Boston Globe*, June 21, 1983, which contains the final quote; Lee Graham, "Women Don't Like to Look at Women," *New York Times*, May 24, 1964; and Steven V. Roberts, "Another First for Nancy," *New York Times*, January 3, 1965. The Wauwatosa Public Library provided valuable research assistance to the author. Obituaries appeared in the *New York Times* and the *Washington Post* on October 19, 1997.

DONNA L. HALPER

DIETRICH, Marlene. December 27, 1901–May 6, 1992. Actress, singer.

Born Maria Magdalena Dietrich in Berlin, the second child and second daughter of police lieutenant Louis Erich Otto Dietrich and Wilhelmina Elisabeth Josephine Felsing, the future icon of enigmatic glamour was reared in a strict Prussian environment. Her father died when she was only six years old, and her mother then married Eduard von Losch, an aristocratic cavalry officer who subsequently perished in the First World War. Dietrich developed a great love for art, literature, and specifically French culture during her years at the Augusta Victoria School in Berlin. She showed musical talent and her mother insisted she pursue a career as a violinist, so Dietrich was enrolled in the Berlin Music Academy. She left in 1921, fascinated by the experimental theater and cabaret life of the city, and was later admitted to Max Reinhardt's Theater School, where she first used the name Marlene Dietrich. She immediately found small parts in revues and stage plays.

On May 17, 1923, she married assistant director Rudolf Sieber. She separated from him in 1939 but never divorced him, despite her publicized affairs with other men (including several co-stars and long relationships with German author Erich Maria Remarque and French actor Jean Gabin) and reportedly with women. Their daughter, Dietrich's only child, Maria Elisabeth Sieber, was born on December 13, 1924. A new family did not hamper Dietrich's ambitions, and she first attracted major attention on the musical stage, singing a duet with the famed cabaret performer Margo Lion in the revue *Es liegt in der Luft (It's in the Air)*.

Dietrich met her influential mentor, film director Josef von Sternberg, in 1929, when he returned from Hollywood to film Heinrich Mann's novel *Professor Unrat*, retitled *Der blaue Engel (The Blue Angel)*, Germany's first sound feature for UFA studios. Although Dietrich had already gained popularity as a singer and had appeared in several films (including a leading role in the 1927 Austrian film *Café Electric*), she always insisted that she had been an innocent, inexperienced theater student who had stumbled unprepared into the audition. In actuality, von Sternberg had long admired her aloof beauty on film and stage, and had insisted on casting her in the pivotal role of the film's cabaret singer, Lola Lola—the leggy, garter-belted, top-hat-wearing siren who tragically alters the orderly life of an aging boys' school teacher. The film premiered in Berlin on April 1, 1930, and was an instant success. Dietrich's songs, particularly her signature melody, "Ich bin von Kopf bis Fuss auf Liebe eingestellt" ("Falling in Love Again"), sold out as recordings. Dietrich and von Sternberg immediately departed for Hollywood, where she signed a seven-year contract with Paramount Pictures.

Dietrich's first American film, *Morocco* (1930), directed by von Sternberg, garnered her an Academy Award nomination for best actress. Among her early Hollywood films, which include *Shanghai Express* (1932), *Blonde Venus* (1932), and *The Devil Is a Woman* (1935), her portrayal of Catherine the Great in *The Scarlet Empress* (1934) is most notable. Her cross-dressing on and off screen added a gender-bending element to her image and also influenced fashion. Nevertheless, Dietrich's typecasting as a decadent femme fatale ultimately did her career more harm than good and eventually she found herself, along with Katharine Hepburn and GRETA GARBO, labeled "box office poison." After seven films with von Sternberg, she finally broke with her possessive director in 1936 and walked out on her Paramount contract, choosing to freelance for other studios instead.

By 1937 the Nazi regime had lost significant film talent to exile following its assumption of power in Germany and subsequent nationalization of the film industry. Propaganda Minister Joseph Goebbels, seeking to reclaim a major international star for German cinema, attempted to lure Dietrich back with a staggering salary and complete script, director, and producer approval. Fervently anti-Nazi, Dietrich rejected Goebbels's offer. She applied for American citizenship in 1937 and received it two years later, incurring the wrath of the Nazi press.

Despite her break with von Sternberg, he convinced her to take the role of Frenchy opposite James Stewart in George Marshall's western, *Destry Rides Again* (1939), and this more accessible Dietrich persona revitalized her career. She interrupted her film career in 1943 to aid the Allied war effort, joining the United Service Organizations (USO) and entertaining, often in uniform, American troops on the front lines in North Africa, Italy, and France. This made her a unique international symbol: she at once represented a "good" Germany as well as the multicultural, immigrant nature of the United States. In appreciation, Dietrich was awarded the U.S. Presidential Medal of Freedom and made a Chevalier (and later an Officer and a Commander) of the French Legion of Honor.

Her sporadic later film roles, especially her performances in Billy Wilder's *A Foreign Affair* (1948) and *Witness for the Prosecution* (1957), Alfred Hitchcock's *Stage Fright* (1950), and Stanley Kramer's *Judgment at Nuremberg* (1961), have gained critical reevaluation since her death, but her postwar career encompassed more than film. Turning to the stage, she appeared in Las Vegas and on Broadway in a highly successful one-woman show. She also toured internationally, but her performances in West Germany in 1960 brought a mixed reaction of adulation and lingering resentment regarding her "treasonous" abandonment of her homeland during the war. Concerned about her appearance and health problems after breaking a leg during a performance in Australia in 1975, she exiled herself from public life. Her two final appearances in film were a heavily veiled cameo in *Just a Gigolo* (1979) and an audio presence in Maximilian Schell's superb documentary of her life and work, *Marlene* (1984).

A recluse at her Avenue Montaigne apartment in Paris, Dietrich resisted seeing journalists, fans, or even her few surviving Hollywood friends, taking legal action against any incursions on her privacy. She died of natural causes in her sleep on May 6, 1992. Services were held at La Madeleine in Paris, and she was buried near her mother's grave at the Friedenau Cemetery in Berlin. Her brave role as a German American in World War II heartened Americans, who also cherished her image as an exotic "Golden Age" Hollywood icon. Her unique look has been emulated by everyone from MARILYN MONROE to Madonna, but she has received less recognition for her progressive influence on women's roles in cinema and society. Recent years, however, suggest a more serious reception of Dietrich: a square in Berlin and a soundstage at the former UFA studios now bear her name, a German postage stamp was issued in 1997 to commemorate her international stardom, and even her direct involvement with the Allied war effort has found a growing appreciation with newer generations of Germans.

Bibliography: Marlene Dietrich insisted that she was born in 1904 (and later dates), although records show 1901 to be the correct year. Her naturalization as a U.S. citizen has also been variously reported as occurring between 1936 and 1939. The Marlene Dietrich Collection at the Stiftung Deutsche Kinemathek in Berlin is an impressive archive of her correspondence with a wide variety of world leaders, artists, and celebrities and includes photographs, scripts, press clippings, and personal items spanning her long career. In 1960, her thoughts on a variety of subjects were collected in a book entitled *Marlene Dietrich's ABC*. Her 1978 autobiography, *Nehmt nur mein Leben (My Life Story)*, and her 1989 version, *Ich bin, Gott sei Dank, Berlinerin (My Life)*, are more creative than factual; the 1993 biography *Marlene* by daughter Maria Riva is detailed and reliable, but often tends toward very subjective criticism. Books on Dietrich abound in several languages, the most important English-language examples being Richard Griffith, *Marlene Dietrich—Image and Legend* (1959); Josef von Sternberg's autobiography, *Fun in a Chinese Laundry* (1965); Leslie Frewin, *Dietrich: The Story of a Star* (1967); and John Kobal, *Marlene Dietrich* (1968). A 1968 illustrated filmography by Homer Dickens, *The Films of Marlene Dietrich*, was revised and reissued in 1992 as *The Complete Films of Marlene Dietrich*. For several decades *Marlene: The Life of Marlene Dietrich* by Charles Higham (1977) was considered the most authoritative exposé. More recent works are *Dietrich* by Alexander Walker (1984), *Sublime Marlene* by Thierry de Navacelle (1984), *Dietrich: Style and Substance* by Patrick O'Connor (1991), the well-researched *Marlene Dietrich: Life and Legend* by Steven Bach (1992), and the somewhat more sensationalist *Blue Angel: The Life of Marlene Dietrich* by Donald Spoto (1992). A particularly useful bibliography of Dietrich's filmography is found in the entry by Robert Pardi in *The International Dictionary of Films and Filmmakers* (4th ed., 2000). Obituaries appeared in the *New York Times* on May 7, 1992, and *Variety* on May 11, 1992.

ROBERT VON DASSANOWSKY

DOUGLAS, Helen Gahagan. November 25, 1900–June 28, 1980. Actress, politician.

Helen Gahagan Douglas, a Democratic congresswoman from California who lost a celebrated U.S. Senate race to Richard Nixon in 1950, held national center stage in the early years of postwar American politics. She was born in Boonton, New Jersey, the middle of five children of Lillian Rose Mussen, a former teacher, and Walter Hamer Gahagan II. She grew up in Brooklyn's posh Park Slope neighborhood; her father, a contracting engineer, owned the Gahagan Construction Company. Her mother insisted on tutors—for dance, languages, piano, horseback riding—and outings to art exhibitions and classical concerts. In 1914 the family bought a summer home in Fairlee, Vermont, which was a refuge for Helen throughout her life.

Helen attended the private Brooklyn girls' school Berkeley Institute. Her poor performance and her fascination with acting led her parents to send her to secondary school at Capen School in Northampton, Massachusetts. After graduating in 1920, she entered Manhattan's Barnard College. In her sophomore year she landed a role in an off-Broadway play. This performance ended college but opened the door to a spectacular Broadway career.

Gahagan worked under top New York producer-managers attracted to her natural talent, dramatic style, uncommon beauty, height, and elegant carriage. Family money allowed Helen to be picky, accepting only starring roles in interesting productions. In 1927 she began operatic voice training. Disappointed after two summers singing in Europe, she returned to New York for David Belasco's *Tonight or Never.* She fell in love with her leading man, the handsome, talented Melvyn Douglas (né Melvyn Hesselburg). They married on April 5, 1931, and moved to Hollywood for Melvyn's film opportunities. The couple had two children: Peter (1933) and Mary Helen (1938). In between she starred in her only film, H. Rider Haggard's *She* (1935). She was also close to Melvyn's son Gregory from his first marriage.

In 1937, Gahagan's life took an extraordinary new direction after a European singing tour exposed her to Nazism. She joined the Hollywood Anti-Nazi League, then chaired the John Steinbeck Committee to Aid Migratory Workers. In 1939, ELEANOR ROOSEVELT invited the Douglases to the White House for an intimate small dinner, cementing Helen's commitment to New Deal politics. She moved her acting talents to the political stage and never looked back.

Her friendship with Eleanor Roosevelt quickly opened doors for Gahagan. In July 1940 she was elected California's Democratic national committeewoman. After campaigning for President Roosevelt in 1940, she was appointed head of the Women's Division for California and vice-chair of the Democratic Party in California, thus holding the three top party positions for women. Gahagan placed her public life at the top of her priorities. A strained marriage became long distance when Melvyn moved to Washington for his war efforts and later joined the army. With Peter in private school and help at home, Helen had the freedom and the money to move energetically into Democratic politics.

In 1944, feeling restless, she filed, under the name Helen Gahagan Douglas, in the primary race for the Fourteenth Congressional District, the seat of retiring New Dealer Thomas Ford. Undaunted by unfamiliarity with this downtown district, right-wing accusations of Communist ties resulting from her and Melvyn's Popular Front activities, and atypical credentials for a female political candidate, she pulled off a narrow win. She moved to Washington with her children and her loyal babysitter and friend, Evelyn Chavoor, who ran her household and office. Melvyn returned to the couple's Los Angeles home after the war.

Douglas joined eight other women in Congress, including MARY NORTON, MARGARET CHASE SMITH, and CLARE BOOTHE LUCE. New Deal rhetoric and President Harry S. Truman's Fair Deal domestic liberalism shaped her ideology of uncompromising morality, reason, and human decency. In the House Foreign Affairs Committee, she pressed for America to lead international peace efforts. Domestically she fought for bettering life for the ordinary American. Douglas early prioritized civil rights. Her interests broadened to Jewish concerns, including the creation of Israel, and civilian control of atomic energy. She co-sponsored the Atomic Energy Act of 1946, her single legislative success. Despite being away from her district and gloomy prospects for Democrats in 1946, she won handily, thanks to her campaign managers, Ruth and Ed Lybeck.

In the Republican-dominated 80th Congress she quickly involved herself in organized labor's vow to return Congress to Democratic hands in 1948. She immersed herself in efforts to extend the wartime Fair Employment Practices Commission, continue consumer price and rent controls, and expand middle-class housing, particularly for veterans. Her flamboyant 1947 "Market Basket Speech," delivered with a basket full of groceries on her arm, made a strong anti-inflationary statement on the House floor. In 1948, her district sent her back by a two-to-one margin.

Eager for change but with little support from party leadership, Douglas announced in October 1949 she would run against aging conservative Democratic senator Sheridan Downey. In March 1950, Downey withdrew, ostensibly for health reasons, and was replaced by Manchester Boddy, editor of the Democratic *Los Angeles Daily News.* In the primary campaign Boddy dubbed Douglas the Pink Lady, but effective support from organized labor, liberal women's groups, blacks, small farmers, organized ethnic groups, liberal intellectuals, and nationally visible Democrats such as Eleanor Roosevelt created campaign momentum, and Douglas easily won the Democratic primary.

Her opponent was Republican congressman Richard M. Nixon. In a climate of worsening cold war tensions, Nixon used his strong anti-communist credentials in the House, particularly with the Alger Hiss perjury case, to imply that Douglas was "pink down to her underwear." Douglas lost handily, receiving half as many votes as Nixon. The race remains one of the worst "red-smear" campaigns in American politics.

Douglas did not let the campaign loss diminish her sense of self, and after the election a semblance of family gradually returned, as did a happier marriage. In 1951 the Douglases moved to Manhattan. Although she refused offers of high-level appointments or opportunities to run for office, the public aura around her never dissipated and she maintained a full schedule of speeches, campaigning, and travel. Disarmament became a major concern in the 1950s, and she spoke out against the Vietnam War a decade later. In the early 1970s, women's movement leaders, particularly those urging women to run for political office, sought her out, and she graced the cover of *Ms.* in October 1973. The Watergate hearings and Nixon's resignation in 1974 brought a rush of attention and reexamination of the 1950 campaign. In 1972 she was diagnosed with breast cancer, and her health gradually deteriorated. Helen Gahagan Douglas died on June 28, 1980, in New York City at the age of seventy-nine.

Bibliography: Helen Gahagan Douglas's papers are found at the Carl Albert Congressional Research and Studies Center, University of Oklahoma, Norman. Additional archival material is located at Bancroft Library, University of California, Berkeley; and the Franklin D. Roosevelt Presidential Library, Hyde Park, New York. Material on her theatrical career is in the Billy Rose Theatre Collection, the New York Public Library for the Performing Arts, Lincoln Center. Her oral history, along with interviews with colleagues and friends, is in the Women in Politics Oral History Project at Bancroft Library; also of interest is Melvyn Douglas's oral history in the Indiana University Oral History Program. Helen Gahagan Douglas's well-written autobiography, *A Full Life* (1982), appeared posthumously. For biographical information, see Ingrid W. Scobie, *Center Stage: Helen Gahagan Douglas, A Life* (1992). See also Colleen Marie O'Connor, "Through the Valley of Darkness: Helen Gahagan Douglas' Congressional Years" (PhD dissertation, University of California, San Diego, 1982). On the 1950 campaign, see Greg Mitchell, *Tricky Dick and the Pink Lady: Richard Nixon vs. Helen Gahagan Douglas—Sexual Politics and the Red Scare, 1950* (1998). An obituary appeared in the *New York Times* on June 29, 1980.

INGRID WINTHER SCOBIE

DOUGLAS, Marjory Stoneman. April 7, 1890–May 14, 1998. Writer, environmentalist.

Marjory Stoneman Douglas was a popular writer who became an ardent environmentalist. Her newspaper columns, fiction, poetry, and nonfiction defined South Florida as a distinctive region, revealed her role as a social activist, and propelled her, late in life, into the leadership of a crusade to save the Everglades.

Born in Minneapolis, Minnesota, Marjory spent her childhood and young adult years in New England. She was the only child of Florence Lillian Trefethen and Frank Bryant Stoneman. Stoneman, who was raised in a Quaker colony in Indiana, attended the University of Minnesota and later became an attorney and a founder and editor of the *Miami Herald.* After attempting several unsuccessful business ventures, Stoneman moved his young family to Providence, Rhode Island. Lillian, a talented violinist, began to suffer nervous breakdowns, and in 1895 she and Marjory moved to her parents' house in Taunton, Massachusetts, where Marjory was cared for by her grandmother and aunt Fanny. Stoneman remained in Providence, later moving to Florida.

Marjory attended the Taunton public schools, graduating from high school in 1908, and entered Wellesley College as a member of the class of 1912. An English major, she studied with KATHERINE LEE BATES and VIDA SCUDDER. EMILY GREENE BALCH cultivated her social conscience; Elizabeth Fisher, her knowledge of geology and geography; and Malvina Bennett, her speaking voice. When discussing her early commitment to women's rights, Douglas wrote, "As Wellesley developed our skills, we also became more convinced of a woman's right to use them" (Douglas, *Voice of the River,* p. 78).

Marjory's first years after college were difficult. Her mother died of cancer soon after commencement. Not wanting to teach or return to Taunton, Marjory lived in Boston that summer, training to teach basic skills to salesgirls in department stores, and then took jobs in St. Louis and Newark, New Jersey. Quite lonely when she landed in Newark, she often frequented the local library, where she met well-mannered Kenneth Douglas, the church and social service editor for the Newark *Evening News,* thirty years her senior. More than ready to accept his attentions, she agreed to marry him three months later in April 1914.

Within months of their marriage, Kenneth was arrested for passing bad checks and sentenced to six months in jail. She rejoined him after his release, but her uncle advised her to leave Kenneth and meet her father in Florida. The childless marriage was dissolved by 1918. Although Marjory kept her married name because she believed it was easier to get along with the title "Mrs.", she felt she had been so completely dominated in her marriage that she never again accepted control by anybody, particularly a man.

Except for service in Europe during World War I, Marjory Stoneman Douglas devoted the rest of her life to presenting the drama and needs of South Florida to the public. Her tools were her pen and her voice. When she arrived in Miami in September 1915, it had fewer than five thousand residents; when she died eighty-three years later, the metropolitan area counted 4.5 million. She was met on her arrival in Miami by her father and his new wife, Lillius Eleanor Shine (Lilla), a native of North Florida, who became her close friend and introduced her to a southern point of view. By then Frank Stoneman was editor of the *Miami Herald.* When the society editor took a leave, Douglas replaced her and began to make the many personal contacts that would help her throughout her career. That spring she testified before the state legislature about the need to ratify the woman suffrage amendment.

With war raging in Europe, Douglas enlisted in the navy as a yeoman first class. Frustrated with clerical assignments, she put in for a discharge and joined the Civilian Relief Department of the American Red Cross, leaving for France in September 1918. During her time overseas, she sent back dispatches about Red Cross relief work in France, Italy, and the Balkans and absorbed disquieting images of the cost of war to civilians, especially refugees. Before she returned home, her father cabled her with an offer to be assistant editor of the *Miami Herald.*

During the three years that Douglas produced her daily column, "The Galley," she expressed her growing social consciousness. Her ballad "Martin Tabert of North Dakota Is Walking Florida Now," about a boy beaten to death in a labor camp, was widely circulated. She started a Baby Milk Fund and began to speak out about the problems arising from Miami's real estate boom, demanding that the growth be managed and that land be set aside for parks and recreation. She also developed an interest in the Everglades, witnessing the nuptial flight of the white ibis early one morning and observing flocks of birds numbering thirty to forty thousand. She served on a committee organized by Ernest F. Coe working to establish Everglades National Park. After the pressure of her schedule led to what a doctor called "nerve fatigue," Douglas decided to leave the *Herald.*

For the next fifteen years Douglas established herself as a regional writer of colorful short stories about South Florida that appeared in popular magazines, in particular the *Saturday Evening Post.* Her characters and plots reflect issues in historical and modern South Florida and often show young people or older women outwitting shady characters. In 1926, with her earnings, Douglas built, and with modest inheritances later completed, the small and beloved house in Coconut Grove where she lived for the next seventy-two years. Her aunt Fanny's death in 1938 and her father's death in 1941 led to another nervous breakdown, but when she recovered, she felt renewed and ready for a new challenge.

What followed was Douglas's most important and first full-length book, *The Everglades: River of Grass* (1947). She was well prepared by her years as a journalist and regional writer and by her passion for the landscape. Realizing she knew very little about the Everglades, even though she served on the parks committee, she asked Garald Parker, the state hydrologist, what the Everglades were. He explained that they were not swamps, as the public thought, but a barely perceptible flow of water running from Lake Okeechobee through miles of saw grass to the sea. This led to the book's conceptual breakthrough: "It is a river of grass." As she wrote in the book's dramatic opening, "There are no other Everglades in the world. They are, they have always been, one of the unique regions of the earth, remote, never wholly known" (p. 5).

Douglas proved to be a formidable researcher and synthesizer. Although her book is a classic example of nature writing, it also reveals the region's human history, especially the role of Indian peoples. She dealt with the importance of the Everglades as the region's watershed and ended with a call for preservation in a chapter prophetically called "The Eleventh Hour." *Reader's Digest* printed the poetic first chapter, and the book was a success. As for the national park, although it was finally established in 1947, the solutions to the Everglades' problems were just beginning.

For the next twenty years, Douglas produced full-length books, both fiction and nonfiction. The theme of her novel *Road to the Sun* (1951) was the human cost of reckless real estate development. Her protagonists were young men in *Freedom River Florida 1845* (1953) and *Alligator Crossing* (1959), the former about three boys (a slave, an Indian, and a Quaker settler) and the latter about a boy outwitting a plume hunter. Her *Key to Paris* (1961) drew on her love for anything French. Two studies for the general public, relying on both historical and scientific research, were *Hurricane* (1958) and *Florida, the Long Frontier* (1967).

Marjory Stoneman Douglas was almost eighty when she began the crusade that is almost synonymous with her name. For the last years of her life, repairing the Everglades became, as she said, "a central force in my existence" (Douglas, *Voice of the River,* p. 224). In 1969 the Miami chapter of the National Audubon Society faced the threat of a proposed jetport in Big Cypress Swamp next to the Everglades. Joe Browder, Audubon president, asked Douglas to make a public statement opposing the jetport. When she responded that she believed protests were more effective if they came from organizations, Browder challenged her to start such a group—and she launched the Friends of the Everglades. They defeated the jetport and, in 1974, convinced Congress to authorize Big Cypress Preserve.

For the last twenty-five years of her life Douglas was a spokesperson for the restoration of the Everglades. She became nearly blind, but still testified before Congress, gave speeches in hundreds of places wearing her trademark wide-brimmed hat, and submitted to interviews by major journals. She saw the whole of South Florida as one ecosystem blocked from its natural functions by canals and channels and subject to agricultural pollution. Her goal was to make the river of grass flow again. In 1985, Douglas attended the groundbreaking ceremony for a project to restore the natural flow of the Kissimmee River into Lake Okeechobee. Although Congress did not pass the

Comprehensive Everglades Restoration Plan until 2000, it was Douglas's Friends of the Everglades that paved the way. She knew the job was not finished. Whenever she was introduced as the woman who saved the Everglades, she would turn to the speaker and say, "They aren't saved at all" (*Atlanta Journal-Constitution,* May 15, 1998).

Marjory Stoneman Douglas died in her sleep at her home in Coconut Grove at the age of 108. The National Park Service scattered her ashes in the park's Marjory Stoneman Douglas Wilderness Area, which had been established in 1978 with more than a million acres.

Bibliography: The Marjory Stoneman Douglas papers are located in the Archives and Special Collections Department of the Otto G. Richter Library, University of Miami, Florida. Rosalie E. Leposky published an extensive bibliography of Douglas's writings and works about Douglas in *The Marjorie Kinnan Rawlings Journal of Florida Literature* 8 (1997), pp. 55–73. When Douglas was in her nineties, John Rothchild assisted her in tape-recording her autobiography, which was published as Marjory Stoneman Douglas, *Voice of the River* (1987). For collections of Douglas's previously published short stories, see *Nine Florida Stories by Marjory Stoneman Douglas* (1990) and *"A River in Flood" and Other Florida Stories by Marjory Stoneman Douglas* (1998), both edited by Kevin M. McCarthy. For a selection of her poems and daily column "The Galley" published in the early 1920s in the *Miami Herald,* see Marjory Stoneman Douglas and Jack E. Davis, *The Wide Brim: Early Poems and Ponderings of Marjory Stoneman Douglas* (2002). Obituaries appeared in the *Miami Herald* and the *New York Times* on May 15, 1998.

POLLY WELTS KAUFMAN

DU BOIS, Shirley Graham. *See* Graham Du Bois, Shirley.

DULLES, Eleanor Lansing. June 1, 1895–October 30, 1996. International affairs expert, federal official, economist.

Eleanor Lansing Dulles was born into a family of middle-class means and ruling-class connections. Her father, Allen Macy Dulles, was an unambitious Presbyterian minister, but her mother, Edith Foster, proved a driven parent, pouring her ambition into the career of her older son, John Foster. Eleanor, seven years younger than Foster and two years younger than her brother Allen, played catch-up her whole life.

As the fourth of five children and a female, Eleanor was not subject to the heavy weight of expectation that shaped her brothers' lives. She was born in Watertown, New York, and graduated from Wykeham Rise School in Washington, Connecticut. Entering Bryn Mawr College in 1913, she quickly distinguished herself as one of the brightest students on campus, despite her poor eyesight. She majored in psychology. Two days after graduation and two months after the United States entered World War I, Eleanor set sail for Paris. Fighting her way to the front, she bravely attempted to help devastated French peasants, staying in Paris at war's end. The Paris Peace Conference was a family conclave. Uncle Robert Lansing was secretary of state, lawyer brother Foster drafted the notorious war guilt clause of the Versailles Treaty, and Allen, also a lawyer, drew up the borders of Czechoslovakia.

Eleanor returned home, a changed New Woman. She openly smoked cigarettes, abandoned the Protestantism of her forefathers, and lived easily on her own. Influenced by two Bryn Mawr professors, Anne Bezanson and SUSAN KINGSBURY, she became a pioneer in the new field of industrial management, accepting a fellowship and studying factory management firsthand by taking entry-level jobs at a steel company and a hair net factory. Fascinated by business, she reluctantly concluded that there was no place for a woman in the industrial landscape of the time.

After scrounging up her passage, she sailed for Britain, where she enrolled in the London School of Economics. Returning to the States in 1924, she entered Radcliffe College to work on a PhD in economics. Her topic, the French franc, could not have been more timely. With the greatest amount of war damage to repair, the French government proved unable to cope with its postwar financial crisis. Her study of this problem, published as *The French Franc, 1914–1928* (1929), was so incisive that no less an authority than John Maynard Keynes declared it the best thesis he had read on monetary inflation. She received her PhD in 1926 and began teaching at Bryn Mawr.

While doing research in Paris, Eleanor met her unlikely husband, David Blondheim, eleven years her senior. The divorced son of orthodox Jews, Blondheim was a philologist who had come to Europe to pursue studies of the Hebrew language and the Talmud. Neither the Reverend Dulles nor the bigoted Foster Dulles could be expected to approve what they saw as a misalliance. And David's parents were no more enthusiastic about a marriage outside their religious fold. Only on December 6, 1932, after the Reverend Dulles died, was Eleanor willing to marry David. Two years later she became pregnant. By this time the Nazi persecution of German Jews was daily intensifying. David, haunted by money troubles and increasingly distraught, committed suicide on March 19, 1934. As if anticipating the fate of most of European Jewry, he died by inhaling poisonous gas.

Foster took charge of the distraught Eleanor's life. Almost as soon as Eleanor gave birth in October, 1934, to a son she named David, Foster convinced her to legally to change her son's last name to Dulles; having kept her name when she married, she became known as Mrs. Dulles. She raised her son and Ann Welsh Dulles, her adopted daughter born in 1937, on her own, while carving out a career for herself, a difficult task for a woman at that time.

From 1936 to 1942, Dulles worked as an economist for the Social Security Board, and then joined the Division of Postwar Planning at the State Department. The end of the war gave her a breakout opportunity to become the staff economist for the U.S. military delegation to Austria. Her years in Vienna were good ones professionally. After that assignment ended, Dulles returned to Washington to work briefly in the Department of Commerce. At the end of 1952, shortly before President-elect Dwight Eisenhower asked her brother Foster to be secretary of state, she became head of the Berlin desk at the State Department. With the news that Allen would become head of the Central Intelligence Agency, foreign policy during the Eisenhower years would be dominated by the Dulles siblings.

During the 1950s, the cold war dominated the international landscape. The conflict over the future of Germany and Berlin in particular lay at the heart of the confrontation between East and West. As head of the Berlin desk, Eleanor Dulles played a major role in determining American diplomatic and military policy during the two Eisenhower administrations, especially during the Berlin crisis of 1960–61 that led to the erection of the Berlin Wall. That the Dulles siblings met at her house in McLean, Virginia, on a regular basis for tripartite conclaves enhanced her influence further.

In April 1959 Foster Dulles resigned as secretary of state; one month later he was dead of cancer. The election of John F. Kennedy in November 1960 meant that Allen would no longer head the CIA. But Eleanor stayed at her post at State, only leaving in 1962 when Secretary of State Dean Rusk requested her resignation. At the age of sixty-six, she resumed her scholarly career, writing books such as *Berlin: The Wall Is Not Forever* (1967) and *One Germany or Two* (1970), teaching at Georgetown University, and serving as a consultant to the State Department. She long outlived her brother Allen, dying in Washington in 1996 at the age of 101.

A woman of much intelligence and kindness, Eleanor Lansing Dulles became an important policy maker at a time when few women had access to influential positions. Only her gender kept her from the highest levels of power. Without her family connections, she would never have risen to prominence at the State Department, and yet she still suffered from discrimination. While proud of her professional accomplishments, she faced the dilemma of caring for her children while occupying a series of challenging jobs. That she was a single mother made her task that much more difficult.

Bibliography: Eleanor Dulles amassed a huge personal and professional archive. Her papers, which also contain extensive papers of her family, are stored at the Dwight D. Eisenhower Presidential Library in Abilene, Kansas; records of her work are found in the State Department archives at the University of Maryland, College Park. In addition, both her brothers preserved voluminous archival collections, which are located in the Department of Rare Books and Special Collections, Princeton University. Biographical information is found in *Current Biography* (1962), pp. 115–17. In addition to her scholarly publications, Eleanor Dulles wrote a detailed memoir, *Chances of a Lifetime* (1980), which covers her family background and professional career. *Dulles: A Biography of Eleanor, Allen and John Foster Dulles and Their Family Network*, by Leonard Mosley, appeared in 1978. An obituary appeared in the *New York Times* on November 4, 1996.

DIANE KUNZ

DUNNIGAN, Alice Allison. April 27, 1906–May 6, 1983. Journalist, civil rights activist.

Throughout most of its history, American journalism has discouraged women from entering its ranks. Alice Allison Dunnigan was one of the pioneers who broke down the barriers, for both her gender and her race, by working as a reporter in the nation's capital. By chronicling the decline of Jim Crow during the 1940s and 1950s, Dunnigan also became a civil rights activist.

Alice Allison was born in a three-room house near Russellville, Kentucky, the daughter of sharecropper Willie Allison and laundress Lena Pittman. Alice had one brother, Richard, who was seven years her senior. From an early age, she displayed an abundance of grit, drive, and persistence. At the age of four, she began walking four miles a day to attend school, becoming such a determined student that she graduated as the valedictorian of her class at her segregated high school.

When Alice Allison was growing up in the rural South, only three occupations were open to African American women: teaching black students, cleaning whites' houses, or working in the fields. She chose teaching, attending West Kentucky Industrial College for one year to earn the minimum credentials to become a teacher. In 1924, she began teaching in a one-room schoolhouse near her hometown.

Meanwhile, Allison struggled in her personal life. In 1926 she married Walter Dickinson, a sharecropper; the marriage lasted four years. A year later, she married Charles Dunnigan, a handyman. In 1932 she gave birth to her only child, Robert William. When the boy was four months old, Dunnigan turned him over to her parents so that she could continue to teach and could complete her degree, which she received from West Kentucky Industrial College in 1932. Her son was raised by his grandparents, and the Dunnigans eventually divorced.

After the United States entered World War II, Alice Dunnigan became the first African American from Logan County, Kentucky, to pass a federal civil service examination. She then accepted a job as a clerk-typist for the War Labor Board in Washington, D.C. After one year, she was promoted to economist for the Office of Price Administration.

In early 1946, Dunnigan left the government to enter the field of journalism. In her new job, she served as the Washington correspondent for the Associated Negro Press, a news agency that provided stories to some hundred black newspapers throughout the United States. The job fulfilled a dream that Dunnigan had harbored for many years. She later wrote that she had promised herself, during her childhood, "When I grow up . . . I'll write for a newspaper and let people know what other people are doing" (Dunnigan, *A Black Woman's Experience,* pp. 27–28).

Dunnigan's first reporting assignment was to cover the ousting of Mississippi racist Theodore Bilbo from the U.S. Senate because of conduct unbecoming to the office. But when Dunnigan arrived at the Capitol, she was told that African American reporters were not allowed to use the Senate Press Gallery. Only by standing in line with tourists for a brief glimpse of the Senate floor from visitors' seating was Dunnigan able to obtain the information she needed to write her story.

The next day, Dunnigan applied for press credentials. Her request coincided with the efforts of Louis Lautier, a correspondent for the *Atlanta Daily World,* to desegregate the congressional press galleries. Lautier's campaign led to a congressional hearing and then to a decision by the Senate Committee on Rules and Administration in March 1947 to change the policy. The senators also said that other African American reporters should have access to the galleries. With her application for credentials already on file, in June 1947 Dunnigan became the first African American woman in history accredited to cover the U.S. Congress. Later in the summer, she used that success as leverage to secure similar credentials to cover the White House, the Supreme Court, and the State Department.

Dunnigan then set out, in earnest, to become the crusading newspaper reporter that she had, for four decades, wanted to be. She saw her journalistic work as a form of civil rights activism, later writing: "While the role of the Black press, like other newspapers, is that of objectively reporting the news as it happens, it has another function equally as important—that of fighting oppression" (Dunnigan, *A Black Woman's Experience,* p. ii).

Dunnigan's stories often were the only ones reporting instances of discrimination. When a six-foot cross, a symbol of the Ku Klux Klan, was burned in a vacant lot in northeast Washington, she documented it; no coverage of the incident appeared in either of the city's two major dailies, the *Washington Post* and *Washington Evening Star.* Another Dunnigan story told of white families filing suit to evict a black family from a house they had purchased in a white neighborhood of Washington; again, neither the *Post* nor the *Star* reported the event. On a federal level, she reported that during a congressional hearing a Georgia congressman had called a civil rights leader a "black son-of-a-bitch"; even though the incident had taken place during a public event, mainstream newspapers failed to report it.

Dunnigan broke another barrier in 1948 by becoming the first woman journalist of color to travel as part of the press corps accompanying a president of the United States. She paid her own way to accompany President Harry Truman on the cross-country train trip as part of his reelection campaign. The last in the long list of barriers that Dunnigan broke was one created by other women. In 1955, she was asked to join the Women's National Press Club, thereby becoming the first African American member.

Dunnigan left journalism in 1961 when Vice President Lyndon Johnson appointed her to the staff of the President's Committee on Equal Employment Opportunity. In 1967, she shifted to the staff of the Council on Youth Opportunity. She retired in 1970 and died in Washington thirteen years later at the age of seventy-seven.

Bibliography: The Alice Allison Dunnigan Papers are located at the Moorland-Spingarn Research Center at Howard University. Dunnigan told her own story in *A Black Woman's Experience: From Schoolhouse to White House* (1974); see also her interview in the Black Women Oral History Project, Schlesinger Library, Radcliffe Institute for Advanced Study, Harvard University. Dunnigan also researched, compiled, and wrote *The Fascinating Story of Black Kentuckians: Their Heritage and Traditions* (1982). For additional information about her life and career, see Rodger Streitmatter, "Alice Allison Dunnigan: An African-American Woman Journalist Who Broke the Double Barrier," *Journalism History* 16, nos. 3–4 (Autumn–Winter 1989), pp. 87–97; and Streitmatter, *Raising Her Voice: African-American Women Journalists Who Changed History* (1994). Obituaries appeared in the *Washington Post* on May 8 and the *New York Times* on May 9, 1983.

RODGER STREITMATTER

DURR, Virginia Foster. August 6, 1903–February 24, 1999. Civil rights activist.

Virginia Heard Foster was born in the parsonage of the Presbyterian church in Birmingham, Alabama, where her father, Sterling Johnson Foster, preached. A member of a wealthy plantation-owning family from Alabama, Foster had married Anne Patterson, whose own planter family stretched back generations in the fertile Tennessee Valley. The couple had three children: Sterling Foster Jr. (1898), Josephine (1900), and Virginia (1903). Foster had enjoyed a privileged upbringing that included schooling at Southwestern Presbyterian University (now Rhodes College), Hampden-Sydney College in Virginia, and Princeton Theological Seminary. His wife raised their three children with the help of several black domestic servants and maintained a busy social schedule in Birmingham and Union Springs, where the family spent holidays and summers at the Foster plantation. As a child, Virginia rarely questioned the rituals of race generated by segregation, though she would grow up to repudiate them.

The Fosters lived in relative affluence, but when Virginia was seven, her father was dismissed from his ministry over a theological dispute and temporarily abandoned his wife and children. Anne moved to Memphis with her children to live with her sister, but within a year the family was reunited in Birmingham; Sterling would spend the rest of his days selling insurance and trying his hand at real estate. Virginia attended segregated public schools in Birmingham until 1918, when, at the age of fifteen, she was sent to a finishing school in New York. In the fall of 1920, she enrolled in the National Cathedral School in Washington, D.C.; she graduated in 1921 and headed off to Wellesley College. Virginia recalled her education there as liberating—she had been exposed to new ideas about the capabilities and ambitions of women and African Americans—but it was cut short by her family's declining fortunes. At the end of her sophomore year, she went home once again to Birmingham.

Her only solace was becoming a debutante in the summer of 1923 and taking a job at a law library. One Sunday in 1925, when Virginia was twenty-one, Clifford Judkins Durr caught her eye in church. Durr was a young lawyer from Montgomery who had been a Rhodes scholar and a fraternity brother of Sterling Foster Jr. at the University of Alabama. He and Virginia began courting, and they married on April 5, 1926. She was not the first Foster girl to marry a lawyer. In 1921 her sister Josephine had married Hugo Black, an attorney who later became a U.S. senator and Supreme Court justice. Virginia and Cliff began a life partnership of personal affection and shared political values of economic justice, racial equality, and resistance against McCarthyism. They also raised four daughters: Ann (born in 1927), Lucy (1937), Virginia ("Tilla") (1939), and Lulah (1947). A son, Clifford, died in 1938 at age three.

Virginia Durr became aware of poverty as a pressing political issue as she witnessed the ravages of the Depression in Birmingham, where she and her husband lived (with her parents) during the first five years of their marriage. She began volunteering with the Junior League and, in 1931, the Red Cross, aiding impoverished children. In 1933, Clifford Durr went to work for the Reconstruction Finance Corporation, a federal government lending agency created in 1932 and expanded during Roosevelt's presidency. The Durr family relocated to Seminary Hill, Virginia. Within a year, immersed in the exhilarating Washington network of New Deal Democrats, Virginia began volunteering for the Women's Division of the Democratic National Committee, where she met ELEANOR ROOSEVELT. The group adopted the abolition of the poll tax as one of its goals, and later several members, including Durr, helped create a separate organization, the National Committee to Abolish the Poll Tax. Beginning in 1941, Durr served as vice chairman.

In November 1938, Durr attended the inaugural meeting of the Southern Conference for Human Welfare (SCHW), an interracial organization of union activists and radicals, educators, and New Dealers devoted to the improvement of economic conditions, voting rights, and race relations in the South. Increasingly committed to the cause of racial and economic equality, Durr continued fighting the poll tax and attending SCHW conventions while, in 1941, Clifford went to work for the Federal Communications Commission (FCC).

As the cold war escalated in the late 1940s, liberals and civil rights supporters were among the many who came under intense scrutiny from the federal government. In 1948, when President Truman invited Clifford Durr to keep his position at the FCC, he declined in protest over the recently implemented loyalty oath, and opened his own law practice, mostly representing people accused of being Communists or fellow travelers. After two financially shaky years, the Durrs moved to Denver; but they soon returned to Alabama.

While Cliff settled into his new practice in Montgomery, Virginia found herself in the crosshairs of Mississippi senator James O. Eastland, notorious segregationist and member of the Senate Internal Security Subcommittee. In 1954 the committee called the Durrs, Aubrey Williams, Myles Horton of the Highlander Folk School, and others to New Orleans to answer questions about their involvement in SCHW (later called the Southern Conference Educational Fund), which had long been attacked from the right as a Communist-influenced group of agitators. Durr stood her ground and vehemently denied membership in the Communist Party.

In Montgomery, the Durrs became part of a network of civil rights activists, including E. D. Nixon, a leader in the local chapter of the National Association for the Advancement of Colored People (NAACP), and Rosa Parks. On the evening of December 1, 1955, after Parks's momentous defiance of a local segregation ordinance on a city bus, Nixon called Virginia and Cliff to accompany him to bail her out of jail. During the bus boycott that followed, Virginia regularly attended mass meetings, became active in the Council on Human Relations, and participated in the carpool for boycotters. With the dawning of the black power movement in the mid 1960s, Durr expressed to friends her disappointment about white civil rights supporters seemingly being shunted aside in favor of a black nationalist agenda. For the rest of her life, however, even after the death of her husband in 1975, she continued the struggle in her own way: giving lectures, doing interviews, and publishing her autobiography in 1985.

In her unique brand of activism, Virginia Foster Durr combined the gentility, wit, and charm of a white southern lady with the "radical" notion that African Americans and the poor should have greater control of their own lives and livelihoods. During a period when civil rights activism and calls for economic justice were seen by many as "un-American" and certainly "un-southern," she demonstrated the courage to renounce and resist in a very public way the values of the racist culture of which she was a product. Virginia Foster Durr died in a Carlisle, Pennsylvania, nursing home in 1999 at the age of ninety-five.

Bibliography: The largest collection of Durr's papers is located at the Schlesinger Library, Radcliffe Institute for Advanced Study, Harvard University. It includes a 1975 oral history interview with Virginia Foster Durr and Clifford Durr. Smaller collections are also held by the Alabama Department of Archives & History in Montgomery. *Outside the Magic Circle: The Autobiography of Virginia Foster Durr* (Hollinger F. Barnard, ed., foreword by Studs Terkel), was first published in 1985. A collection of her letters, *Freedom Writer: Virginia Foster Durr, Letters from the Civil Rights Years*, ed. Patricia Sullivan, appeared in 2003. Her work with the Southern Conference Educational Fund and the Southern Conference for Human Welfare is detailed in several books, including Thomas A. Krueger, *And Promises to Keep: The Southern Conference for Human Welfare, 1938–1948* (1967); Irwin Klibaner, *Conscience of a Troubled South: The Southern Conference Educational Fund, 1946–1966* (1989); and John Egerton, *Speak Now against the Day: The Generation before the Civil Rights Movement in the South* (1994). An obituary appeared in the *New York Times* on February 26, 1999.

STACY BRAUKMAN

DYKES, Eva Beatrice. August 13, 1893–October 29, 1986. Educator, literary scholar.

At Radcliffe College's commencement ceremonies in June 1921, Eva B. Dykes was awarded the PhD. She was the first African American woman to fulfill the qualifications for the PhD and the first black woman to receive a terminal degree in English. Later, she would touch the lives of hundreds of students and college professors.

Martha Ann Howard and James Stanley Dykes welcomed the second of their three daughters, Eva Beatrice, into a family that cherished and promoted education. Eva's maternal grandparents, John and Rebecca Howard, once enslaved on a cotton plantation in Howard County, Maryland, migrated to Washington, D.C., after emancipation. In an era when African Americans struggled just to obtain a primary school education, all of the Howards' four children graduated from high school and two of Eva's uncles attended Howard University. Eva's mother also attended Howard, where she met her future husband, an 1888 Howard University honors graduate, but had to withdraw because of a recurring illness. When Eva was young, her parents divorced and Martha Ann took her three girls to live with her brother, James Howard. A strong promoter of education, Eva's Uncle James would become a strong parental influence in her life.

In an era of legal and customary racial segregation, James Howard created a home environment that refused to let discrimination limit one's dreams. Like other members of the black middle class at the turn of the century, he made sure that the Dykes children played musical instruments, and he arranged for them to take private French lessons at the then-segregated Berlitz language school. In addition to French, Eva learned Greek and Latin. Unlike other African Americans in the segregated South, she also had access to literature and scholarly works.

In 1910, Dykes graduated from M Street High School (later renamed Paul Laurence Dunbar High School). Following in the family tradition, she received a BA in English from Howard University in 1914. A summa cum laude graduate, she left her family and familiar surroundings and moved to Nashville, Tennessee, to teach English and Latin at Walden University.

With her uncle's encouragement, a year later Dykes enrolled at Radcliffe to earn a master's degree. Radcliffe accepted Dykes, but it refused to acknowledge her undergraduate degree. Undaunted, she simply enrolled in additional courses and graduated magna cum laude with honors with a BA in English in 1917. She received her MA in 1918. As a graduate student, she could not live in the dorms or attend social functions with white students. She also faced rejection from archivists, who sometimes barred her from conducting research because of her race. Nevertheless, she refused to let racism deter her from her goals.

In 1921, Dykes satisfied all of the requirements for the PhD in English. Her 644-page dissertation, "Pope and His Influence in America from 1715 to 1815," explored Alexander Pope's attitudes toward slavery and the oppressed and his impact on American writers. Although Dykes was the first black woman to complete her requirements for the PhD, two other African American women, SADIE TANNER MOSSELL ALEXANDER in economics from the University of Pennsylvania and Georgiana Simpson in German from the University of Chicago, received their doctoral degrees earlier in the spring of 1921, because their schools held their graduation ceremonies earlier than Radcliffe's.

In 1920, during her years as a doctoral student, Dykes made a life-changing personal decision to convert to the Seventh-Day Adventist religion. Her faith would be a powerful influence on her personal life and her work as an educator. She once turned down an offer of marriage from a physician because he did not share her faith, and she never married.

After graduation, Dykes taught English and Latin for eight years at her high school alma mater, prestigious Dunbar High School in Washington, D.C., where her students included future physician Charles Drew and future statesman William Hastie. In 1929, she became a member of the Howard University English faculty, where she won numerous teaching awards. Her publications include *Readings from Negro Authors for Schools and Colleges* (1931), co-authored with fellow Howard faculty Lorenzo Dow Turner and Otelia Cromwell; and *The Negro in English Romantic Thought: Or a Study of Sympathy for the Oppressed* (1942), in which she argued that several English Romantic writers of the early nineteenth century championed individual freedom and expressed a desire to see an end to slavery, and that English women were instrumental in promoting the abolitionist movement in Great Britain.

In 1934, the president of Oakwood College, a small Seventh-Day Adventist College in Huntsville, Alabama, offered her a position, but it took Dykes ten years to decide to leave Howard University. In 1944, she joined Oakwood's faculty as an associate professor and chair of the English department. Aside from receiving an administrative position, she also had the opportunity to work in an environment that reinforced her religious faith. She was the school's first professor with a PhD.

While at Oakwood, Dykes directed the English department and helped the college gain accreditation. She also continued to publish in the *Journal of Negro History* and religious magazines such as the *Message*. Although she retired in 1968, the college asked her to return in 1970. Oakwood College recognized her service to the university by naming its new 600,000-volume library after her in 1973. Eva B. Dykes retired in 1975 and died in Huntsville in 1986 at the age of ninety-three.

Bibliography: Manuscript collections pertaining to the life of Eva B. Dykes are found in Special Collections at the Eva B. Dykes Library at Oakwood College in Huntsville, Alabama, and at the Moorland-Spingarn Research Center at Howard University, Washington, D.C. Dykes was interviewed by Merze Tate as part of the Black Women Oral History Project (1979) at the Schlesinger Library, Radcliffe Institute for Advanced Study, Harvard University. Other sources on her life include Dana Brewer Bathurst, *Eva Dykes: A Star to Show the Way* (1989), and DeWitt Williams, *She Fulfilled the Impossible Dream: The Story of Eva B. Dykes* (1985). Also of interest is Catherine Marie Johnson, "Contributions of African American Women to Post-Secondary Education: A Pioneer in the Tradition of Service and Scholarship, Eva Beatrice Dykes, 1893–1986" (MA thesis, Michigan State University, 1992). An obituary appeared in the *Huntsville Times* on November 2, 1986.

SONYA RAMSEY

E

EAMES, Ray. December 15, 1912–August 21, 1988. Designer, artist, filmmaker.

Recognition of Ray Eames's contribution to the most famous design partnership in twentieth-century America was, until recently, given only grudgingly, if at all. A warm but private and modest person, she stood in the shadow of the international reputation of her husband and partner, Charles Eames. Today her talents and contributions, which her husband always acknowledged, are seen as central to their collaboration. Best known as furni-

Eames

ture designers, the couple also designed toys, interiors, exhibitions, buildings, and multimedia shows, and directed approximately a hundred short films.

Bernice Alexandra Kaiser was born in Sacramento, California, to Edna Burr, a housewife, and Alexander Kaiser, an insurance agent. Known as Ray, a name she legally adopted in 1954, she grew up in a loving if overprotective household: an elder daughter had died shortly before Ray was born. Graduating from Sacramento High School in 1931, she showed an early aptitude for art. After one semester at Sacramento Junior College, she and her widowed mother moved to New York State to be near her older brother, who then was a cadet at West Point. Enrolled at the May Friend Bennett School in nearby Millbrook between 1931 and 1933, Ray specialized in liberal and fine arts.

Interested in abstract art, Ray threw her prodigious energies into the avant-garde culture of New York. She studied painting and sculpture at the Art Students League, following her inspirational teacher, German émigré Hans Hofmann, when he left to establish his own school. She joined the American Abstract Artists (AAA) in its founding year (1936), picketed galleries that refused to show nonrepresentational art, took modern dance classes with MARTHA GRAHAM and HANYA HOLM, and developed a passion for film. Her art was exhibited in AAA shows in 1937–41. Thus, when she met her future partner in 1940 at the Cranbrook Academy of Art in Michigan, she was a well-rounded modernist—a fact often ignored by writers who assumed that the Eames aesthetic and interest in film originated with Charles. The couple married in 1941 and moved to Los Angeles. They had no children, although Charles had a daughter from a previous marriage.

Charles and Ray Eames were both perfectionists, and their shared interests and complementary qualities provided the basis of their successful personal and professional collaboration. Charles was trained in architecture, but he also had a strong sense of structure, something Ray also brought from her studies with Hofmann along with her sense of form. They both believed design to be a problem-solving activity, but Ray's approach, rooted in her extraordinary visual sensibilities and well-trained "eye," was often more intuitive. The extremely high quality of her graphics (including covers for *Arts & Architecture*), textile designs, and sculpture—all now greatly sought after by collectors—suggests that, had she not shifted her attentions to design, she could have made significant contributions in these three areas. There is no doubt, however, that as Charles's wife and collaborator she was able to enjoy a highly creative career as a full-time designer and participate in projects at a level rarely available to women at that time, particularly in the field of industrial design.

At Cranbrook, Ray had become familiar with the determination of Eero Saarinen and her soon-to-be husband to use industrial technologies to produce furniture at prices affordable to the majority of the population. Between 1941 and 1946 the Eameses concentrated on the commercial mass-manufacture of low-cost, complex-molded plywood furniture, the best known of which are the chairs with separate back and seat. Ray's interest in structure and her ability to produce dynamic forms in tension (what Hans Hofmann called "push and pull") were central to the sculptural form of these chairs. These objects met with great acclaim when exhibited at the Museum of Modern Art in 1946. Unfortunately for Ray and the other designers who worked in her office, credit was given only to Charles.

Ray's hand can also be strongly seen in their other furniture designs, especially the seating in plastic and metal and the modular storage units of 1950. The latter owe much to her passion for Mondrian and her facility with collage, as did the colorful façade of their own home in Pacific Palisades, a minimalist structure they designed and built between 1945 and 1949 as a "background for life in work" (Kirkham, p. 110). Its interior decoration was one of the few projects for which Ray was given full credit during her lifetime. The Eameses used the term *functioning decoration* to describe carefully arranged "ordinary" and "found" objects such as toys, stones, driftwood, starfish, souvenirs, and masks, many of which were handmade. "Functioning decoration" offered cheap and easily copied ways of personalizing spartan structures, but its emphasis on decoration and density of ornamentation was frowned upon by most designers. Today it is seen as a precursor of postmodernism and is regarded as one of the most innovative aspects of their work.

From the mid 1950s the couple increasingly focused on communications as opposed to products. They approached exhibitions, multimedia, and film as educators, saturating audiences with "information overload" in the belief that viewers were capable of negotiating complex and diverse material, much of it related to making accessible new advances in science and technology, including the computer. Animation, puppet shows, interactive devices, and timelines were among the many devices they used to emphasize that these new developments were "in the service of mankind" (Albrecht, p. 29). In *The Information Machine: Creative Man and the Data Processor*, a 1957 film they made for IBM and shown at the 1958 World's Fair in Brussels, animation and humor helped humanize a technology widely viewed as a means of social control. Fears of "Big Brother" were allayed and computers presented as the best means of solving problems. Sherlock Holmes was featured in an electronically controlled puppet show at the IBM pavilion at the 1964–65 New York World's Fair, which suggested that computers use the same logic as the famous sleuth.

That Ray Eames died in Los Angeles on August 21, 1988, exactly ten years to the day after Charles, is considered by many to illustrate the closeness of this husband-wife team. After Charles's death, Ray oversaw the sorting of the enormous archive in their office. That archive, together with their joint work, offers incontrovertible evidence of the major role Ray played in one of the most creative and influential design collaborations of the twentieth century.

Bibliography: The main archive from the Eames Office is housed in the Manuscripts, Prints and Photographs, and Motion Picture, Broadcasting and Recorded Sound divisions of the Library of Congress. The Vitra Design Museum, Germany, is the main repository of prototypes, furniture, and experimental projects—much of it acquired directly from the Eames Office. Ray Eames helped compile the posthumously published *catalogue raisonné* of their work: John Neuhart, Marilyn Neuhart, and Ray Eames, *Eames Design: The Work of the Office of Charles and Ray Eames* (1989). She wrote an untitled article on "Line and color" for *California Arts & Architecture* (September 1973) and the introduction to Philip and Phyllis Morrison and the Office of Charles and Ray Eames, *Powers of Ten: A Book about the Relative Size of Things in the Universe and the Effect of Adding Another Zero* (1982). Secondary works include Pat Kirkham, *Charles and Ray Eames: Designers of the Twentieth Century* (1995); Donald Albrecht, ed., *The Work of Charles and Ray Eames: A Legacy of Invention* (1997); Arthur Drexler, *Charles Eames: Furniture from the Design Collection, Museum of Modern Art* (1973); and John and Marilyn Neuhart, *Connections: The Work of Charles and Ray Eames* (1976). An obituary appeared in the *New York Times* on August 23, 1988.

PAT KIRKHAM

EAST, Catherine. May 15, 1916–August 17, 1996. Federal official, feminist.

"Midwife to the women's movement" (as Betty Friedan called her), Catherine East spent her career as a federal civil servant, moving from the Civil Service Commission to the new federal bodies created in the 1960s and 1970s to enhance opportunities for women. As a government insider, Catherine East served as the primary conduit of governmental information for feminists across the nation. Determined to see an independent women's movement arise to goad the government into doing more for women, East encouraged Friedan and others to form a new feminist organization—"an NAACP for women"—that could function, unconstrained, outside the government's ambit. In 1966, the National Organization for Women (NOW) emerged to play that role.

Born in Barboursville, West Virginia, to Bertha Woody and Ulysses Grant Shipe, Catherine was the oldest of three surviving children in a troubled family. When she was eleven, her mother suffered an emotional breakdown; her father committed suicide four years later. A good student despite the family's difficulties, Catherine considered teaching her only career option and enrolled in a teacher training program at Marshall College in Huntington, West Virginia. Financial difficulties forced her to leave college eleven credits short of her bachelor's degree, and she went to work. She married Charles East in 1937, and in 1939 she accepted an offer from the U.S. Civil Service Commission for a GS-3 clerk position in Washington, D.C. She finished her degree in 1943 by transferring credits from classes at George Washington University, where her husband studied engineering. Her first daughter, Elizabeth, was born in 1945, followed by Victoria in 1952.

East advanced in the civil service quickly, but she saw few opportunities to raise the issue of equity for women. Sex discrimination, she recalled, was just something you lived with. East greeted the 1961 announcement of the President's Commission on the Status of Women (PCSW) warily, fearful that it would create a hostile environment for the women in government who had been trying to blend in, but in April 1962 she agreed to staff the Commission's federal employment committee as its technical secretary. In 1963, she transferred to the Women's Bureau in the U.S. Department of Labor to serve as executive secretary for the two permanent groups the Commission had recommended to succeed it. She remained at Labor for the next twelve years.

For East, the transition inaugurated the most actively feminist and fulfilling years of her life. Divorced in 1956, when her two daughters were four and eleven, East raised her children as a single parent. Relying on the help of housekeepers and babysitters, she built her life around her career, her feminist work, and her children's activities. Her razor-sharp intelligence made her an imposing figure, despite her short stature, curly hair, and soft West Virginia accent. Throughout her activist years, her Arlington, Virginia, home became a way station for visiting feminists.

As executive secretary of the Interdepartmental Committee on the Status of Women (ICSW) and the Citizens' Advisory Council on the Status of Women (CACSW), groups with very little real power, East had to act carefully. Between 1964 and 1966, she organized three annual meetings of state commissions on women and she began to lobby for an organization that would create outside feminist pressure on government agencies. To kindle indignation, East and Mary Eastwood, a feminist lawyer, wrote a speech for Martha

Griffiths (D-MI) describing the dereliction of the Equal Employment Opportunity Commission (EEOC) when it came to women's rights, which Griffiths delivered on June 20, 1966. East, Eastwood, and feminist attorney MARGUERITE RAWALT disseminated the speech at their own expense. Attendees of the June 1966 Conference of State Commissions on Women in Washington, D.C., sought permission from the presiding federal officials to express disapproval of the EEOC; rebuffed, a group led by Betty Friedan formed the National Organization for Women at a conference luncheon.

East briefed the leaders sub rosa on the issues they should tackle, herself informed by feminists inside the EEOC and other federal agencies. She kept her low profile, not out of concern for losing her job, but for fear of being transferred to a position in which she could do less good. For the next decade, East advised the founders of proliferating new movement groups, such as the National Women's Political Caucus and the Women's Equity Action League, while continuing to staff the CACSW as well as a new independent organization of state commissions and an ad hoc body appointed by President Richard Nixon in December 1969. This Presidential Task Force on Women's Rights and Responsibilities, headed by Virginia Allan, advocated, among other measures, action on the ERA and expansion of federal laws barring discrimination.

In 1975, East left the CACSW for the State Department and the National Commission on the Observance of International Women's Year (IWY). As deputy coordinator, East helped prepare for the United Nations Conference on Women held in Mexico City. She then worked on policy recommendations for the National Women's Conference scheduled for Houston in 1977. But East differed with BELLA ABZUG, who had authored the legislation creating the national conference, about both the representation at the conference and its scope. Abzug believed that every issue is a woman's issue, a stance East thought would dilute the movement's power and dissipate its limited resources. At odds with Abzug and upset by her volatility, East resigned. After her retirement from the federal government, East focused her efforts on the unsuccessful attempt to ratify the ERA in Virginia. She also volunteered with the NOW Legal Defense and Education Fund and the Virginia Women's Political Caucus.

During her career, East steered policy in the covert way of the knowledgeable civil servant. Of her proudest accomplishments, East pointed to the drafting of a position on childbearing leave that would treat it like any other temporary "disability." While working for the IWY Commission, East also oversaw the publication of a series of eye-opening pamphlets describing the legal status of homemakers in each state in the Union. East described her role in Washington as that of a catalyst—knowing who knew what, and where to turn for information. But Betty Friedan in 1976 gave her the credit she was due: East, she said, was "the valiant, incorruptible woman [who] for all these years . . . has been the pivot of the feminist underground in Washington." Catherine East died in Ithaca, New York, at the age of eighty.

Bibliography: Catherine East deposited her personal papers at the Schlesinger Library, Radcliffe Institute for Advanced Study, Harvard University. Further documentation appears in the records of the Citizens' Advisory Council on the Status of Women and the National Commission on the Observance of International Women's Year held by the National Archives. Her writings consist chiefly of testimony to various state and federal bodies and unattributed government publications. East also contributed an extensive oral history interview, conducted by Cynthia Harrison, to the Women in the Federal Government Oral History Project at the Schlesinger Library. Accounts of East's contribution to the women's movement are found in Betty Friedan, *It Changed My Life: Writings on the Women's Movement* (1976), which contains the final quote on p. 77; and Cynthia Harrison, *On Account of Sex: The Politics of Women's Issues, 1945–1968* (1988). This account is based also on conversations with the author over the course of twenty years. An obituary appeared in the *New York Times* on August 20, 1996.

CYNTHIA HARRISON

EDWARDS, India. June 16, 1895–January 14, 1990. Journalist, Democratic Party official.

India Edwards, who served as vice-chair of the Democratic Party and head of its national women's organization in the 1940s and 1950s, was born in Chicago. The older of two daughters of India Thomas and Archibald Walker, she spent her early childhood in Nashville, Tennessee, surrounded by aunts, uncles, cousins, and grandparents. When she was rather young, her parents divorced, but within a few years her mother married Canadian-born Jack Gillespie, whom India and her sister considered their father. Though the family moved to various midwestern cities, India always regarded Nashville as home. After graduating from Central High School in St. Louis, she aspired to study journalism at Columbia University, but Gillespie opposed the idea, suggesting that she attend a school closer to the family.

India opted instead to move to Chicago and search for employment. She soon became a freelance writer for the *Chicago Tribune,* beginning a career that spanned two decades and culminated in her rank as editor of the women's and society pages. Though her ardent support for the Democratic Party clashed with the conservative viewpoint of the *Tribune*'s publisher, Colonel Robert McCormick, she found that he never interfered with her work or her political activities.

In 1917 she married Daniel Sharp, who was killed in World War I only a year after their wedding. In 1920 she married Jack Moffett, an investment banker. They had two children: John (1924), who died in 1943 in a military training accident, and India (1926), to whom she passed on the unusual name she shared with her own mother as well as a great-aunt. India and Moffett separated in 1933. In June 1942 she married Herbert Threlkeld Edwards Jr., who was involved with cultural affairs and documentary films in the Department of State. Soon after their wedding they settled in Washington, D.C., where India Edwards began her career with the Democratic Party.

Edwards received her political initiation in the 1944 Democratic campaign, volunteering her journalism skills to write press releases, speeches, and other publicity. She quickly ascended within the Women's Division of the Democratic National Committee (DNC), serving first as its executive secretary (1945–47) and then as associate director (1947–48) before becoming executive director in April 1948. In 1950 she also became the vice-chair of the DNC. As head of the Women's Division, Edwards had two main responsibilities. "Helping to elect Democrats was my chief occupation," she explained, but "helping to raise the status of women in our party was an important part of my duty" (Edwards, p. 9). To meet these goals, Edwards and her staff sponsored regional conferences, mobilized voters, promoted Democratic candidates, published a monthly magazine, coordinated speakers' visits, produced and circulated educational materials, raised funds, and assisted state and local branches of the party committee. Edwards continued the work begun by EMILY NEWELL BLAIR, who steered the group in the 1920s, and MARY (MOLLY) DEWSON, who turned it into a vital organization in the 1930s.

Promoting women's representation in government became Edwards's mission. Rather than seek a cabinet post or ambassadorship for herself, she tried to get jobs for as many women as possible in the expanding federal bureaucracy. She was deeply loyal to President Truman, who often joked that she was the only person other than himself who believed he could win the 1948 election, and he trusted her advice. Edwards was able to use that close relationship to promote Democratic women collectively and to recognize them for their important contributions to the party's success. Persistent and tenacious, she secured appointments for many women, including GEORGIA NEESE CLARK as treasurer of the United States, Eugenie Anderson as ambassador to Denmark, and BURNITA SHELTON MATTHEWS as the nation's first woman U.S. district court judge.

Edwards's political work put her in the spotlight on numerous occasions. Her televised address before the 1948 Democratic National Convention aired during prime time, earning her national attention for a dramatic speech in which she illustrated the high cost of household goods. Three years later Truman asked Edwards to chair the Democratic Party, but she declined his offer. Believing that the party was not ready to be led by a woman, Edwards also feared that Democratic women would suffer a backlash if she headed the party and it lost the coming presidential election. She later admitted, "Not accepting his offer was one of the great mistakes of my life, but I did what I thought at the time was best for the Democratic party" (Edwards, p. 142). In 1952 her name was placed in nomination for vice president at the Democratic convention. Though she insisted it was simply a gesture, she agreed that it was an important symbol of women's progress.

In January 1953 the DNC chair eliminated the Women's Division and integrated its staff and activities into the DNC as a whole. Edwards was not consulted in advance about the decision, but she expressed public support for the integration even as she confided strong private reservations to her friends. She welcomed the idea of a full partnership within the party, but she sensed that in practice this reorganization would simply make it easier for the men to ignore the women. Several months later, Edwards resigned as director of women's activities, though she claimed her decision was prompted by her husband's resignation from his own job rather than by the changes at the DNC. In 1956, Edwards stepped down from the vice-chair post as well. KATHLEEN (KATIE) LOUCHHEIM succeeded her in both positions.

Edwards remained involved in Democratic Party affairs throughout the 1960s, working on various presidential campaigns and assisting with the national conventions. She briefly directed the Washington office of the New York State Department of Commerce in the late 1950s, and she served as special consultant on youth employment to the secretary of labor in the Johnson Administration, assisting with programs in the War on Poverty. After she left Washington, she and her husband retired to California, where she died on January 17, 1990, at the age of ninety-four.

Bibliography: The Harry S. Truman Library in Independence, Missouri, holds the most valuable archival resources regarding India Edwards's political career. These include the India Edwards papers, which consist of correspondence, speeches, newspaper and magazine clippings (including numerous articles profiling Edwards), memorabilia, and other materials from her years with the Democratic Party; the papers of the Democratic National Committee; the papers of Stephen A. Mitchell, which document the 1953 integration of the Women's Division; and the official and personal papers of President Truman. Additional papers from the DNC in this period are located at the John F. Kennedy Library. Additional material on Edwards can be found in the Martha Ragland and Mary W. Dewson papers, both at the Schlesinger Library, Radcliffe Institute for Advanced Study, Harvard University, and the Katie Louchheim papers at the Library of Congress. Edwards's memoir, *Pulling No Punches: Memoirs of a Woman in Politics* (1977), is an especially valuable resource. Useful oral histories of India Edwards include an interview by Jerry N. Hess on January 16, 1969, located at the Truman Library; an interview by Joe B. Frantz on February 4, 1969, located at the Lyndon B. Johnson Library in Austin, Texas; an interview by Patricia Zelman on November 10, 1975, located at the Truman Library; and an interview by Peg Colton from 1976, located at the Woman's National Democratic Club in Washington, D.C. See also Georgia Cook Morgan, "India Edwards: Distaff Politician of the Truman Era," *Missouri Historical Review* 78, no. 3 (April 1984), pp. 293–310. For discussion of Edwards's efforts to appoint women to government posts, as well as general background on women's political engagement in this period, see Cynthia Harrison, *On Account of Sex: The Politics of Women's Issues, 1945–1968* (1988); and Kimberly Brodkin, "For the Good of the Party: Gender, Partisanship and American Political Culture from Suffrage to the 1960s" (PhD dissertation, Rutgers University, 2001). Obituaries appeared in the *Washington Post* on January 16, 1990, and the *New York Times* on January 17, 1990.

KIMBERLY A. BRODKIN

ELION, Gertrude Belle. January 23, 1918–February 21, 1999. Biochemist, Nobel Prize winner.

Gertrude Belle Elion, one of ten women scientists to win a Nobel Prize in the twentieth century, was the elder of two children born to a Jewish immigrant family in New York City. Her father, Robert Elion, and her mother, Bertha Cohen, were descended from scholarly families in, respectively, Lithuania and what is now Poland. When Elion was a teenager, her grandfather died of cancer and she decided to devote her life to curing the disease. The stock market crash of 1929, however, bankrupted her dentist father, and she was able to attend Hunter College only because her grades were excellent and the highly competitive women's division of City College of New York was free of charge.

Elion, known to friends as Trudy, graduated in chemistry with highest honors in 1937 and was refused financial aid by fifteen graduate schools. Only later did she realize that the reason was gender discrimination. In desperation, she entered secretarial school and for seven years took marginal and temporary jobs to inch her way up into chemical research. At various times, she taught nursing students, volunteered in a chemical laboratory, worked as a doctor's receptionist, and substitute taught. After studying nights and weekends at New York University, she earned a master's degree in chemistry in 1941. Her fiancé, another City College graduate, died unexpectedly of a heart infection, and she never married.

When a shortage of industrial chemists opened opportunities for women during World War II, Elion was hired first by the A&P grocery stores to check food for freshness and then by a Johnson & Johnson laboratory in New Jersey. In 1944, at the age of twenty-six, she applied to a Burroughs Wellcome Company laboratory in Tuckahoe, a suburb of New York City. (Burroughs Wellcome, now part of SmithKlineGlaxo, was a British-owned company run solely to benefit medical research laboratories, museums, and libraries.) George Hitchings, who had a PhD in biochemistry from Harvard University, hired Elion, thus beginning their decades-long association.

Hitchings wanted to develop a rational, scientific approach to drug discovery by studying how cells grow. Little was known about nucleic acids in the 1940s, although Oswald Avery at the Rockefeller Institute had just discovered that DNA (deoxyribonucleic acid) carries genetic information. Hitchings knew that all cells require nucleic acids to reproduce but that the cells of tumors, protozoa, bacteria, and viruses require especially large amounts to sustain their rapid growth. Hitchings thought these cells should be acutely vulnerable to disruptions in their life cycle. Dividing the nucleic acids among his staff, Hitchings assigned the purine bases—adenine and guanine—to Elion. Two years later, Elion published the first of her 225 papers. She also worked part-time on a PhD at Brooklyn Polytechnic Institute until a dean told her only full-time students were permitted.

After only six years of chemical research, she synthesized two closely related compounds that became effective cancer treatments: 6-mercaptopurine and thioguanine. She was thirty-two years old and, ever after, she called 1950 her "Wow! Year." By mixing her two drugs with others, physicians could treat childhood leukemia effectively for the first time. Elion had opened up an entirely new area of research in leukemia therapy. She had also demonstrated that minute chemical changes in a compound can fool malignant cells. As she said later, "The intermediary is the doctor, but the excitement is really yours because you know you gave them the tools" (McGrayne, p. 295).

Less than a decade later, a sophisticated relative of Elion's 6-MP made organ transplantation possible. Surgically, organ transplantation had been feasible for years, but animals with transplants died within days because their bodies' immune response rejected grafts. Elion's drug, azathioprine, marketed as Imuran, kept a collie named Lollipop alive for 230 days with a transplanted kidney. In 1961, a human given Imuran and a transplanted kidney from an unrelated person survived. Since then, more than 100,000 kidney transplants in the United States have used Elion's drug. Elion's next invention was the drug allopurinol in the early 1960s, which combats gout by reducing the body's production of uric acid. Before allopurinol, many radiation and chemotherapy patients died because the rapid destruction of their cancerous tissues made uric acid accumulate. In 1968, the American Chemical Society (ACS) awarded Elion its Garvan Medal, the only ACS award that women were allowed to win. Soon after, she won the first of twenty-five honorary doctoral degrees.

Many scientists still regarded Elion as no more than Hitchings's assistant, however. Then, in 1967, Hitchings retired from active research to become an administrator, and Elion became head of the Department of Experimental Therapy. Two years later, Burroughs Wellcome relocated to the Research Triangle Park in North Carolina. The move was difficult for a confirmed New Yorker like Elion, but she kept her subscription to the Metropolitan Opera. And now, for the first time, she said, she could show what she could do without Hitchings. Scientists thought that any compound toxic enough to damage the DNA of a virus would harm the DNA of healthy cells too. But Elion developed the first effective antiviral drug, a purine compound similar to a compound that the herpes virus needs for reproduction. Called acyclovir and marketed as Zovirax, the drug proved effective against herpes simplex, which causes mouth and genital sores, and against herpes zoster, which causes shingles—a potentially fatal illness in cancer and transplant patients. It is also effective against Epstein-Barr virus, pseudo-rabies in animals, and herpes encephalitis, a brain infection that frequently is fatal in children. Elion called acyclovir her "final jewel. . . . That such a thing was possible wasn't even imagined up until then" (McGrayne, p. 301). Her antiviral drug research helped prepare the pharmaceutical industry to challenge the human immunodeficiency virus (HIV). A year after Elion retired in 1983 and became a company consultant, her staff developed azidothymidine (AZT), the first drug licensed to treat the AIDS virus in the United States.

In 1988, Elion was awarded the Nobel Prize in Physiology or Medicine with George Hitchings and Sir James W. Black of the University of London. The three shared $390,000. The Nobel Prize was awarded not for specific drugs, but for developing a rational approach to drug discovery based on "the understanding of basic biochemical and physiological processes." It was an unusual Nobel, the first for drug research in thirty-one years, and one of a few for cancer treatment. Elion was a seventy-year-old woman from industry with no PhD, and at eighty-three, Hitchings was one of the oldest winners in years. Elion almost did not win the prize with Hitchings, but a university colleague emphasized to the skeptical Nobel Committee that she was first author on their early papers (traditionally the indication of the primary researcher) and that her antiviral work had occurred after Hitchings's retirement.

In addition to working on research and holding forty-five patents, Elion served on the boards of the World Health Organization, National Cancer Institute, and American Cancer Society. She was a National Medal of Science winner in 1991 and a member of the National Academy of Sciences. An avid operagoer, traveler, and photographer, she remained active in research and teaching until the end of her life. Elion died suddenly in Chapel Hill, North Carolina, on February 21, 1999, at the age of eighty-one.

Bibliography: Elion's scientific notebooks are the property of SmithKlineGlaxo, and her personal and scientific papers are held by Jonathan L. Elion, MD, Brown University, Providence, Rhode Island. Sharon Bertsch McGrayne, *Nobel Prize Women in Science: Their Lives, Struggles, and Momentous Discoveries* (1993), contains a chapter on Elion, which draws on interviews with the scientist, her colleagues, and family. See also Margaret W. Rossiter, *Women Scientists in America: Before Affirmative Action 1940–1972* (1995). For more on her Nobel Prize, see Katherine Bouton, "The Nobel Pair," *New York Times Magazine*, January 29, 1989, p. 28. Elion summarized her scientific work in her Nobel Prize Lecture, "The Purine Path to Chemotherapy," which was reprinted in *Science* 244 (April 7, 1989), pp. 41–47. See also George H. Hitchings and Gertrude B. Elion, "Layer on Layer: The Bruce F. Cain Memorial Award Lecture," *Cancer Research* 45, no. 6 (June 1985), pp. 2415–20. Elion is included in Tom Brokaw's *The Greatest Generation* (1998). Richard Kent and Brian Huber offer an appreciation in "Gertrude Belle Elion (1918–99)," *Nature*, April 1, 1999, p. 380. An obituary appeared in the *New York Times* on February 23, 1999.

SHARON BERTSCH MCGRAYNE

ELIOT, Abigail Adams. October 9, 1892–October 29, 1992. Nursery school leader, educator.

From a long lineage of social reformers, Abigail Adams Eliot was a pioneer in the American nursery school movement who influenced and trained many early childhood educators and focused attention on the role of parents in preschool education. Born Abby, after her great-aunt, suffragist and New England Women's Club founder ABIGAIL WILLIAMS MAY, who was known as Abby,

Eliot was later called Abigail professionally. As her names suggest, she was a descendant of the well-known Adams and Eliot families of colonial Massachusetts, the youngest of three siblings. Her father, Christopher Rhodes Eliot, was a Unitarian minister and social worker active in temperance and charity work. Her mother, Mary Jackson May, came from a family of famous educators and women's rights advocates. Her sister, MARTHA MAY ELIOT, became a pediatrician and later headed the federal Children's Bureau.

Personally and professionally, Eliot's life was grounded in the Boston area. Born in Dorchester, Massachusetts, she moved at a young age to Boston's Beacon Hill, near the Bulfinch Place (Chapel) Church, where her father took up a ministry. In 1896, at the age of four, she attended one of Boston's newly instituted public kindergartens, where she recalled being led through rigidly sequenced play routines with Friedrich Froebel's sets of wooden blocks. She then went to a public elementary school and to the private Miss Winsor's School for girls. Although not poor, the family lived on her father's salary, and Eliot was given a scholarship by Elizabeth Winsor Pearson, whose sister directed the school. Pearson, one of the founders of the Women's Education Association, played an important role in Eliot's life and provided guidance and support for many of her endeavors.

Eliot entered Radcliffe College in 1910. Knowing that she wanted to pursue some form of social service, she enrolled in courses in economics, psychology, and social ethics. Following receipt of her BA in 1914, she initially went into social work. While serving as a home visitor in Boston with the Children's Mission to Children from 1914 to 1917, she noticed many children wandering the streets, too young to go to school. In 1918, as district secretary for Associated Charities, she became more concerned about the problems of poor children and their families.

After a year studying at Oxford University in 1919–20, Eliot worked briefly for the Massachusetts Minimum Wage Commission, but soon found her calling in preschool education. In 1921, Elizabeth Pearson asked her whether she would be interested in directing a nursery school the Women's Education Association planned to open. Backed by Pearson and the Association, Eliot returned to England to study for six months at the Rachel McMillan Nursery School and Training Centre, the "open air" nursery school founded by Margaret McMillan in Deptford, a slum south of London. Eliot was very impressed by Margaret McMillan but concerned about her lack of contact with parents. After a harrowing experience being left in charge of 32 two-year-olds during a late-afternoon fog, Eliot decided that smaller class size and shorter hours were critical for young children.

In January 1922, Eliot took over a former day nursery in Roxbury, a section of Boston where many lower-income African American, Irish American, and Jewish families lived, and turned it into the Ruggles Street Nursery School and Training Center, one of the first nursery schools and nursery education programs in the United States. She immediately transformed the drab surroundings, shortened the hours, stopped admitting infants, and established relationships with church, medical, dental, mental health, and other child welfare associations. Eclectic and practical in her educational philosophy and methods, she worked closely with parents, encouraging mothers to visit and volunteer at the school and getting the school's black and white parents together for integrated meetings.

In 1926, with additional funding from the Laura Spelman Rockefeller Memorial, the Permanent Charity Fund, Pearson, and others, Eliot started the Nursery Training School of Boston. Still associated with the Ruggles Street school, the center was housed on Marlborough Street in downtown Boston, where one- and two-year nursery education courses were offered for high school and college students. In 1926, Eliot completed a master's in education at the Harvard Graduate School of Education, under the supervision of Professor George E. Johnson. In 1930 she was among the first women to be awarded a doctorate, at a ceremony at which men mounted the platform to receive their degrees while women stood below. Eliot's dissertation on the relationship between eating habits and personality development in two- and three-year-olds was the first research at the graduate school to deal with preschool-age children.

Eliot became active in promoting nursery schools at the national level. She was a founding member of the National Association for Nursery Education; at the association's conference in October 1933, federal funding was announced for Emergency Nursery Schools during the Great Depression. As supervisor for the New England region and member of the National Advisory Committee, she helped monitor the quality of the nursery schools, intended primarily as work relief for unemployed teachers, and convinced the superintendent of the Massachusetts Board of Education not to admit two-year-olds. During World War II, Eliot offered special courses at the Nursery Training School for directors and teachers in federally funded Lanham Act Children's Centers, which provided child care for women working in war-related industries.

In 1952, at the age of sixty, Eliot resigned from the Nursery Training Center, having helped arrange for it to become a part of Tufts University in 1951, where it is now the Eliot-Pearson Department of Child Study. She moved to Pasadena, California, for two years to be director of the Teacher Education Division at Pacific Oaks Friends School. When she returned in 1954, she taught at the private Brooks School in Concord, Massachusetts, and began what she called her second and third careers, in volunteer work in mental health and services to the elderly. She founded what is now the Eliot Community Mental Health Center and helped establish the Unitarian Community Action Committee for the Elderly, both in Concord.

Eliot remained unmarried and in close contact with her family throughout her long and productive life. She lived with her father until his death, with her sister briefly, and then for thirty-seven years with her companion Anna Eveleth Holman, a high school physics teacher who was a classmate from Radcliffe. Eliot, who died in Concord of a heart attack at the age of one hundred, was modest about her many accomplishments. Forthright and energetic, with thick glasses and hair in a bun, she had the no-nonsense manner and dry wit of a New Englander. An indefatigable activist, Eliot's career spanned education, social work, and psychology, and called attention to the importance of parent education and involvement in nursery schools.

Bibliography: Eliot's extensive, catalogued papers are at the Schlesinger Library, Radcliffe Institute for Advanced Study, Harvard University. They include correspondence, records of the Ruggles Street Nursery School and Training Center and the Nursery Training School of Boston, speeches, writings, tributes, photographs, and other documents. There are references to Eliot in the Martha May Eliot, Anna Eveleth Holman, Evelyn Goodenough Pitcher, and other collections at the Schlesinger Library, and in the Eliot-Pearson Department of Child Study Collection, University Archives Collections, Tufts Digital Library at Tisch Library, Tufts University, Medford, Massachusetts. Eliot's memoirs, *A Heart of Grateful Trust* (privately published in 1982 and transcribed and edited by Marjorie Gott Manning), contain much detail about her personal and professional life. Abigail Eliot, "Educating the Parent through the Nursery School," *Childhood Education* 3, no. 4 (December 1926), pp. 183–89, discusses her educational philosophy. Volume 1 of James L. Hymes Jr., *Early Childhood Education: Living History Interviews* (1978), includes her account of the early days of the American nursery school movement. Her career is discussed in Barbara Beatty, *Preschool Education in America* (1995), and in V. Celia Lascarides and Blythe F. Hinitz, *History of Early Childhood Education* (2000). An obituary appeared in the *New York Times* on November 2, 1992.

BARBARA BEATTY

ELIOT, Martha May. April 7, 1891–February 14, 1978. Pediatrician, federal official.

Martha May Eliot, one of the most influential American pediatricians of the twentieth century, was born into a distinguished Boston family, the second of three children of Christopher Rhodes Eliot, a Unitarian minister, and his wife, Mary Jackson May. Her younger sister, ABIGAIL ADAMS ELIOT, had a distinguished career in child advocacy and education. Despite her privileged background, Martha became aware of poverty at a tender age. A deep concern for child health and welfare would inspire her work as a pediatrician and public servant. Eliot's impact ranged from doing important clinical research on rickets prevention to writing the provisions for dependent and crippled children into the 1935 Social Security Act. Her most innovative effort came at the Children's Bureau during World War II when she organized the Emergency Maternity and Infant Care Program (EMIC) to provide federally subsidized health care for military dependents.

Martha Eliot faced formidable obstacles in building her career. After attending Miss Winsor's School in Boston, she graduated from Radcliffe College in 1913. A year of work as an assistant in the Social Service Department of Massachusetts General Hospital solidified her interest in the social aspects of medicine. When Eliot sought career advice from Professor William Sedgwick of MIT, he urged her to work as a bacteriologist. Then she asked what advice he'd give a young man; his reply was to study medicine. This was the course she pursued, entering Johns Hopkins Medical School in 1914. During the next four years, Eliot took advantage of every opportunity to work in clinics and settlement houses. As she wrote her parents, her desire was to be "some kind of a social doctor."

On receiving her MD with honors in 1918, Eliot found that even impeccable academic credentials were no protection from a pervasive bias against women doctors in postgraduate training. When male interns and residents joined the army in World War I, however, many hospitals accepted females to fill vacant positions on their house staffs. Eliot did a medical internship at Peter Bent Brigham Hospital in Boston and a pediatric residency at St. Louis Children's Hospital.

In the fall of 1920, she opened an office in Boston and sent out notices stating that her practice specialized in the prevention and treatment of diseases of children. The unusual addition of the word *prevention* to this announcement expressed Eliot's vision of what the goal of pediatrics should be. But she soon found her concerns and temperament ill-suited to private practice. Luckily, within months Edwards Park, once her teacher at Johns Hopkins, invited Eliot to join Yale's Department of Pediatrics as chief resident and instructor. Besides providing a supportive mentor, the new job allowed her to establish a home in New Haven with longtime friend and fellow pediatrician Ethel Dunham—a domestic arrangement that became a lifelong partnership.

In 1923, Eliot began to collaborate with Park on

her first project in "social medicine"—a three-year prospective study funded by the U.S. Children's Bureau to discover whether a supervised regimen of cod liver oil and sunbaths could prevent rickets, then a major cause of bone deformation in infants and children. The conclusive results, which Eliot published in 1925, were a landmark in the field and proved the efficacy of this preventive approach.

Eliot found that consulting for the federal Children's Bureau provided a satisfying arena for her social concerns. Like the women reformers who founded the Bureau in 1912, Eliot believed in linking research findings with remedial action to benefit the young. In 1924, with Park's approval, she accepted GRACE ABBOTT's invitation to become part-time director of its Division of Maternal and Child Health and for ten years commuted to Washington monthly, supervising research and community health projects across the nation. In 1934, she accepted an appointment as the Bureau's assistant chief and moved to Washington. Among her first tasks was to draft the Social Security Act's provisions for crippled and dependent children. As she analyzed the Depression's negative effect on youngsters' health and welfare, Eliot concluded that their needs had become even more urgent.

Her grasp of how important medical services for military families would be during World War II inspired Eliot to create a federal program delivering care to the dependents of the lowest-paid enlisted men. The Emergency Maternity and Infant Care Program, begun in 1941 as a small state project, became available nationwide in 1943. Using the Social Security Act's mandate to extend and improve maternal and child health, Eliot persuaded Congress to provide the funds necessary to reach mothers and children in every state. Between 1943 and 1949, EMIC financed the deliveries of 1.2 million babies, one in six American births. Despite bitter opposition from conservative doctors who feared government interference with private practice, EMIC flourished under Eliot's leadership. She proved to be a highly effective politician; her disarming, grandmotherly appearance belied iron purpose and indomitable will.

At war's end, Eliot turned her attention to needy children in Europe and Asia. The only woman who signed the constitution of the newly organized World Health Organization, she subsequently served as a consultant to WHO, UNICEF, and the United Nations Children's Fund. In 1947, she became the first woman elected president of the American Public Health Association. The next year, Eliot was chosen to lead the National Conference on Social Welfare; she also received the prestigious Lasker Prize for establishing and running the EMIC program so successfully. After serving as assistant director general of the World Health Organization in Geneva from 1949 to 1951, Eliot returned to the Children's Bureau as its chief (a presidential appointment) until 1956.

Upon leaving government service, Eliot spent three years as head of the Department of Maternal and Child Health at the Harvard School of Public Health. Active well beyond her retirement, in 1959 she played a key role in establishing the Massachusetts Committee for Children and Youth. This organization modernized the state's health and welfare services. In 1967, Eliot became the second woman (her partner, Ethel Dunham, was the first) to receive the American Pediatric Society's highest honor, the John Howland Award. A passionate concern for children and youth endured until her death in Cambridge in 1978 at the age of eighty-six. In her memory, the American Public Health Association established an annual Martha May Eliot Award for outstanding work in maternal and child health.

Bibliography: Martha Eliot's letters to her parents from medical school, photographs, and an extensive oral history conducted by Jeannette Cheek are in the Martha May Eliot collection at the Schlesinger Library, Radcliffe Institute for Advanced Study, Harvard University. The files also contain letters from her mentor, Edwards Park, which show the depth of the bond they established early in Eliot's career. The Children's Bureau records in the National Archives hold Eliot's extensive professional correspondence. A paper she co-authored, "Four Years of the EMIC Program," *Yale Journal of Biology and Medicine* 19 (1947), pp. 621–36, gives her view of its achievements. Her landmark paper "The Control of Rickets" appeared in the *Journal of the American Medical Association* 85 (1925), pp. 656–63. See also H. E. Harrison, "A Tribute to the First Lady of Public Health: Martha Eliot and the Disappearance of Rickets," *American Journal of Public Health* 56 (1966), pp. 734–37. For Eliot's account of her career, see "The United States Children's Bureau" (Howland Award Address), *American Journal of Diseases of Children* 114 (1967), pp. 565–73. For an appreciation of Eliot's work and that of her partner, see Mary Ellen Avery, "Prematurity and Public Health: A Lecture in Honor of Drs. Ethel Dunham and Martha Eliot," *Harvard Public Health Alumni Bulletin* 36 (January 1980), pp. 4–8. Eliot's longtime colleague, William Schmidt, described her achievements in a tribute entitled "Some Kind of a Social Doctor: Martha May Eliot," *Pediatrics* 63 (January 1979), pp. 146–49. For a view of her early work in New Haven, see Marion Hunt, "'Extraordinarily Interesting and Happy Years': Martha M. Eliot and Pediatrics at Yale, 1921–1935," *Yale Journal of Biology and Medicine* 68 (1995), pp. 159–70. An obituary appeared in the *New York Times* on February 23, 1978.

MARION HUNT

ENTERS, Angna. April 18, 1897–February 25, 1989. Dance-mime, artist, writer.

An innovative concert dancer; author of several volumes of memoirs, a novel, plays, and screenplays; and painter, sculptor, and costume designer, Angna Enters was a fiercely independent creative personality. Her explorations in dramatic movement fed the shape and content of the fledgling modern dance movement in a career that spanned five decades.

Her given name was Anita. She was born and raised in Milwaukee, Wisconsin, then a bastion of German and progressive American culture. Her father, Edward W. Enters, was the fourth child in a large German American family. Her mother, Henriette Gasseur-Styleau, came from Watertown, Wisconsin. German and English, and possibly some French, were spoken among the families. An only child, Enters was taken to the theater and had piano and dancing lessons.

Despite Enters's claim to have been educated primarily at home, she graduated from Milwaukee High School in 1915, then completed the three-year design program at the Milwaukee Normal School, later part of the University of Wisconsin, and stayed on for a fourth year of additional study. She meant to be an artist. Her skills as a painter were put to use with the Wisconsin Players, where she also appeared in plays and dance pageants such as *The Quest of the Soul,* which showcased visiting interpretive dance star Paul Swan. She spent a summer working with stage designer and director Robert Edmond Jones at the Pabst Theater, her first exposure to professional theater.

In the fall of 1919, Enters went to New York City to study at the Art Students League. There she met John Sloan. Though she was his student only briefly, she became a friend and the subject of several of his paintings and many drawings of her dances. In search of a physical activity to take her away from her work as a commercial artist, she began to take dancing lessons with Michio Ito, a Japanese dancer with extensive background in Dalcroze Eurythmics who had devised his own system of interpretive movement. After several student dance concerts with Ito, she became his professional partner, appearing with him in concert programs and on Broadway in the *Pinwheel Revel* (1922).

Enters began to present concerts of her own solo dances in 1923. These self-produced evenings, usually scheduled on a Sunday when theaters were dark and could be rented inexpensively, became popular among artists and intellectuals. Other dancers followed her lead, and concert dance became the seedbed of American modern dance.

Enters's dances, which she referred to as Episodes or Compositions, were fresh and original, more natural movement than abstract musical interpretation. Each short piece was accompanied on piano with music specifically arranged for it and was costumed to vividly evoke the character: a young girl at her first formal dance, a sleepy shepherd boy, a catlike Spanish woman, a medieval madonna. As her work developed, her characterizations became more complex—subtle, often comic, evocations of the contradictions of human behavior. Though some of her characters were male, the vast majority were women in particular moments in history: a turn-of-the-century Parisian streetwalker, a Renaissance court lady, a contemporary French cook. She explored the human face of world politics, religion, popular culture, and societal relations between women and men. By the end of her long career as a concert dancer, she had created more than 250 dance-mime compositions.

One of very few dancers to make her living as a concert performer, Enters began to tour in 1926, crossing the United States more than fourteen times and appearing in London annually until 1939. She performed at the White House for the Roosevelts in 1940, and in 1951 she was invited to appear in Berlin by ANTA (American National Theatre and Academy) and the U.S. State Department. She last performed in New York City in 1960.

Enters's dances and the artwork that she continued to produce throughout her life were infused with intense historical research and her travels abroad. She was awarded two Guggenheim Fellowships, in 1934 and 1935, which enabled her to travel to Greece, Egypt, Lebanon, and Palestine. Her paintings, drawings, and small sculptures were exhibited in annual solo shows at the Ehrich-Newhouse Gallery in New York and in cities along her concert tour route.

Enters's notebooks and correspondence became the foundation of articles on dance and mime, memoirs of her life and travels, a *roman à clef* of life among the avant-garde and theater folk of 1920s New York City, and several plays. *Love Possessed Juana,* an epic play about the Spanish queen Juana La Loca, was published by Twice-A-Year Press in 1939 and produced at the Houston Little Theatre in 1946 with sets and costumes designed by Enters. In 1944, Enters became a contract writer for Metro-Goldwyn-Mayer, contributing story ideas to *Lost Angel* (1943) and *Tenth Avenue Angel* (1948), both starring Margaret O'Brien. She also staged the *commedia dell'arte* sequences for *Scaramouche* (1952).

Enters directed a professional production of García Lorca's *Yerma,* starring Libby Holman and Rose Bampton, at the University of Denver in 1958, and in 1962 directed *The Mad Woman of Chaillot* for the Dallas Theater Center. Throughout the 1950s, Enters taught mime and movement for actors at the Stella Adler Theatre Studio. She was artist-in-residence at the Dallas Theater Center and Baylor University in 1961–62, the Center for Advanced Studies at Wesleyan University in 1962–63, and Pennsylvania State University in 1970–71.

Her life companion was Louis Kalonyme, a journalist and art critic who preferred that their partnership, personal and professional, remain secret. In the early years, he published insightful reviews of her concerts as well as critical commentary on his friends in the modern art world. After 1933, he edited her manuscripts and published nothing in his own name. They may have secretly married in July 1936; they never had children. Only after his death in 1961 did Enters make their relationship public, copyrighting their translation of Edmond Rostand's *Chantecleer* in both their names.

During the 1960s, Enters lived as companion to Albert Lewin, retired film director and producer. She refused his offer of marriage and returned to the apartment she had shared with Kalonyme after Lewin's death in 1968. Enters's health began to deteriorate in the early 1970s, and she lived in an elder care facility in Tenafly, New Jersey, until her death in 1989 at the age of ninety-one.

Bibliography: Angna Enters's papers are in the New York Public Library for the Performing Arts at Lincoln Center, which also contains many photographs of the artist. The papers consist of her extensive correspondence with Louis Kalonyme and others, notebooks, sketchbooks, annotated sheet music, manuscripts and page proofs, contracts, programs, drawings, photographs, and ephemera. The only known record of Enters performing is the kinescope/videotape of "Artist's Life," an episode of *Camera Three,* which was produced by CBS on March 15, 1969; a copy can be found in the New York Public Library for the Performing Arts. Other published writings by Enters are *First Person Plural* (1937); *Silly Girl: A Portrait of Personal Remembrance* (1944); *Among the Daughters* (1955); *Artist's Life* (1958); and *Angna Enters: On Mime* (1965). In addition, she published many articles in journals and magazines such as *Drama Magazine, Hound and Horn, New Masses, New Republic, New Theatre,* and *Twice-A-Year.* The only published biography of Enters to date is Dorothy Mandel, *Uncommon Eloquence: A Biography of Angna Enters* (1986). A doctoral dissertation by Ginnine Cocuzza, "The Theatre of Angna Enters, American Dance-Mime" (New York University, 1986), examines Enters's dance career in depth. Other articles about Enters by Cocuzza include "Angna Enters: American Dance-Mime," *Drama Review,* December 1980, pp. 93–102; and "First Person Plural: A Portfolio from the Theatre of Angna Enters," *Women & Performance,* Summer 1983, pp. 36–39. Published reviews of Enters's work appear in Olive Holmes, ed., *Motion Arrested: Dance Reviews of H. T. Parker* (1982); Walter Sorell, *Looking Back in Wonder: Diary of a Dance Critic* (1986); Walter Terry, *I Was There: Selected Dance Reviews and Articles 1936–1976* (1978); and Louis Untermeyer, *From Another World* (1939). For personal and professional reasons, early in her career Enters changed her birth date to April 28, 1907; however, her birth certificate from the Milwaukee Health Department establishes April 18, 1897, as the correct date. This essay draws on material from the author's interview with Enters on July 31, 1980. An obituary appeared in the *New York Times* on March 1, 1989.

GINNINE COCUZZA

ERTESZEK, Olga Bertram. June 15, 1916–September 15, 1989. Undergarment designer, company owner.

Growing up as the daughter of a Krakow corsetiere in the years after World War I, Otylia Bertram (who changed her name to Olga upon becoming a U.S. citizen) could scarcely have envisioned a future as the design leader and human face of the Olga Company, a $67 million California manufacturer of girdles, brassieres, and lingerie. She achieved that success due to her knowledge and skills in corset design, an unfailing eye for beautiful styling, belief in her own future success, and the complementary business acumen of her husband, Jan Erteszek.

Born in Krakow in what was then Austria-Hungary, Olga was the daughter of Stefania Grossfield, who taught her about corset making, and Bernard Bertram, a writer. Several years after graduating from the local gymnasium, she fled Poland with her future husband in August 1939, just ahead of Hitler's invading army. They married on December 6, 1940. After an odyssey across Russia to Japan, Jan secured a visa to the United States, and Olga followed several months later; they settled in Los Angeles in 1941. A criminal lawyer by training, he found work in sales; she took a job in an apparel factory. They became the parents of three daughters: Victoria (1944), Mary (1945), and Christina (1949).

One day the Erteszeks noticed the ungainly rolled hosiery of a woman boarding a trolley. Olga decided that a pretty garter belt would be a far more appealing way to secure stockings. The couple invested five dollars to rent a sewing machine, another five dollars in material, and Olga designed and made a half dozen lace-trimmed garter belts. The foundations buyer for the elite Bullocks-Wilshire department store ordered two dozen belts, launching the business in 1942. By 1944 the Olga Company had diversified into girdles, followed by bras in 1948, and lingerie, sleepwear, and loungewear in the 1960s.

The Erteszeks had embarked on their business in the right place at an opportune time. From small beginnings in the late 1920s, southern California burgeoned as a center of bra and girdle production. When the Nazi occupation of France ended transatlantic export of couture, Americans were forced to rely on U.S. designers. Equally important for the Olga Company and its California confreres, Hollywood's reputation as the movie capital of the United States lent glamour to locally produced foundations and outerwear.

Inventiveness, as much as a favorable location in Van Nuys, California, helped the Olga Company thrive. Between 1950 and 1973, Olga Erteszek secured twenty-three patents for girdles, brassieres, and lingerie combinations, initially testing the designs on herself. Notable among her patents were a removable crotch in a panty-girdle and several girdle components that molded the abdomen, derriere, and hips while maintaining flexibility and comfort. She also developed several composite garments: a half-slip with panty, a slip-blouse, a bra-slip, and a bra-blouse. Olga's assortment of patented bras featured seamless effects or Lycra components that improved both comfort and fit, even in underwire bras. Though hers were the guiding hand and eye in producing these innovations, she brainstormed with Jan and, as the company grew, several resident designers. "Blue-sky" or creative meetings of the design and administrative staff encouraged fresh thinking about the nature of undergarments.

Astute advertising supported the Olga Company's inventiveness. Jan Erteszek, the family wordsmith as well as the firm's business manager, made important contributions to this phase of operations. While embracing their American identity and becoming citizens in 1946, the Erteszeks attached European names to their products in advertising. The Polonaise girdle appeared in 1950; French Secret bras and girdles followed from 1955 through 1960. Early ads showed a Hollywood starlet endorsing Olga's girdles and garter belts, but the most memorable advertisements centered on Olga herself. Despite her innate reticence, she appeared in company advertisements as early as 1952. The power of her own attractive appearance and individual style was central to the campaign titled "Behind every Olga there really is an Olga," which ran from 1964 through 1978. These ads implied Olga's personal touch in designing products and suggested that women who wore her garments would achieve her sophisticated style.

Inspired by strong Judeo-Christian values, Olga and Jan regarded the company as a common venture and initiated profit sharing in 1954. Through the 1950s and 1960s the company grew, leading its co-owners to take it public in May 1967. Company associates shared in the benefits when times were good and in difficult years, such as 1982, avoided layoffs through a work-sharing arrangement. As a result of this philosophy, in 1984 the Olga Company was ranked as one of the best one hundred companies to work for in America, and Olga and Jan Erteszek were named California Industrialists of the Year in 1985. In 1984, Warnaco purchased the Olga Company for $28 million, a bid Olga and Jan accepted over competing offers because at the time the two companies had congruent philosophies. Shortly thereafter, a hostile takeover of Warnaco drastically altered company culture.

Raised Jewish, Olga and Jan Erteszek became Congregationalists when they settled in the United States. They later joined the Presbyterian church and remained devout and active members throughout their lives. As they prospered, Olga and Jan established the Erteszek Foundation. Olga sponsored language literacy for employees and contributed her talents to fund-raising for the Museum of Science and Industry in California. She assisted with "makeover" programs designed to raise the self-esteem of women with mental illness and supported the Ocean Park Community Center, a social service for battered women.

Jan Erteszek died in 1986, the same year Olga and daughter Christina won the New York Underfashion Club's Femmy award. The Intimate Apparel Council honored Olga with its first Intime Award in 1988. The next year Olga Erteszek succumbed to breast cancer in Brentwood, California. She was seventy-three.

Olga's knack for survival and talent for design led her to become "the first lady of underfashions" and to prosper in a challenging business. She delighted in bringing beautiful, comfortable undergarments to women in the United States and abroad. Her daughter Christina, who designed a young women's line for the company, summarized Olga's message for other women as "believe in yourself" and "don't fear the unknown."

Bibliography: Trade and business publications, such as *Corset and Underwear Review (CUR)*, provide important details about Olga Erteszek and her company; see especially June 1944, p. 11, and April 1968, pp. 33–36. The *Wall Street Journal* documented most company milestones. Consumer advertisements in *Vogue* and *Mademoiselle*, plus trade ads in *CUR*, offer clues to company products and advertising strategies. Patent texts, secured from the Minneapolis Public Library, illuminated Olga's inventions. Robert Levering, Milton Moskowitz, and Michael Katz, *The 100 Best Companies to Work for in America* (1984), analyzed company policies. For an overview of the industry, see Jane Farrell-Beck and Colleen Gau, *Uplift: The Bra in America* (2002). Additional information about Olga and her family was supplied by Christina Erteszek in an interview on August 12, 2002. Obituaries appeared in the *Los Angeles Times*, September 17, 1989; the *New York Times*, September 19, 1989; and *Women's Wear Daily*, September 20, 1989.

JANE FARRELL-BECK

ESAU, Katherine. April 3, 1898–June 4, 1997. Botanist.

Katherine Esau was born in the Ukrainian city of Yekaterinoslav (now Dnepropetrovsk), where her father later became mayor. Her parents,

Margrethe Toews and Johan Esau, were descendants of German Mennonites who had settled in the Ukraine in the nineteenth century. She had one older brother, Paul; two other children had died in infancy. Katherine attended a Mennonite primary school and at eleven entered the gymnasium, graduating at eighteen. Johan Esau was a mechanical engineer and, as a city leader, came under suspicion during the Bolshevik Revolution. The Esaus lived in an area occupied by the German army during World War I and fled with these forces to Berlin at the end of 1918. By this time, Katherine had completed a year at Golitsin Women's Agricultural College in Moscow; she then enrolled in the Berlin Landwirtschaftliche Hochschule. After graduating from this agricultural college in 1921, she studied plant breeding and worked at a model seed-breeding station for wheat in northern Germany.

In 1922, the Esaus emigrated to the United States, settling in Reedley, California, near Fresno, where there was a Mennonite community. Katherine worked as a domestic in order to improve her English and learn American customs. She then found a position with a seed company, finally moving on to the Spreckles Sugar Company in the Salinas Valley where she worked on breeding sugar beets resistant to the virus causing curly-top disease. There she made contact with W. W. Robbins, chair of the Botany Division of what would become the University of California at Davis, and he offered her an assistantship to pursue doctoral studies. In the fall of 1927, Esau arrived at Davis College of Agriculture, where her European training was considered the equivalent of a master's degree. She had planned to continue her field studies on the insect-facilitated spread of the curly-top virus—but the College of Agriculture already had an ongoing project on the breeding of sugar beets, and field studies on the virus might have endangered the healthy plants in the breeding program. So Esau moved from field studies to laboratory work on the anatomical changes caused by the virus. She defended her thesis in December 1931 and received her degree in 1932. (The degree was officially awarded from Berkeley because the Davis campus did not offer a PhD at that time.)

In 1932, Esau became an instructor at Davis. Despite the excellence of her research and teaching, she did not reach the rank of full professor until 1949 at age fifty-one—W. W. Robbins didn't believe in early promotion, and Esau had to spend the full number of years in each rank before promotion to the next. Single by choice, she followed a meticulously structured schedule, rising each morning at 5 AM. Colleagues and friends inevitably commented on the tidy organization of her home and office.

During her years at Davis, where she remained until 1963, Esau studied healthy and diseased plants of a number of species, including celery, tobacco, carrot, and pear. During World War II, she worked on developing more productive rubber plants. Over the years, the focus of a great deal of Esau's research was on the phloem, the system of transport vessels in the stem that conduct sugar from the leaves down to the roots. She studied viruses, like the beet curly-top virus, that damage the phloem and spread through this tissue. She observed that viral particles move from cell to cell by means of plasmadesmata, structures that connect plant cells to each other; this opened a new field of research that is still being explored today at the molecular level. Much of Esau's work during these years involved studies using the light microscope, and she became an expert photographer in order to document her research. The darkroom at Davis was not air conditioned, so when she built a house close to campus, where she lived with her parents, she had a darkroom installed there. During the 1940s and 1950s, she produced all of her own photomicrographs.

In 1963, Esau moved from Davis to the University of California at Santa Barbara in order to continue working on phloem with Vernon I. Cheadle, a former Davis colleague who had become chancellor at Santa Barbara. Esau, who was sixty-five at the time of the move, intended to retire within a few years; instead, she stayed more than two decades and considered those years the most productive and gratifying of her career. Santa Barbara had just installed an electron microscope at the time of her arrival, and this instrument opened up a new world for her. She used it to continue her studies on the phloem, exploring the relationship between structure and function and also revealing more about how viruses affect phloem structure. Her last publication, on structures within plant cells, appeared in 1991.

Esau's work was so significant that she dominated the field of plant anatomy for several decades. Because the graduate program at Davis was small, she trained only fifteen graduate students over the years, but her writings greatly increased her influence. She wrote over 160 articles and six books, including the classic *Plant Anatomy.* Originally published in 1953, this 735-page work is evidence of her breadth of knowledge of her subject. The book created new enthusiasm for the field and influenced a whole generation of graduate students. In addition, Esau was an inspired teacher. She was well organized and able to transmit her enthusiasm for her subject, often through humor. She dubbed a picture of herself standing beside an electron microscope Modern American Gothic, and some of the stories she told in class became known as Esau's fables.

Esau received a number of honors during her long career. She was elected to the National Academy of Sciences in 1957, only the sixth woman to be chosen, and later to the American Academy of Arts and Sciences. In 1951 she served as president of the Botanical Society of America, which five years later presented her with its first Merit Award at its fiftieth anniversary meeting. In 1989 President George Bush presented her with the National Medal of Science. Esau died at her home in Santa Barbara in 1997 at the age of ninety-nine.

Bibliography: A selection of Esau's papers is housed in the Archives at the University of California, Davis; there is also a small collection at the Davidson Library at the University of California at Santa Barbara (UCSB). As part of the UCSB Oral History Program, Esau was interviewed by David E. Russell in 1992. Esau's publications include *Plant Anatomy* (1953, 2nd ed. 1965); *Anatomy of Seed Plants* (1960, 2nd ed. 1977); *Plants, Viruses, and Insects* (1961); *Vascular Differentiation in Plants* (1965); *Viruses in Plant Hosts: Form, Distillation, and Pathologic Effects* (1968); and *The Phloem* (1969). Elizabeth Moot O'Hern, "Profiles of Pioneer Women Scientists: Katherine Esau," *Botanical Review* 62, no. 3 (July–September 1996), pp. 209–72, draws on interviews with her, as well as reminiscences by her friend Celeste Turner Wright; it also includes her father's recollections about his life in the Ukraine. Ray F. Evert has written several essays on Esau and her work, among them (with Dwight U. Beebe) "Photoassimilate Pathway(s) and Phloem Loading in the Leaf of *Moricandia Arvensis* (l.) DC. (Brassicaceae)," *International Journal of Plant Sciences* 153, no. 1 (March 1992), pp. 61–77; and "Commentary: The Contributions of Katherine Esau," *International Journal of Plant Sciences* 153, no. 3 (part 2) (September 1992), pp. v–ix. See also the obituary of Esau he wrote with Jennifer A. Thorsch for *Annual Review of Phytopathology* 36, no. 1 (January 1998), pp. 27–40, which includes a bibliography. Additional obituaries appeared in the *New York Times* on June 18, 1997, and the *American Journal of Botany* 84 (November 1997), pp. 1620–21.

MAURA FLANNERY

F

FARRAR, Margaret. March 23, 1897–June 11, 1984. Crossword puzzle editor.

Margaret Petherbridge Farrar, the pioneering crossword editor who turned a filler puzzle into a daily habit for people all over the world, always described her life's work as an accidental career. She was born in Brooklyn and raised in Manhattan, one of three children of Margaret Elizabeth Furey and Henry Wade Petherbridge, an executive with the National Licorice Company in Brooklyn. After graduating from Berkeley Institute in Brooklyn, she attended Smith College, where she majored in history and graduated in 1919.

Her first job was with a bank in New York City, but in 1921 she became secretary to John O'Hara Cosgrave, Sunday editor of the *New York World.* The crossword became her responsibility after Cosgrave ordered her to get it in shape to run in the paper without any mistakes. The puzzle had been a feature in the paper since December 21, 1913, when its inventor, Arthur Wynne, had introduced it on the Sunday pages. From the outset the puzzle had been plagued by typographical errors, misnumbered clues, outright omissions, and other sloppy work of disgruntled typographers, who didn't like the extra chores involved in setting up the crosswords. Surprisingly, no one had tested the puzzles before they appeared in print. After Margaret solved her first crossword and discovered how sloppy they were, she gradually instituted several improvements: typesetting the puzzles one week in advance, using dictionary words only, tightening the diagrams, eliminating most of the unkeyed letters (those that did not cross with other letters), and setting up rules for constructors so that the puzzles could become more uniform. In so doing, she helped shape the crossword into an increasingly popular feature for the *World.*

Margaret Petherbridge was one of the three editors (with F. Gregory Hartswick and Prosper Buranelli) of the first-ever crossword puzzle book, which was published on April 10, 1924, by a new firm, Simon & Schuster. A crossword craze swept the country that year. Simon & Schuster sold more than 350,000 copies in its first year, and crossword puzzles soon became a regular feature of newspapers. Margaret continued to edit the Simon & Schuster puzzle series for sixty years, through more than 130 volumes, a publishing record that has never been broken.

On May 28, 1926, Margaret Petherbridge married John Chipman Farrar, a publisher and author. She left her job at the *World* but continued to edit the crossword puzzle books for Simon & Schuster. A well-bred, erudite woman who successfully managed to have both a career and a family, she worked from her home on Manhattan's Upper

East Side while raising three children: son John Curtis and daughters Alison and Janice. From 1935 to 1942 she was a member of the Children's Book Committee of the Child Study Association. She also did publicity work for the Red Cross during World War II.

Despite the demonstrated popularity of crossword puzzles, the venerable *New York Times* excluded them until 1942, when Margaret Farrar was hired as its first crossword puzzle editor. Her work began appearing in the Sunday *New York Times* on February 15, 1942; on September 11, 1950, the puzzle became a feature of the daily *Times* as well. Farrar constructed puzzles herself, but more often edited ones submitted by her core of steady contributors, who included a retired violinist, a sea captain, and a few prison inmates, all of whom benefited from her warm encouragement and suggestions. In addition to checking the puzzles for accuracy and freshness, she also made sure that words and definitions were not repeated from one puzzle to the next. Over the years Farrar helped develop the sophisticated modern form of the thematic, often wordplay-oriented puzzle that has become the ultimate standard for American solvers.

Retirement was the only word Farrar could never define. When she left the *Times* in 1969 (because of its then-mandatory retirement policy), she went to work editing puzzles for General Features Syndicate, while continuing to compile crossword books and calendars. Widowed in 1974, she took her husband's place on the board of directors of Farrar, Straus & Giroux, of which he had been a founding member. Beginning in 1978 and continuing until her death, she traveled to every American Crossword Puzzle Tournament to speak and award prizes to the winners. She died at her home in Manhattan on June 11, 1984, at the age of eighty-seven, just two months after celebrating the publication of her 133rd book with friends at New York's Lotos Club.

Margaret Farrar's legacy is immense. She took a puzzle that was thrown together and riddled with errors and made it respectable by devising rules for its elegant construction. The evolution of the crossword from a dry, straightforward challenge into a lively game of witty, literate wordplay, enjoyed by millions, is directly attributable to her influence.

Bibliography: The best introduction to Margaret Farrar's influence on the modern crossword puzzle is to sample one of the many books she edited over her long career. See also Farrar's introductory chapter to Eugene Maleska, *Across and Down: The Crossword Puzzle World* (1984). More information can be found in Robert D. Spurrier, "Puzzledom's Reigning Queen: Margaret Farrar," *Games* magazine, September 1982; Roger Millington, *Crossword Puzzles: Their History and Their Cult* (1975); and Helene Hovanec, *Creative Cruciverbalists* (1988). Biographical information is found in *Current Biography* (1955), pp. 193–95, and in a January 5, 1969, article in the *New York Times* about her retirement. An obituary appeared in the *New York Times* on June 12, 1984.

HELENE HOVANEC AND WILL SHORTZ

FENWICK, Millicent. February 25, 1910–September 16, 1992. Fashion editor, civic leader, U.S. Representative.

The second of three siblings, Millicent Vernon Hammond was born in New York City, the daughter of Mary Picton Stevens, a philanthropist and descendant of the Revolutionary War hero John Stevens, and Ogden Haggerty Hammond, a prominent financier and politician. She grew up on the family estate near Bernardsville, New Jersey. In 1915, while en route to France to establish a hospital for war victims, her mother drowned when the passenger liner *Lusitania* was sunk by a German submarine. Millicent attended Foxcroft School, a boarding school in Virginia, but left to join her family in Madrid when President Calvin Coolidge appointed her father ambassador to Spain in 1925.

After the family returned to New Jersey in 1929, she took courses at Columbia University and studied philosophy with Bertrand Russell at the New School for Social Research. At about the same time, she met Hugh Fenwick, a married man five years her senior. Their romance scandalized her family and friends. After Fenwick's divorce, they married in 1932 and had a daughter, Mary (1934), and a son, Hugh Jr. (1937). In 1938, Hugh Fenwick, who had amassed enormous debts, left for Europe and the marriage ended in divorce.

Rather than seek help from her family, Millicent Fenwick sought work to support her children and pay off her husband's bills. Five feet ten inches tall, slim, and stunningly beautiful, she modeled for *Harper's Bazaar.* Because she lacked even a high school diploma, she was turned down for many positions, but through friends she met publisher Condé Nast and talked her way into an editorial position at *Vogue,* where she worked for more than a decade. *Vogue's Book of Etiquette,* which she compiled, was published in 1948 and sold one million copies. Like Fenwick herself, the 650-page book was a compendium of good taste and straightforward common sense.

After receiving a large inheritance in the early 1950s, Fenwick retired from *Vogue* to her family estate in New Jersey, fully intending, she claimed, to settle down and garden. Within months, however, she was championing causes like prison reform and legal aid, often using her personal fortune to further the work of organizations she supported. Long a staunch advocate of civil rights,

Fenwick later served for sixteen years on the New Jersey Committee of the U.S. Commission on Civil Rights.

Sharing the liberal Republicanism that ran deep in her family, Fenwick also began volunteering in the campaigns of Republican candidates. In 1958, she successfully ran for Bernardsville Borough Council, her first elective office, and was twice reelected. When asked years later if with this election she consciously began to pursue a career in politics, she spoke for many women of her generation when she answered, "No, I think I was sort of gliding in by the unpaid volunteer backdoor route" (Lamson, p. 15). In 1969, Fenwick successfully ran for a seat in the New Jersey General Assembly, where she earned the nickname "Outhouse Millie" because she fought for better working conditions, including portable toilets, for migrant workers. She resigned in 1972 when she was appointed director of New Jersey Consumer Affairs, a position she used to battle deceptive auto advertising and funeral home policies.

In 1974, at age sixty-four, she announced that she would run for Congress on the Republican ticket and, despite the strongly anti-Republican tide in the wake of Watergate, she won. At a dinner at the Washington Press Club where the new members of Congress were introduced, she became one of the most quoted members of her freshman class when she related an exchange with a male colleague in the New Jersey Assembly as they debated the Equal Rights Amendment. He opposed the measure, protesting that "I've always thought of women as kissable, cuddly and smelling good." Fenwick retorted, "That's what I feel about men, too. I only hope for your sake that you haven't been disappointed as often as I have" (*New York Times,* September 17, 1992). Coupled with her legendary frugality and the fact that she smoked a pipe, her wit and understated elegance quickly won over the Washington press; she was often referred to as the "Katharine Hepburn of politics." Fenwick also captured the imagination of cartoonist Garry Trudeau, who caricatured her—to her delight—in his *Doonesbury* comic strip as Congresswoman Lacey Davenport, the slightly eccentric paragon of integrity.

As a liberal Republican in Congress, Fenwick was often at odds with her party, and as a junior member of a minority party she wielded little real power. She was, however, an articulate and passionate advocate for many causes, including gun control, campaign spending limits, and restrictions on capital punishment. She supported a peaceful resolution to the Vietnam War and reductions in the defense budget, and she was especially proud to be a lead sponsor of the resolution creating a commission to monitor the 1975 Helsinki accords on human rights. A staunch supporter of the equal rights amendment and abortion rights, Fenwick was also a forceful member of the Republican Women's Task Force.

Although her positions on issues often seemed aberrant for the wealthy district in New Jersey she represented, Fenwick was reelected to Congress three times by increasing margins. In 1982, she announced her candidacy for the U.S. Senate. Although her opponents in the Republican primary portrayed her as an ultra-liberal and a feminist, she won the nomination. Initially favored to win the Senate seat, she chose to stay at her desk in Washington rather than campaign and refused political action committee money, and she was narrowly defeated by Frank Lautenberg, a wealthy Democrat who portrayed her as an aging eccentric.

In 1983 President Ronald Reagan appointed Fenwick to be the first American envoy to the United Nations Food and Agriculture Organization in Rome. She served in that position for four years, until retiring in 1987 to Bernardsville, New Jersey, where she again became active in local affairs. She died at her home of heart problems on September 16, 1992, at the age of eighty-two. At her insistence, her pallbearers included the local fire chief, as well as sundry governors and senators.

Bibliography: The main collection of Millicent Fenwick's papers is located at the Alexander Library at Rutgers University. A much smaller collection is in the Carl Albert Center Congressional Archives at the University of Oklahoma. In her published collection of open letters to constituents, *Speaking Up* (1982), Fenwick offers insight into her political philosophy and views on issues of the day. *Vogue's Book of Etiquette* (1948) offers her views, and those of her class, on proper behavior in every imaginable social situation. She is profiled in Peggy Lamson, *In the Vanguard: Six American Women in Public Life* (1979). Brief biographies of Fenwick appear in several biographical dictionaries, including *Past and Promise: Lives of New Jersey Women* (1990). Fenwick was the subject of numerous profiles in popular periodicals and newspapers. Obituaries appeared in the *New York Times* and *Washington Post* on September 17, 1992.

KATHRYN ALLAMONG JACOB

FEREBEE, Dorothy Boulding. October 10, 1898–September 14, 1980. Physician, medical educator, women's rights activist.

Dorothy Celeste Boulding was born in Norfolk, Virginia, the third child and only daughter of Florence Ruffin Paige and Benjamin Richard Boulding. Her father worked as a railroad clerk and her mother, a former teacher, volunteered in church and community activities. Her maternal grandfather, Richard G. L. Paige, was an attorney and one of the first black members of the Virginia House of Delegates. When Dorothy was six, her mother's ill health forced her parents to send her to live with relatives in Boston, where she grew up in the midst of the black elite. Her great uncle, Harvard Law School graduate George Ruffin, served as the first black judge in Massachusetts. His wife, JOSEPHINE ST. PIERRE RUFFIN, had started the *Woman's Era,* the first black women's newspaper, and had helped found the National Association of Colored Women.

Dorothy Boulding completed most of her education in Boston, and she excelled in her studies. In 1915 she graduated with honors from the academically rigorous Girls' High School. She spent a year completing college entrance requirements before she entered Simmons College in 1916, where she graduated with honors four years later. Her family nurtured her childhood dream to become a physician, and in 1920 she entered Tufts Medical School. Despite being one of only five women and the only African American in a class of 137, she flourished academically. She was named a member of the women's honor society and elected class historian, but she did not escape racial discrimination at Tufts. Her answers to questions were frequently belittled by physicians, and as she later recalled, "We women were always the last to get assignments in amphitheaters and clinics. And I, I was the last of the last because not only was I a woman, but a Negro, too." She graduated near the top of her class in 1924 but encountered difficulties finding an internship because of her race and gender. She spent a year submitting unsuccessful applications.

Boulding's high score on a civil service examination finally led to an internship in 1925 at Freedman's Hospital, a federally funded hospital affiliated with Howard University School of Medicine. Her internship marked the beginning of a forty-seven-year association with the school. In 1927 she became clinical instructor of obstetrics. While maintaining a limited private practice, she would go on to assume other positions at Howard, including physician to women students in 1929 and director of the Howard University health services from 1949 to 1968. Although the medical world at Howard was black-dominated, it was also male-dominated; and though Boulding actively participated, it was not without some difficulty. She later noted that sexism, rather than racism, had posed a greater professional challenge there.

Shortly after her arrival in Washington, Dorothy began to follow her family's tradition of leadership in racial uplift activities and started to craft a career that combined medicine and social activism. In 1929 she launched a successful campaign to establish a settlement house in the slums of southeast Washington because none of the existing ones admitted black children. She served as president of Southeast Settlement House until 1942.

In the midst of these accomplishments, on July 2, 1930, in a small ceremony in West Chester, Pennsylvania, Dorothy Boulding married Claude Thurston Ferebee, a Columbia University–educated dentist on the faculty at Howard College of Dentistry. Dorothy gave birth to twins, Claude Thurston Ferebee Jr. and Dorothy Boulding Ferebee, the next year. But the Ferebee marriage was not happy; tensions developed around her husband's envy of her success, and the couple led increasingly separate lives. Years later, a tragic personal loss further complicated their relationship. On February 6, 1950, their eighteen-year-old daughter collapsed and died from viral pneumonia while visiting her mother's office. Her death precipitated the end of the long estranged Ferebee marriage. On June 20, 1950, the couple finally divorced.

Having joined Alpha Kappa Alpha (AKA), a black sorority, in 1923, Ferebee spent the summers between 1935 and 1941 heading up the sorority's Mississippi Health Project, a program to bring health care to poor African American communities in Mississippi. By 1940 Ferebee and other AKA volunteers had immunized approximately fifteen thousand children against diphtheria and smallpox and had provided medical care to thousands of adults. Their efforts garnered praise from Surgeon General Thomas Parran. Ferebee served as the national president of AKA from 1940 to 1951 and steered the organization toward increasing its lobbying efforts in health, child welfare, racial justice, and economic security. In 1949 she succeeded MARY MCLEOD BETHUNE as the second president of the National Council of Negro Women and served in the position until 1953.

During this time, Ferebee's influence began to expand beyond domestic black women's organizations. In 1951 the Women's Bureau of the U.S. Department of Labor named her a member of a women's committee to study the postwar status of German women. She later took an active interest in improving the lives of African women and children. By 1970 Ferebee had joined boards of several national women's organizations, including the Girl Scouts, the Young Women's Christian Association (YWCA), and the American Association of University Women (AAUW). Ferebee retired from Howard University in 1972, but continued her activism. In 1971 she had begun a four-year term as the chairwoman of the District of Columbia Commission on the Status of Women. Four years later, she founded the Women's Institute, an organization that sought to improve career opportunities for women by providing educational and training programs and by encouraging research and publications about women's lives.

Contemporaries described Ferebee as elegant and tenacious. The *Washington Post* called her an outstanding American who had helped break down racial and sexual barriers "with a marvelous blend of compassion, cussedness, and class." In 1980 Dorothy Boulding Ferebee died of multiple pulmonary emboli and congestive heart failure at Georgetown University Hospital at the age of eighty-one. Her funeral was held six days later at the Howard University chapel. PATRICIA ROBERTS HARRIS, secretary of the Department of Health and Human Services, delivered the eulogy.

Bibliography: The Dorothy Boulding Ferebee Papers in Special Collections at Moorland-Spingarn Library, Howard University, contain correspondence, clippings, curriculum vitae, speeches, essays, audio recordings, information on the Mississippi Health Project, and photographs. The National Council of Negro Women Archives at the National Archives for Black Women's History, Washington, D.C., include materials on Ferebee's work with the National Council of Negro Women. Information on her work with Alpha Kappa Alpha can be found in the Alpha Kappa Alpha Archives in Special Collections at Moorland-Spingarn Library. A copy of her oral history conducted by Merze Tate can be found in the Black Women Oral History Project, Schlesinger Library, Radcliffe Institute for Advanced Study, Harvard University.

Among her publications are "Planned Parenthood As a Public Health Measure for the Negro Race," *Human Fertility* 7, no. 1 (February 1942), pp. 7–10; "Some Health Problems of College Students at Howard University," *Journal of the American Medical Women's Association* 15, no. 11 (November 1960), pp. 1067–70; and "Some Health Problems in South America and Tropical Africa," *Journal of the American College Health Association* 15, no. 4 (April 1967), pp. 318–25. She also wrote a newspaper column, "Women Looking Forward," which appeared in 1950 and 1951 in the *Afro-American* (Philadelphia, Baltimore, and Washington). Her work with the AKA Mississippi Health Project is analyzed in Susan L. Smith, *Sick and Tired of Being Sick and Tired: Black Women's Health Activism in America, 1890–1950* (1995). See also Vanessa Northington Gamble, "On Becoming a Physician: A Dream Not Deferred," in Evelyn C. White, ed., *The Black Women's Health Book: Speaking for Ourselves* (1990). Obituaries appeared in the *Washington Post* on September 18, 1980 (this contains both quotations), and the *Journal of the National Medical Association* 73 (1981), pp. 900–901. The listed birth date is the one that Ferebee used throughout her life; she acknowledged that it might not be accurate, since she never had a birth certificate.

VANESSA N. GAMBLE

FIERRO, Josefina. 1914–March 2, 1998. Civil rights activist.

During the late 1930s and early 1940s Josefina Fierro served as the executive secretary and key leader of El Congreso de Pueblos de Habla Española (Congress of Spanish-Speaking Peoples), the most progressive and militant Latino political and community organization in the Los Angeles area. At a time when anti-Mexican sentiment during the Great Depression had led to mass deportations and the repatriation of thousands of Mexicans (both persons who were here legally and persons without documents), El Congreso was one of the few Mexican American organizations that courageously stood up to protect the rights and interests of Mexicans in Los Angeles and other parts of the United States. Much of this work was due to the leadership of Josefina Fierro, who was then only in her mid twenties and a Latina woman in a political culture better known for its masculine orientation.

The origins of her leadership were to be found in her family background. She was born in 1914 in Calexico along the U.S.-Mexico border. Her parents were involved in the Mexican Revolution of 1910 and supported the most progressive wing of the Revolution, that of anarcho-syndicalist Ricardo Flores Magón. Josefina later recalled growing up hearing at the dinner table about Magonista politics and the Mexican Revolution.

After her parents separated and her father rejoined the revolutionary forces of Pancho Villa in the interior of Mexico, her mother, Josefa, took Josefina and her younger brother to Los Angeles. There her mother operated a restaurant and made sure that Josefina had an education, even though this meant attending as many as eight schools, owing to the family's frequent moves. Finding it difficult to stay in business in Los Angeles, Josefa decided to operate a traveling food service aimed at helping to feed the thousands of Mexican agricultural workers in California. The family finally settled in Madera, where Josefina finished high school. "Never fall back on your sex," her mother told her, "always rely on yourself, be independent."

Following her graduation, Fierro moved to Los Angeles. Around 1938 she enrolled at UCLA with the hope of becoming a medical doctor. Romance and politics, however, got in the way. Fierro met and later married John Bright, a talented and highly political screenwriter who was involved in a variety of radical movements. Bright introduced Fierro to the progressive political culture of Los Angeles in the late 1930s. Given her own family political history, Fierro did not need much prompting from her husband to begin to participate in community activities, especially around Mexican American issues. Bright was later red-baited and blacklisted for his politics during the McCarthy era. By that point their childless marriage had ended in divorce.

In 1938 Fierro met LUISA MORENO, a top official of the United Cannery, Agricultural, Packing, and Allied Workers of America, a CIO-affiliated union that stressed grassroots organizing across race and gender lines. Moreno's dream was to establish a national organization of Spanish-speaking workers to facilitate union building and to combat racism and discrimination not only at the workplace but in other areas such as schools and public facilities.

As Moreno began to organize what she came to call El Congreso, she recognized in Fierro a talented, articulate, honest, and courageous young woman who would not be intimidated by the men she would have to work with. Fierro accepted the challenge, and at the founding convention of El Congreso in Los Angeles in 1939 she became executive secretary of the new organization and, on a day-to-day basis, its main organizer. Through her leadership as well as that of many other young Mexican Americans, El Congreso became one of the most important Mexican American organizations, being far ahead of its time with its call for unity of all Latino groups in the United States. As another part of its progressive agenda, El Congreso actively recruited women members and integrated them into policy-making positions in the organization.

As the United States entered World War II, Josefina Fierro and the other members of El Congreso encouraged Mexican Americans to support the war effort. Unfortunately, El Congreso disbanded during the war because so many of its members had entered military service. Nevertheless, those who remained, including Fierro, continued to struggle against injustice and discrimination in wartime Los Angeles. In the Sleepy Lagoon Case in 1942, a number of Mexican American young men were unjustly arrested for a gang killing and their rights were violated during their trial. Fierro and other progressive community leaders—both Mexican American and Anglo—led the fight to support the youth through the Sleepy Lagoon Defense Committee. One year later, during the tragic Zoot-suit riots, when hundreds of Anglo military personnel indiscriminately attacked and beat up Mexican Americans dressed in the popular zoot-suit fashion favored by Latino youth, Fierro personally intervened with the Roosevelt administration in Washington to get the military pulled out of the Mexican American barrios as a way to end the riots.

Following the war, Josefina Fierro wanted to restart the work of El Congreso. However, like many other labor and working-class leaders of that time, she fell victim to the McCarthyite red scare. Believing that she would be called before the House Committee on Un-American Activities and possibly arrested or deported, Fierro chose self-exile to avoid implicating colleagues and political associates. As a result the Latino community, indeed the American community, lost a significant leader.

Although she would often return to the United States for visits, Josefina Fierro spent much of the rest of her long life in Mexico. Living in Guaymas, she worked with the poor and working people of that area. Never losing her ideals of social justice, she was as critical of the Mexican ruling elites as she was of the American ones. Wherever people were being denied their rights or suffering discrimination, Josefina Fierro spoke out on their behalf. Josefina Fierro died in 1998.

Bibliography: Biographical information on Josefina Fierro is limited; there is practically none covering the period after she returned to Mexico in 1950. For discussions of her activism in the 1930s and 1940s, see Mario T. García, *Mexican Americans: Leadership, Ideology and Identity, 1930–1960* (1989), which contains the quotation on p. 156; García, *Memories of Chicano History: The Life and Narrative of Bert Corona* (1994); George J. Sánchez, *Becoming Mexican American: Ethnicity, Culture and Identity in Chicano Los Angeles, 1900–1945* (1993); and Albert Camarillo, *Chicanos in California: A History of Mexican Americans in California* (1984). An oral history interview with Fierro conducted by Mario T. García on August 25, 1983, is in the possession of the author.

MARIO T. GARCÍA

FIESER, Mary Peters. May 27, 1909–March 22, 1997. Organic chemist.

Mary Augusta Peters was the first of two daughters born to Julia Clutz and Robert J. Peters. Her father was an English professor at Midland College in Atchison, Kansas, when Mary was born. He later took a position in Pennsylvania and the Peters family moved to Harrisburg. Her mother, who held a BA in English from Goucher College, bought and operated a bookstore there.

The Peterses considered education a virtue regardless of gender and encouraged both their daughters in their studies. Mary and her younger sister Ruth attended a private girls' school in Harrisburg, and upon graduation they enrolled at Bryn Mawr College. Mary began as a premedical student, but soon changed her major to chemistry, and received her bachelor's degree in 1930.

At Bryn Mawr, Mary Peters met Louis Fieser, her mentor, who would later become her husband. Louis Fieser was an assistant professor of chemistry at Bryn Mawr when the two met, but in 1930 he was offered a position at Harvard. He accepted the offer, and Mary moved with him to Cambridge, Massachusetts, where she enrolled as a graduate student in chemistry at Radcliffe College. Mary and Louis were married two years later, on June 21, 1932. They did not have children.

While at Radcliffe, Mary Fieser found that some members of the Harvard chemistry department resisted the entrance of women into chemistry. Certain professors discouraged her from taking their courses, and she was left to carry out her early experiments in an unsupervised basement laboratory. She responded by joining her husband's research group and by opting not to pursue a PhD, ending her formal education with a master's degree in organic chemistry from Radcliffe in 1931. She never received any compensation for her efforts in her husband's group, but the position allowed her to continue her research.

Mary Fieser's research career stretched from 1932 to 1956. During those years she published over forty papers on organic chemistry, the majority of which were the result of research carried out in collaboration with Louis Fieser's research group. The first topic of research in the Fieser group was quinone chemistry, and the group rapidly became a leader in the field. During the Second World War, they received a government contract to develop quinone-based anti-malarials and made significant progress in the endeavor. After the war, the group turned its attention to steroid chemistry. Many of the steroids known at the time were of particular medical interest, including several sex hormones, vitamin K, cortisone, and cholesterol. But steroids were often difficult to produce, and research on the compounds was poorly organized. The Fieser group developed new syntheses that made research on steroids more practical, and Mary and Louis co-wrote a text on steroid chemistry that helped unify the new field.

Although Fieser's laboratory research was well received, her best-known contributions to chemistry were pedagogical and reference works. She began publishing chemistry textbooks in collaboration with her husband in 1944. Their first textbook, *Organic Chemistry,* dominated instruction in introductory organic chemistry for more than a decade. It was renowned for its innovative use of diagrams, its clear prose, and its attention to experimental detail. The Fiesers went on to publish more than half a dozen similarly distinguished texts. The popularity of these texts began to wane only in the 1960s, as more theoretical approaches to teaching organic chemistry were increasingly favored.

Textbooks were not the only products of her collaborations with her husband. In 1960, the couple published *A Style Guide for Chemists.* The book, a veritable Strunk and White for chemists, was an outgrowth of Mary's informal efforts to educate Harvard chemistry students in the fundamentals of good writing. In addition to common rules of English usage, it covered topics such as the pronunciation of chemical terms and how to write clear accounts of experimental procedures. Noting their ability to debate the placement of a comma for upward of an hour, a family member suggested the credit should be "Fieser versus Fieser" rather than "Fieser and Fieser." The style guide was still in print and selling well more than twenty-five years after its first publication.

Nevertheless, the style guide was far outstripped by the Fiesers' most popular work, *Reagents for Organic Synthesis,* which became almost synonymous with their byline. *Reagents* provided organic chemists with a convenient, comprehensive guide to literature on the chemicals and procedures employed in synthetic reactions. Because it spared chemists from having to perform extensive literature searches, which they often found time-consuming and unpleasant, it rapidly became a standard laboratory reference.

The first volume of *Reagents* was published in 1967. Although it was impressively thorough, new volumes were needed to keep up with advances in synthetic chemistry. Updating and revising *Reagents* became the focus of Mary Fieser's later career. She and Louis co-wrote five more volumes of *Reagents* in the ten years before his death in 1977. Thereafter, Mary carried on the series alone, publishing her seventeenth and final volume of *Reagents* in 1994. The series continued to be revised and expanded under new editors in subsequent years.

Mary Fieser enjoyed writing *Reagents,* largely because she never developed her colleagues' distaste for literature searches. Early in Louis's collaborations with Mary, he had noted her unusual ability to find, collect, and absorb material. This ability and her talent for prose composition were the most apparent and distinct of Mary's contributions to the Fieser and Fieser collaborations, although Mary's colleagues emphasized that her role in these collaborations and in Louis's other successes extended well beyond her obvious literary talents.

Still, recognition for Mary Fieser's contributions came relatively late in her life. Harvard did not officially appoint her a research fellow until 1959, after she had basically abandoned the laboratory for the library. The American Chemical Society later acknowledged her "literary achievement in organic chemistry" with the 1971 Garvan Medal. Then in 1996 Harvard University acknowledged her contribution to chemical pedagogy by naming its renovated undergraduate organic chemistry laboratory in honor of Mary and Louis Fieser. It was the last honor she received before her death at the age of eighty-seven on March 22, 1997, at her home in Belmont, Massachusetts.

Bibliography: Mary Fieser's numerous research papers and textbooks can be located using *Chemical Abstracts.* Further information on the research she carried out with the Fieser research group is available in Albert B. Costa's entry on Louis Frederick Fieser in *Dictionary of Scientific Biography,* 17 (1990), pp. 291–95, and in the Louis Fieser collection at the Harvard University Archives. The most comprehensive source for biographical information is Stacey Pramer, "Mary Fieser: A Transitional Figure in the History of Women," *Journal of Chemical Education* 62, no. 3 (March, 1985), pp. 186–91, which draws on two interviews with Fieser. Accounts of her accolades can be found in Lois Decker O'Neill, "Mary Fieser: Garvan Medal," *Chemical and Engineering News* 48 (December 14, 1970), p. 64; "Moving to the Head of the Class," *Harvard University Gazette*, December 12, 1996; and William Shulz, "Harvard's Fieser Laboratory Honors Legacy of Husband-and-Wife Team," *Chemical and Engineering News* 74 (April 29, 1996), pp. 75–76. Obituaries appeared in the *Boston Herald* on March 25, 1997; the *Boston Globe* on March 26, 1997; and the *Harvard Gazette* on March 27, 1997.

JEREMIAH JAMES

FISHER, M.F.K. (Mary Frances Kennedy). July 3, 1908–June 22, 1992. Writer.

When Clifton Fadiman reviewed *How to Cook a Wolf* in the *New Yorker* in 1942, he concluded, "M. F. K. Fisher writes about food as others do about love, but rather better." Charting a new course in American letters by writing in a hybrid genre known as gastronomy, she used food as a metaphor for all human hungers and wrote about the art of eating with nostalgia, humor, and panache.

Born in Albion, Michigan, on July 3, 1908, Mary Frances Kennedy was the oldest of four children (three daughters and a son) born to Edith Oliver Holbrook and newspaper publisher Rex Brenton Kennedy. Both sides of her family were upper middle class and valued education. When Mary Frances was two years old, her father sold his share of the *Albion Evening Recorder* in order to move to Puget Sound. In 1912, he acquired the *Whittier News* and purchased a house in the Quaker community of Whittier. During her childhood and adolescence, Mary Frances excelled as a reader and novice cook, learning very early the power of pleasing with a cake, a perfectly scrambled egg, or a smooth sauce.

Observant and intelligent, but also given to boredom, she did not distinguish herself at Whittier Union High School, the Bishop's School in La Jolla, or Miss Harker's School in Palo Alto except when challenged by a demanding teacher. Her parents, however, insisted that she attend college. After a dismal semester in 1927 at Illinois College in Jacksonville, Illinois, she took courses at Whittier College, UCLA summer school, and spent a year at Occidental College. While at UCLA, Mary Frances met Princeton graduate Alfred Young Fisher; she married him on September 5, 1929. After the wedding they sailed to France, where Fisher began his doctoral studies at the University of Dijon. They rented two small rooms at a pension on the rue du Petit-Potet and adopted a "vie bohème" lifestyle. The Fishers returned to the States in the summer of 1932, settling in California.

M. F. K. Fisher published her first article, "Pacific Village," in *Westways* in 1934. In her spare time she began reading old cookery books in the Los Angeles Public Library and writing short essays on medieval and Renaissance culinary traditions for her own and her husband's amusement. She showed her essays to their neighbor Dillwyn Parrish, whose sister sent them to her editor. Harper Brothers offered M. F. K. Fisher a contract, and *Serve It Forth* was published in 1937.

When Parrish and his young wife separated, he invited the Fishers to join him in Vevey, Switzerland. Within a year, Mary Frances and her husband decided to end their marriage, and he returned to a teaching career at Smith College. Living with Parrish in Switzerland, Fisher enjoyed an idyllic but short-lived period of happiness. In 1938 while traveling in Bern, Parrish suffered an embolism that resulted in the amputation of part of his left leg. During the long days of therapy, Fisher and Parrish wrote a novel together; *Touch and Go* (1939) was published under the pseudonym Victoria Berne. Parrish's frequent hospitalizations and the spread of war across Europe hastened their return to California. After her divorce from Fisher was final, Mary Frances married Parrish on May 12, 1939, and they remodeled an abandoned cabin outside the city limits of Hemet, California. Diagnosed with progressive Buerger's disease, Parrish took his own life on August 6, 1941.

M. F. K. Fisher supported herself by writing *Consider the Oyster* (1941) and *How to Cook a Wolf* (1942), a book dedicated to living well during wartime rationing and food shortages. *Look* magazine featured her as one of the top career women in America, and Paramount Studio offered her a job as a screenwriter. Involved in collaborative scriptwriting, which she did not find satisfying, she had an affair and became pregnant. Under the guise of working for the Office of War Information on the East Coast, Fisher secretly lived in Altadena, California, during the last months of her pregnancy and wrote *The Gastronomical Me* (1943). Her daughter, Anne Kennedy Parrish, was born on August 15, 1943, and Fisher introduced her to family members and friends as her adopted child.

Having broken her contract with Paramount Studio in January 1944, Fisher visited New York City with her daughter in the spring of the following year. She met publisher Donald Friede at a party, and they were married in Atlantic City on May 19, 1945. After spending the summer in New York, they returned to Hemet, where their daughter, Kennedy Mary Friede, was born on March 12, 1946. Although the precipitous marriage proved to be a mistake for both of them, Friede's contacts in the publishing world ushered in the most productive period of Fisher's career. She completed *Here Let Us Feast* in 1946, the novel *Not Now but Now* in 1947, and a wealth of articles and stories, including a series of twenty-six articles for *Gourmet* later published as *An Alphabet for Gourmets* (1949). In 1949, Fisher's translation of Brillat-Savarin's seminal work on gastronomy, *The Physiology of Taste,* was issued by the Limited Editions Club.

In the spring of 1949, the Friedes separated, and Fisher and her daughters moved to Whittier to live with her recently widowed father. After Rex Kennedy died in 1953, they moved to St. Helena, in the Napa Valley. During the next ten years, Fisher concentrated on her daughters' education. Wanting to expose them to other languages and cultures, they lived in Aix-en-Provence in 1954 and 1955, and again from 1959 until 1961. With the exception of *A Cordiall Water* (1961) and the collected edition of her five earlier books of nonfiction called *The Art of Eating* (1954), Fisher did little writing during this time, but the experience of living abroad influenced her future books.

Beginning a long association with the *New Yorker* in 1964, she contributed a series of cookbook reviews, stories, and articles under the title "Gastronomy Recalled," later expanded and published as *With Bold Knife and Fork* (1969). A second *New Yorker* series, "The Enclave," was published as *Among Friends* in 1970. During the 1960s, Fisher joined Michael Field and Julia Child as a collaborator on Time-Life's *The Cooking of Provincial France* (1968). Because of her association with Julia and Paul Child, she met Simone Beck, James Beard, and Judith Jones, who became her editor at Knopf.

In 1971 M. F. K. Fisher moved into a small palazzino on the Bouverie Ranch in Glen Ellen, California, where she continued to write and publish prolifically. As food, travel, and entertaining increasingly seized the public's interest, a growing fascination with the seemingly reclusive Fisher ensued. In the 1980s, North Point Press aggressively began to reprint her early books and Knopf published *As They Were* (1982) and *Sister Age* (1983).

Fisher was diagnosed with Parkinson's disease in the early 1980s, and her health declined steadily. She was plagued with arthritis, eye problems, and hip replacement surgery, which decreased her mobility, but her desire to entertain and greet people continued, and she reserved time each day for work and correspondence with her secretary. In 1988 she published *Dubious Honors,* musings on the various introductions she had written for other books as well as the introductions to her own work. *Long Ago in France* was published in 1991, the same year she was elected to the American Academy of Arts and Letters and the National Institute of Arts and Letters.

Beautiful in old age as in youth, she bewitched, enthralled, and maddened those who sought her out and wrote about her in newspaper and magazine articles as well as in books that assessed her contribution to America's culinary landscape. Through the last difficult years, she worked on her secret project: three books—*To Begin Again: Stories and Memoirs, 1908–1929* (1992), *Stay Me, Oh Comfort Me: Journals and Stories, 1933–1941* (1993), and *Last House: Reflections, Dreams, and Observations, 1943–1991* (1995)—that were published posthumously. She died at her home in Glen Ellen on June 22, 1992, at the age of eighty-three.

Bibliography: The Mary Frances Kennedy Fisher Collection (1929–1996) is in the Schlesinger Library, Radcliffe Institute for Advanced Study, Harvard University. The collection, which has not been processed, consists of unpublished and published material, letters, family documents, photographs, legal papers, audiotapes, and videos. Restricted private collections under the control of literary executor Robert Lescher and M. F. K. Fisher's heirs also exist. Because her work has been reconfigured, anthologized, and often republished in limited editions by small presses like Yolla Bolly, Weatherbird, and Engdahl, many checklists of her books are incomplete. A number of periodical articles and stories also are not listed in standard periodical guides. To date there are no published bibliographies.

Important primary sources are: *A Welcoming Life: The M. F. K. Fisher Scrapbook* (1997), compiled and edited by Dominique Gioia; *M. F. K. Fisher: A Life in Letters* (1997), selected and compiled by Norah Barr, Marsha Moran, and Patrick Moran; and Gioia, ed., *The Measure of Her Powers: An M. F. K. Fisher Reader* (1999). Secondary sources include Jeannette Ferrary, *Between Friends: M. F. K. Fisher and Me* (1991); Betty Fussell, *Masters of American Cookery* (1983); David Lazar, *Conversations with M. F. K. Fisher* (1992); Joan Reardon, *M. F. K. Fisher, Julia Child, and Alice Waters: Celebrating the Pleasures of the Table* (1994); and "M. F. K. Fisher: Essayist," in Audie Tucher, ed., *Bill Moyers: A World of Ideas* (1990). The opening quote from Clifton Fadiman appeared in the *New Yorker,* May 30, 1942, p. 65. An obituary appeared in the *New York Times* on June 24, 1992.

JOAN REARDON

FISHER, Mary Te Ata. *See* Te Ata.

FITZGERALD, Ella. April 25, 1917–June 15, 1996. Singer.

Ella Jane Fitzgerald was born in Newport News, Virginia, to Temperance (Tempie) Williams, a laundress, and William Fitzgerald, a wagon driver. When Ella was three years old, her mother began a relationship with a first-generation Portuguese immigrant, Joseph Da Silva. Da Silva and Williams moved with Ella to Yonkers, New York. By 1923 Tempie gave birth to another daughter, Frances. That same year Ella started public school, where she excelled academically. She sang in church and learned to play the piano, but her first love was dance.

Fitzgerald's life changed dramatically after the death of her mother in 1932. That spring, amid rumors of parental neglect and sexual abuse, Ella was placed in the home of her maternal aunt, Virginia Williams, who lived in Harlem. The once-talented student dropped out of school, began to run numbers, and worked as a lookout for prostitutes in neighborhood brothels. Truant officers eventually caught up with her, and she was sent to the New York State Training School for Girls at Hudson, New York. Fitzgerald most likely left the institution around 1934 and never spoke about her time there. Throughout her life she devoted time and money to organizations devoted to disadvantaged and orphaned children.

Returning to Harlem in the middle of the Depression, the runaway lived hand to mouth, dancing on street corners for money. On November 21, 1934, Fitzgerald entered the amateur contest at Harlem's famed Apollo Theater and walked away with first prize. Success at the Apollo often launched professional careers, but bandleaders found Fitzgerald too unkempt and unglamorous for the professional stage. Not to be dismissed so easily, the young vocalist entered another contest at the Harlem Opera House in 1935. Once again she garnered first prize, and this time she won a weeklong engagement at the theater.

A number of musicians claimed to have introduced Fitzgerald to the formidable bandleader and drummer Chick Webb, but vocalist Charles Linton is the most likely. Even though Webb was put off by her appearance, he took her on as a vocalist after soliciting the opinions of several well-known musicians. Although some sources claim Webb adopted her, there is no evidence of a formal adoption.

In June 1935 Fitzgerald made her first recordings, on Decca Records—"Love and Kisses" and "I'll Chase the Blues Away," which demonstrate the diction and rhythm that would characterize her singing throughout her life. She also had an amazing ability to remember hundreds of song lyrics and melodies. Radio broadcasts and live performances brought her to the attention of the jazz press, although journalists often commented on her weight as much as her singing. By November 1937 she beat BILLIE HOLIDAY as the number one female vocalist in polls by both *Down Beat* and *Melody Maker.*

In 1937 Fitzgerald and Webb signed a contract with Decca, and in 1938 she wrote and recorded "A Tisket a Tasket," her first hit record. It remained on the Hit Parade for nineteen weeks. After Webb's death in 1939, she continued to perform with his orchestra, renamed Ella Fitzgerald and Her Famous Orchestra, but the band broke up in 1942. Her brief marriage to Benny Kornegay, a small-time hustler, was annulled in mid 1942. Never one to miss a beat, Fitzgerald found solace in recording and appeared in her first film: an Abbott and Costello feature, *Ride 'Em Cowboy* (1942), where she sang "A Tisket a Tasket" as well as "Rockin' and Reeling." She is filmed as a jubilant, bouncy, if chubby adolescent. This was also her stage persona—one that she barely outgrew as she went on to become a world-renowned vocalist.

In the early forties Fitzgerald began experimenting with scat singing on Lionel Hampton's "Flying Home" at clubs around New York. Her performance displayed the influence of her growing friendship with a young bebop trumpeter, Dizzy Gillespie. Before Fitzgerald recorded the song in 1945, she had been best known for singing popular tunes with jazz influences; with "Flying Home" she began making the transition from swing to bebop, one of the few artists of her generation to do so. Fitzgerald proved herself an adept and gifted musician, building upon the vocal foundations of Louis Armstrong and the technical innovations of musicians like Gillespie and Charlie Parker to push jazz singing forward.

Fitzgerald began touring with Gillespie's band in 1946. She fell in love with one of the band's musicians, bassist Ray Brown, whom she married on December 10, 1947. The couple adopted Fitzgerald's nephew, whom they renamed Ray Brown Jr., and set up house in Elmhurst, Queens. They sometimes appeared together, but their touring schedules and commitments to their respective careers took a toll, and by 1953 they had parted ways.

The singer's long association with producer Norman Granz began in 1949 when she began to appear at his "Jazz at the Philharmonic" concerts. Although she was a well-paid, well-respected artist, she had not yet achieved superstar status. Their relationship would change her career and influence the direction of American popular music. In 1950 Fitzgerald recorded *Ella Sings Gershwin* for Decca. This set the model for a series of records produced by Granz for his label Verve (Fitzgerald signed with Verve in 1955)—*The Songbook Series,* devoted to major American composers of popular songs, including Cole Porter and Duke Ellington. With lavish arrangements and string accompaniment, the songbooks introduced and endeared Fitzgerald to mainstream, middle-of-the-road audiences. Her popularity soared.

Devoted to providing black artists with the kind of management that had been denied them, Granz also took over her management. In addition to the

Songbook Series, Fitzgerald released one of the best live albums of her career, *Mack the Knife: Ella in Berlin* (1960). While the Songbooks were perfectly rehearsed and produced, the live performance presented Ella at her best—spontaneous, brilliant, in sync with the other musicians, and propelled forward by the audience, with whom she had a lifelong love affair.

As her career began this new phase, Fitzgerald again sought romantic companionship and became involved with a Norwegian named Thor Einor Larsen, but the relationship did not last long. Around this time she appeared in another film, *Let No Man Write My Epitaph* (1960), in which she played a heroin addict. She also released an album of the same title.

In the mid sixties, Fitzgerald ended her relationship with Verve though she continued to be represented by Granz. Her health began to fail, but she continued her unrelenting touring schedule. Even open-heart surgery in 1986 did not slow her pace. Her most successful recordings continued to be her renditions of standards, and audiences around the world flocked to see her.

During the last decade of her life Fitzgerald received numerous accolades. In her lifetime she won thirteen Grammys, including one in 1990 when she was seventy-two years old. Her influence expands beyond the realm of jazz and can be heard in a number of contemporary popular singers who followed her. Perhaps only Frank Sinatra had a longer and more successful career as a serious singer of popular ballads. Bouts with heart disease and diabetes left her almost blind and without either of her lower legs. She died in Los Angeles on June 15, 1996, at the age of seventy-nine.

Bibliography: The best and most thorough biography of Ella Fitzgerald is Stuart Nicholson's *Ella Fitzgerald: A Biography of the First Lady of Jazz* (1994), which also includes an excellent discography prepared by Phil Schaap. Music critic Leslie Gourse has compiled the very valuable *The Ella Fitzgerald Companion: Seven Decades of Commentary* (1998), which includes articles, interviews, and tributes. The following books have excellent chapters on Fitzgerald: Linda Dahl, *Stormy Weather* (1984); Leonard Feather, *From Satchmo to Miles* (1972); and Will Friedwald, *Jazz Singing* (1990). The Ella Fitzgerald Collection, in the Music Division of the Library of Congress, contains scores, lead sheets, and individual musician parts, as well as photographs and videotapes. An obituary appeared in the *New York Times* on June 16, 1996.

FARAH JASMINE GRIFFIN

FLANNER, Janet. March 13, 1892–November 7, 1978. Writer, journalist.

Janet Flanner was born in Indianapolis, Indiana, the second of three daughters of William Frank Flanner, a mortician and sometime social reformer, and Mary Ellen Hockett, who wrote poetry and put on local theatricals. In line with Mary Flanner's cultural aspirations, the daughters were educated at Tudor Hall, a private high school. The family was solidly respectable; all the more shocking, then, when in 1911 Frank Flanner abruptly brought the family home from an intended long stay in Europe and killed himself a few months later, apparently driven by financial problems. His suicide solidified Janet Flanner's youthful agnosticism, a departure from her mother's Quakerism and her father's successive religious allegiances.

Flanner had experienced adolescence under her mother's guidance as personally confining; her brief exposure at age seventeen to European sights and sophistication intensified her yearning for a different path. She entered the University of Chicago in 1912 ambivalently, and never conformed to academic dictates, instead indulging in high jinks, dancing late into the night, and gaining repute for her witticisms. In 1914 she withdrew, worked briefly in a Quaker-run girls' reformatory in Philadelphia, and then landed a job as arts critic for the *Indianapolis Star*.

Back in Indianapolis, Flanner accepted visits from a college friend, William Lane Rehm, from Chicago. The pair married rather unexpectedly on April 25, 1918. Unconventionally, the couple wrote a prenuptial agreement resigning any claim to each other's financial assets if they were to divorce—which they later did. The marriage was childless, and Flanner did not take her husband's name.

The couple took up residence in the midst of the cultural and political ferment of Greenwich Village, where Flanner met artists and writers, including the ironists of the Algonquin "Round Table," whom she impressed with her wit. She became close to the glamorous and openhearted Neysa McMein, a successful illustrator, in whose circle she met Harold Ross and Jane Grant, who later founded the *New Yorker*. In this creative, bohemian milieu, Flanner recognized her attraction to women, which had begun to surface on her trip to Europe. She met the self-named journalist Solita Solano in the winter of 1918, and soon the two were in love, clandestinely, and envisioning life together. In July 1921 when Solano gained an assignment in Greece from *National Geographic*, she and Flanner took the opportunity to leave New York. Sharing a passionate romanticism, they saw themselves as journeying toward freedom and art; nonetheless Flanner felt lifelong remorse about abandoning her husband, who remained cordial and helpful to her.

After Mediterranean travel, Flanner settled with Solano in Paris in the fall of 1922, joining many Americans who sought artistic release there. They took tiny rooms in a poor Left Bank hotel, forgoing middle-class comforts but not good wine, fresh flowers, and cigarettes. Flanner never kept house. She lived, penuriously, on an annuity established by her father's will. After the annuity evaporated in 1931, she supported herself entirely through her writing. She was never rich, yet her elegant appearance—her Chanel or Yves St. Laurent tailored suits and well-shod feet, her (prematurely) silver mass of hair and direct brown eyes, which balanced the prominent "beak" (as she called it) of her nose—was consistently remarked upon, as were her skills as a raconteur and her infectiously cackling laughter.

Paris in the 1920s was a magnet not only for American male "expatriates" but also for lesbian artists and innovators. At gathering places such as NATALIE BARNEY'S salon, Flanner was present at the birth of literary modernism (though she did not adopt it as her own); she circulated among GERTRUDE STEIN and ALICE B. TOKLAS, MARGARET ANDERSON and Jane Heap, Robert McAlmon and KAY BOYLE, Nancy Cunard, Colette, James Joyce, Ernest Hemingway (who became a close friend), and other strong personalities. Flanner always worked with and enjoyed the friendship of men as well as women, living as if gender neutrality in society were possible, as did the heroine of her partially autobiographical novel, *Cubical City* (1926). She fell in love only with women. In 1931 she met Noel Haskins Murphy, a statuesque American widow living outside of Paris, and the two were soon passionately involved, though Flanner continued to be devoted to Solano, who was her secretary-editor till Solano's death. In 1940, visiting in New York, she was magnetized by Italian-born Natalia Danesi Murray, and although this relationship henceforward took precedence, Flanner maintained all three through letters, gifts, visits, and reciprocal solicitousness.

Fortunately, Flanner was deflected from another novel in 1925 by a request from the *New Yorker*, just founded, to report on the Paris scene in the manner of the chatty letters she had been sending to Jane Grant. Under the name "Genêt" (invented by Harold Ross, apparently as a Frenchified "Janet"), she began in October 1925 her regular "Letter from Paris." It would continue for fifty years, broken only by World War II, when Nazi occupation forced her to return to the United States from 1939 to 1944. At first arch jottings on literary events, fashions, art and theater openings, her columns ripened into richly serious political and cultural narratives. In a rare achievement of biculturalism, she thoroughly absorbed and communicated French opinion without losing hold of her American national identity.

Becoming engaged in the drama of European politics by the mid 1930s—and leading the *New Yorker's* interest there—Flanner achieved her mature writing mode. She mastered an omniscient style, full of captivatingly immediate details that conveyed thorough knowledge of the person or situation at hand without ever revealing sources for the information—whether it was how the Musée de Louvre transported priceless canvases to safety during World War II or what Coco Chanel ate before going to bed. Her column as Genêt was complemented by her signed essays, often revelatory profiles of notable figures, including ISADORA DUNCAN, Pablo Picasso, André Gide, Igor Stravinsky, Pablo Casals, and (perhaps most controversially, in 1936) Adolf Hitler.

After 1945—no longer certain, as she had been earlier, that Europe shone the beacon of civilization—she contributed gripping assessments of postwar circumstances from sites such as the Nuremberg war-crimes trials, the former Warsaw ghetto, and a displaced-persons camp, as well as many from Italy. These essays showed her more complex, world-weary assessments of politics as well as her increased sympathy with Jews. The French government recognized her accomplishment by making her a knight of the Legion of Honor in 1948. Later she analyzed deGaullism, the Algerian revolution, and the U.S–Vietnam conflict from her perch (at a slightly better hotel) in Paris, while her antennae continued to draw in informative gossip about writers, artists, musicians, and political newsmakers.

Flanner first published a book of her columns, *An American in Paris: Profile of an Interlude between Two Wars,* in 1940. *Paris Was Yesterday, 1925–1939* (1972) contained more from the interwar years; her subsequent "Letters" were collected in *Paris Journal, 1944–1965* (awarded the National Book Award for 1965) and *Paris Journal, 1965–1971* (1971), and her other writings in *Janet Flanner's World* (1979).

Flanner's best pieces were models of current history written on the spot, remarkably insightful and often prescient. Highly self-critical, she worked very hard, all the time, on her writing; to her intimates she complained of albatross deadlines, but her prime discipline was self-imposed. In 1975 she left France for New York. Continuing her vocation and her many varied international friendships into old age, she died in New York City of a heart attack at the age of eighty-six, attended by Natalia Danesi Murray.

Bibliography: The major collections of papers and photographs are the Papers of Janet Flanner and Solita Solano, 1870–1976, and the Papers of Janet Flanner and Natalia Danesi Murray, 1940–1984, in the Library of Congress Manuscript Division. The *New Yorker* papers are in the New York Public Library. Natalia Danesi Murray published letters Flanner wrote to her in *Darlinghissima: Letters to a Friend* (1985); see also John C. Broderick, "Paris between the Wars: An Unpublished Memoir by Solita Solano," *Quarterly Journal of the Library of Congress* 34 (October 1977), pp. 306–14. Flanner's other essay collections include *Petain: The Old Man of France* (1944), *Men and Monuments* (1957), and *London Was Yesterday, 1934–1939* (1975). The most complete treatment of Flanner's life and work is Brenda Wineapple, *Genêt: A Biography of Janet Flanner* (1989), which includes a complete listing of Flanner's writings. See also Shari Benstock, *Women of the Left Bank: Paris, 1900–1940* (1986); the memoir by William Murray, Natalia Murray's son, who met Flanner when he was fourteen: *Janet, My Mother and Me: A Memoir of Growing Up with Janet Flanner and Natalia Danesi Murray* (2000); Flanner's introduction to Jane Grant's *Ross, the New Yorker, and Me* (1968); and Mary McCarthy, "Conversation Piece," *New York Times Book Review*, November 21, 1965, p. 5. Obituaries appeared in the *New York Times* on November 8, 1978, and the *New Yorker* on November 20, 1978.

NANCY F. COTT

FLEISCHMAN, Doris E. *See* Bernays, Doris E. Fleischman.

FLEXNER, Eleanor. October 4, 1908–March 25, 1995. Historian, feminist.

Born in New York City, Eleanor Flexner was the second of two daughters of Anne Laziere Crawford and Abraham Flexner. Her mother, an 1895 graduate of Vassar College, had an exceptionally successful career as a playwright, with royalties from *Mrs. Wiggs of the Cabbage Patch* (1904) eventually making it possible for Eleanor to devote herself to research and writing. Her father, a graduate of Johns Hopkins and Harvard universities, wrote the immensely influential *Medical Education in the United States and Canada* (1910), which laid the basis for the transformation of the field and led to a career with the Rockefeller philanthropies and the Institute for Advanced Study in Princeton, New Jersey. Though her mother was a Protestant and her father a Jew, Eleanor grew up in a nonreligious household. Both parents, who had marched in a suffrage parade, believed their daughters should have the same opportunities as men. At an early age Eleanor decided to be a writer.

Flexner graduated from the Lincoln School, Teachers College, Columbia University. She attended Swarthmore, where, not asked to join a fraternity because she was considered Jewish, she led a protest to abolish exclusive clubs. She wrote her thesis on Mary Tudor, and in 1930 she graduated Phi Beta Kappa with honors in English and history. With a fellowship from Swarthmore, she studied at Somerville College, Oxford, in 1930–31, though lack of competence in Latin prevented her from earning a degree.

Flexner settled in Manhattan in 1931, horrified by the suffering of others during the Depression but personally protected by her parents' income. Participating in a wide range of radical activities in the city, she turned most of her attention during the decade to radical theater. She immersed herself in Popular Front causes and in 1936 joined the Communist Party. Determined to make her mark as a writer, she authored *American Playwrights, 1918–1938: The Theatre Retreats from Reality* (1938). In the late 1930s she wrote an unpublished novel about unions and anti-fascism that was informed by her work as an organizer and researcher with a textile union. During World War II, Flexner tried unionizing secretarial and clerical women. Working for a placement service for an office workers' union, she paid particular attention to finding jobs for African American women. These and other activities exposed her to the sexual discrimination against working women, including what she personally faced.

After World War II, Flexner continued her engagement with radicalism, increasingly focusing on women's issues. For a year, beginning in September 1945, she worked for the Foreign Policy Association, a peace organization through which she encountered former suffragists. While there she met Helen Terry, who soon became what Flexner later called her "beloved companion of thirty years of a shared home in real harmony and mutual enjoyment." At the instigation of the Communist Party, she served from 1946 to 1948 as executive secretary for the Congress of American Women, the Popular Front feminist organization later driven out of existence by McCarthyism. In the late 1940s and early 1950s, she also did editorial and public relations work for a variety of organizations, and was fired from two of them for union organizing. Especially formative in the shaping of her consciousness of race was her work for the National Association of Colored Graduate Nurses, whose members were denied equal access to education and jobs as well as excluded from the all-white American Nursing Association.

At some point, probably in the 1940s, Flexner heard a speech by ELIZABETH GURLEY FLYNN in which she first learned about the Lowell mill girls and other nineteenth-century women activists. Her failure to find information on them in history books impelled Flexner to research and write their stories. From 1950 to 1954, using pseudonyms such as "Irene Epstein" and "Betty Feldman," she wrote and taught on women's issues in publications and a school sponsored by the Communist Party. In 1956, following several years of disillusionment, she left the party.

In the early 1950s, Flexner began to think about writing a history of women in the United States that made the lives of African American and working-class women central to the stories of conflict she wanted to dramatize. Although W. E. B. Du Bois discouraged her, Herbert Aptheker and later Arthur Schlesinger Sr. urged her on. With money she inherited upon the death of her mother in 1955, she devoted herself full-time to research and writing. In 1957, Flexner and Terry moved to Northampton, Massachusetts, where Terry worked on publications at Smith College and Flexner did research in Smith's Sophia Smith Collection.

Century of Struggle: The Woman's Rights Movement in the United States appeared in 1959. It was the first overview of women in the United States that relied on archival materials and met rigorous professional standards. *Century of Struggle* was pathbreaking in its joining of social, legal, educational, labor, and political history; in its focus on the history of working-class and, more distinctively, African American women; and in its deployment of struggle as a theme that bound the narrative together. When second-wave feminism emerged in the 1960s, Flexner's book, which was translated into six languages, connected a new generation of feminists to women's history.

After *Century of Struggle* appeared, Flexner continued to pursue a career as a writer. Looking for the origins of feminism and supported by a Guggenheim Fellowship, she wrote *Mary Wollstonecraft: A Biography* (1972). She also authored *Women's Rights—Unfinished Business* (1971); *Journey: Poems* (1984); and a revised edition of *Century of Struggle* (1975). She converted to Catholicism, with 1962–70 as the years of her most intense interest. In 1973, continuing her lifelong quest to find an institution and outlook to which she could give loyalty, she joined the Protestant Episcopal Church.

Unpretentious, socially inept, aggressively intellectual, and forthright with her opinions, during her Northampton years she participated in Democratic Party politics and supported a variety of progressive causes such as the environment, women's issues, opposition to the war in Vietnam, racial justice, and reform in the Catholic Church. When feminism revived in the late 1960s, she did not identify with the new generation and called, at times angrily, on its advocates to balance liberation with responsibility. Yet her career underscores the importance of the participation by women in the Communist Party and the Popular Front of the 1930s and 1940s, where Flexner, like others, had their consciousnesses shaped about race, class, and gender.

Distraught that her work was insufficiently recognized, over her failing mental and physical health, and over the death of Terry in 1981, Flexner sold her Northampton house in 1986 and moved to a retirement community in Westboro, Massachusetts. She died in Worcester on March 25, 1995, at the age of eighty-six. *Century of Struggle* continues to influence successive generations of readers.

Bibliography: The Eleanor Flexner Papers are at the Schlesinger Library, Radcliffe Institute for Advanced Study, Harvard University; the quote about Terry is from a typed diary entry dated August 23, 1983. The papers also contain copies of her birth and death certificates. On Flexner, the best published source is Ellen F. Fitzpatrick's foreword to Eleanor Flexner, *Century of Struggle: The Woman's Rights Movement in the United States* (enlarged ed., 1996), pp. ix–xxvii. Also of considerable value are Ellen Carol DuBois, "Eleanor Flexner and the History of American Feminism," *Gender and History* 3 (Spring 1991), pp. 81–90; Carol Lasser, "Century of Struggle, Decades of Revision: A Retrospective on Eleanor Flexner's Suffrage History," *Reviews in American History* 15, no. 2 (June 1987), pp. 344–54; and Sarah Van Beurden, "'The Mother of Us All': Eleanor Flexner and the Writing of *Century of Struggle* (1959)" (MA thesis, Lehigh University, 2002). For interviews, see those by Jacqueline Van Voris (1977, 1982, 1983) and Ellen C. DuBois (1988), all at the Schlesinger Library. Obituaries appeared in the *Boston Globe* and (Northampton) *Daily Hampshire Gazette* on March 27, 1995.

DANIEL HOROWITZ

FLORES, Francisca. December 3, 1913–April 27, 1996. Journalist, community activist, feminist.

For more than forty years, Francisca Flores served the Mexican American community as both writer and activist. Born in a Los Angeles barrio to Maria Montelongo and Vicente Flores, recent immigrants from Mexico, she was the second of six children. Francisca lived most of her childhood in San Diego, where her father earned a living as a prodder in a slaughterhouse and her mother labored in various food-processing industries as a cook and union shop steward.

Hardship was not unknown to the Flores family: Francisca's older brother died from tuberculosis, and at age fifteen Francisca herself was diagnosed with the disease. She lost one lung and remained in a San Diego sanitarium until her twenty-sixth birthday. At the sanitarium Flores began to develop her political consciousness, engaging in long conversations with elderly veteran activists from the Mexican Revolution. Eventually realizing the need for a forum where women could discuss their specific concerns and views about politics, Flores encouraged other female patients at the sanitarium to form a group called the Hermanas de la Revolución Mexicana. As she later told her nephew, William Flores, "I knew that the men didn't take us seriously. They only wanted us to make tortillas. They couldn't accept that we had our own ideas."

Flores moved to Los Angeles after her release from the sanitarium. In 1938 she married Laverne Lynn, a radio technician and union activist. The marriage, which produced no children, ended in divorce around 1954.

Once in Los Angeles, Flores quickly joined the activist scene. Primarily self-educated, she befriended journalist Carey McWilliams and provided research assistance for his book *North from Mexico: The Spanish-Speaking People of the United States* (1948), a pathbreaking work on the history of Mexican Americans in the United States. In 1943 Flores became involved in the Sleepy Lagoon Defense Committee, a group organized to finance the appeal of seventeen youths—all but one of whom were of Mexican or Mexican American ancestry—convicted en masse for involvement in the murder of a young L.A. teen named José Díaz. The committee garnered funds for the cause and, after demonstrating that anti-Mexican sentiment had biased the original trial proceedings, eventually saw the release of the defendants from prison.

Over the years, Flores continued to play a significant role in the politicization of the Chicano community. In the late 1940s she joined the ranks of the Community Service Organization, a grassroots group formed to address the needs of the Mexican American population in Los Angeles. Dedicated to the uplift of her community, Flores walked the Eastside voting precincts, which helped secure the 1949 election of Edward Roybal to the Los Angeles City Council, the board's first Mexican American to serve since the 1880s. She also helped create a political interest group dedicated to lobbying for Mexican American interests and politicians by becoming a founding member of the Mexican American Political Association (MAPA) in 1960.

It was in the City of Angels that Flores also embarked on her long career as a journalist dedicated to exposing injustice and initiating social change. Possessing an innate gift with the pen, the blossoming writer regularly contributed articles to several local publications. Flores's quick mind and sharp tongue earned her a job as editor of a cultural and political magazine for the Mexican American community during the 1960s and 1970s. *Carta Editorial,* later named *Regeneración* after Mexican revolutionary Ricardo Flores Magón's activist newspaper of the early twentieth century, became a definitive voice for the burgeoning Chicano movement and sought an end to inequality of all forms.

Despite her own personal successes, Flores remained acutely aware of the overall second-class status of Chicanas in U.S. society. In 1959 she founded a group to recognize the important contributions made by Mexican American women to their communities. The League of Mexican American Women acknowledged the tireless volunteer efforts of its members and sponsored several banquets to honor those unsung heroines who served the Mexican American population. The organization represented one of the first formal efforts to honor Mexican American women for their pivotal roles in political organizing and community building.

Prioritizing women's issues within the Chicano movement remained a top concern for Flores throughout her career. In 1970, while attending the Mexican American National Issues Conference in Sacramento, she and a group of almost thirty other women founded La Comisión Femenil Mexicana Nacional (CFMN). As CFMN's first president, Flores worked to cultivate the leadership skills of its membership and to broaden the political awareness of Chicanas nationwide. Under her guidance a Los Angeles chapter of the Comisión also formed; over the years, several more local chapters emerged throughout the United States.

Of particular interest to Flores was the issue of employment for Chicanas. Minority women, particularly those who did not speak English, typically were relegated to low-income, unskilled jobs, and there were few governmental aid programs to assist them. Ever mindful of this void, in 1972 Flores founded the Chicana Service Action Center (CSAC) in East Los Angeles. One of the first social service agencies to exclusively serve women of the barrio, the center offered skills training, job placement assistance, and support services to its clientele. Flores and her staff also worked tirelessly to create an atmosphere where patrons could develop a sense of self-confidence and self-worth. The CSAC eventually expanded its services to several centers throughout greater Los Angeles and opened an Eastside shelter for battered women and their families. To this day the CSAC continues to assist Mexican American and other low-income neighborhood women in their struggles for equal opportunity.

Known fondly by CSAC employees as the Lady, Flores left her job as executive director of the center in 1982. Upon retirement, Flores suffered health problems but still devoted time to writing. Having served as a symbol of strength and courage to her community for decades, Flores helped numerous Chicanas develop an active awareness of minority women's issues. She died on April 27, 1996, in San Diego, at the age of eighty-two, leaving a lasting legacy for a new generation of female leadership in the Mexican American community.

Bibliography: Some of Francisca Flores's papers, involving her work with the Comisión Femenil Mexicana Nacional and the Chicana Service Action Center, are located at the

California Ethnic and Multicultural Archives, University of California Libraries, Santa Barbara. The Chicano Studies Research Center at the University of California, Los Angeles, holds additional archival material on the Comisión Femenil de Los Angeles. Various writings by Flores can be found in the following publications: *Regeneración, Mas Gráfica, Comercio,* and the *CSAC News;* she also wrote "Mexican-American Women Ponder Future Role of the Chicana," *Eastside Sun,* July 1, 1971. For more on her role in Chicana history, see Rodolfo Acuna, *Occupied America: A History of Chicanos* (2nd ed., 1981), and Alma M. Garcia, ed., *Chicana Feminist Thought: The Basic Historical Writings* (1997). Birth and death records are available from the State of California Department of Health Services; the birth certificate lists November 3, 1913, but the death certificate confirms the December 3, 1913, date she used throughout her life. Biographical information is scanty; Flores's nephew, William Flores, provided invaluable assistance. A brief obituary appeared in the *Los Angeles Times* on May 18, 1996.

ELIZABETH ESCOBEDO

FOLEY, Martha. March 21, 1897–September 5, 1977. Editor, writer.

Martha Foley was born into an Irish American family in Boston, one of two children of Millicent McCarty, a teacher, and Walter Foley, a doctor. For as far back as she could remember, she had wanted to be a writer. When she was very young, her parents fell ill and were unable to care for her. Seven-year-old Martha survived this bleak period by writing a novel—about a lucky little girl who was sent to boarding school. She also discovered the solace of reading. Foley's early escape into fiction proved, in many ways, an ideal education for her literary work to come. It also gave her a penetrating sympathy into the human condition.

Foley graduated from Boston Girls' Latin School in 1915 and attended Boston University for two years but did not graduate. She spent the next decade as a journalist and foreign correspondent for a variety of newspapers, including the *Boston Herald,* the *San Francisco Record,* and the *New York Daily News.* She met her future husband, writer Whit Burnett, in San Francisco in 1925, and two years later she followed him to Paris, where she worked at the *Paris Herald* and wrote fiction. They were married in Vienna in 1930, and their son, David, was born the following year.

The two were passionately in love with each other and with literature, and in 1931 Martha convinced Whit that they should launch a magazine devoted solely to short stories. At a time when American magazines seemed hungry only for slick commercial fiction, they were vehement in their conviction that both readers and writers were capable of more. Although just 167 mimeographed copies were made of the first edition of *STORY,* the magazine quickly made a name for itself. By 1932, when Martha and Whit moved *STORY* to New York where it could be underwritten by Random House, they had come to know most of the short story writers of the day. With financial backing, they were able to increase subscriptions to twenty-five thousand, offer a readers' literary service, launch a book-publishing program, and, of course, continue to introduce the new writers whose work would come to define the twentieth century, including John Cheever, Richard Wright, CARSON MCCULLERS, and J. D. Salinger. During the thirties, publication in *STORY* meant that you had arrived as a serious writer.

In 1941 Foley's marriage to Burnett broke up and she left *STORY,* a double blow. The couple divorced the following year. After the sudden death of Edward J. O'Brien, the longtime editor of *The Best American Short Stories,* in 1941, Foley agreed to take over the editorship of the annual Houghton Mifflin anthology. It was a job she would perform tenaciously for the next thirty-six years.

By the time she stepped into her new role, Martha Foley was already famous among writers as a passionate advocate for serious literature. Now, as the most powerful and most visible arbiter of taste in short fiction in America, she set out to find stories of literary value that might otherwise remain unknown and forgotten, and to give them permanent publication in book form. Not surprisingly, the *Best American Short Stories* books were beloved by writers themselves, who looked to them to find the work of their peers, their followers, and their idols. Here, writers could discover new voices and, at the same time, see what the masters were up to. Here, the work of some of the country's most serious literary artists could be brought to readers who would appreciate it.

All through the 1940s, 1950s, and 1960s, Martha Foley was solely responsible for reading and judging the two thousand or so stories being published in any given year. As she had done at *STORY,* she continued to distinguish between established writers and new ones just finding their way. Similarly, she paid particular attention to the small regional magazines that nurtured these emerging voices. Her efforts were well rewarded. During her reign as annual editor, she was among the first to recognize the talents of dozens of writers, including Saul Bellow, Eudora Welty, Joyce Carol Oates, and John Updike. The contents page of nearly any volume from these years reveals a similar configuration of authors who would go on to receive wide acclaim, but whose earliest work was read, recognized, and first brought to a larger public by Martha Foley.

Foley remained adamant that the series should reflect her tastes and judgments, and hers alone. For a couple of years in the late fifties and early sixties, however, her son David was listed as her co-editor. After Whit, David was the only other great love of Foley's life, and although she could admit to the bitterness of her failed marriage, she could never really confront the truth about her son, an aspiring painter who never managed to find his way in the world. How much he actually contributed to his mother's books is not known. He died in 1971, as a result of drug addiction.

After David's death, Foley plunged into despair, drank heavily for a time, and became increasingly isolated and lonely. Her family was gone; stories were all she had left. She declined help of any kind—she not only read and kept track of well over a thousand stories a year, and assembled the book, but also handled all of the permissions. Now in her seventies, and increasingly out of touch with the shifting currents in contemporary fiction, Foley was no longer able to bring the kind of vitality to the series that had once made it the bellwether of new literary trends.

Martha Foley spent the last years of her life living alone in a furnished two-room apartment in Northampton, Massachusetts. Barely surviving on the six thousand dollars a year she earned as annual editor of *The Best American Short Stories*, she was in desperate financial straits and plagued by constant back pain. And yet she never considered stepping down from her job. Instead, she put a brave face on her situation, worked each day on her memoirs, and read short stories as she always had.

Martha Foley died in Northampton on September 5, 1977, at the age of eighty. Foley knew real loneliness in the last years of her life, but she had also known great happiness—in her passionate devotion to her work and in the cherished company of the many writers whose lives she touched.

Bibliography: A stimulating introduction to Martha Foley is to scan past volumes of *STORY* and *The Best American Short Stories:* as she often told readers, these were the stories she had liked best herself and she hoped they would agree. Her papers are held at the Howard Gotlieb Archival Research Center, Boston University, and the American Heritage Center, University of Wyoming, Laramie. Her book, *The Story of STORY Magazine: A Memoir,* was published posthumously in 1980, with an introduction and afterword by her friend Jay Neugeboren. An obituary appeared in the *New York Times* on September 6, 1977.

KATRINA KENISON

FONTANNE, Lynn. December 6, 1887–July 30, 1983. Actress.

Lynn (whose birth name was Lillie Louise) Fontanne was born in Woodford Bridge, Essex, England, to Jules Fontanne, of French parentage, and an Irish mother, Frances Thornley. The youngest of four daughters, Lynn subtracted five years from her age, not revealing the true date of her birth until after the death of her husband, Alfred Lunt. Jules Fontanne owned a typesetting business but aspired to cultured leisure. His impracticality frustrated Frances but inspired Lynn, who as a young girl crept out of her room to visit the theater and recited Shakespearean monologues in a voice that rang like a bell.

As a teenager, her dark, thin good looks won Lynn modeling jobs with Royal Academy painters Wilfred and Jane de Glehn, but her real break came with an introduction to the great actress Ellen Terry, who agreed to give her lessons. "Think of the *meaning* of what you are saying," Terry advised, "and let the words pour out of your mouth." Terry's influence resulted in walk-ons, leading to Fontanne's first London speaking part, in *Billy's Bargain* in 1910. Her breakthrough, however, came as the spinster Gertrude Rhead in *Milestones* in 1914. Seeing her in the part, actress Laurette Taylor was so impressed that she asked Fontanne to act with her in America.

Taylor's manager George C. Tyler was at first unimpressed with the awkward, astringent actress with the raucous laugh and turned-in toes. But in *The Harp of Life* (1916) with Laurette Taylor, Lynn played a scene so truly that her exit brought down the house. A new star, said critics, was in the firmament. Meanwhile Tyler called rehearsals for *A Young Man's Fancy.* Lynn was sitting offstage when a young actor opened the door, bowed, and fell down three steps to land at her feet. Alfred Lunt became a star in 1919 in *Clarence;* Lynn Fontanne in 1921 in *Dulcy.* They married in 1922. "I loved him utterly," said Fontanne. "We were in the same profession. We were like twins" (Fontanne interview, "The Bunny Raasch Special," Milwaukee, July 30, 1980). They did not have children. Scholars have called Lunt and Fontanne a famous bisexual acting couple; their friend EDNA FERBER called them double-gaited—without, however, naming other sexual partners, though many of their closest friends were gay. Yet certainly Lunt and Fontanne's public image of an inextricably married couple reflected their private loving devotion.

Acting together and separately, Lunt and Fontanne were largely responsible for the Theatre Guild's golden age in the 1920s and 1930s. Lynn played an earthy Eliza Doolittle in *Pygmalion* in 1926 and in 1928 created the role of Nina Leeds in *Strange Interlude.* Together they gave outstanding performances in *Arms and the Man* (1925), *Goat Song* (1926), and *The Brothers Karamazov* (1927).

Yet it was their 1924 triumph in Molnar's witty *The Guardsman* that made Lunt and Fontanne Broadway stars. (They filmed *The Guardsman* for MGM in 1931.) They became famous for their seamless interplay, nuanced repartee, faultless timing, and erotic love making. Married, they could be more suggestive sexually than other actors. Beginning with *Caprice* in 1929, they acted only together. "No one can be as good as the Lunts," complained an actress. "They rehearse in bed" (Langner, p. 394). Onstage they complemented each other. She was glamorous, subtle, calculating, controlled; he, intuitive, fluid, suave, moody.

Wanting greater control over their plays, Lunt and Fontanne left the Theatre Guild, launching Transatlantic Productions with Noël Coward and John Wilson in 1934. Lunt and Fontanne formed their own company, Lunt directed many of their plays, and each had the last word on production.

Meanwhile they created a beautiful estate on 120 acres in Genesee Depot, Wisconsin, with a main house, studio, and cottage housing their large collection of Swedish, English, and continental antiques. Interiors were handpainted, some by Alfred. Lynn, an exquisite seamstress who created many of her own clothes, made the curtains, bed hangings, spreads, and cushions that gave Ten Chimneys such distinction.

Touring America increased their popularity; playwrights fought to write for them. Robert Sherwood gave them three of their greatest successes in *Reunion in Vienna* (1934), *Idiot's Delight* (1936), and the war play *There Shall Be No Night* (1940). S. N. Behrman wrote or adapted five plays for the Lunts, including Giraudoux's *Amphitryon 38* (1937). Noël Coward wrote *Design for Living* (1933), *Point Valaine* (1935), and *Quadrille* (1952) for his close friends. Lunt and Fontanne were equally acclaimed in London, winning British hearts by living in London in wartime and giving performances punctuated by German bombs.

They were perhaps too successful, too beloved. In the late 1940s and into the 1950s, critics began to fault Lunt and Fontanne for choosing unworthy plays. Their greatest hit—Terence Rattigan's *O Mistress Mine* (1944–49)—was followed by *I Know My Love* (1949), *Quadrille,* and *The Great Sebastians* (1955), indifferent plays expertly acted. Audiences forgot they had played Shakespeare, Jonson, Shaw, O'Neill, Chekhov. But in 1958 they opened Duerrenmatt's grim *The Visit* in the newly remodeled and renamed Lunt-Fontanne Theater in New York. Inimitable in high comedy, Lunt and Fontanne suddenly looked like America's best dramatic actors. Having performed more than 160 roles, Lynn Fontanne and Alfred Lunt retired from the stage after a London production of *The Visit* in 1960.

They made a number of television films: *The Great Sebastians* (1957); *The Old Lady Shows Her Medals* (1963), with Lynn playing an unsentimental Mrs. Dowey and Lunt narrating; *The Magnificent Yankee* (1965); and Lynn as the Dowager Empress in *Anastasia* (1967). Their numerous awards and honors included Emmys for *The Magnificent Yankee,* the Presidential Medal of Freedom in 1964, an honorary Tony Award in 1970 for distinguished service to the theater, and the first National Artist Award of the American National Theater and Academy in 1972. Alfred Lunt died of prostate cancer in August 1977. In 1980 Fontanne appeared on PBS in "The Lunts: A Life in the Theater" and that year was honored by the Kennedy Center for the Performing Arts. Lynn Fontanne died of pneumonia at the age of ninety-five on July 30, 1983, at Ten Chimneys and is buried next to her soul mate, Alfred Lunt, in Forest Home Cemetery in Milwaukee.

Bibliography: Most of Lynn Fontanne and Alfred Lunt's papers are in the Wisconsin Center for Film and Theater Research at the Wisconsin Historical Society, Madison. Other significant sources include the Beinecke Rare Book and Manuscript Library, Yale University; the Billy Rose Theatre Collection, New York Public Library for the Performing Arts at Lincoln Center; the Harry Ransom Humanities Research Center, University of Texas at Austin; and the Theatre Museum in Covent Garden, London. George Freedley's brief theatrical biography *The Lunts* (1959) includes reviews, production photos, and a chronology of their performances. Maurice Zolotow's lively *Stagestruck: The Romance of Alfred Lunt and Lynn Fontanne* (1964) lacks notes and sources but is based on numerous taped interviews with the Lunts and their contemporaries. Phillip M. Runkel's *Alfred Lunt and Lynn Fontanne: A Bibliography* (1978) is a useful source. Jared Brown's biography *The Fabulous Lunts* (1986) is a thorough, scholarly examination of the careers of Lunt and Fontanne. Margot Peters's biography *Lunt and Fontanne: Design for Living* (2003) explores their private and professional lives, using previously unpublished letters and taped interviews, as well as the resources of Ten Chimneys, the Lunts' Wisconsin estate, which was restored and opened to the public in 2003.

For Fontanne on acting, Toby Cole and Helen Krich Chinoy's *Actors on Acting* (1970) is valuable, as are Morton Eustis, "The Actor Attacks His Part," *Theatre Arts Monthly* 20, no. 11 (November 1936), pp. 857–71; Lewis Funke and John E. Booth, *Actors Talk about Acting* (1961); Lawrence Langner, *The Magic Curtain* (1951); and Theresa Helburn, *A Wayward Quest* (1960). The quotation from Ellen Terry appears in Lynn Fontanne and George Schaefer, "The Lunts: A Life in the Theater," PBS television, March 7, 1980. The following published letters and reminiscences are important for personal views of Lynn Fontanne: Kerrison Preston, ed., *Letters from Graham Robertson* (1953); Noël Coward, *Present Indicative* (1937) and *Diaries* (1982); *The Letters of Alexander Woollcott* (1944); S. N. Behrman, *People in a Diary* (1972); Marguerite Courtney, *Laurette* (1968); and Enid Bagnold's *Autobiography* (1969). An obituary appeared in the *New York Times* on July 31, 1983.

MARGOT PETERS

FOSDICK, Dorothy. April 17, 1913–February 5, 1997. Specialist in international relations, federal official.

Dorothy Fosdick was born in Montclair, New Jersey. Her father was the eminent religious leader, the Rev. Dr. Harry Emerson Fosdick, for whom John D. Rockefeller Jr. built the Riverside Church in New York City. Her mother was Florence Allen Whitney. She had one older sister, Elinor Whitney. Fosdick attended Horace Mann School in New York and Smith College, where she received a BA in 1934. She continued her education at Columbia University, where she received a PhD in public law in 1939. She returned to Smith College, where she was as an instructor in sociology and government in 1937–42, and then took a position in the State Department, leaving the academic world behind her for the rest of her life. Within the State Department she became a member of the postwar Planning Division and participated in planning the Dumbarton Oaks and San Francisco conferences that led to the establishment of the United Nations. She then decided to move to a more substantive area and was appointed to the Office of European Affairs. She found this division "tough, man-controlled, and anti-feminist," but she was "able to hold [her] own."

Meanwhile, the new secretary of state, George Marshall, had created a Policy Planning Staff within the department and placed it under the direction of George Kennan. In 1948, at the age of thirty-four, Fosdick was chosen by Kennan to be a member of this nine-person group. She remained to work with his successor, Paul Nitze, participating in the development of the Truman Doctrine, the Marshall Plan, and other policy decisions of the early cold war years.

In 1952 Fosdick became a foreign policy adviser and wrote speeches for Adlai Stevenson, the Democratic presidential candidate. Although Fosdick never married (her sister speculated that she never found a man her equal), Stevenson's intellect, humor, and interests were so appealing that Fosdick had a brief romantic liaison with him. But Stevenson disappointed her both professionally and personally.

When the Republicans came to power in 1953, Fosdick left the State Department. In 1954, the Democrats recaptured the Senate and Henry "Scoop" Jackson, the junior senator from Washington, moved to the Senate Armed Services Committee and the Joint Committee on Atomic Energy while retaining his position on the Government Operations Committee. These committees ultimately gave him tremendous influence over American national security policy. Meanwhile, he met Dorothy Fosdick at a dinner. Impressed by her ability and experience, and clearly undeterred by her gender, he invited her to join his staff. Dorothy Fosdick had found her niche. She served as Jackson's principal foreign policy adviser and alter ego until his unexpected death in 1983. Ironically, like many women, Fosdick simultaneously gained enormous power and disappeared from public view. She wrote books under Jackson's name, prepared speeches he presented, and stood in the background as Jackson gained power and influence over U.S. policy.

In the course of her years with Jackson, Dorothy Fosdick's views meshed well with his. Both were cold war liberals who were committed to government support for social causes at home and strong, intrusive government action abroad. As a young woman, she had never agreed with her father's pacifism, preferring the views of her uncle Raymond Fosdick, an international lawyer and supporter of the League of Nations, and their neighbor Reinhold Niebuhr, whose worldview was diametrically opposed to her father's. She nevertheless worked well with both Kennan and Stevenson, neither of whom was a cold war "hawk." But she respected the views of Paul Nitze and came to agree with the ideas expressed in NSC 68, the quintessential cold war document that sent out a clarion call to battle aggressive communism. She clearly would never have joined Jackson if she had not agreed with his advocacy of a strong military and his fervent anti-communism, both of which seemed unduly bellicose to some observers.

Fosdick and Jackson became indispensable to each other. She not only wrote his speeches but advised him on national security matters. She also organized the series of informational hearings that Jackson began in 1959 examining the policy process in the State and Defense Departments as well as the National Security Council. The final 1961 report, which she wrote, influenced the reorganization of the national security apparatus undertaken by the Kennedy administration. Under her guidance and through her contacts, Jackson gathered a Senate staff of unusually talented and knowledgeable people whom she directed. Events, however, began to leave Jackson behind. Kennedy's test ban treaty and Nixon's search for détente ultimately isolated Jackson, although no president, senator, or world leader could fail to take him (and his superb staff) into account.

Jackson also became indispensable to Dorothy Fosdick. Any woman of her day who chose to spend every waking hour on foreign policy had to have a Henry Jackson out in front. Fosdick clearly admired Jackson, found great satisfaction in helping him achieve his policy goals and developed an almost symbiotic relationship with him. That Jackson valued Fosdick is illustrated by his remarks in a private meeting with President Richard Nixon in 1970. Complimenting her work, he told Nixon that Fosdick was a strong and staunch supporter of his program.

Fosdick was a small woman at five foot one and had been an outstanding athlete at Smith. She was described as warm and friendly as well as peppery and competitive, and as a woman who demanded the same commitment from her staff as she herself willingly gave to promote the cause at hand. Usually the only woman at the meetings held by generals, cabinet secretaries, and senators, she was always "Miss Fosdick," not "Dr. Fosdick," to the titled men around her.

After Jackson's death, Fosdick retired to her home in the Georgetown section of Washington, D.C. Over the years she had gathered many friends but had no family nearby. She left no diaries or personal papers and, with one or two exceptions, declined all requests from scholars for interviews, explaining that she lived in the present and not the past. She died in Washington in 1997 at the age of eighty-three.

Bibliography: There are few primary or secondary sources available about the life of Dorothy Fosdick. The best sources documenting her influence are found in the Henry Jackson papers at the University of Washington, Seattle. Fosdick was the author of two books: *What Is Liberty? A Study in Political Theory* (1939), and *Common Sense and World Affairs* (1955). Those who wish to learn more about her views should consult the speeches and other documents she wrote for Henry Jackson, which are collected in Dorothy Fosdick, ed., *Staying the Course: Henry M. Jackson and National Security* (1987), and Fosdick, ed., *Henry M. Jackson and World Affairs: Selected Speeches, 1953–1983* (1990). She is also mentioned in Robert G. Kaufman, *Henry M. Jackson: A Life in Politics* (2000). The quotation comes from an interview in the possession of the author. Obituaries appeared in the *Washington Post,* February 8, 1997; the *New York Times,* February 10, 1997; and the *Daily Telegraph,* February 19, 1997. The latter contains her birth date.

ANNA KASTEN NELSON

FOSSEY, Dian. January 16, 1932–c. December 26, 1985. Primatologist.

Dian Fossey, the world's leading authority on mountain gorillas, is best known as the first person to fully habituate wild gorillas to the presence of a human observer and for her controversial crusade to save the "greatest of the great apes" from extinction. Born in San Francisco in 1932, Fossey was the only child of Kathryn "Kitty" Kidd, a fashion model, and George Fossey III, an insurance agent. Her parents divorced when she was young. Fossey adored animals from an early age, but the only pet her strict stepfather, Richard Price, a building contractor, would allow her to keep was a goldfish. After high school, she studied pre-veterinary medicine at the University of California at Davis in 1950 but struggled with her requisite science courses. Eventually she transferred to San Jose State College, where, in 1954, she earned a bachelor's degree in occupational therapy. Fossey then took a job at Kosair Crippled Children's Hospital in Louisville, Kentucky. But, as she explained to Peter Gorner in a 1983 interview for the *Chicago Tribune,* something in her life was missing: "I wanted to study gorillas. I had this great urge, this need to go to Africa. I had it the day I was born."

Fossey's career was launched by paleoanthropologist Louis Leakey. Renowned for his hominid fossil discoveries in Kenya, Leakey believed that much could be learned about human evolution from studying the behavior of our closest living relatives, the great apes. In 1960, he initiated a field study of chimpanzees in Tanzania and hired Jane Goodall to oversee the project. He would later sponsor Biruté Galdikas's work with orangutans in Borneo. Leakey believed that, because of their patience and perception, women were the best observers of primate behavior. He also favored the untrained eye, because academics were more likely to be distracted by their own interests.

In 1963, Fossey took out a high-interest loan for $8,000 to finance a safari to East Africa. On this trip she had her first sight of mountain gorillas and met Leakey. In 1966 he visited the United States and suggested she return to Africa to study gorillas. In 1967, with Leakey's backing, she headed for Parc National des Virungas in Zaire (now Democratic Republic of Congo) and set up camp in the Kabara meadow, where American zoologist George Schaller had stayed during his pioneering 1959 gorilla study.

Mountain gorillas live only in the forests atop six dormant volcanoes within the Virungas, a mountain range that spans three countries: Zaire, Rwanda, and Uganda. The climate is damp and chilly, the terrain steep and slippery. Funded by the National Geographic Society and the Wilkie and Leakey Foundations, Fossey's mission was to observe the rare gorillas and record their behavior in detail. Six months into her study, however, she was escorted off the mountain by armed soldiers, a result of growing distrust of outsiders in Zaire. The military detained Fossey for two weeks, until she slipped past her guards and escaped into Uganda. Warned that she would be shot on sight if she returned to Zaire, but determined to press on, Fossey relocated to the Parc National des Volcans on the Rwandan side of the Virungas. Here, in 1967, she established the Karisoke Research Centre, a collection of tin-roofed buildings ten thousand feet up the mountain and accessible only by foot. This was the first facility in the world dedicated to long-term research on gorillas in their natural habitat.

Without training, Fossey spent the next three years tracking gorillas and accustoming them to her presence. She used the unorthodox method of mimicking gorilla actions and vocalizations, a technique that eventually enabled her to observe three generations of gorillas at close range. She and her students catalogued a massive amount of data on the Karisoke population, and Fossey was the first to describe important biological phenomena, such as male infanticide and female transfer, in gorillas. Her work laid the foundation for today's understanding of gorilla behavioral biology. In 1970, Fossey began to study for her doctorate in zoology at Cambridge University, which she received in 1976. In these years her primary base remained Rwanda.

Fossey did not flourish in academia, and after she returned to Karisoke she shifted her focus from research to what she called active conservation. A census would eventually reveal that the gorilla population dropped by 50 percent between 1960 and 1980, largely owing to habitat encroachment and poaching. In 1978, Fossey stepped up her conservation campaign, establishing the Digit Fund, an organization named after her favorite gorilla, who was killed by poachers. Fossey used the Digit Fund to raise money for anti-poaching patrols as well as worldwide awareness about the plight of the mountain gorilla. Despite these efforts, the illegal activities continued. Fossey became obsessed with deterring poaching and even resorted to vigilante tactics, such as assaulting suspected poachers, destroying their property, and kidnapping their cattle and children. Her extreme methods alienated her students, enraged the locals, and resulted in the eventual withdrawal of her funding support. In 1979, the Rwandan government asked her to leave.

Fossey returned to the States and taught at Cornell University from 1980 to 1982. She also participated in a U.S. lecture tour with Goodall and Galdikas and completed her book, *Gorillas in the Mist,* which was published in 1983. Fossey went back to Karisoke in 1983 and was found brutally murdered two years later, on December 27, 1985. Fossey, who never married and was fifty-three at the time of her death, was buried in the cemetery she had created for slain gorillas. A Rwandan court convicted an American researcher and Fossey's Rwandan employee of the crime, but many consider her murder unsolved. The leading consensus is that she was killed by individuals opposed to her gorilla conservation efforts.

A striking woman, Fossey stood over six feet tall with thick, black hair, a slim figure, and a low, husky voice. She had a fondness for designer clothes, men, alcohol, and cigarettes. She remained committed to saving gorillas despite ostracism by peers, death threats, and personal struggles with loneliness, emphysema, and acrophobia. Toward the end of her life, she claimed to prefer the company of gorillas to that of humans. Fossey's grave marker bears her Rwandan nickname Nyiramachabelli (the old lady who lives in the forest without a man) and reads, "No one loved gorillas more."

Bibliography: For a complete list of Dian Fossey's scientific and popular works, see Glenn Hausfater and Kenneth Kennedy, "Dian Fossey," *American Anthropologist* 88 (1986), pp. 953–56. Sources of biographical material include Sy Montgomery, *Walking with the Great Apes: Jane Goodall, Dian Fossey, Biruté Galdikas* (1991); Farley Mowat, *Woman in the Mists: The Story of Dian Fossey and the Mountain Gorillas of Africa* (1987; also published as *Virunga: The Passion of Dian Fossey*); and Peter Gorner, "Acting Out a Dream: Dian Fossey's Life with the Gorillas," *Chicago Tribune,* October 3, 1983, which contains the quotation in the text. Key sources about Fossey's study of gorillas include her 1983 book, *Gorillas in the Mist,* and Michael Nichols, *Gorilla: Struggle for Survival in the Virungas* (1989). *Gorillas in the Mist,* a 1989 film starring Sigourney Weaver, was based on her work. For a discussion of Fossey's impact on the field of primatology, see Virginia Morell, "Called 'Trimates,' Three Bold Women Shaped Their Field," *Science* 260 (1993), pp. 420–25. An obituary appeared in the *New York Times* on December 29, 1985. Analyses of the circumstances surrounding Fossey's death include Nicholas Gordon, *Murders in the Mist: Who Killed Dian Fossey?* (1993); Harold Hayes, *The Dark Romance of Dian Fossey* (1990); and Alex Shoumatoff, *African Madness* (1988).

SONYA M. KAHLENBERG

FRAIBERG, Selma. March 8, 1918–December 19, 1981. Psychoanalyst, clinician.

Selma Horwitz was born into a close-knit Jewish family in Detroit, Michigan, shortly before the end of World War I. She was the oldest of three children of Dorella (Dora) Newman, a Detroit-born housewife, and Jack Horwitz, who was born in Russia, came to Detroit with his family during his childhood, and later worked in his family's poultry distribution business in Detroit's Eastern Market until the 1950s. Family life was warm and welcoming, and the Horwitz siblings blended in with many cousins and with the Jewish community.

An inveterate reader, Selma was always bright and busy with her books; the promise she showed in childhood was realized in her academic achievements. She graduated from Detroit's Central High School in 1935 and began college at seventeen. She received her BA from Wayne State University in 1940 and her MSW in 1945. She completed her psychoanalytic training at the Detroit Psychoanalytic Institute, and in 1971 she was certified to practice psychoanalysis by the Board of Professional Standards of the American Psychoanalytic Association.

While avidly pursuing academic achievements, Selma enjoyed a rich personal life. In 1935, when she was seventeen, she met her future husband, Louis Fraiberg, who was then twenty-three. A serious relationship developed in 1940 when she was working for her master's at Wayne State, where he was a teacher's assistant. They were married in 1945. Their daughter, Lisa, was born in 1956.

As part of a two-career academic couple, Selma Fraiberg held a variety of teaching positions. Her first teaching appointments were as lecturer in mental hygiene and casework at the University of Michigan (1947–52), lecturer in child development at Wayne State University's Department of Psychiatry (1952–58), and instructor and lecturer in normal development of the individual at Wayne State University's School of Social Work (1953–54). She was also very successful at winning grants to support her groundbreaking studies on infant psychiatry and the normal child development process.

In 1958 the family moved from Detroit to New Orleans, where Louis began teaching at Louisiana State University. In 1959 Selma agreed to teach at Tulane University on the condition that she would be finished by noon so she could pick up her four-year-old daughter after nursery school. At Tulane she was an associate professor of social casework in the School of Social Work and a lecturer in the Department of Psychiatry of the medical school. There she began to study the development of blind children, which eventually led to her attachment study. In 1961 she went to Baltimore, where she affiliated with the Baltimore Psychiatric Institute as a lecturer.

In 1963 the family moved from New Orleans to Toledo, Ohio, where Louis became chairman of the English department at the University of Toledo. Selma had a private practice at the time and also began what would become the Child Development Project at the University of Michigan. She was associate professor and then professor of child psychoanalysis in the Department of Psychiatry of the School of Medicine at the University of Michigan and a lecturer in child development at the Michigan Psychoanalytic Institute. She was also director of the Child Development Project in Washtenaw County, Michigan, for children with emotional problems. This was a continuation of the work she had begun at Tulane. At first she commuted one day a week, then two—soon it became obvious that her work in Ann Arbor had become the focus of her career. Louis decided that it was better for him to commute than her. In 1966 they moved to Ann Arbor; he commuted until he retired in 1979.

Fraiberg's writing, always rich and interesting, included more than a hundred articles and three major works. *The Magic Years* (1959), a classic dealing with early childhood, received the Outstanding Book of the Year award from the Child Study Association. It was translated into ten languages and is relevant in many different cultural settings. *Insights from the Blind: Comparative Studies of Blind and Sighted Infants* (1977) was written during the time in Michigan when she led a group of clinicians in work with mothers and their blind infants. Her manner of working with the mother and infant together led to an innovative technique that was helpful for parents who had suffered abuse or deprivation in early childhood. This led to the "Fraiberg Intervention Model," which came to be used in many countries.

Selma Fraiberg was a pioneer in understanding the importance of what transpires between caregiver and infant. She can be understood as a strong developmentalist with some degree of optimism about how changes may take place. In her third book, *Every Child's Birthright: In Defense of Mothering* (1977), Fraiberg entered the emerging controversy raised by feminists' challenge to women's traditional caretaking roles, especially what role the mother should play in the early life of her child. Fraiberg saw herself as an advocate for the infant.

Selma and Louis loved to travel and had wonderful trips to many places, including a sabbatical in Israel in 1977. They enjoyed friendships in many countries and had a close group of liberal friends. Selma was somewhat shy: although she loved teaching and writing, she did not enjoy public appearances. Part of her skill at writing came from her family's interest in and appreciation of a good story.

After Louis Fraiberg retired in 1979, the couple made a final move to the University of California at San Francisco School of Medicine, where Selma took on a new position in the department of psychiatry on July 1, 1979. Two years later she was diagnosed with cancer, which she battled for four months. The brain damage she suffered from the tumors and surgery made it nearly impossible for her to communicate during the period of her illness. Her family and friends noted the sadness and irony of her condition: she who had spent a lifetime helping people who were unable to speak for themselves was unable to speak for herself at the end. Selma Fraiberg died on December 19, 1981, in San Francisco at the age of sixty-three and is buried beside her husband, who died in 1994, in Birmingham, Michigan.

Bibliography: This essay is dedicated to the memory of Albert J. Solnit, MD, who enthusiastically and lovingly began work on it but died in 2002. It has been completed by us in his honor. We are especially grateful to Lisa Fraiberg and Malva Dobriken for their invaluable and generous assistance. Selma Fraiberg's books include *The Magic Years* (1959); *Insights from the Blind* (1977); *Every Child's Birthright: In Defense of Mothering* (1977); and a collection of essays edited by Selma Fraiberg and Louis Fraiberg, *Clinical Studies in Infant Mental Health: The First Year of Life* (1980). For an overview of her clinical work, see the foreword by Robert Emde to *Selected Writings of Selma Fraiberg* (1987), edited by Louis Fraiberg. Additional biographical information is found in two tributes by Robert Wallerstein: "In Memoriam: Selma Fraiberg," ed. David Krogh, University of California Academic Senate Publishers, (1986); and "Tribute to Selma Fraiberg," *Dialogue* 6 (1983), p. 5. An obituary appeared in the *New York Times* on December 22, 1981.

ALICE B. COLONNA AND DOLORES T. GEE

FREDERICK, Pauline. February 13, 1906–May 9, 1990. Journalist, broadcaster.

As the first American woman to become a television news correspondent, by definition Pauline Frederick defied convention. Her pioneering achievement can be summed up by her opinion of women's equal capacity to partake of international politics: "There seems to be a feeling that women can't understand or be interested in the more serious happenings, an assumption that news must be spoon-fed to women. I reject that idea because I reject that women are second-class citizens" (O'Dell, p. 100).

Born in the west-central Pennsylvania coal mining town of Gallitzin, Pauline Annabel Frederick was the middle child of Susan Catherine Stanley, a homemaker, and Matthew Philip Frederick, a postmaster who later worked for the Pennsylvania Department of Labor. Though neither of her parents went to school past their early teens, young Pauline was a bookworm. Self-conscious about her buckteeth and allergies, she towered over the boys her own age. She loved to write so much that she began as a reporter when still in high school, covering social events for several Harrisburg newspapers. Also as a teenager, she had a hysterectomy; this seems to have fostered her willingness to forgo marriage for her career.

After graduating from high school in Harrisburg, in 1926 she enrolled at the recently opened American University in Washington, D.C., intending to get a law degree. Majoring in political science, she won a scholarship to get a master's degree in international law, which she received in 1931. A history professor steered her back toward journalism, advice she was grateful to have followed. More comfortable now with her height and looks, she was the very picture of a handsome "career woman" and always showed professional command of the stories she covered.

The story of Frederick's 1931 entry into political journalism is emblematic of her career. Most politicians would not agree to be interviewed by either an uncredentialed journalist or a woman, so she placed a call to arrange an interview with the Czechoslovakian ambassador's wife. When a badgered secretary asked where the interview would be published, Frederick retorted, "That depends on the story I get" (O'Dell, p. 94). This tactic of side-door entry into political life through diplomats' wives culminated with the publication of her 1967 book, *Ten First Ladies of the World.* While telling women's-magazine-style stories of the innocent childhoods, fateful romances, utter dedication, and invariable charm of women such as Imelda Marcos, Lady Bird Johnson, and Yvonne de Gaulle, Frederick also imparted worldwide political history as she situated each woman within her nation's style of power.

Starting in 1931 and continuing over the next two decades, Frederick built her career with steady hard work. She wrote for the *Washington Star* and *United States Daily* (the predecessor of *U.S. News and World Report*), worked as an editor with the *Federal Register,* then entered radio broadcasting by doing women's features for NBC from 1939 to 1944. As a researcher for radio commentator H. R. Baukhage and feature writer for the North American Newspaper Alliance, she found time to contribute four chapters to a volume published in October 1941 on the readiness of American defense called *America Prepares for Tomorrow.*

As World War II wound down, Frederick took her first opportunities for foreign correspondence. Against Baukhage's advice, in 1945 she set off for a nineteen-country, three-continent tour, and did her first overseas broadcast from China. Quitting her job with NBC, she covered the Nuremberg trials as a freelance writer for the North American Newspaper Alliance and freelance broadcaster. She got on the radio only once, covering Hermann Goering's testimony in place of the first-string male reporter, who was otherwise occupied. She repeatedly approached all three networks to hire her full-time, but with no success. Her biggest break came while she was still a freelancer for ABC, when she was sent to cover a 1948 meeting of the United Nations Council of Foreign Ministers. She would often make the trip to UN headquarters in Lake Success when her male colleagues would not bother.

Network television was just coming into its own. Frederick resisted moving into it, partly from fear of aggravating confusion with an actress who shared her name, but a producer wanted her to interview notable women for the 1948 party conventions in Philadelphia, so she reluctantly trooped over to Elizabeth Arden to learn makeup techniques. At the Democratic National Convention, not only did she interview politician HELEN GAHAGAN DOUGLAS and political wife Esther Stassen, but she did their makeup as well. ABC finally hired her full-time, and she was soon broadcasting six times a week on radio and three times a week on television, including her own weekly *Pauline Frederick's Feature Story.*

In 1953 NBC hired Frederick to cover the beat with which she became synonymous: the United Nations. For twenty-one years, she broadcast from a booth above the General Assembly in New York City, reporting on crises that included the Korean War, the Middle East wars, the Cuban Missile Crisis, and the Vietnam War. She lived nearby on Sutton Place. By 1963 she was the highest-paid woman in television. Famous for her dedication, she once broadcast with a shattered kneecap. Finally free of the confines of the women's beat, Frederick had quickly become a UN fixture. In the 1960s, the two questions most frequently asked on the UN tour were "Where did Khrushchev bang his shoe?" and "Do you ever see Pauline Frederick?"

A well-respected member of the fraternity of foreign affairs reporters, she received just about every major award and honor in her field, from a Peabody Award (she was the first woman to receive one) to the Alfred I. DuPont Award for "meritorious service to the American people." In 1969, at age sixty-three, Frederick married for the first time. Her husband, Charles Robbins, was the former managing editor of the *Wall Street Journal.* Forcibly retired from NBC in 1974, Frederick took to the lecture circuit and hosted a thirty-minute international news roundup on National Public Radio called *Pauline Frederick and Colleagues.* In 1976 she became the first woman to moderate a presidential debate, between Gerald Ford and Jimmy Carter. She finally retired in 1981 when she was seventy-five. Widowed in 1989, she died from a heart attack in Lake Forest, Illinois, in 1990.

Bibliography: Pauline Frederick's papers are housed at Smith College. There is no book-length biography, but major sources about her life include Cary O'Dell, *Women Pioneers in Television: Biographies of Fifteen Industry Leaders* (1997); Marlene Sanders, *Waiting for Prime Time: The Women of Television News* (1988); and David H. Hosley and Gayle K. Yamada, *Hard News: Women in Broadcast Journalism* (1987). Also of interest is Gay Talese, "Perils of Pauline," *Saturday Evening Post,* January 26, 1963, pp. 20–22. Obituaries appeared in the *New York Times, Washington Post,* and *Los Angeles Times,* all on May 11, 1990.

NANCY BERNHARD

FRIEND, Charlotte. March 11, 1921–January 13, 1987. Cancer researcher, tumor virologist.

Charlotte Friend was an astute observer and inventive experimenter. Her discoveries, centered on a mouse leukemia virus, were critical in establishing the causal role of viruses in some cancers, and in demonstrating a link between defective maturation and tumor growth. Her early evidence that immunization with virus materials could protect against later cancer development is the underpinning for efforts to develop vaccines against HIV and other tumor-causing viruses.

Charlotte Friend was born on Houston Street in a crowded Jewish neighborhood on the Lower East Side of Manhattan. Her parents, Cecilia Wolpin and Morris Friend, had emigrated from Russia in 1913, together with many family members. Charlotte was the youngest of three daughters, and a son was on the way when her father contracted bacterial endocarditis and died. Her mother, who was trained as a pharmacist, then moved to the Bronx, where an extensive network of grandparents, uncles, and aunts became an important support for the family, and remained so for much of Charlotte's life. She attended Hunter College High School and then worked as a physician's assistant during the day while attending Hunter College at night. During these years she explored the city, taking advantage of the wealth of activities and offerings, many of them free—the museums, concerts, parks, and ethnic neighborhoods. A consummate New Yorker, for most of her adult life Friend lived not far from where she was born. She never married.

After graduating from Hunter College in 1943, Friend enlisted in the navy and attended Midshipmen's School at Smith College, graduating as an ensign. She helped direct the hematology lab at a naval hospital in California, an experience that reinforced her interest in laboratory science. After her discharge in 1946 with the rank of lieutenant j.g., she was able to return to school thanks to the G.I. bill. Admitted to Stanford Medical School, she instead chose to pursue a PhD in microbiology at Yale, studying the effects of aspirin on antigen–antibody reactions. Even at that stage of her career, she recognized the importance of expert guidance and was fearless in approaching distinguished senior scientists such as Elvin Kabat and Michael Heidelberger with questions about her work. Stimulated by an article in *Time* magazine, she wrote to Cornelius Rhoads seeking a position in the newly established Sloan-Kettering Institute for Cancer Research. In 1950, the year she received her PhD, she was hired to work there in Alice Moore's virology laboratory.

In the cells of a transplantable mouse tumor, she and Cecily Cannon-Selby observed particles in the cytoplasm that Friend recognized as similar to those in virus-infected cells. To determine whether the particles were biologically active, she inoculated cell-free extracts of the tumor into newborn mice, using a technique pioneered by Ludwik Gross for transmission of a mouse leukemia virus. Although the mice appeared healthy, when they were killed she observed that they had enlarged livers and spleens, signs indicative of leukemia. She passed the material, either as cell suspensions or as cell-free filtrates, through several generations of mice until eventually a high percentage of them developed leukemia within a few weeks after inoculation. The disease, unlike the lymphoid tumor described by Gross, was manifest as a tremendous increase in red cell precursors with an associated profound anemia.

Friend reported her findings at the 1956 meeting of the American Association of Cancer Research (AACR), and the storm of controversy that greeted her left her with a permanent degree of insecurity about giving scientific presentations. She joked later that people who maintained belief in tumor viruses were accused of having "either holes in their heads or holes in their filters" (Diamond, p. 131). The published report of this work appeared in 1957 in the *Journal of Experimental Medicine* edited by Peyton Rous. Her findings were confirmed by the distinguished pathologist Jacob Furth. Transplantable solid tumors could be obtained with leukemic tissues from virus-infected mice. Other tumor viruses were soon discovered, and the wave of disbelief was reversed. The Friend leukemia virus (FLV) became and remains a superb but complex model for the study of viral oncology and the pathogenesis of neoplasia.

In 1962 Friend received the Alfred P. Sloan Award for Cancer Research, which enabled her to realize her dream of travel. She used the award to work with scientists around the world—Andre Lwoff in Paris, Leo Sachs in Israel, and Donald Metcalf in Australia. In 1966 she became a professor and director of the Center for Experimental Cell Biology at the newly established Mount Sinai School of Medicine in New York City.

Her next groundbreaking contribution to science was her demonstration that the undifferentiated Friend leukemia cells could be induced to mature and differentiate by exogenous agents into red blood cells, and that with differentiation the tumor cells lost their ability to divide. Thus, the most critical aspect of malignancy, uncontrolled growth, could be reversed. Moreover, the morphological and biochemical events are sufficiently like those of normal maturation that they provide models for studying the regulation of gene expression in cell proliferation and differentiation, as well as in neoplasia. In recognition of her achievements, she was elected to the National Academy of Sciences in 1976, the same year that she served as president of AACR.

The same firmness and conviction that fueled her scientific achievements was evident in her involvement in public affairs. She was outspoken in defense of blacklisted academics in the McCarthy and Nixon periods, a passionate supporter of the State of Israel, and a constant role model for, and generous supporter of, other women in science. She contributed to the scientific community by service on numerous advisory committees and editorial boards.

Personally, Charlotte Friend was warm, lively, and direct. Many of her colleagues and most of her staff worked with her over decades. She did not resemble the public image of a dedicated scientist; as a young woman she was glamorous, and as she aged, she remained slim and elegant. At age sixty she was diagnosed with lymphoma. It was a well-kept secret, and for several years she continued to experiment, publish, attract grant funding, and attend meetings. But the disease progressed, and one of her last public appearances was in a wheelchair to accept an honorary degree from Brandeis in May 1986. Eight months later she died in New York City at the age of sixty-five.

Bibliography: Charlotte Friend's papers, including professional correspondence, research notes, and personal and family material, are found at the archives of the Mount Sinai School of Medicine in New York City. Friend reflected on her career in her presidential address to the American Academy for Cancer Research, which was published as "The Coming of Age of Tumor Virology," *Cancer Research* 37, no. 5 (May 1977), pp. 1255–63. Additional biographical material is found in Leila Diamond's essay for the National Academy of Sciences, *Biographical Memoirs* 63 (1994), pp. 126–48. For a complete bibliography, see Diamond and Sandra R. Wolman, eds., "Viral Oncogenesis and Cell Differentiation: The Contributions of Charlotte Friend," *Annals of the New York Academy of Sciences* 567 (1989), pp. 1–356. An obituary appeared in the *New York Times* on January 16, 1987.

SANDRA WOLMAN

FURNESS, Betty. January 3, 1916–April 2, 1994. Television reporter, consumer advocate.

Betty Furness was born Elizabeth Mary Furness in New York City, the only child of Florence Sturtevant and George Furness. Her upbringing was privileged; her father was an executive for Union Carbon and Carbide, and the family resided on Park Avenue. Betty's early education was at the Brearly School in New York City and, after that, the posh Bennett School for Girls in Middlebrook, New York.

In 1930 her father insisted she do something useful over the summer, so at age fourteen she began working at the Powers modeling agency. After two summers, Powers arranged a Hollywood audition for her. Signed by RKO in 1932 for her ability to look both highly sophisticated and like the girl next door, Furness moved west with her mother and attended school on the lot while acting in movies. In six years, Furness appeared in more than thirty-five films, most of them forgotten. One notable exception was *Swing Time* (1936) with Fred Astaire and GINGER ROGERS.

In Hollywood Furness met her first husband, songwriter Johnny Green; they were married on November 26, 1937. The couple had one daughter, Barbara (Babbie) Sturtevant Green, born in 1940. The Greens divorced in August 1943. From 1945 until his death in 1950, Furness was married to radio announcer Hugh B. Ernst.

In the mid 1940s, fed up with the film scripts from RKO and her overall life in Hollywood, Furness and her daughter returned to New York. The out-of-work actress landed parts in some touring stage productions, and began to appear in the experimental medium of television. She made her first regular appearances in the series *Fashions Coming and Becoming* over the DuMont network in 1945. While appearing in the CBS anthology *Studio One* in 1948, Westinghouse, the program's sponsor, offered Furness an additional $150 to perform the show's live commercials. Furness jumped at the chance.

At that time not only were TV commercials live, but they were performed without cue cards and had to be timed to the second. Furness loved the challenge and thrived in her newfound role of commercial spokesperson. She brought an approachable glamour to the kitchen, and her delivery was both genuine and silky smooth, a refreshing contrast to the often jerky sales pitches of the era. Impressed with her ability to increase sales, Westinghouse signed her to an exclusive contract; by 1950 she was being paid $100,000 a year to sing the praises of Westinghouse appliances.

In 1952, 1956, and 1960, Westinghouse purchased the rights to be the sole sponsor for the Democratic and Republican national conventions. Every Westinghouse commercial that aired during those gavel-to-gavel, televised proceedings featured Betty Furness, who by convention's end had amassed more airtime than any politician or newscaster. Her face, name, and tagline, "You can be SURE, if it's Westinghouse," became known all over America. A famous political cartoon of the era asked of the convention, "Who's ahead now, Pop? Taft? Ike? or Betty Furness?" In addition, Furness hosted various Westinghouse-sponsored TV shows, including the talk show *Meet Betty Furness* in 1953 and the primetime *Best of Broadway* series in 1954. Furness would remain with Westinghouse until 1960, when, by mutual agreement, the two parted ways.

Her appetite for politics having been whetted by her convention appearances, Furness unsuccessfully attempted to obtain jobs in network television journalism. Ultimately she turned to local television, hosting radio and television programs in New York City. She also pursued her interest in Democratic politics. Her involvement in the 1964 campaign gained the attention of President Lyndon Johnson, who sent Furness out on speaking tours promoting VISTA and Head Start.

In February 1967, when Furness was making plans for an August wedding to CBS news executive Leslie Midgley, she was approached by President Johnson to be his special assistant for consumer affairs, replacing ESTHER PETERSON. Despite criticism that she lacked government experience and might be too sympathetic to business, Furness accepted the job, saying "You don't refuse a President." She was sworn in on May 1, 1967. Furness later remembered it as the best decision she ever made.

Furness threw herself into her new job, testifying before Congress only weeks after her appointment and, in the first year, embarking on more than a hundred trips on government business. Her hard work and forthright manner paid off; soon the AFL-CIO and the National Consumers' League, among others, were offering praise. Furness served in her federal role until the end of the Johnson administration in 1969. During her tenure she helped enact regulations related to flameproof fabrics, truth-in-lending laws, and credit card billing.

In 1970, Furness was handpicked by Governor Nelson Rockefeller to become consumer affairs adviser for New York State, a post she resigned after one year because she felt the legislature did not take her recommendations seriously. In 1973, Furness became head of New York City's Department of Consumer Affairs.

In July 1974, the fifty-eight-year-old Furness reentered broadcasting when WNBC in New York hired her as an "on-air Ralph Nader." She was the first television reporter to concentrate exclusively on consumer issues. Furness combined her consumer savvy and name recognition with her peerless television delivery, daring to criticize Sears, Macy's, and Lane Bryant, among others, for their business practices. In 1976, she began contributing consumer-related reports to the *Today* show and also wrote a consumer affairs column for *McCall's* magazine.

Furness continued with her WNBC and *Today* duties full-time until 1990 when, after battling stomach cancer, she truncated her workweek to four days. In 1992, both entities, wanting to take a more tabloid approach to their consumer coverage, used the shortened workweek as an excuse to fire Furness. Claiming age discrimination, Furness publicly criticized her employers for her dismissal and announced that she had no plans to retire from public life. Unfortunately, a recurrence of her cancer prevented yet another professional transformation.

Betty Furness died on April 2, 1994, in New York City at the age of seventy-eight. Her death ended an extraordinarily varied career. Furness had propelled herself from fluffy film roles to the halls of the White House; she began in the pioneering days of television and ended up pioneering the field of consumer journalism. Her remarkable endurance, longevity, and, of course, abilities, influenced not only the worlds of television and government, but, through her consumer advocacy, the lives of many Americans.

Bibliography: The best sources on the life of Betty Furness, especially her career in the federal government, are located at the Lyndon B. Johnson Library, University of Texas, Austin. Biographical information can be found in Cary O'Dell, *Women Pioneers in Television: Biographies of Fifteen Industry Leaders* (1997); Michael C. Keith and Robert L. Hilliard, *The Broadcast Century: A Biography of American Broadcasting* (1992); and *Current Biography* (1968), pp. 134–136. See also Anne Chamberlin, "And Now, for the Consumer, Miss Betty Furness," *Saturday Evening Post,* June 17, 1967, pp. 26–27; "Betty Furness: One Year on the Job," *Washington Post,* May 5, 1968; "Star in Consumer Role," *New York Times,* March 6, 1967; and Albert Morehead, "America's Top Saleswomen: Betty Furness," *Cosmopolitan,* February 1953, pp. 133–37. An obituary appeared in the *New York Times* on April 4, 1994. Additional information was provided by Furness's widower, Leslie Midgley, and by former WNBC producer Rita Satz.

CARY O'DELL

G

GAPOSCHKIN, Cecilia Payne. *See* Payne-Gaposchkin, Cecilia.

GARBO, Greta. September 18, 1905–April 15, 1990. Actress.

The woman who came to be known to audiences worldwide as "Garbo" was born Greta Lovisa Gustafsson in Stockholm, the youngest of three children of Anna Lovisa Karlsson and Karl Alfred Gustafsson. Her mother was a housewife. Her father was a laborer, frequently ill and out of work. By the time of his death in June 1920, Garbo had left school to help support the family. She worked first as a latherer in a barber shop, then as a salesgirl in a department store. Friends remembered the young Garbo as a cheerful and rather plump teenager who was obsessed with the theater.

Her first film appearance was in 1921. Captain Ragnar Ring, who made advertising shorts, cast Garbo in a short entitled *How Not to Dress,* in which she wore a series of ungainly outfits. He next cast her in *Our Daily Bread* (1922), which advertised bakery goods. Garbo can be seen at a table with other young ladies, stuffing her face with pastries. To see the proto-Garbo in these early film appearances is to be struck by how un-Garbo-like she appears. Her hair is frizzy, she is overweight, and her entire essence is different. To the extent that she seems like an actress, she is a comedian, wholly open, smiling, and laughing.

Comedy director Erik Petschler subsequently cast her in a slapstick comedy, *Peter the Tramp* (1922). The comedy proved unimportant, but Petschler's advice—that she seek acting training at the Royal Dramatic Theatre Academy—was crucial. The turning point of Garbo's life came in 1922 when, on the basis of an audition, she was accepted there on a full scholarship.

Garbo's lightning rise from poverty and obscurity to international fame began in 1923 when she became the protégé of Mauritz Stiller, the most respected director in Swedish film. He cast her in a major role in *Gosta Berling's Saga* (1924), based on the Selma Lagerlof novel. Acting as a benevolent Svengali figure, Stiller encouraged her to change her name, taught her to act for the screen, insisted she lose weight, and saw that she cultivated an aura of mystery in her dealings with the press.

Gosta Berling was an international success, and when Louis B. Mayer came to Europe on a talent-hunting expedition, he signed Stiller, who also secured a contract for his protégé. As a parting shot, Mayer told Stiller that Garbo needed to lose more weight. In her last European film, *The Joyless Street* (1925), made for German director G. W. Pabst, she was twenty pounds lighter.

Garbo and Stiller arrived in Hollywood in 1925. Her first film, for the silent master Monta Bell, was *The Torrent,* in which the twenty-year-old actress played a poor girl who rises to become an internationally worshipped diva with remarkable self-possession and maturity. She achieved critical plaudits for her next film, *The Temptress* (1926), in which she was cast as a vamp whose seductive power led men to destruction.

Garbo loathed playing vamps, and when she found that she was cast as another in *Flesh and the Devil* (1927), she considered walking out. Instead she made the picture and fell in love with her co-star, John Gilbert. When presented with yet another vamp assignment, however, Garbo went on strike, demanding a lot more money and more sympathetic roles. Eventually, the box office sensation of *Flesh and the Devil* led MGM to accede to her demands. Garbo still played women whose seductive power was overwhelming and dangerous, but now these women were capable of love and of acts of enormous sacrifice.

This, in a sense, was Garbo's great achievement. She turned the nineteenth-century stereotype of the evil woman into a complicated, human figure, transforming her into a kind of saint without in any way dimming the sexual power of her allure. In doing so, Garbo was acting not on intellectual considerations but on instinct, driven by her own temperamental dislike of playing what she called "bad womens." But the results were profound. Using the almost supernatural iconography of the femme fatale, she gave force to what was, in essence, a generous, openhearted romantic vision. Audiences responded with a devotion that bordered on religious adoration.

Because MGM was reluctant to let the Swedish-accented Garbo go before the microphones, she continuing to make silent films, and these late silents—made when the artistry and technology of the medium were at their height—are among her best work. These include *Love* (1927), *The Mysterious Lady* (1928), and *A Woman of Affairs* (1928).

She made a successful talkie debut in *Anna Christie* (1930) and maintained her enormous popularity through the early thirties, despite the weakness of most of her vehicles. Of her first two years of talkies, only *Grand Hotel* (1932)—in which she uttered her signature line, "I want to be alone" (not "vant," contrary to legend)—holds up today. In 1932, her contract ended, but she re-signed with MGM on the condition that she be allowed to make *Queen Christina* (1933), a pet project. *Queen Christina,* in which Garbo plays a bisexual queen who falls in love with a man at a country inn and spends three days in bed with him, is remarkable testimony to the frankness with which sexuality could be explored in pre-Production Code cinema. It is also, for the bisexual Garbo, the closest thing to a screen autobiography.

Garbo achieved the pinnacle of her art in *Camille* (1936), which is regarded as one of the greatest performances in all of sound film. In 1939, with her popularity on the wane, she made a successful comedy, *Ninotchka* (1939), playing a hardheaded Communist who succumbs to the allure of Paris. Her last film, however, the comedy *Two-Faced Woman* (1941), was an embarrassing critical disaster.

Garbo's retirement in 1942, intended to be temporary, became permanent. She became an American citizen in 1951 and spent the rest of her life as an idiosyncratic socialite. She never married or had children. In 1968, the Museum of Modern Art held a complete retrospective of Garbo's films, and momentum began to accumulate around the notion that she was the American screen's greatest actress. Yet despite the increasing interest in her films, she never submitted to an interview. She was often seen, however, and photographed, walking around the Upper East Side of Manhattan, wearing a hat and sunglasses. She lived at 450 East 52nd Street and took a walk every day. Greta Garbo died of kidney disease at age eighty-four in New York Hospital.

Bibliography: Books about Garbo are numerous, and many are of excellent quality. Karen Swenson's *Greta Garbo: A Life Apart* (1997) stands as the definitive biography, though Barry Paris's *Garbo* (1995) is also very good and captures, with its use of phone transcripts, much of Garbo's whimsical sense of humor. For years John Bainbridge's *Garbo* (1955; revised 1971) was the final word on Garbo. Norman Zierold's *Garbo* (1969) also has value as an intelligent and economical analysis of the actress's life, legend, and historical meaning. Alexander Walker's *Garbo: A Portrait* (1980), which made use of previously unavailable studio documents, cleared up many inaccuracies, false assumptions, and misconceptions surrounding Garbo's years with MGM.

In the critical vein, Richard Corliss's *Greta Garbo* (1974), with its cogent film-by-film analysis of the actress's work, is indispensable. Michael Conway, Dion McGregor, and Mark Ricci, *The Films of Greta Garbo* (1991), is a valuable reference. Charles Affron's frame-by-frame study of key Garbo films, *Star Acting: Gish, Garbo and Davis* (1977), gets obtuse at times, but is worthwhile reading. Mick LaSalle's *Complicated Women: Sex and Power in Pre-Code Hollywood* (2000) contains several chapters on Garbo's work. For an understanding of the nineteenth-century vamp tradition from which Garbo's early films derived, two works are essential: Virginia Mae Allen, *The Femme Fatale: Erotic Icon* (1983), and Bram Dijkstra, *Idols of Perversity: Fantasies of Feminine Evil in Fin-de-Siècle Culture* (1986). Obituaries appeared in the *New York Times* and *Los Angeles Times* on April 16, 1990.

MICK LASALLE

GARLAND, Hazel. January 28, 1913–April 5, 1988. Journalist.

Hazel Barbara Maxine Hill was born in Burnett, Indiana, the eldest of sixteen children of Hazel and George Hill, African American farmers. George Hill was also a coal miner, and in search of greater opportunity, the family left Indiana and moved around western Pennsylvania until settling in Belle Vernon in 1932. Hazel helped her mother rear her younger siblings while attending the local high school. She was a gifted student, but the family suffered financial constraints and her father decided that his oldest daughter should quit school and seek employment. Her disappointment at having to terminate her formal education to work as a maid was slightly eased by the pleasure of having a radio and her own room for the first time in her life. She also developed a love of film and attended the movies every chance she had.

Hazel met her future husband, Percy Andrew Garland, at a local party but fell in love with him at a church program when he performed the trombone solo "Sunshine of Your Smile." A native of McKeesport, Pennsylvania, Percy Garland was an inventor and artist who did the window displays for the large and popular Union Clothing Store; eventually he became an industrial photographer. The Garlands married in January 1935, and their only child, Phyllis T. "Phyl" Garland, was born the following October. Garland stayed home to rear her daughter and became involved in black women's clubs through the influence of her mother-in-law. Garland was deeply affected by this education in the club movement, where she met women who carried themselves with pride, dignity, and grace while they sought to advance the race. Through her involvement with women's clubs, Garland also developed the ability to speak publicly.

Hazel Garland's introduction to journalism was serendipitous, but certainly the result of her activist personality. In 1943 she was on the publicity committee for the McKeesport Young Women's Christian Association (YWCA), which had just hired its first black staff member. The YWCA contacted the *Pittsburgh Courier* to cover the event, but no reporter appeared. Garland wrote a story of her own and sent it in, a portent of her long and influential career with the *Courier.* The editor was impressed and contacted her about working as a stringer and reporting on surrounding Pittsburgh neighborhoods. Quickly establishing a reputation for professionalism, promptness, and fine writing, she was asked to join the paper as a reporter in 1946.

The *Pittsburgh Courier,* established as an African American newspaper in 1910, gained prominence under the leadership of Robert Vann, its editor-publisher, treasurer, and legal counsel. One of the best-selling black papers in the country, it was one of the first to publish both local and national editions, printing fourteen during its heyday. The *Courier* was the mouthpiece for the increasingly activist black community locally and nationally, and from its inception called for improvements in education, housing, health care, and economics, and for political and cultural empowerment of the nation's black citizens.

Garland worked in a variety of capacities for the *Courier,* including general assignment reporter (1946–52), feature editor (1952–60), women's editor (1960–72), entertainment editor (1966–72), city editor (1972–74), and finally editor in chief (1974–77). She wrote two mainstay and popular columns, "Video Vignettes" (weekly television reviews) and "Things to Talk About" (social events and commentary). In 1953 she won a Page One Award for best reporting in western Pennsylvania. The series, entitled "The Three I's: Ignorance, Illiteracy, Illegitimacy," profiled a southern midwife and was so powerful that *Life* magazine did a follow-up story. Another high point occurred in 1976 during her tenure as editor in chief when the *Courier* won the John B. Russworm Award for best black newspaper in the country. The prize was five hundred dollars and a lifetime membership for Garland in the National Association for the Advancement of Colored People (NAACP). In 1979 she was selected as a juror for the Pulitzer Prize, and also served on numerous local and national boards.

Hazel Garland was a true Pittsburgher, marked by a mandatory devotion to the Pittsburgh Steelers football team and a celebration of local folks. She had a unique ability, as a journalist and as a person, to connect with ordinary people as well as with the nation's most educated and powerful leaders. Even when writing the society column, she included people from all walks of life. Garland was a social critic who urged and inspired people to act, motivating readers to make a direct effort to get more positive minority role models on television, or to appreciate the accomplishments of Carter cabinet member PATRICIA ROBERTS HARRIS. "Video Vignettes" indicated she was deeply aware of the importance of popular culture in shaping perceptions. In "Things to Talk About," Garland's life and thoughts were laid out against the backdrop of the African American condition. She wrote as if she were speaking to each reader over a cup of coffee, never condescendingly, but accessibly and warmly. "Did you ever hear the 'Star Spangle [sic] Banner' sung the way 'sassy' SARAH VAUGHAN sang it before the Steelers Raiders football duel last Sunday? And what a range that girl has!" she wrote in "Video Vignettes" (November 11, 1975). Yet she could easily switch gears to communicate informed and serious commentary.

After Garland retired as editor in chief of the *Courier,* she continued to write her columns and remained involved with the paper. One of her greatest joys was in 1985, when she and her husband celebrated their fiftieth wedding anniversary with three hundred family and friends. In 1987,

Garland and national broadcaster Mal Goode lent their names to the Garland-Goode Scholarship for deserving journalism students. Hazel Garland died of a heart attack in McKeesport Hospital on April 5, 1988, while recovering from surgery for a cerebral aneurysm. She was seventy-five.

As a prominent female editor of a national publication, Hazel Garland was a pioneer and voice of wisdom. That, however, is only part of her important legacy. Garland's commitment to the advancement of African Americans, and her warmth and ability to understand, appreciate, and communicate with people of diverse backgrounds and realities, contribute to her unique place in the history of journalism, African Americans, and women.

Bibliography: Hazel Garland's numerous articles can be found in the *Pittsburgh Courier* during the years she wrote for and edited the paper. Biographical and professional information was supplied by her daughter Phyl Garland, professor of journalism at Columbia University, who also contributed the entry to Jessie Carney Smith, ed., *Notable Black American Women, Book II* (1996), pp. 240–43. See also Jean E. Collins, *She Was There: Stories of Pioneering Women Journalists* (1980). Obituaries appeared in the *Pittsburgh Post-Gazette* and *New Pittsburgh Courier* on April 6, 1988; the *New York Times* on April 11, 1988; and *Jet,* April 25, 1988, p. 59.

LIANN TSOUKAS

GELLHORN, Martha. November 8, 1908–February 15, 1998. Journalist, novelist, and short story writer.

Martha Gellhorn was born in St. Louis, Missouri, to a family with a strong ideal of public service. Her probably Episcopal, Mississippi-born grandmother, Martha Ellis, married Washington Fischel, a prominent physician born to observant Czech Jews. Both were social activists who left the religions of their birth to help found the St. Louis branch of the Ethical Culture movement. Gellhorn's parents were also intellectually and politically adventurous. German-born George Gellhorn was a physician who, like his father-in-law, had moved away from his Jewish origins. EDNA FISCHEL GELLHORN was a graduate of Bryn Mawr and a prominent women's suffrage activist whose feminism had her husband's full support.

Martha, the third of four Gellhorn children and the only daughter, followed in her mother's footsteps when she enrolled at Bryn Mawr in 1926. Her characteristic independence asserted itself when she left after her junior year to become a journalist. She worked as a reporter for the *Albany Times Union* and the *St. Louis Post Dispatch,* and published her first signed article in the *New Republic.* Her life really began, she believed, when she arrived in France in 1930. There she pursued her interest in pacifism with journalist-diplomat Bertrand de Jouvenel, who was her partner (some sources say he was her first husband) from 1931 to 1934.

When she returned home in 1934 as an anti-fascist, she published *What Mad Pursuit* (1934), a novel transparently based on her own life, and became a field investigator for the Federal Emergency Relief Administration (FERA), a New Deal agency. Her reports to Harry Hopkins on the Depression's impact on Americans, which included the ravages of child prostitution and hunger, and diseases such as pellagra and syphilis, led to a lifelong friendship with ELEANOR ROOSEVELT. *The Trouble I've Seen* (1936) documents in short stories what Gellhorn had seen in fact. "Ruby," for example, tells of the initiation of an eleven-year-old girl into prostitution. The relation between fact and fiction became more complicated in Gellhorn's subsequent work, but the relation was always there and always crucial.

1936 was a turning point, both for Gellhorn and for the larger world: George Gellhorn died, and the Spanish civil war began in July. On a December trip, Martha, her grieving mother, and her youngest brother stopped in Key West, where they met Ernest Hemingway at a local bar. By March 1937 Gellhorn and Hemingway were in Spain. In the heady camaraderie of that war, Gellhorn's career as a war correspondent for *Collier's* began and her love affair with Hemingway prospered. The congruence of the personal and the professional for both writers was exceptional.

The nine years from 1936 to 1945 were for Gellhorn one continuous war stretching from Spain to the surrender of Germany and Japan. These years coincided exactly with the beginning and the end of the Gellhorn-Hemingway relationship. By the time they married in 1940, their best years together were probably over. They were divorced in 1945.

The war years were as crowded professionally as they were personally. Gellhorn published nearly fifty articles for *Collier's,* two novels, and a collection of short stories. She knew how to seize the moment as a correspondent. Despite the prohibition against women in the front lines, she managed to land on the Normandy beach on D-Day plus one, June 7, 1944. Her most traumatic war experience—confronting the horror of Hitler's concentration camps—was not reflected in her fiction until *The Wine of Astonishment* (1948).

By the end of the war, Gellhorn had come to think of London as "the one fixed point of my nomadic life" (Gellhorn, *The View from the Ground,* p. 73). Her "magnificent mother" was another kind of fixed point that brought her back to America on a regular basis. Her 1949 adoption of an Italian war orphan, George Alexander (Sandy) Gellhorn, did not tame her restlessness; she set up home in places as different and as far apart as Mexico, Italy, Wales, and East Africa. Her second marriage, in 1954, to T. S. Matthews, an American journalist living in London, was dissolved in 1963.

Gellhorn's reputation as a journalist was stronger than her reputation as a fiction writer, although her fiction was regularly reviewed in major newspapers and weeklies and had strong admirers throughout her career. H. G. Wells, an early supporter, wrote a preface for *The Trouble I've Seen.* Other admirers included Graham Greene and John Updike, who selected "Miami–New York," a 1953 story about a man and a woman seated together on a plane bound for New York, for inclusion in *The Best American Stories of the Century* (1999). The interaction between men and women was one of Gellhorn's durable subjects, as it was in her story collection *Two by Two* (1961). In her later work she also showed herself to be a keen observer of the English at home and Americans away from home.

Over the years, aging did not diminish Gellhorn's productivity. Three of her six novels and four of her collections of short stories were published in the postwar period. In addition to her fifteen published volumes, Gellhorn left uncollected articles and stories in publications as diverse as *Harper's, Good Housekeeping,* and the *New Statesman.* Throughout her life she remained a busy working journalist who could live on her earnings. There was one exception to her seamless productivity. The Vietnam War, another Dachau for her, precipitated a case of writer's block "made of solid concrete" that lasted six years (Gellhorn, *The View from the Ground,* p. 328). The war hurt more than the other wars she covered because it was an American war and Gellhorn remained intensely American despite her residence abroad.

In 1988, when Gellhorn turned eighty, two remarkable collections of her journalism appeared, replete with valuable hindsight commentary. A new edition of *The Face of War,* originally published in 1959, contains dispatches from the Spanish civil war to the wars in Central America in the 1980s. Its companion and mirror image, *The View from the Ground,* offers selections from fifty years of "peacetime" reporting ironically steeped in wartime fallout. Ten years after these testamentary volumes, Gellhorn died of cancer in London at the age of eighty-nine. She had aptly described herself as a "special type of war profiteer" (Gellhorn, *The Face of War,* p. 2). Her conscience and her craft matured during her coverage of eight wars. Events and her own ability to shape them to her needs despite the constraints of gender conspired to make her a powerful and astute witness to her war-saturated century.

Bibliography: Biographies include Carl Rollyson, *Nothing Ever Happens to the Brave: The Story of Martha Gellhorn* (1990), and its updated version, *Beautiful Exile: The Life of Martha Gellhorn* (2001); and Caroline Moorehead, *Gellhorn: A Twentieth-Century Life* (2003). See also Jacqueline Orsagh, "A Critical Biography of Martha Gellhorn" (PhD dissertation, Michigan State University, 1978). Biographical material on Gellhorn can be found in Bernice Kert, *The Hemingway Women* (1983). The Gellhorn collection at Boston University's Mugar Memorial Library contains her correspondence with Ernest Hemingway. In addition to the collected essays in *The Face of War* (4th ed., 1993) and *The View from the Ground* (1988), Gellhorn's other nonfiction includes *Travels with Myself and Another* (1978), an account of a trip she took with Hemingway to China in 1940. *The Trouble I've Seen* (1936), *Two by Two* (1958), *Pretty Tales for Tired People* (1965), and *The Weather in Africa* (1978) were collected in *The Novellas of Martha Gellhorn* (1994). Other works of fiction include *What Mad Pursuit* (1934), *A Stricken Field* (1940), *The Heart of Another* (1941), *Liana* (1944), *The Wine of Astonishment* (1948, reprinted as *Point of No Return* in 1989), *The Honeyed Peace* (1953), *His Own Man* (1961), and *The Lowest Trees Have Tops* (1967). An obituary appeared in the *New York Times* on February 17, 1998.

CLAIRE SPRAGUE

GIDEON, Miriam. October 23, 1906–June 18, 1996. Composer, music educator.

Miriam Gideon was born in Greeley, Colorado, the younger of two daughters of Henrietta Shoninger and Abram Gideon. Her father taught philosophy and modern languages at Colorado State Teachers College, and her mother taught in a local elementary school; both of her parents were German American Jews. From 1912 to 1916, the family lived in California, Illinois, and Wyoming while Gideon's father held jobs as a teacher and then a reporter. In 1916 the family settled in Yonkers, New York, where Gideon studied piano with Hans Barth and elementary harmony at the local conservatory.

Her parents were not musicians and did not own a piano or phonograph, but they supported Gideon's interest in music. At her request, when she was fifteen they permitted her to live in Dedham, Massachusetts, with her uncle, Henry Gideon, who was organist, conductor, and music director at the reform synagogue Temple Israel in Boston. Her uncle's home was filled with music. Choirs and singers would often visit, and Gideon accompanied her uncle, who sang sacred and secular works. He arranged for her to study piano with Felix Fox and gave her opportunities to perform in local chamber and choral concerts.

Gideon graduated from Girls' High School in

Boston in 1922 and entered Boston University, where she majored in French, minored in mathematics, and took music courses, including composition and music theory. Although her family and teachers did not encourage her to compose, she became absorbed in composition at the age of nineteen after writing a song. After graduating from BU in 1926, Gideon returned to New York, where she enrolled in New York University's graduate music program, intending to obtain a teaching certificate and teach in the public schools. Not satisfied with her courses in music education, she left NYU after a year to continue her training in composition. From 1931 to 1934, Gideon studied harmony, counterpoint, and composition with Lazare Saminsky, a Russian composer and conductor. In 1935, she began to study with noted composer and pedagogue Roger Sessions.

During the eight years she worked with Sessions, her musical language changed from a somewhat conservative, tonal style, as can be heard in two early songs, "She Weeps over Rahoon" (1939) and "The Too-Late Born" (1939), to a free atonal style. To celebrate the centennial of its founding, Temple Emanu-El in New York commissioned Gideon to compose a work. The result was *The Hound of Heaven* (1945), for voice, oboe, and string trio. Its dissonant style marks a break from her earlier, more conservative writing; Gideon identified it as probably the first piece she composed using her own style.

While completing her formal study of composition with Sessions, she entered Columbia University's graduate program in musicology in 1942. There she studied with Paul Henry Lang and Erich Hertzmann, earning an MA in 1946. She began her teaching career as an instructor of music at Brooklyn College, City University of New York, in 1944, and at City College of New York in 1947. In 1949 she married Frederic Ewen, a tenured faculty member in Brooklyn College's department of English and a scholar of German literature. Both she and Ewen lost their teaching positions at Brooklyn College because of McCarthyism. Ewen took early retirement in 1952 rather than be asked to testify about his colleagues' politics; because of her marriage to Ewen, Gideon was not rehired in 1954. In 1955 she resigned her position at City College, whose administrators were also seeking information about leftist faculty members, and that year she began teaching at the newly formed Cantors Institute of the Jewish Theological Seminary (JTS), headed by Hugo Weisgall. In 1970 she received her Doctorate in Sacred Music at JTS, and the next year she was rehired at City College. She also taught at the Manhattan School of Music from 1967 to 1991. While in her eighties, she suffered from Alzheimer's disease. She died at her home in Manhattan on June 18, 1996, at the age of eighty-nine.

Gideon was particularly gifted at composing vocal music. The bulk of her oeuvre consists of music with text, and includes songs for voice and piano, such as *Songs of Voyage* (1961); works for voice and chamber ensemble, such as *Spirit above the Dust* (1980); choral compositions such as *How Goodly Are Thy Tents—Psalm 84* (1947); synagogue services such as *Sacred Service for Sabbath Morning* (1970); and an opera, *Fortunato* (1958). An unusual feature of some of her compositions is the use of more than one language in a single work, such as the song "Mixco" (1957), which sets a Spanish text by Miguel Angel Asturias and its English translation in subsequent stanzas. Noteworthy instrumental compositions include *Three Biblical Masks* for violin and piano or for organ (1960), *Of Shadows Numberless* for piano (1966), and the Sonata for piano (1977). Gideon's music is marked by keen attention to melodic line, a concentrated use of striking harmonic and melodic cells, and a superb sense of drama.

Miriam Gideon was a prolific and well-regarded composer. She wrote approximately seventy works, many of which have been recorded, and enjoyed an active career for over five decades. Her achievements were recognized during her lifetime by several institutions, including the American Academy and Institute of Arts and Letters, into which she was inducted in 1975, and Brooklyn College, which awarded her an honorary doctorate in 1983. Prominent composers, including Milton Babbitt, George Perle, and Hugo Weisgall, have noted the importance of her music. Although Gideon has been widely quoted as resisting the label "woman composer," her unpublished writings reveal that she sometimes identified herself as such and grappled with its beneficial and deleterious associations. Gideon's compositions establish her as a distinctive and significant presence in twentieth-century composition.

Bibliography: The Miriam Gideon Collection at the New York Public Library for the Performing Arts at Lincoln Center contains manuscripts, published and unpublished scores, sketches, diaries, journals, correspondence, and teaching materials. The archives of Broadcast Music, Inc. hold other important correspondence and documents. A biographical sketch and a list of compositions by Gideon appear in Linda Ardito, "Miriam Gideon," *New Grove Dictionary of Music and Musicians Online* (2001); and Jane Weiner LePage, "Miriam Gideon: Composer, Professor, Humanist," in *Women Composers, Conductors, and Musicians of the Twentieth Century,* vol. 2 (1983), pp. 118–41. An autobiographical statement is published in Deena Rosenberg and Bernard Rosenberg, *The Music Makers* (1979), pp. 62–69. Gideon's life and music are explored in Ellie M. Hisama, *Gendering Musical Modernism: The Music of Ruth Crawford, Marion Bauer, and Mir-*

iam Gideon (2001). Gideon's compositions are examined in Marianne Kielian-Gilbert, "Of Poetics and Poiesis, Pleasure and Politics—Music Theory and Modes of the Feminine," *Perspectives of New Music,* Winter 1994, pp. 44–67; George Perle, "The Music of Miriam Gideon," *American Composers Alliance Bulletin* 7, no. 4 (1958), pp. 2–9; and Barbara A. Petersen, "The Vocal Chamber Music of Miriam Gideon," in Judith Lang Zaimont, Catherine Overhauser, and Jane Gottlieb, eds., *The Musical Woman II: An International Perspective* (1987), pp. 222–55. Important interviews with Gideon include Linda Ardito, "Miriam Gideon: A Memorial Tribute," *Perspectives of New Music,* Summer 1996, pp. 202–14; and Albert Weisser, "An Interview with Miriam Gideon," *Dimensions in American Judaism,* Spring 1970, pp. 38–40. An obituary appeared in the *New York Times* on, June 20, 1996.

ELLIE M. HISAMA

GILPIN, Laura. April 22, 1891–November 30, 1979. Photographer.

Laura Gilpin was born in Austin Bluffs, Colorado, the first of two children of Emma Gosler Miller and Frank Gilpin. Her father, the youngest son of a prominent Baltimore Quaker and pharmaceuticals manufacturer, moved west at the age of eighteen to join an older brother in the ranching business. Emma Miller, an ambitious and well-educated young woman raised in St. Louis, followed her husband west to Colorado following their marriage in 1890. For Frank, the West seemed a place where he might invent himself anew; for Emma it was a place where she could recreate the genteel life of eastern society. Their native-born daughter would eventually come to see the West in a very different way: not as a blank tableau but as a land with a rich history and tradition of its own. In a photographic career lasting more than sixty years, she created a visual record of the southwestern landscape and the cultures of the Pueblo and Navajo peoples that focuses less on change than on what she perceived as the timeless and enduring qualities of a place and its inhabitants.

Her family's shifting financial fortunes meant that Gilpin moved frequently as a girl, between remote ranches and the more urban center of Colorado Springs. Her mother's cultural aspirations helped dictate her schooling. In Colorado Springs, Gilpin attended a private elementary school, and in 1905 she went east to study at the Baldwin School in Bryn Mawr, Pennsylvania. In the fall of 1907, she transferred to Rosemary Hall School in Greenwich, Connecticut, but here, too, she felt uncomfortable. She returned home to Colorado Springs in 1909 and never finished the additional year of work necessary for a high school diploma. In 1910–11, she studied violin at the New England Conservatory of Music, but her father's shifting business fortunes forced her to return home to live with her family on a ranch in the western Colorado community of Austin. Here, Gilpin turned her energies to a poultry business, and for the first time began to study photography in a serious way.

Gilpin had first experimented with photography in 1904 when she used a Brownie camera to document the Louisiana Purchase Exposition in St. Louis. Soon, however, she began to work with autochromes, a relatively new photographic technology that produced delicate color transparencies on glass. The extraordinary still-lifes and portraits Gilpin produced in an ice house at her family ranch between 1911 and 1914 stand out as masterworks in the early history of color photography in the United States.

In the fall of 1916, fueled by a passion for art and supported with money from her poultry business, Gilpin moved to New York to attend the Clarence H. White School of Photography, the country's leading institution for the study of fine arts photography. White was a believer in the principles of "pictorialism," a style and a movement intent upon demonstrating the value of photography as a fine art, not a mere mechanical craft, and he was well known for his support of women artists. Under White's tutelage Gilpin mastered principles of design and printmaking skills.

In early 1918, Gilpin fell victim to the great influenza epidemic, and returned home to Colorado Springs to convalesce. There she came under the care of Elizabeth Forster, a private nurse five years her senior. During the long hours they shared together, the two women formed a friendship that would last until Forster's death in 1972.

After she recovered from her illness, Gilpin supported herself by doing portraiture and other commercial jobs. But her real affection was for the southwestern landscape. She and Forster took frequent camping trips through the region, and Gilpin began to assemble the collection of photographic prints that would bring her considerable critical praise. In the early 1920s she exhibited her work in Europe and the eastern United States, drawing acclaim for her mastery of the platinum printing process and for her success at capturing the monumental spaces of the American West. In 1930 she was elected an Associate of the Royal Photographic Society of Great Britain, and that same year the Library of Congress acquired a collection of her prints for its fine arts photography collection. Her interest in bookmaking led her to produce a series of small photographic booklets, including one on the Pikes Peak region (1926) and another on Mesa Verde (1927).

Despite the critical success, Gilpin's professional life was one of struggle. The Depression put a damper on her commercial photography business and forced her to withdraw from the busy exhibition schedule she had maintained during the 1920s. From 1942 to 1944 she worked as a public relations photographer at the Boeing Company in Wichita, Kansas. In 1945, she moved from her longtime home in Colorado Springs to Santa Fe, New Mexico, finally setting up a home with Forster, her friend of more than twenty years. There she started a new photography business and became involved with various groups devoted to the preservation of regional arts and cultures.

Gilpin most fully explored her interest in the connections between the physical landscape and human culture in *The Enduring Navaho* (1968), a book that reflected more than thirty-five years of work with the Navajo people. Her involvement began in 1931, when Forster took a job as a public health nurse in the reservation community of Red Rock, Arizona. Gilpin became a frequent visitor, using her 8×10 view camera to compile a record of a rural American world overlooked by the better-known photographers later working for the federal government's Farm Security Administration project. After Forster lost her job in 1933, the two women seldom returned to the reservation. In 1950, however, Gilpin determined to bring her pictorial story of the Navajo up to date; the project lasted eighteen years. Nothing after the book came out, she said, meant as much to her as the warm reception it received from her Navajo friends.

Gilpin's lifelong interest in landscape photography distinguished her from other women photographers of her generation, even as her approach to landscape photography set her apart from the men who documented the same subject. Unlike her contemporaries Ansel Adams or Eliot Porter, who celebrated the West as a collection of wilderness landscapes, Gilpin was interested in the land as a historical environment, one that shaped and was in turn shaped by human activity. Her rediscovery by a growing art market in the 1970s coincided with renewed professional recognition for her life's work, including two honorary doctorates and a fellowship from the Guggenheim Foundation (1975) to support her continuing work with platinum printing. At the age of eighty-eight, Gilpin died of heart failure in 1979 in Santa Fe, New Mexico.

Bibliography: The papers, prints, and some forty thousand negatives in the Gilpin Collection at the Amon Carter Museum, Fort Worth, Texas, provide exhaustive documentation of Gilpin's life and work. The principal published source on her life is Martha A. Sandweiss, *Laura Gilpin: An Enduring Grace* (1986), which includes an extensive bibliography of Gilpin's published writings, reviews of her work, and a year-by-year account of her photographic exhibitions. Further information on her early work with the Navajo is found in Martha A. Sandweiss, ed., *Denizens of the Desert: A Tale in Word and Picture of Life among the Navaho Indians/Elizabeth W. Forster and Laura Gilpin* (1988), a publication of the letters Forster wrote from the Navajo reservation during the early 1930s. In addition to *The Enduring Navaho* (1968), Gilpin's other books include *The Pueblos: A Camera Chronicle* (1941); *Temples in Yucatan* (1948); and *The Rio Grande: River of Destiny* (1949). An obituary appeared in the *New York Times* on December 1, 1979.

MARTHA A. SANDWEISS

GIMBUTAS, Marija Birutė Alseikaitė. January 23, 1921–February 2, 1994. Archaeologist.

Marija Birutė Alseikaitė was born in Vilnius, the ancient capital of Lithuania. Her parents were part of the Lithuanian intelligentsia that arose from the farming class during a century of Russian rule. Marija's mother, Veronika Janulaitytė Alseikienė, an intensely brilliant woman, earned her doctorate in ophthalmology at the University of Berlin in 1908, becoming the first Lithuanian woman physician. Her father, Danielius Alseika, earned his medical degree in 1910 at the University of Tartu, Estonia. When Lithuania was liberated from Russia in 1918, her parents established the first Lithuanian hospital in Vilnius. The following year the Vilnius region was invaded by Poland.

Although Marija Alseikaitė grew up under the tension of occupation, her home life was emotionally and culturally nourishing, a gathering place for artists, writers, scholars, and political activists. Marija had an exceedingly quick and inquiring mind, a passionate nature, and poetic sensibility. As a child, her imagination was deeply informed by a wealth of Lithuanian folk songs and stories. She and her older brother Vytautas were given private instruction in music and languages, encouraged to learn academic discipline, and expected to contribute their best efforts to the development of culture.

When Marija was ten years old, her world was shattered when her parents separated; when she was fifteen, her beloved father suddenly died. At his deathbed, she vowed to continue his life by becoming a scholar. She began to investigate ancient Lithuanian beliefs and rituals concerning death, and she joined ethnographic expeditions to rural Lithuania to collect and preserve traditional folklore.

Marija Alseikaitė graduated with honors in 1938 from Aušra Gymnasium, Kaunas, and studied linguistics at Kaunas University in the Department of Philology. At the University of Vilnius (1940–42) she studied archaeology under Jonas Puzinas, as well as linguistics, ethnology, folklore, and literature. In 1941, as the war intensified, she married her boyfriend, Jurgis Gimbutas. In 1942 her master's thesis, "Modes of Burial in Lithuania in the Iron Age," was received with honors. During this period, Lithuania suffered the horrors of Soviet occupation (1940–41), when friends and family members were sent to death camps and to Siberia, and German occupation (1941–43), in which most of the Jewish population perished. She clung to her work to remain sane.

On June 15, 1942, the Gimbutases' first daughter, Danutė, was born, and the following year, as the Soviets invaded again, the young family fled to Vienna, then Innsbruck, and finally to Bavaria. Of this period she said, "Life just twisted me like a little plant, but my work was continuous in one direction" (*Women in Transition,* p. 118). After the war ended, she enrolled at Tübingen University and earned her doctorate in archaeology in 1946 with minors in ethnology and history of religion. Her doctoral dissertation, "Prehistoric Burial Rites in Lithuania," which she translated into German, was published that same year. In 1947 their second daughter, Živilė, was born.

In 1949, the Gimbutas family emigrated to America and settled in the Boston area, where Jurgis found work as a civil engineer. Owing to her impressive credentials and linguistic abilities (with advanced facility in nearly twenty European languages), Marija Gimbutas was accepted at Harvard to do postgraduate research. Her book, *The Prehistory of Eastern Europe* (1956), was the first monograph to make all archaeological research from the Baltic to the Caucasus available to Western scholars. She also wrote *Ancient Symbolism in Lithuanian Folk Art* (1958), *The Balts* (1963), *Bronze Age Cultures in Central and Eastern Europe* (1965), and *The Slavs* (1971), establishing her reputation as a world-class scholar. She maintained active ties with Eastern Europe as an exchange scholar. In Lithuania, where her books were banned by the KGB, they were secretly passed from hand to hand.

The Gimbutas family remained actively involved in Lithuanian intellectual activities and cofounded several cultural and educational programs. They maintained close ties with the artists, writers, and scholars of the émigré community. In 1954 their third daughter, Rasa Julija, was born, and the following year Marija Gimbutas became a Research Fellow of the Peabody Museum, Harvard University.

Marija Gimbutas left Harvard and her marriage and moved to California with her two youngest daughters in 1963 to become professor (later chair) of European Archaeology at the University of California, Los Angeles. Gimbutas initiated the Institute of Archaeology, Indo-European studies, and other programs, and was curator of Old World Archaeology at the Cultural History Museum at UCLA. She was also one of several scholars who co-founded, edited, and promoted the *Journal of Indo-European Studies,* and she contributed to numerous scholarly journals. Her Kurgan Hypothesis, combining archaeology and linguistic paleontology, remains the most accepted and debated solution for the homeland of Proto-Indo-European speakers and the Indo-Europeanization of Europe. She stimulated original research by numerous scholars on the transformation of European cultures between 4500 and 2500 BC by organizing international interdisciplinary conferences and publishing the results.

Between 1967 and 1980 Marija Gimbutas was project director of five major excavations of Neolithic sites in southeast Europe. She focused her research on the vast body of symbolic imagery from the pre-Indo-European cultures of the region, which she named "Old Europe." Her approach was interdisciplinary, combining linguistics, mythology, archaeology, ethnology, folklore, and historical records, a methodology she called archaeomythology. This pioneering research resulted in *The Gods and Goddesses of Old Europe, 7000–3500 b.c.* (1974; renamed *The Goddesses and Gods of Old Europe,* 1982), *The Language of the Goddess* (1989), and *The Civilization of the Goddess* (1991). Her interpretations of female symbolism as expressions of divinity, and Old Europe as peaceful and female-centered, have inspired countless artists, philosophers, linguists, anthropologists, writers, mythologists (notably Joseph Campbell), and thousands of women involved in goddess spirituality. Her interpretations have also sparked a sometimes virulent controversy within the fields of archaeology and anthropology.

For decades, Gimbutas maintained an exhaustive lecture, research travel, and writing schedule. She retired from UCLA in 1989. After a long struggle with cancer, Marija Gimbutas died in Los Angeles on February 2, 1994, at the age of seventy-three. Her ashes were buried next to her mother's grave in Kaunas, and three thousand people paid their respects to their most famous Lithuanian/American scholar. As noted British archaeologist Colin Renfrew concluded, "She was a figure of extraordinary energy and talent. The study and the wider understanding of European prehistory is much the richer for her life's work."

Bibliography: For an introduction to the life and work of Marija Gimbutas, see the biographical sketch by Susan Nacev Skomal and Edgar C. Polomé in their edited volume, *Proto-Indo-European: The Archaeology of a Linguistic Problem, Studies in Honor of Marija Gimbutas* (1987). Other commemorative volumes include Miriam Robbins Dexter and Edgar C. Polomé, eds., *Varia on the Indo-European Past: Papers in Memory of Marija Gimbutas* (1997); and Joan Marler, ed., *From the Realm of the Ancestors: An Anthology in Honor of Marija Gimbutas* (1997), which includes a comprehensive bibliography through 1996. Additional publications by Marler include "A Vision for the World: The Life and Work of Marija Gimbutas," *Comparative Civilizations Review* 33 (Fall 1995), pp. 1–20; "The Life and Work of Marija Gimbutas," *Journal of Feminist Studies in Religion* 12, no. 2 (Fall 1996), pp. 37–52; and "Marija Gimbutas: Tribute to a Lithuanian Legend," in Suzanne LaFont, ed., *Women in Transition: Voices from Lithuania* (1998). For the collected writings by Marija Gimbutas on the Indo-European question, see Miriam Robbins Dexter and Karlene Jones-Bley, eds., *The Kurgan Culture and the Indo-Europeanization of Europe* (1997). An unfinished manuscript by Gimbutas completed and published after her death by her former student Miriam Robbins Dexter is *The Living Goddesses* (1999). Archival material on Gimbutas is found in the Manuscripts Department, Vilnius University, the Library of the Academy of Sciences, and the Lithuanian State Archive for Literature and Art, Vilnius, Lithuania; the Joseph Campbell and Marija Gimbutas Library, Pacific Graduate Institute, Carpinteria, California; and the Institute of Archaeomythology, Sebastopol, California. An obituary in the *Independent,* London, February 23, 1994, contains the final quote from Colin Renfrew. An obituary appeared in the *New York Times* on February 13, 1990.

JOAN MARLER

GISH, Lillian. October 14, 1893–February 27, 1993. Actress.

Lillian Diana Gish was born in Springfield, Ohio, the first of two daughters of Mary Robinson McConnell and James Lee Gish. Her sister DOROTHY GISH, who also became a noted stage and screen actor, was born four and a half years later. Both parents came from solidly middle-class, fifth- or sixth-generation American families of mostly English stock. Their youthful union, however, was ill-fated. After briefly trying his hand at shopkeeping, James Gish succumbed to alcoholism and deserted his family; his wife obtained a legal separation in 1901. To make ends meet, Mary Gish, who was then living in New York City, took in boarders. One of these was an actor who induced the young mother to try her hand at performing as well. In due course, the young Gish girls were also enlisted as performers, playing both separately and together in stage productions in New York City and around the country. Despite the early separations occasioned by their new theatrical endeavors, the Gish women remained exceptionally close. Mary Gish never remarried. Though Dorothy later married, she soon left her husband. Lillian, despite a few serious love affairs, remained single all her life.

Yearning for a more settled life for her children, Mary Gish eventually took on the operation of a series of confectionery shops in New York and in the Midwest, where her family still resided. Lillian was sent to various schools, including the Ursuline Academy convent school in East St. Louis, where, though she was not Catholic, she briefly entertained the hope of becoming a nun. Yet Lillian's striking appearance suited her well for a theatrical career. Small-boned and willowy, she had delicate features and flowing golden hair, which she never cut.

In June 1912, the two Gish girls set off for New York City to resume their work in the theater. Their hope, it seems, was to earn sufficient money to buy a house for themselves and their mother. Their first order of business was to visit a friend from their early theater days who had begun to work in "the flickers" and was now going by the name MARY PICKFORD. While waiting for Mary at Biograph Studios, they were spotted by the company's head of production, D. W. Griffith, who immediately offered them work. Though Lillian would have preferred employment in the more prestigious milieu of the theater, Griffith offered an attractive salary, and the girls accepted, moving to New York with their mother to begin their new careers. All three Gishes were immediately cast in *An Unseen Enemy* (1912), a typical Griffith one-reeler about imperiled maidens rescued by an obliging male. Lillian was eighteen.

In the narrative she told of her life to countless interviewers and biographers, Lillian repeatedly placed Griffith at the center of her existence, going so far as to give her 1969 autobiography the subtitle *The Movies, Mr. Griffith, and Me.* Gish soon became the director's favorite leading lady, appearing in many of his one- and two-reelers and later in his most important features, including *Birth of a Nation* (1915), *Intolerance* (1916), *Broken Blossoms* (1919), and *Way Down East* (1920). She spent most of her evenings with Griffith as well, assisting him with production details and absorbing his ideas about filmmaking. Most biographers believe that their relationship was also romantic, though the puritanical Gish, following a lifelong policy of discretion about her amorous attachments, never admitted this.

Griffith, captivated by Lillian's fragile beauty, was fond of casting his protégé as a young wife and mother. In *Way Down East,* perhaps her finest performance for Griffith, she plays Anna, a young girl tricked into a false marriage who eventually finds happiness with a farmer's son. Gish's stricken expression as Anna learning of the death of her baby is captured in one of Griffith's celebrated long close-ups. Later in the story, a lightly clad Anna is cast out into a blizzard by the disapproving farmer, and the biting cold and wintry blasts she endures are palpable. Years later Gish still suffered pain from having dangled her hand in an icy river to add to the authenticity of the scene. The sequence quickly became part of the Gish legend, which held that she was so dedicated to her craft that she would go to any extreme to add to the credibility of her performances. By this time, she had also persuaded Griffith to hire photographer Henrik Sartov, whose soft-focus, backlit close-ups of her became the prototype for glamour cinematography ever afterward.

At Griffith's behest, Gish directed her sister Dorothy in the now-lost film comedy *Remodeling Her Husband* in 1920. The experience, fraught with tension on the set both with the crew and with Dorothy herself, was not one Gish cared to repeat. But the two sisters starred in a final Griffith production, *Orphans of the Storm,* in 1921, before Lillian abandoned her mentor to pursue more lucrative opportunities. Now a major star, she made a series of films in which she was typecast as a delicate, pure-spirited soul subjected to unwonted tribulations. These films included *The White Sister* (1923), *Romola* (1924), and *The Wind* (1928); in this last she had perhaps her finest role. Audiences increasingly identified her with such characters, leading critics to dub Gish the Duse of the screen, a reference to the great Italian stage tragedian. During this period, Gish appears to have been briefly engaged to her sometime producer Charles Duell. Duell subsequently subjected her to an extended series of court battles over contractual issues, presumably out of bitterness over her rejection of him.

After the coming of sound, the overwrought melodramas Gish had specialized in became less viable, and she found it easier to find suitable employment in the theater. She enjoyed numerous stage triumphs, including the role of Ophelia to John Gielgud's Hamlet. She also later performed on television. A lifelong New Yorker with a taste for literature and the arts, she soon became friendly with many of the intellectuals of the day, including, most notably, drama critic George Jean Nathan, with whom she shared a long intimacy. She later explained her refusal to marry Nathan by saying, "I suddenly thought of my tombstone. I thought of his name on it. That decided me. Not then or since have I found a name which I would rather carry into eternity than Lillian Gish" (Affron, p. 271).

A staunch Republican, Gish was also a committed pacifist who made herself unpopular during the early years of World War II by espousing an isolationist policy for the United States. But her major commitment was to her art, which she tirelessly promoted in lectures, interviews, and television specials. Silent cinema, and especially D. W. Griffith, invariably occupied center stage in these reconstructions. From time to time she returned to Hollywood to perform in films—including *Duel in the Sun* (1946), *Night of the Hunter* (1955), *A Wedding* (1978), and *The Whales of August* (1987), in which she starred at the age of ninety-three with BETTE DAVIS. In all of these activities she maintained a reputation as a consummate professional, disciplined, uncomplaining, always prepared, and ready to make any sacrifice for the sake of the production. In 1971 she was awarded an honorary Oscar, one of many accolades she received throughout her long professional life. She died in New York City on February 27, 1993, at the age of ninety-nine. In keeping with her dedication to artistic achievement, her will provided for a $250,000 bequest for "Excellence in the Arts." The Dorothy and Lillian Gish Prize is named for Lillian and her beloved sister.

Bibliography: The most reliable treatment of Gish's life and art can be found in Charles Affron's elegant and meticulous biography *Lillian Gish: Her Legend, Her Life* (2001), based largely on newly available materials from the Gish estate deposited in the New York Public Library. Gish's autobiography, *Lillian Gish: The Movies, Mr. Griffith, and Me* (1969), written with Ann Pinchot, includes many photographs and stresses the artistic importance of silent cinema and of Griffith in particular. Gish followed up this volume with a picture book, *Dorothy and Lillian Gish* (1973), edited by James E. Thrasher, which includes some behind-the-scenes commentary; and *An Actor's Life for Me!* with Selma G. Lanes (1987), a book intended for young people that focused on her early experiences in the theater. Edward Wagenknecht's early appreciation, *Lillian Gish: An Interpretation* (1927), was published as part of a scholarly series commemorating the achievements of significant contemporary figures such as H. L. Mencken, Sinclair Lewis, and D. H. Lawrence. The laudatory portraits in both Albert Bigelow Paine's *Life and Lillian Gish* (1932) and Stuart Oderman's *Lillian Gish: A Life on Stage and Screen* (2000) were shaped by the narrative line Gish fostered. Analyses of Gish's artistry include James Naremore, *Acting in the Cinema* (1988); Roberta E. Pearson, *Eloquent Gestures: The Transformation of Performance Style in the Griffith Biograph Films* (1992); Richard Dyer, "A White Star," *Sight and Sound*, August 1993, pp. 22–24; and Virginia Wright Wexman, *Creating the Couple: Love, Marriage, and Hollywood Performance* (1993). An obituary appeared in the *New York Times* on March 1, 1993.

VIRGINIA WRIGHT WEXMAN

GOLDHABER, Gertrude Scharff. July 14, 1911–February 2, 1998. Physicist.

Gertrude Scharff was born in Mannheim, Germany, the first of two daughters of Nelly Steinharter and Otto Scharff. Her father had developed an interest in chemistry while he was a teenager, but by the time he was ready for university, his own father's death forced him to abandon science to help manage the family's food-wholesaling business. Gertrude's mother had grown up in Munich, and when the family moved there around 1915, it became Gertrude's home until she left Germany twenty years later.

As a child, Gertrude—or Trude as her friends called her—liked to contemplate the world; her sister Liselotte was much more interested in sports. In the spring of 1930, after graduating from the local girls' gymnasium, Trude started in physics at the University of Munich. Her father had suggested she study law as preparation for joining the family firm, but she wanted to understand how the world worked—natural rather than man-made law. In a common practice of that time, after one semester at Munich she went successively for a semester each to the universities of Freiburg, Zurich, and Berlin. In Berlin in 1931, she joined a proseminar led by Max von Laue, the pioneer of X-ray diffraction; one of the other students, Maurice Goldhaber, was to become her husband eight years later. Thus their first meeting, like the whole life they would lead together, was intimately connected with physics.

Upon returning to Munich in the spring of 1932, she began her doctoral work with Walther Gerlach, studying the effect of stress on magnetization in ferromagnetic materials above the Curie temperature at which ferromagnetism stops. Despite the virulent anti-Semitic program of the new Nazi government, Trude, who was Jewish, attained her PhD in 1935. Not yet twenty-four, she immediately began exploring options for leaving the increasingly hostile environment in Germany. Of the many people with whom she corresponded, the only one who encouraged her was Maurice Goldhaber, who was then a student in Cambridge working on nuclear physics with James Chadwick. She did go to England, settling in London. After many months she obtained a postdoctoral position at Imperial College with G. P. Thomson, whose lab still was centered on electron diffraction. In 1939 Maurice Goldhaber, who had moved to the University of Illinois at Urbana in the previous year, returned briefly to England. Trude and Maurice were married that spring and then went together to Urbana. Their sons Alfred and Michael were born there in 1940 and 1942; both went on to earn doctorates in theoretical physics.

The University of Illinois was the beginning of Trude's experience with anti-nepotism rules. These rules were so rigid at Urbana that the physics department head used to warn new male faculty not to get involved with his daughters because a marriage would mean that either the father or the new husband would have to resign. During her eleven years at Illinois, Trude never held a regular tenure-track position. She began what would be her life's work in nuclear physics in Maurice's lab with no salary and no official recognition. Her most noted paper during that early period, published only after the war because it contained classified information, was the verification that neutrons are emitted during the rather gentle process of spontaneous fission of uranium, not only in neutron-initiated fission.

After the war Trude was appointed research assistant professor. During that period she and Maurice joined in an elegant and definitive experiment on fundamental particles. It was well known that the beta particles emitted in weak nuclear decay processes were experimentally indistinguishable from electrons, but this was not quite proof that betas are electrons. The Goldhabers observed beta rays impinging on lead atoms. By the Pauli exclusion principle, electrons could not come close to the atomic nucleus because other electrons already occupied all those nearby configurations. If the betas were not electrons, however, they could descend to the lowest possible orbit, radiating energetic X-rays in the process. No such radiation was seen, proving that betas are indeed electrons.

In 1950, after several long visits to Brookhaven National Laboratory, the Goldhabers joined the lab and moved to Long Island. For the first time Trude had a regular position. Her research flourished as she focused on the responses of nuclei when they are disturbed slightly enough that they respond collectively, rather than by excitation of individual nucleons. Over more than two decades she perfected what became the variable moment of inertia model, correlating patterns of rotational excitation in nuclei ranging from spherical (which can rotate only if a minimum angular velocity allows them to distort their shape) to deformed (which have an almost fixed shape and hence a fixed moment of inertia for a wide range of angular momenta). The beginning stages of her systematic studies were an important foundation for the unified model combining collective and individual-particle effects that earned Nobel recognition for Aage Bohr and Ben Mottelson.

In the 1970s she and her son Alfred published what may have been the first collaborative papers in physics by a mother and son team. Their work concerned the relation between the shapes of rotating nuclei as inferred from the moment of inertia and from the electric charge distribution. The two kinds of data turn out to be closely linked, though not simply proportional.

In 1972 Gertrude Scharff Goldhaber became only the third woman physicist elected to the National Academy of Sciences. Inside and outside the Academy she was a powerful force for the encouragement of young women (as well as men) to pursue science, working to develop science education and enhance the position of women in science. At Brookhaven, she founded the Brookhaven Lecture Series for scientists to present their work to a general audience and helped launch Brookhaven Women in Science. In 1985 she was invited to Munich for the Jubilee of her doctorate, an occasion that would have seemed inconceivable when she left fifty years earlier.

In 1977 Gertrude Goldhaber was compelled to

retire from Brookhaven under rules that would not apply today. She continued her research as adjunct professor at Cornell and then Johns Hopkins until 1985, when she became a research collaborator at Brookhaven, a position she held until she became housebound with a never-diagnosed syndrome in 1990. Even in that late period she maintained an immense enthusiasm for life, and enjoyed meeting and talking with visitors. She died in Patchogue, New York, in 1998, at the age of eighty-six.

Bibliography: For information on Goldhaber's life, see Peter Bond and Ernest Henley, "Gertrude Scharff Goldhaber," in National Academy of Sciences, *Biographical Memoirs* 77 (1999), pp. 108–21; and Elizabeth Pennisi, "Distinguished Physicists Manifest Lifelong Commitment to Succeed," *Scientist* 4, no. 7 (November 26, 1990), p. 7. Some of Goldhaber's significant publications include "Spontaneous Emission of Neutrons from Uranium," *Physical Review* 70, no. 229 (1946), written with George S. Klaiber; "Identification of Beta Rays with Atomic Electrons," *Physical Review* 73, no. 1472 (1948), written with Maurice Goldhaber; and "The Variable Moment of Inertia (VMI) Model and Theories of Nuclear Collective Motion," *Annual Review of Nuclear Science* 26, no. 239 (1976), written with Carl Dover and Alan Goodman. On anti-nepotism rules at the University of Illinois, see Marianne A. Ferber and Jane W. Loeb, eds., *Academic Couples: Problems and Promises* (1997). The authors profited greatly from the personal recollections of Goldhaber's husband, Maurice, and son Michael. An obituary appeared in the *New York Times* on February 6, 1998.

PETER BOND AND
ALFRED SCHARFF GOLDHABER

GOMEZ, Marsha. December 24, 1951–September 29, 1998. Sculptor, potter, activist.

Marsha Anne Gomez was born in Baton Rouge, Louisiana, the eldest of five children of Anna Lula Bueche and Walter Anthony Gomez Jr. Her mother, who was of Cajun and Choctaw ancestry, managed storage facilities and was a homemaker. Her father, whose family originally came from the Canary Islands, owned his own construction business after working in construction for many years. He inspired his daughter's activism when he squared off with Dow Chemicals in 1959 for dumping toxic chemicals in the Achafalaya Basin. From September 1969 to May 1971, Marsha went to Nicholls State College in Thibodaux, Louisiana, where she received an associate degree in special education with an art education minor. She later attended the University of Arkansas at Fayetteville from 1979 to 1981, where she received a BA in arts education. She was also a doctoral candidate at the American Institute of Holistic Theology.

In 1981 Gomez moved to Austin, Texas, where she devoted her time to her pottery and sculpture, to teaching, and to social-change activism. In her early years in Austin she taught traditional pottery at the Dougherty Arts Center and in the Artist-in-Education program sponsored by the Texas Commission on the Arts and the city of Austin. Many one-woman shows and collective exhibits featuring her artwork were held from 1980 onward, and she received numerous prizes, including the La Pena Rebozo Award for achievement in the Latino Arts Community and the Bannerman Fellowship in 1997.

In 1983 Gomez founded the Indigenous Women's Network together with Janet McCloud, Mililani Trask, Aggie Williams, Nilak Butler, and Winona LaDuke. The network, which grew to include indigenous women from many nations, achieved NGO status and United Nations accreditation. Gomez and other members of the network made the indigenous presence felt at many international conferences, including the UN Decade for Women conferences in Nairobi and Beijing as well as the UN Conference on the Environment in Rio de Janeiro in 1992.

In 1983 Gomez, ever active in the arts community, also founded Artistas Indigenas, an arts organization of indigenous women headquartered in Austin. In 1986 she began working for Genevieve Vaughan in an organization that later became the Foundation for a Compassionate Society. In 1988 she became the director of the foundation's retreat center, Alma de Mujer Center for Social Change. Serving groups every weekend, Alma de Mujer catered particularly to women of color, though a wide variety of groups were welcomed. Marsha was administrator of the facility and inspired the groups that came. Caring for the twenty-two acres of land and the buildings that housed some thirty people, she found time to create an organic garden that fed many of the groups while continuing her sculpture and pottery in a studio she created in one of the outbuildings. In 1994 Vaughan donated Alma de Mujer to the Indigenous Women's Network, and Gomez took full responsibility as its director.

Involved in the many struggles of indigenous peoples through her own path in reclaiming her Choctaw heritage, Marsha Gomez brought global information to the local community, connecting struggles in Big Mountain and Mexico, the Rio Grande Valley, Canada, Central America, and the Caribbean. Always rising to what she called her sweet responsibility, Marsha Gomez was a tireless networker and supporter of her sisters and brothers in struggle who used every occasion to disseminate information and inspire others through the force of her convictions.

In 1987 Genevieve Vaughan commissioned Gomez to create a life-size sculpture to be placed outside the Nuclear Test Site located on Shoshone land at Mercury, Nevada. Installed in a ceremony following the Mother's Day action in 1988, the Madre del Mundo sculpture was soon confiscated by the Bureau of Land Management, which released it only after a legal tug-of-war. Gomez made a number of full-size reproductions of the sculpture, which became an emblem of ecofeminism; the reproductions are now located at strategic points around the country. In 1993 Gomez created a statue of the Egyptian goddess Sekhmet to place in the goddess temple established by Vaughan in Cactus Springs, Nevada. A replica of the sculpture of Madre del Mundo can be seen there as well.

Marsha Gomez was a leader in women's spirituality, giving a spiritual cast of respect for the Creator, Mother Earth, and all her creatures to everything she did. Her activism was an outgrowth of her spiritual convictions, and her openness to be a bridge that crossed all cultural divides made her a popular and potent multicultural activist. Eloquent and outspoken, Gomez was a formidable opponent of injustice. She was an activist in the lesbian community as well, and her sculpture demonstrates her poetic woman-centered approach.

Marsha Gomez was a single mother of a son, Mekaya Gomez, born February 23, 1974. In his early twenties Mekaya began to show signs of schizophrenia. As his condition deteriorated and he became more violent, she continued to seek help from state agencies and private facilities, but little was forthcoming. In and out of jail for various minor offenses, Mekaya was released from jail in 1998 and declared sane by the state-appointed psychiatrist. Two weeks later, on September 29, 1998, he murdered his mother. Tried and found guilty of murder in 1999, Mekaya Gomez died of uncertain causes in prison in 2002.

Marsha Gomez's funeral, held at Alma de Mujer, was a tribute to her powerful presence in the community. People came from Mexico, Hawaii, and Canada as well as from across the United States to pay tribute to her. In her forty-six years she had been the heart of an amazing multicultural community of artists, activists, and people who love the earth.

Bibliography: Material by and about Marsha Gomez, including résumés, lists of exhibitions and awards, personal statements, and clippings, can be found at the La Pena arts organization, Austin, Texas. Writings by Gomez include "Woman of the Earth: Art and Activism on Sacred Land," *La Voz de Experanza* 11, no. 9 (November 1998), pp. 5–6; and "Traditional Plants and Herbs," *Indigenous Woman* 2, no. 6 (1999), pp. 44–46. Local coverage of her son's arrest and subsequent death can be found in the *Austin American-Statesman* on October 1, 1998, and January 15, 2002. Tributes to Gomez include Cherrie Moraga, "Tribute to Marsha Gomez: HOMAGE," *Indigenous Woman* 2, no. 6 (1999), pp. 3–4; "In Memoriam," *Arriba Art and Business News*, October 9–22, 1998, pp. 1, 8; and "Marsha Gomez," *La Pena Newsletter*, November-December, 1998, pp. 2–3. Bridget Gomez Day, Lee Ann LaBar, Cynthia Perez, and Liliana Wilson contributed information for this article, which also drew on the author's association with Gomez.

GENEVIEVE VAUGHAN

GOODRICH, Frances. December 21, 1890–January 29, 1984. Actress, playwright, screenwriter.

One of the most important women in the history of motion pictures, screenwriter Frances Goodrich was born in Belleville, New Jersey, and raised in nearby Nutley. She grew up in an upper-middle-class family, the second daughter of five children of Henry Wickes Goodrich, a Brooklyn-born attorney whose real love was directing amateur plays, and Madeleine Christy Lloyd, an avid reader who often spoke with pride of her Huguenot roots. One uncle, Henry Demarest Lloyd, wrote a muckraking exposé of Standard Oil in 1894; another, David Demarest Lloyd, was an editor of the *New York Tribune* and a successful playwright. The family spent summers in Little Compton, Rhode Island.

After graduating from Passaic Collegiate School in 1908, Frances went to Vassar, where she directed plays. She graduated in 1912, later proudly recalling that she wore a red dress while everyone else was in white, and the following year she briefly attended the New York School of Social Service. She soon embarked on an acting career, starting in the Players Club, one of her father's favorite haunts, on Manhattan's Gramercy Park, and then in stock theater in Northampton, Massachusetts. In 1917 she met and married charismatic actor Robert Ames, but the marriage ended after six years because of career conflicts and Ames's drinking problem. Goodrich never had children.

In these years the always fashionably well put together Goodrich had an active social life chronicled and photographed in the newspapers. She also appeared in many Broadway plays, including *Come Out of the Kitchen* (1916) and *Daddy Long Legs* (1918), and in the early 1920s toured in *Fashions for Men* and *Chains,* sharing an apartment with its star, HELEN GAHAGAN. While performing in *Chains* in Chicago, Goodrich met a young vaudeville actor named Albert Hackett. He did not make a good impression.

In 1925 Goodrich began a relationship with the highly successful Dutch-born author Hendrik Van Loon. Though married, he fell immediately in love with Goodrich and convinced her to marry him after a two-year courtship. Committed to a "companionate marriage," the two writers maintained separate residences in Manhattan, which was the cause of much speculation. They divorced in 1929 but remained lifelong friends. Some have speculated that the subsequent success of Goodrich's writing partnership and marriage to Albert Hackett stemmed from this experiment: the couple wrote separately.

By 1927 Goodrich had written a play called *Such a Lady* but was having some trouble with it. She asked Hackett, whom she knew was also a struggling playwright, for help. The two started a collaboration that was to prove highly successful both on and off the stage. Together they wrote the play *Western Union, Please,* followed by *Up Pops the Devil* for Broadway in 1930. Once the financial success of that play was a certainty, the couple married, on February 7, 1931. She was forty, nine years his senior.

Albert Hackett was called to California to act as dialogue director for the film version, and Goodrich accompanied him. She felt ambivalent about Hollywood and her lack of an obvious role there, and the couple returned to New York City for the mounting of their next play, *Bridal Wise.* In 1932, Goodrich and Hackett received offers from MGM to work as studio scriptwriters, and they moved to Hollywood, where they remained for the next several decades (with interludes in New York).

Though initially skeptical about the movie business, Goodrich and Hackett eventually became major players, both professionally and socially, in what is now regarded as Hollywood's Golden Age. The writing team's breakout success was *The Thin Man* in 1934, adapted from the detective fiction of their friend Dashiell Hammett. Although they received only $10,000 for this huge commercial and critical hit, soon Goodrich and Hackett were among the most sought after and highly paid writers in the movie business, earning $2,500 a week even in the Depression years.

Goodrich and Hackett often fought over the scripts (she did the screaming, she said), but their first drafts were always written separately and then they would collaborate, with each acting out various roles. In addition to the Nick and Nora films, the team created and wrote two of the most famous JEANNETTE MCDONALD/Nelson Eddy musicals, *Naughty Marietta* (1935) and *Rose Marie* (1936); the adaptation of Eugene O'Neill's only comedy, *Ah, Wilderness!* (1935); *Easter Parade* (1948); *Father of the Bride* (1950) and its sequel; and, in 1954, *Seven Brides for Seven Brothers,* which they co-wrote with screenwriter Dorothy Kingsley. They also wrote *Lady in the Dark* (1944), one of the first films to deal with psychoanalysis; *The Virginian* (1946); *A Certain Smile* (1958); and *Five Finger Exercise* (1962), their last movie. Their best-known collaboration is *It's a Wonderful Life,* the Frank Capra Christmas classic from 1946.

Frances Goodrich proved a successful match for ruthless self-made Hollywood moguls. She actively organized and was the secretary for the Screenwriters Guild in the 1930s, and later bucked questions from the House Committee on Un-American Activities about the possible Communist connections and background of her colleagues. She was especially forceful in dealing with producers and cutting good deals, and often the only woman in story conferences. "Perhaps there isn't a 'woman's angle,'" she once said, declaring, "I'll fight for what the gal will or will not do, and I can be completely unfeminine yelling about it" (*The Real Nick and Nora,* pp. 40–41). Stunning, if not traditionally pretty, Goodrich always dressed to suit her looks, wearing beautifully tailored suits, stylish heels, and tasteful jewelry. Her refined demeanor may have been a disarming armor when she clashed with studio and production heads, generally successfully.

Hackett and Goodrich's collaborations were not limited to Hollywood screenplays. After the publication of Anne Frank's best-selling diary in 1952, they spent the next several years adapting the book for Broadway. Their play *The Diary of Anne Frank* debuted in 1955 and won the Pulitzer Prize; they also wrote the script for the 1959 film, which was nominated for an Academy Award. Though they received numerous Writers Guild Awards and Oscar nominations, the Goodrich/Hackett team never won an Oscar. Returning permanently to the East Coast in 1962, the couple settled into an apartment at 888 Central Park West, the scene of many convivial social gatherings. Their lifelong, loving collaboration, which lasted for more than fifty years, was ended only by Frances Goodrich's death from lung cancer at home at the age of ninety-three.

Bibliography: David Goodrich, *The Real Nick and Nora* (2001), provides a nephew's portrait of Frances Goodrich and Albert Hackett drawing on privately held personal papers. The Archives Division of the State Historical Society of Wisconsin holds additional archival material, and the Billy Rose Theatre Collection of the New York Public Library for the Performing Arts at Lincoln Center has the most complete clippings collection. Private letters between Goodrich and van Loon are at the Krock Library at Cornell University. An interview with Frances Goodrich by Ronald Bowers, "Frances Goodrich & Albert Hackett," appeared in the October 1977 *Films in Review,* pp. 463–66. Mark Rowland's interview with Goodrich and Hackett is in Patrick McGilligan, *Backstory: Interviews with Screenwriters of Hollywood's Golden Age* (1986). The Oral History Research Office at Columbia University holds Barbara Hogensen, "Reminiscences of Albert and Frances Hackett" (1983). David Woods, "Interview with Frances Goodrich and Albert Hackett," March 9, 1976, is in Dartmouth College Library's Special Collections. Marsha McCreadie, *The Women Who Write the Movies* (1994), discusses Frances Goodrich, based in part on an interview with Albert Hackett conducted shortly before his death in

1995. Other books with important references to Goodrich are Neil Gabler, *An Empire of Their Own: How the Jews Invented Hollywood* (1989); and Nancy Lynn Schwartz, *The Hollywood Writers' Wars* (1982). Books by or about Goodrich's friends include Sheila Graham, *The Garden of Allah* (1970); S. J. Perelman, *Westward Ha! Or Around the World in Eighty Clichés* (1947); and Prudence Crowther, ed., *Don't Tread on Me: The Selected Letters of S. J. Perelman* (1987). See also Marion Meade, *Dorothy Parker: What Fresh Hell Is This* (1988); Henry Ephron, *We Thought We Could Do Anything* (1977); Gloria Stuart, *I Just Kept Hoping* (1999); and Diane Johnson, *Hammett: A Life* (1983). An obituary appeared in the *New York Times* on January 31, 1984.

MARSHA MCCREADIE

GORDON, Ruth. October 30, 1896–August 28, 1985. Actress, writer.

Ruth Gordon, an actress remembered by generations of audiences for her vivid portrayals on stage, in films, and on television, was also a successful playwright and screenwriter, and the author of one novel and three autobiographies. She was born Ruth Gordon Jones in the Wollaston section of Quincy, Massachusetts. Her father, Clinton Jones, was a factory foreman who had gone to sea at eight. Her mother, Annie Ziegler Jones, had been a secretary but was a housewife when Ruth and her half sister Clare (her father's daughter by an earlier marriage) were growing up.

In 1914, Ruth graduated from Quincy High School, where she had taken a college preparatory course. Her father wanted her to be a physical education teacher, but ever since she had seen Hazel Dawn in *The Pink Lady* at Boston's Colonial Theater in 1913, she was determined to be an actress. He was won over and gave her four hundred dollars (his life's savings) for tuition at a New York City drama school, plus fifty dollars to sustain her until she was employed.

Assuming the stage name Ruth Gordon, she entered the American Academy of Dramatic Arts in October of 1914. At the end of the first term, she was told that she showed no promise as an actress and need not return. Her significant education was to be in the theater itself. She found a few roles as a movie extra in New York, but her first real break came in 1915 when she was cast as Nibs, one of the Lost Boys, in a revival of *Peter Pan.* During its New York run, she wrote to thank theater critic Alexander Woollcott for singling her out in his review. He became a close friend and introduced her to a wide circle of celebrities, including Somerset Maugham, Harpo Marx, ALICE DUER MILLER, DOROTHY PARKER, and DOROTHY and LILLIAN GISH. Throughout her life Gordon was an inveterate letter writer. Among her many correspondents were Thornton Wilder, HELEN HAYES, Noël Coward, and Charles Laughton.

For the decade after *Peter Pan,* she toured with road companies, mainly in the Midwest, while she continued to learn her craft. In 1918, when she was playing the role of the Babytalk Lady in Booth Tarkington's *Seventeen,* she met Gregory Kelly, a fellow actor, whom she married the following year. With Kelly's support, in 1920 she underwent painful surgery to have her bowlegs straightened. From 1922 until his death from a heart attack at age thirty-six in 1927, Gordon and her husband operated the Gregory Kelly Stock Company in Indianapolis.

By 1927 Gordon had already met Jed Harris, famous Broadway producer-director. They were lovers and theater collaborators off and on for the next decade. In October 1929, she gave birth in Paris to Jones Harris (on his birth certificate he was Jones Kelly). His very existence was kept out of the newspapers to protect Gordon's career, and he was raised and educated without publicity here and abroad. Harris and Gordon never married.

As a stage actress she reached her peak in the 1930s, critically well received in a dozen plays in New York during that period. Her range was remarkable. Thought by many to be a comedian, she surprised critics in 1934 by playing one of the accusing women in *They Shall Not Die,* a polemical play about the controversial Scottsboro case. Soon she was back to comedy, playing Mrs. Pinchwife in Wycherley's *The Country Wife.* In 1936 she had the opportunity to repeat the role in London, where, under director Tyrone Guthrie, she was the first American actress to play at the Old Vic. In between the London and New York productions of *The Country Wife,* Gordon played Mattie Silver in an adaptation of EDITH WHARTON's *Ethan Frome.* Continuing to show her versatility, in 1937 Gordon played Nora in Ibsen's *A Doll's House* in an adaptation by Thornton Wilder, whom Gordon considered her guide and mentor.

The turning point in Ruth Gordon's life came in 1941, when she met Garson Kanin, who was to be her husband and writing collaborator for the rest of her life. They were married in 1942; she was sixteen years older than he. Shortly after her marriage, she began her career as a playwright, not that she gave up acting for writing. She wrote a glamorous part for herself in her first play, *Over Twenty-One* (1944), a comedy that ran for 221 performances, and an equally glamorous one in *The Leading Lady* (1948), a melodrama about theater politics that had only eight performances. In between she wrote what is now considered her best play, *Years Ago* (1946).

In the late 1940s, Gordon and Kanin began writing screenplays. They were nominated for an Academy Award for *A Double Life* (1947) and *Adam's Rib* (1949), the first of the Katharine Hepburn–Spencer Tracy romantic comedies. Gordon found herself back on the stage in 1954 when Thornton Wilder wrote the role of Dolly Levi in *The Matchmaker* for her. Not since *The Country Wife* had she had a role so well suited to her comic abilities. Unfortunately, nothing on stage in the 1960s or 1970s rivaled her success in *The Matchmaker.* Even her role in Shaw's *Mrs. Warren's Profession* (1976) received mixed reviews.

Then Hollywood and television and the lecture circuit gave her career a special spin. In her seventies and into her eighties she created memorable characters in films. In 1965 she was nominated for an Academy Award for her role in *Inside Daisy Clover.* In 1968 she won an Academy Award as Best Supporting Actress in *Rosemary's Baby.* Other memorable roles were in *Where's Poppa?* (1970) and *Harold and Maude* (1971), which was not a success at first but later became a cult film. She also appeared on a number of television series and sitcoms, and won an Emmy in 1979 for a role in a *Taxi* episode.

She enjoyed sitcoms, but she enjoyed talk shows even more. During the last twenty years of her life she talked with Phil Donahue, Johnny Carson, and Dick Cavett, among others. When Senator Claude Pepper invited her in 1977 to appear before his Select Committee on Aging, the committee was just another audience for her. In her eighties she appeared at Town Hall in New York and on college campuses across the country, an afternoon or evening of just Ruth Gordon standing alone at a microphone and talking.

Ruth Gordon died of a stroke at age eighty-eight on August 28, 1985, at her summer home in Edgartown, Massachusetts. She who had spoken so eloquently at Thornton Wilder's memorial service in 1976 had requested that there be no funeral. Her epitaph might have been a phrase she used often when she was through with a subject and wanted to move on: "Draw the veil."

Bibliography: The major repository of Ruth Gordon materials is the Manuscript Division of the Library of Congress, Washington, D.C. The collection's six thousand items include general correspondence (1924–67) concerning her career, scripts and screenplays, financial papers, and biographical material. Correspondents include Edna Ferber, Alec Guinness, Vivien Leigh, Anita Loos, and Robert Morse. Her letters to Alexander Woollcott are in the Harvard Theatre Collection, Pusey Library, Harvard University. A good biographical source is Linda Tolman's entry in Alice M. Robinson, Vera Mowry Roberts, and Milly S. Barranger, eds., *Notable Women in the American Theatre: A Biographical Dictionary* (1989). Gordon's three autobiographies—*Myself among Others* (1971), *My Side: An Autobiography of Ruth Gordon* (1976), and *Ruth Gordon: An Open Book* (1980)—are rich if repetitious. Her play *Years Ago* is strictly autobiographical; *Over Twenty-One* has autobiographical elements, as does her novel *Shady Lady* (1981). See also Martin Gottfried, *Jed Harris: The Curse of Genius* (1984); and Kathleen McKenna Groutt, "A Metahealth Analysis of the Lives of Gwendolyn Brooks, Dorothy Day, Ruth Gordon, Anaïs Nin, and Georgia O'Keeffe" (PhD dissertation, University of Maryland, 1986). Telling comments on her long career as a stage actress are included in Alexander Woollcott, *Enchanted Aisles* (1924); Stark Young, *Immortal Shadows* (1948); and Brooks Atkinson, *Broadway* (1970). Judith Trojan provides an overview of her film career in the *Wilson Library Bulletin,* February 1986, pp. 50–51. Exemplary popular appreciations of Gordon's long career are Susan Lydon, "The Faa-bu-lous Long Run of Gordon and Kanin," *New York Times Magazine,* October 5, 1969, pp. 64–65+; and Michael Kernan, "The Gusto That Was Ruth Gordon," *Washington Post,* August 29, 1985. An obituary appeared in the *New York Times* on August 28, 1985. Mel Gussow's appreciation in that newspaper on September 8, 1985, is by far the most inclusive of the many tributes she received.

DORIS ABRAMSON

GRAHAM, Bette Clair McMurray Nesmith. March 23, 1924–May 12, 1980. Inventor, entrepreneur, philanthropist.

Bette Clair McMurray was born in Dallas and raised in San Antonio, Texas, the elder of two daughters of Christine Duval, who owned a knitting shop, and Jesse McMurray, who owned an auto parts business. From an early age, she developed a love of art and the inquisitive, independent temperament that would one day lead her to become an innovative entrepreneur. Her mother, an accomplished artist, taught the young girl to paint and fortified her daughter's talent by paying for art lessons throughout her youth.

By the time she reached high school, McMurray's artistic dreams vied with girlhood fantasies of marriage and family. As World War II loomed, the seventeen-year-old McMurray dropped out of Alamo Heights School in San Antonio to marry her childhood sweetheart, Warren Nesmith, before he headed off to war. Ten months later, in 1942, her husband overseas, she gave birth to her only child, Michael (who became a member of the popular 1960s music group the Monkees and appeared on the television show of the same name).

Like so many hasty wartime marriages, Nesmith's ended in 1946 shortly after her husband returned home. A single mother with no source of income and in desperate need of a job, Nesmith was forced to swap her art classes for business school training in shorthand and typing. She relocated to Dallas in search of more lucrative opportunities and landed a secretarial position at Texas Bank & Trust in 1951.

Ironically, her art training would provide the impetus to turn Nesmith from working mother into entrepreneur. When Nesmith was promoted to executive secretary, her manual typewriter was replaced with one of the newly available electric models. Ever the perfectionist, she was frustrated to find she made more errors on the new machine than she had on her old one. Worse, electric typewriters used carbon ribbons, whose ink smeared when an error was erased. While other secretaries retyped their letters until they were flawless, Nesmith looked for a faster cover-up solution.

Recalling that artists paint over their mistakes, in 1954 Nesmith transformed her kitchen into a laboratory, experimenting with a water-based white tempura paint to cover typographical errors. Before long, other secretaries started borrowing her paint. To improve the product, she found a formula for tempura paint at a local library and tapped the expertise of a high school chemistry teacher; an employee at a paint store showed Nesmith how to mix and grind paint. Her kitchen would continue to serve as her workshop, where she used an electric mixer to blend paint and other chemicals. By 1956, demand for her correction fluid inspired her to start Mistake Out, a company named for the product.

While Nesmith spent her spare time seeking office supply dealers, her son and his friends helped bottle and distribute the product. In the company's early years, Nesmith juggled her day job with filling orders at night, and used her $300 monthly bank salary to buy necessary supplies. Conscious of a bias against women in business, she camouflaged her sex by signing company correspondence "B. Nesmith." Still, when she approached IBM about marketing Mistake Out, they declined.

Nesmith was hesitant to leave the stability and weekly paycheck of her bank job to focus on her new product, but the decision was made for her in 1958 when she was fired for accidentally typing her company's name on one of her boss's letters. Concentrating on Mistake Out full-time, Nesmith processed four hundred orders per month from word-of-mouth referrals and ads placed in office supply magazines. After *The Office* magazine's October issue listed Mistake Out as one of its top product recommendations, more than five hundred secretaries across the United States responded. Other trade magazines, such as *The Secretary,* also began featuring the product. General Electric was her earliest big customer.

Mistake Out started the 1960s operating at a small loss, with Nesmith's home doubling as company headquarters. As the product became an indispensable tool of the secretarial trade, Nesmith relocated production and shipping from her kitchen to a 10×26-foot portable metal structure in her backyard, where packaging, shipping, and production were centered.

With her son grown and her business progressing, in 1962 Nesmith married Robert Graham, who soon joined the company. The pair traveled throughout the southern and western United States peddling the correction fluid. Three years later, the firm was selling forty thousand bottles of Mistake Out a week and moved from Graham's backyard to its own building. In 1967, sales topped one million dollars; a decade later they would reach $38 million. Big changes came in 1968: Graham incorporated the company under the new name Liquid Paper, opened the company's first fully automated plant, and let her husband take over as president while she served as chair of the board.

From the start, Graham ran her company with a unique combination of spirituality, egalitarianism, and pragmatism. Raised a Methodist, Graham converted to Christian Science in 1942 and this faith inspired the development of her corporate "Statement of Policy." Part code of ethics, part business philosophy, it covered everything from her belief in a "Supreme Being" to a focus on decentralized decision making and an emphasis on product quality over profit motive. She also believed that women could bring a more nurturing and humanistic quality to the male world of business, and did so herself by including a greenbelt with a fish pond, an employee library, and a childcare center in her new company headquarters in 1975.

With her marriage ending in a messy divorce, Graham formally retired in 1975, leaving her husband to run the firm. She remained the majority shareholder, however. Meanwhile, at Liquid Paper, Robert eliminated Graham's cherished Statement of Policy and also changed the product's formula in an effort to deprive Graham of her royalties. Shrewd business sense and majority stockholder control enabled Graham to have the last laugh: in 1979, she negotiated the sale of Liquid Paper to Gillette for $47.5 million and a guarantee to restore the old formula and her royalties through the year 2000.

A self-proclaimed feminist, Graham spent the last years of her life helping other women achieve as she had. She created two foundations: the Bette Clair McMurray Foundation (1976) provided career guidance, scholarships, and financial education to mature women, and the Gihon Foundation (1978) fostered women's entrepreneurship. To encourage and celebrate women's artistic endeavors, she also established the Gihon's collection of "Works by Women," including original art by MARY CASSATT, GEORGIA O'KEEFE, LOUISE NEVELSON, and GRANDMA MOSES. Bette Nesmith Graham died in Dallas in 1980 at the age of fifty-six.

Bibliography: The greatest breadth of material on Bette Nesmith Graham is found at the Mary Evelyn Blagg-Huey Library of Texas Woman's University, in Denton; notably, the Texas Women's Biofile in the Woman's Collection contains an entry for Nesmith. The Martha Stuart Papers at the Schlesinger Library, Radcliffe Institute for Advanced Study, Harvard University, contain general information about women business owners as well as the Liquid Paper "Statement of Policy." Other helpful resources include Nancy Goebel, "The Unlimited Potential of Bette Graham," *Texas Woman* 1, no. 6 (July 1979), pp. 46–49; Vivian Castleberry, "Bette Graham: Ethics, People Are Liquid Assets in Her Business Philosophy," *Dallas Times Herald*, May 17, 1977; Nancy Baker Jones, "Bette Clair McMurray Graham," *The New Handbook of Texas*, vol. 3 (Texas State Historical Association, 1996), p. 270; Jean Flynn, *Texas Women Who Dared to Be First* (1999), pp. 67–74; Mary Beth Rogers, Sherry A. Smith, and Janelle D. Scott, *We Can Fly: Stories of Katherine Stinson and Other Gutsy Texas Women* (1983); and Jeannette Oppedisano, *Historical Encyclopedia of American Women Entrepreneurs: 1776 to Present* (2000), pp. 117–19. General overviews of women and entrepreneurship in the postwar period include Angel Kwolek-Folland, *Incorporating Women: A History of Women and Business in the United States* (1998); and Debra Michals, "Beyond 'Pin Money': The Rise of Women's Small Business Ownership, 1945–1980" (PhD dissertation, New York University, 2002). An obituary appeared in the *Dallas Morning News* on May 14, 1980.

DEBRA MICHALS

GRAHAM, Martha. May 11, 1894–April 1, 1991. Dancer, choreographer.

Martha Graham, a groundbreaking artist of the twentieth century, conceived of the human body as an instrument of dramatic expression and thrust the art of dance into a modern world. In her lifetime she choreographed more than 180 dances, creating a language of movement based upon exhalation and inhalation of breath. The dances she created made visible the external emotions existing beneath the surface of conventional culture.

Born in Allegheny, Pennsylvania, Martha Graham was the first of three daughters of Jane Beers and George Greenfield Graham; a son William died when he was almost two. Martha was a sixth-generation American of Scotch-Irish descent (her mother could trace her ancestors back to the *Mayflower*), and the family enjoyed a degree of social and economic privilege. Her father was a graduate of the College of Physicians and Surgeons in Baltimore and a specialist in nervous disorders. George Graham's influence on the young Martha was profound. "Movement never lies," he once told her.

In 1908 the family moved west to Santa Barbara, where Graham completed her high school education in 1913. She then entered the Cumnock School of Expression in Los Angeles to study drama and speech. Graduating in 1916, she began to study dance seriously at the age of twenty-two, enrolling at the Denishawn School in Los Angeles. Denishawn was the joint venture of RUTH ST. DENIS and Ted Shawn, and the first established dance academy in the United States. After an inauspicious beginning, Graham was selected by Shawn to appear with him in the popular Denishawn ballet *Xochitl*. Performing the role of the passionate Aztec maiden quickly established her reputation as a magnetic performer.

In 1923, dissatisfied with her opportunities at Denishawn, Graham left to take a job with the Greenwich Village Follies at the Winter Garden Theater in New York City, and began to explore her potential as an independent artist. She experimented with new ways of moving in classes she taught at the Eastman School of Music in Rochester, New York, and on April 18, 1926, she gave her first concert at the 48th Street Theater in New York City, appearing with three of her students.

Dances on this first program had names like *Claire de Lune, Désir, Danse Languide,* and *Maid with the Flaxen Hair,* and almost certainly were influenced by the flowing and decorative style of her teacher, Ruth St. Denis. Yet within a few years, titles such as *Revolt* (1927), *Immigrant: Steerage, Strike* (1928), and *Poems of 1917* (1928) revealed Graham's commitment to her contemporary world. *Heretic* (1929) presented what critic Margaret Lloyd referred to as "the eternal struggle of the individual with something new to offer, coming up against the blank wall of conservatism in any field" (Lloyd, p. 51), a theme that was repeated often throughout Graham's long and prolific career. As an artist, and particularly as a woman artist, she was a rebel in conventional society. The movement vocabulary she created for *Heretic* cast the body as an instrument of force, a maelstrom of power and mass. The essential aspects of Graham technique, including the centrality of breath, the principles of contraction and release, exhalation and inhalation, compression and explosion of energy, were established.

Graham technique, now a standard, codified method of training dancers, developed from the movement vocabulary she created for each new work. Beginning with a series of exercises on the floor, the dancer refines and strengthens the central core of the body. The technique emphasizes the torso, in contrast to classical ballet's articulation of the limbs.

From 1929 to 1938, Martha Graham worked with an all-female company, crafting her approach to choreography under the demanding gaze of her mentor and lover, the composer Louis Horst. The classic works from this period demonstrate Graham's ever-widening command of her materials. The 1930 solo *Lamentation* explored grief as essence, not representation, and *Primitive Mysteries* (1931) was inspired by the meeting of Indian and Catholic traditions in the American Southwest.

Celebration (1934), an abstract dance for eleven women, to a score by Horst, was influenced by 1930s modernist experiments in architecture. *Frontier* (1935), also to a score by Horst, is a portrait of the American frontier woman. With set design by Isamu Noguchi, the dance marked the beginning of Graham's long and extraordinarily fertile artistic collaboration with the Japanese American sculptor.

The looming of fascism in Europe inspired a number of Graham's dances during the 1930s. The solos *Imperial Gesture* (1935) and *Deep Song* (1937) were made in response to the Spanish civil war, while the large group work *Chronicle* (1936) reflected Graham's fears for the world. Invited to perform in the 1936 Berlin Olympics, she refused because she knew that Jewish members of the concert group would not be welcome in Germany. As she had established through her 1929 work *Heretic,* Graham continued to stand for the rights of the individual.

During these years Graham spent summers at Bennington's Summer School of Dance, where leading modern dancers of the time, including DORIS HUMPHREY, Charles Weidman, and HANYA HOLM, gathered to teach and choreograph under the administration of dance educator MARTHA HILL. Here, on the eve of World War II, Graham premiered *American Document* (1938). The dance revealed her new interest in theatricality, integrating spoken and historical texts with representations of American ethnic and racial diversity, in order to ask the critical question, What is an American? It also revealed Graham's new interest in the male protagonist, signaled by the arrival of Erick Hawkins, later her husband, into the company. Merce Cunningham joined the following year.

Between 1938 and 1944 Martha Graham composed a number of works exploring relationships between women and men and the conflicts and contradictions faced by women artists. *Letter to the World* (1940) drew its inspiration from the poetry of EMILY DICKINSON and her experiences as an artist in a conventional Victorian world, and *Deaths and Entrances* (1943) grew from Graham's fascination with the three Brontë sisters. Yet around the same time she also made *Appalachian Spring* (1944), an ode to the spirit and strength of pioneering women and their families.

Graham's artistic life and her personal life were deeply intertwined. Her relationship with Erick Hawkins, ten years her junior, a classics major at Harvard College and a dancer trained in classical ballet, had a profound effect on the work she now created. Issues of sexuality and identity became central to many of the dance dramas she composed during this period, and Hawkins's classical training began to influence the movement vocabulary. In her struggle with issues of personal and artistic identity, Graham turned to Jungian therapist Frances Wickes; this relationship was reflected in a new cycle of her choreography. *Dark Meadow* (1946) and *Errand into the Maze* (1947) explored the mythological journey into the self; *Cave of the Heart* (1946), based upon the Medea myth, and *Night Journey* (1947), inspired by Sophocles' Oedipus Rex, revealed murderous passions and erotic longings in the female protagonists.

Early on, Martha Graham had a reputation as a serious, uncompromising artist. Less well known was her flair for comedy, revealed in a number of works of the same period: *Satyric Festival Song* (1935), a dance inspired by American Indian Pueblo culture and the clowns who satirize and mock the sacred rituals; *Every Soul Is a Circus* (1940), not a literal circus but the circus of life, of ridiculous situations and behavior; and *Punch and the Judy* (1941), a look at the foibles of married life as embodied by the classic marionettes, in which Hawkins played a pompous and overbearing Punch and Graham his silly, fantasizing wife.

In 1948, Hawkins and Graham married, only to part shortly thereafter during an unsuccessful 1950 European tour. Graham was aging, it was increasingly difficult for her to perform her own phenomenal technique, and now she was alone. Problems with alcohol began. In 1954 Graham and Hawkins were officially divorced.

Despite personal difficulties, Graham continued to create work and to perform, composing two major solos for herself—*Judith* (1950), based upon the biblical heroine, and *The Triumph of Saint Joan* (1951). She found new male partners to replace Hawkins and created classics for the company, such as *Canticle for Innocent Comedians* (1952), *Ardent Song* (1954), and *Seraphic Dialogue* (1955). She made her first film, *A Dancer's World,* in 1957, and in 1958 completed her first evening-length ballet, *Clytemnestra.* Based on *The Oresteia,* the work explores themes of redemption and rebirth and is the culmination of Graham's Greek cycle, demonstrating the choreographer's mastery of total world theater through its synthesis of classical Eastern theater forms, such as Noh and Kabuki, and Western contemporary dance. She maintained her sense of humor: *Acrobats of God* (1960) took a sly look at the creative process of the artist, at Graham herself.

Graham now had an international audience. An extended tour of the Far East in 1955 had established her as a cultural ambassador for the United States, and the company danced to acclaim throughout Europe. Ironically, however, she was losing the battle with alcohol and her technical abilities were severely diminished. For a while, she continued to be the central figure in many dance dramas, splitting her protagonist into two aspects—an older heroine who observed most of the action, and the younger self who did most of the actual dancing. But critics deplored her continued presence on stage in works such as *Legend of Judith* (1962), *Cortege of Eagles* (1967), and *The Lady of the House of Sleep* (1968); they urged her to retire. In 1969, at the age of seventy-five, she gave her final performance, appearing as an elderly nun in *A Time of Snow* (1968).

Graham had always considered herself a dancer first, and for several years following her retirement as a performer she was disinterested in the company, in the act of choreographing, and in life. It is widely acknowledged that her own rebirth at this time was due to the relationship she began with Ronald Protas, a young photographer who first came to the studio in the early 1970s, and who eventually became associate artistic director of the Martha Graham Center. Graham began to choreograph again, creating new work for the company and nurturing and developing a new set of young dancers.

Acts of Light (1981) was hailed by *New York Times* critic Anna Kisselgoff as the beginning of a new era for Graham, a period of neo-classicism. The 1984 *Rite of Spring*, which she created at the age of ninety, received mixed reviews, though some considered it one of Graham's finest works. *Maple Leaf Rag* (1990), her last completed dance, lovingly commented on her relation to the choreographic muse and paid fond tribute both to Scott Joplin's music and to Graham's long association with Louis Horst. "Louis," she says at the beginning of the dance, "play me the Maple Leaf Rag."

During her lifetime, Martha Graham's exploration of theatrical boundaries led her to collaborate with many of this century's most important artists. Dancers who worked with Graham include Jane Dudley, Sophie Maslow, Anna Sokolow, Erick Hawkins, Merce Cunningham, Pearl Lang, Yuriko, Bertram Ross, Paul Taylor, and Glen Tetley, as well as guest artists Margot Fonteyn, Rudolf Nureyev, and Mikhail Baryshnikov. At the Neighborhood Playhouse, she taught expressive movement to actors, including BETTE DAVIS, Madonna, Liza Minnelli, Gregory Peck, Tony Randall, Eli Wallach, Anne Jackson, and Joanne Woodward. The list of modern composers who created musical scores for her includes such luminaries as Samuel Barber, Norman Dello Joio, Aaron Copland, Gian-Carlo Menotti, Wallingford Riegger, William Schuman, Robert Starer, and Carlos Surinach.

Martha Graham died on April 1, 1991, at the age of ninety-six. In her will she left everything she owned to Ron Protas. Protas had never had any real training in dance management, and over the years he had alienated a number of Graham's dancers and members of the board of the Martha Graham Center, the umbrella organization that governed the company and the school. The Center entered a period marked by conflict and financial crisis, including legal battles about the rights to use the Graham name and to perform the Graham repertory. In 2002 the Martha Graham Center, under new leadership, was assigned the rights to a significant number of Martha Graham's works, and the Company was reconstituted. The Center kept the Graham legacy vital and built upon it by performing repertory, developing new opportunities for artistic collaboration, and creating archival resources.

Bibliography: The Dance Collection at the New York Public Library for the Performing Arts at Lincoln Center provides the most substantial collection of archival materials relating to the life and work of Martha Graham, including photographs, programs, critical reviews, oral interviews with many of her dancers, video recordings of a number of the dances, and books and scholarly articles. Another major collection, with new documentation, is housed at the Library of Congress in Washington, D.C., and since the resolution of its legal difficulties, the Martha Graham Center has established Martha Graham Resources to identify and preserve its accumulated archives for use by the Center and by the public.

Martha Graham's *Blood Memory* (1991) is a personal account of the artist's career. See also *The Notebooks of Martha Graham* (1973), and Merle Armitage, *Martha Graham: The Early Years* (1937), a collection of Graham's early writings. Biographies of Martha Graham include Agnes de Mille, *Martha: The Life and Work of Martha Graham* (1991), which includes brief biographies of major dancers in her company, as well as a chronology of her work and a list of the honors and awards Graham achieved; Ernestine Stodelle, *Deep Song: The Dance Story of Martha Graham* (1984), which gives particular attention to major choreographic developments in Graham's career and provides in-depth descriptions of many of the dances; Don McDonagh, *Martha Graham: A Biography* (1973); and LeRoy Leatherman, *Martha Graham: Portrait of the Lady as an Artist* (1966). Information about the development of Graham technique can be found in Alice Helpern, *The Technique of Martha Graham* (Studies in Dance History, vol. 2, no. 2, 1991). Interviews with former Graham dancers appear in Marian Horosko, *Martha Graham: The Evolution of Her Dance Theory and Training 1926–1991* (1991), and Robert Tracy, *Goddess: Martha Graham's Dancers Remember* (1997).

A number of books feature major sections devoted to Graham, including Dorothy Bird, *Bird's Eye View: Dancing with Martha Graham and on Broadway* (1997); and Janet Mansfield Soares, *Louis Horst, Musician in a Dancer's World* (1992), which details Horst's influence on Graham. Significant chapters devoted to Martha Graham and her influence on American dance can also be found in Margaret Lloyd, *The Borzoi Book of Modern Dance* (1949); Marcia B. Siegel, *The Shapes of Change: Images of American Dance* (1979); and Deborah Jowitt, *Time and the Dancing Image* (1988). Ellen Graff, *Stepping Left: Dance and Politics in New York City, 1928–1942* (1997), and Mark Franko, *Dancing Modernism/Performing Politics* (1995), explore the influence of the political left on Graham's early work. A photographic essay by Barbara Morgan entitled *Martha Graham: Sixteen Dances in Photographs* (1941) provides visual documentation of her early dances, while Robert Tracy, *Spaces of the Mind: Isamu Noguchi's Dance Designs* (2000), documents the many collaborations between Graham and Noguchi. An obituary appeared in the *New York Times* on April 2, 1991.

ELLEN GRAFF

GRAHAM DU BOIS, Shirley. November 11, 1896–March 27, 1977. Composer, writer, Pan-Africanist.

Heralded as the most influential woman in Africa by the mid 1960s, Shirley Graham Du Bois was a composer, biographer, and playwright before she became a Pan-Africanist organizer and the celebrated widow of W. E. B. Du Bois. A passionate and brilliant woman, Graham Du Bois had a delicious sense of humor and a fiery temper. Lola Shirley Graham was born in Indianapolis, Indiana, the oldest of five children and only daughter of Etta Bell and David Andrew Graham, a prominent and controversial minister in the AME church. As Reverend Graham often dissented from church policies, he was frequently relocated, so Shirley's elementary school education was scattered among Indianapolis, Chicago, Detroit, New Orleans, and Nashville. When she was thirteen, W. E. B. Du Bois visited the family home, beginning their lifelong connection. Shirley attended several high schools and ultimately graduated from Lewis and Clark High School in Spokane, Washington, in June 1915.

Graham moved to Seattle, working odd jobs until she met and married Shadrach T. McCants in 1921. They had two sons: Robert (1923) and David (1925). McCants owned and operated a dry-cleaning establishment and later published a weekly newspaper. Very little is known about this relationship, and Graham changed her name to McCanns after her divorce in 1927. Wanting to pursue her studies and build a career, Graham left her children in the care of her parents, but she always provided for their financial support.

While her parents were serving as missionaries in Liberia, Graham traveled to Paris and studied at the Sorbonne. Here she was introduced to the West African music that would profoundly influence her work. Returning to the United States, Graham enrolled in Oberlin College's Conservatory of Music. Under commission from the Cleveland Opera, Graham composed and wrote the libretto for an opera, *Tom Tom,* which was a musical fusion of West African and European instruments and forms. It opened to critical acclaim at Cleveland Stadium in the summer of 1932. Meanwhile, Graham completed her studies at Oberlin, earning a bachelor's degree in 1934 and a master's in 1935.

Following a teaching stint at Tennessee Agricultural and Industrial State College in Nashville, Graham headed for Chicago to work in the Federal Theatre Project (FTP). Appointed supervisor of its race- and class-conscious "Negro Unit," she wrote the musical score for the popular production of *Swing Mikado,* but quit when the newly formed House Committee on Un-American Activities went after the FTP, eventually shutting it down. Admitted to the Yale Drama School with a Julius Rosenwald Fellowship in 1938, she stayed until her funding ran out, writing and producing two plays—*Dust to Earth* and *Elijah's Ravens.*

Plagued by poverty, and trying to support her sons, Graham was forced to abandon the momentum of her musical and theatrical career to find salaried work. She landed a job with the USO at Fort Huachuca, Arizona, but lost it in 1942 when she supported an uprising by black troops protesting their segregated treatment. By 1943 she was back in New York City working as a field secretary for the National Association for the Advancement of Colored People (NAACP). She was a superb organizer but stayed at her post only a year. She enrolled in a doctoral program at New York University and had completed all but her dissertation by 1945. Tragedy struck early in 1944 when her oldest son, Robert, became critically ill and died. Overwhelmed with grief, Graham believed that Robert's death was hastened, if not caused, by the racism that had prevented his timely admission to a hospital. He was twenty-one. In many ways Shirley Graham never recovered from this loss.

Graham next launched a highly successful career as a biographer. Between 1944 and 1955 she produced works on George Washington Carver, Paul Robeson, Frederick Douglass, Benjamin Banneker, PHILLIS WHEATLEY, POCAHONTAS, and Booker T. Washington. Her biography of Douglass won the prestigious Julian Messner Award for the Best Book Combating Intolerance in 1947. The money from this award allowed Graham to buy a home in St. Albans, Queens, and created her first sense of financial security.

Having rekindled her friendship with W. E. B. Du Bois, Graham became part of a circle of intellectuals, writers, and artists in and around the U.S. Communist Party, including Eslanda and Paul Robeson, Howard and Betty Fast, William L. and LOUISE THOMPSON PATTERSON, Dorothy and Alphaeus Hunton, and Fay and Herbert Aptheker, among many others. In the late 1940s Graham joined a black women's organization, Sojourners for Truth and Justice, that addressed a global concern for the liberation of women. At about the same time she joined the Communist Party.

Graham and Du Bois became intimate partners and political comrades, but as the cold war and anticommunist purges intensified, they came under increasing government scrutiny and harassment. Du Bois was fired from his post with the NAACP, Graham left the organization, and Du Bois soon found himself under federal indictment, although he was later acquitted. On February 14, 1951, Shirley Graham and W. E. B. Du Bois were married. She was fifty-four and he was eighty-two. The love they shared is evident in all of their correspondence and in their personal, often frolicking interactions. Graham always maintained that she married Du Bois precisely to prolong his life, and until his death she put her own work on hold.

Feted everywhere in the world through the late 1950s, Graham Du Bois traveled with her illustrious husband to China, the Soviet Union, Europe, and Africa. She especially fell in love with China and developed close relationships with Zhou Enlai and others in the Communist Party leadership. In 1961 Kwame Nkrumah, the first president of an independent Ghana, invited Dr. and Mrs. Du Bois to live in Accra to realize Du Bois's lifelong dream to edit a multivolume Encyclopedia Africana. Although his health was failing, he did as much work as he could on the encyclopedia. On August 27, 1963, the day before a quarter of a million people gathered for the historic civil rights march on Washington, Du Bois died in Accra, with Shirley at his side.

His grieving widow remained in Ghana, continuing a political relationship with Nkrumah, who in 1964 appointed her director of television. She had enormous influence on the African continent until February 1966 when Nkrumah was overthrown by a military coup, which Graham Du Bois and others believed to have been engineered by the United States. She was caught in Accra and, because of her close association with Nkrumah, barely escaped with her life. Seventy years old, she found herself effectively stateless, having renounced her American citizenship some years before.

Badly frightened by these events, Graham Du Bois took up residence in Cairo near her son, David. After repeated efforts to obtain permission to enter the United States, it was finally granted in the early 1970s. She taught at the University of Massachusetts in Amherst while touring the country under the auspices of *Freedomways,* a journal she helped launch in 1961, speaking about the situation in Africa. She also resumed her writing, producing an intimate portrait of W. E. B. Du Bois, as well as a novel and biographies of Gamal Abdel Nasser and Julius K. Nyerere.

In mid 1975, Graham Du Bois was diagnosed with cancer, but she did not seek medical attention until a trip to China early in 1976. Treatment offered a temporary reprieve, and she resumed her vigorous travels. She returned to China terminally ill and died in Beijing on March 27, 1977, a few months past her eightieth birthday, with David at her side. Her body lay in state, and following cremation her son took her ashes to Cairo. In 1988 he returned them to Accra for burial beside her beloved Du Bois.

Bibliography: The papers of Shirley Graham Du Bois are housed at the Schlesinger Library, Radcliffe Institute for Advanced Study, Harvard University. The collection includes her personal correspondence, passports from several countries (including her cancelled U.S. passport), manuscripts of books and articles, musical scores, and photographs. Other useful archival collections include the W. E. B. Du Bois Papers, University of Massachusetts–Amherst Library; Shirley Graham File, Oberlin College; Du Bois Papers, Amistad Research Center, Tulane University; Julian Mayfield Papers, Schomburg Center for Research in Black Culture, New York Public Library; NAACP Papers, Library of Congress; Kwame Nkrumah Papers, Howard University Library; Eslanda Robeson Papers, Howard University Library; Herbert Aptheker Papers, Stanford University; and Ella Winter Papers, Columbia University Library. Additional personal papers remain with her son, David G. Du Bois, Amherst, Massachusetts. The only published biography is Gerald Horne, *Race Woman: The Lives of Shirley Graham Du Bois* (2000). There is also a useful dissertation by Robert Dee Thompson, "A Socio-Biography of Shirley Graham Du Bois: A Life in the Struggle" (University of California, Santa Cruz, 1997). Her own book, *His Day Is Marching On: A Memoir of W. E. B. Du Bois* (1971), also contains significant autobiographical material. The author appreciates the assistance of David G. Du Bois in the preparation of this entry. This essay also drew on the author's childhood and young adult friendship with Shirley Graham Du Bois, and the knowledge she acquired as a result of the long relationship between her father, Herbert Aptheker, and Dr. and Mrs. Du Bois. An obituary appeared in the *New York Times* on April 5, 1977.

BETTINA APTHEKER

GRASSO, Ella Tambussi. May 10, 1919–February 5, 1981. U.S. Representative, Connecticut governor.

Ella Rosa Giovanna Olivia Tambussi was born in Windsor Locks, Connecticut, the only child of Italian immigrant parents. Her father, Giacomo Tambussi, was a mill worker when he married Maria Oliva, an assembly line laborer. Shortly after the birth of his daughter, Giacomo Tambussi opened a bakery with his brother and his wife left her job at General Electric to stay home with Ella.

The Tambussis lived in a tight-knit community among family and friends, many of whom had recently immigrated from the Piedmont region of Italy. Devout Catholics, the Tambussis enrolled Ella in school at St. Mary's in Windsor Locks beginning in 1924. An exemplary student, she earned a Rockefeller Scholarship to attend Chaffee School, a private preparatory school, and then a scholarship to attend Mount Holyoke, where she studied economics and sociology. Interested in her ethnic heritage, she also studied Italian, modern European history, and literature. She later credited her years at Mount Holyoke with instilling in her the belief that her gender would not be a liability in her career.

Ella Tambussi graduated Phi Beta Kappa from Mount Holyoke in 1940, staying on to earn a master's degree in economics and sociology in 1942. That summer she married Thomas Grasso, a teacher (and later principal) whom she had met at her family's summer cottage in Old Lyme when she was fourteen. After marrying, she worked for the War Manpower Commission in Connecticut for several years. The couple moved into a house across from her parents; there their daughter, Susane, was born in 1948, followed by James in 1951.

Typical of many college-educated, politically engaged women in the 1940s and 1950s, Grasso threw herself into local politics and political volunteerism. She joined the League of Catholic Women at St. Mary's and the Windsor Locks PTA and was appointed to the state Commission on Education. She was also a member of the Suffield chapter of the League of Women Voters.

In 1952, Grasso, who had switched her party affiliation from Republican to Democratic, was elected to one of the two General Assembly seats from Windsor on a platform that combined liberal social ideology with more conservative fiscal management. Labeled the "housewife politician" by the *Hartford Courant,* Grasso earned the support of women with her work on health, education, and consumer affairs, even as she advanced her reputation for more conservative political frugality.

Grasso was mentored by the powerful Democratic state party chair, John Moran "Boss" Bailey, who was instrumental in Grasso's political success. He remained her mentor, adviser, and confidant until his death in 1975. Under Bailey's tutelage, Grasso was appointed an assistant floor leader of the Democratic Party in her second term. In 1958 she was elected secretary of state, a position traditionally held by a woman. She remained in that job until 1970. Committed to reforming the election process, Grasso welcomed input from her constituents. She also used the office to increase her profile across the state.

As she became more prominent in Democratic Party politics, Grasso considered a run for Congress. In 1970, she was elected a U.S. Representative from Connecticut's Sixth District. A moderate Democrat, Grasso retreated from her formerly public anti-war stance. Adhering to her Catholic upbringing, she maintained her conservative stance on abortion, although she did support gender equity in the workplace and in education. Grasso was symbolically important to the women's movement, but she was not a dedicated political advocate on women's issues. Appealing to her district's more conservative voters, she was reelected to Congress in 1972.

Anxious to return to Connecticut, Grasso decided to run for governor in 1974. She fostered ties to the constituencies that had traditionally supported her, including Catholics, and to voters in urban working-class immigrant neighborhoods in New Haven and Hartford, as well as in the small towns similar to Windsor Locks. Despite a crowded field, she won the Democratic primary.

As a candidate for governor, Ella Grasso remained intent on preserving her reputation as a moderate. She did not ally herself firmly with the women's movement, although she received support from key moderate feminist organizations, including the National Organization for Women and the Women's Equity Action League. Like her Republican opponent, she came out against abortion, busing, and the institution of a state income tax, though she did advocate increased revenue sharing in the state's urban districts and increased spending for education and transportation. Buoyed by the damage done to the Republican Party by Watergate and bolstered by Connecticut's formidable Democratic machine, Ella Grasso won the election by an astounding 200,000 votes. She was the first woman in the nation to have been elected governor in her own right.

However, the battle had just begun. Ella Grasso faced a massive state budget deficit. She met the fiscal crisis with promises of frugality, and a strict plan for government reorganization. Moreover, she vowed to balance the budget without instituting a progressive income tax, promoting instead an increase in the more regressive sales tax.

Ella Grasso's first term as governor was tumultuous. Her conservative fiscal policies alienated the liberal wing of her party, the state's civil servants, women's groups, labor, and constituents in urban areas who soon realized that Grasso could not fulfill her promise to increase spending in their districts. Though the state's fiscal health improved, Grasso faced the possibility that she would be a one-term governor. However, because of her masterful handling of a natural disaster—the blizzard of 1978—her popularity rebounded, bolstered by the fact that the government had gone from deficit to surplus in her first term. She won election to a second term and garnered national attention for her handling of the energy crisis, as well as popular approval for her increased aid to social programs in urban areas.

Over the course of her career, Ella Grasso developed a reputation for being personally compassionate but politically vindictive behind the scenes, and for conducting herself with enormous political savvy in public. She balanced her tough, no-nonsense persona with an equal measure of warm maternalism. As a result, "Mother Ella" was beloved by her political colleagues and constituents alike.

In April 1980, Grasso was diagnosed with ovarian cancer. She resigned as governor on New Year's Eve of that year. She died on February 5, 1981, at the age of sixty-one, and was laid to rest at St. Mary's Cemetery in Windsor Locks, Connecticut.

Bibliography: The most complete biography to date of Ella Grasso is Susan Bysiewicz, *Ella: A Biography of Governor Ella Grasso* (1984). See also *Current Biography Yearbook* (1975), pp. 173–76, and Jon E. Purmont, "Ella Grasso: As She Saw Herself," *Connecticut Review* 17 (Spring 1995), pp. 23–29. For a discussion of the impact of women's education on Grasso's career, see Purmont, "Ella Grasso and Her Preparation for Leadership," *Connecticut History* 36, no. 1 (Spring 1995), pp. 66–77. For a journalist's treatment of Grasso's first months in office, see Bernard Asbell, "In Power and Down and Out," *New York Times Magazine,* July 27, 1975, pp. 4+. Grasso's gubernatorial records are housed at the Connecticut State Archives; a posthumous portrait of Governor Grasso, painted by Herbert E. Abrams, can be found at the Museum of Connecticut History, the Connecticut State Library. An obituary appeared in the *New York Times* on February 6, 1981.

LESLIE J. LINDENAUER

GRAVES, Nancy. December 23, 1940–October 21, 1995. Artist.

Nancy Stevenson Graves was born and raised in Pittsfield, in the Berkshire Mountains of northwestern Massachusetts, the elder of two daughters of a prominent New England family. Her mother, born Mary Augusta Bates, was active in local volunteer work. Her father, Walter Lucien Graves, born in Cambridge, Massachusetts, and descended from Cotton Mather, worked at the Berkshire Museum, a small institution in Pittsfield that combined galleries for fine art and the natural sciences under one roof. The artist later reflected that this combination, which in effect eliminated the hierarchies between art and science, strongly influenced her approach as an artist.

Graves attended Miss Hall's School in Pittsfield and then the Northfield School for Girls. After receiving a BA in English from Vassar in 1961, Graves became one of the first women to enroll in the MFA program at the School of Art and Architecture at Yale University. Highly confident, fiercely independent, and possessing a wry sense of humor, she shared a studio space with nine of her male classmates, including Chuck Close and Richard Serra. She married Serra in 1965, following the year of her graduation. After leaving Yale, Graves received a Fulbright grant to study painting and moved to Paris briefly with Serra before settling in Florence. There Graves began the lengthy journey that would culminate in the creation of the provocative sculptures that launched her career.

Camel VI, VII, and VIII were completed in 1968 in New York—where the artist settled permanently in 1966—and shown soon after at the Graham Gallery. The numerous sculptures she destroyed in the process of making these three works speak to her uncompromising perfectionism. In 1969 the Whitney Museum of American Art organized an exhibition of *Camel IV, V, and VI,* making Graves the first woman to have a one-person exhibition there. At a time when abstract art, most notably minimalist art—characterized by spare, often geometric forms, and the use of industrial materials—dominated American art, Graves's sculptural group consisted of three life-size, startlingly realistic camels she had built using wood, steel, burlap, animal hides, wax, and oil paint. In these sculptures, Graves not only displayed for the first time her stated desire to break down boundaries (in this case, between abstract and representational art), but her strong interest in scientific theories of visual perception, specifically the manner in which a viewer perceives and processes images. The extensive public and media attention lavished on this exhibition instantly made Graves an important figure and one of what was then only a handful of successful women artists.

Like many artists of her generation, Graves experimented in several different media and with a wide variety of materials. Though first and foremost a sculptor, she began in 1970—the year she was divorced from Serra—to move effortlessly between sculpture, painting, drawing, printmaking, filmmaking, and costume and set design. She also routinely began to introduce motifs from one work of art into another, often in different media.

But it was the direct-cast technique of bronze casting that revolutionized Graves's entire approach when she used it for the first time in 1978. Allowing her to make an exact cast of virtually any object without modeling (then scaling it up or down to any size), the direct-cast process gave Graves a way to incorporate natural forms directly into her sculpture. She developed a method of constructing bronze sculptures by juxtaposing casts of wildly disparate objects and welding them into compositions (with an almost surrealist sensibility) that seemed to defy gravity. Ranging in scale from several inches to monumental, her sculpture was further distinguished by riotously colored patinas created by fusing enamel paints onto the bronze surfaces in a technique developed specifically for Graves by the Tallix Foundry. She also began to add three-dimensional elements to what were traditionally two-dimensional media: her paintings now often featured large painted aluminum reliefs projecting from the canvas, and she sometimes added cast paper reliefs to the surfaces of her large-scale prints.

In 1979 Graves was a fellow at the American Academy in Rome. Always a voracious intellectual and tireless traveler, she used her months in Italy to study ancient history and archaeology. That study instilled in the artist a desire to place her own work within the continuum of art history. She spoke of making art from the "shards of art" and began to appropriate an array of figures and icons from the annals of history, religion, and mythology—references that were fed by her extensive travels around the Mediterranean and her continued study of history (Padon, p. 11). Graves built a visual vocabulary made up of images based on various art historical sources ranging from Paleolithic cave paintings to motifs from Egyptian tombs to Italian Renaissance painting. Rather than appropriating these images directly, Graves copied them by hand, retaining only fragments of the originals. Each work contained its own enigmatic visual and metaphorical narrative, made all the more enigmatic by their titles, which Graves derived from fragments of literary passages. She believed that all viewers would be able to relate intuitively to these compositions, with their allusions to the common ties among various cultures and the multiformity of nature.

In the last four years of Graves's life she was married to Avery Smith, a veterinarian and poet. She approached her work during this period with her wonted sense of experimentation, including a series of sculptures featuring glass made in collaboration with the Pilchuck School; two print series in which organic material was embossed directly onto paper; and a large floor mosaic for the Ronald Reagan National Airport in Washington, D.C. In a career spanning twenty-eight years, Nancy Graves developed a highly distinctive body of work in a wide range of media, most notably sculpture and painting. Graves's unique combination of abstract gesture and representational imagery and her unceasing experimentation with materials made her one of the most important women artists of her generation. She died in New York City of ovarian cancer at the age of fifty-four.

Bibliography: The Nancy Graves Foundation in New York City maintains biographical information and archival material. A small artist file at the Museum of Modern Art, New York, contains clippings, small exhibition catalogs, and other ephemeral material related to Graves's work. A series of interviews with the artist conducted by Paul Cummings in 1972 is held at the Archives of American Art at the Smithsonian Institution in Washington, D.C. A full-length biography of Graves has yet to be written, but exhibition catalogs of her work include Linda L. Cathcart, *Nancy Graves: A Survey, 1969–1980* (1980); Debra Bricker Balken, *Nancy Graves: Painting, Sculpture, Drawing* (1986); E. A. Carmean Jr., *The Sculpture of Nancy Graves: A Catalogue Raisonné* (1987); and Thomas Padon, *Nancy Graves: Excavations in Print* (1996). An obituary appeared in the *New York Times* on October 24, 1995.

THOMAS PADON

GRAY, Georgia Neese. *See* Clark, Georgia Neese.

GRAY, Susan Walton. December 5, 1913–December 30, 1992. Psychologist.

Susan Walton Gray was born in Columbia, Tennessee, one of several children of Elizabeth Wolfenden and Daniel Roger Gray. She grew up in Rockdale, a small rural community near Nashville, where her relatives were among the most prominent citizens. Gray's privileged childhood experiences influenced her career, both by encouraging her achievement and by raising questions about social justice. She recalled always feeling as a young child that she was just as good as anybody. Because there were not very many children in the rural area where she grew up, the boys and girls all played together; as the oldest of the group, she was frequently in a leadership role. At the same time, her upbringing in Rockdale, which she later described as a feudal society centered around her uncle's blast furnace, made her conscious of the problems of poverty in contrast to her affluent upbringing.

Gray received a BA from Randolph-Macon Woman's College in Lynchburg, Virginia, in 1935, taking several courses in psychology but majoring in classics. A short stint teaching fourth grade convinced her that she did not want to stay in elementary education. She pursued graduate work in psychology at George Peabody College in Nashville, receiving a master's in 1939 and a PhD in 1941. At Florida State College for Women she filled in for a male faculty member who had enlisted during the war, then she returned to Peabody as a faculty member in psychology in 1945 and remained there until her retirement in 1978. (Peabody College became part of Vanderbilt University in 1979.) For thirteen of those years she was the only female faculty member in psychology, but she always felt her work was treated fairly and taken seriously.

Gray's entire career was marked by a commitment to bringing research to bear on serious social problems; she is best known for her work in early childhood education, especially programs for children from disadvantaged backgrounds. She started her Early Training Project in 1959 in response to concerns of the superintendent of a nearby school district, who observed that the academic performance of poor African American children was progressively worsening over the elementary school years. Gray and her colleague Rupert Klaus decided to focus on preschool children, developing an intervention program consisting of intensive summer preschool programs followed by a series of home visits. Gray's analysis of the program showed that early intervention could increase poor children's IQ scores and improve their school performance. This finding made the Early Training Project an inspiration and model for the federal Head Start program in 1965, as its director Sargent Shriver acknowledged. Over time the Early Training Project became one of the most influential longitudinal evaluations of the lasting effects of early intervention. It influenced not only Head Start, but other federally funded intervention programs in the 1960s and many of the early childhood special education programs of the 1970s.

Gray's seventeen-year follow-up study of the original program's participants was also of national import. She found that children who had participated in the preschool program were more successful in high school than those who had not taken part—fewer were placed in special education classes or had to repeat grades; more graduated from high school and were employed or continued their education; and the girls who became pregnant were much more likely to return to school and earn their diplomas.

While the Early Training Project was under way, Gray also helped create in 1965 the Kennedy Center for Research on Education and Human Development at Peabody, one of the original twelve national research centers on mental retardation. At the Kennedy Center, she founded and directed the Demonstration and Research Center for Early Education (DARCEE), which developed model preschool curricula and parent education materials to help improve the school success of preschoolers from low-income families. DARCEE also served as a training site for thousands of research and early-intervention professionals in the late 1960s and early 1970s. Gray urged the creation of a demonstration school for at-risk preschool children at the Kennedy Center; the school—which was named for her in 1986—serves as a model for the best practices in early childhood special education.

Gray's research often challenged existing paradigms. She pioneered the idea that poverty and social discrimination are key sources of poor school performance and can be affected through well-designed intervention programs. Her work was not restricted to one discipline, but called on the resources of psychologists, sociologists, nutritionists, and educators, and on a variety of research methodologies. When other programs were focused solely on improving children's cognitive and language development, Gray worked to affect attitudes toward achievement as well. She took seriously the idea that mothers are children's "first teachers," recognized that low-income parents are deeply concerned with their children's development, and saw that working with mothers is essential to promoting change. This interest in the role of mothers led Gray to discover the "diffusion effect" of the Early Training Project: mothers in the experimental group shared their knowledge and excitement about their children's educational experiences with their families and with other mothers in the community, resulting in gains even for children who did not themselves attend the early education programs.

Gray also made important contributions to the field of school psychology. In 1957, she and two colleagues established a doctoral education program in school psychology, and obtained the nation's first federal training grant from the National Institute of Mental Health to support such a program. Her 1963 book, *The Psychologist in the Schools,* outlined a role for school psychologists that was influential across the country, and established a model for graduate education in this field. Gray also served as the first female president of the Southeastern Psychological Association in 1963.

Susan Gray retired from Peabody in 1978, but continued to be active professionally. She never married. In her retirement, she created a computerized archive of her data for other researchers to use, and she pursued her interests in photography, classics, and fine arts. She died in Nashville in 1992 at the age of seventy-nine following a stroke.

Bibliography: The Early Training Project is described in two books: Susan W. Gray, Rupert Klaus, J. Miller, and B. Forrester, *Before First Grade: The Early Training Project for Culturally Disadvantaged Children* (1966); and Susan W. Gray, Barbara Ramsey, and Rupert Klaus, *From 3 to 20: The Early Training Project* (1982). Gray's many articles can be found in scholarly journals in psychology and child development. Articles about Gray include Barbara Wallston et al., "Dr. Susan W. Gray," *Psychology of Women Quarterly* 5, no. 1 (Fall 1980), pp. 127–39, which focuses on her career and draws on interviews with Gray and her students; Nelson Bryan, "Gray Day: Dedication of the Susan Gray School for Children," *Peabody Reflector* (Winter 1987), pp. 9–10; and Paul Dokecki and J. R. Newbrough, "The Gray-Hobbs Vision," *Peabody Journal of Education* 71, no. 4 (1996), pp. 25–32. See also "Susan Walton Gray (1913–1992)," *American Psychologist* 48, no. 11 (November 1993), pp. 1150. *Susan Walton Gray: A Memorial Tribute* (1993), a booklet prepared by Peabody College, includes an account of her career as well as excerpts from letters written by students and colleagues on her retirement. Peabody College memos about Gray were provided by the Vanderbilt University Archives and by Jan Rosemergy of the Kennedy Center. An obituary appeared in the *New York Times* on January 1, 1993.

ELIZABETH ROSE

GREEN, Edith. January 17, 1910–April 21, 1987. Educator, U.S. Representative, feminist.

The third of five children born to schoolteachers Julia Hunt and James Vaughn Starrett, Edith Louise Starrett spent her first six years in Trent, South Dakota, before her family moved to Roseburg, and then Salem, Oregon. Before graduating from Salem High School, she won a trip to the White House as Oregon's outstanding high school girl. She taught in Salem's schools between 1930 and 1941 and attended Oregon Normal School and Willamette University, not completing college until 1939, when she earned a BS in English and education from the University of Oregon. Later she did graduate work at Stanford University. In 1933, she married Arthur N. Green, a trailer court operator, and they had two sons: James (1934) and Richard (1941). They divorced in 1963.

In the 1940s, Green helped support the family by working at the trailer court and announcing for radio station KALE in Portland. She gained organizational and government experience as chair of the Oregon Congress of Parents and Teachers for three years and its legislative representative in 1951, and director of public and legislative relations for the Oregon Education Association. She was also active in the League of Women Voters, the National Federation of Business and Professional Women, the United Nations Association, the Urban League, and the First Christian Church. These activities served as an excellent apprenticeship for her political career.

In 1952, Green ran as the Democratic candidate for secretary of state of Oregon, suffering her only election defeat. Two years later, at the age of forty-four, she won election to the U.S. House of Representatives from Oregon's 3rd district, located in and around Portland. After this close race, in which she defeated future governor Tom McCall, voters sent her back to Congress nine times, never with less than 63 percent of the vote. Active in national Democratic politics, in 1960 Green became the first woman to lead her state delegation at the Democratic National Convention, where she seconded the nomination of John F. Kennedy; and she ran presidential primary campaigns in Oregon for both John F. Kennedy (1960) and Robert F. Kennedy (1968). The small, conservatively dressed woman who, journalists observed, looked like a schoolteacher, was considered by many of her colleagues to be difficult, and some congressmen dubbed her "the wicked witch of the West." Yet she was respected for her hard work, intelligence, and candor and her skills as a floor manager.

In Congress, Green made her mark in the areas of education and women's rights. She served for eighteen years on the Committee on Labor and Education, eventually rising to chair of its subcommittee on post-secondary education. Her first bill funded rural library services, and she shaped and helped pass three laws that made the federal government a key provider of facilities and scholarships in higher education: the National Defense Education Act of 1958, the Higher Education Facilities Act of 1963, and the Higher Education Act of 1965.

Having been sidetracked from her aspirations to become a lawyer when her parents urged her to be realistic about women's opportunities, Green was aware of being excluded and condescended to by male colleagues throughout her congressional career. From the beginning, she sponsored measures to ban sex discrimination, using her early support for Kennedy to solidify his backing of the Equal Pay Act of 1963, which she had co-sponsored since 1955. Appointed to the President's Commission on the Status of Women in 1961, she co-chaired its Civil and Political Rights Committee, along with lawyer and feminist MARGUERITE RAWALT. Although keenly aware of sex discrimination, she was the only congresswoman to oppose adding the category "sex" to Title VII of the Civil Rights Act of 1964. Considering racial discrimination much worse than sex discrimination, she did not want to clutter the bill with a provision that might increase opposition. At 1964 congressional hearings on the War on Poverty, even before the resurgence of feminist activism, Green challenged the Johnson administration's neglect of poor women and made sure that the Job Corps included women. By 1970 she came to support the equal rights amendment, no longer confident that equity could be gained through legislation and the courts.

Not surprisingly, Green's most important contribution to women's rights came in the area closest to her heart—education. In 1970, she held subcommittee hearings on sex discrimination in education and then arranged for widespread distribution of the testimony, which included and documented her assertion that colleges and universities were "no bastions of democracy." She sponsored Title IX of the Education Amendments of 1972, the landmark measure banning sex discrimination in every aspect of federally assisted education, from preschool through postgraduate education. Her advice to feminists not to call attention to the measure by active lobbying demonstrated legislative shrewdness as well as her preference not to emphasize conflict between the sexes. Like several other long-serving congresswomen, she opposed formation of a congressional women's caucus on grounds that it would be divisive. And, believing that she had achieved her influence by hard work and seniority, Green opposed affirmative action programs.

Green's fierce independence became more pronounced in her later terms. Already in 1965 she was one of just a handful of Democrats to defy Johnson's call for appropriations to escalate U.S. involvement in Vietnam, and she consistently opposed the war. Although she always considered herself a liberal, in the late 1960s and 1970s she broke with former allies, attacking programs that she believed were expanding federal bureaucracies at the expense of state and local decision making and that taxed the middle class to provide for the poor. She considered busing to achieve integration unworkable, diverting funds necessary to improve conditions in the schools. In the 1970s, Green voted against anti-poverty programs that she claimed had wasted millions of dollars with minimal effect. Instead she advocated vocational training and fair wages, providing key leadership for legislation to cover domestic workers in the minimum-wage law in 1974.

Her influence was diminished by her rightward turn. Democratic colleagues dealt her a humiliating defeat on an education funding formula in 1972, and Green switched to the Committee on Appropriations. In 1974, she made the decision, exceedingly rare among politicians, to retire from her perfectly safe seat in the House. Two years later she helped a former House colleague by cochairing Democrats for Gerald Ford in the 1976 election campaign. During her retirement she taught at Warner Pacific College and served on the Oregon Board of Higher Education. On April 21, 1987, she died of pancreatic cancer in Tulatin, Oregon, at the age of seventy-seven.

Bibliography: Edith Green's extensive papers are at the Oregon Historical Society in Portland, unprocessed. The *Congressional Record* contains her remarks in the House during 1955–74; and her newsletters for those years, "Your Congresswoman Reports" and "The Green Letter," are at the University of Oregon Library. Two of her public lectures have been published: "The Federal Role in Education," in *Education and the Public Good* (1964); and *Fears and Fallacies: Equal Opportunities in the 1970s* (1975). Claudia Dreifus, "Women in Politics: An Interview with Edith Green," *Social Policy* 2 (January/February 1972), pp. 16–22, focuses on her views on women's issues. The most extensive and useful published treatments are Rudolph Englebarts, *Women in the U.S. Congress 1917–1972* (1974); Marcy Kaptur, "Edith Starrett Green," in Kaptur, ed., *Women of Congress: A Twentieth-Century Odyssey* (1996), pp. 111–17; Norman C. Miller, "Rep. Edith Green, a Bareknuckle Fighter," *Wall Street Journal,* December 3, 1969; and Louise Wides, "Edith Green: Democratic Representative from Oregon," *Ralph Nader Congress Project: Citizens Look at Congress* (1972). Substantial obituaries appeared in the *Oregonian,* April 22, 1987, and the *New York Times* and *Washington Post,* both on April 23, 1987.

SUSAN M. HARTMANN

GREENACRE, Phyllis. May 3, 1894–October 24, 1989. Psychoanalyst, psychiatrist.

Of the work produced by American psychoanalysts whose careers were established in the 1930s and 1940s, Phyllis Greenacre's is unrivaled in its clinical sophistication and theoretical creativity. It falls into three categories: clinical papers on development; psychoanalytic training and therapy; and studies of creativity. Greenacre's writings are characterized by beautiful, evocative prose in the service of imaginative and bold theoretical ideas, and sensitive interpretation of clinical material.

Greenacre was born in Chicago, the fourth of seven children of Isaiah Thomas Greenacre, a prominent lawyer, and Emma Leantha Russell. She graduated with a BS from the University of Chicago in 1913 and with an MD degree from Rush Medical College, also in Chicago, in 1916. Determined to study psychiatry, even though at that time opportunities for solid training were scarce, she regarded herself as fortunate to be accepted as a resident at Phipps Clinic, which had recently opened at the Johns Hopkins Hospital in Baltimore. Greenacre remained at Phipps Clinic for eleven years and came under the tutelage of the great Swiss American psychiatrist Adolf Meyer. Her interest in the relationship between physical maturation and psychological development predated her years at Johns Hopkins, but her exposure to Meyer's environmental psychiatry reinforced her conviction that the role of physical growth cannot be ignored in clinical psychiatry. In 1919, three years after arriving at Hopkins, Greenacre married Curt P. Richter, the director of the Psychobiological Laboratory of Phipps Clinic. They had two children, Ann (1921) and Peter (1922). The couple separated in 1927 and were divorced in 1930. Greenacre never remarried.

In late 1927 Greenacre moved to New York and became a psychiatrist to the Department of Public Welfare and a consultant to the Children's Court in Westchester County. In 1932 she joined the department of psychiatry of New York Hospital and Cornell Medical College, and began training at the New York Psychoanalytic Institute, graduating in 1937. Greenacre was not an isolated exception as a woman psychoanalyst: a significant number of American women became psychoanalysts in the interwar period. More significantly, they sought and exercised considerable influence and power within societies and institutes as teachers, training analysts, and members of curriculum and educational committees. The range of positions Greenacre held illustrates this fact: she was president of both the New York Psychoanalytic Institute (1948–49) and the New York Psychoanalytic Society (1956–57); a member for many years of the Institute's powerful Educational Committee, serving as chair when important curriculum reforms were enacted (1957–59); a member of the Board of Professional Standards of the American Psychoanalytic Association; and a member of the editorial board of the influential annual *The Psychoanalytic Study of the Child* from its inception in 1945.

Greenacre was renowned for her clinical skills and much sought after as a supervisor, especially for difficult cases. Her therapeutic work took as its point of departure her conviction of the importance of reconstruction. Thus she paid close attention to screen memories as the path by which early, preverbal experiences could be glimpsed. Her first psychoanalytic paper, "The Predisposition to Anxiety" (1941), which today is regarded as classic, originally was criticized for its exploration of preverbal stages of development and her argument that the roots of anxiety might predate the existence of the ego. She was undeterred and continued to publish papers that explored the role of early trauma in neurotic illness.

In the early 1950s a shift occurred in Greenacre's work. She embarked upon two decades of sustained engagement with the problems of fetishism, early ego development, and the creative individual. Remarkably, this rich period, when papers and books rapidly followed one another, began when she was fifty-nine years old and already the author of many notable contributions. The paper that initiated this phase, "Certain Relationships between Fetishism and the Faulty Development of the Body Image" (1953), made the point that fetishists have an especially mutable body image, together with a tendency to individualize and personalize different body parts. Aware that such descriptions were frequently found in fairy tales and folklore, notably in Lewis Carroll's *Alice* books and in Jonathan Swift's *Gulliver's Travels,* Greenacre was stimulated to write *Swift and Carroll* (1955), an absorbing biographical study that remains an exemplary work of applied analysis. In her first theoretical paper on creativity, "The Childhood of the Artist" (1957), she described the potentially gifted infant as unusually responsive to both internal and external stimuli and as having an enhanced capacity for symbolization and continual access to primary-process thinking. She also proposed a theory that aggression is a manifestation of a positive developmental force—a positive response by the infant to the vicissitudes of its earliest experiences, both frustrating and gratifying.

Greenacre's career offers a model for how psychoanalysts can retain and express their individuality while remaining responsive to the ideas of colleagues and predecessors. It is clear from her writings that she felt free to explore Freud's legacy and was also influenced by the work of other analysts. She openly acknowledged the role of Heinz Hartmann's formulations in ego psychology, Willi Hoffer's description of the body ego, and D. W. Winnicott's foundational papers on transitional objects as contributions that enriched and deepened her thinking on psychological development. Her work on creative individuals was above all a brilliant response to her friendship with the analyst and art historian Ernst Kris, who encouraged her to pursue the subject of creativity.

Though her children and circle of old friends constituted a vital emotional center in Greenacre's life, there can be little doubt that work, especially her writing, was equally necessary to her well-being. The capacity for intimacy so evident in her personal life is also reflected in her writing, where her expressive use of language arouses the reader's curiosity and desire to understand the problems that are so absorbing to Greenacre. Her early personal history perhaps provides a key to understanding the origins of her facility with language. A developmental speech delay prevented her from speaking intelligibly until she was seven years old. Before this time she communicated by writing notes, having learned to read and write at the age of four. Writing then was truly her first form of speech. Greenacre famously described the creative individual as experiencing a "love affair with the world"; this phrase may also serve to epitomize the enduring pleasure, excitement, and deep satisfaction that sustained her own long emotional and intellectual engagement with psychoanalysis and creativity (Greenacre, *Emotional Growth,* vol. 2, p. 490).

At the age of ninety Phyllis Greenacre retired and moved to Garrison, New York. She died on October 24, 1989, from cerebral arteriosclerosis in an Ossining, New York, nursing home at the age of ninety-five.

Bibliography: Greenacre's papers are collected in *Trauma, Growth, and Personality* (1952) and *Emotional Growth: Psychoanalytic Studies of the Gifted and a Great Variety of Other Individuals,* 2 volumes (1971). Her books include *Swift and Carroll: A Psychoanalytic Study of Two Lives* (1955) and *The Quest for the Father: A Study of the Darwin-Butler Controversy, as a Contribution to the Understanding of the Creative Individual* (1963). She also edited *Affective Disorders: Psychoanalytic Contribution to Their Study* (1953). Information about her career can be found in Marjorie Harley and Annemarie Weil, "Phyllis Greenacre, M.D. (1894–1989)," *International Journal of Psychoanalysis* 71 (1990), pp. 523–25. A 1972 videotaped interview with Frank Parcells, MD, is deposited in the Gitelson Film Library of the Institute for Psychoanalysis in Chicago. A comprehensive bibliography of Greenacre's publications is available in the Special Collections of the A. A. Brill Library of the New York Psychoanalytic Institute. For a general survey of women in the psychoanalytic movement, see Lisa Appignanesi and John Forrester, *Freud's Women* (1992). A collective portrait of first- and second-generation American women analysts may be found in Nellie L. Thompson, "American Women Psychoanalysts

1911–1941," *Annual of Psychoanalysis* 28 (2001), p. 29. An obituary appeared in the *New York Times* on October 25, 1989.

NELLIE L. THOMPSON

GREENBERG, Florence. September 16, 1913–November 2, 1995. Record label executive, songwriter, music publisher.

Florence Greenberg founded Scepter Records, one of the most successful independent record labels during the golden age of rock and roll and soul music from the mid 1950s to the early 1970s. During its seventeen-year history, Scepter Records released a string of hit records that ranged across the spectrum of contemporary popular music, from the "girl group" sound to urban rhythm and blues. Although major labels dominated the recording industry and male executives filled its management ranks, Greenberg's astute judgment of talent, tireless promotional efforts, and self-consciously maternal management style made her one of the few female entrepreneurs who prospered in the commercial music business.

Born Florence Rieger in New York City, she was the only child of Augusta Weiss and Walter Benjamin Rieger, a real estate salesman. Growing up in Brooklyn, she lived a somewhat sheltered life. After graduating from high school, her very protective Jewish parents opposed her intention to become a nurse because the profession would require her to touch naked men. On December 31, 1936, Florence married Bernard Greenberg, an accountant, and over the next five years they had two children: Stanley, who was blind, and Mary Jane. By the early 1950s Florence was settled into suburban life with her family in Passaic, New Jersey, where like many middle-class women she participated in a variety of civic groups and service clubs.

Greenberg's decision to enter the record business in 1956 stemmed from her dissatisfaction with her role as a suburban housewife. She was forty-three years old, she later recalled, and anxious to get out of the house. Unlike the few other female record executives of her day, who had worked in some aspect of the entertainment industry before starting their own labels, her only training was as an enthusiastic fan who constantly listened to the radio, particularly rhythm and blues. Greenberg began to frequent the Brill Building's Turf restaurant, a New York City hangout for songwriters, who supplied the New Jersey housewife with tips about the recording industry. Benefiting from the industry's competitive structure and the modest amount of entry capital required, in 1958 Greenberg founded her own independent label, Tiara Records. The name suggested a queen on her throne, the same royal imagery later conveyed by her Scepter label.

Greenberg achieved her first success with the Shirelles (originally known as the Poquellos), a quartet of African American teenage harmony singers who were her daughter's classmates at Passaic High School. Greenberg agreed to manage the Poquellos after hearing the group perform their own composition "I Met Him on a Sunday," which she released in 1958 on her fledgling Tiara label under the name the Shirelles. When the record became a minor hit, Greenberg sold the master recording and the entire Tiara label, along with the Shirelles, to major label Decca Records for four thousand dollars. Decca, however, dropped the Shirelles when the group failed to produce a follow-up hit, and Greenberg established Scepter Records to market their records herself.

In an important move, Greenberg recruited Luther Dixon, a talented African American songwriter and arranger, to produce the Shirelles' records. The group's teenage lead vocal and harmonies, rock rhythms, and lush strings, established the blueprint of the "girl group" sound that dominated the popular music charts in the first half of the 1960s. The Shirelles broke through with their next recording, "Will You Love Me Tomorrow," which quickly rose to the top position in the *Billboard* charts, where it stayed for two weeks in January 1961. After the success of "Will You Love Me Tomorrow," the Shirelles went on to have ten Top 40 singles between 1961 and 1963, including the number one hit "Soldier Boy" (1962), co-written by Greenberg.

Greenberg's influence extended to other genres of contemporary popular music. In 1962, Greenberg launched a subsidiary label, Wand Records, to market rhythm-and-blues records. Her first successful Wand artist was Chuck Jackson. Greenberg's Wand label released several groundbreaking hits by black vocal groups, including the Isley Brothers' "Twist and Shout" (1962), which influenced British Invasion groups and helped define the emerging "soul" music sound. Another sign of her canny ability to discern popular musical tastes came in 1963 when Wand released the garage-band classic "Louie, Louie," by the Kingsmen, who were based in Portland, Oregon. The record became her biggest hit, selling ten million copies worldwide.

By the mid 1960s, Greenberg primarily promoted singer Dionne Warwick, a former backup singer whom she discovered on a Burt Bacharach demonstration record. Warwick's hits would include "Walk On By" (1962), "Do You Know the Way to San Jose?" (1968), and "I'll Never Fall in Love Again" (1969). White Texan singer B. J. Thomas's "blue-eyed soul" represented the final cornerstone of the Scepter sound. Beginning in

1966 with a remake of Hank Williams's "I'm So Lonesome I Could Cry," Thomas charted twelve best-selling records over the next six years, including "Hooked on a Feeling" (1968) and "Raindrops Keep Falling on My Head" (1969).

Greenberg built the Scepter label into a substantial enterprise, with fifty-seven employees, separate gospel and classical divisions, its own music publishing and management firms, and a recording studio and record warehouse. She credited her success to her appreciation of black artists and their music and a management style that drew on her identity as a housewife and mother. Although Greenberg left musical production to others, she alone chose which acts to sign and what records to release. Keenly aware that promotion and marketing held the key to success in the competitive record industry, Greenberg established close relationships with independent record distributors across the United States, and hired a roster of ambitious promoters to plug her records to radio disc jockeys.

Despite her business acumen, Greenberg's Scepter label fell victim to the record industry's merger movement in the mid 1970s, when the major labels acquired most of the independent distributorships on which Scepter depended to place its records into retail stores. Determined to retain her corporate independence, Greenberg repeatedly rebuffed lucrative offers from major labels, including a multimillion-dollar offer from Gulf & Western. In 1976, however, with her company on the verge of bankruptcy, Greenberg sold Scepter for a substantial loss to the Springboard International label, which specialized in repackaging "oldies" records.

Greenberg, who divorced her husband in 1965, spent her final years in retirement near her daughter in Teaneck, New Jersey. When Capricorn Records issued a three-CD overview of the label's greatest hits in 1992, she proudly embraced the revival of interest in her career accomplishments. After suffering a massive stroke, she died on November 2, 1995, in Hackensack, New Jersey, at the age of eighty-two.

Bibliography: The best sources for information on Florence Greenberg can be found in published interviews, including Bill Forman, "Anyone Who Had a Heart: Florence Greenberg and the Scepter Records Story," *NARAS Journal* 3, no. 2 (1992), pp. 3–17; and Diana Reid Haig's liner notes to *The Scepter Records Story* (BMG/Capricorn, 1992). Another valuable source is Linda Lynwander, "Memories of a Rock Music Impresario," *New York Times*, May 2, 1993. For the structure of the postwar record industry and the role of independent labels, see Charlie Gillett, *The Sound of the City: The Rise of Rock and Roll* (2nd ed. 1996), and Brian Ward, *Just My Soul Responding: Rhythm and Blues, Black Consciousness, and Race Relations* (1998). For background on the Brill Building and "girl group" sounds, see Alan Betrock, *Girl Groups: The Story of a Sound* (1982), and Bruce Pollack, *When Rock Was Young: A Nostalgic Review of the Top 40 Era* (1981). For a fond reminiscence on the Shirelles' cultural impact and incipient feminism, see Susan J. Douglas, *Where the Girls Are: Growing Up Female with the Mass Media* (1994). For chart positions of Scepter-Wand hits, see Joel Whitburn, *The Billboard Book of Top 40 Hits* (5th ed. 1992), and Whitburn, *Top Pop Singles, 1955–1999* (2000). Obituaries appeared in the *New York Times* on November 4, 1995, and *Billboard* on November 18, 1995.

DAVID ANDERSON

GREENFIELD, Mary Ellen (Meg). December 27, 1930–May 13, 1999. Journalist, editor.

Meg Greenfield was considered by many to be the most powerful woman in Washington, D.C., throughout the 1980s and early 1990s by virtue of her position as the editorial page editor at the *Washington Post* and as a columnist for *Newsweek.* Mary Ellen Greenfield was born in Seattle, the second of two children and the only daughter of Lorraine Nathan and Lewis James Greenfield. Her mother came from a prominent Chicago family of European Jewish origin and a long line of strong and talented women whose intellectual abilities were encouraged, as were Meg's. Her father, the son of Russian Jewish immigrants, was a well-liked antiques dealer and an auctioneer, entertaining enough to be carried live on a weekly radio show. When Meg was twelve, her mother died, leaving the young girl with an irrevocable sense of loss. A smart and popular student, she attended public schools before transferring in high school to Helen Bush Parkside School, a private girl's school from which she graduated in 1948.

At Smith College she was an English major and a member of Phi Beta Kappa; she graduated summa cum laude in 1952. On a Fulbright scholarship, she went to England to study at Cambridge under the critic F. R. Leavis; when she discovered that he enrolled only men, she turned her attention to William Blake's poetry. Next she went to Rome and spent the next few years traveling in Europe with friends and discussing a novel she never quite got written.

Deciding to live in New York, she chose Greenwich Village and, on the recommendation of her friend Robert Gottlieb, volunteered in Adlai Stevenson's 1956 presidential campaign, where soon she became his director of research for New York State. This position led to her working in the research department of the *Reporter,* a small but influential magazine under the direction of the brilliant and mercurial Max Ascoli, who became her mentor. In record time she became a staff writer on the magazine, and in 1961 she went to work in the Washington, D.C., bureau, where she covered nuclear armaments, civil rights, and politics. She was promoted to Washington bureau chief in 1965.

When the *Reporter* shut down in 1968, Phil Geyelin, editor of the *Washington Post* editorial page, hired her and soon appointed her his deputy, making her, at the time, the only woman on the *Post's* editorial page, where her reputation grew as a brilliant writer and an excellent editor. At his request, she began sitting in on his meetings with the *Post's* publisher, Katharine Graham. During Watergate, Greenfield helped Graham craft and edit her speeches defending her paper's coverage, and the two women formed a close professional and personal friendship.

During a labor strike at the *Post* in 1975, Greenfield worked in the mailroom and answered the phones taking death notices. A year earlier, she had also become a columnist at *Newsweek* magazine. Her writings in this period included commentary on Vietnam, Watergate, civil rights, nuclear arms, and the military establishment. Intellectually rigorous, her work was stylish, always distinctive, and often wry. Her editorials and columns won her a Pulitzer Prize in 1978. Even though she was one of the most influential voices in the country, she disapproved of journalists having celebrity status and rarely appeared on television or in front of audiences. Upon winning the Pulitzer, her only interview was for the in-house *Post* newsletter.

In 1979 Donald Graham, the new *Post* publisher, appointed her editor of the editorial page, which included writing for and supervising the editorial and outside opinion pages. Resisting political labeling, in broad terms she could be characterized as progressive on domestic policy and muscular on foreign policy. Under her leadership and in consultation with Donald Graham, the paper endorsed gun control, affirmative action (but not quotas), and Social Security reform. She supported free speech, including speech that was racially and ethnically offensive. She refused to forgo complexity in favor of her own predilections. A perfectionist, she expected as much from her staff and did not mind expressing herself to them either.

In the 1970s she had little patience with the feminist movement, even as she told how just years earlier she was refused permission to read the ticker tape news wires several feet inside an area banned to women in the Press Club. Douglass Cater, then Washington Bureau chief of the *Reporter*, had been indignant, but she had accepted it as the way things were. Only later did she admit to sympathy with many of the movement's goals as she came to understand the cultural bind that women, especially in Washington, found themselves in, whether working or not.

Although her work consumed her time—even on vacation she remained in constant touch with her office—she also relished her friends and greatly enjoyed parties. A born raconteur, she could be elusive, charming, tough, and raucous. With her infectious laugh, her mischievous gray-blue eyes, she told great stories at her own expense; yet, on occasion she would draw up all five-foot-one of herself and wither the most self-important of personages. Famously private as well as gregarious, she needed time alone to read, to reflect, to write, to watch junk TV. She was a passionate gardener, took up Latin for the fun of it, and never lost her love of literature and history, especially classical and medieval. When her beloved brother died prematurely, she established the Jim Greenfield Scholarship Program in the classics in his memory at the University of Washington. The deaths of her father and her brother, both occurring when she was in her early forties, affected her greatly. Although there were other men in her life, she never married and she sometimes expressed regret about that.

Ten years before she died, she bought a house on Bainbridge Island, a short ferry ride from Seattle, and spent as much time there as she could, immersing herself in her garden and bringing together her Washington, D.C., and Seattle friends. After she was diagnosed with lung cancer, for the next three years she continued, to the extent possible, to live her life as she always had—dividing her time between both coasts, secretly working on her memoirs (posthumously published in 2001), supervising the editorial page with her usual vigor, and writing her columns for *Newsweek* until shortly before her death at her home in Washington, D.C., at the age of sixty-eight.

Bibliography: All of Greenfield's papers were donated to the Library of Congress. The archives of the *Washington Post* and *Newsweek* contain many of her writings. Her memoir, *Washington* (2001), includes a foreword by Katharine Graham and an afterword by Michael Beschloss, which also provide important information. Meg Greenfield also figures prominently in Graham's book, *Personal History* (1997), and is quoted in Dan Wakefield, *New York in the 1950s* (1992). Earlier articles and interviews include pieces in the *Washington Journalism Review* (April 1982) by Roger Piantadosi; and an interview in the *Washington Post* in-house newsletter upon her winning the Pulitzer Prize (1978). Along with many firsthand conversations over several years with Meg Greenfield, personal interviews for this article were conducted with Michael Beschloss, her nephew Jim Greenfield, childhood friend Joe Greengard, and Ann Marks, longtime friend and confidante. Extensive obituaries appeared in the *Washington Post* and the *New York Times* on May 14, 1999. See also the tributes by George Will and Charles Krauthammer in the *Washington Post* on May 17 and 18, 1999, respectively, and Hendrik Hertzberg, "The Wayward Press: The Independent Meg Greenfield," *New Yorker*, June 7, 1999, pp. 92–94.

KATE LEHRER

GREENOUGH, Alice. March 17, 1902–August 20, 1995. Cowgirl, rodeo producer.

One of the top cowgirls of rodeo's Golden Age, Alice Greenough was born on her family's ranch near Red Lodge, Montana. Her father, Benjamin Franklin "Packsaddle Ben" Greenough, was orphaned in Brooklyn, New York, before making his way west in 1886. A true cowboy, he won the first bronc-riding contest in Montana. He also drove a stagecoach, carried the mail, punched cattle, and worked as a hired pack and trail guide into the mountains. Greenough's mother, Myrtle Webb, daughter of a Civil War veteran from Illinois, became acquainted with Ben during his trips to the Midwest to sell horses. After several years of correspondence, she packed a trunk and boarded a train bound for Billings, Montana, where she and Ben Greenough were married on October 22, 1899.

Alice was second in a family of eight siblings who grew up breaking wild horses, hunting, fishing, and helping their father with his packing business. Recalling extended stays in the mountains without her father, Greenough said, "I don't think I was ever frightened one day of my life" (Jordan, p. 218). She attended school until age fourteen, when she began carrying the U.S. mail, riding on horseback more than thirty miles every day for several years. Greenough and her younger sister Marge worked as ranch hands for their father and local ranchers in the 1920s, and competed in impromptu riding competitions where they became interested in professional bronc riding. Alice, Marge, and their brothers Bill and Turk became known as the Riding Greenoughs, owing to their successes in local trick riding and roping contests. Greenough married Ray Cahill on August 7, 1922, and had two sons, E. Jay and Thomas, though the marriage was short-lived and ended after a few years. She was briefly married to rodeo performer and rancher Pete Kerscher in the 1930s.

In 1929, as the stock market crash plunged the U.S. economy into the Depression, Marge and Alice joined a Wild West show. Wild West shows were waning in popularity by the late 1920s, and the Greenoughs traveled with the show for only one season before entering professional rodeo. Rodeo was already a fixture of western life, with large annual events like the Calgary Stampede and the Pendleton Round-Up in Oregon. Greenough lived off her prize money, traveled by horseback, and slept in tents while on the road.

In the early days of Greenough's career, women roped and rode against men in smaller competitions, though there were special events set aside for cowgirls, such as saddle bronc riding, trick riding, and relay races. Saddle bronc riding was Greenough's specialty. A popular event with crowds, saddle bronc riding was a dangerous and exciting sport. Holding both reins in one hand, cowgirls had to ride for eight seconds (cowboys rode for ten) to score points and were disqualified if their free hand touched any part of the horse or the reins. Most cowgirls rode untamed horses. Following the 1929 death of Bonnie McCarroll at the Pendleton Round-Up during a ride, many rodeos eliminated women's saddle bronc competitions on the grounds that they were too dangerous.

Rodeo offered Greenough a unique set of opportunities in the 1930s, including financial independence and travel. Depression-era cowgirls earned incomes far in excess of the national average: leading cowgirl Tad Lucas reportedly earned $12,000 in 1935. Still, Greenough traveled to New York and Boston and even Australia and Europe to ride where the purses were larger. In Spain she awed her fans by riding bulls into major arenas in Madrid and Barcelona before bullfights. She took trophies from top rodeos, including the Boston Garden in 1933, 1935, and 1936; competitions in Sydney, Australia, in 1934 and 1939; and Madison Square Garden in 1941. As one of the top bronc riders, Greenough enjoyed the status of minor celebrity while on tour. She also performed stunts in Hollywood films and endorsed cigarettes—though she did not smoke—to supplement her income. Through her career, Greenough competed in every state but three: Vermont, Maine, and New Jersey, which did not have established rodeos.

In 1936, Greenough and other cowgirls and cowboys founded the forerunner of what is today the Professional Rodeo Cowboys Association in response to mismanaged prize money and rodeo events. The organization regulated rodeo management, including the forced standardization of judging rules, and gave competitors more control over the prize money. It also greatly improved the working conditions at rodeos and helped stem the rampant mismanagement of purses. Within the organization, however, women were nonvoting members and were not treated fairly, though they did enjoy the same protection from dishonest rodeo promoters and judges.

The transformation of American culture brought by World War II changed rodeo. Top cowboys enlisted in the war, and rationing of gas and rubber discouraged fans from traveling to attend events. Competitive rodeo was replaced by the new entertainment business of marketing a cowboy image, and rodeo queen beauty pageants gained in popularity. These contests—which persist today at all levels of rodeo—prized beauty over horsemanship and skill and further marginalized cowgirls to accessory roles. Some cowgirls began to compete in calf-roping contests; others, like Greenough, became increasingly disenchanted with the changes in rodeo competition.

Greenough retired from competition in 1941 and went into the business of producing rodeos and stock contracting with longtime friend Joe Orr. They provided bucking horses for rodeos all over the West, and as far east as Milwaukee. Greenough rode exhibitions in the Greenough-Orr rodeos until her 1958 marriage to Orr. The couple moved to Tucson, where Joe Orr died in 1978. Greenough remained in Tucson, living next door to her sister Marge. She died at home on August 20, 1995, at the age of ninety-three. Greenough was the first inductee into the National Cowgirl Hall of Fame in Fort Worth, Texas, and has also been inducted into the National Cowboy Hall of Fame in Oklahoma City, Oklahoma.

Bibliography: Teresa Jordan's collection of oral histories, *Cowgirls: Women of the American West, an Oral History* (1982), is a strong source of biographical information on Alice Greenough and other cowgirls. For the history of women's rodeo as well as Alice Greenough's involvement, see Andrea Mugnier, "Ridin,' Ropin,' and Rodeoin': Champion Cowgirls of Professional Rodeo, 1930–1945," *Nevada Historical Society Quarterly* 44 (Summer 2001), pp. 166–74. Mary Lou LeCompte, *Cowgirls of the Rodeo: Pioneer Professional Athletes* (1993), is a valuable overview of rodeo history and also makes several references to Greenough's career, as does Le Compte's article, "Home on the Range: Women in Professional Rodeo, 1929–1947," *Journal of Sport History* 17, no. 3 (Winter 1990), pp. 318–46. An obituary appeared in the *New York Times* on August 24, 1995. Additional information was provided by the Carbon County Museum in Red Lodge, Montana, and the National Cowgirl Hall of Fame in Fort Worth, Texas.

AMANDA BIRD

GRIERSON, Margaret Storrs. June 29, 1900–December 12, 1997. Archivist.

Margaret Storrs was born in Denver, Colorado, the only daughter and older of two children of Lucius Storrs, geologist and railroad executive, and Mary Louise Cooper, housewife. Her father's profession required frequent travel, giving her a peripatetic childhood. She attended at least seven different schools before leaving home at fifteen to attend the Misses Masters' School in Dobbs Ferry, New York. She majored in English and received her BA from Smith College in 1922, then went on to earn a PhD in philosophy from Bryn Mawr College in 1929. During the year 1924–25 she studied at University College, University of London. Her dissertation explored the relationship of Thomas Carlyle to Immanuel Kant and Johann Fichte.

After teaching at Bryn Mawr, Storrs returned to Smith College in 1931 as an instructor in the Department of Philosophy, where she taught until 1936. During this period she met Marine Leland, a professor of French at Smith and a pioneering figure in the establishment of Quebec Studies in the United States. The two women forged a friendship and a professional partnership that lasted until Leland's death in 1983. In December 1938, Storrs married Sir Herbert Grierson, Lord Rector of Edinburgh University and an internationally known authority on seventeenth-century English literature, who had been a visiting professor at Smith earlier that year. They lived together briefly in Northampton. Herbert Grierson left in 1939, eventually returning to Scotland. They never divorced, and they maintained a friendly correspondence until his death in 1960. They had no children.

In 1940, just as Grierson was exploring opportunities for nonteaching jobs, Smith College was seeking a college archivist. Grierson, who freely admitted that she lacked training and experience in the field, was appointed to the job. At a time when archives of educational institutions were still in their infancy and professional training was nearly nonexistent, her interest and devotion to the college were considered enough qualification.

In 1941, Smith College president Herbert Davis proposed to the newly established Friends of the Smith College Library that they initiate a project particularly appropriate to a women's college and establish a collection of works by women writers. Grierson was appointed executive secretary of the Friends and director of the Women's Collection in 1942. She eagerly added these two positions to that of College Archivist, describing the triumvirate of jobs as a "three-ring circus."

Within the first year, the influence of historian MARY RITTER BEARD and the scope of donations led to a redefinition of the Women's Collection as a "special historical collection of women's materials, recording women's interests and activities in the course of human history and across the face of the earth" ("Imposing Evidence," p. 4). Beard believed that before women's role in history could be known and taught, primary sources must be made available to historians. Mary Beard's dream was that the work of her recently closed World Center for Women's Archives would be carried on by established institutions. Smith College, under the inspired leadership of Grierson, was the first such institution in the United States with the stated mission to accumulate manuscripts and published materials on women. By 1946, when the collection was growing rapidly and its identity as a unique research source among a community of scholars was solidifying, Grierson decided to name the collection after the founder of Smith College, SOPHIA SMITH.

Mary Beard's vision and crusading energy were crucial to shaping the direction of the Sophia Smith Collection (SSC), but Grierson's long hours, tenacious attention to detail, and political and diplomatic skills are what built the SSC from the ground up. Grierson compensated for her lack of formal training by bringing to the job a superior intellect and delicate perception, both conveyed in her incomparably skillful letters. She created one of the preeminent repositories of primary resources for women's history with the help of many interested Smith alumnae and donors, some of who became lifelong friends won over by her pen and typewriter, social grace, diplomacy, and the hospitality of the Grierson-Leland household. Grierson had less success in furthering Mary Beard's efforts to incorporate women's history into the curriculum at Smith, although Grierson prepared the way for future generations of scholars and teachers with her collection priorities.

By the time Grierson retired in 1965, the SSC contained more than 125 collections of manuscripts and records of organizations, including papers of MARGARET SANGER, CARRIE CHAPMAN CATT, SARAH WILLIS PARTON ("Fanny Fern"), ELLEN GATES STARR, and the Garrison family; and records of the Planned Parenthood Federation of America and the National Board of the Young Women's Christian Association. In 1968 Grierson was awarded the Smith College Medal. She retained a keen interest in the SSC and the Smith College Archives and was ever generous in sharing with her successors her institutional memory and important donor connections. She died of cancer in Leeds, Massachusetts, at the age of ninety-seven. She willed her body to Harvard Medical School.

Belying her imposing stature (nearly six feet) and regal bearing, Grierson was deeply private and modest. She shunned recognition for all her accomplishments, yet discerning people such as Mary Beard "got a sharp sense of [Margaret's] force," a quality that served the fledgling SSC well in an era inhospitable to women's advancement. In 1946, Beard believed that "a truly Great Awakening as to women in history" was taking place at Smith College, due in large part to Grierson's exceptional competence and "wide and peculiarly penetrating mind" (Mary Beard to Alice Lachmund, August 1, 1946, Beard Papers, SSC). From her pioneering contribution to women's history—a field that did not even exist when the SSC was founded in 1942—to the sheer hard work she put in every day to keep her three enterprises afloat, Grierson charted a path for her successors and the scholars who turned to the pursuit of women's history in the ensuing decades.

Bibliography: Primary source materials are at the Smith College Archives (SCA), which contains the papers of Grierson and Nina Browne, records of the SSC and Presidents' Office, and SSC/SCA donor files; and the Sophia Smith Collection (SSC), Smith College, which contains the papers of Mary Beard, the Garrison family, Dorothy Brush, and a number of other donors whose correspondence with Grierson sheds light on the early years of the SSC. Grierson wrote the *Annual Report of the Friends of the Smith College Library* during her tenure from 1940 to 1965 and regular articles about college history and SSC holdings for the *Smith Alumnae Quarterly.* Published sources include "Imposing Evidence," *Smith Alumnae Quarterly* 75, no. 2 (Winter 1984), pp. 2–4; Amy Hague, "'Never Another Season of Silence': Laying the Foundation of the Sophia Smith Collection" in *Revealing Women's Life Stories: Papers from the 50th Anniversary Celebration of the Sophia Smith Collection . . . September 1992* (1995); Mary Elizabeth Murdock, "Exploring Women's Lives: Historical and Contemporary Resources in the College Archives and the Sophia Smith Collection at Smith College," in Suzanne Hildebrand, ed., *Women's Collections: Libraries, Archives, and Consciousness* (1986); and Anke Voss-Hubbard, "'No Documents—No History': Mary Ritter Beard and the Early History of Women's Archives," *American Archivist* 58 (Winter 1995), pp. 16–30. Discussion of Margaret Grierson's collaboration with Mary Beard is included in Nancy F. Cott, ed., *A Woman Making History: Mary Ritter Beard through Her Letters* (1991); and Barbara K. Turoff, *Mary Beard as Force in History* (1979). Grierson's death certificate was supplied by the Massachusetts Registry of Vital Records and Statistics. An obituary appeared in the *New York Times* on December 26, 1997.

AMY E. HAGUE

GRIFFITH JOYNER, Florence. December 21, 1959–September 21, 1998. Athlete, entrepreneur.

Florence Delorez Griffith was born in Los Angeles. Nicknamed "Dee Dee," she was the seventh of eleven children (six boys and five girls) born to Florence Scott and Robert Griffith, both African Americans. Her father worked as an electronics technician, and her mother was a seamstress and teacher. The family was solidly working-class until Robert left his wife and children in 1963, which forced them to relocate to the impoverished Jordan Downs Housing Project in the Watts section of Los Angeles. To counterbalance their rough neighborhood, the mother, a devout Christian, raised her children quite strictly. Florence learned to speak softly and distinctly to disguise a slight lisp, but already as a teenager she cultivated the eccentric and flamboyant fashion style that carried over into her athletic career.

Florence began running in elementary school and won the Jesse Owens National Youth Games at fourteen. After graduating from Jordan High School in Los Angeles in 1978, she attended California State University at Northridge for two years; a track-and-field scholarship enabled her to transfer to UCLA, where she was coached by Bobby Kersee. While in college, she helped set the American record in the World Cup 4 × 100 relay (1981), finished second to Evelyn Ashford in the 200 meters in 1982, and finished second in the 400 meters in 1983 behind Rosalynd Bryant. Griffith left UCLA in 1983 without earning her degree to train in earnest for the 1984 Olympic

Games. At Los Angeles, she won the silver medal in the 200 meters. She attracted just as much media attention for her eel-tight body suits in wild colors, but she was denied a place on the relay team because officials argued that her elaborately manicured nails would impede her passing the baton.

Disappointed by her performance, she temporarily dropped out of track and field; but she became motivated again as the 1988 Olympics drew closer. An important influence on her comeback was her marriage to Alfrederick Alfonzo Joyner, track-and-field jumper and 1984 Olympic medalist, on October 10, 1987, in Las Vegas. Joyner became her workout partner and coach, and his calmer temperament was a steadying influence. At the 1987 World Championship Games in Rome, Griffith Joyner won second place in the 200 meters, introducing the hooded running uniform that was adopted by the 1988 U.S. Olympic Team. At the Olympic trials in Indianapolis, she shattered the U.S. and world records, causing the press to dub her "the fastest woman alive."

The 1988 Olympics Games in Seoul, Korea, were the high point of her career. By now she had emerged as the self-constructed "glamour girl of track," complete with the nickname "FloJo." Her "one-leggers" and "athletic negligees," which created a sensation, introduced an ultra-femininity not seen on the competitive track before, and her six-inch fingernails, decorated in red, white, and blue with gold Olympic rings, garnered as much attention as her record-shattering times. She won three Olympic gold medals: in the 100 meters (10.54, wind-aided), the 200 meters (21.34), and the 400-meter relay (41.98). When she earned silver as a member of the 1,600-meter relay team, she became the first American woman to win four medals in one Olympics.

This stellar performance garnered her countless awards, including designation as athlete/sportswoman of the year by the Associated Press, United Press International, and *Track and Field Magazine.* But it also brought controversy: her impressive musculature and dramatic improvement triggered suspicions that her performances were drug-aided. Darrell Robinson, another former 400-meter runner, told the German magazine *Stern* that he had purchased human growth hormones (steroids) to sell to FloJo at her request. Even when she called him a liar on a popular national talk show, this unproven charge increased public scrutiny and disparagement. Despite countless drug tests throughout her career—all of which proved negative—these charges continued to shadow her to her death.

In the year following her Olympic excellence, Florence Griffith Joyner earned roughly $4 million. She retired from track and field in 1989 and continued to coach her husband Al. Their daughter, Mary Ruth Griffith Joyner (affectionately dubbed "MoJo" by the media), was born in 1990. FloJo attempted a brief comeback as a marathoner in 1992 but was thwarted by a damaged Achilles tendon.

She next turned her considerable talents to entrepreneurship and entertainment. She created new uniforms for the NBA's Indiana Pacers and was the co-owner of New Nails Company and a hair-braiding business. She designed a line of sportswear, produced a fitness tape, and authored a series of children's books featuring a character named Barry Bam Bam. In 1998 she secured an exclusive contract with Lady Foot Locker to market footwear and apparel by Saucony. She also embarked on a successful career as an entertainer, appearing on numerous talk shows and television sitcoms (like *227*) and as a host and commentator at sports events.

In 1993 President Bill Clinton appointed Griffith Joyner co-chair of the President's Council on Physical Fitness and Sports. That same year she received the Distinguished Service Award from the United Negro College Fund and served as spokesperson for the American Cancer Society, Multiple Sclerosis Foundation, and Project Eco-School, an environmental education initiative. In 1994 she and Al co-founded the Florence Griffith Joyner Youth Foundation for disadvantaged children.

In April 1996 on a flight from Los Angeles to St. Louis, Griffith Joyner suffered some sort of seizure, but the family refused to release further information. That incident was forgotten until two years later, when on September 21, 1998, she died in her sleep at home. First medical reports said that she died from a heart seizure, but later her death was attributed to suffocation during an epileptic seizure. Because of the controversy that had always dogged her career, Al Joyner agreed to an autopsy to quell rumors that her death was triggered by steroid abuse. The results were negative. Florence Griffith Joyner, a prominent role model for girls and women, was often quoted as saying, "Don't try to be like me. Strive to be better than me." Only thirty-eight when she died, she was buried in Mission Viejo, California.

Bibliography: Several biographies trace Griffith Joyner's career: April Koral, *Florence Griffith Joyner: Track and Field Star* (1992); Nathan Aaseng, *Florence Griffith Joyner: Dazzling Olympian* (1989); and Mark Stewart, *Florence Griffith-Joyner* (1996). Carrie Boyko and Kimberly Colen, eds., *Hold Fast Your Dreams: Twenty Commencement Speeches* (1996), includes an address by her. Sources for a general background on women and sports include Susan K. Cahn, *Coming on Strong: Gender and Sexuality in Twentieth-Century Women's Sport* (1994); Anne Janette Johnson, *Great Women in Sports* (1996); and Mary Jo

Festle, *Playing Nice: Politics and Apologies in Women's Sports* (1996). Florence Griffith Joyner's career was extensively covered in the popular press, especially in *Sports Illustrated.* See also "A Shocking Death—World Record Holder Florence Griffith Joyner Dies," *Track and Field News,* December 1998, p. 53. Obituaries appeared in the *New York Times, Washington Post,* and *Los Angeles Times* on September 22, 1998.

SUSAN E. CAYLEFF

GRISWOLD, Estelle Trebert. June 8, 1900–August 13, 1981. Activist, Planned Parenthood League official.

Estelle Griswold, a lifelong activist whose name is associated with a landmark 1965 Supreme Court decision legalizing contraception in Connecticut, was born Estelle Naomi Trebert in Hartford, Connecticut. Her father, Frank Trebert, a toolmaker of Irish and German descent, imparted to his daughter a love of vigorous outdoor activity and Native American customs. Estelle described her mother, Jennie Church Trebert, as a placid person, understated and very British, despite her American birth. The youngest of two surviving children, Estelle was raised Roman Catholic, but was not a devout practitioner in later life. Intelligent, dynamic, and mischievous, she finished Hartford Public High School in five years, owing to habitual truancy.

Estelle next pursued singing aspirations, funding herself at the Hartt School of Music. In 1922, against her parents' wishes, she left for Paris and Nice to study voice but came back to America after learning that her mother was seriously ill. Her return was marred by the closely spaced deaths of her parents. Resuming her performing career brought work in traveling productions and on radio.

She fell in love with former schoolmate Richard "Dick" Whitmore Griswold, and they were married on October 20, 1927, in New York City. She ended her singing career after her voice coach died. In 1935, the Griswolds moved to Washington, D.C., where she attended George Washington University, pursuing her interests in medicine. This led to an instructorship at the medical school.

During World War II, Richard Griswold left his business career to work in navy intelligence and then joined the Office of Political Affairs in the State Department. In 1945 his wife decided to follow him on his assignment to Europe and attempted to gain employment with the United Nations Relief and Rehabilitation Agency (UNRRA), the organization created to help thousands of displaced persons migrate from Europe after World War II. Initially, the agency rejected Griswold, who was then forty-five years old. Stymied by the official channels of UNRRA, she circumvented the process by going straight to the top. Her proven ability to lead and make bureaucratic mountains melt away with her personal charm and love of a challenge helped her thrive in the chaos of an agency still organizing its relief efforts. She ended her time in Europe implementing her own resettlement plan of displaced persons to several countries in South America for the Church World Service (CWS).

Returning to the United States in 1950, Griswold left the CWS in mid 1951, frustrated by her colleagues' inability to see that their actions meant life or death for displaced persons. She then volunteered with the newly formed New Haven Human Relations Council. Two years later, her husband's battle with emphysema forced her to look for paid work. Their home in New Haven was next door to the main office of the Planned Parenthood League of Connecticut (PPLC). An office worker at the PPLC, aware of Griswold's prior accomplishments, casually offered her the position of executive director. A formal offer quickly followed, and her tenure began on the first day of January 1954.

Griswold knew little about contraception or the birth control movement. (She and her husband had been unable to conceive children.) The advice of an old friend and the former medical director of the PPLC, Hilda Crosby Standish, persuaded her to accept the challenging directorship. The PPLC was woefully behind the national birth control movement, after decades of unsuccessful attempts to overturn Connecticut's anti-contraceptive statute. This law made it a crime for persons to use contraceptives, provide advice on contraception, or help anyone acquire contraceptive materials. Rarely enforced, the statute still meant pharmacists could not sell contraceptives labeled as such; doctors had to make a personal choice to break the law to prescribe female contraception such as diaphragms; and pro-contraceptive groups could not open a birth control clinic without risking a police raid.

Griswold quickly reinvigorated the PPLC. First, she arranged to transport women to New York and Rhode Island birth control clinics, which violated the statute by helping these Connecticut residents acquire contraception. Next, she decided to file suit on behalf of couples who wanted to practice birth control for health or economic reasons. In *Poe v. Ullman* (1961), the U.S. Supreme Court justices dismissed the case because they perceived the law as a dead letter and the suit as a veiled attempt by PPLC to win the right to open clinics.

Consequently, Griswold decided to open a PPLC clinic in November 1961. By the early 1960s, the Catholic-led opposition to contraception was lessening and population control had gained legitimacy. Despite this, Griswold as executive director, C. Lee Buxton as medical director, the clinic staff, and their patients would be risking arrest under Connecticut's law. When the police investigated the clinic, Griswold welcomed the officers and supplied them with armloads of evidence. Catherine Roraback, a local lawyer and civil rights activist, arranged with the prosecutor to have Buxton, Griswold, and a few patients surrender to police, setting in motion the court case bearing her name.

In 1965, the U.S. Supreme Court ruling in *Griswold v Connecticut* transformed the legal landscape. The case cited a married couple's right to privacy as the reason the law was unconstitutional. This established a precedent for civil rights more far-reaching than anything contraceptive advocates believed possible. Hailed as one of the greatest successes in women's struggle for self-determination, the decision helped overturn laws against unmarried people's access to contraception and also set a precedent for the pro-choice ruling in *Roe v. Wade* (1973). The right to privacy invoked in Griswold is the fulcrum on which personal liberties and state authority are balanced.

Shortly after her triumph, Estelle Griswold resigned from the PPLC, owing in part to internal tensions. After her husband's death in 1966, she went on to fight for legalized abortion and senior citizens' rights. She died in 1981 in Fort Myers, Florida, at the age of eighty-one.

Bibliography: The major source of information on Estelle Griswold is the Planned Parenthood League of Connecticut Papers archived at the New Haven Colony Historical Society, New Haven, Connecticut. The Family Planning Oral History Collection at the Schlesinger Library, Radcliffe Institute for Advanced Study, Harvard University, includes the most extensive interview of Griswold along with the interviewer's research materials. There are references to both the PPLC and Estelle Griswold in the papers of the Planned Parenthood Federation of America (PPFA) in the Sophia Smith Collection, Smith College Library, Northampton, Massachusetts. The Margaret Sanger Papers Project, Department of History, New York University, is an excellent starting point for Margaret Sanger, the PPFA, and references to the PPLC. The most detailed book on the legal battle for reproductive rights, including *Griswold v. Connecticut,* is David J. Garrow, *Liberty and Sexuality: The Right to Privacy and the Making of* Roe v. Wade (1998). See also Susan C. Wawrose, *Griswold v. Connecticut: Contraception and the Right of Privacy* (1996). Gereon Zimmerman, "Contraception and Commotion in Connecticut," *Look,* January 30, 1962, pp. 78–83, profiles Estelle Griswold and other participants in the PPLC campaign. An obituary appeared in the *New York Times* on August 18, 1981.

JENNIFER L. BALL

GUGGENHEIM, Peggy. August 26, 1898–December 23, 1979. Art collector and patron.

Marguerite "Peggy" Guggenheim was born in New York City, the second of three daughters of Florette Seligman and Benjamin Guggenheim. Descended from a Swiss peddler who emigrated to the United States in 1848, her father was one of the Guggenheim brothers, who at the time of her birth were making a fortune in copper smelting. Her mother's family, originally from Bavaria, were bankers. Privately tutored at home and on annual trips to Europe, Guggenheim lived a pampered life in her family's townhouse on the Upper East Side. She attended the Jacoby School, a private academy for wealthy Jewish girls, and later she was taught at home by future labor activist Lucile Kohn, to whom she gave a good deal of credit for her awakening social conscience. She was deeply attached to her father, and when he went down on the *Titanic* in 1912 (the mistress he traveled with survived), Guggenheim was heartbroken.

Her father had left the family firm before his death, and as a result Guggenheim called herself "a poor relation"; but when she turned eighteen, she came into $450,000. She would inherit an equal amount after the 1937 death of her mother, a matron who was culturally, if not educationally, sophisticated. In 1920 she sailed for Europe, not knowing that she would spend the next twenty-one years abroad. In France she lived the life of a rich, reckless expatriate, eventually marrying the talented and eccentric Laurence Vail, a writer and artist known as the King of Bohemia, in 1922. The marriage was stormy, with scenes played out on the terraces of Paris and at their house in the south of France, and resulted in two children: Michael Cedric Sindbad, known as Sindbad (1923), and Pegeen Jezebel, known as Pegeen (1925). The marriage effectively ended when, in 1928, Guggenheim met the charismatic John Holms, a British war veteran, would-be writer, and renowned conversationalist. He and Guggenheim led a wandering life for the next six years, including renting a notable house for two summers in the English countryside. Hayford Hall, or Hangover Hall as the residents called it, saw a steady stream of talented visitors, among them the writer DJUNA BARNES, whom Guggenheim had been supporting financially for a decade. At Hayford Hall, Barnes produced her sapphic modernist novel *Nightwood,* which she dedicated to Peggy and John. Holms unexpectedly died while undergoing a minor operation in 1934.

Though she was versed in the old masters and had never previously bought art, Guggenheim opened a gallery devoted to modern art, Guggenheim Jeune, on London's Cork Street in January 1938. Almost immediately, the gallery became a talked-about *succès d'estime,* attracting young surrealist and abstract artists from France, Spain, and Germany. Marcel Duchamp was a reliable adviser to Guggenheim on acquisitions. She showed such contemporary European artists as Kandinsky, Brancusi, Arp, Moore, Calder, and Tanguy. At the time, Guggenheim—a woman of arresting, angular presence, her looks compromised only by an unusually shaped nose—was enjoying liaisons with a series of men, including Samuel Beckett, with whom she had an intense, on-and-off, eleven-month relationship; Yves Tanguy (they had to dodge his wife); and English surrealist and critic Roland Penrose.

The gallery was not turning a profit, and Guggenheim began to explore the idea of a museum of modern art, appointing as director the art critic Herbert Read. He drew up a list of artists she should see, and Guggenheim returned to France with the idea, she said, of buying a picture a day. War threatened, however, and she reluctantly put the museum idea aside, though she continued to buy art at very low prices. She generally followed the guidelines of Duchamp and Read, but she had the eye of a connoisseur and knew what would and would not fit with her collection.

Having acquired works by an extremely wide range of European artists, Guggenheim escaped Europe for New York City in 1941 with her collection and her future husband, artist Max Ernst. There, on West 57th Street, she opened Art of This Century, a gallery dedicated to abstract and surrealist art where European émigré artists like Duchamp and Gorky mingled with the generation of Americans who came to be known as abstract expressionists. Art of This Century gave Jackson Pollock his first one-person show in the fall of 1943, one of the greatest triumphs of Guggenheim's collecting career. She gave similar encouragement to, among others, William Baziotes, Mark Rothko, Robert Motherwell, and Clyfford Still. Arguably, her gallery and her activities in the 1940s led to the shift of the art world's epicenter from Paris to New York City.

Her marriage to Ernst unraveling and the gallery successfully launched, Guggenheim embarked on writing her memoirs. *Out of This Century* (1946) shocked readers with its candid descriptions of her erotic adventures among the avant-garde; it is also an extremely valuable document of the development of modernism. In 1947, she decamped for Venice, shrewdly anticipating that her collection would be shown to best advantage in a relatively small foreign city with a history of fine art. In 1948 she bought a palazzo on the Grand Canal and hung her art, opening the doors to the public. She continued to patronize artists, but her interests shifted again to Europeans, such as the Italian artists Tancredi and Edmondo Bacci. Her Venice guest books contain the signatures and drawings of writers and artists like Jean Cocteau and Truman Capote.

Guggenheim's uncle Solomon's Museum of Non-Objective Painting—where Pollock worked briefly as a carpenter—opened its doors as the Solomon R. Guggenheim Museum, in New York City, in 1959. Peggy worried about what would become of her collection and her palazzo after her death; eventually she left them to the Guggenheim Museum, after making peace with her conservative family. Today the palazzo is a quiet oasis in crowded Venice, its collection a welcome relief from the preponderance of old masters for which the city is known.

Guggenheim died in a hospital outside Venice in 1979 from complications of stroke at the age of eighty-one. She left a considerable artistic legacy. Opinion within the arts community was often critical of her during her life and after—perhaps because of her exuberant celebration of her sexuality, which continued well into old age, not to mention the power she wielded in the art world. Yet she was a key witness, observer, recorder, and finally shaper of the course of twentieth-century culture.

Bibliography: There is significant Guggenheim correspondence in the Emily Coleman papers, Special Collections Department, University of Delaware Library; in the Djuna Barnes papers, Special Collections, University of Maryland Library; and in the Bernard and Becky Reis papers at the Archives of American Art, Smithsonian Institution, and the Research Library, Getty Research Institute, Los Angeles. The Smithsonian's Archives of American Art contains related correspondence in the papers of William and Ethel Baziotes, Edwin David Porter, and Jane and Louis Bouché, among others. The Guggenheim Museum Archives contains scrapbooks kept by Guggenheim, extensive press clippings, and documentation of the agreement between the Peggy Guggenheim Collection and the Museum. In addition to *Out of This Century* (1946), Guggenheim also published *Confessions of an Art Addict* (1960). Jacqueline Bograd Weld's *Peggy: The Wayward Guggenheim* (1986) is competent biographically but singularly negative and gossipy in tone. Virginia Dortch, ed., *Peggy Guggenheim and Her Friends* (1994), is an invaluable oral and documentary history of the subject. Glossy art books by two relatives give accurate information and supply many photographs of Guggenheim and family and friends (including photographs by Man Ray and Berenice Abbott) and reproductions of works in the Peggy Guggenheim Collection: Karole Vail, *Peggy Guggenheim: A Celebration* (1998), and Laurence Tacou-Rumney, *Peggy Guggenheim: A Collector's Album* (1996). Vail's book reproduces pages from the guest book at the palazzo in Venice. Lesbian poet Eileen Myles never knew Guggenheim personally but wrote a verse tribute to her called "Last Supper" (*School of Fish,* 1997). An obituary appeared in the *New York Times* on December 24, 1979.

MARY V. DEARBORN

H

HALL, Helen. January 4, 1892–August 31, 1982. Settlement house leader, social welfare activist.

Helen Hall, the most outstanding of the second generation of settlement house workers, was born to Wilford Hall, a manufacturer of surgical instruments, and Beatrice Dakin Hall, an artist, in Kansas City, Missouri. Her family, which included a younger sister, soon moved to Westchester County, New York, where she enjoyed a comfortable, secure childhood and attended public schools. Her parents believed that women should have some sort of purpose to their lives besides family responsibilities. As a teenager, she became aware of poor people living nearby and her mother encouraged her to engage in charitable activity.

Her family intended her to become a sculptor and, as preparation, she enrolled at Columbia University in 1912 and 1913. Her real desire, however, was a career in social welfare; she spent 1915 at the New York School of Philanthropy, which later affiliated with Columbia University. She then held various social welfare jobs in Westchester County, organizing Eastchester Neighborhood House and then working in the child welfare and widows' pension areas for the county welfare department. When the United States entered World War I, Hall joined the Red Cross to run recreational units in American military hospitals in France. After the war, she set up a YWCA girls' club in Alsace. Next, she spent a year and a half in China and the Philippines organizing clubs for American servicemen.

Returning to the United States in 1922, Hall accepted a position as head of Philadelphia's University Settlement. She also became active in the National Federation of Settlements. In 1928, Hall embarked on a study of unemployment caused by technological change or work stoppages. Her descriptions of unemployed individuals solicited from settlement houses around the United States were published as *Case Studies of Unemployment* (1931). The timing of the study made Hall a national expert on what, by then, was the country's leading problem. As the Great Depression worsened, she provided congressional testimony and also served as an advisor to the governor of Pennsylvania on unemployment issues.

In 1933, she became director of Henry Street Settlement on New York City's Lower East Side; the following year she assumed the presidency of the National Federation of Settlements. That year, President Franklin Roosevelt appointed Hall to the Advisory Council of his Committee on Economic Security, charged with drafting the landmark Social Security Act of 1935. This legislation established the federal welfare "safety net." Besides social insurance, the law also established Unemployment Compensation and such categorical needs programs as Old Age Assistance, Aid to the Blind, and Aid to Dependent Children. Hall, who had traveled to England in 1932 to study that country's social welfare system, argued for the inclusion of national health insurance as well, but Roosevelt did not want to jeopardize his permanent federal welfare structure in a fight over that issue. In the end, Hall joined seven others in issuing a minority report on behalf of national health insurance. She continued to agitate for such coverage, often in connection with the National Federation of Settlements, for the next several decades. In 1952, she published a report documenting the need for national health insurance among Henry Street Settlement's neighbors; "When Sickness Strikes a Family" appeared in *Building America's Health* (1952), a report by the President's Commission on the Health Needs of the Nation. In 1965 she was among those invited to witness President Lyndon Johnson's signing of Medicare into law.

In addition, Hall was a lifelong advocate of government subsidized housing programs for low-income people and for better welfare programs in general. She used her position as a consultant to New York City's Housing Authority to advocate for more social services for problem residents in public housing. She also was among those settlement house workers who argued for incorporating community space into public housing projects. Under her leadership, Henry Street moved some of its programming into the neighborhood housing projects that she had helped create. She also continued to lobby Congress for improvements in the minimum wage, unemployment compensation, and welfare programs.

Hall was effective in part because of certain personal characteristics. She made it her business to know the people who could help her causes, and she used her position as a settlement leader to lobby for reform. Physically, she was tall and attractive, and she had an imposing personality. Her 1935 marriage to *Survey* editor Paul U. Kellogg added to her influence in social welfare circles. Hall and Kellogg lived together in the head resident's apartment at Henry Street until her husband's death in 1958; she remained there until her retirement. At the end of the 1930s, while she continued to preside over the National Federation of Settlements, Kellogg served as president of the National Conference of Social Work. Theirs was a childless, personally happy, and professionally dynamic relationship.

Hall continued as head of Henry Street Settlement until retiring in 1967, taking a leave of absence in 1942–43 to again work for the Red Cross organizing recreation for servicemen in the South Pacific. From 1936 to 1941 she helped form and head the Consumers National Federation, and she continued to work on consumer issues in the decades that followed. She also established a pioneer mental hygiene clinic at Henry Street, developed a strong program for the elderly poor there, and achieved national significance in initiating Mobilization for Youth in 1957, a federally funded program to bring intensive social services and community organization to the Lower East Side. This program is widely regarded as the prototype for Lyndon Johnson's subsequent War on Poverty.

Her energy and commitment to social welfare causes extended into her retirement. Although she had a vacation home in Cornwall, New York, near the Hudson River, she continued to serve on the boards of so many social service organizations that she found it expedient to maintain an apartment on the Upper East Side of Manhattan. She died there at the age of ninety, having been in bad health for several years.

Bibliography: The Helen Hall Papers and the Henry Street Settlement Records, plus other related collections, are located at the Social Welfare History Archives center, University of Minnesota Libraries. Hall's major publication is her autobiography, *Unfinished Business in Neighborhood and Nation* (1971). For more biographical information, see Janice Andrews, "Helen Hall (1892–1982): A Second Generation Settlement Leader," *Journal of Sociology and Social Welfare* 19, no. 2 (June 1992), pp. 95–108; and "Social Reformer and Settlement Leader: Helen Hall and Her Neighbors," in Janice Andrews, ed., *From Vision to Action: Social Workers of the Second Generation* (1992), pp. 43–57; see also Andrews's biographical sketch of Hall in "Female Social Workers of the Second Generation," *Affilia* 5, no. 2 (Summer 1990), pp. 46–59. Sue Steinwall, who processed Hall material at the Social Welfare History Archives, wrote the biographical entry on Helen Hall in Walter I. Trattner, ed., *Biographical Dictionary of Social Welfare in America* (1985), pp. 343–45. The Social Welfare History Archives also has a copy of Megan H. Morrisey's "The Life and Career of Helen Hall: Settlement Worker and Social Reformer in Social Work's Second Generation" (PhD dissertation, University of Minnesota, 1996). Hall's obituary appeared in the *New York Times* on September 2, 1982.

JUDITH ANN TROLANDER

HAMER, Fannie Lou. October 6, 1917–March 14, 1977. Civil rights activist, community organizer.

Fannie Lou Hamer, who followed the examples set by other leading African American women of her time to play a major role in the civil rights movement, was born Fannie Lou Townsend in rural Montgomery County, Mississippi. She was the youngest of twenty children of sharecroppers Lou Ella Bramlett and James Lee Townsend, who was also a Baptist preacher. When Fannie Lou was two years old, her parents moved to Sunflower County and the child received barely six years of education there. School years for sharecroppers averaged only about four months, and Fannie Lou missed many of those because she had very poor clothing. Remembering her parents' struggle to provide for their children, she later drew a link between blacks' lack of access to the political process and their poor economic status.

At age six she began what looked to be a lifetime of working in the cotton fields. In 1944, plantation owner W. D. Marlow offered her a job as his time- and recordkeeper. That year she married Perry "Pap" Hamer, a tractor driver on the Marlow plantation. For the next eighteen years of her adult life, Fannie Lou Hamer worked as sharecropper and timekeeper on the plantation four miles east of Ruleville, Mississippi, the place where she and Perry made their home. She was unable to bear children (and later, in 1961, was sterilized without her consent during a routine operation), and she and Pap adopted two girls. One, Vergie Ree, had been badly burned as an infant, and the girl's parents could not afford to care for her. They took in another, older child, Dorothy Jean, from an impoverished single mother. Later, after Dorothy Jean died of a cerebral hemorrhage, the Hamers assumed the job of raising her two daughters, Jacqueline and Lenora.

Hamer's life changed dramatically on August 31, 1962, when she was forty-four. Inspired by organizers from the Student Nonviolent Coordinating Committee (SNCC) who were encouraging black Mississippians to claim their constitutional rights, Hamer unsuccessfully attempted to register to vote in the county seat of Indianola. That same day her employer fired her from her position as timekeeper when she refused to back down about her intention to register. Familiar with the physical violence that often followed economic reprisals, and having received physical threats, Fannie Lou Hamer left her family to stay with friends. But the move did not prevent the violence, as Hamer and her friends miraculously escaped rounds of gunshots fired into the friends' home when her presence there was discovered.

Despite being denied the right to vote, and the subsequent physical and economic intimidation she faced, Fannie Lou Hamer became an active member of SNCC in Ruleville. She saw her work with SNCC as being an improved situation for her personally and as a way for her to challenge the general state of poverty for black people in Mississippi. She also reasoned that, now that she and her husband had been ejected from Marlow's land, circumstances could not get much worse. She took the literacy test several times and finally became a registered voter. In 1963 she became a field secretary for SNCC. From this point onward Hamer worked with voter registration drives and with programs designed to assist economically deprived black families in Mississippi, circumstances with which she said she felt especially familiar. Religion was also an important part of her activism, and she was instrumental in starting Delta Ministry, a community development program, in 1963.

In April 1964, Hamer joined other civil rights activists in founding the Mississippi Freedom Democratic Party (MFDP), becoming vice chairperson and a member of its delegation to the Democratic National Convention in Atlantic City, New Jersey, where they challenged the seating of the regular all-white Mississippi delegation. In this capacity she addressed the convention's Credentials Committee, passionately pleading with its members to recognize the biracial representatives of the MFDP as the legitimate delegates from the state of Mississippi. Her live televised speech, in which she told how she had been brutally beaten in 1963 in the Montgomery County jail after being arrested for trying to integrate a bus terminal, stands as one of the most compelling in American history, its cadence and use of American symbols rivaling many of Martin Luther King's most famous speeches. Her political rhetoric and personal authority were so powerful that President Lyndon Johnson called a press conference for the exclusive purpose of interrupting televised coverage of her speech. In the end the 1964 challenge failed, despite a compromise offered through Hubert Humphrey and Walter Mondale that would have seated two nonvoting MFDP members. But the MFDP's actions resulted in an unprecedented pledge from the Democratic Party that at its next convention, in 1968, it would not seat delegate groups that excluded blacks.

In the fall of 1964 Hamer traveled to West Africa with a SNCC delegation at the invitation of the president of Guinea. Also that fall Hamer attempted again to run for Congress. (She had already challenged the incumbent, Jamie Whitten, in the Democratic primary the previous spring, but lost overwhelmingly, hardly a surprising result given that so few blacks could vote.) Because the regular Democratic Party disallowed her name on the ballot, the MFDP conceived a "Freedom Vote," which included both black and white candidates. In this symbolic election Hamer defeated her white opponent, Congressman Whitten, by more than 33,000 votes to 49. In 1965, Hamer, Victoria Gray of Hattiesburg, and Annie Devine of Canton took their case to the U.S. Congress, arguing that it was wrong to seat Mississippi's elected representatives, who were all white, when the state's population was fifty percent African American. Even though the challenge lost, the three women took encouragement in the fact that 148 members of Congress agreed with their appeal.

Hamer remained active in civic affairs in Mississippi for the remainder of her life, working with the Mississippi Freedom Labor Union starting in 1965 and serving as a delegate to the National Democratic Convention in Chicago in 1968. Her founding in 1969 of the Freedom Farms Corporation (FFC), a nonprofit venture designed to help needy families raise food and livestock, showed her concern for the economic plight of blacks in Mississippi. The FFC also provided social services, minority business opportunities, scholarships, and grants for education until it succumbed to financial pressures in 1974. As with Delta Ministry, the FFC also provided an outlet for Hamer's religious zeal. In 1971 Hamer became a member of the original policy council of the National Women's Political Caucus and unsuccessfully ran for the Mississippi state senate.

Initiative, courage, and selflessness best describe the character of Hamer's life, and she received wide recognition for her part in bringing about a major political transition in the South and raising significant questions that addressed basic human needs. Her motivation to make a difference in the freedom struggle is best summarized by her repeated remark: "I'm sick and tired of being sick and tired." Suffering from breast cancer, hypertension, and diabetes, into the 1970s Fannie Lou Hamer continued to give numerous speeches across the country, especially concerning basic human rights for all Americans. She died of cancer on March 14, 1977, in Mound Bayou, Mississippi, at the age of fifty-nine.

Bibliography: The Fannie Lou Hamer Papers at Tulane University's Amistad Research Center in New Orleans contain correspondence, clippings, and biographical and financial information. Additional archival material is found at the State Historical Society of Wisconsin and the Mississippi Department of Archives and History. An oral history conducted by Neil McMillen (April 14, 1972) is part of the Mississippi Oral History Program at the University of Southern Mississippi. Other interviews include J. H. O'Dell, "Life in Mississippi: An Interview with Fannie Lou Hamer," *Freedomways* 5, no. 2 (1965), pp. 231–42, and Jerry DeMuth, "Tired of Being Sick and Tired," *Nation,* June 1, 1964, pp. 548–51. Biographies of Hamer include Chana Kai Lee, *For Freedom's Sake: The Life of Fannie Lou Hamer* (1999); and Kay Mills, *This Little Light of Mine: The Life of Fannie Lou Hamer* (1993). See also Bernice Johnson Reagon, "Women as Culture Carriers in the Civil Rights Movement: Fannie Lou Hamer," in Vicki L. Crawford, Jacqueline Anne Rouse, and Barbara Woods, eds., *Women in the Civil Rights Movement: Trailblazers and Torchbearers, 1941–1965* (1990). For popular articles on Hamer, see Phyl Garland, "Builders of a New South," *Ebony*, August 1966, pp. 27–30, 34, 36–37; Paule Marshall, "Hunger Has No Color Line," *Vogue,* June 1970, pp. 126–27; Joyce A. Ladner, "Fannie Lou Hamer: In Memoriam," *Black Enterprise* 7, no. 10 (May 1977), p. 56; and Eleanor Holmes Norton, "Woman Who Changed the South: Memory of Fannie Lou Hamer," *Ms.*, July 1977, p. 51. General sources on the civil rights movement that discuss Hamer include Clayborne Carson, *In Struggle: SNCC and the Black Awakening of the 1960s* (1981); John Dittmer, *Local People: The Struggle for Civil Rights in Mississippi* (1994); and Charles Payne, *I've Got the Light of Freedom: The Organizing Tradition and the Mississippi Freedom Struggle* (1995). An obituary appeared in the *New York Times* on March 15, 1977, with an additional article on March 21, 1977, describing her memorial service.

LINDA REED

HAMILTON, Grace Towns. February 10, 1907–June 17, 1992. State legislator, civic leader.

Grace Towns Hamilton was the first black woman elected to a state legislature in the Deep South. Representing her newly redrawn Atlanta district in the Georgia General Assembly from 1966 to 1984, she exercised more power as a state lawmaker than any African American before her.

She was born in Atlanta, the second of five children (three girls, two boys) of Harriet Eleanor (Nellie) McNair and George Alexander Towns. (Their first daughter died in infancy.) Her father, a native of Albany, Georgia, was the son of a former slave and the grandson of the unacknowledged half brother of George Washington Towns, a Georgia governor. He was educated from grammar school through college at Atlanta University (AU), an integrated institution primarily devoted to the education of blacks. He received another undergraduate degree in 1900, from Harvard, and then spent the next thirty years at Atlanta University as a professor of English and pedagogy. His wife, a graduate of AU's normal school, taught school for a time but after marriage devoted herself to home and family while engaging actively in her community's civic and church affairs.

Grace Towns inherited her mother's fair skin and fine hair, her strong will and her imperial bent, but her father most influenced her professionally and politically. He was her mentor and idol. Like him, she was educated from grammar school through college at Atlanta University and, as her family home was located on the campus, her formative years were spent entirely in the sheltered environs of an institution that knew no color bar. AU awarded her an undergraduate degree in 1927, and in 1929 she earned a master's degree in psychology at Ohio State University while working in Columbus for the Young Women's Christian Association (YWCA).

Returning to Atlanta, she taught psychology at Clark College and the Atlanta School of Social Work. In 1930 she married Henry Cooke Hamilton, a fellow Atlantan then teaching at LeMoyne College in Memphis, Tennessee. In 1931 she gave birth to their only child, Eleanor. During her decade in Tennessee, she taught psychology at LeMoyne and surveyed black workers for the Works Progress Administration before joining the national staff of the YWCA, for which she developed interracial programs on numerous college campuses. In 1941, when her husband became head of AU's high school program (he would complete his career as head of the Department of Education and Psychology at Morehouse College), she returned with him to Atlanta, where the couple lived and worked the remainder of their lives.

In 1943, Grace Hamilton was appointed executive director of the Atlanta Urban League (AUL); she was one of the earliest women to hold such a post. Under her leadership, the Atlanta league chose not to follow the National Urban League's traditional emphasis on employment, but instead waged intensive campaigns for racial advance within the confines of segregation. Hamilton's campaign successes included a remarkable jump in African American voter registration, an increase in school funding, a new hospital for non-indigent Atlanta blacks (now the Hughes Spalding Children's Hospital), and thousands of new housing units for middle-income blacks. She sidestepped the issue of segregation, however, which eventually brought her into conflict with the National Urban League; in 1960 she lost her Atlanta post.

An interim period of private consulting followed. During that time, the civil rights movement broke upon the nation with militant demands for racial justice, and the Supreme Court abolished Georgia's county unit system (a unique device slighting urban in favor of rural voters) and mandated legislative and congressional redistricting. In 1965, Congress enacted the federal Voting Rights Act empowering the federal government to promote racial equity in the southern electoral process, thus removing the last obstacle to African American representation in the region's legislative bodies. In Georgia, Hamilton captured the Democratic nomination for state representative from her new home district in a special primary election held in May 1965, took the office without opposition in the special general election of June 1965, and was sworn in in January 1966. She was one of seven newly elected African American legislators, the first to enter Georgia's lower house since the end of Reconstruction.

During her eighteen years in the state legislature, Hamilton worked tirelessly to expand political representation for blacks in city, county, and state governments. She was a principal architect of the 1973 Atlanta City Charter, which for the first time brought the city's blacks onto the Atlanta City Council in a number commensurate with their proportion in the population. She was a leader in congressional and legislative reapportionment battles, and in 1972, after white legislators had repeatedly manipulated district lines to thwart him at the polls, Andrew Young credited Hamilton for his election when he became the first African American to represent Atlanta's Fifth District in Congress. After the 1980 census, the Fifth District was the center of another brutal reapportionment battle, in which Hamilton took the side of the white leadership against militant young African Americans who wanted an Atlanta seat made to order for a black candidate. Hamilton vigorously challenged their position, but her opponents won and later went on to help defeat her when she ran for reelection in September 1984. She was succeeded by Mable Thomas, a woman one-third her age.

The Atlanta community continued, nevertheless, to shower her with recognition and awards. She held only one other public post, as an advisor to the U.S. Civil Rights Commission from January 1985 to January 1987. Her departure from that work coincided with the death of her husband on January 2, 1987. When she died on June 17, 1992, at the age of eighty-five, the *Atlanta Journal,* which had called her "an institution in the House of Representatives" (August 3, 1984), ran a front-page obituary. The Georgia Legislative Black Caucus established the Grace Towns Hamilton Leadership Award in her honor, and Grady Memorial Hospital gave her name to its Women's and Infants' Pavilion.

Bibliography: The Grace Towns Hamilton papers, the principal source of information about her life and work, are available at the Atlanta History Center, Atlanta, Georgia. Valuable information on her career up to 1970 is available in Sharon Mitchell Mullis, "The Public Career of Grace Towns Hamilton, a Citizen Too Busy to Hate" (PhD dissertation, Emory University, 1976). The most complete account of her life and work is found in Lorraine Nelson Spritzer and Jean B. Bergmark, *Grace Towns Hamilton and the Politics of Southern Change* (1997). Jean B. Bergmark helped update research for this essay. Profiles of George Alexander Towns and George Washington Towns are found in Kenneth Coleman and Charles Stephen Gurr, eds., *Dictionary of Georgia Biography* (1983). An obituary appeared in the *New York Times* on June 20, 1992.

LORRAINE NELSON SPRITZER

HANCOCK, Joy Bright. May 4, 1898–August 20, 1986. Navy officer, director of the WAVES.

In a career with the navy spanning three wars, Joy Bright Hancock worked to open permanent military careers to women. Born in Wildwood, New Jersey, she was the third child in a family of three girls and three boys. Her father, William Henry Bright, a self-made real estate entrepreneur, was active in local and state politics. Her mother, Priscilla Buck, was a local leader in the woman suffrage movement. Hancock described their marriage as a remarkable partnership. Brought up to believe in female equality and public service, she learned to ride and repair bicycles as a girl, and played sports at Wildwood High School. She was enrolled in a Philadelphia business school when the United States entered World War I.

In the fall of 1918, Joy Bright enlisted in the U.S. Navy as a first-class yeoman, one of the nearly twelve thousand enlisted women who served in the First World War (most, like Bright, in stateside clerical positions). Late in the war, she was transferred to the Naval Air Station at Cape May, New Jersey. This assignment proved momentous, for her personal and professional life in the interwar years was intertwined with the early history of naval aeronautics. In 1919, Lieutenant Charles Gray Little, a Harvard-educated navy pilot, was posted to Cape May, and he and Joy Bright soon agreed to marry. Little was appointed to the crew of the navy's first rigid airship and sent to England for training. In the fall of 1920, the couple married overseas. Joy returned to the States to find a home and wait for the completion of Little's transatlantic flight. Tragically, he never returned, having been killed in a dirigible explosion in 1921.

In 1922, Joy Little took a civilian position in the navy's new Bureau of Aeronautics in Washington, D.C. Her fascination with airships led her to request transfer to the Naval Air Station at Lakehurst, where the navy's ZR-1, the *Shenandoah,* was being assembled. In June 1924, she married Lieutenant Commander Lewis Hancock, a Texan, a former submarine commander, and an executive officer of the *Shenandoah.* In little more than a year, Lewis Hancock was also dead, in the stormy crash of his dirigible.

Joy Hancock was devastated by this second tragedy. She spent nearly a year hospitalized with unexplained temporary paralysis; afterward she lived and traveled abroad. Hancock returned to the States in the late 1920s and enrolled in the Crawford School of Foreign Service, preparing for a career newly opened to women. On two attempts she passed the written examination but failed the oral, a circumstance she later attributed to sex bias. Hancock also undertook flight training, reasoning that if she learned to fly, she would overcome her fear of it.

In 1934, Hancock rejoined the Bureau of Aeronautics as head of the Editorial Research section, the bureau's chief publicist. Hancock edited a newsletter, forerunner of *Naval Aviation News,* and published numerous aviation articles in popular magazines, though she concealed her female identity by publishing under her initials. Publicly she began to promote women, in words that echoed the individualistic feminism of the interwar years: "I feel about women in aviation exactly the same way I feel about women in every field of activity. There is a place for a woman wherever she can do a job as well, or better, than anyone else."

The second half of Hancock's career was dedicated to this proposition. In July 1942, the Women's Reserve of the Navy, known as the WAVES (Women Accepted for Volunteer Emergency Service), was established over the objections of many navy leaders. Hancock was commissioned as a lieutenant in October 1942. During World War II, Hancock served as women's representative for the Bureau of Aeronautics, and liaison to the office of Lieutenant Commander MILDRED MCAFEE, director of the WAVES. McAfee, president of Wellesley College, had no prior experience with the military, and she appreciated Hancock's inside knowledge of the navy. In February 1946, Hancock was appointed assistant director of the Women's Reserve, and was transferred to the Bureau of Naval Personnel; in July she became the third and final director of the WAVES.

Hancock's signal achievement was her role in passage of the Women's Armed Services Integration Act (Public Law 625) in 1948, which established for the first time a permanent status for women in all the armed services. At the close of World War II, despite the outstanding military record of women, many questioned the need for their service in peacetime. Hancock's adroit management of the bill helped secure its ultimate success. In formulating her campaign, she took advantage of both the nation's patriotic gratitude to the WAVES and its growing fear of international communism. To demonstrate the navy's full support, she insisted that top navy men, including Admiral Chester Nimitz, dominate the bill's presentation.

The struggle for the bill took nearly two years, and was complicated by the reorganization of the armed services under the National Security Act of 1947. The bill for the integration of women into the armed services was signed into law by President Truman on June 12, 1948.

The end of the WAVES was by no means the end of Hancock's navy career. Captain Hancock served as assistant chief of naval personnel for women from 1948 until her mandatory retirement in 1953. As the highest-ranking woman in the navy, she oversaw the successful integration of women, developing plans and policies for their selection, training, utilization, housing, and welfare. She supervised the call-up of the Women's Naval Reserve during the Korean War.

In contrast to the wartime chiefs of the women's corps, such as McAfee and OVETA CULP HOBBY, who came from civilian life, Hancock had a career that embodied the future for women in the military. She regarded military service as a viable profession for women. She insisted that women be allowed to contribute their technical and professional expertise to the nation's security on an equal basis with men. A leader well liked by men and women, Hancock was diplomatic but not afraid to be confrontational when necessary.

After retiring, Hancock married her friend of many decades, Ralph Ofstie, a navy vice admiral, in 1954. Ofstie died in 1956 following surgery. In 1972, Hancock published her memoir, *Lady in the Navy.* She died of respiratory arrest in 1986 at the age of eighty-eight and was buried in Arlington National Cemetery.

Bibliography: Joy Bright Hancock's autobiography, *Lady in the Navy: A Personal Reminiscence* (1972), is an informative and highly readable source. A lengthy oral history of Hancock is found in a collection of oral histories published in typescript form in 1971 under the title *The WAVES Vol. 1* by the Oral History Program of the U.S. Naval Institute, Annapolis, Maryland. The major manuscript source is the Joy Bright Hancock papers, University of Georgia, Athens; this collection includes unpublished speeches and reports, drafts of navy legislation, photographs, and working drafts of her autobiography. It also includes the transcript of a 1941 radio interview from *Woman's World,* May 29, 1941, from which the quotation is taken. Hancock was the author of *Airplanes in Action: Planes of the Navy, the Army, the Coast Guard, and Commercial Airlines* (1938), a book for young people. Hancock's contributions to the history of women in the U.S. Navy are extensively discussed in Jean Ebbert and Marie-Beth Hall, *Crossed Currents: Navy Women from World War I to Tailhook* (1993). Obituaries appeared in the *Washington Post* on August 22, 1986, and the *New York Times* on August 25, 1986.

SUSAN ZEIGER

HARDY, Harriet Louise. September 23, 1906–October 13, 1993. Physician.

Harriet Louise Hardy, a clinician distinguished for her vigilant investigation of industrial diseases, was born in Arlington, Massachusetts, the first of two daughters of Harriet Louise Decker, a 1902 Wellesley College graduate, and Horace Dexter Hardy, a lawyer, member of the Massachusetts legislature, and assistant district attorney. After Horace Hardy's death from pneumonia in 1910 at age thirty-three, his widow married Charles Maxwell Sears in 1912; Harriet's half-brother Zenas was born in 1913. Sears was an engineer without secure employment. The Depression prompted the Sears family to settle permanently in Dorset, Vermont, where the family home was turned into a guest house. Hardy visited Dorset throughout her life and is buried there.

Hardy attended the Kent Place boarding school in Summit, New Jersey, and in 1928 graduated from Wellesley College, where she had been class president and voted "most popular" among her classmates. Intent on a medical career despite family opposition, she attended Cornell University Medical School (MD, 1932) and took postgraduate training at Philadelphia General Hospital (1932–34). Her family's financial needs and the satisfactions of clinical work during training determined Hardy's early practice at Northfield Seminary for Girls (1934–39) and Radcliffe College (1939–45). While at Northfield she courageously met medical emergencies during a deadly hurricane in 1938 and believed this stress was the precursor to the chronic debilities she suffered throughout her life.

Hardy made two important connections in 1945 that shaped her practice in what she named "clinical preventive medicine" within the professions investigating industrial diseases. She joined the Division of Occupational Disease in the Massachusetts Department of Labor, working as the first medical consultant to the chemists and engineers who were exploring reports of work-associated sickness. She also accepted an appointment to the Industrial Medical Clinic at Massachusetts General Hospital (MGH), where Drs. Joseph Aub and ALICE HAMILTON carried out research on lead poisoning. Aub encouraged her to study the respiratory complaints of workers, primarily young women, in two lamp factories. After reading the scientific literature on materials used in this industry, listening to employees' accounts of illness, and examining their symptoms directly, Hardy concluded that dust produced from the light metal beryllium used in manufacturing fluorescent lights was a dangerous poison. This evidence was contested by industries using beryllium, insurance investigators, lawyers, and a U.S. Public Health Service publication, but Hardy's carefully documented studies of patients won medical attention and the confidence of Hamilton, author of the defining text on occupational disease, *Industrial Toxicology* (1934). Hamilton asked Hardy to co-author the revised edition (1949), initiating a close professional and personal relationship.

Publication of Hardy's papers on beryllium poisoning prompted meetings with scientists doing atomic research. She spent 1948 at Los Alamos, New Mexico, exhilarated by the natural environment while monitoring potentially dangerous workplace exposures at the Scientific Laboratory, and remained a consultant to the Atomic Energy Commission after returning to Boston in 1949. Hardy expected to enlarge the scope of clinical investigation and teaching at MGH, but soon centered her work at MIT, where she created the Occupational Medical Service. Her reputation established, she received support from the new National Institutes of Health and the Atomic Energy Commission, was invited to lecture in Europe, and founded the national Beryllium Case Registry (1952). She settled in nearby Lincoln, Massachusetts, where she shared a home with her sister, Jane, and young nephew.

Over the next two decades the pace of Hardy's professional life was both exhilarating and exhausting as she fought to secure accountability for workers' disabilities. She maintained connections to the MGH Clinic, extending patient-focused research on diseases caused by exposures to toxic "dust," fumes, and chemicals in coal mining, cotton mills, and factories. Neither personal reserve nor critics' assertions dimmed her confrontations with representatives of industry, insurance, and the law who ignored or denied responsibility for conditions that were dangerous to their employees. New challenges compromised her resolve to spare time for reflection and writing as she continued on the faculty at the Harvard Medical School (1952–73), conducted investigations on benzol, asbestos, cadmium, and the anthrax bacillus, and enjoyed professional recognition including election to the Association of American Physicians (1957) and the New York Academy of Sciences. In her invited Annual Discourse to the Massachusetts Medical Society (1975), she reviewed risks of toxic exposure and charged academic medicine with abetting industry's greed and society's neglect through failure to prepare students for careers in occupational medicine.

While a medical student, Hardy began to keep a journal that illuminates the personal and professional challenges she faced throughout her life as a female physician. She first resolved to practice in a rural area, and the journal reflects her delight in nature—she was an avid bird watcher—particularly in periodic retreats to the country when exhausted by the pressures of her work. Dedicated to the new specialty of occupational medicine, she reflected that "Conflict still remains with me and probably always will as to how best to understand and work out God's Will in me and for me. The direct dealing with individuals sick or approaching sickness will always be my own choice" (January 1, 1948). A few years later she asserted, "For better or for worse I have taken my work as my lover, my husband, my children," and although she once suggested that women were particularly suited for occupational medicine, she also questioned, "Is there a need for special women's interests in medicine? I doubt it & feel keenly one should plan to be a good doctor, not a good male or female doctor" (May 20, 1951, and February 15, 1953).

In the late 1960s new symptoms complicated the fatigue and depression that periodically interrupted her work. Choosing early retirement from

MIT in 1971, Hardy accepted an invitation from friends to become an associate of Dartmouth Medical School. Persistent disabilities led to the diagnosis and removal of a benign brain tumor, and she resigned her positions at Dartmouth and at Harvard. Hardy published her memoir, *Challenging Man-Made Disease,* in 1983 and maintained connections with colleagues and friends, but she never regained the strength to engage professional responsibilities. Hardy and her sister moved to Holyoke after lymphoma was diagnosed; when her strength ebbed, she asked to be admitted to Massachusetts General Hospital, where she died on October 13, 1993, at the age of eighty-seven.

Bibliography: Hardy's papers, including her journal (1931–77) and personal and professional correspondence, are in the Schlesinger Library, Radcliffe Institute for Advanced Study, Harvard University. Her scientific publications include "New Clinical Syndrome: Delayed Chemical Pneumonitis Occurring in Workers Exposed to Beryllium Compounds," *Bulletin of the New England Medical Center* 9, no. 1 (February 1947), pp. 16–24; "Risk and Responsibility: A Physician's Viewpoint," *New England Journal of Medicine* 293 (October 16, 1975), pp. 801–806; and Alice Hamilton and Harriet Hardy, *Industrial Toxicology* (1949, 3rd ed. 1974). Her autobiography, *Challenging Man-Made Disease: The Memoirs of Harriet L. Hardy, MD,* with Emily W. Rabe (1983), includes a bibliography. An oil portrait (1985) hangs in the Francis A. Countway Library of Medicine, Harvard Medical School. Useful information for this article was supplied by John Stoeckle, MD, and David Wegman, MD. Obituaries appeared in the *New York Times* and the *Boston Globe* on October 15, 1993.

BARBARA GUTMANN ROSENKRANTZ

HARRIMAN, Pamela. March 20, 1920–February 5, 1997. Socialite, fund-raiser, ambassador.

Pamela Digby Churchill Hayward Harriman was born Pamela Digby in Farnborough, England, into an aristocratic but financially strapped family. She spent her early years at the family's Dorset estate, Minterne Magna, with her father, Edward Kenelm, Lord Digby; her mother, Constance Bruce Digby (known as Lady Pansy); and three younger siblings. In 1935, she attended Downham, a small boarding school in Hertfordshire where, in 1936, she received a domestic science certificate. After that she spent several months in Paris and Munich for "finishing," returning to London in time to participate in the 1938 debutante season. Although a very self-assured eighteen-year-old, Pamela was not successful as a debutante, in that she did not immediately marry into wealth and social status. For the duration of her life, she would strive to overcome the humiliation of being passed over by suitors because of her plain looks and her rather acerbic personality. As a result, she spent a great deal of effort establishing connections with rich and influential men.

In September 1939, Pamela Digby met Randolph Spencer Churchill, the spoiled and alcoholic son of Winston Churchill, who in May 1940 replaced Neville Chamberlain as prime minister of England. Randolph proposed to her on their first date, reportedly because he was just about to go to war, and they were married almost immediately. Soon pregnant, Pamela moved into 10 Downing Street and developed a very close relationship with her in-laws, a family that allowed her access to the politically elite and moneyed class. In October 1940 she gave birth to a son, Winston, but the marriage was already shaky and the couple separated in 1942 and divorced in 1945.

In 1941, Pamela had met Averell Harriman, President Franklin Roosevelt's special wartime envoy, when he came to London to confer with Churchill. Although Harriman was married, the two began an affair, during which time he supported her. Still, Pamela Churchill continued to seek liaisons with other important men, including Major General Fred Anderson, head of CBS William Paley, renowned reporter Edward R. Murrow, wealthy diplomat John Hay "Jock" Whitney, playboy Prince Aly Kahn, and head of the Fiat auto empire Gianni Agnelli. These affairs earned her a rather dubious reputation as a professional mistress. More charitably, Pamela Churchill was developing into a woman able to move forward when the circumstances demanded it.

After the war, Pamela Churchill traveled to the United States and then to Europe seeking some emotional stability, as well as financial security, through a series of love affairs. In 1958, she met Leland Hayward, Hollywood agent and Broadway producer. They fell in love and Hayward divorced his wife. He and Pamela were married on May 4, 1960. Like all the men in her life, Hayward became her center of focus, and she devoted all her energies to seeing to his needs until his death in 1971. He left her with little money, so Pamela Digby Churchill Hayward once again had to create a new life for herself.

After an unhappy stint back in England, she returned to the United States. At a Washington, D.C., dinner party given by Katharine Graham in honor of Arthur Schlesinger Jr., she again met Averell Harriman, now almost eighty years old and a widower. The two rekindled their romance, and on September 27, 1971, six months after Hayward's death, they were married. Pamela Harriman became a United States citizen and immersed herself in the world of Democratic politics. During the Reagan years, the couple worked to revitalize the Democratic Party, and the aging Harriman turned much of this activity over to his enthusiastic and energetic wife. Pamela Harriman and her political action committee, PamPAC, became a powerful force during the 1980s. In 1986 Averell Harriman died, at the age of ninety-four, and left a considerable fortune to his widow, who now devoted all her activities to Democratic Party politics.

In 1992 she worked tirelessly for the Clinton-Gore campaign, and her PamPAC helped ensure Democratic victory in that crucial election year. In 1993 President Clinton appointed her the first female ambassador to France, the high point in her life. She had gained respectability as well as power, but this time in her own right. Determined to prove that she was not merely a society ambassador but an effective representative of her adopted country, she threw herself wholeheartedly into her work at the embassy in Paris. She acted as a facilitator and concerned herself with the important task of creating a good relationship with the media as well as with the local power structure. As ambassador, she called on her considerable social skills when performing ceremonial duties. She did not attempt to set policy, however; her knowledge of her limitations increased her effectiveness.

Pamela Harriman's final years were marred by legal wrangling with the Harriman family over alleged financial mismanagement of her late husband's estate. The lawsuit with the family was settled when Pamela paid the family and the Harriman trusts approximately $15 million in 1996.

Planning to relinquish her post as ambassador after the 1996 election, Pamela Harriman began to consider her options. She had talked about acting as adviser to President Clinton or possibly working for Al Gore's presidential campaign in 2000. On February 3, 1997, however, she suffered a cerebral hemorrhage while swimming laps at the Ritz Hotel in Paris and died two days later at the age of seventy-six.

Although the identity she created for herself emerged from her connections with such powerful men as Winston Churchill and Averell Harriman, she nevertheless exerted political and social influence in her own right. She succeeded because she did not succumb to the gender restrictions imposed upon her. She managed to function effectively within the limitations that society had placed upon her as a woman, and she was able to survive by making the system work for her. Pamela Harriman, whose life encompassed much of the twentieth century, left behind a legacy not only of survival but of service to her adopted country.

Bibliography: Two biographies treat Harriman's life: Christopher Ogden, *Life of the Party: The Biography of Pamela Digby Churchill Hayward Harriman* (1994); and Sally Bedell Smith, *Reflected Glory: The Life of Pamela Churchill Harriman* (1996). An obituary appeared in the *New York Times* on February 6, 1997.

JUNE HOPKINS

HARRIS, Patricia Roberts. May 31, 1924–March 23, 1985. Lawyer, ambassador, federal official.

Patricia Roberts was born in Mattoon, Illinois, to Hildren Brodie Johnson, a schoolteacher, and Bert Fitzgerald Roberts, a Pullman car waiter. After her father abandoned the family, her mother raised Patricia and her younger brother, Malcolm, alone. When she was six years old Patricia became aware of racism after being called a nigger, but her mother steadfastly refused to let her children be defined by the racist stereotypes that existed in the predominantly white community of Mattoon.

Her family did not have a lot of money, but they believed in education. Patricia graduated from Englewood High School in Chicago in 1942 and then enrolled at Howard University, which was one of several colleges that had offered her a scholarship. While attending Howard, she became active in the early civil rights movement, participating in sit-ins to protest racial discrimination in the District of Columbia's restaurants, hotels, and department stores. In 1945 Roberts graduated summa cum laude from Howard University with a degree in political science and economics. Her civil rights activism helped pave the way for her future entry into public service.

After Howard, Roberts returned to Illinois, where she earned a master's degree in industrial relations at the University of Chicago in 1947. During this time she also worked as program director of the local Young Women's Christian Association (YWCA). In 1949 she returned to Washington, D.C., and enrolled at American University to pursue further graduate studies in public policy. While in Washington, she served from 1949 to 1953 as assistant director of the American Council on Human Rights, managing the agency's political action and national legislative programs. From 1953 to 1959, she served as the executive director of Delta Sigma Theta, a national African American sorority under the leadership of president Dorothy Height.

In 1955 Patricia met and married William Beasley Harris, a Washington lawyer and Howard University law professor. They had no children. With her husband's encouragement, she enrolled at George Washington University School of Law, where she graduated first in her class in 1960. After working briefly as a trial attorney in the U.S. Department of Justice Criminal Division in 1960–61, she joined Howard University School of Law as an associate dean of students and a part-time lecturer. While she was working at Howard, President John F. Kennedy appointed her chairperson of the National Women's Committee for Civil Rights. Although this was an unpaid position, Harris was responsible for creating and coordinating support for new civil rights legislation from women's organizations.

Because of her growing political involvement in Washington, Harris was asked to second the presidential nomination of Lyndon Johnson at the 1964 Democratic National Convention. Johnson later appointed her to the thirteen-member Commission on the Status of Puerto Rico, where he was so impressed with her diplomatic skills that he appointed her ambassador to Luxembourg in 1965. The first female African American ambassador in U.S. history, Harris served in that post until 1967. Her international service also included being an alternate to the 21st and 22nd General Assemblies of the United Nations from 1966 to 1967. In the meantime Harris returned to Howard University School of Law in 1967 as a full-time professor.

In 1969 Harris became the first black woman to be selected as dean of Howard University School of Law; she resigned after thirty days, over disagreements with faculty and the president of the university regarding a student uprising. In 1970 she joined the prestigious law firm Fried, Frank, Harris, Shriver and Kampelman, where she practiced corporate law and continued to be involved in Democratic Party politics. In 1977 President Jimmy Carter appointed her to his cabinet as secretary of Housing and Urban Development (HUD). During the Senate confirmation hearings that year, Senator William Proxmire questioned her empathy for the poor and disadvantaged. Harris responded forcefully: "You do not understand who I am. . . . I am a black woman, the daughter of a Pullman car waiter. I am a black woman who even eight years ago could not buy a house in parts of the District of Columbia. I didn't start out as a member of a prestigious law firm, but as a woman who needed a scholarship to go to school. If you think that I have forgotten that, you are wrong" (Smith, p. 439).

Throughout her career Harris was driven by the need to excel at whatever challenge was before her. Fair-skinned, petite, and of medium height, she was opinionated and possessed a sharp tongue. Many viewed her forthrightness as an admirable characteristic, but others judged it a flaw. Nevertheless, she successfully reorganized the Department of Housing and Urban Development and lobbied Congress for additional funding for HUD's subsidized housing programs. Harris's success in this position led President Carter to appoint her in 1979 as secretary of Health, Education and Welfare (HEW), which was renamed the Department of Health and Human Services (HHS) shortly after her confirmation. She held this position until Carter left office.

Harris remained active in politics and in 1982 ran a bitter and unsuccessful campaign for mayor of Washington, D.C., against the incumbent, Marion Barry. Despite her early association as a civil rights activist, her unyielding support for social programs, her support for legislation for the poor and minorities, and her reputation as an effective administrator, Harris failed to mobilize enough support to challenge the popular mayor, who was considered more in touch with the African American community. She received only 36 percent of the vote.

During her impressive career as an attorney and advocate for civil rights, Harris was awarded more than thirty-two honorary doctorates from colleges and universities around the country. After her unsuccessful bid for mayor, Harris accepted an appointment in 1983 as professor of law at George Washington University. Her husband of twenty-nine years, William Beasley Harris, died unexpectedly of a stroke in November 1984. She died five months later from cancer at age sixty on March 23, 1985, in Washington, D.C., where she is buried.

Bibliography: The papers of Patricia Roberts Harris are found at the Library of Congress. Photographs of Harris are in the Moorland-Spingarn Research Center, Howard University. The few books and popular and scholarly articles on Harris mostly focus on her tenure at HUD. Two of the better analyses are found in Herman Nickel, "Carter's Cactus Flower at HUD," *Fortune,* November 6, 1978, pp. 110–13; and Alex Poinsett, "Patricia Roberts Harris: HUD's Velvet-Gloved Iron Hand," *Ebony,* July 1979, pp. 33–36. See also Laurence E. Lynn Jr. and David deF. Whitman, *The President as Policymaker: Jimmy Carter and Welfare Reform* (1981); and Sheila Hobson and Harvey D. Goldenberg, *Black Americans in Government* (1969). Significant information is contained in memorials published after her death, including J. Clay Smith Jr., "Patricia Roberts Harris: A Champion in Pursuit of Excellence," *Howard Law Journal* 29 (1986), p. 440; and "Memorial Tributes," *George Washington Law Review* 53 (1985), p. 319. Obituaries are found in the *New York Times* and *Washington Post* on March 24, 1985, and the *Chicago Defender* on March 25, 1985.

META K. TOWNSEND

HARRISON, Anna Jane. December 23, 1912–August 8, 1998. Chemist, educator.

Anna Jane Harrison was born in Benton City, Missouri, the younger of two children and the only daughter of Mary K. Jones and Albert S. J. Harrison. Both her parents came from Missouri farm families. Her father died when she was seven; her mother then managed the farm. Anna attended a one-room rural school, where she later taught for two years after her graduation from the University of Missouri in the Depression year 1933. (She had attended Lindenwood College in St. Charles, Missouri, for two years before transferring to the university.) She went on to receive her MA in physical chemistry from the University of Missouri in 1937 and her PhD in 1940.

Realistically, the only jobs for a woman in her field were at women's colleges. Her career in chemical education started in 1940 at Sophie Newcomb College, the women's college affiliated with Tulane University, where she served as instructor and then assistant professor. In 1945, she joined the faculty of Mount Holyoke College, where she rose through the academic ranks and retired as William R. Kenan Jr. Professor in 1979. She became part of Mount Holyoke's long tradition of research on ultraviolet spectroscopy of small molecules (the study of the interaction of ultraviolet light with these molecules) begun by EMMA PERRY CARR and Lucy Pickett. Sabbatical leaves took Harrison to Cambridge University in 1952–53 and to the National Research Council of Canada in 1959–60 to further her own specialty within spectroscopy, the technique of flash photolysis (treating the sample with a short burst of light). At the same time, her unique and effective teaching style had an impact far beyond her own institution. It was recognized with the Manufacturing Chemists Association Award in College Chemistry Teaching in 1969, the James Flack Norris Award for Outstanding Teaching of Chemistry, presented by the Northeast Section of the American Chemical Society in 1977, and the American Chemical Society Award in Chemical Education in 1982.

As time went on, Harrison primarily focused her attention on issues of the impact of science on society, an interest that continued to the end of her life. She became one of the first representatives of a liberal arts college to be appointed to the National Science Board, on which she served from 1972 to 1978. In that capacity, she was part of a group that visited the research facilities in Antarctica supported by the National Science Foundation, including two trips to the South Pole. She served as president and on the board of directors of both the American Chemical Society and the American Association for the Advancement of Science. One of her main goals was to increase public understanding of science so that informed citizens could have a rational basis for value judgments about the impact of science and technology on their lives.

When Harrison became the first woman president of the American Chemical Society in 1978, one of her first comments was that she hoped she would not be the last. (Her wish for women to succeed her in that post has been fulfilled on more than one occasion.) Her 1983–84 tenure as the fourth woman president of the American Association for the Advancement of Science also made history; her immediate predecessor was astronomer Margaret Burbidge, and this was apparently the first time two women in a row had been president of a major scientific society. Harrison was the recipient of twenty honorary degrees.

After her retirement, she and colleague Edwin Weaver wrote a textbook, *Chemistry: A Search to Understand* (1989), that was intended to serve the needs of students whom she characterized as "intellectually curious but not professionally driven." One of the goals that was most important in her life was to give others the opportunity to increase their knowledge. She could make chemistry an intellectual adventure for any student, from the most hesitant to the most dedicated.

Harrison's influence on everyone she met was instantaneous, powerful, and of lifelong duration. She was an important presence in South Hadley, where she continued to live for nineteen years after her retirement. She never married. After the death of her mother and an aunt, she had no family in the area, but she was involved in the local community, especially in activities having to do with horses or gardening. She was a very private person, but deeply engaged with the world around her.

Harrison characterized her love of travel as an addiction. Many of her favorite journeys involved rugged terrain where horses and mules were the means of locomotion. She delighted in every new experience with a pack train. Long experience with balky mules may well have figured in developing another of her greatest skills. She could deflate cant and bombast with devastating effectiveness. Her unyielding common sense could cut to the heart of any matter with an economy of language that verged on the laconic.

She inspired not only generations of chemists, but generations of gardeners. Many gardens in South Hadley and elsewhere have plants that grew from those in Anna Harrison's own truly remarkable wildflower garden. A number of local children had their first jobs doing yard work for her, a tradition that continued up to the summer of her death.

During the summer of 1998, she was busy with plans to speak at an upcoming meeting of the American Chemical Society and then to go on a trip to Russia. Unexpectedly, she suffered several strokes in quick succession and died on August 8, 1998, in Holyoke, Massachusetts, at the age of eighty-five. Her passing was marked by moving tributes from the American Chemical Society, the National Science Foundation, and many of her colleagues and friends. Her ashes were buried in Benton City, Missouri. Her return there was so right. Anna Harrison was from Missouri, literally and figuratively. In so many ways the ultimate pioneer woman, she retained the attitudes of the frontier all her life. The farm and the one-room school remained with her always, as did the lessons in self-reliance and good sense that she learned there. She used the quality of going to the heart of the matter as an integral part of her impact on the world of science.

Bibliography: The files of the chemistry department and the archives of Williston Memorial Library at Mount Holyoke College contain many reports about the life of Anna Harrison. Her professional papers are listed in *Chemical Abstracts.* Obituaries appeared in the *Hampshire Gazette* (Northampton, Massachusetts) on August 11, the *Boston Globe* on August 12, the *New York Times* on August 16, and *Chemical and Engineering News* on August 17, all in 1998. Her colleague Edwin S. Weaver and her niece, Mary Jo (Harrison) Freeman, contributed additional information.

MARY K. CAMPBELL

HAVILAND, Virginia. May 21, 1911–January 6, 1988. Librarian, children's literature specialist, writer.

The distinguished career of Virginia Haviland spanned a golden age in children's literature and helped define children's librarianship as a professional specialty. She was born in Rochester, New York, the first child of William J. and Bertha Esten Haviland, both of whom came from well-established New England families. Virginia spent her first years in Rochester, where her father was a bookbinder, before the family, including younger brother Clarence, moved to Amesbury, Massachusetts, in 1917. As a child, Virginia was an avid reader of traditional books like *Peter Rabbit, Alice in Wonderland,* and *Little Women.* She credited the classic *Heidi* with stimulating an early desire to experience foreign places. At that time children's librarianship was not an established profession, so she did not pursue this interest in books more seriously. Instead, she planned on becoming a teacher. Haviland graduated from Amesbury High School in 1929 and entered Cornell University later that year. She earned a BA in economics from Cornell in 1933.

Unable to find a teaching job after graduation, Haviland responded to an employment notice posted in the Boston Public Library (BPL). She took the entrance exam and was hired immediately. Although Haviland's job was editing annotated lists of new library books, she enrolled in a children's literature class taught by BPL's renowned children's librarian, Alice Jordan. "I was absolutely captivated by children's books, children's literature as she presented it," Haviland recalled in a 1980 interview. "And I decided that that was for me." At BPL, Haviland's career progressed from children's librarian to branch manager to head of readers' advisory services for children. She also began writing professionally in 1946, publishing "Children and Their Friends, the Authors" in *More Books: The Bulletin of the Boston Public Library,* followed in that same year by articles on children's programming in the *Wilson Library Bulletin* and *Library Journal.* In 1952, Haviland became associate editor and reviewer for *Horn Book Magazine,* thriving in the heady atmosphere of the magazine's Boston offices. She continued to review children's books for the next thirty years.

Many of Haviland's professional writings focused on publishing trends and the role librarians played in developing children's literature collections. Lamenting that beautiful and appealing books were overshadowed by mediocre publications, Haviland criticized children's book publishers for using lavish illustrations to disguise weak texts, altering and abridging classics, and producing books based on formulas, not inspiration. Concerned that librarians' book purchases were based on publisher promotions, not critical evaluation, she outlined a theory and method for effective selection. She furthered these ideas regarding professional practice in courses taught at Simmons and Trinity Colleges and, later, in her textbook *Children and Literature: Views and Reviews* (1973).

In 1949, the New England Library Association asked Haviland to deliver their annual Caroline Hewins Lecture on the history of children's literature. Frederic Melcher, president of R. R. Bowker Publishing Company, suggested she discuss children's travel stories, and Haviland's presentation on that topic was subsequently published as *The Travelogue Storybook of the Nineteenth Century* (1950). Although it received mixed reviews, the book began Haviland's literary career. Her next effort was a fictionalized biography of William Penn (1952) commissioned by Abingdon Press.

Haviland began writing fairy tale books in 1959, producing some of her best-loved and most enduring work. She traveled the world collecting traditional stories and then recast them in a simplified yet authentic manner. Commencing with *Favorite Fairy Tales Told in England,* her series covered Germany (1959), France (1959), Ireland (1961), Norway (1961), Russia (1961), Scotland (1963), Spain (1963), Poland (1963), Italy (1965), Sweden (1966), Czechoslovakia (1966), Japan (1967), Greece (1970), Denmark (1971), and India (1973). Her fairy tales were favorably reviewed in professional and popular periodicals, including the *New York Times Book Review,* the *Times Literary Supplement,* and the *New Statesman.*

In 1963, the Library of Congress established a Children's Book Section (now called the

Children's Literature Center) and hired Virginia Haviland as founding director. Under Haviland's visionary administration, the Center gathered some hundred thousand children's books the library had acquired through the U.S. copyright law and launched a campaign to highlight the collection through exhibits, lectures, and publications. In the following two decades Haviland built a national research center for the study of children's books. During that period she also edited an impressive array of bibliographies, exhibit catalogs, and anthologies, including *Children's Literature: A Guide to Reference Sources* (1966) and its supplements: *Books in Search of Children* (1969); *Children & Poetry* (1969); *Children's Books of International Interest* (1972); *Yankee Doodle's Literary Sampler of Prose, Poetry, & Pictures* (1974), co-edited with Margaret Coughlan; *North American Legends* (1979); *The Best of Children's Books, 1964–1978* (1980) and its supplements; and *The Openhearted Audience* (1980).

In her quest to advance children's literature, Haviland became active in professional associations and book competitions at home and abroad. She chaired the Newbery-Caldecott Award Committee (1953–54) and was elected president of the American Library Association's Children's Services Division in 1954. Acting as an ambassador for children's books, she participated in countless international meetings, book fairs, and awards committees, helped establish the International Board on Books for Young People, and served for many years on the International Hans Christian Andersen Book Award Committee.

Haviland's final years at the Library of Congress were marked by honors and accolades. In 1976 she won both the Catholic Library Association's prestigious Regina Medal for "continued distinguished contribution to children's literature" and the American Library Association's Grolier Foundation Award for her "unusual contribution" in promoting reading among the young. She retired from the Library of Congress in June 1981.

Though Haviland was an admitted workaholic, her personal life was enriched by enduring female friendships and an international network of professional colleagues. Not only was she active in numerous library associations, she was also a member of the Society of Women Geographers, PEN, and the Authors Guild. Haviland enjoyed hosting stylish events at the Library of Congress and was a gourmet cook at home. Her extensive travel afforded her enormous personal pleasure in addition to literary inspiration and professional advancement.

On January 6, 1988, Virginia Haviland died of a stroke at her home in Washington, D.C. She was seventy-six. Having never married or had children, she left no immediate heirs, but her legacy continues in the Virginia Haviland Scholarship offered by Simmons College's Children's Literature Program. Committed to research to the end, Haviland donated her body to the George Washington Medical School.

Bibliography: Haviland's professional records can be found in the annual reports for the Children's Literature Section of the Library of Congress and in the Boston Public Library Archives. Other papers are included in the *Horn Book Magazine* and Horn Book, Inc. Records, 1899–1986, at Simmons College Archives. A 1980 interview was conducted with Haviland as part of the New England Round Table of Children's Librarians Oral History Project at the Boston Public Library.

Additional books written or edited by Haviland are *Children's Books,* co-edited with Lois Belfield Watt (1964–1980); *Children's Reading in America, 1776: A Selection of Titles* (1976); *The Fairy Tale Treasury* (1972); *Favorite Fairy Tales Told around the World* (1985); *Ruth Sawyer* (1965); and *Samuel Langhorne Clemens: A Centennial for Tom Sawyer: An Annotated, Selected Bibliography,* compiled with Margaret N. Coughlan (1977). Haviland was also a prolific contributor to professional journals such as *Library Trends, Quarterly Journal of the Library of Congress, Library Journal, Horn Book Magazine,* and *Catholic Library World.*

The best sources of information about Haviland's career are "Ave Necque Vale," *Horn Book Magazine* 57, no. 4 (August 1981), p. 383; John Donovan, "Virginia Haviland: A Tribute," *Quarterly Journal of the Library of Congress* 38, no. 4 (Fall 1981), pp. 200–201; Margaret Hodges, "A Laying On of Hands," *Catholic Library World* 47, no. 1 (July–August 1975), pp. 8–9; and Brigitte Weeks, "Virginia Haviland: The Lady at the Library," *Washington Post,* November 7, 1976. Obituaries appeared in the *Washington Post* on January 8, 1988, and the *New York Times* on January 9, 1988.

DEBRA GOLD HANSEN

HAYES, Helen. October 10, 1900–March 17, 1993. Actress.

Helen Hayes Brown was born in Washington, D.C., the only child of Catherine Estelle "Brownie" Hayes and Francis Van Arnum Brown. Helen's family encouraged her early predilection for the stage. Her mother, who toured as a comedian with stock companies, often left her daughter in the care of her grandmother, "Graddy" Hayes, who took the child to matinees. Her father, a traveling salesman for a meat wholesaler, gave her an appreciation for storytelling.

Helen appeared in dance school recitals from the age of five. At nine, she garnered several roles with the Columbia Players in her native Washington, D.C., and made her Broadway debut in the musical *Old Dutch.* Performing as Helen Hayes Brown, she played several more years with Washington stock companies while still managing to graduate from the Academy of the Sacred Heart in

1917. Five feet tall, Hayes played girls—and boys—younger than she. Then, at seventeen and now known as Helen Hayes, she starred as Pollyanna, the orphan "glad girl" teen, in a coast-to-coast tour. The character's sunny disposition—even after her legs are broken—must have intensified Hayes's own innate optimism.

At twenty, Hayes moved with her ever-present mother to New York City. In a series of roles, she evolved from demure lass to saucy flapper, but always with a winsome and winning inner innocence. Expectations were high when she was cast as the star in *Bab,* but the still-novice actor faltered; some reviewers called her voice shrill and criticized her for working too hard. Hayes, taken aback, undertook disciplined training in elocution in the then popular Delsarte System of Acting, and in dance, fencing, and boxing. Her horizons were further broadened by a cruise to Europe in 1921. She returned to the stage refreshed and technically proficient, in plays such as *The Wren, Golden Days, To The Ladies,* and *We Moderns.* For the rest of her life, her notices were almost always favorable, reviewers observing her charm, warmth, humanity, and seemingly effortless acting in both comedy and serious drama.

In 1924 she moved to classical acting in Oliver Goldsmith's *She Stoops to Conquer* and then, the following year, in Shaw's *Caesar and Cleopatra.* Next came James M. Barrie's *What Every Woman Knows,* which she would often revive.

She began seeing playwright Charles MacArthur, and during a three-year run in *Coquette* her producer canceled one performance so that she could attend the premiere of MacArthur's play *The Front Page,* co-authored with Ben Hecht. Shortly thereafter, in 1928, they were married in an afternoon ceremony. Hayes returned to the stage that evening. MacArthur replaced Brownie as Helen's chief inspiration and critic. In 1930, their daughter, Mary, was born. The following year, Hayes made her first Hollywood film, *The Sin of Madelon Claudet;* the screenplay was written by her husband and she won the Academy Award as Best Actress. Other screen performances included *Arrowsmith* (1931) and *A Farewell to Arms* (1932). The MacArthurs, now both markedly successful, moved to a large Victorian house in Nyack, New York, high above the Hudson River, and this was Hayes's principal residence for the rest of her life. The MacArthurs later adopted a son, James, soon after his birth in 1937.

In 1933 and 1935 respectively, Hayes scored twin regal triumphs on Broadway in *Mary, Queen of Scotland* and *Victoria Regina.* She played Queen Victoria on Broadway and then on tour for three years, aging onstage from diffident princess to dowager queen almost a thousand times.

During the next twenty years Hayes appeared almost constantly on Broadway or on tour, in plays such as *Twelfth Night, Candle in the Wind, Harriet, Alice Sit-by-the-Fire,* and *The Wisteria Trees.* When the Tony Awards were created in 1947, Hayes was the first winner as best actress, although she was then appearing in a lightweight comedy called *Happy Birthday.*

In 1949, Mary MacArthur, just beginning her career on the stage, was touring with her mother in summer stock when she contracted polio and died. Hayes found solace in her work, but her husband withdrew into drink and depression. He died, heartbroken, in 1956. Their son James became a successful stage, film, and television star, appearing several times with Hayes.

Numerous stage triumphs, countless public appearances, U.S. State Department tours, and honors including visits to the White House followed. In addition to her eight theater performances weekly, Hayes often rushed to radio stations where she starred in, and sometimes produced, numerous programs. With the advent of television, she appeared frequently in that medium. She also wrote articles and, with co-authors, six books, mostly anecdotal and inspirational.

Hayes played in far fewer films than plays, and never felt at home in Hollywood. Her lack of pretense disadvantaged her in the Machiavellian and competitive studio system. Moreover, at a time when exotic glamour, midnight supper-clubbing, drugs, and dalliances were in vogue, Hayes was a relentlessly plain woman. She dutifully entertained and was entertained but remained an obdurate outsider. Back in Nyack, she drove herself to Gotham six times a week for Broadway and radio obligations.

With her fame and vigorous willingness to make public appearances, as well as her sincere dedication to public causes, Hayes became an exemplary citizen. Journalists often nominated her "First Lady of the Stage" and "First Lady of the American Theater." Other of her contemporaries, among them Judith Anderson, ETHEL BARRYMORE, and KATHERINE CORNELL, were similarly honored, but Hayes ultimately won the title by virtue of the extraordinary length and breadth of her career. Because of changes in the American theater and its "star system," it is unlikely that any performer will again reign over Broadway and "the road" as she did.

Hayes's Irish temper might flare with a stage director, and she could be stubborn and outspoken for causes—including her own career—but she led her public life as a model of propriety. She remained a devout Roman Catholic although married to a divorced man. Her husband, an acerbic jokester when sober, must have been exasperating when drinking, but Hayes was never less than loving in her public comments about him.

Hayes's method of acting owed something to the pre-Stanislavsky performances she had watched from the wings as a child. Onto their nineteenth-century bravura she grafted her own method, which was rooted in reality devoid of flamboyance. She bypassed psychological theory, abstract sociological analysis, and character deconstruction. Perhaps logically for someone who began a professional career as a young child, her approach combined close observation and replication of details with focused storytelling. She said famously that public transportation was her acting school: watching streetcar passengers come and go, she noted appearance, behavior, and speech traits, and around these fashioned playlets.

An asthmatic reaction to backstage dust forced an end to her theatrical career. However, after her last stage appearance—in *Long Day's Journey into Night* at Catholic University in Washington, D.C., in 1964—Hayes continued her work in film and television, and constantly appeared at cultural and civic events until the end of her life. She died on March 17, 1993, at the age of ninety-two and was buried in Oak Hill Cemetery in Nyack, New York.

Onstage and off, Hayes embodied flinty American endurance and sturdy optimism through the Great Depression, two World Wars, and the untimely loss of her teenage daughter and then her husband. Through triumph and tragedy, her life and acting inspired America.

Bibliography: Papers and memorabilia are found in the Helen Hayes Collection in the Billy Rose Theatre Collection, New York Public Library for the Performing Arts, Lincoln Center. Hayes wrote five volumes of memoirs: *Gift of Joy* (1965), *On Reflection: An Autobiography* (1968), *Gathering of Hope* (1983), *Loving Life* (1987), and *My Life in Three Acts* (1990). Kenneth Barrow's biography, *Helen Hayes: First Lady of the American Theater* (1985), can be supplemented by Jhan Robbins, *Front Page Marriage* (1982), which looks at the Hayes–MacArthur relationship. Donn Murphy and Stephen Moore, *Helen Hayes: A Bio-Bibliography* (1993), offers an extensive annotated bibliography, a list of her performances, and a biographical sketch. Obituaries appeared in the *New York Times* on March 18, 1993, and the *Los Angeles Times* on March 19, 1993.

DONN MURPHY

HAYWORTH, Rita. October 17, 1918–May 14, 1987. Actress.

Rita Hayworth was born Margarita Carmen Cansino in Brooklyn, New York. Her father, Eduardo Cansino, a professional dancer, emigrated from Spain in 1913 with his sister and dancing partner, Elsa Cansino. Her mother, Volga Haworth, of Irish English descent, performed with the Ziegfeld Follies. Eduardo and Volga met and married in 1917, and Volga gave up her career when she had her first child, Margarita Carmen. Two boys, Eduardo Jr. and Vernon, followed. Eduardo Cansino continued to travel with his sister after his marriage. The two performed all over North America and Europe under the name the Dancing Cansinos.

Margarita began studying dance with her father at the age of three, and by the time she was six years old she was dancing in public performances. In 1926, Eduardo, Elsa, and Margarita appeared in their first film, a short musical called *La Fiesta* for Warner Bros.' Vitagraph Studios. Soon convinced of the future of music and dancing in motion pictures, Eduardo moved his family to Hollywood in 1927. He opened a dance studio and choreographed and directed dance numbers for films, while continuing to choreograph and perform for the stage.

Rita, as she was now called, soon replaced Eduardo's sister as his primary dancing partner, performing in the nightclubs and dance halls in Baja, Mexico. Her rigorous schedule kept her from finishing high school, though she did complete the ninth grade at Hamilton High in Los Angeles. A bit part in the film *Cruz Diablo* (1934) led to a background role in *In Caliente* (1935) starring Mexican American actress DOLORES DEL RÍO. In 1935, Fox Studio executive Winfield Sheehan discovered her dancing on stage in Tijuana and offered her a studio contract.

She threw herself into her work, appearing in a string of films in the mid 1930s. In 1935 she had two small roles, in *Dante's Inferno* with Spencer Tracy and *Paddy O'Day,* a comedy in which she played a Russian dancer. Like many other Latinas in Hollywood, her earliest roles were as a beautiful foreigner. She played an Argentine dancer in *Under the Pampas Moon* (1935), an Egyptian beauty in *Charlie Chan in Egypt* (1935), and a "Latin type" named Carmen (the starring role) in *Human Cargo* (1936). In 1936, at the age of eighteen, Cansino married forty-year-old Edward "Eddie" C. Judson, a car salesman who presented himself as a "promoter." Judson took charge of her professional life. He convinced her to raise her hairline and change her style of dressing and arranged hundreds of media interviews. Under Judson's tutelage, she was transformed from "Spanish beauty" into an all-American Hollywood pinup girl. The makeover was completed by Columbia studio head Harry Cohn, who advised her to dye her black hair red and change her name to Rita Hayworth.

In 1939 Hayworth was cast as a supporting actress in *Only Angels Have Wings.* But it was the Warner Bros. film *The Strawberry Blonde* (1941) that brought her to the attention of American audiences. Her roles, and her co-stars, grew larger. She starred opposite Fred Astaire in two films:

You'll Never Get Rich (1941) and *You Were Never Lovelier* (1942). In the 1944 Columbia musical *Cover Girl,* starring Gene Kelly, Rita played a small-time dancer named Rusty Parker who wins a contest to become a *Vanity* cover girl. In a striking parallel to her own real-life experiences, the film tells the story of a dancer who is transformed by clothing and makeup into a famous model and movie star.

In the midst of her growing popularity, her personal life remained rocky. Hayworth separated from Eddie Judson and began an affair with Victor Mature, who starred opposite her in *My Gal Sal* (1942). In 1943 Hayworth divorced Judson; soon after she fell in love with young director Orson Welles. They married that year, and their daughter, Rebecca, was born in December 1944. The relationship was volatile from the start. Although Welles loved her, he was not one to commit himself to marriage. In 1948, while she was still married to Welles, Hayworth met Prince Aly Khan, heir to the throne of the Aga Khan. Khan was separated from his wife, Joan Guinness. That year Hayworth divorced Welles and Khan filed for divorce. The two married on May 27, 1949, and Rita gave birth to their daughter, Yasmin Aga, in December. This marriage was also very unstable, and the couple divorced acrimoniously in 1953. She was also married to Dick Haymes from 1953 to 1955 and film producer James Hill from 1958 to 1961.

Hayworth is probably best remembered for two major roles. Playing the title character in the hugely successful *Gilda* (1946) opposite Glenn Ford, she became Hollywood's foremost femme fatale. Scientists working on the atomic bomb detonated on the Bikini Atoll named the bomb Gilda in her honor. In *The Lady from Shanghai* (1948), Hayworth co-starred with her then-husband Orson Welles, who also directed the film. It was a critical and box office failure, and Hayworth never again achieved the recognition she had from her earlier pictures. Despite her fading popularity, she starred in a number of films over the next decade, including *Champagne Safari* (1952), *Miss Sadie Thompson* (1953), and *Pal Joey* (1957). She also worked in European cinema during the 1960s and 1970s. In 1972 she appeared in her final Hollywood movie, *The Wrath of God.*

Diagnosed with Alzheimer's disease in 1980, Rita Hayworth died in New York on May 14, 1987, at the age of sixty-eight. She was never recognized for her acting ability but instead is best remembered for her sultry, exotic looks. Shy, introverted, and insecure all her life, Rita proclaimed that "every man I have known has fallen in love with Gilda and wakened with me."

Bibliography: There are a number of popular biographies of Rita Hayworth, including John Kobal, *Rita Hayworth: The Time, the Place, and the Woman* (1977); James Hill, *Rita Hayworth, a Memoir* (1983); Joe Morella and Edward Z. Epstein, *Rita: The Life of Rita Hayworth* (1983), which contains the final quotation on p. 11; and Barbara Leaming, *If This Was Happiness: A Biography of Rita Hayworth* (1989). Caren Roberts-Frenzel's *Rita Hayworth: A Photographic Retrospective* (2001) includes more than three hundred photographs of Hayworth. Obituaries appeared in the *Los Angeles Times* on May 15, 1987, and the *New York Times* on May 16, 1987.

JOANNE HERSHFIELD

H'DOUBLER, Margaret Newell. April 26, 1889–March 26, 1982. Dance educator.

Margaret Newell H'Doubler is widely regarded as the founder of dance in the American university, yet she was not a dancer and never took more than a handful of dance classes in her life. H'Doubler's lack of dance experience proved to be a shrewd strategy for success, freeing her to make dance education not only a safe discipline for college women, but a popular and respected one as well.

H'Doubler's family background valued the arts, invention, and social idealism, although neither her mother, who was a Normal School teacher, nor her father, who was a writer, poet, inventor, and photographer, had much formal education. Born in Beloit, Kansas, to Sarah Emerson Todd and Charles Wright H'Doubler (whose name is an Americanized version of the original Swiss family name Hougen-Doubler), Margaret Newell H'Doubler was the second daughter and the third and last child of this middle-class Protestant family. She grew up in Warren, Illinois, until her family moved to Madison, Wisconsin, in 1905. Raised in an environment of privilege with carriages, vacations, private tutoring, and piano lessons, H'Doubler read extensively from an early age.

H'Doubler entered the University of Wisconsin in 1906, intending to study either biology or medicine. When she took her obligatory freshman physical education class, however, she discovered a passion for the physical that would animate her for the rest of her life. There was no such major as women's physical education at the time, so she put together her own comprehensive course of study. Four years later, in May 1910, H'Doubler graduated with a BS in biology, with minors in chemistry and philosophy. She was promptly hired as an assistant physical education instructor.

H'Doubler's search for a model of dance she could teach in the university began as an assignment she was given by Blanche Trilling, the chair of women's physical education. In the summer of 1916, as H'Doubler was about to leave for a year's graduate study in philosophy at Columbia's Teachers College in New York, Trilling asked her to investigate the city's leading dance studios for a form of dance she could bring into the university. She wanted one that was unencumbered by personal style and fixed movement vocabularies. Trilling's assignment ultimately led her to Alys Bentley, an idiosyncratic dance educator who taught children's music and dance classes in Carnegie Hall. Bentley taught by freeing students from gravity by having them move their bodies while lying on the floor and feeling the body's structural possibilities. H'Doubler was also influenced by the philosophy of John Dewey, with whom she studied at Columbia. Dewey's emphasis on learning through experience and the dangers of mind–body dichotomies in education steered her away from stiff and imitative dance that sparked no special experiences or emotional or cognitive discoveries for the students involved in it.

When H'Doubler returned to Madison in the summer of 1917, she inaugurated the nation's first college dance class. In her classroom, dance became a way for the college woman to find her expressive side and explore a physical self that was novel for the majority of women in early-twentieth-century America. Classes began with the students lying on the floor, a radical notion for proper college women at the time. Free from worries about balance and falling, the women (all of H'Doubler's early classes were for women only) began to discover their bodies and movement. Staunchly against the physically injurious training that passed for much ballet in America at this time, H'Doubler gravitated toward creative movement that was like problem solving. To this end she imported from her experience in the sciences a famous prop—a human skeleton—which she used in all of her dance teaching to demonstrate the anatomical logic of how the body moved.

H'Doubler accomplished more than she knew in the classroom, and her initiation of curricular change was equally dramatic. Within a few years of that first summer dance class, other new courses in dance were added rapidly at the University of Wisconsin in response to booming student interest. In 1926 the university granted H'Doubler's request for an undergraduate major in dance education, the first such degree in dance in the nation. Although H'Doubler's emphasis was always on training dance teachers rather than performers, starting in the winter of 1918–19 she oversaw a club for dance performances, which she named Orchesis. Like other facets of her program, Orchesis was emulated by H'Doubler's students in college dance programs around the nation.

H'Doubler was an early example of American professional women who rejected traditional female roles to devote themselves to a career rather than domesticity. She did not marry until August 5, 1934, when she was forty-five. She and her husband, Wayne L. Claxton, a Wayne State University art professor who was twelve years her junior, remained childless. For both of them, their students were their children, and they entertained them frequently at the Door County home that Claxton designed and built. An active horseback rider as well as a very stylish dresser, H'Doubler enjoyed traveling around the country lecturing about her theories of dance education.

By the time she retired from full-time teaching in 1954, H'Doubler had effectively succeeded in franchising dance education across America. H'Doubler's students headed major dance programs in colleges, universities, and public and private schools throughout the country, and her 1940 book *Dance: A Creative Art Experience* remained the most widely used book on dance education in the nation. H'Doubler's approach to movement explorations informed not just college dance, but dance in public schools and the theater as well.

That Wisconsin summer session in 1917 changed the course of dance in the United States. Freed from the negative associations of dance as sinful or promiscuous, H'Doubler helped establish new links between female athleticism, health, and morality. Most importantly, she showed what dance had to offer in the way of lifelong learning, especially how each dance student might use the classroom experiences to help shape her approach to the world outside. Margaret Newell H'Doubler remained active in dance education for several decades after her retirement, dying from natural causes in a retirement home in Springfield, Missouri, in 1982 at the age of ninety-two. Her ashes were scattered on the waters of Green Bay, Wisconsin, outside Waymar, her beloved weekend home.

Bibliography: The major historical study of H'Doubler is Janice Ross's *Moving Lessons: Margaret H'Doubler and the Beginning of Dance in American Education* (2000). This feminist cultural history of H'Doubler and her moment in American education draws extensively on H'Doubler's own papers and photographs of her in the University of Wisconsin–Madison Archives as well as on interviews done with the twelve surviving members of the early years of her program. Other sources are Mary Remley's overview of the early years of H'Doubler's work, "The Wisconsin Idea of Dance: A Decade of Progress, 1917–1926," *Wisconsin Magazine of History* 58, no. 3 (Spring 1975), pp. 178–95. See also Judith A. Gray, "To Want to Dance: A Biography of Margaret H'Doubler" (PhD dissertation, University of Arizona, 1978), a general and affectionate account of H'Doubler's professional career written by a former student. One of the best and most detailed primary resources is University of Wisconsin faculty member Mary Alice Brennan's unpublished 1972 interview with Margaret H'Doubler, on file in the Dance Collection in the New York Public Library for the Performing Arts at Lincoln Center. See also Blanche Trilling's "History of Physical Education for Women at the University of Wisconsin, 1898–1946" (1951) in the University of

Wisconsin–Madison Archives. Also important are H'Doubler's own writings about dance teaching, most prominently *The Dance and Its Place in Education* (1925) and *Dance: A Creative Art Experience* (1940; 2nd ed., 1957). An obituary appeared in *Dance Magazine* in August 1982.

JANICE ROSS

HEAD, Edith. October 28, 1897–October 24, 1981. Hollywood costume designer.

Winning eight Academy Awards and thirty-five Academy Award nominations for film costumes was a remarkable achievement for a woman with no formal education in fashion design. But no one argues that Edith Head wasn't remarkable.

An only child, Edith Claire Posener was born in San Bernardino, California. The future costume designer was given her stepfather's surname, Spare, after her mother, Anna Levy, and her father, Max Posener, divorced. Though as an adult she frequently told the story that she never went to grammar school, a diploma indicates that Edith Claire Spare graduated from a Redding, California, elementary school in 1911 and eventually earned a BA from the University of California at Berkeley and an MA in French from Stanford in 1920. In Los Angeles, Edith Spare became a French and art teacher at Hollywood School for Girls. To keep pace with her precocious students, she enrolled in night classes at Otis Art Institute and later at Chouinard, one of the most respected art schools in the country. On July 25, 1923, she married Charles Head, the brother of an art school chum.

Eager to land a higher-paying job as a sketch artist at Famous Players–Lasky film studio (soon to become Paramount Studios), Head borrowed sketches from fellow students and sold herself based on the specious portfolio. Head was hired in 1923 by Howard Greer, then head of design. She quickly made the transition from sketching to designing. One of her earliest assignments was to assist Greer on a Raoul Walsh film, *The Wanderer* (1926). Head was charged with festooning an elephant in flowers and fruits. Unfortunately, the young designer chose to use real flora, and the pachyderm consumed most of her delicious work.

While Head was suffering with a drunken husband at home, her boss, Greer, also an alcoholic, was let go and replaced by his colleague Travis Banton. Head was named Banton's official assistant. Referring to CLARA BOW as a "sausage" too pudgy to enhance his sleek designs, Banton turned the "It Girl" over to Head, and Bow became her first full-fledged star. Next came MAE WEST, and Head's career was secured.

After being named a full designer in 1933, Head dressed more of Hollywood's stars-in-the-making: Shirley Temple (for her first feature film, *Little Miss Marker*, in 1934), Joan Bennett, Frances Farmer, BETTY GRABLE, and a buxom brunette with the Hollywood-imposed name Dorothy Lamour. Because of her remarkable figure, Lamour was cast in the lead role of *The Jungle Princess* (1936). Assigned to put the actress in a sarong, Head wrapped her in a tropical print that revealed Lamour's voluptuous curves. The costume made both the actress and the designer huge stars. American women longed to look like Lamour, so fan mail poured into Paramount asking for how-to help.

Head realized that self-promotion on her part couldn't hurt. Instantly recognizable by her bangs and round, thick-rimmed glasses, she befriended stars and continued to learn everything she could from her boss, Travis Banton. When he was fired in 1938, Head was named Paramount's top designer. Her first marriage ended in October of that same year—she had had enough of alcoholics. Rather than let rumors continue that she was more than just friends with some of her favorite female stars, on September 8, 1940, Head married one of her best friends, Wiard Boppo "Bill" Ihnen, an art director she had known since they had both worked on *A Cradle Song* (1933). They remained married until his death in 1979. Head had no children in either marriage. Many authors have since included her name in books about Hollywood's lesbians, but the designer never commented publicly on her sexual orientation.

Determined that Hollywood acknowledge the importance of the costume designer to a film, Head worked with other designers to pressure the Academy of Motion Picture Arts and Sciences to establish an Academy Award for costume design. In 1949 the first such Oscars were given, one for costume work in color films of 1948, another for black-and-white. Confident of winning for *The Emperor Waltz,* Head was devastated when she was passed over in favor of Madame Karinska and Dorothy Jeakins, who had designed *Joan of Arc.* The setback was only temporary. Eight Academy Awards eventually celebrated her work in *The Heiress* and *Samson and Delilah* (both 1949), *All about Eve* (1950), *A Place in the Sun* (1951), *Roman Holiday* (1953), *Sabrina* (1954), *The Facts of Life* (1960), and *The Sting* (1973).

In 1966, Gulf and Western bought Paramount, signaling the demise of the studio system that had sustained Head's career. After forty-four years at Paramount, she was on the verge of being laid off because the studio, like most others, no longer had budgets for on-staff costume designers. So in 1967 Head took a job at Universal Studios that her friend Alfred Hitchcock had arranged. Because her name was legendary in Hollywood, her bungalow became a stop on the Universal Studios tour. But her days as Hollywood's most respected designer were over. Her last Academy Award, for *The Sting,* starring Robert Redford and Paul Newman, was disputed by designers who said they had costumed the male leads. She pooh-poohed the controversy, noting that any film that carried her name as costume designer meant she deserved the Oscar. She had weathered the same storms in 1954 when it was a known, if carefully guarded, fact that Audrey Hepburn's most stylish gowns in *Sabrina* were designed by couturier Hubert de Givenchy, the actress's designer of choice.

In 1974 Head's star was embedded on the Hollywood Walk of Fame. Over the course of her life she wrote two books, *The Dress Doctor* with Jane Kesner Ardmore (1959) and *How to Dress for Success* with Joe Hyams (1967), and audiotaped interviews prepared for her autobiography, which was published posthumously as *Edith Head's Hollywood* in 1983.

Head died in Hollywood on October 24, 1981, of progressive bone marrow disease at the age of eighty-three. She had just completed her last assignment, dressing Steve Martin in *Dead Men Don't Wear Plaid* (1982). Prior to Head's burial at Forest Lawn Memorial Park in Glendale, BETTE DAVIS gave the eulogy. Davis also wrote the foreword to Head's autobiography, where she noted, concisely, "Edith Head never failed."

Bibliography: Papers relating to Edith Head's Hollywood career can be found at the Margaret Herrick Library of the Academy of Motion Picture Arts and Sciences, Beverly Hills, and the Wisconsin Center for Film and Theater Research, Wisconsin Historical Society, Madison. An interview, "Reminiscences of Edith Head," conducted by Ann Burk on July 29, 1975, is found at the Library of Congress. Edith Head's books include *The Dress Doctor* (1959), with Jane Kesner Ardmore; *How to Dress for Success* (1967), with Joe Hyams; and *Edith Head's Hollywood* (1983), with Paddy Calistro. See also Virginia Antoinette Hirsch, "Edith Head, Film Costume Designer" (PhD dissertation, University of Kansas, 1973). For more general information on film costume design, see Margaret J. Bailey, *Those Glorious Glamour Years* (1982); Regine and Peter W. Engelmeir and Barbara Eizing, eds., *Fashion in Film* (1997); and Elizabeth Leese, *Costume Design in the Movies: An Illustrated Guide to the Work of 157 Great Designers* (1991). In *The Sewing Circle: Hollywood's Greatest Secret—Female Stars Who Loved Other Women* (1995), Axel Madsen discusses rumors of Head's lesbianism. Obituaries appeared in the *New York Times* and *Los Angeles Times* on October 27, 1981.

PADDY CALISTRO

HEDGEMAN, Anna Arnold. July 5, 1899–January 17, 1990. Civil rights activist, YWCA administrator, federal official.

Anna Marie Arnold was born in Marshalltown, Iowa, the oldest of six surviving children of Marie Ellen Parker and William James Arnold. When she was two, the family moved to Minnesota, where her mother had grown up, and settled in Anoka, where the Arnolds were usually the only black family in the small town and her father, a son of former slaves and a college graduate, ran a harness shop. "Four ideas dominated our family life," Anna later recalled: "education, religion, character, and service to mankind" (*The Gift of Chaos,* p. 5). Her parents, particularly her father, instilled in the children a sense that they were "special people" and that only unintelligent people were prejudiced. A devout Methodist and strict taskmaster, William Arnold selected Hamline University, a Methodist college in St. Paul, for Anna after her graduation from the Anoka public high school in 1918. The school sidestepped the issue of segregation by having her live off-campus with family friends and do her practice teaching at the university itself, rather than in the local school system.

After graduating in 1922, she joined the faculty of Rust College, a Methodist school for African Americans in Holly Springs, Mississippi, where she was shocked by her first experiences of Jim Crow and the overwhelming odds facing the students, many of whom were children of sharecroppers. Deciding she needed to "organize the North to free the Negroes of the South" (BWOHP, p. 40), she returned to Minnesota in 1924, only to discover that no public school would hire her because of her race. Instead she sought employment with the Young Women's Christian Association (YWCA). From 1924 to 1934, Anna Arnold held administrative positions in branches in Springfield, Ohio; Jersey City, New Jersey; Harlem; and Philadelphia. In the YWCA she found a network of impressive black women. Supported by an older generation like EVA D. BOWLES and Cecelia Cabaniss Saunders, Arnold in turn mentored younger women like PAULI MURRAY. At the same time, she strongly opposed YWCA policy that segregated African Americans in separate and invariably under-resourced branches.

In 1933, Anna Arnold married Merritt A. Hedgeman, a concert artist who also held jobs in the private and public sectors. By 1934, the couple settled in New York City; they did not have children. That year, Hedgeman began her career as a public servant working for the city's Emergency Relief Bureau. After the bureau was reorganized as the city's Department of Welfare in late 1937, Hedgeman left to become director of the black YWCA in Brooklyn, where she mobilized the community to challenge local stores' discriminatory hiring practices and to pressure the welfare department to hire African Americans. This activism, combined with a successful campaign to replace the existing branch leadership, made her continued employment untenable and she resigned. She then joined the Office of Civilian Defense at the behest of CRYSTAL BIRD FAUSET, director of the Racial Relations Division and a former YWCA colleague.

A. Philip Randolph invited Hedgeman to join the National Council for a Permanent Fair Employment Practices Committee as its executive director in 1944. Moving to Washington, D.C., she worked with an interracial coalition that included the National Association for the Advancement of Colored People, the Anti-Defamation League, the Congress of Industrial Organizations, and the United Council of Church Women. Following the failure of the campaign in 1946, Hedgeman's resignation was accepted. After working on Truman's 1948 reelection campaign, she was rewarded with an appointment as assistant to the administrator of the Federal Security Agency (FSA), a position she held from 1949 until 1953.

Returning to New York City, she worked on Robert Wagner Jr.'s successful mayoral campaign. In 1954 she was sworn in as his assistant, the first black woman to serve in a New York City mayoral cabinet. Underpaid and frustrated by the administration's failure to engage the black community, she resigned in 1958 to work in public relations for a cosmetic company owned by S. B. Fuller, a black businessman. She also worked as a columnist and associate editor for the *New York Age,* a black paper Fuller owned. The position lasted until the paper ceased publication for financial reasons in 1960.

In the 1950s, Hedgeman became increasingly involved with international activities. While she was still at the FSA, the State Department sent her to India for three months. She also attended international conferences in the Middle East, Europe, and Japan. In 1960, she was a keynote speaker at the first Conference of Women of Africa and African Descent in Accra, Ghana. That year, she made the first of three unsuccessful runs for political office in New York City, running as a reform candidate for Congress from the Bronx. She subsequently ran for city council president in 1965 and in the Democratic primary for the State Assembly in 1968.

One of Hedgeman's most important contributions was her role on the advisory committee for the 1963 March on Washington for Jobs and Freedom. Through a paid position with the National Council of Churches' Commission on Religion and Race, Hedgeman was instrumental in gaining the white Protestant churches' support for the march. Hedgeman was less successful in her efforts to have women's involvement in the movement recognized: no black women's organizations were invited to co-sponsor the demonstration. The day of the march, acknowledgment of women was perfunctory, and she "recognized anew that Negro women are second-class citizens in the same way that white women are" (*The Trumpet Sounds,* p. 180). Her next job was to generate grassroots support for the 1964 Civil Rights Act. Hedgeman was on the original board of directors of the National Organization for Women (NOW) and, along with Pauli Murray, sought in 1967 to force NOW to engage issues affecting poor women.

Reaching retirement age, Hedgeman was forced out of the National Council of Churches in 1967. She and her husband began the Hedgeman Consultant Service, through which Anna Hedgeman spoke and advised on urban affairs and education, especially the then new field of African American studies. She viewed these efforts, along with two autobiographical volumes, as part of the "special mission" that God had for African Americans to educate white America to live up to the idea of "Liberty and justice for all" (ibid., p. 201). In 1988, Merritt Hedgeman died. Two years later, at the age of ninety, Anna Arnold Hedgeman died in New York City.

Bibliography: Anna Arnold Hedgeman wrote two autobiographies: *The Trumpet Sounds: A Memoir of Negro Leadership* (1964), which covers her life up until the 1963 March on Washington, and *The Gift of Chaos: Decades of American Discontent* (1977), which includes reflections on the civil rights movement and African American history as well as her own life. The 1978–79 interviews by Ellen Craft Dammond conducted as part of the Black Women Oral History Project (BWOHP), Schlesinger Library, Radcliffe Institute for Advanced Study, Harvard University, are invaluable, although discrepancies between the oral history and her memoirs dictate using these accounts with care. There are also transcripts of interviews with Hedgeman from 1967 and 1968 at Moorland-Spingarn Research Center, Howard University. The Schomburg Center for Research in Black Culture, New York Public Library, has archival material, mostly from the 1950s through the 1970s, as does the National Afro-American Museum and Cultural Center in Wilberforce, Ohio.

Throughout her life, Hedgeman contributed articles to journals and newspapers, especially the black press: see in particular her column, "One Woman's Opinion," in the *New York Age* from 1958 to 1960. Also of interest is Hedgeman's "The Role of the Negro Woman," *Journal of Educational Sociology* 17 (April 1944), pp. 463–72. Useful context for Hedgeman's activities can be found in Paula F. Pfeffer, *A. Philip Randolph, Pioneer of the Civil Rights Movement* (1990); Linda Gordon, "Black and White Visions of Welfare: Women's Welfare Activism, 1890–1945," *Journal of American History* 78, no. 2 (September 1991), pp. 559–90; James F. Findlay, "Religion and Politics in the Sixties: The Churches and the Civil Rights Act of 1964," *Journal of American History* 77, no. 1 (June 1990), pp. 66–92; and Judith Weisenfeld, *African American Women and Christian Activism: New York's Black YWCA, 1905–1945* (1997). Obituaries appeared in the *New York Times* on January 26, 1990, and the *New York Amsterdam News* on February 10, 1990.

NANCY MARIE ROBERTSON

HEDGES, Elaine. August 18, 1927–June 5, 1997. Literary critic, material culture expert, feminist educator.

Elaine Ryan was born in Yonkers, New York, the eldest of three children of Irish American parents Catherine Mary Ryan and John Aloysius Ryan, who had high school educations and had also been born in Yonkers. Her father worked as an auditor for the Yonkers school system and her mother was a housewife. After graduating from Charles E. Gorton High School in Yonkers in 1944, Elaine worked her way through higher education, first commuting to Barnard College, where she graduated summa cum laude in 1948. In 1950 she received her MA in the History of American Civilization at Radcliffe College. That fall she met veteran and fellow graduate student William Hedges when they were both paper graders for Professor Perry Miller's survey of American literature at Harvard. When the couple married in 1956, she left an appointment at Wellesley College to move with her husband to Baltimore, where her husband had an appointment at Goucher College; Goucher's nepotism rules prevented her from also joining the faculty there. Following the births of her two children, Marietta (1961) and James Leonard (1963), she completed her doctorate at Harvard in the American Civilization program in 1970. Her dissertation was on William Dean Howells and his contemporaries.

Like other academic feminists of her generation, Elaine Hedges worked simultaneously as teacher, scholar, and activist, while she was also a wife and mother. She was one of the few women at the notorious 1968 convention of the Modern Language Association (MLA) to urge the establishment of the Commission on the Status and Education of Women; she served on the Commission from 1970 to 1974 and chaired it in 1972–73.

She joined Towson State University's Department of English in 1969 as an assistant professor, becoming a full professor in 1973. In addition, she led the development of the Department of Women's Studies and served as its director from 1972 until her retirement in 1995. She also co-directed several curriculum transformation projects on that campus and others nearby, and co-founded (with Sara Coulter) the National Center for Curriculum Transformation Resources on Women. She designed and edited its extensive publication program, and wrote *Getting Started: Planning Curriculum Transformation* (1997), which was published just before her death. Brilliant, unflappable, determined, intense, and caring, she was known for her fine teaching, her collegiality, her willingness to team-teach, and her careful mentoring of young faculty and students.

Elaine Hedges worked intellectually as a literary critic and as a theorist of women's culture, particularly sewing and quilts. In the end, these interests came together in exceptionally keen scholarship. Her remarkably prescient reading of nineteenth-century women writers equipped her to become the Feminist Press's most valued consultant, as well as one of the most important editors of the *Heath Anthology of American Literature,* where she was in charge of the period 1865–1910. In 1973, the Feminist Press published *The Yellow Wallpaper* by Charlotte Perkins Gilman with Hedges's terse scholarly afterword. The book became a key text in women's history and women's studies courses across the country, and was later reprinted by several international presses.

Demonstrating her high standards, Hedges valued Gilman as the major intellectual feminist of the nineteenth century, but only *The Yellow Wallpaper* met her criterion for literary excellence. To edit *Ripening: The Selected Writings of Meridel Le Sueur* (1982), still the definitive scholarly volume, she spent five years selecting the texts to be included from, literally, a trunk full of materials plus hundreds of volumes of journals, as well as checking MERIDEL LE SUEUR's version of her life.

In 1976, Hedges wrote a short essay on quilts for a panel at the annual meeting of the MLA. Quickly reprinted in *The Radical Teacher* (March 1977), the essay became central to *In Her Own Image: Women Working in the Arts* (1980), an anthology she compiled with Ingrid Wendt that allowed her to conceive of women's art as originating in domestic work—pots, weaving, sewing, and especially quilts. For twenty years, Hedges researched quilts and other forms of sewing, first as they resounded upon the lives of American women in the nineteenth century, then as tropes that permeated, even "romanced," contemporary feminist theory and culture, as scholars, ignorant of sewing's ambivalence for the lives of American women, abused the image.

Hedges saw quilts and sewing as work that was both significant and oppressive. She entered the "quilt world," attending meetings of quilters and quilt historians, subscribing to and publishing in the *Quilt Journal,* writing historical texts for exhibitions, and, most important of all, collecting quilt slides, each with extensive historical and literary notations, that eventually filled four file drawers. She wrote about quilts whose artistry spoke politically and/or raised large sums of money for a cause, and charted the negative relationship between sewing and literary creativity through the works of twenty-five women writers from the nineteenth century through Sylvia Plath. She left a draft of an essay on quilts as "accusatory" texts and plans for a book on the history of quilts, sewing, and women's literature that moved through two centuries.

Off and on through the last three decades of her life, Hedges worked through periods of depression and exhaustion, including severe anemia that required transfusions. Bedridden in December 1996, she offered to read through twenty-five years of *Women's Studies Quarterly* to select pieces for an anniversary issue. The issue was dedicated to her; she died unexpectedly in Baltimore the following June of septicemia following an arterial blockage at the age of sixty-nine. In a volume of Emily Dickinson's *Selected Letters* (edited by Thomas H. Johnson, 1986), Elaine Hedges left a yellow Post-it on letter 891 (p. 303), marked with the word *aphorism*, beside which she had copied out, "I work to drive the awe away, yet awe impels the work." It marks her work-inspired life.

Bibliography: Much of the information about Elaine Hedges's life comes from remarks of family members and colleagues at three memorials held in June and July, 1997, and from *Elaine Hedges, a Tribute: Family, Colleagues, Students, Friends,* published in 1997 by Women's Studies at Towson State University and the Feminist Press at City University of New York. Other personal information comes from telephone conversations with her sister Dorothy Fay and with her husband, daughter, and son. Elaine Hedges's working files, unpublished manuscripts, published work, and quilt collection, including hundreds of books and journals, are to be archived at Brown University in the Feminist Press/Florence Howe/Elaine Hedges collection. Her most important work in print on quilts, sewing, and two centuries of American history is the monograph-length "Essay" she wrote for *Hearts and Hands: The Influence of Women and Quilts on American Society* (1987). Her most important work in print on quilts, sewing, and women's literature is "The Needle or the Pen: The Literary Recovery of Women's Textile Work," in Florence Howe, ed., *Tradition and the Talents of Women* (1991). Books by Hedges not mentioned in the text include *Listening to Silences: New Essays in Feminist Criticism* (1991), with Shelley Fisher Fishkin; and *Land and Imagination: The American Rural Dream* (1980), with William Hedges. An obituary appeared in the *New York Times* on June 22, 1997.

FLORENCE HOWE

HEFFERNAN, Helen. January 25, 1896–August 26, 1987. Progressive educator, state official.

Helen Heffernan was in charge of elementary education for the California State Department of Education from 1926 to 1965. A follower of John Dewey, she was perhaps the most influential progressive educator at the state level in these years. Along with her close friend Corinne Seeds, the principal of the University Elementary School at UCLA, Heffernan was at the center of a statewide network of progressive teachers and administrators, most of whom were women. Heffernan later became the target of conservative attacks, but even during the cold war she continued to fight for a child-centered approach and for the rights of minority and poor children to an equal education.

Heffernan was born in Lawrence, Massachusetts, the youngest of nine children of Michael John Heffernan, a brick mason, and his wife, Margaret Ann Collins. The son of Irish immigrants, Heffernan had come to the industrial city of Lawrence during the Civil War. Here he met his wife, who had come to Lawrence from Maine to find work in the mills. Michael Heffernan died of cancer when Helen was six years old. When she was ten, she and her mother moved to the mining boomtown of Goldfield, Nevada, where her two older brothers were seeking their fortunes as miners. After graduating from Goldfield High School and Nevada Normal School, she began teaching in 1915, when she was nineteen. She taught in small schools in Nevada, Idaho, and Utah before moving to California. After completing her BA at the University of California at Berkeley (1922) and while working toward her MA (1924), she took a position as rural school supervisor in Kings County, California.

In 1926, although she was only thirty and had been a rural supervisor for only three years, she was invited by the State Board of Education to apply for the vacant position of commissioner of elementary schools. Heffernan later claimed that the only reason she was appointed was that she had spent forty dollars for a new hat to wear at the interview, but it was doubtless her ability that won her the job.

By the late 1920s, Heffernan had become converted to the new movement of progressive education. To publicize this approach, she visited schools, spoke at institutes and conferences, created state demonstration schools, and organized the publication of state educational journals that celebrated the progressive Deweyan approach. Heffernan clearly had a magnetic personality, and the collaborative and child-centered methods she advocated were enthusiastically endorsed by numerous supervisors, teachers, and college professors.

By the mid 1930s, however, conservative groups in California began to resist Heffernan's progressive approach. Depression-era political tensions in the state had been heightened by the influx of migrant farm workers. The children of these workers needed schooling, and Heffernan was vocal in defending the rights of these children and the state's responsibility to provide health and family services as well as schooling. Her speeches condemning the conditions in which migrant families lived and their treatment by growers doubtless contributed to the growing suspicion and animosity toward her shown by local politicians, business leaders, and conservative groups throughout the state.

With the outbreak of World War II, Heffernan

was named state head of the federal project to provide day care for the children of war workers. In 1942, she faced another challenge when California saw the forced removal of Japanese American families, including school-age children, to internment camps. Although the schools established in the camps were under the jurisdiction of the War Relocation Authority and not the state of California, Heffernan remained concerned with the welfare of these children. Unlike her friend Corinne Seeds, who received death threats after organizing a drive to bring food and blankets to the Japanese Americans being held at the internment center at Santa Ana, Heffernan did not speak out publicly against the removal. But her support of radicals like Carey McWilliams and her condemnation of race prejudice made clear her sentiments. After the war, Heffernan was a strong supporter of the United Nations. In the hysterical, anti-communist climate of the early cold war, she came to symbolize progressive and "left-wing" views.

Heffernan never married. Throughout her life she had close relationships with women friends, including a romantic relationship with Corinne Seeds between 1939 and 1946. Beginning in the late 1940s, she shared her house in Sacramento with Afton Dill Nance, her colleague in the Division of Elementary Education.

Throughout her career, Heffernan remained steadfast in her commitment to a democratic education for all children. In the 1940s and 1950s she continued to be active at the state, national, and international level. From 1946 to 1948, she served as elementary schools officer with the U.S. occupation forces in Japan. In the 1950s she defended the right of special-needs children in California to public education and was instrumental in the passage of legislation providing medical and educational support for these children. She wrote a number of children's books and textbooks, and numerous pamphlets issued by the California State Department of Education for teachers and supervisors on a wide variety of topics. She also held conferences promoting bilingual education and the needs of the large Mexican American population in California. In 1961, she conducted workshops in Kenya and Nigeria for African educators on the importance of providing equal educational opportunity for girls and women.

Despite her accomplishments, Heffernan continued to be attacked by conservatives, who accused her of abandoning academic standards. In a 1958 article in the *Atlantic Monthly,* for example, Mortimer Smith, a founder of the conservative Council for Basic Education, accused her and her policies of contributing to the decline of American education. In 1962, Max Rafferty, a conservative Southern California school superintendent, was elected state superintendent of public instruction. He immediately challenged Heffernan's influence and ended many of her progressive initiatives. She remained in office for another three years before retiring in 1966 at the age of sixty-nine. That year, her friends and supporters dedicated a redwood grove in what is now Prairie Creek Redwoods State Park in her honor. Helen Heffernan continued to live in Sacramento until her death in 1987 at the age of ninety-one.

Bibliography: Heffernan's career has received little discussion thus far from historians. Irving Hendrick mentions Heffernan's work in "California's Response to the 'New Education' in the 1930s," *California Historical Quarterly* 53 (Spring 1974), pp. 25–40. Kathleen Weiler discusses her early career in "Women and Rural School Reform: California 1900–1940," *History of Education Quarterly* 34, no. 1 (Spring 1994), pp. 25–47, and in *Country Schoolwomen: Teaching in Rural California, 1850–1950* (1998). See also Ruth Wright Morpeth, "Dynamic Leadership: Helen Heffernan and Progressive Education in California" (PhD dissertation, University of California at Riverside, 1989). Heffernan presented her ideas primarily in speeches and brief articles in the *Journal of Western Education* and the *California Journal of Elementary Education.* A good example of these is Helen Heffernan, "A Statement of the Philosophy and the Purposes of the Elementary School," *California Journal of Elementary Education* 1, no. 3 (February 1933), pp. 109–13. She also wrote a number of pamphlets and curriculum guides. An obituary appeared in the *San Francisco Chronicle* on August 31, 1989.

KATHLEEN WEILER

HEIDE, Wilma Scott. February 26, 1921–May 8, 1985. Nurse, educator, feminist.

Wilma Louise Scott was born in Ferndale, Pennsylvania, the third of four children of Ada Long and William Robert Scott. Trained as a schoolteacher but unable to find work in education, William took a job as a railroad brakeman. Ada, who was also trained as a schoolteacher, chose to be a full-time homemaker after marriage. Of the four children, Wilma shared the strongest bond with her intellectually inquisitive father, particularly enjoying their long discussions on issues ranging from religion to economics.

In 1932 the family moved to Connellsville, Pennsylvania, where Wilma attended junior and senior high school. She was a good student but not bookish. Her passion was sports. She became captain of the girls' basketball team, and after high school she played semiprofessionally. Her first brush with sexism came when she declared her intention to become a Lutheran minister and was informed that women could not be ordained. She received another jolt when her parents refused to let her attend Seton Hill, a Catholic women's college. She had a scholarship and was willing to work her way through, but her parents, who could not afford college for all four children, felt it was unfair for only one to get a higher education.

For several years after high school, Wilma Scott stayed in Connellsville, working as a clerk and playing basketball. In 1940, she took a job at the Pennsylvania state mental hospital in Torrance. The work and clinical conditions were appalling, but the experience sparked her interest in nursing. In 1942 she enrolled in the Brooklyn State Hospital nursing program, returning to Torrance three years later with an RN degree in psychiatric nursing. Dismayed to find that conditions for both patients and staff had worsened, she bucked the hospital administration and instituted changes to improve the work environment and patient care.

She left Torrance in 1948 to enroll at the University of Pittsburgh, where she met Eugene Heide, a sociology student seven years her junior. After a short engagement, she and Gene were married in May 1951. Marriage was not an easy decision for the independent Wilma. The couple agreed that it was important for them to keep a measure of independence and individual identity. Bowing somewhat to convention, she took Gene's name, but also kept her own.

In 1953, Gene was drafted and sent to military bases in South Carolina and Georgia. Wilma continued working as a nurse, but spent much of her free time in the emerging civil rights movement. She joined the National Association for the Advancement of Colored People (NAACP), and as a voter registration volunteer for the League of Women Voters, she caused a stir when she refused to abide by the League rule of registering only whites. In 1955 the couple returned to Pennsylvania, where their first child, Terry Lynne, was born the next year.

For the next several years Heide taught and coordinated a nursing education program, but she felt increasingly unhappy and disengaged from the social change work she wanted to do. In 1959, during her pregnancy with her second daughter, Tamara Lee, she sank into a suicidal depression. Responsibility for her children motivated her to get help, but when the doctor told her the reason she was sick was because she wanted to be a man, she was stunned. The statement shook her out of the depression and into thinking about how society circumscribed women's role in public life. By the early 1960s, Heide was pursuing her own course toward feminism and social change—teaching a college course on mental health and writing a series of award-winning articles called "Poverty Is Expensive." During this period she was instrumental in developing an early prototype of Head Start and served on several state and local civil rights commissions.

In 1967, Heide learned of the newly formed National Organization for Women (NOW). According to biographer Eleanor Haney, she exclaimed, "This is the most important movement of the century. I've been waiting for it all my life" (p. 58). With characteristic zeal she organized a powerful Pittsburgh chapter that, among other things, spearheaded a campaign to desegregate newspaper help-wanted ads. She rose quickly through the leadership ranks, becoming NOW's national membership coordinator in 1968 and chair of the board in 1970.

Described by a friend as someone who "could talk a piece of clay into doing something," Wilma Scott Heide inspired women to take action. One of these actions jump-started the stalled equal rights amendment. In 1970, she and several Pittsburgh chapter members disrupted a Senate committee hearing and demanded that Congress move on the constitutional amendment. Within a few months hearings were held, and two years later Congress passed the ERA resolution.

In 1971, Heide was elected president of the National Organization for Women. Spearheading NOW's campaign against AT&T was perhaps her greatest achievement as president. The Equal Employment Opportunity Commission took NOW's lead on sex discrimination in their suit against AT&T, which resulted in the largest employment discrimination settlement up to that time. By the mid 1970s, NOW was struggling with internal strife and explosive growth. In 1974, exhausted and frustrated at her inability to resolve the organizational conflicts, Heide stepped down from what had become the largest feminist organization in the world.

After Heide became president of NOW, she and Gene realized their lives were going in separate directions and agreed to a divorce. Following her academic interests, after leaving NOW she focused on health care, feminism, and peace issues. She received a doctorate from Union Graduate School in Ohio and chaired the women's studies department at Sangamon State University in Springfield, Illinois. Heide spent her last years lecturing and completing a book, *Feminism for the Health of It* (1985). She died of a heart attack in Norristown, Pennsylvania, in May 1985 at the age of sixty-four, having also battled a brain tumor since 1969. Wilma Scott Heide forcefully voiced a feminist ethic that pushed the health care field to treat women as individuals, and she led a national organization that pressed society to give women a measure of equality.

Bibliography: The National Organization for Women archives at the Schlesinger Library, Radcliffe Institute for Advanced Study, Harvard University, contain Wilma Scott Heide's papers; see also the photographs in the library's

Betty Lane collection. Biographical information can be found in Eleanor Humes Haney, *A Feminist Legacy: The Ethics of Wilma Scott Heide and Company* (1985), while Roberta Stock, *Wilma Scott Heide: Her Embracement of Nurses and Nursing* (1991), focuses on her work in the health care field. Heide's doctoral thesis, "Feminism for the Health of It," was published in 1985 with a foreword by Jessie Bernard. The twelve-part series of articles entitled "Poverty Is Expensive" was published by the *Valley Daily News* and *New Kensington Daily Dispatch* (1965). Most of Heide's other writing included articles for professional journals, chapters in books, and speeches. See, for example, "Women's Liberation Means Putting Sex in Its Place," in Mildred E. Katzell and William C. Byham, eds., *Women in the Work Force: Confrontation with Change* (1972); "Feminism, the Sine Qua Non for a Just Society," *Vital Speeches of the Day* (1972), pp. 403–9; "Why Don't We? A Womanifesto for Change," *Ms.*, June 1976, pp. 88–89; and "Feminism: Making a Difference in Our Health," in Malkah T. Notman and Carol C. Nadelson, eds., *The Woman Patient* (1979). Winifred D. Wandersee's book *On the Move* (1988) includes a lengthy discussion of Scott Heide's involvement in NOW. An obituary appeared in the *Philadelphia Inquirer* on May 12, 1985.

REBECCA M. DAVISON

HELLMAN, Lillian. June 20, 1905–June 30, 1984. Playwright, writer, screenwriter.

One of the most important playwrights of the American theater, and generally acknowledged as the best female playwright of her generation, Lillian Hellman was also a memoirist without peer. She is known for her ability to tell a good story and for the clarity with which she depicted and condemned the moral failings of her protagonists. Though she never thought of herself as a political writer, her work is infused with the social and political issues that informed the creative minds of her generation.

Lillian Florence Hellman was the only child of Max Bernard Hellman and Julia Newhouse Hellman. Her father, the son of poor German immigrants who came to the United States in the mid nineteenth century, was born in New Orleans. Her mother came from a prosperous Alabama family whose wealth, consolidated by marriage, was enhanced by commercial success in the post–Civil War South. Jewish by descent on both sides, Lillian grew up conscious of her Jewish roots but without religious training.

Contrasts abounded in her family life. Hellman's father, self-educated and erudite, never attained business success. After the collapse of a shoe-manufacturing business financed by his wife's family, he became a traveling salesman. Yet he remained a lively figure whose forceful opinions, sturdy sense of humor, and blunt speech deeply influenced his daughter. Her mother, more formally educated (she attended, but did not graduate from, Sophie Newcomb College), was by Hellman's evaluation a dreamy woman who distanced herself from her quick-witted and sometimes temperamental husband. Until Lillian was six, the family lived in the New Orleans boarding house run by Max's adoring sisters, Jenny and Hannah. Then they divided their time between New York City (where Julia's mother had moved to a large West Side apartment) and New Orleans.

The young Lillian attended school in New Orleans and New York, graduating from Wadleigh High School in New York in 1922. Without the financial resources to attend college away from home, she enrolled at New York University. During the summers she took courses at Columbia. An indifferent student, she dropped out in her junior year to take a job at the new and unorthodox publishing company Boni and Liveright. Hellman's sharp opinions and spirited participation in the life of the firm led to lifelong friendships and valuable contacts. There she met Arthur Kober, an aspiring and later successful writer, whom she married in December 1925. Hellman published several short stories while she and Kober lived in Paris for several months in 1926; once the couple settled in Hollywood, she began to develop into the talented movie scriptwriter she would become. But she felt restless, uncommitted to any particular form of writing, unsure of what she wanted to do. The marriage survived several separations, ending finally in November 1930, when Hellman met the already celebrated mystery writer Dashiell Hammett. Kober and Hellman divorced amicably in 1932. Hellman and Hammett never married, but they maintained a devoted relationship, sometimes under the same roof, for thirty-one years, until Hammett's death in January 1961. Neither relationship produced any children.

Hellman attributed her turn to playwriting to Dashiell Hammett's suggestion that she dramatize a century-old Scottish criminal libel suit. *The Children's Hour,* the first of her eight original plays, was produced in 1934 to critical raves and financial success. The play focuses on a young girl who brings disaster on her boarding school when she maliciously accuses the two headmistresses of engaging in "unnatural" acts. Like much of Hellman's later work, *The Children's Hour* explores the devastating effects of the human impulse to tell lies and to do evil. A subsequent play, *The Little Foxes* (1939), creates a southern family, very much like her mother's, whose destructive pursuit of wealth tramples morality at every turn. The search for power undergirded by money is also spotlighted in *Another Part of the Forest* (1946), which takes the family drama back a generation to reveal how it sacrifices love and honor in the service of fortune building.

The struggle between good and evil features as

well in Hellman's political plays. *Watch on the Rhine* (1941), written when Hitler seemed fearsomely close to victory, advocates the morality of active engagement in support of some higher value, even to the point of inflicting death if it will prevent a greater harm. A decade later, when McCarthyism silenced many resistant voices, Hellman returned to this theme in *Autumn Garden* (1951). Toward the end of her playwriting career, Hellman tempered her judgments. *Toys in the Attic* (1960) drew on her father's family to depict a more complex set of human motives, including a character modeled on her mother who took advantage of the fruits of wealth to create a life devoted to compassionate charity.

Hellman was a careful and disciplined writer. She researched thoroughly and, often goaded by Hammett, wrote each play several times. She brought these qualities to the movie screenplays she authored in the 1930s and 1940s for Samuel Goldwyn and to the plays she successfully adapted from the work of other authors. By the late 1930s, she was financially successful, a literary figure to be reckoned with. Critics treated her respectfully, though not always favorably, sometimes deriding the melodramatic quality of her work and chiding her for exaggerating the ruthless manipulations of her greedy protagonists. By nature a powerfully emotional woman with a legendary capacity for expressing anger, Hellman refused to suppress her flair for the dramatic either in her own life or in her stage plays.

Hellman saw her plays as explorations of human character, rather than as efforts to impart political messages. Yet the twenty-seven fertile years when she was at her most productive were also the years in which she committed herself to union organizing and to anti-racist and anti-fascist activity, and in which she, along with Dashiell Hammett, defended the Soviet Union. She went to Spain in 1937 during the Spanish civil war and afterward wrote movingly (some say falsely) about her experience of war; the same year, she traveled to Moscow, afterward defending the Stalinist purges that were then at their height. She organized and became active in the Screenwriters Guild. She made a second, difficult journey to Moscow in 1944, raised money for Soviet relief during and after the war years, and organized intellectuals on behalf of world peace in the early cold war years. These activities led the press to label her a communist. But unlike Hammett, who acknowledged his membership in the Communist Party, Hellman consistently denied that she had ever joined its ranks. She was—she said—a rebel, not a joiner. Still, she never denied her sympathy for the cause represented by the Soviet Union and did not, until late in her life, repent her failure to speak out against Stalinist excesses.

Her finest political moment reflected some of the moral dilemmas about which she had written. Called before the House Committee on Un-American Activities in 1952, she challenged the committee's effort to force her to "hurt innocent people whom I knew many years ago in order to save myself." That strategy, she wrote, in a letter that was circulated during the committee hearings, "is, to me, inhuman and indecent and dishonorable" (Hellman, *Scoundrel Time,* p. 90). Like many others, she avoided naming names by pleading the Fifth Amendment. The favorable publicity surrounding her letter probably saved her a prison term for contempt; it did nothing, however, to prevent the Internal Revenue Service from harassing her, or the Hollywood movie industry from blacklisting her. To pay legal and other bills, Hellman sold her beloved home in Westchester County. More than two decades later, her account of this moment, published in *Scoundrel Time* (1976), drew spirited criticism for foregrounding her own role in a persecution that more fiercely victimized many others.

In the 1960s and 1970s, Hellman turned to lecturing, teaching, and writing three best-selling memoirs. Published between 1969 and 1976, they describe a life lived with courage and honesty, enriched by the camaraderie of literary and entertainment celebrities, and filled with satisfying sexual liaisons and the loyalty and love of faithful friends. The memoirs turned Hellman into a role model for young women and many on the Left. They account both for her resurgent popularity in the seventies and for her persistent notoriety. They are also the sources of persistent and continuing accusations against her for exaggerating her own experiences to the point of lying about them. Many of her acquaintances complained that they recognized neither the persona she constructed nor the stories. They accused her of aggrandizing her achievements, appropriating the life stories of those she admired, and embroidering her past at the expense of others. The ensuing controversies overshadowed her literary reputation in her final years, though they did not dampen her fighting spirit. Lillian Hellman died of cardiac arrest on June 30, 1984, at the age of seventy-nine. She is buried in Abel's Hill Cemetery on Martha's Vineyard.

Bibliography: Hellman's papers are located at the Harry Ransom Humanities Research Center, University of Texas, Austin. To date, Hellman has been the subject of two full-scale biographies: William Wright, *Lillian Hellman: The Image, the Woman* (1986); and Carl Rollyson, *Lillian Hellman: Her Legacy and Her Legend* (1988). Other useful biographical accounts include Bernard Dick, *Hellman in Hollywood* (1982); Joan Mellen, *Hellman and Hammett: The Legendary Passion of Lillian Hellman and Dashiell Hammett* (1996); Robert P. Newman, *The Cold War Ro-*

mance of Lillian Hellman and John Melby (1989); and Diane Johnson, *Dashiell Hammett: A Life* (1983). See also Peter Feibleman, *Lilly: Reminiscences of Lillian Hellman* (1988). The most useful compilations of Hellman's work are Stephen H. Bills, *Lillian Hellman, an Annotated Bibliography* (1979); Mark W. Estrin, *Lillian Hellman: Plays, Films, Memoirs: A Reference Guide* (1980); and Mary Marguerite Riordan, *Lillian Hellman: A Bibliography, 1926–1978* (1980). See also Lillian Hellman, *The Collected Plays* (1972). Hellman's three memoirs are *An Unfinished Woman—A Memoir* (1969), *Pentimento* (1973), and *Scoundrel Time* (1976). She is also the author of a novel, *Maybe* (1980), that some have labeled memoir; and co-author with Peter Feibleman of a cookbook that appeared posthumously as *Eating Together: Recipes and Recollections* (1984). Jackson Bryer, ed., *Conversations with Lillian Hellman* (1986), reproduces some of the most interesting interviews with Hellman. Some of the most significant critiques of her work and her veracity appear in Mark W. Estrin, *Critical Essays on Lillian Hellman* (1989). The most useful published evaluations of her work are Doris V. Falk, *Lillian Hellman* (1978); Alice Griffin and Geraldine Thorsten, *Understanding Lillian Hellman* (1999); and Richard Moody, *Lillian Hellman, Playwright* (1972). An obituary appeared in the *New York Times* on July 1, 1984.

ALICE KESSLER-HARRIS

HERNÁNDEZ, María Latigo. July 29, 1896–January 8, 1986. Political activist, community leader.

In March 1986, during National Women's History Week, María L. Hernández's portrait appeared with those of other prominent U.S. women on a poster titled "Women: Builders of Communities & Dreams." The poster was officially unveiled days after her death. A teacher, midwife, author, and mother of ten, Hernández epitomized the image of a political activist dedicated to women and her culture. Her communities of activism were multilayered—from the plight of Mexican Americans and African Americans to the needs of children and expectant mothers. Her life's work stretched over many decades, serving as a bridge between Mexican Americans in the United States and Mexicans in Mexico, as well as across generations.

Born to Eduardo Frausto and Francisca Medrano Latigo, María was one of six children. She spent her childhood years in Garza García, Nuevo León, Mexico, before the family moved to Monterrey. At the age of fifteen, she graduated from secondary school, and began working as a teacher in the school where her father was superintendent.

The Mexican Revolution forced her family to flee to the United States in 1914, arriving in Hebbronville, Texas, on her eighteenth birthday after a temporary stop in Laredo. The family was placed on a farm, where they had to work in the fields for the first time. She met and married her husband, Pedro B. Hernández, in January 1915.

A growing family did not deter either one of them from becoming active politically and economically in the San Antonio community, where they moved in 1918. Their first son, Pedro Hernández Jr., was born later that year, but died of typhoid as a child. Three other children died in infancy. Six children born between 1919 and 1932, four daughters and two sons, survived, and they adopted a daughter in 1938. Upon their arrival in San Antonio, Hernández and her husband opened a grocery store and bakery. Its success allowed her to pursue training in midwifery in the early 1920s. She delivered babies and provided prenatal care for the next twenty-five years, charging her patients ten dollars when doctors charged twenty-five. Hernández understood her clients' financial situations and often allowed them to pay over the course of the pregnancy.

The husband-and-wife team not only shared a business together, but also challenged the social, economic, and political inequalities facing Mexican Americans in San Antonio. They were especially interested in causes relating to education. They helped found La Liga Pro-Defensa Escolar en San Antonio (School Improvement League) in 1934. La Liga was committed to bridging the gap between Mexican American and Anglo students. Hernández was not just a member of the organization; she also spoke out against racial inequalities in public schools. At one point in 1934, she mesmerized an audience of five thousand with a speech, rallying them to the cause of La Liga. As was her preference, she spoke in Spanish, the language of the majority of her audience.

While Hernández remained true to her adopted country, she also broke new ground when she became one of the first female Mexican American radio announcers with her one-hour program on KABC, *La Voz de las Americas* (*Voice of the Americas*), in the 1930s. She also worked with WOAI radio, another local station that broadcast one-hour Spanish-language programs. In 1939 she served as a goodwill ambassador to Mexico for the Orden Caballeros de America (Order of Knights of America, which she and her husband had established in 1929), meeting with the Mexican president and his wife. As a voice of the community, she also campaigned for President Franklin Roosevelt in the 1930s and 1940s.

During World War II, she discontinued her midwifery duties when her oldest son sent her a letter from overseas asking her to stop because it was too dangerous for her to travel alone. Although she put her practice on hold, she continued to assist women by advocating for additional entitlements for the wives and daughters of Mexican American servicemen fighting overseas. Education and civil rights continued to be her major concerns. In 1968, as secretary of the Orden Caballeros de America, she wrote an impassioned letter to the hearing of the U.S. Commission on Civil Rights, held in San Antonio. The letter raised the issue of the discrimination experienced by Mexican American citizens and citizens of African origin. It offered suggestions to remedy the problems, including an impartial study by the commission, but it also highlighted the idea that once students were engaged in civics lessons and understood their rights as U.S. citizens, their rights were less likely to be violated.

Hernández continued her fiery brand of organizing well into her seventies. Her political work would eventually extend throughout the State of Texas during the height of the Chicano movement. Considered one of the founders of the Raza Unida Party in Texas, she and her husband, Pedro, worked tirelessly at campaigning for Raza Unida Party candidates running for state positions. Hernández summed up her decades of activism, service, and volunteering in this way: "I feel my husband and I have worked very hard since 1924 for the betterment of our people. I feel we have not accomplished very much because of our limited resources. But when a person dedicates all of his life to the movement, that in itself is worth more than money" (Cotera, p. 81).

Pedro Hernández died in 1980. Six years later María L. Hernández died of pneumonia in Lytle, Texas, at the age of eighty-nine. In remembrance of her accomplishments, U.S. Representative Henry B. Gonzales said, "She fought a big fight with a little stick," referring to her work to improve the west side of San Antonio (*San Antonio Light*, January 11, 1986). She is remembered as a spokesperson for the poor and a strong advocate for civic responsibility and equality in education.

Bibliography: For biographical information, see Martha P. Cotera, *Profile of the Mexican American Woman* (1976), and the essay by Cynthia E. Orozco in *The Handbook of Texas Online* maintained by the Texas State Historical Association. Additional information can be found in the María L. Hernández file and vertical files, Benson Latin American Collection, University of Texas Library, Austin. Also of interest are Vicki L. Ruiz, *From Out of the Shadows: Mexican Women in Twentieth-Century America* (1998); Richard A. Garcia, *Rise of the Mexican American Middle Class: San Antonio, 1929–1941* (1991); and Rodolfo Rosales, *The Illusion of Inclusion: The Untold Political Story of San Antonio* (2000). An obituary appeared in the *San Antonio Express-News* on January 11, 1986.

MARY ANN VILLARREAL

HICKEY, Margaret Ann. March 14, 1902–December 7, 1994. Lawyer, feminist, federal adviser.

Margaret A. Hickey was born in Kansas City, Missouri, to Elizabeth Wynne and Charles Lawrence Hickey and was the oldest of four surviving children. Because her father was in the American foreign service, she was educated abroad until the family returned to Kansas City at the advent of World War I. She attended Mt. Marty High School in Kansas City and graduated in 1918. At age sixteen she entered personnel work to support herself at a college (never identified), but dropped out in 1921 to become a reporter, which provided her first introduction to discrimination on the job. She entered the Kansas City University (later University of Missouri) Law School in 1923 and received the LLB degree in 1928. Her law practice was not remunerative, owing to both discrimination against her as a woman and the onset of the Great Depression. Nevertheless, she viewed law as a fitting discipline for women because of its insights into administration and decision making.

Supported by her suffragist mother, and influenced by lawyers FLORENCE ALLEN and LENA MADESIN PHILLIPS, Hickey was increasingly drawn to issues of concern to women, particularly those educated young women who had no job skills. Her first efforts to train unemployed women were through a volunteer program, during the early Depression under the auspices of the Young Women's Christian Association, that centered on skills training, counseling, and job placement. That experience prompted her in 1933 to found Miss Hickey's School for Secretaries, a career school in St. Louis for women secretaries, administrative assistants, and business executives. Hickey ended her law practice to assume full responsibility for the school's administration until she sold it in 1968.

Early in her career Hickey joined the National Federation of Business and Professional Women (BPW); she admired its local leaders, and it provided opportunities for career advancement to members. Her involvement in the BPW eventually led to her election as national president for 1944–46. At the invitation of the State Department, she represented the BPW at the United Nations San Francisco Conference in 1945.

In 1942 Secretary of Labor FRANCES PERKINS, recognizing Hickey's knowledge of problems encountered by employed women in business and industry, suggested her for chair of the Women's Advisory Committee (WAC) of the War Manpower Commission. It was the first of many federal government advisory roles Hickey would have under five presidents from Franklin D. Roosevelt through Lyndon Johnson. As WAC chairman, she presided over a forum of fourteen women who advised the War Manpower Commission on the most effective use of women workers in the war effort. Although the WAC made some headway against discrimination and limitations to the full use of women, Hickey was frustrated that the policy-making potentials of competent women remained underutilized in the federal government.

Thus she joined with associations in the BPW and other women's organizations to promote the postwar appointment of women to policy-making positions. She wrote in 1948 to her close friend LUCY SOMERVILLE HOWORTH, "Well, Lucy, the old battle cry was 'votes for women,' and now it ought to be 'politics for women' if we are to get any place" (Rupp and Taylor, pp. 67–68). Hickey never injected her Democratic Party affiliation into her advocacy for women and was thus able to work with many groups, and maintain ties with many individuals, outside the Party.

From war's end until she was well into her seventies, Hickey served in an advisory or consultant capacity to various federal agencies. They included the UN Commission on the Status of Women, the International Development Advisory Board (President Harry Truman's Point Four program), and the Advisory Committee on Welfare Services for Children. In 1961 John F. Kennedy named her to his President's Commission on the Status of Women, for which she chaired the Committee on Federal Employment Policies and Practices. Her committee helped bring about an end to the system of separate categories for men and women Civil Service applicants. In 1964, President Johnson appointed her chair of the Advisory Council on the Status of Women; in that capacity, she pushed for expanded employment of women in government positions. Hickey enjoyed her government service, but found advisory groups frustrating because they were not able to make policy.

Although Hickey was a strong advocate for career women, from the beginning she valued the homemaker and denounced feminists who disparaged the role of women as housewife, mother, or volunteer. She based her feminism on the belief that women had unique qualities, distinct from those of men, that they should use to their advantage. "The days of the old, selfish, strident feminism are over," she said as early as 1945 (Rupp and Taylor, p. 23), and with passing years she concentrated on the positive aspects of women as achievers in volunteer activities as well as in government and business.

In 1934 Hickey married a St. Louis lawyer, Joseph T. Strubinger, a widower fourteen years her senior with whom she developed a warm and successful relationship. The couple did not have children. Throughout her years of public service she spent three days a week in St. Louis with him and commuted to duties elsewhere for the week's remainder. After she became the public affairs editor of the *Ladies' Home Journal* in 1946, she maintained an apartment in Philadelphia. The job entailed writing about the many conventions and conferences she attended, and soliciting articles on public affairs. In 1973 the couple moved to Tucson, Arizona; Strubinger died there that year. Hickey continued her involvement in government and world affairs. From 1973 to 1976 she served as chairman of the Advisory Committee on Voluntary Foreign Aid for the U.S. Department of State and maintained an active role in the Red Cross at the national and international level, attending numerous national conventions and global conferences.

As an octogenarian she adopted a new advocacy on careers for the elderly but retained her interest in women's issues by serving on the University of Arizona Women's Studies Advisory Council. Finally the disabilities of old age overcame her, and she moved to a nursing home in Tucson, where she died in 1994 at the age of ninety-two.

Bibliography: The Margaret Hickey Papers at the Western Historical Manuscript Collection, University of Missouri–St. Louis, is a massive collection. Some eight hundred folders (in addition to scrapbooks) contain correspondence, speeches, printed documents, press clippings, and photographs primarily related to Hickey's public career. There is little family or personal material. There is a transcript of an oral interview conducted by Ann Lever and Susan Hartmann (1974) and a copy of an analysis of Hickey's rhetoric written by Alice Donaldson. The papers contain Hickey's completed, but unpublished, manuscript "*Seventeen* Career Book for Young Women" (1965). Additional material can be found in the Somerville-Howorth Papers, Schlesinger Library, Radcliffe Institute for Advanced Study, Harvard University. There is no biography of Hickey, but numerous references to her appear in Leila Rupp and Verta Taylor, *Survival in the Doldrums: The American Women's Rights Movement, 1945 to the 1960s* (1987); Susan M. Hartmann, *The Home Front and Beyond: American Women in the 1940s* (1982); and Martha H. Swain, *Ellen S. Woodward: New Deal Advocate for Women* (1995). Obituaries appeared in the *New York Times* on December 10, 1994, and the *St. Louis Post-Dispatch* on December 11, 1994.

MARTHA H. SWAIN

HICKS, Beatrice Alice. January 2, 1919–October 21, 1979. Engineer.

Beatrice Alice Hicks was born in Orange, New Jersey, and decided to become an engineer at age thirteen, after admiring the Empire State Building and George Washington Bridge with her father, William Lux Hicks, himself a chemical engineer. Her family also included her mother, Florence Benedict Neben, and a younger sister, Margaret Lurene. After graduating from Orange High School in 1935, Hicks earned her BS degree in chemical engineering from Newark College of Engineering (now New Jersey Institute of Technology) in 1939. She stayed on at the school as a research assistant, and studied electrical engineering and physics at night.

Taking advantage of opportunities for women during wartime manpower shortages, starting in 1942 Hicks worked on engineering design, production, and testing of quartz crystal oscillators at a Western Electric plant in Kearny, New Jersey. By the time of her father's death in 1946, Hicks had joined Newark Controls Company, a metal-working business established by her father and uncle in Bloomfield, New Jersey. As chief engineer and later as vice president in charge of engineering, Hicks led the firm's work in designing, manufacturing, and selling environmental sensing equipment. In 1949, she received her MS in physics from Stevens Institute of Technology. She also took graduate courses in electrical engineering at Columbia. In 1952, *Mademoiselle* selected Hicks as the magazine's "Woman of the Year in Business."

With her uncle's retirement, she bought control and became president of Newark Controls in 1955. The firm specialized in developing and producing switches and sensors used in missiles, jets, and air force equipment, where the devices had to withstand vibrations, shock, and extreme temperature variations. These controls could anticipate equipment failures, locate problems, and gather information to correct them. Company alarms sounded a warning, for example, when an airplane or missile reached a speed that exceeded its structural safety limit. As a pioneer in this engineering field, Hicks invented and patented a type of gas density monitor that was used in the United States space program, among other functions. To ensure top quality, the company manufactured these instruments under tightly controlled conditions, a purpose for which Hicks designed and helped build a special underground laboratory.

In 1950, female engineers on the East Coast began meeting, officially incorporating in 1952 as the Society of Women Engineers (SWE). An early statement of SWE's objectives read: "To inform the public of the availability of qualified women for engineering positions; to foster a favorable attitude in industry toward women engineers; and to contribute to their professional advancement. To encourage young women with suitable aptitudes and interest to enter the engineering profession, and to guide them in their educational programs." When the new organization named its first officers in 1950, Hicks was chosen as president, and the following year she was elected to a second term. She later served on SWE's first board of trustees, among other leadership responsibilities. In 1963, the society presented Hicks with its highest honor, the SWE Achievement Award, conferred annually to recognize a woman who had displayed outstanding accomplishments in engineering. In 1964, Hicks chaired the First International Conference of Women Engineers and Scientists, organized in New York by SWE.

In this highly visible post as a founding member and first president of SWE, Hicks served as a public representative of the nation's relatively few but increasingly visible female engineers. She also became a role model for younger women considering careers in engineering, traditionally an overwhelmingly male-dominated field. Hicks traveled around the country making speeches, giving interviews, and otherwise promoting the idea, as in her acceptance speech for the SWE Achievement Award in 1963, that "education and work in engineering is both the responsibility and the privilege of *all* whose talents are scientific in nature," including women.

In 1948 Hicks married fellow professional engineer Rodney D. Chipp, engineering director of New York City's DuMont television network. Chipp later became director of engineering for ITT's communications systems and established a consulting business specializing in communications technology. The couple had no children. Hicks and Chipp were chosen from hundreds of applicants to represent the National Society of Professional Engineers on Project Ambassador, a fact-finding and goodwill tour of South America. They spent a month in 1960 touring Brazil, Argentina, Uruguay, Chile, and Peru, discussing how engineers from the United States could work smoothly and productively with colleagues there. After Chipp's death in 1966, Hicks became owner of his firm and decided to sell Newark Controls rather than try to manage two demanding businesses simultaneously. She continued working as an engineering consultant in New Jersey.

As a professional engineer licensed in New Jersey, New York, Pennsylvania, and the District of Columbia, Hicks lectured widely on business management and on the engineering of control technology. Her professional affiliations included membership in the Institute of Electric and Electronic Engineers; the American Society of Mechanical Engineers; the American Society of Heating, Refrigerating and Air Conditioning Engineers; and the Women's Engineering Society of Britain. She served as a United States delegate to the International Management Congress in 1954, 1957, 1960, and 1963.

In 1958, Hobart and William Smith College presented Hicks with an honorary Doctor of Science degree. In 1965, she received an honorary Doctor of Engineering degree from Rensselaer Polytechnic Institute, the first time RPI awarded such a degree to a woman. In 1978, Hicks was chosen to become a member of the National Academy of Engineering, the highest professional distinction for engineers in the United States; she was the sixth woman so honored. Beatrice Hicks died of a heart attack at age sixty in Princeton, New Jersey.

Bibliography: For correspondence, articles, and other papers by and about Beatrice Hicks, see the Society of

Women Engineers Collection in the Walter P. Reuther Library, Wayne State University, Detroit, which includes both quotations from the text. For information on her life and career, see *Current Biography* (1957), pp. 255–57; Marilyn Ogilvie and Joy Harvey, eds., *Biographical Dictionary of Women in Science: Pioneering Women from Ancient Times to the Mid-20th Century* (2000), pp. 595–96; and "Dr. Beatrice Alice Hicks, SWE's First President," *SWE Newsletter,* January–February 2000, p. 35. See also "Wanted by Industry: More Like Her," *Business Week,* April 7, 1951, p. 48; and "National Academy Elects Hicks Member," *SWE Newsletter,* May 1978, p. 14. An obituary with photographs appeared in the *SWE Newsletter,* November–December 1979, p. 5, and a death notice appeared in the *New York Times* on November 14, 1979.

AMY SUE BIX

HILL, Martha. December 1, 1900–November 19, 1995. Dancer, dance educator.

Grace Martha Hill was born in East Palestine, Ohio, the eldest of four children of Grace Todd and Grant Hill, a mining engineer. Her paternal genealogy can be traced to Mennonites who left Switzerland for Ohio in the early 1700s because of religious persecution; her maternal relatives settled during the same period in Pennsylvania. Secretly enamored of a renegade aunt who had taken a dancing job on a Missouri riverboat, Martha defied her Presbyterian upbringing by claiming dance as her vocation of choice, despite her parents' belief that it was a sin to dance, whether for recreation or on the stage. Once in college, she seldom returned home, where her career in dance was never acknowledged.

Trained at Battle Creek Normal School of Physical Education (later the Kellogg School), where she studied folk, aesthetic, and interpretive dancing starting in 1918, Hill's summer studies included ballet with Portia Mansfield, and later Edna McCrae at Perry-Mansfield in Colorado, along with lessons by mail with Louis Chalif. After graduation she became an assistant in dancing and athletics at Kellogg, and from 1923 to 1926 served as director of dance at Kansas State Teachers College.

In 1926 she moved to New York City to study with Anna Duncan and Konstantin Kobeleff, as well as train in Dalcroze eurhythmics, but after seeing MARTHA GRAHAM perform, "it was instant conversion" (Tracy, p. 12), and she immediately found her way to Graham's studio. The following spring, finances depleted, she returned to college teaching at the University of Oregon (1927–1929), moving back to the city to study with Graham in the summers of 1928 and 1929, when Graham asked Hill to join her group. Her career as a dancer (under the name Martha Todd) with Graham's first company of women for the next two years meant exhilarating explorations with the choreographer in her most experimental stage creating *Heretic* and *Primitive Mysteries,* performed in the historic series of Dance Repertory Theatre on Broadway. At the same time, Hill taught at Teachers College's Lincoln School while completing work on a BS degree there in 1929. In the fall of 1930, she accepted a part-time position as director of dance at New York University, where she later earned an MA in 1941. Unable to support herself as a dancer, she devoted her life to dance education.

Robert Devore Leigh, president of a new college to be established in Vermont, saw Hill's work at a symposium held at Barnard College and asked her to join Bennington's first faculty in October of 1932. The department Hill established became the first independent dance program to graduate dance majors in the United States. In 1934, with friend Mary Josephine Shelly, Hill convinced Leigh that it would be possible to create a summer dance school with artists in residence teaching as experts in their field. The result was an unprecedented fervor of dance making that brought together choreographers, dancers, composers, and designers.

Through her leadership at Bennington she fostered "way-breaking" ideas for a new dance at a critical moment in the development of concert dance in the United States. "The Big Four" under her wing included Martha Graham, DORIS HUMPHREY, and Charles Weidman (all having been members of Denishawn under the direction of RUTH ST. DENIS and Ted Shawn before establishing their own careers as choreographer-dancers), and German-born dancer HANYA HOLM. As artistic director supporting their dance making within the college setting, Hill was an important catalyst in the creation of masterpieces such as Graham's *American Document* (1938) and *Letter to the World* (1940), Humphrey's *New Dance* (1935) and *Passacaglia in C Minor* (1938), and Holm's *Trend* (1937), among others created at Bennington.

After four summer sessions at Bennington from 1934 to 1938, the program moved to the Mills College campus in California in 1939, before returning to Vermont as part of Bennington's summer School of the Arts through 1942. Although conditions during World War II put an abrupt halt to the Bennington activity, Hill reestablished the summer school at Connecticut College in 1948. There works such as Graham's *Diversion of Angels* (1948) and José Limón's *Moor's Pavane* (1949) premiered under the name of the American Dance Festival.

Throughout her career Martha Hill encouraged the growth of a field dominated by women in a largely matriarchal environment. Later, important men in dance such as Merce Cunningham, Alwin

Nikolais, and Paul Taylor joined the ranks, teaching and producing work under Hill's direction. As dance grew in popularity among college women, many of her students from Bennington, NYU, and later Juilliard created dance departments in colleges across the United States, infusing Hill's brand of professionalism and encouraging a growing population of dance audiences on college campuses.

In 1951, at the invitation of Juilliard president William Schuman, she left her Bennington and NYU posts (where she had established master's degree programs in dance) to found a dance division within the music conservatory. This time, her dance curriculum championed equal training in both ballet and modern dance—a novel concept at the time—that would be replicated in conservatories and departments as the standard for training contemporary dancers throughout the world. For her faculty she chose her former colleagues Martha Graham, Louis Horst, Doris Humphrey, José Limón, and Anna Sokolow, as well as Margaret Craske and Antony Tudor. With the school's move to Lincoln Center for the Performing Arts in 1969, her division held its position as an important center for dance training in higher dance education, despite ongoing struggles for space with George Balanchine's School of American Ballet, also housed at Juilliard.

In 1952, after a long friendship, Martha Hill married Thurston Jynkins Davies, former president of Colorado College, and later director of Town Hall in Manhattan, who was in charge of the American Pavilion at the Brussels World's Fair in 1958. He died of cancer in 1961.

While at Juilliard, Hill became one of the most revered figures in American dance for the pivotal role she played in developing twentieth-century dance. Her influence extended to leading institutions around the world as an adviser in Australia, Hong Kong, and Israel. Martha Hill held her Juilliard position until 1985, when she became artistic director emerita. She died at home in Brooklyn Heights, New York, after a short illness, weeks short of her ninety-fifth birthday. A nonprofit organization established in her name in 2000, the Martha Hill Fund, presents an annual award honoring a distinguished contributor to the field of dance.

Bibliography: The Jerome Robbins Dance Collection of the New York Public Library for the Performing Arts at Lincoln Center contains many articles and tributes documenting Martha Hill's career, such as Anna Kisselgoff, "The Innovations of Martha Hill," *New York Times*, March 28, 1982. The collection also includes the archival video collection, the Martha Hill Oral History Project, begun in 1990 at the Hong Kong Academy for Performing Arts, and other audio and visual resources. For further information on her career, see Sali Ann Kriegsman, *Modern Dance in America: The Bennington Years* (1981); Janet Mansfield Soares, "Martha Hill: The Early Years," *Ballet Review* 28, no. 4 (Winter 2000), pp. 66–94; and the chapter on Hill in Robert Tracy, *Goddess: Martha Graham's Dancers Remember* (1996). Materials have been drawn from the contributor's firsthand knowledge as her student and colleague, as well as interviews with Hill, her brother Lewis, colleagues, students, and friends in preparation for a biography. An obituary appeared in the *New York Times* on November 21, 1995.

JANET MANSFIELD SOARES

HILL, Thelma. May 26, 1924–November 21, 1977. Dancer, dance educator.

Born and raised in New York City, Thelma Hill became a leading dancer, company co-director, master teacher, and cherished mentor to scores of African American dance artists. Little is known of her childhood or her upbringing. She was an only child, and her parents evidently encouraged her early artistic interests. Hill later said she had always been interested in the arts and had studied music and painting as a child. She turned to dance as a teenager. Her interest in dance solidified when she studied tap dance with Mary Bruce, a noted teacher who ran an important studio in Harlem. She took to dance easily, and according to her contemporaries would occasionally teach class to students her age or older.

As a young woman, Hill worked office jobs during the day, including a stint at the New York City Department of Welfare. She married a man named Doll, but the marriage dissolved quickly, and she rarely referred to him in her adult life. She became serious about dance study around 1949, when she began concentrated ballet classes at the Metropolitan Opera Ballet School. Her passion for the art outweighed her late start in training, and she focused on achieving a professional career in dance. Older than most of the other students at her skill level, Hill was always available for counsel and to offer sage advice. She became a mother figure to the other dancers, and early in her career an affectionate nickname emerged and stuck: Mother Hill.

Despite her late start in ballet, Hill studied assiduously with Maria Nevelska, a former member of the Bolshoi Ballet, and assisted noted Harlem dance studio teacher Sheldon B. Hoskins in his annual dance concerts. She achieved a professional career as a ballerina in the short-lived Les Ballets Nègres, founded in 1955, which became the New York Negro Ballet Company in 1957. Working with company founder Ward Flemyng, Hill assumed an administrative role with the group, and became rehearsal director responsible for maintaining the group's repertory during its landmark 1957 tour to England, Scotland, and Wales. Well received by surprised critics and audiences, the company's tour proved that African Americans could achieve classical ballet technique, a truth long denied by American balletomanes. Hill's invaluable presence confirmed her prescient ability to remember and coach all the roles, along with the fiery intensity she brought to her dancing. An injury to her tendon precipitated the end of her career as a dancer *en pointe*.

Upon returning to New York, she performed in the pickup companies of several artists who combined ballet technique with modern and social dance idioms, including Jean-Léon Destiné (1958), Louis Johnson (1958), Geoffrey Holder (1959), Talley Beatty (1960), and Matt Mattox (1961). She joined the newly formed Alvin Ailey American Dance Theater in 1959, and traveled with that company on their landmark tour of Southeast Asia in 1962 sponsored by the U.S. State Department. She quickly became a confidante to Ailey as his enterprise grew, and in the 1963 season she served as rehearsal mistress for the Ailey company. Although she left the troupe to continue her teaching career in New York, she remained close to Ailey throughout her life and served as an uncredited assistant to him on several engagements, including the Broadway musical *La Strada* (1969), which closed after one performance, and the Leonard Bernstein extravaganza *Mass* (1971), which ran for several performances over two years. Both of these shows included dancers from Ailey's company, many of whom had been Hill's students.

In all of her performances, Hill provided an unassuming emotional maturity, layered with an obvious passion and enthusiasm for the art of dance. She rarely performed leading roles in any of the works she danced, but choreographers, audiences, and other dancers always noted her authoritative presence, even when positioned on the periphery of the stage space. Her contemporaries often noted that she did not have a conventional dancer's body, according to ballet or modern dance standards, but she created a thrilling physical illusion in motion suited to the theatrical moment.

Hill's most sustained teaching engagement began in 1960 when she collaborated with other artists, including Ailey, Charles Moore, and James Truitte, to found a dance-training program at the New York City YWCA on Fifty-First Street near the Broadway theater district. In 1962, the program became the Clark Center for the Performing Arts. Besides studio and performance space, the center provided classes in a variety of techniques and choreographic approaches. In this productive environment, Hill trained innumerable African American dance personalities in dance etiquette, time management, and, remarkably, the Lester Horton technique. Developed over more than a decade, the Lester Horton technique improves fluidity in dancers through strength-building exercises that focus on the abdomen and thighs. It involves repeated lateral balances and tilting gestures of the torso, often performed in a flat-back position. By 1970, the technique was taught in dance studios around the world. Hill learned the Horton technique from Ailey, Truitte, and others who had studied with Horton in California before his death in 1953. She became an expert in the technique, and at the end of her life she was writing a textbook about it for publication.

After her performing career ended, Hill devoted herself to her students' individual growth and to the progress of African Americans into the mainstream of American concert dance practice. Her open personality tempered her serious demeanor as a teacher, and she was famous for sometimes intimidating her students toward heightened achievement. Although she had no children, some say that all of her students were her extended family, and her sage guidance continues to be felt among dancers who came under her gaze. Her numerous teaching affiliations also included the American Dance Festival at Connecticut College, the University of Cincinnati, and the Davis Center for the Performing Arts at City College of New York. She was also active in the Regional Ballet Association and the Delacorte Dance Festival in New York City.

Hill died tragically of smoke inhalation in 1977 during a fire in her New York City apartment. She was fifty-three. That same year, the Arts Center of Brooklyn was renamed the Thelma Hill Performing Arts Center in her honor.

Bibliography: Notwithstanding her extensive influence, there are extremely few published accounts of Thelma Hill's life or times. Dawn Lille Hurwitz details Hill's influence in the New York Negro Ballet in "The New York Negro Ballet in Great Britain," in Thomas F. DeFrantz, ed., *Dancing Many Drums: Excavations in African American Dance* (2002). Kathe Sandler's evocative, short documentary film, *Remembering Thelma* (1981), available from Women Make Movies, includes still imagery and reminiscences by several dance associates, including James Truitte and Carmen de Lavallade. Some of Hill's contemporaries, including Mickey Borde, Delores Browne, and Betty Ann (Thompson) Hubbard, contributed information by phone interview. Obituaries appeared in the *New York Times* on November 23, 1977, and in *Dance Magazine*, February 1978, p. 95.

THOMAS F. DEFRANTZ

HILLIS, Margaret. October 1, 1921–February 4, 1998. Conductor.

Margaret Hillis was a conductor of choral and orchestral groups and the founder of several professional music organizations, but was best known as the founder and longtime conductor of the Chicago Symphony Chorus. Along with Robert Shaw, Hillis had a profound influence on choral singing in the United States, raising expectations and standards far beyond previous levels. Breaking gender-based barriers in a field dominated by men, she helped open the door to women who want to pursue conducting as a profession.

Margaret Eleanor Hillis was the first of four children born to Bernice Haynes and Glen Raymond Hillis in Kokomo, Indiana. Margaret and her three brothers were raised in a wealthy family with servants. Her maternal grandfather, Elwood Haynes, was noted for inventing one of the first horseless carriages, a form of stainless steel, and other useful items. Margaret's mother was a homemaker but had attended college, and her father was a well-known lawyer who eventually ran for governor of Indiana, losing by a narrow margin.

Margaret grew up seemingly unaware of the limitations on women's roles in society. An excellent athlete as a young woman, she became a junior golf champion and bowling instructor. She began her interest in music from an early age, taking piano lessons at age five. Between private study and her ability to teach herself, she learned numerous other instruments as well, including saxophone, French horn, tuba, and double bass. Surrounded by classical music through radio, recordings, and live performances, Hillis dreamed of being a professional conductor of orchestras and operas, ignorant of the fact that such careers were considered the exclusive domain of males.

After graduating from the Tudor Hall school in Indianapolis, she entered Indiana University, but her musical studies were interrupted for a period during World War II. Wanting to serve her country, she trained to get her private and commercial pilot's licenses. Unable to pass the eye exam for a multi-engine rating to enter the WASPs, she instead obtained a civilian instructor's rating and trained other aspiring pilots.

After the war Hillis continued her studies at Indiana University, graduating in 1947 with a degree in composition and dreams of becoming a conductor. Warned that women were not hired as orchestral conductors, she was advised to enter the conducting profession through the "back door" of choral conducting. Matriculating at Juilliard School of Music in New York City, she studied under musicologist Julius Herford and choral conductor Robert Shaw from 1947 to 1949.

She soon began building her own formidable reputation in the New York area, in 1950 founding the Tanglewood Alumni Chorus, which later became the American Concert Choir (and had also been known as the New York Concert Choir)—the first professional resident choir in the United States. Her concerts received superb critical notices, and she soon came to the attention of Fritz Reiner, conductor of the Chicago Symphony Orchestra (CSO), who brought her choir to sing with the CSO on several occasions. When that became cost-prohibitive, Reiner invited her to found the CSO's own resident chorus. Hillis accepted the challenge and in 1957 began the job that would eventually earn her an international reputation. In her position she rehearsed and prepared the chorus for performances with the CSO and its conductors. She not only taught the notes and text, but also suggested approximate tempos, dynamics, and phrasing, insisting on flexibility to follow the different interpretations of any conductor leading the performance. In rehearsals she largely used the same piano and vocal scores that the chorus used, but she also studied the orchestral score, at least the passages where the chorus sang, so there would be no surprises.

The Chicago Symphony Chorus (CSC) was only the second orchestra chorus in the United States. Under Hillis's leadership the CSC developed into one of the world's best, known especially for its power, ensemble precision, and clear diction. Hillis and the Chorus worked under the direction of most of the renowned international conductors, and Hillis herself conducted the CSO and CSC on several occasions, the first woman ever to do so. During the period when Sir Georg Solti served as CSO music director (1969–91), both Hillis and the Chorus reached the pinnacle of their success in performance and recording, by 1994 garnering nine Grammy Awards, a record number for any chorus.

Hillis's most famous personal achievement occurred when on short notice in 1977 she replaced an injured Solti and conducted the Chicago Symphony Orchestra and Chorus in Mahler's Eighth Symphony *(Symphony of a Thousand)* in New York's Carnegie Hall. Learning this complex score in only two days, she conducted the several hundred musicians in a rousing performance, followed by audience pandemonium. She was interviewed by countless media outlets, including NBC's *Today Show,* and appeared on the cover of *Time* magazine and on the front page of the *New York Times.* The subsequent publicity brought her additional invitations to lead other ensembles as a guest conductor.

Over the years, Hillis served at various times as conductor to several regional orchestras, chamber ensembles, and other symphonic and opera choruses, including as choral conductor of the American Opera Society (1952–68) and music director of the Elgin Symphony Orchestra (1971–85). In addition to teaching briefly at Juilliard (1951–53), she also taught at Northwestern University from 1968 to 1977. She was a charter member of what is now Chorus America and used family funds to create the American Choral Foundation in 1954. Hillis received numerous awards in recognition of her musical achievements, and Chorus America's highest ensemble award is named for her.

Margaret Hillis was a striking, no-nonsense woman with a resonant, deep voice. A very insular and reserved person, she focused squarely on her career. She never married, but she did have a small circle of personal friends who became her surrogate family. Her friend Elizabeth Burton, a fellow musician, served as her personal assistant through the 1970s. Jane Samuelson, an editor who had interviewed Hillis and became a close friend, helped care for her during her final illness. Hillis also enjoyed her dogs and cats and loved to travel in what little free time she had.

After thirty-seven years as music director of the CSC, Hillis retired in 1994 to pursue guest conducting. She also hoped to write several books. But soon she was diagnosed with lung cancer. She died on February 4, 1998, in Evanston, Illinois, at the age of seventy-six and was buried in her hometown of Kokomo, Indiana. Musicians around the world mourned her death, and a stunning memorial service followed in Chicago's Orchestra Hall.

Bibliography: Material on Hillis can be found in the Margaret Hillis Collection in the Rosenthal Archives of the Chicago Symphony Orchestra. Of special interest are the printed program from her March 14, 1998, memorial service, which contains a useful chronology of her career, and the CSO program book from September 1994, which includes a tribute by Robert Shaw. The archives also contain interviews with the conductor by Jon Bentz (September 19, 1989) and Norman Pellegrini (October 6, 1997). See also Jeannine Wagar, ed., *Conductors in Conversation: Fifteen Contemporary Conductors Discuss Their Lives and Profession* (1991); and Jane Weiner LePage, *Women Composers, Conductors, and Musicians of the Twentieth Century: Selected Biographies* (1980). For a detailed history of the chorus she shaped, see Stanley G. Livengood, "A History of the Chicago Symphony Chorus, 1957–2000" (DMA dissertation, University of Oklahoma, 2001). Articles about Hillis include Giovanna Breu and Sally Moore's profile in *People,* November 28, 1977, pp. 84, 89; and Jane Samuelson, "For the Love of Music," *Chicago Magazine,* April 1980, p. 193. Additional information for this essay was provided by Elizabeth Burton, Elwood Hillis, and Jane Samuelson. Obituaries appeared in the *Chicago Sun-Times* on February 5, 1998, and the *Chicago Tribune* and *New York Times* on February 6, 1998.

STANLEY LIVENGOOD

HINTON, Carmelita Chase. April 20, 1890–January 16, 1983. Educator, school founder.

Carmelita Chase was born in Omaha, Nebraska, the second of four children and the first daughter of Clement Chase, newspaper editor and bookstore proprietor, and Lula Bell Edwards, socialite and philanthropist in the developing city. Her mother's family was from Kentucky, and her father's from New England. While her father encouraged her interests in sports, camping, and travel, her mother was more concerned with Carmelita's social position. Both parents agreed that Carmelita should attend academically rigorous and socially suitable Bryn Mawr College in Pennsylvania, and to prepare her for entrance examinations they sent her to the Episcopal School for Girls. Chase graduated from Bryn Mawr in 1912, having made her mark participating in athletic pursuits (she excelled at tennis), acting in plays, and singing in the college choir. When she realized during her senior year that she would like to work with children professionally, she took an education course that included readings by William James and Friedrich Froebel, whose theories influenced both her philosophy of life and her philosophy of education. After college, Chase returned home to work for her father, assisting in writing editorials for the weekly newspaper he published. Seeking a less protected position, she moved to Chicago, where she lived at Hull House and worked as a temporary secretary to JANE ADDAMS. Two and a half years later, after being exposed to many of the most innovative educational thinkers of her day, including John Dewey, Chase enrolled at the Chicago School of Civics and Philanthropy.

In 1916, before finishing her degree, she married Sebastian "Ted" Hinton, a patent lawyer and amateur naturalist who invented the wooden Jungle Gym, which would later be a source of family income. The couple had three children: Jean (1917), Bill (1919), and Joan (1921). Frustrated by her own "dreary" school experience, she was determined to create learning environments for her children and others that would be joyfully experiential, including real projects in the arts and crafts; camping, hiking and riding; farming and caring for animals; and work jobs. While her children were young, Hinton began to run a kindergarten, first in her Chicago apartment and then in the backyard of her suburban Winnetka home.

In 1923 her husband committed suicide while staying at the Riggs psychiatric clinic in Stockbridge, Massachusetts, where he had gone to be treated for depression. Carmelita Hinton determined to continue her career in progressive education. After teaching kindergarten at North Shore Country Day School in Winnetka for two years, she moved to Cambridge, Massachusetts, in 1925 when there was an opening to teach second grade at the progressive Shady Hill School. At Shady Hill, where her children then enrolled, she acquired a reputation as an outstanding and innovative teacher who took her children and other boarders to school on horseback through the streets of Cambridge. When there was no longer sufficient room for animals, children, and boarders in her Cambridge home, Carmelita and her children moved to Weston, Massachusetts, where she built a house and a barn and her oldest daughter attended Cambridge School of Weston.

As her children reached high school age, Hinton worried that the excitement they had shown for school would be stifled by the secondary schools then available. With the support of her colleagues at Shady Hill, she decided to create her own school. The Putney School was founded on a hilltop at Elm Lea Farm in Putney, Vermont, in 1935. The town of Putney was already known for unusual and visionary experiments, including the internationalist Experiment in International Living, which in 1933 had attracted Hinton to lead the first group of girls on its summer European program to create international understanding. Indeed, "changing the world" was the reason for the Putney School's existence. Carmelita Hinton strongly believed that it is important to educate children in a way that is compatible with their innately curious and active natures, and that those so educated would be a force for positive change in the world. Both Bill and Joan Hinton would graduate from the school.

Hinton's vision was certainly influenced by the progressive education movement and the theorists she had known in Chicago and Cambridge, but it was also a uniquely personal vision growing out of aspects of her own life: her father's commitment to equal education for his daughters; her memories of shared hikes and camping experiences with her brothers; her experiences with her naturalist husband and his ability to awaken their children's interest in animals through caring for them; her belief in the dignity of work in community growing out of her experience at Hull House; and her experience with European youth movements that emphasized physical fitness through outdoor exercise, and mental fitness through folk dance and song. All of these elements were at the core of the Putney School. Her commitment to internationalism resulted in mandatory summer travel in the first years before the war, and in the hiring of many international faculty during and after the war. Her commitment to community and community governance was also strong. Hinton believed in keeping children busy to help them avoid depression and the risks of alcohol, tobacco, and drugs. She was progressive in education, but not permissive in the behavior she expected from her students.

The Putney School was the first truly coeducational boarding school in the country to survive for the long term. Mrs. H., as she was known by students and faculty, was its dominant force, although a faculty strike in 1948 led to increased roles for teachers in the school's administration. In 1955, at age sixty-five, Hinton retired from its direction, but she stayed on its board until her death. She continued to travel and to promote world peace through the Women's International League for Peace and Freedom, and became deeply interested in China, where two of her children spent extended periods of their lives. After retiring from Putney, she moved to a farm in Pennsylvania, where she lived until ill health forced her to move to be near her daughter in Concord, Massachusetts. She died there in 1983 at the age of ninety-two. Her legacy lives on at the Putney School and through its more than three thousand alumni who have lived her vision of helping to make "a civilization worthy of the name."

Bibliography: Carmelita Hinton's personal papers are in the possession of her family. Material relating to the founding and early days of the Putney School can be found at the school's alumni office, which also maintains a collection of photographs of Hinton. Two important sources are Susan McIntosh Lloyd, *The Putney School: A Progressive Experiment* (1987); and Alan R. Sadovnik and Susan F. Semel, eds., *Founding Mothers and Others: Women Educational Leaders during the Progressive Era* (2002), which contains an expanded biographical essay by Lloyd. Carmelita Hinton wrote an autobiographical essay, "My Education in Teaching," which appeared in the *Bryn Mawr Alumnae Bulletin,* Spring 1951, pp. 4–5+. An essay called "Fundamental Principles" was published in the *Putney School Alumni Supplement* of May 1954. Obituaries appeared in the *Boston Globe* on January 18, 1983, and the *New York Times* on January 23, 1983.

M. KATHRYN TOLBERT

HOBBY, Gladys. November 19, 1910–July 4, 1993. Microbiologist.

Gladys Hobby is best known for her role in the clinical research and industrial development of penicillin and streptomycin—two of the most significant therapeutic milestones of the early antibiotic era—and her career broadly reflects the changing interface between biomedical research and therapeutic innovation in the mid twentieth century. Gladys Lounsbury Hobby was born in the Washington Heights section of New York City, one of two daughters of Flora R. Lounsbury and Theodore Y. Hobby. She attended Vassar College and received her bachelor's degree in 1931 before pursuing graduate education at Columbia University, receiving her master's degree in 1932 and a PhD in bacteriology in 1935.

In the course of her dissertation work, Hobby became involved with a bacteriological research team at the College of Physicians and Surgeons of Columbia University; the team included Martin Henry Dawson and Karl Meyer. While at Columbia, she also developed a professional relationship with Presbyterian Hospital; this dual access—to pathological materials and research subjects at the hospital, and to cutting-edge microbiology on the main Columbia campus—gave her a position uniquely well suited to translational research. In September 1940, one month after Howard Florey and Ernst Chain at Oxford published a paper on the chemotherapeutic potential of penicillin in treating infectious diseases in animal models, the Columbia-Presbyterian group became the context for the first clinical trials of the experimental drug, and Hobby's dual position was essential to the research project. As the sole microbiologist on the team, Hobby would carry penicillin-producing cultures of a strain of *Penicillin notatum* every morning from her Columbia laboratory to the clinical ward of Presbyterian Hospital, where they would be displayed and subsequently injected into patients with serious infections. By early 1941, Hobby's team had demonstrated that penicillin would be effective in the treatment of several infectious diseases if sufficient quantities of the pure drug could be produced.

By the 1930s a string of American women bacteriologists, most notably ALICE EVANS, had already begun to blaze a path for Hobby's generation. Yet Hobby was in several ways particularly well positioned to be at the center of the world-redefining era of antibiotic discovery heralded by the introduction of penicillin. Previously, antibacterial drug therapy was based on the construction of specific poisonous molecules (such as arsenicals and sulfa drugs) that would poison the pathogenic microbe more than they would poison the body of the host patient. As a result, medical bacteriology was almost entirely devoted to the study of pathogenic microbes, while the study of medical uses of nonpathogenic microbes—which was the basis of Hobby's doctoral thesis—was relegated to the periphery of medical bacteriological research. Antibiotics, however, turned this relationship on its head. The founding principle of antibiotic therapy was that nonpathogenic microbes—for example, the bread mold that was the source of Alexander Fleming's first sample of penicillin—were themselves an excellent source for finding molecules that selectively killed other microbes. Overnight, knowledge of non-disease-causing (nonpathogenic) microbes became essential to medical bacteriology and the new process of drug development, with Hobby at its center.

Gladys Hobby's career traces out the complex relationships between academia, government, and industry that came to characterize clinical research in the mid to late twentieth century. In a move that was increasingly common for academics interested in pharmaceutical development, Hobby left Columbia in 1944 for a position in industry with Chas. Pfizer Inc., a company that had developed strong connections with Hobby's team as a supplier of the experimental drug during the early penicillin research. In the same year that Hobby joined Pfizer, the company unveiled the world's first commercial plant for the production of penicillin, able to provide over 5 billion units per month. While at Pfizer, Hobby contributed to the development of the powerful anti-tuberculosis drug streptomycin (along with Selman Waksman) and the broad-spectrum Terramycin, among other antibiotic agents.

In 1959, Hobby made another lateral career shift to become chief of research at the East Orange Veteran's Administration (VA), at a time when the VA was becoming increasingly recognized as a well-organized public resource for conducting clinical trials. She also served as clinical instructor and assistant professor of public health at Cornell University Medical School. Upon her official retirement in 1977, Hobby launched another career as a consultant and freelance science writer, authoring many popular articles and the book-length work *Penicillin: Meeting the Challenge* (1985), which narrated the life cycle of the drug as it moved from laboratory to clinic. This book is still today one of the most insightful explorations of the relationships between clinical research and pharmaceutical companies in the early days of the antibiotic era, and presents a powerful image of the wartime penicillin collaboration as being equal in urgency, scope, and significance to the better-known Manhattan Project.

In addition to that book, Gladys Hobby authored several hundred scientific articles, founded and edited the journal *Antimicrobial Agents and Chemotherapy,* and was a charter fellow of the American Academy of Microbiology. She never married. She died at a retirement community in Kennett Square, Pennsylvania, on July 4, 1993, at the age of eighty-two.

Bibliography: Archival sources and biographical information on Gladys Hobby are limited. The best introduction to her work and significance remains her book, *Penicillin: Meeting the Challenge* (1985), which is based on her meticulous research notes and records from the 1940s. She also published numerous articles, including "Primary Drug Resistance—Continuing Study of Drug Resistance in a Veteran Population within the United States," *American Review of Respiratory Diseases* 110, no. 1 (1974), pp. 95–98. For general sources on microbiology and the history of antibiotics, see Harry F. Dowling, *Fighting Infection: Conquests of the Twentieth Century* (1977); and Patrick Collard, *The Development of Microbiology* (1976). An obituary appeared in the *New York Times* on July 9, 1993.

JEREMY A. GREENE

HOBBY, Oveta Culp. January 19, 1905–August 16, 1995. Federal official, army officer, newspaper publisher.

Oveta Culp Hobby became director of the Women's Army Corps during World War II, first secretary of the Department of Health, Education and Welfare, and head of the *Houston Post.* Oveta was born in Killeen, Texas, the second of seven children of Emma Elizabeth Hoover and Isaac "Ike" William Culp. Her mother taught her about the need to participate in community social welfare efforts, while her father, a lawyer who served a term in the Texas House of Representatives, encouraged his daughter's interest in politics. Oveta attended public schools in Killeen, Austin, and Temple, Texas, where her family moved when she was fourteen. After graduating from Temple High School, she attended Mary Hardin Baylor College in Belton, Texas, and took classes at the University of Texas.

More interested in politics than classroom studies, from 1925 to 1931 she served as parliamentarian of the Texas House of Representatives. A Democrat, she worked in local and regional campaigns, as well as at the 1928 Democratic National Convention, held in Houston. Those efforts led to her appointment as an assistant to the city attorney of Houston in 1930. Her only run for elected office was the same year, when she unsuccessfully ran for the state legislature as the representative from Houston. She was also employed as a legal clerk for the Texas State Banking Commission and in 1937 authored a handbook, *Mr. Chairman,* on parliamentary law for Texas public schools.

In 1931 Oveta Culp married William Pettus Hobby, a fifty-three-year-old widower with no children, former Texas governor (1917–21), and president of the *Houston Post-Dispatch* (later *Post*). After her marriage, Hobby began working for the *Post,* rising from research editor to assistant editor, and in 1938 she moved to the business side as executive vice president, a position created for her. The Hobbys bought the *Post* in 1939, and the company soon included radio and television holdings, including KPRC radio. In addition, she was active on various public and private boards and organizations in Houston and statewide. She served as president of the Texas League of Women Voters and as a member of the board of directors of the Museum of Fine Arts in Houston. The Hobbys had two children: William Pettus Hobby Jr. (1932) and Jessica Oveta "Catto" Hobby (1937), both born on her birthday, January 19.

In 1941, a new Women's Interest Section of the War Department's Bureau of Public Relations was created, and Representative EDITH NOURSE ROGERS submitted a women's army bill to Congress. Hobby was recruited by Secretary of War Henry Stimson to organize the Women's Interest Section, and when President Roosevelt signed the women's army bill on May 15, 1942, establishing the Women's Army Auxiliary Corps (WAAC), Hobby became its first director. The WAAC became the Women's Army Corps (WAC) in 1943, with full U.S. Army status, and Hobby continued as director, holding the ranks of major and colonel.

A small, trim woman who was always impeccably dressed, even in uniform, Hobby asked photographers not to take pictures of her when she was smiling, because she wanted to reinforce the seriousness of her position. Her mandate was to create an organizational and training plan for women's efficient integration into the army. She studied British, Canadian, and French women's services and launched a public relations campaign to persuade women and their families that women's army service was necessary and to counter negative public sentiment and slander about the women recruits. Because she was a southern white woman, Hobby's appointment caused concern in organizations like the National Council of Negro Women. In response, Hobby announced that African American women would be recruited in the same proportion as African American men in the army. Of the first 440 candidates selected for officer training, 40 were black. The WAC was never able to recruit the number of women authorized. By the end of the war, about a hundred thousand women had served as WACs, including approximately four thousand black women, a unit of Puerto Rican women, and a few women of Chinese, Japanese, and American Indian descent. In January 1945, Hobby was awarded the Distinguished Service Medal. She retired six months later.

Returning to Houston, Hobby became director of KPRC radio and KPRC-TV, and continued as executive vice president of the *Post.* In 1952, she was named co-editor and publisher of the newspaper. She continued her work on national and community boards and organizations, both public and private, including leadership positions in the Southern Newspaper Publishers Association, the Advertising Federation of America, the American National Red Cross, and the American Cancer Society.

Although a Democrat, Hobby backed Thomas E. Dewey for president in 1948 and worked to organize Democrats for Dwight D. Eisenhower in 1952. Once elected, Eisenhower chose Hobby to chair the Federal Security Agency. When the agency was reorganized as the Department of Health, Education and Welfare (HEW) on April 11, 1953, Hobby became its first director and the second woman to hold a cabinet-level position. She asked to be referred to as "Mrs. Secretary" not as "Madam Secretary," the title used by FRANCES PERKINS. As head of HEW, Hobby supervised the Social Security Administration, the Public Health Service, and the Office of Education. She oversaw a $1.7 billion budget in 1953, the largest of all cabinet departments except for the Departments of Defense and Treasury. A *Time* magazine cover story devoted to her HEW appointment quoted Lyndon B. Johnson: "She's the type of woman you'd like to have for a daughter or a sister, a wife or a mother, or the trustee of your estate." Among Hobby's accomplishments were a program for the voluntary distribution of the Salk vaccine to prevent polio and the expansion of federal programs to help states and localities build new hospitals, medical rehabilitation centers, and nursing homes. Hobby also established the first White House Conference on Education. She resigned her position in July 1955, because of her husband's illness, and returned to the *Post* as president and editor. William Hobby died in 1964.

In addition to running the *Post,* Hobby continued to serve on numerous public boards, especially for education and the arts, as well as presidential commissions and committees. In 1966, she visited Vietnam with an HEW Vietnam Health Education Task Force. An extremely wealthy woman because of her media holdings, she sat on the board of directors of the Bank of Texas, Mutual of New York, and the Corporation for Public Broadcasting. In 1984 she was named to the Texas Women's Hall of Fame. She died in Houston at the age of ninety, following a stroke, and is buried in Houston's Glenwood Cemetery.

Bibliography: The Papers of Oveta Culp Hobby in the Library of Congress concentrate on her service with the Women's Army Corps and cover the years from 1941 to 1952. The Dwight D. Eisenhower Library in Abilene, Kansas, contains papers from her tenure at the Department of Health, Education and Welfare. The Oveta Culp Hobby Papers at the Woodson Research Center, Rice University, span from 1817 to 1995, with the bulk of them from 1938 to 1985. The collection also contains copies of her handbook, *Mr. Chairman.* There is no full-length biography of Hobby. Information about Hobby's work and the history of the WAC is in Mattie E. Treadwell, *The Women's Army Corps* (1954), and Leisa D. Meyer, *Creating G.I. Jane: Sexuality and Power in the Women's Army Corps during World War II* (1996). *Time* magazine ran a cover story on Hobby, "Lady in Command," May 4, 1953, pp. 24–27, which included the quotation from Lyndon B. Johnson. Obituaries appeared in the *New York Times* and *Houston Chronicle* on August 17, 1995.

MELANIE GUSTAFSON

HOFFMAN, Anna Rosenberg. *See* Rosenberg, Anna Marie Lederer.

HOLM, Hanya. March 3, 1893–November 3, 1992. Choreographer, dance educator.

Hanya Holm was born in Worms, Germany, and baptized Johanna Josepha Eckert in a Roman Catholic ceremony. She was the second child, and first daughter, of Valentin Eckert, a restaurateur and wine merchant, and Marie Mörschell, an amateur scientist and lover of the arts. Hanya Holm (a pseudonym she assumed when her professional career began in 1923) spent her childhood in Mainz in comfortable middle-class surroundings. She was educated at the Konvent der englischen Fräuleine and studied the piano from an early age—study her family hoped would lead to a career in music. She continued musical training at the Hock Conservatory in Frankfurt am Main and at the Jaques-Dalcroze Institutes in Frankfurt and Hellerau, earning a teaching certificate there. Her 1917 marriage to painter and sculptor Reinhold Martin Kuntze ended in divorce in 1921. She retained custody of their son, Klaus Valentin Kuntze, born in 1920.

In 1920 Holm saw a solo concert by Mary Wigman, pioneer of the emerging art of modern dance, and changed her allegiance from music to dance. She was one of Wigman's first students. Energetic, articulate, and keenly intelligent, Holm became an indispensable member of Wigman's faculty; in 1929 she was appointed co-director of the Wigman Central Institute in Dresden. Holm danced in Wigman's first performance group, 1923–28, touring widely through Europe. When the company disbanded, she undertook two independent projects: the staging of Euripides' *Bacchae* in Ommen, Holland, in the summer of 1928; and choreography of Igor Stravinsky's *L'Histoire du Soldat* in Dresden in 1929. In May 1930, she directed the dancing chorus for Wigman's epic *Totenmal,* created for a Dancers' Congress in Munich.

Holm came to New York City in September 1931 to establish and direct a school authorized to teach the Wigman method in the United States. She vitally influenced dance training in the States with teaching that encouraged individual creativity through guided improvisation, exercises in choreography, and discussions of dance theory—a strategy that trained dancers without imposing a codified movement vocabulary. She was a guest teacher and lecturer at many colleges and at America's embryonic modern dance institutions: Perry-Mansfield Camp in Colorado, Mills College in California, and Bennington Summer School of the Dance in Vermont. With the appointment to Bennington at its founding in 1934, the dance community recognized Holm as one of four pioneering American modern dance artists, alongside MARTHA GRAHAM, DORIS HUMPHREY, and Charles Weidman. Lecture-demonstrations of the German modern dance, which she created with advanced students, received wide acclaim.

The rise of fascism in Germany compromised the New York Wigman School, and in 1936 Holm broke her business ties to Wigman and began an independent professional and personal life. She renamed the Wigman School the Hanya Holm Studio, formed a dance company, brought her son out of Germany, and started the process of naturalization. On becoming a citizen of the United States in 1939 she changed her name legally to Hanya Holm.

In 1936 Holm choreographed her first complete concert program, and in 1937 she created a modern dance masterpiece. *Trend,* an abstract work of epic proportions about social destruction and rebirth, won an award for best group choreography of 1937. Her lighthearted *Metropolitan Daily* (1938) was the first dance to be televised in the United States. In 1939 she made two works in response to the crisis in Europe—*They Too Are Exiles,* and *Tragic Exodus,* which won the Dance Magazine Award for best group choreography in modern dance. Other notable dances for her company were *Dance of Work and Play* (1938), *From This Earth* (1941), and *Namesake* (1942). The choreographer handled large groups and small ensembles masterfully, but she was not a strong solo performer.

As she adapted to the needs and temperament of American dancers, Holm made her teaching more structured than the image-driven German training. She also turned to her early training as a musician and began to choreograph to great music in the Western canon. Fun-loving and uncompromising, Holm was a strict disciplinarian who inspired dancers to use their instincts. She mentored many dance artists whom she equipped to develop their own styles—including Valerie Bettis, Alwin Nikolais, Mary Anthony, and Don Redlich.

In 1941 Holm established a summer program of instruction and dance production at Colorado College in Colorado Springs. There she created for her company until it disbanded in 1944, and then choreographed concert works for guest artists and students until the program ended in 1983. From 1975 to 1985 she choreographed four dances for the Don Redlich Dance Company, one of which, *Jocose,* later toured the world with Mikhail Baryshnikov's White Oak Project.

Holm began her Broadway career with three successes in 1948: "The Eccentricities of Davey Crockett," one of three independent sections of the dance-opera *Ballet Ballads,* by composer Jerome Moross and writer John LaTouche; José Ferrer's production of the Karel and Josef Capek play, *The Insect Comedy;* and Cole Porter's *Kiss Me, Kate.* The latter won her a New York Drama Critics Award. In 1950 she choreographed another Cole Porter show, *Out of This World.* Eight other musicals followed, the most memorable being *The Golden Apple* (1954), for which she won three awards; *My Fair Lady* (1956), for which she was again recognized with a Drama Critics' Award; and *Camelot* (1960). Holm built a reputation for crafting dance that sprang in seemingly spontaneous fashion from story and song.

Holm embraced many theater genres and appealed to different audiences. She co-directed, with Edward Levy, the world premiere of Douglas Moore's opera *The Ballad of Baby Doe* (1956) at the Central City Opera House in Colorado, staged Gluck's *Orpheus and Euridice* (1959) in Vancouver and Toronto, choreographed a musical film, *The Vagabond King* (1956), and created works for television. For her contributions to the concert stage and musical comedy, Holm was honored with the Capezio Award (1978), the Samuel Scripps American Dance Festival Award (1984), and the *Dance Magazine* Award (1990).

Holm maintained her New York City studio until 1968 and subsequently taught at the Juilliard School (1973–86) and the Nikolais/Louis Dance Theatre Lab (1972–86). She died in New York City at the age of ninety-nine; her remains were interred in Wilkes-Barre, Pennsylvania.

Bibliography: Most general texts on the history of modern dance contain information on Hanya Holm and her works. The Hanya Holm Collection in the Jerome Robbins Dance Division (JRDD), New York Public Library for the Performing Arts at Lincoln Center, contains correspondence, scrapbooks, personal and publicity photographs, business records, programs, and memorabilia. A biography, *Hanya Holm: The Biography of an Artist,* was written in 1969 by Walter Sorell. Two journals devote issues to essays, photographs, and chronology of her works: Marilyn Cristofori, "Hanya Holm: A Pioneer in American Dance," *Choreography and Dance* 2, no. 2 (1992); and "Hanya Holm: The Life and Legacy," *Journal for Stage Directors and Choreographers* 7, no. 1 (Spring/Summer 1993). A documentary film, *Hanya: Portrait of a Pioneer,* co-produced by Marilyn Cristofori and Nancy Hauser, is distributed in video format by Dance Horizons (1988). Claudia Gitelman's *Dancing with Principle: Hanya Holm in Colorado, 1941–1983* (2001) chronicles Holm's forty-three years of summer teaching and choreography at Colorado College. A transcript ("Dance Art" by Hanya Holm and K. Wright Dunkley) of philosophy Holm delivered while teaching in Colorado is available in the JRDD. Excerpts are published in Sorell's biography and in *The Vision of Modern Dance* (1979), edited by Jean Morrison Brown. An obituary appeared in the *New York Times* on November 4, 1992.

CLAUDIA GITELMAN

HOOBLER, Icie Gertrude Macy. July 23, 1892–January 6, 1984. Chemist, nutrition scientist, research administrator.

Born on her family's farm in Daviess County, near Gallatin, Missouri, Icie Gertrude Macy was the third of four children of Ollevia Elvaree Critten and Perry Macy. Her father, who traced his ancestry to English settlers who immigrated early in the seventeenth century, was the third generation of Macys to farm that land. Icie later recalled an idyllic childhood in which she enjoyed participating in the farm work and observing nature, traits that later served her well as a scientist.

Her early education was in a one-room country school, but at age fifteen she was allowed to accompany her older sister to Central College for Women in Lexington, Missouri. Attending the school for seven years, she majored first in music and later in English and received a BA in 1914. During those years, she began to develop her leadership skills, serving as class and student council president and as editor of the college magazine.

Although Icie wanted to go to the University of Chicago for a science degree, her parents thought she should spend another year in a more sheltered environment, so she enrolled at Randolph-Macon College for Women in Virginia. After a year under the encouraging tutelage of Mary Sherrill, her chemistry instructor, she enrolled in the University of Chicago, majoring in chemistry and minoring in physics, and received her BS degree in 1916. Another encouraging mentor, Julius Stieglitz, helped her obtain a job assisting in first-year chemistry classes at the University of Colorado at Boulder. While there she enrolled in a master's program and also assisted in the physiological chemistry course for medical students. The instructor in that course had studied with Lafayette B. Mendel at Yale University, and he encouraged Macy to follow her interest in physiological chemistry at Yale rather than return to Chicago.

Macy enrolled in Yale's Sheffield Scientific School in the fall of 1918 with a Pi Beta Phi Graduate Fellowship and later the Susan Rhodes Cuttler Fellowship. Her scientific development was influenced heavily by both Mendel and Russell Chittenden. Motivated by wartime concerns about the domestic food supply, she did her research on the toxic compound in cottonseed and how its toxicity might be overcome to improve cottonseed's nutritional value.

Upon completion of her doctoral degree in 1920, Macy chose a position as assistant biochemist at West Pennsylvania Hospital in Pittsburgh. Here she cultivated her growing interest in women's health, but she also experienced significant discrimination because of her sex. Consequently, the next year she accepted a teaching and research position offered by AGNES FAY MORGAN at the University of California at Berkeley. Encouraged by her mentors to take a position closer to her area of interest, in 1923 she relocated to Detroit to become director of the newly created nutrition research laboratory of the Merrill-Palmer School and the Children's Hospital of Michigan in Detroit. In the mid 1920s she also took on the responsibility of raising two nieces, who had been in the care of other relatives since the death of her sister in 1917.

In 1931 the laboratory became the Research Division of the Children's Fund of Michigan, an innovative project created in 1929 "to promote the health, welfare, and happiness of the children of Michigan, and elsewhere in the world." Until 1954, when the fund (as planned) had spent itself out of existence, Macy directed the research of over 150 investigators on the health and nutrition of childbearing women and infants and children. This pioneering work included studies of human milk composition, the physiological changes in women's body during and after pregnancy, and measurements of growth and development in infants and children, as well as some of the biochemical changes accompanying that growth. The research was often conducted in connection with charitable institutions and public health programs responsible for the health of indigent women and children and provided the practical benefit of good nutrition and health care for the subjects of the studies. These collaborations, fostered by Macy's involvement in community organizations, her pleasing personality, and her leadership abilities, usually involved demonstration and education projects as well.

On June 11, 1938, forty-six-year-old Icie Macy married B. Raymond Hoobler, a pediatrician and widower twenty years her senior. After what she describes in her autobiography as the happiest five years of her life, her husband died in 1943 on their wedding anniversary. Later, she built her retirement home in Ann Arbor to be near her stepson and his family.

Over the course of her career, Icie Macy Hoobler received numerous research awards, including the Borden Award (1939) of the American Home Economics Association, the Francis P. Garvan Medal (1946) of the American Chemical Society, and the Osborne and Mendel Award (1952) from the American Institute of Nutrition (now the American Society for Nutritional Sciences). Among her many leadership positions, she was the first woman to head a division of the American Chemical Society and the first to head one of its local sections. In 1940, she was named to the Food and Nutrition Board of the National Research Council, serving as the chair of its Committee on Maternal and Child Feeding; in 1944 she served as president of the American Institute of Nutrition. In 1960 she was appointed by the governor of Michigan to the founding Board of Control of Grand Valley State College.

With the end of the Children's Fund of Michigan, the Nutrition Research Laboratory closed in 1954, but in a long retirement Icie Macy Hoobler remained professionally active for many more years. Her projects included the development of a new course for students at the Merrill-Palmer School and a historical library to house the school's valuable collections. She also enjoyed international travel and collecting Asian art. In 1982 she moved back to her hometown of Gallatin, Missouri, where she died two years later at the age of ninety-one.

Icie Macy Hoobler was an influential mentor and role model for women scientists. Notably, she was the rare example of a woman who headed major research collaborations involving many investigators and major funding. Her research has had lasting influence; the standards she established for normal growth of infants and children, as well as her values for biochemical changes during growth, remain in use in pediatric research programs and practices today.

Bibliography: The Icie G. M. Hoobler papers in the Michigan Historical Collections at Bentley Historical Library, University of Michigan, Ann Arbor, contain correspondence, her scientific reports and publications, photographs, and other materials related to her professional activities. Additional archival material is found in the papers of the Merrill-Palmer Institute and the Children's Hospital of Michigan, both in the Walter P. Reuther Library of Labor and Urban Affairs, Wayne State University. Hoobler wrote an autobiography, *Boundless Horizons: Portrait of a Pioneer Woman Scientist,* with Harold H. Williams and Agnes Gainey Williams (1982). Her major scientific publications include *Nutrition and Chemical Growth in Childhood* (3 vols., 1942–51); (with Harold H. Williams) *Hidden Hunger* (1945); *The Composition of Milks* (1950); and (with Harriet J. Kelly) *Chemical Anthropology: A New Approach to Growth in Children* (1957). Biographical information is found in Harold H. Williams, "Icie Gertrude Macy Hoobler (1892–1984): A Biographical Sketch," *Journal of Nutrition* 114, no. 8 (August 1984), pp. 1351–62. An obituary appeared in the *New York Times* on January 13, 1984.

PATRICIA B. SWAN

HOOKER, Evelyn. September 2, 1907–November 18, 1996. Psychologist, gay rights advocate.

In the 1950s, psychologist Evelyn Hooker published research that challenged the reigning scientific wisdom that homosexuality was a sign of mental illness. She helped legitimate homosexuality as a valid field of social scientific study, and until her death she spoke out openly for gay rights.

Evelyn Gentry was born in North Platte, Nebraska, the sixth of nine children of Edward and Jessie Bethel Gentry. Neither her father, a tenant farmer, nor her mother, a practical nurse, had more than a fourth-grade education. When she was seven or eight, the family moved to eastern Colorado, where they bought a piece of unbroken land and lived in a two-room tarpaper shack. When Evelyn reached her teens, the family moved to Sterling, Colorado, where she could attend a higher-quality high school.

Already an outspoken activist, Hooker won a tuition scholarship to the University of Colorado and supported herself in college as a domestic worker. In her senior year, she won an instructorship that allowed her to pursue graduate education. She earned a BA and MA in psychology at the University of Colorado in 1928 and 1929, and then a PhD in 1932 at Johns Hopkins University, where she studied learning in white rats. After she finished her doctoral work, she taught at a small women's college near Baltimore. In 1934 she was diagnosed with tuberculosis; with the support of friends, she moved to California to stay in a sanitarium. After two years of convalescence, she took a part-time job at Whittier College and then won a fellowship to study psychotherapy in Berlin.

During her university years, Hooker was influenced by University of Colorado professor Karl Muenzinger, who inspired her love of science and also, as she remembered, impressed her with his "passion for social justice and the oppressed" (Humphries, p. 199). Hooker developed her own concern with issues of social justice. In 1937 and 1938, during her stay in Germany, she observed fascism firsthand while she lived with a Jewish family. She visited the Soviet Union and supported the Republicans in the Spanish civil war. She considered joining the Communist Party but decided against it. While she was in Europe, officials at Whittier College sent her a letter inquiring about her left-leaning politics. A year after she returned, she lost her job.

In 1939, Hooker applied for a faculty position in psychology at the University of California, Los Angeles. As Hooker recollected, the department chair informed her that he could not hire another woman and directed her to the University Extension division, which appointed her as a research associate in psychology. Two years later she married Donn Caldwell, a freelance writer. They divorced in 1947. In 1951, she married Edward Niles Hooker, a renowned UCLA professor of English. This happier marriage ended in 1957 with her husband's death. Neither marriage produced any children.

In the meantime, Hooker began to plan her research on homosexuality. In the mid 1940s she befriended a student, Sam From, who took her introductory psychology course. From brought her into his circle of gay friends and eventually urged her to study the gay male population. In 1953, Hooker applied to the National Institute of Mental Health (NIMH) for a six-month grant. Her proposed research differed from most other psychological and psychiatric studies of the era: Hooker planned to study the mental health of homosexual men who were neither patients nor prison inmates. She won the grant, which was renewed repeatedly until 1961, when she won an NIMH Research Career Award. In 1956, she published "A Preliminary Analysis of Group Behavior of Homosexuals," her first article on homosexuality.

Her most influential article, "The Adjustment of the Male Overt Homosexual," appeared in 1957. Hooker conducted standard psychological tests on thirty homosexual and thirty heterosexual men of comparable age, education, and IQ scores. None of the subjects was undergoing psychotherapy, and none showed evidence of severe psychological disturbance. Hooker removed identifying information and asked three clinicians to rate each subject's "overall adjustment." The homosexuals' adjustment ratings did not differ significantly from the heterosexuals' ratings. Hooker also presented two of the clinician judges with matched pairs of Rorschach (inkblot) test results and asked them to identify the homosexual in each pair. The judges could not consistently distinguish homosexuals and heterosexuals. Hooker concluded that homosexuality did not necessarily indicate pathology, tentatively suggesting it might be a deviation in sexual pattern within the normal range psychologically. In the 1950s, when homosexuals were routinely considered mentally ill, this was a bold position.

In obtaining her sample of gay male subjects, Hooker had worked with the Mattachine Society, the homophile (or early gay rights) association founded in Los Angeles in 1951. For the rest of her life, Hooker actively supported the movement for gay and lesbian rights. Although she often described herself as "hopelessly heterosexual," from the late 1940s on much of her social life involved gay men. Among her longtime friends were author Christopher Isherwood and poet Stephen Spender.

In the 1960s, Hooker's research shifted away from individual personality dynamics and toward the social networks of gay men. She conducted research in gay bars and published articles such as "The Homosexual Community" (1961) and "Male Homosexuals and Their 'Worlds'" (1965). In 1967, NIMH appointed her to chair its Task Force on Homosexuality. In 1969, the Task Force issued a report that recommended repeal of sodomy laws, portrayed employment discrimination as a problem, and called for better public education. The report both reflected and promoted a larger trend toward more liberal attitudes concerning homosexuality. Like Hooker's earlier research, it helped lay the groundwork for the 1973 American Psychiatric Association decision to remove homosexuality from its list of mental disorders.

In 1970, Hooker retired from her final position at UCLA as clinical professor at its Neuropsychiatric Institute. For the next decade, she engaged in private psychotherapy practice and clinical supervision. Toward the end of her life, she was honored for her pioneering research. In 1990, the Association of Gay and Lesbian Psychiatrists gave her its Distinguished Service Award, and in 1992 the American Psychological Association presented her with its award for Distinguished Contribution to Psychology in the Public Interest. In the latter part of her life, she suffered from bouts of depression and, after years of smoking, chronic lung disease. In 1996, at the age of eighty-nine, Hooker died in her apartment in Santa Monica, California, of cardiovascular disease.

Bibliography: The Evelyn Hooker Papers are housed in the Department of Special Collections Manuscript Division, Charles E. Young Research Library, UCLA. The collection includes her publications, lectures, speeches, correspondence, photographs, awards, and newspaper and magazine articles written about her. Hooker's most significant publications are "A Preliminary Analysis of Group Behavior of Homosexuals," *Journal of Psychology* 42 (1956), pp. 217–25; "The Adjustment of the Male Overt Homosexual," *Journal of Projective Techniques* 21 (1957), pp. 18–31; "The Homosexual Community," in *Proceedings of the Fourteenth International Congress of Applied Psychology* 2 (1961), pp. 40–59; and "Male Homosexuals and Their 'Worlds,'" in Judd Marmor, ed., *Sexual Inversion: The Multiple Roots of Homosexuality* (1965), pp. 83–107. For accounts of her life, see Evelyn Hooker and Paul Chance, "Facts That Liberated the Gay Community," *Psychology Today,* December, 1975, pp. 52–55+; *Λαυδ* Ηυμπηριεσ, Ιντερϖιεω *ωιτη* Εϖελψν Ηοοκερ, *Alternative Lifestyles* 1, no. 2 (May 1978); Bruce Shenitz, "The Grande Dame of Gay Liberation," *Los Angeles Times Magazine,* June 10, 1990; and the documentary film *Changing Our Minds: The Story of Dr. Evelyn Hooker* (1992). Obituaries appeared in the *New York Times* and *Los Angeles Times* on August 22, 1996.

JOANNE MEYEROWITZ

HOPPER, Grace Murray. December 9, 1906–January 1, 1992. Mathematician, computer scientist, naval officer.

Grace Murray Hopper was a straightforward, extraordinarily inquisitive person whose life centered around teaching, computers, and the U.S. Navy. Early realizing the importance of making computers accessible to a broad range of people, she articulated and implemented early efforts toward that goal. Hopper trained, encouraged, and supported large numbers of young men and women who became leaders in the computer field, and was a tireless speaker and advocate for computers and the navy.

Grace Brewster Murray was born in New York City, the eldest of three children of Mary Campbell Van Horne and Walter Fletcher Murray. The Van Hornes had come to New Amsterdam from the Netherlands in the seventeenth century, the

Murrays to the United States from Scotland in the early nineteenth century. Grace's mother attended a private school for girls in New York and was a housewife; her father graduated from Yale University in 1894 and worked as an insurance broker in New York City. The family spent summers in Wolfeboro, New Hampshire, from the time of her infancy.

After attending the Schoonmaker School in New York City (1913–23) and the Hartridge School in Plainfield, New Jersey (1923–24), Grace Murray entered Vassar College, where she studied mathematics, physics, and economics and was elected to Phi Beta Kappa. Graduating in 1928, she went on for an MA (1930) and a PhD (1934) in mathematics from Yale University. On June 12, 1930, she married Vincent Foster Hopper, an academic who taught English and literature. In 1931 Hopper returned to Vassar, where she taught mathematics until 1944. The Hoppers were divorced in 1945; they had no children.

Eager to participate in the war effort after the United States entered World War II, Hopper taught in an accelerated wartime program at Barnard College during the summer of 1943. She was finally able to enter the United States Naval Reserve (USNR) in December 1943, after having to overcome earlier resistance because of her age (too old), her weight (too light), and her occupation as a mathematics professor (classified as essential to the war effort). After attending the Midshipman's School-W at Northampton, Massachusetts, in May and June 1944, she was commissioned lieutenant (jg) and ordered to the Bureau of Ordnance Computation Project at Harvard.

Hopper had no idea beforehand what her assignment would entail. She discovered that she would be one of the first three people learning to program the Harvard Mark I, the first large-scale digital computer in the United States. This massive electromechanical (as opposed to electronic) computer, technically called the Automatic Sequence Controlled Calculator, was over fifty feet long and about eight feet high. First put into operation at Harvard shortly before Hopper arrived in early July 1944, the Mark I was programmed to solve a wide variety of problems related to the war effort. One of Hopper's major tasks was to edit and write portions of a manual describing procedures for the Mark I.

After the war, Hopper remained in the USNR on a navy contract at Harvard as a research fellow at the Computation Laboratory, where she continued to work on the Mark II and Mark III. Hopper did not coin the computer term *bug*, but while she was working with the Mark II a moth was discovered in the apparatus, possibly the first case of an actual bug found to cause a computer malfunction.

Hopper remained at Harvard until 1949, when she joined the Eckert-Mauchly Computer Corporation in Philadelphia as senior mathematician. The major attraction for her was UNIVAC I, soon to be built as the first commercial large-scale electronic computer, a successor of the ENIAC developed by the company's founders at the University of Pennsylvania. She remained with the company and its successors (Remington Rand and later Sperry Rand) in a variety of positions for nearly two decades. There she did what is generally considered her most influential work, the creation and development of the first compilers—programs that translate mathematical or English-like language into numeric code that a computer can understand.

In the early 1950s Hopper wrote the first compiler, the A-0. Beginning in 1955, Hopper and her team developed FLOW-MATIC, a compiler for data processing that used English-type language and opened programming to a wide range of business users. Often inaccurately described as a coinventor of the business computer language COBOL, Hopper was peripherally engaged in that project, although her earlier work on compilers provided a foundation for the development of COBOL.

In December 1966, Hopper was retired from the navy at the rank of commander. The following August, however, she was recalled to temporary active duty to standardize computer languages for the navy. This assignment turned into nearly two decades of work involving the standardization and validation of software, as well as travel throughout the country and the world promoting computers and their use to military, educational, and industry groups. Hopper was a tireless public relations person promoting new ideas related to computing as well as her own ideas about how to get things done. Her colorful speeches typically included some of her standard phrases: "A ship in port is safe, but that's not what ships are built for"; "Go ahead and do it, you can always apologize later"; and "The grimmest phrase in the English language is 'but we've always done it that way.'"

During her continued active duty with the navy, Hopper was promoted to captain in 1973 and to commodore in 1983, the latter rank renamed rear admiral in 1985. On August 14, 1986, Hopper, at seventy-nine the oldest commissioned officer on active duty, was finally retired from the navy, in a ceremony in Boston Harbor on board the USS *Constitution,* the Navy's oldest commissioned war ship. Hopper was hired by Digital Equipment Corporation less than a month later as a full-time senior consultant.

While working in industry and for the navy, Hopper held various visiting teaching positions or lectureships, including at the University of Pennsylvania and George Washington University. Her nonprofessional interests were persistent and varied. She did crocheting and needlework; was a voracious reader, especially of history; and was a serious genealogist.

The most recognized woman in mathematics and computer science of the twentieth century, Hopper received scores of honors, including nearly fifty honorary degrees from colleges and universities. The Grace Murray Hopper Award, given annually to an outstanding young computer professional by the Association for Computing Machinery (ACM), was established in 1971 by the UNIVAC Division of Sperry Rand. In 1986 she received the Distinguished Service Medal, the highest award given by the Department of Defense. In 1987 the Navy Regional Data Automation Center (NARDAC) moved into new quarters named for Hopper at the Naval Air Station in San Diego. She was awarded the National Medal of Technology in 1991.

Hopper died in 1992 at home in Arlington, Virginia, at the age of eighty-five, and was buried at Arlington National Cemetery with full military honors. More recognition came after her death. Given her devotion to the navy and her determination to always move forward, perhaps the most apt came in 1997 when the USS *Hopper* (DDG-70), a guided missile destroyer, was commissioned in San Francisco. The motto on the ship's coat of arms translates to "Dare and Do," which, the navy notes, "captures the spirit of [Rear Admiral] Hopper in her quest for pushing the limits of conventional thinking and looking beyond the norm for innovative solutions and approaches to problem solving."

Bibliography: The most extensive and accessible archival collection is the Grace Murray Hopper Collection (1944–1965) at the National Museum of American History, Smithsonian Institution. Extensive memorabilia is housed at the Grace Murray Hopper Museum at the Naval Computer and Telecommunications Station, San Diego. Hopper was the author or editor of nearly fifty publications. She edited and contributed significant portions of *A Manual of Operation for the Automatic Sequence Controlled Calculator* (1946). Her important talk "The Education of a Computer" appeared in *Proceedings of the Association for Computing Machinery* (1952), pp. 243–49, and was reprinted in *Annals of the History of Computing* 9, nos. 3–4 (1988), pp. 271–81. An extensive partial list of her publications appears in Amy C. King with Tina Schalch, "Grace Brewster Murray Hopper (1906–)," in Louise S. Grinstein and Paul J. Campbell, eds., *Women of Mathematics: A Bibliographic Sourcebook* (1987), pp. 67–73. There are extraordinarily many sources, of varying degrees of accuracy, about Grace Murray Hopper. The biography by Charlene W. Billings, *Grace Hopper: Navy Admiral and Computer Pioneer* (1989), was written for young readers with Hopper's cooperation. Hopper is one of four women profiled in Kathleen Broome Williams, *Improbable Warriors: Women Scientists and the U.S. Navy in World War II* (2001), and is the subject of Carmen L. Mitchell, "The Contributions of Grace Murray Hopper to Computer Science and Computer Education" (PhD dissertation, University of North Texas, 1994). See also Jean E. Sammet, "Farewell to Grace Hopper—End of an Era!" *Communications of the ACM* 35 (1992), pp. 128–31, which gives an excellent account of Hopper's technical contributions. Several interviews of Hopper are located in the Computer Oral History Collection at the National Museum of American History. The Schlesinger Library, Radcliffe Institute for Advanced Study, Harvard University, holds three interviews, including one for the Women in the Federal Government Oral History Project (1981–83). The last quotation is from the United States Navy. An obituary appeared in the *New York Times* on January 3, 1992. Two of Hopper's nephews, John V. Westcote and William T. Westcote, contributed personal information.

JEANNE LADUKE

HORTON, Mildred McAfee. May 12, 1900–September 2, 1994. College president, director of the WAVES.

Mildred Helen McAfee was born in Parkville, Missouri, the youngest of three daughters of Reverend Cleland Boyd McAfee and Harriet Brown McAfee. Her father taught mental and moral philosophy at Park College and served as the moderator of the General Assembly of the Presbyterian Church. Mildred received her secondary education at the Francis W. Parker School in Chicago, and then enrolled at Vassar College, where she was class president, president of the Christian Association, and a member of the basketball and field hockey teams. She graduated Phi Beta Kappa in 1920.

After graduation, she embarked on a teaching career. She taught English and French at Monticello Seminary in Godfrey, Illinois, and then returned to the Francis W. Parker School to teach eighth grade. Next she taught economics and sociology at Tusculum College in Greenville, Tennessee. While serving as dean of women and professor of sociology at Centre College in Danville, Kentucky (1927–32), she received her MA from the University of Chicago in 1928. She also took graduate courses at Columbia University. In 1932 she was appointed executive secretary of the Associate Alumnae of Vassar and two years later became dean of women at Oberlin College. After a nationwide search, McAfee was chosen to succeed ELLEN FITZ PENDLETON as the seventh president of Wellesley College in 1936. Students quickly nicknamed their new president, who was only thirty-six years old, "Miss Mac."

During World War II, McAfee's extensive experience as an educator and administrator made her an ideal candidate to direct the U.S. Navy's new female reserve program established in 1942 to relieve men for duties where they were more urgently needed. Granted a leave of absence from Wellesley to manage the WAVES (Women Accepted for Volunteer Emergency Services), McAfee took the oath of office on August 3, 1942, becoming a lieutenant commander in the Naval Reserves and the first female officer in the United States Navy. The navy promoted her to the rank of captain in November 1943.

The scale of the job both overwhelmed her and challenged her. She learned early, however, that the navy recruited women because they needed them, not because they wanted them in the reserves. She had to overcome inherent sexism and traditionalism while managing more than 86,000 women reservists, who handled jobs ranging from air traffic controller to aviation mechanic, cryptologist, translator, and weather specialist. In many cases, a single female reservist did the job of two men.

Using her creativity, corporate knowledge, experience, and intellect, McAfee proved to naval leaders and others the worth of having women in the navy. She insisted that naval service did not have to come at the expense of femininity. Her sense of humor, determination, and integrity helped her navigate the sometimes turbulent and difficult currents of the Navy Department in general and the Bureau of Naval Personnel specifically. She traveled throughout the country and to Hawaii to monitor the progress of the WAVES program, always encouraging the female reservists that she encountered. As navy men worked with the WAVES, they came to understand that these women volunteered to serve for many of the same reasons as they did—patriotism and a desire to bring loved ones home sooner. *Time* magazine published her portrait on its March 12, 1945, cover, and she received the Distinguished Service Medal, as well as the American Campaign Medal and the World War II Victory Medal, for her contributions to the war effort.

At various points during the war, navy recruiters could not meet their goals, yet refused to enlist African Americans. McAfee never supported the navy's decision to exclude black women and resisted the earlier recommendations to segregate them. When too few joined the WAVES to be separated, McAfee urged Randall Jacobs, chief of the Bureau of Naval Personnel, to discuss the policies for the training and utilization of African American WAVES with Secretary of the Navy James Forrestal. Forrestal saw a segregated navy as an expensive one; for these reasons and others, he agreed in 1944 that African American WAVES would be integrated into the naval female reserve.

On August 10, 1945, McAfee married Reverend Douglas Horton, a fifty-four-year-old widower with a son and three daughters, in Jaffrey, New Hampshire. Now known as Mildred McAfee Horton, she remained on active duty in the navy until February 1946, although she had already resumed the Wellesley presidency. She left Wellesley in 1949 to follow her husband's career aspirations in New York and Cambridge, where he served as dean of Harvard University's Divinity School. On her own she completed studies of schools and colleges for the Carnegie Fund, UNESCO, and other organizations, and also held pioneering positions on the boards of the New York Life Insurance Company, the National Broadcasting Company, and Radio Corporation of America. In 1953, Secretary of Health, Education and Welfare OVETA CULP HOBBY, who had been McAfee's counterpart in the Women's Army Corps during World War II, proposed her as the U.S. representative to the United Nations Social Commission, but the appointment fell victim to McCarthy-era red tape.

When Douglas Horton retired from Harvard in 1959, he and Mildred settled in Randolph, New Hampshire, where, taking their inspiration from the mountaintop dwellings of Hindu sages and disciples he had toured while visiting India, they started a retreat center at the summit of Pine Mountain in Randolph. Horton was a very caring and supportive wife, stepmother, and grandmother who cherished her family life. The last decades of her life brought more acknowledgment of her contributions to women's education as well as opportunities to advance civil rights. In 1961 Wellesley named a dormitory in her honor. In 1963, she co-chaired the National Women's Committee for Civil Rights with PATRICIA ROBERTS HARRIS and began an eleven-year tenure as a trustee at the University of New Hampshire. She ultimately became its first female chairman of the board. Douglas, her husband and ministry partner, died in 1968.

Mildred McAfee Horton died in a nursing home in Berlin, New Hampshire, on September 2, 1994, at the age of ninety-four. An innovator, coordinator, and catalyst, she exhibited activism, professionalism, and outstanding leadership skills, which like her warm smile, quick wit, and sense of humor inspired men and women alike. Her contributions to her country during World War II earned her national respect.

Bibliography: There is no biography of Mildred McAfee Horton. Material on her Wellesley years can be found at the Wellesley College Archives, which also contains an oral history conducted by Jean Glasscock in 1971. See also the oral history interview by John T. Mason in *The Reminiscences of WAVES, Volume 1* (1971), Operational Archives, Naval Historical Center, Washington Navy Yard, Washington, D.C. The Naval Historical Center also contains biographical information. Linda McGoldrick wrote a profile of Mildred McAfee Horton, "A Salute to Captain Mac," which appeared in *Magnetic North* (Winter 1983). For general information on women's roles in the navy during World War II, see Nancy Wilson Ross, *The Waves: The Story of the Girls in Blue* (1943); Susan H. Godson, *Serving Proudly: A History of Women in the U.S. Navy* (2001); and Winifred Quick Collins with Herbert M. Levine, *More Than a Uniform: A Navy Woman in a Man's World* (1997). Obituaries appeared in the *Boston Globe* on September 3, 1994, and the *New York Times* on September 4, 1994.

REGINA T. AKERS

HOWORTH, Lucy Somerville. July 1, 1895–August 23, 1997. Lawyer, federal official, feminist.

Lucy Somerville was born in Greenville, Mississippi, to Robert Somerville, a civil engineer, and NELLIE NUGENT SOMERVILLE, a temperance and woman suffrage leader of national rank who was the first woman to be elected to the Mississippi House of Representatives. Lucy's father, who attended the University of Virginia, and her mother, a graduate of Martha Washington College in Virginia, were the parents of four children, two boys and two girls, of whom Lucy was the youngest.

Scotch-Irish and stalwart Methodists who enjoyed a solid middle-class standing, both parents determined that their children should be well educated. Lucy attended Greenville's Delta Preparatory College before enrolling at Randolph-Macon Woman's College, where as a freshman she formed an Equal Suffrage League. Following her graduation in 1916, she taught one year at Randolph-Macon before entering Columbia University for graduate work in psychology. She worked as a gauge inspector at a munitions plant in New York City during World War I. During 1918–20 Lucy sought contacts with like-minded women through the national board of the Young Women's Christian Association, for which she conducted industrial research, and the University Women's Club, and later credited her time in New York as critical to her development as a human being.

Denied admission to Columbia University to study law because of her sex, Lucy entered the University of Mississippi Law School and graduated first in her class in 1922. For two years she practiced law as an associate of her brother-in-law in Cleveland, Mississippi. In 1924 the governor appointed the rising young lawyer to the state Board of Law Examiners, and she was named United States Commissioner for the Southern Judicial District, a position bearing the honorary title *Judge*. Henceforth she would be known as Judge Lucy. After her father died, she returned to Greenville to begin a solo practice, and in 1928 she married Joseph Marion Howorth, a law school classmate, and together they opened a law office in Jackson. The couple were devoted to each other and remained together for fifty-two years until Joe's death in 1980. They had no children.

In 1931 Lucy Howorth was elected a Hinds County representative to the state legislature where, as chair of the Public Lands Committee, she helped pass bills that benefited her Depression-blighted state. An ardent Democrat, Howorth campaigned for Franklin D. Roosevelt in 1932 among Mississippi women. For such activity she won an appointment in 1934 to the Board of Appeals of the Veterans Administration (VA) and moved to Washington. Dismissed in 1943 through an administrative decision that only veterans could serve on the board, she gained a higher position in the VA as a legislative attorney. In 1949, after the creation of the War Claims Commission, she became an assistant general counsel, deputy general counsel, and ultimately the general counsel.

A firm believer in the power of organizations to bring about change, Howorth worked steadily for women's rights during her Washington years from inside and outside the government. Widely acclaimed as a dynamic advocate for the appointment of women to positions of authority in governmental and educational entities, she was most remembered for her keynote address in 1944 at the White House Conference on Women in Postwar Policy-Making called by ELEANOR ROOSEVELT. She also advanced women's causes through organizations such as the National Federation of Business and Professional Women and the American Association of University Women (AAUW), both of which she had joined when she lived in Jackson in the 1920s. She chaired the AAUW Committee on the Status of Women from 1947 to 1951 at a time when the organization sought to retain for women gains made during World War II, and she was recognized as a leader in the admission of black graduates to the AAUW in 1949. In 1951 she chaired the Assembly of Women's Organizations for National Security, a clearinghouse for women's initiatives for national defense during the Korean War. In the early 1950s she traveled abroad to bolster the International Federation of University Women.

In 1953 the advent of a Republican administration led to her removal from the War Claims Commission, and she retired from the federal government in 1954. After a brief association with a Washington law firm, Howorth received an appointment to the legal research team of President Dwight Eisenhower's Commission on Government Security (1956–57). At the completion of that work, the Howorths returned to Cleveland, Mississippi, where they practiced law until full retirement.

Never afraid to call herself a feminist, Howorth continued her advocacy for women's advancement. Through her friend MARGARET HICKEY she was named in 1962 to the Task Force on Federal Employment Policies of President John Kennedy's

Commission on the Status of Women. Howorth thus became the only prominent New Deal woman to hold a presidential appointment, even if briefly, under every president from Roosevelt to Kennedy.

Although her Washington positions were not as prestigious as those held by other Democratic women, few other women, if any, remained active in organizations and causes to promote the status of women as long as Howorth did. Through her mother's leadership for suffrage and temperance, Howorth had developed a great admiration for leaders of the women's movement and social reform. Her early skill in parliamentary procedure, her acumen, and her quick appraisal of problems won her leadership positions. Howorth's good humor, southern charm, and femininity offset her candid and sometimes brunt demeanor, and thus she was nonthreatening as she pursued her agenda in politics or reform. She found her short stature and unimposing appearance to be a certain surprise factor that often disarmed potential opposition.

During a retirement spanning forty years, Howorth counseled emerging AAUW leaders in Mississippi and gave financial assistance to women's studies and public affairs programs at Delta State University and the University of Mississippi. She devoted countless hours to assisting historians engaged in writing women's history and edited the letters of her grandfather, published as *My Dear Nellie: The Civil War Letters of William L. Nugent to Eleanor Smith Nugent* (1977). Judge Lucy retained her quick wit, humor, keen intellect, and intense loyalty to women friends until her death at home from heart failure at age 102.

Bibliography: The massive Somerville-Howorth Collection at the Schlesinger Library, Radcliffe Institute for Advanced Study, Harvard University, contains extensive family history, correspondence, over sixty articles and speeches, and photographs. Smaller collections are at Delta State University and the Mississippi Department of Archives and History. Pertinent manuscripts are in the papers of the Women's Division of the Democratic National Committee at the Franklin D. Roosevelt Library, Hyde Park, New York; the Harry S. Truman Library, Independence, Missouri; and in the papers of the national AAUW (microfilm) and the Mississippi AAUW (University of Mississippi). Extensive correspondence with Martha Swain (1977–95) is in the authors' possession. Howorth published articles in the Randolph-Macon Woman's College *Alumnae Bulletin* (1935–88), the AAUW *Journal* (1937–56), and *Independent Woman* (1937–44). Her New Deal activity is discussed in Susan Ware, *Beyond Suffrage: Women in the New Deal* (1981), and her club work in Leila J. Rupp and Verta Taylor, *Survival in the Doldrums: The American Women's Rights Movement, 1945 to the 1960s* (1987). A thesis by Jane Elliot, "Lucy Somerville Howorth: Legislative Career, 1932–1935" (Delta State University, 1975) is very informative, as is the entry in *Current Biography* (October 1951). Extremely useful are the oral interviews conducted by Constance Myers, University of North Carolina, Chapel Hill, 1975; Marjorie Wheeler and Chester Morgan, University of Southern Mississippi, 1983 and 1984; and Allen Dennis (1972–73) and Dorothy Shawhan (1983–1995), Delta State University, Cleveland, Mississippi. Obituaries appeared in the Jackson (Miss.) *Clarion-Ledger* on August 24, 1997; the *Washington Post* on August 26, 1997; and the *New York Times* on September 2, 1997.

DOROTHY S. SHAWHAN
MARTHA H. SWAIN

HUGHES, Russell Meriwether. *See* La Meri.

HUMMERT, Anne. January 19, 1905–July 5, 1996. Advertising executive, radio producer.

Anne Hummert, together with her husband, Frank, was instrumental in the development of the daytime radio drama, or soap operas, as both an entertainment form and a highly successful advertising vehicle. Together, they brought friendship, emotional support, and a little romantic fantasy to millions of lonely, isolated housewives during the economic Depression of the 1930s and the challenges of World War II, while effectively blurring the line between culture and commerce in American popular entertainment.

Born Anna Mary Schumacher in Baltimore, Maryland, she was the daughter of Frederick and Anne Lance Schumacher. Little is known about her family or early life. She graduated Phi Beta Kappa with a degree in history from Goucher College in 1925. While attending college, she changed the spelling of her name to "Anne." Because her father had refused to pay her tuition (he did not believe in higher education for women), she worked her way through school as the Goucher correspondent for the *Baltimore Sun.* Upon graduation she began working full-time for the *Sun.* In the summer of 1926 she sailed to Paris and found a job at the *Paris Herald,* the European edition of the *New York Herald Tribune.* She married fellow reporter John Ashenhurst on July 26, 1926, and resettled in Chicago, home of the Ashenhurst family. A son, John, was born in April 1927. By 1928 they were divorced and Anne found herself looking for work.

Unable to find a steady newspaper job, she wrote to the Chicago advertising agency of Blackett-Sample-Hummert, asking for an interview. In 1930 she was hired as an assistant to Frank Hummert, a gifted but reclusive copywriter who never actually saw clients or even had much to do with other agency employees. The young assistant and her boss, who was twenty years her senior and had initially been opposed to hiring a woman for the job, made something of an odd couple, but they worked together extremely well. After five years of professional collaboration, they married in 1935, following the death of Frank's first wife. They did not have children together, but raised her son from her first marriage.

Radio was still in its infancy in these years, and practices of the time allowed advertising agencies to produce programs for their clients. Frank Hummert saw great potential for his clients, who included makers of household cleaning products, pain remedies, and cosmetics, to provide inexpensive entertainment for their target audience of housewives through daytime programming. Anne shared this vision. They reasoned that women would be interested in entertainment that was modeled on the popular serialized romantic fiction in newspapers and magazines. Their first effort, *The Stolen Husband,* was produced for broadcast in 1931 and was not a success. The Hummerts refined their formula and brought three programs to the airwaves the following year. Two of them, *Betty and Bob* and *Just Plain Bill,* proved to be very popular. *Just Plain Bill* remained on the air until 1955.

The fifteen-minute programs written and produced by the Hummerts were melodramatic, naive, humorless, and moralistic with a focus on family and interpersonal relationships. Crime, amnesia, lunacy, and jealously were abundant, but sex was never mentioned. It soon became apparent that the basic program formula could be expanded indefinitely if they could develop a way to mass-produce the programs. In response the Hummerts pioneered a factory system of writing and production that one radio historian compared to the assembly line techniques of automaker Henry Ford. Anne, either alone or with her husband, usually developed general plot outlines that were then filled out by teams of dialoguers and writers under contract for twenty-five dollars a script. The Hummerts retained tight control over the content, and all scripts had to be approved by them before they were sent to their independent production company, Air Features. Anne also cast all the parts in broadcasts. This technique allowed them to produce almost half of the serials brought to network radio between 1932 and 1937 and close to a third of those introduced between 1937 and 1942. What *Time* magazine called "the Hummerts' Mill" could flood the daytime airways with more than a dozen daily dramas, while other creative serial writers could at best manage two or three programs at a time. Controversial at the time, their practices became the model for later television serial production.

Under constant attack and ridicule by social reformers, educators, and network officials who thought the programs lacked taste, Hummert defended her programs as upholding moral values. She pointed out that her scripts emphasized family life and that bad behavior was never rewarded in the end. As the Hummerts often said, they wrote successful stories about unsuccessful people. Some of their most popular, longest-running dramas were *Ma Perkins* (1933–55), *The Romance of Helen Trent* (1933–60), *Mary Nobel, Backstage Wife* (1935–59), *Lorenzo Jones* (1937–55), *Our Gal Sunday* (1937–59), *Young Widder Brown* (1938–56), and *Stella Dallas* (1937–55). As the longevity of those programs suggests, the constant criticism never broke the loyalty American women felt toward soap operas. Many devoted listeners considered the programs educational.

In 1937, Blackett-Sample-Hummert opened a branch office on Park Avenue in New York City. The Hummerts relocated their writing and production operations there in 1938. In 1943 Blackett-Sample-Hummert dissolved. After the split, Frank and Anne continued to produce serials through their own separate writing and production companies, usually from the seclusion of their Greenwich, Connecticut, estate, connected by telephone and mail to their production studios in New York City. In addition to the numerous daily serial dramas, the Hummerts also produced three popular evening musical variety programs and *Mr. Keen, Tracer of Lost Persons,* an evening serial mystery program.

Neither the Hummerts nor their programs made the transition to television. During the mid 1950s they sold their production company and retired to travel. Always private and reclusive, and extremely well off from their years of radio production, they completely withdrew from public sight. When Frank died in 1966, his obituary in *Variety* complained that his widow's obsessive secrecy obstructed the press from confirming the details for over a month. Anne Hummert returned to Goucher College in 1978 as the first artist-in-residence in communication. She died in her Manhattan apartment on July 5, 1996, at the age of ninety-one and is buried in Chicago's Graceland Cemetery.

Bibliography: Copies of scripts for many of the Hummert broadcasts (1932–58) are in the American Heritage Center at the University of Wyoming. Recordings of numerous programs are in the recorded sound collections of the Motion Picture, Broadcasting, and Recorded Sound Division of the Library of Congress. Descriptions of the programs are in John Dunning, *On the Air: The Encyclopedia of Old-Time Radio* (1998); Jim Cox, *The Great Radio Soap Operas* (1999); and Ronald W. Lackmann, *The Encyclopedia of American Radio* (2000). A substantial interview is included in Isabella Taves, *Successful Women and How They Attain Success* (1943). Discussion of radio serials and the Hummerts' role in their development are found in Jim Cox, *Frank and Anne Hummert's Radio Factory: The Pro-*

grams and Personalities of Broadcasting's Most Prolific Producers (Jefferson, N.C.: McFarland, 2003); Raymond W. Stedman, *The Serials: Suspense and Drama by Installment* (2nd ed., 1977); Francis Chase Jr., *Sound and Fury, an Informal History of Broadcasting* (1942); Robert Metz, *CBS: Reflections in a Bloodshot Eye* (1975); Erik Barnouw, *The Golden Web, 1933–1953* (1968), vol. 2 of *A History of Broadcasting in the United States;* and J. Fred MacDonald, *Don't Touch That Dial! Radio Programming in American Life, 1920–1960* (1979). Michele Hilmes, *Radio Voices: American Broadcasting, 1922–1952* (1997), discusses the importance of serial dramas to women. See also Cynthia B. Meyers, "Frank and Anne Hummert's Soap Opera Empire; 'Reason-Why' Advertising Strategies in Early Radio Programming," *Quarterly Review of Film and Video* 16, no. 2 (1997), pp. 113–32. Birth dates vary in different sources, between 1903 and 1905. An obituary appeared in the *New York Times* on July 21, 1996.

JANET W. MCKEE

HUNTER, Alberta. April 1, 1895–October 17, 1984. Blues and cabaret singer.

Alberta Hunter was born in Memphis, Tennessee, the third child of Laura Peterson, a Knoxville native, and Charles E. Hunter, a Pullman porter. Her oldest sibling, John, died at birth. Charles Hunter abandoned the family soon after Alberta was born, and her mother worked as a maid to support the family. Hunter's early years were difficult: as a child she was molested both by a white landlord's boyfriend and by a black school principal, and she witnessed the abuse of her mother by her stepfather. Her grandmother, Nancy Peterson, took over much of the responsibility for raising of Alberta, her sisters, and her cousins. Hunter was devastated when, sometime around 1909, Peterson left Alberta in Tennessee and moved with the other children to Denver.

In 1911, at age sixteen, she made her way to Chicago on the train with one of her teachers and stayed with a family acquaintance. Hunter's unflagging persistence got her a performing job at a bordello called Dago Frank's. By 1915 she was singing at the Panama Café; in 1917–21 she became a mainstay at the Dreamland Ballroom. She worked with renowned composers such as W. C. Handy ("Saint Louis Blues," "Beale Street Blues"), Maceo Pinkard ("Sweet Georgia Brown"), Porter Grainger ("'Tain't Nobody's Business If I Do"), and Eddie Green ("A Good Man Is Hard to Find"), introducing their music to the public.

At the Panama Café she first met Lottie Tyler, the niece of comedian Bert Williams, who was passing through Chicago on her way back to New York. Hunter and Tyler became lovers off and on for many years, living together between 1925 and 1927 and again from 1929 to 1931. Hunter's primary attachments were to women, although she worked hard to hide the fact. She married once (in 1919 to Willard Townsend), but the couple separated after two months and were divorced four years later. She never had children.

Accompanied by Fletcher Henderson's band, Alberta Hunter made her first recordings for Harry Pace's Black Swan label in May 1921. In July 1922 she recorded for Paramount Records, with which she signed an exclusive contract soon after. In this second session she recorded her first original song, "Downhearted Blues," which she had written and copyrighted with the encouragement and assistance of pianist Lovie Austin. The song became a big hit and was recorded by many other artists, including BESSIE SMITH. Hunter's early accompanists included Eubie Blake, Fats Waller, Louis Armstrong, and Sidney Bechet, and in 1923 she was one of the first black singers to record with a white band—the Memphis Five. While under contract with Paramount she recorded some of the same songs for Harmograph, Silvertone, Famous, Puritan, and Gennett, using such pseudonyms as Josephine Beatty, May Alix, and Monette Moore.

Hunter went on to have a prolific recording career with many different companies, including Okeh and RCA Victor in the mid to late 1920s, the legendary Decca and Bluebird labels in 1939–40, Folkways in 1962, and Columbia CBS in the 1980s. Many of these records included original compositions, such as "Chirping the Blues," "Rough and Ready Man," "Black Man," "I Got a Mind to Ramble," "My Castle's Rocking," "I Got Myself a Working Man," "Will the Day Ever Come When I Can Rest," and "Remember My Name."

Hunter also became involved in musical theater, starting in 1920 with a role in the musical comedy *Canary Cottage* by Shelton Brooks. In April 1923 she made her Broadway debut, creating a sensation with her performance in Eddie Hunter's *How Come?* at the Apollo. She went to Europe in 1927 and landed the leading role of Queenie, playing opposite Paul Robeson, in a 1928–29 production of *Showboat* at the Theatre Royal Drury Lane in London. In 1933 she was back in Europe, where she starred in *Vive Paris!* at the Casino de Paris and in one of the earliest British color films, *Radio Parade of 1935*. Hunter toured extensively in the late 1930s, visiting Denmark, Greece, Egypt, Turkey, England, and the Netherlands. She returned to Broadway in *Mamba's Daughters* (with friend and sometimes rival ETHEL WATERS in the leading role) in 1939–40. Between 1944 and 1953, she toured China, Burma, Korea, India, Egypt, Africa, and Europe with the USO.

Alberta Hunter's mother died in 1954; soon after, Hunter left the music business and enrolled in a practical nursing course at the YWCA Nursing School in Harlem. After graduating in 1956, she worked at Goldwater Memorial Hospital until she was forced to retire in 1977. At the age of eighty-two she made a stunning musical comeback. In addition to performing regularly at the Cookery and on many television programs, she wrote and performed the music for the 1978 film *Remember My Name* and sang for President Jimmy Carter at the White House on February 27, 1979. She died at home in New York City on October 17, 1984, at the age of eighty-nine, and was buried in Ferncliff Cemetery, Hartsdale, New York.

Emerging from a difficult and disadvantaged childhood and realizing her dreams through sheer will and persistence, Alberta Hunter is a model of triumph in the face of adversity. As a young performer, her strength was not in the power of her voice (which was rather thin and warbly) but in her performance style and self-presentation, and in her ability to gauge and engage an audience. In later years, she was an inspiration to musicians and non-musicians alike for the joy and vitality she effused on stage. Like a fine wine, her voice was stronger, gutsier, and more richly textured in her eighties than earlier. Through the performance film *Alberta Hunter: Jazz at the Smithsonian* (1982), one of the only surviving glimpses into the power of the vaudeville blues woman's performances, Alberta Hunter left a legacy for future generations. Of her influence and inspiration, contemporary blues woman Gaye Adegbalola says, "She's just everything to me. I love her persona, her joy, her mischief, her piss and vinegar, and she doesn't take herself too seriously. I want to be Alberta Hunter when I grow up!"

Bibliography: The Alberta Hunter papers, consisting of personal and professional material documenting her singing and nursing careers, are found at the Schomburg Center for Research in Black Culture at the New York Public Library. An interview with Alberta Hunter, "Let It Be Classy," appears in Whitney Balliett, ed., *American Singers* (1979). Secondary sources include Sheldon Harris, *Blues Who's Who: A Biographical Dictionary of Blues Singers* (1979); Frank C. Taylor with Gerald Cook, *Alberta Hunter: A Celebration in Blues* (1987); Daphne Duval Harrison, *Black Pearls: Blues Queens of the 1920s* (1988); and Robert Santelli, *The Big Book of the Blues: A Biographical Encyclopedia* (1993). The quotation is taken from a telephone interview with Gaye Adegbalola by the author on October 23, 2003. Obituaries appeared in the *New York Times* and the *Washington Post* on October 19, 1984.

MARIA V. JOHNSON

HUNTER, Clementine. c. December 1886–January 1, 1988. Artist.

Clementine Hunter, the first of seven children and a descendant of slaves, was born in late December 1886 or early January 1887 near Cloutierville, Louisiana, on Hidden Hill Plantation (now called Little Eva Plantation because, allegedly, it was the inspiration for HARRIET BEECHER STOWE's *Uncle Tom's Cabin*). Her parents, both Creoles, were Mary Antoinette Adams and Janvier Reuben, a field hand. Hunter was baptized at age three months and christened "Clementiam" in March 1887. She was initially called Clemence, but later changed her name to Clementine (pronounced "Clementeen").

While she was still young, her family moved to Melrose Plantation. Melrose, originally called Yucca and located along the Cane River in Natchitoches Parish, boasts a rich cultural history. It flourished under Marie Thérèse Coincoin, a former slave, who established it in 1796, but fell into disrepair after the Civil War. During the twentieth century, white owners Cammie and John Hampton Henry restored it (now called Melrose), and turned it into a veritable artists' and writers' colony, populated by people like William Faulkner and Lyle Saxon. Many came for the impressive library, including writer François Mignon, who stayed on until 1970 as plantation curator. His friendship with Hunter had an extraordinary impact on her art.

Charles Duprée, whom Hunter never married, fathered her first two children, Joseph ("Frenchie") and Cora, before his death in 1914. In January 1924, she wed Emmanuel Hunter, a woodchopper at Melrose. They had five more children: Agnes, King, Mary, and two who were stillborn. Clementine worked in the fields when her children were young, but went into domestic service in the main house in the late 1920s. When Emmanuel became bedridden in the early 1940s and then died in 1944, she was forced to support the family. At this time, she also began her painting career.

Hunter always had a creative flair, evidenced by her imaginative menus, dolls, woven baskets, and appliquéd quilts, and the artistic environment of Melrose fueled her interest in painting. When she showed Mignon the discarded paint tubes she'd found in artist Alberta Kinsey's room, he gave her an old window shade and told her to paint a picture on it. From that point on, she painted on anything she or Mignon could find, including buckets, plywood, cardboard, and plastic bottles. Her paintings were primarily scenes of plantation life, such as cotton picking, pecan harvesting, flowers, and religious events; although scenes are repeated, no two images are exactly alike. Hunter painted at night, brush in one hand, canvas in the other, never using an easel. She found painting more difficult than cotton picking because "to paint you got to sweat yo' mind," yet believed she'd go crazy if she didn't. Her paintings sold for nominal fees. She also charged visitors twenty-five (later fifty) cents to see them, but felt guilty doing so because she didn't consider herself an artist: she believed her paintings were a gift from God.

Both Mignon and another Melrose visitor, James Register, encouraged Hunter's painting; they supplied her with materials, marketed her work, organized exhibitions, and helped her win a Rosenwald Foundation grant in 1945. Her first major exhibition was at the New Orleans Arts and Crafts Show in 1949. Reviews in national publications, and her 1955 solo exhibitions at the Delgado Museum of Art (now the New Orleans Museum of Art) and Northwestern State College gallery, made her one of the best-known self-taught African American woman artists. Around 1955, Mignon suggested that Hunter decorate "African House," an early-nineteenth-century West African style building at Melrose, with large murals of Cane River life.

Scholars claim it was Register who added the "Clemence" signature to Hunter's late 1940s work, since she was illiterate. She neither dated nor titled her paintings, but learned to initial them, first using "CH" around 1950, then turning the *C* backward in the late 1950s, and finally superimposing the *H* over the backward *C* by the mid 1970s. Register also encouraged her to experiment beyond her traditional subject matter. For example, during 1962–63 he gave her colorful abstract collages that she reinterpreted in paint. These "abstracts" are unique among Hunter's oeuvre.

Hunter's art has been popular for its beauty and ability to portray a seemingly uncomplicated lifestyle that has all but disappeared. She has been labeled a folk, self-taught, memory, and primitive artist because of her colorful, simple forms, but also because she never had any formal art instruction. Such labels are adequate, but the art is also important as a historical document of southern rural life. Hunter's images are delightful, but they also reveal the backbreaking labor of cotton picking, the violence of the local juke joints, and women's important social and economic roles. Scholars have found West African influences in her art too, but Hunter dismissed such interpretations. Instead, she emphasized that her pictures were memories of familiar activities: "I paint the history of my people. . . . My paintings tell how we worked, played, and prayed." She was often encouraged by friends to try different styles, but preferred to paint what came into her head.

Melrose was sold in 1970 and became a national historic landmark in 1974. Hunter continued to live there until 1978, when she bought a trailer about fifteen miles upriver. Her work continued to win acclaim and was featured in the New Orleans Museum of Art's *Centennial Salute to Clementine Hunter* (1985) and the traveling exhibitions *Two Centuries of Black American Art* and *Forever Free: An Exhibit of Art by African American Women, 1862–1980.*

Hunter painted until her death on January 1, 1988, in Natchitoches Parish, Louisiana, leaving behind several thousand pictures. In her 101 years, she experienced the plantation system's demise and the public's acceptance of her as an artist. She not only became Melrose's most famous resident, but, importantly, she also rose above expectations of what an illiterate black woman was capable of. She is buried in the mausoleum at St. Augustine's Church, near Melrose, next to her close friend, François Mignon, who died in 1980.

Bibliography: All quotations are taken from Shelby R. Gilley, *Painting by Heart: The Life and Art of Clementine Hunter, Louisiana Folk Artist* (2000). Gilley, along with James L. Wilson, *Clementine Hunter: American Folk Artist* (1988), are the best sources for biographical information, bibliographies, and critical remarks on Hunter's art. Another very useful source is Mary E. Lyons, ed., *Talking with Tebe: Clementine Hunter, Memory Artist* (1998). Hunter was interviewed for the Black Women Oral History Project, Schlesinger Library, Radcliffe Institute for Advanced Study, Harvard University, on November 29, 1979. Interviews, photographs, and other primary source material about the artist can be found in the Archives and Special Collections, Cammie G. Henry Research Center, Watson Memorial Library, Northwestern State University of Louisiana, Natchitoches; the Collection of Mildred Hart Bailey, Natchitoches; and the François Mignon Papers, Southern Historical Collection, Wilson Library, University of North Carolina, Chapel Hill. Hunter's popular, innovative recipes are recorded in the cookbook she and François Mignon authored, *Melrose Plantation Cookbook* (1956); this also contains excellent photographs of Hunter and the Melrose murals. See also Mignon's *Plantation Memo: Plantation Life in Louisiana, 1950–70, and Other Matters,* ed. with an introduction by Ora Garland Williams (1972); and Anne Hudson Jones, "The Centennial of Clementine Hunter," *Woman's Art Journal,* Spring/Summer 1987, pp. 23–27. Two substantial museum catalogs, David C. Driskell, *Two Centuries of Black American Art* (1976) and Arna Alexander Bontemps, ed., *Forever Free: Art by African-American Women, 1862–1980* (1980), include discussions of Hunter. For reviews and commentary, see Charlotte Willard, "Innocence Regained," *Look,* June 16, 1953, pp. 102–5; and Allen Rankin, "The Hidden Genius of Melrose Plantation," *Reader's Digest,* December 1975, pp. 118–22. Official records (baptismal, burial, names that Hunter went by) can be found in the Archives of St. John the Baptist Church, Cloutierville, Louisiana; the Archives of the Chapel of St. Augustine, Isle Breville, Natchitoches, Louisiana; and the Censuses of Natchitoches Parish, 1900 and 1910. An obituary appeared in the *Los Angeles Times* on January 5, 1988.

JESSICA DALLOW

HURLEY, Ruby. November 7, 1909–August 9, 1980. Civil rights activist, NAACP administrator.

Ruby Hurley was born Ruby Ruffin in Washington, D.C., the only child of Alice and Edward R. Ruffin. Her parents' fate and her early childhood remain a mystery. According to United States

Census records, in 1920 Ruby lived in the District of Columbia as a "roomer" with Emma and Percy Ray, both of whom were teachers. She attended public schools and graduated from Dunbar High School in 1926. In the following years she graduated from Miner Teachers College and attended Terrell Law School at night. Instead of becoming a lawyer, Ruby worked at the Industrial Bank of Washington, a black-owned institution, and for the federal government. She married Lieutenant William L. Hurley of the U.S. Army Corps of Engineers, and they had no children.

In 1939, Ruby Hurley began her life's work against racial injustice. After the renowned singer MARIAN ANDERSON was barred from performing at Constitution Hall, Hurley served on a committee that succeeded in getting the concert moved to the Lincoln Memorial. For the next four years she worked with a group to reorganize the D.C. branch of the National Association for the Advancement of Colored People (NAACP) and invigorate its youth council. Her efforts gained attention from the national office of the NAACP, which in 1943 hired Hurley as its youth secretary and brought her to New York City. Under her direction until 1952, youth councils and college chapters swelled from 86 to more than 280, with a total membership of 25,000. Hurley's role in expanding the youth councils would pay rich dividends, for the NAACP youth councils in 1960 helped spark the sit-in movement throughout the South.

Hurley's assignments placed her on the front lines of the major battles waged by the civil rights movement. In 1951, the NAACP sent her on a special mission to Birmingham, Alabama, to oversee membership drives in five southern states: Alabama, Florida, Georgia, Mississippi, and Tennessee (North and South Carolina were later added). The next year, this temporary assignment became permanent when the NAACP named Hurley its southeast regional director. By the late 1960s she supervised more than four hundred chapters. Although women were the backbone of the civil rights movement and operated as leaders in local communities, few held top leadership positions in established national organizations with their bureaucratic structures and male camaraderie. Unlike her contemporary ELLA BAKER, who left the NAACP because of its tightly structured system, Hurley flourished as an administrator.

She became regional director just as the pace of racial change quickened. Following *Brown v. Board of Education* (1954), which declared racial segregation of public schools unconstitutional, Hurley planned strategy with her field staff to implement the ruling. In most cases this proved fruitless, as southern politicians embarked on a campaign of massive resistance to keep black children from integrating the schools, and white supremacist groups employed intimidation and violence against African Americans to reinforce their message. In this hostile climate, Hurley took on a number of dangerous tasks. Living in Birmingham, where the bombing of black homes and churches was commonplace under the administration of Police Commissioner Eugene "Bull" Connor, Hurley received obscene telephone calls and witnessed attacks on her house. A private and restrained person, she suffered from weight loss and fatigue. In 1956, Alabama barred the NAACP from operating in the state, and Hurley was transferred to Atlanta, where she stayed even after the Supreme Court overruled Alabama's stance against the civil rights organization.

Before leaving Birmingham, Hurley investigated several murders in Mississippi, including that of Emmett Till, a fourteen-year-old youth from Chicago visiting his uncle during the summer of 1955. Accused of getting too familiar with a white female store clerk, Till was brutally murdered and his mutilated body was dumped in the Tallahatchie River. Hurley, a tall woman with a slightly freckled face and tan complexion, helped in the investigation by going undercover in rural Mississippi. She donned the clothes of a cotton picker and traveled dusty back roads interviewing witnesses. Hurley's devotion to Christian nonviolence did not falter even when black men armed with shotguns had to watch over her to ensure her safety. Despite her efforts, Till's killers were acquitted by an all-white jury. While mobilizing public opinion around the Till case, she also helped lay the groundwork for the admission of Autherine Lucy as the first black undergraduate at the University of Alabama. In 1956, when Lucy's matriculation led to a campus riot and her immediate expulsion, Hurley received the protection of black taxi drivers who circled her house to keep terrorists away.

As director of the region that witnessed the fiercest battles of the civil rights era, Hurley represented the NAACP's interests in struggles in such hot spots as Greensboro, North Carolina, and Albany, Georgia. A believer in litigation, legislation, and quiet negotiations, she occasionally had to rein in some of her field staff who supported the more militant protest activities of groups like the Student Nonviolent Coordinating Committee (SNCC). This was true with respect to Medgar Evers, the NAACP field agent in Mississippi, but when Evers was assassinated in 1963, Hurley convinced his widow, Myrlie, to have her husband, a World War II veteran, buried in Arlington National Cemetery.

After thirty-five years of employment with the NAACP, Hurley retired on March 31, 1978. An active Methodist throughout her life, she served for several years as president of the United Methodist Women. She also belonged to the interracial Southern Regional Council and performed volunteer work for the YWCA. In 1977, Mayor Maynard Jackson of Atlanta selected her to sit on the city's license review board. She died in Atlanta on August 9, 1980, at the age of seventy. For more than three decades, never seeking the limelight, Hurley toiled tirelessly for racial equality and never abandoned her faith in the NAACP or her commitment to the struggle, a dedication that few could match for so long a time. Her career demonstrates the courage it took for a woman functioning in a man's world of politics and activism to overcome both paternalism and resistance in order to gain freedom.

Bibliography: Ruby Hurley still awaits a biographer. Little is known about her private life, but some information can be found in Robert W. Saunders Sr., *Bridging the Gap: Continuing the Florida NAACP Legacy of Harry T. Moore* (2000). See also Christina Greene, "Ruby Hurley," in Waldo E. Martin Jr. and Patricia Sullivan, eds., *Civil Rights in the United States*, vol. 1 (2000), and William D. Pierson, "Ruby Hurley," in Jessie Carney Smith, ed., *Notable Black American Women* (1992). Both Greene and Pierson, however, have the incorrect year of her birth, the former giving 1910 and the latter 1913. News of her career and retirement can be found in "Mrs. Ruby Hurley Honored," *The Crisis*, February 1969, pp. 88–89; and "Ruby Hurley Retires from NAACP after 35 Years of Service," *Jet*, May 4, 1978, pp. 8–9. Ernest Dunbar, "Inside the NAACP: Ruby Hurley's South," *Look*, August 6, 1957, pp. 58–64, provides an account of Hurley's experiences in the immediate post-*Brown* years. Hurley gave two interviews detailing her career. One appears in Howell Raines, *My Soul Is Rested: Movement Days in the Deep South Remembered* (1977). The other is a more extensive unpublished oral history in the Civil Rights Documentation Project, Moorland-Spingarn Research Center, Howard University, Washington, D.C. Hurley's career with the NAACP is well documented in the organization's papers collected in the Manuscript Division of the Library of Congress. Her work is also noted in Denton Watson, *Lion in the Lobby: Clarence Mitchell, Jr.'s Struggle for the Passage of Civil Rights Laws* (1990), and John Dittmer, *Local People: The Struggle for Civil Rights in Mississippi* (1994). For insights about women, including Hurley, and the civil rights movement, see Belinda Robnett, *How Long? How Long?: African-American Women in the Struggle for Civil Rights* (1997). Hurley's obituary appeared in the *New York Times* on August 15, 1980.

STEVEN F. LAWSON

I

ISHIGO, Estelle. July 15, 1899–February 25, 1990. Artist, writer.

Estelle Peck was born in Oakland, California, the only child of much older parents. All that is known is that hers was a privileged family with an artistic bent. Her father, a Civil War veteran, was a landscape painter, and her mother, who was of French ancestry, was an opera singer. When Estelle was twelve, she moved with her parents to Los Angeles, but she was soon sent to live with a procession of relatives and strangers. One of these guardians raped her and threatened to institutionalize her if she reported the attack. She spent much of her unhappy adolescence on her own, looking for adventure.

After graduating from Manual Art High School in Los Angeles, Estelle was unsure what to do but eventually took a teacher's advice and entered the Otis Art Institute. While she was studying there, she met Arthur Shigeharu Ishigo, a young Nisei (second-generation Japanese American) and aspiring actor who was working as a chauffeur. Because of widespread hostility toward interracial marriage in the United States and because of California's anti-miscegenation laws, Arthur and Estelle married in Tijuana, Mexico, in 1928. Estelle's family disowned her. During the years following their wedding, the Ishigos rented a little house in Hollywood, where Arthur worked for Paramount Studios. They did not have children.

Arthur lost his job following the bombing of Pearl Harbor, when widespread anti-Japanese hysteria peaked on the West Coast. Estelle got a job as a teacher at the Hollywood Art Center only to be told to leave after two weeks because the students and their parents would not accept a teacher with a Japanese name. Arthur, one of the more than 110,000 Japanese Americans interned during World War II, received the order to evacuate to the Pomona Assembly Center in April 1942. Estelle could have remained behind. She felt, however, that this would have been "desertion of my husband in time of distress" (UCLA papers). The Ishigos spent three months at the Pomona Assembly Center, a converted race track, where

Estelle worked on the *Pomona Center News* as an art editor. In August 1942, the Ishigos boarded a train to the Heart Mountain Relocation Camp in Wyoming.

While at Heart Mountain, Estelle composed sketches of camp life, depicting the emotional and physical hardships endured by Japanese Americans during the internment. Many of these sketches were later published in her book, *Lone Heart Mountain* (1972). She also worked with Allen Eaton during her last months at the camp, collecting and recording the various art created at Heart Mountain. When Eaton published *Beauty behind Barbed Wire: The Arts of the Japanese in Our War Relocation Camps* (1952), he included several of Ishigo's watercolors.

The Ishigos boarded the last train from Heart Mountain back to Los Angeles. All of the personal possessions they had left behind in Los Angeles were either lost or stolen, and they were forced to move with the rest of the homeless evacuees to a trailer camp in Burbank. After working for several years at low-paying odd jobs, Arthur finally found full-time employment in 1948. The Ishigos' situation improved, but they were still unable to find a desirable place to live, owing to racial discrimination. In 1948, Estelle traveled to New York to visit friends and tried unsuccessfully to find a publisher for her sketches and writing about Heart Mountain. Despite this failure, she continued to display her sketches and watercolors in small community arts gatherings, including community churches and local art festivals. In 1957 Arthur was diagnosed with throat cancer and died, leaving Estelle alone and almost penniless.

During the years following Arthur's death, Estelle continued to show some of her work. Her Heart Mountain sketches and watercolors were displayed at the "Months of Waiting" exhibit at the California Historical Society in 1972, the year her book was published. She supported herself by teaching art classes and by working for a mimeographic company. In the early 1980s, Ishigo was discovered living alone, destitute, with both legs lost to gangrene. Shortly thereafter, she had a stroke. She spent the remainder of her life in a convalescent hospital in Hollywood, where she died at the age of ninety. Estelle Ishigo's perceptions and political insights live on in the numerous watercolors, sketches, and photographs she composed during and after her three-and-a-half year internment. Her sketches and writing in *Lone Heart Mountain* provide an invaluable historical record of the internment as well as a protest against the prejudice and ignorance that irrevocably damaged and destroyed so many lives.

Bibliography: The Estelle Ishigo papers, a collection of personal papers and artwork donated by Ishigo and collected by the Japanese American Research project, are located in the Department of Special Collections, University of California, Los Angeles. The Japanese American National Museum in Los Angeles also contains a collection of Ishigo's documents, and a variety of photographs taken by her. A taped interview with Ishigo conducted by Bacon Sakatani in 1986 is in his possession. The only biography of Ishigo is Vanessa Hall, "'Perhaps Women Like Me of Another Generation Are a Bridge': A Contextual Study of the Life, Activism, and Art of Estelle Ishigo" (MA thesis, Utah State University, 2000). Ishigo provides additional recollections of what it was like to be married to a Japanese American before and after the war in "*Lone Heart Mountain:* Estelle's Epilogue," *Pacific Citizen,* February 16, 1973. See also the documentary film by Steven Okasaki, *Days of Waiting* (1990), which traces her life as of one of the few Caucasians to be interned along with Japanese Americans during the war.

VANESSA HALL

ITO, Miyoko. April 1918–August 18, 1983. Artist.

When New York City became the center of the art world in the late 1940s and abstract expressionist painters such as Jackson Pollock and Willem de Kooning were heralded for their machismo and individual expression, Chicago-based painter Miyoko Ito was a maverick of a different kind, creating an evolving aesthetic and the distinct palette of a painter who believed in her visual vocabulary of line, color, and shapes.

Ito was born in Berkeley, California. Until adolescence she had a life of constant uprooting and separation. Many details about her family and early life are conflicting or missing. Her father emigrated from Japan as a youth, and married her mother, a schoolteacher, who arrived in the United States around 1914. Despite a degree in psychology from the University of California at Berkeley, her father found it difficult to support his family because of the racism and legal discrimination endemic to California at the time. In 1923 the family (which now included a second daughter) returned to Japan, just before the great Kanto earthquake. Soon afterward her mother gave birth to a stillborn son. These traumatic events incapacitated Ito; she became extremely ill and could not walk.

Young Ito stayed in Japan for five years, mostly in convalescence, intermittently separated from her parents (she mentions being raised by her maternal grandmother). These years were also fruitful, in that her talent for calligraphy laid the foundation for her interest in art. She returned to Berkeley in 1928, eventually enrolling in the local high school. She favored further training at an art school, but her parents wanted her to attend the University of California at Berkeley, where she enrolled in 1938, studying art during the emergence of the "Bay Region" or "Berkeley" school of watercolor. Some of Ito's early influences were Worth

Ryder's art history courses, John Haley's teachings of Hans Hofmann's concepts of color and form, a Pablo Picasso retrospective at San Francisco's Museum of Modern Art in 1939, and her participation in an informal group of painters calling themselves the Corps of Serious Painters. A sepia-toned photograph of Ito taken in 1940 features a young woman with her head tilted, curled long hair and short bangs, thumbs hooked in her front pockets; her stance is confident, musing, and alert. Her paintings likewise strike a balance between introspection and inquisitiveness, homing in on life's sentient exhilarations.

Ito's early paintings, done in watercolor of gouache on paper, were of still lifes of items on a table in front of a window. Using staccato-like brush strokes and small planes of discreet variations of blue through what she called a wet/dry method, the cool and intimate setting of these paintings was reminiscent of the precepts of Hofmann and the later work of fauvist painter Raoul Dufy. Similar to Dufy, she used the window as a framing device to engage the interior and exterior. In her later years, she would return to the interior in such works as *Paintress as a Chair* (1973) and *Chiffonier* (1971).

With the outbreak of World War II during her senior year at Berkeley, Ito and her family were forced into internment camps under Executive Order 9066. Fearful of being separated from her boyfriend (her parents were traditionally conservative first-generation Japanese), she persuaded them to allow her to marry Harry Ichiyasu on April 11, 1942, before entering what she remembered as Camp Rann (most likely Tanforan Assembly Center). Kind-hearted peers and professors such as Erle Loran visited her at the camp; they made sure that she received her Berkeley diploma in 1942 and most likely were influential in helping her receive a scholarship through the Quaker Friends Society to attend graduate school at Smith College in September 1942. Being the only graduate student in the Smith art department, with practically no faculty to work with, she left in 1944 to study at the Art Institute of Chicago. She remained in Chicago for the rest of her life.

Ito was reunited with her husband in 1945, and in 1950 she gave birth to a son, Alan Tomio, followed in 1953 by a daughter, Elissa Harumi. The 1950s were not only the decade of her childrearing, but also the decade in which her style and aesthetic fully burgeoned. The way she arranged entire compositions with overlapping orthogonals and interpenetrating colored planes evoked the synthetic cubist works of Picasso and Braque. Geometric forms transform into organic elliptical shapes and undulating soft curves in paintings such as *Construction* (1955), where a body with elongated arms sits in a cool landscape of teal-colored square mounds. Other planes of ground tones are made palpable through her use of a kind of underpainting with primary colors—green or red—over an underdrawing in charcoal that critic Dennis Adrian describes as being similar to the practice of sixteenth- and seventeenth-century Venetian and Spanish painting.

Perhaps influenced by the Chicago Imagists, Ito's paintings from the 1960s make a gesture toward the surreal. In contrast to her spare handling of paint in the past, the brush strokes and some impasto are visible, underscoring the importance of coruscating gradations of light to Ito's art practice. In the 1970s, Ito synthesized her different palettes of subtle and vibrant colors, combining abstract and representative elements into her composition, giving her paintings more depth and allusion. In 1975 she was selected to participate in the Whitney Biennial, and in 1980 she was given a comprehensive retrospective by the Renaissance Society in Chicago. She died of a heart attack in Chicago in 1983 at the age of sixty-five.

Bibliography: An excellent introduction to Miyoko Ito is Dennis Adrian's essay accompanying the catalogue of her 1980 retrospective at the Renaissance Society in Chicago, *Miyoko Ito: A Review* (1980). Also of interest is an oral history interview conduced by Dennis Barrie at the Oxbow Summer School of Painting, Saugatuck, Michigan, on July 20, 1978; this interview is part of the Smithsonian Archives of American Art. See also Lyn Blumenthal and Kate Horsfield, "Interview with Miyoko Ito," *On Art and Artists Series* (Chicago: Video Data Bank/Art Institute of Chicago, 1978), pp. 2–32. Reviews of her work include Alan Artner, "Ito Comes Up with a Five-Star Exhibition," *Chicago Daily News*, July 8–9, 1972; Regan Upshaw, "Miyoko Ito at the Renaissance Society, Chicago," *Art in America* 69 (January 1981), p. 133; David McCracken, "Ito Exhibit Shows Late Artist's Sensitivity and Sure Touch," *Chicago Tribune*, December 23, 1988; and Devonna Pieszak, "The Wordless Poetry of Color," *Christian Science Monitor*, May 4, 1989.

SUSETTE MIN

J

JACKSON, Edith Banfield. January 2, 1895–June 5, 1977. Pediatrician, psychoanalyst.

Edith Banfield Jackson was born in Colorado Springs to William Sharpless Jackson and his second wife, Helen Fiske Banfield. Her father had left Pennsylvania to settle in the new town of Colorado Springs in 1871, and over the next quarter-century he became both a civic leader and—by virtue of entrepreneurship in the railroading, banking, and silver-mining industries—a millionaire. He had no children with his first wife, the poet, novelist, and Indian reformer HELEN FISKE HUNT JACKSON, who died in 1885. In 1888, he married Helen Jackson's niece and namesake, Helen Fiske Banfield, a Vassar-educated teacher who was twenty-three years his junior. The Jacksons had seven children—Edith was the fifth—in the first ten years of their marriage. On October 18, 1899, just shy of Edith's fifth birthday, Helen Jackson, a gentle, loving woman still grief-stricken from her youngest child's death the previous December, apparently experienced a sudden psychotic episode and killed herself with a bullet to her chest.

Edith Jackson was a pretty, ebullient, precocious child before her mother's death, and she functioned cheerfully and effectively for a quarter-century after that tragedy. At Cutler Academy in Colorado Springs, from which she graduated in 1912, classmates knew her as jolly and studious. After a year at Colorado College, she transferred to Vassar College, where she excelled, graduating cum laude with Phi Beta Kappa honors in 1916. She next won admission to the nation's premier medical school, Johns Hopkins, where only 10 percent of an entering class could be women, receiving her MD in 1921. Then, at a time when internships at university hospitals were notably difficult for women to obtain, Jackson was the only woman among eighteen doctors invited to intern at Iowa University Hospital in 1921–22. The following year she garnered a pediatric internship at Bellevue Hospital in New York.

By the summer of 1923, Jackson, impeccably credentialed and involved in the most serious romantic relationship of her life, seemed poised to enjoy the pleasures of both professional and personal autonomy. But her doctor-beau married another woman, and Jackson struggled to find her professional niche. She tried medical research, working from 1923 to 1928 as a member of the U.S. Children's Bureau rickets study in the Yale Pediatrics Department. She registered for a PhD at Yale in 1926 but never completed the first semester's courses. In 1927 she intended to remodel her house and open a private pediatrics practice, but less than six months later she left New Haven and entered psychoanalysis in Washington, D.C., with a medical school classmate, Lucile Dooley. Soon thereafter she began a residency in psychiatry at St. Elizabeth's Hospital there.

Suffering from enervating depressions in the fall of 1929, Jackson learned from an old friend that Sigmund Freud would soon have a free hour. Jackson went to Vienna in mid December 1929, hoping that analysis and training with Freud himself would enable her to find the professional and personal satisfaction that, at age thirty-five, still eluded her. When Jackson lay on Freud's couch for the first time in January 1930, she anticipated a typical training analysis of six months, but she remained in analysis with Freud for six years. During that period she at last adequately mourned her mother and safely lived past the emotionally fraught age (forty) of her mother's suicide. Equally significant, by 1936 Jackson had become passionately committed to the tenets and therapeutic promise of psychoanalysis by attending seminars at the Vienna Psychoanalytic Institute—most influentially, Anna Freud's on child analysis. She attained membership in the International Psychoanalytic Association and, with it, the authority to psychoanalyze adults and children anywhere in the world.

Professionally adrift and depressed when she began her analysis with Freud, Jackson subsequently enjoyed both a rich, contented personal life as a single woman and, using her psychoanalytic insights and skills, a gratifying, nationally renowned career. Affiliated with the Yale School of Medicine from 1936 to 1959, she began as a clinical instructor in psychiatry and eventually held clinical professorships in both psychiatry and pediatrics. Known affectionately as Edie by doctors, nurses, and residents alike, Jackson published nearly two dozen scholarly articles and mentored a generation of pediatricians and psychiatrists who treasured their professional and personal associations with her.

Jackson is best known for directing the internationally renowned Yale Rooming-In Research Project at Grace–New Haven Hospital from 1946 to 1953. The Rooming-In Project, which implemented and studied the then-radical practice of having mothers and babies room together in the hospital from the moment of birth, placed Jackson in the small vanguard of hospital-based academic pediatricians, child psychiatrists, and obstetricians in the United States (a group that included Benjamin Spock, Erik Erikson, and Grantly Dick-Read) who in the mid twentieth century deplored the impersonality, authoritarianism, and rigidity of "modern," "scientific" medicine and met regularly to discuss how both to "humanize" the delivery of medical care to parturients, infants, and children and to empower parents in caring for their children.

Jackson retired from Yale in 1959, but her pioneering, humanistic work continued in Denver, where she spent her last years. She designed a rooming-in unit for the Colorado General Hospital, and studied and counseled unwed mothers who had made the decision, radical in the 1960s, to keep their "illegitimate" babies instead of putting them up for adoption. She helped launch what became the Denver-based National Center for the Prevention and Treatment of Child Abuse. And in her own living room, Jackson hosted planning meetings for the Colorado Association for the Study of Abortion, whose work spearheaded the legislature's passage in 1967 of the first liberalized abortion law in the United States.

Jackson received two prestigious awards for her pioneering work. In 1964 she was the first recipient of the Agnes McGavin Award from the American Psychiatric Association for her contributions to preventive psychiatry. In 1968 she won the C. Anderson Aldrich Award in child development, an honor the American Academy of Pediatrics subsequently bestowed on Benjamin Spock (1970), Erik Erikson (1971), Anna Freud (1974), and T. Berry Brazelton (1983). Edith Banfield Jackson died at home in her sleep on June 5, 1977, apparently of natural causes associated with her eighty-two years; she is buried in the Jackson family plot at Evergreen Cemetery in Colorado Springs.

Bibliography: The largest collection of Edith B. Jackson's papers is in the Schlesinger Library, Radcliffe Institute for Advanced Study, Harvard University. There are also Jackson papers at the Yale University Library and at the Denver Public Library. Between 1933 and 1956 Jackson authored or co-authored thirty articles, among them "Treatment of the Young Child in the Hospital," *American Journal of Orthopsychiatry* 12 (1942), pp. 56–63; "General Reactions of Mothers and Nurses to Rooming-in," *American Journal of Public Health* 38, no. 5 (May 1948), pp. 689–95; "Pediatric and Psychiatric Aspects of the Yale Rooming-In Project," *Connecticut State Medical Journal* 14, no. 7 (1950), pp. 616–21; and, with Ethelyn H. Klatskin, "Methodology of the Yale Rooming-In Project on Parent-Child Relationship," *American Journal of Orthopsychiatry* 25, nos. 1–2 (1955), pp. 81–108, 373–97. Articles about Jackson's life and career by Sara Lee Silberman include "Pioneering in Family-Centered Maternity and Infant Care: Edith B. Jackson and the Yale Rooming-In Research Project," *Bulletin of the History of Medicine* 64, no. 2 (1990), pp. 262–87; "The Curious Pattern of a Distinguished Medical Career: A Psychoanalytic Portrait of Edith B. Jackson," *Biography* 17, no. 3 (Summer 1994), pp. 221–47; and "Edith B. Jackson, M.D.," *Psychoanalytic Review* 85, no. 1 (February 1998), pp. 95–103. See also Morris A. Wessel and Frederic M. Blodgett, "Edith B. Jackson, M.D. and Yale Pediatrics," *Connecticut Medicine* 26, no. 7 (July 1962), pp. 438–41; and Morris A. Wessel, "Edith B. Jackson, M.D.," *Journal of Pediatrics* 93, no. 1 (July 1978), pp. 165–66. An obituary appeared in the *New York Times* on June 10, 1977.

SARA LEE SILBERMAN

JONES, Lois Mailou. November 3, 1905–June 9, 1998. Artist, educator.

Born in Boston, Massachusetts, Lois Mailou Jones was the younger of two children of Carolyn Dorinda Adams and Thomas Vreeland Jones. Thomas Jones worked as superintendent of a large office building and attended night classes at Suffolk Law School, where he received his law degree in 1915 at the age of forty. His wife was a beautician and homemaker for Lois and her older brother, John Wesley. Both parents encouraged Lois's artistic interests and supported her desire to pursue a career in the arts.

Demonstrating early skill and talent, Jones attended Boston's High School of Practical Arts on scholarship, receiving a diploma in 1923. Determined to excel in the profession, she entered the School of the Museum of Fine Arts in Boston in 1923, where she studied design concepts, life drawing, and portraiture under such artists as Anson Cross, Phillip Hale, Alice Morse, and Henry Hunt Clark. For four years she won the coveted Susan Minot Lane Scholarship in Design, graduating with honors in 1927. During her last year at the museum school, Jones enrolled in evening classes at Boston Normal Art School (now Massachusetts College of Art), receiving a teaching certificate in 1927. That same year, Jones won a scholarship to Designers Art School of Boston, where she did graduate work with Ludwig Frank, an internationally known designer of textiles. She continued graduate study during the summer of 1928 at Harvard University.

With no teaching position available at the museum school for an African American, Jones heeded the suggestions of Henry Hunt Clark and educator CHARLOTTE HAWKINS BROWN, who emphasized the need for young African American men and women to take their talents to the South. Awakened by this challenge, Jones accepted Brown's offer to develop the art department at Palmer Memorial Institute, one of the nation's first preparatory schools for African Americans, in Sedalia, North Carolina. Jones chaired the department and provided instruction to students from 1928 to 1930.

In the fall of 1930, Jones joined the faculty of Howard University at the insistence of James V. Herring, founder and chairman of the Department of Art. There she joined James A. Porter, noted historian, scholar, and painter; and James L. Wells, innovator in the field of printmaking. Together they forged a curriculum unique to historically black colleges and universities. As a professor of design and watercolor painting, Lois Jones taught more than twenty-five hundred students, many of whom would directly or indirectly affect the development of American art through their careers as teachers in the arts, or as professionals in the public or private sector. Jones remained at Howard University until her retirement in 1977.

Desiring to find her niche in the art world, in 1937 Jones took a sabbatical to attend the Academie Julian in Paris. Study in France was a tradition for American artists, and her sojourn there marked a shift in her career from that of designer, illustrator, and teacher to that of painter of great power and directness. She set aside watercolors and began using oil paints exclusively. Her landscapes, still lifes, portraits, and creative compositions revealed that she had absorbed the prevailing aesthetic language of impressionism. Her instructors urged her to submit paintings to the annual Salon de Printemps of the Société des Artistes Français, one of the most important exhibits of the year. Her works were accepted and critiqued favorably in the French periodical *Les Beaux-Arts.*

Back in the United States, her work received high praise, and her reputation grew as she continued to exhibit throughout the country. Shortly after her return to Washington, D.C., she met Alain Locke—Rhodes Scholar, poet laureate of the Harlem Renaissance, and chairman of the Philosophy Department at Howard University. One of the most influential voices on art in the African American community at the time, Locke informed Jones of his plans to include one of her Parisian street scenes in his forthcoming book, *The Negro in Art* (1940). Even more importantly, Locke admonished Jones to produce work that focused on the black subject and the African American community. Jones's response to his challenge came in paintings, such as *Jennie* (1943), *The Pink Table Cloth* (1944), and *Mob Victim* (1944), that presented themes and portraits of African Americans. In 1945 she received a BA in art education from Howard.

On August 8, 1953, Lois Mailou Jones married the noted Haitian artist and designer Louis Vergniaud Pierre-Noel in Cabris, France. Beginning the following year, her life and her art would be transformed. Accepting an invitation from the Haitian government to serve as a guest instructor at the Centre d' Art and the Foyer des Arts Plastiques, the couple resided in Port-au-Prince for several months while she completed her commission. From her first visit, Jones fell in love with the country and its people, and this vision affected her art. Jones's new work drew upon her knowledge of design techniques and her passion for color, while synthesizing diverse religious and ritualistic elements of Haitian life and culture. Jones and Pierre-Noel traveled annually to Port-au-Prince until his death in 1982.

In the 1960s, Jones's work moved toward more abstract, design-oriented compositions. During the height of the Black Arts movement, she received a grant from Howard University to conduct research on contemporary artists in Africa. From April to July 1969, Jones visited eleven African countries, compiling biographical material on artists, photographing their work, conducting interviews, and visiting museums. Throughout the 1970s and 1980s, Jones retained a continuing and passionate interest in Africa.

Lois Mailou Jones pursued two distinct careers: as a professor of art and as a creative artist. In the early days she explored the subdued tonalities of impressionism. Later she was passionate about the bold, brilliant colors and decorative patterns that dominate her canvases on Haiti and Africa. While teaching, communicating, and demonstrating a love of art to generations of students and the public at large, Lois Mailou Jones created a body of work characterized by technical virtuosity, consummate skills, versatility, elegance, design, and clarion color. She died in 1998 in her home in Washington, D.C., at the age of ninety-two after a long illness, and is buried on her beloved Martha's Vineyard.

Bibliography: The work of Lois Mailou Jones is represented in museums, galleries, and private collections, including New York's Metropolitan Museum of Art, the Boston Museum of Fine Arts, the Smithsonian's American Art Museum, and the National Portrait Gallery. Tritobia Hayes Benjamin provides an overview in *The Life and Art of Lois Mailou Jones* (1994), which draws in part on personal interviews with the artist in 1986. See also Nancy G. Heller, "Lois Mailou Jones, American Painter," *Museum and Arts Washington Magazine,* July/August 1988, pp. 42–45. James A. Porter provided prefatory comments to *Lois Mailou Jones: Peintures 1937–1951* (1952). General sources on African American and women's art include Cedric Dover, *American Negro Art* (1960); James A. Porter, *Modern Negro Art* (1969); David C. Driskell, *Two Centuries of Black American Art* (1976), and *Hidden Heritage: Afro-American Art, 1800–1950* (1985); Elsa Honig Fine, *The Afro-American Artist* (1973), and *Women and Art: History of Women Painters and Sculptors from the Renaissance to the 20th Century* (1978); Samella Lewis, *Art: African-American* (1978); Charlotte S. Rubinstein, *American Women Artists from Early Indian Times to the Present* (1982); and *Black Art Ancestral Legacy: The African Impulse in African-American Art* (1989). An obituary appeared in the *New York Times* on June 13, 1998.

TRITOBIA HAYES BENJAMIN

JONES, Mary Cover. September 1, 1896–July 22, 1987. Psychologist.

Mary Elizabeth Cover Jones, a pioneer in the field of behavior therapy and a celebrated developmental psychologist, was born in Johnstown, Pennsylvania, the second of three children of Carrie Louise Higson and Charles Blair Cover. Her mother was an accomplished homemaker, an avid amateur singer, and a member of several community organizations. Born and raised in Johnstown, her father became a prominent businessman and community leader. Despite his success, he regretted his lack of post-secondary education and actively encouraged his children to pursue university degrees.

Mary Cover's love of learning was fostered early by the family's regular summer trips to the Chautauqua Institute on Lake Erie, where she recalled hearing Theodore Roosevelt speak. After graduating from Johnstown High School in 1915, she attended Vassar College, where she took every psychology course offered—except one. Prominent experimental psychologist MARGARET FLOY WASHBURN refused to admit Mary to her senior seminar class because of a mediocre grade in an earlier laboratory course. Despite this, Mary recalled Washburn as an excellent teacher who inspired her interest in psychology.

During her college years, Mary was president of the Vassar Socialist Club and an active suffragist and pacifist. Although brought up in the Lutheran faith, she now abandoned any formal interest in religion. She graduated from Vassar in 1919. Attendance at a weekend lecture given by behaviorist John B. Watson in New York City cemented her desire to pursue graduate work in psychology. Following in the footsteps of her older brother, John, she enrolled at Columbia University in the fall of 1919. She completed her master's degree in psychology under R. S. Woodworth in the summer of 1920.

On September 1, 1920, Mary Cover married fellow psychology graduate student Harold Ellis Jones. Their first child, Barbara, was born in 1922. The following year Jones was appointed an associate in psychological research at the Institute of Educational Research at Columbia University's Teachers College. As part of this appointment, she conducted research at the Heckscher Foundation, a home for temporarily abandoned children. To facilitate this work, the family moved into Heckscher House. Here she undertook her now-famous study of the three-year-old child Peter, inspired by Watson's work on the conditioning of fear in infants.

In this study Jones treated Peter's fear of a white rabbit using a variety of behavioral procedures. She concluded that one of the most successful procedures was "direct conditioning," in which a pleasant stimulus (food) was presented to Peter simultaneously with the rabbit. As the rabbit was gradually brought closer to him in the presence of his favorite food, Peter grew more tolerant of the rabbit and was able to touch it without fear. After publishing these results in 1924, Jones completed her dissertation work on the development of early behavior patterns in young children with a fellowship from the Laura Spelman Rockefeller Memorial, a fund that supported basic and applied research in child development. In 1925 Jones gave birth to her second daughter, Lesley, and the following year received her PhD from Columbia.

In 1927, Harold was appointed research director of the new Institute of Child Welfare at the University of California, Berkeley. The family moved to Berkeley and Mary took a position as research associate. She soon became involved in one of three longitudinal studies of child development conducted through the Institute: the Oakland Growth Study (OGS). Her work on the OGS colored the rest of her career. The study, begun in 1932, was designed to follow a group of two hundred fifth- and sixth-grade students from puberty through adolescence. In fact, as members of the group moved into middle and older adulthood, several follow-up studies were undertaken, expanding the scope of the project to include development across the life span. The study's low attrition rate was largely attributable to Jones's conscientiousness and personal relationships with the project's participants.

Jones published more than a hundred studies using data from the OGS. Among these was a series of papers on the long-term psychological and behavioral effects of early and late physical maturation in adolescence. She also examined the developmental antecedents of problem drinking. Throughout her published work, she was extremely careful to relay a sense of the uniqueness of individual participants. Her work reflected an eclectic theoretical outlook and an emphasis on the whole person in her or his developmental, environmental, and social context.

In 1952, at age fifty-six, Jones was appointed assistant professor of education at Berkeley. (Berkeley's strict anti-nepotism rules precluded her appointment in psychology because of her husband's position there.) In that year, she and Harold produced the first educational television course in child psychology, featuring Mary as the host and instructor. In 1959, one year before her retirement, she was granted a full professorship. In 1960, she served as president of the Division of Developmental Psychology of the American Psychological Association (APA). Tragically, just months into their retirement, Harold suffered a fatal heart attack.

After Harold's death, Mary continued to work productively. In 1968 she received the G. Stanley Hall Award for Distinguished Contributions to Developmental Psychology from the APA. During the 1960s and early 1970s, as the behavior therapy field coalesced, her early work on the deconditioning of fear in children received renewed attention. Considered by many behavioral psychologists as the "mother of behavior therapy" in recognition of her work with Peter, Jones herself emphasized the influence of her *longitudinal* research on her personal and theoretical outlook, stating, "Now I would be less satisfied to treat the fears of a 3-year-old . . . without a later follow-up and in isolation from an appreciation of him as a tantalizingly complex person with unique potentials for stability and change."

Mary Cover Jones died in Santa Barbara, California, on July 22, 1987, after a brief illness. She was almost ninety-one years old and still actively involved in her work. As a result of her lifelong commitment to research and service, and despite the prevailing male privilege in academia that often denied her the institutional recognition she might otherwise have had, she was a pioneer in the field of behavior therapy and made a rich and significant contribution to the understanding of development across the life span.

Bibliography: An oral history interview with Mary Cover Jones conducted by Suzanne B. Riess in 1981–82 is available through the Regional Oral History Office, Bancroft Library, University of California, Berkeley. Another interview, conducted by Milton Senn as part of a project on the history of the child development movement, is at the National Library of Medicine, Bethesda, Maryland. Bettyjane K. Reiss's dissertation, "A Biography of Mary Cover Jones" (Wright Institute, Los Angeles, 1990), was based on extensive interviews with Jones; its appendix contains copies of letters, personal documents, family genealogies, and Jones's curriculum vitae, among other material. A small collection of Jones's papers, including personal and professional correspondence and reflections on the Oakland Growth Study, can be found at the Archives for the History of American Psychology at the University of Akron in Ohio. Jones's classic article "A Laboratory Study of Fear: The Case of Peter" was published in *Pedagogical Seminary* 31 (1924), pp. 308–15. See also Jones, "A 1924 Pioneer Looks at Behavior Therapy," *Journal of Behavior Therapy and Experimental Psychiatry* 6 (1975), pp. 181–87, which contains the final quotation on p. 186. Deana Logan surveyed Jones's personal and professional life in "Mary Cover Jones: Feminine as Asset," *Psychology of Women Quarterly* 5 (1980), pp. 103–15. A brief obituary appeared in the *New York Times* on August 21, 1987. See also the obituary by colleagues Paul Mussen and Dorothy Eichorn in *American Psychologist* 43 (1988), p. 818.

ALEXANDRA RUTHERFORD

JORDAN, Barbara. February 21, 1936–January 17, 1996. Lawyer, civil rights activist, U.S. Representative.

Barbara Charline Jordan was born in Houston, Texas. Her parents, Benjamin Meredith Jordan, a warehouse clerk and later an assistant pastor, and Arlyne Patten Jordan, a maid, had saved enough money to have Barbara delivered at home by a physician. Ben Jordan wanted a son and took the birth of a third daughter hard. Barbara's ebony pigmentation compounded his disappointment, prompting him to ask the doctor why his child was "so dark."

Ben Jordan dominated the household. He revered his step-grandfather, H. C. Cashaw, the senior pastor of Good Hope Baptist Church, and adopted a strict, traditional view of family life. Barbara and her sisters, Rose Mary and Bennie, were not allowed to listen to music, dance, play board games, watch movies, or read for pleasure. For most of their childhood, they shared a fold-out mattress. Arlyne submitted to Ben's rules, but when he refused to buy the girls dresses for Easter services, she hired out as a domestic to earn money to take care of her daughters' wardrobe needs.

Just as Ben Jordan worked to control Barbara's spirit, her maternal grandfather, John Ed Patten, worked to liberate it. Disgusted by what he saw as the overzealous nature of Baptists, John Patten objected so strongly to his daughter's marriage that he did not attend the wedding. As generous and free-spirited as Ben was disciplined, Grandfather Patten provided a stark alternative to the Jordan household. Patten, who had been unjustly imprisoned for shooting a police officer, ran a junkyard, and as a toddler Barbara spent her Sundays bundling tin, newspaper, and scrap metal with him while the rest of the family worshipped at Good Hope. Barbara so adored him that she carried his picture in her wallet, next to her pocket-size copy of the Constitution.

Grandfather Patten gave Barbara the confidence to set academic and professional goals that challenged her family's conventions. Immediately upon entering all-black Phillis Wheatley High School, Barbara decided that she would become Girl of the Year and developed a three-year plan to win the award. In the process, she won national oratorical contests, served as president of the school honor society, and, after hearing EDITH SPURLOCK SAMPSON speak at the Wheatley career-day program, decided to become a lawyer. Her parents and teachers urged caution. Texas historically had resisted legal education for African Americans, and only reluctantly had established a law school at all-black Texas State University (TSU, later Texas Southern University) to prevent African Americans from studying law at the University of Texas (UT).

In 1952, Jordan enrolled at TSU, where she joined the school debate team. She convinced coach Tom Freeman that it was not improper for a woman to travel with her male teammates, and under his tutelage she built a national reputation as an individual debater. In 1953, Jordan not only broke Jim Crow customs at national debating contests but defeated white students from Brown and Yale. By 1954, she had visited Chicago, New York, and Boston and experienced life not defined by the color line. After earning her BA in 1956, she decided to apply to Boston University Law School.

Law school was difficult. TSU had taught her to read, research, and speak, but had not challenged her intellectually. Economic pressures compounded academic ones. Her father scraped together the money for her tuition and living expenses, but Jordan's extremely tight budget required her to spend the entire year in Boston and weigh every expense. She began attending interdenominational services conducted by Howard Thurman, dean of Boston University's School of Theology; his sermons moved her so deeply that she considered leaving law for the ministry. Her father's ecstatic response sobered her back into the law. But Thurman had given her the epiphany she sought: "God . . . doesn't mean for me to be hounded into heaven. He just wants me to live right and to treat other people right" (Rogers, p. 71).

She returned to Houston, passed the bar exam in 1959 (becoming one of only three African American women licensed to practice law in the state), and opened an office in her parents' home. Bitten by the political bug during Kennedy's 1960 campaign, Jordan decided that she would seek elected office. In 1962 and 1964, she lost races to represent Houston's Fifth Ward in the Texas senate. Emboldened by a 1966 court-ordered redistricting plan, she ran in the newly created Senate District 11, and in 1967 she became one of the first African Americans elected to a southern state legislature since Reconstruction.

Determined to make an impact, Jordan worked hard to enter the male cliques dominating state politics. She hunted deer, played poker, drank scotch, and courted votes. Her strategy was successful. By the end of her first year she had blocked a restrictive voter registration bill and been elected Most Outstanding Freshman Senator. In 1969, her efforts helped to extend and raise the Texas minimum wage, an act the *Texas Observer* called a near miracle. She won reelection by a wide margin. Her ability to collaborate with rather than berate colleagues drew the attention of key political leaders such as Speaker Ben Barnes, Robert Strauss, and Lyndon Baines Johnson (LBJ). Louis Welch, the mayor of Houston, took notice and declared October 1, 1971, "Barbara Jordan Appreciation Day." LBJ keynoted the dinner in her honor, telling the audience that wherever Barbara "goes, she is going to be at the top. Wherever Barbara goes, all of us are going to be behind her" (Rogers, p. 158).

When LBJ told Barnes that the greatest thing he could do would be to send Barbara Jordan to Congress, Barnes and Jordan collaborated to design a district (the 18th) supportive of her candidacy. After she won the primary, the senate elected her president pro tempore. The next month, she served as Governor for a Day and was introduced to a packed chamber by Leon Jaworski. Jordan entered Congress in 1973 and, with LBJ's help, secured seats on the Judiciary and Government Operations committees. She sponsored legislation expanding the coverage of the Voting Rights Act; mandating the printing of bilingual ballots; making civil rights enforcement procedures mandatory for the Office of Revenue Sharing and the Law Enforcement Assistance Administration; and amending federal authorization for state fair-trade laws. In July 1974, Jordan became an overnight sensation during the nationally televised Judiciary hearings when she voted to impeach Richard Nixon for high crimes and misdemeanors associated with the Watergate scandal. After telling her peers "my faith in the Constitution is whole, it is complete, it is total," she declared that she was "not going to sit here and be an idle spectator to the diminution, the subversion, the destruction of the Constitution" and thereupon delivered a three-minute lecture on the legal history of impeachment.

Jordan's sudden prominence irritated more-seasoned leaders and piqued jealousies within the Black Congressional Caucus. Her fame and pragmatism encouraged party leaders to appoint her to the Democratic Steering Committee, a position she held until she gave up her congressional seat, and her moral stature encouraged Jimmy Carter to ask her to keynote the 1976 Democratic National Convention. Frustrated with congressional egos and political turf, Jordan decided not to seek reelection in 1978. The next year she joined the faculty of the Lyndon B. Johnson School of Public Affairs at the University of Texas at Austin, where she conducted rigorous Socratic seminars in government relations and ethics. She challenged students to decide whether liberty or equality was the higher principle and to recognize the seven core values of government: equality, liberty, freedom, justice, independence, respect for others, and opportunity.

Jordan loved teaching and never missed a class in the seventeen years she taught at UT. Her move to Austin gave her the opportunity to have her first home. Intensely private, Jordan had never lived outside her parents' house or her cramped Washington apartment. She never married. When her close friend Nancy Earl decided to buy five acres outside Austin in 1975, Barbara asked if she could be a part of the deal. Nancy designed and managed the house, and Barbara visited occasionally until she made it her permanent home when she returned to Austin. There they entertained students (including the UT women's basketball team) and family and shared a rich life together.

Barbara Jordan remained active in national Democratic politics for the rest of her life. In 1987 she spoke out forcefully against the nomination of Robert Bork to the Supreme Court. In 1994 President Clinton awarded her the Presidential Medal of Freedom and the next year, despite declining health, she served as chair of the Commission on Immigration Reform. Barbara Jordan died in Austin on January 17, 1996, at the age of fifty-nine from complications associated with a twenty-year battle with multiple sclerosis and a recent diagnosis of leukemia. She was buried in the Texas State Cemetery in Austin.

Bibliography: Barbara Jordan's papers are housed in the Barbara Jordan Archives at Texas Southern University in Houston, Texas. A transcript of Jordan's interview for the Lyndon Baines Johnson Oral History Collection is available at the Lyndon Baines Johnson Library in Austin. For biographical and career information, see Barbara Jordan and Shelby Hearon, *Barbara Jordan: A Self-Portrait* (1978), and Sandra Parham, *Barbara C. Jordan: Selected Speeches* (1999). Articles by Jordan include "Who Speaks for the Negro?" *Austin American Statesman,* June 16, 1968; and "How I Got There—Staying Power," *Atlantic Monthly,* March 1975, pp. 38–39. See also House Judiciary Committee, *Debate on Articles of Impeachment: Hearings Pursuant to H. Res. 803,* 93rd Cong., 2nd sess., July 24–27, 29 and 30, 1974; House Judiciary Committee, Subcommittee on Civil and Constitutional Rights, Barbara Jordan Testimony, *Hearing on the Extension of the Voting Rights Act,* 94th Cong., 1st sess., serial no. 1, pts. 1 and 2, February 25–March 25, 1975; and Remarks of Barbara Jordan, Senate Judiciary Committee, *Hearings on the Nomination of Honorable Robert H. Bork to Be Associate Justice of the Supreme Court of the United States,* Washington, D.C., September 21, 1987. Valuable secondary sources include James Haskins, *Barbara Jordan* (1977); Barbara A. Holmes, *A Private Woman in Public Spaces: Barbara Jordan's Speeches on Ethics, Public Religion and the Law* (2000); and Mary Beth Rogers, *Barbara Jordan: American Hero* (1998). Obituaries appeared in the *Houston Chronicle* and the *New York Times* on January 18, 1996. See also the tribute by Molly Ivins, "She Sounded Like God," *New York Times Magazine,* December 29, 1996.

ALLIDA BLACK

JOYNER, Florence Griffith. *See* Griffith Joyner, Florence.

JOYNER, Marjorie Stewart. October 24, 1896–December 27, 1994. Entrepreneur, beauty culturist, civil rights activist.

Marjorie Stewart was born and spent her early childhood in the rural Blue Ridge Mountains of Monterey, Virginia. The granddaughter of a former slave, virtually from birth she demonstrated the indomitable spirit and keen survival instinct that would one day motivate her to become a leader in business, education, and racial advancement. One of thirteen children born to Annie Dougherty and George Emmanuel Stewart, only Marjorie and three of her sisters endured the family's harsh conditions of poverty to live past infancy. Her father was an itinerant teacher who traveled throughout the Virginia countryside and once worked with Booker T. Washington; her mother, who married this teacher when she was just fourteen, was a homemaker.

Marjorie Stewart's childhood was marked by upheaval. When she was six years old, her father joined thousands of African Americans seeking greater economic opportunities in the North. In 1904 he relocated the family to Dayton, Ohio, accepting a job at a prep school. Not long after, the marriage dissolved. Annie Stewart moved to Chicago and worked as a domestic, while the young girl spent the next six years raised by relatives and friends in Dayton. Finally, in 1912, she joined her mother in Chicago, the city that remained her lifelong hometown. With money tight at home, Marjorie juggled classes at Johnstown Elementary and later Englewood High School with jobs babysitting, cleaning, or waitressing, but she did not graduate from high school at this point in her life.

Six months short of her twentieth birthday, on April 4, 1916, Stewart married Robert Joyner, a podiatrist she met while roller-skating outside her home. Their relationship lasted fifty-seven years, until his death in 1973. They had two daughters, Ann (1921) and Barbara (birth date unknown), both of whom became educators.

Throughout her adulthood, Joyner refused to accept the limitations imposed on her for her race and gender. When she decided to be a beautician, she repeatedly applied to the only school in town, the white-owned A. B. Molnar Beauty School, until she was admitted. In 1915, weeks after becoming its first black graduate, she opened a beauty parlor in a racially mixed Chicago neighborhood. But her training had focused on white people's hair and a white clientele, and Joyner was ill-prepared for the complicated needs of black tresses. After nearly ruining her mother-in-law's hair, the elder woman paid for Joyner to take classes on black hair care with the doyenne of black beauty culture, millionaire entrepreneur MADAM C. J. WALKER.

The association proved fortuitous. Joyner became a trusted employee and quickly was promoted to national supervisor; by 1919 she was helping to develop and manage more than two hundred Madam C. J. Walker beauty schools. After Walker's death that year, Joyner was promoted to vice president and chief instructor of its fifteen thousand agents; she stayed with the company for more than fifty years. With a powerful message about the opportunities for black women in beauty culture, she increased student enrollment during the difficult years of the Depression and launched beauty culture classes in vocational high schools nationwide. At the same time she maintained her own salon, where her clients included BILLIE HOLIDAY, Dinah Washington, and MARIAN ANDERSON. Showing her entrepreneurial spirit, in 1928 she was one of the first black women to receive a patent. The rights to this invention, a device that offered a quicker way to relax hair, as well as the rights to several other products she developed in the 1930s and 1940s, were controlled by the Walker company and she never personally profited from them.

For Joyner, beauty culture provided not only a professional alternative to domestic service but also a route to racial advancement and an entrée into politics. In 1918 she met prominent educator MARY MCLEOD BETHUNE and became a champion of black colleges and universities, especially Bethune-Cookman College. To prove that black beauticians were as qualified as white, Joyner helped write an Illinois law in 1924 requiring licenses for all beauty schools and practitioners in the state. Two years later, Joyner became the first black woman to receive a license, which she maintained for the rest of her life. She continued to promote professionalism and prestige for black beauticians by founding the United Beauty School Owners and Teachers Association in 1945. In 1954 she led members of Alpha Chi Pi Omega, a beauticians' sorority and fraternity she had founded, on a much publicized trip to France to study the latest techniques.

Joyner also used the beauty salon as a community center to rally black beauticians to political causes. In 1929, she teamed up with Robert S. Abbott, founder of the *Chicago Defender*, the popular black newspaper, to establish the Bud Billikin Day Parade in honor of the mythical figure who protects black children; the parade tradition continued for over seven decades. In 1935 she was a founding member of the National Council of Negro Women, and in the 1940s, at ELEANOR ROOSEVELT's invitation, she worked with the Democratic National Committee. Other political efforts included recruiting beauticians to the civil rights activism of Martin Luther King Jr., and canvassing beauty parlors for John F. Kennedy's election campaign in 1960.

Joyner's life exemplified her faith that education can promote racial equality. She graduated from Chicago Musical College in 1924 with a certificate in dramatic art and expression, received a diploma from Chicago Christian High School in 1935, took courses at Northwestern University, and earned a Bachelor of Science degree from Bethune-Cookman College in 1973 when she was seventy-seven years old. She was active in the Mary McLeod Bethune Foundation and a trustee for Bethune-Cookman College, raising over a million dollars on its behalf. In 1961 she was awarded an honorary doctorate in the humanities from Bethune-Cookman; she cherished this award and thenceforth insisted that she be addressed as Dr. Joyner.

At the end of her life, Joyner had little financially and lived on Social Security, but she was rich in personal and social achievements. Hailed as the "Grande Dame of Black Beauty Culture," she influenced both the professionalism of the beauty business and the greater cause of racial equality, demonstrating through her life the centrality of business and educational opportunities for African Americans. Marjorie Stewart Joyner died of heart failure at her Chicago home in 1994 at the age of ninety-eight.

Bibliography: Marjorie Stewart Joyner's papers are located in the Vivian G. Harsh Research Collection of Afro-American History and Literature at the Chicago Public Library, where archivist Michael Flug is a virtual expert on Joyner's life. The author conducted an oral history with Joyner by telephone in April 1993, in which she talked at length about the connections among beauty culture, racial advancement, and politics. For additional information, see "Beauty Pilgrimage," *Ebony*, August 1954, pp. 38–44; Paul Galloway, "Witness to Chicago's Black History: A Beautician Once, a Leader Always," *Chicago Tribune*, February 4, 1987; and "Living Legend Honored at Woodson," *Chicago Weekend*, October 24, 1993. For books on beauty culture and African American beauty culture, see Kathy Peiss, *Hope in a Jar: The Making of America's Beauty Culture* (1998); and A'Lelia Bundles, *On Her Own Ground: The Life and Times of Madam C. J. Walker* (2001). Obituaries appeared in the *Chicago Tribune* and the *Chicago Sun-Times* on December 29, 1994, and in *Jet*, January 16, 1995, p. 54.

DEBRA MICHALS

K

KALLEN, Lucille. May 28, 1922–January 18, 1999. Television comedy writer, novelist.

Lucille Kallen, born in Los Angeles, was the only child of Samuel Chernos, a Russian-born immigrant, and Esther Kallen, also of Russian ancestry but born in Toronto. Information about Lucille's early life is sketchy. When she was three years old, her parents separated and she moved with her mother to Toronto; after her mother died three years later, she was raised in Toronto by her grandparents and attended Harbord Collegiate High School. From an early age she was trained to be a concert pianist, and at sixteen she moved to New York City to study at Juilliard School of Music. At Juilliard, she discovered two things that ended her musical career: her fingers were too short, and she disliked practicing the piano.

Founding a theater group when she was eighteen, Kallen (she took her mother's name professionally) put together a musical revue for which she wrote songs and sketches. She also played the piano onstage and introduced the sketches she had written. In 1948, her act was seen by producer-director Max Liebman, who invited her to create original material at Camp Tamiment, a Poconos resort famous for its Saturday-night shows. There she teamed with Mel Tolkin, who became her lifetime writing partner. At Tamiment she also met her future husband, Herbert Engel, then a soda jerk and later a successful engineer. They married in 1952 and had two children: Paul (1953) and Lise (1955).

When Max Liebman turned to television, he hired Kallen and Tolkin to write for *The Admiral Broadway Revue,* a comedy-and-music program that was broadcast simultaneously on NBC and the Dumont network from January to June 1949. The program marked the very first teaming of two exceptionally gifted comedians named Sid Caesar and Imogene Coca. When *The Admiral Broadway Revue* ended, Liebman moved most of his exemplary team of writers and performers (headed by Caesar and Coca) into a new ninety-minute comedy-and-music program called *Your Show of Shows,* which premiered on February 25, 1950, as part of the "NBC Saturday Night Revue."

Performed live before a studio audience, the program was received enthusiastically by critics and television viewers, who enjoyed its combination of sophisticated, razor-sharp, and often satirical humor, and its imaginative musical numbers. Most programs were highlighted with hilarious, wickedly on-target parodies of currently popular films, foreign films, or silent films. According to Imogene Coca, it was Kallen who came up with the idea for the first parody, a spoof of the 1951 film *A Place in the Sun. Your Show of Shows* ran for four seasons, in 1951 and 1952 winning Emmy Awards for Best Variety Show from the Academy of Television Arts and Sciences. The final program took place on June 5, 1954.

In addition to head writers Kallen and Tolkin, the writing team for *Your Show of Shows* included Tony Webster and a wildly undisciplined young man named Mel Brooks. As later described by the team, the writers' office was usually sheer bedlam. In a hectic, freewheeling atmosphere that included crumpled paper cups, half-eaten sandwiches, cigar butts, and pools of spilled coffee, the writers worked seven days a week for thirty-nine weeks. They joked, argued fiercely, and came up with some of the best comedy material television would ever see.

Kallen, the only woman in the group, was a center of calm in the storm, taking down the material in pencil on a yellow legal pad as it flew by, all the time contributing her ample share. Carl Reiner later recalled that Kallen was in effect the arbiter: if she didn't like a line, she wouldn't write it down. Getting the team's attention was a difficult task, though—one time the five-foot-one brunette resorted to standing on the tattered sofa, waving her red sweater. She later remarked, "Let's say that gentility was never a noticeable part of our working lives" (Sennett, p. 25).

Although *Your Show of Shows* itself entered the realm of television legend, the team of writers also assumed its own fame as the basis for the 1982 film *My Favorite Year* (which became a short-lived stage musical in 1992) and Neil Simon's 1993 play, *Laughter on the 23rd Floor.* Kallen herself was used by writer Carl Reiner, a featured performer on *Your Show of Shows,* as one of the models for the character of comedy writer Sally Rogers on the situation comedy *The Dick Van Dyke Show.* The other model was comedy writer Selma Diamond.

After the end of *Your Show of Shows,* Kallen turned down a job with *Caesar's Hour* to write for *The Imogene Coca Show,* which lasted for only one season. Choosing to stay in New York rather than relocate to California, where much of television production was centered, she continued as a freelance writer for several more years, writing television specials and such weekly shows as *The Bell Telephone Hour.* With Mel Tolkin, she wrote a short-lived stage comedy, *Maybe Tuesday* (1958). In 1964, she wrote a comic novel entitled *Outside There, Somewhere,* which dealt with the competing demands of career and motherhood. Its English title, *Gentlemen Prefer Slaves,* better captures its early feminist consciousness.

In the late seventies, Kallen began writing a series of mystery novels centering on the character C. B. Greenfield, the sly, curmudgeonly editor of a small Westchester weekly newspaper who solved crimes with the aid of his assistant, Maggie Rome. The first novel, *Introducing C. B. Greenfield,* was published in 1979; it was followed by *The Tanglewood Murder* (1980), *No Lady in the House* (1982), *The Piano Bird* (1984), and *A Little Madness* (1986).

Lucille Kallen died of pancreatic cancer on January 18, 1999, at her home in Ardsley, New York, at the age of seventy-six and was buried at Ferncliff Cemetery in nearby Hartsdale. Warmly remembered by her colleagues, Kallen was one of the few women to have played a significant role in the Golden Age of television. Her quick wit, and her sharply honed sense of the comically absurd in everyday life, contributed hugely to one of television's finest shows.

Bibliography: Materials and documents relating to Kallen's writing career can be found in the papers of Max Liebman at the Billy Rose Theatre Collection, New York Public Library for the Performing Arts at Lincoln Center. An oral history of her writing career is available at the Archive of American Television at the Academy of Television Arts and Sciences in North Hollywood, California. See also Lucille Kallen, "A Comedy Writer Remembers Her Favorite Years," *New York Times,* November 29, 1992. Further information on Kallen can be found in the following books: Ted Sennett, *Your Show of Shows* (expanded ed., 2002); William Holtzman, *Seesaw: A Dual Biography of Anne Bancroft and Mel Brooks* (1979); and Sid Caesar and Bill Davidson, *Where Have I Been?* (1982). Obituaries appeared in the *New York Times,* January 21, 1999; the *Los Angeles Times,* January 23, 1999; and the *Washington Post,* January 25, 1999.

TED SENNETT

KANAHELE, Helen Lake. May 26, 1916–June 12, 1976. Labor organizer.

The labor movement in the Hawaiian Islands in the territorial era before statehood (1898–1959) was a period of increasing class struggle and dramatic change. Power once held tightly in the hands of a very small, Caucasian *(haole)* oligarchy who controlled five interlocked sugar companies, or "factors," was slowly wrested away by a highly diverse plantation-based workforce of native Hawaiians and immigrants from Japan, the Philippines, China, Portugal, and places throughout Asia and the Pacific. In this tumultuous period Helen Lake Kanahele played an important role in organizing workers, particularly women, into the mainstream of Hawaii's restructured political, social, and economic landscape.

Helen was born in Kona, Hawaii. The only known details of her early life are those she later recalled to friends. She remembered that her father was an Englishman who died when she was five, although there is no record of such a man in the 1920 census. Likewise the identity of her Hawaiian mother, who died a year later, is unknown. In the Hawaiian tradition, the young orphan was adopted as a *hanai* child by a woman named Irene Woods.

Early on, Helen demonstrated a talent for Hawaiian dance *(hula)* and song, and soon she was discovered by a professional troupe. By the age of six and a half, she was considered ready to tour with E. K. Fernandez Shows on the first of three trips around the world. She received formal education, only through the eighth grade, at Central Intermediate School in Honolulu. On a later tour, she was deeply affected by the "No Colored" signs she saw in restaurants, in washrooms, and on drinking fountains throughout the southern United States. Most Hawaiians in the troupe were naturally dark-skinned and were understandably surprised and offended to find themselves publicly branded as outcasts in the country they had believed was their own.

In her twenties she married Alfred Kanahele and had two daughters, Mary Jane and Helen, but he deserted her within a few years. As a single parent, she had to support herself and her two children with few resources. Leaving her musical career behind, she finally found regular work in the laundry of Honolulu's Maluhia Hospital in 1948.

In 1949, while Helen Lake Kanahele was living in a Hawaiian Homestead house in Papakolea with her daughters and her *hanai* (adopted) brother, the International Longshoremen's and Warehousemen's Union (ILWU) led a strike for wage parity with West Coast dockworkers. Many supported the strikers, but the newspapers expressed outrage at the inconvenience of the shipping strike and accused union leaders of being communists. Helen went down to the pier to see her brother, one of the striking dockworkers, when about two hundred women, mostly wives, mothers, and daughters of the employers, descended on the ILWU headquarters at Pier 11. Carrying brooms to signify they intended to make a clean sweep of the waterfront, it was obvious that most of these pampered *haole* ladies were holding a broom for the first time in their lives. A counterpicket line of union women was organized, and Kanahele became so excited that she got herself a placard and marched with the union pickets. She continued picketing with the Women's Auxiliary every day after that and became totally committed to the strike, cooking and serving food in the strike kitchens and delivering food to strikers' houses. When the strike was over, she stayed in the Women's Auxiliary and in 1951 was elected president.

Kanahele had been active in the Democratic Party since the age of twelve, and with new fervor she tried to break the nearly complete domination of Hawaii's Republican Party over the territorial legislature. She ran as a delegate to the 1950 constitutional convention with a simple and clear platform: equal rights for women, strong guarantees of individual and minority rights, and the right to a job at a fair wage. In the 1950s she campaigned for an amendment to the Organic Act, which would allow women to serve on territorial juries.

She also was an impassioned opponent of the death penalty. She joined the struggle to save the lives of two Hawaiian youths who had been sentenced to hang for the murder of a Caucasian woman in 1948. After trying without success to convince the governor to commute the sentences, she launched an island-wide petition campaign that collected thousands of signatures. The boys' lives were saved, and their sentences eventually were commuted.

Around this time she began to organize her fellow workers at Maluhia Hospital into a unit of the newly formed United Public Workers (UPW). When her supervisor found out what she was doing, he transferred her to the morgue to punish her. She filed a grievance and was transferred instead to the Department of Public Instruction, where she worked as a custodian at Kalakaua Intermediate School until an injury forced her to retire on a disability pension. She continued to be active in the UPW, serving on grievance committees and holding such offices as territorial secretary-treasurer, Oahu division vice president, member of the territorial and state executive board, and secretary and board member of the political action committee.

During the period of red-baiting in the 1950s, Kanahele stood up for her beliefs no matter how much she was attacked. She publicly supported the "Hawaii Seven," who were jailed in 1953 under the Smith Act, and held a *luau* for the defendants and the defense lawyers at the end of the trial. In April 1954, she was subpoenaed to appear before the Territorial Committee on Subversive Activities, where she was subjected to a grueling inquisition into her beliefs about capital punishment and world peace and her leadership of the ILWU Women's Auxiliary. A committed and unrepentant union activist, she took full responsibility for her actions.

Helen Lake Kanahele was able to accomplish things that few native Hawaiians and still fewer women ever dreamed of in the Hawaii of her time. She died in Honolulu in 1976, after a long illness, at the age of sixty.

Bibliography: Biographical information can be found in Barbara Bennett Peterson, ed., *Notable Women of Hawaii* (1984). See also the New York Times Oral History Project, "History of the United Public Workers Union in Hawaii, No. 11, Helen Kanahele (interview November 19, 1966)," Glen Rock, New Jersey: Microfilming Corporation of America (1975). The interview was one of a series of twenty-five published as part of the Pacific Regional Oral History Program. The *Honolulu Record* provides coverage of labor activities in the late 1940s and 1950s; see especially Amy Clarke, "Mrs. UPW Herself," *Honolulu Record,* October 4 and 11, 1956. An obituary appeared in the *Honolulu Advertiser* on June 21, 1976.

WILLIAM J. PUETTE

KAYE, Nora. January 17, 1920–February 28, 1987. Dancer, artistic director, film producer.

Nora Kaye's professional career spanned nearly fifty years, from childhood performances as an extra with the Metropolitan Opera to soloist with the American Ballet Theatre. Kaye's unflinching portrayal of the female psyche and emotional inner landscape opened new possibilities for women in a ballet world previously populated with sylphs and swans, and it was for her that the term *dramatic ballerina* was coined. Through Kaye's labor, the creative genius of choreographer Antony Tudor was realized. She became his muse, and Tudor became her greatest teacher.

Nora Koreff was born and raised in New York City, and for the rest of her life her broad Brooklyn accent was as much a part of her persona as her intensely dramatic performances. A first-generation American, her parents had fled Russia during the Revolution of 1917. Her father, Gregory Koreff, had been an actor at the Moscow Art Theatre and had studied with Konstantin Stanislavsky; little is known about her mother, Lisa. An only child in a sophisticated, old-country household, the highly intelligent and ever-curious Nora found endless stimulation and a place to belong in America through the study of dance.

She began her training at age five when her mother took her to study with Alexis Kosloff, a graduate of the Russian Imperial Ballet School of Moscow. Her next teacher, Margaret Curtis, taught the classical technique of Enrico Cecchetti to children at the Metropolitan Opera Ballet School. When it became apparent that Kaye had genuine talent, her mother decided that she would study with the master, Michel Fokine, who had been ballet master at the Maryinsky Theatre in St. Petersburg and contributed innovative choreography to Diaghilev's Ballets Russes. Fokine brought his vision of a new classicism to the United States along with a freer, liberated style. The combination of strong technical training in Cecchetti technique and the emotive potential Kaye explored through Fokine's coaching formed the twin foundations upon which Kaye would build her professional life.

In 1935, at the age of fifteen, she signed her first contract as a dancer with the Metropolitan Opera Ballet. Around this time she dropped her family name, Koreff, and adopted the name Kaye. For a brief time in the mid 1930s, Kaye became disillusioned with the Opera Ballet and turned to Broadway, where she confirmed her love for combining dance and acting. But ballet was where she would make her mark.

In 1939, Ballet Theatre, which had been founded by George Balanchine and Lincoln Kirstein four years earlier (and between 1935 and 1939 was known as George Balanchine's American Ballet), became the new resident company at the Metropolitan Opera, and Fokine convinced Kaye to return. A few months later, Antony Tudor arrived from England to choreograph for the nascent company. The coming together of these emerging innovators and performers charged the young venture with creativity. Ballet Theatre offered dancers the opportunity to work with many different choreographers, but for Kaye the unique appeal of the company lay in Tudor's ballets. While relocated Russian artists were restaging the classics, Tudor and his American cast came to carry the contemporary wing of the company. Through determination and hard work, Kaye captured Tudor's attention and earned her signature role.

In 1942, Tudor premiered *Pillar of Fire* and Kaye electrified the dance world with her searing portrayal of Hagar, the tormented heroine. Tudor's special method of intellectually probing a character's emotions and communicating them in dance form resonated with Kaye, who had been familiar with method acting all her life through her father. As Hagar, Kaye was able to establish the character's frustrated emotional state with the simple opening gesture of raising her hand to her cheek. This portrayal earned Kaye the title of prima ballerina and convinced her that she could be an actress through the dance. She continued in many roles, with Tudor and others, that drew on her great ability to commit to the personality of a character with an overwhelming dramatic intensity. She conveyed a totality of expression rather than mere mannerism, while her physical strength allowed her to wed technique with stunning interpretation. She was a modern woman who pushed the boundaries for ballerinas beyond a romantic ideal to a new era of dramatic contemporary roles.

In *Pillar of Fire,* Kaye formed a dancing triangle with Tudor and Hugh Laing that obliquely reflected their vital and volatile working relationships. Often paired with Laing, and other danseurs such as Igor Youskevitch and Jerome Robbins, Kaye took on an astounding number and variety of roles, including such thoroughly contemporary roles as Lizzie Borden in AGNES DE MILLE's *Fall River Legend* (1948) and Blanche DuBois in Valerie Bettis's *A Streetcar Named Desire* (1954). She portrayed more classic heroines in *Giselle* and *Romeo and Juliet,* alternating with ballerinas Alicia Markova and Alicia Alonso. Following a brief stint with New York City Ballet that included her creation in 1951 of the Novice in Robbins's *The Cage,* Kaye returned to Ballet Theatre, where she danced until 1959.

Nora Kaye was married three times and never had children. Her 1943 marriage to Michael Van Buren, a socially prominent New Yorker, was quickly annulled. In 1948 she married violinist Isaac Stern, but that marriage ended in divorce in 1950. In what turned out to be a very successful personal and professional partnership, in 1959 she married director and choreographer Herbert Ross. In 1961 Kaye retired from performing and began dividing her time between the New York dance world and the Los Angeles film scene. With Ross, she continued her immersion in the arts as an executive producer of films such as the dance-driven *The Turning Point* (1977) and *Nijinsky* (1980). She also continued to shape the dance field as assistant artistic director of American Ballet Theatre, and as associate artistic director from 1977 to 1983.

Nora Kaye remained committed to the world of dance until her death from cancer in Santa Monica, California, in 1987 at the age of sixty-seven. The Nora Kaye and Herbert Ross Foundation, a philanthropic organization, memorializes both artists. At Kaye's memorial service in New York City, performers and friends from the worlds of dance and film mourned the great ballerina, as they had at her funeral in Hollywood. In the front row of the chapel sat Kaye's old dance comrades Hugh Laing and a weeping Antony Tudor.

Bibliography: The Dance Collection at the New York Public Library for the Performing Arts at Lincoln Center contains scrapbooks, clippings, photographs, and other material documenting Nora Kaye's career. Critic Edwin Denby offers firsthand accounts of many of Kaye's performances in *Looking at the Dance* (1949). Kaye herself speaks of her time with American Ballet Theatre in Charles Payne's book, *American Ballet Theatre* (1977), which includes many striking photographs of Kaye dancing her best-known roles. See also "Nora Kaye on Nora Kaye: Character and Caring," *Dance Magazine,* September 1987, pp. 54–59, which draws on a 1979 interview by Barbara Newman. Dance historian Selma Jeanne Cohen moderated another interview with Kaye, "Nora Kaye Talks about Working with Antony Tudor," in the *Proceedings of the Society of Dance History Scholars* (1985), pp. 84–90. Kaye's work with Tudor and her character are featured in the following biographies of the choreographer: Donna Perlmutter, *Shadowplay* (1991); Judith Chazin-

Bennahum, *The Ballets of Antony Tudor: Studies in Psyche and Satire* (1994); and Muriel Topaz, *Undimmed Lustre: The Life of Antony Tudor* (2002). The Dance Horizons video *Antony Tudor* (1992) includes footage of Kaye dancing with Hugh Laing in excerpts from *Pillar of Fire* and other dances; Kaye can also be seen dancing with Igor Youskevitch in the 1950 film *Giselle.* In 1978 she collaborated with her husband Herbert Ross on *Filming Ballet,* a prescriptive film that discusses the specific problems in filming dance. Editor William Como and others eulogized Kaye in *Dance Magazine,* May 1987, p. 5, as did John Taras in "Nora Kaye: A Tribute," *Ballet Review,* Winter 1987, pp. 36–48. An obituary appeared in the *New York Times* on March 1, 1987.

MARY ANNE SANTOS NEWHALL

KAYE, Sylvia Fine. August 29, 1913–October 28, 1991. Writer, composer, lyricist.

Sylvia Fine was born in an upper-middle-class Jewish neighborhood of Brooklyn, New York, the eldest of three children of Bessie Wolff, a housewife, and Samuel Fine, a dentist. Both parents were Russian émigrés. Considered a musical prodigy, Sylvia started playing piano at age three; by seven she was writing classical compositions, and by eleven she was studying harmony and theory, composing contemporary music and writing lyrics. Sylvia loved the piano but hated to perform. Her first formal recital caused her such severe stage fright that she vowed never to play in public again. An athletic girl with big shoulders, a big bosom, and a long nose, she was self-conscious about her physique because of her diminutive height (five foot two).

Academics were the first priority in the Fine household, and Sylvia was an avid reader. At Jefferson High, from which she graduated at fifteen in 1928, she was president of her class and wrote songs and skits for class shows. Her father insisted upon her going to college, wanting her to be more than a musician. Sylvia enrolled in Hunter College, transferring to their Brooklyn branch (later Brooklyn College) after her sophomore year because they had a superior music faculty and theater department. She graduated in 1933, a music major.

After college she taught piano and worked at Keit-Engle, a music publishing house. One day her company received a call to send sheet music to a rehearsal studio. Sylvia volunteered to go herself; when she arrived, music in hand, she sat down to play. She was kept on as accompanist at a salary of one hundred dollars a week, and at an audition for *The Sunday Night Varities [sic]* in 1939 she met her husband-to-be, Danny Kaye. (They had attended the same high school but had not known one another.) Kaye sang an audition piece that Sylvia had written for the show's director, Max Liebman. Kaye got the job, and Sylvia was smitten. She saw his potential and would dedicate the rest of her life to writing material that showcased his talents. Prior to meeting Sylvia, Danny had been a tummler, or low-class clown, hired to entertain with pratfalls and mimicry. Sylvia turned him into a more sophisticated performer by giving him witty material with complex lyrics and clever melodies that fit his physical style. They were married on January 3, 1940, in Fort Lauderdale, Florida, with Max Liebman as best man.

Sylvia became Kaye's manager and booked him into a string of high-class nightclubs around the country. In Chicago he was on the bill with Kitty Carlisle, who would eventually marry producer Moss Hart. Soon after, Danny was cast in Hart's Broadway show *Lady in the Dark* (1941). He performed an eleven-minute, tongue-twisting piece entitled "Tschaikowsky" written by Ira Gershwin and Kurt Weill, in which he named fifty-four Russian composers in thirty-two seconds. It brought down the house.

From the beginning of their marriage, Danny and Sylvia were completely dependent on each other, both professionally and personally, although Sylvia always redirected the attention to him. Every detail of his career had to go through her. (Danny was said to remark, "I am a wife-made man" and "Sylvia has a fine head on my shoulders.") Neither one of them was easy: he was demanding and complex; she had a tough exterior that terrified people. She was incredibly protective of Kaye, but came to every performance and criticized his work. He knew she was right, but grew to resent her. The couple separated and reconciled many times during Kaye's life.

Sylvia continued to manage his career, negotiating his deals and protecting the rights to their songs. She brought him to the attention of Sam Goldwyn and got him a five-year movie deal at MGM. Danny's first movie, *Up in Arms* (1944), included "The Lobby Number" and "Melody in 4-F," written by Sylvia and Max Liebman. His second movie, *Wonder Man* (1945), contained songs credited only to Sylvia, like "Otchi Tchorniya" and "Opera Number." Sylvia and Danny became bicoastal, with a big house in Bel-Air and a ritzy apartment in New York, and Sylvia became a big player on the social scene, entertaining often. When he appeared on *Time* magazine's cover on March 11, 1946, she was in the background.

Sylvia gave birth to daughter Dena, the couple's only child, in December 1946. She continued to write material for Danny's movies, including *The Secret Life of Walter Mitty* (1947) and *The Inspector General* (1949), but concentrated on Dena Productions, which she created for Kaye's television and moviemaking operations. She was credited as associate producer on Danny's *Knock on*

Wood (1954), *The Court Jester* (1956), *The Five Pennies* (1959), and *On the Double* (1969), composing "Lullaby in Ragtime" and "All About You," among others.

On television, Sylvia was the associate producer and supervising editor of *See It Now: The Secret Life of Danny Kaye* in 1956. She was producer and writer (including commercials) of the *Danny Kaye Special* in 1960, and the executive producer and writer of special music and lyrics for the *Danny Kaye and Lucille Ball Special* in 1962. All three shows were Emmy-nominated. Sylvia's dominating style created friction, and when Danny did a weekly series from 1963 to 1967, she did not participate. But she later produced his 1975 children's television special *Danny Kaye: Look in at the Met,* for which she won an Emmy.

Many assumed that Sylvia Fine Kaye relinquished her own career to orchestrate that of her husband, but she also wrote and composed on her own. She wrote the lyrics and adapted the music for the main title song for *The Moon Is Blue* (1953), and she wrote lyrics to the main title song for *The Man with the Golden Arm* (1955) with Elmer Bernstein, both of which were nominated for Academy Awards. She also wrote "Life Could Not Better Be" with Sammy Cahn, "Lullaby in Ragtime," "Bali Boogie," and "Happy Ending." She taught courses in the history and analysis of musical comedy theater at the University of Southern California and Yale, which evolved into her crowning achievement: a three-part PBS series, *Musical Comedy Tonight,* which she produced, wrote, and hosted, winning a Peabody Award in 1979. After Danny's death in 1987, she gave a gift of one million dollars to Hunter College Playhouse, which was renamed the Sylvia and Danny Kaye Playhouse. She also endowed the Sylvia Fine Kaye Chair in Musical Theatre at Brooklyn College. Sylvia Fine Kaye died of emphysema in New York City on October 28, 1991, at the age of seventy-eight.

Bibliography: The Danny Kaye and Sylvia Fine Kaye Collection at the Library of Congress contains a comprehensive archive of scripts and compositions, many written for Kaye's film and stage appearances. The Museum of Television and Radio in Los Angeles contains many of Danny Kaye's shows and has two of the three *Musical Comedy Tonight* specials that Sylvia Fine wrote, produced, and hosted. Very little has been written about Sylvia Fine Kaye alone. Martin Gottfried, *Nobody's Fool: The Lives of Danny Kaye* (1994), provides invaluable information, as does Dena Kaye's article about her parents and their home in *Architectural Digest,* November 2001, pp. 296–302. The most valuable and comprehensive material is found in the oral histories preserved by the Dorot Jewish Division of the New York Public Library, especially Edwin Newman's 1981 interview and an interview done by Irene Kahn Atkins (October 8 and 14, 1979), both of which are housed in the American Jewish Committee Oral History Collection of the New York Public Library. Dena Kaye, Suzanne Hertfelder, Kitty Carlisle Hart, Michael Feinstein, Perry Lafferty, Bob McIlvane, and Bobby Zarem generously shared information for this essay. Obituaries appeared in the *New York Times* and the *Los Angeles Times* on October 29, 1991.

SUSAN G. BAERWALD

KEATON, Mabel Doyle. *See* Staupers, Mabel Doyle Keaton.

KELLY, Joan. March 29, 1928–August 15, 1982. Historian, teacher, feminist.

Joan Kelly was born in Brooklyn, New York, the only child of Ruth B. Jacobsen, a Lutheran of Norwegian descent, who was a housewife, and George Vincent Kelly, an Irish Catholic lieutenant in the New York City Police Department. Educated in Brooklyn public schools, she attended St. John's University, earning her way by doing office work. Majoring in medieval studies and philosophy, she graduated summa cum laude in 1953 and won a Woodrow Wilson Fellowship. She entered Columbia University and, supported by fellowships, earned an MA (1954) and a PhD (1963) in history under Garret Mattingly. While in graduate school, she married philosopher Eugene Gadol; the marriage ended in divorce in 1972. The couple had no children.

Kelly's shift to Renaissance studies reflected her detachment from Catholicism. In her search for a coherent, secular worldview, she was strongly influenced by the ideas of Paul Kristeller, Ernest Cassirer, and SUSANNE LANGER. Her dissertation, which Mattingly called the best Columbia dissertation he had ever read, was published in 1969 by the University of Chicago Press. In the elegant and erudite *Leon Battista Alberti: Universal Man of the Early Renaissance,* she argued that Alberti, in defining perspective, profoundly changed the way people thought about themselves, nature, and the cosmos. In her sophisticated analysis of Alberti's significance, Kelly emphasized the way his work expressed a "new orientation of perception and thought," which led to "a comprehensive intellectual transformation . . . a newly harmonious order" (Kelly, *Women, History, and Theory,* p. xii). Alberti's quest for unity of thought and practice was reflected in Kelly's own life and work.

Joan Kelly joined the faculty of the City University of New York (CUNY) in 1956, teaching first at Baruch College, then at City College (CCNY), and, starting in 1977, at the Graduate Center. In 1963 and 1969 she was a visiting professor at Columbia University. In the mid 1960s Kelly was actively involved in protests against the Vietnam War and later in the feminist movement. She was one of the first faculty members at City College to support student demands for open admissions, which made her a controversial figure among the faculty. During this period she also began the serious study of Marxist thought, a subject she later incorporated in her teaching.

On leave from CCNY, she taught at Sarah Lawrence College from 1972 to 1974, where her interest in women's history was awakened and led to the shift in her research and teaching interests that marked the last decade of her life. Characteristically, she carried her new intellectual commitment into practice by serving as co-director, with Gerda Lerner, of the newly established Master of Arts Program in Women's History at Sarah Lawrence College, and by becoming director of the CCNY Women's Studies program in 1976–77.

Kelly soon established herself as an influential scholar in the emergent field of women's history. Her articles "History and the Social Relations of the Sexes" (1976) and "Did Women Have a Renaissance?" (1977) made basic contributions to feminist scholarship in challenging traditional historical periodization as being inapplicable to women and in proposing new ways of conceptualizing the social relations of the sexes and their impact on historical development. Defining herself as a socialist-feminist, Kelly played an important role as a reconciler of various intellectual directions in feminist theory, calling for a "doubled vision" that would resolve the conflicts between sexual/reproductive (private) and socioeconomic (public) explanations of women's oppression. For the rest of her life she focused on developing a Marxist-feminist theory of history. Though her long battle with cancer prevented her from completing a book on this subject, she published an important article, "Early Feminism and the *Querrelle des Femmes*" (1982), which dates the origin of feminist thought much earlier than had previously been accepted. Kelly also co-authored a high school text in family history, *Household and Kin: Families in Flux* (1981). She was active in the movement against sterilization abuse and published articles on that subject. A volume of her essays was published posthumously in 1984.

Joan Kelly's deep commitment to education found expression in her innovative feminist teaching methods, which featured group work by students, team teaching, and close mentoring. Her extraordinary ability to listen to students, treat them with respect, and communicate complex ideas in simple, comprehensible language explains the profound impact she made on several generations of students, many of whom claimed she had changed their lives. As chair of the American Historical Association's Committee on Women Historians in 1975 and 1977, she promoted the publication of popular instructional pamphlets for graduate students and teachers of women's history. The Committee also helped design and co-sponsored with Sarah Lawrence College the first Summer Institute for High School Teachers in Women's History in 1976, which served as a model for similar institutes at Stanford and Brooklyn College.

Equally committed to the advancement of feminist scholarship and the professional status of women, Kelly served in leadership positions of several organizations of women's historians as well as on the boards of the *Feminist Press* (1977–82) and *Signs* (1980–82) in a period when these enterprises were breaking new ground.

A charismatic lecturer, Joan Kelly was regarded as an intellectual leader by feminist scholars. Drawing on her understanding of the Renaissance ideal of the "universal man" as an individual both intellectually and emotionally developed, Kelly attempted to redefine this concept in feminist terms: by fusing theory and practice. She exemplified her ideals also in her role as a critic, blending rigorous criticism with constructive support for the person criticized.

Stricken with cancer in 1979, Kelly continued her writing and teaching. In 1979 she married Martin Fleischer, a political scientist. She died in New York City on August 15, 1982, survived by him and her stepdaughter Eve Fleischer. She was fifty-four.

Joan Kelly's work was characterized by marked shifts in direction, yet it is all of a piece. Whether writing or teaching Renaissance art and culture, the poetry of French troubadours, the rise of the bourgeois family, or the history of modern women, she was primarily concerned with changing ideas and their relationship to economic and political forces. This philosophical bent in her historical work enabled her to raise important theoretical questions in women's history and to exert a decisive influence on a generation of scholars. Her intellectual brilliance was balanced by her organizational talents and her deep commitment to group work. Standing, like Alberti, on a new vantage point, she creatively integrated her professional work into her teaching, friendships, and concern for social change.

Bibliography: Joan Kelly's papers, which include research notes, lecture material, and correspondence, are at the Schlesinger Library, Radcliffe Institute for Advanced Study, Harvard University. She is the author of *Leon Battista Alberti: Universal Man of the Early Renaissance* (1969) and co-author, with Renate Bridenthal, Amy Swerdlow, and Phyllis Vine, of *Household and Kin: Families in Flux* (1981). See also her *Bibliography in the History of European Women* (1973; rev. ed. 1976) put out by Sarah Lawrence Publications. Kelly's shorter pieces include "Universal Man" in Philip P. Wiener, ed., *Dictionary of the History of Ideas* (1973); "Alberti" in the *Encyclope-*

Kent

dia Britannica (1974); and "Tommaso Campanella: The Agony of Political Theory in the Counter-Reformation" in Edward P. Mahoney, ed., *Philosophy and Humanism: Essays in Honor of Paul Oskar Kristeller* (1976). A volume of her essays, *Women, History and Theory: The Essays of Joan Kelly* (1984), was published posthumously. All other material is based on correspondence and personal recollections of the author and on conversations with Martin Fleischer, who holds in his possession all official documents pertaining to Joan Kelly. An obituary appeared in the *New York Times* on August 18, 1982.

GERDA LERNER

KENT, Corita. November 20, 1918–September 18, 1986. Nun, artist, teacher.

Baptized in the Roman Catholic faith as Frances Elizabeth, Frannie, as she came to be called, was the fifth of six children born in Fort Dodge, Iowa, to second-generation Irish parents Edith Genevieve Sanders and Robert Vincent Kent. The family moved when she was three to Vancouver, Canada, and then to Hollywood, where living in rental housing owned by her maternal grandfather and earnings from her mother's work as a seamstress and laundress helped compensate for the frequent unemployment of a poetically gifted but alcoholic father.

Suffering from rickets as a child did not prevent Frannie from progressing at a normal pace through the elementary grades at Blessed Sacrament School in Hollywood, and Catholic Girls (later Bishop Conaty) High School, where an Immaculate Heart of Mary (IHM) nun, Sister Noemi, stayed after class to give the talented young girl private art lessons. Frannie pursued her interest in art by taking classes in drawing and still life at Otis Art Institute in Los Angeles the summer following high school graduation in 1936, but set those interests aside that fall to enter the Hollywood novitiate of the IHM congregation. Her formal reception into the community a few months later, under the name Sister Mary Corita, or "little heart," began a thirty-two-year association with the remarkable group of women, including her older sister, Ruth Cecilia Kent, who sponsored Immaculate Heart College and numerous elementary and secondary schools on the West Coast.

For several years Sister Corita taught in IHM schools in Vancouver, British Columbia, and on a nearby American Indian reservation. She then returned to Los Angeles, where she completed a BA at Immaculate Heart College (1941) and an MFA at the University of Southern California (1951), where she focused on art history to avoid what she experienced as the stifling atmosphere of most studio art courses. She matured rapidly as an artist while on the faculty of Immaculate Heart College between 1951 and 1968, emerging as one of the very few women leaders of the Pop Art movement, and credited with revolutionizing type design and the art of silk screening through her unique use of color, form, and the written word rendered in her unique calligraphy.

Mentored by Sister Magdalen Mary, aptly nicknamed "the P. T. Barnum of the IHMs," and aided in her early use of silk-screening techniques by Mrs. Alfredo Martínez, widow of the Mexican muralist, Sister Corita plunged into the art world of the 1950s and '60s, widening her horizons through an art-finding trip to Spain, Italy, and Egypt; annual visits to New York City museums and galleries; and an ever-growing circuit of lectures and gallery talks. Friends who significantly influenced her art and philosophy were the designer and filmmaker Charles Eames, social realist and graphic artist Ben Shahn, author Harvey Cox, Jesuit poet and anti-war activist Daniel Berrigan, and author ANAÏS NIN.

A teacher whose classroom "happenings" matched her serigraphs for outrageous brilliance, Sister Corita made a practice of including student art with her own, as in a banner exhibit at the National Gallery in Washington, D.C., in 1958, and the holiday lobby display "Peace on Earth" at IBM's corporate headquarters in New York City in 1963. Several of her students became professional artists, notably Franciscan nun Karen Bocarello, who founded the Los Angeles community arts center and gallery Self-Help Graphics, Inc., and the annual street celebration "El Día de los Muertos," with its many reminiscences of Corita's flamboyant style.

Kent loved to have her work appear in conspicuous places where people could see and touch it—on book jackets, stationery, posters, in the pages of *Time* and *Newsweek*, even gas tanks (in Boston in 1971)—and to evoke a shock of recognition in viewers, a sudden glimpse into beauty and spiritual meaning in the commonplace. Encouraged by Berrigan in the mid 1960s to use art as political statement, she embraced printmaking as an effective means of nonviolent protest against war, earning the sobriquets "urban guerilla with a paintbrush" from Harvey Cox and "joyous revolutionary" from Ben Shahn.

Most of the serigraphs that propelled her into celebrity status were produced during the three-week periods in August that separated summer school from the fall semester, when she would resume her six-course teaching schedule at Immaculate Heart College. Few were aware of the time pressures under which she worked, or of the insomnia from which she frequently suffered as she created her seemingly spontaneous prints and murals with their brilliant primary colors and strong social and religious messages.

Looking back on this period of her life, Kent saw it as a time of enormous experimentation and tension. The Sisters' ideas about how to adapt to modern times, as mandated by the Second Vatican Council, brought them into sharp conflict with Cardinal McIntyre of Los Angeles, as well as Vatican authorities. Sister Corita personified all that the cardinal found objectionable about this innovative community, with her playful yet serious critiques—the tomato serigraph, "Mary Mother, the juciest [sic] tomato of them all," being just one of her more provocative works. Her punishing schedule, and the controversies embroiling the IHMs and Cardinal McIntyre, had much to do with her decision in 1968 to resign from the college and the sisterhood, and ultimately to abandon the formal practices of Roman Catholicism.

Corita Kent spent her remaining years living quietly in a Back Bay apartment in Boston, outliving by more than a decade a 1974 prognosis that gave her only a year to live following the detection of ovarian cancer. Touched by a sense of her finiteness and possessed of limited energy between successive surgeries and episodes of therapy, she confined her artistic work to watercolor painting and limited her printmaking to commissions she judged would afford her an opportunity to say something unusually substantive. Among these was the 1984 anti-nuclear billboard campaign for Physicians for Social Responsibility, "We can create life without war," in her opinion the most religious thing she ever did. In 1985 the U.S. Postal Service issued her "Love" stamp, which became the best-selling stamp of all time. She died peacefully on September 18, 1986, in the Watertown, Massachusetts, home of her friends Elinor and Charles Mikulka, at the age of sixty-seven.

Bibliography: Corita Kent's selected papers are at the Schlesinger Library, Radcliffe Institute for Advanced Study, Harvard University; her personal print collection is at the Grunwald Center for the Graphic Arts at UCLA; private documents, watercolors, and some prints are housed in the Corita Art Center, Los Angeles. The Jundt Art Museum at Gonzaga University in Spokane, Washington, holds a substantial collection of her prints.

Publications by Corita Kent include *Footnotes and Headlines: A Play-Praybook* (1967); *Corita,* with Harvey Cox and Samuel Eisenstein (1968); *To Believe in Things,* with Joseph Pintauro (1971); and, posthumously, *Learning by Heart: Teachings to Free the Creative Spirit,* with Jan Steward (1992). For biographical material and a critique of her art, see Kenneth Woodward, "The Nun: A Joyous Revolution," *Newsweek* cover story, December 25, 1967, pp. 45–48. Two documentary films on Kent's life are Baylis Glascock, *Corita: On Teaching and Celebration* (1986), and Jeffrey Hayden, *Primary Colors: The Story of Corita* (1990). See also the 1977 interview recorded under the auspices of the Oral History Program at UCLA. Barbara M. Loste based "Life Stories of Artist Corita Kent (1918–1986): Her Spirit, Her Art, the Woman Within" (PhD dissertation, Gonzaga University, 2000) on extensive interviews with family, friends, and professional colleagues, and on Corita's correspondence. Obituaries appeared in the *New York Times* on September 19, 1986, the *Los Angeles Times* on September 20, 1986, and *Commonweal* on October 24, 1986.

KAREN M. KENNELLY

KENWORTHY, Marion Edwena. August 17, 1891–June 26, 1980. Psychiatrist, pioneer in psychiatric social work.

Marion E. Kenworthy was a lifelong player in the institutionalization of psychodynamic concepts and practices in the United States. An early participant in both residential and outpatient care for the mentally ill and a co-creator of the first "model" child guidance clinics, she also exerted a formidable influence on the development of the curriculum at one of the preeminent schools of social work in the country. Through her participation in the emergent professions of psychiatry and social work she advanced the adoption of psychodynamic concepts into the theoretical training and clinical practice of both disciplines.

Born in Hampden, Massachusetts, Marion was the eldest child of John Kenworthy and his second wife, Ida S. Miller. Marion's father arrived in America from England at age sixteen. He had five children with his first wife, who passed away. By the time he married Marion's mother, he owned a textile mill manufacturing woolen blankets. Ida, born in Shrewsbury and also of English descent, was a schoolteacher before she eloped with Kenworthy, a parishioner in the Methodist church where her father was a clergyman. A second child, Ruth, was born in 1894. Marion Kenworthy later attributed her passion to become a doctor (not a nurse, as her father suggested) to her early awareness of her mother's increasingly fragile health and her untimely death in 1900.

John Kenworthy remarried shortly after Ida's death, but foreclosure proceedings on the textile business left him bankrupt. For the remainder of his life he was employed as a gardener. Marion's affectionate and enduring connection to her father underpinned her own long-standing rural sensibilities. Marion and Ruth experienced their stepmother, however, as stern and demanding, and both left the household as soon as they could arrange financial support to pursue advanced education. Marion graduated from Central High School in Springfield, Massachusetts. In 1909, at age seventeen, she secured a loan from her mother's younger sister and entered Tufts Medical School, which did not require an undergraduate degree. She graduated cum laude with her MD degree in 1913.

Kenworthy's first professional employment was as a junior psychiatrist in charge of three hundred women on the chronic ward of Gardner State Hospital. During that time she spent her weekends studying at Boston Psychopathic Hospital with Dr. Elmer Southard, a pioneer in social psychiatry. There she joined a cadre of professionals who, over subsequent decades, became powerful colleagues and collaborators across various areas of mental health. At Boston Psychopathic she observed the development of the first interdisciplinary teams of mental health care workers by Southard and social worker MARY JARRETT, a model Kenworthy would later replicate. Kenworthy next took a position as senior psychiatrist at Foxborough State Hospital, giving her a total of six years of psychiatric supervisory experience.

At age twenty-seven, realizing that she had reached the pinnacle of career possibilities for women within the state hospital system, Marion Kenworthy took a risk and moved to New York City. Her work in 1920 with Dr. Berman Glueck in Vanderbilt Clinic at the New York State Neurological Institute led Glueck to invite her to lecture at the New York School of Social Work. Kenworthy's relationship with the school became a central feature of her career when its director, Porter Lee, hired her as a full-time instructor. In 1924 Kenworthy was appointed director of their Department of Mental Hygiene, to replace the retiring Glueck.

Marion Kenworthy's qualifications were a good match for a profession looking to embrace a scientific methodology and earn concomitant legitimacy. At the forefront of psychoanalytic psychiatry, she introduced psychodynamic theory into social work. During her tenure (1920–56) the New York School affiliated with Columbia University and became known as Columbia University School of Social Work. Kenworthy, whose title became Professor of Psychiatry, is said to have had decisive control over a significant portion of the curriculum and personally taught several generations of social work students. The first endowed chair at the school is in her name.

Kenworthy's collaboration with Glueck and Porter Lee also included work, from 1921 to 1927, at the Bureau of Children's Guidance, a model clinic for the mental health care of children. That work was summarized in *Mental Hygiene and Social Work* (1929), which Kenworthy co-authored with Lee.

In the early 1920s, Kenworthy was one of the first in the United States to be analyzed by Otto Rank, the last formal training she received in psychoanalysis. She started her private practice soon after she moved to New York City. Although she saw patients of all ages, she was one of the first in the city to provide psychiatric services specifically for children. In 1927 she expanded her analytic practice and continued to see private patients for almost sixty years. Diligent about the need for confidentiality, Kenworthy kept her own records of client appointments. Her contemporaries speculate that her clients included some of the most influential people in the country.

Kenworthy was active in professional and voluntary associations throughout her career. During World War II, she helped create and promote model mental health services for soldiers. In that effort she was instrumental in obtaining official military rating status for psychiatric social workers and supported the establishment of a national standard of mental health care for the military. With her friend JUSTINE WISE POLIER, she worked to include mental health concepts in the juvenile court system in New York City. Other interests included the Citizens' Committee for Children, the Wiltwyck School for Boys, and the wartime Non-Sectarian Committee for Refugee Children.

Her lifelong relationship with social worker Sarah H. Swift, who was independently wealthy, made it possible for Kenworthy to develop a privileged lifestyle, facilitating her ability to focus on her work. The two lived together from 1919 until Swift's death in 1975, and throughout that time Sarah managed the household tasks. In 1926 they bought a summer home in Bedford, New York. For nearly fifty years Kenworthy and Swift traveled between their large Fifth Avenue apartment and their rural retreat in Westchester County.

An imposing woman in stature and manner, Kenworthy received numerous honors for her lifetime of dedication to her professional interests. She died of natural causes in her New York City apartment in 1980 at the age of eighty-eight.

Bibliography: Kenworthy's papers, including material about her tenure at the Bureau of Child Guidance, are in the Columbia University Rare Book & Manuscript Library. In addition to her 1929 book co-authored with Porter Lee, Kenworthy's major publications include "Training for Psychiatric Social Work," *Hospital Social Service* 7, no. 1 (1923), pp. 32-37; "Mental Health in Childhood," *Mental Hygiene* 10, no. 2 (April 1926), pp. 242–52; "Psychoanalytic Concepts in Mental Hygiene," *The Family* 7, no. 7 (November 1926), pp. 213–23; and "The Need for Constructive Planning for Children," *Bulletin of the New York Academy of Medicine* 36, no. 9 (September 1960), pp. 596–603.

Rebecca Sperling surveys Kenworthy's life and career in "A Portrait of Marion Edwena Kenworthy: Psychiatrist in Social Work" (PhD dissertation, Columbia University, 1996). For additional biographical material, see transcribed interviews conducted by Albert Deutsch (1956) and Spafford Ackerly (1971) at Columbia. Surveys of her career are found in Viola W. Bernard, "Profiles of Famous American Psychiatrists: Marion E. Kenworthy, M.D.," *Psychiatric Annals* 9, no. 6 (June 1979), pp. 72–79; and Henry

Brosin, "Marion Edwena Kenworthy, M.D.: An Appreciation," *Group for the Advancement of Psychiatry's Circular Letter,* Spring 1981. An obituary appeared in the *New York Times* on June 27, 1980.

REBECCA L. SPERLING

KENYON, Jane. May 23, 1947–April 22, 1995. Poet.

When Jane Kenyon feared that her husband, poet Donald Hall, was likely to die from cancer, she wrote in "Afternoon at MacDowell": "I believe in the miracles of art, but what / prodigy will keep you safe beside me?" This question, carved on her gravestone in Proctor, New Hampshire, now seems meant for her. Hall recovered from his illness, but Kenyon died from leukemia two years later. She had just been named Poet Laureate of New Hampshire; she had become an award-winning poet; she was forty-seven years old.

Born in Ann Arbor, Michigan, the second of two children, Kenyon came from an artistic family. Her father, Reuel, was a piano player, jazz musician, and music teacher; her mother, Polly, was a singer. Through fourth grade she attended a one-room school on the outskirts of Ann Arbor dominated by an authoritarian teacher. Her subsequent education in the public schools did not nurture her spirit, intellect, or creativity. Her valued teachers would be poets and writers who inspired and influenced her: Keats, Chekhov, Akhmatova, Bishop. By the time she reached high school, Kenyon had rejected the fierce Methodism of her family, embodied in her sin-preoccupied grandmother, and decided that nature would be her God.

Kenyon went on to the University of Michigan at Ann Arbor, receiving a bachelor's degree in 1970 and a master's degree in 1972. As a graduate student she took Donald Hall's poetry workshop, and gradually their relationship evolved from teacher-student to friendship and then to love and marriage in April 1972. At first, the power imbalance made Kenyon's evolution as a poet challenging. When they met, Donald Hall was a tenured professor, a recently divorced father of two children, and an accomplished, celebrated poet. Kenyon was a graduate student in her early twenties, unsure of her poetic gifts. Hall realized he could not criticize her poems because then he became her teacher again, so the couple invited their friend Gregory Orr to become a third discussant of their work, and this arrangement helped them achieve critical equality.

In 1975 Kenyon and Hall moved from Ann Arbor to Wilmot, New Hampshire, and took up residence at Hall's family farm, Eagle Pond. Though at first she was overwhelmed by the thick history of the house, Kenyon began to take herself seriously as a poet, and here she found again the natural world that consoled and inspired her. She took great pleasure in rambles with her dog, working in her garden, and portraying the cycles of nature in her poems. Hall and Kenyon developed a rhythm of work that underlay her creativity, writing during the morning, enjoying the double solitude of working alone, knowing they would meet again in the afternoon.

Assisting Kenyon's development of a poetic voice were two friends, Joyce Peseroff and Alice Mattison. The three women formed a long-distance poetry workshop, sharing work through the mail and meeting occasionally. Kenyon had come of age during the women's movement and found this small female community essential to her creativity. Peseroff and Mattison also helped her shape an identity separate from that of wife of a well-known poet. With Peseroff, Kenyon started a poetry magazine called *Green House* in 1976, publishing work by their literary friends until 1980.

Robert Bly then encouraged her to find a poetic "master" to guide her creative development. When she protested she could not have a man as a master, he suggested Russian poet Anna Akhmatova. Kenyon spent five years working on a translation of Akhmatova's lyric poems, published in 1985. Kenyon later felt that her years of imaginative connection with this female predecessor contributed significantly to her poetic evolution. Her publication record supports this insight. Before the Akhmatova translation, Kenyon had published one book of poetry, *From Room to Room* (1978). Afterward, three books came out in rapid succession: *The Boat of Quiet Hours* (1986); *Let Evening Come* (1990); and *Constance* (1993). Each revealed the deepening of her sensibility and craft and received glowing reviews. The posthumous collection *Otherwise: New & Selected Poems* appeared in 1996.

Like Akhmatova, Kenyon expressed intense emotion through the image. Her poetry explores the connection between inner and outer worlds, spirit and nature, self and soul through concrete details that exist fully in the visible world yet connect us to the invisible. At times her poems delight in simply observing the natural world (in "Heavy Summer Rain," the "poppies / with their black and secret centers / lie shattered on the lawn"); at times, as in "Let Evening Come," she gives her images a slowly growing metaphoric resonance: the slowly fading afternoon light, the fox returning to his "sandy den," the shed going "black inside," lead gently toward an acceptance of death: "Let it come, as it will, and don't / be afraid. God does not leave us / comfortless, so let evening come."

As Kenyon grew more rooted in New Hampshire, she began a spiritual journey that continued throughout her life. She and Hall began attending the local Congregational church, where Kenyon found a spiritual community. Her poetry reveals her deepening awareness of the divine, which she continued to find incarnated in the things of this world.

Kenyon's faith did not redeem, but it gave her the courage to withstand the terrible bouts of depression she suffered throughout her life. Her father had struggled with clinical depression, her mother with bipolar disorder, so Kenyon knew that her illness was a biological inheritance, not a character flaw. When she was in deep depression she could not write, answer the phone, or stay in touch with friends, but when she was emerging from the darkness her creative power returned. During such a period she wrote perhaps the most powerful description of depression in American literature—"Having It Out with Melancholy," a blistering anti-ode to the "unholy Ghost" that plagued her, as it does so many others. Unlike most American illness narratives, "Melancholy" does not end with the speaker's recovery: even when the air clears and "ordinary contentment" returns, she knows that depression will come again. Her consolation is the beauty of the present moment: the early morning June light, the cool air pressing through the screen, the "wild, complex" song of the wood thrush.

"Having It Out with Melancholy" appeared in *Constance,* the last of her books to appear before her death. Kenyon was diagnosed with a virulent form of leukemia in January 1994. In October she and Hall went to Seattle for a bone marrow transplant, and for a few months there was hope. Back at Eagle Pond, the couple worked together on *Otherwise,* Kenyon selecting the poems and Hall photocopying selections from her published books and assembling her unpublished poems. In early April 1995, blood tests showed that the leukemia had returned. Together they faced Kenyon's death, she using her last energies to work on the final collection of her poetry. "There was nothing to do," Hall wrote in the "Afterword" to *Otherwise,* "and she died eleven days later, at home in our bed as she wished."

Bibliography: Jane Kenyon's papers, which include photographs of the poet, drafts of published and unpublished poems, correspondence, journals, notebooks, and other materials are in the Milne Special Collections and Archives, University of New Hampshire, Durham. In addition to *Otherwise: New & Selected Poems* (1996), the most important published source for work by Jane Kenyon is *A Hundred White Daffodils: Jane Kenyon* (1999), which includes essays, newspaper columns, the Akhmatova translations, one unpublished poem, and interviews. The collection also includes the definitive bibliography compiled by Jack Kelleher, covering the published poetry, uncollected poetry, translations, edited work, prose, and sound and video recordings. Literary criticism and biographical reflections include John H. Timmerman, *Jane Kenyon: A Literary Life* (2002); Laban Hill, "Jane Kenyon," in Jay Parini, ed., *American Writers: A Collection of Literary Biographies* (vol. 7); Bert G. Hornback, ed., *Bright Unequivocal Eye: Poems, Papers, and Remembrances from the First Jane Kenyon Conference* (2000); "Jane Kenyon Portfolio," *Meridian: The Semi-Annual from the University of Virginia* 4 (Fall 1999), pp. 37–80; Jeffrey Cramer, "With Jane and Without: An Interview with Donald Hall," *Massachusetts Review* 39, no. 4 (Winter 1998–99), pp. 493–511; and "A Tribute to Jane Kenyon 1947–1995," *Columbia: A Journal of Literature and Art* 26 (1996), pp. 154–81. Video recordings include *A Life Together: Donald Hall and Jane Kenyon* (1994), first broadcast on PBS on *Bill Moyers' Journal* in 1993; and *Jane Kenyon: A Celebration of Her Life and Works* (1995). Obituaries appeared in the *Boston Globe* on April 24, 1995, and the *New York Times* on April 27, 1995.

SHARON J. O'BRIEN

KEYSERLING, Mary Dublin. May 25, 1910–June 11, 1997. Social welfare activist, economist, federal official.

Mary Dublin was born in New York City, the second of four children of Augusta Salik and Louis Israel Dublin. Both parents were Jewish immigrants who became exemplary Progressive reformers. Born in Russia, Augusta graduated from Barnard College and was a settlement house resident before her marriage. Lithuanian-born Louis studied mathematics at City College of New York and earned a doctorate in biology from Columbia University. A gifted statistician, he became vice president of Metropolitan Life Insurance Co. and a renowned public health expert. Mary inherited his mathematical genius and devotion to gathering and publicizing data. From her mother she acquired a commitment to social justice, as well as a conviction that women should not curtail their intellectual pursuits upon marriage.

After graduating from Horace Mann School, Dublin earned a degree in economics and sociology from Barnard College in 1930. At Barnard, and at the Geneva School of International Studies in the summer of 1929, she studied with professors and theorists who were revolutionizing economic thought, including John Maynard Keynes. After working for the Committee on the Costs of Medical Care and the New York State Charities Aid Association, she studied at the London School of Economics (1931–32) and Columbia University (1932–33). With capitalism in international crisis, Dublin was drawn to the Left. In London she organized for the Independent Labor Party, and in the summer of 1932 she visited the Soviet Union to examine the socialist experiment firsthand. After passing Columbia's doctoral examination in economics in 1933, she abandoned her dissertation for a faculty position in economics at Sarah Lawrence College.

In New York City, Mary Dublin maintained a frenetic social and political schedule and developed a reputation in left and liberal circles as a brilliant speaker. In 1938 she became general secretary of the National Consumers' League, a women's organization dedicated to improving labor conditions and wages. Under her leadership, the League influenced the passage of the Fair Labor Standards Act of 1938 and defended the National Labor Relations Act of 1935 (NLRA) from conservative attacks. During the latter project she cooperated with Leon H. Keyserling, who as aide to Senator Robert Wagner had drafted the NLRA. In Leon, who later headed President Truman's Council of Economic Advisers, Mary chose a husband as ambitious and argumentative as herself. After marrying in 1940, the socially minded economists lived in Washington, D.C., for the rest of their careers. They had no children.

During the Second World War, Mary Dublin Keyserling worked for the House Committee on National Defense Migration, the Office of Price Administration, and the Office of Civilian Defense. In confronting home-front challenges through these agencies, Keyserling argued that social justice and high living standards were democracy's best defense. In 1943 the Foreign Economics Administration hired her to work on assistance programs for war-ravaged nations. In 1946 she became chief of the International Economic Analysis Division of the Department of Commerce, where she advanced an internationalist program that included aiding foreign nations by increasing U.S. imports.

Keyserling's career suffered when she was brought before the Department of Commerce Loyalty Board in 1948 and 1951, under the auspices of Truman's loyalty program for government employees, on charges that she had been a communist sympathizer in the 1930s. In 1952 Senator Joseph McCarthy publicly accused both Mary and Leon of communist associations. Mary denied the allegations and was cleared. (Later she rarely discussed the investigation.) She left government service in January 1953, attributing her move to Republican capture of the White House. From 1953 to 1963, Keyserling was associate director of the Conference on Economic Progress, a nonprofit consulting group she and Leon founded. She was a leader of the Women's National Democratic Club and served on the Committee for Protective Labor Legislation of the President's Commission on the Status of Women during the Kennedy administration (1961–63).

In 1964 President Johnson appointed Keyserling to head the U.S. Women's Bureau in the Department of Labor. Under her leadership, the agency defeated attempts to abolish it, stimulated the formation of state commissions on women's status, and fought for women's inclusion in War on Poverty jobs programs. The bureau also continued its decades-long opposition to the equal rights amendment (ERA) because it would have invalidated state wage and hour laws that applied only to women. In 1965 the agency persuaded the new Equal Employment Opportunity Commission that protective labor laws for women did not violate Title VII of the Civil Rights Act of 1964. Although equal-rights feminists thought otherwise, Keyserling was sensitive to sex discrimination. Her speeches debunked stereotypes about women workers and urged men to share domestic responsibilities. Keyserling believed that the keys to advancement for the majority of women were adequate minimum wage laws, strong unions, generous social insurance, and high-quality child care. After the U.S. Supreme Court struck down sex-based labor laws in 1971, Keyserling finally embraced the ERA.

After leaving government service in 1969, Keyserling remained active as a consulting economist. She toured five African nations, speaking on economic development. She conducted studies of child-care programs, including one culminating in *Windows on Day Care* (1972), which won her the Distinguished Service Award of the National Conference on Social Welfare. She held many positions related to child welfare and served on the D.C. Commission on the Status of Women (1971–73). She resumed her activism with the National Consumers' League, testifying before Congress into the 1980s in support of raising the national minimum wage. Near the time of her husband's death in 1987, Keyserling began to suffer from Alzheimer's disease. She died at Arleigh Burke Pavilion in McLean, Virginia, in 1997 at the age of eighty-seven.

An influential economist in the Roosevelt, Truman, and Johnson administrations, Mary Dublin Keyserling belonged to a generation of labor-oriented feminists who nurtured the renaissance of the women's movement in the 1960s. Although her critique of capitalism softened during the cold war, she consistently stressed the limits of the free market, arguing that regulatory and redistributive public policies to increase the purchasing power of the working class and poor were good for the nation's economy as well as its conscience. Recognizing that women and racial minorities were overrepresented among the poor, she advocated public child care and anti-discrimination laws to overcome the extra obstacles these groups faced.

Bibliography: Keyserling's career is well documented in a collection of her papers at the Schlesinger Library, Radcliffe Institute for Advanced Study, Harvard University; included are correspondence, speeches, articles, testimony before Congress, appointment books, and a few photographs. Also at the Schlesinger Library, see her 1982 interview in the Women in the Federal Government Oral History Project; see also her 1968 interview with David G. McComb in the Oral History Collection, Lyndon Baines Johnson Library, Austin, Texas. On her loyalty investigation, see Keyserling's file in Record Group 478 (Office of Personnel Management), National Archives, College Park, Maryland.

Keyserling's published writings include "Maternal Mortality and the Decline of the Birth Rate," *Annals of the American Academy of Political and Social Science* (November 1936); "Good Health for a Sound Nation," *Democratic Digest* (July 1939); *The Economy of Israel: Progress under Freedom* (1959, coauthored with Leon Keyserling); *Who Are the Working Mothers?* (1965); "Women's Stake in Full Employment," part 1 of *Women in the U.S. Labor Force*, edited by Ann Foote Cahn (1979); "Why I Am a Strong Advocate of the Equal Rights Amendment," *Barnard College Alumnae Magazine*, January 1981; and "The First National Consumer Organization," in *Consumer Activists: They Made a Difference—A History of Consumer Action Related by Leaders in the Consumer Movement* (1982).

Willadee Wehmeyer, "Mary Dublin Keyserling: Economist and Social Activist," (PhD dissertation, University of Missouri–Kansas City, 1995), provides an overview of Keyserling's career. Landon R. Y. Storrs, *Civilizing Capitalism: The National Consumers' League, Women's Activism, and Labor Standards in the New Deal Era* (2000), discusses her work in the 1930s. Kathleen A. Laughlin, *Women's Work and Public Policy* (2000), examines her leadership of the Women's Bureau. On Keyserling's encounter with anti-communists, see Storrs, "Red Scare Politics and the Suppression of Popular Front Feminism: The Loyalty Investigation of Mary Dublin Keyserling," *Journal of American History* 90, no. 2 (September 2003), pp. 491-524. An obituary appeared in the *Washington Post* on June 13, 1997.

LANDON R. Y. STORRS

KIRCHWEY, Freda. September 26, 1893–January 3, 1976. Journalist, editor, publisher.

Mary Frederika "Freda" Kirchwey was born in Lake Placid, New York, the youngest of the three living children and the second daughter of Dora Child Wendell and George Washington Kirchwey. Her father was a professor and the dean of Columbia Law School. Before coming to New York City, her mother taught English at Albany High School. Freda grew up in a financially comfortable and politically active family where family dinner table conversations addressed major issues of the Progressive era, such as prison reform, working conditions, and women's rights.

Freda was not a rigorous student, preferring to learn instead from firsthand experiences. After schooling at Horace Mann High School, she graduated from Barnard College in 1915; she wrote both for the high school paper, the *Horace Mann Bulletin,* and for her college paper, the *Barnard Bear.* On November 9, 1915, she married Evans Clark, later the director of the Twentieth Century Fund. She kept her maiden name and continued to work. Of their three children, only one, Michael, born in 1919, survived into adulthood. Brewster, born in 1916, lived only eight months, and Jeffrey, born in 1923, died in 1930.

After brief stints on the short-lived literary publication *Every Week* and on the *New York Tribune,* in 1918 Kirchwey joined the staff of the *Nation,* a liberal journal, where her inclination to reform served her well. Originally hired to clip files for its International Relations section, Kirchwey became the section's head in less than a year. From this beginning she launched her lifelong career on the *Nation* as a prolific political journalist and editor and eventually its owner and publisher.

Her career advanced in stages. She became managing editor late in 1922 and literary editor in 1928. The late 1920s were difficult personal years for her. Her mother died and her son became so ill that she left the *Nation* to take him to a better climate in the hope that he might regain his health. Jeffrey never recovered, and his death left Kirchwey devastated and unable to return to work. Following an almost three-year hiatus, she returned with even more responsibilities on the journal. Kirchwey became the executive editor of a board of four editors in 1933, and she purchased the *Nation* in 1937. She molded the journal until her retirement in 1955.

Kirchwey was politically passionate and used her journal to advance her views. In the 1920s she highlighted issues of special concern for women, including access to birth control information, better treatment for working women, and women's place in a world of changing morality. Twice in that decade she arranged for groups of experts to address these issues in the *Nation.* The first series, "New Morals for Old," was published as *Our Changing Morality* (1924), edited by Kirchwey. Next she asked selected women with established careers to examine their attitudes toward marriage, career, and children. The resulting series, "These Modern Women," appeared in 1926 and 1927. Believing in psychology as the ultimate authority, Kirchwey had the reflections of the women (who were not named) analyzed by a behaviorist, a neurologist, and a Jungian psychoanalyst. She then printed those analyses in the *Nation.*

When Kirchwey became the *Nation's* executive editor in 1933, she put the topic of "modern women" behind her and concentrated instead on the larger world around her, a world beset by the Great Depression and soon to be engaged in World War II. Kirchwey gradually abandoned her (and the *Nation's*) pacifist orientation in favor of support for collective security. Her advocacy of universal military training as part of her stance of "militant liberalism" caused an irreparable breach with the *Nation's* former owner, Oswald Garrison Villard. Soon after the United States entered World War II, Kirchwey designated a special portion of the *Nation* as the "Political War" section, where she gave editorial space to leaders who were fleeing from fascism. A fervent anti-fascist, Kirchwey published early exposés about the Holocaust. At times she had wondered if some of the facts were exaggerated, but years later she observed that the circumstances were much worse than what she had printed. Kirchwey's persistent coverage of the Holocaust, along with her support for the rights of Jewish people to live in peace in an independent state of their own, were some of her lasting contributions to journalism.

During World War II and even after it, Kirchwey took another decisive journalistic stand—she wrote and published sympathetic editorials about the Soviet Union. Kirchwey's belief in journalistic freedom created a unique situation for the *Nation*. The front of the journal (the editorial section) was very pro-Soviet, while the back of the journal (the book review section under the literary editor, Margaret Marshall) was virulently anticommunist. This unusual situation lasted until January 1953 when, for financial reasons, Kirchwey fired Marshall.

From 1943 until 1953 Kirchwey coped with financial losses at the journal by reorganizing the structure of the *Nation*. She transferred ownership to a nonprofit organization called "The Nation Associates" in 1943. The solution did not work, leaving the journal in financial trouble. Because she was preoccupied with raising money for the *Nation*, Kirchwey wrote less during her later years on the journal.

Starting in 1945 when she wrote a scathing editorial, "One World or None," immediately after Hiroshima and Nagasaki, Kirchwey grappled with atomic power's potential. In December of 1945 she hosted a three-day public forum on that topic, which she edited and published as *The Atomic Era: Can It Bring Peace and Abundance?* (1950). Kirchwey credited the conference's demand for civilian control of atomic power as a major influence for creating the Atomic Energy Commission. Freda Kirchwey's last forum in the *Nation* (June 1955) was titled "Atoms for Peace." In September she transferred the editorship to her chosen successor, Carey McWilliams.

After retiring from the *Nation* in 1955, Kirchwey spent her remaining years in relative obscurity. She continued to work for the Women's International League for Peace and Freedom (WILPF), serving as its delegate to the United Nations. She also covered the United Nations as a contributor to the York, Pennsylvania, *Gazette and Daily*. She attempted to write a book about her beloved journal, the *Nation*, but never completed it. By 1970 Kirchwey had retired from public life to care for her ill husband, whose death that year left her distraught. She traveled to Switzerland to be with her son, Michael, but felt more comfortable in the United States, where she lived with her sister, Dorothy Kirchwey Brown, in Boston. When Kirchwey's memory failed her, she was moved to a nursing home in St. Petersburg, Florida, where she died in 1976 at the age of eighty-two.

Bibliography: Freda Kirchwey's extensive papers are housed at the Schlesinger Library, Radcliffe Institute for Advanced Study, Harvard University. There are also relevant manuscript collections in libraries around the country that hold papers of her political friends and foes and colleagues at the *Nation*, the most helpful of which are the Oswald Garrison Villard papers at Harvard's Houghton Library and the Dorothy Kirchwey Brown papers at the Schlesinger. Over the course of her long career, Freda Kirchwey wrote an enormous number of signed and unsigned editorials for the *Nation*. The unsigned *Nation* editorials are in a very fragile state and are housed at the New York Public Library. The only full-scale biography is Sara Alpern, *Freda Kirchwey: A Woman of The Nation* (1987). See also Alpern's essay, "In Search of Freda Kirchwey: From Identification to Separation," in Sara Alpern, Joyce Antler, Elisabeth Perry, and Ingrid Scobie, eds., *The Challenge of Feminist Biography: Writing the Lives of Modern American Women* (1992). Carey McWilliams's moving tribute, "The Freda Kirchwey I Knew," appeared in the *Nation*, January 17, 1976, pp. 38–40. Other obituaries are found in the *New York Times*, January 4, 1976; the *Washington Post*, January 10, 1976; and the *Barnard Bulletin*, January 26, 1976.

SARA ALPERN

KITTRELL, Flemmie Pansy. December 25, 1904–October 1, 1980. Nutritionist, home economist, educator.

Flemmie Pansy Kittrell was born and raised in Henderson, North Carolina, the seventh of Alice Mills and James Lee Kittrell's nine children. The Kittrells, descendants of slaves on both sides of the family, were farmers. Flemmie Kittrell attended a local public elementary school, and then enrolled at the Academy of the Hampton Institute at the age of sixteen. After graduating in 1924, she continued her academic career at Hampton Institute and received her BS degree in home economics in 1928.

Like many other ambitious African American women of her time, Kittrell worked for a number of years before seeking an advanced degree. After college, Kittrell taught home economics at

Bennett College in Greensboro, North Carolina. She then moved to Ithaca, New York, and received a master's degree in nutrition at Cornell University in September 1930. Kittrell requested and was granted a second leave of absence from Bennett College to continue her doctoral work at Cornell in 1933. When Cornell conferred Kittrell's PhD in 1936, she was one of only a handful of African American women to have earned a doctorate. Her dissertation was on African American infant feeding practices and nutrition in Greensboro, North Carolina.

After completing her doctorate, she returned to Bennett College, where she became director of home economics and then later dean of students. In 1940, her alma mater, Hampton Institute, invited her to become dean of women and a member of the faculty. After four years at Hampton, Kittrell once again received an invitation to head a home economics department, this time from Mordecai Johnson, president of Howard University.

It was in Washington, D.C., that Flemmie Kittrell's career began in earnest. Not only did Kittrell direct the home economics department at Howard University, but she also became a missionary for home economics both at home and abroad. Her first foray into international home economics was as a State Department consultant to Liberia in 1947. Kittrell conducted a nutritional evaluation of Liberia and suggested a nutritionally sound diet based on the economic and agricultural resources of most Liberians. President Tubman, on the 1948 centennial of Liberia, recognized Kittrell's contribution to the health of Liberians by bestowing the Liberian Award on her. As a Fulbright professor in 1950 and as a participant in President Truman's Point Four development program from 1953 to 1955, Kittrell established a home economics department at India's Baroda University.

Although Kittrell returned to her duties at Howard University in 1955, she never really left India behind. She regularly corresponded with her colleagues there and encouraged Baroda students to pursue postgraduate training in the United States. She also led a group of Indian women on a 1957 State Department tour of home economic extension programs in Hawaii and Japan. The United Nations sent Kittrell back to India in 1960 to conduct a nutritional survey, and she returned for the last time in 1977 as a Fulbright lecturer.

Kittrell's international work continued when she traveled to Africa as a consultant to the Congo Polytechnic Institute between 1960 and 1965. She helped the Institute develop a home economics program for Congolese women in conjunction with the Women's Section of the Methodist Church of the World. Unlike her other international ventures, this institute was plagued with infighting during its early years, reflecting some of the cultural ambivalence toward women's higher education in developing countries. Kittrell noted this ambivalence in a 1962 *Washington Post* article, commenting, "you have to 'sell' the men first on the need for women to be educated." The Congo Polytechnic Institute, however, did provide jobs for some of her students from Howard University and opportunities for some Congolese women to continue their education in the United States. Throughout her career and well after her retirement in 1973, Kittrell continued working in Africa and Asia for UNESCO, the United Nations, and various federal agencies.

Although Kittrell never married, her work with children kept her active. Always concerned about children, and especially poor children, Kittrell started a new and innovative program for underprivileged children at Howard University's nursery school in 1964; this program was one of the models for Head Start. Through research funded by the Children's Bureau of the Department of Health, Education and Welfare, Flemmie Kittrell and the nursery school program determined the needs of poor families, including child care. Always an advocate for African American women, Kittrell recognized that working mothers and children faced special demands, and that programs like Head Start could relieve some of the burdens poor families bore, in addition to giving inner-city children opportunities that they traditionally lacked. Under Kittrell's direction, more than two thousand Head Start workers were trained at Howard University and eventually started new programs throughout the country. Besides developing local programs, from 1970 through 1976 Kittrell also participated in the "Follow Through" Program in Goldsboro, North Carolina; this program focused on increasing family and community participation in early childhood education. By concentrating on the well-being of families rather than simply on teaching cooking and sewing, Flemmie Kittrell and others helped expand the role of home economists in the academy and society, particularly when working with government agencies.

Kittrell's missionary work was not relegated to home economics, however; she also was active within the Methodist Church. In addition to helping organize the home economics department of Congo Technological Institute, she visited Rhodesia, Mozambique, and Ethiopia as a consultant for Methodist educational missions. She also served on the board of a Methodist hospital and retirement home in metropolitan Washington, D.C. Flemmie Kittrell was a feisty, plain-talking advocate for the rights of women and children in the United States and around the world through her research and work in home economics and nutrition. She died of a heart attack on October 1, 1980, at the age of seventy-five, while working in Washington, D.C.

Bibliography: The Flemmie P. Kittrell Papers, in the Manuscript Department of Moorland-Spingarn Research Center, Howard University, Washington, D.C., include several biographical essays that highlight different aspects of her life. The collection also contains lists of publications, personal correspondence, news clippings, and photographs. An oral history interview with Kittrell from August 1977 can be found in the Black Women Oral History Project records at Schlesinger Library, Radcliffe Institute for Advanced Study, Harvard University. Flemmie Pansy Kittrell, "A Study of Negro Infant Feeding Practices in a Selected Community of North Carolina" (PhD dissertation, Cornell University, 1936), contains a short biography, which emphasizes her early life. See also Elinor Lee, "She's Off to the Congo to Organize a College," *Washington Post,* July 30, 1962. For home economics as a profession, including material on African American home economists, see Sarah Stage and Virginia B. Vincente, eds., *Rethinking Home Economics: Women and the History of a Profession* (1997). An obituary appeared in the *Washington Post* on October 5, 1980.

GABRIELLA M. PETRICK

KNOPP, Fay Honey. August 15, 1918–August 10, 1995. Pacifist, prison reformer.

Fay "Honey" Knopp pioneered a response to sexual and systemic violence that was informed by her peace and justice advocacy. She integrated an encompassing spirituality with a belief that people could change themselves and institutions for the better. Her background and her self-identification as a Jewish Quaker pacifist-feminist-activist framed her life and work; her personal virtues of compassion and independence enabled her to see herself in others without sacrificing her commitment to a just and peaceful world.

Fay Birdie Irving was born in Bridgeport, Connecticut, the third of four children of Mollie Feldman and Alexander Ajolo Irving. Her father was a Russian Jewish émigré who became a dentist in the United States; her mother was a housewife. When Fay was born at home, her father carried her to her mother, saying, "She's a honey!" It stuck for the next seventy-seven years and reflected what seemed to many an inherent sweetness permeating her activism. Her considerable sense of independence was striking for a woman of her era. Valedictorian of her class at Warren G. Harding High School in Bridgeport, Connecticut, in 1935, she won membership in the National Honor Society but was unable to accept a scholarship to college because of diminished family finances during the Depression. Her inability to attend college was probably the one regret of her life.

After high school, she launched into a career as a buyer for a chain of women's fashion stores in Connecticut. This work connected her with her future husband, Burt Knopp (whom she married on August 17, 1941), and helped sustain their family until 1964, when she left the fashion field to devote herself full-time to the peace and social justice movements. In 1945, Honey and Burt had a daughter, Sari, and in 1947 a son, Alex.

"To know beyond all knowing that there really was a Light within me . . . a Light that Lighteth all human beings" was how Honey spoke of the spirituality that led her to become a Quaker and infused all of her efforts. When she joined an American Friends Service Committee Peace Caravan that visited her town in 1939, she was already a Gandhian pacifist, but she did not formally become a Quaker until 1962.

In the mid 1950s, the Knopps moved to California in connection with their business dealings. Honey enrolled in a creative writing course at UCLA, met other Quakers, and helped form an International House. Burt and Honey were musicians and cooks; their home was always a welcoming hotbed of conviviality. They sang with Burl Ives, Pete Seeger, Odetta, Malvina Reynolds, Alan Lomax, and later, Utah Phillips.

With clarity of vision and a compelling eloquence, Knopp anticipated the challenges for "social change agents" (her self-description) in the 1960s and 1970s. In 1962, she was part of a delegation from Women Strike for Peace (WSP) to Geneva, Switzerland, to protest the effects of nuclear testing on children's health. In 1963 Clarie Collins Harvey invited her to Jackson, Mississippi, to work with Womanpower Unlimited to create an interracial dialogue among women. In 1964 she participated in "Wednesdays in Mississippi" and worked with Bayard Rustin, Barbara Barnes, and Ruby Davis. Also in 1964, she infused new life into the World Peace Study Mission, accompanying Japanese survivors of Hiroshima (Hibakusha) on a tour of the United States. She served as acting head of the New York chapter of the American Friends Service Committee (AFSC) from 1965 to 1972, and later as a volunteer for the AFSC's National Peace Education Division in Philadelphia, traveling home on weekends.

Knopp had been visiting prisoners since 1955, but the Vietnam War provided new outlets for her activism. In 1968 she and Bob Horton—the only two people designated to visit all federal prisons in the country by the Federal Bureau of Prisoners—established Prisoner Visitation and Support, an ongoing national service organization to federal prisoners. In federal prisons, she came to recognize the plight of prisoners in general as well as political prisoners. In the early 1970s she founded the Prison Research Education Action Project, which was a project of the Safer Society Task

Force of the New York State Council of Churches. Following up on an AFSC book, *Struggle for Justice* (1971), which urged reforms in criminal justice policies, and the Attica uprising of 1971 and the brutal state response, the Safer Society Task Force convened on weekends at the Knopp home to examine core issues of crime and punishment, finally producing *Instead of Prisons: A Handbook for Abolitionists* (1976). It provided innovative models of nonpunitive alternatives to incarceration and programs of community empowerment. Honey was also on the board of the Central Committee for Conscientious Objectors.

In the last decades of her life, much of Knopp's activism focused on issues of sexual abuse and the treatment of sexual molesters. Soon after moving to Vermont in 1979, she visited every one of the twenty-two sex-offender treatment programs inside and outside of prisons and published the first nationwide survey in 1986. She wanted to create an alternative to prison for the "toughest" cases, which she identified as sexual molesters and abusers, especially of children. She believed there was no way finally to abolish prisons unless more effective alternatives could be devised for all the people in them.

Knopp's concern was always for all the people hurt—the victim, the offender, the families, and the community. She believed prisons took responsibility away from sex offenders by removing them from society and shutting them away without treatment, and that if they were released without treatment, they would offend again. Instead she embraced and promoted a model of restorative justice based on a relapse prevention model of treatment, teaching intervention and self-control skills to sex offenders and insisting that offenders take responsibility for their actions.

Until 1993, Knopp served as the director of the Safer Society Program and Press, which published books, research studies, manuals, and training videos dealing with the treatment of sex offenders and prevention of sex-related crimes. She died two years later of ovarian cancer in Shoreham, Vermont, at the age of seventy-six. Notes of condolence came from prisoners, sexual abuse survivors, prison wardens, academicians, peace workers, social workers, Quakers, artists, musicians, and citizens from Europe, Asia, and Israel, all of whose lives she had touched.

Bibliography: The primary sources for this article are Fay Honey Knopp's papers, which are in the possession of her husband, Burton, and her daughter, Sari Knopp Biklen. Her long correspondence with Daniel and Phillip Berrigan and Elizabeth McAlister is in the Cornell Archives. Her contributions to the Consortium on Peace Research, Education and Development are documented in the Swarthmore College Peace Collection. The quotation in the text is from Knopp's plenary speech at a Friends General Conference Gathering in 1994. For more on her philosophy, see her books and articles, particularly: *Instead of Prisons: A Handbook for Abolitionists* (1976); *Researching Your Local Jail: A Citizen's Guide for Change* (1981); *Remedial Intervention in Adolescent Sex Offenses: Nine Program Descriptions* (1982); *Retraining Adult Sex Offenders: Methods and Models* (1984); *When Your Wife Says No: Forced Sex in Marriage* (1994); and *A Primer on the Complexities of Traumatic Memory of Childhood Sexual Abuse* (with A. R. Benson) (1994). Interviews with Burt and Sari Knopp, Faith Lowell, Euan Bear, Brenda Burchard, and Louise Ransom provided useful information for this essay, which also drew on earlier interviews with the Rev. Virginia Mackey, Clare Regan, Margaret Stinson, and Charlotte Frantz. Tributes to Fay Honey Knopp include David Dellinger and David Gilbert, "Loving Abolitionist," in *Toward Freedom* 44, no. 6 (November 1995); and Scott Christianson, "In Memoriam: A Remembrance of Fay Honey Knopp and the Origins of the Abolition Movement in *Instead of Prisons*," in *The Justice Professional* (1998). An obituary appeared in the *New York Times* on August 16, 1995.

JUNE LICENCE AND NANCY JOHNSON

KNUTSON, Coya Gjesdal. August 22, 1912–October 10, 1996. U.S. Representative, farming advocate.

Coya (short for Cornelia) Gjesdal was born in Edmore, North Dakota, the second of four daughters of Christian and Christine Anderson Gjesdal, Norwegian immigrant farmers. Her father, active in the Nonpartisan League, was a believer in farmers working together for fair crop prices, and his enthusiasm for tax relief and state-owned grain elevators made a lasting impression on his daughter. She attended rural school until age thirteen, and then, because her parents were fairly affluent, she attended high school in Edmore. Although a nominal student, Cora was involved in many activities, particularly music—where her strong voice made her a popular soloist both in school and in her Norwegian Lutheran Church. Her ambition was to be a second KATE SMITH.

In 1934, Cora Gjesdal graduated from Concordia College in Moorhead, Minnesota, where she was a member of the prestigious Concordia College Choir. In 1935, she was accepted at Juilliard, but despite having the talent and the dedication to succeed, after one summer's work she determined that she had begun her professional training too late.

During the Depression, jobs were at a minimum, but she worked as a school teacher in Penn, North Dakota, and later in Plummer, Minnesota. After marrying Andrew Knutson, a farmer near Oklee, Minnesota, in 1940, she quit her job because married women were discouraged from teaching. She then worked on the family farm and for the U.S. Agricultural Adjustment Administration, visiting farm families and delivering speeches to encourage food production for the war effort.

A 1942 radio broadcast by ELEANOR ROOSEVELT inspired Knutson to enter public life. Her first step was to help organize a neighborhood Rural Electrification Association (REA) to provide electricity for their township. In 1944, when Coya resumed teaching in Oklee, the Knutsons sold their farm and purchased a hotel. Renamed Andy's Hotel, the business became their permanent residence. In 1948, at Coya's instigation, they adopted seven-year-old Terence from a St. Paul orphanage. Andy, who had a history of alcohol abuse, seemed to resent Terence's presence and had little to do with raising him. Increasingly, Knutson looked to her career and her son for personal fulfillment: home became wherever her work was located.

In 1948, Knutson became the Red Lake County Democratic-Farmer-Labor Party (DFL) chair. In 1950, she was elected to the state legislature, defeating a three-term incumbent. She was reelected in 1952. While serving in the House, she worked for state aid for education, health care, and welfare legislation, bills aimed at improving farm economy, and legislation to improve the working conditions for minority and migrant workers. Along with her heavy schedule, Knutson wrote a column called "Coya's Capital Chat" for her district's six newspapers.

In 1954, Knutson, a charismatic campaigner who loved public life, surprised the DFL by defeating their endorsed candidate and three others in the primary for the 9th district congressional seat. She went on to defeat six-term Republican incumbent Harold Hagen in a stunning upset to become the first congresswoman elected from Minnesota.

Having won a coveted seat on the Agriculture Committee, Knutson introduced twenty-four farm bills, including programs for farm improvement and expansion, soil conservation, enlargement of the federal school lunch program to solve farm surplus problems, and price supports for farmers. In her first speech on the House floor, she pleaded for maintaining farm supports, arguing that adequate farm income was necessary for the economic health and welfare of the country.

Coya Knutson's greatest legislative achievement was passage of the section of the Title II Defense Bill that enabled thousands of students to go to college by borrowing money from the Federal Student Loan Fund. She based her legislation on Norway's plan for funding higher education. Passed in the House without a dissenting vote, Title II of the National Defense Education Act of 1958 (H. R. 5479) was signed into law by President Eisenhower. That year she also initiated a bill (H. R. 12331) to fund cystic fibrosis research at a time when the disease was the third leading cause of death among children. The $1 million appropriation was the first federal grant to support cystic fibrosis research.

In 1956, Knutson came into conflict with the Minnesota DFL when she co-chaired Estes Kefauver's campaign for the Democratic candidacy for president. Knutson's objection to Adlai Stevenson, the DFL choice, was based on his lack of a farm program. Knutson's campaign illustrated her ability to sway voters when Kefauver won the Minnesota primary by over 60,000 votes, but ultimately her stand undermined her political career when she lost the support of the Hubert Humphrey–led DFL.

As the 1958 campaign began, Knutson and the 9th District were rocked by a letter released by Knutson's husband who said that he wanted her at home and not in Congress. Actually the Knutsons had not had a home together for several years and were married in name only. Still, the infamous "Coya Come Home" letter created an avalanche of publicity, and Knutson was defeated in the fall, though only by 1390 votes. The letter's source has never been definitively established, but Knutson's husband testified at a 1958 congressional hearing that he was told by DFL operatives to write the letter.

Knutson did not "go home" but instead stayed in Washington, working for the Office of Civil Defense. She divorced Andy in 1962 and returned to Minnesota in 1972 to live with Terence and his family until her death in Minneapolis in 1996 at the age of eighty-four. "Coya, Come Home" reflected the climate of opinion in the 1950s—a whole set of traits, attitudes, obligations, and restrictions that characterized what people thought proper for women at that time. This attitude in part determined the outcome of Knutson's career, in which this single defeat nearly overshadowed her accomplishments.

Bibliography: The principal source of information is Gretchen Urnes Beito's biography of Coya Knutson, *Coya Come Home* (1990), which contains excellent photos of Knutson throughout her life. Knutson's congressional career is also covered in the 1954–58 *Congressional Record.* "Coya's Capital Chat" column is available in the archives of the *Thief River Falls* (Minnesota) *Times.* Knutson also authored "Protect the Family Farm Now," *Better Farming,* June 1955. Obituaries appeared in the *Minneapolis Star Tribune* on October 11, 1996, and the *New York Times* on October 12, 1996.

GRETCHEN URNES BEITO
DIANE DRAKE

KOMAROVSKY, Mirra. February 5, 1905–January 30, 1999. Sociologist.

Mirra Komarovsky, a pioneer in the sociology of gender, was born in Akkerman, Russia, the first of two daughters of Anna Steinberg and Emmanuel

Borisavich Komarovsky. Landowning Jews and ardent Zionists, the Komarovskys were driven from their home by the czar's police when Mirra was a child. They eventually settled in Baku, on the Caspian sea, where Emmanuel, known as Mendel, became a banker. Educated for the most part by tutors, Mirra grew up speaking Russian, Hebrew, French, and English, reading widely, and practicing the piano several hours a day. This privileged world collapsed in the years following the Russian Revolution. In 1921, amidst growing anti-Semitism, dwindling food rations, and Bolshevik persecution of the middle class, the Komarovskys fled to Wichita, Kansas, where several members of Anna's family had previously settled. Mirra entered Wichita High School in the middle of the 1921–22 academic year and graduated after one semester.

Ambitious for his elder daughter and convinced that Kansas held little opportunity for her, Mendel Komarovsky persuaded his wife to move to Brooklyn. Mendel supported the family as an accountant, writer, and translator, while Mirra began what was to be a lifelong association with Barnard College. Majoring in economics and sociology, she studied with anthropologists RUTH BENEDICT and Franz Boas, psychologist Henry Hollingworth, and sociologist William Ogburn. Komarovsky always praised Barnard for its high intellectual standards, but she never forgot Ogburn's discouraging words when she told him she wanted to teach sociology. "Not a realistic plan," he responded. "You are a woman, foreign born, and Jewish. I would recommend some other occupation" (Komarovsky, "Women Then and Now"). He nonetheless recommended her for a one-year graduate fellowship, which, following her election to Phi Beta Kappa and graduation in 1926, she used at Columbia. She earned an MA in 1927 under his direction.

When Ogburn left for the University of Chicago at the end of the year, Komarovsky faced an uncertain future. For two years she taught at Skidmore College, until a university fellowship made it possible to return to Columbia to complete course work for her PhD (1929–30). To support herself while she looked for a dissertation topic, she took a series of research jobs. Not until she joined New York's Institute for Social Research in 1935, however, did Komarovsky find a methodology and subject that suited her. Working with Paul Lazarsfeld, a mathematician and pioneer in survey research who had just emigrated from Vienna, she wrote *The Unemployed Man and His Family* (1940), an intensive study of fifty-nine families, modeled on work Lazarsfeld had just completed in Europe. Columbia awarded Komarovsky a PhD for her work in 1940.

In *The Unemployed Man,* as in all her subsequent work, Komarovsky built on Ogburn's theory of "cultural lag," according to which cultural attitudes lag behind technological change. The Depression offered a case in point. The economic crisis hit blue-collar occupations harder than it hit service jobs; as a consequence, working-class men often found it harder to find work than their wives did. And yet, traditional views of masculinity prevented many men from sharing breadwinning responsibilities: "I would rather turn on the gas and put an end to the whole family than let my wife support me," one man told her (Komarovsky, *The Unemployed Man,* p. 76).

By 1940, Komarovsky was an experienced sociologist, but reaching her full potential took the inspiration of two people: Marcus Heyman, a businessman she married in 1940, and Millicent McIntosh, who succeeded VIRGINIA GILDERSLEEVE as dean of Barnard in 1947. Komarovsky had been married once before, from 1933 to 1935, to Leo Horney, a dentist, but Horney had wanted a housewife who would cater to him, not a woman bent on a career, and the marriage ended in divorce. Heyman, by contrast, encouraged Komarovsky's ambition until his death in 1970. Neither marriage produced any children. Millicent McIntosh, for her part, quickly identified Komarovsky as a key resource in her effort to retain Barnard's reputation for intellectual achievement in a period of postwar anti-feminism. Komarovsky had returned to Barnard as a part-time lecturer in 1935, had won promotion to instructor in 1938, and ever since had been conducting research on Barnard students and the role conflicts the female students faced. As of 1947, however, she had advanced only to the rank of assistant professor. The new dean promoted her to associate professor in 1948 and full professor in 1954.

An attractive, dark-haired woman of medium height, Komarovsky intimidated some students with her intense intellectuality and Russian accent, but she inspired many more with her innovative research. At a time when Talcott Parsons dominated American sociology with his functionalist faith in social equilibrium, Komarovsky emphasized dysfunction, conflict, and change. In 1953 she published *Women in the Modern World: Their Education and Dilemmas,* a book that anticipated by ten years Betty Friedan's *The Feminine Mystique* (1963). Challenging Parsons's belief in the naturalness of conventional gender roles, she pointed to the conflict her students experienced as they "played dumb" to catch husbands and then as full-time mothers wondered "what is wrong with me that home and family are not enough?"(pp. 77, 127). Komarovsky urged that all students be prepared for careers, that good nursery schools be made universally available, and that men accept their fair share of domestic work—goals she was still advocating three decades later in *Women in College: Shaping New Feminine Identities* (1985).

Though most of Komarovsky's research centered on white, middle-class, educated women, she also examined class differences and masculinity in *Blue-Collar Marriage* (1964), a study of white, working-class, Protestant couples, and *Dilemmas of Masculinity* (1976), which examined how the cultural revolution of the 1960s affected the men at Columbia College.

Komarovsky never taught on Columbia's graduate faculty, but she came to play a more prominent role in sociology than many who did. In 1973, in recognition of her pioneering challenge to the functionalist approach in sociology, she was elected president of the American Sociological Association. She retired from Barnard in 1970, but the college named her professor emeritus, and she continued to teach part-time until 1992, including chairing the newly created Women's Studies Program in 1978–79. Through the years, a steady stream of honorary degrees and professional awards, including the Distinguished Career Award from the American Sociological Association in 1991, celebrated her contributions. She died at the age of ninety-three in her apartment on the Upper West Side of Manhattan.

Bibliography: Though Mirra Komarovsky spent her career studying the intimate details of others' lives, she was an intensely private person who avoided discussing her own life, and she destroyed her personal papers. The Barnard College Archives has copies of her major publications, some materials related to her research and teaching, a few letters, a Mendel Komarovsky essay on the 1905 Akkerman pogrom, copies of passports, a few newspaper clippings, several interviews conducted with friends and family, memorial tributes, and a few pictures. Sources disagree on many dates, especially on Komarovsky's date of birth and birthplace; the essay relies on her family's 1921 passport, her death certificate, and the recollections of her sister, Dolly Cheser. Komarovsky kept a diary in Russian from June through October 1918, which has been translated into English and gives a vivid picture of her precocious intellect.

In addition to the publications cited in the text, Komarovsky's major works include *Leisure: A Suburban Study* with George Lundberg and Mary Alice McInery (1934); "Cultural Contradictions and Sex Roles," *American Journal of Sociology* 52, no. 3 (November 1946), pp. 184–89; "Functional Analysis of Sex Roles," *American Sociological Review* 15, no. 4 (August 1950), pp. 508–16; and "Some Persistent Issues of Sociological Polemics," *Sociological Forum* 2, no. 3 (Summer 1987), pp. 556–63. For details about Komarovsky's life and career, see her article "Women Then and Now: A Journal of Detachment and Engagement," *Barnard Alumnae Magazine*, Winter 1982, pp. 7–10; Shulamit Reinharz, "Finding a Sociological Voice: The Work of Mirra Komarovsky," *Sociological Inquiry* 59, no. 4 (Fall 1989), pp. 374–95; and "Remembering 'Barnard's Best,'" *Barnard Alumnae Magazine*, Spring 1999, pp. 28–29. Mirra Komarovsky's sister, Dolly Cheser, and her niece, Ana Cheser Silbert, granted interviews and shared family papers and memorabilia. Obituaries appeared in the *New York Times* on February 1, 1999, and the *Washington Post* on February 2, 1999.

ROSALIND ROSENBERG

KOONTZ, Elizabeth Duncan. June 3, 1919–January 6, 1989. Education leader, federal official, feminist.

Elizabeth Koontz, the first black president of the National Education Association (NEA), was born Elizabeth Duncan in Salisbury, North Carolina. She was a product of the segregated South, but born into a family that appreciated the role of education. Her father, Samuel E. Duncan, was a high school principal; her mother, Lena Bell Jordan, was an elementary school teacher; and her brother Samuel later served as president of Livingstone College in Salisbury. The youngest of seven, she was able to read by the age of four. Much like other members of her family, her own interest in teaching was piqued when, in grade school, she helped her mother assist adults in developing their literacy.

After graduating from Price High School as salutatorian, Koontz pursued education as a profession. In 1938 she received her bachelor's degree in English and elementary education from Livingstone College. Shortly thereafter, she moved to Harnett County, North Carolina, and began her first position at a training school in which she taught children with learning difficulties. In 1940 she was dismissed because she had protested the excessive boarding charges the teachers had to pay to the school-owned boarding house. After her dismissal, she began graduate work at Atlanta University, where she earned a master's degree in education in 1941. She further studied at Columbia University, Indiana University, and North Carolina College in Durham (later North Carolina Central University). In 1941–42 she taught in an all-black school in Landis, North Carolina, and in 1942–45 she taught in an all-black school in Winston-Salem, North Carolina.

In 1945 she returned to Salisbury to teach at Price Junior-Senior High School. She married a math educator, Harry L. Koontz, in 1947. They had no children. During her time in North Carolina, she began focusing her teaching on the needs of students in special education classes. She also began to extend her professional interests beyond the classroom.

In an effort to meet the needs of students and teachers, Koontz became actively involved with local and state-level teachers' organizations. As she stated in an autobiographical essay, "My goal was more or less to change the system. These organizations provided the means to do that" (Gilbert and Moore, p. 130). In particular, her activity in the National Education Association began in 1952 when the organization, in an effort to become more racially inclusive, created a new policy that allowed blacks limited participation in its proceedings. As a member of the North Carolina Negro Teachers Association (later known as the North Carolina Teachers Association) she was admitted into the North Carolina chapter of the NEA. Locally, she was president of the North Carolina Teachers Association of Classroom Teachers (NCACT) from 1959 to 1963, during which time the NCACT published its first edition of *Guidelines for Local Associations of Classroom Teachers.*

Her national leadership began when she was appointed to the NEA Commission. She was later appointed to the advisory committee of the NEA-DCT (NEA Department of Classroom Teachers) and eventually was elected as secretary of the NEA-DCT for two years. During her tenure with the NEA-DCT, she served as vice president and president-elect. In 1964 she was elected president of the Department of Classroom Teachers, the largest organization within the NEA.

In 1967, Koontz was elected president of the NEA. During her 1968–69 tenure she took the conservative and rural-oriented organization in a more liberal direction. In her inaugural address, "A Time for Educational Statesmanship," which she presented in Dallas, she called for more "teacher power" to move beyond teachers' status as "second-class citizens": "This nation recognizes . . . power. . . . But let it be clearly understood, we will use our power . . . [to] remove every imposed restriction that interferes with the full exercise of professional civil and human rights of educators everywhere" (*Current Biography,* p. 245).

Two U.S. presidents took notice of her leadership abilities and appointed her to roles in their administrations. In 1965, Lyndon B. Johnson appointed her to the National Advisory Council on the Education of Disadvantaged Children. In 1969, though she was a Democrat, she left the NEA presidency to join Richard M. Nixon's administration as director of the Women's Bureau in the Department of Labor.

As head of the Women's Bureau, she fought for equal pay for women. In writing about her views on the rights of women, she stated, "I believe that what women must have is freedom—the freedom to choose different life styles, the freedom to fulfill the best that is in them. A philosopher once said: 'The great law of culture is: Let each become all that he was created capable of being.' I do not think we ask for more than that. I am convinced we cannot settle for less" ("Women as a Minority Group," p. 86).

When she was not reappointed for President Nixon's second term, Koontz returned to North Carolina in 1973 to work for the Department of Human Resources as coordinator of nutrition programs. She served as assistant state school superintendent from 1975 until her retirement in 1982. Her husband died in 1986.

Koontz was known as a soft-spoken woman possessed of a quiet, almost serene self-confidence. Her personal interests included reading and sports such as tennis and basketball. She was affiliated with the African Methodist Episcopalian (AME) Church and was a member of Zeta Phi Beta sorority.

Koontz lived a life that exemplified her desire to bring about change in education locally and nationally. She had a sincere love for the profession of teaching and a desire for excellence and equity for all. She was especially interested in equity—in schools for teachers and the students they taught, and for women in society. Elizabeth Koontz died of a heart attack at her Salisbury home in 1989 at the age of sixty-nine.

Bibliography: A collection of Elizabeth Koontz's papers is held in the Thomas F. Holgate Library, Bennett College, Greensboro, North Carolina. An autobiographical essay by Koontz appears in Lynn Gilbert and Gaylen Moore, eds., *Particular Passions: Women Who Have Shaped Our Times* (1981). For her educational philosophy, see Koontz, "Why Teachers Are Militant," *Educational Digest* 33 (January 1968), pp. 12–14; and "New Priorities and Old Prejudices," *Educational Digest* 36 (May 1971), pp. 32–33. Also of interest is Koontz's article, "Women as a Minority Group," in Mary Lou Thompson, ed., *Voices of the New Feminism* (1970). Biographical material is found in *Current Biography Yearbook* (1969), pp. 244–46. Obituaries appeared in the *Washington Post* on January 7, 1989, and the *New York Times* on January 8, 1989.

SHERYL COZART

KRASNER, Lee. October 27, 1908–June 19, 1984. Artist.

As if to validate the abstract expressionist dictum that the artist and the art are inseparable, Lee Krasner's paintings and collages reflect aspects of her life and character. "I think my painting is so biographical," she remarked to writer Cindy Nemser in 1973, "if anybody can take the trouble to read it." However difficult and disturbing it often was, such revelation is crucial to an art that places the highest value on individual authenticity—a quality with which Krasner was amply endowed.

A native of Brooklyn, New York, Lena (later Lenore, then Lee) was Joseph and Anna Krassner's fifth surviving child, and the first of the immigrant Russian Jewish couple's six children to be born in the United States. Her parents managed a fish and produce store and kept an Orthodox home. Krasner (who changed the spelling of her family name in the 1940s) was observant during her childhood, but soon she manifested an aversion to dogma. Later, art would become her equivalent of religion, and she embraced it with the fervor of a convert. After finishing grammar school, for reasons that always remained unclear to her, she decided to become an artist. Her parents neither encouraged nor discouraged her, as long as she was willing to make her own way, which evidently suited her perfectly.

Her early training was at Cooper Union, which she attended from 1926 to 1928, after which she enrolled in the National Academy of Design. Her headstrong, independent character often set her at odds with her instructors at the conservative academy, where she nevertheless received a thorough grounding in drawing, painting, and design. After graduating in 1932, Krasner took college courses toward a teaching certificate and worked as a model and waitress. In spite of the onset of the Depression, she did not give up hope of becoming a full-time professional artist. That goal seemed more attainable when the New Deal created art patronage programs. Like many of her contemporaries, she would depend on government work, principally for the Works Progress Administration's Federal Art Project (FAP), until the agencies were disbanded in 1943. In the mid 1930s, under FAP auspices, she painted street scenes, still lifes, and other conventional subjects, and experimented briefly with surrealism.

Despite her professional validation by the FAP, Krasner was dissatisfied with her development. In 1937 she returned to art school, this time at the Eighth Street atelier of the celebrated German émigré Hans Hofmann, who transmitted principles of modernism from Munich and Paris to New York. Under Hofmann's guidance, she developed a neo-cubist style, exhibited with the American Abstract Artists, and rapidly gained credence as a younger-generation modernist. Intense, serious, and ambitious, she prided herself on knowing all the notable members of the city's minuscule avant-garde, so when she was invited to participate in an important group exhibition, she was surprised that the name of one fellow exhibitor, Jackson Pollock, was unfamiliar to her. Impulsively, she went to his studio and asked to see his work. As she later recalled, she was amazed by the creative vigor and emotional intensity of his paintings. Their meeting in late 1941 proved to be decisive for both artists, resulting in a romantic attachment that would lead to their marriage four years later and a mutually enriching professional relationship, although no children.

During their early years together, Krasner underwent a profound reappraisal of her artistic direction. "I was much more struck by what he was about; it opened a new channel, a new avenue for me," she told the journalist Grace Glueck ("Scenes from a Marriage," p. 59). Nevertheless, although she acknowledged Pollock's superior gifts, she did not become his follower. The intuitive nature of Pollock's approach helped free Krasner's art from formalist strictures, while her discerning eye and keen judgment—as well as her single-minded dedication to promoting his career—proved invaluable to his success.

After she and Pollock married in October 1945 and moved from New York City to a homestead in The Springs, a hamlet in the town of East Hampton, Long Island, Krasner used a small upstairs room as her primary studio. Devoting much of her time and energy to Pollock, she had only two solo exhibitions and two group shows before a 1955 exhibition of large-scale collages at the Stable Gallery in Manhattan reestablished her as one of the foremost abstract artists of her generation.

The following year Krasner abruptly changed direction, adopting a sensuous painterly style in which human, animal, and plant forms play prominent roles. Often alluding to the natural world's cycle of birth and death, the canvases are simultaneously seductive and ominous, life affirming and morbid. One such painting, later titled *Prophecy*, was on her easel in July 1956 when she left for a trip to Europe. Her relationship with Pollock was in ruins: he was drinking heavily and had taken a lover; and he was no longer painting, while her work was progressing rapidly. At this crisis point, Pollock was killed in an automobile accident and Krasner was left with the emotional aftermath. Many of these conflicts and their subsequent confrontation and resolution are reflected in her work, which often seems to have served as an antidote to her conscious grief, as in her lyrical *Earth Green* series of 1957–59, and an outlet for her repressed anger, as in the subsequent *Night Journey* series.

Krasner's progress was interrupted in late 1962 when she suffered a near-fatal brain aneurysm; this and subsequent bouts of ill health hampered her work for nearly two years. By this time she had established a residence in Manhattan, but she spent several months a year in The Springs, where she now worked in Pollock's former studio. In the 1960s and 1970s Krasner continued to refine the nature-derived imagery she had first explored in the gestural arabesques of the *Earth Green* paintings, emphasizing their calligraphic qualities and later sharpening their edges to resemble cutout collage elements.

Following major solo exhibitions, including a retrospective at the Whitechapel Gallery in London (1965) and the Whitney Museum of American Art in New York (1973), together with important exposure in commercial galleries, she emerged from her sometimes stifling role as Mrs. Jackson Pollock and achieved recognition for her own contributions to modern American art. Chief among them is her singular collage aesthetic. In 1976 she made another major collage series, this time incorporating drawings from her days as a Hofmann student nearly forty years earlier. With titles based on conjugations of the verb *to see,* the series alludes to vision and revision, forcefully affirming the cyclic nature of Krasner's art and life.

That life ended in June 1984 in New York Hospital, where Krasner, who had been in ill health for several years, died at the age of seventy-five. The previous October her first full retrospective exhibition in the United States had opened at Houston's Museum of Fine Arts. Sadly, she did not live to see the show travel to New York's Museum of Modern Art in December 1984. Under the terms of Krasner's will, the bulk of her estate was used to establish the Pollock-Krasner Foundation, a philanthropic agency that gives financial support to visual artists. A separate provision enabled the Stony Brook Foundation to operate her Springs property as the Pollock-Krasner House and Study Center, a historic site and research collection. In 1994, in recognition of both artists' outstanding contributions to American culture, the National Park Service designated the property a National Historic Landmark. Thus, in addition to her art, Krasner left a living legacy that benefits succeeding generations of artists, and a home and studio that continue to inspire admiration for her and Pollock's achievements.

Bibliography: Krasner's personal papers are held by the Archives of American Art, Smithsonian Institution, Washington, D.C. The collection also contains transcripts of interviews with Krasner by Dorothy Gees Seckler (1964, 1967–68), Barbara Rose (1966), Dolores Holmes (1972), and others. The interview with Cindy Nemser, quoted above, was published in "A Conversation with Lee Krasner," *Arts Magazine,* April 1973, pp. 43–48. See also Grace Glueck, "Scenes from a Marriage: Krasner & Pollock," *Art News,* December 1981, pp. 57–61. Additional statements are included in Eleanor Munro's *Originals: American Women Artists* (1979). A catalogue raisonné of Krasner's work, compiled and annotated by Ellen G. Landau, with a detailed biographical chronology by Jeffrey D. Grove, was published by Harry N. Abrams in 1995. Its archive is in the collection of the Pollock-Krasner Study Center, which also contains photographs, publications, oral histories, and other documentary material related to Krasner. In her book *Einstein's Wife: Work and Marriage in the Lives of Five Great Twentieth-Century Women* (1995), Andrea Gabor offers a brief, colorful, and strongly partisan account of Krasner's life. Robert Hobbs's monograph, *Lee Krasner* (1993), is an excellent introduction to Krasner and her work, while the same author's more recent monograph, also titled *Lee Krasner* (1999), features a detailed analysis of her artistic, psychological, and philosophical development. An obituary appeared in the *New York Times* on June 21, 1984.

HELEN A. HARRISON

KUHLMAN, Kathryn Johanna. May 9, 1907–February 20, 1976. Evangelist, faith healer, writer.

Kathryn Johanna Kuhlman, who was born in or near Concordia, Missouri, became globally known as a controversial yet much beloved evangelist and healer. In the last decade of her life, she was widely regarded as the most sought-after healing evangelist in the country, her only close competitor being Oral Roberts. Kathryn was the third of four children of Joseph Adolph Kuhlman, a farmer and the mayor of Concordia, and Emma Walkenhorst Kuhlman, both of whom descended from German immigrants. After finishing the tenth grade at Concordia High School, Kathryn began traveling with her older sister and brother-in-law in their itinerant ministry in the western United States. Eventually, conflicts within her sister's marriage, along with Kuhlman's dislike for her brother-in-law, led her to branch out in a ministry on her own, accompanied by her faithful pianist Helen Gulliford. It appears that while out West, despite her later disavowing any theological education, Kuhlman briefly attended two Bible schools: Simpson Bible Institute in Seattle, Washington (1924–26), and Lighthouse of International Foursquare Evangelism (LIFE) Bible School in Los Angeles, California, run by AIMEE SEMPLE MCPHERSON (1926).

Though raised amid Baptist and Methodist influences, Kuhlman despised denominational boundaries and strove to reach people from all walks of life with her gospel of a miracle-working God. The first major phase of her evangelistic career began at the age of twenty-six, when she settled in Denver in 1933. She first preached in the Kuhlman Revival Tabernacle; within two years she was holding services in the 2,000-seat Denver Revival Tabernacle. During these years she also developed a radio ministry, which helped her become well known beyond the bounds of her own auditorium. In 1938, her ministry was nearly destroyed by her marriage to fellow evangelist Burroughs Allen Waltrip, who left his first wife and children to marry her. Many of her supporters, believing the union to be adulterous, turned against her; more were dismayed when she and Waltrip separated and then divorced in 1947. She never remarried or bore any children, and throughout the rest of her life she refused to discuss the events of those years.

The second phase of Kuhlman's ministry started in 1947, when she launched a new healing ministry in Franklin, Pennsylvania, where she had been ministering alone since leaving Waltrip. In 1948, she moved to Pittsburgh and began holding regular religious services in Carnegie Hall and the local First Presbyterian Church. In these years, in which she continued to speak daily on the radio, her services came to focus especially on healing. Like other faith healing evangelists such as William Branham and Oral Roberts, Kuhlman called out diseases that she believed were being healed in certain locations of the audience. Participants often swooned as she pointed her arm in their direction or prayed for them, and many testified joyously to her healing presence. Although she maintained that she was simply an ordinary person who loved God, her studied gestures, theatrical cadences, frizzy red hair, tall slender frame, and signature long white dresses lent her a spectacular, almost ethereal, mystique. She first received national notice in 1950 with an admiring piece published in *Redbook,* and other media attention (both positive and negative) followed. As her fame grew, Kuhlman traveled virtually nonstop, visiting cities and towns across the nation as well as overseas.

The third phase of her ministry commenced in 1965, when she began hosting regular services in the 2,500-seat Pasadena Civic Auditorium and then, when that venue proved too small, the 7,000-seat Los Angeles Shrine Auditorium, which she filled for ten years. She retained her Pittsburgh residence during this time, however, and continued holding frequent miracle services there as well. That same decade of cross-country travel also witnessed the continuation of Kuhlman's radio broadcasts—four thousand radio programs in all—and the launching of her highly successful television show, *I Believe in Miracles,* which aired on CBS. During the 1960s and early 1970s, Kuhlman also wrote several best-selling books, including *I Believe in Miracles* (1962), *God Can Do It Again* (1969), and *Nothing Is Impossible with God* (1974).

Kuhlman's popularity rose at the same time as American Protestantism and Catholicism saw the rise of the charismatic movement—an ecumenical child of Pentecostalism that emphasized ecstatic religious experience, prophecy, and healing within more traditionally staid worship settings. In a movement that tutored women to be submissive to husbands and male pastors, Kuhlman's prominence as a female leader was unique and unquestionably contributed to the aspersions cast upon her throughout her career. Yet her self-deprecating manner—she described herself as a "yielded vessel" of God—and repeated assurances that she was not usurping male power enabled many leading charismatic men to support her (and thus receive desirable airtime on her radio and TV broadcasts) as an exemplar of Christian womanhood. Besides the claims of miracles received through her prayers, thousands of people were "slain in the spirit" (a Pentecostal and charismatic term for a kind of holy trance) as she touched their foreheads or simply waved her arm in their direction.

Like many faith healers and flamboyant evangelists, Kuhlman was often attacked by critics in the press, as well as the church, as a trickster and a phony. Long scandalized by her ill-fated marriage to Waltrip, she was lambasted by critics for her luxurious lifestyle, the lawsuits filed against her by former staff members, and her supposed sexual trysts. Ever in search of gloomy accounts of people who had faked healings or who had otherwise not been healed in her religious services, members of the press frequently seized upon her as an imposter out to swindle the naive out of their hard-earned cash. Yet countless numbers remained devoted to Kuhlman as a paradigm of Christian love, and they lauded her for her unfailing energy and willingness to touch and sit among the sick, poor, and forgotten of American society. For many years she was the most visible woman in all of American religion, and her impact on other religious women wishing to serve in public ministry was and is immense. Along with Phoebe Palmer and Aimee Semple McPherson, she was one of the most prominent female evangelists in modern history.

In late 1975, Kuhlman's grueling schedule caught up with her. Diagnosed with heart disease, she underwent surgery at Hillcrest Medical Center in Tulsa, Oklahoma. Less than two months later, on February 20, 1976, she died there at the age of sixty-eight. The Pittsburgh-based Kathryn Kuhlman Foundation continues to support missions, churches, and other religious projects established or aided by Kuhlman across the world. Her body is buried at Forest Lawn Memorial Park in Glendale, California.

Bibliography: Kuhlman's papers are located in the Billy Graham Center Archives at Wheaton College in Wheaton, Illinois. This collection, called the Kathryn Kuhlman Foundation Records, includes correspondence, personal calendars, photographs, an oral history interview, videotapes, audiotapes, films, slides, scrapbooks, newspaper and magazine clippings, articles, memorabilia, news releases, and release forms relating to the work of the foundation and Kathryn Kuhlman. Several popular biographies, most of them hagiographical in tone, have been published; these include Helen Kooiman Hosier, *Kathryn Kuhlman* (1976); Jamie Buckingham, *Daughter of Destiny* (1976); Roberts Liardon, *A Spiritual Biography of God's Miracle Working Power* (1990); and Wayne E. Warner, *Kathryn Kuhlman: The Woman behind the Miracles* (1993). Doctoral dissertations on Kuhlman include Katherine Jan Leisering, "An Historical and Critical Study of the Pittsburgh Preaching Career of Kathryn Kuhlman" (Ohio University, 1981); and Todd Vernon Lewis, "Charismatic Communication and Faith Healers: A Critical Study of Rhetorical Behavior" (Louisiana State University and Agricultural and Mechanical College, 1980). Articles in popular magazines written during Kuhlman's life include William A. Nolen, "In Search of a Miracle," *McCall's,* September 1974, pp. 82–83, 101–8; and Louise Farr, "Divine Ms. K.," *Ms.*, January 1975, pp. 12–15. For a general discussion of charismatic and evangelical women during the years of Kuhlman's prominence, see R. Marie Griffith, *God's Daughters: Evangelical Women and the Power of Submission* (1997). Earlier contextual information may be gleaned from Janette Hassey, *No Time for Silence: Evangelical Women in Public Ministry around the Turn of the Century* (1986), and Edith L. Blumhofer, *Aimee Semple McPherson: Everybody's Sister* (1994). An obituary appeared in the *New York Times* on February 22, 1976.

R. MARIE GRIFFITH

KUHN, Irene Corbally. January 15, 1898–December 30, 1995. Journalist.

Journalistic pioneer Irene Corbally Kuhn worked in several mass media over seven decades and on five continents. She interviewed Charlie Chaplin in Paris, showed MARGARET SANGER around Shanghai, and covered the Lindbergh baby murder trial. Born in New York City, Irene Corbally grew up in a capacious Greenwich Village brownstone, doted on by an extended Irish American family headed by her maternal grandfather, who operated a prosperous cooperage. When her mother, Josephine Connor, had married Patrick Corbally, a cooper from County Cork, the groom had moved in with the Connors. Patrick died suddenly when Irene was twelve and her sole sibling, Clarence, was four; Irene's grandparents, two single aunts, and four uncles (before each brother married and moved out) helped raise her.

Winning top prize in a citywide essay contest at age twelve sold the star St. Veronica's School student on journalism. She attended Marymount College from 1917 to 1918 and also studied at Columbia University before becoming a cub reporter at the *Syracuse Herald.* A short stint at the *New York Daily News* followed before she landed a job writing ad copy in Paris in 1921. When that job fizzled, she rebounded as fashion editor of the *Chicago Tribune* Paris edition.

Incurable wanderlust sent her sailing to China that December with colleague Peggy Hull. Irene snagged a job as a feature writer on Shanghai's English-language *Evening Star,* the afternoon counterpart of the *China Press.* In Shanghai she thrived amid the lively social scene of the International Settlement where pampered foreigners clustered. On June 12, 1922, she wed *Press* news editor and former Chicago newspaperman Bert L. Kuhn. She temporarily abandoned journalism and China for housewifery in Hawaii after she became pregnant, but boredom and finances impelled her to work as Honolulu correspondent for the International News Service. Three days before the birth of her only child, Rene Leilani Kuhn (March 2, 1923), Irene scooped the world about a devastating tidal wave, feigning labor pains to persuade a nervous telegraph officer to let her file her story. Kuhn's world collapsed, however, when Bert died mysteriously in Shanghai in February 1926, while she was visiting the United States with their baby. She was convinced but unable to prove that Bert's death resulted from his shadowy work for U.S. naval intelligence.

Work proved to be the despairing Kuhn's salvation. "You can never tell from the good face a woman presents to the world by day when she has to front it alone for her child," she wrote years later, "how she has agonized through the night, fighting the horrid shapes her imagination conjures up—poverty, dependence, possible illness or injury" (*Assigned to Adventure,* p. 408). The next two decades she ricocheted between coasts and media in jobs that capitalized on her versatility. She immediately returned to the *New York Daily Mirror* but rejoined the *Daily News* in 1927. In 1929 she finally got some respite from covering murders and scandals, and from her own grief, by taking a six-month leave to write a beach column for the *Honolulu Star Bulletin;* then she boomeranged back to the *News* as New York's only female "rewrite man." A Fox Films contract next lured her to Hollywood, where her most memorable script was *The Mask of Fu Manchu* for MGM in 1932.

Kuhn missed the straightforwardness of newspapers, however; in 1933 to 1936 she wrote features for the *New York World-Telegram and Sun* and freelanced magazine features. Her short-lived second marriage, to *World-Telegram* features editor Gerald B. Breitigam, whom she wed on December 28, 1935, prompted her to write in six weeks her best-selling memoir *Assigned to Adventure* (1938) after he absconded with her life savings. In 1939, over brunch at the Algonquin Hotel, Kuhn co-founded the Overseas Press Club with eight fellow foreign correspondents. She twice served as vice president of the organization, which sponsors a scholarship in her name.

In 1924 Kuhn had made what was probably the first radio broadcast in China, and in the late 1930s she resumed her radio career. She hosted one of the first interview shows, *Irene Kuhn's Feature Page of the Air,* for the Mutual Broadcasting Company in 1938–39. At NBC, where she became director of program promotion in 1940, she originated *Good Neighbor* programs about Latin America and worked as assistant director of information from 1944 to 1948. During sabbaticals in 1940 and 1944, she served as associate director of publicity for Thomas E. Dewey's presidential campaigns. In the waning days of World War II, she flew to Chungking as an NBC war correspondent. On September 21, 1945, she became the first person to broadcast from newly liberated Shanghai, aboard the radio ship USS *Rocky Mount.* After the war, Kuhn teamed up with daughter Rene on the

NBC talk show *The Kuhns* from 1946 to 1948, and she continued a solo show through 1949.

Irene Kuhn left NBC in 1950 to resume writing. Her conservative column on world issues was nationally syndicated for nearly a quarter century, though it went through several title changes: "The Way Things Are" (1956–61); "Straight Talk" (1961–62); and "It's My Opinion" (1963–78). Into her nineties, despite failing eyesight, Kuhn pounded out dozens of travel articles on a Royal manual typewriter in the book-lined Greenwich Village apartment she inhabited from 1938 to 1993.

Besides possessing a robust sense of humor and an occasionally sharp temper, the five-foot-five, brown-eyed brunette was an excellent listener who all her long life kept the many friends she made in the newspaper, book, magazine, movie, and radio businesses. Kuhn's adventurous life, however, belied her conservative nature. She proclaimed women unfit for major political office and preached to single career women what she never practiced: true fulfillment could be found only as a full-time wife and mother. Her sentiments were typical of the first generation of post-suffrage women who refocused from collective gender goals to individual careers, largely renouncing feminism to fit into male-dominated professions. Her fervent anti-communism in the 1950s also reflected the times, as when, in a widely circulated and controversial article in the *American Legion Magazine,* she accused the *New York Times Book Review* of promoting communism. When she died of a stroke at ninety-seven in the Concord, Massachusetts, nursing home where she lived the last year of her life, Kuhn's friends and colleagues recalled "her humanity and integrity in a ruthlessly competitive business."

Bibliography: The Irene Corbally Kuhn Papers (1875–1986), which include photographs and audio recordings, are at the American Heritage Center at the University of Wyoming, Laramie. In addition to *Assigned to Adventure* (1938), Kuhn wrote two book chapters: "They Wanted the Vote," in Overseas Press Club, *The Inside Story* (1940); and "Tea and Ashes," in Overseas Press Club, *Deadline Delayed* (1947). She also wrote articles in such magazines as the *American Mercury, Good Housekeeping, Cosmopolitan, Reader's Digest, Gourmet, Travel/Holiday,* and the *Citizen* (the official journal of the Citizens Councils of America, a white supremacist group), and co-wrote Raymond de Jaegher's memoir, *The Enemy Within: An Eyewitness Account of the Communist Conquest of China* (1952). Her article accusing the *New York Times Book Review* of promoting communism appeared in the *American Legion Magazine,* January 1951, pp. 18–19, 53+. Biographical information on Kuhn is found in Ishbel Ross, *Ladies of the Press* (1936); Julia Edwards, *Women of the World: The Great Foreign Correspondents* (1988); and Elinor Griest, "Irene Corbally Kuhn," *Overseas Press Club Bulletin,* February 1996, p. 5, which contains the final quotation. See also Linda Lumsden, "'You're a Tough Guy, Mary—and a First-Rate Newspaperman': Gender and Women Journalists in the 1920s and 1930s," *Journalism and Mass Communication Quarterly* 72 (Winter 1995), pp. 913–21. Rene Kuhn Bryant supplied additional biographical information in a telephone interview. An obituary appeared in the *New York Times* on December 31, 1995.

LINDA J. LUMSDEN

KUHN, Margaret Eliza (Maggie). August 3, 1905–April 22, 1995. Political activist, feminist.

Margaret Eliza "Maggie" Kuhn, founder of the Gray Panthers and self-styled "wrinkled radical," was born in Buffalo, New York, the elder of the two children of Minnie Louise Kooman and Samuel Frederick Kuhn. The Kooman family was part of Buffalo's Dutch community, while the Kuhns were recent German immigrants to East Aurora, a town near Buffalo. Minnie Kooman, who had attended business college after high school, helped run the family dry-goods store in Buffalo prior to her marriage. Samuel Kuhn left high school to work for the Bradstreet Company credit firm as an office boy and rose to the position of manager.

Shortly after Maggie's birth, the family moved to Memphis, Tennessee, where Samuel Kuhn managed a branch office of Dun and Bradstreet. Her brother, Sam, was born in 1908. At an early age Kuhn absorbed her mother's disdain for racial segregation. Samuel Kuhn was an active Presbyterian, deeply involved in local church affairs, which he regarded as a civic duty. This thread of church-centered work would run through Maggie Kuhn's life as well.

Kuhn's father was transferred several times during her childhood, and by her high school years, the family resided in Cleveland. She graduated from West High School in 1922 and attended Flora Stone Mather College, the women's college at Cleveland's Western Reserve University. While there, she organized a college chapter of the League of Women Voters.

Kuhn's years at college also signaled the emergence of her unconventional side. In her junior year, she conducted a sexual relationship with her minister's son, the first of a number of passionate affairs during her life. Cautioned by her Gamma Delta Tau sorority sisters about the potential scandal of a pregnancy, Kuhn secured a diaphragm, a bold act for a single woman at that time.

Kuhn graduated from Mather College with a degree in sociology in 1926 and began a twenty-year career with the Young Women's Christian Association (YWCA), first as a volunteer and then as a paid staff member. In Cleveland and later Philadelphia, where her family relocated in 1930, Kuhn actively recruited young working women for

YWCA classes and activities. She also led a class on marriage and human sexuality, which featured frank discussions on birth control, sexual pleasure, and the satisfactions of single life. During those years Kuhn maintained her sexually active lifestyle: "I enjoyed male companionship immensely and felt free to enjoy sex. I enjoyed a good love affair, but when it was over I was never devastated by the breakup" (Kuhn, *No Stone Unturned,* p. 73).

During World War II, Kuhn moved to New York to be the YWCA's program coordinator for its division of the United Service Organizations (USO), providing services for civilian women who toiled in defense plants. After the war ended, Kuhn organized USO job fairs and counseling sessions on work and unemployment relief for the rising numbers of jobless women.

By 1950, both of her parents were in their eighties and her brother had been hospitalized for mental illness. Kuhn moved back to Philadelphia, but commuted to New York City, where she was the assistant secretary of the United Presbyterian Church's Social Education and Action Program, which she described as the church's social conscience. Kuhn edited the journal *Social Progress,* which educated church members on social and political issues, and in 1954 wrote a pamphlet called *The Christian Woman and Her Household,* which encouraged women to conduct consumer boycotts against businesses that treated workers unfairly. Through the 1950s and 1960s, Kuhn sought to raise the consciousness of church officials, ministers, and the laity on issues including civil rights for African Americans, women's rights, and U.S. participation in the Vietnam War. On January 15, 1968, Kuhn participated in the Jeannette Rankin Brigade, the first organized women's protest against the Vietnam War.

In 1970, Kuhn's outrage at her forced retirement at age sixty-five provided the impetus for the founding of the Gray Panthers. "Something clicked in my mind," she recalled, "and I saw that my problem was not mine alone. I came to feel a great kinship with my peers and to believe that something was fundamentally wrong with a system that had no use for people like us" (ibid., pp. 129–30). She called a meeting of five other women who were in the same position. This caucus of social activists called a series of meetings that culminated in the formation of the Gray Panthers, a political action association of elders devoted to the pressing social issues of the time. The group drew on the Black Panthers' name and its philosophy that, according to Kuhn, "social change must be systematic and societal" (Gilbert and Moore, p. 104).

Direct actions became one of the organization's hallmarks. In 1971, Kuhn marched to the White House with seventy-five delegates of the Black House Conference on Aging, which addressed the disproportionate problems of African American elders in the United States. Police on horseback broke up the march, and Kuhn was knocked to the ground. The action drew attention to the group, and their issues were added to the agenda of the Second White House Conference on Aging, which also agreed to more minority representation.

By 1972, thanks to Kuhn's media savvy, the Gray Panthers became nationally known, with Kuhn its most recognized spokesperson. She forged alliances with consumer advocate Ralph Nader, TISH SOMMERS of the Older Women's League, Benjamin Spock, and U.S. Representative Claude Pepper of Florida, and spoke out for national health care, nursing home reform, alternatives to nursing homes for the elderly, an end to negative stereotyping of the aged in the media, and open discussions on the sexuality of people over sixty. At its peak in the 1980s, the Gray Panthers had more than sixty thousand members in its 120 chapters and at large. Kuhn continued to be active and visible in the organization through the mid 1990s, serving as the Gray Panthers' convener despite being increasingly incapacitated by arthritis, osteoporosis, and loss of vision. She died at home in Philadelphia at the age of eighty-nine.

Maggie Kuhn's unique approach to age discrimination, shaped by the civil rights movement of the 1950s and the liberation and anti-war movements of the 1960s, was to combat it utilizing collective, public action by old and young, women and men together. Her vision of the Gray Panthers as a radical, integrated organization, whose members took up issues of broad social significance, as well as her own public life, redefined the role of elders, and older women in particular, in the United States.

Bibliography: The Gray Panthers Papers are held at the Urban Archives, Temple University, and Maggie Kuhn's papers are located at the Presbyterian Historical Association, both in Philadelphia. Kuhn's major works include *The Christian Woman and Her Household: Four Study Programs on the Economic Responsibilities of Christians* (1954); *Get Out There and Do Something about Injustice* (1972); "Gray Panthers," in George L. Maddox, ed., *Encyclopedia of Aging* (1987); *No Stone Unturned: The Life and Times of Maggie Kuhn,* with Christine Long and Laura Quinn (1991); and *You Can't Be Human Alone: Handbook on Group Procedures for the Local Church* (1956). See also Dieter Hessel, ed., *Maggie Kuhn on Aging: A Dialogue* (1977). Other sources of interest include "Alumni Profile: Kuhn," *Reserve,* Spring 1980; "Age Springs Eternal: Hold That Gray Panther!" *Washington Post,* December 4, 1981; and Lynn Gilbert and Gaylen Moore, *Particular Passions: Talks with Women Who Have Shaped Our Times* (1981). An obituary appeared in the *New York Times* on April 23, 1995.

SUSAN ENGLANDER

KUROSE, Aki. February 11, 1925–May 24, 1998. Peace activist, teacher.

Akiko "Aki" Kato was born in Seattle's International District, the third of four children of Harutoshi Kato and Murako Kawamura Okamura. After immigrating to the United States from Japan in the early 1900s, her father worked as a porter on the railroads on the Pacific Coast and in the restaurant industry while her mother finished her college education in Washington state. Aki attended Seattle public schools, but her senior year at Garfield High School was interrupted when, on February 19, 1942, President Franklin Delano Roosevelt signed Executive Order 9066, which ordered the wartime internment of 120,000 Japanese Americans, including her family. Behind barbed wire and armed guards in the "assembly center," Aki finished her high school education at the Puyallup Fairgrounds in Washington. Later, she and her family were moved to a "relocation center" in Minidoka, Idaho.

A bright high school student, Aki was eligible for the Student Relocation Service offered by the American Friends Service Committee (AFSC), which arranged for her to attend Friends University in Wichita, Kansas. Floyd Schmoe, a Quaker peace activist who worked for the AFSC, arranged for her to go to college. After the war she returned to Seattle, where she assisted Schmoe in running the Seattle branch of AFSC. She also accompanied him on his mission to Hiroshima after the war to rebuild houses. In 1949 Aki married Junelow "Junx" Kurose, a Boeing machinist, and between 1950 and 1959 they had six children—Hugo, Ruthann, Rolland ("Rollie"), Guy, Marie, and Paul—as well as several foster children.

In the late 1940s, Kurose worked on anti-war projects and cared for the women known as "Hiroshima maidens"—victims of the bombing in Hiroshima who had come to Seattle for treatment. In the postwar era, she worked on civil rights campaigns and at Head Start, a child development program that served low-income children and their families. Working at Head Start motivated her to return to school, and in 1972 she obtained her bachelor's degree in physics from the University of Washington. In 1981 she received her master's degree in education there at age fifty-six.

Kurose first worked as a teacher at the Martin Luther King Jr. Elementary School in the Central Area. When a federal mandate ordered teacher desegregation in public schools, she was transferred from her mostly African American school to the largely white Laurelhurst Elementary School, where she was the first nonwhite teacher. Using "unconventional" pedagogical strategies to teach science, Kurose stimulated the students' enthusiasm and interest. Surrounded by telescopes, aquariums, and tangrams, Kurose would test her class projects in her Madrona home. Many parents initially feared their children would adopt a Japanese accent from Kurose but eventually the teacher's and students' love of learning dispelled the parents' doubts.

Kurose helped transform the school's curriculum by integrating multicultural and peace education, using the classroom to teach the younger generation about using nonviolence against oppression. Her Quaker faith reinforced these views. She once declared, "It's not just going out and saying 'peace, peace, peace,' but really working to make sure that there's justice for all" (Narasaki, p. 1). Her mission for peace was also influenced by her having been deprived of her constitutional rights as a United States citizen when she was interned during her teen years. Kurose insisted that to achieve justice for all people, she must try to change the conditions that breed injustice. Like Martin Luther King, she believed that justice cannot be obtained without peace, and she passed this vision on to her students.

Untainted by the politics of the Seattle school system, Kurose transcended years of racism and doubts about her credentials to be hailed as the "Mother Teresa" of Seattle's public schools. Throughout most of her teaching years, this benevolent, saintly individual faced another challenge: fighting against multiple cancers in her breasts, bones, and lungs. Kurose retired from Seattle Public Schools in 1996, and four years later she was the first Asian American woman to have a Seattle Public School named in her honor.

Oral historian Studs Terkel profiled Kurose as one of seventy outstanding older Americans in his book *Coming of Age: The Story of Our Century by Those Who've Lived It* (1995) and honored her work in education and community activism. The trauma of being imprisoned in an internment camp during World War II and being racially stereotyped as a teacher in Seattle's schools did not break her spirit. Throughout her life, Kurose not only possessed a deep, subtle understanding of oppression, but also realized that resistance is both collective and personal. She often said, "If you don't have peace within yourself, learning cannot take place. Let there be peace, and let it begin with me" (Bock, p. 1). Aki Kurose continued to seek greater peace and justice until her death in Seattle in 1998 at the age of seventy-three.

Bibliography: Sources on Aki Kurose include Paula Bock, "Activist Aki Kurose Spent Her Life Working for Peace," May 26, 1998, and Rebekah Denn, "School Name Honors Teacher Who 'Believed in Peace,'" November 2, 1999, both in the *Seattle Times.* See also articles in the *Northeast Asian Weekly* by Jason Truesdell, "'We Would Have to Tell Martin' . . . Years after Civil Rights Leader Dies, His Legacy a Troubled One" (January 22, 1994), and Diane Narasaki, "May Aki Kurose's Work for Peace and Justice Bloom for Generations to Come" (May 30, 1998). The American Friends Service Committee memorialized Kurose in a newsletter article, "Minute of Love and Appreciation for Aki (Akiko) Kurose," June 27, 1998. See also Kevin Ervin, "Sharples School May Be Renamed after Aki Kurose," *Seattle Times*, November 2, 1999. Other information was provided by Ruthann Kurose in interviews on December 3 and December 10, 2001. An obituary appeared in the *Northeast Asian Weekly* on May 30, 1998.

RAHPEE THONGTHIRAJ

KUSHNER, Rose. June 22, 1929–January 7, 1990. Journalist, breast cancer activist.

Perhaps the most dramatic moment of Rose Kushner's life occurred in 1974 when a surgeon told her that she had breast cancer. Furious that Kushner had convinced him to do only a biopsy without a mastectomy, he rattled the rails of her hospital bed. Kushner, puzzled about why this doctor was so confrontational at a time that required compassion, concluded that there was something very wrong with the predominantly male medical profession. For a journalist who, by her own admission, had a streak of stubbornness and a loud voice, she believed she had only one choice: to become a breast cancer activist.

Rose Rehert was born in Baltimore to a middle-class Jewish couple, Israel Rehert, a Latvian-born tailor, and Fannie Gravitz, a housewife originally from Lithuania. Kushner was the youngest of their four children. She would draw on this Jewish heritage throughout her years as an activist.

Kushner was extremely bright, graduating from P.S. 49 in Baltimore in 1946 and then matriculating at McCoy College of Johns Hopkins University as a premedical student. Like many women of her generation, she did not complete her education. She married Harvey Kushner, who later became a business executive, on March 18, 1951. The couple had three children: Gantt (1952), Todd (1956), and Lesley (1958). Throughout these years, Kushner maintained an interest in medical subjects. But when she finally earned a degree, from the University of Maryland in 1972, it was a BS in journalism. One of the topics covered by Kushner during her early years as a journalist was the Vietnam War, which she opposed.

Whether it was generals or physicians, Kushner had little use for authority figures. Thus, when she noticed an "elevation" in her left breast in June 1974, she traveled to several libraries, seeking knowledge about breast cancer. What she learned surprised and horrified her: American surgeons continued to perform the disfiguring Halsted radical mastectomy, a nearly century-old operation that removed the breast, lymph nodes, and chest wall muscles on the side of the cancer. In addition, doctors made the decision to proceed with this operation when their women patients were under anesthesia. If the results of an intraoperative breast biopsy showed cancer, the surgeon simply completed the mastectomy. Women awoke from surgery without knowing if they had lost a breast.

Having also learned that breast surgeons in other countries had begun to perform less extensive procedures in two steps, Kushner decided that she would not have a one-step radical mastectomy if she had cancer. But finding a physician who was willing to follow her unconventional demands was not easy (hence, the response of the surgeon who rattled her bed rails). Kushner consulted nineteen surgeons before finding one who was willing to perform a modified radical mastectomy, which left her chest wall muscles in place.

Rose Kushner had stumbled into the story of her journalistic career. "Vietnam will have to wait," she announced in typical fashion, "while I finish a crusade to tell American women—and through them their doctors—what I have learned" (Kushner to John Cushman, August 11, 1974). By 1975 she had established the Breast Cancer Advisory Center, a counseling service, and had published *Breast Cancer: A Personal History and an Investigative Report*. In an era before such illness narratives were common, Kushner's book frankly described being diagnosed with cancer and losing her breast. But more importantly, she discussed and evaluated the scientific literature. Too many physicians, she argued, had the science all wrong.

In her early years as a breast cancer activist, Kushner was highly confrontational. Gaining access to medical meetings as a journalist, she relentlessly challenged respected physicians, many of whom responded angrily. Upon learning in October 1974 that First Lady Betty Ford was to undergo a one-step operation and possible radical mastectomy, Kushner called the White House to try to change her mind. When Kushner was told, "The President has made his decision," she was livid. "That line," she fumed, "has got to be engraved somewhere as the all-time sexist declaration of no-woman rights" (Kushner to Pat Sweeting, October 2, 1974).

In challenging the authority of the male medical profession, Kushner's actions placed her squarely in the second-wave feminist movement of the 1970s. Yet she was no radical. Happily married to a supportive husband and living in suburban Kensington, Maryland, Kushner rejected the strategies of certain other activists, who called doctors butchers, favored broader social change, or exposed their mastectomy scars on posters. Indeed, Kushner preferred to see herself less as a feminist than as a civil libertarian and consumer advocate.

Women, she believed, deserved to know that some physicians were better informed and more respectful than others. Only these doctors deserved their business.

By the late 1970s, Kushner had become America's best-known breast cancer activist, more an insider than an outsider. In 1979, she was the only nonphysician on a National Cancer Institute consensus panel that declared the one-step Halsted radical mastectomy obsolete. The next year, President Jimmy Carter named her as the first lay member of the National Cancer Advisory Board. As the 1980s progressed, Kushner worked tirelessly with Bernard Fisher and other physicians doing randomized controlled trials of less disfiguring breast cancer treatments, such as lumpectomy. Better science, she predicted, would give women better answers. This belief became one of the basic principles of the National Breast Cancer Coalition (NBCC), the highly successful advocacy organization founded in 1991. In publicizing breast cancer, raising hundreds of millions of dollars for research, and placing laywomen on scientific review panels, the NBCC has built on Kushner's ideas.

Unfortunately, Kushner did not live to see the NBCC. In 1982, she found a skin nodule, indicating that her cancer had spread. Although she took tamoxifen and later underwent radiation therapy, Kushner, in typical fashion, declined chemotherapy, which she believed would do more harm than good. Kushner lived for nine more years, dying of metastatic breast cancer in Washington, D.C., in 1990 at the age of sixty. She lobbied until her death for mammography and other innovations that might spare future women her fate.

Bibliography: Rose Kushner's papers are deposited at the Schlesinger Library, Radcliffe Institute for Advanced Study, Harvard University; the two letters quoted in the text are found there. Books by Kushner include *Breast Cancer: A Personal History and an Investigative Report* (1975); *If You've Thought about Breast Cancer* (1979); *Why Me?* (1982); and *Alternatives* (1984). *If You've Thought about Breast Cancer* continues to be updated and reprinted by Harvey Kushner. Articles and books about Kushner include Ursula Vils, "One Victim with a Mind of Her Own," *Los Angeles Times*, October 16, 1975; Nan Robertson, "A Woman's Crusade against 'One-Step' Breast Surgery," *New York Times*, October 22, 1979; Carol Cancila, "'Mrs. Breast Cancer' Keeps Up the Fight," *American Medical News*, October 11, 1985; Barron H. Lerner, "No Shrinking Violet: Rose Kushner and the Rise of Breast Cancer Activism," *Western Journal of Medicine* 174 (May, 2001), pp. 362–65; and Lerner, *The Breast Cancer Wars: Hope, Fear, and the Pursuit of a Cure in Twentieth-Century America* (2001). An interview with Harvey Kushner, March 18, 1998, also provided significant biographical information on Rose Kushner. An obituary appeared in the *New York Times* on January 10, 1990.

BARRON H. LERNER

L

LA FOLLETTE, Suzanne. June 24, 1893–April 23, 1983. Libertarian feminist, editor, journalist.

Named Clara at birth, Suzanne La Follette was born on her family's thousand-acre ranch in Washington's Snake River Canyon. She was the eldest of seven children of Mary Tabor and William LeRoy La Follette, a wheat rancher, stock farmer, fruit grower, and politician. Convinced that individuals should live free and equal, unfettered by political or social restrictions, La Follette embraced first feminism and then radical libertarianism. La Follette went on to help found the conservative *National Review* in the 1950s and organize the Conservative Party in the 1960s, defying the assumption that feminism is the exclusive province of liberals or radicals on the left.

When Suzanne was in her teens, her family retired from farming and moved to nearby Pullman. In 1910 her father was elected to the U.S. House of Representatives as a progressive Republican; he served until his vocal opposition to American entry into World War I scuttled his reelection bid in 1918. While in Washington, D.C., Suzanne finished her education at Trinity College in 1915 and immersed herself in politics, working in her father's congressional office as well as the senatorial offices of his first cousin, Senator Robert M. La Follette of Wisconsin, the famous progressive. When Senator La Follette moved in with Suzanne's family, the shared household became a classroom in a progressive politics that challenged capitalist excesses and the political privilege of big industry. All the La Follette adults saw themselves as feminists and supported Suzanne's participation in the suffrage movement.

When her family returned to Washington State after her father left Congress, Suzanne La Follette launched an independent career. In 1919 she joined the staff of the liberal weekly the *Nation* and worked under the supervision of well-known libertarian writer Albert Jay Nock, her most important mentor and philosophical inspiration. At the *Nation,* La Follette first developed her stellar reputation as an energetic editor renowned for elegant prose and devotion to grammatical propriety.

In 1920, Nock recruited La Follette to his new publication, the *Freeman,* which championed classical liberalism and radical individualism. At this point La Follette retreated from the progressive partisan politics practiced by her family and began measuring society by the liberty it provided to individuals, especially women. Believing that the state would be unable to prevent class exploitation, she championed free markets and equal opportunity to maximize liberty for men and women alike.

After the *Freeman* folded in 1924, La Follette published *Concerning Women* (1926), a book that extended libertarian principles to feminism and challenged both sex stereotypes and traditional feminist strategies, especially the crusade for political rights. She wrote: "It is a misfortune of the woman's movement that it has succeeded in securing political rights for women at the very period when political rights are worth less than they have been at any time since the eighteenth century" (p. 268). Arguing that industrial regulation had simply exacerbated female economic dependence, she asserted that only an unregulated marketplace featuring complete economic freedom would ameliorate sex-based economic inequalities. Echoing anarchist feminist EMMA GOLDMAN, La Follette also attacked state regulation of marriage, arguing that it reduced women to chattel. Utterly committed to her work, La Follette herself never married or had children.

The publication of *Concerning Women* attracted scant attention, which La Follette attributed to a dwindling concern for the "woman issue." More likely, La Follette's iconoclasm left her outside the debates on sex and gender ideology that raged through the 1920s. With her demands that marriage be abolished and that the state be reduced to its barest functions, La Follette would have had little patience for discussions that parsed the best strategies for politically empowering women or reconciling the demands of marriage, motherhood, and careers.

La Follette's experience with *Concerning Women* did not deter her from embarking on her next book project, a history of American art and architecture from colonial times to the 1920s. *Art in America* (1929) grew out of a year she spent in France studying art with American painter and critic Walter Pach. Though the onset of the Great Depression overshadowed its publication, *Art in America* eventually became a classic in its field. In 1930, La Follette resuscitated the ideology of the *Freeman* in a new publication that soon collapsed under financial difficulties. Throughout the 1930s, she decried the growth of the New Deal welfare state in the United States and the advance of totalitarianism abroad in pieces for *Scribner's Magazine,* the *New Republic,* the *Nation,* and *Current History.*

In the late 1930s, at the invitation of philosopher John Dewey, La Follette served as secretary for the Committee for the Defense of Leon Trotsky, which was formed in the wake of the Moscow trials to investigate Stalin's charges against Trotsky and other former comrades. After coauthoring the Dewey Commission's final report, *Not Guilty* (1938), La Follette found herself exhausted and disillusioned, stripped of any vestige of sympathy for the Soviet Union. After this ordeal La Follette won a Guggenheim grant and spent 1937 to 1941 researching a book on the economics of art, a work she never finished. In 1940 she returned to the magazine world and served as managing editor of *American Mercury.*

Anti-communism became La Follette's overwhelming concern in the years after the Trotsky commission. From 1943 to 1945 she worked as director of foreign relief programs for the American Federation of Labor, striving to ensure that reconstruction efforts would exclude communists. In 1950 she revived the *Freeman* for a third time, though anti-communism rather than libertarianism dominated this publication. La Follette used its pages to defend Senator Joseph McCarthy and attack those who minimized the communist threat, departing the publication in 1953 after political clashes with other staff members. Two years later she joined William F. Buckley Jr., whom she had helped recruit to the *Freeman,* to start the *National Review,* which knit together conservatives with widely divergent priorities. No publication was more important to the ascendance of conservative intellectualism in the late twentieth century. La Follette retired as managing editor in 1959.

La Follette divided her retirement years between the Chelsea Hotel in New York City and Bucks County, Pennsylvania. In 1964, she ran for Congress on the Conservative Party ticket, garnering more than fourteen hundred votes in New York's Nineteenth District. To a reporter who wondered how she reconciled her conservative loyalties with her progressive pedigree, she declared that her politics had not changed over the years: "I haven't moved. The world has moved to the left of me." After a long illness, she died in California at the Stanford University Hospital Nursing Home at the age of eighty-nine and was buried near her parents and siblings in Colfax, Washington.

Bibliography: Suzanne La Follette's papers can be found in the La Follette Family Collection at the Library of Congress. Alice S. Rossi, *The Feminist Papers: From Adams to de Beauvoir* (1973), provides a short biography of La Follette accompanying an excerpt from *Concerning Women* (1926). James L. Cooper and Sheila McIsaac Cooper, *The Roots of American Feminist Thought* (1973), also provides biographical information and a thorough analysis of her philosophy; it also contains the final quotation on p. 261. In *The Grounding of Modern Feminism* (1987), Nancy F. Cott places La Follette's writings in the larger context of the 1920s. La Follette describes Albert Jay Nock's influence on her writing in the introduction to Nock's *Snoring as a Fine Art and Twelve Other Essays* (1958). Other writers touch on her magazine career: Susan J. Turner, *A History of* The Freeman (1963); John Chamberlain, *A Life with the Printed Word* (1982); and John B. Judis, *William F. Buckley Jr., Patron Saint of the Conservatives* (1988). Obituaries appeared in the *New York Times* on April 27, 1983, and the *National Review* on May 13, 1983.

KIRSTEN DELEGARD

LA MERI. May 13, 1898–January 7, 1988. Dancer, teacher, dance scholar.

La Meri is remembered as one of the world's greatest ethnological dancers, who brought cultures of the world to the United States through her art. She traveled to every continent except Antarctica, learning dances in their native environment. La Meri influenced dance through her ethnological dance school, performances, lectures, and books on the art, history, and instruction of ethnic dancing.

She was born Russell Meriwether Hughes in Louisville, Kentucky, the second of two daughters of Lily Allen, a homemaker, and Russell Meriwether Hughes, an entrepreneur from a wealthy Virginia family, for whom she was named. From an early age, Meriwether was exposed to theater and dance. At the age of four, her family moved to San Antonio, and in public school as well as private lessons she studied the violin, drama, voice, painting, and creative writing. When she was twelve, she discovered dance.

San Antonio's vibrant theater scene introduced Meriwether to many well-known performers, including dancer LOIE FULLER and musical theater star LILLIAN RUSSELL. In 1912, when she attended an Anna Pavlova performance at San Antonio's Grand Opera House, she decided to pursue dance as a career. In 1914 RUTH ST. DENIS, Ted Shawn, and the Denishawn Dancers appeared in town. Swept up into the alluring mysticism of Orientalism, Meriwether propelled herself into researching distant lands. Yet it wasn't until after a performance by La Argentina, a neoclassical Spanish dancer, that she received her first lesson in ethnic dance. She then began to explore the Spanish and Latin American influences in San Antonio.

After her father's death in 1914, she went to New York City to pursue a career as a writer. There, according to her autobiography, she saw MARTHA GRAHAM perform a Javanese dance in the Greenwich Village Follies. She soon returned to Texas, however, and again concentrated on studying ethnic dance; she created her infamous "Peacock Dance," originally inspired by pictures of Gertrude Hoffman. Beginning in 1916 with her enrollment in the College of Industrial Arts (later Texas Woman's University) in Denton, Texas, Meriwether devoted some time to formal education; over the next seven years she also briefly attended Columbia University and Our Lady of the Lake College in San Antonio. But she never obtained a degree, opting instead for the world of dance.

In 1924 Meriwether joined a traveling variety show that staged prologues to cinematic films. She wound up back in New York City, where she performed in vaudevillian acts and Shubert's *Night in Spain.* She soon tired of the subway circuit and hired an agent, Guido Carreras, an Italian impresario who became her husband in 1931. Carreras secured an engagement in Mexico. Billed as Meri Russell Hughes, she toured cabarets and local theaters. Mexican critics, who could not pronounce her name, dubbed her La Meri. This became her stage name for the rest of her career.

On returning to New York, La Meri made her solo debut at the John Golden Theatre on May 6, 1928, and soon began touring in earnest. Wherever she visited, she studied indigenous dances from masters. In her European tour of 1929, La Meri met Mary Wigman and performed with her inspiration, Anna Pavlova. In Paris, she studied with Uday Shankar, enthralled by the vast possibilities of Indian dance. Before introducing any piece into her repertoire, she performed for these gurus what she had learned. La Meri gathered costumes and traditional music on her travels, guaranteeing that her performances would accurately convey the customs of the cultures she investigated. Many countries hailed her as an outsider who could perform with the flair of a native, earning her the respect of those who held these dances closest to them. La Meri's pursuits earned her the title "Queen of Ethnologic Dance." Moorish dance, the Shawl Dance, the Tamborito, Incan dances, dances of the American Hopi, Burmese dances, and the Bharata Natyam were among the forms she studied. By the end of the 1930s, La Meri had seen the world.

Returning to the States in 1939, she began lecturing on ethnic dance, and she met fellow dancer Ruth St. Denis, whose earlier work had been influenced by Eastern cultures. In 1940, the two founded the School of Natya in New York City; master classes, lecture-demonstrations, and performances became regular features in the education of budding dance ethnologists. Their first student was Jack Cole, jazz dance pioneer and choreographer. In 1942, she became a teacher at Jacob's Pillow, the renowned dance school in Massachusetts. The following year La Meri renamed her school the Ethnologic Dance Center and expanded the curriculum to include courses in music, choreography, philosophy, and history of dance.

La Meri educated audiences through her concerts, teachings, and writings. She preceded each performance with an explanation of the dance's significance and the cultures from which it was derived. She changed costumes onstage to retain the audience's attention while showing the intricacy involved in the donning of exotic attires. Her school also became a popular study spot, training dancers such as Peter di Falco, who later became La Meri's dance partner.

In 1944, La Meri and Carreras, who had no children, divorced. That year, La Meri choreographed her rendition of *Swan Lake,* an Indian-infused production. This was her first experimentally ethnic piece—the choreography was a blend of tradition and artistic interpretation. In 1945 she founded the Ethnologic Dance Theater, followed by the Young Artists Series in 1947. Financial difficulties shut down the Ethnologic Dance Center in 1956. In 1959 La Meri moved to Cape Cod, where she wrote several books on dance. She continued to teach at Jacob's Pillow, where she was on the board of directors and had long been a featured performer.

Throughout her career, she was invited to teach at many schools and universities, as well as write numerous articles for newspapers and magazines (including *Arabesque,* devoted to ethnic dance). In 1970 La Meri publicly reemerged, opening the Ethnic Dance Arts company. She was honored at Columbia University, received the Capezio Award in 1972, and was a faculty member at Iowa State University. She spent her last years raising show dogs and teaching dance. La Meri died in 1988 at the age of eighty-nine, in San Antonio, the town where as a child she had explored the exotic world of distant lands and dance.

Bibliography: The archives of the Jerome Robbins Dance Division of the New York Public Library for the Performing Arts at Lincoln Center contain numerous pictures and articles written by and about La Meri. The most useful source on La Meri is her own *Dance Out the Answer: An Autobiography* (1977). The August 1978 issue of *Dance Magazine* devotes a fourteen-page section to La Meri. Her published poetry includes *Poems* (1917), *Marching to France and Other Texas Rhymes* (1917), *Mexican Moonlight* (1921), *Poems of the Plains* (1922), *The Star Roper* (1925), and *Songs and Voyages* (1938). Her scholarly works on dance include *Dance as an Art Form: Its History and Development* (1933); *Gesture Language of Hindu Dance* (1941); *Spanish Dancing* (1948); *A Curious and Wonderful Gymnastic,* co-authored with Morroe Berger (1961); *Dance Composition: The Basic Elements* (1965); and *Total Education in Ethnic Dance* (1977). General works on dance ethnology include Franziska Boas, *The Function of Dance in Human Society* (1972); Theresa J. Buckland, *Dance in the Field: Theory, Methods and Issues in Dance Ethnography* (1999); and Judith Lynne Hanna, *To Dance Is Human: A Theory of Nonverbal Communication* (1987). An obituary appeared in the *New York Times* on January 21, 1988.

JENNIFER BISHOP AND DARA MILOVANOVIC

LANCEFIELD, Rebecca Craighill. January 5, 1895–March 3, 1981. Microbiologist.

Rebecca Craighill Lancefield, a pioneer microbiologist, was born Rebecca Craighill in Fort Wadsworth, New York, the third of six daughters of Colonel William E. Craighill and Mary Wortley Montague Byram. Although her mother did not attend college, she steadfastly encouraged her daughters to obtain an education. Her father, a West Point graduate, was a career army officer, and the family moved frequently during her childhood. As a result, Rebecca attended many different schools, both public and private, and was sometimes tutored at home. She entered Wellesley College in 1912. At first she considered a major in French or English, but she chose zoology after her roommate persuaded her to try a course in that department.

Rebecca graduated from Wellesley in 1916, the year her father died. Money was short, and she therefore spent her first year after graduation teaching mathematics at a girls' boarding school in Vermont rather than entering graduate school as she had hoped to do. The following year she won a scholarship for daughters of army and navy officers to Teachers College of Columbia University. This enabled her to study bacteriology at Columbia College of Physicians and Surgeons.

In the spring of 1918, Rebecca Craighill received her master's degree in bacteriology from Columbia, and married Donald Lancefield, a graduate student in Columbia's department of genetics working under Thomas H. Morgan, the famous drosophila fly geneticist. That year she was hired by bacteriologists O. T. Avery and A. R. Dochez at Rockefeller Institute for Medical Research (now Rockefeller University), who were investigating strains of bacteria isolated from an outbreak of serious streptococcal infections in the army in Texas. The group successfully isolated several specific types of streptococci, and the results were published in 1919 in a paper that includes

Rebecca Lancefield's name among its authors, a recognition seldom accorded technical assistants at the time. This work shaped the course of her lifelong research on hemolytic streptococci, an especially fortuitous happenstance because Rockefeller had been the only place that had answered her letter when she applied for positions in 1918. Funding for this research at Rockefeller ended after World War I, and in 1919 she returned briefly to Columbia to work as a research assistant on drosophila genetics.

By 1921, Donald Lancefield had completed his doctoral work and accepted a faculty position at the University of Oregon. Rebecca accompanied him and obtained a position there as an instructor in bacteriology. One year later, both Lancefields returned to Columbia University, Donald to accept a faculty position in Professor Morgan's department of biology and Rebecca to resume her doctoral studies. At the suggestion of her dissertation supervisor, Hans Zinsser, she carried out her doctoral research at Rockefeller Institute working on rheumatic fever in Homer Swift's laboratory. Her dissertation work established that "green," or "viridans," strains of streptococci, suspected as the agents causing rheumatic fever, were not responsible for this illness.

When she was awarded her PhD in immunology and bacteriology by Columbia in 1925, she remained at Rockefeller and resumed her work on hemolytic streptococcus, the organism on which she had first worked with Avery. She gradually rose through the ranks at Rockefeller, becoming a full member and professor in 1958. Avery remained her friend and mentor throughout his life.

At the time Rebecca Lancefield began her streptococci work, rheumatic fever, scarlet fever, and acute nephritis were still common and serious ailments. It was unknown how many strains of streptococci existed, which strains were dangerous to humans, or how they did their damage. Her research in the ensuing years provided the basis for answering those questions, for the development of effective diagnosis and treatment, and for understanding the immune response to these organisms. In particular, her meticulous work enabled her to classify and type the numerous strains of streptococci, to identify their most significant antigens, and to determine their disease-producing properties. As a result, she was recognized worldwide for the Lancefield classification system of streptococcal bacteria.

There are indications that Rebecca Lancefield was at times aware that she encountered obstacles because she was a woman, but she apparently never made an issue of such matters; such a stance was common to women of her generation and undoubtedly was a survival mechanism at a time when women in science faced enormous barriers. She preferred honors that came to her without reference to her sex and did not want to be known as the first woman to accomplish this or that. She was elected president of the Society of American Bacteriologists in 1943 and served as president of the American Association of Immunologists in 1961. When in 1970 she was elected to the National Academy of Sciences, this selective body had very few women members.

The Lancefields had one child, Jane, born in 1929. Their daughter looked back on a happy childhood with her scientist parents, who lavished a great deal of affection and attention on her. Jane remembered being aware and very proud of the fact that her mother was "different" from other suburban mothers. Her father, unlike most fathers of the period, actively shared domestic responsibilities and was very involved with his daughter. Her parents had a large circle of colleagues, students, and friends whom they often entertained at home. Rebecca Lancefield's students and colleagues referred to her affectionately as Mrs. L. Her juniors viewed her as a caring, generous mentor and a model of meticulous science. The Lancefields spent summers as a family in Woods Hole, Massachusetts, where the renowned Marine Biological Laboratory was located.

Rebecca Lancefield officially retired in 1965. Although she suffered from osteoporosis in her later years, she maintained her laboratory until she broke her hip in late 1980, an accident from which she never recovered. She died at her home in Douglaston, Queens, on March 3, 1981, at the age of eighty-six; her husband died the following August. The Lancefields, lifelong atheists, are buried in the Church of the Messiah Cemetery in Woods Hole.

Bibliography: The collected papers of Rebecca Lancefield are housed at the Rockefeller Archive Center in Sleepy Hollow, New York. Additional materials are located at the Marine Biological Laboratory in Woods Hole, Massachusetts, and at Rockefeller University in New York City. For overviews of her career, see Maclyn McCarthy, "Rebecca Craighill Lancefield, January 5, 1895–March 3, 1981," *Biographical Memoirs, National Academy of Sciences* 57 (1987), pp. 226–46, which also includes a bibliography of her major papers; and Elizabeth M. O'Hern, "Rebecca Craighill Lancefield, Pioneer Microbiologist," *American Society for Microbiology News* 41, no. 12 (1975), pp. 805–10. See also J. N. Schwartz, "Mrs. L.," *Research Profiles,* Summer 1990, pp. 1–6, and E. H. Kone, "Biography of Rebecca Craighill Lancefield," *News from the Rockefeller University,* December 1971. Lancefield's daughter, Jane Lancefield Hersey, provided additional information in two interviews in the fall of 2002 at her home in New Haven, Connecticut. An obituary appeared in the *New York Times* on March 4, 1981.

ELGA R. WASSERMAN

LANGER, Susanne K. December 20, 1895–July 17, 1985. Philosopher.

Susanne Katherina Knauth was born in New York City, the second of five children (three girls and two boys) in an affluent German American family. Her father, Antonio Knauth, an attorney and partner in the banking firm Knauth, Nachod, and Kuehne, had emigrated from Germany in the 1880s with his wife, Else Uhlrich Knauth. Educated at the Veltin School near her home in Manhattan, as a child Susanne spoke primarily German. Nurtured in a culturally rich environment, she developed the interest in aesthetic forms that would mark her philosophy. Her father, while he opposed education for girls, fostered a love of classical music, and she played cello throughout her life. Her mother encouraged her writing of poetry.

In 1916, after her father's death, she entered Radcliffe College, graduating in 1920. In 1921, she married William Leonard Langer, a fellow German American and a Harvard student who would later become a prominent historian. Together they studied at the University of Vienna in 1921–22. They had two sons, Leonard Charles Rudolph (1922) and Bertrand Walter (1925).

Langer received her master's from Radcliffe College in 1924 and her doctorate in 1926; while studying for her MA, she published an illustrated children's book, *The Cruise of the Little Dipper and Other Fairy Tales* (1923). More significantly, during this period she published articles in the *Journal of Philosophy* and *Mind,* studied logic with Henry M. Sheffer and Alfred North Whitehead, and wrote her dissertation, "A Logical Analysis of Meaning."

While a tutor at Radcliffe College (1927–42), Langer wrote three books. *The Practice of Philosophy* (1930) lays groundwork on the nature of revolutionary thinking, anticipating paradigm theories of science. *An Introduction to Symbolic Logic* (1937) considers logic as a concept central to philosophy, extending beyond tautology to meaning. In *Philosophy in a New Key: A Study in the Symbolism of Reason, Rite, and Art* (1942), her best-known work (over 650,000 copies in print), Langer focuses on the symbolic as the defining mark of humanity. She develops a systemic theory that founds symbolic action in feeling rather than logic and frees "the deadlocked paradoxes of mind and body, reason and impulse, autonomy and law" (p. 25). According to *Philosophy in a New Key,* from the flux of bodily sensation, the sense data, our minds constantly abstract the forms that affect us. Symbols serve for more than just communication or description of the empirical world; the human brain endlessly makes them, as evidenced by dreams. Symbols then work as both an end and an instrument, a human characteristic and need. While the biological and social origins of the symbolic are inflected differently in myth, religion, art, or science, the human drive to symbolize is present in all forms, and they are equally human acts of meaning-making.

In 1942, the Langers divorced and she left Radcliffe. She held a series of teaching appointments, including at the University of Delaware, Columbia University, and the University of Washington, before accepting a permanent appointment in 1954 in the philosophy department at Connecticut College for Women, where she remained until 1962.

With all this turmoil, it was ten years before this productive scholar published her next book. *Feeling and Form: A Theory of Art* (1953) builds on the nascent theory of art in *Philosophy in a New Key.* She extends the earlier example of music to develop an aesthetic theory that includes painting, sculpture, architecture, literature, music, dance, drama, and film. She argues that art is a symbolic form that by "its dynamic structure can express the forms of vital experience that language is peculiarly unfit to convey" (p. 32). Language—limited by its discursive, sequential form—cannot express the emotional content as well as can presentational forms such as music and painting. The creation of aesthetic forms, however, is not an emotional experience; it is an intellectual one of understanding and objectifying emotions.

Langer's philosophy was influenced by Alfred North Whitehead, Bertrand Russell, the early Wittgenstein, and Ernst Cassirer. Though they were friends and she translated Cassirer's *Language and Myth* (1946), sometimes their ideas are allied too closely. Simplistic associations reduce both philosophies. Langer developed a full aesthetic theory. Unlike Cassirer, who values science over art and reason and numbers over feeling and language, Langer offers a nonhierarchical model of symbolic forms, one based in biological evolution, and she avoids a communicative model of language, instead conceiving of language as forming and expressing concepts.

As a faculty member at Connecticut College for Women, Langer published the edited collection *Problems of Art* (1957); *Reflections on Art: A Source Book of Writings by Artists, Critics, and Philosophers* (1958); and *Philosophical Sketches* (1962). These books solidified and extended her aesthetic theory. Next, she wrote *Mind: An Essay on Human Feeling,* published in three volumes (1967, 1973, 1982). This series of inquiries into the gulf that separates the human mind from the animal mind draws on biology, biochemistry, and psychology in ways that puzzled her contemporaries but placed her in the forefront of philosophy of science. Its concern with consciousness prefigures the work of Stephen Jay Gould and places her corpus in American philosophical naturalism. Without this final project, Langer would have been known as a logician and an aesthetic philosopher, but *Mind* marks her as a naturalist and a philosopher of science.

During the writing of this final project, she lived alone in a farmhouse in Old Lyme, Connecticut. By this time in her life, she had been honored with many degrees, the Radcliffe Alumnae Achievement Award, and election to the American Academy of Arts and Sciences (1960). She died at her home in Old Lyme at the age of eighty-nine, only three years after the final volume appeared.

Langer's own influence has been significant, if under-recognized. While women philosophers faced resistance in the mid twentieth century, Langer's books were widely read; *Philosophy in a New Key* still sells well. Her work remains vital to aesthetic philosophy, and references to her work continue in anthropology, psychology, education, and communications. At least two current intellectual schools, biological semiotics and media ecology, acknowledge her work as pathbreaking.

Bibliography: Langer's papers are housed at Houghton Library, Harvard University. A large collection of her annotated books are archived at Connecticut College. Winthrop Sargent's "Philosopher in a New Key," *New Yorker,* December 3, 1960, pp. 71–96, presents a wonderful character sketch and fine introduction to her life and thinking. See also *Current Biography* (1963), pp. 233–35. Donald Dryden offers a fuller picture of her intellectual life in *Dictionary of Literary Biography, 270: American Philosophers before 1950* (2003), pp. 189–99. For a good bibliography, see Rolf Lachmann, "Der Philosophische Weg: Susanne K. Langer (1895–1985)," *Studia Culturologica* 2 (1993), pp. 65–114. A centennial retrospective symposium on Susanne K. Langer appears in *Transactions of the Charles S. Peirce Society* 33, no. 1 (Winter 1997), pp. 131–200. An obituary appeared in the *New York Times* on July 19, 1985.

ARABELLA LYON

LAPE, Esther. October 8, 1881–May 17, 1981. Educator, World Court champion, health care activist.

Visionary, activist, organizer, Esther Everett Lape led the battle for U.S. participation in the Permanent Court of International Justice between 1923 and 1935 and then struggled to create a national health care program. Brilliant and forceful, she used her genius for friendship to create a network of allies to promote women's rights, a viable World Court, and quality medical care and health security for all Americans.

Born in Wilmington, Delaware, into a Quaker family, Esther Lape was the daughter of Esther E. Butler and Henry Lape. Little is known about her family or upbringing. She attended public schools in Philadelphia and received a scholarship to Bryn Mawr College but transferred to Wellesley College, from which she graduated in 1905. After graduation she taught English composition at Arizona State University, Swarthmore College, Columbia University, and Barnard. While teaching, she also wrote freelance articles, concentrating on immigration rights and workers' needs.

During World War I her journalism attracted the attention of Edward Bok, publisher of the *Ladies' Home Journal,* who invited her to do a series on immigration and education for citizenship. In 1923, he invited her to chair the Bok Peace Prize Committee, which sought practical plans for achieving and preserving peace in the world. Under Lape's direction, the $50,000 Peace Prize became a national publicity adventure to stir America's imagination regarding international relations. More than twenty-two thousand plans were submitted, to widespread acclaim and controversy. The winning plan recommended immediate adherence to the Permanent Court of International Justice and cooperation with the League of Nations. Lape and her associates were called before a congressional committee dominated by isolationists, who opposed cooperation with an "un-American" institution. After Lape's brilliant testimony, the hearings fizzled.

Lape's core committee was stellar, and included her lifetime colleagues in the campaign for world peace and internationalism: HELEN ROGERS REID, Narcissa Cox Vanderlip, Elihu Root, Judge Learned Hand, Henry Stimson, Roscoe Pound, and ELEANOR ROOSEVELT. From the beginning Lape was Roosevelt's mentor, guide, and confidante, suggesting that she join the newly established League of Women Voters and chair its national legislation committee. Roosevelt worked even more closely with Lape's life partner, Elizabeth Fisher Read (1872–1943), an attorney and a pioneering international legal scholar. Read became Roosevelt's personal attorney, tax accountant, and fiscal adviser. During the 1920s, Roosevelt dined once a week with Lape and Read at their Greenwich Village home, and together they wrote countless articles for a weekly bulletin, *City, State and Nation,* which Lape and Read edited. In her 1937 autobiography, *This Is My Story,* the first lady credited them with "the intensive education of Eleanor Roosevelt" (p. 325).

In 1925, Bok created the American Foundation to continue the fight for the World Court, with Esther Lape as director ("member in charge"). Elizabeth Read was director of research, and Eleanor Roosevelt was an active member of the board. In 1925 the House voted for U.S. participation in the World Court, but the Senate remained opposed to "foreign entanglements." In 1927, President Calvin Coolidge designated Lape an informal envoy to Europe's capitals to elicit practical suggestions to renegotiate Senate demands concerning the World Court. Lape was to report to the president himself, received ambassadorial treatment in London and Paris, and returned hopeful about prospects for international cooperation.

She was even more hopeful in 1933, when President Franklin D. Roosevelt encouraged the American Foundation to publish a study of public opinion concerning U.S. recognition of the Soviet Union. That study, combined with a 1933 report authored by Lape and Read, "The Relations of Record between the U.S. and the Soviet Union," persuaded FDR to recognize the USSR—which he was eager to do, in part to counter Nazi Germany's growing power. But even as public interest in international law as an alternative to war intensified, the Senate failed by seven votes in 1935 to endorse U.S. adherence to the World Court.

A defeated but steadfast public citizen, Lape next focused the American Foundation on the cruel state of America's health care, which deprived so many of even rudimentary medical attention. Like the right-wing assault against international law, anti–New Dealers condemned any national consideration of health care as "state medicine," "communistic and un-American." To counter the opposition of the American Medical Association (AMA) to all public efforts to ensure health care, Esther Lape assembled 2,100 leading physicians to consider the need for essential changes. Under the direction of Lape, Read, Dr. Hugh Cabot of the Mayo Clinic, and many others, the American Foundation published a startling and important study, *American Medicine: Expert Testimony Out of Court* (1937). Focused primarily on the potential use of medical schools and training hospitals to provide public health services throughout the country, it presented dramatic evidence that doctors believed health care is a legitimate concern of the government and that a national public health policy should be formulated. Although Esther Lape was disappointed that FDR did not do more to promote her crusade for national health security, he included the right of every citizen to "adequate medical care and the opportunity to achieve and enjoy good health" in his 1944 State of the Union address.

Subsequently President Harry Truman called for national compulsory health insurance, and Lape's crusade was more fully advanced by President Dwight Eisenhower, who established the Department of Health, Education and Welfare under the direction of OVETA CULP HOBBY. Eisenhower envisioned a full-fledged health care package for every household, just like in the military. The president relied upon Esther Lape and associates, including Eleanor Roosevelt and Helen Rogers Reid, to help build public support. Their two-volume study, *Medical Research: A Midcentury Survey* (1955), detailed new trends in medical and scientific developments, and the need to improve health care throughout the country. The study had a vast impact on research and medical school practices, but the goal to democratize public health was again thwarted by AMA lobbying. According to Patricia Spain Ward, when Eisenhower gave the pen with which he signed the compromise Health Reinsurance Act to Esther Lape, she waved it before the press conference and said: "NOW! This represents a puny little bone in the vertebrae of what I had in mind!"

Esther Lape was a great-hearted woman with hardworking friends dedicated to the public good. After Elizabeth Read died in 1943, Lape lived with Helen Gavin, who had been Read's physician. Lape retired from the American Foundation in 1955, dividing her time between New York City and Salt Meadow, her country home in Westbrook, Connecticut, which was later designated a wildlife refuge and donated to the National Park Service. Unable to understand why Americans agree that its citizens might be publicly educated while their health remained deprived, she continued to lobby for national health care for all Americans until her death in New York City in 1981 just months before her hundredth birthday.

Bibliography: A collection of correspondence, reports, clippings, and printed material is found in Esther Lape's papers at the Franklin D. Roosevelt Library, Hyde Park, New York. There is additional material on the American Foundation in the Helen Reid Rogers papers at the Library of Congress and the papers of Narcissa Cox Vanderlip at Columbia University. Over the years Patricia Spain Ward and Lape's friends Harold Clark and Burt Drucker shared notes, papers, research, and stories about Esther Lape with the author. Especially helpful is Lape's unpublished memoir covering the years 1927–72, "Salt Meadow: From the Perspective of a Half Century." In addition to the publications mentioned in the text, see Lape, ed., *Ways to Peace* (1924). See also Blanche Wiesen Cook, *Eleanor Roosevelt*, vol. 1 (1992) and vol. 2 (1999); Gilbert Kahn, "Presidential Passivity on a Non-Salient Issue: Franklin Delano Roosevelt and the 1935 World Court Fight," *Diplomatic History* 4, no. 2 (Spring 1980), pp. 137–59; and David S. Patterson, "The United States and the Origins of the World Court," *Political Science Quarterly* 91, no. 2 (Summer 1976), pp. 279–95. Patricia Spain Ward's writings on Lape include "In Recognition of Esther Everett Lape," *Women and Health* 5 (Summer 1980), pp. 1–3; "Medical Maverick: Hugh Cabot," *Humanities*, March–April, 1994, pp. 39–42; and "*U.S. v. American Medical Association, et al.*: The Medical Antitrust Case, 1938–1943," *American Studies* 32, no. 1 (Spring 1991), pp. 123–54. An obituary appeared in the *New York Times* on May 19, 1981.

BLANCHE WIESEN COOK

LARSON, Louise Leung. February 16, 1905–October 1, 1988. Journalist.

Louise Leung Larson, who in 1926 became the first Chinese American woman and the first Asian American reporter on a mainstream U.S. daily newspaper, was born Mamie Louise Tom in Los Angeles, the third child and second daughter of immigrant Chinese parents. Her family called her Mamie, but she adopted her middle name, Louise, professionally. Louise's father, Tom Cherng How, who later adopted the business name Tom Leung and converted the family name from Tom to Leung, and her mother, Wong Bing Woo, were born in 1875 into comfortable and learned households in Gum Jook, Guangdong Province, China. Their marriage in 1898 was arranged. Louise's father emigrated to the United States in 1899. He returned to China in 1901 to bring his wife the next year, and they settled in Los Angeles, where three daughters and five sons were born between 1902 and 1917. (Their firstborn son had died in China as an infant.) Tom Leung was an herbalist; his skills and trade were largely self-taught. His extensive and prominent practice served both white and Chinese clients.

Tom Leung's economic success provided the family with an upper-middle-class lifestyle, which was atypical of Chinese American households of the first half of the twentieth century. Louise grew up in a fifteen-room home outside of Chinatown, with the first floor reserved for the herbalist business. The household was also atypical in its interracial relations. White women served as receptionists in the herbalist business, Chinese and black cooks prepared the family meals, white nannies assisted with child care, and "colored" women did the laundry. Her youth was a mixture of Chinese and American lifestyles, with holidays and food from both cultures. The children took music lessons and went to beach resorts, and their home was a center for typical American youth activities, especially parties with dancing to live bands. In spite of her parents' efforts to have their children learn Chinese (they hired a series of tutors), one of Louise's lifelong regrets was that she never mastered the language.

Like other Chinese Americans, the family experienced racism and xenophobia. Her father and other herbalists were hounded by the police, arrested, and required to pay fines for practicing medicine without a license. Louise and her friends were turned away from a dance hall and treated with suspicion and mistaken for being Japanese during the World War II years. Other siblings were denied employment opportunities because of their race.

Louise graduated from Los Angeles High School in 1922 and enrolled at the University of Southern California, graduating Phi Beta Kappa in 1926. According to her own account, she stumbled into journalism by accident. Short a few credits to complete her degree in English at USC, Louise took some journalism classes and discovered that she liked interviewing people and writing up stories. Having previously sold articles to a morning newspaper, she displayed enormous initiative and approached the *Los Angeles Record* after graduation. The newspaper bought a story about the Chinese customs accompanying the celebration of her nephew's having reached one month of age, and then offered her a job. After filling in for a drunken reporter who failed to show up for work one morning, she began a three-year assignment covering the activities of the Los Angeles courts, from the county jail to the coroner's office, including civil and criminal cases.

During the 1930s and 1940s she covered national stories for such newspapers as the *San Francisco News,* the *Chicago Daily Times,* the *Los Angeles Times Sunday Magazine,* and the *Los Angeles Daily News,* and reported on major events, including Al Capone's 1931 tax-evasion trial, Albert Einstein's national crusade for peace and disarmament, and Madame Chiang Kai-shek's 1942 U.S. trip to raise funds for China's defense against Japan's invasion. She wrote under various names, first as Mamie Louise Leung and Louise Leung, and later as Louise Larson. She also wrote under pen names (such as Jane Logan and Hilda Hoover), which was the practice then of some newspapers, to make it appear that they had more reporters or to allow various reporters to assume more than one persona. Louise wrote about celebrities, including ANNA MAY WONG, AIMEE SEMPLE MCPHERSON, and Charlie Chaplin, and covered the society murder trials of the day. In her *Los Angeles Times Sunday Magazine* articles, Louise provided in-depth coverage about aspects of Chinese American life, ranging from the visit to Los Angeles Chinatown of Kang Yu-Wei, trusted adviser to the Chinese emperor, to Chinese movie extras in Hollywood.

After moving to Chicago in 1929, Louise married fellow journalist Arnold "Wolf" Larson, who was white, without her family's knowledge. Interracial marriages were uncommon, and Louise thought her parents would disapprove. Their first son, Stanley, was born in 1930. They returned to California around 1931 or 1932, and in 1940 moved to Topanga, then a remote area in Los Angeles County. Eventually two more children were born: Jane (1945) and Daniel (1948). The couple divorced in 1950. To help support her children and to rebuild her life after her divorce, Larson returned to journalism in 1958 and created a new beat, writing about local political issues in the Malibu and Topanga area for the *Santa Monica Eve-*

ning Outlook. She also provided editorial commentary to newspapers after her retirement in 1975.

Larson's writings contributed not only to mainstream culture but to the early history and tenor of Chinese American life. Although she led an acculturated "American" life, Louise was encouraged by her husband to explore her Chinese background. She was among the first Chinese Americans to visit China (her first trip of four was in 1976), and in 1977 she fulfilled her wish to visit her parents' village. She also wrote a family memoir, *Sweet Bamboo* (1989, reprinted 2002), that provides detailed descriptions of a multi-generational privileged Chinese American household from the 1900s to the 1950s. Its title is the English translation of *Gum Jook,* the name of her parents' ancestral village.

Louise Leung Larson believed that her "big break" into journalism at the *Los Angeles Record* was due to her being female and Chinese—she was able to bring a unique perspective to the profession. Later, as the only Chinese American woman reporter in the nation, Larson made an asset out of what many deemed a liability: people were willing to be interviewed by her and remembered her. Race and gender got her in the door, and then she proved she could do the job. Louise Leung Larson died from a stroke at age eighty-three at her home in Topanga. She had received many awards recognizing her career as a journalist and a pioneering woman and Asian American.

Bibliography: Louise Leung Larson's memoir of the lives of her parents, siblings, and other relatives, her upbringing, and the family's lifestyle of abundance and subsequent struggle out of poverty after the death of her father in 1931 was published as *Sweet Bamboo: A Memoir of a Chinese American Family* (1989). Her daughter, Jane Leung Larson, has a collection of her private papers and copies of many of her early newspaper and magazine articles. See also the archives of the various newspapers where she worked for copies of her published stories. An oral history of Louise Leung Larson conducted in 1979 is available at the Reading Room of the Asian American Studies Center, University of California, Los Angeles. See also an interview with Louise Leung, "Chinese Writer Finds Her Race an Asset," *San Francisco News,* September 6, 1930. Obituaries appeared in the *Santa Monica Evening Outlook* and the *Topanga Messenger.*

SHIRLEY HUNE

LASKER, Mary Woodard Reinhardt. November 30, 1900–February 21, 1994. Philanthropist, birth control activist, patron of medical research and the arts.

Mary Woodard was born in Watertown, Wisconsin, to a prosperous banker and Watertown native, Frank Elwin Woodard, and Sara Johnson, an Irish-born civic leader. Raised in a comfortable home with her younger sister, Alice, Mary was educated at Milwaukee Downer Seminary and entered the University of Wisconsin in 1918 to study English literature and psychology. Forced by an anemic condition to leave early in 1920, she entered Radcliffe College in the fall, focusing on art history. She graduate cum laude in February 1923, then traveled abroad and took courses at Oxford. When she returned to the States, she took jobs soliciting advertising for the *Social Calendar* and working at the Ehrich Galleries in New York City.

By January 1924 she was working at the Reinhardt Gallery, where her eye for modern art was rewarded with expanded curatorial responsibilities. Within months she was arranging exhibitions, including the first American showing of Marc Chagall, and supervising the gallery's publicity. She also developed a close relationship with the gallery's owner, Paul Reinhardt, whom she married on May 23, 1926. On their honeymoon in London and Paris, Mary Reinhardt started purchasing modern French art. Upon her return, she settled into a life of arranging exhibitions, taking art-buying trips to Europe, and enjoying an active social life.

She developed her business skills as Paul Reinhardt increasingly left the gallery's business affairs to his more competent wife. Her financial acumen was demonstrated when she sold her stocks immediately after the initial stock market crash of October 1929, losing relatively little. She prudently used her still significant profits to purchase more art. But the subsequent Depression hurt the gallery's profits, and Paul Reinhardt, a hard drinker who had curtailed his intake after meeting Mary, began drinking again. He also increasingly resented his wife's control of the gallery. In 1931 he asked her to stop working there. Mary Reinhardt acceded to his request, and by 1932 she and a friend had launched Hollywood Patterns, a Vogue-made line of dress patterns based on clothes worn by movie stars. The business became profitable and was eventually purchased by Condé Nast. When her husband continued his heavy drinking, Mary Reinhardt finally gave up on her childless marriage; she obtained a divorce in Reno, Nevada, on December 19, 1934.

Reinhardt spent the next several years taking various industrial design jobs, running Hollywood Patterns, and pursuing the busy life of a socialite. But for the daughter of civic activists this was not enough. In 1938, after meeting MARGARET SANGER, Reinhardt began working with the Birth Control Federation of America (BCFA), noting, "I always felt that information about birth control or planned parenthood was basic to the life of the adult individual and to solving world population problems, basic to the decent living standards" (personal autobiography). She joined its executive committee in 1939 and became vice-chair of its public information committee and BCFA secretary in 1940.

On April 1, 1939, Reinhardt was lunching with a friend when she was introduced to forty-one-year-old Albert D. Lasker, a German-born, twice-married father of three, who owned a successful Chicago advertising agency. Lasker was taken with the attractive divorcée and began to court her. The two were married at New York's City Hall on June 21, 1940.

Her new marriage brought her emotional security and great wealth, but it did not slow her commitment to birth control. Lasker continued to work with BCFA (renamed Planned Parenthood Federation of America in 1942), serving as a vice president of the Federation in 1947 and as an honorary vice president in 1948. She also persuaded her husband to fund the Federation's "Negro Project," an effort to bring birth control services to rural African American families.

Mary Lasker lost both her parents to strokes and close friends to cancer. These losses led to her growing commitment to medical research. Beginning in 1943 she used her money and her administrative talents to transform the American Cancer Society from a small underfunded doctor-run organization into a successful lobbying and research organization. Committed to changing government policy, in addition to supporting voluntary groups, in 1948 she provided financial support and helped lobby for expanded federal funding for the National Cancer Institute and the National Heart Institute. Soon she became one of the most influential laypersons in cancer and heart research, serving as trustee on a host of medical research foundations. Working closely with her fellow lobbyist Florence Mahoney and publicist Mike Gorman, Mary Lasker led the way in expanding government support for the National Institutes of Health (NIH), whose funding grew from $2.8 million in 1946 to over $1.4 billion in 1972, transforming it into one of the world's richest and most widely respected medical research centers. Lasker also supported mental health research through the establishment of the National Committee for Mental Hygiene in 1944 and the National Institute of Mental Health in 1946.

After Albert Lasker's retirement, Mary persuaded her husband to embrace her commitment to improving medicine and health care. In 1942 the couple established the Albert and Mary Lasker Foundation to further medical education and research. Beginning in 1944 the Foundation instituted the Lasker Awards to recognize organizations and individuals for their contributions to basic and clinical research. The awards, soon referred to as America's Nobels, for the number of recipients who went on to win the Nobel Prize in medicine, became the most prestigious and coveted awards in medical science. After Albert Lasker's death from cancer in 1952, Mary Lasker replaced her husband as president of the Lasker Foundation and continued to support an array of health issues, from blindness and cerebral palsy to AIDS. During the 1960s she worked for passage of Medicare, and in the 1970s she prodded President Nixon and Senator Edward Kennedy into uniting behind a "national war on cancer" through the National Cancer Act of 1971.

Long active in urban beautification programs, Lasker funded the planting of hundreds of thousands of flowers in city parks and traffic islands, and tulips along New York's Park Avenue. In the 1960s she worked on urban beautification with Lady Bird Johnson. She also lent her time, name, and money to a variety of cultural and educational institutions, including the John F. Kennedy Center for the Performing Arts and the Museum of Modern Art. With her husband, she had amassed an impressive private collection of modern French masters, which she eventually sold to help fund her philanthropic projects. Mary Lasker died of cardiac arrest in Greenwich, Connecticut, at age ninety-three, having become a hugely influential force in medical research.

Bibliography: No biography of Mary Lasker exists. Her papers, including a private personal autobiography, were donated to Columbia University's Rare Book and Manuscript Library. See also "Reminiscences of Mary Lasker, 1965 and 1982," in the Columbia Oral History Project. Additional archival material is found in "Minutes of the Birth Control Federation of America" in the Margaret Sanger Papers and in the Planned Parenthood Federation of America Papers, both at the Sophia Smith Collection, Smith College Library, Northampton, Massachusetts; the Margaret Sanger Papers at the Library of Congress; and the Lasker Foundation, New York City. The National Library of Medicine, History of Medicine Division, NIH, Bethesda, Maryland, holds the Albert and Mary Lasker Foundation Lasker Award Archives, 1944–87; the Committee for the Nation's Health Records, 1939–56; the Mike Gorman Papers; and the Florence Mahoney Papers. There is also Lasker correspondence in the Margaret Sanger Papers Microfilm: Collected Documents Series (1997). On her role in medical research, see Elizabeth Brenner Drew, "The Health Syndicate: Washington's Noble Conspirators," *Atlantic,* December 1967, pp. 75–82; Stephen P. Strickland, *Politics, Science and Dread Disease: A Short History of U.S. Medical Research Policy* (1972); Paul Starr, *The Social Transformation of Modern Medicine* (1982); and James T. Patterson, *The Dread Disease: Cancer and Modern American Culture* (1987). An unpublished memoir of Sara J. Woodard in the National Library of Medicine provided additional family background. Also of interest is Lasker's appearance on Edward R. Murrow's show *Person to Person* on May 22, 1959, available at the UCLA Film and Television Archive. An obituary appeared in the *New York Times* on February 23, 1994.

ESTHER KATZ

LAWRENCE, Myrtle Terry. July 27, 1891–May 9, 1980. Sharecropper, labor organizer.

Myrtle Lawrence's life embodied the hardships of many rural white women during the early part of the twentieth century, especially those who lived in the South as sharecroppers. She was born Myrtle Terry in the Alabama hill country near Sulligent, the youngest of four children of Nancy Susie Taylor and Christopher Columbus Terry, whose ancestors were Lamar County pioneers. The family fell upon hard times, owing mostly to untimely deaths and the low price of cotton. Orphaned at age three, Myrtle was sent to live with various relatives, as were her brother and two sisters. She never had a stable home until after she married.

Detailed information about Myrtle Terry's early life is elusive. She reported that she had only two weeks of school as a child and began work hoeing and picking cotton at age six. She gave birth to her first daughter, Geneva Snowbank Lawrence, in 1908 and married Benjamin Franklin Lawrence on May 10, 1909. She had five additional children: James Ollin (1912), Elvin Shields (1914), Bennie (1917), Allen Dewell (1919), and Icey Jewell (1926); Bennie died within his first year.

Like most southern sharecroppers, the Lawrences moved often. Myrtle desperately wanted her own farm, and she and her husband purchased forty acres near Sulligent, Alabama, but lost it when Ben became ill. By 1937 the family had made twenty-seven crops in Lamar County, Alabama; Amory, Mississippi; Colt, Arkansas; and Saint Francis County in the Arkansas Delta. Saint Francis County produced the second highest yield of cotton of any county in the country, and this fact, along with Myrtle's brother having already moved there, led the Lawrences westward toward perceived opportunity in 1926. This move also set the stage for her national prominence.

In 1934 the biracial Southern Tenant Farmers' Union (STFU) was formed in nearby Tyronza, Arkansas, to combat evictions and to redress sharecroppers' grievances over landowners' abuse of the New Deal's Agricultural Adjustment Administration, which had been created in 1933 during Franklin D. Roosevelt's first hundred days in office. The STFU introduced liberals like Reinhold Niebuhr, Sherwood Eddy, ELEANOR ROOSEVELT, and Norman Thomas to southern rural poverty and the economic and social realities of life for agricultural workers and sharecroppers. For these powerful shapers of public opinion, the STFU became an icon of the fighting rural poor in the 1930s.

Myrtle Lawrence paid no attention to the union at first, thinking of it as just another church. The cotton-planting strike of 1936, however, captured her attention and stirred her imagination. She joined that spring, bringing in her large extended family and a network of neighbors. According to STFU leader and co-founder H. L. Mitchell, she quickly emerged as the most effective female cotton organizer in the STFU. She was especially accomplished at organizing African Americans. In her words, "They eat the same kind of food that we eat; they live in the same kind of shacks that we live in; they work for the same boss men that we work for. . . . Why shouldn't they belong to the same union that we belong to?"

By 1937 the STFU had spread to six states and had 25,000 members. In the spring of that year, Lawrence appeared before thousands at the first National Sharecroppers Week meeting in New York City, sharing the stage with senators Robert LaFollette and Robert Wagner and Socialist Party leader Norman Thomas. Lawrence laughed loudly and dipped snuff, a common custom among rural women of the South. Uninhibited even before large audiences, she carried her pink-wrapped spit can onto the stage that night and unselfconsciously continued spitting during the multiple speeches. Although she was popular with the audience, after this evening H. L. Mitchell curtailed her appearances at such events, saying that he did not want STFU members to be identified as "Tobacco Road" characters.

That summer Vassar professor CAROLINE WARE, who taught at the Southern Summer School for Women Workers in Industry, encouraged the STFU to send an outstanding agricultural woman to the twelve-week session at Black Mountain, North Carolina. Mitchell chose Lawrence. Although she had taught herself to decipher script well enough to read letters from her son, she remained functionally illiterate. At Black Mountain she learned to write well enough to communicate her thoughts, but her letters remained difficult to read. Ware recognized Lawrence's intelligence, strength, and curiosity and presented her star student to writers, reformers, college youth, and visiting dignitaries interested in reform in the South. Lawrence especially stood out for her embrace of racial equality, a phenomenon rare among the school's students.

At Black Mountain, Lawrence met Priscilla Robertson, a journalist and Vassar graduate, whom she invited, along with photographer Louise Boyle, to Arkansas to report on the efforts of the STFU. During ten days in September 1937 the two recorded and photographed Lawrence's home, work, and STFU activities in a stunning testimony to her activism.

Although Mitchell curbed her national appearances, Myrtle Lawrence remained active in the STFU at the local and regional levels until sometime around 1943 when she and her husband moved to Tampa, Florida. After working there as a janitor in the ladies' lounge of a shipyard for six months, she retired from work outside the home. She later informally adopted two mentally handicapped children. Widowed in 1970, she became blind and died in Tampa at the age of eighty-eight, having endured multiple physical difficulties.

As an icon of the fighting Arkansas sharecropper, Myrtle Lawrence defied the mournful images in DOROTHEA LANGE's photographs or the passive, blank faces of James Agee and Walker Evans's Alabama sharecroppers in *Let Us Now Praise Famous Men* (1941). Three decades later a 1937 oil painting done of Lawrence and her younger daughter, not one of Evans's or Lange's haunted faces, was chosen to characterize sharecroppers as "representative Americans" for the 1976 Bicentennial Freedom Train Exhibition that traveled the country.

Bibliography: The most comprehensive material on Myrtle Lawrence's life is the Louise Boyle Collection at the School of Industrial and Labor Relations, Cornell University, Ithaca, New York. The Caroline Ware Papers, located at the Franklin D. Roosevelt Library in Hyde Park, New York, and the Priscilla Smith Robertson Papers at Vassar College, also contain material, as does the Southern Tenant Farmers' Union Collection, Southern Historical Collection, University of North Carolina, Chapel Hill. For an institutional history of the STFU, see Donald L. Grubbs, *Cry from Cotton: The Southern Tenant Farmers' Union and the New Deal* (1971). See also H. L. Mitchell, *Mean Things Happening in This Land: The Life and Times of H. L. Mitchell, Cofounder of the Southern Tenant Farmers' Union* (1979). Elizabeth Anne Payne, "The Lady was a Sharecropper: Myrtle Lawrence and the Southern Tenant Farmers' Union," *Southern Cultures* 4, no. 2 (Summer 1998), pp. 5–27, describes Lawrence's difficulties with STFU male leaders and includes her quote on p. 22; the article also contains reproductions of Boyle's photographs and the 1937 painting by artist Virginia Donaldson Gower. Robert B. Duncan, "Notes from Arkansas," *New Masses*, December 21, 1937, pp. 17–19, is based on an interview with Lawrence at Black Mountain.

ELIZABETH ANNE PAYNE

LEACOCK, Eleanor. July 2, 1922–April 2, 1987. Anthropologist, feminist.

Eleanor Burke Leacock conducted influential research on the impact of colonialism and capitalist development on indigenous peoples, and on pedagogy in racialized and class-stratified contexts. Her theoretical contributions include foundational work in feminist anthropology and the anthropology of education, and critical reevaluations of social evolutionist thought.

Eleanor Burke was born in Weehawken, New Jersey, the second of three daughters. Her mother, Lily Mary Batterham, earned a master's degree in mathematics and taught secondary school; her father, prominent social philosopher and literary critic Kenneth Burke, never finished college. Their Greenwich Village apartment and small farm in New Jersey were salons for political radicals, writers, and artists. Until she won a scholarship to the Dalton School, Burke attended New York City public schools. On scholarship, she went to Radcliffe College in 1939, where she took her first courses in anthropology and met her future husband, fellow New Yorker Richard Leacock, a budding filmmaker whom she married on December 27, 1941. In 1942, after Radcliffe authorities asked her to leave because of curfew violations, she transferred to Barnard College. Soon after, Richard was drafted for the duration of World War II.

Graduating from Barnard in 1944 with a degree in anthropology, Leacock sought war-related work in Washington, D.C. Anthropologists RUTH BENEDICT and Rhoda Metraux approved Leacock's employment by the Office of War Information, but the FBI refused to grant her a security clearance. Returning to New York City, she enrolled in graduate school at Columbia's anthropology department, where Marian Smith became her advisor.

Richard was discharged in 1945, and their daughter Elspeth was born in 1946. Pregnancy and infant care did not deter her from her studies, but her earlier encounter with the FBI made Leacock cautious about disclosing her Marxist perspective. She passed her master's exam in 1946. Ruth Benedict arranged a small grant that permitted Leacock to shoot several short films comparing child socialization in Switzerland and Italy while her husband shot films on human geography in Europe. Leacock then traveled to Paris to undertake archival research on the Montagnais-Naskapi (as the Innu of Labrador were known in the literature of the time).

Upon her return to Columbia, Leacock secured departmental funding for field research. In the summer of 1951 she left Elspeth with her father and stepmother (Richard was filming in Latin America) and took her second child, infant Robert, "on her hip" to Labrador. With contemporary evidence to complement the archival data, she challenged the reigning characterization of hunting-gathering groups and the Innu in particular. Leacock found that even hundreds of years after the introduction of commodity trade, basic resources among the Innu remained communal: only rights to trapping lines and pelts had become privatized. She also showed that Innu postmarital residence remained flexible, even as she found evidence that in the past there had been a greater degree of matrilocality. Moreover, she described arenas in Innu life that showed distinct egalitarianism between women and men.

Funded by the Wenner-Gren Foundation, Leacock returned to Labrador in the summer of

1952. She transcribed Innu stories and gave copies to community leaders. At the time, the notion that anthropologists should share research results with the communities they study was virtually without precedent.

Back in New York, Leacock gave birth to her third child, David, shortly before defending her dissertation in 1952. The American Anthropological Association selected her dissertation for their prestigious Memoirs series (1954). Professional kudos, however, did not produce employment. Leacock was a mother and a committed leftist in McCarthy-era America, factors that she believed weighed equally against her in academic job searches. In fact, eleven years would pass before she obtained her first full-time position in anthropology. In the meantime Leacock accepted jobs that she considered anthropologically relevant and had her fourth child, Claudia. After her first marriage ended in 1962, she became involved with James Haughton, an African American labor organizer who became her second husband in 1966. The interracial marriage lasted until Leacock's death in 1987.

Finally, in 1963, the Brooklyn Polytechnic Institute hired her for a full-time anthropology position. That same year Leacock published a critically acclaimed reevaluation of Lewis Henry Morgan's *Ancient Society* and its view of egalitarian societies and cultural evolution. With her greater job security, her scholarly productivity increased dramatically. In keeping with her abiding activism against racism, she wrote *Culture of Poverty: A Critique* (1971), which examined the class and racial bias of that widely accepted theory. Leacock's concern for emancipatory pedagogy brought her to the attention of authorities in newly independent Zambia, who invited her in 1970 to help decolonize their primary school curricula.

In 1972 City College of CUNY invited Leacock to chair and rebuild the anthropology department. Her edition of Engels's *The Origin of the Family, Private Property, and the State* appeared the same year; Leacock's critical introduction influenced a generation of emerging Marxist-feminist scholars. For the rest of her career Leacock remained at City College, where she was beloved as a teacher and valued as a mentor for both graduate students and junior faculty. Her immense publication record (ten books and more than eighty articles) considered different sources and facets of racism, class stratification, and gender hierarchies, and forms of cultural resistance to them. Leacock's last field research was in Western Samoa, investigating the relationship between capitalist development and an alarming increase in adolescent suicide. As a result of a massive stroke suffered while in the field, she died in Honolulu on April 2, 1987, at the age of sixty-four.

Leacock was attacked as an evolutionist, but careful reading reveals that she always emphasized historical transformation, replete with local resistance and unexpected contingencies, rather than any sort of inevitability and certainly without any implication of progress. Her pathbreaking works in feminist anthropology include *Women and Colonization* (1980), co-authored with Mona Etienne, which stresses local resistance to colonial impositions in a range of societies as a major reason for the uneven quality of gender hierarchies; and *Women's Work: Development and the Division of Labor by Gender* (1986), which compares gender and labor during capitalist transformations and underscores the importance of women's organizing in shaping development efforts.

Leacock always wrote for disparate audiences. She was as eager to convince her Marxist colleagues of the problems created by ignoring gender oppression as she was to convince feminist audiences that class and race were as important as gender in shaping exploitation and reservoirs of resistance. Leacock's *Myths of Male Dominance* (1981) collects a number of her writings that dispute a range of arguments that women have always and everywhere been oppressed.

Bibliography: Eleanor Burke Leacock's papers are housed at Fairleigh Dickinson University Library. This essay includes material from an interview the author conducted with Leacock on January 26, 1986. More information about Leacock can be found in Ute Gacs, Aisha Khan, Jerrie McIntyre, and Ruth Weinberg, eds., *Women Anthropologists: A Biographical Dictionary* (1988). Constance Sutton, ed., *From Labrador to Samoa: The Theory and Practice of Eleanor Burke Leacock* (1993), a memorial anthology that analyzes Leacock's contributions to feminist anthropology, includes an autobiographical sketch written by Leacock, "Becoming an Anthropologist." Kenneth Burke's eulogy, "My Daughter, 'Happy,'" was printed in *Dialectical Anthropology* 14, no. 3 (1989), pp. 239–40. In addition to the works cited in the text, see also Leacock, "Women in Egalitarian Societies," in Renate Bridenthal and Claudia Koonz, eds., *Becoming Visible: Women in European History* (1977); "Interpreting the Origins of Gender Inequality: Conceptual and Historical Problems," *Dialectical Anthropology* 7, no. 4 (February 1983), pp. 263–84; Leacock and June Nash, "Ideologies of Sex: Archetypes and Stereotypes," *Issues in Cross-Cultural Research* 285 (1977, special issue ed. Leonore Loeb Adler), pp. 618–45; and Leacock and Helen I. Safa, eds., *Women's Work: Development and the Division of Labor by Gender* (1986). An obituary appeared in the *New York Times* on April 7, 1987.

CHRISTINE GAILEY

LEE, Jane Kwong. April 24, 1902–April 18, 1989. Community activist, journalist.

Jane Kwong Lee is best known in the Chinese community of San Francisco as a community worker and journalist who advocated for Chinese nationalism, American patriotism, and Chinese American feminism in the 1930s and 1940s. Because of her bilingual skills, bicultural background, college education, and Christian contacts, she was well respected in the community and was often called upon to do translations, give speeches, write editorials, and represent women and the Chinese community at various local and national events.

Jane Kwong Lee was born in Op Lee Jeu village, Toishan District, Guangdong Province, China, the second daughter of three children. Because her parents had wanted a son, they chose to name her Lin Hi, meaning "Link to Young Brother," and indeed, a son did follow her. Her father, Kwong Sam Been, was a businessman in Australia and her mother (whose name is not known) was a housewife. Growing up in China at the time of the 1911 Revolution, which advocated social and political reform, including women's rights, Jane was able to attend True Light Seminary in Canton, a boarding school sponsored by the Presbyterian Missionary Board in the United States. There she studied both English and Chinese and became exposed to Western culture and ideas of democracy and feminism. She changed her Chinese name to Lin Jin, "Link to Precious," was baptized as a Presbyterian, and adopted the Western name Jane. In 1920 she completed her last year of middle school at the coeducational Canton Christian College.

Although she had wanted to become a medical doctor, her father's remittances from Australia were not enough to support her higher education as well as that of her brother. Not happy with her options of factory work or marriage at the time of graduation, Jane persuaded her mother to sell some of the family's land so that she could pursue a college education in the United States and, hopefully, return home to a prestigious academic post.

With a student visa in hand, she arrived in San Francisco in 1922. She attended Mills College on a scholarship and worked part-time teaching Chinese to children and English to adults at the local Chinese churches in Oakland, California. During the summer she also worked at a Chinese-owned fruit cannery. She earned her BA in sociology in 1926. Soon after, she married James Lee, who operated a meat market in Oakland, and they had two children, Priscilla (1927) and James Jr. (1931). Dissatisfied with being a housewife, she returned to Mills College and received her MA in sociology and economics in 1933. By then, her mother had passed away and, despite the racial prejudice that prevented Jane from finding a well-paying job in white establishments, she decided to stay in the United States rather than return to China.

Through her contacts in the Chinese community of San Francisco, Jane Kwong Lee eventually secured the position of community worker and was promoted within two years to coordinator of the Chinese Young Women's Christian Association (YWCA). For the next ten years, Lee worked tirelessly for women in Chinatown. She provided assistance to foreign-born women regarding immigration, health and birth control, housing, domestic problems, and financial aid. For the American-born generation she organized classes (bridge, sewing, cooking, and Chinese language) and clubs that met their specific social needs. Because of her bilingual skills, Lee was successful at making home visits and utilizing the local press to publicize and promote the YWCA's services. To supplement her income, she also taught at the Hip Wo Chinese Language School in the evenings. And thanks to her supportive husband James, she did it all without neglecting the needs of her family.

During the 1930s Jane Kwong Lee helped Chinese families find jobs and apply for federal relief, and translated at medical clinics. After war broke out between Japan and China in 1937, she mobilized women in the Chinatown community to do their part to support the war effort in China—fund-raising through door-to-door solicitation and Rice Bowl parties, supporting boycotts against Japanese products and U.S. exportation of scrap metal to Japan, and collecting medical supplies and clothing for refugees in China. As a member of the Chinese War Relief Association's propaganda committee, she worked diligently to host receptions for dignitaries from China, sponsor speakers at the YWCA, give speeches at political rallies, and write newspaper editorials and plays that promoted both Chinese nationalism and women's equality. "If we Chinese women can work with the men at the war front as well as behind the lines, then who can look down on us? Who will dare say women are not equal to men?" she wrote in the *Chung Sai Yat Po* (*Chinese American Daily Newspaper*) on May 3, 1940. After Japan attacked Pearl Harbor in 1941, she taught classes on civil defense and nutrition, and led women in Red Cross work, selling war bonds, sponsoring a weekly USO dance at the Chinese YWCA, and writing Congress to repeal the Chinese Exclusion Act of 1882, which had barred the Chinese from immigrating and becoming naturalized U.S. citizens.

In 1944 Jane Kwong Lee resigned from the YWCA out of sheer exhaustion and moved back to the East Bay to live. She became a naturalized U.S. citizen and commuted to San Francisco to work at the Chinese YWCA for a few more years after the war. She also worked as a journalist, translating news articles into Chinese for the *Chung Sai Yat Po* and reporting for the *Chinese Times.* During the 1950s and 1960s, she took a full-time job as a translator and reporter with *Chinese World,* a bilingual newspaper that was critical of both Chiang Kai-shek's Nationalist Party and Mao Tse-tung's Communist Party. She particularly appreciated the opportunity to stay informed of world events, cover such important news as Stalin's death and President Kennedy's assassination, and have some of her Chinese poems published in the newspaper.

When the newspaper folded in 1969, she helped her husband operate his grocery and liquor store in Oakland until a series of robberies and burglaries forced them to sell the business and retire to El Cerrito, California. With more time on her hands, she wrote a 400-page autobiography, "A Chinese American," which was never published. Her husband James Lee died in 1984, and Jane Kwong Lee's death came just a week before her eighty-seventh birthday in 1989.

Bibliography: Jane Kwong Lee's unpublished autobiography, "A Chinese American," photographs, plays, and other writings are in the possession of her children, Priscilla Holmes and James Lee Jr. Two oral history interviews that were conducted with her by Judy Yung on October 22 and November 2, 1988, at her home in El Cerrito, California, are in the possession of the interviewer. Her life story, a few photographs, excerpts from her autobiography, and some of her newspaper articles are included in Judy Yung's *Unbound Feet: A Social History of Chinese Women in San Francisco* (1995) and *Unbound Voices: A Documentary History of Chinese Women in San Francisco* (1999). An obituary appeared in the *Oakland Tribune* on April 20, 1989.

JUDY YUNG

LEE, Sue Ko. March 9, 1910–May 15, 1996. Labor organizer.

Sue Ko Lee was born in Honolulu, Hawaii, and grew up in Watsonville, California. Both her parents were born in China and migrated to Hawaii, where they were married. Her father, Ko Kan San, was a clerk and her mother, Ing Shee, was a housewife. As the eldest of ten children, Sue was needed at home to do the housework and care for her younger siblings, so she left school after grammar school. She later earned her GED by passing the high school equivalency exam in Berkeley, California. In 1926, she married Lee Jew Hing, a bookkeeper at the National Dollar Stores in San Francisco who had emigrated from China five years earlier. They made their home in San Francisco's Chinatown, where they had two sons, Mervyn (1927) and Stanley (1929).

Because of her husband's family connections, Sue Ko Lee was able to find a job at the National Dollar Stores sewing factory as a buttonhole machine operator, earning piece-rate wages that averaged 25 cents an hour. Her husband continued to work as a bookkeeper there, making $125 a month, enough to support his family and send money back home to China. Knowing that there were few jobs available to Chinese women at the time and with two young children on her hands, she was grateful for a job that allowed her to work flexible hours. Moreover, in all of Chinatown, the National Dollar Stores factory, which specialized in women's light apparel, was the largest, cleanest, and most modern, and it supposedly offered the best wages.

Yet in 1938, at the tail end of the Depression, the Lees and 106 other Chinese garment workers found themselves caught in a labor dispute over obtaining steady employment and increased wages. Frustrated with the management's unfair labor practices and backed by the 1935 Wagner Act, which guaranteed labor's right to collective bargaining, they decided to form the Chinese Ladies' Garment Workers' Union (Local 341 of the International Ladies' Garment Workers' Union [ILGWU]) and go on strike. The fifteen-week strike turned out to be the longest strike in the history of San Francisco Chinatown and the first time Chinese women took a stand against poor working conditions in the garment industry. Lee Jew Hing became vice president of Local 341 and wrote all the Chinese leaflets and press releases. Sue Ko Lee walked the picket line and attended the steering committee meetings. Thanks to the organizing skills of JENNIE MATYAS of the ILGWU, the support of leftist organizations in Chinatown, and the workers' determination to win, an agreement was finally reached. Sue Ko Lee remembered speaking up for the first time at the meeting to vote on the contract, which close to half of the workers found inadequate: "At least that's something to begin with. You had to start someplace. . . . If you take longer, people are not going to stay around. They can't afford to."

The new contract was good for one year and, conveniently, the sewing factory went out of business at the end of that year, claiming financial losses. The ILGWU, however, was able to find jobs for many of the Chinese workers in union shops downtown, which offered them better wages and working conditions. "The strike was the best thing that ever happened," declared Sue Ko Lee. "It changed our lives." Sue and her husband were successfully placed as machine operator and cutter, respectively, in one of the union shops outside Chinatown. Later, when Koret Corporation took over the small shop in which Sue worked, she was promoted to quality control.

Mentored by Jennie Matyas, Sue Ko Lee went on to become the first Chinese American business agent and secretary of both Local 101 and the San Francisco ILGWU Joint Board. She proudly represented the Local Board in 1947 at the 26th National ILGWU Convention in Cleveland, and in 1957 at the California State Labor Convention in

Oakland. After twenty years as a union organizer, however, she became discouraged by the greed of Chinatown contractors and the apathy of Chinese garment workers. "They want the benefits but they wouldn't work for them," she said. She left the ILGWU and went to work for the state of California in employment services, retiring in 1975. Her husband Lee Jew Hing died in 1985, followed by Sue Ko Lee in 1996 in El Cerrito at the age of eighty-six.

Bibliography: Sue Ko Lee's scrapbook of news clippings, newsletters, bulletins, and photographs of the 1938 National Dollar Stores strike and her work with the ILGWU has been deposited at the Labor Archives and Research Center, San Francisco State University. An oral history interview that was conducted with her by Judy Yung on October 26, 1989, at her home in El Cerrito, California, is in the possession of the interviewer; all quotations are from that source. Her life story, photographs, excerpts from the oral history interview, and a history and analysis of the 1938 strike are included in Judy Yung's *Unbound Feet: A Social History of Chinese Women in San Francisco* (1995) and *Unbound Voices: A Documentary History of Chinese Women in San Francisco* (1999).

JUDY YUNG

LE GALLIENNE, Eva. January 11, 1899–June 3, 1991. Actress, theater director, writer.

Because she was born in 1899, Eva Le Gallienne liked to say that she was a step ahead of the century. A consummate character actor, her art was a combination of the dazzling theatricality of Sarah Bernhardt and the deep inner truth of Eleonora Duse, the first modern actor. In a career that spanned the twentieth century, Le Gallienne's pioneering contributions and professional credentials were without parallel in the American theater.

The only child of Julie Nørregaard, a Danish journalist, and Richard Le Gallienne, an English poet and writer, Eva Le Gallienne was born in London, England. After her parents separated when she was four, she was raised by her mother and educated in Paris and London. Julie Nørregaard had been profoundly influenced by playwright Henrik Ibsen (she had been present at the world premiere of *A Doll's House*), and she raised her daughter to be self-sufficient. An extremely precocious and perceptive child, Le Gallienne learned to read at five, and by the time she was seven she could speak and write French, English, and Danish. Although her father was absent, his books, his photograph, and a framed poster of his best-selling novel, *The Quest of the Golden Girl* (1896), were always on display in their home.

After seeing Sarah Bernhardt perform and then meeting her when she was fourteen, Le Gallienne decided to dedicate her life to the theater. She studied for nine months at Tree's Academy (later the Royal Academy of Dramatic Art), but her formal education ended in 1915, when, accompanied by her mother, she moved to New York City to pursue a theater career. In just five years, she played fifteen roles in a variety of plays on Broadway; for two of those years she toured with ETHEL BARRYMORE's company. In 1920, she had her first Broadway hit in Arthur Richman's *Not So Long Ago,* followed by starring roles as Julie in Ferenc Molnar's *Liliom* in 1921 and Alexandra in Molnar's *The Swan* opposite Basil Rathbone in 1923. In 1925, she made her Paris debut at the Theatre de l'Odeon in *Jehanne d'Arc.* That same year she formed her own acting company and produced, directed, and starred in Ibsen's *The Master Builder* and *John Gabriel Borkman* on Broadway and on tour.

Not content with Broadway stardom and long runs in popular hits, she used her celebrity and personal savings and the financial backing of wealthy patrons MARY CURTIS BOK, Alice De Lamar, and Otto Kahn to create in the United States the equivalent of the national theaters she had grown up with in Europe. In 1926, the same year she became an American citizen, she founded the Civic Repertory Theatre on Fourteenth Street in New York City, where she functioned as leading actor, director, and producer. She introduced American audiences to Chekhov and Ibsen, premiered new American work such as SUSAN GLASPELL's Pulitzer Prize–winning *Alison's House* (1930), and adapted Lewis Carroll's *Alice in Wonderland* (1932). Among her memorable moments on stage, she was the first Peter Pan to fly out over the audience. Keeping forty productions alive in rotating repertory, she proved that a subsidized, nonprofit repertory theater playing at low prices could flourish downtown and attract a diverse audience. The Civic Repertory Theatre united a young American theater tradition with a rich European heritage and laid the groundwork for off-Broadway and the regional theater movement that began following World War II. For the rest of her life she championed nonprofit theater and called the lack of government support for the arts a national scandal.

Even though she loathed self-promotion and refused to "market" herself, Le Gallienne quickly won acclaim in her new country. In 1928 President Calvin Coolidge selected her, along with Charles Lindbergh, as one of the outstanding persons of the year, and at age thirty she appeared on the cover of *Time* magazine. Because of her high cheekbones, her wide-set blue eyes, and the slim elegance of her five-foot four-inch figure, Le Gallienne was often praised for her beauty, but her real loveliness lay in the mobility of her expressions and the grace of her movements. In May

1931, a propane hot water heater exploded at her home in Weston, Connecticut, and Le Gallienne almost died from her injuries. Severe burns on her hands were treated with skin grafts and reconstructive surgery, and she developed an intricate stage makeup to hide the scarring. After a year off, she went back to work and took the Civic Repertory Company on a national tour, but after seven successful years the Civic closed, a victim of the Depression.

Le Gallienne returned to Broadway stardom, but continued her advocacy of a national repertory theater. During a career that lasted more than seven decades, she founded or supported a variety of noncommercial theater companies, including the short-lived American Repertory Theatre (1946–47), the National Repertory Theatre, and the Association of Performing Artists. In the 1950s and 1960s, she directed and acted on Broadway and on tour in a number of roles, including Queen Elizabeth in the Phoenix Theatre production of *Mary Stuart* (1957), directed by Tyrone Guthrie; *The Seagull* (1965); *The Madwoman of Chaillot* (1965–66); *Ghosts* (1962); *The Trojan Women* (1965–66); and *Exit the King* (1968). In addition to her calling as a working actor, Le Gallienne had a distinguished literary career. Her translations of twelve of Ibsen's plays were published by Modern Library in two volumes in 1951 and 1961. In 1961, Norway gave her their highest honor, the Grand Cross of the Order of Saint Olav, for her commitment to Ibsen.

Just as Le Gallienne had the courage to reject the status quo in her professional life, she was equally courageous in her personal life. In a closeted society, she loved and lived openly with women. A loyal lover, if not particularly faithful, Le Gallienne juggled several long-term relationships throughout her life and attracted devoted friends like philanthropist Alice De Lamar, her patron for sixty years, who left her a million dollars in 1982. While Le Gallienne fully accepted her sexuality, she refused to be defined by it. She was a theater artist, and in the Dionysian world of theater, all categories, divisions, groupings, and titles—including, she believed, those of sexual orientation, gender, class, and race—were antithetical to art.

Despite advancing age, Le Gallienne continued to work during the 1970s and 1980s. She delighted Broadway and national audiences with her portrayal of theater matriarch Fanny Cavendish in *The Royal Family* in 1975–76, and at eighty-three she literally flew back onto the Broadway stage as the White Queen in her own production of *Alice in Wonderland* (1982). Her final professional performance was in 1984 playing a character drawn from her own life on an episode of NBC's *St. Elsewhere.* Two years later she received the National Medal of Arts. She died of heart failure at her home in Weston, Connecticut, at the age of ninety-two.

Bibliography: Le Gallienne's personal papers, diaries, photographs, and correspondence are at the Library of Congress in Washington, D.C. Her Civic Repertory papers are held at the Beinecke Rare Book and Manuscript Library, Yale University. Her letters to her cousin Mogens Nørregaard are at the Det Kongelige Bibliotek in Copenhagen. Le Gallienne wrote two autobiographies, *At 33* (1934) and *With a Quiet Heart* (1953); *Flossie and Bossie* (1949), a children's story; and best-selling translations of Hans Christian Andersen stories, including *Seven Tales* (1959), *The Nightingale* (1965), and *The Little Mermaid* (1971). Her 1966 biography of her theatrical mentor, Eleonora Duse, *The Mystic in the Theatre,* drew on her firsthand observations and friendship with the legendary actor. A complete and comprehensive source, which draws on Le Gallienne's unpublished papers, letters, diaries, and manuscripts, is Helen Sheehy's biography *Eva Le Gallienne* (1996). An obituary appeared in the *New York Times* on June 5, 1991.

HELEN SHEEHY

LENYA, Lotte. October 18, 1898–November 27, 1981. Singer, actress.

Lotte Lenya, a celebrated Austrian-born singer and actress who promoted and interpreted the music of her first husband, composer Kurt Weill, for American audiences, rose from a childhood of poverty to sustain a sixty-year international stage, film, and recording career. Born Karoline Wilhelmine Charlotte Blamauer in Penzing, a working-class district of Vienna, she was the second of four surviving children of Johanna Teuschl, a laundress, and Franz Paul Blamauer, a coach driver. Karoline, who was raised Roman Catholic, showed natural stage talent at an early age by singing and dancing in an amateur circus. After the girl finished Bürgerschule (middle school) at age fourteen, her mother encouraged her to live with an aunt in Zurich, where she apprenticed in the ballet company of the Zurich Stadttheater and took private acting lessons with stage director Richard Révy. During her seven-year association with the Stadttheater and the Schauspielhaus she appeared in over ninety theater, dance, and opera productions of new and standard-repertory works by Shakespeare, Shaw, Strindberg, Tolstoy, and Wedekind, among others. In 1920 she began using a stage name, Lotte Lenja; she changed the spelling to "Lotte Lenya" after emigrating to the United States and preferred to be called Lenya by her friends.

In 1921 Lenya moved to Berlin, where several years later she met composer Kurt Weill while working as an *au pair* for the expressionist playwright Georg Kaiser. They married in a civil ceremony in 1926, much to the initial dismay of Weill's devoutly Jewish parents. They did not have children.

In 1928 Weill convinced Bertolt Brecht to cast Lenya in the small, mostly nonsinging part of the prostitute Jenny in their new play-with-music, *Die Dreigroschenoper (The Threepenny Opera),* in a commercial run at the Theater am Schiffbauerdamm in Berlin. The unprecedented success of this production made theater history and launched Lenya's career as an actress. For the next several years she played leading roles in many of Berlin's prominent theaters as well as the expanded part of Jenny in the 1931 film version of *Die Dreigroschenoper,* directed by G. W. Pabst, in which she created her signature song with a riveting performance of "Seeräuberjenny" (Pirate Jenny). Soon after Weill and Lenya separated; she moved to Vienna, and he became the target of attacks from Nazi sympathizers and was forced to flee to Paris in March 1933. They divorced later that year.

In June 1933 Lenya premiered the leading role of Anna I in Weill's *Die sieben Todsünden (The Seven Deadly Sins),* choreographed by George Balanchine, in Paris and London. In 1935 Weill and Lenya traveled to New York for the premiere of *The Eternal Road,* a massive biblical pageant directed by Max Reinhardt with a libretto by Franz Werfel and music by Weill. Lenya played the part of Miriam. Lenya and Weill remarried in January 1937 and decided to stay in the States to build new careers. Lenya, still speaking heavily accented English, struggled to find a market for her special talents as Weill became a successful Broadway and Hollywood composer. Her few stage appearances during the 1940s met with mixed to negative reviews, but she aided the U.S. war effort by making several propaganda recordings for broadcast across enemy lines in Germany. Lenya became an American citizen in 1944.

Kurt Weill's untimely death in 1950 empowered Lenya to revive his German stage and concert works, which had been burned by the Nazis and were virtually unknown in America and to the new generation of postwar Germans. In July 1951 Lenya married magazine editor George Davis, who acted as a trusted partner in redefining her career, negotiated for productions and recording contracts, and wrote many of the articles that appeared under Lenya's name until his death in 1957. A concert version of *The Threepenny Opera* in an English adaptation by Marc Blitzstein and conducted by Leonard Bernstein at Brandeis University led to a low-budget staged production in New York's Greenwich Village in 1954 with Lenya playing Jenny. This was one of the first shows to establish off-Broadway as a viable theater venue. Lenya won a Tony Award for her performance, and the show played until 1961, holding for many years the record for the longest-running off-Broadway show, at 2,611 performances. The cast album appeared on MGM records in 1954. Lenya then recorded the most popular of Weill's German stage works for Columbia Masterworks, even though her aging voice required musical transpositions and adaptations that distorted dramatic characterizations and altered musical forms. Lenya then turned to the concert stage and performed legendary evenings of Weill's music in New York and Germany, the personification of the spirit of Weimar Berlin. She later established the Kurt Weill Foundation for Music to sustain his legacy.

Having devoted ten years to Weill's music, Lenya embarked on the third, and probably most fulfilling, stage of her career, including a long run in *Brecht on Brecht* and the title role in Brecht's *Mother Courage.* John Kander and Fred Ebb conceived the role of Fräulein Schneider in *Cabaret* for Lenya and wrote five songs for her to sing, leading to a 1967 Tony nomination for best actress in a musical. Film audiences came to know Lenya from her Oscar-nominated performance in *The Roman Spring of Mrs. Stone* (1961) and as the woman with the knife in her shoe in the James Bond thriller, *From Russia with Love* (1963). From 1962 until his death in 1969, she was married to Russell Detwiler, an artist. A brief (1971–73) marriage to documentary filmmaker Richard Siemanowski ended in divorce.

Lotte Lenya died in New York City on November 27, 1981, at the age of eighty-three and is buried in Mount Repose Cemetery in Haverstraw, New York. After her death a number of singers, including Gisela May, Martha Schlamme, and Ute Lemper, attempted to imitate her performance style and repertory. Others, such as Patti Smith and Marianne Faithfull, acknowledge being inspired by her art. Music critic John Rockwell summed up both Lenya's vocal limitations as a singer and her enduring appeal: "Through her shaky failings, or perhaps even because of them, she projected an individuality, a vulnerability and a defiance that her more technically adroit successors were hard put to match." This combination of vulnerability and survival encapsulates neatly both Lenya's life and her stage personae.

Bibliography: The Weill-Lenya Research Center in New York City has the most comprehensive collection of unpublished material related to Lenya, including letters and historical documents, autobiographical writings, documentation about performances, interviews, photographs, paintings, films, videotapes, audio recordings, artifacts, memorabilia, and oral histories. Of equal importance, especially for access to early documents, photographs, and the musical arrangements that Lenya used in performance, are the Weill-Lenya Papers at the Yale University Music Library. David Farneth, ed., *Lenya, the Legend: A Pictorial Autobiography* (1998), presents a collection of Lenya's autobiographical notes and correspondence, illustrated with three hundred photos, and includes an extensive chronology. *Speak Low (When You Speak Love): The Letters of Kurt Weill and Lotte Lenya* (1996), edited and translated by Lys Symonette and Kim H. Kowalke, tells the story of Lenya and Weill's unconventional and often troubled marriage. Donald Spoto, *Lenya: A Life* (1989), is the only book-length biography, although most biographies of Kurt Weill also cover Lenya quite extensively. The Hessischer Rundfunk made a video documentary about Lenya's life, *Lenya, ein erfundenes Leben*, in 1994. See also David Beams, "Lotte Lenya," *Theatre Arts* 46, no. 1 (June 1962), pp. 11–18, 66–72, which draws on extensive interviews with the singer. For a study of her interpretive style, see Guy Stern, "Lotte Lenya's Creative Interpretation of Brecht," in James K. Lyon and Hans-Peter Breuer, eds., *Brecht Unbound* (1995). An obituary in the *New York Times* on November 28, 1981, contains the final quotation from John Rockwell.

DAVID FARNETH

LEONE, Lucile Petry. January 23, 1902–November 25, 1999. Nursing leader, Cadet Nurse Corps chief.

Lucile Petry was born in Lewisburg, Ohio, the only child of Dora Murray, a homemaker, and David Petry, a high school teacher and principal. When Lucile was a child, her father was a strong influence in her life and instilled in her a reverence for education and a sense of responsibility. Diminutive, attractive, and energetic, she felt driven to succeed and always knew she wanted a career. The Petry family moved to Delaware in 1921, and Lucile attended Selbyville High School. After graduation, she enrolled at the University of Delaware as a chemistry and English major, working at a variety of jobs to pay for her education. Though fascinated by science, she "longed to experience chemistry in human bodies, not in test tubes" (Robinson, p. 9). After graduating from Delaware with honors in 1924, she entered the prestigious nurse training program at Johns Hopkins Hospital, where she graduated first in her class in 1927.

Though her father and her professors at Delaware were disappointed that she had not chosen a field with more status, Petry was drawn to the way nursing connected the basic, social, and behavioral sciences. She disapproved, however, of how schools exploited students. Most schools were operated by hospitals, and nurses' training consisted of working long hours on the wards with little or no formal education about health, disease, or nursing therapeutics. Petry also noted that once they graduated, nurses frequently lacked the institutional support they needed to practice nursing the way she envisioned. Because of these problems, Petry believed, patients did not get the best possible nursing care.

After practicing briefly at Hopkins, Petry attended Teachers College, Columbia University, receiving a master's degree in 1929. Graduate school gave Petry the intellectual armamentaria to articulate her vision for nursing as a national force in health, the importance of nursing research, and nurses' need for an education that inculcated critical thinking skills and balanced apprenticeship with theoretical principles of nursing and health.

After graduate school, Petry taught briefly at Yale School of Nursing before spending 1929 to 1941 at the progressive University of Minnesota School of Nursing, where she rose from instructor to assistant professor to assistant dean. She spent another year doing course work at Columbia while on sabbatical in 1935–36. Her students revered her as a teacher who, although lively and fun, challenged them to become broadly educated, independent thinkers. She transformed Minnesota's curriculum by building bridges between the school of nursing and other university departments. Her hard work did not go unnoticed. In 1941 Petry was recruited to serve as a consultant on nursing education for the United States Public Health Service (USPHS), where she remained for two years.

Though cyclical nursing shortages plagued the United States throughout the late nineteenth and early twentieth centuries, World War II sparked a pressing need for nurses during a time when women were needed throughout the labor market. In 1943 Petry was asked to take charge of the Cadet Nurse Corps, a federal initiative designed to increase the number of nurses by providing housing and tuition subsidies to civilian schools of nursing. Adept at balancing political realities and pressure from hospitals as well as nursing and medical organizations with her own vision, Petry sought to upgrade nursing education by demanding that schools meet certain criteria in order to qualify for federal funds, thereby forcing many programs to improve their curricula. As the public face of the Cadet Nurse Corps, Petry traveled the nation using her personal warmth, charisma, and leadership skills to market the advantages of a free, federally sponsored nursing education to America's young women, spearheading an intensive recruitment campaign that ultimately yielded 180,000 new nurses. The program was so successful that there was no need to draft nurses to fill wartime needs.

Not only did the Cadet Nurse Corps program give Petry a platform to articulate her vision for nursing education, it also afforded her the opportunity to view health care from a national perspective. Petry believed that one of the Corps' most important contributions was that it made nurses and their societal contributions more visible to the American public and initiated a national dialogue about nursing education and the undervalued role of the nurse in the American health care system.

After the Cadet Nurse Corps program ended in 1948, Petry was appointed chief nurse officer of the USPHS and given the rank of assistant surgeon general in the PHS Commissioned Officers Corps; she was the first woman to be so named. This new position gave Petry a forum to develop her interest in international health. She was a delegate to the first World Health Assembly of the World Health Organization (WHO) in 1948 and later a member of the WHO's Expert Committee on Nursing. She continued to speak and publish prolifically on issues related to nursing manpower, health care quality, and public health. She married PHS researcher Nicholas Leone in 1952. They had no children and divorced in 1967.

Throughout the 1950s and early 1960s Leone played a major role in advancing her ideals of a well-educated nursing workforce and helped enact a major piece of legislation that facilitated reaching this goal, the 1964 Nurse Training Act. She played a leadership role in many professional organizations, served on the boards of many prestigious public and private foundations, and won numerous awards for her national service.

Leone retired from the USPHS in 1966 and moved to Dallas to be the associate dean of Texas Woman's University School of Nursing. In 1971 she moved to San Francisco and joined the faculty at the University of California, San Francisco. Until just before her death in San Francisco at the age of ninety-seven, she continued to teach and mentor nursing students. Throughout her sixty-year career, Lucile Petry Leone's leadership and clarity of vision helped forge the integrated model of nursing practice, education, and research that represents the highest standard of contemporary nursing practice.

Bibliography: The majority of Lucile Petry Leone's papers are in the History of Nursing Archives, Special Collections, Boston University Library, but there are also relevant materials in the archives of the Division of Nursing, United States Public Health Service, located at the National Archives in College Park, Maryland. Biographical materials relevant to Leone's life and work are also located in the Historical Reference Files, Office of the Public Health Historian, USPHS, which also houses photographs of her. Leone published dozens of articles in nursing and health care journals. The article that best summarizes her vision for the nursing profession is "The Art of Nursing," *Journal of the American Medical Association* 157 (April 1955), pp. 1381–83. Additional biographical materials can be found in David W. Brueggemann, "Remembering Lucile Petry Leone," *American Association for the History of Nursing Bulletin* 65, no. 6 (Winter 2000), pp. 9–10; Delores J. Haritos, "Lucile Petry Leone," in Vern L. Bullough, Alice P. Stein, and Lilli Sentz, eds., *American Nursing: A Biographical Dictionary*, vol. 2 (1992); Shirley H. Fondiller, "The Indomitable Lucile Petry Leone: Nursing's Valiant Leader," *Nursing and Health Care Perspectives* 21 (November–December 2000), pp. 275–77; Thelma M. Robinson, "Lucile Petry Leone (1902–1999) As We Remember Her," *American Association for the History of Nursing Bulletin* 65 (Winter 2000), p. 9; and Edna Yost, "Lucile Petry Leone," *American Women of Nursing* (1955). A brief autobiographical reflection on her life and work can be found in Thelma M. Schorr and Anne Zimmerman, eds., *Making Choices, Taking Chances: Nurse Leaders Tell Their Stories* (1988). See also Joan E. Lynaugh and Barbara L. Brush, *American Nursing: From Hospital to Health System* (1996), and Cynthia Connolly, "Prevention through Detention: The Pediatric Tuberculosis Preventorium Movement in the United States, 1909–1951" (PhD dissertation, University of Pennsylvania, 1999). An obituary appeared in the *New York Times* on December 5, 1999.

CYNTHIA CONNOLLY

LE SUEUR, Meridel. February 22, 1900–November 14, 1996. Writer, radical activist, feminist.

Meridel Le Sueur was a major radical writer of the 1930s who wrote persistently throughout her long life, filling more than 140 journal volumes in addition to her publications. Equal parts writer and socialist-feminist activist, she participated in both the Old Left and the New Left and the feminist movements of both the early and the late twentieth century. She was blacklisted during the 1940s and 1950s red scare just as her family had been tormented for being Socialists during and after World War I. She lived to be celebrated by the young radicals and feminists of the 1960s and 1970s, becoming something of an icon. She published her last novel, *The Dread Road* (1991), after she was ninety.

Born in Murray, Iowa, to Mayme "Marian" Lucy and William Winston Wharton, an itinerant Disciples of Christ minister, she was the eldest of three children. When Meridel was ten, her mother left her husband and fled with the children to live with her mother, Mary Antoinette Lucy, in Perry, Oklahoma. Both of these women were left-wing public activists, her grandmother a Woman's Christian Temperance Union (WCTU) worker, her mother a traveling Chautauqua-tent public speaker on sex equality, birth control, women's education, and woman suffrage. When Meridel was fourteen, her mother moved the family to Fort Scott, Kansas, to head the English department at the new People's College led by Socialist Party leader Eugene Debs. There Marian met Arthur Le Sueur, head of the law department, a supporter of the Socialist Party and the Industrial Workers of the World (IWW) who had been a Socialist mayor of Minot, North Dakota. Le Sueur and Marian Wharton married in 1917, and Meridel and her brothers took Le Sueur's name.

People's College did not survive, and with World War I looming, the Le Sueur family moved to St. Paul, Minnesota, where Marian and Arthur worked with the Nonpartisan League and their household became a way station for Socialists, Wobblies, labor organizers, anarchists, and others on the political left. Meridel went to Central High School in St. Paul, but left school permanently in the ninth grade. She lived in Chicago briefly, studied acting in New York City (living in an anarchist group with EMMA GOLDMAN), and then worked as a Hollywood movie extra. By 1928 she was back in St. Paul and a member of the American Communist Party.

Sometime in 1926, Le Sueur married Harry Rice, born Yasha Rubonof in Russia, a Communist Party organizer in St. Paul. While in jail for demonstrating against the executions of anarchists Nicola Sacco and Bartolomeo Vanzetti, Meridel decided to have a child as a deliberate affirmation of life in the face of what she saw as social and political death around her. Rachel was born in 1928, Deborah within two years, but their parents soon divorced.

Initial recognition for Le Sueur's writing came when her short story "Persephone" was published in the *Dial* in 1927. As the title suggests, hers was a midwestern retelling of the Greek rite-of-spring myth of Persephone and Demeter, where the daughter is kidnapped to the underworld and redeemed by her mother's offering grain to the earth for springtime rebirth. Later, Le Sueur fully Americanized this myth with Native American women's voices and native corn and drew upon it often, titling a 1975 collection of poetry *Rites of Ancient Ripening* and using *Ripening* as the title for the 1982 anthology from the Feminist Press that brought her writing back into circulation.

From 1927 until after World War II, Meridel Le Sueur was much in the public eye. She wrote journalistic pieces for *New Masses,* and published poetry, short fiction, and essays, such as "Corn Village" (*Scribner's,* August 1931), that laid out the core imagery and ideas with which she would work for seventy more years—her passionate rendering of people's suffering in poverty and struggling against unfair labor conditions, and her lyrically expressed hope for renewal symbolized by women's birthgiving and the earth's cycles of regeneration. Her work was anthologized in *O. Henry Prize Stories* and *O'Brien Best Stories.* Her 1935 story "Annunciation," based on her pregnancy with her first daughter, Rachel, was called "a small American masterpiece" (*Ripening,* p. 8).

The 1930s were years of political success as well as literary accolades for her. At the 1935 American Writers Congress, she was the only woman among twenty-eight speakers. In 1937 she was elected one of the vice presidents of the League of American Writers along with Van Wyck Brooks, Langston Hughes, Ernest Hemingway, and others. Her piece "I Was Marching," about the 1934 Minneapolis truckers strike, was reprinted three times. A collection of her works, *Salute to Spring,* was published in 1940, followed by a regional oral folk history, *North Star Country,* in 1945.

Placed on the House Committee on Un-American Activities' Communist suspect list after World War II, she was deserted by publishers, her books banned. Between 1947 and 1954, only Alfred Knopf would publish the biographies for children from which she made a meager living, supplemented with teaching, writing, factory work, and waitressing. During this bleak period, her daughters were her primary support system. She had been involved with Robert (Bob) Brown, an artist, for twenty-five years until his death in 1954, but the two were not always mutually supportive. In the 1950s, traveling by bus and dividing her time between the Southwest and Minnesota, she became active on behalf of Native American land rights.

By the end of the 1960s, the new radicalism and the women's movement gave Le Sueur a fresh audience of admirers. Her opposition to the Vietnam War led her to send a poem of solidarity, "Dòan Kêt" (1975), to the North Vietnamese Women's Union. In the 1970s and 1980s, even into her nineties when she was suffering from spinal deterioration, she wrote daily and traveled all over the country, doing poetry workshops supporting women's and working people's causes. When she was not chosen as a delegate to the World Conference on Women, held in 1985 in Nairobi, she went anyway and was prominent among the world's women in her bright flowing scarves and silver and turquoise Native jewelry.

On November 14, 1996, at the age of ninety-six, Meridel Le Sueur died in Hudson, Wisconsin, the town in which she had lived with her daughter Rachel.

Bibliography: Meridel Le Sueur's papers are at the Minnesota Historical Society, St. Paul, Minnesota. The collection includes 133 volumes of the more than 140 journals she kept from her teens through her nineties, plus letters, audiotapes, published and unpublished manuscripts, clippings, and photographs. Most of her personal library, copies of her books, and a few boxes of miscellaneous papers are at the Augsburg College Library, Minneapolis. A small collection of correspondence and annotated copies of poetry and stories is in the University of Delaware Library Special Collections Department.

There is no complete published bibliography of Le Sueur's works, but the list compiled by Lara Friedman-Shedlov that is included in the collection at the Minnesota Historical Society is extensive. For an introduction to Le Sueur's published work, see *Salute to Spring* (1940) and *Ripening: Selected Work, 1927–1980* (1982), which also contains a very useful overview of Le Sueur's career by Elaine Hedges. Le Sueur published a joint biography of her mother and stepfather called *Crusaders* (1955). Her novel *The Girl,* originally written in the 1930s, was published in 1978. Two dissertations have been devoted to her work: Neala Schleuning Yount, "'America: Song We Sang without Knowing'—Meridel Le Sueur's America" (University of Minnesota, 1978); and Nora Ruth Roberts, "Three Radical Women Writers: Meridel Le Sueur, Tillie Olsen, Josephine Herbst—A Marxist-Feminist Discussion" (City University of New York, 1995). See also Constance Coiner, *Better Red: The Writing and Resistance of Tillie Olsen and Meridel Le Sueur* (1995). In 1976, the Twin Cities Women's Film Collective made a 16mm film, "My People Are My Home," from her works and featured her voice. An obituary appeared in the *New York Times* on November 24, 1996.

GAYLE GRAHAM YATES

LEVERTOV, Denise. October 24, 1923–December 20, 1997. Poet, teacher, activist.

Priscilla Denise Levertoff (who later changed the spelling of her last name) was born in Ilford, Essex, into a family with a rich cultural and religious heritage. Her father, Paul Philip Levertoff, was a Russian Jew who had converted to Christianity and emigrated to England, where he became an Anglican priest and a distinguished scholar and activist. Denise's Welsh-born mother, Beatrice Adelaide Spooner-Jones, was a writer and teacher. Denise had one older sister, Olga, born in 1914.

Olga and Denise were educated privately by their mother, with mornings devoted to lessons at home and afternoons and evenings to museum visits, concerts, and reading aloud from nineteenth-century English and Russian poets and novelists. Sundays were passed in church, with services led by their father. By age five, Denise knew that she wanted to be an artist; when she was twelve, she sent some poems to T. S. Eliot, who replied with a letter of advice. By the time she was twenty-one, she had completed the poems that were to be published in 1946 in her first book, *The Double Image.* In these poems, she displays the sensitivity to nature and the respect for mystery that were to mark most of her future work.

Levertov came of age during World War II. Her family remained in London during the Blitz and were leaders in providing sanctuary for Jews fleeing from Hitler. From 1941 to 1944, she worked in hospitals as part of the Civil Nursing Reserve. On December 2, 1947, Levertov married American novelist Mitchell Goodman, and in 1948 she moved with him to New York City. Behind her was the old European world of her family; before her, the new American world of her husband.

As a poet, Levertov thrived in America, encouraged by the friendship of poet Robert Creeley, who published her work in *Origin* and *Black Mountain Review.* In William Carlos Williams, with whom she developed a father-daughter relationship, she found her most important mentor, and through her interaction with him, she developed her own poetics. In 1955, Levertov was naturalized as an American citizen, and the following year she published her first American book, *Here and Now.* With the appearance of the luminous and celebratory poems in her third and fourth books, *With Eyes in the Back of Our Heads* (1960) and *Jacob's Ladder* (1961), she came into her own as an American poet.

The 1950s also brought changes in Levertov's personal life. Her only child, Nikolai Gregor Goodman, who would become a writer, was born in June 1949. The Goodmans lived in New York City for most of the 1950s, with two extended periods abroad. In December 1950, they moved to Europe (France and Italy), where they remained until February 1952. In January 1956, the Goodmans and Levertov's recently widowed mother moved to Mexico. Levertov, Goodman, and Nikolai returned to New York at the beginning of 1958, but Mrs. Levertoff remained in Mexico for the last two decades of her life.

In the early 1960s, Levertov entered a place of shadows from which she was not to emerge for almost two decades. The somber tone was due in part to personal losses. In 1964, her sister Olga, only fifty years old, succumbed to lingering illness. Her beloved Welsh mother, alone in Mexico, gradually became a shell of herself. In 1973, Levertov's marriage crumbled, and she and Goodman divorced in 1975. These three events were incorporated into her poetry. Among her finest poems are the elegies for her sister, the "Olga Poems," which move from their shared childhood to the deathbed when "pain and drugs / quarreled like sisters in you." Her frequent visits to her mother, who had been her first teacher and best friend, were also occasions of self-examination and reflection. In "The 90th Year," Levertov creates a portrait of an old woman struggling to read *War and Peace* with a magnifying glass, a woman who as a young mother had taught her to see the flowers and had read Tolstoy aloud to her family.

Another factor in the darkness of Levertov's work during the 1960s and 1970s was her outrage over American participation in the Vietnam War. In the 1960s, she began a series of visiting appointments at American universities, and found herself energized by her students. She and her husband became national leaders in protests against the war, and in 1968 Goodman was convicted for violating laws related to the draft. In 1972, in the company of MURIEL RUKEYSER and Jane Hart, Levertov traveled to Hanoi, and on her return she spoke on numerous campuses about her conviction that nature and the most vulnerable human beings were being destroyed by greed, racism, and sexism, and by the institutionalization of these in capitalism. Her anguish can be tracked in the titles of her books: *The Sorrow Dance* (1967), *Relearning the Alphabet* (1970), *To Stay Alive* (1971), *The Freeing of the Dust* (1975), and *Life in the Forest* (1978). In the "Life at War" sequence, in angry and occasionally self-righteous tones, she vividly represents the atrocities of war. The critical response to Levertov's political poems has been mixed. Many feel that these poems represent a falling off in her poetic gift, a failure in sympathy and vision, the very areas in which she had previously excelled. This stressful period in American history left her exhausted.

The 1980s and 1990s were for Levertov a period of recovery and retrieval. In her personal life and in her poetry, she was able to make a fresh start that was simultaneously a movement forward and a return to her roots. Widely honored as one of America's best poets, she received numerous awards and honorary doctorates and was elected to the American Academy of Arts and Letters. In 1981, she became a professor at Stanford, where she remained until retiring in 1994.

The single most important factor, however, in her recovery from despair was the reclaiming of her Christian heritage. Her poetry flowered anew, characterized by technical mastery, spiritual depth, and tempered joy. Her attention to spiritual life is suggested by the titles of her last volumes: *Candles in Babylon* (1982); *Oblique Prayers* (1984); *Breathing the Water* (1987); *A Door in the Hive* (1989); *Sands of the Well* (1996); and *This Great Unknowing* (1999), published posthumously.

Denise Levertov died in Seattle in 1997 from complications of lymphoma. She was seventy-four. She had lived a life of uncompromising integrity and made immense contributions to modern poetry. She was both spiritual and pragmatic, Jewish and Christian, European and American, Romantic and modern, and in holding these opposites in fruitful balance, she created the poems that secured her place in American literature.

Bibliography: Denise Levertov's papers, assembled by the poet herself, are in the Cecil H. Green Library at Stanford University. They include family records and correspondence with her parents, her sister, her husband, and her son, as well as Levertov's notebooks and manuscripts and her correspondence with public figures and other poets, including William Carlos Williams. Beinecke Rare Book and Manuscript Library at Yale University contains her letters to Williams, and Houghton Library at Harvard University contains the papers of James Laughlin, her editor at New Directions for nearly four decades. Levertov published more than twenty-five books of poetry (including small limited editions), most of which were combined into the following collections: *Collected Earlier Poems 1940–1960* (1979); *Poems 1960–1967* (1983); *Poems 1968–1972* (1987); and *Poems 1972–1982* (2001). See also *The Selected Poems of Denise Levertov* (2002). Levertov published several volumes of prose, including *The Poet in the World* (1973); *Light Up the Cave* (1981); and *New and Selected Essays* (1992). She wrote a number of brief autobiographical pieces, collected in *Tesserae: Memories and Suppositions* (1995). *The Letters of Denise Levertov and William Carlos Williams,* edited by Christopher MacGowan (1998), preserves an important intergenerational dialogue in modern poetry; her interviews, collected in *Conversations with Denise Levertov,* edited by Jewel Spears Brooker (1998), reveal the progression of her thinking about poetry, teaching, and politics.

Reviews, criticism, and bibliography are collected in Albert Gelpi, ed., *Denise Levertov: Selected Criticism* (1993). Harry Marten, *Understanding Denise Levertov* (1988), is an overview of her life and work through the mid 1980s. Linda Wagner, *Denise Levertov* (1967), is an early assessment, and Wagner's collection of essays, *Denise Levertov: In Her Own Province* (1979), contains valuable mid-career commentary. A bibliography of Levertov's work through the mid 1980s may be found in Liana Sakelliou-Schultz, *Denise Levertov: An Annotated Primary and Secondary Bibliography* (1988). Obituaries appeared in the *Seattle Times* on December 22, 1997, and the *New York Times* on December 23, 1997.

JEWEL SPEARS BROOKER

LEWIS, Lucy Martin. c. 1895–March 12, 1992. Potter.

Lucy Martin Lewis was born to Lola Santiago and Martin Ortiz of the isolated Acoma Pueblo in northwestern New Mexico, where she lived throughout her life. She had two brothers, Joseph and Albert. At the time of her birth (she did not know the exact date or year, but celebrated on November 2), Acoma Pueblo was one of the most isolated of the twenty surviving Indian Pueblos of the American Southwest; even today, most Acoma people speak a Western Keresan dialect as their first language. When Lucy was a child, Spanish was the second language, English was spoken by relatively few Acoma people, and formal schooling often ended, as in her case, in the third grade. As a child, she learned to make pottery in the traditional Pueblo way—by observing the work practices of an accomplished artist to whom she was related, helping that person prepare clays and paints and fire the vessels, and herself making and painting countless pottery containers as play and for practice. Her great-aunt Helice Vallo was her mentor and critic, and in later years Lucy Lewis also served in those capacities to some of her own children and grandchildren.

She and Toribio Lewis (or Luis, also known as Hashkaya), also of Acoma, were married in about 1915 and had nine children (seven daughters and two sons) between 1919 and 1947. Five of her children—Anne, Andrew, Emma, Mary, and Delores—became accomplished potters in the Acoma tradition. Her oldest child, Ivan, who had moved to the Cochiti Indian Pueblo after his marriage to a Cochiti woman, also made pottery but in the tradition of his new community. Her other children were Margaret, Cecilia, and Carmel.

Acoma Pueblo ("Sky City"), which has been continually occupied since about AD 1200, is located atop an isolated, sheer-walled sandstone mesa, four hundred feet above the desert floor. Until after the middle of the twentieth century, it was inaccessible by road and had no running water, so that its beautifully painted, strong, lightweight pottery jars (ollas) were essential for hauling and storing water atop the waterless mesa. Most Acoma women and even a few men had always been part-time potters and pottery painters, and their wares were widely traded throughout New Mexico, but their products slowly became functionally obsolete after the 1880s when the Santa Fe railroad brought inexpensive industrially made goods to the region. For decades afterward, Acoma people depended on pottery sales to tourists for a significant portion of their cash income. Their pottery became a major market commodity that enabled the cash-poor society to participate in the economic system of the industrial world.

Lucy Lewis was a prolific artist who, early in her life, not only made utilitarian vessels for use in her Pueblo but also made thousands of small curio pieces to be sold to passengers on the Santa Fe Railroad and, after the 1930s, to tourists at roadside stands. Still, she remained anonymous outside of her Pueblo until she first entered a competitive art exhibition at Gallup, New Mexico, in 1950. There she received an Award of Merit, the first of many honors that came to her in the latter part of her life. And for the first time she was exposed to the influential dealer- and collector-dominated Indian art market. She soon signaled her newfound knowledge of that market by signing her work (she may have been the first Acoma potter to do so regularly), thereby raising the potential status of her pottery from "souvenir curio" to "fine art."

That new status was confirmed in 1958, when she first brought her work to the most prestigious of all Indian art exhibitions, the Southwestern Indian Art Market in Santa Fe. She won the Outstanding Exhibit Award, securing her reputation as a major traditional Indian artist and attracting the attention of major Indian art patrons, including photographer LAURA GILPIN and Indian Art Curator Kenneth Chapman of Santa Fe's Laboratory of Anthropology and Indian Arts Fund. Her success and new status helped inspire younger Acoma pottery artists to participate in that art market and by that means develop a vigorous new tradition of Acoma art pottery based upon the millennium-old utilitarian painted pottery traditions of the Pueblo world.

At Acoma and the other Pueblos, painted pottery was not only utilitarian; it also carried symbolic values, and these seemed to remain largely unchanged even after the transformation of pottery into a modern fine art. Pottery making was usually a woman's art. It used earthen materials and came to symbolize complex relationships among Pueblo women, the Earth Mother, and fertility. At Acoma it also symbolized life-giving water and therefore clouds, rainfall, and ancestral spirits. And, as at many other Pueblos, it was also a gift to the dead. At Acoma, many generations of men had collected pottery shards from ancestral Pueblo villages to be ground up and incorporated into the fabric of new vessels by their pottery-making relatives. The fragmentary paintings on those shards were often integrated into new designs in what seems to have been a self-conscious reiteration of their past by new generations of potters.

When Lucy Lewis was introduced to ancient Pueblo pottery by the museum curators and fine arts collectors she had met, she was one of the first modern Acoma potters to see and touch whole vessels that had been made by her ancestors. Perhaps for the first time she saw fragmentary designs as complete paintings, and these she translated into modern terms. Soon enough, books illustrating ancient southwestern vessels came to her attention, and her repertory expanded. From then on, she created elegant new forms inspired by ancestral wares, and virtually every vessel she made after about 1960 was both a thing of beauty and a subtle statement of ethnic pride and continuity with the past. Her husband died in 1966, but she remained active into her nineties, dying in Acoma, New Mexico, in 1992.

Bibliography: The only published biography of Lucy Lewis is Susan Peterson, *Lucy M. Lewis, American Indian Potter* (1984). It includes many fine photographs of the artist and her work. After 1974, beginning with the Maxwell Museum of Anthropology's *Seven Families in Pueblo Pottery* (1974), she is mentioned with regularity in group exhibition catalogues, one-person exhibition catalogues, and short articles. Judging from the increased frequency throughout the 1990s of published discussions of her work, her reputation within the limited circle of Indian art scholars, collectors, and dealers grew after her death, but there is little awareness of her or her work in any wider art context. The literature on the ancient history of Acoma Pueblo and the Southwest is rich, but much of it is either technical or superficial. Velma Garcia Mason's chapter on Acoma Pueblo in Alfonso Ortiz, ed., *Handbook of North American Indians*, vol. 9 (1979), pp. 450–66, remains the best accessible source, but see also Ward Allen Minge, *Acoma: Pueblo in the Sky* (1976). An obituary appeared in the *New York Times* on March 26, 1992.

J. J. BRODY

LIBBY, Leona Woods Marshall. August 9, 1919–November 10, 1986. Nuclear physicist.

Leona Woods was born on a small farm in La Grange, Illinois, the second of five children (three girls and two boys) of Mary Holderness and Wreightsill Woods. Her father was a lawyer. Her mother ran the farm; she depended on her children for help after her husband's death. During World War II, Leona Woods would bring her colleagues from the Chicago Metallurgical Laboratory at the University of Chicago, including its director Enrico Fermi and his wife Laura, to help with the harvest.

Leona Woods became an athletic young woman able to do sustained physical labor, necessary traits in her early scientific training. She attended the University of Chicago and graduated, at the age of nineteen, in 1938 with a BS in chemistry and began work on a PhD. Passing her qualifying examinations quickly, she asked James Franck to be her adviser. Leona had taken his course on quantum chemistry, completing a report on Louis Brillouin's band theory of solids. Franck accepted, but warned that as a woman going into science she might well starve. Leona had no intention of starving, so she turned to Robert Mulliken, also a Nobel Laureate, and in 1943 completed an experimental dissertation, "On the Silicon Oxide Bands. II. Note on Spin Doubling Sigma States of 1 Positive Ion of Carbon-Monoxide," under his guidance and that of recently arrived Polish physicist Stanislaw Mrozowski.

At Chicago, Leona Woods was the only woman on Fermi's team experimentally investigating whether a nuclear chain reaction could be sustainable and controllable. In December 1943 these experiments demonstrated that a bomb using fissile materials was at least possible. Her skills with vacuum tube technology were indispensable in the building of the neutron detectors used to monitor the chain reaction in the carbon and uranium "pile." As a member of the group Leona Woods worked intensely, both in physically helping to build the reactor and on the night shifts monitoring the pile in a bitter Chicago winter. At the same time Fermi lectured the group on the latest developments in nuclear physics; assigned to take notes, she rapidly learned the most up-to-date nuclear physics. Also in the group was PhD physicist John Marshall, who had migrated from Columbia University with Fermi in 1941. In July 1943 he and Woods married.

After the nuclear reactor went "critical" and the knowledge that a controlled nuclear fission reaction was secured, Leona and John Marshall moved with Fermi to construct similar experiments at Argonne National Laboratory, a more remote location south of Chicago. Any physicist with Leona Marshall's talents was rare and highly valued, whether female or male. Fermi even helped her hide her first pregnancy, counseling her to wear baggy clothing, until two days before her first son, Peter, was born in 1944. She returned to work at Argonne one week later, while her mother, and on occasion Fermi's assigned bodyguard, took care of Peter. Soon thereafter the Marshalls moved to Hanford, Washington, to build reactors to produce plutonium. John Marshall, however, spent the rest of the war in Los Alamos, New Mexico, joining Robert Oppenheimer's team that designed and built the first nuclear bombs. Leona Marshall's main responsibilities remained at Hanford, producing fuel and plutonium for the bombs.

After the war the Marshalls returned to the University of Chicago, and Leona became a fellow at Fermi's Institute for Nuclear Studies; she became an associate in 1947, and finally assistant professor in 1954. The Institute's work was dominated by Fermi's research priorities, although he encouraged Leona's work. In 1949 the Marshalls' second son, John, was born. After Fermi died in 1954, Institute personnel began to leave, and the Marshalls separated. John Marshall returned to Los Alamos; Leona accepted a position as a fellow at the Institute for Advanced Study at Princeton.

Over the next several years her career advanced through a series of appointments, including visiting scientist at Brookhaven National Laboratory (1958–60) and associate, then full, professor at New York University (1960–63). In this period she described herself as a single mother, separated from her husband, and trying to raise two children. She also managed to stay at the center of a very competitive field, and at the center of the organizational and technical changes within experimental physics: from small to large teams, and from the laboratory bench to ever more powerful accelerators, as research shifted from the nucleus to fundamental particles. She worked in teams of increasing size, on ever more complex experiments, analyzing the results and publishing a steady stream of co-authored papers, while simultaneously training graduate students. The analytical aspects of her research continued after she moved to the University of Colorado in 1963; at that time she also served as a consultant to Los Alamos, TRW Space Systems Group, and the Rand Corporation, where she was a staff member from 1966 to 1970.

In 1966 she divorced John Marshall and married recently divorced Willard Frank Libby, a UCLA chemist she knew at the Institute for Nuclear Research and a 1960 winner of the Nobel Prize in Chemistry for the development of radiocarbon dating. Leona Marshall Libby continued her own work in particle physics at Colorado, moving closer to her husband by joining UCLA as a visiting professor of engineering in 1970. She finally severed her ties with Colorado in 1972. This geographical shift marked a change in her research toward ancient climates and cosmology.

While working in high-energy physics, Leona

Marshall Libby published papers and edited or contributed to volumes with others. Later she published her insightful but sometimes inaccurate reminiscences of Fermi and the Manhattan Project. As her research shifted to using radioactivity as a historical indicator, she published two books and co-authored many papers. After Willard Libby died in 1980, she edited his papers with Rainer Berger (seven subject volumes published as five) and edited a posthumous volume of his writings on solar physics and chemistry. She became an advocate for nuclear power and environmental issues. The fact that she was a Fellow of the American Physical Society and the Royal Geographical Society reflects the breadth of her interests and the depth of her technical abilities. She never led a research project yet was a pivotal member of many research teams. She died at age sixty-seven in Santa Monica, California, in 1986, just two years after her last paper on quasi-stellar objects.

Bibliography: Leona Marshall Libby published three books: *The Uranium People* (1979); *Carbon Dioxide and Climate* (1980); and *Past Climates: Tree Thermometers, Commodities and People* (1983). For biographical information, see the essay by Ruth H. Howes in Louise S. Grinstein, Rose K. Rose, and Miriam H. Rafailovich, eds., *Women in Chemistry and Physics: A Biobibliographic Sourcebook* (1993), which also contains a detailed bibliography of Libby's technical publications. Laura Fermi, *Atoms in the Family: My Life with Enrico Fermi* (1954), contains reminiscences of Leona Woods Marshall. An obituary appeared in the *Los Angeles Times* on November 13, 1986.

ELIZABETH GARBER

LISTON, Melba. January 13, 1926–April 23, 1999. Jazz trombonist, arranger, composer.

Jazz trombonist and arranger Melba Doretta Liston was born in Kansas City, Missouri, in the wake of that city's now legendary jazz scene. Too young to participate directly, she did reap the influences of growing up in a major jazz hub through her family, who passed along their love for the music. The only child of Lucille Clark, an office worker, and Frank Liston, a laborer, Liston spent her early years crossing back and forth between Kansas City, Missouri, where she was raised by her mother, and Kansas City, Kansas, where she was under the care of her maternal grandparents. Liston recalled a lonely childhood, relieved only by music, usually on the radio. When she asked her mother for a trombone at the age of seven, some of her relatives were opposed, considering it a boy's instrument. Nonetheless, in the midst of the Great Depression, her mother managed to buy the horn. Encouraged by her mother and her grandfather, a guitarist, Liston began teaching herself how to produce sound on the horn, and to play familiar melodies, inventing her own notation system to help her remember songs that she heard on the radio and in church. She rejected the teacher her mother found for her, preferring to play by ear. At age eight, she performed on the radio.

Liston and her mother moved to Los Angeles in 1937, joining her maternal grandmother and aunts, who had already relocated, in hopes of finding better opportunities. She was soon immersed in formal music training at McKinley Junior High School, and in a remarkable children's orchestra sponsored by the Parks and Recreation Department and led by drummer and celebrated music educator Alma Hightower. Among Liston's bandmates were tenor saxophonist Dexter Gordon and alto saxophonist Vi Redd. She continued to play with Hightower's group while attending Jefferson High School and when she later transferred to Los Angeles Polytechnic High School.

In 1942, at age sixteen, Liston joined local 767, the black local of the segregated American Federation of Musicians union in Los Angeles. Almost immediately, she secured a regular trombone position in the Lincoln Theater band under Bardu Ali. The musicians played for vaudeville acts and also performed in skits as needed. Some acts lacked proper arrangements, so Liston began writing for them as well as playing the shows. The following year, some of Bardu Ali's musicians, Liston among them, were wooed away by trumpet player and composer-arranger Gerald Wilson. Liston worked as Wilson's copyist in a six-year apprenticeship that helped her develop as an arranger and a composer. In addition, Wilson introduced her to leading figures such as Count Basie, Duke Ellington, and Dizzy Gillespie, each of whom would go on to hire her.

Liston's school friend, tenor saxophonist Dexter Gordon, called her for her first recording date in 1947. Both takes of "Mischievous Lady" were released on Dial Records, complete with solos by Liston. Her education in bebop accelerated when she and Wilson joined Dizzy Gillespie's orchestra in New York in the late 1940s; the brilliant group of young musicians included tenor saxophonist John Coltrane. When Gillespie's band broke up after a year, Wilson gathered together many of the musicians, including Liston, for a southern tour with BILLIE HOLIDAY. Unfortunately, audiences were sparse, the tour was a disaster, and Liston was discouraged enough to quit the band business and take a job as bookkeeper. Although she didn't play during this four-year period, she continued to write.

Liston was married and divorced three times in her life. None of the marriages produced children, and little is known of them because she seldom discussed her life outside of music. She did tell one interviewer that whenever she was married, she became a wife and ceased to be a trombonist—when musicians saw her with her trombone again, they would know that another marriage had ended.

In 1956, Dizzy Gillespie hired her as trombonist and arranger for his State Department tour to the Middle East, followed by a subsequent tour to South America. Liston was often the only woman in the band and endured the skepticism of male musicians. She described the loneliness she felt as a single person where many of her colleagues had wives and children, as well as the extra work of sewing and cooking that would default to her as the only woman.

Her career blossomed during her tenure with Gillespie. After hearing her solo with Gillespie's band on her own arrangement of Claude Debussy's "My Reverie," pianist-composer Randy Weston initiated a long-term collaboration that has often been compared to that of Duke Ellington and Billy Strayhorn. Their first effort, an album entitled *Little Niles* (1958), was a critical success. That same year, she recorded her only album under her own name, *Melba Liston and Her Bones,* which showcased her writing and playing with six other leading trombonists and a rhythm section. She then toured Europe with another renowned bandleader, Quincy Jones, in 1959.

During the 1960s and 1970s, Liston worked on a wide range of projects, including bassist Charles Mingus's Town Hall Concert, trumpet player Clark Terry's concert with the Buffalo Symphony, and for Motown Records, working with Marvin Gaye, Diana Ross, and Ruth Brown. In 1973, she conducted the Randy Weston Big Band at the Newport Jazz Festival, then took a hiatus from performing. For more than five years she lived in Jamaica, where she taught at the University of the West Indies and served as director of Afro-American Pop and Jazz at the African-American Division of the Jamaica School of Music in Kingston. In 1979, Liston returned to the United States to play for the Women's Jazz Festival in Kansas City and for the New York Salute to Women in Jazz. This homecoming inspired the formation of Melba Liston and Company, first as an all-woman group and later as a mixed group.

A stroke put an end to Liston's trombone career in 1985, but she was determined to keep writing. Fellow musicians threw a benefit to buy her a computer, and she learned to use her left hand and a composing program. In 1987, she received an American Jazz Master Award from the National Endowment for the Arts. Her later collaborations with Weston included *Spirits of Our Ancestors* (1992) and *Volcano Blues* (1993). In 1993, she was honored at the first International Women's Brass Conference in St. Louis. Liston died in Los Angeles of heart disease on April 23, 1999, at the age of seventy-three.

Bibliography: The Melba Liston Collection at the Center for Black Music Research, Columbia College, in Chicago, contains lead sheets and scores with meticulous scope notes. Oral histories of Liston are collected at the Smithsonian Jazz Oral History Program and the UCLA Oral History Program. An edited version of the latter appears in Clora Bryant et al., *Central Avenue Sounds: Jazz in Los Angeles* (1998). Other sources include the vertical files at the Institute of Jazz Studies, Dana Library, Rutgers University. Articles devoted to Liston and her music include Erica Kaplan, "Melba Liston: It's All from My Soul," *Antioch Review* 57, no. 3 (Summer 1999), pp. 415–25; Pat Mullan, "Melba Liston: Jazz Master," *Newsletter of the International Women's Brass Conference,* October 1995, pp. 1–2 (reprinted from *Jazz Now* magazine); W. Royal Stokes, "The Big Band Sound of Melba Liston," *Ms.,* January 1983, pp. 99–101; Dalia Pagani, "Melba Liston: Interview," *Cadence,* May 1984, pp. 5–12; and Stan Woolley, "Melba Liston," *Jazz Journal International,* February 1987, pp. 20–21.

There are substantial references to her in histories of women in jazz, including Linda Dahl, *Stormy Weather: The Music and Lives of a Century of Jazz Women* (1989); Sally Placksin, *American Women in Jazz* (1982); and Leslie Gourse, *Madame Jazz: Contemporary Women Instrumentalists* (1995). See also Bette Yarbrough Cox, *Central Avenue—Its Rise and Fall (1890–c. 1955)* (1993). For more on her work with Dizzy Gillespie, see Gillespie and Al Fraser, *To Be or Not to Bop* (1979). For more on her own music education and philosophy of improvisation, see Paul Berliner, *Thinking in Jazz: The Infinite Art of Improvisation* (1994). Obituaries appeared in the *Los Angeles Times* on April 28, 1999, the *New York Times* on April 30, 1999, the *Guardian* on May 18, 1999, and *Down Beat,* August 1999, p. 20.

SHERRIE TUCKER

LIVINGSTONE, Mary. June 23, 1906–June 30, 1983. Radio and television comedian.

Mary Livingstone, a key member of comedian Jack Benny's radio and television casts for nearly thirty years, was born Sadie Marks in Seattle, the second of the three children of Esther Wagner and David Marks. She was raised in Vancouver, British Columbia, where her father, a Romanian immigrant who had married an American, was a successful businessman and a prominent leader in the Jewish community. During the family's sojourn in Vancouver, they regularly entertained performers appearing at the Orpheum Theater. Among these guests was Jack Benny (born Benjamin Kubelsky), a rising vaudeville star, who came to a Passover seder in 1921. He paid no attention to Sadie.

After Marks graduated from King George High School, her family moved back to the United States and settled in Los Angeles. She took a job working in the hosiery department at May Company Department Store in Hollywood. During this period she was reintroduced to Benny, who was twelve years her senior. He courted her by appearing at her counter every day, and after a short acquaintance they were married on January 14, 1927. (Their meeting at the May Company would later become part of the radio show; when she insulted him, he would threaten to send her back there.) Although she had no show business aspirations, she traveled with him on the Orpheum circuit, and when the female partner in his comedy act became ill, she agreed to fill in, taking the name Marie Marsh. Despite her lack of experience, their act received rave reviews, and theater managers advised Benny to hire her instead of his previous partner. He did, and after their tour the couple made one well-reviewed short film together, *Bright Moments,* in 1928. Her only other film appearances were in *Mr. Broadway* (1933) and *This Way Please* (1937). In 1934, they adopted their only child, an infant daughter they named Joan Naomi.

Benny credited his wife with encouraging him to try the new medium of radio. After a guest spot on Ed Sullivan's show, he was offered his own program, which first broadcast on May 2, 1932. Benny and his writers soon invented a character to be played by Marks: Mary Livingstone, an eccentric fan from Plainfield, New Jersey. The Mary character, the president of Jack's fan club, read Jack a terrible poem expressing her undying love, but also revealed that her mother hated him and his show. On the air, Marks cleverly punctuated Mary's lines with nervous laughter. Benny wrote later that she was "simply fantastic," and that her "delicious rippling silver laughter" made the character come to life (Joan Benny, pp. 79–80). Listeners apparently agreed, as letters demanding a return of "the girl who laughed from Plainfield, New Jersey" poured in. Responding to this feedback, the writers decided to make Mary a permanent member of the cast, and Marks soon changed her name legally to Mary Livingstone Benny.

Radio comedy was in its infancy, and Benny and his staff were influential in shaping the genre. Benny recognized that instead of telling jokes, he could create humor through the development of characters and ongoing story lines. His other innovation was to make himself the butt of jokes from his cast, which included an announcer, a bandleader, a tenor singer, and a valet, in addition to Mary. Although she was introduced as a stereotypical "dizzy dame," by 1934 she had been redefined as Jack's secretary, and as a witty, wisecracking, and astute deflater of Jack's pretensions and bad behavior. Yet Livingstone's distinctive high-pitched voice always exuded warmth and good-humored affection for Jack, even as she delivered her barbs.

Mary Livingstone was the only major recurring female character on the show, and many listeners mistakenly understood her to be Jack's girlfriend. Livingstone played her as a smart, independent, irreverent resister of Jack's authority, who openly expressed interest in many attractive men. The character, who was not unlike the feisty heroines of 1930s "screwball" comedies, was presented as an equal member of the on-air "family."

Livingstone's excellent comic timing, wry delivery, and infectious laugh enlivened the comedy sketches and parodies of popular films for which the Sunday night show became very popular. Mary's character was developed further through two important running gags: to Jack's annoyance, she recited hilarious poems about him, and she read letters from her "mother in Plainfield" that combined ridicule of Jack with zany stories of her fictional relatives' responses to the Depression and war.

In 1948, Livingstone informed Benny that after many years of enduring "mike fright" she could no longer take the strain of weekly live performances. To continue her contribution to the program, the producer recorded her lines at home, then edited them into the performance taped by the rest of the cast. Mary also appeared intermittently on Benny's various television shows, debuting in 1951, but she was not a regular, and by the early 1960s she had retired.

Livingstone's performance was crucial to the long-running success of the radio program, but unlike her friend GRACIE ALLEN, she was never billed equally with her husband. Livingstone wrote that when the couple made personal appearances together, promoters wanted to advertise them as "Benny and Livingstone," but she refused. "In truth, in my own mind, there were never two careers in our family. . . . Jack was the star. I was always a featured member of his company" (Benny and Marks, p. 68). This self-assessment was accurate. Livingstone was a talented and admired comic actress, but she was never interested in an independent show business career or stardom beyond her important supporting role on Benny's programs.

Livingstone and Benny were married for forty-seven years, until his death in 1974. She was a popular, stylish Hollywood hostess, and the socially active couple had many enduring friendships with show business colleagues, but some later criticized what they saw as her insecurity and status-seeking. After her husband's death, Mary Livingstone became more reclusive and lived quietly in Holmby Hills, California, where she died in 1983 at the age of seventy-seven. She is buried next to Benny at nearby Hillside Memorial Park.

Bibliography: Mary Livingstone's professional and personal papers (including radio and television scripts, recordings, scrapbooks, correspondence, and photographs) are part of the Jack Benny Papers Collection at the University of California, Los Angeles. Recordings of the radio and television shows are widely available commercially. Livingstone's biography of her husband, *Jack Benny*, coauthored under the name Mary Livingstone Benny with her brother Hilliard Marks, with the assistance of Marcia Borie, was published in 1978. Joan Benny integrated her father's unpublished memoirs into her own account of her parents' lives and careers in *Sunday Nights at Seven: The Jack Benny Story* (1990). Several other Benny biographers and friends discuss Livingstone's personal and professional life extensively; see Benny manager Irving Fein's *Jack Benny: An Intimate Biography* (1976); radio writer Milt Josefsberg's *The Jack Benny Show* (1977); and George Burns's unflattering accounts of Livingstone in *Gracie: A Love Story* (1988) and *All My Best Friends* (1989). Scholarly accounts of the show and its performers, as well as synopses of many programs, can be found in *Jack Benny: The Radio and Television Work* (1991), published by the Museum of Television and Radio in Beverly Hills. See also Margaret T. McFadden, "'America's Boy Friend Who Can't Get a Date': Gender, Race, and the Cultural Work of the Jack Benny Program, 1932–1946," *Journal of American History* 80, no. 1 (June 1993), pp. 113–34. Obituaries appeared in the *New York Times* on July 1 and 2, 1983.

MARGARET T. MCFADDEN

LOGAN, Onnie Lee Rodgers. ca. 1910–July 10, 1995. Midwife.

Onnie Lee Rodgers's birth outside Sweet Water, Alabama, was attended by an unlicensed, untrained midwife, as were one-half of all U.S. births that year. Her exact date of birth is not known, because accurate vital statistics were not maintained in many rural areas, particularly for African Americans, until the 1930s. She was the fourteenth of sixteen children born to Len and Martha Rodgers, one of the few landowning black families in Marengo County. Onnie Lee's values were shaped by a Baptist upbringing, with church on Sundays and family prayer meetings during the week. In *Motherwit: An Alabama Midwife's Story,* the 1989 autobiography that introduced her to a national audience, she remembered, "We lived a happy, comfortable life to be right outa slavery times" (p. 17).

Onnie Lee Rodgers completed the tenth grade in the segregated school in Sweet Water, but left school after her mother's death when she was around eighteen. Like her mother and maternal grandmother, she chose midwifery as a vocation in response to a divine calling. As a sickly child who couldn't help in the fields, she cooked, sewed, and attended deliveries with her mother, learning that midwifery encompassed more than just assisting with the delivery. Following a profoundly altruistic ethic of service, her mother often worked without pay or for farm produce, and provided a range of assistance including child care, cooking, cleaning, and washing.

In 1930 Onnie Lee Rodgers married Elmo Watkins, a railroad worker. Their son Johnnie was born the next year. At age twenty-one, she took the first steps toward becoming a midwife, when while working as a maid she was called in to assist in the delivery of her employer's baby. The attending doctor was amazed at her natural ability to coach the mother through labor and care for the mother and baby afterward. He told her she would make not only a good midwife, but a good doctor. She began to attend deliveries with other local midwives.

Around 1934 she and her husband moved from Magnolia, Alabama, to Mobile, working as a maid in addition to caring for their son. Within a few years her husband left her, and she learned that the marriage had never been legal because Watkins had never divorced his first wife. Widowed from a second marriage to Homer George, her final marriage to Roosevelt Logan around 1951 lasted until her death.

After Logan's first marriage broke up, she took another job as a live-in maid for a physician and his wife. She worked for the Mears family for over forty years, and credited Dr. Mears for encouraging her as a midwife. Besides asking her to discuss her deliveries and telling her she would have made a good doctor, the Mearses granted Logan the flexibility to leave work at will in order to attend deliveries.

Logan received her midwifery license in 1947 after she completed a nine-month training program at the Mobile County Board of Health, which supervised midwives and authorized annual renewal of their permits. Alabama then had the nation's highest maternal mortality rate, and midwives attended one-fifth of all births and one-half of black births. Patients of midwives were required to receive prenatal care from a doctor in order to be released for home delivery, and midwives had to call the doctor for assistance in the event of complications.

During the first ten years of her career, Logan's clients were mainly black families living in extreme poverty. Some houses were so unsanitary that she had to bring her own soap and sheets to put on the bed. If there were no clothes for the new baby, Logan sewed them from an old skirt in between contractions. After the delivery, she returned with needed supplies and sometimes cooked breakfast and dinner as well. Despite these obstacles, of the hundreds of births Logan attended, only four infants died—three infants were stillborn and one died shortly after birth.

According to Logan, most miscarriages were caused by pregnant women doing hard field labor and eating inadequate diets, not by midwives' lack of skill or knowledge. She acknowledged that she and her patients benefited from modern prenatal care and nutrition, and credited midwife training classes for teaching her to prepare sanitary pads for delivery, scrub her hands, tie the umbilical cord, put silver nitrate in the baby's eyes to prevent blindness, and pack a bag with sterile instruments and supplies. "But so many things that I have run into that the classes did not teach me. . . . Two-thirds of what I know about deliverin, carin for mother and baby, what to expect, what was happenin and was goin on, I didn't get it from the class. God gave it to me. So many things I got from my own plain motherwit" (ibid., p. 90).

Until the mid 1960s, Logan's clients were typical for granny midwives: poor families in the black neighborhoods of Mobile and outlying rural areas who could not afford doctor-attended births in hospitals or who feared prejudicial treatment in white-run health institutions. As public maternity clinics expanded to reach poor rural and urban patients, maternal and infant mortality decreased significantly. The Maternal and Infant Care clinic in Mobile was originally patronized mainly by whites, but by the 1970s both blacks and whites used the clinic. This change eroded Logan's patient base. She began to cater to white fundamentalists who wanted a biblical home birth with a midwife. Malpractice liability and economic competition reduced the number of doctors willing to authorize home births, and in 1976 Alabama outlawed lay midwifery. The Board of Health allowed Logan to continue practicing until 1984, when she was the last granny midwife in Mobile and one of the last in Alabama.

Despite such trends, the feminist health movement of the 1970s promoted the resurgence of midwifery by encouraging women to seek female practitioners and take a proactive role in their own health care. Feminist health activists rejected the traditional obstetrical view of childbirth as a disease requiring medical intervention with drugs, instruments, and surgery. Instead, activists saw labor and delivery as a natural process that should be allowed to progress with a minimum of interference in a supportive, all-female environment. Many schools of nursing established certified nurse-midwife programs. By the time of Logan's death in Mobile in 1995, American childbirth had been transformed to incorporate many of the patient-centered, non-interventionist practices long advocated by Logan and other midwives.

Bibliography: Much of the biographical information on Logan can be found in Onnie Lee Logan as told to Katherine Clark, *Motherwit: An Alabama Midwife's Story* (1989). Useful secondary sources include E. H. Beardsley, *A History of Neglect: Health Care for Blacks and Mill Workers in the Twentieth-Century South* (1987); Darlene Clark Hine, *Black Women in White: Racial Conflict and Cooperation in the Nursing Profession, 1890–1950* (1989); Jacqueline Jones, *Labor of Love, Labor of Sorrow: Black Women, Work, and the Family from Slavery to the Present* (1985); Judith Walzer Leavitt, *Brought to Bed: Childbearing in America, 1750 to 1950* (1986); Susan Smith, *Sick and Tired of Being Sick and Tired: Black Women's Health Activism in America, 1890–1950* (1995); and Karen Kruse Thomas, "'Law Unto Themselves': Black Women as Patients and Practitioners in North Carolina's Campaign to Reduce Infant and Maternal Mortality, 1935–1953," *Nursing History Review* 12 (2003), pp. 47–66. An obituary appeared in the *New York Times* on July 13, 1995.

KAREN KRUSE THOMAS

LONGWORTH, Alice Roosevelt. February 12, 1884–February 20, 1980. Politician, journalist, Washington hostess.

Known in her youth as "Princess Alice" and later as "the other Washington Monument," Alice Roosevelt Longworth was born in New York City, the eldest child of Theodore Roosevelt (TR), twenty-sixth president of the United States, and ALICE LEE. Her mother was from an upper-class Boston family; her father was the Harvard-educated son of a wealthy New York reformer. During her father's two terms as president, Alice was the archetypal New Woman whose modern behavior and witty tongue made her the first political celebrity of the twentieth century. She was a presence at virtually every Republican convention from 1908 until her death and, with her brother Ted, the self-appointed heir to her father's political legacy. Increasingly conservative over time, politically she is best characterized as having had independence and a willingness to speak her mind. Although she never ran for office, she was a political player who brokered candidacies for other women, such as Illinois congresswoman RUTH MCCORMICK. A valuable ally and a fearsome enemy who was courted by presidents and presidential aspirants from both parties, by her own count she averaged three White House dinners a year after World War I.

Alice's childhood was remarkable for the personal freedom and independence she was permitted by her parents and her Aunt Anna "Bamie" Roosevelt. Her mother died of Bright's disease two days after Alice's birth, and Alice saw little of her father until his remarriage in 1886 to EDITH CAROW and the birth of Theodore Jr. in 1887. In 1898, as TR prepared to embark for Cuba with his regiment of Rough Riders, Alice and the equally ungovernable Ted were removed to Bamie's, while the younger siblings Archie, Kermit, Quentin, and Ethel remained at the family home at Oyster Bay, New York.

When Theodore Roosevelt became president in 1901 after the assassination of William McKinley, Alice was a high-spirited, blue-eyed teenager and, as her mother's only heir, independently wealthy. Schooled at home, she acquired a political education under the tutelage of her father, who required her to learn something every evening and repeat it at breakfast. Though she never described herself as a feminist, she became symbolic of the new social freedoms that modern women claimed. She drank, she danced, and she drove from Washington to New York in an open car; when TR thundered that his daughter would not smoke under his roof, she perched on top of the White House and puffed away. Their struggles were legendary, but laced with humor: when Owen Wister asked Roosevelt why he did not discipline Alice, the president responded that he could "run the country or control [Alice]," but he "could not possibly do both" (Felsenthal, p. 400). As commercial products appeared in "Alice Blue," and songs such as "Alice, Where Art Thou" and "Alice Blue Gown" became popular dance tunes, Princess Alice enhanced her father's presidency in a way that "first daughters" Margaret Truman, Lynda and Lucy Johnson, and Julie and Tricia Nixon would replicate more sedately.

Surprisingly, while other women fought for suffrage, access to the smoke-filled back room, and elected office, Alice entered politics as a wife. On tour in Asia in 1905, she met Nicholas Longworth, a Republican congressman from Ohio, and they married at the White House on February 17, 1906. Alice was an enthusiastic campaigner, a presence in the gallery in the House of Representatives, and a practiced dinner-party politician. She worked tirelessly behind the scenes to promote her husband, whose alliances were to the right of her father's. In 1912, these differences surfaced as TR split the party with his Bull Moose candidacy and Longworth, a Taft Republican, lost.

Without portfolio until her husband returned to Congress in 1914, Longworth became a regular in the Senate gallery, and was soon publicly allied with Idaho progressive William Borah. During World War I and the battle over peace terms, Longworth turned her political energies to helping her husband, Borah, and Henry Cabot Lodge defeat the League of Nations. Throughout the Republican 1920s (her husband was speaker of the house from 1925 to 1931), her home was filled with policymakers and presidents whose agendas were defined by isolationism and Prohibition. The Longworths' only child, Paulina, was born in 1925.

Her husband's death in 1931 ended Longworth's hope of returning to the White House; watching her Hyde Park relatives take office in 1933 was a second blow. Although Franklin and ELEANOR ROOSEVELT continued to issue invitations, Alice was vocally opposed to the New Deal, publicly referred to FDR as "Feather Duster," and by the end of the 1930s had become a member of the isolationist America First organization. This period also saw her emergence as an author. In 1936, she followed the success of her 1933 memoir *Crowded Hours* with "Capital Comment," a syndicated column designed as a witty, anti–New Deal response to Eleanor Roosevelt's socially conscious "My Day." However, much of her humor, including nasty imitations of cousin Eleanor that she was famous for into old age, was unprintable and did not translate well into a daily column, and she gave up the column less than two years later.

During World War II and the cold war, Longworth attended Republican conventions as a delegate from Ohio; as a journalist, she often reported on the Democratic conventions as well. In 1956, she was mysteriously absent from both, later admitting that she had been hospitalized for breast cancer surgery. In 1957, Paulina died suddenly, having taken an overdose of prescription medications. Ironically, this tragedy led to the great friendship of her life when she assumed the guardianship of granddaughter Joanna Sturm.

Throughout her life, Alice Roosevelt Longworth remained a fixture in popular culture. The model for George S. Kauffman's *First Lady* (1935), she was always good for a quote, and was sought after by aspiring Republicans much as Eleanor Roosevelt was by Democrats. To the end of her life, she occupied the house on Massachusetts Avenue in Washington, D.C., where she and Longworth had plotted a presidential run. Surrounded by her father's hunting trophies and mementoes of a life in politics, she died of bronchial pneumonia on February 20, 1980, at the age of ninety-six.

Bibliography: The Alice Roosevelt Longworth Collection of diaries and letters is held at the Library of Congress, Washington, D.C. Her memoir, *Crowded Hours: Reminiscences of Alice Roosevelt Longworth* (1933), was written in middle age; a gossipy oral history, Michael Teague's *Mrs. L.: Conversations with Alice Roosevelt Longworth* (1981), supplements this volume. She has inspired three full-length biographies: James Brough, *Princess Alice: A Biography of Alice Roosevelt Longworth* (1975); Carol Felsenthal, *Alice Roosevelt Longworth* (1988); and Howard Teichmann, *Alice: The Life and Times of Alice Roosevelt Longworth* (1979). In *The Roosevelt Women* (1998), Betty Boyd Caroli includes Longworth in a generational biography. Longworth's vivid youth makes her prominent in modern accounts of the years up to and including her father's presidency. Such accounts include Hermann Hagedorn, *The Roosevelt Family of Sagamore Hill* (1955); Edmund Morris, *The Rise of Theodore Roosevelt* (1979) and *Theodore Rex* (2001); and Edward J. Renehan Jr., *The Lion's Pride: Theodore Roosevelt and His Family in Peace and War* (1998). A reserved account of Alice's marriage to Nicholas Longworth can be found in Clara Longworth Chambrun, *The Making of Nicholas Longworth: Annals of an American Family* (1933). Jerry Israel provides context for the 1906 Pacific tour in "'For God, for China and for Yale'—The Open Door in Action," *American Historical Review* 75, no. 3 (February 1970), pp. 796–807. Obituaries appeared in the *Washington Post* on February 21 and 24, 1980, and the *New York Times* on February 25, 1980.

CLAIRE BOND POTTER

LOOS, Anita. April 26, 1888–August 18, 1981. Screenwriter, novelist.

The East Coast view of Anita Loos is that she charmed New York's intellectual heavyweights with *Gentlemen Prefer Blondes,* her witty 1925 novel about the gold digger Lorelei Lee. The West Coast view is that she sold her first screenplay in 1912, worked with D. W. Griffith, and then wrote screenplays for silent films and talkies that helped make stars out of Douglas Fairbanks, Constance Talmadge, Clark Gable, and JEAN HARLOW. More than either coast realized, Anita Loos managed to work better in the different genres of screenwriting, fiction, and playwriting than almost any other writer of her times.

Corinne Anita Loos was born in Sissons (now Mount Shasta), California, the second child of Minerva Smith and R. Beers Loos. Her father moved around California opening and closing newspapers and starting amateur dramatic societies. He was something of a scoundrel, the type of man Loos later found herself both attracted to and wanting to write about, most notably in parts she wrote for Clark Gable. He put Anita on the stage as a child, and she frequently supported the family while he was absent. Her schooling was somewhat erratic, but young Anita read voraciously, filling notebooks with comments about philosophers she read, and she graduated from San Diego High School in 1907.

While living in San Diego, she began writing scenarios for motion pictures. Her first produced script, *The New York Hat,* a satire of small-town provincialism starring MARY PICKFORD, was produced by the Biograph company in 1912. In 1914 she met Biograph's leading director, D. W. Griffith, in Los Angeles, where she now settled. He was enchanted with her, at least partly because she was small (four foot ten inches) and looked like she was still in her teens. Griffith, who had left Biograph, hired her as a full-time writer. Loos later gave the impression that she wrote most of the titles for Griffith's epic *Intolerance* (1916), but only a few show her distinctive wit.

Loos continued to crank out screenplays, many of which remained unproduced. Douglas Fairbanks and John Emerson, two New York actors, were brought into Griffith's studio, and Emerson found some of Loos's unproduced screenplays in the director's files. Though Griffith thought the scripts' humor depended too heavily on titles, he allowed Emerson to direct Fairbanks in one, *His Picture in the Papers* (1916). To Griffith's surprise, it was a hit and established Fairbanks as a movie star. Loos wrote eight other Fairbanks films, placing her wit and satire at the service of Fairbanks's acrobatic skills: "My chief requirement in writing scripts for all those first Fairbanks movies was to find a variety of spots from which Doug could jump" (*A Girl Like I,* p. 216). Emerson collaborated on many of the Fairbanks films, and became Loos's second husband in 1920. (An ill-fated early marriage to songwriter Frank Pallma had ended in divorce.) Emerson had difficulty dealing with Loos's success, and they separated often, but the marriage lasted until his death in 1956. They had no children.

Their association with Fairbanks ended when the actor's ego was bruised by a magazine article crediting Loos with his rise to stardom. Producer Joseph Schenck hired Loos and Emerson to make his sister-in-law Constance Talmadge a star just as they had done for Fairbanks. Talmadge had charmed audiences as what Loos called a "Babylonian flapper" in *Intolerance,* but her career floundered until Loos began writing scripts for her that allowed her delightful and charming personality to emerge on screen.

The Talmadge pictures were made in New York, and Loos relocated there, where she met many of the leading East Coast literary figures. Once she noticed H. L. Mencken and George Jean Nathan making fools of themselves over a not particularly bright blonde. To amuse herself on a train trip, Loos wrote a short piece about such a blonde, whom she named Lorelei Lee. She later showed it to Mencken, who insisted that it be published. He felt she was the first American author to make fun of sex, suggesting she send it to Henry Sell of *Harper's Bazaar.* Sell liked it enough to ask her to do additional stories. On a trip to Europe, she wrote about Lorelei's adventures abroad in diary form (on meeting her, Sigmund Freud recommends that she cultivate some neuroses), sending the manuscripts back to Sell, who published them in serial form.

By the time she returned to New York, the stories had been so successful Mencken suggested she publish them as a book. Her husband feared that such a "naughty" book would damage her reputation, but instead it turned into a widely successful best-seller, *Gentlemen Prefer Blondes.* Loos wrote a sequel, *But Gentlemen Marry Brunettes,* in 1928 (she herself was a brunette), and though it sold well, it did not match the literary and financial success of its predecessor.

In the early 1930s, her savings depleted because of the Depression, Loos returned to Hollywood to work at MGM. One of her first assignments, *Red-Headed Woman* (1932), helped define Jean Harlow as a witty vamp but was so racy that it is considered responsible, along with MAE WEST, for the development of the stricter censorship code in the film industry after 1932. Loos wrote the screenplay for the enormous hit *San Francisco* (1936), which helped establish Clark Gable as a box office star, followed by another Gable vehicle, *Saratoga* (1937). One of her last major screen credits was the wickedly funny 1939 adaptation of CLARE BOOTHE LUCE's play, *The Women.*

Loos eventually returned to New York City, where she lived for the rest of her life. In 1949 she adapted *Gentlemen Prefer Blondes* for its stage musical version starring Carol Channing. (She was not involved in the 1953 film that showcased MARILYN MONROE.) In 1951, she adapted the Collette novella *Gigi* for the stage, which made the young Audrey Hepburn a star on Broadway. Writing novels and memoirs now became her major focus. *A Mouse Is Born* (1951) satirized Hollywood through an actress-character named Effie Huntress; *No Mother to Guide Her* (1961), based on an incident in the life of silent film star CLARA BOW, gave a nostalgic look at old Hollywood. She followed with a two-volume autobiography, *A Girl Like I* (1966) and *Kiss Hollywood Good-By* (1974), as well as a memoir about New York, *Twice Over Lightly* (1972), which she co-authored with HELEN HAYES. An energetic fixture on the New York social scene until shortly before her death, Anita Loos died there on August 18, 1981, at the age of ninety-three.

Bibliography: The most accurate book on Anita Loos is Gary Carey's biography, *Anita Loos* (1988). More entertaining but less accurate are Loos's memoirs. The first volume, *A Girl Like I* (1966), deals with her life up to the publication of *Gentlemen Prefer Blondes;* a second volume, *Kiss Hollywood Good-By* (1974), covers the thirties in Hollywood. *A Cast of Thousands* (1977) is primarily a picture book, with text by Loos. *The Talmadge Girls* (1978) is Loos's memoir about Norma, Constance, Natalie, and their mother Peg Talmadge and captures the friendships of the women of the early movie business; it also includes an incomplete script for *A Virtuous Vamp,* one of the silent films Loos wrote for Constance. The script for *San Francisco* was published (1979) with an afterword by Loos on the writing of the film. In her later years Loos became a source of information about early Hollywood, and quotes from her appear in Kevin Brownlow, *The Parade's Gone By* (1968) and *Hollywood: The Pioneers* (1979), and Richard Schickel, *D. W. Griffith: An American Life* (1984). Filmed interview material with Loos appears in the Thames Television documentary *Hollywood: The Pioneers* (1979) and the documentary *D. W. Griffith* (1993). Cari Beauchamp, *Without Lying Down: Frances Marion and the Powerful Women of Early Hollywood* (1997), gives a very good sense of how the working women of early Hollywood, including Loos, collaborated and supported each other. Many photographs of Anita Loos are in the New York Museum of Modern Art's Film Stills Archive. An obituary appeared in the *New York Times* on August 19, 1981.

TOM STEMPEL

LORDE, Audre. February 18, 1934–November 17, 1992. Poet, activist.

"Black, lesbian, mother, warrior poet," Audre Geraldine Lorde was born in New York City. Author of seventeen books of poetry and prose that have been translated into scores of languages, Audre Lorde was an educator, community healer, bridge builder. Her work and words inspire and galvanize activists everywhere to continue the struggle for civil liberties, human rights, racial justice, the freedom to love, the right to learn.

Audre's mother, Linda Gertrude Belmar, worked in her family's grocery store in Grenada, where she met Frederick Byron Lorde, the tall (six foot three) traveling constable from Barbados. They married in Grenada and moved to New York just before the economic crash of 1929. Although poor during the Depression years, they were among the first black realtors in Harlem, enterprising and bold. Their daughters, Phyllis (born 1928), Helen (born 1931), and Audre, went to Roman Catholic elementary schools. Audre, uniquely gifted and competitive, went to Hunter College High School, at that time a girls' school, where she flourished. In 1949, her first poems were published in *Seventeen* magazine.

At nineteen, Audre Lorde took a leave from Hunter College to study at the National University of Mexico and live in Cuernavaca. There she had an epiphany about words and nature. One morning on the mountain she felt she understood the mysteries and vagaries of life and the power of words to translate feeling into poetry. From that moment, she knew that she was primarily a poet. After graduating from Hunter in 1959, she published poetry in major journals and pathbreaking collections, including Paul Breman's London-based *Sixes and Sevens: An Anthology of New Poetry* (1962), and *New Negro Poets: USA* (1964), edited by Langston Hughes, with a foreword by Gwendolyn Brooks. In 1967, Diane di Prima began the Poets Press, which published Lorde's *The First Cities* the next year.

In 1961, Audre Lorde received a master's in library science from Columbia University, where she met the man who would be her husband, Edwin Ashley Rollins, a white attorney who devoted his life to public service law and the Legal Aid Society. They married in 1962. Their daughter, Elizabeth Lorde-Rollins, was born in 1963, and their son, Jonathan Frederick Ashley Rollins, was born in 1964. The Lorde-Rollinses had a complicated, profoundly honest marriage, and bumpy, although durable, friendship. Arguably, their marriage ended when Audre realized that liberation for her generation meant in part that one did not in fact have to do it all. Specifically, it ended in 1968 when Lorde was invited to be poet-in-residence at Tougaloo, the historically black college outside Jackson, Mississippi.

Audre Lorde's summer at Tougaloo changed her life. There, she understood that she needed to teach, and to lead. While at Tougaloo, she wrote most of the poems in *Cables to Rage* (1970) and met Frances Clayton, the woman who would become her partner for more than twenty years. Clayton was a visiting exchange professor of psychology from Brown University when Lorde arrived at Tougaloo. In 1970 Audre divorced Ed, and Frances left her position at Brown for a new career as psychotherapist and a new family in New York.

At the same time, Yolanda Rios Butts, one of Audre's great friends, gave *First Cities* to Mina Shaughnessy, then director of City College's SEEK (Search for Education, Elevation, and Knowledge) program, a compensatory open-enrollment program. Shaughnessy offered Lorde her first CUNY position. From there, she went to John Jay College of Criminal Justice in 1970, where she fought to build a significant Black Studies program. In 1981, she accepted the distinguished Thomas Hunter chair offered by Donna Shalala, then Hunter College's president.

Pioneering and prolific, Audre Lorde published almost a book a year—poetry, essays, and *Zami: A New Spelling of My Name* (1982), a memoir she called a biomythography. She lectured throughout the United States, Europe, and Africa. Everywhere she went, she built and enhanced movements and connected them all to each other. Throughout the peace and civil rights movements, there was sexism and homophobia; in the women's movement, homophobia and racism. But "Sister Outsider" never flinched. She was the first to insist on the unity of all our differences, and activists from BARBARA DEMING to Angela Davis acknowledged the courage she gave them.

Over time, many of Audre Lorde's words have become book titles, and banners to march with: "Your Silence Will Not Protect You." "We learn to work when we are tired, so we can learn to work when we are afraid." "The Master's Tools Will Never Dismantle the Master's House." "Poetry Is Not a Luxury." "Death Is Not a Disease." Her love poems are ardent and sexy; her political words are fierce and prophetic.

Audre Lorde inspired and helped build enduring institutions and organizations. In 1980, she created Kitchen Table: Women of Color Press with Barbara Smith, Rosie Alvarez, Leota Lone Dog, Susan Yung, and others. Lorde was involved with each step of the publishing process; she was particularly involved with Kitchen Table's Freedom Organizing Pamphlet Series, which published Angela Davis, Merle Woo, Barbara Omolade, and several of her own essays.

On October 14, 1979, Audre Lorde was a featured speaker at the first national march and rally for lesbian and gay rights in Washington. She forged important alliances with gay black men and encouraged them to build institutions of their own. Internationally, Lorde joined Gloria Joseph, Johnnetta Cole, and other "founding mothers" to create SISA (Sisters in Support of Sisters in South Africa). With Dagmar Schultz, Ika Hügel, May Optiz, and others, Audre Lorde rallied Afro-German women, beginning with her students at Berlin's Free University, to tell their stories and forge alliances. In the end, Lorde worked especially to connect the peoples of the African diaspora.

In 1978 Audre Lorde was diagnosed with breast cancer. Determined to live as fully as ever, she confronted her situation with courage and creativity. *The Cancer Journals* (1980) became a blueprint for countless women similarly besieged. Lorde's conviction that the environmental and economic poisons of pharmaceutical and industrial greed ravaged the lives of people who were everywhere sacrificed by careless disregard forged another ever-growing movement. Her journey through the maze of limited U.S. medical options to homeopathic alternatives, then mostly limited to Europe, changed the way health activists organized. A second book of essays, *A Burst of Light* (1988), highlighted her response to liver cancer: "Our battle is to define survival in ways that are acceptable and nourishing to us, meaning with substance and style. Substance. Our work. Style. True to ourselves" (pp. 98–99).

Lorde received many prizes and grants, including the Manhattan Borough President's Award for Excellence in the Arts (1988) and the Walt Whitman Citation of Merit, which named her New York State Poet Laureate for 1991–93, as well as honorary doctorates from Haverford, Oberlin, Hunter, and the University of Osnabruck, Germany.

In the course of Audre Lorde's journey for health and life, she preferred the healing warm waters of the Caribbean and the soft breezes of Judith's Fancy on the island of St. Croix to the cold of New York or the damp of California. This meant, also, a lifetime shift in allegiances. She left Frances Clayton for her new partner, Gloria Joseph, activist and sociologist, whom she had met during the 1970s at Hampshire College. Lorde thrived in St. Croix, wrote poetry and essays, made extraordinary macramé necklaces for all her beloveds, continued her political work, and took a new name, Gamba Adisa, "Warrior: She Who Makes Her Meaning Clear." Then Hurricane Hugo devastated the island and her sense of well-being. In her final struggle against pain and fatigue, she made several extraordinary trips, including to Hawaii for the full eclipse of the sun. She died at home on St. Croix on November 17, 1992, at the age of fifty-eight. Her voice resonates now louder than ever, and her legacy grows on every continent.

Bibliography: Audre Lorde's papers and journals are at Spelman College in Atlanta; selected copies are in the Lesbian Herstory Archives in New York City. Published poetry by Audre Lorde not mentioned in the text includes *From a Land Where Other People Live* (1973); *The New York Headshop and Museum* (1974); *Coal* (1976); *Between Ourselves* (1976); *The Black Unicorn* (1978); *Chosen Poems, Old and New* (1982); *Our Dead Behind Us* (1986); *Undersong: Chosen Poems, Old & New* (1992); *The Marvelous Arithmetics of Distance* (1993); and *The Collected Poems of Audre Lorde* (1997). Her other published prose includes *Uses of the Erotic: The Erotic As Power* (1978); *Sister Outsider: Essays and Speeches* (1984); *I Am Your Sister: Black Women Organizing across Sexualities* (1985); *Apartheid USA* (1986); and *Need: A Chorale for Black Woman Voices* (1990).

Audre Lorde is captured on several documentary films: Ada Gay Griffin and Michelle Parkerson, *A Litany for Survival: The Life and Work of Audre Lorde* (1996); Jennifer Abod, *The Edge of Each Other's Battles: The Vision of Audre Lorde* (2000); and Margaret Wescott, *Stolen Moments* (1998), featuring lesbian pioneers Judy Grahn, Leslie Feinberg, Audre Lorde, Joan Nestle, and Georgia Ragsdale.

Among the secondary sources on Lorde are Angela Bowen, "Who Said It Was Simple: Audre Lorde's Complex Connections to Three U.S. Liberation Movements, 1952–1992" (PhD dissertation, Clark University, 1997); Gloria Joseph and Jill Lewis, *Common Differences: Conflicts in Black & White Feminist Perspectives* (1981); Lester C. Olson, "On the Margins of Rhetoric: Audre Lorde Transforming Silence into Language and Action," *Quarterly Journal of Speech* 83, no. 1 (February 1997), pp. 49–70; Olson, "Liabilities of Language: Audre Lorde Reclaiming Difference," *Quarterly Journal of Speech* 84, no. 4 (November 1998), pp. 448–70; and Townsand Price-Spratlen, "Negotiating Legacies: Audre Lorde, W. E. B. Du Bois, Marlon Riggs, and Me," *Harvard Educational Review* 66, no. 2 (Summer 1996), pp. 216–30. An obituary appeared in the *New York Times* on November 20, 1992.

BLANCHE WIESEN COOK AND CLARE M. COSS

LOUCHHEIM, Kathleen (Katie). December 28, 1903–February 11, 1991. Democratic party official, writer.

Kathleen Scofield Louchheim was born in New York City, the only child of Adele Joseph and Leonard B. Schoenfeld. Both parents were of German Jewish (with some Austrian) ancestry. Her father changed the family name to Scofield during World War I because his birth name sounded too German. Known throughout her life as Katie, she had little to say about her father, whom she described as a kind of broker. He was not very successful in business; the family lived with her maternal grandparents, who were a major influence on her childhood.

The extended family lived prosperously in a large townhouse, maintained by servants, on Manhattan's Upper East Side. In 1917 her uncle paid Katie's tuition to Rosemary Hall, a boarding school in Greenwich, Connecticut. One of only three Jews admitted to her class, she was happy and popular at school. But when she graduated in 1921 there was no more money for tuition, so she went to secretarial school instead of Smith College.

Katie worked for several companies until the spring of 1926, when the family went to Germany. Her beau, Walter C. Louchheim Jr., four years older and also of German Jewish ancestry, soon followed; they were married in Hamburg on June 25, 1926. Returning to New York, her husband worked on Wall Street in his father's successful brokerage house, but did not like it. They lived in Shrewsbury, New Jersey, where their two daughters, Mary and Judith, were born in the early 1930s. When President Roosevelt appointed Joseph P. Kennedy head of the new Securities and Exchange Commission in 1934, Katie persuaded Walter to ask for a job. They moved to Washington, D.C., in October 1934 and stayed for almost forty years.

Although her birth family had been "moderate Republicans and nominal Jews" (Louchheim, *By the Political Sea*, p. 4), Louchheim began volunteering at the Democratic National Committee (DNC) in the late 1930s. For the 1940 election she raised money for Roosevelt's campaign and was successful enough to be introduced to the president and ELEANOR ROOSEVELT. When World War II created a manpower shortage, she went to work for the United Nations Relief and Rehabilitation Administration, largely doing press and public relations. After the war ended in 1945, she was sent to Germany to set up an information program on displaced persons camps.

Returning home to Washington, she immersed herself in partisan politics, and found herself a delegate to the 1948 Democratic National Convention from the District of Columbia. DAISY HARRIMAN, Democratic National Committeewoman from D.C. since 1924, tapped Louchheim to become her alternate and attend DNC meetings as her stand-in. (Louchheim would succeed her in 1956.) At a DNC meeting in September 1953, Chairman Steve Mitchell asked Louchheim to become head of women's activities. She succeeded INDIA EDWARDS, who had made the Women's Division a powerful component of national headquarters until Mitchell abolished it after the Democrats lost the White House in 1952. Party women wrote so many letters in protest that Mitchell created an Office of Women's Activities

(OWA) in its place. Unlike the Women's Division, the new office had neither staff nor budget. Louchheim's first job was raising money. Her second task was creating a women's program suitable for a party out of power.

Even though women's advocate was not a job she had asked for or wanted, she plunged in. For seven years at the DNC, Louchheim pursued three goals: increasing women's participation in grassroots politics, involving them in national fund-raising, and bringing more women into party councils and public service. Louchheim's OWA produced a regular newsletter, "For and About Women," ran numerous regional meetings, sponsored biannual campaign training schools, and developed numerous fundraising gimmicks including "Teas for TV" and the revival of Democratic Women's Day (September 27). The Democratic Congressional Wives Forum, organized by her to do the work formerly done by staff, produced the only official *History of Democratic Women* (1960).

The presidential campaign of 1956 was the height of Louchheim's political career. She ran the women's program at the convention, was elected vice-chairman of the DNC, and traveled with Democratic candidate Adlai Stevenson. On December 12, 1958, Louchheim and her Republican equivalent Clare Williams appeared on the cover of *U.S. News and World Report* for the story "What Women Do in Politics." Louchheim always insisted that the "woman's vote" or "women's issues" were myths that only served to keep women on the sidelines. But she realized that far too often women—in both parties—were ignored or not taken seriously as campaign operatives, even though they did 80 percent of the work.

Although dismayed when campaign manager Robert Kennedy booted her from the DNC in 1960, she campaigned for his brother and was rewarded with a job in the State Department. Starting as "special assistant for women's affairs," a position without staff or duties, she soon moved to Public Affairs, where she felt more useful. Following the pattern of her years at the DNC, Louchheim catered to the concerns of foreign service wives. She ended her eight years as Deputy Assistant Secretary of State for Educational and Cultural Affairs, the first woman to hold such a post. In 1968, President Johnson appointed her U.S. Ambassador to UNESCO, but the Democrats lost the election and her term was short. She retired to pursue her first love—writing books and poetry.

Louchheim was the most important Democratic party woman in the 1950s. She had worked hard for Democratic women as well as candidates, no small feat during an era of anti-feminism and for a party not in power. Like her Republican counterparts, she kept party women in the news when the domestic, not the political, realm was considered women's proper place. A prickly character, the well-dressed and distinguished-looking Louchheim was opinionated and strong, cutting quite a figure in Washington's political and social circles.

In the last three decades of her life, Louchheim contributed to several newspapers and published two books of poetry: *With or without Roses* (1966) and *Observe the Lark* (1985). She also published a political memoir, *By the Political Sea* (1970), and a popular history, *The Making of the New Deal: The Insiders Speak* (1983). Widowed in 1973, she married Donald S. Klopfer, a co-founder and former chairman of Random House, in 1981. He died in 1986. Louchheim died of pneumonia and complications related to a stroke on February 11, 1991, at her home in New York City, at the age of eighty-seven.

Bibliography: The Katie Louchheim papers are in the Library of Congress. They include family papers, letters, her journals, interviews, unpublished speeches and writings, photographs, memorabilia, and scrapbooks. Her memoir, *By the Political Sea* (1970), is the most complete account of her career and observations about politics. See also "What Women Do in Politics," *U.S. News and World Report*, December 12, 1958, pp. 72–80. On women in the Democratic party, see Jo Freeman, *A Room at a Time: How Women Entered Party Politics* (2000), and Kimberly Brodkin, "For the Good of the Party: Gender, Partisanship, and American Political Culture from Suffrage to the 1960s" (PhD dissertation, Rutgers University, 2001). Louchheim also recorded several oral histories, including for the Jewish Division of New York Public Library (1983), the John F. Kennedy Library (1968), and the Lyndon Baines Johnson Library (1969); the Schlesinger Library at Radcliffe Institute for Advanced Study has transcripts of oral histories conducted in 1969, 1972, 1973, and 1978. Obituaries appeared in the *New York Times* and the *Washington Post* on February 12, 1991.

JO FREEMAN

LOVE, Nancy Harkness. February 14, 1914–October 22, 1976. Aviator, commander of the Women's Auxiliary Ferrying Squadron.

Nancy Harkness Love, commander of the Women's Auxiliary Ferrying Squadron (WAFS) during World War II, was born Hannah Lincoln Harkness in Houghton, Michigan, the only daughter and second child of Alice Graham Chadbourne, a homemaker, and Robert Bruce Harkness, a physician. Her father disliked his sister-in-law, for whom his daughter was named, and decided to call her Nancy. As a teenager she was sent away to Massachusetts to attend Milton Academy. In August 1930, when she was sixteen, Nancy spotted a biplane flying near her home and wangled a ride. Captivated by flight, she convinced her

Love

father to let her take flying lessons. She soloed on August 31 and by September 10 she had the ten hours necessary for her private pilot's license. Her mother thought flying improper for a young girl, but not her bemused, doting father—who for the rest of his life kept a scrapbook of his daughter's aviation exploits.

After graduating from Milton in 1931, Nancy entered Vassar College. In addition to her studies, she earned her limited commercial license in 1932 and transport license in 1933. A reversal in Dr. Harkness's finances required that she leave Vassar in January 1934. She tried a secretarial job in New York, hopped passengers from New York to New Jersey, lived on tomato soup, and finally, having three hundred flying hours to her credit, landed a job as a salesperson at a Beechcraft sales agency out of East Boston Airport.

Her next job came courtesy of the New Deal, when veteran aviator PHOEBE OMLIE chose her to work with the Bureau of Air Commerce's Airmarking Project. Throughout 1935, she traveled the eastern states, convincing city leaders that the name of their town painted on the roof of a prominent building would serve as a navigational aid to pilots. On January 11, 1936, she married fellow pilot Robert M. Love, her employer, who owned Boston's Inter City Airways. The next year Gwinn Aircar Company hired her to help test and sell its revolutionary vehicle with a tricycle landing gear (now the norm in aircraft).

By May 1940, Love had more than a thousand hours and a seaplane rating. She ferried a single-engine aircraft to Canada for shipment to Europe for the war effort, and this, her first crack at ferrying, gave her an idea. Pilots were in short supply. She wrote to Colonel Robert Olds that she knew of more than fifty women pilots capable of ferrying aircraft for the army. The time wasn't right, but the idea resurfaced in June 1942. The United States was now at war. Colonel William H. Tunner, commander of the Ferrying Division of the Air Transport Command (ATC), desperately needed pilots to ferry airplanes from the factories to training fields or to the docks for shipment abroad.

Bob Love, an Army Air Corps reservist before Pearl Harbor, was now Major Love, deputy chief of staff at ATC headquarters in Washington, D.C. Nancy worked for the ATC in Baltimore. Aviation fuel was easier for ATC employees to obtain than gas for an automobile, so Nancy flew rather than drove from Washington to Baltimore daily. Colonel Tunner's and Major Love's offices were in close proximity. Over the water cooler, Tunner learned that Love's wife flew to work. Realizing that women pilots could fill the void, he got in touch with her. Their meeting led to the formation of the WAFS.

On September 5, 1942, Love sent telegrams to eighty-three American women pilots, ages twenty-one to thirty-five, with at least five hundred hours, a commercial license, a 200-horsepower engine rating, and recent cross-country flying experience, asking them if they were available immediately to join a group of women pilots under the Air Transport Command to perform domestic ferrying duties. By January 25, 1943, twenty-eight women had answered their country's call, qualified, and were busy ferrying small single-engine aircraft, thereby releasing male pilots for combat duty. Dividing them into four groups, Love established three more squadrons to handle additional volunteers.

In November 1942, renowned aviator JACQUELINE COCHRAN—backed by Army Air Forces commander General H. H. "Hap" Arnold—had established a flight school in Texas to train women pilots for the army. A total of 1,074 eventually graduated. In July 1943, Cochran convinced the army to merge the school and the ferrying squadrons, with Cochran as Director of Women Pilots. On August 5, 1943, all women flying for the army became known as Women Airforce Service Pilots (WASPs). Love retained command of the women in the Ferrying Division, and by mid 1944 her squadrons were ferrying 65 percent of the high-powered fighter aircraft delivered in the United States.

Love, a hazel-eyed beauty who was going prematurely gray in her twenties, did not seek power or celebrity. Never a joiner, she was shy of speaking in public and disliked being in the limelight. She had no patience with politics and hated paperwork. Though she resented Cochran's interference, Love chose to work within the system rather than buck it. To keep the peace in the male-dominated military, she kept her mouth shut, went along, and kept her women flying. She is credited with being the first woman to fly the P-51, P-38, B-25, C-47, and B-17, among others.

The WASPs flew until they were deactivated December 20, 1944, a move fraught with controversy—the waste of a trained resource (the women pilots) versus accusations that the women were taking men's jobs. Male pilots were coming back from combat tours, and public opinion dictated they should be retrained to ferry the army's planes and perform the other flight-related duties women now were handling. The WASPs were sent home.

When the war was over, Nancy Love did not continue to make aviation history. She did what most young American women of that generation did: she went home and started a family. The Loves had three daughters—Hannah (1947), Margaret (1949), and Alice (1951)—and settled on Martha's Vineyard in 1952. Love never again took on anything like the WAFS, but she continued to fly into the 1970s. She died of cancer at age sixty-two in Sarasota, Florida.

Bibliography: The WASP Archive at the Blagg-Huey Library, Texas Woman's University in Denton, is the best resource for information on the WAFS and WASPs. Nancy Love left no writings of her own, and her biography has yet to be written. Love's existing collection of papers, letters, and photographs is currently in the hands of her daughter, Margaret "Marky" Love, of Middleburg, Virginia. Sarah Byrn Rickman, *The Originals: The Women's Auxiliary Ferrying Squadron of World War II* (2001), draws on interviews with two of Nancy Love's daughters, Allie and Marky, as well as interviews with nine pilots from Love's original WAFS squadron. Other secondary sources about the WASPs that include information on Love and the WAFS include Sally Van Wagenen Keil, *Those Wonderful Women in Their Flying Machines: The Unknown Heroines of World War II* (1979; rev. ed., 1990); and Marianne Verges, *On Silver Wings: The Women Airforce Service Pilots of World War II, 1942–1944* (1991). See also Deborah G. Douglas, *United States Women in Aviation, 1940–1985* (1991). Obituaries appeared in the *Vineyard Gazette* on October 26, 1976, and the *WASP Newsletter* in December 1976.

SARAH BYRN RICKMAN

LUCE, Clare Boothe. March 10, 1903–October 9, 1987. Writer, U.S. Representative, ambassador.

Clare Boothe was born in New York City, the daughter of William F. Boothe and Ann Clare Snyder (after whom she was named Ann Clare). Her father, a sometime businessman and professional musician, often worked on theatrical productions. Her mother was an unsuccessful dancer and actress who never lost her taste for the fast, itinerant life of the show business world. Although she and Boothe had two children together (a son, David, had been born a year before Clare), they never married.

Clare's unstable childhood was marked by the family's continually precarious finances, frequent moves, and her parents' eventual separation. New social possibilities opened up once her mother married a prosperous physician, Albert Austin, and returned to New York State. After an erratic early education at schools in Chicago and Memphis, Clare eventually graduated from Miss Mason's School in Tarrytown. Traveling frequently (and lavishly) to Europe with her mother and stepfather, she quickly became a fixture of the social world of the wealthy and privileged. In 1923, she met George Tuttle Brokaw, a socially prominent heir to a clothing fortune twenty-three years her senior. They married later that year, and their daughter Ann was born in August 1924. The marriage was a disaster almost from the beginning. Clare had large ambitions, which a conventional social marriage thwarted. George was a serious and boorish drunk, with few interests beyond riding, golf, and gambling. They divorced in 1929, at which point Clare—financially secure as a result of her divorce settlement—moved out of the social aristocracy and began searching for a career.

For four years, she did editorial work on various magazines, rising to become managing editor of Condé Nast's glamorous *Vanity Fair* in 1933. But she bridled at the anonymity of editorial work and in 1934 left Nast's employ to become a playwright. Her first play, *Abide with Me* (apparently based on her marriage to George Brokaw), opened on Broadway in 1935. It was not a success. A year later, however, her play *The Women* (a scathing picture of the lives of rich society matrons) was an immediate and enduring popular success. Subsequent plays—*Kiss the Boys Goodbye* (1938) and *Margin for Error* (1940)—also thrived at the box office. All three subsequently became motion pictures.

In 1934, she met Henry Robinson Luce, the founder and editor of *Time, Fortune,* and later *Life* magazines, at a party in New York City. Luce developed an immediate and intense infatuation with her, divorced his wife of twelve years, and married Clare late in 1935. Within a year, however, their briefly passionate relationship had become something akin to a marriage of state—formal, highly public, emotionally cool, but nevertheless enduring. Both partners gained something from the relationship—Harry an intellectually challenging and socially prominent wife who helped speed his transformation into a major public figure; Clare an enormously wealthy and influential husband who provided her with entrée into worlds she might never otherwise have entered.

By the late 1930s, Clare Boothe Luce had become interested in politics and world affairs, things in which she had taken little interest in the past. In 1940 her husband acceded to her request to write a series of articles about the deteriorating international climate in Europe for *Life.* Too long in the end for the magazine, the articles were published as a successful book, *Europe in the Spring* (1940), which established her as a prominent commentator on international issues. That fall, she campaigned actively for Wendell Willkie, the Republican nominee, as an outspoken advocate of preparation for war. In 1942, she ran for and won a congressional seat from the district in southern Connecticut where she and her husband maintained a country house.

As a member of Congress, Luce soon emerged as one of the most outspoken voices of the Republican party's right wing—combining her support for the war effort with strong opposition to the kind of internationalism she suspected the Roosevelt administration had in mind for after the war, which she once famously described as "globaloney." She was a powerful, witty, and engaging speaker who attracted particular attention because she was one of the very few women in Congress. In 1944, she became the first woman to give the keynote address at the Republican National Convention.

Luce's political career was relatively brief. She won reelection to Congress in 1944, but declined to run again in 1946. Her political ardor had dimmed considerably after the sudden death of her only child, Ann, in an automobile accident in 1944. Finding public life too difficult, she turned to religion—and in 1946 became a convert to the Catholic church.

For the next several years, Luce seemed to live many, parallel lives. She was active in the church, published several books, and wrote a new play as well as a screenplay for a Hollywood film. One of the best-known women in America, she campaigned for Dwight Eisenhower in 1952 and even made some unsuccessful overtures toward a race of her own for the Senate from Connecticut. Instead, early in 1953, the new president appointed her American ambassador to Italy—by far the most important diplomatic post yet occupied by a woman.

She was, by any measure, the most visible American ambassador in the world during her three years in Italy. Accompanied by her powerful husband, who set up an office for himself in Rome and helped her fund a lavish regime of entertainment in the embassy, she traveled widely in Italy and became enormously popular with many Italians but not with the Italian left, which despised her strident anti-communism. She resigned as ambassador in 1956 to return to private life, but in 1959 Eisenhower nominated her again, this time to be American ambassador to Brazil. She was confirmed by the Senate, but resigned before ever taking up her post.

That was the end of Luce's official career, but she hardly disappeared from public view. She remained an active and popular figure within the Republican Party and an active champion of its conservative wing. In 1964 her husband retired as editor-in-chief of Time Inc., and they began spending much of their time in Phoenix, Arizona, where—in February 1967—Harry suddenly died of a heart attack. After that, Clare became far less visible, living for fifteen years in Hawaii before finally moving to Washington, D.C., in 1983, where she was a popular social figure in the Reagan years. An icon to some of the early years of the modern Republican right and to others a pioneer among women in public life, Clare Boothe Luce died in Washington on October 9, 1987, at the age of eighty-four.

Bibliography: Clare Boothe Luce's voluminous papers are in the Manuscripts Division of the Library of Congress. In addition to the plays mentioned in the text, she is the author of *Child of the Morning* (1951) and *Slam the Door Softly* (1970). Her other books include *Stuffed Shirts* (1931), a collection of satirical essays, and *Saints for Now* (1952). Luce is the subject of a short, impressionistic study by her friend Wilfrid Sheed, *Clare Boothe Luce* (1982), and Sylvia Jukes Morris's much more thorough study, *Rage for Fame: The Ascent of Clare Boothe Luce* (1997), which follows her life up to 1942. Ralph G. Martin's *Henry and Clare: An Intimate Portrait of the Luces* (1991), Stephen Shadegg's *Clare Boothe Luce* (1970), and Alden Hatch's *Ambassador Extraordinary* (1955) are geared more toward popular audiences. An obituary appeared in the *New York Times* on October 10, 1987.

ALAN BRINKLEY

LUMPKIN, Grace. *See* Lumpkin, Katharine Du Pre.

LUMPKIN, Katharine Du Pre. December 22, 1897–May 5, 1988. Writer, scholar, social critic.

Katharine Du Pre Lumpkin, author of *The Making of a Southerner* (1946), was born in Macon, Georgia, the youngest of seven children of Annette Caroline Morris and William Wallace Lumpkin. Descended from a prominent slave-owning family, her father fought with the Confederacy and then helped undermine Reconstruction as a member of the Ku Klux Klan. Her mother came from plainer stock. Orphaned during the war, she was brought up by wealthy relatives in Augusta, Georgia, and taught school briefly before she married. Reduced to working for the railroad and exiled to Columbia, South Carolina, William Lumpkin devoted himself to the movement to enshrine the memory of the Lost Cause. Above all, he sought to instill in his children loyalty to white supremacy and to the southern past.

Katharine first came into intimate contact with the black and white rural poor when the Lumpkins moved to a farm in the Sand Hills, South Carolina's poorest and most desolate region. By the time she left for college, at the age of fifteen, she had begun to distance herself from her father's romantic views of the antebellum past. In 1915 she graduated from Brenau College in Gainesville, Georgia, with a BA in history, having been introduced to the Social Gospel by the Young Women's Christian Association (YWCA). Lumpkin went north to graduate school at Columbia University (1918–19), but she was disappointed by what she found. Studying with noted sociologist Franklin H. Giddings, she was drilled in the tenets of social

Darwinism, which taught that racial mores lie beyond the reach of reason or legislation. In response, she struck out on her own, beginning a pattern she would follow throughout her life. She wrote a master's thesis entitled "Social Interests of the Southern Woman," and in 1920 she became the YWCA's national student secretary for the southern region, a position she held for five years.

Lumpkin left the South again in 1925, this time to pursue her twin interests in class and race at the University of Wisconsin, where she studied sociology and labor economics with some of progressivism's leading lights. Her dissertation on delinquent girls was directed by Edward A. Ross, and she received her PhD in 1928. On the cusp of the Great Depression, Lumpkin took a one-year replacement position at Mount Holyoke College. There she met radical economist Dorothy Wolff Douglas. By the time the year ended, they had moved together to nearby Northampton, Massachusetts, where Douglas taught at Smith College. They had also committed themselves to a partnership that would last for almost thirty years. After a year of research supported by a Social Science Research Council fellowship, Lumpkin joined Douglas in founding the Council of Industrial Studies at Smith College, which Lumpkin directed from 1932 to 1939. She directed a series of studies on the economic history of the Connecticut River Valley, and (with Douglas) published a book on child labor. From 1940 to 1953 she headed the independent Institute of Labor Studies in Northampton.

The Depression meanwhile had inspired a new left-wing political movement, known broadly as the Popular Front, which Lumpkin and Douglas embraced wholeheartedly. Lumpkin's move to the left was shared—and influenced—by a network of radical southerners that stretched back to her YWCA days. Among them was her sister, Grace Lumpkin. Born in 1891, Grace too had attended Brenau College, then traveled to France as an emissary for the YWCA during World War I. By the time the stock market crashed in 1929, Grace had aligned herself with the Communist movement. She had also fallen in love with Michael Intrator, a handsome, self-educated Jewish immigrant and a battling member of the Fur and Leather Workers. She married him on May 4, 1932. Grace based her first and best-known novel, *To Make My Bread* (1932), on an international cause célèbre, the Gastonia, North Carolina, textile strike of 1929. In it she traced the travails of the rural poor as they experienced the shock of factory work and then sought out new ways of understanding the world. She wrote three other novels, as well as a number of short stories.

As the thirties gave way to the war years, Katharine Du Pre Lumpkin "came out" as a southerner, first in *The South in Progress* (1940), which condemned segregation and portrayed interracial industrial unions as the best hope for regional change, and then in 1946 in *The Making of a Southerner*, the autobiography that became her most enduring work. One of a spate of autobiographies published by white southerners in the 1930s and 1940s, *The Making of a Southerner* showed how a child absorbed her society's assumptions about race, class, and gender and how change could occur from within. Neither elegiac reminiscence nor savage attack, Lumpkin's work represented her liberation not as a rejection of a regional heritage, but as a rereading of southern history that stressed dissent, conflict, and change.

Reviewed favorably in both the South and the North and chosen as a Book-of-the-Month Club selection, *The Making of a Southerner*'s success helped Lumpkin win a Houghton Mifflin Literary Fellowship to write a historical novel from the point of view of a black Reconstruction leader. The manuscript, however, was rejected by Houghton Mifflin, and she painfully put it aside. At the same time, she was caught in the riptide of McCarthyism. In 1953 Robert Gorham Davis, a Smith College English professor, testified before the House Committee on Un-American Activities (HUAC) that Lumpkin and Douglas had been members of a Communist Party faction within the American Federation of Teachers. Subpoenaed by HUAC, Douglas cited the Fifth Amendment. By then, Grace Lumpkin had renounced her earlier radicalism and become an outspoken anti-communist and right-wing critic of the emerging struggle against segregation. She testified before Senator Joseph McCarthy's Permanent Investigating Subcommittee of the Government Operations Committee. Behind the scenes, she willingly named names, even implicating her sister and Dorothy Douglas in conversations with the FBI.

Katharine Du Pre Lumpkin never spoke publicly about this experience, but it shattered her personal and professional worlds. She and Douglas eventually left Northampton and parted ways. Lumpkin wanted to return to the South, but she was unable to secure a position in a black college and unwilling to teach in a segregated institution. In 1957 she joined the sociology department at Wells College in Aurora, New York, where she taught until 1967. Upon retirement she moved with her companion, Elizabeth Bennett, to Charlottesville, Virginia, where Lumpkin published her final book, a biography of the pioneering abolitionist feminist Angelina Grimke, with whom she deeply identified. Grace Lumpkin meanwhile was living in obscurity in King and Queen Courthouse, Virginia. The fraught relationship between the two sisters entered a new stage as Grace's health and financial situation declined. Grace died in 1980, in a retirement home in Columbia, South Carolina, where much of her family still lived. Katharine lived out her final years in Chapel Hill, North Carolina, and died in 1988 at the age of ninety.

Bibliography: Katharine Du Pre Lumpkin's papers, including an interview by Jacquelyn D. Hall, are in the Southern Historical Collection, University of North Carolina at Chapel Hill. Her other publications include *The Family: A Study of Member Roles* (1933) and *The Emancipation of Angelina Grimke* (1974). For her career, see Darlene O'Dell, *Sites of Memory: The Autobiographies of Katharine Du Pre Lumpkin, Lillian Smith, and Pauli Murray* (2001); Hall, "'To Widen the Reach of Our Love': Autobiography, History, and Desire," *Feminist Studies* 26 (Spring 2000), pp. 231–47; Hall, "You Must Remember This: Autobiography as Social Critique," *Journal of American History* 85 (September 1998), pp. 439–65; Hall, "Open Secrets: Memory, Imagination, and the Refashioning of Southern Identity," *American Quarterly* 50 (March 1998), pp. 110–24; Fred Hobson, *But Now I See: The White Southern Racial Conversion Narrative* (1999); and Darlene Clark Hine's foreword to a reprint of *The Making of a Southerner* published by the University of Georgia Press (1991). Grace Lumpkin's papers are in the South Caroliniana Library at the University of South Carolina in Columbia. Her publications include *A Sign for Cain* (1935), *The Wedding* (1939, reprint 1976), and *Full Circle* (1976). For her career, see Jacquelyn D. Hall, "Women Writers, the 'Southern Front,' and the Dialectical Imagination," *Journal of Southern History* 69, no. 1 (February 2003), pp. 3–38; Richard Gray, *Southern Aberrations: Writers of the American South and the Problems of Regionalism* (2000); and Suzanne Sowinska's introduction to a reprint of *To Make My Bread* (1995). Katharine Du Pre Lumpkin's obituary appeared in the *Chapel Hill Newspaper*, May 6, 1988, and Grace Lumpkin's in the *Columbia State*, March 24, 1980.

JACQUELYN D. HALL

LUPINO, Ida. February 4, 1918–August 3, 1995. Actress, film director

Ida Lupino, the most prolific American woman director in history, was born in London, England, the daughter of Connie Emerald, a tap dancer and actress, and Stanley Lupino, a music hall comedian and actor from one of England's most celebrated theatrical families. As a child, Ida and her younger sister Rita acted in a model theater built by her beloved father. At the age of twelve she performed in London's Tom Thumb Theatre. By thirteen she was already enrolled in one of England's most prestigious acting schools, the Royal Academy of Dramatic Art.

She wasn't there long before she was plucked for her first film. Her youthful-looking mother was auditioning for a part in *Her First Affaire* (1933), but director Allan Dwan took greater interest in Emerald's daughter, Ida, who appeared older than her years. The young Lupino plucked her eyebrows, dyed her hair blond, and became known as "the English Jean Harlow." As a result of her next film, *Money for Speed* (1933), Lupino caught the attention of a Hollywood talent scout. Moving to the United States (she became a citizen in 1946), she appeared in a string of mediocre films for Paramount Pictures, usually playing syrupy young ingénues. In 1938 she married actor Louis Hayward.

Lupino came to her film roles the same way she came into life, with a chip on her shoulder and something to prove. With her tiny five-foot two-inch frame, dusky voice, dark hair, and large, wide-set, luminous eyes, she always seemed ready to face the fate life posed for her. Breaking out of her vapid roles to play serious dramatic characters, she finally found success in films such as *The Light That Failed* (1939), where she played a vengeful Cockney prostitute opposite Ronald Colman, and *They Drive by Night* (1940), where she portrayed an adulterer-turned-murderer. Now under contract to Warner Brothers, she reached her full potential in film noir pictures such as Raoul Walsh's *High Sierra* (1941), where she co-starred as Humphrey Bogart's loyal girlfriend; *The Sea Wolf* (1941); *Ladies in Retirement* (1941), one of her favorite roles; and *The Hard Way* (1942), for which she won a New York Film Critics Award. While Hayward served in the armed forces, Lupino was active in the Hollywood war effort, but the couple divorced in 1945.

Her experience of powerlessness as an actress drove her to want to control her own career, and hence to directing. In 1949 Lupino teamed up with her second husband, Collier Young, whom she had married in 1948, to form her own company called Filmmakers. Their first feature, *Not Wanted*, appeared in 1949, Lupino having taken over as the (uncredited) director after Elmer Clifton fell ill. Over the next five years, Lupino wrote and directed five features for the company, while starring in six features directed by others. Additionally, she directed and starred in one more: *The Bigamist* (1953).

Virtually the only woman directing in Hollywood then, Lupino chose social issues for the themes of her movies—bigamy, polio, unwed motherhood—and she handled these topics at a time when they elicited controversy. Like life, her films posed problems, though not necessarily solutions. Something unexpected would interrupt the flow of her characters' day, and their lives were suddenly changed: in *Outrage* (1950), a bookkeeper walking home alone gets raped; in *The Hitch-Hiker* (1953), her biggest critical and box office success, a traveler whom two vacationers innocently pick up turns out to be a psychopath. Her films were unlike any American movies of their time. They were low budget (made for less than

$160,000), they starred unknown actors, and they were shot without studio backing.

After the demise of her company in 1954, Lupino was suddenly in great demand for the new medium of television, which occupied her for most of the rest of her career. If producers wanted a director who could handle westerns, violence, and the tough subjects, they called Ida Lupino. By her own count, she directed literally hundreds of episodes for shows such as *Thriller, Gunsmoke, Have Gun–Will Travel,* and *The Fugitive.* Norman Macdonnel, longtime producer of *Gunsmoke,* noted that he hired Lupino when he had a story that had to be hard-hitting. She became known as "the female Hitch," as in Hitchcock, for her talent in creating suspenseful, action-oriented drama.

On the set, however, everyone from actors to stagehands called Lupino "mother," a name she relished. Even her director's chair proclaimed her "Mother of All of Us." She made it a point to never shout orders, learning to get results through other means. "You don't *tell* a man," she said; "you *suggest* to them, 'Let's try something crazy here. That is, if it's comfortable for you, love.' . . . And they do it—they just go and do it." As much as she loved being called "mother" by her many male colleagues, she often made no bones about the fact that she did not like to work with other women.

In 1951, Lupino divorced Collier Young and married Howard Duff. In 1952 she gave birth to a daughter, Bridget Mirella. In addition to her directing, she appeared as a regular on *Four Star Playhouse* from 1953 to 1956. In 1957–58 she and Duff co-produced and appeared in a television situation comedy called *Mr. Adams and Eve,* which was about two married movie stars not unlike themselves.

Deferring more and more to Duff's career, Lupino acted and directed less and less, a decision she seems to have regretted. In 1966 she directed her last Hollywood film, *The Trouble with Angels.* After years of marital problems, the couple separated in the early 1970s but did not divorce until 1984. Out of the public eye, Lupino was rediscovered in the 1970s and 1980s by film historians and feminist scholars who were drawn to the unconventional choices she made as a director. Lupino, however, was more than a little averse to being aligned with the feminist cause. "Keeping a feminine approach is vital," she said. "Instead of saying, 'Do this,' I tried to make everybody a part of it. Often I pretended to a cameraman to know less than I did. That way I got more cooperation." Earlier her reputation had rested on her acting skills, but now she was hailed for her distinctly female perspective on film noir.

On August 3, 1995, when she was seventy-seven years old, Ida Lupino suffered a stroke and died at her home in Burbank, California. Her pioneering efforts paved the way in a field that would not open its doors again to women for another forty years.

Bibliography: Archival material documenting Ida Lupino's career as an actress and director can be found at the Margaret Herrick Library of the Academy of Motion Picture Arts and Sciences, Beverly Hills, California. Included among these are unpublished papers on Lupino by Mary Ann Anderson, executor of Lupino's estate and Lupino's closest colleague up until her death. Other collections are held by the UCLA Film & Television Archive; the University of Southern California Cinema-Television Library; and the Wisconsin Center for Film and Theater Research, Madison. Lupino discusses her directorial style in "Me, Mother Directress," *Action,* May–June 1967, pp. 14–15, which contains the quotations found in the text. For an overview of her life, see William Donati, *Ida Lupino: A Biography* (1996). Annette Kuhn, ed., *Queen of the 'B's: Ida Lupino behind the Camera* (1995), offers scholarly appraisals of Lupino's career, while Ally Acker, *Reel Women: Pioneers of the Cinema, 1896 to the Present* (1991), surveys Lupino in the larger context of Hollywood history. Interesting reassessments of Lupino's career include Carrie Rickey, "Lupino Noir," *Village Voice,* October 29–November 4, 1980, pp. 43–45; Ronnie Scheib, "Ida Lupino, Auteuress," *Film Comment,* January–February 1980, pp. 54–64; and Louise Heck-Rabi, *Women Filmmakers: A Critical Reception* (1984). An obituary appeared in the *New York Times* on August 5, 1995.

ALLY ACKER

LUSCOMB, Florence. February 6, 1887–October 27, 1985. Suffragist, peace activist, labor organizer, civil libertarian.

Florence Hope Luscomb was born in Lowell, Massachusetts. Her father, Otis Luscomb, aspired to be an artist but supported himself as a clerk and dressmaker. Her mother, Hannah, a native of St. Louis, Missouri, was reared in an anti-slavery and temperance family with Yankee and Scots-Irish ancestral roots in Boston and Blandford, Massachusetts. In 1889, Hannah Luscomb left her son, Otis Kerrshaw, born in 1881, in temporary custody of her husband and moved to Boston with her daughter. Able to support herself with income from property she inherited in St. Louis, Hannah Luscomb devoted herself to Bellamy Nationalism, the labor movement, and the Massachusetts Woman Suffrage Association. Describing herself as a born reformer, she raised her daughter in a comfortable but modest middle-class home focused on outdoor exercise and political activities. Florence's most important personal relationship was with her mother; she saw her father rarely and believed he had no influence in her upbringing. Reared as a feminist, she never reconciled her desire for heterosexual romance with her thirst for personal independence and never married. Nor did she, as far as is known, have a romantic relationship with a woman.

Florence attended the private academy Chauncy Hall, but finished her last two years of high school at Brighton High, graduating in 1905. She was among a handful of early-twentieth-century women to enroll in the Massachusetts Institute of Technology, where she earned a degree in architecture in 1909. She and another MIT graduate, Ida Annah Ryan, launched the first women's architectural practice in the United States in Waltham, designing modest housing and public buildings. But Luscomb was soon drawn into woman suffrage activism, speaking at one of the first open-air meetings in Massachusetts and selling the *Woman's Journal* near the Statehouse. Recruited to work in suffrage campaigns in Ohio, Virginia, and New York, she took a leave from her firm during World War I and never worked in architecture again. On the road for suffrage in 1915, she gave 222 speeches in fourteen weeks and also learned to drive and repair her party's touring car. As a member of the Appalachian Mountain Club, she became an experienced hiker and camper in the White Mountains.

After suffrage, Luscomb worked as a paid employee for the Boston League of Women Voters, the Massachusetts Civic League, the Anti-Saloon League, and the Women's International League for Peace and Freedom (WILPF). She ran for the Boston City Council in 1922, losing by a few thousand votes, but neither mainstream political party appealed to her. Hannah Luscomb's death in 1933 coincided with the depth of the Depression and the collapse of many civic organizations. Having resigned from her position at WILPF, Luscomb could find no salaried employment. Now in her mid forties, she was in the ranks of the middle-aged unemployed and never found another salaried position.

Luscomb turned next to the labor movement. As president of the Boston AFL local of the Bookkeepers, Stenographers and Accountants Union, she led her union into the CIO in 1937, where it became the United Office and Professional Workers of America. A vigorous supporter of the Popular Front, she joined other Boston leftists in anti-fascist organizing, the Scottsboro Defense Committee, the struggle to support Republican Spain, and on union picket lines. Although she visited the Soviet Union in 1935, she refused to join the Communist Party on the grounds that she was too independent to follow a party line.

Freedom of speech and thought were linchpins of Luscomb's beliefs. She joined the Civil Liberties Union of Massachusetts shortly after its founding in 1919 and was a lifelong member, leading coalitions against loyalty oaths and the expulsion of leftists from the American Civil Liberties Union. Identified as a "fellow traveler" by the Massachusetts Commission to Investigate Subversive Organizations in 1938, Luscomb was also subpoenaed by a similar state commission in 1955. When her name appeared on its blacklist, she sued the commission, and civil libertarians credited her partially successful lawsuit with derailing the anticommunist crusade in Massachusetts.

Having joined the National Association for the Advancement of Colored People (NAACP) during the woman suffrage campaign, Luscomb was a tireless supporter of civil rights and a promoter of interracial cooperation in all the organizations to which she belonged; she was elected to a vice presidency of the Boston NAACP for 1948. In the same year she became an ardent advocate of the Progressive Party candidacy of Henry Wallace. She opposed American intervention in Korea and ran for Congress on the Progressive Party ticket in 1950 and for governor in 1952. Her faith in the American system of democracy reached a low point in the early 1960s. Her passport was seized by the State Department, publications sent to her from China and Canada were confiscated, and many of the organizations to which she belonged were on the U.S. attorney general's blacklist.

Forced to support herself with a small inheritance from her mother, she faced steady inflation in Boston's tight housing market. In 1940 she had built a modest cabin on a small piece of land in Tamworth, New Hampshire, with no running water or electricity. Except for some years of World War II, she stayed in Tamworth each summer, where she received guests, grew a vegetable and flower garden, and, until the late 1960s, climbed nearby Mount Chocorua at least once a year. She was an early participant in cooperative living in Boston, moving among a series of student households with her dwindling stock of 1930s furniture. Her appearance remained constant over many decades. Years of hiking and walking the streets of Boston kept her vigorous and healthy. She was five feet six inches tall, brown-eyed, slim, and unpretentious in dress and manner. Her friendly smile and firm handshake conveyed much of her open and emphatic personality.

When the Vietnam War crisis reached a peak in the late 1960s and the women's liberation movement emerged from the New Left, Luscomb was welcomed as a speaker at political protests and teach-ins by a new generation of political activists. A member of the Boston Community Church since the 1920s, she continued to bring controversial speakers to its pulpit, many of them socialists and radicals. Her religion, she once said, was the "brotherhood of man," and her class the "class of women." She died in a nursing home in Watertown, Massachusetts, on October 27, 1985, at the age of ninety-eight; her ashes were scattered by friends at her Tamworth cabin. In 1999 she was one of six women memorialized in sculptural relief at the Massachusetts Statehouse for their contributions to the state's political history.

Bibliography: Taped and transcribed interviews, correspondence, photographs, memorabilia, political pamphlets, and speeches are in the Florence Hope Luscomb Papers at the Schlesinger Library, Radcliffe Institute for Advanced Study, Harvard University. An edited version of interviews and a brief biographical portrait are in Ellen Cantarow with Susan Gushee O'Malley and Sharon Hartman Strom, *Moving the Mountain: Women Working for Social Change* (1980). Strom, *Political Woman: Florence Luscomb and the Legacy of Radical Reform* (2001), considers her mother and grandfather and places Luscomb's life in its broader historical context; the quotations in the text appear on pp. 75 and 272. On Luscomb and suffrage, see Strom, "Leadership and Tactics in the American Woman Suffrage Movement: A New Perspective from Massachusetts," *Journal of American History* 62, no. 2 (1975), pp. 296–315; and Sara Hunter Graham, *Woman Suffrage and the New Democracy* (1996). On Luscomb's run for city council, see Sarah Deutsch, *Women and the City: Gender, Space, and Power in Boston, 1870–1940* (2000). An obituary appeared in the *Boston Globe* on October 28, 1985.

SHARON HARTMAN STROM

LYND, Helen Merrell. March 17, 1896–January 30, 1982. Sociologist, social philosopher.

Helen Merrell was born in La Grange, Illinois, outside Chicago. Her father, Edward Tracey Merrell, who had attended Hartford Theological Seminary, edited a small Congregationalist magazine, *The Advance,* and when it failed, shifted from one job to another. Her mother, Mabel Waite Merrell, had studied at Mount Holyoke for two years and had taught school in Chicago. After marrying, she participated in church work and took in boarders to boost the family's modest income. The first of three daughters, Helen Merrell grew up in a pious atmosphere. Following her graduation from Lyons Township High School in La Grange, her father changed jobs, and the family moved to Framingham, Massachusetts. Helen Merrell entered nearby Wellesley College.

Wellesley struck her as an "ingrown place in many ways" but it provided "an emancipating experience" (*Possibilities,* p. 21). A commuter for her first two years, Merrell became a college leader and, as a senior, student government president. Inspired by her favorite professor, Mary S. Case, who introduced her to Hegel, she developed a passion for philosophy. Case and her father, she later commented, were the great influences in her life. Helen Merrell graduated from Wellesley in 1919, a member of Phi Beta Kappa, and taught for two years at girls' private schools in Westchester, New York. On September 3, 1921, she married Robert Staughton Lynd, a student at Union Theological Seminary, whom she had met two summers before. Helen studied history at Columbia University from 1921 to 1922, when she received her MA. In 1923, the Institute of Social and Religious Research of the Rockefeller Foundation hired Robert Lynd to head a study of the religious life of a typical American community. He selected Muncie, Indiana, which became the subject of the Lynds' classic works in sociology: *Middletown: A Study in Contemporary American Culture* (1929) and *Middletown in Transition: A Study in Cultural Conflicts* (1937).

Helen and Robert Lynd began research in Muncie in January 1924 and remained through June 1925, assisted by a staff of three. The Lynds decided to follow the method of anthropologists, which determined their focus on such topics as "Getting a Living," "Making a Home," and other fundamental areas of life. Neither of the Lynds had a social science degree, and the study's goals kept shifting. "Some of the most interesting material came from things that couldn't have been charted in advance," Helen recalled (ibid., p. 37). A half-time research associate, she worked on the local press, organizational records, and interviews with Muncie residents. The Lynds shared the labor of writing the study; as co-authors, each rewrote the other's chapters. When Robert Lynd later submitted part of the work for his dissertation at Columbia, where he taught from 1931 on, the couple tried to delete the sections that Helen Lynd had written; in her view this proved impossible.

Finding the completed study uninteresting and not sufficiently devoted to religion, the Rockefeller Institute declined to publish it, but Harcourt Brace did. Met by widespread acclaim, *Middletown* won front-page reviews and best-seller status. Exploring the industrial revolution that since 1890 had transformed one small city, and by extension American culture as a whole, it showed how industrial progress had divided Muncie's population into a "business class" and a "working class," and it traced the decline of community spirit, which gave way in the 1920s to consumer culture. Written in a detached and ironic tone, *Middletown* conveyed a critical spirit that appealed to the Lynds' contemporaries, as it has to generations of readers and scholars ever since.

Even before *Middletown's* success, Helen Lynd found an academic post. In 1928 she took a part-time job at Sarah Lawrence College in Bronxville, New York. Founded that year, the new progressive college developed a student-centered tutorial program that suited her. Lynd taught there for almost four decades, never with a full-time salary. In 1929–30 she held a concurrent position as a lecturer in economics at Vassar. Early in her teaching career the Lynds had two children: Staughton Craig (1929) and Andrea Merrell (1934).

Unbound by divisions among academic disciplines, Lynd pursued a range of interests that included history, psychology, and what she called social philosophy, her main field of teaching at Sarah Lawrence. Her publications reflected her diverse interests. The second Middletown book, researched by Robert Lynd but written by both Lynds, assessed the impact of the Depression on the changes under way in Muncie. Helen Lynd's dissertation at Columbia, where she earned a PhD in history in 1944, explored the history of ideas. Written for the doctoral seminar of Carlton J. H. Hayes, it became a book called *England in the Eighteen-Eighties* (1945). Subsequent publications included *Field Work in College Education* (1945), which promoted off-campus projects in the arts and sciences, and *On Shame and the Search for Identity* (1958), an insightful study of personality development.

An admired teacher, Helen Lynd was also a social activist. After the American Legion complained to college officials that she was "a Communist or something in their opinion indistinguishable from it" (ibid., p. 48), she was among twelve Sarah Lawrence faculty members called before Senator William Jenner's Internal Security Subcommittee in March 1953. Accompanied by her lawyer, Telford Taylor, Lynd told the subcommittee that she had never been a Communist, although she subsequently regretted, she claimed, that she had not refused to answer on constitutional grounds.

Retiring from teaching in 1964 and widowed in 1970, Lynd continued to pursue her interest in psychology and explored the sources of creativity. She died of a stroke in Warren, Ohio, on January 30, 1982, at the age of eighty-five. A versatile and innovative academic, Helen Merrell Lynd advanced the quest for self-knowledge in several fields. Like many other ambitious women of her generation who entered professions in the 1920s, she combined marriage and family with career. Distinctively, because of *Middletown* and its enduring impact, the Lynds' reputations as scholars were largely intertwined.

Bibliography: Manuscript sources are in the Papers of Robert Staughton and Helen Merrell Lynd (1895–1968) at the Manuscript Division of the Library of Congress and in the Helen Merrell Lynd Papers (1904–1980) at the Sarah Lawrence College Archives. The Oral History Research Office at Columbia University contains interviews with Helen Merrell Lynd from 1973 and 1974. Parts of the interviews appear in a volume by Lynd in collaboration with her son, Staughton Lynd, called *Possibilities* (1978), which includes some work from her final years. Bert James Loewenberg, ed., *Toward Discovery* (1965), contains segments of Helen Lynd's unpublished and published work, including three articles that appeared in the 1940s and 1950s. For information about the Lynds and the *Middletown* books, see Maurice R. Stein, *The Eclipse of Community* (1960); Dwight W. Hoover, *Middletown Revisited* (1990); Richard Wightman Fox and T. J. Jackson Lears, eds., *The Culture of Consumption* (1983); and Daniel Horowitz, *The Morality of Spending* (1985). An obituary appeared in the *New York Times* on February 1, 1982.

NANCY WOLOCH

M

MACY, Icie Gertrude. *See* Hoobler, Icie Gertrude Macy.

MADAR, Olga Marie. May 17, 1915–May 16, 1996. Labor leader, feminist.

Olga Marie Madar was born in Sykesville, Pennsylvania, the ninth of thirteen children. Both of her parents were Czechoslovakian immigrants. Her father, Paul Madar, was a coal miner and later owned a grocery store, which he ran with his wife, Anna Seman Madar. When he lost the store and his savings at the start of the Great Depression, the family in 1930 followed several of Madar's older siblings to Detroit, where they had moved in search of work.

Madar attended Northeastern High School, graduating in 1933. That summer she was hired as a temporary seasonal worker on the assembly line at the Chrysler Kercheval plant. The experience taught her the importance of unionism. She later recalled that the line moved so fast that she could never keep up. She also was appalled to discover that Chrysler retained her because she had earned a citywide reputation as a great softball player, and the company-sponsored women's softball team needed quality players. Working in auto plants during the summer months, Madar, the first in her family to attend college, put herself through Michigan Normal School (now Eastern Michigan University) in Ypsilanti. She graduated in 1938 with a BS in physical education.

After graduation, Madar taught history, biology, and physical education in Flat Rock, Michigan. In 1941, she took a better-paying job as a small-parts assembler at a defense plant operated by the Ford Motor Company in Willow Run, Michigan. Many of the thousands of women and men employed at the plant in the production of bombers and other defense-related goods were migrants to southeast Michigan, and they and their families overwhelmed the social services available in the Ypsilanti area. The United Auto Workers (UAW), which represented the Ford employees, stepped into the void and provided community assistance, housing information, and a variety of classes. An active participant in UAW Local 50, Madar put to use her training and skills as an athlete, physical education teacher, and coach by organizing recreation programs for workers and their families at Willow Run. The local union soon hired her as director of recreation, social services, and women's activities, an appointment that defined her own sense of purpose for the rest of her life.

Madar was offered a job on the international staff of the UAW in October 1944. She served as director of the union's Recreation Department until she was elected to the International Executive Board (IEB) in 1966. During those two decades, the UAW developed a broad vision of its responsibilities to union members and to society, seeking to improve the lives of auto workers in and out of the workplace. Olga Madar helped implement and fulfill this idea of social unionism. Her first significant accomplishment as an international officer came in 1952, when the American Bowling Congress and the Women's International Bowling Congress dropped their "white only" membership policies. Championing the union's retired workers and the UAW's concern to extend its reach into communities, Madar saw to the establishment of senior citizen centers and, as Detroit Parks and Recreation commissioner, eliminated racially discriminatory hiring practices.

The UAW also innovated in the postwar era by advancing the idea of gender equality in the workplace and the union hall. The pace of change was slow, however, and in 1964 a group of female international representatives, including Madar, sought the election of a woman to the IEB to highlight the increased importance of women in the ranks and their continued exclusion from leadership positions. The group failed in 1964 but succeeded two years later when a new at-large seat was created. Although Madar had little collective bargaining experience—a distinct liability for a board member—she was elected board member-at-large at the UAW convention in May 1966.

Reelected to the IEB in 1968, Madar was elected to the first of two terms as international vice president in 1970. Her responsibilities expanded to include the new Department of Consumer Affairs and Department of Conservation and Resource Development, as well as the reorganized Department of Recreation and Leisure-Time Activities; she also serviced the union's technical, office, and professional workers' locals. Madar used her position to press for greater employment of women on the international staff and to establish leadership training programs for UAW women. On the national stage, Madar facilitated the UAW's endorsement of the equal rights amendment (ERA) in 1970, an unprecedented action by a labor union. Madar also was a founding member of the National Women's Political Caucus, the Women's Equity Action League, and the Network for Economic Rights.

Madar retired from the UAW in 1974, having spent thirty years on the international staff. She turned her attention to the formation of a new national organization for union women. More than three thousand women from fifty-eight unions attended the founding convention of the Coalition of Labor Union Women (CLUW) in March 1974. The largest single contingent was from the UAW, and Madar was elected president of the new group. Madar's own feminist commitments were evident in the organization's goals and purposes. CLUW vowed to organize women workers, to demand sex-blind treatment in the workplace, and to encourage women to become more active and to gain a larger share of power and influence in the unions. Declaring that "A woman's place is in her union," CLUW asserted the importance of unionism as the principal vehicle for improving the status of working women. The formation of CLUW encouraged labor movement women to integrate their commitments to unionism and feminism, and helped widen the base of the women's movement.

Olga Madar stepped down as president of CLUW in 1976 but remained active in union and civic organizations, including CLUW, the Democratic Party, the National Committee on Pay Equity, and the National Council of Senior Citizens. Madar never married or had children; she kept her romantic life private and left no record of it. She epitomized the socially conscious unionist whose devotion to the labor movement and working people was complete and personally rewarding. Madar died of heart failure at her Detroit home one day before her eighty-first birthday.

Bibliography: The principal sources on Olga Madar are her personal papers held by the Archives of Labor and

Urban Affairs, Walter P. Reuther Library, Wayne State University, Detroit. The Olga Madar Collection includes correspondence, reports, minutes, news clippings, publications, and other material reflecting her career with the UAW and her work on behalf of women, senior citizens, and other community groups. An oral history interview with Madar from May 21, 1994, can be found in the UAW Oral Histories at the Archives of Labor and Urban Affairs. Another interview from August 1976 is available at the Michigan Historical Collections, Bentley Historical Library, University of Michigan, and as a microfilm supplement to the Twentieth Century Trade Union Woman: Vehicle for Social Change oral history project, sponsored by the Program on Women and Work, Institute of Labor and Industrial Relations, University of Michigan and Wayne State University. A videotape of a 1990 interview conducted by Sue Carter is available at the Michigan Women's Historical Center and Hall of Fame in Lansing. Biographical sketches include Fran Harris, *Focus—Michigan Women, 1701–1977* (Michigan Coordinating Committee of the National Commission on the Observance of Women's Year, 1977), p. 105; and Amy Beth Aronson, "Olga Madar," in Jennifer Scanlon, ed., *Significant Contemporary American Feminists: A Biographical Sourcebook* (1999), pp. 174–80. More information about the UAW is in Nancy Gabin, *Feminism in the Labor Movement: Women and the United Auto Workers, 1935–1975* (1990). On women and organized labor in the postwar era, see Dennis Deslippe, *"Rights, Not Roses": Unions and the Rise of Working-Class Feminism, 1945–1980* (2000.) Obituaries appeared in the *Detroit Free Press*, May 17, 1996; the *New York Times*, May 18, 1996; and the *AFL-CIO News*, June 10, 1996.

NANCY GABIN

MAHLER, Margaret. May 10, 1897–October 3, 1985. Psychoanalyst.

Margaret Schönberger was born in the small Hungarian village of Sopron, close to the Austrian border. Her father, Gusztav Schönberger, a Hungarian Jew and a graduate of the medical school of Vienna University, was a general practitioner and the chief public health officer for the district; her mother, Eugenia Wiener, was a beautiful, pampered girl who gave birth to her first child at age nineteen, only nine months and six days after she married. Margaret very strongly felt herself to be her father's daughter and always felt unwanted by her mother, who, she believed, favored her younger sister Suzanne. Although early in childhood she turned to her father's world of intellect, science, and medicine, she always longed for a closeness to her mother that she did not have, and never quite came to terms with not having been properly cared for by her.

Margaret left home at sixteen to attend Gymnasium in Budapest, where she found excitement and intellectual stimulation. She was especially close to and influenced by psychoanalysts Sandor Ferenczi and Michael Balint, who sparked her early interest in psychoanalysis. Her education took place at a succession of institutions: the University of Budapest (1917–19), the University of Munich (1919–20), and the University of Jena (1920–22). She also spent a semester at the University of Heidelberg. After receiving her medical degree from the University of Jena in 1922, she worked as a pediatrician in two clinics in Vienna, where she observed firsthand the importance of the mother-infant bond. She began psychoanalytic training in 1922, completing it in 1933.

In 1936, at age thirty-nine, Margaret Schönberger married Paul Mahler, a chemist. She and her husband fled Vienna and the Nazis in 1938, arriving in New York City after a brief stay in London. They did not have children. Paul had difficulty making an adequate living after emigrating, but Margaret Mahler continued her work as a psychoanalyst of both children and adults. The couple eventually divorced in 1953. She accepted an invitation to teach at Philadelphia Psychoanalytic Institute, which became a home away from home as she continued her clinical work in New York. She later taught at Columbia University's College of Physicians and Surgeons (1941–55) and Albert Einstein School of Medicine (1955–74).

The turning point in Mahler's career occurred when she, together with Manuel Furer, opened Masters Children's Center in Manhattan. The center received its first funding in 1959, but Mahler and Furer had begun working there in 1957. Here in 1959, long before such research became popular, she began her observational research project on mother-infant pairs. Masters Children's Center was located in a brownstone in Greenwich Village; the basement housed a large playroom arranged with large action toys and a mothers' sitting area on one side. The idea to observe normal mother-infant pairs in a naturalistic playground-like setting grew out of Mahler's previous analytic work with psychotic children, as well as her long-standing interest as a pediatrician in observing normal babies and their caretakers. She hypothesized that the core disturbance in psychotic children was their inability to perceive and internalize the mother as a beacon of orientation—and that because they were not able to establish a symbiotic relationship with a caretaker, the mother, they were not able to become separate individuals with separate self and object representations. Mahler asked herself how normal babies develop into separate individuals in the caretaking presence of their mothers. She hypothesized that all normal children go through a process of psychological birth—the separation-individuation process—and she believed that this intrapsychic process could be inferred from observations of mothers and their infants and toddlers in a natural setting.

In this research project, Mahler and colleagues observed a group of mothers and their babies, beginning when the infants were four months of age, three to four times a week. Participant observers mingled with both mothers and children to observe processes of separating and reuniting as these developed through age three. Detailed records were kept, and the results of the study were published in a number of papers authored by Margaret Mahler and colleagues, and eventually in her most influential book, *The Psychological Birth of the Human Infant* (1975), co-authored with Fred Pine and Anni Bergman. Follow-up studies of these original subjects still continue, and many of the subjects of the original study have remained in contact with the researchers.

While this research project turned Mahler's interest from pathology to normal development, she nevertheless remained involved with questions raised by severely disturbed autistic or psychotic children who were not able to undergo a normal process of separation-individuation. She felt that such children could be helped only by doing intensive treatment with the mother-child pair so that a more normal attachment could develop between them. This was the beginning of mother-infant psychotherapy, treating mothers and their young children together, which has since become a major treatment modality.

While Margaret Mahler was passionate about her ideas and her findings, she was open to the new findings of infant research, even if they appeared to contradict some of her theories. As a result of these new findings, she gave up her early idea that infants normally go through an autistic phase in early development, and she invited both pediatrician Berry Brazelton and infant psychiatrist Daniel Stern to regular exchanges of ideas and findings at Masters Children's Center.

Interestingly, Mahler needed constant companionship and never liked to work alone. This proved to be of great importance, because she was able to create a community of devoted colleagues and students who participated in her work and shared the excitement of coming together to think, search, and observe, always profiting from her incisive ways of understanding and conceptualizing. Mahler was demanding both of herself and of others, but she was also enormously generous in the way she provided for her friends and colleagues. For many years she owned a small house in Connecticut, which she loved dearly and where she loved to entertain. Margaret Mahler remained intensely involved in her work to the end of her life, dying in New York City in 1985 at the age of eighty-eight. The Margaret S. Mahler Psychiatric Research Foundation outside Philadelphia continues active research on her pathbreaking ideas.

Bibliography: Archival material is found in the Margaret Mahler Collection at the Yale University Library Archives and at the Margaret S. Mahler Foundation in Wynnewood, Pennsylvania. The best source of information on Margaret Mahler's life is *The Memoirs of Margaret S. Mahler* (1988), compiled and edited by Paul E. Stepansky. Much of the information contained in the memoir comes from interviews done by Doris Nagel for the Columbia University Oral History Collection. In addition to *The Psychological Birth of the Human Infant: Symbiosis and Individuation* (1975), Mahler was co-author (with Manuel Furer) of *On Human Symbiosis and the Vicissitudes of Individuation* (1968). See also J. Aronson, ed., *Selected Papers of Margaret S. Mahler* (2 vols., 1979). Follow-up studies to Mahler's original research appear in Anni Bergman, *Ours, Yours, Mine: Mutuality and the Emergence of the Separate Self* (1999). Also of interest is John B. McDevitt and Calvin F. Settlage, eds., *Separation-Individuation: Essays in Honor of Margaret S. Mahler* (1971). An obituary appeared in the *New York Times* on October 3, 1985. See also Anni Bergman, "Tribute to Margaret S. Mahler," *Psychoanalytical Inquiry* 7 (1987), pp. 307–10; and Fred Pine, "Margaret S. Mahler, M.D.: In Memoriam," *Psychoanalytical Psychology* 3 (1986), pp. 101–4.

ANNI BERGMAN

MANLEY, Effa. March 27, 1897–April 16, 1981. Baseball owner and business manager, civil rights activist.

Effa Manley, Negro League baseball team co-owner and manager, was born in Philadelphia, Pennsylvania. Her mother, Bertha Ford, a German immigrant who was half Asian Indian, was married to Benjamin Brooks, who was African American. They had four children before Effa was born. When Effa was older, her mother told her that she was the result of an affair with John Marcus Bishop, a wealthy white financier who had a seat on the New York Stock Exchange, whom Bertha met through her work as a seamstress. Bertha and Benjamin Brooks had divorced soon after the affair; Brooks sued John Bishop and won $10,000 for the alienation of his wife's affections. Bertha married a second time, to a black man named B. A. Cole. They had two children.

Effa graduated from William Penn High School in Philadelphia in 1916 and moved to New York City, where she passed as a white woman to earn higher wages. She returned home at night to the black community and she lived a segregated life. She married Mr. Bush (first name unknown) and they later divorced. Effa was a great fan of the legendary New York Yankee Babe Ruth. While attending the 1932 World Series in New York City, she met her second husband, Abraham (Abe) Manley, whom she married on June 15, 1933, in

New York City. On their marriage certificate, Effa listed her race as colored. She believed herself to be white, but would likely not have been able to marry Manley, a black man twelve years her senior, if she had identified herself as a white woman. The marriage brought Effa respect in the Harlem community of Sugar Hill, where most of her acquaintances believed she was a very light-skinned black woman. She never disputed this assumption until very late in her life. Abe and Effa had no children.

In 1935, Abe Manley purchased a Negro League team, the Brooklyn Eagles, with $100,000 earned from his work as a "numbers banker." (A common game at the time in black communities, playing the numbers involved bets on anything with numbers, such as the daily figures of the Stock Exchange.) Effa Manley was the co-owner and business manager of the successful Negro League baseball team for thirteen years, the second woman owner of a major league team. Though Abe had made the decision to purchase the Eagles, Effa soon came to dominate the business of running the team. Without any formal training, she controlled the club's day-to-day business operations, including hotel arrangements, payroll, equipment, and publicity. Manley was active at the league level; though her husband held the title of league treasurer, she did virtually all of the work. The team first played in Brooklyn's Ebbets Field, but then moved to Ruppert Stadium in Newark, New Jersey, where they became the Newark Eagles and played in the minor league stadium of the Bears, a Yankee farm team.

The Negro League teams were a central part of black communities, and the Newark Eagles were no exception. In 1946, the Newark Eagles won the Negro League World Series; it was a very proud moment for Manley. Her teams included future major league players such as Larry Doby, Monte Irvin, and Don Newcombe. Manley served as a mother figure to some of her players, and she called them her "boys." She was later accused of having affairs with her players, a charge she denied.

Manley was a well-known beauty with a head for business who also maintained a commitment to the black community. In 1935, she was a founding member of the Citizens League for Fair Play, a group that organized picket lines and forced the desegregation of department stores with slogans such as "Don't Trade Where You Can't Work." She also served as the treasurer of the New Jersey chapter of the National Association for the Advancement of Colored People (NAACP). The Newark Eagles sold "Stop Lynching" buttons along with team merchandise at their games and held fund-raisers on behalf of anti-lynching campaigns.

On April 15, 1947, Jackie Robinson integrated the major leagues as an infielder for the Brooklyn Dodgers. Other players, including several of the Eagles, soon followed suit. Manley's business acumen came through when she demanded that the major league teams pay Negro League owners for their players, a practice unheard of until she set a precedent by demanding $5,000 (a cheap price) for Monte Irvin. With many players moving to the major leagues over the next few years and black fans following their successes, the Negro League teams quickly declined, and the Manleys sold the Newark Eagles in 1948. After Abe Manley's death in 1952, Effa returned to Philadelphia, where her extended family still lived. She moved to Los Angeles in 1968 and married again, this time to musician Charles Alexander, an old flame. The marriage was short-lived and she later admitted it to be a mistake.

In the last decades of her life Manley became an activist for her "boys," fighting for recognition of the Negro League players and taking up the cause of convincing the National Baseball Hall of Fame and Major League Baseball to include more Negro League players in the Hall of Fame. When the Special Committee on Negro Leagues disbanded in 1977, after only nine Negro League players had been inducted, Manley began a letter-writing campaign with the goal of creating another committee that would honor players by listing their names on a special plaque. With Leon Herbert Hardwick, she published *Negro Baseball . . . Before Integration* in 1976 to record the history of Negro League players and to offer her suggestions of the greatest players.

As her health began to fail, Effa Manley moved into a rest home run by former Negro Leaguer Quincy Trouppe. She continued to enjoy jazz, her extended family, and correspondence with some of her old players. Manley died of a heart attack on April 16, 1981, in Los Angeles after a diagnosis of colon cancer and the development of peritonitis after surgery; she was eighty-four. She was buried in the Catholic Holy Cross Cemetery and Mausoleum in Culver City, California. Her gravestone reads: "She Loved Baseball."

Bibliography: There are two main manuscript collections on Effa Manley. The first is at the National Baseball Hall of Fame Museum and Library in Cooperstown, New York. This collection includes an Abe and Effa Manley "Officials" file, an Effa Manley "Personal File, Ashland Collection" and "Professional File, Ashland Collection," a "Newark Eagles Subject File," and Effa Manley's scrapbook. The files include copies of the marriage certificate and obituaries of Abe and Effa Manley as well as a Hall of Fame questionnaire from 1973. The second collection of manuscript material is at the Newark Public Library in Newark, New Jersey. Boxes of business records, which had been left behind in a house owned by the Manleys, were recovered and given to the library. They are available on microfilm.

Secondary works on Manley's life include Gai Ingham Berlage, "Effa Manley: A Major Force in Negro Baseball in the 1930s and 1940s," *Nine: A Journal of Baseball History and Social Policy Perspectives* 1, no. 2 (Spring 1993), pp. 163–84; a section in Berlage, *Women in Baseball: The Forgotten History* (1994); Amy Essington, "'She Loved Baseball': Effa Manley and Negro League Baseball," in William M. Simons, ed., *The Cooperstown Symposium on Baseball and American Culture, 2000* (2001); and James Overmyer, *Queen of the Negro Leagues: Effa Manley and the Newark Eagles* (1998). Manley also appears in several oral histories: Allen Richardson, "A Retrospective Look at the Negro Leagues and Professional Negro Baseball Players" (MA thesis, San Jose State University, 1980); Art Rust Jr., *Get That Nigger off the Field: An Oral History of Black Ballplayers from the Negro Leagues to the Present* (1992); William Marshall, "Effa Manley interview," October 19, 1977, for the A. B. "Happy" Chandler Oral History Project, University of Kentucky Library. She is interviewed in two documentaries: *Only the Ball Was White* (1992) and *There Was Always Sun Shining Someplace: Life in the Negro Baseball Leagues* (1983). The Social Security Index and an obituary in the *Los Angeles Times* on April 18, 1981, list her birth date as 1897, although the year 1900 is also attributed as her birth date and appears on her gravestone.

AMY ESSINGTON

MARACCI, Carmelita. July 17, 1908–July 26, 1987. Dancer, choreographer, teacher.

Carmelita Maracci was born in Goldfield, Nevada, the youngest of three children of Joseph Maracci, a gambler and restaurant owner, and Josephine Gaus, a pianist. The family moved to San Francisco and then to Fresno, California. Listening to her German French mother practice Schubert and Schumann, Maracci nurtured a natural musicality. She had an oval face of unconventional beauty and glistening ebony hair often twisted into a Spanish knot, and she acquired her mother's perfectionist nature and refined aesthetic taste. She was petite with exquisite proportions for dancing—sloping shoulders, straight but well-shaped legs, feet with beautiful high arches, and natural flexibility.

Inspired after seeing Anna Pavlova perform, Maracci at about age twelve began ballet studies with Anna Haloise and later with Anita Peters. She studied Spanish dancing with Hippolita Mora and later was influenced by Helba Huara. She practiced technique by day and created dances by night.

As a child, Maracci attended convent schools in San Francisco. She was an intellectual who studied everything from the Greek classics to the Renaissance to contemporary culture. After graduating from the Mildred Lee Lynch School for Girls in Fresno in 1924, she moved to Los Angeles, accompanied by her German grandmother, to continue her dancing lessons.

After studying for less than two years with Ernest Belcher, Maracci opened the Hollywood Bowl season as a soloist in the Faust Ballet from *The Phantom of the Opera* on July 3, 1926. She then studied privately in New York City with Enrico Zanfretta, an austere Italian ballet master, and occasionally with Luigi Albertieri. Her extraordinary ballet technique enabled her to jump weaving her limbs (entrechat huit), turn nine to seventeen revolutions (pirouettes), and balance effortlessly.

After touring with a revue of Alexis Kosloff, she became disillusioned with the superficiality of dance as entertainment. She withdrew from professional engagements and returned to California to teach and study dance more profoundly. Delving into her father's part-Spanish heritage, she utilized zapateado (heel beating), castanets, and flawless ballet technique to create dances. Maracci made her debut of original dances using music by Ravel, de Falla, Granados, and Schumann at the Los Angeles Philharmonic on April 22, 1930, presented by L. E. Behymer. To enhance her exotic allure, publicity materials listed her birthplace as Montevideo, Uruguay.

Around this time Lee Freeson, a theater actor and associate director with Nachum Zemach (founder of the Moscow Habima Theater), encountered Maracci while she was practicing in a Hollywood studio and was captivated by her singing castanets. He became her stage manager, confidant, and soul mate. They lived together for thirty years before marrying in 1965. They had no children.

On April 11, 1937, in New York, Benjamin Zemach gave up his performance at the 92nd Street Y so Maracci and her ensemble could dance for an audience of artists and intellectuals. In June, Maracci danced *Cante Jondo* (Deep Song), *Viva tu Madre* (Live for the One Who Bore You), and *Dance of Elegance* in an impromptu private performance in her small Hollywood studio for dance critic John Martin. Overwhelmed by her dances, he was compelled to write in his review: "once in a generation can one expect to find a young dancer so manifestly destined for a great career" (*New York Times*, June 27, 1937). Her first Broadway appearance was at the St. James Theatre on December 31, 1939, for the Holiday Dance Festival.

Maracci then toured across the country for four seasons presented by Columbia Concerts Corporation. Impressed by notices that referred to her as a "tornado," Sol Hurok engaged Maracci in January 1946 and presented her at Carnegie Hall. Maracci's touring contract with Hurok ended after an incident in St. Paul, Minnesota, when she walked off the stage because of a rowdy audience. Already limited by her refusal to dance in Franco's Spain, touring became financially impossible after local managers dropped her. She rehearsed with her small company, performing infrequently until the mid 1950s and appearing at the Brooklyn Academy of Music in 1954.

Maracci's dancing was deeply personal and an innovative art form. With fiery, passionate individuality and deep political and social convictions, she created dances inspired by Goya's war drawings, Federico García Lorca's poetry, and Unamuno's philosophy. Her dances could be satirical, witty, or flirtatious; a passionate protest of inhumanity or a celebration of human spirit; a plunge to deepest sorrow or an expression of joy. Proclaiming herself a non-bomb-throwing anarchist, she wanted to help change the world through the theater. The Spanish civil war had awakened her to the interconnectedness of the world and inspired *La Pasionaria.* Contributing proceeds from her performances to Spanish refugee aid, her compassion extended beyond the footlights. Her friends included Edward Weston, who photographed her in 1937, AGNES DE MILLE, Muriel Stuart (protégé of Pavlova), and Igor Stravinsky.

Her artistic reputation led to projects such as Walt Disney's *Three Caballeros* (1945); American Ballet Theatre's *Circo de España* (1951), with sets and costumes by her friend Rico Lebrun; and Charlie Chaplin's *Limelight* (1952). All were commercially successful but personally unsatisfying. She found more fulfillment in her own small portraits, such as *Nightingale and the Maiden.* Inspired by a poem written in 1500, she imagined and realized the sweet singing trills of the nightingales with her virtuoso playing of castanets.

Incapable of compromising her principles for financial gain, which limited her performing, teaching gave her more autonomy. Always struggling to make ends meet and in later years debilitated by severe arthritis, Maracci taught until several months before her death. Her reputation attracted students such as Jerome Robbins, Paul Godkin, Donald Saddler, Allegra Kent, and Cynthia Gregory. Rejecting ballet's regimentation and mannered formalities, Maracci inspired students to seek their individual creative voice. She imbued technique with poetry. The whole body danced from the heart, not just the feet, through the fingertips fluttering like raindrops. Maracci provoked her students to feel, think, smell the wisteria, and ask questions. Her teaching included politics, poetry, music, and cooking as a way to nurture the art of dance as an integral part of a student's journey of life.

Carmelita Maracci was a groundbreaking dancer, choreographer, intellectual, and teacher who had a unique blend of artistry, fiery passion, and social consciousness. She died following a heart attack in Los Angeles in 1987 at the age of seventy-nine. Her dances have vanished due to the ephemeral nature of her art, but Maracci's legacy continues through her students and other individuals she inspired.

Bibliography: The Jerome Robbins Dance Division, New York Public Library for the Performing Arts at Lincoln Center, contains materials related to Carmelita Maracci, including personal papers, scrapbooks, announcements, programs, drawings, photographs, oral history, costume designs (Robert Tyler Lee), and videos. Biographical and descriptive information can be found in Agnes de Mille's *Portrait Gallery* (1990), *America Dances* (1980), *Book of the Dance* (1963), and *Dance to the Piper* (1951), as well as in Carol Easton, *No Intermissions* (1996). Photographs of Maracci are found in Merle Armitage, *Dance Memoranda* (1947), and John Martin, *The Dance* (1946). Articles written by Maracci include "The Symbolic and Psychological Aspects of the Dance," in Walter Sorell, ed., *The Dance Has Many Faces* (1951); and "The Portrait—The Individual Voice," *Impulse,* 1961, pp. 14–15. See also the following articles in *Dance Magazine:* Donna Perlmutter, "Carmelita Maracci: An Appreciation," November 1987, pp. 32–33; Tobi Tobias, "William Carter: An Interview," June 1975, pp. 44–52; Jocelyn Knowles, "Lessons with Carmelita Maracci," May 1964, pp. 38–41; and Allegra Kent, "Carmelita Maracci," January 2001, p. 68. The birth year of 1908 is determined by the 1910 U.S. Census; her birth certificate was destroyed by the "Great Fire" of 1923 in Goldfield, Nevada. Obituaries appeared in the *Los Angeles Times* on July 30, 1987, the *New York Times* on August 3, 1987, and *Variety* on August 19, 1987.

ELSPETH KUANG

MARSHALL, Catherine. September 27 1914–March 18, 1983. Inspirational writer and lecturer.

The catalyst for Catherine Marshall's career as a Christian writer was the premature death of her husband, the Reverend Peter Marshall, in 1949. When the popular rector of Washington's historic New York Avenue Presbyterian Church and chaplain of the U.S. Senate succumbed to a second heart attack at age forty-six, his thirty-four-year-old widow was left with few financial resources to raise their nine-year-old son. Devastated but undaunted, she determined to extend her husband's ministry by editing some of his more than six hundred sermons. The resulting book of sermons and prayers, *Mr. Jones, Meet the Master* (1949), landed on the *New York Times* best-seller list for almost a year.

Her second book—and second best-seller—has become a Christian classic: *A Man Called Peter* (1951) limns Marshall's "God-guided" rise from the working classes of dour Coatbridge, Scotland, to a prominent Christian ministry in America. Not least among the appeals of *A Man Called Peter* is its account of the three-way romance among God, Peter, and Catherine—as well as the glimpses provided the reader of Catherine's own spiritual growth. The film version starring Richard Todd and Jean Peters was one of the top-grossing films of 1955.

The author was born Sarah Catherine Wood in Johnson City, Tennessee, oldest of the three children of the Reverend John Ambrose Wood and his wife, Leonora Haseltine Whitaker. She was brought up in Presbyterian manses in small southern towns, and her family environment was richer in love and support than in material possessions. After graduation from high school in Keyser, West Virginia, Catherine set her sights on Agnes Scott College, a women's college in Decatur, Georgia. Though college was difficult for the family to fund during the Depression, she was enabled to enroll in 1932 by a small work scholarship, the usual minister's daughter's discount, and a timely federal contract awarded to her mother to write the history of their county. A history major at Agnes Scott, Catherine wrote poetry that she later credited with honing her writing skills.

Visiting Peter Marshall's Westminster Presbyterian Church in nearby Atlanta her sophomore year, she fell immediately in love. Entries in the journals she began at this time reflect her intensifying passions for the pursuit of a spiritual life—and for a life as the wife of Peter Marshall. Her father officiated at their wedding on November 4, 1936; she would draw on the memories of her marriage for many years and books to come.

Catherine Marshall's life was shaped by being a minister's wife. In 1937 her husband became pastor of the prestigious New York Avenue Presbyterian Church in Washington, D.C., and she was thrust into her new role of helpmate to her husband's career. Their only child, Peter John, was born in 1940. An extended illness from 1943 to 1945 from a form of tuberculosis (a harbinger of the debilitating lung disease that was to persist throughout her adult life) was but one of the young wife's trials. She also struggled with her resistance to her husband's dedication to his ministry, which she often resented because he was frequently absent and because she believed he was risking a heart attack, which is what eventually claimed his life.

Luckily for her as she forged her new life as an inspirational author, the 1950s were sympathetic to religion. She edited additional volumes of sermons and prayers for McGraw-Hill, including *Let's Keep Christmas* (1953), *The Prayers of Peter Marshall* (1954), and *The First Easter* (1959). The autobiographical *To Live Again* (1957) provides a narrative sequel to *A Man Called Peter.* Determined to sublimate her grief into a productive ministry of writing, she explores with frankness and sensitivity the intimate anguish that widows and widowers know well—and offers reassurance of rebirth and renewal. In *Beyond Our Selves* (1961), she suggests ways to discern God's will in matters of loss and grief. Her father's death in 1961 provides the faith-affirming conclusion to this book.

Although not always sympathetic to Peter Marshall's conservative views on the role of women, she found herself after his death believing that her own definition as a woman depended on marriage. On November 14, 1958, she married Leonard Earle LeSourd, the executive editor of *Guideposts,* an inspirational magazine published by Reverend Norman Vincent Peale. She became stepmother to three children, Linda, Leonard, and Jeffrey, and lived in suburban Chappaqua, New York.

The LeSourds' personal alliance was a productive author-editor partnership of twenty-three years. He reviewed her manuscripts with care; she served *Guideposts* as roving editor. With Elizabeth and John Sherrill, they founded Chosen Books, a publishing house dedicated to Catherine's works and to other inspirational books intended for a Christian audience, and organized a prayer group called "The Intercessors." Her past and present family life, which grew to include Peter's wife Edith and their two children, Mary and Peter, provided material for her exploration of personal and spiritual relationships in *Something More* (1974), *The Helper* (1978), and *Meeting God at Every Turn* (1980).

Two novels written years apart created an enthusiastic audience for Marshall, particularly among secondary students. *Christy* (1967), set in 1912, is based on the experiences of Leonora Whitaker, Marshall's mother, who at nineteen taught in a mission school in remote Cutter's Gap in the Great Smoky Mountains of Tennessee. Produced as a television series in the 1990s by CBS, the show received awards for its values from religious organizations like the Southern Baptist Convention, but it also garnered praise from secular sources for its artistry and professionalism. *Julie* (1984), although prompted by Marshall's fascination with both the Johnston Flood of 1889 and the inner workings of small-town newspapers, was set in the 1930s and paralleled many of her own girlhood experiences.

Following Catherine Marshall's death at Boynton Beach, Florida, on March 18, 1983, at the age of sixty-eight, Leonard LeSourd drew on his wife's copious journals and correspondence for several posthumous volumes concerning her later years—including her doubts and depressions—that he edited and published in her name. Twenty years after her death, Catherine Marshall's numerous books of Christian guidance have sold more than eighteen million copies and been translated into more than thirty-five languages. Her claim on her Christian audience has endured; all but a few of her books remain in print.

Bibliography: Catherine Marshall's own essays and books provide a logical resource for biographical facts, especially *A Man Called Peter* (1951), *To Live Again* (1957), *Beyond Our Selves* (1961), and *Meeting God at Every Turn* (1980). Volumes edited by Leonard LeSourd are also helpful: *A Closer Walk* (1986) and *Light in My Darkest Night* (1989) develop details of her second marriage, relationships with her stepchildren, and her final illnesses. See also Paul Boyer, "Minister's Wife, Widow, Reluctant Feminist: Catherine Marshall in the 1950s," *American Quarterly* 30, no. 5 (Winter 1978), pp. 703–21. Agnes Scott College houses Catherine Marshall's papers, including journals, manuscripts, galley proofs, and correspondence. The collection also contains thirty-one audiotapes made between 1973 and 1983 that record interviews with Marshall and Leonard LeSourd, her speaking engagements, and the interviews she conducted for research purposes. An obituary appeared in the *New York Times* on March 19, 1983.

LINDA L. HUBERT

MARSHALL, Leona Woods. *See* Libby, Leona Woods Marshall.

MARTIN, Gloria. June 3, 1916–November 22, 1995. Socialist feminist organizer, activist.

Gloria Martin pioneered the fusion of women's liberation with socialism. She was an inventive and down-to-earth organizer, a free-spirited bohemian, and a passionate orator. Her lifetime of activism provided a bridge between the Old Left of the 1930s and the New Left of the 1960s.

Born in St. Louis, Gloria was adopted at infancy by Beulah Radford and William Seeger, along with an unrelated younger child, Mary Lee. The family's early years were spent in Asheville, North Carolina. Seeger was a florist, but in 1919 he operated a café near the childhood home of one of Gloria's favorite writers, Thomas Wolfe. The family moved back to St. Louis when Gloria was eight.

Her upbringing in a white, working-class family in the Jim Crow South shaped Gloria's emerging political ideology, especially her critique of capitalism and all forms of bigotry. At age fourteen, she had to quit high school to work in a department store to help her family's finances, and that was the end of her formal education. But she continued to read voraciously, developing a deep knowledge of the world and a special love of literature and the arts. In her early twenties, Gloria joined the Young Communist League (YCL) and participated in a drive to end segregation in St. Louis. She quit the group during the 1940s out of disgust with its embedded sexism and in disillusionment with the shifting allegiances of the Soviet Union during wartime.

In the mid 1930s Gloria married George Adrian Dick, a postal worker, with whom she had three children: Gloria Adrian (1936), David (1938), and Michael (1941). After the couple divorced, she married James P. Martin, a magazine salesman, and had three more children: Denise (1943), Terrence (1945), and Kevin (1949). In 1950, having divorced Martin, she moved to Seattle, where she entered into a significant relationship with Thomas Eugene Warner, a plumber. Their children, Thomas and Jonathan, were born in 1952 and 1953. In these years she became involved with the Congress of Racial Equality and the National Association for the Advancement of Colored People (NAACP) in Seattle and supported herself and her family through such varied jobs as janitor, leather crafter, and chicken plucker.

After her years of activism around issues of class, race, and sex, Martin was more than ready for feminism's explosion in the 1960s. She forged links between female Marxists and women of the New Left through her popular, pioneering class "Women in Society," which she launched in 1966 at Seattle's Free University. In these classes, she formed an especially strong bond with Clara Fraser, a daughter of radical Jewish immigrants who had been involved in the Socialist Workers Party since the 1940s. In 1966, Fraser helped lead the Seattle local in an exodus that created the Trotskyist and feminist Freedom Socialist Party (FSP). The new party differed from the parent organization in support for the black movement, advocacy of female leadership, and dedication to internal democracy.

Martin and Fraser, who was a prolific writer and a political theorist as well as an organizer, became lifelong friends and collaborators in developing an activist integration of Marxism and feminism. They worked with members of Students for a Democratic Society (SDS) to found Radical Women in 1967. Radical Women's goal was (and is) to provide a radical voice within the feminist movement and to teach women the leadership skills, social history, and class consciousness they were denied in male-dominated organizations.

Soon after Radical Women was launched, Martin joined the fledgling Freedom Socialist Party. She served as FSP organizer from 1973 to 1978, decisive years when the party developed from a lone Seattle local into a national entity with a quarterly newspaper, the *Freedom Socialist.* Also during this period, Radical Women and the FSP formally affiliated as autonomous organizations with a shared commitment to women's rights, revolutionary socialism, and principled politics. Martin's account of these action-filled years is told in her history, *Socialist Feminism: The First Decade, 1966–76* (1986), which details numerous campaigns, including efforts for divorce reform, abortion, and child care, community organizing against police brutality, mobilizing welfare recipients, and a groundbreaking strike at the University of Washington.

Gloria Martin's unflappable presence in helping stand off a police raid on the local Black Panther Party is still warmly remembered by then-Panther leader Elmer Dixon. Martin forged strong alliances with Janet McCloud, Ramona Bennett, and other women leaders in the Native American movement through her energetic participation in anti-poverty, child welfare, and sovereignty struggles. Martin, Fraser, and African American feminist Nina Harding helped spearhead early mobilizations for abortion rights by low-income women of color. Martin also displayed a strong affinity with the lesbian and gay movement, having witnessed the trauma and violence suffered by her adoptive father because he was gay.

In 1990, at age seventy-four, Martin was elected organizer of Radical Women's Seattle branch. Interviewed by the *Seattle Times* on the occasion of her inauguration, Martin said, "We have to fight for survival issues—better pay, benefits, abortion rights, child care. But then we have to go further. We have to change the system" (July 5, 1990).

In her home life, Martin was a gifted gardener, friend of stray cats, and tireless archivist of memorabilia from the civil rights and feminist movements. She maintained close friendships with artist Robert LaVigne and photographer Edmund Teske. In her sixties and seventies, she managed and then owned Shakespeare & Martin Booksellers (later Shakespeare & Co.), which specialized in women's literature and rare books. During this period, she made several trips to Europe to see literary landmarks; some of the friends she made on these trips would later travel all the way to Seattle to visit her bookstore.

The last Radical Women meeting she attended featured the classic labor film *Salt of the Earth* (1954), and Martin regaled the gathering with tales of her adventures with the Communist union organizers portrayed in the film, Virginia and Clinton Jencks. Gloria Martin, the salty-tongued feminist revolutionary, died of brain cancer in 1995 in Bellevue, Washington, at the age of seventy-nine.

Bibliography: Information on Gloria Martin's political organizing is located in Special Collections at the University of Washington and in private archives at the Seattle headquarters of Radical Women and the Freedom Socialist Party. In addition to Martin's *Socialist Feminism: The First Decade, 1966–76* (1986), see her essay, "Where Matters Stand with Me," *Committee for a Revolutionary Socialist Party (CRSP) Pre-Conference Discussion Bulletin,* October 1, 1978. See also Clara Fraser, *Revolution, She Wrote* (1998); and *The Radical Women Manifesto: Socialist Feminist Theory, Program and Organizational Structure* (2001). Obituaries appeared in the *Seattle Times,* November 26, 1995; *Seattle Post-Intelligencer,* December 1, 1995; *Los Angeles Times,* December 2, 1995; *St. Louis Dispatch,* December 8, 1995; *Sojourner* (January 1996); and *Freedom Socialist* (January–March 1996).

HELEN GILBERT

MARTIN, Marion Ella. January 14, 1900–January 9, 1987. Republican Party leader, state labor official.

Born in Kingman, Maine, to Florence McLaughlin and William Henry Martin, both of whom had grown up in small northern Maine communities, Marion Ella Martin was the youngest of their two children and the only daughter. Her father was a prominent wholesale potato dealer, and the family became wealthy. Her mother was active in community groups and progressive causes, including the Federation of Women's Clubs and the Episcopal Church. They moved to Bangor in the early 1920s.

Martin attended elementary school in Kingman and secondary school from 1913 to 1917 at Bradford Academy in Massachusetts. She entered Wellesley College in 1918, majoring in chemistry, but left after two years because she had contracted tuberculosis of the throat. She returned home to Bangor and was a semi-invalid for about eight years. When health permitted, she engaged in golf and riding, both lifelong passions, and in 1926 she took a trip around the world with friends. Martin said the years of illness gave her time to select what she wanted out of life. She was nearly thirty when she recovered her health and began her career. She chose to remain single.

In 1930, the Maine Republican Party sought a candidate to challenge the incumbent Democratic legislator. Both of her parents were asked to run, but declined. Martin agreed to run and was elected to the Maine House of Representatives in 1930 and 1932 and the Maine Senate in 1934 and 1936. She served on the Legal Affairs Committee and became its first woman and its first nonlawyer chair. Serving on the committee with numerous male lawyers convinced her to finish her education. She said she "could get just so far in an argument, then I'd hit a stone wall of legal phraseology—so I studied law in self-defense" (*Portland Press Herald,* 1972). In 1933, she enrolled at the University of Maine, majored in economics, and graduated Phi Beta Kappa in 1935. She attended Yale University Law School in 1935–36 and a summer session at Northwestern University Law School in 1937.

Martin, an attractive woman with prematurely gray hair and sparkling eyes, soon gained a reputation in Maine GOP circles as a well-informed legislator and effective campaigner. Her abilities and northern Maine constituency led to her election in 1936 as Republican National Committeewoman from Maine. In 1937, RNC Chairman John Hamilton named her assistant chairman and head of the women's division. She spent her first year contacting and organizing Republican women's clubs, culminating in a 1938 convention in Chicago where the National Federation of Women's Republican Clubs was formed. Martin is credited as the founder of the group and served as its first director. Before her efforts, Republican women's groups operated independently of one another, reducing the potential power of the GOP women's vote. Martin, known as a dynamic speaker, traveled to nearly every state, sometimes giving two or three speeches a day. Martin believed that women could educate themselves and others about politics and that they had particular interests, especially in national and family security, that were not being met by the New Deal. She wanted women to succeed in the party and beyond, on their merits alone, and helped gain equal representation of women in regular committees of the RNC, but thought they should not compete with men.

Even though the efforts of Martin and the revitalized Republican women's clubs helped the GOP to regain control of Congress in 1946, shortly after the election the new RNC chairman, Carroll Reece, asked for Martin's resignation, surprising and angering many in the party. Speculation was that Reece wanted a Taft supporter in the job and that Katherine Kennedy Brown of Ohio, a Taft supporter, had been seeking Martin's ouster for some time. Martin espoused neutrality for the women's groups until the party had nominated a candidate.

After efforts to get Martin appointed to the Federal Communications Commission failed, she returned to Maine and was named commissioner of labor and industry by Governor Horace Hildreth in 1947. She was the first Maine woman to head a major government department and the only woman in the country at the time to head a labor and industry department. She said she liked the state administrative job because she could take responsibility for both mistakes and accomplishments. She remained in the job for twenty-five years, reappointed and praised by both Republican and Democratic governors. Martin reorganized the Department of Labor and Industry, dividing it into relatively autonomous divisions. She supported and worked for increased safety regulations, a living minimum wage, equal pay, protective legislation for women, child labor laws, and programs to help women become entrepreneurs. Governor Kenneth Curtis called her a pioneer in industrial safety. In 1958, she attended the International Labor Organization meeting in Geneva as the only state-level official to serve as a delegate. After her retirement in 1972, Rep. William Hathaway (D-Maine) said, "She has never let labels—whether they be Republican, Democrat, labor or management labels—get in the way of meeting the needs of people" (*Kennebec Journal,* September 23, 1972).

A moderate Republican, she remained active in Republican Party politics in Maine and was mentioned from time to time as a possible candidate for elective office, but she never ran again. A strong supporter of mediation to solve disputes, she continued to work as a mediator after her retirement. She died at her home, in Hallowell, Maine, in 1987, five days short of her eighty-seventh birthday.

Bibliography: There are no manuscript collections. Most information about Martin is in the form of newspaper clippings about her activities. Her own scrapbook collection of clippings, mostly about speeches, is at the National Federation of Republican Women, Alexandria, Virginia. A newspaper clipping file that covers much of Martin's career is on file at the *Portland Press Herald,* Portland, Maine. The Margaret Chase Smith Library, Skowhegan, Maine, has numerous clippings about Martin as well as several photographs, mostly from the 1930s and 1940s. The Maine State Library has a small file about Martin and information about the Department of Labor and Industry. Information about issues supported and opposed by Martin is available at the Maine State Archives and Maine Legislative Library, although neither resource has a collection specifically dedicated to Martin. The Wellesley College Archives has an extensive clipping file about Martin, mostly from the 1930s and 1940s, as well as alumni reports that list her activities, and Wellesley College reunion notes. Jo Freeman's *A Room at a Time: How Women Entered Party Politics* (2000) contains a brief discussion of Martin's activities at the Republican National Committee. See also Catherine E. Rymph, "Forward and Right: The Shaping of Republican Women's Activism, 1920–1967" (PhD dissertation, University of Iowa, 1998). Martin's nephew, William H. Martin of Bethesda, Maryland, and former Maine governor John H. Reed of Washington, D.C., supplied additional information. Her obituary appeared in the *Portland Press Herald* on January 9, 1987; the *New York Times* on January 11, 1987; and the *Washington Post* on January 12, 1987.

CANDACE A. KANES

MARTIN, Mary. December 1, 1913–November 3, 1990. Actress.

Mary Virginia Martin was born in Weatherford, Texas, the second of two daughters of Preston Martin, an attorney, and Juanita Presley, a violin teacher at Weatherford Seminary (later Weatherford College). She spent two years at Weatherford High School before her parents sent her to Ward Belmont, a finishing school in Nashville, Tennessee. Here she took voice and dance lessons, but after only two and a half months she returned to Weatherford and completed high school. On December 1, 1930, she married Benjamin Jackson Hageman, an older boy she had been dating since she was fourteen. They had a son, Larry, born in 1931. (He later changed his name to Larry Hagman and earned television fame as J. R. Ewing on *Dallas.*) The couple divorced in 1937, and three years later she married Paramount story editor Richard Halliday, who would also be her manager for thirty-three years and father of their daughter, Mary Heller Halliday, born in 1941.

Martin moved back to Weatherford in 1931 before the birth of her son and opened a dance school. A successful venture for several years, the school was destroyed by fire in 1937, and Mary set out for California. Her proverbial "big break" came when Laurence Schwab heard her sing at the Trocadero in Hollywood and brought her to New York in the fall of 1938. On November 9, 1938, Martin sang "My Heart Belongs to Daddy" in Cole Porter's *Leave It to Me!* and her dream was fulfilled. She soon appeared on the cover of *Life* magazine and signed a contract with Paramount. Martin appeared in a string of films between 1939 and 1943, including two with Bing Crosby, *Rhythm on the River* (1940) and *Birth of the Blues* (1941).

Her first love remained the theater, however, and in 1943 she went back to Broadway in *One Touch of Venus.* Though the part was originally planned for MARLENE DIETRICH, it gave Martin her first star billing, and she toured in the CHERYL CRAWFORD production in 1945. The hit shows followed with hardly a stumble. The following season, *Lute Song* offered "Mountain High, Valley Low." In 1947 she opened the national tour of *Annie Get Your Gun* in Dallas. She not only received a special Tony Award in 1948, but she discovered that she loved to tour. The role of a lifetime came in April 1949, as Nellie Forbush in Rodgers and Hammerstein's *South Pacific.* Martin received her second Tony and reprised the role in London. She loved needlepoint, and, as an expression of gratitude to the legendary duo, she stitched a special pillow for each of them.

Another milestone in her stage career came on October 20, 1954, when *Peter Pan* opened at New York's Winter Garden. She won her third Tony and would forever be associated with the title character. In November 1959, she reunited with Rodgers and Hammerstein in *The Sound of Music.* Fellow cast member John Randolph recalled that during the run, Mary Martin never let down. She was awarded her fourth Tony, against formidable competition: ETHEL MERMAN in *Gypsy.*

Her theatrical career endured for two more decades. The 1965 international tour of David Merrick's *Hello, Dolly!* settled in for a London run. Her last happy Broadway run was in Merrick's *I Do! I Do!,* which opened in December 1966 with one of the smallest casts in Broadway history: Mary Martin and Robert Preston. It enjoyed a sold-out run and subsequent tour. Her final Broadway triumph came on October 20, 1985, in *Our Hearts Belong to Mary.* She toured in *Legends!* in 1986, but the show never opened on Broadway. Asked why by a fan, she replied, "Darling, you're not seventy-three!" Her last standing ovation was in New York on June 12, 1988, at *A Cabaret for Cole.*

Mary Martin also became one of the first Broadway stars to conquer television. In 1953, she and Ethel Merman performed a historic duet on *The Ford 50th Anniversary Television Show.* On March 7, 1955, Martin brought *Peter Pan* to NBC so successfully that a second live performance was mounted the following January. She did a show for CBS with Noel Coward, *Together with Music,* in 1955. With John Raitt, Martin brought *Annie Get Your Gun* to NBC in 1957, and in 1959 she starred in two specials for the network: *Magic with Mary Martin* and *Music with Mary Martin.* In 1961 she and Bob Hope celebrated 25 *Years of* Life. In 1967 she co-hosted the first televised Tony Awards show with Robert Preston on ABC. Her final television appearances included a December 1989 interview with Larry King and the Kennedy Center Honors.

Mary Martin loved living in grand style, maintaining homes in Connecticut and New York City and a meticulously appointed farm in Brazil. After her husband's death, she settled in Rancho Mirage, California. Martin did not collect her own memorabilia, but Richard Halliday had devoted a wall in their New York home to displaying his favorite "Mary memorabilia," which became known as Richard's wall. Its focal point was a needlepoint of clasped hands that Mary had made—hands that symbolized their love for each other. Martin died in Rancho Mirage at the age of seventy-six. As she once said, "Thank you all for the spirit of my life. It will never end, because when I go, I'll be swinging up there on a star."

Bibliography: Mary Martin wrote two autobiographies, *Mary Martin's Needlepoint* (1969) and *My Heart Belongs* (1976). Her life and career have been definitively researched by Barry Rivadue in *Mary Martin: A Bio-Bibliography* (1991). Martin's personal papers, including correspondence from Richard Rodgers, Ethel Merman, and Janet Gaynor, are in the Mary Martin Collection at the Weatherford Library in Weatherford, Texas. The final quote is from the cover of a tribute held in her memory in New York City on January 28, 1991. Obituaries appeared in the *New York Times* on November 5, 1990, and *Variety* on November 12, 1990.

AL F. KOENIG JR.

MARTINEZ, Maria Montoya. c. 1881–1887–July 20, 1980. Potter.

Maria, as she was so often called, was the most famous of all American Indian potters. She was born to Reyecita Pena and Thomas Montoya at San Ildefonso Pueblo near Santa Fe, New Mexico, the first of their five daughters. Many American Indians did not publicly record birth dates or keep written records, but she was likely born between 1881 and 1887. Her sisters, Maximiliana, Desideria, Juanita, and Clara, were also well-known potters; Clara lived with Maria all her life and assisted her in pottery. Maria attended St. Catherine's Indian School in Santa Fe for one year, which she remembered to be the second grade. She spoke English and Spanish as well as her native Tewa, in which her name was Maria Poveka, or Pond Lily.

In 1904 Maria married Julian Martinez, who also lived on the pueblo, and the two spent that summer demonstrating pottery making at the St. Louis World's Fair. Maria and Julian had four sons: Adam (1905), Juan Diego (1915), Antonio (1921), and Phillip (1925). Julian and his artistic son Adam decorated walls of Santa Fe's La Fonda Hotel, and their canvas and paper works hang in museums. Adam married Santana Roybal, who was from a family of accomplished potters. Adam and Santana lived with Maria and Julian and were devoted caretakers all their lives. Santana apprenticed to Julian, learning his methods of decorating and designs; when Julian died in 1943, Santana painted pottery for Maria. After serving in World War II, Antonio returned to make his own pottery and to paint designs for his mother under the name of Popovi Da. By the 1950s Adam and Santana began signing pottery together.

Maria was, as she so often said of herself, the most famous Indian after Geronimo. Her skill at making large pots was particularly well known. In their early years Maria and Julian worked in their pueblo's traditional painted pottery, called polychrome, with designs from the Spaniards; it was made of red clay with an overcoating of liquid buff clay, polished with a cloth, and decorated with black, iron-rust red, and titanium-orange bird and feather pictorials. The natural clay was prospected on pueblo land and mixed half and half with local volcanic ash, which Maria called blue sand.

Maria was taught the old way of pottery making by her aunt Nicolassa. She never used a potter's wheel. She began a pot by forming a pancake of clay between her palms and laying it in a bowl-like vessel which was the bottom of a broken pot, called a puki. Coils of clay, rolled between the potter's palms, were added one on top of the other, building a cylinder that could be expanded into a rounded shape by use of gourd tools. The round pot could remain an inwardly curved or open bowl, or more coils could be added to build a bottle or a water jar.

A 1908 archaeological excavation near the pueblo, headed by Edgar Lee Hewett, director of the Museum of New Mexico in Santa Fe, changed Maria's life. Two-thousand-year-old black pottery shards were unearthed. The archaeologists asked Maria to reconstruct the forms and told Julian how other indigenous societies had smoked clay to make it black. Maria and Julian experimented several years to perfect the shiny jet-black firing that made them famous. As Maria said, "Black goes with everything."

They continued making polychrome, red ware, and black ware. After finishing the pot shape, for red or black pots Maria scraped, sanded the surface, and applied an iron-bearing clay slip, which she polished to a high shine with a water-smoothed stone. Julian spent time in the museums, researching his pueblo's designs, and abstracted them in his sketchbooks. Using a yucca frond brush, he decorated the surface of Maria's pots with a more refractory clay that would remain matte against the polished shiny pottery background. Pots were stacked on an iron grate over juniper wood for the fuel, surrounded by dried cow chips for insulation. A forty-five-minute open fire rendered the finished pots an oxidized iron-red color; an additional forty-five minutes of smothering the fire with wild horse manure and wood ash smoked the pots black. Although they are fragile at this low bonfire temperature, these pots can endure forever.

Maria and her design painters Julian, Santana, and Popovi, won prizes for fifty or more years at Santa Fe Indian Market and the Gallup pow-wow. Maria claimed to have attended every World's Fair, and in particular remembered the 1939 Treasure Island, San Francisco Fair, attended by more than 10 million visitors. She also spoke often of the seemingly endless year (1914) the family spent in San Diego at the Panama-California Exposition Fair, where they were to live and demonstrate. When they arrived, Maria found the buildings were in the multi-storied design of Taos Pueblo, not the single-storied design of San Ildefonso Pueblo. Though they were disappointed in their dwellings, Maria and her family honored the agreement they had made and stayed the full period.

Maria was unusually gregarious and loved receiving the many honors that came to her in her lifetime. She claimed to have laid the cornerstone of Rockefeller Center in New York City and "laid her hands on the glass" for the dedication of Dulles International Airport outside Washington, D.C. Her portrait was sculpted by MALVINA HOFFMAN. In 1978 the Smithsonian American Art Museum's Renwick Gallery mounted an exhibition, "Maria and Her Five Generations," which lasted six months. In addition, Maria and her family gave hundreds of students San Ildefonso pottery courses during summer sessions at the University of Southern California's Idyllwild campus.

On July 20, 1980, Maria died at the Pueblo. She was said to have been more than a hundred years old. Potters in San Ildefonso, including her great-granddaughter Barbara Gonzales and great-great-grandson Cavan, continue to make polychrome, red, and black pottery to this day.

Bibliography: For information about Maria Montoya Martinez, see Alice Lee Marriott, *Maria: The Potter of San Ildefonso* (1948), which is illustrated with drawings by Margaret Lefranc; and Richard L. Spivey, *Maria* (1979). Susan Peterson, *The Living Tradition of Maria Martinez* (1977, reissued 2002), contains 195 color and 135 black-and-white photographs; these are the only published photographic representations of Maria and her family's life and work. See also the exhibit catalogue *Maria Martinez: Five Generations of Potters* (1978), edited by Peterson. Maria was featured in the exhibition "Pottery by American Indian Women" at the National Museum of Women in the Arts, Washington, D.C., in 1997. The Heard Museum in Phoenix, Arizona, holds Peterson's Maria Martinez archive, which includes hundreds of black-and-white and color negatives and prints of Maria and her family at San Ildefonso Pueblo, with notes and drafts of Peterson's manuscripts made when Maria was alive. An obituary appeared in the *New York Times* on July 22, 1980.

SUSAN PETERSON

MASSEY, Estelle. *See* Osborne, Estelle Massey Riddle.

MATTHEWS, Burnita Shelton. December 28, 1894–April 25, 1988. Judge, lawyer, feminist.

Burnita Shelton Matthews was born in Copiah County, Mississippi, the second of five children and the only daughter of Lora Barlow and Burnell Shelton. In 1949, after nearly thirty years in the practice of law, Matthews became the first woman in the nation to serve as a life-tenured federal trial court judge.

Burnita Shelton developed an affinity for the law at a young age, winning an oratory contest at the age of eleven. As a child, she accompanied her father to the courthouse, where he served as clerk of the Chancery Court for Copiah County, and often sat in on trials. Her father, however, firmly opposed his daughter's plan to pursue a legal career. Respecting his preference, she attended the Cincinnati Conservatory of Music, where she received a teaching certificate.

Still determined to become a lawyer, Burnita returned to Mississippi, but no law school in the state then accepted women. She supported herself for several years by teaching music and piano. In 1917, she married Percy Matthews, whom she had first met in high school. Born in New Orleans, Percy had attended Millsaps College in Jackson, Mississippi, and received a law degree from Chicago-Kent College of Law in 1916. Shortly after their marriage, Percy enlisted and served in World War I as a pilot. Although they remained married for fifty-two years, until Percy's death in 1969, they lived apart for much of their marriage. Percy served as a lawyer in the Judge Advocate General's Corps of the U.S. Army and was frequently stationed elsewhere. The couple had no children.

After Percy's departure for war, and during the height of the suffrage movement, Matthews moved to Washington, D.C., motivated by the prospect of law school admission there. Recognizing his daughter's unflagging passion for the law, Burnell Shelton offered to cover her law school tuition, but Matthews preferred to pay her own way. She attended law classes at night at National University (now George Washington University) while holding down a day job at the Veterans Administration. She earned an LLB in 1919, followed by LLM and Master of Patent Law degrees in 1920. Weekends, she picketed the White House with other suffragists. Later, she recalled that during those protests "you could go to the front of the White House, and you could carry a banner, but if you spoke you were arrested for speaking without a permit. So when they asked me why I was there, I didn't answer" (*Third Branch*, p. 6). The banner she carried declared her purpose. And no arrest record impeded her admission to the bar.

When Matthews graduated from law school, no law firm in the District of Columbia would hire her. Even the Veterans Administration, where she had previously worked, declined to consider her for a position in its legal department because she was a woman. Wasting no time on anger, resentment, or self-pity, she devoted her energy to establishing a practice of her own. Believing the Nineteenth Amendment incomplete, she also served as counsel to the National Woman's Party (NWP), the group responsible for introducing in 1923 the idea and the original text of an equal rights amendment. The Woman's Party also urged legislators to repeal protective labor laws that applied only to women and other laws that restricted women's opportunities. Matthews wrote in those early days: "It is, of course, disappointing to women, that men of the legal profession are unable to see equality as equity when applied as between men and women. But then it is not surprising when one remembers that this defective vision, this regard of discrimination as 'protection' is traditional" (Matthews, "Women Should Have Equal Rights with Men," p. 120). Matthews helped change that tradition.

The D.C. bar knew Matthews as a skilled practitioner and an expert in the field of eminent domain. When the federal government condemned the headquarters building of the National Woman's Party near the Capitol in 1927 to make way for the current Supreme Court building, Matthews's representation led to the largest condemnation award the United States had yet paid. Her success did not please then–chief justice William Howard Taft, who grumbled that the "blackmailing members" of the NWP had attempted to "use every method possible to squeeze up the amount they are to derive from the Government." Unfazed, the NWP used the settlement to purchase the historic Sewall-Belmont House nearby.

In addition to working with the National Woman's Party and practicing law independently, Matthews was active in the Women's Bar Association of D.C., the American Bar Association, and the National Association of Women Lawyers. She served as the Mississippi delegate to the International Woman Suffrage Alliance in Paris in 1926. And she taught evidence at Washington College of Law from 1933 to 1939.

After a nationwide lobbying effort and a personal plea from INDIA EDWARDS, head of the Women's Division of the Democratic National Committee, President Truman named Matthews to the Federal District Court for the District of Columbia in 1949. Her colleagues on the bench were initially less than welcoming, assigning her the most technical and least rewarding motions. One District of Columbia jurist was reported to have commented: "Mrs. Matthews would be a good judge, [but there is] just one thing wrong: she's a woman" (*New York Times,* April 28, 1988). The president disagreed: "This was one appointment about which I had no misgivings, only genuine satisfaction" (*Third Branch,* p. 8).

Matthews's firm hand in managing each case identified the great lady from Mississippi more than her fine lace collar and cuffs, her slim size and soft voice. She presided over major trials, including a criminal trial of Teamsters leader Jimmy Hoffa and a suit brought by Black Muslims for the right to conduct religious services in a local prison. At a time when women faced much professional hostility, Judge Matthews showed her confidence in women lawyers by hiring only women as law clerks. Her colleagues, in the main, would hire no women, so she attracted clerks of a different, enriching life experience and extraordinary talent.

After nearly twenty years on the District Court, Judge Matthews took senior status in 1968 and thereafter sat regularly on court of appeals panels until the early 1980s. She rejoiced in President Carter's decision to change the face of the U.S. judiciary by appointing women in numbers to the bench. Throughout her life, she remained a caring counselor to women lawyers and judges, and a constant voice favoring the adoption of the equal rights amendment. Matthews died of a stroke in Washington in 1988 at the age of ninety-three and was buried in her birthplace of Copiah County, Mississippi.

Bibliography: Papers extensively documenting the professional career of Burnita Shelton Matthews are found at the Schlesinger Library, Radcliffe Institute for Advanced Study, Harvard University; her personal and family papers are at the Mississippi Department of Archives and History, Jackson, Mississippi. An oral history with Matthews conducted by Amelia R. Fry, April 29, 1973, is located at the Regional Oral History Office, Bancroft Library, University of California at Berkeley (1975). See also "Leader of Women's Rights Movement Recalls Suffrage Fight and Appointment to Bench," *Third Branch* 17, no. 3 (March 1985), pp. 1, 6–9. Writings by Matthews include "Women Should Have Equal Rights with Men: A Reply," *American Bar Association Journal* 12 (February 1926), pp. 117–20; and "The Woman Juror," *Women Lawyers Journal* 15, no. 2 (April 1927). Biographical material on Matthews is found in Lee Berger Anderson, "Judge Burnita Shelton Matthews: Lawyer and Feminist," *Women Lawyers Journal* 92 (Summer 1973); Kate Greene, "Torts over Tempo: The Life and Career of Judge Burnita Shelton Matthews," *Journal of Mississippi History* 56, no. 3 (August 1994), pp. 181–210; Rebecca Mae Salokar and Mary L. Vocansek, eds., *Women in Law: A Bio-bibliographical Sourcebook* (1996); and Ruth Bader Ginsburg and Laura W. Brill, "Women in the Federal Judiciary: Three Way Pavers and the Exhilarating Change President Carter Wrought," *Fordham Law Review* 64 (November 1995), pp. 281–90. The quote from Taft is taken from correspondence in the archives kept by the Supreme Court's curator. Obituaries appeared in the *Washington Post* and the *New York Times* on April 27 and 28, 1988, respectively.

RUTH BADER GINSBURG

MATYAS, Jennie. September 27, 1895–January 26, 1988. Labor organizer and educator.

Jennie Matyas, whose birth name was Zsofia, was born in Nagysajo village in Hungarian Transylvania, the third of six children of Abraham Matyas and his second wife, Sarah Eckstein. Growing up in an impoverished household that also included four half-brothers and -sisters, Jennie was accustomed to a meager diet, crowded conditions, and child-care responsibilities. Her father emigrated to the United States, and then arranged for the passage of his wife and children to New York in September 1906. Jennie did not find their frugal existence in a three-room flat on Manhattan's Lower East Side unusual. Soon she was bringing to her mother small sums earned doing housework, and at the age of fourteen, two years before she was legally employable full-time, she started working part-time in the garment industry. To her great regret, she had to stop attending school, but she took advantage of night school classes, especially to improve her skills in English.

A fast learner in the dressmaking industry, Jennie dutifully gave over her pay to her struggling mother, who did laundry work to supplement the small sums her husband made teaching Hebrew. Persistent tensions with her devout, elderly father contributed to Jennie's departing from Orthodox Judaism. Influenced by co-workers who had participated in the labor strikes of 1909–10 known as the Uprising of the 20,000, and shocked by the 1911 Triangle Shirtwaist Fire, she became an avid believer in labor union membership in order to combat sweatshop conditions.

By 1911 she was a member of Local 25 of the International Ladies' Garment Workers' Union (ILGWU), and she quickly moved into leadership positions. She was an active supporter of ILGWU efforts to provide education, health, and recreational services for its members, and by 1915 she succeeded in bringing the first black women into Local 25 membership. Like many ILGWU activists, Matyas found appeal in the credo of socialism. A member of the Socialist Party executive committee in the New York area during the mid 1910s, she especially admired the ideas of Morris Hillquist and Eugene V. Debs. She also supported woman suffrage. A scholarship from Local 25 enabled the dynamic four-foot eleven-inch activist to attend the Rand School of Social Science in 1916. A skilled public speaker, she made an ILGWU-sponsored speaking tour to northeastern cities in 1919 to raise money for striking steelworkers.

Disillusioned by Communist inroads into her union, Matyas dropped out of the ILGWU in 1922 to pursue further education. After attending James Millikin College, Western Reserve, and the University of Wisconsin, and only a year short of completing a bachelor's degree, she decided in 1925 to marry a longtime friend, printing pressman John Charters, who lived in San Francisco. They had no children. After nine years of working as a private seamstress, she reentered the union movement in 1934 as an ILGWU organizer and director of education in San Francisco on the invitation of President David Dubinsky, who remembered her earlier activism and shared her views on Communist infiltration.

By now an enthusiastic supporter of New Deal programs, Matyas took advantage of the opportunities for union organizing that opened with passage of the 1935 National Labor Relations Act. In the late 1930s she spearheaded many organizing successes in the San Francisco area, none more pathbreaking than those among Chinese American women garment workers. Especially notable was her performance during the fifteen-week strike in 1938 of Chinese Workers Local 341 against the National Dollar Stores. The year before she had led women workers at the Spirella Corset Factory in Emeryville in a successful fight for union recognition, increased wages, and shorter hours by orchestrating a forty-two-day sit-down strike, a strategy new to the San Francisco area. From 1935 to 1941 she belonged to a group of San Francisco–area liberals and labor leaders who sponsored a one-month Pacific Coast School for Workers held in Berkeley each summer. She also was associated with the adult education projects of Alexander Meiklejohn and his wife Helen, such as the San Francisco School of Social Studies, from 1934 to 1942.

Matyas took a leave from the ILGWU in August 1942 to serve as one of the eleven members of the Women's Advisory Committee, which advised War Manpower Commissioner Paul V. McNutt on women's part in the war effort. She also completed enough courses at the University of California to graduate cum laude with a degree in economics in 1943. Upon resuming ILGWU work, she became an international vice president (May 1944) and thus a member of the general executive board. For the next fifteen years she followed in the ILGWU tradition of being the lone woman who sat on this most influential body in the ILGWU. In the San Francisco area, she was responsible for establishing and overseeing the health insurance and retirement benefit programs of the ILGWU locals. Her work in negotiating labor-management contracts together with the union's business agent, representatives of the garment industry, and an impartial chairman resulted in wage increases linked to cost-of-living statistics; progress toward pay equality for women; a thirty-five-hour week for all garment workers; increases in employer payments to the retirement fund; and improvements in the piece-rate settlement system and in the apprenticeship program. As a result of her activism, the ebullient, articulate Matyas became a well-known public figure in the San Francisco area and in the California labor movement.

Among the three hundred people attending Matyas's retirement banquet, held September 17, 1959, during a national AFL-CIO convention in San Francisco, were longtime New York associates like David Dubinsky and ROSE SCHNEIDERMAN, California labor leaders like John F. Shelley and C. J. Haggerty, and local ILGWU members. In her late sixties, Matyas took classes to qualify for a teaching credential and was employed by the San Francisco School District from 1964 to 1983, teaching courses in current events to senior citizens until she was eighty-seven years old. A widow since 1945, Matyas moved into a retirement home

Maxwell

in San Francisco in 1974, where she died in 1988 at the age of ninety-two.

Bibliography: The most important materials on Jennie Matyas's labor union career are in the ILGWU collections at the Kheel Center for Labor-Management Documentation & Archives, Cornell University, and in the Labor Archives and Research Center (LARC), San Francisco State University. Additional material on her worker education efforts can be found in the Meiklejohn collection at Bancroft Library, University of California at Berkeley, and the papers of the San Francisco School of Social Studies at the LARC. The ILGWU organ *Justice,* especially Matyas's occasional articles published in 1934–59, provides useful orientation.

The best source on Matyas's youth is an oral history conducted in 1955: *Jennie Matyas and the ILGWU,* interview by Corrine L. Gilb, Regional Oral History Office, Bancroft Library, 1957. There is supplementary information in a 1975 interview of Matyas by Doris H. Linder, in a tape recording at the LARC. Regarding Matyas's service on the Women's Advisory Committee (WAC) of the War Manpower Commission (WMC) in 1942–44, the best source is the minutes of WAC meetings in the official records of the WMC, Record Group 211, National Archives. Oral histories of Paul St. Sure, Matthew B. Tobriner, Louis Goldblatt, and Julia Gorman Potter at Bancroft Library include useful comment about Matyas, as does the Sonia Kaross oral history in the Women's History Collection of the California Historical Society, San Francisco. Judy Yung's *Unbound Voices: A Documentary History of Chinese Women in San Francisco* (1999) provides insights on Matyas's organizing work among Chinese American garment workers. In the record of Matyas's entry into the United States at Ellis Island on September 23, 1906, she is identified as Zsofia Matyas, age nine (List of Alien Passengers for the U.S. Immigration Officer, Arriving from Fiume aboard the *S.S. Ultonia,* Microfilm Roll 707, National Archives). No birth certificate exists to confirm that her birth year was the 1895 she always used as an adult, rather than 1896. Her death certificate is available from the Department of Public Health, City and County of San Francisco.

DORIS H. LINDER

MAXWELL, Vera. April 22, 1901–January 15, 1995. Designer of women's apparel.

In a career that spanned the 1930s through the 1980s, sportswear designer Vera Maxwell offered American women a relaxed alternative to the more dressed up mid-century styles of Paris-dictated fashions. Known for softly tailored women's fashions, Maxwell's mid-market price point, easy styling, and durable construction won her an immediate and loyal following. Vera Maxwell customers ran the gamut from working women to urban socialites to screen star (and later princess) Grace Kelly, who was one of Maxwell's staunchest admirers and a lifelong client. LILLIAN GISH, MARTHA GRAHAM, and First Lady Pat Nixon were also loyal clients.

She was born Vera Huppé in the Bronx, the middle of three children and second daughter of Irma Honthumb and Bernard Alexander Felix Von Huppé. Her father was an Austrian immigrant and her American-born mother was of Bavarian descent. Vera was raised in a cultured family of modest means and was educated in public schools in New York and Leonia, New Jersey. In her late teens, she joined the Metropolitan Opera Ballet, inspired by a childhood infatuation with Russian ballerina Irina Pavlova, whom her grandmother had taken her to see perform. Throughout her career as a fashion designer, Maxwell regularly referred to dance as a source of inspiration for the sense of freedom, ease, and body awareness that her clothing reflected. Another major influence was the work of French fashion designer Gabrielle "Coco" Chanel, who also believed that women's fashion could be functional and feminine without being conventionally decorative.

In 1923, she met and married Raymond J. Maxwell, a businessman who worked on Wall Street, with whom she had her only child, Raymond John Jr., in 1924. (The dates of her relationship with Maxwell do not have firm documentation; she may have married him as early as 1921.) By the late 1920s, however, the couple had separated, and Maxwell, needing work, capitalized on her still youthful appearance and dancer's figure by working first as a model at B. Altman and then as a fit model for William Badger—a Seventh Avenue manufacturer of furs, woolens, tweeds, and riding clothes.

Unable to resist making suggestions and alterations while modeling the samples she wore for the pattern makers, Maxwell's flair for fashion eventually landed her a job in Badger's fitting rooms. Soon she was producing her own designs. New to the technical aspects of the design and cutting rooms, she attended trade courses at night in tailoring techniques, pattern grading, and wholesale construction methods that added to her already keen sense of line and fit. During the next decade Maxwell worked for several Seventh Avenue sportswear manufacturers (including Adler & Adler, Glenhunt, and Max Milstein) before opening her own business, Vera Maxwell Originals, in 1947.

One of Maxwell's most widely recognized contributions to American fashion was her mid-1930s formula for interchangeable separates, which she termed the "Weekend Wardrobe." Consisting of a jacket, blouse, and varying length skirts or pants, the four- or five-piece mini collections were color and fabric coordinated for maximum interchangeability and responded to what Maxwell rightly recognized as the American woman's need for carefree travel wardrobes in an age of increased air and business travel. Her 1935 "Einstein Jacket" was inspired by a meeting with the legendary physicist: Maxwell copied his practical gray tweeds into a pocket-laden, loosely constructed jacket and skirt ensemble that blurred the lines between suiting and outerwear—once again bringing to women's wear the freedom and practical ease generally associated with men's clothing. Despite this, Maxwell's designs were never masculine in tone; she often added a splash of whimsy and indulgence to her ensembles by lining the jackets and evening coats with the same printed fabrics the dress was cut from—a luxurious but sensible touch that became one of her signature details. A 1940s cotton overall uniform designed for war workers at the Sperry Gyroscope Corporation was an early incarnation of the jumpsuit that enjoyed popularity nearly three decades later.

Insistent that American women's bodies were not always best represented by a professional fit model, Maxwell struggled with department stores, which were reluctant to offer and advertise clothing that she specifically designed and cut in larger sizes. True to form, Maxwell always graded her patterns up to sizes 18 or 20 in order to accommodate those women (like herself) who were not—and felt no need to be—a perfect size 8. Her use of wrap-and-tie closures and supple wool jerseys offered a more personalized fit and ensured a longer wear time as a woman's body weight underwent inevitable fluctuations.

By 1938, Maxwell had divorced her first husband (though she kept his name throughout her career) and had married architect Carlisle Johnson. This marriage produced no children, and by 1945 the couple lived separately. Most sources cite this date for their divorce, but it was not finalized until 1957.

Maxwell's career reached its peak in the 1950s, at which time her designs were being sold in nearly seven hundred stores nationwide. Her popularity began declining by the 1960s, when her more traditional tailored looks began to be eclipsed by the modern-edged work of designers such as Mary Quant in Britain and Pierre Cardin in France. In 1970, in an attempt to infuse and reenergize her line, Maxwell entered into a production and distribution partnership with Morton Milstein, which allowed her to remain in business until 1985. In 1986, Maxwell was contracted freelance to design a collection for the Peter Lynne division of Gulf Enterprises. This was to be her last full line of commercially available mass-produced fashions.

Maxwell won the highly coveted Coty American Fashion Critics' Award in 1953 and the Neiman-Marcus Award in 1955, and two full-scale retrospective exhibitions of her work were mounted during her lifetime: at the Smithsonian Institution in 1970, and at the Museum of the City of New York in 1980.

Vera Maxwell spent her last years with her son and daughter-in-law, dividing her time between Gilgo Beach, Long Island, and Puerto Rico. She lived to the age of ninety-three, succumbing to health complications caused by a mild stroke on January 15, 1995, in Rincon, Puerto Rico. She is buried in a family plot in Castine, Maine.

Bibliography: Photos, press releases, and clippings of Maxwell and her work are located in the Costume Institute at the Metropolitan Museum of Art in New York City. Information about Maxwell's life and career is found in Valerie Steele, *Women of Fashion* (1989); Caroline Rennolds Milbank, *New York Fashion: The Evolution of American Style* (1989); and Eleanore Lambert, *World of Fashion* (1976). Milbank also includes Maxwell in her *Couture: The Great Designers* (1985). See also *Current Biography* (1977), pp. 291–94. Maxwell discusses her theory of clothing that can be designed to accommodate a size 6 or a size 16 with equally appealing results in "Stylist Admits Women Change," *Boston Herald,* January 15, 1963. The *New York Times Magazine,* October 4, 1942, featured an article by Virginia Pope, "Fashions for War Workers," pp. 28–29, on Maxwell's designs for female war workers. In 1962, Maxwell published a small run of pamphlets to commemorate her twenty-fifth year in business under her own name; these included ensembles from past and current collections with an emphasis on their timeless style. Copies can be found in the library of the Costume Institute as well as in the costume collection of the Museum of the City of New York. An obituary appeared in the *New York Times* on January 20, 1995.

PAT KIRKHAM AND KOHLE YOHANNAN

MAYER, Ellen Moers. *See* Moers, Ellen.

MAYNOR, Dorothy. September 3, 1910–February 19, 1996. Operatic soprano, music and arts educator.

A gifted, hardworking singer with a notably beautiful tone, Dorothy Maynor also left a lasting legacy in arts education. Born Dorothy Leigh Mainor in Norfolk, Virginia, she was the third child and second daughter of the Rev. John J. Mainor, a minister in the African Methodist Episcopal Church, and Alice Jeffries Mainor. Music was important in the Mainor household, and reportedly the infant Dorothy could sing before she could walk. She also studied piano from an early age.

She was a short (four-foot-eight), plump woman with coloring that reflected her mixed ethnic heritage, primarily black and American Indian. Her photos show, and the reports of those who knew her confirm, a cheerful, intelligent personality. Her early education was in the Norfolk public schools. In 1924, at the age of fourteen, she entered Hampton Institute in nearby Hampton, Virginia, as a boarding student. Founded in 1868 for the education of African American (and, later, American Indian) youths, Hampton Institute provided a high-quality education in a time and place where Jim Crow still ruled.

Mainor was serious about her studies and her music, and soon came to the attention of the choir director, noted composer and arranger R. Nathaniel Dett. At the age of sixteen she was a soloist when the school choir performed at Carnegie Hall; a year later, she was garnering rave reviews from critics in Boston and Philadelphia. She graduated from Hampton in 1933 with a degree in home economics, and subsequently won a scholarship to Westminster Choir School (now Westminster Choir College) in Princeton, New Jersey, where she was the sole black member of, and a featured soprano soloist with, the Westminster Choir. Mainor completed her course requirements in just two years, and received a BA in choral conducting in 1935.

With financial aid from Harriot S. Curtis, a former dean of women at Hampton Institute, Mainor went to New York, where she studied voice and attended concerts and the opera on inexpensive standing-room tickets. She conducted a church choir in Brooklyn to earn money, and changed the spelling of her surname to Maynor. In the summer of 1939, she got her big break. Curtis and others arranged for her to audition for conductor Serge Koussevitzky, then music director of the Boston Symphony Orchestra, at the orchestra's summer home at Tanglewood. Initially Koussevitzky was reluctant to hear her, but when he did he was enthusiastic, proclaiming her "a musical revelation!"

Koussevitzky immediately invited her to sing the next day at his annual picnic for the musicians and his friends. These included Noel Straus, a music critic for the *New York Times,* who wrote about the new discovery. Dorothy Maynor was on her way. Her debut in New York's Town Hall, on November 19, 1939, was highly anticipated. The audience included a notable assortment of music managers and conductors and black singer-activist Paul Robeson. The reaction was almost overwhelmingly positive; Olin Downes of the *Times* called her singing "phenomenal for its range, character and varied expressive resources."

Both then and later, the soprano was notable for the wide variety of music she performed, from German lieder to assorted operatic arias (including her trademark, "Depuis le Jour" from Charpentier's *Louise*) to spirituals. Ironically, some critics complained about her performances of spirituals because her high soprano lacked the darkness found in the singing of contralto MARIAN ANDERSON and Paul Robeson, and thus sounded insufficiently "Negroid" to their ears.

High-profile singing engagements—recitals, broadcasts, and performances with major symphony orchestras—followed the recital, as did a series of recordings. Her twenty-five-year career took her to Europe, Australia, and South America, and on numerous transcontinental tours. In 1949 she became the first African American ever to sing the national anthem at a presidential inauguration, when she did the honors for Harry S. Truman. In 1953, she repeated the role at the inauguration of Dwight D. Eisenhower. In 1963, she formally retired from her professional singing career.

Maynor never made it to the stage of the Metropolitan Opera; she was not even accorded the courtesy of an audition. This was partly owing to residual racism at an institution that had welcomed Marian Anderson as its first black singer only in 1955 at the end of her career; it was also partly owing to the sweet, light nature of her voice, which was not best suited for filling a large house. (In 1975, she became the first black member of the Met's board.) Although Maynor encountered racism during her career, she seems to have been philosophical about it. In the 1940s, she had done research into the origins of spirituals, taking a tape recorder to the then-untouched islands off the South Carolina coast. In 1974, she put the songs she found to use, founding the Heritage Society Chorus to perform the spirituals unaccompanied.

In 1942, Maynor married the Rev. Shelby Albright Rooks, then a university professor and, beginning in 1943, the pastor of St. James Presbyterian Church in Harlem. They had no children. Although she was often on the road, the two were close, and she was involved with the church when at home. Mrs. Rooks, as she was known at the church, was largely responsible both for the idea of building a community center next to the church, and for paying for it. With her retirement, Maynor became even more involved with the church, becoming its choir director. When Rooks had the idea of beginning a music school in the community center, his always-energetic wife took up the idea and ran with it. She started in 1964 as the sole teacher—of piano, music theory, and music appreciation—for 20 students. Those numbers grew; soon there were 325 students and a faculty of twelve, plus Maynor and support staff.

For what eventually became the Harlem School of the Arts, Maynor assembled a glittering group of supporters, including Leonard Bernstein, George Balanchine, Marian Anderson, Artur Rubenstein, AGNES DE MILLE, Leontyne Price, Samuel Barber, and Vladimir Horowitz. For minimal fees, the school taught instrumental and vocal music, dance, drama, and art, lending or renting instruments to students who did not own them. In 1977, a new and larger building was opened; today, the school serves more than three thousand students. Maynor served as the school's executive director until she retired in 1979. She died in West Chester, Pennsylvania, in 1996 at the age of eighty-five.

Bibliography: The main source on Maynor is William F. Rogers Jr., *Dorothy Maynor and the Harlem School of the Arts: The Diva and the Dream* (1993). For additional biographical information, see *Current Biography* (1951), pp. 419–21. Also of interest is an oral history conducted in 1976, "The Reminiscences of Dorothy Maynor," for the Oral History Research Office, Columbia University. See also Jon Michael Spencer, *The New Negroes and Their Music: The Success of the Harlem Renaissance* (1997); and Deena Rosenberg, "The Music Makers," *Opera News*, February 1993. The *New York Times* covered her singing career and her work at the Harlem School of the Arts; the obituary, which appeared on February 24, 1996, contains the two quotations from the text.

SARAH BRYAN MILLER

McAFEE, Mildred. *See* Horton, Mildred McAfee.

McAULIFFE, Christa. September 2, 1948–January 28, 1986. Teacher. **RESNIK, Judith.** April 5, 1949–January 28, 1986. Astronaut.

When the space shuttle *Challenger* exploded on January 28, 1986, seven crew members lost their lives, including Christa McAuliffe, the first teacher in space, and Judith Resnik, who was making her second shuttle flight after becoming the second American woman in space in 1984. McAuliffe and Resnik both symbolized the new opportunities for women in the space program, but they came to that fateful flight from very different backgrounds.

Sharon Christa Corrigan was born in Boston, Massachusetts, to Edward and Grace George Corrigan while her father was a sophomore at Boston College. Her mother stopped modeling to take care of Christa, the first of five children. The name Sharon was dropped almost immediately, and she was called Christa throughout her life. Within three years her father, whose education had been interrupted by World War II, completed college and found a job with Jordan Marsh department stores. He soon moved his family to Framingham, a suburb west of Boston, where Christa attended public school and where her ambitions were shaped by a junior high school career class that taught that women could become teachers, nurses, or airline stewardesses.

Christa switched to Marion, a private coeducational high school run by the Boston archdiocese, where, in tenth grade, she met Steven McAuliffe. Within months they had agreed to marry after they both finished college. In 1970 Christa graduated from Framingham State College with a certificate in education. In her classes she discovered the diaries of pioneer women on the Oregon Trail and found new heroes in Margaret Thatcher and Indira Gandhi.

As agreed, the McAuliffes married the summer after college. They moved to Washington, D.C., where Steve studied law at Georgetown University and Christa taught history at a suburban junior high school and waited tables at Howard Johnson's to pay the bills. Their first child, Scott, was born in 1976, and two years later Christa earned a master's degree in educational administration from Bowie State College in Maryland. In 1978 they moved to New Hampshire, where Christa taught junior high until her daughter, Caroline, was born in 1979. She returned to work at Bow Memorial School two years later, then found a new job at Concord High School where she could teach social studies the way she had always wanted to, including field trips to courts and prisons, and readings from the diaries and journals of pioneer women. Outside the classroom she led a scout troop, taught Catholic doctrine to children in her parish, and welcomed inner-city children into her home during summer vacations.

She was brimming with imagination, and her ambition was piqued when the National Aeronautics and Space Administration (NASA) announced in 1984 that they would send a teacher into space. She got the application but procrastinated for weeks until her husband's encouragement and literary talents enabled her to complete it and mail it in. In her essay she explained: "I cannot join the space program and restart my life as an astronaut, but this opportunity to connect my abilities as an educator with my interests in history and space is a unique opportunity to fulfill my early fantasies. I watched the Space Age being born, and I would like to participate" (*Challengers,* p. 158).

More than eleven thousand teachers applied for the Teacher in Space program. McAuliffe survived the statewide competition and two rounds of the national competition. When the penultimate cut left ten candidates, Christa and the other nine went to the Johnson Space Center in Houston for more tests. By the time McAuliffe learned in the summer of 1985 that she had been selected, she was already a public figure. As the chairman of the New Hampshire selection committee said, "NASA wasn't looking for the teacher who communicated the most effectively with students. It wanted the teacher who communicated most effectively with *everyone*" (Hohler, p. 66).

She left Steve in charge in New Hampshire while she lived alone in a furnished apartment near the Space Center in Houston. Her closest friend in Houston was Barbara Morgan, her backup as teacher-in-space. Christa also befriended Judy Resnik, the other woman who would fly on *Challenger.*

Judith Arlene Resnik was born in Akron, Ohio, the first of two children of Sarah Polen and Marvin Resnik. Her father had immigrated from Israel after Israel's war of independence and became an optometrist; her mother was a legal secretary. Like Christa, Judy grew up the oldest child and daughter in a religious home. Like Christa she had a boyfriend in college, Michael Oldak, whom she married after graduating.

Resnik had been an outstanding student in math and science at Firestone, Akron's excellent public high school, where she was encouraged by her teachers as well as her father to become whatever she wanted to be. A gifted pianist, she rejected Juilliard to be one of the few women at Carnegie Tech (now Carnegie Mellon University) in Pittsburgh, graduating in 1970. Like the McAuliffes, Resnik and her new husband set off for Washington, D.C., where he would eventually study law while she earned a doctorate in engineering from the University of Maryland in 1977 and worked at the National Institutes of Health (NIH). The childless Resnik marriage fell apart after six years.

Resnik was at NIH in the summer of 1976 when she learned that NASA would be selecting the first new class of astronauts in a decade and for the first time would accept applications from women. She had never contemplated becoming an astronaut but realized that she met the qualifications and decided to apply. She was one of the initial six women selected in 1978. She had never been a feminist, and after she became an astronaut she refused an interview with the Jewish magazine *Hadassah,* explaining that she did not want to be thought of as a "first woman" or a "first Jewish" astronaut.

McAuliffe and Resnik were not political activists, but both benefited from demands that the astronaut corps mirror a broader spectrum of American society. NASA knew the shuttle would need scientists, engineers, and physicians in addition to the test pilots who manned the Mercury, Gemini, and Apollo missions, so it broadened the qualifications. NASA called these new astronauts mission specialists. Christa McAuliffe, who was neither pilot nor scientist, was a payload specialist, an astronaut who usually flies a single mission because she or he has skills not found in the astronaut corps. Her specialty was education. She planned to keep a journal of her flight like the pioneers' journals she assigned as reading for her students.

While training, McAuliffe often appeared on television and made a place for herself in America's households. When the *Challenger* exploded seventy-three seconds after its launch on January 28, 1986, the crew's compartment fell for two and a half minutes before it reached the ocean. Resnik's and McAuliffe's remains were the first recovered. A public opinion poll taken eighteen hours after the disaster showed that 98 percent of Americans knew who McAuliffe was.

Christa McAuliffe is buried in a Catholic cemetery in New Hampshire, and Judith Resnik's remains lie in a Jewish cemetery in Ohio. Both are memorialized at Challenger Space Centers, dedicated to science education. In addition, lunar craters and asteroids are named for each of the *Challenger* astronauts. As the second American woman in space, Judith Resnik represents the beginning of the regular participation of women in the greatest adventure of the twentieth century. As the first teacher in space, Christa McAuliffe embodies the respect and affection Americans feel toward their teachers, many of whom have been women.

Bibliography: NASA's public relations office has excellent photographs, as do the archives at the Smithsonian's National Air and Space Museum. The first biographies of both women appeared in *Challengers: The Inspiring Life Stores of the Seven Brave Astronauts of Shuttle Mission 51-L,* an excellent description of the entire episode written by the staff of the *Washington Post* and published in 1986. Since then there have been several biographies of Christa McAuliffe, including *I Touch the Future—: The Story of Christa McAuliffe* (1986), by Robert T. Hohler, the reporter who covered her story from the start and accompanied her to Houston for her hometown newspaper, the *Concord Monitor. A Journal for Christa,* written by her mother, Grace G. Corrigan, came out in 1993. See also Colin Burgess, *Teacher in Space: Christa McAuliffe and the* Challenger *Legacy* (2000). A critical account of McAuliffe's flight can be found in Constance Penley's *NASA/Trek: Popular Science and Sex in America* (1997). There is no single biography of Judith Resnik, although many newspaper articles are available at the archives of the NASA history office. Additional information was provided by Marvin Resnik and Barbara Morgan. A posthumous profile of Judith Resnik appeared in the *New York Times* on February 9, 1986, followed by one of Christa McAuliffe on February 10, 1986.

BETTYANN HOLTZMANN KEVLES

McBRIDE, Katharine. May 14, 1904–June 3, 1976. College president, educator, psychologist.

The daughter of Thomas Canning McBride, a mechanical engineer and prize-winning inventor, and Sally Hulley Neals, Katharine Elizabeth McBride was born in Philadelphia and grew up in Germantown, Pennsylvania, attending first Stevens School and then Germantown Friends School. After graduating cum laude from Bryn Mawr College in 1925, she entered the college's graduate program as a student and part-time reader in psychology, receiving her MA in 1927. Following a year of graduate study in neurology at Columbia University, she accepted a full-time salaried position on a research team working in Philadelphia-area hospitals. While conducting studies of disturbances in language and thinking among patients, McBride collected data for her dissertation. She then returned to Bryn Mawr Graduate School, completing her doctorate in psychology in 1932. With Theodore Weisenburg, she published *Aphasia: A Clinical and Psychological Study* (1935) and, with Anne Roe as an additional co-author, *Adult Intelligence: A Psychological Study of Test Performances* (1936).

In 1935 McBride was appointed lecturer in education at Bryn Mawr, where she also directed a guidance center and clinic for area schools. In 1936, she became an assistant professor of education and psychology; in 1938, an associate professor and assistant to the dean. In 1940, she went to Radcliffe College as its new dean. Working with President ADA COMSTOCK, whom she greatly admired, McBride learned to pay close attention to the relationship between higher education and society. In 1942, thirty-eight-year-old McBride became the fourth president of Bryn Mawr College, making her one of the youngest college presidents in the country. When she announced her plans to retire in 1970, a writer for the *New York Times* called her the "dean of women college presidents," lamenting Bryn Mawr's choice of a male as her successor.

Tall and very slim, with a low voice and self-effacing manner, McBride was popular with the Bryn Mawr College community. As poet MARIANNE MOORE (Bryn Mawr '09) put it: "O fortunate Bryn Mawr with her creatively unarrogant President / unique in her exceptional unpresidential constant: a liking for people as they are." Responding to the challenges of World War II and to student unrest in the 1960s, McBride successfully negotiated with student leaders to adapt Bryn Mawr traditions of self-government to changing times. Her other achievements included expansion of the Graduate School from 133 students to more than 600, of whom 20 percent were male; the establishment of a separate social work school offering professional certification and graduate degrees; and the founding of a laboratory nursery school and the Child Study Institute. During her tenure the undergraduate student body grew from 700 to 900, including an increase in the number of scholarship students.

Throughout her career, McBride sought to preserve and extend access to a rigorous liberal arts education. Her visibility and success on the national scene were made possible by her reputation as a moderate progressive; while conceding that promoters of radical transformations in higher education had correctly identified problems, she advocated a slower and more thoughtful pace of change. During World War II, for example, McBride added technical and vocational courses to the curriculum to meet government demands for workers, but she pointed out that mathematics, science, and foreign languages had significant contributions to make in reshaping the postwar world. In the 1940s and 1950s, McBride acknowledged criticism that women's liberal arts education was poor preparation for marriage and family life, but argued successfully against the establishment of a distinctive "women's" curriculum. In the 1960s and 1970s, she supported demands for the expansion of higher education to new and larger populations of students, but warned of the financial burdens ahead. In 1960, she received the Alumnae Association's highest honor, the M. Carey Thomas Award.

McBride also took politically courageous positions. In 1959 she testified before Congress against loyalty oaths for faculty, and she refused to allow Bryn Mawr to participate in a federal loan program that required such oaths of undergraduates. Despite considerable pressure, she did not withdraw the faculty appointment of radical historian Herbert Aptheker, who taught at Bryn Mawr from 1969 to 1973. In 1970, she joined more than thirty college presidents in asking President Nixon to end American involvement in the war in Southeast Asia. She recommended that the college once again decline government-sponsored financial aid, owing to a new requirement to report student protesters. Faculty and alumnae helped her raise funds to make up for the lost revenue.

As was befitting her stature as one of the nation's leading educators, McBride served on numerous commissions. President Eisenhower appointed her to the Committee on Education Beyond the High School, and President Kennedy appointed her to the National Science Foundation. She chaired the College Entrance Examination Board from 1949 to 1952, and was on the board of trustees of the Educational Testing Service from 1949 to 1964. In 1955–56 she chaired the American Council on Education; she also served on the Carnegie Foundation Commission on the Future of Higher Education from 1967 to 1973. On the state and local level, McBride worked with the Philadelphia Commission on Higher Education, the Pennsylvania State Council of Higher Education, the Philadelphia Child Guidance Clinic, and Bryn Mawr Hospital. She was awarded twenty-three honorary degrees.

Although McBride claimed to be too busy for hobbies, she took time for long walks, enjoyed the company of a series of household pets, and entertained frequently at the college. She never married, and she remained close to her family. She bought a summer home in the Poconos near her brother and sister-in-law's, and had close relationships with her two nieces. In the 1950s, her parents lived with McBride in her residence at the college.

In retirement, McBride continued her active involvement in national organizations. In 1971 she delivered the prestigious Horace Mann Lecture, entitling her talk "Higher Education and the Pace of Change." She taught "Social Foundations of Education" at Bryn Mawr and consulted with local clinics on cases of speech disturbance in children. Katharine McBride died of a heart ailment in Bryn Mawr Hospital in 1976 at the age of seventy-two.

Bibliography: The papers of Katharine McBride's administration are found in the Archives of Bryn Mawr College. The Archives also contain a list of McBride's organizational memberships, and awards, and transcripts of "memorial minutes" following her death. The entire issue of the *Bryn Mawr Alumnae Bulletin,* Spring 1970, is devoted to discussions of McBride's presidency. Also useful are Cornelia Meigs, *What Makes a College: A History of Bryn Mawr* (1956); Patricia Hochschild Labalme, ed., *A Century Recalled: Essays in Honor of Bryn Mawr College* (1987); and personal information obtained from Mabel Lang, professor emerita of Greek, Bryn Mawr College. See also "Bryn Mawr Raises Its Torch," *Fortune,* April 1943, p. 107; "Bryn Mawr College Head Hailed by Marianne Moore," *Philadelphia Inquirer,* March 2, 1967 (which contains the lines of poetry in the text); and Fred M. Hechinger, "In the College Presidencies: More and More a Man's World," *New York Times,* August 24, 1969. For McBride's own writing, see "What Is Women's Education," *Annals of the American Academy of Political and Social Science* 251 (May 1947), pp. 143–52; "The Key to Teaching: Put Students First," *Christian Science Monitor,* November 22, 1965; and "Higher Education and the Pace of Change," Horace Mann Lecture (1971). Lorett Treese, archivist at Bryn Mawr, provided invaluable assistance to the author. An obituary and an editorial concerning her work appeared in the *New York Times* on June 4, 1976.

LYNN D. GORDON

McBRIDE, Mary Margaret. November 16, 1899–April 7, 1976. Radio and television host, journalist.

Mary Margaret McBride was born on a farm in Paris, Missouri, the eldest of five children, and the only daughter, of Elizabeth Craig and Thomas Walker McBride. Like many other farm families in the "Little Dixie" area of Missouri, her parents were transplanted southerners. Her father's family, originally from Ireland, settled first in South Carolina, then Tennessee; her mother's Scottish ancestors migrated from Virginia by way of Kentucky. The family moved often in Mary Margaret's youth, because her mercurial father would trade anything from a mule to a farm in the hope of making a better deal. Money was always tight, and yet Mary Margaret remembered a youth of plentiful food, outdoor adventures, and strong family ties, especially to her beloved mother.

At age eleven, Mary Margaret was sent to boarding school in Fulton, Missouri, through the intercession of a wealthy great-aunt who wanted her to train as a teacher and eventually take over the school, which later became William Woods College. McBride wanted to be a writer instead. When her great-aunt refused to pay her college tuition, she worked her way through the University of Missouri, graduating with a BA in journalism in 1918.

After a brief stint in Washington, D.C., McBride landed a job at the *Cleveland Press,* where a story she filed about an interfaith religious convention led to a job offer in New York handling publicity for the group. There she met her lifelong friend and business manager, Estella H. "Stella" Karn. When the Interchurch World Movement folded soon after, McBride was hired as a feature writer at the New York *Evening Mail,* where her career flourished until the paper was sold in 1924. At Karn's insistence, she turned to freelance magazine writing, forging a lucrative career writing for national magazines such as the *Saturday Evening Post, Cosmopolitan,* and *McCall's.* Fulfilling a childhood ambition, she brought her mother to New York for a vacation, and later took her to Europe. During her twenties, McBride was engaged to a Missouri classmate but consciously chose career over marriage. Her friendship with Stella Karn was her most significant personal relationship.

Like many other Americans in the 1920s, McBride played the stock market; when the market crashed, she lost all her savings and found herself totally broke. The years 1930 to 1934 were the most difficult of her life, as magazine assignments dried up and her self-confidence (always rather shaky) plummeted. Then a chance audition for a daytime radio show changed the direction of her life. She knew nothing about radio, but her journalistic experience, plus a good radio voice (Karn said it pushed itself up against you), got her the job.

McBride premiered as the host of the *Martha Deane Show* in 1934, playing a fictional grandmother who was supposed to chat about household matters and other fluff. That lasted about three weeks before McBride confessed to her live radio audience (and shocked sponsors) that she wasn't a grandmother, that she wasn't even married, and that she would much rather talk to them about interesting places she'd been and people she'd met than how to sew clothes from old curtains. Instead of being fired, she found an enthusiastic and loyal audience that eventually reached six to eight million listeners daily. She broadcast a half-hour show as Martha Deane on WOR from 1934 to 1940, while also hosting a fifteen-minute talk show on CBS from 1937 to 1941 under her own name. From 1941 to 1950 she broadcast forty-five minutes on NBC ("It's one o'clock, and here is Mary Margaret McBride" opened every show), then switched to ABC from 1950 to 1954. The "First Lady of Radio" celebrated her tenth anniversary on the air in 1944 by filling Madison Square Garden and her fifteenth at a nearly sold-out Yankee Stadium.

Mary Margaret (everyone called her that, even ELEANOR ROOSEVELT, her favorite guest) was a superb interviewer: served by a phenomenal memory, she used her newspaper training to develop an ad-lib interview style that put even the most nervous guests at ease. She especially enjoyed literary and theatrical types, but also welcomed explorers, ministers, florists, indeed anyone she thought would interest her homebound audience, mainly women. Unlike other daytime shows that dispensed only recipes and chitchat, Mary Margaret took her audience seriously and never talked down to them.

An important part of the program was "doing the products." McBride accepted no sponsor unless she could personally vouch for the product. As part of her sales pitch, she often enthusiastically consumed favorite products like Dolly Madison Ice Cream on the air. Her love affair with food added pounds to her short, stout, and always corseted frame, but she never lasted long on a diet. Her loyal listeners responded by buying her products, which kept her on the air.

In addition to her demanding radio schedule, McBride wrote magazine articles, inspirational pieces, children's books, and four autobiographical volumes. She even tried television, taping a thirteen-week nightly series in 1948, although like many radio personalities she failed to make the transition. McBride was a perfectionist, and despite her cheerful broadcasting tone, she often succumbed to deep feelings of insecurity. In 1954 she gave up her national radio show, mainly because Stella Karn was ill with the cancer that would cause her death three years later. From 1953 to 1956 McBride wrote a nationally syndicated newspaper column and made guest appearances on radio and television, but she missed having a regular radio slot. In 1960 she began broadcasting three times a week on station WGHQ in Kingston, New York, near the West Shokan farm in the Catskills that Karn bought in the 1940s, where Mary Margaret lived in a converted barn. Slowed in 1970 by a broken hip that left her quite frail, she broadcast until just a few months before her death in April 1976 at the age of seventy-six.

Mary Margaret McBride realized the cultural and political importance of talk radio, and she was one of the first to exploit its potential. The magazine-style radio format that she pioneered—in-depth, ad-libbed interviews by a host personality with multiple sponsors—served as a model, albeit uncredited, for successful shows like *Today* and the *Tonight Show,* and her serious discussion of books and ideas anticipated the appeal of public radio. The phenomenal bond she formed with her listeners is critical to understanding the history of radio and twentieth-century popular culture.

Bibliography: The Mary Margaret McBride papers at the Library of Congress contain correspondence, photographs, and approximately twelve hundred hours of McBride's radio broadcasts, primarily from the 1940s and early 1950s. McBride wrote four autobiographical volumes: *Here's Martha Deane* (1936); *How Dear to My Heart* (1940); *A Long Way from Missouri* (1959); and *Out of the Air* (1960). *Tune in for Elizabeth* (1945) and *The Growing Up of Mary Elizabeth* (1966) were directed toward juvenile readers. Other books included *Jazz,* with Paul Whiteman (1925); *Charm,* with Alexander Williams (1927); *Paris Is a Woman's Town* (1929), *London Is a Man's Town (But Women Go There)* (1930), *New York Is Everybody's Town* (1931), and *Beer and Skittles: A Friendly Guide to Modern Germany* (1932), all with Helen Josephy; and *America for Me* (1941). She edited *How to Be a Successful Advertising Woman* (1948) and *Harvest of American Cooking* (1957). The Associated Press carried her nationally syndicated column "Mary Margaret McBride Says" from 1953 to 1956. Susan Ware, *It's One o'Clock and Here Is Mary Margaret McBide: A Radio Biography* (2004), analyzes her career. Jacqueline D. St. John provided an early assessment of her importance in "Sex Role Stereotyping in Early Broadcast History: The Career of Mary Margaret McBride," *Frontiers* 3, no. 3 (1978), pp. 31–38; see also Michele Hilmes, *Radio Voices* (1997). Obituaries appeared in the *New York Times,* the *Washington Post,* and the *Poughkeepsie Journal,* all on April 8, 1976.

SUSAN WARE

McCARTHY, Mary. June 21, 1912–October 25, 1989. Writer, critic.

Mary Therese McCarthy was born in Seattle, the first of four children and the only daughter of Therese "Tess" Preston and Roy Winfield McCarthy, a lawyer. Until Mary was six, her family lived in the benevolent shadow of her maternal grandparents, Augusta Morgenstern and Harold Preston, a prominent Seattle attorney. In 1918, the year of the worldwide influenza epidemic, the McCarthys traveled by train to Minneapolis to resettle near Roy's parents, Elizabeth Sheridan and J. H. McCarthy, a wealthy grain-elevator merchant. By the time they arrived, Roy and Tess had caught the flu; they died soon after. Their deaths, and the fact that for days Mary's paternal grandmother tried to keep the news from the children, were the defining events in Mary McCarthy's life. Within a short time, her experience was transformed from one of remembered harmony to a trial of deprivation and torment with a spiteful great-uncle and great-aunt, Myers and Margaret Shriver, in whose care the orphans were placed in Minneapolis. For years thereafter, McCarthy battled to preserve her delight in beautiful things and to resist the debilitating emotion of self-pity.

Another pivotal event occurred when she was eleven, when her grandfather Preston rescued her and took her back to Seattle. (She wouldn't see her brothers, who were sent to a Catholic boarding school in Minnesota, for the next six years.) In Seattle, Mary was enrolled in Forest Ridge Convent, where she underwent a series of "endless reenactments of that conflict between excited scruples and inertia of the will," which McCarthy describes in *Memories of a Catholic Girlhood* (1957); that conflict became a lifelong trait (p. 21). Her romance with the Ladies of the Sacred Heart led to a series of attachments to intellectual women: Dorothy Atkinson at Annie Wright Seminary, where she went next; Helen Sandison and Anna Kitchel at Vassar College; political philosopher HANNAH ARENDT in middle life. Meanwhile, Mary's complicated relationship with her Jewish grandmother (her mother had converted to Catholicism) inspired the final chapter of *Memories*, "Ask Me No Questions." Like most of the other chapters, it first appeared in the *New Yorker*, where McCarthy's memoirs were often read as fiction.

In Seattle, Mary had her first affair, at fourteen, with a man twice her age. That, and her introduction to Seattle bohemia a year later, marked the onset of a taste for sexual adventure and the clandestine life, which was reinforced by being the teenage ward of elderly grandparents. This period is revisited in McCarthy's autobiography, *How I Grew* (1987). When she arrived at Vassar in 1929, the rudiments of contrary Mary, as she was called in later years, were in place. She intimidated many classmates with her boldness and intellectual self-assurance but confided her loneliness to favorite professors. Her contempt for Vassar's social elite, some of whom became her roommates, was mingled with fascination and envy.

Vassar was influenced by the left-wing politics of the Depression, but McCarthy saw herself as a literary girl. With a group of classmates that included poet ELIZABETH BISHOP, she founded a campus literary magazine, *Con Spirito*. But she was also introduced to the left-leaning *New Republic*, where she published her first book review shortly after graduation; and to the work of John Dos Passos, whose *U.S.A.* trilogy introduced her to the Sacco and Vanzetti case. The execution of two Italian immigrants unjustly convicted of murder and robbery touched her deeply. As an orphan, she later wrote, she felt herself a victim of class oppression at the hands of her wealthy Minneapolis grandparents, and that sense gave her a lively sympathy for victims of injustice. But it was a sympathy for persons, not for a class, race, or sex. The difference helps explain McCarthy's lack of empathy for the women's movement, which she charged with sins not unlike the ones she battled in herself: self-pity, greed, envy. She strove to establish herself as an exception to any group. And yet there was always a man at Mary McCarthy's side: over the years she had four husbands and many lovers.

At Vassar, McCarthy made Phi Beta Kappa and graduated cum laude in 1933 and surprised her friends by immediately marrying the actor Harold Johnsrud, whom she had known for several years. With him she plunged into the cultural life of New York City (described in McCarthy's best-selling novel *The Group*, 1963) and began writing reviews for the *Nation*. Her first book, a series of autobiographical sketches called *The Company She Keeps* (1942), contains her best-known story, "The Man in the Brooks Brothers Shirt," which had been published by *Partisan Review* (*PR*) in 1941 after other journals rejected it as "immoral." The story established McCarthy's talent for rendering the human comedy of sex in startling detail.

By then, McCarthy had divorced Johnsrud, had a serious affair with *PR* editor Philip Rahv, and had a fling with Trotskyism. She had become *PR*'s theater reviewer, and in 1938 she married the distinguished critic Edmund Wilson. McCarthy credited Wilson with getting her to write fiction, but the two fought bitterly, starting with a blowup over Mary's pregnancy with their son Reuel (she wanted the baby, he did not), which led to her brief psychiatric commitment at New York's Payne Whitney Clinic (another event written up in *The Group*). Reuel Wilson, McCarthy's only child, was born on Christmas Day, 1938. The marriage lasted until 1945, and McCarthy drew liberally on its travails in several stories and in the novel *A Charmed Life* (1955).

In the summer of 1945 McCarthy met a group of émigré thinkers from war-torn Europe led by anarchist journalist Nicola Chiaramonte. McCarthy's attempt to start a magazine called *Critic* fell through the cracks with a generation that was becoming increasingly polarized. Progressives like playwright LILLIAN HELLMAN, who were sympathetic to the Soviet Union, were shunned by intellectuals whose anti-Stalinism had hardened into organized anti-communism. McCarthy, and her close friends Hannah Arendt and critic Dwight Macdonald, who were driven mainly by moral convictions, stood outside both camps. When the Vietnam War arrived, they sided with the youthful anti-war movement. McCarthy traveled to Saigon and Hanoi in 1967 and 1968 for the *New York Review of Books* and wrote about the Watergate hearings a few years later.

McCarthy's 1946 marriage to writer and teacher Bowden Broadwater was productive and generally happy. But in 1955 McCarthy was invited by a European art journal to write a book about Venice. Thus began her love affair with the early Renaissance, which led to a second book on Florence. Both sold more copies than any previous book, but the long intervals in Europe weakened her marriage.

In 1960, while on a lecture tour sponsored by the State Department, McCarthy met James West, a foreign service officer attached to the U.S. Embassy in Warsaw. Almost overnight they decided to marry, despite the fact that they were both already married and West had three young children. After getting their divorces and marrying in Paris in 1961, they set up housekeeping on the Rue de Rennes; starting in 1967, they spent summers in Castine, Maine. The success of *The Group* in 1963 had turned Mary McCarthy into a celebrity (although not without a pummeling from fellow writers Norman Mailer and Elizabeth Hardwick), and her Paris salon swarmed with distinguished visitors. In Paris, she wrote two more novels, *Birds of America* (1971) and *Cannibals and Missionaries* (1979), neither of which, in the opinion of critics, matched the wit and style of the best of her earlier fiction.

As a fiction writer, McCarthy has been criticized for relying too much on facts drawn from private life. Parodies of her affairs and marriages had a curative effect on the author, but for readers they sometimes read like period pieces. Yet as a chronicle of bohemian life in the 1930s, 1940s, and 1950s, McCarthy's work is unequaled. And few have matched her sometimes savage brilliance as a critic. But it is as a woman whose intellectual life was played out on the literary and political battlefields of the twentieth century that McCarthy made her mark. A contrarian, who was sued by Lillian Hellman in 1980 for calling her a liar on the *Dick Cavett Show*, she relished a good fight; especially a fight for truth, about which, McCarthy writes in *How I Grew*, "I have always been monotheistic" (p. 199). Mary McCarthy died in New York City in 1989 at the age of seventy-seven.

Bibliography: Mary McCarthy's extensive papers are in Special Collections at Vassar College. In addition to the books mentioned in the text, her other works of fiction include *The Oasis* (1949), *Cast a Cold Eye* (1950), and *The Groves of Academe* (1952). Important nonfiction titles are *Venice Observed* (1956), *The Stones of Florence* (1959), *On the Contrary* (1961), *Mary McCarthy's Theatre Chronicles, 1937–1962* (1963), *The Seventeenth Degree* (1974), *The Mask of State: Watergate Portraits* (1974), *Ideas and the Novel* (1980), and *Intellectual Memoirs: New York 1936–1938* (1992). She is the subject of three biographies: Carol Gelderman, *Mary McCarthy: A Life* (1988); Carol Brightman, *Writing Dangerously: Mary McCarthy and Her World* (1992); and Fran Kiernan, *Seeing Mary Plain* (2000). McCarthy's confrontation with Lillian Hellman is explored by Nora Ephron in *Imaginary Friends*, a play produced on Broadway in 2002. An obituary appeared in the *New York Times* on October 26, 1989.

CAROL BRIGHTMAN

McCLINTOCK, Barbara. June 16, 1902–September 2, 1992. Geneticist, cytologist.

Barbara McClintock was born in Hartford, Connecticut, the third of four children of Sara Handy, a homemaker, and Thomas Henry McClintock, a physician. Her parents were New Englanders, though her father's parents were British immigrants; her mother descended from blue-blooded Yankee stock. They named their youngest daughter "Eleanor," but soon decided that "Barbara" suited her better. (McClintock changed her name legally as an adult.) In 1908, the family moved to Brooklyn, New York, where Barbara grew up and attended Erasmus Hall High School. In 1919 she enrolled in the agricultural college of Cornell University. She received all of her post-secondary education there, taking a bachelor's degree in 1923, a master's in 1925, and a PhD, under the direction of the cytologist Lester Sharp, in 1927.

In the 1920s, cytologists studied chromosomes and geneticists studied heredity. To be sure, the two fields had fused in the work of Thomas Hunt Morgan and his students, who, in 1910, began one of the most successful research projects in the history of biology. The Morgan school used *Drosophila*, the fruit fly, to examine the material basis of heredity. The core of their work was to identify mutations—genetic changes—in flies and map them to specific sites on the chromosomes. Morgan is considered second only to Gregor Mendel among the founders of genetics. But nearly twenty years after Morgan had begun his *Drosophila* studies, relatively little cytogenetic work was being done with other organisms.

McClintock did for maize—Indian corn—what Morgan did for fruit flies. By 1925, corn was well studied by geneticists. But the maize chromosomes are so small that no one had been able to count them accurately, let alone distinguish them from one another. As a graduate student and young postdoctoral fellow, McClintock adapted existing microscopic and histological techniques to maize chromosomes and developed new ones. Combining these with her remarkable powers of observation, she was able to identify the correct chromosome number (ten), distinguish the chromosomes from one another, and map groups of genes to specific chromosomes. Her work made possible an explosion of new interest in maize genetics. The beginning of what has been called the golden age of maize genetics can be dated to the publication of her PhD thesis in 1929.

During this period, McClintock, together with George Beadle (who went on to win a Nobel Prize in 1958), Marcus Rhoades, Charles Burnham, and professor Rollins Emerson, helped make Cornell one of the top two centers for plant genetics in the country. This young group—all save Emerson were graduate students and postdoctorates—published paper after stunning paper, outlining the major problems in maize genetics, many of which continue to interest plant molecular biologists today.

The Depression was a difficult time to be a scientist of either gender, but it was particularly hard on women. McClintock might have obtained a teaching position, as did her friend and colleague Harriet Creighton, but she was unwilling to give up research time and detested academic politics. Instead, she went along on research assistantships, a National Research Council fellowship, and then a Guggenheim. These took her from Cornell to the California Institute of Technology to Berlin and back. During these years she endured financial hardship but enjoyed immense personal and scientific freedom—by far the more important commodity to her. Then and for the rest of her career, McClintock preferred to work alone. Though she conferred extensively with trusted colleagues and enjoyed informal mentorships of young, pliable scientists, her perfectionism and need for autonomy made it impossible for her to work closely with anyone for long periods of time.

In 1936, she took a faculty position at the University of Missouri in Columbia. She was never happy there and resigned in 1939, despite the apparent imminence of a promotion with tenure. She developed a reputation for irreverence, wit, compassion, and a hot temper. Friends and colleagues either loved or feared her, and sometimes both. She had many loyal friends, but seemingly no intimates. She never married and had few if any romantic involvements past college.

In 1941, she took a summer position at Cold Spring Harbor on New York's Long Island, at the Carnegie Institution of Washington's Department of Genetics. It was an ideal post for her, with no teaching or administrative duties. Within a year, the position became permanent; she remained there until her death.

In 1944, during an experiment designed to create new mutations for purposes of mapping genes to sites on chromosomes, she discovered numerous so-called mutable genes, which turn on and off spontaneously as the plant develops from embryo to adult. Patterns in the pigmentation and other characters of the leaves and kernels of these plants suggested to her that the on-off switching was not random. She decided there must be some new type of element controlling the action of the genes. By 1946 she had identified two new genetic elements—not genes, she said, but gene-controllers—that were necessary for the control. In early 1948 she found that these elements could transpose, or move from place to place in the chromosomes, while the plant was developing. Wherever they landed, these "controlling elements" seemed to alter the action of nearby genes. Through coordinated transposition, she believed, controlling elements executed the genetic program of development, much as the hammers on a player-piano execute the program encoded on a piano roll.

But where was the piano roll? Transposition in maize was confirmed immediately and repeatedly by other researchers. Few scientists, however, could accept her notion that the movements were coordinated; neither had she proved it, nor could they imagine where the seat of control might lie. To most geneticists in the 1950s and 1960s, transposition seemed a curiosity, a random phenomenon with no obvious biological function, though it had some experimental utility.

A research project in Central and South America, begun in 1957 and continued for over twenty years, exposed McClintock to evolutionary changes in maize chromosomes. All the while, she pursued her studies of controlling elements at Cold Spring Harbor. Late in her career, she integrated these two lines of research into a sweeping theory of organic change. She came to see evolution and embryological development as aspects of a common process, one that must be mediated by genes. The keys to both processes lay in the control—in the patterns—of gene action on different time scales. Such ideas are now at the forefront of both experimental biology and the philosophy of science.

Meanwhile, during the 1970s, transposition was discovered in bacteria, and its biochemistry was explained in terms of DNA sequences and enzymatic action. Soon, transposition—more broadly defined now—was found to be nearly universal in the living world and was linked to medical fields such as cancer, virology, and immunology. McClintock experienced a scientific renaissance. Her theories of genetic control—never widely accepted and by this time rejected outright—were forgotten. A younger generation of scientists reframed her as the discoverer of transposition. She won, unshared, the 1983 Nobel Prize in Physiology or Medicine, "for her discovery of transposable genetic elements."

Winning the Nobel Prize was bittersweet for McClintock. Though glad for the recognition from her peers, she believed that the prize missed her most important ideas. She wanted to be known for the discovery of genetic control. Her model for how that control was executed—by movable elements switching the genes on and off—turns out to apply only in rare special cases. But being wrong on that mechanism should not exclude her from the pantheon of experimentalists and thinkers of modern biology.

McClintock stayed current with new results in biology until she died, on September 2, 1992, in

Huntington, New York, at the age of ninety. Younger colleagues were by that time sufficiently deep into efforts to sequence the human and other genomes to offer her new hope that heredity, development, and evolution—the three greatest questions of twentieth-century biology—might soon be integrated.

Bibliography: The primary repository of McClintock's correspondence, unpublished writings, and research notes is the library of the American Philosophical Society (APS) in Philadelphia, Pennsylvania. Also at the APS are tapes and transcripts of interviews with McClintock and many of her friends and colleagues, conducted by Evelyn Fox Keller and by Nathaniel Comfort, as well as many photographs of McClintock, her colleagues, and her corn. Other important collections include the Marcus Rhoades papers, at the Lilly Library of Indiana University; and the George Beadle papers, at the California Institute of Technology, in Pasadena, California. Most of McClintock's most important published scientific papers have been collected as *The Discovery and Characterization of Transposable Elements: The Collected Papers of Barbara McClintock* (1987). A lively collection of reminiscences and scientific and personal memoirs of McClintock may be found in Nina Fedoroff and David Botstein, eds., *The Dynamic Genome: Barbara McClintock's Ideas in the Century of Genetics* (1992). Evelyn Fox Keller's *A Feeling for the Organism: The Life and Work of Barbara McClintock* (1983; Tenth Anniversary Edition 1993) was the first biography of McClintock and made McClintock into something of an emblem of feminine science. Nathaniel Comfort, *The Tangled Field: Barbara McClintock's Search for the Patterns of Genetic Control* (2001), is the first to exploit McClintock's research notes; its first chapter provides references to the most important scholarly, popular, journalistic, and juvenile writing on McClintock. Short versions of different aspects of McClintock's life and career may also be found in Comfort, "'The Real Point Is Control': The Reception of Barbara McClintock's Controlling Elements," *Journal of the History of Biology* 32, no. 1 (1999), pp. 133–62; Comfort, "From Controlling Elements to Transposons: Barbara McClintock and the Nobel Prize," *Trends in Biochemical Sciences* 26, no. 7 (July 2001), pp. 454–57; Nina Fedoroff, "How Jumping Genes Were Discovered," *Nature Structural Biology* 8, no. 4 (2001), pp. 300–301; and Carla Keirns, "Seeing Patterns: Models, Visual Evidence and Pictorial Communication in the Work of Barbara McClintock," *Journal of the History of Biology* 32, no. 1 (1999), pp. 163–96. An obituary appeared in the *New York Times* on September 4, 1992.

NATHANIEL COMFORT

McCOY, Esther. November 18, 1904–December 30, 1989. Architectural historian and critic, writer.

Esther McCoy was born in Horatio, Arkansas, the second of four children of Katie Mae and James L. McCoy. Although her parents were midwesterners, she traced most of her ancestors back to pre-revolutionary New England. Esther was raised in Coffeyville, Kansas (sometimes erroneously given as her birthplace), until age thirteen, when she went away with her older sister Ruth to Central College for Women, a preparatory boarding school in Lexington, Missouri. McCoy attended a number of colleges—Baker University in Kansas, the University of Arkansas, and Washington University in St. Louis—before settling down at the University of Michigan at Ann Arbor. In 1926, she left Michigan shortly before graduating, when some of her transfer credits were not accepted, and headed to New York City.

After an assortment of short-term jobs and residences, she found work as a researcher and reader of manuscripts for writer Theodore Dreiser and, traveling now in avant-garde literary circles, moved in among other writers on Patchin Place in Greenwich Village. In 1928 McCoy went to Paris for nine months. There, she later recalled, she was introduced to Freudianism and surrealism and the man with whom she had her first serious romantic relationship, John Mitchell. While in Paris, McCoy began to write fiction, mostly short stories, and in 1930 she and Mitchell moved to Key West, Florida, for five months, each to work on a novel. Although McCoy's novel, entitled *Blackberry Winter,* was never published, a shortened version of it won honorable mention in a Scribner's novella competition. Upon returning to New York, she struggled to find work as a writer in the worsening Depression.

In 1932, McCoy fell ill with double pneumonia, and as part of her recovery a friend arranged for her to spend a month in Santa Monica, California, with Ida and Wilbur Needham, who owned a bookshop and were willing to put her up in return for some help with selling. McCoy found much more than books and good health in Southern California. She became so enamored of the region that she essentially never left. She concentrated particularly on the local architecture, reading about it voraciously and visiting houses under construction, where she often made the acquaintance of the architect. She also turned the leftist sympathies she had developed earlier in New York into more active engagement in radical politics, which included writing for socialist and communist newspapers and magazines and undertaking slum housing surveys.

In 1941, McCoy married Berkeley Greene Tobey. They had no children, and the marriage lasted until his death in 1962. When the United States entered World War II, McCoy, like many women, sought to help out with the war effort and entered a job-training program at Douglas Aircraft to become an engineering draftsman. In 1944 she applied these skills to her growing passion for architecture and got a job doing drafting work for architect Rudolph M. Schindler. When the war ended, McCoy sought a career as an architect, but she was discouraged from applying to the architecture school at the University of Southern California because of her gender and age. Instead McCoy began to write architectural history and criticism, bringing her novelist's sensitivity for character, plot, and scene to her nonfiction prose. Her first article on architecture, "Schindler: Space Architect," was published in 1945 in the journal *Direction;* this was soon followed by regular writing on the subject for *Arts & Architecture, Progressive Architecture, Mademoiselle* (as architecture scout), the *Los Angeles Times,* and many other newspapers and architectural journals.

McCoy proved herself an astute analyst of the architecture of Southern California, bringing its history to light and particularly arguing for its unique contribution to modern architecture. Where others had written off twentieth-century California architects as either provincials or simple copiers of the European international style, McCoy argued for their importance as modernist innovators. Her first major book, *Five California Architects* (1960), traced in the work of California architects Bernard Maybeck, Irving Gill, Charles and Henry Greene, and R. M. Schindler a distinctly California style of modern architecture influenced by indigenous sources such as stuccoed Spanish Colonial missions and adapted to the region's sunny mild climate. That year she published a second book on another California architect, Richard Neutra. Later in her life her commitment to protecting the legacy of California's modernist architects led her to catalogue Neutra's papers at the University of California at Los Angeles.

Another way McCoy championed the significance of California's modern architecture was by giving attention to the Case Study Houses project, initiated in 1945 by *Arts & Architecture* magazine under editor (and good friend) John Entenza. Until 1966, prominent Los Angeles architects were invited to build small, single-family, servantless "case study houses" to prove that well-designed modern homes could provide affordable housing for the middle class. McCoy's *Modern California Architecture: Case Study Houses* (1962) helped popularize these experiments. Into the last decade of her life, McCoy's productivity showed little sign of flagging. In 1979 she published *Vienna to Los Angeles: Two Journeys,* on the correspondence between Neutra and Schindler, and in 1984, *The Second Generation,* a successor of sorts to her first book on California architects, this one devoted to J. R. Davidson, Harwell Hamilton Harris, Gregory Ain, and Raphael Soriano.

McCoy ensured that her message reached a wide public by writing for newspapers, teaching and lecturing, participating in preservation campaigns such as the unsuccessful effort to save Irving Gill's Dodge House in West Hollywood, and helping to organize numerous museum exhibitions, which over her career ranged from the *R. M. Schindler Retrospective* (1954) and *Roots of California Contemporary Architecture* (1956) to, in the last year of her life, *Blueprints for Modern Living: History and Legacy of the Case Study House* (1989). McCoy also developed expertise in Mexican and Italian arts and architecture, which involved her in developing an exhibition, *Ten Italian Architects* (1967), for the Los Angeles County Museum of Art and in writing frequently for Mexican and Italian architectural periodicals.

In 1985 Esther McCoy received the American Institute of Architects' National Honor Award for excellence. She died four years later of emphysema at her home in Santa Monica at the age of eighty-five. Although not an architect, McCoy became appreciated by many as "the mother of Modern California architecture," a writer who used her talents to elucidate the unique path of architectural modernism in the American West.

Bibliography: The Esther McCoy Papers at the Smithsonian Institution's Archives of American Art are extensive, and contain correspondence, fictional and architectural writings, taped interviews, research notes, lectures, clippings, photographs, slides, and ephemera. Particularly noteworthy is the transcript of a 1987 interview with her by Joseph Giovannini. In addition to the books mentioned above, she wrote *Craig Ellwood* (1968). *Modern California Houses: Case Study Houses* (1962) was reprinted in 1977 as *Case Study Houses.* She wrote or contributed to numerous exhibition catalogues, including *Memorial Exhibit: Works of R. M. Schindler, Architect, 1916 to 1953* (1954); *Roots of Contemporary Architecture* (1956); *Felix Candela* (1957); *Irving Gill* (1958); *Juan O'Gorman* (1964); *Ten Italian Architects* (1967); *Natives and Visionaries* (1975); *A. Quincy Jones: A Tribute* (1980); *Home Sweet Home: The California Ranch House* (1983); Whitney Museum of American Art, *High Styles: Twentieth Century American Design* (1986); and Elizabeth A. T. Smith, ed., *Blueprints for Modern Living: History and Legacy of the Case Study Houses* (1989). Her voluminous articles and reviews on architecture most frequently appeared in *Arts & Architecture, Progressive Architecture,* the *Los Angeles Times,* and the Italian architectural periodicals *Zodiac* and *Lotus.* Two helpful portraits of her are Michael McDonough, "First Lady of L.A. Architecture," *Metropolitan Home,* August 1989, p. 38, and Robert Venturi and Denise Scott Brown, "Re-evaluation: Esther McCoy and the Second Generation," *Progressive Architecture* 71, no. 2 (February 1990), pp. 118–19. An obituary appeared in the *New York Times* on December 31, 1989. Probing discussions of her influence that appeared after her death include Paul Goldberger, "Learning to Take California Seriously," *New York Times,* January 14, 1990; Joseph Giovannini, "Esther McCoy," *Progressive Architecture* 71, no. 2 (February 1990), p. 22; and Michael McDonough, "An American Saga," *Metropolis* 9 (March 1990), pp. 38–43, 60–61.

LIZABETH COHEN

McLEAN, Barbara. November 16, 1903–March 28, 1996. Film editor.

Barbara McLean, one of only two people ever to be nominated seven times for an Academy Award for film editing, started learning her trade in grade school. She was born in Palisades Park, New Jersey, the daughter of Charles Pollut (some sources list his name as Anton Pollu), the owner of a film laboratory. Nothing is known about her mother or any siblings. During her breaks from school, young Barbara would work in the lab, patching together release prints of the films of the adjacent E. K. Lincoln studio.

In 1924 she married J. Gordon McLean, a projectionist and later a cameraman, and they moved to Los Angeles. The couple had no children and divorced in the late forties. Based on her lab experience, McLean got a job at Fox studios, then moved to First National and became an assistant editor. She worked on films during the transition from silent to sound films both at First National and later at United Artists, where she helped cut MARY PICKFORD's first talkies.

As an assistant to Alan McNeil, she worked on the first films of a new company called Twentieth Century, which was releasing its films through United Artists. Her first solo credit was *Gallant Lady* (1933), and soon she was cutting several pictures a year for Twentieth Century. McLean received her first Academy Award nomination for *Les Miserables* (1935). A 1945 article in the *Los Angeles Times* noted that she was one of only eight women film editors in the industry in her time.

In 1935, Twentieth Century merged with the older Fox company to become Twentieth Century Fox. By then, her work had impressed Darryl F. Zanuck, the head of the studio, and she became his chief cutter. Zanuck's focus was on telling stories on film, and McLean's editing kept the stories flowing. In the script for *Jesse James* (1939), the train robbery scene has several amusing diversions that McLean cut out of the film to keep the scene moving. The humor of the scene is still there, but there is not one shot in the sequence that is not needed to tell the story.

Her skill as a film editor can be seen in the variety of films she cut in the 1940s. Her credits include the musical *Down Argentine Way* (1940), the war film *A Yank in the RAF* (1941), the pirate movie *The Black Swan* (1942), and the religious picture *The Song of Bernadette* (1943). For all her focus on keeping the narrative moving, McLean's editing could dazzle if called for. In *A Bell for Adano* (1945), she took material director Henry King shot on the return of the Italian POWs to their village and put it together with such a sure sense of emotion that when she cut at exactly the right moment to King's overhead shot of the prisoners and villagers coming together in the square, the cut was more heart-stopping than conventional close-ups would have been. Part of her success in this scene, and she felt as a film editor in general, came from having studied music as a child. Due to her sense of rhythm, she could cut the numbers in a musical just by the visuals alone, without having to listen to the music and vocal sound tracks.

Because of Zanuck's faith in her, McLean's suggestions and requests were followed. She frequently asked directors to shoot material, especially close-ups, to help her improve the rhythm of the scene. Directors too often wanted to leave the scene in just the master shot, but she wanted shots to cut in if necessary. Not that she did not hold on a long take if it worked. In *12 O'Clock High* (1949), she lets a one-take scene King had shot run nearly five and a half minutes without a cut. She also discussed with Fred Sersen, the studio special effects man, what shots were needed for special effects sequences. Sersen said, "If we put Bobbie [her nickname] on this picture, we'll save a lot of money." McLean helped Sersen prepare the material for his special effects shots for such films as *The Rains Came* (1939) and *Wilson* (1944). On the latter, she also had to cut down the enormous amount of footage shot of the 1912 Democratic convention into a workable sequence, and she condensed several bill-signing scenes into montage sequences. She won her only Oscar for her work on *Wilson*.

She also made suggestions on casting, helping King convince Zanuck that young Tyrone Power could become a star. She was also not afraid to voice her opinion about the costumes. She was the only woman in the projection room, but neither she nor Zanuck saw her simply as representative of the female audience, although she believed she brought her "woman's" point of view as part of their everyday discussions. Frequently Zanuck and others would disagree with her, and she would say, "I don't care. Don't ask me. If you're going to ask me, then listen to me." They did.

McLean worked closely with other directors on the lot. King not only wanted her to cut all his pictures (she cut twenty-nine of his), but had her come down to the set to discuss which shots were needed and which were not, as did Edmund Goulding. Elia Kazan was dazzled when McLean took several shots of the peasants beating rocks to warn of the danger to Zapata in *Viva Zapata!* (1952), duplicated them, reversed them, and built a scene into a sequence. Kazan said, "Where in the hell did you get all that film?"

In 1951 McLean married Henry King's longtime assistant director and later a director himself, Robert D. Webb. She was the co-producer on his 1955 film *Seven Cities of Gold* and associate producer on his 1956 film *On the Threshold of Space.* The marriage lasted until Webb's death in 1990.

McLean was made the chief of Fox's editing division in 1949, a job title that simply confirmed her status as the top editor on the lot. Her editing credits after 1949 include the classic western *The Gunfighter* (1950); *All About Eve* (1950, her last Academy Award nomination); *The Snows of Kilimanjaro* (1952); the first CinemaScope movie, *The Robe* (1953); and *Niagara* (1953), in which she was forced by the censors to use the less provocative long take of MARILYN MONROE walking away from the camera. In 1960 McLean was made head of the feature editorial department, a job that involved her in more administrative details. She retired from the studio in 1969 and died in 1996 in Newport Beach, California, at the age of ninety-two.

Bibliography: There is not yet a biography of Barbara McLean. Ally Acker's *Reel Women* (1991) contains a brief biographical sketch of her. Sam Staggs's *All About "All About Eve"* (2000) is one of the few "making of" books that actually has a section on the editing of a film, and it presents a nice portrait of McLean at work, giving a flavor of her personality. Mel Gussow's biography of Darryl Zanuck, *Don't Say Yes until I Finish Talking* (1971), has only a few references to McLean, as does George F. Custen's *Twentieth Century's Fox: Darryl F. Zanuck and the Culture of Hollywood* (1997). In David Shepard and Ted Perry's collected oral history interviews with Henry King, *Henry King Director: From Silents to 'Scope* (1995), King does discuss his working relationship with McLean. *Elia Kazan: A Life* (1988) mentions the "rock sequence" in *Viva Zapata!* but Kazan only says that Anthony Quinn suggested the action; there is no mention of what McLean did in the editing room. An extensive oral history interview with McLean was done by the author at the American Film Institute in 1970; this was the source of information in Acker's, Staggs's, and Custen's books, as well as for the quotes in this essay. Obituaries appeared in the *Los Angeles Times* on April 2, 1996, and the *New York Times* on April 7, 1996.

TOM STEMPEL

McNEILL, Bertha Clay. November 12, 1887–September 21, 1979. Peace activist, educator.

Bertha McNeill dedicated her life to improving race relations, furthering blacks' education, and working for peace and international understanding. Like the African American club women and internationalists who came before her, including MARY CHURCH TERRELL and Addie Hunton, McNeill worked on all of these concerns simultaneously because she believed that improving race relations at home created the climate for world peace.

Bertha McNeill was born in Southport, North Carolina, the eighth child of Lucy A. Reaves and Henry C. McNeill. Little is known about her family or upbringing. For her early education she attended Gregory Normal Institute in Wilmington, North Carolina, which had been founded by the American Missionary Association. As a young woman she moved to Washington, D.C., and attended Howard University, graduating in 1908. McNeill undertook graduate work at Columbia University and the University of Chicago, and later earned a master's degree in English from Catholic University in 1945.

Reflecting the strong tradition of middle-class black women's dedication to personal and community development through maintaining and improving educational institutions, McNeill worked as a teacher in traditional black institutions and helped create new black educational resources. In Washington she taught English and journalism at the famous M Street School, which later became Dunbar High School, named after black poet Paul Laurence Dunbar. After retiring from Dunbar in 1957, McNeill taught as a visiting professor of English at Howard University.

Bertha McNeill played a strong role in maintaining educational associations for African American women. In April 1910 she joined other African American women leaders in education from the Washington, D.C., area, among them Mary Church Terrell, Dr. Sara Brown, Mary Cromwell, and Dr. Georgianna Simpson, in founding the College Alumnae Club. In 1923 the group expanded the organization and by 1924 incorporated it as a national organization, renaming it the National Association of College Women (NACW) (it later became the National Association of University Women). LUCY DIGGS SLOWE, dean of Howard University, became the NACW's first national president. McNeill also served as a charter member of the Howard University Women's Club and was a fifty-year member of the Alpha Kappa Alpha Sorority.

Next to education, working for peace played the most important role in McNeill's life. A long-standing member of the Women's International League for Peace and Freedom (WILPF), she joined the organization in the 1930s. McNeill served the organization in various executive capacities and represented WILPF at four international congresses. She continued the work of linking African American causes to the work for world peace and bringing the talents and insights of African American women to the cause of peace.

In WILPF her worked spanned the local, national, and international scenes. In 1935 Bertha McNeill became the chair of WILPF's Interracial Committee, which had been directed by prominent black club woman and peace activist Addie Hunton since 1928. In December 1937 the committee's name changed to the Committee on Minorities and Race Relations and its purpose expanded to reflect world and national developments, in effect becoming an umbrella committee addressing civil rights, anti-Semitism, and refugee rights. During World War II, McNeill worked actively in conjunction with the National Association for the Advancement of Colored People (NAACP) and the Alpha Kappa Alpha sorority to defeat the Austin-Wadsworth Bill, introduced in 1943, which proposed mandatory wartime noncombatant conscription of women ages eighteen to fifty. She later served on the national executive board of WILPF in the 1940s and 1950s and as national vice president in 1948–49 and 1953. In the heat of the McCarthy-era red scares, McNeill chaired the Committee on the Special Problems of the Branches, designed to respond to cold war antipathy toward peace groups. She was also on the board of the Jane Addams Peace Association, the educational arm of WILPF. In 1954 she became president of the Washington, D.C., branch of WILPF.

McNeill represented the U.S. section of WILPF at four international WILPF congresses. When in 1946 she attended the Tenth International Congress of WILPF, held August 4–9 in Luxembourg, she wrote about the Congress for the *National Notes* of the National Association of Colored Women (NACW). In her reflections, she shared with readers the experience of sailing to Luxembourg with ten other U.S. WILPF members aboard the steamship *Brazil,* a former luxury liner that had been commissioned as a troop transport ship during World War II. Once in Luxembourg, McNeill joined two hundred women from twenty-two countries who had gathered to rebuild the organization, provide war relief to Europe, and plan for future peace and freedom.

For decades Bertha McNeill lived at 2645 15th Street N.W. in Washington, D.C., joined there in her final years by her brother, Oliver McNeill, and her sister, Beulah McNeill Nurse. From 1964 to 1969 she wrote a weekly column covering congressional developments for the North Carolina *Wilmington Journal.* McNeill never married. She frequently hosted gatherings of visiting clubwomen, educators, and peace activists from around the country. She was also a long-standing member of the Lincoln Congregational Temple, United Church of Christ. Bertha McNeill died in 1979 at the age of ninety-one at the Wisconsin Avenue Nursing Home in Washington, D.C.

Bibliography: The papers of Bertha C. McNeill are found at the Swarthmore College Peace Collection. Her papers include minutes from the WILPF committees she chaired and a daily diary, along with two important articles: "Women's League Fights War Profits Bill," *Philadelphia Record,* February 16, 1938, which describes McNeill's peace speeches; and Bertha McNeill, "An International Congress," *National Notes,* March–April 1947, which details her trip to the WILPF Tenth International Congress. General sources on WILPF include Gertrude Bussey and Margaret Tims, *Pioneers for Peace: The Women's International League for Peace and Freedom, 1915–1965* (1980); Catherine Foster, *Women of All Seasons: The U.S. Section of the Women's International League for Peace and Freedom, 1915–1946* (1995); and Linda Schott, *Reconstructing Women's Thoughts: The International League for Peace and Freedom before World War II* (1997). For the experiences of African American women in WILPF, see Joyce Blackwell-Johnson, "African American Activists in the Women's International League for Peace and Freedom, 1920s-1950s," *Peace and Change* 23, no. 4 (October 1998), pp. 466–82.

MELINDA PLASTAS

McQUEEN, Thelma (Butterfly). January 8, 1911–December 22, 1995. Actress.

Thelma McQueen was born in Tampa, Florida, the only child of Mary Richardson, a domestic worker, and Wallace McQueen, a stevedore. When Wallace and Mary separated in 1916, Mary left Florida with her daughter and looked for work to support the two of them. Thelma attended school at St. Benedict's Convent in Augusta, Georgia, while her mother searched for a job up and down the East Coast. When she was hired as a cook in Harlem, she sent for Thelma, who by then was living with an aunt in Augusta. They first lived in Manhattan, and in 1924 moved to Babylon, New York, on Long Island, where Thelma graduated from high school.

After high school, McQueen attended nursing school at the Lincoln Training School in the Bronx. Before she could complete her training, however, she became involved with the theater. Motivated by a nursing school instructor, Thelma decided to try her hand at performance. She began as a dancer in Venezuela Jones's Negro Youth Group under the auspices of the Works Progress Administration (WPA). She studied dance with Janet Collins, Katherine Dunham, and Geoffrey Holder; Adelaide Hall was her voice teacher. Her stage debut came in 1935, when she danced in the "Butterfly Ballet" in Jones's adaptation of *A Midsummer Night's Dream.* The name "Butterfly" stuck.

McQueen first appeared on Broadway in 1937 playing a maid in *Brown Sugar,* directed by George Abbot. According to the review in the *New York Times,* she was about the only thing the show had going for it—it closed after only four performances. Her strong reviews encouraged Abbot to cast her in more shows, particularly *Brother Rat* (1937) and *What a Life* (1938). Her inimitable high-pitched and somewhat squeaky voice lent itself to comedy, and she used it to great effect in *What a Life.*

As an African American actress in the 1930s,

McQueen faced a difficult decision: either to act in roles she considered stereotypic and demeaning, or not to act in Hollywood. During the touring show of *What a Life,* she auditioned and was eventually cast as Prissy in David O. Selznick's 1939 film, *Gone with the Wind.* Here McQueen would find the role that would define her for the rest of her life. Although she was at first considered too old to play the part of teenage Prissy, Selznick preferred to cast an experienced actor in the role. McQueen recalled in an interview for the documentary, *The Making of a Legend: Gone with the Wind* (1989), that the role itself surprised her; she didn't think, in the late 1930s, that she would be playing a slave. Other black actors cast in the film also had qualms about their roles, and some complained to Selznick about explicitly racist elements in the script. Though the film still suffered from considerable racist overtones, it is to the credit of the black actors (and to Selznick as well) that *some* elements were changed during production. For her part, McQueen refused to be slapped or to eat watermelon on screen. Her resistance prompted co-star HATTIE MCDANIEL to warn McQueen that she would never get anywhere in Hollywood if she continued to complain.

Though McQueen would get more roles in Hollywood films, they were often as maids, as in *The Women* (1939), *Cabin in the Sky* (1943), *Mildred Pierce* (1945), and *Duel in the Sun* (1946). Her last film of the 1940s was *Killer Diller* (1948), in which she played "Butterfly." Frustrated with being typecast, she abandoned moviemaking in 1949. And though she declared that she would never work in television, she ended up doing *The Beulah Show* from 1950 to 1952, after having earlier worked on the show when it was on radio. Afterward, McQueen made good her promise to leave Hollywood and return east.

The years between 1952 and 1970 (when she would appear in a film again), were filled, though not always with acting. While living in Hollywood, McQueen had attended classes at UCLA and City College of Los Angeles. From time to time, she would appear in the theater, her first love, but McQueen now pursued education, taking classes at Southern Illinois University, Queens College, and New York University. In 1975 she earned her bachelor's degree from City College of New York, where she studied Spanish. Community activism was an important part of her life; she was a longtime member of the National Council of Negro Women and received awards for her work in several fields. McQueen was admitted to the Black Filmmakers Hall of Fame in 1975. She also worked a variety of jobs after leaving Hollywood, including taxi dispatcher, domestic, and department store saleswoman. She also owned a restaurant in Augusta.

In 1951 she created the first of several one-woman shows and musical reviews; her last one was created in 1976. The 1970s saw McQueen return to the screen, both big and small. In 1979 she received an Emmy Award for her role in *The Seven Wishes of Joanna Peabody.* She appeared in two different television versions of *The Adventures of Huckleberry Finn* (1981 and 1985). Her last film role was Ma Kennywick in *The Mosquito Coast* (1986). A longtime atheist, she won the Freethought Heroine Award from the Freedom From Religion Foundation in 1989. After filming *The Mosquito Coast,* she returned to her volunteer position at P.S. 153 in Harlem.

McQueen never married, and as an only child she had few living relatives by 1986, when she began spending winters in her home in Augusta. There, in December 1995, a housefire started while she was attempting to light a kerosene heater. She managed to escape the house, but she suffered severe burns and died on December 22 at the age of eighty-four.

Bibliography: There is no substantial biography of McQueen. The most significant sources on her life and work are Donald Bogle's *Toms, Coons, Mulattoes, Mammies, and Bucks: An Interpretive History of Blacks in American Films* (1973), and *Blacks in American Films and Television: An Encyclopedia* (1988). John Stark's interview, "Lawd, Miss Scarlett, Look at What Butterfly McQueen Is Up to Now," *People Weekly,* December 1, 1986, pp. 72–75, is also good and is quoted in many obituaries. There is a short piece in Richard Lamparski, *Whatever Became Of . . . ?, Second Series* (1968), which is brief but informative. There are six photographs of her at the Schomburg Center for Research in Black Culture, New York Public Library. The Edward Mapp Collection at the Academy of Motion Picture Arts and Sciences in Los Angeles also has material on McQueen. Obituaries appeared in the *New York Times,* December 24, 1995, and the *New York Amsterdam News,* December 30, 1995.

LISA M. ANDERSON

MEAD, Margaret. December 16, 1901–November 15, 1978. Anthropologist.

Margaret Mead—anthropologist, scientist, reformer, museum curator, public intellectual, college professor, and popular lecturer and writer—was born in Philadelphia, the eldest child of Emily Fogg Mead and Edward Sherwood Mead. Four other children were born: Richard, in 1903; Katherine, in 1905 (she died nine months after she was born); Elizabeth, in 1909; and Priscilla, in 1911.

Mead traced her family on both sides to colonial ancestors whose descendants migrated in the early nineteenth century from New England and Pennsylvania to the Midwest. Her father, born in Ohio to a middle-class family of Methodists and high school educators, was a professor at Wharton

School of Finance and Commerce at the University of Pennsylvania. Her mother, born in Chicago to an upper-middle-class family of Unitarians and progressive reformers, was a leader of the women's rights movement in Pennsylvania. Anticipating a career as a college professor that she never achieved, she wrote a pathbreaking master's essay on the immigrant Italian community of Hammonton, New Jersey.

Mead's strong-willed parents were often at odds, and her sister Katherine's death was a trauma from which the family never entirely recovered. Mead became close to her paternal grandmother, Martha Ramsey Mead, a retired schoolteacher and progressive educator who lived with them, taught the children at home during grade school, and took care of the domestic responsibilities for Mead's mother, who hired servants to do most of the work. Mead attended Doylestown High School and New Hope School for Girls, graduating in 1919, and then spent a year at DePauw University in Indiana, her father's alma mater. Barnard College, to which she transferred her sophomore year, was unique in its emphasis on the social sciences, and given its connection to Columbia University, Mead studied with some of the major scholars in the field. She became a campus leader and organized her apartment mates into a group called the Ash Can Cats, who remained her lifelong friends. During her childhood she had participated in the Victorian culture of homoerotic friendships between girls, and at Barnard she became intimately involved with her classmates Marie Eichelberger and Leone Newton and, along with Leone, was part of a secret homosexual circle. Her world fell apart, however, when Marie Bloomfield, a hanger-on to her lesbian circle, committed suicide. Feeling responsible, Mead broke with Leone.

RUTH BENEDICT, a Columbia PhD in anthropology fifteen years older than Mead and her section leader in a course in anthropology taught by Franz Boas her senior year, persuaded her to enter the Columbia PhD program in anthropology after her graduation from Barnard in 1923. They established a lifelong friendship, becoming lovers several years after they met. While working on her PhD (which was formally awarded in 1929), Mead also completed a master's degree in psychology. Her master's thesis challenged racist IQ testing by proving that tests given to Italian high school students in Hammonton were culture-bound. In 1923 she married Luther Cressman, an Episcopal priest, and kept her maiden name. In 1928 she divorced Cressman and married Reo Fortune, a New Zealand anthropologist. Divorcing Fortune in 1935, the next year she married Gregory Bateson, an English anthropologist, whom she divorced in 1950. Her daughter, Mary Catherine Bateson, was born in 1939.

Between 1923, when Mead entered anthropology, and 1939, when World War II began, she did fieldwork in tribal indigenous societies in the South Pacific, including Samoa (1925–26); Manus (1928–29); three societies in Papua, New Guinea: the Arapesh, the Mundugumor, and the Tchambuli (1931–33); and Bali (1936–39). Aside from Samoa, these ventures were collaborations with her husbands (except for Cressman) in which she studied the women and the children in the societies and they studied the men. Her study of adolescent sexuality on Samoa, *Coming of Age in Samoa* (1928), published when she was twenty-seven, made her famous.

A public intellectual, Mead wrote popular accounts of her fieldwork, including *Growing Up in New Guinea* (1930) about the Manus, and *Sex and Temperament in Three Primitive Societies* (1935) about the three Papua New Guinea societies she studied. A scientist, she wrote detailed scholarly ethnographies of a number of these societies, as well as scholarly articles about theory and methodology that were often discounted by her critics in anthropology. A reformer, she advocated freer sexuality and communal childrearing, although she gave up the socialism of her college years to follow John Dewey in espousing progressive education. She also joined Franz Boas in arguing for cultural relativism against the racism of conservative evolutionary thinking. A museum curator, she remained at the American Museum of Natural History in New York City from her hiring in 1926 until her death. Like Ruth Benedict and Léonie Adams, the renowned poet who was her close friend, she wrote poetry in the 1920s that she published in the day's popular small poetry journals.

Long before Derek Freeman in 1983 attacked her Samoan research as false, famed linguist and anthropologist Edward Sapir, shocked by her free-love views when they had an affair, published similar charges. He did not refer to her by name, but he spread the belief that she was incompetent. Restudies of her Samoa and New Guinea fieldwork, however, demonstrate that she was a brilliant observer who pioneered in using social science methodology. She was, however, hampered by employing Benedict's configurationist approach, which allowed her to study deviancy but focused on cultures as unitary systems. Stung by the criticism, in 1942 Mead articulated an almost postmodern position when she characterized her previous ethnography as a "fiction" and called for fieldworkers to disclose their own personalities in writing up their ethnographies.

Yale social psychologist John Dollard and Lawrence Frank, the administrator of the Laura Spellman Rockefeller Fund, converted Mead to a neo-Freudian point of view. Frank also introduced her to the small-conference format and to interdisciplinary networking. He was one of a number of mentors she adopted, including Benedict, Boas, Bateson, and British anthropologist Alfred Radcliffe-Brown. Mead was a controversial scholar among anthropologists and sociologists, but her studies of childhood and adolescence and her cultural relativism brought her a major reputation in the field of psychiatry. In 1946 she became an adjunct professor in psychiatry at the University of Cincinnati and in the 1950s at the Menninger Foundation in Kansas, visiting each institution for several weeks each year.

She brought her neo-Freudianism into anthropology in the culture and personality school, which she and Benedict shaped into a vehicle for studying the character of contemporary societies in order to help the government in its espionage and morale-building programs during World War II and also to further internationalism after the war. From 1942 to 1945, Mead served as executive secretary of the National Research Council's Committee on Food Habits. In that position she studied food distribution and nutrition, while touring the country and promoting the formation of local councils. At the end of the war Benedict took the lead in establishing their joint Research in Contemporary Cultures project at Columbia University, which eventually involved 120 individuals studying fourteen cultures. Beginning in 1940 Mead lived in the ground floor apartment in Lawrence Frank's Greenwich Village brownstone, and Frank's wife Mary, along with Marie Eichelberger, helped look after Mary Catherine and her own children. During this period Mead spent summers in New Hampshire, along with Gregory Bateson and numerous academic friends, in a compound Frank established.

The post–World War II period marked another turn in Mead's life and career. She divorced Bateson in 1950, and she studied subjects as varied as cybernetics, psychosomatic medicine, mental health, the family, education, extrasensory communication, and gender. Between 1953 and 1971 she restudied the Manus people numerous times. By the 1950s she became involved in civil rights, speaking out against racism, and in the 1960s she positioned herself as a critic and defender of rebellious youth to the older generation. During that decade she participated in the ecumenical movement in religion, particularly through the Episcopal Church, which she had joined as a child. In 1961 she began writing a popular column in *Redbook* magazine, with the assistance of her partner, Rhoda Métraux.

Throughout her career Mead was critical of the feminist movement for downplaying motherhood and domesticity and for an anti-male bias. Yet as the offspring of a careerist grandmother and a women's rights mother, she incorporated their insights to honor women's special skills derived from motherhood that they could exercise in the home or bring into the professions. That point of view was furthered with the birth of Mary Catherine and Mead's enthusiastic espousal of motherhood, as she became a major advocate for natural childbirth and breast-feeding. She also embraced the new sociobiology, which emphasized the differences between women and men, that became popular after World War II. Yet as much as she criticized mothers in the United States for poor mothering, she recommended that talented women enter the professions, and she called on fathers to help with home chores and on scientists to create a technology that could eliminate housework. She articulated these ideas in her major work on gender, *Male and Female: A Study of the Sexes in a Changing World* (1949). Her later thought combined a concern over the future of democracy with support for a global world order. Identifying progress with complex ethnic societies like the United States and with the Western critical tradition, she wanted to harness Westernization and technology to positive ends before their destructive potential, evident in the atom bomb, destroyed the world.

With a protean intelligence and endless energy, Mead stands astride the twentieth century as a controversial model of dynamic womanhood. She was subjected to criticism in academic journals and to ridicule in the popular press for her assumption of male roles and her endless flow of opinions. Many of her stances—like the culture-and-personality combination—are now out of fashion, although she is acclaimed for having founded the field of visual anthropology in her work on Bali with Gregory Bateson. She was awarded many honors, including being elected president of the American Anthropological Association (1960) and of the American Association for the Advancement of Science (1975), as well as election to the National Academy of Sciences. She became an adjunct professor of anthropology at Columbia in 1954 and chaired the anthropology department at Fordham University between 1969 and 1971. Yet although she was appointed an assistant curator of ethnology at the American Museum of Natural History in 1926, she wasn't promoted to the associate level until 1942, sixteen years later. She was appointed a lecturer at Teachers College of Columbia University between 1947 and 1951, although she didn't officially join the Columbia graduate faculty in anthropology until 1954, when she became adjunct professor.

Throughout her adult life Mead had intimate relationships with both women and men. She was confused over whether she was homosexual or heterosexual until her mid thirties, when she decided for bisexuality. With an extraordinary talent for friendship and seduction and a belief in free love, she formed intimate relationships with ease, although her relationships with Ruth Benedict and Gregory Bateson were special, and she remained close to her college friend Marie Eichelberger, an acolyte who took care of her personal needs. In her writings on gender she criticized male aggressiveness—whether on the part of heterosexual or homosexual men who took the active role in sex—while she also focused on male insecurity. She derived her most radical theories about gender from her observations of pre-state societies, while she was influenced by the "constitutional type" school of physical anthropology to conclude that body type and personality characteristics varied by individuals and not by sexual anatomy. Because Hitler used those theories to support his racist ideology, she obfuscated them in her writings. Aside from her argument for bisexuality and breaking down gender categories in *Sex and Temperament in Three Primitive Societies,* she never produced the book she intended to write on gender and constitutional types.

A tiny woman, five feet two inches tall, weighing less than 100 pounds in the 1920s, Mead neither exercised nor played sports, and although she often tried to diet, she grew increasingly stout as she aged. Prone to accidents, often suffering from neuritis in her right arm, in her later years she adopted a trademark thick stick for walking, appropriate to the role of grandmother/guru that she affected in the 1960s and 1970s as she positioned herself as a bridge between the rebellious young and the older generations. She died in New York City in 1978 of pancreatic cancer at the age of seventy-seven, continuing to write and travel until nearly the end.

Bibliography: The Mead Papers at the Library of Congress were fully opened to researchers in 2001. The Benedict papers at Vassar College have now also been fully opened. The first biography to appear based on the new material is Lois W. Banner, *Intertwined Lives: Passion and Intellect in the Lives of Ruth Benedict and Margaret Mead* (2003). On Mead's life, Jane Howard's *Margaret Mead: A Life* (1984) is still useful, as is Hilary Lapsley's *Benedict and Mead: A Kinship of Women* (1999), although neither author used all the Mead letters, which were then restricted. The numerous interviews with Mead's family and friends that Howard did for her biography are at Columbia University Special Collections. Also of interest is Mary Catherine Bateson's memoir, *With a Daughter's Eye: A Memoir of Margaret Mead and Gregory Bateson* (1984); Derek Freeman, *Margaret Mead and Samoa: The Making and Unmaking of an Anthropological Myth* (1983); and Freeman, *The Fateful Hoaxing of Margaret Mead: A Historical Analysis of Her Samoan Research* (1999). The most recent examination of the controversy, which supports Mead, is James Côté, ed., "The Mead-Freedman Controversy in Review," special edition of the *Journal of Youth and Adolescence* 29 (2000).

In addition to the books mentioned in the text, other publications by Mead include *And Keep Your Powder Dry* (1942); *New Lives for Old: Cultural Transformations—Manus, 1928–53* (1956); *Continuities in Cultural Evolution* (1964); and the edited works *Cooperation and Competition among Primitive Peoples* (1937), *Childhood in Contemporary Cultures* (1955), and *Letters from the Field, 1925–1975* (1977). Mead also published two biographical works on Ruth Benedict, which include excerpts from Benedict's writings: *An Anthropologist at Work: Writings of Ruth Benedict* (1959) and *Ruth Benedict* (1974). An extensive, though not exhaustive, bibliography of Mead's work is Joan Gordan, ed., *Margaret Mead: The Complete Bibliography, 1925–1975* (1976). In addition, Mead published a best-selling autobiography *Blackberry Winter: My Earliest Years* (1972). An obituary appeared in the *New York Times* on November 16, 1978.

LOIS W. BANNER

MEEK, Lois Hayden. *See* Stolz, Lois Hayden Meek.

MENDIETA, Ana. November 18, 1948–September 8, 1985. Performance and minimalist artist, feminist.

Ana Mendieta was born in 1948 in Havana into a family with important Cuban social and political ties. Her father, Ignacio Mendieta, was a lawyer who took part in the 1959 revolution that brought Fidel Castro to power. Her mother, Raquel Oti, was a housewife. Even before the United States broke off relations with Cuba on January 3, 1961, it was widely rumored that Castro planned to send the children of middle- and upper-class families out to the countryside to live with the peasantry. In the panic that ensued, thousands of Cuban children were separated from their parents and sent to the United States. At age twelve, Ana and her older sister Raquel went to Iowa under "Operation Peter Pan," a 1960–62 program carried out by the Catholic Diocese of Miami. Arriving in the United States in 1961, the girls did not see their mother or younger brother for five years, or their father for eighteen.

Although Ana had initially been excited about coming to the United States for a little while, being suddenly extracted from her privileged, white upbringing in Cuba and relocated to Iowa was difficult. Against the backdrop of the civil rights movement, Ana and Raquel were abruptly recoded as "dark" and subjected to the anxiety and racism of the times. When their mother finally joined them, she was determined to get U.S. citizenship so she could get her husband out of Cuba; Ana, by this time less enamored of American politics, only reluctantly agreed to citizenship so that she would have more freedom to travel. In this way, the United States political climate had prepared Mendieta for her own explicit self-identification as a third world woman artist.

Ana Mendieta attended the University of Iowa, where she received a BA in 1969 and an MA in painting in 1972. Influenced by the 1970s explosion of minimalist earth and body art as well as performance art, Mendieta staged several protest "rape" scenes and initiated her frequent use of blood in *Blood Writing* (1974) and *Blood Sign No. 2* (1974), where, dragging hands and forearms dipped in blood over canvases, she left behind mute but disturbing trails. Her growing interest in Santería, a syncretic practice combining Catholicism and African religious images and practices, led to her series of earth/body sculptures called *Siluetas;* more than two hundred were documented in film and photographs. Her *First Silueta* was executed in 1973 in Oaxaca at a Zapotec grave site; she photographed herself lying on the floor of a tomb, covered with long white flowers that seemed to grow not only from the ground but from her body. Although she was a small woman, her use of her own body in her works invested them with a mute, monumental appeal. She would continue to explore similar themes through the early 1980s: in her 1976–77 *Tree of Life* series, where she positioned her mud-covered, nude body against trees; her 1977 *Fetish Series,* in which she molded sand or mud "women" inscribed or affixed with symbolic signs; and her 1981 *Rupestrian Sculptures* in Cuba, a series of primitive female figures carved in limestone cliffs and caves. Works such as these were meant to be ephemeral, the only documents of them photographs and the occasional video, in keeping with Mendieta's ideas about the evanescent and simultaneously eternal presence of life, death, and the importance of ritual.

Mendieta's work derived a large part of its energy from the openings in art practice and theory created by feminist activists. In 1978, Mendieta moved to New York City, where she joined the first feminist art gallery in New York, the SoHo A.I.R. (Artists in Residence) Gallery. Beginning in the late 1960s, feminist activists had been central in making visible the work of women artists, through groups like Women Artists in Revolution (WAR), the Ad Hoc Women Artists' Committee, and the Women's Art Registry.

Like other women artists of the seventies and early eighties, Mendieta transformed the mostly masculinist language of minimalism and of "dematerialization." Women artists challenged minimalist assumptions about the universal masculine nature of artist and spectator, as well as about the equality of everyone's access to "art." By infusing their minimalism with a politicized and feminist sensibility, women artists of the 1970s and 1980s imbued their work with a sexual politics that was anything but neutral. Ana Mendieta's growing sense of herself as a third-world woman of color meant that her feminism of necessity found itself at the intersection of gender and race.

The turning point of Mendieta's art had already come in 1972, when she realized that "my paintings were not real enough for what I wanted the images to convey, and by real I mean I wanted my images to have power, to be magic" (Barreras del Rio, p. 28). Mendieta's references in her molded mud, earth, wood, and sand art to female figures in Santería, Taíno Indian, and Meso-American religious beliefs brought a racialized and gendered awareness together with a third-world perspective. Repetitive and ritualistic, politically informed, and using earth, blood, fire, gunpowder, wood, and ashes, Mendieta's pieces were less a protest against patriarchy than an invitation to the restorative powers of nature, especially for women. Her attraction to Santería came in part because it, like her own art, contained extensive healing imagery, but using Santería also allowed Mendieta to investigate her own dislocation from Cuba to the United States. She brought these issues together in 1981, writing that her art was "a direct result of my having been torn from my homeland. . . . This obsessive act of reasserting my ties with the earth is really the reactivation of primeval beliefs . . . the after-image of being encompassed within the womb, is a manifestation of my thirst for being" (Perrault, p. 10).

In 1983, Mendieta received a fellowship from the American Academy in Rome. There, she worked for the first time in a studio, creating bas-relief works molded and baked from mud or sand, painting more formalized shapes on leaves and bark paper, and burning such shapes with gunpowder into carved wood slabs. In 1985, she married the minimalist sculptor Carl Andre. Before she could complete her next major project, an installation commissioned by the city of Los Angeles, she fell from the thirty-fourth-story window of their Greenwich Village apartment under suspicious circumstances. Her husband was charged with second-degree murder but acquitted in 1988. Ana Mendieta's small but important oeuvre remains an influential part of the 1970s explosion in committed feminist art.

Bibliography: Writings by Mendieta include "Self Portraits" (MA thesis, University of Iowa, 1972); "Siluetas" (MFA thesis, University of Iowa, 1977); and "Venus Negra, Based on a Cuban Legend," *Heresies* 4, no. 1 (1981), p. 22. Petras Barreras del Rio and John Perrault, eds., *Ana Mendieta: A Retrospective* (1987), a valuable aid to Mendieta studies, includes a brief but helpful chronology, a detailed bibliography of critical works on Mendieta through 1987, an exhibition history of her art, an essay by Perrault, "Earth and Fire: Mendieta's Body of Work," and an essay by Barreras del Rio, "Ana Mendieta: A Historical

Overview." Jane Blocker, *Where Is Ana Mendieta? Identity, Performativity, and Exile* (1999), is an excellent book-length study of Mendieta's work by an art historian. Other secondary works that treat Mendieta's work include Melissa E. Feldman, "Blood Relations: Jose Bedia, Joseph Beuys, David Hammons, and Ana Mendieta," in Dawn Perlmutter and Debra Koppman, eds., *Reclaiming the Spiritual in Art: Contemporary Cross-Cultural Perspectives* (1999); and Mary Jane Jacob, "*Ashé* in the Art of Ana Mendieta," in Arturo Lindsay, ed., *Santería Aesthetics in Contemporary Latin American Art* (1996). Susan L. Stoops, ed., *More Than Minimal: Feminism and Abstraction in the '70s* (1996), is an excellent introduction to some of the key debates surrounding women's minimalist art in the 1970s; see especially Whitney Chadwick, "Balancing Acts: Reflections on Postminimalism and Gender in the 1970s." See also two pieces by Lucy R. Lippard, "The Pains and Pleasures of Rebirth: Women's Body Art," *Art in America* 64, no. 3 (May–June 1976), pp. 73–81, and "Quite Contrary: Body, Nature, Ritual in Women's Art," *Chrysalis* 2 (1977), pp. 31–47. A documentary film directed by Kate Horsfield, Nereyda Garcia-Ferraz, and Brenda Miller, *Ana Mendieta: Fuego de Tierra,* appeared in 1987. Coverage of her death appeared in the *New York Times* on September 10, 1985.

TACE HEDRICK

MENTSCHIKOFF, Soia. April 12, 1915–June 18, 1984. Lawyer, law professor, dean.

Soia Mentschikoff was born in Moscow, one of three children of Eugenia Ossipov and Roman Sergei Mentschikoff, both of whom came from elite Russian families. Her father, an American citizen who had returned to Russia for a time, moved with his family back to the United States in 1917, settling in New York City, where Soia attended public school. She earned her BA at Hunter College in 1934, and her LLB in 1937 from the Columbia Law School.

Within her chosen profession—the law—Soia Mentschikoff was a pathbreaker. She was, for example, the first woman partner in any Wall Street law firm, the first woman to be offered a permanent position on the Harvard Law School faculty, the first woman faculty member at the University of Chicago Law School, the first woman president of the American Association of Law Schools, and the first woman dean of the University of Miami Law School. The recipient of numerous honorary degrees and other honors, she was included in a short list of "Lawyers of the Twentieth Century" by the *American Lawyer,* and her name appeared on lists of candidates for the United States Supreme Court.

During her first year at law school, Mentschikoff met the brilliant commercial law scholar and legal philosopher Karl N. Llewellyn. Mentschikoff was Llewellyn's student and research assistant; their relationship deepened over the years, and they were married in 1946. The Llewellyn-Mentschikoff personal and professional partnership is at the heart of Soia Mentschikoff's story; their collaboration on the majestic Uniform Commercial Code (UCC) was at the heart of their relationship. Until Llewellyn's death in 1962, Mentschikoff not only pursued her own career goals but also dedicated herself to her husband's professional interests (which, indeed, became hers) and to his personal needs.

After graduating from Columbia in 1937, Mentschikoff sought a position with the New York law firm of Scandrett, Tuttle and Chalaire, making it clear that she would accept only an offer that included the opportunity to do litigation. Despite the fact that there were at the time no women lawyers at the firm, she was hired, and despite the fact that women lawyers were rarely if ever welcomed as litigators, litigation was part of the package. From 1941 to 1947 she practiced mainly labor law at the Wall Street firm of Spence, Windels, Walser, Hotchkiss and Angell, becoming a partner in the firm in 1945.

In 1941, she had her "first accidental involvement" in the process that resulted in the creation of the UCC when she assisted Karl Llewellyn in drafting various commercial law statutes. When Llewellyn became chief reporter for the revision of the Uniform Sales Act, he asked Mentschikoff to help out. She asked her firm for four months' leave of absence, and she became assistant reporter.

On her return to the firm, Mentschikoff continued her involvement with commercial law drafting projects, most notably the Uniform Commercial Code, which, as its name suggests, attempted to unify the whole body of state commercial law, covering sales, negotiable instruments, documents of title, security interests in personal property, and more. As revised and amended through the years, this joint effort of the American Law Institute and the National Conference of Commissioners on Uniform State Laws was, in the end, adopted by every state except Louisiana, and by the District of Columbia, and is widely accounted the most successful code ever written in the United States. Llewellyn's appointment of the relatively unknown Soia Mentschikoff as associate chief reporter "was soon recognized as a brilliant appointment. . . . She was shrewd and formidable in handling people; she had extraordinary technical ability and facility in drafting and her capacity for calm, lucid presentation in committee or on a public platform has become legendary" (Twining, pp. 283–84).

Mentschikoff's burgeoning reputation in the world of commercial law led to an invitation, in 1947, to go to Harvard Law School as a visiting professor. She taught commercial law and commercial arbitration at Harvard for two years; during the second year she was offered a permanent faculty position. This was, in a word, astonishing: Harvard did not even admit women as students until 1950. But the university did not extend an offer to Llewellyn, and Mentschikoff rejected the offer.

Columbia University, which did have women students, was not about to appoint a woman to the law faculty. Thus, when two offers arrived in 1951 from the University of Chicago Law School, Karl and Soia accepted. Existing nepotism rules are said to have barred tenure for both, with the result that Karl became a tenured professor, Soia a professorial lecturer with voting privileges. This relegation to a lower status neither troubled Mentschikoff nor kept her from becoming and remaining for many years a highly influential member of the law faculty. While there, she directed some of her considerable energy to a major empirical study of commercial arbitration, funded by the Ford Foundation.

Llewellyn died in 1962. Mentschikoff continued teaching at Chicago until 1973, when she accepted the deanship of the University of Miami Law School, where she had spent several semesters as a distinguished visiting professor. In the eight years of the Mentschikoff deanship at Miami, the law school grew considerably in stature, gaining national recognition for the improvements in faculty, curriculum, student body, and physical plant that had been initiated and implemented by the determined, energetic, and, to some, overwhelming dean.

Mentschikoff's qualities of mind, character, and temperament combined to produce a powerful impression on those who knew her. Possessed of an incisive, powerful intelligence and an indomitable will, she was self-assured, with a firm belief in herself and in her capabilities that enabled her both to take risks and to ignore career constraints. Her down-to-earth, candid, outspoken, no-nonsense manner captivated all whom it did not intimidate (and no doubt some of those it did). Mentschikoff was, at the same time, a loyal, responsible, and caring family person: she and Karl opened their home to her parents, and, having no children of their own, raised her brother's two young daughters.

In retirement, Mentschikoff kept working at projects as long as she could. She died of cancer at her home in Coral Gables in 1984 at the age of sixty-nine.

Bibliography: The Soia Mentschikoff Papers at the University of Miami include personal papers, correspondence, memoranda, and speeches, files from the Chicago and Miami periods, Uniform Commercial Code files (1940s–60s), Arbitration Project materials (1956–60), Rand Corporation papers, Westinghouse Case Files, law journal reprints, books, photographs, awards, and graduation robes. Mentschikoff published a number of scholarly pieces and also edited two casebooks: *Commercial Transactions: Cases and Materials* (1970), and, with Irwin P. Stotsky, *The Theory and Craft of American Law: Elements* (1981). For her recollections on drafting the UCC, see "Reflections of a Drafter," *Ohio State Law Journal* 43 (1982), pp. 535, 537. She has been the subject of a number of bibliographic studies, including Dawn Bradley Berry, *The 50 Most Influential Women in American Law* (1996); and Zipporah Batshaw Wiseman, "Soia Mentschikoff (1915–1984)," in Rebecca Mae Salokar and Mary L. Volcansek, eds., *Women in Law: A Bio-Bibliographical Sourcebook* (1996). See also Connie Bruck, "The First Woman Everything," *American Lawyer,* October 1982, pp. 32–37, which gives the reader a superb sense of the woman. Some works about Karl Llewellyn contain information about Mentschikoff, especially William L. Twining, *Karl Llewellyn and the Realist Movement* (1973), and James J. Connolly, Peggy Pschirrer, and Robert Whitman, "Alcoholism and Angst in the Life and Work of Karl Llewellyn," *Ohio Northern University Law Review* 24, no. 1 (1998), pp. 43–124. Whitman, "Soia Mentschikoff and Karl Llewellyn: Moving Together to the University of Chicago Law School," *Connecticut Law Review* 24 (1992), pp. 1119–30, is especially informative. Tributes that appeared on her death include Irwin P. Stotzky, "Soia's Way: Toiling in the Common Law Tradition," *University of Miami Law Review* 38 (1984), pp. 373–79, written by a close colleague, friend, and admirer. An obituary appeared in the *New York Times* on June 19, 1984.

BARBARA ARONSTEIN BLACK

MERMAN, Ethel. January 16, 1906–February 15, 1984. Singer, actress.

The singer known to audiences as Ethel Merman was born Ethel Agnes Zimmermann in her grandmother's house in Astoria, New York. She was the only child of German accountant Edward Zimmermann and Scottish mother Agnes Gardner. She graduated from New York's William Cullen Bryant High School, where she had been an editor of the *Owl,* in 1924. From school, Merman would often walk to Ross Music on Steinway Avenue, Astoria, in the days when it was a common custom to give complimentary sheet music to aspiring singers.

Her career began at Brooklyn Paramount Theater, where Broadway impresario Vinton Freedley discovered Merman and cast her in his new Gershwin musical, *Girl Crazy.* The show opened at the Alvin Theater on October 14, 1930—Merman sang "I Got Rhythm" in the first act and returned as a star after intermission. The great hits followed. In *George White's Scandals* (1931) she sang to Depression-era audiences "Life Is Just a Bowl of Cherries." *Take a Chance* (1932) brought another Merman standard entitled "Eadie Was a Lady." On November 21, 1934, was the premier of *Anything Goes,* the first of five shows written for Merman by Cole Porter; Ethel was soon affectionately dubbed the Merm. *Red, Hot and Blue!* (1936) teamed Merman with Jimmy Durante and

Bob Hope; *DuBarry Was a Lady* (1939) had her pledging "Friendship" with an insecure Bert Lahr. It was his *Panama Hattie,* however, that was special to Merman. She received her first solo star billing on October 30, 1940. "Oh, I even took a picture of it," she quipped—and the marquee remained lit for 501 shows. Merman saluted World War II with Porter's *Something for the Boys* (1943) under the aegis of producer Michael Todd. The Irving Berlin musicals were the next chapter in the story of Merman's achievements on Broadway: *Annie Get Your Gun* (1946) gave Merman her longest run—1,147 performances—and she played Mrs. Sally Adams in *Call Me Madam* (1950) without missing a show.

Though Merman was hugely successful on the stage, Hollywood stardom eluded her. She made three Berlin film musicals, *Alexander's Ragtime Band* (1938), *Call Me Madam* (1953), and *There's No Business Like Show Business* (1954), all for Fox. But Broadway was her home, and she returned for *Happy Hunting,* which opened December 6, 1956, at the Majestic Theater.

Merman's personal life was as much a whirlwind as her stage career. Her first marriage, to William Smith in November 1940, had been immediately deemed a mistake. Merman became pregnant during her courtship with Robert Levitt, who soon married her (the date is uncertain). Levitt was the father of both of her children: Ethel (1942) and Robert Levitt Jr. (1945). Her daughter died in 1967. By 1960, Merman's third marriage (March 9, 1953), to Continental Airlines chairman Robert Six, had failed. Her final union, with actor Ernest Borgnine (June 1964), was short-lived and never discussed publicly by Merman.

On May 21, 1959, Merman began her epic turn as Rose in *Gypsy.* The titanic score by Jule Styne and Stephen Sondheim gave the world "Everything's Coming Up Roses" and Merman reason to rush to the theater every night for 702 performances. She said that after *Gypsy* there would be no more shows, which turned out to be only partially true. Merman helped open Lincoln Center on September 22, 1963, performing "They Say It's Wonderful" and "Blow, Gabriel, Blow." There was a limited-engagement revival of *Annie Get Your Gun* there, and on March 28, 1970, she became Dolly Gallagher Levi for another limited run in David Merrick's *Hello, Dolly!* The show closed after the Sunday matinee on December 27, 1970. Merman received a special Tony Award for lifetime achievement in 1972.

Beginning in 1975 Merman would divide her time between television and concerts. She celebrated the bicentennial with a concert conducted by Arthur Fiedler. Merman was especially proud of her work at Nashville's Grand Ole Opry in September 1976. She teamed with MARY MARTIN on May 15, 1977, for *Together on Broadway,* an unqualified triumph for both—and took the Carnegie Hall stage alone on May 10, 1982. Her last encore that night was "Someone to Watch over Me," by George and Ira Gershwin, the team who had started it all on October 14, 1930, five blocks south at the Alvin Theater. After the performance she received the Pied Piper Award from the American Society of Composers, Authors, and Publishers (ASCAP) in honor of her lifetime achievements.

Merman lived on Central Park West, and in the Berkshire and Surrey Hotel apartments, where she proudly displayed memorabilia, always in a colorful setting. On her white mantel chimed a gold clock inscribed "Civic Light Opera, November 12, 1971" for her appearance there with Gwen Verdon. She collected 117 acetates of her live performances, beginning with the July 13, 1937, Gershwin memorial. Each song from a television appearance was noted in her hand on the label. Merman's annotated scripts were carefully filed, and she had a collection of inscribed photos from the royalty of show business, commencing with GINGER ROGERS from *Girl Crazy,* who wrote: "Your success, my happiness."

Merman's last year was quiet. She was suddenly debilitated by the effects of a brain tumor on April 8, 1983, as she was leaving her home for the Academy Awards, after hastily writing a note to producer Marie Marchesani: "Will be in touch upon my return. Leaving in about two minutes." She died less than a year later, at the age of seventy-eight, in her apartment. The voice of Broadway had been silenced. No more would she take a bow after "Rose's Turn" from *Gypsy* and catch the eye of conductor Milton Rosenstock, who would mouth words in cadence: "Do we have to do this thing again tonight?" No more would Merv Griffin say, "Only one, there's only one like the woman I'm about to present . . . Ladies and gentlemen, here to sing for you is the incomparable Ethel Merman." During her final year at home, she was cared for by her nurses Kathryn Shreve and Ona L. Hill. When she was still able, she would visit them in Kenilworth, New Jersey, and had a red maple tree planted on the Hill property. It is stalwart and blooms in vivid red—who could ask for anything more?

Bibliography: On September 1, 1994, when the United States Postal Service dedicated a stamp to Merman, the year of her birth was given as circa 1909. High school records indicate that 1906 is accurate. She co-authored her memoirs first with Pete Martin in *Who Could Ask for Anything More* (1955) and later with George Eells in *Merman—An Autobiography* (1978). See also "Porter on Panama," *Time,* October 28, 1940, pp. 65–67; and "Ethel Merman and Her Magic," *Newsweek,* December 31, 1956, pp. 35–38. She is featured in the definitive Broadway reference book, Louis Botto's *At This Theatre: 100 Years of Broadway Shows, Stories and Stars* (2002). Merman's own scrapbooks, located at the Museum of the City of New York, include voluminous newspaper clippings. Al Koenig's column in *Joslin's Jazz Journal,* "On with the Show," has featured Merman since 1997. Koenig also wrote the liner notes for the 1990 compact disc release of Merman's *You're the Top.* All unattributed quotations can be found in material in the author's possession. Obituaries appeared in the *New York Times* on February 16, 1984, and *Variety* on February 22, 1984.

AL F. KOENIG JR.

MIN, Mollie Hong. October 18, 1887–November 9, 1979. Community activist.

Mollie Hong Min exemplified the spirit of the pioneer generation of Korean women who immigrated to Hawaii. While many prominent male political leaders grabbed the spotlight with their involvement in the Korean independence movement in the early years of immigration, Korean immigrant women patiently carved out their place in the realm of community activism and service, and contributed their resources and time to the well-being of the Korean communities in the new land.

Mollie Hong was born in Pyongyang, Korea, the second child and first daughter of Marjorie Lee and In Taik Hong, a landowner. Mollie led a relatively well-to-do life as a young girl. When she was thirteen, she was recruited by American Christian missionaries to teach in their Sunday school, an experience that profoundly shaped her commitment to education and community service. Several years later she and her brother Chi Pum, who was five years older, were asked by Dr. William Noble, one of the leading Christian missionaries in Korea at the time, to become missionaries for Korean immigrants in Hawaii. Not wanting to be separated from their children, their parents sold and gave away their properties and land in Korea and left for Hawaii as a family in 1903 when Mollie was sixteen.

Christianity continued to dominate Mollie Hong's life upon her arrival in Hawaii. In the early years of Korean immigration to Hawaii, Methodists wielded the most influence among recent Korean immigrants, who had arrived to work as sugar plantation laborers. Hong embraced the Methodist faith and took advantage of its power and influence within the community to better herself. The Methodist Women's Mission Board, impressed by her academic ability, paid the tuition for her to attend the elite Kawaiahao Seminary Girls' School in Hawaii, where she was the only Korean student. With the endorsement and financial support of church leaders, she next gained admission to Methodist Deaconess Theological College in San Francisco, graduating in 1913.

Mollie Hong's status in the community was elevated even higher through her match-made marriage to Reverend Chan Ho Min on June 4, 1913, in San Francisco. Reverend Min, who had graduated from the well-known Methodist Pae Chai School in Seoul and co-founded the Young Men's Christian Association in Korea, had immigrated to Hawaii in 1905, at the age of twenty-seven, to become the minister of the Korean Methodist Episcopal Church in Honolulu. Having left that post, Reverend Min was pursuing further education at the University of Southern California. Reverend Min's scholarships paid for his education but did not provide enough to live on, so Mollie Hong Min was the family breadwinner during this time, making money by giving talks at churches about the state of Christianity in Korea. During the most difficult times, she also cleaned houses for wealthy families; she was ashamed of this and kept it a secret. Reverend Min was appointed as a Methodist elder in Long Beach, California, in 1917. He finished his studies in 1919.

As was not uncommon for women of her generation, Mollie Hong Min decided to dedicate her life to supporting her husband. Being a minister's wife gave Min respectability and a platform for her activism, while Reverend Min's career benefited immeasurably from his having an educated (and attractive) wife. Their first child, Paul, was born in 1914, followed by Thomas (1917), Phillip (1919), Jessie (1921), and Andrew (1923).

Mollie Hong Min's career as a community activist and organizer began as a volunteer in the Los Angeles chapter of the Red Cross during World War I. Having lived in both Korea and Hawaii, Min could easily weave in and out of the worlds of the Korean immigrant community and the larger American society. Min eventually became the representative for Korea of the Red Cross, a highly visible spot in the larger society outside the Korean community in Los Angeles. She and her husband were also active participants in the Korean independence movement through their association with both the Korean Methodist Church and the Korean National Association in Los Angeles. In 1918 Reverend Min was chosen by the Korean immigrant community as an unofficial delegate to the Paris Peace Conference. Although the trip never took place, owing to visa and financial complications, Min's selection made them the most prominent couple in the Los Angeles Korean community at a significant moment in the Korean independence movement at home and overseas.

When the Mins moved back to Hawaii in 1919, Reverend Min became the minister of the Korean Christian Church. Mollie Min's influence on the Korean community and beyond was felt most palpably after her husband became superintendent of the new Korean boarding school, the Korean

Christian Institute. Min was asked to teach, serve as an administrator, and help recruit qualified teachers from the wider Hawaiian community. In addition to her work at the school, she was active in the Pan Pacific Southeast Asia Association, the YWCA, the Red Cross, and the Korean Women's Relief Society.

Min continued her community work well after Korea gained its independence on August 15, 1945, and she was active with relief work during the Korean War. Min received numerous awards for her community service and activism, including the Award of Merit from the Republic of Korea in 1973. In 2003, she was also posthumously honored as one of the twenty-seven outstanding Korean Americans in Hawaii. A member of the pioneer generation of Korean immigrant woman, Mollie Hong Min took advantage of the opportunities that were opened to her both through her connections to Christianity and through her marriage to Reverend Min. She, in turn, enriched the Korean community and the larger communities of Los Angeles and Hawaii with her community service and volunteer work in the pre-1965 years of Korean immigration. Widowed in 1954, Mollie Hong Min died in Honolulu, Hawaii, at the age of ninety-two.

Bibliography: Mollie Hong Min's autobiography is in the possession of her daughter-in-law, Betty Min. For general biographical information, see Roberta W. S. Chang, "Mollie Min and the Reverend Chan Ho Min: Indelible Figures in the History of Koreans in Hawaii," an unpublished paper delivered at the Koreans in Hawaii Conference, Center for Korean Studies, University of Hawaii, January 13–15, 2000; and the entry by Jessie M. Martin in Barbara Bennett Peterson, ed., *Notable Women of Hawaii* (1984). Bruce Cumings, *Korea's Place in the Sun: A Modern History* (1997), and Carter J. Eckert, *Korea Old and New: A History* (1990), provide introductions to Korean history. For the experience of Koreans in America, see Hyung-chan Kim and Wayne Patterson, *The Koreans in America, 1882–1974: A Chronology and Fact Book* (1974); Warren Y. Kim, *Koreans in America* (1971); and Patterson, *The Korean Frontier in America: Immigration to Hawaii, 1896–1910* (1988).

LILI M. KIM

MITCHELL, Joan. February 12, 1926–October 30, 1992. Artist.

Joan Mitchell's career as an abstract painter spanned nearly five decades, a remarkable success when one considers that between the 1960s and the 1980s, her abstract expressionist style, itself typically associated with male painters such as Jackson Pollock and Willem de Kooning as well as a "masculine" sensibility, was well out of favor in the art world. Despite these challenges, Mitchell remained committed to her unique combination of processes and goals, creating a coherent yet varied body of work that has transcended fleeting tastes and ideologies.

Mitchell's childhood provided her with ample financial security and many artistic role models. Born in Chicago, Joan was the second child of Marion Strobel and James Herbert Mitchell. Her mother co-edited the journal *Poetry* with Harriet Monroe, bringing T. S. Eliot, Ezra Pound, and other major modern poets to American readers, often for the first time. James Mitchell was a graduate of Rush Medical School at the University of Chicago who later served as the president of the American Dermatological Association. Despite his medical career, Joan's father involved her in his amateur art making, teaching her to draw and watercolor and taking her to Chicago museums. He once told her that she could never be as good an artist as he was because she was a woman, and Mitchell later remarked that she sometimes felt that she painted (and painted abstractly) to exorcise the ghost of his criticism.

A significant force in her artistic development was the midwestern landscape of her youth. Throughout her life, Mitchell focused primarily on landscapes and nature as inspirations for her nonrepresentational paintings. Even when living in Paris and New York, Mitchell would remember the violence of Lake Michigan during a storm, or the quiet, obscuring, all-encompassing snows on the prairies, and use these memories as generators of feelings from which to paint. The majority of her titles, nearly always assigned after the painting was finished, allude specifically to plants and animals (*Ladybug*, 1957, and *Straw*, 1976) or generally to water, land, sky, or some combination of these features (*Blue Territory*, 1972, or *Land*, 1989).

After two years at Smith College, Mitchell received a scholarship to the School of the Art Institute of Chicago in 1944, earning her BFA degree in 1947 along with a fellowship for travel to Europe to continue her work. As an undergraduate, she enhanced her studies with regular trips to the Art Institute to see favorite works by Paul Cézanne, Henri Matisse, and Wassily Kandinsky, later citing these artists as significant influences upon the development of her own unique style. After graduation, Mitchell moved to New York with Barney Rosset, a classmate from her high school years at the progressive Frances W. Parker School. In the spring of 1948, she and Rosset traveled to Europe, she on her fellowship and he to market his documentary film, *Strange Victory*, in Czechoslovakia. The couple eventually settled in an unheated apartment in Paris's Left Bank before moving to a rented villa in Provence. They remained there until the winter of 1949, at which time they married and returned to New York.

The city in 1950 had just become the new capital of the art world, and its leading currency was abstract expressionism. In the exciting atmosphere of Greenwich Village, hundreds of American and expatriate European artists rejected the previously dominant styles of social realism, cubism, and surrealism to try a more painterly, less geometric style that increasingly omitted representational forms of any kind. Although Mitchell had been exposed to works by Jackson Pollock, Hans Hofmann, and Arshile Gorky before her trip to Europe, it was not until her return to New York in 1950 that she fully opened herself to the possibilities of total abstraction. She became increasingly active in the art scene, befriending Willem and ELAINE DE KOONING, Michael Goldberg, Franz Kline, and Miriam Schapiro. Maintaining her nearly equal love for poetry, she also formed a strong bond with poet and art critic Frank O'Hara.

Her initially informal attendance at meetings of the predominantly male Eighth Street Club, a gathering of the leading avant-garde artists of the time, resulted in an official membership in 1951. The fact that all the key female abstractionists of the time were included (such as Helen Frankenthaler, Grace Hartigan, LEE KRASNER, and Elaine de Kooning) should not occlude the fact that membership for women in this community was rare. Mitchell impressed this elite circle of artists, as well as critics like O'Hara and Thomas B. Hess, with her intellectual acumen and her aesthetic sensibilities as well as her personal toughness, sharp tongue, and ability to keep up with the men in their renowned alcoholic proclivities. Throughout this period, she and Rosset (now founder of Grove Press) were often apart and eventually divorced in 1952, perhaps in part due to her turbulent affair with Michael Goldberg.

Freeing herself from both the social restrictions of her upper-class upbringing and the artistic restrictions of representation, Mitchell began painting large (six- to eight-foot) abstract canvases. In 1950, she had her first solo exhibition, at the Saint Paul Gallery and School of Art in Minnesota; more significantly, she participated in the 1951 "Ninth Street Show," where her *Untitled* (c. 1950) drew praise from critics and fellow painters, including Willem de Kooning, whose own recent work offered inspiration for this new direction in Mitchell's painting. Later that year her work was chosen for the Whitney Museum of American Art's "1951 Annual Exhibition of Contemporary American Painting." Numerous solo and group exhibitions followed in Europe and the States, and the Whitney purchased Mitchell's *Hemlock* (1956) in 1958.

In 1955, Mitchell began alternating her time between her studio on St. Mark's Place and Paris, where she moved permanently in 1959, settling into a studio on the rue Frémicourt and later purchasing a permanent home in Vétheuil, northwest of Paris. Moving away from the New York art world allowed Mitchell greater freedom to continue to paint in the abstract expressionist vein, rather than be caught up in the ever-changing styles of New York painting. In France, she befriended a number of artistic and literary artists, most significantly French Canadian painter Jean-Paul Riopelle, who became her lover and sometime domestic partner until their breakup in 1979. Mitchell never had children, and despite her numerous friendships, she seemed to form her strongest emotional attachments to her many dogs, naming paintings after them and describing them as integral to her artistic process.

Mitchell's lifelong interests in poetry and nature were increasingly commingled with a contradictory desire for isolation and fear of abandonment. Particularly from the 1960s on, Mitchell was troubled by a nearly obsessive fear of death and loss, exacerbated by the deaths of many of her most significant friends, including Frank O'Hara, her psychoanalyst and friend Edrita Fried, and her entire immediate family. Additionally, she confronted reminders of her own mortality with the diagnosis of jaw cancer in 1984 (both her mother and her sister had died of cancer) and two hip replacement surgeries. Mitchell often described painting as the only balm against her fears, her abstractions operating as imaginary utopias in which she was whole, at one with nature, and fully alive. Ultimately her final battle with cancer, this time in her lungs, would cause her death in Paris on October 30, 1992, at the age of sixty-six.

Bibliography: Focused, comprehensive studies of Mitchell's life and work are available in two monographs written by authors personally familiar with the subject: Judith Bernstock, *Joan Mitchell* (1988), and Klaus Kertess, *Joan Mitchell* (1997). The biographical chronology assembled by Debbie Taylor in Kertess's book is the most thorough and accurate available. Françoise S. Puniello and Halina R. Rusak have compiled a more recent bibliography in *Abstract Expressionist Women Painters: An Annotated Bibliography* (1996). The Archives of American Art at the Smithsonian Institution holds audiocassettes of an interview with art historian Linda Nochlin (from April 1986), as well as photographs and letters in the files of Michael Goldberg, among others. Exhibition catalogues that focus on Mitchell exclusively are Joan Mitchell, *My Five Years in the Country* (1972); Marcia Tucker, *Joan Mitchell* (1974); Yves Michaud, *Joan Mitchell: New Paintings* (1986); and Barbara Rose, *Joan Mitchell: The Bedford Series, a Group of Ten Lithographs* (1981). More readily available are numerous exhibition catalogues and broader texts on modern art that contain brief entries on Mitchell. See particularly Dore Ashton, "The Adventures of the New York School," in *American Images: The SBC Collection of Twentieth-Century American Art* (1996); Elsa Honig Fine, *Women and Art: A History of Women Painters and Sculptors from the Renaissance to the 20th Century* (1978); Eleanor Munro, *Originals: American Women Artists* (1979); Frank O'Hara, *Art Chronicles: 1954–1966* (1975); and Irving Sandler, *The New York School: The Painters and Sculptors of the Fifties* (1978). Bill Scott's postscript, "In the Eye of the Tiger," *Art in America* 84 (March 1995), pp. 70–71, contains a lively personal account of Mitchell's last years and impact on younger artists. Obituaries appeared in the *New York Times* on October 31, 1992, and the *Washington Post* on November 1, 1992.

KIRSTIN RINGELBERG

MITFORD, Jessica. September 11, 1917–July 23, 1996. Writer, political activist.

Jessica Mitford targeted her sharp wit and intolerance of the absurd at the funeral industry in 1963 with her best-selling book *The American Way of Death.* In doing so she not only earned herself the title of muckraker but also brought the burial industry to its knees. This was not Mitford's first bit of rabble-rousing, but it was one with which the public could identify.

Jessica Lucy Freeman Mitford was born in Batsford, Gloucestershire, England, the sixth of seven children and one of six daughters. Her parents were British aristocrats, and the children were raised in the English countryside and London neighborhoods, with pets, servants, and governesses. Her father, David Mitford, was the Second Lord Redesdale. Her mother, Sydney Bowles, a cousin of Winston Churchill, did not believe in formal schooling for girls, and the sisters were tutored at home by a series of governesses. Jessica (always known as "Decca") resented her mother's attitude toward formal education, although the method used to teach the girls encouraged them to investigate and inquire.

The Mitford children took widely divergent political paths as adults. Tom, the only son, was killed in the Second World War. Nancy became a writer best known for *The Pursuit of Love* (1945) and *Love in a Cold Climate* (1949). Diana married Sir Oswald Mosely, the leader of the British Union of Fascists. Unity was an ardent follower of Adolph Hitler who shot herself in the head when it became obvious that Germany and England were going to war. Pamela and Deborah pursued their love of horses and country life. And Jessica devoted her life to left-wing political causes and writing.

In January 1937, Jessica met Esmond Romilly, a nephew of Winston Churchill. Seeking adventure and knowing of Esmond's anti-fascist activities, she asked if she could accompany him to Spain. They left almost immediately and were married May 18; she was nineteen and he eighteen. Her father cut her out of his will. When they returned to England a few months later, Jessica was pregnant. They lived in a small rented flat, and Mitford worked for a short time as part of a market-research team. During this period, she came into close contact with the working class for the first time. For the rest of her life she never stopped pursuing working-class interests.

Their baby, Julia, was born in December 1937 and died four months later of complications from measles. After a three-month stay in Corsica, the couple returned to England and jumped into the political fray. Mitford raised money to fight fascism in Spain, sabotaged the marches of Diana's husband Oswald Mosely, and participated in trade-union marches and in the Labor Party. In February 1939 Mitford and Romilly emigrated to the United States. She would not live in England again, although she visited there frequently.

A series of low-paying jobs and the generosity of friends and strangers kept them fed. They met and befriended liberal New Dealers, including civil rights lawyer Clifford Durr, his wife VIRGINIA FOSTER DURR, and Katharine Meyer, the daughter of Eugene Meyer, owner of the *Washington Post.* (Katharine married Phillip Graham, future publisher of the *Post,* the following year.) When England entered the war against Germany, Romilly enlisted in the Royal Canadian Air Force. A pregnant Mitford moved in with the Durrs, and stayed for two and a half years. Constancia Romilly was born in February 1941. On December 2 of that year, Mitford received a telegram informing her that Esmond Romilly was missing in action after his plane went down in the North Sea.

In wartime Washington Jessica Mitford went to work for the Office of Price Administration (OPA), where she met left-wing labor lawyer Robert Treuhaft. They were married in Guerneville, California, on June 21, 1943. Following a brief stint in San Francisco, they moved to Oakland, where they spent the rest of their married lives. Their son Nicholas was born in May 1944, followed by Benjamin in October 1947. When Nicholas was ten, he was hit and killed by a bus while bicycling around his paper route.

Meanwhile Mitford's political allegiances were traveling further leftward. In 1944 Mitford became both a U.S. citizen and a member of the Communist Party. Treuhaft had become a member the year before. Increasingly active in civil rights activism, Mitford was subpoenaed in 1951 by the California State Committee on Un-American Activities for her involvement in the East Bay Civil Rights Congress. She took the Fifth Amendment and was dismissed as an uncooperative witness. Treuhaft and Mitford remained in the Party until 1958, finally resigning because they believed that the American Communist Party had lost touch with its working-class goals. Mitford later described these years with characteristic wit in *A Fine Old Conflict* (1977).

In addition to her work for civil rights and other radical causes, Mitford increasingly devoted her attention to writing. Her 1960 memoir of Mitford family life, *Daughters and Rebels* (published in England as *Hons and Rebels*), already showed her extraordinary humor and take-no-prisoners attitude. Then in 1963 she published *The American Way of Death*, a pointed but often hilarious exposé of the funeral industry. The genesis of the book was her husband's discovery from his union work that the cost of a funeral most often equaled the exact amount available to the widow for burial purposes. Mitford and Treuhaft spent five years researching the book, which upended the public's attitude toward burial practices and led to a Federal Trade Commission investigation of the industry. In *Kind and Usual Punishment: The Prison Business* (1973), she exposed sentencing procedures, prison conditions, and the use of prisoners for medical experiments. Then came *Poison Penmanship: The Gentle Art of Muckraking* (1979), which included among its targets Elizabeth Arden's Maine Chance spa, the Sign of the Dove (a high-priced New York restaurant), and the Famous Writer's School, which closed shortly after her investigation. Her final book looked at the high cost of childbearing in *The American Way of Birth* (1992).

Mitford died of cancer on July 23, 1996, at her home in Oakland at the age of seventy-eight. At the time of her death, she was working on a revised version of *The American Way of Death.* Given her strong attitudes about the funeral industry, she requested that her body be cremated.

Bibliography: The extraordinary Mitford family has attracted its share of chroniclers and biographers, the most recent being Mary Lovell, *The Sisters: The Saga of the Mitford Family* (2001). Also of interest is Jonathan and Catherine Guinness, *The House of Mitford* (1985). In addition to the books mentioned in the text, Mitford was the author of *Lifeitselfmanship* (1956), a privately printed booklet about members of the Communist Party; *The Trial of Dr. Spock, the Rev. William Sloane Coffin, Jr., Michael Ferber, Mitchell Goodman, and Marcus Raskin* (1969); *Faces of Philip: A Memoir of Philip Toynbee* (1984); and *Grace Had an English Heart* (1989). *The American Way of Death Revisited* was completed by Robert Treuhaft and published in 1998. An obituary appeared in the *New York Times* on July 24, 1996.

JANET BEYER

MOERS, Ellen. December 9, 1928–August 25, 1979. Educator, writer, literary critic.

Pioneering feminist literary critic Ellen Moers was born in New York City, the second of two daughters of Celia Lewis Kauffman and Robert Moers. Her father, a graduate of New York University Law School, worked as a lawyer in New York City. Her mother, a 1910 graduate of Syracuse University who also studied at the University of Grenoble and was a suffragist, worked as a teacher in New York City high schools. Ellen and her older sister, Mary, grew up on West End Avenue in Manhattan in a solidly upper-middle-class community. Both girls achieved significant academic success, and they followed the same pattern of education: undergraduate study at Vassar, followed by graduate work at Radcliffe and Columbia. Mary studied social anthropology and law; Ellen studied comparative literature.

After receiving her BA in 1948 from Vassar, where she was elected to Phi Beta Kappa, Ellen Moers went on to get her MA at Radcliffe College. Weeks after her graduation, she married Martin Mayer on June 23, 1949, in a ceremony at the Pierre Hotel in New York City. Mayer, a 1947 Harvard graduate, forged a career as a well-known freelance writer, working mainly on the subjects of economics, business, and finance. The couple had two sons: Thomas Moers Mayer (1955) and James Moers Mayer (1958). For the rest of her life, Moers (who kept her given name professionally) and her family lived in Manhattan during the academic year and spent their summers on Shelter Island, New York.

Moers went on to study for her PhD in comparative literature at Columbia University, finishing her dissertation in 1957. Her thesis, on the rise of dandyism in England and France, later served as the basis for her first book, *The Dandy, Brummel to Beerbohm* (1960). The book, which combined scholarly rigor with public appeal and illustrated its survey with plates depicting eighteenth- and nineteenth-century fashion excesses, was met with critical acclaim and was widely read, and was translated into many languages, including Japanese. In 1962 Moers was awarded a Guggenheim Fellowship to study the works of Theodore Dreiser. *The Two Dreisers,* Moers's discussion of Dreiser's most famous books, *Sister Carrie* and *An American Tragedy,* was published in 1969.

While caring for her young family, Moers worked intermittently at local colleges and universities, including part-time teaching at Hunter College and Columbia University. In later years, she taught at Barnard College, Brooklyn College, the Graduate Center of the City University of New York, and the University of Connecticut at Storrs, where she served as visiting university professor starting in 1976. She reached many students through her teaching and was an active participant in New York City's literary and intellectual circles.

In the 1960s, riding the wave of the nascent women's liberation movement, Moers was frequently asked to lecture and write on women's literature. Her first article on the subject, "The Angry Young Women," appeared in *Harper's* magazine in December 1963, the same year that Betty Friedan published *The Feminine Mystique.* This article presented Victorian women writers as models for the budding feminist movement in their constructive use of anger. Between lecturing and serving on panels at conferences on women, Moers wrote further articles on LOUISA MAY ALCOTT, WILLA CATHER, and Mary Wollstonecraft. One of her most influential contributions was the concept of the "female gothic," which she first defined in 1974 in the *New York Review of Books* in an article of the same name.

The recipient of a National Endowment for the Humanities fellowship in 1972, Moers decided to put her research and study on this topic into a book, which became *Literary Women* (1976). She considered it a "dialogue" on the subject of women writers: "The new wave of feminism, called women's liberation, pulled me out of the stacks and made the writing of this book much more of an open-air activity than a bookish person like myself could otherwise have expected" (p. xiii). A huge undertaking and one of the first of its kind, *Literary Women* chronicles, cross-culturally, the work of women writers from the seventeenth through the twentieth century. In it Moers concluded that the historical existence of a segregated tradition of women's writing had been an advantage to women rather than a detriment. Widely read and discussed, *Literary Women* inspired praise and interest for its unprecedented scope, and energetic debate for its controversial omissions.

In 1978, Moers published *Harriett Beecher Stowe and American Literature,* and at her death she was working on a book about the interrelationships among British and American literary figures of the last century. Stricken with cancer, she died in New York City on August 25, 1979, at the age of fifty.

Ellen Moers loved books and libraries, but her writing was far from dry or dull. She was a sharp, accurate critic, never afraid to praise or blame a writer's work. Her lasting contribution to women's literature may lie not so much in her pronouncements or judgments as in her emphasis on the importance of gender in studying literature written by women. That discovery helped lay the groundwork for ensuing generations of feminist and literary scholars.

Bibliography: Literary papers and related correspondence of Ellen Moers are at the Rare Book and Manuscript Library in Columbia University's Butler Library. There are more than fourteen thousand items in the collection, mainly letters and typescripts related to her professional career. In addition to the books mentioned in the text, Moers also wrote extensive literary criticism for the *New York Times, New York Review of Books, American Scholar,* and many other scholarly journals; "The Female Gothic" appeared in the *New York Review of Books* 21, no. 4 (March 21, 1974), and 21, no. 5 (April 4, 1974). An issue of *Signs: Journal of Women in Culture and Society* 24, no. 3 (1999), is dedicated to *Literary Women* and its influence on literary theory. An obituary appeared in the *New York Times* on August 27, 1979.

GIORDANA MECAGNI

MONGAN, Agnes. January 21, 1905–September 15, 1996. Curator, art historian.

Agnes Mongan was born in Somerville, Massachusetts, the second of four children of Eliza Teresa O'Brien, a homemaker, and Charles Edward Mongan, a physician. Her family traced its ancestry to Ireland, although both her parents were born in the Boston area. At age thirteen she told her father she wanted to learn all about the objects in her parents' collections of Persian carpets, English silver, and antique furniture. He later sent her to Bryn Mawr College, where she studied art history and English literature. After graduating in 1927, she spent a year abroad with a Smith College Seminar program; on returning home, she received a master's degree from Smith.

In 1929 she took her first job at Harvard's Fogg Art Museum, where she would spend virtually the rest of her life, even after her official retirement in 1975. She started as a research assistant under Paul Sachs, the great collector, banker, and associate director of the Fogg. Sachs trained Mongan's eye and paved the way for her in social and scholarly circles.

The Fogg's collection was particularly rich in French drawings, and that became Mongan's specialty, with a particular focus on Jean-August-Dominique Ingres. But she was at Harvard during the brief moment when the university was also the epicenter of contemporary art in America. She was a founding member of the Institute of Contemporary Art in Boston and active with the Museum of Modern Art in New York. Both institutions grew out of the interests of a remarkable group of Harvard undergraduates, including Lincoln Kirstein, the Filene's heir who would co-found the New York City Ballet and was Mongan's great friend.

Mongan published extensively. Her magnum opus was *David to Corot: French Drawings in the Fogg Art Museum* (1996). Her loyalty to the university was legendary. "I won't give advice to collectors unless they're willing to do something for Harvard," she once said. They didn't necessarily have to do something predictable. After she told Harvard alumnus Melvin R. Seiden that Al Hirshfeld was the finest living draftsman in America, Seiden bought Hirschfeld with a passion. The result was a collection of hundreds of the artist's drawings and prints that Seiden gave to the Harvard Theatre Collection. Seiden also endowed the I Tatti Mongan Prize, named for the Fogg curator and her sister, Elizabeth (1910–2002), a distinguished print curator.

Despite her dedication to Harvard, in her early years at the university Mongan couldn't walk down the front steps of Widener Library after 6 PM or join the faculty club because of her sex. Male colleagues asked her to do their typing, which she avoided by never learning how, and she was regularly paid half their salaries. Harvard also only hired male curators, so, although carrying a full curatorial load, she was called Keeper of Drawings until she became the Fogg's first female curator in 1947. In 1951 she became assistant director of the Fogg, then associate director in 1964. Ultimately, she became the Fogg's first female director, a job she held from 1969 to 1971. She also held an appointment as a lecturer in the Department of Fine Arts, where her classes and seminars from the 1950s through the 1970s trained and influenced many of the country's leading curators. William Robinson, who took his first course in the field with Mongan and later became curator of drawings at the Fogg, remembered her as an inspired and inspiring teacher.

Mongan was something of a sleuth, hunting down important drawings, making important attributions. An ace connoisseur, she once identified a series of sixteenth-century portraits as the work of François Clouet. The artist was in the employ of Catherine de'Medici; Mongan recognized the handwriting of Catherine's secretary on the pictures. As a southpaw, Mongan had a particular interest in the work of left-handed artists, which she identified by the slant of their strokes. Her study of dogs in Italian painting convinced her that seeing-eye dogs were used in the fifteenth century. She encouraged the Fogg to collect forgeries, both to get them off the market and to sharpen the eyes of her students. She added immensely to the quality and quantity of the Fogg's holdings, and although her specialty was French drawings, she was catholic in her acquisitions.

The biggest adventure of her career was a secret attempt to buy the world's greatest cache of drawings, those of the Albertina Museum in Vienna. In 1936, though, they were still in the hands of a Habsburg archduke who intended to sell them to pay his enormous debts. Mongan and Sachs spent months in Vienna working on the scheme, but it ultimately failed when the story broke and the Austrian government confiscated and nationalized the drawings.

She was a stickler on certain subjects. Woe to the journalist who referred to an entire show as an exhibit. The phone would ring, and Mongan would remind the writer that an exhibit is one object in an exhibition. As a woman who had had such a hard time in her profession, she became a mentor to a younger generation of female scholars. Personally elegant and impeccably dressed, "She was not unlike the work of her favorite artist," former Harvard Art Museums director James Cuno once remarked, "because she, like Ingres, offered a twist on the traditional that in the end was more than modern." She never married. At the end of her life, she moved into a retirement home in Cambridge, where she enjoyed taking fellow residents on personal tours of the Fogg.

Two years before her death in Cambridge at the age of ninety-one, the Fogg opened the Agnes Mongan Center for the Study of Prints, Drawings and Photographs, where the museum's hundred thousand works on paper were finally consolidated in one place and made accessible to all. Said Mongan at the opening, "They should have done it years ago."

Bibliography: The best source for Mongan's background and early career is the transcript of interviews conducted in 1991 by Anne A. Meyer for the Schlesinger Library, Radcliffe Institute for Advanced Study, Harvard University. The oral history also contains the most complete bibliography of Mongan's academic writings, as well as a complete list of her honors and awards to that point. For another account of her career, see Nicholas Fox Weber, *Patron Saints: Five Rebels Who Opened America to a New Art, 1928–1943* (1992). See also articles by Christine Temin in the *Boston Globe* on April 22 and 23, 1994, and September 17, 1996, which contain the quotations in the text. An obituary appeared in the *New York Times* on September 17, 1996.

CHRISTINE TEMIN

MOODY, Helen Wills. October 6, 1905–January 1, 1998. Athlete.

Helen Wills dominated American women's tennis from the early 1920s through the 1930s. During her fifteen-year career, she amassed nineteen Grand Slam singles titles, including eight Wimbledon titles and seven U.S. Open singles titles. Between 1927 and 1934 she maintained her ranking as the number one female singles player in the world. Wills was one of the most celebrated female athletes of her time, and among the first American-born women to garner international athletic fame.

Helen Newington Wills, an only child, was born in Centerville, California. Her father, Clarence A. Wills, was a surgeon, and her mother, Catherine Anderson, was a housewife. Both had grown up in California and graduated from the University of California at Berkeley, Clarence from the medical school and Catherine with a bachelor's degree in social science. Helen Wills began playing tennis as a child, and, with the support of her parents, quickly became part of a robust California tennis culture in which women were encouraged to compete and achieve. She attended high school at the private Anna Head School in Berkeley, graduated in 1923, and went on to study art at UC-Berkeley. She was elected to Phi Beta Kappa, although her studies were frequently interrupted by her tournament play and she did not earn a degree.

Wills arrived on the tennis scene at a fortuitous time. By the early 1920s, when she first stepped into the public eye, athletes were gaining new prominence in American popular culture, and a string of charismatic female tennis stars—most notably France's Suzanne Lenglen—had drawn particular attention to women's tennis. In 1923, seventeen-year-old Wills stunned the tennis world by defeating six-time U.S. champion Molla Mallory to capture the U.S. singles championship. Admiring press coverage, which emphasized both her striking good looks and her growing string of victories, spread her fame throughout the country, winning her so many admirers that one New York editor famously remarked that "all the males in America . . . are a little in love with her" (Engelmann, p. 293).

Wills became an international figure in 1926 when she traveled to the French Riviera in quest of a match with Suzanne Lenglen, then considered the greatest female player of all time. The prospect of a meeting between the world's two best women players drew dozens of newspaper reporters from throughout Europe and the Americas. The rivalry became front-page news around the United States, and coverage took on a nationalistic note, as reporters contrasted the young, wholesome "American Girl" with the more worldly Lenglen. Though Wills lost to Lenglen that year, she would soon replace the Frenchwoman as the world's best female player. Between 1927 and 1933 she racked up a 180-match winning streak, defeating such notable players as Alice Marble and Helen Jacobs. A back injury forced her to cut back play in 1933, but she returned in 1935, winning two more Wimbledon titles before retiring from tournament play in 1938.

Like many female athletes of her era, Wills reflected the complexities of changing times in her play and demeanor. She played a powerful, relentless game, and her style was frequently compared to men's. Her loose, calf-length tennis skirts departed from women's traditionally enveloping athletic garb. But she was classically beautiful, and she eschewed many of the fashion trends that characterized the nation's controversial flappers, wearing her hair long and avoiding makeup. The combination of "modern" skill with "old-fashioned" modesty proved immensely appealing, and she was credited with sparking new interest in sports among American women, as well as with helping to usher in more athletically oriented standards of female beauty.

She showed little emotion on the court, earning herself the nickname Little Miss Poker Face. The serious pursuit of a career, let alone an athletic career, was an unusual endeavor for privileged women such as Wills, and in her autobiography she tended to downplay her talents, adopting a breezy style and frequently devoting as much attention to her interest in art and details of her travel and acquaintances as to her tennis achievements. She insisted that she played tennis largely for pleasure, writing, "I have always thought of it as a diversion, and not as a 'career'" (*Fifteen-Thirty*, p. 3). Still, the drive that lay behind her achievements was unmistakable. In 1931, she told historian Will Durant: "The only thing that I know I really want, is some means of exercising the restlessness which seems to be continually in my heart. Tennis, painting—almost anything will do. . . . It is the reason why I have played tennis so fast and furiously for so many years" (Durant, pp. 98–99, 105).

Wills also took artistic and literary endeavors seriously. At the height of her fame, she mounted several shows of her paintings and the *Saturday Evening Post* and the *New York World* commissioned drawings from her, although critics agreed that such attention was due more to her celebrity than to her artistic skill. She published two works of nonfiction, an instruction manual entitled *Tennis* (1928) and the autobiographical *Fifteen-Thirty: The Story of a Tennis Player* (1937), as well as a mystery novel, *Death Serves an Ace* (1939).

Despite her public acclaim, Wills remained a private, somewhat enigmatic person. She married twice. Her first marriage, on December 23, 1929, to stockbroker Fred Moody, ended in divorce in 1937. Two years later, on October 28, 1939, she married Aidan Roark, a well-known Irish polo player. The couple divorced in the 1970s. She had no children.

After her retirement from tournament play in 1938 she lived a quiet, largely reclusive life in California, where she played tennis into her eighties. After several years of failing health, she died at age ninety-two in a Carmel convalescent home. Her ashes were scattered at sea, off the coast of the state where she had lived her entire life.

Bibliography: Helen Wills's work includes *Fifteen-Thirty: The Story of a Tennis Player* (1937), which recounts the bulk of her tennis career and describes her other activities and her developing life philosophy; and *Tennis* (1928), in which she describes the mechanics of tennis play, illustrated by her own drawings, and offers perspectives on psychology and strategy, as well as fashion and etiquette. Susan Cahn's *Coming on Strong: Gender and Sexuality in Twentieth-Century Women's Sport* (1994) contains a chapter that thoughtfully relates the public images of female athletes, including Wills, to the cultural shifts of the 1920s. Will Durant, *On the Meaning of Life* (1932), is a compilation work that includes a candid eight-page letter by Wills.

The standard biographical work on Wills, with copious details on her life and career, is Larry Engelmann, *The Goddess and the American Girl: The Story of Suzanne Lenglen and Helen Wills* (1988). Obituaries appeared in the *New York Times* and the *Los Angeles Times* on January 3, 1998.

PAMELA GRUNDY

MORENO, Luisa. August 30, 1907–November 4, 1992. Labor leader, civil rights activist.

Luisa Moreno was the most recognized Latina labor leader in the United States during the 1930s and 1940s. She remains the only transcontinental Latina union organizer, as her work carried her from the garment shops of New York City to canneries in Los Angeles. A Guatemalan immigrant, she was the first Latina vice president of a major union—the United Cannery, Agricultural, Packing, and Allied Workers of America (UCAPAWA)—which in its heyday was the seventh largest CIO affiliate. But her most notable "first" was in 1939 as the driving force behind El Congreso de Pueblos de Habla Española (the Spanish-speaking Peoples Congress), the first national Latino civil rights assembly.

Born Blanca Rosa Rodríguez López in Guatemala City, Moreno had a most unlikely childhood for a labor activist. One of four children, she grew up surrounded by wealth in her native country. Her mother, Alicia López Sarana, was a prominent socialite married to Ernesto Rodríguez Robles, a powerful coffee planter. At the age of nine, she attended school at the Convent of the Holy Names in Oakland, California.

Returning home, Luisa desired a university education but soon discovered that women were barred. She organized her elite peers into Sociedad Gabriela Mistral to push for greater educational opportunities for women. But with success in sight, she ran away to Mexico City. The young Latina flapper supported herself as a journalist as she consorted with the likes of Diego Rivera. In 1927 she published a volume of verse, *El Vendedor de Cocuyos (Seller of Fireflies).*

In this heady atmosphere, she married Guatemalan artist Miguel Angel de León, a man sixteen years her senior. They wed on November 27, 1927, and on August 28, 1928, they arrived in New York City. By the time their daughter, Mytyl Lorraine, was born that November, they were living in a crowded tenement in Spanish Harlem. Moreno found herself laboring over a sewing machine. In 1930 she joined the Communist Party and soon began to mobilize her peers on the shop floor into La Liga de Costureras. At a time when only a few male unions had "ladies auxiliaries," Moreno organized a male auxiliary charged with the task of fund-raising.

Leaving an abusive husband and the Communist Party, Moreno in 1935 was hired by the American Federation of Labor (AFL) to work with cigar rollers in Florida. Her superiors believed the Ku Klux Klan would think twice before harming a woman organizer. Her fair complexion also afforded her added protection. Slender and only four foot ten, Moreno possessed a delicate beauty, which belied her steely determination. Her organizing days in Florida signaled the birth of "Luisa Moreno." Deliberately distancing herself from her past, she chose the alias "Moreno," a name diametrically opposite her given name Blanca Rosa. At this time Luisa decided to board her daughter with a pro-labor family. From the time she was seven until almost thirteen, Mytyl lived with informal foster families; some treated her well, others abused her.

Although Moreno negotiated a solid contract covering thirteen thousand cigar workers, she clashed with AFL officials. In 1938 she joined the fledgling UCAPAWA, a CIO-affiliated union dedicated to grassroots leadership and to organizing across race and gender. Her first task was to take charge of the pecan shellers' strike in San Antonio, Texas, where the secretary of the Texas Communist Party, EMMA TENAYUCA, had emerged as the fiery local leader. Moreno was sent to help move the affiliate from street demonstrations to a functioning trade union. She organized the strikers into a disciplined force that employers could no longer ignore, and management agreed to arbitration.

El Congreso de Pueblos de Habla Española was the first national civil rights assembly for Latinos in the United States. More than a thousand delegates assembled in Los Angeles on April 28–30, 1939. With the help of local activists such as JOSEFINA FIERRO, Moreno drew upon her contacts with labor unions, mutual aid societies, and other community groups. Delegates drafted a comprehensive platform, calling for an end to segregation in public facilities, housing, education, and employment.

In 1940 Moreno briefly accepted a desk job with the union in Washington, D.C., in order to reunite with her daughter, now almost a teenager. By 1941, however, she had taken a new assignment—to consolidate organizing among southern California cannery workers in Local 75, many of whom were Mexican and Jewish women. Moreno, as the newly elected union vice president, threw herself into this task, earning the nickname "The California Whirlwind." Capitalizing on the gendered networks on the shop floor, Moreno harvested unparalleled success as cannery workers under the UCAPAWA banner significantly improved their working conditions, wages, and benefits. Moreno encouraged women's leadership. In 1943, for example, Mexican women filled eight of the fifteen elected positions of the local. The local also provided benefits that few industrial unions could match—free legal advice and a hospitalization plan.

Moreno rose in the ranks of the California CIO, becoming the first Latina to serve on a state CIO Council. This professional success, however, masked personal turmoil. In 1941 Moreno married dry cleaner Jacob Shaffer, but Mytyl refused to accept him. The marriage lasted less than three months. Mytyl continued to be a rebellious teen, eloping at sixteen with Edward Glomboske, a returning veteran.

Moreno's greatest professional challenge would begin in August 1945 as the union launched a campaign among northern California cannery workers. A year earlier UCAPAWA had changed its name to the Food, Tobacco, Agricultural, and Allied Workers of America (FTA). Directing an ambitious drive, Moreno and the union won a National Labor Relations Board (NLRB) election covering seventy-two plants. In February 1946, however, the NLRB rescinded the results. The rival Teamsters immediately began a campaign of sweetheart contracts, rampant red-baiting, and physical assaults. The FTA lost by less than two thousand votes in the second tabulation. This defeat marked the beginning of the end for FTA.

In 1947 Luisa Moreno retired and married Gray Bemis, a union colleague she first met in New York. A year later, she faced deportation proceedings for her radical past. Accompanied by her husband, she left the United States in 1950 under terms listed as "voluntary departure under warrant of deportation" on the grounds that she had once belonged to the Communist Party. She died in her native Guatemala on November 4, 1992, at the age of eighty-five.

Bibliography: The Southern California Library for Social Studies & Research in Los Angeles contains the most expansive primary materials on Luisa Moreno, including a small Luisa Moreno collection, the Mytyl Glomboske papers, and the Robert Kenny collection (Kenny was Moreno's close friend and attorney). These collections contain a number of photographs of Moreno, particularly in her youth. Her only publication in English was the text of a speech, "Caravans of Sorrow," that she delivered to the 1940 conference of the American Committee for the Protection of the Foreign Born, a document reprinted in David Gutiérrez, *Between Two Worlds: Mexican Immigrants in the United States* (1996). For more biographical information, see Vicki L. Ruiz, "Una Mujer Sin Fronteras: Luisa Moreno and Latina Labor Activism," in Ruiz and Virginia Sánchez Korrol, eds., *Latina Legacies* (2004); Ruiz, *From Out of the Shadows: Mexican Women in Twentieth Century America* (1998); and Albert Camarillo, *Chicanos in California* (1984). This essay draws on interviews with Luisa Moreno conducted by Camarillo and Ruiz between 1976 until 1985 and by Ruiz with her daughter Mytyl in 2001.

VICKI L. RUIZ

MORRISSY, Elizabeth. March 2, 1887–April 16, 1981. Economist, Catholic educator and activist.

Elizabeth Morrissy was born in Elkhorn, Wisconsin, the fourth of six children of John Morrissey and Elizabeth O'Connor. Both parents were of Irish Catholic heritage and were raised in Wisconsin. Soon after Elizabeth's birth, the family surname was changed from Morrissey to Morrissy. Christened Lilian Elizabeth, she was known after 1908 simply as Elizabeth. Her mother died in 1889, her father remarried, and two more children were born. John Morrissy's blacksmith business provided a middle-class living standard for the large family.

In 1904 Morrissy graduated from Elkhorn High School. She attended Beloit College in Beloit, Wisconsin, on a scholarship, majoring in history and earning her BA degree, graduating Phi Beta Kappa in 1908. For the next twelve years she taught history in public high schools in Michigan, Idaho, and Iowa. Morrissy wanted to pursue a graduate degree, and to this end had taken courses at the University of Wisconsin in the summer of 1916. But the need to earn her living slowed her progress toward that goal.

The year 1920 proved to be a turning point in her life. A wage dispute prompted her to resign from her Iowa teaching position and move to Baltimore, Maryland. There she enrolled in the PhD program in political economy at Johns Hopkins University, and, with the help of a university administrator, secured a full-time teaching position at the College of Notre Dame of Maryland, a neighboring Roman Catholic women's institution. The School Sisters of Notre Dame, who conducted the college, provided Morrissy with campus housing, a convenient teaching schedule, and transportation to and from her Johns Hopkins classes. With this unusual support, Morrissy earned her MA in 1922 and her PhD in 1930. She was one of the first women to receive a PhD in economics from Johns Hopkins University. Her master's essay, "Graft in the Building Trades," and her doctoral thesis, "Unemployment Insurance in American Trade Unions," concentrated on labor issues, an interest that continued throughout her life. She never married.

At the College of Notre Dame and also at Johns Hopkins, Saint Louis, and Catholic Universities where she taught summer courses over the years, Morrissy gained the respect and affection of faculty colleagues and students alike. A brilliant teacher, she impressed upon her students that educated women had an obligation to assume leadership roles in the public sector as well as in business and the professions. Her own career, which combined teaching and public service, offered them a compelling role model.

The pervasive social distress of the 1930s drew Morrissy into the public sector. A loyal Democrat, she assisted in the development of New Deal programs in the areas of employment, labor rights, and social security. Her federal appointments in the 1930s and 1940s included membership on the National Advisory Council on Economic Security, the National Advisory Council of the National Youth Administration, the Consumers' Advisory Council, and the Board of the National Association of Consumers. In addition, Morrissy widened her influence as an educator by participating in various forums for adults, including lecture series, civic study groups, social action conferences, radio programs, and labor institutes.

Morrissy's public service also extended to the level of local government. During her tenure on the Baltimore City Board of School Commissioners (1948–60), she was prominent in the battle for racial integration of Baltimore public schools. The cause of racial equality also consumed her at Notre Dame, where, as a member of the college's advisory board, she campaigned hard for the college to admit African American students, an objective that was finally achieved in 1951.

A dedicated Roman Catholic, Elizabeth Morrissy worked ceaselessly and effectively to raise the social consciousness of the large American Catholic community. In an era when few women played public leadership roles within the church, she became a distinguished exception. From the 1930s through the 1950s she held key offices in many important church organizations, including the National Council of Catholic Women, the Catholic Conference on Industrial Problems of the National Catholic Welfare Conference, the Catholic Association for International Peace, and the National Conference of Christians and Jews. In 1955 she received the Medal of the Cross of Honor *Pro Ecclesia et Pontifice,* a papal decoration awarded for outstanding service to church and society.

Morrissy pressed Catholic women in particular to honor in action the social teachings of their church as found in the papal encyclicals, *Rerum Novarum* (1891) and *Quadrigesimo Anno* (1931). In a powerful address before the 1948 convention of the National Conference of Catholic Women, she boldly challenged the traditional Catholic view that woman's place was in the home. According to Morrissy, all women, whether mothers or not, are called to social motherhood, or "service to humanity." She called upon the many middle- and upper-class homemakers who were wasting their leisure time in selfish pursuits to enter the public sector to fight for legislative reform in the areas of housing, public education, and social services. Although this "radical" message dismayed church conservatives, Catholic laywomen greeted it enthusiastically.

In 1964 Elizabeth Morrissy retired from the College of Notre Dame as professor *emerita* after forty-four years of teaching. She died of cardiac arrest in April 1981 at the age of ninety-four in St. Joseph's Nursing Home, Catonsville, Maryland. Her body was cremated and her ashes were interred in the Sisters' Cemetery at the College of Notre Dame of Maryland.

Bibliography: A substantial collection of primary and secondary materials on Elizabeth Morrissy, including a 1973 oral interview and excellent photographs, may be found in the archives of the College of Notre Dame of Maryland. Family-held letters, papers, and interviews form the basis for a brief, privately printed tribute by Alice E. H. Ayres, *Character, Decency, and Joy: The Life of Elizabeth Morrissy* (1998), but this source should be used with caution. Most of Morrissy's publications appeared in the form of pamphlets and reprinted speeches. Among them are *What Laws Must We Have?* (1937); "The Status of Women: 'To Be Equal Does Not Mean to Be Identical,'" *Vital Speeches of the Day,* November 1, 1948, pp. 55–60; "God's Will in Society," *Catholic Action* 34, no. 10 (October 1952), pp. 4–7; and "Social Action's Challenge to Women," *Catholic Action* 32, no. 5 (May 1950), pp. 13–14. An essay, "Current Changes and Post-War Teaching," appears as a chapter in *Fifty Golden Years: A Series of Lectures on the Liberal Arts College* (1946), edited by the College of Notre Dame of Maryland. Morrissy's obituary appeared in the *Baltimore Sun* on April 18, 1981.

MARY J. OATES

MORTON, Nelle Katharine. January 7, 1905–July 14, 1987. Christian educator, feminist theologian.

Nelle Katharine Morton was born in a logging camp cabin on Holston Mountain in Sullivan County, Tennessee. She was the eldest of three daughters of Jonathan Morrell Morton, a bookkeeper and merchant, and Mary Katherine Mol "Kate" O'Dell, a housewife. When she was four, the family moved from the logging camp to her mother's home near Bluff City, Tennessee, and lived there until she was twelve. This farm, which had been in her mother's family for five generations, provided a sense of stability and continuity for the family. Then the family moved to Kingsport, Tennessee, where she graduated from Dobyns-Bennett High School. Late in her life, Morton described her family's circumstances as poor, yet with enough shelter, clothing, and food so that she had not felt poor.

In 1925 Morton graduated with a BA in art from Flora Macdonald College for Women in Red Springs, North Carolina. Following graduation, she began to teach art at Kingsport's Jackson Elementary School. A religious woman, Morton's college dream was of doing Christian missionary work in Africa. Her dream led her to attend the Presbyterian School of Christian Education (1926–27) in Richmond, Virginia, but she found the program to be too pious and theologically constrictive. After a year of studies, she returned home to teach in Kingsport.

In 1929, she left Tennessee for New York City, where she attended the Biblical Seminary of New York. After completing her master's in religious education in 1931, she began her professional career as a religious educator in Brooklyn, with the Plymouth Congregational Church, but was fired for speaking out against racism. She then moved to the First Presbyterian Church in Stanton, Virginia. Following this she was employed by the Presbyterian Church U.S. (South) Board of Education in Richmond, Virginia, as its assistant director of youth work.

During these years she developed curricula for anti-racism work among high school and college students, focusing much of her work toward instigating social change within the southern church. She became a member of the Fellowship of Southern Churchmen (FSC), a radical, interdenominational organization with a mission of promoting civil rights and full integration for the South's black citizens. In 1944, she became the general secretary of the FSC, a position she held until December 1949. She guided the FSC in all of its integration activities and edited its journal, *Prophetic Religion.*

Finding that she had breast cancer in 1948 created a personal crisis of awareness, causing her to sink her roots deeper into family and friends. Less than a half year after her mastectomy, she resigned her leadership position with the Fellowship of Southern Churchmen and returned home to her family's farm in Tennessee to live with her aging widowed father. She lived in Tennessee until 1956, financially supporting herself by doing freelance writing for Protestant church publications. Her early books (*Living Together as Christians,* 1952; *My Camp Book,* 1952; *Making Our Group Christian,* 1953; *The Church We Cannot See,* 1953; and *The Bible and Its Use,* 1955) were all published during these years. She also continued to work with the FSC by running integrated summer camps for children on the farm.

The second phase of her life's work began at this time when she started teaching mentally retarded children in Bristol, a city on the Tennessee-Virginia border. Recognizing that traditional ways of working with retarded children were not effective, she began to experiment with her own ways of reaching them. She became so successful that both states asked her to teach other teachers about her methods.

Vigorously recruited by the Theological School of Drew University for an open position in religious education, she joined its faculty in 1956, where she taught until 1971. These faculty years overlapped the early moments of the second wave of the feminist movement. While at Drew, Morton read feminist literature and became friends with Mary Daly, a young feminist philosopher and theologian. In their discussions, they developed an awareness that the word *God,* in theological discourse, could not be encompassed as a noun but rather needed to be represented as a verb manifested in the actions of being and doing.

During a 1962–63 sabbatical, Morton traveled to the University of Geneva in Switzerland, where she studied with child development specialist Jean Piaget. Much of her later academic work on the topic of language, metaphor, image, and symbol in God-talk drew on insights she gained from her work with retarded children and from this later time of intensive study.

In 1968, Morton's "Equipping the Laity: Women, Theology and Language" was one of the first specifically feminist theology courses taught in the United States. Following her retirement from Drew, Morton lectured about feminist theology in many theological schools. During these years she befriended and mentored many young feminist scholars in religion, biblical studies, and theology, but sternly rejected their attempts to name her as the foremother or mother of feminist theology, saying, "I am not a mother; I am not your mother; I am your sister."

While in retirement at Pilgrim Place in Claremont, California, Morton wrote her last book, *The Journey Is Home* (1985). In this book she documented ten years (1970–80) of scholarship in feminist spirituality and feminist theology. Specifically, she documented her personal encounters with the Goddess. About the moment of her own awakening to experiencing God as SHE, Morton writes, "this is the first time I experienced a female deity. I had conceptualized one before but I had not experienced one directly. . . . Not until that moment did I realize that women had no cosmic advocate in any of the five major patriarchal religions of the world" (p. 157).

Throughout her life Morton formed and cultivated intense personal friendships with men and women. She never married. Her friends described Morton's personal style as having a confrontational edge. She did not tolerate the continuing presence of racism, heterosexism, ageism, or sexism in any of her enduring personal relationships.

During the last years of her life, Morton was diagnosed with sideroblastic anemia. She died of complications following surgery in Pomona, California, on July 14, 1987, at the age of eighty-two. She was cremated, and her ashes were taken to her ancestral burial grounds in Shipley Cemetery, Bluff City, Tennessee.

Bibliography: Archival material is found in the Nelle Morton Archives at the Presbyterian Historical Center in Montreat, North Carolina, which has an oral history done in 1984 by Tina Blair. There is additional material in the Fellowship of Southern Churchmen Records, which contain an oral history done on June 25, 1983, by Dallas Blanchard and which are part of the Southern Historical Collection, University of North Carolina at Chapel Hill. In addition to the books mentioned in the text, Morton authored numerous articles in various religious magazines and feminist journals. See also the Lumiere/Presbyterian Church USA documentary video, *The Journey Is Home: A Film about Nelle Morton* (1988). Articles that treat Morton's life and work include Elizabeth Francis Caldwell, "Nelle Morton: A Radical Journey," in Barbara Ann Keely, ed., *Faith of Our Foremothers: Women Reshaping Religious Education* (1997); Don Donohue, "Prophets of a New Social Order: Presbyterians and the Fellowship of Southern Churchmen, 1934–1963," *Presbyterian Survey* 74 (Fall 1996), pp. 209–21; and Catherine Keller, "Goddess, Ear and Metaphor: On the Journey of Nelle Morton," *Journal of Feminist Studies in Religion* 4 (Fall 1988), pp. 51–57. Tributes include Carter Heyward, "Nelle Morton Journeys Home," *Christianity and Crisis*, September 14, 1987, p. 276; and Betty Thompson, "Nelle Morton: Journeying Home," *Christian Century*, August 26–September 4, 1987, pp. 711–12. An obituary appeared in the *Claremont Courier* on July 18, 1987.

RUTH E. KRALL

MUDD, Emily Hartshorne. September 6, 1898–May 2, 1998. Marriage counselor, family planning advocate.

Emily Hartshorne Mudd was a pioneering marriage counselor, family planning advocate, researcher, and educator, and a significant collaborator and consultant for Alfred C. Kinsey's sexuality research. She was born Emily Borie Hartshorne in Merion, Pennsylvania, the second of the four surviving children of Clementina Rhodes and Edward Yarnell Hartshorne. Her Quaker-raised father had wanted to be a doctor, but he followed his father into employment with the Lehigh Valley Railroad as a purchasing agent and later became a banker. Both parents were active in civic community work. Emily often recalled feeling horror at learning that her maternal grandmother had borne thirteen children, of whom only eight survived, and that, of her own suffragist mother's children, the first was born spastic and another had died in infancy.

Educated in private schools, she entered Vassar College in 1917, but her college days were shortened by her wartime volunteer work and the typhoid fever she contracted while working as a "farmerette" with Vassar's unit of the Woman's Land Army. Instead of returning to college, she spent several years studying at Lowthorpe School of Landscape Architecture in Groton, Massachusetts, earning a degree in 1922. She met her future husband, Harvard-educated microbiologist Stuart Mudd, in Boston; they were married in Bryn Mawr, Pennsylvania, on September 12, 1922. After living briefly in New York City, the couple moved to the Philadelphia area, settling in Haverford. Their first child, Emily Borie, was born in 1923, followed by Stuart Harvey in 1927, Margaret Clark in 1930, and John Hogden in 1939.

Stuart Mudd was an admirer and defender of birth control activist MARGARET SANGER, and a friend of millionaire international birth control advocate Clarence J. Gamble. Emily Mudd shared her husband's interests in both medicine and birth control, and she became his unpaid research assistant, co-authoring fourteen articles on the microbiology of spermatozoa and spermatoxins, first at Harvard, later at Rockefeller Institute in New York (with grant money from Margaret Sanger), and then at Henry Phipps Institute in Philadelphia. Stuart Mudd later joined the faculty of the medical school at the University of Pennsylvania, eventually chairing its department of microbiology for seventeen years.

In 1927, the Mudds helped found the Maternal Health Center, a birth control clinic just outside Philadelphia. Five years of client work and volunteer counseling convinced Mudd that failed contraceptive negotiations, patriarchal erotic dynamics, and relationship conflicts underlay unwanted and unplanned pregnancy. She reasoned that sound relationship counseling might address those conflicts and might prevent family planning problems. In 1933 Mudd became a founding director of the Marriage Counsel (after 1947, Marriage Council) of Pennsylvania, one of only three such marriage counseling centers in the United States at the time. In 1936 she earned an MSW from the University of Pennsylvania and became executive director of the organization. For the next three decades, until her retirement in 1967, she worked with its large, predominantly female clientele as a counselor, researcher, and administrator.

Her casework research and a prolific body of publications on men, women, and relationship conflicts during the Depression and World War II years brought her to the attention of clinicians and researchers, such as pioneer gynecologist Robert Latou Dickinson, mentor of Indiana University zoology professor Alfred C. Kinsey's human sexual behavior research. Dickinson introduced Mudd and Kinsey in 1944, resulting in a unique collaboration where Kinsey and his research team spent several months in Philadelphia, interviewing Mudd's clients and numerous contacts in the medical and other professional communities. Kinsey asked Mudd to join his research team, and she worked as an editorial consultant on both the "Kinsey Reports"—*Sexual Behavior in the Human Male* (1948) and *Sexual Behavior in the Human Female* (1953). She often referred to their collaboration as a highlight of her career. Yet she also presented him with a grave methodological challenge: namely, that two partners in any given sexual relationship or incident would give different accounts, especially of coital frequency and duration, a problem that could be redressed only through paired reporting and careful, contextual analysis. She believed that Kinsey eventually accepted her point, however reluctantly, despite its devastating implications for some of his previous findings, which were based on the account of one partner, not both partners. Their joint plan for a successor volume on sexual adjustment in marriage was ended by his premature death in 1956.

Awarded her PhD in sociology from the University of Pennsylvania in 1950, Mudd was appointed assistant professor in psychiatry there. Soon after, the Marriage Council affiliated with the University of Pennsylvania Medical School. When she came up for tenure six years later, she was promoted simultaneously to full professor, becoming the first woman at this rank in the school's history. Her sole- and co-authored books and edited anthologies included *The Practice of Marriage Counseling: An Experience Study and Guide for Teachers, Leaders and Counselors* (1951); *Man and Wife: A Sourcebook of Family Attitudes, Sexual Behavior, and Marriage Counseling* (1957); and *Success in Family Living* (1965).

Emily Mudd spent an active retirement. She was a founding emerita women's studies faculty member, a critical feminist reviewer of the Masters and Johnson dual-sex therapy training methods and operations, co-chair of the contentious Pennsylvania Abortion Law Commission in 1972, and director of a university hospital clinic for pregnant African American teenagers and their younger sisters. She and her husband also traveled widely as tireless international birth control volunteers for Clarence J. Gamble's Pathfinder Fund, which promoted family planning services throughout the world, especially in developing countries. Widowed in 1975, Mudd married book publisher Frederick Gloeckner in 1980 and continued to provide private counseling until she was in her eighties. Regarded as a giant in the field she helped create, she was also an avid and creative landscape gardener. She died at her home in Haverford, Pennsylvania, on May 2, 1998, just months shy of her one hundredth birthday.

Bibliography: The Emily Borie Hartshorne Mudd Papers are held at the Schlesinger Library, Radcliffe Institute for Advanced Study, Harvard University. Interviews with Mudd from May 21, 1974, and August 3, 1974, are part of the Family Planning Oral History Project at the Schlesinger Library. For additional biographical information, see *Current Biography* (1956), pp. 453–55. In addition to the books mentioned in the text, Mudd's publications include "The Historical Background and Ethical Considerations in Sex Research and Therapy," in William H. Masters, Virginia E. Johnson, and Robert C. Kolodny, eds., *Ethical Issues in Sex Therapy and Research* (1977). For an example of her methodological critique of Kinsey, see Emily Mudd, Marvin Stein, and Howard E. Mitchell, "Paired Reports of Sexual Behavior of Husbands and Wives in Conflicted Marriages," *Comprehensive Psychiatry* 2, no. 3 (1961), pp. 149–56. An obituary appeared in the *New York Times* on May 6, 1998.

JUDITH ALISON ALLEN

MURRAY, Anna Pauline (Pauli). November 20, 1910–July 1, 1985. Writer, human rights activist, lawyer, priest.

The caption accompanying a stern-faced portrait of Anna Pauline Murray in the 1926 Hillside High School Yearbook reads: "The best I can do to help others is to be the best I can myself." This prophetic inscription, penned when she was only fifteen, aptly characterizes a life of personal achievement and social activism that spanned the better part of the twentieth century. From a childhood marked by the sudden death of her mother in 1914, the murder of her father nine years later in a mental hospital, and the embrace of a proud circle of elder kin, Murray inherited an abiding compassion for the helpless, an unyielding commitment to social justice, and a lifelong hunger for knowledge. Her writings, her labor and civil rights work in the 1930s and 1940s, and her advocacy for gender justice in education, employment, and religious life helped lay the foundation for the contemporary American civil rights and feminist movements.

Murray was born in Baltimore, the fourth of six children of Agnes Georgiana Fitzgerald, a nurse trained at Hampton Institute, and William Henry Murray, a teacher educated at the Howard University College Preparatory Department. After her mother's death when she was three, she went to live in Durham, North Carolina, with her maternal grandparents, Robert and Cornelia Fitzgerald, and her mother's oldest sister, Pauline Fitzgerald Dame. Grandmother Cornelia was the daughter of Sidney Smith, a lawyer from a prominent white North Carolina family, and a part-Cherokee slave named Harriet owned by the Smiths. Grandfather Robert was a teacher, as was Aunt Pauline, who became Murray's adoptive mother. In this aunt's classroom Murray began school as an underage onlooker.

Murray was a bright and strong-willed girl whose willingness to challenge the status quo was evident early. An honors graduate, president of the literary society and editor of the yearbook, she declined a scholarship to highly regarded, historically black Wilberforce College. Murray's opposition to racially segregated schooling, along with financial constraints, led her to Hunter College—a public, tuition-free school for women in New York City. To satisfy the college's academic and residency requirements, Murray moved in with relatives in Queens so that she could attend Richmond Hill High, from which she earned her second diploma with honors in 1927.

Murray worked for a year before entering Hunter in 1928. There she concentrated in English and history, was invited to membership in Sigma Tau Delta (a national English fraternity), and joined the journalism and international student clubs. She also took Pauli as her official first name. Because Murray worked her way through school, she was often exhausted and ill. Her academic performance suffered, and she left school to work full-time after her sophomore year. She married William Roy Wynn in 1930, but this brief relationship was later annulled. Returning to college, she graduated with a BA in 1933. She never had children.

Murray's first professional job after Hunter was as a field representative for *Opportunity* magazine, the official publication of the National Urban League. From 1935 to 1939, she worked for the Works Progress Administration (WPA)—initially as a remedial reading teacher, then with the Workers' Education Project. During her tenure with the WPA, she was introduced by labor and civil rights activists to a philosophy of human rights that linked racial and economic oppression in the United States with the persecution of Jews in Germany and the repression of African and Asian peoples by European colonial powers. This philosophy became part of a personal worldview to which Murray later added the subjugation of women.

In 1938, Murray was denied admission to the graduate school of the University of North Carolina (UNC) at Chapel Hill on racial grounds. The injustice of the university's decision was compounded by the fact that her black relatives paid state taxes that subsidized the school, and her white ancestors, the Smiths, were among its generous benefactors. Although Murray did not have the resources to challenge UNC in court, she garnered the support and attention of several people who became advisers and lifelong friends. Among these were ELEANOR ROOSEVELT; Thurgood Marshall, NAACP counsel and future associate justice of the U.S. Supreme Court; William Hastie, Howard University Law School dean and future federal judge; and Leon A. Ransom, Howard University law professor and member of the NAACP legal brain trust.

Murray's relationships with Marshall, Hastie, and Ransom proved timely, for she had long dreamed of becoming a lawyer. Not until two events in 1940, however, was the course set to realize this goal. The first was her arrest in Petersburg, Virginia, for disorderly conduct and violation of a state statute requiring segregation in public transportation. During a Greyhound bus trip to Durham, Murray and a friend, Adelene McBean, were directed by the driver to move to a rear seat. They complied, but their reluctance and questioning attitude provoked an arrest and incarceration. Despite the efforts of a superb defense team, Murray and McBean were found guilty of disorderly conduct. In a tactical move, the prosecution dropped the segregation violation charge.

The second event to move Murray toward a career in law was her assignment as the Workers Defense League's field secretary for the Odell Waller campaign. Waller was a twenty-three-year-old black sharecropper who was convicted by an all-white jury of first-degree murder in the shooting death of his white landlord. Waller never denied shooting his landlord, but he believed, as did Murray, that he had acted in self-defense. The two-year appeal that ended in Waller's execution brought Murray into a national debate about the interconnection of race, poverty, and judicial fairness. It also brought her to a close friendship with Eleanor Roosevelt, who waged an eleventh-hour battle on Waller's behalf inside the White House.

With recommendations from Thurgood Marshall and Leon Ransom, Murray was admitted to Howard University Law School on a tuition scholarship in the fall of 1941. Over the next three years, she set precedents in and out of the classroom. The only woman enrolled during most of her time there, she was class president and graduated with the highest overall grade average. She also served as legal adviser and co-organizer for two student-led boycotts of Jim Crow restaurants in Washington, D.C. In this capacity, she devised training procedures and field strategies that were adapted by civil rights activists in the 1960s.

In 1944 Murray received a Rosenwald Fellowship and applied to Harvard Law School for graduate study. The arrival of a letter indicating that she was "not of the sex entitled to be admitted," along with the slights she had endured as a female student at Howard, convinced her that the struggle for civil rights had multiple fronts. Racial discrimination and "Jane Crow" (Murray's term for sex prejudice) were insidiously similar. And most women of color, she argued, faced both. Murray launched a letter-writing campaign, hoping to persuade Harvard officials to reverse their decision. Even President Roosevelt, at the First Lady's urging, sent an inquiry to the school's president, but Harvard refused to change its admissions policy.

Murray subsequently entered Boalt Hall School of Law at the University of California at Berkeley in the fall of 1944. Concentrating in labor studies, she earned a Master of Law degree a year later. When her thesis, "The Right to Equal Opportunity in Employment," appeared in the *California Law Review* (1945), it was one of the earliest to address women's employment rights.

After a brief appointment as a deputy attorney general for the state of California, Murray returned to New York City, where a fierce bias against women attorneys made it virtually impossible for her to secure a job in a law firm. She clerked for male attorneys until the experience of being overworked, humiliated, and unfairly undercompensated inspired her to open her own law practice in 1949. Seven years later Murray was recommended by a friend, Lloyd K. Garrison, great-grandson of abolitionist William Lloyd Garrison, for a position as an associate with the prestigious firm of Paul, Weiss, Rifkind, Wharton, and Garrison in New York City. She became the only black attorney, and one of only three women attorneys, in the firm.

The practice of law was never completely satisfying or financially profitable for her, and in 1960 Murray left to teach at the newly established Ghana Law School in Accra, where she developed a course on constitutional law. She also coauthored a textbook on African law, *The Constitution and Government of Ghana* (1961), with Leslie Rubin. Prompted by political unrest and an invitation to pursue a doctorate in law at Yale University, Murray returned to the States after only a year. She completed her dissertation, "Roots of the Racial Crisis: Prologue to Policy," in 1965 and was awarded the Doctor of Judicial Science degree.

Murray's advocacy for women's rights intensified over the next two decades. She served on the Committee on Civil and Political Rights of the President's Commission on the Status of Women that was chaired by Eleanor Roosevelt until her death. Murray drafted the pivotal "Memorandum in Support of Retaining the Amendment to H.R. 7152 to Prohibit Discrimination in Employment Because of Sex," which was distributed to key senators when the Civil Rights Act of 1964 was under consideration. With Betty Friedan and others, she was also a founder of the National Organization for Women in 1966.

After Yale and a stint as consultant to the Equal Employment Opportunity Commission, Murray entered higher education and held posts at Benedict College (1967–68) and Brandeis University (1968–73). The course of her teaching career was altered, however, by an irrepressible call to the ministry and the death in 1973 of her intimate friend, Irene Barlow. Murray resigned her tenured position as Louis Stulberg Professor of Law and Politics at Brandeis and enrolled at General Theological Seminary in New York City. She earned the Master of Divinity degree with honors in 1976. The following year she became the first black woman to be ordained as a priest in the history of the Episcopal Church. After serving congregants in Baltimore, Washington, D.C., and Pittsburgh, she retired in 1983. She died of cancer in Pittsburgh in 1985 at the age of seventy-four.

Writing was Murray's deepest passion, but this creative yearning was often frustrated by economic hardship, poor health, family obligations, and an irresistible inclination toward activism. Nevertheless, she produced a substantial body of work, including a collection of poetry, *Dark Testament and Other Poems* (1970); a family memoir, *Proud Shoes: The Story of An American Family* (1956); and an award-winning, posthumously published autobiography, *Song in a Weary Throat: An American Pilgrimage* (1987). Less well known are Murray's political essays, sermons, and legal works, such as *States' Laws on Race and Color* (1951), a compilation that Thurgood Marshall referred to as the bible for civil rights attorneys.

Because Murray was a brilliant woman who often took an uncompromising stance and was temperamentally a loner, she did not function well in groups. For this reason, her contributions to civil rights in the 1940s are often overlooked by scholars who have focused on the movement's organizational leadership, the majority of whom were men. Feminist scholars acknowledge Murray's pioneering work as a theoretician and activist, yet the importance of her early emphasis on the intersection of race, class, and gender deserves greater attention. Murray's deepest emotional attachments were to women, yet her autobiographical writings skirt this issue. Given the milieu of black middle-class respectability in which she was reared and the social-historical context in which she functioned, it is not surprising that her passion is revealed primarily in her poetry and private writings.

Pauli Murray is without question one of the most important figures in the history of twentieth-century America. The scope of her influence, which crosses the literary, political, and religious landscapes, is all the more remarkable given the lack of resources and barriers she faced throughout her life.

Bibliography: Pauli Murray's appreciation of history is evident in the voluminous collection of materials she assembled and bequeathed to the Schlesinger Library, Radcliffe Institute for Advanced Study, Harvard University. This wide-ranging collection of papers, interviews, photographs, and audiovisual recordings documents Murray's multiple careers, personal life (although she purged a portion of these materials), health concerns, as well as a lifelong correspondence with friends, family, and political figures. Interviews and related papers are also housed in the

Southern Historical Collection at the University of North Carolina, Chapel Hill; the Eleanor Roosevelt Papers at the Franklin D. Roosevelt Presidential Library in Hyde Park, New York; and the Moorland-Spingarn Research Center at Howard University.

No critical biography of Murray has been published, and her family memoir and autobiography (which was reissued as *Pauli Murray: The Autobiography of a Black Activist, Feminist, Lawyer, Priest, and Poet* in 1989) remain the best treatments of her life. She is the subject of several biographies in-process and a growing body of scholarship linked to various aspects of her life. Notable works include Jean M. Humez, "Pauli Murray's Histories of Loyalty and Revolt," *Black American Literature Forum* 24, no. 2 (Summer 1990), pp. 315–35; Darlene O'Dell, *Sites of Southern Memory: The Autobiographies of Katharine Du Pre Lumpkin, Lillian Smith, and Pauli Murray* (2001); and a compendium of essays edited by Susan Ware, "Pauli Murray's Notable Connections," *Journal of Women's History* 14, no. 2 (Summer 2002), pp. 54–87. An expanding list of PhD dissertations includes Flora Renda Bryant, "An Examination of the Social Activism of Pauli Murray" (University of South Carolina, 1991); Regina E. Mooney, "Transgression as Transformation: An Investigation into the Relationship between Mystically Religious Experience and Moral Experience in the Lives of Dorothy Day and Pauli Murray" (Claremont Graduate University, 1992); Doreen Marie Drury, "'Experimentation on the Male Side': Race, Class, Gender, and Sexuality in Pauli Murray's Quest for Love and Identity" (Boston College, 2000); and Elaine Sue Caldbeck, "A Religious Life of Pauli Murray: Hope and Struggle" (Northwestern University, 2000). Obituaries appear in the *New York Times* and the *Washington Post* on July 4, 1985, and in *Jet* on July 28, 1985, p. 51.

PATRICIA BELL-SCOTT

MURRAY, Madalyn Mays. *See* O'Hair, Madalyn Mays Murray.

MUSKRAT, Ruth. *See* Bronson, Ruth Muskrat.

N

NASH, Ruth Cowan. *See* Cowan, Ruth Baldwin.

NAUMBURG, Margaret Jeannette. May 14, 1890–February 26, 1983. Progressive educator, art therapist.

Margaret Naumburg made major contributions to two fields: she founded Walden School, a progressive educational institution for students from preschool through high school, and then went on to become a founder of art therapy in the United States. Her work in both areas was built on psychoanalytical principles.

Margaret Jeannette Naumburg was born into an upper-middle-class family in New York City, the third of four children and youngest daughter of Therese R. Kahnweiler and Max Naumburg. Her father, a German Jewish clothing merchant, emigrated from Bavaria as a child. Her mother was born in Wilmington, North Carolina. Margaret attended P.S. 87, the Horace Mann School, and the Sachs School. She matriculated at Vassar College in 1908 but transferred to Barnard College at the end of the year. There she majored in philosophy and economics, studied with John Dewey, and was elected president of the Socialist Club.

Following her 1912 graduation from Barnard, Naumburg enrolled at the London School of Economics. In the spring of 1913 she joined the first English-language training course conducted by Maria Montessori in Italy. After receiving her diploma, she returned to New York to open a Montessori class at the Henry Street Settlement (1913–14). She underwent analysis with Jungian analyst Beatrice Hinkle, a very bold move for an educated woman of her time. Naumburg later underwent a second analysis with Freudian A. A. Brill, the parent of a Walden School student, whose work she had read earlier in her career.

In 1914 Naumburg began a modified Montessori class at the Leete School with her friend Claire Raphael. This was the beginning of the Children's School, where the philosophy and practices were based on psychoanalytic theory. At Naumburg's request, art director Florence Cane and many of the teachers underwent analysis as a means of better understanding themselves and their students. Naumburg planned a program that gave affective development parity with cognitive development. The curriculum was designed to evolve from the needs of the children and emphasized the importance of the environment and self-education. Materials were easily accessible to the children at all times.

During the summer of 1914, Naumburg studied "organic education" with Marietta Johnson in Fairhope, Alabama. She also studied the Jaques-

Dalcroze Method of Rhythmic Gymnastics (called Eurhythmics). Influenced by teachers and theorists such as F. Matthias Alexander, Alys Bentley, and Dr. Yorke Trotter, she incorporated their major tenets into the program. She found specific correlations between physical coordination and analytic psychology in their belief that the adult must find the deeper cause for a child's physical or mental problems and assist the child in the reeducation process. From 1914 to 1916 she did postgraduate work at Columbia University.

Naumburg became a part of the group of artists and intellectuals who lived, worked, and socialized in Greenwich Village and on the West Side of Manhattan. She was able to call upon some of these individuals to serve as guest instructors at the school. Through her contacts with this group, she met and fell in love with author and *Seven Lively Arts* editor Waldo Frank. They married in 1916, and their son Thomas was born in May 1922. In 1923, as the marriage was disintegrating, Margaret met Waldo's protégé, Nathan Jean Toomer, an African American writer. Their relationship continued when Margaret and Thomas moved to Reno in preparation for her divorce from Waldo. Between 1924 (when she returned to New York) and 1928, Naumburg and Toomer, as disciples of philosopher Georges Ivanovich Gurdjieff, engaged in self-study, wrote book manuscripts on subjects they knew well, and attended dance performances and lectures led by Alfred R. Orage. When Naumburg broke with Toomer in 1928, she shifted her allegiance from Gurdjieff to the medium Eileen Garrett.

Margaret Naumburg's careers occurred in two distinct time periods, separated by the years spanning her pregnancy, the birth of her son, and her divorce. Between 1914 and 1921 she founded and actualized the Children's School (later renamed Walden School at the request of the students). In 1921 she became the advisory director, and in 1924 she ended her administrative ties to the school. Thereafter she is listed as "founder" in Walden School publications. Naumburg's first book, *The Child and the World: Dialogues in Modern Education* (1928), was the synthesis of her experiences as director of the Children's School and her interactions with other members of the "new schools" movement in New York and around the country.

Naumburg's second career began in the 1930s, as she sought a new direction within the field of psychology through her work at Bellevue Hospital. In 1941 she became a special research worker in the Department of Clinical Psychiatry at New York State Psychiatric Institute and Hospital and started her research on the art expression of "behavior problem children" and adolescent schizophrenics. The work, done over a six-year period, is considered by many to be the beginning of art therapy in the United States. Her 1943 monograph, "Children's Art Expression and War," was the first in a series of books and articles describing the use of spontaneous art expression as a means of diagnosis and therapy. She espoused analytically oriented art therapy, a therapeutic approach emphasizing the projection of spontaneous images as a direct communication from the subconscious. It encouraged the use of spontaneous art productions as a nonverbal form of communication between pupil and art teacher or patient and art therapist.

Naumburg joined the Graduate Faculty at the New York University (NYU) Department of Art Education in 1958. She drew upon both her educational and her therapeutic backgrounds to guide students who were learning to use the spontaneous art and case study methods. She mounted a number of exhibitions, accompanied by talks and workshops, sometimes with the assistance of her students and former students. Naumburg became certified as a psychologist in New York State in 1961 and lectured at numerous symposia and conferences around the world. When NYU did not reappoint her in the spring of 1965, she transferred her course to the New School for Social Research.

Naumburg maintained a full schedule of teaching, writing, and lecturing until the late 1960s. In September 1973 she moved to Brookline, Massachusetts, to be near her son and his family. She was beginning to have memory loss and was frustrated by her inability to actively continue her work and her writing. Margaret Naumburg died in Needham, Massachusetts, on February 26, 1983, at the age of ninety-two.

Bibliography: The extensive Margaret Naumburg Papers at the Department of Special Collections, Van Pelt-Dietrich Library Center, University of Pennsylvania, cover all the phases of her professional life. See also the Waldo Frank Papers at the University of Pennsylvania and the Jean Toomer Papers, Beinecke Rare Book and Manuscript Library, Yale University, for her relationships with these men. Naumburg's books include *The Child and the World: Dialogues in Modern Education* (1928); *Studies of the "Free" Art Expression of Behavior Problem Children and Adolescents as a Means of Diagnosis and Therapy* (1947), republished as *An Introduction to Art Therapy* (1973); *Schizophrenic Art: Its Meaning in Psychotherapy* (1950); *Psychoneurotic Art: Its Function in Psychotherapy* (1953); and *Dynamically Oriented Art Therapy: Its Principles and Practices* (1966). She also published numerous journal articles, monographs, and book chapters, including: "Maria Montessori, Friend of Children," in *The Outlook* (1913); "The Walden School" in the *Twenty-Sixth Yearbook of the Society for the Study of Education: Part I: The Foundations and Technique of Curriculum-Construction* (1926); and a series of articles on the Gary, Indiana, schools. Naumburg is one of two women profiled in Paul Rosenfeld's *Port of New York: Essays on Fourteen American Moderns* (1924). For additional information, see Robert H. Beck, "American Progressive Education, 1875–1930" (PhD dissertation, Yale University, 1942), and Dana Leigh Buck, "The Origins of Art Therapy: The Contributions of Florence Cane and Margaret Naumburg" (MA thesis, Massachusetts College of Arts, 1985). See also Blythe Hinitz, "Margaret Naumburg and Walden School" in Alan R. Sadovnik and Susan F. Semel, eds., *Founding Mothers and Others: Women Educational Leaders during the Progressive Era* (2002); Thomas Frank, "Margaret Naumburg, Pioneer Art Therapist: A Son's Perspective," *American Journal of Art Therapy* 22, no. 4 (July 1983), pp. 112–15; and Judith A. Rubin, "The Significance of Florence Cane and Margaret Naumburg for Art Education," *American Journal of Art Therapy* 22, no. 4 (July 1983), pp. 120–22. Additional verification was provided by Dr. Thomas and Kate Frank. An obituary appeared in the *New York Times* on May 6, 1983.

BLYTHE S. FARB HINITZ

NEARING, Helen Knothe. February 23, 1904–September 17, 1995. Writer, homesteader, organic gardener.

Helen Nearing was born Helen Knothe in Ridgewood, New Jersey, the second of three children of Maria Obreen and Frank Knothe. Her Dutch-born mother was an artist and a quiet beneficent influence. Her father, a New York City businessman, served as president of the local board of education and the Unitarian Men's Club, and loved music. The Knothes were socially active and aware, and raised their children as intellectuals, vegetarians, theosophists, and Unitarian Universalists.

As a child, Helen was introverted and bookish, but she blossomed at age thirteen at a girls' camp in New Hampshire, where she read the classics, wrote poetry, and became one with nature. She also fell in love with the violin, and her family foresaw a possible career in music. When she graduated from Ridgewood High School in June 1921, her parents gave her a choice of going to college, to the Boston Conservatory for music, or to Europe to study violin. The free-spirited Helen jumped at the opportunity to go abroad. At seventeen, she heard Hindu philosopher Jiddu Krishnamurti speak at the International Convention of the Theosophical Society in Paris. Helen and Krishnamurti soon became friends. For the next several years she traveled around the world, stopping in Vienna to study the violin and continuing on to Switzerland, India, and Sydney, Australia.

"Some time in my youth or childhood, I must have done something good," Helen sang from *The Sound of Music* when she reminisced about meeting two famous and extraordinary men, Krishnamurti and Scott Nearing. Helen had met Scott briefly when she was seventeen and later reconnected with him through a fortuitous phone call in 1928. Nearing was a well-known economist and social critic who had been blacklisted from teaching at the University of Pennsylvania for his radical views. When Scott, aged forty-five, and Helen, twenty-four, reconnected, they framed their early relationship as a working partnership and friendship. Scott was separated from his wife, Nellie, but was not divorced. Helen and Scott's partnership evolved into marriage in 1947 when Nellie died. Scott had two sons from his first marriage, and he and Helen had no plans to have more children.

Starting out in New York City, the couple had no money and no prospects. Scott's head was full of ideas and Helen's head was full of music. She brought to the partnership her youth, enthusiasm, secretarial skills, and natural ability to hustle, and he brought experience and a philosophy. They moved to Pike Valley outside Jamaica, Vermont, in 1932 because there they could grow their own food. Vermont was an experiment for them where they planned a nonexploitive, socially just lifestyle. Helen knew nothing about living responsibly off the land and looked to Scott for guidance in all practical skills. Scott in turn looked toward Helen for spiritual guidance.

Through a small legacy given to Helen, they were able to buy another parcel of land, with maple trees, and these became their cash crop. In 1950, Helen and Scott co-authored *The Maple Sugar Book,* which chronicled their maple-sugaring techniques. Soon people were coming to Forest Farm to learn about their innovative techniques of homesteading, organic gardening, and maple sugaring. When the ski industry invaded their simple existence on Stratton Mountain in 1952, they moved to Harborside, Maine, on Cape Rosier. Author PEARL BUCK, who encouraged them to write what became their most famous book, *Living the Good Life,* bought their Vermont property.

At the second Forest Farm, in Maine, Helen took the lead and Scott receded. (Helen was then forty-eight, and Scott was sixty-nine.) In 1954, they co-authored *Living the Good Life: How to Live Simply and Sanely in a Troubled World,* which they published through Scott's Social Science Institute, a publishing company founded by the Nearings after repeated rejections from mainstream publishers. They also established a blueberry cash crop, kept open house, and divided their days into three equal segments. One-third of the day was devoted to labor, one-third to community service, and the last third to self-improvement. They traveled the United States on the lecture circuit and co-authored *USA Today: Reporting Extensive Journeys and First Hand Observations* (1955). During the 1960s they wrote a regular column for *Mother Earth News* and continued to travel and lecture internationally.

In 1970 the Nearings became even more famous when Schocken Books reprinted *Living the Good Life.* By now, the Nearings' alternative lifestyle was reaching into the mainstream. Thousands of visitors from around the world traveled to their remote farm hoping to catch a glimpse of the good life in action. Photographers, television crews, and an international documentary film crew heralded the Nearings as celebrities of the back-to-the-land movement. The Nearings took their guru celebrity in stride and co-authored several more books, including *Continuing the Good Life: A Half Century of Homesteading* (1979) and *Our Home Made of Stone: Building in Our Seventies and Nineties* (1983), which chronicled the building of their final home, which they continued to call Forest Farm, from 1974 to 1978.

By 1980, Helen and Scott were winding up their life together, and they knew it. In 1983 Scott died a conscious, controlled, at-home death at age 100 with the aid of Helen and a friend. Helen, seventy-nine and now alone, continued to lecture about aging and dying and maintained the farm and her lecture schedule with help from two close women friends. In her tribute to Scott, *Loving and Leaving the Good Life* (1992), she recounted their fifty-three-year partnership. She never used the word *God* and believed that the whole of manifestation was an experience of some great purpose. "Life is all a tremendous unity," she said, "and a learning unity and an evolving unity, and we're lucky to be part of it."

In 1995, Helen Nearing published *Light on Aging and Dying.* She was tired and looked forward to death because she believed in reincarnation. On a stormy day in September 1995, while she was driving to a movie, her car sped off a windy road near Harborside and collided with a tree. She died instantly, stunning friends, family, and the good-life public. She was ninety-one. Her impact and legacy live on through her books and the Good Life Center at Forest Farm, where people continue to learn about practicing a simple, purposeful life living off the land.

Bibliography: Archival material can be found in the Scott Nearing Papers, Swarthmore College Peace Collection; the Scott and Helen Nearing Papers, Mugar Memorial Library, Boston University; and the Scott and Helen Nearing Papers, Thoreau Institute at Walden Woods in Lincoln, Massachusetts. Two documentary films distributed by Bull Frog Films introduce the couple and their philosophy: *Living the Good Life with Helen and Scott Nearing* (1977), produced by Bull Frog Films, and *Helen Nearing: Conscious Living/Conscious Dying* (2000), co-produced by Andrea Sarris and Polly Bennell. The quotations in the text are from the 2000 film. See also Ellen LaConte, *On Light Alone: A Guru Meditation on the Good Death of Helen Nearing* (1996); and John Saltmash, *Scott Nearing: An Intellectual Biography* (1991). An obituary appeared in the *New York Times* on September 19, 1995.

ANDREA SARRIS

NEEL, Alice. January 28, 1900–October 13, 1984. Artist.

Born in Merion Square, Pennsylvania, Alice Hartley Neel was the fourth of five children of George Washington Neel, a clerk for the Pennsylvania Railroad, and Alice Concross Hartley, a housewife descended from a signer of the Declaration of Independence. Shortly after Neel's birth, the family moved to Colwyn, Pennsylvania. Upon graduating from Darby High School in 1918, she worked as a stenographer for the Army Air Corps and held other civil service jobs. Enrolled in evening art courses at the School of Industrial Art in Philadelphia, by 1921 she had decided on full-time study at the Philadelphia School of Design for Women (now Moore College of Art).

In 1924 at the Chester Springs summer school of the Pennsylvania Academy of the Fine Arts she met Carlos Enríquez, an upper-class Cuban artist whom she married on June 1, 1925. In 1926 the couple moved to Havana, Cuba, where their daughter Santillana del Mar Enríquez was born in December. Socializing with Cuban avant-garde writers and artists, Neel embraced the syncretic mulatto culture of Cuba and developed an expressionist figurative style. She exhibited at the XII Salón de Bellas Artes, but in May 1927 she returned to Pennsylvania with Santillana.

When Enríquez joined her that fall, they first moved to West 81st Street in Manhattan, then to Sedgwick Avenue in the Bronx. In December Santillana died of diphtheria, and shortly thereafter Neel again became pregnant; Isabella Lillian Enríquez (called Isabetta) was born in November 1928. Although Enríquez's parents sent some money so they could continue painting, their poverty put a strain on the marriage. One solution was to move to Europe, where they could live cheaply. Enríquez left for Cuba with Isabetta to seek funds for their European sojourn, but, to Neel's chagrin, he left Isabella with his sisters and traveled to Paris alone.

Depressed by the absence of her husband and child, Neel threw herself into making art, but soon her depression overwhelmed her. She lost weight, ran out of money, and had to return to her parents' home in Colwyn. Unable to persuade her mother to raise Isabetta, who was still in Cuba, and torn by her desire to continue painting, Neel suffered a nervous breakdown on August 14, 1930, and she was hospitalized at the Orthopedic Hospital in Philadelphia. In January 1931 Enríquez returned to the United States, visited Neel in the hospital, took her home to her parents, and left. She attempted suicide and was rushed to a local hospital, then returned to Orthopedic Hospital, and finally admitted to the suicide ward of Philadelphia General Hospital. She spent the summer of 1931 at Gladwyne Colony, a private sanatorium, where the director encouraged her to draw.

Back in Colwyn by September 1931, she resumed painting. In 1932 she moved to Greenwich Village with Kenneth Doolittle, a sailor with a temper who would later destroy many of Neel's paintings in a fit of jealousy. At the first Washington Square Art show in 1932 she met John Rothschild, a wealthy Harvard graduate who became a sometime lover and lifelong supporter. She never again saw Carlos Enríquez, but they never divorced. Isabetta visited Neel at the Jersey shore during the summers of 1934 and 1939, but was raised by her Havana relatives.

Between December 1933 and April 1934 Neel was enrolled on the Public Works of Art Project (PWAP), a government relief project set up to help destitute artists; in August 1935 the Federal Arts Project of the Works Progress Administration was launched, and Neel joined the easel division. During the late 1930s she participated in the activities of the Artists' Union and the American Artists' Congress and painted expressionistic social-protest street scenes. She became friends with bohemians, communists, and radical writers, such as Joe Gould, Samuel Putnam, poet Kenneth Fearing, and *New Masses* editor Mike Gold, all of whose portraits she painted. Neel was proud that she later provided the model for a character—the cheerfully eccentric artist, Louise Patterson, living amid a clutter of furniture, painting equipment, and rambunctious children—in Fearing's detective thriller, *The Big Clock* (1946).

In 1935 Neel met José Santiago, a nightclub singer; they lived together in the Village and eventually moved to Spanish Harlem, where her son Richard Neel was born in September 1939. Santiago left Neel in December, and that winter she met Sam Brody, a filmmaker who had been a member of the communist Workers Film and Photo League. She lived with him intermittently for almost two decades. In September 1941 she gave birth to Hartley Stockton Neel.

When the Federal Arts Project was phased out in 1943, Neel and her sons were helped with funds from public assistance and supportive friends. During the 1940s and 1950s, as she struggled to support her children and obtain scholarships for their education, she never stopped painting. Many of her paintings from that period are portraits of her Spanish Harlem neighbors and her sons.

Three factors contributed to the blossoming of Neel's art in the late 1950s and early 1960s. She began to see a therapist who helped her develop the ego strength she needed to survive in the art world; her two sons left for college; and she started attending artists' meetings in the Village. Neel played a role in Robert Frank and Alfred Leslie's 1959 underground film *Pull My Daisy* (1959), starring Gregory Corso, Allen Ginsberg, Peter Orlovsky, and Larry Rivers, with narration by Jack Kerouac. In 1964 she was freed from financial worries by a yearly stipend of $6,000 from Muriel Gardiner, a wealthy American psychoanalyst.

During the 1960s and 1970s she painted art world personalities, such as Frank O'Hara, Robert Smithson, Henry Geldzahler, Andy Warhol, celebrities such as Linus Pauling and Virgil Thompson, along with neighbors, her sons, and their young families. Nancy Greene, whom Richard married in 1963, assisted her when requests came in for loans and photographs. Nancy and her children also became the models for some of Neel's finest paintings; *Pregnant Woman* (1971) shows the lived experience of Nancy nude, bulgingly pregnant, hot, uncomfortable, and distracted as she lies on a bed.

During the 1970s the women's movement featured Neel in exhibitions, and feminists hailed her as an art world "survivor." In 1974 the Whitney Museum of American Art exhibited her portraits; in 1975 the Georgia Museum of Art presented a major retrospective. She showed in many prestigious group shows, and in 1979 the Women's Caucus for Art gave her and three other artists an award for outstanding achievement in the visual arts. Frequently invited to speak at colleges across the country, she both amused and confounded audiences. Her white hair topped by an elegant turbanlike hat, her twinkling blue eyes, and her sweet grandmotherly grin contrasted with her witty, salty tongue that aimed tart jibes at the art world. She continued painting until just before her death from cancer at her home on Manhattan's Upper West Side at the age of eighty-four.

Bibliography: Neel wrote few letters, but other archival materials, photographs, and artworks are housed at Neel Arts Inc., New York City. The Archives of American Art, Smithsonian Institution, Washington, D.C., has some papers. The Robert Miller Gallery in New York has published many profusely illustrated exhibition catalogues and handles sales from the estate. More than twenty hours of audiotaped interviews between Patricia Hills and Alice Neel conducted between 1979 and 1982 formed the basis for Patricia Hills, *Alice Neel* (1983). Other interviews with Neel, conducted by Richard M. Polsky during 1981, are housed in the Columbia University Oral History Collection, New York City. Exhibitions in the 1970s that brought renewed interest to Neel included *Alice Neel* (Whitney Museum of American Art, 1974) and *Alice Neel: The*

Woman and Her Work (Georgia Museum of Art, 1975). The scholarly catalogue for the exhibition celebrating Neel's centenary is Ann Temkin, Susan Rosenberg, and Richard Flood, *Alice Neel* (Philadelphia Museum of Art, 2000).

Other secondary sources include Pamala Allara, *Pictures of People: Alice Neel's American Portrait Gallery* (1998); Gerald L. Belcher and Margaret L. Belcher, *Collecting Souls, Gathering Dust: The Struggles of Two American Artists, Alice Neel and Rhoda Medary* (1991); Eleanor Munro, *Originals: American Women Artists* (1979); Cindy Nemser, *Art Talk: Conversations with Twelve Women Artists* (1975); Linda Nochlin, "Some Women Realists: Painters of the Figure," *Arts Magazine* 48 (May 1974), pp. 29–33; and Piri Halasz, "Alice Neel: I Have This Obsession with Life," *Art News* 73 (January 1974), pp. 47–49. An obituary appeared in the New York Times on October 14, 1984.

PATRICIA HILLS

NEVELSON, Louise. September 23, 1899–April 17, 1988. Sculptor, painter, printmaker.

Louise Nevelson was born in the village of Pereyaslav near Kiev in tsarist Russia. Named Leah, she was five and a half when she was brought to America by her mother, Minna Ziesel Smolerank, along with an older brother and a younger sister, to join her father, Isaac Berliawsky, who had settled in Rockland, Maine, a few years earlier. It was there that Louise's youngest sibling, another sister, was born. Starting out as a junk dealer, Isaac eventually pulled his family out of poverty by investing in various properties, but because the Berliawskys were foreigners and Jews, the family was ostracized in the provincial Protestant town. Louise's proud but illiterate mother, who was homesick for Russia and always ill and unhappy in Maine, encouraged the aspirations of her talented eldest daughter. Louise's social isolation underscored her early artistic identity and fed simultaneous feelings of inferiority and superiority, which enabled her to endure years of being ignored as an artist.

Louise's art teachers also encouraged her, and in 1918 she graduated from the commercial course at Rockland High School. Tall and dark like her mother, as well as very beautiful, Louise soon met a wealthy New Yorker in the shipping business who was visiting Rockland. His younger brother and business partner was Charles S. Nevelson, whom she would marry at Boston's Copley Plaza Hotel in June 1920.

Young Mrs. Nevelson planned to study art in Manhattan, but she was diverted by her new bourgeois milieu and by the 1922 birth of her son, Myron "Mike" Irving Nevelson. Although her husband and his circle criticized her flair for the dramatic and her desire for independence, she took voice, acting, and art lessons. When Nevelson turned thirty in the fall of 1929, she enrolled in the Art Students League in New York City to study painting and drawing with Kenneth Hayes Miller and other artists.

At the League, Nevelson heard about Hans Hofmann, a famous German teacher of modern art. She sent young Mike to stay with relatives in Rockland and sailed for Europe in the fall of 1931. Disappointed by Hofmann's class, she worked as an extra in German films and traveled to Italy and then Paris, where an exhibition of African carvings ignited her interest in primitive art. Returning to New York the following fall, she enrolled again in the Art Students League and studied drawing and painting with George Grosz. She left her husband, who had lost his money in the stock market crash; after a marriage that had been disappointing from the start, they divorced in 1941.

In the 1930s Louise Nevelson created cubist semi-abstract figurative sculptures in clay, working with sculptor Chaim Gross and later at the Sculpture Center in New York. Always possessed of exuberant energy, she studied modern dance and investigated religions, metaphysics, and spiritualism. Living an impoverished but gregarious bohemian life, she had many friends and lovers, including Mexican muralist Diego Rivera, who encouraged her interest in pre-Columbian sculpture. (Decades later she would visit Mexico to study Mayan carvings, totemic sculptures, and temple sites.) She earned money by teaching art through the Works Progress Administration and painting portraits using heavily applied and incised oil paint. She also began to exhibit her drawings, paintings, and sculpture in group shows, notably in a 1935 exhibition of twenty young sculptors at the Brooklyn Museum of Art.

In 1941 Nevelson went to see German art dealer Karl Nierendorf, who immediately offered her a show, her first one-artist exhibition, in his prestigious New York gallery. Influenced by Dada and surrealism, she used detritus from junk shops to create circus figures for a show at Jimmy Ernst's Norlyst Gallery in 1943; that same year art collector PEGGY GUGGENHEIM included her in a show of women artists. In 1945 relatives in Maine bought a brownstone on East 30th Street to give her space to make, store, and display her rapidly growing body of work.

Nierendorf continued to exhibit her drawings and blocky, fanciful, painted sculptures until his unexpected death in 1947. Because she was now without a dealer, the art establishment ignored Nevelson, and she was excluded from a big exhibition at the Museum of Modern Art in 1951. She was dismissed partly because of her flamboyance, flirtatiousness, and disinterest in intellectualizing about art, but also because of her gender. In 1952 she joined the National Association of Women

Artists in an attempt to band together against the prevalent sexist attitudes around her. Nevelson's visual thinking was highly intuitive: she avoided logical reasoning as unnatural and antithetical to creativity and reveled in what she called flash thinking—the rapid assimilation of mental images and perceptive leaps. Desperate and determined to succeed, she worked untiringly and joined numerous organizations with annual shows. Meanwhile, she also experienced a painful burden of creativity: the repeated unearthing and exposing of her deepest perceptions in the face of probable neglect, an experience that led to recurrent periods of drinking and despair.

During the 1950s Nevelson began to concentrate on collecting debris from gutters, such as moldings, finials, chair legs, and other pieces of discarded wood. After painting them matte black, she created assemblages within boxes and then arranged the boxes into large walls. The boxes and walls integrated visual memories as disparate as Maine's tar-blackened piers and Mayan hieroglyphics. By transforming found objects into art, she also vindicated her father's vocation as a junk dealer. She built her walls with passion and urgency, especially after her home was condemned for urban renewal. From 1955 to 1958, Colette Roberts exhibited these black environments as well as etchings in a series of solo shows at Grand Central Moderns.

Finally, Nevelson began to win recognition. In 1956 the Whitney Museum acquired *Black Majesty,* and in the next two years other sculptures were accepted into the collections of the Brooklyn Museum of Art and the Museum of Modern Art. In 1959, when Nevelson was almost sixty, she created a chalk white assemblage for a show of sixteen "young" artists at the Museum of Modern Art. Two years later she had an exhibition of gold-painted pieces at New York's Martha Jackson Gallery.

In 1964 Arnold Glimcher first showed Nevelson's work at his Pace Gallery in New York, and their successful business alliance lasted the rest of her life. The Whitney Museum honored her with a major retrospective in 1967. Two years later Princeton University commissioned her first monumental outdoor steel sculpture, and during the next decade she would create many more, including seven pieces at Louise Nevelson Plaza in lower Manhattan. By now Nevelson had found not only the artistic recognition that had so long eluded her but celebrity status as well. Dressed in theatrical assemblages of designer clothes and ethnic jewelry for the cameras, she reveled in the attention attracted by her flamboyant persona.

At the age of eighty Nevelson was elected to the prestigious American Academy of Arts and Letters. Her unique iconography was highly regarded for the way it combined cubism and expressionism in ordered exteriors and emotive interiors. The power of her work as well as its massive scale also shattered conventional ideas about the work of women artists. Nevelson died of metastasized lung cancer at her home on Spring Street in lower Manhattan on April 17, 1988, at the age of eighty-eight.

Bibliography: Quotations are from Nevelson's writings and interviews as cited in *Louise Nevelson: A Passionate Life* by Laurie Lisle (1990). Other sources include Jean Lipman, *Nevelson's World* (1983); Laurie Wilson, *Louise Nevelson: Iconography and Sources* (1981); Louise Nevelson, *Dawns + Dusks: Taped Conversations with Diana MacKown* (1976); and Arnold Glimcher, *Louise Nevelson* (1976). Many exhibition catalogs exist, notably the Whitney Museum's *Louise Nevelson: Atmospheres and Environments* (1980). Reviews of Nevelson's work can be found in art magazines and newspapers beginning in the 1930s. Personal papers (including letters, photographs, exhibition catalogs, and other materials) and oral histories are at the Smithsonian's Archives of American Art in Washington, D.C., and in the Louise Nevelson Archive at the Farnsworth Art Museum, Rockland, Maine. An obituary appeared in the *New York Times* on April 18, 1988.

LAURIE LISLE

NEWMAN, Pauline. October 18, c. 1890–April 8, 1986. Labor activist, union official.

Pauline Newman was a die-hard union loyalist from her teenage years into her nineties. A tough Lithuanian Jewish immigrant with an acerbic tongue, slicked-back hair, and a penchant for tweeds, Newman negotiated with male unionists, middle- and upper-class women reformers, and government officials to improve the lives of working women. She left a lasting imprint on each of these very different worlds.

Newman was born into a world in transition, that of poverty-stricken but deeply religious Jews in Kovno, Lithuania, around 1890. (The exact date of her birth was lost with the family Bible when she emigrated.) The youngest of four children, three girls and a boy, of Theresa and Meyer Newman, Pauline was launched on her activist career at a tender age when she demanded to know why Jewish girls did not receive the same religious education as boys. Her father, a Talmud teacher, accommodated her desire to learn, teaching her to read Hebrew and Yiddish. Newman would later claim that her childhood resentment at the privileges accorded men and boys in Jewish education and worship sparked a lifelong commitment to fight sex discrimination wherever she found it.

When her father died in 1901, Newman, her sisters, and her mother left Kovno for New York, where her brother had settled a few years earlier. Newman began work at a hairbrush factory before moving to the Triangle Shirtwaist Factory in Greenwich Village. Powerfully drawn to the labor socialism espoused by older workers in her shop, and ever hungry for education, Newman organized reading groups for the teenage girls she worked with. These young immigrant girls sparked a series of wildcat strikes and walkouts and, in 1907, a rent strike on Manhattan's Lower East Side that eventually involved more than ten thousand families.

Hailed by newspapers as the "Lower East Side Joan of Arc," the young Newman continued to organize women garment workers, paving the way for the 1909 general strike that came to be known as the Uprising of the 20,000. During the long cold months of the strike, Newman played two important roles. Through inspiring speeches at street corner rallies and in the union halls of Lower Manhattan, she kept up the spirits of the strikers. She also fund-raised among New York's wealthiest women, even drawing some elite women onto picket lines, who participated in the hope that their presence would diminish police brutality against the strikers. These "mink brigades" won the strike its first positive press in the city's mainstream newspapers.

In recognition for all she had done, the International Ladies' Garment Workers' Union (ILGWU) appointed the still-teenage Newman as its first woman general organizer. She spent the next four years traveling the country, organizing garment strikes in Philadelphia, Cleveland, Boston, and Kalamazoo, Michigan. By decade's end, these strikes would bring more than 40 percent of all women garment workers into trade unions, a remarkable percentage for workers in any trade and a clear refutation of union leaders' oft-repeated assertions that women could not be organized. Still, a frustrated and often lonely Newman felt that the male union leadership undermined and undervalued her work.

Newman nearly collapsed under the weight of her grief when the Triangle Shirtwaist Factory burned on March 25, 1911. One hundred forty-six young workers lost their lives, most of them Jewish and Italian women, and many of them friends Newman had come to cherish in her years at Triangle. Desperate to do whatever she could to prevent such disasters in the future, Newman accepted a post in 1913 inspecting industrial shops for the Joint Board of Sanitary Control established by New York State in the aftermath of the fire. At the same time, Newman worked as a lobbyist for the Women's Trade Union League (WTUL) of New York, pushing for passage of wage, hour, and safety legislation for women workers. She also campaigned for woman suffrage in immigrant neighborhoods and through the Socialist Party. Through her work as a factory inspector, Newman met FRANCES PERKINS, then an activist for the National Consumers' League and later Franklin Roosevelt's Secretary of Labor, as well as future New York governor Al Smith and future senator Robert Wagner. These friendships convinced Newman that working through government was as important to the future of working women as grassroots organizing. She never abandoned union work, but she now divided her energies among organizing, education, and lobbying.

In 1917, the WTUL dispatched Newman to Philadelphia to build a new branch of the league. There she met a young Bryn Mawr economics instructor named FRIEDA MILLER, who enthusiastically left academia to join Newman in "the movement." The two were soon living together, beginning a turbulent relationship that would last until Miller's death in 1973. In 1923 the two women moved to Greenwich Village, where, as part of a community of politically active women couples, they raised Miller's daughter, Elisabeth. Happy to take a job in New York after more than a decade of traveling, Newman became educational director for the ILGWU Union Health Center, the first comprehensive medical program created by a union for its members. She would retain that position for the next six decades, using it to promote worker health care, adult education, and greater visibility for the concerns and needs of women workers.

Newman remained an organizer into the 1930s, reaching out to African American and Afro-Caribbean women through WTUL campaigns to unionize laundry, hotel, and domestic workers. She also continued her government work, consulting for New York State on minimum wage and safety standards, and serving as a member of the U.S. Women's Bureau Labor Advisory Board and the International Labor Organization Subcommittee on the Status of Domestic Workers.

She was a fixture and a legend at ILGWU headquarters into the 1980s, writing and lecturing on trade union history. She was also a devoted mentor to younger women trade unionists. Often a thorn in the side of male union officers, Newman came to be venerated by both leaders and the rank and file as a living embodiment of the union's history. In addition, Newman was hailed by the Coalition of Labor Union Women as a foremother of the women's liberation movement. She left an important legacy through her writings as one of the few working-class women of her generation to chronicle the political activism of immigrant and native-born working women.

Pauline Newman died in New York in 1986, at approximately ninety-six years of age. She had forged a political career that addressed her complex identity as a Jewish working-class woman; her life illuminates the tensions among gender, class, and ethnicity that both powered and fractured alliances within the American labor and women's movements. Organizer, writer, government investigator, mentor to three generations of trade union women, Pauline Newman made herself into one of the most important women in the history of American labor.

Bibliography: For a fuller treatment of Pauline Newman's life, see Annelise Orleck, *Common Sense and a Little Fire: Women and Working-Class Politics in the United States, 1900–1965* (1995). Ann Schofield has done an insightful short sketch of Newman's life in *"To Do and to Be": Portraits of Four Women Activists, 1893–1986* (1997). An early and important article including information about Newman is Alice Kessler-Harris's "Organizing the Unorganizable: Three Jewish Women and Their Union," *Labor History* 17, no. 1 (Winter 1976), pp. 5–25. A brief interview about Newman's childhood is one of the oral histories contained in Joan Morrison and Charlotte Fox Zabrisky, eds., *American Mosaic* (1982). Pauline Newman's personal papers are held at the Schlesinger Library, Radcliffe Institute for Advanced Study, Harvard University. Additional materials can be found in the Papers of the Women's Trade Union League and Its Principal Leaders, 1855–1964 (University Microfilms International), as well as in articles Newman wrote for the *New York Call, Progressive Woman,* the WTUL magazine *Life and Labor,* the *Ladies Garment Worker,* and the ILGWU newspaper *Justice.* An obituary appeared in the *New York Times* on April 10, 1986.

ANNELISE ORLECK

NIGGLI, Josefina. July 13, 1910–December 17, 1983. Playwright, writer, educator.

Josefina Maria Niggli was born in Monterrey, the capital of the state of Nuevo León in Mexico, during the first year of the Mexican Revolution. In many ways she is more truly a child of the Mexican struggle for social equality than Frida Kahlo, who changed her year of birth to 1910 to declare solidarity with Mexican independence. As a child, Niggli twice was sent to live in Texas for her safety during the many years of struggle. She eventually remained in Texas, but the culture and community spirit of Mexico greatly influenced her writing. Niggli was one of the first Latina writers to publish creative works dealing with specific aspects of Mexican culture. Unlike most women writers of the early twentieth century, she also distinguished herself in a variety of literary genres.

Niggli's grandparents on her father's side, of Swiss and Alsatian heritage, immigrated to Texas in 1836—the year Texas proclaimed its independence from Mexico. Her father, Frederick Ferdinand Niggli, had moved to Mexico with his bride in 1893. Josefina's mother, Goldie Morgan, was a violinist of Irish, French, and German descent. Josefina was their only child. Her father worked as the manager of a cement plant in Mexico, and her mother home-schooled Josefina. Josefina was ready for college at age fifteen, and her family chose the College of the Incarnate Word in San Antonio. Niggli majored in philosophy and minored in history, and became interested in writing as a career. She was guided and mentored by the head of the English department, who entered one of her stories in a national contest. By the time she graduated in 1931, Niggli had taken first and second prizes in the National Catholic College Poetry Contest and second prize in the *Ladies' Home Journal* College Short Story Contest. In 1931 she published a poem, "Tourist in a Mexican Town," in the *Denver Echo.* This and other poems were self-published in Texas in a book titled *Mexican Silhouettes* around this time. In addition, in the late 1920s and 1930s, Niggli became popular in San Antonio for writing and producing shows for KTSA Radio.

After studying playwriting at the San Antonio Little Theatre, in 1935 Niggli decided to join the Carolina Playmakers, a graduate program in drama at the University of North Carolina at Chapel Hill. Her thesis consisted of a three-act play, *Singing Valley,* and she graduated in 1937 with a master's degree in drama. She later studied advanced playwriting at Stanford University, radio writing and production at New York University, journalism and film at Columbia University, and poetic forms at the National University of Mexico (UNAM).

While it seems unusual to find Mexican culture depicted in North Carolina in the 1930s and 1940s, it was a happy coincidence for Niggli's work. Had she remained in the Southwest, where the Mexican American population suffered more severely during the Great Depression, she might not have found as many opportunities for publication and staging. Her move to the Carolina Playmakers helped develop her playwriting and provided the opportunity to seek fellowships. In 1936 and 1938, she received Rockefeller Fellowships in Playwriting; she also received a National Theatre Council Fellowship, and another for the Breadloaf Writers' Conference, where she developed her first novel. Her early plays were included in the anthologies *The Carolina Play-Book* (1936), *The Best One-Act Plays of 1938,* and *Contemporary One-Act Plays* (1938). That year she also published her own anthology, *Mexican Folk Plays.*

In 1945, Niggli published her first novel, *Mexican Village,* which is her best-known and considered her most influential work. It consists of ten related stories about the people in a small village called Hidalgo and the factory that is their principal place of work. Reviews at the time called her novel a convincing portrayal of Mexican village life, depicting the tensions between traditionalism and modern society, and between Spanish and Indian cultures. In 1946, she received the Mayflower Cup for the best book written during the previous year by a North Carolinian.

In the late 1940s and early 1950s, Niggli was hired as a scriptwriter for Twentieth Century Fox and Metro-Goldwyn-Mayer in Hollywood, where she contributed to *Sombrero* (1953) based on *Mexican Village.* She also wrote for radio and television, including such shows as *The Twilight Zone* and *Have Gun Will Travel.* Although Niggli's first name was originally spelled "Josephine," she used "Josephina" from early childhood, and during her working life had migrated to "Josefina," more appropriate to her Latina culture. In 1956 she was hired to teach English and drama at Western Carolina University. She also chaired the theater department and remained there until her retirement in 1975.

Latino critics consider Niggli a landmark writer of the early twentieth century. Gloria Anzaldúa in *Borderlands/La Frontera* (1987) describes Niggli's writing as that of a consciousness caught between borders. By writing in English, Niggli taught the English-speaking world about Mexican cultural heritage in plays such as *The Fair God* (1936) and *Azteca* (1936). She also elaborated Mexican politics and class struggle in *The Cry of Dolores* (1935) and later works.

One of Niggli's strongest contributions was the portrayal of the Mexican woman character, especially that of the "soldier-woman," or *soldadera,* who is not afraid to fight for a cause alongside the men. The *soldadera* (also called Adelita in Mexican culture, after the name of a heroic woman depicted in a popular corrido or ballad commemorating the Revolution) is an important symbol for Mexican and Chicana women. Niggli's full-length, one-act play of 1938, *Soldadera,* represents an innocent and sweet Adelita who by her courage and sacrifice becomes the symbol of the revolutionary cause. Niggli helped bring the Adelita image to English-language society, and to this day an "Adelita" is a symbol of struggle and freedom for the U.S. Chicana.

Josefina Niggli died in 1983 at her home in Cullowhee, North Carolina, at the age of seventy-three. She never married or had children. Although she lived most of her adult life in North Carolina, she is buried alongside her father and mother in San Antonio, Texas.

Bibliography: A collection of Josefina Niggli's documents and personal papers is found at Western Carolina University. A (selected) list of her plays and the years they were first produced includes *Tooth or Shave* (1935); *The Cry of Dolores* (1935); *Soldadera* (1936), published in Margaret Mayorga, ed., *The Best One-Act Plays of 1937* (1938); *Azteca* (1936); *The Fair God* (1936); *Singing Valley* (1936); *Mexican Folk Plays* (1938, reprinted 1976); *This Is Villa* (1938), published in Mayorga, *The Best One-Act Plays of 1938* (1939); *Red Velvet Goat* (1936); *Sunday Costs Five Pesos* (1936) in Robin Malan, ed., *Play Workshop: Ten One-Act Plays* (1972); *Miracle at Blaise* in Betty Smith, ed., *25 Non-Royalty One-Act Plays for All-Girl Casts* (1942); *The Ring of General Macías* in Smith, ed., *20 Prize-Winning Non-Royalty One-Act Plays* (1943); and *This Bull Ate Nutmeg* in Esther E. Galbraith, ed., *Plays without Footlights* (1945). Niggli's novels include *Mexican Village* (1945); *Step Down, Elder Brother* (1947); and *A Miracle for Mexico* (1964), for juvenile readers. She also published *Pointers on Playwriting: The Writer* (1945; revised and enlarged edition published as *New Pointers on Playwriting,* 1967); *Pointers on Radio Writing; The Writer* (1946); and *Sombrero* (1953; screenplay, with Norman Foster).

Gloria Anzaldúa's *Borderlands/La Frontera* (1987) and Tey Diana Rebolledo's *Women Singing in the Snow: A Cultural Analysis of Chicana Literature* (1995) consider Niggli's work in broad context; see also Alicia Arrizon, "Soldaderas and the Staging of the Mexican Revolution," *TDR: The Drama Review: A Journal of Performance Studies* 42, no. 1 (Spring 1998), pp. 90–112. Doctoral dissertations that discuss Niggli's work include Suzanne Michelle Bost, "Mulattas and Mestizas: Mixed Identity in Women's Writing of the Americas, 1850–1996" (Vanderbilt University, 1997); Rita Keresztesi Treat, "Strangers at Home: Ethnic Modernism between the World Wars" (University of California, Santa Cruz, 1999); and Gloria Louise Velasquez Treviño, "Cultural Ambivalence in Early Chicana Prose Fiction" (Stanford University, 1985).

ELIZABETH COONROD MARTÍNEZ

NIN, Anaïs. February 21, 1903–January 14, 1977. Novelist, diarist.

Anaïs Nin was born in Neuilly, France, the oldest of three children and the only daughter of Rosa Culmell and Joaquin Nin y Castellanos, both Cuban musicians. Joaquin, a composer and concert pianist, earned a living performing and giving lessons; Rosa was a singer of French Danish descent, born in Cuba. Anaïs lived a sophisticated life with her parents near Paris, enjoying the company of other artists and traveling in Europe. When she was eleven years old, her mother emigrated to the United States with Anaïs and her two brothers after her father abandoned the family in the south of France after a series of extramarital affairs. Despite her father's neglect, Anaïs continued to yearn for his attention and hoped for his return to the family. She started her diary as a letter to him during her ocean voyage to the States; thus began her lifelong obsession with recording her thoughts and experiences in detail. This literary exercise developed into a body of work that filled sixty-nine bound and loose volumes over her lifetime and ultimately overshadowed her novels and other work.

Once in the United States, Nin's mother managed to earn a meager living by giving music lessons and taking in boarders, and the family moved several times. Anaïs found New York City overwhelming and dirty. She attended public schools, leaving Wadleigh High School in Harlem in 1919, at age sixteen, having learned enough English to continue her self-education by reading material from the public library. She also worked as a part-time artist's model to help her mother support the family.

Nin met Hugh Parker Guiler in his parents' home when she was eighteen, and they married in Cuba on March 3, 1923, when she was twenty. In 1924, they moved to Louveciennes, near Paris, where Guiler was transferred by his firm, the National City Bank. Here, Anaïs existed in the conservative circle of businessmen until her own interest in writing eventually put her in contact with artistic and literary figures, including Henry Miller, his wife June, Lawrence Durrell, and Antonin Artaud. She had begun writing stories, and the publication of her *D. H. Lawrence: An Unprofessional Study* (1932) brought her some positive attention. Nin and Miller inspired each other's writing, and they began an eight-year affair and a lifelong friendship.

Nin and Guiler managed a mutually dependent relationship that survived many of Nin's liaisons. Guiler's wealth enabled Nin to live elegantly, travel, self-publish, and support other artists. Under the name Ian Hugo, Guiler worked as a copper engraver, art filmmaker, and book illustrator (he did illustrations for several of Nin's books), while continuing to work as a financial adviser. Nin cultivated her life as an artist, moving freely in the seamier areas of Parisian life; she paid particular attention to her costume and makeup, creating an exotic persona. Her lifestyle stimulated the content of her diary, characterized by a self-conscious surrealistic prose that was constantly being rewritten. Because she and her associates were not able to find publishers for their work, they founded Siana Editions (for *Anaïs* spelled in reverse).

Nin received positive reviews in Europe for her novels *House of Incest* (1936) and *Winter of Artifice* (1939), but her work was not well received when she and her husband returned to the United States to avoid the war. Eventually, a positive review by Edmund Wilson in the *New Yorker* brought her some critical attention, but for the most part her work was ignored. With the help of Gonzalo More, a Peruvian Marxist she had known in France, she purchased a hand-operated letter press, founded Gemor Press, and sold her own imprints.

Nin's interest in psychoanalysis led to her intense processing in writing of her experiences and conflicts. Her first analyst was René Allendy, and later she studied under Otto Rank, a student of Freud. Nin, in fact, worked as a psychoanalyst in New York for about six months under Rank, who became her lover and suggested she abandon her diaries to seek a more objective way to achieve self-acceptance. She rejected that advice. Her self-interpretation and details of affairs continued to dominate her diaries and stories, as she attempted to create a more fully realized self. Having rejected motherhood and aborted a pregnancy, she often wrote about how the role of nurturer conflicted with the self as artist. She felt her creations were the men in her life and her writings: "Nature connived me to be a man's woman. Not a mother to children, but to men."

Nin desired acceptance as an artist who had created a new genre of writing, but publishers for the most part continued to dismiss her until the first volume of her diaries was published in 1966. The diaries intrigued readers with their hinted-at omissions, explicit sexual experimentation, and discussions of the life of the artist. Her erotic poetic stream of consciousness, especially in light of the women's movement, appealed to a sizable audience in the late 1960s and early 1970s; she was seen as producing a new type of women's writing. Subsequently, however, the accuracy of the diaries came to be debated. Critics who defend Nin suggest that she intentionally confused fiction and autobiography, and that studying the diaries as a new type of fiction is appropriate and would have been acceptable to Nin herself. Whether she is inventing the subject of the diaries as a character of fiction seeking "a poetic truth" or whether she is inventing a self out of psychological need continues to generate critical study. Her posthumously published erotica, though popular, has diminished her stature as a feminist writer.

In 1947 Nin met, and later bigamously married, Rupert William Pole, a teacher fifteen years her junior, with whom she traveled to California. She lived on each coast to maintain relationships with both husbands. Nin taught creative writing and was invited to speak at many colleges and universities through the 1960s and 1970s. She also acted in several underground art films. Pole cared for her until her death from cancer in Los Angeles on January 14, 1977, at the age of seventy-three. According to her wishes, her ashes were scattered on the Pacific Ocean.

Bibliography: There are collections of Nin's papers at the University of California at Los Angeles, Special Collections, given by her brother Joaquin Culmell-Nin; and at Northwestern University. The University of Tulsa contains one box of correspondence (1969–92) between Nin and colleagues and her literary agent, Gunther Stuhlman. Seven volumes of her diary, covering the years 1931–74, were published between 1966 and 1980. After the death of Guiler in 1985, there appeared new versions that included previously omitted material: *Henry and June: From 'A Journal of Love': The Unexpurgated Diary of Anaïs Nin, 1931–32* (1986), *Incest: 'A Journal of Love': The Unexpurgated Diary of Anaïs Nin, 1932–1934* (1992), and *Fire:*

From 'A Journal of Love': The Unexpurgated Diary of Anaïs Nin, 1934–1937 (1995). Her other fiction includes *This Hunger* (1945), *Ladders to Fire* (1946), *Children of the Albatross* (1947), *The Four-Chambered Heart* (1950), *A Spy in the House of Love* (1954), and *Solar Barque* (1958); *Cities of the Interior* (1959) contains some of the above-listed novellas. Short story collections by Nin include *Under a Glass Bell* (1944), *Collages* (1964), *Waste of Timelessness, and Other Early Stories* (1977), *Delta of Venus* (1977), and *Little Birds* (1979); the last two collections of erotica were published posthumously. She also published nine volumes of nonfiction, including *Realism and Reality* (1946), *The Novel of the Future* (1968), and *In Favor of the Sensitive Man and Other Essays* (1976). Biographies include Deirdre Bair, *Anaïs Nin: A Biography* (1995); Wendy DuBow, ed., *Conversations with Anaïs Nin* (1994); and Noel Fitch Riley, *The Erotic Life of Anaïs Nin* (1993). An obituary (which contains the quotation in the text) appeared in the *New York Times* on January 16, 1977.

SUSAN PIZZOLATO

NORDSTROM, Ursula. February 1, 1910–October 11, 1988. Children's literature editor, publisher.

Ursula Nordstrom was born in New York City, the only child of actors Henry E. Dixey (sometimes spelled "Dixie") and Marie Ursula Nordstrom. (A few records inexplicably list her father's surname as Litchfield.) Her parents married shortly before her birth and divorced when she was seven. After that, Nordstrom rarely saw her dashing father; she spent most of the year in boarding schools and her vacations with her mother and, later, her stepfather, businessman Elliott R. Brown.

She was educated at Winnwood School in Lake Grove, New York, and then at Northfield Seminary in Massachusetts. Despite teachers' recognition of young Ursula's literary talent (at sixteen, she stated an intention of becoming a writer), she proceeded not to college but, at her family's behest, to business school for secretarial courses. An interest in publishing led her in 1931 to a job at Harper and Brothers (later Harper and Row, and now HarperCollins), where after five years she found a congenial berth in the Department of Books for Boys and Girls as the assistant to the director, Ida Louise Raymond. Having little ambition for the department, the publishing house casually passed the directorship to Nordstrom after Raymond's departure in 1940. The directorship was to be Nordstrom's for thirty-three years, and in that time the department became legendary. Also at Harper she met Mary Griffith, who would be Nordstrom's companion until her death.

Her whole-souled consecration to finding and nurturing creative talent led to discovery after discovery: she recognized the gifts of John Steptoe, author-illustrator of *Stevie* (1969), when he was a teenage art student and Shel Silverstein, author of *The Giving Tree* (1964), through his work for *Playboy*. With copious correspondence, she elicited and shaped landmark book after landmark book, from Margaret Wise Brown's *Goodnight, Moon* (1947) and E. B. White's *Charlotte's Web* (1952) to Maurice Sendak's *Where the Wild Things Are* (1963) and Louise Fitzhugh's *Harriet the Spy* (1964). Under her guidance, books challenged taboos in children's literature, with Fitzhugh's *The Long Secret* (1965) discussing menstruation, John Donovan's *I'll Get There, It Better Be Worth the Trip* (1969) depicting a homoerotic encounter, and Maurice Sendak's *In the Night Kitchen* (1970) featuring a gleefully naked young boy as protagonist. Her interests were broad, leading her to develop books for children from infancy to young adulthood; she also ushered in the genre of the beginning reader with Harper's I Can Read Books series, starting with Else Minarik's *Little Bear* (1957), illustrated by Maurice Sendak. She tempered her devotion to creativity with a pragmatism about marketing that allowed her to shape both books and marketing approaches to maximum effect; she cajoled salespeople and cultivated major retailers, and she wisely sought out expert testimony to preempt criticism on controversial titles.

Some of her colleagues felt that her books were too far ahead of their time, and that may have limited their appearance on the important American Library Association's annual Notable Children's Books list. Nevertheless, they received a total of three Newbery Medals and two Caldecott Medals, plus numerous other awards. Nordstrom herself was the recipient of the Woman's National Book Association's Constance Lindsay Skinner Award in 1972. Though she was uncomfortable about her own writing, her book *The Secret Language* (1960) was named an American Library Association Notable Children's Book and became a popular favorite with many young readers, who relished the exotic details (taken from Nordstrom's own youth) of life at a girls' boarding school.

Though Nordstrom is probably the single most significant editorial figure in the field's twentieth-century evolution, she was not a phenomenon in isolation. Many women in publishing houses were relegated to the children's division—but the institutional market (schools and libraries) for children's books and for creative talent in works for youth was blooming, and such "relegation" gave many gifted women, who refused to accept the judgment of their literature as unimportant, the opportunity for considerable achievement and reward. All the same, Nordstrom's "firsts" were often dual: she was, in 1960, the first female vice president at Harper and the first from the children's division; she was the first female recipient, in 1980, of the Association of American Publishers' Curtis

Benjamin Award, as well as the first children's publisher to be so honored. Nordstrom, a self-described "ardent feminist," was eventually offered a "chance to move along (or up) to the adult field" (Marcus, *Dear Genius,* p. 326), after having proven herself satisfactorily in what was considered lesser work, but she summarily and indignantly rejected this opportunity in favor of what she considered the far more interesting and important work of publishing "good books for bad children."

The fierce devotion she lavished on her books meant that she had little tolerance for competing editors and disapproving critics. Nordstrom was famously at odds, for instance, with Anne Carroll Moore, the powerful superintendent of children's work at the New York Public Library, who had disparaged both *Stuart Little* and *Charlotte's Web.* Though life for her assistants and junior colleagues wasn't always peaceful, several talented individuals among them went on to their own luminous careers in publishing and spoke with respect and awe of Nordstrom's abilities.

As the decades wore on, publishing became less a creative and more a bottom-line business. This fact may have contributed to Nordstrom's decision, in 1973, to trade the position of director of the department, with its attendant administrative obligations, for that of senior editor, under her own imprint of Ursula Nordstrom Books, until her retirement from Harper in 1979. She and her partner Mary Griffith traded the bustle of New York City for the quiet of rural Bridgewater, Connecticut. Nordstrom died in nearby New Milford, after a long fight with ovarian cancer, on October 11, 1988, at the age of seventy-eight. She was posthumously inducted into the Publishing Hall of Fame in 1989, but her real memorial lies in the continuing impact of the books she brought into the world and the literature she shaped.

Bibliography: The single most significant source for information on Nordstrom is Leonard S. Marcus's collection of her letters, *Dear Genius: The Letters of Ursula Nordstrom* (1998), which is prefaced by a detailed biography and an overview of Nordstrom's career and includes a bibliography of some depth. Marcus's interview with William C. Morris (director of library promotion and advertising at Harper), "An Interview with William C. Morris," *Horn Book* 71, no. 1 (January–February 1995), pp. 37–46, contains some of the most significant professional reflections on Nordstrom's career. Nordstrom's own interview with Roni Natov and Geraldine De Luca, "Discovering Contemporary Classics: An Interview with Ursula Nordstrom," *The Lion and the Unicorn* 3, no. 1 (January 1979), pp. 119–35, is also enlightening, as is her chapter "Editing Books for Young People" in Betsy Hearne and Marilyn Kaye's *Celebrating Children's Books: Essays on Children's Literature in Honor of Zena Sutherland* (1981). HarperCollins retains Nordstrom's professional papers. Additional information was provided by Barbara Dicks, Betsy Hearne, Leonard S. Marcus, William C. Morris, and Charlotte Zolotow. An obituary appeared in the *New York Times* on October 12, 1988.

DEBORAH STEVENSON

NORWOOD, Rose Finkelstein. September 10, 1890–September 25, 1980. Labor organizer and leader.

Rose Finkelstein was born in Kiev, Russia, the second of eight children of Henry Finkelstein, a distillery worker studying to be a rabbi, and Fanny Shafferman. Her parents, planning to emigrate to Brazil, crossed the Atlantic with one-year-old Rose and her older sister, but other travelers convinced them to disembark in New York. The family settled in Boston, where Henry Finkelstein made his living as a tailor while his wife ran a small grocery store. Irish American youth regularly shrieked "Christ Killer" at Rose as she walked to school, and pelted her with bricks. She sustained a serious head wound during one of these attacks, for which her assailant was sent to prison. This experience, which forced her family to move to a less hostile neighborhood in Roxbury, strongly influenced Rose to later assume a leading role in labor's campaign against fascism, and to fiercely embrace Zionism.

Finkelstein left high school in her senior year to become an operator for New England Telephone, one of a very few Jews employed in a company that systematically discriminated against them. In 1912, at the request of the Women's Trade Union League (WTUL), the International Brotherhood of Electrical Workers (IBEW) organized the Boston Telephone Operators Union (TOU). Finkelstein joined as a charter member. She quickly became a member of the executive boards of both the TOU and the Boston WTUL, and she helped lead the 1919 New England telephone strike. Called by the female operators over the objection of the IBEW leadership, and joined by the male telephone workers only on the third day, the strike completely shut down telephone service in five states and ended in victory for the strikers.

Frequent moves had disrupted Rose's schooling, and she enthusiastically participated in the burgeoning workers' education movement after World War I. Finkelstein was determined to acquire both a broad cultural education and the writing and speaking skills trade unionists required to bargain effectively with highly educated managerial officials. She was part of a large delegation of telephone operators in the first class at the Bryn Mawr Summer School for Women Workers in Industry in 1921. The Boston Trade Union College's executive secretary called her one of the most consistent attendants at classes from the school's opening in 1919 until it closed in 1931.

Finkelstein left the telephone service to marry Hyman Norwood on December 25, 1921. Her wedding gown was made at the Boston WTUL's dress shop, which it had established to finance labor organizing. Her husband, a Jew born in Simna, Russia, owned a small tire and battery shop in Roxbury, and was a motorcycle racer and former streetcar man. During World War II, he was employed in the Hingham shipyard, and later worked in gas stations and tire shops. The couple had two children, Bernard (1922) and Barbara (1926). Because of the anti-Semitic harassment she had suffered as a child, Rose vowed to raise her children in an all-Jewish neighborhood, and the family resided in Mattapan. At Brookwood Labor College summer institutes in 1928 and 1935, she studied not only organizing techniques, but how to raise the "trade union child." This led her to found, and assume the presidency of, a Child Study Association group in Boston.

For almost a quarter century after 1933, Norwood was one of the principal woman field organizers in the American labor movement, relating easily to workers in a broad range of industries. She was a powerful extemporaneous speaker, highly effective at organizing meetings and strike rallies. After directing several successful campaigns among telegraphers, in 1937 she became business agent of the Laundry Workers Union in Boston, leading a series of bitterly contested strikes. At Lewandos Laundry in Watertown, she was arrested in a picket line brawl. Norwood challenged the company's practice of paying blacks lower wages than whites. Because of her prominence in interracial labor organizing, the Boston branch of the National Association for the Advancement of Colored People (NAACP) appointed her to its advisory board in 1942.

As an officer of the Boston WTUL during the 1930s, and as its president from 1941 to 1950, Norwood spearheaded campaigns in Boston against fascism and anti-Semitism, including lectures by close friend and exiled Jewish Social Democratic Reichstag deputy Toni Sender. In 1937, Norwood rallied support on the Boston docks for British seamen on the *Linaria,* who had staged a sit-down strike when they learned the ship's cargo included war materiel for Franco's forces in Spain. As a leader of the Massachusetts Citizens Committee for Racial Understanding, Norwood mobilized opposition to the wave of brutal beatings of Boston's Jews during World War II by Irish American youth. After the war, Norwood lobbied for legislation to permit displaced persons, many of them Holocaust survivors, to enter the United States. She also championed the right of married women to retain their jobs during the Depression and after World War II. She campaigned against the Boston School Committee rule requiring a female teacher to resign when she married, and for a bill to grant women teachers pay equal to that of their male counterparts. As Boston WTUL president, she urged organized labor to protect women's employment after the war ended.

From 1939 until her retirement in the mid 1950s, Norwood was an organizer for the International Ladies' Garment Workers' Union, the International Jewelry Workers Union, the American Federation of State, County, and Municipal Employees, the Retail Clerks International Union, and the Building Service Employees International Union, on numerous campaigns across New England and Pennsylvania. Police dogs and clubs, tear gas, and inclement weather never deterred her. Norwood's activism on behalf of Boston's senior citizens during the 1970s led Boston mayor Kevin White to appoint her to the advisory council to his Commission on the Affairs of the Elderly. She died of a heart attack in Boston on September 25, 1980, at the age of ninety, having survived her husband by twenty-three years.

Bibliography: The Rose Norwood Papers are in the Schlesinger Library, Radcliffe Institute for Advanced Study, Harvard University. They consist mostly of a small amount of correspondence and scrapbooks of newspaper clippings. Letters from Rose Norwood are in the National Women's Trade Union League Papers, Library of Congress, Washington, D.C. See also Stephen H. Norwood, *Labor's Flaming Youth: Telephone Operators and Worker Militancy, 1878–1923* (1990); Norwood, "Reclaiming Working-Class Activism: The Boston Women's Trade Union League, 1930–1950," *Labor's Heritage* 10, no. 1 (Summer 1998), pp. 20–35; and Sari Roboff, *Boston's Labor Movement: An Oral History of Work and Union Organizing* (1977). Obituaries appeared in the *Boston Globe* on September 28, 1980, and in the *Boston Herald-American* on September 27, 1980. The Hamburg Emigration Lists suggest that Rose Norwood was born in 1890. The 1900 federal census lists her year of birth as 1889. She gave 1891 as her year of birth.

STEPHEN H. NORWOOD

NYRO, Laura. October 18, 1947–April 8, 1997. Singer-songwriter, feminist.

Laura Nyro was a prodigiously talented artist whose music was an ingenious melding of R&B, pop, doo-wop, jazz, and Broadway. Her songwriting first brought her to the attention of the music business as a teenager when she wrote a series of catchy pop songs that better-known artists made into top ten hits. Soon Nyro was defying pop conventions with her own breathtakingly original recordings, which influenced generations of musicians from Joni Mitchell to Ricki Lee Jones, from Kate Bush to Tori Amos.

Nyro was born Laura Nigro in New York City, where she was raised by her Jewish mother and Italian father. She and her younger brother Jan grew up in a Bronx neighborhood where her family straddled the line between working and middle class. Her father, Louis Nigro, was a jazz trumpeter who eventually turned to piano tuning for steady work; her mother, Gilda Mirsky, worked as a bookkeeper at the American Psychoanalytic Association. Nyro's influences ran the gamut from high to low culture, from the city's museums and concert halls to the Catskill hotels where her father played jazz. While she was growing up, she listened to the popular music of the day—especially R&B and the girl groups that flourished in the early sixties—but also to jazz artists, from John Coltrane and Miles Davis to BILLIE HOLIDAY. A precocious child, by the age of eight she was writing songs on her family's Steinway grand piano. By sixteen, while a student at Manhattan's High School of Music and Art, she was singing doo-wop with a group of Puerto Rican boys on the street corners of her neighborhood.

After graduating from high school, Nyro sold her first song, "And When I Die," to the folk group Peter, Paul, and Mary for $5,000. Trying on various stage names as a teenager, she eventually settled on Laura Nyro (pronounced "Nero"). In 1966, at eighteen, she recorded her first album, *More Than a New Discovery.* Although the album failed to register on the charts, it contained four songs that over the years became hits for others—"Wedding Bell Blues" and "Blowin' Away" for the Fifth Dimension, "And When I Die" for Blood, Sweat and Tears, and "Stoney End" for Barbra Streisand. Nyro's first break as a performer came when she was invited to the 1967 Monterey Pop Festival. Monterey showcased the free-form psychedelic rock coming out of San Francisco, and Nyro, whose act was more nightclub than hippie, met with a chilly reception. Nyro was not booed off the stage, as legend has it, but she wasn't embraced either, and her experience there apparently undermined her confidence in herself as a performer. She struggled with stage fright for the rest of her career, and often chose smaller, cozier venues where she would be surrounded by sympathetic fans.

By 1967 Nyro was widely regarded as one of the hottest songwriters around, and her Lower East Side look—the long, black gypsy hair and self-dramatizing poses—was unique in the rock world. The following year Columbia Records signed her to a $4 million record contract. Her first record with her new label, *Eli and the Thirteenth Confession,* pushed the envelope of pop music with its harmonic complexity and quirky, often enigmatic lyrics. Once again, others hit gold with her music—Three Dog Night with "Eli's Comin'," and the Fifth Dimension with "Stoned Soul Picnic." Her 1969 follow-up, *New York Tendaberry,* was more experimental, and some found it self-consciously arty. For *Christmas and the Beads of Sweat* (1970) Nyro chose to work with a number of veteran R&B musicians and the result was decidedly more listenable, but no less passionate, than her previous effort. This album marked Nyro's first effort to tackle the political upheavals of the day, including the government's repression of the Black Panthers. Her next album, *Gonna Take a Miracle,* which she recorded in 1971 with the R&B trio Labelle, consisted entirely of remakes of soul and doo-wop classics.

Nyro usually wrote about romantic love, although her love of New York City, which she described in "New York Tendaberry" as "looking like a city, but feeling like a religion," seemed to loom almost as large. If Nyro's music often suggested that romantic love was the central fact of a woman's life, she also bristled against women's subordination. As early as 1968, in "The Confession," she exhorted her lover to "super ride inside my lovething" and sang, "you were born a woman not a slave." And in "Emmie," she wrote, albeit obliquely, of a woman's love for another woman.

Nyro had a large cult following, but little enthusiasm for the business of selling records. She refused to change a single note or word in her songs, even when producers argued that such tweaking could allow her to have a hit record of her own. In 1971, at the age of twenty-four, she left New York and the music industry to marry a carpenter, David Bianchini, and moved to a small Massachusetts fishing town. Her disenchantment with the business owed quite a lot to her disillusionment with her manager, David Geffen, whose phenomenal success began when he started managing Nyro in 1967. In the end, both her marriage and her retirement were short-lived. Her marriage ended in early 1974, and in 1976 she recorded *Smile,* an ambitious jazz-inflected album that was a commercial disappointment. In 1978, she gave birth to her only child. Although her son, Gil Bianchini, has her ex-husband's surname, his birth father was a man from India named Harindra "Hari" Singh with whom Nyro was briefly involved. In 1983 she began a relationship with painter Maria Desiderio, with whom she lived for the rest of her life in rural Connecticut.

Nyro did not tour for ten years after her son's birth, but she did record three more albums of original music: *Nested* (1978), *Mother's Spiritual* (1984), and *Walk the Dog and Light the Light* (1993). Although Nyro's music became overtly political—she wrote about the environment, feminism, love between women, and animal rights—she did not find favor with critics, even feminist critics, who suspected that her kind of feminism, which put great emphasis on women's mothering, reinforced dominant cultural assumptions about women. None of this seems to have deterred Nyro, who didn't miss the limelight, and who said of her ten-year break from performing, "Sometimes you trade one success to find another" (Romanowski, p. 141). Nyro died of ovarian cancer (the same disease that had claimed her mother's life) at the age of forty-nine in Danbury, Connecticut, soon after the release of her two-CD career compilation, *The Best of Laura Nyro: Stoned Soul Picnic.*

Bibliography: Michelle Kort, *Soul Picnic: The Music and Passion of Laura Nyro* (2002), is the one biography of the singer. Robert Christgau, *Christgau's Record Guide* (1981), contains a discography. Patricia Romanowski, "Laura Nyro," in Barbara O'Dair, ed., *Trouble Girls: The Rolling Stone Book of Women in Rock* (1997), and Jon Pareles and Patricia Romanowski, eds., *The Rolling Stone Encyclopedia of Rock & Roll* (1983), include biographical information and assessments of Nyro's musical career. See also Gillian Garr, *She's a Rebel: The History of Women in Rock & Roll* (1992). Articles that treat her significance and legacy include Deborah Sontag, "An Enigma Wrapped in Songs," *New York Times,* October 26, 1997; Stephen Holden, "Tribute to Laura Nyro: Inside the Heart of an Earth Mother," *New York Times,* October 30, 1997; Peter Marks, "An Elusive Folk Star Who's Ripe for Rediscovery," *New York Times,* April 22, 2001; and Neil Strauss, "The Times Are A-Changin'," *New York Times,* September 27, 2001. Obituaries appeared in the *New York Times* and the *Washington Post* on April 10, 1997.

ALICE ECHOLS

O

O'CONNOR, Jessie Lloyd. February 14, 1904–December 24, 1988. Labor journalist and activist, pacifist.

Jessie Lloyd was born in Chicago. Her father, attorney William Bross Lloyd, was known as one of the "millionaire socialists" whose family wealth derived in part from a controlling interest in the *Chicago Tribune.* Her mother, Lola Maverick Lloyd, was heir to a Texas cattle fortune and a founder of the Woman's Peace Party. Her paternal grandfather was noted reformer Henry Demarest Lloyd, best known for his social critique of American capital, *Wealth against Commonwealth* (1894). Given this dual inheritance of wealth and a family tradition of reform and activism, Jessie Lloyd O'Connor dedicated her life to the quest for social justice. Not an ideologue, she never committed to one party or political persuasion. Rather, she was first and foremost a humanist, albeit with a radical bent and, at times, a stinging wit.

The oldest of four children, Jessie grew up in the well-to-do Chicago suburb of Winnetka, where she attended local private and public schools. In 1915, at age eleven, she traveled with her mother to Europe on Henry Ford's controversial Peace Ship; her lifelong pacifism was rooted in this firsthand encounter with the carnage of World War I. After graduating from New Trier High School in 1921, she went on to her mother's alma mater, Smith College, graduating magna cum laude with a degree in economics in 1925.

Jessie Lloyd traveled in Europe, somewhat restlessly, for several months after graduation as she sought to shape her life's work. She soon found her calling in journalism, first as a stringer for both the *London Daily Herald* and her family's paper, the *Chicago Tribune.* Initially assigned to write what she considered "fluff" pieces around the League of Nations sessions in Geneva in 1926, she wanted instead to expose injustices, hoping that this would encourage others to work for social change. Before returning to the United States in 1928, she spent more than a year in the Soviet Union, observing and reporting on the successes and failures of the Russian Revolution. In addition to several nonfiction pieces she published upon her return to America, she also wrote an unpublished, semi-autobiographical satirical novel variously titled "Polly Goes to Russia" or "A Flapper in the Soviet Union."

After several months spent trying to market her novel, in 1929 Lloyd joined the staff of the labor-oriented Federated Press (FP), an alternative news service. She was soon involved in a passionate love affair with her editor, Harvey O'Connor, and equally passionate about her first major assignment for the FP—the lengthy and bitter textile workers' strike centered in Gastonia, North Carolina. In dramatic but simple prose, Lloyd reported on the horrid living conditions, the dangerous work environment, and the legal persecution of union organizers. She would use that same style of reportage when she covered the equally violent miners' strike in Harlan County, Kentucky, in 1931.

In between those two strikes, Jessie Lloyd and Harvey O'Connor married in June 1930. Decades later, they would title the unpublished version of their autobiography "The Contumacious Couple." These two seemed an unlikely pair—she an heiress and he the adopted son of working-class parents, a former logger, and a member of the Industrial Workers of the World. In addition to their commitment to each other, they shared a commitment to working for social justice, never denying that it was Jessie's money that allowed them to dedicate their lives to social action work.

In 1931 the O'Connors moved to Pittsburgh. Now writing as Jessie Lloyd O'Connor, she continued to report on the growing labor strife in the Depression-rocked steel industry. O'Connor also grew increasingly alarmed at the rise of fascism and was an early and ardent supporter of the American League Against War and Fascism. In 1932 the O'Connors went to the Soviet Union, where for several months they joined their old friend ANNA LOUISE STRONG on her English-language newspaper, the *Moscow Daily News.* The start of the New Deal in 1933 saw the couple back in Pittsburgh, where they continued their writing and their activism, interspersed with travel around the United States and abroad.

By the late 1930s, the O'Connors had returned to Jessie's birthplace, Chicago. From 1937 to 1943, she was secretary and then president of the Chicago chapter of the League of Women Shoppers, a pro-labor, anti-fascist consumer group that urged women, "Use Your Buying Power for Justice." From 1939 to 1945 they were residents of the famed settlement Hull House. There, O'Connor threw herself into increasingly localized social action work, organizing women neighbors into the Stop and Go Light Mothers Club and investigating substandard housing for the Metropolitan Housing Council. Even as World War II raged, O'Connor remained true to her pacifist upbringing, maintaining throughout an active membership in the organization her mother had helped form, the Women's International League for Peace and Freedom. During this period the O'Connors also started a family, adopting eighteen-month-old Stephen in 1942 and eleven-month-old Kathleen in 1943.

In 1948 the family moved to Little Compton, Rhode Island, and there O'Connor would live the rest of her life, active almost until her death. Despite their frequent public denials, both O'Connors had long been suspected of being members of the Communist Party. Twice during the 1950s, Harvey was called to testify before the House Committee on Un-American Activities Committee but refused to name names, and both lost their passports for several years. Their response was to provide financial assistance to victims of the anti-communist witch hunts through an organization called the National Committee to Abolish HUAC. As the civil rights movement accelerated in the 1950s, the O'Connors also provided financial assistance as well as opened up their oceanfront home to activists in need of rest. Ever the pacifist, Jessie Lloyd O'Connor was an early and outspoken critic of the war in Vietnam, taking part in anti-war demonstrations well into her sixties. Slowed in her later years by an eye condition that left her nearly blind, O'Connor nonetheless continued to protest the impact of Reaganomics at home and U.S. militarism abroad. A year after her husband of almost sixty years passed away, Jessie Lloyd O'Connor died in a hospital in Fall River, Massachusetts, at the age of eighty-four. She was throughout her life a fighter for peace and an advocate of social justice.

Bibliography: The Jessie Lloyd O'Connor Papers are at the Sophia Smith Collection, Smith College Library, Northampton, Massachusetts, and include correspondence, published and unpublished writings, O'Connor's FBI records, birth and death certificates, and photographs. In addition, Lola Maverick Lloyd's papers, which include a great deal of material relating to O'Connor, are part of the Schwimmer-Lloyd Collection at the New York Public Library. See also Harvey O'Connor, Jessie Lloyd O'Connor, and Susan M. Bowler, *Harvey and Jessie: A Couple of Radicals* (1988). Obituaries appeared in the *Providence* (R.I.) *Journal Bulletin* on December 27, 1988; the *Chicago Tribune* on January 8, 1989; and the *Guardian* on January 18, 1989.

KATHLEEN BANKS NUTTER

O'HAIR, Madalyn Murray. April 13, 1919–c. September 1995. Atheist.

"America's most hated woman" was born Madalyn Evalyn Mays, the second child and only daughter of Lena Christina Scholle and John Irvin Mays, an ironworker, in booming Pittsburgh, where the family tempered prosperity with Presbyterian practice. After the Depression hit the steel industry, the Mayses lived nomadically, shifting across America's heartland. Madalyn graduated from Rossford (Ohio) High School in 1936 and then attended college sporadically.

In 1941 Mays eloped with John Roths, a steelworker. Within two years, he shipped out to the Pacific and she shipped out to Europe and North Africa as a cryptographer in the Women's Army Corps. The separation effectively dissolved their marriage. Indeed, when Lieutenant Roths returned home pregnant after the war, she was hoping that William Murray—the father, a fellow officer, and a Roman Catholic—would get a divorce and marry her. He refused. Unbowed, she divorced Roths, and her forgiving parents refolded her into the family. In return, this professed atheist had her son, William Murray III, baptized after his May 1946 birth.

Within weeks, the single-mother veteran matriculated at Ashland, a local Christian college in Ohio, where she completed its required two-year Bible study course and graduated with a BA in history in 1948. After fitful attempts at graduate study and yet another family move, Madalyn Mays settled in Houston, earning an LLB in 1952 from South Texas College of Law, which then lacked American Bar Association accreditation. The ever-nomadic, raucous Mays clan left the Texas oilfields for Baltimore.

Mays became pregnant in early 1954 and chafed under parental and community scrutiny for withholding the father's identity. Following the birth of Jon Garth Murray that November, she assumed the name Murray, gained employment as a social worker, and relied on her family for child care, in repayment for which she attempted conformity. Despite her family's spiritual convictions, however, she remained an unabashed atheist. An outsider who monitored McCarthy-era politics vigilantly, Murray identified with those deemed "un-American," so much so that, in August 1960, she attempted to defect to the USSR at its Paris consulate, young sons in tow.

Murray returned to America, and fortune intervened, as what mattered most to her personally—family, atheism, individual rights—converged politically in October 1960. Upon hearing of her son Bill's discomfort during compulsory classroom prayers and Bible study, the educated yet feisty Murray took action, demanding that his Baltimore public school halt mandatory religious practices. She then took Bill out of school when the district refused to allow him to leave the classroom during school prayers. From her kitchen table, she wrote other atheists and civil rights champions, such as the American Civil Liberties Union, for support. The Murrays' suit was first heard in Baltimore Superior Court that December, then in the Maryland Court of Appeals. In May 1962, the U.S. Supreme Court agreed to hear *Murray v. Curlett,* pairing it with *Schempp v. Abington,* a suit brought by a Pennsylvania family. In an 8–1 decision announced June 17, 1963, the Supreme Court deemed organized prayer in the schools unconstitutional.

The victory created fame and infamy, catapulting Madalyn Murray into the media's crosshairs. Her family was ostracized, physically assaulted, and subjected to death threats. Nonetheless, she took her intellectual argument to the duplication machine, devising *American Atheist* from the files of the *Free Humanist* newsletter, and printed the first monthly issue in July 1963. Supported by other atheists and civil rights advocates, Murray now endeavored to achieve two goals: to have all religious matters removed from public schools and government, and to have atheism accorded due respect.

Murray and her sons fled to Hawaii. Within a year, she married Richard O'Hair and they moved to Austin, Texas, intending to create a respected community for atheism. To this end, she founded the Society of Separationists, devoted to First Amendment causes, and the American Atheist Center. The same year, after publishers rejected *Why I Am an Atheist,* she created the American Atheist Press and in quick succession published *Why I Am an Atheist* (1966), *The American Atheist* (1967), *An Atheist Epic* (1968), and *An Atheist Speaks* (1970). She took to the airwaves as well, broadcasting "Atheist Point of View" (June 1968) and "Dial-an-Atheist" while suing for equal time to rebut religious speakers. Meanwhile, O'Hair provided a home for Robin Murray, the infant child of William and Susan Murray, and legally adopted her in 1974.

Articulate and knowledgeable, O'Hair reveled in debating theology, a subject she knew well from college days and home life. In the turbulent world of the 1960s and 1970s, she became a popular media figure. She continued to assail the laws, hoping to strengthen individual freedoms and challenging deistic slogans on coins ("In God We Trust") and in oaths ("One Nation Under God"). In the early 1970s the O'Hairs bought doctorates of divinity to gain IRS tax exemption. Under O'Hair's stewardship, the American Atheists expanded nationally and internationally, developed radio and television programming, and built its own library and archive.

Madalyn O'Hair became "the Atheist." Yet not all members of her group admired her confrontational style or approved of her organizational nepotism, particularly the fast-track promotions of Jon Murray to executive director and Robin Murray-O'Hair to editor. In 1980, William Murray publicly repudiated his role in *Murray v. Curlett* and, in an act of revenge against his mother, embraced evangelical Christianity. In response O'Hair tightened ties with those around her.

On August 26, 1995, Madalyn Murray O'Hair, Jon Murray, and Robin Murray-O'Hair disappeared under suspicious circumstances. Their remains were uncovered in Camp Wood, Texas, and identified in early 2001. Investigators believe they had been kidnapped, extorted, and then murdered.

Although the media portrayed Madalyn Murray O'Hair as anti-American, anti-woman, immoral, and intolerant, the reality of her life contrasted mightily. She cherished her extended family, prized democracy and its individual rights, and championed women's rights, especially the right to control one's own body. O'Hair was volatile, secretive, and self-aggrandizing in turn. She never opposed religion, only its intrusion into the public domain. "I just want three words on my tombstone: Woman, Atheist, Anarchist. That's me."

Bibliography: Unpublished materials—journals, letters, photographs—are found in the American Atheists library and archives and in the private collection of Jim Nassbourn. Among Madalyn Murray O'Hair's prolific outpourings not mentioned in the text, notable volumes include *What on Earth Is an Atheist?* (1969), *Women and Atheism: The Ultimate Liberation* (1979), and *The Best of Dial-an-Atheist* (1982), all published by American Atheist Press; and *Freedom under Siege* (1974). O'Hair's ideas can also be traced in the *American Atheist Newsletter* and the *American Atheist Magazine,* starting in 1963. "American Atheists: A History" (available from the organization) pinpoints her early and continuing efforts, while Conrad F. Goeringer, "The Murray O'Hair Family: Generations in Service to Atheism and the Separation of Church and State," *American Atheists* Newsletter, June 2000, captures her worth. Various insights into O'Hair's character can be found in *Current Biography* (1977), pp. 328–30; "Letter to the Editor: I Am the Maryland Atheist," *Life,* April 13, 1963, p. 63; and Robert Liston, "Mrs. Murray's War on God," *Saturday Evening Post,* July 11–18, 1964, pp. 83–86. Bryan F. Le Beau, *The Atheist: Madalyn Murray O'Hair* (2003), offers an overview of her life, quoting material from O'Hair's private journals and material from her FBI file, heretofore unpublished. The final quote appears in an interview with O'Hair in *Freedom Writer* 5, no. 2 (March/April/May 1989). Standard obituaries did not appear; see Ross Milloy, "Bodies Identified as Those of Missing Atheist and Kin," *New York Times,* March 16, 2001. Stephen Bates, "The Unfaithful," *Washington Post,* July 29, 2001, reconciles O'Hair's public and private personae. Susan L. Pizzolato provided bibliographic assistance, and Ellen Johnson, president of American Atheists, supplied archival information.

HARRIETTE L. WALKER

O'KEEFFE, Georgia. November 15, 1887–March 6, 1986. Artist.

The first internationally acclaimed American woman artist, Georgia O'Keeffe emerged in the twentieth century as one of the cultural icons of her time. Known as much for her fiercely independent spirit as for her pioneering accomplishments in American modernism, O'Keeffe conducted life on her own terms. Georgia Totto O'Keeffe was born in Sun Prairie, Wisconsin, the second of seven children, and she spent her childhood on the prosperous dairy farm of her parents, Ida Totto and Francis Calyxtus O'Keeffe. Both parents were offspring of European immigrants (Hungarian and Irish, respectively) who had come to Sun Prairie in the mid nineteenth century to homestead on the American frontier. Georgia's exceptional natural talent surfaced quickly, and her parents encouraged her with private lessons in drawing and watercolor painting. By the time O'Keeffe left the family farm at age thirteen to attend Sacred Heart Academy near Madison, she had resolved to become an artist.

In 1902, the O'Keeffe family moved to Williamsburg, Virginia, but Georgia and her older brother stayed behind to attend high school in Madison, where they lived with their aunt. The next year, she joined her family in Virginia and was sent off to Chatham Episcopal Institute, a private girls' boarding school not far from Lynchburg. O'Keeffe focused on art studies and graduated in 1905, the only art major in her class.

During her twenties, she solitarily pursued her goal of establishing a career—an unusual focus for women of her day. In the academic year 1905–06, she attended the School of the Art Institute of Chicago, intent upon becoming an art teacher. That summer she returned to Williamsburg and was stricken with typhoid, forcing her into a long period of convalescence. Episodes of long-term illness would plague her in early adulthood, interrupting the flow of her life and sometimes changing its course.

In 1907, O'Keeffe moved to New York City to attend the Art Students League, where her instructors included the flamboyant William Merritt Chase, whose exciting ideas about brushwork stimulated the artist's technical development. She also was invigorated by the intellectual and creative ferment of the New York cultural scene. The period was one of heady revolution in the arts, and the innovative photographer and gallery proprietor Alfred Stieglitz was a leading voice. A tireless proselytizer, Stieglitz aimed to introduce the best of European avant-garde art to the United States and to provide a center for the promotion of progressive American artists. Slightly more than ten years would pass before Georgia O'Keeffe joined the Stieglitz circle as its only female member.

In the intervening years, O'Keeffe struggled to find her own voice in her art. For several years, beginning in 1908, she stopped painting altogether, pursuing instead a career in commercial art and advertising in Chicago. A change of heart came in 1912 when she attended a summer art class at the University of Virginia in Charlottesville given by Alon Bement, who introduced her to Arthur Wesley Dow's radical approach to art education, which stressed fundamental principles of design, not replication of nature, as the primary tools of artistic expression. Dow's teachings pointed O'Keeffe for the first time in the direction of abstraction.

With renewed enthusiasm, O'Keeffe returned to her former goal of teaching art. In 1912 she took a position at a high school in Amarillo, Texas, where she first encountered—and fell in love with—the American West. For two years,

O'Keeffe taught in Amarillo and spent her summers assisting Bement in his classes at the University of Virginia. The classes eventually led her to study with Dow himself at Columbia Teachers College in the fall of 1914; this initiated a period of intense artistic and personal growth. Often with her Columbia classmate Anita Pollitzer, O'Keeffe visited Stieglitz's exhibitions, and at Pollitzer's urging she supported women's suffrage. By this stage in her life, O'Keeffe's unique personality had fully emerged. She was a new kind of woman—intense, direct, and often severely dressed in tailored black clothes and men's shoes. She was uninhibited and unafraid to chart her own course.

In the pivotal year 1915, O'Keeffe accepted a one-year teaching assignment in Columbia, South Carolina, in part because it allowed her more time to pursue her own work. Although now removed from the avant-garde New York scene, O'Keeffe kept up with its developments through periodicals and a vibrant correspondence with Anita Pollitzer. In October, O'Keefe experienced an artistic breakthrough when she embarked upon a series of bold experiments in abstraction. She produced a remarkable set of abstract charcoal drawings that laid the foundation for the highly personal vocabulary of line, movement, and shape O'Keeffe employed for the rest of her life. She was one of the earliest artists to explore pure abstraction, and her exceptional virtuosity emerged while she was a schoolteacher working in virtual isolation in South Carolina.

Excited by her discoveries, O'Keeffe sent a packet of the drawings to Pollitzer in New York in early 1916 with strict instructions not to show them to anyone. Pollitzer, however, took the drawings to Stieglitz, who categorized O'Keeffe's art at first glance as an unabashed expression of female sexuality and promptly exhibited the works without notifying her. The painter's visit to New York in the spring of 1916 finally brought her face to face with Stieglitz. At first angered and then flattered by Stieglitz's appropriation of her work, O'Keeffe agreed to let him keep the drawings for future exhibitions. In the fall of 1916, O'Keeffe returned to Texas as head of the art department at West Texas State Normal College in Canyon and resumed her abstract experiments. She also painted watercolors based upon the vast expanses of the Texas plains, successfully integrating the objective with the nonobjective to produce some of the most important works of her career.

When she contracted severe influenza in early 1918, O'Keeffe temporarily left her job in Canyon to recuperate. Stieglitz, concerned for his protégée's health, offered her the opportunity to paint full-time if she quit her job and moved to New York. O'Keeffe accepted, and her life as an independent artist began. Her personal life also changed drastically; Stieglitz, who was twenty-three years her senior, was now at its center. Soon after O'Keeffe arrived in New York, he left his wife to live with O'Keeffe in a little studio belonging to his niece. Stieglitz began photographing O'Keeffe regularly, creating during this period some of the most erotic and private images in what would eventually become a composite "portrait" of her comprising more than three hundred images. Stieglitz and O'Keeffe married in 1924, and for the next twenty years he exhibited, promoted, and sold her work in his prestigious galleries.

From 1918 to 1929, O'Keeffe returned to oils and painted many of her masterful and best-known works: the lyrical, emotionally charged abstractions inspired by music and the sensual flower close-ups, both of which invited sexual interpretations despite her objections; her visionary pictures of Manhattan skyscrapers and East River panoramas; and the luscious renderings of fruit, leaves, and trees often painted during summer visits to the Stieglitz family vacation home at Lake George, New York. Her range of subjects was defined by the seasonal routine of the life she shared with Stieglitz: he insisted on spending the winter months in Manhattan and the summer months at Lake George. A private person, O'Keeffe frequently felt overwhelmed by the unremitting influx of her husband's family and New York friends.

During the 1920s, O'Keeffe achieved her first significant professional successes: a series of exhibitions at the Stieglitz galleries and record-setting prices for her works. Despite this, the decade was tumultuous. The constraints of the Manhattan–Lake George orbit bored her, and increasingly she found little in either place to stimulate her artistic needs. Her health suffered, and her childless marriage to Stieglitz faltered. O'Keeffe's self-esteem was especially wounded in the late 1920s when Stieglitz began a romantic involvement with his young gallery manager, Dorothy Norman.

Seeking an escape from the tensions of her life as well as a source of new artistic inspiration, O'Keeffe decided in 1929 to take a trip to New Mexico with artist Rebecca Strand, wife of photographer Paul Strand. They stayed with MABEL DODGE LUHAN, a former New York salon hostess, in her adobe compound in Taos. O'Keeffe remained in Taos for five months, thrilled by the new world of subjects now opened up to her. Her experience yielded her first important group of Southwest canvases: the brooding Penitente crosses, sun-drenched adobe churches, and colorful landscapes of red, blue, and black hills. From that point, she succumbed to the pull of the high desert. For the next twenty years, from 1929 to 1949, she established her own seasonal circuit between New Mexico and New York—a routine separate from that of Stieglitz, who would not leave the East. The body of work she created in the 1930s and 1940s established a relationship between herself and the New Mexico landscape so personal that her paintings have been seen as consummate interpretations of the American Southwest.

Among the most original, and enigmatic, of O'Keeffe's southwestern motifs are what she called her symbols of the desert—pictures of animal bones and skulls that she began to paint on her second trip to Taos in the summer of 1930—but the northern New Mexican landscape, particularly the area near Ghost Ranch, remained her most enduring theme. She discovered the area in 1934, after a three-year hiatus from the Southwest, during which time she suffered a nervous breakdown and was unable to paint for more than a year. Beginning in 1937, she rented a small adobe house on the ranch. She bought the house in 1940, and its stunning views became O'Keeffe's place of artistic and spiritual renewal for the rest of her life. In 1945, O'Keeffe bought a second New Mexico property in the Hispanic village of Abiquiu, twelve miles southwest of Ghost Ranch.

In 1946 the Museum of Modern Art mounted a retrospective of her work, the first solo show there to honor a woman. That July, Alfred Stieglitz died, and O'Keeffe spent the next three years mostly in New York, settling his estate. In 1949, at age sixty-one, the painter moved permanently to New Mexico, now dividing her time between Abiquiu (winters and springs) and Ghost Ranch (summers and falls). Although she continued to make frequent trips to New York, she had essentially closed the door on that phase of her life.

Throughout the 1950s and 1960s, O'Keeffe painted in an increasingly spare and more geometric manner. She produced three important late series: the patio pictures based upon the courtyard of her Abiquiu house, the images of the winding road outside her bedroom window at Ghost Ranch, and the paintings of clouds and rivers viewed from the air, which were inspired by her extensive airplane travel abroad in the 1950s. An exhibition at the Whitney Museum of American Art in 1970 introduced her to a new generation of art historians, critics, and enthusiasts. She became a celebrity icon and, for the emerging feminist movement, a cultural heroine. Ironically, O'Keeffe did not subscribe to late-twentieth-century feminism, but she nonetheless became a role model for countless women searching for validation of their own individuality.

In 1971, now eighty-four years old, O'Keeffe completed her final series of paintings, in which she depicted solitary black rocks balanced upon stumps. Soon after, the onset of macular degeneration destroyed her central vision, and she would never again produce quality paintings. Undaunted by the loss of her essential vision, she experimented well into her nineties with other media, primarily producing hand-built clay pots. In this process she was encouraged by young sculptor Juan Hamilton, whom she had hired in 1973 to help her with her artwork, exhibitions, and publications. He became her assistant and manager for the remainder of her life. In 1984, almost completely blind and in failing health, O'Keeffe moved to Santa Fe, where she lived with Hamilton and his family until her death there in 1986 at age ninety-eight. She requested no funeral or memorial service, and her ashes were scattered over her beloved landscape of northern New Mexico. When once asked to explain her extraordinary life, she said quite simply, "I've always known what I've wanted—and most people don't."

Bibliography: Archival sources include the Stieglitz-O'Keeffe Archives, Yale Collection of American Literature, Beinecke Rare Book and Manuscript Library, Yale University; the Georgia O'Keeffe Foundation Archives, Abiquiu, New Mexico; and the Georgia O'Keeffe Museum Research Center, Santa Fe, New Mexico. Biographical information on Georgia O'Keeffe can be found in many sources, including Laurie Lisle, *Portrait of an Artist: A Biography of Georgia O'Keeffe* (1980); and Roxana Robinson, *Georgia O'Keeffe* (1989). Also of interest is O'Keeffe's unconventional autobiography, *Georgia O'Keeffe* (1976). Anita Pollitzer, *A Woman on Paper: Georgia O'Keeffe* (1988), draws on their close friendship; see also Jack Cowart, Juan Hamilton, and Sarah Greenough, *Georgia O'Keeffe: Art and Letters* (1987). Perry Miller Adato produced a documentary film, *Georgia O'Keeffe,* for WNET, New York City, in 1977. Exhibition catalogues include Lloyd Goodrich and Doris Bry, *Georgia O'Keeffe* (1970); Georgia O'Keeffe, *Georgia O'Keeffe: A Portrait by Alfred Stieglitz* (1978, rev. ed., 1997); and Charles C. Eldredge, *Georgia O'Keeffe: American and Modern* (1993). Nancy G. Heller, "Georgia O'Keeffe: Pioneer," *Museum & Arts Washington,* November–December 1987, contains the final quote on p. 38. Other sources include Katharine Kuh, *The Artist's Voice: Talks with Seventeen Artists* (1962, rev. ed. 2000); and Wanda M. Corn, *The Great American Thing* (1999). An obituary appeared in the *New York Times* on March 7, 1986.

SARAH L. BURT

OLIVAREZ, Graciela. March 9, 1928–September 19, 1987. Civil rights activist, federal official, entrepreneur.

Graciela Olivarez devoted her life to civil rights activism and civil service as a passionate advocate for the rights of the Chicano/Latino people of the United States, a high-ranking official in the Carter administration, and an entrepreneur. She was born Graciela Gil in the small town of Sonora, Arizona, one of five children in a working-class family. Her father, Damian Gil Valero, an immigrant from Spain, was a machinist who worked in the copper mines; her mother, Eloisa Solis, of Mexican descent, was a homemaker who would often teach piano to make ends meet. When Graciela and her family moved to Phoenix, she dropped out of high school to help her family and began working at a variety of jobs while taking courses at a local business school. She earned her high school equivalency diploma in 1950 at the age of twenty-two; two years later she joined Spanish-language radio station KIFN, where she worked as an announcer, engineer, and women's program director. She also became the first woman disc jockey, with a talk show that focused on the Mexican American community's needs and interests. In 1958 she married Alfred Paul Olivarez; her son, Victor, was born in 1959. The couple divorced in 1961.

Her radio program on KIFN often informed the community on issues such as jobs, neighborhood safety and awareness, education, and health and Social Security, and Olivarez became increasingly active with the social and political movements of the time. In 1962, at the invitation of philanthropist and activist Robert Choate, she joined the Choate Foundation in Phoenix as a staff specialist, and worked on programs targeted for youths and families in the Mexican American and African American communities. In 1963, with the support of the President's Committee on Juvenile Delinquency and Youth Crime Control, she planned and conducted the first national conference on educational and bilingual problems of Mexican American students.

Her work and opinions were noticed as far as the Arizona state capital, and as a result she was appointed state director of the Office of Economic Opportunity (OEO) in 1965. As the OEO project representative she worked with the Departments of Labor and Health, Education and Welfare on the development of employment projects and was responsible for organizing Community Action Programs throughout Arizona. This former high school dropout wrote proposals for funding, trained staff, evaluated programs, formed a state coordinating committee for all federally funded social welfare programs, gave lectures and speeches, participated in a civil rights seminar in England as a guest of the Ditchley Foundation, and advised the governor of Arizona on OEO regulations and policies.

On one of her many business trips, she was seated next to Father Theodore Hesburgh, president of the University of Notre Dame. She reportedly spoke intently about how difficult it was for Mexican American communities to get quality education and health care, and shared her frustrations over the limitations of her OEO position. He was so impressed by her intelligence and enthusiasm, and her commitment to civil rights and the advancement of Chicanos/Latinos, that he invited her to attend the university's law school, offering to waive the entry requirements and supply a fellowship to cover her tuition.

Despite her lack of formal educational training, Olivarez entered law school, received the John Hay Whitney Fellowship, and in 1970, at the age of forty-two, became the first woman to graduate from the University of Notre Dame Law School. She next worked as a consultant with the National Urban Coalition on Mexican American affairs. A year later she testified before Congress regarding deficiencies in federal food distribution, and by 1972 she was appointed vice-chair of the President's Commission on Population and the American Future.

Soon after, Olivarez decided to return to the Southwest, accepting a position as law professor at the University of New Mexico (UNM) in Albuquerque. She continued her role in the civil rights movement and worked in various local and state government positions. At UNM she became the director of the Institute for Social Research and Development. In 1975, Governor Jerry Apodaca appointed her New Mexico's state planning officer.

In May 1977 President Jimmy Carter named her director of the Community Services Administration, the successor of the Office of Economic Opportunity. She became the highest-ranking Latina in his administration, and the third highest ranking woman in federal government. During her tenure she became known as a fervent proponent of economic, health, and educational policies that sought to improve conditions for working-class and ethnic communities. Frank and energetic, Olivarez was considered a tireless leader who was quick-witted and outspoken. Sargent Shriver referred to her as the pepper of one commission they both served on, to which she allegedly responded, "He better hope that I never become the chili."

In 1980 she resigned her post in Washington because she wanted to return to her home in New Mexico, and because the financial burden of maintaining two households had become too great. She became a senior consultant with United Way of America, built a private business as a political and public relations consultant, and had a Saturday morning radio show in Albuquerque. Olivarez always held that her most rewarding and inspiring times were her days as a radio talk show host, because they kept her in direct contact with the communities she worked to help. As an entrepreneur, Olivarez became interested in other forms of media, founding Olivarez Television Company Inc. in the mid 1980s and securing a television broadcasting license. Before this project could come to fruition, she died of cancer in Albuquerque in 1987 at the age of fifty-nine.

Graciela Olivarez was a firm believer in the importance of Latino unity, and in the uniqueness of the various groups that compose the broadly defined category "Hispanics" in the United States. She was a fearless advocate for the working poor, and her work and steadfast commitment to the struggle for human and civil rights in the United States still serves as a model for Latinas and Latinos of all backgrounds.

Bibliography: Coverage of Graciela Olivarez's career can be found in various newspapers and magazines, including the *Albuquerque Journal* and the *Washington Post.* See especially Jacqueline Trescott, "Opening a Door for the Poor: Graciela Olivarez, the Administration's Viceroy of Social Engineering," *Washington Post,* September 16, 1978, which contains the quotation. Also of interest is an interview with Olivarez, "The Poor Are an 'Easy Target' at Budget-Cutting Time," *U.S. News & World Report,* January 22, 1979, pp. 24, 27; and "Graciela Olivares *[sic]*: Depression-Era Child Helps Nation's Poor," *New York Times,* March 26, 1977. Biographical material is found in Gale Hardy, *American Women Civil Rights Activists: Bibliographies of 68 Leaders, 1825–1992* (1993); Diane Telgen and Jim Kamp, eds., *Notable Hispanic American Women* (1993); and Matt S. Meier, *Mexican American Biographies: A Historical Dictionary, 1836–1987* (1988). Additional material was supplied by Raquel Velasquez, a close friend of Graciela Olivarez, in an interview on September 1, 2003. An obituary appeared in the *Washington Post* on October 1, 1987.

BÁRBARA O. REYES

OLMSTED, Mildred Scott. December 5, 1890–July 2, 1990. Social worker, civil libertarian, peace activist.

Mildred Scott was born in Glenolden, Pennsylvania, the second of three daughters of Henry J. Scott, a lawyer, and Adele Brebant Hamrick, daughter of a well-to-do Philadelphia family. Mildred, a sometimes lonely but bright child, attended Friends Central School and graduated from Smith College in 1912.

At Smith she became interested in sociology after hearing Wellesley professor VIDA SCUDDER speak about social reform and settlement work. When she discovered that her father was not willing to send her to law school, she accepted a job at College Settlement in Philadelphia. While there, she enrolled in courses at the Philadelphia Training School for Social Work, a precursor of the Pennsylvania School of Social Work. Subsequently she completed a survey of the needs of juveniles for the Seybert Institute, marched in a 1913 suffrage parade, and volunteered in a suffrage tearoom. Her first major job was with the Main Line Federation of Churches, organizing the first social service department for Bryn Mawr Hospital. She also volunteered with the Main Line Birth Control Clinic. In 1918 she worked for the Girls Protective League near an army camp in Laurel, Maryland.

In 1919 Scott accepted a position with the American Red Cross in Paris, supervising recreation for the troops who had not been demobilized. She next worked with the Quakers doing reconstruction work in the Argonne. In January 1920 she went to Germany with Ruth Mellor, a friend from Smith College, to work in the child-feeding program run by the American Friends Service Committee (AFSC). Here she first met representatives of the newly formed Women's International League for Peace and Freedom (WILPF), an organization that grew out of the International Conference of Women at the Hague in 1915—which, under the leadership of JANE ADDAMS, had attempted to bring a negotiated peace to end World War I. The newly constituted WILPF was made up of sections in many countries as well as international committees.

Returning to Philadelphia in 1920, Scott took a job with the White-Williams Foundation, working on juvenile delinquency, while she volunteered with WILPF. In September 1922 she became executive secretary of the Pennsylvania branch of the organization, a job she was to hold for more than forty years. Working for WILPF exactly suited her devotion to peace as well as her faith in women's ability to solve problems. She believed firmly in progress, and felt the time would come when international law would govern conflicts between nations. In later years she became increasingly devoted to the Gandhian concept of nonviolent direct action, especially as it related to issues of civil rights.

On October 30, 1921, Mildred Scott married Allen Olmsted, who pursued a career in the law and served as county judge. Their first son, Peter, was born in April 1924; they adopted a daughter, Enid, in November 1927, and a second son, Anthony, in December 1930. In 1924, the couple moved to Thunderbird Lodge in Rose Valley, a Philadelphia suburb. Here they spent the rest of their lives, helping to develop a progressive school (the School in Rose Valley) on land adjacent to theirs, and enjoying the creation of an extensive garden. Allen and Mildred Olmsted shared many political and social values, and were supportive of each other's endeavors. Nevertheless, their marriage was sometimes stormy, complicated by Mildred's deep attachment to Ruth Mellor, who sometimes lived with them and often accompanied them on their world travels.

At WILPF, Olmsted recruited new members so vigorously that the Pennsylvania branch accounted for one-third of the total U.S. membership. Her skills soon came to the attention of the U.S. national board, and in 1934 she was named national organization secretary. She was promoted to national administrative secretary in 1946 and to executive secretary in 1963. She served also on the international executive committee of WILPF from 1937 to 1953, attending international congresses and traveling for WILPF. One of her more demanding trips took her into Nazi Germany in 1934 to investigate the status of an imprisoned WILPF member. Throughout the WILPF organization she was known for her courage, enthusiasm, hard work, and colorful hats.

From her position at WILPF, Mildred Olmsted worked with many coalitions on issues of race, peace, and civil liberties. She was appointed to several White House Conferences and served for a time on the Pennsylvania board of the National Youth Administration.

Among the many highlights of Mildred Olmsted's long career with WILPF were organizing a conference of American and Mexican women in 1928 and the Women's Committee to Oppose Conscription in 1943. At the first postwar international conference of WILPF, her optimistic speech was a turning point in the decision to keep the organization going. In 1961 she organized a conference of U.S. and Soviet women held at Bryn Mawr College. Throughout her career she wrote extensively for WILPF publications, always reminding her readers that small groups of determined people can change the world.

Mildred Olmsted retired from WILPF in 1966 at the age of seventy-six, but continued to be active in the organization, and served on several boards and committees of AFSC and the Society of Friends. She continued to serve on the board of SANE, an anti-nuclear-proliferation organization she had helped found, and on the board of the Pennsylvania branch of the American Civil Liberties Union. Many honors came to her in her later years, including a Lifetime Achievement Award from WILPF in 1986.

Mildred Scott Olmsted bore the loneliness and discomforts of old age valiantly. Her husband died in 1977; Ruth Mellor became mentally incapacitated and died in 1989. Despite a broken hip that did not mend properly, she continued to attend meetings and entertain guests until the end of her days. Often she exhorted her many visitors to social action. She had suffered a heart attack at age forty and had been warned to slow down, but she had never heeded the warning. Finally on the night of July 2, 1990, just five months short of her hundredth birthday, her heart gave out. A memorial service was held at the Providence Friends Meeting House in September, and Mildred Scott Olmsted's ashes were buried on her property in Rose Valley, beside those of her husband and her son Peter.

Bibliography: Most of the materials on Mildred Scott Olmsted are at the Swarthmore College Peace Collection. These include the Papers of Mildred Scott Olmsted and of Allen S. Olmsted II. The former contain fourteen interviews with Mildred Olmsted taped by Margaret Hope Bacon. Also at the Peace Collection, there are many references to Mildred Olmsted in the WILPF Papers, U.S. and International; the Jane Addams papers; the Dorothy Detzer Papers; and the Women's Committee to Oppose Conscription Papers. For her writing, see *Fellowship Magazine,* November 1938, pp. 7–8; *The American Friend,* December 8, 1938, pp. 524–25; and numerous issues of *Four Lights,* the publication of WILPF. Educational records can be found in the archives of Friends Central School and of Smith College. A biography by Margaret Hope Bacon, *One Woman's Passion for Peace and Freedom: The Life of Mildred Scott Olmsted,* was published in 1993. See also Gertrude Bussey and Margaret Tims, *Pioneers for Peace: Women's International League for Peace and Freedom, 1915–1965* (1965); Dorothy Detzer, *Appointment on the Hill* (1948); and Catherine Foster, *Women for All Seasons: The Story of the Women's International League for Peace and Freedom* (1989). Also of interest is Grace Rotzel, *The School in Rose Valley* (1971). Obituaries appeared in the *Philadelphia Inquirer* on July 4, 1990, and the *New York Times* on July 7, 1990.

MARGARET HOPE BACON

ONASSIS, Jacqueline Lee Bouvier Kennedy. July 28, 1929–May 19, 1994. First Lady, reporter, editor.

Jacqueline Lee Bouvier was born in Southhampton, Long Island, the first child of Janet Lee and John "Black Jack" Vernou Bouvier III. Her younger sister, Caroline Lee, was born March 3, 1933, and the sisters shared an intense intimacy and rivalry throughout their lives. Her parents both came from elite, wealthy New York families, whose earlier generations had not been above embellishing their lineages to ease their acceptance into society. This illusion of noble ancestry, fabricated by both families, enhanced Jacqueline's sense of the dramatic and her instinctive understanding of the power of an image, which she used to advantage in crafting her own image as First Lady.

Jacqueline inherited her beauty from her father, an extraordinarily handsome man. A magnet for scores of women throughout his life, his sexual attractiveness was matched only by his self-indulgence. His myriad affairs led to a failed marriage with Janet; they divorced in 1940. Her parents' angry quarrels developed Jacqueline's ability to tune out unpleasant things—a skill she would employ in her own marriages—and her penchant to escape into literature, art, fantasy, and horses. Her parents' divorce left her with deep insecurities and a gnawing emptiness that haunted her, fueling her needs to purchase extravagantly and to marry men of wealth.

On June 21, 1942, her mother married the wealthy, twice-divorced stockbroker Hugh D. Auchincloss II, heir to a Standard Oil fortune. Jacqueline and Lee resided with them at Auchincloss's two comfortable estates, Merrywood in McLean, Virginia, and Hammersmith Farm in Newport, Rhode Island. Janet's second marriage gained her and her daughters unlimited access to polite society and produced two half siblings, Janet (1945) and James (1947). Jacqueline's combined families provided a powerful social network that she utilized successfully throughout her life.

Jacqueline Bouvier was educated at Miss Chapin's in New York and Holton-Arms in Washington, D.C., where she displayed extraordinary intelligence and an artistic and literary prowess. At fifteen, she enrolled in Miss Porter's School in Farmington, Connecticut. She entered Vassar in 1947 and spent her junior year abroad at the Sorbonne in Paris, cultivating her love of French culture and language and traveling extensively in Europe. She completed her education at George Washington University, graduating in 1951.

Her interest in publishing began that year when she won *Vogue*'s Prix de Paris contest; the prize was a year's apprenticeship as junior editor at the magazine's offices in Paris and New York. Instead she decided to seek a job as "Inquiring Photographer" at the *Washington Times Herald,* a position she secured with the help of her stepfather.

In 1951, she met John Fitzgerald Kennedy, then a Massachusetts congressman about to run for the Senate, and they began a courtship in 1952. Their wedding took place in Newport, Rhode Island, on September 12, 1953. Jacqueline deeply loved her husband; his first love was politics. His constant womanizing brought tension and pain to the relationship, but conditioned by her own father's example, she appears to have accepted this behavior as a part of the marriage. She ignored all but his most blatant infidelities, which continued until his death.

After suffering a miscarriage in 1955, she delivered a stillborn baby girl in 1956. Daughter Caroline Bouvier Kennedy was born November 27, 1957, and son John Fitzgerald Kennedy Jr. on November 25, 1960. Despite her discomfort with politics, she had campaigned with her husband during his presidential bid in 1960 until pregnancy curtailed her activities. A third child, Patrick Bouvier Kennedy, was born August 7, 1963; his death of hyaline membrane disease on August 9, caused intense grief for both parents.

After her husband's inauguration as the nation's thirty-fifth president, Jacqueline Kennedy's exceptional knowledge of art, history, and literature gave her the self-assurance to undertake the restoration of the executive mansion. Her families' social and political connections provided her with the personal access to accomplish her goal. Bringing together a prestigious Fine Arts Committee of art historians, antiques experts, and directors of leading American galleries and museums, she directed a restoration of the White House that filled the house with historic furniture, portraits, and fine period antiques. On February 14, 1962, she presented the restored White House to a nationwide audience of fifty million viewers in a historic, hour-long tour with Charles Collingwood on CBS television. She established the White House Historical Association to continue the mansion's preservation and successfully promoted legislation that established the White House as a national historic site under the National Park Service.

Both John and Jacqueline Kennedy possessed an elegance of mind and manner, but she especially understood the connection between pomp and power, ceremony and compelling historical drama. Her exquisite taste recast the image of the White House as a brilliant stage on which her husband conducted politics and diplomacy, and where leading artists highlighted American cultural achievements. At these events the First Lady deftly lobbied the artists to press her husband for the creation of a cabinet position for arts and culture.

John Kennedy's growing appreciation of her singular contributions to his presidency, and his recognition of her popularity, brought him to seek her help with campaigning, a move that shifted the dynamics of their marriage. She accompanied her husband on a pre-campaign foray to Dallas, Texas, where Kennedy was assassinated on November 22, 1963. Having structured the image of his presidency, Jacqueline Kennedy now shaped the pageantry of his funeral, imbuing his tragic death with dignity in carefully orchestrated ceremonies. After his death, she further shaped his presidential legacy in an interview with author Theodore White, fixing the Kennedy administration in the American collective memory as "Camelot."

Shattered by the assassination, the thirty-four-year-old widow struggled with depression, with making a life for herself, and with bringing up her children as a single parent. Although she distanced herself from the Kennedy clan to raise her children with privacy and discipline, she instilled in them a fierce pride in their heritage. In September 1964, she relocated to New York City, where she directed her children's schooling and worked on plans for the Kennedy Library. During this time, she was linked romantically with several prominent men.

The assassination of Robert F. Kennedy in 1968 intensified her fear for the safety of her children in the United States. She soon agreed to marry Aristotle "Ari" Onassis, a Greek shipping tycoon, whose wealth provided her and her children with a secure life. However, her remarriage on the Greek island of Skorpios in October 1968 shattered her iconic status with the American public, and the couple's initial delight in each other soured. She increasingly spent time with her children in New York City, and he resumed his affair with his longtime mistress, opera singer MARIA CALLAS. Evidence suggests that Onassis planned to divorce his wife, but he died from myasthenia gravis in 1975 without having signed divorce papers. She inherited $20 to $26 million from the Onassis estate.

After his death, Jacqueline Kennedy Onassis returned to New York to carve out a life on her own. She resumed her publishing career, first as an editor at Viking Press and then, starting in 1978, as a senior editor at Doubleday. She edited a number of prestigious books and brought noted authors and their works to the press.

Now past fifty, she found happiness in a personal relationship with diamond merchant Maurice Tempelsman, whom she had known from Democratic campaigns since the late 1950s. Later he became her financial adviser. In 1982, he moved into her New York apartment, where they lived together until her death from non-Hodgkins lymphoma on May 19, 1994, at the age of sixty-four. She is buried beside President Kennedy at Arlington National Cemetery in Virginia.

Jacqueline Kennedy's beauty, glamour, and clothing made her a widely emulated fashion icon. So close was the bond she forged with the American people that the First Lady was always referred to by the familiar and affectionate name Jackie until the end of her life. Her significance in American history rests with her role in historic preservation and in structuring the image of the Kennedy presidency, funeral, and legacy. Her White House restoration and unique entertainments, highlighting the vitality of the nation's artistic achievement, promoted an American cultural hegemony that accompanied the country's postwar economic and military might. After her tenure, no presidential spouse could be a successful First Lady without a significant national project. Her time in the White House marked a watershed in redefining the First Lady's role in the last half of the twentieth century.

Bibliography: The papers on Jacqueline Kennedy Onassis at the John F. Kennedy Library, Boston, are only partially open for research, although the notes from Theodore White's *Life* magazine interview with her after Kennedy's death are accessible. The East Hampton Library on Long Island holds newspapers and archives relating to the Bouvier family. See also John H. Davis, *The Bouviers: Portrait of an American Family* (1969) for more family background.

As one of the most admired and written about women of her times, Jacqueline Kennedy Onassis has been the subject of numerous scholarly and popular books. See, for example, C. David Heyman, *A Woman Named Jackie* (1994); Ellen Ladowsky, *Jacqueline Kennedy Onassis* (1997); Edward Klein, *Just Jackie: Her Private Years* (1998); Barbara Leaming, *Mrs. Kennedy: The Missing History of the Kennedy Years* (2001); Sarah Bradford, *America's Queen: The Life of Jacqueline Kennedy Onassis* (2000); and Hamish Bowles, *Jacqueline Kennedy: The White House Years: Selections from the John F. Kennedy Library and Museum* (2001). Also of interest is Carl Sferrazza Anthony, *As We Remember Her: Jacqueline Kennedy Onassis in the Words of Her Friends and Family* (1997). General sources on First Ladies that touch on Jacqueline Kennedy's importance to the role include Anthony, *First Ladies: The Saga of the Presidents' Wives and Their Power*, vol. 2 (1991); Lewis L. Gould, ed., *American First Ladies: Their Lives and Their Legacy* (1996); Kati Marton, *Hidden Power: Presidential Marriages That Shaped Our Recent History* (2001); and Edith Mayo, ed., *The Smithsonian Book of the First Ladies: Their Lives, Times, and Issues* (1996). Obituaries appeared in the *New York Times* and the *Washington Post* on Mary 20, 1994.

EDITH P. MAYO

OPPENHEIMER, Jane Marion. September 19, 1911–March 19, 1996. Embryologist, historian of science.

Jane Marion Oppenheimer achieved international distinction as an embryologist and a historian of science. Educated when few women received the PhD and even fewer had postdoctoral training, she devoted her research career to understanding the embryology of the fish embryo and to the history of embryology.

An only child, she was born in Philadelphia to Sylvia Stern and James H. "Harry" Oppenheimer. Her early years were heavily influenced by her much loved physician father, whom she credited for showing her the ways of the mind and of science. To build his daughter's physical strength and stamina, he devised a daily regimen of exercises and insisted that she engage in sports at school. Her father also saw to it that her education included private tutoring in French, and she later confided to a close friend that when she was a child her role model was Joan of Arc. First inspired by a cherished piano teacher, Jane was also devoted to classical music. She supported and regularly attended concerts of the Philadelphia Orchestra and was a guarantor of the Bethlehem Bach Festival for many years. A strong-willed, outspoken, yet intensely private person, her friends knew her as a lover of fine food, spirited conversation, and first-class travel. She never married.

Oppenheimer graduated from Bryn Mawr College in 1932 with a major in zoology and minor in chemistry. While still an undergraduate, she attended summer classes at Woods Hole Marine Biological Laboratories in Woods Hole, Massachusetts, where she made the acquaintance of John Spangler Nicholas and her future experimental subject—the embryo of *Fundulus heteroclitus* (the common minnow or killifish). She continued her scientific training as a graduate student at Yale University, where she studied with Nicholas, whom she credited with encouraging her to explore both experimental embryology and its history. While at Yale, she was also strongly influenced by Ross Granville Harrison, the most prominent American embryologist of the time.

As Nicholas's PhD student, Oppenheimer independently pursued work on *Fundulus,* while Nicholas pursued other interests. Nicholas had previously devised a method for removing the outer covering of fish embryos, thus making it possible to perform on teleost embryos precise experimental manipulations similar to those done previously on amphibians by Harrison and by Hans Spemann in Germany. After receiving her PhD in zoology from Yale in 1935, Oppenheimer received fellowships, including one from the American Association of University Women, for three consecutive years of postdoctoral studies at Yale and the University of Rochester. Although postdoctoral training in the sciences is now the norm, it was quite unusual at the time, and even more so for a woman PhD.

In 1938, Oppenheimer took an appointment as an instructor in biology at Bryn Mawr College, where, except for a number of visiting professorships, she would spend the rest of her career. When she retired from the Bryn Mawr faculty in 1980, she was the William R. Kenan Jr. Professor of Biology and History of Science. Known to her students as "Miss Op," she inspired feelings of both awe and fear. Kind and generous to those who earned her respect, she had high expectations of those around her, and if she thought they were not trying hard enough, her critiques were daunting.

Oppenheimer made a number of important contributions to teleost embryology. A group of seven papers she published from 1934 to 1937 is especially noteworthy, as they demonstrated both similarities and differences between fish and the amphibian and avian species studied by others. These early papers provide a wealth of information about the early development of the fish embryo, which was of great interest to contemporary researchers exploiting the genetic potential of zebrafish *(Danio rerio)* to study development. Throughout her career as an embryologist, Oppenheimer used the methods of experimental embryology to explore questions of embryonic inductions, differentiation capabilities, and regulation. One of her last *Fundulus* projects involved sending embryos into space on the 1975 Apollo-Soyuz joint space mission to study the effects of zero gravity on embryonic development.

As a historian of science and medicine, Oppenheimer wrote numerous articles and book reviews, many on the origins of embryology. Her writing ability earned her the admiration and respect of her scientific colleagues. She enjoyed intellectual history and was motivated to write about her library discoveries, believing that "life in our laboratories is made more meaningful to us when we know something about our intellectual forebears." A topic of special interest to her was the relationship of embryological data to evolutionary theory. She also relished telling dramatic stories about early physiological and surgical discoveries. Together with Benjamin H. Willier, she co-edited *Foundations of Experimental Embryology* (1964), a collection of reprinted landmark articles in developmental biology. Her translation of the "Organizer" paper by Spemann and Mangold made that critical work accessible to countless students and investigators who lacked the ability to read German.

Oppenheimer belonged to numerous professional and scholarly societies that noted her accomplishments as both an embryologist and an historian of science. She served as president of the American Society of Zoologists in 1973 and was a fellow of the American Association for the Advancement of Science. Her many honors included election to the American Philosophical Society, of which she was secretary from 1987 to 1992, and the American Academy of Arts and Sciences. In 1981 she was named a Distinguished Daughter of Pennsylvania. She died of cancer on March 19, 1996, at her home in Philadelphia at the age of eighty-four.

Jane M. Oppenheimer was an exacting scholar whose attention to detail was noteworthy. She regarded herself as an intellectual fox, not a hedgehog, and colleagues who were creative and imaginative as well as precise gained her admiration. As both scientist and historian, she took pains to get all her facts right and to place them in the context of broader intellectual issues. If the situation also involved some high drama, it delighted her even more. By recasting a sentence from her review of a biography of Theodor Boveri, we can say of her what she said of Boveri: The qualities of Oppenheimer's work were inseparable from those of her person.

Bibliography: Information about Jane Oppenheimer's work and life was obtained from copies of her curriculum vitae and list of publications on file at Bryn Mawr College, and from firsthand knowledge. For reflections on her career, see the introduction to her *Essays in the History of Embryology and Biology* (1967), which contains the quotation on p. v. The second edition of *Foundations of Experimental Embryology,* which she edited and expanded, appeared in 1974. Important scientific publications include "The Development of Isolated Blastoderms of *Fundulus heteroclitus,*" *Journal of Experimental Zoology* 72 (1936), pp. 247–69, and "Transplantation Experiments on Developing Teleosts *(Fundulus* and *Perca),*" *Journal of Experimental Zoology* 72 (1936), pp. 409–37. An obituary written by June Z. Fullmer appeared in *Isis* 88, no. 1 (1997), pp. 181–83. Photographs of Oppenheimer at various stages in her career are in the Bryn Mawr College Archives. The author is pleased to acknowledge Professors Ernst Berliner, Viktor Hamburger (deceased), and Anthony Kaney, who shared their remembrances of Oppenheimer. Obituaries appeared in the *Philadelphia Inquirer* on March 22, 1996, and the *New York Times* on March 23, 1996.

MARGARET HOLLYDAY

ORDWAY, Katharine. April 3, 1899–June 27, 1979. Botanist, conservationist, philanthropist.

Only after her death did more than a handful of people know the full extent of Katharine Ordway's historic contribution to conservation. The fourth of five children, and the only daughter, Katharine Ordway was born in St. Paul, Minnesota, to Jessie Cornwell Gilman and Lucius Pond Ordway. Her Brooklyn-born father grew up in Providence, Rhode Island, and migrated to St. Paul after graduating from Brown University. The English ancestors of both Katharine's parents had emigrated to Massachusetts in the seventeenth century. As a founder of Minnesota Mining and Manufacturing (3M), Lucius Pond Ordway became a leading and wealthy St. Paul entrepreneur.

From 1914 to 1917 Katharine Ordway attended Westover Preparatory School for Girls in Middlebury, Connecticut. In 1924 she graduated cum laude from the University of Minnesota with a liberal arts degree in botany and art. She returned to college when she was in her fifties to study biology and land-use planning at Columbia University. Disliking Minnesota's harsh winters, she established her primary home in the wooded hills of southwestern Connecticut, maintaining a winter residence in Arizona and a summer cottage among the dunes and marshes of Long Island. In addition to her focus on conservation, she was an avid art collector and world traveler. She never married.

Ordway loved nature, although she was not a typical outdoors enthusiast. Small in stature and thin, with fragile health, her sensitive skin forced her to carry a parasol while in the sun. As a child growing up in Minnesota, she was thrilled by the prairie's unbroken sea of waving grass. She became engrossed in studying the plants and animals inhabiting the prairie.

The tallgrass prairies of the Great Plains were at one time North America's largest ecosystem, four hundred million acres, covering almost a fifth of the continent. They originally were home to eighty species of mammals, as well as a vast variety of brilliant wildflowers and a host of pharmaceutical plants. Being on the avian Central Flyway, the Great Plains prairie waters support migratory species and provide nesting habitat for other birds. Now less than 1 percent of that once-vast ecosystem remains.

Ordway was greatly distressed by the thought that the prairies might vanish. When she was in her fifties she inherited a substantial fortune from her father that enabled her to take action. Along with the money came the self-confidence she had lacked while in the shadow of her four brothers.

At the age of sixty she established the Goodhill Foundation, a personal grant-making entity, to fund her primary interest of buying up tracts of undeveloped open land. She achieved this goal by funneling grants through the Nature Conservancy, a national group dedicated exclusively to saving undisturbed segments of natural land as examples of various ecotypes. The Nature Conservancy ranked prairies as the least protected and most in need of preservation, and its staff prepared a list of prairie properties for her to consider for acquisition. She chose several small Minnesota sites for her first preserves. One piece had never even been plowed. She personally toured each tract of land prior to agreeing to fund its purchase.

Soon Ordway realized that surviving prairies elsewhere also needed protection. Shy and always seeking anonymity, she next underwrote the acquisition of small preserves in Nebraska, South Dakota, Kansas, and Missouri. But what she really wanted was to preserve a huge expanse of tallgrass prairie—one where nothing but prairie grass stretched to the horizon, without power lines, houses, or roads anywhere in sight. In 1971, after years of work by her colleagues at the Nature Conservancy, such a preserve became a reality in the Flint Hills of eastern Kansas. The Flint Hills had escaped cultivation because they are rocky and steep, and they might be the only place where thousands of acres of natural tall grass still exist. This Konza Prairie Research Natural Area (later renamed the Konza Prairie Biological Station), which encompasses more than 8,500 acres, has been designated by the United Nations as an International Biosphere Reserve and serves as a laboratory for ecological research by scientists studying the complex interactions among invertebrates and other organisms found in the root system.

Having now found her sense of purpose, Ordway provided the money for the Nature Conservancy to procure large prairie preserves elsewhere in the Plains states. A 7,500-acre mixed-grass prairie in South Dakota acquired for $1.5 million became the Samuel H. Ordway Memorial Prairie, commemorating her cousin. When Ordway died in 1979, the Ordway Prairie Preserve System included more than 31,000 acres in the midwestern states—the most extensive sanctuary system of its type in the world.

As a botanist, Katharine Ordway understood the value of prairies and grasslands, whose complex ecosystem, mostly out of sight underground and storing fertility for thousands of years, produced the rich North American soils that have helped feed the world. In addition to preserving tallgrass prairies, Ordway used her inheritance to acquire tidal marshes, barrier islands, scrub forests, nature reserves, wilderness areas, a Pacific Flyway link in Oregon (critical nesting habitat for threatened bird species), and a unique palmetto prairie in Florida.

While she was alive she made grants from her personal resources, leaving the money in her Goodhill Foundation for use after she died. Following Ordway's instructions, within five years of her death the directors distributed the foundation's assets to preserve natural areas. The Nature Conservancy used foundation resources to add 40,000 acres of tallgrass prairie to the Flint Hill system. Eleven million dollars went to save prairie and forest habitat along twenty-two miles of northern Nebraska's Niobrara River, the only remaining long stretch of wild river in the Great Plains. The foundation dedicated $10 million to saving 192,000 acres of various ecosystem types from New England to Hawaii that were at risk of being lost forever to development. The foundation directors also set up the Ordway Endangered Species Conservation Program. Directly and through the Goodhill Foundation, Katharine Ordway gave at least $64 million for conservation—at that time ranking second only to the much wealthier John D. Rockefeller Jr. She died in New York City at the age of eighty.

Bibliography: Biographical information can be found in William D. Blair Jr., *Katharine Ordway: The Lady Who Saved the Prairies* (1989); and Mary Joy Breton, *Women Pioneers for the Environment* (1998). For information about her father, see Virginia Brainard Kunz and John M. Lindley, "The Financial Angel Who Rescued 3M: The Life and Times of Lucius Pond Ordway," *Ramsey County History* 36, no. 3 (Fall 2001), pp. 4–31. *The Katharine Ordway Collection* (1983) catalogues the collection of art she left to Yale University Art Gallery. For a discussion of the prairie ecosystem, see Douglas H. Chadwick, "What Good Is a Prairie," *Audubon*, November/December 1995, pp. 38–46, 114–16. Her descendants John G. Ordway Jr., John G. Ordway III, and Richard Nicholson provided helpful information. Obituaries appeared in the *New York Times* on June 28, 1979, and the *St. Paul Pioneer Press* on June 30, 1979.

MARY JOY BRETON

ORKIN, Ruth. September 3, 1921–January 16, 1985. Photographer, photojournalist, filmmaker.

Ruth Orkin was born in Boston but grew up in southern California. She was the only child of former silent film star Mary Ruby and Samuel Orkin, an inventor who built toy boats. Mary Ruby's movie career lasted only from 1913 to 1917, but she was a dedicated fan of Hollywood and regularly took her young daughter to movie premieres and stars' funerals. At age ten Ruth was taking photographs using a thirty-nine-cent Univex still camera; two years later she was developing these images in a makeshift darkroom and operating a primitive 16mm movie camera. Many of Orkin's lifelong subjects—urban and natural landscapes, narratives of celebrity and street life—were established in her earliest images of the Hollywood foothills, strangers on the street, family members, and movie stars.

Her parents' encouragement of Orkin's interest in pushing boundaries continued despite the family's often precarious financial situation. But the real world was less indulgent than her parents, and the inner drive that inspired a cross-country bicycle trip at age seventeen would not help her overcome all the obstacles before her. After attending Beverly Hills High School and Eagle Rock High School, graduating in 1939, she spent a year at Los Angeles City College. In 1943, at the age of twenty-two, a dearth of employable males during World War II inspired MGM Studio to hire Orkin as its first messenger girl. There she met—and photographed—directors, stars, and technicians who taught her much about filmmaking and encouraged her to pursue her goals. When she tried to follow the job trajectory into more ambitious realms, such as shooting features, Orkin was greeted with laughter by the head of the Cinematographer's Union, which did not admit women. A subsequent stint in the Women's Auxiliary Army Corps (WAAC) was supposed to lead to schooling in making training films, but her sex again stood in the way. Orkin would have to defer her dream of making movies for another decade.

In 1944, she moved to New York City, where she worked as a nightclub photographer and met fellow photographers such as Stanley Kubrick, Arnold Newman, Weegee, and Edward Steichen. All the while she pursued her private art of making visual poetry of the prosaic, photographing neighbors' kids, impromptu street scenes, or sudden miniature melodramas in her neighborhood. Soon she was doing small jobs for money. A *New York Times* assignment to photograph young Leonard Bernstein for a 1945 profile led to increasingly frequent appearances in the major weeklies of the period, including *Life, Look, Collier's, Ladies' Home Journal,* and *Coronet.* Her work was popular with readers and her peers; Edward Steichen, for example, praised the "human expression" (Orkin, *A Photo Journal,* p. 31) in her photojournalism and included her work in all of his Museum of Modern Art group photography shows.

Much of Orkin's work from this period takes the form of sequences, a then-radical technique she perfected in such Manhattan street-scene series as "Jimmie Tells a Story" and "The Cardplayers" (both 1947), and theatrical and musical series showing artists and entertainers in intimate, sometimes comical, often poignant moods and situations. This technique can be seen as an outgrowth of Orkin's fascination with movies; indeed, it is arguably her version of the sequential images in film that she was denied access to at the time. The sense of intimacy and candor she obtains from her subjects can be traced to her unabashed immersion in the process and her passion for breaking the rules. For her "How America Lives" assignments for *Ladies' Home Journal,* she lived with and photographed a "typical American family" for two weeks. In another innovation, Orkin overcame her editors' indifference to the naturalness of 35mm color photography by convincing *Ladies' Home Journal* to run the first color cover based on this format—the March 1950 shot of a young woman in a market for the magazine's "Undiscovered American Beauties" series.

New York City was Ruth Orkin's base during this time, and she is remembered as a preeminent chronicler of Manhattan's vibrant street life of the 1940s and '50s. Increasingly, though, her assignments took her across the country and to more far-flung destinations like Israel, South America, and, most memorably, Florence, Italy, where she shot her most famous image, "American Girl in Italy" (1951). This widely influential work captures Jinx Allen, a New York friend, harried but stoic as she walks, clutching her shawl, through a gauntlet of leering, transfixed Italian men. The image's combination of narrative power, compositional elegance, humor, and humanity represents both a high point and a summation of the Orkin style. The image, which looks candid but was to some extent staged, also inspired a debate about artistic manipulation of material that continues today.

In 1952, Orkin became a filmmaker, combining talents with fellow photographer Morris Engel, whom she married that year. Their first effort, *Little Fugitive* (1953), which is considered the first low-budget, independent feature shot entirely on location to break into the mainstream, brilliantly records a young boy's odyssey through Coney Island. Orkin and Engel shared most of the tasks, with Orkin co-writing, co-directing, and editing the film. Francois Truffaut hailed *Little Fugitive,* with its gritty-poetic images, sense of spontaneity, and do-it-yourself attitude, as the major inspiration for French new-wave cinema, and the film received an Academy Award nomination and the Venice Film Festival's Silver Lion. A second collaboration, *Lovers and Lollipops* (1956), also won praise.

In 1959, Professional Photographers of America named Orkin, along with DOROTHEA LANGE and MARGARET BOURKE-WHITE, among the "Top Ten Women Photographers in the U.S." Now responsible for raising two children, Andy and Mary, born in 1959 and 1961, Orkin retired from filmmaking to resume still photography, shooting most frequently from the window of her Central Park West apartment. These images formed the basis of two well-regarded books, *A World through My Window* (1978) and *More Pictures from My Window* (1983).

Orkin spent much of her later years doing lecture tours, cataloging her work, and exhibiting it at such venues as the Metropolitan Museum of Art and Nikon House, with forays into teaching at New York's School of Visual Arts (1976–78) and the International Center of Photography (1980). This pioneer who humanized celebrities and found the extraordinary in ordinary life died in New York at the age of sixty-three after a long battle with cancer.

Bibliography: Ruth Orkin's autobiographical *A Photo Journal* (1981) offers an overview of her career. Miles Barth's *Ruth Orkin: A Retrospective* (1996) and Patricia Bosworth's *Ruth Orkin: Above and Beyond* (1999) feature representative samples of her work. An interview with Orkin in *Darkroom Photography,* September–October, 1982, pp. 18–25, and a retrospective in *Popular Photography,* June 1977, pp. 100–109+, are also informative. Her daughter Mary runs the Ruth Orkin archive, and she made a short documentary, *Ruth Orkin: Frames of Life,* narrated by one of Ruth's subjects, actress Julie Harris, in 1995. An obituary appeared in the *New York Times* on January 17, 1985.

GARY MORRIS

ORR, Alice Greenough. *See* Greenough, Alice.

OSBORNE, Estelle Massey Riddle. May 3, 1901–December 12, 1981. Nurse, nursing administrator.

Estelle Osborne was a leader in struggles to eliminate racial discrimination in national professional nursing organizations and in society as a whole. She fought to eliminate exclusionary practices for blacks in nursing at a time when rigid patterns of segregation and discrimination in nursing education and employment for blacks existed across the United States. Osborne worked tirelessly for forty-three years to ensure that future black nurses would be experientially and educationally prepared to assume higher positions in nursing and would have the opportunity to do so.

Estelle Massey was born in Palestine, Texas, the eighth of eleven children of Hall and Bettye

Estelle Massey. Her father was a handyman and farmer who raised vegetables and livestock; her mother was a domestic who earned money cleaning white people's homes, although she never allowed her daughters to do so. Neither parent was educated, but they determined that their children would be. All of the Massey children completed at least two years of college.

After high school, Estelle Massey followed in two of her siblings' footsteps and graduated as a teacher from Prairie View State College, but after two years of teaching she desired a change. While working as an assistant to her brother, a St. Louis dentist, Estelle confided in him her desire to become a dentist as well. Instead Edward Massey filled her head with stories of the new nurses' training program at a nearby hospital. After meeting with the superintendent, she agreed to become a student in City Hospital No. 2's first nursing class. Initially she was not very happy with her training, but after learning nursing procedures she discovered she liked nursing.

After her graduation in 1923, Massey was immediately hired as a head nurse at the hospital where she had trained. She was the first African American head nurse at City Hospital, a position she held for almost three years. But when opportunities for advancement to supervisor were posted, Massey was never encouraged to apply. When she realized she would always have to work under white supervision there, she resigned and went to work for the St. Louis Municipal Visiting Nurses. The job site was different, but attitudes among whites remained the same. Six months from the day she arrived, she resigned and moved to Kansas City, Missouri.

In Kansas City, Massey was hired as an instructor at Lincoln School of Nursing. After a brief period at Lincoln, she believed she needed more education. With the school administrator's blessings and his signature on her bank loan note, in 1927 Estelle Massey enrolled in the first of three summer sessions she attended at Teachers College, Columbia University. In 1929 she resigned from Lincoln, obtained a Rosenwald Fund scholarship, and completed her course work for her bachelor of science degree in nursing. Encouraged by members of the Rosenwald Fund, she returned to Teachers College and in 1931 became the first black nurse awarded a master's degree in nursing education.

After graduation, she was appointed educational director at Freedman's Hospital (currently Howard University School of Nursing) in Washington, D.C. Next she served on a team studying the health and welfare of blacks in the South, funded by the Rosenwald Fund. Then, at the invitation of the board of directors of Homer G. Phillips Hospital (formerly City Hospital No. 2) in St. Louis, Massey was invited back to be director of nurses at her alma mater; she was the first black person to hold this position there. By this time, Osborne was the best-known African American in nursing, having served five successive years, starting in 1934, as president of the National Association of Colored Graduate Nurses (NACGN), an association established to promote professionalization, education, and practice opportunities for black nurses throughout the country. MABEL KEATON STAUPERS, who also went on to a distinguished nursing career, served as her executive secretary and collaborator.

In 1943, Massey was hired as consultant to the National Nursing Council for War Service. The first black appointee, Massey was responsible for working with politicians and professional organizations to change discriminatory policies, practices, and customs in white nurse-training schools and the armed services that effectively excluded black nurses from military service. After only two years, the number of schools admitting both black and white students had grown from eighteen to thirty-eight, the Cadet Nurse Corps had enlisted two thousand black students and was providing monies for their education, and the U.S. Army and Navy had lifted their bans on accepting black nurses in their service.

With the end of the war and the growing number of black students enrolled in training schools across the country, Massey's efforts now concentrated on opening doors to higher education for black nurses. In 1945, she was the first African American to join the nursing faculty of New York University. The following year she married Herman Osborne. An earlier marriage to a physician named Riddle had ended in divorce. Neither marriage produced children. In eight years at NYU, her leadership position on campus provided her the opportunity to mentor numerous black students and nurses.

With experience gained in integrating nursing education, nursing service, community health work, and nursing administration, the only other area in nursing left to integrate was the professional nursing organization hierarchy. In 1948 Osborne ran for election to the board of directors of the American Nurses Association and won. She served until 1952.

When seven nursing organizations came together to form the National League for Nursing, the consensus to invite Osborne to join their administrative staff was based on her years of experience in all areas of nursing. She accepted. Working for the League was a job in which Osborne could wield influence in the causes to which she had dedicated her life. She remained at the League for twelve years (from 1954 to 1966); she retired with the titles Associate General Director and Director of Services to State Leagues.

Estelle Massey Riddle Osborne was an outstanding black leader who made tremendous gains in the profession of nursing. Seeking out and conquering racial prejudices at all levels in professional nursing, she gave blacks in nursing the tools to rise above adversities and helped shape the history of professional nursing. Osborne died in 1981 in Oakland, California, at the age of eighty.

Bibliography: Important writings about Estelle Massey Riddle Osborne's life and accomplishments can be found in Edna Yost, *American Women of Nursing* (1965); Darlene Clark Hine, *Black Women in White: Racial Conflict and Cooperation in the Nursing Profession, 1890–1950* (1989); M. Elizabeth Carnegie, *The Path We Tread: Blacks in Nursing Worldwide 1854–1994* (1995); Mabel Keaton Staupers, *No Time for Prejudice: A Story of the Integration of Negroes in Nursing in the United States* (1961); and Gwendolyn Safier, *Contemporary American Leaders in Nursing: An Oral History* (1977). See also the interview of Osborne conducted by Dr. Patricia Sloane (June 21, 1976) found at the M. Elizabeth Carnegie Nursing History Archive, Hampton University School of Nursing, Hampton, Virginia.

Osborne was a prolific writer. See "Negro Nurses: The Supply and Demand," *Opportunity: Journal of Negro Life*, November 1937, pp. 327–29; "The Negro Nurse Student," *American Journal of Nursing* 33, no. 6 (June 1933), pp. 534–36; "The Negro Nurse Student," *American Journal of Nursing* 34, no. 8 (August 1934), pp. 806–10; "Sources of Supply of Negro Health Personnel, Section C: Nurses," *Journal of Negro Education* 6 (July 1937), pp. 483–92; "The Training and Placement of Negro Nurses," *Journal of Negro Education* 4 (January 1935), pp. 42–48; and "Status and Contribution of the Negro Nurse," *Journal of Negro Education* 18 (Summer 1949), pp. 364–69. See also Estelle Massey Riddle and Josephine Nelson, "The Negro Nurse Looks toward Tomorrow," *American Journal of Nursing* 45, no. 8 (August 1945), pp. 627–30; and Mary E. Carnegie and Estelle M. Osborne, "Integration in Professional Nursing," *Crisis* 69, no. 1 (January 1962), pp. 5–9. Additional information was supplied by Alice Royal and Dr. M. Elizabeth Carnegie. An obituary appeared in the *New York Times* on December 17, 1981.

MARIE O. PITTS MOSLEY

OTERO, Katherine Stinson. *See* Stinson, Katherine.

OWINGS, Margaret Wentworth. April 29, 1913–January 21, 1999. Environmental activist, artist, writer.

Margaret Wentworth was born in Berkeley, California, the second child and only daughter of Jean Baird Pond and Frank Wesley Wentworth. Reared in an upper-class Republican family—her father owned an office furniture business and both parents came from distinguished New England lineages—Margaret Wentworth had what she later described as a happy childhood, despite the early onset of diabetes. She started her education in public schools and Anna Head School in Berkeley, then transferred to Bradford Academy, a private school in Massachusetts, to complete her high school education. All signs pointed to her then attending her mother's alma mater, Smith College. But these were the early 1930s, a period of economic distress. Her father was a trustee of Mills College in Oakland, and Mills needed students; therefore Margaret Wentworth attended a women's college in California rather than in Massachusetts. This choice proved to be a happy one, because at Mills she encountered one of the great figures of the Bay Area at the time, the college's president, Aurelia Reinhardt.

A dedicated educator and a fount of energy, Reinhardt drew visiting scholars and artists of national prominence to enrich student life. At Mills, Margaret Wentworth heard George Gershwin perform, met Carl Sandburg, and became acquainted with the noted photographer IMOGEN CUNNINGHAM. An art major, Margaret graduated in 1934 and then spent the next year pursuing graduate study at the Fogg Museum at Harvard University. While in Massachusetts, she met the man who would become her first husband, Malcolm Millard.

Returning to California after her graduate studies, Margaret worked briefly for museums in San Francisco before marrying Millard in August 1937. The young couple established a household in his native Illinois, where he began to practice law. There their only child, Anne Wentworth Millard (always known as Wendy), was born in 1940. Although the couple shared interests in common—they both loved the landscapes of New Mexico and California's Big Sur coast, for example—Margaret was, according to her later recollection, deeply depressed. At this low point of her life, the writings of John Muir gave her a sense of purpose and enabled her to go on. With a home in Carmel, too, by this time, she joined the Point Lobos League, and in 1947 she and the League fought successfully to protect an important stretch of California coast.

In 1952 the marriage ended in divorce and Margaret moved to New Mexico with her daughter to pursue her art. In New Mexico, she soon met Nathaniel Owings, who would become her second husband and her staunch supporter in all her activities. Another strong personality, Nathaniel was one of the nation's leading architects and a partner in Skidmore, Owings, and Merrill. In December

1953 Margaret and Nathaniel married, having between them a number of residences in several states from which to choose a domicile. They decided, however, to build a spectacular home (Nathaniel's first residential design) chiseled into a cliff on the Big Sur coast. This decision proved to be fateful because Wild Bird (the name Margaret bestowed on the home) gave her an opportunity to observe the coastal wildlife at close hand. She was soon seeing such things as a sea lion that had been killed by a heedless hunter, a spectacle she found intolerable.

In hindsight, there were many factors pointing her toward a passionate commitment to the natural world. Her father had been active in the Save-the-Redwoods League. At summer school at the University of California at Berkeley, Margaret had studied with and been inspired by Chiura Obata, one of the outstanding artists of Yosemite. In addition to reading John Muir, she had fallen under the spell of RACHEL CARSON. The list goes on. In the late 1950s all of these influences came together, and she found her life's work when she organized the Committee to Save the Sea Lions.

Over the ensuing decades she poured energy into protecting redwood trees and mountain lions, in addition to the sea lions, and she worked on behalf of the Environmental Defense Fund. She served on California's State Park Commission from 1963 to 1969. President Lyndon Johnson appointed her to the National Parks Foundation for 1968–69. (By this time, she had become a Democrat.) But probably her most noteworthy achievement was the role she played in founding the Friends of the Sea Otter (FSO) in 1968.

Owing to its dense pelt, the sea otter had been aggressively hunted in the nineteenth century. Believed to be extinct as of the early twentieth century, otters were rediscovered along the California coast in 1938. They were a small and still endangered group, but they were still the bane of, and in danger from, abalone fishermen, who resented otters because they fed on the prized mollusks. Joined by James Mattison, a local surgeon, Margaret Owings took on the abalone fishermen and any other threats to the sea otter she could identify. FSO is widely recognized to have played an indispensable role in protecting the sea otter, although the species is still embattled.

Toward the end of her long life, Margaret Owings collected many awards and honors, such as the Audubon Medal from the National Audubon Society and in 1998 the Society's designation as one of the top 100 American champions of conservation. Having been widowed in 1984 and deprived of the emotional support of her devoted husband, she nonetheless fought on until the end. Because she poured so much time and energy into her activism, she spent relatively less time on her art than she might have otherwise—though she did make charming sketches of the animals she was trying to protect for organizational publications, and had six one-woman shows of her paintings and stitchery. In late 1998 the Monterey Bay Aquarium Press published a compilation of her writings and artwork, *Voice from the Sea: Reflections on Wildlife and Wilderness.* Just weeks after its publication, Margaret Owings died at her cliffside home in Big Sur at the age of eighty-five.

Bibliography: The chief source for Margaret Owings's life is a very full oral history interview conducted by Suzanne Riess and Ann Lage of the Regional Oral History Office, Bancroft Library, University of California, Berkeley, entitled "Margaret Owings: Artist, and Wildlife and Environmental Defender" (1991). See also Anne LaBastille, *Women and Wilderness* (1980), which contains a chapter on Owings. There are photographs of Owings in the Bancroft Library and also at the Friends of the Sea Otter in Monterey, California. Obituaries appeared in the *San Francisco Chronicle* on January 25, 1999, and the *New York Times* on January 31, 1999.

GLENNA MATTHEWS

P

PAGE, Ruth Marian. March 22, 1899–April 7, 1991. Dancer, choreographer.

Ruth Marian Page helped establish the ballet as an integral part of American culture. She was born and raised in Indianapolis, the second of three children of Marian Heinly and Lafayette Page. Her mother, who had studied to be a concert pianist, was a moving force in the founding of the Indianapolis Symphony Orchestra. Her father, a prominent physician, was instrumental in establishing what is today known as the Riley Hospital for Children. Encouraged in her artistic development by her mother, she was impelled to dance by her own abundant physical gifts, poetic yearnings, energy, and ambition in a period of international female soloists—ISADORA DUNCAN, RUTH ST. DENIS, and Anna Pavlova.

Page studied ballet with Serge Oukrainsky, Jan Zalewsky, Adolph Bolm, and Enrico Cecchetti. In 1914 she auditioned for Pavlova, who was passing through Indianapolis on one of her North American tours. The celebrated ballerina encouraged her to study in Chicago and eventually took the young dancer into her company, though not before Ruth had received her diploma from the Tudor Hall School for Girls in 1916 and begun studies at Miss Williams' and Miss McClellan's French School for Girls in New York. In 1918–19 Page, accompanied by her mother, spent a year in South America, touring with Pavlova. Returning to the United States, she performed as Adolf Bolm's partner in his Ballet Intime, receiving rave reviews for her performance in *The Birthday of the Infanta* at the Chicago Opera in 1919. From 1922 to 1924 she starred and toured in Irving Berlin's *Music Box Revue*. Page, a white woman, discovered African American jazz dancing during this Broadway excursion.

In 1925 Page married Thomas Hart Fisher, a young Harvard-educated lawyer, forming an enduring partnership with a man who acted—zealously—as her legal adviser, agent, promoter, fellow aesthete, and companion. During their honeymoon, they stopped in Monte Carlo, where, warmly encouraged by the great ballet master Cecchetti, Page auditioned for Diaghilev. She was the first American to be accepted into the Ballets Russes, but she soon left, sensing a lack of opportunity for quick advancement. Home base became Chicago, where her husband would eventually take over his father's law practice. The couple had no children.

Early in her career, Page formed a number of enduring collaborative friendships, two of which were particularly important: with designer (and co-scenarist) Nicolas Remisoff, whom she met as first ballerina of Chicago Allied Arts (1924–27), and Isaac van Grove, conductor of the Chicago Symphony Orchestra, with whom she worked as ballet director and first dancer at the Ravinia Opera Festival (1926–31). Page also collaborated with the German modern dancer Harold Kruetzberg on a series of joint performances in the United States, Canada, and Japan (1933–36), and performed and choreographed with the elegant and vernacular-savvy Bentley Stone for over two decades, starting in 1935. Throughout her career she exhibited a profound understanding of the collaborative, interdisciplinary essence of the ballet.

Like the modern dancers, Page created her choreography on her own body, imbuing the ballet with motor impulse, drive, and weight. Her themes, often of obsession and compulsion expressed in sexual terms, rendered in metaphor her own lifelong love affair with dance. She often incorporated spoken words into her choreographies: "Most choreographers seem to think that your voice leaves you once you get into toe shoes" (1948 speech reprinted in *Page by Page*). Page's fascination with dance from different cultures gave her an especially good eye for vernacular dance. For the 1933 Chicago World's Fair she choreographed *La Guiablesse* to music by African American composer William Grant Still, dancing with an almost all-black cast, including the twenty-one-year-old Katherine Dunham. In a time of racial segregation, when blacks were not permitted to dance in classes alongside whites or to perform with white companies, Page made opportunities for black dancers like Dunham and Talley Beatty, who would go on to become choreographers in their own right.

Page's first masterpiece as a choreographer was *Frankie and Johnny* (1938, created in collaboration with Bentley Stone), a bawdy convergence of African American dance, modern dance, and ballet idioms that provoked and scandalized audiences from Boston to Paris. In creating *Frankie and Johnny* Page was motivated, as were other American choreographers of the time, by the idea of creating a distinctly American ballet genre. Her works in this vein were inventive and innovative rather than stylistically sublime: *Hear Ye! Hear Ye!* (1934), about a murder trial to music by Aaron Copland; *Americans in Paris* (1936, originally *An American in Paris*), to George Gershwin's music score; *An American Pattern* (1937, with Bentley Stone), about a woman who tries to escape from a conventional life; *The Bells* (1946), which evoked Edgar Allan Poe's poem; and *Billy Sunday* (1948), based on the revival meetings of the famous evangelist.

In the late 1940s and early 1950s Page achieved international recognition as a choreographer, setting works of the Ballet Russe de Monte Carlo and assembling a company called Les Ballets Américains to perform a program of distinctive American ballets in postwar Paris. She triumphed with *Revanche* (1951, Revenge) and *The Merry Widow* (1953, originally *Vilia*). A 1954 appointment as ballet director of the Lyric Theatre of Chicago (later the Lyric Opera of Chicago) held the promise, never quite realized, of a resident ballet company that could be subsidized through an opera season along with independent touring. After a highly successful New York engagement, Columbia Artists Management contracted Ruth Page's Chicago Opera Ballet to tour the United States in 1956–57. The company continued its extensive tours (later as Ruth Page's International Ballet) through 1969 to great acclaim. Through these venues Page constructed a substantial repertory of ballets, perfecting the form of opera-into-ballet with ballets like *Camille* (1959) and *Carmen* (1960, 1962, 1972). As part of her campaign to bring ballet into the mainstream, Page also gave lecture-demonstrations throughout the public schools of Chicago. In 1971 she established the Ruth Page Foundation, which instituted under its umbrella a school of dance, co-directed by Larry Long.

Ruth Page and Thomas Fisher led a cosmopolitan life, maintaining a summer home in St. Tropez, and combing the opera houses, performing-arts festivals, museums, and ruins of Europe. In 1969 her husband of forty-four years died after a long struggle with amyotrophic lateral sclerosis. In 1983 she married André Delfau, her longtime set and costume designer. In later life she focused upon documenting and preserving her legacy, including giving a vast archival collection to the New York Public Library for the Performing Arts. Ruth Page died in Chicago in 1991 at the age of ninety-two. Succeeding as a choreographer in the ballet world, a prerogative usually reserved for men, Page inscribed her figurative voice as well as her literal one on ballet in America.

Bibliography: The New York Public Library for the Performing Arts at Lincoln Center houses extensive collections related to Page's career: the Ruth Page Collection, a vast collection of personal and professional manuscript materials, including correspondence, manuscripts, notebooks, publicity material, and business records; the Ruth Page Video Archives, consisting of 129 videotapes, including two television documentaries of Page's career, made-for-television productions of her ballets, documentary videotapes of her choreographies, and extensive on-camera interviews; and costume and set designs, music scores, posters, programs, films, photographs, clippings, and scrapbooks related to her ballet productions. Andrew Mark Wentink has written an excellent finding aid for the manuscript collection: "The Ruth Page Collection: An Introduction and Guide to Manuscript Materials through 1970," *Bulletin of Research in the Humanities* 83, no. 1 (Spring 1980), pp. 67–162. The Newberry Library in Chicago also holds materials on Ruth Page. *Page by Page*, edited by Andrew Mark Wentink (1978), is a fascinating collection of Page's writings, including previously published accounts of the status of dance in countries she visited on tour, speeches, statements of her choreographic process, and reminiscences. See also Wentink's second edited collection of Page material: *Class: Notes on Dance Classes around the World, 1915–1980* (1984). John Martin had access to Page's personal diaries for his biography *Ruth Page: An Intimate Biography* (1977). See also George Dorris, "*Frankie and Johnny* in Chicago and Some Problems of Attribution," *Dance Chronicle* 18, no. 2 (1995), pp. 179–88; and Jack Anderson, *The One and Only: The Ballet Russe de Monte Carlo* (1981). An obituary appeared in the *New York Times* on April 9, 1991.

JOELLEN A. MEGLIN

PARRISH, Essie. November 29, 1902–July 9, 1979. Spiritual and political leader of the Kashaya Pomo Indians, basket maker.

Essie Nellie Parrish was born, in her words, "in an old shack between the redwood trees and the acorn trees," on Charlie Haupt's ranch in northern Sonoma County, California, where the Kashaya made their home while they worked on Haupt's ranch and neighboring ranches as farm laborers. Her Indian name was Pewoya (the Stirrer). Born the fifth of nine children to Emily Colder and John Fiske Pinola, both Kashaya Pomo, she was raised by her maternal grandmother, Rosie Jarvis, and attended Stewart's Point schoolhouse through the sixth grade.

Essie began "dreaming" when she was four years old, and not long after her people recognized her as the last of the four Dreamers promised to the Kashaya people in 1871 by their first Dreamer, Jack Humbolt. In 1872 a revivalist religion known among the various Pomo tribes as the *Bole Maru*, or Dream Dance, swept through north central California, producing Dreamers, who reorganized and revitalized their respective tribes according to the dictates of their Dreams. By 1943, when Essie took over as leader from her predecessor, Annie Jarvis, the Dream Dance religion had greatly diminished among other Pomo tribes, but Essie, a powerful leader, galvanized the Kashaya Pomo around her Dreams and would continue to do so until her death in 1979.

About 1914 the federal government bought the "homeless" Kashaya Indians a forty-two-acre parcel on a remote mountaintop east of Stewart's Point. This plot of land became the Kashaya Pomo Reservation, locally known as Stewart's Point Reservation. It became the place Essie called home, where she would conduct religious activities in the Roundhouse, the religious center of the Kashaya Pomo, and where she would raise her thirteen children. Marriage to Daniel Scott, a Kashaya Pomo, produced four surviving children: Ernest, Pearl, Bernice, and Aaron. In 1928 she married Sidney Parrish, a Point Arena Pomo, and with Sidney, her husband until his death in 1978, she had nine surviving children: Vernita, Violet, Warren, Otis, Sidney Jr., Vivian, Ronnie, Morris, and Vanadene.

Like all Dreamers, Essie Parrish possessed the gift of prophecy. She could "see" future events in her Dreams. She foresaw "jets," fast airplanes that would crisscross the skies. She foresaw massive fighting and knew that in that huge war—World War II—Kashaya men would be drafted. The Spirit told her to weave a pair of protective handkerchiefs for each Kashaya man entering the war. Essie instructed the young men to wear the handkerchiefs over their chests in battle; she told their mothers or wives to "dance the mate handkerchief" in the Roundhouse. More than twenty Kashaya men went to war. All returned alive except for the one whose mother did not dance his handkerchief.

Parrish's dreaming was inextricably tied to her doctoring. She was a medicine woman of the first order, using herbs, special songs, as well as hand power to counter illness. But she went further, developing what she called a spiritual instrument in her throat for sucking out pains. Among the Pomo people and throughout much of California, sucking doctors were valued by the native peoples as the most valuable doctors. Along with her good friend, Cache Creek Pomo medicine woman and basket weaver Mabel McKay, Parrish would be the last of the sucking doctors in California—and probably the last in the entire country.

In addition to serving her tribe as spiritual and political leader and as a greatly sought after medicine woman, Essie Parrish became a world-renowned Pomo basket maker. The Pomo are generally regarded as the world's finest basket weavers, and early in her life Essie distinguished herself among the finest of the Pomo artists. Her baskets are held in numerous national museums, including the Smithsonian. She could play several musical instruments and earned herself a position as manager at an apple cannery where she worked for several years. Essie used to say, "there's no such a word as 'can't.'" Her life is testimony.

In her later years, Parrish was recognized for her many accomplishments. Famous anthropologists, Alfred Kroeber and Samuel Barrett among them, worked with her. With the anthropologists she made over twenty films, and one of them, *Chishkale (Beautiful Tree),* which describes the preparation of acorns as food, won a Cannes Film Festival award in 1969 for best documentary. Starting in the late 1950s, she worked with Berkeley linguist Robert Oswalt to create a dictionary of the Kashaya Pomo language. She also helped him prepare *Kashaya Texts* (1962), which records many Kashaya legends as well as Parrish's own stories and experiences.

In 1971 Essie Parrish gave testimony that influenced the U.S. government to turn over a former Central Intelligence Agency (CIA) property to all of the Indians of Sonoma County. She renamed the place Ya-Ka-Ama (Our Land) and told the various Indian tribes who would be sharing the buildings and land to "come together here." She lectured in dozens of schools and universities, including the University of California at Berkeley and the New School for Social Research. When Robert Kennedy visited the tiny reservation in 1968 while investigating Indian schools, Essie met him as "head of state" for the Kashaya tribe and took him into the Roundhouse, where she presented him one of her beautiful baskets. Later, she sadly told her people that he would not live long. Several months later he was assassinated in Los Angeles.

Several years after Essie Parrish's death in 1979 at the age of seventy-six, the National Organization for Women selected her (along with Gloria Steinem and SOJOURNER TRUTH) as one of a dozen American women to be honored on their poster celebrating National Women's History Month. She is buried next to her husband, Sidney, in the Kashaya Pomo cemetery under redwood and oak trees.

Bibliography: The numerous films collected at the University of California at Berkeley as part of the Kashaya Documentary Film Project offer the best introduction to the life of Essie Parrish. See especially *Chishkale* (1965) and *The Sucking Doctor* (1963). Additional information can be found in Robert Oswalt, ed., *Kashaya Texts* (1962); Jenny Goodrich, Claudia Lawson, and Vana Lawson, *Kashaya Pomo Plants* (1980); and Greg Sarris, *Mabel McKay: Weaving the Dream* (1994). This essay drew on personal communications with Essie Parrish before her death. Additional information was provided by Vana Lawson, Essie Parrish's daughter.

GREG SARRIS

PARSONS, Betty. January 31, 1900–July 23, 1982. Art dealer, artist.

The art dealer Betty Parsons was born Elizabeth Beirne Pierson in Manhattan, where she would achieve her greatest fame, in the first month of the new century. She was the second of three girls born to Suzanne Miles, who came from a well-known family of southern planters and politicians, and J. Fred Pierson Jr., heir to a line of New York manufacturers and inventors. This family tradition of wealth and prestige surely led to Betty's emphasis on status and socializing—though Pierson, who had none of his brigadier general father's military discipline, managed to gradually but permanently deplete the family's resources.

From 1910 to 1915, Betty attended Miss Chapin's School. In 1913 she visited the art exhibition at the 69th Infantry Regiment Armory—the infamous "Armory Show" that brought avant-garde European art to many American eyes for the first time. Unlike most attendees, Betty was bewitched by what she saw. Determined to take part in this new, radical art world, Betty requested that her parents let her attend college at Bryn Mawr; not wishing to "spoil" her for marriage with an education, however, they would send her to Mrs. Randall MacKeever's Finishing School instead. Betty compromised: she would go to MacKeever's if she could also take sculpture classes with Gutzon Borglum, later director of the Mount Rushmore project.

When Betty's parents divorced after World War I, she met sophisticated, wealthy Schuyler

Livingston Parsons, ten years her senior. The lively couple married on May 8, 1920, but suddenly, on their honeymoon, found each other unbearable. Within two years, during which Betty studied sculpture with Mary Tonetti in Manhattan and became a regular visitor to Alfred Stieglitz's 291 gallery, tensions led to a seemingly mutual divorce in Paris in May 1923.

In Paris, Parsons enrolled in classes at the Académie de la Grande Chaumière. Eventually studying under her idol Bourdelle, as well as Ossip Zadkine and Arthur Lindsey, Parsons began to develop the ideas about art that she would espouse and promote for the rest of her life: spirituality, expressivity, freedom from traditional techniques and subjects, intuitive and spontaneous processes, and the centrality of the artist's vision. She also began keeping a journal that she carried with her constantly, sketching, writing poems, and including clippings that chronicled her experiences and interests.

Supported by Schuyler's alimony payments, Parsons formed friendships with the most important cultural figures of the time, including the tight-knit lesbian and bisexual expatriate community that included JANET FLANNER, ROMAINE BROOKS, NATALIE BARNEY, and Adge Baker. Parsons soon fell in love with Baker and subsequently moved into a small house behind the Montparnasse cemetery with her, where they lived for eight years.

In 1933, Parsons broke up with Baker and returned to the United States, driven in part by financial necessity (both her ex-husband and her family had been bankrupted by the stock market crash and could no longer support her) and in part by expectations of family and friends that she lead a more conventional life. She lived in Santa Barbara, California, for two years, teaching art, recommending wines at a liquor store, and painting portraits. Parsons also developed a lifelong pattern of deftly accepting just enough support from friends to avoid poverty and maintain an appropriately cosmopolitan lifestyle.

Parsons moved back to Manhattan in November 1935 and exhibited her watercolors at Midtown Galleries that winter. The owner, impressed by her clear passion for proselytizing art, gave Betty her first "real" job, installing and selling art. She was subsequently sought for other Manhattan gallery positions, including at Mrs. Cornelius J. Sullivan's gallery. Parsons began to develop a small stable of as-yet-unrecognized artists like Joseph Cornell, Hedda Sterne, Adolph Gottlieb, and Barnett Newman.

When Brandt's gallery closed in 1946, Parsons borrowed funds from her friends to take over and renovate the space, which became the Betty Parsons Gallery. She had already started to bring exposure to abstractionists and surrealists whose work was too radical for the few other galleries in New York at the time, but in 1947, when PEGGY GUGGENHEIM left for Europe permanently, Parsons took on her stable of artists, including Clyfford Still, Mark Rothko, and Jackson Pollock. Most of these artists had their first one-person show at Parsons's gallery, where the unusual setting—spare, with white walls and bright lighting—was ideal for larger, bolder works. When Pollock, Rothko, Newman, and Still approached her to deal in their work exclusively, feeling that she was allowing too many, and too many subpar, artists into her roster, Parsons refused and lost them to another dealer, Sidney Janis.

Such setbacks were always temporary for Parsons, who continued to run her gallery with the unpopular notion that more artists, working in a variety of styles, were better than fewer. Although most famous for essentially launching the careers of most of the New York school of abstract expressionists, Parsons also gave important early support to Robert Rauschenberg, Ellsworth Kelly, and Agnes Martin. Martin and Sterne were just two of more than twenty women artists Parsons supported, including Barbara Chase-Riboud.

Throughout her nearly fifty years as an art dealer, Parsons continued to make her own art, moving through a number of different styles from abstract painting to found-object sculpture. Never quite as well known as those she nurtured, Parsons nonetheless had significant success with her work, which was featured in dozens of solo exhibitions and group shows between 1933 and 1977.

Parsons remained single and childless for the rest of her life, although she enjoyed many romantic affairs. She stayed in contact with her first love, Adge Baker, throughout her life. Parsons died at her Long Island cottage in Southold after suffering a stroke in 1982 at the age of eighty-two.

Betty Parsons's life and experiences spanned the history of avant-garde modernism in America, from her visit to the Armory Show as an impressionable teen through her presentation of the abstract expressionists' works when no one else would and later as a supporter of minimalist and conceptual artists. Inarguably the most important art dealer at the most important time in modern American art, Parsons had a democratic openness and commitment to the next risky new style, if seriously and personally felt, that opened the door to America's ascendance as leader of the contemporary art world.

Bibliography: The only biographically complete study of Parsons's life and work is Lee Hall, *Betty Parsons: Artist, Dealer, Collector* (1991). The majority of Hall's research came from Betty Parsons's own idiosyncratic journals as well as interviews with Parsons, her friends, associates, and family members. Much of this material is otherwise unavailable. The Archives of American Art at the Smithsonian Institution holds numerous materials on Parsons, including detailed files from the Betty Parsons Gallery, correspondence, financial records, announcements, photographs, artists' files, and sales records. There are also several interviews with Parsons herself, personal papers, and correspondence.

The only exhibition catalogue that focuses on Parsons's own art was published by the Montclair Art Museum, Montclair, N.J., in 1974: *Betty Parsons Retrospective: An Exhibition of Paintings and Sculpture*. Her collection of the art of others is documented in the exhibition catalogue *Betty Parsons: Paintings, Gouaches and Sculpture, 1955–1968* (1968). Articles on exhibitions at her gallery are too numerous to mention, but some articles on and interviews with Parsons herself include: Lawrence Alloway, "Diary of an Art Dealer," *Vogue*, October 1963, pp. 157, 216–17; Rosalind Constable, "The Betty Parsons Collection," *Art News*, March 1968, p. 6; and Grace Lichtenstein, "Betty Parsons: Still Trying to Find the Creative World in Everything," *Art News*, March 1979, pp. 52–56. Numerous broader texts on modern art contain brief entries on or mentions of Parsons. See particularly Brooke Bailey, *The Remarkable Lives of 100 Women Artists* (1994), and Charlotte Streifer Rubinstein, *American Women Artists* (1982). An obituary appeared in the *New York Times* on July 24, 1982. For assessments of her career after her death, see John Russell's brief feature, "Betty Parsons: An Artist Both in Life and Art," *New York Times*, August 15, 1982; Cleve Gray, "Betty Parsons: 'The New Was Her Nourishment'" in *ART News*, October 1982, p. 103; and Edith Newhall, "A Portrait of the Artist . . . and the Dealer and the Bon Vivant," *New York*, May 13, 1991, p. 29.

KIRSTIN RINGELBERG

PATTERSON, Louise Alone Thompson. September 9, 1901–August 27, 1999. Communist labor and community organizer, civil rights activist.

Born in Chicago, Louise Alone Thompson was raised by her mother, a domestic worker who never wavered in her support of her daughter's radical activities. Beyond that, little is known about her family background. Growing up in a variety of far western towns, Louise later attributed her racial awareness to the alienation, discrimination, and humiliation she experienced growing up in communities without a strong or cohesive black presence. She graduated from Oakland (California) High School in 1919, and she was one of the first African American women to graduate from the University of California at Berkeley, where she received a degree in economics, cum laude, in 1923. After a brief stint in graduate school, she accepted teaching positions in Pine Bluff, Arkansas, and at Hampton Institute in Virginia. One of the few African American faculty members at a school for black students, she condemned Hampton for cultivating racism in the form of "white philanthropy." Her outspoken support for a student strike hastened her departure from the teaching staff.

With the aid of an Urban League fellowship, she enrolled at the New York School for Social Work in 1927. Working with black families in Hell's Kitchen, she was troubled by the high dropout rate among black teenagers and the channeling of young African American women into traditional occupations such as domestic service and nursing. Striving to understand the systemic causes of poverty, she was once again embittered by what she perceived as institutional racism. Abandoning social work, she obtained a position with the Congregational Educational Society, a liberal organization that involved itself with social issues and labor and race relations.

During these years, Thompson began her association with the Harlem Renaissance, for which she remains best known. Her friendship with Alain Locke drew her to the attention of the influential philanthropist Charlotte Osgood Mason, the movement's pivotal "Godmother." Although she was grateful for the financial support provided by white patrons like Mason, Thompson was uncomfortable with what she perceived to be Mason's desire to direct the work of black artists into stereotypical paths. Securing a position as literary secretary for Langston Hughes and ZORA NEALE HURSTON, she began a lifelong (and possibly romantic) relationship with Hughes, who dedicated his 1942 collection of poems, *Shakespeare in Harlem*, to her. With sculptor AUGUSTA SAVAGE, Thompson organized a literary and social group known as the Vanguard. Left-wing but not openly Communist, the group aimed to expose black intellectuals to progressive ideas.

Thompson was not yet a Communist, but her leftward progression was apparent; the process was hastened by her deepening commitments to civil rights and labor activism. She strove to educate herself in Marxist theory by attending the Marxist Workers' School in downtown Manhattan. Already a skilled and persistent organizer, in 1931 she invited a group of associates among the Harlem intelligentsia to form a chapter of the Friends of the Soviet Union (FOSU), an organization whose goal was to educate Americans about life within the USSR. Especially appealing to Thompson was Soviet treatment of national minorities.

As secretary of the Harlem chapter of the FOSU, Thompson involved herself in a much publicized project: the 1932 voyage of twenty-two black artists and intellectuals (including Hughes and writer DOROTHY WEST) to the USSR to make a Soviet-sponsored film about African American life. In her essay "With Langston Hughes in the USSR," Thompson contrasted the treatment the group received there with the sting of discrimination encountered by black Americans in their own land. The ultimate cancellation of the project caused dissension among participants; some called Thompson "Madame Moscow" for her overly trusting and fulsome regard for her Soviet hosts.

The trip appears to have been a turning point for Thompson. Upon her return, she gave a celebrated interview to the *New York Amsterdam News* where she explained why she preferred Russia to living in America. Inspired by the idea of an international crusade against racism and the promise of a revolutionary society where racism disappeared, she formally joined the Communist Party in 1933 and remained a member until her death. From that point, she was centrally involved in Party activities. In May 1933 she organized a highly successful march on Washington to draw attention to the Scottsboro case, a key issue in galvanizing support for the Party, especially in Harlem. Shortly after, she joined the International Workers Order (IWO), a Communist-sponsored social services organization whose work was especially important as the Depression worsened. She was also one of several leaders called upon to present a detailed defense of Communist actions during the Harlem riot of 1935. During the Spanish civil war she traveled to Spain and later helped develop a support network in Harlem for the Loyalist cause.

Thompson's interest in cultural activities reflected Communist concerns at the time. Under the aegis of the IWO, she and Langston Hughes organized the Harlem Suitcase Theatre in 1938. With its focus on portability, the name reflected the group's goal of making theater accessible to the masses. Theater historians credit Hughes with developing the concept for the group, but laud Thompson for her efforts in managing and holding it together, a pattern that has been called typical of her life.

Described as beautiful, vivacious, and intelligent by associates and contemporaries, Thompson had a brief and unhappy marriage to writer and intellectual Wallace Thurman in 1928. In 1940 she married prominent African American lawyer, journalist, and Communist organizer William L. Patterson. Their daughter, Mary Louise, was born in 1943. With her husband, Patterson was one of the founders of the Civil Rights Congress (CRC), which aimed to focus national and international attention on civil liberties violations in American society. She was among the signers of its controversial "We Charge Genocide" petition, a document delivered to the United Nations in 1951 that charged the U.S. government with officially sanctioning genocidal treatment of African Americans. In the 1950s Patterson was one of the organizers of Sojourners for Truth and Justice, a black woman's auxiliary of the CRC. In later years she remained active in a host of radical causes: campaigning against the execution of the Rosenbergs, active in defense activities for accused Communist revolutionary Angela Davis, and speaking out against the threat of nuclear war. Louise Alone Thompson Patterson died at the Amsterdam Nursing Home in Manhattan in 1999 just weeks short of her ninety-eighth birthday.

Bibliography: Thompson reminisced about her life and career in a lengthy interview (November 16, 1981) given to Ruth Prago as part of an Oral History of the American Left, a transcript of which is housed in the Tamiment Institute, New York University. Biographical sketches appear in Mark Solomon, "Rediscovering a Lost Legacy: Black Women Radicals Maude White and Louise Thompson Patterson," *Abafazi: The Simmons College Review of Women of African Descent* 6 (Fall/Winter 1995), pp. 6–13; and Margaret B. Wilkerson, "Excavating Our History: The Importance of Biographies of Women of Color," *Black American Literature Forum* 24 (Spring 1990), pp. 73–84. Thompson's article on the Soviet film project appears in David Levering Lewis, ed., *The Portable Harlem Renaissance Reader* (1994). References to her life may be found in William L. Patterson's autobiography, *The Man Who Cried Genocide* (1971), and she is quoted and mentioned frequently in biographies of key figures of the Harlem Renaissance. Her own recollections of Langston Hughes appear in the PBS video series *Voices and Visions* (1988). On the Soviet film project, see Robert S. Boynton, "The Red and the Black," *New York Times Magazine,* January 2, 2000, p. 22. Secondary sources that refer to her activities include Mark Naison, *Communists in Harlem during the Depression* (1983), and Gerald Horne, *Communist Front? The Civil Rights Congress, 1946–1956* (1988). Obituaries appeared in the *New York Times* on September 2, 1999, and the *Los Angeles Times* on September 19, 1999.

MARIE MARMO MULLANEY

PAUL, Alice. January 11, 1885–July 9, 1977. Suffragist, feminist.

In the United States and internationally, Alice Paul was a leader in the struggle for equal rights for more than seven decades. As a suffragist Paul developed a nonviolent civil disobedience campaign that spurred passage of the Nineteenth Amendment. In the post-suffrage era she raised public awareness of the need for complete equal rights under the law regardless of gender through her advocacy of the equal rights amendment (ERA). Paul's leadership style was marked by total dedication to the cause. She was a strong strategist but shy, precise in her diction but quiet-spoken, physically small but intellectually gigantic. No one who came in contact with her denied her charismatic leadership.

Born in Moorestown, New Jersey, an area that had been largely Quaker for centuries, Alice Paul was the first of four children of Tacie Parry and William Mickle Paul. Her father, a prominent Quaker business leader, was president of the Burlington County Safe Deposit and Trust Company. Her mother was on the board of the Moorestown Hicksite Friends School. Alice grew up in a large, comfortable house on a working farm and as a child gathered eggs in the chicken house to sell to townsfolk, keeping track of her earnings in a small ledger. A prodigious reader from an early age, she treasured her family's huge library, especially the writings of Dickens.

The family—loving, capable, and well-off—had for many generations been a part of the more liberal Hicksite Quakers (officially the Society of Friends). Alice went to the Moorestown Hicksite Friends Meeting and attended the Quaker grammar school and high school that her parents helped found and support. From her Quaker upbringing, she learned the value of economic independence and that it was better to practice one's beliefs than to talk about them. Sex equality also was one of the basic, indisputable tenets practiced by Friends in business and professional life, as basic as the practice of trying to reach one's "Inner Light." When her father suddenly died from pneumonia in 1902, Alice's grief was exceeded by her concern about her mother, whom she saw as unprepared to run a farm and house.

After excelling in both academics and athletics, at age sixteen she entered Swarthmore College intent on a science career. But when a professor in the new field of social science joined the faculty in her senior year, she switched her path. After graduating from Swarthmore in 1905, she worked for a year as a social worker on New York's Lower East Side and then earned an MA in sociology from the University of Pennsylvania in 1907. Still interested in social work, later that year Paul went to England to work among the poor for the Charity Organization Society. She also took courses at the London School of Economics.

Paul remembered going to Quaker suffrage meetings with her mother as a child, but she had not shown much interest in the cause until she went to England. Greatly influenced by militant tactics of the Pankhursts (Emmeline and her daughters Christabel and Sylvia), Paul enthusiastically campaigned for suffrage through their Women's Social and Political Union. When London rowdies caused a riot in Parliament Square in 1908, the suffragists were arrested, Alice among them, although she was not imprisoned. Several arrests later she did land in jail, where she promptly went on a hunger strike until released. During one of her arrests, she met LUCY BURNS, a Brooklyn-born Vassar graduate, and the two became close allies. After a third hunger strike, Paul's weak health forced her to return home in 1910 to recuperate. She aimed again at her original goal of a PhD and a faculty appointment, and in 1912 completed the requirements for the degree at the University of Pennsylvania. Her doctoral dissertation examined women's legal status in Pennsylvania. She never married.

Once back in the United States, Paul was inevitably drawn into suffrage circles, but she found the main suffrage organization, the National American Woman Suffrage Association (NAWSA), conservative and timid compared to British suffrage militancy. She especially fretted over the NAWSA's lack of support for a federal suffrage amendment (Paul's preference); the NAWSA favored focusing on whichever state legislatures were considering woman suffrage.

In 1913 Paul and former fellow inmate Lucy Burns became chairs of NAWSA's Congressional Committee, where they attempted to introduce some of the lessons they had learned in England to the American movement. Most spectacularly, Paul and Burns organized a massive suffrage parade in the nation's capital to coincide with the inauguration of President Woodrow Wilson in March 1913. For the upcoming congressional elections in 1914, Paul sent organizers to western states, many of which already had equal suffrage, to warn their congressional candidates that if they did not support a federal amendment, women voters could "hold the party in power responsible," as the suffragists in England had done under their parliamentary system. This strategy further estranged Paul from suffrage leaders. Finding it impossible to work within the NAWSA, Paul and Burns organized their own parallel Congressional Union in 1914, which became the National Woman's Party (NWP) in 1916.

In January 1917 the NWP at Paul's instigation began picketing the White House, a militant stance that appalled mainstream suffrage leaders. As "silent sentinels" outside the White House fence, well-dressed women sedately carried beautifully sewn banners with slogans like "Mr. President, How Long Will Women Have to Wait for Liberty?" When the United States entered World War I in April, the pickets pointed to the hypocrisy of fighting to "make the world safe for democracy" while denying the right to vote to half its citizens. In a political climate increasingly intolerant of dissent, the suffragists were harassed, physically assaulted, and then arrested. Paul herself was arrested in October. Sent to the Occoquan Workhouse in Virginia, she was placed in solitary confinement. When she went on a hunger strike, she was forcibly fed, which was both dangerous and humiliating. As public objections about the treatment of the suffragists rose, Paul was finally released along with other suffrage martyrs. She recuperated at her Moorestown home, satisfied that the suffragists were winning the war of public opinion. In 1919 Congress passed the Suffrage Amendment and on August 26, 1920, the Nineteenth Amendment was ratified, the result of both the National Woman's Party's militancy and pressure and the NAWSA's organizational work and larger membership.

Although some suffragists dropped out of politics after 1920, Alice Paul entered phase two of her political career: securing passage of a federal equal rights amendment to the U.S. Constitution to complete women's legal equality. Her initial draft of an amendment, which read "Men and women shall have equal rights throughout the United States and in every place subject to its jurisdiction," was introduced in Congress in 1923. (The wording was later changed to the more familiar "Equality of rights under the law shall not be denied or abridged by the United States or any State on account of sex.") Instead of energizing the suffrage coalition with a new goal, the ERA split it badly, with many activists opposed to the amendment because it would end protective legislation for women workers, an important goal of many Progressive Era reformers. The two sides remained deadlocked for decades.

In addition to her ERA advocacy, Paul received a law degree from Washington College of Law in 1922 and a PhD in law from American University in 1928. She spent much of the 1930s abroad, especially in Geneva, trying to persuade women of other nationalities to join her in submitting an equal rights treaty to the League of Nations. Even though that effort was unsuccessful, as was her attempt to convince the Pan-American Conference to support a similar treaty, she was pleased when international women's groups, including the NWP, lobbied successfully for the insertion of equal rights for women and men in the United Nations preamble after the war—with the ironic result that most emerging nations incorporated in their constitutions the very words the United States was loath to adopt.

Alice Paul's name and that of the National Woman's Party are so closely linked as to seem almost synonymous, but she held no official position in the organization, except for a few years during the 1940s. There never was any question about who was in charge, however. Living in Belmont House, the NWP headquarters in Washington, she dominated the organization just as much as she had during the suffrage campaign. In the 1950s and 1960s, long before feminism reappeared on the national agenda, she continued to press for equal rights for women. Her decades of advocacy began to pay off in 1964, when Title VII of the Civil Rights Act banned discrimination on account of sex in employment. Still focused entirely on legal equality, Paul was dubious about parts of the feminist agenda developed by the National Organization for Women and other emerging women's organizations, but she felt vindicated when Congress finally passed the ERA in 1972 and sent it to the states for ratification. In 1974 Paul suffered a serious stroke and moved to a Quaker nursing home in her birthplace of Moorestown, New Jersey, where she died three years later at the age of ninety-two.

Bibliography: The Library of Congress holds the National Woman's Party papers, which are the primary archival sources on Alice Paul. The Schlesinger Library, Radcliffe Institute for Advanced Study, Harvard University, also has material in its Alice Paul and Women's Rights collections. An illuminating oral history, "Conversations with Alice Paul," was conducted by Amelia R. Fry (in 1971–73) as part of the Suffragists Oral History Project at the Bancroft Library of the University of California at Berkeley. General historical studies of the suffrage and ERA periods of Paul's career include Christine Lunardini, *From Equal Suffrage to Equal Rights: Alice Paul and the National Woman's Party, 1910–1928* (1986); Linda Ford, *Iron-Jawed Angels: The Suffrage Militancy of the National Woman's Party, 1912–1920* (1991); Susan D. Becker, *The Origins of the Equal Rights Amendment: American Feminism between the Wars* (1981); Nancy F. Cott, *The Grounding of Modern Feminism* (1987); Leila J. Rupp and Verta Taylor, *Survival in the Doldrums: The American Women's Rights Movement, 1945 to the 1960s* (1987); and Rupp, *Worlds of Women: The Making of an International Women's Movement* (1997). See also Amelia R. Fry, "Alice Paul," in Carol and John Stoneburner, eds., *The Influence of Quaker Women on American History: Biographical Studies* (1986); and Fry, "Breaking the Chains: Alice Paul and the ERA," *Social Education* 59 (1995), pp. 285–89. Obituaries appeared in the *New York Times* and the *Washington Post* on July 10, 1977.

AMELIA ROBERTS FRY

PAYNE, Ethel L. August 14, 1911–May 28, 1991. Journalist, human rights and civil rights activist.

Ethel L. Payne, who was dubbed "first lady of the black press," occupied what she called her box seat on history for four decades. The granddaughter of slaves, she rose to prominence in a segregated America that forced blacks to attend separate but unequal schools and women to occupy inferior positions in the male-dominated newspaper business. Born in Chicago, Ethel Lois Payne was the daughter of William Payne, a Pullman porter, and Bessie Austin Payne, a housewife. Payne grew up in a home of limited income but strong values. She had five siblings—three older sisters, an older brother, and a younger sister. Her father died when she was twelve, a trauma that engendered in her a sense of responsibility to her family and others, and a determination to protect the weak.

Payne sandwiched her education in between jobs, graduating from Lindbloom High School, but never received a college degree. She wanted to attend law school, but lack of money and discrimination thwarted that goal. Instead she worked as a clerk for the Chicago Public Library. She never married. Despite a persistent suitor,

Payne chose adventure over family life, often saying that she was married to her work.

In 1948, the year President Harry S. Truman signed an executive order desegregating the armed forces, Payne entered Army Special Services and became a hostess at the quartermaster depot in Tokyo, Japan. Here she planned recreation for black troops on the base. Her mother had encouraged an interest in writing, and she began keeping a diary. When Alex Wilson, a black journalist with the *Chicago Defender,* visited her in Tokyo, he asked to take her diary notes about black GIs and Japanese women and share these with "the folks back home." At this point Payne had no serious thoughts of a journalism career. Wilson rewrote her diary notes, and the *Defender,* then a nationally distributed weekly, published them emblazoned with the headline "GIs Abused, Amused and Confused." Circulation boomed because people didn't know about army life for blacks in the Far East. That front-page story helped Payne get her first newspaper job, but not before she was castigated by Army officials for allegedly disrupting the morale of the troops. The truth was that President Truman's order for integration of the armed forces was not being carried out, and the article shone a bright light on a dirty secret.

Payne began her career with the *Chicago Defender* in 1951 and became the Washington correspondent two years later; she was the second black woman to be accredited to the White House press corps. When the Interstate Commerce Commission handed down an opinion in 1954 that segregation in interstate travel should be ended, she asked President Eisenhower, "When can we expect that you will issue an executive order ending segregation in interstate travel?" Eisenhower drew himself up to full military posture and "barked" at Payne: "What makes you think I'm going to do anything for any special-interest group? I'm the President of all the people, and I'm going to do what I think is best for all the people." That afternoon, the *Washington Star* carried a box on the front page, "Negro Woman Reporter Angers Ike." The ICC finally banned segregation on buses and trains in 1961.

Payne found that the duties of her position required aggressiveness and a thorough indoctrination in the ways of Washington. The job was so demanding that she routinely worked until 2 or 3 AM before taking a taxi to the post office and mailing her stories to Chicago. At White House press conferences, Payne strove to ask questions that dealt with issues of vital concern to African Americans. She saw herself as a conduit through which black citizens, whose interests were largely ignored, could have access to presidential thinking about their concerns.

Payne was raised by a deeply religious mother but did not attend church on a regular basis as an adult. A short, solidly built woman who occasionally wore the African garb she acquired on her many trips abroad, Payne spoke in a low voice but asked penetrating questions. Her Washington, D.C., apartment was decorated with books, posters, and figurines from China and Africa. She had a wide network of friends and journalists who became her Washington family. As more blacks began to work as reporters in the mainstream media, she became a mentor to many African American women working for white newspapers.

From 1951 to 1973, Payne covered Washington as the *Chicago Defender's* political correspondent. She covered seven presidents and all of the presidential campaigns from 1956 to 1988. She was the first black female war correspondent, reporting the treatment of segregated U.S. troops in Korea, the Vietnam War, and the Nigerian civil war, and events in every major country except Russia and Australia. In 1955, her publisher sent her to Bandung, Indonesia, to cover the first conference of Third World countries. She covered Africa's liberation movements, from Ghana's independence in 1957 to Namibia's freedom from South Africa in 1990, and interviewed such heads of state as Ethiopia's Haile Selassie, South Africa's Nelson Mandela, and Uganda's Idi Amin.

In 1972, Payne became the first black female commentator on network television, working for six years with the CBS television and radio series *Spectrum.* Called back to Chicago to head the *Defender's* local coverage in 1973, she remained on the staff there until 1978. Returning to Washington and her beloved national and international reporting in 1980, Payne wrote and self-syndicated a column for several black newspapers. She also served as a distinguished visiting professor of journalism at Fisk and Jackson State universities. Payne said that although the black press was hampered by limited resources, it had always performed a unique role advocating against racism and discrimination on behalf of African Americans. She often advised young journalists to "agitate, agitate, agitate."

Because of her longtime coverage of Africa, the National Association of Black Journalists established the Ethel Payne Fellowships in 1993. Every year, two black journalists travel to Africa to observe and report on the continent's culture and citizenship for an American audience. The woman the *New York Times* called "the nation's pre-eminent black female journalist" died in Washington, D.C., on May 28, 1991, just weeks shy of her eightieth birthday.

Bibliography: A good introduction to Ethel Payne is Rodger Streitmatter, *Raising Her Voice: African-American Women Journalists Who Changed History* (1994). The main repository of her papers is the Library of Congress; additional material is found at the New York Public Library's Schomburg Center for Research in Black Culture, and Howard University. An oral history of Payne conducted by Kathleen Currie is located in the Women in Journalism Oral History Project of the Washington Press Club Foundation, on deposit at the Oral History Collection of Columbia University and the National Press Club library, Washington, D.C. The Eisenhower quotation is taken from session two of the Currie interview, p. 22. An obituary appeared in the *New York Times* on June 1, 1991.

DOROTHY GILLIAM

PAYNE-GAPOSCHKIN, Cecilia. May 10, 1900–December 7, 1979. Astronomer, astrophysicist.

Cecilia Helena Payne was born in Wendover, England. She was the oldest of three children of Emma Pertz, an artist and poet, and Edward John Payne, a historian and lawyer. From an early age she was fascinated with the natural world and the night sky; her earliest memories were of a meteor shower she observed with her mother while out in her carriage. Her father died suddenly when she was only four years old, leaving her mother very limited means with which to raise the young family. In 1912 they moved to London. Though Cecilia excelled in school, she also sought information about botany, chemistry, and physics from relatives, tutors, and the many books in her family's library. She enjoyed a particularly close relationship with her Aunt Dorothea, from whom she first learned of the possibility of higher education and careers in the sciences for women. After graduation from St. Paul Girls' School, she won a full scholarship to study at Newnham College of Cambridge University.

Cecilia Payne entered Cambridge in 1919, at first pursuing a course of study in the natural sciences. At the end of her first year, after hearing a lecture by Sir Arthur Eddington about his research on eclipses and the implications of his findings for the theory of relativity, she decided to become an astronomer. Though it was too late for her to officially change her course of study, she began attending courses and lectures taught by such influential astronomers as William Smart, Edward Milne, and Leslie Comrie in addition to her regular course work in the natural sciences.

After graduating from Newnham College in 1923, Payne realized there were few opportunities for a woman astronomer in England, beyond perhaps teaching at a girls' school. At the advice of her professors, she sought a fellowship to study astronomy and astrophysics at Harvard University; since the late nineteenth century, unique circumstances at the Harvard College Observatory had allowed women such as ANNIE JUMP CANNON and ANTONIA MAURY to play important, although limited, observational and computational roles there. Having secured a Pickering Fellowship from Newnham College for one year of study at the Harvard College Observatory, she worked closely with its head, Harlow Shapley, who was impressed by her talent and dedication and immediately put her to work using existing photographic slides in the observatory's collection to make interpretations and measurements about the sizes and locations of stars.

Relishing the intellectual community and personal freedoms afforded her at Harvard, Payne remained in the graduate program with the help of a small stipend from the observatory, and the project evolved into her influential PhD dissertation on the origin of line spectra and the physics of stellar atmospheres. Payne became the first graduate student granted a PhD in astronomy (as distinct from physics) at Radcliffe College or Harvard University. Her dissertation, published in 1925 as *Stellar Atmospheres: A Contribution to the Observational Study of High Temperature in the Reversing Layers of Stars*, included her unexpected observation (still accepted today) that stars are primarily made up of hydrogen and helium. Her dissertation was widely praised for both its innovation and its accuracy by the international astronomical community, and it cemented her position as an important astronomer. Otto Struve, one-time head of the International Astronomical Union, described *Stellar Atmospheres* as "undoubtedly the most brilliant PhD thesis ever written in astronomy."

In 1925, with the aid of a National Research Council fellowship, Payne committed to stay at Harvard to continue the research that would become her second book, *Stars of High Luminosity* (1930). This work was the first comprehensive and systematic explanation of existing observations of these stars, and also offered important new interpretations. At the same time, she had to accept a poorly paid academic position on the observatory staff. This allowed her to teach courses and advise graduate students, but she was barred from holding an official university appointment because she was a woman. She remained in this position until 1938, when the Harvard Corporation appointed her Phillips Astronomer and lecturer in astronomy. She became a U.S. citizen in 1931.

In 1933, devastated after the tragic deaths of four close friends and miserable after a brutal rebuff from a love interest, Payne undertook an extended trip to Europe, where she visited all the major observatories on the Continent and attended the annual meeting of the Astronomische Gesellschaft in Germany. There she met a young Russian astronomer named Sergei Gaposchkin, a brilliant man whose political beliefs barred him from returning to the Soviet Union and whose nationality made remaining in Nazi Germany extremely dangerous. Payne managed to secure an academic position for him at the Harvard College Observatory, despite cutbacks there due to the Depression. Their personal relationship deepened, and in March 1934 they eloped to New York City, where they were married by a justice of the peace. The couple lived and worked together in Cambridge for the rest of their lives and had three children, Edward (born 1935), Katherine (1937), and Peter (1940), all of whom inherited a love for astronomy and were at one time employed by the Harvard College Observatory as lecturers and researchers.

Now known as Cecilia Payne-Gaposchkin, she began a long collaboration with her husband on the study of variable stars and galactic structure. They jointly published *Variable Stars* in 1938. A lifelong pacifist, she worked prodigiously during World War II, believing that a scholar's place in wartime was to continue research and pursue international cooperation as much as possible. In 1956 she was finally named to the Harvard faculty as a professor of astronomy and chairman of the Department of Astronomy, more than twenty-five years after she began performing the duties of a faculty member.

Cecilia Payne-Gaposchkin continued her research and published widely in the field of astronomy throughout her career, authoring or coauthoring more than three hundred scientific papers and eight major books, including *Stars in the Making* (1952), which grew out of her Lowell Lectures at Harvard, and the textbook *Introduction to Astronomy* (1954), which was the standard in the field for decades. She also edited several volumes produced by the Harvard College Observatory. Payne-Gaposchkin was one of the first women to be elected to many of the major professional societies of scientists and academics, including the American Academy of Arts and Sciences and the American Philosophical Society. After retiring in 1966, she accepted an emerita appointment from Harvard University, and remained involved in professional astronomy almost until her death thirteen years later in Cambridge from lung cancer at the age of seventy-nine.

Bibliography: The best source on Cecilia Payne-Gaposchkin's life and career is *Cecilia Payne-Gaposchkin: An Autobiography and Other Recollections* (1984), edited by her daughter Katherine Haramundanis. This volume contains several scholarly essays assessing the historical significance of Payne-Gaposchkin's life and work, as well as "The Dyer's Hand," Payne-Gaposchkin's autobiographical memoir. See also Owen Gingerich, "The Most Brilliant Ph.D. Thesis Written in Astronomy," in A. G. Davis Philip and Rebecca Koopmann, *The Starry Universe: The Cecilia Payne-Gaposchkin Centenary* (2001); and Peggy A. Kidwell, "Cecilia Payne-Gaposchkin: Astronomy in the Family," in Pnina G. Abir-Am and Dorinda Outram, *Uneasy Careers and Intimate Lives: Women in Science, 1789–1979* (1987). The quotation from Otto Struve is found on p. 220 of Struve and Velta Zebergs, *Astronomy of the 20th Century* (1962). An obituary appeared in the *New York Times* on December 8, 1979.

DEBORAH LEVINE

PEACE PILGRIM. See Ryder, Mildred Norman

PEARL, Minnie. October 25, 1912–March 4, 1996. Actress, comedian.

Sarah Ophelia Colley Cannon, better known as Minnie Pearl, was country music's most famous comedian and one of the best-known comedy actresses of the second half of the twentieth century. Sarah was born in Centerville, Tennessee, the last of five children born to Fannie Tate House and Thomas K. Colley, proud, conventional southern parents and themselves native Tennesseans, who embraced Victorian culture. Thomas Colley owned a lumber business in Centerville, and Fannie was active in the town's civic and cultural affairs and supported many middle-class reforms, including woman suffrage.

As a teenager, Sarah took "expression lessons," an early term for acting lessons, and after graduating from Hickman County High School in 1930, earned a degree in dramatics in 1932 from Nashville's prestigious women's finishing school, Ward-Belmont College. Beginning in 1934, she spent six years traveling the southern vaudeville circuit as a producer and director for the Wayne P. Sewell Company. During this time, Sarah began to develop the character of Minnie Pearl, at first as a means of attracting publicity in towns where the company was performing, but later as a permanent fixture in her comedic repertoire.

When Sarah was asked to audition for the radio show *The Grand Ole Opry* in 1940, it had been on the airwaves for fifteen years. The Nashville radio show, representative of the barn dance genre, evoked for a national audience an idealized front-porch community where people worked hard, praised God, and sang old-time music. In this program, gossips played a critical role, forging relationships on stage through the telling of tales about various characters in order to promote a familiarity between performers and the listeners who tuned in. Gossips were also typically old maids; after all, the ultimate joke in a genre that lauded marriage and family was an unmarried woman. In this role of gossip and spinster, the character of Minnie Pearl flourished, though not without some initial concern on the part of advertisers that Sarah was too sophisticated to portray a simple country girl. They encouraged her to be more boisterous, to exaggerate her character, and to go for "boffo laughs."

By 1943, Pearl was a critical player on the *Opry*'s national show. Soon, and for decades after, audiences came to know and love her for her down-home dresses, her hat with an ever-present price tag dangling from the brim, and a welcoming holler, "Howdee! I'm just so proud to be here." Her jokes played on assumptions bound up in the character: Minnie's old age, her unattractiveness, and her inability to find a man. She lived in a fictional town called Grinder's Switch where residents lived and worked in "traditional" ways. Pearl and the other characters simultaneously poked fun at and reinforced stereotypes of hillbillies and country folk. Listeners tuned in every Saturday night to hear about Brother (who was once arrested, Minnie said slyly, for driving while ignorant), Aunt Ambrosy, Uncle Nabob, and many others. Much of the show's humor focused on residents who lived clean, wholesome lives, played games such as Pin the Tail on the Donkey, and questioned modern gadgets, values, and inventions. Minnie's Mammy, for example, told Brother that "it's all right to flirt with the girls that wears the *lipstick,* but always marry one that can push a *broomstick.*"

Marriage to Henry R. Cannon, a World War II fighter pilot, in 1947 did not slow her career. Instead, Henry took over management of Minnie Pearl. The couple never had children, and Sarah was consequently able to pursue a variety of entrepreneurial activities while maintaining a busy schedule of entertaining audiences on the *Opry* and later on television. Sarah began writing her own fan newspaper in 1944 called *The Grinder's Switch Gazette,* sold Minnie Pearl dolls, and opened a chain of chicken restaurants that eventually went bankrupt.

In 1968 some of the *Opry* cast began performing on the syndicated television show *Hee Haw,* which would end up airing for twenty years. Minnie, Roy Clark, Grandpa Jones, and a host of others performed acts similar to those they staged on the *Opry,* yet the emphasis was more on rube characters and caricatures of hillbilly life than on the mix of rural nobility and hillbilly silliness Minnie and others presented on the *Opry* stage. Ironically, it is because of *Hee Haw* that most Americans know Cousin Minnie Pearl.

Sarah also used the Minnie Pearl character in a variety of political and charitable causes. Dressed as Minnie Pearl, she announced to an Alabama rally in 1958, "I'm as happy as a dead pig in the sunshine to introduce your next governor, George Wallace" (*Wall Street Journal,* May 6, 1958). She was also a longtime activist in promoting cancer research because her sister died from cancer in the late 1960s and Sarah herself had a double mastectomy in 1985. After her mastectomy and in typical Minnie Pearl fashion, Sarah joked that, from the waist up, she was once again eighteen years old. At her death, her fortune endowed the Minnie Pearl Cancer Foundation.

Her proudest moment was, of course, being named to the Country Music Hall of Fame in 1975. Not long after celebrating her fiftieth anniversary on the *Opry* in 1990, Sarah suffered an incapacitating stroke, and she remained in a Nashville nursing home until her death from another stroke at the age of eighty-three. She was buried in the Mount Hope Cemetery in Franklin, Tennessee. In a fitting tribute, the *Nashville Tennessean*'s political cartoonist drew a halo with a price tag reading "Priceless."

Bibliography: There are two major collections of material devoted to Sarah Colley Cannon. The first is at the Country Music Foundation in Nashville, Tennessee, which has an extensive clipping file, including columns she wrote for the Nashville *Banner* entitled "Minnie's Memories" and obituaries from local and national papers. It also has an entire run of the *Grinder's Switch Gazette* (1944–46). Gaylord Entertainment (the owner of the *Grand Ole Opry*), also in Nashville, has Sarah's costumes, articles from the 1940s and 1950s, and bound copies of her radio scripts from the same period. Gaylord has an extensive collection of Minnie Pearl pictures, but relatively few of Sarah Cannon, as well as oral interviews conducted with Sarah for her autobiography, *Minnie Pearl* (co-written with Joan Dew, 1980). Both collections focus primarily on the character, Minnie, and not on the woman, Sarah, who created her. Sarah helped produce a variety of videos and albums, including the video, *Minnie Pearl: Old Times* (1988), and record albums *Lookin' Fer a Feller* (1998) and *Country Music Hall of Fame, 1975* (1998). Finally, Sarah published several books, among them *Minnie Pearl's Diary* (1953) and *Minnie Pearl Cooks* (1970, rev. ed. 1971). She also wrote a children's book, entitled *Minnie Pearl's Christmas at Grinder's Switch* (1963).

Two secondary articles treat Minnie Pearl: Pamela Fox, "Recycled 'Trash': Gender and Authenticity in Country Music Autobiography," *American Quarterly* 50, no. 2 (June 1998), pp. 234–66; and Kristine Fredriksson, "Minnie Pearl and Southern Humor in Country Entertainment," in Charles K. Wolfe and James E. Akenson, ed., *Country Music Annual 2000* (2000), pp. 75–88. Details about her life and work can also be found in Mary A. Bufwack and Robert K. Oermann, *Finding Her Voice: The Saga of Women in Country Music* (1993). An obituary appeared in the *New York Times* on March 6, 1996. See also coverage in the *Nashville Tennessean* and the *Nashville Banner* for March 5–7, 1996; the "Priceless" cartoon ran on March 6, 1996.

KRISTINE MCCUSKER

PEPLAU, Hildegard E. September 1, 1909–March 17, 1999. Nurse educator, pioneer in psychiatric nursing.

One of the first nurse theorists and a specialist in psychiatric care, Hildegard E. Peplau laid the foundation for modern nursing. Best-known for her 1952 book, *Interpersonal Relations in Nursing,* Peplau treated nursing as an applied science, thereby elevating it to a profession at a time when it was struggling to find a role in the wake of the scientific and technological changes transforming health care. By developing the concept of a nurse-patient relationship, she positioned nurses as equal participants in a professional health care team rather than as the handmaidens of physicians.

Hildegard Elizabeth Peplau (known from childhood as Hilda) was born in Reading, Pennsylvania, the second child and second daughter of six children of Ottylie Elgert and Gustav Peplau. Her father, from a German-speaking part of Poland, emigrated to the United States in 1899 and settled into life shoveling coal as a fireman for a railroad. Hilda's mother, born in Poland, emigrated to America in 1903 to escape an arranged marriage. After meeting and marrying in Bristol, Connecticut, in 1907, the couple remained part of the working-class poor in Reading, where Ottylie stayed at home to care for the children. When the railroad periodically shut down because of labor strife, she would bake goods, clean houses, or find employment in a shirt factory.

As the child of a poor family, Hilda had limited professional choices after her 1928 graduation from Reading Evening High School. She had been interested in health care since the influenza epidemic of 1918, and nursing paid a small stipend, so she enrolled in Pottstown Hospital School of Nursing in 1928. The hospital lacked interns or residents, so bright nurses, including Peplau, were chosen by the physicians to assist in surgeries. By the time she graduated in 1931, she had had a number of experiences that most nurses never received. Peplau became the operating room supervisor at Pottstown and later headed the staff of the Bennington College infirmary.

At Bennington, she caught the attention of the president and received a full scholarship. Introduced to interpersonal theory, she graduated with a BA in interpersonal psychology in 1943 at the age of thirty-three. Determined to serve her country during World War II, Peplau enlisted in the U.S. Army Nurse Corps and was assigned to the School of Military Neuropsychiatry in England, where she came into contact with the world's top psychiatrists. After leaving the service, Peplau attended Teachers College of Columbia University in New York City and received an MA in the teaching and supervision of psychiatric nursing in 1947. In January 1945, while still in England, Peplau had given birth to a daughter, Letitia Anne. She was deeply concerned about the negative social attitudes toward unwed mothers at that time but eager to raise her child. Her dilemma was resolved when her brother Walter agreed to adopt the baby, casting Peplau in the more acceptable role of a single woman raising her "niece."

After a brief stint as a staff nurse in the Bellevue Psychiatric Department of the New York City Women's Disturbed Service, Peplau returned to Teachers College as an instructor in nursing education. There she became one of the first nurse educators to advocate baccalaureate education for nurses in order to encourage women's scholarship and leadership. She directed the graduate program of psychiatric nursing at Teachers College from 1948 to 1953 and developed classes that strongly emphasized direct clinical experience with mental patients. She received an EdD in curriculum development from Teachers College in 1953. Peplau started as an instructor at Rutgers University in 1954 and eventually became a full professor and headed both the Department of Psychiatric Nursing (1954–74) and the Graduate Program in Psychiatric Nursing (1956–74). She developed the first graduate program devoted exclusively to the preparation of clinical specialists in psychiatric nursing. Prior to this program, graduate nurses had to prepare as administrators or teachers.

Experience as a nurse in both general and psychiatric hospitals convinced Peplau of the need for nurses to improve their relations with patients. While in New York, she completed her book *Interpersonal Relations in Nursing,* but publishers refused to release it without a physician co-author. Peplau finally found a willing publisher in 1952 and the book quickly became a classic. Instead of presenting nursing as an art, Peplau emphasized its scientific aspects. She focused on exploring and understanding the needs, feelings, attitudes, and beliefs of both the patient and the nurse, with the aim of providing a partnership to promote health. Peplau's theory was revolutionary in that it encouraged nurses to work with patients instead of working for them.

Throughout her articles, lectures, and workshops, Peplau followed the assumption that it is a function of nursing to foster personality development in the direction of maturity. After laying the foundation for psychiatric nursing, she continued to build on her theory of illness as a learning experience. She worked as a private-duty psychiatric nurse in New York City from 1953 to 1955, which produced data for her 1955 article on loneliness. She later developed a model for anxiety, one of the most important concepts in psychiatric nursing. In 1954, the William Alanson White Institute in New York City certified her in psychoanalysis, and she maintained a part-time private psychotherapy practice from 1958 until 1974. She served as executive director of the American Nurses Association in 1969–70, and then as its president in 1970–72.

A prolific writer and straightforward woman, Peplau once observed that much of her work did not get attributed to her. In part, this is because many of her theories now appear to be common sense; but Peplau also had the generous habit of sharing her thoughts with anyone who wrote to her. Deriving most of her satisfaction in life from using her head, Peplau never could resist solving human puzzles and remained active into her final years. Following retirement from Rutgers in 1974, the professor emerita moved to Sherman Oaks, California, to spend time with family members, including Letitia Anne. Hildegard Peplau succumbed to a stroke in Sherman Oaks on March 17, 1999, at the age of eighty-nine, and her remains were scattered at sea off the coast of California.

Bibliography: The Hildegard E. Peplau Papers in the Schlesinger Library, Radcliffe Institute for Advanced Study, Harvard University, are an extensive source of correspondence, published and unpublished writings, syllabi, lectures, clippings, and oral histories covering the period 1923–84. Barbara J. Callaway, with the cooperation of Peplau, produced a biography, *Hildegard E. Peplau: Psychiatric Nurse of the Century* (2002). Peplau provided a video interview in *Portraits of Excellence: Hildegard Peplau* (1988). Among her most important works are: "Interpersonal Techniques: The Crux of Psychiatric Nursing," *American Journal of Nursing* 62 (June 1962), pp. 50–54; "A Working Definition of Anxiety," in Shirley F. Burd and Margaret A. Marshall, eds., *Some Clinical Approaches to Psychiatric Nursing* (1963), pp. 323–27; "Therapeutic Nurse–Patient Interaction," in Anita Werner O'Toole and Sheila Rouslin Welt, eds., *Interpersonal Theory in Nursing Practice: Selected Works of Hildegard E. Peplau* (1989), pp. 192–204 (the volume also includes some of Peplau's unpublished papers); and "Nursing Science: A Historical Perspective," in Rosemarie Rizzo Parse, ed., *Nursing Science: Major Paradigms, Theories, and Critiques* (1985), pp. 13–30. Letitia Anne Peplau provided generous assistance, as did Grayce M. Sills and Shirley A. Smoyak. An obituary appeared in the *New York Times* on March 28, 1999.

CARYN E. NEUMANN

PEREZ, Selena Quintanilla. *See* Selena.

PETERSON, Esther. December 6, 1906–December 20, 1997. Labor lobbyist, federal official, consumer activist.

In 1961, Esther Peterson, then a labor lobbyist, became director of the Women's Bureau and assistant secretary of labor, making her the most influential woman in the Kennedy administration. From that position, she fought for women's rights and helped create the institutions that fostered the birth of the women's movement. She served subsequently as a champion of working women and consumers in the administration of every Democratic president during the rest of the twentieth century. Carrying on the legacy of ELEANOR ROOSEVELT, Peterson often quoted her admonition to "compromise, but compromise up!" In 1981, Esther Peterson received the Medal of Freedom from President Jimmy Carter.

Born in 1906 to a Mormon Republican family in Provo, Utah, Esther Eggertsen was the fifth of the six children of Annie Nielson and Lars Eggertsen, both of Danish descent. Both her parents had graduated from Brigham Young Academy, and her father was superintendent of schools in Provo; Esther herself graduated from Brigham Young University in 1927. After a two-year stint as a teacher in Cedar City, Utah, she headed for New York City, where she earned a master's degree in 1930 at Columbia University Teachers College. There she met Oliver Peterson, a young radical from North Dakota, whom she married in 1932. Oliver, who worked for the Brooklyn YWCA, exposed Esther to the conditions of the urban poor and to the strategies of labor organizing and socialism for ameliorating them. After she graduated, Esther moved to Boston to teach physical education at the Winsor School, an elite private school for girls. In 1934, Oliver joined her in Massachusetts, studying sociology at Harvard and organizing education services for workers. At Oliver's urging, Esther volunteered at the YWCA rather than the Mormon Relief Society, teaching current events, gymnastics, and dancing to immigrant working girls. Although she retained an affectionate connection to her Mormon origins, she distanced herself increasingly from its formal observance, offended particularly by the church's long-standing dogma concerning racial inferiority.

Peterson's initiation as a labor activist came when she joined her students on the picket line in the early 1930s. Some of the young women she taught at the YWCA were garment workers who had gone on strike to resist an increase in work without an increase in pay. Peterson recruited support from middle-class women in the National Women's Trade Union League and the YWCA, and within a few weeks the women had organized a local of the International Ladies' Garment Workers' Union. While teaching at the Winsor School, she served as recreation director at the Bryn Mawr Summer School for Women Workers in Industry. After leaving Winsor in 1936, Peterson became an organizer for the American Federation of Teachers, establishing three teachers' locals in New England.

Throughout her career, Peterson dealt both personally and professionally with the challenge of combining paid work and family care. In 1938, when Oliver's job with the Works Progress Administration took them back to New York, she gave birth to her first child, Karen, and in 1939 took a job as an assistant director of education for the Amalgamated Clothing Workers Union (ACWU) in New York, a post she held until 1944. After war broke out, the ACWU's president Sidney Hillman, citing her ability to speak English without a stigmatizing immigrant accent, asked Peterson to organize workers sewing military uniforms in Virginia, Pennsylvania, and Delaware. She helped organize six locals and, with Bessie Hillman, helped support the integration of black and white workers. In 1944, when Oliver was working for the Office of Price Administration, the family moved to Washington, D.C., and in 1945 Esther became the ACWU's Washington legislative representative. Now raising three children (Eric and Iver having followed Karen in 1939 and 1942), she worked on the minimum wage raise and gave birth to her fourth child, Lars, in 1946. At the same time, she became active in the coalition with other labor women and the U.S. Women's Bureau to protect women workers from discrimination in the workplace and from the threat to labor legislation for women posed by the newly invigorated equal rights amendment. Not entirely comfortable with a woman lobbyist, in 1947 the staff assigned her to a lightweight congressional newcomer from Massachusetts, John F. Kennedy.

In 1948, Oliver accepted a position as labor attaché in Sweden, and the Petersons spent the next nine years in Europe. Esther soon created a substantive role for herself by studying Swedish labor regulations for domestic service workers and attending international conferences on behalf of the American labor movement.

As industrial unionists and socialists, both Esther and Oliver had considered and rejected appeals to join the Communist Party. In 1952, Oliver accepted a posting in Brussels, but he was summoned home to face charges of Communist affiliation, as alleged in FBI reports that also implicated Esther. Although cleared, Oliver returned to Brussels much scarred by the experience. The Petersons came home in 1957, and shortly afterward Oliver was diagnosed with cancer of the lymph nodes. He continued to work for the State Department, but they henceforth declined foreign assignments.

As a lobbyist for the Industrial Union Department of the AFL-CIO, Peterson threw her support early behind Senator John Kennedy's quest for the presidency. After the 1960 election, Kennedy asked Peterson what position she wanted and she replied: "The Women's Bureau." He gave her that post, but within the year he elevated her to assistant secretary of labor for labor standards. She was now the most powerful woman in his administration, readily recognizable by her wide smile and her distinctive braided hair coiled on her head.

Peterson devised Kennedy's agenda on behalf of women's rights, proposing that the president name the first national commission on the status of women, which he did in 1961. ELEANOR ROOSEVELT chaired the commission but Peterson, as executive vice-chairman, ran it. The prestigious commission and its seven subcommittees prompted the appointment of similar state commissions. Thus, by 1963 a national network of women activists had appeared, engaged in enhancing the status of women. In addition, acting on Peterson's advice, Kennedy issued an order barring selection by sex in civil service jobs, and Congress passed the Equal Pay Act (1963). Peterson also tried to improve the circumstances of black women workers, household workers, and domestic migrant workers. In order to include the women's perspective in the battle for civil rights legislation, Peterson organized the National Women's Committee on Civil Rights.

After Kennedy's assassination, Lyndon Johnson asked Esther Peterson to remain in her position at the Department of Labor. In addition, Johnson appointed her a special assistant to the president for consumer affairs, another Kennedy initiative. Attacked by consumer groups as unqualified, by the end of her tenure she had helped establish a national consumer education program. A campaign against deceptive advertising earned her the label "the most pernicious threat to advertising today" (*New York Times,* December 18, 1996). Feeling undermined by powerful presidential aides Jack Valenti and Joseph Califano, she resigned her White House consumer post in 1967 but retained her position as assistant secretary of labor.

She remained at all times an advocate for women. When Congress passed the Civil Rights Act of 1964, which barred discrimination in employment based on sex as well as race, Peterson finally reversed her position on special laws for women only and persuaded the president to add "sex" to the executive order barring race-based discrimination by federal contractors and requiring affirmative action. When the National Organization for Women appeared in 1966, she advised administration officials to pay careful attention to the new movement.

With the election of a Republican president in 1968, Peterson left the White House. After a brief sojourn with the ACWU as a lobbyist, an offer from the president of Giant Foods, a major Washington, D.C., supermarket chain, led the sixty-three-year-old Peterson in 1970 to begin a new career as a consumer advocate inside a major consumer industry. Promised a free hand, Peterson put Giant on record behind a "consumer bill of rights." Using it as a bargaining tool, Peterson got Giant to lead the way on open-dating, unit-pricing, and nutritional labeling. In 1977, Peterson left Giant Foods and returned to the White House as special assistant for consumer affairs to Democratic president Jimmy Carter. Although the attempt to unify the various federal consumer offices under one umbrella agency failed, Carter did sign an executive order requiring the U.S. government to list all products banned in the United States, making it easier for foreign countries to refuse their sale abroad. President Reagan withdrew the order barely a month after his inauguration.

Oliver Peterson died in 1979, and Carter's defeat the following year left Esther free to undertake new ventures. At the request of Rhoda Karpatkin, executive director of the Consumers Union and president of the International Organization of Consumers Unions (IOCU), Peterson represented the IOCU at the United Nations. In that position, she lobbied successfully to have the UN produce its own list of products banned by any country, an effort the United States alone stoutly resisted. Ralph Nader credited the adoption of the United Nations Guidelines for Consumer Protection in April 1985 to Peterson's work. In 1993, at age eighty-six and in a wheelchair, she accepted an appointment from yet another Democratic president: Bill Clinton named her as U.S. Delegate to the United Nations General Assembly. She died in Washington, D.C., at the age of ninety-one.

Throughout her life, as a teacher, union organizer, government official, and corporate executive, this consummate negotiator forged alliances and crafted compromises that benefited workers of both sexes and all races, and consumers in the United States and abroad. A mother and wife, she fought for the right of other women to meld paid work and family care. Committed to working within the Democratic Party, Esther Peterson looked for the "half a loaf." Her colleague CATHERINE EAST commented that Peterson, "a very savvy politician," taught her how to get things done in government: "She played a very active role, very quietly."

Bibliography: Esther Peterson deposited her extensive collection of personal papers at the Schlesinger Library, Radcliffe Institute for Advanced Study, Harvard University. The documents cover most of her career, particularly her role in shaping federal policy on women's issues and consumer concerns. Further documentation appears in the records of the U.S. Department of Labor held by the National Archives; in the records of the President's Commission on the Status of Women, which can be found at the Schlesinger Library, the Kennedy Library, and the National Archives; in the records of the National Consumers League and in the papers of Michael Pertschuk, both at the Library of Congress. Peterson did oral history interviews for the Kennedy, Johnson, and Carter presidential libraries; for the Schlesinger Library; for the "Twentieth Century Trade Union Woman" project (University of Michigan, Wayne State University, and Schlesinger Library); for the Columbia University Oral History Research Office; and for Foreign Service Spouse Oral History. Catherine East, in her own oral history interview for the Schlesinger Library's Women in the Federal Government Oral History Project, also credits Peterson with much of the progress made inside government in the 1960s. With the assistance of Winifred Conkling, Peterson wrote a memoir, *Restless: The Memoirs of Labor and Consumer Activist Esther Peterson* (1995). Obituaries appeared in the *Washington Post* on December 21, 1997, and the *New York Times* on December 22, 1997. See also a warm appreciation by Ralph Nader in the *Washington Post* on January 24, 1998. This account is based on the author's conversations with Peterson over the course of twenty years.

CYNTHIA HARRISON

PETRY, Ann. October 12, 1908–April 28, 1997. Writer, children's author.

A descendant of four generations of African American New Englanders from Connecticut, writer Ann Petry was born Ann Lane in Old Saybrook, Connecticut, the youngest of three daughters of Bertha James and Peter Clark Lane. The oldest daughter died in infancy. Her family was one of the few black families in Old Saybrook. Petry's father owned the local drugstore, where he worked as a pharmacist. Her mother was a licensed chiropodist, as well as a beautician, a barber, a manufacturer, and an entrepreneur. After graduating from Old Saybrook High School in 1925, Ann received a degree in pharmacy from the Connecticut College of Pharmacy in 1931. She worked in her family's drugstores in Old Saybrook and Old Lyme for the next seven years. Drugstores provide the setting for a number of her short stories and at least one novel.

On February 22, 1938, she married George D. Petry, a New York mystery writer who originally hailed from New Orleans. Shortly thereafter, the bride moved to Harlem with her husband. That same year, she began to work as a salesperson and reporter for the *Amsterdam News,* one of the nation's most influential African American newspapers. Thus began her association with a network of black newspapers and magazines that would greatly influence her fiction and her career. In 1939 Petry's first short story, "Marie of the Cabin Club," published under the pseudonym Arnold Petri, appeared in the Baltimore *Afro-American.*

When her husband entered the armed services during World War II, Ann Petry became fully engaged in Harlem's vibrant cultural and political life. From 1941 to 1944 she worked as a reporter and women's editor for Adam Clayton Powell Jr.'s militant newspaper, *The People's Voice,* where she wrote a society column called "The Lighter Side" as well as feature-length stories. In Harlem, Petry helped organize Negro Women Inc., a community action and consumer group for working-class women. Petry also studied painting at the Harlem Art Center, took piano lessons, and acted in *On Striver's Row,* a production by the American Negro Theatre, then the center of radical Negro theater. She later recalled that her work in the theater allowed her to learn firsthand how dialogue in a play furthers action. She used this device in her Harlem fiction, which is characterized by quick pacing that seems to mirror the teeming streets of northern Manhattan.

For two years starting in 1943, Petry took Mabel Louise Robinson's workshop and course in creative writing at Columbia University. This experience would change the direction of her career. In 1943 her story "On Saturday the Siren Sounds at Noon" was published in the *Crisis,* the magazine of the National Association for the Advancement of Colored People. This is when publishing house Houghton Mifflin discovered her and encouraged her to write a novel. She was encouraged to apply for and eventually won Houghton Mifflin's prestigious literary fellowship in 1945. A year later, they published her first novel, *The Street,* the story of Lutie Johnson, an ambitious working-class single mother, a resident of Harlem, who finds herself defeated by racism, sexism, and lack of economic opportunity.

The Street became the first novel by an African American woman to sell over a million copies, and it continues to be Petry's best-known work. No other black woman before her had achieved this level of literary success. Along with MARGARET WALKER, Gwendolyn Brooks, and DOROTHY WEST, Ann Petry helped initiate an important new strain in American letters: a voice of a newly emergent black woman, as attentive to literary form as she was to presenting complex portrayals of usually poor and working-class African Americans, especially women and children.

Petry's *Country Place,* a melodramatic tale set in a small New England town and centered around the lives of a cast of white characters, was published in 1947. Tiring of her newfound literary celebrity, Petry and her husband returned to Old Saybrook in 1948, where she devoted her time to raising her daughter, Elisabeth Ann, who was born in 1949, and writing fiction for children as well as a number of short stories.

Ann Petry wrote only one more novel, *The Narrows* (1953), which was published in the shadow of Ralph Ellison's *Invisible Man* (1952) and James Baldwin's *Go Tell It on the Mountain* (1953). Though it has been forgotten by later generations of readers, many scholars consider it to be Petry's masterpiece. Set in the fictional New England town of Monmouth, Connecticut, *The Narrows* is the story of Link Williams, a Paul Robesonesque scholar-athlete and graduate of Dartmouth College, and his affair with a wealthy married white socialite, Camilla Sheffield. A complex meditation on black masculinity, intra-racial class conflict, and cold war politics, in many ways the novel anticipates Toni Morrison's *Song of Solomon* as well as a number of other works by black women writers who would emerge almost twenty years later.

In these years Petry continued to publish short stories, which might be roughly divided into three categories: integrationist race-relation stories set in New England; the Harlem implosion stories where racial frustration leads to violence turned within the black community; and at least one jazz story, "Solo on the Drums." They were later collected in *Miss Muriel and Other Stories* (1971). Petry also became an acclaimed writer of works for children and teenagers, including *The Drugstore Cat* (1949); *Harriet Tubman, Conductor on the Underground Railroad* (1966); *Tituba of Salem Village* (1964); and *Legends of the Saints* (1970). With HARRIET TUBMAN and Tituba, Petry sought to address the need for children's books about African American figures, especially heroic black women.

Ann Petry died on April 28, 1997, at the age of eighty-eight in Old Saybrook, Connecticut, after a brief illness. In the last decade of her life she was discovered by a new generation of scholars, students, journalists, and readers, received a number of honors and accolades, and found much of her fiction in print once again.

Bibliography: Ann Petry's papers are housed in Special Collections at Mugar Memorial Library, Boston University. Earlier letters, publications, reviews, and photographs are also in the James Weldon Johnson Memorial Collection of Negro Arts and Letters, Beinecke Rare Book and Manuscript Library, Yale University. In addition to the books mentioned in the text, Petry authored two autobiographical statements: her entry in *Contemporary Authors: Autobiography Series,* vol. 6 (1988); and "My Most Humiliating Jim Crow Experience," *Negro Digest* 4, no. 8 (June 1946), pp. 63–64. The most comprehensive reference work on Petry's life and writings is Hazel Arnett Ervin, ed., *Ann Petry: A Bio-Bibliography* (1993), which includes a thorough chronology of the author's life; a critical introduction to her work; a comprehensive listing of Petry's own fiction, poetry, nonfiction, and journalism; a bibliography of secondary reviews and critical essays about Petry; and six interviews conducted with Petry over the course of her career. The only full-length critical study of Petry's work is Hillary Holladay, *Ann Petry* (1996). Lindon Barrett's *Blackness and Value: Seeing Double* (1999) devotes two chapters to Petry's novels. Gladys Washington focuses on Petry's short fiction in "A World Made Cunningly: A Closer Look at Ann Petry's Short Fiction," *CLA Journal* 30, no. 1 (September 1986), pp. 14–29. An obituary appeared in the *New York Times* on April 30, 1997.

FARAH JASMINE GRIFFIN

PETRY, Lucile. *See* Leone, Lucile Petry.

PHILLIPS, Marjorie Acker. October 25, 1894–June 19, 1985. Artist, museum director.

Marjorie Acker was born in Bourbon, Indiana, while her parents, Alice Beal and Charles Ernest Acker, were visiting relatives. Marjorie's father, a chemical engineer, inventor, and manufacturer, had left a job with Western Electric in Chicago and the couple had stopped in Bourbon to visit his parents while en route to their new home in East

Orange, New Jersey. Marjorie was the second of their six children.

During Marjorie's early years, the family lived a well-to-do lifestyle in East Orange and Niagara Falls, New York, where her father built a chemical plant. After a financial setback in 1907 severe enough to lead the family to move to New York City to live with Alice's parents, Acker founded a nitrogen company in 1909 in Ossining-on-the-Hudson, New York, which became the family home.

Marjorie was exposed to art at an early age. Her uncles, Gifford and Reynolds Beal, were noted American painters, and during her youth Marjorie spent summers with the Beal family at their home, "Wilellyn," in Newburgh, New York, where her uncles had a studio on the top floor. While living in Niagara Falls, Marjorie often visited Buffalo, where she saw the 1901 Pan American Exposition and frequented Albright Art Gallery. Similarly, in New York City she visited numerous museums and galleries.

She began experimenting with art at age five, and in 1911, at age sixteen, she decided she wanted to become an artist, despite her father's initial disapproval. After attending Miss Fuller's School for Girls in Ossining in 1915, Marjorie and her older sister, Eleanor, began commuting to the Art Students League in New York, where they took classes with instructors Boardman Robinson and Kenneth Hayes Miller. With Robinson, Marjorie focused on the study of design and pattern; with Miller, she studied oil painting. She became well versed in the art movements of the day, visiting modern art galleries and KATHERINE DREIER's Société Anonyme. Marjorie thought of herself as a realist painter and emulated the techniques of European painters Vincent Van Gogh, Paul Cézanne, and Pierre Bonnard. The latter was one of her favorite artists.

Marjorie met collector and museum founder Duncan Phillips at an exhibition displaying Phillips's collection at the Century Club in New York in January 1921. Introduced through Gifford Beal, the couple immediately felt an intellectual and artistic bond. After a brief courtship, they married in Ossining on October 8, 1921, and settled in Washington, D.C., where Phillips had recently opened the Phillips Memorial Art Gallery. (Its name has changed over the years, to Phillips Memorial Gallery, then the Phillips Gallery, and today the Phillips Collection.) Heir to a Pittsburgh steel fortune, Phillips had gained notoriety in the art world as a collector of contemporary American and modern European art. In Marjorie, he had found a soul mate whose artistic creations he admired and whose advice he sought on the formation and development of his museum.

In Washington, Marjorie devoted her time to motherhood (she gave birth to a daughter, Mary Marjorie, in 1922, and a son, Laughlin, in 1924), her art, and the administration of the museum. Duncan Phillips appointed her associate director of the Phillips Memorial Gallery in 1925. In that role, she helped select paintings, traveled to meet with dealers and museum directors, and assisted in exhibition planning. Marjorie was credited with being one of the influences on Duncan Phillips that made him more receptive during the mid 1920s to avant-garde trends in modern art; her "artist's eye" helped him visualize and understand more challenging styles in art.

Having originated in 1921 as a single room in the Phillips family home in the Dupont Circle area of Washington, D.C., the museum expanded in size during the 1920s, until the entire residence was given over to the museum in October 1930. At that time, the Phillips family moved into their new home, "Dunmarlin" (designed by John Russell Pope), on the outskirts of Washington, D.C., on Foxhall Road. From the 1930s through the 1960s, Marjorie and Duncan Phillips worked together to create the identity of the Phillips Memorial Gallery as a museum of modern art and its sources. The museum's collections and exhibitions focused on late-nineteenth- and early-twentieth-century American and European art in addition to selected examples of old-master art that represented a stylistic affinity with modern art. The museum, with its art school (1930–45), also became an influential center for local artists of the Washington, D.C., Virginia, and Maryland areas.

Despite her involvement with the Phillips Memorial Gallery, Marjorie Phillips continued to paint prolifically, working in her studio every morning. Her works, painted with expressive brushstrokes and vivid color, are predominantly still lifes, landscapes, and various scenes from her daily life. An avid sketcher, Marjorie even took her art materials with her to the baseball games she attended with her sports-enthusiast husband. A resulting painting, *Night Baseball* (1951), one of her most famous works, depicts the Washington Senators playing against the New York Yankees, as seen from the Phillips' seats behind first base. Her husband became the most vocal supporter of her art, and he worked diligently to display her work at his museum and at New York art galleries. One-woman exhibitions of Marjorie Phillips's work were held at the Phillips Memorial Gallery in 1926, 1927, 1948, and 1955. She also had solo exhibitions at a variety of other venues.

After Duncan Phillips's death in 1966, Marjorie became director of the Phillips Collection. During her tenure, she continued to pursue the goals that she and Duncan had set for the museum. She organized several exhibitions of work by D.C.-area artists, including Sam Gilliam in 1967, as well as a major retrospective of the art of Paul Cézanne in 1971. During these years, she also wrote a biography of her husband.

She retired as director in 1972, passing the baton to her son, Laughlin, who remained as the museum's director until 1991. After her retirement, Phillips focused on her art and writing her autobiography. Marjorie Acker Phillips died at her home in Washington, D.C., of pulmonary failure on June 19, 1985, at the age of ninety.

Bibliography: Correspondence by and concerning Marjorie Phillips can be found in the Phillips Collection Papers, Archives of American Art, Smithsonian Institution, Washington, D.C., and in the Archives of the Phillips Collection, Washington, D.C. The most complete account of Marjorie Phillips's life can be found in her autobiography, *Marjorie Phillips and Her Paintings* (1985), edited by her niece Sylvia Partridge. Other key sources include Marjorie Phillips, *Duncan Phillips and His Collection* (1970, rev. ed. 1982); Erika D. Passantino et al., *The Eye of Duncan Phillips: A Collection in the Making* (1999); Grayson Lane, "Duncan Phillips and the Phillips Memorial Gallery: A Patron and Museum in Formation, 1918–1940" (PhD dissertation, Boston University, 2002); and Paul Cummings's interview with Marjorie Phillips, June 27, 1974, Archives of American Art, Smithsonian Institution. Exhibit catalogues of her work include Thomas C. Howe, *Marjorie Phillips* (California Palace of the Legion of Honor, 1959); Edward W. Root Art Center, Hamilton College, Clinton, New York, *Paintings by Marjorie Phillips* (Hamilton College, 1965); and Susan Drysdale, *Marjorie Phillips* (Marlborough Fine Art, Ltd., 1973). Obituaries appeared in the *Washington Post* on June 20, 1985 and the *New York Times* on June 21, 1985.

GRAYSON HARRIS LANE

PICCARD, Jeannette Ridlon. January 5, 1895–May 17, 1981. High-altitude balloonist, Episcopal priest.

Forty years after she became the first woman to ascend to the stratosphere, in 1974 the Rev. Dr. Jeannette Ridlon Piccard became the first woman ordained an Episcopal priest. Indomitable and fascinated by everything but housekeeping, she had pursued her "call" to the priesthood for seven decades, once explaining, "There are many ways to wait."

Jeannette Ridlon was born in Chicago and baptized in an Episcopal church two weeks later. She was the seventh of nine children of Emily Caroline Robinson and John Ridlon, an orthopedic surgeon, and grew up in privileged circumstances, although her twin sister's death at age three permanently scarred her own life. Devout even as a child, at eleven she told her horrified mother she wanted to become an Episcopal priest. Her mother promptly burst into tears and ran out of the room, the only time Jeannette ever saw her Victorian mother run.

Jeannette Ridlon was educated in Chicago, but young women of her class background were expected to make good marriages rather than pursue higher education. Overcoming Victorian notions of propriety, she convinced her father to support her going to Miss Shipley's School and then to Bryn Mawr College in Pennsylvania. Once there, president M. CAREY THOMAS assured her that the Episcopal priesthood would certainly be possible by the time she graduated, and encouraged Jeannette to take philosophy and psychology. She received her BA in 1918.

After deciding against joining a convent, she moved to the University of Chicago to study organic chemistry. There she met Swiss professor Jean Felix Piccard, eleven years her senior. She received her MS in chemistry from the University of Chicago in 1919 and married Piccard on August 19, 1919. They moved to Switzerland, returning to the States in 1926. During these years, they had three sons: John Auguste (1921), Paul Jules (1924), and Donald Louis (1926). Donald, who first ascended in a balloon with his mother at age seven, later popularized the modern sport of hot-air ballooning.

With high-altitude ballooning in its infancy, Jean Piccard and his twin brother Auguste cooperated closely in designing and constructing the experimental balloons. In 1931, Auguste ascended to the stratosphere. Three years later, in 1934, Jean and Jeannette Piccard followed, studying cosmic rays and breaking Auguste's altitude record. In preparation for their historic flight into the stratosphere, Jeannette Piccard became the first female licensed balloon pilot, explaining simply that her husband needed a balloon pilot, so she went out and learned how to be one. In the family-designed balloon with its pressurized gondola (now exhibited at the Museum of Science and Industry in Chicago), the Piccards ascended from Dearborn, Michigan, into the stratosphere to an altitude of 57,579 feet—more than ten miles high. Although they long dreamed and struggled to return to the risky and mysterious stratosphere, they never did. Such piloted balloon flights utilizing pressurized gondolas were precursors to later piloted space flights, and Jeannette Piccard held the female altitude record until Soviet cosmonaut Valentina Tereshkova's 1963 space flight.

In 1936 they moved to Minnesota, where Jean Piccard became a professor of aeronautical engineering at the University of Minnesota. The family lived in a stucco house along the high banks of the Mississippi River for forty-five years. In 1942, at forty-seven, Jeannette earned her PhD in education from the University of Minnesota with a dissertation entitled "The Housing of Married Students at the University of Minnesota, Fall Quarter, 1939–1940." After Jean Piccard's 1963 death, the

National Aeronautics and Space Administration (NASA) hired her as a publicity consultant to the Manned Spacecraft Center in Houston. A 1965 photograph shows her in a fur stole by a mockup of the Apollo Command Module; she consulted for NASA until 1970 and remained intensely interested in balloons her entire life.

Long an active Episcopalian and never forgetting her priestly call, she was ordained a deacon in 1971, only a year after women were fully accepted as deacons. From then on, she was the assistant at the predominantly African-American St. Philip's Episcopal Church in St. Paul, Minnesota. In 1972–73, in her late seventies, she enrolled in classes at General Theological Seminary in New York City; in 1977, Hobart and William Smith College awarded her the Doctor of Divinity degree.

On July 29, 1974, at Church of the Advocate, an African American church in Philadelphia, Piccard—at seventy-nine, well past retirement age—and ten other women were joyfully but controversially ordained Episcopal priests. In honor of the fact that she had waited the longest, Jeannette was ordained first. Recognizing that canon law was not fully followed but believing that the sacrament of ordination had occurred, supporters argued that the ordinations were "irregular but valid." Opponents strenuously disagreed. Protestant churches had had women ministers for many decades. But the Episcopal church, like the Catholic and Orthodox churches, believes in apostolic succession—that through the sacrament of their ordination every priest's spiritual lineage traces through a male line back to Jesus Christ—and in the centrality of the sacraments, which only priests (and bishops) are allowed to celebrate. Ordaining women priests then fundamentally shifted church power both symbolically and politically. Most significantly, and this is the source for much of the aversion toward women as priests, their ordination broke with the traditional image of God as a solely male deity.

The ordination of the Philadelphia Eleven and later the Washington Four, along with their subsequent public celebrations of the Eucharist—a strictly priestly function—such as Piccard and two of the other Philadelphia Eleven celebrated at Riverside Church in New York City on October 27, 1974, threw the Episcopal Church into an uproar. Piccard later remembered this as a very painful time. That crisis forced considerable debate and political strife before the church recognized women as priests at its 1976 national convention. In January 1977, the Rev. Drs. Jeannette Piccard and Alla Bozarth-Campbell, both from the Diocese of Minnesota, were publicly welcomed as Episcopal priests in good standing. Piccard became associate rector at St. Phillip's Church and in 1981 became an honorary canon of the Diocese of Minnesota St. Mark's Cathedral.

Jeannette Piccard died on May 17, 1981, in Minneapolis, and was buried at Lake Vermillion, Minnesota. Her years of witness and contention bore fruit. She had shown the same determination to become an Episcopal priest that she had shown finding a way to ascend to the stratosphere. "I'm not going to have it said there's anyplace I can't go. . . . If you can't do it, it's something you've got to do."

Bibliography: The Piccard Family Papers, which primarily cover the years from 1926 to 1983, are found at the Manuscript Division of the Library of Congress, Washington, D.C. The collection includes her 1916 college essay, "Should Women Be Admitted to the Priesthood of the Anglican Church?"; the Library of Congress also has a film of Jean and Jeannette Piccard's 1934 stratosphere flight and photographs. For a detailed but very critical analysis of the Piccards' flights, see David H. DeVorkin, *Race to the Stratosphere: Manned Scientific Ballooning in America* (1989). Heather Huyck, "To Celebrate a Whole Priesthood: The History of Women's Ordination in the Episcopal Church" (PhD dissertation, University of Minnesota, 1981), provides an overview as well as significant material on Piccard. See also Mary Donovan, *Women Priests in the Episcopal Church* (1988); and Catherine M. Prelinger, ed., *Episcopal Women: Gender, Spirituality and Commitment in an American Mainline Denomination* (1992). For further ecclesiastical details, see the *Episcopal Clerical Directory* (1979 edition), which listed her priestly ordination as January 1977, when her orders were "regularized," rather than July 1974, when she was "irregularly ordained." This essay draws on additional information provided by her sons, John Piccard and Donald Piccard, as well as the author's interviews with Piccard between 1974 and 1981, the source of the opening quotation. The final quote is from a 1979 videotaped interview in the family's possession. Obituaries appeared in the *New York Times* and the *Washington Post*, both on May 19, 1981.

HEATHER A. HUYCK

PICKFORD, Mary. April 8, 1892–May 29, 1979. Actress.

Mary Pickford was the most famous and successful female film star of the silent era. Her nickname, America's Sweetheart, reflects the enormous affection in which she was held. Her box office strength has never been equaled by any other woman: during her more than twenty years of stardom, *Photoplay* magazine ranked her "number one" fifteen times.

Pickford was born Gladys Smith in Toronto, the oldest of three children of Charlotte Hennessey and John Charles Smith. Her father, a poor provider who held jobs as a printer and occasionally as a bartender, died when she was a child, leaving her family penniless. Desperate for money, Charlotte took a friend's suggestion to make ends meet by putting her children on the stage. Although Gladys was only five years old, she made her first appearance at the Toronto Princess Theatre in September 1898 and immediately felt at home. Soon she was touring and mastering the acting craft, although at the expense of her formal schooling, which was extremely limited. As a teenager, she went to work on Broadway for the great theatrical impresario David Belasco, who changed her name to Mary Pickford. In the spring of 1909, when the family faced the financial pinch of the summer season, when theaters, not yet air-conditioned, would be closed, Charlotte sent her daughter to find temporary work in the new medium of motion pictures. Pickford took a trolley car to Biograph Studios in New York City, a bustling film production center, where she was told that actresses were paid five dollars a day, a large sum at the time. Claiming she was a "Belasco actress," she demanded "at least ten" and a "guarantee of no less than twenty-five per week." Suitably impressed, the great D. W. Griffith hired her, and on April 20, 1909, Mary Pickford debuted in *Her First Biscuits.*

Pickford rose rapidly to fame in the movies. Shrewdly grasping the security that film stardom could bring her family, she embarked on a busy career. She made forty-two films in 1909 and another thirty-two in 1910, the year in which she moved to Hollywood, the emerging capital of American moviemaking. By 1912, she was a major motion picture star. Pickford had the intelligence to adapt her acting style, first learned in theater, to the intimacy of the motion picture camera. Teaching herself how to hold an audience's eye, and how to use her entire body to suggest specific meanings, she learned to "live" in front of a camera. As a result, she became a spontaneous, believable, and radiant movie presence. Contrary to the stereotype of her as a sentimental, cloying figure who always masqueraded as a child, Pickford usually played sassy young girls, not children, and her characters were optimistic and self-confident, with an amazing ability to survive. Their feisty, frequently naughty antics made people laugh.

Audiences loved Pickford's comic gifts. Plots were sometimes paused so she could perform her almost Chaplinesque routines. In *Through the Back Door* (1921) she straps wet brushes onto her feet and "skates" across a dirty kitchen to clean it. In *Pollyanna* (1920), one of her biggest hits, she perfectly executes a comedy routine in which her muddy-footed young heroine tries to walk across expensive carpets without leaving tracks.

Although she was essentially a comedian, she also became a capable dramatic actress, and her best films showcase both abilities. A definitive example is her hugely successful 1918 movie *Stella Maris,* in which she plays two unrelated people: the title character, a young, wealthy, disabled woman, and Unity Blake, a deformed servant girl. As Stella, she is pretty, sunny, and well groomed. As Unity, she is dull-skinned, sallow, and downright ugly. It is not just that they don't look like the same person: Pickford generates a totally separate inner life for each girl, and creates two individuals who are emotionally as well as physically different. In *Little Lord Fauntleroy* (1921), she plays both a little boy and his beautiful mother. In the movie's excellent double exposures, in which both the child and mother appear together, it is difficult to believe that a single, mature actress is performing both roles.

Pickford's many movies included two versions of *Tess of the Storm Country* (1914 and 1922); *Poor Little Rich Girl, The Little Princess,* and *Rebecca of Sunnybrook Farm* (all in 1917); *Amarilly of Clothesline Alley* (1918); *Suds* (1920); *Sparrows* (1926); and many others. Her last silent film was *My Best Girl* in 1927, which paired her with Charles "Buddy" Rogers, who would become her last husband. Pickford made a successful sound debut in 1929 in *Coquette,* for which she won the Oscar for Best Actress, but her career was virtually over. Always a shrewd businesswoman, she opted to step away from her career. She was no longer young, and the arrival of sound had irrevocably changed filmmaking. Pickford understood instinctively that her type of films was going out of style. She was forty-one years old in 1933 when her final movie, *Secrets,* was released. She then retired to private life at her Hollywood mansion, Pickfair, remaining active by doing charity work and producing films.

Pickford married three times, always to actors: Owen Moore in 1911 (divorced in 1920), Douglas Fairbanks Sr. in 1920 (divorced in 1933), and Rogers in 1937. Her marriage to Fairbanks, who was her male counterpart in fame, was an unprecedented pairing of celebrity power for the times. They were the top male and female stars of the day, and as a romantic couple they inspired an almost lunatic fan adulation. On their four-week honeymoon in Europe they were mobbed everywhere they went. The Pickford-Fairbanks marriage, unquestionably a love match, ended in the 1930s after both had passed their prime as stars. No one knows for certain what went wrong between them, as they maintained a silent dignity on the subject. Rumors of Fairbanks's infidelity, however, are assumed to have been a major factor. He and Pickford had no children, but Pickford and Buddy Rogers adopted two children, Ronald Charles and Roxanne, in the early 1940s.

Throughout her career, Pickford was famous for her hard work and dedication to quality. Her enormous stardom, particularly when paired with her legendary marriage to Fairbanks, guarantees her a place in movie history, but her managing of her own career marks her as exceptional. She involved herself in all aspects of the business, learning everything about the making of movies. A tough negotiator who had supported her family from childhood onward, she made a series of smart moves that increased her earning power and, more important, ensured her control over her own career. In 1915, she became the first actress to have her own production company, Pickford Film Corporation, which meant that she could choose her own directors and supporting casts. She had approval over advertising, a vote on the film's final cut, and the right to question any role she did not like. In addition to her famously large salaries, she negotiated a guarantee of 50 percent of the profits and final ownership of her films by having the copyright revert to her after a five-to-six-year period of distribution. Early in 1919, when the company releasing her movies was rumored to be merging with another powerful corporation, Pickford understood at once that she might lose her hard-won controls. Acting swiftly, she formed a business alliance with Fairbanks, D. W. Griffith, William S. Hart, and Charles Chaplin to create their own company, United Artists. This not only increased her profits but maintained her full right to control her career in a way that few actresses have ever pursued, much less achieved.

Pickford spent the final years of her life out of the spotlight, somewhat reclusive and rumored to be an alcoholic. Her last official appearance was in March 1976, when she was filmed at home receiving her honorary 1975 Oscar. She died on May 29, 1979, with her husband of forty-two years, Buddy Rogers, at her side. Writing about her in 1955, her contemporary Cecil B. DeMille (who had directed her in two 1917 movies, *The Little American* and *Romance of the Redwoods*) made a definitive statement about her life and career: "There have been hundreds of stars. There have been scores of fine actresses in motion pictures. There has been only one Mary Pickford."

Bibliography: Mary Pickford's autobiography, *Sunshine and Shadow* (1955), lacks detachment but is worthwhile for its revelations about her basic philosophies of work and life. There are two major biographies: Scott Eyman, *Mary Pickford: America's Sweetheart* (1990), and Eileen Whitfield, *Pickford: The Woman Who Made Hollywood* (1997). Both have interesting points of view on Pickford's career, and both contain comprehensive bibliographies and filmographies. See also Cari Beauchamp, *Without Lying Down: Frances Marion and the Powerful Women of Early Hollywood* (1997), for its insights into Pickford's personality, her overall career, and her working relationship with another strong and successful career woman. Kevin Brownlow's *Mary Pickford Rediscovered: Rare Pictures of a Hollywood Legend* (1999) is the best book on Pickford's screen persona. Jeanine Basinger recreates the early years of Hollywood in *Silent Stars* (1999), which contains chapters on Pickford and Douglas Fairbanks; the quotations from DeMille and on being a Belasco actress are from pages 15 and 20, respectively. Archival material is located at the Library of Congress (films and papers); UCLA Film & Television Archive (films); the George Eastman House in Rochester, New York (films); Bison Archives, Hollywood, California (photos); the Mary Pickford Foundation in Los Angeles (films, photos, papers, and video copies of films); the Margaret Herrick Library at the Motion Picture Academy of Arts and Sciences (over 50,000 photos, Pickford's personal scrapbooks, and papers); and the Library of Moving Images in Hollywood (Pickford's home movies, private photographs, and films). An obituary appeared in the *New York Times* on May 30, 1979.

JEANINE BASINGER

PICON, Molly. February 28, 1898–April 6, 1992. Actress.

Molly Picon was an engaging performer for more than eighty years. She won an international following, first with her starring roles in Yiddish theater and film and later in English on stage, film, radio, and television. Born Margaret Pyekoon, she was the first child of Jewish immigrants who settled on New York's Lower East Side. Her mother, Clara Ostrovsky (later Ostrow), and her large family had fled pogroms that threatened their small village near Kiev, and arrived in Philadelphia in 1890. Louis (or Lewis) Pyekoon (later Picon) abandoned a wife and three children in Poland when he left for the United States, where he met and married Clara. It was only after the birth of Molly's younger sister and only sibling, Helen, that Clara discovered her husband's bigamy. Although she never divorced him, he soon drifted out of their lives.

Clara returned to Philadelphia with her young daughters and began working as a seamstress. She made costumes for the actresses from the nearby Columbia Theatre, which housed a Yiddish repertory company headed by Michael Thomashefsky and his wife, Fanny. Molly began her stage career at age five when, at Fanny's urging, Clara entered her in an amateur night contest at a local burlesque house. Molly's victory as "Baby Margaret" was the first of many amateur-night successes. She performed as a child actor with Thomashefsky's troupe, for which her mother served as wardrobe mistress, first at the Columbia and then at the Arch Street Theater. After struggling to balance the demands of work and school, Picon opted for performing and left William Penn High School in 1915 after her sophomore year. When her appearances in local variety shows did not prove sufficiently lucrative, she auditioned for a vaudeville promoter, who cast her as "Winter" in "The Four Seasons," an English-language vaudeville act. Traveling with trained seals, a group of acrobats who taught her tumbling, and a drunken rooster act, among others, Picon crisscrossed the country from San Francisco to Boston, where the tour abruptly ended. It was winter 1918–19 and the influenza pandemic, which had already killed thousands in Boston, had closed the theaters.

The Grand Opera House, which housed a Yiddish theater troupe managed by Jacob "Yonkel" Kalich, an émigré and former rabbinical student from Poland, remained open. Kalich had seen Picon perform in Philadelphia and offered her a contract with his company, which she promptly accepted. When he proposed marriage to her a few months later, they celebrated their engagement on the Grand Opera House's stage. They married in Philadelphia on June 29, 1919, with Picon in a gown her mother had fashioned from a theater curtain. Their personal and professional partnership would last for fifty-six years.

Kalich's determination to make his wife a star matched her own career aspirations. The era wanted large, buxom female performers, however, and the diminutive Picon stood only four feet eleven inches and weighed only ninety-five pounds. Convinced that her size could work to her advantage, Kalich created a series of roles that would capitalize on her energy, insouciance, vivaciousness, and charm, while allowing her to play a wide range of characters. From motherless adolescent waifs to pert ingénues with mischievous eyes, to glamorous—even sexy—women, the spirited Picon delighted audiences with her animated songs and dances, as well as her somersaults, splits, and cartwheels. Beginning with the eponymous "Yankele" (Little Yankel), which she first played in Boston and claimed to have performed more than three thousand times in her career, transgressive behavior became her signature.

In her second season in Boston, Picon performed until the seventh month of her first, and only, pregnancy. Her daughter was stillborn on August 13, 1920, and Picon's grief was compounded by the knowledge that she would be unable to bear more children. (She and Kalich eventually cared for four foster children, who did not live with them but whom they supported financially over the years.) With characteristic resilience, she and Kalich left for Europe, where they would spend the next two years. Back in New York, they collaborated with composer Joseph Rumshinsky to create a successful series of Yiddish stage musicals in the 1920s, such as *Mamele, Raizele, Oy Is Dus a Meydl* (Oh, What a Girl), and *Mazel Bruch* (Good Luck). At New York's Second Avenue Theatre, whose management they had assumed, and on tour throughout the country, they played to crowded houses. "Our Molly" was then the highest-paid Yiddish stage performer in the world.

In 1929 Picon made her Broadway debut in vaudeville in English at the Palace, still the nation's most prestigious vaudeville house. With the stock market crash later that year, Picon and Kalich lost their savings and their theater. Yet they managed to lease another space, which they renamed the Molly Picon Theatre and opened in September 1930. They continued to create new works for the Yiddish theater and performed them on tour in the United States and Europe. In Poland, Picon starred in two highly acclaimed Yiddish musical films for director Joseph Green: *Yidl mitn Fidl* (Yiddle with His Fiddle) in 1936, which became the first truly international Yiddish hit, and *Mamele* (Little Mother) in 1938.

The indomitable Picon spent the 1940s working tirelessly in a variety of venues, including radio, on which she had first appeared in 1936. She and Kalich created a radio show sponsored by Maxwell House Coffee that ran for almost two decades. During World War II, she and Kalich gave benefit concerts to help the war effort and toured army camps entertaining American troops. At war's end, they returned to Europe to bring some solace to survivors of the Holocaust and were among the first American entertainers to visit displaced persons camps. There were more wartime performances for American troops in Korea and Japan in the 1950s, as well as frequent trips to Israel, for which they had became dedicated fund-raisers.

In addition to nightclub appearances and concert tours, Picon also tried television (an eight-week program for Rokeach Soap in 1949) but preferred performing before live audiences. Despite being told that she was "too Jewish" to play to mainstream audiences, she still sought recognition on the non-Yiddish stage. In 1959 she appeared in the London production of *A Majority of One* as Mrs. Jacoby, a role she had lost on Broadway to GERTRUDE BERG. When her performance in England proved a critical and popular success, Picon began receiving offers for American stage productions.

In 1961, she created the role of spirited widow Clara Weiss in the Broadway musical *Milk and Honey*. Still doing her signature somersaults and flips, she captivated audiences with her performance, was nominated for (but did not win) a Tony Award, and was thrilled to finally be a legitimate Broadway star. She also took on film roles, appearing in *Come Blow Your Horn* (1963), for which she received an Oscar nomination, as Yente the Matchmaker in *Fiddler on the Roof* (1971), and in *For Pete's Sake* (1974), to mostly positive reviews. She continued to do the occasional television show but was increasingly focused on her beloved husband, who died in 1975. Within four months after his death, Picon was working again. In 1979 she appeared in a one-woman show, *Hello Molly,* in which she reflected on her many years in the Yiddish theater and delighted audiences with her anecdotes. The next year she published her autobiography, *Molly!*

Elected to the Broadway Hall of Fame in 1981, Picon lived in Manhattan with her widowed sister, Helen, with whom she spoke only Yiddish, and continued to perform well into her eighties. Proud of her Jewish heritage, devoted to Jewish causes, and dedicated to the audiences she loved, the irrepressible Picon finally succumbed to Alzheimer's disease, dying in Lancaster, Pennsylvania, on April 6, 1992, at the age of ninety-four.

Bibliography: Molly Picon's papers have been deposited at the American Jewish Historical Society at the Center for Jewish History in New York. The extensive collection consists largely of material relating to Picon's career as a performer, especially in the Yiddish theater. It includes manuscripts of Yiddish and non-Yiddish plays, numerous radio and television scripts, programs and announcements for Picon's performances, and personal memorabilia such as correspondence, photographs, and scrapbooks. In addition, there is a great deal of musical material such as songbooks, handwritten lyrics, and sheet music, much of it in Yiddish. Related materials are also available at the YIVO Institute for Jewish Research Archives and Library in New York City. There are films and film clips at the National Center for Jewish Film at Brandeis University, and limited holdings at the National Yiddish Book Center in Amherst, Massachusetts. Published sources on Picon's life and career include Molly Picon, with Jean Bergantini Grillo, *Molly! An Autobiography* (1980); Picon, as told to Eth Clifford Rosenberg, *So Laugh a Little* (1962); and a children's book by Lila Perl, *Molly Picon, a Gift of Laughter* (1990). An obituary appeared in the *New York Times* on April 7, 1992.

BARBARA WALLACE GROSSMAN

PICTOU, Anna Mae. *See* Aquash, Anna Mae.

PILPEL, Harriet Fleischl. December 2, 1911–April 23, 1991. Lawyer, women's reproductive rights advocate, civil libertarian.

Harriet Fleischl was born in New York City, the eldest of three daughters of Ethel Loewy and Julius Fleischl. Both her parents were born in the United States. Her paternal grandfather had emigrated from Prussia at age fifteen and later founded Emil Fleischl & Sons, a wholesale dairy that sold eggs and dairy products to restaurants, hotels, and retail stores. Harriet's father worked there; her mother, who graduated from normal school, worked for a time as a teacher.

While still in Evander Childs High School, Harriet determined the two values central to her identity: the power to decide for herself whether and when to have children, and the freedom to speak her mind. She was on the high school debate team and throughout her life was an effective public speaker. When she graduated in 1928, her yearbook picture was captioned "A Budding Portia." She enrolled at Vassar College, where she received a bachelor's degree in 1932. She continued her studies at Columbia University, first taking a master's degree in international relations and public law in 1933, followed by a law degree in 1936. At Columbia, she was selected as articles editor for the prestigious Columbia Law Review and graduated near the top of her class.

In 1933, she married Robert Pilpel, an executive for nonprofit organizations, who strongly supported his wife's career throughout their more than fifty years of marriage. During World War II, he spent part of his time at the Joint Distribution Committee offices in New York, and part in Europe, helping to smuggle Jews out. The couple had two children: Judith (1939) and Robert (1943).

As a lawyer, Harriet Pilpel was brilliant, eclectic, and determined not to be held back by discrimination against women in the field of law. In 1936 she joined the law firm of Greenbaum, Wolff and Ernst, which specialized in First Amendment issues; she became a partner in the mid 1940s. Firm leader Morris Ernst, a founder of the American Civil Liberties Union and an active civil libertarian, was equally forward-thinking when it came to hiring and promoting women. When the firm disbanded, she became counsel to Weil, Gotschal and Manges in 1982. Her practice included family law and copyright, as well as First Amendment and reproductive freedom issues.

For five decades, Pilpel was a preeminent strategist, advocate, and organizer for reproductive freedom and free speech. She was general counsel to the Planned Parenthood Federation of America (PPFA) and active on the boards of many organizations, including the Alan Guttmacher Institute and the National Abortion Rights Action League. Beginning in 1962, she held leadership positions in the American Civil Liberties Union. She also was a member of the President's Commission on the Status of Women in the Kennedy administration, as well as a member of the task force on the status of women for Lyndon Johnson's Citizens Advisory Commission.

Between 1937 and 1991, Pilpel participated in twenty-seven cases before the U.S. Supreme Court. Throughout her career, she litigated and wrote perceptively on matters of free expression, family law, and copyright. In 1961, the Supreme Court rejected her initial effort to secure married people's constitutional right to use contraception. Justice John M. Harlan dissented, however, relying on a law review analysis that Pilpel had coauthored. Four years later, in *Griswold v. Connecticut* (1965), the Court held that the Constitution protects the right of married couples to use contraceptives. Over the next decade, Pilpel played a leading role in crafting the claims to expand rights of reproductive choice. In 1972, in *Eisenstadt v. Baird,* she helped persuade the Court to extend the right to contraceptive choice to single people. In 1973, Pilpel represented PPFA in *Roe v. Wade* and *Doe v. Bolton,* the landmark cases that established a woman's right to abortion. She later played a pivotal role in a series of cases in the 1970s in which the Court struck down regulatory measures that had the practical effect of burdening access to abortion.

Pilpel made particularly powerful contributions to establishing minors' rights to contraception and abortion. She led litigation efforts, beginning with *Carey v. Population Services International* in 1977, which recognized a minor's right to obtain contraceptives without parental consent. She wrote prolifically on this subject, explaining complex issues to family planning providers, legislators, parents, and teenagers. Her scholarly work was frequently cited by the Supreme Court and in legislative debate, and she often presented her views in public forums such as William F. Buckley Jr.'s television show, *Firing Line*.

In the years following *Roe v. Wade,* Pilpel was a wise mentor to the lawyers who litigated whether payment for abortions for poor women could be excluded from the otherwise comprehensive Medicaid program. Even though the Supreme Court rejected the constitutional challenge to the Medicaid exclusion in 1981, under Pilpel's leadership these lawyers persevered politically and legally to ensure that in the states where most poor women in the United States reside, the state still pays for abortions. Her reproductive freedom work continues through the Harriet Pilpel–Planned Parenthood Fellowship in the Arthur Garfield Hays Civil Liberties Program at New York University Law School.

Pilpel understood that the development of constitutional principles is a multifaceted and political process. She was a brilliant legal tactician with a deep knowledge of the nuance of doctrine, but she was also acutely attuned to political opinion, organizational politics, the press, religious feeling, and the broad cultural forces that shape constitutional principles. Her imposing manner could be intimidating when it suited her purposes, but that distance was quickly dissipated by her wit, her relish for shared gossip, and her eagerness to engage the hardest questions. Most of all, she had an enormous capacity for friendship. Widowed in 1987, she married Irving Schwartz, a hospital administrator, in 1989. She died at her New York City home in 1991 of a heart attack at the age of seventy-nine, just days after she had received an award from the New York Civil Liberties Foundation.

Bibliography: A small collection of Harriet Pilpel's papers is found at the Schlesinger Library, Radcliffe Institute for Advanced Study, Harvard University, which also holds an oral history interview done by Eleanor Jackson Piel between 1972 and 1975. Pilpel published books and articles on family law, copyright law, minors' rights to contraception and abortion, birth control, and general constitutional issues related to free expression and reproductive freedom. See especially Harriet Pilpel, *Your Marriage and the Law* (1952), written with Theodora Zavin, a pioneering effort when the practice of matrimonial law was on the brink of widespread change; *A Copyright Guide* (1960), written with Morton David Goldberg; and Abraham Stone and Mrs. *[sic]* Harriet F. Pilpel, "The Social and Legal Status of Contraception," *North Carolina Law Review* 22 (1944), pp. 212–25, which was cited by the Supreme Court in recognizing the constitutional right to contraception. Pilpel was one of twelve lawyers profiled in Elinor Porter Swiger, *Women Lawyers at Work* (1978). An obituary appeared in the *New York Times* on April 24, 1991. See also Sylvia Law, "A Tribute: Harriet Fleischl Pilpel," *Family Planning Perspectives* 23, no. 4 (July–August 1991), pp. 182–83.

SYLVIA A. LAW

POLIER, Justine Wise. April 12, 1903–July 31, 1987. Judge, juvenile justice and child welfare authority.

Justine Wise was born into a family strongly committed to social justice. Her first three years were spent in Portland, Oregon, where her father, Stephen S. Wise, was the rabbi of Temple Beth-El. Her mother, Louise Waterman, raised in New York City's wealthy German Jewish community, was a painter and child welfare advocate whose family had opposed her marriage on the grounds that Wise came from a Hungarian family of modest means, was a rabbi, and was a Zionist. Their opposition reflected the ethnic, class, and political divisions among American Jews at the turn of the century.

In 1906, Justine's family moved to New York City, where her father established the Free Synagogue (renamed the Stephen Wise Free Synagogue after his death). She and her older brother James were raised in a vibrant, intellectual home in which many of the nation's politicians and religious leaders gathered. She often recounted a defining childhood memory of her parents inviting a group of prominent New Yorkers to meet H. O. Tanner, a black painter who had returned from self-exile in Paris. When a white guest protested that he would not sit down for dinner with a black man, Rabbi Wise, who signed the 1909 call to establish the National Association for the Advancement of Colored People (NAACP), showed him the door. In 1918, Rabbi Wise founded the American Jewish Congress, which was committed to defending Jewish rights.

Justine Wise's concerns for economic and racial justice deepened during college. A graduate of Horace Mann High School, she studied social and economic problems at Bryn Mawr for two years before transferring in 1922 to Radcliffe, where she lived and worked at the Elizabeth Peabody Settlement. She spent her last year of college at Barnard, where she was involved in a research study on women and industrial injuries.

Upon finishing college, Justine went to work in a textile mill in Passaic, New Jersey, to pursue her interests in the rights of workers. Though ultimately blacklisted, she described the experience as a very important year in her life. Encouraged by her father, she began Yale Law School in 1925, intending to acquire skills in constitutional, labor, and administrative law. When the textile strike broke out in Passaic in 1926, she commuted between Yale and Passaic to support the strike effort.

At the end of her second year, Justine Wise married Leon Arthur Tulin, one of her law professors. Her first son, Stephen, was born in 1928, a month before the bar examination. The family later moved to New York City, where Arthur had a post at Columbia University and Justine worked for the New York State Labor Department as the first woman referee in the Workmen's Compensation Division.

After her husband's untimely death from leukemia in 1932, she became involved with the International Juridical Association (IJA). At the IJA she worked with another young lawyer, Shad Polier, whom she married in 1936. They raised two more children, Trudy and Jonathon. The couple continued to work together and hold leadership positions in a range of civic organizations, including the American Jewish Congress, until his death in 1976.

When Fiorello LaGuardia became mayor of New York City in 1934, he asked Justine Polier to direct the Workmen's Compensation Division of the Corporation Counsel's Office. As a referee she had seen the ways in which workers' rights were abused and so used her new position to implement reforms, including a program for city workers to choose their own doctors and get impartial medical testimony. In 1935 LaGuardia appointed Polier a judge in the Domestic Relations Court (the predecessor to Family Court), the first woman to hold a judicial office above magistrate in the state of New York. She served as a Domestic Relations Court judge for thirty-eight years, except for a leave of absence in 1941–42 to serve as special counsel at the Office of Civil Defense under ELEANOR ROOSEVELT.

Early in her tenure as a Domestic Relations Court judge, Polier identified racial and class discrimination in the legal and social service system. She set out to challenge discriminatory practices in the court and expand social services for the city's poor children. She spearheaded a preventative and rehabilitative approach to juvenile delinquency and introduced psychiatry into the courts, schools, and social service institutions. Along with Eleanor Roosevelt, she became a leading supporter of the Wiltwyck School for Boys, the first nonsectarian agency in the East for neglected and delinquent African American boys between the ages of eight and twelve.

Polier challenged institutional racism in two landmark cases: In *In the Matter of Skipwith and Rector* (1958), hailed as the first northern decision against de facto segregation, she ruled in favor of African American parents conducting a school boycott and charged the New York City Board of Education with offering Harlem junior high school children inferior educational opportunities by reason of racial discrimination. Frustrated after finding no suitable agency willing to place a young black Protestant girl, Polier helped initiate *Wilder v. Sugarman* (1974), a class action suit against the discriminatory practices of city, state, and voluntary adoption agencies.

Active in communal affairs throughout her life, Polier served on the boards of various Jewish, legal, juvenile rights, and philanthropic organizations, including the American Jewish Congress, the Free Synagogue, the Citizens' Committee for Children, and Louise Wise Services, an adoption and child-care agency founded by her mother in 1916. When she was attacked by a congressional committee during the McCarthy era because of her association with the Field Foundation and its supposed links to organizations listed as subversive by the attorney general, Polier asserted her credentials as a liberal anti-communist who had led the drive to expel Communist-dominated groups from the American Jewish Congress in the early 1950s.

Upon retiring from the bench in 1973, Polier took up the fight for children's rights across the country and became the director of the juvenile justice division of the Children's Defense Fund. Throughout her life, Polier wrote numerous articles, books, reports, and speeches in the field of juvenile justice. She also wrote and spoke on issues related to labor, race relations, Israel, and Jewish identity. Referred to by friends as a gentle warrior, Justine Polier lived and practiced her convictions throughout a life that reflected and affected local, national, and international events of the twentieth century. She died in New York City in 1987 at the age of eighty-four.

Bibliography: The Justine Wise Polier Papers at the Schlesinger Library, Radcliffe Institute for Advanced Study, Harvard University, include almost fifty boxes of personal and professional papers that span her lifetime and include oral histories, newspaper clippings, and photographs. In addition, the American Jewish Historical Society (in New York City and Waltham, Massachusetts) has a small collection that includes correspondence with Eleanor Roosevelt and materials pertaining to the World War II Jewish refugee problem. Oral histories of Polier are available in the American Jewish Committee Oral History Collection, Dorot Jewish Division of the New York Public Library; Columbia University Oral History Research Office; and the New York Public Library. See also "Woman Lawyer in the Depression: An Oral History," *Guild Practitioner* 39, no. 4 (Fall 1982), pp. 121–28. In addition to numerous articles, reports, and legal decisions, Polier wrote three books: *Everyone's Children, Nobody's Child: A Judge Looks at the Underprivileged Children in the United States* (1941); *The Rule of Law and the Role of Psychiatry* (1968); and *Juvenile Justice in Double Jeopardy: The Distanced Community and Vengeful Retribution* (1989). Joyce

Antler includes a portrait of Polier in *The Journey Home: Jewish Women and the American Century* (1997) and has an essay entitled "Justine Wise Polier and the Prophetic Tradition" in Pamela S. Nadell and Jonathan D. Sarna, eds., *Women and American Judaism: Historical Perspectives* (2001). Polier's obituary appeared in the *New York Times* on August 2, 1987.

ADINA BACK

PONSELLE, Rosa. January 22, 1897–May 25, 1981. Operatic soprano, arts administrator.

Dramatic soprano Rosa Ponselle was a singer of prodigious natural talent and strong work ethic whose relatively brief but highly acclaimed career made her one of America's most prominent and enduring vocal greats. Most of that career centered in New York City at the famed Metropolitan Opera. In addition to her innate musicality and vocal range, Ponselle was an all-American diva notable for the unconventional path she took to the Met: she born in the United States and did not travel to Europe to train, despite her era's belief that European training was a necessity for American singers.

She was born Rosa Ponzillo in Meriden, Connecticut, the youngest of three children of Maddalena Conte and Bernardino Ponzillo, Italian immigrants from southern Italy. Her father owned several small businesses, including a saloon, a bakery, a coal business, and a small farm. All the Ponzillo children worked from a relatively young age, and Ponselle never finished high school. Her earliest musical training came in the form of piano and singing lessons from Anna Ryan, the music director and organist at the Ponzillos' parish church, who also taught Rosa's older sister, Carmela, and brother, Tony. Rosa's primary stage experience prior to her Met debut was the vaudeville act she had with her sister.

Though Carmela's move to New York City to pursue a theatrical career had been vigorously opposed by their father, Rosa encountered less resistance when she joined her sister in the big city, possibly because financial difficulties plagued the family at the time. Carmela had already been on the vaudeville circuit for a while when she got the idea in 1915 to create a sister act with the young Rosa. Together they successfully traveled the popular Keith circuit.

Through their new singing teacher, William Thorner, the Ponzillo sisters met the famous tenor Enrico Caruso, who pronounced that one day Rosa would sing with him. By his arrangement she auditioned with the Metropolitan Opera, and several months later, on November 15, 1918, the twenty-one-year-old singer who had never sung in an opera made her Metropolitan Opera debut—opposite Enrico Caruso. Although many American artists were encouraged to change their names to more European-sounding monikers, the general manager of the Met, Giulio Gatti-Casazza, encouraged Rosa to adopt the more generically Continental "Ponselle" over "Ponzillo."

Rosa Ponselle came to the Met at the right time with the right voice. With World War I still raging, the Met had limited options for importing new talent. Here, however, was a homegrown product whose voice perfectly fit the revival Gatti-Casazza was most hoping to showcase: Verdi's masterpiece, *La forza del destino,* which had not been heard in New York City for almost four decades. Though Ponselle's overwhelming attack of nerves nearly kept her from getting out on stage—her anxiety about her lack of formal training dogged her entire career—she quickly calmed down and an overnight sensation was born.

Indeed, Ponselle's debut had all the classic American Cinderella elements, and embodied the immigrant dream as well: a girl from a working-class family, with strong Catholic roots, and no previous operatic experience or knowledge, thrust into the spotlight alongside one of the most famous and talented tenors in the world on an international stage—and she triumphed. She would remain a mainstay of the Met's roster for almost twenty years, singing difficult and sometimes rare repertory, such as *Don Carlos, La Gioconda, La vestale, Norma,* and *La traviata.* She had to painstakingly learn each complex role as it came, preparing with her coach, Romano Romani. She would also find success on the radio (including live Saturday broadcasts from the Met on NBC starting in 1931) and in concert work, though she rarely performed outside of the United States for fear of hostile audiences.

Rosa Ponselle would finally set foot on European soil in the summer of 1924, when she traveled to her parents' homeland to study with famed conductor Tullio Serafin. A kind and nurturing man, Serafin proved the perfect mentor for the skittish soprano. Under his tutelage, Ponselle began to grow as a dramatic singing actress, which would be a hallmark of her career.

In 1935 Ponselle failed to win over the critics with her interpretation of the role of Carmen, and in 1937 she split with the company that had been her home, when the Met's management refused her request to mount a production of Cilea's *Adriana Lecouvreur.* The Met felt that it would not sell well even in the best of times, let alone in the Depression, despite Ponselle's name value. Stubborn to the end, Ponselle removed herself from the roster and turned her attention to her married life; she had wed Carle A. Jackson, the son of Baltimore's mayor, in 1936.

The couple eventually settled in Green Spring Valley, just outside Baltimore, so that Jackson could rejoin the family insurance business. Rosa busied herself with decorating the house that she affectionately dubbed Villa Pace, after her famous aria "Pace, pace" from *Forza.* The childless marriage, however, had been shaky from the start and further deteriorated when Jackson enlisted in the navy during World War II. Ponselle filed for divorce in 1950 but stayed in her newly adopted city. At about the same time, she became involved with the Baltimore Civic Opera, first as director of auditions, and later as artistic director, one of the few women to hold such a high administrative position, especially at that time. She also turned to teaching and coached a number of singers who would go on to prominent careers, including Beverly Sills, Sherrill Milnes, and James Morris. Her own voice remained as wondrous as ever, as evidenced by a series of RCA recordings from the 1950s and by later accounts, from those who heard her sing live, of the magical sound, still glorious and effortless after all the years.

Her later years were touched by illness, and she died at her beloved Villa Pace on May 25, 1981, at the age of eighty-four. She was buried next to her older sister, Carmela, in Druid Ridge Cemetery in Baltimore. Though her career was neither widely international nor particularly lengthy, Ponselle's vocal legacy in one of the most difficult repertoires endures, and she did it in her native land, on her own terms.

Bibliography: The Metropolitan Opera Archives has many visual resources, such as photographs, a painted portrait, and costumes of Ponselle, as well as contracts, reviews, performance records, and some correspondence. The Music Division of the New York Public Library for the Performing Arts at Lincoln Center houses a collection of Ponselle's papers and scrapbooks. The most useful sources for information on Ponselle's life are the two major biographies of Ponselle published in 1997 to coincide with the centenary anniversary of her birth: Mary Jane Phillips-Matz, *Rosa Ponselle: American Diva* (1997), and James A. Drake, *Rosa Ponselle: A Centenary Biography* (1997), both of which include useful bibliographies and discographies. Drake also collaborated with Ponselle on an earlier version of her life story in *Ponselle: A Singer's Life* (1982). Vivid portraits can also be found in Peter G. Davis, *The American Opera Singer* (1997), and John Briggs, *Requiem for a Yellow Brick Brewery: A History of the Metropolitan Opera* (1969). An obituary appeared in the *New York Times* on May 26, 1981.

RONA M. WILK

PORTER, Dorothy. *See* Wesley, Dorothy Porter.

PORTER, Katherine Anne. May 15, 1890–September 18, 1980. Writer.

Katherine Anne Porter was born in the small community of Indian Creek, Texas, to Mary Alice Jones and Harrison Boone Porter, a farmer. She was the fourth of five children, one of whom had died in infancy. Originally named Callie Russell, she changed her legal name to Katherine Anne in 1915, in tribute to her strong-willed paternal grandmother, Catherine Porter.

As an adult, Porter created an impression that she had come from an aristocratic, if not wealthy, family. Her Porter forebears had in fact belonged to the smaller slaveholding class in Kentucky before the Civil War, but her own origins were humble. By the time she was born the family had much less land and little income. A sense of reduced status and means would trouble Porter throughout her life, possibly impelling her acquisition of beautiful accoutrements of cultivated living in her later years.

Shortly before Porter was two years old, her mother died, and her father descended into prolonged mourning and lassitude. He moved his family to their Grandmother Porter's small house in Kyle, Texas, a few miles south of Austin, and essentially surrendered his parental duties. Known locally as Aunt Cat, this upright and severe grandmother provided a model of female strength traceable in the assertive females of Porter's fiction. Harrison Porter openly blamed his children for their mother's death, and his unreliable affection seems to have hinged on his daughters' prettiness at any given moment. Porter would retain a lifelong concern with physical beauty and a troubled preoccupation with masculine attention.

After Grandmother Porter died in 1901, the family moved around to various Texas towns, with the older children often working to support their father. In San Antonio, Porter was able to add a year of secondary schooling to the few years of grammar school she had had in Kyle. That was the full extent of her formal education. She was self-educated through her reading.

Porter was married multiple times. Indeed, it is uncertain whether there were three, four, or five marriages. When she was only sixteen she married John Henry Koontz, a salesman and the son of a ranching family near Victoria. She converted to Catholicism at that time. The marriage was turbulent and ended in divorce nine years later. Porter was married to Eugene Pressly, a U.S. State Department Foreign Service employee, from 1933 to 1938 and to Albert Erskine, an editor, from 1938 to 1942. What was thought to have been a brief marriage to a British painter named Ernest Stock in 1925 was probably not formalized. But an additional marriage, soon after her first divorce and quickly annulled, has been discovered. There may have been others. In addition, she had numerous tumultuous love affairs. She never had children.

Porter's early adulthood was also troubled by a bout with tuberculosis and a near-death experience in the flu epidemic of 1918–19 (recounted in her novella "Pale Horse, Pale Rider") while she was working as a reporter and columnist for the

Rocky Mountain News in Denver. In 1920 she left the newspaper and went to New York seeking to become a serious writer. In 1921 she left for Mexico, where she spent six months embroiled in the political intrigues of the Mexican Revolution. She would return to Mexico for three additional stays in the next decade. Her first mature short story, "María Concepción," published in 1922, and some of her early nonfiction reflect her observations and experiences in Mexico. In 1931, having been awarded a Guggenheim Fellowship, she went to Berlin, then on to Paris, where she lived until 1936.

In 1930, when Porter was forty years old, her first volume of short stories, *Flowering Judas and Other Stories,* appeared. It was republished in 1935 in an expanded edition that attracted an award from the Book of the Month Club. "Hacienda," a novella pondering the frustration of political aspirations in Mexico, saw journal publication in 1932. *Pale Horse, Pale Rider* (including, besides the title story, "Old Mortality" and "Noon Wine") appeared in 1939 and *The Leaning Tower and Other Stories* in 1944. All these works were highly esteemed by a small circle of writers and critics, but attracted little popular readership or financial reward. It was Porter's striking beauty, shown to advantage in published photographs by George Platt Lynes, that made her a public figure in the 1930s and beyond.

With the long-awaited publication of her one novel, *Ship of Fools,* in 1962, and its making into a successful motion picture, she at last gained a secure income and a popular following. The novel's long gestation, traceable to a journal she kept during her voyage to Germany in 1931, had begun in 1937. She first intended it as a novella but by 1939 realized it would be novel. Its publication was announced in 1941, but only after twenty-one years of struggle did it appear, on April Fool's Day, 1962. It attracted mixed reviews. Her *Collected Stories* (1965), on the other hand, won both a Pulitzer Prize and the National Book Award.

Porter has been generally admired as a stylist and symbolist and a defining figure of literary modernism, primarily on the basis of her short fiction. Her nonfiction, published in 1970 in *The Collected Essays and Occasional Writings,* has been less studied. In recent years, Porter has also been seen as an important figure in cultural studies, providing insight into the artistic and social currents of her times. For example, an unfinished and unpublished novella, "The Man in the Tree," illustrates her response to the changing race relations and racial uneasiness of the period. Her scrutiny of the rise of the Nazi Party during her residence in Berlin in 1931 and 1932 captures the political unrest preceding World War II. Her flirtation with communism and later defection trace a pattern common to American intelligentsia in the 1930s. And the curious contrast between her development of strong female characters and her expressed dislike of feminist currents in the 1960s and '70s demonstrates the tensions of changing gender roles.

Katherine Anne Porter's last published work, *The Never-Ending Wrong* (1977), commemorated the fiftieth anniversary of the execution of Sacco and Vanzetti. In failing health after a stroke, she died in Silver Spring, Maryland, at the age of ninety. Porter's enormous correspondence provides an important resource for the study of modernist literary circles, the business of letters, and social developments during a large swath of the twentieth century. But it is primarily for her keenly crafted short stories and novellas that Katherine Anne Porter will retain a niche in American literary history.

Bibliography: Porter's letters and other personal papers are for the most part located at the University of Maryland, which also has an extensive collection of photographs. Her correspondence with politically radical novelist Josephine Herbst is at the Beinecke Rare Book & Manuscript Library, Yale University. In addition to works mentioned above, see Ruth M. Alvarez and Thomas F. Walsh, ed., *Uncollected Early Prose of Katherine Anne Porter* (1993); Darlene Harbour Unrue, ed., *"This Strange, Old World" and Other Book Reviews by Katherine Anne Porter* (1991); and Unrue, ed., *Katherine Anne Porter's Poetry* (1996). Important scholarly works about Porter include Jane Krause DeMouy, *Katherine Anne Porter's Women: The Eye of Her Fiction* (1983); Joan Givner, *Katherine Anne Porter: A Life* (1982; rev. ed. 1991); Kathryn Hilt and Ruth M. Alvarez, *Katherine Anne Porter: An Annotated Bibliography* (1990); Janis P. Stout, *Katherine Anne Porter: A Sense of the Times* (1995); Unrue, *Truth and Vision in Katherine Anne Porter's Fiction* (1985); and Walsh, *Katherine Anne Porter and Mexico: The Illusion of Eden* (1992). An obituary appeared in the *New York Times* on September 19, 1980.

JANIS P. STOUT

PORTER, Sylvia. June 18, 1913–June 5, 1991. Syndicated financial columnist, writer.

Pioneering columnist Sylvia Porter began life as Sarianni "Sylvia" Feldman, the younger of two children born to Louis and Rose Maisel Feldman. She was born on Long Island, in Patchogue, New York, but by the time she entered school the family was living in Brooklyn. Her parents were Russian Jewish immigrants—her father was a physician, and her mother a housewife—and she and her older brother John had a comfortable childhood. Despite this traditional home life, Sylvia was strongly encouraged by her mother to go to college and pursue a career.

Encouragement was replaced by example after her father died suddenly of a heart attack in 1925, leaving his wife and children in financially precarious circumstances. Mrs. Feldman, who changed the family's name to Field, worked at a variety of jobs before opening a successful hat shop. A brilliant student, Sylvia earned her diploma from James Madison High School in Brooklyn and, at age sixteen, entered Hunter College in Manhattan in the fall of 1929.

Within weeks, the American stock market crashed, and her mother was among the hundreds of thousands of investors who lost their savings in the panic. The scope and mystery of the event seized young Sylvia Field's imagination, and she promptly shifted her attention from English and history to the study of economics. She later told a writer that she had wanted to understand how people could be rich on Monday and poor on Tuesday.

In 1931, as a student, she married Reed Porter, an attractive young bank employee. The following year, just before her nineteenth birthday, she graduated from Hunter magna cum laude and Phi Beta Kappa. She would later say that her Phi Beta Kappa key unlocked the door to her first job: an idiosyncratic money manager got a glimpse of it when she showed up looking for a job and hired her on the spot. Thereafter, she worked at several small brokerage firms, learning the vocabulary and machinery of the stock and bond markets in the male-dominated world of Wall Street, while studying business at night at New York University School of Business Administration.

Along the way, Porter wrote freelance articles for a few Wall Street publications, using the ambiguous byline "S. F. Porter." By early 1934, not yet twenty-one, she was writing a weekly column about government securities for the *American Banker.* But she wanted a larger role in financial journalism, which in that era was written almost exclusively by and for men. She would later frequently mention being denied a job by an Associated Press editor who told her that the AP had never hired a woman for its financial department and never would. In August 1935, after a monthlong trial doing three pieces a week, she finally became a full-time financial reporter for the *New York Post.* In 1938, she began writing a daily column, initially called "Financial Post Marks" but later labeled "S. F. Porter Says." Not until 1942 was the column's name changed to "Sylvia Porter Says."

Porter's style was clear and conversational, often humorous and occasionally blunt, and her topics revealed a passion for fair play. Economic issues were urgently important to the lives of all Americans, she argued, and should be explained in ways people could easily understand. That approach would govern her work throughout her long, prolific career. Her flagship was her column, nationally syndicated in 1947; it reached more than 40 million Americans, year in and year out, until her death. She also generated popular radio shows, newsletters, speeches, magazine articles, and books. Her influence with American consumers during World War II was such that Treasury officials sought her advice about marketing war bonds. Less memorably, she led a citizens' advisory panel on inflation for President Gerald Ford in 1974 and 1975.

Her first book, published in 1939, was called *How to Make Money in Government Bonds* and was notable for being both understandable and authoritative. Indeed, in 1940 she famously scolded Treasury Secretary Henry Morgenthau for his handling of Treasury bond auctions. In 1941, with America still officially neutral, she published *If War Comes to the American Home,* a prescient and practical guide to the likely effects of a wartime economy. In *The Nazi Chemical Trust in the United States* (1942) she examined the German chemical companies that were supporting Hitler.

Her postwar books were forerunners of the consumer advice genre—titles such as *Managing Your Money,* co-authored with J. K. Lasser (1953), *How to Get More for Your Money* (1961), and *How to Get a Better Job* (1981). She is perhaps best known for *Sylvia Porter's Money Book,* first published in 1975. It sold more than one million copies and remained a perennial best-seller in its subsequent updated editions. In the 1980s, she launched *Sylvia Porter's Personal Finance Magazine,* but that venture was less successful and later closed.

Porter has been recognized as one of the most influential business journalists of the twentieth century. She established a lonely beachhead for women in a region of journalism that had long excluded them, although few followed in her wake until at least the early 1980s. More significantly, with her emphasis on clear, accessible writing free of the obscure jargon she called bafflegab, she helped create a new vision of how business journalism could contribute to the economic literacy of American consumers. Yet in the early decades of her long career, the vivacious and attractive Porter was typically portrayed in the media, not as a pioneer, but as an oddity, a woman out of place in a man's world, while later profiles frequently stressed the burden her lucrative career placed on her personal relationships. One editor, quoted anonymously in a 1960 *Time* cover story, simply said, "Sylvia's a non-woman" (p. 47).

Her marriage to Reed Porter ended in 1941. In May 1943, she married G. Sumner Collins, a widowed newspaper industry executive, with whom she raised a daughter, Cris Sarah, whom they adopted in 1949, and a stepson, Sumner C. Collins, who was ten at the time of the marriage. She was widowed in 1977. In January 1979 she married James F. Fox, a public relations adviser. After a long illness, she died from complications of emphysema in 1991, at her country estate in Pound Ridge, New York. She was cremated and her ashes were scattered on her daughter's property in Maine.

Bibliography: Sylvia Porter's extensive collected papers and a biographical sketch are in the Western Historical Manuscript Collection at the University of Missouri in Columbia. Her daughter, Cris Collins Del Cuore, provided helpful insights. An interview with Porter appears in Lynn Gilbert and Gaylen Moore, *Particular Passions: Talks with Women Who Have Shaped Our Times* (1981). Magazine and newspaper articles that touch on her career include Wambly Bald, "The Girl behind the Low-Down on High Finance," *New York Post,* September 26, 1947; Ruth Hawthorne Fay, "Women at the Top," *Cue Magazine,* November 19, 1949, p. 16; Jana Guerrier, "Wall Street Woman," *Coronet,* January 1954, pp. 26–29; "Sylvia & You," *Time,* November 28, 1960, pp. 46–52; Joseph Wershba, "Friend of the Consumer," *New York Post Magazine,* July 29, 1962, p. 2; *Current Biography,* 1980, pp. 324–27; and Elizabeth Whitney, "Sylvia Porter: Living Legend Becomes an Institution," *St. Petersburg Times,* February 26, 1989. An obituary appeared in the *New York Times* on June 7, 1991.

DIANA B. HENRIQUES

POST, Marion. *See* Wolcott, Marion Post.

POTTER, Clare. 1903– January 5, 1999. Fashion designer.

Clare Potter, one of the first American fashion designers to be known by name, is remembered for her remarkable sense of color and for designing stylish, practical, comfortable, and affordable clothes. Distinguished by their simplicity of line, easy fit, and sensible cut, Potter's designs in the 1930s and 1940s, along with those of CLAIRE MCCARDELL, VERA MAXWELL, and a small group of other American designers, were promoted as the "American Look." Potter helped redefine not only the U.S. fashion industry but also the idea of American fashion itself.

Born Clare Meyer, she grew up in Jersey City, New Jersey. Little is known about her upbringing, except that she had an older sister and that her family was reasonably well off. Self-reliant and talented at art from an early age, she served as art editor for her high school paper. A high school art teacher was an early mentor, encouraging her to attend evening classes at the Art Students League in midtown Manhattan.

Certain that she would become a professional artist, Clare enrolled in the fine arts program at Pratt Institute in Brooklyn in the early 1920s. There the clothes she designed and made for herself attracted the attention of the director, who suggested she build upon her highly individual feel for color and line and study costume design. She shifted classes and took outside courses in draping to catch up, but left Pratt before graduating to take up employment with one of the leading New York wholesale dress manufacturers, Edward L. Mayer. She stayed there for three years honing her skills at cutting, draping, and designing midmarket sportswear.

Living in Mexico for six months opened up a whole new color palette for Clare, one she described as subtle and sophisticated. Once back in New York, she reentered the fashion industry. After working briefly for a wholesale firm, she found employment in 1930 with one of the leading ready-to-wear firms, Charles W. Nudelman Inc. of Seventh Avenue. Nudelman's firm specialized in mass-produced, good-quality fashionable clothing at affordable prices. Around this time she married J. Sanford Potter, an architect and engineer. The couple lived on a farm in West Nyack, New York, and commuted into the city. They had no children.

Designers who worked for a large ready-to-wear company usually were not acknowledged by name, but Potter was fortunate enough to be taken up by DOROTHY SHAVER, vice president of the Lord & Taylor department store, and promoted as a name designer. At a time when Paris dominated the world fashion scene and American fashion was considered inferior, Shaver campaigned ceaselessly for the recognition of American design and designers. After 1936, when her work was featured in Lord & Taylor's "American Look" campaign, Potter achieved fame as a designer of what had then become identified as "sportswear," a type of clothing regarded as a uniquely American contribution to world fashion. Her work was regularly featured in *Vogue, Town and Country,* and *Harper's Bazaar,* and she was honored in 1938 with the Lord & Taylor Award for distinguished sportswear for women and the Coty Award in 1946 for her casual clothes and use of color.

One of the first fashion designers to respond to the lifestyle shift to greater informality then taking place in the United States, Potter aimed her designs at real women with active and varied lives. Her clothing moved with the wearer, and she favored materials such as jersey and rayon that not only hung well in and of themselves but also facilitated ease of movement. In a turn away from traditional wholesale design production methods, Potter abandoned sketching as a way of working out her ideas. Instead she preferred to work directly on a human model—cutting, draping, pinning, and basting in the material in which the items were to be mass produced. This method guaranteed that she would know exactly how a material would hang and whether or not a design would prove comfortable once it was commercially produced. It also allowed her to manipulate color, one of her most distinctive traits. Paying little attention to conventional color combinations, she mainly worked in solid colors dyed to her specifications and liked to use a different color for each item in an ensemble. For example, the colors of a chocolate brown bolero and matching slacks with a pale blue waistband from 1945 were offset by touches of pink from the brassiere top underneath.

During the 1930s and 1940s, Potter explored the entire panoply of sports and leisure wear, becoming known for beautifully cut trousers, bathing suits, sundresses, and evening separates. She catapulted lounging pajamas into high-style fashion and teamed tapered trousers with Eastern-style tunics, bringing the pajama look to the mass market. Given the era's greater informality of life and leisure, many of her pajamas, low-back sundresses, and low-neck sweaters were sufficiently elegant to wear at night. Additionally, Potter is credited with inventing the "evening sweater" that took a woman from daytime pursuits to evening events, and also with a two-piece bathing suit of bloomer pants and brassiere top.

In 1948, shortly after Dior's New Look was revealed, Potter started a ready-to-wear business named Timbertop after her West Nyack farm where the company was based. At first she was in partnership with Martha Stout, a former magazine editor, but by the mid 1950s she was on her own, assisted by her husband, who drafted the patterns from which her designs were cut. The clothes she designed in the 1950s and early 1960s were somewhat dressier than those she had done earlier, and in later years included more suits, tailored dresses, and evening separates. Despite this late career transition to more dressed-up styles, Clare Potter is best remembered for casual, but still alluring, designs that gave American women well-cut clothes at reasonable prices.

In the late 1950s, Potter and her husband moved to a Japanese-style house he had designed on Lake Nebo in Fort Ann, New York. There she grew camellias and raised Dalmatians. An avid sportswoman throughout her life, she especially enjoyed horseback riding. Upright, serene looking, and elegantly slender, Potter had a distinguished profile and prematurely gray hair that conjured up the image of an American aristocrat. Clare Potter died at home at the age of ninety-five in 1999.

Bibliography: Clare Potter's design career is remarkably undocumented. For general overviews of Clare Potter's life and work, see Beryl Williams, *Fashion Is Our Business* (1945); Valerie Steele, *Women of Fashion: Twentieth Century Designers* (1991); and Caroline Rennolds Milbank, *New York Fashion: The Evolution of American Style* (1989). Fashion publicist Eleanor Lambert includes Potter in her *World of Fashion* (1976). Clippings, several press releases, and photographs are in the collection of the Costume Institute at the Metropolitan Museum of Art in New York City. Clare Potter's designs are featured on the covers of both *Vogue* (July 1943) and *Harper's Bazaar* (June 1953). An obituary appeared in the *New York Times* on January 11, 1999.

PAT KIRKHAM AND KOHLE YOHANNAN

PRIMUS, Pearl. November 29, 1919–October 29, 1994. Dancer, choreographer, anthropologist.

Known for her gravity-defying jumps, Pearl Primus hurdled racial barriers in the dance world that had cut short the careers of earlier African American dancers. Along with Katherine Dunham, Primus fused modern dance with African dance, creating a public forum for African American women in the arts.

Born in Port of Spain, Trinidad, Pearl Eileene Primus came to New York City with her family when she was two. Her father, Edward Primus, held a variety of jobs, from merchant seaman in Trinidad to building superintendent, carpenter, and war plant employee in New York, while her mother, Emily Jackson Primus, stayed at home to raise Pearl and her two younger brothers. The healing profession early claimed Primus's interest; because she excelled at Hunter College High School, she set her sights on becoming a doctor. In 1940 she graduated from Hunter College with a degree in biology and sought work to save money for medical school at Howard University. Denied a job as a laboratory technician because of racial discrimination, Primus turned to the National Youth Administration (NYA) for assistance, which placed her in a NYA dance group. She first worked in the wardrobe department, but soon found herself on stage in *America Dances,* replacing a dancer who did not show up. Short and sturdy with powerful legs, Primus relied on her background as a track-and-field athlete to make up for her lack of dance training. She later recalled that the production awakened the dancer inside her.

After the NYA project was discontinued, when the United States entered World War II, Primus received a scholarship from the New Dance Group, a school that offered classes in a variety of techniques, from those of MARTHA GRAHAM and HANYA HOLM to the dances of her homeland taught by Trinidadian Beryl McBurnie. The New Dance Group also introduced Primus to the politics that infused modern dance. Not content to let art reside in a removed world of abstraction and beauty, dancers associated with the New Dance Group advocated for a social purpose for dance, with widening the opportunities for black dancers being one way to implement that goal. Primus's performances throughout the early 1940s, beginning with her professional debut on February 14, 1943, at the 92nd Street Y (Young Men's Hebrew Association) and continuing in an ongoing engagement at Barney Josephson's Café Society, reflected her growing political conscience. Primus began to view the arts as another form of healing. When she shared with John Martin, the leading dance critic of the era, her dilemma about having to choose between remaining in dance or going to medical school, he responded that art may have even greater curative power than medicine.

Assuaged, Primus devoted herself to dance. Through dances such as *Strange Fruit* (1943), a solo to the song by Abel Meeropol (made famous by BILLIE HOLIDAY) about a lynched body hanging from a tree, Primus expanded her association with artists who had similar political concerns, such as Teddy Wilson, Hazel Scott, Lena Horne, Billie Holiday, and Paul Robeson. During the war years she joined them in Negro Freedom Rallies that promoted the fulfillment of democracy at home as well as around the world. Primus was more confrontational than earlier African American dancers, and her quick rise and battling attitude attested to the changes that had occurred in the dance field and beyond. Primus trained with white dancers, performed with them, and appeared in the same institutions where most white modern dancers produced their shows. Primus benefited from the success of such dancers as Martha Graham and DORIS HUMPHREY in establishing modern dance as a women's arena in the 1930s, but she extended that achievement by using her notoriety to protest more vocally against the limitations African Americans continued to face—in the dance world and in society at large.

Primus's concern for the plight of African Americans led her to an investigative trip to Georgia, Alabama, and South Carolina in 1944 during which she posed as a migrant worker and picked cotton. That same impulse to understand African Americans' place in the world prompted her to begin researching African dance, and she choreographed dances based on both pursuits such as *Hard Time Blues* (1943), about the ravaged conditions in which African Americans lived, and *Fanga* (1949), a West African ritualistic dance of welcome that opened her performances. Even as Primus danced, choreographed, and toured in the musical *Show Boat,* she continued her schooling, switching from medicine, to psychology, and finally, to anthropology. Anthropology brought together her concerns for a better understanding of her heritage that would lend a different perspective on the plight of peoples of the African diaspora. In 1948 she received a Rosenwald Foundation grant for $4,000 that allowed her to travel to Africa to test her book learning with fieldwork. The trip set the agenda for her life's work: spreading and preserving African dance traditions and the belief that the arts were an integral part of life and the community.

Primus pursued these goals accompanied by Percival Borde, a dancer she met in Trinidad on a visit there in 1953. They married in 1954, and she bore a son, Onwin Borde, a year later. Primus and Borde worked together, founding the Primus-Borde School of Primal Dance in New York City and often performing together, until his death in 1979. Borde even served as Primus's assistant in her largest endeavor, the establishment of the African Performing Arts Center in Monrovia in 1959, a task for which she was presented the "Star of Africa" by the President of the Republic of Liberia. Primus's work in preserving African dance fused with her devotion to education in the 1950s and 1960s, particularly in advocating for including the arts in the public school curriculum. She continued her formal education at the same time and completed her doctorate at New York University in 1978 in educational sociology and anthropology. Throughout her life Primus was a sought-after educator in dance, anthropology, and African studies, exemplifying the necessity of understanding the arts for their social function as well as their aesthetic principles. She held various college residencies, and she received the American Dance Festival's first Distinguished Teaching Award in 1991. That same year she was awarded the National Medal of Arts. She died in her home in New Rochelle, New York, at the age of seventy-four.

Bibliography: Photographs, videos, clippings, and programs concerning Primus are held at the New York Public Library: in the Jerome Robbins Dance Division of the Library of the Performing Arts at Lincoln Center, and at the Schomburg Center for Research in Black Culture. The recent documentary *Free to Dance* (2001) features Primus—including a re-creation of her dance "Strange Fruit"—and places her contributions within the history of African Americans in dance in the twentieth century. A useful bibliography is Adele R. Wenig, *Pearl Primus: An Annotated Bibliography of Sources from 1943 to 1975* (1983). Important books that discuss Primus are John O. Perpener III, *African-American Concert Dance: The Harlem Renaissance and Beyond* (2001); Julia L. Foulkes, *Modern Bodies: Dance and American Modernism from Martha Graham to Alvin Ailey* (2002); Lynne Fauley Emery, *Black Dance from 1619 to Today* (1988); and two collections of short essays edited by Gerald Myers and put out by the American Dance Festival as part of its project to research and preserve African Americans' contributions to modern dance: *The Black Tradition in American Modern Dance* (1988) and *African-American Genius in Modern Dance* (1994).

Articles and dissertations specifically on Primus include Beverly Anne Hillsman Barber, "Pearl Primus: In Search of Her Roots 1943–1970" (Ph.D. dissertation, Florida State University, 1984); Jean R. Glover, "Pearl Primus:

Cross-Cultural Pioneer of American Dance" (MA thesis, American University, 1989); Ric Estrada, "Three Leading Negro Artists and How They Feel about Dance in the Community: Eleo Pomare, Arthur Mitchell, and Pearl Primus," *Dance Magazine* 42, no. 2 (November 1968), pp. 45–60; and Richard C. Green, "Pearl Primus and 'The Negro Problem' in American Modern Dance," *UCLA Journal of Dance Ethnology* 19 (1995), pp. 68–76. A special issue of *Talking Drums! The Journal of Black Dance* 5 (January 1995) was in memory of Primus. An obituary appeared in the *New York Times* on October 31, 1994.

JULIA L. FOULKES

PROSKOURIAKOFF, Tatiana. January 23, 1909–August 30, 1985. Artist, epigrapher, archaeologist.

Tatiana Avenirovna Proskouriakoff, an epigrapher and archaeologist who revolutionized studies of Maya hieroglyphs, was born in Tomsk, Siberia, the second of two daughters of Avenir Proskouriakoff, a chemical engineer, and Alla Nekrassova, a physician. When her father was commissioned as a wartime weapons purchasing agent in the United States for the czar's government, the Proskouriakoff family emigrated from Russia in 1916. After the Russian Revolution the next year, the family decided to stay permanently and became naturalized U.S. citizens in 1924. Proskouriakoff, known as Tania, grew up in the Philadelphia area, where she graduated from Lansdowne High School in 1926. She attended Pennsylvania State University, where in 1930 she received a BS degree in architecture, at that time a male-dominated field. Between 1930 and 1932 she took courses in anthropology and archaeology at the University of Pennsylvania.

After her graduation, Proskouriakoff returned to Philadelphia where, owing to the Depression, jobs in architecture were few. Instead, she worked at a studio, designing and painting original needlepoint designs. During this time (out of boredom, according to her) she volunteered at the University of Pennsylvania Museum, a decision that forever changed the course of her life. In exchange for library privileges, she did illustrations for the museum, and soon progressed to producing drawings for Linton Satterthwaite, a Mayanist at the museum. Her drafting talent was clear, and in 1936 Satterthwaite invited Proskouriakoff on her first trip to Central America, as a member of an expedition to the Maya site Piedras Negras, Guatemala, where she would survey the site and produce drawings. Proskouriakoff spent two field seasons (1936 and 1937) at Piedras Negras, and the monuments of this site would later inspire her greatest discovery.

In 1939, archaeologist Sylvanus Morley of the Carnegie Institution of Washington (CIW) was impressed by Proskouriakoff's drawings of Piedras Negras, which pictured what that urban center might have looked like at its apogee, and he offered her a job. Her remarkable architectural reconstruction drawings, which she had executed in her spare time using her earlier training as well as measurements and observations from the field, formed the body of Proskouriakoff's *Album of Maya Architecture* (1946). Proskouriakoff carried out additional fieldwork at the sites of Copán (1939), Chichén Itzá and Puuc sites (1940), and Mayapan (1951–55), as well as other research trips to Mexico and Guatemala.

When first hired by Morley, Proskouriakoff was employed as a draftsperson and illustrator with the CIW's Division of Historical Research (later renamed the Department of Archaeology), a position she held from 1939 to 1942. She was a full staff member from 1943 until the dissolution of the department in 1958. Remaining a research associate of the Carnegie Institution, Proskouriakoff then moved her office to the Peabody Museum of Harvard University. From 1958 to 1970 she was a research associate in Maya Art at the Peabody, and in 1970 she became curator of Maya Art at the Peabody. During the late 1960s and the 1970s she taught courses on Maya iconography, art, and religion in the fine arts and anthropology departments at Harvard. In 1976 she was a visiting Mellon Professor at the University of Pittsburgh.

Proskouriakoff's research contributions combined her knowledge of art with her studies of archaeology and the Maya. Her *Study of Classic Maya Sculpture* (1950) resulted from a collegial disagreement with Morley about the dating of monuments. Proskouriakoff suggested, and proved, that Maya monuments could be ordered and dated on the basis of style and morphology. Proskouriakoff's most important work was the groundbreaking "Historical Implications of a Pattern of Dates at Piedras Negras, Guatemala," published in *American Antiquity* in 1960. In this article she examined patterns of hieroglyphic dates on as yet undeciphered monuments and concluded that, contrary to the prevailing views of the day, the content of the inscriptions recorded real, historical events in the history of the Maya. This view revolutionized the study of Maya hieroglyphs and has been borne out in subsequent decades of study. Proskouriakoff devoted much of the rest of her academic career to the study of the jades from the Cenote of Sacrifice at Chichén Itzá; this painstaking and careful work culminating in her 1974 publication, *Jades from the Cenote of Sacrifice.* At the end of her life, she was working on *Maya History,* published posthumously in 1993.

Proskouriakoff was recognized for her outstanding contributions to the field of Maya studies, and especially the study of Maya hieroglyphs—despite her never having obtained an advanced degree. In 1962 she received the Alfred Vincent Kidder Award for Eminence in the Field of American Archaeology, an award for which she had designed the medal. In 1983 she was elected a member of the American Philosophical Society for her research contributions. Perhaps most significantly, Proskouriakoff was honored in 1984 by the country of Guatemala, the location of her most important research, with its highest tribute: the Order of the Quetzal.

Proskouriakoff was known as an opinionated, independent, and critical individual, marked by intellectual dedication and curiosity throughout her life. Colleagues remember her as challenging accepted notions in the field of archaeology, and thinking outside the accepted paradigm. Privately, she was sometimes shy, and her diaries suggest bouts of self-doubt. Her willingness to take on challenges and embrace hardship was reflected in her adaptation to difficult living circumstances while working in the field and in a foreign culture, and, more profoundly, in her role as a woman in a largely male field.

Proskouriakoff died in 1985 at the age of seventy-six in a nursing home in Watertown, Massachusetts, where she was suffering from Alzheimer's disease. Her ashes are buried at the site of Piedras Negras. Though she never married, she left behind a close community of colleagues, friends, and a small circle of students; her devotion to these individuals mirrored the formative relationships she had with her own mentors (especially Sattherthwaite, Morley, Kidder, and Alfred Tozzer). Her finest contributions to the field of Maya archaeology are both her insightful discoveries about the nature of Maya inscriptions, and her pioneering spirit as an early example, and an inspiration to her intellectual descendants, of a woman working in field archaeology.

Bibliography: Important and rich archival sources on Tatiana Proskouriakoff, including her personal diaries and some papers, are found at the Harvard University Archives. The Peabody Museum Archives holds papers, letters, photographs, and research notes, as well as a scrapbook about Proskouriakoff put together by her colleague Ian Graham. The museum archives also house a variety of drawings, maps, plans, and field diaries from Proskouriakoff's expeditions and archaeological work. See also Char Solomon, *Tatiana Proskouriakoff: Interpreting the Ancient Maya* (2002), a biography written by a former Peabody Museum volunteer who worked with Proskouriakoff. Ian Graham's obituary of Proskouriakoff in *American Antiquity* 55, no. 1 (1990), pp. 6–11, includes a full list of her publications. An obituary appeared in the *New York Times* on September 11, 1985.

SARAH E. JACKSON

PUKUI, Mary. April 20, 1895–May 21, 1986. Hawaiiana expert, translator.

Mary Pukui was born Mary Kawena Wiggin in Kau, Hawaii, at Haniumalu, the only child of Henry Nathaniel Wiggin and Mary Paahana Kanakaole. Young Mary was known as Kawena in Hawaiian circles, and her complete given Hawaiian name was Kawena-ula-o-ka-lani-a-Hiiaka-i-ka-poli-o-Pele-ka-wahine-ai-honua, which translates as "the rosy glow in the sky made by Hiiaka in the bosom of Pele, the earth-consuming woman." Her New England–born father, who spoke fluent Hawaiian in addition to English, worked as an overseer *(luna)* on a sugar plantation in Naalehu owned by Hutchinson Sugar Company. Her mother was a descendant from the sacred line of native Hawaiian high priestesses who served the volcano goddess Pele and from kahunas who were experts in using herbal medicines for cures. This dual heritage exposed Mary to the richness of both cultures, and she spoke both languages fluently.

Mary was adopted *(hanaied)* at birth by her grandmother Naliipoaimoku (Poai), a sacred high priestess who was pleased by the respect shown her by her Western son-in-law. Mary was raised as a *kapu* (especially protected) child and as a *punahele* (most cherished). As the descendant of a long and intricate tradition of high-ranking chiefs and priestesses, it was natural for Mary Kawena to continue in her family's traditional role of studying the complicated genealogy, language, lore, and customs of ancient Hawaii. She trained her strong retentive mind and memory by listening to long detailed stories told by her elders. When her grandmother died when she was nine, Mary felt compelled to continue in her line of protecting native culture.

Mary knew the value of a Western education as well as a native Hawaiian one. She understood early on that she could become the *kumu* (source) for accurate Hawaiian knowledge if she mastered research techniques and both English and Hawaiian languages. She attended schools first in Kau, then Waiaohinu, Mountain View, and Hilo; after the family moved to Honolulu, she attended Central Grammar School and later boarded as a student at Kawaiahao Seminary. Her family encouraged her to remain bilingual. At fifteen Mary left high school to care for her uncle; later, when she was twenty-eight years old, she completed high school at Hawaiian Mission Academy.

Mary was rooted in many faiths. Baptized by an Episcopal bishop when he toured Kau, she never forgot the ancient Hawaiian gods and religion taught to her by her grandmother. After her marriage to Kalolii Pukui in 1913, she became a Mormon. He had been born in Keauhou, Kona, Hawaii in 1875, and when he was thirteen he had moved with his family to Utah. After he returned to Hawaii, he worked as a salesman and later as a researcher of land titles. They adopted two children: Patience, a Japanese child whose parents had died in an influenza epidemic, and Faith, a Hawaiian Japanese child. In 1931 she gave birth to their daughter Asenath Henrietta Pelehonuamea Napuaala-o-Nuuanu, nicknamed Pele. All of her daughters studied and danced the hula under her guidance and went on to outstanding careers in preserving Hawaiian culture.

A neighbor, Laura Green, was so impressed with Mary Pukui's knowledge of Hawaiian lore that she introduced her to the research world of the Bishop Museum in Honolulu. In 1921 Pukui met Dr. Martha Beckwith, an anthropology professor at Vassar in ethnology and folklore who was doing research there. Beckwith and Pukui collaborated in recording *Hawaiian Stories and Wise Sayings* (1923), and Vassar published Pukui's *Hawaiian Folktales* in 1933. Their shared research interests launched a long, productive cooperation translating Hawaiian newspapers and manuscripts, including the writings of early Hawaiian scholars Samuel Kamakau and John Papa Ii. In addition, Mary Pukui and Laura Green published *The Legend of Kawelo and Other Hawaiian Folk Tales* in 1936.

Pukui was formally hired as a translator of Hawaiian language at the Bishop Museum in 1937, but she also worked as a researcher, recorder of Hawaiian lore, consultant, and teaching scholar. Anthropologist E. S. C. Handy became her mentor at the museum, and Pukui collaborated with him on *The Outline of Hawaiian Physical Therapeutics* (1934). She accompanied Dr. Handy and his anthropologist wife, Willowdean Chatterson Handy, to her native region, where Pukui learned the art of field studies and the Handys gathered materials for the shared publications *The Hawaiian Planter* (1940) and *The Polynesian Family System in Ka'u Hawaii* (1958). During World War II she was consulted as a Hawaiiana expert and worked as a foreperson in a U.S. Army Corps of Engineers unit to camouflage military installations. Her husband worked with her and died suddenly in 1943.

Mary Pukui pioneered oral history in the islands by taping conversations with elderly Hawaiians who recalled the old Hawaiian ways and events. A vast collection of these tapes dating from the 1950s to the 1980s is located in the Bishop Museum. Pukui could think and write in both Hawaiian and English, and this gave her a tremendous advantage in explaining Hawaiian culture. Her reputation of wisdom as the *kumu,* or source, spread widely. She taught Hawaiian language classes at the museum and the Honolulu YWCA and gave hula demonstrations at public sites like the Kamehameha schools.

Mary Pukui became interested in preserving the accurate meanings of Hawaiian language during World War II and collaborated with Henry Judd and John Stokes to produce *Introduction to the Hawaiian language with the English-Hawaiian, Hawaiian-English Dictionary* (1943), which became the standard for the native Hawaiian language. This was later expanded into the *Hawaiian-English Dictionary* (1957), co-authored with well-known linguist Samuel H. Elbert. Her *English-Hawaiian Dictionary,* co-authored with Elbert, appeared in 1964, and the *Hawaiian Dictionary: Hawaiian-English, English-Hawaiian* with Elbert was published in 1971. Pukui's *Place Names of Hawaii,* published with Elbert and Esther T. Mookini, appeared in 1974. In 1979 she again collaborated with Elbert, on *Hawaiian Grammar,* which was adopted for use in the schools. Her fascination with the native Hawaiian tongue led her to write Hawaiian songs, and her lifelong interest in hula offered her opportunities to collaborate with hula musical archivist-entertainers Iolani Luahine, Fred Beckley Kahea, and Lokalia Montgomery. In 1980 she collaborated on the publication of *Hula: Historical Perspectives.*

Her motto was "Knowledge to me is life," a code that she strove to live by and entice others to follow. Mary Pukui gave life and knowledge to native Hawaiians as they resurrected their culture in the Hawaiian Renaissance of the 1970s that continues to this day. She died in Honolulu in 1986 at the age of ninety-one.

Bibliography: The Bishop Museum's Library and Archives in Honolulu hold the personal papers, manuscripts, oral history tapes, translation work, photographs, biography file, and published books of Mary Pukui. The Pukui collection of oral history tapes at the museum is cataloged by the name of the person (usually native Hawaiian) interviewed. These audiotapes also contain interviews with Pukui from 1959, 1960, 1961, and 1971. The Bishop Museum also holds the personal correspondence between Pukui and her assistant Eleanor Williamson, who aided her in recording oral histories. For biographical information, see Eleanor Lilihana-a-I Williamson's introduction to Mary Pukui's *Olelo No'eau: Hawaiian Proverbs and Poetical Sayings* (1983). See also Clarice B. Taylor, "The Childhood of Mary Kawena Pukui," *Honolulu Star-Bulletin,* July 1956, pp. 3–27; Jeanette Lam, "Island Profile: Mary Kawena Pukui," *Paradise of the Pacific* 70, no. 1 (1958), pp. 24, 32; Aldyth Morris, "The Pukui-Elbert Hawaiian Dictionary," *Paradise of the Pacific* 70, no. 1 (1958), pp. 22–23; Pat Pitzer, "Sharing from the Source," *Honolulu Magazine* 18, no. 5 (1983), pp. 109–13, 178–89; "Mary Pukui Preserved Hawaiian Culture," *Historic Hawaii,* July 1986, pp. 10–11; and Samuel H. Elbert, "Kawena: A Personal Reminiscence," *Honolulu Magazine,* November 1, 1989. An obituary appeared in the *Honolulu Star-Bulletin* on May 22, 1986.

BARBARA BENNETT PETERSON

Q

QOYAWAYMA, Polingaysi. Spring 1892–December 6, 1990. Educator, writer, potter.

Polingaysi Qoyawayma, the renowned Hopi educator and writer, was born in the Second Mesa Village of Oraibi on the Hopi Reservation sometime in the spring of 1892. Her exact birth date is unknown because her people at that time did not celebrate or keep a record of birthdays. She was born a member of the Coyote Clan of her mother (Hopi lineage is through the mother), and a child of the Kachina Clan (through her father). Following Hopi traditions, her navel cord was tied to a stirring stick and thrust into the ceiling to mark her birthplace, her ears were pierced as an infant, and she was given the name Polingaysi, which means "butterfly sitting among the flowers in the breeze," in a Hopi naming ceremony on the twentieth day of her life.

Polingaysi was raised in the traditional Hopi way by her culturally conservative parents, Qoyawayma (called Fred) and Sevenka. Her early years were spent playing and learning with her siblings and other children in the village. Polingaysi was one of eight children born to Fred and Sevenka. Two of the children, a boy and a girl, died young.

Polingaysi was exposed early to Christianity, Western education, and white culture because her father worked for H. R. Voth, a Mennonite missionary to the Hopi. Polingaysi attended church services and learned to sing hymns though she could not speak English. Upon entering school, Polingaysi was given the name Bessie, which she later changed to Elizabeth. On hearing her daughter's new name, her mother said to her, "You were named in the Hopi way. Your true name is Polingaysi. That will always be your true name" (*No Turning Back*, p. 28).

Unlike her siblings and friends who were rounded up and forced to attend the Christian (Mennonite) school, Polingaysi volunteered because she was curious about school and the non-Indian world. This decision upset her more traditional parents. Reluctantly they agreed to let her attend the Mennonite school, and in 1906 at the age of fourteen, Polingaysi entered the Sherman Institute in Riverside, California, where she spent four years. While at Sherman, Polingaysi worked in the home of a white family and saved money for a house she hoped to build someday. During this time, the conflict over white influence upon Hopi life came to a head between Hopi progressives (those who welcomed whites) and Hopi traditionalists (those who wanted to expel whites). In the end, the progressives were driven out by force from Oraibi, and as a result, Polingaysi's family moved to a village that became known as New Oraibi.

After graduation from Sherman in 1910, Polingaysi returned home but found it hard to fit in. Once she had embraced Western culture, it was difficult to fit back into traditional Hopi life. She did not want to marry and have children like most Hopi women her age; this preference was difficult for her mother, who had prepared traditional plaques for her daughter's marriage. Her journey was problematic for her family, who did not always understand her position. In fact, some Hopi referred to her as the "the little one who wanted to be a white man" (ibid., p. 3).

Sensing that Polingaysi's white ways were presenting problems, her father arranged for her to live with a missionary family, the Freys. They wanted Polingaysi to help convert Hopis to Christianity. To prepare for this, she took several trips to the Midwest and later decided to attend Bethel Academy in Newton, Kansas.

Soon after her return from Bethel Academy in 1914, Polingaysi realized that missionary work did not suit her. She saw a great deal of worth in the Hopi way of life even though she had embraced many non-Indian ways, a view most missionaries did not share. In 1924, Polingaysi was offered a job at the Indian school in the Hopi community of Hotevilla as a housekeeper and later as a teacher. She had previously worked, though briefly, in Indian education. In 1918, Polingaysi was hired as a temporary assistant at the Kayenta Indian Boarding School. Later, she served as a substitute teacher at Tuba City Boarding School. In 1931, after she had been transferred to teach on the Navajo reservation, she married Lloyd White, another teacher who was part Cherokee and part white. The marriage was brief and ended in divorce because of different interests and the importance of independence to Polingaysi. She never remarried or had children.

As an educator, Polingaysi strongly believed in making education culturally relevant for her students, which was an innovative idea for that time. She used the Hopi language and culture to teach English and other subjects, drawing on familiar stories and objects to make points about concepts. Polingaysi felt it was easier for her pupils to learn if they started from something they could relate to. Indians and non-Indians criticized her teaching techniques, but Polingaysi was committed. In time, most people realized the value of her teaching philosophy, which was "reach them, then teach them" (ibid., p. 127). When John Collier became commissioner of Indian Affairs in 1933, one of his emphases was on the value of Indian students and their culture, which supported Polingaysi's teaching methods. She retired in 1954 after thirty years of teaching on the Navajo and Hopi reservations and was recognized for her service by the United States Department of the Interior with the Distinguished Service Award.

Returning to the Hopi reservation, Polingaysi continued to counsel Hopi people, especially those wanting to pursue higher education. To assist students, she founded the Hopi Student Scholarship Fund at Northern Arizona University. Polingaysi also embarked upon pottery making and writing. Over time, she gained recognition for her pottery designs, which used old Hopi methods, and inspired other Hopi artists such as her nephew, Al Qoyawayma. In her lifetime Polingaysi wrote or collaborated on three books: *The Sun Girl* (1941), the true story of Dawamana, a Hopi maiden, and how she learned the butterfly dance; her autobiography, *No Turning Back: A Hopi Indian Woman's Struggle to Live in Two Worlds* (1964); and *Broken Pattern: Sunlight and Shadows of Hopi History* (1985), the life story of the Hopi maiden Sevansi.

Polingaysi Qoyawayma died on December 6, 1990, and is buried at Pumpkin Seed Hill cemetery at Kykotsmovi with a headstone just below Old Oraibi, where she was born.

Bibliography: The best introduction to Polingaysi's life is her autobiography, which was told to Vada F. Carlson: *No Turning Back: A Hopi Indian Woman's Struggle to Live in Two Worlds* (1964). The full title of her first book is *The Sun Girl: A True Story about Dawamana, the Little Hopi Indian Maid of Old Oraibi in Arizona and of How She Learned to Dance the Butterfly Dances at Moencopi* (1941). Her final book, *Broken Pattern: Sunlight and Shadows of Hopi History* (1985), was written with Vada F. Carlson. Gretchen M. Bataille and Kathleen Mullen Sands, *American Indian Women, Telling Their Lives* (1984), examines personal narratives of American Indian women, including Polingaysi Qoyawayma. Additional biographical information is found in Bataille, ed., *Native American Women: A Biographical Dictionary* (1993), and Liz Sonneborn, *A to Z of Native American Women* (1998). Al Qoyawayma provided additional information for this essay.

MARY JO FOX

QUIMBY, Edith Hinkley. July 10, 1891–October 11, 1982. Biophysicist.

Edith Hinkley Quimby was a pioneer in the use of radionuclides in medicine and the development of standards for radiation protection. Her seventy-five articles outline major research contributions to biophysics, and her books trained a generation of radiologists and established the basis for modern health physics. *Physical Foundations of Radiology* (1944, and later editions), written with Otto Glasser, L. S. Taylor, and James Weatherwax but known simply as Quimby, became the "bible" for thousands of students studying for the American Board of Radiology's physics exam.

Edith's father, Arthur S. Hinkley, earned his living as a farmer although he was trained as an architect. He and his wife, Harriet (whose family name was also Hinkley), had a son and two daughters. Born in Rockford, Illinois, Edith Smaw Hinkley and her family moved several times before settling in Idaho, where she attended Boise High School. Both her father and a high school teacher encouraged her questions about science and taught her to seek her own answers in books and the laboratory.

Edith Hinkley received a four-year scholarship to Whitman College in Walla Walla, Washington, where she became the first woman to undertake the mathematics/physics major. After receiving her BS in 1912, she took a two-year appointment to teach high school physics and chemistry in Nyssa, Oregon. In 1914, a fellowship allowed her to pursue a master's degree in physics at the University of California at Berkeley, where she met fellow graduate student Shirley Leon Quimby. They married on June 9, 1915, and she received her MA in physics in 1916.

Shirley Quimby taught high school in Antioch, California. In 1918, when he enlisted in the navy, his wife replaced him at the school. In 1919, he accepted a position as an instructor at Columbia University and began work on a doctorate in physics. The instructorship paid $1,200 a year, which wasn't enough to live on in New York, so Edith Quimby went looking for a job. Through physics department connections, she landed an interview with Gioacchino Failla, who was looking for an assistant to work on medical uses of radiation in his laboratory at Memorial Hospital. Failla interviewed the young, blond, cheerful woman and, according to Quimby, said, "Well, I never thought of having a woman for an assistant, but I don't mind trying it for six months."

In this way, Quimby joined Failla in a collaboration that lasted for more than thirty years and produced creative and fundamental research on the biological effects of radiation. In 1919, radiation, primarily in the form of radium and its radioactive daughter, radon, was being used as a cure for cancer and as a therapy for other diseases. The doses were measured by erythema, reddening of the skin. Quimby and Failla attempted to standardize doses by using a "faint erythema" that could be detected without attempting to compare degrees of redness. They related this biological effect to source strength and the distance of the source from the patient.

Eventually Quimby thought of using strips of

film as radiation detectors and relating the dosage at a given location to the shadowing of the film there; this was the origin of the standard film badges used to document the exposure of modern radiation workers. Failla and Quimby developed sensors to approximate radiation doses in tissues by techniques such as embedding radon-filled tubes in butter. They found that beeswax absorbs and scatters radiation nearly the same as human tissue, so it could be used to investigate the behavior of radiation in human tissue. In this way, Failla and Quimby mapped out techniques for treating human tumors with radiation and later X-rays while keeping medical personnel safe.

At Memorial Hospital, Quimby served as assistant physicist (1919–32) and associate physicist (1932–43); at Cornell Medical School she was an assistant professor of radiology from 1938 to 1943. In 1943, she followed Failla to the College of Physicians and Surgeons at Columbia University as an associate professor of radiology. Her academic career was unusual for a woman and a non-physician, as well as someone without a doctorate. During this period, she worked part-time on the wartime Manhattan Project studying the biological effects of radiation exposure. In 1954, Columbia appointed her full professor and, in 1960, awarded her emeritus status. Throughout her career and for several years after retirement, she continued research on the clinical use of radioactive isotopes. Her laboratory provided isotopes for clinical use to the medical personnel of Columbia and its associated hospitals.

By the early 1950s, the use of radioactive isotopes in medicine had become so widespread that Quimby developed a course for physicians in the physics and biological effects of radiation. This course gave rise to her widely used publications: *Radioactive Isotopes in Clinical Practice* (1958), with Sergei Feitelberg and Solomon Silver, and *Safe Handling of Radioactive Isotopes in Medical Practice* (1960). Her influence on radiation safety was ensured by her pioneering role in training both physicians and health physicists in its use. Columbia offered both a master's degree in radiological physics and a doctorate in biophysics, and Quimby continued to teach in the program for several years after her nominal retirement.

Quimby's contributions earned significant public recognition. In 1940, she was the first woman to receive the Janeway Medal of the American Radium Society, and in 1941 she was awarded the Gold Medal of the Radiological Society of North America. Many other awards and honors followed. Quimby was a fellow of the American Physical Society and the American College of Radiology and served as president of the American Radium Society in 1954. In addition, she was a member of the Advisory Committee for Medical Uses of Isotopes of the Atomic Energy Commission and served as a consultant on radiation therapy for the U.S. Veterans Administration.

In addition to her professional success, Quimby had a busy personal life. Her husband, a successful professor of physics with interests ranging from the Mayan calendar to the dimensions of racing yachts, supported and guided her career. She had no children but enjoyed reading detective stories, going to the theater, playing bridge, and "domesticity." She was active in the Episcopal Church, the Democratic Party, and the League of Women Voters. She had a gift for friendship and remained a happy, attractive woman, standing five feet eight inches tall and sporting gray eyes and gray hair. She died at her home in New York City in 1982 at the age of ninety-one.

Bibliography: An interview with Edith H. Quimby, videotaped on July 11, 1977, and transcribed, was published by Lauriston S. Taylor and Kelly G. Sauer in 1984 as *Vignettes of Early Radiation Workers;* see pp. 229–41, which contain the quotation from Failla. This material is part of the Human Radiation Experiments (HREX) Archive maintained by the Decision and Information Services Division of Argonne National Laboratory. Margaret (Betsy) G. Ott, "Edith Smaw Hinkley Quimby," in Louise S. Grinstein, Carol A. Biermann, and Rose K. Rose, eds., *Women in the Biological Sciences: A Bibliographic Sourcebook* (1997), pp. 413–23, contains a complete bibliography of Quimby's publications as well as a thorough discussion of her life and work. "Edith H(inkley) Quimby," *Annual Obituary 1982,* pp. 495–97, presents a compact summary of Quimby's career. Harold H. Rossi, "Edith Hinkley Quimby," *Physics Today* 35, no. 12 (December 1982), pp. 71–72, provides another summary of Quimby's career, written by a professional colleague. Shirley B. McDonald, "Edith Smaw Hinckley [*sic*] Quimby (1891–1982): Biophysicist," in Benjamin F. Shearer and Barbara S. Shearer, eds., *Notable Women in the Life Sciences: A Biographical Dictionary* (1996), pp. 335–39, provides a readable summary of her career and life. An obituary appeared in the *New York Times* on October 13, 1982.

RUTH H. HOWES

R

RADNER, Gilda. June 28, 1946–May 20, 1989. Comedian, actress, writer.

Gilda Susan Radner was born in Detroit, Michigan, the second of two children of Henrietta Dworkin and Herman Radner (originally Ratkowsky), a well-to-do realtor and businessman. The name Gilda was taken from the title of her mother's favorite RITA HAYWORTH movie. From childhood, Radner loved show business. Her father, an amateur magician and tap dancer, encouraged her to perform, taking Gilda to Detroit's Riviera Theater to see touring productions of Broadway shows. During winters, the family relocated to Florida because of Henrietta's aversion to the cold, but Radner, shy and overweight, found it difficult to make friends. Her weight became a catalyst for her career as a comedian. Knowing that she was not going to make it on looks, she decided to be funny.

Radner's performance talents were honed at the Liggett School for Girls in Detroit, where she sang in school choir, acted, and directed. Her father's death when Gilda was fourteen was devastating; her lifelong battle with eating disorders began at this time. After graduating from high school in 1964, Radner attended the University of Michigan in Ann Arbor, majoring in public speaking and oral interpretation. She was active in the university's theater department and the Ann Arbor Civic Theater, but she did not yet see theater as a profession; instead she intended to teach emotionally disturbed children. Repeatedly dropping out and re-enrolling, she did not graduate.

In 1969, Radner moved to Toronto. Working at the box office of a local avant-garde theater rekindled her enthusiasm for dramatics. In 1972 she performed in a Toronto production of *Godspell.* A year later, she was cast in the Toronto company of Second City, a Chicago-based improvisational comedy troupe. Through Second City she met comedians John Belushi, Dan Akroyd, and Bill Murray, as well as Lorne Michaels, a young television producer who would become the founding father of *Saturday Night Live,* the television show that was the catalyst for Radner's career. Radner also acted in several television productions for children and had an uncredited part in the film *The Last Detail* (1973).

In 1974, Radner moved to New York to write and perform for the *National Lampoon Radio Hour,* a spinoff of the satirical magazine *National Lampoon,* and then for the *National Lampoon Show,* an off-Broadway cabaret show. The following year she became the first cast member chosen by Lorne Michaels for the "Not Ready for Primetime Players," the ensemble troupe of actor-comedians who formed the cast for *NBC's Saturday Night* (later *Saturday Night Live [SNL]*). The ninety-minute, late-night, live telecast premiered on October 11, 1975. Capturing the imagination of a youthful audience weary of 1960s-style protests and ready to be entertained, its wild, irreverent antics and political and cultural satire made *SNL* a surprise hit. The combination of its hip audience and its innovative performance style represented a seismic shift in television comedy.

With her roster of lovable but eccentric characters, Radner was the heart and soul of the *SNL* ensemble. Most memorable were Emily Litella, the dowdy media analyst known for her malapropisms ("Soviet jewelry" and "too much violins on television") and catch phrase "Never mind"; lispy newscaster Roseanne Roseannadanna ("It's always something"); Baba Wawa, her wicked parody of television journalist Barbara Walters; nerdy adolescent Lisa Loopner; and Rhonda Weiss, a Long Island Jewish "princess." In 1978 her portrayal of these characters won her an Emmy from the National Academy of Television Arts and Sciences for "outstanding continuing performance by a supporting actress in music or variety."

Radner never saw herself as a feminist, or an "-ist" of any sort, but she always spoke up for the few women in the cast and on the staff of the notoriously male-heavy show. Her sense of loyalty was strong, and she was beloved by her colleagues for her warmth and generosity. When NBC executives, who considered her to be the next LUCILLE BALL, offered her a variety show of her own, she refused because she thought it would break up the *Saturday Night* family.

Following the success of co-stars Chevy Chase, Dan Akroyd, and Jon Belushi as independent performers, Radner developed her own one-woman show. *Gilda Radner—Live from New York,* which opened at the Winter Garden theater on Broadway in August 1979, drew mixed reviews from critics who did not appreciate the carryover of her *SNL* personae to Broadway. The following year, the show was released by Warner Brothers as a feature film, with Mike Nichols directing. It bombed, but Radner continued to work with Nichols, who directed her in Jean Kerr's *Lunch Hour* on Broadway that year. Gilda left *SNL* in 1980.

In 1984, Gilda Radner wed for the second time. After a brief (1980–82) marriage to *SNL* guitarist G. E. Smith, she married the love of her life, actor-director Gene Wilder, whom she met on the set of the film *Hanky Panky* in 1981. She co-starred with Wilder in *The Woman in Red* (1984) and *Haunted*

Honeymoon (1986). Though her films were far less successful than her television work, her marriage was fulfilling.

Radner's hunger to have a family of her own led her on a troubled and lengthy quest. She battled infertility, and ultimately had a natural pregnancy that ended in a miscarriage. Meanwhile, her health began to decline, and in 1986 her symptoms were finally diagnosed as ovarian cancer. Radner fought the disease for two and a half years, enduring chemotherapy, radiation, and other treatments, finally finding solace with the Wellness Community, a support group in California for people with cancer. Her open battle against ovarian cancer greatly increased public awareness of this long-dormant woman's health issue.

In 1988, after a seven-year hiatus from television, Radner appeared on *It's Garry Shandling's Show* for what would be her last appearance. With Wilder by her side, she died in her sleep in Los Angeles on May 20, 1989, at the age of forty-two. After her death, Wilder and Radner's friends established Gilda's Club, an organization, now worldwide, that provides support for people and families living with cancer.

Bibliography: Gilda Radner's autobiography, *It's Always Something* (1989), chronicles her struggles with cancer. Former *Saturday Night Live* writer Alan Zweibel brings her to life in *Bunny Bunny: Gilda Radner, A Sort of Love Story* (1994), a series of touching dialogues that chronicles their friendship. With Zweibel, she wrote *Roseanne Roseannadanna's "Hey, Get Back to Work!" Book* (1983). Radner's effect on the *SNL* cast and staff is discussed in Tom Shales and James Andrew Miller, *Live from New York: An Uncensored History of* Saturday Night Live (2002). Also see David Saltman's sentimental biography, *Gilda: An Intimate Portrait* (1992), written by a longtime friend. Radner's performances are recorded on video in *Gilda Live* (1980), the filmed version of her Broadway show, and *The Best of Gilda Radner* (1989). In addition to *SNL* videos, archival footage is also available in the television biographies *Gilda Radner: The E! True Hollywood Story* (1997); *Gilda Radner: It's Always Something* (2002); and *Funny Women of Television* (1991). Biographical information appears in *Current Biography* (1980), pp. 327–29. An obituary appeared in the *New York Times* on May 21, 1989.

LAUREN ANTLER

RAND, Ayn. February 2, 1905–March 6, 1982. Writer, political philosopher.

Of all the writers who came in the great migrations from Russia to America, Ayn Rand was the one who seized most violently its license for self-invention. Born Alisa Rosenbaum in St. Petersburg, she was the eldest of three daughters of Fronz Rosenbaum, a prosperous chemist, and his wife Anna, a housewife. The Russian Revolution, which began when Alisa was twelve, ended the family's bourgeois existence. After studying history at the University of Petrograd from 1921 to 1924, she became determined to emigrate to the United States, which she did, alone, in 1926 at the age of twenty-one. With her Remington-Rand typewriter under her arm, she stayed briefly in New York and Chicago before heading to Hollywood with a new name and her long-nurtured vision of a world of heroic rationalism and passionate purposefulness. In 1929, her visa expiring and her work as a movie extra ending, she married bit-part actor Frank O'Connor and acquired an American identity, which was one of her most prized possessions. By her choice the couple never had children.

During her years in the film industry in Hollywood and New York, Rand began writing fiction. Her first public success was the 1935 play *The Night of January 16th,* which featured an outlaw hero brought to trial before an audience-jury who could vote to convict or acquit. *We the Living* (1936) is a semi-autobiographical treatment of the young Alisa's experiences in Soviet Russia; its heroine dies on the border between the war-torn and imaginatively frozen country of origin and the promised land creatively imaged as "abroad." Her next book, the fable *Anthem* (1938), found only an English publisher.

Rand hated the Marxist Revolution and the Stalinist aftermath with its totalitarian Nazi twin. But it was really nineteenth-century Russia, its religious and political collectivism, its literary and philosophical admiration of suffering, that she rejected. And it was an ideal of nineteenth-century America, inventive and contentious, fearlessly and ruthlessly (one of her favorite words) building and destroying along the trajectory of an intuited Destiny, that she admired and promulgated. A "Romantic Realist," Rand celebrated human volition and reason's power to search out and reach the object of desire or of political logic as it reaches a correct result in mathematics, her favorite subject as a child. Like the heroic characters in her novels, she delighted in the designation "materialist"; secular humanism was her religion.

The publication of *The Fountainhead* (1943) brought Rand the international sensation she had hoped for. Meagerly printed because of the wartime paper shortage, by 1945 *The Fountainhead* was selling a hundred thousand copies a year. The story was and remains controversial, especially for its depiction of a heroine whose loathing for a corrupt world is so fixed that she can enter it only through rape and battle, and a hero whose ego-investment in creative freedom leads him to dynamite the housing project he himself has designed. But its portrait of the heroic ego in service to absolute value touched a human, and eventually a cold-war, nerve.

When Howard Roark is asked by media mogul Gail Wynand whether society's indifference or persecution made him want to start a movement and change the world, *The Fountainhead's* hero demurs: "It didn't make me want to rule people. Nor to teach them anything. It made me want to do my own work in my own way and let myself be torn to pieces if necessary" (p. 554). Rand believed this, but the postwar world and her new eminence brought temptations to teach and rule as well. In 1946 Rand wrote "Screen Guide for Americans" alerting producers how to detect "Communist" ideas in submitted screenplays, and the following year she testified in the same vein before the House Committee on Un-American Activities. In 1951 she and O'Connor moved permanently to New York City, where she supported herself as a writer and lecturer.

In 1957 Rand published *Atlas Shrugged* as an epic drama and philosophical "summa"; in it a mysterious hero named John Galt fights to create a utopian future to replace a mass culture Rand sees as based in intellectual death. She seems to have expected that the novel would catalyze a social change to match the personal change that readers of *The Fountainhead* affirmed. But the protean and pluralist country of her adoption, though privately fascinated, was not publicly persuaded by her fiction. Her teaching turned much more didactic.

In the quarter century after *Atlas Shrugged,* Rand wrote no more novels, but spoke and wrote vivid controversialist prose both within and around the movement of Randian political philosophy and social psychology that came to be called Objectivism. The titles of her collections, including *The Virtue of Selfishness* (1964), *Capitalism: The Unknown Ideal* (1966), and *The Romantic Manifesto* (1969), suggest the element of audacity in her defense of nineteenth-century values. Though she forcefully critiqued leftist political thought, she reveled in an age where debate on great ideas held the world stage. That debate diminished in the mid 1970s, and in 1974 she was diagnosed with lung cancer; these elements contributed to a decline toward pessimism and creative paralysis that, with some recoveries and moments of productivity, lasted until her death in New York City in 1982 at the age of seventy-seven.

The paradox hinted at in the exchange between Howard Roark and Gail Wynand in *The Fountainhead* eventually shadowed the personal life of Ayn Rand. Like Roark, she desired her integrated life to reflect her integrated philosophy, to lead by example and not by fiat. But as the support group around her became an institution, publishing a newsletter, offering courses, attracting both strong and weaker personalities to the cause, Rand's often bracing dogmatism became more troublingly autocratic. As the 1960s climaxed, the group, in a sad reflection of her homeland's history, became subject to personal and political loyalty tests, and finally to purges. After her death a biography by Barbara Branden and a memoir by Branden's ex-husband, founder of the Objectivist Nathaniel Branden Institute and a former lover of Rand's, disclosed a painful history of humans who were not equal to the utopian vision of *Atlas Shrugged.* Yet the legacy of urgent individuality contained in her novels, a sense of life both joyous and responsible for consequences, continues to find legions of appreciative though sometimes wary readers, despite the revelations of human weakness.

Bibliography: All four of Ayn Rand's novels remain in print, as do the collections of her essays published during her life. In addition to the ones mentioned above, they include *For the New Intellectual* (1961), *The New Left: The Anti-Industrial Revolution* (1971), and *Philosophy, Who Needs It* (1982). Rand's will in 1982 designated Leonard Peikoff as heir to her papers, manuscripts, and unpublished writings. Selections published from these papers include Leonard Peikoff, ed., *The Early Ayn Rand: A Selection from Her Unpublished Fiction* (1984); Michael S. Berliner, ed., *The Letters of Ayn Rand* (1995); and David Harriman, ed., *The Journals of Ayn Rand* (1997). Other selections are being edited under Peikoff's direction. Important biographical works include Barbara Branden, *The Passion of Ayn Rand* (1986), and Nathaniel Branden, *My Years with Ayn Rand* (1999). See also Mimi Reisel Gladstein, *The New Ayn Rand Companion* (1999); Chris Matthew Sciabarra, *Ayn Rand, the Russian Radical* (1995); and Gladstein and Sciabarra, eds., *Feminist Interpretations of Ayn Rand* (1999). An obituary appeared in the *New York Times* on March 7, 1982.

JUDITH WILT

RAWALT, Marguerite. October 16, 1895–December 16, 1989. Lawyer, feminist.

Marguerite Rawalt was born in Prairie City, Illinois, the oldest of three children and only daughter of Viola Bell Flake, a housewife, and Charles Rawalt, who operated a farm and a flour mill. The family lived in Oklahoma, New Mexico, and Kansas before finally settling near Corpus Christi, Texas, where Charles sold farm equipment. Marguerite obtained a classics-oriented high school education at Bayview College, graduating at the top of her class. In 1914, the tall, extroverted eighteen-year-old matriculated at the University of Texas in Austin, but left after just one year when family funds ran out.

Rawalt taught high school math for the next two years in Lorena, Texas, and then worked as a secretary and attended business school in San Antonio. There she met Army Air Corps Master Sergeant Jack Tindale, whom she married in 1918. Handsome and outgoing, he failed to establish a successful career, and Marguerite supported him through nine years of marriage. They did not have children. From 1921 to 1924 she worked as secretary and assistant to Texas governor Pat M. Neff, who nourished her interest in government, connected her with important Texans, and supported and encouraged her in the formative years of her career.

Upon her divorce in 1927, Rawalt resumed her maiden name and accepted Neff's invitation to become his secretary at the U.S. Board of Mediation in Washington, D.C. Without an undergraduate degree, she enrolled in George Washington University's law school and began attending evening classes. She earned both a bachelor's and an LLB in 1933, and an LLM in 1936.

In 1933 the Democrats' capture of the White House and her Texas connections helped Rawalt obtain employment in the office of the chief counsel of the Bureau of Internal Revenue; she was the only woman in a group of thirty newly hired lawyers. Having to insist at the outset that she was hired as a tax attorney, not a docket clerk, she worked in several divisions until her retirement in 1965. Although she strove for top-level positions, Rawalt believed that sex discrimination kept her from advancing beyond the post of assistant division head or receiving a judicial appointment or other federal appointments for which she lobbied strenuously.

In 1937, Rawalt married Harry Secord, a widower and retired army officer. She said of him and her mother that they were "my complete friends and my partners" (Patterson, p. 146). Because he too was a federal employee, they kept the marriage secret for two years so as not to run afoul of a policy that limited the employment of married women in the government. Eleven years Rawalt's senior, Secord enthusiastically supported her public ambitions, which she increasingly realized through a series of professional and women's organizations.

In 1942, she was elected president of the National Association of Women Lawyers and campaigned hard to become the first woman president of the Federal Bar Association and the first woman member of the American Bar Association's House of Delegates in 1943. Thereafter turning her attention to women's organizations, she joined the National Woman's Party, the General Federation of Women's Clubs, and Zonta International, all of which gave her means to exercise her feminist energies. From 1954 to 1956, she served as president of the 165,000-member National Federation of Business and Professional Women, endeavoring to shape it into a leading voice for women's rights and establishing a related foundation to promote research on women's status.

By 1960 Rawalt was an avid supporter of the proposed equal rights amendment (ERA) to the Constitution, and she was frustrated by the failure of traditional women's organizations to attack sex discrimination, especially in contrast to the escalating civil rights movement. Consequently, she was thrilled when John F. Kennedy appointed her to his President's Commission on the Status of Women (PCSW) in 1961, where, as the only member to support the ERA, Rawalt negotiated a compromise in the commission's report that kept the possible need for the amendment alive. She served on the PCSW's successor, the Citizens Advisory Council on the Status of Women, through the Johnson administration, deepening her ties with such feminists as PAULI MURRAY and CATHERINE EAST and lobbying to include sex in Title VII of the Civil Rights Act of 1964 and then to secure its enforcement.

Retiring from the IRS in 1965 and recently widowed, at the age of seventy Rawalt took on women's rights as a virtually full-time job. In Washington, she plotted strategy and lobbied officials with an expanding group of feminists, including Martha Griffiths, Mary Eastwood, Phineas Indritz, Betty Friedan, and KATHRYN CLARENBACH, while using her connections with women's organizations to stir activity at the grass roots. She helped plan the organizing meeting of the National Organization for Women (NOW) in October 1966, chaired its legal committee until 1969, and established and served as treasurer of NOW's Legal Defense and Education Fund from 1970 to 1973. In 1968 she also joined the more conservative Women's Equity Action League, whose focus on legal reform was more compatible with her mainstream feminism, and served on its advisory board.

Rawalt worked on several suits challenging discriminatory treatment of women under state laws. She threw herself into the campaign for passage and ratification of the ERA as a co-founder of Women United and the ERA Ratification Council, a member of the board of ERAmerica, and an indefatigable public speaker for the cause. In 1973, she began teaching courses on women and the law at George Washington University. She attended the first International Women's Year Conference, in Mexico City in 1975, and helped plan the National Women's Year Conference in Houston in 1977.

Marguerite Rawalt formed a critical link between an older women's rights generation and second-wave feminism. With younger feminists she picketed the White House and the men-only Oak Room restaurant, and she came to support decriminalization of abortion. Yet she considered sexuality a private concern and resisted efforts by more radical feminists to claim such issues as lesbian rights, which, she felt, threatened support for the movement and distracted it from its crucial role of achieving equality for women through legal reform. She continued to promote women's rights until 1988, when she moved back to Corpus Christi, where she died of complications following hip surgery at the age of ninety-four.

Bibliography: Marguerite Rawalt's extensive papers are at the Schlesinger Library, Radcliffe Institute for Advanced Study, Harvard University. In addition to correspondence and speeches, they contain articles she wrote for legal and other periodicals. With Rawalt's cooperation, Judith Paterson published a full-length biography, *Be Somebody: A Biography of Marguerite Rawalt* (1986). The Columbia University Oral History Research Office has an oral history of Rawalt conducted by John T. Mason Jr. in 1980. See also Elizabeth Shelton, "Fightin' Marguerite Rawalt Is on Law-Path for Women's Rights," *Washington Post,* August 29, 1968; and Lisa Myrick, "At 90, Lawyer-Feminist Rawalt Keeps on Fighting," *Legal Times,* May 5, 1986, p. 11. An obituary appeared in the *Washington Post* on December 22, 1989.

SUSAN M. HARTMANN

RAY, Dixy Lee. September 3, 1914–January 2, 1994. Marine biologist, federal official, governor of Washington.

That Dixy Lee Ray would head a major federal agency and subsequently become the governor of Washington says less about her own accomplishments than about politics in the 1970s. A woman who never fit traditional gender roles and had no interest in feminism, Ray was nominated to federal office by a president who was openly hostile to the women's movement. Having limited political experience and a difficult personality, she was elected governor because she was an outsider and outspoken nonconformist.

Born in Tacoma, Washington, Ray was the second of five daughters born to Frances Adams and Alvis Marion Ray. Her father's family were southern Baptists from Tennessee who moved west in the 1880s. Her mother's family had migrated from the Plains. Neither parent finished high school; instead Alvis Ray went to work in his father's printing business, which provided his family with a modest middle-class lifestyle. Although Ray's given name was Margaret, it was her nickname "the Little Dickens," or "Dicks," that stuck. At the age of sixteen she legally changed her name to Dixy Lee, an acknowledgment of both her southern background and her admiration for the Confederate general. Ray's other early role models included Bertha Landes (socialist mayor of Seattle from 1926 to 1928) and AMELIA EARHART.

An excellent student, Ray graduated from Stadium High School in Tacoma and attended Mills College in Oakland, California, on a scholarship. Her choice of zoology as her major stemmed from her love of the outdoors and her years spent exploring the coastline of her native Puget Sound. She received a BA in 1937 and an MA, also in zoology, the following year. At that point, having no money to pursue another degree, Ray took the option typically available to educated women and began teaching in the Oakland public schools. When America's entry into World War II created a dearth of qualified male graduate students, Ray was able to obtain financial support to pursue her PhD in biology at Stanford University; she received her doctorate in 1945.

That year Ray took a faculty position at the University of Washington, where she was one of two women in the natural sciences. Her research on marine invertebrates subsequently led to a Guggenheim Fellowship, several scientific papers, research support from the U.S. Navy, and an edited volume, *Marine Boring and Fouling Organisms* (1959). She attained the rank of associate professor in 1957 but was never promoted to full professor, which was a source of disappointment for her. Despite her success in forging a university career, Ray ultimately preferred public to academic forums. A skilled speaker, in 1957 Ray was asked to develop a series of public television programs on marine biology. In 1963 she became the first director of Seattle's Pacific Science Center, a new museum dedicated to popularizing science.

Dixy Lee Ray achieved national fame in 1972 when President Nixon nominated her to serve on the Atomic Energy Commission (AEC), despite her lack of background in either physics or nuclear issues. As she acknowledged, the impetus for her appointment came from the pressure on Nixon to nominate a woman. Presumably Ray's experience in explaining science to a lay audience also recommended her at a time when public fear of nuclear power was rising. Ray was the second woman to serve on the commission (MARY INGRAHAM BUNTING was the first) and the first to be appointed to a full term; just six months later, she was promoted to chair, making her one of the highest ranking women in the federal government. But the press was equally fascinated by the fact that she had never married, lived in a custom-built motor home, wore kneesocks, and insisted on taking her two dogs to the office.

Ray's brief tenure as head of the AEC (1973–75) was marked by turmoil. Soon after assuming the chairmanship, she learned of the administration's plans to eliminate the commission. In an effort to save her agency, Ray pushed through a reorganization plan, alienating many agency staffers and powerful federal legislators in the process. Ray also became a strident supporter of the controversial breeder reactor, which drew the ire of environmental groups and prompted consumer advocate Ralph Nader to dub her Ms. Plutonium, a gendered epithet that stuck. Ray could be equally dismissive of her environmental critics, calling them ignorant, crazy, and opposed to human progress. Asked to author the Nixon administration's energy plan in the wake of the 1973 oil crisis, Ray produced *The Nation's Energy Future* (1973), which ardently advocated the rapid development of nuclear power and paid little attention to solar energy and conservation. Predictably, it angered environmentalists. With her current job slated to be abolished, Ray did not receive an energy appointment in the Ford administration. Instead she was offered a scientific advisory position in the State Department, a post that she resigned after only six months.

Ray then turned her attention to electoral politics. Although she claimed to be an Independent, Ray ran for governor of Washington State in 1976 as a Democrat. Like Jimmy Carter, she ran as a political outsider—a status reinforced by her gender and her motor home. Only the second woman (after ELLA GRASSO) to win a governorship who was not succeeding her husband to the office, her election attracted national attention. Ray was elected, and her policies were decidedly conservative. She favored lower property taxes, smaller government, and the development of nuclear power, while opposing growth control and restrictions on oil supertankers in Puget Sound. In the end, all but the most sympathetic observers labeled her administration a failure. Many of Ray's problems stemmed from her inexperience, but her combative style, distaste for the political process, and ability to alienate even close supporters made her wildly unpopular among politicians of both parties, the press, and eventually the public. In 1980 she became the first incumbent governor to lose in a primary election.

As the seventies ended, so did Ray's public career. She retired to Fox Island in Puget Sound, and from there she continued to consult on nuclear power issues and lend her support to charitable and conservative political causes. She also coauthored two anti-environmentalist jeremiads with friend and journalist Lou Guzzo: *Trashing the Planet: How Science Can Help Us Deal with Acid Rain, Depletion of the Ozone and Nuclear Waste (Among Other Things)* (1990) and *Environmental Overkill: Whatever Happened to Common Sense?* (1993). Dixy Lee Ray died at her home on January 2, 1994, at the age of seventy-nine.

Bibliography: Most of Ray's papers documenting her tenure as director of the Pacific Science Center and her federal and state service are housed at the Hoover Institution at Stanford University; the collection includes both official and personal correspondence, as well as numerous photographs of Ray and tape recordings of her speeches. The official records from her gubernatorial years reside in the Washington State Archives in Olympia. Useful biographical information is found in Louis Guzzo, *Is It True What They Say about Dixy? A Biography of Dixy Lee Ray* (1980), a sympathetic biography based primarily on interviews with Ray and her sister Marion Reid. For a more scholarly treatment, see Kurt Kim Schaefer, "Right in the Eye: The Political Style of Dixy Lee Ray," *Pacific Northwest Quarterly* 93 (Spring 2002), pp. 81–93. Useful published interviews with Ray appear in Jennifer James-Wilson and Brenda Owings-Klimek, eds., *Making a Difference: A Centennial Celebration of Washington Women,* vol. 2 (1990); "Profile: Dixy Lee Ray," *BioScience* 24 (September 1974), pp. 489–91; and "A Conversation with Dixy Lee Ray," *Science,* July 11, 1975, pp. 124–27. See also articles in the Seattle *Post-Intelligencer,* October 5, 12, and 19, 1969; the *Christian Science Monitor,* February 23, 1973; and *Time,* December 12, 1977, pp. 26–35. Some interesting material on her early scientific work is contained in Lynn and Gray Poole, *Scientists Who Work Outdoors* (1963), and Iris Noble, *Contemporary Women Scientists of America* (1979). Obituaries appeared in the Seattle *Post-Intelligencer* and the *New York Times* on January 3, 1994.

LINDA NASH

REES, Mina S. August 2, 1902–October 25, 1997. Mathematician, federal official, university administrator.

Mina Spiegel Rees was born in Cleveland, Ohio, the youngest of the five children of Alice Louise Stackhouse and Moses Rees. Her father, who was an insurance agent, was born in New York of German parents; her English-born mother emigrated to the United States in 1882. By the time Rees was of school age her family had moved to New York City, and she attended public school in the Bronx. In 1919 she graduated as valedictorian from Hunter College High School, a selective college preparatory public school for girls in Manhattan, and went on to Hunter College, at that time a women's college that charged no tuition. While at Hunter, Rees was deeply involved in student activities, particularly student government. She graduated summa cum laude as a mathematics major in 1923.

Upon graduating from Hunter, Rees took a job teaching at her old high school and also began full-time graduate studies in mathematics at Columbia University. Believing women to be unwelcome in Columbia's PhD program, she finished her master's courses at Columbia's Teachers College in 1925. The following year she accepted a position as an instructor at Hunter College. Three years into her instructorship, Rees took a leave of absence to study for a doctorate in abstract algebra with L. E. Dickson at the University of Chicago. She did most of the work for her dissertation independently because Dickson had switched his interest from abstract algebra to number theory. Rees received her PhD in 1931 and returned to

Hunter College. She was promoted to assistant professor the following year and to associate professor in 1940.

In 1943 Rees took a leave of absence from Hunter to serve the war effort as technical aide to Warren Weaver, chief of the Applied Mathematics Panel (AMP) of the National Defense Research Committee in the Office of Scientific Research and Development. The AMP promoted the involvement of civilian mathematicians in war-related research, and Rees was responsible for much of its operation, first as Weaver's only technical aide and later as his executive assistant and secretary to the panel. In addition, Rees supervised those contracts issued by the AMP that involved the development of electronic computers. For her work with the panel, Rees received Great Britain's King's Medal for Service in the Cause of Freedom in 1948 and the President's Certificate of Merit in 1958.

Rees had intended to return to Hunter when the Applied Mathematics Panel was disbanded in 1946, but instead she accepted an appointment as head of the Mathematics Branch of the newly established Office of Naval Research (ONR). At ONR Rees established policies for government funding of scientific research, policies that later inspired the design of the National Science Foundation. Rees remained with ONR until 1953, serving as director of the Mathematical Sciences Division from 1949 and as deputy science director during her last year.

Starting as early as 1951, Mina Rees publicly encouraged women to engage in scientific research. Although she later expressed reservations, probably grounded in her own self-doubts, about the likelihood that women would produce much high-quality mathematical research, she eventually understood that there were women who could be successful research mathematicians, provided they received the same opportunities as men.

When Rees left the federal government in 1953, she returned to Hunter College as a professor of mathematics and dean of the faculty. She did not completely sever her relationship with the government, however. While at Hunter she served as a consultant to, or on, advisory committees to such federal agencies as the National Bureau of Standards, the National Science Foundation, the Bureau of the Census, and the Department of Defense. On June 24, 1955, Rees married Leopold Brahdy, a physician she had known for almost twenty years. They lived together in New York City, sharing many recreational and cultural interests, including art, until his death in 1977. In addition to her love of mathematics, Rees was an accomplished painter.

In 1961 Rees left Hunter College to become dean of graduate studies at the newly formed City University of New York (CUNY). Once again she was in charge of setting policy for a newly founded entity, overseeing the start of new doctoral programs, and coordinating the existing graduate programs at the four senior colleges of CUNY: Brooklyn, City, Hunter, and Queens. Rees's commitment to the graduate education of women was evident in the policies set up by CUNY, and she spoke with particular pride of the provision for part-time study and the policy that took child-care expenses into account for financial aid. In 1965, Rees, the only woman dean of a graduate school in a coeducational institution, was presented with the American Association of University Women's Achievement Award.

Rees was named provost of the Graduate Division in 1968 and the following year became the first president of the Graduate School and University Center. In 1970 she was the first woman to chair the Council of Graduate Schools in the United States, and in 1971 served as the first woman president of the American Association for the Advancement of Science (AAAS), when the organization first gave Vietnam War–era dissidents the right to express their political views at its annual meeting.

In 1972 Rees retired from CUNY as president emeritus of the Graduate School and University Center. After her retirement Rees published many papers. Some were descriptions of the place of mathematics in federal government programs during World War II and the postwar era; others concerned the role of graduate education in a changing society. Although these and her other publications give a clear picture of Rees's scholarly approach to her writing, they do not fully capture her extreme dedication to education and the advancement of women. Associate Joan Byers summed up her friend by referring to her love of students, minorities, and women, and her desire to help "the under class" because of her own family background.

In April 1983, when Rees was eighty, the National Academy of Sciences awarded her the prestigious Public Welfare Medal. Two years later CUNY dedicated the library at the Graduate School as the Mina Rees Library. Rees died in 1997 at the Mary Manning Walsh Home in Manhattan at the age of ninety-five.

Bibliography: Autobiographical information on Mina Rees appears in the transcript of a 1978 panel discussion, "Women Mathematicians before 1950," *Newsletter of the Association for Women in Mathematics* 9, no. 4 (July–August 1979), pp. 9–18, and in an interview in Donald J. Albers and G. L. Alexanderson, eds., *Mathematical People: Profiles and Interviews* (1985), pp. 255–67. Rees is one of four women profiled in Kathleen Broome Williams, *Improbable Warriors: Women Scientists in the U.S. Navy in World War II* (2001). Two doctoral dissertations about

Rees appeared after her death: Marimi Matsushita, "A Woman Mathematician and Her Contributions: Mina Spiegel Rees" (EdD dissertation, Teachers College, Columbia University, 1998), and Amy Elizabeth Shell, "In Service to Mathematics, The Life and Work of Mina Rees" (DA dissertation, University of Illinois at Chicago, 2000). Both contain extensive appendixes that include details of her career, her publications, and honors bestowed on her. An appendix in the Matsushita dissertation includes a 1996 interview with Joan Byers. See also Phyllis Fox, "Mina Rees (1902–)," in Louise S. Grinstein and Paul J. Campbell, eds., *Women of Mathematics: A Biobibliographic Sourcebook* (1987), pp. 175–81; Judy Green, Jeanne LaDuke, Saunders Mac Lane, and Uta C. Merzbach, "Mina Spiegel Rees (1902–1997)," *Notices of the American Mathematical Society* 45 (1998), pp. 866–73; and F. Joachim Weyl, "Mina Rees, President-Elect 1970," *Science* 167 (February 20, 1970), pp. 1149–51. Archival sources include the Mina Rees Collection, Archives of the CUNY Graduate School and University Center; Women in the Federal Government Oral History Project, Schlesinger Library, Radcliffe Institute for Advanced Study, Harvard University; and the Applied Mathematics Panel General Records (Record Group 227, Office of Scientific Research and Development), National Archives 2, College Park, Maryland. An obituary appeared in the *New York Times* on October 28, 1997.

JUDY GREEN

REID, Margaret Gilpin. January 27, 1896–October 25, 1991. Economist, home economist, educator.

Margaret Gilpin Reid was born on a farm near Cardale, Manitoba, outside Winnipeg, to Scottish parents of Presbyterian heritage. Her parents, Martha Louise Sparling and John Clements Reid, were farmers. The Reid homestead was established on a quarter section of unbroken prairie, and she was schooled at the local schoolhouse. When she completed her secondary education in Oak River, she trained at the Normal School in Regina and became a schoolteacher.

To Reid, as to many of her counterparts in the American Midwest and the Canadian Prairie, the local agricultural college represented an almost unimaginable opportunity for higher education. In 1916, she registered in the diploma program in home economics at Manitoba Agricultural College, intending to gain new practical skills to take back to her rural students as a high school teacher. While she was a student, a new degree program in home economics was established, and Reid decided to stay on until 1921 to qualify for a bachelor's degree in that subject. Reid did very well academically, and participated in basketball and student government. She was Lady Stick, the equivalent of student body president, representing the women registered in the Faculty of Home Economics, alongside the Senior Stick who represented the men in the Faculty of Agriculture.

Returning to rural Manitoba as a high school teacher no longer appealed to Reid, who never married. Instead she took her new degree to the University of Chicago, where she enrolled in the economics department and wrote a dissertation under the supervision of HAZEL KYRK. After spending the 1929–30 academic year teaching at Connecticut College, Reid returned to her intellectual roots in the Midwest. She earned her PhD in 1931, and after expansion and revision, her thesis was published in 1934 as *The Economics of Household Production.* Starting in 1930 as an assistant professor, she lectured on consumption economics in the department of economics and sociology at Iowa State College in Ames, where she was a colleague of renowned economist Elizabeth Hoyt. She became a naturalized U.S. citizen in 1939 and was promoted to full professor in 1940.

During World War II, Reid moved to Washington to participate in the war effort. In 1943–44, she worked as an economist in the Division of Statistical Standards in the Bureau of the Budget. From 1945 to 1948, she was head of the Family Economics Division in the Bureau of Human Nutrition and Home Economics of the Department of Agriculture. In 1948, she returned to academe as a professor of economics at the University of Illinois at Urbana-Champaign. In 1951 she joined the University of Chicago as a professor of economics; she would remain affiliated with that university until her late eighties.

Margaret Reid, Hazel Kyrk, and Elizabeth Hoyt together believed that home economists understood consumer issues better than other economists and worked to better the lives of ordinary families. In this spirit, Reid's book *Consumers and the Market* (1938) educated consumers about such issues as advertising, labeling, credit, legal protection, and the state's responsibility to protect consumers. By the time Reid returned to Chicago in 1951, her publications were appearing consistently in economics, rather than home economics, journals.

Reid's contributions to the analysis of household production were strikingly original. She was one of the first to recognize that the economics of time allocation in the household could be systematically studied. She tackled the conceptually difficult problem of distinguishing between household production and consumption, and claimed that unless housework is understood as productive work with associated labor costs, neither the contributions women make to the economy nor their labor market decisions can be understood.

Reid considered four alternative methods of valuing the household production of goods and services: opportunity cost, retail price, the cost of hired workers, and the cost of boarding services.

All had weaknesses. Opportunity cost measured the value of potential earnings foregone because of time spent on household production. This method was particularly useful for understanding labor-market decisions made by women; however, it was not especially helpful for putting a value on the goods produced in the household, because it implied that the value of a service provided by an individual who could earn a great deal in a different field was greater than the value of a superior service provided by someone without such alternative earning opportunities. In *Food for People* (1943), Reid estimates the value added by household production by subtracting the cost of purchased inputs from the prices of market substitutes for household-produced goods and services. The third and fourth methods she used for valuing household production used the wage that would be required by individuals hired to do the work, such as domestic servants, or the prices that would be charged by boarding houses for similar goods and services. Ultimately, Reid explained household production as a function of income, geographical differences, race, tastes, and stages of the life cycle.

In 1961 Reid retired from the University of Chicago. In 1962 she published her influential *Housing and Income,* which used Milton Friedman's permanent income hypothesis (PIH) to explore the relationship between housing expenditures and income. Friedman publicly credited Reid as a major influence on his theoretical work, as did Franco Modigliani. In 1980 Reid became the first woman to be designated a Distinguished Fellow by the American Economics Association, in recognition of both her pioneering work on consumer and household behavior and her having inspired a subsequent generation of Nobel Prize winners at the University of Chicago.

In retirement Reid turned her attention to a book on the relationship between health and income; this occupied most of her attention until the late 1980s. The book, which was never completed, included a detailed consideration of related variables such as education level, income security, changes in health care techniques, and changes in permanent income related to position in the life cycle. Margaret Reid died in Chicago in 1991 at the age of ninety-six after a long illness. A major influence on the empirical tradition at the University of Chicago, she left most of her estate to that institution to encourage the study of consumption economics by young economists.

Bibliography: Margaret Gilpin Reid's personal papers and manuscripts are located at the University of Chicago Library. She was a very prolific writer and presented many of her statistical results at economics conferences. A reasonably representative list of her writings can be found in the entry on Reid by Evelyn L. Forget in Robert W. Dimand, Mary Ann Dimand and Evelyn L. Forget, eds., *A Biographical Dictionary of Women Economists* (2000). In 1996, Nancy Folbre and Michele Pujol edited a special issue of *Feminist Economics* (vol. 2, no. 3) in honor of Margaret Reid. This journal issue contains several articles on her work, photographs of the young Margaret Reid, and a newspaper likeness from 1960 when the University of Manitoba awarded her an honorary degree. Franco Modigliani's tribute to Margaret Reid can be found in his Nobel lecture, published as *Life Cycle, Individual Thrift and the Wealth of Nations* (1985). Milton Friedman's appreciation is made clear in *A Theory of the Consumption Function* (1957).

EVELYN L. FORGET

RESNIK, Judith. *See* McAuliffe, Christa.

REYNOLDS, Bertha Capen. December 11, 1885–October 29, 1978. Social work educator and practitioner, political activist.

Bertha Capen Reynolds was born in Brockton, Massachusetts, to Mary Capen, a secondary school teacher, and Franklin Reynolds, an organ builder and tuner. Her English ancestors were among the earliest settlers of the Plymouth and Massachusetts Bay colonies. Traumatic losses of an infant and a three-year-old to illness before Bertha was born left her mother unwilling to emotionally attach herself to Bertha out of fear that she too would die young. When Bertha was only eighteen months old, her mother gave birth to her brother Frank, whose fragile health absorbed all of her mother's care and attention, and within the next year Bertha's father died of tuberculosis. These losses may well have contributed to the feelings of unworthiness and guilt that, combined with a deep desire for religious fulfillment, would eventually lead Bertha to seek justification for her existence in doing "good works."

After the death of her husband, Mary Reynolds returned with her children to live at the Capen family homestead outside Stoughton, Massachusetts, with Bertha's grandfather and elderly relatives. Reynolds considered her children too delicate to be sent to school, and insisted on educating them at home. This insular life left Bertha painfully shy and lacking in social skills. Born and raised a practicing Methodist, the church was her primary link to the world outside her isolated family. Methodism offered her the hope of spiritual fulfillment, but Bertha's repeated failures to experience religious conversion only compounded her feelings of guilt, rejection, and anxiety. In addition to her mother, a secondary school teacher of Latin and chemistry, Bertha was also influenced by her aunt Bessie Capen, headmistress of the Capen

School for Girls in Northampton, Massachusetts, where she attended high school. Reynolds graduated from Smith College in 1908 at the age of twenty-two with a Phi Beta Kappa key and a determination to save the world that she would never outgrow.

After a disheartening year of teaching in the high school department of exclusively black Atlanta University, Reynolds returned home to Stoughton with a growing sense of despondency about her future. On the advice of one of her mother's friends, she underwent psychotherapy with noted psychiatrist James Putnam, one of the first proponents of Freudian theory in the United States. Putnam's recommendation of the one-year certificate program at the Boston School for Social Workers at Simmons College, in which Bertha enrolled in 1912–13, opened a new world for her, providing her with the conversion she could not achieve in Methodism, and validating her as a person with a calling as social work moved from philanthropy to a profession.

Reynolds's first paid social work position (1913–18) was at the Boston Children's Aid Society (BCAS), where she witnessed a new concern with the causes and treatment of mental illness, and rising public awareness of psychiatry and mental health issues. In 1918, Reynolds entered a formal training program in psychiatric social work at Smith College. Freudian theory met her intellectual need for a scientific basis for understanding human behavior, but she objected to the tendency of the medical model of social work practice to locate pathology within the individual. She began viewing behavior as an adaptive response to the transactions between the person and the social system in her or his environment.

From 1918 to 1925, Reynolds was at the cutting edge of the child welfare, mental hygiene, and psychiatric social work movements. She immersed herself in her work and began to develop a philosophy of practice that addressed itself to the natural forces of life adjustment and growth. Her growing reputation in the field led to an appointment in 1925 as associate director of the prestigious Smith College School for Social Work, a citadel of psychiatric social work.

While Reynolds was at Smith, a student introduced her to the writings of Marx and Engels. The Great Depression inspired her search for radical political solutions to the plight of the poor. As a response to the deteriorating work conditions, overwhelming caseloads, and devastation social workers seemed powerless to help their clients contend with, she became a strong and active force in the movement to unionize "rank and file" social workers. In 1934, she wrote the first of her four books, *Between Client and Community* (which first appeared in *Smith College Studies in Social Work* and was not published as a book until 1973). Her unionism, Marxism, and unwillingness to compromise her political and professional beliefs in the face of the changing political climate in the United States separated her from a large segment of her professional constituency and created an irreconcilable rift in her relationship with Everett Kimball, director of Smith College School for Social Work. In 1938, at age fifty-three, she resigned her position.

After leaving Smith, Reynolds spent several years as an itinerant consultant and teacher, and wrote her second book, *Learning and Teaching in the Practice of Social Work* (1942). In 1943, she was hired as the United Seamen's Service Representative in the Personal Service Department of the National Maritime Union, a position that gave her an opportunity once again to work closely with workers in the labor movement. It would be the last professional appointment she would hold. By 1948, with a reputation as a Soviet sympathizer and supporter of the union movement, she was ostracized from the traditional cadres of the social work profession.

Unable to find a job in her field, she returned once more to the family homestead in Stoughton to keep house with her brother Frank. She never married. The remaining years of her life centered around the roles of writer, critic, and thinker that had supported her professional life. She wrote two more books: *Social Work and Social Living* (1951) and an autobiography, *An Uncharted Journey* (1963). She was actively involved in the civic and religious life of the town and wrote a series of essays on religion, Marxism, and ethics, as well as a number of papers, articles, and poems. Through these efforts she attained a measure of success in piecing together the diverse forces of religion, social work, and politics in her life, observing that for the first time she felt whole. She died of natural causes in her Stoughton home at the age of ninety-two, leaving behind a rich heritage of creative and integrative scholarly writings.

Bibliography: The most comprehensive collection of Bertha Capen Reynolds's papers, correspondence, published and unpublished manuscripts (including her 1958 "Informal Autobiography"), diaries, speeches, and other memorabilia can be found in the Sophia Smith Collection, Smith College Library, Northampton, Massachusetts. Another source of informal papers and correspondence is at the American Institute for Marxist Studies in New York. In addition to the books cited in the text, see Bertha Capen Reynolds, "Re-Thinking Social Casework" (pamphlet, 1938) and "The Social Casework of an Uncharted Journey," *Social Work* 9, no. 4 (October 1964), p. 13. Sharon Freedberg, "Bertha Capen Reynolds: A Woman Struggling in Her Times" (PhD dissertation, Columbia University, 1984), describes Reynolds's life and its significance for the field of social work. See also Freedberg, "Religion, Profession, and Politics: Bertha Capen Reynolds's Challenge to

Social Work," *Smith College Studies in Social Work* 56, no. 2 (March 1986), pp. 95–110; and Penina Migdal Glazer and Miriam Slater, *Unequal Colleagues: The Entrance of Women into the Professions, 1890–1940* (1987).

SHARON FREEDBERG

RIGGS, Lutah Maria. October 31, 1896–March 8, 1984. Architect.

Lutah Maria Riggs had a long and successful architectural career centered in Santa Barbara, California, where she specialized in residential design. Born in Toledo, Ohio, she was the only child of Lucinda C. Barrett and Charles B. Riggs, a physician. While Lutah was still a young girl, her father moved to California to recuperate from a lung ailment. Once there, his involvement with the Esoteric Fraternity, a quasi-monastic religious group, distanced him from his family, who remained in Ohio. After Charles Riggs died in August 1905, Lucinda married Theodore Dickscheidt. By this time, Lutah was in grammar school in Middletown, Ohio. By 1912, the family had relocated to Indianapolis, where Riggs attended the Manual Training High School, graduating in 1914.

Later that year, Riggs and her mother moved to Santa Barbara to join Dickscheidt, who had traveled west looking for employment. After briefly attending the local teachers' college, in 1917 she won a scholarship to the University of California at Berkeley, where she entered an architecture program modeled closely on the system of architectural education at the École des Beaux-Arts in Paris. Student assignments covered a range of building types in a variety of historical vocabularies, but all emphasized the plan as the starting point of the design process. Riggs excelled in draftsmanship, producing compelling architectural renderings of great beauty. When she received a BA in architecture in 1919, she became one of forty-two women to be awarded an architecture degree at the University of California before 1920.

Riggs remained at Berkeley taking classes until 1921, when she returned to Santa Barbara, in part to be closer to her mother who was in ill health. With perseverance, she secured a drafting job in the architectural office of George Washington Smith, who enjoyed a thriving practice designing large Spanish Colonial Revival villas for elite residents of Santa Barbara and Montecito, where his office was located. Smith and Riggs worked well together, and she traveled with his family to Mexico in 1922 and to Europe in 1924 on architectural study trips. By 1924, she was officially a partner in the firm and held the title of chief draftsman, although Smith gave her a free hand in much design work; she earned her architectural license in 1928. Smith also helped Riggs finance the purchase of land and the construction of "Clavelitos," the Spanish Colonial Revival house that the younger architect designed for her own use in 1926. When Smith died suddenly of a heart attack in 1930, Riggs and another Smith employee, Harold Edmondson, formed a partnership to continue the work of the office, but Riggs dissolved the partnership in 1931.

During the balance of the 1930s and early 1940s, Riggs worked alone, conducting her practice in the studio that had housed the Smith office. During these years, her biggest project was an expansive Mediterranean-inspired country estate for Baron Maximilian von Romberg in Montecito (1937–38), although she also began to design more modest houses as well, including a number of single-story houses for Rolling Hills (1939–40), a suburban community on the Palos Verdes peninsula that was under the management of an old friend, landscape artist A. E. Hanson. When private construction ceased during World War II, Riggs worked for MGM and later Warner Brothers as a set designer on films, including *The Picture of Dorian Gray* (1943) and *The White Cliffs of Dover* (1943).

After the war, Riggs returned to architectural practice in a partnership with Arvin B. Shaw III that lasted from 1945 to 1951. Working from the converted garage at Clavelitos, Riggs and Shaw were busy with many house remodelings, as well as with the design of the Alice Erving house in Montecito (1949–51). In contrast to the historical revival styles that characterized Riggs's prewar work, this was a modern house with exposed framing, large expanses of window glass, and an open plan. Admired for its sensitive siting, the house provided mountain views while protecting the owner's privacy; these qualities were enhanced by the landscape design provided by Thomas Church, one of California's preeminent modernist landscape architects.

From the early 1950s, Riggs maintained her architectural practice with the support of two or three draftsmen. Although one of her best-known works of this period is the Temple of the Vedanta Society of Southern California (1954–56), a Montecito building inspired by South Indian wooden temples, she continued to specialize in domestic architecture. These domestic buildings included both relatively modest modern houses (like the C. Pardee Erdman house of 1957–59 in Montecito), as well as more extensive estates in pared-down versions of the historical revival vocabularies she had used before the war (like the Wright S. Ludington house, "Hesperides," of 1957–59, also in Montecito).

Although Riggs continued to practice throughout the 1970s (including another Montecito house for Ludington, "October Hill," completed in 1973), the last decades of her career were increasingly devoted to other professional activities. Twice president of the Santa Barbara chapter of the American Institute of Architects (AIA) (1941 and 1953), she served as the preservation officer for the local chapter from 1955 into the 1960s and on the AIA's National Committee on Preservation of Historic Buildings in 1955. When in 1960 she was made a Fellow of the AIA, she was one of three women among the 317 architects inducted into the College of Fellows since its establishment in 1952. At the state level, she joined the Professional Advisory Council to the School of Architecture at the University of California in 1958, served on the State Board of Architectural Examiners between 1961 and 1964, and in 1961 acted as a juror for the architectural competition for a new governor's mansion. At the local level, Riggs was a founding member in 1960 of the Citizens Planning Association of Santa Barbara County Inc. She was also a founding member of the city's Advisory Landmark Committee, and she served from 1960 on the County Historic Preservation Commission.

While willing to speak out on architectural and planning issues, Riggs was a private person with a reserved demeanor who never married. She worked best in small groups, often consulting closely with her clients. She remained active as an architect until 1980, and the end of her career overlapped with early feminist efforts to recover the histories of women in the profession. Like others of her generation, however, Riggs did not welcome this focus on her gender, feeling that it undermined an appreciation for the quality of her work. Lutah Maria Riggs died in Santa Barbara on March 8, 1984, from complications of a perforated duodenal ulcer, at the age of eighty-seven.

Bibliography: The Lutah Maria Riggs archives are located in the Architecture and Design Collection of the University Art Museum at the University of California, Santa Barbara, and include drawings, photographs, business and personal correspondence, daily calendars, and taped interviews with Riggs. The most thorough study of her work is David Gebhard, *Lutah Maria Riggs: A Woman in Architecture, 1921–1980* (1992), which reproduces photographs and drawings of many of her architectural projects and provides a selected list of her designs (built and unbuilt) and an extensive bibliography; especially useful are references to articles about Riggs's work in sources that are not well indexed, such as the *Santa Barbara News-Press,* the *Los Angeles Times,* and *Sunset* magazine. A. E. Hanson offers a firsthand account of working with Riggs in David Gebhard and Sheila Lynds, eds., *An Arcadian Landscape: The California Gardens of A. E. Hanson, 1920–1932* (1985). Among the articles about Riggs's work published in professional architectural journals and national shelter magazines are "Estate of Mr. and Mrs. Allen Breed Walker, Montecito, California," *Country Life,* July 1936, pp. 58–60; "Project for a House in Santa Barbara" (Burton G. Tremaine Jr. house, unbuilt), *Arts and Architecture,* March 1949, pp. 26–29; "Glass Tent: A Santa Barbara House" (Alice Erving house), *House and Home,* September 1952, pp. 114–19; Curtis Besinger, "How to Take Full Advantage of Your Site" (Alice Erving house), *House Beautiful,* May 1961, pp. 102–9, 160, 163–64; and "A House Full of Adaptable Ideas," *House and Garden,* November 1962, pp. 220–25, 269–70. An early example of feminist scholarship that discusses Riggs in the context of women in the architectural profession is Harriet Rochlin, "A Distinguished Generation of Women Architects in California," *Journal of the American Institute of Architects* 66 (August 1977), pp. 38–42. Obituaries for Riggs appeared in the *Santa Barbara News-Press,* March 9, 1984; the *Los Angeles Times,* March 21, 1984; *Progressive Architecture,* May 1984, p. 29; and *Architecture,* May 1984, p. 378.

ABIGAIL A. VAN SLYCK

RINCÓN DE GAUTIER, Felisa. January 9, 1897–September 16, 1994. Political activist, mayor of San Juan.

Felisa Rincón was born in Ceiba, Puerto Rico, the daughter of Enrique Rincón Plumey, a lawyer, and Rita Marrero Rivera, a schoolteacher. The oldest of nine children, she was often sent to live with relatives; this practice exposed her to a variety of experiences at an early age. Before the age of ten she had spent three years with her mother's sister, who was married to a poet. When she was twelve years old, in the year of her mother's death, her father sent her to San Lorenzo to live with his brother Francisco, a pharmacist. She later moved with her father to San Juan, where she attended Central High School. Her father remarried, had a son, and divorced his second wife. He then asked Rincón to leave school to help take care of the house and her siblings in Vega Baja. At the age of seventeen Rincón returned to San Juan, where she met, among her father's friends, the leaders of Puerto Rico's Liberal Party, which favored independence for the island.

Although her father was a member of Puerto Rico's upper class, Rincón had already had considerable contact with the island's poor. While she lived in Vega Baja she had contact with the *jíbaro,* the Puerto Rican peasants who worked the fields of the large plantations owned by people like her father. In San Juan she saw the city's impoverished people struggling to survive in a growing urban center. In 1925, she moved temporarily with one of her sisters to New York City and worked briefly as a seamstress in the garment industry.

In 1932, when women got the right to vote in Puerto Rico, she defied her father and registered. When she expressed to Antonio Barceló, a friend of her father's and leader of the Liberal Party, her disappointment that so few women were taking advantage of the opportunity to become politically active, he made her the party's representative for the registration of women. In this capacity, she went from house to house in San Juan, telling women about their rights and encouraging them to register to vote. She ventured into the slums, particularly La Perla, where she witnessed the living conditions of San Juan's poor. In La Perla she saw the rickety shelters built to and beyond the water's edge; the lack of paved streets, sewers, and public sanitation; the pollution from a nearby slaughterhouse; and children without shoes. These issues would later become the focus of her political career.

The 1932 elections proved disappointing: widespread vote buying by the incumbent party prevented the opposition Liberals from gaining much support. The same pattern of vote buying during the 1936 election campaign led Rincón and fellow activist Luis Muñoz Marín to advocate a boycott, but this position brought them into conflict with the Liberal Party leadership and they were eventually expelled from the party. In 1938 she joined Muñoz in founding the Partido Popular Democrático (Popular Democratic Party, or PPD), which supports commonwealth status as a special relation between the United States and Puerto Rico. In March 1940 she married Genaro A. Gautier, a lawyer who was the PPD's secretary general. The couple had no children.

Widely touted as a possible mayor of San Juan, Rincón initially declined offers to run for office. In 1944 the PPD's Roberto Sánchez Vilella was elected mayor, but he resigned two years later. With his endorsement, Rincón was appointed mayor of San Juan on December 5, 1946. She decided to run for the 1948 elections and won. She was reelected mayor of San Juan four times and served in the position until January 13, 1969.

Affectionately known as Doña Fela, Rincón pioneered many policies that worked to improve the conditions of San Juan's poorest residents. She oversaw the construction, near the city center, of low-cost housing with public spaces, basketball courts, and medical clinics; she pioneered the use of public schools as shelters for those whose homes were destroyed during hurricanes. Rincón also created elder-care centers and a program of legal assistance centers. Her administration instituted the distribution of food and shoes to poor children. To maintain connections with her constituents, she held weekly open office hours and established a system of community representatives that continues to be used.

Rincón also worked to encourage women to participate in the economy. In 1949 she established a program of preschool child-care centers to allow women to find employment outside the home; this program later was a model for the federal Head Start Program in the 1960s. She encouraged the establishment of garment and canning centers that employed women and participated in the creation of various women's organizations, such as the Union of American Women, which in 1954 declared her "Woman of the Americas."

Her terms in government encouraged the conservation of culture in the form of architecture, the arts, and popular festivities. Her administration created the Historical Monument Commission, which successfully preserved much of San Juan's colonial architecture. She rescued the *Actas del Cabildo de San Juan,* the city's colonial Spanish laws, from a rotting basement and published them. San Juan's Tapia Theater was reconstructed in 1949. The plazas of San José, Caleta las Monjas, and Parque de las Palomas were restored in 1961. She helped organize Little League baseball teams, and Hiram Bithorn Stadium was constructed in 1962.

In 1964, Rincón again ran and won San Juan's mayoral elections. During this term, however, she increasingly came under fire from a new generation of politicians within her own PPD, and she declined to seek reelection in 1968. Nevertheless, she remained an active political figure. In 1992, at the age of ninety-five, she was a delegate to the Democratic National Convention in New York City. She died in San Juan on September 16, 1994.

Bibliography: The best sources of information about Felisa Rincón can be found in two locations in Puerto Rico. In 1985 Rincón donated her personal documents to the Archivo General de Puerto Rico, where they are housed as the Felisa Rincón de Gautier Collection. In addition, the Felisa Rincón de Gautier Foundation maintains a museum located in Old San Juan that displays many of her awards, photographs, and personal belongings.

Felisa Rincón's career has attracted little scholarly attention. There are, however, a few popular treatments and books aimed at young readers. Such works include Ruth Gruber, *Felisa Rincón de Gautier: The Mayor of San Juan* (1972); Lawrence Swinburne, *Felisa Rincón de Gautier* (1990); and Magali García-Ramis, *Doña Felisa Rincón de Gautier: Mayor of San Juan* (1995). Perhaps most comprehensive is the lists of awards and accomplishments compiled and published in Leonardo Rodríguez Villafañe's *Felisa Rincón de Gautier: Una Mujer al Servicio de su Pueblo* (1986). Rodríguez provides a quick introductory overview of her life and calls for a more substantive biography. Obituaries appeared in *El Nuevo Día* on September 18, 1994, and the *New York Times,* the *Washington Post,* and the *San Juan Star* on September 19, 1994.

MARIOLA ESPINOSA

ROBINSON, Julia B. December 8, 1919–July 30, 1985. Mathematician.

Julia B. Robinson was an outstanding mathematician who made her greatest contributions in the fields of logic and number theory. She is best known for theorems she discovered and proved that eventually played an essential role in solving Hilbert's Tenth Problem.

Julia B. Robinson was born Julia Bowman in St. Louis, Missouri, the second of two daughters of Helen Hall and Ralph Bowers Bowman. (A third sister was born after her father remarried.) Ralph Bowman, a middle-class owner of a machine tool and equipment company, had completed his secondary education. Helen Bowman had attended business school. Julia's mother died when she was two, so her father sent Julia and her sister to live with their paternal grandmother in Arizona. Ralph Bowman joined his daughters and then married Edenia Kridelbaugh, whom Julia eventually thought of as her mother. When Julia was nine years old she contracted scarlet fever and then rheumatic fever, which caused her to have to be isolated from everyone except her father for long periods of time. Eventually, she missed more than two years of school, but through tutoring she was able to catch up with her peers in the ninth grade.

At San Diego High School, Julia preferred mathematics to all other subjects and, though the only girl in her classes, continued taking mathematics through her senior year. At age sixteen she entered San Diego State College, now San Diego State University, where she majored in mathematics. During her sophomore year, her father committed suicide, and although the family financial situation was difficult, Julia did succeed in remaining in school.

After her junior year, she was able to transfer to the University of California at Berkeley, where she took a number theory course taught by Raphael Robinson. She received her BA in 1940 and her MA the following year, but had difficulty finding a job using mathematics. Therefore, she obtained a position as a teaching assistant at Berkeley and continued her studies. Meanwhile, Julia and Raphael Robinson's relationship developed on a more personal level, and in December 1941 they were married.

Because she wanted a family, Robinson was excited when she finally became pregnant but severely disappointed when she miscarried. During a bout with viral pneumonia, Robinson found out that her childhood rheumatic fever had left her with scar tissue in the mitral valve of her heart. Her doctor advised her never to attempt to have children again and predicted that her heart would fail prematurely. Crushed by this news, she tried to divert her attention by returning to her study of mathematics.

After spending the 1946–47 academic year at Princeton, Julia and Raphael returned to Berkeley, where she began to work toward a PhD with Alfred Tarski. She completed her thesis, entitled "Definability and Decision Problems in Arithmetic," and received her PhD in 1948. During this time she also began working on the most famous problem she is associated with, the tenth problem on David Hilbert's list of twenty-three unsolved problems. (Hilbert, a prominent late-nineteenth-century German mathematician, challenged his fellow mathematicians at the Second International Congress of Mathematics in 1900 to solve twenty-three problems that he believed were important to the development of mathematics.) She began working on the problem only because it was appealing to her, and she later admitted that she probably would not have taken it on had she known that it was on Hilbert's list.

During Raphael's sabbatical year in 1949–50, Julia did research at the RAND Corporation in Santa Monica. At RAND, she was able to solve George Brown's "fictitious play" problem, which some people at the time believed to be one of the most important theorems to date in elementary game theory. She published her results in the paper "An Iterative Method of Solving a Game" (1951). In 1950, Robinson presented a paper on her work on existential definability at the first post-war International Congress of Mathematics at Harvard. There she met and began a collaboration with Martin Davis and Hilary Putnam that eventually led to many discoveries of significant pieces to the solution of the Tenth Problem.

During the 1950s, Robinson did some work on hydrodynamics at Stanford under Al Bowker. Though she worked very hard, she was not able to develop any significant results, but she never hid this fact because she believed that a person's failures should be included along with her successes. Nepotism rules at Berkeley did not allow members of the same family to teach in the same department, so Robinson was relegated to the rank of part-time lecturer in mathematics during the 1960s and 1970s.

Soon after a joint paper with Davis and Putnam was published, Robinson began to have trouble with her heart, just as the doctor in San Diego had foretold. In 1961 she had surgery to remove obstructions in her mitral valve, followed by two other major operations in the 1960s. Although these medical problems slowed her down somewhat, her rehabilitation allowed her to enjoy for the first time activities such as biking, hiking, and canoeing.

Though very frustrated at not being able to find a solution to Hilbert's Tenth, Robinson continued on in this work throughout the 1960s and eventually came close to a solution except for missing an important Diophantine relation. Then in February 1970, after reviewing one of her papers, a twenty-two-year-old Russian mathematician named Yuri Matijasevich proved the relation that was needed to solve Hilbert's Tenth Problem. In the next few years, Robinson and Matijasevich collaborated to improve and extend the solution.

In 1975, Julia Robinson became the first woman mathematician to be elected to the National Academy of Sciences. With the accolades came, finally, an appointment at Berkeley as a full professor that same year. In 1982, she was nominated for the presidency of the American Mathematical Society (AMS). Her husband wanted her not to accept the nomination, so that she could preserve her energies for mathematics, but others convinced her that as a woman and a proven mathematician she should. Robinson had always tried to encourage talented women to become research mathematicians, and her position as president of the AMS allowed her to have even greater influence. Other honors quickly followed, including election to the American Academy of Arts and Sciences and a generous grant from the MacArthur Foundation.

In August 1984, as she presided over the AMS summer meeting, Julia Robinson learned during an emergency hospital visit that she had leukemia. Less than a year later, she died from the disease in Berkeley at the age of sixty-five.

Bibliography: At the end of her life, Julia Robinson collaborated with her sister, Constance Reid, on "The Autobiography of Julia Robinson," which appeared in *College Mathematics Journal* 17, no. 1 (1986), pp. 3–21. Reid put this article, along with a collection of writings from some of Julia's friends and colleagues, into a book, *Julia: A Life in Mathematics* (1996). See also Yuri Matijasevich, "My Collaboration with Julia Robinson," *Mathematical Intelligencer* 14, no. 4 (1992), pp. 38–45.

Julia Robinson published many papers during her mathematical career, all of which can be found in Solomon Feferman, ed., *The Collected Works of Julia Robinson* (1996). She also coauthored a number of other papers. An obituary appeared in the *Los Angeles Times* on August 5, 1985. See also the *Notices of the American Mathematical Society* 32 (October 1985), pp. 739–42 for an obituary and remembrances by colleagues.

SARAH L. NORDMANN

ROCHE, Josephine. December 2, 1886–July 29, 1976. Industrialist, federal official, social welfare and labor activist.

Born to the business class in Neligh, Nebraska, Josephine Aspinwall Roche was the only child of John J. and Ella Aspinwall Roche. Both parents graduated in 1873 from Wisconsin's State Normal School and taught briefly before making a life in Nebraska. They lavished on their daughter the finest education available, first at Gates Academy in Nebraska and then at Vassar College. By Roche's graduation in 1908, her parents had moved to Denver, where her father officiated in one of Colorado's major coal-producing enterprises, the Rocky Mountain Fuel Company (RMF).

Between 1908 and 1915, Roche developed commitments that drove her long and varied career. These convictions grew from her immersion in two extraordinary reform communities. One was in New York City, where as a graduate student in political science at Columbia University she hardened her commitment to social science research as the basis for social reform and earned her MA in 1910. The other was in Denver, where the early enfranchisement of women exposed her to the bruising battles of partisan politics. In 1912, Roche joined Denver's police force at the urging of the police commissioner. Her zeal for the force's anti-prostitution campaign aroused such opposition from local businesses, however, that she soon resigned and intensified her work for the new Progressive Party. This partisan vehicle attacked the interests opposed to her police work and promoted national legislation for old age and disability pensions as well as the right of workers to organize. In 1913, Roche became the party's organizer for women and secretary of the Colorado Progressive Service. The party died in 1916, but its platform lived on in Josephine Roche.

The next decade broadened Roche's experience. From 1915 to 1918, she directed the Girls Department of Denver's Juvenile Court; from 1919 to 1923 she ran the U.S. Foreign Language Information Service (FLIS). On July 2, 1920, Roche married Edward Hale Bierstadt, a writer who was also an associate director in FLIS. Ultimately, the pair proved more passionate about FLIS's mission to integrate immigrants into the American nation than about each other. The marriage lasted only two years and produced no children. From 1923 to 1925, Roche managed the Editorial Division of the Children's Bureau in the federal Department of Labor. In 1925, she returned to Denver because of her father's failing health and acted as referee in the Juvenile Court.

With her father's death in 1927, Roche's life took a dramatic turn toward a field where she would make one of her deepest marks: the coal industry. Inheritor of her father's holdings in RMF, Roche amassed enough additional shares to become majority stockholder. She then recreated RMF as an experiment in relations between labor and capital. Astonishing her anti-union competitors, she invited the United Mine Workers of America (UMW) to organize the company's workers. In August 1928, Rocky Mountain Fuel signed a historic contract with the UMW, which laid one foundation stone for nationwide collective bargaining in the coal industry. As a woman running a major industrial concern, Roche was unique. As an industrialist intent on using her company equally to serve consumers, workers, and investors, she pursued a rare vision.

Her progressive approach to industrial management did not go unnoticed. When Franklin D. Roosevelt assumed the U.S. presidency in 1933, he tapped Roche to help set standards in the coal industry under the National Industrial Recovery Act. A committed New Dealer, Roche ran in the Democratic primary for governor of Colorado in 1934 with the slogan, "Roosevelt, Roche, and Recovery." She lost that bid for elective office, but when Roosevelt immediately appointed her assistant secretary of the Treasury, she became the second-highest ranking woman in the federal government after Labor Secretary FRANCES PERKINS. In the Treasury, Roche supervised the Public Health Service and served on the President's Committee on Economic Security, which drafted recommendations for the 1935 Social Security Act. She also chaired the executive committee of the National Youth Administration, and eventually the President's Interdepartmental Committee to Coordinate Health and Welfare Activities. From these positions, Roche helped design U.S. welfare policy in the 1930s and, presciently, helped draw up a blueprint for national health policy that shaped federal programs finally created in the 1960s.

The 1940s brought a change of venue for this restless daughter of privilege. In response to problems at RMF, she left the Treasury in 1937. From 1939 to 1944, she served as president of the National Consumers' League. Rocky Mountain Fuel continued to face serious financial problems, and it declared bankruptcy in 1944; she resigned as president and director in 1950. By this time, she occupied a more effective position from which to attempt humanizing the coal industry: in 1948, she became director of the UMW's Health and Welfare Fund. Here, Roche developed a health and welfare system for miners that closely tracked her earlier suggestions for government-sponsored programs. The Fund delivered health care even to remote valleys of Appalachia, where miners and their families had rarely visited a doctor before. Roche directed this model enterprise until 1971, when violent rivalries among union leaders finally pushed her out at age eighty-five. She died five years later in Bethesda, Maryland.

As a female executive in heavy industry and a director of agencies staffed by men, Josephine Roche stood in the vanguard of women's advancement during the twentieth century. Promoting women was not, however, her primary interest: her life's work was motivated by her desire to minimize class differences without abandoning capitalism. As an architect of health and welfare policies, Roche set an agenda for state development that shaped federal legislation well into the 1960s, and she helped design social welfare programs that sustained literally millions of Americans. Fittingly, such a remarkable career earned her many honors, including the designation by *American Women* in 1936 as one of the ten outstanding women in the United States. Probably her most cherished recognition came in a note attached to an award from the American Labor Health Association in 1958. Penned by John L. Lewis, president of the UMW, the cover letter read: "A tribute, worthy of a goddess, coming from the hearts of men."

Bibliography: The most important sources on Roche's life are two manuscript collections in Norlin Library at the University of Colorado, Boulder: the Josephine Roche Papers, which contain the closing quotation, and the Records of the Rocky Mountain Fuel Company. In addition, the National Archives houses records of Roche's work at the Department of the Treasury and in the Department of Labor. Her leadership of the Interdepartmental Committee to Coordinate Health and Welfare Activities is documented in the Franklin D. Roosevelt Presidential Library in Hyde Park, New York, and her service to the United Mine Workers is revealed in the archives of the United Mine Workers of America Health and Retirement Fund at West Virginia University in Morgantown. Many popular publications covered Roche during her lifetime. Although they sometimes contain errors of fact, they give some sense of her personality and reputation. See George Creel, "Josephine Roche of the Denver Police," *Woman's Journal* 44, no. 28 (July 12, 1913), p. 218; Creel, "Up from Riches," *Colliers,* June 15, 1935, pp. 14+; Millard Milburn Rice, "Roosevelt, Roche and Recovery," *Literary Digest* 118 (September 1, 1934), p. 8; and "She's a Tender-Hearted Battler," *Rocky Mountain News,* May 25, 1934. On her groundbreaking work at Rocky Mountain Fuel, see Mary Van Kleek, *Miners and Management* (1934) and "A Coal Company Looks Forward," *New Republic,* September 19, 1928, pp. 119–21. No full-length biography analyzes Roche's life, but several articles rehearse elements of her life story. These include Marjorie Hornbein, "Josephine Roche: Social Worker and Coal Operator," *Colorado Magazine* 53 (1976), pp. 243–60; and "Josephine A. Roche: Champion of the 1930s Working Class," *Colorado Heritage* (1994), pp. 45–46. Richard Mulcahy has ably narrated the history of the UMW Health and Welfare Fund in *A Social Contract for the Coal Fields: The Rise and Fall of the United Mine Workers of America Welfare and Retirement Fund* (2000). An obituary appeared in the *New York Times* on July 31, 1976.

ROBYN MUNCY

ROEBLING, Mary G. July 29, 1905–October 25, 1994. Banker, financier.

Mary G. Roebling, one of the first women to head a major commercial bank, was born Mary Gindhart in West Collingswood, New Jersey, the daughter of Mary Wilhelmina Simon, a music teacher, and Issac Dare Gindhart Jr., a telephone company executive. Mary, the oldest of four children, attended Moorestown High School but did not finish, leaving in 1921 to marry Arthur Herbert, a New York banker and musician. The following year, she gave birth to a daughter, Betty Herbert. After Arthur abruptly died of blood poisoning in 1924, she returned with her young daughter to live with her parents before moving to Philadelphia to work as a salesgirl at Blum's department store. From there she took a job at a Philadelphia brokerage firm, working first as a secretary and then as a customer's consultant (not to be mistaken for the more prestigious position of broker, which was not open to women). In the evenings she took courses at the Wharton School at the University of Pennsylvania, studying merchandising and business administration. Sometime during this period she also remarried, to Hugh D. Graham. They were soon separated and presumably divorced. In 1933, she met and married Siegfried Roebling, a banker and owner of Trenton Trust Company and the great-grandson of Brooklyn Bridge designer John Roebling. With Siegfried, she had a son, Paul, born in 1934.

When Siegfried unexpectedly died of a heart attack in 1936, his estate passed to his son Paul, with Mary to act as trustee. The estate, however, was essentially insolvent, the Depression having reduced the value of his Trenton Trust stock to practically nothing. Mary Roebling would later say that she had inherited an opportunity and nothing more. She quickly involved herself in the affairs of the bank and by the end of 1936 had herself and her father appointed to the board of Trenton Trust. The following year she declared herself its president. Of all bank presidents in the country at that time, Mary Roebling was one of the youngest (age thirty-one) and one of the few women.

To rebuild Trenton Trust's assets, Roebling emphasized the services offered by the bank. She insisted on a more "homey" and personalized approach, transforming the bank into a "family." While publicly pursuing what might be considered more "feminine" business methods—focusing on the needs of the customer by making banking more comfortable—Roebling sharpened her skills by commuting to New York City to take economics courses at New York University. One of her adversaries on Trenton Trust's board noted that she was a very powerful woman who could be ruthless when necessary. In 1958 she was the first woman elected governor of the American Stock Exchange, a position in which she served until 1962.

Roebling's business success can be attributed to her aggressive and innovative business practices, her philanthropic efforts, her political connections, and her decision to devote her entire life to her career. To Roebling's mind, banks were "department stores of finance," and with this perspective she emphasized service, opening branches at train stations and promoting drive-in and walk-up banking. She used a wide variety of marketing gimmicks to attract customers, like periodically redecorating the main bank to reflect a particular theme. Realizing women's untapped economic significance, she sought to tailor bank services to women's needs, establishing a women's division and offering special services for women's clubs and groups. She pursued philanthropy as yet another way to market her bank. An early purchaser of Israel Bonds, Trenton Trust was the first city bank to appoint a Jew to its board of directors. As whites moved into the suburbs, Roebling built herself an elegant townhouse in downtown Trenton, saying that she believed people should live where they made their living.

Politically she was a loyal Republican and a fierce supporter of capitalism. A friend to Presidents Eisenhower, Nixon, and Reagan, she was profoundly anti-communist. She championed a strong military, served under several administrations as an aide to the secretary of the army, and founded the Army War College Foundation to raise money for the war college in Carlisle, Pennsylvania.

When Trenton Trust was acquired by National State Bank of New Jersey in 1972, its assets had grown from $17 million to over $200 million. Roebling was quickly elected chairman of the combined institutions. During her tenure she also helped found the Women's Bank N.A. of Denver, which opened in 1978. As chairman of the board of the Women's Bank, Roebling went out of her way to avoid the mistakes made by the organizers of the ill-fated First Woman's Bank of New York, which lost money during its first two years and closed after losing close to a million dollars. Roebling made sure that those directing the Denver bank had financial experience, and she downplayed the feminist goals of the enterprise by insisting that the bank would be a bank for everyone.

Roebling believed that women had an even greater stake than men in the free enterprise system. Her political conservatism was tempered by a nod to liberal feminism wherein she advocated economic inclusion and equal opportunity. Women, she argued, must financially empower themselves and push for equal pay for equal work. Title VII of the Civil Rights Act of 1964 had presented women with an opportunity to gain entry into new economic positions and they must seize the moment. She was, however, focused on material security as the way to female liberation. She objected to the second-wave feminist philosophy that "the personal is political," and to the lumping together of issues like abortion and lesbianism with what she believed to be the more important economic issues, like equal pay. Arguing that capitalism frees women, she summed up her economic feminism when she wrote in 1966 that "women, even more than men, have reason to feel indebted to the American Free Enterprise system."

When Mary Roebling retired as chairman of the board of National State Bank in 1984, it reported assets of $1.2 billion. Active in civic and philanthropic circles until the end of her life, she died in 1994 at her home in Trenton at the age of eighty-nine.

Bibliography: Mary Roebling's papers are available at Special Collections and University Archives, Rutgers University Libraries, New Brunswick, New Jersey. The most complete biographical account is by Patricia Rooney Faulk, "Gender and Power in the 20th Century: Mary G. Roebling, Pioneer Woman Banker" (PhD dissertation, University of Pennsylvania, 1992). See also *Current Biography* (1960), pp. 342–44, and Women's Project of New Jersey Inc., *Past and Promise: Lives of New Jersey Women* (1990). Also of interest is Mary Roebling, "Women's Stake in the Free Enterprise System," *Manage Magazine* 18, no. 10 (1966), pp. 37–44, which contains the final quotation. An obituary appeared in the *New York Times* on October 27, 1994.

SUSAN M. YOHN

ROGERS, Ginger. July 16, 1911–April 25, 1995. Actress, dancer.

Ginger Rogers, whose dancing and acting talents delighted audiences in Hollywood's heyday, was born Virginia Katherine McMath in Independence, Missouri, to Lela Emogene Owens, a secretary from Council Bluffs, Iowa, and William Eddins McMath, an electrical engineer from Scotland. Their first child had died in infancy, and Eddins and Lela separated before Virginia, their second child, was born. They later divorced. The constants in Rogers's often unsettled life—she was twice abducted by her estranged father—were her devotion to her mother and her devotion to Christian Science, which she shared with her mother. In Lela, Rogers also inherited an activist mother who championed prison reform and enlisted in the marines during World War I. Lela's second husband, John Logan Rogers, an insurance agent, never legally adopted Virginia, but he gave her his name and a new life in Fort Worth, Texas, where the indefatigable Lela soon found work as a theater critic. Rogers, who went by the name Ginger from an early age, attended the Fifth Ward Elementary School. By the time she was fourteen, however, her theatrical career began to take off, and her formal education ended; her real schooling took place backstage of the Majestic Theater, watching and mimicking some of the acts her mother was sent to review.

In 1925, Rogers won the Texas state Charleston contest and began a month's tour of the southern vaudeville circuit that lasted three years and eventually brought her to New York City. She made her Broadway debut in December 1929 in *Top Speed*. Ten months later she was starring in George Gershwin's *Girl Crazy*, a musical that featured "Embraceable You," the aching ballad written expressly for her. Under contract with Paramount, she made movies whenever she wasn't performing in Broadway shows. In 1931 she broke her contract with Paramount, signed a new one with RKO, and left New York, her mother by her side, for Hollywood.

Movie stardom, unlike her Broadway success, did not come at top speed. Her obliging Anytime Annie in *42nd Street* (1933), who famously only said "No" once and then didn't hear the question, and her breezy pig-Latin rendition of "We're in the Money" to open *Gold Diggers of 1933* (1933) did catch the public eye, but not until she was paired with Fred Astaire in *Flying Down to Rio* (1933) did Rogers, after nineteen movies, become a screen presence who commanded more than passing, amused attention. Fred and Ginger, as they are affectionately remembered, would make nine movies for RKO between 1933 and 1939. The best of them, *The Gay Divorcee* (1934), *Top Hat* (1935), *Swing Time* (1936), and *Carefree* (1938), were enlivened by Roger's gift for conveying, then surmounting, female wariness before the elegant but importunate male. *The Barkleys of Broadway*, made for MGM in 1949, was the coda to their screen partnership.

The incandescent magic of their pairing is easier to marvel at than describe. Katharine Hepburn quipped that Astaire gave her class and she gave him sex appeal. David Thomson was struck by how "her robustness rubbed off on his remoteness so that he seemed warmed by her, just as she gained cool in his draft" (Thomson, p. 645). Her sexual charm is undeniable, but what entrances is the cleverness and heart that move her to respond, often reluctantly, to Astaire's summons to the dance floor, where her own transfiguration awaits her. Arlene Croce celebrates the resulting metamorphosis: "She was a hot mama at the age of twenty-two. . . . Astaire would turn her into a goddess" (Croce, p. 22).

Her comic gravity matured into a moral outlook in the films she made without and after Astaire. An amused skepticism grounded her Academy Award–winning portrayal of Kitty in *Kitty Foyle* (1940), a role she accepted only after insisting that the script eliminate what she deemed objectionable sexual material. What might be prudish in the performer is sublimated in her screen character, who was born and arguably fully developed in *Stage Door* (1937), but persisted in her sympathetic portraits of resilient young women of integrity and resolve: a prostitute's daughter in *The Primrose Path* (1940); Polly Parrish, a salesgirl who loses a job but acquires a foundling in the socially adventurous *Bachelor Mother* (1939); the tender-hearted class interloper in *Fifth Avenue Girl* (1939); and a disillusioned working girl trying to go home in Billy Wilder's pseudo-pedophilic comedy, *The Major and the Minor* (1942). She is at her most lively and determined in *Vivacious Lady* (1938), but her freest performance is as the cheerfully vulgar Roxie Hart in the movie of the same name, which appeared in 1942 and was the basis for the musical *Chicago*.

She was the highest-paid female star in 1945, but already there were fewer roles that made credible, humane use of her defensive wit and emotional stamina. Except for the prankish fun she shares with Cary Grant in *Monkey Business* (1952), many of her later films bore titles hinting at waning or depressed spirits: *Perfect Strangers* (1950), *Storm Warning* (1951), *Forever Female* (1953), *Tight Spot* (1955), *Twist of Fate* (1954), and the implausible *Black Widow* (1954), in which Rogers for the first and only time played a femme fatale, literally. Her nature was to be not a killer, but a survivor. She survived five marriages, none of which produced any children: the first to fellow dancer Edward Jackson Culpepper, which lasted only a few months in 1929 (the divorce was finalized in 1931), then longer runs with actor Lew Ayres (1934–41); Jack Briggs, a serviceman she met at a war-bond rally (1943–49); Jacques Bergerac, a French lawyer and aspiring actor almost sixteen years her junior (1953–57); and William Marshall, a producer and director (1961–67).

Her final film was 1965's *Harlow*, but both financial need and love of performing kept her from well-deserved retirement. She ended her career as a still leggy blonde, appearing on television, touring with *The Ginger Rogers Show*, and headlining revivals of such Broadway standards as *Hello, Dolly!* and *Mame* from Europe to Australia. Rogers revisited her own life in her 1991 autobiography, *Ginger: My Story*. She died of natural causes at her home in Rancho Mirage, California, at the age of eighty-three, and is buried next to her mother in Oakwood Memorial Park in Chatsworth, California.

Bibliography: Sheridan Morley's amply illustrated *Shall We Dance: The Life of Ginger Rogers* (1995) is the only biography of Rogers; it takes little issue with Rogers's own account of her life, *Ginger: My Story* (1991). The best writing on her art as a dancer is Arlene Croce, *The Fred Astaire & Ginger Rogers Book* (1972). For her film work in general, the books to consult are John Kobal, *Gotta Sing, Gotta Dance: A Pictorial History of Film Musicals* (1971); Homer Dickens, *The Films of Ginger Rogers* (1975); and Joycelyn Faris, *Ginger Rogers: A Bio-Bibliography* (1994). David Thomson offers a brisk and shrewd summary of her film career in his indispensable and highly readable *A Biographical Dictionary of Film*, 3rd ed. (1994). Rogers is featured in James Robert Parish, *The RKO Gals* (1974); Parish and Michael R. Pitts, *Hollywood Songsters* (1991); and David Shipman, *The Great Movie Stars 1: The Golden Years* (1995). Fans of Rogers and students of mother–daughter psychology might find passing interest in Lela Rogers's *Ginger Rogers and the Mystery of the Scarlet Cloak: An Original Story Featuring Ginger Rogers, Famous Motion-Picture Star, as the Heroine* (1942). Obituaries appeared in the *New York Times* and the *Los Angeles Times* on April 26, 1995.

MARIA DIBATTISTA

ROLLE, Esther. November 8, 1920–November 17, 1998. Actress, dancer.

A pioneering actress and a strong advocate in the fight against stereotypical portrayals of African Americans in the media, Esther Rolle gained national recognition during the 1970s in television sitcoms for her supporting role as Florida Evans on *Maude*, and later for her starring role on *Good Times*. Ironically, she often played one of the roles that she fought against in the media—domestics. As a dark-skinned, stout actress, Rolle admitted that this kind of role "was the reality for women with my physical appearance." She recognized that many black women were indeed maids and domestics, but she detested the stereotypical image of the maid with "the rolling eyes who doted on her white charges but ignored her own children," and she struggled to provide more enlightened portrayals over the course of her career.

Esther Rolle was born the tenth of eighteen children to Elizabeth Dames and Jonathan Rolle in Pompano Beach, Florida. Her parents were vegetable farmers who had migrated from the Bahamas. They encouraged several of her older siblings to organize a dramatic and musical group to perform at local churches and community organizations, but the group had disbanded by the time Esther was old enough to join. Two of her sisters, Rosanna Carter and Estelle Evans, would pursue professional acting careers.

Esther Rolle attended Booker T. Washington High School in Miami and then moved to New York City to live with her sister Rosanna. Little is known about her personal life in this period. She studied at Spelman College in Atlanta in the 1940s, and also at Hunter College and the New School for Social Work in New York City. She found work in New York's garment district and was briefly married to a pants presser. This only known marriage ended in divorce with no children.

In the late 1950s, Esther and sister Rosanna performed with the Asadata Dafora Dance

Troupe, where Esther became a principal dancer. Asadata, a Sierra Leone–born choreographer/dancer, was a prominent figure in dance circles from the 1930s to the late 1950s. Esther Rolle also danced with the Shogola Obola Dance Company, but her emerging focus on acting took precedence over her career as a dancer.

After appearing in two off-Broadway plays, *Ballet behind the Bridge* and *Ride a Black Horse,* she made her first major off-Broadway appearance in Jean Genet's *The Blacks* in 1961. She toured in *Purlie Victorious* in 1962, and in 1964 made her Broadway debut in James Baldwin's *Blues for Mr. Charlie.* As one of the founding members of the renowned New York–based Negro Ensemble Company (NEC), she performed in seven of the company's productions from 1968 to 1971, with her most notable performance being in *Happy Ending.* She continued her off-Broadway career in such shows as *Rosalie Pritchett* in 1972. During the 1970s she launched into television, where she appeared on the police series *N.Y.P.D.* and as Sadie Gray in the daytime drama *One Life to Live.*

In 1972, while performing the role of Miss Maybelle in Melvin Van Peebles's musical *Don't Play Us Cheap,* she attracted the attention of TV producer Norman Lear. Esther Rolle joined Lear's sitcom *Maude* in the role of the outspoken maid Florida Evans in the household of a liberal white employer played by Bea Arthur. Rolle initially rejected the role until she was assured that the character of Florida Evans would not be a stereotypical black maid. She also insisted on having a voice in the development of the character. Esther Rolle proved to be such a hit on *Maude* that Lear spun off the sitcom *Good Times* in 1974 to showcase her talents.

Good Times, created by African American writer Eric Monte, portrayed a black two-parent family with three children confronting the harsh realities of urban life in a southside Chicago housing project. One of Rolle's conditions in accepting the part was to be able to alter any objectionable dialogue in the script. Considered a groundbreaker, *Good Times* was the first black family sitcom of the 1970s. It was a huge success and one of the highest rated shows on television. *Good Times,* however, received severe criticism from various segments of the African American community, which accused the show of perpetuating stereotypes. During the early years of the sitcom, Rolle defended the program in various articles. But in 1977, upset that the image of her son J. J. (played by Jimmie Walker) was a poor example for black youth, Rolle left the show. After changes in J. J.'s character, Rolle was persuaded to resume her role the following season, but the show ended in 1979.

After *Good Times,* Rolle continued her television and film career. In 1978 she won an Emmy for her role in the movie *Summer of My German Soldier.* She starred in such films as *I Know Why the Caged Bird Sings* (1979) and *Driving Miss Daisy* (1989), and as narrator for Marlon Riggs's 1987 documentary *Ethnic Notions.* She also created a one-person show about SOJOURNER TRUTH.

In 1990 Rolle barely escaped death when she was involved in a car accident that shattered several of her ribs and severely damaged her left eye. With expert medical care and a strong will, she recovered, although not completely.

During the 1990s, Rolle continued her fight to shatter black stereotypes in the media. In 1990 she became the first woman to receive the NAACP Chairman's Civil Rights Leadership Award for promoting positive images of African Americans. She also developed a one-woman show based on the life of MARY MCLEOD BETHUNE. One of Rolle's favorite parts was that of Lena Younger in LORRAINE HANSBERRY's drama *A Raisin in the Sun,* and she performed the classic at the Kennedy Center to record audiences in 1987 and in the 1989 television production. She would recreate the role for the play's thirty-fifth anniversary at the Alliance Theatre in Atlanta in 1994.

In 1997, Esther Rolle was featured in the film *Rosewood,* and was a host in various educational films as well. Poet Maya Angelou directed Esther Rolle's last major film, *Down in the Delta* (1998). Just before the film's release, Rolle died of complications from diabetes in Los Angeles at the age of seventy-eight.

Bibliography: Biographical information and the opening quotation were drawn from a personal interview with Esther Rolle on October 11, 1994, in Atlanta, Georgia. Material on Rolle's performing career can be found in Donald Bogle, *Blacks in American Films and Television: An Illustrated Encyclopedia* (1988); Edward Mapp, *Directory of Blacks in the Performing Arts* (1990); James Haskins, *Black Dance in America* (1990); Richard A. Long, *The Black Tradition in American Dance* (1989); and Allen Woll, *Dictionary of the Black Theatre* (1983). Useful articles include Lewis Shawn, "Esther Rolle," *Ebony,* May 1978, pp. 91–96; and Leisha Stewart, "Good Times Continue for 'Good Times' Star," *Ebony,* June 1991, pp. 64–66. Additional information was obtained from her longtime friend and publicist, Larry Calhoun. Theater photos can be found at the New York Public Library for the Performing Arts at Lincoln Center. Obituaries appeared in the *Los Angeles Times* on November 18, 1998, and the *New York Times* on November 19, 1998.

KATHY A. PERKINS

ROME, Esther. September 8, 1945–June 24, 1995. Feminist health activist, author.

Esther Rome, born Esther Rachel Seidman in Norwich, Connecticut, was the fourth child of

Rose Deitsch, who emigrated from Poland as a child, and Leo Seidman, a native of Brooklyn, New York. Along with her older siblings, Esther was raised in Plainfield, a small industrial town in Connecticut where the Seidmans ran a five-and-ten-cent store. From an early age, Esther expressed an active interest in medicine, but soon received the message that in the conservative social climate of postwar America women didn't become doctors. In 1962, Esther graduated from Norwich Free Academy and entered Brandeis University, where she earned a BA in art in 1966.

Shortly before graduating, Esther met Nathan Rome, a woodworker, whom she married on December 24, 1967. The couple lived in Cambridge, Massachusetts, until 1977, when they moved to Somerville. Their son Judah was born in 1977, followed by Micah in 1982. In 1968, Rome received her Master of Arts in Teaching from Harvard, and she briefly taught art at a junior high school in Attleboro, Massachusetts. Dissatisfied with her teaching experiences, she left the profession in 1969 and discovered what would become her life's work: women's health advocacy.

By the late 1960s, the women's health movement had just begun to emerge in major urban centers nationwide. Drawing on the ideas and practices of radical feminism, community health reform, and 1960s counterculture, women's health advocates strove to increase women's autonomy over their health, bodies, and sexuality and transform their health care services. Following a Boston women's liberation conference held in the spring of 1969, Rome and the thirteen other women who founded the group that would become known as the Boston Women's Health Book Collective began meeting regularly to discuss issues relating to women's health and bodies from a feminist perspective. Inspired by their conversations, the women developed short papers on topics such as sexuality, childbirth, and reproduction, articles in which they combined their personal experiences with information gleaned from medical literature. First compiled in 1970 as a cheap newsprint booklet, these essays formed the basis of the Collective's groundbreaking health manual, *Our Bodies, Ourselves.* Having undergone several substantial revisions and expansions since its original incarnation, *Our Bodies, Ourselves* has become a feminist classic and an invaluable resource for women worldwide, selling millions of copies in nineteen languages. Rome's contributions to the various editions included chapters on postpartum depression, female anatomy and physiology, sexually transmitted diseases, and food and nutrition.

An active member of the Collective for over twenty-five years, Rome worked in the Collective's office and served on its board of directors. A diligent and pragmatic presence in the group, she helped keep the Collective focused on its immediate and long-term goals. Her approach to women's health activism was marked by resourcefulness and creativity. In 1977 she authored the Collective's menstruation brochure—printed in red ink—which included her innovative techniques for menstrual massage. She also created an anatomically correct Raggedy Ann doll that the Collective used in public lectures and demonstrations on female anatomy. Practicing what a fellow Collective member described as "applied feminism," Rome was dedicated to creating practical solutions and distributing sensitive, accessible, and accurate information that women could use in their everyday lives.

Her commitment to these goals was reflected in her passionate advocacy regarding two major women's health issues: tampon safety and silicone breast implants. In 1980, the Centers for Disease Control reported evidence of a strong link between the use of high-absorbency tampons and toxic shock syndrome, a newly discovered bacterial infection that causes serious illness and sometimes death. As part of a task force established in 1982 by the American Society for Testing Materials, Rome vigorously campaigned for accurate labeling and uniform standards for tampon absorbency. Despite continued resistance from manufacturers, her tireless efforts prevailed, and in 1990 the Food and Drug Administration (FDA) instituted requirements for standardized tampon labeling.

From 1988 onward, Rome grew increasingly concerned about the safety of silicone breast implants and the information women received about such devices. As a representative of the Collective, she served on an FDA committee that produced educational materials for women considering breast implants. In 1992, the FDA declared a moratorium on the use of silicone-gel implants. Along with her actions on the federal level, Rome organized a Boston-area support group for women with breast implants, wrote articles for a local newspaper, and spoke to local and national media outlets about the continued controversy surrounding the subject.

Throughout all her activist work, Rome emphasized that women's health issues are inextricably linked to larger social, economic, and political contexts. Her philosophy is perhaps best illustrated in her final work, *Sacrificing Ourselves for Love,* a collection of articles written with Jane Hyman. Published posthumously in 1996, the book analyzes the ways many women jeopardize their health and well-being in order to meet societal standards for female appearance and behavior. In her essays on body image and cosmetic surgery, Rome argued that medical interventions posed costly and inadequate solutions to women's discontentment with their looks, a problem that she believed required larger changes in American culture and society.

An observant Jew and devoted mother, Esther Rome skillfully combined her commitments to faith and family with her dedication to women's health advocacy. Her interest in nutrition was inspired by her adherence to kosher guidelines, and she enjoyed celebrating religious holidays with friends, family, and feasts. She and her family were actively involved in Temple B'Nai Brith in Somerville. In her life and work, Rome maintained an unswerving commitment to the principal goals of the women's health movement, seeking to inform and empower women in their health care decisions. After a protracted struggle with breast cancer, Esther Rome died in 1995 in her Somerville home at the age of forty-nine. Shortly before her death, she remarked that, besides her family, the Collective was the best thing that ever happened to her.

Bibliography: Many of Esther Rome's articles, letters, and other papers can be found in the Boston Women's Health Book Collective Archives, 1973–1991, Schlesinger Library, Radcliffe Institute for Advanced Study, Harvard University. See also Boston Women's Health Book Collective, *Our Bodies, Ourselves for the New Century* (1998); and Jane Hyman and Esther Rome, *Sacrificing Our Selves for Love: Why Women Compromise Health and Self-Esteem . . . and How to Stop* (1996). Additional information was supplied by Wendy Sanford, Paula Doress-Worters, Nathan Rome, and Judah Rome. Obituaries appeared in the *Boston Globe* on June 25, 1995, and the *New York Times* on June 27, 1995.

ABIGAIL BASS

ROSENBERG, Anna Marie Lederer. July 19, 1902–May 9, 1983. Public relations counsel, federal official.

Entering public relations in the early 1920s, Anna Rosenberg developed a specialty in manpower and personnel issues that made possible a career that straddled the public and private sectors. After a succession of government posts during the New Deal and World War II, she became U.S. assistant secretary of defense in 1950, the first woman to reach so high a post in the Pentagon. Even though she preferred to be regarded simply as a public official, she recognized the obstacles faced by women and tried to nurture other women's careers. "Men bend backward not giving women a chance," she said in a 1943 interview. "So if women don't give women a chance, it's bad."

Anna Marie Lederer was born in Budapest, Hungary. Her parents, Albert Lederer, a furniture manufacturer, and Charlotte Bacskai, a writer and illustrator of juvenile fiction, already had one daughter, Clare, born two years earlier. In 1912, the family emigrated to the United States, settling in New York City. At Wadleigh High School, her quick intelligence and high energy made her a leader. In 1917, when the United States entered World War I, she cut back on her classes to run the recreation room of a debarkation hospital and sell Liberty Bonds. She later left school entirely to work full-time for the war effort. In the fall of 1919 she was naturalized and married infantryman Julius Rosenberg, who later became a rug merchant. In 1920 they had a son, Thomas.

A speech Rosenberg gave on woman suffrage at the Amsterdam Democratic Club brought her to the attention of Tammany Hall leader James Hagan, and soon she was helping manage local political campaigns. Recognizing her own talents for organization, in 1924 she opened a public relations firm. She put together events for Jewish philanthropies and helped firms with their labor issues in southern factories.

Like many other women, Anna Rosenberg took advantage of opportunities opened by the New Deal to move into government administration. Working first as the chief assistant to Nathan Straus Jr., regional director of the National Recovery Administration (NRA), Rosenberg set up New York State's NRA offices and secured board members to draft local NRA codes. When Straus resigned in 1934, she succeeded him, becoming the only female NRA regional director in the country. After the Supreme Court struck down the NRA in 1935, Rosenberg became regional director of the newly created Social Security Board, a post she held until 1943. Again the lone regional female administrator, she directed a large staff that implemented and interpreted the Social Security Act to the public. During the 1930s she also served New York City Mayor Fiorello La Guardia in labor negotiations. Controversially, throughout her government service she continued to do public relations and consulting on the side, insisting that they did not interfere with her official positions.

Rosenberg's expertise in manpower issues was even more in demand during wartime. In 1941, after the United States entered World War II, she became regional director in the Office of Defense Health and Welfare Services, for which she developed government training programs for defense workers. As regional director of the War Manpower Commission (1942–45), she set up employment services and government child-care programs. In July 1944 President Roosevelt sent her to Europe as his personal representative to report on military personnel matters. The following summer she again went to Europe, this time to identify the needs of demobilized soldiers for President Harry S. Truman. She was instrumental in encouraging presidential support for the GI Bill.

In 1945, upon the recommendation of General Dwight D. Eisenhower, she became the first recipient of the Medal of Freedom, a civilian decoration. In 1946 she received the Congressional Medal of Honor and in 1947 the United States Medal for Merit.

The culmination of her government service came in 1950 when Secretary of Defense George Marshall nominated her as assistant secretary of defense. After controversial confirmation hearings in which she cleared herself of charges of being a communist (the main witness had confused her with another Anna Rosenberg), she held this post until 1953. Her chief task was to develop plans for the universal military service and training of eighteen-year-olds. When the Democrats lost the White House in 1952, she returned to New York and the private public relations firm, Anna M. Rosenberg Associates, that she had founded in 1945. After divorcing her first husband in 1962, she married Paul Gray Hoffman, a Republican who had been the first administrator of the Marshall Plan after World War II and was then head of the Ford Foundation. He died in 1974.

In a 1966 essay on women and careers, Rosenberg concluded that career opportunities for women had barely improved during her lifetime. Press reports repeatedly contrasted her public roles with society's gender expectations. They emphasized her petite and trim stature and penchant for fashionable hats, expensive perfumes, and gold bangles and charm bracelets. Critics accused her of using her sex to ease relations with the difficult men she often worked with. For her part, she believed in looking her "best" but insisted that her dress had nothing to do with her ability in a job.

Rosenberg was often called Seven-Job Anna. When asked how she could hold so many jobs at once, Rosenberg answered, "I delegate authority to other people in whom I have confidence and who do not come running to me with every little problem." Her keen business skills, efficiency, and friendly manner won her many admirers, and she continued to work for her public relations firm until just a month before her death from cancer and pneumonia in New York City on May 9, 1983, at the age of eighty.

Bibliography: Manuscript material is located in the Anna Rosenberg papers (1879–1983) at the Schlesinger Library, Radcliffe Institute for Advanced Study, Harvard University. Additional material on her government career is found at the Franklin D. Roosevelt and Harry S. Truman presidential libraries. An oral interview conducted June 7, 1957, is part of the Herbert H. Lehman Project, Columbia University Oral History Research Office. Biographical material can be found in *Current Biography* (1943), pp. 631–34, which contains both quotations, and *Current Biography* (1951), pp. 538–40. Sources vary on Rosenberg's birth date, some giving June, others July 19, 1899 or 1902. Because she was born in Hungary, her birth certificate is inaccessible to American scholars. See also Jacqueline McGlade, "Establishing Mediation as Enterprise: The Career of Anna Rosenberg," *Business and Economic History* 25, no. 1 (Fall 1996), pp. 242–51. Popular articles about her career include S. J. Woolf, "A Woman Sits in Judgment for NRA," *New York Times Magazine,* March 31, 1935, p. 18; "Outgoing Directrix," *New Yorker,* September 15, 1945, pp. 20–21; and "Busiest Woman in U.S.: Anna Rosenberg Runs Country's Manpower," *Life,* January 21, 1952, pp. 79–87. For her thoughts on women and careers, see Anna Rosenberg Hoffman, "A New Look at Woman's Work," in Robert M. Hutchins and Mortimer J. Adler, eds., *The Great Ideas Today 1966* (1966), pp. 44–55. Obituaries appeared in the *New York Times* and the *Washington Post* on May 10, 1983.

ELISABETH ISRAELS PERRY

ROSS, Nellie Tayloe. November 29, 1876–December 19, 1977. Wyoming governor, federal official.

Nellie Davis Tayloe, who as Nellie Tayloe Ross would later become the first woman governor in the United States, was born near St. Joseph, Missouri. Her father, James Wynns Tayloe, a merchant and gentleman farmer, and mother, Elizabeth Blair Green, were descended from wealthy southern slaveholding families. After her mother's death in 1884, Nellie was raised by her father and three older brothers, and educated in public and private schools in Missouri, Kansas, and Nebraska. After graduation from a teachers' training school in Omaha, she taught kindergarten for two years before her marriage, in 1902, to attorney William Bradford Ross.

Starting married life in Cheyenne, Wyoming, William built a thriving law practice and became active in Democratic Party politics while Nellie devoted herself to being a wife and mother. The Rosses had four sons: twins George Tayloe and James Ambrose (1903), Alfred Duff (1905), and William Bradford (1912). Tragedy struck the family when, at the age of ten months, baby Alfred died when his perambulator tipped over and he suffocated before he could be rescued. Ever afterward Nellie Ross would speak passionately about motherhood as woman's highest calling.

William Ross began his rise in Wyoming politics in 1904, when he was elected county attorney. When he determined to run for governor as a Progressive Democrat in 1922, his wife at first opposed his decision, worrying about the financial costs of abandoning his practice and hating his long absences from home. He was victorious, but served only two years of his term before dying, from complications from appendicitis, in 1924.

Widowhood transformed forty-eight-year-old Nellie Tayloe Ross from a privacy-loving homemaker into a public figure. Only days after William's death, Democratic Party officials asked Ross to run for governor in the upcoming special election. She agreed to do so to carry on her husband's legacy as a supporter of workers' rights, occupational safety, Prohibition, and a federal amendment to outlaw child labor.

As the first state to enfranchise women, Wyoming had a long-standing tradition of women's rights and an active and vocal feminist movement. Ross had never been affiliated with women's causes, and had not even been an advocate of woman suffrage. She nonetheless accepted the enthusiastic support of both Republican and Democratic women activists who welcomed the possibility of electing the nation's first woman governor. At the same time, her campaign literature assured voters that she would take full responsibility for her decisions—the fact that she was a woman would in no way alter her obligation to the people. She was elected by a margin of more than eight thousand votes.

Ross was aware that her administration would be scrutinized as a test of whether women were fit to govern. Feminists were disappointed when she distanced herself from their causes, although the press lauded Ross as the epitome of both femininity and political ability, a woman with cameo features, a beautiful smile, and enough fortitude to govern wisely. During her two years as governor, she championed mine safety legislation, fought for state control of lands adjoining Yellowstone National Park, promoted a state severance tax on mineral development, and did her best to uphold the Eighteenth Amendment.

By 1926, Ross was ready to seek reelection. Wanting to run on her record, she refused to appeal directly to women voters and thus alienated Republican women who had voted for her in 1924 either out of sympathy for her widowhood or in hopes of a feminist administration. Running as a Democrat in a traditionally Republican state, as a "dry" in a state where Prohibition was nearly impossible to enforce, and as incumbent in a time of economic trouble, Ross also faced organized opposition from the Ku Klux Klan. She lost by 1,365 votes, although she ran ahead of all other Democratic candidates in the state.

A year later, Ross admitted in *Good Housekeeping* that if she had overcome her distaste for "the woman issue," recruited women advisers, and confronted the persistent charge that women were unfit to govern, she probably could have been reelected. Despite her earlier hesitancy, she had by this time become a national feminist icon. An excellent public speaker, she lectured on the popular Chautauqua circuit. By 1928 she was serving as a vice-chairman of the Democratic National Committee and co-directing (with ELEANOR ROOSEVELT) the women's effort for Democratic presidential nominee Al Smith.

By 1932, Ross had become a major figure in Democratic women's circles. She made speeches for the Roosevelt campaign and was convinced that the key to Democratic victory lay in aggressively courting women voters, who made up half of the electorate. When Roosevelt was elected, she was appointed director of the Mint. During her twenty-year tenure in that office, she presided over the greatest expansion of mint production to date, including the construction of the gold depository at Fort Knox. She held this position until 1953, when she retired from public office.

Like other women in public life, Ross faced the dilemma of affirming both her femininity and her equality. Ross had tried to set an example for women politicians by being ladylike but also asserting her capacity to wield power. Many women, Republican and Democratic, would follow her lead. In 1958, Senator MARGARET CHASE SMITH wrote Ross, "Well do I remember the days when you were Governor and my admiration for you. . . . I have through the years tried to emulate you—to do my job as well as any man could without losing my femininity." Nellie Tayloe Ross died in Washington, D.C., on December 19, 1977, at the age of 101, and lay in state in the rotunda of the Wyoming state capitol in Cheyenne before burial in Lake View Cemetery.

Bibliography: The papers of Nellie Tayloe Ross are archived at the American Heritage Center, University of Wyoming at Laramie, and in the Wyoming State Archives in Cheyenne. Material on her involvement in Democratic politics is found in the papers of the Women's Division of the Democratic National Committee, Franklin D. Roosevelt Presidential Library, Hyde Park, New York. Ross wrote numerous speeches but published little. The main statement of her political strategies and principles is in a three-part magazine article: Nellie Tayloe Ross, "The Governor Lady," *Good Housekeeping*, August–October, 1927. Studies of Ross's career include Barbara J. Aslakson, "Nellie Tayloe Ross: First Woman Governor" (MA thesis, University of Wyoming, 1960); William Dubois and Mabel Brown, "Wyoming Citizen of the Century: Nominee Nellie Tayloe Ross," Citizen of the Century Program, American Heritage Center; and Virginia Scharff, "Feminism, Femininity and Power: Nellie Tayloe Ross and the Woman Politician's Dilemma," *Frontiers: A Journal of Women Studies* 15, no. 3 (1995), pp. 87–106, which contains the quote from Margaret Chase Smith on p. 103. See also Mabel Brown, ed., *First Ladies of Wyoming, 1869–1990* (1990), and T. A. Larson, *History of Wyoming* (1965). Obituaries appeared in the *New York Times* and *Washington Post* on December 21, 1977.

VIRGINIA SCHARFF

ROSS, Ruth. February 1, 1930–August 5, 1986. Magazine editor, journalist.

As the first editor in chief of *Essence* magazine and the person who gave that groundbreaking publication its name, Ruth Ross helped supplant prevailing stereotypes of Aunt Jemima and Sapphire with compelling images of black beauty and pride.

A feisty, sophisticated woman who balanced substance with style, Ruth N. Ross was born in Manhattan at the twilight of the Harlem Renaissance. Like many other black strivers, her parents had come to New York City in search of opportunity. Her mother, Florence, was from Oklahoma, where she had been trained as a teacher. Her father, Edgar Lee Ross, had been born in the South and had worked as a cook on merchant ships before becoming a lawyer, eventually securing an appointment as commissioner of weights and measures in New York. The youngest of three children, "Ruthie" shared her parents' taste for education and travel, becoming an avid reader and swimmer and spending vacations in Italy with a cousin who lived there.

Educated in New York public schools, Ross graduated from Hunter College in 1957, then launched her career as a journalist. At that time, African Americans generally were not welcome in mainstream media and worked only for the black press, but Ross was one of the few to break through the barriers. By the mid 1960s she had become an assistant editor at *Newsweek* magazine. Being both black and female, she was an early "two-fer" in the lingo of affirmative action, for newsmagazines rarely employed women of any color above the level of researcher, a situation that led to a 1970 class action suit at *Newsweek*.

Meanwhile, Ross maintained strong ties with other black journalists. She helped found Black Perspective, the first organization in New York to address issues of race in the media and to serve as a support group for those who were integrating the mainstream. When Ross met Leandra Abbott, a young magazine journalist, at one of their meetings, she set up an interview that got the newcomer a job at *Newsweek* and then attentively mentored Abbott as she learned to navigate the work culture there. Indeed, Ross coached and encouraged all black journalists who came to work at *Newsweek* because she wanted them all to do well. Ross also scrutinized the magazine's coverage of the numerous racial conflicts of that period, questioning editors on matters of slant and tone. At times she irritated them, but they often made the changes she suggested.

Given her background, Ross seemed an excellent prospect in 1969 when four young African American men, who called themselves the Hollingsworth Group, approached her about the possibility of becoming editor in chief of a new magazine for black women. They had little financing and no experience in publishing, and they were operating out of a sparsely furnished rented room in midtown Manhattan. But all had quit promising jobs in business and finance to devote full time to this project. Upon meeting Ross, they were convinced that she could provide the editorial direction they needed. Ed Lewis, who later became CEO of Essence Communications, recalled: "It was her passion for the magazine, her passion to be a voice for black women. She had a historical grounding in the role black women had played."

Ross understood the risk in leaving *Newsweek* for a start-up, but the promise of fulfilling an unmet need was so great that she accepted the job. Her reasons surfaced in a February 11, 1970, story in the *New York Times* announcing the debut of *Essence:* "No longer would she have to hear the familiar, 'But Ruth, we already have one black story in the back of the book,'" she was quoted as saying. Yet her editors at *Newsweek* suggested that she could come back if things did not work out.

The first problem for the fledgling magazine was its name: the male founders intended to call it *Sapphire.* They cited the definition of a sapphire as a semi-precious stone, but focus groups of black women recoiled at the idea, associating it with the stereotype of the overbearing African American woman as well as the name of Kingfish's haranguing wife in *Amos 'n' Andy,* a minstrelsy-derived comedy popular among whites but long an irritant to blacks. A research firm failed to produce a suitable title after hundreds of names were suggested. But when Ross came up with "Essence," the others immediately knew it was right.

The stunning inaugural issue in May 1970 featured articles by leading black writers and scholars on topics related to relations between women and men and other relevant issues, all highlighted by beautiful illustrations under the supervision of photographer Gordon Parks. In keeping with the spirit of the times, the cover article and much of the content had a militant tone. Ross not only had come up with a serious Afrocentric publication, but also had broken away from the superficial cast of traditional women's magazines.

The public responded enthusiastically to this bold new magazine, but white critics said it was too radical and too black. *Time,* known as a conservative media publication, was particularly harsh in its review, while a Madison Avenue newsletter suggested that advertisers might not respond well to such an approach. Unnerved by these comments and intent on reassuring their investors, the

Hollingsworth Group dismissed Ross after that first issue and subsequently took a lighter, "less black" approach.

Ross's break with *Essence* was bitter, made worse when the spot she had left at *Newsweek* closed up behind her. She continued to work there, but was limited mostly to special projects rather than news. Recognition eluded her. From 1980 to 1983, Ross served as director of public affairs for the New York City Department of Employment, then became a freelancer. In 1986, she became ill and soon learned that she had advanced cancer. She died on August 5 of that year in New York City at the age of fifty-six.

Throughout her life, Ruth Ross was a very private person, though she enjoyed entertaining friends at her home, which they remembered was like a little jewel. Although she never married nor had children, Ross was so generous in mentoring young people that many considered her "the mother of black journalists in New York."

Bibliography: Very little information is available on Ruth Ross. Background on the founding and evolution of *Essence* can be found in the lavishly illustrated *Essence: 25 Years Celebrating Black Women* (1995), edited by Patricia Mignon Hinds and with text by Audrey Edwards. See also Philip H. Dougerty, "Advertising: A Magazine for Negro Women," *New York Times,* February 11, 1970. Most of the information in this article came from interviews with those who knew Ross as a colleague and friend, among them: Dr. Phyllis Harrison-Ross, her sister-in-law; Leandra Abbott, former *Newsweek* researcher; Pheobe Tribble, friend of the Ross family; Ed Lewis, CEO of Essence Communications; Osborn Elliott, former editor in chief of *Newsweek;* C. Gerald Fraser, co-founder of Black Perspective; Earl Caldwell, journalist and friend; and Rose Jourdain, a journalist and author who worked briefly with Ross on planning the first issue of *Essence.* This essay also draws on the author's recollections of a luncheon meeting with Ed Lewis and Jonathan Blount, another founder, in 1969 before the magazine made its debut. A short obituary appeared in the *New York Times* on August 7, 1986.

PHYL GARLAND

ROUNTREE, Martha. October 23, 1911–August 23, 1999. Radio and television producer, journalist.

Martha Rountree, the co-creator and first moderator of *Meet the Press,* was born in Gainesville, Florida, the second of five children of Mary Jane Tennant, a homemaker, and Earle S. Rountree, a lawyer and real estate agent. Her family later moved to Columbia, South Carolina, where Martha grew up. While studying briefly at the University of South Carolina, Rountree worked as a reporter for the *Columbia Record* to help pay for her tuition. She left college without graduating, however, and returned to Florida to write for the *Tampa Tribune.* There she worked as a general reporter and eventually a sports columnist, writing under the name M. J. Rountree. On one occasion she wrote a humorous piece that caught the interest of the local CBS manager, who was astonished to find that "M.J." was tall, blonde, and female.

In 1938 she moved to New York and worked as a freelance editor and journalist with the intention of becoming a radio producer. Soon after, Rountree and her sister Ann formed a production company, Radio House, which eventually developed a new program, *Leave It to the Girls,* to be broadcast by the Mutual Broadcasting System. *Leave It to the Girls* was first conceived as a serious discussion of male-female problems by career women, with one male joining a panel of women to answer questions submitted by listeners, but it soon changed to a more humorous format. Premiering on radio in 1945, the program first aired on local New York television in 1947 and moved to the NBC network from 1949 to 1954. It was brought back briefly in 1962 as a syndicated weekday program.

The show that Rountree is most associated with, *Meet the Press,* premiered in 1945 as a radio show, also employing a panel format. It was created with Lawrence E. Spivak, whom Rountree had met when she submitted articles to *American Mercury,* which he was then editing. Spivak was familiar with her radio work, and they discussed a radio program he was sponsoring that dramatized articles published in the magazine. Together they came up with the concept for *Meet the Press.* It moved to television in 1947. Rountree was the original television moderator until 1953; Spivak was a regular panelist and occasional moderator. In 1952 *Meet the Press* won the George Foster Peabody Award for television news.

Meet the Press was the first unrehearsed, panel interview show with politicians and other notable figures of the day to appear on television. The format was unique, and Rountree had a remarkable ability to get important newsmakers to appear on air. She was actively involved in each week's discussions and brought other women on air, such as former First Lady ELEANOR ROOSEVELT. The format set the standard for political interview shows that is still used today. In commenting on *Meet the Press,* Rountree said, "I think it is important that the public should hear its elected officers speak out and take their stand in answer to direct questions without preparation or oratory. There is nothing so refreshing as unadorned conviction" (*New York Times,* March 10, 1946).

In 1951, Rountree and Spivak produced *Keep Posted* (later renamed *The Big Issue*) for the Dumont network. In a format that foreshadowed contemporary programs such as CNN's *Crossfire,* panelists discussed controversial issues and responded to questions from a panel of expert citizens. Another joint production for Dumont, *Washington Exclusive,* presented six former senators from rival political parties who discussed the affairs of the nation; the program lasted six months.

Martha Rountree described herself as "a blunt speaking, down-to-earth, television news reporter and I'm proud of it" (*Current Biography,* p. 482). With her extensive radio and television work, she showed that women were capable and influential participants in broadcast news at a time when it was barely acceptable for women to appear on air. In 1953 Rountree sold *Meet the Press* and *The Big Issue* to Spivak for a reported $125,000. Under a clause in her sales contract, she was prevented for two years from producing a program that was similar to *Meet the Press,* so she went on the lecture circuit.

In 1941 Rountree had married Albert N. Williams Jr., a magazine and radio writer; the childless marriage ended in divorce in 1948. In 1952 she married Oliver M. Presbrey, an advertising agency executive, with whom she had two daughters, Martha (1953) and Mary (1955). The family lived in Washington, D.C., where Rountree, who loved to entertain, threw large parties and invited many politicians who also appeared on *Meet the Press.*

In 1956, Rountree and Presbrey became partners in Rountree Productions with Robert Novak. They produced *Press Conference,* a program that invited a newsworthy subject to answer questions in front of sixteen reporters with Rountree moderating. At the end of the program, she summarized the key points for the viewers. The show moved to ABC in the fall of 1956. In April 1957, the name of the program was changed to *Martha Rountree's Press Conference.* The last show aired in July 1957. *Capitol Closeup,* a daily news radio show, began in 1959 and was broadcast from her home in Washington, D.C. Interviews included Vice President Richard Nixon, FBI chief J. Edgar Hoover, Speaker of the House Sam Rayburn, and Attorney General William Rogers.

In 1965 Rountree founded the Leadership Foundation, a nonprofit political research organization. Its purpose was to educate the public on current issues and events and to establish special projects for its members through polls and surveys of their interests. She served as president until 1988. She was also a member of the National Press Club and the Women's National Press Club. Martha Rountree died in Washington, D.C., in 1999 at the age of eighty-seven of complications from Alzheimer's disease.

Bibliography: There is no biography of Martha Rountree. *Current Biography* (1957), pp. 480–82 provides a small amount of biographical information and discusses her career in broadcasting. Rick Ball, *Meet the Press: Fifty Years of History in the Making* (1998), chronicles the history of *Meet the Press,* including Rountree's contributions. See also the chapter on Rountree and Spivak in Dan Nimmo and Chevelle Newsome, eds., *Political Commentators in the United States in the 20th Century: A Bio-critical Sourcebook* (1997). Diana Gibbings, "A Lady Producer," *New York Times,* March 10, 1946, highlights Rountree's role as one of the few women producers in radio. Other useful secondary sources include Marion Marzolf, *Up from the Footnote: A History of Women Journalists* (1977); and Donna L. Halper, *Invisible Stars: A Social History of Women in American Broadcasting* (2001). An obituary appeared in the *New York Times* on August 25, 1999.

MARY E. BEADLE

RUDOLPH, Wilma. June 23, 1940–November 12, 1994. Athlete.

Wilma Glodean Rudolph, one of the twentieth century's greatest track stars and an inspiration to African American and female athletes alike, was born in St. Bethlehem, Tennessee. Her father, Edward Rudolph, had been previously married before he wed her mother, Blanche, and Wilma was the twentieth child in a family of twenty-two. Her parents did not have much, but they were able to provide for their large family. Her father was a railroad porter and tradesman; her mother was a domestic worker in the local community.

A premature baby, Wilma turned into a sickly child, enduring measles, mumps, scarlet fever, chicken pox, and double pneumonia. Then her mother noticed that her left leg was not developing at the same rate as her right. Doctors told the Rudolphs that Wilma had polio and that her leg would continue to deteriorate, leaving her unable to walk. Blanche Rudolph refused to accept this diagnosis and received a second opinion offering a more optimistic prognosis. Thereafter mother and daughter traveled ninety miles each week to Meharry Hospital at Fisk University in Nashville for heat, water, and massage treatments, supplemented by an exercise routine that they continued at home. After two years of intense therapy, Wilma was able to walk with the aid of a metal leg brace. By age twelve, she could walk free of crutches, a brace, or corrective shoes.

Owing to Wilma's various childhood illnesses, her mother tutored her at home in basic academic fundamentals. Finally unfettered by physical ailments, Rudolph enrolled in the local, segregated Burt High School, and there she discovered her athletic abilities. Following her older sister's example, she joined the basketball team. During a local tournament, renowned track coach Edward Temple of Tennessee State University (TSU) noticed the tall, lanky guard and asked the sophomore if she would like to attend the university's summer sports camp. Temple was already known for his talents as the sociology-professor-cum-pro-bono-coach of the TSU "Tigerbelles," whose team members dominated women's track and field in this era, producing numerous Amateur Athletic Union and Olympic champions. Wilma Rudolph accepted his invitation without hesitation.

Before eventually entering TSU as a full-time scholarship student, Rudolph worked out with the team, attending Temple's daily college practices while still a student at Burt. At age sixteen, Rudolph won her first medal (bronze) as a member of the 4×100 relay team at the 1956 Olympics in Melbourne, Australia. In her next Olympic appearance, in Rome in 1960, Wilma Rudolph made her mark, becoming the first American woman to take gold three times in the international meet. She beat her competitors in the 100-meter dash and the 200-meter dash, and anchored her team's victory against Germany in the 4 × 100 relay, setting or equaling Olympic or world records in all three events. The 1960 Olympic games were the first to be televised, and Rudolph's victories, coupled with her inspirational story of having overcome physical and societal barriers to compete, produced a surge of interest in women's track and field.

When Rudolph returned from Rome, Tennessee governor Buford Ellington, who had won election on a segregationist platform, planned to head the welcome celebration for the young sprinter. Rudolph refused to attend any segregated event. Given their star participant's repudiation, program organizers opened the parade and banquet to all, making Wilma Rudolph and the Tigerbelles' homecoming the first integrated public event in her hometown of Clarksville.

Rudolph took a year off from her studies to make public appearances and compete in other international track events. Her last competitive race was in 1962. She returned to TSU after her travels and completed her BA in education in 1963. That same year she married Robert Eldridge, whom she had dated in high school and with whom she had her first daughter, Yolanda, in 1958. The couple had three more children: Djuana (1964), Robert Jr. (1965), and Xurry (1971). The two divorced in 1976. A brief previous marriage to Willard Ward had ended in divorce in 1962.

After retiring from track (there was no money for amateurs and no professional track circuit to compete on then), Rudolph taught at Cobb Elementary in Clarksville and coached the Burt High School track team. She moved on to coach track, first in Maine and then at DePauw University in Indiana. She continued to speak nationally on the topic of women and athletics, serving as a role model for future track-and-field stars such as FLORENCE GRIFFITH JOYNER, Jackie Joyner-Kersee, and Evelyn Ashford. Rudolph also served as a sports commentator on national television and as the co-host of a radio show and penned her autobiography, simply titled *Wilma* (1977). Her work in "Operation Champ"—an athletic outreach program for underprivileged youth in sixteen major U.S. cities, sponsored by Vice President Hubert Humphrey in 1967—continued when she created in 1981 what she called her greatest accomplishment, the Wilma Rudolph Foundation, a not-for-profit, community-based amateur sports program.

In the last year of her life, Wilma Rudolph made few public appearances. After fainting during a speech in July, she was diagnosed with brain cancer and was in and out of hospitals for treatment. The physical strength that propelled her to break the ribbon three times during the 1960 Summer Olympics in Rome was depleted, and she now depended on her coach and mentor Edward Temple as she took his arm on their daily walks around the track at her alma mater, Tennessee State University. On November 12, 1994, the native Tennesseean succumbed to brain and breast cancer at her home in Brentwood at the age of fifty-four. Shortly after her death, the National Women's Athletic Association marked Wilma Rudolph's importance to her sport by electing her to their Hall of Fame.

Bibliography: Wilma Rudolph's autobiography, *Wilma*, was published in 1977. General biographies include Tom Biracree, *Wilma Rudolph* (1988); Wayne R. Coffey, *Wilma Rudolph* (1993); Victoria Sherrow, *Wilma Rudolph: Olympic Champion* (1995); Alice K. Flannagan, *Wilma Rudolph: Athlete and Educator* (2000); and Amy Ruth, *Wilma Rudolph* (2000). For general sources on women and sports, including the Olympics, see Joan Ryan, *Contributions of Women in Sports* (1975); Karen Christensen, Allen Guttmann, and Gertrude Pfister, eds., *International Encyclopedia of Women and Sports* (2001); Janet Woolum, ed., *Outstanding Women Athletes* (1992); Joseph Layden, *Women in Sports* (1997); Jane Leder, *Grace and Glory: A Century of Women in the Olympics* (1996); and Martha Ward Plowden, *Olympic Black Women* (1996). Obituaries appeared in the *New York Times* and the *Los Angeles Times* on November 13, 1994.

LYDIA CLAIRE CHARLES

RUKEYSER, Muriel. December 15, 1913–February 12, 1980. Poet, writer, political activist.

"Breathe-in experience, breathe-out poetry," wrote Muriel Rukeyser as a young woman of less than twenty in *Theory of Flight* (p. 11). Published in 1935, this first volume of poetry won the Yale Younger Poets award and began her prolific career as a poet and political activist. By her very essence, Rukeyser defied categorization, but three central themes emerge from her work: witness, body, and transformation.

Born in New York City to Myra Lyons and Lawrence B. Rukeyser, Muriel was the older of two daughters in a second-generation, upwardly mobile, secular Jewish family. Her father, originally from Wisconsin, co-founded a cement-mixing company at a profitable time in the building of New York City. Her mother, from Yonkers, worked for a lock company before marriage. Affluence, tension, and misery characterized family life, and the "silence at home" first moved Muriel to write poetry (*The Poet's Craft,* p. 116). She attended Manhattan's School of Ethical Culture and the Fieldston School before entering Vassar College in 1930. She adored her newfound intellectual and political freedom in college, where she edited the leftist *Student Review,* took flying lessons, and became active politically. Aligned with the Communist Party, she went to Alabama for the Scottsboro trials, and was arrested and jailed for interviewing black reporters.

In 1932 her father's bankruptcy ended Rukeyser's time at Vassar, and she returned to New York City. For the next forty-eight years, she pursued writing and political activism while supporting herself through a variety of jobs, including writing, publishing, translating, editing, scriptwriting, journalism, and teaching. At regular intervals of one to two years, she published new volumes of poetry and prose, the only exception being during her early years of motherhood. Her life's published works include fourteen volumes of poetry, three biographies (two of scientists), as well as shorter biographical prose/poems, a treatise on the theory and practice of poetry, plays, scripts, and essays, six children's books, one work of fiction (a blend of memoir and fantasy), and translations of Spanish, German, and Swedish poets.

Rukeyser was in Barcelona reporting on the 1936 People's Olympiad when the Spanish civil war ignited. This experience profoundly deepened her vision of poet as witness with a responsibility to the world. The same year, she wrote an epic poem, "The Book of the Dead," about West Virginia's Gauley Bridge, where silicone miners were dying. She worked for the Writers' War Board during World War II but thereafter became a pacifist who participated in anti-war movements, including a wartime trip to Hanoi in 1972. In 1974 she went to South Korea to protest the pending execution of a dissident poet. Always, the need to witness informed her actions and poetry.

Rukeyser also wrote of identity and self, as in this 1944 poem: "To be a Jew in the twentieth century / Is to be offered a gift. If you refuse, / Wishing to be invisible, you choose / Death of the spirit, the stone insanity. / Accepting take full life" (*Beast in View,* p. 62). Although she was not an observant Jew, her understanding of the world as a place of contradictions and connections can be seen as integral with Jewish intellectual traditions. Later, she wrote more of her heritage in "Akiba," one of her biographical poems.

In addition to her written words, Rukeyser made an impact on people through her physical presence. A large woman who carried her head and body with powerful grace, she spoke in a deep voice and had an arresting smile. She was comfortable in her body. Ignoring long-held standards of female modesty (particularly for poets), she wrote openly about pregnancy in "Nine Poems for the Unborn Child" (1948); about creativity, making love, and giving birth in "To Enter That Rhythm Where the Self is Lost" (1962); and about her struggles after suffering a stroke in "Resurrection of the Right Side" (1978). The power of her words lay in the textured, rooted details of her poetry as well as in her vision.

Underlying her work is a belief in the human capacity "to make change in existing conditions;" she saw poetry's "transfer of human energy" as one element of such change (*The Life of Poetry,* p. xi). How people evolve, shift consciousness, and interconnect permeates her writing. Her 1942 biography of nineteenth-century scientist Willard Gibbs was motivated by her own search for a language of transformation, such as he created for physics. Her mind simply did not accept standard conceptual divisions, whether between art and science, passion and technology, power and gender, or peace and violence.

She also rejected accepted standards in her everyday living. In 1945, after moving from New York to San Francisco to teach at the California Labor School, she experimented with marriage for less than two months (with painter Glyn Collins). Two years later, she chose to give birth to William Lawrence Rukeyser as a single mother—a controversial decision for a woman at that time. She never named the father, and her own father disinherited her. Yet her words consistently celebrated a delight in her son. By 1955, they moved back to New York City, and she taught at Sarah Lawrence for twelve years, surviving a red-baiting attack in the late 1950s.

As a woman, she continually broke barriers, writing of women's sexuality and women's actions. She dared to speak of erotic feelings, including her love for both women and men. In 1968, she asked in a poem, "What would happen if one woman told the truth about her life? / The world would split open" (*The Speed of Darkness,* p. 103). Little surprise that Rukeyser was celebrated by the women's movement, by feminist writers such as ANNE SEXTON and Erica Jong, Alice Walker and Adrienne Rich, among others. Yet the depth of her woman-centeredness preceded the second wave of feminism.

By the late 1960s, Rukeyser began to have

strokes. She recovered from the first and continued her poetry and activism. As the strokes worsened, she slowed down but never stopped writing. She died on February 12, 1980, in New York City at the age of sixty-six.

Muriel Rukeyser was a bard poet, often compared to Whitman, her words suggesting a vision of a future as well as a reflection of experiences tied to a present. Throughout her life, her poetry evoked extreme reactions. She wrote of the dark and bright sides of humanity, of oppression and empowerment; she affirmed a full spectrum of sexuality as the human condition, and spoke of erotic feelings as well as love. She gave voice to a pithy humor, particularly at the end of her life. The power and keenness of Rukeyser's insights as well as her lyrical poetry are only beginning to be fully recognized.

Bibliography: Muriel Rukeyser's papers at the Library of Congress contain literary notes, notebooks, literary manuscripts, typescripts, production materials (for books and plays), diaries, and correspondence plus other materials. Two anthologies provide valuable introductions to her work: Kate Daniels, ed., *Out of Silence: Selected Poems/ Muriel Rukeyser* (1992); and Jan Heller Levi, ed., *A Muriel Rukeyser Reader* (1994, with an introduction by Adrienne Rich). Important volumes of poetry include *Theory of Flight* (1935); *U.S. 1* (1938); *Beast in View* (1944); *The Green Wave* (1948); *Waterlily Fire* (1962); *The Speed of Darkness* (1968); and *The Gates* (1976). See also her *The Life of Poetry* (1949; 2nd ed., 1996) and *The Orgy: An Irish Journey of Passion and Transformation* (1967; 2nd ed., 1997), which contain informative and reflective introductory essays by Jane Cooper and Sharon Olds, respectively. Anne F. Herzog and Janet E. Kaufman, eds., *How Shall We Tell Each Other of the Poet? The Life and Writing of Muriel Rukeyser* (1999), is a marvelous collection of essays and poems about and inspired by Rukeyser. See also Louise Kertesz, *The Poetic Vision of Muriel Rukeyser* (1980), and Kate Daniels, "The Demise of Delicate Prisons," in Jack Myers and David Wojahn, eds., *A Profile of Twentieth Century American Poetry* (1991), for additional context. For Rukeyser's own reflections on her life and work, see Cornelia Draves and Mary Jane Fortunato, "Craft Interview with Muriel Rukeyser," in William Packard, ed., *The Poet's Craft: Interviews from the New York Quarterly* (1987); Rukeyser, "The Education of a Poet," in Janet Sternburg, ed., *The Writer on Her Work* (1980); Louise Bernikow, "Muriel at 65: Still Ahead of Her Time," *Ms.*, January 1979, pp. 14+; and Judith McDaniel, "A Conversation with Muriel Rukeyser," *New Women's Times Feminist Review* 10 (April 25–May 8, 1980), pp. 4–5, 18–19. An obituary appeared in the *New York Times* on February 13, 1980.

MAIDA SOLOMON

RUUTTILA, Julia Evelyn. April 26, 1907–April 5, 1991. Labor journalist, writer, activist.

Julia Ruuttila stood less than five feet two, but her presence in the Oregon Left and the union movement was imposing. She was born Julia Evelyn Godman in Eugene, Oregon, the first of two children of Ella Blossom Padan and John Burwell Godman. She was primarily schooled at home, drilled in writing by her mother, a former schoolteacher, and taught history by her father, a graduate of Marietta College in Ohio. He worked in construction and as a foreman in logging camps and sawmills and was an active member of the Industrial Workers of the World (IWW, or Wobblies). Her mother was also an activist: a suffragist, secretary of the local Socialist Party, and a door-to-door distributor of illegal birth control information. The Godman home was frequented by Wobblies and other radicals. Julia eavesdropped on their heated discussions and absorbed their ideas.

At age fifteen, Julia married a sawmill worker named William Clayton Bowen; they were divorced after ten months. Although her second marriage, to Maurice "Butch" Bertram, on July 6, 1926, was unhappy, it gave her her only child, Michael Jack, born in June 1928, and led her to her life's work. Butch was working in a sawmill outside Portland, Oregon, when the surge of union organizing hit in 1934. Julia and Butch recruited at the mill to organize a woodworkers' union; Julia founded and headed the ladies' auxiliary. In 1937 the union bolted from the American Federation of Labor (AFL) for the Congress of Industrial Organizations (CIO); as the International Woodworkers of America (IWA), it precipitated an eight-and-a-half-month lockout. Under Julia's leadership the auxiliary successfully fought to obtain community support, welfare benefits, and birth control so the men could afford to maintain solidarity until they won their case before the National Labor Relations Board.

Realizing there were many former Wobblies in the new woodworkers' union, Julia enlisted the support of the union to organize the Free Ray Becker Committee in 1936. Ray Becker was the last Wobbly in prison following the tragic events of November 11, 1919, in Centralia, Washington, when the American Legion attacked the IWW Hall. The Wobblies fought back, resulting in the deaths of four Legionnaires, the lynching of one Wobbly, and the imprisonment of seven more. Julia had been writing poetry and fiction since her teens and had taken courses at the University of Oregon, so to publicize Becker's case, she began writing for the woodworker's union paper, *The Timberworker.* Soon she was Oregon editor, continuing until 1940 when the union became embroiled in a red hunt and she quit in protest. By this time she was also writing for the *People's World.*

On May 6, 1943, shortly after divorcing Bertram, she married Ben Eaton, a seaman. They lived together only a few months and she divorced him in 1946. In May 1948, Vanport, the wartime housing city on the edge of Portland, was destroyed in a flood. At the time Julia was employed as a stenographer for the State Public Welfare Commission, so she wrote under her pen name Kathleen Cronin when she reported for the *People's World* on the flood and the inadequacies of the Housing Authority's and the Welfare Commission's responses. Her identity was discovered and she was fired. A high-profile but futile hearing ensued.

She next went to work for the International Longshoremen's and Warehousemen's Union (ILWU), first as a publicist during a strike and later as the secretary to the international representative for the Northwest, Matt Meehan. She was already working as a stringer for the ILWU newspaper, *The Dispatcher.* She was also a correspondent for Federated Press, the labor and farm news service until its demise in December 1956. In addition, she was active in the Democratic Party as a precinct committeewoman, interrupting her service only to work for the Progressive Party during Henry Wallace's 1948 presidential campaign.

Following her marriage on Jan 3, 1951, to Oscar Ruuttila, a warehouseman and ILWU and Communist Party activist, Julia moved to Astoria, Oregon, where she worked for the Columbia River Fishermen's Protective Union and organized an ILWU Ladies Auxiliary and a Committee for Protection of Oregon's Foreign Born. The latter activity sparked a subpoena for her to testify at a House Committee on Un-American Activities hearing on "Communist Political Subversion" in Seattle in December 1956. Though Ruuttila was not a member of the Communist Party, she refused on principle to testify, claiming the protection of the First and Fifth Amendments to the U.S. Constitution.

About a year after their marriage, Julia and Oscar took in her grandson Shane, born May 7, 1949. Following Oscar's death in 1962, Julia adopted Shane. The next year she returned to Portland, where she joined the Portland ILWU Ladies' Auxiliary and chaired their Legislative Committee. She was active in Vietnam War protests and helped draw the labor movement into the anti-war struggle. Though plagued with asthma, ulcers, arthritis, and angina, she could frequently be found on picket lines.

Julia Ruuttila claimed she had been arrested for the first time in the 1930s during a strike. In 1973 she was arrested for the last time for sitting in at the electric company offices in protest of rate hikes. She retired from *The Dispatcher* at age eighty and moved to Anchorage, Alaska, to live with Shane and his family. She died in Anchorage on April 5, 1991, following a severe heart attack in early February. She had testified at a town meeting against the Gulf War the previous December.

Ruuttila saw herself as carrying on her father's IWW tradition and was proud when her grandson also became a union leader. Though she had received many honors, she most valued having been made an honorary lifetime member of the International Woodworkers of America. Never forgetting her father's history lessons, she often published labor history articles for union papers, but was proudest of her investigative reporting. She was always on the side of the underdog and the worker and never could understand why anyone but a capitalist would not oppose the capitalist system.

Bibliography: Julia Ruuttila's papers and oral history are at the Oregon Historical Society, Portland. The records of the Free Ray Becker Committee are housed there as well. There are additional oral history tapes at the Tamiment Institute Library, New York University. Ruuttila wrote numerous stories for *The Timberworker,* Federated Press, *People's World,* and *The Dispatcher,* as well as occasionally for *Mainstream* and the *Oregon Labor Press.* Of particular interest is her "Life and Death of an American Town" by Kathleen Cronin (Julia Ruuttila), *Mainstream* 11, no. 8 (August 1958). Her poetry can be found in her self-published volume, *This Is My Shadow* (n.d.). A biography by Sandy Polishuk, *Sticking to the Union: An Oral History Biography of Julia Ruuttila,* was published in 2003. An obituary appeared in the *Portland Oregonian* on April 17, 1991.

SANDY POLISHUK

RYDER, Mildred Norman (Peace Pilgrim). July 18, 1908–July 7, 1981. Spiritual teacher, pacifist.

Mildred Lisette Norman was born on a small poultry farm in Egg Harbor City, New Jersey, the oldest of three children of Josephine Marie Rauch and Ernest Norman. The family was poor but well respected in the German immigrant settlement their ancestors founded in 1855 after fleeing Germany to escape conflict and militarism. Her father, a carpenter, and her mother, a tailor, instilled a strong peace ethic in their children, encouraging discussion of social, political, and moral questions, but did not provide religious training.

Mildred was precocious and a gifted student, but limited finances led her to take on secretarial work after graduating from Egg Harbor City High School in 1926. In 1933 she married Stanley Ryder, a businessman. The marriage was strained from the start, and the couple did not have children. In 1938, determined to find a more meaningful life and uncomfortable about having so much while others were starving, she underwent a life-changing spiritual experience. At the end of an all-night walk, she felt "called" to give her life to something beyond herself. For the next fifteen years, Mildred Norman Ryder searched, prayed, and prepared herself physically, emotionally, and mentally to find that calling.

In 1939 she moved with her husband to Philadelphia, but they separated in 1942 after strong disagreement over Stanley's participation in World War II. The couple divorced in 1946. Searching for the service she felt called to undertake, she worked with the elderly and individuals with emotional disturbances, and then volunteered in peace organizations—the American Friends Service Committee, the Women's International League for Peace and Freedom, and later the United Nations Council of Philadelphia. She radically simplified her life, divesting herself of her possessions and avoiding frivolous activities. She became a vegetarian and learned to live on ten dollars a week. She joined the Endurance Hiking Club, undertaking wilderness treks to strengthen herself and to live simply. Walking, meditating, and praying, she struggled to achieve inner peace by overcoming what she called her self-centered nature (ego) to reach her "higher, God-centered" nature (conscience). Her intermittent glimpses of "the realization of the oneness of all creation" gradually became more frequent and longer. By fall 1952, after becoming the first woman to hike the entire Appalachian Trail in one season, she achieved total inner peace.

The idea to become a peace pilgrim arrived in a vision at the end of this hike. After walking five months and 2,050 miles, living completely outdoors with one set of clothes, a blanket, and two plastic sheets, and consuming only minimal provisions, she confirmed her ability to live simply, at need level, for long time periods, in all weather conditions.

On January 1, 1953, at age forty-four, Mildred Norman Ryder adopted the name Peace Pilgrim, slipped on canvas sneakers, dark blue slacks, and a blue tunic with her new name sewn on (she chose blue because it is the international color of peace), and set out to walk from Pasadena to New York. Carrying only a toothbrush, a comb, a pen, and three peace petitions, she took a vow to walk penniless and to remain a wanderer until humankind had learned the way of peace. She had no organizational backing, accepted no money, and owned only what she wore.

She never approached anyone, but waited for people to approach her. She walked five thousand miles that first trip, urging peace among nations, groups, and individuals, and urging people to seek that very important inner peace, because she believed that is where peace begins. Her message was a simple one: overcome evil with good, hatred with love, and falsehood with truth. She preached that people should tend to their own inner peace first, and with that in hand, they could better influence peace in the broader society and world. Her philosophy of spiritual maturity was later collected in *Steps toward Inner Peace,* a thirty-two-page pamphlet first printed in 1966.

For twenty-eight years, from 1953 to 1981, she crossed the country seven times, including trips to Mexico and Canada. On her second pilgrimage in 1955, she walked at least 100 miles in each state, visiting every state capital. In 1957, she walked 1,000 miles in Canada, crossing ten provinces, walking 100 miles in each. In 1964, arriving in Washington, D.C., she completed 25,000 miles on foot for peace and stopped counting. But she continued walking for another seventeen years. She began her fourth pilgrimage in 1966; her fifth in 1969; her sixth in 1973. In 1976, she visited Alaska and Hawaii. In 1978, she began her final pilgrimage.

Endowed with boundless energy and robust health, Peace Pilgrim averaged twenty-five miles a day, moving north in summer and south in winter to avoid cold weather. She seldom missed more than a few meals before someone fed her. Shelter was provided most nights, but if not, she slept in fields, under bridges, in haystacks and drainage pipes. She had several dangerous experiences, which she called opportunities, including near-death in a desert snowstorm. She was arrested for vagrancy twice, but when she was jailed, she found receptive female audiences for her philosophy and songs.

Though Peace Pilgrim was only five foot two, she was a spellbinding, forceful orator, commanding absolute attention in a room. She spoke in thousands of community centers, churches, schools, and homes, and was usually booked a year in advance. She was also a frequent guest on radio and TV stations, and corresponded with thousands by letter and her "Peace Pilgrim's Progress" newsletter.

On July 7, 1981, as she was being driven to her next speaking engagement, Peace Pilgrim was killed in a car accident outside Knox, Indiana. She was eleven days shy of her seventy-third birthday. Her ashes were interred in the family cemetery plot in Galloway Township, New Jersey.

When Peace Pilgrim stepped out alone in 1953, the cold war, the Korean War, and McCarthyism were her backdrop. It was a daring, groundbreaking feat that required enormous moral courage. Her sustaining it fearlessly for nearly three decades inspired all who met her, but especially women who could not imagine themselves walking alone through the desert at night or unmolested on inner-city streets. Like Gandhi, she lived the change she wanted to see. Her life was her message, and it created a spiritual chain reaction wherever she went.

Bibliography: Peace Pilgrim, Her Life and Work in Her Own Words, compiled posthumously by five friends and first published in 1982, is based on words gathered from her "Peace Pilgrim's Progress" newsletters, taped speeches, personal letters, interviews, and news articles over twenty-eight years; the quotations in the text are found on pages 8 and 21. Researchers will find additional source materials and her letters in the Swarthmore College Peace Collection, Swarthmore, Pennsylvania. Ann Rush, "Peace Pilgrim, an Extraordinary Life," *Advanced Development* 4 (January 1992), traces Peace Pilgrim's development from her early life to her gradual spiritual transformation to a life of commitment and total service. *Peace Pilgrim: Spirit of Peace* (1997) is a documentary film containing interviews with those who knew Peace Pilgrim and those who were inspired by her message. *Peace Pilgrim: An American Sage Who Walked Her Talk* (2000) is a documentary film that includes photos and footage from her early life and pilgrimages as well as interviews with family members and friends who knew her. *Friends of Peace Pilgrim Newsletter* is a semi-annual newsletter put out by Friends of Peace Pilgrim to disseminate the work of Peace Pilgrim and news from people who continue to be influenced by her.

MARTA DANIELS

S

SADKER, Myra Pollack. March 3, 1943–March 18, 1995. Feminist, educator, writer.

Myra Pollack Sadker's contribution to helping teachers understand the ways schools discriminate against girls was a breakthrough that challenged the myth that America provides equal education for all. Through her research, teaching, writings, and public speaking, Sadker worked tirelessly to educate Americans about the academic, psychological, physical, and professional costs of sexism and gender bias in education. Born in Portland, Maine, she was the oldest of the two children of Shirley Shilling and Louis Pollack. Her father, born in New York City, was a linotypist with three years of college; her mother, a native of Maine, worked as a secretary for the state after high school. On both sides of her family, Myra Pollack was descended from Polish and Russian Jews who migrated to the United States in the early twentieth century.

Myra was raised in very modest circumstances in Augusta, Maine, where she attended Farrington Elementary School and graduated from Cony High School in 1960. Her early years were marked by a strong motivation to learn and achieve, often within the context of academic institutions that devalued her accomplishments because she was female. After high school, she enrolled in Boston University, where she received a BA in English in 1964. Though her family had few financial resources, Myra lost a college scholarship to a far wealthier male student because, as a professor explained, the male student would need to support a family someday. This incident set the stage for her later graduate and professional research on the many ways girls and women experience discrimination in education.

In 1965 Myra Pollack married David Miller Sadker. The couple had met while pursuing master's degrees in teaching at Harvard University. After receiving the MAT degree in 1965, Myra Sadker began a series of teaching positions in Virginia, Maine, Massachusetts, and Thailand. The Sadkers formed a deep personal and professional partnership, researching gender issues as a team and authoring numerous books and articles together throughout their careers in education. The couple had two daughters: Robin (1970) and Jacqueline (1975).

A turning point in Myra Sadker's career occurred in 1968 at the University of Massachusetts in Amherst. Though she had received a fellowship to the PhD program in English, Myra transferred into the less prestigious EdD program, where her husband was enrolled as a doctoral student. Though multicultural education was a significant focus of the university at the time, Myra and David Sadker grew increasingly aware of gender bias throughout the institution. For instance, their co-authored articles and proposals were considered "David's work." Women were often quieter and less influential in male-dominated classroom discussions. As an editor of the campus newspaper, Myra Sadker wrote an editorial on sexism at the university entitled "The Only Socially Acceptable Form of Discrimination." This article led to her landmark 1973 book, *Sexism in School and Society,* co-authored with Nancy Frazier and published two years after Sadker received the EdD degree.

After two years as an assistant professor at the University of Wisconsin–Parkside, Myra Sadker joined the faculty of American University in 1973. She had a twenty-two-year career there, as professor, dean, and co-director of several projects devoted to teacher and principal effectiveness and the analysis of gender bias. Sadker was also a prolific writer. Her books defined a field and showed the interconnections between contemporary gender bias and the historical struggle for the educational rights of women and girls. Through numerous articles and more than a dozen federally funded research grants, Myra and David Sadker exposed the lack of awareness to gender bias prevalent in teacher training and wrote new textbooks that addressed the issue.

Throughout the 1980s and the early 1990s, Myra and David Sadker's research focused on classroom interaction. Their conclusion—that from primary school to graduate school, male students consistently received more attention from teachers than female students did—culminated in their book *Failing at Fairness: How America's Schools Cheat Girls* (1994). They also argued that while girls are consistently shortchanged educationally, boys too suffered the costs of sexism through pressures that undervalue their future family roles as husbands and fathers. Along with her husband, Myra Sadker offered presentations and workshops in more than forty states and overseas, and took their findings to popular audiences through guest appearances on network television. Though the Sadkers' research was denounced and criticized by conservative groups, Myra Sadker bravely advocated for the educational rights of children and encouraged parents to challenge the debilitating effect of sexism in schools.

The many honors she received in her lifetime reflect the range of Myra Sadker's accomplishments and the impact she made on the field of education. Among them were the Eleanor Roosevelt Award (1994) for education research and development presented by the American Association of University Women, and the 1994 Educational Achievement Award for research and writing on behalf of girls' education, presented by the National Coalition of Girls' Schools.

Myra Sadker died on March 18, 1995, at Georgetown University Hospital in Washington, D.C., after undergoing a bone marrow transplant as treatment for breast cancer. She was fifty-two years old. Myra Sadker Advocates for Gender Equity, a nonprofit organization founded in her memory, continues her dedication to promoting equity in and beyond schools.

Bibliography: The best introduction to Myra Sadker is through her research, starting with *Sexism in School and Society* (1973), co-authored with Nancy Frazier. She was the co-author with David Sadker of *Now upon a Time: A Contemporary View of Children's Literature* (1977); *Teachers Make the Difference: An Introduction to Education* (1980); *Sex Equity Handbook for Schools* (1982); *Teachers, Schools and Society* (1988); and *Failing at Fairness: How America's Schools Cheat Girls* (1994). A special issue of *Equity and Excellence in Education* 33, no. 1 (April 2000), on gender equity in education, appeared in her memory; see especially David Sadker's "Myra and Me" (pp. 4–8). David Sadker also provided invaluable assistance. Obituaries appeared in the *Washington Post* on March 20, 1995, and the *New York Times* on March 21, 1995.

SHERYL A. KUJAWA-HOLBROOK

SAGER, Ruth. February 7, 1918–March 29, 1997. Geneticist.

Ruth Deborah Sager was born in Chicago, the only child of Deborah Borovik and Leon Sager, a business executive. After her mother died in the flu epidemic of 1918, her maternal grandparents took over many aspects of her early upbringing until 1922, when her father married Hannah Schulman, with whom he had two more daughters, Esther and Naomi. The connection with the Borovik family remained strong throughout Sager's life.

Hannah and Leon were very involved with social and cultural issues and encouraged this interest in their daughters. After graduating at age sixteen from New Trier High School in Winnetka, Sager enrolled at the University of Chicago. She began as an English major but changed to the biological sciences after taking a course with charismatic physiologist Anton J. Carlson; she graduated in 1938 with a BS degree.

While touring in Palestine with her family in the summer of 1938, Sager became impressed with the spirit of independence and self-sufficiency of kibbutz members, and for several years after college graduation she became involved with the kibbutz movement in the States. She also began a graduate program in plant physiology at Rutgers University, where she earned a master's degree in October 1944 with a thesis on tomato-seedling nutrition.

In 1944 Ruth Sager married Seymour Melman and in 1945 they moved to New York City, where she enrolled at Columbia University, a world-renowned center for genetics research during this period. Her husband later became a professor of industrial economy at Columbia, but their childless marriage ended in divorce in 1960. Sager's doctoral thesis on corn genetics was completed in 1948 under the direction of Marcus Rhoades. Although her dissertation had focused on nuclear genes, her interest was drawn early to the nontraditional area of cytoplasmic inheritance, in part owing to Rhoades's research on pollen sterility.

After obtaining her doctorate, Sager received a Merck postdoctoral fellowship (1949–51) to work in the laboratory of Samuel Granick at Rockefeller Institute. Prior to starting at Rockefeller, Sager spent the summer at Stanford's Hopkins Marine Biology Station, where, in what she remembered as one of the great scientific intellectual experiences of her life, she took a microbiology course given by Cornelius Van Niel. Searching for a model microorganism that would be amenable to studying mutations affecting the chloroplast, she was given a sample of the single-celled green alga *Chlamydomonas reinhardi* by Gilbert Morgan Smith, a world-renowned algologist. During the six years Sager worked at Rockefeller Institute, first as a postdoctoral fellow and then as an assistant biochemist with Granick, she published classic papers on nutritional regulation of *Chlamydomonas* and began studying chloroplast structure and cytoplasmic mutations.

Unable to obtain a permanent position at Rockefeller, Sager returned to Columbia in 1955 as a research associate, working in lab space provided by Francis Ryan. In 1961 Sager and Ryan co-authored *Cell Heredity: An Analysis of the Mechanics of Heredity at the Cellular Level,* which is considered the first textbook on molecular genetics. Although without a faculty position and therefore unable to have graduate students, she obtained her own support for her salary and research through grants from the National Science Foundation, the American Cancer Society, and the National Institutes of Health. When Ryan died in 1965, she was faced with finding a new position and was appointed professor of biology at Hunter College, where she stayed until 1975. Though not a research university, Hunter was able to provide laboratory space for Sager's work. Her research at Rockefeller, Columbia, and Hunter was reported in over fifty papers and was largely on the biology and genetics of *Chlamydomonas* chloroplast genes. Many of these publications were co-authored with her research associate Zenta Ramanis, with whom she wrote more than twenty papers between 1963 and 1976.

Sager is credited with overcoming two major technical obstacles in working in the formerly intractable area of cytoplasmic genes—the difficulty of obtaining mutations, and the problem of using segregation and recombination analysis with genes that have a pattern of maternal inheritance. In overcoming these obstacles, she was able to provide both a conceptual framework and the experimental methods for work on cytoplasmic genes. Her second book, *Cytoplasmic Genes and Organelles* (1972), summarized the work on cytoplasmic genes in the chloroplasts and mitochondria of *Chlamydomonas,* yeast, fungi, and higher plants. Sager's work on chloroplast genetics (along with the work of others on mitochondrial genetics) made a major contribution to the current view of the evolution of eukaryotic cell organelles by the endocytosis of symbiotic bacteria.

In the early 1970s, Sager began to shift her interest from chloroplast genetics to the genetics of cancer. She spent a year (1972–73) as a Guggenheim Fellow in the laboratory of Sir Michael Stoker at the Imperial Cancer Research Laboratory in London, where she concentrated on learning techniques for culturing animal cells. In 1973 Sager married Arthur Pardee, a biochemist at Princeton University, and two years later they both moved to the Sidney Farber (now Dana-Farber) Cancer Research Institute in Boston, where Sager was appointed professor of cellular genetics and chief of the Cancer Genetics Division at Harvard Medical School. Sager and Pardee maintained separate but related research programs and were co-authors on several papers.

In the field of cancer genetics, Sager is known for her pioneering studies on tumor suppressor genes such as the mammary serpin, maspin. In addition, she developed culture methods to compare normal and cancerous cells, used cell hybrids to demonstrate tumor suppression, provided evidence for the increase of genetic instability in cancer cells, and pioneered in the identification of genes in cancer cells that were functionally altered by changing their rate of expression but whose DNA was not modified by mutation.

In addition to her two books, Sager published more than two hundred research papers. Sager's success was due to her brilliance as an experimentalist, her persistent hard work over five decades, her outstanding training, and the support and mentoring she received from a series of scientists, including Marcus Rhoades, Francis Ryan, and Arthur Pardee. Not unlike other notable women scientists of this era, Sager obtained her first faculty position at a women's college at age forty-seven and her first independent faculty position at a research university ten years later. Ruth Sager was elected to the National Academy of Sciences in 1977, the American Academy of Arts and Sciences in 1978, and the Institute of Medicine in 1992. She died of bladder cancer at her home in Brookline, Massachusetts, in 1997 at the age of seventy-nine.

Bibliography: Ruth Sager's archives, which include lab notebooks, correspondence, photographs, and videos, are housed at the library of the Marine Biological Laboratory in Woods Hole, Massachusetts. Biographical information can be found in *Biographical Memoirs of the National Academy of Sciences* 80 (2001), pp. 276–89, which includes Arthur B. Pardee's brief but detailed synopsis of Sager's scientific contributions. See also *Current Biography* (1967), pp. 367–70; and the essay by Carol A. Biermann in Louise S. Grinstein, Carol A. Biermann, and Rose K. Rose, eds., *Women in the Biological Sciences* (1997), pp. 467–76, which provides a more complete list of Sager's publications. Some of the information for this essay came from an unpublished interview with Sager by Bonnie Spanier, and from unpublished research by Gail K.

Schmitt. An excellent contextual analysis of Sager's contributions to chloroplast genetics can be found in Jan Sapp, *Beyond the Gene: Cytoplasmic Inheritance and the Struggle for Authority in Genetics* (1987). Some of Sager's early papers are classic and highly cited: see especially, "Nutritional Studies with *Chlamydomonas*" (with Samuel Granick), *Annals of the New York Academy of Sciences* 56 (1953), pp. 831–38; "Nutritional Control of Sexuality in *Chlamydomonas reinhari*" (with Granick), *Journal of General Physiology* 37 (1954), pp. 729–42; and "Mendelian and non-Mendelian inheritance of streptomycin resistance in *Chlamydomonas reinhardi*," *Proceedings of the National Academy of Sciences* 40 (1954), pp. 356–63. For reviews by Sager of her later work, see "Tumor Suppressor Genes: The Puzzle and the Promise," *Science*, December 15, 1989, pp. 1406–12; and "Expression Genetics in Cancer: Shifting the Focus from DNA to RNA," *Proceedings of the National Academy of Sciences* 94 (1997), pp. 952–55. Mary J. C. Hendrix, ed., *Maspin* (2002), is dedicated to Sager and includes a review of work on maspin done in Sager's lab. An obituary appeared in the *New York Times* on April 4, 1997.

PATRICIA STOCKING BROWN
AND GAIL K. SCHMITT

SAMPSON, Edith Spurlock. October 13, 1897–October 8, 1979. Lawyer, state official, judge.

Edith Lucille Spurlock was one of eight children of Louis and Elizabeth McGruder Spurlock. Born in Pittsburgh, she attended Lincoln Elementary and graduated from Peabody High School in 1915. Her father managed a cleaning and dyeing company during the day and worked nights as a waiter for a large catering establishment. Her mother, a housewife, helped out with a part-time millinery and false hair business. Neither of her parents had more than a grade school education. Spurlock described her mother as being very ambitious and participating in various community affairs such as the Lucy Stone Suffrage League. Their family lived modestly, with the children contributing to the household income on occasion. Edith's first job was in a fish market after school, scaling and pounding fish, when she was fourteen.

During high school, Spurlock set her sights on becoming a schoolteacher, until contacts she made through her church enabled her to gain employment with the Associated Charities of Pittsburgh as a social worker. She went on to further her education at the New York School of Social Work. While in New York, she was given a small indication of what the future held for her. In a criminology class led by Professor George Kirchwey, a professor at Columbia University law school, Spurlock distinguished herself as a promising legal scholar. After an examination on which Spurlock made the highest grade among her classmates, Kirchwey asked her what vocation she intended to pursue. When she answered social work, he replied that she had the earmark of one who should study law.

After completing her studies in New York, Spurlock returned to Pittsburgh, where in May 1919 she married Rufus Sampson, the northern representative of Tuskegee Institute. Shortly after their marriage, they moved to Chicago, where she became a social worker for the Illinois Children's Home and Aid Society. As luck would have it, her path crossed once again with Professor Kirchwey. This time she took his advice and enrolled in night classes at John Marshall Law School while keeping her day job placing dependent children in new homes and finding adoptive homes for the neglected. Compounding this rigorous schedule, Sampson took over the care of two small children, left by a sister who died. Most of her studying was done on streetcars between jobs and family duties.

In 1925, Sampson received her law degree but failed to pass the Illinois State bar. She passed on the second try, but in the meantime became the first woman to receive a master's degree in law from Loyola University in 1927. Sampson began her legal career by working simultaneously as a lawyer in private practice and as a referee in Cook County Juvenile Court. During these years Sampson learned the practical side of the law. Sometime during the early 1930s she and Rufus Sampson divorced. In 1934, she married Chicago attorney Joseph Clayton, to whom she remained happily married until his death in 1956.

Sampson (as she continued to be known) practiced law out of her South Side office in Chicago, where she dealt mostly with criminal and domestic relations cases, gaining a reputation for helping those who would have difficulty getting legal advice elsewhere. In 1938, she, along with fellow John Marshall Law School alumnae Georgia Jones Ellis and Sophie Boaz, another Chicago attorney, broke the color bar of the National Association of Women Lawyers.

Appointed assistant state's attorney of Cook County in 1947, the arena of Sampson's work expanded in 1949 when she was invited to travel as a representative of the National Council of Negro Women, along with representatives of twenty-six other national organizations, on a world tour sponsored by America's Town Meeting of the Air. The purpose of the tour was to lecture and debate about the political issues of the day. At every stop of the tour, Sampson was questioned about the status of black Americans. Each time, she admitted to the horrible injustices directed at the black community, yet she continually pointed out how democracy, properly practiced, could lead to racial equality. At the end of this seventy-two day trip, which she paid for herself, the delegates agreed to make their group permanent, thereby organizing the World Town Hall Seminar. They elected Sampson president of the group and initiated a nationwide speaking tour.

Further drawing her away from her law practice and into world affairs, in 1950 President Truman appointed her to serve as alternate United States delegate to the fifth regular session of the United Nations General Assembly, becoming the first African American to be appointed a United Nations delegate. The committee to which she was appointed focused on the social, cultural, and humanitarian problems of the world. She personally debated such issues as land reform, reparation of prisoners, and the repatriation of Greek children. Sampson was reappointed in 1952.

From 1955 to 1962, Sampson served as assistant corporation counsel of the City of Chicago under Mayor Richard Daley, who was her political ally, and concurrently served as member-at-large for UNESCO during the Eisenhower administration. In 1961, Vice President Lyndon B. Johnson appointed her to serve on the U.S. Citizens Commission on the North Atlantic Treaty Organization. In 1964 and 1965 she was a member of the U.S. Advisory Committee on Private Enterprise in Foreign Aid.

In 1962, the local Democratic Party in Chicago nominated her to fill an unexpired term as a circuit court judge. She won the judgeship in a landslide, becoming the first black woman so elected in the United States. Throughout her years in the city's municipal court system, she presided over divorce courts, traffic courts, and landlord-tenant relations courts and received acclaim for her humanistic approach, her strong personality, and her warmth. She won reelection to the Circuit Court of Cook County in 1964 and 1970, and retired from the bench in 1978. Edith Spurlock Sampson died the following year in Chicago at the age of eighty-one.

Bibliography: Edith Spurlock Sampson's papers are at the Schlesinger Library, Radcliffe Institute for Advanced Study, Harvard University. The bulk of the collection pertains to her career as a judge and her work with the United Nations. Papers concerning her work with the National Council of Negro Women are in the National Archives for Black Women's History, Washington, D.C. For her philosophy about democracy and civil rights, see "I Like America," *Negro Digest,* December 1950, pp. 3–8. Articles about Sampson include "Lady Lawyers: Seventy Carry on Battle for Sex and Race Equality in Courts," *Ebony,* August 1947, pp. 18–21; *Current Biography* (1950), pp. 511–513; "Thorn in Russia's Side," *Negro Digest,* September 1951, pp. 3–7; and "Justice—Edith Sampson Style," *Reader's Digest,* November 1968, pp. 167–174. Sampson's birth date sometimes appears as 1901, but 1897 is confirmed by the Register of Wills, Pittsburgh, Pennsylvania, as well as the Office of Pupil Affairs, Peabody High School, Pittsburgh. Obituaries appeared in the *Chicago Tribune* on October 10, 1979, and the *New York Times* on October 11, 1979.

CECILY B. MCDANIEL

SARTON, May. May 3, 1912–July 16, 1995. Poet, writer.

May Sarton's publishing career began in 1930 and ended the year after her death with the publication of her last journal, *At Eighty-Two* (1996). Sarton's writing has spoken to people the world over—men and women, young and old, the highly literate and the casual reader. Of special value to women, she demonstrated that more than one model for life exists. To all she revealed the value of solitude. By reveling in the beauty of nature and the power of friendship and love in her writings, she emphasized aspects of the human condition often overlooked.

Born in Wondelgem, Belgium, Eleanore Marie Sarton was the only child of extraordinary parents. (A younger brother died in infancy.) Her father, George Sarton, founded the discipline of the history of science, publishing the first issue of *Isis,* the journal of the history of science and civilization, in 1912, the year May was born. Coming to the United States in 1915 as a refugee, George Sarton was soon established at Harvard University and as an associate of the Carnegie Institute. He was joined by his wife and daughter in 1916. Sarton would continue his work in Cambridge until his death in 1956. Her mother, Eleanor Mabel Elwes Sarton, an Englishwoman educated in Belgium, was an artist and designer, a passionate gardener, and although afflicted with ill health, the mainstay for the unworldly George's life's work. May Sarton's own character contained elements of both parents'—her father's strong, often blind, devotion to his work and her mother's love of the natural world. Both parents gave her unusual encouragement and leeway in her life and choice of a career.

Despite her wide reading and her intelligence, Sarton was not an intellectual. She had little formal education. The most important educational institution in her life was the experimental Shady Hill School in Cambridge. Here her talents for writing, especially poetry, were nourished. Here too she was exposed to gifted teachers, one of whom became her first "Muse." (Throughout her career, Sarton believed that she needed the influence of a greatly admired woman, who might or might not be a lover, to inspire her poetry.) Sarton moved from Shady Hill to Cambridge High and Latin School, from which she graduated in 1929, but did not accept the Vassar College scholarship she won. Instead she joined EVA LE GALLIENNE's Civic Repertory Theatre in New York City. When that troupe disbanded in 1933, Sarton ran her own Apprentice Theatre at the New School for Social Research until 1935. Her theater training, combined with her innate sense of the dramatic, made her a skilled performer when in later years she traveled the country reading her poetry.

After initial acclaim for her first book of poetry, *Encounter in April* (1937), and her first novel, *The Single Hound* (1938), Sarton was largely neglected by the critical world. She never belonged to any school of literature, nor did she participate in the experimental methods of the literary avant-garde. A steady and prolific writer, she continued to have popular success, though her enjoyment of it was blighted by the slight notices given her by the literary establishment. In addition to poetry and fiction, her stories and essays appeared in the *Ladies' Home Journal, Vogue,* and *Redbook,* as well as the *New Yorker.* In 1959 she published *I Knew a Phoenix: Sketches for an Autobiography,* the first of her many volumes of journals and memoirs. Sarton considered her poetry primary, but these books—close observations of the life around her, reflections, and narratives of her neighbors and herself—brought her many readers who came to believe they knew her personally through the intimate details of her life: her pets, her gardening and love of flowers, her friends, her struggles with breast cancer, a stroke, and depression.

In 1965 Sarton published *Mrs. Stevens Hears the Mermaids Singing,* a novel that presented the lesbianism of the protagonist openly, a daring statement at a time when lesbianism was usually mentioned obliquely if at all. Sarton resisted labeling and preferred not to be called a lesbian writer, believing that she wrote of human love of many kinds. Her frank treatment of love between women, however, created ripples that extended throughout the entire publishing world. She herself had many relationships with women, some of whom she regarded as her Muses, and had a longtime relationship with Judith Matlack, a teacher of English at Simmons College. They shared an apartment in Cambridge from 1945, the year they first met, until 1958, when Sarton moved to Nelson, New Hampshire. Even after that separation, they spent holidays and vacations together, until Matlack's failing mind prevented such occasions.

Despite her productivity and prominence with the reading public, Sarton was largely ignored by academic critics until the early 1970s, when Columbia University professor Carolyn G. Heilbrun began to correspond with her. In 1974 *Mrs. Stevens Hears the Mermaids Singing* was republished with a critical introduction by Heilbrun. By then the women's movement had discovered Sarton and her books were increasingly read in colleges and universities. Sarton was very much aware of this new phase of her life, which came as she herself was moving toward old age. As she continued to publish memoirs and journals, new readers discovered her, often by word of mouth.

In 1973, Sarton left New Hampshire and moved to York, Maine, to the house by the sea she described in her late journals. By the end of the decade, Sarton's health began to fail. She suffered from breast cancer, and although she had many other afflictions in later years, cancer caused her death in York in 1995 at the age of eighty-three. Her ashes were buried in Nelson Cemetery, under the stone figure of her totem, the phoenix that had stood in the garden of her Maine house.

May Sarton was a complex and often difficult woman, arousing either extreme devotion or extreme dislike in acquaintances. Slim and distinguished-looking in her youth, in middle age she cut a substantial figure, usually elegantly dressed, with her snow-white hair fashionably styled. A few wise friends could compass all the layers of Sarton the woman and appreciate the value of Sarton the writer, who brought solace and inspiration to so many readers. She did not fail to make a myth of her life, nor did she despair.

Bibliography: Lenora P. Blouin, *May Sarton: A Bibliography* (2nd ed., 2000), is the definitive bibliography. The major archives reside at Amherst College; Harvard University; the Berg Collection of the New York Public Library; Scripps College; and Westbrook College of the University of New England, Biddeford, Maine. The latter is particularly rich, containing much of Sarton's personal library, including video and audiotapes and photographs. Fourteen individual volumes of poetry were published before Sarton's *Collected Poems* appeared in 1993. A volume of new poems, *Coming into Eighty,* was published in 1994. Of her nineteen novels, *Mrs. Stevens Hears the Mermaids Singing* (1965) and *As We Are Now* (1973) may be the best known, but some of the earlier novels, in particular *The Bridge of Years* (1946) and *Faithful Are the Wounds* (1955), are often considered her best. Her finest prose may be found in her three memoirs: *I Knew a Phoenix: Sketches for an Autobiography* (1959), *Journal of a Solitude* (1973), and *A World of Light: Portraits and Celebrations* (1976). Less carefully crafted but with wide appeal are her journals, among them *Plant Dreaming Deep* (1968), *The House by the Sea* (1977), and *Endgame* (1992). In addition, Sarton wrote children's stories, plays, short stories, magazine and newspaper articles, translations, and film scripts. Her letters are being collected and edited by Susan Sherman; the first volume, *May Sarton: Selected Letters, 1916–1954,* appeared in 1997. In 1972, Agnes Sibley published *May Sarton* in the Twayne's United States Author Series. The first full-length critical treatment of Sarton was a collection of essays edited by Constance Hunting, *May Sarton: Woman and Poet* (1982). Hunting also edited essays and speeches from Westbrook College's National Conference "May Sarton at Eighty" in *A Celebra-*

tion for May Sarton (1994). A biography by Margot Peters, *May Sarton*, was published in 1997. An obituary appeared in the *New York Times* on July 18, 1995.

NANCY MACKNIGHT

SÁNCHEZ, Maria Clemencia Colón. January 3, 1926–November 25, 1989. Community activist, Connecticut state representative.

Maria Clemencia Colón was born in the small mountain town of Comerio, Puerto Rico, one of six children and a twin. When farm work could no longer sustain the family, her parents decided to move closer to the city to seek work. Although they taught their children the importance of getting an education, Maria was forced to leave school in the eighth grade and became chief housekeeper and caretaker for her younger brother. Determined to make a life for herself after her mother refused to allow her to join a convent, Maria decided instead to go to Hartford, Connecticut, to visit an aunt. Years later, in 1954, Hartford would become her permanent home.

Shortly after moving to Hartford, she married a man named Sánchez. In 1955 she gave birth to a daughter who lived for less than a week. She never had any more children, and she remained in the turbulent marriage until her husband's death. To support herself, Maria Sánchez went to work in the tobacco fields and quickly earned the respect of her fellow workers as crew leader. She later worked in a meatpacking company in New Britain, Connecticut, where she remained for the next several years. Upon her return to Hartford, she saved enough money to buy a newsstand there while still managing to send a portion of her salary to her mother in Puerto Rico.

Maria Sánchez's Hartford community became her family. She quickly became involved in the Catholic Church, beginning with her local parish of the Sacred Heart on Ely St. While at Sacred Heart, she was instrumental in organizing a group of Puerto Rican community activists who worked to get the first Spanish-speaking priest in their church and to move the Spanish Mass from the isolation of the basement to the main vestibule.

During the 1950s the Puerto Rican population in Connecticut increased steadily. The first visible Puerto Rican community in Hartford grew around the Clay Hill area, and "Maria's News Stand" was located in the heart of it. The newsstand became the launching pad for political and other community activism. It was also situated down the street from an elementary school, and Sánchez took every opportunity to speak about the importance of an education to the young people who stopped by on their way to and from school. To many Puerto Ricans in her community, Sánchez was the "madrina," the godmother. She functioned as a one-woman social service operation, interceding with city hall on behalf of her largely poor neighborhood regarding housing, education, and welfare issues. She also became the link between the politicians and the people they purportedly represented, holding voter registration drives outside of her store and getting out the vote on election day. Loyal relationships were formed between local politicians eager to be seen as "Maria's friend" and a woman who still struggled with her English but who wielded the ability to sway the vote in her community.

Sánchez made many other contributions to her community. She helped create community organizations such as the Puerto Rican Day Parade Committee, La Casa de Puerto Rico, the Society of Legal Services, the Spanish American Merchants Association, and the Community Renewal Team. She also founded the Puerto Rican Coronation Ball, a special event designed to raise funds for the church. In 1964 she helped found the Puerto Rican Day State Parade.

By the mid 1960s, Sánchez was an active participant in Hartford politics. In 1966, she became treasurer of the Puerto Rican Democratic Club of Hartford and was an active member of the Latin American Action Project. She then sought and won a seat on the Hartford Democratic Committee. Her mission was the same as in the previous decade—to gain recognition and support for the issues in her community. These commitments, however, began to take their toll on her health. Often it would be midnight before she realized she had not eaten or taken the medicine to control her diabetes.

Sánchez's fight for bilingual education, the cause for which she is best known, came to fruition in 1972 with the establishment of the Ann Street School, which began a pilot program that drew children from all over the city. Hartford's first groups of bilingual educators were mostly Puerto Ricans trained at the Ann Street School through a Teacher's Corps program.

In 1973, Sánchez began her sixteen-year tenure as an elected member of Hartford's school board. She was the first Puerto Rican woman to hold public office in that city. Not always following party lines, she voted for what she considered to be in the best interest of the community's children, such as supporting the appointment of Herman LaFontaine, the first Puerto Rican superintendent of schools.

In 1988, Sánchez successfully challenged Abraham L. Giles for the State House of Representatives to become the first Puerto Rican woman elected to the Connecticut General Assembly. The Sixth District represented the central and northeast sections of Hartford, an area that was gradually becoming more Latino and African American. Sánchez fought for the rights of Puerto Ricans at the state level in Hartford with the same vigor she had brought to all her community activism, but her political career ended prematurely. In 1989, just one year into her term, Maria Sánchez died at her Hartford home at the age of sixty-three, most likely from complications of diabetes. She was buried beside her parents in Comerio, Puerto Rico. In 1991 the Maria C. Sánchez Elementary School on Babcock Street in Hartford was named in her honor, and two years later she became the first Puerto Rican named to the Connecticut Women's Hall of Fame.

Bibliography: Sources on Maria Sánchez are limited. A paper by Helen Ubinas, "The Life and Times of Maria Clemencia Colón Sánchez: Hartford's Puerto Rican Community's Matriarch, 1926–1989," for the Hartford Studies Project at Trinity College offers an overview of her life. For her political influence, see "An Institution Called Sánchez: Politician, Role Model, Refuge," *Hartford Courant*, January 15, 1981. For general background on Puerto Rican political mobilization and ethnicity, see José E. Cruz, *Identity and Power: Puerto Rican Politics and the Challenge of Ethnicity* (1998), and Andrés Torres and José E. Velázquez, eds., *The Puerto Rican Movement: Voices from the Diaspora* (1998). See also Robert E. Pawlowski, *La Gente, La Casa: The Development of Hartford's Puerto Rican Community*, a publication of La Casa de Puerto Rico found at the University of Connecticut, and Ruth Glasser, *Aqui me Quedo: Puerto Ricans in Connecticut* (1997). Magalie Rodríguez, of the Sánchez Elementary School, provided valuable assistance to the author. Obituaries appeared in the *Hartford Courant* on November 26 and 29, 1989, and the *New York Times* on November 27, 1989.

LINDA C. DELGADO

SCHARRER, Berta Vogel. December 1, 1906–July 23, 1995. Neuroscientist.

Berta Vogel was born in Munich, Germany, the eldest of four children of Johanna Greis, a homemaker, and Karl Phillip Vogel, a judge who served as vice president of the federal court of Bavaria. Berta grew up in a prosperous middle-class family and had a happy childhood filled with art and music. She attended the girls' gymnasium in Munich, where she developed an interest in biology and decided early that she wanted to become a research scientist. Upon passing the gymnasium examinations, she entered the University of Munich and became a student of Karl von Frisch, the well-known expert in bee behavior and 1973 Nobel Laureate in Physiology or Medicine. She earned her PhD from the University of Munich in 1930.

While Berta Vogel was a doctoral student in Professor Frisch's laboratory, she met a fellow student, her future husband, Ernst Scharrer. They married in 1934, when Ernst had completed a medical degree in neuroanatomy and a PhD in zoology. Berta and Ernst remained close scientific collaborators until Ernst's untimely death in 1965. Ernst Scharrer had discovered that certain hypothalamic neurons of a fish had secretory activity similar to that of an endocrine gland cell, which was a controversial, unexpected, but very significant finding in 1928. The Scharrers jointly pursued this finding. Ernst studied these cells in vertebrates while Berta searched for similar phenomena in invertebrates.

The Scharrers decided at the outset of their careers that Ernst would find paid positions and that Berta would find space and work as an unpaid researcher in the same laboratory so that they would not run afoul of anti-nepotism rules. They did not have children because Berta believed that she could not continue her scientific work while raising children on one academic salary. In 1934 Ernst Scharrer accepted a position as director of the Edinger Institute for Brain Research in Frankfurt, where Berta Scharrer obtained laboratory space but neither title nor salary. The Scharrers, neither of whom was Jewish, had hoped that the Institute might remain insulated from political events and the rise of Nazism, but they soon encountered increasing pressure to shun Jewish colleagues and to join Nazi organizations. Finding the Nazi system increasingly intolerable, in 1937 the Scharrers left Germany for the United States, leaving behind their work, their friends, and their families.

Ernst accepted a one-year fellowship at the University of Chicago, while Berta obtained an unpaid position as research associate. She was given no research funds but managed to find her experimental subjects—cockroaches—at no cost in the basement of her laboratory building. The following year, the Scharrers moved to New York, her husband as visiting investigator at the Rockefeller Institute for Medical Research, Berta as unpaid research associate, the first of numerous relocations. In 1940 her husband joined the faculty at Western Reserve University (now Case Western Reserve University) while Berta was appointed an instructor and fellow in anatomy. In 1945 both Scharrers became U.S. citizens.

In 1946 Berta Scharrer followed her husband to the University of Colorado Medical School in Denver. There she won a Guggenheim Fellowship and a U.S. Public Health Service Special Fellowship, but she still had no title. In 1950, when invited to organize an international symposium in Paris, she asked the dean of the medical school to give her a title so she could list it on the program. He appointed her "Assistant Professor (research), unsalaried."

Finally, in 1955, Berta Scharrer obtained her first paid position as tenured professor of anatomy at the newly opened Albert Einstein College of Medicine of Yeshiva University in the Bronx, where her husband had been recruited to become chairman of the anatomy department. At Einstein she taught medical school classes and became a key mentor to the medical students, but she still received only half a salary. Berta Scharrer's life changed abruptly in 1965 when Ernst died tragically, caught in the undertow while swimming in the ocean in Miami where the Scharrers were attending the annual meeting of anatomists. Berta herself narrowly escaped the same fate. After her husband's death, Berta Scharrer agreed to serve as acting chair of the anatomy department until a successor for her husband could be found, but she refused to be considered for permanent chair. For the first time in her career she now received full salary. In 1967 she was elected to the National Academy of Sciences, one of the first few women scientists to be so honored, as well as the American Academy of Arts and Sciences. In 1978, at age seventy-two, Berta Scharrer was appointed distinguished university professor emerita, and in 1983 she received the National Medal of Science from President Reagan. Her stellar research career continued until she died on July 23, 1995, in New York City at the age of eighty-eight.

The Scharrers jointly opened up the entirely new field of neuroendocrinology, an experimental and clinical science that explores the relationship between an organism's central nervous system and its internal secretions. Berta Scharrer's experiments with insects, specifically the cockroach, provided the most convincing early proof of the physiological significance of neurosecretion. In the 1980s her research placed neurosecretion in a wider evolutionary and biological framework. Throughout her life she remained an important spokesperson for the broadest view of the significance of the neuropeptides. In her late eighties, despite increasing physical handicaps, she moved into yet another new field, comparative neuroimmunology, and together with colleagues showed that the interaction of neurosecretory cells and neuropeptides with the immune system in invertebrates is strikingly similar to that in analogous vertebrate systems.

Science was Berta Scharrer's life. She had enormous physical stamina. While in Colorado, Berta and her husband enjoyed a vigorous life of mountaineering and skiing. Colleagues, students, and friends remembered her for her openness, warmth, and consideration and as a nurturing, attentive teacher. Friends describe her as a private, unobtrusive, scrupulously honest person. Berta Scharrer encountered much hostility as a woman, but in the words of one of her colleagues, "Berta persevered and more than succeeded in her scientific and personal goals where others might easily have given up."

Bibliography: Sources of information about Scharrer include Dominic P. Purpura, "Berta V. Scharrer," *Biographical Memoirs* 74 (1998), pp. 288–307; Birgit H. Satir and Peter Satir, "Berta Vogel Scharrer (1906–1995)," in Louise S. Grinstein, Carol A. Biermann, and Rose K. Rose, eds., *Women in the Biological Sciences: A Bibliographic Sourcebook* (1997), which includes a list of Berta Scharrer's scientific publications; and "On Journeys Well Traveled," in S. K. Millen, ed., *Einstein*, Spring/Summer 1989, pp. 3–6, which is based on an interview with Berta Scharrer. See also Steven Wissig, "A Tribute to Berta Scharrer," *Anatomical Record* 249, no. 1 (September 19, 1997), pp. 1–5; and Karen Young Kreeger, "Pioneering Neuroscientist Berta Vogel Scharrer Dies," *Scientist* 9, no. 17 (September 4, 1995), p. 17. "Berta V. Scharrer Memorial," *Einstein Quarterly Journal of Biology and Medicine* 12 (1996), pp. 142–51, contains reminiscences by colleagues and former students from the memorial service held at Albert Einstein College of Medicine in September 1995; the final quotation appears on p. 149. Scharrer discusses her career in a video documentary, *Berta Scharrer: A Partner in the Discovery of Neurohormones* (1987), available at the U.S. National Library of Medicine, Bethesda, Maryland. Additional archival material about Scharrer is located at the Department of Anatomy of the Albert Einstein College of Medicine, Bronx, New York. An obituary appeared in the *New York Times* on July 25, 1995.

ELGA R. WASSERMAN

SCHIFF, Dorothy. March 11, 1903–August 30, 1989. Newspaper owner and publisher.

Dorothy Schiff was born and reared in the house on Manhattan's Fifth Avenue that her grandfather, prominent German Jewish investment banker and philanthropist Jacob Henry Schiff, had given her father, Mortimer, when he married Adele Neustadt. Her mother's family inhabited the same social circles as the Schiffs. Dorothy and her younger brother had a materially privileged but emotionally austere childhood in which, she later told her biographer, "there was no joy, none" (Potter, p. 50).

After graduating from Brearley School in 1920 and spending one academically disastrous year at Bryn Mawr, she married the charming but impecunious socialite Richard B. W. Hall on October 17, 1923. They had two children: Mortimer (1924) and Adele (1925). Schiff later said their union had been based on her desire to leave home and his to marry money, and she divorced him in 1932 after her parents' deaths left her an heiress.

By then she had already entered an entirely different world with the man who became her second husband, writer George Backer. They were married on October 21, 1932; their daughter Sarah-Ann was born in 1934. Backer, a minor member of the Algonquin Circle, was active in New Deal politics, and through him she became involved in social welfare work, which led to a state post in President Roosevelt's 1936 campaign and a friendship with both Roosevelts. (Her 1976 authorized biography caused a rumpus by broadly hinting that her relationship with the president had been sexual, but she insisted readers were misinterpreting a simply flirtatious friendship.) She later credited her involvement in liberal politics, a dramatic break with her family's traditional Republicanism, with helping her overcome a severe anxiety neurosis that intensive psychoanalysis had not cured.

In 1939, George Backer asked Schiff to bankroll his purchase of a tatterdemalion afternoon paper, the *New York Post,* notable only for its longevity—founded by Alexander Hamilton in 1801, it was the country's oldest daily—and its rarity as a pro-Roosevelt organ when most publishers opposed the president. Within three years, tired of losing money, Schiff took over the paper herself, becoming the first female publisher in New York. With the support of her features editor, Theodore Olin Thackrey, whom she married on July 29, 1943, a week after divorcing Backer, she remade the paper as a tabloid, maintaining its staunch liberalism but adding more pictures, features, and local news. But the couple's political and other disagreements (in 1948 Dorothy supported Thomas E. Dewey and Ted endorsed Henry Wallace in dueling *Post* columns) led in 1949 to Schiff's third divorce.

The paper entered its golden age in the 1950s under editor James A. Wechsler. Profitable at last, it gained a reputation as the intellectual's tabloid, covering civil rights and labor as assiduously as nightlife and crime; its motto, quipped the press critic A. J. Liebling, was "*Lux et Sex.*" It hired talented young reporters and published a huge roster of liberal columnists, including Max Lerner and Murray Kempton. Schiff herself wrote a regular column that roved from gossip about political dinners to outrage over the racially motivated murder of Emmett Till.

The *Post*'s investigative series were famously fearless, taking on such sacred cows as Robert Moses, Senator Joseph McCarthy ("Smear, Inc." preceded Edward R. Murrow's landmark CBS documentaries by two years), and J. Edgar Hoover. McCarthy retaliated with an investigation of Wechsler, and Hoover, as Schiff cheekily reported in a bylined story, tried a menu of pressure tactics to have the series killed. The *Post* broke the story of Richard Nixon's campaign "slush fund" under the typically extravagant headline "Secret Rich Men's Trust Fund Keeps Nixon in Style Far Beyond His Salary." In 1958, after the *Post* had unenthusiastically endorsed Averell Harriman for New York governor, Schiff changed her mind and in the last edition before election day urged readers to vote for Nelson Rockefeller instead. Schiff's switch was widely credited with electing Rockefeller, but many furious readers denounced what they saw as her treachery.

Schiff again showed an independent streak during the printers' strike that shut down New York's seven major dailies in 1962–63. After eighty-six days, fearing for her paper's survival and feeling marginalized by her six stronger colleagues, she broke ranks and resumed publication. The strike was finally settled after 114 days, but by 1967 its aftershocks helped kill off four of the other six struck papers. Theodore Kheel, the city's mediator, later eulogized Schiff in the *Post* as "the only publisher in New York with balls."

But the *Post* too was struggling in the chilly newspaper climate of the 1960s and 1970s, despite (or, as some longtime readers believed, because of) Schiff's decision to appoint a "softer" editor in 1961 and name herself editor-in-chief in 1962. The *Post*'s coverage grew steadily frothier, its news budget stingier, and its influence flabbier. Though few were surprised that in 1976 the *Post* was scooped on its own biggest story, Schiff's sale of the paper for an estimated $30 million, the buyer was a shock: Australian press magnate Rupert Murdoch, the avatar of "boobs and bums" journalism. Although he insisted he would not change the paper's character, Murdoch soon steered it toward aggressive conservatism and "Headless Body in Topless Bar" raucousness. Schiff's stated reasons for selling varied: either the paper was losing too much money or she wanted to save her heirs from large inheritance taxes.

Schiff married her fourth husband, Baltimore industrialist Rudolf Sonneborn, on August 18, 1953, and divorced him in 1974 after years of separation. She resumed her birth name after her third divorce, but used "Mrs." instead of "Miss" at her brother's urging that "Mrs." was seemlier for a woman with children. (She strongly disapproved of "Ms.") Schiff died of cancer in 1989 at her Manhattan apartment at the age of eighty-six.

Raised in a wealthy and conservative family that had prepared her only for wifehood, the accidental newspaperwoman emerged as an unlikely but forceful voice for little-guy liberalism in an era when its champions were both rare and endangered. Impatient with abstractions, famously imperious, often called eccentric (not always with fondness), Schiff relished her reputation as one of New York's most powerful women but proudly confessed to loving gossip and sharing her readers' popular tastes. In her inaugural column on September 30, 1951, she described her goal: to "share with like-minded people the excitement and stimulation that keep me burning and active as publisher of a militantly liberal newspaper, in a world seething with despair and discontent, but at the same time, in many places, aspiring toward the stars."

Bibliography: The large collection of Dorothy Schiff Papers at the New York Public Library includes Schiff's letters, office memoranda, photographs, clippings, and other personal and family papers, as well as the *Post's* editorial, operational, business, and legal files. Her column, for most of its life entitled "Dear Reader," ran frequently but irregularly from 1951 to 1958. Jeffrey Potter, *Men, Money and Magic: The Story of Dorothy Schiff* (1976), based largely on his interviews with Schiff, emphasizes her romances, marriages, and friendships with the famous. For A. J. Liebling's assessment, see "New York Revisited," *New Yorker,* October 29, 1955, pp. 106+. On the postwar New York press in general, see Liebling, *The Press* (1961, rev. 1975). The seventeen-part series "Smear, Inc." began in the *Post* on September 4, 1951, and James Wechsler's *Age of Suspicion* (1953) includes his account of McCarthy's investigation. The slush fund story appeared in the *Post* on September 18, 1952; Schiff's "My Secret Life with J. Edgar Hoover" ran October 5–6, 1959. On the decline of the *Post,* see Jack Newfield, "Goodbye, Dolly! A Reminiscence of the *New York Post,*" *Harper's,* September 1969, pp. 92–98. The article on Schiff in *Contemporary Authors* 121 (1987) includes a 1985 interview. Obituaries appeared in the *New York Times* and the *New York Post* on August 31, 1989.

ANDIE TUCHER

SCHÖNBERG, Bessie. December 27, 1906–May 14, 1997. Dancer, dance educator.

Calling herself a meddler rather than a teacher, Bessie Schönberg molded the course of concert dance in the twentieth century with her broad-minded teaching methods and watchful tutelage. She inspired and mentored so many in the dance world that the annual New York Dance and Performance Awards presented by Dance Theater Workshop in New York City are called the Bessies.

Bessie Schönberg was born in Hanover, Germany, in 1906. Her mother, Rose Elizabeth McGrew, an American opera singer, had met her father, an engineering student from Dresden named Schönberg (first name unknown), when she came to Germany to study voice. The youngest of three girls, Schönberg grew up surrounded by the arts, her father serving as her mother's accompanist in rehearsals and her companion to museums and performances in Dresden. The idyll soon shattered, first when Schönberg's mother returned to the United States before World War I, then with her father's military service, beginning in 1914. Living in Dresden with her father's sister, a photographer, Schönberg found consolation in the arts, modern theater, poets, music, and painters—and particularly dance. She began lessons in Dalcroze, a kind of rhythmic gymnastics, and was so entranced that she grew distracted in her other studies. When her father returned from the war, he abruptly ended the lessons. He considered dance a profession suitable only for the lower class, and Bessie took no more dance classes while in Germany. Instead, she stood in front of a store window staring at a photograph of Mary Wigman, the German dancer just then beginning to define a modern style of concert dance.

Schönberg's mother came back to Germany in 1926 and took Bessie back with her to Eugene, Oregon, where she was teaching in the music department of the University of Oregon. Here Schönberg took courses in painting and sculpture, and, finally, dance. Her classes there did not inspire her, however. Movement reminiscent of ISADORA DUNCAN was too sentimental and loose for Schönberg; stately and solid herself, she desired more discipline and weight to the body. She finally found what she had been seeking for so long in the classes of a newly hired teacher from New York City, MARTHA HILL.

Hill was fresh from classes with MARTHA GRAHAM, who was then assembling a technique that featured bodies laden with force and meaning. When Hill left Oregon to return to New York City in 1929, Schönberg went with her and arrived in the middle of a dance revolution. Modern dance solidified in the decade following the passage of women's suffrage in 1920. Graham, DORIS HUMPHREY, HELEN TAMIRIS, and other women were eschewing the confines of both ballet and show dancing and creating expressive movement imbued with the social and political issues of the day. Female modern dancers did not ardently embrace specific goals about changing the status of women, but their roles as choreographers, performers, teachers, and directors of companies placed them in the middle of ongoing debates about what women were capable of, the differences and similarities between men and women, and the role of women as creators of and commentators on American culture.

Schönberg placed herself at the forefront of these changes by aligning herself with Martha Graham. She took classes and performed some of Graham's groundbreaking early works, including *Heretic* and *Primitive Mysteries,* until a knee injury in 1931 sidelined her and eventually forced her to give up a performing career. Martha Hill offered her an alternative—a teaching position. Although Schönberg was still bitter and unsure what to do, she accepted a job as Martha Hill's assistant at Bennington College in 1933, finished her BA degree there the next year, and then pieced together a variety of teaching jobs in Connecticut, Philadelphia, and New York City, before settling at

Sarah Lawrence College in 1938. She became director of theater and dance there in 1956 and stayed until her mandatory retirement in 1975, after which she continued teaching at a variety of schools in the New York City area until her death.

Although trained in Graham technique, Schönberg did not subscribe to one particular dance method. Instead, she developed courses based on principles of movement—space, pressure, gravity, time, rhythm—that often sounded more like courses in physics. She devised problems that students would have to figure out (some remembered them as diabolical), such as showing a day's weather through movement. This approach bred an open-mindedness and breadth that allowed students to flourish across a variety of aesthetic trends in dance. In the 1960s and 1970s, when dancers eschewed technique, employed pedestrian movement, and broke with theatrical conventions, she acknowledged that even a walk could have an artistic intent. Schönberg recognized the fragility of creation, and her capacity to look, judge discreetly, and prod gently made her an ideal companion in the process of making art.

Although married to Dimitry Varley, a Russian-born economist and potter, for fifty years (from 1934 until his death in 1984), Schönberg had no children of her own. She devoted her life to nurturing through teaching and gardening. She received many awards, including her own "Bessie" for lifetime achievement in 1988, and the American Dance Festival's Balasaraswati/Joy Ann Dewey Beinecke Endowed Chair for Distinguished Teaching in 1997. Her legacy lives on in her students, Meredith Monk and Lucinda Childs among them, who continue to pay tribute to her. Schönberg died on May 14, 1997, from an apparent heart attack at her home in Bronxville, New York, at the age of ninety. She was scheduled to teach at Juilliard that day.

Bibliography: The archives of Sarah Lawrence College hold the largest collection of materials concerning Schönberg, including biographical materials, correspondence, photographs, and records of her activities and performances at the college. Photographs, videos, clippings, and an extensive oral history conducted in 1976–77 are held in the Jerome Robbins Dance Division of the New York Public Library for the Performing Arts at Lincoln Center. The documentary *Bessie* (1998) features tributes to Schönberg by students such as Meredith Monk and Ronald K. Brown, interspersed with her own reminiscences. Besides the documentary, Schönberg has not been the subject of any extended study, although most dance history books mention her impact as a teacher and mentor. Published interviews include "A Lifetime of Dance," *Performing Arts Journal* 4, nos. 1 & 2 (1979), pp. 106–17; and Deborah Jowitt, "A Conversation with Bessie Schönberg," *Ballet Review* 9, no. 1 (Spring 1981), pp. 31–63, which primarily discusses her interaction with Martha Graham. Other articles include Norton Owen, "A Tribute to Our Collective Mother: Remembering Bessie Schönberg," *Dance/USA Journal* 15, no. 1 (Summer 1997), pp. 16–17, 22; Anne Tobias, "Bessie's Way," *Dance Ink* 4, no. 4 (Winter 1993/94), pp. 38–42; Deborah Jowitt, "The Original Bessie," *Dance Magazine* 65, no. 9 (September 1991), pp. 46–49; and Doris Hering, "To Teach the Unteachable," *Dance Magazine* 36, no. 8 (August 1962), pp. 24–27. Obituaries appeared in the *New York Times* on May 15, 1997, and in *Dance Magazine* 71, no. 8 (August 1997), pp. 40–42.

JULIA L. FOULKES

SCHULTZ, Sigrid Lillian. January 5, 1893–May 15, 1980. Journalist, war correspondent.

Sigrid Schultz, who issued prophetic warnings about the rise of Nazism from her post as a foreign correspondent in Berlin during the 1930s, was born in Chicago. She was the only child of Herman Schultz, a well-known portrait painter of Norwegian descent, and his seventeen-year-old wife, Hedwig Jaskewitz, whose background was Russian, Polish, French, and German. Her father, who had studios in Paris, Cairo, London, and Berlin, frequently traveled abroad to paint the portraits of royalty, government officials, and upper-class Europeans, often bringing his family with him. Sigrid spent her first eight years in Chicago and then the family moved to Paris. In 1911 she graduated with high honors from the Lycée Racine, and in 1914 she earned a degree at the Sorbonne. In addition to studying history and international law, she also aspired to be an opera singer but was unable to afford vocal training.

In 1914 the family moved to Berlin. When World War I broke out, both her parents were too ill to travel, and the stranded family fell on hard times. Fluent in German, English, French, and Norwegian, Sigrid Schultz increasingly became the primary breadwinner for her family, landing a series of jobs as a French and English tutor to German families. When the United States declared war on Germany in 1917, the Schultz family were considered "enemy aliens." Adding to the distress of the time, Sigrid's Norwegian fiancé died at sea when a German submarine torpedoed his ship.

In 1917, Schultz answered an advertisement to become the interpreter for an Iraqi diplomat, Reouf Chadirchi, who was stationed in Berlin. Her job exposed her to German politics at high levels, and when the war ended in 1919 she became an interpreter for Richard Henry Little, the Berlin correspondent for the *Chicago Tribune*. Schultz soon graduated to freelance cub reporter; her first stories on the Weimar Republic included coverage of the Kapp Putsch and violent rioting in Tiergarten. In 1925, Schultz became the bureau chief for Central Europe for the *Chicago Tribune*, based in Berlin. At the time, DOROTHY THOMP-

SON came to Berlin as the bureau chief for Central Europe for the *Philadelphia Public Ledger.* Schultz and Thompson were the first women to head major foreign bureaus for American newspapers.

In 1930, when the Nazis took an unprecedented number of seats in the Reichstag, Schultz became one of the first journalists to warn of the dangers of Nazism. Enjoying more access to the Nazi leadership than most American reporters, she was able, in 1931, to arrange a series of interviews with Hitler, where she became convinced of his ruthlessness and witnessed his power to persuade and control people. When Hitler became chancellor in 1933 and the persecution against the Jews intensified, Schultz quietly began helping Jews leave the country, a fact she revealed in an interview late in life.

Sigrid Schultz was not known as an especially fine writer, but by the mid 1930s she had acquired a reputation as an expert news-gatherer and one of the most astute press observers in Germany. In 1937, Schultz began to publish articles reporting on Nazi ideology and brutality in the *Chicago Tribune* under the by-line John Dickson, adopting a pseudonym to avoid the risk of being expelled by German authorities for her frank reporting. In 1938, when it became evident that war would break out, she returned to the United States and established a residence in Westport, Connecticut, where her mother could live. Returning to Berlin, Schultz began a weekly radio broadcast on the Mutual Broadcasting network, giving penetrating political observations on the unfolding events in Germany to American audiences over the next two years. On her way to one of her last broadcasts, her left knee was permanently damaged by shrapnel from a British air raid over Berlin.

In the summer of 1939, Sigrid Shultz was part of one of the biggest stories of her times. On July 13, 1939, under the by-line John Dickson, Schultz reported in the *Chicago Tribune* that Berlin negotiators had been dispatched to Moscow to discuss plans for Soviet-German cooperation. Dickson predicted that German and Russian leaders would soon be allies. All this was conjecture until August 22, when the *Tribune* ran a front-page story under the by-line of Sigrid Schultz that a German-Soviet non-aggression pact was about to be signed. When the German Army invaded Poland on September 1, 1939, signaling the beginning of the World War II, Schultz continued her reports, often sneaking out of Germany to file them.

The wartime situation for foreign correspondents worsened, and in February 1941 Schultz returned to Connecticut. She was suffering from typhus contracted on her travels, and her extended recovery, plus the unwillingness of German authorities to let her back in the country, kept her in the United States through most of the war years. From 1941 to 1944, Schultz lectured throughout the United States and wrote *Germany Will Try It Again* (1944), a history of German aggression that warned against trusting German propaganda about wanting peace. In 1944 Schultz finally returned to Europe, traveling abroad as a journalist for *McCall's, Collier's,* the *Chicago Tribune,* and Mutual Broadcasting. Present at the liberation of Buchenwald concentration camp, she returned to the United States determined to write all she knew of Nazism and its crimes. In 1945, she resigned her job at the *Tribune,* unable to tolerate the extreme isolationist politics of her boss, Colonel Robert R. McCormick. She went on to report on the Nuremberg war trials for other periodicals.

Although Schultz spent less time abroad after the war, she wrote prolifically on international affairs over the next three decades, providing political and historical analyses of Germany and the aftermath of the war. She never married, and she cared for her mother at their Westport home until her mother's death in 1960. One of the founders of the Overseas Press Club, she edited *The Overseas Press Club Cookbook* (1962), which included recipes along with anecdotes about the political circumstances of memorable meals. Even as her health failed as a result of a heart attack, crippling arthritis, and later lymphatic cancer, Sigrid Schultz remained alert and astute. At the time of her death in Westport in 1980 at the age of eighty-seven, she was working on a history of German anti-Semitism.

Bibliography: Biographical material can be found in the Sigrid Schultz papers at the State Historical Society of Wisconsin Archives in Madison, which contain correspondence, clippings, speeches, diaries, and unpublished memoirs. A number of books on women, journalism, and World War II discuss Schultz, including Maurine Hoffman Beasley and Sheila J. Gibbons, eds., *Taking Their Place: A Documentary History of Women and Journalism* (1993); Barbara Belford, *Brilliant Bylines: A Biographical Anthology of Notable Newspaper Women in America* (1986); Julia Edwards, *Women of the World: The Great Foreign Correspondents* (1988); David H. Hosley and Gayle K. Yamada, *Hard News: Women in Broadcast Journalism* (1987); Marion Marzolf, *Up from the Footnote: A History of Women Journalists* (1977); Nancy Caldwell Sorel, *The Women Who Wrote the War* (1999); and Lilya Wagner, *Women War Correspondents of World War II* (1989). For a history of war correspondents, see Michael Emery, *On the Front Lines: Following America's Foreign Correspondents across the Twentieth Century* (1995); and Frederick S. Voss, *Reporting the War: The Journalistic Coverage of World War II* (1994). See also Cynthia Charmaine Chapman, "Psychobiographical Study of the Life of Sigrid Schultz" (PhD dissertation, Florida Institute of Technology, 1991). An obituary appeared in the *Chicago Tribune* on May 17, 1980.

JEANNE HOUCK

SEKAQUAPTEWA, Helen (Tuwawisnöm). c. 1898–March 24, 1991. Writer.

Helen Sekaquaptewa was born in Orayvi (Oraibi), Arizona, located on Third Mesa on the Hopi Indian Reservation. Her mother was Sihaynöm and her father was Talashongniwa. Sekaquaptewa was a member of her mother's clan, Eagle. At her naming ceremony three weeks after her birth, Sekaquaptewa was named Tuwawisnöm, which means "trail marked by sand." She was the third of five children. Her father became a leader of the "Hostile" faction of Orayvi, which opposed U.S. government intervention in Hopi life, including mandatory schooling for Hopi children. The "Friendlies" supported a more accommodating approach to the growing U.S. presence. Throughout her life, Sekaquaptewa had to negotiate the tensions between the two (sometimes called Traditionals and Progressives).

Sekaquaptewa spent the first years of her life learning Hopi customs. She also took part in the "hide and seek" match between the Orayvi Hostiles and the U.S. military forces sent to round up children for school. In 1906 an internal dispute between the Hostile and Friendly factions at Orayvi resulted in the expulsion of the Hostiles from the village. Sekaquaptewa went with her family to an encampment that later became the village of Hotvela (Hotevilla). Her family survived the first winter with little food or shelter.

Sekaquaptewa describes being "kidnapped" in that same year and sent to boarding school in Keams Canyon, Arizona, forty miles away. Here, she was named Helen. She was lonely and often teased by others for being the daughter of a Hostile. She endured the harsh treatment typical of Indian boarding schools, including physical punishment. Sekaquaptewa spent four summers at school because government agents feared she would not return if she was sent home. She finally returned to Hotvela in 1910. During this year, she continued to learn Hopi "women's skills," including corn grinding, cooking, and making piki bread (a traditional paper-thin bread). She returned to school when troops came to Hotvela in 1911 to round up students.

Although Sekaquaptewa was homesick, she was also a serious student. She was a good reader and enjoyed learning. In 1915 she finished the sixth grade. She begged her parents to send her to Phoenix Indian School for further education. When her parents refused, she obtained permission from the Keams Canyon Agency superintendent.

Her school experience reveals how Sekaquaptewa managed cultural and family conflict through personal choices. She was often an outsider. At school she was teased because she was the child of a Hostile. At home she faced conflict because she wanted to continue school. She made the decision that fit her personal values, such as love of learning. While at Phoenix Indian School, Helen met her future husband, Emory Sekaquaptewa, who was also a student. In 1918, she completed the eighth grade and returned to Hotvela. She was soon busy caring for villagers during the influenza epidemic of 1918 and 1919. Her mother and a brother died during the epidemic.

In 1919, she married Emory, who had returned to the reservation. They had a traditional Hopi ceremony and were also married "by license" on February 14. She and Emory initially tried to live in the family home, which now belonged to her older sister. There was not enough room, and tension caused the young couple to move to the Hotvela school, where Emory worked. In the summer of 1919, they moved to Lapwai, Idaho, on the Nez Perce Reservation. Helen was a cook and seamstress at the school, and Emory worked in the physical plant.

In May 1920, they returned to Hotvela. Helen's first of ten children, Joy, was born around this time, but she died a year later from dysentery. Her son Wayne was born soon after. Her other children were born approximately two years apart: Eugene, Emory Jr., Abbott, LeRoy, Allison, Selwyn, Marlene, and Edward. Life was often difficult for Sekaquaptewa in Hotvela because of her modern ways. She dressed in Anglo clothing. She had her children immunized and took them to the government hospital for care. Gossip and criticism in the village could be intense, but Sekaquaptewa was secure in her decision to take the best from both Hopi and Anglo culture.

She and Emory built a home on a ranch nine miles southwest of Hotvela, and they began spending summers there. They moved permanently in the mid 1940s to get away from the village and to grow more corn. They adopted a young Navajo, Milton, in the 1940s, and a Hopi boy, Loren, in the 1950s. Helen required all of her children to attend school, and she even spent six years (1954–60) in Phoenix to make a home for her younger children while they attended school.

In the 1950s, Helen became a Mormon. She noted the similarities between Hopi and Mormon religious philosophy, including kindness and industry, which conformed to her own values. She participated in the Relief Society, where she enjoyed singing and quilting.

She also began to tell stories to her Anglo friend, Louise Udall, who wrote the stories down. They eventually became the basis for her autobiography, *Me and Mine* (1969), which was a critical success and gave Sekaquaptewa a certain respect in the Hopi community. In the 1970s she returned to the village of Kiqötsmovi (Kykotsmovi), where she was active in village and Eagle Clan activities.

She also participated in cultural preservation projects, such as the recording of stories and lullabies. She died there in 1991.

In *Me and Mine,* Sekaquaptewa describes a determination to choose the best parts of Hopi and modern American culture. All of her decisions were based on a clear personal vision of what it meant to be a Hopi woman in a rapidly changing world: hard work, kindness, and a commitment to the well-being of her family and others. In *Me and Mine,* Sekaquaptewa concludes, "The years have passed by with cycles of planting and cultivating the corn and other crops, and then the harvest. The days have brought their routine tasks—cooking, sewing, cleaning, and helping with the outside work when necessary. . . . While it has taken more pages telling of my childhood, school days, and marriage, those years were only laying the foundation for wifehood and motherhood—the best years of my life, the real living" (p. 246).

Bibliography: A note on spelling: Hopi has not been a written language until very recently. Consequently, the spelling of Hopi words is inconsistently based upon phonetic interpretation by non-Hopi speakers. Several scholars have developed competing schemes to spell Hopi words. The spellings in this essay are based upon the most complete Hopi orthography to date: *Hopi Dictionary/Hopìikwa Lavàytutuveni: A Hopi-English Dictionary of the Third Mesa Dialect* (1998). The most commonplace names are also provided in parentheses.

Family members dispute the 1898 birth date. There is no birth certificate on file, which is common for Native Americans at this time. Several of her children think she was born a few years earlier because her memories of the Orayvi split in 1906 are so vivid. Sekaquaptewa left no collection of personal papers. The main source of information about her life is her autobiography, *Me and Mine* (1969). She is also the subject of two biographical sketches: "Helen Sekaquaptewa" in Liz Sonneborn, *A to Z of Native American Women* (1998), and Kathleen Sands, "Helen Sekaquaptewa," in Gretchen Bataille, ed., *Native American Women: A Biographical Dictionary* (1993). An analysis of her autobiography can be found in Gretchen Bataille and Kathleen Sands, "Two Women in Transition," in *Native American Women: Telling Their Lives* (1984). Sekaquaptewa is featured in the film *Hopi: Songs of the Fourth World* (1983). She also contributed her knowledge of Hopi stories and lullabies to *Iisaw: Hopi Coyote Stories,* a videotape in the series *Words and Place: Native Literatures from the American Southwest* (1981); and Kathleen Sands and Emory Sekaquaptewa, "Four Hopi Lullabies: A Study in Method and Meaning," *American Indian Quarterly* 4, no. 3 (August 1978), pp. 195–210. The author would like to thank the Sekaquaptewa family, especially Marlene and Emory, for providing information and insight into the life of their mother.

WENDY HOLLIDAY

SELENA. April 16, 1971–March 31, 1995. Singer.

Selena, a singer who introduced the Tejano sound into the national lexicon of music, was born in Freeport, Texas, the youngest of three children of Abraham Quintanilla Jr., who had been raised in the south Texas port city of Corpus Christi, and Marcella Ofelia Samora, who was from Washington State. Both parents' forbears had been part of the twentieth-century migration of Mexican farm workers into the United States. Selena and her siblings, Abraham III ("A.B.") and Suzette Michele, grew up in Lake Jackson and Corpus Christi, Texas, in a patriarchal household where the strict discipline of their father and their Jehovah's Witness faith instilled a strong sense of obedience and respect as well as a tight-knit family structure. Selena's mother anchored the family as nurturer and counselor.

As a young adult, Selena's father had been a member of a band, *Los Dinos,* and to compensate for his lost dreams of a music career he sought fulfillment through his children. Under his tutelage, Selena's brother learned the bass guitar, her sister trained as a drummer, and Selena developed a strong talent for singing and performing. In 1982 the Quintanillas moved to Corpus Christi in search of new opportunities for their group, now named *Selena y los Dinos.* The city was a center of Tejano, the type of music that had become the major source of the band's popularity. Originating on the Texas-Mexico border in the early twentieth century, Tejano evolved as a hybrid of sounds from the region's past. Its lively, bouncy beat drew on the polka and accordion music of German immigrants, the twang of a Mexican twelve-string guitar, sounds of the big swing bands, Latin rhythms, Mexican lyrics, and later, pop and rhythm and blues.

The band performed at weddings, parties, urban clubs, and rural dance halls, wherever Quintanilla could arrange bookings. Although Selena made good grades at West Oso Junior High School, the constant travel disrupted her schooling. After eighth grade she enrolled in a correspondence school for artists, the American School in Chicago, from which she received a high school diploma in 1990.

By the mid 1980s Selena began to gain recognition in the Tejano music world, even though a lead female singer was considered less of a draw than a male singer. In 1987 two of Selena's single recordings became regional hits and helped her win Female Vocalist of the Year at the Tejano Music Awards. In 1989 she signed a recording contract with Capitol-EMI Latin Records, who planned to make Selena a star in the international Latin music world and then introduce a crossover album that would secure *Selena y los Dinos*'s place in the mainstream English popular music market. Recognizing the importance of language in her career plan, Selena, who grew up speaking English, finally began to study Spanish.

Selena's performances had always been characterized by high energy and a voice with an emotional range that went from a soft, vulnerable sweetness to a robust ferocity. Although she created a sexy stage persona with her long, flowing black hair, dark eyeliner, and red lipstick, and her signature costume of spandex tights, bare midriff, and sequined bustier, she still managed to be viewed as the wholesome "girl next door" with family values, an image that broadened her appeal.

Each year of the 1990s brought further success. Her 1990 album, *Ven Conmigo,* reached the top of the *Billboard* regional Mexican chart and stayed there fifty-six weeks, a first for a Tejano artist, male or female. A 1992 single recording duet with Alvaro Torres, "Buenos Amigos," reached number one on the *Billboard* Latin chart, as did the album *Amor Prohibido* in 1994. That year Selena won a Grammy for the album *Selena Live!* and *Texas Monthly* named her one of the Twenty Most Important Texans of the year. Outgrowing dance halls, Selena increasingly performed in concert halls and arenas.

In 1990, Christopher Perez, a hard-rock guitarist from San Antonio, joined the band, and he and Selena courted secretly for months because they expected her father to object. On April 2, 1992, the couple eloped; they were married by a justice of the peace at the Nueces County courthouse. They eventually moved into a home next door to Selena's parents in the working-class Molina subdivision of Corpus Christi.

Selena often made fashion sketches and hand-decorated her own costumes. Turning her hobby into a business, she hired a designer to create a line of clothing to sell under her own label, and in January 1994 she opened a Corpus Christi fashion boutique and beauty salon called Selena, Etc. The following September she established a second boutique in San Antonio. Selena enjoyed working in her boutique, and when on tour she turned many of her responsibilities over to her devoted fan club president, Yolanda Saldivar, who also was hired as a general manager to oversee both of the shops.

By early 1995 there were complaints that Saldivar was failing to pay bills, poorly managing the company, and neglecting her fan club responsibilities; there was also evidence of possible theft and embezzlement. Selena and other family members confronted Saldivar and asked her to return missing financial records. Several weeks later Selena met with Saldivar at her Corpus Christi motel room with the intention of obtaining the records and terminating her employment. Following an argument, Saldivar shot Selena in the back. Selena rushed to the motel's lobby before collapsing; she died shortly thereafter from internal bleeding and cardiac arrest caused by the gunshot wound.

Within hours of the death of the twenty-three-year-old singer, thousands of mourners gathered outside the motel and Selena's home; in San Antonio five thousand people attended a candlelight vigil. Two days later more than sixty thousand filed by her casket at the Corpus Christi convention center, and dozens of memorials were held across the country. Governor George W. Bush declared her birthday, April 16, Easter Sunday, as Selena Day.

For most people in the States, Selena became established nationally as a musician and a cultural symbol through the sensational circumstances of her death. Her long-planned crossover album, *Dreaming of You,* was released posthumously in July 1995, debuting at number one on the *Billboard* Top 200 Album Chart—the first time a Latin artist had achieved that honor. Ironically, it was the Tejano and not the English music on this and her other albums that created her national popularity. The "Selenamania" that ensued involved a media blitz, extensive sales of memorabilia and records, public shrines (including some of a religious nature), as well as a 1997 motion picture of her life story. The broad interest in Selena's music also encouraged many Latinos in an unabashed articulation of cultural pride. She represented a Tejana version of the American dream: by hard work she went from poverty and obscurity to wealth and fame, but she never abandoned her origins or heritage. Selena was for many "una mujer del pueblo"—a woman of the people—just as the origins of the music she introduced also were "del pueblo."

Bibliography: The most thorough biography of Selena, which includes a full discography, is Joe Nick Patoski, *Selena: Como la Flor* (1996). Other biographies are Clint Richmond, *Selena! The Phenomenal Life and Tragic Death of the Tejano Music Queen* (1995); Veda Boyd Jones, *Selena* (2000), written for a young audience; Maria Celeste Arraras, *Selena's Secret: The Revealing Story behind her Tragic Death* (1997); and Himilce Novas and Rosemary Silva, *Remembering Selena: A Tribute in Pictures and Words* (1995), a photo essay of her life. *Selena: Her Life in Pictures, 1971–1995,* a commemorative issue of *People Magazine,* was published in the spring of 1995, and a biographical essay by Cynthia E. Orozco appears in *The Handbook of Texas* (1997). Articles about Selena that discuss her status as a cultural symbol and icon include Ana Castillo, "Selena Aside," *Nation,* May 29, 1995, pp. 764–66; Ilan Stavans, "Dreaming of You," *New Republic,* November 20, 1995, pp. 24–25; Larry Rohter, "A Legend Grows, and So Does an Industry," *New York Times,* January 12, 1997; and Jennifer L. Willis and Alberto Gonzalez, "Reconceptualizing Gender through Intercultural Dialogue: The Case of the Tex-Mex Madonna," *Women and Language* 20, no. 1 (Spring 1997), pp. 9–12. Selena's impact on the music world is discussed in Diana A. Terry-Azios, "Tejano Music Queen: Selena Quintanilla's Untimely Death Came before her Crossover Success," *Hispanic,* March 31, 2000, p. 28; and Tony Cantu, "Cashing in on Selena: How the Tejano Queen's Murder Caused an Economic Phenomenon," *Hispanic*, June 30, 1996, p. 18. This essay draws on telephone interviews with Suzette Quintanilla Arriaga, Selena's sister, and Bob Peña, manager of Q Productions, the Quintanillas' recording company. Obituaries appeared in the *New York Times*, the *Los Angeles Times*, and the *Washington Post* on April 1, 1995, and in *Newsweek* and *Time* on April 10, 1995.

MARILYNN WOOD HILL

SHARAFF, Irene. January 23, 1910–August 16, 1993. Broadway and Hollywood costume designer.

In a career spanning nearly fifty years, Irene Sharaff was an innovative, award-winning costume designer who was head designer on more than forty films and sixty Broadway shows. She was born in Boston, but little is known about her parents, siblings, or upbringing until her graduation from Wadley High School in New York City. Originally aspiring to be a painter, she studied at the New York School of Fine and Applied Art and at the Art Students League. She then spent 1931 studying in Paris at the Grande Chaumière, impressed most by the haute couture designs of Chanel and Elsa Schiaparelli. For a time she did fashion illustrations for *Vogue*, *Harper's Bazaar*, and other magazines, and throughout her career she was noted for her masterful costume sketches. She never married, and she divulged few details about her personal life.

Sharaff began design work as assistant to ALINE BERNSTEIN, designer for New York's Civic Repertory Theatre. She first attracted attention in 1932 when she designed both the costumes and the scenery for EVA LE GALLIENNE's Civic Repertory Theatre production of *Alice in Wonderland*, drawing on Tenniel's illustrations. In 1934 the Ballets Russes de Monte Carlo, which had always employed Russian designers, commissioned Sharaff to design the scenery and costumes for two ballets, Leonide Massine's *Union Pacific* and Stravinsky's *Poker Game*. She subsequently designed costumes for the American Ballet Theatre and the New York City Ballet, including Balanchine's *Scheherazade* and *Slaughter on Tenth Avenue*.

After a decade of designing on Broadway, Sharaff began working in Hollywood in the early 1940s, although she still considered New York City her home. A ballet sequence in MGM's 1951 production of *An American in Paris* won Sharaff her first Academy Award for scenery and costume design. At seventeen minutes, with five complex scenes each styled after a different painter (Dufy, Manet, Gauguin, Van Gogh, and Toulouse-Lautrec), the ballet is a visual extravaganza of great intelligence.

Sharaff received sixteen Oscar nominations over her lifetime, winning the award in 1956 for her contrasts between British imperial gowns and Thai court dress in *The King and I;* for the flamboyantly colored Puerto Rican gang garb in contrast to the jeans of the rival Jets in *West Side Story* in 1961; for ancient Egyptian designs imaginatively adapted from source statuary for *Cleopatra* in 1963; and for the dowdy garb of the university professors in *Who's Afraid of Virginia Woolf?* in 1966. Her creative capacity to blend historical inspiration with contemporary lines is exemplified by her use of hooded windbreakers to approximate the male silhouette of the Italian Renaissance as traced through gang street clothes in *West Side Story*. Other notable Sharaff designs include the turn-of-the-century dresses and suits for Vincente Minnelli's *Meet Me in St. Louis* (1944). One concession made to wartime sensibilities was a military allusion in some of the dresses, including double rows of buttons and braid trim. Another was to fabricate the lace for the dress white gowns the family wears to the world's fair at the end out of inexpensive tuile decorated with appliqués. Sharaff marked the end of the war not with extravagance, but with highlighting the distinction between classes and various ethnic groups through costuming as veterans return home in *The Best Years of Our Lives* (1946).

Sharaff had an impeccable sense of color design for early Technicolor, knowing how to mute and combine colors to best effect for the characteristics of the three-color technology. One can trace the evolution of film stock and lighting by exploring the ever brighter colors she chooses once the film stock will, for example, accept the cyan blues without bleeding. Her designs for Minnelli's *Brigadoon* (1954) turn the gowns of the village girls into shades reminiscent of "Heather on the Hill" and add to the dreamlike atmosphere throughout.

In addition to her film success, she continued to work on Broadway. In 1951 she won a Tony Award for the stage production of *The King and I*, which was also the occasion of one of her most famous quotes: "The first act finale of *The King and I* will feature Miss Lawrence, Mr. Brynner and a Pink Satin Ball Gown." Her stylized Thai costumes stimulated an haute couture and ready-to-wear emulation that precipitated a boom in the silk industry in Thailand.

Leaving MGM to freelance, Sharaff designed *Guys and Dolls* (1955) for Sam Goldwyn, where she contrasted actress Jean Simmons's Salvation Army costume with the slinky dresses of the gangster's molls. *Porgy and Bess* (1959) followed, allowing her to create costumes that, while realistic for the period, afforded the African American cast a greater measure of dignity appropriate to the times. She designed *Can-Can* for Twentieth Century Fox in 1960, which gave her many chances to rework the can-can skirts briefly used in *An American in Paris.* Returning to Goldwyn, she made *Flower Drum Song* in 1961, and a series of films starring Elizabeth Taylor, which in addition to *Cleopatra* and *Who's Afraid of Virginia Woolf?* included Minelli's *The Sandpiper* (1965), for which she simulated Carmel, California, dress at the Billancourt studios in Paris, and Franco Zeffirelli's *The Taming of the Shrew* (1967), for which she did elaborate Elizabethan costumes with a decidedly Italian Renaissance influence as the film was shot in Rome. Barbra Streisand's *Funny Girl* (1968) and *Hello, Dolly!* (1969) were two of her most elaborate later efforts, and she ended her career doing the retrospective costumes for a fictional JOAN CRAWFORD in *Mommie Dearest* (1981), giving her the chance to imitate the designs of the other famous designers who defined Crawford's transformations, including Adrian, who preceded her at MGM.

In 1976 Sharaff published a lively autobiographical memoir, *Broadway and Hollywood: Costumes Designed by Irene Sharaff* (1976), which detailed her manner of working, including careful historical study of period and setting, as well as close attention to the music and choreography when working on musicals. In the last years of her life she battled emphysema. She died of congestive heart failure in New York City in 1993 at the age of eighty-three.

Bibliography: Sketches and designs by Irene Sharaff are found at the National Art Library, Victoria and Albert Museum, London; the Shubert Archive, New York City; and Special Collections at the Yale School of Drama Library, New Haven, Connecticut. The best introduction to her career is Sharaff's *Broadway and Hollywood: Costumes Designed by Irene Sharaff* (1976). Also of interest is Meredith Brody's interview with Sharaff in *Interview* 19, no. 8 (August 1989), pp. 127–29. For more general background on costume design on Broadway and in Hollywood, see Margaret J. Bailey, *Those Glorious Glamour Years* (1982); Elizabeth Leese, *Costume Design in the Movies* (revised ed. 1991); W. Robert LaVine, *In a Glamorous Fashion: The Fabulous Years of Hollywood Costume Design* (1980); and Tony Lewenhaupt, *Crosscurrents: Art, Fashion, Design, 1890–1989* (1989). An obituary appeared in the *New York Times* on August 17, 1993.

MAUREEN TURIM

SHARP, Zerna Addas. August 12, 1889–June 17, 1981. Educator, reading consultant, textbook editor.

Zerna Addas Sharp, a textbook editor known as the "mother of Dick and Jane," was born in Hillisburg, Clinton County, Indiana. She was the first of five children (two girls and three boys) born to Charlotte Smith and Charles Sharp. Her father was a merchant who operated a general store in nearby Scircleville, and her mother was a homemaker. Her father died in 1915, and her mother remarried, to Charles Heady, in 1923.

Zerna taught herself to read at age five and graduated from high school at sixteen. After taking a course at Marion Normal College, she received her teaching license in 1906. She began her teaching career as a kindergarten and first grade teacher, later becoming an elementary school principal. She never graduated from college, but during her career she audited summer classes at Columbia and Northwestern universities.

In 1924 Sharp was hired by Scott, Foresman and Company, the Chicago publishing firm, as a reading consultant. As she traveled to schools across the Midwest, she was distressed to find that children were not reading well and disliked their textbooks. The problem, she believed, was that children were being given too many new words at once, which kept them from becoming interested in the material in the primers. Sharp's reports back to Scott, Foresman recommended that the firm develop a new reading primer for children that would be more engaging and accessible. Eventually, in 1928, the publisher asked her to come work in the Chicago office to create the format for a new primary reader.

Sharp's ideas for a new approach to reading texts coincided with the views of William S. Gray, dean of the College of Education at the University of Chicago, who was hired by Scott, Foresman in 1929. While Sharp's opinions derived from classroom experience and observation, Gray drew on the theories of John Dewey and other leaders of the progressive education movement. The progressive educators believed in teaching children to read whole words, and having them read for meaning, deemphasizing phonics. They also stressed the importance of engaging students' interest in reading, and teaching at their level of readiness. Gray's work was also shaped by the trend toward scientific study of how children learn to read.

At Scott, Foresman, Sharp joined forces with Gray, Harry Johnston (the new head of the reading department), illustrator Eleanor Campbell, and other staff to initiate what would become the twentieth century's most successful American reading series. In 1930, this team introduced the characters Dick and Jane in the first of the Elson Basic Readers. Sharp did not write any of the books herself (in later years she refused to sign copies because she hadn't written them) but her input was fundamental to the readers. She developed the basic format, which became known as the picture-story method, invented and named the characters, and even decided what they would wear. In the early years, clothing styles were patterned after those in the Sears and Montgomery Ward catalogs.

In their day, the books were a radical departure from typical reading primers. They used fresh material by leading children's authors, brightly colored illustrations, and simplified vocabulary and sentence structure and provided wide supplementary reading and extensive teachers' guides and study aids. The books also introduced new words gradually. The first volume introduced only one new word per page, and the first three volumes used a total of only fifty-eight words. The linguistic patterns familiar to the 85 million children who learned to read from the series between the 1930s and the 1970s—"Look, Dick. Look, Jane. Look and see"—originated with Sharp's own observations of children playing together. Despite their limited vocabulary, these stories contained more action, humor, and suspense than previous readers.

Later editions of the books updated the characters, including the family pets: Spot the terrier became a cocker spaniel by the 1940s; by the 1960s Mother was drying clothes in the dryer, not on a clothesline; and car models changed along with fashions. Later a new edition of the series was created with a multiethnic cast of characters in response to criticisms that the characters were all white and that female characters reflected gender stereotypes. Sharp, who considered herself a pioneer feminist and hired many women to her staff at Scott, Foresman, was irate that the media and the women's movement saw Jane and Mother as subservient to Dick and Father. "It never bothered the children," she responded. "That's an adult's viewpoint."

Beginning in the mid 1950s, with Rudolf Flesch's *Why Johnny Can't Read* (1955), advocates of a phonics-based approach to reading questioned the series' pedagogy. Others criticized the limited vocabulary and what had come to be perceived as stilted language. By the early 1970s, the series—viewed as revolutionary at its initiation and reactionary at its decline—had run its course. But Dick and Jane, Sally, Spot, and Puff lived on in the memories of millions of baby boomers, and the out-of-print books became widely traded as memorabilia.

Sharp never married—primarily, she later said, because she never found a man she thought she could live with. She was close to her family in Indiana, and she returned to Clinton County frequently during the years she lived in Chicago, and helped many members of her family financially. Her nephew described her as very strict and strong-willed, but generous. She was also frugal; while he was attending college in Chicago (with tuition paid by her), she once invited him to her apartment for breakfast and then asked him to return a bag of lightbulbs for a refund because she believed they had burned out too quickly.

After Sharp left Scott, Foresman in 1964, she retired to Seal Beach, California, where she remained active, traveling abroad well into her eighties. In 1978 she moved back to a retirement home in Frankfort, Indiana, where she died of liver and kidney failure three years later at the age of ninety-one.

Bibliography: A collection of documents related to Zerna Addas Sharp is at the Clinton County Historical Society in Frankfort, Indiana. It includes family photographs; Sharp's birth and death records, high school diploma, and teaching and principal's licenses; and newspaper articles. Family background and anecdotes were supplied by Nancy Hart, curator of the Clinton County Historical Society, and Robert Sharp, Zerna Sharp's nephew. A 1993 video documentary, *Whatever Happened to Dick and Jane?*, produced by David Thompson for WTVP 47 in Peoria, Illinois, includes audio excerpts from a 1959 interview with Sharp. See also the popular treatment in Carole Kismaric and Marvin Heiferman, *Growing Up with Dick and Jane: Learning and Living the American Dream* (1996). Information about the development of the Elson Basic Readers, the role of William S. Gray, and the place of the Dick and Jane series in the history of reading education appears in Miriam Balmuth, *The Roots of Phonics* (1982); Jeanne S. Chall, *Learning to Read: The Great Debate* (1967); and Nancy A. Mavrogenes's thirty-three page analysis of Gray's series for the Chicago Board of Education, "William S. Gray and the Dick and Jane Readers" (1985). The obituary in the *New York Times* on June 19, 1981, contains Sharp's rejoinder about Dick and Jane.

ILENE KANTROV

SHAVELSON, Clara Lemlich. 1886–July 12, 1982. Labor activist.

Clara Lemlich Shavelson was the most famous of the *fabrente Yidishe meydlekh,* the fiery Jewish immigrant girls whose militancy and dedication to the ideal of bread and roses helped galvanize the early-twentieth-century U.S. labor movement. In 1909, at the age of twenty-three, the young shirtwaist-maker delivered an impassioned speech at New York's Cooper Union that sparked an "uprising" of twenty thousand to forty thousand garment workers. Lemlich's role as the catalyst for the 1909 strike ensured her place in histories of the labor movement, immigration, and American Jewry, but telescoping her long activist career into one cameo appearance oversimplifies her complex legacy.

Lemlich was born in 1886 (date unknown) in Gorodok, Ukraine, to deeply religious Jewish parents. Like most girls in late-nineteenth-century East European Jewish villages, she was taught to read and write Yiddish but was offered no further Jewish schooling. When Clara was denied admission to Gorodok's only public school because she was a Jew, her parents reacted angrily, banning Russian language, books, and music from their home. Undaunted, Lemlich read and collected revolutionary texts by Lenin, Trotsky, and Marx, among others. By 1903, when the Kishinev pogrom convinced her parents to emigrate, sixteen-year-old Clara was a committed socialist.

Already experienced in needlecrafts, Lemlich quickly found work in a Lower East Side garment shop after her arrival in New York City in 1905. Firmly rejecting the idea that women and unskilled workers could not be organized, Lemlich organized a series of strikes in garment shops around New York in 1907 to 1909, laying the groundwork for a general strike to improve wages, hours, and conditions in the shirt and dress trades. Despite warnings from American Federation of Labor president Samuel Gompers and middle-class reformers in the Women's Trade Union League that young women workers could not sustain a general strike, Lemlich called on her fellow waist- and dressmakers to come to a meeting in the Great Hall of the People at New York's Cooper Union in November 1909. After a series of labor leaders urged caution, Lemlich jumped on the stage and began exhorting the crowd of young women workers in Yiddish. "I am one of those who feels and suffers from the things pictured. I move that we go on a general strike," she shouted. The New York garment uprising that followed sparked similar strikes in Philadelphia, Cleveland, Chicago, Iowa, and Kalamazoo, Michigan, resulting in an unprecedented 40 percent of women garment workers being organized into unions by 1919.

Lemlich's name and face were well enough known after the 1909 strike that she was blacklisted from the garment trades. For a few years she channeled her considerable energies into suffrage activism, helping to found and sustain the Wage Earner's League for Woman Suffrage. Here again, Lemlich's uncompromising nature got her in trouble, this time with historian MARY BEARD, who controlled funds earmarked by affluent suffragists to pay a working-class suffrage organizer. In 1912 Beard fired Lemlich for refusing to moderate her radical politics to suit the vision of cross-class sisterhood espoused by middle-class women reformers.

Retiring briefly into the role of wife and mother, Lemlich married printer's union activist Joe Shavelson in 1913 and moved to the Brooklyn immigrant neighborhood of Brownsville, where she gave birth to three children–Irving (c. 1914), Martha (c. 1917), and Rita (c. 1926). Almost immediately, Clara Shavelson began organizing wives and mothers around the primary issues affecting their workplace—the cost of food and housing. In 1917 she organized kosher meat boycotts to protest price increases in staple foods. After World War I, she led a rent strike movement that swept New York's immigrant neighborhoods.

In 1926, Shavelson brought her community organizing skills into the Communist Party USA, helping to found the United Council of Working Class Housewives, which provided aid to striking workers by raising funds, opening community kitchens, and establishing collective child-care arrangements so that women workers could walk the picket lines. In 1929, Shavelson and her neighbor Rose Nelson decided that working-class women needed a movement of their own, and they cofounded the United Council of Working-Class Women (UCWW). Through the UCWW, Shavelson led rent strikes and anti-eviction demonstrations; meat, bread, and milk boycotts; and sit-ins and marches on Washington calling for controls on the costs of housing and staple foods, for the construction of more public housing, and for more public schools.

The peak of the UCWW's influence came in 1935, when the group forged coalitions with a wide range of progressive women's groups, mothers' leagues, neighborhood groups, and union auxiliaries to protest the high cost of living. In 1935, Shavelson and Nelson led a nationwide meat boycott that shut down 4,500 butcher shops in New York City alone before spreading to Chicago, Detroit, Los Angeles, Minneapolis, Cleveland, St. Louis, and Seattle, soon involving women of many racial, religious, and ethnic backgrounds. After the strike, the group changed its name to the Progressive Women's Councils; Shavelson led the group during the World War II years. After the war, housewife organizers conducted two more nationwide meat boycotts, and led annual marches on Washington to lobby elected officials on matters of concern to working-class housewives, such as rent control and federally funded public housing, paving the way for the modern tenant and consumer movements. Long before the 1960s women's movement, Shavelson knew and made sure that other working-class activists understood that the personal was deeply political.

At the age of fifty-eight, Clara Shavelson returned to the garment shop floor when her husband Joe became too ill to continue working. She quickly became active in a range of union causes and spoke regularly against nuclear weapons and the intensifying arms race. Her passport was revoked after a visit to the Soviet Union in 1951. That same year, shortly after the sudden death of her husband, Shavelson was subpoenaed to testify before the House Committee on Un-American Activities (HUAC). In 1954, when Shavelson retired from the International Ladies' Garment Workers' Union (ILGWU), the unrepentant radical was denied a pension on a technicality. After a long battle she was awarded two honorary stipends by ILGWU president David Dubinsky, but she never received the pension she had earned from the union she had helped found—and that hailed her as a pioneer on every major anniversary.

Shavelson found love a second time with an old labor movement acquaintance named Abraham Goldman. The two were married in 1960 and lived together until his death in 1967. At age eighty-one, beginning to suffer from Alzheimer's, Shavelson moved into the Jewish Home for the Aged in Los Angeles, the city where her children Martha and Irving now lived. Remaining feisty into her nineties, she helped organize the home's orderlies into a union. Clara Lemlich Shavelson, who was once described by her friend and political collaborator Rose Nelson as a sparkplug who set off conflagrations wherever she was, died on July 12, 1982, at the age of ninety-six.

Bibliography: Clara Lemlich Shavelson's life is traced in full in Annelise Orleck, *Common Sense and a Little Fire: Women and Working-Class Politics in the United States, 1900–1965* (1995). There is also information about her life and suffrage activism in Meredith Tax, *The Rising of the Women: Feminist Solidarity and Class Conflict, 1880–1917* (1980); and Mari Jo Buhle, *Women and American Socialism, 1870–1920* (1981). For a description of her Cooper Union speech, see *New York Call,* November 23, 1909. A small collection of papers is held at the Catherwood Library, Cornell University. Papers and interviews with colleagues are in the possession of her grandson Joel Schaffer.

ANNELISE ORLECK

SHEPPERSON, Gay Bolling. August 14, 1887–November 17, 1977. Social worker, New Deal administrator.

Gabrielle "Gay" Bolling Shepperson was born at Cottage Hill, a tobacco farm in rural Charlotte County, Virginia, one of six children, and the fourth daughter, of Mary Burton and John Daniel Shepperson. Her father was from an "old stock" Virginia family of tobacco growers and slaveholders, and her mother was a direct descendant of Jane Rolfe, the daughter of POCAHONTAS. Her parents' economic situation steadily declined during her childhood, and her mother's frequent illnesses exacerbated the family's misfortunes. Shepperson attended a two-room log cabin school and county high school many miles from their farm. When her mother moved to Richmond for medical treatment and into the household of the wealthy uncles and aunts of the Bolling family who had raised her, Gay joined her, attending a fashionable finishing school, Miss Virginia Ellett's School (later St. Catherine's) for two years. She took summer courses at a local university, and at age twenty Shepperson became a self-supporting high school teacher, eagerly escaping dependence on her relatives.

Her family's financial decline, her mother's poor health, and the separation of her parents taught Shepperson the uncertainty of life, and poignantly demonstrated the particularly vulnerable position of women in society. For six years, Shepperson taught in Richmond schools and volunteered through a local Presbyterian church to organize club and recreational activities for white girls living in the city's slums. In 1913 she became an apprentice with the Associated Charities in Washington, D.C., but interrupted her training to work in the War Department in 1917. After the armistice, she completed her apprenticeship and secured a position with the American Red Cross (ARC) as a field representative in the Gulf Coast states. She became acquainted with Harry Hopkins, a fellow ARC worker, in New Orleans, and the two developed a tremendous personal and professional regard for one another. This relationship served both Shepperson and Hopkins after he became head of the Federal Emergency Relief Administration (FERA) during the New Deal.

In 1923, Shepperson received what she called the real training of her career at the New York School of Social Work, but she attended that school only briefly because advocates of child welfare reform in Richmond were eager to secure her services at home. A new division, the Children's Bureau, had been created in the Virginia Department of Public Welfare as a result of intense lobbying by leaders of the state's women's suffrage movement, notably Adele Clark and Nora Houston. The legislation specifically called for hiring a woman to direct the division, and Shepperson accepted the position in 1923.

Shepperson reorganized Virginia's public welfare programs for indigent children with the help of a biracial staff, which she assembled by hiring professional white female social workers, largely trained in the North, and by retaining and hiring experienced local black social workers, male and female. But low salaries, staff cuts, racial prejudice, and a conservative political climate hampered the work. In 1927, Shepperson resigned and accepted a similar post in the Division of Children and County Organization in the Georgia Department of Public Welfare (GDPW).

In Atlanta, Shepperson joined the GDPW's staff of social workers who were seeking to alter the state's public welfare system, and especially to address the needs of indigent African Americans as well as poor whites. Local black activists such as LUGENIA BURNS HOPE, white woman suffrage leaders such as Josephine Wilkins, and the Commission on Interracial Cooperation, headquartered in Atlanta, whose staff included JESSIE DANIEL AMES and Arthur Raper, were all involved in this effort. Among this interracial network was a white social worker from Charleston named Louisa FitzSimons. In 1928, Shepperson and FitzSimons met and formed what became a life partnership.

In the midst of the Great Depression, Shepperson was appointed executive secretary of the Department of Public Welfare in 1931. Her office assisted with the disbursement of federal Reconstruction Finance Corporation funds, and in 1933 she was appointed executive secretary of the Georgia Emergency Relief Commission under the auspices of Governor Eugene Talmadge. As federal New Deal assistance programs expanded, Shepperson repeatedly complained to Harry Hopkins, director of FERA, about Talmadge's interference and efforts to use relief funds for patronage purposes. After a heated face-to-face argument with Talmadge, Hopkins federalized Georgia's FERA and Civil Works Administration, placing Shepperson in sole charge of the programs.

Convinced that the problems of poverty in Georgia were systemic, and not simply the product of the economic depression, Shepperson's administration embraced the theme of "reconstructing Georgia" and moved quickly to reorganize the entire county-based state relief system. By putting professional social workers in charge of county offices, Shepperson kept such programs free from political influence and earned her administration a reputation for honesty and effectiveness. When the Works Progress Administration (WPA) was introduced in 1935, Franklin Roosevelt appointed Shepperson chief administrator of Georgia's federalized program; she was the only woman in the nation appointed chief administrator of a state WPA. By 1937, she directed 4,500 relief personnel and her administration provided jobs for 105,000 destitute Georgians. Within the limits of her position, Shepperson leveraged the federal power she possessed in ways that challenged economic structures of racial and gender discrimination. But she could not control policies set by Washington, especially the low region-based wage scales for government projects that particularly disadvantaged southern labor. She also faced strong resentment for being a woman in a powerful government position.

In 1938 Louisa FitzSimons accepted a position with the U.S. Children's Bureau in Washington, D.C. Shepperson's plans to join her were sidetracked when disgruntled planters and politicians charged her with using her administration for patronage purposes. After an investigation exonerated her, President Roosevelt accepted her resignation in 1939. Shepperson, having served longer than any state New Deal administrator in the nation, relocated to the farm she and FitzSimons had purchased in McLean, Virginia.

With the dramatic changes in government agencies in wartime Washington, Shepperson and FitzSimons secured a variety of welfare-related positions. In 1940 and 1941, Shepperson briefly served as chief assistant to HARRIET ELLIOTT, the only woman appointed to the eight-member National Defense Advisory Commission. After a brief tenure with the District of Columbia Board of Public Welfare in 1941 and 1942, Shepperson became assistant to the chief of the U.S. Children's Bureau (Katharine Lenroot) in 1943 and in 1944 director of its Social Service Division. Shepperson retired from government service in 1946, followed by FitzSimons in 1955. The two pioneer southern social workers moved back to Richmond, where they lived together until FitzSimons's death in 1968. Gay Shepperson died in Richmond in 1977 at the age of ninety. Her career exemplifies the difficulties and contributions of women in public service and provides an extraordinary perspective on the evolution of social work, public welfare, and federal power.

Bibliography: The Gay Bolling Shepperson Papers, which include several clippings files, are located at the Atlanta History Center, Atlanta, Georgia. FERA States Files (1933–36) on deposit at the National Archives II, College Park, Maryland, are a rich source of material concerning Shepperson's work in Georgia during the New Deal, as are Lorena Hickok's reports to Harry Hopkins, found in the Harry Hopkins Papers at the Franklin D. Roosevelt Presidential Library, Hyde Park, New York. Michael Holmes, *The New Deal in Georgia: An Administrative History* (1975), which drew on Shepperson's personal recollections, chronicles the power struggles and enormous challenges that defined her tenure. See also Sarah Wilkerson-Freeman, "The Creation of a Subversive Feminist Dominion: Interracialist Social Workers and the Georgia New Deal," *Journal of Women's History* 13, no. 4 (Winter 2002), pp. 132–54. Shepperson's niece, Philippa Armstrong, provided important insights into her aunt's personal life and character.

SARAH WILKERSON-FREEMAN

SHERIF, Carolyn Wood. June 26, 1922–July 23, 1982. Social psychologist.

Born in Loogootee, Indiana, the youngest of three children of Bonny Williams, a homemaker, and Lawrence Anselm Wood, a teacher, Carolyn Wood later recalled her parents as encouraging any ambition she and her siblings set for themselves, including pursuing a college education. Carolyn graduated from West Lafayette High School in 1940. Although the family had been hit hard by the Depression, her father's job as supervisor for teacher training in agricultural education at Purdue University enabled the Wood children to attend the university. Like her siblings, Carolyn worked part-time jobs in college that ranged from singing in a Methodist Church quartet to working at the school bookstore.

At Purdue, Carolyn was a member of the second class of an experimental program for women that was designed to encourage careers in science. Her many extracurricular activities focused on her keen interests in music, theater, and radio. She later recalled that the course of her life was markedly affected by the start of World War II during her second year in college, simultaneously sparking her interest in working for a better world and later offering her opportunities for graduate study and employment that otherwise would have been less open to her as a woman.

After graduating from Purdue with a BS in science (with highest distinction) in 1943, she went on to the University of Iowa to pursue graduate work in psychology. She earned her MS in just one year. Along the way, she read Muzafer Sherif's *The Psychology of Social Norms* (1936) and immediately decided that that was the kind of social psychologist she wanted to be.

After graduating from Iowa, Carolyn Wood moved to New Jersey and accepted a job as a research assistant to the director of Audience Research, Inc. She was soon disappointed because it did not have the rigor she expected of work purporting to be scientifically based. Her dissatisfaction, which was also spurred by incidents of sexual harassment on the job, prompted her to write to Hadley Cantril, a noted psychologist at Princeton, for advice about graduate study. Within a week he telephoned her and offered her a research assistant position with Muzafer Sherif. She was enthusiastic and eager to work with the rising star. Though quite different in age and background (sixteen years her senior, Muzafer, who had earned a PhD in the United States, permanently immigrated from Turkey in 1944 after being jailed for his outspoken criticism of the Nazi movement), they married in December 1945. She recalled later that her romantic notions of a relationship in which the couple shared commitments to social justice, gender equity, and social psychology made Muzafer powerfully attractive to her. The first of their three daughters, Sue, was born in 1947. Joan followed in 1950, and Ann in 1955.

Carolyn Wood Sherif took a few graduate courses at Columbia and began to work with Muzafer, defining a distinctive Sherifian approach to social psychology that focused on the self-system, intergroup conflict and cooperation, and social judgment. Despite the Sherifs' openness about the cooperative nature of their work, Carolyn's contributions were often unrecognized or misattributed because of Muzafer's eminence.

Collaborative projects produced some of the Sherifs' most important works, including one of the best-known field studies in psychology, the Robbers Cave experiment, which demonstrated the effectiveness of superordinate goals as a means of reducing intergroup conflict. It was published as *Intergroup Conflict and Cooperation* in 1961. *Reference Groups: Exploration into Conformity and Deviation of Adolescents* (1964) reported a study of natural adolescent groups in five American cities. Sherif's ingenious use of children's and adolescents' sport activities in studying natural group processes contributed to her national reputation in sport psychology.

In 1958 the couple realized that in order for Carolyn's work to be recognized in its own right, she would need the PhD. Not wanting to be a student where Muzafer was a member of the standing faculty, Carolyn decided to study with Wayne Holtzman at the University of Texas, where Muzafer took a position as visiting research professor. They continued research at the Institute of Group Relations, which Muzafer had established at the University of Oklahoma. Carolyn recalled those years as tough—not only because she was a full-time mother of three and a full-time graduate student, but also because of the complications regarding her status vis-à-vis faculty and other students, since she was already the co-author of several books and articles, including a well-known social psychology textbook. She completed her PhD in psychology with a minor in sociology in 1961.

Sherif's PhD did make a difference, and she was offered a visiting appointment at the University of Oklahoma, which she held for two years. Soon, though, the couple sought opportunities that could lead to tenured positions for them both. In 1966, Pennsylvania State University offered Muzafer a position in sociology and Carolyn a position in psychology. Despite the quantity and impact of her work, she was not promoted to full professor until 1970.

Carolyn Sherif was an outsider in a male-dominated department, one of two women out of a faculty of about thirty. This isolation, combined with her long-standing interests in gender issues, was a major influence in the last decade of her life. She credited her participation in the first graduate seminar on the psychology of women at Penn State in 1972 with crystallizing her research and professional commitment to these concerns. Soon after she helped launch the women's studies program at Penn State.

Sherif joined Division 35 (Psychology of Women) of the American Psychological Association (APA) as soon as it was formed and served in many different capacities, including as division president (1979–80). Applying her earlier work, she advocated analysis of gender identity from the perspective of the self-system, reasoning that it offers a more broadly based, process-oriented conceptualization of the construct than do traditional role-bound definitions. Her work was recognized with the Association for Women in Psychology's Distinguished Publication Award (1981), and the

American Psychological Foundation's Distinguished Teaching of Psychology Award (1982).

After a brief fight with cancer, Carolyn Wood Sherif died in 1982 in State College, Pennsylvania, at the age of sixty. Her legacy is honored by the APA's Division 35 Carolyn Wood Sherif Award, given annually for major contributions to the field of the psychology of women through scholarship, teaching, mentoring, and leadership.

Bibliography: An incomplete collection of their papers as well as news clippings and other material for both Carolyn Wood Sherif and Muzafer Sherif (1906–88) are located in the Special Collections Room of Paterno Library at Pennsylvania State University. A brief but revealing autobiographical sketch appears in Agnes N. O'Connell and Nancy Felipe Russo, eds., *Models of Achievement: Reflections of Eminent Women in Psychology* (1983). An interview with the Sherifs appears in Richard I. Evans, *The Making of Social Psychology: Discussions with Creative Contributors* (1980). In addition to works cited above, Carolyn Sherif's principal co-authored publications include *Groups in Harmony and Tension* (1953) and *Attitude and Attitude Change* (1965). Single-authored publications of note include *Orientation in Social Psychology* (1976); "Bias in Psychology," in Julia A. Sherman and Evelyn Torton Beck, eds., *The Prism of Sex: Essays in the Sociology of Knowledge* (1979); and "Needed Concepts in the Study of Gender Identity," *Psychology of Women Quarterly* 6, no. 4 (Summer 1982), pp. 375–98. Obituaries by Martha T. Mednick and Nancy Felipe Russo for the *Psychology of Women Quarterly* 8 (Fall 1983), pp. 3–8, and by Leigh S. Shaffer and Stephanie A. Shields in *American Psychologist* 39, no. 2 (February 1984), pp. 176–78, pay tribute to Sherif as a scholar and colleague.

STEPHANIE A. SHIELDS

SHERMAN, Esther Luella. *See* Devi, Ragini.

SHIELDS, Laurie. *See* Sommers, Tish.

SHORE, Dinah. February 29, 1916–February 24, 1994. Singer, television entertainer.

Singer and television personality Dinah Shore connected with audiences for over six decades by seeming to be truly enjoying herself while performing. Born Frances "Fanny" Rose Shore in Winchester, Tennessee, she was the second child of Russian immigrants Solomon A. Shore and Anna Stein. Before age two, she contracted polio, an affliction she was able to overcome, though she retained a slight limp for about ten years. Later she said that surviving polio gave her the drive to go into sports and entertainment.

In 1924, the Shores, a Jewish family, moved to Nashville, where Fanny Rose Shore began singing in her father's department store. At fourteen, she also sang at a club called the Pines without informing her parents, who nevertheless attended her debut, having been alerted by a friend about their daughter's early passion to sing before a bigger audience. After her mother's death in 1934, her older sister, Elizabeth ("Bessie"), who had moved to St. Louis after marrying, returned to Nashville with her husband to help raise the teenager.

After graduating from Hume Fogg High School as "best-all-around-girl" in 1934, Shore attended Vanderbilt University in Nashville, majoring in sociology, though her heart was already set on music. While at Vanderbilt, she sang on WSM radio and tried her luck in New York City with little success. After graduating in 1938, she returned to New York and received a number of assignments, starting with singing for free ("for no") on WNEW radio along with Frankie Laine, Dennis Day, and Frank Sinatra. When Martin Block and Jimmy Rich of WNEW forgot her name after she sang "Dinah" at her audition, they referred to her as that Dinah person, and that's how Frances Rose Shore became Dinah Shore.

After completing several radio assignments and making her record debut with Xavier Cugat, Dinah Shore's big break came in October 1940 when she became a regular on Eddie Cantor's radio show, *Time to Smile,* sponsored by Sal Hepatica. On the Cantor show, Shore developed her signature talent and trademark style of pleasing the audience, a skill Cantor was quick to nurture. Her success led NBC to offer her a fifteen-minute radio program, which ran through 1942 on the Blue network.

At this time Dinah Shore was also enjoying success on the record charts. Her rendition of "Yes, My Darling Daughter" sold more than a half million copies, and she earned $115,000 in 1942. In 1946, she had six songs at the top of the charts. Hollywood also beckoned, and she made her film debut in 1943 with *Thank Your Lucky Stars.* She made several other films the next year (for example, *Up in Arms, Belle of the Yukon,* and *Follow the Boys*), but the movies were not to be her medium. A few years later, that privilege would go to television.

Meanwhile, Dinah Shore responded to the war effort in the 1940s by becoming a tireless entertainer of the troops. She met her husband, actor George Montgomery, at the Hollywood Canteen. They became engaged on December 4, 1943, and were married a day later. While Montgomery continued to serve his country, GIs all over wanted to hear Dinah Shore sing "I'll Walk Alone" and her other hits. She responded by doing numerous USO tours, including entertaining twelve thousand troops at Versailles, and received a USO award as the first entertainer to visit GIs on the front lines. Not forgetting her Tennessee roots, she also appeared at various defense rallies in her home state; at one event she helped raise $387,475, singing her signature song "Yes, My Darling Daughter" among others.

After making her television debut in 1950 on the Ed Wynn show singing "Blues in the Night," on November 27, 1951, she premiered her own NBC television show, a live, twice-weekly, fifteen-minute musical variety program during which she encouraged viewers to "See the USA in your Chevrolet." At the end of a show to fill time, she blew the audience a kiss. The kiss became her trademark. Among her many distinctions, Shore, who had sung gospel as a child, fought to present black performers, such as MAHALIA JACKSON, Nat King Cole, and ELLA FITZGERALD, to her vast American audience. In 1955 she won the first of her ten Emmy Awards from the Academy of Television Arts and Sciences, and in 1957, her hour-long show premiered in color. The show remained on the air until 1962.

George Montgomery and Dinah Shore remained married for almost twenty years. Their first child, Melissa Ann, was born in January 1948. Their second child, John David ("Jody"), was adopted in 1954. The couple divorced in 1962, and the next year Shore entered into a short-lived marriage to Palm Springs tennis player Maurice Fabian Smith, which ended in divorce within a year.

A new chapter in Dinah Shore's career, and her love affair with television, began in 1970, when she started a four-year run with her talk show *Dinah's Place.* On this show she met and began her convention-defying four-year relationship with actor Burt Reynolds, almost twenty years her junior. Her later talk shows included *Dinah!* from 1974 to 1979 and *Dinah & Friends* from 1979 to 1984.

Dinah Shore, who had always played tennis and whose golf handicap was 21, pioneered and sponsored a prestigious Ladies Professional Golf Association tournament (the Dinah Shore Classic) in Palm Springs, California, in the later phase of her life. She also wrote best-selling cookbooks (*Someone's in the Kitchen with Dinah,* 1971; *The Dinah Shore Cookbook,* 1983; and *The Dinah Shore American Kitchen,* 1990) and did another talk show, *Conversations with Dinah,* on the Nashville Network from 1989 to 1991. She endowed her alma mater, Vanderbilt, with a scholarship fund and supported many causes, including Jerusalem's Hebrew University.

A knowledgeable businessperson and entrepreneur, Shore was appointed to the board of directors of MGM/UA in 1985; she was one of the few women entertainers to serve in such a capacity. A Peabody Award winner, Dinah Shore was inducted in the Television Academy's Hall of Fame in 1992. Two years later she died of ovarian cancer at her home in Beverly Hills at the age of seventy-seven.

Bibliography: The Jewish Federation of Nashville has articles and information about Dinah Shore's Tennessee roots. The Museum of Television and Radio (formerly the Museum of Broadcasting) in Beverly Hills, California, has tapes of Dinah Shore's radio and television shows. Bruce Cassidy, *Dinah! A Biography* (1979), provides useful biographical information, as does *Current Biography* (1966), pp. 376–78. *Dinah Shore—Sealed with a Kiss,* a one-hour television documentary (1998), provides many clips of her as a performer and also includes interviews with family members, friends, and colleagues. Gregory Koseluk, *Eddie Cantor: A Life in Show Business* (1995), and Eddie Cantor with David Freedman and Jane Kesner Ardmore, *My Life Is in Your Hands and Take My Life: The Autobiographies of Eddie Cantor* (2000), provide information and anecdotes about Dinah Shore's early days in radio. Obituaries appeared in the *New York Times* and *Los Angeles Times* on February 25, 1994.

PHILIPPE PEREBINOSSOFF

SHOUSE, Catherine Filene. June 9, 1896–December 14, 1994. Philanthropist, Democratic party activist, patron of the arts.

Catherine Filene was born in Boston, the elder of two children of Thérèse Weil and A. Lincoln Filene, a wealthy department store owner. Her grandfather, William Filene (Filehne), immigrated from Germany and founded Filene's Department Stores. Her mother, an inveterate entertainer as well as an accomplished musician, was an avid supporter of the Boston Symphony Orchestra and the Boston Music Settlement in the North End. The Filenes divided their time between Boston and their country house in Weston, Massachusetts.

Influenced by her father, Catherine inherited a strong interest in careers for women and the belief that a woman could do what she wanted provided she worked for it. Known to her friends as Kay, she attended Bradford Academy (later Bradford College) from 1911 to 1913, and then spent the following year at Vassar College, where her housemate was EDNA ST. VINCENT MILLAY. She graduated with a BA from Wheaton College in Norton, Massachusetts, in 1918. Straightforward and adventurous, Catherine arranged her classes at both Vassar and Wheaton so that she could attend symphony concerts in New York and Boston. During her junior year at Wheaton she became the director of the Bureau of Vocational Opportunities and organized their first intercollegiate conference on opportunities for college women.

Upon graduation, she took a trip with her uncle to Washington, D.C., and returned home with three job offers. She took the one that paid the most ($1,400 per year), as assistant to the chief of the Women's Division of the U.S. Employment Service of the Department of Labor in Washington, D.C. In 1919, she returned to Boston, became active in state Democratic politics, and enrolled at Radcliffe College as a graduate student. In 1920, when the Harvard Graduate School of Education opened, she transferred there, becoming the first woman to earn a degree (M.Ed., 1923). During this time, she also did career counseling for women at both Wheaton and Cornell and was commissioned by Houghton Mifflin to edit *Careers for Women* (1920), made up of chapters written by women who were leaders in their respective fields. She edited an expanded version in 1934.

In 1921, Catherine Filene married Alvin E. Dodd, an economist; their only child, Joan, was born in February 1923. During the 1920s, the Dodds lived in Washington, D.C., where Alvin helped establish the U.S. Chamber of Commerce and Catherine was active in Democratic politics. Along with FLORENCE JAFFRAY HARRIMAN, she was a founder of the Woman's National Democratic Club in 1925 and edited its bulletin from 1929 to 1932. In 1926, she chaired the board of the Federal Prison for Women, where she instituted a job-training and rehabilitation program. In 1929, with the help of social scientist and Smith College professor Chase Going Woodhouse, she founded the Institute of Women's Professional Relations. The institute, which she chaired until 1945, sought to raise the level and number of women in professional positions and held national conferences on opportunities for women.

After Alvin's term at the U.S. Chamber of Commerce ended in 1929, he and Catherine separated. She divorced him in 1930 and two years later married Jouett Shouse, whom she had met through her political work. A lawyer and businessman who had been a congressman from Kansas and assistant secretary of the Treasury under President Coolidge, Jouett was serving as chair of the Democratic National Executive Committee. The Shouses spent a great deal of time at Wolf Trap Farm, fifty-three acres that Catherine had bought in Fairfax, Virginia, in 1930 with what was left of her inheritance after the stock market crash. There they hunted, raised and bred boxers, and hosted fund-raising events. Soon after their marriage, the couple informally adopted a boy, whom they named William Filene Shouse.

Well-known for her organizational acumen and her fund-raising success, Catherine Filene Shouse was active in civic and cultural affairs in the Washington area. Having been exposed to music early in life, she maintained a lively interest in the performing arts and took many trips to Europe for musical events and festivals. While traveling in Germany after the war, Jouett and Catherine Shouse became interested in the General Clay Fund, which supported the U.S. Army's German Youth Activities Program to retrain German youth about democracy and social and political involvement. Beginning in 1947, Shouse lent her considerable expertise to organizing donations and fundraising for the enterprise and regularly toured its centers until the 1960s. In addition, at the invitation of former president Herbert Hoover, she helped organize the Hungarian Relief Fund in 1956, raising $500,000 within a month.

Shouse broadened her involvement in the music world when, in 1957, she was appointed chair of the President's Music Committee's People-to-People Program; she served until 1963. Through this organization she produced annual calendars of performing arts events, and organized the first International Jazz Festival (1962) in the Washington area. In 1958 Eisenhower appointed her to the board of the National Cultural Center (renamed the John F. Kennedy Center for the Performing Arts), where she remained until 1980. She also served on the board of the National Symphony Orchestra from 1949 to 1968.

In 1966, Catherine Filene Shouse donated a portion of her Wolf Trap estate to the Department of the Interior to create a performing arts park within the National Park Service, as well as the money to build an open-air amphitheater to be called the Filene Center. Her donation, a unique public/private partnership for the arts, was accepted by an act of Congress in October 1966. Wolf Trap Farm Park for the Performing Arts became her best known and crowning achievement. She then established the Wolf Trap Foundation to manage the park, arrange programming, and raise funds, maintaining an active role in the foundation into her nineties. The ground-breaking ceremony for the Filene Center took place in 1968, and the gala opening on July 1, 1971. When the center burned to the ground in 1982, she had a new amphitheater designed; it reopened in 1984. In 1977 President Gerald Ford gave her the Presidential Medal of Freedom, and she was one of twelve to receive the National Medal of Arts in 1994. Jouett Shouse died in 1968, and Catherine Filene Shouse died in Naples, Florida, on December 14, 1994, at the age of ninety-eight.

Bibliography: The papers of Catherine Filene Shouse are located at the Schlesinger Library, Radcliffe Institute for Advanced Study, Harvard University. For additional biographical information, see the Wolf Trap commemorative program book for June 9, 1995. See also Barbara Gamarekian, "Capital Grande Dame with Whim of Iron," *New York Times,* June 7, 1981. Shouse's grandson, Dave Robertson, provided valuable information for this essay. Obituaries appeared in the *Washington Post* and the *New York Times* on December 15, 1994.

GLYNN EDWARDS

SIMKINS, Mary Modjeska Monteith. December 5, 1899–April 5, 1992. Civil rights activist, community organizer.

Mary Modjeska Monteith was born and raised in Columbia, South Carolina, the oldest of eight siblings. Named for an aunt and the Polish actress Helen Modjeska, she was known as Modjeska from primary school on. Although her parents were both the grandchildren of slaves, Henry Clarence Monteith, a construction foreman, and his wife, Rachel Evelyn Hull, a former schoolteacher, enjoyed middle-class status and sent all their surviving children to college. Besides reading her children the tales of Hans Christian Andersen, Modjeska's mother also read them tracts about the Niagara Movement and other current racial affairs, offering them a political education from a young age. Once when an armed mob surrounded and fired on his home, Henry Monteith fought back; his return of fire dispersed the crowd and saved his family. Their eldest daughter remembered both of her parents as fearless during the early years of the twentieth century, a particularly violent period known as the nadir of American race relations.

Modjeska Monteith attended primary and secondary schools attached to Benedict College, and then earned her BA from the school in 1921. She accompanied her mother, who was more politically active than her husband, to local meetings of the National Association for the Advancement of Colored People (NAACP). After graduation, she taught at Booker T. Washington School in Columbia, specializing in mathematics, until her marriage in 1929 to black businessman Andrew Whitfield Simkins, a widower with five children who was sixteen years her senior. Her husband had worked for North Carolina Mutual Insurance before he bought a Columbia gas station and liquor store, and became prosperous in local real estate. Like her mother before her, Modjeska Simkins was forced to retire from teaching once she married—she was not even allowed to finish out the school year following her December wedding.

In 1931 Simkins became the first director of Negro Work for the South Carolina Tuberculosis Association. She was sent for training to Michigan State Normal School (now Eastern Michigan University) before going out into the field, where she became a popular and effective organizer. With great pride, she explained that her husband supported her career, and that they employed a housekeeper to take care of domestic activities while she was out on the road. Their Columbia home was a place where South Carolina blacks, for whom there were limited opportunities for public accommodation in the state's capital, might find overnight hospitality, something Simkins credited to her husband's generosity and sociability.

Simkins had tremendous success with her public health programs, but in 1942 she was asked by her employers to withdraw her membership from the South Carolina branch of the NAACP, for which she served as corresponding secretary. She refused and was summarily fired. Simkins, who spent most of her adult life as an unpaid volunteer for civil rights, next channeled her considerable energies into the NAACP in South Carolina. She spearheaded campaigns for pay equity for black teachers in Columbia (won in 1945) and the dismantling of the state's all-white election primary (achieved by court victories in 1947 and 1948), and several other grassroots campaigns. Especially important was her work in championing South Carolina desegregation lawsuits, including *Briggs v. Elliot* (1951), which eventually became part of the *Brown v. Board of Education* cluster of cases ruled on by the Supreme Court in 1954.

Although Simkins published an editorial column, "Palmetto State," in the Norfolk *Journal and Guide* from 1946 to 1948, most of her energy and activism cannot be gleaned from her published writings. Devoted to working within neighborhoods and rural communities, she organized meetings, strategized with co-workers, and rallied the troops, making speeches throughout the South—from Birmingham, Alabama, to Richmond, Virginia, from Highlander, Tennessee, to Durham, North Carolina. She was a dynamic force within grassroots organizations such as the Commission on Interracial Cooperation, the Southern Regional Council, the Southern Negro Youth Congress, and the Southern Conference for Human Welfare, to name but a few of the half-dozen organizations for which she was a mainstay. In 1956 she was hired as public relations director for the Victory Savings Bank in Columbia; she was then promoted to branch manager and eventually elected to the board of directors.

By the late 1950s her unwillingness to repudiate Communist leaders working for social justice—comrades such as James and Esther Jackson, and Herbert Aptheker—caused her to break with several organizations. She became disaffected and dropped her affiliation with the NAACP. Although raised a Baptist, Simkins became alienated from the institutional African American church, complaining that too many black ministers provided too little support for civil rights agitation. She also suggested that the civil rights movement mirrored the gender politics within the twentieth-century black church: men were given control of the leadership, and women were expected to perform most of the actual work.

Although she had a formidable reputation within her own state and was recognized as a "matriarch" of South Carolina's civil rights movement along with her good friend and Charleston colleague, SEPTIMA POINSETTE CLARK, Simkins's reputation was limited to local, southern networks.

When put forward for a leadership role, however, Simkins recoiled, suggesting, "if I'm up here as president I can't do a thing but preside. . . . I can raise a whole lot of more hell from the floor." And hell-raising was Simkins's specialty, as she took public and vocal stands against prisons putting black women prisoners in South Carolina chain gangs, poor conditions at the Palmetto State Hospital for Negroes, the prevalence of police brutality, and other injustices.

Mary Modjeska Simkins cast herself as a renegade within the movement for racial uplift and social reform, and her combative posture remained legendary. "I just like a fight," she confided to an interviewer. "I don't feel good when I am not in a fight." Simkins died in Columbia in 1992 at the age of ninety-two. In 1995 a portrait of her was hung in the South Carolina state house in honor of her long career as a crusader for justice.

Bibliography: A wealth of material is available in the Modjeska Monteith Simkins Papers at the South Caroliniana Library at the University of South Carolina, Columbia. Equally useful is an interview with Modjeska Simkins (July 28–31, 1976) conducted by Jacquelyn Hall, available in the Southern Oral History Program Collection, University of North Carolina at Chapel Hill, which is the source of all the quotations. See also Barbara Woods, "Black Woman Activist in Twentieth Century South Carolina: Modjeska Monteith Simkins" (PhD dissertation, Emory University, 1979), and Woods, "Modjeska Simkins and the South Carolina Conference of the NAACP, 1939–1957," in Vicki L. Crawford, Jacqueline Anne Rouse, and Barbara Woods, eds., *Women in the Civil Rights Movement: Trailblazer and Torchbearers, 1941–1965* (1990).

CATHERINE CLINTON

SMITH, Hazel Brannon. February 5, 1914–May 14, 1994. Journalist, newspaper publisher.

Hazel Brannon Smith's columns and editorials opposing racial violence and speaking out against white extremists in Mississippi during the turbulent civil rights movement of the 1950s and 1960s earned her a national reputation. In 1964 she became the first woman to win the Pulitzer Prize for Editorial Writing.

Born in Alabama City, Alabama, near the Etowah County seat of Gadsden, she was the firstborn child of Georgia Freeman, a housewife, and Dock Boad Brannon, a steel mill worker and electrical contractor. She attended public elementary schools and graduated from Gadsden High School in 1930 at age sixteen. Too young for college, she worked for the weekly *Etowah Observer* for two years, writing personal items and selling advertisements, then entered the University of Alabama in 1932 to study journalism. She was an editor of the student newspaper and a member of Delta Zeta sorority, and graduated with a BA in 1935.

In 1936 Brannon purchased the 600-subscriber *Durant News* in Holmes County with a $3,000 loan. She successfully boosted subscriptions, increased advertising revenue, and paid off the loan in four years. On April 8, 1943, she announced her purchase of the *Lexington Advertiser,* a weekly with 1,800 subscribers, in the Holmes County seat with the front-page headline "Welcome to Lexington Miss Hazel Brannon." She later acquired the Jackson *Northside Reporter* and the *Banner County Outlook* in Flora, Mississippi.

In 1946, Brannon's six-month law-and-order editorial campaign against bootlegging and gambling led to numerous indictments and a citation for contempt of court in retaliation for her criticism of public officials. The Mississippi Supreme Court overturned the citation in 1947. Meanwhile, the *Lexington Advertiser* prospered, allowing its editor to indulge in the lifestyle of a coquettish southern belle with a penchant for stylish clothes and white Cadillac convertibles. "Honey, I had the most eligible bachelor in Durant and the most eligible bachelor in Lexington," she told the Jackson, Mississippi, *Clarion-Ledger* in 1986, "and my only trouble was that I couldn't have them both. That's true. I was something" (Kaul, p. 240). She returned from a sea cruise in 1949 engaged to the ship's purser, Walter Dyer ("Smitty") Smith, and they married on March 21, 1950. They had no children.

As an editor Hazel Brannon Smith was outspoken and often controversial, but still a southern white woman who supported the status quo in race relations. When the United States Supreme Court declared on May 17, 1954, in *Brown v. Board of Education* that segregated public schools were unconstitutional, Smith acknowledged three days later in her front-page column, "Through Hazel Eyes," that the court "may be morally right" even though "we know that it is to the best interest of both races that segregation be maintained in theory and in fact" (Kaul, p. 241).

Smith's concern for the law surfaced again that summer in her coverage of the shooting of a twenty-seven-year-old black man by the Holmes County sheriff and her call for the sheriff to resign. The sheriff responded to her editorial crusade with a libel lawsuit. The Holmes County Circuit Court awarded him a $10,000 judgment, but the Mississippi Supreme Court reversed the conviction in 1955. Smith reported her legal victory with this comment: "I am a firm believer in our Southern traditions and racial segregation, but not at the expense of justice and truth" (Newman, p. 68). Despite considering herself a segregationist, she refused to join the Holmes County Citizens' Council as part of the southern-wide mobilization to impede implementation of the 1954 *Brown* decision.

Retaliation for her stands came in a variety of ways. Her husband was fired in 1956 as administrator of the forty-five-bed county hospital he had served since 1950. When her photograph appeared in a November 1957 *Ebony* magazine article, anonymous circulars appeared in Holmes County declaring her an integrationist, a charge she denied. Her moderate law-and-order editorial pleas for equal justice stopped short of an outright endorsement of racial integration even though she was routinely castigated as a "liberal" and "integrationist" in the inflammatory context of Mississippi's closed society and resistance to civil rights.

The most significant challenge came with the 1958 founding of a rival newspaper, the *Holmes County Herald,* for the sole purpose of driving the *Lexington Advertiser* out of business. Supported by many of Holmes County's most prominent citizens, many with strong connections to the Citizens' Council, the *Herald* succeeded in siphoning subscribers and advertising revenue, including legal and public notices, from Smith's newspapers. Soon the economic pressure and political intimidation took a toll. The plight of Smith and her newspapers gained national attention when the International Conference of Weekly Newspaper Editors and Southern Illinois University awarded her the Elijah P. Lovejoy Award for Courage in Journalism in July 1960. A besieged Smith continued to editorialize against racial violence and the growing intransigence of white southerners.

In May 1964, Smith became the first woman to win the Pulitzer Prize for Editorial Writing, the Pulitzer committee citing her "steadfast adherence to her editorial duties in the face of great pressure and opposition." By then she had become more publicly aligned with the emerging civil rights movement in Mississippi and the nation, supporting the Civil Rights Act of 1964. A bomb exploded in the *Northside Reporter* in August 1964 while she was covering the Democratic National Convention. The notoriety that came with the Pulitzer Prize provided income from speaking tours that sustained her struggling newspapers, but to meet her mounting debts she was still forced to mortgage personal property, cut her staff, and sell two newspapers she had acquired in the 1950s. For the next two decades she continued to borrow money to support the *Lexington Advertiser* and to finance construction of her Greek-revival mansion on the outskirts of Lexington, which she called Hazelwood. Her health deteriorated and her behavior became erratic, signs later recognized as Alzheimer's disease. Her husband died on November 20, 1982.

The last edition of the *Lexington Advertiser* appeared on September 19, 1985. Two weeks earlier, the rival *Herald* published a legal notice that Smith had filed for bankruptcy. Banks repossessed her home, her furniture was auctioned, and in February 1986 a relative took the penniless Smith back to her hometown of Gadsden, Alabama. A made-for-television movie based on her life, *A Passion for Justice,* appeared on ABC a month before she died of cancer in a nursing home in Cleveland, Tennessee, at the age of eighty. She was buried in Forrest Cemetery in Gadsden, Alabama.

Bibliography: Affidavits, reports, and newspaper clippings about Smith are in the files of the Mississippi Sovereignty Commission, Mississippi Department of Archives and History, Jackson, Mississippi. Academic and scholarly accounts of Smith's career include Mark Newman, "Hazel Brannon Smith and Holmes County, Mississippi, 1936–1964: The Making of a Pulitzer Prize Winner," *Journal of Mississippi History* 54 (February 1992), pp. 59–87; and Arthur J. Kaul, "Hazel Brannon Smith and the *Lexington Advertiser,*" in David R. Davies, ed., *The Press and Race: Mississippi Journalists Confront the Movement* (2001). Newspaper and magazine accounts of her life include Rick Friedman, "The Weekly Editor: Women's Angle," *Editor & Publisher,* October 24 and 31, 1964; T. George Harris, "The 11-Year Siege of Mississippi's Lady Editor," *Look,* November 16, 1965, pp. 121–28; Lee Freeland, "Time Closes Lexington Newspaper That Battled Racism," *Clarion-Ledger,* January 5, 1986; Fred Grimm, "Hazel Smith, Champion of Civil Rights, Fights Final Battle Alone and Forgotten," *Chicago Tribune,* March 27, 1986; and Dudley Clendinen, "Delta Blacks Rally for 'Woman of Principle,'" *New York Times,* March 31, 1986. Jerry Mitchell, "Fighting Editor Hazel Brannon Smith Faces Last Battle," *Clarion-Ledger,* May 7, 1994, reported on the ABC-TV film of Smith's life. Obituaries appeared in the *Clarion-Ledger* on May 15, 1994, and the *New York Times* on May 16, 1994.

A. J. KAUL

SMITH, Hilda Worthington. June 19, 1888–March 3, 1984. Workers' education specialist, federal official.

Hilda "Jane" Worthington Smith was the oldest of three children and first daughter of Mary Helen Hall and John Jewell Smith. She had an older half sister, Ella Smith Sexton, from her father's first marriage to Henrietta de Groot Smith. Hilda was born in New York City, where her prosperous and well-connected family resided. Her father owned and operated a steam heating company. Her mother had been a public school teacher before marriage.

Smith attended the Horace Mann School and the Veltin School, a private girls' high school in New York City, graduating in 1906. As a self-confessed tomboy, she did not make friends easily and preferred to spend time reading, writing poetry (which she did all her life), playing with her siblings, and riding her pony at her family's Hudson Valley summer home. When she was in her early teens, she met the headmistress of Saint Faith's House, a school for unwed mothers in Poughkeepsie, New York. Her mother became a trustee of the school, though she disliked having Hilda spend much time there. But spend time there she did. In contrast to the Veltin School, where she felt out of place among the posh New York City girls, at Saint Faith's she could cook, clean, care for the babies and the girls, be in the countryside she loved so much, and enjoy a modicum of independence and responsibility. This was probably her first exposure to girls whose station in life was very different from her own, and to the value of the work that social workers could do.

Bryn Mawr College also played an important role in her emerging social philosophy. She graduated from Bryn Mawr College in 1910 with a BA, and stayed on for a master's degree in ethics and psychology, which she received in 1911. Interested in social work after volunteering with factory workers at a Philadelphia settlement house, she received a second master's in 1915 from the New York School of Philanthropy (later the New York School of Social Work) and returned to the town of Bryn Mawr, where she directed a community center. In 1919 she was appointed a dean at the college.

In 1921, Bryn Mawr president M. CAREY THOMAS, just back from a trip to Europe, where she had seen schools for women workers firsthand, asked Smith to start and manage one at Bryn Mawr. From 1921 to 1933, Smith ran the Bryn Mawr Summer School for Women Workers, a decidedly left-leaning summer program where women workers—many of them immigrants working in the garment industry—learned labor economics, drama, literature, history, and social psychology, and enjoyed fresh air, healthy companionship, three square meals a day, and spontaneous learning. Many of these workers later became leaders and activists in the labor movement, in education, and in other public service professions. The school affected the careers of teachers too. ESTHER PETERSON, recruited by Smith to teach physical education, went on to become a leading consumer advocate and presidential adviser. Hilda Worthington Smith had found the cause that shaped the rest of her career. In 1926 she was one of the founders of the Affiliated Schools for Workers, a network of workers' education schools that later became the American Labor Education Service.

Despite support from the Women's Trade Union League and the Young Women's Christian Association, Bryn Mawr decided it could no longer support the school, partly because of its controversial activities. Smith moved it near her summer estate in West Park, New York, renamed it the Vineyard Shore School for Women Workers in Industry, and recruited Ernestine Friedman to run it, but it closed during the Depression. Smith tried again some years later to operate a coeducational workers' school, the Hudson Shore Labor School, and it remained in business until the early 1950s.

In 1933 Smith caught the eye of Harry Hopkins, and he started her on her career in government service. Hired as a specialist in workers' education for the Federal Emergency Relief Administration (FERA) and later the Works Progress Administration (WPA), she initiated and ran teacher-training programs in their Emergency Education Program. She also worked to promote workers' education (which, with its emphasis on the needs of citizens as workers, she saw as distinct from adult education) in the FERA and WPA. From 1934 to 1937 she developed a small program of educational camps for women on relief, which the press nicknamed "she-she-she" camps, a reference to the Civilian Conservation Corps (CCC), which excluded women.

In Washington, D.C., and the states, Smith's idealistic plans for labor education often clashed with the New Deal's pragmatic focus on temporary relief. By 1942, Smith was employed by the Federal Public Housing Authority, where she advised regional and local housing projects on community programs and prepared training materials. She later worked with the National Committee for the Extension of Labor Education and served as a consultant for state commissions on the elderly.

Smith's career in government service was not over, however. In 1965 she was appointed to the Office of Economic Opportunity (OEO). During the seven years she spent with the OEO, she held many varied assignments, mostly overseeing training projects for community action programs. She retired from the OEO in 1972 when she was eighty-three, but continued to consult on elderly affairs for two more years. During the last ten years of her life, she suffered from a broken hip and other injuries that sidelined her for short periods of time. She died of leukemia in 1984 in a Washington, D.C., nursing home at the age of ninety-five. Her siblings, including her sister Helen, with whom she was especially close, had all died by then.

Smith was single-minded in her devotion to work and, aside from writing poetry, had few other outside interests. Though she had several lifelong friendships, she never formed any serious romantic attachments and never married. By her own accounting, as she noted in her autobiography, *Opening Vistas in Workers' Education* (1978), "I was not in the least depressed by this absence of male companions or by the evident lack of marital prospects. . . . Each year I watched the men I knew marry other women, and found that I did not care" (p. 91).

While she spent many years devoting her energies to workers' education, Hilda Smith believed that her most significant contribution was in fighting for the underdog, the less fortunate, and those eager to better themselves. She won admiration from generations of government colleagues and made loyal friends. Her capacity for leadership guided many nonprofit and government organizations to successfully fulfill their missions.

Bibliography: The major collection of material on Hilda Worthington Smith is located at the Schlesinger Library, Radcliffe Institute for Advanced Study, Harvard University. Additional material is found at the Franklin D. Roosevelt Library, Hyde Park, New York; the State Historical Society of Wisconsin in Madison; and Cornell University, Ithaca, New York. Smith's publications include *Women Workers at the Bryn Mawr Summer School* (1929); *Education and the Worker-Student* (1934), with Jean Ogden; *Poems* (1964); and *Opening Vistas in Workers' Education: An Autobiography of Hilda Worthington Smith* (1978). She is profiled in Joyce L. Kornbluh, *A New Deal for Workers' Education: The Workers' Service Program, 1933–1942* (1987). See also Kornbluh and Mary Frederickson, eds., *Sisterhood and Solidarity: Workers' Education for Women, 1914–1984* (1984), and the 1986 documentary film by Suzanne Bauman and Rita Heller, *The Women of Summer.* An obituary appeared in the *New York Times* on March 14, 1984.

DIANE HAMER

SMITH, Kate. May 1, 1907–June 17, 1986. Singer, radio star.

Kate Smith, one of America's most admired and beloved popular singers, was born Kathryn Elizabeth Smith in Washington, D.C. Her mother, Charlotte Yarnell Hanby, was a homemaker, and her father, William Smith, owned the Capitol News Company, which distributed newspapers and magazines in the greater District of Columbia area. The youngest of three daughters (the middle child died in infancy), Smith grew up in a close-knit family. Her earliest musical influences were her mother, a pianist at her Presbyterian church, and her father, who sang in the choir at his Roman Catholic church. She attended Business High School in Washington, D.C., most likely graduating in the class of 1924. She then attended classes at George Washington School of Nursing for nine months before withdrawing to pursue a career in show business.

Kate started out as a natural, untrained performer, with her earliest performances on amateur nights at vaudeville theaters in the Washington, D.C., area. Composer-showman Eddie Dowling brought her to New York City in 1926 to appear in his new Broadway musical comedy, *Honeymoon Lane.* The volume of her singing and the five-foot-ten, 200-pound performer's agile Charleston dance routine stopped every show. When *Honeymoon Lane* closed after two seasons, Smith toured with the road company. Back in New York in 1928, she played in blackface in *Hit the Deck.* In 1930 she co-starred with comedian Bert Lahr in the hit musical comedy *Flying High,* again on Broadway, where her powerful contralto voice caught the attention of Columbia Records executive Joseph M. "Ted" Collins. He became her personal manager, telling her, "You do the singing and I'll fight the battles" (Hayes, p. 17). The agreement, on a handshake, endured for thirty-four years, until Collins's death in 1964.

Collins convinced CBS president William S. Paley to give Smith a sustaining radio series in 1931. On the air she was the "Songbird of the South," and her theme song, "When the Moon Comes Over the Mountain," whose lyrics she had written in a poem as a girl, became one of 1931's biggest hits. In 1932 Smith made a cameo appearance in the Paramount motion picture *The Big Broadcast,* and she was signed by Paramount to star in her own picture late that year. Titled *Hello Everybody!* (her opening signature on the radio), it was semi-autobiographical but a failure at the box office.

More successful was the 1933 vaudeville show Collins put together called "Kate Smith's Swanee Revue." After opening in New York, the show toured the country. Her charm lay in her folksy manner, her girl-next-door image, and the quality of her voice. She was proficient at a variety of singing styles, including opera, country, and sacred, although her forte was the slow popular ballad, ending in an impressive high note. Smith, who never had a singing lesson in her life, had a rich range of two and a half octaves.

Missed by her radio audience, in 1934 she debuted *Kate Smith's New Star Revue,* a radio series sponsored by Hudson motor cars. The next season she was singing on *Kate Smith's A&P Coffee Time.* In 1937 she signed with General Foods for *The Kate Smith Hour,* which lasted eight seasons. Collins next decided to test the waters for a daytime commentary show, and in April 1938 *Kate Smith Speaks* made its debut at noon. The top-rated series lasted until 1951, first on CBS, and later on Mutual. Smith spoke of current events and recommended new plays, movies, and good books; Ted Collins read the news.

On the November 10, 1938, program, Smith introduced a patriotic anthem originally written by Irving Berlin in 1918 and slightly revised to commemorate the twentieth anniversary of the armistice that ended the World War. "God Bless America" would forever be associated with Kate Smith.

Berlin regarded it as his most important composition, and he and Smith donated all proceeds from its performances to the Boy and Girl Scouts of America. Kate recreated her radio introduction of the anthem in the 1943 motion picture, *This Is the Army,* an all–Irving Berlin musical that starred Ronald Reagan.

When America went to war again, Kate Smith was a significant force on the home front. She sang many morale-boosting songs, such as her million-selling "The White Cliffs of Dover," "Comin' in on a Wing and a Prayer," and "I'll Be Seeing You." *The Kate Smith Hour* went on a tour of military bases and centers of war work in 1943, with expenses borne by the Kated (Kate-Ted) Corporation. Smith also conducted several eighteen-hour radio war bond marathons, being personally responsible for the sale of some $600 million in bonds. So successful were her appeals that Columbia University published a psychological study of her technique titled *Mass Persuasion.* Her wartime activities are largely responsible for President Reagan's giving her the Medal of Freedom in 1982.

Critics predicted that Kate Smith would never succeed in television because of her weight, which at times topped three hundred pounds. Collins took that as a challenge, and Smith became a pioneer in daytime television, hosting a critically acclaimed live variety hour on NBC from 1950 to 1954. Her warm personality, hearty laugh, and singing style won her a new generation of admirers. Her last TV series, *The Kate Smith Show,* aired Mondays on CBS in 1960, although she continued to make frequent guest appearances on *The Ed Sullivan Show* and other variety programs.

Smith was a recording artist for nearly fifty years, with some 580 songs to her credit. Her most prolific period was from 1963 to 1968 with RCA Victor, beginning with a live concert album at Carnegie Hall. Her million-selling albums included the sacred LP *How Great Thou Art.* Raised as a Presbyterian, she converted to Catholicism after Ted Collins's death. She never married. In the mid 1970s, Smith gained added fame as something of a good luck charm for Philadelphia's professional hockey team, the Flyers. She was invited to sing "God Bless America" before crucial games, in which the team was invariably victorious; the Flyers won the Stanley Cup in 1974 and 1975, and a statue of Kate Smith was dedicated outside Spectrum Arena in 1987.

Kate Smith's favorite place on earth was Lake Placid. She discovered the Adirondack village in 1932 and soon bought an island vacation home, Camp Sunshine, where she would spend forty summers. She loved to swim, drive her speedboat, and shop for antiques. At Lake Placid she could be herself; the locals loved her. Chronically overweight, in her mid sixties she developed diabetes, eventually losing a leg below the knee and becoming an invalid. On June 17, 1986, she died in Raleigh, North Carolina, where she lived near her sister Helena and a niece. She was seventy-nine.

When she first spoke of "God Bless America" that November day in 1938, she predicted, "Here is a song that will be timeless—it will never die—others will thrill to its beauty long after we are gone" (Hayes, p. 52). Her mortal remains repose in a pink granite mausoleum at St. Agnes Cemetery in Lake Placid, but her voice lives on in her many recordings, especially the Berlin anthem to her beloved America.

Bibliography: Kate Smith's career memorabilia are in the Howard Gotlieb Archival Research Center at Boston University. Additional materials, including two pre-1931 career scrapbooks, recordings, numerous radio and television programs, personal correspondence, and photographs, are owned by the Kate Smith Commemorative Society in Cranston, Rhode Island. Kate Smith wrote two autobiographies: *Living in a Great Big Way* (1938) and *Upon My Lips a Song* (1960). She also wrote a cookbook, *Kate Smith's "Company's Coming" Cookbook* (1958), and a children's book, *Stories of Annabelle* (1951). Robert K. Merton, *Mass Persuasion: The Psychology of a War Bond Drive* (1946), analyzes Smith's success selling bonds in a 1943 drive. Secondary sources include Richard K. Hayes, *Kate Smith: A Biography with a Discography, Filmography and List of Stage Appearances* (1995), and Michael R. Pitts, *Kate Smith: A Bio-Bibliography* (1988). Obituaries appeared in the *New York Times* and the *Los Angeles Times* on June 18, 1986.

RICHARD K. HAYES

SMITH, Margaret Chase. December 14, 1897–May 29, 1995. U.S. representative and senator, Republican Party official.

Margaret Chase Smith, the first woman to serve in both houses of Congress and the first woman to seek the nomination of a major political party for the presidency of the United States, was born Margaret Chase in Skowhegan, Maine, the eldest of six children of Caroline Murray and George Emery Chase. Her father was a barber who worked only sporadically because he suffered from migraine headaches. Her mother waited tables and worked in a shoe factory. While still in school, Margaret contributed to the family income as a store clerk and a night telephone operator. Following graduation from Skowhegan High School in 1916, and after a brief experience teaching in a one-room country school, she took a series of clerical jobs in her hometown.

At the same time, she became passionately involved in women's clubs, especially the Federation of Business and Professional Women, where she encountered a community of ambitious young women like herself. She founded the local chapter in 1922, and by 1925 was president of the Maine State Federation. These activities functioned as an apprenticeship for public life, training her in poise, organizing, fund-raising, public speaking, and politics. Before long, she graduated into partisan political organizations, joining the Skowhegan Republican Committee in 1926, becoming its secretary in 1928, and winning election to the Maine State Republican Committee in 1930.

Margaret Chase remained unmarried into her thirties, but she had been "keeping company" with a prominent local businessman and politician, Clyde Harold Smith, since high school. Twenty-one years her senior, Smith was a divorced man who wanted to cap his long and distinguished political career as governor of Maine, and they married on May 14, 1930. They had no children.

Though Clyde Smith was never to be governor, his wife helped him win election to Congress from Maine's second district in 1936. Margaret Chase Smith (she used both names because of her own prominence in Maine politics) worked as her husband's campaign manager and secretary. When his health began to fail shortly after arriving in Washington, she was his liaison with his constituents at home. Near the end of his second term, Clyde Smith suffered a series of heart attacks. Before he died on April 8, 1940, he dictated a press release urging his constituents to "support the candidate of my choice, my wife and partner in public life, Margaret Chase Smith." Despite significant party opposition, she easily won election to his unexpired term and the next full term that fall.

Representative Smith swiftly established her independence from party orthodoxy by approving President Roosevelt's defense policies and favoring social security and labor measures. Such independence found favor at home, and she was reelected by a large majority in 1942. In perhaps the most important stratagem of her career, Smith resisted assignment to committees assumed appropriate for women and secured a seat on the House Naval Affairs Committee. A key committee in wartime, Naval Affairs fostered her development of expertise in military matters, facilitating her ability to surmount gender assumptions and appear tough enough to handle hard issues. Although she consistently distanced herself from feminism, Smith's sensitivity to gender discrimination, heightened through many years in the workplace, led her to pursue a series of measures during and after the war to equalize opportunities for women. She pressed for fair wages, child care, workplace equity, and the equal rights amendment. Through her position on Naval Affairs, Smith relentlessly pressed for rank and regular status for military women, first for nurses and ultimately for all women in the armed services, culminating in the Women's Armed Services Integration Act of 1948.

In 1948, Smith decided to risk her extremely safe seat as Second District representative to launch a campaign for the U.S. Senate, a first for a woman. She did it with the able assistance of William C. Lewis Jr., legislative counsel to the Naval Affairs Committee. Lewis was fifteen years her junior and possessed the legal education Smith lacked. He managed her successful campaign and afterward signed on as her administrative assistant, a post he held until she left office in 1973. Smith never remarried, and Lewis was also unmarried. They were intensely devoted to one another, but neither was willing to risk her political career for a romantic attachment. Lewis remained her devoted aide and companion until he died of a heart attack in 1982.

Although Smith's election to the Senate was greeted with great expectations of imminent political equity for women, she served most of her twenty-four years in the upper house as the only woman. Smith was a petite woman with silver hair and a firm chin, whose physical attractiveness was the source of relentless mention in the press. As she struggled to fit into the masculine ethos of the Senate, she wore plain dark suits with a single feminine touch, a fresh rose in her lapel that soon became her trademark and an easy shorthand for reporters and cartoonists who found it more interesting than her political opinions.

Building a reputation for hard work and perfect attendance, she attacked extremism on both the left and the right. The most dramatic example was her June 1, 1950, speech on the Senate floor, a riveting "Declaration of Conscience" against the depredations of her colleague, Senator Joseph McCarthy, and the willingness of the leaders of her party to put up with them. Though the speech attracted favorable media attention, it did little to restrain McCarthy, who was not censured by his peers until four years later. The speech extracted a price from Smith, however. She immediately lost some prized committee assignments, and the Old Guard Republican leadership never forgave her, a serious hardship in an institution where so much depends on interpersonal relationships.

On domestic issues, Smith was moderate, even liberal, endorsing civil rights, federal aid to education, and social security. But as a hard-line anticommunist, she was frequently critical of President Eisenhower's, and later John F. Kennedy's, conciliatory cold war policies. The Soviet press referred to her as an "amazon war monger," an epithet she proudly trumpeted when she launched a bid for the Republican nomination for president in 1964. Her odd campaign was known most for what it lacked: staff, headquarters, and money. She made modest showings in primaries in New Hampshire and Illinois, but was never a serious contender. At the Republican National Convention, she became the first woman to be placed in nomination for a major political party and gathered twenty-seven first-ballot votes.

Smith returned to the Senate, where seniority had elevated her to ranking member on two key committees, Armed Services and Appropriations. As the Vietnam War escalated, she never wavered from her firm defense policy, despite increasing entreaties from her constituents. In 1970, she made a second Declaration of Conscience speech criticizing the extremist tactics of student militants as well as the Nixon administration's attempts to repress dissent.

After a campaign marked by serious altercations with anti-war students and activist women, Smith lost her bid for a fifth term in 1972. She returned to her hometown of Skowhegan, where she and Lewis established a research library. She devoted her final years to the Margaret Chase Smith Library, while a sympathetic media gradually transformed her into a symbol of all that was good about a Maine that was rapidly fading away. She died at her home following a massive stroke at the age of ninety-seven.

Bibliography: The Margaret Chase Smith Library in Skowhegan, Maine, contains over 300,000 documents, 3,000 photographs, dozens of audio and videotapes, forty-three volumes of statements and speeches, and nearly 500 scrapbooks of clippings and personal items. This article draws on Janann Sherman, *No Place for a Woman: A Life of Senator Margaret Chase Smith* (2000); the quotation from Clyde Smith is on p. 42. Other biographies include Patricia L. Schmidt, *Margaret Chase Smith: Beyond Convention* (1996); Patricia Ward Wallace, *Politics of Conscience: A Biography of Margaret Chase Smith* (1995); Alice Fleming, *The Senator from Maine: Margaret Chase Smith* (1969); and Frank Graham Jr., *Margaret Chase Smith: Woman of Courage* (1964). William C. Lewis Jr., ed., *Declaration of Conscience* (1972), is a collection of Smith's essays and speeches. On women of Smith's era, see Irwin N. Gertzog, *Congressional Women: Their Recruitment, Treatment, and Behavior* (1984). More contemporary women in Congress are discussed in Linda Witt, Karen M. Paget, and Glenna Matthews, *Running as a Woman: Gender and Power in American Politics* (1994). A detailed survey of the Women's Armed Services Integration Act of 1948 appears in Janann Sherman, "'They Either Need These Women or They Do Not': Margaret Chase Smith and the Fight for Regular Status for Women in the Military," *Journal of Military History* 54 (January 1990), pp. 47–78. Obituaries appeared in the *New York Times*, the *Washington Post*, and the *Los Angeles Times* on May 30, 1995.

JANANN SHERMAN

SMITH, Mary Louise. October 6, 1914–August 22, 1997. Republican Party official, feminist.

Mary Louise Smith, longtime Republican Party official and feminist, was born in Eddyville, Iowa, the second daughter of bank president Frank Epperson and homemaker Louise Jager Epperson. In 1929, Epperson's bank failed and the family moved to Iowa City, where Mary Louise attended high school and the State University of Iowa (later the University of Iowa). While at the university, she met Elmer Smith, a medical student, whom she married on October 7, 1934.

After graduating in 1935 with a degree in social work administration, Mary Louise Smith helped support the couple by working for the Iowa Emergency Relief Association and gave birth to the couple's three children: Robert (1937), Margaret (1939), and James (1942). From 1937 to 1940, Elmer practiced medicine before entering military service during World War II. Mary Louise later credited her sense of independence and self-worth to the five years she spent raising her children while Elmer was away in the military.

In 1945, the family moved to Eagle Grove, Iowa. Always a Republican voter, Smith now embarked on her active involvement with the party. Club work was the main avenue for women's involvement in party politics during the 1950s, but Smith went further, using her club experiences and networks to move into the county Republican Party organization.

In 1963, the Smiths moved to Des Moines. Her children grown and her husband retired, Smith felt able to take on more responsibility within the party. That year, she also read Betty Friedan's *The Feminine Mystique* and, like millions of other women, resolved to continue to pursue ambitions beyond her role as a wife and mother. In 1964, making use of the statewide network of support she had established through club work, Smith successfully bid to become Iowa's Republican national committeewoman, a springboard to state and national prominence. She helped develop a system of precinct organization in Iowa that became a model for later national efforts. In 1969, she was named to the Republican National Committee (RNC) Executive Committee, where George H. W. Bush became her mentor.

In 1972, the Republican and Democratic national conventions were both under pressure to promote greater participation by women and minorities. As a middle-aged, economically comfortable woman, Smith initially doubted that the new feminist movement had anything to offer her. But younger Republican women persuaded Smith that her rights were tied to those of all women. Smith became an ardent supporter of the equal rights amendment (ERA) and reproductive freedom, positions she viewed as fully in keeping with her strong commitment to Republican traditions of individualism. At the GOP convention, Smith helped maneuver the planks endorsed by the National Women's Political Caucus into the GOP platform. After the convention, she served as one of two vice-chairs of the RNC's Rule 29 Committee, which was charged with drafting proposals for bringing more women and minorities into active participation in the party.

In 1974, President Ford named Smith to succeed George Bush as RNC chairman; she was the first woman to hold that position. Although some noted her lack of leadership experience, she was appealing as a trusted party person, an experienced grassroots organizer, and a known feminist at a time when the new women's movement seemed to have broad appeal. Although the GOP lost the presidency in 1976, Smith was widely credited with having helped revive the party in the critical post-Watergate years. She served as RNC chairman (her word) until January 1977.

Smith, like other GOP feminists, was dismayed by the increasing influence of Reagan Republicans in the party. In 1980, delegates passed a platform that ended the GOP's long support of the ERA and called for a constitutional ban on abortion. Smith responded by promoting party unity, believing she could work for feminist reforms from within. Despite criticism from many in the women's movement, she actively campaigned for Reagan in 1980 and headed a Women's Policy Advisory Board to advise the campaign on women voters. Smith's decision was consistent with her strong Republican identity and her understanding of partisan politics. She had always championed the two-party system and believed it was necessary to work through that system, rather than outside it. Smith was rewarded with an appointment to the U.S. Commission on Civil Rights, where she served in 1982 and 1983. But her support for affirmative action and school busing conflicted with the positions of the Reagan administration and she was eventually removed from the commission.

In 1984 Smith ended her twenty-year career as Iowa's Republican national committeewoman. By this time she was a widow, Elmer having passed away in 1980. In the 1980s and 1990s, she increasingly reached out into other areas, including peace and women's issues. She served on the boards of Planned Parenthood, the Iowa and U.S. Institutes of Peace, and ecumenical religious organizations. Smith did not remove herself from party work, however. From 1988 to 1994, she served as national co-chair of the Republican Mainstream Committee (an organization of moderate Republicans), was active in Republicans for Choice, and campaigned for her old friend and mentor George H. W. Bush in 1988 and 1992.

In the last years of her life, Smith took on projects that promoted the study of women. With Des Moines art collector Louise Noun, Smith founded the Iowa Women's Archives at the University of Iowa, a repository for the papers of Iowa women and women's organizations, which opened its doors in 1992. And at Iowa State University in 1995, she lent her name to a chair in women and politics.

The gray-haired, elegantly coiffed Smith was a gifted and sought-after public speaker who inspired listeners, men and women, young and old, across the political spectrum. She was at times criticized for the partisan loyalty that defined her public career and her private identity, especially as the GOP drifted further from the issues of equality and diversity that Smith embraced. Indeed, because of this intense partisanship, Smith's commitment to feminism never exceeded her commitment to the two-party system. As she once told an interviewer, "there is never any real 'woman power' until women understand the system through which that power flows. And that is the political party system." Smith died in Des Moines on August 22, 1997, of lung cancer at the age of eighty-two.

Bibliography: Mary Louise Smith's papers are held by the Louise Noun–Mary Louise Smith Iowa Women's Archives at the University of Iowa. This extensive collection relates primarily to her public career. It includes her RNC chairman files, as well as correspondence, newspaper clippings, photographs, videotapes, and Republican memorabilia from the mid 1960s through the mid 1990s. Additional materials on Mary Louise Smith and the Republican National Committee are located in the White House Central Files held by the Gerald R. Ford Library, Ann Arbor, Michigan. Louise Noun's *More Strong-Minded Women: Iowa Women Tell Their Stories* (1992) contains an interview with Smith. Suzanne Schenken, who conducted extensive interviews with Smith as part of a planned biography, provided additional family information. Tanya Melich's *The Republican War against Women: An Insider's Report from behind the Lines* (1996) includes a number of references to Smith. General sources on women and the Republican Party include Jo Freeman, *A Room at a Time: How Women Entered Party Politics* (2000), and Catherine E. Rymph, "Forward and Right: The Shaping of Republican Women's Activism, 1920–1967" (PhD dissertation, University of Iowa, 1998). Smith attracted much media attention, and numerous profiles appeared during the 1970s–90s in magazines and newspapers. The quotation is taken from Janet Ellis, "Mrs. Smith Goes to Washington," *MD's Wife,* January 1975, p. 9. Obituaries appeared in the *Washington Post* and the *Des Moines Register* on August 24, 1997, and in the *New York Times* on August 25, 1997.

CATHERINE RYMPH

SNOWDEN, Muriel. July 14, 1916–September 30, 1988. Community leader, civil rights activist.

Muriel Sophronia Sutherland Snowden, cofounder and co-director of Freedom House, a pioneering organization committed to community activism in Roxbury, Massachusetts, was born the second of three children of Reiter Lucinda Thomas, a homemaker, and William Henry Sutherland, a graduate of Howard University and a successful dentist. In 1919 the Sutherlands moved from their black neighborhood in Orange, New Jersey, where Muriel was born, to the wealthy all-white community of Glen Ridge, New Jersey. Motivated by Reiter Sutherland's increasing anxieties about her children growing up in an urban ghetto, the family moved into a thirteen-room house in one of the most exclusive neighborhoods in the country. Voted "most scholarly" and "most brilliant" by her white classmates at Glen Ridge High, Sutherland graduated as the valedictorian of her class in 1934 and went on to Radcliffe College, where in 1938 she received her BA in Romance languages.

The transition from Glen Ridge High to Radcliffe College was difficult. When she arrived, she was shocked to learn that because she was African American she could not live in a dormitory. Commuting between Belmont and Cambridge, Muriel felt disconnected from campus life and struggled to do well in her courses. In her second year, after her mother convinced the dean of the college to provide Muriel a single room in one of the dorms, she began to excel. As a sophomore, she joined Alpha Kappa Alpha, a black sorority, and became active in the League of Women for Community Service. Mentoring and teaching French to underprivileged young black girls, Sutherland became interested in community activism and social work.

Upon completion of her degree, Sutherland took a job (against her parents' wishes) as a social investigator for the Essex County Welfare Board in Newark, New Jersey. Working in Newark's third ward opened her eyes to African Americans who, unlike her family, had not escaped the poverty and racism of urban ghettos. After five years of investigating applications for relief, she concluded that systematic change could be more readily effected through community organization than by individual casework, so in 1943 she entered the New York School of Social Work at Columbia University on a National Urban League Fellowship to study community organization with a focus on race relations.

On May 28, 1944, she married Otto Phillip Snowden, a graduate of Howard University. Following the birth of their only child, Muriel Gail, in July 1945 and her husband's discharge from the service, the couple returned to Boston in 1946, where Otto Snowden resumed his work as director of St. Mark's Social Center in Roxbury, a predominantly black community in which his family had lived for thirty years. Muriel Snowden spent two years as a volunteer at St. Mark's, working to set up one of the first interracial nursery schools in Boston. Committed to maintaining Roxbury's stability as an economically diverse and racially mixed neighborhood, Otto Snowden resigned as director of St. Mark's in 1948 and began working to organize a nonsectarian community center, while Muriel took a position as executive director of the Cambridge Civic Unity Committee (CCUC), a local public agency charged with promoting better community relations, to support the family financially. With the responsibilities of motherhood and a full-time job, she found it impossible to complete her master's in social work.

In 1949, the Snowdens founded Freedom House, an interracial center committed to new ideas and methods for coping with community problems and racial tensions. Not long after, Muriel sadly resigned as director of CCUC to co-direct the newly founded organization. Otto admitted that Muriel was an equal partner of Freedom House but was insistent that the public image had to be of a single head, so Muriel reluctantly accepted the title of associate director while he carried the title of executive director. Not until 1972 did Snowden officially change her title to co-director.

The diversity of programs that Freedom House offered between 1949 and 1984 reflected the Snowdens' dual commitment to addressing the immediate needs of Roxbury and to promoting organized community activism to bring about larger institutional and systemic changes throughout Boston. While encouraging citizen participation in the residential renewal of the Washington Park section of Roxbury, struggling with desegregation and the improvement of the Boston public school system, and aggressively dealing with business and industry over the issue of affirmative action, Freedom House at the same time was organizing neighborhood clean-up campaigns, establishing a preschool and a credit union, creating travel/study opportunities, running SAT workshops, and helping recent graduates apply for jobs.

During the civil rights movement of the 1960s, the Snowdens came under heavy criticism from young black militants who found Freedom House's commitment to black self-help problematic. Labeled as "by-passed moderates" and "Mr. and Mrs. Thomas who run Freedom House, that cabin in the cotton," the Snowdens spent much of the 1960s defending Freedom House, but also rethinking the organization's relationship to the African American community. Indeed, Freedom House was transformed during the decade and played an increasingly critical role in the struggle for civil rights in Boston. During the Boston race riot of June 1967, the Snowdens joined militants in meetings around unity and strategy, opened up lines of communications between the rioters and city authorities, and made Freedom House an emergency medical station. The Snowdens were also actively involved in the push to desegregate Boston public schools in the early 1970s.

In addition to managing Freedom House, Snowden taught community organization part-time at Simmons College School of Social Work from 1958 to 1970 and served on the boards of many organizations, including the University of Massachusetts, the Boston Museum of Science, and the Board of Overseers of Harvard College. The first African American and woman to serve on many of these boards, she brought the concerns of both groups to the table.

A soft-spoken woman with a persuasive personality, Muriel Snowden convinced Boston businesses to participate in affirmative action programs, challenged university boards to think seriously about minority admissions and the treatment of female faculty, and gave voice to the concerns of Boston's black community. In 1984 the Snowdens announced their joint retirement from Freedom House. In 1987 Muriel Snowden received a five-year grant from the John D. and Catherine T. MacArthur Foundation, but she died the following year of cancer at her home in Dorchester at the age of seventy-two.

Bibliography: The Muriel S. and Otto P. Snowden Papers, 1911–1990, in the Archives and Special Collections Department, Snell Library, Northeastern University, Boston, contain correspondence, speeches, articles by and about the Snowdens, family photographs, and videotapes. Muriel's personal files contain biographical information and genealogical charts for the Sutherland family, as well as correspondence with her brother William Sutherland, peace activist in the United States and Africa. Professional files document her work outside of Freedom House, including her directorship of the Cambridge Civic Unity Committee, her teaching at Simmons School of Social Work and Wellesley College, and her active involvement on the boards of a number of local and nation civic organizations, as well as many of her speeches given as co-director of Freedom House and as a community organizer. The Freedom House, 1941–1996, records are also in the Archives and Special Collections Department at Northeastern University. Snowden was among the seventy-two women interviewed for *The Black Women Oral History Project*, vol. 9 (1991). Her articles include "Citizen Participation: The Boston Washington Park Story," co-authored with Otto Snowden, in the *Journal of Housing* 20, no. 8 (September 30, 1963), pp. 435–39; "A Team and a Dream: The Story of Freedom House" (May 1965) and "Woman to Woman" (December 1984) in *Radcliffe Quarterly;* and "Some Personal Reflections and Observations on the Negro Middle Class" in C. Eric Lincoln, ed., *Is Anybody Listening to Black America?* (1968). Obituaries appeared in the *Boston Globe* on October 1, 1988, and the *New York Times* on October 3, 1988.

CRYSTAL FEIMSTER

SOLANAS, Valerie. April 9, 1936–c. April 25, 1988. Writer, feminist provocateur.

Valerie Jean Solanas was born in Atlantic City, New Jersey, the elder of two daughters of Dorothy Biondi and Louis Solanas, a bartender. Raised in an ethnically diverse blue-collar neighborhood near the boardwalk, Valerie attended both public and parochial schools and lived for a time with her maternal grandparents after her parents divorced. In an attempt to discipline her volatile behavior, she was sent to Holy Cross Academy, where she first experimented with lesbianism. Within a year, however, she was ejected for hitting a nun. She then moved to Washington, D.C., to live with her mother and graduated from Oxon Hill High School in June 1954.

Solanas first found like-minded souls as an undergraduate at the University of Maryland, where she joined a circle of students interested in jazz, poetry, and art. In an era of Peter Pan collars and mandatory heterosexuality, Valerie was openly lesbian and wore dungarees and men's workshirts. She majored in psychology and graduated in 1958. The next year, she dropped out of the master's program in psychology at the University of Minnesota to travel cross-country, living with various men. As she explained later, "Everyone likes a change once in a while" (Harron, p. xv). It is possible that she bore a son in this period or later, although she denied having any children and certainly did not raise a child herself. Indeed, Solanas's desire to constantly reinvent herself complicates any portrait of her life.

By 1965, Solanas had moved to Greenwich Village, where she tried to earn a living as a writer and befriended a group of lesbians, transsexuals, and drag queens. In 1966 a men's magazine called *Cavalier* published "A Young Girl's Primer, or How to Attain to the Leisure Class," in which Solanas suggests panhandling and charging men for conversation as means to survive in the big city. About the same time, she gained entrée to the Factory, Andy Warhol's studio, where she met a variety of writers, artists, and actors who hoped to find refuge and fame there.

In 1966–67, Valerie Solanas's dreams of artistic recognition seemed within reach. She gained a small part in a Warhol film, *I, A Man;* met Olympia Press publisher Maurice Girodias, who paid her a $500 advance for what became her feminist tract, the *SCUM Manifesto;* and completed a play, *Up Your Ass*. In the *SCUM Manifesto,* Solanas built upon ideas generated in her psychology courses and her experience on the streets. Claiming that life in this society is largely irrelevant to women, the manifesto declared, "there remains to civic-minded, responsible, thrill-seeking females only to overthrow the government, eliminate the money system, institute complete automation and destroy the male sex" (*SCUM Manifesto,* p. 1). Arguing that men hate themselves and seek to claim all of women's virtues—"emotional strength and independence, forcefulness, dynamism, decisiveness"—as their own, she demanded that women eliminate all men except those who "do good" (ibid., pp. 2, 15). British filmmaker Mary Harron later described the manifesto's tone as "deadpan, icily logical, elegantly comical: a strange juxtaposition, as if Oscar Wilde had decided to become a terrorist" (Harron, p. viii).

Solanas's vision riveted some feminists and the manifesto inspired many to action, including Roxanne Dunbar-Ortiz, who moved to Boston and launched a "female liberation front." Other feminists, however, found Solanas's ideas politically naïve and her language nearly pornographic. When publisher Girodias claimed that SCUM was an acronym for the Society for Cutting Up Men (something Solanas never seems to have intended), he reinforced the idea that the manifesto was part of a movement of man haters.

To many, feminists and non-feminists alike, the violent implications of the *SCUM Manifesto* came to life when Solanas shot Andy Warhol on June 3, 1968. To Solanas the motives were quite distinct. Warhol had lost one of the only copies of her play, *Up Your Ass,* and refused to produce it. Convinced that Warhol was stealing her ideas, she tracked him down at the Factory, shot him at close range, and then turned herself in to a police officer. When Warhol survived the shooting, Solanas was charged with attempted murder. She soon became a *cause célèbre* among such radical feminists as Ti-Grace Atkinson and Florynce Kennedy, a feminist lawyer who offered to serve as her counsel. Solanas was examined by psychiatrists at Elmhurst Psychiatric Hospital and then incarcerated in Mattewan State Hospital until December 1968. Moved to the Women's State Prison at Bedford Hills, she pled guilty to first-degree assault in February 1969. In June, she was sentenced to three years at Bedford Hills, with credit for time served.

After her release, Solanas moved between New York City and San Francisco, living in poverty and trying to sell her writings to passersby. She published a new version of the *SCUM Manifesto* in 1977, which led to a brief flurry of interviews and attention. A decade later, however, she had once again disappeared. On April 25, 1988, she was found dead in her room at a welfare hotel in San Francisco's Tenderloin district. The landlord had gone to collect overdue rent and discovered her body, which had probably lain there for several days. No obituaries noted her passing.

Rosalyn Baxandall has called Valerie Solanas "our movement's Victoria Woodhull." Flaunting a queer sexuality before the category existed, producing provocative political manifestos, and surrounded by scandal, Solanas, like Woodhull, has served as a lightning rod for feminists. The *SCUM Manifesto* remains a political touchstone. It has been reprinted at least ten times in English, excerpted in half a dozen major feminist anthologies, posted on numerous Web sites, and translated into German, French, Spanish, Italian, and Czech.

Bibliography: No biography exists of Valerie Solanas, nor are her papers collected in any archive, but there are abundant primary sources, most notably her writings and numerous interviews. Some primary materials are housed at the Andy Warhol Museum in Pittsburgh, Pennsylvania. The *SCUM Manifesto* has been reprinted most recently in Mary Harron and Daniel Minahan, *I Shot Andy Warhol* (1995), the shooting script for their 1996 independent film of the same name. A first-person account of Solanas's impact is provided by Roxanne Dunbar-Ortiz, "From the Cradle to the Boat: A Feminist Historian Remembers Valerie Solanas," *San Francisco Bay Guardian,* January 5, 2000. Important interviews can be found in the following sources: Judy Michaelson, "Valerie: The Trouble Was Men," *New York Post,* June 5, 1968, p. 57; Robert Marmorstein, "Scum Goddess: A Winter Memory of Valerie Solanis *[sic],*" *Village Voice,* June 13, 1968, pp. 9–10, 20; and Howard Smith and Brian van der Horst, "Valerie Solanas Interview," *Village Voice,* July 25, 1977, p. 32. The results of her court case are noted in "Warhol's Assailant Gets Up to 3 Years," *New York Times,* June 10, 1969. Also of interest is Liz Jobey, "Solanas and Son," *Guardian Weekend,* August 24, 1996. The two most informative and insightful secondary sources are Mary Harron's introduction to *I Shot Andy Warhol,* pp. vii–xxxi; and Dana Heller, "Shooting Solanas: Radical Feminist History and the Technology of Failure," *Feminist Studies* 27, no. 3 (Spring 2001), pp. 167–189. On the general context for Solanas's life and writings, see Alice Echols, *Daring to Be Bad: Radical Feminism in America, 1967–1975* (1989), which contains the Baxandall quotation on p. 105.

NANCY A. HEWITT

SOMMERS, Tish. September 8, 1914–October 18, 1985. Civil rights activist, feminist, co-founder of Older Women's League.

Letitia Innes was born in Cambria, California, and grew up in the Sierra Madre Mountains and San Francisco, the daughter of Murray Innes, an upper-middle-class Scotch-Irish mining engineer, and Catherine Dorsch, who was from a lower-class background and had worked as a teacher before her marriage. When her parents divorced in 1926, Tish (as she was known all her life) gained an insider's view into the economic hardships faced by older divorced women as she watched her mother try to raise her and her two older brothers while working as a salesperson.

With generous help from wealthy relatives, Tish studied dance with well-known modern dancer Mary Wigman in Germany from 1933 to 1936. There her political naiveté bumped up against the anti-Semitism and racism of the Nazi Third Reich. When she returned to California in 1936, she continued her education at UCLA, joined the Communist Party, and worked as a youth organizer. In 1938 she married Sidney Burke, a radical writer. They had no children and divorced in 1943. During these years, she organized professional dancers in Hollywood and created the Pan American Dance Troupe, a racially and culturally integrated youth group, in East Los Angeles. In 1948 she became the Southern California youth group leader for the Henry Wallace presidential campaign.

In 1949, she married Joe Sommers, a union organizer, and converted to Judaism; eight years later she adopted Bill, a one-year-old boy from Appalachia, whom she raised while she worked for the Progressive Party in New York City and agitated for civil rights in Birmingham, Alabama. A lifelong community activist, Tish Sommers worked as a volunteer for a Seattle poverty program in the mid 1960s. In 1971 she settled in Berkeley, California, and lived in a collective feminist home—a newly separated, soon-to-be-divorced, fifty-seven-year-old woman now preoccupied with problems encountered by older women. With Ruth McElhinney, she founded the Women's Action Training Center in Oakland, which focused on women's employment problems, and wrote *The Not-So-Helpless Female* (1973), a manual on organizing. At the same time, she chaired the National Organization for Women's Task Force on Older Women, when "older women" were defined, tellingly, as women over thirty.

In 1974, she and newly widowed Laurie Shields organized the Displaced Homemakers Network, which turned into a national grassroots movement that addressed the problems encountered by women affected by divorce or death of a spouse. In California, Shields and Sommers began to press for legislative and political support for "displaced homemakers," a term coined by Sommers. In 1975, activist lawyer Barbara Dudley drafted a bill to provide displaced homemakers with job training and counseling in California. When the governor opposed the legislation, Sommers threatened to stage a sit-in with hundreds of elderly women. The legislature passed the bill, providing funds for a pilot project housed at Mills College in Oakland. Widely copied all over the country and coordinated by the Washington, D.C., Displaced Homemakers Network, such training programs provided midlife women with the opportunity to recognize the skills they had already gained and to receive education to achieve economic independence.

Fueled by grassroots activists, the movement rapidly swept across the nation. By 1977, twelve states had passed legislation to help displaced homemakers. In the late 1970s, Shields and Sommers founded the nonprofit Older Women's League Education Fund (OWLEF), which published "Gray Papers" on such policy issues as social security, pensions, welfare, and health care. In 1980, in preparation for an upcoming White House Conference on Aging, Shields and Sommers held a regional conference at which they founded the Older Women's League (OWL). In the first two years, the organization boasted more than seventy chapters and five thousand members who focused on social security reform, pension rights, and health care insurance. The national office of OWL, established in Washington, D.C., in 1982, provided expert testimony before Congress and published educational materials on older women's issues. Within a decade, the discrimination and invisibility faced by older wives, their need for support, job training, and education, and for planning for "a good death," had all been redefined as feminist issues.

Together, Tish Sommers and Laurie Shields forged a remarkable political partnership. Sommers, a tall, slim, and graceful woman, was the visionary who came up with ideas for job training, counseling, older women's co-housing, living wills, and hospice care. Her direct sense of injustice struck a resonant chord. Her motto, inspired by the labor activist Joe Hill's famous last words, "Don't Mourn for Me, Organize" was "Don't Agonize, Organize." Sommers knew how to change the consciousness of older women. A typical OWL poster announced, "For men, they created retirement plans, medical benefits, profit sharing and gold watches. For women, they created Mother's Day." Reflecting her lifelong commitment to economic and social justice, Sommers's last campaign focused on access to health care. Her slogan, "Health care is a right, not a privilege," reflected her lifelong commitment to economic and social justice and inspired future health care activists.

Shields, shorter and stouter, was an exceptional organizer, blessed with an ability to reach out to people, and with the endless energy to travel and speak all over the country. Some people thought they were lovers; others are certain they were not. Whatever the nature of their relationship, it was, by all accounts, emotionally intimate and mutually supportive. As Sommers's health began to fail, Laurie Shields, her partner, companion, housemate, and caregiver, was by her side. In 1987, two years after Sommers's death in Oakland at the age of seventy-one, Shields published *Women Take Care: The Consequences of Caregiving in Today's Society,* a prescient work on the experience of death, dying, and the burden of caretaking that usually falls to women. When

Shields died in 1989, she was buried next to Tish Sommers in Oakland, California.

Like many middle-aged leaders of NOW, Tish Sommers brought the values she had embraced in the Old Left, union, and civil rights movements into the modern women's movement. Like other feminists, she excavated a common but invisible problem—the financial, emotional, and health discrimination faced by older women. By "naming" the problem, Sommers not only gave middle-aged divorced women the more dignified term *displaced homemaker*, but also created a grassroots movement that successfully, case by case, gained greater equality for older women in social security and in pensions.

Bibliography: The best biographical source is Patricia Huckle, *Tish Sommers, Activist, and the Founding of the Older Women's League* (1991). Sommers's papers, photographs, publications, testimony, and material on aging can be found in Special Collections at Love Library, San Diego State University. Also see Kathleen M. Kautzer, "Moving against the Stream: An Organizational Study of the Older Women's League" (PhD dissertation, Brandeis University, 1988). For greater depth on OWL, see Laurie Shields, *Displaced Homemakers: Organizing for a New Life* (1981). Ruth Rosen, *The World Split Open: How the Modern Women's Movement Changed America* (2000), places the revival of feminism in a wider historical context. Media coverage that brought OWL to public notice included Cynthia Gorney, "The Discarding of Mrs. Hill," *Ladies' Home Journal*, February 21, 1976, pp. 58+, and a series of articles on the Older Women's League written by Judy Klemesrud in the *New York Times* between October 10, 1980, and December 5, 1981. Obituaries appeared the *Los Angeles Times* and the *New York Times* on October 19, 1985. See also the obituary for Laurie Shields in the *New York Times* on March 4, 1989.

RUTH ROSEN

SPIVEY, Victoria Regina. October 15, 1906–October 3, 1976. Blues singer, record producer, promoter.

Victoria Spivey, among the most successful and prominent performers during the heyday of female blues singers in the 1920s, was one of eight children born to Addie Smith and Grant Spivey in Houston, Texas. Her father was a laborer who played in a local string band, and her mother was a nurse who sang classical and religious music in church. Victoria, who had no formal schooling, began piano lessons when she was about ten years old and began playing for silent movies by twelve. Houston was rich with musical talent in the African American community during that period. House parties, whorehouses, and gambling houses provided opportunities for string bands, blues pianists, singers, and guitarists to hone their skills while earning money. Galveston, Houston, and Dallas served as Spivey's training ground until she left in 1926 for Moberly, Missouri, just outside of St. Louis, where she began writing her own blues. Among them was "No. 12 Let Me Roam," a poignant expression of her ambivalence about leaving south Texas, which she dearly loved.

Spivey was a staff writer for a music company during her tenure in Missouri, and she worked with a wide range of entertainers. Among them were her older sisters, Addie, a comedian known as Sweet Peas(e), and Elton, the "Za-Zu Girl," who were popular vaudeville performers. Spivey's first recording was "Black Snake Blues," produced in 1926 for General Phonograph's OKeh label. At twenty she was already an ambitious, seasoned performer with the gumption to press for her compositions to be heard. Spivey's piano style was clearly Texan, but over the years her subject matter ranged from mournful to brassy. She could lament the ravages of drug addiction in "Dopehead Blues" and the sorrows of losing her father in "Grant Spivey," and in the next breath sing "One Hour Mama."

Spivey worked in many different arenas within the music business. She enjoyed a featured role in King Vidor's *Hallelujah* (1929), the first sound movie with an all-black cast produced by a major Hollywood studio. And, unlike many of the singers of the classic blues era of the 1920s, Spivey crossed over to religious and jazz songs when the opportunities arose. Some of the most accomplished jazz artists recorded with her, among them Louis Armstrong and Porter Grainger. She toured with the *Hellzapoppin* revue and other black variety shows in New York, the Midwest, and Canada during the 1930s. But New York City was her love, and she made her home there with her first husband, Reuben Floyd, to whom she was married from 1928 until the early 1930s. Dancer William "Billy" Adams became her second husband around 1934 and her manager in 1937, and she toured with various shows in the Midwest under his management. Spivey performed in some of the same Chicago clubs as Memphis Minnie, Big Bill Broonzy, and Tampa Red during the late 1930s, when blues from the Delta region became the blues of choice. The nightclub circuit in New York, Chicago, Cincinnati, and Cleveland in the late 1930s and the 1940s gave Spivey continuing opportunities to perform.

By the late 1940s and the 1950s, Spivey's main venues were small jazz clubs in and around New York City. She eventually dropped the club scene and began playing for her church in Brooklyn in the late 1950s. After a hiatus of about ten years, however, Spivey returned to performing in nightclubs on a regular basis, in spite of poor health. By that time, Victoria had teamed up with Leonard Kunstadt, a young white man who was captivated by her as a singer and as a woman. Although he was nearly twenty years her junior, they became lovers and business partners. His companionship and devotion to her and the music were the impetus for her renewed energy and return to performing in New York in the 1960s. Kunstadt was editor of *Record Research Magazine;* Spivey contributed the column "Blues Is My Business," which offered news and notes about blues and jazz musicians, as well as firsthand accounts of her performances and personal relationships with artists such as Louis Armstrong, Roosevelt Sykes, and Lonnie Johnson.

In 1962, she started her own record label, Spivey Records. The first release on the Spivey label was *Basket of Blues* with two of her old friends, Lucille Hegamin and Hannah Sylvester. Subsequent releases were reissues of her "TBs Got Me" (the 1926 original was titled "TB Blues"), the erotic "Organ Grinder Blues," and "Murder in the First Degree." This was a remarkable feat, because most artists of that era had no rights to their own compositions. She then recorded new renditions of some of her most famous blues in 1962. This release, *Victoria and Her Blues,* though not widely distributed, became a collector's item and demonstrated that she was still a superb musician. Willie Dixon, the Chicago blues musician and producer, helped Spivey expand her label with releases that included Memphis Slim, Big Joe Williams, Lonnie Johnson, and Roosevelt Sykes. She also encouraged and recorded new musicians who were just hitting the blues and jazz circuit. Among them were James "Sugar Blue" Whiting, Lucille Spann, and Muddy Waters and his band. Young Bob Dylan made his first recording on the Spivey label, after being encouraged to sit in on sessions with many of the blues artists who performed at Gerde's Folk City in New York in the early sixties.

The American mania for folk and blues festivals in the 1970s gave Spivey new audiences across the United States and in Europe. Audiences had shifted mainly from black listeners to white college students and hippies. But Spivey's entrepreneurial spirit led her to contact friends such as Sippie Wallace, Roosevelt Sykes, and Little Brother Montgomery, who were gratified by the renewed appreciation for the music to which they had devoted their lives. Spivey was a phenomenal performer and businessperson whose perseverance and devotion to her music, and to the women and men who played it, inspired her to strive for the recognition they all so justly deserved. She remained active until shortly before her death from chronic liver disease on October 3, 1976, at Brooklyn's Beekman-Downtown Hospital, just short of her seventieth birthday.

Bibliography: Daphne Duval Harrison, *Black Pearls: Blues Queens of the 1920s* (1988), weaves biographical information with texts of Spivey's songs and recordings. John Cowley and Paul Oliver, eds., *The New Blackwell Guide to Recorded Blues,* provides a discography of new releases of Spivey's recordings along with brief commentary. See also Tony Russell, *The Blues: From Robert Johnson to Robert Cray* (1997); Angela Y. Davis, *Blues Legacies and Black Feminism* (1998); and David Jasen, "*The Blues Is Life: Victoria Spivey,*" liner notes, 1976. *Melody Maker Magazine,* a music magazine published in England, often has more information on blues than American sources. Obituaries appeared in the *New York Times* on October 7, 1976, *Rolling Stone* on November 18, 1976, and *Melody Maker* on October 23, 1976.

DAPHNE DUVAL HARRISON

SPOTTED ELK, Molly (Mary Alice Nelson Archambaud). November 17, 1903–February 21, 1977. Performing artist, dancer.

Her life began on Indian Island, heart of the Penobscot Reservation in Old Town, Maine. The priest at the old Catholic mission church christened her Mary Alice, but all four hundred Penobscots tied to the small river island pronounced it the "Indian way"—Molly Dellis. In her teens she adopted the stage name Neeburban, the Penobscot word for Northern Lights, and at age twenty-one she invented herself anew as Molly Spotted Elk. Under this name she won international acclaim for her spellbinding performances of Native American dances. With unusual grace and resilience, Molly strove to resist assimilation while building a bridge between cultures.

Her family, like many others on Indian Island in the early 1900s, survived primarily on income from sweetgrass and woodsplint baskets. Her father, Horace Nelson, gathered and prepared the raw materials, and her mother, Philomene Saulis Nelson, did the weaving. Horace, who had attended Dartmouth College for a year (1901), later served two years as tribal representative to the Maine state legislature (1921–22) and another two as tribal chief (1939–40). Otherwise he spent most of his adult life hunting, fishing, gardening, canoe-building, and helping his wife with basket production and sales. Molly, the oldest of eight children, helped support her siblings. Although she attended the Catholic mission primary school on the island and secondary school on the mainland, starting at age fifteen she traveled with Indian vaudeville troupes each summer and sent most of her modest earnings home. Passionate about dancing, she was well versed in Penobscot dances and also pursued ballet—scrubbing floors to pay for classes.

Throughout her life Molly showed keen interest in tribal traditions. As a child, she prompted elders to tell her Penobscot legends by offering to do their chores in exchange for stories. As a young woman in 1924–25 she took anthropology classes at the University of Pennsylvania, encouraged by Professor Frank Speck, whose extensive Indian research included long sojourns at Indian Island. At Penn she relished researching various Native American dance traditions and giving lecture-dance recitals. Short of funds, however, she left school to join the Miller Brothers' 101 Ranch Wild West Show. Based in Oklahoma, 101 resembled Buffalo Bill's Wild West, with rodeo stunts, souped-up Indian dances, and mock Indian massacres. Turned off by 101's circus atmosphere, Molly quit the show in 1925 and soon after moved to New York City. Now known as Molly Spotted Elk, she modeled for several well-known artists and danced in Broadway revues and nightclubs. At TEXAS GUINAN's famous speakeasy she gained celebrity status, dancing in an eagle-feather headdress—and little else—and captivating the club's wealthy crowd.

By 1928 Molly had grown weary of being "an injun in the flesh parade" (McBride, *Molly Spotted Elk,* p. 136) and jumped at an offer to play the female lead in *The Silent Enemy,* a serious docudrama about Ojibwa Indians. She spent a rugged year on location in the woods of northern Ontario along with co-stars Buffalo Child Long Lance and Chauncey Yellow Robe and an all-Native cast featuring a hundred Ojibwa who still lived a traditional hunting life. Released in 1930, the movie won critical acclaim, but fared poorly at the box office as a silent film eclipsed by the new "talkies." (After her death, it was reissued on video and has become something of a classic.) Molly also played bit parts in a half dozen Hollywood films, including *Ramona* (1936), *Lost Horizon* (1937), and *The Good Earth* (1937).

In 1931, at the age of twenty-eight, Molly ventured to Paris to give the opening performance for the International Colonial Exposition. She spent several years in Europe, drawn by sophisticated and appreciative audiences. Soon after arriving, she fell in love with French journalist Jean Archambaud. In 1934 she returned to the States to give birth to their daughter (also named Jean). A host of challenges kept Molly from going back to France until the summer of 1938. In 1939, the couple married and had a second daughter, who lived just two weeks. A year later, World War II and the German occupation of France forced Jean into hiding and sent Molly fleeing on foot over the Pyrenees Mountains with their little girl. Mother and child made it back to the reservation in Maine, but Jean died in a refugee camp in France in 1941. This loss sent Molly into a long-term emotional spin, culminating in a year at Bangor State Mental Hospital (1948–49). Once released, she passed most of the rest of her life as a recluse on the reservation, making Indian dolls and baskets. She died there, after taking a bad fall, in 1977 at the age of seventy-three.

The subject of many newspaper articles throughout the 1920s and 1930s, Molly Spotted Elk wrote extensively herself. Before going to France, she published a few poems, and while abroad she and her husband co-authored articles about Indian traditions and outdoor life. Over the years, she wrote down the legends she had learned as a child, eventually completing a 230-page manuscript. In late 1939 she signed a contract with a French publisher for this work, but the agreement soon fell apart owing to the war. Some sixty years later the stories were finally published by the Maine Folklife Center.

Ranging between her home island and cosmopolitan centers, Molly Spotted Elk wrestled with questions of cultural identity and chronicled her struggles in a series of diaries spanning forty years. These detailed records of her public and private experiences may be her greatest legacy, offering a rare insider's look at Native American life on and off the reservation. In particular, they shed light on the pressures Native entertainers (including two of her sisters) endured in having to act out white stereotypes of "Indians" as savages or romantic icons of nature in order to succeed.

Born at a time when America's indigenous cultures seemed doomed, she lived to see the start of their revitalization in the 1970s—an era when young Penobscots came to her to ask about ancestral traditions and legends. In 1980, three years after Molly Spotted Elk died, her people regained a fraction of their aboriginal land and sovereignty through the Maine Indian Claims Settlement. Today they cherish her memory, and a new generation of Penobscot storytellers performs the time-honored legends that she gathered up as a child.

Bibliography: Diaries of Molly Spotted Elk covering selected years from 1920 to 1959, along with her correspondence and other papers, are found at the Maine Folklife Center, University of Maine, Orono. Her writings were published in *Katahdin: Wigwam's Tales of the Abnaki Tribe* (2003). The main biographical source is Bunny McBride, *Molly Spotted Elk: A Penobscot in Paris* (1995), which contains an exhaustive bibliography of primary and secondary materials relating to Molly's life. McBride, *Women of the Dawn* (1999), surveys the lives of Maine Indian women, with Molly Spotted Elk as one of the four major characters. See also McBride, "The Spider and the WASP: Chronicling the Life of Molly Spotted Elk," in Jennifer Brown and Elizabeth Vibert, eds., *Reading beyond Words: Contexts for Native History* (1996). Information about the 1931 International Colonial Exposition is found in the National Archives, College Park, Maryland.

BUNNY MCBRIDE

STAFFORD, Jean. July 1, 1915–March 26, 1979. Writer.

Jean Stafford, fourth child and third daughter of Mary Ethel McKillop and John Richard Stafford, was born in the small California town of Covina, a short distance from Los Angeles, where her father's mother, an ardent supporter of woman suffrage and an occasional writer, resided. John Stafford graduated from Amity College, and his Missouri-born wife had been a teacher. By the time Jean was born, her parents, along with Jean's older sisters Mary Lee and Marjorie and her adored brother Dick, had moved to a small walnut ranch in Covina. Vividly portrayed in Stafford's best novel, *The Mountain Lion* (1947), the Covina house contained a Victrola, an *Encyclopaedia Britannica,* and books by Shakespeare, Dickens, Balzac, and Mark Twain, as well as a Western called *When Cattle Kingdom Fell,* published by Jean's father in 1910. Although Stafford later alluded to the "pastoral serenity" (Hulbert, *The Interior Castle,* p. 8) of her early years, she also described herself as lonely and afraid.

The Covina life ended abruptly when Jean's father sold the ranch and moved his family to San Diego in 1920. He soon lost almost all his savings in the stock market, and the Staffords moved again, first to Colorado Springs and then to Boulder, where his wife ran a boarding house for female university students while he wrote stories and articles that usually remained unpublished. Although Jean was an excellent student, she later described her own education in the Boulder public schools and at the University of Colorado as a shabby affair. In need of money, the tall, slender, and very pretty Jean modeled for art classes; too poor to join a sorority, she belonged to a group of intellectuals who met regularly to drink beer and discuss modernist writers like Joyce and D. H. Lawrence. The suicide of a friend during her junior year of college haunted her for the rest of her life, as did memories of her parsimonious mother and her misanthropic father.

Although *The Mountain Lion* and many of Stafford's short stories are set in Colorado, she was ambivalent about the West. In her "Author's note" to her collected short stories, she wrote, "I could not wait to quit my tamed-down native grounds. As soon as I could, I hotfooted it across the Rocky Mountains and across the Atlantic Ocean" (Stafford, *Collected Short Stories,* p. xi). She graduated with both a BA and an MA from the University of Colorado in 1936 and left for Germany, having been awarded a fellowship to study philology at Heidelberg University. Stafford's year abroad provided material for a number of short stories set in Germany during the rise of Hitler, a novella called "A Winter's Tale" (1954), and several articles.

In the summer of 1937 Stafford returned temporarily to Boulder as assistant to the director of the university's annual Writer's Conference. There she met writers and literary critics, some of whom helped launch her literary career; she also befriended an aspiring poet named Robert Lowell, scion of the prominent Lowell family of Boston. After an unhappy year teaching English at Stephens College in Missouri, she briefly attended graduate school at the University of Iowa, but unhappy there, too, she left precipitately for Massachusetts to live with a college friend named John Robert Hightower, who also had been in Heidelberg. Deciding that she was not in love with Hightower and was infatuated with Robert Lowell, she moved to Concord to write. In Boston for the Christmas holiday, Lowell, with Stafford beside him, drove his car into a wall. Injuries to her back and face would plague her for the rest of her life. Her short story "The Interior Castle" draws on her hospital experience after the accident. Despite the fact that, to pay her medical bills, she sued Lowell for the injuries she had sustained, she married him on April 2, 1940.

The eight years Stafford spent as wife of the volatile Lowell launched her as a writer but damaged her emotionally. In Baton Rouge, while Lowell attended graduate school, she served as secretary at the prestigious *Southern Review,* which was publishing short stories by such women writers as Eudora Welty and MARY MCCARTHY. Subsequently, while Stafford and Lowell were living in Connecticut following a summer she had spent at Yaddo, Stafford's *Boston Adventure* (1944) appeared. The novel traces the growth and development of a poor young woman who becomes the secretary of a rich Boston dowager. During this period she also published short stories in such important journals as *Sewanee Review, Partisan Review,* and *Harper's.* In 1945 she was awarded a grant from the National Institute of Arts and Letters as well as a Guggenheim Fellowship in fiction. (She would receive a second one in 1948.)

With earnings from *Boston Adventure* Stafford purchased a house in Maine's Damariscotta Mills, where she worked on her second novel, *The Mountain Lion,* a poignant coming-of-age tale about an adolescent boy and his disaffected younger sister, Molly, who aspires to be a writer. A revealing short story called an "Influx of Poets," published in the *New Yorker* in 1978, reflects Stafford's own frustrations in Maine as she tried to combine her life as a writer and her life as spouse of a poet who expected her to entertain his cronies. By the time *The Mountain Lion* was published in 1947, Stafford had separated from Lowell; they later divorced. Suffering from depression and alcoholism, she was hospitalized for almost a year in Payne Whitney Psychiatric Clinic at New York Hospital, where Robert Lowell also would become a patient several years later.

Two other marriages followed, the first to *Life* magazine editor Oliver Jensen from 1950 to 1953, the second to *New Yorker* writer A. J. Liebling from 1959 to 1963. She never had any children. During these years, Stafford published many award-winning short stories, most of them appearing in the *New Yorker*, whose fiction editor, KATHARINE WHITE, became a close friend. Stafford's third novel, *The Catherine Wheel* (1952), and three collections of short stories, *Children Are Bored on Sunday* (1953), *Bad Characters* (1964), and *The Collected Stories* (1969), also were published during this period. Praised for their style, some of these works are written in the lapidary prose of a Henry James or an EDITH WHARTON, others in the colloquial manner of Mark Twain. *The Collected Stories of Jean Stafford* won the Pulitzer Prize for Fiction in 1970, and she was inducted into the National Institute of Arts and Letters.

Following Liebling's death in 1963, Stafford remained in their home in The Springs, Long Island, writing occasional essays and reviews, as well as a book about the mother of Lee Harvey Oswald, *A Mother in History* (1966). After a stroke in 1976 and suffering from emphysema, Stafford, a chain-smoker and an alcoholic, died on March 26, 1979, in White Plains, New York. She was sixty-three. Today Jean Stafford is best remembered for her novel *The Mountain Lion* and her brilliant portraits of perceptive, outspoken, and often misunderstood female characters, many of whom resemble their creator.

Bibliography: The Collected Papers of Jean Stafford are located in Special Collections at the University of Colorado in Boulder. This collection includes correspondence, juvenilia, drafts of manuscripts, photographs, and some of Stafford's books. Correspondence between Stafford and Robert Lowell is in the Houghton Library at Harvard University. *Jean Stafford: A Comprehensive Bibliography* by Wanda Avila (1983) is a valuable guide to her published novels, short stories, essays, and articles. *Shenandoah* 30 (Autumn 1979) contains reminiscences about her by Peter Taylor, Wilfrid Sheed, Dorothea Strauss, and others. Critical biographies include David Roberts, *Jean Stafford: A Biography* (1988); Charlotte Margolis Goodman, *Jean Stafford: The Savage Heart* (1990); and Ann Hulbert, *The Interior Castle: The Art and Life of Jean Stafford* (1992).

An early assessment of Stafford is in Louis Auchincloss, *Pioneers and Caretakers: A Study of Nine American Women Novelists* (1965). Another early article championing Stafford is Olga Vickery's "The Novels of Jean Stafford" in *Critique* 5, no. 1 (Spring–Summer 1962), pp. 14–26. Critical assessments of Stafford's writing include Mary Ellen Williams Walsh, *Jean Stafford* (1985), and Maureen Ryan, *Innocence and Estrangement in the Fiction of Jean Stafford* (1987). A comprehensive survey of Stafford as a short story writer is Mary Ann Wilson, *Jean Stafford: A Study of the Short Fiction* (1996). Discussions of Stafford's depiction of the West include Goodman, "Jean Stafford," in *Updating the Literary West* (1997), and three chapters on Stafford in Susan J. Rosowski, *Gender, Creativity, and the West in American Fiction* (1999). The first of a number of fine feminist discussions focusing on questions of gender is Blanche H. Gelfant's "Revolutionary Turnings: *The Mountain Lion* Reread," *Massachusetts Review* 20 (Spring 1979), pp. 117–25. Thomas Carl Austenfeld, *American Women Writers and the Nazis: Ethics and Politics in Boyle, Porter, Stafford, and Hellman* (2001), includes one chapter on Stafford's depiction of Germany in her short stories and articles. An obituary appeared in the *New York Times* on March 29, 1979.

CHARLOTTE MARGOLIS GOODMAN

STANWYCK, Barbara. July 16, 1907–January 20, 1990. Actress.

The actress who captured Depression-era and wartime audiences as Barbara Stanwyck was born Ruby Katherine Stevens in Brooklyn, New York, the last of five children of the Scotch-Irish couple Byron and Catherine McGee Stevens. She was orphaned as a young child, losing her mother to a streetcar accident at age three and her father, a laborer, at sea soon after. By the age of five, Stanwyck was being raised in several foster homes and later by her older sister. She left school at thirteen, working as a telephone operator, department store wrapper, pattern cutter for *Vogue*, and file clerk. Combined with her ambition to rise above her family tragedy, these varied experiences no doubt gave her the realistic, even hopeful, edge that makes her screen performances so communicative and compelling.

At age fifteen, she fled the workaday world to dance in New York nightclubs. She joined the Ziegfeld Follies in 1922 and later toured with the company when she was not appearing in small roles in musical comedies. She was cast in her first dramatic stage role at age nineteen in *The Noose* in 1926. Inspired by a poster for a play featuring English actress Jane Stanwyck, she changed her name to Barbara Stanwyck and made her film debut in *Broadway Nights* (1927) in a small dancing part.

Comic actor Frank Fay became the first of her two husbands on August 26, 1928. The notoriously embattled marriage, which gave Stanwyck her adopted son, Dion Anthony Fay, in 1932 reportedly inspired the script for the film *A Star Is Born*. Stanwyck divorced Fay in February 1935.

Despite her two failed films, Harry Cohn, head of Columbia Pictures, cast her in Frank Capra's *Ladies of Leisure* (1930). She was subsequently put under nonexclusive contract with both Columbia and Warner Brothers, and continued her work with Capra, who molded her early image of moral strength in such films as *Forbidden* (1932) and *The Bitter Tea of General Yen* (1933). But her career did not command attention until she joined Lux Radio Theater and started freelancing. Her title role in *Annie Oakley* (1935) added the quality of independence to her fledgling star image, and King Vidor's *Stella Dallas* (1937) secured her fame. With world war fast approaching and female survivalists becoming a trend in film, Stanwyck's intelligent performances found even more favor. Comedy only sharpened her rational quality, which often hinted at a distrust of the cinematic fatalism in the roles she played. Nowhere is this as evident as in Howard Hawks's *Ball of Fire* (1941) and Preston Sturges's *The Lady Eve* (1941), where she wrests multidimensional realism from screwball comedy.

Although Stanwyck had been romantically linked with Frank Capra and actor William Holden (whose career she helped launch and with whom she co-starred in his 1939 debut film, *Golden Boy*), she married a longtime friend, screen idol Robert Taylor, on May 14, 1939, at the behest of MGM boss Louis B. Mayer. She would divorce him in 1951. Stanwyck's move into film noir seemed inevitable given her sultry intensity, and her tour-de-force performance as amoral siren Phyllis Dietrichson in Billy Wilder's *Double Indemnity* (1944) manages to parody the blonde screen goddess while it also presents cinematic evil in a disturbingly human dimension. That year she was named the highest-paid woman in the United States.

Sexual frustration begins to color her performances by the mid 1940s—she had already suggested masochism in DeMille's *Union Pacific* (1939)—and Stanwyck's characters seemed to hit a glass ceiling as the postwar era reestablished female social repression. Her doomed, bed-ridden invalid railing against dehumanization and murder in *Sorry, Wrong Number* (1948) can easily be understood as an allegory of the era's female rage. Melodramas like *The Strange Love of Martha Ivers* (1946), *The Lady Gambles* (1949), *All I Desire* (1953), and *Executive Suite* (1954) allowed Stanwyck to revisit different aspects of her career persona such as the moralist, the femme fatale, and the frustrated neurotic. Her Westerns, among them *The Furies* (1950), *Cattle Queen of Montana* (1954), and *Forty Guns* (1957), avoided the camp quality that consumed other mature female stars in the genre, such as JOAN CRAWFORD and MARLENE DIETRICH. But age and rugged roles increased her sexually ambiguous aura and she became a gay icon, an aspect exploited by director Edward Dmytryk, who cast her as a lesbian madam in *Walk on the Wild Side* (1962).

Although she understood how to survive in the Hollywood star system, Stanwyck also foresaw the demise of the great studios and helped pioneer the concept of independent film development by forming Barwyck Production Company in 1956. As the choice film roles dwindled, she moved to television, where she first hosted her own short-lived series, *The Barbara Stanwyck Show* (1960–61), and then returned to the Western as the silver-haired matriarch of *The Big Valley* (1965–69). Her elegantly powerful character not only enshrined her star status (she was billed as "Miss" Barbara Stanwyck, Hollywood's "title" of respect for its legendary female actresses), but won her a new generation of fans in the era of the nascent women's movement. Nominated for four Academy Awards for Best Actress, Stanwyck was finally honored with a Special Academy Award in 1982. She also received three Emmy Awards.

Misfortune beset her later years: she became estranged from her adopted son, lost a kidney to illness in 1971, and lost her house and film memorabilia to fire in 1985. Her final appearances, however, include major roles in the popular television mini-series *The Thorn Birds* (1983) and in the *Dynasty* spin-off *The Colbys* (1985–86). Stanwyck died of congestive heart failure in Santa Monica, California, on January 20, 1990, at the age of eighty-two. Her ashes were scattered near Sequoia National Park, at Lone Pine, California.

With a reputation for being a true professional and a "director's actress" among the dominant leading ladies of Hollywood's Golden Age, Barbara Stanwyck contributed most significantly to the humanization of the female cinema image in her time. She inhabited her roles with intelligence and self-realization, qualities that continue to inspire audiences and that certainly influenced the changing social perceptions of women in mid-twentieth-century America.

Bibliography: Material on Barbara Stanwyck is included in one of the earliest studies on women and film, Marjorie Rosen's *Popcorn Venus: Women, Movies and the American Dream* (1973), but the first serious exposé on her life and work was the 1974 book, *Starring Miss Barbara Stanwyck*, by Ella Smith (rev. ed. 1985). This was followed by Jerry Vermilye's and Al DiOrio's *Barbara Stanwyck* biographies (1975 and 1983, respectively) and the illustrated *The Films of Barbara Stanwyck* (1984) by Homer Dickens. Jane Ellen Wayne's *Stanwyck* followed in 1985, and in 1994 Axel Madsen published his biography on the actress—also titled *Stanwyck. Current Biography* (1947) offered details on Barbara Stanwyck in mid-career, but one of her rare interviews from late in her life, "Stanwyck Speaks" with Bernard Drew in *Film Comment* (March–April 1981), pp. 43–46, is important to film historians. Among significant articles, Gene Ringgold essayed the actress in "Barbara Stanwyck" in *Films in Review* 14, no. 10 (December 1963), pp. 577–602. A special section devoted to Stanwyck is found in *Film Comment*, March–April 1981, pp. 33–47. Stanwyck's biographical notes are found in all cinema reference sources, with a succinct summation of her unique quality in a biography/filmography entry by Arthur Nolletti Jr. and Maria DiBattista in volume 3 *(Actors and Actresses)* of the *International Dictionary of Films and Filmmakers*, 4th ed. (2000). The Margaret Herrick Library at the Academy of Motion Pictures Arts and Sciences in Beverly Hills holds a biography file of media clippings of Stanwyck. Obituaries appeared in the *New York Times* on January 22, 1990, and in *Variety* on January 24, 1990.

ROBERT VON DASSANOWSKY

STAUPERS, Mabel Doyle Keaton. February 27, 1890–September 30, 1989. Nursing leader and activist.

Mabel Eloise Doyle was born in Barbados, West Indies. Her mother, Pauline Lobo, was a seamstress, and her father, Thomas C. Doyle, was a dentist. She and her mother arrived in New York City on April 21, 1903. The following year her father reunited with the family, which eventually included another daughter. They were naturalized in 1917.

Forced to repeat the sixth and seventh grades when she transferred into the New York public schools at thirteen, Mabel completed secondary education at P.S. 119 in 1914. She immediately entered Freedmen's Hospital School of Nursing in Washington, D.C. (now Howard University College of Nursing) and graduated with honors in 1917. Nursing attracted young, upwardly mobile black women in search of greater autonomy and opportunity to serve their communities, but like many black nurses she began her career as a private duty nurse. In 1918, she married a physician she had met during her training, James Max Keaton of Asheville, North Carolina. The marriage was short-lived and ended in divorce two years later.

In 1920, Mabel Doyle Keaton returned home to Harlem, where she soon demonstrated passion and proficiency in health care advocacy work, community organizing, and nursing administration. That year she joined forces with two physicians, Louis T. Wright and James L. Wilson, to open the first black-owned and -managed health care facility in Harlem, the Booker T. Washington Sanitarium. In 1921, Keaton moved to Philadelphia, where she served first as director of nurses at Mudget Hospital, then as resident nurse at the Home of St. Michael and All Angels for Crippled Children, an Episcopal Church-sponsored institution. Later that year she accepted a fellowship from the Henry Phipps Institute to study in the area of tuberculosis social work. She completed a course at the Pennsylvania School for Health and Social Work and was offered a position as a medical social worker at Philadelphia's Jefferson Hospital Medical College.

When Keaton learned in 1922 of an opening at New York's Tuberculosis and Health Association, she was not only qualified but eager to return home. In this new position she conducted a survey of black health care needs in Harlem that led to her appointment as the executive secretary of the newly established Harlem Committee of the New York Tuberculosis and Health Association. Over the course of the next twelve years Keaton became a prominent figure known for organizing health education public lectures, establishing fresh-air summer retreats for children, and developing health services that included free examinations and dental care for schoolchildren and prenatal clinics for pregnant women. She also agitated for the appointment of black physicians to tuberculosis clinics and hospitals in the city.

The first phase of her professional life involved a series of positions that provided essential administrative experience and enabled her to network with black male physicians and white nursing leaders. In 1931 she married Fritz C. Staupers, a native of Barbados, and now became known as Mabel Keaton Staupers. Neither of her marriages produced children.

The second phase of her career commenced in 1934 when she became the first salaried executive secretary of the National Association of Colored Graduate Nurses (NACGN), which had been founded in 1908 to facilitate the professional development of black women nurses and to challenge the exclusionary practices of the American Nurses' Association. Depression-era funding from the Rockefeller Foundation and the Julius Rosenwald Fund enabled the NACGN to become an established organization with permanent headquarters in Rockefeller Center in New York City, where all the major national nursing organizations had offices.

An ardent integrationist and feminist, as NACGN's executive secretary Staupers set as her goal nothing less than the full integration of black women into the mainstream of American nursing. Her collaborator in vigorous pursuit of this equal-rights agenda was NACGN president ESTELLE MASSEY RIDDLE OSBORNE. The wartime nursing shortage aided their efforts, underscoring the consequences of official policies that limited by quota or excluded altogether black nurses from service. When Ohio congresswoman and nursing advocate FRANCES PAYNE BOLTON introduced legislation in 1943 to create the Cadet Nurse Corps, the NACGN supported an amendment to the Bolton Bill to ensure that black student nurses would be able to join the corps. More than two thousand had done so by the war's end.

Staupers's simultaneous fight to eliminate quotas established by the U.S. Army Nurse Corps was a model of interracial cooperation and political maneuvering. After a series of frustrating meetings with top military officials, Staupers sought assistance from First Lady ELEANOR ROOSEVELT, and enlisted the black press, black and white nurses, friends throughout the civil rights activist community, and the general public to protest the racial quotas and blatant discrimination practiced by military medical agencies. In January 1945 the Army Nurse Corps began accepting nurses without regard to race and the Navy Nurse Corps opened its doors to black women, thus ending discriminatory practices in one of the most important institutions in America.

In 1946 Staupers resigned as NACGN executive secretary, but she continued to fight for full integration of professional nursing associations, and she was later elected president of the organization. In 1948 the American Nurses Association House of Delegates announced that all nurses, regardless of race, were welcome to membership. Three years later, the members of the NACGN, with encouragement from president Mabel Staupers, voted the organization out of existence. The dissolution of the NACGN signaled the triumph of Staupers's life quest for equality of opportunity and social justice: "The doors have been opened, and the black nurse has been give a seat in the top councils," Staupers declared. "We are now a part of the great organization of nurses, the American Nurses' Association."

In 1951 Staupers received the prestigious Spingarn Medal from the National Association for the Advancement of Colored People. At the age of seventy-one, she published *No Time for Prejudice: A Story of the Integration of Negroes in Nursing in the United States* (1961), a detailed chronicle, infused by her indomitable spirit of optimism, of how black women overcame racial, gender, and class obstacles in the health care profession. After her husband died in 1949, Mabel Keaton Staupers lived with her sister in Washington, D.C., where she died of pneumonia in 1989 at the age of ninety-nine.

Bibliography: Manuscript collections include the Mabel Keaton Staupers Papers at Amistad Research Center, Tulane University, New Orleans; the Staupers Papers at the Moorland-Spingarn Research Center, Howard University, Washington, D.C.; the National Association of Colored Graduate Nurses Collection at the Schomburg Center for Research in Black Culture, New York Public Library; and the Records of the Surgeon General's Office of the U.S. Army, and the Records of the War Department, General and Special Staff, both at the National Archives Research Center in Suitland, Maryland. See also Darlene Clark Hine, "Black Professional and Race Consciousness: Origins of the Civil Rights Movement, 1890–1950," *Journal of American History* 89, no. 4 (March 2003), pp. 1279–94; Hine, "Mabel K. Staupers and the Integration of Black Women into the Armed Forces," in John Hope Franklin and August Meier, eds., *Black Leaders of the Twentieth Century* (1982), pp. 241–57; and Marie Oleatha Pitts Mosley, "Mabel K. Staupers: A Pioneer in Professional Nursing," *Perspectives on Community: Leaders from Nursing's History* (Official Publication of the National League of Nursing) 16, no. 1 (January/February 1995), pp. 12–17. See also Hine, *Black Women in White: Racial Conflict and Cooperation in the Nursing Profession, 1890–1950* (1989), which contains the quotation from Staupers on pp. 184–85, and Mary Elizabeth Carnegie, *The Path We Tread: Blacks in Nursing, 1854–1984* (1986). An obituary appeared in the *New York Times* on October 6, 1989.

DARLENE CLARK HINE

STERN, Edith Rosenwald. May 31, 1895–September 11, 1980. Philanthropist, civic leader.

Edith Rosenwald was the third of five children of Augusta Nusbaum and Julius Rosenwald, both of whom were of German Jewish descent. She was born in Chicago and spent her childhood years there while her family acquired immense wealth as her father helped build the Sears-Roebuck empire in the early 1900s. As an adult, she lived in New Orleans, where she channeled funds to African American education, political reform, civil rights, and the arts.

The Rosenwalds followed a philanthropic ethos informed by Jewish tradition. Believing strongly in the value of education, they made substantial donations to the University of Chicago, JANE ADDAMS's Hull House, and Tuskegee Institute. The Julius Rosenwald Fund, established in 1917, helped build more than 5,200 African American schools in the South. Edith was strongly influenced by her father's philanthropic interests, and she also followed his favored method of issuing challenge grants.

Edith Rosenwald attended John Dewey's laboratory school at the University of Chicago but never completed high school. In 1910–11 she went to a finishing school in Dresden, Germany. In 1913 she married Germon Sulzberger, whose family owned a Chicago meatpacking business. After a European honeymoon, they settled in New York City. By 1917, the marriage had fallen apart, but Edith did not obtain a divorce until 1920, after she met and fell in love with Edgar Stern, a wealthy New Orleanian of German Jewish descent. Edgar was a Harvard graduate who joined his father's cotton brokerage firm, Lehman, Stern and Company; later he pursued interests in banking, publishing, and real estate. The couple married in 1921 and had three children: Edgar Jr. (1922), Audrey (1924), and Philip (1926).

While her children were young, Edith Stern concentrated on education. She helped establish the New Orleans Nursery School (later called the Newcomb Nursery School), taking an active part in its administration as well as providing financial assistance. In the late 1920s, she was instrumental in the creation of a private school for school-age children, Metairie Park Country Day School in Metairie, a New Orleans suburb. Both schools are still in existence.

Edith and Edgar Stern named their New Orleans house Longue Vue after the Hudson River inn where the couple became engaged. In the late 1930s, Edith hired nationally known landscape architect Ellen Biddle Shipman to redesign her gardens and then decided to build a new home on the same property. At Shipman's suggestion, Stern hired prominent New York architects William and Geoffrey Platt. The new Longue Vue was Greek Revival in style, and Shipman's landscape plan drew on seventeenth- and early-eighteenth-century English as well as Spanish sources. In the early 1970s, Stern began opening the gardens to the public on a limited basis. In 1978, having moved out of the house, she turned the property into a public facility that would host educational programs focusing on decorative arts, landscape architecture, and gardening for children and adults.

During World War II, Edith Stern worked with the Red Cross on membership drives and war bond sales, in both New Orleans and Washington, D.C., where her husband took a government position as a "dollar-a-year" man. After the war, she became involved with New Orleans politics as part of a successful women's grassroots effort to elect reform mayoral candidate DeLesseps S. "Chep" Morrison in 1946. With brooms donated from Sears, she and the "Women's Broom Brigade" promoted their "Clean Sweep" motto, aiming to rid the city of its infamous machine politics. Through her involvement in Morrison's campaign, she became interested in vote fraud and helped organize the Voters' Registration League. At Morrison's request, she also served on the city's Parkway and Park Commission. A tireless and determined volunteer, she was active in the League of Women Voters and in the national Democratic Party.

Like many southern white liberals at the time, Edith and Edgar Stern sought to improve education and living conditions for African Americans, but challenged segregation only indirectly. In the 1930s, Edgar served as Walter White's primary white contact for the National Association for the Advancement of Colored People (NAACP) in New Orleans and ran the fund-raising campaign for the merger of two African American schools, New Orleans University and Straight College, into Dillard University; he served on Dillard's board until his death, when Edith took over the spot. Although not active in grassroots civil rights organizing, Edith and her husband, through the family foundation, provided important funding for the movement, including the Voter Education Project of the Southern Regional Council. The Stern-owned television station, WDSU, broadcast editorials in favor of integration and the growing movement.

Edith Stern was also a patron of the arts, and after her husband's death in 1959 she devoted more time to that cause. She served on the board of the New Orleans Museum of Art and was instrumental in helping the museum build its Latin American art collection. A classical music lover, she was also a major benefactor of the New Orleans Symphony. President Kennedy appointed her to the National Cultural Center Advisory Committee on the Arts.

Because of her wealth and family standing, Edith Stern occupied a high place in the New Orleans social hierarchy. But because Edith and her husband were Jews, even though neither of them was religious, they were excluded from the most significant social activities in the city—the balls and other events surrounding Carnival and Mardi Gras—and often left town during this time of the year. Their civic and philanthropic efforts, however, received local acclaim: both (Edgar in 1930 and Edith in 1964) won the Times-Picayune Loving Cup, a prestigious award for community service. Edith Stern became a strong supporter of Israel and was also active in the National Council of Jewish Women. Perhaps Edith Stern's most enduring legacy was the Stern Fund, a family foundation modeled on her father's Rosenwald Fund that supported civil rights, civil liberties, campaign finance reform, public interest law, consumer advocacy, women's rights, and social justice until it disbanded in 1986.

Edith Stern's health declined over the last two years of her life, and owing to circulatory problems, she used a wheelchair most of the time. She died in New Orleans on September 11, 1980, at the age of eighty-five and was buried beside her husband at Longue Vue House and Gardens.

Bibliography: Collections of Edith Stern's papers are found at Longue Vue House and Gardens, and in the Stern Collection at the Will W. Alexander Library, Dillard University, in New Orleans. Gerda Weissmann Klein, *A Passion for Sharing: The Life of Edith Rosenwald Stern* (1984), commissioned by Stern's friends, is full of valuable information (including long quotes from family papers) but often sketchy regarding exact dates. Further details about Stern's family background and her father's philanthropic efforts can be found in M. R. Werner, *Julius Rosenwald: The Life of a Practical Humanitarian* (1939). See also the entries on Edgar and Edith Stern in Glenn R. Conrad, ed., *Dictionary of Louisiana Biography,* vol. 2 (1988). Adam Fairclough, *Race and Democracy: The Civil Rights Struggle in Louisiana, 1915–1972* (1995), places the Sterns' civil rights contributions in context, and James Gill mentions the Sterns' annual Carnival departure in *Lords of Misrule: Mardi Gras and the Politics of Race in New Orleans* (1997). Obituaries appeared in the *New York Times* and *New Orleans Times-Picayune* on September 12, 1980.

KAREN TRAHAN LEATHEM

STIEBELING, Hazel Katherine. March 20, 1896–May 18, 1989. Nutritionist, federal official.

Hazel Katherine Stiebeling was born on a farm in Haskins, Ohio. Her father, Adam Stiebeling, had immigrated to northern Ohio from Saasen, Germany; her mother, Elizabeth Brand, was born in Ersode, Germany. The family had six children—four girls and two boys—of whom Hazel was the second child. The Stiebelings were a farm family and almost entirely self-supporting. Hazel remembered being a lively child who played with her brothers and performed household and farm tasks.

Hazel showed academic promise at an early age, and her mother took an active interest in her education, sending her to live with grandparents in Findlay, where the schools were better. Stiebeling began studying domestic science in high school and in 1915 completed a two-year course in it at Skidmore College in New York. After graduating from Skidmore, Stiebeling was appointed domestic science teacher at the high school in Findlay she had attended. She taught for three years while studying part-time at the local college, and then she enrolled at Columbia University's Teachers College in New York to pursue a BS degree, which she received in 1919. Upon graduation, she was appointed head of teacher training in domestic arts at Kansas State Teachers College in Emporia. Two years later, she became head of the department of home economics there.

After three years in Kansas, Stiebeling returned to Columbia for graduate work, receiving an MA in 1924. At Columbia, as the assistant and a student of well-known nutrition researcher Mary Swartz Rose, she specialized in nutrition. Stiebeling also worked with nutrition researcher Henry C. Sherman, who had helped her get a research assistantship. In 1928, she received her doctorate in chemistry from Columbia. Her research helped establish the importance of Vitamin D in children's diet by working out dietaries for lab rats that proved that Vitamin D is necessary to bone growth. Her first publication, which she cowrote with Sherman, "Quantitative Studies of Responses to Different Intakes of Vitamin D," was published in the *Journal of Biological Chemistry* in 1929.

While still working at Columbia, Sherman told Stiebeling that the United States Department of Agriculture (USDA) had a good record for appointing women to interesting positions, so she took the Civil Service exam. In 1930 a position opened up, and LOUISE STANLEY, head of USDA's Bureau of Home Economics, appointed her senior food economist at an annual salary of $4,600. In her position as head of the Section on Food Economics in the Food and Nutrition Division, her job was to study food consumption and the purchasing practices of housewives. Natural and economic catastrophes intervened, however, steering her work in a slightly different direction. Responding to the drought of 1930 and then to the widespread Depression, Stiebeling worked with the Red Cross, the Public Health Service, and the national Extension Service to create menus for many budget levels that would supply adequate nutrition as well as a degree of palatability for low cost.

At the USDA, Stiebeling took up work begun by Wilbur Olin Atwater, compiling information about Americans' eating habits and nutrition. Atwater had helped establish the Bureau of Home Economics within the USDA and was one of the early leaders of the home economics movement. In 1931, Stiebeling wrote the USDA bulletin *Adequate Diets for Families with Limited Incomes.* This bulletin was based on research performed by USDA staff and addressed the specific problems of feeding families during the early years of the Great Depression. Other USDA bulletins written by Stiebeling dealt with nutrition and cost in family diets (1933), nutrition and pellagra in South Carolina (1932), and iron content in fruits and vegetables (1932). Later in the 1930s she wrote popular articles on these subjects for the *Woman's Home Companion.*

Stiebeling also represented the United States at various international conferences. In 1936 she went to Scotland to join agricultural economists at an international conference on food consumption. She then attended the League of Nations Conference on Nutrition as the U.S. representative. As nutrition consultant for the Health Section of the League of Nations, she traveled to Hungary, Yugoslavia, and Czechoslovakia to give advice to nutrition programs. In 1939, Stiebeling attended another League of Nations conference on nutrition in Buenos Aires. After the war she continued this work with the United Nations Food and Agriculture Organization.

Stiebeling's expertise in nutrition and food conservation was especially sought after during World War II. In 1942 she became assistant chief of the Bureau of Human Nutrition and Home Economics, and in 1944 she was promoted to chief. In 1952, President Harry Truman conferred on her the Distinguished Service Award of the USDA for her contributions to the improvement of American nutrition. Stiebeling became director of Human Nutrition and Home Economics in 1954, as part of the reorganized Agricultural Research Service (ARS), which replaced the Bureau of Home Economics. In 1957, following additional reorganization, Stiebeling was made director of the Institute of Home Economics within the ARS. She and colleague Callie Mae Coons directed important research on family nutrition. In 1959, President Dwight Eisenhower presented her with a Distinguished Civilian Service Award, and a journalist at the awards ceremony noted that her excitement at receiving the award was infectious. After thirty-three years of service, Stiebeling retired from the USDA in 1963. At that time her title was Deputy Administrator for Nutrition and Consumer Use Research.

Biographer Edna Yost described Hazel Stiebeling as "a positive person" who was persuasive rather than pushy, as "her soft-spokenness, her un-tenseness, her almost serenity make it inevitable that she gets what she wants." Throughout her career as a civil servant, Stiebeling was more interested in doing the right thing than winning glory for herself. She was tall and slim, never married, took an active role in the Lutheran Church, and after retirement became an amateur watercolorist. She died on May 18, 1989, at the Goodwin House in Alexandria, Virginia, at the age of ninety-three.

Bibliography: Material on Stiebeling can be found in the USDA History Collection, Special Collections, National Agricultural Library, Beltsville, Maryland. See also Jacqueline L. Dupont and Alfred E. Harper, "Hazel Katherine Stiebeling (1896–1989)," *Nutrition Reviews* 60, no. 10 (October 2002), pp. 342–48; Edna Yost, *American Women of Science* (1943, rev. ed. 1955; quotation appears on p. 176 of the original edition); *Current Biography* (1950), pp. 548–50; and Sarah Stage and Virginia B. Vincenti, eds., *Rethinking Home Economics: Women and the History of a Profession* (1997).

MEGAN ELIAS

STINSON, Katherine. February 14, 1891–July 8, 1977. Aviator.

A slight young woman (she claimed to weigh a hundred and one pounds, and was very particular about that one extra pound), Katherine Stinson was one of the first and most famous women aviators of the early twentieth century. During her brief career—approximately seven years—and less than a decade after the invention of the airplane, she was known as the most daring woman stunt pilot of her generation. "It didn't occur to me to be *afraid*," she wrote. "Other people were doing it. If they could, certainly I ought to be able to."

Katherine Stinson was born in Fort Payne, Alabama, the oldest of four children of Edward Anderson Stinson and Emma Beavers. The Stinsons were an aviation-minded family: Katherine's mother incorporated the Stinson Aviation Company in 1913 in Hot Springs, Arkansas. In 1915 the family established Stinson Field (later, Stinson Municipal Airport) in San Antonio, Texas. That same year, Katherine, her younger sister Marjorie, who was a pioneer aviator in her own right, and their brother Edward taught at a flying school founded by her mother there. Edward and her other brother, Jack, later organized the Stinson Aeroplane Company.

Katherine decided to learn to fly because she dreamed of being a music teacher and thought that the prize money she could earn as a pilot would enable her to fulfill her desire. In 1912 she had her first ride in a Benoist aircraft piloted by Tony Jannus, a well-known pilot of the time, in St. Louis. Eventually she went to Chicago and took lessons with pilot Max Lillie at Cicero Field. On July 16, 1912, she took her qualifying flight for a license, and was granted Aero Club of America Certificate No. 148 on July 24, reportedly the fourth woman in the United States to become a licensed pilot. In Cincinnati, Ohio, in July 1913 she began her flying career, which in the days before World War I primarily meant exhibition flying in meets and competitions all over the country. In September of that year she became the first woman commissioned to fly mail from the Helena, Montana, fairgrounds to downtown Helena. For the rest of 1913 and during 1914, Stinson made flying appearances throughout the United States.

In 1915, after the death of noted aviator Lincoln Beachey, Stinson purchased the engine from his aircraft and had it installed in an aircraft that was being constructed for her by the Partridge and Keller Aeroplane Company. In July of that year she became one of the first women in the world to perform the loop-the-loop (Ruth Law had already executed a similar stunt), an aerial maneuver in which an aircraft in level flight climbs steeply in a circle without turning, until at the top of the circle it is flying upside-down. It then dives down to complete the loop until it is flying level again. In November 1915 she added to her repertoire the "dippy twist" loop, in which the aircraft does a vertical banking maneuver, permitting it to fly wingtip-over-wingtip at the top of the each loop. She eventually became proficient at doing eighty consecutive loop-the-loops in a row, flying inverted for a half minute at a time, and doing a series of spiral spin maneuvers in which the aircraft dove and spiraled simultaneously.

On the night of December 17, 1915, she made what was undoubtedly her most dramatic flight in view of a select audience of twenty-five persons at Griffith Park in Los Angeles. Stinson was determined to outdo Art Smith, a famous male aviator known as the Bird Boy, who had flown a loop at night trailing fire in his wake. Using magnesium flares on her aircraft, she flew a series of aerial maneuvers to spell out the letter "CAL" (presumably for California), then "she looped; flew upside down, and dropped in a mad tumble to within a hundred feet of the earth all the while being showered with the drippings from the burning lights on her biplane" (*Aerial Age Weekly,* January 17, 1916, p. 424).

In December 1916, she leased an aerobatic aircraft called the Laird Looper, from E. M. "Matty" Laird, a well-known pilot and aircraft builder, and set off on a six-month tour of Japan and China. She was the first woman to fly in Asia. A crowd of twenty-five thousand people was present at her first appearance on Tokyo's Aoyama Parade Ground, and she quickly became a role model for Japanese women.

On June 24, 1917, she made a 670-mile fundraising flight for the Red Cross from Buffalo, New York, to Washington, D.C., stopping along the way at Albany, New York City, and Philadelphia; the flight garnered $50,000 in donations. On December 11, 1917, she flew 610 miles from San Diego to San Francisco in nine hours, ten minutes, setting records for distance and duration. In the following year, on May 23, 1918, she made another distance and duration record-setting flight of 601.763 miles from Chicago to Binghamton, New York. In the summer of that year she went to Canada, where she flew in numerous exhibitions and set a Canadian distance and duration record, while being the first woman to fly the airmail in that country.

Disappointed that she was not allowed to fly as a military pilot during World War I, she went to England and France, where she was an ambulance driver in the Red Cross Overseas Motor Corps. After the war, bouts with influenza and tuberculosis forced her to retire from flying. In 1928 she married Miguel A. Otero Jr., a World War I aviator and attorney who was later a judge of the First Judicial District, New Mexico. They had no children. The couple settled in Santa Fe, and Stinson worked for the Red Cross and restored old Santa Fe residences. She died there in 1977 at age eighty-six after a long illness.

Bibliography: The Marjorie Stinson Papers at the Manuscript Division of the Library of Congress contain two boxes (35–36) of biographical materials on Katherine Stinson. A collection of Stinson family letters and related papers are located in the Evans Memorial Library, Aberdeen, Mississippi. Biographical material on Katherine and Marjorie Stinson is also contained in the Early Birds of Aviation, Inc. Collection, and the general biographical files of the Archives Division, National Air and Space Museum, Smithsonian Institution, Washington, D.C. Although quoted extensively in the popular press, Stinson seems to have written only one article, "Why I Am Not Afraid to Fly," in *American Magazine,* January 7, 1919, pp. 36–37+, in which the quotation in the opening paragraph appears. Useful secondary sources include Debra L. Winegarten, *Katherine Stinson, The Flying Schoolgirl* (2000); John W. Underwood, *The Stinsons: The Exciting Chronicle of a Flying Family and the Planes That Enhanced Their Fame* (1969); and Claudia M. Oakes, *United States Women in Aviation through World War I* (1978). Valerie Moolman, *Women Aloft* (1981), contains a photographic essay about Stinson's tour of the Orient. Obituaries appeared in the *New York Times* on July 11, 1977, and the *Washington Post* on July 16, 1977.

DOMINICK PISANO

ST. JOHNS, Adela Rogers. May 20, 1894–August 10, 1988. Journalist, novelist, screenwriter.

Adela Rogers St. Johns was born in Los Angeles, California, the daughter of Earl Rogers, a famous criminal defense attorney, and Harriet Greene, a housewife who originally came from upstate New York. Her parents divorced, remarried, and divorced again, all by the time Adela was in her teens. She consistently sided with her father and lived with him in Los Angeles after her parents' final split, while her younger brother moved to New York with her mother. Her father later remarried and had two sons, whom Adela helped raise after her stepmother's death.

Adela attended various schools, but never graduated from high school. Instead, she received an informal education in her father's law office and in court. When St. Johns turned eighteen, she told her father she wanted to be an attorney but he suggested that instead she become a newspaper reporter, a career that opened up to women in the early twentieth century. In 1913, he persuaded William Randolph Hearst to hire her as a reporter, either for the *San Francisco Examiner* or the *Los Angeles Herald* (her own writing and several biographical sketches are inconsistent about this). She covered the city beat and used her father's connections to get several local scoops. She was soon promoted to feature writing.

In 1914 she married copy editor William Ivans "Ike" St. Johns. They had a daughter, Elaine, in 1918 and a son, William (Bill), a year later. The couple led a hectic life, with late-night poker games, drinking, and busy careers. This caused a great conflict for St. Johns, who called the modern woman's career, marriage, and children "trying to drive three mules" at once (St. Johns, *The Honeycomb,* p. 13). In 1920, St. Johns began to write magazine fiction and screenplays for Hollywood so she could work at home. She also wrote profiles for the new fan magazine *Photoplay.* Her frankly admiring writing style and lively parties made her a favorite among Hollywood's leading stars, and she gained many exclusive interviews through personal connections.

Conflict over family duties and money led to divorce in 1929. St. Johns married Richard Hyland and had her third child, Dick, probably around 1930. They divorced in the early 1930s. In 1935, while covering the trial of Bruno Richard Hauptmann for kidnapping and murdering the

Lindbergh baby, Hyland sued for custody of their son, claiming that St. Johns was an unfit mother. St. Johns won custody, but this incident reinforced her conflict over parenthood and career. So bitter were her feelings that she refused to even name Hyland in her autobiography. St. Johns adopted another son, McCullah (Mac), probably in the late 1930s. He was a childhood friend of her son Bill who had lived with the family on and off since the 1920s. She also married for a third time, to a Cleveland airline executive named Francis Patrick O'Toole, but that marriage also ended in divorce in the early 1940s.

Throughout the 1930s, Adela Rogers St. Johns practiced a combination of feature writing, interviews, trial coverage, and investigative journalism for the Hearst news syndicate. St. Johns covered all the major stories of her day, including the Hauptmann trial, the early New Deal years in Washington, the assassination of Huey Long, and the abdication of Edward VIII. She even covered sports, from the "woman's angle." In the early days of the Depression, she posed as an unemployed woman for a week, struggling to get assistance from Los Angeles charities and welfare agencies. She herself said that she practiced "sob sister" reporting, or getting at the human stories beneath the headlines. Her writing has been criticized as emotional and propagandistic, but even her critics acknowledge her craftsmanship and uncanny ability to gain access to newsmakers.

During World War II, St. Johns had problems selling stories to popular magazines. At one point, she was $17,000 in debt, drinking heavily, and attempted suicide. She moved to New York City, but still had a difficult time until the *Ladies' Home Journal* hired her to write a serial on wartime Washington, which was titled "Government Girl." RKO bought the movie rights, which made her solvent again. After her oldest son, a pilot, was killed in action, she moved back to California where she wrote screenplays and served as a script doctor at MGM. In 1948 she received her final assignment from Hearst, a eulogy of Gandhi. Hearst died soon thereafter and St. Johns retired from reporting. She spent the rest of her career writing fiction, an autobiography, and several other books of anecdotes and reminiscences. She also taught journalism for several years at the University of California, Los Angeles.

After struggling with alcohol for decades, as had her father, St. Johns gave up drinking in the 1960s. She also became a minister in the Church of Religious Science, a non-denominational spiritual movement founded by Ernest Holmes in Los Angeles in the 1920s. In 1970, she was awarded the Medal of Freedom by Richard Nixon, whom she had supported politically and known since he was a grocery delivery boy in Whittier, California. St. Johns died at the age of ninety-four in 1988 in Arroyo Grande, California.

The theme of her autobiography captured the difficulties faced by many Anglo, middle-class women of the early twentieth century. St. Johns loved newspaper work and the camaraderie of the city room, yet she also wanted a family, and often felt guilt over spending time away from them. She was proud of the fact that she could work as hard as any male reporter at chasing a story, but she also wholeheartedly embraced the "sob sister" label and the "woman's angle." She remained ambivalent about feminism, supporting suffrage but also calling modern women failures for stooping to the level of men and neglecting their duties at home. Nevertheless, she paid homage to the prominent women of the twentieth century, such as ELEANOR ROOSEVELT and MARGARET SANGER, in writings such as *Some Are Born Great* (1974). If she was personally ambivalent about the challenges faced by women in the twentieth century, her career and her writings visibly celebrated women's new opportunities and achievements in public life.

Bibliography: St. Johns left no collection of personal papers. A clipping file about her is available at the Billy Rose Theatre Collection, New York Public Library for the Performing Arts at Lincoln Center. The most extensive biographical material can be found in her own writing, starting with her autobiography, *The Honeycomb* (1969). *Final Verdict* (1962), an account of her father's law career, contains much valuable information about her childhood. She also wrote a Hollywood memoir, *Love, Laughter and Tears* (1978), although it contains little personal material on her own life. She describes her career and her struggle with alcoholism in a 1981 interview in *Contemporary Authors* (1983), which also contains the most complete list of her books, stories, and screenplays. Her novels include *The Skyrocket* (1925), *The Single Standard* (1928), and a spiritual novel, *Tell No Man* (1966). Her screenplays include *Inez from Hollywood* (1924), silent westerns such as *The Arizona Wildcat* (1927), and *What Price Hollywood?* (1933). St. Johns receives a brief treatment in Ishbel Ross's *Ladies of the Press* (1936). For general treatments of women in journalism, see Phyllis Leslie Abramson, *Sob Sister Journalism* (1990); Maurine H. Beasley and Sheila J. Gibbons, *Taking Their Place: A Documentary History of Women and Journalism* (1993); and Robert Downs and Jane B. Downs, *Journalists of the United States: Biographical Sketches of Print and Broadcast News Shapers from the Late 17th Century to the Present* (1991). Obituaries appeared in the *New York Times*, the *Los Angeles Times*, and the *Chicago Tribune* on August 11, 1988.

WENDY HOLLIDAY

STOLZ, Lois Hayden Meek. October 19, 1891–October 24, 1984. Early childhood educator.

Lois Hayden Meek was born in the nation's capital, where her father, Alexander Kennedy Meek, was a lawyer for the U.S. Senate. She was the second child of Meek and his wife, Fannie Virginia Price. When she was a young child, her parents separated, and she and her brother were raised by her father and her paternal grandparents. She spent many summer vacations on the Tennessee farm where her father grew up, which was part of the land owned by his Scotch-Irish ancestors since the American Revolution.

As a teenager, Meek focused on becoming a proper young lady, but her father, who believed every woman should be able to earn her own living even if she never had to work, insisted that she continue her education. Despite her initial resistance she enrolled in Washington Normal School in 1910, where, with the help of some inspiring teachers and the encouragement of friends, she excelled in her studies and graduated at the top of her class in 1912.

As she liked to put it, Meek became a teacher in spite of herself. Upon graduation she began working in the Washington, D.C., public schools. After four years of teaching first grade, the school district promoted Meek to "model teacher," which meant supervising other elementary school teachers, a position she held until 1921. In the afternoons and evenings, Meek began working toward her BA in educational sociology from George Washington University, which she earned in 1921. Meek's involvement with the Progressive Education Association, which began in these years, led to early experiments with activity-based, individualized learning with her second-graders.

Deciding to pursue a graduate degree in education, in the fall of 1921 she enrolled in the most prestigious graduate program in education, Teachers College at Columbia University. Her adviser thought women should be taking care of the home rather than pursuing graduate degrees, so Meek selected her own course of study, enrolling in whatever courses caught her attention. She took classes from leaders in the field of education and psychology, such as John Dewey, William Heard Kirkpatrick, PATTY SMITH HILL, and Edward Thorndike.

Having earned her doctorate in child psychology in 1925, Meek accepted a job with the American Association of University Women (AAUW) in Washington, D.C., to set up a national adult education program in child development. Her role was to inspire and encourage college-educated women to pursue education and careers in child development. While working for the AAUW, Meek's former professor and mentor, Patty Smith Hill, asked her to be the first chairman of the Committee on Nursery Schools, organized to promote the newly formed nursery school movement. The National Association for Nursery Education (NANE), which later became the National Association for the Education of Young Children (NAEYC), emerged from this committee and Meek served as its first president from 1929 to 1931.

Having now established herself as one of the leaders in the growing field of child development, Meek returned to Teachers College in 1929 as professor of education and associate director of the Child Development Institute. In March 1930 she succeeded HELEN THOMPSON WOOLLEY as the institute's director, a role she remained in until 1939. She also continued her active involvement in the Progressive Education Association, serving on its executive committee from 1930 to 1935.

Meek's leadership in the field of child development caught the attention of the Roosevelt administration as it struggled to deal with the massive unemployment wrought by the Depression. Many credit Meek with helping to convince Harry Hopkins, administrator of the Federal Emergency Relief Agency and later the Works Progress Administration, to initiate, starting in 1933, government-sponsored nursery schools staffed by unemployed teachers, nutritionists, and others. Meek served on the advisory board and worked tirelessly to make sure the government's nursery school program remained education-centered, mobilizing students and other faculty at Teachers College to teach in and supervise these schools.

In 1938 during a visit to the Institute of Child Welfare Research at the University of California at Berkeley, she met Dr. Herbert Rowell Stolz, the Institute's director. The two fell in love, prompting Meek to relocate to California, and they married that same year. She had had an earlier, brief marriage in 1924 that had ended in divorce.

During World War II, Governor Culbert Olson asked Stolz to serve as his special assistant in charge of the Care of Children in Wartime program. Even though she had spent most of her career as an academic, Stolz also had experience in organizing and implementing day-care programs; consequently she was an excellent choice to coordinate and inspire local California communities to request Lanham Act child-care funds, which had been approved in 1942 as part of the nation's war effort. For the next six months she worked indefatigably to see that public child-care programs were established throughout the state.

Just as she was becoming frustrated by the lack of response and the administrative red tape, Stolz received a phone call from Edward Kaiser, the son of Henry J. Kaiser and general manager of his two Portland, Oregon, shipyards. Kaiser asked her to help him establish child-care centers at the shipyards, which employed roughly twenty-five thousand women. As director of the Kaiser Child Service Centers, Stolz played an integral role in the center's design—suggesting that the centers include an infirmary and that they remain open twenty-four hours a day. At one point the two centers served as many as a thousand children a week. Stolz would later recall this as one of the most thrilling projects of her career.

When the centers closed at the end of the war, Stolz returned to her longtime passion, teaching students and conducting research. In 1945 she filled a last-minute vacancy in the psychology department at Stanford University; this became a permanent position in 1947. Stolz helped establish Stanford's first child development program and founded the Stanford Village Nursery School. Her research explored the parent–child relationships of children born while their fathers were fighting abroad during World War II.

Stolz officially retired from Stanford in 1957, but she remained an active researcher, consultant, and teacher in her role as professor emerita. From 1957 to 1960 she conducted a major study for the AAUW on the effects of maternal employment on children. She also served her community as a consultant to the Palo Alto Public School District, as a member of the Santa Clara Head Start Committee, and as a teacher trainer for Head Start. Widowed in 1971, Stolz remained active until her death at her home in Palo Alto in 1984 at the age of ninety-three.

Bibliography: The Lois Meek and Herbert Rowell Stolz Papers (1917–1984) are located in the History of Medicine Division, National Library of Medicine, NIH, Bethesda, Maryland. For biographical information on Stolz, see Julia Grant, "Lois Meek Stolz," in Maxine Schwartz Seller, ed., *Women Educators in the United States* (1994). Interviews with Stolz include James Hymes, "The Kaiser Child Service Centers: An Interview with Lois Meek Stolz," in *Living History Interviews: Book 2: Care of the Children of Working Mothers* (1978); Ruby Takanishi, "An American Child Development Pioneer," UCLA Academic Senate Research Committee, 1979, Department of Special Collections, UCLA Library; Milton J. E. Senn, "Interviews with Leaders in the Child Guidance and Clinic Movement" (1968), History of Science and Technology Collection, Bancroft Library, University of California, Berkeley; and Margo Davis, "Lois Meek Stolz: An Interview" (1977), Stanford Oral History Project, University Archives, Stanford University.

Major publications by Stolz include *Preschool and Parental Education: Twenty-Eighth Yearbook of the National Society for the Study of Education* (1929); *Personal-Social Development of Boys and Girls* (1940); *Your Child's Development and Guidance* (1940, rev. ed. 1950); *Somatic Development of Adolescent Boys* (1951), with Herbert Rowell Stolz; *Father Relations of War-Born Children* (1954); *Influences on Parent Behavior* (1958); and "The Effects of Maternal Employment on Children: Evidence from Research," *Child Development* 31 (1960), pp. 749–82. An obituary appeared in *Young Children*, January 1985, p. 24.

NATALIE FOUSEKIS

STRAUSS, Anna Lord. September 20, 1899–February 23, 1979. League of Women Voters president, United Nations delegate.

Anna Lord Strauss, the second of three daughters of Albert and Lucretia Lord Strauss, was born in New York City. Her father, who was of German and Jewish descent, had attended City College of New York but dropped out because of financial difficulties. Answering an ad from J. & W. Seligman and Company, he joined the banking firm and rose rapidly. In time he became vice-governor of the Federal Reserve Board. Her mother was a granddaughter of LUCRETIA MOTT, and the family was strongly influenced by her Quaker heritage.

Strauss remembered a childhood of freedom, sports, and warm family life where outdoor activities overshadowed school. Her sisters were Bryn Mawr graduates who went on to professions; she, instead, went to the New York School for Secretaries and found jobs with the Federal Reserve Board, where she worked until her father joined the Board, and the U.S. Shipping Board. When her father served as a financial adviser at the Versailles Peace Conference in 1919, he took her along, a trip she sometimes described as her substitute for college. Family lore has it that on the ship one night she borrowed a sailor's garb and climbed to the crow's nest, a spontaneous act that typified her adventurous, almost tomboyish, spirit.

After she returned from France, Strauss was still puzzled about what to do with her life. Following a series of State Department jobs, she joined the staff of *The Century* magazine in 1923. In six years she moved from secretary to managing editor. During the Depression she felt it wrong to take a paying job from someone who needed it, so she turned to volunteer work. For a while she worked with immigrants at Ellis Island and then from 1931 to 1933 she organized the library at the New York State Department of Labor.

Still looking for satisfying volunteer possibilities, in 1934 she joined the New York City League of Women Voters, a step that would shape her future life. She worked her way to president, and in 1944, when the national League of Women Voters was in the throes of a revolution brought about by local members who wanted more say in the organization's policies and projects, she was persuaded to accept nomination as president. When the biennial convention chose her instead of the handpicked successor of the outgoing president, most of the staff and all the continuing board members resigned. She moved into an empty office with a tiny all-new board and two staff people.

Faced with this challenge she hired a number of enthusiastic young women and recruited additional board members who shared her views about the League's future. Over the next six years she demonstrated a gift for organization and for identifying talent. Anna Strauss's style was Quakerly—she treasured simplicity, consensus, and brevity—and she transformed the hitherto hierarchical, specialist-ridden organization into one that depended on members doing their own reading and thinking rather than listening to authorities. The membership grew rapidly as the national office built strong relationships with local leagues and undertook to educate whole communities about the issues facing the postwar United States. With integrity and common sense she managed a sometimes fractious organization of able, mostly college educated, mostly young women. The League became an increasingly important force in hundreds of local communities, and a voice heard in Congress as well as in the White House.

In 1950 she turned over the leadership of what was by then a highly effective organization to Percy Maxim Lee, who had joined the Board in 1944, and went on to new opportunities created by the reputation for competence and leadership she had earned as League president. In 1951 President Truman appointed her to the Commission on Internal Security and Individual Rights, and in 1951–52 she served as a delegate to the United Nations General Assembly. When the House Committee on Un-American Activities (HUAC) and Joseph McCarthy were on the rampage, with others she organized a Freedom Agenda and raised money for publications to remind citizens of what the Bill of Rights was about.

Many governmental and private bodies also discovered her ability to work effectively with women of many different cultures, and she made numerous trips to other parts of the world for this purpose. When the League established the Carrie Chapman Catt Memorial Fund (later renamed the Overseas Education Fund) to work with women in other countries, she joined its board. In the summer of 1953 she spent four months in Southeast Asia under the auspices of the United Nations. An adventurous traveler, she seized every opportunity for new experiences whether they were part of her official program or not. During these trips she wrote long revealing letters to be circulated to friends and colleagues.

Believing strongly in the concept of the public interest, she was disturbed by the increasingly important role of special interests in politics, although she recognized that there were plenty of differences about what constituted the public interest. She worried about the role of money in campaigns, and believed that if enough people would learn from the methods of the League of Women Voters the government could become a real democracy.

She never lost her interest in sports, and in her sixties she took up scuba diving. Her energy was legendary: once in Japan she visited twenty-three towns in twenty-one days. Throughout her life she was a person of extraordinary, but very quiet, generosity. She had inherited a considerable income and believed in using it to help friends, relatives, and the organizations in whose work she most believed. Her papers bear witness to the number and careful design of her gifts. When she was trekking around the world, she made sure friends were invited to use her country house in Newtown, Connecticut.

Strauss was a splendid example of a woman who turned voluntary work into a major career in public service, and she inspired many others to do likewise. She never married, though her male friends were numerous and among the most interesting men of her time. After a few years of declining health, Anna Strauss died in New York City at the age of seventy-nine.

Bibliography: Voluminous papers dealing with her work and a small collection of private papers are at the Schlesinger Library, Radcliffe Institute for Advanced Study, Harvard University. There are also personal papers, including diaries, still in the possession of her family. The Oral History Research Office, Columbia University, holds an oral history conducted by Kitty Gellhorn in 1971–72 entitled "The Reminiscences of Anna Lord Strauss." The papers of the League of Women Voters of the United States in the Library of Congress contain full and detailed records of her years as national president. For background on the League of Women Voters, see their publication *Forty Years of a Great Idea* (1960); Louise M. Young, *In the Public Interest: The League of Women Voters, 1920–1970* (1989); and Barbara Stuhler, *For the Public Record: A Documentary History of the League of Women Voters* (2000). Three family members offered invaluable assistance in researching Strauss's life: Janet French Cramer, and Lucretia and Fred Mali. Obituaries appeared in the *New York Times* on February 24, 1979, and the *Washington Post* on February 25, 1979.

ANNE FIROR SCOTT

STREETER, Ruth Cheney. October 2, 1895–September 30, 1990. Colonel, U.S. Marine Corps Reserve.

Ruth Cheney Streeter, whose sense of duty and sacrifice for her country during World War II paved the way for women in the armed forces, was born Ruth Cheney in Brookline, Massachusetts, the second of three children and the only daughter of Mary Ward Lyon and Charles Paine Cheney. Her parents were affluent and well-established Episcopalian New Englanders. Her mother, a graduate of Wellesley College and a philanthropist, provided for her family after Ruth's father, a Harvard graduate and banker, died of tuberculosis in 1900. Ruth credited her mother for being an example of political and social activism and her brothers for imbuing in her a tomboy spirit.

Ruth and her brothers spent their early childhood traveling all over the country and Europe with their attractive and wealthy widowed mother and vacationing every summer in Peterborough, New Hampshire, where their mother built a country estate. Around 1905, however, the family moved back to Boston to ensure Ruth's proper education with private tutors. Three years later her mother married Harvard professor William Henry Schofield, and the family settled in Cambridge.

In 1910, Ruth attended the Château de Dieudonné, a finishing school in France, and then Miss May's School in Boston. She came out as a debutante in 1913 and engaged in activities reserved for the daughters of the upper crust, including the Junior League. In 1914 she entered Bryn Mawr College but, lacking the desire to finish college, in 1916 she returned to Boston, where she fell in love with Thomas Winthrop Streeter, a Harvard-educated lawyer and businessman. They were married in 1917, and their first son, Frank Sherwin, was born in March 1918.

In 1918 the family moved to Washington, D.C., where her husband landed a wartime job with the Department of Purchase, Storage and Traffic. Ruth Streeter contributed to the war effort by volunteering with several organizations to support her two brothers, who were sent overseas with the army. When her younger brother, William Halsall Cheney, was killed while flying over Italy, Streeter eased her grief by immersing herself even more in volunteer work. She and her mother later created the Air Force "Cheney Award" in honor of her brother.

Following the end of the war the family moved to New York City. Declaring it an unsuitable place to raise a family after two more sons, Henry Schofield (1920) and Thomas Winthrop Jr. (1922) were born, the Streeters moved to Morristown, New Jersey, where their daughter Lillian was born in 1927. Streeter followed her mother's example and became an active member of the Morristown community, volunteering with the League of Women Voters and the New Jersey Women's Republican Club, and founding the Junior League of Morristown.

The Streeters were not immune to the financial woes that befell the United States during the Depression, and this uncertainty inspired Streeter to donate her time to social welfare work. She was elected president of the Morris County Welfare Board in 1932 and was the only woman appointed in 1932–33 to the State Relief Council, where she campaigned to help raise money for the poor.

As the United States prepared to enter World War II, Streeter felt her call to duty. The death of her brother had inspired her interest in aviation, and with all three of her sons contemplating military service, Ruth felt compelled to help her country in some way. At the age of forty-five, she completed an aeronautics course at New York University and began taking private flying lessons. In 1941 she became the only woman on New Jersey's Defense Council on Aviation and in 1942 earned her commercial pilot's license. She joined the Civil Air Patrol in New Jersey with the understanding that her job would be to patrol the Atlantic Ocean. Furious when told she could only organize the men's flying schedules, not fly herself, she then tried five times to join the Women's Airforce Service Pilots (WASPs) but was rejected for being twelve years over the age limit.

Ruth Streeter's opportunity to join the military came when the Marines decided to recruit Women Reservists to free men for combat duty. Upon the intercession of a family friend, President Roosevelt offered her the newly created position of director of the Women's Reserve. Thrilled with the prospect of serving her country, Streeter accepted an appointment as major (the first woman to hold that rank in the U.S. Marine Corps) in January 1943, and took over as director on February 13, 1943. She moved to Washington, D.C., where she would lead one thousand officers and approximately eighteen thousand enlisted women. Her tasks included recruiting across the country and overseeing the Women Marines' various duties, such as clerical work, parachute rigging, and transportation and mechanical jobs.

Ruth Cheney Streeter excelled in her duties as director and was promoted to the rank of lieutenant colonel on November 12, 1943, and colonel in 1945. In dealing with the wartime military bureaucracy, she looked to the women who held similar posts in other branches of the service—OVETA CULP HOBBY (WAC), MILDRED MCAFEE (WAVES), and Dorothy Stratton (U.S. Coast Guard Women's Reserve)—for advice and morale. On December 7, 1945, after two years of hard work, travel, and having rarely seen her family, Streeter retired from her post. In 1946 she was awarded the Legion of Merit for outstanding service.

Upon her retirement, Streeter returned to her civic duties. She joined the New Jersey Veterans Council (1946–53) and the U.S. Defense Advisory Council for Women in the Service. She and her husband, who became a historian after his retirement, were extremely active in historical preservation through the New Jersey Historical Society and the New Jersey Historical Sites Council. After her husband's death in 1965, she moved to a small cottage in Morristown where she spent her final years enjoying her many grandchildren and great-grandchildren and attending Marine Corps and

Bryn Mawr events. Ruth Cheney Streeter died of congestive heart failure on September 30, 1990, at her home in Morristown, just shy of her ninety-fifth birthday. She was buried in Peterborough, New Hampshire, where she had spent summers as a young girl.

Bibliography: Reminiscences of Colonel Ruth Cheney Streeter, Director of Women Marines (1979), a discussion of her service in the Marines and her family life, is located at several depositories, including the Schlesinger Library, Radcliffe Institute for Advanced Study, Harvard University. Ruth Cheney Streeter, *Tales of an Ancient Marine* (n.d.), provides an in-depth look into her life in the military. The only available copy of this memoir is at the Joint Free Public Library of Morristown and Morris Township in Morristown, New Jersey. The Women's Project of New Jersey, in Special Collections and University Archives, Alexander Library, Rutgers University, contains photographs and other memorabilia of Streeter during World War II. *Current Biography* (1943), pp. 744–46, is also helpful. Obituaries appeared in the *New York Times* and *Boston Globe* on October 2, 1990.

KATHRYN N. LOSAVIO

SWENSON, May. May 28, 1913–December 4, 1989. Poet.

Anna Thilda May Swenson was born in Logan, Utah, to first-generation Swedish immigrants, Anna Margareta Elizabeth Hellberg and Dan Arthur Swenson. Inspired by the Mormon missionaries who helped save his father's family from financial destitution, Dan Swenson attended Utah State Agricultural College (now Utah State University), where, in 1912, he began a lifelong career as a teacher and woodworker in the Department of Mechanical Arts. Resourceful and determined, Margaret Swenson worked hard as a young wife to make a comfortable home, canning her own fruits and vegetables, pressing her own cider, keeping bees for their wax and honey, and making most of her family's clothes. The eldest of ten children, May assisted her mother with these domestic duties and helped raise her siblings. It is no surprise, then, that Swenson's success as a poet owes as much to her fierce self-sufficiency as it does to raw talent: a single woman who began her career at the end of the Depression, Swenson became one of the most prolific and respected American poets of the twentieth century, with eleven volumes of poetry (plus four posthumous titles) and several prestigious awards to her name.

Swenson was beloved by her many siblings, who remember both her intense creativity and her quiet reserve. This description of Swenson's character is a fitting forecast of what was to come in her poems: exuberant and stylistically playful, Swenson's poems are also sinewy with self-restraint, a combination made especially apparent in her three books of riddle poems. Indeed, a tension between rapture and reserve courses through Swenson's writing as a whole, nurturing her remarkable capacity for revealing likenesses where most see only oppositions. In this vein, Swenson repeatedly bridged the worlds of art and science in her work, an effort she articulates brilliantly in her essay "The Experience of Poetry in a Scientific Age" (1966). For Swenson, keen observation of the world in which we live was a matter of spiritual consequence; hence, her claim as a young adult that "[religion is] not for me. . . . It seems like a redundancy for a poet" (Knudson and Bigelow, p. 34). Baptized into the Mormon Church, she did not practice the religion as an adult.

A gifted storyteller, Swenson was encouraged by her grade school teacher to pursue her talents as a writer. As a student at Logan High School, from which she graduated in 1930, and later at Utah State University, Swenson wrote for the school newspaper, entered various literary competitions, and published poems in *Scribble,* the literary magazine she helped edit. After graduating from college in 1934, she and her cousin Sunny headed east in the summer of 1936. Swenson knew she would never return to Utah for good; like many young writers, she was drawn to New York City, where she held a variety of jobs to support herself.

In 1947 Swenson moved to 23 Perry Street in Greenwich Village, where she lived for nineteen years. Working as a typist for trade publications in the drug industry, she lived frugally, eventually saving enough money to dedicate one full year to writing and publishing her poems, a strategy she refined in coming years. Her breakthrough came in 1949 when James Laughlin selected several of her poems for inclusion in volume 11 of *New Directions in Prose and Poetry.* A few years later, Swenson began working for Laughlin as a manuscript reader at New Directions.

With the 1950s came several milestones for Swenson: in 1950 her lover, Pearl "Blackie" Schwartz, moved into the Perry St. apartment, where she would remain for the next sixteen years; "Snow by Morning," the first of Swenson's fifty-nine poems to appear in the *New Yorker,* was accepted for publication; and on her fortieth birthday, Swenson sold her first book, *Another Animal* (1954), to Charles Scribner's Sons. Swenson's literary debut also included an invitation to Yaddo, the writers' and artists' colony in Saratoga Springs, New York, where she met fellow poet ELIZABETH BISHOP, with whom she shared a close friendship until the latter's death in 1979. Their correspondence is rich with commentary on particular poems, matters of style and craft, and the literary world at large.

In 1960 Swenson quit her job at New Directions. Able to live on the money she earned from a

Guggenheim Foundation Grant and an Amy Lowell Traveling Scholarship, she and Pearl camped throughout France, Spain, and Italy for the year. After the publication of her third book, *To Mix with Time* (1963), Swenson returned to an early interest: playwriting. Funded by a theater associates grant from the Ford Foundation in 1964, she spent the year writing a one-act play, "The Floor," which was given eighteen performances in 1965 and 1966.

Despite Swenson's discomfort in large groups, along with her conviction that the writing of poems cannot be taught, she accepted several short teaching jobs in the years ahead. One such position, writer-in-residence at Purdue University in Indiana in 1966–67, led to her friendship with Rozanne "Zan" Knudson, a fellow faculty member who would become Swenson's most significant life partner. The two women shared a love of poetry, birding, and the outdoors, and soon purchased a house together in Sea Cliff, Long Island, where they lived for almost two decades.

Although Swenson spent her adult life in the East, her poems always remained loyal to their western roots; a wide-eyed love of wild nature, a playful yet plain-spoken diction, and a hearty resistance to staid convention summon repeatedly the adventurous girl who always preferred her chores out-of-doors to those that kept her inside. Big-hearted and open to risk, May Swenson was a pioneer of her craft, a fact attested to by the many major awards she earned in her last decade of life, including the Bollingen Prize (1981), a MacArthur Fellowship (1987), and an honorary doctorate from her alma mater, Utah State University (1987). For all Swenson's professional good fortune throughout the 1980s, however, her life was fraught with failing health. Plagued increasingly by bouts of debilitating asthma, Swenson and Zan Knudson began spending winters away from Long Island, first in Arizona, and then in Los Angeles. Eventually Zan built a house in Ocean View, Delaware, where Swenson died from a heart attack brought on by severe asthma in 1989 at the age of seventy-six.

Bibliography: May Swenson's manuscript materials and the majority of her letters are located in Special Collections, Olin Library, Washington University, St. Louis. Of particular interest are the 268 letters exchanged between Swenson and fellow poet Elizabeth Bishop, fourteen of which (by Swenson) may be found in *Made with Words* (1998), edited by Gardner McFall. See also Kirstin Hotelling Zona, ed., *Dear Elizabeth: Five Poems & Three Letters by May Swenson* (2000). For in-depth discussion of this correspondence, see Zona's *Marianne Moore, Elizabeth Bishop, and May Swenson: The Feminist Poetics of Self-Restraint* (2002); and Richard Howard's essay, "Elizabeth Bishop-May Swenson Correspondence," *Paris Review* 36 (Summer 1994), pp. 171–86. Swenson published twelve volumes of poetry (including one book of translations) in addition to those named above: *A Cage of Spines* (1958); *Poems to Solve* (1966); *Half Sun Half Sleep* (1967); *Iconographs* (1970); *More Poems to Solve* (1971); *The Guess and Spell Coloring Book* (1976); *New and Selected Things Taking Place* (1978); *In Other Words* (1987); *The Love Poems of May Swenson* (1991); *Nature: Poems Old and New* (1994); and *May Out West: Poems of May Swenson* (1996). In addition to her books of poetry, Swenson published short stories, reviews, and essays, the best of which is "The Experience of Poetry in a Scientific Age," in Howard Nemerov, ed., *Poets on Poetry* (1966).

Scholarship on Swenson is steadily growing; one of the most substantive studies of her poetry to date is John Hollander's *The Work of Poetry* (1997). Several excellent interviews with Swenson have also been published, such as "A Conversation with May Swenson" by Lee Hudson, in Hudson, *Literature in Performance* (1983). Additional biographical information on Swenson may be found in Knudson, *The Wonderful Pen of May Swenson* (1993), and Knudson and Suzzanne Bigelow, *May Swenson: A Poet's Life in Photos* (1996). Though his list of secondary sources is somewhat outdated, Kenneth E. Gadomski's *Bibliography of Primary and Secondary Sources* (1986) on Swenson provides a thoroughly comprehensive listing of Swenson's archival holdings and publications. An obituary appeared in the *New York Times* on December 5, 1989.

KIRSTIN HOTELLING ZONA

T

TALLMOUNTAIN, Mary. June 19, 1918–September 2, 1994. Poet, writer, teacher.

Mary TallMountain often described herself as an "Inbetween," and she saw it as her most important work to do justice to being always "between" vastly different cultures, accepting contradictions, and healing through a vision that transcended one-sided worldviews. The life that brought her to honor all that she was is the subject matter of her writing—her childhood in Alaska, her suffering as a displaced person, the hope and beauty she found in Franciscan and native spirituality, the languages that met in her, and her knowledge of poverty, illness, rage, and reconciliation.

Mary TallMountain was born Mary Demoski in

the Koyukon village of Nulato, Alaska, just below the Arctic circle. Her mother, Mary Joe Demoski, Athabascan and Russian, attended the Catholic mission school; her father was Clem Stroupe, an Irish American soldier stationed in Nulato. Her parents lived together because the Catholic Church and the army forbade them to marry.

When Mary was six, her mother became too ill with tuberculosis to look after her children and her father was transferred. Nulato's white missionary doctor and his wife wanted to adopt Mary and her younger brother Billy, but the village council chose only Mary to be sent "Outside." Shortly after, without being able to say good-bye, the child, now called Mary Randle, was taken away. She never saw her mother or brother again. Her mother, to whom she continued to write, died two years later; Billy died of tuberculosis at fourteen. The probability that she herself would have died, had she not been sent away, finally reconciled her to her mother's decision, although only after years of conscious healing.

After her adoption came what Mary called "years of shadow" (TallMountain, *The Light on the Tent Wall,* p. 23). She had been molested by her adoptive father in Nulato, she was forbidden to speak Athabascan, and she was ridiculed by Oregon schoolmates for being Indian. She became so self-destructively wretched that the Randles returned north to the Aleutians, where they lived until she was fourteen. Her adoptive mother, Agnes Randle, a schoolteacher, lightened her misery by continuing to teach her, walking twilight beaches sharing Wordsworth and other writers aloud. Mary published her first story at age ten and began writing a novel, but it was not until 1968, after near death from cancer, that she considered publishing her work again.

During the Depression, the Randles lost everything and became migrant farm workers. Her adoptive father died just after she graduated from high school in 1935. At eighteen, she married Dal Roberts, who died three years later. They had no children. Agnes Randle died in 1944, and, bereft again and alone in the world, Mary left for Reno. There she met jazz musician Reuel Lynch, the love of her life, who reintroduced her to Catholicism. After Lynch also died, she moved to San Francisco, where she worked as a legal secretary and stenographer. In 1959, after studying Catholicism, she became a Franciscan lay worker. Her "Inbetweenness" found expression in the intense mysticism of Franciscan practice, combined with the earth-rooted spirituality of her Athabascan upbringing.

Through the shadow years from age six into her forties, Mary TallMountain carried a silent and self-destructive rage that never left until she stopped "pushing away my roots" (Bruchac, p. 14). Forgetting took the form of secret drinking, contemplation of suicide, and illness—disasters she finally overcame with a conscious choice to live, which her poem "Schizophrenia" graphically displays. She stopped drinking, and for the next several years she found a new freedom running her own stenography business, only to lose health, business, and home to cancer in 1968. She moved to the poorest section of town, the Tenderloin, resumed writing her childhood journals, and began publishing poetry as Mary Randle.

Seeking help with her writing, Mary met writer and teacher Paula Gunn Allen in 1974, and the two became friends. Mary TallMountain had at last found someone who understood the pain of her split between cultures, the desolation of not belonging anywhere—someone who offered support and creative answers. Meeting once a week for a year and a half to read her poems, Mary discovered she could reclaim her roots and heal her own and others' wounds through writing. Simon Scanlon of Friars Press published her first chapbook, *Nine Poems,* in 1977. In 1978 Paula persuaded Mary to return to Nulato, after an absence of fifty-four years; there she found herself both a stranger and rooted in the land. The visit deeply affected her writing.

After confronting cancer again in 1976, Mary found her father, who was in his eighties, by looking up his name in a Phoenix phone book. She cared for him until his death in 1978, reconciling with him and sharing stories. That year, she published a folded broadside, "Good Grease," with New York's Strawberry Press, and began using the name TallMountain (a rough translation of her maternal grandmother's name, Matmiya). She continued to publish prolifically in journals and anthologies, and in 1980 clearly emerged as a Native American literary renaissance writer when *Blue Cloud Quarterly* dedicated an issue to *There Is No Word for Goodbye;* the title poem won a Pushcart Prize in 1981.

But Mary TallMountain was more than a writer: she was deeply involved in healing and teaching. From 1978 on, with a grant from Alaskan poet Geary Hobson, she traveled regularly to Alaska, reading her poetry and teaching in often isolated community centers, schools, and prisons, where she offered Inbetween knowledge to those still being colonized by white culture. In 1987, with Wendy Rose, she was a founding member (and spiritual grandmother) of the Tenderloin Women Writers Workshop, where women from all walks of life shared stories of hardship and joy, helping each other write and publish.

By the time she became ill again in the late 1980s, Mary TallMountain was reading and teaching all over the country. In 1991, she suffered a stroke that left her liable to forget words. Her great humor helped her through this tragedy too. She died in Petaluma, California, in 1994 at age seventy-six. Although much of her writing is scattered in journals and anthologies, her work is known and loved by teachers and students for its earth-centered compassionate heart and spiritual depth, and especially for her refusal to be anything but an Inbetween.

Bibliography: Mary TallMountain's papers, including her complete journals, are at the Elmer D. Rasmuson Library, University of Alaska, Fairbanks. Paula Gunn Allen discusses her work in *The Sacred Hoop* (1986), *Off the Reservation* (1998), and her foreword to TallMountain's *The Light on the Tent Wall: A Bridging* (1990). See also Gabrielle Welford, "Mary TallMountain's Writing: Healing the Heart—Going Home," *Ariel: A Review of International English Literature* 25, no. 1 (January 1994), pp. 136–54, and "Reflections on the Writing of Mary TallMountain: Facing Mirrors," *Studies in American Indian Literatures* 9, no. 2 (Summer 1997), pp. 61–68. A very helpful interview with Joseph Bruchac III, "We Are the In Betweens: An Interview with Mary TallMountain," *Studies in American Indian Literatures* 1 no. 1 (Summer 1989), pp. 13–21, contains her description of herself as an "Inbetween." She is also included in *I Tell You Now: Autobiographical Essays by Native American Writers,* edited by Brian Swann and Arnold Krupat (1987). A 1989 video with Bill Moyers, *Ancestral Voices,* from the series *The Power of the Word* was published as part of *The Language of Life* (1995). There is extensive commentary on her role in the Tenderloin Women Writers Workshop in Carol Heller, *Until We Are Strong Together* (1997). Her published work includes *There Is No Word for Goodbye* (1981), *Green March Moons* (1987), *Continuum* (1988), *The Light on the Tent Wall* (1990), *Matrilineal Cycle* (1990), *A Quick Brush of Wings* (1991), and *Listen to the Night* (1995). Most of her work appeared in anthologies, such as Andrea Lerner, ed., *Dancing on the Rim of the World: An Anthology of Contemporary Northwest Native American Writing* (1990); Duane Niatum, ed., *Harper's Anthology of 20th Century Native American Poetry* (1988); and Geary Hobson, ed., *The Remembered Earth: An Anthology of Contemporary Native American Literature* (1979, 1981). Her work also appeared in journals such a *Calyx, Zyzzyva, Wicazo Sa Review, The Way of St. Francis, Bitterroot,* and *Akwesasne News.* This essay draws on conversations with Mary TallMountain from 1992 and 1993. A complete bibliography and reprints of TallMountain's works are available from the TallMountain Circle/Freedom Voices of San Francisco. An obituary appeared in *Calyx* 15, no. 3 (1994–95), p. 119.

GABRIELLE WELFORD

TALMA, Louise. October 31, 1906–August 13, 1996. Composer, pianist, music instructor.

Louise Juliette Talma was born in Arcachon, France, an only child of American parents, both of whom were professional musicians. Her father, Frederick Talma, a pianist and his wife's opera coach, died when Louise was an infant. Louise was brought up by her mother, Alma Cecile Garrique, an opera singer who was singing in France at the time of her daughter's birth. Louise's mother gave up her career to nurture her daughter's musical aspirations. In the summer of 1914, the two moved to New York City, where Louise graduated from Wadleigh High School in 1922, after earning a Greek Prize and the John G. Wright Scholarship for the best academic record. In 1931 she received a Bachelor of Music degree from New York University while simultaneously attending the Institute of Musical Arts (the present-day Juilliard School of Music), studying music theory with George Wedge, ear-training with Helen Whileyand and Franklin Robinson, counterpoint with Percy Goetschius, and composition with Howard Brockway. In 1933 she received an MA from Columbia University.

Perhaps her more significant training, however, was at the Fontainebleau School of Music in France, where starting in 1926 she studied piano with Isadore Philipp. While in France her interests broadened to include composing, and in 1928 she spent the first of many summers studying composition with Nadia Boulanger, who remained a close friend and colleague for years. Through her friendship with Boulanger, Talma became the first American to teach at Fontainebleau. Boulanger's admiration of Stravinsky exerted a strong influence on Talma's early compositional style. It was Boulanger's profound religious faith, however, that exerted the greatest influence on Talma. After being raised a Protestant, and then embracing atheism, Louise converted to Catholicism in 1934, with Boulanger assuming the role of godmother. Religion soon became the basis of Talma's life and work.

Talma's output of finely written yet technically demanding compositions comprises more than forty major works, the greatest portion of which are vocal compositions based almost entirely upon sacred or spiritual texts, but also including four orchestral pieces and a full-scale, three-act opera, *The Alcestiad* (1955–59), first performed at the Frankfurt Opera House in 1962 with a libretto by her close friend Thornton Wilder. Her compositions have been performed by the Baltimore, Milwaukee, and NBC symphonies, and the Buffalo and Los Angeles philharmonics, among others. Widely acclaimed for her work in music, she was honored with two Guggenheim Fellowships (1946, 1947), a Fulbright Grant (1955), two grants from the National Endowment for the Arts (1966, 1975), as well as election to the National Academy of Arts and Letters (1974). In 1963 she became the first American woman to receive the Sibelius Medal for composition. For fifty-one years starting in 1928, Talma taught music theory and musicianship at Hunter College in New York City. She was promoted to full professor in 1952, professor emeritus in 1976, and visiting distinguished professor from 1976 to 1979.

Talma's compositional output divides into three major periods: "neo-classical" (1939–53), serial neo-tonality (1954–72), and non-serial atonality (1973–96). Her music is motivic but nondevelopmental; her works are predominantly polyphonic, sparsely textured compositions that make extensive use of counterpoint. Imitation is a common technique in almost all her choral and early instrumental compositions, though not as common in her later instrumental works.

First-period neo-classical works, among which are *Four-Handed Fun* (1939), *The Piano Sonata no. 1* (1943), *Toccata for Orchestra* (1944), and *Alleluia in the Form of Toccata* (1945), reveal the influence of Stravinsky's forceful rhythms. Melodies in the first-period compositions are short, and generally stepwise or triadic in nature, intertwined with a strong rhythmic motive, the latter often emerging as the more prominent aspect. Tonality in Talma's first period does not follow the lines of traditional tonal linearity. *Pastoral Prelude* for piano (1949) is just one of many compositions employing tonal centricity, in which certain pitches assume greater importance over others, and serve as tone centers for the composition in part, or as a whole.

The *String Quartet* (1954) was Talma's passage into serial composition and her second style period. Talma did not relinquish tonality with the adoption of serial technique but incorporated it into the row. In the *String Quartet* and *Six Etudes* for piano (1954), the twelve-tone row is arranged into tonally related subsets that Talma employs to emphasize tonal elements. Some works—*Six Etudes* and *Three Duologues* for clarinet and piano (1968)—are strictly serial; others—*Piano Sonata no. 2* (1955) and *Sonata for Violin and Piano* (1962)—are more loosely assembled, with the twelve-tone row acting merely as a source of motivic and intervallic construction.

Talma's third-period instrumental compositions are athematic and atonal, though the vocal works continue to maintain their connection with tonality—for example, *Thirteen Ways of Looking at a Blackbird* (1979) and *Infanta Marina* (1990). *Summer Sounds* for clarinet and string quartet (1973) contains a twelve-tone row that Talma uses as a source of motives and intervals. Talma abandons the row in the later third-period works, such as *The Ambient Air* for flute, violin, cello, and piano (1983). A tonally structured twelve-tone row appears again, however, in *Seven Episodes* for flute, viola and piano, which although written in 1986–87, embodies the stylistic traits of the second period.

Talma was a deeply spiritual woman with a strong religious faith reflected in her numerous settings of sacred texts. She was not attracted to the feminist movement and preferred to be considered a composer, rather than a female composer. She never married. Talma was well known in the New York City composers' circle and was good friends with MIRIAM GIDEON, who lived in the same apartment building. Strongly devoted to her roles as teacher and composer, Talma consequently spent less time promoting her own works, which resulted in her often not hearing her compositions until many years after they were written. She spent much time composing at various artist colonies and was working on a song cycle with chamber accompaniment at Yaddo in Saratoga Springs, New York, when she died in 1996 at the age of eighty-nine. In her will, she bequeathed close to $1.3 million, as well as the royalties from her music, to the MacDowell Colony, another artist colony she strongly believed in and loved.

Bibliography: Luann Dragone, "Structural Consistency amidst Stylistic Diversity in the Music of Talma" (PhD dissertation, CUNY Graduate School, 2003), analyzes six major works (two from each period) and compares them to other works of that period. Susan Teicher, "The Solo Works for Piano of Louise Talma" (PhD dissertation, Peabody Institute of Johns Hopkins University, 1983), discusses Talma's piano compositions up to and including *Textures* (1977). Christine Ammer, *Unsung: A History of Women in American Music* (1980), gives an overall summary of Talma's compositions up until 1973. Jane Weiner LePage, *Women Composers, Conductors and Musicians of the Twentieth Century* (1980), provides biographical information as well as a good picture of Talma. An obituary appeared in the *New York Times* on August 15, 1996.

LUANN REGINA DRAGONE

TANDY, Jessica. June 7, 1909–September 11, 1994. Actress.

Jessie Alice Tandy was born in London, the youngest of three children of Jessie Helen Horspool, the headmistress of a school for children with mental retardation, and Harry Tandy, who worked for a rope manufacturing firm. Her father died when she was twelve, and her mother took on clerical jobs and adult classes to supplement the family income. Tandy attended Dame Alice Owen's girls' school in London, but bouts with tuberculosis (from which she eventually recovered) kept her at home much of the time.

She began to take classes in Shakespeare, and soon began drama classes on weekends. In 1924 she entered the Ben Greet Academy of Acting, and three years later, at the age of eighteen, made her professional acting debut in *The Manderson Girls*, a tiny workshop production. This role was followed by an engagement with the Birmingham Repertory Theatre. In 1929 she made her West End debut in *The Rumour* by C. K. Munro and from then on worked steadily on the London stage. In 1930, she made a brief trip to the United States, where she made her Broadway debut in *The Matriarch.* In New York, Lee Shubert, the powerful theatrical impresario, convinced her to change her name professionally to Jessica.

Tandy returned to London, and to the London stage. In 1932 she won acclaim as schoolgirl Manuela in Christa Winsloe's *Children in Uniform.* That same year, she married actor Jack Hawkins; in 1934 their daughter, Susan Phillida, was born. From 1934 to 1938 she appeared in a number of important London productions, playing Ophelia in John Gielgud's production of *Hamlet,* and later Cordelia in his production of *King Lear.* She also appeared with Laurence Olivier in *Henry V* and played the role of Viola in Tyrone Guthrie's production of *Twelfth Night.*

In 1940, Tandy moved to New York with her six-year-old daughter, hoping to find work on Broadway and in Hollywood. While appearing in a production of *Jupiter Laughs* by A. J. Cronin, she met a young Canadian actor, Hume Cronyn. She divorced Hawkins in 1942 and married Cronyn the same year. Shortly after that, the couple moved to Hollywood, where their son, Christopher, was born in 1943, followed by daughter Tandy in 1945. Hume Cronyn worked fairly steadily in films and had a contract with MGM, and Jessica Tandy soon secured a contract with Twentieth Century Fox. Her early films included *The Seventh Cross* (1944) with Spencer Tracy and *Forever Amber* (1947), but she found her film roles unsatisfying and was eager to get back to the theater.

In 1946, Cronyn cast his wife in a studio production of *Portrait of a Madonna* by Tennessee Williams, which turned out to be a major turning point in her professional life. Knowing that Williams and director Elia Kazan were looking for an actress to play Blanche in Williams's new play *A Streetcar Named Desire,* Cronyn urged them to come and see the production. Williams recalled later, "It was instantly apparent to me that Jessica was Blanche." The 1947 Broadway production of *A Streetcar Named Desire,* with Jessica Tandy and Marlon Brando, became one of the landmark productions in the history of American theater. Tandy stayed with the role for two years, winning the Tony Award for Best Actress. Not only did the play become an instant classic, but the acting in the production became a model for young American actors. (Tandy herself became an American citizen in 1954.) She was passed over, however, for the film version of the play, when the studio insisted on having a film star and gave the part to Vivien Leigh. Still, *Streetcar* had established Tandy as a formidable talent.

She and Cronyn soon began to act together on the stage. Their success in the two-character *The Fourposter* (1951) encouraged critics to liken them to LYNN FONTANNE and Alfred Lunt, a comparison that delighted them. Although they still continued to make films, Tandy and Cronyn committed themselves primarily to theater in the 1950s and 1960s. They helped launch Tyrone Guthrie's first season in the regional theater in Minneapolis, and Tandy performed as well in other regional theaters around the country. But she remained a major Broadway star, appearing in the classics as well as in new work, including *A Delicate Balance* by Edward Albee. She also appeared in Alfred Hitchcock's film *The Birds* in 1963.

The 1970s and 1980s were an especially productive time for Tandy and Cronyn. In 1972, they traveled to Paris with director Alan Schneider to meet with Samuel Beckett and to propose a Beckett Festival at Lincoln Center. Later in such Beckett plays as *Not I* and *Happy Days,* Tandy established herself as a master of that playwright's work. Tandy starred as well in many new Broadway plays in these years, notably *The Gin Game* (with Cronyn), which won the Pulitzer Prize and for which Tandy again won a Tony Award (1978), and *Foxfire* (1982), written by Cronyn and Susan Cooper, for which Tandy won her third Tony. She won an Emmy in 1988 for her performance in the television version of the play. In 1983, she played Amanda in an important revival of Tennessee Williams's *The Glass Menagerie.* Both *The Gin Game* and *Foxfire* had begun in regional theaters and demonstrated the growing importance of such theaters in the development of new plays.

From the 1970s through the early 1990s, Tandy remained much in demand as an actress. Her film appearances included *The World According to Garp* (1982), *Cocoon* (1985), and *Batteries Not Included* (1987). In 1989 Tandy starred in the film *Driving Miss Daisy* with Morgan Freeman, for which she won an Oscar as Best Actress. The film, which also won an Oscar as Best Picture, was a much-heralded example of the success of the independent film movement. Indeed, Tandy may have had her greatest influence as she grew older with her portrayals of aging in America as a dynamic and vital process. Films such as *Cocoon* and *Driving Miss Daisy* became successful anomalies in a youth-driven cultural scene.

Tandy continued acting into the 1990s. Shortly before her death, she completed three films, including *Nobody's Fool,* starring Paul Newman. She died at her home in Easton, Connecticut, on September 11, 1994, of ovarian cancer, after one of the most enduringly successful careers in the history of American stage.

Bibliography: There is no biography of Jessica Tandy and no available collection of her papers, but Hume Cronyn's autobiography, *A Terrible Liar* (1991), contains an account of their life together. Milly S. Barranger, *Jessica Tandy: A Bio-Bibliography* (1991), contains a list of her theatrical and film appearances through 1990 and a bibliography of theatrical books and articles in which she is mentioned. The *New York Times* obituary from September 12, 1994, which includes the quotation from Tennessee Williams, provides an extensive account of her life and career.

EVANGELINE MORPHOS

TAUSSIG, Helen Brooke. May 24, 1898–May 20, 1986. Pediatrician, cardiologist.

Helen Brooke Taussig, who is known as the founder of pediatric cardiology for her innovative work on blue baby syndrome, was born in Cambridge, Massachusetts, the youngest of four children of Edith Guild and Frank William Taussig. Her father was the Henry Lee Professor of Economics at Harvard University and a co-founder of the Harvard School of Business Administration. When Helen Taussig was eleven years old, her mother died of tuberculosis, and Frank Taussig became her strongest influence. Although the young Taussig was inspired by the intellectual climate of Harvard's college community, she struggled at school because she suffered from undiagnosed dyslexia (the condition was unknown at the time). Her work gradually improved and, on completing high school at Cambridge School for Girls in 1917, she was admitted to Radcliffe College, where her mother was an early graduate. After two years of study, she transferred to the University of California at Berkeley to enjoy a year of independence away from home. She decided to stay and complete her BA degree there, graduating in 1921.

When Taussig returned to Massachusetts, she told her father that she wanted to become a physician. He recommended public health as a more suitable career for a woman, and suggested she enroll at Harvard University's new School of Public Health. Although women were accepted as students, they were not permitted to earn degrees. When Taussig asked the dean why any woman would study under such an unfair system, he said he hoped that none would. "I'll not be the first to disappoint you," she replied. Having proven to her father that public health was no more welcoming to women than medicine, she gained his support to go to medical school. After a brief trip to Europe with the family and two courses at Harvard, Taussig moved to Boston University, where she could earn credits toward a degree. In 1924 she enrolled at Johns Hopkins University School of Medicine; she graduated with her MD in 1927.

In 1928, Taussig began her internship in the pediatric department of Johns Hopkins Hospital, where Edwards A. Park had been appointed chief. She worked at the new Cardiac Clinic of the Harriet Lane Home, established by Park, and in 1930 he appointed her physician-in-charge, a position she would hold until 1963. Taussig began to specialize in babies with birth defects of the heart, in part because other physicians were not very interested in these apparently hopeless cases.

Taussig had lost her hearing after suffering from whooping cough as an intern, but she learned to feel with her fingers the heart murmurs caused by various defects. She became interested in a congenital heart condition that causes blue baby syndrome, or anoxemia, in which the patient's blood has insufficient oxygen. Using a new X-ray technique, fluoroscopy, to confirm her diagnoses, Taussig established the cause of the syndrome. She found that the birth defect creates an underdeveloped artery leading from the heart to the lungs and may also produce a leaking septum (the wall separating the chambers of the heart).

Taussig became convinced that it should be possible to correct this condition surgically. She spoke to Alfred A. Blalock, the eminent thoracic surgeon newly arrived at Johns Hopkins Hospital, about developing surgical methods for improving the flow of blood to the lungs. Vivien Thomas, Blalock's extraordinarily talented African American technician, perfected the surgical technique by conducting more than two hundred experimental procedures on dogs. Thomas and Blalock took two years to develop the techniques before performing their first operation on a child with anoxemia on November 29, 1944. The child, who had only been able to live in an oxygen tent, was able to go home for Christmas. After repeating the successful treatment on two more patients, Blalock and Taussig published their results in the *Journal of the American Medical Association.* The technique was named the Blalock-Taussig operation, and was used worldwide to prolong and improve the lives of children. The procedure is also considered an important step in the later development of open-heart surgery for adults.

Taussig continued her research on cardiac birth defects and, as founder of the new field of pediatric cardiology, trained many others to diagnose the condition and perform the blue baby operation. She documented her extensive experience with heart conditions from her work in the cardiac clinic, and in 1947 published her comprehensive guide, *Congenital Malformations of the Heart.* She also taught at Johns Hopkins School of Medicine, becoming an associate professor of pediatrics in 1946 and finally a full professor in 1959, the first woman to hold that rank at the university.

In 1962 Taussig traveled to Germany to investigate the role of thalidomide in a wave of birth defects appearing there and in the United Kingdom. Sold as a sleeping tablet since 1958, the drug was suspected of causing extensive malformations of the fetus when used during pregnancy. Taussig reported her findings to the American College of Physicians and the American Pediatric Society, and wrote a series of editorials requesting that the Food and Drug Administration (FDA) deny approval for thalidomide's use in the United States. Her findings and the concern she generated helped Frances O. Kelsey, medical officer at the FDA, institute her requested ban on the drug. In 1964, Taussig received the Presidential Medal of Freedom for preventing a potential tragedy and in recognition of her contributions to medicine. In 1954 she had received the Albert Lasker Award for her work on the blue baby operation, and in 1965 she became president of the American Heart Association, the first woman to hold that post.

Although Taussig formally retired from Johns Hopkins University in 1963, nearly half of her most important works were published after this point. She was researching cardiac defects in birds at the University of Delaware when she was killed in a car accident near her retirement home in Kennett Square, Pennsylvania, in 1986, just days before her eighty-eighth birthday. Taussig never married but she was a beloved member of a large extended family of patients and colleagues, who dedicated the Helen B. Taussig Children's Heart Center at Johns Hopkins Hospital to her in 1970.

Bibliography: Taussig's personal papers, including correspondence, personal photograph albums, research materials concerning patients and their long-term follow-up results, and certificates, medals, and awards, are kept at the Alan Mason Chesney Medical Archives of Johns Hopkins University. The first published description of the 1944 operation appears in Alfred Blalock and Helen Brooke Taussig, "The Surgical Treatment of Malformations of the Heart in Which There Is Pulmonary Stenosis or Pulmonary Atresia," *Journal of the American Medical Association* 128, no. 3 (May 19, 1945), pp. 189–202. For Taussig's own account of the development of the operation and her later career, see the oral history "Helen Brooke Taussig, M.D. Interviewed by Charles A. Janeway, M.D.," Schlesinger Library, Radcliffe Institute for Advanced Study, Harvard University; and W. P. Harvey, "A Conversation with Helen Taussig," *Medical Times* 106 (November 1978), pp. 28–44. For Taussig's analysis of the thalidomide tragedy, see "Dangerous Tranquility," *Science*, May 25, 1962, p. 683, and "The Thalidomide Syndrome," *Scientific American*, August 1962, pp. 22, 29–35. Biographical material, including an extensive bibliography, is available in Dan G. McNamara, James A. Manning, Mary Allen Engle, Ruth Whittemore, Catherine A. Neill, and Charlotte Ferencz, "Helen Brooke Taussig: 1898 to 1986," *Journal of the American College of Cardiology* 10, no. 3 (March 1987), pp. 662–71. Useful tributes include A. McGehee Harvey, "Helen Brooke Taussig," and Mary Allen Engle, "Dr. Helen B. Taussig, the Tetralogy of Fallot, and the Growth of Pediatric Cardiac Services in the United States," both in *Johns Hopkins Medical Journal* 140 (April 1977), pp. 137–41 and 147–50. See also Joyce Baldwin, *To Heal the Heart of a Child: Helen Taussig, M.D.* (1992), a biography for young readers, and the chapter on Taussig in Sherwin B. Nuland's *Doctors: The Biography of Medicine* (1988). An obituary appeared in the *New York Times* on May 22, 1986.

MANON S. PARRY AND ELIZABETH FEE

TAUSSKY-TODD, Olga. August 30, 1906–October 7, 1995. Mathematician.

Olga Taussky-Todd, a mathematician noted for her work in number theory and for helping to make matrix theory better known, was born in Olmutz (later Olomouc in Czechoslovakia), then part of the Austro-Hungarian Empire. Olga was the second of three daughters born to Ida Pollach and Julius David Taussky; all three sisters pursued careers in science. In 1909 the family moved to Vienna, Austria, and later to Linz. Her father, a self-educated man, was by profession an industrial chemist. Her mother was a housewife who cared for home and family with warmth and affection while her husband often was on trips outside the country as a consultant. It may be that Olga's parents' harmonious marriage was a model for her own.

In elementary school Olga did well in grammar and essay writing. At the age of fourteen she entered the Mittelschule in Linz, followed by the Gymnasium Koernerschule (for girls only) a year later. She used her writing ability for both prose and poetry while her father, who managed a vinegar factory, posed mathematics problems to her related to his job, such as arranging all his magazines in chronological order or figuring out the formula to maintain a particular level of acidity in vinegar. Her father's encouragement of her mathematical interests influenced her choice of career.

During her last year in the Gymnasium her father died. Despite uncertain family finances, Olga was still able to enroll at the University of Vienna, where she initially majored in chemistry but succumbed to mathematics when she took a course in number theory from her adviser, famous German theorist Philip Furtwanger. In 1930 she received her doctorate for a thesis in number theory, which was published two years later. Her record at Vienna led the esteemed mathematician Richard Courant to recommend her for a job in Göttingen as editor of David Hilbert's collected works on number theory. Warned not to return to Göttingen after 1932 because of the German political situation (Taussky's family was Jewish), Olga returned to Vienna and then spent the academic year 1934–35 on a fellowship at Bryn Mawr, where she worked with noted mathematics professor Emmy Noether, one of the few senior women in the field at the time, and a woman whose strong personality intimidated Olga at times. A high point at Bryn Mawr was accompanying Noether on her weekly trip to lecture at Princeton.

In 1935 Olga began a Yarrow Fellowship at Girton College, a women's college at Cambridge University. She next took a teaching position at the University of London, where at an intercollegiate seminar she met John (Jack) Todd, an Irish-born mathematician who was teaching at another London college. He nurtured the relationship by posing a mathematics problem for her to solve, and they were married in London on September 29, 1938. Not only did the Todds share cultural interests like concerts and hiking, but they shared a love of mathematics. Throughout their fifty-seven years of married life, they worked in separate offices near one another, working on mathematics, sometimes in collaboration, sometimes individually. They had no children.

The outbreak of war in Europe in 1939 dramatically affected the recently married couple, who moved eighteen times during World War II, including a stint in Belfast. When they relocated to London, Olga did research using differential equations for the British Ministry of Aircraft Production. This was her introduction to matrix theory (essential to understanding wing flutter in airplanes), which became her major focus for the rest of her career. In 1947 the couple took a yearlong position at the National Bureau of Standards in Los Angeles, their first introduction to the state that would be their home for almost four decades. After returning briefly to a still-devastated London, they emigrated permanently to the United States, where they worked for the National Bureau of Standards in Washington, D.C., from 1949 until 1957. As analyst, Jack had the official job of figuring out how to use then-new high-speed computers for problem solving. Olga's title was consultant in mathematics.

In 1957, when the California Institute of Technology invited both of them back to academic life, they accepted the offer. Jack had a full professorship, and she had a position as a researcher, there being no historical precedent for women on the faculty at Caltech. Olga gave graduate seminars and directed doctoral students. In 1963 she became the first woman to gain tenure at Caltech, and in 1971 she was named a full professor; it was a moment of great satisfaction for her. Over the course of her career, Taussky-Todd authored more than two hundred scientific papers and served as an editor for four mathematical journals. She was a member-at-large of the Council of the American Mathematical Society and also served on the Committee on Tables of the National Academy of Sciences. Reaching mandatory retirement in 1971, she continued to advise students and play an active role in the Caltech community.

Among colleagues Olga Taussky-Todd was equally noted for her devotion to mathematics and her kindness and generosity to young mathematicians. A superb teacher and mentor, she insisted on meeting with her graduate students once a week, whether or not they had any progress to report. She and Jack loved to travel and enjoyed opening their home to visiting mathematicians, young and old, male and female. To celebrate a special publication or presentation, Jack made a practice of bringing her a gift, perhaps silver Jefferson cups or beautiful amber jewelry. The couple also generously endowed a number of visiting professorships and lectures at Caltech in recognition of the institution's importance to both their careers. Professionally active into her eighties, Olga Taussky-Todd died of complications from a broken hip at her home in Pasadena at the age of eighty-nine.

Bibliography: Olga Taussky-Todd wrote a memoir at the request of the Oral History Project of the California Institute of Technology Archives, portions of which were published as "An Autobiographical Essay" in Donald J. Albers and G. L. Alexanderson, eds., *Mathematical People: Profiles and Interviews* (1985). The Caltech Archives also contain some of Olga's letters, a copy of her dissertation, various photographs, and other personal items. Correspondence between the Todds and Mary Ann McLoughlin is found at the College of Saint Rose, Albany, New York. Transcripts of interviews with the Todds, their colleagues, and friends by Mary Ann McLoughlin, as well as photographs and other archival materials, are also deposited there. Secondary sources include Edith H. Luchins, "Olga Taussky-Todd" in Louise S. Grinstein and Paul J. Campbell, eds., *Women of Mathematics: A Biobibliographic Sourcebook* (1987); and Luchins and McLoughlin, "In Memoriam: Olga Taussky-Todd," *Notices of the American Mathematical Society* 43, no. 8 (August 1996), pp. 838–47. See also Mary Ann McLoughlin, "Olga Taussky-Todd: Grande Dame of Mathematics" (PhD dissertation, Rensselaer Polytechnic Institute, 1996), which discusses her contributions to the field of mathematics and contains a full bibliography of her scholarly publications. An obituary appeared in the *Los Angeles Times* on December 3, 1995.

MARY ANN MCLOUGHLIN

TE ATA. December 3, 1895–October 26, 1995. American Indian folklorist and performance artist.

Despite solemn promises to the contrary, the United States forced the Chickasaws twice in less than a century to relinquish their tribal domain to land-hungry Americans. The Chickasaws left their southeastern homelands beginning in 1837 for Indian Territory. In 1893, Congress established the Dawes Commission to negotiate for the termination of all land titles, specifically with the so-called Five Civilized Tribes (Chickasaw, Choctaw, Creek, Seminole, and Cherokee). The Chickasaws refused even to meet with the commissioners, so Congress authorized the commission to begin surveying the land and preparing tribal rolls for land allotments. At this transition toward what the U.S. government hoped would be tribal extinction, Te Ata was born on December 3, 1895.

Christened Mary Frances Thompson, she was born in the family's home in Emet, Oklahoma. Mary was an enrolled Chickasaw but with Choctaw lineage as well. She attended a tribal boarding school before the family moved to the nation's capital of Tishomingo. Mary was the second child of eight born to Alberta Freund and Thomas Benjamin Thompson. She had an older half-sister born to Thomas and his first wife, Belle Gardner. Six of the children lived to adulthood.

Mary's mother, called Bertie, was mainly of German extraction; though she was not educated beyond the fourth grade, she was a tireless worker and an unconditional Christian. Mary's father, Thomas, a mixed-blood Chickasaw, dropped out of high school a year before graduating to go to work; later he acquired a general store. He grew up speaking Chickasaw but would not teach his children the language, thinking it would be a handicap for them in mainstream American culture. But he was proud of his tribe and served as its last treasurer before the tribal government ceased functioning in 1907. Fortunately, he passed along to his children a few Chickasaw and Choctaw stories that had survived the cultural upheaval of the past century.

As a youngster, Mary learned the stories and acted them out for her family. From this very modest beginning culturally, she became the preeminent interpreter and performer of Indian folklore of the twentieth century. This resulted from a combination of talent, creativity, inquisitiveness, passion, and some critical influences on her life and career. When she was about seven, her aunt Mary Harkins gave her the name Te Ata, which the little girl understood to mean "bearer of the dawn." One of her Tishomingo high school teachers, Muriel Wright, encouraged her to expand her base of Indian stories. Wright was a Choctaw scholar and the longtime editor of the history periodical *The Chronicles of Oklahoma,* and she became Mary's early role model.

At Oklahoma College for Women from 1915 to 1919, Te Ata was introduced to the theater by Frances Davis, who refined her talent and contributed to the knowledge and poise she would need to launch a career. Davis also sent her protégée off to Carnegie Institute of Technology for graduate training and encouraged her to get experience performing on the Chautauqua circuits, which she did from 1919 through 1922. There Te Ata developed the ambition and grit needed to overcome her shyness and to challenge the social mores holding that a woman's proper place was in the home. Traveling about America, Te Ata visited Indian communities and began building a repertoire of Indian stories that she would continuously expand and adapt as a performance artist for a variety of audiences.

She moved to New York City in 1922 and began presenting artistic programs of American Indian folklore. She was five feet seven, slender, beautiful. At times she accompanied herself by shaking a gourd rattle or beating a drum. Wearing traditional Indian clothing (usually deerskin), she performed with an economy of movement and always with grace and fluidity. In her programs, she assumed widely disparate roles, ranging from a bumptious young brave to an old woman at the end of her trail.

She caught the attention of several prominent people who helped promote her career because they believed she was an exceptional artist. One sent her to London to entertain there. Another, ELEANOR ROOSEVELT, intermittently through the 1920s invited Te Ata to entertain guests at her Greenwich Village apartment and the New York governor's mansion. She had Te Ata entertain at the White House in 1933 at the Roosevelts' first state dinner, and at the Roosevelts' 1939 Hyde Park picnic honoring the king and queen of England.

Another who befriended her and encouraged her career in the early 1930s was Dr. Clyde Fisher, an eclectic scientist with the American Museum of Natural History and founding director of the museum's Hayden Planetarium. In 1933 they were married at Bacone Indian College in Muskogee, Oklahoma. Te Ata and Clyde, a striking and compelling couple, were recognized as part of New York's intellectual and cultural elite throughout their marriage, which ended with Clyde's death from heart disease in 1949. They had no children.

Te Ata's career took her all over America, from great stages to school auditoriums to Indian reservations. But irrespective of venue or degree of sophistication of the audience, Te Ata never compromised her integrity or her material. Her mission was to entertain and educate, enlighten and inspire, and she willingly accepted this honor and responsibility from the 1920s through the late 1970s, a period when the dominant white society was relatively unreceptive to minorities. Over her career's last twenty years, she helped bring about the modern era of tribal self-determination, not politically but by presenting the ageless beauty and wisdom of tribal folklore to successive generations of Americans, thousands of whom were positively and permanently influenced by her.

She lived her last years in Oklahoma, where she was named to the Chickasaw National Hall of Fame and the Oklahoma Hall of Fame. In 1987, she was named Oklahoma's first official State Treasure. Te Ata died in Oklahoma City on October 26, 1995, just short of her hundredth birthday. According to her instructions, she was cremated and her ashes were scattered with wildflower seeds along Pennington Creek in Tishomingo.

Bibliography: The only published account of Te Ata's life is Richard Green, *Te Ata, Chickasaw Storyteller, American Treasure* (2002). In addition to hundreds of newspaper clippings covering her career from the 1920s through the 1970s, the book draws on interviews with her few surviving contemporaries, family members, and several Chickasaw tribal members. Te Ata's private papers are still held by the family, although a small amount of material was donated to the University of Oklahoma Western History Collections. There is also material at the Chickasaw Council House Museum in Tishomingo, Oklahoma. Another important source of information is an unpublished memoir by Te Ata with Jane Werner Watson. An obituary appeared in the *Daily Oklahoman* on October 28, 1995.

RICHARD GREEN

TENAYUCA, Emma. December 21, 1916–July 23, 1999. Labor and civil rights activist.

Mexican American activist Emma Tenayuca gained national distinction during the 1930s as an organizer for labor and civil rights and as an intellectual within the Communist Party. Born in the Westside area of San Antonio, Texas, she was descended on her mother's side from Spanish settlers and on her father's from Native Americans. One of eleven children, Tenayuca was raised by her maternal grandparents in a devout Catholic household, where her grandfather exposed her at a young age to a range of ideas as well as to the everyday experiences of the Mexican worker.

Tenayuca's first labor-organizing experience was in 1933 at age sixteen. During the Finck Cigar Company strike she joined the picket lines with the women strikers and was jailed. During that strike, she met Mrs. W. H. Ernst, with whom she later organized San Antonio chapters of the Communist-affiliated Workers' Alliance of America. In the meantime Tenayuca graduated from Brackenridge High School in 1934 and obtained a job as an elevator operator in downtown San Antonio. In 1934 and 1935 she helped organize garment workers at the Dorothy Frocks Company as well as helped organize two branches of the International Ladies' Garment Workers' Union in San Antonio against some of the region's most powerful financial interests.

In 1935, as secretary of the Westside Unemployed Council, Tenayuca held mass meetings to protest the elimination of Mexican families from the city's relief roles. The next year, she set up additional chapters of the Workers' Alliance; with a membership of more than three thousand, it was one of the strongest in the country. In 1937, she became general secretary for the ten chapters of the Workers' Alliance of America in San Antonio and was appointed to the National Executive Committee of the Workers' Alliance of America. During this time, the group staged protests against relief conditions and the beatings of Mexican immigrants by agents of the U.S. Border Patrol. Tenayuca also fought for a minimum wage, the right to strike, and equal rights for Mexican-born workers, and against arbitrary deportations. In 1937, the year she joined the Communist Party, Emma Tenayuca married Homer Brooks, a prominent figure in the Texas Communist Party. They had no children.

On January 31, 1938, Tenayuca led more than ten thousand pecan shellers in a strike, the largest in San Antonio history and the largest community-based strike by Mexican Americans in the 1930s. The police arrested her and several organizers from the United Cannery, Agricultural, Packing and Allied Workers of America (UCAPAWA) on charges of communist agitation. Upon her release, she resumed her strike work despite repeated threats on her life. By then the CIO had taken an interest in the strike, but only if Tenayuca did not participate further in strike activities. Too much attention had been focused on her open ties to communism. The Texas Industrial Commission began public hearings of the strikers' grievances, but the strike gains eroded within a few months when the pecan industry mechanized.

In 1938, the Texas Communist Party nominated Emma Tenayuca as its candidate for the U.S. Congress from San Antonio, and the next year she was elected chair of the Texas Communist Party. Her article on Mexicans and the question of nationalism, "The Mexican Question in the Southwest," co-authored with her husband, was published in *The Communist* in March 1939. The Tenayuca-Brooks article marked the first political essay written by a Mexican American that argued for the rights and status of Mexicans in the United States. Written at the height of the pecan strike, Tenayuca's piece expanded upon Marxist theories of nationalism, liberation, and citizenship. The "Mexican Question" was originally a national Anglo query into the rights, lands, and status of Mexicans that became significant with the signing of the Treaty of Guadalupe Hidalgo in 1848, which is the historical point with which Tenayuca began her essay. Tenayuca argued that the Mexicans of the Southwest do not constitute a separate nation but are inextricably connected not only to each other by race and land, but also to Anglo-Americans. Further, Tenayuca argued that, with the emergence of Mexicans in civic culture, Mexican Americans are central to modern notions of American capitalism and democracy.

On August 25, 1939, the Texas Communist Party was ousted from its state convention at the Municipal Auditorium in San Antonio when approximately five thousand rioters stormed into the auditorium throwing rocks and bricks. Tenayuca escaped safely, but she was singled out for death threats long after the riot. Her remaining credibility as a community organizer was destroyed by the announcement that the Soviet Union and Nazi Germany had signed a non-aggression pact ushering in the German invasion of Poland and the start of World War II. In 1939 Emma Tenayuca divorced Homer Brooks.

Ostracized after the Municipal Auditorium riot and blacklisted for her affiliation with the Communist Party, Emma Tenayuca was unable to find work in San Antonio. She worked briefly as a secretary and bookkeeper for a garment manufacturer before moving to Houston and then San Francisco. During World War II she tried to enlist in the Women's Army Corps, but her application was rejected, most likely because of her involvement in the Communist Party. Tenayuca spent the war years in San Francisco. In 1952 she graduated magna cum laude from San Francisco State College, where she obtained teacher certification. She also gave birth to a son, Frank. Tenayuca returned to San Antonio and taught reading in the local elementary schools of the Harlandale school district for many years, earning a master's degree in education from Our Lady of the Lake University in 1974. She retired from teaching in 1982. Following a long illness, Emma Tenayuca died in San Antonio on July 23, 1999, at the age of eighty-two.

Bibliography: There is no biography of Emma Tenayuca, but information about her Texas organizing can be found in Zaragosa Vargas, "Tejana Radical: Emma Tenayuca and the San Antonio Labor Movement during the Great Depression," *Pacific Historical Review* 66 (November 1997), pp. 553–80; David Lewis Filewood, "Tejano Revolt: The Significance of the 1938 Pecan Shellers Strike" (master's thesis, University of Texas, Arlington, 1994); Victor Nelson-Cisneros, "UCAPAWA Organizing Activities in Texas, 1930–1950," *Aztlán* 9 (Spring–Fall 1978), pp. 71–84; and Raúl Ramos, "Así Fue: La Huelga de los Nueceros de San Antonio, Texas, Febrero 1938" (senior thesis, Princeton University, 1989). See also Julia Kirk Blackwelder, *Women of the Depression: Caste and Culture in San Antonio, 1929–1939* (1984); Roberto Calderón and Emilio Zamora, *Chicana Voices: Intersections of Race, Class, and Gender* (1986); and Mario T. García, *Mexican Americans: Leadership, Ideology, and Identity, 1930–1960* (1989).

ZARAGOSA VARGAS

THADEN, Louise. November 12, 1905–November 9, 1979. Aviator.

Iris Louise McPhetridge, whose career in aviation as Louise Thaden was marked by numerous "firsts" for women, was born in the small northwest Arkansas town of Bentonville, the older of two children of farmers Edna Hobbs and Roy Fry McPhetridge. Although she indicated in her autobiography, *High, Wide and Frightened* (1938), that "from the time when I was seven and jumped off the barn under an oversized umbrella, I've wanted to fly" (p. 21), she was over twenty before she got the opportunity to fly. After graduating from Bentonville High School, she enrolled at the University of Arkansas in Fayetteville in 1921. Majoring first in journalism, then switching to physical education, she dropped out in her junior year to work for the J. H. Turner Coal and Building Materials Company in Wichita, Kansas. Turner was a major investor in Walter Beech's Travel Air aircraft company, and Louise found aviation much more interesting than building materials.

Eager to counter the perception that aviation was dangerous, several airplane manufacturers during this period hired women pilots to showcase their planes. As Thaden once put it, "Nothing impresses the safety of aviation on the public quite so much as to see a woman flying an airplane." If a woman could handle it, she said, "the public thinks it must be duck soup for men" (Corn, p. 75). In 1927, Beech offered her a job with his Pacific Coast distributor and a chance to make a living flying. She soloed later that year and promptly set an altitude record (20,260 ft), an endurance record (22 hours, 3 minutes, and 28 seconds) and then a speed record (156 mph) in a Beech Travel Air.

Beech built her a special plane for the first Women's Air Derby in 1929, a grueling 2,700-mile race from Santa Monica, California, to Cleveland, Ohio. As the twenty competitors gathered on the flight line, Will Rogers remarked that it looked like a "powder puff derby" and the name stuck. Thaden crossed the finish line ahead of the field. In Cleveland, Thaden and competitors PHOEBE OMLIE, AMELIA EARHART, Gladys O'Donnell, RUTH NICHOLS, and Blanche Noyes decided to celebrate their camaraderie with a permanent organization. The Ninety-Nines (named for the number of charter members) was open to any woman with a pilot's license; its purpose was to foster "good fellowship" and jobs for female pilots. Thaden served as de facto president until the organization was formalized, then as national secretary until 1936.

Right after the Derby, Louise left competitive aviation and moved to Pittsburgh with her new husband, Herbert von Thaden, a pilot and aeronautical engineer whom she married in 1928. She planned to settle down and raise a family, but the switch to domesticity was difficult. Her son Bill was born in 1930, but two years later she was back setting aviation records. In August 1932, she and Frances Marsalis decided to set a new endurance record. In a Curtiss Thrush biplane, which reporters dubbed the Flying Boudoir, the women circled Long Island for 196 hours, made seventy-eight air-to-air refueling contacts and twice-daily radio broadcasts, breaking the old record of 123 hours.

After the celebration was over, Thaden returned to home and family. Her daughter Pat was born in 1933. Throughout her career, Thaden struggled to balance her love for family and her passion for aviation, which she saw as incompatible and perhaps even pathological. "To a psychoanalyst, a woman pilot, particularly a married one with children, must prove an interesting as well as an inexhaustible subject. Torn between two loves, emotionally confused, the desire to fly an incurable disease eating out your life in the slow torture of frustration—she cannot be a simple, natural personality" (Thaden, p. 139).

When Pat was two years old, Thaden again took to the skies as assistant to Phoebe Omlie, then with the Bureau of Air Commerce, in launching an innovative National Air Marking Program in 1935. The plan called for twelve-foot letters and symbols to be painted on the roofs of barns, factories, warehouses, and water tanks at fifteen-mile intervals, marking the direction and mileage to the nearest airport. As part of the Works Progress Administration, air marking provided thousands of jobs for unemployed men, and, thanks to Omlie, jobs for female pilots in administering the program.

While working in Texas, Thaden and Blanche Noyes decided to compete for the prestigious Bendix Trophy in 1936. The purse was $7,000, an enormous prize during the Depression; moreover, Bendix had decided to offer a consolation prize of $2,500 for the first woman to cross the finish line regardless of her position in the race itself. Having no time to build a special racer, Thaden, with Noyes as her co-pilot and navigator, entered the race in a stock Beech Staggerwing. Plagued by weather and navigation problems, Thaden and Noyes were convinced they had no chance to finish in the money when they landed in Los Angeles. In fact, they had won the race, which entitled them to both the $7,000 purse and the $2,500 consolation prize. Later that year, at the peak of her game, Thaden was awarded the Harmon Trophy from the Federation Aeronautique Internationale for the outstanding female aviator of the year.

In 1938, Thaden retired from competitive aviation. During World War II, she became active in the Civil Air Patrol and served with Ruth Nichols in Relief Wings, a humanitarian air service. She devoted the rest of her life to her family, the family business (Thaden Engineering Company), and promoting women's aviation through a wide variety of civic and aviation organizations. She died of a heart attack in High Point, North Carolina, in November 1979, three days shy of her seventy-fourth birthday.

Though often publicly overshadowed by tales of Amelia Earhart, Louise Thaden continues to be celebrated by aviators. She is featured in the National Aviation Hall of Fame as well as halls of fame in Arkansas, Virginia, Tennessee, and North Carolina. Her Beech Travel Air, winner of the 1929 Derby, has found a permanent home at the Museum of Women Pilots in Oklahoma City. And in 1991, Thaden's leather flying helmet was taken aboard the *Atlantis* space shuttle by Mission Specialist Linda Goodwin.

Bibliography: Louise Thaden's personal and professional papers are housed in the Arkansas Aviation Museum, Fayetteville, Arkansas. Additional documents are found at the Louise M. Thaden Office and Library Building, Staggerwing Museum, Tullahoma, Tennessee; the National Air and Space Museum, Smithsonian Institution, Washington, D.C.; and the archives of The Ninety-Nines, Inc., Museum of Women Pilots, Oklahoma City. Louise Thaden's autobiography, *High, Wide and Frightened* (1938), colorfully describes many tense moments, failed engines, and near misses, her frustrations with the constraints imposed upon female pilots, and her guilt over her failure to wholeheartedly embrace domesticity and motherhood. Also of interest are Jean Adams and Margaret Kimball, *Heroines of the Sky* (1942); Joseph J. Corn, *The Winged Gospel: America's Romance with Aviation, 1900–1950* (1983); Kathleen Brooks-Pazmany, *United States Women in Aviation, 1919–1929* (1991); Dean Jaros, *Heroes without Legacy: American Airwomen, 1912–1944* (1993); Lu Hollander, Gene Nora Jessen, and Verna West, *The Ninety-Nines, Yesterday, Today, Tomorrow* (1996); and Gene Nora Jessen, *The Powder Puff Derby of 1929* (2002). Additional information was obtained from Patricia Thaden Webb through the National Aviation Hall of Fame.

JANANN SHERMAN

THOMPSON, Louise Alone. *See* Patterson, Louise Alone Thompson.

THORNTON, Willie Mae. December 11, 1926–July 25, 1984. Blues singer.

Willie Mae "Big Mama" Thornton was the fifth child born to Mattie Hughes and George Thornton in Montgomery County, Alabama. Thornton's father was a preacher, and her mother was a singer who participated in services, as did their children. Willie Mae sang in church as a very young child. She ventured into solo performances for a local talent show and won when she was about ten years old. This spurred her desire to perform in one of the itinerant tent shows that traveled throughout the South during the interwar years. At the age of fourteen, the same year her mother died, she left home to join Sammy Green's Hot Harlem Revue. Here she sang, danced, performed comedy routines, and learned to play the neck-rack harmonica and the drums, which she often played simultaneously as she sang foot-stomping blues.

Around 1948 Thornton left the show and moved to Houston, Texas, where she played in local clubs. Donald Robey, the owner of the Peacock Lounge, saw her perform and began recording her on his Peacock Record label in 1951; she remained with the label until 1957. In Houston, Thornton adopted the nickname Big Mama, apt for a woman nearly six feet tall and three hundred pounds; one of her first records was "They Call Me Big Mama." Johnny Otis, a well-known band leader, also took an interest in her belting style of singing and included her in his Rhythm and Blues Caravan that toured the United States in 1951–52. She worked in several lounges and clubs in Houston before moving to Los Angeles in the early 1950s. She continued performing in local clubs in the Watts and Central Avenue areas of town. A trip to the East Coast and a stint at New York's Apollo Theater in 1952 were the high point of this period. Thornton's powerful voice and comedic talent earned respect from many of the blues and R&B musicians with whom she performed and recorded, among them Esther Phillips, Margie Evans, and Etta James.

Her most successful Peacock recording, "Hound Dog," with Otis's band, was released in 1953 and became her only recording to reach the *Billboard Magazine*'s Top 40 rhythm and blues charts. Though Johnny Otis and Thornton claimed authorship of the song, the songwriting team of Jerry Leiber and Mike Stoller successfully disputed the claim and earned royalties for decades. Royalty disputes were common for blues singers because of their "trust" in record companies. Tragically for Thornton, Elvis Presley recorded "Hound Dog" and subsequently rose to exceptional fame and fortune after performing it on *The Ed Sullivan Show,* while her earnings never matched her immense talents. From the late 1950s to the mid 1960s the majority of her appearances were in small clubs up and down the West Coast with local rhythm and blues bands. She still recorded occasionally on minor labels, such as Irma, Bay-Tone, and Sotoplay. Her alcoholism plagued her health, and some found her tough, intractable personality alienating.

The era of student protests and sit-ins, marches, and folk festivals ushered in by the mid 1960s brought Thornton the greatest acclaim of her career. She was selected to join the American Folk Blues Festival in 1965 and toured the United States and Europe with other blues greats such as Muddy Waters and Otis Spann. Other jazz and folk festivals attracted a new audience of young people who were exploring a variety of musical styles. Arhoolie Records began to record Thornton during this period and produced her most famous blues song, "Ball and Chain." It became the most financially successful of any of her recordings because JANIS JOPLIN, a young white Texan, emulated Thornton's brassy, hard-driving style and made it her signature piece as the finale of her concerts. This renewed interest in Thornton, and she returned to the circuit.

Jazz and blues festivals in Monterey, San Francisco, Houston, and Dallas provided the most exposure in the late 1960s and the 1970s. Thornton never had the kind of success enjoyed by Joplin and other young white singers who began their careers as hers was fading, but she was highly respected by critics and loved by audiences who attended the festivals that soon became a yearly affair in cities on the West Coast and in Texas, the Delta, and the Midwest. Her last performance at the San Francisco Blues Festival in 1979 brought a standing ovation and the festival's award for her contributions to the blues. By then the tall, hefty, big-boned woman had become gaunt and frail; she had to remain seated while performing, but the audience's overwhelming response gave her the energy to belt out an amazing rendition of "Ball and Chain." According to one critic, Big Mama "sang, moaned, yelled and did about everything there is to do to the song."

Her personal life is scarcely known; she never married or had children. The lyrics to some of her songs and the manner in which she performed them, however, imply that her decision to be an irreverent, hard-drinking, tough "mama" may have been her way of coping with her sexual identity. Thornton had long dressed in overalls and cowboy hats, and sometimes in men's suits and ties, which lent an air of sexual ambiguity. In July 1984, Willie Mae Thornton was found dead in a rented room in Los Angeles, at the age of fifty-seven, her body emaciated from the ravages of alcoholism. Johnny Otis, who had championed her career from early on, preached at her funeral. She was buried in the Inglewood Park Cemetery in California. That same year, she was inducted into the Blues Foundation Hall of Fame, honored as a formidable singer and musician and an important influence on a generation of younger artists, including Janis

Joplin, Angela Strehli, Aretha Franklin, and Taj Mahal. An African American woman who was subject to the constraints of racism and sexism from her birth to her death, Big Mama Thornton's boisterous spirit and her musical gift remained intact in the face of tragic exploitation.

Bibliography: Though there is no full-length biography of Willie Mae Thornton, biographical information can be found in Johnny Otis, *Upside Your Head! Rhythm and Blues on Central Avenue* (1993), in which he also shares his personal feelings about Thornton; and Sheldon Harris, *Blues Who's Who: A Biographical Dictionary of Blues Singers* (1979), which cites numerous dates and locations of Thornton's appearances until the mid 1970s. For background on earlier blues singers, see Daphne Duval Harrison, *Black Pearls: Blues Queens from the 1920s* (1988), and Angela Y. Davis, *Blues Legacies and Black Feminism* (1988). Michael Erlwine, Vladimir Bogdanov, Chris Woodstra, and Cub Koda, eds., *All Music Guide to the Blues* (1996), give a brief review of her recordings. John Cowley and Paul Oliver, eds., *The New Blackwell Guide to Recorded Blues* (1996), reviews "Hound Dog—The Peacock Recordings." The quotation appears in Richard Cohen, "San Francisco Blues Festival," *Living Blues* 44 (Autumn 1979), p. 29. Obituaries appeared in the *New York Times* on July 28, 1984, and *Rolling Stone* on September 13, 1984.

DAPHNE DUVAL HARRISON

TILLMON, Johnnie. April 10, 1926–November 22, 1995. Welfare rights leader, community activist.

Johnnie Tillmon, a leading advocate for poor women, began her organizing activities well before she became executive director of the National Welfare Rights Organization in 1972 and continued them long after the organization's demise. Born in Scott, Arkansas, to John Percy, a sharecropper, and Gussie Danfort, a homemaker and field hand, Johnnie was the oldest of three children. Her family moved frequently during her childhood as her father sought the best arrangement from plantation owners. She began to pick cotton when she was only seven years old. Despite segregation, she recalled playing with the children of the poor white sharecroppers. The relatively easy relationships she had with whites, beginning in childhood, shaped her multiracial approach to political activism and kept her focused more on class than on race issues.

In order to attend high school, she moved to an aunt's in Little Rock, attending school by day and working the night shift at a local munitions factory. When night jobs were no longer available at war's end, she quit high school and went to work in a laundry, where she engaged in her first organizing experience, mobilizing the workers to demand a half-cent-per-hour raise. She continued to work in that nonsegregated laundry for the next fifteen years. A short-lived marriage to James Tillmon produced three children between 1948 and 1952 (Marsha, Ronald, and Auluvance), but she left him when she was pregnant with the third child. Between 1954 and 1961, she had three more children (Josalyn, Tanya, and Caffie) whom she raised on her own, working in a laundry to support them, while relatives or neighbors cared for them.

In 1960, Tillmon moved to Los Angeles to join her brothers and immediately went to work in a large unionized laundry. When the shop steward quit, the other workers asked Tillmon to represent them. By this time, she had moved into the Nickerson Gardens Housing Project in Watts and had become active in the local improvement group and community politics.

After learning of her daughter's chronic school truancy, Tillmon decided that it would be best to remain at home to supervise her children. She applied for public assistance, and within months of collecting benefits she began her welfare rights organizing. Spurred to action when she overheard a slight about welfare recipients, Tillmon called a meeting of other women in the housing project, ostensibly to discuss housing arrangements. Out of this initial mid-1963 meeting, a core group of eight women formed ANC Mothers Anonymous of Watts (named for the Aid to Needy Children program under which they received benefits), the first known welfare mothers group in the country. Although they feared reprisals from the welfare authorities, they nevertheless went public in 1965 when Tillmon was invited to speak on a radio program.

From the start, Tillmon had a broader agenda, believing that welfare mothers should be trained or receive an education if they wished, and should have quality child care available. Tillmon's early start in organizing ANC Mothers eventually catapulted her in 1972 into the top leadership position of the National Welfare Rights Organization (NWRO), which was founded in 1966 by George Wiley, an African American former academician who had previously served as associate director of the Congress of Racial Equality. Elected first to the newly formed Los Angeles County Welfare Rights Organization (WRO), and then to the presidency of the California WRO, Tillmon was elected temporary chairman at a meeting of the National Coordinating Committee in February 1967; the following August she was elected to a full two-year term. In that capacity she worked closely with George Wiley in formulating policy and traveled widely helping to organize local groups and mediate problems. She was reelected in 1969, after being challenged for office, and in 1971 moved to Washington, D.C., to take the position of associate director. When Wiley resigned as executive director in 1972, Tillmon took his place.

Her ascendancy to the top post in NWRO was

not a natural progression, but instead resulted from gradual shifts in the organization as the women welfare recipients sought to wrest control, first from the largely white professional staff, and then from the black men who replaced them. By the time Tillmon assumed the directorship, she already had begun to forge ties with the women's movement, particularly through her relationship with Aileen Hernandez, the black former president of the National Organization for Women (NOW). At Gloria Steinem's urging, Tillmon wrote "Welfare Is a Women's Issue" for the newly launched *Ms.* magazine (Spring 1972). This article had a significant impact on the largely middle-class feminist movement, as it sought to build a broader base and reach out to working-class women and women of color. In turn, Tillmon increasingly viewed the NWRO as being part of a broader women's movement. Some describe NWRO as a black women's organization, but Tillmon insisted that it was a poor women's organization, for women of all colors. With her charisma and no-nonsense style, she also carried her message to other groups, drawing on both the statistics and the lived experiences of poor women to forge ties between anti-poverty and civil rights activists, including Martin Luther King Jr.

The changes in the NWRO led to a growing disaffection among the early supporters and funders Wiley had cultivated. Unable to recover from a growing debt and stifled from pursuing its agenda in the changed political climate of the 1970s, NWRO closed its doors in Washington, D.C., in 1974. Tillmon returned to Los Angeles, where she resumed her local community organizing and went to work for a city councilman on whose campaign she had earlier served. In 1979 she married local blues musician Harvey Blackston, known as Harmonica Fats.

The demise of the NWRO did not ring the death knell for welfare rights activism. Tillmon remained a key player in a loose network of women in local recipient groups, many of whom came together at the 1977 International Women's Year Conference in Houston. Forging coalitions with other groups there, they successfully garnered support for their substitute "Women, Welfare, and Poverty" platform resolution.

Tillmon remained active in the Watts community and continued to respond to phone queries from welfare recipients until 1991, when diabetes caused her health to fail. Even then, she retained her reputation as a leading welfare rights advocate and was still serving on the Los Angeles County Welfare Advisory Committee up to the time of her death there in 1995 at the age of sixty-nine.

Bibliography: Personal interviews with Tillmon constitute one of the major sources of biographical information, particularly the twelve-hour oral history conducted by Sherna Berger Gluck in 1984 and 1991 (on deposit at Special Collections, California State University, Long Beach). Other short, journalistic interviews include John Mitchell, "A Dreamer and Her Dream Lose Ground," *Los Angeles Times,* July 9, 1995, and Brian Lanker, *I Dream a World: Portraits of Black Women Who Changed America* (1989). Tillmon's only attributed published writing is her Spring 1972 *Ms.* essay, "Welfare Is a Women's Issue," pp. 111–12, 114–16. Her personal papers were lost or destroyed in a flood, and the records of ANC Mothers were destroyed in a fire. The records of the NWRO are on deposit at Moorland-Spingarn Research Center, Howard University, Washington, D.C. Informal conversations with Tim Sampson, a founding staff member of NWRO and social worker–organizer in Southern California, provided additional insights into Tillmon's early organizing in Los Angeles. Guida West, *The National Welfare Rights Movement: The Social Protest of Poor Women* (1981), with its extensive interviews of Tillmon and many other players, remains the most exhaustive study of women's work and experiences in the NWRO and their relationship both to other women's organizations and to civil rights organizations. See also Felicia Kornbluh, "A Right to Welfare? Poor Women, Professionals, and Poverty Programs, 1935–1975" (PhD dissertation, Princeton University, 2000), which offers a broad contextual analysis of women's welfare organizing. Kori Kelly, "Conflict and Strategy in the National Welfare Rights Movement," *Berkeley McNair Research Journal* 8 (Winter 2000), further explores the gender politics and conflicts in the organization, drawing on the NWRO papers. Obituaries appeared in the *Los Angeles Times* on November 25, 1995, and the *New York Times* on November 27, 1995.

SHERNA BERGER GLUCK

TINSLEY, Beatrice Muriel. January 27, 1941–March 23, 1981. Astronomer.

Beatrice Muriel Tinsley is noted for her contributions to the study of galaxy evolution. This field of astronomy is of wide importance because galaxies are extremely bright and visible at enormous distances and therefore are some of the few landmarks astronomers can use to map the whole universe. Tinsley's personal story is both exhilarating and tragic. She was active in the very male world of the physical sciences during the 1960s and 1970s, a time when widely voiced feminist ideals came into stark conflict with traditionally male patterns of career and personal life. Tinsley tried to do what her male peers did: combine the career of a first-rank research scientist with family life, spouse, and children. She certainly succeeded in the career, facing and surmounting a daunting succession of professional obstacles to earn tenure at Yale and an international reputation as a leader in her field. But she did so at great personal cost. Her success came only after divorce and separation from her children, causing her such stress that she blamed it for the cancer that took her life at forty.

Beatrice Muriel Hill was born in Chester, England, and grew up in New Zealand. Her father, Edward Owen Eustace Hill, was an Anglican vicar. He later became mayor of New Plymouth. Her mother, Jean O'Hagen Morton, wrote inspirational romances. The parents instilled a strong sense of mission in their three daughters: they should concern themselves with Great Things. Beatrice, the middle child, excelled at music, mathematics, and science. She seems to have translated her parents' religious mission into rationalistic form. As an undergraduate at the University of Canterbury in New Zealand, she decided to pursue cosmology, the study of the universe as a whole.

She took her BSc degree in 1961 and married Brian A. Tinsley, a graduate student in atmospheric physics. The Tinsleys remained at Canterbury until Brian finished his PhD in 1963. They then moved to Dallas, Texas, where Brian had found a rare nonmilitary job in atmospheric physics with the Southwest Center for Advanced Studies, which soon became the University of Texas at Dallas. Beatrice first hoped to study cosmology in Dallas, but this proved unworkable, so in 1964 she began the PhD program in astronomy at the University of Texas, Austin, a four-hundred-mile weekly commute. She received her PhD in 1967.

Tinsley's dissertation research was an ambitious study of how a galaxy's light changes as its stars age. This is important, because light travels at a finite speed. As we look out in space, we look back in time. We see faraway galaxies not as they are now, but as they were in infancy. To use those distant galaxies as landmarks, we must know their true light output. There are no young galaxies nearby, however, to let us see what light young galaxies emit. Tinsley, therefore, made computer simulations that tracked light output of many different kinds of stars over their billion-year life spans, adding up the light to calculate the evolution of light from a whole galaxy. On the basis of her simulations, she argued that young galaxies are brighter and bluer than old ones.

Tinsley's work was pathbreaking. When she started work in the mid 1960s, almost everything she needed to make her models—from computer resources to knowledge of what mix of stars populates galaxies—was barely up to the job. One of Tinsley's key contributions was surely her conviction that the time for this work was ripe. Her results were the first of their kind that astronomers considered realistic enough to impact the cosmological debate.

Successful graduate work often leads directly to a job or postdoctoral fellowship. Instead, the Tinsleys adopted children, Alan (in 1966) and Teresa (in 1968), and Beatrice spent most of the next five years raising them. She published several articles based upon her dissertation, and when both children were in preschool, she looked for a job. Because Brian was established in his laboratory, she looked in Dallas and Austin, but she found only part-time and temporary appointments.

Tinsley's articles brought professional recognition. She first received research funding from the National Science Foundation in 1971 and began to publish a flood of papers extending her work in new directions. She collaborated with prominent astronomers, including James Gunn of Caltech and Richard Larson of Yale. She was a visiting researcher at Mount Wilson and Palomar observatories and at the University of Maryland. In 1974 she, Gunn, Richard Gott, and David Schramm collaborated on a landmark paper, "An Unbound Universe?" Evaluating various cosmological arguments, they concluded (iconoclastically) that the universe will probably expand forever. Widely cited and debated, the paper was popularized in *Scientific American,* giving it enormous readership. In 1974 Tinsley received the ANNIE J. CANNON Prize in support of research by women in astronomy. Still, neither Dallas nor Austin offered a real job. Tinsley's disappointment was bitter, and it is hard to untangle the personal and professional factors that led to the Tinsleys' divorce in 1974. Beatrice sought jobs outside Texas, soon receiving offers from top-tier institutions, including Chicago and Yale. She chose Yale, for its New England atmosphere and to work with Larson.

At Yale after 1975, Tinsley enjoyed a smooth professional path and she became a full professor in 1978. A decade's work indicated that galaxies are much more complicated than she had assumed in the mid 1960s, and she turned more to galaxies themselves, and less to their implications for cosmology. One of Tinsley's accomplishments was to help turn galaxy studies from an esoteric specialty into a recognized field. Her broad interests had led her to develop an extraordinary array of contacts and collaborators. By organizing a still-remembered 1977 conference drawing together astronomers working on related but uncoordinated problems, she transformed her personal network into a group with a public identity.

In 1978 Tinsley was diagnosed with melanoma, a virulent skin cancer that took her life three years later in New Haven at the age of forty. She is remembered with the American Astronomical Society's Beatrice M. Tinsley Prize for innovative research, and by a visiting professorship at the University of Texas, Austin.

Bibliography: For biographical information, see Edward Hill, *My Daughter Beatrice: A Personal Memoir of Dr. Beatrice Tinsley, Astronomer* (1986); and Richard Larson and Linda Stryker, "Beatrice Muriel Hill Tinsley," *Quarterly Journal of the Royal Astronomical Society* 23 (1982), pp. 162–65. For her work in context see Joann Eisberg, "Making a Science of Observational Cosmology: The Cautious Optimism of Beatrice Tinsley," *Journal for the History of Astronomy* 32 (2001), pp. 263–78. For a racy overview of her milieu, see Dennis Overbye, *Lonely Hearts of the Cosmos: The Scientific Quest for the Secret of the Universe* (1991). Her major contribution to cosmology appeared in J. Richard Gott, James E. Gunn, David N. Schramm, and Beatrice M. Tinsley, "An Unbound Universe?" *Astrophysical Journal* 194 (1974), pp. 534–53, popularized as J. Richard Gott et al., "Will the Universe Expand Forever?" *Scientific American* (March 1976), pp. 62–73. Tinsley summarized her final understanding of galaxies in Beatrice M. Tinsley, "Evolution of the Stars and Gas in Galaxies," *Fundamentals of Cosmic Physics* 5 (1980), pp. 287–388. The latter provides an extensive bibliography, including Tinsley's own most significant articles. Her papers are found at the Astronomy Department, Yale University. The author has a collection of taped interviews with Tinsley's friends and colleagues.

JOANN EISBERG

TOGASAKI, Kazue. June 29, 1897–December 15, 1992. Physician.

Gynecologist and obstetrician Kazue Togasaki was born in San Francisco, the second of eight children, and oldest daughter, of Japanese immigrants Kikumatsu Togasaki, owner of a wholesale equipment supply firm, and Shige Kushida, homemaker and temperance advocate. A ninth child was born to Kikumatsu and his second wife, Sugi Hida, a college professor.

The Togasakis were devout Christians who, with their children in tow, regularly greeted immigrants arriving from Japan and invited them to live with them temporarily. Sometimes there were as many as twelve extra people sleeping on floors in their house. In the aftermath of the 1906 San Francisco earthquake, Shige took over a local church and created a makeshift hospital for the Japanese immigrants, enlisting nine-year-old Kazue to help. Shige often sent her daughters to accompany immigrant women to the doctor to translate for them.

The children's activities meshed with the family ethic. After morning Bible reading and a full day of school, the daughters were dispatched to care for ill or needy families. Sometimes Kazue extended this mandate to include lecturing errant fathers who had the audacity to come home drunk. Kazue's parents imparted a sense of self-reliance and self-respect to their children. This childhood of charitable work was perhaps the greatest influence on the daughters, leading to their careers in medicine.

Initially, Kazue earned her bachelor's degree in zoology in 1920 at Stanford University. She received her RN at the Children's Hospital School of Nursing in 1924. She continued her education at the University of California School of Public Health Nursing, received her degree in 1927, and went to work as a nurse. Spurred on by her independent outspoken mother and her father's belief in education, Kazue decided to become a physician. She applied to medical schools, at a time when there were quotas restricting not only women but also Japanese Americans, and was accepted at Women's Medical College of Pennsylvania. In 1933, she and Megumi Shinoda became the first women of Japanese ancestry to receive an MD in the United States. Kazue completed her internship at Children's Hospital of San Francisco and began her private practice there in 1935.

Described by her family as strong-willed, sometimes domineering, Kazue charted the course for her five younger sisters. In short order, fourth-born Mitsuye Togasaki Shida (1902–73) became a registered nurse; fifth-born Yoshiye Togasaki (1904–99) received her MD in pediatric public health from Johns Hopkins University School of Medicine in 1935; sixth-born Chiye Togasaki Yamanaka (1905–95) obtained an RN in public health nursing from the University of California in 1929; seventh-born Teru Togasaki (1907–90) graduated in 1936 with an MD from the University of California Medical School; and eighth-born Yaye Togasaki Breitenbach (1908–) went into psychiatric nursing with the Veterans Administration. None of the Togasaki physician sisters married. Strong-willed, independent, ardent advocates, they were sometimes intimidating to men in their social circle. The Togasaki brothers—Kiyoshi, Susumu, and Shinobu—were equally accomplished, pursuing careers in journalism, political activism, and computer science.

World War II interrupted the lives and careers of every person of Japanese ancestry living on the West Coast. This close-knit family ended up in widely separated War Relocation Authority (WRA) camps. Brother Kiyoshi, who was working in Japan, and sisters Mitsuye, living in Hawaii, and Yaye, in the armed forces, escaped the forced incarceration. Kazue was named director of medical services at Tanforan Assembly Center in San Francisco, until she, her father, and brother Shinobu were transferred into permanent detention at Topaz in central Utah. A take-charge person accustomed to getting things done, she ignored the army when setting up the clinic at Tanforan. "Rules? I'm not here for rules; I'm here to be a doctor" (Shinobu and Gordon Togasaki oral history, p. 39).

Sister Teru was imprisoned with her brother Susumu's family at Poston, Arizona, where she practiced for a time in the hospital. Yoshiye, a public health physician in Los Angeles, volunteered to set up the medical unit at Manzanar on the condition that her family join her. Citing a critical shortage of health care professionals, the chief medical officer said they could not afford to put her and her highly trained sisters in one place. When Yoshiye became ill, the WRA decided to allow her to join her sisters Chiye and Kazue now at Tule Lake. After Kazue and Dr. George Hashiba performed a hysterectomy on her, Yoshiye returned to the pediatric wards within five days.

The male chief medical officer at Tule Lake considered Kazue and Yoshiye too disruptive when they made rounds and ordered treatment, so after six months he transferred them to Manzanar. There, advised that things were not going to improve and realizing they could not be effective in camp, both departed to complete their residencies, Kazue to Chicago for training in obstetrics and Yoshiye to Bellevue Hospital in New York.

In 1947, Kazue returned to postwar San Francisco and resumed her practice. After Bellevue, Yoshiye volunteered to minister to refugees with the U.N. Relief and Rehabilitation Administration. When she returned home, she joined the California State Health Department and later, in 1951, Contra Costa County Health Department, where she retired in 1972 as chief of preventive medical services and deputy health officer.

After the war, Chiye first went to work for the San Francisco Visiting Nurse Association, then joined her husband in Hiroshima, Japan, and worked for the Atomic Energy Commission until 1959. Teru decided not to return to her prewar general practice in Sacramento, but practiced in Honolulu for thirteen years. Noted in the family as the best diagnostician of the three sisters, her experiences as a prison physician induced her to fight successfully for a new women's prison. In the mid 1960s, Teru returned to San Francisco. Yaye, then a colonel in the U.S. Army, became an expert in psychiatric nursing and helped set up the VA psychiatric hospital in Salt Lake City. She later returned to work in New York.

Kazue devoted herself to her practice, delivering more than ten thousand babies, including entire families and several generations, and became a pillar in the Japanese American community. She never took a vacation, partly because she did not want her patients to deliver with someone else, and treated families whether or not they could afford to pay. As a woman obstetrician who could speak Japanese, she saw many Japanese American women, though later she extended her practice to a diverse group of people.

Throughout her career, she invited unwed mothers to stay with her; she delivered their babies and helped with adoptions. She cared for terminally ill people, hosting them in her own house. Every Sunday Kazue opened her home to Japanese American students from the University of California, and she regularly cooked for friends and family. The *San Francisco Examiner* named her one of the ten "Most Distinguished Women of 1970" for her years of community service.

When her memory began to fail, Kazue closed her practice and endured Alzheimer's disease for more than twenty years before it claimed this remarkable woman at the age of ninety-five. Kazue Togasaki pioneered a place in medicine for women of Japanese ancestry and faced down a climate of anti-Asian discrimination with determination and a strength she brought to every aspect of her life.

Bibliography: Published family biographical information exists in Bill Hosokawa, *Nisei: The Quiet Americans* (1969); John Tateishi, *And Justice for All: An Oral History of the Japanese American Detention Camps* (1984); Dennis L. Breo, "WWII 'internment' still haunts MD," *American Medical News* 24, no. 38 (October 9, 1981), pp. 3, 23–24; Stan Yogi, "Yoshiye Togasaki," *ACLU News*, July–August 2001; and Fusako Yamamoto, "The Togasaki Family: Remarkable Pioneers," *Pacific Citizen*, December 2002, pp. 70–71. Unpublished reports in author's possession include Louis Fiset, "Licensed Nikkei MDs WWII Era, All Physicians in USA" (2002); Margaret Ohwa, "Dr. Yoshiye Togasaki" (1988); and Kikumatsu Togasaki, "As the Lord Led Me" (n.d.).

Unpublished oral histories consist of audiotapes of "Kazue Togasaki, interview on her life in Japanese American relocation centers and her medical career" (1974), conducted by Sandra Waugh and Eric Leong for the Combined Asian American Resources Project, archived at the Bancroft Library, University of California, Berkeley; transcripts of audiotaped interviews with Yoshiye Togasaki, conducted in 1993 by Eizo and Mary Kobayashi for the Diablo Chapter of the Japanese American Citizens League; and an oral history with brother Shinobu and nephew Gordon Togasaki and an oral history with nephew David Togasaki, conducted by Gwenn Jensen for the Japanese American Medical Association (2002), archived at the Japanese American National Museum, Los Angeles. Obituaries appeared in the vernacular newspaper *Hokubei Mainichi*, March 10, 1990 (Teru), December 22, 1992 (Kazue), and December 8, 1999 (Yoshiye).

GWENN M. JENSEN

TOMITA, Teiko. December 1, 1896–March 13, 1990. Poet.

Teiko Matsui was born in Kasuga, Osaka prefecture, Japan, the second of nine children (five daughters and four sons) of Mine Terahara and Eitaro Matsui. Teiko's father had been adopted as heir to the Ichisaburo Matsui family because they did not have children of their own. Teiko had fond memories of her grandparents, who lived nearby and who were supportive of her studies, as was her father. Eitaro Matsui, who was a member of the village council, farmed part of his large acreage and had sharecroppers farming the rest. He also operated a pawnshop, and Teiko helped her father with the bookkeeping.

Teiko graduated with highest honors from Sakurai Koto Jogakko, an elite girls' high school in Nara prefecture. While in high school she learned to write *tanka,* a traditional Japanese poetic form consisting of thirty-one syllables arranged in five successive lines of five, seven, five, seven, and seven syllables. Her first tanka teacher gave her a pen name, Yukari, which she continued to use throughout her writing career. Aspiring to be a high school teacher, Teiko was accepted to the prestigious Nara Municipal Normal School. Owing to her mother's worsening health and her older sister's marriage, however, her father asked her to return to help the family. Despite these family obligations, she managed to earn a certificate to teach at the elementary school level from a nearby women's normal school, Tennoji Joshi Shihan Gakko in Osaka, and taught for six years at area elementary schools.

Although Teiko would have been happy to continue teaching the rest of her life, her parents urged her to get married, and a relative served as a go-between to arrange a marriage for her with Masakazu Tomita, who was from the neighboring prefecture of Nara. Masakazu had emigrated to the United States a decade earlier to join his older brother, who was farming on the Yakama Indian Reservation in Washington State. Teiko got to know Masakazu through the letters they exchanged before he returned to Japan to marry her in 1920. They traveled in Japan before leaving for the United States in February 1921. Soon after her arrival in the Yakima Valley town of Wapato, Washington, she began working in the fields and cooking for the farm workers. They later worked at a nursery.

Teiko and Masakazu Tomita had five children. Three were born in the Yakima Valley: daughter Kiku (1923), son Jun (1926), and daughter Kay (1928). In 1929 the Tomitas moved to Sunnydale, outside of Seattle, to start a nursery. Two more children were born there: daughter Yae (1931) and son Joe (1935). The tragic disappearance of Yae in 1933 led Teiko to seek spiritual solace in religion, and she became a devout member of the Japanese Presbyterian Church in Seattle.

Tomita continued to write tanka that chronicled her life in the United States. In 1939, she joined the Seattle Tanka Club and sent poems monthly for discussion and critique. Many of her poems were published in Japan.

Just as their nursery business was finally taking hold, war broke out between their land of birth, Japan, and their adopted land, the United States. Because Japanese immigrants were denied the right to become naturalized citizens of the United States on the basis of race, they were considered permanent aliens; with the outbreak of war they became enemy aliens. Fearing that her poems written in Japanese might be viewed as suspect, Teiko painfully burned her manuscripts. In 1942, in one of the most massive violations of civil rights in American history, more than 110,000 Japanese immigrants and their citizen children were rounded up and forcibly removed from their West Coast homes to be placed in temporary detention centers and then incarcerated in inland concentration camps. Teiko and her family were removed to the assembly center at Pinedale near Fresno, California, then incarcerated at Tule Lake in northern California, and later transferred to Heart Mountain, Wyoming. In those bleak years she took solace in composing poems and attending lectures and classes in Japanese poetry.

In July 1945 the Tomitas secured a work release to take a job with a large nursery near Minneapolis, Minnesota. Teiko cleaned and cooked for the owner's family. After the war ended, the Tomitas returned to their Sunnydale nursery to start over once again. Teiko took a job as a garment worker sewing in a factory employing a multiethnic workforce.

After much struggle they were able to rebuild their business and build a new home. All of their children graduated from college and had active careers. Teiko believed that her years of struggle had borne fruit in the limitless future of her children. But just as she and her husband felt contentment in their final years, in 1967 their land was condemned by eminent domain to accommodate the expansion of Seattle-Tacoma International Airport. They moved in with their daughter Kay and her family in Seattle, and spent the rest of their lives in this intergenerational extended family.

Throughout the postwar years Tomita continued to write and publish poems. In 1956 her poems were published in a collection of immigrant tanka, *Renia no yuki* (Snow of Rainier). She regularly contributed her poems to the Seattle Japanese language newspaper *Hokubei Hochi.*

Widowed in 1977, Tomita recovered from a stroke she suffered in 1983 but did not publish any further poetry. She died in Seattle in 1990 at the age of ninety-three and was buried at Washelli Cemetery in Seattle.

Teiko Tomita recorded her life and innermost thoughts through her poetry. Using traditional poetic form and traditional metaphors, she created new meanings expressing the immigrant experience in a land and life so different from Japan and also created new metaphors, images, and vocabulary in adapting the content and language of the tanka while maintaining its ancient form. Her poetry reflected the imagery, feelings, and sensibilities of an immigrant generation taking root in a new land and offers a better understanding of the

Japanese immigrant experience in the United States.

Bibliography: The best source of information on Teiko Tomita is Gail M. Nomura, "Tsugiki, a Grafting: A History of a Japanese Pioneer Woman in Washington State," in Karen J. Blair, ed., *Women in Pacific Northwest History* (1988, rev. ed. 2001). See also Nomura's essay in Elizabeth Jameson and Susan Armitage, ed., *Writing the Range: Race, Class, and Culture in the Women's West* (1997), and a shortened version in *Women's Studies* 14, no. 1 (1987), pp. 15–37. A short biographical entry by Emily Lawsin appears in Brian Niiya, ed., *Japanese American History, An A-to-Z Reference from 1868 to the Present* (1993, rev. ed. 2001). The best published collection of Tomita's poems is found in the anthology *Renia no yuki* (Snow of Rainier) (1956), edited by Mihara Senryu et al. Her poems also appear in Kazuo Ito, *Hokubei hyakunen zakura* (North American Hundred Years Cherries) (1969) and *Zoku hokubei hyakunen zakura* (North American Hundred Years Cherries, Supplement) (1972). Ito's book *Hokubei hyakunen zakura* was translated into English by Shinichiro Nakamura and Jean S. Gerard as *Issei: A History of Japanese Immigrants in North* America (1973). A short video on Tomita is found in the *Celebrate Women* series by KCTS-TV, Seattle. Photographs are found at the Japanese American National Museum in Los Angeles. Oral history excerpts are found in Eileen Sunada Sarasohn, *Issei Women, Echoes from Another Frontier* (1998). Additional information was provided in an interview with Teiko Tomita on July 26, 1983, and in phone interviews with Kay Hashimoto in May and June 2003. Obituaries appeared in the *Seattle Post-Intelligencer* on March 15, 1990 and the *Seattle Times* on March 15 and 19, 1990.

GAIL M. NOMURA

TRAMBLEY, Estela Portillo. January 16, 1927–December 29, 1998. Dramatist, writer, educator.

Estela Portillo Trambley was a Texas writer whose early nontraditional portrayals of women helped establish an important feminist presence within Chicano literature. Blending topics that addressed the challenges of life along the Texas-Mexico border with philosophical discussions on nature and spirituality, her stories and plays offered rich and complex depictions of women's experiences that confronted the stereotypical images of Chicanas as weak or submissive and urged readers to pay greater attention to their social concerns.

Born in El Paso to immigrant parents, Delfina Fierro and Francisco Portillo, a piano teacher and a railroad mechanic, Estela spent the early part of her youth with her grandparents. With their influence she developed a fondness for nature and an appreciation for her cultural heritage that later became strong themes in her work. Estela lived with her grandparents until she was twelve and they passed away. She then rejoined her parents and two brothers and a sister, and attended El Paso High School.

In 1947, Portillo married Robert Keith Trambley, a local car salesman, and began her own family. Throughout a period spanning more than twenty years, she balanced a busy teaching career with the roles of wife and mother of seven children: Luz (1947), Naurene (c. 1949), Joyce (1951), Eugenie (1955), Tracey (1957), and twins Roberta and Robert (1961). She earned a BA degree at the University of Texas, El Paso, in 1950, and then taught English at El Paso Technical High School and served as English department chair from 1959 through 1966. Although Trambley's combined occupations as homemaker and professional might have seemed progressive for most women of her era, she viewed her life as quite traditional and expressed dissatisfaction with its limitations. Motherhood was further complicated by the loss of her only son, a nine-month-old twin. In pain over his death, Trambley turned to a long period of intensive reading and ultimately produced a utopian work entitled *After Hierarchy.* Although by her own measure the book was terrible, the experience refreshed her life perspective and planted the desire to write.

Trambley's creative expression took root when it collided with the rising political activism of the late 1960s. As her interests in exploring cultural origins and demanding social justice converged, creative opportunities for depicting both flourished. In particular, within the Chicano community, public forums such as *floricantos* and *teatro campesino,* which combined elements of music, poetry, and performance with political conscious raising, offered many emerging Chicana/o artists the ideal venues for self-expression.

In Trambley's case, the inspiration to write arose from her involvement in the bilingual community troupe Chicano Theater. In 1968, when the group found itself in need of new material, Trambley volunteered to compose a play. She soon became captivated by the world of theater production and playwriting. In 1971 she produced *The Day of the Swallows,* a play that explored lesbianism and critiqued the cultural demands of marriage placed on Mexican women. Sensing its importance, a friend submitted the work to the Chicano literary journal, *El Grito,* which quickly accepted it for publication. The strong critical acclaim and interest that followed helped mark a turning point in Trambley's burgeoning writing career. The play began to be widely performed and was soon included in several anthologies. *The Day of the Swallows* played a significant role in Trambley's winning the prestigious Quinto Sol Award for literature in 1972.

In 1969 Trambley was approached by a local El Paso radio station and asked to host a talk show, *Estela Says.* Taking a temporary leave from teaching, she next hosted *Cumbres* (Peaks), a Spanish-language television program that focused on the visual and performing arts. Following her media stint, Trambley returned to writing and in 1973 became a resident dramatist at El Paso Community College. Having completed five plays, she took advantage of her tenure and staged productions at the local Chamizal National Theatre as well as at the California State University, Los Angeles campus. In 1976, the production of her musical, *Sun Images . . . Los Amores de Don Estufas*, attracted Hollywood's interest, and Montezuma Esparza Productions optioned the work for two film projects, although a screen version never materialized. The play also elicited criticism from some Chicano critics who felt its comedic style and emphasis on entertainment departed from the more urgent tone and politically driven nature of most early Chicano theater.

As Trambley evolved as a writer and playwright—first by completing a master's degree in 1977 in creative writing at the University of Texas, El Paso, and then by spending time in Mexico studying playwriting at Universidad Nacional Autónoma de Mexico—her differing views on the purpose and goals of Chicano literature and her own self-identification as a Chicana became significantly apparent. She resisted the more explicit social protest rhetoric present in some Chicano works and, rather than citing other writers of color as influences and allies, she more often emphasized the impact that European philosophy and English and Euro-American classics had on her writing.

While some eventually came to view her as elitist and conservative, Trambley remains highly regarded by many feminist scholars. As a female pioneer on the literary scene, she helped bring attention to other Chicana writers by editing the first all-women's issue of a major Chicano journal, the 1973 September issue of *El Grito*. Similarly, Trambley's own work relentlessly argued for a more just society for women. Ranging over such topics as domestic violence, drug abuse, and capitalist exploitation, her stories typically traced a character's search for selfhood through a deeply rooted spirituality, and her plots emphasized the rejection of traditional roles and expectations for women by vividly illustrating how binding and unfulfilling they could be.

Trambley's concern for women's issues was always equally matched to her commitment for education, which was reflected in her many affiliations with academic institutions. She served as a visiting professor at the University of California, Riverside, in 1973 and held the Presidential Chair in Creative Writing at the University of California, Davis, in 1995. During the final two decades of her life, Trambley continued to write while working in El Paso as a teacher for homebound children with physical, emotional, and learning problems. Estela Portillo Trambley died of cancer on December 29, 1998, in her hometown of El Paso at the age of seventy-one.

Bibliography: There is some discrepancy over Trambley's birth year, with several sources listing it as 1936; however, 1926 appears to be the most accurate date. Her self-compiled archive is located in the Nettie Lee Benson Latin American Collection, General Libraries, University of Texas at Austin. It is limited mainly to a few local newspaper and magazine interviews, an audiotaped discussion with the author, and some critical essays on her stories, but it also includes several drafts of her plays, short stories, essays, and poetry. Other works by Trambley not mentioned in the text include *Rain of Scorpions and Other Writings* (1975, rev. ed. 1993), *Sor Juana and Other Plays* (1983), and *Trini* (1986). Paula W. Shirley's comprehensive essay on Trambley's life and writing appears in the *Dictionary of Literary Biography: Chicano Writers*, 3rd series, volume 209 (1999), pp. 212–21. In addition, there are three critical interviews with her: Juan Bruce-Novoa, *Chicano Authors: Inquiry by Interview* (1980), pp. 163–81; Faye Nell Vowell, *MELUS* (Winter 1982), pp. 59–66; and Karin Rosa Ikas, *Chicana Ways: Conversations with Ten Chicana Writers* (2002). See also Maythee Rojas, "Following the Flesh: Embodied Transgressions in the Work of Four Chicana Writers" (PhD dissertation, Arizona State University, 2001). Cordelia Candelaria discusses Trambley's short story "La Yonfantayn" in Arturo J. Aldama and Naomi H. Quiñonez, eds., *Decolonial Voices: Chicana and Chicano Cultural Studies in the 21st Century* (2002).

MAYTHEE ROJAS

TREE, Marietta. April 12, 1917–August 15, 1991. Diplomat, political hostess.

Mary Endicott Peabody, known from childhood as Marietta, was born in Lawrence, Massachusetts, the oldest of five children, and the only daughter, of Mary Parkman and Malcolm Peabody. Her father, son of the redoubtable Endicott Peabody, founder and rector of Groton School, was an Episcopal minister. Her mother, a stern and strong woman, was the dominant partner in the household.

In 1925 the Peabody family moved to Philadelphia when Malcolm Peabody was offered a church in Chestnut Hill; in 1938 he was elected bishop of central New York, and the family moved again to Utica and later to Syracuse. Marietta meanwhile went to St. Timothy's, a Maryland finishing school, graduating in 1934. She then spent a year at La Petite École Florentine in Florence. Though most of her schoolmates aspired to marriage and children, Marietta, a tall (five foot ten) blonde beauty, when asked how she saw her future, replied, "Parties, people and politics" (Seebohm, p. 14).

She went on in 1936 to the University of Pennsylvania, leaving college after three years without completing her bachelor's degree. On September

2, 1939, she married Desmond FitzGerald. A lawyer, seven years older, FitzGerald introduced his young bride to sophisticated life in New York City. Their one child, a daughter named Frances, was born in October 1940.

Three months after Pearl Harbor, Desmond FitzGerald enlisted in the army and Marietta went to work as a volunteer for Nelson Rockefeller's Office of Inter-American Affairs. Soon, with her friend Dorothy Paley, the wife of William Paley of CBS, she became involved in the civil rights movement, helping to revitalize and integrate the Sydenham Hospital in Harlem.

By 1943 she was a researcher for *Life,* Henry Luce's picture weekly. She shared an office with Earl Brown, a black journalist, who enlarged her contacts in Harlem. She became a shop steward for the Newspaper Guild and turned into an ardent Roosevelt Democrat, serving as a vice chairman of the CIO-PAC, the political action committee of the Congress of Industrial Organizations. "My entire life was indeed changed by the job," she later wrote. "I would never have become militant in the opening battles for civil rights, never become a shop steward in the CIO, never become a Democrat, never known the difference between a Trotskyite and a Stalinist . . . and never fallen in love" (ibid., p. 128).

She led a glittering evening life in the war years. An especially intense friendship was with the gifted film director John Huston. When Desmond FitzGerald returned from the war, the marriage was essentially finished, though they did not divorce until July 1947—a divorce regarded with great maternal disapproval. By this time John Huston in a drunken moment had married a Hollywood actress, and Marietta had fallen in love with Ronald Tree, an Anglo-American (his grandfather was Marshall Field of Chicago) and a Churchill Tory in British politics.

Marietta and John Huston remained friends; he cast her in two of his movies. In *The Misfits* (1961) she is the divorcee who tries to tempt Clark Gable with her laundry in St. Louis; in his posthumously released *Mr. North* (1988), she is, more appropriately, a character based on Mrs. Vanderbilt. As for Desmond FitzGerald, he disappeared into the Central Intelligence Agency and died in 1967.

Marietta FitzGerald married Ronald Tree on July 26, 1947. Their only child, Penelope, was born in New York in December 1949. The Trees had initially tried living in England, but Marietta's political earnestness had not played well, and champions of Tree's first wife systematically snubbed her. Back in the United States, Marietta Tree plunged into reform Democratic politics in New York City and, through a growing friendship with Governor Adlai Stevenson of Illinois, became a figure in the national party. She took an active role in organizing volunteers for Stevenson's 1952 and 1956 presidential campaigns. Her dinners in the Tree's elegant house on East 79th Street were noted for impassioned discussion of politics and policy.

By 1960 her friendship with Stevenson turned into a love affair. When President Kennedy appointed Stevenson ambassador to the United Nations in 1961, Stevenson named Tree the American representative on the United Nations Human Rights Commission. Tutored by the first woman to hold the job, ELEANOR ROOSEVELT, Tree became a competent and effective diplomat. In 1964 Stevenson promoted her to the Trusteeship Council with ambassadorial rank. Stevenson's sudden death in 1965, as he strolled with Marietta along a London street, ended her formal diplomatic career.

She retained her interest in domestic politics and served as a delegate to the New York State Constitutional Convention in 1967. Her concern with urban race relations led her to take courses in city planning at Columbia and to meet an English city planner, Richard Llewellyn-Davies. Her marriage had meanwhile become tiresome on both sides and was doomed by her husband's bisexuality. A series of strokes preceded Ronald Tree's death in July 1976.

Her friendship with Llewellyn-Davies blossomed into an active partnership in his global planning firm and soon became a love affair. His death in 1981 was a grave blow to her. She then served as chair of the Citizens Committee for New York City. Marietta Tree died of cancer—an illness she stoically kept secret from friends and relatives except for her older daughter—in New York on August 15, 1991, at the age of seventy-four.

Marietta Tree had sprung from a long line of Puritans—Peabodys, Parkmans, Endicotts. Her Massachusetts ancestors had been ministers, abolitionists, educators, reformers. The blood had not run thin. She had the New England passion to improve the world, a belief that, as the daughter of privilege, she owed society kindness and service. But she did not dedicate herself in the Boston fashion to plain living as well as high thinking. She united two contrasting American traditions—a New Yorker in her style, a New Englander in her soul. Her ideal, she once said, was to be a combination of CAROLE LOMBARD and Eleanor Roosevelt.

Marietta Tree was a woman of intelligence, beauty, and ambition who was born too soon. Hers was the story of a generation of women struggling at some psychic cost to free themselves from the old domestic concept of women's role and to embark on their own trajectories of self-realization. Succeeding generations of American women benefited from their struggles.

Bibliography: Marietta Tree's papers, including correspondence, notebooks, appointment books, scrapbooks, and an oral history, are in the Schlesinger Library, Radcliffe Institute for Advanced Study, Harvard University. Caroline Seebohm, *No Regrets: The Life of Marietta Tree* (1997), is well-researched and intelligent, though somewhat given to unsympathetic psychological speculation. An obituary appeared in the *New York Times* on August 16, 1991.

ARTHUR M. SCHLESINGER JR.

TRILLING, Diana Rubin. July 21, 1905–October 23, 1996. Cultural and literary critic.

Diana Trilling was above all else a critic: of books, culture, and the society she inhabited. She and her husband, literary critic and Columbia professor Lionel Trilling, were among a group of people in the 1930s, 1940s, and 1950s who have been called the New York intellectuals. This passionate and committed circle of activists and thinkers also included Irving Howe, MARY MCCARTHY, Philip Rahv, HANNAH ARENDT, Sidney Hook, and Dwight McDonald. Many of these intellectuals wrote for the *Partisan Review*, the magazine that best represented Diana Trilling's social and intellectual world.

Diana Rubin was born in New York City, the youngest of three children, and the second daughter, of Helene Forbert and Joseph Rubin. Both parents were immigrant Polish Jews. Her father was a manufacturer of straw braid, and the family, though not wealthy, was comfortable. As the youngest child Diana believed she should not outdistance her older siblings and felt a strong competition for her mother's affections. A fearful and anxious child, throughout her life she was haunted by fears of separation and the unknown. As an adult, a trip to a friend's country home could cause her to become weak with anxiety. She recognized that her fears were unfounded, but she could not overcome them.

A bright student, she attended Erasmus Hall High School in Brooklyn and then Radcliffe College, from which she graduated in 1925. She majored in fine arts but later regretted that she went through college without having read Dante, Homer, or Chaucer. After graduation she returned to New York City, where she lived for the rest of her life. Unable to find a job in art history, she worked as an assistant to the writer of a children's program for the National Broadcasting Company.

Her mother had always encouraged her to foster her talent for singing, and after her mother's death in 1926 she studied music seriously. She was encouraged by her teacher to pursue a career in this field but realized that her talents were not that strong. In 1929 she was operated on for severe thyroid dysfunction. The operation took an emotional and physical toll, and although it did not affect her voice, she never sang again.

She met Lionel Trilling at a speakeasy in 1927 and they were married in 1929, just months before the stock market crash. Both their families were financially destroyed by the ensuing Depression. Diana and Lionel lived on his small salary as a beginning instructor at Columbia University, and she became part of his world of intellectual friends. Disturbed by the attitude of people who considered her simply her husband's mate, she nevertheless considered her first role to be that of Lionel's wife. For the rest of their marriage she had to deal with being overshadowed by her more famous husband.

The 1930s were a time of intense political and economic ferment, and many intellectuals became Communists or fellow travelers. Trilling was sympathetic to the injustices caused by capitalism and actively supported causes that would help those people who needed it, but unlike many from their intellectual circle, she did not join the Communist Party. In 1932 Trilling had volunteered at the National Committee for the Defense of Political Prisoners, which she later identified as a Communist front organization. She joined, she wrote, because of her increasing fear of being alone and her need to be with people, not out of political conviction. By 1933 she had left the organization, disillusioned by the tactics and ideology of the group's leaders. As Stalin ruthlessly consolidated his political power in the Soviet Union, she and her husband became identified as staunch anti-communists.

Diana Trilling did not begin her public career as a writer and critic until she was in her mid thirties. In 1941 Margaret Marshall, the literary editor of the *Nation*, called Lionel looking for a writer for the literary notes column, and Diana offered herself for the job. Soon she was reading a book and a half of fiction a day for the column. On July 22, 1948, the Trillings' only child, James, was born; her approaching forty-second birthday and a desire to be serious about the future had spurred her decision to become pregnant. She left the *Nation* in 1949 to become a freelance writer. The first of her many essays for the *Partisan Review* (a review of MARGARET MEAD's *Male and Female*) appeared in 1950. Her essays also regularly appeared in the *New Yorker*, the *Atlantic*, *Harper's*, *Dissent*, *Redbook*, *Esquire*, and the *Saturday Review*.

Starting in 1964, her essays and criticisms began appearing in collections, all published by Harcourt Brace, that chronicled her wide-ranging literary and cultural interests. *Claremont Essays* (1964) treats subjects ranging from Norman Mailer and Alger Hiss to political scandals in England; *We Must March My Darlings: A Critical Decade* (1977) concerns the women's movement and other aspects of contemporary cultural protest; and *Reviewing the Forties: Commentaries on Culture in the 1940s* (1978) collects many of her fiction reviews for the *Nation.* Her only book of social history, as opposed to reviews or commentaries, was *Mrs. Harris: The Death of the Scarsdale Diet Doctor* (1981), a popular treatment of the trial of Jean Harris, the Madeira School headmistress accused of murdering her lover, Dr. Herman Tarnower.

After Lionel Trilling's death in 1975, she edited a twelve-volume edition of his work. With macular degeneration robbing her of her sight, she was forced to dictate her memoirs, *The Beginning of the Journey: The Marriage of Diana and Lionel Trilling,* which was published in 1993. In her ninetieth year, she wrote a seventy-five-page article on Goronwey Rees, a Welsh literary figure, and then headed for her summer home on Cape Cod. Shortly before her death she finished an account of an evening the Trillings spent at the Kennedy White House. Diana Trilling died in New York City on October 23, 1996, at the age of ninety-one.

Bibliography: Manuscripts and other material relating to Diana and Lionel Trilling are in the Butler Library of Columbia University. In her memoirs, *The Beginning of the Journey: The Marriage of Diana and Lionel Trilling* (1993), she writes about her childhood and life with Lionel Trilling through 1950. Additional information can be found in Stephen L. Tanner, *Lionel Trilling* (1988). In addition to the books mentioned in the text, Diana Trilling edited *The Viking Portable D. H. Lawrence* (1947) and *Selected Letters of D. H. Lawrence* (1958). In 1971 she received a grant from the National Endowment for the Humanities to interview the self-described New York intellectuals from the 1930s to the 1960s; the project was never finished, but ninety-three tapes and unedited transcripts were deeded to Columbia University's Oral History Research Office. An obituary appeared in the *New York Times* on October 25, 1996.

JANET BEYER

TUCHMAN, Barbara Wertheim. January 30, 1912–February 6, 1989. Historian, writer.

Barbara Wertheim was born in New York City, the second of three daughters of Alma Morgenthau and Maurice Wertheim. Both families were wealthy, assimilated German Jews distinguished for their public service and philanthropy. Her German-born maternal grandfather, Henry Morgenthau Sr., rose to a position of political influence during World War I; as ambassador to Turkey, he assisted Palestinian Jews and was a hero to Turkish Armenians. Barbara was close to her grandfather, from whom she absorbed her passion for geopolitics. Although not a college graduate, her mother was an avant-garde "new woman" whose passion was American music. She founded the League of American Composers and the Cos Cob Press, and supported the work of Aaron Copland, Virgil Thompson, and others. Barbara's father, a third-generation German Jewish immigrant, was a Harvard graduate, an investment banker, a philanthropist, and a patron of the arts. Her parents' artistic friends filled her Cos Cob, Connecticut, home in her childhood; ISADORA DUNCAN gave her dancing lessons. She attended Walden School, which her mother co-founded. By the time she graduated, her parents were divorced.

In 1929, she enrolled at Swarthmore. She did not want to take a required chemistry course, and she also objected to the sorority system there and its refusal to admit Jews. She transferred to Radcliffe, where she became a history and literature major and graduated in 1933. She regarded her honors thesis, "The Moral Justification for the British Empire," as "the single most formative experience of my career" (Tuchman, *Practicing History,* p. 15). She did not undertake graduate study, a decision she never regretted, as she thought it saved her writing style from becoming stultifyingly academic.

Instead, her preparation was in international affairs and journalism. She made excellent use of the opportunities provided by her family position. After graduation, she went to London with her grandfather to attend an international monetary conference and then worked in Tokyo for the American Council of the Institute of Pacific Relations. Back in the States, she wrote for *The Nation,* which her father briefly owned, and for which she reported on the Spanish civil war from Madrid. The defeat of the Spanish Republicans, she later wrote, "cracked my heart, politically speaking, and replaced my illusions with recognition of *realpolitik*" (ibid., p. 6).

On June 18, 1940 (the day Hitler entered Paris), Barbara Wertheim married Lester Tuchman, a New York City internist and eventually professor at Mount Sinai Medical School. Their first daughter, Lucy, was born in 1941. While Lester served as an army physician, Barbara made use of her knowledge of Japan by working with the Office of War Information. After the war, with the birth of two other daughters, Jessica (1946) and Alma (1948), Tuchman stayed home and began to write. Prodigiously disciplined, she wrote in the mornings while the children were small and then all day when they went to school. She gave credit to the domestic help she was able to hire. Nonetheless, "it was a struggle. I had three small children and no status whatever," she later recalled. "That was very difficult, particularly when you were, well, just a Park Avenue Matron" (*Greenwich News,* February 9, 1989). In the 1960s, she and her husband briefly divorced but then remarried.

Bible and Sword was rejected by numerous

publishers before it appeared in 1956. Inspired by the founding of the state of Israel, she examined the long historic relationship between England and Palestine, and provocatively argued that British support for a Jewish homeland in Palestine rested on a long-standing English philo-Semitic tradition. Subsequent books appeared rapidly thereafter and to much wider acclaim. *The Zimmermann Telegram* (1958) focused on the U.S. entry into World War I. *The Guns of August* (1962), which addressed the immediate precipitants of the First World War, won Tuchman the Pulitzer Prize for best work of general nonfiction and an immense and devoted audience.

As postwar America's most widely read historical author, Barbara Tuchman had an uneasy relationship with academic historians, who gave her books uneven reviews. Although a painstaking researcher, she insisted that she was more a writer than a historian. She characterized her own approach to history as narrative rather than analytic. Instead of emphasizing large social forces, she concentrated on individual human action, contingency, and character. Nonetheless, many a younger historian remembers reading and being inspired by Barbara Tuchman. "To write history so as to enthrall the reader and make the subject as captivating and exciting to him as it is to me has been my goal," she wrote in *Practicing History* (p. 17).

Tuchman believed that the past had lessons to teach the present and was inspired by contemporary developments in her historical choices. Just as the United States reopened relations with China in 1971, she published *Stillwell and the American Experience in China, 1911–1945,* for which she won a second Pulitzer. During the 1960s, she wrote many articles on two issues of great concern to her: support for the State of Israel, and criticism of American involvement in Vietnam. Although she insisted that she was not a Zionist, she visited and wrote enthusiastically about Israel after its 1967 victory in the Six Day War. She was also an early and vociferous advocate of U.S. withdrawal from Vietnam and one of the first public figures to call for Richard Nixon's impeachment.

As for another political development of the period, the rise of feminism, Tuchman appreciated its historic importance but did not become personally involved and found the clamor of the movement at times irritating. Like other high-achieving women of her generation, she believed that it was more useful for talented, determined women like herself to achieve success on the basis of their own merits. She was ferociously independent and individualistic. She liked being a mother, was proud that she did not let her writing interfere with her childrearing, and thought that motherhood gave women a certain superiority to men.

Tuchman received numerous awards, honors, and honorary degrees, including from Yale, Hebrew Union College, Columbia, and Harvard. She was a trustee of Radcliffe College, which all three of her daughters attended, and of the New York Public Library, where she wrote her later books. To honor her father, she endowed the Wertheim Study at the 42nd Street Building, a special room for serious authors regardless of academic status. She was the first woman president of the American Academy of Arts and Letters.

Barbara Wertheim Tuchman died in Greenwich, Connecticut, in 1989 at the age of seventy-seven of complications from a stroke. She is buried at Temple Israel Cemetery in Hastings-on-Hudson.

Bibliography: Yale University holds a large collection of Barbara Tuchman's professional papers. Her private papers are in family hands. There is a taped interview at the Greenwich, Connecticut, Public Library and a transcript of an interview done by her cousin in the American Jewish Committee Oral History Collection at the New York Public Library. A privately published pamphlet, "In Memoriam: Barbara Wertheim Tuchman," includes a biography, testimonials, and a comprehensive bibliography. *Current Biography* (1963), pp. 426–28, includes a long article on her authorial achievements. In addition to the books cited, Tuchman also published *The Lost British Policy: Britain and Spain since 1700* (1938); *The Proud Tower* (1966), a study of social life on the eve of World War I; *Notes from China,* a collection of essays (1972); *A Distant Mirror,* on fourteenth-century Europe (1978); *Practicing History: Selected Essays* (1981), which features several autobiographical essays; *The March of Folly: From Troy to Vietnam* (1984); and *The First Salute,* on the American Revolution (1988). An obituary appeared the *New York Times* on February 7, 1989. Lucy Tuchman Eisenberg provided additional information.

ELLEN CAROL DUBOIS

U

UCHIDA, Yoshiko. November 24, 1921–June 21, 1992. Children's author, activist.

Yoshiko Uchida was born in Alameda, California, the second of two daughters of Iku Umegaki and Takashi "Dwight" Uchida. Her father, the son of a samurai, emigrated from Japan to the United States territory of Hawaii in 1903 when he was nineteen. In 1906, he moved to the West Coast and later managed a Japanese-based import-export business. In 1916 a common acquaintance arranged a marriage between him and Iku Umegaki, who moved to the United States to marry him. Dwight and Iku shared in common their Protestant faith and degrees from Doshisha University, a Christian university in Kyoto, Japan. Although both daughters were American citizens because they were born in the United States, neither parent ever became a naturalized citizen.

A lower-middle-class family, the Uchidas rented a home in Berkeley, California, and were active in the community. Although all family members spoke English, they primarily spoke Japanese at home. Yoshiko ("Yo") and her older sister Keiko ("Kay") spent their childhood playing with other children in the neighborhood, attending school, and going to church. Nonetheless, as a Japanese American and a racial minority in the United States, Uchida did not fully feel accepted into American society. Of her years as an adolescent, she recalled that she "wanted more than anything to be accepted as any other white American. . . . I saw integration into white American society as the only way to overcome the sense of rejection I had experienced in so many areas of my life" (*Desert Exile*, p. 40).

Influenced by her mother's poetry and her father's letter writing, Yoshiko wrote stories from the age of ten. She excelled in her studies and completed University High School in Oakland in two and a half years, graduating in 1938. At the age of sixteen, Uchida entered the University of California at Berkeley, where she majored in English, history, and philosophy. Yoshiko was particularly active in the Japanese Women's Student Club, of which she served as president.

The war abruptly interrupted the lives of Uchida and her family. In 1942, President Franklin D. Roosevelt issued Executive Order 9066 authorizing the removal of all persons of Japanese ancestry from certain regions in the western states. The FBI immediately sought out leaders in Japanese American communities, and her father was taken to a prisoner-of-war camp in Missoula, Montana. In May 1942, Uchida, her mother, and her sister received ten days' notice that they would be evacuated from Berkeley to the Tanforan Racetrack Assembly Center in San Bruno, California. Uchida would not be able to graduate with her classmates, and completion of her studies at Berkeley would be delayed. The Uchida family was eventually reunited, then moved to the internment camp in Topaz, Utah.

While the family made a life with other Japanese American families in Topaz, Uchida's sister Kay received a release to teach preschool children at Mount Holyoke College in South Hadley, Massachusetts. Uchida, who taught school children in the camp for a year, received a full fellowship from Smith College in Northampton, Massachusetts, that allowed her to leave the camps as well. Uchida received her master's in education from Smith in 1944 and then joined her parents (who had also finally gained release) in Philadelphia, where she taught elementary school. The family then moved to New York City to join her sister; Uchida worked as secretary in order to focus on her writing.

After Uchida had little success getting her stories published, an editor suggested that she write from her Japanese American experience. Uchida's first book for children, *The Dancing Kettle and Other Japanese Folk Tales,* was published in 1949. In 1952, Uchida received a grant from the Ford Foundation to study the Japanese Folk Art movement in Japan. She wrote several articles about Japanese arts for Japanese and U.S. publications, and also authored a book about Japanese artist Kanjiro Kawai. Upon her return from Japan, Uchida moved to Oakland, California, where she cared for her parents until their deaths. In 1971 she moved to Berkeley, where she lived for the rest of her life. She never married.

The experience of growing up in between American and Japanese cultures, along with her subsequent experience living in Japan, significantly shaped Yoshiko Uchida's purpose in writing. In addition to learning much about her own heritage and ancestral culture, Uchida also became friends with the people Americans had viewed as enemies during the war. She increasingly emphasized the need for understanding and communication between peoples in order to work toward a peaceful future. Throughout her numerous books for young adults, Uchida addressed themes of belonging, self-acceptance, and the courage to be oneself in the face of adverse circumstances. Her later books increasingly examined the specific perspective of Japanese American immigrants and their children who were trying to fit into American society. This change in focus was motivated by her mother's death in 1966.

Journey to Topaz: A Story of the Japanese-American Evacuation (1971) was her first book addressing the internment of Japanese Americans during World War II. Her sequel, *Journey Home* (1978), relates what happens when the Japanese American family returns from Topaz to their original home in Berkeley, California. While these works clearly reflect aspects of her own and her family's experiences, *Desert Exile: The Uprooting of a Japanese American Family* (1982) is written as autobiography and is her most personal narrative of her life and internment. When asked why she wrote the *Journey* series, Uchida stated, "I wrote it for the young Japanese Americans who seek a source of continuity with their past. But I wrote it as well for all Americans, with the hope that through knowledge of the past, they will never allow another group of people in America to be sent into a desert exile again" (*Desert Exile*, p. 154).

Yoshiko Uchida devoted much energy to that goal, speaking in public about her own experience of being a Japanese American during the war. Those who met and knew her thought highly of her as a gracious and generous woman. Uchida is credited with only one adult novel, *Picture Bride* (1987), but her books have made the first- and second-generation Japanese American experience accessible to all ages. The final book she saw published was *The Invisible Thread* (1991), an autobiography for young adults. Yoshiko Uchida died in 1992 in Berkeley after a stroke at the age of seventy.

Bibliography: The largest collection of Yoshiko Uchida's papers is in the Bancroft Library, University of California, Berkeley. Additional papers are at the University of Oregon Library, Eugene. Her manuscripts for *In-Between Miya* and *Mik and the Prowler* are part of the Kerlan Collection of Children's Literature, Children's Literature Research Collections, Andersen Library, University of Minnesota, Minneapolis. The most comprehensive listing of Uchida's published works is in Daniel Jones and John D. Jorgenson, eds., *Contemporary Authors, New Revision Series*, vol. 61 (1998), pp. 449–52. The most comprehensive collection of reviews and articles about Yoshiko Uchida's work can be found in Lawrence J. Trudeau, ed., *Asian American Literature: Reviews and Criticism of Works by American Writers of Asian Descent* (1999), pp. 458–70. Other critical analyses of Uchida's work include Danton McDiffett, "Prejudice and Pride: Japanese Americans in Young Adult Novels of Yoshiko Uchida," *English Journal* 90, no. 3 (2001), pp. 60–65; Rocio G. Davis, "Itineraries of Submission: Picture Brides in Recent Japanese American Narratives," in Esther Mikyung Ghymn, ed., *Asian American Studies: Identity, Images, Issues Past and Present* (2000); Violet Harada, "Caught Between Two Worlds: Themes of Family, Community, and Ethnic Identity in Yoshiko Uchida's Work for Children," *Children's Literature in Education* 29, no. 1 (March 1998), pp. 19–30; Hideyuki Yamamoto, "Japanese American Families in the Works of Yoshiko Uchida," *AALA Journal* 2 (1995), pp. 39–46; and Masamui Usui, "Regaining Lost Privacy: Yoshiko Uchida's Story Telling as a Nisei Writer," *Studies in Culture and the Humanities* 3 (1994), pp. 1–22. Obituaries appeared in the *San Francisco Chronicle* on June 23, 1992, and the *New York Times* on June 24, 1992.

KAREN LEONG

UNDERHILL, Miriam O'Brien. July 22, 1898–January 7, 1976. Mountaineer.

"My feet just naturally took me uphill," reflected Miriam O'Brien Underhill, one of the greatest American mountaineers of the twentieth century. Miriam O'Brien was born in Forest Glen, Maryland, the older of two children. Her father, Robert Lincoln O'Brien, was a Harvard graduate and editor of the *Boston Transcript.* He also chaired the U.S. Tariff Commission and worked as an assistant to President Grover Cleveland. Her mother, Emily Young, was one of the first women to graduate from Boston University Medical School. Both parents loved the outdoors, and they introduced Miriam to the mountains of northern New Hampshire when she was very young. Throughout her life, she would seek wild places.

Miriam first saw the Alps in 1914, when she went with her mother and seven-year-old brother on a European tour. In Chamonix, France, Miriam tasted rock climbing on a small peak in the Mont Blanc range, but never dreamed she would one day stand on, and even ski down from, some of the surrounding summits.

Miriam O'Brien received a BA in math and physics from Bryn Mawr College in 1920 and stayed on to earn a master's in psychology in 1921. She continued her graduate work at Johns Hopkins, studying physics from 1923 to 1925. For several summers after World War I, the O'Briens returned to the Alps, and Miriam continued dabbling in fairly easy mountain climbing. When she was at home, she and friends in the Boston-based Appalachian Mountain Club (AMC) practiced the rock climbing they had learned in Europe. They also found that winters in New Hampshire's White Mountains provided rigorous conditions for alpine climbing. Her success performing there and her belief that her physical endurance knew no limits inspired her toward more challenging mountaineering.

In May 1926 she traveled to the Alps with the express intent of doing hard rock climbing, and from that summer until the mid 1930s she was unstoppable. Her skills, style, and determination grew with every new peak. She covered snow and ice with ease, but her specialty was difficult rock, where tiny finger- and toeholds require agility, balance, timing, and strength. At first she climbed with expert guides. Recognizing her singular talent, one of them took her up the south wall of the

Torre Grande, one of the most difficult pinnacles in the Dolomites. She was the first amateur to make this ascent, now called Via Miriam. In the summer of 1926, she and her guide became the first ever to climb the Aiguille de Roc, a sheer tower in the Mont Blanc range. This true first ascent whetted Miriam's appetite for more ambitious goals.

Soon she was going first on the rope, with the guide providing support as needed from behind. Going first meant solving the "problems" climbers face, such as finding a route on a seemingly smooth rock face, tackling a long, vertical crack, or getting up and over an overhanging ledge. The next step in improving her climbing was dispensing with guides altogether—a practice frowned upon by the professionals and many of their clients as very risky. Among her partners on guideless climbs was an increasingly close friend, Robert L. M. Underhill, a Harvard philosophy instructor and expert mountaineer she had met on AMC trips back in the States. They climbed often and well together, and soon realized that the chemistry linking them was not restricted to high icy cliffs. They married in 1932.

Despite her success climbing with Robert and other men, Miriam realized that in their company it was not really possible for her—or any woman—to fully expand her mountaineering skills. Even if women led, in the event of emergency men would insist on taking over; only by climbing manless, she reasoned, could a woman truly experience all of the responsibilities of leadership. Miriam was not the first who climbed without men, but it was she who best articulated the reasons for doing it.

Miriam climbed *en cordée féminine,* as the French Alpinists put it, with the best American and European mountaineers of her day. In August 1929 she and Frenchwoman Alice Damesme jolted the male-dominated climbing community by scaling the Grépon, one of the most difficult rock climbs of all. In 1931 she and Micheline Morin, another Frenchwoman, climbed the Mönch and the Jungfrau, two of the classic climbs in the Oberland. A year later, she and Damesme made the top of the Matterhorn, a feat considered the apex of Alpine achievement.

Over the next few years, Underhill's attention became focused on the home front. She gave birth to two sons, Bobby in 1936 and Brian in 1939. After World War II, Miriam and Robert turned to the Rocky Mountains for new adventure. Leaving their young boys behind, they explored the Sawtooth Mountains in Idaho and the Mission, Swan, and Beartooth Ranges in Montana on horseback and foot, and put up numerous first ascents. By 1951, the boys were old enough to try some rock climbing, and the family resumed its summer trips to Europe. The following year Miriam and Robert climbed the Matterhorn; for Miriam it was her third and final time. A year later her sons did it.

Meanwhile, Underhill had become an active member of the Appalachian Mountain Club. She edited its journal, *Appalachia,* from 1956 to 1961, and again in 1968. In the mid 1950s the Underhills started spending summers in Randolph, New Hampshire, a small community in the shadow of the Presidential Range that was a magnet for climbers and hikers. They moved there permanently in 1960. During the short summers at the highest altitudes of the White Mountains, Underhill assembled a collection of photographs of alpine flowers. These were published in 1964 in the AMC's *Mountain Flowers of New England.*

Miriam and Robert were charter members of an AMC subsection for those who climbed all forty-eight White Mountain peaks over four thousand feet. Together they initiated a challenging variation on this so-called Four Thousand Footer Club—climbing the same mountains in winter. Fastidious on detail, the Underhills insisted the climbs be done only in the winter calendar months, when the days are shortest and the weather most severe. They climbed Mt. Jefferson, their last winter four-thousand-footer, on December 31, 1960. Miriam was sixty-two years old and Robert seventy-one. They were the first AMC members to complete the winter list.

Miriam Underhill died on January 7, 1976, after a debilitating bout with cancer, in a hospital in Lancaster, New Hampshire. She was seventy-seven.

Bibliography: Underhill's biography, *Give Me the Hills,* is the best source for details about her climbing career. First published in England in 1956, it was expanded and reissued by the Appalachian Mountain Club in 1971; the opening quote is found on p. 248. Underhill's essays on climbing in Europe and in the American West appear in various issues of the *Ladies Alpine Club Journal* and *Appalachia,* the biannual journal of the AMC. Her most significant essay on climbing manless is "Without Men," *Appalachia* 19 (December 1932), pp. 187–203. Her wildflower photographs appear in *Mountain Flowers of New England* (1964). A memoriam by Christopher Goetze appeared in *Appalachia* 41 (June 1976), pp. 125–27; see also Nea Morin, "Miriam Underhill," *Alpine Journal* 82 (1977), pp. 272–73. Sections devoted to Underhill can be found in Julie Boardman's *When Women and Mountains Meet* (2001) and Rebecca A. Brown's *Women on High: Pioneers of Mountaineering* (2002). Cicely Williams in *Women on the Rope* (1973) also describes her achievements, and Sir Alfred Lunn credits her significance in *A Century of Mountaineering* (1957). An obituary appeared in the *New York Times* on January 9, 1976.

REBECCA A. BROWN

UNDERHILL, Ruth Murray. August 22, 1883–August 15, 1984. Anthropologist, Bureau of Indian Affairs educator, writer.

Ruth Murray Underhill was born in Ossining-on-the-Hudson, New York, the eldest of four children (three girls and a boy) in an upper-middle-class Quaker family. Her father, Abram Sutton Underhill, worked as a lawyer in New York City, fifteen miles from the family farm. Her mother was Anna Taber Murray. Both parents came from Anglo-American stock. Underhill attended the Ossining School for Girls, and the Preparatory School for Bryn Mawr, but enrolled instead at Vassar College, from which she graduated in 1905 with a BA in English.

After graduating from Vassar, her choices were marriage or teaching. Both looked tame, so she took a job as an agent for the Massachusetts Society for the Prevention of Cruelty to Children in Boston, where she worked with Italian families. She next traveled to Europe, taking classes at the London School of Economics and the University of Munich. She returned enriched by her language study, which eventually included fluency in five languages: French, German, Italian, Spanish, and Papago. Subsequently she settled in New York City, where she worked for several different social work agencies, including the Charity Organization Society. When World War I began in Europe, she secured an appointment with the American Red Cross and was sent to northern Italy. From 1915 to 1918 she cared for orphans of Italian soldiers; from 1918 to 1920 she served as an administrator of an Italian orphanage.

Following the war, Underhill returned to New York City and was employed by social work agencies for the rest of the decade. She also tried her hand at writing for newspapers, magazines, and advertising agencies. In 1920 she published her first novel, *White Moth,* about a successful businesswoman who must negotiate the strict gender roles of the workplace. Sometime in the 1920s she married Charles Crawford, but the marriage was unsatisfying, childless, and brief. In 1930 Underhill enrolled for graduate study at Columbia University, searching for a department that could help her to understand people. She landed in the office of anthropologist RUTH BENEDICT. Now in her forties with two decades of social work experience, Underhill was hardly a typical student, but she felt an immediate attraction to anthropology, which she sustained for the rest of her life.

At Columbia, Underhill's primary mentors and teachers were Benedict and Franz Boas, who promoted anthropological studies that endorsed cultural relativity and scientific objectivity. Boas encouraged his female students to work with native women in the field in order to discover aspects of female ritual and life inaccessible to men. Beginning in 1931 Underhill traveled each summer to Arizona, where she lived and worked with an older Papago (Tohono O'Odham) woman, Maria Chona, using Spanish to communicate with her interpreter. Underhill attributed her successful studies of Papago culture to her Quaker upbringing: she knew how to listen quietly and participate unobserved. During the academic year she worked as an assistant in anthropology at Barnard College under the supervision of GLADYS REICHARD, another mentor. In 1937 Underhill finished her dissertation, "Social Organization of the Papago Indians," and received her PhD.

An important result of her Papago fieldwork was her essay "The Autobiography of a Papago Woman," which was published in the *Memoirs of the American Anthropological Association* in 1936. Throughout the narrative Underhill expresses her interest in women's issues by emphasizing Chona's perspective as a woman. Because of Underhill's heavy-handed editorial work, many critics have questioned the ethnographic accuracy of this text. Others, however, praise her efforts at cross-cultural communication and admire the literary qualities of the autobiography. The text's collaborative nature, its explicit feminist agenda, and recently added contextual material continue to compel teachers and students of anthropology, life writing, women's studies, cultural studies, and Native American studies. Republished in 1979 as *Papago Woman,* Maria Chona's autobiography remains one of the most popular ethnographic texts.

Unable to find a teaching job because of her age and gender, and the Great Depression, in the summer of 1934 Underhill participated in the Hogan School, a school funded by the Bureau of Indian Affairs (BIA) that aimed to teach Navajos their own language. She also taught applied ethnology to BIA employees, most of whom were non-Indian. Underhill was next hired as an anthropologist for the U.S. Indian Service, the educational branch of the BIA. She held the position of associate supervisor of Indian education from 1938 to 1944, based out of Santa Fe, and supervisor from 1944 to 1948, based out of Denver. In these years she traveled extensively across the United States studying North American Indians, writing educational materials for the BIA, assisting reservation teachers with curriculum development, and presenting workshops about Indian culture to BIA personnel. Underhill also wrote several popular books during this period, including an illustrated ethnography of the Pueblo Indians, *First Penthouse Dwellers of America* (1938); a collection of translated Indian songs, *Singing for Power: The Song Magic of the Papago Indians of*

Southern Arizona (1938); and a novel, *Hawk Over Whirlpools* (1940). All of her works reached a wide popular audience.

Underhill retired from government service in the fall of 1948 and took a position as professor in the department of anthropology at the University of Denver. She retired in 1952, but later taught at New York State Teachers College in New Paltz and at Colorado Women's College. She also continued to publish books about North American Indians, including *Red Man's America: A History of Indians in the United States* (1953) and *Antelope Singer* (1961). In addition to reaching general readers, many of her books were adopted as textbooks by Indian school districts.

In 1979 the chairman of the Papago (Tohono O'Odham) tribe invited Underhill to a special ceremony on the reservation. Over a four-day period, ceremonies were held in her honor and she rode as grand marshal at the head of the parade. Because she understood the Papago people, the Papagos considered Underhill their friend and advocate. For the remainder of her life Ruth Underhill continued to travel, write, and consult. In 1984 she died in her southeast Denver home a week short of her 101st birthday.

Bibliography: Ruth Underhill's papers are located in the Denver Museum of Natural History. For a detailed biography and bibliography based on a 1981 interview with Underhill, see Joyce Griffen's "Ruth Murray Underhill," *Women Anthropologists: Selected Biographies* (1989), pp. 355–360. Griffen notes that many sources have misprinted Underhill's birth year as 1884; the correct date is 1883. Barbara A. Babcock and Nancy J. Parezo's entry in *Daughters of the Desert: Women Anthropologists and the Native American Southwest, 1880–1980: An Illustrated Catalogue* (1988), pp. 72–75, and *Current Biography* (1954), pp. 617–19, include lists of honors she received and reviews of her significant books. Underhill's preface to *Papago Woman,* pp. ix–x, provides a brief but candid overview of her work up to 1979. Catherine Jane Lavender, "Storytellers: Feminist Ethnography and the American Southwest, 1900–1940" (PhD dissertation, University of Colorado at Boulder, 1997), includes a chapter that analyzes the feminist agenda in Ruth Underhill's ethnography. An obituary appeared in the *New York Times* on August 18, 1984.

BECKY JO GESTELAND MCSHANE

V

VARE, Glenna Collett. *See* Collett, Glenna.

VAUGHAN, Sarah. March 27, 1924–April 3, 1990. Jazz singer.

The only child of African American migrants from Virginia, Sarah Lois Vaughan was born in Newark, New Jersey. Her father, Asbury Vaughan, was a carpenter and amateur blues guitarist, and her mother, Ada, was a laundress and church organist and vocalist. Sarah played piano and organ in Newark's First Mount Zion Baptist Church, but she preferred to sing. Her straitlaced father forbade her to go to dances, so she sneaked out of the house at night to go to clubs. A skinny girl with buckteeth and no sense of style, at age fifteen she shocked her parents by finding a job singing and playing piano at the USO. After dropping out of Arts High School for gifted children, in 1942 she decided to try her luck in the Apollo Theater's amateur night contest in Harlem. Her intense stage fright made the emcee think she might faint. But her beautiful interpretation of the ballad "Body and Soul" won her the ten-dollar first prize and the promise of a week's work.

Swing-era bandleader Earl "Fatha" Hines was amazed when he heard her sing at the Apollo in 1943: "Is that girl singing, or am I drunk or what?" (Gourse, p. 19). Her rich, smoky voice had a range of two and a half to three octaves, and she could give the impression of singing even higher. Hines hired her and bought her a pretty, white gown with a peplum. On the road, she tolerated the rigors of travel and segregated living and earned her nickname, Sassy, by standing up for herself in the midst of wild, mischievous jazz musicians. Vaughan worshipped Billy Eckstine, the band's starring baritone. She learned the rhythmic and harmonic innovations of the new style of jazz, bebop, from her band mates, alto saxophonist Charlie "Bird" Parker, and trumpeter Dizzy Gillespie, who told people, "Sarah can sing notes that other people can't even hear" (ibid., p. 20).

Leaving Hines, Vaughan sang with Eckstine's bebop band and then began a solo career. Though naive about business, she got herself a recording contract with Musicraft. While singing at Café Society in Greenwich Village, she met George Treadwell, the house trumpeter, whom she married on September 16, 1946. Treadwell became her manager, taught her stagecraft, and took her on the road. In 1947, she recorded "The Lord's Prayer." MARIAN ANDERSON, Sarah's idol, sent a congratulatory message, even though critics who were unaccustomed to Vaughan's style called her bebop-inspired embellishments eccentric. But Vaughan, who knew the quality of her work, told a writer for *Ebony* in 1949 that she would not be satisfied until she was singing on the concert stage.

She and Treadwell worked doggedly to get her lucrative bookings. Dave Garroway, whose midnight radio show, *The 11:60 Club*, was broadcast coast-to-coast from Chicago, dubbed her the Divine One. He used her recording of "Don't Blame Me" as his eerily atmospheric theme song. "It's Magic" was her first big hit for Musicraft. Then Vaughan switched to Columbia in 1949, and her moody version of "Black Coffee" reached number thirteen on Billboard's pop song list. Estimates of her income ranged from $150,000 to $250,000, and she acquired a taste for marathon partying with cognac, marijuana, cocaine, cigarettes, and jam sessions. Her relationship with Treadwell was stormy. The more successful Sarah Vaughan became, the less she wanted a boss.

In 1951, Vaughan's group went to Europe for the first time. By 1953, traveling with an illustrious jazz trio, she wished she could record more jazz, not just pop tunes. Treadwell switched her to the Mercury label and its subsidiary EmArcy in 1954, which allowed her to record both popular and jazz songs. She worked at least ten months of the year in concert halls and clubs. In 1958 her recording of the pop tune "Broken Hearted Melody" earned her a Grammy nomination. But it didn't help her marriage, and she filed for divorce. She married twice more, and with her second husband, Clyde B. Atkins, adopted a daughter, Debra Lois, in 1961. (Debra later changed her name to Paris Vaughan.) All of her marriages and long-term relationships failed, undermined by Vaughan's difficulty in separating her personal life from her demanding profession (her husbands and lovers doubled as her managers) and her single-minded focus on her career.

The late 1960s and early 1970s were dark days for jazz, as rock and roll reigned in the pop music world, but Sassy's voice ensured her survival. In 1974, Michael Tilson Thomas, the classical music conductor, invited her to sing a Gershwin program with the Los Angeles Philharmonic at the Hollywood Bowl. The Gershwin concert, a great success, was followed by more concerts with Thomas and others. In 1981 Vaughan won an Emmy Award for Individual Achievement, for a Gershwin concert with the New Jersey Symphony Orchestra that had been broadcast on PBS. In 1982 she performed Gershwin again with Thomas at the Dorothy Chandler Auditorium, accompanied by the Los Angeles Philharmonic and her trio. A CBS recording of the concert, *Gershwin Live!*, earned her first Grammy.

At the Monterey Jazz Festival in 1984, Vaughan sang "Send in the Clowns," a trademark song that showcased everything for which she had become famous—vocal acrobatics, playfulness, and her gorgeous, supple voice. Now earning $30,000 for single concerts and $40,000 for a week in a club, she kept traveling. Songs such as "Misty" and a cappella renditions of "Summertime" and "The Lord's Prayer" brought her standing ovations. She had the mysterious power to move people to tears with her singing.

Diagnosed with lung cancer in 1989, she performed in public for the last time at the upscale Blue Note Club in New York before returning to the Hidden Hills home in Los Angeles that she had purchased in the 1970s. She died there days after celebrating her sixty-sixth birthday. Her recording of "Ave Maria" was played at her funeral service at the Mount Zion Baptist Church in Newark, and her coffin was borne on a chariot drawn by two white horses to Glendale Cemetery in Bloomfield, New Jersey. With her genius for improvisation and rhythmic swing, Vaughan left behind a legacy of peerless recordings, and she won worldwide respect for performing jazz singing as high art.

Bibliography: The only full-length biography is Leslie Gourse's *Sassy: The Life of Sarah Vaughan* (1993), which draws on personal interviews with Vaughan's friends and colleagues and contains a discography as well as a complete list of her films, awards, and videos. See also Denis Brown, *Sarah Vaughan: A Discography* (1991). Collections of clippings exist in the Institute of Jazz Studies at Rutgers University, as well as in the morgue of the *New York Times*, with especially interesting articles by John S. Wilson. Many of the best-known jazz critics wrote about her, including Whitney Balliett, *American Singers: Twenty-Seven Portraits in Song* (1988). Pioneering jazz critic and historian Martin Williams offered a retrospective critique of Vaughan's recording career in the *Saturday Review*, August 26, 1967, p. 81. Obituaries appeared in major publications from coast to coast and abroad, including the *New York Times* and the *Los Angeles Times*, on April 5, 1990.

LESLIE GOURSE

VREELAND, Diana. July 29, 1903–August 22, 1989. Fashion magazine editor and curator.

Diana Vreeland was born Diana Dalziel in Paris. She was the eldest of two daughters of Emily Key Hoffman, an American, and Frederick Y. Dalziel, a Scot. Socially prominent and pleasure-loving, the couple included their children in their very active social lives. While Diana and her younger sister, Alexandra, accompanied their parents to European resorts and attended gatherings at their parents' Paris salon, the girls were not given access to traditional studies, and Diana's formal education was erratic.

In 1914, spurred by the onset of World War I, the Dalziels moved to New York City. Diana was enrolled at the Brearley School for Girls, but she soon proved incapable of standard academic studies and never again returned to a traditional learning institution. Instead, Diana began classes at the Fokine School of Ballet. Michel Fokine, the legendary Russian choreographer, was a significant influence in her life, imparting a strong sense of discipline and allowing free rein to her flamboyant imagination.

Diana made her social debut in 1922, and, as she matured, gained new grace and confidence. This poise represented a change for the plain girl who had been terribly shy and suffered from an astigmatism that had left her slightly blind. Despite her lack of physical attractiveness, Diana had a penchant for all things beautiful, as well as a remarkable gift of verbal expression.

In 1923, Diana Dalziel met T. Reed Vreeland, a Yale-educated banker descended from a respected Dutch colonial family. He was tall, handsome, and beautifully dressed. Diana's attraction was immediate, and the couple was married on March 1, 1924, in New York City. The newlyweds moved to Albany, New York, where their first son, Thomas R. Vreeland Jr., was born in 1925; a second son, Frederick Dalziel Vreeland, was born in 1927. The Vreelands returned to New York City, and shortly before the stock market crash of 1929 the family moved to London. Long after her many successes, Diana Vreeland counted her marriage, which lasted until her husband's death in 1966, among her greatest achievements.

Diana Vreeland's life in London was marked by elegance and extravagance. Much of her time was spent being fitted for clothes at prestigious fashion houses in Paris, such as Schiaparelli and Mainbocher. Vreeland's original sense of style caught the attention of these designers, and they offered her clothes well below cost in exchange for her chic visibility. She dressed in perfectly tailored suits and gowns that showed off her small and well-proportioned figure. Her choice of monochromatic neutrals served as a simple backdrop for her outrageous headwear and jewelry that would become the Vreeland hallmark.

This luxurious lifestyle ended in 1936 when Reed Vreeland was transferred back to New York. It soon became clear that her husband's salary could not provide for the family, let alone support Diana's standard of living. A chance encounter with Carmel Snow, editor in chief of one of the world's leading fashion magazines, *Harper's Bazaar,* led to Diana Vreeland's first job offer. Though she had never held a professional position, two gifts—an unerring eye and her witty bons mots—facilitated her ascension in fashion's ranks. Her life of privilege would also provide American woman of the Depression era a glimpse into a world of fantasy and romance.

Vreeland first applied her rarefied knowledge and offbeat point of view to a column entitled "Why Don't You?" Her suggestions included what to wear when taking tea with Hitler at the Carlton Hotel in Munich or how to decorate a newly constructed staircase from the library to your bedroom. Ironically, her often absurd suggestions proved to be cheerful diversions to readers and have become famed as "Vreelandisms." But she also offered practical ways for women to brighten their lives as she suggested five-and-dime-store trimmings to embellish a limited wardrobe. Her columns were widely read and even affectionately satirized. Vreeland quickly cemented a reputation for taste and daring and, by 1939, was working as the full-time fashion editor. For the next two decades, Diana Vreeland remained at *Harper's Bazaar,* where she redefined the role of fashion editor.

In 1962, *Vogue* magazine appointed Vreeland associate editor, and the next year she became editor in chief, the most prominent position in American fashion journalism. Immediately, she recognized that new trends in music, clothes, and attitudes were emanating from teenagers and the counterculture. After coining the term *youthquake,* she chose to celebrate the most unusual-looking young beauties in *Vogue,* be they models or debutantes, and turned some into celebrities. "Lifestyle" profiles became in-depth and featured glimpses into the homes of fashionable personalities, and articles that discussed aspects of grooming—from fitness to plastic surgery—were pioneered.

Though ostensibly aiming for a broad audience, Vreeland never ventured far from the privileged world of what she called the beautiful people. Rather than report on the latest fashions from Paris or New York, she sought to present some of the historically most dramatic images in fashion. Specially commissioned clothes that could not be purchased in any store were photographed in far-flung locations. Such images were to become legendary, but *Vogue*'s revenues began to drop sharply, and in 1971 Vreeland was fired.

That same year, the Metropolitan Museum of Art's Costume Institute was planning to reopen its revamped galleries. Desperately needing greater visibility and urged by her well-connected friends, the museum hired Vreeland as a special consultant. What she lacked in scholarship Vreeland more than made up for in terms of hard work and imagination as a curator. Starting in 1973, she organized popular exhibitions that drew fashion aficionados as well as the general public. Attendance soared, as did participation in the Costume Institute's annual fund-raising benefit gala—an event that became known as the party of the year. Vreeland continued to work until shortly before her death in New York City on August 22, 1989, from a heart attack.

Diana Vreeland remains a legendary fashion figure whose work as an arbiter of style and influential magazine editor served as a link to earlier eras in which extravagantly stylish women reigned. Her remarkable individuality seems all the more striking when contrasted with today's age of casual fashion and homogeneous marketing and presentation.

Bibliography: The best introduction to Vreeland's life is Eleanor Dwight, *Diana Vreeland* (2002). Vreeland's numerous articles and editorial spreads appeared consistently in *Harper's Bazaar* and *Vogue* magazines from the late 1930s to the early 1970s; for a compilation, see John Esten and Katherine Betts, *Diana Vreeland: Bazaar Years* (2001). In the files of Conde Nast, the parent company of *Vogue* magazine, are hundreds of memos issued by Vreeland throughout the 1960s. Her autobiography, *D. V.*, edited by George Plimpton and Christopher Hemphill, was published in 1984. See also her earlier book with Hemphill, *Allure* (1980). Vreeland was also the author and stylist of many other books and catalogues that were published to coincide with her numerous exhibitions at the Metropolitan Museum of Art. The more noteworthy works include *The World of Balenciaga* (1973); *Hollywood Costume: Glamour, Glitter, Romance* (1976); *Inventive Paris Clothes: 1909–1939* (1977); *Imperial Style* (1980); *Yves Saint Laurent* (1983); and *Man and the Horse: An Illustrated History of Equestrian Apparel* (1984). Vreeland was always evasive about her exact birth date (many sources cite 1906), but Social Security records confirm July 29, 1903. An obituary appeared in the *New York Times* on August 23, 1989.

PATRICIA MEARS

W

WADE, Margaret. December 30, 1912–February 16, 1995. Basketball coach, physical education teacher.

Lily Margaret Wade was the youngest of eight children born to Bittie Veal and Robert Miller Wade in McCool, Mississippi. Wade established and honed her athletic skills at a very young age, as her older brothers were exceptional athletes and often included her in their activities. Wade's advanced athletic skills and her height (five feet eleven) were put to use when she entered Cleveland (Mississippi) High School in 1927 and joined the girls' basketball team.

The relatively new game of basketball (developed in 1891) caught on quickly in Mississippi and other parts of the South because it was inexpensive and could be played outdoors throughout most of the year. Wade was attracted to the game because it required a balance of both physical skill and mental sharpness. Wade and her female teammates played basketball with six rather than five players per team, with the court divided into halves or thirds. Players were permitted to run only within their half or third of the court. Basketball's rigorous nature prompted physical education leaders to develop and promote these modified rules early in the twentieth century, as fears persisted that five-player basketball was too strenuous for girls and women. Despite these restrictive rules, Wade quickly became a team leader and was named to the all-conference team in 1928 and 1929.

Upon graduation from high school in 1929, Margaret Wade took her athletic talents to Delta State Teachers College to play basketball and pursue a degree in health and physical education. While at Delta State, Wade was elected to the all-conference teams in each of her first three years in college and captained the squad during her sophomore and junior years. She was given the team's Most Valuable Player Award during her junior year. Prior to Wade's senior year at Delta State, officials decided to eliminate the women's basketball program. The decision by school leaders was a response to the ever-present criticism that female participation in competitive basketball, even under the more restrictive six-player rules, was unfeminine and potentially physically harmful, thus inappropriate. Wade and her teammates were so upset with the school's decision that they held a ceremony to burn and bury their uniforms.

Wade earned her degree from Delta State in 1933 and began a short-lived career as a semi-professional basketball player with the Tupelo Red Wings. Semi-professional and industrial league sport, especially basketball, became very popular in the 1920s and 1930s; it gave working women an opportunity for recreation and provided the public with a relatively cheap and exciting form of entertainment. The Red Wings, like many women's amateur and semi-professional teams, traveled extensively to compete. In less than two years with the team, Wade helped the squad win state and regional championships.

A serious knee injury in 1935 ended her playing days. By this time Margaret Wade's outstanding coaching career had already begun. For over two decades, beginning in 1933, Wade coached girls' high school basketball at Marietta, Belden, and Cleveland high schools in Mississippi. She compiled an outstanding win-loss-tie record of 453–89–6. During her seventeen-year tenure as coach of her alma mater, Cleveland High, Wade directed her team to the state finals for three straight years. In addition, she coached its girls' track-and-field team to consecutive Mississippi State championships in 1958 and 1959. In 1959 Margaret Wade returned to Delta State as an assistant professor and chair of the Women's Physical Education Department. In 1973 Delta State President Aubrey Lucas announced that the women's basketball program was returning to campus, forty-one years after Wade and her teammates burned their uniforms. At age sixty, Wade agreed to be Delta's new head coach, despite having battled cancer and living with constant arthritic pain in her knees. In 1973–74, their inaugural season with Wade as coach, the Lady Statesmen won sixteen of eighteen games and the Mississippi State Championship. Wade's championship team was quite different from the Delta State team she played on in the early 1930s. Five-player rules, rather than the two-court, six-player game, now governed women's basketball, and the campus and the team had become integrated, allowing African Americans the opportunity to participate in and contribute to Delta's success.

Over the course of the next three seasons, Delta State women's basketball success helped bring the sport to the nation's attention. Wade's team amassed an amazing ninety-three wins to only four losses from 1975–77, winning three Association for Intercollegiate Athletics for Women (AIAW) national championships, and putting together a winning streak of fifty-one games. By the 1978 season, Delta State's success and subsequent fan support were evident as they played in front of several thousand spectators each game, becoming role models to girls and boys across Mississippi. The team's success was attributable to Wade's coaching style: a combination of grandmotherly compassion with a preoccupation for detail, simplicity, and perfection. Her devotion to the women she coached went well beyond their four years of athletic eligibility.

Although Delta State enjoyed winning seasons and earned a spot in the AIAW postseason playoff tournament during the 1977–78 and 1978–79 seasons, it became increasingly difficult for small colleges to stay competitive. As more money poured into women's intercollegiate athletic programs in the late 1970s as a result of Title IX, larger institutions with better facilities and other enticements were more successful at recruiting top high school players. Margaret Wade retired from coaching after the 1978–79 season. In 1980 she co-authored a book about basketball techniques entitled *Basketball* with Delta State's men's coach Mel Hankinson. She continued to teach basketball coaching classes at Delta State until her retirement from the faculty in 1982. She never married.

In 1978 it was announced that the Wade Trophy, in honor of Margaret Wade, was to be given annually to the best collegiate female basketball player in the nation. The award has become the most prestigious honor bestowed on a female basketball player, drawing comparisons to the Heisman Trophy in college football. Margaret Wade was inducted into the Mississippi Sports Hall of Fame, the Delta State Hall of Fame, the Mississippi Coaches Hall of Fame, Naismith Memorial Basketball Hall of Fame (the first woman so honored), and the Women's Basketball Hall of Fame. She died on February 16, 1995, in Cleveland, Mississippi, at the age of eighty-two. For over fifty years Margaret Wade devoted herself to women's basketball, developing players and the game and helping propel women's athletics to the place it holds in early twenty-first-century America.

Bibliography: There are limited sources available detailing the life of Margaret Wade. Two interviews conducted with Wade are located in the Capps Archives and Museum, Delta State University in Cleveland, Mississippi. The first is dated December 3, 1981, and the second, undated, appears to have been given after Wade's retirement from Delta State. Jacqui Salmon's account of Wade's life and career in "Margaret Wade: A Prize Coach," *Women's Sports* 4, no. 5 (May 1982), pp. 40–42, is a short, but solid, overview. See Sarah Pileggi's article, "New Era for Delta Dawns," in *Sports Illustrated,* March 31, 1975, pp. 67–68, for a review of Delta State's upset national championship victory over reigning Immaculata College. An exhaustive synopsis of women's basketball history, including Delta State's successes in the 1970s, is provided in Joan S. Hult and Marianna Trekell, eds., *A Century of Women's Basketball: From Frailty to Final Four* (1991). On semi-professional and industrial league sport, see Susan K. Cahn, *Coming on Strong: Gender and Sexuality in Twentieth-Century Women's Sport* (1994); Lynne Emery, "From Lowell Mills to the Halls of Fame: Industrial League Sport for Women," in D. Margaret Costa and Sharon R. Guthrie, eds., *Women and Sport: Interdisciplinary Perspectives* (1994); and Pamela Grundy, *Learning to Win: Sports, Education, and Social Change in Twentieth-Century North Carolina* (2001). For more on Title IX and its impact on women's sports, see Mary Jo Festle, *Playing Nice: Politics and Apologies in Women's Sports* (1996). A replica of the Wade Trophy is located in the Walter Sillers Coliseum on

Delta State's campus. An obituary appeared in the *Bolivar Commercial* on February 16, 1995, and the *New York Times* on February 17, 1995.

RITA LIBERTI

WALKER, Margaret. July 7, 1915–November 30, 1998. Poet, novelist, educator.

Margaret Abigail Walker was the first of four children born to Marion Dozier and Sigismund C. Walker in Birmingham, Alabama. Reverend Walker, originally from Jamaica, was a Methodist minister and a professor of philosophy and religion at New Orleans University (later Dillard University). Marion Walker, from Pensacola, Florida, was a pianist and teacher. In New Orleans, where the Walkers moved when Margaret was ten, Margaret and her siblings were brought up in an environment that emphasized religion, civic activism, music, and reading. Margaret's mother initiated her interest in poetry and the literary classics at an early age, reading the work of Paul Laurence Dunbar and Shakespeare, among others. As early as age eleven, Walker was reading the poems of Langston Hughes and Countee Cullen. When she was twelve her father gave her a journal for her poems and other writing. She also grew up hearing the stories of her grandmother, Elvira Ware Dozier, who lived with the family and told the youngster about her own mother, a former slave and a survivor of the Civil War who later would be the model for Walker's only published novel, *Jubilee* (1966). Walker's creative writing was profoundly influenced by the oral tradition, the rhythms of biblical literature, and the experience of being a black woman in the segregated South.

Walker graduated from Gilbert Academy in New Orleans in 1930. She attended New Orleans University for two years, but in 1932, on the advice of Langston Hughes, she transferred to Northwestern University; she graduated in 1935 with a degree in English. In her creative writing class there, Walker wrote about one hundred pages of *Jubilee,* but she concentrated more on her poetry. After graduation, Walker worked on Chicago's North Side for the Federal Writers' Project, continued writing poetry, and developed a literary friendship with the emerging writer Richard Wright. These years proved invaluable; Walker found herself among other young writers who were also honing their skills, including Arna Bontemps, Willard Motley, Frank Yerby, Fenton Johnson, and the dancer Katherine Dunham. The works she published in magazines and journals included her poem "For My People," published in the prestigious journal *Poetry* in 1937. "For My People," which has become Walker's best-known poem, offers a panoramic view of black people animated but suspended in their dead-end activities and asserts that revolutionary change, even violence, is necessary.

In 1939 she returned to academia, enrolling at the University of Iowa Writers' Workshop for an MA degree. Walker graduated in 1940 and completed the manuscript of poems that became her first book of poetry, *For My People* (1942). This volume won the Yale Younger Poets award in 1942 and established Walker as a significant literary voice. She was the first African American woman honored in this prestigious national literary competition.

The 1940s, 1950s, and 1960s were significant decades for Walker both professionally and personally. She began her career in university teaching at Livingstone College in Salisbury, North Carolina, in 1941, and at West Virginia State College the following year. In June 1943 Walker married Firnist James Alexander, a soldier and later an interior decorator. Three of the couple's four children were born before the decade ended: Marion Elizabeth (1944), Firnist James Jr. (1946), and Sigismund Walker (1949). Firnist Alexander was extremely supportive of his wife's work. When she won a Rosenwald Fellowship for creative writing in 1944 to continue her research for *Jubilee,* the couple returned to Livingston College. In 1949 they moved to Mississippi and Jackson State College (later Jackson State University), where she taught until her retirement in 1979. During these years, Walker raised her family (her fourth child, Margaret Elvira, was born in 1954), published essays, was an activist in her community, and earned a PhD.

The work on *Jubilee,* begun during the 1930s, stretched to thirty years of writing, researching, and revising before it was completed as Walker's PhD dissertation in creative writing at the University of Iowa in 1965; it was published the following year. Written in traditional narrative style, the novel recreated slaves' experiences on southern plantations, the upheaval of the civil war, and African Americans' efforts to establish themselves as free people in the aftermath of emancipation and war. Walker extensively researched archives to achieve historical accuracy in the novel, but her dedication to creating a convincing folk environment through the incorporation of stories, sermons, songs, proverbs, and the characters' black southern speech powerfully anchors the novel to its period. A few black historical novels had appeared before *Jubilee,* most notably Arna Bontemps's *Black Thunder* (1936), the story of Gabriel Prosser's slave insurrection in Virginia. Walker's book, however, set the standard for the proliferation of black historical novels (such as Alex Haley's *Roots,* 1976) and neo-slave narratives (such as Toni Morrison's *Beloved,* 1987) that followed.

Throughout most of her working life, Walker balanced four significant jobs—writer, college professor, wife, and mother. Imparting to her children the traditions and love that she had known as a child required considerable time. Moreover, having four children demanded that Walker be a wage earner; she could not enjoy the luxury of writing full-time. As she wrote in her essay "On Being Female, Black, and Free," the writer needs "a piece of time; a peace of mind; a quiet place; and a private life," and "nobody writes to full capacity on a full-time teaching job." Nevertheless, Walker's published volumes of poetry, essays, and short stories; her biography *Richard Wright, Daemonic Genius: A Portrait of the Man, A Critical Look at His Work* (1993); and *Jubilee* established her as a significant voice in African American letters.

Walker died of cancer at her daughter Marion's home in Chicago on November 30, 1998, at the age of eighty-three. Jackson State University recognized her service on its campus with the Margaret Walker Alexander National Research Center. Her work has been the subject of numerous books, dissertations, and scholarly conferences, as well as a documentary. The city of Jackson renamed the street of her residence in her honor, and the governor of Mississippi proclaimed July 12, 1980, Margaret Walker Alexander Day in the state that she had called home for nearly fifty years.

Bibliography: Walker's papers from 1940–98 are archived at the Margaret Walker Alexander National Research Center at Jackson State University. Her poetry includes *For My People* (1942); *Prophets for a New Day* (1970); *October Journey* (1973); and *This Is My Century: New and Collected Poems* (1989). Among her collections of essays, the most notable are Maryemma Graham, ed., *How I Wrote* Jubilee *and Other Essays on Life and Literature* (1990); and Graham, ed., *On Being Female, Black, and Free: Essays by Margaret Walker, 1932–1992* (1997). Biographical information can be found in Eugenia Collier, "Fields Watered with Blood: Myth and Ritual in the Poetry of Margaret Walker," in Mari Evans, ed., *Black Women Writers: A Critical Evaluation, 1950–1980* (1984). Graham, ed., *Conversations with Margaret Walker* (2002), is a collection of previously published conversations with the author arranged chronologically, beginning with an excerpt from a 1974 conversation between Walker and Nikki Giovanni and ending with a 1996 interview. See also the documentary film, *For My People: The Life and Writing of Margaret Walker* (1998). For additional information, see Graham, ed., *Fields Watered with Blood* (2001); Joyce Pettis, "Margaret Walker: Black Woman Writer of the South," in Tonette Bond Inge, ed., *Southern Women Writers: The New Generation* (1990); Janet Sternburg, *The Writer on Her Work* (1980), which contains the quotation on pp. 100–101; and Eleanor Traylor, "Music as Theme: The Blues Mode in the Works of Margaret Walker," in Evans, ed., *Black Women Writers.* An obituary appeared in the *New York Times* on December 4, 1998.

JOYCE PETTIS

WALLACE, Lila Bell Acheson. December 25, 1888–May 8, 1984. *Reader's Digest* co-founder, philanthropist.

Lila Bell Acheson was born Eliza Bell in Virden, Manitoba, the third child of five and the youngest daughter of Mary Eliza Huston and Reverend Thomas Davis Acheson. After completing his theological studies in Canada, Lila's father moved the family first to Lewistown, Illinois, where Lila attended high school, and then to Tacoma, Washington, where he worked as a Presbyterian minister. Shortly after their arrival in the United States, Lila and her family became U.S. citizens.

She attended Ward Belmont (later Belmont University), a two-year Presbyterian college in Nashville, Tennessee, before moving on to the University of Oregon, where she graduated with a BA in 1917. After college, Lila worked as an English teacher for two years in Eatonsville, Washington. During summers, she assisted with the management of a Young Women's Christian Association (YWCA) home on an island in Puget Sound. At the outbreak of World War I, she attended a short training session given by the U.S. Department of Labor and was assigned to improve working and living conditions for women laborers at a large munitions plant in Pompton Lakes, New Jersey.

A determined and promising social worker, Lila Acheson was busy focusing on a career, not romance, when she received a holiday greeting card from DeWitt Wallace, one of her brother Barclay's classmates from Macalester College in St. Paul, Minnesota, whom she had once met briefly. After college, DeWitt had remained in St. Paul, struggling to keep a job in publishing and trying unsuccessfully to secure backing to launch his own magazine. When Lila was sent to Minneapolis to help establish a YWCA in 1920, the two struck up a relationship.

Lila Bell Acheson and DeWitt Wallace were married on October 15, 1921, in Pleasantville, New York, with Reverend Barclay Acheson officiating. This personal union was the catalyst for one of the most successful professional unions of editorial and business talent in the twentieth century. Lila understood how to stimulate and organize DeWitt's creativity, and from her career in social work, she understood the American public as well. DeWitt's idea of condensing only the best articles, those "of lasting interest," from other prominent publications and gathering them in one pocket-sized booklet for the ease and delight of American readers, thrilled Lila. DeWitt wanted to call it the *Reader's Digest.*

The couple moved into an apartment at 1 Minetta Lane in New York's Greenwich Village. After sending out their first mailings offering subscriptions for three dollars, they left for their honeymoon. Upon returning home, DeWitt was discouraged by what he thought to be a poor showing of interest in the magazine, given the number of subscription orders they received. But Lila saw things differently. Her enthusiasm persuaded her hesitant husband to go ahead, and five thousand copies of the first issue of *Reader's Digest* appeared in February 1922. By 1935, circulation of the monthly magazine had passed one million. Today, in addition to publishing books, records, and foreign-language editions in offices all over the world, *Reader's Digest* has one of the largest magazine circulations in the United States.

The success of *Reader's Digest* soon caused it to outgrow its cramped quarters in Greenwich Village. The Wallaces moved the company to a suburban space in Westchester County and moved themselves into a small apartment in Pleasantville, New York. In the 1930s the rapidly expanding publication established a large Georgian-style office park and surrounding grounds in the neighboring town of Chappaqua, keeping Pleasantville as the official address of *Reader's Digest* headquarters because it had such an ideal ring for their all-American publication.

The enterprising couple, who never had children, built a castle-like home, called "High Winds," near the office complex in a community called Mount Kisco. While supporting DeWitt's editorial vision and protecting him from outside demands, Lila worked to design a company that was not only inspirational in theory but aesthetically pleasing in reality. Her day-to-day interaction with *Reader's Digest* employees was limited, however, because she mainly worked out of their home and communicated her ideas by memo. The magazine's cover was her artistic territory from day one, and she took great care in choosing just the right sketch or watercolor. She chose the color schemes and design for *Digest* property as well and worked with top interior decorators to construct company offices all over the world. It was Lila who decided that Pegasus should become the symbol of the *Reader's Digest* because, according to Greek mythology, the winged horse's hoof struck a fountain that was a source of artistic inspiration.

A fervent patron of the arts, Lila Acheson Wallace gave millions to the Metropolitan Museum of Art, the Juilliard School of Music, and the restoration of Monet's house and gardens at Giverny, France, and she oversaw the purchase of the *Digest*'s extensive art collection. Humane and well-traveled, Wallace also supported the New York Zoological Society and the restoration of the temples at Abu Simbel in Egypt. By far her greatest philanthropic passion was the restoration of America's eighteenth-century Hudson River mansion Boscobel. Her money rescued the dilapidated relic from the brink of destruction, and her artistic expertise and direction returned Boscobel, renewed, to the American public.

In 1972 President Richard M. Nixon presented Lila Acheson Wallace and DeWitt Wallace with the Presidential Medal of Freedom, the highest honor given to American civilians. Both Wallaces retired from active management of the company in 1973, though they remained involved in the Reader's Digest Association, Inc. Although she did not work in the public eye or flaunt her philanthropic efforts, Wallace's generosity and professional achievement left a strong legacy. With the death of her husband in 1981 at age ninety-one, Lila came to own almost all of the company's voting stock. Although she continued to make large donations to her favorite charities, her health was deteriorating and internal unrest and uncertainty over what would happen to the privately held *Reader's Digest* clouded her last years. Lila Acheson Wallace died of heart failure at her home in Mount Kisco, New York, on May 8, 1984, at the age of ninety-five.

Bibliography: Memorabilia and some personal correspondence are in the Special Collections of the DeWitt Wallace Library at Macalester College, St. Paul, Minnesota. Books about *Reader's Digest* include John Heidenry, *Theirs Was the Kingdom* (1993); Samuel A. Schreiner Jr., *The Condensed World of the* Reader's Digest (1977); James Playsted Wood, *Of Lasting Interest: The Story of the* Reader's Digest (rev. ed. 1967), which contains quality color portraits of both Lila and DeWitt Wallace; and John Bainbridge, *Little Wonder or,* The Reader's Digest *and How It Grew* (1946). An obituary appeared in the *New York Times* on May 9, 1984.

ANNIE LIZA BERGEN

WALLACE, Phyllis Ann. June 9, 1921–January 10, 1993. Economist.

Though Phyllis Ann Wallace was not the first African American woman to receive a PhD in economics, she was among the first to have had a significant impact on labor market policy in the United States. As first research director at the Equal Employment Opportunity Commission (EEOC), she developed a research agenda for quantifying the amount and impact of discrimination in the labor market. Later, she joined the faculty of Massachusetts Institute of Technology (MIT), where she maintained a high level of activity on corporate and government advisory boards, as well as in civic organizations. She had no role models, but she possessed an unshakable belief in her ability to make a difference, an amazing ability to define herself regardless of the preferences of family, friends, or social conventions, a fierce independence, and a commitment to transcend the stereotypes of race and gender.

Phyllis Wallace was born Annie Rebecca Wallace in Calvert County, Maryland, the eldest child of Stevella Parker and John L. Wallace. Called Becky by her six siblings, she legally changed her name to Phyllis Ann while she was in high school. She graduated first in her class at Frederick Douglass High School in Baltimore, but could not attend the University of Maryland because of her race. Instead she attended New York University with support from the state of Maryland, which paid African American students to leave the state if they wanted to major in something offered at the University of Maryland but not at one of the state's historically black colleges. Wallace joked that she compared the catalogues of Morgan State College and the University of Maryland to ensure that she would be able to escape.

At New York University, Wallace majored in economics. She graduated from NYU magna cum laude and Phi Beta Kappa in 1943, and entered Yale University's economics program that fall. Prevented by her race and gender from working as a teaching assistant, she deflected the slight by saying it left her more time for research. She received her master's degree in 1944, and her doctorate in 1948; she was the first African American woman to earn the PhD in economics from Yale. Proficient in four foreign languages (German, Russian, Spanish, and French), she focused her research on international trade and commodity relationships. Perhaps because of her fierce independence and her commitment to her career, Phyllis Wallace never married. During her life, she enjoyed a close relationship with her mother and siblings, and took a keen interest in the education of her nieces and nephews.

Wallace taught part-time at City College of New York and worked at the National Bureau of Economic Research before joining the faculty at Atlanta University (1953–57), but the heavy teaching load made it difficult for her to do research. In 1957, she joined the CIA as a researcher on trade matters. Her willingness to work at the CIA was consistent with her fierce independence and her desire to pursue a rewarding research career, but she was not forthcoming about her work there until later. Professionally visible on Soviet economic issues, she published an authored comment on industrial growth in the Soviet Union in 1959 and testified before the Joint Economic Committee of Congress on Soviet economic power in 1962. At a time when few African Americans testified before Congress, and then largely on civil rights matters, Wallace shared her expertise on a key international economic issue.

When the Civil Rights Act of 1964 established the Equal Employment Opportunity Commission, Wallace became its the first chief of technical studies. The EEOC research budget was sparse, but the agency was rich in data sets. A pioneer in research on the economics of discrimination, Wallace provided government data to graduate students and young academicians for analysis that was the basis for findings on the pattern and practice of labor market discrimination. Wallace is known for bringing together an interdisciplinary team of academics to develop EEOC guidelines on employment testing. Prior to the development of these guidelines, employment tests did not have to be directly relevant to job requirement or performance and some tests could be used to implement discriminatory practices. This work influenced the outcome of *Griggs v. Duke Power* (1971), an early employment discrimination case.

Wallace left the EEOC in 1969 to join the New York–based Metropolitan Applied Research Center (headed by sociologist Kenneth B. Clark) as vice president for research. She focused on urban poverty issues, especially as they affected African American girls. She maintained a research relationship with the EEOC as well, contributing some of the research that charged AT&T, the nation's largest private employer, with sexual and racial discrimination. The resulting 1973 consent decree was the largest and most comprehensive civil rights settlement at that time.

Phyllis Wallace's career took yet another turn when she joined MIT's Sloan School of Management as a visiting professor in 1972 and earned tenure there in 1975, the first African American woman to attain full professor status at the Sloan School. She was extremely productive in her years at MIT, writing or editing six books and more than a dozen working papers on aspects of employment discrimination. Her *Black Women in the Labor Force* (1980), co-authored with Linda Datcher and Julianne Malveaux, was one of the first studies to look at the status of African American women in the labor market. Wallace was also a founding board member of the Committee on the Status of Women in the Economics Profession (1972–75) and the first woman, and the first African American, to serve as president of the Industrial Relations Research Association (1988). In her inaugural remarks to that body, she encouraged researchers to deconstruct the barriers to advancement that exist for minorities and women in internal labor markets. She also reiterated her strong support for employment and training programs.

Phyllis Wallace retired from MIT in 1986, but remained active in university and Sloan School activities. Always passionately interested in the arts, in retirement Wallace continued to serve as an overseer of Boston's Museum of Fine Arts and helped establish its Nubian Gallery. After her unexpected death at her Boston home at the age of seventy-one, Lester Thurow, dean of MIT's Sloan

School, noted, "Professor Wallace widened all our knowledge and made everyone wiser about the issues of women attempting to advance in the business world."

Bibliography: Biographical information about Phyllis Wallace is sparse. See Julianne Malveaux, "Tilting against the Wind: Reflections on the Life and Work of Phyllis Ann Wallace," *American Economic Review* 84, no. 2 (May 1994), pp. 93–97. A Festschrift Conference, "New Developments in the Labor Market," was held in June 1987 at the Industrial Relations Section, Sloan School, MIT; it featured a talk by Alice Rivlin on Phyllis Wallace's work, as well as papers from colleagues and friends. Phyllis A. Wallace's published work includes *Unemployment among Black Teenaged Females in Urban Poverty Neighborhoods* (1972); *Pathways to Work: Unemployment among Black Teenage Females* (1974); *Equal Employment and the AT&T Case* (1976); *Women, Minorities, and Employment Discrimination* (1977); *Black Women in the Labor Force* (1980); *Women in the Workplace* (1982); and *MBAs on the Fast Track* (1989). This essay draws on conversations with Wallace's sister Lydia Mills, colleagues, and associates, and the author's personal communications with Wallace from 1974 until 1993. Obituaries (which include an incorrect birth year of 1923) appeared in the *New York Times* and the *Boston Globe* on January 13, 1993, and the *Baltimore Sun* on January 15, 1993. See also the January 13, 1993, article in MIT's student newspaper, *The Tech,* which contains the final quotation.

JULIANNE MALVEAUX

WALTERS, Sister Annette. May 18, 1910–February 22, 1978. Catholic nun, psychologist, feminist.

Born to middle-class Lutheran parents in Elmwood, Wisconsin, Margaret Anna Walters was the second of two children and the only daughter of Anna Berglund and Emil A. Walters. Her German-born father was a jeweler and part owner of Cohen and Walters Jewelry. Her American-born mother grew up in Minnesota in a well-educated, middle-class family. After a devastating flood during Walters's early years, the family moved to Minneapolis, where her mother ran a large catering business that supported the family while her father served in World War I and later after their divorce.

Bright and energetic, Walters attended public schools until her busy mother became concerned about her popular daughter's unsupervised activities and transferred her to St. Margaret's Academy run by the Sisters of St. Joseph of Carondelet (CSJ). Interested in the sisters' lives and appreciating their kindness during her high school years, Walters enrolled at the College of St. Catherine in St. Paul in the fall of 1927. By her sophomore year she had converted to Catholicism, and in February 1929 she became a CSJ postulant. Later that summer, she was received into the community and given the religious name Sister Annette.

Demonstrating unusual intellectual promise, Walters was mentored by the indomitable Sister Antonia McHugh, who in her role as dean and later as president steered the women's college toward academic excellence. Walters completed her BS in chemistry at St. Catherine's in 1933 and two years later an MA in educational psychology at the University of Minnesota. Groomed to return to the faculty at St. Catherine's, she continued graduate work at Minnesota and was awarded a PhD in experimental psychology in 1941. This was a unique and remarkable achievement, because, with the exception of educational psychology, the field of psychology was still viewed with suspicion at most Catholic institutions. During her graduate work at Minnesota she was mentored by young psychology professor B. F. Skinner. Although very different in their approach to psychology, religion, and life, these kindred spirits corresponded, visited each other's homes, and maintained their unique professional friendship for more than thirty years.

From 1941 to 1960, Walters chaired the psychology department at St. Catherine's, developing her reputation as a researcher and clinician. In 1948 she became a licensed diplomate in clinical psychology and four years later was awarded a Fulbright Scholarship at the University of Louvain in Belgium. During her Fulbright year she, in collaboration with Sister Kevin (Mary) O'Hara, wrote and published *Persons and Personality: An Introduction to Psychology* (1953). This book was part of the highly esteemed Century Psychology Series edited by Richard M. Elliott, and became the most extensively used undergraduate text in Catholic higher education for almost a decade.

After publication of this textbook, Walters began a twenty-five-year professional career that would expand and define her reputation as a psychologist, educator, feminist, and human rights activist. In 1954, Walters received a grant from the Hamm Foundation to co-found St. John's Mental Health Institute for Clergy at St. John's University in Collegeville, Minnesota. The institute was unique because of its mission and its ecumenical staff. For almost two decades, Walters counseled thousands of male clerics and conducted hundreds of workshops. In 1971, she resigned her position after the institute persistently refused to allow other women to attend. Chiding the institute for its "hopelessly passé and middle class" approach, she challenged the male board to "catch up with the dynamics of women's liberation" (Gillespie, p. 77).

It was also during the 1950s that she began presenting and writing for the Sister Formation Conference (SFC), beginning a twenty-year collaboration with Sister Ritamary Bradley (1916–2000), editor of the organization's *Bulletin.* Founded in 1954, the SFC was a national, grassroots organization developed and led by Catholic sisters, and in 1960 the charismatic Walters became its executive secretary. Unprecedented in its time, the SFC's purpose was to broaden the educational and professional expertise of nuns working at all levels of education, health care, and social service. Using the *Bulletin* to disseminate cutting-edge ideas and promote discussions, the SFC succeeded in creating dialogue among sisters of many religious orders (including Anglican) and, in some cases, male clerics. Its phenomenal success in expanding the power base and autonomy of Catholic sisters eventually led to Walters's and Bradley's removal in 1964. Threatened by the sisters' independence and expertise, Vatican officials subsequently suppressed the organization and renamed it a "committee," placing it under the more conservative Conference of Major Superiors of Women.

This event was an inspiration to Walters, who spent the next fourteen years expanding her social activism, embracing feminism, and advocating for human rights. In 1966, with the support of her CSJ community, she accepted a faculty position to begin a psychology program at St. Ambrose College in Davenport, Iowa. This allowed her to continue working with Bradley, who was on the English faculty. Their Davenport home became a refuge for nuns caught in the aftermath of the Second Vatican Council (1962–65) and political activists attacking sexism, racism, and the Vietnam War. In 1968 Walters joined protesters at the Democratic National Convention in Chicago and became involved in numerous national and regional women's rights organizations. Active in the National Coalition of American Nuns and the ecumenical Institute for Women Today, Walters advocated for women's ordination, participated in a program to assist women incarcerated in Alderson Prison, and in 1977 was an Iowa delegate to the National Women's Conference in Houston.

As the capstone to her professional career, she had been working on a book manuscript that would have been the culmination of over thirty years of clinical experience in psychology. She intended to do the final writing of *Psychology of Conscience and Moral Development* after receiving a research fellowship from Yale University to support this important scholarship. At age sixty-four, she was denied a faculty sabbatical by St. Ambrose University and instead was given a one-year, final contract. She was then replaced by a male faculty member in his thirties who had only a BA. She filed a sex and age discrimination suit, but died of cancer at St. Mary's Hospital in Minneapolis before the successful completion of her case, never having had the time to complete the book. Sixty-seven years old at the time of her death, Sister Annette Walters was the prototype of the twentieth-century activist nun who lived what she taught and believed.

Bibliography: The Archives of the Sisters of St. Joseph of Carondelet, St. Paul Province, holds information about Walters's college life and faculty career, religious activities, correspondence with superiors, materials related to the St. John's Mental Health Seminars, and some audiotaped interviews and other materials and artifacts. Marquette University Archives contains all materials involving her official duties as executive secretary of the Sister Formation Conference, as well as an extensive collection of personal correspondence, presentations, and articles, particularly from 1960 to 1978. Walters also co-authored *The Nursing of Children* (1948) with Gladys Sellew and wrote *Prayer: Who Needs It?* (1970). Pathbreaking articles include numerous writings published in *New Catholic World, Catholic Educational Review, Religious Education, Sponsa Regis* (*Sisters Today*), and the *Sister Formation Bulletin.* C. Kevin Gillespie devotes a chapter to Walters in *Psychology and American Catholicism* (2001). Judith Ann Eby's dissertation, "A Little Squabble among Nuns: The Sister Formation Crisis and the Patterns of Authority and Obedience among American Women Religious, 1954–1971" (St. Louis University, 2000), describes the SFC, including the years of Walters's achievements as executive secretary. Information also came from interviews conducted with Sr. Mary O'Hara, Eileen Gavin, and Sr. Ritamary Bradley, and with archival assistance from Phil Runkel, Srs. Mary Kraft, Margery Smith, and Alberta Huber. Obituaries can be found in the *Quad City Times* (Davenport, Iowa), February 23, 1978; the *St. Paul Pioneer Press-Dispatch,* February 24 & 25, 1978; and the *Minneapolis Star-Tribune,* February 24, 1978.

CAROL K. COBURN

WARE, Caroline Farrar. August 14, 1899–April 5, 1990. Historian, consumer activist.

Caroline Farrar Ware was born in Brookline, Massachusetts, the daughter of Henry Ware, a lawyer, and Louisa Farrar Wilson. The firstborn of two children, Ware came from a prominent, old-stock Unitarian family with an abolitionist tradition. She attended the Winsor School in Boston and graduated in 1920 from Vassar College. After a year of study at Oxford, Ware did graduate work at Radcliffe College, earning her doctorate in history in 1925. Because of her gender, teaching positions in major research universities were closed to her, so she joined the faculty of Vassar. In 1927 she married her life partner, Gardiner C. Means, a textile entrepreneur and graduate of Harvard Business School; they had no children. In 1929 her dissertation won the Hart, Schaffner, and Marx Economics Prize; it was published as *The Early New England Cotton Manufacture* in 1931.

Ware taught history at Vassar until 1934, with a two-year leave in 1931–33 to direct a research project that led to the publication of her second book, *Greenwich Village, 1920–1930* (1935). In these two major historical studies, Ware pioneered what she later came to call "the cultural approach to History." Her study of the New England cotton textile manufacture devoted equal attention to the Yankee farm daughters who worked in the mills and the Boston investors who owned them. Her study of Greenwich Village focused on the neighborhood's varied immigrant and working-class groups rather than the more famous (and far fewer) bohemians. This emphasis on ordinary lives anticipated by a generation the 1960s call for "history from the bottom up."

Franklin Roosevelt's New Deal opened opportunities for both Caroline Ware and Gardiner Means in Washington, D.C., and the city became their base for the rest of their lives. In 1933 Means became an economic advisor to Agriculture Secretary Henry Wallace, and Ware became a special assistant on the staff of the Consumer Advisory Board of the National Recovery Administration (NRA). Beginning a lifelong identification with consumer issues, she articulated consumer interests in the drafting of the NRA's industry-wide "codes of fair competition." In 1938 Ware began working full-time in the federal government as a social science analyst for the Industrial Section of the National Resources Committee. This activist bent continued during World War II, as Ware served as a deputy to the consumer commissioner of the National Defense Advisory Commission and in the consumers division of the Office of Price Administration.

Ware did not totally cut herself off from academe, however. She commuted to a part-time appointment at Sarah Lawrence College from 1935 to 1937 and also taught at American University. In addition, she served as a lobbyist for the American Association of University Women. In 1942 she joined the faculty at Howard University, where she taught history and, later, social work. Ware was also deeply committed to the field of women's labor education. Between 1922 and 1944, she taught at five summer sessions at the Bryn Mawr Summer School and the Southern Summer School for Women Workers in Industry. Drawing on that experience, in 1946 she authored a study that surveyed this field, *Labor Education in Universities.*

In the postwar period Ware increasingly focused on Latin American development issues. Combining her interests in teaching and social activism, she taught social work at the University of Puerto Rico for four successive summers. Fluent in Spanish and Portuguese, she was an articulate advocate for community education and participation in the development process, advising a number of international organizations such as the United Nations, the Pan American Union, and UNESCO. She was active in the Overseas Education Fund of the League of Women Voters and participated in many international conferences.

At the same time, Ware continued to be concerned with issues of social justice in the United States. Her decision to take a full-time position at a predominantly black institution reflected her broader commitment to racial equality in American society. At Howard she supported student protests against Jim Crow laws and picketed a segregated cafeteria. When several Howard students were arrested in 1944 for breaking Virginia's segregation laws covering public transportation, she posted their bail and arranged for NAACP lawyers to take the case. As a white woman, she felt that her constitutional rights were being violated if she was forced to sit apart from her African American friends. This reasoning underlay Ware's unwavering commitment to civil rights.

In 1935 Ware and Means had bought a seventy-acre farm in Vienna, Virginia, still well outside the ring of Washington, D.C., suburbs. PAULI MURRAY, who met Ware at Howard in the 1940s, called the farmhouse "a sanctuary for city-weary students and government workers, intercontinental travelers on diplomatic missions, writers, professionals, and leaders of various humanitarian causes." Panamanian-born labor activist Maida Springer Kemp recalled that the hospitality she received at the Ware-Means farm in 1945 kept her from snapping under the strain of the capital's strict segregation customs.

Just as the New Deal had drawn Caroline Ware into federal service, so did the election of John F. Kennedy in 1960. She served on the President's Commission on the Status of Women (1961–63), the Citizens Advisory Council on the Status of Women (1964–68), and the Consumer Advisory Council (1962–64), contributing to the emergence of revitalized women's and consumer movements in the late 1960s. In accepting an award from Radcliffe College in 1967, she connected developments in the United States with broader events in world history: "In these years, workers have moved toward becoming people, not merely hands to be bought by the piece or adjuncts to the machine. Negroes in the United States, Untouchables in India, Indians in the high Andes have all moved toward first class citizenship, and women toward full partnership; colonial status is becoming a thing of the past; the war on poverty calls not only for the elimination of material deprivation but for 'representation' of the poor." Ware saw a basic commonality in these dramatic changes.

A small, energetic woman known to close friends as Lina, Ware struggled with worsening eyesight as she aged. Gardiner Means had poor hearing, so just as they had all their lives, they complemented each other. Means died in 1988, and Ware died of a heart condition on April 5, 1990, in a retirement community in Mitchellville, Maryland. The farm they had bought for a song during the Depression was now worth millions, and in a final gesture of stewardship they donated the land to the Northern Virginia Park Authority.

Bibliography: The major collection of Ware papers is held by the Franklin D. Roosevelt Presidential Library, Hyde Park, New York. Additional materials are found in the papers of the National Consumers' League at the Library of Congress. The Schlesinger Library, Radcliffe Institute for Advanced Study, Harvard University, has two oral history transcripts of particular interest: Susan Ware, "Interview with Caroline F. Ware—Women in the Federal Government Project," January 1982, and "Maida Springer Kemp on Caroline F. Ware," a supplement to the Black Women Oral History Project. For the South Carolina experiences of her forbears, see Elizabeth Ware Pearson, ed., *Letters from Port Royal, 1862–1868* (1969; originally published in 1906). A secondary source of interest is Ellen Fitzpatrick, "Caroline F. Ware and the Cultural Approach to History," *American Quarterly* 43 (June 1991), pp. 173–98. Pauli Murray, *Song in a Weary Throat: An American Pilgrimage* (1987), offers evidence of Ware's commitment to racial justice; the quotation about the farm is on p. 198. For an overview of her broader motivations, see Caroline Ware, "Revolution of Rising Participation," *AAUW Journal*, January 1968, pp. 54–57, which contains the quotation about world history. Other books she wrote or to which she contributed include *The Cultural Approach to History* (1940), *The Consumer Goes to War: A Guide to Victory on the Home Front* (1942), and *Consumer Activists: They Made a Difference—A History of Consumer Action Related by Leaders in the Consumer Movement* (1982). An obituary appeared in the *Washington Post* on April 7, 1990.

THOMAS DUBLIN

WARREN, Elinor Remick. February 23, 1900–April 27, 1991. Composer, pianist.

Elinor Remick Warren's seventy-five-year career, one of the longest in American musical history, early established her as a successful woman composer of serious music at a time when men dominated her field. Born in Los Angeles, she was the only child of talented musical amateurs James Garfield Warren, a successful businessman with a fine tenor voice, and Maude Remick Warren, an accomplished pianist who had studied with a pupil of Franz Liszt.

Well before she began music study at age five, Warren began composing songs, which her mother copied into a notebook. She credited her first teacher, Kathryn Montreville Cocke, with giving her a solid foundation for her future in music, as well as with helping her overcome a shyness so acute that she would cry if a stranger spoke to her.

Her father's involvement in Los Angeles choral groups, as well as his personal interest in solo singing, fueled his daughter's interest in art song and choral writing. During her sophomore year at Westlake School for Girls, she studied theory and harmony with a well-known local composer, Gertrude Ross. At Ross's suggestion, she sent one of her compositions, *A Song of June*, to G. Schirmer, a major New York publisher. Schirmer accepted her composition for publication while she was still in high school. After graduating from Westlake, Warren spent one year at home, studying with Ross and taking piano master classes with Harold Bauer and Leopold Godowsky.

In 1919, she entered Mills College, renowned for its music school. After completing the freshman year, however, Warren felt she had exhausted the resources the school could offer her. She prevailed upon her extremely reluctant parents to let her go to New York City. During her four and a half years in New York, Warren studied accompanying with the most celebrated accompanist of the day, Frank LaForge; piano technique with Ernesto Berumen, a well-known Mexican pianist; and the larger compositional forms with Clarence Dickinson, eminent musical director of the Brick Church and professor of music at Union Theological Seminary.

Almost immediately, New York publishers showed an interest in Warren's compositions. In 1922 alone, major music firms published eleven of her songs for solo voice and chorus. Through LaForge, she met many Metropolitan Opera stars, who programmed her songs for their national tours. She also began her career as an accompanist to singers such as Lawrence Tibbett (whom she had known in California), Richard Crooks, Florence Easton, and Margaret Matzenauer. Billed as "assisting artist," she would perform a group of solo piano works in their recital programs.

In 1923 and again in 1925, Warren recorded a highly successful series of solo piano pieces for OKeh Records. Also in 1923, she appeared at the Hollywood Bowl as piano soloist with the Los Angeles Philharmonic in Mozart's *Concerto in D minor*, repeating the performance in 1926 at the orchestra's regular subscription series in Philharmonic Auditorium.

In 1925, Warren married a Los Angeles physician, Raymond Huntsberger. In 1928, they became the parents of a son, James. There had been problems in the marriage from the start, however, and a year after her son's birth, Warren began divorce proceedings.

On April 14, 1936, Warren's first major work with orchestra, *The Harp Weaver* for women's chorus and baritone soloist, set to a text by EDNA ST. VINCENT MILLAY, premiered at New York's Carnegie Hall with ANTONIA BRICO conducting. Though only the composer's first attempt at a work in the larger form, *The Harp Weaver* was a resounding success. Eight months later, on December 12, 1936, Warren married Zachary Wayne Griffin, like her father a talented amateur tenor, who had achieved national success as producer of the *Burns and Allen* radio show, starring George Burns and GRACIE ALLEN. The Griffins had two children: Zachary Wayne Jr. (1938) and Elayne (1940).

Following her success with *The Harp Weaver,* Warren now began to write extensively in the larger forms; during the early 1940s she gave up solo piano appearances and touring with singers to allow more time for composing. Her next work with orchestra, a choral symphony, *The Passing of King Arthur* (renamed *The Legend of King Arthur* in a later edition), for mixed chorus and baritone and tenor soloists, premiered March 21, 1940, at a Los Angeles Philharmonic performance broadcast over national radio. It won Warren international recognition and remains today one of her best-loved works.

Warren is best known for her more than sixty-five published art songs and for her compositions in the larger forms. Her love of the natural beauty she experienced growing up in the American West is notably heard in orchestral works such as *The Crystal Lake* (1946), *Along the Western Shore* (1954), *Suite for Orchestra* (1954, rev. 1960), and the song cycle with orchestra, *Singing Earth* (1950, rev. 1978). Mysticism is a prominent theme in her large works for chorus and orchestra, such as *The Legend of King Arthur* (1939, rev. 1974), *The Harp Weaver* (1932), *Abram in Egypt* (1959), and *Requiem* (1965).

Throughout her career, Warren made highly individualistic choices that tended to remove her from America's musical mainstream but allowed her to remain creatively independent. Rather than remain permanently in New York, she chose instead to spend her creative life in Los Angeles, where she had earlier found her inspiration. Unlike many American composers, she waited until 1959, when she was well established in her career, to go to Paris for nearly three months of intensive private study with Nadia Boulanger. With many composers adopting a more avant-garde style, she remained true to her neo-Romantic vision, which remarkably mirrored her own personality. Nonetheless, her compositions, accessible to audiences and characterized by a carefully crafted style that is emotionally intense and powerful, received significant premieres during her lifetime by important orchestras and artists, to generally favorable reviews.

Petite, beautiful, with a shy nature that turned to warmth and humor with friends, Warren was humble about her gifts and unable to accept a compliment easily. Devoted to husband and family, she believed that being a wife and mother nurtured rather than impeded her life as a composer. Though aware of the difficulties facing women in her profession, Warren preferred, instead, to proceed along the path she had chosen, believing that there was no gender in music.

Warren continued working into her nineties, including participation in a series of recordings of her major works. She died from cancer at her Los Angeles home in 1991. In 1996, her family established the Elinor Remick Warren Society, dedicated to projects that perpetuate her musical ideals and legacy.

Bibliography: Elinor Remick Warren's principal publishers include Ditson, Carl Fischer, Flammer, Galaxy, Lawson-Gould, Theodore Presser, E. C. Schirmer, G. Schirmer, and Masters Music. Her catalogue contains more than two hundred published compositions, including works for orchestra, chorus and orchestra, chamber ensemble, piano, voice, and chorus. Warren's family has donated the composer's correspondence, memorabilia, manuscripts, scores, and recordings to the Library of Congress, Washington, D.C. Other repositories containing partial collections include UCLA, the Fleisher Collection at the Free Library of Philadelphia, the New York Public Library, and the Los Angeles Public Library. Two basic sources dealing with Warren's life and music are *Elinor Remick Warren: Her Life and Her Music* (1987) and *Elinor Remick Warren: A Bio-Bibliography* (1993), both by Virginia Bortin. Important discussions of the composer's career are included in Christine Ammer, *Unsung: A History of Women in American Music* (1980); Susan Pearl Finger, "The Los Angeles Heritage: Four Women Composers, 1918–1939" (PhD dissertation, UCLA, 1986); Jane Weiner LePage, *Women Composers, Conductors, and Musicians of the Twentieth Century: Selected Biographies* (1983); and Ellen Lerner, *The Music of Selected Contemporary American Women Composers: A Stylistic Analysis* (1978). A brief obituary appeared in the *New York Times* on April 30, 1991.

VIRGINIA BORTIN

WASHINGTON, Fredi. December 23, 1903–June 28, 1994. Actress, civil rights activist.

Fredericka Carolyn Washington was born in Savannah, Georgia, the eldest of five children of Hattie and Robert T. Washington. Both parents were African American, although Washington's light complexion and blue-gray eyes made her racial identity a subject of speculation throughout her life. After her mother's death in 1915, Fredericka ("Fredi") and her sister Isabel were placed at St. Elizabeth's Convent for African American and Native American children in Cornwell Heights, Pennsylvania.

At sixteen, Washington moved to Harlem to live with her maternal grandmother, a housekeeper, and was later joined by Isabel. Washington attended Julia Richmond High School, but left before graduation to work in a dress company stockroom. She pursued further studies at the Egri School of Dramatic Writing and the Christophe School of Languages.

In 1921, Washington was working as typist and bookkeeper for Black Swan Records when the prospect of doubling her income persuaded her to audition for the chorus of the groundbreaking all-black musical, *Shuffle Along.* When the *Shuffle Along* tour ended, Washington joined the chorus at New York's Club Alabam', and in 1927 formed a ballroom act with one of the Club's male dancers, Al Moore. As Fredi et Moiret, they became the first African American artists to perform at the St. Regis Hotel in New York, following that engagement with a European tour. Returning to the United States in 1928, Fredi et Moiret performed in nightclubs and cafes, and in several musicals. As a solo artist, Washington danced in two musical shorts for major Hollywood studios: *Black and Tan* (1929), featuring Duke Ellington and his orchestra, and *Mills Blue Rhythm Band* (1934), featuring Hamtree Harrington and the Three Deuces.

As her career as a dancer flourished, Washington sought more serious dramatic roles. She made her Broadway debut in 1926 opposite Paul Robeson in *Black Boy*, playing the first of several "tragic mulatto" roles. (She initially appeared under the stage name Edith Warren, but soon reverted to her given name.) Although *Black Boy* ran only a few weeks, Washington attracted favorable critical attention. In 1930, she received praise for her performance as Lola, faithful follower of a Garvey-esque black nationalist, in *Sweet Chariot.* In 1931, Washington and Isabel created a sensational sister act in *Singin' the Blues.*

By 1933, Fredi Washington had become a sought-after young actress. That year she appeared in the musical short *Hi-De-Ho* with Cab Calloway; the feature film *The Emperor Jones* with Paul Robeson; and the play *Run Little Chillun,* which brought Washington glowing notices from critics and congratulatory letters from African American leaders. *The Emperor Jones* prompted the Motion Picture Producers and Distributors of America (which tightly regulated the content of films) to insist that Washington, playing a Harlem hussy, wear dark makeup to ensure that her love scenes with Robeson did not give the appearance of interracial romancing. In 1933 she also filmed in Jamaica a steamy tale of interracial passion and vengeance, *Drums in the Jungle,* released outside the United States as *Crime of Voodoo* in 1935 (and in 1936 as *Love Wanga* or *Ouanga*).

Her burgeoning fame soared with her next screen role in one of the era's most controversial films, *Imitation of Life* (1934). She garnered international attention for her compelling performance as Peola Johnson, a young African American woman who passes for white. Although co-star Louise Beavers's submissive servant role evoked considerable criticism, Washington's character aroused even more debate on the explosive topic of racial passing. Washington rallied to the occasion by becoming an avid spokesperson for race pride, speaking out against racial prejudice and the pressure to pass in Hollywood. During the run of her next film, *One Mile from Heaven* (1937), Washington expressed her goals as an actress in political terms: to portray realistic black characters, and to serve as a role model for other African American actors.

In 1939 Washington appeared onstage with ETHEL WATERS in the critically acclaimed *Mamba's Daughters.* Washington's pride in this artistic triumph was marred by protests surrounding its engagement at a segregated theater in Washington, D.C. When the *Mamba* tour ended, she gave up acting to take a full-time job on the *People's Voice,* a militant newspaper founded by her brother-in-law, Adam Clayton Powell Jr. Hired to do public relations, Washington became theatrical editor in 1943. She used her columns to protest racism and to exhort her peers to political activism. As her writing became increasingly critical of America's socioeconomic system, charges of un-Americanism haunted the newsroom. Although Washington denied that she was a member of the Communist Party, assistant managing editor Marvel Cooke claimed that she and Fredi Washington were both communists, and they were both fired in 1947.

Washington returned to performing in 1946–50, appearing in a string of plays notable for non-traditional casting, non-stereotyped roles, and commercial failure: *Lysistrata; A Long Way from Home; How Long Til Summer; The Triumph of the Egg;* and *Soldadera.* In 1949, she made her television debut on *The Goldbergs,* playing an atypically competent housekeeper who intimidates her employer. During these years, Washington also worked as registrar for the Howard Da Silva School of Acting and as an adviser to producers in casting such stage productions as *Porgy and Bess* and *Carmen Jones.*

Until her retirement from public life in 1952, Washington remained an outspoken advocate for racial justice. Having already co-founded and served as the first executive secretary of the Negro Actors Guild of America in 1937, during the 1940s and early 1950s she continued working with the National Association for the Advancement of Colored People (NAACP), the Hollywood Mobilization Emergency Committee, the Joint Actors Equity Theatre League Committee on Hotel Accommodations, the National Negro Congress, and the World Congress for Peace.

In her personal life, Washington manifested values instilled by the nuns of St. Elizabeth's and her grandmother. She dressed conservatively, preached monogamy and sobriety, and shunned late nights and narcotics. Her 1933 marriage to trombonist Lawrence Brown was childless and ended in divorce in 1951. The following year, she married dentist Hugh Anthony Bell; the marriage lasted until his death in 1984. Washington died from pneumonia in Stamford, Connecticut, in 1994, at the age of ninety. Her contributions to the cultural and social life of the nation were recognized by her induction into the Black Filmmakers Hall of Fame in 1975, and a 1981 award from the Audience Development Company (AUDELCO), a New York–based nonprofit group devoted to preserving and promoting African American theater.

Bibliography: The Fredi Washington Papers at the Amistad Research Center at Tulane University, New Orleans, and at the Schomburg Center for Research in Black Culture, New York Public Library, contain correspondence, clippings, scripts, programs, and photographs, primarily from the 1920s through the 1940s. Additional materials (clippings and photographs) are located at the New York Public Library for the Performing Arts at Lincoln Center. Information on Washington's life and career may be found in Donald Bogle, *Brown Sugar: Eighty Years of America's Black Female Superstars* (1980); Thomas Cripps, *Slow Fade to Black: The Negro in American Film, 1900–1942* (1977); "Oh Sister!: Fredi and Isabel Washington Relive '30s Razzmatazz," *Essence*, September 1978, pp. 98–99+; and Cheryl Black, "Looking White, Acting Black: Cast(e)ing Fredi Washington," *Theatre Survey* 45, no. 1 (May 2004). Obituaries appeared in the *New York Times* on June 30, 1994, and the *London Independent* on July 4, 1994.

CHERYL BLACK

WATERS, Ethel. October 31, 1896–September 1, 1977. Singer, actress.

Born in Chester, Pennsylvania, and raised primarily by her maternal grandmother, Sally Anderson, Ethel Waters was conceived when John Wesley Waters, a pianist and playboy, raped Louise Tar Anderson when she was only twelve. His mother, Lydia Waters, who probably passed for white, forbade her brown-skinned son from acknowledging paternity. Louise Anderson soon married Norman Howard, and their daughter Genevieve was born fifteen months after Ethel, who grew to resent her half sister because she was lighter-skinned and lived with their mother. A child of abject poverty, Ethel practically raised herself in the red-light district of Philadelphia as a foul-mouthed ringleader and a practiced thief with unorthodox religious convictions (drawn from Catholicism, Pentecostalism, and the Baptist Church) that persisted throughout her life.

Around 1909, Ethel was illegally married to Merritt "Buddy" Purnsley (she was thirteen, and the minimum marrying age was eighteen). She left him a year later because of his infidelity and abuse. She married Clyde Edward Matthews in 1928 and left him in 1933. Later in her career she married jazz musician Edward "Eddie" Mallory. With no children of her own, she pacified agonizing memories of her childhood by acting as a surrogate mother to dozens of young girls, including her half sister's only child, Ethel's namesake, who died young from illness.

Ethel adopted her father's family name onstage. Waters's first appearance lasted two weeks in 1913 at the Lincoln Theatre in Baltimore, where she was billed as "Sweet Mama Stringbean," a tall, lean, and skillful shimmy dancer performing songs like "Shim-Me-Sha-Wabble." To distinguish her act, she obtained written permission to become the first woman to sing "St. Louis Blues," and audiences compared her droll wit to that of Bert Williams as she toured the vaudeville and T.O.B.A. circuits from Atlanta to Chicago. (The initials stood for the white Theater Owners' Booking Agency, although black actors dubbed it Tough on Black Asses.) Ironically, Waters later became the first African American entertainer (other than Bert Williams in the *Ziegfeld Follies*) to move successfully from vaudeville and nightclubs to what blacks called the white time without wearing blackface.

Around 1919, she moved to Harlem, where she captivated black audiences at Edmond's Cellar, a top gathering place for musicians. In 1921, she made her recording debut on Cardinal records with "New York Glide" and "At the New Jump Study Ball." That same year, Harry Pace and W. C. Handy hired her to sing blues-oriented popular songs for Negro-owned Black Swan Records. Her first sides, "Down Home Blues" and "Oh Daddy," saved the label from ruin, selling 500,000 copies in six months and reaching both black and white audiences. Black Swan arranged for her to tour the South, accompanied by Fletcher Henderson. In 1925, Waters, now hailed as the "Queen of the blues," had an international hit on Columbia Records with "Dinah." Columbia, which paid her fee of $250 a record, never identified her in its catalogue as African American, epitomizing the enigmatic nature of her career and her life. She went on to record more than 250 sides combined for Black Swan, Columbia, and other labels between 1921 and 1963, championing an extensive array of popular songs that included spirituals and Tin Pan Alley tunes. She recorded with accompanists Pearl Wright and Reggie Beane and an extraordinary list of jazz instrumentalists including James P. Johnson, Coleman Hawkins, Fats Waller, Glenn Miller, Tommy and Jimmy Dorsey, Benny Goodman, Benny Carter, and Count Basie.

Ethel Waters was an unsurpassed popular singer and stylist, influencing musicians of various backgrounds including the elder SOPHIE TUCKER (who paid to study her style), Adelaide Hall, Ivie Anderson, Bing Crosby, PEARL BAILEY, Connee Boswell, Bix Beiderbecke, and BILLIE HOLIDAY. She had perfect pitch and never read music or formally studied diction, yet she excelled at risqué blues-inflected tunes and subtle jazz phrasing sung in a sweet and refined style that contrasted with BESSIE SMITH and GERTRUDE "MA" RAINEY, the classic blues shouters of the day. In 1933's "I Got Rhythm," she foreshadowed scat-singing devices later employed by Louis Armstrong and ELLA FITZGERALD, and generally drew on her own experience to become an exceptional storyteller through song on record and on stage.

Ethel Waters's acting career was set in motion with her Broadway debut in the all-Negro revue *Africana* (1927) and her film debut playing herself as a clear-cut jazz singer in *On With the Show* (1929), where she sang "Am I Blue?" Later, Irving Berlin spotted Waters in a commanding performance of "Stormy Weather" at the Cotton Club backed by Duke Ellington and his orchestra and signed her to join *As Thousands Cheer* (1933). Waters became the first African American to share equal billing with whites on Broadway, singing the showstoppers "Heat Wave," "Harlem on My Mind" (portraying JOSEPHINE BAKER), and the controversial "Supper Time," a heartrending song about lynching. Other stage appearances include *Blackbirds* with Eubie Blake (1930), *Rhapsody in Black* (1931), and *Mamba's Daughters* (1939), where she was the first African American to headline a dramatic Broadway play. Her film credits include *Rufus Jones for President* with Sammy Davis Jr. (1933); *Cairo* (1942); *Stage Door Canteen* (1943); and the all-black musical *Cabin in the Sky* with Eddie "Rochester" Anderson and Lena Horne (1943).

As one of the highest paid entertainers, earning $1,000 a week for *As Thousands Cheer* in 1933 and $10,000 for the film *Tales of Manhattan* in 1942, Ethel Waters gained influence over scripts and casting that was unprecedented for a black actress. Yet her remarkable contributions have been obscured by the stereotypical roles she played, roles that recalled southern mammies and television's "maid-coms" (situation comedies starring a black maid). Still, her acting led to pathbreaking achievements. She received an Academy Award nomination for best supporting actress for her performance in *Pinky* (1949) and won the New York Drama Critics Award for best supporting actress in *Member of the Wedding* (1950), a part she successfully reprised in the film version in 1952. She also starred in the first nationally broadcast television series featuring an African American in the leading role as ABC's cheerful maid *Beulah* (1950–52), a role later taken over by HATTIE MCDANIEL and Louise Beavers. Waters quit following pressure from black and white critics who viewed the role as a betrayal of her past accomplishments. Later she became the first African American actress to earn an Emmy Award nomination, for playing a dying blues singer on CBS's *Route 66* (1961).

Ethel Waters was one of the most powerful African American female entertainers of her time, bringing nuances and contradictions to the limiting roles available. She titled her rags-to-riches, best-selling autobiography, *His Eye Is on the Sparrow* (1951), after a favorite hymn. She retired to her home in California soon after, taking on occasional film and television roles until 1972 and regularly participating in evangelist Billy Graham's "crusades." She died in Chatsworth, California, in 1977 at the age of eighty, and was commemorated in a 1994 U.S. Postal stamp series devoted to popular singers.

Bibliography: Ethel Waters wrote two autobiographical books, *His Eye Is on the Sparrow* (with Charles Samuels, 1951), and *To Me It's Wonderful* (with an introduction by Eugenia Price and Joyce Blackburn, 1972). For biographical information, see Donald Bogle, *Toms, Coons, Mulattoes, Mammies, and Bucks: An Interpretative History of Blacks in American Films* (4th ed. 2001); Gary Giddins, *Visions of Jazz: The First Century* (1998); Sheldon Harris, *Blues Who's Who: A Biographical Dictionary of Blues Singers* (1979); Dwandalyn Reece King, "A Performance Biography of Ethel Waters (1896–1977)" (PhD dissertation, New York University, 2000); Tom Lord, *The Jazz Discography* (2000); Henry Pleasants and Barry Kernfeld, "Ethel Waters," in Kernfeld, ed., *The New Grove Dictionary of Jazz* (2nd ed. 2002); and Carl Van Vechten, "Negro 'Blues' Singers: An Appreciation of Three Coloured Artists Who Excel in an Unusual and Native Medium," *Vanity Fair*, March 1926, pp. 67, 106, 108. An obituary appeared in the *New York Times* on September 2, 1977.

KYRA D. GAUNT

WAUNEKA, Annie Dodge. April 11, 1910–November 10, 1997. Navajo leader, health care activist.

Annie Dodge Wauneka, who was born in a dirt-floored hogan in Sawmill (Deer Springs), Arizona, has been called "a one-woman Peace Corps for the Navajos." Her father was charismatic Navajo leader and tribal chairman Henry "Chee" Dodge. Her mother, Kee' hananba, a sheepherder, had been married to Chee for a short time but had separated from him by the time Annie was born. Annie was raised in her father's household, where she had an older half-sister and two older half-brothers.

At the time Chee Dodge added Annie to his

household, he was fifty years old, a wealthy rancher, and extremely active in tribal affairs. The Dodge home saw a constant stream of both Navajo and white visitors. Frequently the little girl fell asleep to the lull of adult voices assessing the meaning of some new policy and how it might affect the Navajo. No one, least of all her father, would have guessed that the seed of political awareness and public service was being planted in Annie as she lay bundled in her blankets.

But it was this relationship with her father—indirectly as a child and more intensely as a young adult—that nurtured her desire to work for her people. Although Chee Dodge treated Annie less well than his other children when she was small, making her herd sheep while he sent her half-siblings to private, off-reservation schools, he eventually enrolled her in the Bureau of Indian Affairs (BIA) school in Fort Defiance, Arizona. While there she was baptized in the Roman Catholic church, which she attended all her life, although she also retained her traditional Navajo spiritual beliefs. She also attended the Albuquerque Indian School in New Mexico through the eleventh grade. On October 22, 1929, a year after she left school, she married George Wauneka, a handsome Navajo athlete she had met there, and the young couple was sent to manage Chee's ranch at Tanner Springs, Arizona. Between 1931 and 1950 they had ten children (Georgianne, James Henry, Marvin, Henry Chee, Irma Lydia, George Leonard, Timothy, Franklin, Lorencita, and Sullie Shirlene), nine of whom survived infancy.

During the 1930s and 1940s, Chee urged Annie to get involved in local tribal politics. He took her with him as he traveled the reservation and ultimately passed his legacy for leadership to her on his deathbed in 1947. Annie Dodge Wauneka was elected to the Navajo Tribal Council in the next election in 1951, representing Klagetoh and Wide Ruins. The only previous woman council member had served just one term. Having a woman in a position of authority, however, was not unusual for Navajos. Women were actively involved in decision making at home and in lower levels of tribal government. The Waunekas still had children at home when Annie took her seat on the council, but George and various relatives pitched in to care for the children while she concentrated on her new career.

At this time tuberculosis was running rampant through the Navajo Tribe at a level nine times that in the general American population. Doctors with the Bureau of Indian Affairs, the wing of the Department of the Interior responsible for federal programs for American Indians, struggled to deal with the epidemic. In the mid 1950s, frustrated at being unable to bring it under control, they asked the Navajo Tribal Council for help. The council in turn appointed its one woman member to look into it.

Wauneka took this assignment seriously, and it defined most of the rest of her professional life. First she studied with the BIA doctors until she understood the disease. Then she drove her pickup truck throughout the Southwest, visiting all the hospitals where Navajos were treated. She also sought out infected Navajos and convinced them to go the hospital for treatment. She skillfully managed to get the traditional medicine men and the BIA doctors to work together by bringing the medicine men to the clinics where they could learn about TB, and by helping the government doctors learn in what instances the traditional doctors were more effective. For her work on tuberculosis and other Navajo medical problems, Annie Wauneka was one of thirty-one distinguished Americans selected for the Presidential Medal of Freedom in 1963.

After new drugs brought TB more under control, Wauneka turned her attention to Navajos' need for better nutrition with a weekly Navajo-language radio program. She also targeted child health, with an annual baby contest at the Inter-Tribal Fair in Gallup and with free layettes for any mothers who had their newborns checked by government doctors. In the 1960s she worked to bring Head Start to the Navajos. She even worked to bring a medical school to the reservation, but was unable to get financing for this dream.

Throughout her life, Wauneka served as a bridge between her people and white government officials. She traveled to Washington, D.C., repeatedly to give testimony before congressional committees, usually around budget time, reminding the legislators of their responsibility to appropriate enough funds to meet Navajo medical and educational needs. She was famously outspoken when she thought white government officials were not living up to their obligations. Wauneka attracted attention when she traveled, in part because she always wore traditional Navajo outfits—long gathered skirts and velvet tunics, silver and turquoise necklaces and bracelets, and her hair pulled back in a two-looped bun bound with white yarn.

Annie Wauneka served on the Navajo Tribal Council for twenty-seven years. She lost her last election by thirteen votes in 1978, partly because some of her constituents thought she was too focused on national politics. She continued to work on boards and as a counselor to younger Navajos and remained active well into her seventies, when she was slowed by age and Alzheimer's disease. Wauneka died on November 10, 1997, and was buried in a remote location on the Tanner Springs Ranch in Arizona. The Navajo Tribal Council closed for a day to mourn her passing.

Bibliography: An overview of Wauneka's life can be found in Carolyn Niethammer, *I'll Go and Do More: Annie Dodge Wauneka, Navajo Leader and Activist* (2001); the opening quote is found on p. 140. See also Mary Carroll Nelson, *Annie Wauneka: The Story of an American Indian* (1972), and Virginia Hoffman and Broderick H. Johnson, "Annie Dodge Wauneka," in their *Navajo Biographies* (1970). Wauneka's articles include "The Dilemma for Indian Women," *Wassaja,* September 1976, p. 8; and "Helping a People to Understand," *American Journal of Nursing,* July 1962, reprinted in Pamela J. Brink, ed., *Transcultural Nursing: A Book of Readings* (1990), pp. 234–40. Her activities are well documented in the *Navajo Times* (Window Rock, Arizona) and the *Gallup Independent* (New Mexico) between 1951 and 1978. Her speeches from her twenty-seven years in the Navajo Tribal Council are available on microfiche in the Navajo Tribal Council Office of Records in Window Rock, Arizona. A funeral program was provided by her daughter Irma Bluehouse, who also shared additional information. Other information was provided by Ellouise DeGroat, Abe and Mildred Chanin, and her grandson, Milton Bluehouse Jr. The Navajo Nation Museum in Window Rock has many photographs of Annie Wauneka and her family. An obituary appeared in the *New York Times* on November 16, 1997.

CAROLYN NIETHAMMER

WAY, Katharine. February 20, 1902–December 9, 1995. Physicist.

Katharine Jones Way, a pioneer in developing techniques for the collection, evaluation, and dissemination of data in nuclear physics, was born in Sewickley, Pennsylvania, to William Addison Way, a lawyer, and Louise Jones, a housewife. She was christened Catherine, but later changed her name to Katharine, and was known as Kay to her friends and colleagues. She was the second of three children, with an older brother and a younger sister. Her mother died when Way was twelve, and her father remarried shortly thereafter. Her stepmother was an ear and throat specialist, and impressed Way early in her life with the realization that women can play an important role in the professional world.

Way's pre-college years were divided between Miss Hartridge's boarding school in Plainfield, New Jersey, and Rosemary Hall boarding school in Greenwich, Connecticut. The latter school was noted for its emphasis on intellectual development, and Way thrived on the demanding curriculum. Way enrolled at Vassar College in 1920, but dropped out after completing only two years of study because of illness, diagnosed as possible tuberculosis. Following a two-year convalescence at Saranac Lake, New York, she attended Barnard College for two semesters in 1924–25. Still unsure of her career goals, she took off several more years, and when she resumed her college studies it was at Columbia University, where she studied mathematics. There, Professor Edward Kasner instilled in her an interest in mathematics, and her first published paper was co-authored with Dr. Kasner. Way attended classes at Columbia between 1929 and 1934, and continued her education at the University of North Carolina (UNC), Chapel Hill. Here she met John Wheeler, a physicist who stimulated her interest and enthusiasm for physics in general and nuclear physics in particular. Way was Wheeler's first graduate student, and he became a mentor and remained a valued friend throughout her career. She never married.

After obtaining her PhD in nuclear theory at UNC in 1938, Way held a Huff Research Fellowship at Bryn Mawr college in 1938–39, followed by a position at the University of Tennessee as instructor from 1939 to 1941 and then as assistant professor in 1941–42. By then World War II was creating unprecedented opportunities for women in science, including in physics. John Wheeler helped her obtain a research position with the Manhattan Project, which was secretly developing the atomic bomb. She worked first in Chicago, where she collaborated with Eugene Wigner (Nobel Laureate, 1963) and developed what became known as the Way-Wigner formula for fission-product decay. Then she moved to Oak Ridge National Laboratory (then called Clinton Laboratories) in Oak Ridge, Tennessee. Wartime research efforts produced vast amounts of data on nuclear decay, and in her Oak Ridge years Way specialized in the collection and systematization of these data, which became the focus of the rest of her career.

In 1949, Way moved to the National Bureau of Standards in Washington, D.C., to continue her evaluation work. In 1953, with the goals of putting her evaluation efforts on a more permanent footing and simultaneously achieving a wider dissemination of the results, Way approached the National Academy of Sciences National Research Council with a proposal to form a research group devoted to the evaluation and dissemination of nuclear data. She assembled a group of physicists, and under her leadership this group, known as the Nuclear Data Project (NDP), began regular publication of loose-leaf sheets of evaluated data that became known as the Nuclear Data Sheets. Feeling the need for a closer association of her team with an active research center, Way arranged for the project to move to Oak Ridge National Laboratory in 1964. At the same time, Way took dissemination of the ever-increasing amounts of evaluated data on nuclear-level properties and radioactive decay characteristics one step further by establishing a new two-part journal, *Nuclear Data,* published by Academic Press. Section B continued the Nuclear Data Sheets; Section A, titled *Nuclear Data Tables,* included other physics compilations. Way was the editor, and the editorial board included John Wheeler. Section A's first issue appeared in December 1965, Section B's appeared in February 1966.

Way is best known for her work with the NDP, and she remained its head until her retirement in 1968, when she moved to Durham, North Carolina, and became an adjunct professor at Duke University. She continued to edit the journal *Nuclear Data Tables* and in 1973 expanded the coverage to include compilations in atomic data. Way remained as editor of the expanded journal *Atomic Data and Nuclear Data Tables* until 1982.

Throughout her life Way never hesitated to speak out or act when she encountered unfairness, whether to individuals or in the context of larger social issues. While at graduate school in North Carolina, Way joined in efforts to provide food and clothing to textile workers who had lost their jobs as a result of strikes. In 1946 she and Dexter Masters co-edited *One World or None,* which focused on the threat to world peace posed by the atomic bomb and the need for international atomic weapons control. Including contributions by leading scientists such as Hans Bethe, Niels Bohr, and Albert Einstein, the book sold a hundred thousand copies and was translated into several languages. As McCarthyism surfaced in the postwar scientific community, Way reacted strongly against the investigations directed at some of the scientists who had been accused based on innuendo, rumor, and gossip. Way and another physicist wrote to the Atomic Energy Commission complaining about the proceedings. In the early sixties, Way took part in marches and other activities in support of the civil rights movement.

In person, Way was friendly but demanding. Those who worked directly with her quickly learned to appreciate her periods of intense concentration. During her retirement years in Durham, Way became interested in the health problems of the aged. She organized talks, researched materials pertaining to health or financial issues of seniors to help members of local senior groups keep abreast of new developments, and formed an ad hoc committee, Durham Seniors for Better Health in the City of Medicine. In 1974 Way was named a University of North Carolina Distinguished Alumnus. The award was a tribute to a distinguished career in which intellectual honesty and original thinking were mixed with equal parts of love for friends and care for those less fortunate than herself. Katharine Way died in Chapel Hill at the age of ninety-three.

Bibliography: The personal details in this essay were obtained by the author from several interviews with Way. For further information on Way, including a list of most of her published papers and sources for other publications, see the article by Murray J. Martin, Norwood B. Gove, Ruth M. Gove, and Agda Artna in Louise S. Grinstein, Rose K. Rose, and Miriam H. Rafailovich, eds., *Women in Chemistry and Physics: A Biobibliographic Sourcebook* (1993). There is a brief biographical sketch, written by Way, in *American Men and Women of Science* (19th ed., 1995/1996). An obituary, including a photograph, appeared in *Physics Today* 49 (December 1996), p. 75.

MURRAY MARTIN

WEDEL, Cynthia Clark. August 26, 1908–August 24, 1986. Church worker, educator, volunteer.

The eldest of four children of Elizabeth Snow Haigh and Arthur Pierson Clark, Cynthia Clark was born in Dearborn, Michigan, her mother's hometown. She, her brother, and twin sisters grew up in St. Louis, Buffalo, and Evanston, Illinois, as the family followed her father's moves as a civil engineer for steel companies. Mrs. Clark, a graduate of Kalamazoo College, brought her children up as active Episcopalians.

After graduating from Evanston Township High School in 1925, Cynthia attended Northwestern University as a day student. She took her BA in history magna cum laude in 1929; with a fellowship from Northwestern she completed her MA in 1930. In 1931 she became director of Christian education at her parish church, St. Luke's Evanston. Having discovered that she was inadequately prepared for a position dealing primarily with children and young adults, she took courses at Garrett Theological Seminary in Evanston.

Clark secured a position at the New York headquarters of the Episcopal Church in 1934, and in 1935 she became the national director of youth work. In 1939 she married the Rev. Theodore O. Wedel, the church's general secretary for college work. He was a widower sixteen years older than she with two teenage children, Carl and Gertrude. The Wedels moved to Washington shortly after their marriage when he became dean of the College of Preachers at the National Cathedral, a program of continuing education for clergy. Within a few years they were recognized as one of the most prominent couples in the church. They encouraged and supported one another throughout their happy marriage.

In Washington, Wedel became an active volunteer in the church's Woman's Auxiliary locally and nationally, and also in the Red Cross, the Girl Scouts, and local welfare organizations. She taught part-time at the National Cathedral School for Girls from 1939 to 1949. Her Red Cross work, which began during World War II, continued for many years; she focused on the recruitment, training, and placement of volunteers.

Wedel's work in the Women's Auxiliary led to the achievements for which she was most widely known. She served on its national board from 1946 to 1952, and as president from 1953 to 1955. Her interest in ecumenism was heightened by involvement in United Church Women in Washington and at the national level. When the National Council of Churches (NCC) and the World Council of Churches (WCC) were organized in the early fifties, both Wedels were active participants. The devastating effects of the Depression, fascism, and World War II had persuaded many Christians that they should renew the movement toward unity that had begun in the 1920s. They wanted to cross denominational lines to relieve social and economic problems and to prevent future wars, as well as pursue the ideal of one church. The WCC was founded in 1948, and the NCC two years later. Because none of the denominations allowed women to hold leadership positions, United Church Women was formed as a female support group for the NCC.

After 1950, Wedel was much in demand as a speaker at church meetings of all denominations, voluntary organizations, and colleges and universities. At the same time she published a number of pamphlets, study guides, and articles for the NCC, Church Women United, and the Episcopal Church, including *Citizenship, Our Christian Concern* (1952), *What of the Women?* (1953), *Women in the Church* (1955), and the prescient *Employed Women and the Church* (1959). Her work with women's organizations, volunteers, and ecumenical groups was the basis for her publications and speeches. Her constant refrain was that as the world changed, organizations must change also or disappear. In particular the role of women was changing, as women could now pursue careers, including the ordained ministry. The mass of female volunteers was no longer available; organizations needed to recognize this and adjust. She urged her readers and listeners to embrace change, and to acknowledge the equal importance of men and women in the work of the church and all other groups.

In the early fifties Theodore Wedel urged his wife to return to graduate school to prepare for a paying career. She received a PhD in psychology from George Washington University in 1957. Her dissertation was on social dynamics, which the Wedels had found to be a useful tool for their work. She served as a lecturer in psychology at American University for the next three years. Following Theodore's retirement in 1960, the couple moved to New York, where they lived for most of the remainder of the decade. When they returned to Washington, she became the associate director of the Center for Voluntarism of the Institute for Applied Behavioral Science, serving from 1969 to 1973.

Cynthia Clark Wedel was actively involved in a variety of social causes throughout the 1960s and 1970s. She was appointed to the President's Commission on the Status of Women from 1961 to 1963, and served from 1963 until 1968 as a member of the Citizens' Advisory Council on the Status of Women. She also actively campaigned for the rights of the poor, against capital punishment, and against the Vietnam War.

Her ecumenical activism increasingly took her to roles of national leadership. She was assistant general secretary of the National Council of Churches from 1962 to 1965 and associate general secretary from 1965 to 1969. In 1969 she was the first woman elected president of the NCC. All previous white male presidents had been elected unopposed; Wedel's nomination was challenged by a black man. She refused to withdraw and was elected by a wide margin. Although a strong supporter of racial equality, she believed that women too had been victims of discrimination and regarded her election as a belated recognition of their importance in the church. A delegate to the World Council of Churches assemblies in the fifties and sixties, she later was elected one of the six presidents of that organization from 1975 to 1983. At the time of her death, Wedel was the only woman to have served as president of both organizations.

Wedel was the consummate woman volunteer, with "a fondness for controversy" and a willingness to be a "pretty obstreperous" token (oral history interview, 1982). She attributed her leadership to her skill at pulling things together and making them work. Friendly, outgoing, generous of her time and advice, she was admired in her own denomination and beyond. After her husband's death in 1970, she continued to live at Goodwin House, an Episcopal retirement center in Alexandria, Virginia, until her death from cancer in August 1986 at the age of seventy-seven.

Bibliography: Transcriptions and tapes of two 1982 oral history interviews with Wedel are in the archives of the Episcopal Women's History Project at the archives of the Episcopal Church, Austin, Texas. The archives also contain folders of her speeches and articles on a variety of topics. Papers relating to her various positions can be found in the archives of the World Council of Churches and the National Council of Churches in New York, the archives of the American Red Cross in Falls Church, Virginia, and the archives of the Diocese of Washington. In addition to the pamphlets mentioned in the text, she was the author of "The Ordained Woman Today" in Sarah Bentley Doely, ed., *Women's Liberation and the Church: The New Demand for Freedom in the Life of the Christian Church* (1970), *Changing Patterns for Church Women* (1962), *Faith or Fear and Future Shock* (1964), *Ecumenical Rivalry and Cooperation* (1970), and *Reflections on Ministry* (1976). She was co-editor with William P. Greenspun of *Second Living Room Dialogues* (1967). Obituaries appeared in the *New York Times* on August 28, 1986, and the *Washington Post* on August 29, 1986.

BARBARA BRANDON SCHNORRENBERG

WEGLYN, Michi Nishiura. November 29, 1926–April 25, 1999. Writer, civil rights activist.

Michi Nishiura Weglyn was the first American woman to write a comprehensive book about the internment camps in the United States during World War II. Titled *Years of Infamy: The Untold Story of America's Concentration Camps* (1976), the book won wide acclaim for its originality and the depth with which it examined the subject. That Weglyn herself had been confined behind barbed wire lent authenticity to the book, but it was her painstaking eight-year-long research in repositories like the Franklin D. Roosevelt Presidential Library and the National Archives, culling once-impounded documents, that gave the book its authority and its rightful place in the narrative of American history.

An attractive woman, petite, often in frail health, Weglyn impressed friends and colleagues with the passion with which she undertook her pursuits. Born in Stockton, California, she was the eldest of two daughters of Tomojiro Nishiura, who had emigrated from Japan in 1916, and Misao Yuwasa Nishiura, who had come in 1922. Michi spent her girlhood on a tenant farm in Brentwood, California, where the entire family, the girls included, worked in the fields and orchards, raising fruit and vegetables on nearly five hundred acres. Weglyn once said she had ruined her health by trying to work harder than her male counterparts in order to compensate for not being the boy her parents had wanted.

Life on the farm abruptly ended for the Nishiura family with the cataclysmic events of December 7, 1941, and the ensuing Executive Order 9066 issued on February 19, 1942, by President Franklin D. Roosevelt. In effect, the Order authorized the removal of all persons of Japanese ancestry from the West Coast—approximately 112,000 persons, two-thirds of whom were U.S. citizens—to concentration camps around the country. The Nishiura family ended up in a sun-scorched, dust-whipped, camp in Gila Rivers, Arizona, one of ten such camps. Michi was fifteen years old, three years younger than the median age of the *nisei,* the first U.S.-born generation of Japanese. Of this she wrote: "In our immaturity and naïveté, [we] believed that this, under the circumstances, was the only way to prove our loyalty to a country which we loved" (*Years of Infamy,* p. 21).

In camp, like most internees, Michi strove for a sense of normalcy. She became a good student, gaining inspiration from an extraordinarily committed English teacher, and graduated from Butte High School in camp in 1944. Soon afterward, released from camp but still barred from returning to California, the bright student with a literary-artistic bent left to enroll in Mount Holyoke College in Massachusetts. Unfortunately, a bout with tuberculosis forced her to withdraw without finishing. But this self-described "college dropout" would later be awarded an honorary doctorate from Mount Holyoke.

In 1945, the author's parents also relocated across the country—to Seabrook Farms in New Jersey, a large food-processing operation that had recruited internees for employment. Michi joined them there, but later in the decade she moved to New York City. She took courses in fashion design and later became a costume designer for the popular *Perry Como Show,* a position she held for eight years.

Sometime during the late 1940s, she met Walter Weglyn when both lived at Columbia University's International House. They married in 1950 and did not have children. Significantly, her husband, a perfume chemist, had been a Holocaust survivor, and that horrifying experience led to him to be an ardent supporter of his wife's book project, spurring her on, editing, and advising her to be honest at all cost.

When the book was finally published in 1976, Japanese Americans had special cause to cheer, for it offered indisputable evidence that the decision to herd them into camps had been, not a military necessity as wartime authorities had claimed, but a policy based on racial prejudice, economic and political interests, and an irrational, excessive response to war by government officials. (A government commission investigating the issue in 1988 would come to a nearly identical conclusion.) Weglyn also reached the startling conclusion that Japanese Americans, as well as large numbers of Latin American Japanese (the latter having been hijacked from their homes and brought to the States), had been congregated in the camps as a "hostage reprisal reserve" that could potentially be exchanged for U.S. prisoners in the Pacific.

Buoyed by the author's findings, in 1978 Japanese Americans revived a stuttering movement they had mounted earlier in the decade to seek redress from Congress for the deprivation of their constitutional rights, their material losses, and the abasement they had endured in the years of their incarceration. A decade later, after intensive lobbying, letter writing, public education, and government investigative hearings, Congress enacted the Civil Liberties Act of 1988 requiring payment of $20,000 to each former internee. The act also included a formal apology from the president of the United States and established a fund to educate the public about the camps, emphasizing ways to prevent such an egregious breach of civil and human rights from recurring.

Most former internees expressed gratitude, feeling that their honor had been vindicated and their faith in democracy restored. But Weglyn—

the mother of redress, as she had been called—was not totally satisfied, mindful that thousands of others who had also suffered at the hands of the U.S. government during the war had not been included in the redress: the Pacific railroad workers and mine workers who had been fired from their jobs at the behest of the government, and the former internees abducted from Latin America. She continued to advocate for them in speeches, letters, and articles. She lived to see victory only in the case of the railroad and mine workers.

In 1993, California State Polytechnic University at Pomona established the Michi Nishiura and Walter Weglyn Endowed Chair for Multicultural Studies. Walter Weglyn died in 1995. Overwhelmed by this loss, Michi Weglyn continued her work for justice, but her health was declining. She died of cancer in New York City in 1999 at the age of seventy-two. A salient appraisal of Michi Weglyn's significance came from Paul LeClerc, president of Hunter College, when the college conferred on her an honorary doctorate in 1992: "You have contributed to our understanding of our history and of each other."

Bibliography: The best way to trace Michi Weglyn's life is through articles in the archives of the language newspapers: *Nichi Bei Times,* and *Hokubei Mainichi,* San Francisco; *Rafu Shimpo,* Los Angeles; and the *New York Nichibei.* Of special interest are articles by Kenji Taguma, editor of *Nichi Bei Times* and Phil Tajitsu Nash (*Nichi Bei Times,* April 26 and April 27, 1999). The final quotation is taken from a certificate presented to Weglyn when the honorary doctorate was conferred. Papers and photographs of the author exist in the collection of longtime friend and fellow researcher Aiko Yoshinaga-Herzig, Falls Church, Virginia. Voluminous correspondence, photographs, and records of the Weglyns are in the collections of Cedrick Shimo, Los Angeles, and Kiku Funabiki, San Francisco. John Fuyuume of Seabrook, New Jersey, has a collection of photographs and memorabilia of Weglyn's stay at Seabrook Farms. There is also some material in the Mount Holyoke Archives. A comprehensive account of the American wartime camps can be found in *Personal Justice Denied: Report of the Commission on Wartime Relocation and Internment of Civilians* (1983), available in reprint by University of Washington Press (1997). An obituary appeared in the *New York Times* on May 2, 1999.

MEI T. NAKANO

WEISBORD, Vera Buch. August 19, 1895–September 6, 1987. Labor organizer, radical.

A leader in pivotal labor struggles of the 1920s, Vera Wilhelmine Buch grew up as the second of two daughters of German American woodcarver John Casper Buch and his wife, Nellie Amelia Louisa Crawford, who was descended from English colonists in Connecticut and New York. Born in Forestville, Connecticut, at age four Vera moved with her family to New York City. She attended Hunter High School and graduated as valedictorian of her class in 1912. Despite her family's modest means, she won a scholarship and enrolled in Hunter College, where she took classes. In 1916, she was diagnosed with tuberculosis and went to a sanitarium to recover. There she encountered socialism and began to study political thought. After she left the sanitarium, Buch found a job as a secretary and quietly joined the Industrial Workers of the World in 1919 and the Workers' Party (later the Communist Party of the United States) in 1920.

Buch first became active in communist labor organizing during the 1926 Passaic, New Jersey, textile strike. A citywide labor conflict that lasted nearly a year, the Passaic strike was a pivotal moment for the American Left, marking the emergence of communist-led labor unions in a key industry and demonstrating the strength of worker discontent in the workplace in a decade noted for its quiescence. The strike was organized by charismatic union leader Albert Weisbord, the son of Russian Jewish immigrants and a graduate of Harvard Law School. Weisbord was passionately committed to the workers' cause and believed in inclusive and democratic union leadership. He quickly tapped Buch, then a member of his staff, to aid him in strike activities. Soon the relationship between Buch and Weisbord became personal as well as professional, although they did not marry until 1938. They never had children.

After the Passaic strike was lost, owing to a leadership struggle with the American Federation of Labor–affiliated United Textile Workers, Vera Buch was assigned to organizing efforts in Philadelphia, Detroit, and the Pennsylvania coal fields. While Albert Weisbord worked as a Communist Party political organizer in Detroit, Buch played a central role in communist efforts to organize the automobile industry. Editing shop papers such as the *Ford Worker,* she penned a women's column and did party work among women. The stirring of worker organization in the textile industry brought the couple back to the East Coast for a New Bedford, Massachusetts, strike. In 1928 they helped form the National Textile Workers Union. Soon after, Vera Buch was sent south to support a mass strike at the Loray Cotton Mill in Gastonia, North Carolina.

Pitting underpaid and exploited southern textile workers against the massive Manville-Jenckes Company, Gastonia took on legendary proportions and became the subject of several labor novels and historical studies. Workers at the Loray Mill had been hit with a series of wage cuts and "stretch-outs" (when workers were assigned additional machines). The strike, which drew in thousands of textile workers, quickly escalated with company and police violence. When vigilantes attacked the union hall one night, they physically attacked Buch and other labor organizers on site. Along with clubs and fists there were rifle shots, and the local sheriff was killed. Buch and fifteen others were arrested and charged with murder and conspiracy. After a mistrial, Buch and nine others were released, while the remaining leaders still faced charges. The murder trials and local repression (including the murder of southern labor organizer and songwriter Ella Mae Wiggins) caused the strike to collapse. With the defeat in Gastonia, the hope of organizing the southern textile industry faded.

Disputes over Communist Party conduct during the Passaic and Gastonia strikes, and disagreements over the direction of party organization, led Vera Buch and Albert Weisbord to leave the party and form the Communist League of Struggle, which lasted from 1931 to 1937. During that time, Buch served as associate editor of its journal, *Class Struggle,* and wrote essays on such topics as labor, feminism and revolution, and women and war. When the League began to decline in 1935, Vera and Albert moved to Chicago, where they organized among the unemployed and black workers on the South Side. Buch characterized these efforts, and her long-standing commitment to radical social change, as "the long wait," noting that engagement in these struggles had meant "living on the fringes of society, never integrated into it, never having more than a toehold."

Organizing on the margins, however, led Buch to some of the most important social justice struggles of the twentieth century. She worked for integration in the Congress of Racial Equality in the 1940s, participated in the broader civil rights struggle in the 1950s and 1960s, and took part in the women's movement of the 1970s. If Vera Buch was politically marginal, however, it was owing not just to the choice of political issues but also to the place of women on the Left. As she wrote, "In general the situation of women in the Party—and of wives in particular—was an ignominious one." With passion and insight, Buch argued that women's problems went beyond their roles as workers and must be seen as part of the larger class struggle.

Vera Buch Weisbord's feminist engagement had an experiential base. An early lesbian relationship, periodic strain in her marriage, and an infection from an abortion that physically handicapped her brought home issues of sexuality and gender discrimination. Continuing health problems allowed her to be only intermittently active in politics during the 1940s and 1950s. In 1952, however, she fulfilled a lifelong ambition and took art classes at the Art Institute of Chicago. In the next twenty years, she produced more than four hundred paintings. In 1976, Vera Buch and Albert Weisbord were present in Passaic, New Jersey, for the fifty-year commemoration of the textile strike. In 1977, the same year her husband died, she published her autobiography, *A Radical Life.* A decade later, in 1987, Vera Buch Weisbord died of heart failure at the age of ninety-two in Chicago.

Bibliography: The best biographical source on Vera Buch Weisbord is her autobiography, *A Radical Life* (1977), which focuses on her radicalism in the 1920s and 1930s and includes a timeline of her activism. The quotations in the text are found on p. 318 and p. 144, respectively. Vera Buch and Albert Weisbord did not donate personal papers to a repository, but selections from their writings were reprinted in *Class Struggle* (1968) as part of the Greenwood Press series on radical periodicals in the United States. For historical context on Weisbord's activism, see John A. Salmond, *Gastonia, 1929: The Story of the Loray Mill Strike* (1995); Kathleen Brown and Elizabeth Faue, "Social Bonds, Sexual Politics and Political Community on the U.S. Left, 1920s–1940s," *Left History* 7, no. 1 (Spring 2001), pp. 7–42; and Edward P. Johanningsmeier, "The Trade Union Unity League: American Communists and the Transition to Industrial Unionism, 1928–1934," *Labor History* 42, no. 2 (May 2001), pp. 159–178. Obituaries appeared in the *Chicago Tribune* on September 9, 1987, and the *New York Times* on September 13, 1987.

ELIZABETH FAUE

WEISS-ROSMARIN, Trude. June 17, 1908–June 26, 1989. Editor, writer, educator.

For nearly all of Trude Weiss-Rosmarin's life, women were not permitted to ascend the rabbi's pulpit. Aware of this limitation, Weiss-Rosmarin fashioned her own pulpit—the editorial page of the *Jewish Spectator,* a monthly and later quarterly journal that she edited for fifty-three years.

Trude Weiss was born in Frankfurt-am-Main, Germany, to Salina Mulling, a homemaker, and Jacob Weiss, a prosperous wine merchant. The family affiliated with Orthodox Judaism, but like many other middle-class German Jews, they strongly identified with German culture. From an early age, Weiss resented that her Orthodox upbringing restricted girls from gaining a full education and participating in synagogue life. As a young girl, she embarked on her own path of Hebrew study, supplemented by classes at the Hebräische Sprachschule under the strict and demanding Yosef Yoel Rivlin. During her youth, she also furtively attended an Eastern European synagogue where she learned Yiddish.

In 1917, at age nine, she joined a German Zionist youth group, Blau-Weiss, and enjoyed the easy contact between boys and girls. In 1922, she ran away from home to a *hakhshara* farm near Berlin where she, along with other youths, trained to become agricultural pioneers in Palestine. Before her training was over, she was diagnosed with a case of pneumonia and brought home by her mother to convalesce.

After shelving her pioneer dreams, she focused on gaining a Jewish and secular education. When her parents refused to foot the bill for her missed school year, she financed her own secondary education by securing a teacher and director position at the Hebrew language school in Duisburg. While she completed her secular studies, she also studied Jewish topics at Franz Rozenzweig's historically significant but short-lived (1920–26) Freie Jüdische Lehrhaus.

In 1927, Weiss enrolled at the University of Berlin. In 1929 she continued her education at the University of Leipzig. Finally, in 1931, at the age of twenty-two, she earned her doctorate in Semitics, archaeology, and philosophy from the University of Würzburg. Her dissertation was entitled "The Mention of the Arabs and Arabia in Assyrian-Babylonian Texts."

Weiss quickly realized that career options in Assyriology were severely limited in Germany. In 1931 she married Aaron Rosmarin, a Russian-born scholar with American citizenship, and she and her new husband immigrated to New York City. In an era when most women simply adopted their husbands' last name as their own, Weiss-Rosmarin decided, anticipating many later feminists, to hyphenate her name. After receiving the disappointing news that Depression-era universities could not afford to hire new faculty, Weiss-Rosmarin redirected her career toward educating Jewish women.

In October 1933, Weiss-Rosmarin and her husband founded the School of the Jewish Woman under the sponsorship of Hadassah. Weiss-Rosmarin served as director and teacher at the Upper West Side school. She drew upon her experience at Rozenzweig's Lehrhaus as a model for the curriculum. Single and married women took courses in Bible, Hebrew, and Jewish history. The school folded in 1939, in part because of the impending war but also because Hadassah had withdrawn its support three years earlier.

In 1938, Weiss-Rosmarin gave birth to her only child, Moshe, but refused to interrupt her professional life to become a full-time mother. Lacking support from her husband, Weiss-Rosmarin paid for the services of a maid and nursemaid from her own earnings. In the 1940s she and Aaron Rosmarin divorced, and she later married Nesim (legally known as Nesip) Seven. Her son became a rabbi and moved to Israel.

The legacy of the School of the Jewish Woman continued to live on in the shape of the *Jewish Spectator*. In late 1935, students received volume 1 of a monthly school newsletter. It was renamed the *Jewish Spectator* in February 1936 under the joint editorship of Weiss-Rosmarin and her husband. The magazine included Jewish news, short stories, and expositions on traditional Hebrew sources. Although its earlier issues were clearly directed toward women, including recipes, children's sections, and a guide to Kosher food, the magazine was always committed to intellectual content. Within its first year of publication the work of well-known authors, such as Ludwig Lewisohn and Chaim Nachman Bialik, filled its pages.

In 1943 Weiss-Rosmarin became sole editor of the magazine and continued to infuse her own personality into the "Editor's Quarter." Her editorial comments ranged from incisive interpretations of traditional Jewish texts to critical commentary on contemporary issues. She never shied away from controversy and often raised the ire of established Jewish organizations and denominational bodies. Three key topics recurred throughout her editorial remarks: Zionism, feminism, and Jewish survival.

Although Weiss-Rosmarin was an ardent supporter of a Jewish state, she believed that Zionist ideals had to be squared with pragmatic measures. She recommended that Jews accept the 1947 U.N. Partition Plan because it was a viable path for saving Jewish lives. Later, she was one of the earliest Jewish leaders to recognize Palestinian nationalism as a true and legitimate movement.

Although Weiss-Rosmarin never argued that biology was destiny, her brand of feminism maintained that women were "different, physiologically *and* psychologically" from men ("Jewish Women in a Man's World," *Jewish Spectator*, May 1950, p. 7). Her goal was to give all women the opportunity to become knowledgeable about Judaism. Starting in 1940, she published the *Jewish People's Library* series, which provided accessible, inexpensive books about Jewish history, texts, and practices. Weiss-Rosmarin believed that only through serious Jewish education could the Jewish people continue to survive. If American Jews learned about their own distinctiveness and came to feel pride in their unique heritage, philosophy, and ethics, they would want to remain actively and energetically Jewish.

Beyond being skilled with the pen (a prolific writer, she published many books), Weiss-Rosmarin was also a talented orator. To help fund her magazine, she embarked on lengthy lecture tours throughout the country. In addition, she continued to study Assyriology and was a member of the American Academy of Religion and the Society for the Scientific Study of Religion.

In 1978, Weiss-Rosmarin moved the offices of the *Jewish Spectator* to Santa Monica, California. Early in the summer of 1989, Weiss-Rosmarin wrote her last editorial, introducing her readership to Robert Bleiweiss, her handpicked editorial successor. On June 26, 1989, she died of cancer there at the age of eighty-one. After her death, an outpouring of elegiac letters flooded the *Jewish Spectator.* People from all over the country considered her a mentor and a teacher. Trude Weiss-Rosmarin was a woman who crossed many boundaries and barriers without ever compromising her fiery convictions.

Bibliography: Trude Weiss-Rosmarin's papers are housed at the American Jewish Archives at Hebrew Union College in Cincinnati, Ohio. The archives contain correspondence, scrapbooks of Weiss-Rosmarin's articles, and records from the *Jewish Spectator.* Aside from decades' worth of editorials and articles published in the *Jewish Spectator,* Weiss-Rosmarin published a wide array of books, including *Religion of Reason: The Philosophy of Hermann Cohen* (1936), *Jewish Women through the Ages* (1940), *The Oneg Shabbath Book* (1940), *What Every Jewish Woman Should Know* (in collaboration with Miriam Isaacs) (1940), *Judaism and Christianity: The Differences* (1943), *Jewish Survival: Essays and Studies* (1949), and *Jewish Expressions on Jesus: An Anthology* (1977). She also published a regular column entitled "Letters from New York" in the London *Jewish Chronicle* from 1963 to 1966.

As of yet, there is no biography of Weiss-Rosmarin. For an excellent meditation on her intellectual development, see Deborah Dash Moore, "Trude Weiss-Rosmarin and the *Jewish Spectator,*" in Carole S. Kessner, ed., *The "Other" New York Jewish Intellectuals* (1994). Also see Elliot B. Gertel, "My Friend, Trude Weiss-Rosmarin," *Jewish Spectator* 54 (Fall 1989), pp. 11–17; and Estelle Gilson, "Trude's a Holy Terror," *Present Tense,* Winter 1978, reprinted in the *Jewish Spectator* 54 (Fall 1989), pp. 6–10. *Moment* magazine's interview with Marie Syrkin and Weiss-Rosmarin also offers valuable reminiscences in Weiss-Rosmarin's own words (September 1983, pp. 37–44). See Moshe Kohn, "Two Veteran Journalists," *Jerusalem Post,* August 15, 1989, for her obituary.

LILA CORWIN BERMAN

WERTHEIMER, Barbara Mayer. November 7, 1925–September 20, 1983. Labor educator and activist, historian, feminist.

Barbara Mayer Wertheimer was among the first American labor educators to wonder why so few women held leadership positions even in unions that were mostly female, and to ask what could be done to change that. As a scholar, she found inspiration in the past efforts of women to organize and join unions, and as a labor educator and activist, she created the research institutes and adult education programs women needed to become union leaders. She undertook her best-known study, *We Were There: The Story of Working Women in America* (1977), to fill the huge gap in the literature on working women, and she had just begun to write the second volume in this planned multivolume series when she was diagnosed with lung cancer.

Born to Max David Mayer, the American-born son of German Jewish immigrants, and Eleanor Sanford, the daughter of a family from Oak Park, Illinois, that traced its origins to the *Mayflower,* Barbara Mayer spent all of her childhood and most of her adult life in New York City. Her parents met in Vienna while studying psychoanalysis. Both her father and her paternal grandfather were physicians, and her Wellesley-educated mother, a pioneer in industrial psychology, held several professional positions in New York City agencies, including the Department of Welfare. Barbara's younger brother, David, was born in 1929.

Growing up on the Upper West Side of Manhattan in an apartment filled with books and music, and where the dinner guests included such people as MARGARET MEAD, Franz Boaz, and Karl Llewellyn, Barbara became an avid reader and critical thinker. She attended P.S. 165 and Columbia Grammar Preparatory School and divided her summers between sleep-away camp and a country house in Southbury, Connecticut. Shortly after her father's death in 1943, when Barbara was a freshman at Oberlin College, her mother moved to the Southbury house and devoted herself to raising and training show dogs.

After graduating from Oberlin in 1946 with a degree in psychology, Barbara abandoned the idea of becoming a missionary in Africa and went to work instead as a union organizer for Amalgamated Clothing Workers of America (ACWA), later to become the Amalgamated Clothing and Textile Workers Union (ACTWU). She split that first paid union position, and its meager salary, with her husband, Valentin Wertheimer, whom she had met at Oberlin and married shortly after graduation. After eighteen months of organizing garment workers in the Scranton, Pennsylvania, area the Wertheimers returned to Manhattan, where Barbara became associate education director for the ACWA, and Val, after completing law school at Columbia University, became a union attorney and high-ranking officer. While working at Amalgamated, she had two children: Ellen (1953) and David (1955).

By the time she left the ACWA in 1958 to attend New York University, she was the acting national education director, the first woman in the union's history to hold that position. (She always suspected that the "acting" part of her title had something to do with her gender.) In 1960, she graduated from New York University with a master's degree in adult education. Throughout these years, the family lived in the Seward Park Houses, a union cooperative on Manhattan's Lower East Side, and was active in the labor and civil rights movements.

From 1961 until 1966, when she became a senior extension associate (labor relations specialist) at Cornell University's School of Industrial and Labor Relations in New York City, Wertheimer worked as a community services consultant for the New York State Division of Housing and Community Renewal. At Cornell, she developed innovative programs in adult education around such topics as "Labor Explores the Arts" and "Women as Leaders." Ford Foundation–funded research she undertook about the barriers to women's participation in trade unions led directly to the establishment in 1972 of the Trade Union Women's Studies program, which she co-directed with Anne Nelson, a former roommate at Oberlin. For this program, she designed a series of undergraduate-level courses specifically and exclusively for women workers, on the theory that trade union women needed to be trained, at least initially, separately from the men in their organizations. It became the model for other extension credit programs developed for adult, nontraditional students, including Cornell's Off-Campus College.

In 1977 she was appointed an associate professor in the Extension Division. She founded and directed the Institute for Women and Work, which had a research focus and won major funding from unions, corporations, and prestigious foundations, including Carnegie, Ford, and Rockefeller. Her research and work at Cornell during these years broke new ground in the field of labor and adult education and received worldwide recognition. In 1983, she was appointed a full professor.

Throughout her years at Cornell, Wertheimer was active in the National Organization for Women and the National Commission on Working Women. In 1974 she was a founding member of the Coalition of Labor Union Women (CLUW), the first inter-union advocacy and policy group to function within the traditional labor movement to increase the number of women in leadership positions and to promote women's issues within unions, at the collective bargaining table, and in the legislature. A prolific writer, as well as fiercely competitive and a self-described workaholic, she contributed many articles about working women to a wide variety of journals and anthologies and co-authored, with Anne H. Nelson, *Trade Union Women: A Study of Their Participation in New York City Locals* (1975). Her writings continue to be assigned in trade union and college courses across the country.

Throughout her life, Barbara Wertheimer took a profound interest in her students and colleagues and supported in numerous ways their efforts to climb up the union, academic, and corporate ladders. With her help, many of these women became high-ranking leaders in their trade unions and other organizations. This mentoring infused every aspect of her research, teaching, and writing as she carved new space for working women, and helped define the agenda for gender equality during the heady days of the women's liberation movement.

Her husband died in 1978. Two years later Barbara met Robert Simpson, an architect, and the two developed a close and loving relationship. Her children were at her side at her country home in Lakeville, Connecticut, when she died of lung cancer at the age of fifty-seven on September 20, 1983. She left unfinished the second volume of *We Were There,* which she planned to call *Our Century, Our Time: The Story of Working Women, 1914 to the Present.*

Bibliography: The Archives of Labor and Union Affairs, Walter P. Reuther Library, Wayne State University, in Detroit has an interview with Wertheimer done by Bette Craig in 1980 as part of the University of Michigan's oral history project "The 20th Century Trade Union Woman: Vehicle for Social Change." Wertheimer is best known for her groundbreaking history *We Were There: The Story of Working Women in America* (1977), and for the study she co-authored with Anne H. Nelson, *Trade Union Women: A Study of Their Participation in New York City Locals* (1975). She also edited a collection of essays entitled *Labor Education for Women Workers* (1981) and contributed to Alice Cook, Val Lorwin, and Arlene Kaplan Daniels, eds., *Women and Trade Unions in Eleven Industrialized Countries* (1984). An obituary appeared in the *New York Times* on September 22, 1983.

DOROTHY FENNELL

WESLEY, Dorothy Porter. May 25, 1905–December 17, 1995. Librarian, historian.

At a time when African American women had few professional opportunities, Dorothy Porter Wesley chose to become a librarian. For more than four decades, she worked at what is now the Moorland-Spingarn Research Center at Howard University in Washington, D.C. There she built a collection of materials by and about people of African descent; starting from a few thousand scattered books in 1930, the collection grew to tens of thousands of items by her retirement in 1973. Scholars have relied on the published and unpublished materials Dorothy Porter Wesley gathered to produce a voluminous literature reconstructing and interpreting black history, culture, and life.

Dorothy Louise Burnett was born in Warrenton, Virginia, to Hayes Joseph Burnett Sr., a physician, and Bertha Ball, a homemaker and tennis enthusiast. The oldest of four children, Dorothy grew up in Montclair, New Jersey, a suburb of New York City, where her father established his practice after graduating from Howard University's medical school. Dorothy lived in an Irish Catholic neighborhood and attended a predominantly white high school before moving to Washington, D.C., to attend Miner Normal School (later Miner Teachers College), where she received a teaching diploma. During her last year at Miner, she ran the library while the librarian was on extended sick leave and decided that she preferred librarianship to teaching. When the librarian returned, Dorothy enrolled at Howard University, where she worked as a student assistant in the library and, in 1928, received her BA.

In 1929, Dorothy Burnett married artist and art historian James Porter, who taught at Howard University. The couple had one child, Constance, born in August 1939. When they married, Dorothy Burnett Porter was working at the Howard University library during the school year and at a branch of the New York Public Library during the summer. Determined to have a career as a professional librarian, she enrolled at Columbia University, where she received a BS in library science in 1931. The next year she received a Julius Rosenwald Fund scholarship in support of graduate work; in 1932 she became one of the first African American women to earn a master's degree in library science. Offered permanent professional employment by the New York Public Library, Porter chose instead to return to Howard University.

In 1930, at the university administration's behest, Dorothy Porter had begun to create what would become a world-class black history collection by gathering together some three thousand long-ignored items donated in 1914 by Howard trustee Jesse Moorland, some anti-slavery material abolitionist Louis Tappan had given in 1873, and scattered books by and about blacks that Porter found on the main library's shelves. Referred to as the Moorland Foundation, a Library of Negro Life and History, the collection marked a strong beginning, but Porter struggled in the early years to build on that basis with no budget for new acquisitions. What she lacked in financial resources, however, she made up for in creativity and persistence. Recognizing that Howard University itself played a significant role in African American history, Porter established its archives, saving the records of the institution and the personal libraries and papers of its faculty. Her commitment to preserving Howard's past led her to raid office trash cans and drop in on the families of deceased faculty members to retrieve files and records.

Her ability to develop the collection required strategic action and a wide network of knowledgeable friends. She sometimes used her own money at rare book auctions and donated her purchases to the collection. Scholars who used the growing Moorland Foundation collection usually sent her signed copies of their resulting publications, which she added to the collection. On other occasions, she showed up at the right place and time to claim an overlooked or under-appreciated bounty. When one of her friends, civil rights advocate MARY CHURCH TERRELL, left her papers to the Library of Congress, Porter found six boxes of manuscript material Library of Congress officials had missed at Terrell's home and added that material to Howard's collection. Similarly, when Porter heard that the Washington, D.C., branch of the National Association for the Advancement of Colored People was cleaning out its office files, she sent a university truck to haul the records to the library.

Eventually Dorothy Porter did win a budget from the university with which to expand and enhance the collection. In 1946, she made her most significant purchase: attorney Arthur B. Spingarn's personal collection of approximately five thousand books, pamphlets, manuscripts, and sheet music by black authors and composers. In 1958 Spingarn's world-renowned collection of black music was added. By the late 1950s, the Moorland Foundation included the Oswald Garrison Villard Collection of Anti-Slavery Papers, the books and papers of Professor Alain Locke, and the papers of Angelina Weld Grimké, among many others.

In 1958, Howard University Press issued the 398-page *Catalogue of the African Collection in the Moorland Foundation, Howard University Library*, compiled by students in the Program of African Studies under Dorothy Porter's supervision and editorship. She also compiled other standard reference sources, including *The Negro in the United States: A Selected Bibliography* (1970), *Early Negro Writing, 1760–1837* (1971), and *Afro-Braziliana: A Working Bibliography* (1978). Such work, as well as her long and close association with collectors such as Spingarn and historians such as Carter G. Woodson, gave Porter an encyclopedic knowledge of the publishing record of the African diaspora. She served as an adviser to a number of major commercial publishing projects and as a consultant to libraries in the United States and Africa, while also pursuing her own research. By the time she retired in 1973, historian Benjamin Quarles said, "there hasn't been a major Black history book in the last 30 years in which the author hasn't acknowledged Mrs. Porter's help" (Madison and Wesley, p. 18).

In 1970, James Porter died. Nine years later she married a longtime friend, historian Charles H. Wesley, who died in 1987. Throughout both marriages, Dorothy Porter Wesley supported and contributed to her husbands' success while also achieving her own. In late 1995 she left Washington to live with her daughter in Ft. Lauderdale, where she died a month later at the age of ninety.

Bibliography: The personal books and papers of Dorothy Porter Wesley are in the African-American Research Library and Cultural Center of the Broward County (Florida) Library. Her unprocessed administrative records are housed with the Howard University Archives at the

Moorland-Spingarn Research Center, Howard University, in Washington, D.C. Her publications include "Sarah Parker Remond: Abolitionist and Physician," *Journal of Negro History* 20, no. 3 (July 1935), pp. 287–93; "The Organized Educational Activities of Negro Literary Societies, 1828–1846," *Journal of Negro Education* 5, no. 4 (October 1936), pp. 555–76; "David Ruggles, an Apostle of Human Rights," *Journal of Negro History* 28, no. 1 (January 1943), pp. 23–50; and "Black Antiquarians and Bibliophiles Revisited, with a Glance at Today's Lovers of Books and Memorabilia," in Elinor Des Verney Sinnette, W. Paul Coates, and Thomas C. Battle, eds., *Black Bibliophiles and Collectors: Preservers of Black History* (1990), pp. 3–20. A helpful history of the Moorland-Spingarn Research Center is Thomas C. Battle, "Moorland-Spingarn Research Center," *Library Quarterly* 58, no. 2 (April 1988), pp. 143–51. Dorothy Porter offered reminiscences in "Introduction: Fifty Years of Collecting," in Richard Newman, *Black Access: A Bibliography of Afro-American Bibliographies* (1984), pp. xvii–xxviii; and in Avril Johnson Madison and Dorothy Porter Wesley, "Dorothy Burnett Porter Wesley: Enterprising Steward of Black Culture," *Public Historian,* Winter 1995, pp. 15–40. Articles about her include Helen H. Britton, "Dorothy Porter Wesley: Bibliographer, Curator, and Scholar," in Suzanne Hildenbrand, ed., *Reclaiming the American Library Past: Writing the Women In* (1996), pp. 163–86, which provides a bibliography of her publications; and Thomas C. Battle, "Dorothy Porter Wesley: Preserver of Black History, May 25, 1905–December 17, 1995," *Black Issues in Higher Education,* January 25, 1996, pp. 22–23. Obituaries appeared in the *New York Times* on December 20, 1995, and the *Washington Post* on December 31, 1995.

CHERYL KNOTT MALONE

WEST, Dorothy. June 2, 1907–August 16, 1998. Short story writer, novelist, journalist.

On Dorothy West's ninetieth birthday, first lady Hillary Rodham Clinton hailed the gifted writer of the Harlem Renaissance as a "national treasure." Beginning in the 1920s, West claimed the domestic genre for her fiction. In it, she gave voice to the complications of color and racial identity as she knew them from her own experience. Born in Boston's South End, Dorothy was raised in an extended family of maternal aunts and cousins, including poet Helene Johnson. Her father was Isaac Christopher West, the only child of slaves from Richmond, Virginia, who moved to Boston and became a successful fruit wholesaler. Her mother, Rachel Benson, was the sixth of nineteen children of Helen Pease and Benjamin Benson of Camden, South Carolina. The mixed-race offspring of white slave masters and house servants, they raised their children with white middle-class values. Rachel inherited the belief that a person with light skin and a higher social class would experience less racial prejudice. This belief was borne out in the experience of her only child, Dorothy, who felt the difference her own darker skin made.

Dorothy West's formal education, though typical of young white women of her day growing up in Boston, was unconventional for a young black woman. She attended public schools through high school graduation in 1925. According to most sources, West was tutored privately by Monroe Trotter's sister, attended Martin School in Boston's Mission Hill District, and Girls Latin School, graduating in 1925. But more important was the nourishing of West's artistic sensibility, and her greatest early influences were her mother, a vivid storyteller, and in all likelihood her cousin Helene, a poet. West admired her cousin's literary gifts and in 1926 followed her to New York City, where both participated in literary contests and took writing classes at Columbia University. Her instinct as a writer was to tell her family story, and it became her lifelong ambition.

West's professional career began in 1926 with a series of important publications. *Opportunity* published "The Typewriter" (reprinted in *Best Short Stories of 1926*). At the magazine's annual banquet, where Jean Toomer awarded the story second prize (she shared the prize with ZORA NEALE HURSTON), Dorothy and cousin Helene met writers Hurston, Countee Cullen, Langston Hughes, Bruce Nugent, and Wallace Thurman. That year, Thurman founded the short-lived experimental literary magazine *Fire!!,* which later inspired West to start her own magazine, *Challenge.* Also in 1926, as editor of the *Messenger,* Thurman published her short story "Hannah Byde," and *Copy,* Columbia's literary magazine, reprinted West's story "An Unimportant Man," which had originally appeared in Boston's *Saturday Evening Quill.* These revealing portraits of color and class tensions within black families challenged the aesthetics of the New Negro movement, which held that the role of the arts was to create a positive image of the black race. With the exception of Hurston's play *Color-Struck* (1925) and Thurman's *Blacker the Berry* (1929), few black writers published works that dealt with the effect of intra-racial color bias.

In 1932, together with Langston Hughes and artist Mildred Jones, West spent eleven months in the Soviet Union, where she participated in *Black and White,* an unfinished propaganda film about U.S. race relations. Back in New York in 1934, she founded the literary quarterly *Challenge.* James Weldon Johnson's introductory essay in the inaugural issue noted that the quarterly was intended to rejuvenate the spirit of the Harlem Renaissance. The magazine published such writers as Hughes, Hurston, Cullen, Helene Johnson, and Claude McKay, and newer voices like PAULI MURRAY and Mae Cowdery. Responding to criticism from Chicago's South Side Writers that *Challenge* was politically conservative, West hired

Richard Wright as assistant editor. Renamed *New Challenge* by West in the spring of 1937, the revamped quarterly published MARGARET WALKER, Ralph Ellison, and Wright's "Blueprint for Negro Writing." West stopped publication with the fall 1937 issue because of editorial and financial difficulties.

West remained in New York until the end of World War II, struggling to write while also working as a welfare investigator and then for the Federal Writers Project. By 1945 she had moved to Oak Bluffs on Martha's Vineyard, where her family had vacationed every summer, to live with her mother. There, nearing forty, she completed her first novel, *The Living Is Easy* (1948). Set in pre–World War I Boston, this autobiographical work reveals the nature of West's own childhood. It tells the tragic story of the upwardly mobile "outlander" Cleo Jericho and her disastrous marriage to Bart Judson; the characters were modeled on West's mother and father. Using the daughter's perspective, West critiques the color dynamics of black middle-class striving. In this text, the narrative voice comes to recognize the damage done to women like Cleo who imitate northern (white) values when removed from the nurture of their own southern communities. Along with JESSIE FAUSET's novel *Comedy American Style* (1933), *The Living Is Easy* anticipates texts of the 1960s that reveal the negative effects of intra-racial color bias. Significantly, West herself neither married nor had children of her own.

West never stopped writing short stories, her favorite genre. Between 1940 and 1960, the *New York Daily News* published two of her stories every month, including the highly acclaimed "Jack in the Pot" (1940). West also worked at the *Vineyard Gazette*, a job that lasted some thirty years and eventually included writing her own Oak Bluffs social column from 1973 to 1993.

In 1995, more than four decades after *The Living Is Easy*, West published *The Wedding*, though not without difficulty. She had stopped working on the manuscript in the 1960s, fearing that the radicalized civil rights movement would not welcome her book about the black bourgeoisie. Years later, Doubleday editor and Gay Head resident JACQUELINE KENNEDY ONASSIS, to whom *The Wedding* is dedicated, reportedly encouraged her to finish it. Set in Martha's Vineyard in the 1950s, *The Wedding* explores the complicated genealogies of the white and black sides of Shelby Coles's family. In the *dénouement*, two family members, one black and one white, reconcile the divisions of the Shelbys and the Coleses. The novel boldly represents the power of love to transcend divisions of color, race, class, and family. These themes have run through West's writing since the 1920s, and continue to resonate with readers.

Finally achieving best-seller status, Dorothy West became a celebrity at eighty-eight. Nowhere was her eminence more apparent than at her ninetieth birthday party, prompting the naming of Dorothy West Avenue on Martha's Vineyard and a stirring performance by soprano Jessye Norman. A year later, many of the same admirers—Vineyard neighbors, political, academic, and arts celebrities—attended her memorial after her death in Boston at the age of ninety-one.

Bibliography: Dorothy West's papers are collected at the Schlesinger Library, Radcliffe Institute for Advanced Study, Harvard University, and in Special Collections at Boston University. Her letters are included in various author folders in the James Weldon Johnson Memorial Collection, Yale Collection of American Literature, Beineke Rare Book and Manuscript Library, Yale University, along with personal contributions such as first drafts in pencil of "Jack in the Pot" and "Mammy" given by West in 1942. The documentary *As I Remember It: A Portrait of Dorothy West* was released in 1991 and written, directed, and produced by Salem Mekuria. See also Dorothy West, *The Richer, The Poorer: Stories, Sketches, and Reminiscences* (1965); and Lionel C. Bascom, *A Renaissance in Harlem: Lost Voices of an American Community* (1999). James Robert Saunders and Renae Nadine Shackelford have collected many of West's articles in *Dorothy West's Martha's Vineyard: Stories, Essays, and Reminiscences by Dorothy West Writing in the* Vineyard Gazette (2001). Interviews with West include David Levering Lewis, "Dorothy West" (October 1976) in "Voices from the Renaissance," Special Collections, Schomburg Center for Research in Black Culture; Genii Guinier, "Interview with Dorothy West," *Black Women Oral History Project* (May 6, 1978), vol. 10, ed. Ruth Edmunds Hill (1991); Deborah McDowell, "Conversations with Dorothy West" (June 22–26, 1984; June 26–30, 1985), in Victor Kramer, ed., *The Harlem Renaissance Re-examined* (1987); and Katrine Dalsgard, "Alive and Well and Living on the Island of Martha's Vineyard: An Interview with Dorothy West, Oct. 29, 1988," *Langston Hughes Review* 12, no. 2 (Fall 1993), pp. 28–44. West is featured in Abby Arthur Johnson and Ronald Maberry Johnson, *Propaganda and Aesthetics: The Literary Politics of Afro-American Magazines in the Twentieth Century* (1979); Eleonore van Notten, *Wallace Thurman's Harlem Renaissance* (1994); Karen R. Veselits, "'Prologue to a Life': Dorothy West's Harlem Renaissance Years, 1926–1934" (PhD dissertation, College of William & Mary, 2001); Mary Helen Washington, "I Sign My Mother's Name: Maternal Power in Dorothy West's Novel, *The Living Is Easy*," in Washington, ed., *Invented Lives: Narratives of Black Women, 1860–1960* (1987); and Sharon L. Jones, *Rereading the Harlem Renaissance: Race, Class, and Gender in the Fiction of Jessie Fauset, Zora Neale Hurston, and Dorothy West* (2002). Obituaries appeared in the *New York Times* (containing the opening quotation from Hillary Rodham Clinton), the *Washington Post*, and the *Vineyard Gazette* on August 19, 1998.

KAREN R. VESELITS

WEST, Mae. August 17, 1893–November 22, 1980. Actress, writer.

Mae West, a woman who "invented" herself just as surely as Henry Ford "invented" the Model T, was born in Brooklyn, New York. Her mother, Matilda "Tillie" Delker Doelger, came to the United States from Bavaria in the 1880s and married an Irish boxer, John Patrick West. Mary Jane, soon known as Mae, was the eldest of three children. Mae's father took her to the prize rings and gyms, but her mother brought her to local amateur contests as "Baby Mae—Song and Dance." On the stage almost continually after the age of seven, Mae West appeared in local repertory companies called "the subway circuit." Although stage mothers were virtually a backstage fixture of vaudeville theaters, Mae went out alone on the Keith circuit at seventeen, dancing and singing with Frank Wallace, the son of a Lithuanian tailor from Queens. She and Wallace were secretly married in Milwaukee, Wisconsin, on April 11, 1911, although documents confirming the marriage (which West initially denied) were not discovered until 1935. A divorce was granted in 1942. She never had children.

West played the "tough girl" in early Broadway revues such as *A La Broadway* (1911), *A Winsome Widow* (1912), and *Sometime* (1918), attracting notoriety for doing the "shimmy" but no starring roles. By the time she was thirty, she knew she would have to write her own material to get the attention she wanted. For a woman with little or no formal schooling, her output was astonishing, and it continued throughout her career. Considering its sheer volume, it is surprising she is remembered primarily as an actress.

Three amateur scripts—*The Ruby Ring* (1921), *The Hussy* (1922), and *The Chick* (1924)—were never produced, but in 1926, with money she borrowed from her mother, she wrote, produced, and starred in *Sex* as a good-hearted prostitute named Margy LaMont. *Sex* ran from April 1926 through March 1927 before it was raided by the police and prosecuted for obscenity, earning West a ten-day sentence in the Women's Prison on Welfare Island and scads of free publicity. The belated police raid and the jail sentence were really directed at West's new play about gay men, *The Drag* (1927), which had drawn attention at out-of-town previews for its salacious jokes and cross-dressed actors.

West set aside *The Drag* to write and star in *Diamond Lil* (1928), earning her first good reviews for playing what became her most memorable character, a tough-talking, voluptuous 1890s Bowery saloon hostess. Following that success, she wrote *The Pleasure Man* (1928), keeping most of the gay cast of *The Drag* hidden behind a bizarre story of an unscrupulous Lothario who seduces a country girl and is castrated by her avenging brother. When *Pleasure Man* was raided and prosecuted as obscene, West put up bail for the entire cast and went to court. The jury failed to reach a verdict and charges were dropped, but she incurred substantial legal fees defending a play in which she never appeared. With the theater industry already feeling the effects of the Depression, she next revised her novel *Babe Gordon* (1930) for the stage, calling it *The Constant Sinner.* The story dealt with a white woman and a black mobster, but she quickly found that no theater would open a play with a biracial cast. Her old friend George Raft, now playing celluloid gangsters, urged her to leave New York and try Hollywood.

Starting in 1932, West's signature comedy drew film audiences eager to shrug off the despair of hard times. Her first role, in *Night after Night* (1932), contains the kinds of sexual innuendo and double entendres that the public quickly began to associate with the swaggering blond actress: to the hatcheck girl who remarks, "Goodness, what beautiful diamonds," she answers, "Goodness had nothing to do with it, dearie." Her next hit was *She Done Him Wrong* (1933), an adaptation of *Diamond Lil* that featured a young actor named Cary Grant. In *I'm No Angel* (1933), also starring Grant, West utters the memorable self-appraisal, "When I'm good, I'm very good, but when I'm bad, I'm better."

In the midst of the Depression, Mae West commanded an annual income of $480,833, making her the highest-paid woman in America. She wielded considerable power in Hollywood, but also drew opposition from the Catholic League of Decency and from Joseph Breen, who was charged with enforcing the industry's Production Code governing acceptable material on screen. *Belle of the Nineties* sneaked through in 1934, but dialogue in *Klondike Annie* (1935) was changed in order to receive the Seal of Approval. William Randolph Hearst still denounced Mae West as a "menace to the Sacred Institution of the American Family" and forbade his newspapers from mentioning her name (Pierpont, p. 90). One last brush with censors occurred in 1937 when she appeared on NBC's Chase and Sanborn radio show in a skit opposite Edgar Bergen's dummy Charlie McCarthy. The comedy dealt with Adam and Eve and the snake in the Garden of Eden, and although the lines were innocent enough, radio accented the pauses and the double entendres, and West's tongue-in-cheek delivery sent shock waves through Sunday evening audiences.

Mae West kept making movies, including *Go West Young Man* (1936) and *My Little Chickadee* (1940) with W. C. Fields, but her movie career stalled. Mike Todd produced her new play, *Catherine Was Great,* in 1946 and she took *Diamond Lil* to London in 1948 and to Broadway in 1949. In the 1950s she put together a popular Las Vegas nightclub act, complete with musical numbers featuring four male body builders. She also published her autobiography, *Goodness Had Nothing to Do with It* (1959). West returned to Hollywood in Gore Vidal's *Myra Breckinridge* (1970). At a time when her later performances were shrinking into self-parody, she was "discovered" by new voices in the theater. Younger audiences recovered her classic films of the 1930s, and gay audiences found her flamboyant style suited to camp comedy. She herself was an indefatigable performer, appearing in her last movie, *Sextette* (1978), at the age of eighty-three.

Critics disagree about Mae West's impact on the stage, some finding her little more than an animated shape, but the hourglass figure and its brassy display were costumed accessories. She will be remembered for her wit. An unschooled writer, hardly a trained playwright, West left her mark on stage plays, novels, an autobiography, and a dozen screenplays. She understood America's gothic taste for gangsters and gunmen, and gave audiences a new cast of heroines who never paid "the wages of sin" and always had the last laugh. "Haven't you ever met a man who could make you happy?" "Sure, lots of times." The smart-mouthed barbs dismantled Victorian morality when the censors weren't looking. The French writer Colette said of her, "She alone out of an enormous and dull catalogue of heroines, does not get married at the end, does not die, does not take the road to exile" and is "in her style, as solitary as Chaplin used to be" (Virmaux and Virmaux, pp. 62–63).

Over the years West supported her extended family in California and managed to keep much of her wealth through her long career, although in her last years she was a recluse and in ill health. Paul Novak, a former member of her nightclub act, was her companion for the last twenty-five years of her life. Diagnosed with diabetes in her seventies, she suffered a stroke and died at her home in Los Angeles on November 22, 1980, at the age of eighty-seven. She was buried in Brooklyn.

Bibliography: Manuscripts of Mae West's stage plays are held in the Manuscript Division of the Library of Congress. *Sex* and *The Drag* were copyrighted under the pseudonym Jane Mast. Lillian Schlissel, *Three Plays by Mae West* (1997), contains *Sex, The Drag,* and *The Pleasure Man,* as well as an appendix with the incomplete records of the criminal prosecutions of *Sex* and *The Pleasure Man* found in the Municipal Archives of the City of New York. The Roger Richman Agency of Beverly Hills, California, representing the receivership estate, governs rights to her writings. *The Constant Sinner* (1931) is part of the Shubert Archive in New York City, which also holds scripts of early Broadway revues in which she appeared. Newspaper clippings and memorabilia can be found in the Billy Rose Theatre Collection, New York Public Library for the Performing Arts at Lincoln Center, and in theater collections at Harvard University, the Stanley Musgrove Collection at UCLA, and the Harry Ransom Humanities Research Center at the University of Texas, Austin. Mae West's films are in the Paramount Collection at the Margaret Herrick Library of the Academy of Motion Picture Arts and Sciences in Beverly Hills. The most reliable and inclusive biography is Emily W. Leider, *Becoming Mae West* (1997). Other standard works include George Eels and Stanley Musgrove, *Mae West* (1982); Jon Tuska, *The Films of Mae West* (1973); and Carol M. Ward, *Mae West: A Bio-Bibliography* (1989). Also important are Maurice Leonard, *Mae West: Empress of Sex* (1991); Tim Malachosky, *Mae West* (privately published, 1993); Marybeth Hamilton, *When I'm Bad I'm Better* (1995); and Richard Helfer, "Mae West on Stage: Themes and Persona" (PhD dissertation, City University of New York, 1990). See also Claudia Roth Pierpont, *Passionate Minds: Women Rewriting the World* (2000), and Alain and Odette Virmaux, eds., *Colette at the Movies: Criticism and Screenplays* (translated by Sara W. R. Smith, 1980). An obituary appeared in the *New York Times* on November 23, 1980.

LILLIAN SCHLISSEL

WHITE, Katharine. September 17, 1892–July 20, 1977. Magazine editor.

As a fiction and poetry editor for the *New Yorker* for thirty-two years—and as friend, cheerleader, and adviser to several generations of writers—Katharine White was a significant force in twentieth-century American literature. She was born Katharine Sergeant in Winchester, Massachusetts, the last of three daughters of Elizabeth Blake Shepley, a homemaker, and Charles Sergeant, a railroad company executive. The family, whose ancestors on both sides had lived in New England since the seventeenth century, were nominally Congregationalists but were not observant. When Katharine was six (by which time the family had moved to Brookline), her mother died. Afterward, her father's sister Caroline—a graduate of Smith College and a former headmistress of a girls' school—came to live with her brother and nieces. In her intellectual and literary interests, she was an important influence on Katharine.

Katharine attended Miss Winsor's School in Boston and, starting in 1910, Bryn Mawr College, from which her sister Elizabeth had graduated. The summer before her freshman year, she became engaged to Ernest Angell, a Harvard senior whose family had spent summers near the Sergeants for many years. She graduated fourth in a class of seventy-nine in 1914, and a year later, after Ernest Angell had graduated from Harvard Law School, they married and settled in Cleveland. In 1916, Katharine gave birth to a daughter, Nancy; in 1919, the family moved to New York. A son, Roger, was born the following year.

In the early 1920s, Katharine began to have some success as a freelance writer, placing articles and reviews in the *New Republic,* the *Atlantic Monthly,* and the *Saturday Review of Literature.*

In summer 1925, acting on the recommendation of a friend on the staff of a new magazine called the *New Yorker,* she applied for, and got, a job as a part-time manuscript reader. Within weeks she was a full-time editor; not long after that she was the most trusted colleague of the magazine's founder, Harold Ross.

On the surface, Ross and Katharine Angell were the most mismatched pair imaginable. He was a rough-hewn westerner, a high school dropout, and an erstwhile newspaperman who revered humorists like DOROTHY PARKER and Ring Lardner but had no interest in "literature." She was a proper Bostonian who loved Jane Austen and wore wool suits, Sally Victor hats, and her hair in a bun. But they made a formidable team. As a colleague later wrote, "Ross, though something of a genius, had serious gaps. In Katharine, he found someone who filled them . . . what he lacked, she had; what she lacked, he had. She complemented him in a way that, in retrospect, seems to me to have been indispensable to the survival of the magazine."

The colleague was Elwyn Brooks White, known professionally as E.B., who started contributing to the *New Yorker* in 1926 and shortly afterward was recognized, by Ross and Katharine Angell, as one of the magazine's most important and gifted writers. He and Katharine were married in 1929, less than a year after she and Ernest Angell divorced. In 1930, they had a son, Joel. The marriage lasted until Katharine's death.

Ross had started the *New Yorker* as a humor magazine with a New York focus, but in the late twenties and through the thirties, it broadened and deepened; by the end of that period, in addition to the funny essays and cartoons, it was publishing serious short stories, poems, journalism, and criticism. More than any other single person, Katharine White was responsible for the change. It was less that she had a conscious plan to alter the character of the magazine than that she personally and enthusiastically responded to ambitious writers and pieces of writing and championed them to Ross, who, as often as not, had the intelligence and good sense to go along with her. And so, in this period, White encouraged and escorted into the pages of the *New Yorker* such writers as Sally Benson, LOUISE BOGAN, KAY BOYLE, Morley Callaghan, John Cheever, Nancy Hale, John O'Hara, and Sylvia Townsend Warner.

In 1938, prompted by E. B. White's desire to leave New York City, the Whites moved to North Brooklin, Maine, where they had bought a summer house four years earlier. Katharine worked half-time editing *New Yorker* fiction, and, with her husband, edited an anthology, *A Subtreasury of American Humor* (1941). She developed an interest in gardening, which eventually led to a series of articles for the *New Yorker,* published posthumously as a book in 1979, *Onward and Upward in the Garden.* Other than a handful of sketches and short poems, her only other published writing was a semi-annual review-essay of new children's books, which she contributed to the *New Yorker* from 1933 to 1948.

In winter 1943, with the *New Yorker* staff depleted by the war, Ross summoned the Whites back to New York. As before, E. B. White wrote for the magazine and Katharine White edited. In the forties and fifties, she helped the *New Yorker* become a more international and self-consciously literary magazine, working closely with such authors as ELIZABETH BISHOP, Nadine Gordimer, MARY MCCARTHY, Vladimir Nabokov, JEAN STAFFORD, Peter Taylor, Niccolo Tucci, and John Updike. Although White had a formal, sometimes imposing demeanor, she was devoted to her writers, with a concern and a loyalty that went beyond the professional level. Many of them became close friends.

In 1957, Katharine retired (although she continued an informal relationship with the *New Yorker* for the rest of her life) and the Whites moved permanently to Maine. White was afflicted in her later years by a series of infirmities, the most galling of which was a degeneration in her eyesight that made it difficult for her to read and impossible to write. She died of congestive heart failure in Blue Hill, Maine, on July 20, 1977, at the age of eighty-four. William Shawn, Ross's successor as editor of the *New Yorker,* wrote an unsigned tribute to her in the magazine, observing, "More than any other editor except Harold Ross himself, Katharine White gave the *New Yorker* its shape, and set it on its course."

Bibliography: Katharine White's papers, including a large selection of her personal and professional correspondence and her collection of books by *New Yorker* authors, are at the Bryn Mawr College Library. In addition, the New Yorker Records, at the New York Public Library, contain several thousands of letters exchanged between her and *New Yorker* contributors. The only biography of White is Linda H. Davis, *Onward and Upward: A Biography of Katharine S. White* (1987). See also Emily Herring Wilson, ed., *Two Gardeners: Katharine S. White and Elizabeth Lawrence—A Friendship in Letters* (2002). The quotation from E. B. White is found in "The Art of the Essay, I," *Paris Review* 12, no. 48 (Fall 1969), p. 85. A valuable and insightful essay about her is Nancy Franklin, "Lady with a Pencil," *New Yorker,* February 26 and March 4, 1996, p. 172. Roger Angell's "The King of the Forest," *New Yorker,* February 21, 2000, p. 120, is mainly about his father, Ernest Angell, but sheds significant light on his mother as well. For a history of the *New Yorker,* see Ben Yagoda, *About Town: The New Yorker and the World It Made* (2000). This article benefited from an e-mail correspondence with Roger Angell. Obituaries appeared in the *New York Times* on July 22, 1997, and in

"Katharine Sergeant White," the *New Yorker,* on August 1, 1977, p. 72, which contains the final quotation.

BEN YAGODA

WHITNEY, Ruth. July 23, 1928–June 4, 1999. Magazine editor.

Ruth Reinke was born in Oshkosh, Wisconsin, the youngest of three children and the second daughter of Helen Deistler, a homemaker, and Leonard G. Reinke, a partner in a family-owned firm that made cemetery monuments. She grew up in a modest bungalow and never forgot her midwestern roots. Ruth's mother suffered from mental illness and was often hospitalized, and Ruth and her siblings were raised largely by their father. Ruth graduated in 1945 from Oshkosh High School, where she edited the school newspaper and won honorable mentions in national competitions. She obtained a scholarship to Northwestern University, where she majored in English literature. In college she met journalism student Daniel Whitney, whom she married after her graduation in 1949. They had one child, Philip, born in September 1963.

Ruth Whitney's first job was with Time Inc., in Chicago, where she wrote sales-promotion letters to motivate and train college subscription agents. When her department was moved to New York City, she and her husband relocated. Once in New York, Daniel launched what would become a prominent advertising agency, Whitney & Whitney. Ruth continued to work in sales-promotion as a copywriter until she was fired from her position at Time Inc., for, as she later remembered, her lack of enthusiasm about her work. Her supervisors encouraged her to apply for other openings within the company, but having decided that she wanted to move from the sales to the editorial side of the magazine business, Whitney realized she would find few opportunities in the male-dominated world of news magazines. She took an editorial position at *Better Living,* a supermarket magazine for homemakers. After only three years there, she took over as editor in chief. She later surmised that she had been offered the position primarily so that the owners had someone to steer the magazine through its demise; it folded shortly after she assumed editorship.

Once Ruth Whitney had worked at that level of experience and responsibility, she hoped to find a comparable position. Many women's magazines still had male editors; women's fashion magazines stood out as an arena in which professional women congregated and excelled. Accepting an associate editor position at *Seventeen,* Whitney discovered that she liked working for a young audience and with other women. She stayed at *Seventeen* for eleven years before taking over the helm at *Glamour* in 1967.

When Whitney took the position at *Glamour,* she inherited a fashion magazine and quickly transformed into something more, rapidly decreasing fashion features from half the magazine's content to a quarter. She spoke of her readers as educated, smart, and open to new ideas. Within the first year she had made her mark, featuring an African American woman on the magazine's cover, making *Glamour* the first major women's magazine to do so. Combining style with serious news coverage, Whitney's *Glamour* would tackle topics as controversial as abortion rights and feminism and pave the way for other women's magazines to do the same. After watching the 1991 Supreme Court confirmation hearings of Clarence Thomas, she reconfigured the issue then in production to include Anita Hill, who had publicly accused Thomas of sexual harassment, as one of the featured women of the year. "Ruth used a mix of fashion, art, and a big wallop of feminism," said longtime rival, *Cosmopolitan* editor Helen Gurley Brown. "She was very pro-choice, bless her heart, along with sex and love and careers" (Finkel, p. 1).

Whitney's approach created controversy. In one case, many readers cancelled their subscriptions after *Glamour* published an article on a lesbian couple who attended their high school prom. Whitney was undeterred. Despite the criticism, Whitney's progressive stance won her reader loyalty and garnered many accolades, including four peer-generated National Magazine Awards, two for general excellence and one each for personal service and public interest. She was presented with the American Society of Magazine Editors' Hall of Fame Award in April 1996 and received a Lifetime Achievement Award from the Magazine Publishers Association in 1998.

Ruth Whitney had her own vision for the magazine, but she always checked in with and respected her readers. Her staff conducted focus groups, editorial research, and readership surveys. Whitney read all the reader mail that related to the magazine's content or approach, which she estimated amounted to ten thousand letters a year. She loved the mail so much that she once called it the next best thing to a paycheck. As a deputy editor of *Glamour* put it, "The fingerprint of the reader was on every page" (Finkel, p. 1).

Whitney also brought *Glamour* tremendous financial success, making it Condé Nast's most profitable and most widely read publication. Industry lore posited that no matter how profits fluctuated within Condé Nast, losses could be covered by *Glamour.* Despite her success, Ruth Whitney was removed as *Glamour*'s editor in September 1998 after thirty-one years, singled out in part because of her age and her remarkable longevity in a business marked by rapid turnover. The National Council of Women's Organizations, a Washington-based coalition of more than a hundred groups, protested Whitney's termination to S. I. Newhouse Jr., the CEO of Advance Publications, which owns Condé Nast. She was replaced with *Cosmopolitan* editor-in-chief Bonnie Fuller, whose tenure at *Glamour,* more in keeping with industry standards, was brief.

Despite her success and the glamour that surrounded her job, Ruth Whitney was, as one journalist put it, a woman of substance rather than of style. An extremely hard worker and a very private person, she always considered herself a journalist, not a fashion person. Contrary to industry practice, she did not run an editor's note with her photo in the magazine. She also refused parties at the magazine for her twentieth, twenty-fifth, and thirtieth anniversaries. She preferred the privacy of the home her brother designed for her and her husband in Irvington, New York, to Manhattan's social scene. Whitney was an avid swimmer and speed walker. Widowed in 1995, she spent a good deal of time with her son, Philip. Ruth Whitney died at the age of seventy at her home on June 4, 1999, of Lou Gehrig's disease.

Bibliography: There is no collection of Ruth Whitney's personal papers. The author thanks Philip Whitney for his assistance with this article. The best introduction to Whitney is to scan the issues of *Glamour* she edited from 1967 to 1998. Other sources include Rebecca Finkel, "Friends Remember the Legacy of Ruth Whitney," *Medialife Magazine,* June 1999; Catherine Fitzpatrick, "Longtime Editor Whitney Is a Woman of Substance," *Milwaukee Journal Sentinel,* January 15, 1998; Robin Pogrebin, "The Long-Term Low Profile Behind the Buzz at Glamour," *New York Times,* September 8, 1997; and Alex Kuczynski, "An Editor Who Cared for Issues, not Clothes," *New York Times,* September 1, 1998. For general sources on women in the media in this period, see Cynthia M. Lont, *Women and Media: Content, Careers, and Criticism* (1995); Ellen McCracken, *Decoding Women's Magazines: From* Mademoiselle *to* Ms. (1993); Janice Winship, *Inside Women's Magazines* (1987); Mary Ellen Zuckerman, *A History of Popular Women's Magazines in the United States, 1792–1995* (1998); and Nancy A. Walker, ed., *Women's Magazines, 1940–1960: Gender Roles and the Popular Press* (1998). An obituary appeared in the *New York Times* on June 5, 1999.

JENNIFER SCANLON

WICKENS, Aryness Joy. January 5, 1901–February 2, 1991. Statistician, economist, federal official.

Aryness Joy Wickens, who created and refined numerous federal economic statistics, was one of the foremost American female statisticians in the twentieth century. She was born in Bellingham, Washington, the only child of Elizabeth Chapman and Oliver Hodgson Joy. Her father was born and raised in Albion, California, and her English-born mother came to the United States at age three. Trained as a schoolteacher, Elizabeth quit work after marrying Oliver Joy in 1899.

Oliver Joy worked in a lumber mill in Bellingham until, after a severe hand injury, he started an employment service for the local lumber and fishing industries. During Aryness's freshman year of high school, he shifted his business to the expanding logging industry near Vancouver. Rather than follow him to Canada, Elizabeth and Aryness lived with the extended Chapman family in Seattle, where Aryness could attend Seattle's rigorous Lincoln High School.

In 1918, Aryness Joy entered the University of Washington, where she met several people who heavily influenced her career. Chief among these was Dorothy Wolfe Douglas (wife of economist Paul H. Douglas), who taught Joy in a year-long sociology course. After Joy graduated Phi Beta Kappa from Washington in 1922 with a major in sociology and a minor in economics, Paul Douglas offered her a research assistantship at Chicago's Graduate School of Economics and Business, where she could pursue a master's degree. Sensitive to her parents' fears about Joy living unchaperoned in a large city, the Douglases also invited her to live with them. Although it was an intense, competitive, and largely male environment, Joy succeeded admirably; after completing her degree in 1924, she took a position teaching finance, sociology, and economics at Mount Holyoke College. In 1928, she left Mount Holyoke to join the research staff of the Federal Reserve Board, beginning a career with the federal government that would last more than four decades.

Aryness Joy had worked on federal statistical projects intermittently since graduating from the University of Washington. In the summer of 1922, she served as a field agent for the U.S. Children's Bureau; during the summers of 1926 and 1927, she worked with the Federal Reserve Board's Division of Research and Statistics, helping to develop and refine several economic statistics, including a new index of industrial production. After joining the Board full-time in 1928, she continued improving various economic indicators and industrial statistics.

At the onset of the Great Depression, controversies about the level of unemployment revealed the inadequacies of the government's existing economic statistics. Once Franklin D. Roosevelt took office in 1933, the federal government embarked on a wholesale reform of its statistics, which in turn led to the formation of the Committee on Government Statistics and Information Services, an independent review organization staffed by members of the American Statistical Association and the American Economic Association. Joy worked with this group, and the experience helped propel her from a narrow focus within the Federal Reserve Board to a wider acquaintance with a broad group of government officials and federal statistics. From 1934 to 1938 she worked in several New Deal agencies, gradually shifting from creating statistics to compiling and synthesizing economic data for policy reports. In 1938 she joined the Bureau of Labor Statistics in the Department of Labor, serving as special assistant to the commissioner, Isador Lubin. She would spend the rest of her career within the Department of Labor, where she would earn a reputation for statistical acumen, efficient management, and sharp debating skills.

The mid 1930s brought important changes in Joy's professional career and a transformation in her personal life. In 1935 she married David L. Wickens, an economist with the Department of Agriculture, with whom she had two sons: David (1939) and Donaldson (1942). David L. Wickens continued his own career in the federal government for many years, before retiring to manage the family's farms in Vienna, Virginia, and Avon, South Dakota. Though David's work on the South Dakota ranch forced the couple to spend substantial amounts of time apart, they remained married until his death in 1970.

Wickens's work in the Bureau of Labor Statistics established her reputation as an eminent government statistician. Foremost among her responsibilities as chief of the Prices and Cost of Living branch during the 1940s was calculation of the Bureau's Cost-of-Living Index (later renamed the Consumer Price Index). With the Roosevelt administration focused on limiting wartime inflation, the Index became a key part of both federal price and wage controls, thereby drawing the ire of national labor officials. Claiming that the Index underestimated the rise in living costs, the American Federation of Labor and the Congress of Industrial Organizations issued their own, much larger estimate of the change in the cost of living during the war. Wickens helped orchestrate the Bureau's response, winning praise from her fellow statisticians but antagonizing union leaders, who often accused Wickens of being anti-labor.

According her own account, Wickens was a candidate for commissioner of the Bureau in 1945, but she removed herself from consideration, stating that her obligations to her family required a less demanding schedule. Instead, she served as assistant commissioner to Ewan Clague, a fellow University of Washington graduate, until 1954, when she temporarily took over as acting commissioner during the search for a permanent replacement. She was highly regarded by her fellow statisticians, and in 1952 she served as the second female president of the American Statistical Association. From 1955 until her retirement in 1970, she held a number of top positions in the Department of Labor, including economic adviser to the secretary of labor. In 1961, she was honored as one of the first six recipients of the Federal Woman's Award for outstanding service in the federal government. Even after retirement, Wickens continued to serve in an advisory role, spending several years with the Commission on Federal Paperwork.

Although Aryness Joy Wickens contributed little to statistical theory, she developed and improved many federal economic statistics and garnered praise for her efficient management of government agencies. As one of the most prominent female civil servants, Wickens forged a career path through a largely male domain, relying on her technical and administrative skills to earn the respect of her colleagues. Wickens died on February 2, 1991, in Jackson, Mississippi, at the age of ninety.

Bibliography: The Schlesinger Library, Radcliffe Institute for Advanced Study, Harvard University, holds a small collection of Wickens's personal papers, photographs, numerous clippings and reprints, and papers related to her post-retirement work. The records of the Department of Labor and the Bureau of Labor Statistics in the National Archives also contain extensive correspondence related to Wickens. The best sources of biographical information are the transcripts of two oral history interviews with Wickens: "The Reminiscences of Mrs. A. J. Wickens" (1957), Oral History Research Office, Columbia University; and "Aryness Joy Wickens" (1982), Women in the Federal Government Oral History Project, Schlesinger Library. Transcripts of a third oral history interview with Wickens (1978) are housed in the Historical Office of the U.S. Department of Labor in Washington, D.C. For an overview of Wickens's views on government statistics, see her presidential address to the American Statistical Association, "Statistics and the Public Interest," *Journal of the American Statistical Association* 48, no. 261 (March 1953), pp. 1–14. She also occasionally published in academic journals such as the *American Journal of Sociology, American Economic Review, Journal of the American Statistical Association, Journal of Political Economy.* The most extensive existing account of the World War II cost-of-living controversy (in which Wickens played a central role) is Kathryn Smul Arnow, *The Attack on the Cost of Living Index* (1951). An obituary appeared in the *New York Times* on February 8, 1991.

THOMAS A. STAPLEFORD

WILKE, Hannah. March 7, 1940–January 28, 1993. Artist.

Hannah Butter was born in New York City and lived there nearly all of her adult life. She had one sibling, her older sister, Marsie. Her parents, Emanuel and Selma Butter, also born in New York, came from eastern European Jewish fami-

ganic gardening, the rituals of spring, finding food in the wild, preparing for winter, living on a limited income, and keeping marriages healthy (Stamberg, p. 272). She promoted earth-friendly, simple living, a philosophy described in her *Book of Uncommon Sense: A Practical Guide with 10 Rules for Nearly Everything* (1986): "I think everyone should live a little more gently on the earth. Some of our wants and desires are causing cruel gashes on this sweet planet, which is a beautiful place" (*Middlesex News,* March 22, 1986). With her independence, her disregard for social constraints, and her commitment to living "gently on the earth," she recalled the hippies of the 1960s (whom she credited with freeing her from girdles, china sets, and matching crocodile bags and shoes) and anticipated the environmental awareness that marked the 1980s and 1990s.

In May 1986, Kim Williams was diagnosed with ovarian cancer. After one unsuccessful surgery, she chose to forgo any further treatment. In this, she followed her own guidelines for dying that she had presciently outlined in her *Book of Uncommon Sense* and became an advocate for an individual's right to control her or his own death. "I wish to die in peace, not in pieces," she wrote. "I don't want my body to be a battlefield" (*Uncommon Sense,* pp. 163, 169). In an interview from her home, she explained, "I am ready to go. I've had a good life; I've done what I set out to do, and now it is time to move on" (*Missoulian,* July 13, 1986). She died in her home at the age of sixty-two, and Mel scattered her ashes over the hills near Missoula. Her death was mourned nationwide: commentaries appeared in *Time,* the *New Yorker,* and numerous local newspapers. The Kim Williams Trail, running along the Clark Fork River, was named for her in 1987, and the Kim Williams Graduate Fellowship was instituted to fund journalism students at the University of Montana.

Bibliography: Published works by Kim Williams include *High Heels in the Andes* (1959), *Eating Wild Plants* (1970), *The Kim Williams Cookbook and Commentary* (1983), and *Kim Williams' Book of Uncommon Sense: A Practical Guide with 10 Rules for Nearly Everything* (1986). She also published poems in such publications as *Living Wilderness, Christian Science Monitor, Denver Post,* and *Oregonian.* The Kim Williams papers, housed at the University of Montana, contain diaries from 1958 to 1970, extensive correspondence, speeches, NPR material, unpublished stories and poems, notes on topics of interest to Williams, financial records, and numerous newspaper articles on Williams. Another source of information is "Kim Williams, R.I.P." in Susan Stamberg, *Talk: NPR's Susan Stamberg Considers All Things* (1993). Additional information was provided by her sister Froni Crane and friends Leo Lott, Nancy Wendel, and Lois Dodge. Obituaries appeared in the *New York Times* and the *Missoulian* on August 7, 1986.

JILL BERGMAN

WILLIAMS, Mary Lou. May 8, 1910–May 28, 1981. Jazz composer, arranger, pianist.

Musician Mary Lou Williams was born Mary Elfrieda Scruggs in Atlanta, Georgia, the second of seven children born to Virginia Riser Burley. She was raised by her mother and her stepfather, Fletcher Burley, and did not meet her father, Joseph Scruggs, until her late twenties.

Around 1915 her family moved north to the East Liberty section of Pittsburgh, seeking a better life. "Smoketown," as Pittsburgh was then called, provided a hardscrabble existence for the growing Burley family. Her mother worked as a laundress, while Fletcher Burley was a laborer in the steel mills; together they sought relief from drudgery in drink and music. A child prodigy, Williams began playing as a toddler by imitating her mother as she practiced hymns on a storefront church harmonium. By age seven or eight, Williams accompanied her stepfather, who liked to gamble, to taverns, where for tips she played requests—everything from the blues, ragtime, and pop songs to bits of operettas, Irish ballads, and waltzes. When Fletcher Burley acquired a player piano, Williams practiced tirelessly.

Soon she was known as "the little piano girl of East Liberty." Her white teachers took her to hear opera and European classical music, but Williams was more interested in listening to African American pianists like Jack Howard, Louie Austin, Earl Hines, James P. Johnson, and Fats Waller. (She learned to read and write music years later on her own.) When her stepfather became too ill to work, Williams left high school and took a job accompanying a black vaudeville act called "The Hits and Bits." It was a precarious and unsavory livelihood for a fourteen-year-old girl, but she loved being around musicians and sent home money when she could. Even at that young age, Mary set no personal limits on her professional life, deflecting the resistance to her gender of many in the music business with stubborn determination, humor, hard work, and impeccable musicianship.

On May 10, 1926, Mary, an attractive, shapely, brown-complexioned and high-strung yet introverted sixteen-year-old African American woman, married the "Hits" bandleader, saxophonist John Overton Williams. It was more a marriage of convenience than romance, but the two supported each other professionally. After the vaudeville act folded, they headed for Memphis, John's hometown. When John was hired in 1928 by an excellent "territory" band in Oklahoma called the Clouds of Joy, Mary followed, but not as a musician. She acted as chauffeur and gofer, until her skillful arrangements and original composition at an audition so impressed a record producer that he insisted she, rather than the band's regular pianist, play on the recordings. In 1931 she got the piano chair permanently and quickly became the key member of the band. A brilliant soloist, writer, and arranger, Williams was in demand as a writer during the Swing Era for many big bands. She wrote the hit "Roll 'Em" for Benny Goodman, receiving her usual fee of $15—"silk stockings," as she dryly put it.

Having divorced John in 1942 and eager to pursue a career on her own, Williams left the Clouds of Joy. Later that year, on December 10, she married trumpeter Harold "Shorty" Baker, with whom she led a combo until Baker took a job with Duke Ellington's orchestra in 1943. At loose ends, Williams accompanied him on the road, writing arrangements for the band at Ellington's request, including "Trumpets No End." Although she and Baker soon parted, they never divorced; he died in 1966.

Settling in New York City in late 1943, Williams was extremely busy for the next twelve years. She became a fully accomplished modernist, and a mentor to younger players such as Dizzy Gillespie, Thelonious Monk, and Bud Powell. She was a featured performer at Café Society Downtown, hosted her own radio program, wrote music for other radio shows, performed in many revues, and appeared on Broadway in the short-lived show *Blue Holiday.* She premiered an extended work of twelve tone poems called *The Zodiac Suite* for a chamber-jazz ensemble at Town Hall in 1945. The following year, she presented fresh arrangements of sections of *Zodiac* for symphony orchestra at Carnegie Hall, a first both for a female and for an African American jazz composer.

Williams also tried to educate people about her concept that jazz had developed from the roots of slavery. Her "history of jazz" commentary with music, which she first presented in a concert at Cornell University in 1946, would later become an important part of her repertoire.

After a busy and tumultuous sojourn to Europe in 1953–54, Williams withdrew from the hectic life of nightclubs—what she called nite life. She concentrated intensely on spirituality, taught children at Harlem storefronts, and helped raise a troubled sister's son—who was like the child she had wanted but hadn't had. After she was baptized as a Roman Catholic in 1957, attracted by the Church's rituals and the progressive Catholics she befriended, such as DOROTHY DAY, Lorraine Gillespie (Dizzy's wife), and pianist Hazel Scott, she began to write music with a strong spiritual component, including *Black Christ of the Andes,* also known as *St. Martin de Porres,* and three jazz masses. Alvin Ailey choreographed *Mary Lou's Mass* for his company in 1971–73 and it was widely performed, notably at St. Patrick's Cathedral in 1975 and 1979.

Williams gradually began to play in public venues in the late 1950s. By the 1970s, she often performed at the Cookery in New York and began recording more often, including the brilliant self-produced *Zoning* (1974). From 1977 to 1981, she was artist in residence at Duke University; her jazz history classes became sellouts on campus. With her personal manager, Peter O'Brien, SJ, a Catholic priest, she toured extensively. Even when diagnosed with bladder cancer in 1978, Williams did not let up the pace professionally. She worked on her last major composition, the unfinished *History of Jazz for Wind Symphony* and set up the Mary Lou Williams Foundation to provide scholarships for gifted poor young musicians to study with established jazz artists. She died at her home in Durham, North Carolina, at the age of seventy-one.

Mary Lou Williams was acclaimed by admirers as an extraordinary musician and presence, celebrated for her rare command of the successive styles of jazz she lived through, from stride to avant-garde. In an almost completely male-dominated profession, she achieved the highest respect for her mastery of the music, which is all the more impressive given the odds against her. Although she received many honorary degrees and awards, her most cherished prize, she said, was Duke University's Trinity Award, given by the students to the best-loved faculty member. Above all, she wanted to keep the heritage of jazz music alive.

Bibliography: The Mary Lou Williams Archive, housed at the Institute of Jazz Studies, Rutgers University, Newark, New Jersey, contains her correspondence, diaries, recordings, photographs, and other memorabilia, as well as music manuscripts. A good part of Williams's compositions and arrangements in her archive have not been published or recorded. Among published writings, Williams collaborated with editor Max Jones on "Mary Lou Williams: My Life with the Kings of Jazz," eleven autobiographical articles first published in *Melody Maker* magazine from April to June 1954, and republished subsequently, including in Ben Sidran, *Talking Jazz* (1992). The Williams Archive contains drafts of her unpublished partial autobiography, *Zoning the History of Jazz.* Writings on Williams include Whitney Balliett's long piece about her importance, "Out Here Again," *New Yorker,* May 2, 1964, pp. 52–54+. Joanne Burke made a documentary film about her, *Music on My Mind* (1981), and Linda Dahl's biography, *Morning Glory* (2001), includes a full-scale treatment of her life and work, an extensive bibliography, and a discography. An obituary appeared in the *New York Times* on May 29, 1981.

LINDA DAHL

WILLS, Helen. *See* Moody, Helen Wills.

WINSTON, Ellen Black. August 15, 1903–June 19, 1984. Sociologist, welfare policy expert.

Ellen Black Winston, a sociologist who became the country's first federal commissioner of welfare, was born Ellen Black in Bryson City, North Carolina, the first of four children of Marianna Fischer and Stanley Warren Black. Both parents originally hailed from Illinois. Winston's father was an attorney and banker, and her mother opened and ran the first library in their town. Ellen attended public school in Bryson City, and graduated from Swain County High School. She received a BA from Converse College in Spartanburg, South Carolina, in 1924, and then went to the University of Chicago, where she pursued an advanced degree in sociology. She was awarded her MA in 1928, the same year she married sociologist Sanford Richard Winston, and her PhD in 1930.

After finishing graduate school, Ellen Winston taught high school in the Raleigh, North Carolina, public school system, while her husband served as professor and department chair at North Carolina State University. The couple remained married until his death in 1969 and had no children. During the Depression, however, she began commuting to Washington, D.C., to conduct research on social conditions for the Federal Emergency Relief Administration (FERA) and the Works Progress Administration (WPA). She then returned to academia as chair of the department of sociology and economics at Meredith College (1940–44) in Raleigh.

Winston wrote extensively about social and economic programs. Early in her career, she focused her research on the incidence and correlates of mental illness. Her interests later shifted toward social welfare and policy, and she became involved in many large-scale studies of the social conditions of needy populations. This research generated several co-authored books, including *Seven Lean Years* (1939), a study of rural relief problems; *The Plantation South* (1940), an analysis of the social aspects of the plantation system; *Foundations of American Population Policy* (1940); and *The Negro's Share* (1943), a study of living conditions and relief problems among African Americans. Her articles appeared in academic journals, such as the *American Sociological Review* and the *American Journal of Sociology*, as well as in technical publications on public relief.

Throughout her career in social policy, Winston advocated public welfare programs that emphasized preventive, protective, and rehabilitative services. The objective of welfare programs, she believed, was to help people become self-sustaining as quickly as possible. She emphasized giving children opportunities for education and training that would prevent the perpetuation of poverty from generation to generation. She opposed benefit cuts, believing that families, especially those on Aid to Families with Dependent Children (AFDC) rolls, needed adequate grants to live decently if they were ultimately to move themselves out of dependency groups.

Winston was appointed North Carolina's welfare commissioner in 1944 and held the position for eighteen years, during which time she was the highest-ranking woman in state government. With hard facts and statistics she defended the state welfare system against reluctant legislators. She fought against popular perceptions of welfare as a drain on the economy by promoting her vision of welfare as an investment in children. Winston was a hands-on administrator who took a comprehensive view of welfare. She insisted on personally visiting North Carolina's counties to meet with local administrators in order to achieve an understanding of local needs that could not be gained by sitting behind her desk in the state capitol.

Winston believed in preventive and rehabilitative services for families who did not qualify for cash grants. Under her administration, North Carolina increased the number of licensed daycare centers from a handful to more than 350, and the number of foster homes from 87 to 1,500. During her tenure, the state's adoption program more than doubled. And she implemented a program for the aging that resulted in the licensing of more than five hundred family care homes. Winston also worked to keep children out of jails and detention centers while they waited for court hearings, developing programs that allowed them to stay in their own homes or foster homes. Urging county welfare superintendents to accept full responsibility for the welfare of children in trouble, she placed many of the social workers in North Carolina on twenty-four-hour call with the sheriffs and juvenile courts.

In 1963, at age fifty-nine, she was appointed as the first United States Commissioner of Welfare, a position she held until 1967. A reorganization in the Department of Health, Education and Welfare had established a new Welfare Administration with a budget of $3 billion and responsibility for administering the department's public assistance programs. The new agency oversaw the Bureau of Family Services, which administered the federal and state programs for old age assistance, medical assistance for the aged, AFDC, Aid to the Permanently and Totally Disabled, and aid to the blind. As commissioner, she introduced progressive innovations in the federal programs overseeing public assistance, medical care, and child welfare services. Her expansive vision of welfare influenced many important legislative developments, including Medicaid.

In 1966, Winston published her long-range ideas in a pamphlet entitled "Social Development—Key to the Great Society." Winston was concerned that only the middle classes were enjoying improved opportunities for educational and cultural self-fulfillment. She saw the provision of public assistance grants as rooted in the recognition of public responsibility for meeting the financial needs of citizens. The concept that such assistance was a "right," argued Winston, was one of the great philosophical contributions of the public assistance program. Throughout her career, however, she was also acutely aware that greatly increased appropriations would be necessary before the implementation of the programs fully supported the tenets of social welfare. Her efforts were rewarded by a number of honorary degrees, as well as her election as president of the National Conference on Social Welfare in 1965–1966.

At her death at age eighty, on June 19, 1984, one editorial writer said: "No woman in North Carolina—and perhaps no man—understood better than she the complicated ways of social change." Winston was, as another commentator noted, a "practical sociologist," who "knew how to connect policy to the daily lives of the people."

Bibliography: Collections of Ellen Winston materials are held by Special Collections at the North Carolina State University Libraries, and by The Woman's Collection at the Walter Clinton Jackson Library, University of North Carolina at Greensboro. Both include personal and professional correspondence, photographs, newspaper and periodical clippings, and family histories. There is also an oral history by James B. Carey, "Interview with Ellen Black Winston," March 28, 1972, in Special Collections at the University of Chicago. Winston was the author or co-author of numerous books and articles, including: "A Statistical Study of Mental Disease" (PhD dissertation, University of Chicago, 1930); "The Assumed Increase of Mental Disease," *American Journal of Sociology* 40, no. 4 (1934), pp. 427–39; with Frank Lorimer and Louise K. Kiser, *Foundations of American Population Policy* (1940); "Social Problems of the Aged," *Social Forces* 26, no. 1 (1947), pp. 57–61; "Values of the Aid to Dependent Children Program," *Social Forces* 28, no. 1 (1949), pp. 50–53; *Social Work Education and Social Welfare Manpower* (1965); with Gladys O. White, "Simplifying Need Determination in Public Assistance," *Welfare in Review* 5, no. 8 (1967), pp. 1–4; and *Social Welfare Education and Careers in the South* (1975). The final quotations are found in Jack Aulis, "As Welfare Commissioner, She Saw Every Social Upheaval of the Century," *Raleigh News and Observer,* December 29, 1991. An obituary appeared in the *Washington Post* on June 21, 1984.

CHRISTA MCGILL AND VIRGINIA NOBLE

WISE, Brownie. May 25, 1913–September 24, 1992. Home party sales pioneer, Tupperware executive.

Brownie Mae Humphrey Wise, a pioneer in home party sales, was born in Buford, Georgia, the only surviving child of Walker Carlton Humphrey and Rossa Belle "Rosie" Stroud. Her father, a plumber, was one of six children in a family of farmers and blacksmiths in Forsyth County, Georgia. After Brownie's parents divorced when she was young, her mother worked as a hatmaker, and then as an organizer for the hatmakers' union. Because her job required extensive travel and physical risk, she left Brownie for months and years at a time with her older sister, Pearl, who was a dressmaker near Atlanta; there Brownie grew up with an extended group of cousins. She was a good student, but her schooling probably ended after eighth grade. She was more interested in fashion and dressing up, and boys, and had a knack for getting her way. In her early teens, Brownie left her cousins' home and accompanied Rosie on the road.

Brownie dreamed of being a writer and illustrator. In 1936, she won a contest to paint a mural at the Texas Centennial in Dallas. While there, she met Robert W. Wise, who was working at the Ford Motor Company exhibit. Brownie and Robert married in Dallas on December 15, 1936, and moved to Detroit shortly afterward. Their only child, Jerry, was born in 1938. While Jerry was an infant and toddler, Brownie was a frequent contributor to the *Detroit News*'s "Experience Column," writing long, carefully crafted descriptions of her life for the other contributors under the pen name Hibiscus. What she wrote, however, was wishful thinking. She told her column friends how homesick she was for her big mansion in Natchez, Mississippi, when she'd actually grown up in a family of extremely modest means in Georgia. She described her house in Dearborn as "Lovehaven," and her husband "Yankee" as loving and devoted, but Robert Wise was a violent drunk.

After Brownie and Robert Wise were divorced in 1942, she worked as a salesperson in a clothing shop and as a secretary for Bendix Aviation. In an effort to earn extra income, she became involved in selling Stanley Home Products—cleaning aids and brushes—at home party demonstrations. Stanley was a pioneer in home party selling, and the job was a perfect fit for her personality. She had drive and ambition and charm, and she quickly became one of the top Stanley sellers.

In the late 1940s, Brownie Wise saw some Tupperware, a new polyethylene product that was being sold, with limited success, at department stores. Along with several other Stanley branch managers around the country, she figured out that Tupperware should be sold at home parties because users needed to learn how to "burp" the airtight Tupper seal correctly in order to understand why Tupperware was such a major improvement in food storage containers. Wise switched from Stanley Home Products to Tupperware, recruited dealers and managers, and thrived selling Tupperware at home parties.

In 1950, Brownie moved to Florida with her son Jerry and her mother Rosie. Wise started a company she called Tupperware Patio Parties and was selling far more Tupperware than the department stores and hardware stores. Her success caught the eye of Earl Tupper, the reclusive, eccentric inventor of Tupperware, who had unsuccessfully started a home party division at his company. He asked her to be vice president in charge of Tupperware Home Parties Inc. in Kissimmee, Florida. From that time on, Tupperware was sold exclusively on the home party plan.

Wise took what she'd learned in Stanley and improved on it tenfold. She had an intuitive grasp of selling, consumer culture, and the remarkable hodgepodge of fantasies shared by many Americans in the 1950s. She started Tupperware's "Homecoming Jubilee," a four-day sales meeting that mixed learning with cornball entertainment, amazing prizes, and elaborate participatory costumed theme nights. Wise knew how to inspire her managers and dealers to work harder—and to believe in themselves. She was a good (if sentimental) writer and an excellent speaker. She offered women the opportunity to earn extra money, to travel, and to be part of an organization that pulled out the stops and did everything first class. She recognized women who got very little recognition elsewhere in their lives, bestowing upon them trophies, luxury goods, and applause. And she taught others in the company how to do the same.

Earl Tupper hated the limelight; Brownie Wise loved it. With Tupper's blessing, the company's public relations staff decided to put Brownie up on a pedestal as a wonder-woman salesperson. Female executives were rare in the 1950s, and the strategy worked. As the company grew, Wise appeared on talk shows, was quoted by newspapers, and appeared on the cover of numerous magazines (she was the first woman ever featured on the cover of *Business Week*). But when the press suggested that Brownie Wise was responsible for Tupperware's success, and that she could be equally successful selling any product, Earl Tupper couldn't stand it. Over time, Wise had become increasingly high-handed, and she was less patient with Tupper's style of micro-management and unpredictable temper. In 1958, Tupper unceremoniously and abruptly fired her, booting her from the multimillion dollar company she had helped build; she had no company stock and was given just one year's salary. Within a year's time, Tupper sold the company, eventually moving to Costa Rica.

Brownie Wise spent the rest of her life starting home party cosmetics companies that failed to thrive. She was a consultant to direct sales companies, she dabbled a bit in Florida real estate, and toward the end of her life she worked in ceramics, especially in raku. She died in Kissimmee, Florida, in 1992 at the age of seventy-nine.

Although Brownie Wise's time as the head of a large corporation was brief, her impact was huge. Tupperware Home Parties became the gold standard for home party selling. Many other large companies, like Mary Kay Cosmetics, copied the formula that she figured out. Building on her understanding that the heart of any direct selling company is its sales force, she nurtured and rewarded thousands of lower-middle-class women without college educations—women who would otherwise have had very few opportunities in life.

Bibliography: The extensive unpublished papers of Brownie Wise (including personal and business correspondence, photos, audio recordings, and press clippings) are at the Archives Center of the National Museum of American History, Smithsonian Institution. Also housed there are the papers of Earl Silas Tupper. Other information for this article came from the vital records offices of Dallas County, Texas, Wayne County, Michigan, and the state of Florida, and from approximately two hundred interviews conducted in the course of making the film *Tupperware!* (2004). The only book Brownie wrote (with a ghostwriter) was *Best Wishes, Brownie Wise: How to Put Your Wishes to Work* (1957), which was put together quickly from speeches she had given. The only serious work done on Brownie Wise to date has been Alison Clarke, *Tupperware: The Promise of Plastic in 1950s America* (1999). For an overview of the direct selling industry and its history, see Nicole Woolsey Biggart, *Charismatic Capitalism: Direct Selling Organizations in America* (1989).

LAURIE KAHN-LEAVITT

WOLCOTT, Marion Post. June 7, 1910–November 24, 1990. Photographer.

Marion Post was born in Montclair, New Jersey, the daughter of Marion Hoyt, a trained nurse, and Walter Post, a physician. She had one sibling, Helen, three years her senior. The Posts were affluent, owing to her father's successful medical practice, but the troubled marriage ended in divorce when Marion was thirteen. This unhappy home situation made her a quiet, withdrawn girl. Marion received her early education in the Montclair public schools, then finished high school at Edgewood School, a progressive, private, coeducational school in Greenwich, Connecticut. At Edgewood, Marion felt herself growing, opening up to new ideas and friendships, and maturing. For the rest of her life, she would be a strong advocate of progressive education.

While Marion was at Edgewood, her mother moved to Greenwich Village and began working with birth control activist MARGARET SANGER. Young Marion's weekends and summers were spent in the stimulating atmosphere of bright, creative people, such as composer Aaron Copeland and painters Stefan Hirsch and George Ault. She made extra money posing nude for artists, and learned to sneak into the back of theaters to catch plays from the wings. She also took classes at the New School for Social Research and New York University and held a succession of teaching jobs.

On a visit to Europe in 1932 she heard Adolph Hitler address a huge crowd and was horrified by his message of race elitism and hatred. In 1933, in Vienna to study child psychology, she acquired her first camera and began to photograph under the encouragement of a locally successful portrait photographer, Trude Fleischmann. The next year, she and her sister (who was also studying photography) helped Fleischmann, who was Jewish, get out of Vienna and resettle in New York City. Soon Post was back in New York herself, trying to take pictures for a living but finding it very difficult because no one had any money. Many of her early pictures were taken backstage at various theaters, including shots of Lee Strasberg, Elia Kazan, and Clifford Odets.

From early 1937 until July 1938 she worked for the Philadelphia *Evening Bulletin* to make ends meet, but she found the male staff condescending and resented being relegated to covering "women's page" stories. Post wanted to use her camera to make a difference, to have an impact on the troubling age in which she found herself. In 1938 she found her niche. With an introduction from Paul Strand and Ralph Steiner, whom she had met through the New York Photo League, she showed a portfolio of her work to Roy Stryker, director of the Historical Section of the Farm Security Administration (FSA) in Washington, and was hired. Her reputation as a major social documentary photographer of the 1930s is based on the work she accomplished over the following three years.

The FSA was a small New Deal agency that had been created to meet the needs of the poorest American farmers, especially tenants or sharecroppers who lived on land far too poor to support them and their families. The FSA adopted an experimental approach to rural poverty that included small loans to purchase better farm equipment, nutritional aid to farm women and their families, clean camps for migrant workers, and even some collective farms. It was all fairly controversial, particularly in the South. As a result, a small group of highly skilled photographers, including DOROTHEA LANGE and Walker Evans, was enlisted to photograph farm problems and the programs that were being developed to deal with them. Their job was to create propaganda, but it was honest propaganda. Photographers were encouraged to get to know their subjects, gain their cooperation, and then simply photograph their ordinary routines in fields, farmyards, and homes.

Marion Post was twenty-eight and a strikingly beautiful woman when she went to work for the FSA. Her early assignments, mostly in the deep South, tended to be more in the nature of public relations than the sort of substantive visual investigation of rural problems that she wanted to do. Her immediate superior, Roy Stryker, realized that she could visit an agricultural project, take a few pictures, and go on her way leaving a smile on every male face in the area. It was certainly a misuse of her talents, but she found ways to make more serious images as well. Within a year, Stryker had accepted her much more fully as a professional and gave her more serious work to do.

One of Post's most successful assignments involved working with MARGARET JARMAN HAGOOD and Howard Odum at the University of North Carolina's Institute for Research in the Social Sciences. There she spent much of the fall of 1939, returning in September 1940, exploring ways the camera could be used to underscore and highlight the social realities that the social scientists were studying. Her work with Hagood focused especially on the problems of women in the South and is a powerful and useful body of images.

In May 1941, Marion met and fell in love with Leon Oliver "Lee" Wolcott, an official in the Department of Agriculture. Six weeks later, on June 6, 1941, they were married. Lee, a widower, had two young children, four-year-old Gail and two-year-old John. Within a year, their first child, Linda, was born, and a second, Michael, arrived in 1945. Marion resigned from the FSA in 1942 and gave up professional photography, although she continued to photograph for her own personal reasons for the rest of her life. Lee, a strongly dominant man, refused to consider any suggestion of her accepting photographic assignments, and Marion was ready for a new role as wife and mother. Over the next thirty years, she followed her husband's career, first as a successful farmer and later with the State Department, living in various parts of the United States as well as in Iran, Egypt, and India, before settling permanently in California.

In 1975, Marion Post Wolcott's work was "rediscovered" by Lee Witkin, founder of the Witkin Gallery in New York City, and in 1976 she had several photographs in a show on FSA photography curated by the gallery. From that time until her death, she was increasingly in demand. In 1985 she received the Dorothea Lange Award from the Oakland Museum in California. She died of lung cancer in Santa Barbara, California, in 1990 at the age of eighty.

Bibliography: Marion Post Wolcott's photographic images from 1938 to 1942 are part of the FSA Collection in the Division of Prints and Photographs at the Library of Congress. Paul Hendrickson, *Looking for the Light: The Hidden Life and Art of Marion Post Wolcott* (1992), explores many personal aspects of Wolcott's life and especially her complex relationship with Lee Wolcott. F. Jack Hurley, *Marion Post Wolcott: A Photographic Journey* (1989), provides more coverage of her professional career and her changing relationship with Roy Stryker. See also Hurley, *Portrait of a Decade: Roy Stryker and the Development of Documentary Photography in the Thirties* (1972); and Roy Stryker and Nancy Woods, *In This Proud Land: America as Seen in the FSA Photographs* (1973). More recent works include Carl Fleischhauer and Beverly Brannan, *Documenting America, 1935–1943* (1988); and Nicholas Natanson, *The Black Image in the New Deal: The Politics of FSA Photography* (1992). An obituary appeared in the *San Francisco Chronicle* on December 1, 1990.

F. JACK HURLEY

WOLFF, Helen. July 27, 1906–March 28, 1994. Publisher.

Helen Wolff's tastes led her to discover and publish some of the finest authors of the twentieth century. Her facility with languages made her an excellent editor for European authors, and her understanding of all phases of publication from production to marketing allowed her to develop a market in the United States for many authors whom other publishers felt would have only critical success. Though the authors she published celebrated her discernment and her taste, she saw herself as "a practical woman, not a great intellect." This focus on publishing as a practical matter explains her ability to find and succeed with authors who might appear to have little market value, including Italo Calvino, Karl Jaspers, and Umberto Eco.

She was born Helen Mosel in Uskob, Macedonia, the second of four children of Ludwig Mosel, a German engineer who had been stationed there by the electrical engineering firm Siemens to help electrify Turkey, and Josefa Fischof, a cultivated woman who had little formal education but worked as an occasional correspondent for German newspapers. Her mother's multinational heritage (both Hungarian and Austrian) and the mixture of peoples and religions in Macedonia fostered Helen's ease with languages, love of books, and firm commitment to tolerance. The family left Macedonia during the Balkan Wars between 1912 and 1913, and eventually her mother moved the children to the German countryside. Helen was educated mainly by tutors until she entered the Schondorf School in Bavaria as a day student when she was fifteen. The only girl in the all-boys school, she continued to excel in languages, reading Shakespeare in English and learning Italian and French as well.

She began her training as a publisher in 1927 at Kurt Wolff Verlag, a firm founded by her future husband, Kurt Wolff, that began issuing titles in 1913. Wolff published important German avant-garde authors, including Heinrich Mann, Max Brod, and Franz Kafka, during the 1910s and 1920s. When Helen interned there, she was assigned to work on an international art series, called Pantheon, where she handled translations, correspondence with authors, editing, and production. In 1929, a French publisher bought the series and she left Kurt Wolff's firm in Munich to work in Paris for Pegasus Press. Later, she left Pegasus to work as a translator for the Institut International de Coopération Intellectuelle, a branch of the League of Nations. Throughout this time, she remained in contact with Kurt Wolff. In the early 1930s, Kurt Wolff divorced his first wife and, anxious about the rise of Nazism, dissolved his firm and left Germany. Helen and Kurt married in London in 1933, and their son, Christian, was born the next year. They spent the 1930s in France and Italy, barely escaping the German occupation of France through Portugal on their way to America in 1941.

They arrived nearly penniless in New York, dependent on Helen's facility with English to guide the couple and their seven-year old son. In 1942, Kurt and Helen attracted a few investors and formed a new publishing firm, Pantheon Books, which they ran out of their apartment on Washington Square. There, Helen did everything from contacting authors to developing a line of children's books to copy editing to shipping. Jacques Schiffrin joined the firm in 1943, and together the three published a wide array of now-classic European fiction and nonfiction writers, including André Gide, André Malraux, Carl Jung, and Albert Camus. They also published such commercially successful works as Anne Morrow Lindbergh's *A Gift from the Sea* (1955), Boris Pasternak's *Doctor Zhivago* (1958), and Giuseppe Tomasi di Lampedusa's *The Leopard* (1960). Never limiting themselves to European works, the Wolffs developed their varied tastes into an eclectic list that included historical novels such as Mary Renault's *The King Must Die* (1958), spiritual works such as Alan Watts's *The Way of Zen* (1957), and nature writing such as Joy Adamson's *Born Free* (1960).

Helen and Kurt resigned from Pantheon in 1961 and soon afterward created their own imprint, "A Helen and Kurt Wolff Book," at Harcourt Brace Jovanovich. The joint names on that imprint indicated the level of the partnership between them; neither dominated the firm, and thus they put their names in alphabetical order. As she explained in 1982, "I never felt that I was in my husband's shadow; I always felt that I was in his light." Helen proved the mutuality of their partnership after Kurt's unexpected death in 1963. She continued to improve the reputation of their imprint, publishing eighteen to twenty new volumes a year, developing critical interest in authors that the firm had already issued, including Georges Simenon, Uwe Johnson, Max Frisch, and Günter Grass, as well as adding new authors such as Amos Oz and Stanislaw Lem. Although she published a great deal of serious fiction, she always searched for authors who exhibited what she called playfulness of mind.

Her treatment of Simenon is typical of her commitment to managing the public perception of authors. By publishing his psychological fiction, such as *The Bells of Bicêtre* (1964), and developing Simenon's reputation, Wolff was able to issue the Inspector Maigret novels without having critics dismiss him as simply a mystery writer. As a result, according to Wolff, Simenon was taken seriously and strongly reviewed. At the same time, Wolff remained committed to publishing authors who might appear to have no market but who would become classics. As she explained to the *New Yorker* in 1982, "It requires a special effort to put European authors on the map here. . . . Very often, I feel that I am swimming against the stream." In addition to her own publishing duties, she mentored other women in publishing, including literary scout Maria Campbell, and formed strong friendships with writers as diverse as Anne Morrow Lindbergh, ANITA LOOS, Iris Origo, and HANNAH ARENDT. Honored for her support of German authors and German culture abroad, Helen Wolff retired from publishing in 1986 and died from a heart attack in Hanover, New Hampshire, in 1994 at the age of eighty-seven.

Bibliography: Helen Wolff's papers are located at the Beinecke Rare Book and Manuscript Library at Yale University. For profiles of her life, see Herbert Mitgang, "Imprint: Helen Wolff," *New Yorker*, August 2, 1982, pp. 41–73, which contains all the quotations in the text; and Thomas Weyr, "Helen Wolff," *Publishers Weekly*, February 5, 1973, pp. 30–32. Information about the early years of Pantheon Books can be found in Andre Schiffrin, *The Business of Books* (2000). Wolff's friendship with Anne Morrow Lindbergh is discussed in Susan Hertog, *Anne Morrow Lindbergh: Her Life* (1999); for her friendship with Hannah Arendt, see Arendt's letters, especially the collection edited by Lotte Kohler and Hans Saver (translated by Robert and Rita Kimber), *Hannah Arendt/Karl Jaspers Correspondence, 1926–1969* (1992). Also of interest is Michael Ermarth, ed., *Kurt Wolff: A Portrait in Essays and Letters* (1991). Other biographical details of her life were obtained in an interview with her son Christian Wolff on May 5, 2003. An obituary appeared in the *New York Times* on March 30, 1994.

CATHERINE TURNER

WOLFGANG, Myra Komaroff. 1914 [?]–April 12, 1976. Labor leader.

Myra K. Wolfgang, a pioneer in organizing low-wage service workers, was born Mira Komaroff in Montreal, Canada, to European Jewish parents. (She changed the spelling of her first name in October 1941 to encourage a different pronunciation.) The exact date is unknown, but her birth year most likely was 1914. Her father, Abraham Komaroff, emigrated from Russia as a young man and married Ida Ipp, a Jewish immigrant from Lithuania. After the birth of their third and youngest child, the family moved to Detroit, Michigan, where Abraham Komaroff earned a comfortable middle-class living as an insurance broker and later as a real estate agent. Although not strictly religious, the Komaroffs identified strongly with their Jewish culture. They were active members of the Jewish community in Detroit and sympathized closely with the labor movement, to which many Jewish workers belonged.

In part because of financial pressures and in part because she was seduced by the radical politics of the time, Wolfgang left college after one year as an art student at Carnegie Institute in Pittsburgh and returned in 1932 to Detroit, where she lived and worked for the rest of her life. She joined the Proletarian Party and earned a reputation as a fiery orator. Through such activities she met Louis Koenig, secretary-treasurer of the Detroit Waiters Union, Local 705, who hired her as an office assistant. She remained associated with that union local her entire adult life.

Wolfgang's activities in Local 705 expanded quickly. Following a recent amalgamation with the Detroit Waitresses Union, she began organizing women workers in restaurants, bars, hotels, and private clubs. In 1934 Wolfgang was elected to the executive board of Local 705 and to the Detroit Joint Board of the Hotel and Restaurant Employees and Bartenders International Union (HREBIU, the forerunner of the Hotel Employees and Restaurant Employees International Union), and was the youngest woman delegate from any union to the American Federation of Labor national convention. She was only twenty years old.

Myra Wolfgang was an inspiring organizer—relentless, creative, and media-savvy. In 1937 she helped conduct the first sit-down strike among service workers at a downtown Detroit Woolworth's. She organized activities among the young female strikers, brought in speakers, and arranged for press coverage, which included a favorable article in *Life* magazine. After Woolworth's capitulated and signed a union contract, Local 705 grew rapidly.

In 1938 Myra met her husband, Moe Wolfgang, an attorney in private practice who often represented poor workers. They married on August 31, 1939, and had two daughters: Laura (1942) and Martha Debora (1946). Moe was an observant Jew, and Myra followed Jewish religious traditions for his sake. Moe championed his wife's work until his death in 1963, often caring for their children alone when Wolfgang's increased responsibilities took her around the country. In 1950 Wolfgang was appointed vice president of the HREBIU executive board, the only woman at that level in the union, and in 1960 she became the secretary-treasurer of Local 705 after Louis Koenig's death. She achieved these positions against difficult odds; women constituted less than 18 percent of union members in the United States in 1952, and only a handful of unions had even one woman vice president.

Wolfgang fought to improve the condition of working women by negotiating contracts that increased wages, eliminated wage kickbacks for choice jobs, created pensions, and reduced harassment on the job. Perhaps her most celebrated effort was in spearheading the drive to unionize the waitresses known as bunnies in Hugh Hefner's Playboy clubs. When a club opened in Detroit in 1963, Wolfgang sent her seventeen-year-old daughter to apply for a job. In spite of her age the Playboy Club offered her the position, but without pay, telling her that her salary would come from tips. Launching an organizing drive that criticized Playboy's economic and sexual exploitation of these young women, Wolfgang lambasted their employment policies as "a gross perpetuation of the idea that women should be obscene and not heard" (Pitrone, p. 124). The Detroit Playboy Club was organized in August 1964.

From the mid 1930s to the 1960s Wolfgang was appointed to numerous public commissions in Michigan and Washington that investigated and advised on matters affecting working women. A tireless lobbyist for state and federal legislation that protected women workers and increased minimum wage laws, she fought to extend those laws to restaurant workers. Her political agenda included civil rights and opposition to the Vietnam War. As early as 1949, she encouraged members of Local 705 to serve black customers, and in 1957 she served on an NAACP committee that investigated violations of Michigan's Equal Public Accommodations Law. In 1963 Wolfgang went to Selma, Alabama, to support the civil rights demonstrations and that year became a member of the National Committee of Women for Civil Rights. In 1965 Wolfgang testified at a congressional hearing against the Vietnam War.

Friends and coworkers remembered Myra Wolfgang as a devoted and extremely effective advocate for workers, women, and minorities. Five feet six inches tall, a regular drinker of scotch whiskey, and a heavy smoker, Wolfgang battled a weight problem for most of her adult life. Her manner was often as abrasive with employers as it was with her own office staff, and she was not above engaging in rough-and-tumble politics to maintain her position of power. In one union election, she fired two staff members who ran an opposition slate against her allies.

Wolfgang supported the principle of equal pay for equal work, but also advocated limits to the hours women could work and the amount of weight they were required to lift on the job. Though she joined middle-class feminists like Betty Friedan in advocating access to abortion and the establishment of child-care centers, Wolfgang vigorously opposed the equal rights amendment, fearing it would abolish protective labor legislation for women. She and Friedan clashed publicly and frequently on the issue. Wolfgang continued to lead as a working-class feminist in co-founding the Coalition of Labor Union Women (CLUW) in 1974. At this time, only nine unions had women in top leadership positions. CLUW worked to expand the organizing of women in many industries, supported the elevation of women officers in unions, and promoted a feminist agenda within the labor movement. Two years after CLUW's founding, Wolfgang died of cancer in Detroit on April 12, 1976, at the age of sixty-one.

Bibliography: A small collection of Myra Wolfgang's papers are housed in the Union Archives, Walter P. Reuther Library, Wayne State University in Detroit, Michigan. Included are newspaper clippings, correspondence, speeches, and statements. The most extensive treatment of Wolfgang's life is Jean Maddern Pitrone, *Myra: The Life and Times of Myra Wolfgang, Trade-Union Leader* (1980). See also Dorothy Sue Cobble, *Dishing It Out: Waitresses and Their Unions in the Twentieth Century* (1991), and *The Other Women's Movement: Workplace Justice and Social Rights in Modern America* (2004). There is a short biographical sketch of Wolfgang in a pamphlet published by the Union Women's Alliance to Gain Equality (WAGE), *'You Can't Scare Me . . .': Labor Heroines: 1930s–1980s* (1981). Myra Wolfgang published a monthly article in Local 705's newspaper, the *Hotel-Bar Restaurant Review*, from April 1937 until the mid 1970s. The March 22, 1937, issue of *Life* magazine makes no mention of Wolfgang but has over a dozen photographs from the Detroit Woolworth's sit-in. An obituary appeared in the *New York Times* on April 13, 1976. See also obituaries in the May 1976 edition of the *Catering Industry Employee* and the April 19, 1976, edition of the *Hotel Voice*.

DAN KATZ

WOOD, Elizabeth. March 4, 1899–January 16, 1993. Public housing administrator, urban planner.

Ruth Elizabeth Wood was born in Nara, Japan, the third of four children of Mary Isabelle Cokely and Frank Elmer Wood. The Woods were temporarily living in Japan while Frank was the representative of an international ministry of men, the Brotherhood of St. Andrew. While there, Elizabeth's mother became an authority on Japanese flower arrangements.

Elizabeth Wood was raised in a family where education was encouraged and religion was important. She grew up in Bloomington, Illinois, where her father became a professor of biology at Illinois Wesleyan University. Graduating from Bloomington High School, Elizabeth enrolled in Illinois Wesleyan's College of Liberal Arts in 1916, declaring biology as a major in her sophomore year. She finished her education at the University of Michigan, receiving a BA in 1921 and an MA in 1922, both in rhetoric. After graduation, Wood taught English at Vassar College from 1922 to 1926. She then pursued graduate studies in English at the University of Chicago, but after a year withdrew because of disappointment in the curriculum and financial constraints. She later returned to the university to take classes in social case work.

Wood moved from academia to a series of jobs in private and public social welfare and housing agencies in Chicago as economic depression and Franklin D. Roosevelt's New Deal programs were reshaping the political and urban landscape. Chicago had long been a center for progressive reform and good-government groups. Wood came to know Walter H. Blucher, executive director of the Chicago-based American Society of Planning Officials, and Louis Brownlow, who created the Public Administration Clearinghouse at the University of Chicago. Both played key roles in the housing division of the New Deal's Emergency Administration of Public Works, known as the Public Works Administration (PWA), and helped lay the groundwork for a federal public housing program.

In the early 1930s, Wood worked first as a case worker for United Charities, a private agency that administered programs through the Illinois Emergency Relief Commission. Wood then advised homeowners and did editorial work for the Bureau of Home Modernization. The building where she worked housed a national association of contractors, whose head, a building contractor, mentored Wood on materials and construction. In 1934, she consulted with the Public Works Administration in planning housing developments. Between 1933 and 1937, the PWA succeeded in financing and building 21,000 units in fifty projects in thirty-five cities; three projects were in Chicago. The PWA's low-rise buildings were championed for their architecture, community facilities, tenant leadership, and participation in social programs, but the agency often ignored local mayors and city councils. Lawsuits challenged the federal government's power of eminent domain and led to the passage of the U.S. Housing Act in 1937, authorizing federal funds to local housing authorities who became responsible for management.

Amid these unfolding events, Wood's expertise in housing grew. From 1934 to 1936 she served as secretary of the Housing Committee of the Council of Social Agencies; from 1934 to 1936 she was the first executive director of the Metropolitan Planning Council (then called the Metropolitan Housing Council, or MHC). The MHC consulted with the Illinois State Housing Board, where she served as executive secretary from 1935 to 1937 and where she helped write state enabling legislation setting up the Chicago Housing Authority (CHA). In 1937, Mayor Edward J. Kelly appointed Wood the first executive secretary of the Chicago Housing Authority, a position she held until 1954.

As executive secretary, Wood implemented ideas that early housing reformers, many of them women, and the PWA advocated. She promoted social management that encouraged tenants to build a sense of community, planned at a scale large enough to eliminate gridiron streets and to recover land for parks and play areas for children and provide sitting areas for mothers, all the while using the best materials to build durable housing. Kelly and the CHA, however, angered the Board of Aldermen because location decisions were made without their input. The issue was whether to build in already built-up areas or on vacant sites in outlying areas in white neighborhoods. With the pressure of housing returning veterans, Kelly directed Wood to build on city-owned sites, mostly in white areas. The rampant racial strife in Chicago thus was exacerbated. Anti-black riots occurred in white neighborhoods wherever public housing sites were selected. Wood, already controversial because of her views of integration, became a lightning rod for opponents. Despite personal attacks and public vilification, Wood remained committed to selection policies that resulted in residential diversity by race and income. During much of her term, Wood had been joined in her fight for integrated housing by Robert R. Taylor, an African American who served as a CHA commissioner and as chairman from 1943 to 1950.

The real estate mentality that had opposed public housing from the start replaced a not well entrenched social welfare agenda. In Chicago, the 1947 election of Mayor Martin H. Kennelly signaled a political change, and local aldermen regained power to implement a new urban redevelopment policy that emphasized the role of private business and downplayed the role of the CHA. Needing the aldermen's approval to build at all, Wood reluctantly carried out their preferences for building high-rises in overcrowded slum areas instead of racially integrated, scattered site housing. In 1954 Mayor Richard J. Daley reorganized the CHA, created an executive director position, and stripped the executive secretary of any powers. Always a fighter, Woods resigned in protest.

Following her ouster at the CHA, Wood moved

to New York City, where she consulted with agencies such as the Citizens Housing and Planning Council and received Ford and Guggenheim Foundation grants to study international housing programs. From 1965 to 1972, she was a staff member of the U.S. Department of Housing and Urban Development (HUD), coordinating public housing with the Office of Economic Opportunity's social and economic programs.

Elizabeth Wood deeply believed that public housing was a way to replace slums, create permanent affordable housing, build community, and promote integration to the extent possible. She steadfastly fought interests that favored real estate over people. But from its earliest days public housing lacked popular support, and the underfunded and under-maintained projects soon became seen as slums. Broader changes in public housing policy ultimately undermined Wood's efforts, but her accomplishments remain part of the history of early reformers, many of them women, who argued for a strong social welfare agenda in housing; Wood referred to this period as the beginning years. During her last decades, Elizabeth Wood, who never married, moved to Alpharetta, Georgia, and then to Wesley Woods Health Center in Atlanta, where she died in 1993 at the age of ninety-three.

Bibliography: Elizabeth Wood summarized her philosophy in *The Beautiful Beginnings, The Failure to Learn: Fifty Years of Public Housing in the United States* (1982), which also contains brief biographical notes. See also her *Social Planning: A Primer for Urbanists* (1965), and *Social Aspects of Housing and Urban Development* (1967). Additional information on Wood's life was obtained from archivists at Illinois Wesleyan University, the University of Michigan, Vassar College, the University of Chicago, Cornell University, the Brotherhood of St. Andrew, and the Episcopal Church. For analysis of Chicago public housing that also includes biographical material and Wood's role, see Martin Meyerson and Edward C. Banfield, eds., *Politics, Planning, and the Public Interest: The Case of Public Housing in Chicago* (1955); Arnold R. Hirsch, *Making the Second Ghetto: Race and Housing in Chicago 1940–1960* (1983); and Adam Cohen and Elizabeth Taylor, *American Pharaoh: Mayor Richard J. Daley: His Battle for Chicago and the Nation* (2000). In 1976, Elizabeth Wood delivered a lecture at Columbia University, "Ideals and Realities in Subsidized Housing Since 1934," which was reprinted in Richard Plunz, ed., *Housing Form and Public Policy in the United States* (1980). For overviews of public housing and urban life, see Gail Radford, *Modern Housing for America: Policy Struggles in the New Deal Era* (1996); Nicholas Lemann, *The Promised Land: The Great Black Migration and How It Changed America* (1992); and Sudhir Alladi Venkatesh, *American Project: The Rise and Fall of a Modern Ghetto* (2002). Obituaries appeared in the *New York Times* on January 17, 1993, and the *Chicago Sun Times* on January 24, 1993. See also the tribute in the *Journal of Housing* 50, no. 3 (March–April 1993), pp. 124–25.

JACQUELINE LEAVITT

WOODHULL, Nancy. March 1, 1945–April 1, 1997. Editor, journalist, news executive.

Most people in the world of journalism thought the Gannett media company was crazy when it launched a new national newspaper called *USA Today* in 1982. Longtime editor and journalist Nancy J. Woodhull saw the potential of the innovative new publication, however, and signed on as its first managing editor for news.

Nancy Jane Cromwell was born in Perth Amboy, New Jersey, one of two daughters of Mertie May Post and Harold S. Cromwell. She began her journalism career in her home state in 1964 when she left school after a year at Trenton State College to work at the *Perth Amboy Evening News*, which became The *News Tribune* in Woodbridge, New Jersey. She later worked at the *Detroit Free Press* from 1973 to 1975. Woodhull began working for Gannett in 1975 when she became the night city editor at the Rochester, New York, *Times Union*. During the 1970s she was married to Charles Woodhull; they divorced in April 1976. In September of that year she married fellow journalist William Douglas Watson, and their only child, Tennessee Jane, was born in 1981.

Woodhull was managing editor at the Rochester *Democrat & Chronicle* when she was recruited to join the *USA Today* development team. Gannett CEO Al Neuharth, who had the original idea for the new newspaper, said its goals were to inform and entertain the millions of TV-generation individuals who didn't usually read newspapers. To staff the new publication, Neuharth hired people climbing the journalism ladder, people looking for adventure, and many women and minorities who had bumped against the glass ceiling. In the face of almost universal criticism of the publication idea and its concise writing style, Woodhull recalled that Neuharth's unwavering belief in the project inspired them all.

Woodhull had more responsibilities than a typical managing editor because *USA Today* was a completely new concept. She was one of the ten top planning editors for the new publication, and was in charge of story selection for page one of the newspaper and for the entire news section. Woodhull also edited news stories and had a hand in the innovative new design of the paper, which allowed stories to carry equal importance on the front page.

After three years as *USA Today* managing editor, Woodhull became a senior editor at the newspaper in 1985. She had also been named vice president of news for Gannett New Media Services, the company's research and development arm for electronic distribution, when it was organized in August 1984. In 1986, Woodhull became president of Gannett New Media Services and was now responsible for all news, marketing, sales, and development. She remained a senior editor at *USA Today* during this time. In 1987 she took on additional duties as president of Gannett News Service, the company's national wire service for its eighty-three papers at that time. In 1990 she left Gannett when she was named vice president and editor in chief of Southern Progress, a Time Warner division based in Birmingham, Alabama, that published magazines such as *Southern Living* and *Progressive Farmer*. When she left Gannett, she was the highest-ranking woman executive in the company.

In 1990 Woodhull was named a trustee of the Freedom Forum, a nonprofit organization founded by Al Neuharth that focused on free speech, free press, news media history, and newsroom diversity issues. In 1991 she left Time Warner and began her own consulting firm, which helped businesses develop better relationships between men and women in the workplace and marketplace. One of her first clients was a division of Time Warner. Of her venture, Woodhull said, "Both the corporate world and the woman's world need a clearer vision of where women are and will be in the marketplace and the workplace" (*USA Today*, October 30, 1991).

Throughout her career Woodhull pushed for women in leadership positions in the public and private sectors. After moving to Washington, D.C., to work at *USA Today*, she became involved with the Women's Center in northern Virginia, which helped thousands of women through counseling and workshops. She later started the Information and Career Advisory Network (I CAN) for the center to provide mentoring for women with funding from the Gannett Foundation. Woodhull was also an early member of the Journalism & Women Symposium. Concerned about the content of media and its lack of representation of women, in 1988 she and Betty Friedan founded Women, Men & Media, a research and outreach project investigating gender issues in the newspaper, magazine, film, and broadcast industries. Besides being active in these organizations, she often helped arrange key funding for their projects. For example, when she learned that the Women's Hall of Fame in Seneca Falls, New York, was floundering financially, she obtained a grant from the Gannett Foundation to rescue it. She later served as president of the Women's Hall of Fame.

"Do something to help another woman every day" was one of Woodhull's most deeply held convictions. Beginning in 1992, she served as scholar-in-residence at the University of Rochester while continuing her work with the Freedom Forum. Nancy Woodhull continued to lead, mentor, and nurture other women journalists until her death on April 1, 1997, of lung cancer at her home in Pittsford, New York, at the age of fifty-two.

Bibliography: Gannett's Public Affairs Department provided archived press releases from 1982 to 1990. Additional biographical information on Nancy Woodhull is found in the various articles that tracked her career, including Judy Mann, "A Friend of Women Moves On and Up," *Washington Post*, September 7, 1990; Mann, "Newspapers and the Invisible Woman," *Washington Post*, April 19, 1996; and "Woodhull opens firm," *USA Today*, October 30, 1991. For background on the Gannett organization, see Al Neuharth, *Confessions of a S.O.B.* (1989), and Peter Pritchard, *The Making of McPaper: The Inside Story of USA Today* (1987). Obituaries appeared in the *Los Angeles Times*, *Washington Post*, and *New York Times*, all on April 2, 1997. See also tributes by Deborah Tannen, "In Memory of Nancy Woodhull," *American Journalism Review*, May 1997, p. 17, which contains the final quotation; and Judy Mann, "Women and the Media Lose a True Leader," *Washington Post*, April 4, 1997. Assistance with research was provided by William D. Watson, Nancy Woodhull's husband.

BETH HALLER

WORMINGTON, Hannah Marie. September 5, 1914–May 31, 1994. Archaeologist.

Hannah Marie Wormington was born in Denver, Colorado, the only child of Adrienne Roucolle and Charles Watkins Wormington. She had a half brother and a half sister by her father's previous marriage. Her father, a businessman, was born in Worcester, England, and her mother, a writer, was born in Toulouse, France. Hannah was nine years old when her father died, and she was raised in a bilingual home by her mother and maternal grandmother. The early death of her father, combined with her international and intellectual family ties, shaped Marie Wormington's creative and disciplined approach to the study of North American prehistory.

After graduating from East High School in Denver in 1931, Marie Wormington began an undergraduate degree at the University of Denver (DU). In her sophomore year, anthropology professor Étienne B. Renaud introduced her to archaeology. Renaud was a key scholar in American Paleo-Indian studies, particularly in using stone spear point designs to develop a time-sensitive tool typology. Wormington had been acquainted with fellow anthropology undergraduate student John Lambert Cotter since junior high, and they began a lifelong friendship. In 1934, at Professor Renaud's suggestion, Cotter and Wormington volunteered to work at the Colorado Museum of Natural History (now the Denver Museum of Nature and Science). Here Wormington was introduced to Museum Director Jesse D. Figgins, another leading Paleo-Indian scholar. Wormington graduated from DU in 1935.

After graduation, Marie Wormington and her mother went to Europe, where Wormington spent several months in France, England, and Spain meeting archaeologists and visiting sites. In England Wormington met Dorothy Garrod, her model of a woman archaeologist. She also met the American Paleo-Indian scholar E. B. Howard. Throughout her trip Wormington was asked by European archaeologists to exchange American for European photos and drawings of Paleo-Indian/ Paleolithic artifacts. Her bilingual facility and strong social skills, experience with the Paleo-Indian collections and scholars, and excellent memory and organizational ability had placed her on the brink of becoming a recognized scholar and Paleo-Indian expert as a young woman.

When Marie Wormington returned from Europe she took the photo exchange proposal to Figgins, and the director and museum trustees supported it. During the winter of 1935–36, she and fellow DU alumnus Betty Holmes catalogued, photographed, and developed a projectile point classification system for all the museum's Paleo-Indian collections. These included materials from Folsom, Finley, and Lindenmeier (excavated in 1935 by Cotter) as well as a five-hundred-piece surface collection from Yuma and nearby counties in eastern Colorado. This study, particularly the work with the avocational Yuma collection, resulted in Wormington's identification of point facial flaking pattern (for example, fluting as opposed to oblique, parallel collateral, or indeterminate flaking) as reflecting different periods in Paleo-Indian chronology. Radiocarbon dating of archeological sites was still in the future, and the question of the contemporaneity of people and now-extinct animals was a controversial issue. In 1937, E. B. Howard invited Wormington and Holmes to give a presentation on their Paleo-Indian classification scheme at the International Symposium on Early Man, in Philadelphia, and in 1939 Wormington published her first edition of *Ancient Man in North America.* By its fourth edition in 1957 the book had become the internationally recognized standard for North American Paleo-Indian point typology.

In 1937 Marie Wormington was appointed curator of archaeology at the Denver Museum, and she served in that capacity until 1968. Throughout that period ornithologist Alfred M. Bailey was the museum director, and he was not supportive of either women scholars or archaeology. The trustees, however, were. In 1937–38 Wormington had a scholarship to Radcliffe College, where she enrolled in a graduate program that, with stops and starts, resulted in her earning a master's degree in 1950 and a PhD in 1954; both degrees were in anthropology, with course work in both archaeology and geology. She was one of the first women to be allowed to participate in anthropology classes at Harvard University, and Harvard's Clyde Kluckhohn and Kirk Bryan were her mentors.

Marie Wormington always respected avocational archaeologists, and she was involved with the Colorado Archaeological Society (CAS) throughout her career. Her groundbreaking Paleo-Indian publications were written as popular works, as was her *Prehistoric Indians of the Southwest* (1947). During the late 1930s through the early 1950s she conducted fieldwork with the help of avocational archaeologists in western Colorado, which resulted in her dissertation research and two technical publications on the Fremont Culture and (with Robert H. Lister) the Uncompahgre Plateau. She was a charter member of the CAS Denver Chapter in 1947.

Other than occasional terms teaching at schools in Arizona or Minnesota, Marie Wormington lived her entire life in Denver. In 1940 she married George D. "Pete" Volk (1909–80), a petroleum engineer who was supportive of and often assisted with her archeological research. Volk was in the U.S. Army Corps of Engineers during World War II, and Wormington joined him on several assignments, volunteering with the Red Cross. When Volk returned at the end of the war, Wormington had a miscarriage. She then returned to her prewar round of excavation, graduate school, research, and publications and, eventually, teaching.

Marie Wormington was a small, good-looking, and energetic woman who was an excellent cook and a gracious hostess. She always resented her 1968 termination from the Denver Museum, which coincided with the museum's acquisition of the Crane ethnographic collection and the passing of supportive trustees. Having to remain in Denver because of her husband's ties to that city, she was left without any strong institutional affiliation just when her 1966–67 excavations at the Frazier site and her 1968–69 work (with Joe Ben Wheat) at the Jurgens site meant she needed graduate students, a research laboratory, and computer support. She did not finish those projects.

Wormington pursued her Paleo-Indian interests in Mexico, Russia, China, and Alberta as well as the United States during her career. She served as the (first woman) president of the Society for American Archaeology in 1968–69 and received the Society's Distinguished Service Award in 1983. She was working on another revision of her world-renowned book on Paleo-Indian studies when she died in a fire in her Denver home in 1994 at the age of seventy-nine. Marie Wormington was an important model for women interested in interdisciplinary Americanist archaeology, and for nurturing working relationships and respect between avocational and professional workers in the field.

Bibliography: The primary source for Marie Wormington's manuscripts and correspondence is the National Anthropological Archives, National Museum of Natural History, Smithsonian Institution, Washington, D.C. Archival materials at the Denver Museum of Nature and Science include the transcript of a 1983 talk by Wormington as a Colorado Pioneering Archaeologist, a 1987 oral historical interview, a 1994 letter from John Cotter, and a 1994 interview with Betty Holmes Huscher Bachman. The Volk Christmas letters (1958–89) are on file at the Colorado State Historical Society Library, Denver. Published biographical material, written before Wormington's death, includes Ute Gacs, Aisha Khan, Jerrie McIntyre, and Ruth Weinberg, eds., *Women Anthropologists: Selected Biographies* (1989); Cynthia Irwin-Williams, "Women in the Field: The Role of Women in Archaeology before 1960," in G. Kass-Simon and Patricia Farnes, eds., *Women of Science—Righting the Record* (1990); and Linda Cordell, "Women Archaeologists in the Southwest," in Nancy J. Parezo, ed., *Hidden Scholars: Women Anthropologists and the Native American Southwest* (1993). A biographical article, written by Jeanne Varnell in *Women of Consequence: The Colorado Women's Hall of Fame* (1999), includes the erroneous claim that her parents had divorced. Scholarly obituaries, which derive most of their information from personal knowledge and records, include Dennis Stanford's in *American Antiquity* 61, no. 2 (1996), pp. 274–78, which contains a full bibliography and photos; Marcia Tate's in *Southwestern Lore* 60 (1994), p. 1; and Jane Stevenson Day's in *Anthropology Newsletter* 35, no. 6 (September, 1994), p. 73. An obituary appeared in the *New York Times* on June 2, 1994.

RUTHANN KNUDSON

WRINCH, Dorothy Maud. September 12, 1894–February 11, 1976. Mathematician, philosopher, theoretical biochemist.

Dorothy Maud Wrinch was born in Rosario, Argentina, the only child of Ada Minnie Souter and Hugh Edward Hart Wrinch. Her father was an engineer for a British firm; both her parents were English. During her adolescence the family moved to England, where she attended Surbiton High School, a public day school in the suburbs of London, while her father worked at the local waterworks. In 1913 she received a scholarship to Girton College, a residential women's college at Cambridge University. At Cambridge she studied mathematical logic with philosopher Bertrand Russell and in the 1920s wrote a dozen papers on the philosophy of science. In 1916 she won the title of Wrangler in mathematics by scoring the highest grade in the final examination. After receiving her BA in 1917 and an MA in 1918, she taught mathematics at University College, London, while completing her MSc (1920) and her DSc (1922).

In 1922 Dorothy Wrinch moved to Oxford and married John William Nicholson, who studied atomic spectra and was recently appointed director of studies in mathematics and physics at Balliol College, Oxford University. She taught mathematics on a per-term basis at Oxford's five women's colleges and earned another MSc in 1924. Their only daughter, Pamela, was born in 1928. The next year Dorothy Wrinch became the first woman to receive a DSc from Oxford University. The marriage was not happy, and the couple separated when Nicholson was institutionalized for alcoholism in 1930. That year Wrinch left Oxford and became a single mother, determined to raise her daughter and keep her career. Her marriage to Nicholson was finally dissolved in 1938.

Pamela was the great joy of Dorothy Wrinch's life. In the preface to her sociological study *Retreat from Parenthood* (1930), which she published under the pseudonym Jean Ayling, Wrinch stated that "in spite of strenuous efforts, the author can see no essential conflict between the children of the mind and the children of the body; she feels, on the contrary, that the good life flourishes best in the presence of both these joys." The book contained utopian plans for reorganizing medical service, home design, child care, and labor laws to make childrearing compatible with professional careers for both women and men.

The year 1930 was also when Dorothy Wrinch began to expand her professional studies to include biology and chemistry in a series of fellowships at the Universities of Vienna, Paris, Prague, and Leiden. In 1934 she applied mathematical physics to chromosome mechanics, and by 1936 she began publishing her cyclol theory of protein structures. Beginning with the single hypothesis that the peptide chains would be polymerized into sheets by links between the CO and NH groups, Wrinch deduced that the sheets would fold into a series of closed octahedrons that she called cyclols. The series was described by the general formula $72 \times n^2$, where n is the number of amino acid residues. Wrinch felt her hypothesis was proven in 1937 when egg albumin was shown to have 288 (72×2^2) residues in the molecule. This deduction created excitement in the newly emerging world of molecular biology, with Irving Langmuir emerging as her principal advocate and Linus Pauling as her leading critic. The controversy became so heated that her young daughter wrote Pauling asking him not to attack her mother any more without proof. Unfortunately for Wrinch, these proteins did not contain cyclols, but her ideas stimulated much thought and work. Wrinch made the theoretical jump from a linear model of amino acid monomers in proteins to two- and three-dimensional models. She vigorously argued her theories and made many enemies.

Dorothy and Pamela Wrinch came to the United States in 1935, when Wrinch began a five-year Rockefeller Foundation Fellowship. Stranded by the outbreak of war in Europe, she eventually found a position in 1941 as a visiting professor at Amherst, Smith, and Mount Holyoke colleges, with the help of Otto Charles Glaser of the Amherst biology department. Wrinch and Glaser were married on August 20, 1941, and settled permanently and happily in Massachusetts. She became a United States citizen in 1943.

After a year of giving seminars at all three colleges, Wrinch began a thirty-year association with Smith College. She had a few graduate students, conducted seminars for students and faculty, lectured, and continued her research. In the summers she lectured and taught with her husband at the Marine Biological Laboratories at Woods Hole on Cape Cod. In the 1940s she concentrated on developing techniques for interpreting X-ray data of complicated crystal structures, including the protein X-ray data she got from experimentalists. This research led to her monograph *Fourier Transforms and Structure Factors* (1946). She studied mineralogy because she saw an analogy between the morphologies of protein crystals and certain minerals. She filled notebooks with her criticisms and ideas drawn from many branches of science. Her total list of publications eventually reached 192.

In 1954 the cyclol structure was found in the ergot alkaloids. Ergot is a parasitic fungus that lives on cereals and is a starting material for many pharmaceutical preparations. The ergot alkaloids can be considered simple versions of proteins. Dorothy Wrinch told colleague Marjorie Senechal, "First they said my structure couldn't exist. Then when it was found in nature they said it couldn't be synthesized in a laboratory. Then when it was synthesized, they said it wasn't important anyway" (Kass-Simon and Farnes, eds., p. 368). The first major breakthrough in understanding the three-dimensional structure of biological molecules came with the 1953 helical DNA structure described by James Watson and Francis Crick on the basis of X-ray photographs taken by Rosalind Franklin.

Otto Glaser died of nephritis on February 8, 1951, and Wrinch moved to faculty housing on the Smith College campus until her retirement in 1971. She then settled in Woods Hole, where her daughter, Pamela Wrinch Schenkman, died tragically in an accidental fire in 1975. Heartbroken and very weak, Dorothy Wrinch died ten weeks later on February 11, 1976, in Falmouth, Massachusetts, at the age of eighty-one.

Dorothy Wrinch's contribution to science was to apply mathematical techniques to biology, which helped spur the rise of molecular biology. She remained a controversial and somewhat confrontational figure. Restless and often embittered, she was constantly frustrated by the job market and difficulties in getting research funding. Yet she passionately loved her work and constantly looked to the future. Nobel Laureate Dorothy Hodgkin said, "I like to think of her as she was when first I knew her, gay, enthusiastic and adventurous, courageous in the face of much misfortune, and very kind" (Hodgkin, p. 564).

Bibliography: Dorothy Wrinch's papers are in the Sophia Smith Collection, Smith College Library, Northampton, Massachusetts, and consist of more than twenty large boxes of correspondence, papers, notes, and miscellaneous items. A complete bibliography is found in Marjorie Senechal, ed., *Structures of Matter and Patterns in Science: Inspired by the Work and Life of Dorothy Wrinch, 1894–1976* (1980), which grew out of a symposium held at Smith on September 28–30, 1977. Wrinch's publications include "On Certain Methodological Aspects of the Theory of Relativity," *Mind* 31 (1922), pp. 200–204; *The Retreat from Parenthood* (1930), published under the pseudonym Jean Ayling; *Fourier Transforms and Structure Factors* (1946); and *Chemical Aspects of the Structure of Small Peptides* (1960). For additional biographical material, see Maureen M. Julian, "Women in Crystallography," in G. Kass-Simon and Patricia Farnes, eds., *Women of Science: Righting the Record* (1990); and Pnina G. Abir-Am, "Synergy or Clash: Disciplinary and Marital Strategies in the Career of Mathematical Biologist Dorothy Wrinch," in Abir-Am and Dorinda Outram, eds., *Uneasy Careers and Intimate Lives: Women in Science, 1789–1979* (1987). An obituary appeared in the *New York Times* on February 15, 1976. See also Dorothy Crowfoot Hodgkin's tribute in *Nature* 260 (April 8, 1976), p. 564.

MAUREEN M. JULIAN

WU, Chien-Shiung. May 31, 1912–February 16, 1997. Physicist.

Chien-Shiung Wu, known professionally as C. S. Wu, was born in Liuhe near Shanghai, China, the second of three children and the only daughter of Fan Fuhua, a housewife, and Wu Zhongyi, the founder of the Mingde School, the region's first school for girls, and a strong supporter of equal rights for women. Chien-Shiung, who translated her name as "Courageous Hero," completed the first four grades of her father's school by age nine and began boarding at Soochow Girls School in nearby Suzhou. After Wu graduated as Soochow's valedictorian in 1930, she studied physics at the elite National Central University in Nanjing, where she was active in the underground student movement that opposed the growing militarism of Japan. After graduating as National Central's valedictorian in 1934, Wu taught for a year at a provincial university before doing research for another year at the National Academy of Sciences in Shanghai.

Because China had no postgraduate physics training, Wu embarked for the United States in 1936, her way paid for by a wealthy uncle. Originally destined for the University of Michigan, Wu enrolled instead at the University of California at Berkeley, where the physics department was at the height of its fame. Nuclear physics was the most exciting field in science, and Wu became a student of future Nobel Prize winner Emilio Segrè. She studied both the electromagnetic energy given off when a particle going through matter slows down and the radioactive inert gases emitted when the uranium nucleus fissions. Wartime and political conditions prevented her from returning home until 1973.

Wu received a PhD in 1940 and spent two years as a research assistant at Berkeley. Although she was recognized nationally as a fission expert, U.S. anti-war hysteria about Asians was at a peak and none of the nation's top twenty research universities employed a woman physics professor. As a result, she could not get a research job in a university or in the Manhattan Project, which was developing the atomic bomb.

In 1942 Wu married another Chinese-born physicist, Yuan Chia-liu, who anglicized his name to Luke Yuan. The couple moved to the East Coast, where Wu taught briefly at Smith College until the wartime shortage of physicists opened up jobs for her first at Princeton University and then at Columbia University in New York City, where the U.S. Division of War Research was developing sensitive radiation detectors for the atomic bomb project. After the war, Columbia asked Wu to remain as a research associate; Yuan commuted to Long Island to a job at Brookhaven National Laboratory. Although Wu was a fiercely competitive and hardworking perfectionist, she did not receive a regular faculty position at Columbia until 1952. Their son, Vincent Wei-chen Yuan, was born in 1947, and his parents became U.S. citizens in 1954. Wu, who was dignified and rather formal, retained her Chinese style of dress until late in life. She later listed the requisites for a successful married woman in science as a supportive husband, good child care, and a home close to work. Fortunately, she had all three.

Searching for a research topic at Columbia, Wu chose beta decay, a type of radioactivity in which a neutron inside the nucleus turns into a proton, releasing an electron and a neutrino. The electron and neutrino burst out of the nucleus at tremendous speeds and rid the nucleus of excess energy. The proton remains inside a new, more stable nucleus. Enrico Fermi had theorized in 1934 that most of the electrons would burst out of the nucleus at very high speeds, yet early experiments produced many *slow* electrons. In a series of exceedingly difficult and precise experiments conducted between 1946 and 1952, Wu showed that previous experimentalists had used radioactive materials of uneven thicknesses. Using uniformly thin material, Wu confirmed Fermi's prediction and established her reputation as a brilliant scientist.

Wu's research took a new turn in 1956 when two young Chinese American physicists, Tsung Dao Lee at Columbia and Chen Ning Yang at the Institute for Advanced Study in Princeton, suggested that a newly discovered particle, the K-meson, might decay in two different ways. Lee and Yang suspected that more particles might emerge from one side of a nucleus than another. If so, the particles sometimes violated basic laws of parity and symmetry, which said that molecules, atoms, and nuclei behave symmetrically.

To investigate the idea, Wu quickly formed a team with cold-temperature experts at the National Bureau of Standards in Washington, D.C. Like all forms of matter, atomic nuclei move constantly in every direction as a result of their heat energy. Wu planned to eliminate as much of this random heat energy as possible. She used helium gas cooled to a liquid and cerium magnesium nitrate crystals to cool radioactive cobalt nuclei to within a few thousandths of a degree of absolute zero. Then she aligned a powerful magnet with the slow-moving nuclei long enough for the team to detect whether the radioactive nuclei were ejecting most of their electrons one way, as Lee and Yang had suggested. Even today the experiment would be challenging, but with 1950s technology it was extraordinarily difficult.

As Wu and the National Standards team analyzed their results in January 1957, they realized that more electrons did indeed come out one side of the nuclei and that the law of parity could sometimes be violated. The experiment eventually provided a key to the understanding of strong, weak, and electromagnetic forces.

Wu was outspoken about the role of women in science: "Bringing a womanly point of view may be advantageous in some areas of education and social science, but not in physical and mathematical sciences, where we strive always for objectivity. I wonder whether the tiny atoms and nuclei, or the mathematical symbols, or the DNA molecules have any preference for either masculine or feminine treatment. . . . I sincerely doubt that any open-minded person really believes in the faulty notion that women have no intellectual capacity for science and technology" (McGrayne, p. 279). Appointed the first Pupin Professor of Physics in 1973, she retired from the Columbia faculty in 1981. Never losing her zest for physics, she continued to travel, lecture, and teach, as well as encourage women to consider careers in science. Wu died of a stroke in New York City at the age of eighty-four.

Bibliography: Wu's personal and scientific papers are expected to reside at either Columbia University or Nanjing University. Her two most important scientific papers are C. S. Wu, E. Ambler, R. W. Hayward, D. D. Hoppes, and R. P. Hudson, "Experimental Test of Parity Conservation in Beta Decay," *Physical Review* 105 (February 15, 1957), pp. 1413–15, and Wu, "Recent Investigation of the Shapes of Beta-Ray Spectra," *Reviews of Modern Physics* 22 (October 1950), pp. 386–98. See also Wu, "One Researcher's Personal Account," *Adventures in Experimental Physics* (1973). Wu explained her parity experiment for general audiences in "Subtleties and Surprises: The Contribution of Beta Decay to an Understanding of the Weak Interaction," *Annals of the New York Academy of Sciences*, November 8, 1977, and "The Discovery of the Parity Violation in Weak Interactions and Its Recent Developments," Nishina Memorial Foundation, April 1983. Biographical information is found in Sharon Bertsch McGrayne, *Nobel Prize Women in Science: Their Lives, Struggles, and Momentous Discoveries* (1993; 2nd ed. 1998), which is based on interviews with Wu and numerous colleagues and family members. For more on Wu and the position of women in science, see Lynn Gilbert and Gaylen Moore, *Particular Passions: Talks with Women Who Have Shaped Our Times* (1981); Gloria Lubkin, "Chien-Shiung Wu, the First Lady of Physics Research," *Smithsonian*, January 1971; Jacquelyn A. Mattfeld and Carol G. Van Aken, eds., *Women and the Scientific Professions: The MIT Symposium on American Women in Science and Engineering* (1965); Emilio Segrè, *From X Rays to Quarks: Modern Physicists and Their Discoveries* (1980); and Edna Yost, *Women of Modern Science* (1959). According to Wu, her date of birth was May 31, rather than the commonly accepted date of May 29. An obituary appeared in the *New York Times* on February 18, 1997.

SHARON BERTSCH MCGRAYNE

WYNETTE, Tammy. May 5, 1942–April 6, 1998. Country music singer and songwriter.

Born Virginia Wynette Pugh in Itawamba County, Mississippi, Tammy Wynette became a legendary singer and songwriter whose music in the late 1960s and 1970s helped redefine Nashville and women's place in country music. She was the only child of Mildred Russell and William Hollice Pugh, both of whom worked on the six-hundred-acre farm of her grandfather, Chester Russell, in the rich bottomland of the northeastern Mississippi hill country. When Wynette (as she was known) was still an infant, her father died of a brain tumor, and her mother moved to Memphis to work in a war plant, leaving her with her grandparents. No stranger to hard work, she grew up picking cotton and doing chores around the farm.

Wynette went to junior high and high school in nearby Tremont, Mississippi, but dropped out one month before graduation to marry construction worker Euple Byrd. While he moved from job to job in Mississippi and Alabama, she enrolled in beauty school and eventually became a licensed beautician. The couple had three children: Gwendolyn (1961), Jacquelyn (1962), and Tina (1965). After several years of unhappiness over her husband's unstable employment and moody temperament, she filed for divorce in 1965.

Between working in beauty shops and raising her children, Wynette also pursued her lifelong dream to become a musical performer. She had been brought up in the Baptist church and the Church of God (she attended both regularly), and had always sung in the choir and in the cotton fields, and mastered the piano at a young age. In 1965, Wynette began performing on a local Birmingham, Alabama, television morning show, *Country Boy Eddie*, where she made contacts with country music disc jockeys and began making regular trips to Nashville's Music Row in an effort to land a recording contract. After numerous rejections, her door-to-door approach finally paid off in 1966 when she walked into producer Billy Sherrill's office, borrowed his guitar, and sang a handful of songs for him. Sherrill instantly agreed to record her.

In addition to guiding Wynette through her first foray into the country music business, Billy Sherrill gave the singer a new name. He warned her that Wynette Pugh lacked commercial appeal, and suggested Tammy Wynette, which stuck. Her first single, "Apartment #9," came out in the fall of 1966 and received moderate airplay but failed to crack the country Top 40. The following year, however, she began a remarkable string of more than three dozen top ten singles, twenty of which went to number one, starting with her duet with David Houston, "My Elusive Dreams."

From the late 1960s through the 1980s, Tammy Wynette popularized songs about women dealing with rocky relationships, troubled men, hard times, and heartache. Singles such as "Your Good Girl's Gonna Go Bad" (1967), "I Don't Wanna Play House" (1968), "D-I-V-O-R-C-E" (1968), her signature song, "Stand By Your Man" (1969), and "Kids Say the Darndest Things" (1973), reflected a new sensibility for female country singers. Much like the feisty, independent-minded songs of Loretta Lynn, who reached superstardom around the same time, Wynette's music expressed the ambivalence of loving imperfect men, as well as the resolve to overcome romantic loss and family suffering. As a singer and a songwriter, she combined vulnerability and strength, dependence and autonomy, in a voice that was uniquely emotional and compelling, especially to female audiences.

In the midst of her immense success, Tammy Wynette suffered through two more failed marriages. In 1967, the same year she won a Grammy for "I Don't Wanna Play House," she wed guitarist Don Chapel, but the couple divorced the same year. In 1968, while touring with her girlhood idol, George Jones, the two fell in love; they married in February 1969. After being named the Country Music Association (CMA) Female Vocalist of the Year in 1968, Wynette won a Grammy Award for "Stand By Your Man" and a second consecutive CMA Award for Female Vocalist of the Year in 1969, a feat she repeated for a third time in 1970. She also gave birth to a daughter, Tamala Georgette Jones, in 1970. Tammy Wynette and George Jones performed and recorded together, and became an enduring, almost mythologized couple, even after their marriage dissolved. During the 1970s, their duets, most notably "We're Gonna Hold On" (1973) and "Golden Ring" (1976), topped the charts and became country standards. George Jones's legendary drinking did not deter Wynette, and she went into the marriage believing that she could help him quit. When his extended drinking binges and violent outbursts took their toll, she divorced him in 1975.

As the 1970s wore on, Wynette's chart success waned, though she continued touring extensively. At the same time, the ongoing turmoil of her personal life played out in the public eye like a bad country song. In 1976 Wynette made the ill-advised decision to marry Nashville real estate executive Michael Tomlin, a marriage that lasted all of two months. Suffering from chronic stomach pains, appendicitis, and intestinal problems, she underwent many surgeries, and developed painful adhesions as well as a mean dependence on painkillers, all of which plagued her to the end of her life.

Her 1978 marriage to longtime friend, producer, and songwriter George Richey was her last. He became her manager as well, eventually controlling her touring and recording schedule and her finances with a tight fist. She released more than a dozen albums during the 1980s, some greatest hits collections and others that featured new material. But Wynette did not match the heights of her earlier success until she recorded a novelty song, "Justified and Ancient," with British dance duo The KLF in 1992. The following year she released the album *Honky Tonk Angels* with Loretta Lynn and Dolly Parton, and a new generation of fans discovered her music.

At the age of fifty-five, Tammy Wynette died in her sleep at home in Nashville on April 6, 1998, allegedly from a blood clot in the lung. Hundreds of country singers, songwriters, and musicians packed the Ryman Auditorium, the original home of the Grand Ole Opry, to pay tribute to a woman who had co-written one of the greatest country songs of all time, and whose career had proved to skeptical industry insiders that "girl singers" could sell millions of albums, headline concert tours, and appeal to women fans.

Bibliography: Tammy Wynette's autobiography, *Stand By Your Man*, with Joan Dew, appeared in 1979. Her daughter, Jackie Daly (with Tom Carter), published *Tammy Wynette* (2000), a biography and reminiscence that is also an indictment of George Richey's controlling relationship with her mother. In it Daly points to his possible role in perpetuating Wynette's drug addiction and, eventually, causing her death. In early 1999, she and two of her sisters had their mother's body exhumed and an autopsy performed; the results were inconclusive. For more information on the case, see *USA Today*, February 11, 1999. On Tammy Wynette's place within country music, see Joan Dew, *Singers & Sweethearts: The Women of Country Music* (1977); and Mary A. Bufwack and Robert K. Oermann, *Finding Her Voice: The Saga of Women in Country Music* (1993). Obituaries appeared in the *New York Times* on April 7, 1998, the *Atlanta Journal and Constitution* on April 8, 1998, and *Billboard* on April 18, 1998.

STACY BRAUKMAN

Y

YONEDA, Elaine Black. September 4, 1906–May 26, 1988. Labor organizer, radical.

Elaine Black Yoneda, whose birth name was Rose Elaine Buchman, was born on the Lower East Side of New York City, the first of two children of Nathan Buchman and Mollie Kvetnay, Marxist labor activists from czarist Russia. Her father emigrated to the United States in 1902; her mother joined him in October 1905 in New York City. Her brother Abraham ("Al") was born when they lived in Waterbury, Connecticut. In 1910 the family moved back to New York, settling in Brooklyn, where her father opened a four-chair, unionized barbershop. By then her parents had joined the Socialist Party. In September 1919 her parents became charter members the Communist Party, which formed that month in Chicago.

Despite the labor agitation and government repression around her and being raised in a politically leftist, working-class, and secular Jewish household, Elaine appeared oblivious to her surroundings. By the time she had finished eighth grade, she was smoking cigarettes, unbeknownst to her parents. Her mother, who did not like her growing breasts, bound them with towels to flatten them. In 1920 the family moved to Lemon Grove, near San Diego, California.

It was there, as the sole Jewish pupil in her school, that Elaine first experienced anti-Semitism from her schoolmates. Her parents soon moved to San Diego, where her father bought a clothing store. In 1921 the teenage Elaine attended her first political meeting, one supporting the Russian Revolution.

The independent-minded Elaine dropped out of San Diego High School in her senior year after her parents refused to let her apply to nursing school. The family moved to Los Angeles, where she worked at the elegant Darby Hotel, whose prosperous clientele impressed her. At her parents' urging, she began attending meetings of the Young Workers League, where she met Edward Francis Russell Jr., a machinist. On January 12, 1925, Elaine married "Young Ed." The newlyweds were more interested in romance than politics. Their daughter, Joyce, was born in 1927.

During a 1930 visit to a local Communist Party office to visit a friend, the couple ended up being detained during a violent police raid. Asked their names, Elaine said "Black," after Blackie, her husband's nickname. The name stuck. Outraged at the raid, she joined the labor movement, becoming the district secretary and later the Pacific Coast vice president of the International Labor Defense, which provided legal aid for workers. Bailing out a badly beaten Japanese American from jail in 1931, she ended up falling for Karl G. "Hama" Yoneda, who had been a communist since 1927. She herself joined the Communist Party in October 1931, an affiliation she kept for the rest of her life. She and Karl began a relationship as she grew apart from Russell, whom she divorced in January 1934.

In San Francisco, where Karl and Elaine ended up, they began living together. As Karl Yoneda, who became the editor of the party's Japanese-language newspaper there, would later explain it, a California law barring interracial marriage prevented their getting married. Hoping to make their affair legal, they took the train to Washington State, where on November 5, 1935, they found a Methodist minister in Seattle who was willing to marry them. They later had a son, Thomas Culbert, who was born in 1939 in San Francisco.

An early feminist who argued for equal pay for equal work, Elaine Yoneda became legendary in San Francisco for her militancy and fighting spirit on the side of workers and immigrants in the 1930s. She was the only woman on the Longshore Strike Committee of the San Francisco General Strike in 1934. She was convicted of "vagrancy" at another protest, although appellate judges later overturned her conviction, ruling that she was convicted just because she was a communist. The San Francisco police called her the Red Angel for bailing out those arrested during protests and strikes, and the San Francisco *Call Bulletin* labeled her Tiger Girl for mobilizing farm workers during the 1936 lettuce strike in Salinas, California. For many years, she was president of the ladies' auxiliary of the International Longshoremen's and Warehousemen's Union. The FBI kept her under surveillance, putting her on a detention list to be activated in a national emergency.

In November 1939, she ran unsuccessfully with the Communist Party's endorsement for a nonpartisan spot on the San Francisco Board of Supervisors, receiving an astounding 20,506 votes. Then thirty-three years old, she advocated free day care for working mothers, low-cost housing, an end to racial discrimination, and protection of civil rights, and she pledged to "Keep America out of Imperialist War." Decades later, the board of supervisors would adjourn a meeting to mourn her passing.

Despite opposing Japan's expansionist war in Asia, the Yonedas, with infant son Tommy, were incarcerated at Manzanar Relocation Center in California for eight months in 1942 during World War II. Not being of Japanese ancestry, Elaine Yoneda was not subject to Executive Order 9066 that authorized the massive roundup, but she felt the family should stay together. At Manzanar, they came under violent harassment from pro-Japan fellow internees, who were upset at their support for the U.S. war against Japan. Elaine and her son even had to seek refuge in the administration building from attacking pro-Japan internees at one point. By then Karl Yoneda had already left to join the U.S. Army Military Intelligence Corps.

After the war, the Yonedas ran a chicken farm in northern California near Petaluma. Elaine remained politically active, becoming chair of the Sonoma County chapter of the Civil Rights Congress, a nationwide group supporting victims of racist terror. In 1960 they sold the farm and returned to San Francisco, where she worked for the pension fund of the International Longshoremen's and Warehousemen's Union-Pacific Maritime Association until her retirement in 1973. Elaine Yoneda also organized pilgrimages to Manzanar and in August 1981 testified before the U.S. Commission on Wartime Relocation and Internment of Civilians as part of her efforts to seek redress and reparations.

On May 26, 1983, the couple celebrated their

fiftieth anniversary together with six hundred people at the longshoremen's union hall in San Francisco. Despite failing health, she remained active in women's, peace, and labor struggles. On May 25, 1988, at a presidential campaign rally in San Francisco, the eighty-one-year-old activist shook hands with Democratic candidate Jesse Jackson. She died at home in San Francisco the next morning. In their memory, the Southwest Labor History Association annually gives an Elaine and Karl Yoneda Memorial Award.

Bibliography: The most important materials about Elaine Yoneda's political activism are in the Elaine Black Yoneda Collection at the Labor Archives and Research Center, San Francisco State University. They include correspondence, research material used for a biography of her, a transcript of an interview by Lucy Kendall in 1976 about her 1930s militancy, hundreds of pages of FBI documents on her, and her testimony to the U.S. Commission on Wartime Relocation and Internment of Civilians. Important sources for her own recollections of the internment experience are oral history interviews with her by Betty E. Mitson (March 2, 1974) and Arthur A. Hansen (March 3, 1974), archived at the Center for Oral and Public History at California State University, Fullerton. Vivian McGuckin Raineri's biography, *The Red Angel: The Life and Times of Elaine Black Yoneda, 1906–1988* (1991), is the most complete survey of her life. See also Karl G. Yoneda's autobiography, *Ganbatte: Sixty-Year Struggle of a Kibei Worker* (1983), and his papers at the Young Research Library, University of California, Los Angeles, which are especially useful for material relating to the Yonedas' internment during World War II. Elaine Yoneda's testimony to the relocation commission appears in *Only What We Could Carry: The Japanese American Internment Experience* (2000), edited by Lawson Fusao Inada. Susan Musicant profiled her in "Working Women's History: Elaine Black Yoneda," *Union W.A.G.E.* 55 (September–October, 1979), p. 13. Obituaries appeared in the *San Francisco Chronicle* on May 27, 1988, the *New York Times* on May 29, 1988, and the *Los Angeles Times* on May 30, 1988.

DANIEL C. TSANG

INDEX OF BIOGRAPHIES BY FIELD

Index of Biographies by Field

Engineering/Technology

English/Literary Theory

Fashion/Textile Design

Feminism

Film

Index of Biographies by Field

Food

Gardening

Government: Appointed Officials (State and Federal)

History

Home Economics. *See* Nutrition

Housing Reform

International Affairs

Journalism

Labor

Index of Biographies by Field

Index of Biographies by Field

Psychiatry/Psychoanalysis/Psychiatric Social Work

Psychology

Public Health/Women's Health

Publishing/Editing

Radicalism/Socialism

Radio/Television

Religion/Spirituality

Social Work

Socialite/Hostess

Sociology

Sports/Physical Education/Recreation

Theater/Vaudeville/Comedy

INDEX OF CONTRIBUTORS

Index of Contributors

Index of Contributors